AMERICAN NATIONAL BIOGRAPHY
Supplement 2

AMERICAN NATIONAL BIOGRAPHY

GENERAL EDITOR

Mark C. Carnes
Ann Whitney Olin Professor of History, Barnard College

EDITORIAL ADVISORY BOARD

AMERICAN
NATIONAL BIOGRAPHY

Supplement 2

Published under the auspices of the
AMERICAN COUNCIL OF LEARNED SOCIETIES

Editor

Mark C. Carnes

With a Cumulative Index by Occupations and Realms of Renown

OXFORD
UNIVERSITY PRESS

2005

OXFORD

UNIVERSITY PRESS

Oxford University Press, Inc., publishes works that further
Oxford University's objective of excellence
in research, scholarship, and education.

Oxford   New York
Auckland   Cape Town   Dar es Salaam   Hong Kong   Karachi
Kuala Lumpur   Madrid   Melbourne   Mexico City   Nairobi
New Delhi   Shanghai   Taipei   Toronto

With offices in
Argentina   Austria   Brazil   Chile   Czech Republic   France   Greece
Guatemala   Hungary   Italy   Japan   Poland   Portugal   Singapore
South Korea   Switzerland   Thailand   Turkey   Ukraine   Vietnam

Published by Oxford University Press, Inc.
198 Madison Avenue, New York, New York 10016
http://www.oup.com

Oxford is a registered trademark of Oxford University Press

Library of Congress Cataloging-in-Publication Data

(Revised for Supplement 2)

American national biography / general editors, John A. Garraty, Mark C. Carnes
p.   cm.
"Published under the auspices of the American Council of Learned Societies."
Includes bibliographical references and index.
1. United States—Biography—Dictionaries.   I. Garraty, John Arthur,
1920–   . II. Carnes, Mark C. (Mark Christopher), 1950–   .
III. American Council of Learned Societies.
CT213.A68   1998   98-20826   920.073—dc21   CIP
ISBN-13: 978-0-19-522202-9 (Suppl. 2)
ISBN-10: 0-19-522202-4 (Suppl. 2)

Printing number: 9 8 7 6 5 4 3 2 1

Printed in the United States of America
on acid-free paper

EDITORIAL AND PRODUCTION STAFF

MANAGING EDITORS
Paul Betz and Jonathan Wiener

COPYEDITORS
Jean Kaplan, Marion Laird

FACTCHECKERS
Lisa Chensvold, Christine Guyonneau

PROOFREADER
Publishing Synthesis, Ltd.

DIRECTOR OF EDITORIAL DEVELOPMENT AND PRODUCTION
Timothy J. DeWerff

PUBLISHER
Casper Grathwohl

CONSTITUENT SOCIETIES OF THE
AMERICAN COUNCIL OF LEARNED SOCIETIES

African Studies Association

American Academy of Arts and Sciences

American Academy of Religion

American Anthropological Association

American Antiquarian Society

American Association for the Advancement of Slavic Studies

American Comparative Literature Association

American Dialect Society

American Economic Association

American Folklore Society

American Historical Association

American Musicological Society

American Numismatic Society

American Oriental Society

American Philological Association

American Philosophical Association

American Philosophical Society

American Political Science Association

American Psychological Association

American Schools of Oriental Research

American Society for Aesthetics

American Society for Eighteenth Century Studies

American Society for Environmental History

American Society for Legal History

American Society for Theatre Research

American Society of Church History

American Society of Comparative Law

American Society of International Law

American Sociological Association

American Studies Association

Archaeological Institute of America

Association for Asian Studies

Association for Jewish Studies

Association for the Advancement of Baltic Studies

Association of American Geographers

Association of American Law Schools

Bibliographical Society of America

College Art Association

College Forum of the National Council of Teachers of English

Dictionary Society of North America

Economic History Association

German Studies Association

Hispanic Society of America

History of Science Society

International Center of Medieval Art

Latin American Studies Association

Law and Society Association

Linguistic Society of America

Medieval Academy of America

Metaphysical Society of America

Middle East Studies Association

Modern Language Association

National Communication Association

National Council on Public History

Organization of American Historians

Renaissance Society of America

Sixteenth Century Society and Conference

Society for American Music

Society for Cinema and Media Studies

Society for Music Theory

Society for Ethnomusicology

Society for French Historical Studies

Society for the Advancement of Scandinavian Study

Society for the History of Technology

Society of Architectural Historians

Society of Biblical Literature

Society of Dance History Scholars

PREFACE

This is the second supplement to the twenty-four-volume *American National Biography*, which was published in 1999. After the contents of the print edition were issued in an online format (www.anb.org) in the spring of 2000, articles were added to the website. The first supplement was published in 2002.

Under the general editorship of John A. Garraty and Mark C. Carnes, the *ANB* was designed to provide broad coverage of notable figures in American history, from the earliest recorded contact of Europeans in North America to the near present. The 1999 print edition included only those who died before 1996. The three-year lag was partly dicatated by practical considerations, but also by the need to assess subjects from an historical perspective. This is especially so when the person has died at a young age or is in the midst of his or her career.

The American Council of Learned Societies and Oxford University Press conceived of the *ANB* as an active enterprise. The first print supplement included figures who, for various reasons, were omitted from the initial set as well as, although not comprehensively, people who died from 1996 through early 2001. The subjects in the present volume represent a similar mix of figures from the past and the recently deceased.. Among the subjects of new articles are the notables one would expect to find, such as Steve Allen, Gwendolyn Brooks, Ray Charles, Katharine Graham, Katharine Hepburn, Yehudi Menuhin, Tito Puente, Ronald Reagan, and Eudora Welty. As in the base set, a concerted effort has been made to profile individuals from all walks of life—biochemists and religious leaders, economists and business executives, philosophers and political operatives. A few people of admittedly ephemeral significance appear in these pages, too, but the aim is to show how they were representative of American popular culture at a given moment in the country's history.

The present book includes figures who were omitted from the earlier volumes. Among them are Adolph Coors, Casey Jones, Audre Lorde, Eugene Ormandy, and Ritchie Valens. In the interest of completeness, several state governors, American Indian leaders, and first ladies who failed to make it into the 1999 edition of the *ANB* and its first supplement are now subjects of articles.

Following the articles in this volume is an updated Index by Occupations and Realms of Renown, which is in a somewhat different format from the one found in the 1999 edition of the *ANB*. Although the specific occupational categories are largely unchanged, they have been grouped under general headings, such as Art and Architecture, Government and Politics, and Science and Technology. Thus the reader can more easily identify subjects in related fields, as in the case of Nurses, Pharmacists, Physicians, and Surgeons General, who are listed, along with other types of health-care workers, under the rubric of Health and Medicine.

Updates of the *ANB Online* and further print supplements will be issued at regular intervals. We welcome suggestions of other notable figures of the past who have not yet entered the pages of the *ANB*. Although we have gone to considerable lengths to ensure the accuracy of the articles already published, we also welcome corrections of inadvertent errors, which can be readily rectified in the online edition.

As a collective biography of the American nation in all its diversity, the *ANB* will remain a dynamic resource for historians, students, and the general reader.

Mark C. Carnes

AMERICAN NATIONAL BIOGRAPHY
Supplement 2

A

ADAMS, Alice (14 Aug. 1926–27 May 1999), writer, was born in Fredericksburg, Virginia, the daughter of Nicholson Barney Adams, a professor of Spanish at the University of North Carolina, and Agatha Erskine Boyd Adams. An only child, Adams grew up in a Chapel Hill, North Carolina, farmhouse. As Adams recalled in a July 1996 talk at the University of California, Davis (UCD), "I was one of those really horrible children who wrote poetry. I came from an extremely literary little town, Chapel Hill, so writing was considered a marvelous thing to do. For me to become a writer was not the least rebellious, it was conformity." She described her family as "three difficult, isolated people" and her mother as a depressed person and failed writer. "My mother read all the time so I thought: 'If I'm a writer, maybe she'll like me'" (quoted in *Current Biography Yearbook*, p. 7).

Adams left home at age sixteen to attend Radcliffe College. At Harvard she took Kenneth Kempton's writing class. "Miss Adams, you're a very nice girl," he advised her. "Why don't you forget about this writing and go get married?" (quoted in *Dictionary of Literary Biography*, p. 5).

After graduating in 1946, Adams worked at a publishing company in New York City but was fired for taking too much time off to visit her fiancé, Mark Linenthal, Jr. Less than a year after graduation, they married; they had one son together. The couple lived in Paris for a year while Linenthal studied at the Sorbonne. In 1948 they moved to San Francisco, where Linenthal taught English at San Francisco State University. Adams loved San Francisco, and the city became her permanent home.

But Adams's marriage was not a happy one. Because society frowned on divorce, she instead saw a psychoanalyst, who advised her to stop writing, the second authoritarian male to do so. In 1958 Adams divorced. "I was writing in only the most spasmodic, desperate way. . . . [Peter, her son] was difficult then, I disliked my husband, and we didn't have any money" (quoted in *Current Biography Yearbook*, p. 7). A year later her first short story, "Winter Rain," was published in *Charm* magazine.

"I didn't start publishing immediately, it took forever," said Adams. "I was terribly old, or so it seemed at the time. I was over thirty before I published anything." Over the next several years she struggled to raise her son, holding a variety of low-paying clerical jobs. "It was very boring but I thought I could conserve energy for writing," she told her UCD audience. "And most of those jobs, which were in medical settings of one sort or another, supplied fodder for my fiction."

Adams wrote short stories as a sideline and had a series of love affairs, one of which became the wry subject of her marginally successful first novel, *Careless Love*, published in 1966. Three years later she made her first sale to a national literary magazine with the *New Yorker*'s November 1969 publication of "Gift of Grass," about an unhappy teenage girl's sudden empathetic understanding that adults can be miserable, too. In 1964 Adams began a long-term relationship with Robert McNie, an interior designer. Adams and McNie never married. Adams's second novel, *Families and Survivors*, was published in 1974. This book, like much of her work, is based on her personal experiences. While her sophisticated literary style was praised by many critics, others found her range of subjects to be limited and superficial. But when her first collection of short stories, *Beautiful Girl*, was published in 1979, Susan Wood, a reviewer from the *Washington Post Book World* (21 Jan. 1979), likened her work to that of F. Scott Fitzgerald.

Adams's second collection of short stories, *To See You Again* (1982), was a critical success. Reviewers praised her satirical eye, sense of humor, and social observations. In these stories, as in so much of her work, the constant theme was falling in love, falling out of love, and all stages in between. She also wrote about women struggling to find their place in the world, as had she. That year, in recognition of the twelfth consecutive appearance of her work in *Prize Stories: The O. Henry Awards*, Adams won a special award for continuing achievement, joining the ranks of previous winners Joyce Carol Oates and John Updike. Her third collection of short stories, *Return Trips*, was published in 1985. In 1990 Adams published her only collection of nonfiction essays, a travelogue, *Mexico: Some Travels and Travelers There*, that received uneven reviews.

From 1991 to 1997 Adams wrote five novels. Her last novel, *After the War* (2000), was published posthumously, bringing her body of work to eleven novels, five collections of short stories, and numerous uncollected works. Her final collection of short stories, *The Last Lovely City*, was published shortly before her death. Adams died in her Victorian home in the affluent Pacific Heights section of San Francisco.

Adams's place on the American literary spectrum has not yet been determined. For one thing, critics haven't reached consensus on whether to label her a short-story writer or a novelist. For most of her career, Adams was celebrated as a writer of short stories, but in the 1990s she devoted herself primarily to writing novels. Four were published during this, the last decade of her life, and her final novel, *After the War*, was published the year after her death. Additionally, critics have not always praised her work. Still, in 1992 Adams was awarded the Academy and Institute Award in Literature by the American Academy and Institute of Arts and Letters. As Elizabeth Davis of UCD has observed, Adams's "elegant, sparse style influenced a whole generation of American women writers. Her satirical eye, her complicated, fast-talking characters, her social commentary on class and personal relationships—all of these elements made her fiction immensely exciting for writers and readers alike" (personal communication, 2002).

• A detailed article by Christine Ferguson that describes and critiques most of Adams's work appears in *Dictionary of Literary Biography* 234 (2000), pp. 3–15. An unsigned article in *Current Biography Yearbook* (1989), pp. 6–10, also is informative. David Kippen, book editor for the *San Francisco Chronicle*, writes about Adams's connection to San Francisco in "A Street Named Alice Adams," 3 June 1999. Adams gave a reading at the University of California, Davis, in July 1996, which was videotaped for the English department (available from the UCD Media Distribution Lab under the title *Women Writers of Northern California: Alice Adams*). While several sources list the day of Adams's death as 26 May, her death certificate lists 27 May. Obituaries are in the *San Francisco Chronicle* and the *New York Times*, both 28 May 1999.

ELISABETH SHERWIN

AGRONSKY, Martin (12 Jan. 1915–25 July 1999), broadcast journalist and commentator, was born Martin Zama Agronsky, the son of Isador Agronsky and Marcia Dvorin Agronsky, Jewish immigrants from Minsk, Russia (now Belarus). Born and raised in Philadelphia, he attended public schools and studied journalism at Rutgers University, where he received a bachelor of science degree in 1936. On graduating, Agronsky traveled to Jerusalem to take a job as a reporter with the *Palestine Post*, an English-language newspaper owned by his uncle. A year later he departed for Europe, where he freelanced stories from the battle fronts of the Spanish Civil War.

At the outbreak of the Second World War in 1939, the National Broadcasting Company (NBC) expanded its limited European news operations. Agronsky, though lacking radio training or experience, was hired as a correspondent in 1940. NBC's coverage of the war is usually overshadowed in the history books by the bravura work of its broadcasting rival CBS. Agronsky, however, was a bright spot for NBC, distinguishing himself under fire in the Balkans, North Africa, and the Middle East.

With the entry of the United States into the conflict following the Pearl Harbor attack, NBC transferred the young but seasoned war correspondent to the Pacific, attaching him to the forces of General Douglas MacArthur. Here, Agronsky covered the bloody Allied retreat from the Asian mainland; he was among the passengers on the last airplane out of Singapore before the arrival of the Japanese. Not yet thirty, Agronsky had gained a considerable reputation among his colleagues and the listening public for daring battlefield journalism on three continents. In 1943

he returned to the United States and married Helen Smathers; the couple had four children and remained together until her death in 1969. Agronsky married Sharon Hines circa 1972, and the couple had one child. The union ended in divorce after some fifteen years.

As Agronsky was making a name for himself as a war correspondent, a corporate shift was taking place in the radio industry that would greatly affect his career. In 1943, the U.S Supreme Court upheld a ruling that in effect forced the Radio Corporation of America (RCA) to divest itself of one of its two radio networks (known as "NBC-Red" and "NBC-Blue"). Agronsky's contract was among the assets assigned to the Blue network, which was sold off and reorganized into a new company, the smaller and weaker American Broadcasting Company (ABC). As a result, after the war, while many of his colleagues were poised to move into lucrative positions in the television news services created by the dominant NBC and CBS networks, Agronsky found himself in the Washington bureau of ABC, which would not be able to field a competitive television news operation for decades.

Nonetheless, Agronsky continued to distinguish himself as a radio journalist for ABC. In 1952, he received the George Foster Peabody Award for his coverage of Senator Joseph McCarthy's "anti-Red" campaign. Though only bits and pieces of the Agronsky radio programs survive, a January 1952 recording contains the following remark, which shows little of the fear that silenced many of his colleagues during this period: "Copies of the Senate subcommittee report questioning the ethics and honesty of Wisconsin Senator McCarthy go to the Justice and Internal Revenue Departments today, where it will be seen if the government's federal agencies have any more courage than Mr. McCarthy's Senate colleagues" (courtesy of the Media Archives and Peabody Awards Collection, University of Georgia Libraries).

Agronsky's stance on McCarthyism caused a number of sponsors to pull their advertising from his program, and he received a substantial amount of hate mail, some of it anti-Semitic. At one point he was called to network headquarters, fully expecting to be fired. Struggling ABC, however, was in no position to lose an award-winning correspondent. According to the journalist's son, David Agronsky, "they instead congratulated him and took him to lunch," and Agronsky always considered his McCarthy broadcasts the accomplishment of which he was proudest. It is worth noting that Agronsky's radio challenge to McCarthy predated by two years the more widely remembered criticisms of McCarthy delivered on television by Edward R. Murrow of CBS.

With television now established as the nation's dominant public news medium, and ABC still lagging far behind its competitors, Agronsky left the network to rejoin NBC News in 1957. His reputation for accurate, insightful reporting continued to grow, His coverage of the nine-month Jerusalem trial of Nazi war criminal Adolf Eichmann, broadcast in segments on NBC's daily news program *The Huntley-Brinkley Report*, won him the Alfred I. DuPont Award. Moving to CBS News in 1964, he did stints for the network as its Paris bureau chief and as host of the Sunday interview series *Face the Nation*. His prime-time television documentary "Justice [Hugo] Black and the Bill of Rights" won an Emmy Award in 1968.

Having worked for all three commercial networks, however, Agronsky decided to look elsewhere to pursue the hard-hitting analytic journalism that he felt was missing from American television. In 1969 he took what seemed to be a backward career step by joining the news department of WTOP, a local Washington, D.C. station. He agreed to anchor WTOP's daily evening newscast in return for hosting a weekly series, *Agronsky and Company*, which he described as "a bull session among first-class reporters." The program debuted in October 1969, featuring Agronsky in dialogue with Washington columnists Hugh Sidey, Carl Rowan, and Pete Lisagor. In a matter of months the show was considered so successful by WTOP's owner, the Post-Newsweek Company, that Agronsky was released from his obligation to anchor the local news.

In 1971 Agronsky again broke with the conventions of American broadcast journalism by splitting his time between commercial and noncommercial television news operations. *Martin Agronsky: Evening Edition*, which aired daily on WETA from 1971 to 1974, was among the first daily news programs on American public television. Ironically, after decades of work on the three coast-to-coast networks, this local newscast did much to make Agronsky an influential national figure. As the succession of scandals known as Watergate broke, Agronsky became the key television voice that brought the news each day to the "inside-the-Beltway" audience. President Richard Nixon was an avid viewer, frequently having critical memos sent to Agronsky concerning the particulars of a broadcast.

Meanwhile, *Agronsky and Company* was developing into a local institution in Washington. "Everybody who is in public life watched Agronsky," Senator Edward Kennedy recalled. In 1976 the show went before a national audience. Under a novel syndication system, it was aired on Post-Newsweek's commercial stations and, where no such stations existed, on noncommercial PBS affiliates across the rest of the country. The series also indicated the shape of things to come in American journalism by turning relatively unknown print reporters into "media personalities." Agronsky regulars Sidey, Rowan, Lisagor, James Kilpatrick, Elizabeth Drew, and George Will all became household names and faces, with Will emerging as, perhaps, the first news analyst "superstar."

To many critics, this kind of media savvy is not normally thought of as compatible with journalistic excellence. However, Agronsky retained the high standards he had established early in his career. Reuven Frank, for many years the head of NBC News, admired the "low decibel" style that Agronsky maintained for himself and his opinionated guests, adding that the show's "repertory company had the assignment of covering a story for at least a couple of days that week. They knew what they were talking about, so you got more than their opinion." Presidents Jimmy Carter and Ronald Reagan were regular viewers, each making personal telephone calls on multiple occasions to Agronsky or his guests in direct response to remarks made on the program.

After more than a half century in print, radio, and television, Agronsky announced his retirement in 1988. He spent his retirement playing golf and pursuing personal interests. He was a founding trustee of the National Theatre Company in Washington and a member (and past president) of the Congressional Radio and Television Correspondents' Association. He died at his Washington home.

Though novel in format, *Agronsky and Company* proved to be the model for successful television news analysis programs, such as *The McLaughlin Group*, *The Capital Gang*, and many others. While *Agronsky and Company*'s national audience was commercially insignificant by mass broadcasting standards, the program's targeted demographic appeal presaged the cable era, winning it a fiercely loyal following among the group that would later be characterized as "news junkies." During the final broadcast of *Agronsky and Company*, columnist Tom Oliphant of the *Boston Globe* told the host, "You've been one of the few people who fought the battle for the news and for seriousness against commercialism and schlock."

• See Edward Bliss, Jr., *Now the News: The Story of Broadcast Journalism* (1992) for perspective on Agronsky's career.Detailed obituaries are in the *Washington Post*, 26 July 1999, the *New York Times*, 27 July 1999, and most major newspapers.

DAVID MARC

ALBERT, Carl (10 May 1908–4 Feb. 2000), politician, was born Carl Bert Albert in McAlester, Oklahoma, the son of Ernest Homer Albert, a coal miner and farmer, and Leona Ann Scott Albert. He attended a two-room school and worked in cotton fields, where he sometimes carried a sack under one arm and a book under the other. At McAlester High School he excelled as a debater, became president of the student body, and graduated in 1927. That year, Albert entered the University of Oklahoma, where he majored in political science and excelled as a public speaker, winning the National Oratorical Championship in 1928. Albert, who had arrived in Norman with just $20, waited tables and did odd jobs to finance his undergraduate education. After graduating Phi Beta Kappa in 1931, he studied on a Rhodes Scholarship at Oxford University, earning a B.A. in jurisprudence in 1933 and a B.C.L. a year later. He was admitted to the bar in Oklahoma in 1935 and practiced law in Oklahoma City.

Albert entered the U.S. Army Air Force in 1941. He served in the Pacific theater during World War II. By 1946 he had attained the rank of lieutenant colonel and won the Bronze Star. He married Mary Sue Greene Harmon in 1942; they had two children.

Having risen from poverty, Albert strove to expand economic opportunities for others. During the 1930s he identified himself as a New Deal Democrat. Albert won a seat in the U.S. House of Representatives in 1946, when Democrats were losing their long-held majority, and represented the western portion of Oklahoma for the next thirty years. A Cold War liberal, he backed President Harry S. Truman's policies to contain Soviet expansionism as well as such domestic measures as public power, public housing, farm price supports, and federal aid to education. Because his district was poor, Albert saw federal aid as a "deliverer," not a "demon" (Albert and Goble, p. 156). Devotion to district, party, and the House hierarchy defined Albert's early congressional career.

By the 1950s, Albert, known as the "Little Giant from Little Dixie," was emerging as a powerful member of the House. Representing a securely Democratic district, he gained seniority and caught the attention of Speaker Sam Rayburn of Texas, who made him majority whip in 1955. "I can tell big timber from small brush," Rayburn joked, in reference to Albert's five-foot, four-inch, 150-pound frame (*Washington Post*, 6 Feb. 2000). Quiet and self-effacing, Albert followed Rayburn's advice to "work hard, go along, and get along" (Peters, p. 158). The Speaker, in turn, remarked that nobody studied legislation as thoroughly as Albert. Yet others noticed a "certain smarminess" in the freckle-faced Oklahoman's "teacher's pet" demeanor that had "served him well on the way up" (Farrell, p. 264). Even as a schoolboy, Albert once admitted, he noted his instructors' "likes and dislikes" and then "told them what they wanted to hear" (Albert and Goble, p. 39).

Following Rayburn's death in 1961, John W. McCormack of Massachusetts became Speaker, and Albert succeeded McCormack as majority leader. In addition to handling the day-to-day chores of leadership, Albert, who sat on the Education and Labor Committee, worked to enact President Lyndon B. Johnson's Great Society legislation. Civil rights, a concern of liberals by the 1950s, vexed the Oklahoman, whose constituents were conservative on racial matters. He belatedly endorsed the weak Civil Rights Act of 1957, then played a major role in passing the landmark Civil Rights Act of 1964, siding with his party's national leadership against the wishes of white Oklahomans. The majority leader also rallied votes for the Economic Opportunity Act of 1964, which funded Johnson's War on Poverty. With Congress approving a spate of liberal reforms, Albert recalled his years as majority leader, from 1962 to 1971, as the most satisfying period of his career.

Yet there were lapses in Albert's leadership. Despite the large number of Native Americans in Oklahoma, he did not push "self-determination" for tribes. Listening to Indian leaders in his district, who had assimilated into Anglo society, Albert instead helped Native Americans advance economically and join the American mainstream. "Red Power" advocates, who wanted Indians to retain their unique identity, rejected such a policy. During the 1968 Democratic National Convention in Chicago, Albert was embarrassed when, standing at the podium, he failed to quiet rowdy delegates. President Johnson, watching the spectacle on television, immediately telephoned Dan Rostenkowski, a burly, jowly congressman from Chicago, who took the gavel from Albert's hand and brought the hall to order. In his personal life, Albert, a chronic worrier, suffered a heart attack in 1966 and drank heavily at Washington parties, though not at work. Nevertheless, he retained his leadership position and, following McCormack's retirement in 1971, became Speaker of the House.

Albert's tenure as Speaker, from 1971 to 1977, was a difficult one. President Richard M. Nixon often vetoed legislation passed by Congress, and House Democrats bickered among themselves. Older leaders, products of the existing seniority system, supported the U.S. war effort in Vietnam and remained conservative on race. Younger Democrats, critical of ongoing involvement in Vietnam and liberal on civil rights, wanted to diminish the power of committee chairs and open the House to new voices. Albert, a part of the established House hierarchy, a hawk on Vietnam, and a proponent of busing, chose to unite his party by stressing economics. But his championing of New Deal–like programs, including expanded public works and a higher minimum wage, underscored Albert's own seniority and lack of fresh ideas. The Speaker gradually sided with reformers by taking power from committee chairs, curtailing the seniority system, and opening committee proceedings to public scrutiny.

Watergate placed the Oval Office within Albert's reach. During the scandal, the United States was on two occasions without a vice president, making the Speaker first in line to become president. Following the resignation of Vice President Spiro T. Agnew in 1973, Nixon, in a fit of bipartisanship, purportedly offered the vice presidency to Albert, who declined the honor, affirming that his place was in Congress. When Vice President Gerald R. Ford became president following Nixon's resignation in 1974, the Speaker was again next in line to become president. As the crisis climaxed, with the House considering Nixon's impeachment, Albert won widespread praise by insisting that the president be treated fairly. Thereafter House Democrats tired of Albert's less-than-dynamic leadership.

Albert retired from Congress in 1977 and returned to McAlester, where he kept an office. His hometown named a parkway, a junior college, and a lake in his honor. The former Speaker wrote speeches and worked on his memoirs. He died in McAlester.

Albert took pride in his humble roots and liberal outlook. Like his successor, Speaker Tip O'Neill, he believed that all politics was local and that an active state, promoting economic opportunity, could enhance the station of poor Americans, whether northern or southern, white or black, Anglo or Indian. "Not as a matter of economics, nor logic, nor common decency, nor in fairness to future generations, can we justify excluding the American poor from the mainstream of American life," Albert told the House in 1964 (*Congressional Record*, 88th Cong., 2nd sess. [1964]: 18277). Upon his death, leaders in both parties lauded Albert's statesmanship.

• Albert's papers are housed at the Carl Albert Congressional Research and Studies Center, University of Oklahoma, Norman. Albert's memoir (with Danney Goble) is *Little Giant: The Life and Times of Speaker Carl Albert* (1990). A favorable view of Albert and Indian rights is W. Dale Mason, "The Carl Albert Collection: Resources Relating to Indian Policy, 1963–1968," *Chronicles of Oklahoma* (Winter 1993–1994), 422–37. A critical account is Dean J. Kotlowski, "Limited Vision: Carl Albert, the Choctaws, and Native American Self-Determination," *American Indian Culture and Research Journal* (2002). For Albert's relationship with his colleagues, see D. B. Hardeman and Donald C. Bacon, *Rayburn: A Biography* (1987); Tip O'Neill (with William Novak), *Man of the House: The Life and Political Memoirs of Speaker Tip O'Neill* (1987); John A. Farrell, *Tip O'Neill and the Democratic Century* (2001); and James M. Cannon, *Time and Chance: Gerald Ford's Appointment with History* (1994). Also valuable is Ronald M. Peters, Jr., *The American Speakership: The Office in Historical Perspective*, 2d ed. (1997). Obituaries are in the *New York Times* and the *Washington Post*, both 6 Feb. 2000.

DEAN J. KOTLOWSKI

ALLEN, Steve (26 Dec. 1921–30 Oct. 2000), comedian, author, songwriter, was born Stephen Valentine Patrick William Allen in New York City, the son of vaudeville comedians Carroll William Allen and Isabelle Donohue, who performed under the stage names Billy Allen and Belle Montrose. Literally born into show business, Allen toured the vaudeville circuit with his parents from infancy until his father died suddenly when Allen was only eighteen months old. Because his mother chose to continue her career, she left her young son in the care of her eccentric family in Chicago. In his first autobiography, *Mark It and Strike It* (1960), Allen characterized the Donohue family as "argumentative, popular, wild, and unruly. . . . The only thing that made the endless bickering at all tolerable was the sense of humor with which the family was blessed" (pp. 4–5). Despite Allen's unsettled childhood, during which he attended eighteen different public schools, he credited his years with the Donohues as being the foundation for his wry worldview and keen sense of comedy, which would serve him unfailingly throughout his life.

In 1941 Allen enrolled at Drake University on a journalism scholarship. But plagued by asthma, he transferred to Arizona State Teacher's College. However, he dropped out of school following his sophomore year to work as a wisecracking disk jockey at Phoenix radio station KOY. In 1942 Allen was drafted into the army but was soon discharged because of frequent asthma attacks. During his brief army service, he married his college sweetheart, Dorothy Goodman, with whom he was to have three sons. Allen re-

turned to KOY in 1943, expanding his radio presence to include duties as announcer, writer, producer, and music director. Throughout his years at KOY, Allen honed his abundant natural talent as an entertainer, which seemed to flow to him from an inexhaustible font of creativity.

In 1945 Allen gathered his family and his life's savings of $1,000 and moved to Los Angeles to try his luck on the national radio scene. After working as a disk jockey at two obscure stations, he successfully pitched his premise for a daily comedy show called "Smile Time" to the Mutual Broadcasting Company. At the end of his two years with Mutual, Allen felt as if he "had completed a four-year college course in radio comedy. I knew almost every old joke ever written, had learned how to write new jokes on every conceivable subject; and the business of performing five times a week had given a certain professional polish to my work" (*Mark It*, p. 123).

Allen gained serious notice in Hollywood in 1948 when he developed a program for CBS affiliate KNX in a new format called a "talk show." Given free creative reign, he cut back on recorded music, increased ad-lib comedy, read his mail on the air, and initiated celebrity interviews—one of the first major opportunities for stars to promote their own work on the air. On one memorable evening when scheduled guest Doris Day did not show up, Allen carried a heavy floor microphone into the standing-room-only studio audience and treated his listeners to twenty-five minutes of innovative banter with ordinary people. The show was a lights-out hit, and Allen had, in effect, invented modern talk radio. More importantly, he impressed CBS enough to invite its multitalented employee to New York for a shot at the new medium of television.

On Christmas Day, 1950, "The Steve Allen Show" debuted. In his trademark horn-rimmed glasses, Allen displayed his comedic and musical skills to rave reviews. He was soon invited to join the panel of the popular quiz show "What's My Line?" and he emceed a clever musical series called "Songs for Sale." The break that catapulted him to national prominence came in 1953 when NBC's New York flagship station WNBC asked Allen to host a live talk show from 11:30 p.m. to 1 a.m. Television experts predicted failure for this untried format, but they had not counted on the transcendent appeal of Allen's talent. With the same blend of piano music, informal banter, high-profile guests, and zany sketches punctuated by his cackling laugh that had captivated radio audiences, "The Steve Allen Show" became so popular in New York City that NBC decided to change its name to "Tonight" and broadcast it coast to coast beginning in the fall of 1954. The bedtime habits of millions of Americans were changed forever. Allen would do almost anything for a laugh. In perhaps his most memorable stunt during this experimental period, he rushed out of the Hudson Theatre dressed as a policeman, hailed a cab, threw a three-foot Hebrew National salami in the back seat, and ordered the startled driver to take it to Grand Central Terminal.

During Allen's years at the helm of "Tonight" (1954–1957), he introduced all the staples of the late-night talk show: the opening monologue, the studio orchestra with a flaky leader, the host's desk, the free-form interview, musical guests, and digressions into spontaneous comedy during goofy skits like "The Question Man," the "Man on the Street" interviews, and a regular spot called "Crazy Shots." Many of these serendipitous (and sometimes dangerous) stunts and set pieces influenced later network talk show hosts, including Johnny Carson, David Letterman, and Jay Leno. Allen also devoted time to serious subjects like the plight of migrant workers and the dangers of drinking and driving (he downed six double vodkas on that show to dramatize the point).

In his second autobiography, *Hi-Ho, Steverino* (1992), he proudly recounts the night he turned "Tonight" into a documentary on organized crime and the Mafia's impact on New York politics. A few nights later, Allen remembers, the mob sent thugs to the theater, slashed his car's tires, and released stink bombs in the balcony, which "resulted in one of the funniest shows we had done in months" (*Hi-Ho*, p. 138).

In 1952, while Allen's star was skyrocketing through the world of entertainment, his first marriage ended in divorce. In 1954 he finally stabilized his personal life when he wed renowned stage and screen actress Jayne Meadows, who became her husband's creative and business partner for the rest of his life. They would have one son.

In 1955, while still airing "Tonight" three evenings a week, NBC revived "The Steve Allen Show" on Sundays in prime time to compete with CBS's dominant "Ed Sullivan Show." In contrast to Ed Sullivan's wooden format, Allen's freewheeling style included gags like featuring 21-year-old Elvis Presley singing "Hound Dog" to a real basset hound. For three years, Allen matched Sullivan's ratings and helped launch the careers of Andy Williams, Steve Lawrence and Eydie Gorme, Don Knotts, Louis Nye (whose cheerful greeting "Hi-Ho, Steverino!" became a 1950s catch phrase), Tom Poston, the Smothers Brothers, Jackie Mason, Don Adams, Bill Dana, Jim Nabors, Jonathan Winters, and the Muppets. With all the pressure of starring in two network shows, Allen somehow still found time to play the title role in a feature motion picture, *The Benny Goodman Story* (1955), and managed to write half a dozen books and hundreds of original songs.

In 1960, after winning a Peabody award as creator of the best television comedy show, Allen left NBC. For the next seventeen years, he spread his endless creative energies all over the entertainment map. He produced another weekly comedy hour for ABC (1961–1962), and a late-night syndicated show from Hollywood (1962–1964); he hosted "I've Got a Secret" for CBS (1964–1967); performed with Meadows in several syndicated comedy shows from 1968 to 1972; and hosted the syndicated "Steve Allen's

Laughback" (1976–1977). During these prolific years, he also wrote a dozen more books, most notably *Letter to a Conservative* (1965), *A Flash of Swallows* (poetry, 1969), an illustrated children's book, *Princess Snip-Snip and the Puppykittens* (1973), and *Schmock! Schmock!* (1975). He wrote the music and lyrics for a Broadway musical, *Sophie* (1963), and produced an autobiographical play, *The Wake* (1971). He also became more socially active, authoring the pamphlet *Morality and War* (1961), confronting William F. Buckley in a series of debates, "Dialogues in Americanism" (1964), and turning his ongoing support for migrant farm workers into a respected book, *The Ground Is Our Table* (1966).

In 1977 Allen initiated his most ambitious project, the *Meeting of Minds* series, which he had been developing for eighteen years. The conceit was for actors, in a round table discussion, to portray famous personages throughout history. His purpose, he said in the introduction to volume two of the *Meeting of Minds* scripts (1979), was "to awaken greater popular interest in the great debates of our cultural, intellectual, theological, and political history" (pp. 2–3). Allen eventually wrote twenty-four one-hour scripts, produced by PBS, aired from 1977 to 1981, and published by Prometheus Books as a complete set in 1989. Spectacularly distinguished panels included Christopher Columbus, Karl Marx, Ulysses S. Grant, and Marie Antoinette; Martin Luther, Voltaire, Plato, and Florence Nightingale; and Frederick Douglass, dowager empress of China Tz'u-hsi, Cesare Beccaria, and the Marquis de Sade (discussing the topic of torture). Allen himself hosted all twenty-four programs, and Meadows played most of the female parts. The series received high critical praise, including Emmy, Peabody, and TV Critics Circle awards, and was endorsed by the National Education Association. Historian Will Durant called *Meeting of Minds* "a conception of originality and courage . . . a masterpiece of presentation."

Throughout the 1980s and 1990s Allen starred in television series including "The Steve Allen Comedy Hour" (1980–1981); "Life's Most Embarrassing Moments" (1984–1985); "Inside Your Schools" (1985); "Steve Allen's Music Room" (1984–1986); "The Start of Something Big" (1985–1986); and "Host-to-Host" (1989–1991); and he made guest appearances on many popular prime-time programs, including "Diagnosis Murder," "The Love Boat," "The Simpsons," and "St. Elsewhere." He and Meadows toured the country in A. R. Gurney's two-person play *Love Letters*, and he even acted the lead in Gilbert and Sullivan's *The Mikado* (1995).

Although Allen will be best remembered as a pioneering television personality, he had a generous gift for music. His training was limited to three years of piano lessons, and he never learned to read music. Nevertheless, he built a distinguished career as a composer, lyricist, pianist, conductor, and singer. Among his most recognized tunes are "This Could Be the Start of Something Big," "Gravy Waltz," "Pretend

You Don't See Her," and the Louis Armstrong holiday classic "Cool Yule." He wrote lyrics or music for many Hollywood films: the theme from *Picnic, Houseboat, On the Beach, Sleeping Beauty*, and *Bell, Book and Candle*. He also wrote the songs for CBS's acclaimed musical miniseries "Alice in Wonderland" in 1985, and that same year he composed "Ten Feet Tall," a march played each season for the enshrinees at the Professional Football Hall of Fame. Over the years, Allen produced more than seventy-five record albums and CDs, including the widely admired *Steve Allen Plays Jazz Tonight* (1993) and *The Songs of Steve Allen* (1996). He made hundreds of appearances with symphony and pop orchestras, many featuring his own compositions. Moreover, dozens of major artists have performed his music. The list includes Armstrong, Ella Fitzgerald, Bing Crosby, Judy Garland, Nat King Cole, Tony Bennett, Mel Tormé, Count Basie, Sarah Vaughan, and Aretha Franklin.

On top of all this activity, in the last twenty-five years of his life Allen greatly expanded his range as an author. He wrote a series of nine mystery novels, many centering on fictionalized versions of himself and his wife as amateur detectives. The books began with *The Talk Show Murders* (1982) and ended with *Murder in Hawaii* (1999). He published collections of short stories: *The Public Hating* (1990) and *The Man Who Turned Back the Clock* (1995). In a total departure from escapist fiction, in 1982 he penned *Beloved Son*, a sensitive personal reflection on his son Brian's venture into the world of religious cults.

Allen traveled widely, and inspired by Jayne Meadows's background in Asia as the daughter of missionaries, he wrote *Explaining China* (1980). He wrote more plays, a musical comedy called *Seymour Glick Is Alive but Sick* (1982), and another children's book, *The Bug and the Slug in the Rug* (1995). Naturally, he produced many books and articles on comedy, most notably *Funny Men* (1956), *Bigger than a Breadbox* (1967), *Funny People* (1981), *How to Be Funny* (1987), *Make 'Em Laugh* (1993), and *Steve Allen's Private Joke File* (2000).

Allen's astonishingly varied career is difficult to summarize. The long list of his accomplishments is almost as broad as it is deep, documented by a string of successes in almost every entertainment medium. He was fortunate enough to be present at the dawn of the Golden Age of television, but he took full advantage of this good fortune. He was one of the most durable personalities in the history of television, contributing regularly as a performer, writer, producer, and/or composer for nearly sixty years. He can justifiably be called the father of the television talk show, and he was equally comfortable interviewing Lincoln biographer Carl Sandburg, Bob Dylan, or beat comic Lenny Bruce.

His talent as a comedian was legendary, and he spread it thick on radio, television, in print, and on stage and screen. One of live television's first great ad-libbers, when someone in a studio audience once asked him, "Do they get your program in Boston?"

he quickly replied, "They see it, but they don't get it." Allen was inducted into the Television Academy's Hall of Fame in 1986, and the first telecast of the American Comedy Awards presented lifetime achievement awards to only five comics: Sid Caesar, Jonathan Winters, Mel Brooks, Woody Allen, and Steve Allen. Allen appeared in a dozen motion pictures, and he composed more than 9,000 songs, earning recognition by *Guinness Book of World Records* as the modern era's most prolific songwriter.

Yet this same man who could run around in a fake mustache crying, "Schmock! Schmock!" and who thought nothing of diving into a nine-foot bowl of Jell-O, could also host the Emmy Awards show, write snappy dialogue for the likes of Socrates, Aristotle, and Thomas Jefferson, and produce a treatise titled *Steve Allen on the Bible, Religion, and Morality* (1990). Allen maintained a strong social conscience throughout his career, passionately expressing his liberal views on issues such as civil rights, freedom of speech, capital punishment, and nuclear policy in a variety of major media outlets. When Jayne Meadows warned him that speaking out so publicly on political issues could hurt his television ratings, he said that he was more worried about the ratings of mankind.

In assessments of his complex legacy, Allen has been called "a one-man creative conglomerate," "the thinking man's comic," and "entertainment's renaissance man." Stories about him often quote his friend Andy Williams's aptly humorous remark: "Steve did so many things, he's the only man I know who's listed on every one of the Yellow Pages." Part of Allen's genius was undoubtedly his ability to work efficiently on many diverse projects at once, and everything he produced, from the broadest slapstick humor to the most scholarly essay or personal poem, displayed an insatiable curiosity grounded in a kind and unerring intelligence. Seemingly awed by the sheer volume of his achievement, Allen once mused, "The world has already let me do about 28 times more than I thought I was gonna be able to do at the age of 21—so, thanks to the universe" (CNN.com). In 1979, he told *People* magazine, "It kills me that someday I'll have to die. I don't see how I'll ever get it all done" (qtd. in Tresnioski and Weinstein). When he died in Encino, California, he had gotten most of it done.

• The scripts from Allen's early radio and television work are housed in the University of Southern California's Doheny Library, and many of the manuscripts of his books, articles, and songs are in Bowling Green University's Library of Popular Culture. Unfortunately, NBC destroyed thousands of its early kinescopes, films, and tapes, including most from the original "Tonight" show. The largest collection of Allen's extant tapes from radio and television, along with his personal papers, are owned by Meadowlane Enterprises, run by Allen's son Bill in Van Nuys, California. Some of its holdings are on deposit in the UCLA Film and Television archives. Allen wrote fifty-four books, including the posthumous *Vulgarians at the Gate: Trash TV and Raunch Radio* (2001), which expressed his dismay over the ugliness and immorality of much of popular culture. Not content to be just another critic of declining standards, Allen offers some eighty pages of remedies for coarsening entertainment values. Other socially conscious books by Allen are *Ripoff: The Corruption that Plagues America* (1979), *Passionate Nonsmokers' Bill of Rights* (1989), and *Dumbth: The Lost Art of Thinking* (1998). Allen is mentioned in many scholarly studies on the early history of television. See Harry Castleman and Walter J. Podrazik, *Watching TV: Six Decades of American Television* (2003), Richard Marschall, *The History of Television* (1986), and Gerald Nachman, *Seriously Funny: The Rebel Comedians of the 1950s and 1960s* (2003). Two of the best tributes to Allen are Larry Gelbart, "In Memoriam," *Emmy*, Dec. 2000, and Paul Kurtz, "A Tribute to Steve Allen," *Skeptical Inquirer*, Jan. 2001. See also Alex Tresnioski and Fannie Weinstein, "King of Comedy: A Prankster and a Poet, Steve Allen Pioneered the Wacky Late-Night TV Talk Show," *People Weekly*, 13 Nov. 2000. Obituaries are in the *Los Angeles Times* and the *New York Times*, both 1 Nov. 2000, and *Entertainment Weekly*, 10 Nov. 2000.

BRUCE L. JANOFF

ANFINSEN, Christian B. (26 Mar. 1916–14 May 1995), biochemist and Nobel laureate, was born Christian Boehmer Anfinsen, Jr., in Monessen, Pennsylvania, the son of Christian Boehmer Anfinsen, a mechanical engineer, and Sophie Rasmussen Anfinsen. Both parents were from Bergen, Norway, and taught Christian Jr. Norwegian customs and language. The family lived in Charleroi, a small town near Pittsburgh, until the 1920s when they moved to Philadelphia.

In 1933 Anfinsen entered Swarthmore College on a scholarship; there he played football and worked as a dining hall waiter. He received his B.S. in chemistry in 1937. In 1939 he earned an M.S. in organic chemistry from the University of Pennsylvania. That year he traveled to the Carlsberg Laboratory in Copenhagen on a fellowship to develop new ways of analyzing the chemical structure of complex proteins under the guidance of Kaj Ulrik Linderstrøm-Lang, whose lab was home to many innovators in protein chemistry. This fellowship was cut short by the onset of World War II.

In 1941 Anfinsen married Florence Bernice Keneger. They had three children. In 1943 he earned a Ph.D. in biological chemistry from Harvard. In 1943–1950 he was instructor and eventually assistant professor of biochemistry at Harvard Medical School. He also worked at Harvard in 1944–1946 for a study on malaria funded by the Office of Scientific Research and Development (OSRD), a temporary wartime agency.

Anfinsen left Harvard in 1950 (he returned for one year in 1962–1963) to work at the National Institutes of Health (NIH), where he became the chief of the Laboratory of Cellular Physiology of the National Heart Institute. Attracted by both the free time to pursue his scientific interests and the doubling of his salary, Anfinsen worked at NIH for the next thirty years, moving in 1963 to head the Laboratory of Chemical Biology at the National Institute of Arthritis, Metabolism, and Digestive Diseases.

At NIH he studied the amino acid structure of proteins, seeking to explain why proteins fold into distinct three-dimensional structures. Inspired by Frederick Sanger, a future Nobel laureate, Anfinsen applied Sanger's technique used to discover insulin's amino acid sequence to his own research on the three-dimensional structure of an enzyme and began experiments with bovine pancreatic ribonuclease (RNase, which breaks down RNA). Soon Anfinsen anticipated that Stanford Moore and William H. Stein, who were conducting similar research at the Rockefeller Institute, would determine the amino acid sequence of RNase first, which they did by 1960. Anfinsen concentrated on the ribonuclease's disulphide bonds. Observing the enzyme's ability to reform its structure after taking apart the bonds forcibly and then returning the enzyme to its original environment, he postulated that the protein's folding structure is entirely determined by its amino acid sequence. This breakthrough also yielded Anfinsen's thermodynamic hypothesis of protein folding, which explained the nature of a given amino acid structure: the shape of the protein that the amino acid structure created was a response to the thermodynamic stability of its environment. Fully formed by 1962, Anfinsen's ideas were first met with skepticism by the scientific community but later served as the foundation for which he, Moore, and Stein were awarded the 1972 Nobel Prize for chemistry.

In 1959 Anfinsen published *The Molecular Basis of Evolution*, which promoted the link between protein chemistry and molecular genetics and "the possibilities of integration of these fields toward a greater understanding of the fundamental forces underlying the evolutionary process" (Prologue, p. vii). The book, which included science, theory, and philosophy, showcased Anfinsen's ability to elucidate the larger implications of his research and that of his peers while also attempting to bring attention to his field, which lagged behind the more popular quest of cracking the DNA code.

After receiving the Nobel Prize, Anfinsen began work on interferon, a protein that stimulates the human body's attack on viruses and other disease agents. Using affinity chromatography, a technology he had used to great effect with the bacterium staphylococcus aureus (a common cause of food poisoning) in the 1960s, Anfinsen purified interferon to obtain large amounts of it and then determined its amino acid sequence. Based largely on his groundbreaking research, interferon became a major ingredient of drugs designed to fight certain cancers, tumors, and other serious illnesses.

By 1980 Anfinsen's professional and personal life had undergone serious changes. He divorced his wife in 1978 and married Libby Ester Shulman Ely the next year; they had no children. He also converted to Orthodox Judaism. Leaving the National Institutes of Health, Anfinsen went to work in Israel as the chief scientist at Taglit, a company formed by the business division of the Weizman Institute, where Anfinsen had been on the board of governors since 1962. Taglit's funding fell through, however, and the Anfinsens soon returned to the United States.

In 1982 Anfinsen accepted an offer to be a professor of biology at Johns Hopkins University. For the next twelve years, his research centered on pyrococcus furiosus, thermophilic bacteria that live in the ocean near tectonic plate vents. In a funding request letter, he wrote, "These crazy animals seem to enjoy life at 350° C and 300 atmospheres and should have some fascinating proteins and nucleic acids in them." His last work on these organisms was aimed at creating enzymes from the bacteria that could detoxify hazardous waste dumped in oceans.

Throughout his career, Anfinsen was a strong advocate of human rights, and he also engaged in political activism. He led a movement within the NIH in support of Nobel Laureate Linus Pauling's petition to ban atmospheric nuclear testing, which contributed to the 1963 Nuclear Test Ban Treaty. He wrote numerous letters attempting to gain better treatment of scientists in the Soviet Union, and he used his Nobel laureate status to implore President Richard Nixon to encourage greater scientific exchange between Soviet and American scientists. In 1981, he traveled to Argentina to rescue twelve scientists facing domestic coercion charges. From 1981 to 1989, Anfinsen was the chairperson of the National Academy of Scientists' Committee for Human Rights.

Anfinsen was an editor of *Advances in Protein Chemistry* and published over 200 scientific journal articles. He was awarded honorary degrees from more than ten universities. In his spare time, he played viola and piano. An avid and reputably fearless sailor, Anfinsen often sailed out on the Chesapeake Bay and along the East Coast. He remained active and professionally employed until his death. He died in Randallstown, Maryland.

Anfinsen expressed his views on concerns relating to ethical responsibility and science. In a speech about genetic engineering, he said, "The qualities that characterize and motivate a good scientist do not necessarily have any bearing on the ethical or sociological sequelae of discovery. An investigator who is worth his salt will attack an interesting problem for its own sake."

• Anfinsen's papers are in the History of Medicine Division Reading Room at the National Library of Medicine, Bethesda, MD. Overviews of his career can be found in *Nobel Prize Winners*, ed. Tyler Wasson (1987), pp. 24–26; *Notable Twentieth-Century Scientists*, ed. Emily J. McMurray (1995), pp. 53–54; and *Nobel Laureates in Chemistry* ed. Laylin K. James (1993), pp. 532–37. For professional and personal overviews see Evangelos N. Moudrianakis, an Anfinsen colleague at Johns Hopkins, "From Protein Coagulation and Reversible Denaturation to the Protein Folding Problem: Chris Anfinsen Defining the Tradition," *FASEB Journal* (Jan. 1996): 179–83; Alan N. Schechter, "Christian B. Anfinsen," *Structural Biology* (Aug. 1995): 621–23. An obituary also written by Evangelos N. Moudrianakis appeared in the *Independent* (London), 24 May 1995.

JOSH MCILVAIN

ATANASOFF, John Vincent (4 Oct. 1903–15 June 1995), inventor and computer scientist, was born near Hamilton, New York, the son of Ivan Atanasoff, a Bulgarian immigrant and self-taught electrical engineer, and Iva Purdy Atanasoff, a schoolteacher. John Atanasoff was precocious; by age nine he had corrected faulty home wiring, become fascinated with his father's slide rule and logarithms, and been tutored to college algebra–level mathematics by his mother. One of his mother's books introduced him to nondecimal number bases, a nontraditional concept that served him well later in his pursuit of automatic calculation. He attended Mulberry High School in Florida. In 1925 he received a B.S. degree in electrical engineering from the University of Florida and an M.S. in mathematics from Iowa State College (now Iowa State University) the following year. Also in 1926 he married Lura Meeks; they had three children and divorced in 1949. In 1949 he married Alice Crosby.

In 1930 Atanasoff completed his physics Ph.D. at the University of Wisconsin and returned to Ames to join the Iowa State faculty. Throughout his graduate years, he had found that solving simultaneous equations was an obstacle to his research. A mechanical calculator helped for simple formulas, but repetitive solutions proved to be prohibitively tedious. In investigating ways to automate this task, he became the first to distinguish between an "analog" computer (like a slide rule) and a "proper" (digital) computer. Analog devices he regarded as imprecise and too awkward for data input and output.

In late 1937, he experienced an epiphany involving several key novel ideas relating to automatic computing: all-electronic design for speed; binary arithmetic; logic operations for computing; separation of data and arithmetic; and low-cost dynamic storage. He also invented the concepts of a central clock synchronizing all operations, and the use of many processing elements operating in parallel for higher speed. As an electrical engineer he realized that vacuum tubes could function like electromechanical relays but faster and more reliably.

Atanasoff enlisted the help of a talented graduate student, Clifford Berry. Together they devised a prototype that operated on 12-bit numbers. In 1939, Atanasoff obtained funding from Iowa State College for a full-scale system, the Atanasoff-Berry Computer (ABC). The ABC had 50-bit (15-decimal) precision and enough parallel processors to solve twenty-nine equations simultaneously.

In 1940 Atanasoff met John Mauchly, a physics professor at Ursinus College in Pennsylvania, at a scientific conference. Mauchly told Atanasoff of his interest in using analog devices to analyze data to predict the weather. Atanasoff explained his work in building a computing device and invited Mauchly to Ames to see the ABC. In June 1941 Mauchly spent four days as Atanasoff's houseguest and learned about the ABC, including the concept of digital computing. Atanasoff told Mauchly not to reveal the concepts because the patent application had not yet been filed.

In the following months, Mauchly and Atanasoff exchanged letters about computing. Mauchly expressed interest in building an ABC variant at the University of Pennsylvania but failed to inform Atanasoff that he had secretly begun to build a much larger machine, the ENIAC, using U.S. Defense Department funding. By June 1942, Atanasoff went on leave to Maryland to direct the Naval Ordnance Laboratory, interrupting work on his computing project. His students scattered to start their own careers. Iowa State hired patent lawyer Richard Trexler to help Atanasoff complete the ABC patent application. The application required additional time and investment. Iowa State's unwillingness to spend funds stalled the patent application process, unknown to Atanasoff.

Atanasoff corresponded with IBM, suggesting that they consider using his ideas in their business machines. IBM's polite response was that they saw no future in electronic computing. Mauchly continued consulting Atanasoff about computing. In 1944, Mauchly revealed to Atanasoff that he was building an electronic computer but refused to elaborate. When the ENIAC was announced with great fanfare in 1946, Atanasoff suspected Mauchly had appropriated his ideas without permission or credit. The ENIAC developers filed several patents on the concept of electronic digital computing, which were granted seventeen years later to Sperry Univac Corporation, the ENIAC commercial descendant.

Iowa State's orphaned ABC was dismantled in 1947 to make room for another project. Only a memory drum and a logic unit were preserved (both now at the Smithsonian Institution in Washington, D.C.). On a 1948 visit to Ames, Atanasoff discovered the ABC had been destroyed, which ended his hope of resuming the patent process. He never returned to Iowa State. Instead he founded the Ordnance Engineering Corporation (1952), which in a short period employed 100 workers. In 1956 he sold it to Aerojet, where he served as vice president till 1961. From 1961 to 1982 he served as president of Cybernetics, Inc., in Frederick, Maryland.

In 1964, when Sperry demanded patent royalties from competitors, intellectual precedence issues resurfaced. Honeywell general counsel Henry Hanson recalled Atanasoff's work and enlisted Atanasoff as a witness in one of the longest and most expensive court cases in history. It ended in 1973, with Judge Earl Richard Larson concluding that ENIAC developers "did not themselves first invent the automatic electronic digital computer, but instead derived that subject matter from one Dr. John Vincent Atanasoff." There was no appeal. Sperry was denied patent rights, and as a result no one holds the patent on the invention of the electronic digital computer.

Atanasoff's contribution to computing was made independently of concurrent work on electromechanical computers by Howard Aiken at IBM, George Stibitz at Bell Labs, and Konrad Zuse in Germany. Zuse independently recognized the value of binary numbers, logic operations, and separate memory. Atana-

soff was first in realizing the advantage of all-electronic operation.

Atanasoff's limited budget forced him to find inexpensive ways to store data. The modern DRAM (dynamic random-access memory) is a direct descendant of the capacitor arrays he used in his computer. He was the first to refer to computer data storage as "memory." His economy also led him to find clever ways to use the same logic for multiple functions; consequently, the ABC required only 600 vacuum tubes. The complexity of Atanasoff's computer resembled that of the first commercial microprocessor, the Intel 4004.

Atanasoff had a restless, creative mind. He patented thirty-two diverse inventions. He recognized the need for a universal binary computer alphabet for all human languages, an idea that anticipated ASCII and Unicode. Atanasoff envisioned digital communication to avoid errors inherent in analog communication, another idea decades ahead of its time.

After the 1973 court decision, Atanasoff was belatedly recognized for his seminal work. He received Bulgaria's highest science award and was a member of the Bulgarian Academy of Science. He also was awarded four honorary degrees. Knowledge that the ENIAC developers claimed undue credit as innovators has slowly propagated through the scientific community. In 1990 President George H. W. Bush awarded Atanasoff the National Medal of Technology. Iowa State's Ames Laboratory completed a working replica of the ABC soon after Atanasoff's death in 1995.

Though trillions of times faster, modern computers stem from Atanasoff's original ideas. Communication of his ideas to the ENIAC developers led to one of the most contentious arguments in the history of inventions but resulted in an earlier start to the digital computer revolution than would have otherwise occurred.

• Atanasoff's own description of the ABC computer can be found in *The Origins of Digital Computers: Selected Papers*, edited by B. Randell (1982). A complete record of the court case exists in the archives at the Iowa State University Library. A detailed biography on Atanasoff is Clark Mollenhoff, *Atanasoff: Forgotten Father of the Computer* (1988). An account that emphasizes the issues of intellectual precedent of the ABC is provided by ENIAC engineer Arthur Burks and his wife Alice Burks in *The First Electronic Computer: The Atanasoff Story* (1988). A similarly hardware-centric article is "Dr. Atanasoff's Computer" in *Scientific American* (Aug. 1988). Many mysteries surrounding the ABC were solved only in the process of building its replica, and these are detailed in Raúl Rojas and Ulf Hashagen, eds., *The First Computers—History and Architecture*. The irony of the misplaced credit is continually rediscovered, as documented in Jeffrey Young's "John Vincent Atanasoff: Father of the Computer?" in *Forbes*, 7 July 1997. The *New York Times* and the *Washington Post* published Atanasoff obituaries on 17 June and 19 June 1995, respectively.

JOHN L. GUSTAFSON

AVERY, R. Stanton (13 Jan. 1907–12 Dec. 1997), inventor and entrepreneur, was born Ray Stanton Avery in Oklahoma City, Oklahoma, the son of Oliver Perry Avery, a Congregationalist minister, and Emma Dickinson Avery. Avery's early life was largely shaped by his family's religious and humanitarian interests. (Avery's mother was the daughter of a Congregationalist minister, and his brother became a minister.) Although "Stan" rebelled against the family profession, he continued to be drawn to its secular message. As a student at Pomona College from 1926 to 1932, he worked at a Los Angeles skid row mission. During a year-long trip to China (1929–1930), he spent several months at a missionary-run famine relief center. In 1932 he graduated from Pomona and took a job with the Los Angeles County Department of Charities. In later years he always insisted on the highest ethical standards in business relationships.

During the Great Depression, Avery was also attracted to various left-wing movements. "I was pretty radical in my thinking," he recalled (quoted in Clark, p. 10). His involvement in the People's Educational Center led to contacts with communists and other radicals. However, he gradually became disillusioned and by the late 1930s had disavowed communism and political activism in general.

By that time Avery had developed other interests that dominated his life. As a youth he had been fascinated by a small printing press his father used to publish sermons and church bulletins. At Pomona he was well known for his ad hoc inventions, such as a combination phonograph and alarm clock that enabled him to wake up to music. In 1933 his reputation as a tinkerer won him a job as production manager at the Adhere Paper Company, a small firm owned by a Pomona classmate. The company made self-adhesive signs and tags, and Avery was assigned to improve the primitive machinery.

Although Adhere Paper soon failed, Avery continued to experiment. He took a job at a Los Angeles nursery that allowed him to use its shop for his after-hours work. He borrowed $100 from his fiancée Dorothy Durfee and bought an old washing machine motor and other cast-off equipment and built a machine that combined paper and adhesive to make self-adhesive labels. Users did not have to glue or wet the labels. Durfee helped him sell these labels to gift and antiques shops. The response was encouraging, even though Avery's labels were more expensive than conventional labels. In 1935 Avery and Durfee married. They had three children. They gradually expanded sales to include drug, hardware, and furniture stores. By 1936 Avery was a full-time manufacturer with a small plant and several employees. He called his company Kum Kleen Products, later Avery Adhesives.

From the beginning Avery devoted most of his time to machinery and production problems. Apart from his fascination with mechanical devices, he had little interest in business and was too shy to make speeches or public appearances. Yet he recognized his limitations and recruited capable associates to handle the tasks he disliked. His wife performed those functions until their daughter was born in 1938. Avery then turned to Pomona classmates and friends. His most influential colleague, Russ Smith, was a Pomona graduate and a brother of one of Avery's classmates.

As the label business grew in the late 1930s and the early 1940s, Avery had to overcome formidable obstacles. In 1938, for example, his plant burned, destroying most of the machinery and materials. Fortunately Avery had recently purchased insurance and was able to save the stock of finished labels. While he continued to meet customers' needs, the insurance money allowed him to buy new and better machinery and improve his operations. Two years later he became involved in a patent fight with the Dennison Company, the leading manufacturer of gummed labels. Though Dennison eventually won the suit, Avery and the Dennison managers agreed to share the technology. As a result of these contacts, moreover, Dennison asked Avery to supply it with self-adhesive labels, which it later sold under its own brand name. Avery, who had feared that Dennison would force him out of business, now supplied materials to other manufacturers, an activity that soon overshadowed his own label business.

A few months later, after Pearl Harbor, Avery learned that his supply of synthetic rubber, a critical component of adhesive, would be cut off because his operation was not essential to the war effort. He recalled: "I literally broke down. I cried. I couldn't even talk. That was probably the company's lowest point" (quoted in Clark, p. 24). Again, however, an apparent setback led to new opportunities. Avery developed a series of industrial labels applicable to war production and found new markets. He built a new plant in 1942 and by 1945 had fifty employees.

At the end of the war Avery quickly positioned his company to take advantage of its enhanced position. In 1946 he incorporated the firm as the Avery Adhesive Label Company and hired Russ Smith as general manager. Smith had a varied background in finance and marketing and became the architect of the company's organizational evolution. Together Avery and Smith recruited other executives, many with ties to Pomona College, and gave them wide latitude in managing the business. Avery continued to devote most of his attention to technical issues, accumulating many patents, but his influence extended to every facet of the company's operations. The firm's informal atmosphere, devotion to quality and service, and technical leadership were examples of his impact.

The Avery Company's postwar expansion was largely based on two strategic initiatives: a growing emphasis on production for other manufacturers (institutionalized in 1954 with the creation of the Fasson Division for this purpose, located in Painesville, Ohio), and a larger international presence, primarily in Europe. Avery left the implementation of these policies to Smith and other executives, though in 1958, when the Fasson managers plotted to buy out the division, Avery moved to Painesville for a year, put down the rebellion, and installed new managers.

Charles D. Miller, the manager of European operations in the 1960s, eventually succeeded Avery and Smith as chief executive.

In the 1960s Avery boasted that his company would not follow others in diversifying and artificially accelerating its growth. In fact it expanded rapidly and developed a broad and diverse product line. When the energy crisis and severe recession of the mid-1970s hobbled many fast-growing corporations, Avery suffered a humiliating setback. By 1975 it had too much production capacity, shrinking profits, and a collapsing stock price. Anticipating retirement, Avery had already begun to turn over his responsibilities to Miller. The crisis reinforced his desire to leave and to insist that Smith step down as well. Miller renamed the company Avery International in 1976 and merged it with Dennison to create Avery Dennison in 1990.

By the 1970s Avery had become a well-known community figure in southern California. In retirement he was an active fundraiser for Pomona College and for the California Institute of Technology, and he served on the boards of the Huntington Library and the Los Angeles Museum of Art. His wife died in 1964, and in 1965 he married Ernestine Onderdonk. Avery died in Los Angeles.

• Avery's business career is summarized in a company-sponsored history, David L. Clark, *Avery International Corporation 50-Year History, 1935–1985* (1988), and in a booklet, R. Stanton Avery and Charles D. Miller, *Avery International: Fifty Years of Progress* (1985). He was one of the subjects of a feature article in the *New York Times,* 29 July 1979. An obituary is in the *New York Times,* 22 December 1997.

DANIEL NELSON

B

BAD HEART BULL, Amos (01 Jan. 1869?–1913), folk artist, was born on the Pine Ridge Indian Reservation in what is now Wyoming, the son of Bad Heart Bull (the elder). His mother's name is unknown. Amos, also known as Eagle Lance, Amos Bad Heart Buffalo, Amos Bad Heart Buffalo Bull, and Tatanka Cante Sice, was also the nephew of Sioux chief He Dog and cousin of the renowned Sioux warrior Crazy Horse.

Bad Heart Bull's relatives said that he "had no schooling. His education was almost entirely that which he received, after the manner of primitive tradition from his father and uncles" (Blish, p. 8). His father and uncles (He Dog, Only Man, Little Shield, and Short Bull) were warlike, unwilling to accommodate themselves to the encroaching whites and the U.S. government, and his father was with Crazy Horse at the Battle of Little Bighorn in 1876 when General George Armstrong Custer and 200 soldiers were killed. The Sioux also engaged in internecine wars with other tribes, most notably the Crows and Shoshones. However, Amos Bad Heart Bull was too young to take part in the last wars with enemies, both white and other tribes, and his temperament was more contemplative. In addition, the 1890 massacre of Sioux tribesmen, including women and children, at Wounded Knee, South Dakota, marked the end of the Indian Wars.

Amos Bad Heart Bull had several occupations, including cowboy, Indian policeman, army scout, and tribal historian, but it is for his drawings and paintings of tribal life and events of the Oglala Sioux during a period of dramatic change that he is principally remembered. This artwork now exists only in reproduction; the original notebook containing the drawings was interred with the body of his sister Dollie (Mrs. William) Pretty Cloud, who died in 1947, in accordance with tribal custom, and the sister's family refused repeated requests by historians for exhumation in order to retrieve the ledger. Fortunately, University of Nebraska Native American art historian Hartley Burr Alexander had photographed each page of the notebook twenty years before, and it is these black-and-white and color images that were assembled by Alexander's one-time graduate student Helen Blish into a book published in 1967 by the University of Nebraska Press, *A Pictographic History of the Oglala Sioux.*

Bad Heart Bull taught himself to draw, as well as to read and write (in both English and Lakota). The Sioux had a long and lively tradition of "picture-writing," telling the story of the tribe in its great and small events, rituals, and celebrations through pictures that were often painted or etched on rocks (pictographs). In many instances, these pictographs served as calendars. Although the U.S. government increasingly forbade the age-old rituals, Bad Heart Bull sought out the stories of his tribe, encouraged by his uncles who longed for the old buffalo hunting days.

Where he distinguished himself from earlier pictographers was his detachment, artistic skills, and interest in documenting a way of life that he understood was waning. Bad Heart Bull's contribution was to instinctively assume the role of anthropologist, who, with insider knowledge, expressed his views through graphic arts. He used a variety of materials over the years—pencils and brushes, crayons, colored ink and watercolors—that were likely taken from army supplies or that he may have purchased on his own.

His active artistic career dates from 1890, when he enlisted as a scout in the U.S. Army at Fort Robinson, Nebraska. It was then that he bought from a clothing dealer in Crawford, Nebraska, a used ledger that had originally contained 300 pages. He filled up this notebook with more than 400 pictures (half of the drawings were on other sheets of paper inserted into the notebook) of his tribe's daily life, its celebrations, and past exploits based on his own observations and what others told him over the remaining twenty-three years of his life. Along with the drawings, Bad Heart Bull wrote sometimes lengthy captions that described what was taking place.

Perhaps because of his concomitant membership in the tribe and service in the army, he developed an understanding not only of his native people but of how these natives were perceived by the larger, increasingly white society. Bad Heart Bull began to collect treaties involved in Indian-federal government relations—probably to develop his own understanding of recent American Indian history—but his artwork and captions chronicled his native people.

Bad Heart Bull's drawings differed from other Sioux pictographs in a number of respects: the first is the quantity of cultural and historical detail. Rather than freeze a particular moment, he told an entire story in a drawing. His depiction of the death of Crazy Horse, for instance, shows Crazy Horse and others at the guard house where the Sioux warrior was stabbed in the back. These figures were placed at the center of the image in close-up, while soldiers in formation and Sioux tribesmen are shown in miniature and at more than one vantage point. Piecing together the various elements in the image, the viewer identifies the story of what brought Crazy Horse to Fort Robinson and how a misunderstanding led to his death. Bad Heart Bull's drawing was realistic, moving beyond the

stylized figures of much tribal and primitive art to capture the personalities of specific people. His work was
also unique in his balanced composition, use of color,
and sense of perspective (often slightly to the side and
above the heads of the individuals depicted, sometimes directly overhead). These drawings and paintings, however, are not championed by art historians
but by sociologists who find that his images corrob-
orate other evidence about Sioux tribal life.

Like the original art itself, much of the history of
American Indians and of Amos Bad Heart Bull is interred with their bones. In his patrilineal society, we
know the name of his father but not his mother; the
year of his birth is only approximate, and there was
no obituary. Bad Heart Bull is remembered solely for
his drawings, saved from oblivion by a few scholars
who saw in them something unique and valuable.

• Apart from Helen Blish's *A Pictographic History of the
Oglala Sioux* (1967), there is little written about Amos Bad
Heart Bull, although he is the subject of brief entries in a
number of publications. Among these are Hartley Burr Al-
exander, *Sioux Indian Painting* (1938); J. J. Brody, *Indian
Painters and White Patrons* (1971); Frederick J. Dockstader,
Great North American Indians: Profiles in Life and Leadership
(1977); Dorothy Dunn, *American Indian Painting of the
Southwest and Plains Areas* (1968); Oscar B. Jacobson and
Jeanne d'Ucel, *American Indian Painters* (1950); Patrick Lester, *The Biographical Directory of Native American Painters*
(1995); Mari Sandoz, *These Were the Sioux* (1961); and
Jeanne O. Snodgrass, *American Indian Painters: A Biograph-
ical Directory* (1968).

DANIEL GRANT

BARBONCITO (before 1825–16 Mar. 1871), Navajo headman, was born in lower Canyon de Chelly,
Arizona, to a Navajo woman of the Ma'iides- gizhnii
(Coyote Pass or Jemez clan) and an unknown father.
His war name was Hashke Yich'i'adehyilwod, "He
Ran Down toward the Enemies in Anger." He was
also known by a number of sobriquets during his lifetime, one of which, Hastiin Daghaa'i, "Mr. Mustache," gave rise to his Spanish-English name. Little
is known of his early life except that he had at least
three brothers. He had two wives; how many children
is not recorded.

While the names Barboncito, Barbon, and El Barbon, variants of a not uncommon name in Navajo,
lead to some uncertainty in identifying individuals in
the historic record, Barboncito appears to have
achieved some prominence by the early 1850s. He is
said to have gained recognition as a warrior while he
was young, but he was better known for his eloquence
as an orator and as an advocate of peace in his later
years. He knew various ceremonies, including Bless-
ingway and Evilway.

Barboncito is known to have attended several meetings of headmen with government officials, including
visits to Santa Fe. In 1853 he was reported living at
Encino Gordo on the Chinle Wash, about midway between Canyon de Chelly and the San Juan River. He
was probably one of the seven Navajo headmen who

received medals from Governor David Meriweather
in Santa Fe in 1853.

In 1858 the Navajo and the military at Fort Defiance became embroiled in a dispute, and the soldiers
killed some livestock belonging to the headman Manuelito. At Manuelito's request, Barboncito traveled to
Santa Fe to obtain compensation for the lost animals.
Barboncito's efforts failed, and relations between the
tribe and the whites led to open hostilities in the same
year. Dixon S. Miles led a campaign in a war for which
neither the army nor the Navajo were prepared. Both
sides were nearing exhaustion when Barboncito approached Miles near the mouth of Canyon de Chelly
and requested peace. Seven days later a truce was negotiated near Fort Defiance, and Barboncito was one
of those who signed on behalf of the tribe. A treaty
was concluded on Christmas day, but a severe snowstorm prevented Barboncito's presence.

The following year was one of uncertainty and
preparations for war on both sides. Barboncito, then
living at Pueblo Colorado near present-day Ganado,
worked to preserve peace, but to no avail. War resumed early in 1860. In May the Navajo, reportedly
organized by Herrero and Barboncito, attacked Fort
Defiance in force. But Barboncito soon realized the
futility of the war, and in June and July he made unsuccessful attempts to open negotiations for peace. As
the war was winding down later in the year, the government tried to identify the various Navajo leaders,
and they drew up lists including the names Barbon
and Barboncito. Early in February 1861 a treaty at
Fort Fauntleroy (present-day Fort Wingate) was
signed by forty-eight headmen, among whom were
several named Barbon and Barboncito. Either a "Barbon de Chelli" or a Barboncito may have been the
well-known leader.

The peace negotiated at Fort Fauntleroy was tenuous, disrupted in part by the beginning of the Civil
War, the closing of several forts in or near Navajo
country, and the incursion of raiders from New Mexico seeking livestock and captives who could be sold
as slaves in the settlements. In May 1862 two Navajo
envoys were sent by the "principal chiefs," identified
as Armijo, Cayetano, and Barboncito, under a flag of
truce to ask for peace. The same leaders sent another
delegation to Cubero in August. The bands of these
headmen were reported to have separated from the
rest of the tribe and to have remained at peace since
1861. The Navajo agent John Ward tried to settle
these bands near Fort Wingate in November. James
H. Carleton, recently appointed military commander
in New Mexico, in December met in Santa Fe with
Barboncito and Delgadito and informed them that, if
they desired peace, they must relocate to Fort Sumner
at the Bosque Redondo on the Pecos River. They refused this request, as they did similar repeated demands by Carleton in the spring and summer of 1863.

Eventually Carleton ordered Christopher "Kit"
Carson to suppress the Navajo, but Barboncito and
his associates appear to have moved south to the Datil
and Rito Quemado region in hopes of avoiding the

war. However, in September Pueblo Indians attacked the Navajo and subsequently claimed to have killed a Barboncito, probably a mistaken identity. In the following month a delegation including Barboncito's brother Sordo arrived at Fort Wingate and offered to assist the army in catching thieves and rebels, probably Navajo of other bands.. Carleton, however, refused to exempt these Navajo from the punitive military campaign. The Navajo finally sent a delegation to Fort Sumner to observe conditions there. About the same time troops operating near Rito Quemado attacked some Navajo and killed Sordo.

In February 1864 a man identified by government officials as "Barbon No. 2" visited Fort Canby and, after consulting with Herrero, decided to bring his people in to surrender. Whether or not he did so is not known, and whether or not he was the same man as Barboncito is uncertain. In May a report from Fort Canby noted that El Barbon No. 1 and El Barbon No. 2, sons of "old Barboncito or Cla," were waiting to be sent to Fort Sumner. In August a detachment of troops encountered Barboncito on his way from Canyon de Chelly to Fort Canby and escorted the group to the fort, from whence they were soon sent on to Fort Sumner.

In July, during a council held as part of an investigation of conditions at Fort Sumner, several Navajo leaders presented their complaints. Barboncito, the last called upon, compared the sterility of the land, water, and vegetation with the productivity of the Navajo country, saying: "I own nothing but my own body. I have no stock. Before I get too old, I would like to see my children in their old country as they were before." Nothing came of this meeting.

In April 1868 Barboncito was a member of a group who visited Washington to present its case to President Ulysses S. Grant. Late in May General William T. Sherman and Colonel Samuel Tappan negotiated the final Navajo treaty. Barboncito was the spokesperson for the Navajo in these negotiations. Chosen for his eloquence, Barboncito described the injunctions and values of Navajo religious beliefs, the harsh realities of exile and captivity, and the Navajo hopes and desires for a future of peace and prosperity. Even the skeptical Sherman found these arguments persuasive, and the commissioners agreed to allow the Navajo to return to their land. The treaty was signed on 1 June 1868. Seventeen days later the Navajo began the journey home.

The return to Navajo country took place too late for planting in the high desert, and the people were forced to rely on rations, wild foods, and the help of some Navajo who had maintained herds in the farthest reaches of their lands. For several years the struggle to overcome their poverty led to more raids to steal livestock.

Barboncito, who had been appointed head chief, was expected to keep the peace despite raids by the Utes and conflicts with Hispanic settlers moving westward in New Mexico and Mormons expanding their frontiers to the south in Utah. In addition Navajo families wanted the return of their women and children who were being held as servants in New Mexico. Despite his declining health, Barboncito lectured his people to control raiding. He also went on expeditions to restrain those who would steal livestock, to seek return of captive relatives, and to negotiate peace with representatives of the Mormons. Finally, following an illness of over eighty days, Barboncito died. The place of his death is not known with certainty.

• The most productive sources for information on Barboncito's life are the Correll papers in the Navajo Nation Library in Window Rock, Arizona, and the records of the War Department and the Bureau of Indian Affairs in the National Archives in Washington, D.C. J. Lee Correll, *Through White Men's Eyes: A Contribution to Navajo History* (1979), is the most thorough compilation of both documentary and contemporary published sources. Correll, "Barboncito–Navajo Naat'aanii," *Navajo Times Tourist Edition* (1966), pp. 28 ff., is the best published biography, despite its brevity. The chapter on Barboncito in Virginia Hoffman, *Navajo Biographies* (1974), is overly popularized. Richard F. Van Valkenburgh, "Navajo Naat'aani," *Kiva*, vol. 13 (1948): 14–23, provides data on native names but errs in the date of Barboncito's death. More extensive Navajo oral tradition is in Broderick H. Johnson, ed., *Navajo Stories of the Long Walk Period* (1973). Lawrence Kelly, *Navajo Roundup* (1970), presents complete transcripts of much of the correspondence of the Carson campaign and is a useful source on that period, while Gerald Thompson, *The Army and the Navajo: Bosque Redondo Reservation Experiment, 1863–1868* (1976), has detailed data on the Fort Sumner exile. Several sources describe the negotiations of the final treaty. The most complete is Correll (1979), cited above, which in vol. V includes sources on events leading up to the negotiations (pp. 23–35), the negotiations (pp. 35–46), proceedings of the council (pp. 129–39), and the text of the treaty (pp. 91–100). A somewhat imaginative account of Barboncito's meeting with a representative of the Mormons is in Paul Bailey, *Jacob Hamblin, Buckskin Apostle* (1948).

DAVID M. BRUGGE

BARNETT, Jackson (01 Jan. 1856?–29 May 1934), wealthy American Indian, was born in the Creek Nation, Indian Territory, the son of Siah Barnett, an African-Creek farmer, and Thlesothle, a Creek woman. During his childhood the Civil War violently split the Creek people, and the countryside was ravaged. Siah Barnett fled to Kansas with the Loyal Creeks. Thlesothle died in a refugee camp near Fort Gibson as the war ended. Given into the care of maternal relatives, the orphaned Jackson spent much of his youth and early adulthood transporting people and goods across the Arkansas River at John Leecher's ferry above Muskogee. While working as a ranch hand, Barnett fell from a horse and sustained a head injury. In the 1880s or early 1890s, Barnett relocated westward to the central Creek Nation, where he built a small cabin and established himself in a network of paternal kin. A shy man with a beaming smile, Barnett formed no romantic relationships with women. He spoke both English and Creek, but he had no schooling and led an obscure life as an unskilled laborer.

The Curtis Act of 1898, which forced the partition of communally held Creek lands and resources and subordinated the Indians to the state of Oklahoma, resulted in the dissolution of the Creek Nation. These were hard times. Between 1895 and 1912 Barnett, who owned little more than a horse and a saddle, became a homeless, itinerant laborer moving from farm to farm among Creek friends and relations. He was among the Creeks who supported the failed uprising led by Chitto Harjo (Crazy Snake) between 1900 and 1909 to restore treaty-based sovereignty and to block the division of Creek lands. In 1903 Barnett received title to 160 acres in Creek County, Oklahoma, as his share of the Creek estate, but he had little understanding or regard for private landownership; the deed was filed under the roof of his employer's shed. In 1906 Congress passed the Burke Act to protect vulnerable Indians like Barnett. According to this act's provisions, the Interior Department assumed managerial responsibility for "restricted" Indians, holding their property in trust.

In 1912 the discovery of the Cushing oil field in Creek County brought a dramatic reversal in Barnett's fortunes. The Interior Department supervised the negotiation of a lucrative oil lease on his behalf, but only after his mental competency was contested by self-interested parties in politicized hearings. The Okmulgee County Court succeeded in establishing jurisdiction, and a local guardian was appointed to oversee the affairs of the "incompetent" Barnett. A homestead was purchased for Barnett outside Henryetta suitable to his modest needs. During World War I rising demand for oil and spectacular strikes in the Cushing field brought Barnett's fortune to $47,000 a month, and he was crowned the "wealthiest Indian in the world" by the *New York Times*. The Barnett fortune, roughly equivalent to $30 million in 2002 dollars, was a magnet for dozens of schemers, including those empowered as his guardians. Childless and illiterate, the elderly Barnett was described by federal judge John Knox as the "shuttledore in a game of battlecock, in which the stakes were high" (*Barnett v. Equitable*, 1927). In 1919 lobbying efforts from Oklahoma churches to convey Barnett's "surplus" funds to philanthropic purposes met with the approval of the Indian Bureau. Plans for the Jackson Barnett Hospital in Henryetta, however, were suspended when the gold digger Anna Laura Lowe (1881–1952) persuaded the compliant Barnett to marry her after one meeting. Failing to secure a wedding license in Oklahoma, the couple was married on 23 February 1920 in Coffeeville, Kansas. They had no children from this marriage. Efforts by the Indian Bureau and the Oklahoma guardian to nullify the marriage were unsuccessful. In late 1922, with Barnett's approval, Commissioner of Indian Affairs Charles Burke, arch foe of the Oklahoma guardianship system, brokered an agreement in which two trusts were created, splitting the estate between Anna Barnett and Bacone Indian College, a Northern Baptist institution.

The Barnetts, freed from the Oklahoma guardian, immediately relocated to Los Angeles, California. A colonial-style mansion on Wilshire Boulevard in the elegant Hancock Park neighborhood, befitting the millionaire Indian, became the Barnetts' new home. During his last years Barnett enjoyed a comfortable standard of living, engaging in his favorite pastimes of riding ponies and directing traffic at the busy intersection opposite his home. The genial, wealthy Indian became a Los Angeles icon.

From 1923 to 1929 a whirlwind of controversy swirled around the legitimacy of the Indian Bureau's action in creating the trusts. Vigorous opposition came from Barnett's Creek relatives (for whom no provision had been made) as well as Barnett's guardian, politicians, lawyers, and judges within Okmulgee County, who believed the federal government had overstepped its authority by giving away the estate of a mentally enfeebled Indian to a woman of poor moral character. These disgruntled Oklahomans generated a storm of litigation over the trusts and instigated a sequence of humiliating congressional investigations into the Burke administration's mismanagement of Indian affairs. The educational endowment to Bacone was revoked after Barnett was judged incompetent by a 1927 federal court decision, *Barnett v. Equitable*. Another federal court ruling annulled the Barnetts' fourteen-year consensual marriage and denied Anna Barnett any right to Jackson Barnett's property, including the family home. Soon afterward Jackson Barnett died in Los Angeles. The estate was divided among approximately three dozen Creek claimants and their lawyers.

Barnett achieved celebrity status in the popular culture for his fairy-tale life as a fabulously wealthy Indian, and the saga of his contested fortune made his story the most significant Indian policy case of the 1920s. This simple, imperturbable man was the still center of a violent struggle pitting the Justice Department against the Interior Department and federal power against state power. The Barnett scandal brought intense public scrutiny to many undemocratic aspects of law and policy, such as the Indian Bureau's abuse of authority over restricted Indians' property, which was underpinned by the belief in Indians' cultural and intellectual inferiority. The battle over Barnett's fortune emblematized the way law and prejudice combined to permit the legal robbery of Indians' lands and resources nationally in the postallotment era. The notorious Barnett case added considerable momentum to the reform spirit building in Congress in the 1920s that culminated in the reform legislation of the Indian New Deal in the 1930s.

• The richest sources for Barnett's life are government documents, especially those preserved in Record Groups 21, 48, 60, 75, and 118, depositions, exhibits, newspaper articles, and other primary documents, that are part of the public record in the extensive litigation over the Barnett fortune. They are held in facilities of the National Archives and Records Administration in Fort Worth, Texas, Laguna Niguel, California, College Park, Maryland, and New York City. Another excellent source is the Justice Department's exhaustive research published in the U.S. Senate Subcommittee on Indian Affairs's *Survey of Conditions of the Indians in the United States*, 70th Congress, 2d sess. (microfilm; 1928–1944). Relevant court decisions available online include two Supreme Court opinions at FindLaw (see links below) and various others through the subscription-based service LexisNexis, including *United States v. McGugin* (1928), Lexis 1441; *United States v. McGugin* (1940), Lexis 3628; *Barnett v. Equitable* (1927), Lexis 1374; and *United States v. Mott* (1929), Lexis 1309.

Tanis C. Thorne, *The World's Richest Indian: Jackson Barnett* (in press), assesses Barnett's place in transforming twentieth-century Indian policy and law. A thumbnail sketch of Barnett is Donald Fixico, "Jackson Barnett and the Allotment of Muscogee Creek Lands," in *The Invasion of Indian Country in the Twentieth Century: American Capitalism and Indian Natural Resources* (1998). Barnett's first biographer, Benay Blend, framed the Barnett case's significance in terms of its reform of the Oklahoma probate system in "Jackson Barnett and the Oklahoma Indian Probate System" (master's thesis, Univ. of Texas at Arlington, 1978). A shorter article by Blend was published under the same title in *Essays in History: E. C. Barksdale Student Lectures* 7 (1978–1979): 5–39. The first historical assessment of Barnett was a brief analysis in Angie Debo, *And Still the Waters Run: The Betrayal of the Five Civilized Tribes* (1940; repr., 1984), which contextualizes the case in terms of Oklahoma's sad history of exploitation of the Five Civilized Tribes.

TANIS C. THORNE

BATES, Peg Leg (11 Oct. 1907–8 Dec. 1998), tap dancer, was born Clayton Bates in Fountain Inn, South Carolina, the son of Rufus Bates, a laborer, and Emma Stewart Bates, a sharecropper and housecleaner. He began dancing when he was five. At twelve, while working in a cotton-seed gin mill, he caught and mangled his left leg in a conveyor belt. The leg was amputated on the kitchen table at his home. Although he was left with only one leg and a wooden peg leg his uncle carved for him, Bates resolved to continue dancing. "It somehow grew in my mind that I wanted to be as good a dancer as any two-legged dancer," he recalled. "It hurt me that the boys pitied me. I was pretty popular before, and I still wanted to be popular. I told them not to feel sorry for me." He meant it. He began imitating the latest rhythm steps of metal tap shoe dancers, adding his own novelty and acrobatic steps. He worked his way from minstrel shows and carnivals to the vaudeville circuits. At fifteen, after becoming the undisputed king of one-legged dancers, able to execute acrobatic, graceful soft shoe and powerful rhythm-tapping all with one leg and a peg, he established a professional career as a tap dancer.

In 1930, after dancing in the Paris version of Lew Leslie's *Blackbirds of 1928*, Bates returned to New York to perform as a featured tap dancer at such famous Harlem nightclubs as the Cotton Club, Connie's Inn, and the Club Zanzibar. On Broadway in the 1930s, he reinvented such popular tap steps as the Shim Sham Shimmy, Susie-Q, and Truckin' by enhancing them with the rhythmic combination of his

deep-toned left-leg peg and the high-pitched metallic right-foot tap. As one of the black tap dancers able to cross the color barrier, Bates joined performers on the white vaudeville circuit of Keith & Loew and performed on the same bill as Bill "Bojangles" Robinson, Fred Astaire, and Gene Kelly. In 1949 Bates sang and danced the role of the swashbuckling pirate Long John Silver in the musical review *Blackout*s. "Don't give up the ship, although you seem to lose the fight; life means do the best with all you got, give it all your might," he sang in the Ken Murray musical that played for three years at the Hollywood and Vine Theatre in Hollywood, California. Wearing a white suit and looking as debonair as Astaire, Bates made his first television appearance in 1948 on "This Is Show Business" (a show hosted by Clifton Fadiman and Arlene Francis), performing high-speed paddle-and-roll tapping and balancing on his rubber-tipped peg as though it were a ballet pointe shoe. On the *Ed Sullivan Show* on television in 1955, Bates strutted his stuff as he competed in a tap challenge dance, countering Hal LeRoy's wiggly steps with airy wing steps. "You're not making it easy," Bates chided as he tossed off heel clicks and soared into a flash finish with trenches (where the body leans forward on the diagonal and the legs kick high to the back). Bates made over twenty appearances on the *Ed Sullivan Show*, last appearing in a tap challenge dance with "Little Buck" on 22 August 1965.

While television gave him greater fame than ever before, Bates continued to pursue a variety of performance venues. In 1951 he invested his earnings and with his wife, Alice, purchased a large turkey farm in New York's Catskill Mountains and converted it into a resort. (The date of his marriage to Alice is not known; it lasted until her death in 1987. They had one child.) The Peg Leg Bates Country Club, in Kerhonkson, New York, flourished as the largest black-owned-and-operated resort in the country, catering to a largely black clientele and featuring hundreds of jazz musicians and tap dancers. "During the prejudice years, country clubs were not integrated," said Bates, "and I started thinking how blacks might like to have a country resort just like any other race of people." After selling the property in 1989, Bates continued to perform and teach. He appeared before youth groups, senior citizens, and handicapped groups, spreading his philosophy of being involved in spite of life's adversities and encouraging youngsters to be drug free and pursue an education. "Life means, do the best you can with what you've got, with all your mind and heart. You can do anything in this world if you want to do it bad enough," he often said.

Bates's tap dancing was melodically and rhythmically enhanced by the combination of his deep-toned peg, made of leather and rubber-tipped, and the higher-pitched metallic tap shoe. He was also accomplished in acrobatics, flash dancing (executing spectacularly difficult steps involving virtuosic aerial maneuvers), and novelty dancing. He consistently proved himself beyond his peg-legged specialty, surpassing other two-legged dancers to become one of the finest rhythm dancers in the history of tap dancing.

In 1992 Bates was master of ceremonies at the National Tap Dance Day celebration in Albany, New York, where he received a Distinguished Leadership in the Arts award. In 1991 Bates was honored with the Flo-Bert Award by the New York Committee to Celebrate National Tap Dance Day. Bates died in Fountain Inn, South Carolina, just a mile and a half from the place where he lost his leg.

• Bates is interviewed in Rusty Frank's book *Tap! The Greatest Tap Dance Stars and Their Stories, 1900–1955* (1990; rev. ed., 1994). In 1992 Constance Valis Hill conducted an oral history interview with Bates, which is in the archives of the National Museum of Dance in Saratoga, New York. That same year, Hill wrote a feature article on Bates, "Tap Day to Receive a Peg Leg Flourish," for the *Albany Times Union*, 22 May 1992. In 1991 Bates was the subject of an hour-long documentary, *Dancing Man: Peg Leg Bates*, produced by Amber Edwards of New Jersey Public Television. His "Solo Dance" on the 17 July 1960 broadcast of the *Ed Sullivan Show* can be seen on tape. An obituary is in the *New York Times*, 8 Dec. 1998.

Constance Valis Hill

BECKER, Abraham Jacob (25 Feb. 1872–15 Jan. 1953), and **Magdalena Hergert Becker** (4 Aug. 1878–7 July 1938), missionaries, were born in Russia and Kansas, respectively. Abraham Becker was born in Wohldemfuerst, Kuban, Russia, the son of Jacob P. Becker, a farmer and minister and a founder of the Mennonite Brethren branch of the Mennonite Church, and Margaretha Wiens Becker. Magdalena Becker was born Magdalena Hergert in Hillsboro, Kansas, the daughter of Wilhelm and Magdalena Hergert, farmers. The Jacob Becker family emigrated to America in 1875 and settled in central Kansas among other Germans from Russia. In 1893 Abraham Becker claimed a homestead in the Cherokee Outlet of Oklahoma, near Fairview. The following year the Hergert family moved to Fairview.

In 1896 the Mennonite Brethren Church of North America began missionary work among the Comanche Indians of Oklahoma Territory. Abraham Becker helped the missionary Henry Kohfeld build a chapel at the newly opened Post Oak Mission. This experience inspired Becker to enter the ministry. On 27 October 1897 Abraham Becker and Magdalena Hergert married. For two years Abraham Becker received training at McPherson College in Kansas. In October 1901 the Mennonite Brethren Foreign Mission Board appointed Abraham Becker a missionary to assist Kohfeld at Post Oak. The Beckers arrived on the field on 7 March 1902. They spent the rest of their lives among the Comanches.

Located on the Kiowa-Comanche Reservation about twenty miles west of Fort Sill, Post Oak was the first "foreign" mission established by the denomination. The mission had an inauspicious start, and after twelve years Kohfeld could not claim a single baptized convert. The turning point came in 1907, when Abraham Becker was named head missionary. After securing the services of a respected government interpreter, Herman Asenap (Greyfoot), the Beckers began holding services at Indian encampments and lived with the Indians for weeks at a time. Soon seven converts were baptized, marking the birth of a Comanche Mennonite Brethren Church.

The impediments to successful mission work were many. The Comanches were content with their traditions and were suspicious of the white people. They were impoverished, frustrated by the corrupt allotment system, and demoralized by the government's insensitive acculturation program. The Beckers had to cope with the effects of gambling, alcoholism, spousal abuse, and other problems endemic to reservation life. They also were confronted with polygamy, the use of peyote, and the strong role of traditional beliefs and medicine men. However, the progressive chief Quanah Parker did not discourage his Quahada band members from participating in the mission program. Through tenacity and ingenuity, the couple slowly overcame the many hurdles they faced.

In 1904 Magdalena Becker accepted a half-time position as field matron in the Indian service. This proved critical to the success of Post Oak Mission. For twenty-eight years she trained Indian women in the skills of good housekeeping, financial management, child care, preventive health practices, cooking, sewing, quilting, gardening, and canning. This was in addition to her responsibilities as a missionary and mother of six children. She became fluent in the Comanche language and obtained the trust of the families in their area. In one year Magdalena Becker traveled 3,000 miles, mostly by horse and buggy, made 480 family visits, nursed 135 sick Indians, helped compose 550 letters, conducted 26 sewing sessions, and registered scores of births and deaths. This demanding work broke down barriers and made the Comanches amenable to the Beckers' religious message. After Magdalena became a field matron, church attendance rose significantly.

Medical services were minimal, and the death rate was high among the Indians. Hundreds came to "Mother" Becker to be treated for illnesses, often camping on the grounds until they either improved or died. When the Beckers first came to the reservation, the Comanche buried their dead in the Wichita Mountains. The Beckers encouraged them to use the mission cemetery instead. During his tenure Abraham Becker buried six hundred people at Post Oak and built the coffins for about half of those.

Quanah, although a polygamist and follower of the peyote religion, developed great respect for the Beckers. He had the grave of his white mother, Cynthia Ann Parker, removed to Post Oak Cemetery and reserved a plot for his own tomb. Two of his seven wives participated in Magdalena's training classes, and one of his wives, To-pay, eventually became a member of the church. When Quanah was near death, he called for the missionary couple, but he died before they arrived. On 26 February 1911 Abraham Becker conducted the funeral of this famous and last chief of the Comanches. An imposing granite monument marked Quanah's resting place in the mission cemetery.

After Magdalena Becker retired from the Indian service in 1932, the mission outreach was expanded to the Mexican-American community in Lawton, Oklahoma. When the seemingly indefatigable Magdalena succumbed to liver disease in Chickasha, Oklahoma, fifteen hundred people attended her funeral at Post Oak Cemetery. Abraham retired three years later and moved to Lawton. However, he maintained contacts with "his" Indians and continued to exert influence. He married Katharina Poetker on 30 November 1941. In the months before his death, Becker worked to prevent Fort Sill from acquiring Post Oak and adjacent lands for a missile range. The plans were dropped temporarily, but in 1957 the army won. The historic mission and cemetery were relocated to nearby Indiahoma.

Abraham Becker died in Lawton and was buried at Post Oak Mission next to Magdalena. The historian William T. Hagan wrote that this Mennonite couple "had come to make a life among [the Comanches]— and to rest among them when that life ended." Their achievement "was the development of the Post Oak Mission into, arguably, the most successful one in western Oklahoma." Abraham Becker baptized over 425 converts. But as Hagan noted, "the Beckers' concern was not only for their souls. They were dedicated to helping the Comanches achieve a more healthy and productive way of life. They were there to help at all stages, from birth to death." "They became one of us," stated Asenap, their lifelong interpreter.

Unlike many missionaries and Indian bureau officials, the Beckers did not insist that the natives cast off their "Indianness" in order to become Christianized and "civilized." However, the Beckers' sensitivity to cultural expressions did not extend to dancing, an activity condemned by Mennonites. This caused some resentment. Abraham Becker supported the efforts of the Indians to escape mission status and to establish their own independent Mennonite Brethren congregation. That they ultimately succeeded and that their church still existed in the early twenty-first century is tangible evidence that the Beckers' ministry was a success.

• The Beckers' correspondence with their Foreign Mission Board, much of it in German, is in the files of the General Conference of the Mennonite Brethren Church of North America, Center for Mennonite Brethren Studies, Fresno, Calif. Magdalena Becker's Field Matron Reports, Kiowa Agency, are in the Archives-Manuscripts Division, Oklahoma Historical Society, Oklahoma City. A valuable collection of her daily record books is in the Center for Mennonite Brethren Studies, Hillsboro, Kans. A comprehensive account of the Beckers and Post Oak Mission is in Marvin E. Kroeker, *Comanches and Mennonites on the Oklahoma Plains: A. J. and Magdalena Becker and the Post Oak Mission* (1997). William T. Hagan has provided two important works on the Comanches, *United States–Comanche Relations: The Reser-vation Years* (1976; repr. 1990) and *Quanah Parker, Comanche Chief* (1993).

MARVIN E. KROEKER

BELANGER, Mark (8 June 1944–6 Oct. 1998), baseball player and union leader, was born in Pittsfield, Massachusetts, the son of Ed Belanger, a factory worker and technician, and Maria Bianchi Belanger. An excellent all-around athlete, Belanger stood out in basketball as well as baseball at Pittsfield High School, once scoring 41 points in a basketball game that gave his school the Western Massachusetts championship in 1962. After being scouted by Frank McGowan and Joe Cusick, he signed with the Baltimore Orioles as a free agent and began his professional career with Bluefield (West Virginia) in the Rookie League. Under the tutelage of manager Billy Hunter, the right handed hitter and thrower averaged .298 at the plate with 3 home runs and 23 runs batted in. In 1963 Belanger entered the Army and served one year, after which he returned to the minor leagues with Aberdeen (South Dakota) in the Northern League. He was named "Rookie of the Year" in 1964 despite only hitting .226. He advanced to Elmira (New York) in the Eastern League the following year and, despite a weak batting average of .229, was named to that league's all-star team.

Despite his lack of offensive prowess, Belanger shone with his play at shortstop, and his glove earned him his major league debut with the Orioles in August of 1965. After spending most of the following year at Rochester (New York) in the International League, he earned another call-up to the majors at the end of 1966, where he witnessed the Orioles' first World Series triumph. In 1967 Belanger joined the Orioles for good, and after splitting his time between second base and shortstop, he settled in at the latter position. The Orioles demonstrated their faith in Belanger's abilities by trading regular shortstop Luis Aparicio to the Chicago White Sox. On 25 November 1967 he married Daryl Anne "Dee" Apple; they had two sons.

Belanger's arrival coincided with the emergence of some of the greatest teams in the Orioles' history. Playing in the same infield as third baseman Brooks Robinson and second baseman Davey Johnson, Belanger—nicknamed "Blade" for his thin frame as much as for his uncanny ability to snuff out opponents' rallies—became a key component of a franchise that regularly visited postseason play, including three straight trips to the World Series (1969–1971). During his tenure with the Orioles, he won a total of eight Gold Gloves (including six in a row between 1973 and 1978) and ended his career with an overall fielding percentage of .977. Although Belanger never developed offensive skills to match his defensive prowess (hitting only .229 lifetime with 20 home runs and 389 runs batted in), he occasionally surprised opposing teams with a timely hit. Paradoxically, Belanger often enjoyed his greatest success at bat against star pitchers such as Denny McClain and Nolan Ryan.

He was a leader in the clubhouse as well as on the field. Belanger's family also contributed to the team's success; when the Orioles switched from organ music to recorded music in 1975, his wife's suggestion that John Denver's song "Thank God I'm a Country Boy" be played during home games was an immediate success among fans. Despite the apparent incongruity of using a country-flavored tune in the Northeast, the song eventually became a standard during the seventh-inning stretch.

After finishing his major league career in 1982 with the Los Angeles Dodgers, Belanger—who had long served as the Orioles' player representative with the Major League Baseball Players Association—went to work for the union full time. In his capacity of assistant to union head Donald Fehr, Belanger served through some of the most tumultuous labor problems that the major leagues had ever experienced. Having endured an early season strike in 1972 while still a player, he played a key role in events that led to the mid-season strike of 1981. Belanger took his duties as the Orioles player representative seriously, noting during negotiations that "what we are trying to do . . . is avoid a strike any way we can." He also earned high marks from teammate Brooks Robinson, who said, "Doug [DeCinces, the Orioles' third baseman and American League player representative] and Belanger enjoyed being part of that [negotiating team] more than anyone else."

Although unsuccessful in preventing a strike that wiped out much of the 1981 season, Belanger continued to work with the union through additional periods of labor unrest, including a brief two-day strike in 1985, a thirty-two day owners lockout in 1990, and a late season strike in 1994 that eventually forced the cancellation of that year's World Series.

A heavy smoker for years, Belanger was diagnosed with lung cancer and died from the disease in New York City. He was memorialized by his former boss Fehr, who said, "Players . . . owe a debt of gratitude to him. I personally miss the wisdom and insight he provided on virtually every important decision the MLBPA has made over the last three decades."

While the average baseball fan appreciated Mark Belanger for his on-field skills, his most lasting legacy will be the advancement in major league salaries that resulted from his yeoman work with the Players Association. Belanger's work on behalf of players was often performed out of the public eye but had a lasting impact on major league baseball and, by extension, all professional sports in North America.

• The Baseball Hall of Fame in Cooperstown, New York, maintains a file on Belanger's career. The best source of information on his post-playing career is James Edward Miller, *The Baseball Business: Pursuing Pennants and Profits in Baltimore* (1990). Also useful for understanding the context of baseball labor difficulties are Kenneth M. Jennings, *Balls and Strikes: The Money Game in Professional Baseball* (1990); and Andrew Zimbalist, *Baseball and Billions: A Probing Look Inside the Big Business of Our National Pastime* (1992). An obituary is in the *Baltimore Sun*, 7 Oct. 1998.

EDWARD L. LACH, JR.

BELL, Alfred H. (28 June 1895–10 Apr. 1977), petroleum geologist, was born Alfred Hannam Bell in Simcoe, Ontario, the son of Walter Bell and Nuala Dunly Bell, teachers. In 1912 Bell began work on a B.S. degree at the University of Toronto, majoring in chemistry and mineralogy. In 1917 his degree was granted *in absentia* because he had become a member of the Canadian Overseas Expeditionary Force. From 1916 to 1919 he served in France, Belgium, and Germany.

After his tour of duty abroad, Bell resumed his geological studies in summer fieldwork stints for the Geological Survey of Canada (Peace River district) in British Columbia, the Mackenzie River district of Northwest Territory, and the Whitehorse district of Yukon Territory. In the winter of 1920–1921 he was the National Research Council of Canada Scholar. In 1922 he studied geology and paleontology at the University of Toronto and the next year at the University of Chicago. From 1924 to 1926 Bell interrupted those courses of study to work for the Texas Company out of a Kansas office. In 1926 he received his Ph.D. from the University of Chicago for his dissertation "The Geology of Whitehorse District, Yukon Territory." That year, he was hired to the oil and gas section of the Illinois State Geological Survey (ISGS).

In 1930 Bell became head of the oil and gas section of the ISGS, holding that position of distinction until his retirement in 1963. His work as a petroleum geologist in that capacity is unsurpassed. He authored or coauthored more than 100 publications, mainly on the theme of petroleum geology. For example, Bell's initial contribution to the ISGS's own *Illinois Petroleum* bulletin series, inaugurated in 1926, had for its title (issued 24 July 1926) "Oil Prospects in Central Pike County" (pp. 7–10). Subsequent releases of that bulletin quite often included articles by him, a highly readable as well as highly useful one to oil operators being "The Dupo Oil Field" (2 March 1929). The field itself was discovered by the Ohio Oil Company in 1928 on the northward extension of St. Clair County's Waterloo anticline (bordering the Mississippi River near St. Louis).

However, Bell's greatest contributions to petroleum geology and to oil and gas prospecting comprise four publications: (1) his classification map of 1930, by which he ranked the regions of Illinois according to their likelihood of producing oil and gas, with the Illinois basin beneath Wayne County as the most likely source, its sedimentary rock strata of the Paleozoic age (from which any oil and/or gas would have to come), bottoming out at a depth from the surface of 14,000 feet; (2) his article, first delivered as a paper before the annual meeting of the Illinois State Academy of Science in 1930, "The Relation of Geology to the Development of the Petroleum Industry in Illinois," *Transactions of the Illinois State Academy of Science* 23 (March 1931), in which Bell demonstrated the value of deeper drilling in the Illinois basin, particularly from the so-called "Fairfield basin," named after the county seat of Wayne (his prognostication was confirmed in 1937); (3) his "Role of Fundamental Geologic Principles in the Opening of the Illinois Basin," *Economic Geology* 36 (December 1941): 774–85, in which Bell summarized succinctly salient aspects of oil and gas discoveries that ushered in the greatest boom for oil output ever in Illinois, from 1937 to 1942 a total of 514,700,000 barrels; and (4) his "Oil Resources and Possibilities," *Illinois Petroleum* 72 (1955): 1–12, in effect a status report for prairie state oil production up to 1955.

The classification map of 1930 prompted the Pure Oil Company, which had two years previously (1928) found oil in the Michigan basin, similar in geologic type and configuration to the basin in Illinois, to explore Illinois in the mid-1930s.

Under Bell's guidance the ISGS's oil and gas section collected one of the fullest mineralogical records of oil and gas drilling anywhere in the nation. Moreover, Bell enhanced the ISGS's reputation among state geological surveys by amassing carefully detailed data on such matters as statistics of annual oil output, total wells drilled per year, and new field discoveries, all of which he made available to the American Institute of Mining, Metallurgical, and Petroleum Engineers; the American Association of Petroleum Geologists; and the National Scouts and Landsmen's Association. Over the years Bell also promoted effectively a better understanding, as well as a more efficient use, of secondary recovery methods (particularly that of water flooding), which added greatly to Illinois's cumulative oil production.

Bell called repeatedly for oil operators of Illinois to drill for deeper "horizons," particularly below the McClosky "sand," to be reached in the central basin at a depth of 3,120 feet (that rock formation being within the Valmeyeran of the Mississippian System of the Paleozoic Era).

In the 16 June 1938 *Oil & Gas Journal*, Bell recommended much more testing of the St. Peter sandstone, to be found in association with a major unconformity in rocks of Ordovician age not far below the "Trenton" limestone, some 6,220 feet down in the "heart" of the Illinois basin. Until his 1963 retirement from the ISGS, Bell predicted that paying quantities of oil would be found at the St. Peter basin, though as of the new millennium no such amounts have yet been "hit." Younger geologists such as L. L. Sloss have acknowledged Bell's work in publications dealing further with the gas and oil potential of the Illinois Basin.

Perhaps this geological prediction, like others by him, will come true. Throughout his distinguished career he was more often right than wrong. Major geological unconformities have often delivered sizable quantities of oil. Bell died in Champaign, Illinois.

• The best primary sources for Bell's works are at the Illinois State Geological Survey in Urbana/Champaign. Representative of Bell's pleas for ever deeper drilling in Illinois are "Possible Producing Strata Below the McClosky in Illinois," *Oil & Gas Journal* 37 (16 June 1938): 30–31, 108, and two collaborative articles: with George V. Cohee, "Recent Development in Illinois with Discussion of Producing Formations Below McClosky 'Sand,'" *Bulletin of the American Association of Petroleum Geologists* 23 (June 1939): 807–22, and, with L. E. Workman, "Deep Drilling and Deeper Oil Possibilities in Illinois," *Bulletin of the American Association of Petroleum Geologists* 32 (Nov. 1948): 2041–62.

Robert H. Dott, Sr.'s tribute to Bell can be found under "Memorials," *Bulletin of the American Association of Petroleum Geologists* 62 (Mar. 1978): 469–70, to be supplemented by George V. Cohee and John C. Frye's "Memorial to Alfred Hannam Bell," Geological Society of America *Memorial* 9 (Nov. 1978): 1–4. To give an overall context, not only for Bell's "place in the picture" but also for "Table I: Illinois Crude Oil Production, 1905-1980" (pp. 164–65, important for a fuller appreciation of the prairie state's contribution to America's "oil picture"), consult Keith L. Miller's "Petroleum and Profits in the Prairie State, 1889–1980," *Illinois Historical Journal* 77 (Autumn 1984): 162–76.

KEITH L. MILLER

BERNE, Eric (10 May 1910–15 July 1970), psychiatrist, was born Eric Lennard Bernstein in Montreal, Quebec, the son of David Hillel Bernstein, a general physician, and Sara Gordon Bernstein, a writer and editor. When Eric was eleven, his father died from tuberculosis, leaving his mother to provide for him and his younger sister. Eric studied mathematics and physics at McGill University, where he graduated with a B.A. in 1931. The intense playfulness that would later characterize Berne's writing and work was evident in his youth; as an undergraduate he wrote for several McGill newspapers under the pseudonyms Lennard Gandalac, Ramsbottom Horseley, and Cynical St. Cyr, a pen name that reappeared in his adult life as Cyprian St. Cyr. Under the pen name Lennard Gandalac, Esq., he failed to publish a novel, *Ramsbottom Horseley*, but he did publish a humorous article titled "Who Was Condom" for the journal *Human Fertility* (1940).

Berne remained at McGill for both his M.S. in surgery and M.D. degrees, completed in 1935. He then moved to the United States, where he interned at the Yale Psychiatric Clinic in New Haven from 1936 to 1938 and began psychoanalytic training with Paul Federn. Berne became a U.S. citizen in 1939 and changed his name legally to Eric Berne in 1943. In 1942 he married Elinor McRae. They had two children.

During World War II Berne interrupted his analytic training to serve with the U.S. Army Medical Corps. Like many psychiatrists during the war, Berne was required to assess the mental fitness of "nervous" soldiers. He soon distinguished himself with his ability to make quick and accurate diagnoses, and he later published a series of articles on the role of intuition in clinical diagnosis. He also began doing group psychotherapy with soldiers at Bushnell General (Army) Hospital in Ogden, Utah. In 1945 he and his first wife divorced amid considerable ill will and charges that he abused her.

When Berne was discharged from the military he joined the staff at Mt. Zion hospital in San Francisco and resumed psychoanalytic training at the San Francisco Psychoanalytic Institute with Erik Erikson. In 1949 he met and married Dorothy De Mass Way. They had two children. He published his first book on psychoanalysis, *The Mind in Action*, in 1947 (revised in 1968 as *Mind in Action*), and he became a leading group therapist at several hospitals in the San Francisco bay area. Berne departed from mainstream psychoanalysis when his application for membership in the San Francisco Psychoanalytic Institute was denied. According to Warren D. Cheney, Berne, who had completed more than ten years of analytic training, was "devastated" when his application was turned down. But the rejection "spurred him to intensify the long-standing ambition to add something new to psychoanalysis" ("Eric Berne: Biographical Sketch," *Transactional Analysis Journal* 1 [1971]: 18). Berne began revising Paul Federn's psychoanalytic ego-state model. By 1957 the rudiments of his new Transactional Analysis (TA) were appearing in such articles as "Ego States in Psychotherapy" (*American Journal of Psychotherapy* 11 [1957]: 735–43) and "Transactional Analysis: A New and Effective Method of Group Therapy" (*American Journal of Psychotherapy* 12 [1958]: 293–309).

Most of the concepts of Transactional Analysis are elaborations of Federn's ideas in vernacular language and with practical aims for group therapy. TA studies both the ego-states of an individual and the manner in which those ego-states shape his or her social interactions (transference). The first phase of TA is Structural Analysis, "the study of the relationships within the individual of three types of ego states" (Berne, "Transactional Analysis" [1958], p. 743). These three sets of ego-states are the Parent, Adult and Child (mapping loosely onto the superego, ego, and id). The Child relies on childlike reasoning; the Parent is a "borrowing" of perceived parental attitudes; and the Adult is capable of accurate reality-testing. The second phase of TA, Transactional Analysis, studies the use of these ego-states in communication strategies—in Transactions, Scripts, and Games. The Transaction, the most basic unit of social analysis, "consists of a single stimulus and a single response, verbal or nonverbal" (Berne, *What Do You Say After You Say Hello?* [1972], p. 20). Scripts are "complex sets of transactions, by nature recurrent." They are blueprints for real-life dramas, set in childhood, that determine the "destiny and the identity of the individual" (Berne, "Transactional Analysis" [1958], p. 742). Games are agreed-upon (although not always conscious) rules of transacting in which there is always a pay-off to one of the parties. There are four therapeutic goals of TA: to help the individual gain "social control," to achieve symptomatic relief, to cure the transference, and ultimately to achieve a "script cure." In Berne's words, "While every human being faces the world initially as the captive of his script, the great hope and value of the human race is that the Adult can be dissatisfied with such strivings when they are unworthy" (*Transactional Analysis in Psychotherapy* [1961], pp. 125–126).

His *Transactional Analysis in Psychotherapy* (1961), *The Structures and Dynamics of Organizations and Groups* (1963), and *Games People Play* (1964) became the seminal books of Transactional Analysis. Many of his TA ideas crystallized in his Tuesday evening seminars, which began in 1951 as informal professional gatherings, developed in 1958 into the San Francisco Social Psychiatry Seminars, and expanded in 1964 with the founding of the International Transactional Analysis Association. In the midst of the rising popularity of TA, Berne divorced his second wife in 1964.

It is largely through the widespread popularity of *Games People Play* that Berne and his concepts of games, scripts, strokes, and transactions entered the vernacular. *Games* was reviewed in virtually every major newspaper and magazine in the United States, and Berne was interviewed widely on television. In 1967 he married his third wife, Torre Rosecrans, a "beautiful intelligent conscientious courteous affectionate Aphrodite with long blond hair" (letter from EB to "Moe," 16 July 1967), but the marriage ended in divorce in early 1970. At the time of his death from a heart attack, Berne was at work on two TA books, *Sex in Human Loving* (1970) and *What Do You Say After You Say Hello?* (1972).

Berne's professional accomplishments as the founder of Transactional Analysis are widely recognized; as for his personal life, his friends have reflected on the extreme paradoxes of his personality. He could be spontaneous and charming at one moment, then authoritarian, demanding, and cruel at another. Two of his biographers explain that Berne was "a master at wrapping himself in a cloak of mystery, in keeping his personal life guarded and compartmentalized so that when he shifted from one of his compartments to another, he appeared an entirely different person" (Jorgensen, p. x). The reasons for the failure of Berne's three marriages remain unclear, but his friend Claude Steiner has suggested that Berne's early death was embedded within his own life-script: he "died of a broken heart," having not been able to sustain love and to allow himself to be loved by others (quoted in Stewart, p. 15).

The legacy of Berne's Transactional Analysis is mixed. The International Transactional Analysis Association boasts more than 7,000 members, and the European Association for Transactional Analysis, founded in 1974, has more than 4,000 members. Students and followers of Berne have continued to innovate and promote TA; perhaps the most popular of these efforts was Thomas Harris's *I'm OK, You're OK* (1967) (whose title was playfully spoofed in Wendy Kaminer's 1992 *I'm Dysfunctional, You're Dysfunctional*). However, TA has not enjoyed as much popularity in the broader world of psychotherapy. Berne's biographer Ian Stewart notes that Berne's acknowledged influence among practitioners outside of TA circles has been minimal.

• Berne's papers are held at the archives of the University of California, San Francisco. The two extant biographies of Berne were written by practitioners of TA: *Eric Berne: Master Gamesman* (1984), by Elizabeth Watkins Jorgensen and Henry Irvin Jorgensen, and *Eric Berne* (1992), by Ian Stewart. Stewart's book is less a biography than a review of Berne's contributions to the theory and practice of psychotherapy. References to and remembrances of Berne appear in the writings of numerous TA practitioners, most notably in a 1971 Eric Berne memorial issue of the *Transactional Analysis Journal*, which also includes an annotated bibliography of Berne's writings. Additional remembrances can be found in Claude Steiner's *Interview: On the Early Years of Transactional Analysis* (1991); Irvin Yalom, *The Theory and Practice of Group Psychotherapy* (1970); and Jacqui Schiff, "One Hundred Children Generate a Lot of TA," in G. Barnes, *Transactional Analysis after Eric Berne: Teachings and Practices of Three TA Schools* (1977). An obituary is in the *New York Times*, 7 July 1970.

RACHAEL I. ROSNER

BERRY BROTHERS, dancers, consisted of Ananias "Nyas" Berry (18 Aug. 1913–5 Oct. 1951) and James Berry (c. 1915–28 Jan. 1969), both born in New Orleans, Louisiana, and Warren Berry (25 Dec. 1922–10 Aug. 1996), born in Denver, Colorado, the sons of Ananias Berry and Redna Berry, whose occupations are unknown.

In 1919, Nyas and James first began performing together, touring the church circuit in Chicago as elocutionists reciting poems by Paul Laurence Dunbar. After the family moved to Denver, the two elder brothers branched out and began playing carnivals. Their father, a very religious man, had forbidden them to dance, but Nyas had memorized dances he had seen other performers do, and had built upon them himself. He persuaded his father to let him enter an amateur dance contest, in which he floored the audience. The theater manager offered Nyas $75 a week; the elder Ananias insisted that Nyas and James continue as a team.

They then put together an act based on the widely acclaimed Bert Williams and George Walker, the most famous African-American show business performance team of their time. Nyas and James named their act "The Miniature Williams and Walker." In the mid-1920s the Berry family moved to Hollywood, California, where James danced at parties given by silent film stars such as Mary Pickford and Clara Bow. They also appeared in Our Gang comedies. Toward the end of the decade they opened as a duo, "the Berry Brothers," with the already legendary Duke Ellington at Harlem's Cotton Club. Although the famous nightclub would remain their home base for the next four and a half years, they toured and performed in other groundbreaking shows. In 1929 they traveled to London and were featured performers in Lew Leslie's popular and highly acclaimed all-African-American revue *Blackbirds of 1928*. They were the first African-American act at the Copacabana in 1929. They appeared in "Rhythmania" at the Cotton Club and "Rhapsody In Black" in 1931. When Radio City Music Hall had its grand opening on 27 December 1932, the Berry Brothers were on the bill.

In 1934 Nyas Berry left the act and married Valaida Snow, a popular African-American entertainer. It was during this time that Warren Berry, the youngest brother, was pulled out of school and formal dance classes and drafted into the act. James Berry taught his younger brother every move of the Berry Brothers' act, and soon this new duo was performing steadily. When Nyas's marriage dissolved, he talked his brothers into forming a Berry Brothers act with three Berrys. Nyas also persuaded them to move back to Hollywood. The Berry Brothers enjoyed tremendous success in their newly formed trio and appeared extensively throughout the United States on stage, in clubs, and in film, as well as throughout Europe. The brothers possessed three distinct personalities and styles: Nyas was the king of the strut, James was the comedian and singer, and Warren was the solid dancer/acrobat. Their act remained virtually unchanged for over twenty years. In addition to their work in the 1941 musical film *Lady Be Good*, the Berrys also appeared in *Panama Hattie* (1942), *Boarding House Blues* (1948), and *You're My Everything* (1949). Their club engagements over the years included the Apollo Theatre, the Zanzibar Café, and the Savoy Ballroom in New York, the Moulin Rouge in Paris, and the Rio Cabana in Chicago.

In 1938, at the downtown Cotton Club, a legendary competition took place between the Berry Brothers and the Nicholas Brothers, another great dance act. The Berrys devised a memorable finish in which Nyas and James ran up side stairways onto an elevated balcony and took a flying leap twelve feet out and over the heads of the entire Cab Calloway orchestra, while Warren, on the stage below, completed a flip-flop twist. On the last note of the music, all three landed simultaneously in splits. "People talked about that for a long time!" recalled Warren Berry (Frank, 1990/1995).

The secret of the Berry Brothers' success was timing, precision, and dynamics. They were masters of the "freeze and melt," the sparkling contrasts between posed immobility and sudden flashing action. The act that the three brothers perfected stayed their act for over twenty years. This repetition was common throughout vaudeville, when acts toured the country year after year. During that time, audiences wanted to see exactly the same familiar act with no changes. When the Berry Brothers contemplated using a new song or creating a new dance routine, the bookers dissuaded them. Resigned, the Berry Brothers kept their act intact until Nyas's death of heart failure at the age of thirty-nine, in New York. Warren and James performed together and then as solo acts individually for a time. But then Warren's hip injury that he had suffered as a teen finally disabled him. In 1969 James Berry died in New York of complications of arteriosclerosis. Warren worked for over fifteen years as a film editor for Screen Gems in New York City. During his last years he worked in Los Angeles on several unpublished scripts; he died in Los Angeles.

The Berry Brothers are remembered as one of the greatest dance acts in the history of the American stage and cinema in the twentieth century. At a time when tap dancers were "a dime a dozen," these brothers combined their talents to form a unique act that remains unsurpassed. Ironically, they never wore taps on their shoes because the work that they did with the canes and acrobatics required leather-soled shoes for safety. Their mixture of the Cakewalk's Strut, tap dancing, thrilling acrobatics, and amazing cane work was a winning and lasting formula.

• For further reading on the Berry Brothers, see Jean and Marshall Stearns, *Jazz Dance, The Story of American Vernacular Dance* (1968/1994), which provides information on the content of their dance act. Rusty E. Frank, *TAP! The Greatest Tap Dance Stars and Their Stories 1900–1955* (1990/1995), contains the last published interview with Warren Berry. Obituaries for Ananias, James, and Warren Berry appear respectively in the *New York Age*, 13 Oct. 1951; the New York *Amsterdam News*, 8 Feb. 1969; and the *Los Angeles Times*, 16 Aug. 1996.

RUSTY E. FRANK

BLASDEL, Henry Goode (20 Jan. 1825–26 July 1900), first governor of Nevada, was born near Lawrenceburg, Indiana, the son of Jacob Blasdel, a merchant, and Elizabeth Weaver Blasdel. His father's family settled in New England late in the seventeenth century; his mother's family was among the early arrivals in Virginia. Blasdel shared their Methodism, abstinence, and antislavery views. He entered the seminary at age fourteen, but when his father died two years later, Blasdel turned to farming. On 9 December 1845 he married Sarah Jane Cox, the daughter of a neighboring farmer and Blasdel's sister-in-law; they had three children who survived to adulthood. Blasdel worked as a farmer and storekeeper, shipped farm produce to New Orleans, and operated a riverboat.

Blasdel joined the quest for wealth in the West, migrating to California with the gold rush in 1852. Like many other arrivals, he found prospecting less profitable than providing services to other miners, and he returned to shipping goods. He then invested in the grain business but went bankrupt. In 1861 Blasdel crossed the Sierra Nevada to the Comstock Lode, where he wielded political and economic influence during one of the West's biggest mining booms. That year the legislature appointed him one of the first three county commissioners and first recorder of Storey County, where Virginia City is located. He helped found the town's first Masonic lodge. The owner of several mining claims, he worked as a mine and mill superintendent and won attention for quitting one job because he objected to requiring miners to work on Sunday.

Most residents of Nevada Territory were loyal to the Republican party and its Civil War offshoot the Union party. This helped power the drive for statehood, which culminated on 31 October 1864 with Nevada's admission as the thirty-sixth state. Blasdel was a member of the Republican party, which nominated him for governor. He defeated the Democrat David Buell 9,834 votes to 6,555, as Republicans won every state office. In 1866 Blasdel defeated the Democrat John D. Winters 5,125 votes to 4,105 amid Democratic claims that Blasdel's supporters, though not necessarily the governor, threw out enough votes to affect the outcome. The charges were probably untrue.

The governor's salary of $4,700 a year made Blasdel Nevada's highest-paid public official. Power was another matter. Nevada's governor was and remains a plural executive. Other state officials ran separately, and the governor's authority was limited. However, Blasdel used his office as a bully pulpit, encouraging passage of the constitutional amendments "to rid the nation of the curse of slavery" (Thirteenth Amendment), to define citizenship (Fourteenth Amendment), and to guarantee black male suffrage (Fifteenth Amendment). He encouraged construction of a state home for orphans and legislative support for a state capitol building. While he was in office, all state officials worked in rented quarters.

During Blasdel's tenure, Congress approved legislation to expand Nevada east and south. Blasdel urged the legislature to recognize the boundary changes and to redraw county lines. Hoping to establish a county government and to scout mining investments, Blasdel visited the Pahranagat Range along the Utah border. He and his party took a more southern route than previous travelers and nearly died of starvation. Blasdel and an associate went ahead to find help, returned, and brought their group to its destination, where the population proved smaller and the mining less profitable than the governor hoped. He returned to Virginia City looking, a local journalist wrote, "mighty rough and dirty."

Blasdel distinguished himself as a counterpoint to the rollicking mining society in which he lived. He became known as the "coffee and chocolate governor" for serving nothing more potent at official receptions. Also he firmly opposed gambling, following in the footsteps of his equally opinionated but less abstemious predecessor, the territorial governor James Nye. In 1865 the state legislature overwhelmingly passed a law against gambling, which Blasdel signed. In 1867, when gambling advocates sought less-stringent regulations, the legislature approved them but without the two-thirds majority required to override a veto. In a veto message quoted in many Nevada history texts, Blasdel declared: "Gambling is an intolerable and inexcusable vice. It saps the very foundations of morality, breeds contempt for honest industry and totally disqualifies its victims for the discharge of the ordinary duties of life."

In 1869 the legislature not only passed a bill legalizing gambling but overrode Blasdel's veto. State officials wanted the revenue that regulating and taxing gambling would provide. In his final message as governor, Blasdel called the measure "a blot and a stain upon the state." Nevertheless gambling remained legal in Nevada until 1910, when Progressive Era reformers abolished it temporarily.

Blasdel also dealt with issues and problems growing out of Native-white relations. During his first term, Blasdel and the state militia rode to Reese River in central Nevada to confront Shoshones upset with the influx of miners into the area. Blasdel negotiated with tribal leaders, settled the dispute without bloodshed, and won their respect.

As a politician Blasdel had to get along with Nevada's most powerful industrialists, the mining executives. In his first legislative session, he sought property taxes to give the state a sound economic footing, and the resulting legislation favored mining property over others. Later he called a special session of the legislature to adjust state taxes in the industry's favor. Yet Blasdel also stood up to Nevada's most powerful force, the mining and banking executive William Sharon, when he vetoed a bill supporting construction of Sharon's Virginia and Truckee Railroad. The legislature overrode him.

After leaving office, Blasdel never reentered politics. He returned to Virginia City and invested in mines there and in other parts of Nevada. In 1874 he moved to northern California to work in San Francisco, probably in business and land development. Residing in Oakland, he settled on a twenty-five-acre tract later called "Fruitvale." He eventually built a seventeen-room mansion, where he resided until his death in Oakland.

Blasdel might seem little more than a trivia question about Nevada's governors. However, he was a consequential figure who helped establish the state government during a historic mining boom. He took an unusually strong moral stand on the issues of his time, more so than many of his successors, and carved a niche as one of the few Nevadans to publicly and strongly oppose gambling.

• Some of Blasdel's papers are in the Nevada State Archives in Carson City, Nev., and in the Henry E. Huntington Library in San Marino, Calif. His annual messages to the legislature are in the *Journal of the Senate*. Biographical material is in Myrtle Tate Myles, *Nevada's Governors: From Territorial Days to the Present, 1861–1971* (1972). On the territorial government, see Andrew J. Marsh, *Letters from Nevada Territory 1861–1862*, edited by William C. Miller, Russell W. McDonald, and Ann Rollins (1972). The reference to his salary is in the *Las Vegas Review-Journal*, 31 Oct. 1997. Several references to Blasdel are in Walter Van Tilburg Clark, ed., *The Journals of Alfred Doten, 1849–1903* (1973), which includes a description of him on 8–12 June 1866, page 889.

Older texts referring to Blasdel are Myron F. Angel, ed., *Reproduction of Thompson and West's History of Nevada, 1881: With Illustrations and Biographical Sketches of Its Prominent Men and Pioneers* (1958); James G. Scrugham, ed., *Nevada: A Narrative of the Conquest of a Frontier Land* (1935); and Effie Mona Mack and Byrd Wall Sawyer, *Here Is Nevada: A History of the State* (1965). Biographical material appears in Myrtle Tate Myles, *Nevada's Governors: From Territorial Days to the Present, 1861–1971* (1972). Three state history

texts that deal briefly with Blasdel are Russell R. Elliott and William D. Rowley, *History of Nevada* (1987); James W. Hulse, *The Silver State: Nevada's Heritage Reinterpreted* (1998); and Hulse, *The Nevada Adventure: A History* (1981), a junior high school text. Two studies of a key issue in Blasdel's time are Phillip I. Earl, "Veiling the Tiger: The Crusade against Gambling, 1859–1910," *Nevada Historical Society Quarterly* 28, no. 3 (Fall 1985): 158–74; and Ralph J. Roske, "Gambling in Nevada: The Early Years, 1861–1931," *Nevada Historical Society Quarterly* 33, no. 1 (Spring 1990): 28–40. Blasdel's electoral totals are in *Political History of Nevada 2000*, a publication of the Nevada Office of Secretary of State (2000). Two fine discussions of Blasdel's time and place are Rodman W. Paul, *Mining Frontiers of the Far West, 1848–1880* (2001); and Ronald M. James, *The Roar and the Silence: A History of Virginia City and the Comstock Lode* (1998). See also Leslie Burns Gray, *The Source and the Vision: Nevada's Role in the Civil War* (1989). Obituaries are in the *Virginia City Daily Territorial Enterprise*, 27 July 1900, and the *San Francisco Chronicle*, 27 July 1900.

MICHAEL GREEN

BLOCH, Bernard (18 June 1907–26 Nov. 1965), linguist, was born in New York City, the son of Albert Bloch, a painter and professor of art, and Hortense Altheimer Bloch. Bernard Bloch spent ten years of his childhood in Munich, Germany, where his father associated with Der Blaue Reiter group that included Paul Klee (1879–1940) and Wassily Kandinsky (1866–1944). In 1923 Bernard's father returned to the United States and took the family to Lawrence, Kansas, where he continued his career at the University of Kansas. There Bernard completed high school and went on to major in English at the university, earning a bachelor of arts degree in 1928 and a master of arts in comparative literature in 1929. His course of study focused on literature but also included Latin, Greek, German, Gothic, Old and Middle English, and the history of the English language.

For the next two years Bloch studied at Northwestern University. There he took his first course in linguistics with Werner F. Leopold (1896–1984), who was so impressed by Bloch's knowledge of phonetics that he recommended him as a field worker on the linguistic atlas project being developed by Hans Kurath (1891–1992), at the time a leading authority on the dialects of American English. Training took place in New York at the 1931 summer Linguistic Institute of the Linguistic Society of America, and Bloch then undertook field work to determine and record in phonetic transcription the pronunciations used in New England dialects. At the same time he held a half-time position as instructor of English at Mount Holyoke College in South Hadley, Massachusetts, where he met Julia Evelyn McDonnell, an assistant in the English department. They married the following year and ten years later had one child.

With the completion of active field work, in 1933 the Blochs moved to Providence, Rhode Island, and Bernard enrolled as a graduate student at Brown University, studying under Kurath. He received a doctoral degree in English and general linguistics in 1935 with a dissertation on the sound *r* in New England speech. From 1937 to 1943 Bernard Bloch served as instructor and then assistant professor of English at Brown, teaching German for one semester in 1939. Through much of this period Bernard and Julia Bloch worked on the editorial staff of *The Linguistic Atlas of New England* (1939–1943), which Kurath directed and edited. Bernard was assistant editor of the atlas, and Julia assisted in the preparation of its 700 dialect maps. In addition, for the *Handbook of the Linguistic Geography of New England* (1939), Julia compiled and edited the data for the chapter on "Communities and Informants," and Bernard wrote the two chapters on what Kurath called "the tools of the language geographer" —the phonetic alphabet and other symbols used to record pronunciation and the worksheets that guided the field workers' interviews with local speakers and on which responses were recorded. These volumes were the first and remain the most complete account of words and pronunciations used in any American English regional dialect.

Editorial work on the *Atlas* project and frequent professional contact with the senior leadership of the Linguistic Society of America at annual winter meetings and summer Linguistic Institutes led to Bloch's election as editor of the Society's journal *Language*, a post he held from 1940 until his death. Despite the enormous workload involved in selecting, editing, and sometimes rewriting extensively the articles and reviews for more than 100 issues of the journal, as well as numerous special publications sponsored by the Linguistic Society, Bloch managed to publish a body of important research that gained him universal recognition as one of the leading American linguists. His published writings can be divided into three intersecting categories: linguistic analyses of Japanese, theoretical work on phonology, and formal syntactic study.

Bloch's work on phonology is best known, in particular the papers "Phonemic Overlapping," *American Speech* 16 (1941): 278–84; "A Set of Postulates for Phonemic Analysis," *Language* 24 (1948): 3–46; and "Contrast," *Language* 29 (1953): 59–61. He formulated principles of phonemic theory with such clarity that these articles became a standard source for later accounts of the views of the American generation of linguists known variously as structuralists, descriptivists, Bloomfieldians, and post-Bloomfieldians, whose work, in the 1940s and 50s, concentrated on the synchronic description of languages, with a focus on the development of procedures for data collection and analysis. Bloch's special theoretical concern was to establish that the "basic assumptions that underlie phonemics . . . can be stated without any mention of mind and meaning" (1948: 5), although he repeatedly made clear that linguists could, should, and nearly always did use meaning as a practical procedure in gathering data and establishing preliminary analyses.

Bloch put his phonological principles to the test in "Studies in Colloquial Japanese IV: Phonemics," *Lan-*guage 26 (1950): 86–125. This was the culmination of eight years of work on Japanese, begun in 1942 at Brown when Bloch was placed in charge of Japanese language instruction, an urgent national need following the outbreak of the Second World War. In association with efforts to develop teaching materials for Japanese instruction, Bloch, along with George L. Trager (1906–1992), produced *Outline of Linguistic Analysis* (1942), a booklet designed "to present in brief summary the techniques of analysis which are necessary for learning a foreign language by the method of working with native speakers and arriving inductively at the grammatical system of their language" (p. 4). The text actually was more of a guide for linguists engaged in creating language teaching materials than for students, and it became a highly regarded introduction to linguistic analysis within the Bloomfieldian framework; Leonard Bloomfield contributed the chapter on syntax.

In the fall of 1943 Bloch moved to Yale University as assistant professor of linguistics. There he directed instruction in Japanese for the Army Specialized Training Program and Civil Affairs Training School and, following the techniques presented in the *Outline*, he developed the textbook *Spoken Japanese* (1945), coauthored with Eleanor Harz Jorden and native speakers of Japanese who served as linguistic consultants. Bloch became a pioneer in the American linguistic analysis of the Japanese language, publishing studies on phonology, morphology, and syntax.

Bloch's "Studies in Colloquial Japanese II: Syntax," *Language* 22 (1946): 200–48, was one of the few extended syntactic analyses ever presented by an American descriptivist; descriptivists, as a rule, concentrated on phonology and morphology. Here he determined the syntactic categories and the constituent structure of major Japanese sentence types. In a companion paper, "Syntactic Formulas for Japanese," *Studies in Linguistics* 5 (1947): 1–12, less well known but equally important, Bloch suggested an alternative representation of Japanese syntactic structure. Using notations inspired in part by the Danish linguist Otto Jespersen in *Analytic Syntax* (1937), Bloch presented formulas that provided structural descriptions in the form of labeled bracketing of constituent structure. This work foreshadowed aspects of Noam Chomsky's *Syntactic Structures* (1957), and it therefore is not surprising that Bloch accepted an extended review of that important book for the journal he edited (Robert B. Lees, rev., *Language* 33 (1957): 375–408).

Chomsky's work, usually referred to as generative grammar and focused on linguistic theory and the explanation of linguistic universals, raised many questions about the validity of the descriptivist approach that Bloch had helped to develop, but Bloch never used his editorship to prevent publication of views that differed from his own. Early in his career he continued to accept conservative, philological articles even as descriptivism was assuming prominence in the field of linguistics, and later he kept *Language* open to both descriptivist and generative approaches as the latter gained primacy. He was an exemplary editor, a statesman rather than a gatekeeper.

Bernard Bloch's contributions to linguistics and to the Linguistic Society of America were recognized with his election to the presidency of that society in 1953, and he and Julia Bloch are remembered through the Bernard and Julia Bloch Memorial Fund, which supports the appointment of a Bloch Fellow at the biennial Linguistic Institute. Julia Bloch died on 22 October 1960 in New Haven, Connecticut; Bernard Bloch died five years later, also in New Haven.

• Bloch's papers are at Yale University (Bernard Bloch Papers). Four of his articles are included in Martin Joos, ed., *Readings in Linguistics: The Development of Descriptive Linguistics in America since 1925* (1957). Three articles on phonological theory are reprinted in Valerie B. Makkai, ed., *Phonological Theory: Evolution and Current Practice* (1972). Five papers on Japanese, including two on syntax, are reprinted in Roy Andrew Miller, ed., *Bernard Bloch on Japanese* (1970), which contains an introductory essay on Bloch's contributions to Japanese studies. A bibliography of Bloch's publications is in *Language* 43 (1967): 18–19. An obituary by Martin Joos is in *Language* 43 (1967): 3–18; another obituary is in the *New York Times*, 29 Nov. 1965.

JULIA S. FALK

BLOCH, Konrad E. (21 Jan. 1912–15 Oct. 2000), biochemist, was born in Neisse, Upper Silesia (then part of Germany), the son of Fritz Bloch, a mechanic, and Hedwig Striemer Bloch. His father, whose family had been in the province since 1800, ran the family drapery business. While on a summer vacation during World War I, Bloch joined his father, a German officer, at the quiet German-Danish front and enjoyed the beaches on the Baltic Sea. During his *Gymnasium* (high school) studies, where he found most of the teachers to be "martinets," Bloch thought that he would pursue a career in metallurgy, influenced by his reading on the new alloy inventions, especially stainless steels.

At the Technische Hochschule (technical university) in Munich, Bloch found the metallurgy course "uninspiring," but quickly found his field after taking Hans Fischer's course in organic chemistry. For the next two years he spent long hours in Fischer's laboratory, synthesizing compounds to be used by graduate students in Fischer's research group. In 1934, Fischer denied Bloch's application to work with him as a graduate student because he thought the political climate would not allow him to take on a Jewish student. Fischer, an "ardent patriot" but not a Nazi, naively tried to obtain a graduate position for Bloch at universities in the "Free City of Danzig" and Utrecht, where he was turned down; months later Danzig became part of the Reich, and Utrecht was overrun by the Nazis at the outset of World War II. Finally sensing that he might be in jeopardy but unable to emigrate to the United States, where his future wife had already fled, Bloch, with Fischer's help, obtained a position at a research institute at Davos in the Swiss Alps, the setting Thomas Mann had chosen for *The Magic Mountain* and the site of many tuberculosis sanatoria.

Frederic Roulet, the institute research director, asked Bloch, who had no previous research experience, to investigate the claim of Bloch's predecessor at the institute that he had found cholesterol among the lipids of human tuberculosis bacilli, in contradiction of earlier reports. Unaware then of how important cholesterol would be in his future research, Bloch discovered the flaw in his predecessor's work and confirmed that no cholesterol was present in these lipids. Bloch's next project came from Roulet's finding that both live and dead human and bovine TB bacilli, as well as their organic solvent extracts, all elicited the same response when injected into the skin. Bloch isolated phosphatidic acids from these bacilli and needed to test their activity. Fifty years later, he "jokingly" showed an interviewer the scars on both his arms, the marks of the young researcher's willingness to serve as an experimental animal.

After unexpectedly receiving a response from a letter he had written to Yale's R. J. Anderson, the American expert on the TB bacilli, Bloch asked Anderson for assistance in coming to the United States. Anderson arranged for an appointment as an assistant in biochemistry at Yale, a position that did not have a stipend. It was enough for the American consul in Frankfort to issue an immigration visa; Bloch arrived in New York in late 1936 with only $100 and began searching the *New York Times* for a job in the chemical industry. He also contacted Anderson at Yale, who discouraged him from coming there but suggested that he work for Hans T. Clarke at Columbia. With financial assistance from a private foundation arranged by Clarke, Bloch completed his Ph.D. in 1938, his thesis in part drawing on some of the work he had published while in Davos.

In 1941 Bloch married Lorna Teutsch; they had two children. He stayed at Columbia until 1946, first as a postdoctoral fellow with the brilliant Rudolf Schoenheimer, a pioneer in the use of radioisotopes to study biochemical metabolism. After Schoenheimer's suicide in 1941, Bloch and two other postdocs were told that funds were available to continue projects developed by their deceased mentor. There were three major areas of research, and the postdocs had worked in all of them. The final division was determined by drawing lots, and it fell to Bloch to continue in the area of fatty acids and cholesterol, which became a lifelong focus.

When new faculty appointments opened up after World War II, Bloch moved to the University of Chicago as an assistant professor. "Once independent," he said, "an investigator may choose to play it safe by continuing . . . earlier research, or . . . may venture in new directions. The decision is a matter of temperament and imagination, not necessarily of intelligence. I decided to temporize and play it safe. . . ." By 1954 his work in cholesterol biosynthesis had garnered sufficient attention that he received "out of the blue" a letter that said simply, "Dear Mr. Bloch. We are pleased to appoint you professor of biochemistry." It was from the Department of Chemistry at Harvard University. Bloch moved to Harvard that year with appointments in both chemistry and biochemistry, which he laughingly said allowed him to vote in two departments. He later served as chairman of both, which he dismissed as being no special honor because the chairman is simply "the faculty representative who reports to the dean."

His lifelong devotion to cholesterol resulted in the sharing in 1964 of the Nobel Prize in Medicine or Physiology with Feodor Lynen "for their discoveries concerning the mechanism and regulation of the cholesterol and fatty acid metabolism." In making the presentation, Professor S. Bergström of the Nobel Committee commented: "Mainly through the basic biochemical work of this year's prize winners do we know today in detail how cholesterol and fatty acids are synthesized and metabolized in the body. . . . Derangements of this complicated mechanism of formation and metabolism of lipids are in many cases responsible for the genesis of some of our most important diseases, especially in the cardiovascular field. A detailed knowledge of the mechanisms of lipid metabolism is necessary to deal with these medical problems in a rational manner."

"Whatever the motives," Bloch said many years later, "whether curiosity or ambition—usually a combination of both—only near the end does one fully appreciate the rewards and privileges that go with a career in science. So much the better if the results should have some degree of permanence. Science is indeed a glorious enterprise, and has been for me, I admit, glorious entertainment." Bloch died in Burlington, Massachusetts.

• For an autobiographical account, see *Annual Review of Biochemistry* 56 (1987): 1–9. An extensive oral history conducted in 1993 is on file at the Chemical Heritage Foundation in Philadelphia (see http://www.chemheritage.org/HistoricalServices/Abstract/bloch.htm). An obituary is in the *Washington Post*, 17 Oct. 2000.

JAMES J. BOHNING

BLUNDEN, Jeraldyne (10 Dec. 1940–22 Nov. 1999), dancer and choreographer, was born Jeraldyne Kilborn, in Dayton, Ohio, the daughter of Elijah Kilborn, an insurance agent, and Winifred Keith Kilborn, who worked at Wright Patterson Air Force Base. Her mother played the piano and her father had an artistic nature, which included writing poetry and soft-shoe dancing. Although Dayton was geographically divided along racial lines at the time, she attended Irving Public School, which was not segregated, and Roosevelt High, which was all white when she entered and fully integrated by the time she graduated. Segregation had never been the official policy of Dayton, and African Americans freely shopped in department stores, although there were no black employees except for cleaning help. Blunden's grandmother was one of the first blacks to build her own home.

Beginning at the age of eight, Blunden trained in classical ballet with Josephine Schwartz, who, with her sister Hermene, was considered the premier dance teacher in Dayton. Their company, the Dayton Ballet, was one of the first regional ballet companies in the United States. A group of mothers had previously invited "Miss Jo" to teach at Linden House, a black community center, where she conducted classes three days a week, thereby breaking racial boundaries. She and her sister were to become Blunden's role models and greatest supporters. Choreography, improvisation, and modern dance were part of the training given by the Schwartz sisters, and Blunden actually started to create dances while still in elementary school. Eventually the Schwartzes helped Blunden obtain scholarships to study dance outside of Ohio. When Schwartz formed the Linden Dance Company, Blunden was one of ten girls in the group, which rehearsed in a church on Saturday mornings. The ballet company rehearsed at the same time and place.

At thirteen Blunden was a well-trained and obviously talented dancer, and she went to the Schwartz sisters' main studio, where, although she was African American, she was accepted by the other students because of her abilities. Even before *Lincoln's Portrait*, a racially integrated production of the sisters, she danced with the Dayton Ballet Company, but always as a guest and never with a partner. For several years she came to New York City to take the annual Christmas course at the School of American Ballet. At fifteen she danced and briefly toured with Karamu, a black company from Cleveland. Blunden enrolled at Connecticut College, choosing it because of its dance program, but returned home after three weeks. She attended Central State College for two years, planning to major in elementary education, but did not graduate. In 1959 she married Charles Blunden; they would have two children. She spent the summers of 1958 and 1959 at the American Dance Festival in Connecticut on a scholarship. Here she was exposed to the Horton, Graham, Cunningham, and Limón modern dance techniques, saw the three latter companies perform, and learned repertory from Helen Tamiris. The first year she was the only black student; the second year there was one other. During this time she also came to New York City on weekends to study ballet with Karel Shook.

While still in college Blunden taught dance classes at the Linden Center. In 1963 she was asked to direct the program. This formed the basis for her own school, Dayton Contemporary Dance, which she modeled on that of her mentors. She sent her young students to study on scholarship at the American Dance Festival, the Alvin Ailey American Dance Center, and the Dance Theatre of Harlem. The small performing group, which was started as an outlet for these students, turned professional in 1968. When the company performed her ballet *Flite* at the Northeast Regional Ballet Association in 1973, the Dayton Contempory Dance Company became the first African-

American troupe to gain membership in that organization.

Her company performed works by invited artists Eleo Pomare, Talley Beatty, Donald McKayle, Ulysses Dove, and Lynn Taylor Corbett, among others, with an emphasis on preserving works that were in danger of being lost, particularly those by black choreographers. Hers was the first predominantly black company in the nation to acquire a dance by Merce Cunningham. The company performed throughout the United States, receiving recognition for its vitality and varied repertoire.

Blunden, who gave up performing to devote herself to teaching, felt that ballet is the basis for all dance. When she herself taught, however, it was a modern class based on the Horton technique, borrowing from Martha Graham, José Limón, and others.

Blunden died in Dayton. She was honored with a MacArthur Foundation grant (1994), the Dance Magazine Award (1998), a Lifetime Achievement Award from the National Black Arts Festival (1998), and a Dance USA Honors Award (1999). These accolades were for her energy, her warm humor, and her fierce determination to showcase the contributions of black choreographers and performers to American modern dance. Jennifer Dunning noted that Blunden had mixed feelings about that role: "What I do is from a black perspective. But people who are sure of themselves don't bother with that," she quoted Blunden as saying. Before her death she arranged for her daughter, Debbie Blunden-Diggs, and Kevin Ward to take over as co-directors of the Dayton Contemporary Dance Company.

• There are numerous reviews of the Dayton Contemporary Dance Company, along with videotaped performances, in the Jerome Robbins Dance Collection of the New York Public Library at the Lincoln Center, and the company also has its own archives in Dayton. Blunden wrote about her company's application to the National Association for Regional Ballet in "Remembering The Membership Evaluation," *Dance Magazine,*Oct. 1944, pp. 60–61; and she discusses her decision to found her dance company in the column "Board Spotlight," *Dance/USA Journal* 2, no. 1 (Summer 1994): 10. The best article on Blunden is by Doris Hering, "The Future of Dance Is In Dayton?" *Dance Magazine*, Dec. 1993, pp. 66–69. Some of the material in this article was taken from an unpublished interview with Blunden by the author (New York City, 14 Oct. 1996). Jennifer Dunning's obituary in the *New York Times*, 24 Nov. 1999, used some material from an earlier feature article she had written (*New York Times*, 13 Oct. 1996).

DAWN LILLE

BOORDA, Jeremy Michael (28 Nov. 1938–16 May 1996), admiral and chief of naval operations, was born in South Bend, Indiana, on 26 November 1938, the son of Herman Boorda, a clothing merchant, and Gertrude Frank Wallis Boorda. At the age of sixteen he dropped out of high school and enlisted in the navy after lying about his age. Thereafter he took readily to discipline and was assigned to the Naval Air Technical School in Norman, Oklahoma. In March 1957 he married Bettie Ray Moran; they had four children.

Over the next five years Boorda rose steadily through the enlisted ranks and, as a chief petty officer, attended officer candidate school in 1962. That year he was commissioned an ensign and fulfilled a number of routine assignments both at sea and ashore. In 1964–1965 Boorda saw active duty in Vietnam aboard several destroyers and subsequently attended the Naval War College and the University of Rhode Island, where he obtained a bachelor's degree in 1971. He resumed destroyer duty off Vietnam for two years before assuming command of the destroyer *Farragut* in 1975. In 1977 Boorda came ashore as executive assistant with the naval secretariat for manpower and reserve affairs, returning to sea in 1981 as commander of Destroyer Squadron 22. Two years later he served as executive assistant to the chief of naval personnel, and in 1984 he became executive assistant to the chief of naval operations. Here he enhanced his reputation as a competent, politically astute officer yet one who enjoyed a strong rapport with enlisted personnel.

Boorda continued to fulfill positions of increasing prestige and importance as rear admiral and commander of Destroyer-Cruiser Group 8 in 1984, commander of Battle Force Sixth Fleet in 1987, and, the following year, chief of naval personnel. In December 1991 he advanced to four-star admiral; in this capacity he served as commander, Allied Forces South Europe, and commander, U.S. Naval Forces Europe.

Boorda's most significant service occurred in February 1994 when he ordered American and allied air strikes against Serbian forces in Bosnia. These missions constituted the first ever offensive action by forces belonging to the North Atlantic Treaty Organization (NATO); the performance of naval air units under his command was regarded as outstanding. Bombing runs were continuously conducted in all weather conditions,frequently in the face of heavy and accurate Serbian anti-aircraft fire, yet inflicted heavy damage on armored formation with little loss. On 23 April 1994 President Bill Clinton appointed him the twenty-fifth chief of naval operations, and Boorda also made history by becoming the first chief of naval operations to have risen from the enlisted ranks. The appointment generated some controversy in naval circles owing to Boorda's lack of direct combat experience, but his political savvy and popularity within the service were held as greater assets in the post-Cold War period.

Boorda inherited a service boasting great technical competence and military prowess but one also buffeted by recent internal problems. These included a spiraling crash rate for expensive and elaborate F-14 jet fighters and a cheating scandal at the U.S. Naval Academy. The navy had also suffered political and public fallout as a consequence of the Tailhook incident of 1991, which made the service appear hostile to women sailors. (The incident involved a highly publicized Las Vegas convention where female personnel were physically assaulted by navy flyers.) Furthermore, as the Cold War ended, the armed services endured a period of fiscal austerity and cutbacks. As CNO, Boorda did his best to preserve long-range strategic spending while also seeking pay raises and other benefits to retain skilled personnel. He proved particularly effective in lobbying Congress for newer and better ships, aircraft, and highly sophisticated technical systems to enhance combat effectiveness. In this respect, Boorda was considered an effective spokesman for naval interests. However, he was criticized within the senior ranks for appearing too willing to compromise navy tradition and esprit de corps in favor of "political correctness" with respect to gender issues. Such dissension was never mollified during his two years in office.

Boorda's tenure as CNO was suddenly and unexpectedly interrupted over the seemingly innocuous issue of service medals. The admiral had previously worn combat valor pins suggesting that he had been personally under fire during his Vietnam service. However, Boorda never experienced direct combat, and therefore wearing such decorations was technically illegal. In 1995 the Office of Awards and Special Projects decided that he did not merit combat pins. When it became apparent that *Newsweek* magazine was about to break the story, Boorda committed suicide in his office. He left a brief suicide note addressed to "his sailors" in which he apologized for these transgressions, characterizing them as an "honest mistake." Subsequently an April 1998 memorandum issued by naval secretary John Dalton, backed by the authority of the retired admiral Elmo Zumwalt, concluded that Boorda was, in fact, entitled to wear combat pins. Speculation is rife as to the motives behind his death; the most plausible seems to be his fear that media scrutiny would ravage the naval image he had fought so hard to uphold. Boorda was interred with full military honors at Arlington Cemetery.

• There is no single depository of Boorda papers extant, however several of his letters appear in the Paul J. Kern Papers, Military History Institute, Carlisle Barracks, Pa., and the Joseph C. Strasser Papers, Naval War College Archives, Newport, R.I. Also, the Nimitz Library, U.S. Naval Academy, Annapolis, Md., has a videotaped interview. Discussion of Boorda's policies can be found in Nicholas A. Trongale, "Changes in Navy Leadership Theory and Practice: Post-Vietnam" (Ed.D., University of San Diego, 2001), and Robert H. Gooch, "Women and Men in the New Navy: Life Since Tailhook" (Ph.D., Salve Regina University, 2001). Coverage of Boorda's career and denouement appears in Dan Howard, "What Price Leadership?" *Proceedings of the U.S. Naval Institute* 122 (July 1996): 8–9. For a more critical assessment, consult Peter J. Boyer, "Admiral Boorda's War," *New Yorker* 72, 16 Sept. 1996, pp. 68–86. An overview of the navy in Boorda's time is in Gregory L. Vistica, *Fall from Glory: The Men Who Sank the U.S. Navy* (1997), while the issue of misused medals is adequately addressed in Bernard G. Burkett, *Stolen Valor: How the Vietnam Generation Was Robbed of Its Heroes and Its History* (1998). A superior obituary is in the *Washington Post*, 17 May 1996, and a brief obituary on the same date is in the *New York Times*.

JOHN C. FREDRIKSEN

BOUDREAU, Lou (17 July 1917–10 Aug. 2001), baseball player, was born Louis Boudreau in Harvey, Illinois, the son of Louis Boudreau, a machinist, and Birdie Trent Boudreau. His parents divorced when he was seven. His father, a semiprofessional player, taught him baseball, but basketball was Boudreau's main sport in high school and college. He attended the University of Illinois on a basketball scholarship and led his team to a Big Ten co-championship as a sophomore, a feat he surpassed with the champion Illini baseball team that year as a third baseman. After his sophomore year Boudreau signed a deal with the Cleveland Indians, who paid his parents each a small sum in return for Boudreau agreeing to join the Indians organization after he graduated. Word of the agreement was leaked (by a jealous stepfather, according to *Baseball: The Biographical Encyclopedia*) and in 1938, midway through his junior basketball season, the Big Ten suspended Boudreau, abruptly ending his collegiate career. Though he did persevere and earn his bachelor's degree in physical education in January 1940, he launched his professional baseball career in the summer of 1938.

Just before reporting to Cedar Rapids in the class B Three-Eye League, Boudreau married his long-time sweetheart Della DeRuiter; they were to have four children. Boudreau hit .290 playing third base for Cedar Rapids, but with the star Ken Keltner ahead of him at Cleveland, he shifted to shortstop in 1939, when he moved up to triple A Buffalo. There he batted an impressive .331 and in August, at age twenty-two, won a call-up to the parent club. He was a fixture in Cleveland for the next twelve seasons, earning a reputation as an excellent fielder and a dangerous hitter. Though he was of average size (5 feet 11 inches, 185 pounds) and had a mediocre arm and below-average speed, Boudreau had lightning reflexes, was highly competitive, and possessed an outstanding baseball mind. In 1940, his first full season, he drove in 101 runs with a .295 batting average and 46 doubles and won an All-Star Game berth. Though his offensive production declined the next year, he still led the league with 45 doubles.

Following the 1941 season, the Indian manager Roger Peckinpaugh, who as a twenty-three-year-old fill-in for the New York Yankees at the end of the 1914 season had been the youngest major league manager ever, was fired. Boudreau, a natural leader in high school and college, applied for the open position and, at age twenty-four, became the youngest permanently appointed manager in major league history to that date. Bob Dolgan of the *Cleveland Plain Dealer* wrote that he "looked as though he was in charge of everybody from the players to the umpires to the groundskeepers and ushers." As a player-manager, the young shortstop found greater success playing than managing. With the Hall of Fame pitcher Bob Feller in the military most of the 1942–1945 stretch, the Indians struggled and finished no higher than third place.

Boudreau suffered from arthritic ankles that kept him out of the service, but he regularly led the league in fielding and in 1944 led the league in hitting at .327. With the war over and Feller back, Cleveland had high hopes in 1946, but poor hitting condemned them to a sixth-place finish.

When the colorful maverick Bill Veeck bought the club in late 1946, Boudreau was in trouble. Although Veeck regarded Boudreau as the best shortstop in baseball, he did not rate Boudreau's managerial skills highly and hoped to sign Casey Stengel to manage the team. The highly popular Boudreau said he would not play in Cleveland for another manager, and Veeck reluctantly signed him to another year as leader. In the 1947 season the shortstop hit .307 and led the league in doubles but only piloted the Indians to a fourth-place finish. Veeck worked out a deal to trade Boudreau to the St. Louis Browns, but it fell through. Veeck maintained that last-minute Browns financial demands torpedoed the deal, but the popular impression was that a wave of protest in Cleveland forced him to back down. The reprieved skipper demanded a two-year contract and got it.

That settlement paved the way for the crowning season of Boudreau's career. In 1948 he batted .355, drove in 106 runs, struck out only 9 times in 560 at bats, and piloted the Indians to a tie with the Red Sox for the American League pennant. He then unexpectedly selected the left-handed rookie ace Gene Bearden to face lefty-laden Boston on one day's rest for the one-game playoff, and the young man pitched a complete-game 8–3 win, helped by Boudreau's clutch 4 hits, including 2 homers. The Indians then beat the Boston Braves in six games to win the World Series, the first Cleveland title since 1920. He climaxed his season by easily winning the league's Most Valuable Player award.

Boudreau's bad ankles contributed to his slowing down the next two years, as Cleveland slipped behind Stengel's new Yankee dynasty. Boudreau hit .284, then .269, and new team owners sacked him as manager after the 1950 season. Released as a player, he caught on with the Red Sox and played about half-time in 1951 before being asked to take over the team's leadership in 1952 as player-manager. He barely played again, but he managed Boston for three seasons with modest success. He then managed Kansas City without distinction in 1955, 1956, and part of 1957, the last year shortened by his firing. At that point he moved to the broadcast booth with the Chicago Cubs, his boyhood favorites, where he served as a popular announcer for thirty years. This new career was interrupted only briefly in 1960, when he swapped jobs with manager Charlie Grimm for most of the season and barely avoided the cellar.

Boudreau's career record as a player includes a .295 batting average, 8 times leading the league in fielding, 7 All-Star appearances, and election to the Hall of Fame in 1970. As Cleveland's manager he sensitively oversaw the integration of the American League with Larry Doby in 1947, developed the Boudreau shift in 1946 to combat Ted Williams's fearsome bat (he moved everyone but the left fielder to the right of second base to slow the notorious pull hitting of Williams), and converted third baseman/outfielder Bob Lemon into a Hall of Fame pitcher. Boudreau finished managing with a career 1,162-1,224 won-lost record. He died in Olympia Fields, Illinois.

• Boudreau (with Ed Fitzgerald) wrote the autobiographical *Player-Manager* (1949, updated 1952). Bill Veeck, *Veeck as in Wreck* (1962), offers colorful insights; and *Baseball: The Biographical Encyclopedia* (2000), ed. David Pietrusza et al., provides a reasonably comprehensive sketch. An informative obituary by Bob Dolgan is in the *Cleveland Plain Dealer*, 12 Aug. 2001. The 11 Aug. 2001 issue of the *New York Times* has an obituary as well.

JOHN R. M. WILSON

BOWERMAN, Bill (19 Feb. 1911–24 Dec. 1999), track coach, was born William Jay Bowerman in Portland, Oregon, the son of Jay Bowerman, president of the Oregon state senate, and Lizzie Hoover Bowerman. The Bowermans were divorced in 1913 and the children were placed in the custody of their mother.

From 1913 to 1921 Bill Bowerman lived in Fossil, Oregon, where his mother taught school. Later, she and her four children lived for two years in Ashland, Oregon, and one year in Seattle before settling in Medford, Oregon, in 1924. Bill was considered to be an unruly child, and in 1924 he was sent to Hill Military Academy in Portland. The next year he attended Medford High School, where his incorrigible ways caught the attention of Superintendent of Schools E. H. Hedrick. In a session that Bowerman later credited with changing his life, Hedrick sharply reprimanded him for his behavior and suggested that he channel his energy into athletics. Bowerman did just that, going out for football, basketball, and tennis.

After completing high school in 1929, Bowerman attended the University of Oregon, where he played left end on the varsity football team. When his football eligibility was completed, he competed in track at the 440-yard distance for two seasons. He graduated with a Bachelor of Science degree in business administration in 1934. Having joined the Reserve Officers Training Corps (ROTC) while a student at Oregon, he became a second lieutenant in the army reserve upon graduation. He was hired by Franklin High School in Portland as football coach and biology teacher but left after a year to return to Medford as football and basketball coach. In 1938, his first year as Medford football coach, his team was unbeaten and won a state title. The following year he started a track team and as track coach enjoyed spectacular success; his teams won several state titles and took the prestigious Hayward Relays seven times in eight attempts.

Bowerman married Barbara Young in 1936; the couple would have three sons. In December 1941 Bowerman entered the U.S. Army. He served until 1945, mostly in the Tenth Mountain Division, as quartermaster and supply officer. An eye problem kept him out of combat. The division fought in Italy in 1944, and one of Bowerman's jobs was to collect the bodies of soldiers killed in action. He reached the rank of major before leaving the army in 1945.

The following year Bowerman resumed his duties as track and football coach at Medford. In 1948 he left to become track coach and freshman football coach at the University of Oregon in Eugene; he disliked his football duties, however, and resigned after four years, continuing as track coach and assistant athletic director. He quickly built a winning track program, and the University of Oregon enjoyed tremendous success in that sport until his retirement in 1973. His teams won four National Collegiate Athletic Association (NCAA) track and field championships. He coached forty-four all-American athletes and nineteen Olympians. One of his earliest and most famous all-Americans, middle-distance runner Bill Dellinger, eventually succeeded him as track coach at Oregon. Among the other track athletes he coached were Steve Prefontaine, Kenny Moore, Dyrol Burleson, Jim Grelle, and Jim Bailey.

Bowerman is perhaps most famous for his role in popularizing running as a lifelong activity. In 1964 he took a team of athletes to New Zealand, where he met Arthur Lydiard, who had made running something of a way of life for mature persons in that country. Bowerman considered himself in good physical condition at age fifty-two, but when he accompanied a group of Lydiard's mature runners he found himself unable to keep up. This inspired him to organize a jogging club when he returned to Eugene; the sport soon became extraordinarily successful there. He prepared a pamphlet, the watchword of which was "train—don't strain." This was followed in 1967 by a small book, *Jogging*, written with physician Waldo E. Harris, that became the "bible" of recreational runners in the United States. In it he described the practical and physiological advantages of recreational running, provided programs and tips, and urged women to take up the sport.

Throughout his long career as track coach at Oregon, Bowerman constantly worked at improving procedures and equipment. He made pioneering experiments with artificial track surfaces, timing clocks and apparatus, aids for hurdlers and throwers, and movie-making as an aid to coaching track. Especially critical of American-made track shoes, he founded the Blue Ribbon Sports Company to import and distribute shoes from Adidas in Germany and Onitsuka Tiger in Japan. Blue Ribbon was the forerunner of the Nike sports shoe empire, which Bowerman cofounded in 1972 with Phil Knight, one of his former runners. He experimented tirelessly with athletic shoes, seeking to make them lighter but more supportive. Famously, he invented the waffle sole in his kitchen, using his wife's waffle iron as a template. He eventually poisoned himself by using hexane as a solvent for rubber in insufficiently ventilated spaces, and the effects on his nervous system resulted in his having to walk with a brace for the rest of his life.

Bowerman has been characterized as being highly organized with a strain of unpredictability—an intense person who concentrated on every detail of the track-coaching and teaching experience. He tended to work his athletes somewhat less than most coaches, with the result that they progressed steadily and were not often injured. He was opinionated and did not take contradiction easily. His relationship with the NCAA was often stormy, but less so than his experience with the American Athletic Union (AAU). An incident in 1959 in which the AAU slighted Dellinger incurred Bowerman's anger and was partially responsible for his role in the founding of the U.S. Track and Field Federation (USTFF) in a sport that had been dominated by the AAU. When Bowerman was selected as head track coach to the 1972 U.S. Olympic Team, he soon found himself at odds with Olympics officials, who wanted the coaches to agree to television interviews. Bowerman regarded such events as "inquisitions." Discouraged by the bombing at the 1972 Olympics in Munich, Germany, biased judging, and other incidents, Bowerman retired from coaching the next year to devote himself to his business interests.

Bowerman was elected to the National Track and Field Hall of Fame in 1981 but characteristically refused induction because his coach at Oregon, Bill Hayward, had never been chosen. He considered his greatest achievement to be the popularization of running with the American public. He died in a retirement home in Fossil.

• Bowerman's books, in addition to *Jogging*, include *Coaching Track and Field* (1974) and *High Performance Training for Track and Field* (1990). The indispensable source on Bowerman is William H. Freeman's 1972 Ph.D. dissertation at the University of Oregon, *A Biographical Study of William Jay Bowerman*. A shorter, more accessible source, also by Freeman, is "Renaissance Man of the Olympics," *Christian Science Monitor*, 13 Mar. 1972. Other articles include Kenny Moore, "Fishing in the Rivers of Men's Minds," *Sports Illustrated* 37, no. 7 (14 Aug. 1972): 30–34, and Joe Henderson, "A Coach and a Tradition," *Track and Field News* 22, no. 9 (1 June 1968): 20–21. A booklet that deals with Bowerman's business career is K. E. Greenberg et al., *Bill Bowerman and Phil Knight: Building the Nike Empire* (1997). An Internet site that provides articles on Bowerman, and photographs, is www.billbowerman.com. Obituaries are in the *New York Times*, 27 Dec. 1999, and *Runner's World*, Apr. 2000.

LUCKETT V. DAVIS

BRADLEY, Wilmot Hyde (4 Apr. 1899–12 Apr. 1979), federal geologist, paleolimnologist, and science administrator, was born in Westville, Connecticut, the son of John Lucius Bradley, a dentist, and Anna Miner Hyde Bradley, who gave him an abiding interest in electrical-mechanical phenomena and natural history. In 1916 "Bill" Bradley passed from high school in nearby New Haven to Yale's Sheffield Scientific School, where he studied mechanical engineering, then chemistry, and, in his senior year, geology with Alan M. Bateman and Adolph Knopf.

After receiving a bachelor of philosophy degree in 1920 Bradley joined the U.S. Geological Survey (USGS) for a season's mapping with fuels geologists in the Wasatch Mountains before beginning graduate studies at Yale. Similar work in the Uinta Mountains during the next two summers led in 1922 to full-time employment with the USGS, his marriage to Catrina van Benschoten, and their move to Washington, D.C. The couple had two children.

Encouraged by Chief Geologist David White, Bradley added studies of composition, origin, history, and microfossils to geologic mapping of strata in the Eocene Green River Formation, including those in Colorado's Naval Oil Shale Reserve No. 1. Bradley recognized varves (annual deposits) in the Green River sequence, for which he estimated a six-million-year duration. In 1927 Yale accepted as Bradley's dissertation his study of the formation's lakeshore phases, published as USGS *Professional Paper* 140-D (1926).

Also in the 1930s Bradley investigated geology and natural gas resources in New York, evaluated the Alcova and other dam sites in the West for the Bureau of Reclamation, and led USGS colleagues in analyzing the geology and biology of graded beds in Pleistocene abyssal cores from the North Atlantic. He also studied strategic-mineral deposits both before and after Pearl Harbor, some for Bateman's division of the Board of Economic Warfare.

In June 1942 USGS Director Walter C. Mendenhall and Chief Geologist Gerald F. Loughlin shifted Bradley to full-time management. Bradley had helped William W. Rubey's earlier efforts to make geology, geologists, and the USGS more useful to the war effort, before Rubey returned to strategic-minerals studies. Bradley completed Rubey's negotiations with the Army Corps of Engineers by forming the Military Geology Unit of civilian geologists, geomorphologists, ground water hydrologists, soils and beach scientists, botanists, cartographers, and other specialists drawn from the USGS, other federal agencies, academe, and industry, to provide the corps with terrain and related engineering intelligence about designated strategic areas in the style of German *Wehrgeologie*. The MGU demonstrated its usefulness by aiding the planning for the U.S. Seventh Army's campaign in Sicily. After the Normandy landings the MGU prepared tank trafficability maps for the U.S. Third Army's advance across France and Germany, but its more than 100 scientists and supporting staff continued to concentrate almost exclusively on work for or service in the Pacific theaters.

In July 1944 Director William E. Wrather and his deputy Thomas B. Nolan began to fit USGS branches for the postwar years by replacing Loughlin with Bradley, the youngest person yet to become chief geologist. Like his predecessors White and Mendenhall, Bradley strongly supported attaining a balanced program of applied and fundamental research. From Clarence King's founding directorate (1879–1881), this view held that "to apply science to human needs, there must be science to apply" (Mendenhall, USGS

Fiftieth Annual Report [1929], pp. 11–12). Bradley quickly remade the geologic branch consistent with that goal by dividing it into two groups of sections. He appointed Rubey and Harold M. Bannerman to lead, respectively, the new Divisions of Basic Sciences and Economic Geology. Bradley also established sections to undertake functions recognized as increasingly important in recent years—engineering geology, foreign geology, military geology, geochemistry, and geophysics. Encouraged by Wrather and Nolan, Bradley chose younger geologists to manage these units to combine innovative ideas with technological advances such as airborne surveys of magnetism and radioactivity, photogrammetry in geologic mapping, and, later, electron microscopes, mass spectrometers, and electronic computers.

Personable, witty, and unpretentious, Bradley gently but firmly led the geologic branch (renamed a division in 1949) in war and peace for the next fifteen years, an interval far longer than any of his predecessors, during which funds more than quadrupled and the staff more than doubled. Bradley's scientists applied multidisciplinary techniques in investigating uranium and other rare-element deposits, expanded military and foreign geology efforts worldwide, assessed Alaska's Naval Petroleum Reserve No. 4 and other energy-rich sedimentary basins, evaluated highway, dam, and other construction sites, examined underground nuclear test sites, investigated volcanoes and radioactive waste and their hazards, began studies of lunar geology, tektites, and impact craters, and strove to extend geologic mapping of the nation at a scale of 1:24,000 to aid resource and land appraisals. Like White, Bradley encouraged younger scientists to find projects that interested them, to improve themselves, and to support each other's work. He laughed easily, even when some responded to his talk about Eocene coprolites by saying he was certainly full of his subject. The USGS Pick and Hammer Club players initially burlesqued Bradley's "streamlining" the geologic division but in their annual review of agency foibles for 1956 spurned any other employment—deciding that (as in the popular song) their hearts belonged to Bradley for "he treats us so well." The mixed results of his division's struggles with the "evils of prostitution," its ever-increasing dependence on outside funding, did not significantly decrease that loyalty. Seventeen of the 105 USGS scientists in the National Academy of Sciences joined the geologic division during Bradley's managerial years. The academy elected Bradley in 1946, the same year Mendenhall and Wrather sponsored Bradley's membership in the capital's Cosmos Club.

In August 1959, at Bradley's request, he returned to full-time research on past and present algal-ooze lakes and their cyclical sediments—especially those in Florida's Mud Lake—as analogues to the Green River strata, similar sequences, and their energy resources. His interpretation of varved sediments formed in permanently stratified freshwater lakes, rather than playa lakes, held for most of the Green River sequence.

Bradley continued to serve as an associate editor (1945–1974) of the *American Journal of Science*, and the periodical honored him with a festschrift on his sixty-first birthday in 1960; Yale had awarded him an honorary D.Sc. thirteen years earlier, on the occasion of Sheffield's centennial. In 1965 he also presided over the Geological Society of America, whose Penrose Medal he received seven years later from his citationist and close friend Nolan (who had succeeded Wrather as director in 1956). After Bradley retired from the USGS in 1969, he moved to a fifty-acre farm on Maine's coast near Milbridge. There, he continued his scholarly activities until he died following a stroke. In 1984, the USGS geologic division renamed for Bradley its yearly series of distinguished internal talks to emphasize their multidisciplinary nature.

• Record Group 57 at the National Archives and Records Administration's Archives II facility in College Park, Md., holds Bradley's public papers, except for the sixty-five notebooks and eight map groups from his work in the West (1919–1957) and Northeast (1934–1955) that are kept in the USGS Field Records Library at Denver, along with some 500 of his images in the adjacent USGS Field Photographs Library. For a finding aid to these collections, see Renée M. Jaussaud's 679-page "Inventory of the Records of the United States Geological Survey Record Group 57: In the National Archives [1999]," in Clifford M. Nelson, ed., "Records and History of the United States Geological Survey," *U.S. Geological Survey Circular* 1179 (2000, CD-ROM). *USGS Bulletin* 823 (1931): 68, 545, 937 (1944): 116-17, 1049 (1957): 110, 111, 1195 (1965): 203; and the cumulative indexes of the *Bibliography and Index of Geology* list most of Bradley's publications. These citations also are available on CD-ROM and on the Web as part of the American Geological Institute's "GeoRef" online bibliographical database. A six-page bibliography and a seven-page partial transcript of an informal oral history of Bradley by Ellis L. Yochelson and Clifford M. Nelson in 1976, both unpublished, are at the USGS National Center Library in Reston, Va. Biographical articles about Bradley include those by USGS geologists Wendell P. Woodring, Bradley Memorial Volume, *American Journal of Science* 258-A (1960): 1–5; George V. Cohee, *Journal of Paleontology* 46 (1972): 608–09; Preston [E.] Cloud [Jr.], *American Philosophical Society Year Book for 1980* (1981): 534–39; Vincent E. McKelvey [Chief Geologist, 1971; Director, 1971–1978], *Geological Society of America Memorials* 11 (1981): 7 pp. (with bibliography); and McKelvey, *National Academy of Sciences Biographical Memoirs* 54 (1983): 75–88 (with bibliography). See also Donald H. Williams, *Cosmos Club Bulletin* 38, no. 12 (Dec. 1985): 6-9. Obituaries are in the *Washington Post*, 19 Apr. 1979, and the *New Haven Register*, 23 Apr. 1979.

CLIFFORD M. NELSON

BRAGG, Janet (24 Mar. 1907–11 Apr. 1993), aviator, nurse, and nursing home proprietor, was born Janet Harmon in Griffin, Georgia, the daughter of Cordia Batts Harmon and Samuel Harmon, a brick contractor. The Batts family had long been established in Griffin. Bragg's maternal grandfather was a freed slave of Spanish descent, and her maternal grandmother was a Cherokee. Bragg's grandfather had built the house in which she and her siblings were born; her mother had been born in the same house. Bragg, the youngest of seven children, had a happy childhood, enjoying sports and games and excelling at school. In an interview conducted at the University of Arizona as part of a project called African Americans in Aviation in Arizona, Bragg reminisced: "We were a very happy family. We were not a rich family, only rich in love."

Independence was encouraged in the Harmon household. The children were allowed to attend any church they chose. They were also encouraged to achieve their potential educationally, regardless of gender. In her autobiography, *Soaring above Setbacks* (1996), Bragg recalled her father saying, "If Jack can do it, so can Jill." This statement bolstered Bragg's courage, leading her to believe, "I could do anything I set my sights on." Bragg transferred from public elementary school to St. Stephens Episcopal School, which provided a better education in those days of strict segregation. She chose to attend an Episcopal boarding school, Fort Valley Episcopal High School, in Fort Valley, Georgia, where she did well in math, science, and sports.

Bragg next attended Spelman Seminary (now Spelman College), an all-black women's college in Atlanta, Georgia, where she majored in nursing. Her training took place at MacBicar Hospital on the Spelman campus. MacBicar's nursing program was selective and demanding. Bragg was one of two out of an entering class of twelve who survived the probationary period. The hospital had no interns, so nursing students assisted in operations and performed other procedures customarily handled by interns. As a result they received first-rate training. Bragg received her registered nurse (R.N.) degree in 1929.

After her graduation from Spelman, Bragg worked as a nurse in a segregated department of a Griffin hospital, but she left after a month because of the inferior care offered to black patients. She moved to Rockford, Illinois, to live with a sister. While there, she passed the Illinois nurses' license test. Unable to find professional employment in Rockford, she moved to Chicago, where she became a nurse at Wilson Hospital. About 1931, while working at Wilson, she met and married Evans Waterford; they had no children. The marriage lasted only a few years (five according to one source), but she kept the name Waterford until she married again.

In 1933 Bragg's father died. Bragg took on the support of her mother and two nieces, who moved into her Chicago home. She left the hospital for a better-paying nursing job in a medical office. Graduate work in pediatric nursing at the Cook County School of Nursing and a graduate certificate in public health administration from Loyola University led to a more lucrative position as health inspector for the Metropolitan Burial Insurance Company. She could now afford to pursue her dream of learning to fly.

In her autobiography Bragg wrote: "I saw a billboard with a bird . . . nurturing her young fledglings into the flying world. It read, 'Birds Learn to Fly. Why

Can't You?' . . . It was so beautiful." In 1933 she enrolled in Aeronautical University ground school. Her instruction by the black aviation pioneers John Robinson and Cornelius Coffey was in meteorology, aeronautics, aircraft maintenance, and aircraft mechanics. Because the school owned no airplanes, it could not provide actual flight instruction. Flight instruction cost $15 an hour at the time, so Bragg decided it made more sense financially to purchase her own plane, which she could then rent to others. The plane, costing $600, was the first of three she would own.

Finding an airfield where she and other aspiring black flyers would be permitted to learn to fly proved impossible. Black pilots were not allowed to fly out of airports used by whites. If they truly wanted to fly, they needed to build their own airfields. The class at the ground school, with the aid of Robinson and Coffey, formed the Challenger Aero Club. The group purchased land and built an airfield with their own hands in the small, all-black town of Robbins, Illinois. In the spring of 1934, in her own plane and from the airfield she had helped build, Bragg learned to fly. After thirty-five solo hours, she passed the test for the private pilot's license. In addition to her other activities, in the 1930s Bragg wrote a weekly column, "Negro Aviation," in the *Chicago Defender* under the byline Janet Waterford.

In 1939 the federal government announced the Civilian Pilot Training Program (CPTP) for whites only. Black pilots, civil rights organizations, and prominent politicians successfully lobbied to have the race restriction removed. African Americans would be trained, but separately from whites and in different facilities.

In 1943, during World War II, Bragg and several other black women applied for appointments with the Women's Auxiliary Service Pilots (WASPS). The interviewer rejected Bragg outright, and her appeal was unsuccessful. She then applied to the military nurse corps but was informed that the quota for black nurses was filled.

Unable to join the war effort, Bragg went to the CPTP school at Tuskegee, Alabama, to obtain her commercial pilot's license. After successfully completing her written work, she took and passed her flight test, but a bigoted instructor refused to issue her license. Bragg returned to Chicago, where she passed the test with ease, the first black woman to do so.

Flying was a hobby, and Bragg continued to work as a health inspector until an opportunity arose to start her own business. Bragg and her brother had arranged to purchase a property, but her brother backed out. A friend suggested she turn the property into a health care facility for patients on welfare. With the aid of cousins from Georgia, Bragg's venture grew into a nursing home business that eventually housed sixty patients. She married Sumner Bragg late in 1951, and he joined her in running the business. They operated several nursing homes successfully until their joint retirement in 1972. They had no children.

Bragg befriended several Ethiopian students studying in the United States, traveling with them and showing them around. For her helpfulness she was invited to Ethiopia to meet the emperor, Haile Selassie, in 1955. In the 1970s she traveled widely in Africa, leading tour groups. In 1986, after the death of Sumner Bragg, she moved permanently to Arizona, where the Braggs had been spending their winters.

Bragg's achievements were recognized during her later years. Invited to appear at aviation events around the country, she received many awards and honors. She was also active in such civic organizations as the Tucson, Arizona, Urban League, Habitat for Humanity, and the Adopt-a-Scholar Program at Pima College in Tucson. She died in Blue Island, Illinois, a suburb of Chicago. She wrote in her autobiography, "I think I've had a wonderful life."

• The best source of information on Bragg is her autobiography. Darlene Clark Hines, *Black Women in America* (1993), focuses on Bragg's aviation career, while Jim Haskins, *Black Stars: African American Entrepreneurs* (1998), concentrates on her work as a nursing home administrator. A revealing interview with Bragg conducted in 1989 is part of *African Americans in Aviation in Arizona: A Report of African American History Internship Project* (1989). Rufus Hunt, "A Page from Chicago's Aviation History," *Chicago Defender*, 2 May 1981; and A. S. Young, "She's Mother to Ethiopians," *Chicago Defender* (n.d.), explore various facets of Bragg's life. Obituaries are in *Jet*, 5 May 1993, and the *Chicago Defender*, 15 April 1993.

MIRIAM SAWYER

BRANNAN, Charles F. (23 Aug. 1903–2 July 1992), attorney and cabinet member, was born Charles Franklin Brannan in Denver, Colorado, the son of John Brannan, an electrical engineer, and Ella Louise Street Brannan. On graduating from nearby West High School in 1921, he attended Regis College before transferring to the University of Denver, where he studied law and was active in both student government and athletics. After receiving his LL.B. in 1929, he began practicing law in his hometown, specializing in irrigation and mining issues. On 29 June 1932 Brannan married Eda Seltzer, a schoolteacher whom he had met while they were both attending the University of Denver; the couple had no children.

An avid supporter of President Franklin D. Roosevelt's New Deal, Brannan entered government service in 1935 when he was appointed assistant regional attorney in the USDA's Resettlement Administration. Already an expert in water and conservation issues, Brannan helped arrange the purchase of drought-stricken lands in the western states. In 1937 he became regional attorney in the USDA's Office of the Solicitor, where he helped form irrigation districts and other cooperative agricultural projects. Brannan became regional director in the Farm Security Administration (later the Farmers Home Administration and now known as the Farm Service Agency) for the states of Wyoming, Colorado, and Montana, where he administered loan programs for water facilities and supervised credit for individual farmers.

After briefly serving as an assistant administrator in the FSA (April–June 1944), Brannan was appointed assistant secretary of Agriculture by President Roosevelt. While assistant secretary he administered the department's programs in flood control and water supply management and its efforts in managing timber and grazing lands within the public domain. He also served for several years as vice chairman of the department's Policy and Program Committee, which made recommendations to Congress concerning long-term agricultural programs and policies. During the mid-1940s Brannan also acted as the agricultural advisor to the U.S. delegation to the United Nations (1945) and acted in a similar capacity to the American delegate to the United Nations Economic and Social Council. While handling these various duties Brannan also was a vice chairman of the Commodity Credit Corporation.

In 1948 Secretary of Agriculture Clinton P. Anderson resigned to run for the U.S. Senate from New Mexico and recommended that Brannan replace him. On gaining his confirmation from the Senate in May of that year, Brannan urged Congress to take immediate action on the long-range farm program, arguing that a "strong, productive agriculture" was critical to world peace and prosperity. One of Brannan's first challenges after taking office was helping President Harry S. Truman win an uphill battle for election. A tireless campaigner, Brannan took to the stump and made countless speeches in which he deflected Republican criticism of low farm prices by charging that the Republican-dominated Congress had sabotaged farm price supports by failing to provide adequate storage facilities for surplus grain. Brannan's support helped Truman carry several farm states.

Brannan's most notable action as secretary came in 1949, when he proposed what became known as the Brannan plan to solve a complex set of problems that dogged American agriculture. As fewer farmers produced more crops on farms that increasingly began to resemble production facilities, the sector was persistently plagued by low prices and falling real income. Designed to keep farm income at its record wartime levels while allowing supply and demand to determine commodity prices, Brannan proposed guaranteed price supports (from 90 percent to 100 percent of parity) on 75 percent of the various commodities produced by American farmers—an increase from 25 percent—which he hoped to accomplish by including such previously excluded perishable items as eggs and milk. To help preserve family farms, Brannan advocated direct payments to farmers (not to exceed $26,000 apiece). While admitting that his program was expensive, he argued that since depressions were "farm-led and farm-fed," the cost was more than justified by the resulting stability in the national economy; furthermore, the resulting lowered prices of foodstuffs would result in increased consumer consumption levels and better nutritional levels, particularly among the poor.

While Brannan's plan was supported by liberal farm organizations like the Farmers Union and labor unions such as the Congress of Industrial Organizations (which thought that lower commodity prices would benefit workers), it drew immediate opposition from conservative farm organizations like the National Grange and the American Farm Bureau Federation—which termed the plan "left wing"—as well as a host of conservative organizations such as the National Association of Manufacturers. Congressional Republicans soon joined in the chorus of opposition voices, variously condemning the plan as either too costly or an attempt to "regiment" American agriculture. In the face of extensive opposition, Brannan's plan was ultimately defeated during the course of Congressional deliberations.

On leaving office in 1953, Brannan returned to Denver and practiced law. He also served as the general counsel for the Farmers Union before finally retiring around 1990. Having earlier served as president of the University of Denver Alumni Association, Brannan spent his later years as vice president of the Harry S. Truman Library Institute for National and International Affairs (1981–1992). He died in Denver.

Although thwarted in his attempts to bring progressive solutions to the seemingly intractable problems of American agriculture while in office—thus sharing in the fate of much of the domestic portion of President Truman's Fair Deal—Brannan did live to see many of his agricultural price proposals adopted into law in 1973. Ahead of his time in terms of public policy, even his far-reaching proposals did not solve the myriad problems that resulted in a decline in the number of American farmers in the late twentieth century.

• Brannan's papers are held at the Harry S. Truman Presidential Library in Independence, Missouri. His plan to revive American agriculture received its fullest coverage in John Rose Kerr, *The Brannan Plan: A Proposed Farm Program* (1950), and Reo M. Christenson, *The Brannan Plan: Farm Politics and Policy* (1959). An obituary is in the *Washington Post*, 5 July 1992.

EDWARD L. LACH, JR.

BREGER, Dave (15 Apr. 1908–16 Jan. 1970), cartoonist, was born Irving David Breger in Chicago, Illinois, the son of Benjamin Breger, a butcher, and Sophie Passin Breger, within a few weeks of their arrival in the United States from the Ukraine. Young Breger earned his high school diploma in 1926 at Crane Technical School, where he drew cartoons signed "Irving Breger" for the school newspaper. He studied architecture at the University of Illinois but switched to medicine when he entered Northwestern University. Before graduating in 1931 with a degree in abnormal psychology, he served as editor-in-chief of the campus humor magazine, the *Purple Parrot* (c. 1930), for which he drew cartoons in the geometric manner of John Held, Jr. Unable to find employment as a psychologist during the Great Depression, he freelanced cartoons and sold enough to finance a trip abroad, visiting his parents' homeland and Africa. After two years, he returned to Chicago and became office manager in his father's sausage factory at the stockyards, where he coined the slogan, "Our Wurst Is the Best." On a 1937 vacation trip to New York, Breger took cartoons around to magazine cartoon editors and sold one to the *Saturday Evening Post*. Shortly thereafter, he left Chicago for New York to pursue a cartooning career. He achieved modest success, selling his work to such magazines as *Collier's, Esquire, Parade, This Week,* and others, in addition to the *Saturday Evening Post.*

Early in 1941, Breger was drafted into the army and shipped to Camp Livingston in Louisiana, where he was assigned to repairing trucks. In his off hours, he continued to draw cartoons, working, at first, in the bakery, which was the only place where lights were on all night. "Even during maneuvers," he later wrote, "I managed to carry on, sketching in the back end of a truck" by the light of the taillight extension draped over his shoulder. Among the cartoons he did were some based on his own experiences in the army, in which he drew a round-faced freckled and spectacled version of himself as the protagonist, a well-meaning misfit. The *Saturday Evening Post* began publishing these single-panel semiautobiographical efforts on 30 August 1941 as a series under the heading *Private Breger*. When the army realized Breger's talent, he was transferred to the Special Services Division and sent to Fort Dix, New Jersey. On 9 January 1942, he married Dorathy Lewis of Brooklyn, New York; they had three children. (It was Breger's second marriage; his first, to a fashion model named Evelyn, lasted five years and produced no children.)

In the early spring of 1942, Breger was assigned to the New York staff of *Yank, the Army Weekly,* which was about to be launched. The editors asked him to do a cartoon like the *Post*'s *Private Breger* but with a different name, and by the time of the magazine's first issue on 17 June 1942, Breger had reincarnated his alter ego as "GI Joe" (last name, Trooper), thereby coining a generic name for the ordinary infantryman that endured beyond the years of World War II. (During World War I, "GI" stood for "galvanized iron" and designated garbage cans; in the WWII armed forces, "GI" was standard argot for "government issue.") That summer, Breger was sent to cover the American military presence in England, becoming one of the first two correspondents from *Yank.*

Breger's cartoon persona soon attracted the attention of King Features newspaper syndicate, and on 19 October 1942, *Private Breger* debuted in scores of the nation's newspapers. Henceforth, in addition to his weekly cartoon for *Yank,* Breger produced a daily panel cartoon for domestic syndication while also fulfilling his other obligations at the army magazine—taking photographs and doing miscellaneous artwork.

"He's a busy soldier," wrote Ernie Pyle, the famed WWII correspondent, who also pointed out that Breger made five sets of photostatic copies of his cartoons, filing one set with the army's public relations office and sending three to King Features in New York ("to be sure at least one gets there") and one, by special request, to Supreme Allied Commander General Dwight D. Eisenhower. This requirement at first nearly paralyzed the cartoonist: "My production of cartoons came almost to a standstill," he recalled, "because of my concern that the General would take offense at most of my gibes at Army life." But Eisenhower's aide reassured Breger: "Don't worry about it—the General said he just wants to make sure of one laugh a day out of the War."

Promoted to second lieutenant in March 1943, Breger was promptly banished from *Yank,* which published only the work of enlisted men. *GI Joe* appeared thereafter in the military newspaper, *Stars and Stripes,* until the spring of 1944, when it was discontinued in order to eliminate "duplication of efforts" (as Breger diplomatically put it). *Private Breger* continued in newspaper syndication on the home front, and for *Stars and Stripes* Breger produced another cartoon, *GI Jerry,* which satirized Nazi philosophy in a military setting through the device of what Breger called "an unpleasant German soldier." With the end of the war, Breger left the army and so did his cartoon character: "Private Breger" became "Mister Breger" and continued syndicated life for the next two decades until the cartoonist's death in Nyack, New York, after a short illness.

The "Private Breger" cartoon incarnation is an almost childlike naif, meek and a little clumsy, confused but wholly undismayed by the alien environment into which he has been plunged by his local draft board. In his vague bafflement, he is every conscripted American of the time, who, unused to the highly regimented life of the military, tries, in the best spirit but with sometimes risible results, to adapt. Much of the cartoon's humor arises from this juxtaposition of civilian attitude and military custom. In his barracks, Private Breger hangs a "Home Sweet Home" placard and faces disciplinary action for "inciting to mutiny." Carrying a violin case, he is admonished by his sergeant, "I don't care how they do it in the movies. Take your rifle out of that violin case!" Another time, Private Breger sends his weapon out to a professional laundry to be cleaned. The military's institutional mind-sets are often ridiculed. Standing in ranks and looking askance at a stack of picks and shovels that suggests his next task, Private Breger is advised by his sergeant to "wipe that opinion off your face." On another occasion, his commanding officer sends him off with the following: "Here are your secret orders where to go. You are not to open them until you reach your destination safely." Later, he is given another order: "Arrange these documents alphabetically and then burn them." But throughout his military adventures, Private Breger exercises considerable ingenuity and enthusiasm for the work. On a long march, rather than shoulder his rifle, he puts the butt in a roller skate and trails the weapon alongside, saying to an irate sergeant, "Well, they do it in the artillery, don't they?"

Breger's drawing style, achieved without benefit of any art instruction (like that of many cartoonists), employs straightforward unadorned outline, no linear variation or stylistic pyrotechnics except solid blacks and gray tones strategically placed to enhance the clarity of the composition. His gags often demand detailed pictures of equipment and setting, and Breger was adept at drawing whatever is needed from virtually any angle. Pyle observed a visual rhetoric in the cartoons: "Breger always makes officers bigger than privates. And he always makes officers' jaws jutting and privates' jaws rounded. That's to show 'authority' and 'obedience,' he says."

In postwar civilian life, Mister Breger remains the well-meaning victim of his circumstances. The cartoonist assigned his character to any and all occupations, wherever his search for a gag took him. As a result, Mister Breger is more prop than personality except for his eternal haplessness. On an automobile trip with his wife, they run out of gas, and he walks to the nearest town; when he returns with a can of gasoline, his wife tells him that she played the radio to pass the time and now the battery is dead. In another strip, Mister Breger plants a roof garden, and the roots come through his ceiling.

In the 1960s, Breger developed and taught a course in general cartooning for New York University, one of the first of its kind on the college level, and translated his experiences into a book, *How to Draw and Sell Cartoons* (1966). During World War II, his cartoons embodied the fundamental clash of civilian and military ways of life, but his lasting contribution to American culture is in christening the common foot soldier "GI Joe."

• Many of Breger's cartoon originals and papers are at Syracuse University. His wartime cartoons have been collected in four books: *Private Breger: His Adventures in an Army Camp* (1942; reprinting *Saturday Evening Post* cartoons), *Private Breger in Britain* (1944), *Private Breger's War* (1944), and *The Original "GI Joe" ("Private Breger")* (1945). Breger edited and provided commentary for a collection of rejected magazine cartoons entitled *But That's Unprintable* (1955) and wrote *How to Draw and Sell Cartoons* (1966). Biographical information is supplied in the introductions to some of the books and in Ron Goulart, ed., *The Encyclopedia of American Comics: From 1897 to the Present* (1990). Many of his cartoon originals and papers are at Syracuse University. The *New York Times* published an obituary on 17 Jan. 1970.

ROBERT C. HARVEY

BRIGGS, Ansel (3 Feb. 1806–5 May 1881), pioneer and first governor of Iowa, was born in Shoreham (Addison County), Vermont, the son of Benjamin Ingley Briggs, a farmer, and Electa Trippman Briggs. His biographer reports that he received a "fair education in the common schools" in Vermont, supplemented by a term at the Norwich Academy. In the early 1820s his family moved to Guernsey County,

Ohio, where they farmed; young Briggs took an interest in the stagecoach business and hauled freight in the area. Sometime between 1825 and 1828 Benjamin Briggs died in an accident while driving a wagon loaded with salt. The family then moved to Cambridge, a town in Guernsey County, where Ansel Briggs became head of the household.

In 1830 Briggs married Nancy M. Dunlap, whose birth date, according to the Briggs family bible, was the same as Ansel's. She was probably his first wife (although several biographies indicate an earlier wife who also shared his birthdate). The couple, who remained together until her death in 1847, had eight children, three of whom survived infancy. Her father, Major James Dunlap, a hero of the War of 1812, introduced Briggs to politics (probably Whig) in the area. Briggs was elected constable in 1831, served as deputy sheriff and jailer of Guernsey County, and in 1836 ran unsuccessfully for county treasurer as a Whig. With a partner he opened a store in Cambridge around this time.

Briggs probably moved to the Iowa Territory in 1839—not, as tradition has it, in 1836. On his arrival in Iowa, Briggs lived first in Davenport, where he contracted with the U.S. government for mail routes out of Dubuque and Davenport and likely hauled freight in conjunction with the mail business. In 1841 he moved to Jackson County; there he ran a mill while maintaining ownership of his mail routes, subcontracting them out to Thomas Dillon and George Atherton of Davenport. In the summer of 1842 Briggs and his partner, John Francis, bought at auction for $2,000 the newly surveyed town of Andrew, which was to be the county seat of Jackson County. For the next decade Briggs bought and sold town lots in Andrew.

In August 1842 Briggs was elected to the Fifth Territorial Assembly as Jackson County's representative. As such he served on the Committee on Enrolled Bills and chaired the Committee on Territorial Affairs. In 1843 he served as deputy treasurer of Jackson County and may have opened a store in Andrew with a partner. In 1844–1845 he served a term as Sheriff of Jackson County. In Iowa, the Whigs, narrowly the minority party, were able to forestall passage of an 1844 constitutional plebiscite, motivated by the belief that their party would soon gain a majority and therefore be able to control how the new state of Iowa was set up. But in May 1846 the Democratic party finally won voter acceptance of a constitution for the proposed state. Briggs's own Jackson County returned the highest percentage of yes votes of any county. Although he was well established and well known in Jackson County, Briggs had not much experience in territorial politics, nor had he participated in either of the constitutional conventions. Despite this and his lack of education, the Democratic party nominated Briggs as their candidate for governor of Iowa as it sought statehood in 1846.

Banking was the most important issue separating Whig from Democrat in Iowa in this period; the Democrats had outlawed banking in the new state constitution. Some days before the 24 September Democratic convention in Iowa City, Briggs offered at a banquet the toast, "No banks but earth, and they well tilled." This endeared him to the Democrats and became the anti-Whig slogan of the gubernatorial campaign. Briggs was nominated at the convention on the first ballot, receiving 62 votes while his opponents, Judge Jesse Williams of Jefferson County and William Thompson of Henry County, received 32 and 31 votes, respectively. In the election on 26 October, Briggs defeated his Whig opponent, Thomas McKnight, a Dubuque lawyer, by 247 votes out of 15,005 cast.

The chief accomplishment of Briggs's administration was laying the groundwork for Iowa's school system. Normal schools were chartered at Mount Pleasant, Oskaloosa, and Andrew, as was the University of Iowa in Iowa City, with branches in Dubuque and Fairfield. But these monuments of education were erected in the shade of partisan politics. In the regular session of the first General Assembly in April 1848, James Harlan, a Whig, defeated Charles Mason, a Democrat, for election as state superintendent of public instruction. However, through a technicality, Briggs refused to issue Harlan a "certificate of election." In a special session of the General Assembly that same month, Harlan again ran, this time against Thomas Hart Benton, Jr., whom he also defeated. But again Governor Briggs and Secretary of State Elisha Cutler had the election invalidated, this time through the subterfuge of interpreting different spellings of Harlan's name as votes for different individuals.

Other achievements credited to the Briggs administration are the settlement of the Iowa/Missouri boundary dispute; the appointment of Charles Mason as head of a commission to draft the first law code of the state (the "Code of 1851"); the planning and development of roads, bridges, and railroads in Iowa; and Iowa's full support of the Mexican War (1846–1848).

During most of his administration Briggs lived in Andrew, remote from the capital in Iowa City. Here he pursued his various business interests, avoided Iowa City's influence-seekers and river climate, and looked after his ailing wife. In October 1849 he married Frances Carpenter, the widowed mother-in-law of his friend Philip Bradley; the couple remained together until her death in 1859. Briggs stayed in Andrew until 1854, maintaining his business interests and staying involved in county politics. He then moved west to Council Bluffs, Iowa, where he engaged in land development and speculation around Omaha.

In 1860 Briggs set out with his son John Shannon Briggs in the wave of mining enthusiasts headed for Colorado, where he filed at least one claim. After a return to Andrew, Briggs, with his two surviving sons, went to Montana to mine in 1863. In 1865 he returned to the Council Bluffs area. From 1869 to 1874 he moved between Jackson County and the Council Bluffs area. After that he moved permanently to Omaha, where he died.

• The State Historical Society of Iowa in Iowa City contains most of the primary papers pertaining to Ansel Briggs and his governorship; some official letters are located in the Historical Society branch in Des Moines. This account depends heavily on a work by Loren N. Horton and Timothy N. Hyde, *Report: Ansel Briggs Project* (1975), a preliminary biographical study and recommendations for state memorials, which was commissioned from the Iowa State Historical Department by the Iowa State Legislature. This well-researched revision of the chronology and detail of numerous earlier biographies found in Iowa county histories and newspaper and other ceremonial accounts includes a thorough bibliography. An obituary is in the *Omaha Daily Herald*, 6 May 1881.

KATHRYN LORIMER KOKEN

BROOKS, Gwendolyn (7 June 1917–3 Dec. 2000), poet and novelist, was born Gwendolyn Elizabeth Brooks at her grandmother's home in Topeka, Kansas, the daughter of David Anderson Brooks, a janitor, and Keziah Wims Brooks. When she was two months old, the family settled in Chicago, where she would live the rest of her life. Brooks and her brother had a sheltered upbringing in a cheerful, orderly household. (She would later draw on memories of those years for her poem "a song in the front yard" [1945].) At Forrestville Elementary School, where she learned that light skin and fine hair were valued, this shy child with dark skin and coarse hair felt socially isolated. Her mother, however, encouraged her interest in writing, and Brooks published her first poem in *American Childhood* magazine in 1930.

Later, to escape further isolation at a mostly-white high school, she transferred to an all-black school; finally at the somewhat more integrated Englewood High School she found a peer group and teachers who encouraged her writing. From then on, she was constantly publishing—in national periodicals and regularly in Chicago's African-American newspaper, the *Defender*. With her mother's encouragement, she showed her work to poets James Weldon Johnson, whom she found cold and distant, and Langston Hughes, with whom she established a long friendship.

Her family struggled financially during the Great Depression, but the year she finished high school Wilson Junior College opened with a low tuition that made it possible for her to earn an associate's degree. After college, Brooks endured a series of dead-end jobs, including a humiliating position as a domestic; she later fictionalized that experience in her poem "Bronzeville Woman in a Red Hat" and in a chapter of her novel *Maud Martha*. She also worked several months for a charlatan spiritual healer operating out of the Mecca Building, a once-fashionable apartment building that had decayed into a tenement; her experiences therein would later become the basis of her long narrative poem "In the Mecca." Active in the Youth Council of the NAACP, she cofounded a club for young black artists and writers. Through the

NAACP, she met fellow poet Henry Blakely, whom she married in 1939; they had two children. Blakely died in 1996.

Brooks's mature style developed after 1941 when she and her husband joined a South Side poetry workshop run by white socialite Inez Cunningham Stark. Brooks credited Stark with introducing her to the artistic possibilities available in poetic form and forcing her to submit her work to more rigorous aesthetic judgment. She began winning poetry contests, and book publishers encouraged her to develop more poems about African-American life. The title of her first book, *A Street in Bronzeville* (1945), refers to the *Defender*'s name for the African-American section of Chicago; the book includes some of her most admired poems, such as "The Sundays of Satin-Legs Smith," a portrait of a Bronzeville dandy; "The Mother," a bold and compassionate poem about abortion; and two poems that present African-American perspectives on World War II: "Negro Hero" and "Gay Chaps at the Bar."

Working on poetry, fiction, and book reviews while her son attended school, Brooks wrote *Annie Allen* (1949), which loosely follows the life of the title character, an intelligent, sensitive African-American woman. The centerpiece is the poem "The Anniad"; the title alludes to Virgil's ancient epic *The Aeneid*, and the language strives for Virgilian complexity, suggesting the extraordinary heroism and ingenuity it takes to get through an ordinary life. For that book, she became the first African American to receive a Pulitzer Prize.

Ironically, as Brooks was receiving high literary honors, her family was having trouble finding suitable housing. The tiny apartments they lived in are described in many of her poems. Housing for African Americans in Chicago was then limited to one area on the South Side; it had expanded very little over the decades while its population had increased, nearly doubling in the 1940s. Part of her motivation for writing a novel, therefore, was to earn enough of an advance to be able to put a down payment on a house. The resulting autobiographical novel, *Maud Martha* (1953), is now considered a classic of African-American literature, with its intimate, affectionate, and sometimes infuriated view of urban African-American life in mid-century, before the rise of the Civil Rights movement. It portrays, through a series of lyrical scenes and frequent linguistic play, the childhood and young adulthood of an African-American woman in Chicago.

Brooks's next collection, *The Bean Eaters* (1960), took an explicitly political turn with such poems as "The Ballad of Rudolph Reed," about the tragic result of a black family moving into a white neighborhood. Her most popular and most often reprinted poem, "We Real Cool," in eight short, infectiously rhythmic lines, introduces seven dropouts bragging about their wild lives despite their expectation of early death. She came to consider this poem her most successful combination of artistry with popular appeal, since, with its

clarity and catchiness as well as its frequent inclusion in anthologies, it has spoken to an unusually broad audience.

In 1963, she was offered a teaching position at Chicago's Columbia College. Throughout the 1960s and 1970s, she would go on to teach also at Elmhurst College, Northeastern Illinois University, and the University of Wisconsin at Madison, among other schools.

Brooks identified 1967 as the turning point in her career. Attending a Black Writers Conference at Fisk University, she was impressed by the contrast between the formal respect for her and the enthusiasm for the more radical Amiri Baraka. That striking contrast indicated to her a shift in African-American culture from liberal integrationism toward a more militant black nationalism. Returning home, she was asked by writer and community organizer Walter Bradford to lead a workshop for some members of the Blackstone Rangers street gang who were interested in writing. Although she eventually turned that workshop over to Bradford, she started meeting with black college students (including Don L. Lee [later Haki R. Madhubuti] and Carolyn Rodgers) for workshops in her home. Both these groups resisted Brooks's attempts to teach traditional poetic forms and high cultural aesthetics, insisting rather on a populist aesthetic in tune with their radical politics. That same year, Brooks read at the dedication of a mural depicting African-American cultural heroes, including herself. Afterward, some of her workshop students led her into a local bar, where they gave an impromptu poetry reading, much to the appreciation of the patrons. The literary ambitions of the gang members and the warm reception of the tavern customers opened Brooks's eyes to an audience she had neglected. The events of that year initiated her commitment to the Black Power movement and black cultural nationalism, as well as the Black Arts Movement, which in the late 1960s and early 1970s encouraged black artists and writers to reject European-derived aesthetics and the production of works for white audiences in favor of African and African-American themes and forms for a specifically African-American audience.

In 1968 she succeeded Carl Sandburg as Poet Laureate of Illinois, and, using her own funds, she established an award for young writers in the state. That same year, Harper and Row, Brooks's publisher since 1945, brought out *In the Mecca* (1968), which includes, among other pieces, her narrative poem set in the Mecca Building, as tributes to martyred heroes such as Malcolm X and Medgar Evers, and a sequence of poems about the Blackstone Rangers. Starting with *Riot* (1969), however, she published new work only with black presses. Dudley Randall's small but influential Broadside Press in Detroit began publishing chapbooks of her new poetry, two anthologies she edited, and her unconventional autobiography *Report from Part One* (1972), which, rather than providing a straightforward narrative of her life, offers a collage of anecdotes, comments on her own and others' writing, interviews, photographs, and commentary on her work by other writers. She would publish other chapbooks and the collection *To Disembark* (1981) through Madhubuti's Third World Press and her own imprints.

In 1969, she and her husband separated, and she felt a renewed sense of freedom. She traveled on her own to East Africa, an experience that influenced her sense of American blacks as Africans in the New World. During this period, she also wrote the first volume of her autobiography and began editing an annual periodical, *The Black Position* (1971–1974). Her mother, however, encouraged the couple to reconcile, which they did in 1973; in part to celebrate that reunion, they traveled together to Ghana.

In 1976 Brooks became the first black woman elected to the National Institute of Arts and Letters. She was appointed, in 1985, poetry consultant to the Library of Congress. By this point, however, much of her early work, except for *Selected Poems* (1963), was out of print, so she self-published her collected works, *Blacks* (1987). Over the years, she received numerous awards, including over fifty honorary doctorates. She died in Chicago.

With passion, clarity, and rich literary craft, Brooks's writings present and comment on urban African-American life in the mid- to late twentieth century. As the struggle for racial justice heated up, she became a more overtly political public figure. She was the most prestigious African-American poet of her generation, so her conversion in the late 1960s to a radical black politics was an important endorsement of that position. Her decision to publish only with black presses restricted the audience for her later work, but it made concrete her commitment to African-American readers and cultural institutions. She successfully married political engagement with the highest quality of artistry and in the latter part of her career sought to present poetry as a cultural practice available to everyone, not just the literary elite. A major figure in American poetry, she used her personal prestige to support and inspire young black writers and to establish publishing institutions that would serve the specific cultural interests of African Americans.

• Brooks's papers are at the Bancroft Library, University of California, Berkeley. *Selected Poems* (1963) is her most widely available collection, but it includes none of her later work. *Report from Part One* (1972) and *Report from Part Two* (1996) contain autobiographical essays and sketches, interviews, and commentaries on her own and other writers' works. *Blacks* (1987) is the most comprehensive collection of her work, including nearly all the poems from her earlier books as well as *Maud Martha* and a broad sample of her later poetry. Her books for children include *Bronzeville Boys and Girls* (1956), *Aloneness* (1971), and *The Tiger Who Wore Gloves* (1974).

George E. Kent, *A Life of Gwendolyn Brooks* (1990), gives an account of her life through 1987. The most thorough critical commentary is D. H. Melhem, *Gwendolyn Brooks: Poetry and the Heroic Voice* (1987). B. J. Bolden, *Urban Rage in Bronzeville: Social Commentary in the Poetry of Gwendolyn Brooks* (1998), discusses her early career. There are two collections of essays on Brooks: *A Life Distilled: Gwendolyn Brooks, Her Poetry and Fiction* (1987), ed. Maria K. Mootry and Gary Smith, and *On Gwendolyn Brooks: Reliant Contemplation* (1996), ed. Stephen Caldwell Wright. Two other books pay tribute to Brooks's art and influence: *To Gwen, with Love* (1971), ed. Patricia L. Brown, Don L. Lee, and Francis Ward, and *Say That the River Turns: The Impact of Gwendolyn Brooks* (1987), ed. Haki R. Madhubuti. Some significant interviews include Gloria T. Hull and Posey Gallagher, "Update on *Part One*: An Interview with Gwendolyn Brooks," College Language Association Journal 21, no. 1 (1977): 19–40, and Martha H. Brown and Marilyn Zorn, "GLR Interview: Gwendolyn Brooks," *Great Lakes Review* 6, no.1 (1979): 48–55. An obituary is in the *New York Times*, 4 Dec. 2000.

JAMES D. SULLIVAN

BROWER, David (1 July 1912–5 Nov. 2000), editor and environmentalist, was born David Ross Brower in Berkeley, California, the son of Ross John Brower, an instructor in mechanical drawing at the University of California, and Mary Grace Barlow Brower. After dropping out of the University of California in 1931, Brower worked as a clerk in a Bay Area candy store and did publicity work for the Curry Company in Yosemite National Park, where he also filled in as an occasional tour guide. An accomplished mountain climber, he participated in first ascents of seventy peaks in the Sierra Nevada range and led the first ascent of Shiprock in New Mexico in 1939. Brower joined the Sierra Club in 1933 and eight years later was named a member of the club's board of directors. In 1943 Brower married Anne Hus, an editor with the University of California Press, which had hired Brower as an editor in 1941. The Browers had four children. As a member of the Tenth Mountain Division in Italy during World War II, Lieutenant Brower was awarded the Bronze Star for service as a combat intelligence officer during the final assaults on German positions in the Apennines.

His publicity and publishing experience seemed to make Brower the ideal choice, in 1952, as the Sierra Club's first executive director. At the time, many Sierra Club members crusaded against the proposals of the Bureau of Reclamation to construct two dams within Dinosaur National Monument in Utah as part of its massive Colorado River Storage Project. While some members of the Sierra Club supported or were undecided about the proposals, Brower was unequivocally opposed. A joint emergency committee, which included Brower and representatives from the Wilderness Society and the Isaak Walton League, initiated a campaign to educate the public through pamphlets, articles, speeches, and films.

At congressional hearings in January 1954, Brower compared Dinosaur to the Hetch Hetchy Valley within Yosemite National Park, which had been dammed in the early twentieth century. While this project had provided water and power for the city of San Francisco, the reservoir behind the Hetch Hetchy dam had also obliterated a pristine valley and failed to live up to grandiose predictions of its potential for recreation. Brower also pointed out errors in the Bureau of Reclamation's calculations on evaporation at one of the Dinosaur dam sites, demonstrating that an alternative location—Glen Canyon, farther downstream—would be more efficient.

In the spring of 1956 the Colorado River Storage Project received congressional authorization, but without a dam in Dinosaur National Monument. The Dinosaur victory set the tone for keeping dams out of Kings Canyon in California, the Grand Canyon, and elsewhere. However, to keep Dinosaur dam-free, Brower and fellow conservationists agreed not to protest the building of Glen Canyon Dam. For years Brower felt guilt-stricken about the compromise. He hoped this perceived mistake could be rectified by draining Lake Powell.

Brower's style and tactics, displayed to maximum effect during the Dinosaur campaign, transformed the Sierra Club into a potent national organization. Under Brower, the Sierra Club branched out, moving beyond parks and wilderness towards policies on wildlife, pollution, and pesticides. His provocative Sierra Club books and bold full-page newspaper advertisements had immense impact upon conservation campaigns. During the 1960s, for instance, Brower authorized the "battle ads," the most famous of which, concerning an especially inane rationalization for damming the Grand Canyon, asked if the Sistine Chapel should be flooded so that tourists could get closer to the ceiling.

Brower's innovative and abrasive style, while important to many key conservation victories, simultaneously alienated more staid members of the Sierra Club. Tension simmering over many years finally boiled over in 1969 in what Sierra Club historian Michael Cohen called "The Brawl." Some influential members were concerned over the costs of Brower's coffee-table books. More serious was a flap over the loss of the organization's tax-exempt status, which the Internal Revenue Service revoked after publication of the Grand Canyon advertisements allegedly brought the Sierra Club into direct involvement with congressional legislation. In 1967 photographer Ansel Adams, who had sponsored Brower's membership in 1933, officially withdrew his support for Brower's continued tenure as executive director. In 1969 a contentious club election resulted in the defeat of Brower and his colleagues. That year Brower resigned during a board meeting at which he was going to be fired.

Along with much of the Sierra Club's staff, Brower immediately formed Friends of the Earth, which quickly emerged as an influential lobbying group for environmental causes. Its Brower-penned motto, "Think globally, act locally," became standard bumper sticker fare for activists worldwide. The organization added arms control, nuclear proliferation, and population growth to more customary green debates concerning natural resources and environmental degradation. In 1986 Brower left Friends of the Earth, too, because of disagreement over the group's increasing emphasis on lobbying and legislation and a planned move from San Francisco to Washington, D.C. Moreover, as with the Sierra Club in 1969, he concluded that the organization's radicalism had dissipated.

In 1982 Brower was reelected to the Sierra Club board, only to resign in May 2000 due to his perception of the organization's passivity in the face of global environmental crises. He remained the director of Earth Island Institute, which he founded in 1982, until his death. On the international scene, Brower founded Friends of the Earth International and many Friends of the Earth organizations around the world. He received Japan's Blue Planet Prize in 1998 and was thrice nominated for the Nobel Peace Prize (in 1978, 1979, and, with Paul Ehrlich, 1998). He died in Berkeley.

Brower played a key role in transforming the apolitical, genteel conservationism of the early Sierra Club into the comprehensive and savvy environmental activism of the postwar era. Brower was in the vanguard of the dramatic battles waged by the Sierra Club and other groups for the integrity of national parks and the preservation of wilderness during the 1950s and 1960s. Without his efforts, national treasures such as the Grand Canyon, the Redwoods, and Dinosaur National Monument would have been irrevocably altered if not completely destroyed. In his long post–Sierra Club career, he remained a principled and uncompromising advocate of wilderness and ecological values. Reviled by many on the opposite sides of debates over dams and progress, respected and admired by both moderates and radicals within environmentalism, Brower was arguably the most influential environmental activist of the twentieth century.

• Archival materials pertaining to Brower include the Sierra Club Records, Friends of the Earth Collection, and the David Ross Brower Papers housed at the Bancroft Library on the University of California campus at Berkeley, and collections held by the Sierra Club in San Francisco. The Regional Oral History Office at the Bancroft Library also possesses the transcript of an interview with Brower conducted by Susan R. Schrepfer in 1980. A two-volume autobiography, *For Earth's Sake: The Life and Times of David Brower* (1990) and *Work in Progress* (1991), mixes his recollections of growing up, climbing mountains, and fighting bureaucrats with reprinted book forewords, articles, and congressional testimony. John McPhee, *Encounters with the Archdruid* (1971), is a rollicking account of a year spent with Brower as the conservationist sparred with a geologist, resort developer, and his archnemesis, Bureau of Reclamation commissioner Floyd L. Dominy. Michael P. Cohen, *The History of the Sierra Club, 1892–1970* (1988), provides a comprehensive survey of Brower's years as executive director of the Sierra Club. Obituaries are in the *New York Times*, 7 Nov. 2000, and *Sierra*, Jan.–Feb. 2001.

FRANK VAN NUYS

BROWN, Eddy (15 July 1895–14 June 1974), violinist and radio pioneer, was born in Chicago, Illinois, the son of Jacob Brown, a tailor and amateur violinist from Austria, and Rachel "Ray" Brown (maiden name unknown) from Russia. His mother, who had a keen interest in Christian Science, named him after Mary Baker Eddy. The Brown family moved to Indianapolis when Eddy was four. He took his first violin lessons from his father and then studied with Hugh McGibney at the Metropolitan School of Music (later Butler University's Jordan College), giving his first public recital at the age of six. In 1904 he traveled to Europe and entered the Royal Conservatory of Music in Budapest to study violin with Jenö Hubay. His teachers there included Béla Bartók, Zoltán Kodály, and cellist David Popper. In 1906 Brown won the Budapest Concerto Competition. (Finishing second was a young violinist and fellow Hubay student named Jenö Blau, who later changed his name to Eugene Ormandy and became a famous conductor.) The next year Brown opened the new hall at the Liszt Conservatory with a performance of the Mendelssohn concerto.

In 1909 Brown graduated from the Royal Conservatory with an artist's diploma and the Premier Prix. That year he made his official Budapest debut with a performance of the Beethoven concerto. David Popper called it the best performance of the concerto that he had heard since Joseph Joachim. Brown continued his studies that summer with Hubay in Ostende and in October made his London debut at Albert Hall, playing the Tchaikovsky concerto with the London Philharmonic under Sir Landon Ronald. The renowned violin teacher Leopold Auer encouraged Brown to study with him in Russia. Brown agreed. After an extensive tour of England, Brown made his Russian debut and entered Auer's class at the St. Petersburg Conservatory the same month as did another prodigy, Jascha Heifetz. Brown stayed on with Auer for five years as one of his star pupils, making his Berlin debut in 1910 playing the Brahms concerto with the Berlin Philharmonic under the direction of Artur Nikisch.

In 1916 Brown returned to the United States. His debut took place on 17 January in his hometown, Indianapolis, where he played the Beethoven concerto with the New York Symphony conducted by Walter Damrosch, repeating the program at the Metropolitan Opera House in New York City that same week. He also made his New York recital debut at Aeolian Hall on 19 January. It was so successful that he gave four more recitals there in as many weeks and made his Boston debut on 2 April. That was followed by appearances with all the leading orchestras. In Philadelphia, a critic said, "In emotional eloquence, sincerity and pervasive appeal, his playing comes closer to that of Kreisler than any other violinist of the younger generation." After a performance of the Tchaikovsky concerto with the Chicago Symphony, another critic wrote that Brown "simply electrified the well-seasoned orchestra habitués who, accustomed to great performances, seldom are surprised out of their composure by any artist, however sensational." On 11 November 1917 Brown gave the United States premiere of the Debussy violin sonata

at Carnegie Hall, and when Leopold Auer came to the United States in 1918, he made a point of attending one of Brown's Carnegie Hall recitals. Brown had joined Maud Powell and Albert Spalding as part of the first wave of great American-born concert violinists.

Columbia Records quickly signed up the young sensation, issuing his first recordings in the summer of 1916, and Carl Fischer, Inc., published a series of his violin transcriptions. Brown even followed in the tradition of Fritz Kreisler and Efrem Zimbalist, Sr., by composing a musical called "Roly-Boly Eyes" with Louis Gruenberg (who also served as piano accompanist for several Brown recordings). The musical opened in 1919 and ran on Broadway for two years at the Knickerbocker Theater. Brown called it the most profitable thing he ever did. In 1921 he married Polish actress Halma Bruzovna. They had no children and quickly divorced. In 1926 he married the American opera singer Beth Lydy, who starred in many Broadway musicals under the stage name Lyda Betti. They also had no children.

Brown continued to tour abroad, making appearances with conductors such as Wilhelm Mengelberg, Felix Weingartner, Hans Richter, and Max Fiedler. He recorded for German Odeon in the 1920s, including an acoustic Mendelssohn concerto with Friedrich Weissmann and unissued performances with Wilhelm Furtwangler. He also formed a string quartet with violinist Edwin Bachman, violist William Schubert, and cellist Lajos Shuk and established the Chamber Music Society of America. In 1956 *Musical America* magazine declared that his work with the Society "anticipated the present boom in chamber orchestras and the Baroque and early Classic repertoire by several years," and "laid the foundation for the cultivation of public taste in these fields."

In 1930 Brown's career took a new direction: he became one of the pioneers of American radio when, after mentioning the possibilities of cultural education through radio at a dinner party, he was named musical director of the Mutual Broadcasting Corporation radio station WOR in New York. In his new post at WOR, Brown launched an innovative series of programs: a Sunday evening chamber music series, a series devoted to "Famous Women Pianists," and a series devoted to modern American orchestral music. Brown's wife Beth Lydy wrote many of the scripts for these programs. Brown also performed much of the violin repertoire in a weekly series called "Masters of the Bow" that ran for three years. He performed sonatas by modern American composers, often with the composer at the piano, and gave the first radio performance of all ten Beethoven sonatas with pianist Clarence Adler.

After several years, WOR came under a management less committed to classical music. In 1936 Brown resigned and became director of WQXR, a fledgling new station in New York. Under his direction, it became the first radio station in the United States to devote itself exclusively to classical music. His example paved the way for the type of cultural programming now found on National Public Radio. He remained director of WQXR until 1942; he sold his interest in the station in 1949.

Brown's involvement with radio largely put a halt to his touring career as a soloist. Virtually none of his hundreds of radio broadcasts survive, although he made a series of recordings for the Royale label in the late 1930s (including his only sonata recordings: the Grieg G Major, with Clarence Adler, and John Powell's "Sonata Virginianesque," with the composer at the piano). He also recorded compositions by American composers Daniel Gregory Mason and Albert Stoessel, as well as Baroque duos with violinist Roman Totenberg and a dashing performance of Henri Leonard's nineteenth-century bon-bon "Serenade Humoristique," with violinists Mischa Mischakoff and Benno Rabinoff (another Auer pupil).

In 1949 Brown and his wife returned to Europe at the behest of the U.S. State Department to establish cultural ties between the United States and European countries. While there, they also founded, with the aid of the Italian government, the Accademia Internazionale di Bel Canto, a school and theater for young singers in Bordighera, a town on the Italian Riviera. His ties with the State Department and the new school culminated in the establishment of the American Opera Auditions, which allowed young American singers to perform in Europe and study at the Accademia. Brown's interest in opera was long-standing. As early as the 1930s, he had collaborated with his wife in producing summer productions of Mozart in Connecticut.

In 1956, Brown and his wife became artistic coordinators and master teachers at the University of Cincinnati College-Conservatory of Music in Ohio. He continued to champion American music. His only LP recording was of the violin concerto by American woman composer Mana-Zucca, which he called "the most outstanding violin concerto written by an American." He returned to Indianapolis in 1971 as Artist-in-Residence at Butler University—the place where he had begun formal violin lessons some seventy years earlier. He died unexpectedly in Abano, Italy, while en route to Budapest to speak at the Liszt Academy.

Brown, though largely forgotten a quarter century after his death, contributed enormously to the development of classical music in the United States. Recordings of his violin playing confirm that he was one of Auer's finest pupils.

• For interviews with Brown, see Frederick H. Martens, *Violin Mastery* (1919), pp. 25–37; "New Transcriptions Made by Eddy Brown for Second Tour," *Musical America* (30 Sept. 1916): p. 16; Olin Downes, "Eddy Brown on the Qualities that Ensure Artistic Success," *Musician* (Aug. 1917): 573–74; and Hazel Gertrude Kinscella, "All-'Round Musical Training Vital for Solo Artist, Says Eddy Brown," *Musical America* (27 July 1918), p. 17. Profiles of Brown include Victor Kuzdo, "America's 'Envoy Extraordinary to the Kingdom of Violinists,'" *Musical America* (15 Jan. 1916): 41; Robert Sabin, "New Cincinnati Coordinators Have Been Pioneers in Music," *Musical America* (Apr. 1956); Susan Len-

nis, "Eddy and Lyda Betti Brown: Keeping Alive Musical Tradition," *Indianapolis Star Magazine*, 27 Feb. 1972, pp. 24–31; and Henry Roth, "Eddy Brown Centenary," *The Strad* (July 1995): 708. An essay by Jackson Wiley, "Honoring the Life of Eddy Brown," appeared in a memorial program at Butler University, 3 Nov. 1974. A brief biographical sketch appears in Alberto Bachmann, *An Encyclopedia of the Violin* (1926). A more substantial biographical entry is included in David Ewen, *Living Musicians* (1940). Brown is also discussed in Henry Roth, *Great Violinists in Performance* (1987). Carl Fischer, Inc. published a number of his violin transcriptions; he recorded for Columbia, Odeon, Royale, Sonora (as a conductor), and Bradime-Disques. An originally unissued performance of the Tchaikovsky concerto for Odeon was released on a limited edition LP in the 1970s by Thomas Clear (TLC-2586). On compact disc, several of Brown's recordings have been reissued in *The Recorded Violin: The History of the Violin on Record*, vol. 2 (Pearl BVA II) and *The Auer Legacy*, vol. 2 (Appian CDAPR 7016). Booklets accompanying these CDs contain biographical sketches of Brown. For a complete list of his recordings, see James Creighton, *Discopaedia of the Violin* (1974). Obituaries are in the *New York Times*, 18 June 1974, and *Variety*, 26 June 1974.

JOHN ANTHONY MALTESE

BROWN, George E., Jr. (6 Mar. 1920–15 July 1999), congressman, was born in Holtville, Imperial County, California, the son of George Edward Brown, an orange picker, and Bird Alma Kilgore Brown. He attended local public schools and then graduated from Holtville Union high school (1935) and nearby El Centro Junior College (1938). He then entered the University of California at Los Angeles, where as president of the student housing association he became the first to integrate university housing by taking an African-American roommate. A pacifist who was an early critic of internment of Japanese-Americans after the attack on Pearl Harbor, Brown spent the early part of World War II as a conscientious objector in a Civilian Conservation Corps camp in Oregon before joining the Army in 1944. After enlisting as a private, he eventually rose to the rank of second lieutenant in the infantry.

After leaving military service, Brown continued his education at UCLA, where he earned a degree in industrial physics in 1946. While Brown spent the next decade in a variety of engineering and personnel positions with the City of Los Angeles, he also embarked on what would become his life's work—politics. He first ran for public office in 1954 when he was elected to the City Council in Monterey Park. In the following year he became the town's mayor and served in that capacity until 1958, when he was elected to the California State Assembly as a Democrat. While in the Assembly he introduced a bill to ban the use of lead in gasoline—the first such measure in the nation.

In 1962 Brown ran for and won a seat in the U.S. House of Representatives. He served for more than three decades and ended his tenure as the longest-serving congressman in California history. Consistently liberal in his views, Brown was among the earliest opponents of American involvement in Vietnam.

In the face of increasing commitments in Southeast Asia, Brown drew accusations of disloyalty when he claimed that President Lyndon Johnson believed that the "peace of mankind can be won by the slaughter of peasants in Vietnam." In 1966 Brown was the only member of Congress to oppose military appropriations bills, and he even withheld support for civil defense funds, claiming that they "created a climate in which nuclear war becomes more credible."

Equally liberal in his domestic views, Brown voted for the 1964 Civil Rights Act, and for years he proudly displayed a photograph of himself standing next to Dr. Martin Luther King as President Johnson signed the bill into law. Convinced that he could make a greater impact on world events in the Senate, Brown gave up his seat in Congress in 1970 and entered the California Democratic primary. After a bruising campaign, Brown lost the nomination to fellow Representative John V. Tunney, a moderate whom he had derided during the contest as the "lightweight son of the heavyweight champ."

Determined to reenter public life, Brown ran for Congress in 1972 in a newly created House seat that included San Bernardino County. Reelected to the next thirteen sessions of Congress, he resumed his own unique style of liberal activism. Long concerned with environmental matters, he took the lead on issues such as alternative fuels and solar energy and was a leading supporter of the creation of the federal Environmental Protection Agency. In 1980 he bowed to political reality and voted for the B-1 bomber. "If the B-1 was being built in some other state and I didn't have two Air Force bases and a lot of retired military people who feel strongly about the B-1, I'd probably have voted the other way," he explained. Brown then returned to his former pattern of general opposition to military matters. He was a harsh critic of President Ronald Reagan's so-called "Star Wars" anti-missile defense system and later opposed deployment of American troops in the Middle East during the Persian Gulf War.

Despite his hostility to military deployment in outer space, Brown was a staunch supporter of peacetime space exploration. Especially fond of unmanned space programs, he was one of the National Aeronautics and Space Administration's greatest supporters in Congress, and he took a leading role to preserve funding for the manned space station program. Although he served on a number of committees and subcommittees during his tenure in Congress, Brown's proudest moment came in 1990, when he assumed the chairmanship of the Committee on Science, Space and Technology. Long noted for his bipartisan commitment to science, he served as the ranking Democrat on the committee following the Republican takeover of Congress in 1994.

Although increasingly targeted by Republicans during his last few election campaigns, Brown remained in office in no small measure because his constituents recognized his commitment to their concerns; his 1992 campaign received special help in the form of a fundraising letter from a group of scientists who testified that "the scientific and technical community rarely has had a person so perfectly fit to represent its interests and concerns in Congress."

In 1988 he married Marta Macias. He had two sons with her and was stepfather to four of her children. Brown was still serving in the House when he died in Bethesda, Maryland.

Among the longest-serving members in the history of Congress, Brown remained steadfast in his devotion to liberal ideals, even when they seemed to fall out of fashion. Although he championed myriad causes during his public career, he will no doubt be best remembered for his support of environmental concerns and space exploration.

• George Brown's papers are held at the University of California–Los Angeles. Brown awaits a biographer, and secondary information on his life and career is scarce and must be gleaned from sources such as daily newspapers and the *Biographical Directory of the United States Congress, 1774–Present*. Obituaries are in the *Los Angeles Times* and the *New York Times*, 17 July 1999.

EDWARD L. LACH, JR.

BROWN, Les (14 Mar. 1912–4 Jan. 2001), bandleader, was born Lester Raymond Brown in Reinerton, Pennsylvania, the son of Ray Winfield Brown, a baker, and Hattie Mae Nye Brown. His father played the soprano saxophone in a saxophone quartet and was also skilled on the trombone; he was known locally as the "March Prince," playing the John Philip Sousa repertoire. He also taught woodwinds and cornet to Les, who by the age of fourteen was considered a talented musician. Les recalled that he focused on music so that he could spend less time in the family bakery.

From 1926 to 1929, three of his high school years, Brown attended the Ithaca Conservatory of Music, where he studied classical music—including harmony, theory, and composition—as well as clarinet and bassoon. Because he played in the conservatory orchestra, he was eligible for a full scholarship. In 1927, before he graduated, Brown played in a band called the Rainbow Men. It was a "big" band—four saxophones, four brass, and four rhythm. Brown did the arrangements.

On graduation from Ithaca in 1929, Brown received a full scholarship to attend New York Military Academy. His friend Bob Alexy played trumpet there and helped arrange the scholarship. Brown excelled as a student, though he often would sneak away to the fraternity houses to listen to big bands on the radio. Paul Whiteman, Mildred Bailey, and the Coon-Sanders orchestra were among his favorites. In 1932 he graduated as valedictorian from the New York Military Academy. Though he won an appointment to the U.S. Military Academy, Brown instead joined the Rainbow Men on a tour of New England. He never attended West Point.

In an example of the good timing that characterized Brown's life, in the summer of 1930 the Duke Blue Devils (Duke University's college band) heard the Rainbow Men playing at Revere Beach, Massachusetts. As a result, Duke offered Brown a much-needed music scholarship; his father's bakery was not doing well at that time. At Duke he majored in French, joined the Blue Devils, and in 1933, his sophomore year, became the band's leader. In 1936, during his final summer gig with the Blue Devils at Budd Lake, New Jersey, he met Georgia Claire DeWolfe, whom he nicknamed "Cluny." In 1938 they married and moved to New York City. They had two children.

By this time Brown was becoming a key figure in swing music, arranging for such notable bandleaders as Larry Clinton, Red Nichols, and Isham Jones. Brown's arrangements and his own band's reviews attracted two "angels": Eli Oberstein of RCA Victor Records and Joe Glaser. Oberstein booked Brown for an engagement at the Hotel Edison on Broadway, which was broadcast live nationally each night by NBC, while Glaser landed the bandleader a recording contract on Bluebird Records, a subsidiary of RCA Victor. The bookings, the broadcasts, and the recordings combined to make the Les Brown dance band famous. Brown then hired talented vocalists, which increased his fame.

Timing certainly worked in Brown's favor in New York in 1940, when he met Doris Day, a former dancer. He hired her as his vocalist on the spot. At the time he was the bandleader for the World's Fair Dancing Campus. In the fall they began their tour, and Brown had a national audience. In the meantime, Day decided to leave the band and return to Cincinnati to marry Al Jordan, one of Jimmy Dorsey's trombonists. In 1944 Brown persuaded Day, whose marriage had ended, to return to the band. He paid for her and her infant son and mother to travel to New York City for recording and performing dates at the Hotel Pennsylvania. The following year she toured widely with the band.

In 1942 songwriter Ben Homer told Brown that he had started on a good tune. After reviewing the song, Brown made some revisions and called Buddy Morris, his publisher. Morris, who was unsatisfied with the first two lyricists' attempts, approached Bud Green, the composer of "Flatfoot Floogie," who further revised the tune. Morris supplied the song's title, "Sentimental Journey," and Day sang it to everyone's immense satisfaction. However, the Musicians' Union had imposed a recording ban, and "Sentimental Journey" was not released until 1945. The song was number one on the radio show "Hit Parade" for sixteen weeks, largely because, as one writer explained, it evoked "the eagerness of GIs returning to see their loved ones again" (*New York Times*, 6 Jan. 2001).

Despite the increasing popularity of Les Brown and his Band of Renown (a name coined by a radio announcer during a live broadcast in 1942), many jazz reviewers were critical. In 1940 Barry Ulanov, writing for *Metronome*, a big band magazine, found the band inconsistent, characterized by the two-beat "jumping" mode pioneered by Jimmie Lunceford and Benny Goodman; however, he found that the Brown ballads were treated with novel tonal shadings and harmonic variations. Critic George Simon observed that Brown's band was skilled musically but lacked audience rapport.

In 1943 Frank Comstock took over as principal arranger, and the band improved. After World War II, Brown moved to Beverly Hills to balance his family life and music making. He had also agreed to be Bob Hope's back-up band, a gig that lasted more than fifty years. Initially the agreement put the band in a studio for Hope's radio broadcasts, but soon it joined him in his popular tours to entertain U.S. troops stationed overseas. Then the world of national television broadcasts became the band's stage. Later the Band of Renown backed Steve Allen and Dean Martin on television.

Brown was astute about the economics of the big band business, which enabled him to select the best musicians. By 1950 his players earned $8,000 a year from the Bob Hope work, exploited other recording and weekend opportunities, and spent most of the year with their families. He expected them to be capable of fast, accurate sight-reading, but mostly Brown sought "that big, warm round tone that . . . gives our band a sound unlike any other" ("What I Seek in a Musician," *Down Beat*, 6 May 1953). He also expected his musicians to be "neat," "well-groomed," and not into alcohol or drugs. Among his most important musicians were Butch Stone, a long-time highlighter of the band; Dave Pell, tenor saxophone; Ray Sims, trombone; Geoff Clarkson, piano; Wes Hensel, trumpeter-arranger; and Tony Rizzi, a guitarist who gave Comstock the opportunity to write lead parts for guitar. From 1952 to 1958 Brown and the Band of Renown annually received the *Down Beat* award for best dance band.

Critics now praised the band's high standards, teamwork, and pride in its organization. In 1951 *Down Beat* found the band to be "a genuinely 'happy' band." Brown was a founding member of the Recording Academy (later the National Academy of Recording Arts and Sciences), and in 1954 he helped bring the Grammy Awards to television by recruiting Bob Hope, Frank Sinatra, and Bing Crosby to appear on the first broadcast.

Although Brown had announced his intention to retire several times over the years, he continued leading his band, although less frequently, until a few months before his death. "Cluny" Brown died in 1996, and in 1998 he married Evelyn Hutter, a long-time family friend. The Band of Renown survived its founder, led by Les Brown, Jr., and managed by Clyde "Stumpy" Brown, Brown's younger brother. Brown died at his home in Pacific Palisades.

Brown's career exhibited a gift for impeccable timing. A consummate musician and savvy businessman, he was recognized in 1996 by the *Guinness Book of World Records* for "leading the longest-lasting musical organization in the history of pop music." His recorded legacy comprises more than fifty albums, featuring such titles as "Alexander the Swoose," "Joltin' Joe DiMaggio," and such favorites as "Sentimental Journey" and "I've Got My Love to Keep Me Warm."

• The archives of the Institute of Jazz Studies, Rutgers University, Newark, N.J., contain early reviews and profiles of Brown from publications including *Down Beat*, *Metronome*, and *Jazziz* as well as photographs and other research material. George T. Simon, *The Big Bands* (1967), is an excellent first-hand report of the era that includes lively forewords by Frank Sinatra and the author. "Band Businessman," *Time*, 25 Feb. 1952, p. 60, is an excellent profile of Brown. See also Gunther Schuller, *The Swing Era: The Development of Jazz, 1930–1945* (1989). Christian Batchelor, *This Thing Called Swing: A Study of Swing Music and the Lindy Hop, the Original Swing Dance* (1997), is a uniquely informative publication written from the viewpoint of what dance style was popular with the public and the bands that met the demand, rather than the viewpoint of the "great leaders and players." An obituary by Richard Severo is in the *New York Times*, 6 Jan. 2001.

MELINDA SCOTT

BROWN, Willa (22 Jan. 1906–18 July 1992), pilot and aviation educator, was born Willa Beatrice Brown in Glasgow, Kentucky, the only daughter of Hallie Mae Carpenter Brown and Eric B. Brown, a farm owner. After 1910 the family, as part of the internal migration of African Americans from the rural South to northern cities, moved to Terre Haute, Indiana, hoping for greater opportunities in employment and education. There her father worked in a creosote factory; he was also pastor of the Holy Triumphant Church in 1920 and the Free Church of God in 1929.

At Wiley High School, Brown was one of only seven black students in the 100-member chorus. During her high school years she also did part-time domestic work. Brown graduated in 1923 and entered Indiana State Normal School, a teacher training school that is now part of Indiana University. She majored in business subjects, minored in French, and joined the Alpha Kappa Alpha sorority. In September 1927, Brown, ready to begin her teaching career, headed for Gary, Indiana. The home of U.S. Steel, Gary was also known for its innovative school system (swimming pools, laboratories, adult education) and served as a model for other American cities. Called the "City of the Century," it experienced a building boom and a population surge of Eastern Europeans and African Americans who came for employment in the steel mills.

Gary's population statistics for black children of school age were 267 in 1916, 1,125 in 1920, and over 4,000 in 1930. The influx of African Americans generated resentments among whites. When eighteen blacks were admitted to Emerson High School, over 600 white students walked out. This led to the opening in April 1931 of Roosevelt School, a state-of-the-art high school for black students. There, Brown chaired the commercial department, which taught typewriting and stenography; she also taught those subjects in the evening school for adults. She introduced a typewriting club, which produced the *Annex News* (vol.1, no.1, 15 Oct. 1927), perhaps the only student newspaper in Gary's schools.

On 24 November 1929 Brown married Wilbur J. Hardaway. A graduate of Tuskegee Institute and newly elected alderman of the Fifth Ward, he was one of Gary's first black firemen when its "colored" fire station was created two years earlier. Brown continued to teach, using four summer vacations to complete her bachelor's degree, which she received in August 1931. The Hardaways' stormy marriage ended a few months later, but Brown remained to the end of the school term the following June.

Brown then moved to Chicago and chose positions where she could put her skills to good use during the Great Depression. From 1932 to 1939 she worked for the federal government as well as in private venues. Her employers included Dr. Julius H. Lewis, the first African-American faculty member of the University of Chicago's medical school (1937–1938); Dr. Theodore K. Lawless, a renowned African-American dermatologist and philanthropist (1938–1939); and Horace Cayton, coauthor of *Black Metropolis* (1939). While working as a drugstore cashier in 1934, she met John C. Robinson, a pilot. She joined the Challenger Aero Club, founded by Robinson in 1931, and found herself in a circle of African-American aviation enthusiasts. Being at Chicago's Harlem Airport was exhilarating for Brown, who "was always an outdoor person." She began preparatory courses at the Aeronautical University, established in 1929 by the Curtiss-Wright Flying Service. That there were classes for African Americans at all was due to the outstanding performances of Robinson and Cornelius R. Coffey, who had had to threaten legal action before they were admitted some years earlier. They then were hired to teach other African Americans.

On 13 May 1934 Brown was seriously injured in a car accident while returning from a Mother's Day visit. She was hospitalized with a broken arm, several broken ribs, and a fractured vertebra (*Chicago Defender*, *Gary American*, both 19 May 1934). Recovered and continuing her enthusiasm for flying, she earned a student license in 1937 and a private pilot license in 1938. Brown's charisma, energy, and talent for attracting attention were evident when she arrived at the *Chicago Defender* to request coverage of an air show that a group of thirty flyers planned to stage. An editor, Enoch P. Waters, reported that the older reporters "polished their eyeglasses to get an undistorted view . . . [Brown] made such a stunning appearance in white jodhpurs, white jacket, white boots, that all the typewriters suddenly went silent." The flyers got their publicity.

Waters suggested forming a national organization as a clearing house for information about African Americans' aviation activities. On 16 August 1937 the National Airmen's Association of America (NAAA) received its charter, with the *Chicago Defender* providing the mailing address. Some other charter members included Cornelius Coffey; Chauncey Spencer, a pioneer pilot and civil rights activist; and Janet Bragg, also a pioneer pilot. Brown, as secretary, assumed public relations duties. Her letters, flying visits to black colleges, and radio addresses helped the group grow and establish chapters in other cities. For the next decade, her life became one of ceaseless and aggressive effort for the inclusion of blacks into the aviation mainstream and the country's war mobilization. Chauncey Spencer (author interview, 3 June 1995) said, "Willa was persistent and dedicated. She was the foundation, framework, and the builder of people's souls. She did it not for herself, but for all of us." Brown and Coffey founded the Coffey School of Aeronautics in 1938, with Coffey as president and chief flight instructor and Brown as director.

In 1939 Brown became the first African-American woman to receive a commercial pilot license, with a ground instructor rating, and a radio license. That same year, as war approached, the Civilian Pilot Training Program (CPTP) was launched to provide a source of trained manpower. Although CPTP was working through colleges only, the Coffey school wanted certification as a training center. Brown successfully conducted separate demonstrations of college and noncollege students for government officials, to prove "Negroes" could absorb technical education, a point in doubt since a 1925 War Department report. An article in *Time* magazine (25 Sept.1939) reported that " [Brown] has labored mightily to whip up interest in flying among Negroes, get them a share in the . . . training program." About 200 pilots were trained, and many went on to secondary training at the segregated Tuskegee (Alabama) Army Air Field, which produced America's black air corps, the Tuskegee Airmen.

Brown was appointed federal coordinator for the Chicago unit of CPTP in February 1940 and remained until 1943. In 1942 she became the first African-American member of the Civilian Air Patrol (CAP) in Illinois, one of 400 pilots accepted of the 1,560 who had applied in Illinois. As lieutenant of the segregated squadron, she had charge of 25 pilots, several light planes, and four army training biplanes. The Coffey school closed at war's end, and on 7 February 1947 Coffey and Brown married. This union also was short-lived, ending in divorce. Brown was married for the third time in 1955, to the Reverend J. H. Chapell, whom she met while they were both employed at the Great Lakes Naval Training Base in Waukegan. She had no children with any of her husbands. Brown returned to teaching aeronautics and commercial subjects in high school in 1962 until her retirement in 1971. That year she became the first black woman appointed to the Federal Aviation Administration's Women's Advisory Committee on Aviation, serving until 1974.

In recognition of her leadership, Brown was invited to speak at the Tuskegee Airmen's fourth annual convention in August 1974. She was unable to attend, but in remarks read at the meeting, she wrote, "We desperately wanted blacks to fly and we desperately wanted them to be accepted into the Army Air Corps as cadets . . . we threw the word 'I' out of our vocabulary altogether. We needed everybody's help. . . .The YMCA, the Chicago Urban League, the Chicago Board of Education, NAACP, the Eighth Regiment Armory, civic-minded individuals in all walks of life, other flying schools in the area, and, of course, churches of all denominations supported the effort." Brown was the first black woman to make aviation her career and to tirelessly promote opportunities for other African Americans in the field. She was honored as a pioneer in the "Black Wings" exhibition at the National Air and Space Museum in 1982. She died in Chicago.

• A lengthy biographical article on Brown appears in Betty Kaplan Gubert, Miriam Sawyer, and Caroline Fannin, *Distinguished African Americans in Aviation and Space Science* (2001). Other books to consult are Jesse J. Johnson, *Black Women in the Armed Forces, 1942–1974: A Pictorial History* (1974), and Enoch P. Waters, *American Diary: A Personal History of the Black Press* (1987). A videotape, *Willa Brown—An American Aviator*, was written by Severo Perez and produced by the California Department of Education, 1997. An obituary is in the *Chicago Sun Times*, 20 July 1992.

BETTY KAPLAN GUBERT

BROWNING, John M. (23 Jan. 1855–26 Nov. 1926), gun inventor, was born John Moses Browning in Ogden, Utah, the son of Jonathan Browning, a blacksmith and gunsmith, and Elizabeth Caroline Clark Browning. Jonathan Browning, a disciple of Joseph Smith, had twenty-two children by three wives; Elizabeth Clark was his second wife. The inventor of two percussion cap repeating rifles, the elder Browning served as armorer to the Mormon column on its trek from Illinois to Utah in 1846–1847. John attended Ogden's public school until he was fifteen but mostly apprenticed himself to his father. At fourteen he built a clever slide rifle and was soon foreman in his father's blacksmith shed.

On 10 April 1879 Browning married Rachel T. Child; they had eight children. On 12 May, Browning filed his first patent, for a single-shot rifle that improved on an older Sharpe falling-breech block principle. In 1880 on receipt of his patent, Browning, his brother Matthew, and his half-brothers Sam, George, and Ed founded J. M. Browning & Brothers," a "factory" that would eventually turn out some 600 rifles, together with a sporting goods business that would quickly dominate western markets. Impressed by the rifle, T. G. Bennett, head of Winchester Repeating Arms, traveled to Ogden in 1883, bought the rights to the gun (to be sold as the Winchester Model 1885), and optioned the inventor's next idea, for a high-caliber (big game) repeater.

Browning's brilliant designs were made possible by new steel alloys for breeches and barrels and new metallic cartridges as they evolved into gas-tight containers for high-velocity propellants. In 1884, Browning traveled to New Haven to deliver the prototype for the famous Winchester Model 1886, whose flawless lever action removed a spent shell and loaded a second while ingenious vertical sliding locks sealed the chamber. Browning accepted $50,000, and agreed to design the first successful repeating shotgun (Model 1887). A lackluster tour (1887–1889) as a Mormon missionary in Georgia did not interrupt the flow of new guns from the hunter-inventor in Utah. To protect its monopoly in sporting rifles, Winchester bought 44 Browning patents but manufactured only ten. The company requested specific features, wrote and filed Browning's patents, and refined his ideas. For the Model 1894, Bennett asked for a lever-action that could withstand new high-pressure smokeless powders, and he furnished Browning with new nickel steel barrels. Instantly popular, this gun was followed by the Model 1895, which featured a box magazine or a military clip for jacketed sharp-nosed cartridges.

Around 1889, Browning became interested in the machine gun invented by Hiram Stevens Maxim, and he retraced the steps by which Maxim in 1883 had devised a recoil-driven hinged toggle link system for automatic fire. Browning's variation used gas from an exploding cartridge to eject the shell and load and fire the next. He may not have seen Maxim's omnibus patent of 1884 advancing claims for twelve different systems of gas-actuated automatic fire, but Winchester's patent office was probably cautious. In any case, Browning offered his gas prototype to Colt, which, in an attempt to circumvent Maxim's claims, patented the Colt Model 1895 automatic machine gun. Maxim accused Colt of piracy.

Browning then turned to the semi-automatic pistol, already invented in Europe but not yet perfected. Learning from Maxim, Browning in 1895–1896 filed broad patents for pistols featuring blow-back action and various locking recoil systems. The results were a series of handguns, of which the .22 Colt Woodsman, favorite of target shooters, and the Model 1911 .45 automatic, with its amazing "parallel ruler" operating slide, are among the finest ever made. Browning's pistols gained him entry to a European market for weapons far larger than an isolationist United States could provide. The first pistol, a .32 caliber, he sold to Fabrique Nationale d'Armes de Guerre of Belgium, which brought it out in 1899. When Winchester balked at paying royalties (instead of buying exclusive rights) for his new auto-loading shotgun, Browning in 1902 made the first of sixty-one trips across the Atlantic to deal with Fabrique Nationale directly. Wealthy from investments in real estate, cattle, and sporting goods, Browning could now underwrite his innovations; his sporting goods company placed an order for 10,000 of the new shotguns as part of the contract he signed with Fabrique Nationale to make them. Belgium knighted the inventor in 1914 because the manufacture of his designs transformed Fabrique Nationale into one of the world's largest arms corporations. Even so, he continued to license new pistols

and sporting rifles to American companies such as Colt, Stevens, and Remington.

Although the U.S. Navy bought 200 Colt Model 1895 machine guns, the U.S. Army in 1904 adopted the Maxim Model 1901, then, bowing to pressure, allowed Colt to manufacture Maxim guns under license. In 1916, when Maxim died, Colt patented Browning's improved .30 caliber recoil machine gun. The following year, after the United States entered the Great War, the army adopted it and the more original .30 Browning automatic rifle (BAR), for which the inventor brought gas operation to perfection; Browning waived most royalties to secure the contract. The army asked for a .50 caliber model, and then for a 37mm cannon to replace its Maxim pom-pom guns. The latter was never manufactured, but the superb .50 caliber machine gun served American land, sea, and air forces through much of the twentieth century.

Browning spent his final years supervising assembly lines in Connecticut and Belgium. His last major design, the superposed shotgun, aligned two barrels vertically to facilitate aiming. After his death in Herstal, Begium, his family incorporated the J. M. and M. S. Browning Company in Utah, and manufactured the shotgun at its subsidiary, the Browning Arms Company.

In 1977, Fabrique Nationale bought Browning Arms, but virtually every gun manufacturer now copies Browning's familiar magazines, actions, and locks. Pistols incorporating his designs outnumber all others combined; that is probably true of his sporting rifles as well. For those reasons, Browning ranks with Maxim in genius and Mikhail Kalashnikov in influence, and exceeds both in versatility.

• The only full-length biography, though hagiographic and reticent on the troubled history of Browning's machine gun, is John Browning and Curt Gentry, *John M. Browning, American Gunmaker: An Illustrated Biography of the Man and His Guns* (1964). George Chinn, *The Machine Gun* (1951), though informative, is mistaken in many details. Dolf L. Goldsmith, *The Devil's Paintbrush: Sir Hiram Maxim's Gun* (1989), is the most accurate account of the Browning-Maxim patent disputes. Of several histories of Winchester Repeating Arms, the most authoritative on Browning's models are R. L. Wilson, *Winchester: An American Legend* 1991), the sixth edition of *The History of Winchester Firearms, 1866-1992*, ed. Thomas Henshaw (1993), and R. Bruce McDowell, *Evolution of the Winchester* (1985); the latter reproduces some patent drawings. Donald B. Bady, *Colt Automatic Pistols, 1896-1955* (1956), is excellent on Browning sidearms, and Robert Q. Sutherland and R. L. Wilson, *The Book of Colt Firearms* (1971) provides technical specifications for the machine guns. Comment on the implications of Browning's automatic weapons can be found in Roger Ford, *The Grim Reaper: Machine-Guns and Machine Gunners in Action* (1996). An obituary is in the *New York Times*, 27 Nov. 1926.

JOSEPH W. SLADE

BRUGGER, Kenneth C. (16 June 1918–25 Nov. 1998), textile engineer and monarch butterfly researcher, was born Kenneth Charles Brugger in Kenosha, Wisconsin, the son of Oswald Brugger, an auto parts salesman and farmer, and Carrie Linderman Brugger. Following high school, he attended the Milwaukee School of Engineering. Brugger served in the Army Signal Corps during World War II and was assigned to work on cryptology at Fort Monmouth, New Jersey. He married Mary K. Frye in 1942; the couple had three children.

After the war Brugger was employed for some time at the Simmons mattress factory in Kenosha and subsequently worked as a junior supervisor with the underwear manufacturer Jockey International, also in Kenosha. Although he lacked a college degree, his mathematical and technical skills led to his promotion to chief engineer for Jockey's knitting processes. He designed and developed new textile machinery, notably a machine, referred to as a compactor, for the manufacture of nonshrinking fabric; it produced a cotton fiber product so compressed that the fabric's rebound during washing overcame the inevitable shrinkage. In the 1950s Brugger investigated various devices, ranging from cruise control to graduated eye lenses. For some years, his avocations were breeding and racing homing pigeons and rose gardening.

Brugger's marriage ended in divorce in 1966. He left Kenosha and then traveled in Mexico and worked as a consultant textile engineer (especially with the Rinbros underwear manufacturing company) in Mexico City. He also became involved in a program to track migrations of monarch butterflies to discover their wintering sites in Mexico. Brugger was in the habit of driving with his dog through the countryside surrounding Mexico City and at one time had encountered a mass of butterflies in the pine-covered volcanic mountains west of the city.

For decades entomologists had sought to locate the winter home of the monarch butterfly of eastern North America. The leaders in this program, Fred A. Urquhart at the University of Toronto and his wife, Norah Urquhart, had assembled a corps of individuals who tagged the butterflies in their more northern locales in order to track the migrations southward. The Urquharts hypothesized that the overwintering site was somewhere in southern Mexico or Central America, and a plea for information was placed in Mexican newspapers.

On 26 February 1973, Brugger responded to Urquhart's published notice and was persuaded to undertake a further search—efforts which in time were supported by an Urquhart grant from the National Geographic Society. Brugger's girlfriend, Catalina "Cathy" Aguado, who had grown up in the area involved in the investigation, joined him in the search. They married in 1974 and had one child.

The Bruggers sighted large numbers of monarchs, including a November 1973 sighting of butterflies knocked from the sky by hail. On 2 January 1975, as the couple ascended to10,000 feet at Cerro Pelón, they found the Oyamel fir trees covered with millions of butterflies, thus solving the mystery of where the monarchs spend the winter. Within the year, they discovered at least one other nearby site. In about 1987 the Bruggers divorced.

The Urquharts did not visit the area until January 1976, and Brugger accompanied them to the site. On that occasion, discovery was made of a tagged butterfly from Minnesota, confirming the location as the overwintering site of the eastern migrating monarchs. On his own, Brugger had found at least two tagged insects earlier, in 1975, from Missouri and from Texas. He visited the young boy who had tagged the Texas specimen and wanted to invite him to the Mexican site, but Urquhart would not allow that kind of publicity or recognition for someone who was not part of his own volunteer corps. Urquhart noted Brugger's discovery of the overwintering site in his newsletter, but a public announcement was not made until August 1976 when Urquhart published an account in *National Geographic*; even so, it was not specific as to the exact location of the butterfly settlement. After his initial discovery, Brugger assisted the Urquharts in tagging insects in Mexico, an effort that helped confirm that the monarchs undertake a return from Mexico in the spring; they reproduce in the southern United States, and these descendants finally make their way to the north.

Brugger, who was color-blind, was unable to see the bright orange and black of the swarming insects that he uncovered to the world. His crucial role in the discovery of the overwintering of the monarch was the outcome of a combination of his life circumstances and personal qualities. The pursuit of the site of the monarch grew from his inherent curiosity and problem-solving interests rather than any special knowledge of or interest in butterflies. He accepted the role of discoverer but avoided the controversies that arose from the Urquharts' attempt to guard the secret of the place. Many others have subsequently made their way to Cerro Pelón—including troops of tourists—and in doing so raised the question of how to balance knowledge with the protection of a fragile environmental area. What Brugger, engineer and problem solver, thought of these matters is not recorded; he left the writing to others. He died in Austin, Texas.

• No manuscript resources or publications by Kenneth Brugger are known. Biographical information can be culled from general articles on the monarch butterfly migration and overwintering, of which the first was Fred A. Urquhart, "Found at Last: The Monarch's Winter Home," *National Geographic* 150, no.2 (Aug. 1976): 160–73. Lincoln P. Brower, "Understanding and Misunderstanding the Migration of the Monarch Butterfly (Nymphalidae) in North America: 1857–1995," *Journal of the Lepidopterists' Society* 49, no.4 (1995): 304–85, gives a historical overview of the study of the migration phenomenon and includes an account of Brower's controversy with Urquhart. Alex Shoumatoff, "Flight of the Monarchs," *Vanity Fair* 471 (Nov. 1999): 268–72, 295–300, and Sue Halpern, *Four Wings and a Prayer: Caught in the Mystery of the Monarch Butterfly* (2001), also include useful information on Brugger and his role in the discovery. I am especially grateful to Katharine Brugger Carroll for information and remembrances of her father. An obituary of Brugger is in the *New York Times*, 12 Dec. 1998.

CLARK A. ELLIOTT

BUDGE, Don (13 June 1915–26 Jan. 2000), tennis player, was born John Donald Budge in Oakland, California, the son of John "Jack" Budge, a Scottish ex-professional soccer player who managed a laundry in Oakland, and Pearl Kincaid Budge. Don's older brother Lloyd, later a tennis instructor, taught him the rudiments of the game, but the preteenager preferred baseball, football, and basketball. Although he was only five feet six inches tall, at University High School in Oakland he became a forward on the varsity basketball team.

In June 1930 Lloyd Budge goaded Don into entering his first tennis tournament, the California State Boys (under age fifteen) Championship, which he won. Exhilarated, he was determined to become a champion. Among Northern California juniors (under age eighteen) he ranked fourth in 1931 and first in 1932. A right-hander, he used steady, slow-paced ground strokes and quick court covering, which he improved constantly.

Following high school graduation in 1933, he won the U.S. Junior Championship at Culver, Indiana, defeating Gene Mako, the favorite. Afterward, the two became doubles partners and close lifetime friends. Amazingly, Budge grew six inches during the next twelve months, and by 1935 he was almost six feet two inches tall, a sinewy beanpole who never weighed more than 155 pounds during his amateur career.

Budge entered the University of California in late 1933 but left in the spring to join the U.S. Davis Cup auxiliary team and tour Eastern tournaments. His Western forehand grip was effective on hard courts, but he lost repeatedly on Eastern grass, where balls bounced lower and faster. He redeemed himself partially at the U.S. championships at Forest Hills, New York, by upsetting Bitsy Grant, the tireless retriever, before losing to Vernon Kirby, a South African left-hander. Back in California he almost beat Fred Perry, the world's best player, in the Pacific Southwest Championship final. The U.S.L.T.A. ranked him ninth for the year.

In need of expert coaching, Budge spent three California winters learning and practicing with Tom Stow, a veteran professional instructor. This training improved Budge's game. During the 1934–1935 off-season, Stow changed Budge's forehand grip from Western to semi-Eastern with resultant improvement in his forehand drive. They also worked on net play essentials and physical training. Improved results followed during 1935. Abroad with the U.S. Davis Cup team, the freckled redhead conquered Henner Henkel and Baron Gottfried von Cramm, of Germany, in the Interzone Final but lost to Perry and Bunny Austin, as England retained the cup. At Wimbledon, Cramm stopped Budge in a semifinal. Budge won the Newport Invitation tournament but was defeated by Grant

in the U.S. nationals. Budge's American singles ranking rose to second, behind Wilmer Allison. With Mako, he rated second in doubles.

Budge worked on getting to net more swiftly, behind fast-paced ground strokes, and he also sharpened his already excellent net skills. Command of his short-court attack showed in his Davis Cup triumphs over Jack Crawford and Adrian Quist during the U.S. loss to Australia. Budge lost on grass surfaces only twice in 1936, both times to Perry, at Wimbledon, and in the U.S. Championships. The U.S.L.T.A. ranked Budge first.

During the 1936–1937 off-season Snow taught Budge to master hitting ground strokes early, only six to eight inches above the bound, leaving opponents out of position and scrambling. Although he lost two early-season contests to Grant, Budge thereafter dominated, winning all twelve of his Davis Cup singles and doubles matches.His victory over Cramm was memorable. Trailing 1–4 in the final set, he won 8–6, causing the United States to defeat Germany and proceed to take the Cup from England. Budge also bested Cramm in the Wimbledon, U.S., and Pacific Southwest finals. He now ranked first in the world. The Budge-Mako team won the doubles title at Wimbledon.

Budge was a good-natured champion, with impeccable court manners and sportsmanship. He turned down a lucrative offer to turn professional so that he could help the United States retain the Davis Cup. In 1938 in the Challenge Round, he beat Jack Bromwich and Quist, of Australia. He also was the first to accomplish tennis's "Grand Slam" by winning all four of the world's major singles titles: the Australian, the French, Wimbledon, and the United States. In the finals, he overcame Bromwich at Adelaide, Roderich Menzel at Paris, Austin at Wimbledon, and Mako at Forest Hills. At year's end, he kept his number one world ranking.

In November 1938 Budge turned professional, prevailing over professional stars like Ellsworth Vines, Perry, Bill Tilden, Bobby Riggs, Frank Kovacs, and Les Stoefen. After enlisting in the U.S. Air Force in 1942, Budge tore a right shoulder muscle and never again swung as powerfully as before. Afterward he lost to Riggs but continued competing until 1957. He won the U.S. Professional Championships of 1940 and 1942. He worked, in 1941, as fellow-player Sidney Wood's partner running a laundry service in New York City. Budge won the James E. Sullivan Award as the best American amateur athlete of 1937, and the Associated Press poll named him the best athlete of 1938. The International Tennis Hall of Fame enshrined him in 1964. Budge was the dominant star of 1937–1942, best remembered for his "Grand Slam" in 1938. At his peak, he controlled punishing deep first and second serves, crisp punched volleys, sure overheads, and steady, powerful ground strokes, especially his lightning-fast backhand, which his contemporaries called the greatest shot in tennis.

In 1941 Budge married Deidre Conselman; they had two sons. The marriage ended in divorce. In 1967 he married Loriel McPherson; they had no children. After retiring from competition, he coached the sport and conducted a tennis camp for children in Jamaica; later, in Virginia, he did consulting and promotion activity for sporting goods manufacturers and made guest speeches. The Budges lived at "Firethorne," a mansion in Dingman's Ferry, Pennsylvania. He died in a Scranton, Pennsylvania, hospital as a result of internal injuries received in a one-car accident in the Pocono Mountains.

• Autobiographical accounts are *Don Budge: A Tennis Memoir* (1969) and, in *American Lawn Tennis*, "The Early Days," Dec. 1958, pp. 17–19, and "Reminiscences," Mar. 1958, pp. 40–41, and Apr., 1958, pp. 38–40. Trustworthy biographies are by Allison Danzig in *Budge on Tennis* (1939), pp. 1–37, and Herbert Warren Wind, "The Sports Scene: Budge and the Grand Slam," *The New Yorker*, 15 Feb. 1988, pp. 75–89. Steve Flink, *The Greatest Tennis Matches of the Twentieth Century* (1999), details the match generally regarded as Budge's greatest in "Don Budge vs. Baron Gottfried Von Cramm, Davis Cup, 1937," pp. 29–36. Descriptions of Budge's style of play and evaluations of his all-time greatness are treated perceptively by Julius D. Heldman, "Style of the Great V: Don Budge," *World Tennis*, Apr. 1960, pp. 36–39; Paul Metzler, *Tennis Styles and Stylists* (1969), pp. 106–110, 193–94; Tom Stow, "The Greatest of Them All—Don Budge," *World Tennis*, Feb. 1954, pp. 36–37; and Ellsworth Vines and Gene Vier, *Tennis Myth and Method* (1978), pp. 21–33. Obituaries are in the *New York Times* and the *Washington Post*, 27 Jan. 2000.

FRANK V. PHELPS

BUELL, Marjorie Henderson (11 Dec. 1904–30 May 1993), cartoonist known as "Marge," was born Marjorie Lyman Henderson in Philadelphia, Pennsylvania, the first of the three daughters of Horace Lyman Henderson, an attorney, and Bertha Brown Henderson. Marge grew up on the 60-acre family farmstead on Hershey Mill Road in Malvern. She attended the Friends' School in West Chester and received her high school diploma from the Villa Maria Convent (or Academy) in 1921. She and her sisters drew throughout childhood, doing elaborate comic pictures for birthdays and special family events. Marge launched her commercial artistic career at the age of eight, selling drawings to her friends. While still in high school, she sold cartoons to the *Philadelphia Ledger*, working out of her own studio, a converted chicken coop. An early mentor was Ruth Plumly Thompson, author of many of the Oz books after L. Frank Baum's death in 1919; years later, Marge illustrated Thompson's *King Kojo* and some of her short stories in magazines. Encouraged to pursue cartooning as a vocation, she submitted single-panel gag cartoons signed "Marge" by mail and sold them to the humor magazines *Life* and *Judge*, and to *Country Gentleman*, *Collier's*, and the *Saturday Evening Post*. By 1929 she had produced at least two regular features of flapper follies—"The Boy Friend," a syndicated newspaper strip, around 1925–1926, and, for magazine publication, "Dashing Dot," which recorded in verse and drawings the mundane machinations of one of the era's curly-headed, long-legged sweet young things. She also wrote humorous chatty articles, some of which she illustrated.

Marge's cartoons were appearing in nearly every weekly issue of the *Saturday Evening Post* when in early 1935 she was asked to invent a successor to one of the magazine's popular recurring features, a single-panel pantomime cartoon by Carl Anderson called "Henry." Anderson's mute (and mouthless) bald-headed boy was leaving the *Post* for national newspaper syndication by King Features. Marge devised a female version of Henry, an equally silent and resourceful and slightly anti-authoritarian apple-cheeked little girl with corkscrew curls and a red dress. "I wanted a girl," Marge told a newspaper interviewer five years later, "because a girl could get away with more fresh stunts that in a small boy would seem boorish. Lulu's curls, I guess, were reminiscent of the way my hair looked when I was a youngster, but her face and the dress were just accidents." Christened "Little Lulu Moppet" by the *Post* editors, this child (who was, Marge later said, a little more than seven years old and a little less than nine) debuted in the "Henry" slot on the penultimate page in the magazine on 23 February 1935 and reappeared every week for the next ten years.

In her inaugural appearance, Lulu is a member of the wedding party, a picture of innocence who leads the bridesmaids down the aisle scattering not rose petals but banana peels behind her as she goes; the bridesmaid immediately behind Lulu is slipping and falling, but Lulu displays a perfectly innocent expression. Lulu's subversive tendencies were revealed in deadpan pantomime over the next few weeks. In her third appearance, she stands in a line of men to attend a theatrical event for "Men Only," wearing a phony moustache. In another she brings a cat to a dog show. In sitting for a family photograph, she grimaces and frowns while all the rest of the family smiles. Sometimes Lulu is simply clever or inventive. Lining up to take the required cold shower before entering the swimming pool, she wears rain gear and carries an umbrella. To take her pet dog on the trolley, she drapes the animal across her shoulders like the woman next to her who is wearing a fox fur. Lulu is often an irritant to her male playmates. She enters the boys' model airplane flying contest with a bird disguised as a model airplane. But Lulu's forte as a conscience-free scamp is usually without sexist bias. She puts an "I.O.U." in the collection plate at church. Standing next to a fisherman being photographed with his catch, Lulu holds her catch aloft—an old boot. She wears muddy galoshes to a shoe-shine stand. In a library festooned with "Silence" signs, she blows her nose loudly. At first, Lulu seemed more nine years old than seven: she had the long, spindly legs of a teenager. But as the years rolled by, Marge made the moppet cuter by shortening her legs and stature and making her head proportionately larger, so that the character was more infantlike and, thus, more appealing. By the end of the feature's run in the *Post*, Lulu often acted in four-panel comic strips, two panels stacked on another two in the shape of a square single-panel cartoon.

Lulu was almost immediately a hit. Her popularity with *Saturday Evening Post* readers prompted the Rand McNally Company to publish a collection of her *Post* cartoons in 1936, before the feature was two years old. Five more collections would be published by David McKay, 1939–1944. Composer Julia Smith wrote "Waltz for 'Little Lulu'" in 1937, and in 1939 the Knickerbocker Toy Company was manufacturing Little Lulu dolls that the *Post* and *Ladies' Home Journal* offered as premiums with a two-year subscription. Lulu's success as a promotional ploy resulted in her most remembered role: in 1944 Marge signed a contract for Lulu to star in advertising cartoons for Kleenex tissues. The editors at the *Post* were not pleased at this development, but since Marge owned the copyright on Lulu, she could do as she wished with the character; the *Post*, however, could decide what to do with the cartoon, and it was discontinued. "We parted amicably," Marge recalled in later years. The last Lulu cartoon in the *Post* was published on 30 December 1944, but Lulu continued to appear in the magazine—in Kleenex ads, which, for the next fifteen years, made Lulu nearly ubiquitous in newspapers and magazines and on billboards and display cards in trolleys and subways and department stores, even, in 1949 and 1957, in an electronic display in New York's Times Square.

On 30 January 1936 Marge married Clarence Addison Buell, an executive with Bell Telephone of Philadelphia, and the couple moved into a house built in 1684 on the family estate in Malvern; they had two sons. In 1943 Famous Studios produced the first eight of twenty-eight Lulu animated cartoons, and in 1945 Western Publishing Company brought out the first *Marge's Little Lulu* comic book, initially drawn and written by Western staff cartoonist John Stanley. Working with Marge's supervisory consent, Stanley refined Lulu's personality somewhat, making her feistier and more assertive and giving her fat boyfriend the name Tubby Tompkins (Marge had called the character "Joe"). Faced with the need for stories with plots, Stanley created the necessary conflict by pitting Lulu against her male playmates; no longer just mischievous, Lulu emerged as a crusading feminist (before the term had been invented), besting the boys at every turn. For the next decade or more, Stanley wrote the comic book stories and Irving Tripp drew them, working from Stanley's page layouts and pencil sketches. The comic books, eventually published throughout the world in a half-dozen foreign languages, were reportedly second only to Disney comic books in sales and distribution. In 1950, a Little Lulu newspaper comic strip was produced by Western and syndicated by the Chicago Tribune–New York Daily News Syndicate, starting June 6 and continuing for the next twenty years under many hands, including cartoonists Woody Kimbrell, Roger Armstrong, Ed Nofziger, and writers Al Stoffel and Del Connell.

By the late 1940s, Marge was managing a merchandising empire that fostered a horde of products—phonograph records, games and puzzles, bean bags, balloons and assorted toys, greeting cards and children's apparel, candy and confections, cosmetics and toiletries, towels and frabrics featuring Lulu and her milieu, and so on. While Marge approved all the Lulu appearances from the comic book and comic strip to coloring books and dolls, she drew Lulu only for the Kleenex campaign, often assisted by one or the other of her sisters, who inked her drawings. In 1971, Marge sold her rights to Western and retired, moving shortly thereafter to Oberlin, Ohio; she died in nearby Elyria.

Although many women grew up with the assertive and self-reliant Lulu as a role model, Marge was not a crusader for women's rights. According to her older son, Lawrence, "She knew she had created a feisty character and liked it, and she was very proud of having created a popular nonviolent cartoon. But she was not a conscious feminist. She didn't see life that way." She was most pleased, he said, at being an entrepreneurial success as a woman cartoonist. But Marge did more than create a merchandising empire: whether she intended it or not, she also created an icon for America's young girls.

• The most complete albeit brief biography of Buell is the entry by Eva M. Maddox in *The Scribner Encyclopedia of American Lives, Vol. 3: 1991–1993* (2001). Buell is also mentioned and "Dashing Dot" illustrated in Trina Robbins, *A Century of Women Cartoonists* (1993). The Little Lulu cartoons of the *Saturday Evening Post* have been collected in *Little Lulu* (Rand McNally, 1936) and in five similar volumes from David McKay: *Little Lulu and Her Pals* (1939), *Little Lulu on Parade* (1941), *Laughs with Little Lulu* (1942), *Oh, Little Lulu* (1943), and *Fun with Little Lulu* (1944). *Marge's Little Lulu* comic books were published in 1945–1984, 275 issues altogether (with "Marge's" dropped from the title with No. 207 in 1972), while *Marge's Tubby*, 1952–1962, numbered 49 issues. From 1943 through 1947, Famous Studios produced 26 animated cartoons that were distributed by Paramount; two more were created in 1961–1962, and a new series was developed for HBO television in 1995. Two live-actor television specials were aired on ABC-TV in 1978 and 1979, starring Lauri Hendler as Lulu. In the 1980s, Gladstone Publishing Company produced the *Little Lulu Library*, a series of 18 slip-cased volumes reprinting John Stanley's Little Lulu stories from the comic books. The only comprehensive exhibition of Buell's work during her lifetime was curated in 1982 by John and Susan Edwards Harvith, art historians at Syracuse University, who worked with Buell. Obituaries in the *New York Times*, 3 June 1993, and in the *Daily Telegraph*, 12 June 1993, though short, are fairly comprehensive and helpful.

ROBERT C. HARVEY

BULLARD, Eugène Jacques (9 Oct. 1895–12 Oct. 1961), combat pilot, was born Eugene James Bullard in Columbus, Georgia, the son of William Octave Bullard, a laborer and former slave, and Josephine Thomas. Both parents were of African American and

Creek Indian descent. In 1906 Bullard, the seventh of ten children, ran away from home, ending his formal education. He lived for a time with a band of gypsies, who taught him to ride racehorses. He then worked as a horse handler, jockey, and laborer in several southern states. Bullard gained the respect of several employers by his quiet insistence on treatment with dignity and equality, an ethos instilled in him by his father and strengthened by his sojourn with the tolerant, English-born gypsies.

Early in 1912, Bullard made his way to Norfolk, Virginia, where he stowed away on a freighter bound for Europe. Set ashore in Aberdeen, Bullard worked his way south, joining a traveling vaudeville troupe, Freedman's Pickaninnies, in Liverpool later that year. There he also trained as a prizefighter and won his first fight, on points, in early 1913. A good but not exceptional fighter, Bullard fought under the auspices of African-American welterweight champion Aaron Lester Brown, "the Dixie Kid." On 28 November 1913, Bullard first fought in Paris, achieving a twenty-round win not reported in local boxing papers. Bullard discovered in Paris his ideal milieu, where people of all races and nationalities found acceptance and equal opportunity. The following spring, after touring the Continent with Freedman's Pickaninnies, Bullard settled in Paris. Adept at languages, he earned his living both as a fighter and as an interpreter for other fighters. At about this time he began to use the Francophone version of his name, Eugène Jacques Bullard (pronounced Bull-*ar*).

In August 1914 war broke out in Europe. On 19 October 1914, shortly after his 19th birthday, Bullard enlisted in the French Foreign Legion. He saw action as a machine gunner in some of the bitterest fighting on the Western Front. Following crippling losses along the Somme in April 1915, three Foreign Legion regiments were consolidated into one.

Late that summer, Bullard's father wrote to the U.S. secretary of state, pleading that his son, not yet twenty, be "freed at once and sent home" from the war. "He must have made a mistake when he enlist [*sic*]," William Bullard wrote, and enclosed a document certifying that his son's birth date as recorded in their family Bible was 9 October 1895. (In his autobiography, Bullard himself several times gave his birth year as 1894, from which has stemmed ongoing confusion.) The American ambassador in Paris was notified of the elder Bullard's request, but under French law a nineteen-year-old was not underage; neither the American nor the French government took further action (quoted in Lloyd, pp. 41–42).

After heavy fighting in the Champagne in autumn 1915, Bullard and other surviving Legionnaires were transferred to regular French regiments, Bullard to the 170th Infantry, a crack unit known to the Germans as the "swallows of death." Early in 1916, the 170th was sent to Verdun, a sector notorious for its savage fighting. In early March Bullard sustained a crippling thigh wound, for which he received the Croix de Guerre.

Unable to continue ground fighting, Bullard requested a transfer to aviation gunnery. His recuperation complete, he began training in October 1916. He soon transferred to fighter pilot training and on 5 May 1917 received pilot's license number 6950 from the Aéro Club de France. Moving on to advanced pilot training, in August Bullard was assigned to squadron 93 of the Lafayette Flying Corps, a group of American fighters under French command. With squadrons 93 and 85, Bullard flew at least twenty missions over the Verdun sector. He reported shooting down at least two enemy planes; as happened to other flyers, however, there was no corroborating evidence, so these were not scored as official "kills."

A competent pilot appreciated by his comrades, Bullard nevertheless was abruptly removed from aviation and returned to the 170th infantry as a noncombatant. Circumstantial evidence suggested that, while other pilots of the Lafayette Flying Corps were transferred to the American Army Air Corps, Bullard was remanded because of his race. The United States would not commission an African-American aviator until 1942.

Bullard was discharged from the military on 24 October 1919, nearly a year after the Armistice. Since his war wounds prevented serious resumption of his boxing career, he instead became a jazz drummer and later was central to the management of Le Grand Duc, one of the most noted Parisian jazz clubs between the wars. Ada Louise Smith, known as Bricktop, first headlined there before opening her own Montmartre club. The roll call of musicians and guests at Le Grand Duc included the most celebrated names in Paris in the 1920s. Bullard also became the proprietor of Gene Bullard's Athletic Club and owner of another celebrated jazz club, L'Escadrille, in the 1930s.

In 1923 Bullard married Marcelle Straumann, daughter of a socially prominent family. The couple had two daughters and also a son, who died in infancy. Bullard's deep commitment to his businesses was incompatible with his wife's society interests. They separated after eight years and divorced in 1935; Bullard retained custody of his two daughters.

At the outset of World War II, Bullard assisted French counterintelligence by reporting information gleaned from the conversations of Nazi visitors to his establishments. When Germany invaded France in May 1940, Bullard, with many others, left Paris to fight. Unable to reach the 170th Infantry to the east, Bullard volunteered with the 51st Infantry at Orléans. He was severely wounded in June. His French commanding officer, who had also been his superior at Verdun, ordered him to flee south, fearing that Bullard would be executed if captured. Making his way overland to Spain, Bullard eventually reached New York, medical treatment, and involvement with Charles de Gaulle's Free French movement. During and after the war, Bullard lived in Harlem and was active with New York's French community. He returned briefly to France in 1950–1951, while unsuccessfully seeking compensation for the loss of his Parisian businesses.

At the invitation of the French government, in 1954 he assisted at the relighting of the eternal flame at the Arc de Triomphe. In 1959 he was made a chevalier of the Legion of Honor, France's highest award; he received fifteen medals in all from the French government. Bullard died in New York and is buried in the French War Veterans' plot, Flushing Cemetery, Queens, New York.

For many years after World War I, the conventional stance of American authorities was that blacks did not have the mettle or the intellect to fly. In France, Bullard was widely recognized as an athlete, war veteran, and leader in Parisian expatriate society. However, his achievement in daring to train and fly as a combat pilot—which African Americans in the United States would struggle for decades to be allowed to do—was given little recognition in the United States until well after his death. In 1989, Bullard was inducted into the Georgia Aviation Hall of Fame. He is depicted on the noteworthy "Black Americans in Flight" mural at the St. Louis International Airport, dedicated in 1990. A memorial bust at the Smithsonian Institution's National Air and Space Museum was unveiled in 1991. On 14 September 1994, Bullard was posthumously commissioned as a second lieutenant in the U.S. Air Force.

• Craig Lloyd, *Eugene Bullard: Black Expatriate in Jazz-Age Paris* (2000), reconstructs Bullard's life through painstaking examination of contemporary sources to verify and amplify Bullard's unpublished autobiography, *All Blood Runs Red: My Adventurous Life in Search of Freedom* (completed 1961). The latter is in the possession of Bullard's daughter and grandson. An earlier biography, P. J. Carisella and James W. Ryan, *The Black Swallow of Death* (1972), also quotes extensively from Bullard's memoir and includes photographs of Bullard throughout his life. Tyler Stovall, *Paris Noir: African Americans in the City of Light* (1996), discusses Bullard's years in Paris. Articles by Jamie H. Cockfield, who was influential in securing Bullard's posthumous commission, include "The Black Icarus," *Over the Front* 9, no. 4 (winter 1994), pp. 362–67, and "All Blood Runs Red," *Legacy: A Supplement to American Heritage* (Feb./Mar. 1995), pp.7–15. Obituaries are in the *New York Times*, 14 Oct. 1961, and the *New York Amsterdam News,* 21 Oct. 1961. Correspondence and manuscript relating to the writing of Bullard's autobiography are part of the Louise Fox Connell Papers, Schlesinger Library, Radcliffe College.

CAROLINE M. FANNIN

BULLOCH, James Dunwoody (25 June 1823–7 Jan. 1901), Confederate naval officer, was born near Savannah, Georgia, the only child of James Stephens Bulloch and his first wife, Hester Amarintha Elliott. Major Bulloch had been one of the owners of the *Savannah*, a ship that in 1819 made the first steam-assisted crossing of the Atlantic. Hester Bulloch's father was a U.S. senator, and her mother belonged to the prominent Dunwody family. (J. D. Bulloch changed the spelling of his middle name to Dunwoody.)

J. D. Bulloch joined the U.S. Navy as a midshipman in 1839. The Annapolis naval academy did not yet exist, so he immediately went to sea. At one point he served under David Farragut, the future Union admiral. In 1844–1845 Bulloch studied at a naval school in Philadelphia, and he graduated second in his class. At the time of the Mexican War, he was assigned to the Pacific squadron. During 1849–1851 he was employed in the coast survey. After this, he was one of the naval officers assigned to command government-subsidized mail steamers. In 1851 he married Elizabeth Caskie of Richmond. They had no children, and she died three years later. Bulloch was captain of the *Black Warrior* when the authorities at Havana seized its cargo in an incident that brought Spain and the United States close to war. In October 1854 Bulloch left the navy, having attained the rank of lieutenant. Promotion was slow, and he could expect better pay as a merchant marine officer.

Bulloch made his home in New York City, where his half sister Martha lived. Martha had married the elder Theodore Roosevelt, a wealthy glass importer, and was the mother of the future president. In 1857 Bullock married Harriet Cross Foster, a widow and the daughter of a career army officer from Maryland who served in the Union army during the Civil War. They had five children before she died in 1897.

It was out of principle that the Georgia-born sailor supported secession. Bulloch later pointed out: "I had become completely identified with the shipping enterprises of New York. I had no property of any kind in the South." He emphasized: "my personal interests were wholly, and my personal friendships were chiefly, in the North" (Bulloch, vol. 2, p. 32). Nevertheless on 8 May 1861 he reported to the secretary of the Confederate navy for assignment. The Confederate navy immediately sent Bulloch overseas as a naval purchasing agent. The South, which lacked the resources to construct a modern navy on its own territory, hoped to acquire ships in Britain and France.

On 4 June 1861 Bulloch arrived in Liverpool, a major cotton entrepôt and shipbuilding port where the South enjoyed widespread sympathy. Although he lacked ready money, the firm of Fraser, Trenholm advanced him credit. Bulloch quickly signed a contract for building the commerce raider *Florida* and later contracted for the construction of the better-known *Alabama*. Intended for use against unarmed merchant ships, these wooden corsairs were built for speed and, by combining sail with steam, were relatively independent of coaling stations. Bulloch's Liverpool solicitor advised him that British law allowed foreign governments in need of warships to build vessels at British dockyards and to purchase existing ones provided the ships were not armed in the queen's jurisdiction. The Foreign Enlistment Act also prohibited recruiting sailors on British soil for service on foreign warships.

In the fall of 1861 Bulloch returned to the United States [the Confederacy] on the *Fingal*, a blockade-runner carrying military supplies. After landing at Savannah, he traveled to Richmond, where he met with the naval secretary, who awarded him the rank of commander in the Confederate navy. Bulloch returned to Liverpool on 10 March 1862 and spent the remainder of the war in Britain and occasionally in France. During 1862 the *Florida* and the *Alabama* slipped out of British waters to be equipped elsewhere for war. Bulloch had been promised both commands, but in the end the Confederate secretary of the navy regarded him as indispensable as a naval agent. In 1864 Bulloch purchased the *Shenandoah* for use against whalers. Irving Stephens Bulloch (1842–1898), J. D. Bulloch's half brother, served aboard the *Alabama* and the *Shenandoah*. Bulloch also tried to build ironclads in Britain and France to smash the Union blockade. Only the *Stonewall*, purchased from Denmark, reached American waters during the last days of war.

Excluded from the general pardon at the end of the Civil War, Bulloch remained in Liverpool, where he made his living as a cotton broker in the firm of Bulloch and Robertson. By the time of the 1871 census he was a British subject. He secretly visited his half sister's home in New York City in the winter of 1871. In his autobiography Theodore Roosevelt confirmed the visit of two Bulloch uncles (the other being Irving Bulloch). Roosevelt visited his "Uncle Jimmy" in England several times. Roosevelt encouraged his uncle to write his memoir, *The Secret Service of the Confederate States in Europe; or, How the Confederate Cruisers Were Equipped*, which was published in Britain in 1883 and in the United States in 1884.

Apparently Bulloch fell into financial difficulties. In 1888 Roosevelt wrote to Henry Cabot Lodge, enclosing "a letter from my dear old uncle, Capt. Jas. D. Bulloch," to find out whether Bulloch was eligible for a Mexican War pension. "It is literally everything to him" (Roosevelt, 1925, vol. 1, p. 73). As evidence of his comparative impoverishment, his probated estate amounted to only 200 pounds. Toward the end of his life Bulloch lived with his married daughter. He served as a director of the Liverpool Nautical College and the Orphan Boys Asylum. Bulloch died in Liverpool of cancer and cardiac arrest shortly after his nephew was elected vice president of the United States. On Bulloch's grave at Toxteth in Liverpool an inscription reads, "an American by birth, an Englishman by choice."

• Much of Bulloch's official correspondence is in the U.S. Department of the Navy, *Official Records of the Union and Confederate Navies in the War of the Rebellion*, ser. 2, vol. 2 (1894–1927). Other Bulloch letters are in the microfilm collection *Civil War and the Confederacy: The Business Records of Fraser, Trenholm, and Company of Liverpool and Charleston, South Carolina, 1860–1877*, from the Merseyside Maritime Museum, Liverpool (13 reels, Adam Matthew Publications, 1998). Apparently Bulloch's private papers do not survive. Bulloch's memoir, *The Secret Service of the Confederate States in Europe; or, How the Confederate Cruisers Were Equipped* (1883; 1884), includes little about his private life. Philip Van Doren Stern added an introduction, notes, illustrations, and other supplements in a 1959 reprint (reissued in 2001). For a contemporary obituary notice, see *Liverpool Daily Post*, 8 Jan. 1901. A good sketch of Bulloch's life, written with the help of his younger daughter, is by James Morton Callahan,

"James Dunwody Bulloch," in the *Dictionary of American Biography*, vol. 2, edited by James Truslow Adams (1940), pp. 257–58. Warren F. Spencer added a few details in "James Dunwoody Bulloch," *Dictionary of Georgia Biography*, vol. 1, edited by Kenneth Coleman and Stephen Gurr (1983), pp. 136–38. For another account see Charles Grayson Summersell, "Bulloch the Builder," in *CSS* Alabama: *Builder, Captain, and Plans* (1985). Frank J. Merli offers a succinct interpretation of Bulloch's career in "James Dunwoody Bulloch," *Encyclopedia of the Confederacy*, edited by Richard N. Current et al., vol. 1 (1993), pp. 239–41, and greater detail in *Great Britain and the Confederate Navy, 1861–1865* (1970; repr. 2004 with a foreword by Howard Jones) and *The Alabama, British Neutrality, and the American Civil War*, edited by David M. Fahey (2004). Virginia Bullock-Willis provides an intelligent reading of Bulloch's memoir in "James Dunwoody Bulloch," *Sewanee Review* 34, no. 4 (Oct.–Dec. 1926): 386–401. His famous nephew mentioned Bulloch in Theodore Roosevelt, *Theodore Roosevelt: An Autobiography* (1920) and *Selections from the Correspondence of Theodore Roosevelt and Henry Cabot Lodge, 1884–1918* (1925).

DAVID M. FAHEY

BURKE, Arleigh (19 Oct. 1901–1 Jan. 1996), admiral and chief of naval operations, was born Arleigh Albert Burke in Boulder, Colorado, the son of Oscar A. Burke and Claire Mokler Burke, farmers. After being educated at numerous preparatory schools, Burke gained admittance to the U.S. Naval Academy, Annapolis, in 1919. He graduated four years later, 71st in a class of 413. On his graduation day in 1923 he married Roberta Gorsuch; they had no children. Over the next two decades Burke fulfilled routine naval service duties ashore and at sea; in 1931 he received a master's degree in chemical engineering from the University of Michigan. Following a two-year tour with the navy's bureau of ordnance in 1937, he became executive officer of the destroyer *Cravin* and commenced a long association with that class of warships. In 1939 Burke became lieutenant commander of the destroyer *Mugford*; he trained his crew to a razor's edge and won the coveted Destroyer Gunnery Trophy for 1939. Following the attack on Pearl harbor in December 1941, he immediately sought a combat command; however, his technical expertise was much in demand and he served instead in the less glamorous but equally important billet as ordnance inspector at the Naval Gun Factory in Washington, D.C.

Burke remained stateside until March 1943, when he transferred to the Pacific theater. There he assumed command of Destroyer Division 43 aboard the *Walter* and within days sank a Japanese destroyer near the Solomon Islands on his first sortie. Promoted to captain the following May, he transferred his flag to Destroyer Squadron 23 on board the *Charles Ashburne* and gained a reputation as the finest destroyer tactician in the navy. During the November 1943 battles of Empress Augusta Bay and Cape St. George, Burke's vessels rapidly closed with enemy flotillas, fired scores of well-aimed torpedoes, and sank several more Japanese warships without loss. Consequently, Destroyer Squadron 23, nicknamed the "Little

Beavers" after a cartoon character, became the most celebrated destroyer formation of the war. Up to this point, U.S. Navy forces were at a disadvantage in-nighttime engagements owing to tactical inflexibility and superior Japanese weaponry. Burke, however, im-provised his own tactics, splitting his division in two, thereby granting his captains greater flexibility. He thus became the only American naval officer to achieve operational parity with Admiral Razio Ta-naka, the great Japanese destroyerman. Admiral Wil-liam F. Halsey, having learned of these exploits, chris-tened him "Thirty-one-knot Burke" on account of his high-speed tactics, and the sobriquet stuck. When the Solomon Islands campaign concluded, the Little Beavers had conducted twenty-two surface actions, had sunk or disabled one Japanese cruiser, nine de-stroyers, and a submarine, and had destroyed thirty aircraft.

In March 1944 Burke transferred as a commodore to serve as chief of staff to Vice Admiral Marc A. Mitscher's Fast Carrier Task Force 58. In this capac-ity, he helped plan and coordinate some of the largest naval encounters of the war, with victories at Leyte Gulf in 1944 and Okinawa in 1945. During this last engagement, waves of Japanese kamikaze forced Burke and his staff to abandon the carriers *Bunker Hill* and *Enterprise* before finally settling aboard the *Ran-dolph*. He was recalled to Washington, D.C., after thirty-one months of continuous combat, and in July 1945 he became director of research at the Bureau of Ordnance. Among his thirteen wartime decorations were a Distinguished Service Medal, the Navy Cross, the Legion of Merit, and the Silver Star.

From 1945 to 1947 Burke functioned as chief of staff to the Atlantic Fleet, and in 1948 he led the *Hunt-ington* on a goodwill cruise of the Mediterranean. The following year he was posted to the chief of naval operations office (CNO), where his behavior engen-dered considerable controversy. The postwar period was a difficult time of transition for the armed ser-vices; they were forced to compete against each other for declining revenues and resources. In concert with CNO Louis Emil Denfield, Burke emerged as a stri-dent opponent of the Air Force's new Convair B-36 intercontinental bomber, which many admirals felt would be acquired at the expense of naval aviation. Furthermore, Burke strongly seconded Denfield in championing creation of a new class of super aircraft carriers to expand the navy's strategic capabilities. Such outspokenness displeased members of the Harry S. Truman administration and in 1949 Burke found himself deleted from the list of officers slated for pro-motion. Fortunately, President Truman decided to overlook Burke's role in the so-called Admirals' Re-volt, and in July 1950 he arranged his promotion to rear admiral. Burke subsequently commanded Cruiser Division 5 during the Korean War and in 1951 went ashore as part of the Military Armistice Commission. He served for three more years as di-rector of the Strategic Planning Division of the Navy Department. In 1955 President Dwight D. Eisen-hower rehabilitated Burke's reputation by appointing him chief of naval operations.

Burke's nomination occasioned controversy, as he was selected over the heads of fifty-seven naval offi-cers who had more seniority. He thus became vice admiral at 53, the youngest officer to serve as chief of naval operations. Throughout his tenure, Burke be-came closely identified with the navy's struggle to re-define itself in an age of nuclear deterrence and lim-ited conflict. He proved instrumental in promoting such new technologies as nuclear propulsion for sub-marines and surface vessels, the *Polaris* ballistic mis-sile system, and the large *Forrestal*-class attack carri-ers. Burke also orchestrated deployment of naval assets throughout a host of Cold War confrontations that ranged from the Quemoy-Matsu incidents off Taiwan in 1957 to marine landings in Lebanon in 1958. His success can be gauged by the fact that he served no less than three two-year terms as CNO, longer than any other incumbent. He retired in 1961 after refusing an offer by President John F. Kennedy to serve an unprecedented fourth term. Burke sub-sequently settled in Fairfax, Virginia, where he served on the boards of several companies. In 1984 the navy paid him considerable tribute by naming an entire class of vessels, the expensive and highly sophisticated *Arleigh Burke* guided missile destroyers, in his honor. This was followed in 1991 when the first ship of this class, the *Arleigh Burke* (DDG-51), was commis-sioned while he was still alive. Burke died at Bethesda Naval Hospital.

• There is no single cache of Burke correspondence, but scattered materials are in the Bernard L. Austin, Julius A. Furer, and Frank Kowalski Papers, Manuscript Division, Li-brary of Congress. Other collections exist at archives of the Naval War College, Newport, R.I., the U. S. Naval Institute, Annapolis, Md., and the Operations Branch, Naval Histori-cal Center, Washington, D.C. A collection of printed war-time dispatches, admonitions, and reflections is Arleigh Burke, *The Best of Burke* (1986). For an essay by Burke on Cold War policy, see Frank R. Barnett, William C. Mott, and John C. Neff, eds., *Peace and War in the Modern Age: Prem-ises, Myths and Realities* (1965). Published biographies in-clude Ken Jones, *Admiral Arleigh (31-Knot) Burke* (2001); James C. Bradford, ed., *Quarterdeck and Bridge: Two Cen-turies of American Naval Leaders* (1997); and Elmer B. Potter, *Admiral Arleigh Burke* (1990). Critical examinations of his later career are Robert W. Love, ed., *The Chiefs of Naval Operations* (1980), and John P. Madden, "Operation Bumpy Road: The Role of Arleigh Burke and the U.S. Navy in the Bay of Pigs Invasion" (master's thesis, Old Dominion Uni-versity, 1988). Shorter but equally useful accounts are David H. Rosenberg, "Officer Development in the Interwar Navy: Arleigh Burke—The Making of a Professional," *Pacific His-torical Review* 44, no. 4 (1975): 503–26, and Eugene Wolfe, "Derailing the Last Tokyo Express," *Naval History* 10, no. 2 (1996): 34–39. Obituaries are in the *New York Times* and the *Washington Post*, both 2 Jan. 1996.

JOHN C. FREDRIKSEN

BURKE, Billie (7 Aug. 1885–14 May 1970), actress, was born Mary William Ethelbert Appleton Burke in

Washington, D.C., the daughter of William Burke, a singing clown, and Blanche Beatty Hodkinson, a widow from New Orleans. Her father performed with a circus and had a penchant for quoting Shakespeare, this in the days before clowns wore red noses and flap shoes. Most of Burke's childhood was spent touring the United States, Europe, and Russia with her parents.

Burke received little formal education. In 1893 she briefly attended the Misses Baillie's School when, after the Billy Burke's Barnum and Great London Circus Songsters act failed to catch on, her family settled in London. At her mother's insistence, Burke began taking lessons in singing, ballet, elocution, and fencing. As part of her training, she also appeared in music halls and pantomimes. (In her first autobiography Burke claimed that she had no wish to become an actress. "The dream was entirely my mother's," she added [Burke, 1949, p. 24].)

In 1903 the fledgling performer with waist-length red hair made a hit singing "Mamie, I Have a Little Canoe" in "The School Girl," produced by the great Charles Frohman. The show ran for two years at the Prince of Wales Theatre, and Burke became a minor celebrity. Comfortable with performing by now, she decided to pursue straight comedy parts and was given her first chance by Sir Charles Hawtrey in *Mr. George*, which opened in 1907 at the Vaudeville Theatre on the Strand. Burke scored a hit, although the play did not. Thinking her ready for Broadway, Frohmann brought her to New York that year to appear in *My Wife* opposite John Drew.

Burke became a true star in her next Broadway play, *Love Watches*, which opened at the Lyceum Theatre in 1908. The reviewer for the *New York Times* described Burke as "the daintiest imaginable picture, wistful, alluring, bright, vivacious, and full of life and go" ("A Dainty Comedy at the Lyceum," 28 Aug. 1908). Burke had found her niche in light comedy. Enrico Caruso and Mark Twain were among her admirers. In 1909 she took the play to London's Haymarket Theatre then toured in it throughout the United States. Over the next four decades Burke would often appear on Broadway then lead the company on a national tour. She appeared as Mrs. Worthley in *Mrs. Dot* (1910), as Lily Parradell in Sir Arthur Wing Pinero's *The 'Mind the Paint' Girl* (1912), and as Violet in W. Somerset Maugham's *Caesar's Wife* (1921). She was also seen in Booth Tarkington's *Rose Briar* (1922) and Noël Coward's *The Marquise* (1932). In the part of Lily Parradell, Burke felt she had been accepted as a dramatic actress. "Up to now," she said, "the critics had regarded me as a cream puff" (Burke, p. 112).

On 11 April 1914, Burke married showman Florenz Ziegfeld, Jr.; the couple had a daughter. In 1915 Ziegfeld acted as Burke's agent when she signed a contract with film pioneer Thomas H. Ince, whose studio was in Santa Monica, California. This was partly an act of defiance on Burke's part. The Frohman organization, which previously had treated her like the most delicate of flowers, disapproved of her marriage to Ziegfeld and punished her, she felt, by arranging a grueling tour for her in *Jerry*. She signed a contract with Ince at a salary of $10,000 a week. Burke played opposite William Desmond in *Peggy* and then went on to make about a dozen films for the Famous Players–Lasky organization back in New York—among them a film version of Victorien Sardou's *Let's Get a Divorce* (1918), a fluffy Belle Epoque comedy.

The stock market crash of 1929 forced Burke and her husband to abandon their opulent lifestyle. After Ziegfeld died in 1932, leaving a large number of debts, Burke's friend director George Cukor gave her the part of the mother in *A Bill of Divorcement* with John Barrymore and newcomer Katharine Hepburn. This was Burke's first nonsilent film. She decided not to return to New York but to stay in California, which had what she called "a wonderful climate for geraniums and actresses" (Burke, p. 253). Having signed a contract with Metro-Goldwyn-Mayer, Cukor cast her in one of the best films of the Thirties, the all-star *Dinner at Eight* (1933), an adaptation of the play by George S. Kaufman and Edna Ferber, with Jean Harlow, Marie Dressler, Wallace Beery, and both John Barrymore and Lionel Barrymore. Burke played Mrs. Oliver Jordan, a society matron who learns to take it on the chin like everyone else in the Depression of the 1930s, but not before Burke, in her tremulous, chirping voice, rants about the servants, a ruined aspic, and the unsuitability of crab meat for her grand dinner. As a character actress, Burke's trademark became the dithering, daffy, frequently rich older woman.

Two years later, Burke appeared in *Becky Sharp*, the film adaptation of Langdon Mitchell's stage version of William Makepeace Thackeray's *Vanity Fair*. She portrayed Lady Bareacres and was directed by Rouben Mamoulian. *Becky Sharp* was "the first full-length photoplay produced in the three-component color process of Technicolor" (Andre Sennwald, "The Radio City Music Hall Presents 'Becky Sharp,'" *New York Times*, 14 June 1935). She also played the hapless Mrs. Topper in Hal Roach's popular Topper series, beginning with *Topper* (1937), followed by *Topper Takes a Trip* (1939), and finally *Topper Returns* (1941).

Burke was nominated for an Academy Award in 1938 for her performance in *Merrily We Live* in the part of Mrs. Emily Kilbourne. Immortality was conferred upon her the following year when, as Glinda, the Witch of the North, in *The Wizard of Oz* (1939), she asked Judy Garland, as Dorothy, "Are you a good witch or a bad witch?" Among her notable films from this period are *The Man Who Came to Dinner* and *In This Our Life*, both released in 1942, *The Cheaters* (1945), and *The Barkleys of Broadway* (1949) starring Fred Astaire and Ginger Rogers, written by Betty Comden and Adolph Green, with music and lyrics by George Gershwin and Ira Gershwin.

In 1949 Burke published her autobiography *With a Feather on My Nose* and another, *With Powder on My Nose*, in 1959. From 1944 to 1946, she had starred on her own radio show, "The Billie Burke Show," and also in the *Doc Corkle* television series in 1952 (which lasted only three weeks on the air). She was now living happily and comfortably in West Los Angeles near her daughter and grandchildren, still doing a few films and summer stock. Burke played Doris Dunstan, Elizabeth Taylor's character's prospective mother-in-law in the huge success *Father of the Bride* (1950), directed by Vincente Minnelli, and in the sequel, *Father's Little Dividend* (1951). Her last films of note were *The Young Philadelphians*, starring Paul Newman (1959), and John Ford's *Sergeant Rutledge* (1960).

Burke easily transitioned to film acting and worked with a number of pioneers in the early days of Hollywood. In addition to her many films, television, and radio appearances, she wrote two volumes of memoirs, kept her marriage together while married to a world-class womanizer, and also raised a child successfully. A trouper's trouper, she once said, "To survive in Hollywood, you need the ambition of a Latin American Revolutionary, the ego of a grand opera tenor and the physical stamina of a cow pony" (quoted in *Women in World History*, vol. 3, p. 216). She died in Los Angeles and was interred at Kensico Cemetery in Valhalla, New York.

• Burke's autobiography, *With a Feather on My Nose* (1949), provides a candid assessment of her life, her marriage, and her career through the 1940s. Other informative sources include David Shipman, *The Great Movie Stars: The Golden Years* (1970), and *Women in World History*, vol. 3 (1999), pp. 214–17. For dates of Burke's Broadway appearances, see Daniel Blum, *A Pictorial History of the American Theatre 1860–1980* (1981). There is a lengthy obituary in the *New York Times*, 16 May 1970, and one in *Variety*, 20 May 1970 (*Variety Obituaries*, vol. 7). Both the *New York Times* and the *Variety* obituaries give Burke's birth date as 1886, whereas most other sources give it as 1885.

ANDREA WEEVER

BURNETT, Peter Hardeman (15 Nov. 1807–17 May 1895), first governor of California, was born in Nashville, Tennessee, the son of George Burnet, a carpenter and farmer, and Dorothy Hardeman Burnet. He grew up in modest circumstances and moved with his parents first to a farm around age four and later, in fall 1817, to Howard County, Missouri. In 1826 he returned to Tennessee, where he clerked at a hotel for $100 a year and later at a store for double that amount. It was around the same time that he added a second "t" to his surname—making it "more complete and emphatic"—and was followed in his example by his brothers. Burnett married Harriet W. Rodgers on 20 August 1828; the couple had six children.

Although successful enough to buy out his employer in the spring of 1829, he spent the next several years struggling to achieve permanent success in business. Burnett then returned to Missouri, settling at Liberty; the change in scenery, however, did little to change his luck in commerce. While possessing little in the way of formal education, Burnett had studied law on his own and in the spring of 1839 turned to the legal profession in a desperate attempt to erase debts that had accumulated from years of entrepreneurial setbacks. Although he succeeded in being named prosecuting attorney for his district several months later, his financial troubles continued and he suffered the added burden of caring for an ailing wife.

In the spring of 1843, weary of his financial struggles, Burnett decided to make a fresh start out West. After obtaining permission from his creditors, he left Independence, Missouri, on 22 May 1843 in a party of 875 men, women, and children, with Oregon Territory as their goal. Upon reaching Whitman's Mission the following October, Burnett continued on to Fort Vancouver and took up farming near the mouth of the Willamette River.

Finally settling on another farm near present-day Hillsboro, Oregon, Burnett soon became a leader in his adopted community. Named one of nine members of the legislative committee of Oregon in 1844, by the following year he was serving as a judge on the Supreme Court. In 1848, following the establishment of a formal territorial government, Burnett was elected to the legislature and in August of that year was named as one of the territory's Supreme Court justices by President James K. Polk. Burnett did not learn of his presidential appointment for several months because in September 1848 he, ever in search of new opportunities, led a party of 150 men to California with the gold mines of Yuba as their goal. The party arrived in early November, but Burnett did not remain in the mining business for long; by year's end he had swapped the uncertain fortunes of a prospector for employment as the attorney and general agent of John A. Sutter.

In 1849 Burnett left Sutter. On August 13 of that year territorial governor Bennet Riley appointed Burnett a judge of the superior tribunal of California. Burnett took a leading role in the movement for California statehood. On 13 November of that year he was elected territorial governor; the new state's constitution received ratification during the same election. After briefly serving as military governor, on 21 March 1850 he was inaugurated in San Jose (then serving as the temporary capital). During his inaugural speech Burnett recommended that free African Americans be banned from the new state, an idea that had also been popular in Oregon and which he had taken a leading role in incorporating into that state's laws in 1844. Although California formally joined the Union on 9 September 1850, Burnett had grown tired of his position and resigned as governor on 9 January 1851; his lieutenant governor, John McDougall, succeeded him and finished out the remainder of his term. .

After leaving the governor's office, Burnett practiced law for a number of years and in 1854 moved to San Jose. In early 1857 he was appointed to the state supreme court, where he served until October 1858. Having long since satisfied his creditors back East, he was free to develop new interests and in 1863 moved to San Francisco, where with Joseph W. Winans and Sam Brannan he founded the Pacific Bank of

San Francisco. Burnett served as president of the firm until 1880, when he retired from business. In that same year he also published his memoirs, *Recollections and Opinions of an Old Pioneer*. He died at his home in San Francisco.

Although he never remained in one position long enough to make a real difference, Burnett was the first governor of the state of California. An unexceptional man, he was one of hundreds who survived a variety of personal and professional setbacks back East and managed to enjoy success while contributing to the development uof the American West.

• Burnett's papers are held at the California State Archives in Sacramento, California. In addition to his memoirs, he was also the author of *The Path Which Led a Protestant Lawyer to the Catholic Church* (1859). His life and career received attention in Andrew F. Rolle, *California, A History* (5th ed., 1998), and Robert G. Cleland, *From Wilderness to Empire: A History of California, 1542–1900* (1944). An obituary is in the *San Francisco Chronicle*, 18 May 1895.

EDWARD L. LACH, JR.

BURNHAM, Louis Everett (29 Sept. 1915–12 Feb. 1960), journalist, activist, and radical, was born in Harlem, New York, the son of Charles Breechford Burnham, a building superintendent, and Louise St. Clair Williams Burnham, a hairdresser. His parents had emigrated from Barbados to the United States in search of a better livelihood, and they bought their own property in Harlem and began providing rooms for new Caribbean immigrants. Burnham attended New York City public schools and graduated from Townsend High School in 1932. In the fall of 1932 he enrolled in City College. He became actively involved in student political activities, serving as president of the Frederick Douglass Society and vice president of the student council. Affable, charismatic, and a powerful orator, he often spoke on campus about racial injustice, the threat of fascism to world peace, unemployment, and the plight of American youth. He graduated from City College in 1936.

Burnham became caught up in two protest movements that swept through depression-era Harlem. One sought to free the Scottsboro boys, nine African-American adolescents who were falsely accused and sentenced to death for raping two white women in Alabama in 1931. Another protested the 1935 Italian invasion of Ethiopia. In the mid-1930s Burnham joined the Communist Party, USA, and the Young Communist League because of their active involvement in the Scottsboro case, support for racial equality, opposition to fascism, and connections to a worldwide, left-wing political movement.

After his graduation Burnham became southern director of the American Student Union (ASU), a left-wing organization that sought to build mass youth movements around civil rights, antifascism, and increased government spending for education and jobs. He organized ASU chapters on black college campuses. Burnham joined the National Negro Congress (NNC), an umbrella organization of African-American civic, labor, and religious groups, founded in 1935. During the late 1930s he emerged as a well-respected Communist activist in Harlem.

In 1939 Burnham joined the Southern Negro Youth Congress (SNYC), a left-led civil rights group formed in 1937 by James E. Jackson, Jr., Christopher Alston, and Edward E. Strong. That year the SNYC relocated its headquarters from Richmond, Virginia, to Birmingham, Alabama, the center of southern industry and a hothouse of segregation. In 1941 Burnham became the SNYC's organizational secretary. He assisted in coordinating campaigns for African-American voting rights and the desegregation of public accommodations, and he helped plan black cultural events in Birmingham and across the South during and after World War II. In 1940 he married Dorothy Challenor, a Brooklyn native, who was also involved in progressive political organizing.

After the war Burnham became involved in new campaigns for racial equality. In 1946, inspired by the teachings of Mohandas Gandhi, he led nonviolent marches of black veterans through the streets of Birmingham to demand the right to vote. In response to the resurgence of white supremacy after the war, he wrote *Smash the Chains* (c. 1946), a pamphlet that vividly detailed lynchings and other forms of racial injustice in the postwar South. In 1948 he became southern director of the Progressive party and headed the presidential campaign of Henry Wallace in the South.

Burnham fell victim to anticommunism and resurgent white supremacy as the Cold War escalated. In 1948 the Birmingham commissioner of public safety, Eugene "Bull" Connor, an ardent segregationist and anticommunist, targeted Burnham for his effort to bring Wallace's running mate, Senator Glen Taylor (R.-Idaho), to an integrated SNYC conference in the city. Upon Connor's orders, police investigators whisked Burnham to Connor's office, where the police chief threatened a possible Ku Klux Klan attack at the SNYC conference if Taylor attended. The Klan did not attack the symposium, but local police did forcibly prevent Taylor from attending the conference. In this repressive political climate, the SNYC lost its support in the African-American community and among organized labor. The organization dissolved in 1949, and Burnham moved with his family back to New York that year.

Burnham continued to engage in left-wing political activities during the McCarthy period. He served as editor of *Freedom*, a progressive newspaper he co-founded in 1951 with the athlete, actor, and activist Paul Robeson. The paper featured articles by Louis Burnham, Paul Robeson, Eslanda Robeson, W. E. B. Du Bois, Shirley Graham Du Bois, and Lorraine Hansberry, among others, about civil rights struggles in the United States and independence movements in Africa, Asia, and the Caribbean. The paper also vocally criticized the Korean War and McCarthyism.

Government repression forced the newspaper to shut down in 1955.

Burnham turned his attention to chronicling the emerging civil rights movement. His pamphlet *Behind the Lynching of Emmett Louis Till* (1955) is an account of a fourteen-year-old African-American who was lynched in Mississippi for allegedly whistling at a white woman. "In all the foul record of human oppression, few crimes have matched in unbridled savagery, the kidnap-murder" of Till, Burnham wrote (*Freedomways*, Winter 1962, 10).

In 1958 Burnham joined the staff of the *National Guardian*, a New York–based radical newspaper, and served as its "national liberties and civil rights" editor. The following year he was elected to the American Communist party's National Committee. At the same time he, along with the veteran activist Esther Cooper Jackson, initiated discussions to found what became *Freedomways* magazine. First published in the spring of 1961, the journal chronicled black freedom movements in the United States, Africa, and the Caribbean. While delivering a lecture at a Negro History Week event in February 1960, Burnham suffered a massive heart attacked and died later that evening in New York City.

Scholars and activists have taken interest in Burnham's life and activism. In 2001 his family and friends founded the Louis E. Burnham Award. Granted each year, the award recognizes the work of scholars and journalists committed to racial justice and the advancement of the African-American community.

• Burnham's personal papers are in the possession of his wife, Dorothy Burnham, in Brooklyn, N.Y. Information about him is in the Esther I. Cooper Papers, Southern Negro Youth Congress Papers, and Edward E. Strong Papers at the Moorland-Spingarn Research Center, Howard University, Washington, D.C. For writings by Burnham, see *Smash the Chains* (c. 1946) and *Behind the Lynching of Emmet Louis Till* (1955) at the University of Illinois at Urbana-Champaign Library, Rare Books and Special Collections. Burnham helped cowrite Hugh Mulzac's *A Star to Steer By* (1963). Articles by or about Burnham are in the *Birmingham World*, *Birmingham Age-Herald*, *Birmingham News*, *Daily Worker*, *Freedom*, and *National Guardian*. Information about his life and work is in Erik S. McDuffie, *Long Journeys: Four Black Women and the Communist Party, USA, 1930–1956* (2003); Diane McWhorter, *Carry Me Home: Birmingham, Alabama, the Climatic Battle of the Civil Rights Revolution* (2001); Esther Cooper Jackson, ed., *Freedomways Reader: Prophets in Their Own Country* (2000); Robin D. G. Kelley, *Hammer and Hoe: Alabama Communists during the Depression* (1990); and Mark Naison, *Communists in Harlem during the Depression* (1983). *Freedomways* ran a tribute to Burnham in its Winter 1962 issue. The Federal Bureau of Investigation kept files on Burnham's political activities from the early 1940s until his death. Obituaries are in the *Worker*, 21 Feb. 1960, and the *National Guardian*, 14 Feb. 1963.

ERIK S. McDUFFIE

BURRIS, Samuel D. (1808–c. 1869), antislavery activist and conductor on the Underground Railroad, was born in Kent County, Delaware. Little is known of his early years except that his mother was a free woman of color, but as a young adult he moved to the Philadelphia area, became a farmer, married, and started a family. (No information about his wife and children is available.) In the mid-1840s he became involved in the antislavery movement and began assisting slaves who were on the run attempting to make it to freedom. Burris welcomed fugitives into his home, hid them for a day or two, supplied them with food and water, and sent them on their way. He became friends with leading black abolitionists, including Charles Purvis, one of the founders in 1833 of the American Anti-slavery Society, and William Still, best known for his post–Civil War book titled *The Underground Railroad, a Record of Facts, Authentic Narratives, Letters, &c.*, detailing the loosely knit group of antislavery activists—black and white—who devoted their time, energy, and money to helping slaves escape from bondage.

In 1847, Burris expressed his fear about the dangers of helping runaways. If caught, especially in certain states, he noted, black conductors might be sold into slavery. In Delaware, for example, helping slaves escape "was a crime next to murder if committed by a colored man." Burris not only welcomed fugitives into his home but also during the late 1840s ventured into Kent County, Delaware, to guide blacks out of slavery. In June 1847, while attempting to lead Maria Mathews across the Pennsylvania line, he was arrested, jailed, tried, and convicted of helping slaves to escape. He was fined five hundred dollars. Unable to pay, he was kept in jail for ten months. Later, he was sentenced to be sold into slavery for fourteen years. "When the hour arrived, the doomed man was placed on the auction-block," William Still explained, "Two traders from Baltimore were known to be present; how many others the friends of Burris knew not." The usual opportunity was given to traders and speculators to examine the human property, and Burris's head, arms, legs, and extremities were all closely scrutinized. When the bidding began Burris expected to be sold to the Deep South. The final bidder, however, was Isaac Flint, a Quaker, who had learned about Burris's plight, raised five hundred dollars to purchase him, and disguised himself at the auction. In fact, Flint represented a group of Burris's friends, abolitionists from Pennsylvania and northern Delaware. Burris did not know until after he was "knocked down" that Flint was a friend. The two men promptly returned to Pennsylvania.

In the family's effort to raise funds to help Flint purchase Burris, they had gone deeply into debt and lost their farm, becoming nearly destitute. They tried to regain some of their economic well-being but were unable to do so. In 1851, the Burris family emigrated to California, where gold had been recently discovered. Settling in the San Francisco area, Burris took an active role in racial uplift. In 1862 he led a drive to raise relief funds for "contraband" (as slaves fleeing into Union lines were called) in Philadelphia. In the same year, he signed a petition (with ten others) to improve schools for African-American youngsters in the San Francisco area. There were three hundred black children in the city but their school only accommodated sixty pupils. "We need another, better and larger place," he and the others said; "a building convenient, healthful and capable of holding" 150 pupils. He also pointed out that the black children needed "a school of a higher grade" and "additional teachers." It is not known where Burris died.

• The best source on Burris is William Still, *The Underground Railroad, a Record of Facts, Authentic Narratives, Letters, &c.* (1872); see also William H. Williams, *Slavery & Freedom in Delaware, 1639–1865* (1996); *The Liberator*, 30 June 1848; Rudolph M. Lapp, *Blacks in Gold Rush California* (1977).
LOREN SCHWENINGER

BURROUGHS, Stephen (01 Jan. 1765?–28 Jan. 1840), rogue, imposter, and author, was born in Hanover, New Hampshire, the son of Eden Burroughs, a Presbyterian minister, and Abigail Davis Burroughs. Burroughs recalled in his autobiography that he was "the terror of the people where I lived, and all were unanimous in declaring, that Stephen Burroughs was the worst boy in town, and those who could get him whipped were most worthy of esteem." When not perpetrating pranks on his neighbors, Burroughs spent his time reading novels and daydreaming, and at the age of fourteen he ran away from home to enlist in the Continental army. His father derailed his plan to enlist, but in characteristic fashion Burroughs tried again and again, eventually succeeding. After taking part in several skirmishes, however, Burroughs's military ardor cooled, and his father managed to obtain his son's discharge.

Burroughs then returned home to Hanover and began studying for admission to nearby Dartmouth College. He enrolled in 1781 but soon clashed with administrators and teachers and left shortly afterward. Casting about for some calling, he set out for the coast and boarded a ship bound for France. In the first of many impostures, he passed himself off as a physician.

After several military engagements aboard a privateer, Burroughs again went home to his father. There he took up teaching, a vocation to which he would repeatedly return. Yet he soon left home once more, but not before stealing several sermons written by his father, who was an influential and widely admired religious figure. Heading south, he auditioned as a preacher in faraway towns, using his father's words as his own. Though he found employment for a short time, he was soon unmasked and pursued by an angry mob in Pelham, Massachusetts. In his autobiography Burroughs recalled these and other impostures with considerable delight, laughing at his successes and bewailing the inevitable failures. At the same time, a deeper current ran through his writings, one that linked his own self-fashioning with a general erosion of respect for authority and tradition characteristic of the revolutionary era.

It was perhaps appropriate that Burroughs's next scheme took place against the backdrop of Shays' Rebellion. Thanks to the shortage of coin, a growing number of counterfeiters began operating in Massachusetts at this time. Burroughs joined them, enthralled by the prospect of making a fortune. In what became a common refrain in his memoirs, he recalled that "the mania of wealth had taken strong possession of our minds, and we listened with eagerness to her calls." But after trying to pass some of the counterfeit coin, Burroughs was arrested in 1785 and sent to prison for three years. The authorities eventually incarcerated him at Castle Island, a jail in the Boston harbor. There he led a group of convicts in a complicated escape. He and his associates tunneled out of the prison and then kidnapped the sentry guarding the boats and rowed to the mainland. The initial attempt was successful; a later attempt ended in failure. But his managing to flee to the mainland for a short time only added to his reputation.

Burroughs eventually served out his time and returned home to his father. In 1789 he married his cousin Sally Davis; they had two boys and one girl. He tried to make a fresh start, teaching school in Charlton, Massachusetts. But by his own admission he had sexual relations with one of the teenage girls in his class, an episode that eventually led to a criminal trial for rape. The court found Burroughs guilty, and it ordered him whipped in public and sentenced to prison. He nonetheless managed to escape, most likely with the connivance of neighbors sympathetic to his version of events. Burroughs later recalled that by this time his reputation had assumed a life of its own, and he found himself blessed and cursed with folk-hero status. People began to attribute crimes and impostures to Burroughs, regardless of whether he had done the deed in question. Perhaps in response, he fled to Long Island, where he began teaching school under an assumed name. He nonetheless clashed with local authorities over which books would be included in a circulating library, and he pushed for more secular texts, an act of defiance that opened him to persecution.

After several costly lawsuits, Burroughs moved to Georgia, where he became enmeshed in the Yazoo land speculations of the 1790s. By his account he grew wealthy and became an agent of financier Robert Morris. Burroughs eventually lost his fortune shortly after his employer went bankrupt, and he returned to his father's home once more. There he penned the first volume of his widely read autobiography, *The Memoirs of Stephen Burroughs* (1798); a second volume documenting his life in Long Island and Georgia appeared in 1804. The same year his memoirs appeared, Burroughs and his family moved to the township of Stanstead in Lower Canada (now Quebec). Though ostensibly a farmer, Burroughs quickly acquired fame as a counterfeiter of notes issued by banks in the United States. Despite several attempts to prosecute him, Burroughs evaded capture. Thanks to his exploits, he became the real and imagined source of every counterfeit note in circulation in the United States, a reputation that only added to the appeal of his memoirs, which went through multiple editions in the early 1800s.

Burroughs's career as a counterfeiter came to an end when he was captured by Quebec authorities in 1810. Though originally condemned to be transported to Botany Bay, he secured a pardon and moved to the small town of Trois Rivières on the St. Lawrence River. There he rebelled one last time, becoming a devout Roman Catholic (encouraged, perhaps, by the conversion of his daughter, who went on to become the mother superior of the local Ursuline Convent). He himself became a much-admired tutor and teacher, and by all accounts abandoned his life of crime. He lived out the final decades of his life in relative obscurity, in spite of the phenomenal popularity of his autobiography, which went through additional editions. And while in those same memoirs he would complain that his life had been a "continued course of tumult, revolution and vexation," he found in his later years a measure of stability and even respectability. He died after a brief illness in Trois Rivières.

An extreme version of the self-made man, Burroughs came to symbolize the challenges to authority unleashed during the revolutionary generation. "I am so far a republican," wrote Burroughs, "that I consider a man's merit to rest entirely with himself, without any regard to family, blood, or connection." It was a philosophy that continued to gain currency in the early republic, and both Burroughs and his writings achieved iconic status, often earning favorable comparison with Benjamin Franklin's *Autobiography*. Burroughs remained a household name until the mid-nineteenth century, at which point his written works, like his reputation, sank into obscurity.

• No organized collection of Burroughs's papers exists, though scattered court papers at the National Archives of Canada document his life in crime in Quebec. The best source on his life remains his memoirs, the most complete of which was published in 1811 and eventually republished with minor alterations in 1988 by Northeastern University Press. Burroughs also published two additional pamphlets. The first, *Stephen Burroughs's Sermon, Delivered in Rutland, on a Hay Mow, to his Auditory the Pelhamites* (1798), offers a fictional "sermon" delivered while impersonating a minister. Toward the end of his life Burroughs also penned a petition to the British authorities seeking financial relief titled *A View of Practical Justice as Administrated in Lower Canada* (1836).

Though no biography of Burroughs exists, he is treated in several secondary sources. See, e.g., Larry Cebula, "A Counterfeit Identity: The Notorious Life of Stephen Burroughs," *The Historian* 64 (2002), 317-33; Robert A. Gross, "The Confidence Man and the Preacher: The Cultural Politics of Shays' Rebellion," in Gross, ed., *In Debt to Shays: The Bicentennial of an Agrarian Rebellion* (1993), 297-320; Christopher W. Jones, "Praying upon Truth: 'The Memoirs of Stephen Burroughs' and the Picaresque," *Early American Literature* 30 (1995), 32-50; Linda Kealey, "Punishment at Hard Labor: Stephen Burroughs and the Castle Island Prison, 1785-1798," *New England Quarterly* 57 (1984), 249-54; Stephen Mihm, "The Alchemy of the Self: Stephen Bur-

roughs and the Counterfeit Economy of the Early Republic," *Early American Studies* 2 (2004), forthcoming; Aurelia Grether Scott, "The Strange Case of an Early Long Island Schoolmaster," *Journal of Long Island History* 7 (1967), 10-23; and Daniel E. Williams, "In Defense of Self: Author and Authority in the Memoirs of Stephen Burroughs," *Early American Literature* 25 (1990), 96-122.

STEPHEN ANDERSON MIHM

BURTON, Richard (10 Nov. 1925–5 Aug. 1984), actor, was born Richard Walter Jenkins, Jr., in Pontrhydyfen, South Wales, the son of Richard Walter Jenkins, a coal miner, and Edith Maude Thomas Jenkins. Burton was the twelfth of thirteen children. He was two years old when his mother died, and he was sent to live with his married older sister in the nearby industrial city of Port Talbot. A good student and athlete, Burton attended the Port Talbot Secondary School. At age fifteen he made his first stage appearance in a school play. In 1941 Burton left school for financial reasons to work in a clothing store. While employed at the store, he joined the local squadron of the Air Training Corps, a program designed to prepare teenagers for military service, and his participation in a corps-produced radio documentary gave him the idea to become an actor. In the fall of 1942 Burton returned to the Port Talbot Secondary School, where he came under the tutelage of the English instructor Philip Burton, who strongly encouraged his interest in the theater. Philip Burton became his legal guardian in 1943. Assuming his guardian's last name instead of Jenkins, Burton, aided by Philip Burton's theater world connections, made his professional stage debut in a minor role in *The Druid's Rest*, a comedy by the Welsh playwright Emlyn Williams. The production premiered in Liverpool in late 1943 and opened in London in early 1944. Later in 1944 Burton attended a special wartime six-month course at Exeter College, Oxford, then entered the Royal Air Force.

After finishing his military service in late 1947, Burton settled in London and quickly established himself as a rising young acting talent in supporting roles in stage productions, including Christopher Fry's 1949 verse drama *The Lady's Not for Burning*, directed by John Gielgud. In 1950 Burton made his American stage debut when *The Lady's Not for Burning* was presented on Broadway. Burton's first screen appearance came in the British-produced *The Last Days of Dolwyn* (1949), the story of a Welsh village flooded to build a reservoir. While making the film, Burton met Sybil Williams, a Welsh-born actress who had a small part in the film. The couple married in 1949 and had two children. Burton spent the summer of 1951 at the Shakespeare Memorial Theater in Stratford-upon-Avon, giving well-received performances as Prince Hal in *Henry IV*, Parts 1 and 2; as Caliban in *The Tempest*; and in the title role in *Henry V*.

Of medium height with dark hair, piercing green eyes, an athletic bearing left over from his rugby-playing days, pockmarked skin that gave him a rugged look, and a deep, sonorous voice, Burton drew the attention of Twentieth Century–Fox Pictures in Hollywood, which signed him to a contract in 1952. He made a strong impression in his first American film, *My Cousin Rachel* (1952), a mystery based on a novel by Daphne DuMaurier, and he earned an Academy Award nomination for best supporting actor. Burton became a fully fledged movie star with *The Robe* (1953), a lavish religious drama about Christians in ancient Rome. *The Robe* was the first movie made in the CinemaScope wide-screen technique and was a huge success at the box office.

Burton then appeared in several mediocre films, some of which sold enough tickets to keep him among the first rank of Hollywood stars. The most significant of these films is the screen version of John Osborne's trendsetting play *Look Back in Anger* (1959). Burton had greater success on stage during this period. He spent the 1953–1954 theatrical season with London's Old Vic Company, where he played the title roles in *Hamlet* and *Coriolanus* and also had principal parts in *King John, Twelfth Night,* and *The Tempest.* During the 1955–1956 Old Vic season, he played the title role in *Henry V* and alternated with the actor John Neville the roles of Iago and the title role in *Othello.* In New York Burton costarred with Helen Hayes in Jean Anouilh's romantic comedy *Time Remembered* in 1957. In 1960 he enjoyed one the biggest successes of his career as King Arthur to Julie Andrews's Guinevere in Frederick Loewe and Alan Jay Lerner's musical *Camelot,* for which he won the Tony Award for best actor in a musical.

Burton left the cast of *Camelot* in the fall of 1961 to play Mark Antony in the film *Cleopatra,* a gargantuan Hollywood epic made in Rome with Elizabeth Taylor in the title role. While making the film, Burton and Taylor commenced a brazenly adulterous affair that provided much fodder for gossip columns. After divorcing their spouses, Burton and Taylor married in 1964. For the next decade the couple's lavish lifestyle and tempestuous relationship was minutely detailed by the press. Burton and Taylor, who adopted a daughter, divorced in 1974, remarried in 1975, and divorced permanently in 1976. After *Cleopatra,* released in 1963, Burton made nine more films with Taylor, most notably *Who's Afraid of Virginia Woolf?* (1966), a film version of Edward Albee's play about a bitterly quarreling married couple. Burton's films without Taylor during the 1960s include *Becket* (1964), the story of the friendship between Thomas Becket, played by Burton, and Henry II, played by Peter O'Toole; *The Night of the Iguana* (1964), based on a play by Tennessee Williams, with Burton as a defrocked clergyman living in Mexico; *The Spy Who Came in from the Cold* (1965), an espionage thriller starring Burton as a British secret agent; and *Anne of the Thousand Days* (1969), with Burton as a lusty Henry VIII dealing with his young wife Anne Boleyn, played by Genevieve Bujold.

In 1964 Burton returned to the stage to play the title role in a Broadway production of *Hamlet* that opened with much hoopla in the wake of his marriage to Taylor. The production, which was done in modern dress on a nearly bare stage, was well received. Howard Taubman of the *New York Times* called Burton's portrayal of Hamlet "notable for its masculinity . . . full of the temperament of a man in prime physical and mental health." This production was Burton's last significant stage appearance. His abandonment of the stage disappointed critics, who felt he had sold out to the fame and fortune of Hollywood and failed to live up to the promise he had shown on stage in the 1950s, when he was expected to eventually join the ranks of Britain's premiere stage actors.

Burton made no apologies for his career choices and frankly enjoyed his luxurious, jet-setting lifestyle. A heavy drinker and smoker all of his adult life, Burton by the late 1970s began to suffer from a variety of ailments, including stomach ulcers and spinal problems. Stiff, gaunt, and gray-haired, with his still strong voice the only remnant of his once powerful acting equipment, he continued to appear regularly in films, but most were poorly received. In 1976 he briefly returned to the stage to take over the role of a psychiatrist treating a disturbed teenager in Peter Shaffer's drama *Equus,* and the following year he repeated the role in the screen version. Though the film was neither a critical nor a commercial success, it earned him a seventh and final Academy Award nomination for best actor. In 1976 Burton married Susan Hunt, a fashion model. They divorced in 1983 and had no children. Later in 1983 Burton married Sally Hay, a film production assistant, with whom he had no children. Burton, who had long maintained his primary residence in Switzerland, died at a hospital in Geneva.

• Burton is the author of the brief childhood memoir, *A Christmas Story* (1964). Tyrone Steverson, *Richard Burton: A Bio-Bibliography* (1992), is the most complete source of information on Burton's career. For a biography that incorporates excerpts from Burton's diaries, letters, and journals, see Melvyn Bragg, *Richard Burton: A Life* (1988). A shorter biography is Hollis Alpert, *Burton* (1986). An obituary is in the *New York Times,* 6 Aug. 1984.

MARY C. KALFATOVIC

BUTLER, David (15 Dec. 1829–25 May 1891), first state governor of Nebraska, was born near Bloomington, Monroe County, Indiana, the son of George W. Butler, a farmer, and Nancy Christy Butler. One of ten children, his formal education was limited to intermittent attendance at local district schools. After losing his father at an early age, Butler supported his family by farming, engaging in mercantile pursuits, and cattle dealing. He married Mary Paulina Smith on 22 April 1852; it is not known how the marriage ended.

Butler had accumulated a sizable fortune before losing it all in the Panic of 1857. In 1858, seeking a fresh start in the West, Butler moved to the Nebraska Territory, where he settled in Pawnee City and resumed cattle trading. He also reentered retail trading and at the same time began studying law. On 25 January 1860 he married Lydia Story; they had eight children, four of whom survived to adulthood. In 1861 he was admitted to the bar and elected to the territorial legislature. Butler moved up to the territorial senate in 1863. In 1866 he was elected the first governor of the state on Nebraska's admission to the Union. In a hard-fought campaign fraught with charges of fraud, Butler, a Republican, edged out the future secretary of agriculture and Arbor Day founder J. Sterling Morton, the Democratic candidate, by 145 votes. He was sworn into office on 27 March 1867.

As the state's first executive, Butler was handicapped by the state constitution of 1866, which in seeking to minimize the power of government had provided for little government at all; it limited the governor's salary to $1,000 annually and that of state legislators to $3.00 a day for a maximum legislative session of forty days. Despite limited resources, Butler set about building up the state. He encouraged the development of railroads and in 1869 urged the establishment of a Bureau of Immigration, which the legislature founded in 1870.

The most divisive issue facing Butler was the location of the state capitol. Originally in Omaha, the matter had been hotly contested by Nebraskans living south of the Platte River, who felt underrepresented in state government. The legislature passed a bill creating a commission, consisting of Butler, Secretary of State Thomas P. Kennard, and State Auditor John Gillespie, to select a new site and have the area prepared for development as the new state capitol; the site would also include the new state university, the state penitentiary, and the state insane asylum.

After scouting various sites, the Commission ignored its original mandate to place the new capitol on state lands and instead accepted the offer of a small village named Lancaster to become the new capitol; they designated it "Lincoln." The commissioners were swayed in their decision by uncertainty over land titles as well as the commercial possibilities of nearby salt deposits (a hope that later proved ephemeral). Faced with slow land sales after the new territory was surveyed, the commissioners brought in phony buyers to bid up the price of the land. The ploy worked, and soon lots were selling for market value. Despite lack of local materials and disinterest on the part of area architects (only one bid was submitted), the commissioners also pushed through the construction of the new state capitol building. Budgeted at $40,000, it cost $75,000 and was so poorly constructed that it required replacement within twelve years.

Despite criticism of Butler's methods by Democrats and anti-Lincoln factions within the state, his actions were approved by the legislature in 1869. For his part, Butler was reelected in 1868, and although he failed in an attempt to gain a U.S. Senate seat in 1869, his prospects seemed solid. Soon, however, charges of malfeasance—including illegal speculating on land lots, one-bid construction contracts on university and insane asylum buildings, and bribery—were leveled against him. Although Butler won reelection in 1870, the number of his enemies was growing; in 1871 Edward Rosewater, a Republican legislator from Omaha, asked Butler to account for money collected from the federal government for school lands that had been sold off prior to the state's admission to the Union. Butler replied that he had collected the funds—totaling $16,881.26—and deposited them with the state treasurer. When an audit revealed no such deposits, Butler admitted he had kept the money but had secured it with mortgages on land in Pawnee County.

On the basis of the new evidence, the state House of Representatives voted eleven articles of impeachment against Butler on 6 March 1871. The subsequent trial revealed a pattern of extreme laxity in state financial management, with Auditor Gillespie also being impeached but not convicted and new state treasurer James Sweet coming under heavy criticism for commingling state funds in his own bank. In June the state senate voted to convict Butler on the sole charge of misappropriating state funds. The other ten charges were dropped. Sentenced to removal from office, Butler returned to Pawnee City and resumed his cattle trading business. In 1874 a state commission took out deeds on various lands in Pawnee, Gage, and Jefferson counties in order to settle claims against Butler; by the time the final sale of the lands was consummated in 1895, the debt was more than recouped. In 1877, after numerous unsuccessful attempts, Butler's supporters succeeded in having his impeachment proceedings expunged from official state records, and Butler himself mounted a political comeback in 1882, when he was elected to the state senate as an independent. After finishing a poor third in the 1888 governor's race as the Union Labor party candidate, Butler retired from public life. The father of eight children, he died on his farm near Pawnee City.

Although David Butler's place in history is secure as a result of his serving as the first governor of Nebraska, he must also bear the stigma of an impeachment proceeding that was as much a result of poor judgment as of malfeasance.

• Butler's papers are held at the Nebraska State Historical Society in Lincoln, Nebraska. The best secondary treatment of his life and career is James C. Olson, *History of Nebraska* (1966); he was also the subject of an unpublished manuscript by David Hodwalker, "Public Career of David Butler, First Governor of Nebraska" (1938), which is on deposit at the Nebraska State Historical Society. An obituary is in the *Omaha Daily Bee*, 26 May 1891. E. A. Kral assisted with research for this article.

EDWARD L. LACH, JR.

BUTLER, William Allen (20 Feb. 1825–9 Sept. 1902), lawyer and writer, was born William Howard Allen Butler in Albany, New York, the son of Benjamin Franklin Butler, an attorney, and Harriet Allen Butler, sister of Lieutenant William Howard Allen, a naval hero in the War of 1812. His family moved to Washington, D.C., in 1834 when his father was appointed attorney general by President Andrew Jackson, and Butler studied at private schools in Georgetown and Hudson, New York. When his father became attorney general in the cabinet of Martin Van Buren in 1837, Butler entered the grammar school of the newly established University of the City of New York. The next year his father retired from the cabinet and went into private practice in New York City, where he helped establish the law school of the City University and collaborated on the preparation of *The Revised Statutes of the State of New York.* Butler graduated in 1843, and, as the law school at the university had not yet opened, he prepared for a career in the field by studying with his father. Three years later he was called to the bar. At that time, according to his daughter, he dropped "Howard" from his name "as the signature was inconveniently long" (p. 87, fn.) and embarked on a seventeen-month tour of Europe. On his return in 1848, he joined his father in practice.

Butler & Butler, which in 1849 became Barney & Butler, was among the most successful law firms in New York City, and, although they represented a wide variety of clients, their main activity related to the burgeoning city's growth as a port. Butler's association with admiralty law, growing initially from his mother's family connections with the navy, was reinforced by his marriage in 1850 to Mary Russell Marshall, the daughter of an agent and part owner of the Black Ball Line of Liverpool packets. Ten children were born to the couple. Butler came to be recognized as a leading expert in admiralty law and was made chief counsel of the Board of Pilot Commissioners, an association created by the New York State Legislature in 1853 for the licensing and regulation of pilots, whose consitutionality he successfully defended. He later represented the Board in the case of *People v. Vanderbilt* (26 N.Y. 287), winning it security from encroachments by private steamship lines on the public piers in the Harbor of New York. He served as president of the American Bar Association in 1886 and of the Association of the Bar of the City of New York in 1886–1887, and he was appointed to Governor Samuel Tilden's commission to prepare a plan of government for the cities of New York State.

Butler was devoted to letters throughout his life. He was named Class Poet in 1843, and the animated descriptions of the Old World he sent home from his travels appeared in the *Literary World.* After entering law practice, he was a frequent contributor to the *Democratic Review* and other journals. Several of his memorial addresses were published, and his legal writings include *Lawyer and Client: Their Relation, Rights, and Duties* (1871), described by George C. Hoyt as "a most admirable statement of the rules of professional ethics" (Butler, p. 412), and *The Revision of the Statutes of the State of New York and the Revisers* (1889). His biography of his father's close friend, *Martin Van Buren, Lawyer, Statesman, and Man* (1862), was the first printed memorial of the eighth president. Butler also wrote two novels: *Mrs. Limber's Raffle, or, A Church Fair and Its Victims* (1876), a humorous tale dramatizing his conviction that church raffles were technically in violation of the gambling law, and *Domesticus* (1886), a mild satire on the frivolity of social life and the servant problem. Neither was a success.

It was his poetry that established Butler's reputation as a man of letters and made him, for a time, one of the literary lions of New York, and indeed caused him to observe wryly in his memoirs, "[A]fter many years of toil to attain a desired place in my profession, my chief, if not my only, claim to public reputation has been the writing of a few pages of society verse" (p. 274).

His *Nothing to Wear: An Episode of City Life,* first published anonymously in the seventh issue of *Harper's Weekly* on 7 February 1857 and issued as a separate volume later that year, was a sensational popular success. Its 329 lines describe the plight of Miss Flora M'Flimsy of Madison Square, a vain, self-indulgent society belle who, although she spends a fortune on her wardrobe, is sunk "in utter despair / Because she has nothing whatever to wear." Widely reprinted in America and England and, in translation, in Germany and France (with no financial benefit to its author, who received a total of $50 for it), it was the most popular poem of its decade, far outselling Walt Whitman's *Leaves of Grass.* It spawned numerous imitations, including *Nothing to Do* (1879) by a youthful Horatio Alger, dedicated to Butler and featuring the same antiheroine. William Dean Howells, in a review of Butler's collected poems in 1899, said of it, "[P]rairie fire suggests a feeble image of the swift spread of Mr. Butler's poem. . . . I prefer a train of gunpowder" (p. 654). The bitter sarcasm with which Butler treats his subject is leavened by the deftness and ingenuity of his rhymes. "Nothing to wear!" exclaims his narrator. "Now as this is a true ditty, / I do not assert—this, you know, is between us— / That she's in a state of absolute nudity, / Like Powers' Greek Slave or the Medici Venus" (ll. 57–61). He concludes his diatribe on a more serious note, calling on the "spoiled children of fashion" to consider the plight of their less fortunate sisters in the city's garrets "where wretches, the young and the old, / Half-starved, and half-naked, lie crouched from the cold" (ll. 310–311). Butler felt that "the power of the poem" was derived from the moral it pointed (p. 281), and many critics agreed that, in Howells's words, it was "that touch of heart" that reclaimed it from mere satire (ibid).

In the years that followed *Nothing to Wear,* Butler continued to turn out satirical verse, as well as children's poems and some serious lyrics, of which the most ambitious was *Oberammergau* (1890), a poem of over 400 lines about the passion play he had seen while traveling in Germany. Although his writing was generally well received, he never repeated the popular success of his 1857 triumph, whose title had entered the language. Throughout his life, Butler was devoted to community service. He was a trustee of the New York Public Library and was closely associated with the University of the City of New York, where for many years after his graduation he taught courses in admiralty law and served on its council. In 1865 he moved to Yonkers, where he contributed both legal assistance and money to hospitals and such causes as the Women's Institute, which he was instrumental in establishing. His sight failed in his final years, but he continued in both his vocation and his avocation until his sudden death from gastritis in his residence, Round Oak, in Yonkers. Honored equally for the lucidity and perceptiveness of his legal writings and for the wit and trenchancy of his light verse, he enriched American literature with a small classic whose message, Howells predicted, would be as applicable at the end of the twentieth century as it was at the end of its own.

• Butler provided a detailed account of his early life in *A Retrospect of Forty Years, 1825–1865*, edited by his daughter Harriet Allen Butler and published in 1911. His career in the law and in letters is examined in George C. Hoyt, *Annual Report of the Association of the Bar of the City of New York* (1904), reprinted in Butler's *Retrospect*, pp. 391–423. The brief and modest preface to his collected verse, *Nothing to Wear and Other Poems* (1899), makes an interesting comment on his literary efforts, and that volume received an appreciative review by William Dean Howells in *Harper's Monthly*, suppl. 2, Sept. 1899, p. 654. An obituary is in the *New York Times*, 10 Sept. 1902.

DENNIS WEPMAN

C

CADMUS, Paul (17 Dec. 1904–12 Dec. 1999), artist, was born in New York City, the son of Egbert Cadmus and Maria Latasa Cadmus, artists. His father was a lithographer and painter of watercolors who had studied with Robert Henri; his mother illustrated children's books. Egbert Cadmus was of Protestant Dutch ancestry and a self-proclaimed atheist; his wife, of Spanish descent, was an observant Roman Catholic. The resulting tension in the household led their son to separate himself from all religious doctrines. But he did acquire from them a precocious ability to draw the human figure. He later recalled that by the time he was ten years old he knew he wanted to become a painter. Cadmus attended local public schools until 1919, when he dropped out of Townsend Harris High School and enrolled in drawing and printmaking classes at the National Academy of Design in Manhattan. After seven years of study in various media at the academy he enrolled for further training at the Art Students League, also in Manhattan.

Following the completion of his studies in 1928, Cadmus worked for three years as a commercial illustrator for Blackman and Company, a New York City advertising agency. By 1931 he had saved enough money to travel to Europe with a fellow painter, Jared French. That summer they toured France and Spain on bicycles, with visits to major art museums the focus of their travels. Cadmus was especially drawn to Italian Renaissance art, in particular works by Mantegna, Signorelli, and Caravaggio, and was also captivated by the Dutch painter, Hieronymus Bosch. In the fall the two men settled on the island of Mallorca, off the Spanish coast in the Mediterranean, and remained there to paint for two years. In the summer of 1932 they toured museums in Austria, Germany, and Italy.

During his stay abroad Cadmus began producing what he considered his first adult work, beginning with *Jerry* (1931), a portrait of Jared French, and *Self-Portrait: Mallorca* (1932). He also painted several Mallorcan coastal scenes, but these seemed somewhat incidental to the portraits he made there, including several boldly colored canvases of local fishermen, as well as *Bicyclists* (1933), one of his best-known works. This study of two passing cyclists evoked his own recent travels; its oversized rounded figures and ocher-tinged palette also paid homage to the Renaissance painters he admired. Most notably while on Mallorca, he called upon memories of home to produce two paintings set in New York City that are also among his most famous: *Shore Leave* (1933), which depicts sailors making pickups in Riverside Park, and

Y.M.C.A. Locker Room (1933), a frieze of male bodies, young and old, engaging in horseplay and other displays of male camaraderie. In these two paintings Cadmus established his distinctive realistic style, adapting the draftsmanship of Renaissance masters to produce sardonic caricatures of American life.

Returning to New York in 1934, Cadmus settled in Greenwich Village and secured employment with the Public Works of Art Project (PWAP), a federally financed program intended to help artists during the Depression; it subsequently became part of a larger government agency, the Works Progress Administration (WPA). About this time he became friendly with Lincoln Kirstein, the noted ballet, theater, and art impresario who later married Cadmus's sister, Fidelma. His imagination fed by seedy surroundings, Cadmus painted *The Fleet's In!*, a companion piece to *Shore Leave* that depicted drunken and carousing sailors. The painting was initially accepted for a PWAP show at the Corcoran Art Gallery in Washington, D.C., but before the show's formal opening U.S. Navy officials succeeded in having it withdrawn because of its adverse depiction of American seamen. Cries of censorship ensued, and Cadmus's story was publicized throughout the country. Virtually overnight he became nationally known, his art deplored by the conservative establishment but championed by progressive critics who likened him to William Hogarth, the eighteenth-century English painter and engraver known for his savage satire.

That same year Cadmus painted two canvases in a similar vein: *Greenwich Village Cafeteria*, a scene of rowdy patrons at a local hangout, and *Coney Island*, a portrait of humanity at its ugliest crowded onto a city beach, the famous amusement park visible in the background. Henceforth, grotesque elements appeared frequently in Cadmus's work, beginning with his nude male figure paintings *Horseplay* and *Gilding the Acrobats* (both 1935). His series *Aspects of Suburban Life* (1935–1936), intended as preliminary studies for a mural in a Long Island post office, was ultimately rejected by government authorities as unsuitable because of its savage visual commentary on U.S. life. Cadmus's career nevertheless flourished despite—or perhaps because of—his notoriety. He became a frequent exhibitor at New York's recently founded Whitney Museum, and in 1937 the city's prominent Midtown Galleries gave him his first one-man show. In a pamphlet for that show Cadmus published his "Credo," in which he declared that the most "living and vital" art was inspired by contemporary life. Cadmus continued to exhibit periodically with Midtown Galleries for the rest of his life.

Perhaps for economic reasons, Cadmus suppressed his satiric eye in creating *Pocahontas and John Smith* (1938), a mural dramatically depicting Smith's fabled rescue by the Indian princess. Commissioned as a WPA project, the mural was inspired by Lincoln Kirstein's production of the ballet *Pocahontas* on the New York stage, and it was subsequently hung in a Richmond, Virginia, postal facility—after Cadmus made changes in an Indian loincloth earlier deemed too "provocative." Along the same noncontroversial lines, Cadmus created drawings of ballet positions for Kirstein's book *Ballet Alphabet: A Primer for the Layman*, published in 1939.

Cadmus returned to his earlier style with *Sailors and Floosies* (1938), another sardonic look at the navy, and *Seeing the New Year In* (1939), which depicts a drunken gathering on New Year's Eve. In *Hinky Dinky Parley Voo* (1939), whose title is the refrain of a World War I doughboy drinking song later favored by aging veterans, five figures, including a soldier and two prostitutes, cluster drunkenly around a bar. These and other paintings completed between 1935 and 1939 were produced using a so-called mixed technique that combined underpainting with oil, varnish, and glazing; Cadmus had shifted to the mixed technique after working initially in conventional oils. In 1940, with the encouragement of French, Cadmus began using egg tempera on pressed wood, a method favored by Italian Renaissance painters; this remained his preferred medium, although he sometimes used acrylic paints later on as well.

Cadmus had his first major museum exhibition at the Baltimore Museum of Art in 1942 and a year later had sixteen of his works included in a major exhibition of realistic art organized by Kirstein at the Museum of Modern Art in New York City. In the 1940s Cadmus began spending summers at Fire Island with Jared French and his wife, and during their years there the trio made a series of photographs of one another that was published half a century later. The beach at Fire Island also became the backdrop for many of his paintings, including *Fantasia on a Theme by Dr. S.* (1946), a grotesque study of the human figure that received mixed reviews. In the postwar era Cadmus's particular representational style, known as Magic Realism, as well as his subject matter were beginning to seem passé as the New York art world embraced Abstract Expressionism, and the rest of the country, inspired by renewed patriotism, no longer seemed receptive to his social critiques. Not surprisingly, therefore, his unsettling series *The Seven Deadly Sins* (1945–1949) met largely with rejection even among those who had professed admiration for his earlier work.

Cadmus drew consolation at this time from friendships with the British poet W. H. Auden, whom he met on Fire Island, and with another Briton, the writer E. M. Forster, with whom he had begun corresponding during the war; Forster and Cadmus exchanged letters and visits until Forster's death in 1970, and during a trip to England in 1950 Cadmus drew a portrait of the writer. In the early 1950s Cadmus left New York to work and travel in France and Italy. His experiences produced two especially notable canvases: *Bar Italia* (1955) and *Night in Bologna* (1958), both of which are disturbing depictions of Americans abroad but vary in their presentation. Typical Cadmus grotesques crowd the canvas of *Bar Italia. Night in Bologna*, which received wider critical praise (and which Cadmus later identified as his favorite work), features only three figures—a predatory soldier, a seductive female, and a male tourist—captured in shadowy archways.

In the 1960s Cadmus relocated his studio to Brooklyn Heights and began making a series of drawings of the male nude using a single model, a singer and dancer named Jon Anderson who became his lifetime companion. The series became a major ongoing project for Cadmus, and he continued to work on it until a few years before his death. In 1975 he moved to a studio in Weston, Connecticut, a favorite rural location for New York painters and illustrators. There he completed another major painting, the largest (46 by 92 inches) of his career: the satirical *Subway Symphony* (1976), in which he rightly claimed to have captured "all the horror of the [New York] subway." By this time, however, Cadmus had become largely ignored outside New York, where Midtown Galleries continued to show his work.

A rediscovery of Cadmus by a wider audience began in the 1980s, initiated by a 1981 exhibition of his paintings; organized by the Miami University Art Museum in Ohio, the show traveled to several regional museums in the eastern half of the nation. Three years later Kirstein published the first edition of *Paul Cadmus*, an illustrated biography of the painter that also offered a cultural assessment of his work and its significance; a revised edition was published in 1992. Cadmus was also the subject of a 1984 documentary by the filmmaker David Sutherland: *Paul Cadmus: Enfant Terrible at 80. The Drawings of Paul Cadmus*, with an introduction by the writer Guy Davenport, was published in 1989. Four years later Midtown Galleries sponsored Cadmus's last major show.

Cadmus's rediscovery in the 1980s undoubtedly proceeded from an emerging public acknowledgment and acceptance of homosexuality. Although Cadmus never publicly discussed his sexual preference—nor did Kirstein touch directly on the artist's sexuality in his biography—it has been widely assumed that Cadmus was gay. As early as 1976 the national gay magazine *The Advocate* had praised Cadmus as a homosexual artist. Proclaiming that supposition, Pridefest America, a gay cultural festival held annually in Philadelphia, awarded him its first international arts award in the summer of 1999. Homosexual references, some oblique, some more overt, appear in many of his paintings, beginning with the suggestive interchange depicted in *Bicyclists*, and his numerous depictions of idealized male nudes suggest a reverence for the male body that led many prominent members of the homosexual community to praise him as one of their own. He died at his home in Weston.

Although Cadmus is not a major painter, he is considered a significant proponent of the realist tradition in American art; he can thus be placed squarely in a long line that includes, most notably, Thomas Eakins and also embraces such Cadmus near-contemporaries as Ivan Albright, Reginald Marsh, and Jack Levine. Cadmus's work is included in a number of major U.S. collections, including the National Museum of American Art in Washington, D.C., and New York's Whitney Museum of American Art.

• Biographical information is available in Lincoln Kirstein's *Paul Cadmus*, rev. ed. (1992), which also includes illustrations, many in full color, of nearly all of Cadmus's work, as well as an extensive bibliography and a reprint of Cadmus's "Credo." See also Brant Mewborn, "Paul Cadmus: Portrait of the Artist as a Gentle Man," *After Dark*, Mar. 1978, pp. 46–53; and Raymond J. Steiner, "Profile of Paul Cadmus," *Art Times*, May 1986, p. 10. For a discussion of Cadmus's early notoriety, see especially Harry Salpeter, "Paul Cadmus: Enfant Terrible," *Esquire*, July 1937, pp. 105–11. Biographical information is also included in Guy Davenport's introduction to *The Drawings of Paul Cadmus* (1989) and in Diane Casella Hines, "The Figure Drawing of Paul Cadmus," *American Artist*, Nov. 1972, pp. 28–33 ff. For a selection of Cadmus's work in another medium, see Margaret French and Jared French, *Collaboration: The Photographs of Paul Cadmus, Margaret French and Jared French* (1992). Especially useful overviews of the American realist tradition in painting can be found in Oliver Larkin, *Art and Life in America*, rev. ed. (1960), and Barbara Rose, *American Art since 1900: A Critical History* (1967; rev. and expanded ed., 1975). See also Dorothy C. Miller and Alfred H. Barr, Jr., *American Realists and Magic Realists* (1943, repr. 1969). An obituary is in the *New York Times*, 15 Dec. 1999.

ANN T. KEENE

CALDERÓN, Alberto P. (14 Sept. 1920–16 Apr. 1998), mathematician, was born in Mendoza, Argentina, to a physician and his wife (their names are unknown). Encouraged by his father, Alberto showed an unusual precocity in mathematics and the sciences and was fascinated by mechanics. At the age of twelve he was sent to school in Zurich, Switzerland, to prepare for that city's famed engineering school, the Eidgenössische Technische Hochschule (ETH), whose former students included Albert Einstein. After two years abroad, however, he returned to Argentina to complete his secondary education. During this time he became increasingly interested in mathematics as a vocation, but on graduating he enrolled at the University of Buenos Aires to study civil engineering, which his father believed would offer a more suitable and practical career. Calderón maintained his interest in the field by participating in seminars at the university's Institute of Mathematics.

After earning his university degree in 1947, Calderón became a researcher in geophysics at Argentina's state-owned oil corporation, YPF. The job, which drew upon his mathematical skills, was satisfying, but friction soon developed with his supervisor,

and Calderón resigned. He returned to the university to become an assistant in the engineering school and do research at the Institute of Mathematics. The institute was in fact a two-man department within the school of engineering, led by Professor Julio Rey Pastor, considered the founding father of modern mathematics in Argentina, and his assistant, Dr. Alberto Gonzalez Dominguez. During Calderón's student days Gonzalez Dominguez had become an important mentor, and he would remain a lifelong friend.

In 1948 the prominent Polish-born mathematician Antoni Zygmund, a professor at the University of Chicago, came to the institute to conduct a seminar in mathematical analysis, the branch of mathematics that comprises calculus, infinite series, and the analysis of functions. The half-dozen participants included Gonzalez Dominguez as well as Calderón, who impressed Zygmund by modestly proposing an original, alternate proof to a theorem discussed in Zygmund's classic work *Trigonometrical Series* (1935). The impressed Zygmund promptly invited him to come to the University of Chicago for further study, and Calderón accepted. A fellowship from the Rockefeller Foundation enabled him to move to Chicago the following year.

Initially Calderón felt overwhelmed by his new surroundings and was tempted to return to Argentina. The University of Chicago mathematics department, which included at that time André Weil, Marshall Stone, and other superb mathematicians, was considered by many to be the best in the world. A developing friendship with Weil, sparked by Calderón's interest in the work of Weil's "Bourbaki" group, together with Zygmund's pleadings, convinced Calderón that he should remain. Further encouragement from department chairman Stone led Calderón to enroll in the doctoral program, which he completed in one year. For his dissertation, Calderón submitted three separate papers on ergodic theory and harmonic analysis, each of which offered solutions to long-standing problems.

Calderón received his Ph.D. in 1950 and that same year married Mabel Molinelli Wells, a fellow mathematician whom he had met as an undergraduate at the University of Buenos Aires; the couple had two children. That fall he moved with his wife to Ohio State University, where he had been appointed associate professor of mathematics, but he continued to work closely with Zygmund until Zygmund's death in 1992. The most celebrated result of their collaboration was "On Singular Integrals," a paper published in the journal *Acta Mathematica* in 1952. In that groundbreaking work they formulated what became known as the Calderón-Zygmund theory of singular integrals—mathematical objects that look infinite but are in fact finite. They continued to work together on singular integrals over the following decades, attracting other mathematicians to the university to work in the same field, and in doing so created the so-called Chicago school of mathematical analysis. Calderón and Zygmund and their colleagues demonstrated links between Fourier analysis and partial differential equations, providing solutions to problems in physics and engineering, including the movement of heat and sound waves; they also made significant contributions to the development of probability theory.

Calderón moved to New Jersey in 1953 to become a visiting fellow for two years at the Institute for Advanced Study in Princeton. In 1955 he joined the faculty of the Massachusetts Institute of Technology. In 1959 he returned to the University of Chicago as professor of mathematics. In 1972 he went back to MIT, where he taught for three years before returning permanently to Chicago in 1975 to become University Professor of Mathematics. During the next decade he served several years as department chairman before his retirement in 1985. In the 1970s and early 1980s Calderón also taught classes as an honorary professor at the University of Buenos Aires and served as director of the Instituto Argentino de Matematica in that city. Throughout his years in the United States Calderón maintained strong ties with his native country and encouraged many gifted young mathematicians there; a number of them came to study with him in the United States. He also encouraged the development of mathematics in Spain following the demise of the Franco regime in the mid-1970s.

Calderón's wife had returned to Argentina in the late 1960s, and she died there in 1985. In 1989 he married the mathematician Alexandra Bagdasar Bellow, a professor at Northwestern University; Bellow, a former wife of the novelist Saul Bellow, had met Calderón when they both taught at MIT some years earlier. Calderón's last two published papers were written jointly with Bellow, a renowned expert in ergodic theory.

As a leading mathematician of the twentieth century, Calderón was awarded many honors, including the 1989 Wolf Prize, considered the highest award in mathematics. He also received a National Medal of Science from the U.S. government in 1991—five years after the same award was bestowed on Zygmund. As a teacher, Calderón, who was multilingual, was known for his warmth, enthusiasm, and encouragement of his students. In private life, he was a gifted pianist and an accomplished tango dancer who enjoyed a wide variety of music; he also derived pleasure from fixing all sorts of mechanical devices, especially small home appliances. Indeed, practical applications of mathematical and scientific knowledge were always of great interest to Calderón, and he took great satisfaction from the fact that his theoretical work in mathematics was essential to important developments in signal processing, geophysics, and tomography.

Calderón died at a Chicago hospital following a brief illness.

• For biographical information, see Michael Christ, Carlos E. Kenig, and Cora Sadosky, eds., "Introduction," in Har-

monic Analysis and Partial Differential Equations:Essays in Honor of Alberto P. Calderón (1999). See also "Obituary: Alberto Calderón," *The University of Chicago Chronicle*, 30 Apr. 1998. An obituary is in the *New York Times*, 17 Apr. 1998.

ANN T. KEENE

CAMPBELL, John (1653–04 Mar. 1728), journalist, evidently born in Scotland, was probably the son of Duncan Campbell, the postmaster of Boston. His mother's identity is unknown. In 1702 John Campbell succeeded the deceased Duncan Campbell and became, with the approval of Governor Joseph Dudley, postmaster of Boston. As postmaster, Campbell was commissioned by the Massachusetts General Court not only to deliver the handwritten "public letters" but also to circulate maritime and mercantile information and political news (mostly from Europe) to other postmasters and to regional leaders. Following the model of the English newspaper press, especially the *London Gazette*, Campbell began, on 24 April 1704, to print the *Boston News-Letter*. Printed every Monday, the *News-Letter* was timed to take advantage of the arrival of the weekly post and was mailed with Campbell's franking privileges.

Campbell produced the *Boston News-Letter* as an effort, in the phrase of Arthur Schlesinger, to "improve and commercialize" the flow of public, if mostly maritime, information. The news published in the *News-Letter* was aimed principally at the economic, political, and social elite of Massachusetts. As the economy was so dependent on the sea, the news, primarily in the form of accounts simply lifted from the London papers and reprinted, featured European wars and alliances, piracy, poor weather, the movement of ships more generally, events in the Caribbean, domestic events, and market conditions in London. Comparatively little news came from the American colonies.

The *News-Letter* was a printed half-sheet (about 12″ by 8″ with two columns on each page) that followed closely the physical appearance (including the organization of the content) of the *London Gazette*. Though not the first attempt to produce a newspaper (Benjamin Harris's *Publick Occurrences* appeared briefly in Boston as a broadsheet before being suppressed in 1690), Campbell's enterprise was to become the first successful newspaper in North America. Campbell noted that his newspaper was "published by authority," and he was careful not to give offense to his governmental patrons. Nevertheless, through the *News-Letter*, he transformed what was essentially private correspondence into a public activity of gathering and disseminating the news to whoever wanted to pay for it. In so doing, he created the institution of the newspaper in North America. The *News-Letter*, surviving until 1776, focused initially, to be sure, on events in London and the other European capitals, but it was firmly fixed as well on providing useful information to those who had no other ready source of such information.

While not an "official" publication, Campbell's *News-Letter* appears to have been published with the approbation of the royal governor and seems to have served official needs on occasion by publishing proclamations and official notices, even publishing stories that reflected an official point of view, such as publicizing punishment of a drover who did not keep the Sabbath. The General Court often did not reimburse Campbell fully for publishing official notices, and on at least one occasion in 1722 (when he was no longer postmaster but still publishing the *News-Letter*) it refused to reimburse him at all. The *News-Letter* was first printed (until 1707) by Bartholomew Green, who used pica types; the publisher for the first few issues was Nicholas Boone, until Campbell later included his own name in the notice at the end of each issue.

The *News-Letter* was not well written. It was published weekly, and accounts of political developments in Europe were reprinted generally in chronological order, in order to provide a "thread of occurrences." Some maritime news from the colonial American ports and a few brief local items were also included. There was little advertising (often no more than one or two advertisements per issue in the early years), though the use of blank pages (or at least blocks of blank space) allowed readers space for writing their own letters. Initially the *News-Letter* was two printed pages but soon (by 1705) expanded to four before reverting by 1707 back to two.

The *News-Letter* remained two pages until 1719, when Campbell sought to make his "thread of occurrences" more current by producing both supplements and four-page numbers. As Campbell himself observed in a notice in the issue of 10 August 1719, "It was impossible with half a Sheet a Week to carry on all the Public Occurrences of Europe, with those of this, our Neighboring Provinces, and the West Indies." The expanded editions continued well into 1720; soon after, his newspaper resumed its two-page appearance. It was a constant struggle for Campbell to find sufficient subscribers (he complained in 1719 that he could not find 300 subscribers, compared to the "thousands" who read English newspapers).

Green was succeeded as printer of the *News-Letter* by John Allen, who published it for four years, from 10 November 1707 through 1 October 1711; Campbell's post office and Allen's printing shop were then consumed in the great fire of 2 October 1711. With the following issue, Bartholomew Green resumed printing the newspaper, adding his name as printer to the imprint in 1715.

In 1718 Campbell was replaced as postmaster (thereby losing considerable advantage of using the mails to circulate his newspaper free of postage), and his successor as postmaster, William Brooker, started a rival newspaper, the *Boston Gazette*, which was printed by James Franklin. Brooker's tenure as postmaster was brief, and when he was replaced by Philip Musgrave, the printing of the *Boston Gazette* went to Samuel Kneeland, nephew of Bartholomew Green. Soon thereafter, in 1720, Campbell printed the *News-Letter* on half a sheet, advising his customers to use the other half for their own correspondence, thereby saving money by combining the newspaper and the letter for only one postage charge. In this way, Campbell sought to minimize the competitive edge that he had lost when he was removed as postmaster. The appearance of the *Gazette* precipitated the first journalistic controversy in British North America when Brooker attacked Campbell and his newspaper for being unresponsive to the needs of its readers. If readers were pardonably bored with its details, the controversy nonetheless heralded a new age of journalism in the colonies.

In 1721 a third newspaper, the *New England Courant*, was started in Boston by James Franklin, who promptly criticized Campbell's newspaper for its dullness. Campbell was quick to respond and waged battle with Franklin for the duration of his tenure as publisher of the *News-Letter*. Indeed, Campbell supported Cotton Mather against Franklin in the smallpox inoculation controversy of 1721, briefly publishing a full sheet weekly before reducing it back to a half sheet, like the *Gazette* and the *Courant*. By the end of 1722, Campbell had turned the *News-Letter* over to Bartholomew Green, who had remained as its printer since resuming that activity in 1711.

Campbell held a number of civic positions, including justice of the peace. He was married twice, perhaps three times, and his surviving spouse was Mary Clarke Pemberton. He appears to have died in Boston.

Campbell deserves historical attention as publisher of the first successful newspaper in the British North American colonies, however marginal its financial standing. Campbell's initiative was quickly imitated, and within a generation New England was home to a number of newspapers.

• The recent work of Charles E. Clark has broadened understanding of the advent of newspapers in British North America and provides the broad context for Campbell's career and achievement. Clark, "The Newspapers of Provincial America," in the American Antiquarian Society, *Proceedings*, vol. 100 (1991), pp. 367–89, is an excellent and compact summary that blends the broadest developments with recent historiography, while his more recent *The Public Prints: The Newspaper in Anglo-American Culture, 1665–1740* (1994) provides a wider political and cultural context in which to set Campbell's pathbreaking activity. Information about Campbell may be gleaned from a variety of sources, including Clarence S. Brigham, *History and Bibliography of American Newspapers, 1690–1820* (2 vols., 1947); Isaiah Thomas, *The History of Printing in America*, repr. ed. (1970); Joseph T. Buckingham, *Specimens of Newspaper Literature* (1850); and John T. Winterich, *Early American Books and Printing*, repr. ed. (1974). A source of conveniently compiled information is Benjamin Franklin V, ed., *Boston Printers, Publishers, and Booksellers, 1640–1800* (1980).

WILLIAM L. JOYCE

CAPEZIO, Salvatore (13 Apr. 1871–6 Jan. 1940), theatrical and dance shoe manufacturer, was born in Muro Lucano, a small town near Potenza in southern

Italy. His father was a construction engineer, but his parents' names do not appear in readily available sources of information. Not wishing to enter his father's profession, he emigrated to the United States. According to Capezio company information on the Internet and in most reference sources, the teenaged Capezio arrived in 1887 and opened a shoe repair shop on West Thirty-ninth Street in New York. In fact, the company is known as "The Dancer's Cobbler since 1887." The date of his arrival, however, varies in public records: 1890 (1900 census), 1889 (1910 census), and 1883 (1920 census.) The discrepancies may reflect Capezio's difficulty with the English language or someone else's having incorrectly supplied the information. Perhaps most authoritative are the Ellis Island passenger records; they show the 21-year-old Capezio arriving on 30 April 1892 on the *Anglia*, which sailed from Palermo. The ship's manifest also listed 11-year-old Giuseppe Capezio, who may have been his brother, since when he died it was reported that he was survived by his brother, Joseph. Under the heading "Calling," both were marked "shoemakers." Possibly Capezio's first entrance into the United States went unrecorded, and this may have been a subsequent voyage to accompany the child Giuseppe. The earliest appearance of the establishment in New York City directories is 1894.

Whatever the correct date of its founding, the shop was favorably located. Across the street from the Metropolitan Opera House at Broadway and Thirty-ninth Street, it was in the midst of the theater district. At first Capezio repaired only street shoes, but through his friendship with Italians working in the Metropolitan's wardrobe department, he soon learned the techniques of theatrical shoemaking. One day the renowned tenor Jean de Reszke rushed into the shop needing replacement shoes for that evening's performance of *Romeo and Juliet*. Capezio quickly fashioned a pair of shoes for de Reszke. Word spread, and from then on Capezio made shoes for the singers and corps de ballet of the Metropolitan, as well as for the dancers of the Ziegfeld Follies and the companies of other theaters.

In 1902 Capezio married a dancer, Angelina Passone (Dalva 1987) or Pasione (*Italian-American Who's Who* 1938). Trained at La Scala in Milan, she danced at the Hippodrome, located on Sixth Avenue between Forty-third and Forty-fourth Streets. Called the world's largest theater, the Hippodrome was famous for its productions of opera and extravaganzas, which might feature dancing elephants or water ballets in a huge elliptical tank. The couple had no children.

When the famous Russian ballerina Anna Pavlova made her first U.S. tour in 1910, she and Angelina Capezio struck up a friendship. Soon Capezio was creating her shoes, by hand. Dancers' shoes, especially those for dancing *en pointe*, appear to be delicate, but their complicated construction employs principles of physics and engineering. Capezio also consulted with choreographers and designers. On 27 February 1915, Pavlova wrote in a letter, "Your theatrical shoes are indeed the best I've ever had." She also let others in the world of dance know about "the dancer's cobbler." Her endorsement of Capezio's craftsmanship strengthened the company's image and consequently its revenues.

Although he had no children of his own, Capezio ran his establishment as though it were a large family. He carefully trained the shoemakers in the special art of making dance shoes, and many staff members remained for decades. (A prime example is Ben Sommers, who at fourteen started working for the company as an errand boy in 1920. He became president of the Capezio Corporation in 1940 when Capezio died, a post he still held in 1962.)

During World War I (1914–1918), when Italy was allied to the United States, Capezio's New York factory was given a contract to make leggings for the Italian army's uniforms. By 1920 Capezio was living alone on Grove Street in East Paterson, now Elmwood Park, New Jersey. He remained there until his death. According to the 1920 U.S. Census, he was divorced. However, that may not be true, given that he was a Catholic and that other information from the census, such as his age (forty) and date of arrival in the United States (1883) is questionable. He became a U.S. citizen in 1921, and he was a Democrat. His awards included a gold medal at the General Commercial Exposition, Paris, 1925, and the Cross of Honor, Florence, 1929.

Between 1928 and 1935 Capezio held eight U.S. patents for the manufacture of tap soles, ballet shoes, and a toe shield. Among the many dancers he made shoes for were Marilyn Miller, Eleanor Powell, and Vera Zorina. Other performers who wore his shoes were Enrico Caruso, Lillian Russell, John Barrymore, and Ethel Barrymore. The Boston and Chicago Opera companies as well as Radio City Music Hall were his clients.

A modest man about whom there is little personal information, Capezio was a superb craftsman and a charismatic figure. As a young man he created an enterprise that is still thriving more than one hundred years later. Moreover, it continues to be run by the descendants of his extended family as well as by other longtime employees who are not related. Now known as Capezio/Ballet Makers, Inc., they make dance clothing as well as shoes. During the late 1930s the company entered the field of fashion offstage and gained a vast new audience. Designer Claire McCardell showed Capezio ballet flats with her new collection in 1941, which featured capri pants. Boots, in all fabrics and colors, were introduced soon after.

The Capezio Dance Award was instituted in 1952 to honor important figures in the dance world. Fred Astaire, Bob Fosse, and Rudolph Nureyev were among the winners. In 1987 the Salvatore Capezio Scholarships were established to commemorate the founder by assisting ballet students with their tuition.

• The articles with the most information on Capezio, but more specifically on the company, are by William Como, "A

Diamond for Capezio," *Dance* magazine, Oct. 1962, pp. 46–49, and Nancy Vreeland Dalva, "Capezio Centenary: Family Affairs," *Dance* magazine, May 1987, pp. 90–94. *Italian-American Who's Who: A Biographical Dictionary of Italian-American Leaders* (1938) is helpful. Obituaries are in the *Paterson* (New Jersey) *Morning Call*, 8 Jan. 1940, and in the *New York Times*, 10 Jan.1940.

BETTY KAPLAN GUBERT

CARDOZO, Michael H. (15 Sept. 1910–20 Oct. 1996), lawyer, educator, and government adviser, was born Michael Hart Cardozo IV in New York City, the son of Ernest Abraham Cardozo, a lawyer, and Emily Rebecca Wolff Cardozo. He was a first cousin of United States Supreme Court Justice Benjamin Cardozo. Cardozo attended the Berkeley-Irving School in New York City and then, from 1924 to 1928, Phillips Academy, Andover, Massachusetts. In 1928 he entered Dartmouth College, where in 1932 he received an A.B. degree. He then went to Yale Law School, served on the editorial board of the *Yale Law Journal*, and in 1935 received an LL.B. degree.

On graduating from Yale, Cardozo became an associate in the law firm of Parker & Duryee (then known as Parker, Finley & Benjamin). In 1937 he married Alice Corneille; they had three children. (Michael Cardozo V served as deputy counsel to President Jimmy Carter.)

In 1938 Gerhard Gesell, a Yale classmate and special counsel with the Securities and Exchange Commission, invited Cardozo to join him with the Temporary National Economic Committee investigating life insurance (interview, 29 May 1975, pp. 2–3. "I didn't necessarily prepare for a Government career," Cardozo recalled. "The atmosphere at the Yale Law School in those days was very likely to encourage somebody to get into Government. William Douglas, Thurman Arnold, Charles Clark and Walton [Hale] Hamilton were all people who, at one time or another, had a lot to do with Government. So, it wasn't surprising that a lot of us did go into it" (interview, 29 May 1975, p. 2). In 1940–1942, he was an attorney with the Justice Department, Tax Division, and through Oscar Cox, a Justice Department official and also general counsel for lend-lease, he entered the international arena (interview, 29 May 1975, p. 4).

In 1942 Cardozo was with the Office of Lend-Lease Administration, Office of the General Counsel. In 1943–1944 he served as U.S. lend-lease representative to Turkey and then was with the Foreign Economic Administration. Cardozo noted that his experience in lend-lease was important in developing his expertise in foreign aid programs (interview, 29 May 1975, p. 10). In 1945–1952, he was with the U.S. Department of State in the Office of the Assistant Legal Adviser and in 1950–1952 served as assistant legal adviser for economic affairs. Cardozo negotiated and drafted war account settlement agreements, including lend-lease, educational and cultural agreements such as Fulbright, military assistance legislation and agreements such as NATO, and postwar economic assistance programs such as the Marshall Plan. He was named officer of the Order of Orange-Nassau, the Netherlands.

From 1952 to 1963 Cardozo was a professor of law at Cornell Law School; he taught public and private international law and admiralty. In 1958–1959 he was a Fulbright and Guggenheim fellow in Belgium. As a consultant to the Senate Committee on Foreign Relations in 1960–1961, he was involved in drafting the Mutual Educational and Cultural Exchange Act of 1961. In the following year he was a visiting professor of law at Northwestern School of Law. He wrote numerous articles on foreign aid and international law and was editor of the "Proceedings of Summer Conferences on International Law" at Cornell (1957, 1958, 1960, 1962). Based on his government experience and his research as a Guggenheim and Fulbright awardee is *Diplomats in International Cooperation: Stepchildren of the Foreign Service* (1962), in which he argued that the complexity of American diplomacy necessitated a new type of diplomat in the multinational organizations—one who "is the catalyst in government and diplomacy, coordinating the work of many agencies and groups" (p. 89). In a subsequent essay, "Intervention: Benefaction as Justification" (Stanger, ed.), he argued that it was improper for the United States to threaten to cut off economic aid to force other countries to change policies in fields unrelated to that aid, and recommended that aid be channeled through international organizations as a means to prevent such manipulation.

From 1963 to 1973 Cardozo was the first executive director of the Association of American Law Schools. He was also a visiting professor of Law at the University of Pennsylvania, Howard University, and Georgetown University; a member of the faculty of the Salzburg Seminar in American Studies (summer 1968); and a delegate to the American Council of Learned Societies. Cardozo continued to write; served as editor of *PREVIEW of United States Supreme Court Cases* (1965–1975, 1981–1983); was on the board of editors of *The Practical Lawyer*, and wrote the *Association Process, 1963–1973* (1975). Cardozo was a prime advocate for the reform of legal writing.

In 1973 he went into private practice in Washington, D.C. Cardozo represented educational entities and nonprofit groups and was involved in issues such as fair use of copyrighted material. He also served as a government consultant, held leadership positions in legal and educational organizations, and continued with his scholarship. As a consultant to the Administrative Conference of the United States, his analysis "The Federal Advisory Committee Act in Operation" was published in the *Administrative Law Review* (1981). Cardozo was visiting professor of law at George Washington University and American University, president of the Washington Foreign Law Society (1976), a founder and president of the Fulbright Alumni Association (1982), a member of the American Law Institute (life member, 1989), secretary of the American Society of International Law (1978–

1994), and editor of the *Journal of Supreme Court History* (1988–1992). Active in numerous educational groups, especially the Dartmouth alumni, he related the value of his undergraduate education in "Reflections of Four Years on Fifty: Earning the Style of Human Being" (Ferry, ed.). Well-versed in his family's history, Cardozo took on the role of curator of the family tree. His keen interest in Jewish history led to the founding of the Gomez Foundation (of which he was president) for Mill House near Newburgh, N.Y., the oldest standing Jewish residence (ca. 1714). Cardozo died at his home in Washington, D.C.

Admired and well liked for his tolerance of different viewpoints and his achievements in government, education, and legal scholarship and practice, he is most remembered for his respect for and commitment to a tradition of law as a profession of public service before the "bottom line" became an overriding preoccupation for many in the field.

• Cardozo's papers and other personal and professional archival material are in the possession of the Cardozo family in Washington, D.C. Transcripts of the Michael H. Cardozo interview by Richard D. McKinzie, 29 May 1975, for the Truman Library Oral History Project, contain important information about his career in government and about some of his publications emanating from his government experience. Transcripts of the Cardozo interview by Ellen M. Scholle, 11 Apr. 1991, for the American Jewish Committee Oral History Library Project (American Jews of Sephardic Origin), contain information about his family life and some limited information on his career. Other sources of family and biographical information include Michael H. Cardozo, *Portrait of Emily: Her Short Life and Ernest's Lifelong Love* (1978), and Frances Nathan Wolff, *Four Generations: My Life and Memories of New York for Over Eighty Years* (1939). Reflections on his family life and his professional career are noted in Michael H. Cardozo, V, "Michael H. Cardozo," and Arthur Power Dudden, "Michael H. Cardozo, IV," in "In Celebration of the Life of Michael Hart Cardozo, IV, 1910–1996" (Memorials, 27 Oct. 1996, Washington Hebrew Congregation, Washington, D.C.). In addition to his publications as editor of professional journals cited in the article, Cardozo's works include *Diplomats in International Cooperation: Stepchildren of the Foreign Service* (1962); "Intervention: Benefaction as Justification," in *Essays on Intervention*, Roland J. Stanger, ed. (1964), pp. 63–85; *The Association Process, 1963–73: Decision Making in the Association of American Law Schools* (1975); "The Federal Advisory Committee Act in Operation," *Administrative Law Review* 33, no. 1 (Winter 1981): 1–62; and "Reflections of Four Years on Fifty: Earning the Style of Human Being," *Warming up for Fifty Years*, W. H. Ferry, ed. (1982), pp. 204–209. An obituary is in the *New York Times*, 22 Oct. 1996.

MARILYN TOBIAS

CAREY, James Francis (19 Aug. 1867–31 Dec. 1938), Socialist politician, was born in Haverhill, Massachusetts, the son of James Carey (1814–1889), a day laborer and sometime shoemaker, and Mary Moriarty Carey (1834–1891). His parents had emigrated from Ireland at the time of the Great Famine.

Carey's birthplace, Haverhill, was a prominent shoemaking city that specialized in women's "slippers," or dress shoes. During Carey's childhood, Haverhill had undergone the transition from handcraft to factory. Multistory shoe shops sprouted throughout the downtown, and the population of the city grew rapidly with an infusion of Irish and French-Canadian immigrants and Americans from the northern New England states. In later years, Carey underscored his blue collar roots by claiming that he ended his formal education at ten years of age to join his older brothers and sisters in the shoe shop. The passage of time may have affected his memory, for the 1880 federal census states that twelve-year-old James was "at school."

The Carey family moved frequently, perhaps as the number of children increased. Yet, the city directories of Haverhill for the 1870s and 1880s indicate that James Carey was the homeowner at each address. So future Socialist James F. Carey grew up in an atmosphere of private property but also of collective earnings. The 1880 federal census noted that there were seven wage earners in the house. Three sons were heel cutters, two daughters were shoe stitchers, a son-in-law was a shoe heeler. The father, James, was still a day laborer but the combined pay checks provided a modicum of security.

James F. Carey joined his older brothers as a heel cutter in the Haverhill factories. Cutters were among the better paid of shoe workers, as their work demanded precision. Carey moved to Ward Five in Haverhill, where Haverhill's newest immigrants found employment in the shops. The area became a polyglot, multiethnic enclave of Italians, Armenians, Greeks, Poles, Lithuanians and eastern European Jews who joined the earlier Irish and French-Canadian residents. This was the area in which James F. Carey would nurture and develop his political talents.

Carey's baptism into political action was through the local Nationalist club. Nationalists had been inspired by the reform ideas of Edward Bellamy, author of the utopian novel *Looking Backward*. They supported a collectivism that had more in common with the English Christian Socialism than with Marx's "scientific" socialism. They called for municipal ownership of public services and for such election reforms as the initiative, the referendum, and the recall. The Nationalists endorsed the People's Party, or Populists, a product of Midwestern agrarian movements. By 1893 Nationalists were in control of the Populists in Massachusetts and had added a workingman's agenda to what had been a predominantly agriculturalists' movement.

In 1892 Carey presided over the Bay State Populists as they absorbed the local Labor party. A year later, he made his first appearance on the ballot on a Populist slate in the state elections, running for state representative. In 1894 a Reform Coalition including the Populists won the Haverhill mayoral election, though neither Carey nor his fellow Populists were successful in their individual races. The campaign did demonstrate, though, that their hard-hitting campaign with a focus on local problems could undercut the Republicans and Democrats in town.

In December 1894 Carey was propelled into the forefront of local attention during a major strike among the city's shoe workers. He gave speech after speech, traveled the state to raise funds for the strikers, and took a leadership position in discouraging violence. Though supported by the local press, the strike failed. And so, too, did the People's Party in Haverhill. Carey, however, had discovered that he was a gifted orator who could stir his audiences.

A local judge had referred to Carey as a "Socialist" during the strike, and now Carey gladly took on that title. In 1896 he ran for mayor of Haverhill as the candidate of the Socialist Labor Party of Daniel De Leon. He received about 10 percent of the vote. The local press thought that number was "significant." The next year he ran for a seat in the Common Council from Ward Five. Carey's platform reflected his pragmatic form of socialism and he was persistent in pursuing these same causes in each of his succeeding campaigns despite demands from the national and state party leaders to hew to the more ideological party line. Carey pushed for municipal ownership of some public utilities, public works projects, abolition of unguarded railway crossings, and free clothing for children who would otherwise be unable to attend school. He received over 900 votes (the Socialist candidate for mayor, John Chase, received 950 votes running citywide), and won every precinct in his ward. When the major parties deadlocked over the presidency of the Common Council, they turned to Carey to take up the gavel. His evenhanded leadership won praise from the local Republican press. More importantly, he won national recognition as the first Socialist to be elected to a municipal office. Carey, a skilled politician, chose his issues carefully and wisely and took a public stand only when he knew he had public support. He had little success in getting his program approved, though many of the issues would be incorporated into a Progressive Republican platform a decade later.

The tension between the national Socialist Labor Party and its Haverhill branch escalated to the point of separation in 1898. The national party wanted rigid conformity. The Haverhill group wanted local autonomy. Carey and his fellow Socialists found a more receptive home in the new Social Democratic Party led by Eugene Debs.

In 1898 Carey ran for a seat in the state legislature under the banner of the Social Democrats. He soundly defeated three opponents and polled almost 60 percent of the vote from his district. Another Haverhill Socialist, Louis Scates, won a seat from another district to join Carey in Boston. They were the first Socialists in the Massachusetts General Court, as the legislature was called. Emboldened by their success, local Socialists put up a full ticket in the municipal elections several weeks later. John C. Chase, a Socialist, was elected mayor of Haverhill and was joined by three Socialist aldermen and three Socialist members of the Common Council.

Carey was reelected to state office from 1899 to 1903. He proposed legislation, made stirring speeches, and won national acclaim for his unique status, but he seldom prevailed. The State House reporter for the *Boston Traveler* lamented that Carey was not a Republican. "If he was it would mean that many of the excellent ideas which come from him would be adopted in the Legislature with a whoop. The Republicans in the Legislature are afraid of Mr. Carey's political designation."

In 1903 Carey married Clara L. Stevens, a shoe stitcher who was an active member of the Socialist Party. Carey, who had become alienated from the Catholic Church, was married in a private home by a Unitarian minister active in Socialist politics. The "Socialist wedding" omitted the word "obey" in the vows. The couple went to the bride's home in East Surry, Maine, for their wedding trip. The Maine farm became a second home to Carey.

In 1903 the Catholic Church, an increasingly conservative and divided shoe workers union, union pioneer Samuel Gompers, and a revived Republican Party targeted Carey for defeat. The candidate himself, perhaps taking his constituents for granted, did not campaign very hard. Instead, he spent the weeks before the election working for the election of the state ticket. Carey's district, known as "the Gibraltar of Socialism," fell to the Republicans by 150 votes. Carey accepted defeat with the resigned comment that "everything will happen for the best." He now gave his full attention to the state Socialist Party and played a major role in the national party. In 1900 he had evolved the strategy that would unify the Social Democrats and lead to the formation of the Socialist Party of America. He was in great demand as an orator, traveling throughout the East and Midwest to speak at party gatherings. He served on the National Executive Board of the Socialist Party and was secretary of his state party. In 1908 a movement began to nominate Carey for president, but he withdrew his name from consideration to serve as chairman of the convention. Carey was nominated many times in the century for the post of governor of Massachusetts. In 1912 he returned to Haverhill to run in the municipal election, after an absence of a decade from local politics. He lost the election, moved to Surry, Maine, and aside from periodic lecture tours and some involvement in Maine socialism, ceased to take an active role in Socialist politics. In 1919 Carey retired completely from politics. His last years were plagued with illness. He died in Lawrence, Massachusetts.

Carey's place in history rests primarily on his title as the first Socialist elected to a municipal office in America. Yet he was not a doctrinaire Socialist. He fought attempts to bring divisive issues such as religion, class consciousness, and the destruction of private property into the Socialist program. He insisted that the party focus on politics, on the winning of elections, rather than on ideology. And for years he was successful in shaping the Massachusetts party to this perspective. He was a skillful orator whose emotional pleas for the poor and the working class earned him the derisive nickname of "Weeping James." But he also knew how to use humor and to win over a crowd of people by talking about issues that mattered to them. Oratory, not writing, was his preferred mode of communication. The only writings extant under his name are transcriptions of speeches.

• The Haverhill (Mass.) Public Library Special Collections has a limited clipping file on Carey and a five-volume file on "Haverhill Labor Problems." There are four available pamphlets of Carey's speeches and debates: *Child Labor* (1899); *The Menace of Socialism* (1911), a debate with Rev. Thomas Gasson, president of Boston College; *Socialism, the Creed of Despair* (1909), a debate with George Hugo; and *Debate on Socialism Held at Faneuil Hall* (1903), a debate with Frederick J. Stimson. Carey plays a featured role in Henry Bedford's *Socialism and the Workers in Massachusetts, 1886–1912* (1966). Bedford also wrote "The 'Haverhill Social Democrat': Spokesman for Socialism," *Labor History* (Winter 1961), and "The Socialist Movement in Haverhill," *Essex Institute Historical Collections*, vol. 99, no. 1 (Jan. 1963). Carey's obituary is in the Haverhill *Sunday Record*, 1 Jan. 1939, and in the Haverhill *Evening Gazette* on 3 Jan. 1939.

PATRICIA TRAINOR O'MALLEY

CARLEBACH, Shlomo (14 Jan. 1925–21 Oct. 1994), Jewish spiritual leader and pioneer of the movement Return to Tradition, was born in Berlin, Germany, the son of Paula Cohn Carlebach and Rabbi Naftali Carlebach. His father, grandfather, and uncles were known rabbis, members of the German-Jewish movement of return to tradition, which attempted to be loyal to the *halacha*, the Jewish Law, at the same time that it strived to embrace European culture. The Carlebach rabbis had received university degrees in addition to rabbinical education. Shortly before the Nazi rise to power, the Carlebachs moved to Austria, where Carlebach's father found a position as a rabbi. After the Nazis' march into Austria in 1938, the family moved to New York, where Naftali Carlebach became the rabbi of Kehilat Jacob, a small Orthodox congregation on the Upper West Side of New York that was affiliated with Young Israel, a liberal Orthodox American movement.

Disillusioned with the Enlightenment-oriented neoorthodoxy, and finding it to be unsatisfactory both spiritually and intellectually, young Carlebach decided to explore the world of ultraorthodox Eastern European Jewry, which never embraced the ideals of the Enlightenment. Ultraorthodox institutions and communities in America grew significantly during the 1940s and 1950s as the result of the arrival of thousands of refugees from Eastern Europe, among them prominent Torah scholars and Hasidic leaders. Carlebach took advantage of the new opportunities and enrolled in an Eastern European rabbinical academy, the Beth Midrash Govoha, a newly established yeshiva in Lakewood, New Jersey. There he became a disciple of Rabbi Aaron Kotler, one of the more prestigious ultraorthodox scholars of his day. Striving for more spirituality and spontaneity in the expression of

Jewish devotion, Carlebach, together with his twin brother, Eli Haim, joined Lubavitch, a Hasidic group whose leaders came to America as refugees at the beginning of World War II. Carlebach became a follower of the sixth Lubavitch rebbe, Rabbi Joseph Isaac Schneersohn, who recruited him in 1949 to become a *schaliach*, outreach messenger, to spread the teachings of Hasidism among American Jews.

Carlebach and Zalman Schachter, who became a lifelong friend of Carlebach's, were the first messengers sent by the Lubavitch Hasidic group to make inroads into the secular American Jewish community. Their mission was revolutionary. Lubavitch had had a network of messengers from its early days, but the messengers' initial mission had been to keep the connection between the rebbe, the spiritual leader of Lubavitch, and his followers alive and, at times, to make recruits for the Lubavitch brand of Judaism among observant Jews. Carlebach and Schachter's mission was different. They aimed to convince unobservant Jews, many of whom grew up in secular or liberal households, that Hasidic Judaism was a preferred way of life that could offer greater spiritual and intellectual meaning.

Starting as an emissary of Lubavitch, Carlebach soon became independent and pursued his outreach mission on his own. Departing from Lubavitch's norms, he taught mixed crowds of men and women, and gave concerts to mixed crowds, turning his musical talents into a means of outreach. Influenced by country and gospel music, Carlebach composed throughout the years hundreds of melodies to Jewish prayers and biblical verses. In his music and stories, Carlebach promoted a message that relationships between human beings should be based on love, compassion, and forbearance. "If you see a fellow human being, created in the image of God, how come you do not embrace him?" he would ask. Departing from Lubavitch theology, he welcomed non-Jews who wished to explore the Jewish tradition. In his teachings, sermons, and music, Carlebach promoted the idea that an accepting, loving God was still guarding His people, and that the Jews had a rich spiritual tradition, which was at least as good as that of other cultures. Relying on the teachings of Rabbi Nachman of Braslav, an early nineteenth-century Hasidic mystic, Carlebach emphasized joy as a means of getting closer to God.

Carlebach's understanding of Judaism and his outreach mission, which he saw as a calling to bring "lost" Jewish souls into the fold, were strongly influenced by the Holocaust. The Holocaust also shaped his understanding of the course of Judaism within modern society. Rejecting the Enlightenment's ideals of rational humanity, he embraced the supernatural and advocated the need of human beings to seek the help of a loving God.

During the late 1960s and early 1970s, Carlebach's emphasis on love, joy in worship, the supernatural, and an accepting God found friendly audiences among adherents of the counterculture, whose ideals were in some ways similar to those of Carlebach. In 1967, Carlebach established the House of Love and Prayer in San Francisco, an outreach center and semi-commune that amalgamated Hasidic Judaism with hippie styles and tastes. He and his disciples opened a branch of the House of Love and Prayer in Jerusalem, Israel, where some of the West Coast neo-Hasids found their home. A yeshiva intended for returnees to tradition, influenced by Carlebach's hippie-orthodox style, started in Jerusalem at the same time. While some Orthodox Jews were taken aback by Carlebach's tolerance of hippie styles and manners, others, including major Hasidic leaders, such as the Amshinover rebbe, supported his mission. Carlebach, however, never established an organization, and influenced spiritual inquirers on a one-on-one basis, making hundreds of converts throughout his lifetime. His inclusive and nonjudgmental outreach style, which allowed potential converts to study Judaism at their own pace and on their own terms, served as an example and inspired a larger Orthodox Jewish outreach movement, and gave rise to an influential movement of Return to Tradition.

In 1967, Carlebach's message acquired a messianic overtone. He became convinced that the Israeli victory in the Six-Day War against Egypt, Jordan, and Syria was no accident, and the surprising Israeli conquest of Judea and Samaria had a purpose in God's plans. He encouraged his disciples to emigrate to Israel and build homes there. In 1976 he established a neo-Hasidic village in Israel, Meor-Modiin, which is still inhabited by his followers. In 1973 Carlebach married Neila Glick, a disciple who shared his neo-Hasidic vision; they had two daughters. Carlebach continued to travel, preach, and sing throughout the world. Following the death of his father, Carlebach and his brother took over the spiritual leadership of their father's old congregation in New York, turning the synagogue, which became known as the Carlebach Shul, into a fashionable uptown yuppie-Hasidic center. The waves of nostalgia and belated appreciation that followed Carlebach's death in October 1994 revitalized and enlarged the neo-Hasidic movement. His followers established dozens of Carlebach-style synagogues and prayer groups in North America and Israel and published compilations of his tales and songs.

• A small but good archival collection on Carlebach is the Carlebach Nearprint File at the Jacob Rader Marcus Center of the American Jewish Archives in Cincinnati. A series of books published by Carlebach's disciples after his death provides material on Carlebach's outreach mission, thought, and life. These include Shlomo Carlebach with Susan Yael Mesinai, *Shlomo Stories: Selected Tales* (1994); *The Holy Beggar Banquet: Traditional Jewish Tales and Teachings of the Late, Great Reb Shlomo Carlebach and Others in the Spirit of the 1960s, the 1970s, and the New Age*, ed. Kalman Serkez (1998); and *Holy Brother: Inspiring Stories and Enchanted Tales about Rabbi Shlomo Carlebach* (1997). An analytical essay on Carlebach and the neo-Hasidic movement is Yaakov Ariel, "Hasidism in the Age of Aquarius: The House of Love and Prayer in San Francisco, 1967–1977," *Religion and American Culture* 13, no. 2 (summer 2003), 139-65.

YAAKOV ARIEL

CARNAHAN, Melvin Eugene (11 Feb. 1934–16 Oct. 2000), governor of Missouri, was born in Birch Tree, Missouri, the son of Albert Sydney Johnson Carnahan, who served in the U.S. House of Representatives (1945–1947 and 1949–1961), and Mary Kathel Schupp Carnahan, a teacher. Because his father was in Congress, Mel Carnahan spent much of his youth in Washington, D.C., completing his secondary schooling there in 1950. That fall he enrolled at George Washington University, where he graduated in 1954 with a degree in business administration. That same year he married his high school sweetheart, Jean Carpenter; the couple had four children. With an ROTC commission, Carnahan spent the next two years in the air force but failed the physical exam required for all pilots. In 1956 he returned to Missouri and entered the law school at the University of Missouri–Columbia. In 1959 he graduated with the school's highest honors.

After law school Carnahan and his wife moved to Rolla, Missouri, where he set up private practice. In 1961, at the age of 26, he was elected municipal court judge in Rolla. The next year he was elected to the Missouri House of Representatives and served for two terms. During his second term he served as the majority leader and guided the state's first civil rights legislation through the General Assembly. His fast track up the Missouri state political ladder was abruptly halted by his defeat for a seat in the state senate in 1966. During the next fourteen years, he focused on his family and his law practice in Rolla. Nevertheless he remained involved in local politics, serving as president of the school board, where he supervised the construction of a new high school. In 1980 he again ventured successfully into the political arena and won handily the state treasurer seat. As treasurer, Carnahan revamped the operations of his office and instituted modern accounting systems. In 1984 his desire for higher office was thwarted when he came in second in the Democratic primary for governor. Again he returned to his Rolla law practice.

In 1988 Carnahan ran for lieutenant governor. Although John Ashcroft had no difficulty retaining the governorship, Carnahan ran a strong campaign and won by almost 100,000 votes. As one of the few Democratic officeholders, Carnahan was kept on the political sidelines during Ashcroft's second term. In 1992 Carnahan was ready to try again for governor. He bested St. Louis Mayor Vincent Schomehl in the Democratic primary and then went on to win in the fall against Republican Attorney General William Webster, garnering nearly 60 percent of the vote.

For Carnahan the single overriding issue of his first term was passage in 1993 of the Outstanding Schools Act, financed with a $310 million tax increase. It sought to reduce class size while at the same time raising state aid to the poorer school districts, thereby providing more equality in education throughout Missouri. In a flurry of legislation passed in his first two years, he persuaded the General Assembly to implement one of the nation's first welfare-to-work programs, reorganized the state government, established lifetime sentences for sexual predators, and increased the number of prison beds. He vetoed a concealed weapons law and resisted any further restrictions to the state's abortion laws. In 1996 Carnahan was re-elected with 57% of the vote over Republican auditor Margaret Kelly. During his second term he focused on tax issues. The General Assembly eliminated the food sales tax, and Carnahan signed into law more than $650 million in tax cuts. He continued to find more money for early childhood education and school aid and also pressed for passage of a children's health insurance plan. At the other end of the age spectrum he tripled spending for in-home health care for seniors and advocated better regulation of nursing homes. A staunch advocate of the death penalty, Carnahan was asked in January 1999 by Pope John Paul II to spare the life of a death-row inmate. The Pope had visited St. Louis and had spoken out strongly in support of the Church's pro-life position and against all forms of capital punishment. After John Paul left, Carnahan acceded to his wish, although the governor knew this decision would be controversial.

Limited to two terms by Missouri law, Carnahan announced that he would challenge Senator John Ashcroft in 2000. Both men had been two-term governors and had held numerous statewide offices. It was a bitterly fought contest between two men who loathed each other. The outcome remained unknown in the final weeks. On the way to a campaign event with his son Randy and a top aide, Chris Sifford, Carnahan's twin-engine Cessna crashed near St. Louis, killing all aboard. Carnahan posthumously won the election and his widow was selected to serve in his stead for two years until a special election could be held.

Supporters of Mel Carnahan often wore gold lapel pins shaped like straight arrows, a symbol that fit the man. As governor, his greatest concern was the welfare of Missouri's children, and his proudest achievement was the passage of the Outstanding Schools Act. Though lacking charisma, this quiet, confident, and determined man applied his innate common sense and goodwill toward solving his state's problems. In a state where conservative ideology dominated the rural areas and more liberal thinking resided in the cities, Carnahan crafted a middle ground. Although he tasted political defeat more than once, he always came back for another try, reflecting his heartfelt belief that he could be a leader for progressive change in Missouri.

• Carnahan's papers are maintained at the Missouri State Archives, Jefferson City. Jean Carnahan provides valuable biographical information in the last chapter of her *If Walls Could Talk: The Story of Missouri's First Families* (1998) and in *Don't let the Fire Go Out!* (2004). Carnahan's governorship is surveyed in Liz Sharp, Rob Crouse, and Robyn Burnett, *Missouri: Meeting the Challenge of a New Millennium: The Carnahan Administration, 1993–2000* (2001). An obituary is in the *New York Times*, 18 Oct. 2000.

EDWARD A. GOEDEKEN

CARNERA, Primo (26 Oct. 1906–29 June 1967), world heavyweight boxing champion, was born in Sequals, a town in northern Italy known for its mosaic industry, the son of Sante Carnera, who worked in that industry, and Giovanna Mazziol Carnera. Primo Carnera's native tongue was the Friulian dialect of northern Italy. His formal education having ended in the third grade, he had limited ability in reading and writing. In his early teens he left home to work for an uncle who lived in Le Mans, France, and earned his living there by performing menial tasks in the building trade. Tall—almost six feet seven inches—and powerfully built, he was working for a traveling circus by the time he was twenty-one years old; he was billed as "Juan the Unbeatable Spaniard," and daily met the challenges of all comers in boxing, wrestling, and weight-lifting.

In March 1928 Carnera was noticed by Paul Journée, a former French heavyweight champion, who persuaded him to leave the circus and begin serious training as a boxer. Three months later, Carnera was presented to Léon Sée, a journalist and manager of boxers, under whose direction he would rise to fame. Sée, who had experienced a brief, disappointing career as a boxer, decided to build up the confidence of his pupil by matching him against opponents who were paid to lose. In a book that he later wrote (*Le Mystère Carnera*), Sée disclosed that the outcomes of most of Carnera's fights, through 1931, were arranged, a claim that he never retracted, but the details of which are open to debate.

Carnera's great size and apparent success in the ring quickly attracted attention. Fighting mostly in Paris, he won fourteen of fifteen fights within a year, his only loss coming on a foul. He was then matched against Young Stribling, a famous American heavyweight, the two to fight first in London and then in Paris. According to Sée, an arrangement was made so that Stribling would foul Carnera and lose the first fight, and Carnera would lose the second fight in a similar manner. For the first time, Carnera was made aware that his fights were not honestly contested, but he proved to be a good actor and convincingly fouled Stribling to lose the return fight.

Early in 1930 Carnera arrived in the United States. Although the details are uncertain, it is clear that his management was soon taken over by two New York City mobsters who also managed boxers, Bill Duffy and Owen Madden, but Sée was permitted to remain on the scene as Carnera's friend and confidant. Carnera's American debut was in Madison Square Garden—a one-round knockout of Clayton (Big Boy) Peterson—and sportswriters strongly hinted that the fight had been fixed. This was followed by a barnstorming tour of the states and a long series of pre-arranged knockout victories. However, according to

Sée's book, the fight with Carnera's most formidable opponent, heavyweight contender George Godfrey, was honestly fought, Carnera winning on a foul; and there were two genuine fights near the end of 1930 with heavyweight contenders, a loss to Jim Maloney and a win over Paolino Uzcudun. Thereafter nearly all of Carnera's fights are thought to have been "sincère," to use Sée's term.

In 1931, Carnera defeated another contender, King Levinsky, but lost a great fifteen-round fight to future heavyweight champion Jack Sharkey in Brooklyn, New York, in which Carnera was knocked down twice but displayed great bravery and considerable skill. In 1932, Carnera won twenty-four of twenty-six fights, and his first fight in 1933 was a knockout victory over contender Ernie Schaaf. Schaaf died five days later, but an autopsy revealed that he had entered the ring with a blood clot on his brain, suffered in a previous fight.

Carnera was distraught over Schaaf's death, but he had become the leading contender for the heavyweight title, which Sharkey now held. On 29 June 1933, the two met for the title in Long Island City, New York, and Carnera dominated the fight, winning by a knockout in the sixth round after landing a terrific right uppercut to the jaw. This was followed by two successful defenses of the title, in which he defeated Paolino Uzcudun in Rome and Tommy Loughran in Miami, both by fifteen-round decisions.

Carnera is probably the most denigrated fighter in history. American sportswriters were hostile to him almost from the first because so many of his early fights were faked, his American managers were mobsters, and he usually enjoyed an advantage of six inches or more in height and forty to eighty pounds in weight over his opponents. He was commonly referred to as a "freak," and this abuse persisted long after Carnera's ring career had ended, as seen in an article by Arthur Daley that appeared in the *New York Times* the day after his death. Yet Carnera outside the ring was naive, unassuming, and even gentle. His managers took advantage of him and generally gave him only enough money to keep him well fed, clothed, and entertained, but somehow he sent home enough money to build his family a fine villa. As a boxer, Carnera seldom punched to the limit of his size and strength, but he had an effective left jab and moved with surprising speed and nimbleness despite his giant frame.

On 14 June 1934 Carnera lost his heavyweight title to Max Baer and received a terrific beating in the process. He was knocked down in the first round and suffered torn tendons in his right ankle. He arose and fought on despite the pain and loss of mobility, but Baer knocked him down twelve times and the referee finally stopped the fight in the eleventh round. To add to the cruelty of the loss, Baer clowned and mimicked his opponent throughout.

Although he had a few more good victories, and even attempted a comeback after World War II, Carnera's career was nearly over. His most notable fight after losing his heavyweight title was his knockout by Joe Louis on 25 June 1935. He returned to Italy and married Giuseppina Kovacic, a Yugoslav, in March 1939. From 1940 to 1942 he was an actor in Italian films and was privately tutored by his wife. The remaining war years were spent living quietly in Sequals.

After a failed boxing comeback in 1945 and 1946, Carnera became a professional wrestler. In July 1946 he arrived in the United States and soon was touring the country, making good money in a sport that was mostly acting and acrobatics and which no one took seriously. His wife managed him shrewdly and he received an immigrant's visa to the United States, finally becoming an American citizen in 1953 along with his wife and two children. The family resided in Hollywood, California.

Carnera continued to wrestle until the late 1950s. He had appeared in a successful American film, *The Prizefighter and the Lady*, with Myrna Loy and Baer in 1933, and he resumed his acting career in 1949. Among other movies, he appeared in *Mighty Joe Young*, *On the Waterfront*, *Prince Valiant*, and *Casanova's Big Night*. In 1956 he was the inspiration for the character of the exploited heavyweight Toro Moreno in Budd Schulberg's *The Harder They Fall*, best known for being Humphrey Bogart's last film.

In his later years Carnera, always fond of drink, turned to alcohol more heavily than before. In 1967 he collapsed and had to be hospitalized; suffering from diabetes and liver cirrhosis, he returned to Sequals, where he died.

Carnera's boxing career was undoubtedly the most scandalous in the history of boxing. Although a dutiful son and a loving husband and father, he was a naive and uneducated Italian peasant who was exploited and vilified unmercifully by the press, largely because of his formidable appearance. Yet he was a successful boxer, wrestler, and actor.

• By far the best reference on Carnera and his career is Frederic Mullally, *Primo: The Story of "Man Mountain" Carnera, World Heavyweight Champion* (1991). His major fights are described in *Ring* magazine and the *New York Times*. A short biography by John D. McCallum is in *The Encyclopedia of World Boxing Champions since 1882* (1975). The veracity of Léon Sée's *Le Mystère Carnera* (1934) is doubtful. Carnera's obituary is in the *New York Times*, 30 June 1967, and an article on him by Arthur Daley titled "A Gigantic Hoax" appeared in the same issue.

LUCKETT V. DAVIS

CASEY, Robert (9 Jan. 1932–30 May 2000), attorney and governor, was born in Jackson Heights, Queens, New York, the son of Alphonsus L. Casey, attorney, and Marie Cummings Casey. Shortly after his birth, his family returned to their native town of Scranton, Pennsylvania, where his father practiced law, often representing working men against powerful moneyed interests; Casey later attributed his own political philosophy to his father's influence. After graduating from nearby Scranton Prep, he entered the

College of Holy Cross on a basketball scholarship and graduated with an A.B. degree in 1953. Later that year he married Ellen Theresa Harding. The couple had eight children.

After completing law school at George Washington University in Washington, D.C., in 1956, Casey returned to Scranton and opened his own law practice. In 1962 he ran as a Democrat for an open seat in the state senate and was elected. Frustrated with his party's minority status, Casey entered the Democratic gubernatorial primary in 1966, only to be narrowly edged out by millionaire businessman Milton Shapp. Undaunted, Casey was elected as a delegate to the state constitutional convention in 1967 and in the following year successfully ran for the position of state auditor. In his new position, he eliminated the practice of forced political contributions from state employees and also kept a close eye on expenditures within the 501 state school districts. After losing another bid for the Democratic nomination for governor in 1970 to Shapp (in part because he angered Philadelphia Mayor James Tate, a major player in Democratic party circles), Casey was reelected as state auditor in 1972 despite a general Republican landslide.

Casey left office in 1976 and made yet another attempt at the governor's office in 1978, but he fell victim to a campaign "dirty trick" when an unknown businessman with the same name as his entered the Democratic primary for lieutenant governor. The "impostor" Casey won the primary but lost the geneeral election. Following the campaign, Casey spent several years working for the Philadelphia law firm of Dilworth, Paxson, Kalish & Kauffman. In 1986, with the prospect of an open seat in the governor's race, Casey decided on one last try for office. With the help of established political veterans like Pat Caddell and two then-unknowns (James Carville and Paul Begala), Casey won a rough primary battle against Philadelphia district attorney Ed Rendell. In the no-holds-barred general election, Casey overcame the financial backing and name recognition of his Republican opponent, William Scranton, III (a son of a former governor), with a well-run campaign that included a controversial "guru" television advertisement that reminded voters of Scranton's years of involvement with transcendental meditation. Casey won an upset victory.

Casey endured a rough start to his administration. His attempt to reform state property taxes met with a crushing defeat at the polls; he also had to undergo quadruple bypass surgery following a heart attack. Nevertheless, his first term held some solid accomplishments: a recycling law that made Pennsylvania the largest state in the nation to require trash recycling; the creation of CHIP (Children's Health Insurance Program), a program that expanded health care coverage for children of working families unqualified for welfare but unable to afford health insurance; Pennvest, another program that made grants and loans available to rural areas to upgrade water and sewer facilities; and automobile insurance reforms.

Perhaps his most controversial act was the 1989 signing into law of the Pennsylvania Abortion Control Act, which required a 24-hour waiting period for abortion and which successfully survived a court challenge from Planned Parenthood.

Despite predictions that his stance on restricting abortion would hurt him politically, Casey breezed to reelection in 1990, carrying 66 of the state's 67 counties over his Republican opponent Barbara Hafer, who had derided Casey as a "red-neck Irishman from Scranton." Casey's second term was marked by efforts to stave off the effects of a nationwide recession in Pennsylvania, which forced him to implement a $3 billion tax increase in order to balance the state budget. Casey drew heavy criticism for his actions and suffered another defeat in 1993 when his plan to introduce major health care reforms (which paralleled similar efforts by President Bill Clinton on the national level) failed. By that time, however, Casey had other concerns. Diagnosed in 1991 with a rare hereditary disease called familial amyloidosis, Casey suffered declining health until a combined heart-liver transplant operation in June 1993 led to an eventual full recovery.

Casey's antiabortion stance often placed him at odds with the leadership of his own party, most notably at the 1992 Democratic National Convention when he was denied the opportunity to address the assembly. Casey's dogged insistence that the Democratic party had lost its way on the issue led to further problems in 1994, when he refused to campaign on behalf of Mark Singel, his lieutenant governor and the Democratic gubernatorial nominee, or Harris Wofford, who had been appointed to the U.S. Senate by Casey and who was then seeking reelection; both men eventually suffered narrow defeats.

On leaving office in 1995, Casey considered running for president but withdrew from the race when it became apparent that his health might be an issue. He resumed his legal practice and became a spokesperson for organ donations. He founded the Campaign for the American Family, Inc., a lobbying organization, and the Fund for the American Family, Inc., a foundation. He died in Scranton after a brief illness.

Despite suffering numerous political and physical setbacks, Casey held a firm belief in his own vision and made a solid contribution to the welfare of his state. Once derided as the "three-time loss from Holy Cross," he stunned observers with a political comeback late in life, and his courage in the face of illness earned him the respect even of his political foes.

• Casey's papers are at the Pennsylvania State Archives in Harrisburg, Pennsylvania. The best source of information on his life and career is his candid autobiography, *Fighting for Life* (1996). Obituaries are in the *New York Times* and the *Pittsburgh Post-Gazette*, both 31 May 2000.

EDWARD L. LACH, JR.

CASHIN, Bonnie (28 Sept. 1908?–3 Feb. 2000), fashion designer, was born in Oakland, California, the daughter of Karl Cashin, a photographer and inventor, and Eunice Cashin, owner of a dress shop. Supposedly named after her grandmother's horse (*Tribune*, 23 Apr. 1970), Cashin said she was born in 1915, one year before her brother Richard. Some published statements support her claim; however, other sources suggest probably 1908. For example, an article on her costume work at the Grenada Theater and Metropolitan in Los Angeles, published in the Oakland *Tribune*, 12 Sept. 1926, described Cashin as the "flapper school girl of 17 last year." This suggests she was born in 1908 or 1909. The same article noted that Cashin graduated from Hollywood High "a year ago," confirmed by yearbooks in the Hollywood High archives.

Much like Coco Chanel, Bonnie Cashin was a little beauty and the best model for her own work. Of French and Armenian descent, she was described as "dainty and winsome, with a fair skin, violet-grey eyes and a heavy mass of black bobbed hair. She cannot be much more than five feet tall. . . ." (*Tribune*, 12 Sept. 1926). According to most accounts, before she graduated from high school she showed her sketches to the director of a ballet company in Los Angeles and was hired to make the costumes for the company's performances. Soon after her graduation, she joined the company full time as its designer. In 1934 the ballet company moved to New York's Roxy Theater, where she made about seventy-two costumes a week for all their performances. She considered the Roxy her "formal schooling in design" and credited the experience with giving her the ability to create attractive garments for moving figures. There too she started designing sportswear for Adler & Adler.

When the United States entered the Second World War, Cashin was appointed to a committee designing uniforms for women in the armed services. But, frustrated with the fabric and trim restrictions imposed on civilian use, she soon returned to the freedom of costume design and moved to Hollywood. After she moved back to California, she married Robert Sterner, an illustrator who worked for Disney; their marriage was brief and ended in divorce. They had no children.

Cashin joined Twentieth Century–Fox in 1943 and created costumes for more than 30 major films, the best known of which were *Laura* (1944) and *Anna and the King of Siam* (1946). Her work on the latter film is notable for its historical authenticity.

In 1949 Cashin returned to New York, where she concentrated on casual, layered apparel that soon caught the attention of American women. In 1952 she started her own business, Bonnie Cashin Designs, and received her first Coty Award. In 1968 she won her second Coty Award and in 1972 she was inducted into the Coty American Fashion Critics Hall of Fame.

Cashin was one of the few women in the postwar years to make an important contribution to American fashion when Parisian designers dominated the runways. She believed in clean lines and uncomplicated styles. In 1967, she was quoted as saying, "Good clothing should be comfortable, mobile and without undue obsolescence" (*Tribune*, 5 Oct. 1967). Traveling in Japan, she admired the practice of layering garments so that they could be discarded according to temperature and climate. She was noted for mixing unusual fabrics; she liked to work with canvas, jersey, leather, poplin, suede and tweed. She was credited with innovations such as the "pocketbook" pocket (a pocket with a clasp and the look of a pocketbook), the "dog leash" skirt, and canvas raincoats, hooded jersey dresses, industrial zippers, grommet closures, jumpsuits, and lightweight capes and ponchos.

For two decades Cashin designed canvas, jersey, leather, and tweed clothing for Philip Sills. She also created rainwear for Modelia, gloves for Crescendoe-Superb, and handbags for Coach Leatherware. In the 1970s she designed knitwear that was knitted to shape instead of cut and sewn, and she invented the roomy turtleneck that did not need a zipper to fit over the head. In 1972 Cashin established The Knittery, a company specializing in limited-edition hand knits, and, around 1980, the Innovative Design Fund, a foundation for nurturing adventurous designers. In the 1960s, Bonnie met Curtis Kellar, husband of Amy Vanderbilt and head counsel for Mobil Oil. The two instantly became friends, and after his wife's death Kellar and Cashin were constant companions, though they did not marry.

As a designer, Cashin retained her independence, probably her most important accomplishment. She created designs for the sake of her art, then found someone to make and market them for her. She was truly one of the great designers of the twentieth century. Cashin died in Manhattan after undergoing open-heart surgery. In 2001 she was inducted into the Fashion Hall of Fame.

• For the basics on Bonnie Cashin, see Mary Picken, *The Fashion Dictionary* (rev. and enl. ed., 1973). See also, thanks to Ms. Kathleen Leles DiGiovanni, librarian at the Oakland History Room, insightful articles from the Oakland *Tribune*, including "Girl Designs Dresses for S.F. Theater," 12 Sept. 1926; "Bright Bonnie," 5 Oct. 1967; and "Golden Stitches," 23 Apr. 1970. Other sources include the 1925 yearbook in the Hollywood High School library, Curtis Kellar, Stephanie Day Iverson, whose biography of Cashin was scheduled for publication in fall 2002, and the *New York Times* obituary on Cashin, 5 Feb. 2000.

SAMANTHA PETERSON

CHAFEE, John H. (22 Oct. 1922–24 Oct. 1999), governor, secretary of the navy, and U.S. senator, was born John Hubbard Chafee in Providence, Rhode Island, the son of John Sharpe Chafee, a tool manufacturer, and Janet Hunter Chafee. After completing his studies at the Deerfield Academy in Deerfield, Massachusetts, Chafee enrolled at Yale University in 1940. When the United States entered World War II, Chafee, who was a sophomore, left Yale to enlist in the U.S. Marine Corps as a private. In 1942, on his twentieth birthday, he was fighting on Guadalcanal. Commissioned as a second lieutenant, Chafee later served with the Sixth Marine Division in the April 1945 battle of Okinawa.

After the war ended, Chafee returned to Yale and in 1947 received his B.A. degree. He then enrolled in Harvard University's law school, completing his course work for a law degree in 1950 and heading home to Providence to set up a law practice. On 4 November 1950 he married Virginia Coates; they had six children. In March 1951, however, Chafee was recalled to the marines to fight in Korea. Now a captain, he commanded a rifle company with the First Marine Division. Released from active status in June 1953, Chafee reestablished his law practice in Providence and soon entered the local political arena. In 1956 he won election to the Rhode Island House of Representatives and was returned in 1958 and 1960.

In 1962 Chafee set his sights on higher office and gained the nomination as the GOP standard bearer for governor. His opponent, John A. Notte, Jr., was a first-term Democrat in a state that had become increasingly Democratic, while Chafee represented the old Yankee Republican establishment. Nevertheless, Chafee campaigned vigorously and squeaked out a victory—by only 398 votes out of about 325,000 cast—to become only the third Republican governor in thirty years. During his three terms as governor, Chafee promoted a liberal agenda and signed antidiscrimination legislation in housing and employment and a health care plan for the state's elderly (both of which preceded similar federal legislation). He also supported the construction of Interstate 95, acquisition of land for state woodlands and waterfront parks, and the expansion of the state vocational training program. Reelected in 1964 and 1966 by large margins, Chafee met defeat in 1968, primarily because of his call for a state personal income tax. In 1968, he had also become involved in national Republican politics when at the Republican convention he openly criticized the Republican civil rights plank and then—to the chagrin of Richard Nixon—openly supported presidential candidates George Romney and Nelson A. Rockefeller and just as openly opposed Spiro T. Agnew as Nixon's running mate. The November 1968 defeat was compounded by the loss earlier in the year of his fourteen-year-old daughter, who died from a horseback-riding accident.

Despite Nixon's personal feelings, Chafee's eastern liberal credentials made him an attractive candidate to balance the conservatives in the new Nixon cabinet. He was appointed secretary of the navy and served during most of Nixon's first term, from January 1969 until April 1972. As navy secretary Chafee focused on maintaining the fighting capabilities of the navy and marine corps during a time of increased demand for military downsizing as the United States withdrew its forces from the Vietnam War. He is perhaps best remembered for his decision in May 1969 to block the court martial of the commander of the *Pueblo*, which had been captured by the North Koreans in 1968.

Chafee resigned in 1972 to run for the U.S. Senate against Claiborne Pell but lost despite Nixon's landslide that fall. He returned to private law practice and geared up for another run in 1976. This time he was successful and became Rhode Island's first Republican senator in forty-six years. He was reelected in 1982, 1988, and 1994, when he garnered 65 percent of the vote. Chafee's Senate voting record falls in the ideological center—a little more liberal on cultural and social issues and a little more conservative on foreign and defense policy. Chafee became known for his bipartisanship and constantly worked to broker agreements with Democratic colleagues. As the Senate became more bitterly partisan in the Clinton years, Chafee's influence waned, and he often became a lone voice in the middle crying out for reasoned discussion and compromise on contentious issues. During the Reagan years, for example, he chaired the Senate Republican Conference from 1985 to 1990, but as his party shifted rightward he quietly resisted the trend and was dumped in favor of the more conservative Thad Cochran of Mississippi.

Despite being out of his party's mainstream for the final decade of his career, Chafee remained very much a legislative force in the Senate. He was a staunch and tireless supporter for environmental legislation. From 1980 onward he had a guiding hand in the passage of numerous environmental laws, including: the Superfund Toxic Waste Cleanup Program (1980), the Clean Air Act (1986), the Oil Spill Prevention and Response Act (1990), and the Safe Drinking Water Act (1995). From 1994 he chaired the Senate Environmental and Public Works Committee; he also served on the finance and intelligence committees and the Joint Committee on Taxation. Chafee's liberal leanings were reflected in his sustained efforts to expand Medicaid to include maternal care, child health programs, and community health centers for the uninsured and the disabled. In the early 1990s, he was a leading advocate for national health care insurance, but his efforts to foster a bipartisan compromise with the Clinton White House over a national health plan withered before the partisan warfare that erupted in 1994. In March 1999 Chafee announced that he would not seek a fifth term; he died at Bethesda Naval Hospital in Bethesda, Maryland.

Reared in a family imbued with a sense of political noblesse oblige, Chafee devoted his considerable energies toward fostering a better environment for his fellow citizens by improving their health care and protecting their natural world. In all his endeavors, Chafee sought common ground with his opponents, discovering compromise where it often seemed none existed. His sense of decency, pragmatism, and fair play won him admiration from friend and foe alike and helped him succeed in the Washington political wars where others had failed. His environmental legacy, of which he was justly proud, will long survive his passing.

• Chafee's papers are maintained in the Special Collections Department of the University of Rhode Island Kingston Library. Congress published a memorial volume titled *Memorial Tributes Held in the Senate and House of Representatives of the United States together with Memorial Services in Eulogy of John H. Chafee, Late Senator from Rhode Island* (1999). Chafee's service as navy secretary is recounted by Paul B. Ryan, "John Hubbard Chafee," in Paolo E. Coletta, ed., *American Secretaries of the Navy*, vol. 2 (1980), pp. 981–1002. James Brady details Chafee's military exploits in *The Coldest War: A Memoir of Korea* (1990). An obituary is in the *New York Times*, 26 Oct. 1999.

EDWARD A. GOEDEKEN

CHAMBERLAIN, John (28 Oct. 1903–9 Apr. 1995), journalist, literary critic, and author, was born John Rensselaer Chamberlain in New Haven, Connecticut, the only son of Robert Chamberlain, a furniture store owner, and Emily Davis Chamberlain. He was educated in New Haven's public schools, and his family spent summers at Morris Cove, near New Haven's harbor, where he learned to sail. When Chamberlain reached the seventh grade, his father decided to send him to a new private academy, the Loomis Institute, located in Windsor, Connecticut. At Loomis, Chamberlain played football and served as editor in chief of the *Loomis Log* and the school's yearbook. Graduating from the academy at age sixteen, Chamberlain—whose father believed him too young to go on to college—traveled west with a school friend, Collin Stevens, and eventually found work in a Pomona, California, orange grove. Later Chamberlain earned $30 a week doing piecework at a Claremont, California, orange-packing house.

Returning home to Connecticut in the summer of 1921, Chamberlain wanted to attend Princeton University. A post–World War I depression, however, necessitated his attendance at nearby Yale University, where he took a number of mathematics classes to achieve his ambition of becoming a civil engineer. "I soon found I was over my head," Chamberlain recalled in his memoir, and he switched his studies to history and economics on the advice of his faculty adviser, Richard Newhall. Although influenced by H. L. Mencken's iconoclastic periodical the *American Mercury* and the works of such Midwestern literary figures as Theodore Dreiser and Carl Sandburg, Chamberlain later said that during his college days innocence was "a better word than apathy to describe our political state" (Chamberlain, *A Life with the Printed Word*, p. 12). Hoping to follow in his father's footsteps (Robert Chamberlain had been art editor for the *Yale Record*, the university's humor magazine), John Chamberlain submitted several drawings, complete with verses and jokes, to the *Yale Record*. Although the magazine's editors rejected his drawings, his prose contributions were accepted. Chamberlain made the *Record*'s board of editors by the end of his freshman year and served as chairman during his junior year. During his time at the university, he also contributed to the *Yale Literary Magazine*.

After graduating from Yale in 1925 with a bachelor of philosophy degree, Chamberlain sought but failed to find a job as a reporter on a New York newspaper. He instead became a copywriter with the Thomas F.

Logan Company, a New York advertising firm. With the help of the *New York Sun* columnist Sir Frederick Cunliffe-Owen, who wrote him a letter of introduction to the *New York Times* acting managing editor Freddie Birchall, Chamberlain joined the *Times* as a cub reporter on 2 January 1926. During his early years on the newspaper, he wrote feature articles, worked part-time for the *Times* Washington, D.C., bureau, and did some book reviews. On 22 April 1926 Chamberlain married Margaret Sterling; they would have two children. Two years later Chamberlain became assistant editor of the *New York Times Book Review*. Margaret Chamberlain died in 1955. On 29 June 1956 Chamberlain married Ernestine Stodelle; they had one child.

In 1930 the Liveright, Inc., publishing firm gave Chamberlain, a contributor to such publications as the *New Republic* and *Common Sense*, a $400 advance for a biography on the British critic and philosopher George Henry Lewes. Obtaining a leave of absence from the *Times*, Chamberlain traveled to England to do research for his book. While in England, Chamberlain decided that, instead of a book on Lewes, he should work on a volume "clarifying for myself the strange fact that a depression could happen in America" (Chamberlain, *A Life with the Printed Word*, p. 40). In 1932 Liveright published Chamberlain's *Farewell to Reform: The Rise, Life, and Decay of the Progressive Mind in America*. The book explored the development of progressive thought, literature, and politics in America through examinations of such figures as Hamlin Garland, Upton Sinclair, Thorstein Veblen, Charles Beard, Theodore Roosevelt, and Woodrow Wilson. Chamberlain, who in the 1932 presidential election supported the Socialist Party candidate Norman Thomas, called the book a "radical critique of Progressive history" (Chamberlain, *A Life with the Printed Word*, p. 52).

After a short stint with the *Saturday Review of Literature*, Chamberlain in 1933 returned to the *New York Times* as the newspaper's first daily book review columnist, a position he held until 1936. His friend and fellow critic Clifton Fadiman said of Chamberlain's work that it was "analytic, more like monthly periodical journalism than like the hurried product of the daily grind" (*Current Biography*, 1940, p. 154). In February 1936 Chamberlain accepted an invitation from Archibald MacLeish to join the staff at Henry Luce's business magazine *Fortune*. Chamberlain became a "workhorse" for the periodical, sometimes producing three articles per issue. In reporting on such companies as Electric Autolite, Westinghouse Electric, and Beechnut, Chamberlain soon discovered that "none of the fashionable liberal stereotypes covered the world of business." His reading of three books—Isabel Paterson's *The God of the Machine* (1943), Rose Wilder Lane's *The Discovery of Freedom* (1943), and Ayn Rand's *The Fountainhead* (1943)— also influenced his move to libertarian and conservative political beliefs.

Chamberlain left *Fortune* in late summer 1941 to become an associate professor at the Columbia University School of Journalism. During World War II he offered his expertise on charts and graphs on a part-time basis to William "Wild Bill" Donovan's Office of Strategic Services. Following the war, Chamberlain worked as New York editor and editorial writer for *Life* and helped organize and edit the *Freeman*, a magazine whose original intention, according to Chamberlain, was to "fight the Leftish intellectual weeklies—the *New Republic* and the *Nation* on their own ground." (Chamberlain, *A Life with the Printed Word*, p. 145). Chamberlain's career in journalism also included work as an editor for *Barron's Financial Weekly*, articles and book reviews for the *Wall Street Journal*, lead book reviews for the *National Review*, and a regular column distributed nationwide by King Features Syndicate from 1962 to 1985. Along with *Farewell to Reform*, his books include *John Dos Passos: A Biographical and Critical Essay* (1939), *The American Stakes* (1940), *The Roots of Capitalism* (1959), and *The Enterprising Americans: A Business History of the United States* (1963). He also wrote the introduction to William F. Buckley's *God and Man at Yale: The Superstitions of "Academic Freedom"* (1951). Chamberlain, who lived in Cheshire, Connecticut, died at the Yale–New Haven Hospital.

• Chamberlain explored his multifaceted journalism career in his memoir, *A Life with the Printed Word* (1982). His book reviews for the *Freeman* are collected in *The Turnabout Years: America's Cultural Life, 1900–1950* (1991). A profile of Chamberlain is in *Current Biography* (1940), and the reporter's career is featured in a tribute by William F. Buckley, "John Chamberlain, RIP," *National Review*, 1 May 1995, p. 24. Obituaries are in the *Washington Post*, 12 Apr. 1995, and the *New York Times*, 13 Apr. 1995.

RAY E. BOOMHOWER

CHARLES, Ray (23 Sept. 1930–10 June 2004), pop and jazz singer, pianist, and composer, was born Ray Charles Robinson in Albany, Georgia, the son of Bailey Robinson, a laborer, and Aretha Williams. Williams, a teenage orphan, lived in Greenville, Florida, with Robinson's mother and his wife, Mary Jane Robinson. The Robinson family had informally adopted her, and she became known as Aretha Robinson. Scandalously, Aretha became pregnant by Bailey Robinson, and she briefly left Greenville late in the summer of 1930 to be with relatives in Albany for the baby's birth. Mother and child then returned to Greenville, and Aretha and Mary Jane shared Ray Charles's upbringing. He was deeply devoted to his mother and later recalled her perseverance, self-sufficiency, and pride as guiding lights in his life. His father abandoned the family and took another wife elsewhere.

An early involvement in African-American gospel music at the New Shiloh Missionary Baptist Church was central to the musical development of R. C. Robinson, as he was known in childhood and early in his professional career. He listened to the *Grand Ole Opry*

and other country music shows on the radio and frequented the Red Wing Café, a local general store that had both a jukebox with blues recordings and a piano. The café's owner, Wylie Pitman, tutored Robinson in the boogie-woogie piano style.

At five Robinson began experiencing symptoms of a disease that was almost certainly glaucoma, and over the course of two years he went blind. In 1937 his mother secured financial support from the state to enroll him in the Colored Department of the Florida School for the Deaf and Blind in St. Augustine. Soon thereafter he suffered unremitting pain in his right eye, and a doctor was obliged to remove it. During his eight years in school Robinson learned to read braille, and he received instruction in classical piano and clarinet. He listened extensively to recordings by the leading jazz artists of the day and taught himself to play alto saxophone while continuing to develop his interests in blues and country music. In his early teens Charles spent some portions of the summers with family friends in Tallahassee, and there he became involved in professional performances. Upon returning to school, he played in St. Augustine. Around this time he taught himself to arrange and compose by dictating parts to fellow musicians.

Aretha Robinson died in mid-1945, and Charles left school in the fall of that year to attempt a career as a musician. Initially he lived with family friends in Jacksonville, contributing to their household with his small income as a pianist. He spent several months as a pianist, singer, and arranger for a big band in Orlando in 1947 and also played in small groups there. While based in Tampa later in 1947, Charles toured regionally, first as the pianist in a rhythm and blues group and then as both the pianist and an occasional singer in an otherwise white country and western band, the Florida Playboys. This activity foreshadowed his revolutionary foray into country and western music in the early 1960s. Charles remained in Tampa into 1948, playing in other rhythm and blues combos. Sometime during this period he was made aware of his uncomfortable facial appearance on stage, one eye missing and the other often encrusted, and he permanently adopted his trademark dark wraparound sunglasses.

In March 1948 Charles traveled to Seattle, deliberately leaving Florida as far behind as possible. In Seattle he formed a cooperative group, the McSon Trio—"Mc" taken from the trio's bass player Gosady McGee and "Son" from Robinson. During his years in Florida, Charles had experienced considerable success copying the styles of Nat Cole's trio and the singer and pianist Charles Brown, and the McSon Trio carried on in this style.

The McSon Trio made its first recordings in Seattle for the Down Beat label in February 1949. In the list of personnel on the label, to avoid confusion with the famous boxer Sugar Ray Robinson, the company's owner Jack Lauderdale dropped Robinson's surname and made him Ray Charles. Lauderdale also mangled the group's name, making it Maxin. That year the

McSon or Maxin Trio found modest regional success, touring and broadcasting in the Northwest. Around this time, in the course of one of his countless unmarried relationships, Charles fathered his first child, with Louise Mitchell. Also while in Seattle he became a heroin addict.

To avoid a suit brought by *Down Beat* magazine, the Down Beat label was renamed Swing Beat Records in October 1949 and Swing Time Records in the spring of 1950. Charles traveled to Los Angeles, where the company was based, to record again, and in 1950 he moved there. He made numerous further recordings and at Lauderdale's instigation toured the Southwest and the South in 1950 and 1951 as the intermission soloist for the blues singer and electric guitarist Lowell Fulson. Charles became Fulson's pianist and the group's music director, arranging songs and leading rehearsals. In April 1951 Charles signed with the Billy Shaw Agency in New York, as did Fulson. Charles married Eileen Williams on 31 July 1951. They had one child and divorced in 1952.

Charles recorded "Baby Let Me Hold Your Hand" in late November 1950, and it became a hit in 1951. This disc and others attracted the attention of Ahmet Ertegun, co-owner, with Herb Abramson, of the emerging record company Atlantic. They purchased Charles's contract from Swing Time in 1952. Charles then toured the Northeast with Fulson, and he went across the Southwest and the South again as the pianist and arranger for the rhythm and blues trumpeter Joe Morris. In 1953 Charles mainly toured as a freelance soloist based in Houston and New Orleans.

Early in 1954, frustrated with the mediocrity of his ad hoc accompanists, Charles insisted on receiving support for his own band, which he formed in Texas. The group comprised two trumpets, tenor and baritone saxophones, piano, bass, and drums, with Charles adding a third line to the reed section by playing alto sax when not on piano or singing. The septet first appeared as accompanists to the rhythm and blues singer Ruth Brown, but soon thereafter it went out on its own. Charles remained a bandleader for fifty years.

In November 1954 the septet recorded Charles's controversial, secularized, sexually oriented adaptation of a gospel song as "I Got a Woman," with words by his trumpeter Renald Richard. Notable among his band members at this time were Don Wilkerson on tenor saxophone and David "Fathead" Newman on baritone sax. "I Got a Woman" reached number two on the rhythm and blues charts in mid-March 1955, and it heralded a new genre, soul music. Subsequent hit recordings, mainly his own compositions, included "A Fool for You," "This Little Girl of Mine" (based on the well-known gospel song "This Little Light of Mine"), and "Hard Times" in April 1955; and "Drown in My Own Tears" (composed by Henry Glover) and "Hallelujah I Love Her So" in November 1955. These discs continued his manner of modifying rhythm and blues, most notably through the use of characteristic gospel chord progressions and through

Charles's raw voice, delivering spoken interjections and complicated twisting melodic lines after the manner of a preacher. In 1956 "Drown in My Own Tears" reached number one on the rhythm and blues charts. During this period Charles came to be known as "Brother Ray," a nickname symbolizing the ways his music evoked the church.

In Dallas on 5 April 1955 Charles married Della Beatrice Howard. They had three children. For many years he proclaimed his was a happy family life and marriage, but he was rarely at home. He toured incessantly and spent most of his time in the office when he was not on the road. He fathered seven more children outside of marriage, and in his autobiography he candidly admitted that he hired sexually compliant women for his female vocal quartet the Cookies or, as they became better known after 1959, the Raelets.

Charles moved his family from Dallas to Los Angeles in 1958. That year the quality of his band improved with the addition of the trumpeter Marcus Belgrave and the saxophonist Hank Crawford. Crawford also became Charles's music director. Leroy Cooper, another notable saxophonist, had spent a period with Charles in 1957, and in 1959 he joined for an extended stay. Phil Guilbeau, a trumpet soloist, joined in 1960. With Newman on tenor saxophone and Charles on piano, this collection of powerful and individualized improvisers made Charles's group into one of the best bands of its era.

Charles's career blossomed, and his repertory broadened in unprecedented ways. He displayed an ability to shatter notions of style by making nearly any nonclassical music into soul music. In 1957 and 1958 Charles recorded two albums, *Soul Brothers* and *Soul Meeting*, as the coleader, with the vibraphonist Milt Jackson, of a jazz group. Charles mainly played piano but appeared on three of these tracks as the group's alto saxophone soloist.

Charles broke through to larger audiences with "What'd I Say?" a 45-rpm disc divided into two parts. Although "What'd I Say?" seems tame from the perspective of modern-day rap music, it was for its time sexually explicit, with a grunting "unnh" and "ooh" interchange between Charles and his Raelets, and the tune was banned on some radio stations. Recorded in February 1959, "What'd I Say?" reached number one on the rhythm and blues charts and number six on the pop charts later that year.

In May 1959 Charles recorded *The Genius of Ray Charles*, an album of American popular ballads sung to orchestral accompaniment, including versions of "Don't Let the Sun Catch You Cryin'," "Am I Blue?" and "Come Rain or Come Shine." Later that month a promoter taped a concert in Atlanta, and the resulting Atlantic album, *Ray Charles in Person*, offers special insights into the magical rapport between Charles and his audiences and a definitive version of "Drown in My Own Tears." In June 1959, at his last session for Atlantic, Charles indicated his coming direction by recording a version of the country music classic "I'm Movin' On," a composition by Hank Snow.

Charles left Atlantic early in 1960, when ABC-Paramount offered him an unmatchable contract that allowed him to retain the permanent rights to his new recordings, which were merely leased to ABC-Paramount, with an exceptionally high percentage of royalty income going to Charles. Their first collaboration, *Ray Charles Hits the Road*, recorded in March 1960, was a collection of tunes associated with place-names. This album included a devastatingly emotional interpretation of "Georgia on My Mind," which became, as a separately released single, the first of his recordings to reach number one on the pop charts and the first to secure a Grammy Award for the year's best pop song.

In June 1961 Charles recorded *Ray Charles and Betty Carter*, an album of duos with the jazz singer Betty Carter, including a playful version of "Baby, It's Cold Outside" that appeared to mixed reviews but later came to be regarded as a classic. At this time Charles fulfilled a long-term desire when he expanded his group from seven or eight pieces, as it had been since 1954, into a sixteen-piece big band. In July 1961 Charles, the Raelets, and his big band made their first visit to Europe, performing in the south of France at the Festival Mondial de Jazz de Antibes–Juan-les-Pins. In October 1961 they held a triumphant five-day engagement in Paris. For the remainder of his life, Charles toured worldwide on a regular basis, making numerous returns to Europe, visiting the Far East from 1964 onward, and performing in South America and Australia from the 1970s.

In October 1961 Charles reached number one on the pop charts for the second time with "Hit the Road, Jack," a composition by Percy Mayfield that featured a comical interplay between the Raelet Margie Hendricks, kicking "Jack" out of her life, and Charles, begging to be forgiven. "Unchain My Heart," featuring a catchy Latinesque dance beat, reached number nine on the pop chart in January 1962.

Charles's greatest success in the studio came in 1962, when he went against the advice of ABC-Paramount and ventured into a realm normally closed to African Americans. *Modern Sounds in Country and Western Music* topped the pop album charts for more than three months that year, and in a reversal of the normal practice of the day, abridged 45-rpm singles were then extracted from the album, such was the demand for the music. "I Can't Stop Loving You" rose to number one in June 1962, and "You Don't Know Me" reached number two in September. "Born to Lose" was among the album's other memorable tracks. As a consequence of the success of this LP, Charles made another such album, *Modern Sounds in Country and Western Music*, volume two.

Charles was arrested for narcotics possession in Philadelphia in November 1955 and again in 1958 and in Indianapolis in November 1961, but he managed to wiggle out of the charges each time. By mid-1963, when Charles released a new country-oriented single that reached number four on the pop chart, its title, "Busted," had taken on an additional and ironic autobiographical meaning. Late in 1964 another drug arrest in Boston was incontestable. Charles ceased performing in public, and in July 1965 he took a forced retirement from music to enter St. Francis Hospital in Lynwood, California, to cure his addiction. Pleading guilty to a charge of possession of drugs, he received a suspended sentence and probation.

In 1965 Charles was a multimillionaire, the head of Ray Charles Enterprises and RPM International (a clever acronym, in the context of 45-rpm singles, for Recordings, Publishing, and Management). The staff and holdings of his corporations included Charles; the Raelets; a big band; the RPM recording studio; Tangerine Records; the publishing companies Tangerine Music and Racer Music; Racer Management; a transportation department comprising cars, buses, and airplanes with full-time drivers and pilots; and associated managers, lawyers, accountants, and subsidiary workers. But success did not soften Charles. If anything, he became a harder man than ever before, miserly, vindictive, unfeeling, and self-absorbed, at times to the point of abusive and warped behavior. He maintained a glossy public image and continued to put on fabulously entertaining shows, but he drove many fine musicians from his band. Long-term relationships with several of his unofficial "wives" disintegrated, replaced by a new set of long-term relationships with unofficial "wives," and he lost two paternity suits. Much can be forgiven in light of the experience of growing up blind and black and broke, but for Charles the ultimate result was an innately ugly and exploitive personality that stands in stark contrast to the musical beauty he brought to the world.

In the fall of 1965, after his release from St. Francis Hospital, Charles recorded the lamenting love song "Crying Time," which reached number six on the pop charts early in 1966, and "Let's Go Get Stoned," with its amusing lyric in light of his troubles with drugs. In 1966 Charles resumed performing, and the single "Crying Time" received two Grammy Awards in 1967. That year also brought the release of the film *In the Heat of the Night*. Singing the title song on the soundtrack, Charles provided, in collaboration with his longtime colleague, the composer and arranger Quincy Jones, an unforgettable example of his ability to translate into sound both the tense flavor of race relations in the rural South and the atmosphere of a languid southern summer.

Charles continued to tour at a breakneck pace, nine or ten months of every year, always to packed venues and, through the mid-1970s, to generally enthusiastic reviews. He recorded prolifically but without much success. In 1974 Charles left ABC-Paramount, and Tangerine Records became Crossover Records. This maneuver failed to produce new hits, but in 1976 his rendition of "America the Beautiful," recorded in 1971, reached vast audiences after it was picked up as the music for a pairs skating team for their routine at the Winter Olympics.

In 1977 Charles's wife Della, having finally given up on trial separations, obtained a divorce. Concurrently Charles's public appearances began to suffer, with band members cycling through a revolving door and audiences no longer filling venues to capacity. Despite these problems, Charles maintained a positive presence in other ways. He became involved in film and television as an actor, arranger, composer, and performer, including well-received appearances as the host of an episode of the television show *Saturday Night Live* in 1978 and as Ray in the film *The Blues Brothers* in 1980. He found success performing as a soloist with pop string orchestras rather than his own band. Through the early 1980s he reoriented his recordings toward activities in Nashville, and in 1985 he reached the top of the country music charts with "Seven Spanish Angels" from his album *Friendship*. He sang "America the Beautiful" at the Republican convention in 1984 and at Ronald Reagan's second inauguration in January 1985. Charles also became a prominent spokesman in advertising campaigns, most notably for Diet Pepsi in the early 1990s. Buoyed by renewed popularity, Charles maintained a busy performing schedule for another dozen years. He died of acute liver disease in Beverly Hills, California.

Charles was one of the most important musicians of the twentieth century. In the mid- to late 1950s he was the seminal figure in the emergence of a new genre that later became known as soul music. In the early 1960s he achieved the double feat of bringing an African-American musical conception into country and western music and bringing country and western music into the mainstream of American pop music. More broadly he was a pioneering musical postmodernist. Genre meant little to Charles. Instead, musical process was everything, and he applied his personalized musical vision to whatever material he took up. Like all great singers, he had an inimitable, immediately recognizable voice. Above all, that voice had a searing intensity that somehow captured the specificity of his experiences, conveying the tragic circumstances of his upbringing while celebrating the joyousness and catharsis of his having overcome obstacles through music.

• Charles's appropriately titled autobiography *Brother Ray: Ray Charles' Own Story* (1978; rev. ed. 1992), in collaboration with David Ritz, presents a heavily filtered and self-edited story despite Charles's protestations of raw honesty. Even though Ritz could not crack through Charles's wall of privacy, that in itself revealed something of the essence of Charles's personality, and Ritz through his interviews successfully captured details of many of the central events of Charles's career. Michael Lydon's *Ray Charles: Man and Music* (1998) is one of the best biographies ever written in the realm of pop music and jazz—meticulously researched, entertaining to read, and filled with both new information about Charles's experiences and deep insight into his character. For a concise but penetrating assessment of Charles's musical achievements, see David Marsh, "Ray Charles," in *The New Grove Dictionary of American Music*, ed. Stanley

Sadie and H. Wiley Hitchcock (1986). Joshua Paxton supplies an equally brief but revealing analysis of Charles's piano playing in "The Gospel Style of Ray Charles," *Piano Today* 18 (Spring 1998): 33–35. Some of the complexities of his life and personality are captured in a television documentary from the *American Masters* series, "Ray Charles: The Genius of Soul," directed by Yvonne Smith (1991). Louie Robinson celebrates Charles's success as a corporate head in "Blues Becomes Big Business: Singer Ray Charles Parlays Voice into Multi-Million Dollar, National Enterprise," *Ebony* 18 (Apr. 1963): 34–36, 38–41, and "The Enduring Genius of Ray Charles," *Ebony* 29 (Oct. 1974): 125–28, 130, 132, 134, with a number of magnificent photos of Charles and his entourage in both articles. Obituaries are Richard Cromelin and Randy Lewis, *Los Angeles Times*, 11 June 2004, which includes a list of hit singles and Grammy Awards; and Jon Pareles and Bernard Weinraub, *New York Times*, 11 June 2004.

BARRY KERNFELD

CHERRY, Don (18 Nov. 1936–19 Oct. 1995), jazz cornetist, multi-instrumentalist, and bandleader, was born Donald Eugene Cherry in Oklahoma City, Oklahoma, of mixed African-American and Choctaw Indian heritage, the son of Ulysses Cherry, a bartender, and Daisy Lee McKee. Cherry spent his earliest years in Kenner, Oklahoma, and Oklahoma City. In 1941 the family moved to Los Angeles, where Cherry's father took a job as the bartender at the Plantation Club. Cherry became immersed in music. He listened to the jazz and rhythm and blues musicians who performed at that club and to his grandmother and mother, who played piano, which became his first instrument. In 1950, while in junior high school, he took up trumpet, and during this period he appeared with his sister as a dancer at parties his father gave.

Cherry learned to play a number of different brass instruments at Freemont High School, and he also traveled without permission during the school day to play in the big band at Jefferson High School under the renowned African American music educator Samuel Brown, many of whose students became famous jazz musicians. This act of truancy led to his being sent to Jacob Reece detention school, where he met the drummer Billy Higgins.

In the early 1950s Cherry began working professionally, often as a pianist, including a period in a trio with Higgins on drums and another as a member of the trumpeter Art Farmer's quartet. Around 1955 Cherry married Carlotta Hewitt. They had two children, both of whom became professional musicians.

Around 1956 Cherry formed a bop quartet, the Jazz Messiahs, with the alto saxophonist George Newman, a longtime schoolmate. They traveled to Vancouver, British Columbia, for performances at a local jazz society. The tenor saxophonist James Clay then began working with the group in place of Newman. This version of the Jazz Messiahs played at the Cellar in Vancouver in August 1957. Through Clay both Newman and Cherry began rehearsing with the visionary avant-garde alto saxophonist Ornette Coleman in Los Angeles. Later in 1957 Coleman and

Cherry had their first job together in Vancouver. Coleman secured a recording contract in Los Angeles, and the resulting quintet album, *Something Else! The Music of Ornette Coleman*, has historic value as both Coleman's and Cherry's first recording. But for Cherry and his fellow sideman Higgins this album mainly documented their considerable talents in the then-prevailing bop style.

In the fall of 1958 Coleman, Cherry, and Higgins played for six weeks at the Hillcrest Club in Los Angeles in a quintet led by the pianist Paul Bley, with Charlie Haden on bass. Haden then began rehearsing with Coleman, Cherry, and Higgins, and the saxophonist's first historic quartet was born. By this time Cherry was doubling on trumpet and pocket cornet. The latter is a compact version of the normal cornet, with tightly wound tubing that made it about half as long; Cherry called it a "pocket trumpet."

Three members of the Modern Jazz Quartet, John Lewis, Percy Heath, and Connie Kay, were impressed by Bley's group and helped Coleman secure a contract with the Atlantic label. In Hollywood in May 1959 the quartet of Coleman, Cherry, Haden, and Higgins recorded the pioneering free-jazz album *The Shape of Jazz to Come*, notable for its nearly complete avoidance of conventional harmony and for its intermittent disruptions of the regular rhythmic pulse associated with bop. From Cherry's perspective, the startling difference was that the saxophone and pocket cornet lines, whether in unison or in harmony, became intentionally ragged, with a bop-based aesthetic of melodic coordination, precision, and clarity giving way to sloppier, heterophonic statements. This celebration of a folk-like aesthetic, turning conventional professional musicianship on its head, pointed the direction for Cherry's music for the remainder of his life.

In August 1959, under the sponsorship of Lewis, Heath, and the Atlantic recording executive Nesuhi Ertugen, Coleman and Cherry spent three weeks at the School of Jazz in Lenox, Massachusetts. In October the quartet recorded another album, *Change of the Century*, in Hollywood, California. In November the group traveled east to begin a now-legendary two-and-a-half month engagement at the Five Spot in New York, while critical arguments raged over the value of their departures from the jazz tradition. The ensuing period, extending to March 1961, brought Cherry and Coleman considerable success with further lengthy club dates in New York, nationwide touring, and several more important albums, including the December 1960 landmark "double-quartet" improvisation *Free Jazz* (that is, with four reed and brass players, two bassists, and two drummers). Cherry also recorded a quartet album, *The Avant Garde*, as coleader with the tenor saxophonist John Coltrane in late June and early July 1960.

Cherry's career was influenced by his heroin addiction, which severely disrupted the quartet, as did the addictions of Higgins and Haden. Owing to previous arrests in California, mainly for drug problems, Higgins was denied a "cabaret card," a license to perform in New York venues serving alcohol, in April 1960. In September, Haden was obliged to leave the group for similar reasons. After he recorded the quartet albums *Ornette* (Jan. 1961) and *Ornette on Tenor* (Mar. 1961), Cherry was jailed on a narcotics conviction, the details of which are unknown. He lost his cabaret card, and his affiliation with Coleman ended.

In November 1961 Cherry recorded the album *Evidence* as a member of the soprano saxophonist Steve Lacy's quartet. In mid-1962 Cherry and Higgins began working with the tenor saxophonist Sonny Rollins, recording the album *Our Man in Jazz* in late July. Toward the end of his nine months with Rollins, Cherry first went to Europe, touring from Scandinavia to Italy early in 1963. Cherry was allowed to work in New York City again and played at the club Birdland before leaving Rollins's group.

In summer 1963 Cherry formed the New York Contemporary Five as coleader with the saxophonists Archie Shepp and John Tchicai. The quintet recorded the album *Future I* in New York. While in Copenhagen, Denmark, in the autumn of 1963, the group held a five-week engagement at the Montmartre, recorded again, and made a film short, *Future One*. The members then returned to New York, where they disbanded early in 1964.

In summer 1964 Cherry joined the most radical of the avant-garde saxophonists, Albert Ayler, whose quartet went to Copenhagen in September. The group recorded the album *Ghosts* that same month, and it performed at the Montmartre into the fall. Cherry remained in Copenhagen and played with the South African expatriate pianist Abdullah Ibrahim (then known as Dollar Brand) before setting off on a period of musical hoboing, which culminated with two months in the Moroccan village of Suzuka.

Cherry and Hewitt divorced early in the 1960s, and Cherry's mother, Daisy McKee, raised their two children in Los Angeles during these years of his international touring. In December 1964 Cherry married the Swedish artist Moki Karlsson. They lived in Stockholm before settling in a converted schoolhouse in Tagarp in southern Sweden, where they ran an organic farm. Cherry raised his stepdaughter, born Neneh Mariann Karlsson, who developed a prominent career in pop music as Neneh Cherry. Their son Eagle Eye Cherry became an actor and well-known pop musician.

In the mid- to late 1960s Cherry used a full-sized cornet rather than the pocket instrument. From 1965 through autumn 1966 he led a small group whose principal members were Gato Barbieri, tenor saxophone; Karl Berger, vibraphone; Jean-François Jenny-Clark, string bass; and Aldo Romano, drums. Lacy took Barbieri's place when the group appeared in the Italian film short *Appunti per un film sul jazz* (1965), and Bo Steif was the bassist when the quintet recorded at the Montmartre early in 1966. Cherry brought some of these musicians to New York to make three albums that rank among the most important sessions of free jazz, *Complete Communion* (Dec. 1965) in a quartet with Barbieri, the bassist Henry Grimes, and the drummer Ed Blackwell; *Symphony for Improvisers* (Sept. 1966) with the saxophonist Pharoah Sanders, Berger, and Jenny-Clark added to the group; and *Where Is Brooklyn?* (Nov. 1966) by a quartet including Sanders, Grimes, and Blackwell. Cherry also recorded in groups led by the expatriate jazz composer George Russell in Stuttgart, Germany, in August 1965 and by the Italian pianist Giorio Gaslini in Milan in February 1966.

At the jazz festival in Berlin in November 1968, Cherry made a pioneering foray into the incorporation of diverse ethnic instruments and musical procedures into jazz, adding instruments from the Balinese gamelan ensemble to a standard combination of brass, reeds, vibraphone, and rhythm section. Cherry played cornet, producing his characteristically compact tone and alternating between wild flurries of sound and forthright melodic motifs drawn from both the gamelan tradition and modern jazz. He doubled on four types of flutes, Haitian gourd, and bells while also vocalizing. The album *Eternal Rhythm* captures this historic band in concert, and it includes prominent passages in which Cherry plays a bamboo flute and a Bengali wooden flute simultaneously in harmony.

Cherry recorded in a quartet led by the South African expatriate bassist Johnny Dyani in Copenhagen in 1968 and then worked in a trio with Dyani and the Turkish percussionist Okay Temiz from 1969 to 1970. In 1970 Cherry recorded on cornet, flugelhorn, and bamboo flute under Haden's leadership for the album *Liberation Music Orchestra*.

By the 1970s Cherry was delving more and more deeply into non-Western cultures. He took up Tibetan Buddhism. He studied the *berimbau* (a single-stringed Brazilian musical bow with a gourd resonator) with Nana Vasconcelos, with whom he worked in Europe throughout the mid-1970s. He also added the *doussn'gouni* (a Mali "hunter's guitar" with six strings, a gourd resonator, and a rattle) to his arsenal of instruments. Cherry played both of these instruments informally as an itinerant street musician. He taught music in Mexico, made a documentary with bedouins in Tunisia for German television, and in July 1973 traveled to India to study that country's classical music. By 1975 Cherry was dividing his time between the farm in Tagarp and New York City, and he was once again working with Higgins.

In October 1976, for the Black Saint label, Cherry, the tenor saxophonist Dewey Redman, Haden, and Blackwell recorded the album *Old and New Dreams*, in part to revive the style of Coleman's now-classic free-jazz quartet. The quartet adopted Old and New Dreams as a group name for international touring from 1978 into the early 1980s, and for the ECM label it made another album of that same name in August 1979 as well as the album *Playing*, recorded in concert in Bregenz, Austria, in June 1980.

In 1978 Cherry formed the cooperative multi-instrumentalist trio Codona with Vasconcelos and Colin Walcott. The group's three albums (recorded in 1978, 1980, and 1982) are disappointing, displaying a pan-genre blandness that characterized much of what later came to be known as "world music," but in live performance Codona was capable of delivering spectacular hour-long improvisations, with Cherry transferring melody or rhythm seamlessly from cornet to flute to piano to *doussn'gouni* to percussion to voice and his companions doing likewise on their arrays of Western and non-Western instruments.

During this period Cherry performed outside of jazz contexts as a soloist with the rock guitarist, singer, and songwriter Lou Reed. He continued to work as a street musician in diverse contexts, and in 1982 he was awarded a grant from the National Endowment for the Arts to teach music and dance to children in the Watts district of Los Angeles. From 1982 he recorded and then toured with Haden's reconstituted Liberation Music Orchestra. When Walcott died in a bus crash in 1984, Codona disbanded, and Cherry formed a quintet, Nu, that included Vasconcelos.

In August 1988 Cherry recorded the album *Art Deco* as the leader of a quartet with Clay, Haden, and Higgins. That fall he made the first of several appearances at the annual San Francisco Jazz Festival with a Berkeley group, the Hieroglyphics Ensemble, led by the saxophonist and keyboard player Peter Apfelbaum. In 1989 Cherry moved to San Francisco to strengthen that association. Using members of the Hieroglyphics Ensemble, including Apfelbaum, Cherry also formed his own quartet, Multikulti, which toured internationally.

In 1995 Cherry's health failed. He left San Francisco to spend his final months with his family at Neneh Cherry's home in the Spanish countryside near Malaga, where he died.

• A fine musicological essay on Cherry's role in avant-garde jazz by Ekkehard Jost is in Jost's book *Free Jazz* (1974), pp. 133–62. Details of Cherry's first two decades of recordings are in Mike Hames and Roy Wilbraham, *Don Cherry on Disc and Tape* (1980). Information on Cherry is scattered through newspapers, magazines, and record liner notes. Among the best of these essays are Amiri Baraka (as LeRoi Jones), "Don Cherry: Making It the Hard Way," *Down Beat* 30 (21 Nov. 1963): 16–17, 34; Mike Hennessey, "Cherry's Catholicity: The Kaleidoscopic View of Jazz," *Down Beat* 33 (28 July 1966): 14–15; Keith Knox, "Don Cherry's Symphony of the Improvisers," *Jazz Monthly* 13 (Aug. 1967): 5–10; Peter Occhiogrosso, "Emissary of the Global Muse: Don Cherry," *Down Beat* 42 (9 Oct. 1975): 14–15, 39; Howard Mandel, "The World in His Pocket: Don Cherry," *Down Beat* 45 (13 July 1978): 20–22, 54–55; Lee Jeske, "Don: The Cherry Variations," *Down Beat* 50 (June 1983): 18–20; and Joseph Hooper: "Not Your Average Family: Three Talented Cherrys—Don, Neneh, and Eagle-Eye—and How They Grew," *New York Times Magazine,* 10 Dec. 1989, pp. 48–50, 54, 58–59, 122. John Gray identifies further such articles in his book *Fire Music: A Bibliography of the New Jazz, 1959–1990* (1991), pp. 139–42. A detailed account of Cherry's affiliation with Ornette Coleman is in the biographical appendix to David Wild and Michael Cuscuna, *Ornette Coleman, 1958–1979: A Discography* (1980), pp. 58–66. Obituaries are by Claudia Levy, *Washington Post,* 20 Oct. 1995, and Peter Watrous, *New York Times,* 21 Oct. 1995.

BARRY KERNFELD

CHILDS, Marquis (17 Mar. 1903–30 June 1990), Pulitzer Prize–winning journalist, columnist, and author, was born in the Mississippi River community of Clinton, Iowa, the son of William Henry Childs, an attorney, and Lilian Malissa Marquis Childs. As a teenager, Marquis Childs decided that he wanted to become a newspaperman. He said he discovered the "power of the printed word" while attending the 1920 Clinton County Fair in DeWitt, Iowa, where his father was campaigning for county attorney (quoted in Childs, *Witness to Power,* p. 1). Childs paid a barnstorming pilot $5 for a ride in a World War I–era Jenny biplane. Once in the air over the fairgrounds, he tossed out leaflets promoting his father's candidacy, an act that received coverage in the area's newspapers. His father won the election.

After receiving his bachelor's degree from the University of Wisconsin in 1923, Childs became a reporter for the United Press (UP), working in Chicago and other midwestern cities. After a year with the UP, he returned to his home state and earned a master's degree from the University of Iowa in 1925. Childs rejoined the UP's staff that same year and reported to New York—to work, he said, "from one assignment for which I was totally unprepared to another for which I was equally well equipped" (quoted in *Current Biography,* 1943, p. 127). In 1926 he began his longtime connection with the *St. Louis Post-Dispatch,* joining the newspaper as a features reporter. Traveling around the country, Childs usually reported on stories dubbed "cornfield murders," including such oddities as a child born in Tennessee with a tail (quoted in *Witness to Power,* p. 2). He did manage to report from time on time on what later became his specialty: politics.

On 26 August 1926 Childs married Lue Prentiss; the couple had two children. Lue Prentiss Childs died in 1968, and in August 1969 Marquis Childs married Jane Neylan McBain. They had no children.

Taking a leave of absence from the *Post-Dispatch* in the spring of 1930, Childs traveled to Sweden for a housing exposition. Impressed by what he saw, he produced a number of articles for the *Post-Dispatch* and for *Harper's* magazine on the country's democratic socialistic government. His experiences in Sweden formed the basis for his best-known work, *Sweden: The Middle Way,* published in 1936. The book's exploration of Sweden's cooperatives proved to be so compelling that President Franklin D. Roosevelt appointed a commission to study the issue. By the time of his book's release, Childs had been working for two years in the *Post-Dispatch*'s Washington, D.C., bureau. On his return from overseas, tired of his feature-writing duties, he had attempted to be named the newspaper's theater and movie critic. Instead, O. K. Bovard, the *Post-Dispatch*'s managing editor, sent him

to be the third man in the newspaper's Washington bureau to cover the burgeoning agencies created by Roosevelt's New Deal program. "I plunged in with the eagerness of the innocent I was," Childs said, describing the atmosphere of the times as "incandescent" (quoted in *Witness to Power,* p. 4). His coverage of the 1936 presidential campaign resulted in an article for *Harper's* about far-right opposition to Roosevelt, titled "They Hate Roosevelt," that was later reprinted as a book.

Childs traveled again to Europe in 1937, visiting a number of Scandinavian countries to research the subject of collective bargaining for his book *This is Democracy: Collective Bargaining in Scandinavia* (1938). During the trip he also visited Spain and produced a series of articles on the civil war there for the *Post-Dispatch.* Childs continued his travels the next year, journeying to Mexico to report on scandals with the oil expropriation program in that country. His articles on the subject resulted in the call for an investigation of the issue by the U.S. Senate as well as denunciations of Childs by some senators, including Pennsylvania Democrat Joseph F. Guffey, who later apologized to Childs. In 1942 he wrote about his experiences as a correspondent in the nation's capital in the book *I Write from Washington,* which a critic for the *New York Times* called "an intelligent, reasonable and pleasantly breezy book" (quoted in the *New York Times,* 14 October 1942).

In 1944, following the death of syndicated columnist Raymond Clapper, Childs left the *Post-Dispatch* to take over Clapper's national column, distributed by the United Features Syndicate in approximately two hundred newspapers across the country. Childs returned to the *Post-Dispatch* staff in 1954 but continued to produce his column, titled "Washington Calling," along with interviews with such national and international leaders as Dwight Eisenhower, John Kennedy, Jawaharlal Nehru, Harold Macmillan, and Chou En-lai. From 1962 to 1969, Childs served as the chief of the *Post-Dispatch*'s Washington bureau, becoming a contributing editor in 1969. Over the years Childs's column concentrated on such issues as gun control, the reform of mental institutions, the influence of big business on government, civil rights, and arms control. Reflecting on his days as a columnist, Childs noted that he always tried "to get some piece of news to put into any column I write" (quoted in Dudman, *St. Louis Post-Dispatch,* 1 July 1990). In 1970 he received a Pulitzer Prize for commentary, the first time the prize had been awarded for such work.

In addition to his numerous nonfiction books, Childs wrote such novels as *Washington Calling!* (1937), *The Cabin* (1944), *The Peacemakers* (1961), and *Taint of Innocence* (1967). Later in life, he became engaged in a project he had started but abandoned at age twenty-nine, a book on the history of the Mississippi River, published in 1982 as *Mighty Mississippi: Biography of a River.* A member of a number of associations, including the Century, Gridiron, and Washington Press clubs, Childs received honorary degrees from the University of Wisconsin and the University of Iowa. He died in San Francisco and is buried in Clinton, Iowa.

• Childs's papers, including correspondence and original typescripts for many of his books, are located in the Special Collections Department of the University of Iowa Library in Iowa City, Iowa. He explored his experiences as a Washington, D.C., correspondent in the books *I Write from Washington* (1942) and *Witness to Power* (1975). There is a profile of Childs in 1943's *Current Biography*, and the reporter's life is examined in a piece by colleague Richard Dudman, "Journalism Comrade Recalls Years with Veteran Reporter," published in the *St. Louis Post-Dispatch*, 1 July 1990. Obituaries are in the *St. Louis Post-Dispatch*, 1 July 1990, and the *New York Times*, 2 July 1990.

RAY E. BOOMHOWER

CHILDS, Morris (10 June 1902–2 June 1991), Communist official and American intelligence double agent, was born Moishe Chilovsky in Kiev, Ukraine, the son of Joseph Chilovsky, a cobbler, and Anna Chilovsky. Joseph Chilovsky, a Jew, fled Tsarist oppression, arriving in America in 1910; he sent for the rest of his family late the next year. (In 1926 the spelling of their name was Americanized, and Morris became a naturalized citizen the following year.) In 1916 Morris went to work as an apprentice in his father's business; then he became a milkman. In 1919 he joined the Communist party in Chicago. Twice arrested for participating in street demonstrations, he soon became a protégé of future party leader Earl Browder, who in 1929 sent him for training to the Lenin School in Moscow. There Childs befriended future leaders of the communist movement in Russia and abroad.

In 1932 Childs returned from Moscow to serve as the party's district organizer in Wisconsin. In 1935 he was promoted to district organizer in Chicago, one of the CPUSA's most important posts. In 1938, the same year he ran for the U.S. Senate on the Communist ticket, he was elected to the party's Central Committee. In 1945 he suffered a mild heart attack and was briefly sidelined from communist activities. After Earl Browder's removal as party leader in 1945, his successor, Eugene Dennis, asked Childs to take charge of the party's national political work but then appointed him editor of the *Daily Worker*, despite his lack of journalistic experience. In 1947 Childs went to Moscow to cover a conference of foreign ministers. While there he consulted with Soviet officials about whether the CPUSA should support a third-party candidate for president in 1948. During this visit, however, he was disturbed by reports from old friends of the persecution of Russian Jews. In June, shortly after his return to the United States, he was abruptly removed as editor in an effort by Dennis to appease a faction led by William Foster. He also suffered a massive heart attack in that year and was an invalid for several years. His political disgrace and illness saved him from indictment in 1948 when the government convicted the top leadership of the CPUSA, including John Gates, his successor at the *Daily Worker*, for violating the Smith Act by conspiring to teach and advocate overthrow of the government.

Childs recuperated in Chicago, supported by his younger brother Jack, who had been trained in Moscow from 1931 to 1933 before returning to New York to work as a functionary in the party's secret underground apparatus. In late 1951 when the FBI approached Jack, who had been inactive in party affairs since 1948, he provided information to them. At his suggestion, the government agents contacted the bedridden Morris, who was amenable to working for the agency. They also arranged treatment for his heart problems at the Mayo Clinic. In 1952 Morris reestablished his party connections, meeting with Stanley Levison and William Weiner, who were in charge of the CPUSA's financial operations, and William Foster. In 1956, Dennis, after his release from prison, secretly made Morris his deputy for foreign affairs. In April 1958 Childs traveled to Moscow and Peking.

Between 1958 and 1977 Morris Childs made fifty-two trips to Communist countries on behalf of the CPUSA leadership, regularly meeting with top officials of the USSR, China, and Cuba, including Nikita Khrushchev and Leonid Brezhnev. He was present in the office of a top Soviet official when news was received of John Kennedy's assassination; he was able to report on the genuine shock felt in Moscow and the Soviets' insistence that Lee Harvey Oswald, who had earlier defected to the Soviet Union, had not been a Russian agent. Childs also provided early intelligence reports on the Sino-Soviet split.

On his 1958 trip to Moscow, Childs set up the pipeline through which Soviet money was funneled to the CPUSA for the next twenty-two years, an operation in which Jack Childs played a key role. Altogether, more than $28 million was sent, much of it transferred from the KGB to Jack Childs before being given to party leader Gus Hall. Carefully traced by the FBI, this money financed Communist party newspapers, salaries, and political and organizing campaigns, enabling a tiny political organization with fewer than five thousand members to maintain a presence far out of proportion to its size in American life.

The Childs brothers also played a key role in the FBI's surveillance of Dr. Martin Luther King, Jr. Both Jack and Morris told the FBI that Stanley Levison was a major source of secret funds for the CPUSA in the 1950s and also managed the party's reserve fund, investing cash in friendly businesses. Levison emerged as one of King's closest advisors early in 1957, shortly after severing his ties to the CPUSA. When the FBI learned about his relationship with King from Jack Childs in 1962, Attorney General Robert Kennedy authorized telephone and wiretap surveillance of the civil rights leader, concerned that Levison was a Communist agent or that Soviet money directed to the CPUSA was being used to finance the Southern Christian Leadership Conference.

For thirty years, Operation Solo, as it was codenamed, provided the FBI with an unparalleled window into the operations of the CPUSA and the Soviet bloc. Morris, a secret member of the party's Central Committee, engaged in no open party activity in the United States. The FBI set up a sham business in Chicago that was the ostensible source of Morris's income. His frequent trips to Moscow led the Soviets to provide him with his own apartment there. The KGB caused occasional scares when they became suspicious about why American intelligence had not penetrated the Childses' smoke screens. Afraid that the Church Committee that investigated intelligence abuses after the Watergate scandal would expose Solo as it looked into the FBI's wiretapping of King, agents told Senator Frank Church about Morris Childs and elicited a pledge from him not to delve any further. At one point bureau agents wiretapped the Childses to counter suspicions that the brothers might actually be triple agents.

In 1980 Jack Childs died. The following year Operation Solo was shut down and Morris was moved into the witness protection program when a book appeared documenting the operation. Morris Childs, who had received the Order of the Red Banner from Leonid Brezhnev in 1977, was presented with the Presidential Medal of Freedom for Intelligence in 1987. (Jack Childs received the same decorations, the latter posthumously.) Morris Childs died in Miami.

Childs was married three times. His first wife, Helen Lerman, was a fellow Communist. They had one son, Billie, and divorced in 1947 or 1948. After his 1947 heart attack, Childs lived with Sonny Schlossberg, a former party member from Chicago. They married in 1959, but she died soon afterward. He married Eva Lieb in 1962.

• The only full-length account of Morris Childs is John Barron's *Operation Solo: The FBI's man in the Kremlin* (1996). The most careful and detailed story is in David Garrow, *The FBI and Martin Luther King, Jr.* (1981), updated in "The FBI and Martin Luther King," *Atlantic Monthly,* July–August 2002.

HARVEY KLEHR

CHILES, Lawton (3 Apr. 1930–12 Dec. 1998), U.S. Senator and governor of Florida, was born Lawton Mainor Chiles, Jr., in Lakeland, Florida, the son of Lawton Mainor Chiles, a railroad conductor, and Margaret Patterson Chiles, a housewife. A fourth-generation Floridian, Chiles attended Lakeland public schools and graduated from the University of Florida in 1952. While at the university, he was a member of Florida Blue Key, the Hall of Fame, and Alpha Tau Omega fraternity.

On 27 January 1951 Chiles married Rhea Grafton; they had four children.

He left law school to serve in the U.S. Army in 1953–1954 as an artillery officer in Korea. Receiving his LL.B. from the University of Florida Law School in 1955, he was admitted to the Florida bar and began practicing in his hometown. Chiles was elected to the Florida House of Representatives in 1958, served until 1966, and was elected to the Florida Senate (1966–

1970). In the state senate he was chairman of the Florida Law Revision Council, which in 1967–1968 overhauled the old 1885 state constitution. Chiles joined with other progressive state legislators, including Reubin Askew and Bob Graham, to fight the "Pork Chop Gang," a group of twenty or so rural legislators who represented only 17 percent of the voters but controlled the state legislature. Finally, as Chiles later recalled, the "one-man, one-vote" court decisions broke the "strangle-hold of the status quo . . . where vested interests and the lobbyists just exerted almost total control" (Bass and DeVries, 30 Jan. 1974, p. 3).

In 1970 Chiles ran for the U.S. Senate to replace the long-serving Spessard Holland. Clad in hiking boots and khakis, Chiles walked 1,033 miles from Pensacola to Dade County in ninety-two days. Lacking name recognition and money, he thought the trek through the state would be the best way to connect with voters on a one-to-one basis. In his legendary walk, which earned him the nickname "Walkin' Lawton," Chiles projected a down-home, populist image. A television report contrasted his rally featuring buckets of fried chicken with his opponent's black-tie, $1,000-a-plate dinner. Voters responded favorably, and Chiles won with 902,438 votes (53.9 percent) to 772,817 (46.1 percent) for Republican Bill Cramer.

In his three terms in the Senate, Chiles became a strong defender of children and families as well as the environment. He advocated the establishment of the Everglades–Big Cypress National Park (1971) and successfully fought the Cross-Florida Barge Canal (1975–1976). He generally favored government programs such as student loans and child care and supported the establishment of the federal departments of Energy (1977) and Education (1979). While he was against busing, he was a moderate on race. In a speech to the Jaycees in Lake Wales, Florida, in 1972, he deplored the costs of racial prejudice and noted that segregation "still exists in the south and in the north"; he urged that the spotlight be taken from busing and the emphasis placed on equal opportunity for a good education (Lynch, 1972, p. 14). He insisted on "government in the sunshine" and was the chief sponsor of a 1976 federal law requiring regulatory agencies to conduct their meetings in public. Key foreign policy positions included his advocacy of U.S. withdrawal from Vietnam (1971), cosponsorship of the War Powers Act of 1972, and votes for the Panama Canal treaties, SALT I, and the ABM treaty. Chiles was reelected to the Senate in 1976 with 63.1 percent of the vote over Republican John Grady and in 1982 won 61.7 percent of the vote in defeating Republican Van Poole. In his eighteen-year U.S. Senate career, Chiles served as chairman of the Special Committee on Aging and became the first Floridian to serve as chairman of the powerful Senate Budget Committee. While in the Senate, Chiles also championed a balanced budget, favored reduced government bureaucracy, and was the chief proponent of the Federal Paperwork Reduction Act of 1980. He was also a member of the Governmental Affairs, Agriculture, and Appropriations committees.

In late 1987, Senator Chiles stunned supporters by announcing that he would not seek a fourth term in the Senate, giving recurring bouts with depression (later treated with Prozac) as one reason for his decision. He was also frustrated with federal government gridlock. In 1990, however, renewed after a hiatus from politics, Chiles captured the Democratic nomination for governor. As was his custom, he limited contributions to $100 per person, but he nonetheless defeated incumbent Republican governor Bob Martinez by 56.5 percent to 43.4 percent. In 1994 Chiles won a second term with a hard-fought victory over Jeb Bush (son of former President George H. W. Bush) by 50.8 to 49.2 percent. Chiles emphasized his "cracker" roots and Bush's inexperience while overcoming allegations that Democrats made misleading telephone calls to frighten elderly voters.

Chiles's two terms as governor emphasized programs for Florida children that expanded the Healthy Kids program, provided increased health coverage, bolstered prenatal and infant care, and protected children from abuse and neglect. Chiles thought that if Florida focused on children, then the state's future would be secure. He helped establish Enterprise Florida, a public-private partnership to boost economic development, and orchestrated the passage of a public campaign finance law (1991). He vetoed a school prayer bill (1996) as well as tort reform legislation (1998), while insisting on accountability and standards in public education. Governor Chiles won a signal victory in 1997 when the tobacco industry agreed to reimburse the state $11.3 billion over twenty-five years for smoking-related illnesses. The legislature created the Department of Elderly Affairs (1991), established a three-day waiting period for handgun purchases (1991), and established a tenth state university (1991).

Chiles also had to deal with such problems as Hurricane Andrew in 1992, an economic downturn, an influx of Haitian and Cuban immigrants, murders of tourists and abortion doctors, crowded schools, and wildfires. With twenty-four days left in his second term, on 12 December 1998 he died of an abnormal heart rhythm while exercising in the Mansion gym. In thirty-eight years of political contests, Chiles never lost a race and earned a reputation as an astute politician, a man of integrity, and a homespun centrist who communicated with and cared about the people of his state.

• Chiles's senatorial papers (1969–1988; 1,731 cubic feet) are stored in the P. K. Yonge Library at the University of Florida, Gainesville. His gubernatorial papers will be housed at the Bureau of Archives and Records Management, Tallahassee, Fla. The Lawton Chiles Foundation, 116 S. Monroe St., Suite 200, Tallahassee, Fla., continues his work on behalf of children and contains his diary from the 1970 walk. An oral history of interest is by Jack Bass and Walter DeVries, 30 January 1974, at the Southern Oral History Program, University of North Carolina. There is no formal bi-

ography, but secondary sources include Hilda Maness Lynch, "Lawton Chiles," in the Ralph Nader Congress Project's *Citizens Look at Congress* (1972); Stephen C. Craig, "Politics and Elections," in *Government and Politics in Florida*, ed. Robert J. Huckshorn (1991); Jill A. Elish, "Remembering a Real Floridian, Lawton Chiles," *Florida Living Magazine* 19, no. 4 (April 1999): 30–34; Michael Barone and Grant Ujifusa, *The Almanac of American Politics* (1996); Tom Fiedler and Lance de Haven-Smith, *Almanac of Florida Politics, 1998*, Florida Institute of Government; and United States Senate, *A Memorial Service In Honor of Florida's Former Governor and United States Senator: Lawton Chiles* (1999). An obituary is in the *New York Times*, 14 Dec. 1998.

JULIAN M. PLEASANTS

CINQUÉ (c. 1814–c. 1879), slave mutineer, was born Sengbe (also spelled Singbe and Sengbeh) Pieh in the village of Mani, in the Mende territory of Sierra Leone, Africa, the son of a rice farmer. His mother died when he was young, and at about the age of twenty-five he lived with his father, his wife, and his three children. One day while working alone in his rice field, he was seized by four members of the Vai tribe, often employed by Europeans to capture slaves for the market. He was taken to Lomboko, an island at the mouth of the Gallinas River on the coast of Sierra Leone, where he was purchased by Pedro Blanco, a Spanish slave trader, for sale in Cuba. He remained in Lomboko for three months in chains before Blanco filled the ship that was to transport him to Havana.

Slavery was still legal in Cuba, but the trans-Atlantic trade in slaves had been abolished by international treaties in 1820. When Cinqué arrived he was thus technically contraband, but once landed he was legally a slave and was housed with many other recently transported Africans. Within ten days, he was purchased, along with forty-eight other able-bodied African men, by one of the leading Spanish dealers in Cuba, José Ruiz, who paid $450 each for them. Ruiz and a companion, Pedro Montes, who had made the more modest purchase of four children all under 12 years of age, loaded their 53 slaves on the schooner *Amistad* on 28 June 1839 and set sail for Puerto Príncipe, a short distance from Havana. Each slave had been provided with a false Spanish passport in case of search by English authorities while in transit.

Alarmed by the cruel joke of the ship's cook, who communicated to the slaves that they were to be killed and eaten by the crew, Cinqué found a nail while exercising on deck and picked the lock on his iron collar. On the third night out, he freed his fellow slaves, all but three of whom were from Mende territory and spoke the same language. Arming themselves with machetes being shipped to the sugar plantations for cutting cane, the slaves quickly killed the cook and Ramón Ferrer, the captain. The two remaining crew members disappeared, presumably drowned trying to swim for shore. The mutineers, under Cinqué's command, then ordered their former owners Ruiz and Montes to steer the ship back to Africa. Montes, who had been a sea captain, was put at the helm and told to head into the rising sun, but the Spaniard reversed the course every night in hopes of being picked up and freed by Americans or Cubans. This zigzag route continued for sixty-three days, during which ten of the Africans died. At last on 26 August the need for food and water forced Cinqué to order a landing at the next island they saw, which proved to be Long Island, New York.

The vessel was immediately seized by U.S. Navy officers and on 29 August the mutineers were arrested for piracy and murder. Ruiz and Montes were set free; they demanded the return of the ship and its cargo, including the slaves, as their property. Because New York was a free state, Coast Guard Lt. Thomas Gedney, who had seized the schooner, had the *Amistad* towed to Connecticut, where slavery was still legal, hoping to claim it and its 43 surviving slaves as salvage. The Africans, including the four children, were jailed in New Haven while the courts undertook to clarify the local, national, and international issues involved. Lt. Gedney sued for possession of the boat and all its cargo; Ruiz brought a separate suit for the return of his human property; and because Cuba was a possession of Spain, the Spanish government demanded that the slaves be returned to Havana to be tried for murder. President Martin Van Buren, seeking to maintain good diplomatic relations with Spain, supported the claim.

The trial of the Africans in the Circuit Court in Hartford on 17 September 1839 became a national sensation. The proslavery southern states opposed the freeing of the slaves, recognizing the threat to the institution on which their economy depended, and abolitionists in the north saw the case as an opportunity to promote their cause. The handsome, charismatic leader of the mutiny became a hero in the northern press, where his name took the form Cinqué (variously spelled Cinquè, Cinquez, or Cinquenzo, and sometimes embellished with the forename Joseph), and his status in Africa was elevated to royalty. William Cullen Bryant's poem "The African Chief," published in the *Emancipator* on 19 September 1839, said of him, "A prince among his tribe before, / *He could not be a slave*" (italics in the original). In the meantime, the Africans were kept in the New Haven jail, where they were given English lessons and instruction in Christianity. To help defray the costs of their incarceration, they were exhibited to the curious for twelve and a half cents a look. Both dignified and congenial, the Black Prince, as Cinqué was often called in the newspapers, cheerfully consented to perform native dances and turn somersaults on the lawn.

Lewis Tappan, a founder of the New York Anti-Slavery Society, organized an *Amistad* Committee to help free the prisoners and hired the prominent constitutional lawyer Roger Sherman Baldwin for their defense. Baldwin argued that they were not legally slaves but "kidnapped Africans" and that their mutiny was justified by "the inherent right of self defense." Cinqué delivered a speech so dramatically in his native Mende that it moved the audience even before it was translated for them. The Circuit Court found in favor of the Africans and ordered them freed. The Spanish government protested the decision and persuaded Secretary of State John Forsyth to direct the district attorney to appeal the case. President Van Buren issued an executive order to have the defendants transported to Cuba immediately if the appeal succeeded, thus preventing an appeal by the Africans. When the Federal District Court affirmed the Circuit Court's decision in January 1840, the government appealed again; in February of the next year the case was carried to the U.S. Supreme Court. The seventy-three-year-old former president John Quincy Adams, long an ardent supporter of abolition, was persuaded to join the defense, and his legendary eloquence carried the day. On 9 March, after trials that had dragged on for eighteen months, the Africans were once again declared free to return to Africa.

As the government refused to pay the costs of repatriation, several of the Africans went on a speaking tour, organized by the *Amistad* Committee, to raise money for their trip. Speaking in Mende, Cinqué was said to possess "a very graceful and animated manner" and became a popular spokesperson for the abolitionist cause. By November the mutineers, now reduced by death to thirty-five, had raised enough money for the long journey and embarked for Sierra Leone. They arrived in January 1842, accompanied by missionaries planning to establish a mission in Komende (spelled Kaw-Mendi in American sources), near Freetown. Cinqué continued inland to Mani in search of his family but, according to most reports, never saw them again. Little is known of his life after returning to Africa, but some accounts report that he made himself a powerful and prosperous chief among his people and even engaged in slave trading. Other versions have him returning to the mission to serve as an interpreter or returning there only in the last week of his life to die and be buried in the mission cemetery.

The leader of the only successful slave rebellion in American history, Cinqué set in motion a legal battle that was to provide an important precedent in American and international law. The *Amistad* case helped to establish the authority of the courts, and it constituted what historian Howard Jones described as "an historic milestone in the long struggle against slavery and for the establishment of basic civil rights for everyone, regardless of color."

• The principal collections of material related to Cinqué and the *Amistad* case are the Amistad Research Center in New Orleans, La.; the Amistad collection of the New Haven Colony Historical Society Library in Connecticut; and the National Archives in Washington, D.C. Early accounts are John Warner Barber, *A History of the Amistad Captives* (1840, repr. 2000), and Simeon E. Baldwin, *The Captives of the Amistad* (1886). The case is given its most balanced and thoroughly documented examination in Howard Jones, *Mutiny on the Amistad: The Saga of a Slave Revolt and Its Impact on American Abolition, Law, and Diplomacy* (1987, repr. 1998). Among the many fictionalized accounts of the *Amistad* case and its principals, the best known are Williams A. Owens, *Slave Mutiny* (1953), and Barbara Chase-Riboud, *Echo of Lions* (1989). The events of the mutiny and the trial are presented dramatically in Steven Spielberg's film *Amistad* (1997).

DENNIS WEPMAN

CLAIBORNE, Craig (4 Sept. 1920–22 Jan. 2000), food journalist and restaurant critic, was born in Sunflower, Mississippi, the son of Lewis Edmond Claiborne, a cotton grower and local bank officer, and Mary Kathleen Craig Claiborne. His father lost his lands and fortune shortly after Craig's birth and never again held gainful employment. His mother moved the family to the larger town of Indianola and opened a boarding house. She became famous for her high-quality meals, prepared by black cooks using her recipes. Craig grew up savoring outstanding southern cooking. After graduating from Indianola High School, he attended Mississippi State College before moving to the University of Missouri, where he received a B.A. in journalism in 1942.

Claiborne immediately volunteered for the navy and took part in the invasion of Morocco. After attending officers' training school in early 1944, he served on submarine chasers until February 1946. Claiborne spent the next four years in public relations positions in Chicago, interrupted only by a trip to France and Italy in 1949. When the Korean War broke out, Claiborne again volunteered. He later cited several incidents leading to his decision to make cooking his career—his first taste of exotic food, a highly spiced lamb couscous while in Morocco, and his "spiritual revelation" when encountering classic French high cuisine aboard the *Île de France*. Awaiting his discharge from the navy in 1953, he considered his future. Claiborne disliked his previous work but loved food and enjoyed writing: he would become a food writer.

Claiborne used his GI Bill educational benefits to enroll in the famous L'École Hôtelière, the professional school of the Swiss Hotel Keepers Association. He spent a year in Lausanne, Switzerland, earning certificates in classical French cooking and in table and banquet service. During vacations he worked as a waiter at Swiss resort hotels. He became the first American food journalist professionally trained in food preparation and service.

In 1954, Claiborne returned to New York and contributed articles to *Gourmet* magazine on a free-lance basis. In October 1955 he joined the staff of *Gourmet*. Understanding the value of publicity, Claiborne convinced Jane Nickerson, *New York Times* food editor, to publish an interview with a young Mississippian who had just spent a year at a great Swiss cooking school—himself. When Nickerson resigned in 1957, Claiborne applied for the post. No male had ever served as food editor for a major metropolitan newspaper, but executive editor Turner Catledge, impressed by Claiborne's credentials and delighted to reminisce with him about Mississippi State dormitory life, offered Claiborne the position.

Claiborne established what became a widely imitated system of restaurant criticism. He would arrive anonymously accompanied by two or three friends, whose dishes he would sample. Drawing on his Swiss training, Claiborne evaluated the restaurant's food, ambience, and service, rating the establishment on a scale of zero to four stars. Although always favoring classic French cuisine, Claiborne approvingly reviewed Cajun, Chinese, Mexican-American, and Thai restaurants. He shocked purists by giving the Chock Full O' Nuts sandwich shops one star.

Claiborne regularly provided articles on food and restaurants for the daily paper, and recipes for the Sunday magazine section. An avid traveler, he provided articles on new or exotic dishes from places as diverse as New Orleans and Delhi. Claiborne enjoyed discovering young chefs, frequently chronicling innovations of unknown cooks.

While preparing an article on Le Pavillon, which Claiborne considered New York City's best restaurant, he met its head chef, Pierre Franey. They became friends and, after Franey left the restaurant in 1960, collaborated on articles for the *Times*. Claiborne built a beach house in East Hampton, and the two men used Claiborne's enormous professionally equipped kitchen to test recipes before presenting them in the newspaper. Notable amateur and professional cooks prepared signature dishes in his kitchen, which Claiborne described in his columns.

In 1959 the management of the *Times* granted Claiborne full rights to use the paper's name on a cookbook. Published in 1961, the *New York Times Cookbook* would sell over a million copies, making Claiborne wealthy. He compiled over twenty more cookbooks. *Craig Claiborne's Gourmet Diet* (1980), written with Franey after Claiborne developed high blood pressure, taught readers how to limit dietary salt and fat. Claiborne became famous for his elaborate New Year's Eve and birthday parties and for his Fourth of July picnics; the lavishly illustrated *Craig Claiborne's Memorable Meals* (1985) commemorated many feasts prepared in his kitchen. *Craig Claiborne's Southern Cooking* (1987), a tribute to his native cuisine, included many of his mother's recipes, along with others suggested by twenty-eight noted professional and amateur cooks.

Claiborne achieved worldwide notoriety for a lavish November 1975 dinner. As a contribution to an auction benefiting New York City's public television station, American Express offered a dinner for two, without limit on costs, at any restaurant in the world using its credit card. Claiborne submitted the winning $300 bid. Choosing the little-known Chez Denis in Paris, he and Pierre Franey sat down to a $4,000 five-hour, thirty-one-dish meal with nine wines. The *Times* ran Claiborne's account of the meal on page one, generating nearly a thousand letters, mostly critical of spending so much money on a single meal while people around the world were starving. The Vatican termed the event "scandalous."

Always open about his homosexuality, Claiborne described in his autobiography a sexual encounter with his father while an adolescent. Claiborne apparently never entered into a long-term homosexual relationship, often preferring the company of heterosexual men and women.

In 1972 Claiborne left the *Times* to start a food industry newsletter jointly with Franey. When the newsletter failed, Claiborne returned to the *Times* in 1974, remaining until his retirement in 1986. Claiborne continued to write, publishing a revised and updated version of his *New York Times Cookbook* in 1990. He died in a Manhattan hospital, leaving the bulk of his estate, including his books and home, to the Culinary Institute of America.

Purists faulted Claiborne for deviating from classic French methods of food preparation and for welcoming convenient new technologies such as frozen foods and food processors. What his critics found objectionable were actually his strengths. Along with James Beard and Julia Child, Claiborne demystified classic and ethnic cuisines, adapting them for the American kitchen. His restaurant reviews revealed the secrets of famous chefs; his carefully tested recipes tempted readers to try dishes they might otherwise never have tasted.

• The Craig Claiborne Collection at the Culinary Institute of America, Hyde Park, New York, has Claiborne's extensive collection of cookbooks. His autobiography, *A Feast Made for Laughter: A Memoir with Recipes* (1982), details Claiborne's life up to its date of publication. His cookbooks contain brief introductions, often with useful biographical data. The pictorially attractive *Craig Claiborne's Memorable Meals* (1985) has much information on activities in his East Hampton kitchen. Gay Talese describes Claiborne's hiring and work for the *Times* in *The Kingdom and the Power* (1969). Pierre Franey, *A Chef's Tale* (1994), depicts his collaboration with Claiborne. John L. and Karen Hess severely criticize Claiborne for deviating from strict classical French cuisine in *The Taste of America* (1977). Betty Fussell, *Masters of American Cookery* (1983), praises Claiborne's contributions to American cooking. Claiborne's obituary appears in the *New York Times*, 24 Jan. 2000. [*Editor's Note:* An article by Craig Claiborne on the life of Irma Rombauer is available to readers of the *American National Biography*.]

MILTON BERMAN

CLAMPETT, Bob (8 May 1913–2 May 1984), animation artist, was born Robert Clampett in San Diego, California, the son of Robert Caleb Clampett, a grocer, and Mildred Myrtle Clampett. Not much later, the Clampetts moved to Glendale, California, where Clampett attended local schools. While at Glendale High, Clampett won a *Los Angeles Times* cartooning contest. His winning entry, appearing on the front page of the paper's Junior section, attracted the attention of publisher William Randolph Hearst, who signed Clampett for his rival *Los Angeles Examiner*. On Clampett's graduation in 1930, the *Examiner* also sent him to study at the Otis Art Institute in Los Angeles.

Clampett had been making his own home movies since age twelve, and while at the *Examiner* and Otis he free-lanced his ideas around the studios. Clampett joined Charlotte Clark in creating the first Mickey Mouse doll for Walt Disney, whose 1928 "Steamboat Willie," starring a jaunty Mickey, had revolutionized film cartoons. When in 1930 Clampett took one of his original 16mm shorts to a major titling company, its proprietor, Leon Schlesinger, offered the teenager a job in Schlesinger's new film cartooning venture. Schlesinger abandoned his titling business to accept Warner Bros.' offer to supply its animated cartoons; in 1933, Clampett joined this company as an animator and soon was directing its Looney Tunes and Merrie Melodies cartoons.

The director of an animated cartoon provides its imaginative concept, usually first expressed in his own drawings. Clampett's visually anarchic and verbally punning sense of humor was crucial in giving Warner cartoons the biting edge that came to differentiate them from Disney's increasingly realistic-but-sentimental work.

Clampett is credited with streamlining Warners' lovable Porky Pig into a slimmer yet cuter being who ended each cartoon with a stuttered "That's All, Folks." After the success of his cartooned "When's Your Birthday?" in a live-action 1937 Joe E. Brown film, Clampett briefly went on his own in partnership with Edgar Rice Burroughs but soon returned to Warners. He created Daffy Duck, its inspiration being the baseball player "Daffy" Dean, brother of the great pitcher and malapropist Dizzy Dean. He created Tweety Bird (said to have been patterned after a baby picture of himself), and he pioneered the earliest animation of a story by Dr. Seuss (Theodor Seuss Geisel)—"Horton Hears a Who" (1940). In 1955 he married Theota Ann Stone; they had three children and remained married until Clampett's death.

During World War II, when his idol, animator Tex Avery, departed to lead Metro-Goldwyn-Mayer's cartoon unit, Clampett gave full rein to his surrealistic, absurdist slapstick and often black-humorous tendencies. Visually, he pulled his characters out of shape; verbally, he gave them outrageous sounds. He specialized in in-jokes. In "Russian Rhapsody, or Gremlin in the Kremlin," for instance, he managed to include caricatures of a number of Warner Bros. employees. Clampett's satirical enthusiasms (often parodying currently popular films and performers) can partly be inferred from the titles of some of his more famous cartoons: "Tin Pan Alley Cats" (1943), the Bugs Bunny Academy Award tale "What's Cookin', Doc?" (1944), "Bacall to Arms," "The Big Snooze," "Book Revue," and "The Great Piggy Bank Robbery, featuring Duck Twacy" (all 1946). Clampett earned three Emmys and a Grand Shorts Award.

During 1946, at the beginning of the television era, Clampett quit Warners. After a brief stint with Columbia Pictures, he set up his own studio, at first specializing in animated commercials. In 1950, partly boosted by the nationwide success of Burr Tillstrom's Chicago-based television series "Kukla, Fran and Ollie" (Fran was a human, the others were hand puppets), Clampett talked Los Angeles television station

KTTV into commissioning a show featuring hand puppets.

This was "Time for Beany," which ran locally for five years before acquiring nationwide distribution. "Beany" (a gap-toothed boy wearing a beany hat topped by a propeller) led a crew of zany, punning characters, including Cecil the Seasick Seaserpent (voiced by humorist Stan Freberg), Cap'n Hufnstuf (and his ship the Leakin' Lena), Dishonest John, Careless the Mexican Hairless, and Tearalong the Dotted Lion. The show, which attracted a loyal local following including Lionel Barrymore and Groucho Marx, went into syndication in the mid-1950s and became popular nationwide. In 1959 Clampett created "Matty's Funday Funnies," sponsored by Mattel Toys for a national audience. By 1962 this had become "Matty's Funnies with Beany and Cecil." In this incarnation, the characters were no longer puppets but cartoons. Clampett's various shows ran until 1967.

After Beany and Cecil's eclipse and a short period of obscurity during the 1970s, Clampett regained renown. Film critics and historians finally began to take seriously the 10-minute animated cartoon. Clampett was named by *Mediascene* magazine as one of the eight greatest animators of all time. He was a special guest during the first animation exhibition at the Museum of Modern Art in New York, and became a popular figure on college campuses and at comic conventions.

Clampett, a perpetually youthful founding father of one of the twentieth century's distinctive art forms, was in Detroit promoting a new video version of Beany and Cecil when he suffered a heart attack and died. The Clampett studio, headed by his widow, survived. He was central to Warners' golden age, which lasted through World War II, and with the rise of television Clampett went on to become one of its legendary innovators.

• Clampett's archive remains in family hands. Among discussions of Warner Bros. cartoons providing good background on Clampett are Jerry Beck and Will Friedwald, *Warner Bros. Animation Art: The Characters, the Creators, the Limited Editions* (1997), and Steve Schneider, *That's All, Folks: The Art of Warner Bros. Animation* (1988; 1994). Clampett's television creations are covered in Tim Brooks and Earle Marsh, *The Complete Directory of Prime-Time Network TV Shows, 1946-Present* (1979). An obituary is in the *Los Angeles Times*, 4 May 1984. Among subsequent *Times* appreciations is Charles Solomon, "Bob Clampett's Five Decades of Animation," 13 May 1984.

JAMES ROSS MOORE

COLE, John Ralph (14 Dec. 1914–13 Aug. 1958), cartoonist known as "Jack Cole," was born in New Castle, Pennsylvania, the son of DeLace Cole, a dry goods salesman and amateur song-and-dance man, and Cora Belle Cooper Cole, formerly an elementary schoolteacher. The third of six children, Jack at age fifteen enrolled in the Charles N. Landon correspondence school of cartooning, paying for it with his lunch money. Not a sedentary youth, he spent his summers during his high school years hiking and ca-

noeing. Between his junior and senior years he bicycled to California for the 1932 Olympic Games, a 7,000-mile round trip that he described in an article he illustrated for *Boys' Life* magazine in 1935. After he graduated from high school in 1933, Cole went to work at the local American Can factory, and on 7 July 1934 he eloped with Dorothy Marie Mahoney; they had no children.

Settled domestically, Cole freelanced cartoons in his spare time, submitting them by mail to magazines. In 1936, after only modest success through the mails, he borrowed $500 in small amounts from local merchants and friends and moved to New York with his wife. From their apartment in Greenwich Village, Cole made weekly sales visits to magazine editors. His drawing style at the time "belonged to the goofy-school being championed by such successful magazine cartoonists as Bill Holman and Dr. Seuss [Theodor Seuss Geisel]," according to the comics historian Ron Goulart (Goulart, p. 7). Cole sold some cartoons over the next few months but found greater financial security in 1937, when he was hired by Harry "A" Chesler to work for $20 a week in one of the early comic book art "shops." These were factory-model sweatshops, usually large rooms with rows of drawing tables at which cartoonists labored in assembly-line fashion, each producing some aspect of the final product (figures, faces, backgrounds, lettering). Cole, however, did all the drawing, pencils to inks, on his assignments, one-page humorous fillers that he crammed with sight gags, punning signage, and the sort of exaggerated anatomy that earned this style of drawing the name "bigfoot."

Like most young cartoonists in the 1930s, Cole aspired to his own syndicated newspaper comic strip because syndication offered the greatest potential for steady income. In the spring of 1938 he contributed a regular bigfoot comedic feature, "Peewee Throttle," to a comic book devised as a marketing tool by a United Feature official who hoped to form his own syndicate. Entitled *Circus Comics*, it lasted only three issues and sold nothing into syndication. By the end of the year Cole had started producing serious adventure stories drawn in a straight, more-or-less illustrative style. His first, a detective story, "Little Dynamite," about a diminutive cop, debuted in *Keen Detective Comics*, cover dated February 1939. His realistic drawing style employed a thick line and much feathered shadowing, and he used the odd-angle perspectives that later marked his mature manner. During this period Cole freelanced material to several publishers, including Centaur, Hillman, Novelty, and MLJ, producing for the latter several "true crime" stories that demonstrated, as Goulart has pointed out (Goulart, p. 11), that Cole, "unlike many of his contemporaries," realized that comic book pages weren't newspaper strips and therefore required somewhat different visual treatment in layout and narrative breakdown.

Late in 1939 Cole created his first costumed superhero, the Comet, for the first issue of MLJ's *Pep*

Comics (Jan. 1940). About the same time he started editing and drawing for *Silver Streak Comics*, published by Lev Gleason. Working for Gleason through 1940, Cole created several characters and worked on one of the line's stellar costumed heroes, the Daredevil. Cole also continued freelancing with other publishers, and by the close of the year he worked almost exclusively for Quality Comics. There, at the publisher's directive, he created Midnight, a detective character that duplicated another Quality creation, Will Eisner's the Spirit, a crime fighter in mufti who hid the top part of his face behind a domino mask. Midnight debuted in *Smash Comics* number eighteen (Jan. 1941).

In August 1941 Quality inaugurated two new titles, and Cole created features for each. For *Military Comics* he concocted "Death Patrol," a somewhat humorous treatment of a gruesome theme—one member of a team of military flyers dies in each issue of the comic book. For *Police Comics* he invented a costumed superhero, Plastic Man, who was unique in the history of comics. Plastic Man started out as a petty crook named Eel O'Brian who leads his gang in a robbery attempt at a chemical factory, where a vat of acid spills on him, soaking him and leaving him unconscious. When he awakens, he finds he can stretch himself in any direction to virtually any length. He decides to use this power to fight crime and allies with the police as an undercover operative, assuming a variety of disguises by changing his physical appearance. Fans and comics historians often call Plastic Man the "wackiest superhero in comics," but the label is misleading. At first the feature was a straightforward, realistically rendered cops-and-robbers adventure. The only outright comedy was in the astonishment of the hoodlums at the shapes Plastic Man assumed in order to capture them, a reaction Cole was quick to exaggerate for comedic effect. The shape-changing device made Cole's creation popular. By the fifth issue of *Police Comics*, Plastic Man was the cover feature, and the number of pages allotted to him increased steadily, reaching fifteen pages by the nineteenth issue. By this time Cole had hit his stride, producing stories laced with sight gags, exaggerated action, and caricatural criminals.

The evolution was gradual. Beginning with the comical reactions of the crooks to Plastic Man's elasticity, Cole soon caused his rubbery hero, now in a red leotard costume, to assume ever more outlandish disguises. Plas (as he was nicknamed) often took the shape of a piece of furniture or a conveniently positioned objet d'art. For the reader the fun was in discovering which chair in the crook's hideout is red with black and yellow stripes and a yellow diamond, a telltale design that duplicated that of Plas's ornamental belt. Once Plas was a red carpet with a yellow diamond in the middle, another time a red vase with black and yellow stripes. Plas also deployed his pliable propensity to defend himself. Sprayed with deadly poison gas, he converted himself into a giant bellows and blew it all away. Caught in a fog bank, he turned himself into a periscope to see over it. The flood of sight gags proceeded from this visual pranksterism as Cole filled his panels with a maniacal frenzy of incidental pictorial hilarity in the bigfoot style. In *Police Comics* number thirteen (Nov. 1942) Cole introduced Woozy Winks, a short, tubby, small-time crook with a bulbous nose who became Plas's sidekick, the personification of ineptitude. An outright comedy character, Woozy was doubtless the catalyst that completed for Cole the transformation of the feature from serious to humorous and then to seeming slapstick. But Plastic Man was not a comedian.

Cole's masterstroke was in making Plas an entirely sane character in a world of crackbrained criminals. What made the feature seem wacky was the bigfoot cartoon style Cole deployed, a style that produced Plastic Man's unique parody. Many of the characters looked like daffy lunatics, but most took themselves seriously. The crooks plotted their crimes as cannily as criminals in any other comic book, but Cole nonetheless parodied the criminal mind. If his villains' actions seemed somewhat zany, it was because their personalities were wholly defined by their lawbreaking purposes. They were obsessive, and to the normal reader obsessiveness escalates to insanity, hence wacky. Cole made his moral point by making many of his criminals crazily comic in appearance, thereby suggesting that only madmen seek a life of crime. At the same time that Plastic Man veered off into greater visual comedy, so too did Midnight. Cole had found his métier. But he abandoned Midnight with the December 1942 issue of *Smash Comics* (number thirty-eight). His workload with Plastic Man had increased too much for him to maintain both features, and in the spring of 1943 he began to produce additional stories for the occasionally issued *Plastic Man Comics*.

For the remainder of the decade Cole did Plastic Man and, in the early years, a number of short humorous filler features. In 1942 Eisner was drafted into the army, and Cole produced the daily comic strip version of *The Spirit* for a time (18 May–8 Aug). At the end of 1946 Cole returned to Midnight, continuing the feature until *Smash Comics* expired in September 1949. He also created serious material for *True Crime Comics* in the mid-1940s, and he revived his earlier career freelancing single-panel gag cartoons to magazines. By 1951 he was doing only a miscellany of occasional stories for Quality, and in 1953 Cole left comic books altogether to concentrate on magazine cartooning. Within a year he was the star cartoonist in Hugh Hefner's new men's magazine launched in December 1953. For *Playboy*, starting with the fifth issue, Cole abandoned the linear mode he had deployed so skillfully in comic books and produced startlingly accomplished full-page, full-color watercolor cartoon paintings, depicting zaftig young women in various stages of dishabille while in compromising situations with their male admirers. Hefner, a frustrated cartoonist himself, hoped to establish a distinctive "look" for the magazine's cartoons, and Cole supplied it. His painterly approach to cartooning set the fashion for *Playboy* cartoonists. So important was he to *Play-*

boy that Hefner insisted he move from Connecticut to be near the magazine's office in Chicago, and in early 1956 Cole and his wife bought a house in nearby Cary, Illinois.

In early 1958 Cole achieved every cartoonist's dream: he sold a newspaper comic strip to the Chicago Sun-Times Syndicate. *Betsy and Me* began 26 May, and it was as distinctive in execution and concept as Cole's Plastic Man had been for comic books and his panel cartoons had been for *Playboy*. Drawn in the ultramodern abstract style made popular earlier in the decade by UPA animated cartoons, the strip was narrated by Chet Tibbit, the diminutive albeit proud husband of Betsy and father of an unabashed boy genius, Farley. It was a "family" strip, but Cole's storytelling manner made for unusual comedy. The fatuous protagonist and narrator said one thing in the captions accompanying the drawings, but the pictures contradicted what he said, revealing Chet to be a trifle pretentious and wholly delusional, a visual-verbal tour de force.

At the pinnacle of his professional achievement, Cole inexplicably committed suicide by shooting himself in the head with a .22 caliber Marlin rifle on a country road near Cary. Although he left several notes, the one that gave the reasons for his action, addressed and mailed to his wife before he shot himself, was never made public.

Without question or qualification Cole was a cartooning genius, a virtuoso at the craft, an absolute master of the medium. He excelled in three of cartooning's genres, creating and consistently producing unique work in each. In a lengthy appreciation of Cole in the *New Yorker* (p. 80), the Pulitzer Prize–winning cartoonist Art Spiegelman called Plastic Man "the embodiment of the comic book form: its exuberant energy, its flexibility, its boyishness, and its only partially subliminated sexuality." Producing all of his own material, from pencil preliminaries to final script and inks, Cole was the very emblem of cartooning. In each of his masterworks the verbal and the visual blend in authentic cartooning fashion, creating a meaning that neither words nor pictures alone can achieve.

• Cole provided a brief autobiographical glimpse into his career in "Playboy's Hard Worker," *Freelancer*, 1956 (pp. 4-5). Ron Goulart, *Focus on Jack Cole* (1986), approaches a full biography but is lamentably short (just seventy-eight pages, including a thirty-page portfolio of comic book stories and splash pages). Some of the information is repeated in Goulart's more widely available *Encyclopedia of American Comics* (1990). Art Spiegelman's appreciation, "Forms Stretched to Their Limits," *New Yorker*, 19 Apr. 1999 (pages 76–85), was subsequently published in book form as *Jack Cole and Plastic Man: Forms Stretched to Their Limits* (2001). It rehearses Cole's career but not in as much detail as Goulart, and its chief appeal is in Spiegelman's analysis of Cole's storytelling technique in rendering Plastic Man and in Spiegelman's theorizing about Cole's suicide. Less poetic but probably more accurate theorizing is done by the comics historian Clay Geerdes in an unpublished article, "Plastic Man," written in 1991. More in the same vein is in Robert C. Harvey, "The Mystique and Mysteries of Jack Cole," *Comics Journal*, Oct. 1999, 155–161. In "The Long Arm of the Law," a chapter in vol. 2 of *The Steranko History of Comics* (1972), pp. 80–89, Jim Steranko summarizes several Plastic Man stories and reprints the text of Cole's *Boys' Life* article about his cross-country bicycle trip to Los Angeles and back. A special section of several insightful articles on Cole, including reminiscences and interviews with Cole's coworkers and with his youngest brother Richard, is in *Alter Ego*, June 2003.

ROBERT C. HARVEY

COLLEY, Russell (22 July 1897–4 Feb. 1996), inventor, designer, and aeronautical engineer, was born Russell Sidney Colley in Stoneham, Mass., the son of Frank S. Colley, a druggist, and Florence Vesta Hopkins Colley. Russell spent several summers in high school serving as an apprentice electrician. After he revealed his desire to become a women's fashion designer, his art teacher directed him out of her freehand drawing class into what she considered more appropriate, a mechanical drawing class. He was accepted into Wentworth Institute of Technology in Boston, Massachusetts, and in 1918 completed the two-year machine construction and tool design course.

Out of a class of 65, Russell was one of eighteen chosen to go to Kent, Ohio, to work at the Kent Machine Company. He first worked as a machinist and graduated to drafting. Here he designed different-sized concrete mixers, which Kent built and sold. In 1921 he married Dorothy Mae Antle; they had one child.

Around 1928, Colley was persuaded to go to the B. F. Goodrich Company in Akron, Ohio, where he joined the experimental division. "You never know what kind of job you'll be given," he was told. One of his first assignment was to make a golf ball driving machine. "Playing golf by hand, the normal way, was useless to me after that," he later recalled. In the 1930s, Colley became an assistant to Dr. William C. Geer, a past president of Goodrich. Geer sought to develop airplane wing deicers. For testing of pneumatic wing deicers Colley developed one of the largest refrigerated wind tunnels in the United States. He also developed the "rivnut," part rivet and part nut, to fasten the fairing strip to each wing-tip edge of the deicer. His system allowed a single worker to perform a task that had previously required two.

Colley began working on aeronautical problems for James "Jimmy" Doolittle, aviator and U.S. army officer. Doolittle introduced Colley to Wiley Post, a racing pilot. Post had experienced brief periods of flight time in the jet stream, enough to realize that in it a plane could fly much faster. But to stay in the rarified air of the stratosphere, or jet stream, for any length of time, a pilot had to wear a fully pressurized suit. Colley and Post went to the California B. F. Goodrich plant. Colley explained their need for a suit that would stand 2½ pounds of pressure. They made the first suit out of balloon cloth, a rubberized fabric. It was then pressurized with less than one pound of oxygen pressure, but this caused it to rip up the middle.

Colley and Post returned to Akron, and Colley continued to work on the pressurized suit. He observed that a tire with a pressurized inner tube withstood far greater pressure. So Colley designed a sheet metal mold dipped in latex and contoured it to fit Post's body. Since there were no sewing machines at the plant, Colley, used his wife's sewing machine. He made the outer layer of sailcloth. But on the day Post tested the suit, it did not work. Post had gained some weight and it was a hot day. Post couldn't get the suit off. They were forced to take him to the golf ball cold storage room and cut it off him. The third suit, completed in 1934, fit perfectly. On 5 September 1934 Post flew to a reported height of 48,000 feet. Unfortunately, the altimeter froze at 35,000 feet, so he did not set a verified record. Nevertheless, this flight and subsequent ones proved the practicability of Colley's altitude suit and oxygen supply system; it also demonstrated that the winds at the base of the stratosphere increased the airplane's speed tremendously.

In 1942–1944, during World War II, Colley worked with Doolittle to produce high-altitude pressure suits for his crew to use during its raid on Tokyo. Changing the mission from high altitude to low altitude, however, removed the need for pressure suits. Colley had been working on a design he and his team had devised from his observations of the tomato worm. He noticed that the segmented worm performed 90 degree turns without changing pressure anywhere on its body. The team adapted the segmented bellows into the arms and legs of the pressure suit. This gave the pilot the ability to sit and stand and rudimentary mobility while pressurized. These early suits, however, failed later more rigorous tests. One evening at home, Colley began sketching on a piece of paper. His mesmerized family sat around the kitchen table, watching a tiny capsule appear. The capsule was to contain a man. Colley then drew an enormous rocket that was to boost the man and capsule into space. It was a concept almost beyond the family's comprehension. Colley's pressure suit team had been developing several pressure suit models in recent years. He would tell them no more. The program was secret.

By the late 1950s, Colley's team had made phenomenal progress on the Mark series of pressurized suits for astronauts. The Mark II soft suit of lightweight rubberized fabric led directly to the development of the Mark IV, the suit chosen for the Mercury astronauts. Colley received patents on the neck ring, the wrist coupler, the tomato worm effect as applied to the suit, and many others. He received sixty-five patents in the B. F. Goodrich name, for which he was paid only one dollar each. He constantly made things, carving, whittling, painting, constructing, and inventing them throughout his life. Colley is considered the "father of the American space suit" for his part in the development of Wiley Post's successful pressure suit and the Mercury space suit. In 1993, Senator John Glenn presented him with a NASA Honor Award for his contribution to the production of the Mercury space suit. He died in Springfield, Ohio.

• See Lloyd Mallan, *Suited Up for Space* (1971), for coverage of early space suit development. Also see Lillian D. Kozloski, *U. S. Space Gear* (2000), for chronology of design and problem solving. See Stanley R. Mohler and Bobby H. Johnson, *Wiley Post, his Winnie Mae, and the World's First Pressure Suit* (1971), for the complete Wiley Post story. *Outbound (Voyage Through the Universe)* (1989) gives an overview of the development of space suits and life in space. This article also draws on an oral history interview with Russell Colley conducted 9 May 1989 for the National Air and Space Museum. An obituary is in *Time*, 19 Feb. 1996.

LILLIAN D. KOZLOSKI

COLÓN, Jesús (20 Jan. 1901–1974), writer and political and community activist, was born to working-class parents in rural Puerto Rico, whose names are not known. In *A Puerto Rican in New York and Other Sketches*, a compilation of his autobiographical short essays written in English, Colón described his humble childhood in Cayey, a small farming town in a breathtaking mountain range, well known for producing hand-rolled cigars. Cigars were among the most important products for export of this territory acquired by the United States after a successful war against Spain in 1898. In 1917 Puerto Ricans became American citizens. The Puerto Rico of Colón's childhood memories appears free of American influence. His dearest childhood memories belong to the world of tobacco workers, male and female, who spent many hours rolling cigars while listening to the local and international news that a hired reader read aloud to them. According to Colón's memoirs, the reader included literary passages, such as Émile Zola's *Germinal* (1885), Honoré de Balzac's *Le Père Goriot* (1834), and Miguel de Cervantes's *Don Quixote* (1605, 1615). They also heard passages from Karl Marx, Pyotr Alekseyevich Kropotkin, and Errico Malatesta, who exposed them to leftist political ideas. His early contact with the plight of workers created in Colón an interest in socialist and communist ideology.

Colón's family moved to San Juan, but his memoir does not date or explain the reasons for the move to the island's capital. His father, a baker by trade, may have been among the thousands of migrant workers displaced to urban centers who sought work in the industries recently inaugurated throughout the major cities. The island was witnessing a change in social structure, as a pre–World War I technology replaced traditional agricultural industries. Beginning a strong emigration to the United States, a considerable number of workers were lured to northeastern industrial cities, particularly to New York City.

San Juan did not have, however, a major impact on Colón. His sketches include no descriptions of the island's largest city, a jewel of Spanish colonial architecture. Colón must have been familiar with the colonial quarters, known as Old San Juan, since his grammar school was located within the historic district. He did not appear to experience difficulties in acculturation from his former peasant life to growing up in a city that was undergoing major urban renovations.

Colón's remembrances of his experiences in San Juan are limited to his real passions: his interest in literature and his allegiance to the struggling working class. One of his sketches records that his literary debut took place while he was in the eighth grade. His class wrote letters of condolence on the death of a classmate's mother, and only the best letter was to be mailed on behalf of the students. Colón's short letter was the one selected. Although as an adult Colón produced no literature other than his short essays, he wrote for newspapers and translated literary and political writings into English or Spanish.

Colón's early passion to serve people is also visible in his involvement with student groups. For instance, he acted as a spokesperson for his classmates, who had decided to boycott a teacher for an unfair decision. He also helped found a student newspaper, which soon covered heated political and social events experienced by Puerto Rican society at large. The newspaper reported on the emergence of workers' groups (many with socialist inclinations) that often clashed with governmental restrictions on free expression of political discontent. The dockworkers of Puerta de Tierra, a marginal neighborhood outside San Juan where the most important industrial docking piers were located, were among those who took action. The dockworkers organized into strong workers' unions and often defied strict official restrictions on strikes. From the school playground, the young socialist Colón and his schoolmates witnessed a strike, including police brutality that resulted in the deaths of several strikers. The school newspaper, *Adelante* (Let's Go Forward), recorded this open violation of the workers' rights, as Colón remembers in the sketch.

For unstated reasons, in 1918 Colón boarded illegally a cargo ship bound for the United States, where he joined a brother in New York City. He had not finished junior high school, so he had to take several menial jobs. Colón worked hard, long hours in the train and dock systems of the city. His several jobs as a laborer in New York City brought him into contact with workers who, like himself, could barely make ends meet. These individuals represented a variety of ethnic groups, mainly African Americans and Latinos, people of high moral caliber who continuously struggled to survive. Their struggles and their successes (in spite of societal oppression) became lessons in the will to succeed in spite of dire economic conditions.

Colón's life in New York resembled the lives of thousands of other Puerto Ricans who arrived before World War II. Conditions were harsh and even inhumane, though Colón sprinkled his stories of acculturation with humor. This is true of his sketch, "Two Men with But One Pair of Pants," which tells of Colón sharing one pair of working pants with his brother.

As a black man Colón also had to deal with rampant racist attitudes. He vividly remembered that often African Americans and black Latinos suffered from discrimination because of their skin color. This is the theme of his sketch about being denied an office job as a translator despite the fact that he had done excellent translations from his home. The editor withdrew the opportunity after he met Colón in person. Colón's sketches often call for racial harmony, as he recognized that the xenophobia and racism of mainstream society also kept immigrants from organizing into cohesive, powerful social groups.

In *A Puerto Rican in New York and Other Sketches* (1961), a compilation of sketches originally written in English for the Socialist publication the *Worker*, Colón recorded the tremendous socioeconomic changes he witnessed in New York City. Colón was a prolific writer of sketches, which are estimated at more than four hundred (Acosta Belén and Korrol, p. 20), some written for Spanish-language publications in New York and in Puerto Rico. Colón's most common subject matter was the plight of immigrants, particularly Latinos. *A Puerto Rican* also follows the radical transformations of New York City through his detailed descriptions of its many ethnic neighborhoods.

New York City was close to Colón's heart. He discovered the city as a teenage boy and got to know it well through his many jobs. In New York he met Rufa Concepción Fernández, and they married in 1925. She appears often in his sketches as "Concha." In 1958, after Concha's death, Colón married Clara (maiden name unknown), who is also present in his sketches. Colón instructed his Jewish-American wife about Puerto Rico's political conditions through trips to the island and through his anecdotes.

Colón's involvement with Puerto Rican and Latino communities led him into activism and a political career. In 1953 he was a candidate for the New York City Council as a member of the American Labor Party, and in 1969 he ran for New York City controller as the candidate of the Communist Party. In 1959 his membership in the Communist Party attracted the attention of the Walter committee investigating "un-American activities." Colón's statement to this House committee, delivered in New York City on 16 November 1959, is one of his most challenging political declarations of his constitutional right to promote the cause of Puerto Rican independence. "Certainly," he said, "I will never cooperate with the efforts of this committee to take away the few liberties the Puerto Ricans have today nor to set a barrier to the only solution for Puerto Rico and Puerto Ricans: complete and absolute independence" (*The Way It Was*, p. 102). He died in New York City.

Because Colón wrote *A Puerto Rican in New York and Other Sketches* in English, he stood out from other Puerto Rican or Latino writers of his time, who wrote mainly in Spanish. By writing in English, Colón improved the chances for dissemination of his pro–Puerto Rican and Latino opinions. *A Puerto Rican*, published in the early 1960s by a mainstream publishing house, was at the forefront of an incipient Puerto Rican and Latino literature in English. Colón's work offers a rare portrait of a place and a time in the history of New York City of interest to social historians. His strong lobbying on behalf of destitute workers and his proud view of a multicultural New York place him among the earliest proponents of multiculturalism.

• The Jesús Colón Papers Collection at the Centro de Estudios Puertorriqueños at Hunter College, New York City, include his notes and unpublished papers. Colón, *Lo que el pueblo me dice: Crónicas de la colonia puertorriqueña en Nueva York* ("What the People Tell Me: Chronicles of the Puerto Rican Population in New York"), ed. Edwin Karli Padilla Aponte (2001), is a compilation of Colón's articles published in Spanish-speaking newspapers in New York from 1927 to 1944. A short introduction in Spanish traces Colón's active life as a Latino and Puerto Rican activist and follows his campaign in favor of Puerto Rico's independence. Colón, *The Way It Was and Other Writings*, ed. Edna Acosta-Belén and Virginia Sánchez Korrol (1993), a compilation of sketches he left unfinished at his death, was completed by the editors, who used his unpublished papers. An extensive introduction states Colón's literary significance, with emphasis on the ramifications of his political activism on behalf of the Puerto Rican and Latino communities in New York City. Rafael Ocasio, "Colón, Jesús," in *Identities and Issues in Literature*, ed. David Peck (1997), traces Colón's role in the development of a contemporary Puerto Rican literature written in English. Maricela Oliva, "Colón, Jesús," in *Biographical Dictionary of Hispanic Literature in the United States*, ed. Nicolás Kanellos (1989), offers a detailed analysis of Colón's writings with a strong biographical outlook and emphasizes Colón's literary themes and subjects.

RAFAEL OCASIO

COMO, Perry (18 May 1912–12 May 2001), singer of popular music and television entertainer, was born Pierino Roland Como in Canonsburg, Pennsylvania, the son of Pietro Como, a mill hand, and Lucia Travaglini Como, immigrants from Palena, Italy. The seventh of thirteen children, Perry Como earned a few cents a day working after school in a local barbershop in Canonsburg. Later, while attending high school, he operated his own barbershop. Como, performing at wedding receptions and other functions, gained local recognition for his singing ability. One of the few vocalists of his generation to read music, he played both organ and baritone horn.

Vacationing in Cleveland in 1933, Como auditioned for Freddie Carlone's band and was hired at twenty-five dollars a week. That same year Como married his high school sweetheart, Roselle Beline, the daughter of French immigrants; they had three children, whom they sheltered from the celebrity world of show business. "Roselle always stood by me," Como remarked. She died in August 1998, two weeks after celebrating their sixty-fifth wedding anniversary.

Como's popularity skyrocketed in the late 1930s after he became the featured vocalist with the Ted Weems orchestra. When the Weems band broke up in the early 1940s, NBC offered him a contract to share star billing with singer Jo Stafford on the Chesterfield Supper Club, a radio show broadcast Mondays through Fridays. Como usually sang romantic ballads during each broadcast. When that show came to Friday night television in the late 1940s Como continued to be a featured vocalist, supported by the Mitchell Ayres Orchestra and the Fontane Sisters. A smorgasbord of comedy routines, dancing, and singing, the show gave him the opportunity to reveal a captivating personality. His neckties and business suits, however, did not complement his casual style and in later shows he wore cardigan sweaters, dubbed Perry Como sweaters by his fans. The program was soon moved to a half-hour slot on Sundays, competing with Ed Sullivan's *Toast of the Town*. Meanwhile, Como was also performing before enthusiastic and often frenetic audiences at the Paramount Theater in New York City and the Steel Pier in Atlantic City. "Perry Como was the heartthrob of the ladies at that time," remarked David Hamid, Jr., part owner of the Steel Pier.

Hollywood filmmakers lured Como to the silver screen, but his career in the motion picture industry was brief and unrewarding. Three of his movies, *Something for the Boys* (1944), *Doll Face* (1945) and *If I'm Lucky* (1946), remain memorable because they featured Carmen Miranda. "I was wasting their time and they were wasting mine," Como admitted. Television, however, seemed made for his singing style and personality. His baritone voice, intimate and personal, complemented his affability and sincerity. Television viewers liked his friendliness. On 14 May 2001 the *Washington Post* noted in retrospect: "What Perry Como did week after week on his TV shows was not so much sing to his fans as have a continuing conversation with them, a conversation in song."

In 1950 Como signed with CBS, hosting his own program for five seasons. In 1955 he went back to NBC, starring in the weekly *Perry Como Show*, later titled *The Kraft Music Hall*. He remained with NBC until 1963. From the late 1940s through the early 1960s Como was a pioneer in the television variety show genre. His singing style evolved into the popular musical form called easy listening, influencing a generation of lounge singers. Beginning with his first, on Christmas Eve 1948, Como's Christmas specials on ABC-TV became an integral part of the holiday season. These annual events were accompanied by his three Christmas albums (1946–1948) for the RCA Victor label. A fourth Christmas album, recorded for Como's 1993–1994 Irish Christmas television special, was his only non-RCA recording in half a century. When ABC decided to cancel Como's annual Christmas special in 1987, the *Dallas Morning News* mounted a "Save Perry" letter-writing campaign. A fan wrote: "If Perry Como is removed from Christmas, can Santa Claus be far behind?"

Wearing a cardigan sweater and showing a winning smile on television, he appeared so relaxed that his critics believed he lacked ambition. However, his career spanned more than six decades and made him wealthy. "People have always thought that I wasn't ambitious," he said. "They judged by appearances and were fooled. I was competitive. I wanted success and was willing to work for it." In *New Statesman*, 14

May 2001, a music critic wrote, "nobody else was so intensely relaxed."

Como was one of the most successful performers of the twentieth century. Along with nonsense tunes like "Hot Diggity Dog Ziggity Boom," lighthearted songs like "Papa Loves Mambo," and even a rock-and-roll number, "Juke Box Baby," he left an enduring legacy as an interpreter of the romantic ballad. In 1943 in the midst of a strike by the American Federation of Musicians, Como recorded with only vocal accompaniment "Goodbye Sue" for the RCA Victor label. Among his most popular romantic ballads are "Dream Along with Me," "Don't Let the Stars Get in Your Eyes," "Temptation," "Because," "Till the End of Time," "Prisoner of Love," "And I Love You So," and "It's Impossible." Often accompanied by the Mitchell Ayres Orchestra and the Ray Charles Singers, Como sold more than one hundred million records and had fourteen tunes that were ranked number one musical hits. In 1946 he was named top-selling male singer by *Billboard*. As late as 1973 he received a Grammy award nomination as best male pop vocalist for "And I Love You So." His achievements during the rock-and-roll era, when ballad crooners were falling by the wayside, were particularly remarkable.

During the final years of his long life Como spent most of his time at his home in Jupiter Inlet Beach Colony near Palm Beach, Florida, golfing, fishing, and taking long walks with his wife. Near the time of his death he had become a great-grandfather. He devoted himself to various charities, including his annual golf benefits at Duke University in North Carolina, and even found time to visit radio stations that carried *Weekend with Perry*, a weekly program syndicated throughout the United States. In his later years he suffered from Alzheimer's disease.

Combining a gentle voice with a pleasant personality, Como celebrated in life and in song romantic love and lifelong fidelity. He parlayed these values and his ability to express them in song into one of the most successful careers in twentieth-century popular entertainment.

• Perry Como's most important legacy is his music. Unfortunately, many of his albums for RCA are unavailable on compact disc. For Como's career on television see Alex McNeil, *Total Television* (1996). His singing career is examined briefly in Donald Clark, ed, *The Penguin Encyclopedia of Popular Music* (1989). Also see Kathleen J. Edger, ed., *Contemporary Theatre, Film, and Television*, vol. 20 (1999). Obituaries and retrospectives on Como include those in the *Palm Beach Post*, 13 May 2001; the *Washington Post*, 14 May 2001; *USA Today*, 17 May 2001; *Rolling Stone*, 17 May 2001; and the *Dallas Morning News*, 19 May 2001.

SALVATORE MONDELLO

CONKWRIGHT, P. J. (23 Oct. 1905–31 Jan. 1986), book designer, was born Pleasant Jefferson Conkwright in Bristow, located in what was then Oklahoma Territory, the son of Pleasant Jefferson Conkwright and Mildred Fox Conkwright, missionaries. In 1908 the family settled in Salpupa, southwest of Tulsa, where P. J.'s father remained a pastor at the First Baptist Church until his retirement in 1941. In Salpupa P. J. produced Sunday school bulletins on a duplicator for his father. His enthusiasm for printing developed further, and as a teenager he worked part time in a local print shop. He also printed his Boy Scout newspaper on his own small press.

In 1924, P. J. Conkwright enrolled at Oklahoma Baptist University in Shawnee, Oklahoma. During the next four years, he transferred to the University of Oklahoma, the University of Missouri, and ultimately the University of Kentucky. In 1928 he received his Bachelor of Arts in history from the University of Kentucky in Lexington. He then moved back to Oklahoma and taught courses in English and art for the next year. Conkwright began working for the University of Oklahoma Press in 1929. Over the next ten years he worked as a proofreader, art editor, and eventually the press's book designer. In 1934, while in Oklahoma, he married Hazel Dale Boone; they remained together until his death. In 1938 he received his Master of Arts in English and history, with an emphasis on American printing history. In 1939 he became chief book designer at Princeton University Press, where he worked until his retirement in 1970. (From 1960 to 1970, he also taught graphic arts at Princeton.)

Throughout his career, Conkwright had an intense drive for learning; he was specifically interested in typographic history. In September 1956, he received a nine-month Guggenheim Fellowship to study typography and design in Europe. During this time, he and his wife traveled throughout Europe to examine lettering and inscriptions on monuments, buildings, and store fronts. While traveling, he met with some of the top European printers, typographers, and typographic historians of the time, such as John Dreyfus, Herman Zapf, Walter Tracy and Charles Peignot. His previous studies together with the information gathered from this trip furnished him with an in-depth knowledge of inscriptional letterforms.

Perhaps the most impressive contribution that Conkwright made to the world was his ability to bring clean and innovative design to the conservative academic audience of university press books. He was interested in every detail of his projects, from the typesetting and printing to the binding and stamping. His title pages tend to be the focus of the book's design and therefore garner the most attention. They consistently display skill in incorporating text and ornament or image, demonstrating a meticulously planned hierarchy that always appears at ease. The expertise of Conkwright's design lies in its subtlety. His work is, in fact, so sensitively designed that it is difficult for one to imagine it looking any other way. Every title page that he created was exacting and precise and always appropriate to its content, however obscure the subject might be. His contemporaries included Bruce Rogers, William Addison Dwiggins, and Frederic

Warde, director of printing at Princeton University Press (1922–1924).

Conkwright was aware of classic typographic styles and printing techniques, and he steadily applied them to all aspects of his work throughout his career. Due to this interest in the production aspects of publishing, new ties were established between the compositors and printers and the designers and publishers. He also helped to bring attention to the applications of typographic history amid a conformist and hesitant publishing culture. The most prominent of these applications was his research for Princeton's 1950 publication of *The Papers of Thomas Jefferson*. As a result of his earlier studies, and with the aid of Linotype, Conkwright was able to develop a recut of a type from 1800 named Monticello, which was then used for the entire series.

Conkwright received an American Institute of Graphic Design (AIGA) Gold Medal as well as honorary degrees from Princeton University and the University of Kentucky. Between 1942 and 1976 he had a record fifty-two books in the AIGA Fifty Books Show. He was also a member of the Grolier Club and the American Academy of Arts and Letters. He died in Princeton.

Conkwright was an ideal book designer. In addition to his talent for practical design, his interests in typographic history and thorough knowledge of printing created elegant, understated, and always successful results. He was known as "the reader's designer" because he defined communication as the true aim of printing. Warm and friendly, modest and dedicated, he was greatly respected throughout his career and his lifetime.

• The best source for information on P. J. Conkwright is the *Princeton University Library Chronicle* 56, no. 2 (Winter 1995); the entire journal is dedicated to him. Other resources with good descriptions of his work include John Dreyfus, *P. J. Conkwright and University Press Design* (1963), and Dreyfus, "P. J. Conkwright, Style and Tradition: Book Designs 1940–1970," *Princeton University Library Chronicle* 32, no. 2 (Winter 1971). Conkwright's most well-known work, "University Press Book Design," can be found in György Kepes et al., *Graphic Forms: The Arts as Related to the Book* (1949). This was reprinted in the easier-to-locate *Typographers on Type: An Illustrated Anthology from William Morris to the Present Day*, edited by Ruari McLean (1995). Another example of Conkwright's writing is his 1974 book *Some Notes from the Journal of a Book Designer*.

SHELLEY GRUENDLER

CONOVER, Willis Clark, Jr. (18 Dec. 1920–17 May 1996), jazz radio announcer, was born in Buffalo, New York, the son of Willis Conover, Sr., a U.S. Army officer, and Francis Estelle Harris. The family was continuously uprooted by the demands of a military career, and by the time of his graduation from high school Conover had attended more than twenty schools. At the age of fourteen he played the role of a radio announcer for a skit in school. Shortly afterward he initiated a correspondence with the writer H. P.

Lovecraft. After Lovecraft's death, Conover collected these letters as *Lovecraft at Last* (self-published in 1975; published by Cooper Square Press in 2002).

Conover spent two semesters at Salisbury State Teachers College in Maryland and then worked part-time for eight weeks at a local radio station. In 1939 his victory at an amateur announcing contest in Washington, D.C., led to a full-time job as an announcer at station WTBO in Cumberland, Maryland. There he developed a passionate devotion to jazz. Inducted into the army in 1942, Conover mentioned his experience as a radio interviewer, and he was immediately given a job at Fort Meade, Maryland, interviewing inductees. In July 1944 he began working weekends at WWDC, where he presented the only jazz show in the Washington area, and following his discharge in February 1946, he worked full-time at WWDC while also promoting jazz concerts in the city.

In late 1954 the Voice of America (VOA) hired Conover. His program *Music U.S.A.* ran for forty-two years, six nights per week, from 6 January 1955 until a few months before his death. Initially it consisted of two thirty-minute segments, the first presenting classic American popular songs and the second jazz. At some point he focused on the jazz show and presented a separate, twice-weekly program of popular songs. He also prepared musical programs aimed at specific foreign countries with portions of his scripts overdubbed in the appropriate languages.

From 1958 Conover maintained residences in both Arlington, Virginia, and New York City, shuttling between the two. He continued to work for WWDC during the early portion of his affiliation with the VOA, and later he moonlighted for a brief period as a jazz announcer for WCBS in Manhattan.

Conover traveled extensively under the sponsorship of the State Department and the U.S. Information Agency. In 1959 he landed in Warsaw to find hundreds of Poles waiting with flowers, gifts, and jazz instruments. He was stunned to hear thunderous cheers as he disembarked. Conversely, his Polish fans were equally puzzled that Conover was not routinely treated as a famous man. The Polish jazz pianist Adam Makowicz credited Conover with inspiring his own shift from classical music, for which Makowicz was expelled from school and forced to become a homeless runaway in Communist Poland. In 1976, when Makowicz finally went to New York City, he was astonished that few jazz musicians knew of Conover's work and worth. But the VOA was forbidden by law to broadcast within the United States, and hence the only Americans who heard Conover were those who encountered him on local AM radio or in his capacity as master of ceremonies at the summertime Newport Jazz Festival from 1956 to 1960.

In 1964 Conover established the Friends of Music U.S.A. By year's end this informal fellowship had 20,000 members in 76 countries, from Korea to Ghana. Each chapter received a free subscription to *Down Beat* magazine and occasionally free albums. In the course of his worldwide travels Conover acquired local recordings from fellowship chapter members and when appropriate played these on his show.

In the mid-1960s Conover received another tumultuous reception as a guest at the Tallinn International Jazz Festival in Estonia (then in the USSR). He made a number of appearances at the annual International Jazz Jamboree Festival in Warsaw, and in 1978 he received Poland's highest public honor, the Order of Merit. Later, as an expression of his special relationship with Poland, he established a half-hour VOA show, *Music with Friends*, that was broadcast weekly in that country.

In 1983 President Ronald Reagan presented Conover with a citation for his achievements as a representative of American music and implicitly American life. In 1990 Conover received an honorary doctorate from the Berklee College of Music in Boston. Conover's last trip abroad was in late January 1995, when Warsaw-based jazz musicians and the U.S. embassy in Poland organized a three-day celebration in his honor.

Conover's second or third wife was an Arab princess whom he met at the Brussels World's Fair. His fourth wife, circa 1970s, was Shirley Clarke, a publicist. Around 1984 he received a fan letter from Evelyn Tan, a young Chinese writer and artist. They met and soon thereafter married. None of Conover's five marriages produced children, and all ended in divorce. Conover was never eager to give out details about his marriages and divorces, and further information about names and dates is unknown.

A heavy smoker, Conover had a cancerous tumor removed from his neck early in 1985 and thereafter was unable to eat solid foods. His health and eventually his voice declined. He died in Alexandria, Virginia.

Conover presented his programs in a rich baritone voice and with a meticulously careful delivery, stretching out vowels in an effort to accommodate himself to the technical foibles of long-range shortwave broadcasting. Although his deliberate manner of speech made him sound unhip, he was anything but that. Drawing from his own library of some tens of thousands of recordings, he gave his audiences a broad-ranging view of jazz, playing a Dixieland band or a sugary swing orchestra at one moment and John Coltrane the next. His jazz program began with the motto "Time . . . for . . . jazz" followed by the opening of Duke Ellington's 1942 recording of "Take the 'A' Train" and the announcement "This is Willis Conover in Washington, D.C., with the Voice of America Jazz Hour." As the English writer Richard Williams put it, "From Nottingham to Novosibirsk, hearts would beat a little faster" (Williams, p. 17). Communist authorities made vigorous and repeated efforts to jam the broadcasts, and there were times when long bursts of static stretched across Europe on the VOA's shortwave frequencies. But these efforts seemingly had the effect of making the nightly jazz show still more mysterious, appealing, and popular.

Conover's deliberate manner of presentation also derived from his recognition that substantial segments of his audience scarcely understood English. Indeed many listeners later told him that they learned the English language from his show.

In an attempt to defuse accusations that he was a puppet for the Central Intelligence Agency (CIA), Conover worked exclusively as a freelance contractor for the VOA and never as a government employee. An irony of this position was that Conover had no health insurance. In this regard one of America's greatest champions suffered silently from one of the great injustices of American life.

Conover's shows included interviews with famous musicians and informed musical commentary, but he carefully avoided overt political statements, hoping the music would speak for itself. His efforts to distance himself from government affiliation and politics did nothing to alleviate the perceived threat he posed. For example, in 1967 Conover attended a jazz festival in Moscow organized by a Communist Party youth organization, and he invited local musicians to a reception afterward. But the KGB prevented this interaction, telling the young musicians, including the future distinguished saxophonist and composer Aleksey Kozlov, that they would never be allowed to leave the USSR if they attended Conover's party.

Conover's audience was estimated to be in the tens of millions, but his impact is best measured in anecdotal ways. Throughout Eastern Europe jazz fans surreptitiously recorded *Music U.S.A.*, using crude tape recorders or old X-ray film as a phonographic medium. These recordings were circulated through large underground markets. Aspiring Polish bebop musicians recounted the experience of learning American recordings through fearsome, one-shot ear-training exercises whereby, as Conover broadcast a new piece of music, one member of the group memorized bars one through four, the next member bars five through eight, the next nine through twelve, and so forth in tag-team fashion. On his travels across the Iron Curtain, Conover encountered jazz bands proudly performing tunes they had learned in this manner.

If radio played a significant hand in the fall of communism, argued the writer Marc Fisher, then credit for this achievement was due less to the ceaseless hours of heavy-handed propaganda programs broadcast on VOA and Radio Free Europe than to the attractiveness of shows, most notably Conover's programs, that conveyed a slice of American culture. In July 2001 the Willis Conover Jazz Festival was held in Moscow in remembrance of his contributions to the dissemination of American music during the communist era.

• On 16 and 17 Aug. 1994 the jazz pianist Billy Taylor interviewed Conover for the Smithsonian Institution's Jazz Oral History Program. This tape is in the institution's Museum of American History. In 2001 the College Park, Maryland, branch of the National Archives and Records Administration acquired approximately 30,000 tapes from Conover's decades of VOA broadcasts (including more than

500 interviews of musicians) as well as films, videos, and recordings from the Newport festivals and other jazz events Conover hosted or organized. Conover's private library—comprising recordings, correspondence, memos, books, magazines, record catalogs, manuscripts, program notes, memorabilia, photographs, and other personal items—is in the general collection and archives of the Music Library at the University of North Texas.

Conover's career may be pieced together from brief biographical articles, including W. Royal Stokes, "Willis Conover: Voice of Jazz Abroad," *Jazz Times* (July 1986): 12–13, 19; Karen-Lee Ryan, "Win Friends with Jazz," *Houston Chronicle*, 11 Aug. 1987, p. 3; W. P. Hinely, "Willis Conover," *Jazz Forum* [international edition] no. 112 (1988): 4–10; Fernando Gonzalez, "His Voice Frames a World of Music," *Boston Globe*, 14 Sept 1990, p. 41; David Burns, "30 Million Know His Voice—You Don't," *World Monitor* 6 (Feb. 1993): 14–16; Fred Bouchard, "1995 *Down Beat* Lifetime Achievement Award: Willis Conover: The Voice Heard Round the World," *Down Beat* 62 (Sept. 1995): 28; and Gene Lees, "The Man Who Won the Cold War: Willis Conover," in *Friends along the Way: A Journey through Jazz* (2003), pp. 250–67.

Marc Fisher reviewed two books on the impact of short-wave radio during the cold war in "Freedom in the Air," *Washington Post*, 12 Apr. 1998, sec. X, p. 9. "On the Scene—Poland: Willis' Homecoming," *Jazz Forum* [international edition] no. 91 (1984): 19–20, covered one of Conover's trips to Warsaw. A report on the festival established in Moscow in his honor was broadcast on the NPR show *Weekend Edition Sunday* on 8 July 2001; a transcription of this report is at the Proquest Direct Web site. Obituaries are Robert McG. Thomas, Jr., *New York Times*, 19 May 1996; Richard Harrington, *Washington Post*, 20 May 1996; Richard Williams, *Guardian*, 23 May 1996; and Adam Makowicz, *Jazz Times* 26 (Sept. 1996): 47–48, 135.

BARRY KERNFELD

COORS, Adolph (1847–5 June 1929), brewing magnate, was born Adolph Herman Joseph Coors in rural Barmen, Prussia (now Wuppertal, Germany), the eldest child of Joseph Coors, a flour miller, and Helene Coors. When Adolph was a young child, the Coorses moved to the city of Dortmund so that his father could find work. On finishing grammar school at age fourteen, Adolph, with his father's assistance, took an apprenticeship in the business office of the Wenker Brewery, just across the street from the Coorses' home. The next year, in 1862, both parents died of tuberculosis—his mother in April and his father eight months later. Adolph's two siblings, William and Helene, were put into a Catholic orphanage, but Adolph continued his work as bookkeeper and apprentice at the brewery.

Soon Adolph, dazzled by the allure of mechanization and the dawning industrial age, sought a more hands-on position at the brewery. "Young Adolph watched the Wenker Brewery bolt its first steam engines into position and with a clang roar multiply its output. Adolph was entranced. . . . In a career move that would shape everything to come, Adolph abandoned the business of selling beer for the challenge of brewing it" (Baum, p. 5).

In 1868, facing the prospect of being drawn into combat by Bismarck's campaign to forge a unified Germany, Adolph Coors joined the wave of those fleeing the conflict. At age twenty-one he sneaked aboard a transatlantic ship headed for Baltimore. This episode, in singular conflict with his rigid ideal of dutiful self-discipline, was to be a lifelong source of private shame for Coors, but it put him on the threshold of an extraordinary career as an entrepreneur.

After settling in America, Coors was put off by the insular nature of immigrant German communities in Baltimore and New York. Meanwhile, he found factory working conditions repugnant, and the intense pressure to join the fledgling unions offended him. He came to the fateful decision to continue west. He made his way to Chicago, where he took various skilled jobs until he finally acquired his first brewery job in America. However, Coors soon thirsted for greater autonomy and decided to continue further west. He rode the new transcontinental railroad into territorial Colorado, arriving in the young city of Denver in 1872. There he used his savings to buy into a bottling company in the burgeoning town. Within the year, Coors maneuvered himself into sole ownership of the company. However, his interest continued to lie in brewing.

Coors began searching for the perfect site—and the source—of what would become his lasting achievement, Coors Brewing Company. He believed that clean, high-quality water was the fundamental ingredient in creating good beer. This was the main reason he chose to locate on the bank of Clear Creek in the town of Golden. Site located, Coors sold his bottling company and for additional financing took on Denver Candy Shop owner Jacob Schueler as a majority, silent partner. Coors bought brewing equipment, the Clear Creek land, and the run-down tannery on the site he'd staked out. By late 1873, Adolph Coors, at the age of twenty-six, had become part owner of Golden Brewery.

Coors's signature obsession with product quality drove the early success in Golden. A local newspaper reported, "Messrs. Schuler [*sic*] and Coors have leaped to the front rank of brewers in a remarkably short time, and their beer is regularly sold in Denver and the mountain and valley towns" (quoted in *Brewed in America*, p. 250). By mid-1874 Golden Brewery was pumping out 800,000 gallons of beer per day.

In 1879 Coors married Louisa Weber, also a German immigrant. By 1880 he was a father for the first time; four more children were eventually born to the couple. Buying out Schueler's interest that same year, Coors became sole owner of the brewery, immediately renaming it the Adolph Coors Company. He had been frugal enough with his resources to build a malt house, a steam mill, and an ice house to supplement the brewery.

Once repelled by the too-tight-knit German communities of the American East, Coors was comfortable with the ease of communication and the feeling of community of his all-German workforce. He also overcame his disdain for labor unions and allowed workers to unionize. A $16-per-week salary and free beer on the job kept morale high. The motto he wrote for the company was true to form: "The more we do ourselves, the higher quality we have." Coors's commitment to quality would be recognized on a broad stage at the 1893 Chicago World's Fair. His lager was the only beer brewed west of the Mississippi to receive a medal at that international exposition.

The company, for all its success, would face threats. The seeds of public relations problems that would sprout over the following century were sown with Coors's friendship with a prominent supporter of the local Ku Klux Klan. The prohibition movement was gaining force as women's groups became organized and vocal. In response, Coors began investing company capital into diverse industrial areas: cement, real estate, and a pottery house. The most immediate threat to the enterprise came in 1894. On Memorial Day, a flood raged through Clear Creek, threatening to tear apart all that Adolph Coors had accomplished. The strong-willed German's quick action saved the day, however, as, within a matter of minutes, he bought up the houses of families living on the opposite bank of the creek and had his workers dig feverishly, literally bending the river away from the Coors compound. The river still runs that way today. (See Baum, *Citizen Coors*, p. 9.)

Prohibition finally did come to Colorado in 1916, sparking a distrust of government that remained through generations of Coorses. Adolph, painfully, had to order the disposal of three months' beer production. To survive, he oversaw the transition of the company apparatus into making products such as malted milk and a near-beer, called "Mannah," that thoroughly disgusted him.

At seventy, Coors was a millionaire twice over. When the company incorporated in 1913, he named his sons as president, vice president, and general manager. He had laid the foundation for a company that would outlast prohibition and go back into brewing. He himself would not do so. In June 1929 the great entrepreneur visited the Cavalier Hotel in Virginia Beach, Virginia, to recover from the flu. Instead, he jumped from the sixth story of the hotel, ending his life on the very coast that had greeted him sixty-one years before.

• For a thorough account of the entire history of the Coors family business, see Dan Baum, *Citizen Coors: A Grand Family Saga of Business, Politics, and Beer* (2001). For further information on later generations of Coorses, see Russ Bellant, *Coors Connection: How Coors Family Philanthropy Undermines Democratic Pluralism* (1990). For more on the life of Adolph Coors, see the Coors Company–commissioned book by William Kostka, *The Pre-Prohibition History of Adolph Coors Company 1873–1933* (1973); also see Russ Banham, *Coors: A Rocky Mountain Legend* (1998). For background and context on the brewery business, including the Coors Company, see Stanley Baron, *Brewed in America* (1962), and William L. Downard, *Dictionary of the History of the American Brewing and Distilling Industries* (1980). An obituary is in the *Virginian-Pilot*, 6 June 1929.

ELI DANSKY

CORSO, Gregory (26 Mar. 1930–17 Jan. 2001), poet, was born Gregory Nunzio Corso in New York City, the son of Fortunato Corso, a day laborer, and Michelina Corso (maiden name unknown). His parents were poverty-stricken teenagers who consigned their son to foster care at birth. After being beaten by her husband, his mother ran away, and Gregory did not see her again until the year before his death. When he was ten his father, who had remarried, took the boy in. When his father was drafted to fight in World War II, Corso ran away from home. In short order he was arrested for stealing food and at the age of twelve was sent to the notorious Tombs prison in downtown Manhattan. A gang of black convicts tried to rape him, but Gregory fought back. Some Mafia prisoners provided him a degree of protection. Soon in despair, however, he slammed his hands through a window in the Tombs and was sent temporarily to Bellevue Hospital, where he spent three months in a locked ward for the criminally insane.

Corso emerged from the Tombs in 1945. World War II had just ended, and the city was in a state of celebration. In 1947 Corso was arrested again for robbery. This time he was sentenced to five years in Clinton prison at Dannemora in upstate New York. There he was introduced to books and learned to read. He spent much of his time in the prison library and developed a passion for Percy Bysshe Shelley and Homer. This was for him a magical transformation. Putting his new tools to work, he began to write poetry.

In 1950 Corso was released from prison and moved back to the Greenwich Village neighborhood of his childhood. In 1953 he became close friends with the three writers whose names stand alongside his as originators of the "beat generation": Allen Ginsberg, William Burroughs, and Jack Kerouac. Corso and Ginsberg shared a small apartment on the Lower East Side. Although Corso was glad to have found someone who appreciated his poetry, he was repelled by Ginsberg's homosexuality. One night Ginsberg attempted to seduce him. A lifelong tug of emotions began, in which whenever Corso wanted to upset Ginsberg he reminded him of the incident. Shortly thereafter William Burroughs swept into this setting. His express purpose was to work on a book with Ginsberg; his unstated purpose, however, was to consummate a complex passion for Ginsberg, so Burroughs promptly cast Corso out of the apartment. With no money, Corso turned to Jack Kerouac for help. Kerouac, who was trying to extricate himself from an intense affair with a young black woman, offered Corso the couch at her place. When Corso slept with the woman, Kerouac became enraged. He went on a three-day benzedrine-fueled writing binge and wrote *The Subterraneans*, whose climactic scene was based on Corso's "betrayal." Corso then distanced himself from the "beats," but he rejoined them later.

In 1954 Corso moved to Cambridge, Massachusetts, where he became a fixture of the literary underground. Corso's poetry, printed in small magazines and declaimed at local readings, impressed a number of Harvard students and intellectuals, so that a group of them put up the money to have his first collection, *The Vestal Lady on Brattle*, published in a limited edition.

In the summer of 1955 Corso settled in North Beach, the Greenwich Village of San Francisco. That same year Ginsberg moved to San Francisco and wrote his famous poem "Howl." As the beats attained national prominence, the press focused on Ginsberg and on Corso, who gloried in being portrayed as the "bad boy" and made sure everyone knew he had been in prison. He became master of the "put on" and of surrealist gestures: when an interviewer from *Time* magazine asked him what his poetry was about, he replied, "Fried shoes." In 1956 Kerouac joined Ginsberg and Corso in San Francisco. This period is vividly described in Kerouac's second novel, *Desolation Angels*, in which Corso plays a central role; he replaced Neal Cassady, protagonist of *On the Road*, as the exemplary Kerouacian hero characterized by his rhapsodic celebration of angst. In November the trio traveled south to Mexico City.

Each of the beats had a distinct writing style; Corso's was the least affected by the others. As much as he enjoyed Ginsberg's and Kerouac's appreciation of his work, he became wary of their influence and weary of their celebration of poverty. Defiantly leaving them to their slums, he wired a girlfriend for a plane ticket and flew to Washington, D.C., to stay with Randall Jarrell, the poetry consultant to the Library of Congress. Corso spent a week discussing his work with Jarrell before returning to the beats. He then embarked on a writing streak that would continue unabated for five years.

In February 1957 Corso made his way on the SS *America* to France. In Paris he looked up Jean-Paul Sartre, Henri Michaux, Marlon Brando, and Jean Genet, who recognized him as a fellow ex-prisoner. Ginsberg joined him there in April to work on preparing Corso's book *Gasoline* for publication with Lawrence Ferlinghetti's San Francisco–based City Lights. When Burroughs joined them at their cheap hotel two months later, Corso dubbed it the "Beat hotel." While living there he wrote his most famous poem, "Bomb," and the balance of *The Happy Birthday of Death*.

When Ginsberg returned to the United States in March 1958, Corso and Burroughs remained in Paris, where they shared an equal, collaborative relationship, which Corso would later describe as being as close to "love" as anything he had ever known. Because Burroughs was a heroin addict, however, Corso started using the drug. In the fall, City Lights published *Gasoline* and, as a broadside, "Bomb." Both publications rapidly sold out several printings, but Corso and Ferlinghetti soon had a falling-out. Corso sent his work to New Directions, the most prestigious avant-garde publisher in the United States, and they took him on.

In January 1959 Corso returned to New York to act in Robert Frank's underground film *Pull My Daisy*. He also gave a series of highly publicized readings with Ginsberg that spread the doctrine of the "beatniks," The paranoid American political climate frightened Corso (his fears were substantiated years later when his F.B.I. files revealed that he had been under surveillance throughout his visit). In March he stole a television set and some furniture from Ginsberg's apartment and sold them to pay his fare back to France.

In 1960 the seminal Grove press anthology *The New American Poetry: 1945–1960*, edited by Donald Allen, established Corso's reputation. In June, New Directions brought out *The Happy Birthday of Death*; its success established Corso as a world poet. It contains a series of long poems with singular titles ("Marriage," "Bomb," "Police," etc.) that inject subversive street humor into meditations challenging national subjects. The book stands as Corso's equivalent to "Howl," *On the Road*, and *Naked Lunch* and remained in print for more than forty years. In 1962 Corso's *Selected Poems* was published by Eyre & Spottiswode in Britain, the country where his work got the most attention and polarized the poetry community. And *Long Live Man*, written during the preceding two years, was published by New Directions in America. With this book Corso became the poet of American pop history, writing about events as they happened.

Corso's work is based upon juxtapositions of a desired state with reality. In "Greece," for example, he starts out by informing us, "They've reached the moon and I've reached Greece," then immediately brings us down to earth with the second line: "and New York children are murdering each other."

Corso's career fell off sharply in 1963 and, despite publishing two more splendid collections of poetry (*Elegiac Feelings American* [1970], *Herald of the Autochthonic Spirit* [1981]) and a fine volume of selected poems, *Mindfields* (1989), Corso never regained the momentum of his great period. By 1963 he had become, and would remain, a heroin addict and alcoholic. In the same year the four original members of the beat generation went their separate ways, never regaining their personal closeness. Corso, whose inability to trust people had been imprinted by his traumatic childhood, was devastated. Indeed, for the next twenty years he poured as much energy into building and destroying families as into writing poetry.

In 1963 Corso married Sally November, with whom he had a daughter. He abandoned them in 1965. In 1968 he married Belle Carpenter. He abandoned her in 1970. In 1972 Corso had a relationship with a woman named Jocelyn, with whom he had a son out of wedlock. She abandoned them. In 1973 Corso married Lisa Brinka, with whom he had a daughter; in 1976 he abandoned them. (The marriages to November, Carpenter, and Brinka eventually ended in divorce.) In 1980 Corso started living with

Kaye Macdonnah in San Francisco. In 1982 they had a son, Nile; in 1983 they separated, and Corso moved back to New York. In 1984 he discovered he had a fifth child whom he had fathered during a one-night affair in Los Angeles in 1953.

Corso's life shifted into its final phase in 1983 when a couple he had known for years, Roger and Irvyne Richards, offered him his only permanent home in their apartment in Greenwich Village at 15 Horatio Street. In 1992 a wealthy Japanese artist, Hiro Yamagata, was convinced by Allen Ginsberg to support Corso on $5,000 a month for the remainder of his life. Corso moved into an apartment across the hall from the Richards. In 1999 he was diagnosed with prostate cancer. He died in Brooklyn Park, Minnesota. His ashes were buried next to the grave of his favorite poet, Percy Bysshe Shelley, in Rome.

From the time the beat generation emerged in the mid-fifties until his death, Corso was often as controversial as Allen Ginsberg, the movement's mercurial mastermind; as William Burroughs, its visionary, satirical brain; as Jack Kerouac, its chronicler and heart. The group's original impact cannot be grasped without Corso's particular assistance. Burroughs, Ginsberg, and Kerouac imprinted the beat lifestyle on the public consciousness. Corso, especially, acted it out for everyone. He was the "angel headed hipster" Ginsberg described in *Howl*; the man in Kerouac's *On the Road* who wanted to "burn burn burn"; the surreal junkie whose portrait Burroughs memorably drew in the Nova trilogy. Corso's work is easy to understand, even blunt. It addresses everyday subjects: marriage, power, fear, the H-bomb. Less formally educated than his peers, Corso was nevertheless the chosen poet of the group.

• Given the longevity of his career and staying power of his poetry, which has been widely anthologized and published in translation in many countries, relatively little has been written about Gregory Corso. Gregory Stephenson, *Exiled Angel: A Study of the Work of Gregory Corso* (1989), is the only book-length work. There is also a good chapter on Corso in Stephenson's *The Daybreak Boys: Essays on the Literature of the Beat Generation* (1990.) Other useful documents are "Biographical Note" in *The New AmericanPoetry: 1945–1960*, ed. Donald Allen (1960); *Gregory Corso, Writings from Unmuzzled Ox Magazine*, ed. Michael Andre (1981); and Robert Wilson, *A Bibliography of Works by Gregory Corso, 1954–1965* (1966). An obituary is in the *New York Times*, 19 Jan. 2001.

VICTOR BOCKRIS

COTTER, John L. (6 Dec. 1911–5 Feb. 1999), archaeologist, was born John Lambert Cotter in Denver, Colorado, the son of John Aloysius Cotter, a technician who installed telephone exchanges, and Bertha Becker Cotter. John grew up as an only child, a brother having died in infancy before John's birth. Because his father's job required him to move from town to town in several western states, John attended public schools not only in Denver but also in Spokane, Washington, Longmont, Colorado, La Mesa, California, and Butte, Helena, and Livingston, Montana. After graduating from high school in Denver, Cotter began studying journalism at the University of Denver, but he soon switched to anthropology, specializing in archaeology. After receiving a B.A. in 1934 and an M.A. in 1935, he began work toward a Ph.D. at the University of Pennsylvania but left in 1937, before completing all the degree requirements, to become director of the Archeological Survey of Kentucky under the aegis of the Works Progress Administration (WPA).

Accepting a position as archaeologist with the U.S. National Park Service (NPS) in 1940, Cotter began a career as an administrator and research archaeologist that spanned 37 years. His first NPS appointment was as custodian of Tuzigoot National Monument, Arizona. While there he married Virginia Wilkins Tomlin in 1941; they had two children. In 1943 Cotter took a leave of absence from the park service when he was inducted into the U.S. Army. Serving with the 357th Infantry Regiment of the 90th Division during the Normandy invasion in June 1944, he was wounded by shrapnel and was awarded the Purple Heart.

After mustering out of the army in 1945, Cotter returned to Tuzigoot as superintendent, remaining there until being transferred to Tupelo, Mississippi, in 1947 to direct an archaeological survey of the Natchez Trace. The old road from Natchez, Mississippi, to Nashville, Tennessee, an early-nineteenth-century wagon road constructed over an ancient Indian trail, was being developed into the Nachez Trace Parkway, a unit of the national park system. He recorded and evaluated archaeological sites situated along the Trace as an aid in interpreting its prehistory and history.

From 1950 to 1954 Cotter was stationed in Washington, D.C., as the park service's acting chief archaeologist, after which he directed a major field project at Jamestown, Virginia. In 1957 he was transferred to Philadelphia to become regional archaeologist of the park service's northeast region, a position he held until his retirement in 1972. After retirement he continued as a consultant to the park service until 1977.

In terms of research interests, Cotter's career divides cleanly into two distinct, contrasting phases: an earlier period (1935 to 1954) when he excavated numerous prehistoric sites in Colorado, Kentucky, Tennessee, Alabama, and Mississippi, and a later period (1954 until his death in 1999) when his research focused almost entirely on historic Euro-American sites on the Atlantic seaboard.

Cotter's earliest field work of importance was at two Paleo-Indian sites in the western United States: a component of the Folsom complex at the Lindenmeier site, Colorado, in 1935, and the Blackwater Draw site, New Mexico, type site for the Clovis complex, where in 1936 and 1937 he helped Edgar B. Howard carry out exploratory excavations. The work at Lindenmeier was sponsored by the Denver Museum of Natural History; that at Blackwater Draw was sponsored by the Academy of Natural Sciences of

Philadelphia. As Cotter had taken most of the field notes at Blackwater Draw, Howard assigned preparation of a final report on their excavations to Cotter. His report, published in the Academy's *Proceedings*, established Cotter's reputation as an authority on Paleo-Indian archaeology. It included the first description of the material culture of the Clovis people and demonstrated for the first time that Clovis predated Folsom.

From 1937 to 1954, Cotter redirected his research domain from the western to the southeastern United States, but his interests remained primarily with pre-Columbian archaeology, particularly that of the Hopewellian and Mississippian cultures. His best-known publications during this period were of his excavations at the Gordon site, the Emerald mound, and the Bynum mounds (the latter coauthored with John M. Corbett), all in Mississippi.

His exploration from 1954 to 1957 of the archaeological remains of seventeenth-century Jamestown, the first permanent English settlement in North America, exposed Cotter to research problems different from those he had faced previously at pre-Columbian sites, and different strategies were needed to deal with them. Historical archaeology was just beginning to evolve into a specialized field at the time, and Cotter had to learn many things as he went along. He became acquainted with seventeenth-century material culture and learned how to use historical documents as sources of data to complement the archaeological data. He developed specialized strategies for locating and studying archaeological features at the site.

Cotter became so captivated by this experience that he discontinued his long-standing involvement with prehistory and devoted the rest of his career to historical archaeology. His published report on the Jamestown project firmly established his reputation as a leading advocate for historical archaeology. As the first comprehensive description of major archaeological excavations at an English colonial site in America, it set a standard of descriptive and interpretive content that was widely followed by archaeologists reporting their work at other English colonial sites. He returned to his studies at Penn in 1957 and was awarded the Ph.D. in 1959. He then became adjunct professor at the University of Pennsylvania and taught a seminar in historical archaeology, the first such course in the United States. He continued to teach the seminar every year until 1979, inspiring a generation of students, some of whom became professional historical archaeologists. He held a field school every summer during this period where his students excavated historic sites in the Philadelphia area. He was curator for American Historical Archaeology at the University of Pennsylvania museum from 1972 to 1980 and remained curator emeritus until his death at home in Philadelphia.

Cotter was a cofounder of the Society for Historical Archaeology, served as its first president, and edited the first edition of its bulletin, *Historical Archaeology*.

He was awarded the prestigious J. C. Harrington Medal by the Society for Historical Archaeology and the David E. Finley award for Outstanding Achievement in Historic Preservation by the National Trust for Historic Preservation. The John L. Cotter award was established in his honor by the Society for Historical Archaeology in 1999.

• Cotter was author or coauthor of several books and more than 200 journal articles and reviews. His best-known publications are *Archaeology of the Bynum Mounds, Mississippi* (with John M. Corbett), *Archeological Research Series*, no. 1, U.S. National Park Service (1951), *Archeological Excavations at Jamestown, Virginia* (*Archeological Series*, no. 4, U.S. National Park Service (1958), and *The Buried Past: An Archaeological History of Philadelphia* (with Daniel G. Roberts and Michael Parrington) (1992).

A detailed biographical sketch by D. G. Roberts, "A Conversation with John L. Cotter," appeared in *Historical Archaeology* 33, no. 2 (1999): 6–50. Obituaries include those by E. B. Jelks in *Society for American Archaeology Bulletin* 17, no. 3 (1999): 35, and D. G. Roberts in *Historical Archaeology* 33, no. 4 (1999): 6–18. The latter includes a complete bibliography of all Cotter's publications.

EDWARD B. JELKS

COVERDELL, Paul (20 Jan. 1939–18 July 2000), U.S. senator, was born in Des Moines, Iowa, the son of Eldon P. Coverdell, an insurance man, and Vonis Wagner Coverdell. The family settled in Georgia during Paul's teenage years. After graduation from Lees Summit High School in Missouri, Coverdell attended Georgia State University and then the University of Missouri, Columbia, from which he graduated with a degree in journalism in 1961. He spent two years in the army on Okinawa, in Taiwan, and in Korea and rose to the rank of captain. Following his discharge, he worked in the family's insurance business until 1968. Coverdell married Nancy Nally in 1972; the couple had no children.

John F. Kennedy's example in the early 1960s persuaded Coverdell to participate in politics, albeit as a Republican. The death of Senator Robert Kennedy in June 1968, despite their very different ideological views, acted as catalyst for Coverdell to take the plunge into a Georgia senate race. Although Coverdell lost, he became well acquainted with his district. This laid the basis for his election to the Georgia senate in 1970. The Republican delegation in that heavily Democratic legislature was small, and in 1974 Coverdell became the minority leader in the upper house.

During fourteen years as a lawmaker, Coverdell concentrated on building his party in Georgia . As one of his friends put it, "he and I were Republicans when being Republicans wasn't cool" (Black and Black, *The Rise of Southern Republicans*, p. 315). Coverdell forged alliances with black and white politicians in his state. He joined Newt Gingrich and other younger Republicans in campaigns to increase the GOP presence. Following an unsuccessful race for Congress in 1976, he concentrated on the legislature, where he supported reform of the state's pension laws and legislation to curb drunk driving and raise the legal age for drinking.

Coverdell met George Herbert Walker Bush in the late 1970s. In 1988, when Bush, then vice president, announced for the presidency, Coverdell ran Bush's successful campaign in Georgia. In early 1989, Bush appointed Coverdell director of the Peace Corps. During his two and a half years as director of the agency, Coverdell sponsored the World Wise School program to link school children in the United States with Peace Corps volunteers. When he stepped down to run for the Senate in September 1991, President Bush praised his efforts to recruit "a wider representation of volunteers from all backgrounds and regions of the country" (statement announcing the resignation of Paul Coverdell as director of the Peace Corps, 4 Sept. 1991, bushlibrary.tamu.edu/papers/1991/91090406.html).

In 1992 Coverdell challenged the incumbent Democrat, Wyche Fowler, Jr., in the Georgia senate race. Through a series of ads in which he did not appear in person, Coverdell argued that Fowler was too liberal and out of touch with the people of Georgia. Fowler won with 49 percent of the vote to 48 percent for Coverdell. Georgia law mandated, however, that to win a statewide office a candidate had to secure a majority of the popular vote. A runoff took place three weeks later. Without the higher turnout of the presidential election to help him, Fowler went down to defeat before Coverdell's well-organized campaign. The Republican won a narrow but significant victory, 51 percent to 49 percent.

An unassuming individual with a high forehead and prominent glasses, Coverdell was not a media senator. Behind the scenes he took on the routine assignments that endeared him to the Republican leadership. With few hobbies outside of politics, Coverdell soon emerged as a significant if unheralded figure in the Senate hierarchy. He was pro-choice on abortion but otherwise advocated lower taxes and a reduced role for the federal government. On policy issues, he was identified with the enactment of education savings accounts, which allowed the withdrawal of funds tax-free to pay educational expenses. These accounts have since been named after him. In foreign policy Coverdell sought harsher penalties for drug smugglers, and he sponsored additional funds to help Colombia deal with the problems of drug trafficking. Most of Coverdell's important work occurred out of public view. He was not a gifted speaker, but he won the esteem of colleagues in both parties. At home he had constructed an effective network of Republicans across Georgia who supported his reelection.

Coverdell campaigned in 1998 on the slogan "Coverdell Works," and he had a large financial war chest. His opponent, Michael Coles, was a wealthy cookie maker. Coverdell noted that he was "on the Reagan-Bush team" while his rival was "on the Kennedy-Clinton team" (Black and Black, *Southern Republicans*, p. 316). In a year when other Republicans experienced reverses in both the House and Senate,

Coverdell romped to victory with 52 percent of the vote to 45 percent for Coles. With a secure base, Coverdell seemed likely to become an even more influential Republican in the Senate during his second term. By 1999 he had signed on with the presidential candidacy of Texas governor George W. Bush and was poised to play a prominent role in the national Republican campaign as the link between the Bush team and the party in the Senate.

In mid-July 2000, Coverdell complained of severe headaches and was admitted to an Atlanta hospital. Tests revealed that he had suffered a cerebral hemorrhage and he was rushed into emergency surgery. He died the next day. "He was a workhorse . . . and not a showhorse," said Ted Stevens, a Republican colleague from Alaska ("Lawmakers remember Sen. Coverdell as a skilled, kind-hearted colleague," CNN.com, July 19, 2000). Not until Coverdell's papers are opened and a biography is written will it be possible to understand fully his role in the development of the Republican party in the South in the 1970s and 1980s as well as his place in the Senate during the 1990s. His contributions to the growth of the Republican party in the South and to the effectiveness of the GOP in the Senate in education and tax policy were substantial and important, and he is likely to be judged as an important figure in the rise of the Republican party in the South during the last three decades of the twentieth century.

• Paul Coverdell's papers, which are not yet open for research, are housed at the Ina Dillard Russell Library at Georgia College and State University in Milledgeville, Georgia. The William Russell Pullen Library at Georgia State University in Atlanta has three helpful and detailed oral history interviews with Coverdell about his early years in Georgia politics. The George H. W. Bush Presidential Library at Texas A&M University has source material (also not yet open for research) on Coverdell's Peace Corps service and his friendship with the Bush family. Although Coverdell did not write much, some of his speeches have autobiographical features. The *New York Times*, 19 July 2000, has a good obituary.

LEWIS L. GOULD

CRAIGHEAD, Frank Cooper, Jr. (14 Aug. 1916–21 Oct. 2001), naturalist, was born, with his twin John, in Washington, D.C., the son of Frank Craighead, Sr., a forest entomologist with the U.S. Department of Agriculture, and Carolyn Jackson Craighead, a biologist technician. Frank traced his curiosity and esteem for the natural world to his father, who ferried his family to the countryside outside Washington to observe the local flora and insect and mammal populations. In their teens, the twins became absorbed with birds of prey, especially falcons. In 1934 they traveled west to study and snare falcons and hawks, which they described in a lively article, "Adventures with Birds of Prey," in *National Geographic Magazine* (July 1937).

In 1939 the twins graduated with A.B. degrees in science from Pennsylvania State University, and they received their Ph.D. degrees in ecology and wildlife management from the University of Michigan in 1949. K. S. Dharmakumarsinjhi, an Indian prince, read their article in *National Geographic* and in 1940 invited them to be his guests and train falcons. "Life with an Indian Prince" (*National Geographic*, May 1940) relates their experiences in India. With the outbreak of World War II the twins returned home. They established a survival training program for U.S. Navy personnel stranded in a strange country and prepared a manual, *How to Survive on Land and Sea* (1943). By the war's completion they trained Office of Strategic Service (OSS) agents in survival tactics and were readying themselves to be dropped into enemy territory.

In November 1943 Frank Craighead, on a leave from the navy, married Esther Stevens, whom he had met at the University of Michigan. The couple had three children. In 1987, following the death of Esther in 1980, Frank married Shirley Cocker. After the war Frank and John returned to the University of Michigan to continue their graduate educations and in 1950 received doctorates from the Wildlife Management Institute. Their dissertation, *Hawks, Owls, and Wildlife*, was published in 1956.

In 1952, for the first time in their careers, the twins chose to follow separate paths. While John opted for an academic career as a professor of zoology at the University of Montana, Frank became an itinerant naturalist, accepting a variety of positions. In 1955 Frank founded the Craighead Research Institute (in 1980 renamed the Craighead Environmental Research Institute). He was also manager of the Desert Bighorn Game Range in Nevada and was wildlife biologist with the U.S. Forest Service.

In 1959 the twins resumed their earlier career relationship for a privately funded, team-based study of the grizzly bear population in the Yellowstone National Park ecosystem. Over the roughly twelve-year span of the study (inspired in part by the bear's complete lack of arteriosclerosis despite a fat-producing diet), information was assembled on the bears' social organization, feeding habits, herd and individual range sizes, litter size, mortality rates, and hibernation patterns. To study the movements and habits of such large, aggressive animals, the Craigheads immobilized the bears and looped radio tracking collars around their necks. The Craigheads designed both of these techniques, perhaps their most significant contributions to the field of wildlife biology. (In all between 1961 and 1969 twenty-four different bears were instrumented by the Craigheads and their team.)

The twins' study came to an unexpected halt after a dispute with the park administration. In 1967 two women camped miles from each other were attacked and killed by two different bears. The park administrators blamed the camp food dumps for attracting the bears and concluded that the offending dumps should be closed as soon as practicable. The Craigheads favored the gradual closing of the dumps while the grizzlies were weaned from their recently acquired taste

for campers' garbage and reintroduced to their wild food. The Craigheads lost out in this increasingly bitter bureaucratic conflict, and park officials terminated their study. (As Frank and John had predicted, the bears continued to raid the closed dumps and threaten campers, necessitating the grizzlies' destruction.)

Despite the frustrating outcome of their five-year war with the Yellowstone National Park bureaucracy, the Craigheads' research on grizzlies was regarded as groundbreaking. "It was all brand new," declared Chuck Schwartz, head of the Interagency Grizzly Bear Study team. "They were pioneers not only in the study of bears," Schwartz continued, "but in the science of working with large carnivores" (*Los Angeles Times*, 26 Oct. 2001). And according to Harry Reynolds, president of the International Bear Association, the Craigheads helped form the public's view of bears as a crucial and integral part of the environment (*International Bear News*, p. 3). Indeed many young biologists were attracted to the field by the research efforts of the Craigheads. Chris Servheen, for instance, who was responsible for the conservation of grizzlies for the U.S. Fish and Wildlife Service, recalled as a youngster watching a National Geographic television special on the Craigheads' work with grizzlies. "From that point on, I wanted to do what I do today," declared Servheen. "I know so many people who have the same story I have. They got into conservation because of what the Craigheads did" (*AP Worldstream*, 24 Oct. 2001).

While widely known for his field studies of grizzlies, Frank Craighead was actually "one of the nation's most versatile naturalists," asserted the *Denver Post* (26 Oct. 2001). The broad scope of his expertise is indicated by the more than seventy scientific papers he published and the five books he co-authored, *Hawks in Hand* (1939), *A Field Guide to Rocky Mountain Wild Flowers* (1940), the aforementioned *How to Survive on Land and Sea* and *Hawks, Owls, and Wildlife*, and *Track of the Grizzly* (1979). Frank Craighead's last book, *For Everything There Is a Season* (1994), of which he was the sole author, even more impressively displays the wide range of his knowledge of nature. He unearths for readers of *For Everything There Is a Season* the hidden, albeit predictable, rhythms of the northern Rockies ecosystem. During the late winter and early spring, for instance, robins, red-winged blackbirds, and starlings appear, the latter greedily feeding on the "masses of wood ticks" swarming over "sick and dying moose, elk and bison—casualties of the winter" (p. 9). Methodically but at times almost poetically, Craighead carries the story through the summer and early fall and the beginning of the avian retreat to Central and South America. By late November nature has closed down and, in Craighead's words, "the Southward migration is largely over and most animals are now where they will remain throughout the winter" (p. 159).

Further evidence of the breadth of Frank Craighead's interests lay in his advocacy of the preservation of rivers as much as possible in their wild state. Committed to this endeavor, he became one of the "principal architects" of the 1968 Wild and Scenic Rivers Act (*Los Angeles Times*, 26 Oct. 2001). This Act protects rivers with great geologic, wildlife, and scenic values, and the areas immediately surrounding them, for the enjoyment of future generations and to protect water quality. Some twenty years after the passage of the law Craighead was diagnosed with Parkinson's disease, and he died at St. John's Living Center in Jackson, Wyoming.

• Most of Frank Craighead's personal papers were destroyed when his house burned down in 1978. What was salvaged from the fire, including some of his original writings and slides, is at the Craighead Environmental Research Institute in Moose, Wyoming. The fullest account of Craighead's life is in Frank C. Craighead, Jr., *Craighead Environmental Research Institute* (2001). Perhaps the best way to trace Frank and John's early careers is through the essays they contributed to the *National Geographic*, among them "We Survive on a Pacific Atoll," Jan. 1948, and "Wildlife Adventuring in Jackson Hole," Jan. 1956. Useful material is also in the *International Bear News* 2 (Feb. 2002): 8–9; the *Los Angeles Times*, 26 Oct. 2001; and *AP Worldstream*, 24 Oct. 2001. An obituary is in the *New York Times*, 4 Nov. 2001.

RICHARD HARMOND

CRAM, Donald J. (22 Apr. 1919–17 June 2001), organic chemist, was born Donald James Cram in Chester, Vermont, the son of William Cram, a lawyer and farmer, and Joanna Shelley Cram. His family relocated to nearby Brattleboro when he was two, and he received his early education in local one-room schools. His father's death when Cram was only four placed the family in strained circumstances, and they dispersed when he was sixteen. Cram briefly attended school in Lake Worth, Florida, before finishing high school in 1937 at Winwood, a private school in Long Island, New York, where he worked as a factotum for his tuition and board. During his senior year he developed an interest in chemistry and won a scholarship to Rollins College in Winter Park, Florida.

In 1941 Cram graduated from Rollins with a B.S. in chemistry. He married Jean Turner on 22 December 1941; the couple had no children. Having been challenged at Rollins by a chemistry professor who claimed Cram would never be successful in academic research, Cram was determined to do just that. He entered the University of Nebraska, where he worked with Norman O. Cromwell. In 1942 Cram received an M.S. in organic chemistry. Following graduation he worked at Merck & Company in New Jersey, where he conducted research on penicillin. Immediately following the end of World War II, Cram entered Harvard University on a National Research Council Fellowship, where he worked under the direction of L. F. Fieser and the Nobel Prize winner Robert B. Woodward. Cram received his Ph.D. in organic chemistry in 1947.

Following a brief postdoctoral stint at the nearby Massachusetts Institute of Technology (MIT), Cram headed west and joined the faculty of the University of California–Los Angeles (UCLA) as an instructor; he spent the rest of his professional career there. After receiving promotion to assistant professor in 1947, he rose through the ranks as an associate professor (1950), full professor (1956), and university professor (1988). He also served from 1985 until 1995 as the Saul Winstein Professor of Chemistry. He retired in 1990.

During the 1950s Cram became interested in the field of artificial enzymes. Enzymes are proteins that act as catalysts in certain chemical reactions, and the development of artificial substitutes that offered greater stability and that could be produced more quickly and cheaply than their natural counterparts was an industrial priority. The biggest problem he faced was that of molecular recognition; enzymes, like most other naturally occurring compounds, are selective about reacting with other types of molecules.

Cram closely followed the work of his fellow researcher Charles Pedersen, a chemist at DuPont Corporation. In 1967 Pedersen published a paper concerning the artificial synthesis of a type of molecule called crown ethers, so named because the molecules, formed from a chemical group known as ethers, physically resembled crowns. The paper suggested two significant developments. First, it described the first artificial compound with the ability to form stable bonds with alkali metal ions, such as sodium and potassium. Second, it suggested that the physical shape of a molecule was as important in the bonding process as its electrostatic charges.

Using Pedersen's work as a foundation, Cram and his colleagues spent hours assembling Corey-Pauling-Koltun molecular models in an attempt to determine the most efficient shape of potential synthetic molecules. After determining that a three-dimensional molecule would offer greater contact potential, Cram focused on developing a variety of "host" molecules, each of which would accept only one type of "guest" molecule. He dubbed this type of research "host-guest chemistry." By 1987, when he shared the Nobel Prize for chemistry with Pedersen and the French chemist Jean-Marie Lehn, Cram had developed over five hundred different host molecules. Possible applications include antigens that can recognize antibodies, the development of chemical sensors that can detect specific metals or chemicals in the environment, and the development of drug delivery systems.

While conducting groundbreaking research, Cram also made notable contributions to the development of UCLA's chemistry department. During a career that spanned more than four decades, he published over four hundred research papers and wrote several books on organic chemistry, including one he co-wrote with his second wife, Jane Lewis Maxwell, whom he married in November 1969 after his first marriage ended in divorce the previous month. Cram did not have children in any of his marriages. In addition to guiding over two hundred graduate students in their studies, Cram taught some eight thousand undergraduates as well, entertaining students on the last day of class by playing folk songs on a guitar. After winning the Nobel Prize, Cram explored new avenues of research, and late in his career he developed carcerands, a type of hemispherical molecule that bonded together at the rim, thereby creating a type of "prison cell" with the potential to "trap" other molecules.

In addition to the Nobel Prize, Cram also received the three American Chemical Society Awards, including the Society Arthur C. Cope Award for Distinguished Achievement in Organic Chemistry (1974), the Newby McCoy Award (1965 and 1975), and the California Scientist of the Year Award (1974). A member of both the National Academy of Sciences (1961) and the American Academy of Arts and Sciences (1967), Cram also consulted for a number of industrial concerns, including Upjohn, Eastman Kodak, and Union Carbide. He served as university professor emeritus from 1990 until his death at his home in Palm Desert, California. Following the death of his second wife in May of 2000, Cram had married Catherine Collett Cook in September of that year, nine months before he died.

One of five UCLA scientists to have won the Nobel Prize, Cram is remembered for his groundbreaking work in organic chemistry and his humanity. He was as comfortable riding a surfboard with friends as he was conducting research that earned him the title "the father of host-guest chemistry."

• Cram's papers are in the UCLA archives in Los Angeles, Calif. Cram wrote several textbooks, most notably *Fundamentals of Carbanion Chemistry* (1965), *Elements of Organic Chemistry*, with John H. Richards and G. S. Hammond (1967), and *Essence of Organic Chemistry*, with J. M. Cram (1978). He was the subject of articles in the *New Scientist*, 22 Oct. 1987 ("Pedersen's Crowning Achievement," by Lionel Milgrom, pp. 31–32); and *Science*, 30 Oct. 1987, vol. 238 ("Chemistry in the Image of Biology," by Roger Lewin, pp. 611–612). Obituaries are in the *New York Times*, 20 June 2001, and the *London Daily Telegraph*, 22 June 2001.

EDWARD L. LACH, JR.

CRUMIT, Frank (18 May 1888–7 Sept. 1943), entertainer, was born in Jackson, Ohio, the son of Frank Crumit, a banker, and Mary C. Poor Crumit. Educated locally and at Culver Military Academy near South Bend in Indiana, he continued his studies in electrical engineering at the University of Ohio (now Ohio University) in Athens, Ohio, graduating in 1910.

Although he had no formal musical background, Crumit was attracted to the variety stage, and by 1913 he was performing as a song-and-dance man. Eventually he formed a partnership with Paul Beise, vocalizing with Beise's small groups. By 1918 Crumit had played a juvenile lead on Broadway, where he enjoyed occasional successes for the next ten years. He continued his variety performances for several years, typically strolling onstage, ukulele in hand, and telling the pit orchestra to join the pinochle game backstage.

In 1919 Crumit recorded his first songs; in 1923 his "My Little Bimbo Down by the Bamboo Isle," made

for Columbia records, set a pattern for idiosyncratic, typically humorous songs sung in an engagingly laconic, clear voice. He signed with Victor records later that year, accompanying himself or working with the jazz-based orchestra assembled by Nat Shilkret, Victor's musical director. The band was sometimes headed by Leonard Joy. Crumit's career lifted off.

During the 1920s he had one hit after another, many of which he wrote himself. Perhaps the catchiest of the ones he performed was Percy French's "Abdul Abul Bul Amir," the comically sad tale of Abdul, a doer of heroic deeds, who was brought low by Ivan Skavinsky Skavar. Crumit's ten-inch shellac recording of "Abdul" and "Frankie and Johnny" sold more than two million copies. "Abdul," which reflected Crumit's roots in variety (listeners could sing along with the repeated refrains), represented one strain of his repertoire. In the same vein was the song-tale "The Gay Caballero," which along with "Abdul" was eventually honored by a sequel, although Abdul had to be resurrected from the dead.

Crumit was also interested in traditional American music of the nineteenth and early twentieth centuries, and he recorded such songs as "Frankie and Johnny," "Little Brown Jug," "The Pig Got Up and Slowly Walked Away," "Granny's Old Armchair," "My Grandfather's Clock," "Wake Nicodemus," "Henry Clay Work," and others. Crumit became a kind of walking, chatting songbook; at one time his repertoire was estimated at 10,000 tunes. His enthusiasm for the folk song was far in advance of the folk song revival of the 1930s; it laid the foundation for later work by Pete Seeger and others. Crumit also adapted and recorded Irish folk tunes.

Although Crumit never appeared in Great Britain, his popularity on recordings was almost as strong there as in the United States. For most of the 1920s Crumit combined his recording career with occasional returns to Broadway productions, none more successful than *Tangerine* (1921), a long-running musical comedy in which he costarred with Julia Sanderson and added a hit song to the score, which was otherwise by Monte Carlo and Alma Sanders. Sanderson was already and perhaps unknowingly part of musical theater history for having introduced Jerome Kern's "They Didn't Believe Me" to America, the song's long melodic line constituting the true beginning of a golden age of American songwriting.

Sanderson and Crumit often appeared together. After their road tour of George Gershwin and Ira Gershwin's *Oh, Kay!* (1927), they married and temporarily "retired" from show business. They remained married until Crumit's death; they had no children. In 1928 they ended their retirement, appearing on radio's variety program sponsored by Blackstone Cigar. The hallmark of any Crumit-Sanderson show was its deceptive urbanity, as the pair moved through topicalities to "plain talk" with other guests. In this respect they helped set a pattern for the informal husband-wife radio talk shows of the 1930s and 1940s.

In 1930 Crumit and Sanderson coined "The Battle of the Sexes," a quiz show, for WABC. The questions were real and the competition strong, but the all-male and all-female teams were rarely contentious. The show moved to NBC's network in 1938, during the era's collective quiz show mania. It sometimes aired five times a week. From 1929 to 1943 it ranked among the most popular shows on American radio. Crumit and Sanderson rarely recorded together, but their "Would You Like to Take a Walk?" (1943) showcased their affectionate partnership.

"The Battle of the Sexes" also provided opportunities to present their kind of music, increasingly the contemporary repertoire of Richard Rodgers and Lorenz Hart, the Gershwins, Irving Berlin, Vincent Youmans, and Cole Porter. The show's popularity never waned; it ended only when Crumit suddenly died of a heart attack at the Hotel Gotham in New York. The previous afternoon's show had gone on as usual and Crumit's last number was Alec Wilder's "It's So Peaceful in the Country," inspired by the couple's home across the river in New Jersey.

Between 1935 and 1939 Crumit was the president of the Lambs Club in New York. He was an original talent, often undervalued, who entertained two generations of Americans and finally came to personify some of early radio's easygoing, here-are-some-friends-in-the-house-to-help-us-through-the-day charms.

• There is no known Crumit archive. Among obituaries, the most useful is in the *New York Times*, 8 Sept. 1943. Even more helpful are Kevin Daley's liner notes for *The Return of the Gay Caballero* (ASV Living Era AJA 5012, 1982). Bill Owen and Frank Buxton, *The Big Broadcast: 1920–1950* (1972), contains detail on Crumit's radio career.

JAMES ROSS MOORE

CURRIE, Lauchlin (8 Oct. 1902–23 Dec. 1993), economist, was born in the small fishing village of New Dublin, Nova Scotia, Canada, the son of Lauchlin Bernard Currie, who operated a fleet of merchant ships, and Alice Eisenhauer Currie, a schoolteacher. His father died four years later and his family moved to the nearby town of Bridgewater. Most of his schooling was in Bridgewater, but he also briefly attended schools in Massachusetts and California, where he had relatives. After two years at St. Francis Xavier's University, Nova Scotia (1920–1922), he studied at the London School of Economics and received his B.Sc. in 1925. There his teachers included Edwin Cannan, Hugh Dalton, A. L. Bowley, and Harold Laski.

In 1925 he moved to Harvard, where his chief inspiration was Allyn Abbott Young, then president of the American Economic Association. In 1931 he received his Ph.D. for a dissertation on banking theory and monetary policy. He remained at Harvard until 1934 as assistant to, successively, Ralph Hawtrey, John H. Williams, and Joseph Schumpeter. There, he constructed the first money supply and "income ve-

locity" series for the United States. He also attacked the Fed's "commercial loan theory" of banking (or "real bills" doctrine), blaming it for monetary tightening in mid-1929, when the economy was already declining, and then for its passivity during the next four years in the face of mass liquidations and bank failures (in his book *The Supply and Control of Money in the United States* [1934]). In a January 1932 Harvard memorandum on antidepression policy, Currie and fellow instructors Harry Dexter White (a close friend since 1925) and Paul T. Ellsworth urged large fiscal deficits coupled with open-market operations to expand bank reserves, as well as the lifting of tariffs and the relief of interallied debts (see Laidler and Sandilands, 2002).

In 1934 Currie became an American citizen and joined Jacob Viner's "freshman brain trust" at the U.S. Treasury. There he outlined an "ideal" monetary system for the United States, which included a 100-percent reserve banking plan to strengthen central bank control over the money supply by preventing member banks from lending out their demand deposit liabilities, while at the same time removing reserve requirements on genuine savings deposits with low turnover. Later that year Marriner Eccles moved from the Treasury to become governor of the Federal Reserve Board. Eccles took Currie with him to the Fed as his personal assistant. White, another "freshman brain trust" recruit, became a top adviser to treasury secretary Henry Morgenthau, and for some years he and Currie worked closely in their respective roles at the Treasury and the Fed.

At the Fed, Currie drafted what became the important 1935 Banking Act. He also constructed a "net federal income-creating expenditure series" to show the strategic role of fiscal policy in complementing monetary policy to revive an economy in acute, persisting depression. When, after four years of recovery, the economy declined sharply in 1937 he was able to explain to President Franklin D. Roosevelt, in an unprecedented four-hour interview, that the declared aim of balancing the budget "to restore business confidence" had damaged the economy. This was part of the "struggle for the soul of FDR" (Stein, 1969) between the cautious Secretary Morgenthau and the expansionist Governor Eccles. At first FDR sided with Morgenthau and disaster followed. In April 1938 the president at last asked Congress for major appropriations for spending on relief and public works. In May 1939 the rationale was explained in theoretical and statistical detail by Currie (dubbed "Mr. Inside" by James Tobin [1976]) and by Harvard's Alvin Hansen ("Mr. Outside") in testimony before the Temporary National Economic Committee to highlight the role of government budgets in the recovery process.

Named FDR's White House economist in July 1939, Currie advised on taxation, social security, and the speeding up of peacetime and wartime production plans. In January 1941 he was sent on a mission to China for discussions with Generalissimo Chiang Kai-shek and Chou En-lai, the Communist representative in the Chinese wartime capital of Chungking. On his return in March he recommended that China be added to the lend-lease program. He was put in charge of its administration under the overall direction of FDR's special assistant Harry Hopkins.

Currie was also asked to expedite the Flying Tigers program, in which U.S. Navy pilots were released for combat as mercenaries under Claire Chennault who commanded the Chinese air force in the war with Japan. He also helped organize a large training program in the United States for Chinese pilots. In May 1941 he prepared a paper on Chinese aircraft requirements for General George C. Marshall and the Joint War Board. The document, accepted by the Board, stressed the role an air force in China could play in defending Singapore, the Burma Road, and the Philippines against Japanese attack, but it also pointed to its potential for strategic bombing of targets in Japan itself. These activities, together with Currie's work in helping to tighten U.S. sanctions against Japan, are said to have played a part in provoking Japan into attacking Pearl Harbor later that year.

Currie returned to Chungking in July 1942 to try to patch up the very strained relations between Chiang and General Joseph W. Stilwell, commander of U.S. forces in China. Currie was one of several of FDR's envoys who recommended Stilwell's recall and reassignment. Back in Washington, Roosevelt asked Currie to put this case to General Marshall, but the general dismissed the idea. Only much later did Marshall concede that his protégé's continued presence in China was indeed a mistake. Stilwell was recalled in October 1944.

In 1943–1944 Currie ran the Foreign Economic Administration, and in early 1945 Roosevelt appointed him to head a tripartite (U.S., British, and French) mission to Bern to persuade the Swiss to freeze Nazi bank balances and stop further shipments of German supplies through Switzerland to the Italian front. He was also closely involved in loan negotiations with the British and the Russians, as well as in preparations for the 1944 Bretton Woods conference —staged primarily by Harry Dexter White—that led to the creation of the International Monetary Fund and the World Bank.

After the war Currie was one of those blamed for "losing" China. It was also alleged by Elizabeth Bentley, an ex-Soviet agent, that Currie and White had participated in wartime Soviet espionage (see Sandilands, 2000, and Boughton and Sandilands, 2002). Though she had never met them herself, she claimed that White and Currie had passed on information to other Washington economists who were consciously abetting her own espionage activities, and that Currie and White probably knew where the information was ultimately destined. White and Currie were, of course, heavily involved in official wartime cooperation with the Soviet ally, but she put a sinister interpretation on these activities. White and Currie demanded to appear together before the House Committee on Un-American Activities in August 1948 to rebut Bentley's

charges. Their testimony appeared to satisfy the Committee at that time, though the strain contributed to the fatal heart attack that White suffered immediately after the hearing.

No charges were ever laid against Currie, and in 1949 he was selected to head the first of the World Bank's comprehensive country surveys. This was to Colombia. After Currie's report was published in Washington in September 1950, he was invited by the Colombian government to return to Bogota as adviser to a commission established to implement the report's recommendations. He has been falsely accused (for example by Haynes and Klehr, 1999, p. 150) of fleeing the United States to avoid McCarthyite charges of disloyalty. In fact he returned in December 1952 to appear before a grand jury in New York that was investigating Owen Lattimore's role in the famous Amerasia case that involved the publication of secret State Department documents by that magazine.

When Currie, as a naturalized U.S. citizen, attempted to renew his passport in the poisonous atmosphere of 1954, this was refused, ostensibly on the grounds that he was now residing abroad. However, the reality was probably connected with the then top-secret "Venona" project, which had decrypted some wartime Soviet cables that mentioned Currie's name (see Haynes and Klehr, 1999, and Sandilands, 2000). He had recently been divorced from his first wife, Dorothy Bacon, whom he married in 1927 and with whom he had two sons; in 1954 he married a Colombian, Elvira Wiesner, with whom he later had a son and a daughter. After a military coup in Colombia in 1953 he retired from his economic advisory work and devoted himself to the raising of Holstein cattle on a farm outside Bogota. He developed the highest-yielding dairy herd in the country.

With the return of civilian government in 1958, President Alberto Lleras personally conferred Colombian citizenship upon him and he returned to full-time advisory work for a succession of presidents. Between 1966 and 1971, though, he served as a visiting professor in North American and British universities: Michigan State (1966), Simon Fraser, Canada (1967–1968 and 1969–1971), Glasgow (1968–1969), and Oxford (1969). He returned permanently to Colombia in May 1971 at the personal behest of President Misael Pastrana to prepare a national plan of development known as the Plan of the Four Strategies, with focus on urban housing and export diversification. The plan was implemented, and the institutions that were established in support of the plan played a major role in accelerating Colombia's urbanization.

Currie remained as chief economist at the National Planning Department for ten years, 1971–1981, followed by twelve years at the Colombian Institute of Savings and Housing until his death in 1993. There he doggedly defended the unique housing finance system (based on "units of constant purchasing power" for both savers and borrowers) that he had established in 1972. The system thus continued to boost Colombia's growth rate and urban employment opportunities year by year. Currie was also a renowned adviser and writer on urban planning, and he played a major part in the first United Nations Habitat conference in Vancouver in 1976. His "cities-within-the-city" urban design and financing proposals (including the public recapture of land's socially created "valorización," or "unearned land value increments," as cities grow) were elaborated in his book *Taming the Megalopolis* (1976). He was a regular teacher at the National University of Colombia, the Javeriana University, and the University of the Andes, and was also publishing widely in international journals. His writings were heavily influenced by his old Harvard mentor Allyn Young. A paper on Youngian "endogenous" growth theory was published posthumously (*History of Political Economy* 29 [1997]: 413–44). He was still teaching when he died. On the day before his death he was awarded Colombia's highest honor, the Cruz de Boyaca, by President Cesar Gaviria for services to his adopted country.

• Currie's very extensive collected papers are archived at Duke University's Special Collections Library (http://scriptorium.lib.duke.edu). His China papers are also archived at the Hoover Institution, Stanford University. His most influential early work on monetary theory, policy, and statistics is *The Supply and Control of Money in the United States* (1934). His long Harvard memorandum (with Harry Dexter White and Paul T. Ellsworth), dated January 1932, on antidepression policy is published in *History of Political Economy* 32, no. 2 (Summer 2002) with a foreword by David E. Laidler and Roger J. Sandilands that explains its significance as a forerunner of what has become known as the Chicago School's monetary tradition. A comprehensive biography of Currie is Roger J. Sandilands, *The Life and Political Economy of Lauchlin Currie: New Dealer, Presidential Adviser, and Development Economist* (1990), which includes a comprehensive bibliography of Currie's writings. Discussion of Currie's work in the New Deal is in Herbert Stein, *The Fiscal Revolution in America* (1969); James Tobin, "Hansen and Public Policy," *Quarterly Journal of Economics* 90: 32–37; and Ronnie J. Phillips, *The Chicago Plan and New Deal Banking Reform* (1995). Appraisals of the significance of the "Venona" papers—decrypts of Soviet cables that passed between Moscow and New York during the war—and whether they support the allegations that Currie was a Soviet spy are in John Earl Haynes and Harvey Klehr, *Venona: Soviet Espionage in America in the Stalin Era* (1999); Roger J. Sandilands, "Guilt by Association? Lauchlin Currie's Alleged Involvement with Washington Economists in Soviet Espionage," *History of Political Economy* 32, no. 3 (Fall 2000): 473–515; and James M. Boughton and Roger J. Sandilands, "Politics and the Attack on FDR's Economists: From Grand Alliance to Cold War," *Intelligence and National Security*, 17, no. 2 (Summer 2002). Obituaries are in the *New York Times*, 30 Dec. 1993, and the London *Times*, 10 Jan. 1994.

ROGER J. SANDILANDS

CURTIS, William Buckingham (17 Jan. 1837–30 June 1900), champion amateur athlete and "father" of amateur athletics in America, was born in Salisbury, Vermont, the son of Henry Harvey Curtis, a Presbyterian minister and college president, and Elizabeth "Betsey" C. Deming. Betsey Curtis died from tuberculosis a year after Bill's birth, and by 1840 his father married Julia Ann Roberts. From 1841 to 1862, the year Bill's father died, the family moved for church assignments in Ohio, Indiana, and Illinois. This strong Christian home environment eventually influenced Curtis's philosophy of life and set the general pattern for his later efforts to "purify" sport.

In 1847 young Curtis and his father were influenced by Henry Ward Beecher, a popular preacher and promoter of "muscular Christianity," who, in addition to possessing a fine physique and enormous energy, increased their Indiana church membership with numerous revivals and sermons on the evils of gambling. The following year, in another effort to purify the community of unclean influences, Bill's father bought the land next to his church to prevent the construction of a theater on the adjacent site. These examples of Christian commitment to follow "truth" rather than falsehoods accompanied Curtis throughout his life. From 1861 to 1863 he fought in the Civil War for the principles of abolition, and from 1866 to 1900 he attempted to purify sport of fraud and money corruption.

When Curtis was about ten years old, he contracted tuberculosis, and his parents sent him to the cool, dry mountains of Manchester, Vermont, where his stepmother's clan still lived. He enrolled in Burr's Seminary and strengthened himself through a regimen of mountain climbing, walking, and outdoor sports. Eventually his chiseled muscles filled out a frame that was five feet, nine inches, and two hundred pounds, accompanied by blue eyes and a long sandy beard.

In 1850 Curtis moved with his family for his father's assignment at Chicago's First Presbyterian Church. Unable to gain admission to West Point, he privately followed the entire West Point course of study, which sharpened his math and engineering skills. By 1851 he entered Wabash College in Crawfordsville, Indiana, where he led other young men in athletic games, swimming, ice-skating, and "cross country tramps." By 1852 he began a 20-year unbroken string of victories in the 100-yard dash, and at age 40 he still ran the 100 in 10.8 seconds. In 1852, after a small disagreement with a French professor, he left Wabash College and enrolled at Bell's Commercial College in Chicago, where he studied business and regularly attended nearby athletic clubs. While working as a bookkeeper for his brother's fish business, Curtis continued to excel in multiple sports, and his national reputation grew. He added gymnastics, weight lifting, and rowing to his list of sports, which included such feats as harness lifting 3,239 pounds.

In 1860 Curtis's father assumed the presidency of Knox College in Galesburg, Illinois. That same year the campus was host to the Lincoln-Douglas debates in which Abraham Lincoln first framed his moral opposition to slavery. By June 1861, after the first volleys of gunfire in the American Civil War, Curtis joined the Nineteenth Illinois Volunteers, eventually earning honors for his service as chief of staff to General John

Basil Turchin. The general was court-martialed for the "minor" sacking of Athens, Alabama, in May 1862, but Curtis remained loyal and rejoined Turchin after President Lincoln reinstated the general.

In 1866 Curtis moved to New York City and founded the prestigious New York Athletic Club (NYAC) in 1868. He continued to advise and help create "pure amateur" model clubs across the country. He opened new sport clubs in Chicago, including the Chicago Athletic Club in 1872, designed after Ottignon's Metropolitan Gymnasium in Chicago, which Curtis helped establish in 1860 with Hubert and Charles Ottignon. Ottignon's was a clearinghouse that verified national sport records and set early national rules standards according to the rigorous Curtis criteria. A much-requested referee of many national sporting contests, both professional and amateur, Curtis learned firsthand the difficulties gambling money created for "the business of sport." Eventually he declined to judge professional contests because his "honest" and "fair" decisions created too many ugly confrontations with financial backers of the losers, especially if the "stake" money was in the thousands and betting was heavy.

In 1870 Curtis moved back to Chicago. Among his friends was Louis Sullivan, a prominent architect who mentored Frank Lloyd Wright. Sullivan credited Curtis with influencing his life with a regimen of physical discipline and intellectual study at the Calumet River Lotus Club that included boating, swimming, river ice-skating, and multiple field activities, such as the shot put and the hammer throw. Sullivan recalled that, when Curtis walked along the Calumet River boat pier prior to a swim, "he was a sight for the Greeks," and Sullivan was "enraptured at the play of light and shade" on Curtis's sharply defined musculature (Twombly, *Louis Sullivan: His Life and Times*, p. 52). Curtis summered on his houseboat docked at the Calumet River and also kept boats at Bath Beach in Brooklyn, New York.

In 1879 Curtis permanently moved back to New York City to edit the sporting newspaper *Spirit of the Times*. To escape the foul air of lower Manhattan after long hours at the *Spirit* offices, Curtis went hiking and ice-skating at the Fresh Air Club, which he founded soon after relocating. Fresh Air Club members took long train rides into the country every weekend, but first, during the week, Curtis scouted the route by hiking or skating it himself, earning the name "Pathfinder," with which he signed *Spirit* reports.

Curtis publicly rejected the artificial and elitist social boundary between amateur and professional sportspeople as developed by British sporting traditionalists. He objected to the NYAC becoming dominated by rich people who were more concerned with socializing than participating in the science of sport. He believed that personal honesty and character were more important than a person's professional or amateur athletic status, but he insisted that "pure" amateur sport could help athletics attain higher moral standards by eliminating gambling and fraudulent "show" business aspects from so-called "sporting" events.

From 1870 to 1898 Curtis played a significant role in stifling the spread of the "fancy" ice shows, which contained elements of theater, dance, and music, by promoting a form of figure skating that required skaters to etch precise figures rather than entertain spectators. Figure skating was easier for him to measure and judge as "sport" than the "art" of theatrical "fancy" performances. By 1870, vowing he would never serve again as a judge for a "fancy" contest, he predicted the type of scandal that plagued the ice dancing of the 2002 Winter Olympics, when judges were found guilty of corrupted decisions. He favored speed skating because winners could be scientifically measured with a stopwatch.

Curtis's relentless campaign against impure sport included numerous editorial attacks against minor sporting violations. His language was so strong that his friends likened it to using a "cannon to kill a mosquito" (*N. Y. Times* obituary, 8 July 1900). He became more mellow late in life, since he had come to grudgingly accept that the business of professional sport was winning over amateur sport. His writing style was particularly sharp toward "money-grabbing" athletes who wrote disagreeable letters to the *Spirit*, which he published in full and then criticized in accompanying editorials. For example, Curtis denounced one letter from a disgruntled speed skater as "an uncivil answer to a generous offer [that] can only be classed as an ungrateful grunt from a hyperborean hog . . . a tirade of ignorant insolence which no gentleman could have written" (*Spirit of the Times*, January 24, 1885, p. 803). Although Curtis was a founder of the Amateur Athletic Union (AAU) in 1888, he became critical of its leadership by 1895 and wrote numerous editorials typified by the following statement: "Because the little boys of the Amateur Athletic Union have declined to let anybody else play in their backyard," this rule change, which denied unregistered amateur athletes from outside the New York region a chance to compete, is "the most absurd, mischievous and cowardly law ever promulgated by the AAU," and is "in direct opposition to all traditions of manly sport" (*Spirit of the Times*, January 16, 1897, p. 11). The AAU eventually became an autocratic and unforgiving institution headed by James E. Sullivan, who was more of a social climber than a "pure" sportsman according to Curtis standards.

Never married, Curtis was generous and kindhearted. He had no interest in the sport of boxing, revolted at the idea of battering another person with his fists, yet he did not hesitate to engage an adversary at close quarters. He once threw a bully off a train for harassing a black man. Another time, in his typically heavy-handed fashion, he reprimanded an inconsiderate driver of a horsecar, concluding with the gentlemanly offer, "Now, my friend, if you'll come down off that wagon, I shall be pleased to give you a sound thrashing" (Seida, *"Father Bill" Curtis: Father of*

American Amateur Athletics, p. 153). The man remained seated.

Curtis supported the inclusion of Native Americans in sport but stopped short of openly encouraging women in sport. As his *New York Times* obituary stated: "In spite of his fondness for children and his evident appreciation of family life, he never married, and it is believed by his friends that he had been the victim of an unhappy love affair in early life. Occasional hints which he dropped, together with his well-known aversion to frivolous women, tend to support this supposition." Never one to dress in high fashion style, Curtis sometimes deliberately dressed like a poor farmhand and loved to expose "fakes" and "charlatans" who assumed from his attire that he was uneducated.

On 30 June 1900, at age 63, Curtis attempted to climb the summit of the 6,288-foot Mount Washington in New Hampshire with members of his Fresh Air Club and the Appalachian Mountain Club. Because of his active and energetic lifestyle—his body likely produced a high metabolic rate and much heat even in the coldest weather—Curtis never wore an overcoat. Never fully accepting his physical limits, he ignored warnings from descending climbers that severe cold weather was above, and he continued to ascend the route. A blinding ice-storm grew worse and after a severe struggle on slippery rocks, evident from dents and bruises on his head, he died from exposure a short distance below the summit house.

• Curtis's handwritten letters to Albert Sullivan, the brother of Louis Sullivan, are in the archives of the New York Athletic Club (NYAC) in New York City. The Appalachian Mountain Club archives contain an evaluation report of the accidental circumstances of his death. Curtis's views on gambling are in "The Increase of Gambling and Its Forms," *Forum*, Oct. 1891, pp. 281–92. Microfilm copies of the *Spirit of the Times* contain published letters from his antagonists and supporters and Curtis's personal responses. A comprehensive but uncategorized chronological source is by the Chicago boat historian Lowell M. Seida, *William Buckingham "Father Bill" Curtis: Father of American Amateur Athletics* (2001). Also helpful is a journal article by Joe Willis and Richard Wettan, "William Buckingham Curtis: The Founding Father of American Amateur Athletics, 1837–1900," *Quest*, Monograph 27 (1977). A surprisingly revealing look is in an NYAC memorial publication, *Constitution and By-Laws of the National Amateur Skating Association of America* (1904). A brief but pointed insight into Curtis's persona is the 1863–1864 diary of Nadine Turchin, *A Monotony Full of Sadness*, ed. M. E. McElligott (1977). See also Caspar Whitney, "The Sportsman's View-Point," *Outing* Aug. 1900, p. 557; Robert Korsgaard, *A History of the Amateur Athletic Union of the United States* (microform, 1952); Fred G. Jarvis and Bob Considine, *First Hundred Years: A Portrait of the NYAC* (1969); and Robert Twombly, *Louis Sullivan: His Life and Work* (1986). For context on the Curtis period, see Stephen Hardy, "Entrepreneurs, Structures, and the Sportgeist: Old Tensions in a Modern Industry," *Essays on Sport History and Sport Mythology*, ed. Donald G. Kyle and Gary D. Stark (1990). Obituaries are in the *New York Times*, 8 July 1900, and *Spirit of the Times*, 7 July 1900.

PAUL DELOCA

D

DALITZ, Morris B. "Moe" (24 Dec. 1899–31 Aug. 1989), developer, casino operator, and rumored organized crime associate, was born Morris Barney Dalitz in Boston, the son of Barney Dalitz, who ran a laundry business, and Anna Dalitz (maiden name unknown). The family moved to Detroit when Dalitz was a child, and his father owned several laundries there.

During Prohibition Dalitz became involved in illegal activities. He worked with Detroit's Purple Gang to protect his family's laundry from union organizers. Caught between two rival criminal groups, he branched out from Michigan, forming partnerships with Sam Tucker, Morris Kleinman, Ruby Kolod, Frank Rosen, and Louis Rothkopf, and an alliance with Meyer Lansky. He opened bars and casinos near Cincinnati and Youngstown and across the Ohio River in Kentucky, and he supplied liquor to other operators. He also invested in such legal enterprises as laundry, steel, real estate, ice cream, and a railroad. He had a brief marriage that ended in divorce.

After the Twenty-First Amendment repealed Prohibition, Dalitz and his partners continued bootlegging by supplying molasses through their Molaska Corporation to illegal distillers from Ohio to New Jersey. During World War II, he enlisted in the army and received a commission to run the quartermaster's laundry, taking advantage of his residence at the Hotel Savoy-Plaza in New York City to scout new business opportunities. After the war, he invested in land and a laundry in Tucson, illegal bookmaking in Phoenix, and casinos in Reno. He also married Toni (her maiden name is unknown), whom he divorced in the early 1950s; they had one son.

His greatest opportunity came in Las Vegas in the late 1940s. Wilbur Clark, a onetime manager of gambling ships off the California coast and owner of the El Rancho Vegas, the first hotel on the Las Vegas Strip, ran out of money building his dream hotel, the Desert Inn. After a long quest for financing, he turned to Dalitz, who brought in partners Kleinman, Tucker, and Allard Roen; finished the hotel for its 24 April 1950 opening; and ran it. Clark served as the hotel's public face or front man. Dalitz preferred to avoid notoriety, as demonstrated by his resistance to testifying before Senator Estes Kefauver's committee investigating organized crime. (When Kefauver accused him of getting rich bootlegging, Dalitz replied, "Well, I didn't inherit any money, Senator. . . . If you people wouldn't have drunk it, I wouldn't have bootlegged it.") The published report of the hearings includes no references to Dalitz, who seems to have struck the committee as less objectionable than some of the others they interviewed.

In Las Vegas, Dalitz pursued legal casino investments. He and his partners bought out Clark and built the Desert Inn Country Club, correctly expecting it to be a major tourist attraction. For several years, it hosted the Professional Golf Association's Tournament of Champions. The Desert Inn group received a contract to operate the casino at the Showboat Hotel, built in 1954, and became co-owners of the Stardust, which opened in 1958. He was the landlord for a downtown Las Vegas property, the Sundance, later called Fitzgerald's. In 1954, he married Averille (maiden name unknown); they had a daughter and divorced in 1964.

Unlike many of his counterparts from organized crime, Dalitz invested his profits in many legitimate, noncasino businesses. He and Roen joined local builders Irwin Molasky and Mervin Adelson in their Paradise Development Company. They built the first large private hospital in Las Vegas, Sunrise Hospital, now part of Humana; the Las Vegas, International, and Winchester Country Clubs; numerous housing tracts; and office buildings both downtown and closer to the Strip. In several cases, they received financing from the Teamsters Central States Pension Fund, thanks in part to Dalitz's having known union leader Jimmy Hoffa for several decades.

Dalitz became heavily involved in charitable giving, often anonymously. He helped found the local United Way. He donated to Nevada Southern University, later the University of Nevada, Las Vegas, one of 14 organizations to which he left substantial sums in his will. He chaired the United Jewish Appeal and fundraising committees for the construction of a new building for Temple Beth Sholom, then the only local synagogue. He contributed money and land to the Catholic Church to build the Guardian Angel Cathedral next to the Desert Inn. His favorite charity was the Variety Club, a fundraising group for handicapped children. He also gave $50,000 to UNLV to name its Center for Economic Education for its longtime director Barbara Schick, a UNLV graduate and Dalitz's companion for two decades until her death in 1986.

Dalitz also played a role in desegregating Las Vegas. In 1960, local NAACP leader Dr. James McMillan threatened a boycott of local casinos unless they began serving African Americans. Although Dalitz shared the racism of most Las Vegas businessmen, casino and otherwise, fearing that customers from segregated areas would refuse to gamble alongside blacks, Dalitz eventually agreed to accede to the NAACP's demands, and sent word to McMillan that segregation was over.

Not only a leader in business and charitable activities, Dalitz became active in political campaigns. In 1962 he joined other Strip operators in spending hundreds of thousands of dollars to defeat the gubernatorial campaign of local publisher Hank Greenspun, who was critical of Dalitz's organized-crime ties and local influence. In 1966, Dalitz and his partners contributed heavily to the gubernatorial campaign of Republican Paul Laxalt, whose opponent, incumbent Grant Sawyer, had appointed gaming regulators who imposed more restrictions on them.

In 1967, Dalitz sold the Desert Inn to Howard Hughes but remained a consultant. He sold his interest in the Stardust in 1969 to Lansky associate Albert Parvin. Meanwhile, he and his partners in Paradise Development continued to build the city. In the late 1960s, they opened the Boulevard Mall and began raising money to build the Rancho La Costa resort in California. *Penthouse* later published an article claiming that they built the spa with Teamsters money as an organized crime resort. They sued for libel. The judge ruled that Dalitz and Roen were public figures, making libel hard to prove. They dropped their case, but Molasky and Adelson won an apology from the publisher.

In his later years, Dalitz won numerous accolades from his adopted community. He received B'nai B'rith's Torch of Liberty Award and the City of Peace Award for aiding the Bonds for Israel program. He won plaudits for supporting a new synagogue, the YMCA, and UNLV. But he still faced accusations of ties to organized crime, although even some critics agreed that he had sought legitimacy but proved unable to sever his old connections. He also dealt with his son's death in a plane crash in 1972 but remained close to his daughter.

When Dalitz died, in Las Vegas, the city mourned him as a community builder. Whatever his previous activities and associates, he had been a highly successful businessman and land developer who changed Las Vegas's appearance and contributed to the community. He was a crucial figure in Las Vegas's growth in the 1950s and 1960s, reaping and increasing the benefits of the postwar boom and helping to set the stage for the growth in the 1990s that followed his death. He also reflected the contradictions of many in Las Vegas's past: seemingly a legitimate businessman involved in his community, but never free of old ties to organized crime, and possibly more deeply involved than anyone will ever know.

• Moe Dalitz left behind no personal papers, although numerous references to him appear in other collections in the Department of Special Collections, Lied Library, University of Nevada, Las Vegas, which also maintains an extensive biography file on him. The *Las Vegas Review-Journal* and *Las Vegas Sun*, the two daily newspapers throughout Dalitz's time in Southern Nevada, contain a wealth of articles about him and his activities.

Dalitz is the subject of several brief biographies and appears as a key figure in several books. More favorable analyses of him are Alan Balboni, "Moe Dalitz: Controversial Founding Father of Modern Las Vegas," in Richard O. Davies, ed., *The Maverick Spirit: Building the New Nevada* (1999), 24–43; John L. Smith, "Moe Dalitz and the Desert," in Jack E. Sheehan, ed., *The Players: The Men Who Made Las Vegas* (1997), 35–47; Smith, "Morris B. 'Moe' Dalitz: The Double Life," in A. D. Hopkins and K. J. Evans, eds., *The First 100: Portraits of the Men and Women Who Shaped Las Vegas* (1999), 122–24. Less favorable analyses appear in Sally Denton and Roger Morris, *The Money and the Power: The Making of Las Vegas and Its Hold on America, 1947–2000* (2001); Ronald A. Farrell and Carole Case, *The Black Book and the Mob: The Untold Story of the Control of Nevada's Casinos* (1995); and Ed Reid and Ovid DeMaris, *The Green Felt Jungle* (1963). Hank Greenspun tells his side of the story in Hank Greenspun and Alex Pelle, *Where I Stand: The Record of a Reckless Man* (1966). How Dalitz and his partners affected local growth and development can be found in Eugene Moehring, *Resort City in the Sunbelt: Las Vegas, 1930–2000*, 2d ed. (2000). Extensive obituaries are in the *Las Vegas Review-Journal* and the *Las Vegas Sun*, 1 Sept. 1989, with additional stories about his funeral and reminiscences over the following week.

MICHAEL GREEN

DANGERFIELD, Rodney (22 Nov. 1921–5 Oct. 2004), comedian and actor, was born Jacob Cohen in Babylon, Long Island, New York, the son of Phillip Cohen, a vaudeville comedian. His mother's name is not known. Dangerfield's father abandoned his family soon after Dangerfield was born. Struggling against poverty, Dangerfield's mother moved her two children among several low-rent areas in Long Island and the Bronx. In his 2004 autobiography, *It's Not Easy Bein' Me: A Life of No Respect but Plenty of Sex and Drugs*, Dangerfield characterized his mother as "cold-hearted and selfish" (Dangerfield, 2004, p. 8). "On my birthdays, I never got a present, a card, nothing" (Dangerfield, 2004, p. 6). Starved for affection and often unsupervised, Dangerfield was five when a man paid him a nickel to go to an office and be kissed. Dangerfield recalled going back to earn more nickels and titled chapter one of his autobiography "I Was a Male Hooker."

Living in Far Rockaway, Long Island, Dangerfield at age ten sold ice cream on the beach. He saved $100, which his mother put in the bank. A few months later it was gone, and he was deeply hurt when his mother perfunctorily explained that she "needed the money." Twice a year he took a train to Manhattan to spend an hour with his father, now a stockbroker. "My father saw me two hours a year; that's what it amounted to," Dangerfield said in an interview with Terry Gross recorded in July 2004.

Dangerfield spent most of his teenage years in Kew Gardens, an upscale neighborhood in Queens. Because his family was poor, he never fit in. He experienced anti-Semitism, seldom had enough money to join school activities, and worked delivering groceries to the back doors of friends' homes, which humiliated him. Virtually every childhood experience left emotional scars and convinced Dangerfield that he was a loser. However, this inferiority complex became a rich source for the comic material that made him famous.

After he finished high school, Dangerfield worked as a soda jerk, fish truck driver, theater barker, and singing waiter at the Polish Falcon nightclub in Brooklyn. During this period he began to smoke marijuana and to write jokes. "I was trying to forget reality with jokes. I was always depressed, but I could tell a joke and get a laugh" (Dangerfield, 2004, p. 31). He officially changed his name to Jack Roy, performed in amateur shows, and was sporadically booked in the Catskills' "borscht belt," where he worked for $12 a week plus room and board. For the next ten years he collected hundreds of jokes in a duffel bag, but he was discouraged at every turn. "I played one club that was so far out," he quipped, "that my act was reviewed in *Field and Stream*" (McLellan, p. B8).

In 1948, at age twenty-eight, Dangerfield decided to quit show business. "To give you an idea of how well I was doing at the time I quit," Dangerfield remembered, "I was the only one who knew I quit" (Dangerfield, 2004, p. 63). In 1948 he married the singer Joyce Indig and went into the aluminum siding business. The couple had one child but divorced in 1949. After twelve years and one short stint in jail when his accountant cooked his books, Dangerfield in 1961, at age forty, decided to make a comeback. "Show business was my escape from life. . . . It was like a fix. I needed it to survive" (Dangerfield, 2004, p. 77). In 1963 he remarried Joyce Indig, and they had another child. But again the couple quickly separated, and they divorced in 1970.

Early in his comeback Dangerfield was booked in New York's Inwood Lounge, where he had many old friends. Worried that he would bomb, he asked the lounge's owner, George McFadden, to bill him under any name except Jack Roy. At showtime McFadden made the introduction, "Here's Rodney Dangerfield!" The new act brought down the house, and the name stuck.

Dangerfield's big break came in 1966, when he appeared on *The Ed Sullivan Show*. Ed Sullivan loved Dangerfield's act and asked him back six more times. These television appearances forced Dangerfield to develop another key element of his comic persona. Because he had no taste in clothes, he chose a safe outfit, a red tie, a white shirt, and a black suit, which became his trademark uniform for the next forty years. The shirt and tie are in the Smithsonian Institution in Washington, D.C.

Dangerfield became a regular on television with appearances on the Merv Griffin, Joey Bishop, and Mike Douglas variety shows. He made a deal with *The Dean Martin Show* to write skits and appear with Martin for twenty-eight weeks. When the Academy Award–winning movie *The Godfather* (1972) sparked Americans' fascination with the Mafia concept of "respect," Dangerfield quickly realized the line "I don't get no respect" fit his lovable loser's image. Writing rapid-fire jokes off that line, he created a comic persona even the great comedian Jack Benny envied.

Dangerfield's signature routine began: "I tell ya, I don't get no respect. No respect at all." He followed with jokes like: "My mother never breast fed me. She told me she liked me as a friend." "When I was a kid I got no respect. I played hide-and-seek. They wouldn't even look for me." "I remember the time I was kidnapped and they sent back a piece of my finger to my father. He said he wanted more proof." "What a dog I got. His favorite bone is my arm." "I'm a bad lover. Once I caught a peeping tom booing me." "My wife likes to talk during sex. Last night she called me from a motel." "With my doctor, I don't get no respect. I told him I wanted a vasectomy. He said with a face like mine, I didn't need one." After hearing Dangerfield's act, Benny remarked, "Rodney, I'm cheap and I'm 39, that's my image, but your 'no respect' thing, that's into the soul of everybody. Everybody can identify with that" (Shales). Rodney Dangerfield became a household name in 1969, when he appeared with Johnny Carson. Over the next decade he made seventy appearances on *The Tonight Show*, a record. Carson's successor Jay Leno called Dangerfield "the greatest stand-up comedian of all time" ("Rodney Dangerfield Paid the Ultimate Respect").

Dangerfield now had more work than he could handle. He was a headliner in Las Vegas, made commercials, and was a prized guest on television shows, but he needed to be near his children in New York City. In September 1969 he opened a nightclub called Dangerfield's on First Avenue that became a hot spot on the Manhattan club scene. In 1985 he made a deal with HBO to showcase new talent from his nightclub's stage and introduced edgy young comics such as Jerry Seinfeld, Roseanne Barr, Bob Saget, Louie Anderson, Tim Allen, Rita Rudner, Robert Townsend, Andrew Dice Clay, Jeff Foxworthy, Sam Kinison, and Jim Carrey.

In 1980 Dangerfield became a movie star with his portrayal of a nouveau riche boor in the movie *Caddyshack*. His first starring role was in *Easy Money* (1983), but the movie failed at the box office. In 1986 Dangerfield wrote, coproduced, and starred in *Back to School*, which grossed more than $100 million. From 1971 to 2002 he appeared in more than a dozen motion pictures, including a straight dramatic role as an abusive father in *Natural Born Killers* (1994), which critics argued deserved an Oscar nomination. He won a Grammy in 1981 for his comedy album *No Respect*, and he even entered the world of rap music with "Rappin' Rodney" (1984). With his bassett hound face, French horn voice, and forlorn, bug-eyed stare, Dangerfield knew he projected a cartoonlike character. In 1991 he parlayed this image into the animated feature musical *Rover Dangerfield*, which he wrote and produced. He also provided the voice-over for Rover and cowrote the songs.

In 1982, to correct a lifetime of bad habits, Dangerfield checked into the Pritikin Longevity Center in Santa Monica, California. He stopped smoking and lost weight, and he met Joan Child, a Mormon thirty years his junior. The couple married in 1993.

In the last dozen years of Dangerfield's life, his health deteriorated. He created jokes about his mythical physician, Doctor Vinnie Boom Batz. "Doc, every morning when I look in the mirror, I feel like throwing up. What's wrong with me?" He said, "I don't know, but your eyesight is perfect" (Dangerfield, 2004, p. 252). In reality Dangerfield had the best medical care and was among the great late bloomers in Hollywood. He was fifty-nine when he made *Caddyshack*, and he enjoyed his greatest popularity between ages sixty and eighty-two. He suffered a heart attack on his eightieth birthday, but in 2001 he made a triumphant return at New York's prestigious Avery Fisher Hall. Because he said nothing political or topical and used nothing from the headlines, he appealed to audiences of all ages and from every walk of life. His timeless jokes were about the vulnerability of human nature, and his subject was usually the exquisite humiliation of being Rodney Dangerfield. Often frank about sex and drugs, he did not offend audiences because they identified with his sweaty, tie-tugging existential Everyman.

Even at the height of his popularity, Dangerfield was never able to fully assimilate his celebrity. He was a kind and generous man, but millions probably loved him more than he loved himself. In the "Foreword" of *It's Not Easy*, Jim Carrey observed, "From all the hundreds of comedians he has helped and inspired, and from anybody who digs great comedy, he gets nothing but love and respect" (Dangerfield, 2004, p. xii). In 2003, before undergoing brain surgery, Dangerfield delivered his last great joke. When asked how long he would be in the hospital, he said: "If things go right, I'll be there about a week. If things don't go right, I'll be there about an hour and a half." Things did go right that day. Dangerfield died the following year in the University of California, Los Angeles (UCLA) Medical Center from complications after heart valve replacement surgery.

• Because *It's Not Easy Bein' Me* was published in the year of Dangerfield's death, the autobiography covers his entire life, including a candid discussion of his drug use and final illnesses. Dangerfield wrote three other books playing on his lovable loser persona, *I Couldn't Stand My Wife's Cooking, So I Opened a Restaurant* (1972), *I Don't Get No Respect* (1982), and *No Respect*, with Eric Teitelbaum and Bill Teitelbaum (1995). Dangerfield wrote, produced, provided voice-over, or acted in more than twenty motion pictures, including *The Projectionist* (1971), *Ladybugs* (1992), *Meet Wally Sparks* (1997), *Little Nicky* (2000), *My 5 Wives* (2000), and *The 4th Tenor* (2002). Terry Gross's interview with Dangerfield is "Remembering Rodney Dangerfield," *Fresh Air*, National Public Radio, 6 Oct. 2004. In 1997 he discussed his lifelong battle with depression on a PBS episode of *Healthweek* (Program 121). His biography, *Rodney Dangerfield: Respect at Last*, appeared on the History Channel. He is featured in scholarly works on comedy, including Albert Goldman, *Freakshow: Misadventures in the Counterculture* (1971), and Asa Berger, *Jewish Jesters* (2001). See also Tom Shales, "Rodney Dangerfield Beating Troubles to the Punch," *Washington Post*, 7 Oct. 2004; and Erik Hedegaard, "Gone to Pot," *Rolling Stone*, 10 Oct. 2004. Many of Dangerfield's jokes are in Ronald L. Smith, *Who's Who in Comedy* (1992); in Ronald L. Smith, comp., *The Comedy Quote Dictionary* (1992); and on Dangerfield's Web site,

www.rodney.com. See also Dennis McLellan, "Comic Icon Built a Career on Getting 'No Respect,'" *Los Angeles Times*, Home Edition, 6 Oct. 2004, B8. Jay Leno is quoted in a review of Dangerfield's funeral, "Rodney Dangerfield Paid the Ultimate Respect," PR Newswire Association, 14 Oct. 2004. Obituaries are in the *Los Angeles Times*, 6 Oct. 2004, and *Daily Variety*, 6 Oct. 2004.

BRUCE L. JANOFF

DANIEL, Clifton (19 Sept. 1912–21 Feb. 2000), journalist, was born Elbert Clifton Daniel, Jr., in Zebulon, North Carolina, the son of Elbert Clifton Daniel, a pharmacist, and Elvah Jones Daniel. He began submitting stories to his local newspaper as a boy and then worked at the Zebulon *Record* until his graduation from the Wakelon School in his hometown. In 1929 Daniel entered the University of North Carolina, where he was an editor on the *Carolina* magazine. After graduating in 1933, he was a reporter and columnist from 1934 to 1937 for the Raleigh *News and Observer* under Josephus Daniels. Daniel moved on as a correspondent for the Associated Press in Washington and Europe (1937–1944). He joined the *New York Times* in February 1944 as a war correspondent and covered the end of the fighting in Europe. By then he was professionally known as Clifton Daniel.

After World War II, Daniel reported on the first decade of the Cold War in the Middle East, London, Bonn, and finally Moscow, where he was the only permanent correspondent of a non-Communist newspaper from 1954 until November 1955. A stomach ulcer forced him to return to the United States for treatment and ended his overseas career. A thin, handsome man, Daniel was something of a dandy who knew the precise gradations of formal wear in high society; in London he was known as "The Sheik of Fleet Street" (*Growing Up with My Grandfather*, p. 29). As an eligible bachelor, he was sought after for New York dinner parties. In late 1955, at one of these affairs, he met Margaret Truman, the daughter of former president Harry S. Truman, and within a few months the couple was engaged. As shrewdly noted by managing editor Turner Catledge, Daniel's boss at the *Times*, "both were from small towns and each was the only child of adoring parents" (Catledge, *My Life and the* Times, p. 204). They were married on 21 April 1956; the couple had four sons.

In 1957 Daniel became Turner Catledge's assistant and then rose to assistant managing editor in 1959. Five years later, Daniel was named managing editor with responsibility for the news department. He believed that the *Times* needed improvement in its reporting, and he devoted his four years in the post to that task. He wanted more "good stuff," by which he meant "illuminating flashes of color, description and background that can be obtained only by first-hand original reporting and skillful writing" (Shepard, *The Paper's Papers*, p. 204). He lifted the quality of the obituaries, broadened coverage of the arts, and promoted Charlotte Curtis to women's news editor. A speech that Daniel made to the World Press Institute in 1966 about the way that the *Times* covered the Bay of Pigs in 1961 attracted wide attention for its revelations about decision making within the newspaper (*New York Times*, 2 June 1966).

Daniel's tenure as an executive was not on the whole a successful one. He was happiest dealing with the marginal areas of the news. "He seemed to lack fire," wrote Max Frankel, the paper's main Washington correspondent, "devoting himself to improving society news and other peripheral features and complaining oddly about his lack of authority over the staff" (Frankel, *The* Times *of My Life*, pp. 304–05). Beneath his suave exterior, Daniel was "a man with sharp edges, sometimes abrupt and short-tempered," according to Turner Catledge (*My Life and the* Times, p. 205).

Daniel had a well-developed sense of his own importance to the *Times* and in 1968 found himself in a confrontation with the publisher, Arthur Ochs Sulzberger. The issue was the long-running testy relationship between the Washington bureau and the main office in New York City. Daniel and others in *Times* management wanted to replace Tom Wicker as the Washington bureau chief with James I. Greenfield from New York. The proposed change aroused the ire of Pulitzer Prize–winning columnist James Reston, who regarded the Washington bureau as his personal preserve. After extensive protests from Wicker and Reston, Sulzberger decided not to make the contemplated changes, much to the surprise of Catledge, Daniel, and their allies. The incident roiled the *Times* and left bruised feelings. So incensed was Daniel that he refused to speak to Sulzberger for several weeks. The two men then had a stormy meeting at which very harsh words were exchanged. The incident ended in Daniel's losing Sulzberger's trust, and within a year he was out as managing editor, replaced by A. M. "Abe" Rosenthal.

For the next eight years, Daniel played out his string with the *Times*. He served as a commentator on the newspaper's radio station WQXR and then returned to Washington to cover national politics as head of the Washington bureau. There he covered the end of Richard Nixon's presidency and the beginning of Gerald R. Ford's administration. He retired from the *Times* in 1977; he continued to write his memoirs, which appeared in 1984, and edited "Chronicles of the Twentieth Century," published in 1987. He and his wife lived in Washington and Manhattan. He died at his home.

Daniel was an excellent reporter who enjoyed great professional success in the 1940s and 1950s. His marriage to Margaret Truman made him a celebrity journalist as well. In his role as editor of the *New York Times*, he proved to be a transitional figure between the sober, nonanalytic journalism of the Turner Catledge regime and the more abrasive and confrontational style of his successor A. M. Rosenthal.

• The Margaret Truman Daniel and Clifton Daniel Papers are housed at the Harry S. Truman Library and have information on family matters. The *New York Times* archives in New York City are a rich source for details of Daniel's journalistic career. The Turner Catledge Papers at Mississippi State University are also important for Daniel's rise at the *Times*. Daniel contributed an interesting oral history memoir to the Truman Library and also wrote an anecdote-rich account of his friendships in *Lords, Ladies and Gentlemen: A Memoir* (1984). Clifton Truman Daniel, *Growing Up with My Grandfather: Memories of Harry S. Truman* (1995) is a memoir by one of Daniel's sons. Daniel is discussed in Turner Catledge, *My Life and the* Times (1971), and Max Frankel, *The* Times *of My Life and My Life with the* Times (1999). Daniel is a major figure in Gay Talese, *The Kingdom and the Power* (1969), a journalistic history of the *Times*. Important documents about Daniel can be found in Richard F. Shepard, *The Paper's Papers: A Reporter's Journey through the Archives of the* New York Times (1996). There is a biographical essay on Daniel in *Current Biography*, 1966, pp. 66–69, and an obituary in the *New York Times*, 22 Feb. 2000.

LEWIS L. GOULD

DANIELIAN, Leon (31 Oct. 1920–8 Mar. 1997), American dancer, teacher, and choreographer, was born in New York City, the son of Frank Danielian and Varsik Koolidganian Danielian, recent émigrés from Armenia. His mother was born in Tiflis, Georgia, and his father in Harpout, Armenia. They settled first in Bridgeport, Connecticut, where his older sister Hercelia was born. When the family moved to New York, his mother was active in the Armenian community; she taught the Armenian language in all five boroughs and was a gifted Armenian actress as well. His father was a rug dealer who bought and sold oriental rugs that he imported or found at auctions and private sales.

Leon and his sister began studying dance in New York with Madame Seda Suny, a family friend, after she took them along with her one afternoon to observe as she gave a dance lesson in their neighborhood. At first, Leon was not overjoyed with the idea of taking lessons, but he stuck with it. When he was eight his family moved to Atlantic Highlands, New Jersey. By then Mme. Seda (as she was known) was very impressed with Leon's potential and traveled to New Jersey once a week to continue with the lessons, staying overnight and teaching him the following day as well. When he reached the age of twelve, Mme. Seda recommended that he study with her former teacher, the Russian dancer Mikhail Mordkin, one of Anna Pavlova's partners.

Returning to New York City at age thirteen, Danielian lived in Manhattan and continued studying with Mordkin. He later studied with others, including Michel Fokine, Igor Schwezoff, and Vecheslav Swoboda. As a young teenager Danielian began performing Armenian and Russian dances with his sister in church halls and film houses. He made his professional debut in the Mordkin Ballet in 1937, performing in such venues as Lewisohn Stadium.

In 1939 Danielian joined Ballet Theatre (later known as American Ballet Theatre), at its inception, as a soloist along with eight other Mordkin Ballet dancers. Performing the ballets of Fokine, Anton Dolin, and Antony Tudor, as well as Mordkin, he remained in Ballet Theatre through the end of 1941. During this time the ballet world preferred Russian training, Russian stars, and Russianized names. For example, in the Mordkin Ballet's printed programs Danielian was listed as Leo or Leon Danieloff. Danielian was one of the first two American-born dancers to achieve principal rank, the other being John Kriza.

In 1942 Danielian joined Colonel de Basil's original Ballet Russe company as premier danseur and remained with it until their South American tour. While most of the dancers stayed in South America during the Second World War years, Danielian became principal dancer with the New York–based Ballet Russe de Monte Carlo in 1943, an association that lasted until 1958. He also danced in the Broadway production of *I Married an Angel* (1938) and the operetta *Song of Norway* (1944), both choreographed by George Balanchine, and took part in productions by opera companies in Pittsburgh and St. Louis.

Danielian took periods of leave from the Ballet Russe de Monte Carlo to perform as guest artist with Roland Petit's Ballet des Champs Elysées in Paris (1951–1952) and go on tour in southern France and northern Africa with Yvette Chauviré. He served as principal guest artist with the San Francisco Ballet in 1957–1958, touring internationally.

Early in his dance career Danielian decided to teach, and he served on the faculty of the School of Ballet Russe de Monte Carlo in New York City from 1948 to 1965. He also had his own school in White Plains, New York during the 1950s and early '60s. He presented his students dancing in his own choreography as the Leon Danielian Ballet Group. The Ballet Russe de Monte Carlo and the Louisville Civic Ballet also performed his choreography between 1953 and 1961.

Danielian had suffered from degenerative osteoarthritis since his early thirties, years later undergoing hip replacement surgery. By the late 1950s he was disabled to the extent that he no longer performed, but he continued his career as a master teacher, choreographer, and coach. In 1966 he became director of the American Ballet Theatre School in New York, a post he held until 1980. In 1982 Danielian moved to Austin, Texas, where from 1984 he held the Susan Menefee Ragan Regents Professorship of Fine Arts at the University of Texas, retiring in 1991. A dance studio in the Winship Drama Building was named in his honor in 1993; at the same time an endowed scholarship was established in his name. In February 1997 Danielian moved to a nursing home in Connecticut, where he died of heart failure the following month.

Danielian was known for a virtuoso style, in both classical and *demi-caractère* roles, characterized by exceptional rapidity, cleanness of line, drama, and lyricism. Critics wrote of his perfect *tours en l'air*, exceptional beats, high *grands jetés*, and his elegance and carriage. He was the first American dancer to perform an *entrechat huit (a* jump with eight beats of the legs while in the air). In classical roles Danielian was an elegant partner of such renowned ballerinas as Alexandra Danilova, Nathalie Krassovska, Anna Istomina, Mary Ellen Moylan, Ruthanna Boris, Yvette Chauviré, and Moscelyn Larkin. He was considered an exemplar of classical style for the male dancer. His principal roles included Siegfried in *Swan Lake*, Harlequin in *Carnaval*, the Rose in *Le Spectre dela Rose*, and the male partner in "Bluebird Pas de Deux," *Les Sylphides*, and *Don Quixote*. Of his *demi-caractère* roles he was best known for his portrayals of the Peruvian in *Gaîté Parisienne*.

Major company tours made Danielian nationally and internationally known. His firsthand knowledge of and experience in the works of Fokine, Léonide Massine, Mordkin, Dolin, Balanchine, Eugene Loring, and Tudor made him an invaluable company member, ballet master, coach, and master teacher. His interest in the teaching of dance enabled him to remain active after an early end to his performing career. He trained many principal dancers in such companies as the Ballet Russe de Monte Carlo and American Ballet Theatre. His expressive approach to the teaching of technique and style, his exacting standards of performance, and his keen sense of humor were among his distinguishing characteristics.

• Primary source material at the Dance Collection, New York Public Library, includes photographs, audio and video tapes, and motion pictures. Biographical information can be found in Jack Anderson, *The One and Only: The Ballet Russe de Monte Carlo* (1981), and Edwin Denby, *Looking at the Dance* (1949). Focusing on his teaching are Joseph Gale, *Behind Barres: The Mystique of Masterly Teaching* (1980), and R. Gold's article "Leon Danielian and the American Ballet Theatre School," *Dance Magazine*, Jan. 1975. See also Alice Helpern, "Leon Danielian," *International Dictionary of Ballet* (1993), and an interview with Danielian in John Gruen, *The Private World of Ballet* (1975). Obituaries appear in the *New York Times*, 12 Mar. 1997, and the *Austin American-Statesman*, 11 Mar. 1997.

ALICE HELPERN

DEBENEDETTI, Charles Louis (27 Jan. 1943–27 Jan. 1987), historian, was born in Chicago, Illinois, the son of Louis Albert DeBenedetti, a bread delivery truck driver, and Clementine Caroline Diero DeBenedetti, a legal secretary. "Chuck," as DeBenedetti liked to be called, attended Mendal Catholic High School and graduated in 1960. Reared in a strong Italian-Catholic family, DeBenedetti applied to and was accepted at the Jesuit-run Loyola University in Chicago, from which he graduated in 1964. On 29 August 1964 he married Sandra Kisala from Chicago. They had two children. DeBenedetti then enrolled in the graduate history program at the University of Illinois. In 1968 he was awarded his Ph.D. His dissertation, "American Internationalism in the 1920's: Shotwell and the Outlawrists," supervised by Norman Graebner, revealed an intense effort to connect historical studies to the issues of war and peace and to eliminate or at least restrict armaments, conscription, nuclear proliferation, colonialism, racism, sexism, and war.

In 1968 DeBenedetti accepted a teaching position at the University of Toledo. The expanding movement against the Vietnam War played a pivotal role in the development and expansion of the Conference for Peace Research in History (CPRH), now the Peace History Society. Formed in December 1963 at the American Historical Association meetings in Washington, D.C., and led by the historians Merle Curti and Edwin Bronner, the CPRH sought to "communicate its findings to the public at large in the hope of broadening the understanding and possibilities of world peace" ("Minutes of CPRH By-Laws"). From 1972 to 1985 DeBenedetti served on the CPRH National Council, of which he was secretary-treasurer (1977–1979), and he was coeditor of the organization's journal *Peace and Change* (1984–1985) In 1979 he was elected president, a position he held for four years. His inaugural message set the tone and direction as the organization approached a new decade: "We must at least work to maintain CPRH's visibility and influence . . . through active participation in the historical profession at large . . . [and] we must become more aggressive in solidifying the Conference's role as a most useful satellite in the international peace movement. . . . It means projecting what we know beyond campus and profession" (*CPRH Newsletter,* Fall 1979, pp. 4–5). Under his leadership CPRH sponsored numerous panel sessions at the annual meetings of the American Historical Association, the Organization of American Historians, and the Society for Historians of American Foreign Relations. He also organized peace history conferences at various universities, initiated the project culminating in the groundbreaking publication of the *Biographical Dictionary of Modern Peace Leaders* (1985), and supported efforts that led to the establishment of the National Peace Academy (1985).

Coupled with his administrative leadership in CPRH, DeBenedetti also published widely in the field of peace history. In his early years at the University of Toledo, he published articles in journals such as *American Studies, World Affairs, Peace and Change,* and the *Historian* and an important chapter in Charles Chatfield's edited work *Peace Movements in America* (1973). DeBenedetti's first major book, *Origins of the Modern American Peace Movement, 1915–1929* (1978), revealed that, after the start of World War I, American peace workers were the first to combine radical social criticism with a commitment to active nonviolence. In his examination of internationalists, legalists, and social progressives, DeBenedetti insisted that peace seekers "were the first to recognize that the same modernizing processes that made war so total and peace so necessary also intensified the egocentric power of mass nationalism and, with the spread of social revolution, the virulence of international class conflict" (DeBenedetti, *Origins of the Modern American Peace Movement,* p. ix). Despite taking issue with his thesis that the modern peace movement began between 1915 and 1929, Curti noted in his review in the *Journal of American History* that DeBenedetti's research was "far-reaching and intensive" and that his exposition was "clear and forceful" (Curti, p. 722).

DeBenedetti's teaching, research, and emerging role as a leader in the CPRH led to his promotion, in 1978, to full professor. In an effort to update Curti's classic book *Peace or War: The American Struggle, 1636–1936* (1936), DeBenedetti offered his own observations on the historical evolution of the peace movement in *The Peace Reform in American History* (1980). The central theme of *The Peace Reform,* and indeed of all DeBenedetti's scholarly writings, was that peace was a social process, one "of reconciling peoples by means of democratic structures developed through self-conscious human planning" (DeBenedetti, *The Peace Reform,* p. 106). Chronologically organized, *The Peace Reform* evaluates peacemaking ideologies and movements from the establishment of Quaker settlements in Pennsylvania in the seventeenth century to the conclusion of the Vietnam War. Insisting that peace is more than the absence of war, DeBenedetti's survey points out that peacemakers have been as essential to the American reform tradition as abolitionists and women's rights advocates. Equally important, peace reformers had been at it for over two hundred years, and their "guiding faith in self-governance and right conduct forged in them a determination to seek social and policy change through highly-charged but non-violent methods" (DeBenedetti, *The Peace Reform,* p. 198). Not all peace historians, however, agreed with DeBenedetti's central thesis. Arthur A. Ekirch, Jr., for instance, noted the "chameleon-like quality to reform" and lamented that the "limited influence and parochial nature of peace reform give little basis for complacency to those of us who continue to hold an irreconcilable animus against all militarism and war" (Ekirch, pp. 71, 73).

DeBenedetti spent the early 1980s on two projects. The first was an effort to bolster the role of twentieth-century peace advocates in contrast to popular military figures. The result was an edited work, *Peace Heroes in Twentieth-Century America* (1986), a collection of essays by historians in the field that discusses peace activists, such as Jane Addams, Eugene Debs, Norman Thomas, A. J. Muste, Martin Luther King, Jr., Philip Berrigan, and Daniel Berrigan among others. In a lengthy introduction, moreover, DeBenedetti defended his notion of peace heroes, insisting that "citizen peace seekers must hammer home the reality that a century of peace activism in the United States has verified: that people must take risks for peace with the same tenacity and sacrifice that they invest unquestioningly in war and war preparations" (DeBenedetti, *Peace Heroes,* p. 19).

DeBenedetti's second project was a major endeavor to examine the anti–Vietnam War movement. In August 1986 he received a large grant from the Social Science Research Council to complete an oral history on elite dissent and foreign policy making during the conflict in Southeast Asia. Sadly, shortly after he received the grant DeBenedetti was stricken with brain cancer, which took his life a few months later. However, the unpublished manuscript was placed in the hands of his close friend and fellow peace historian Chatfield. Chatfield saw the manuscript through to publication in 1990 as *An American Ordeal: The Antiwar Movement of the Vietnam Era*. It was DeBenedetti's crowning achievement in the profession. *An American Ordeal* highlights the diverse coalitions formed against the war and how radical elements dominated the movement in the late sixties only to be replaced by a much larger consensus of liberal and pacifist groups in the early seventies. Tellingly this massive work represents "an account of the conflict in the American interior—in church meeting halls, city streets, college campuses, editorial offices, electoral campaigns, congressional halls, and divided families—where most Americans struggled among themselves over the Vietnam War" (DeBenedetti, *An American Ordeal*, p. 1). The book was awarded the Stuart Bernath Prize by the Society for Historians of American Foreign Relations.

DeBenedetti died in Toledo, Ohio. At the time of his death, he was serving as president of the Society for the Study of Internationalism. One tribute in particular describes his contributions as scholar and person: "Chuck conveyed a personal concern that was genuine and unbounded. He was a rock of quiet strength. A man of warmth and good humor, enthusiasm and engagement, generosity and scholarship, Charles DeBenedetti was a sustaining force in the field and in many lives" (*CPRH Newsletter*, 3 Mar. 1987, p. 3). In May 1990 the Vietnam Antiwar Movement Conference held in Toledo, Ohio, was a memorial to DeBenedetti as well as a celebration of the posthumous publication of *An American Ordeal*. In his memory the Peace History Society awards, on a biannual basis, the Charles DeBenedetti Prize for the best article published in the field of peace history.

• The *Council on Peace Research in History Newsletter* (1971–1986), on file at the Swarthmore College Peace Collection, contains numerous references to DeBenedetti's various roles within the organization. DeBenedetti's inaugural speech to the CPRH is in *CPRH Newsletter*, Fall 1979. The "Minutes of CPRH By-Laws" (1971, 1972) are in the Swarthmore College Peace Collection, Document Group 94. DeBenedetti's published books include *Origins of the Modern American Peace Movement, 1915–1929* (1978); *The Peace Reform in American History* (1980); as editor, *Peace Heroes in Twentieth-Century America* (1986); and with Charles Chatfield, *An American Ordeal: The Antiwar Movement of the Vietnam Era* (1990). Two reviews are Merle Curti, *Journal of American History* (Dec. 1980): 722; and Arthur A. Ekirch, Jr., "Review Essay," *Peace and Change* 7 (Spring 1981): 71–73. Melvin Small and William D. Hoover, eds., *Give Peace a Chance: Exploring the Vietnam Antiwar Movement* (1992), is dedicated to DeBenedetti's memory. An editorial comment on DeBenedetti's contributions to peace history and his passing is in *CPRH Newsletter* (3 Mar. 1987), 3. An obituary by his mentor Norman Graebner is in *Perspectives, the Newsletter of the American Historical Association* 25 (Oct. 1987): 15.

CHARLES F. HOWLETT

DEDERICH, Charles (22 Mar. 1913–28 Feb. 1997), reformed alcoholic and founder of Synanon, was born Charles Edwin Dederich in Toledo, Ohio, the son of Charles Edwin Dederich, a promoter, and Agnes Kountz Dederich, a singer. When Dederich was four years old, his father, an alcoholic, was killed in an automobile accident. Dederich graduated from high school and entered the University of Notre Dame. Eighteen months later, he dropped out because of poor grades. Returning to Ohio, Dederich enrolled in the University of Toledo but flunked out there as well. After securing work at Gulf Oil's Toledo office, he married a woman whose name is unknown and had one son. Dederich worked at Gulf as a traveling salesman. In 1944 he was diagnosed with meningitis and fell into a coma for two weeks. Through the experimental use of penicillin, he revived. Still, he suffered from some facial paralysis and loss of hearing and was convinced that he was dying. He quit his job and moved with his family to Los Angeles. In California, Dederich divorced his wife, married Ruth Jason (the date is unknown), and had a daughter. He found work at Douglas Aircraft but had difficulty maintaining employment because of his drinking and dependence on benzedrine.

In 1956, when his addictions had incapacitated him, Dederich joined Alcoholics Anonymous, attending his first meeting in Beverly Hills. By his account, Dederich became a "frantic and fanatical Alcoholics Anonymous member" (quoted in Gerstel, p. 35). During his initial recovery through A.A., he also took part in an experiment at the University of California Berkeley that used LSD to treat alcoholics. His experience with LSD is said to have brought about a personality change, giving him new levels of confidence.

Dederich's second wife divorced him shortly after he became a committed A.A. member, and he promptly embarked on a new personal mission to treat alcoholics, turning his Ocean Park apartment into a forum for group therapy. Dederich's therapeutic arsenal consisted largely of long discussions of Ralph Waldo Emerson's essay on self-reliance and innovative confrontation tactics in which group members barraged one another with criticism and profanity until their defenses were broken and they confronted their demons. This confrontational conversation-in-the-round evolved into what would be known in Synanon parlance as "the game." By 1958, Dederich had moved his band of reforming alcoholics and drug addicts into an Ocean Park storefront, where he won a battle among the reformed alcoholics for control of the group. Dederich desired a more formal, hierarchical organization, with himself at the helm. The narcotics addicts supported him, and Synanon, the first ex-addict–run therapeutic community for drug abuse, was incorporated on 15 September 1958 with forty members. The term is said to come from one of the participating addicts who "stumbled over the words seminar and symposium, gave up and called them synanon" (quoted in Van Gelder, p. 369).

Synanon's history is typically divided into three parts. The early years of Synanon were as tumultuous as Dederich's life. Having moved his growing facility to an old National Guard armory in Santa Monica, California, Dederich fought great community resistance from neighbors who were distressed by the proximity of illegal drug addicts. Dederich spent a short time in jail after the city pressed charges against him for running a hospital without a license and failing to vacate the Synanon headquarters. Throughout the controversy, the press seemed to side with Dederich, portraying him as an iconoclastic underdog waging war with the establishment for the benefit of society's downtrodden addicts. By 1965, Synanon, the novel therapeutic community, and Dederich had become the subject of books, articles, television shows, and eventually a major motion picture, *Synanon*, starring Edmond O'Brien as Dederich and Eartha Kitt as Dederich's third wife, Betty Coleman Dederich. It was in these early years that Dederich created the saying "Today is the first day of the rest of your life."

Synanon's resident population grew from 500 in 1964 to 1,400 in 1969. Between 1958 and 1968, an estimated 6,000 to 10,000 addicts passed through the institution. The recovery process was said to take two years. Addicts quit "cold turkey," slowly earning more responsibility within the community. Staying clean and either acquiring a job and living spot outside Synanon or remaining within the institution were the treatment goals. The effectiveness of Dederich's methods of encounter group analysis ("the game") and self-reflection remains unclear, but Synanon set up chapters across the country and Synanon-model drug treatment programs were established at the federal prison in Terminal Island and at the Nevada State Prison. Dederich also established Synanon "game" clubs for nonresidents who desired to participate in the encounter groups. These nonaddicts payed club "fees" and were referred to as "squares." Dederich and his fellow Synanon leaders proved adept businesspeople, requiring Synanon community members to "hustle" donations of materials and services, as well as selling the Synanon story through public talks.

During the late 1960s and early 1970s, Dederich concluded that addicts could not return to society and remain clean, and that nonaddict club members should be allowed to join the community and live an alternative style of life. Dederich called this new group the "lifestylers," and they gradually came to supplant the original addicts. Synanon continued to use the image of addict rehabilitation to garner financial and material support from the American business community, but addict reform became increasingly less significant. Synanon now implemented loyalty tests and banned tobacco, sugar, alcohol, and any drugs with psychotropic effects. These measures alienated many of the addicts. By now, Dederich's Synanon had become a multimillion-dollar operation.

In 1974 Synanon's board of directors declared that Synanon Foundation, Inc. was a religion; its new goal was to run a church. This religious orientation ushered in other changes. Soon Synanon's wealth was privatized by the Dederich family, who lived an ever more luxurious lifestyle. Synanon modified its antiviolence stance so that "enemies" inside and outside the group could be punished through the new Synanon paramilitary force (bands of members chosen to protect the church's interests, essentially thugs). Synanon made ever stronger efforts to control the members of the congregation: their hair was sheared; pregnant women were asked to have abortions; men were expected to have vasectomies if they had lived in the community for more than five years (Dederich exempted himself); and in 1977, married couples were asked to divorce and change partners. Some have suggested that Synanon's transformation mirrored Dederich's increasingly disorganized mental state. His wife died in 1977, and he returned to drinking.

In 1978 Dederich ordered two members of Synanon to place a rattlesnake in the mailbox of a lawyer, Paul Morantz, who had won a court settlement against Synanon. All three were charged with conspiracy to commit murder. In 1978 they pleaded no contest. Dederich avoided a jail sentence but resigned as the group's leader, and Synanon faced its most besieged period, complete with lawsuits, exposés by former members, a Pulitzer prize–winning investigative report, and a government review of the group's financial activities. In 1991 Synanon lost its tax-exempt status. The church disbanded shortly thereafter, though branches of the community remained in existence. Dederich died of cardiorespiratory failure in Visalia, California.

Overweight, alcoholic, a failure at school and in business, Dederich was an unlikely figure to start and steward one of the most innovative, controversial addiction treatment programs of the twentieth century. Yet he was by all accounts a commanding presence. From Synanon's founding in 1958 to his death in 1997, the man and the institution were inextricably linked. Dederich was a charismatic, egotistical visionary responsible for several innovations in the addiction treatment field, chiefly the creation of a modern therapeutic community complete with its culture of rehabilitation and the use of former addicts as drug rehabilitation counselors. Dederich appears to have seen himself as a messianic leader for the reforming addict, but in the course of his life, the power he acquired seemed to transform him into a deranged and despotic leader of a religious cult.

• Biographical sketches of Dederich appear in William L. White, *Slaying the Dragon: The History of Addiction Treatment and Recovery in America* (1998); Ellen Broslovsky, "Just to Breathe: Personal Recollections of Synanon Founder, Charles E. Dederich," *Communal Societies* 20 (2000): 95–108; and David U. Gerstel, *Paradise Incorporated: Synanon* (1982). An obituary is Lawrence Van Gelder, "Charles Dederich, 83, Synanon Founder, Dies," *New York Times*, 4 Mar. 1997.

SARAH TRACY

DE LATOUR, Georges (20 Oct. 1856?–28 Feb. 1940), California wine maker, was born Georges Marie Joseph de Latour in the village of Daglan near Sarlat in France's Perigord region. Although hardly a mystery man, biographers, obituarists, and even descendants are unsure of the year of de Latour's birth (some sources give 1858) and unable to provide the Christian names of his parents, although it is agreed that they were landed gentry who died when he was very young.

The orphan was raised in Sarlat by family friends named de Boisson and attended elementary school in Sarlat before enrolling in the École Centrale in Paris, where he picked up a knowledge of chemistry as well as a liberal arts education. The "adventuresome" Frenchman, as contemporaries described him, sailed to New York around 1883. He apparently mined for gold in California's Tuolumne County, in the Sierra Nevada's Mother Lode, only to lose what francs he had managed to save in the Old Country. De Latour is then believed to have picked cherries in the San Joaquin Valley.

By 1892 de Latour was residing in a San Jose hotel, the Lake House, which was the headquarters for his infant California Tartar Works. Cream of tartar, used to stabilize egg white foams and in baking powder, was a by-product of wine making, developed from what had been waste products, argols. These were naturally occurring crystalline deposits of a potassium tartrate compound that encrusted the insides of wine casks and tanks. The young entrepreneur collected argols by horse and wagon from Northern California wineries to either sell to chemical companies or to refine himself. He sold the processed product to the manufacturers of baking powder. As late as 1898, the *San Francisco Call* described the tartar industry as unique to California. The state was producing half a million pounds yearly, worth 20 cents a pound. De Latour also began to make use of another wine by-product, distilling brandy from the pomace, or pulp, left over from the pressing of grapes. But as yet he had grown no grapes and made no wine.

De Latour and an associate, de Guigné, engaged in sales of tartar to the East Bay's Stauffer Chemical Company, where he met Fernande Romer, a secretary in the firm. The couple married in April 1898 in San Francisco's Notre Dame des Victoires Church and made a home nearby; they had two children.

In 1896, de Latour became a naturalized citizen; he was now a director of Stauffer. In 1897 San Jose residents, complaining of the strong odors issuing from his plant, filed suit against him. He closed the plant and moved to Sonoma County the next year to reestablish his tartar works and distillery in Healdsburg. But the lure of Napa Valley drew him in 1899 to sell the Healdsburg properties and buy land from Charles P. Thompson at Rutherford, just south of St. Helena. He now owned four acres—of orchard, vineyard, and wheat fields, plus a Victorian house and outbuildings—in the heart of America's premium wine country.

Because French prunes and even raisins were still local rivals of wine grapes, de Latour diversified by adding a fruit dryer. More important, he began to import millions of bench-grafted *Vitis vinifera* vines from France on *Vitis rupestris St. George* rootstock that was resistant to the aphidlike plant louse *Phylloxera vastatrix*. The grafted vines made it possible to replant the vineyards of the Napa Valley, which by the late 1880s had been ravaged by *Phylloxera* infestation. Although not the first Napan to introduce bug-proof stock, he so dominated the trade that he was hailed as the savior of Valley viticulture and enology. As early as 1900 he may have purchased bulk wine to sell in San Francisco for altar use. In 1903 he finally entered the grape-growing and wine-making business. He bought 128 more acres of the Thompson ranch and returned to France to buy choice grafted vines. He first bought good and heavy-bearing varieties but quickly learned to upgrade his vineyards with the very best varietals such as cabernet sauvignon and pinot noir. By 1909 he had 450,000 fine French vines.

Not till 1906 did de Latour incorporate the Beaulieu Vineyard and Winery, also called BV, that made him world-famous. He rented the old John Thomann cellar in St. Helena for his first crush, converted his tartar works to a winery, and leased the Harris Ranch's winery for storage while securing 146 acres surrounding it. He also purchased land in nearby Oakville. His Thompson Ranch land became Beaulieu Vineyard #1; the Harris Ranch, Beaulieu #2. (In 1921 he bought 110 acres of the St. Joseph Agricultural School on the Silverado Trail for BV #3.) During 1908 he built a new distillery and planted muscat grapes to take advantage of a boom in the sale of dessert wines, which he fortified with his brandy. In 1910 he purchased a carbonization machine to make sparkling wines to satisfy a growing fad for the "bubbly."

In 1923 de Latour completed the piecing together of his Beaulieu operation by buying the old (1882) Seneca Ewer Winery on four acres across the road (now Highway 29, California's *Route du Vin*) from his hospitable estate with its formal gardens. He enlarged and modernized the fine stone cellar designed by Hamden D. McIntyre, the "Palladio" of California winery architecture. By 1933 it held a million gallons of wine from almost 600 acres of vines.

Prohibition (1919–1933) crippled California's wine industry—except for Beaulieu. As other wineries closed and vineyards converted to prune and pear orchards, de Latour prospered because in 1908 he had secured the custom of the San Francisco Roman Catholic Archdiocese for its sacramental wine. All through the Dry Years, he was the major supplier of altar wine, nationally. A visionary, he anticipated the end of the Great Experiment and expanded operations in 1930, adding another 200,000 gallons of wine.

When Repeal came in 1933, de Latour was practically the only vintner with vast vineyards in prime condition, a huge stock of wine properly aged, an efficient plant, and sales representatives. For a time, he had no rivals. BV was *the* California wine.

A good judge of character with a passion for quality in wine, de Latour chose subordinates well. When his wine briefly slipped in quality, he hired André Tchelistcheff from the National Institute of Agronomy in Paris as his wine maker. The Russian soon put things right, and in 1939, at the Golden Gate International Exposition's competitive tasting, de Latour won, over some 100 rivals, the grand prize for his burgundy; he also won gold medals for his cabernet sauvignon and muscat de frontignan. He died in San Francisco.

De Latour is remembered as the key figure—the essential link—connecting the pioneer period of California wine making (1860–1900) with the modern (post-Repeal) period. He literally kept wine-grape growing and wine making viable during the dark Prohibition years, hastening the industry's renaissance after World War II.

• The nearest thing to a biography of de Latour is Rod Smith, "*Private Reserve*," 2000, a History of Beaulieu. Also useful with scattered references are James T. Lapsley, *Bottled Poetry* (1996); Charles L. Sullivan, *Napa Wine: A History from Mission Days to the Present* (1994); William F. Heintz, *California's Napa Valley* (1999); and Leon D. Adams, *The Wines of America* (1990). For an obituary, see the *St. Helena Star*, 1 Mar. 1940; see also a retrospective appreciation in the *Napa Register* of 30 Mar. 1963.

RICHARD H. DILLON

DEL RÍO, Dolores (3 Aug. 1904–11 Apr. 1983), actress, was born María Dolores Asúnsolo López-Negrete, in the city of Durango in Chihuahua, Mexico, the daughter of Jesús Leonardo Asúnsolo, a banker, and Antonia López Negrete y López. Both parents were from wealthy, socially connected families. As a child, del Río enjoyed the privileges that wealth and status afforded, including dance, music, and art lessons. In 1910, however, the family's life was disrupted by the outbreak of the Mexican Revolution. Her father escaped to the United States while she and her mother fled to Mexico City. There they were protected by her mother's distant cousin Francisco Madero, the first president of postrevolutionary Mexico. In Mexico City, she continued her ballet studies and attended the Colegio Francés, a traditional French convent school located in the capital city.

On 11 April 1921, at the age of seventeen, she married 35-year-old Jaime Martínez del Río, the son of a prominent and wealthy family who had been educated in England. The newlyweds traveled to Europe for their honeymoon and for two years enjoyed the life of high society, socializing with royalty and the international "jet set." In 1924 the couple returned to Mexico and settled on their ranch in Chihuahua. Compared to their whirlwind life in the capital cities of Europe, they found rural life very dull. After a number of personal and financial crises, including a miscarriage,

they moved to Mexico City. Here, they again enjoyed a busy social life. At a party in 1925 Dolores was introduced to the American film director Edwin Carewe and his wife, Mary Atkins, who were vacationing in Mexico. Carewe, impressed by her beauty and by her dancing ability, invited the couple to visit him in Hollywood.

In August of 1925 the del Ríos arrived in Los Angeles. Already a number of Mexicans worked there as actors in the film industry, including Lupita Tovar, Lupe Velez, Delia Magana, Gilbert Roland (whose original name was Luis Alonso), and Ramón Novarro, a distant cousin of Dolores. Carewe immediately offered her a contract and a "professional" name: Dolores del Río (an abbreviation of her married name, Dolores Asúnsolo de Martínez del Río). Her first roles included bit parts in Carewe's *Joanna* (1925), *High Steppers* (1926), and *The Whole Town's Talking* (1926). In 1926 she was selected as one of the "WAMPAS Baby Stars," an annual beauty pageant put on by the Western Association of Motion Picture Advertisers that promoted young actresses. The 1926 starlets included Mary Astor, Fay Wray, Joan Crawford, and Janet Gaynor.

Del Río's first major part was in First National's *Pals First* (1926) opposite Lloyd Hughes; but it was the lead role as Charmaine, a French barmaid, in Raoul Walsh's *What Price Glory?* (1926), that catapulted her to cinematic fame. After her box-office success in Walsh's film, she appeared in an adaptation of Leo Tolstoy's *Resurrection*, directed by Carewe in 1927; *The Loves of Carmen* (1927, R. Walsh); *The Trail of '98* (1928, Clarence Brown); *Ramona* (the third film version of Helen Hunt Jackson's popular nineteenth-century novel) in 1928, directed by Carewe; and *Revenge* (1928, UA). In addition to her film roles, del Río was featured regularly in fan magazines such as *Photoplay* and in the *New York Times*. In 1933, *Photoplay* declared that the young Mexican star had the "most perfect feminine figure in Hollywood."

When the industry introduced sound technology in 1929, the careers of many stars of silent films failed. However, del Río survived the transition owing to her exceptional beauty and her ability to speak English with an accent, which suited her to roles as a foreigner. Her first sound films included *Evangeline* (Carewe, 1929); the musical *The Bad One* (1930); and King Vidor's South Seas tragic romance, *Bird of Paradise* (1932), in which she starred as the Polynesian princess. She also starred in three Latin American musicals—RKO's *Girl of the Rio* (1932), *Flying Down to Rio* (1933), and *In Caliente* (1935)—as well as a number of romantic melodramas such as *Devil's Playground* (1937), *Ali Baba goes to Town* (1937), *Lancer Spy* (1937), and *International Settlement* (1938).

While del Río enjoyed phenomenal success in her public life, there were problems in her private life. Her marriage ended in divorce in 1928 amid persistent rumors of a long-term affair with Carewe. Jaime del Río died later that year in Europe after a brief illness. In

August 1930, she married Cedric Gibbons, supervising art director at Metro-Goldwyn-Mayer, who built a beautiful home for her in Santa Monica. Although the couple was often featured in the local society pages, stories circulated about marital difficulties. In 1931, del Río fell ill and it was reported that she had suffered a nervous breakdown. In 1940 she finally divorced Gibbons and immediately began a relationship with the much younger director Orson Welles, while he was filming *Citizen Kane* (1941). Welles cast her in the leading role in his espionage film *Journey into Fear* (1942). The film was reedited by RKO and released to disparaging reviews.

By this time, del Río's career was in decline. She was approaching forty, old by Hollywood standards, and could not compete with rising young stars. In 1941, after Welles abandoned her for the younger actress Rita Hayworth, del Río returned to Mexico with her mother and settled in the fashionable neighborhood of Coyocan in Mexico City. For the next twenty years, she enjoyed a career as a Mexican movie star in the "Golden Age" of Mexican cinema. In Emilio Fernández's film about the revolution, *Flor Silvestre* (1943), del Río starred as Esperanza, a young Indian woman who falls in love with the son of a wealthy landowner. Later that year, she received an Ariel (Mexico's Oscar) for best female actress in Fernández's film *María Candelaria* (1943), which was also the first Mexican film recognized at Cannes.

Del Río returned to Hollywood occasionally—once in 1947 to star in John Ford's *The Fugitive*, an adaptation of Graham Greene's novel *The Power and The Glory*; again in the 1960s to play the role of an older Indian woman opposite Elvis Presley in *Flaming Star* (1960, Don Siegel); and again in John Ford's *Cheyenne Autumn* (1964). Del Río married American businessman Lewis Riley in 1959 and lived in Mexico until her death in Newport, California. She is still remembered as one of the most beautiful actresses in the history of Hollywood and Mexican cinema.

• There are a number of biographical works in Spanish on Dolores del Río, including David Ramón's three-volume set *Dolores del Río* (1997) and Aurelio de los Reyes and García Rojas, *Dolores del Río* (1996). For a critical study of del Río's role as a Mexican icon, see Carlos Monsiváis, "Dolores del Río: The Face as an Institution," in *Mexican Postcards*, trans. John Kraniauskas (1997). See also Joanne Hershfield's scholarly study of del Río's Hollywood career, *The Invention of Dolores del Río* (2000). An obituary is in the *New York Times*, 13 Apr. 1983.

JOANNE HERSHFIELD

DE MAN, Paul (6 Dec. 1919–21 Dec. 1983), literary theoretician and critic, was born in Antwerp, Belgium, the son of Robert de Man, a prosperous manufacturer of X-ray equipment, and Magdalena de Brey de Man. Young Paul enjoyed a comfortable upper-middle-class upbringing. After local schooling, Paul de Man enrolled at the University of Brussels in 1939 as a chemistry student. He pursued his studies over the next three years as World War II raged in

Europe and Belgium came under German occupation. During this time, according to the biography he made available later in his career, he also pursued an interest in literature by writing reviews and articles for unspecified French and Flemish publications.

On leaving the university in 1942, the multilingual de Man—fluent in German, Dutch, and English as well as French and Flemish—abandoned his studies and began earning his living as a translator for publishers in Brussels and Antwerp while continuing to write for Belgian publications. In 1947, two years after the war, a virtually penniless de Man emigrated to New York, settled in Greenwich Village, and worked for a while as a bookstore clerk in Grand Central Terminal. He quickly became acquainted with Manhattan literati, among them the writer and critic Mary McCarthy, who found translation jobs for him. In 1949, at McCarthy's recommendation, he was hired as a teacher of French literature at Bard College, some eighty miles north of the city. De Man's charming manner and obvious erudition gained him prestige and influential friendships at Bard, and in 1950 he married Patricia Kelley, one of his students. At the instigation of English department chairman Theodore Weiss, de Man moved to Boston in 1951 with the intention of taking graduate courses in literature as a nonmatriculated student at Harvard, in nearby Cambridge. Over the next few years de Man and his American wife had two children; he supported his new family as a teacher at a Berlitz language school.

In 1954 de Man was admitted to Harvard's prestigious Society of Fellows, which paid him a small stipend for limited teaching duties while allowing him to pursue formal graduate study in comparative literature and literary criticism. At Harvard, de Man developed close associations with other Harvard fellows who would go on to distinguished careers, among them Donald Hall, John Hollander, and Noam Chomsky, and he also became a protégé of professors Harry Levin and Reuben Brower. De Man was especially interested in the New Criticism, a text-centered, formalist approach to the study of literature, developed in the United States in the 1940s by Brower and others, that had now emerged as the predominant academic mode of literary criticism. The New Criticism had as its central tenet that a precise meaning of any text can be determined by careful reading and that the text alone, independent of historical and biographical information, should be employed to arrive at that meaning.

As de Man continued his studies, he developed his own approach to critical theory, combining principles of the New Criticism with the philosophical insights of Martin Heidegger and Friedrich Nietzsche as well as Maurice Blanchot and other continental literary theorists. During this time de Man began contributing articles to French literary journals, including "Les exégèses de Hölderlin par Martin Heidegger" (1955), an important early essay that explored ironic oppositions in Heidegger's analysis of the poetry of Friedrich Hölderlin. A year later, in another important early article, "Impasse de la critique formaliste," de Man took a step beyond the New Criticism, isolating the text still further by dismissing the value of any aesthetic considerations of literature and arguing that formalist criticism ultimately failed to explicate the ambiguity of poetry.

At Harvard, de Man quickly emerged as a star pupil, and his years there were marred by only one incident. In early 1955 the chairman of the comparative literature department received an anonymous complaint alleging that de Man had been associated with the occupying Nazi Party during World War II in Belgium. But after de Man firmly and indignantly denied the charges, the matter was dropped and his studies continued. After he earned master's (1958) and doctoral (1960) degrees, he was hired by Cornell University and taught there for six years. In 1966, at a seminal international conference on literary theory held at Johns Hopkins University, de Man met the French philosopher Jacques Derrida, a fellow participant. At that conference, Derrida introduced the term "deconstruction" to describe a new form of criticism that was strikingly similar to de Man's approach. In essence, the theory of deconstruction stated that taking apart—"deconstructing"—any text reveals that there are multiple meanings and therefore an absence of any single "true" or "correct" interpretation. De Man's and Derrida's mutual discovery that they were both raising questions about the reliability of language, and that furthermore they were at that very moment applying those questions to independent studies of the same obscure text by Jean-Jacques Rousseau, forged a bond of sorts between them.

A year after the Johns Hopkins conference, de Man joined the Johns Hopkins faculty, and his growing reputation as a brilliant literary theorist led to his appointment in 1970 as a professor of comparative literature at Yale University. The following year de Man's preeminence in his field was established virtually overnight with the publication of his first book, *Blindness and Insight*. This collection of essays sets forth de Man's arguments against all traditional forms of literary criticism and argues that critics are, as he put it, "blind" to the "paradoxical discrepancy" between the statements they make about literature and the actual results of their interpretations: "Their findings about the structure of texts contradict the general conception that they use as their model" (preface to *Blindness and Insight*). The book became required reading for graduate students in literature departments at major American universities, along with collections of essays by Jacques Derrida, which had recently begun to appear in English translation. The similarities in their respective approaches to the study of literature, as well as de Man's own commentaries on Derrida's writings, led to public identification of de Man as the leading exponent of deconstruction in the United States.

During the 1970s deconstruction itself moved beyond academia to become a household word, a catchy term adopted even by people who had never read Derrida or de Man—and who would have found their stylistic complexity forbidding—but who latched onto what was widely perceived to be its larger meaning: the implicit rejection of traditional authority in the post-John F. Kennedy era of youth-generated social and political protest—of the Vietnam War, of civil rights abuses, and of perceived limitations on personal freedoms. In such a context, de Man enjoyed not only academic prestige but widespread public recognition in the national press, along with Derrida, a charismatic figure in his own right who was now lecturing frequently in the United States.

Despite excessive media attention, de Man continued to teach, to mentor students, and to publish a second collection of essays, *Allegories of Reading* (1979), which focused on Romantic and post-Romantic writers and was enthusiastically well received in academia. A third book followed in the spring of 1983, a revised edition of *Blindness and Insight*, which included a new foreword and three additional essays. Already ill with cancer at the time of publication, de Man died the following December in New Haven and was mourned as a much-beloved figure by students and faculty alike.

Over the next few years, two posthumously published works by de Man burnished his reputation: *The Rhetoric of Romanticism* (1984) and *The Resistance to Theory* (1986). In the summer of 1987, as a third posthumous volume, *Aesthetic Ideology* (1988), was being assembled for publication, rumors began circulating of evidence that de Man had been a Nazi collaborator during World War II. A Belgian graduate student at the University of Louvain, doing research for a thesis on de Man, had discovered numerous essays and reviews written by de Man between 1940 and 1942 for the pro-Nazi Brussels newspaper *Le Soir* and had found that many of them expressed pro-Fascist opinions and varying degrees of anti-Semitism. Word quickly spread to the American academic community, but the story was not broken publicly until 1 December 1987 in an article in the *New York Times*.

The *Times* article created an uproar as numerous publications in the United States and abroad picked up the story, and in the public mind the revelations abruptly dethroned de Man as an academic paragon. As a further consequence, deconstruction itself, which had already garnered a sizable number of detractors in academia, now came under mortal attack by many who speculated whether de Man had deliberately promoted deconstruction as a self-serving defense of his wartime journalism. Had de Man lived, critics wondered, might he have argued that the controversial articles did not in fact mean what they appeared to say? Supporters said that de Man had understandably accommodated himself to the occupying regime in order to survive, and they pointed out that he had abandoned journalism—and by implication collaborationist activities—several years before the war ended. Friends and supporters also asserted that they had never heard any anti-Semitic or profascist comments from him and indeed had assumed him to be left of center politically.

Prominent scholars argued back and forth over the matter as more revelations came to light. Additional wartime articles written by de Man for collaborationist Belgian publications, both French and Flemish, were discovered, making a total of 290, spanning the period 1939 to 1943. De Man's personal life came under attack as well when he was accused of being a bigamist. Researchers discovered that he had married a Belgian woman, Anaide Baraghian, in 1943 and had three sons with her before emigrating to the United States in 1947. Apparently abandoned by de Man, the family had moved to South America, but it was unclear whether de Man had ever divorced her. Furthermore it was discovered that de Man had claimed, with apparent pride, in correspondence with Harvard in the early 1950s that he was the son of Hendrik de Man, a prominent Belgian Fascist during the war, when in fact he was Hendrik's nephew. Other detractors spread the word that de Man had initially failed his doctoral exams, though the relevance of this information to the present controversy was unclear. At a long-planned international conference on de Man held in Antwerp six months after his death, participants learned more damaging details of de Man's life, including reports of shady financial dealings during the war and an impending arrest for fraud at the time he immigrated to the United States.

Many longtime supporters deserted de Man, dismissing any possible value in his work now that his clouded past had been revealed. But a core of friends and disciples stood by him, most prominently the critic and scholar Jonathan Culler, who published several articles in defense of both the man and his work and subsequently inherited de Man's mantle as the leading proponent of deconstruction in the United States. Somewhat ironically, Jacques Derrida—an Algerian-born secular Jew—came to de Man's defense as well, though some observers commented that he was understandably most interested in defending deconstruction itself as a viable theory.

During the year following de Man's death, public interest in the controversy gradually died out, but the debate over the merits of deconstruction persisted for many years in academic circles because the man and his work seemed inextricably linked. The posthumous publication of three more collections of de Man's essays—*Fugitive Writings* (1988), *Critical Writings, 1953–1978* (1989), and *Romanticism and Contemporary Criticism* (1993)—did not seem to allay the controversy. Fairly or not, de Man's reputation was posthumously destroyed, though it is difficult to believe that his career would have been saved had he lived to defend his wartime pursuits. The 1987 revelations came, after all, at a time when the Holocaust had recently emerged, decades after war's end, as a new focus of both national and international attention, and any behavior even tangentially associated with support for the Nazi regime and its attendant anti-Semitism was no longer defensible. As for the fate of deconstruction itself, even at the time of de Man's death its hegemony was already being challenged by new modes of critical thought that have largely supplanted it. Nevertheless, though deconstruction was permanently tainted by its association with de Man, it continues to have a strong core of supporters in the academic community.

• For biographical information on de Man, see David Lehman, *Signs of the Times: Deconstruction and the Fall of Paul de Man* (1991); and James Atlas, "The Case of Paul de Man," *New York Times Magazine*, 28 Aug. 1988, pp. 36ff. Lehman's book is a biography as well as an assessment of deconstruction and of de Man's writings; a respected scholar, Lehman is a harsh critic of de Man, but his sources are unimpeachable. The Atlas article is primarily a middle-of-the-road view of the controversy itself but offers biographical information as well. Readers should be cautioned against reliance on "Paul de Man: A Chronology, 1919–1949," a preface to Werner Hamacher, Neil Hertz, and Thomas Keenan, eds., *Responses: On Paul de Man's Wartime Journalism* (1989); ostensibly a factual chronology of de Man's first thirty years, it contains many errors. Jonathan Culler's essay, "Paul de Man," in *Dictionary of Literary Biography*, v. 67, *Modern American Critics since 1955* (1988), has limited biographical details and was prepared before news of de Man's wartime activities was circulated, but it has an excellent explication of his theories. For Culler's defense of de Man, see "It's Time to Set the Record Straight about Paul de Man and His Wartime Articles," *Chronicle of Higher Education*, 13 July 1988, sec. 2, p. 1. Jacques Derrida's multiple defenses of de Man and deconstruction are included in his *Mémoires: For Paul de Man*, rev. ed. (1989). Hamacher, Hertz, and Keenan, eds., *Wartime Journalism, 1939–43* (1988), is supposedly a complete collection of de Man's Belgian newspaper articles, though many, including all those in Flemish, are not translated. For the initial public disclosure of de Man's wartime articles, see "Yale Scholar's Articles Found in Nazi Paper," *New York Times*, 1 Dec. 1987, sec. 2, p. 1. For a post–de Manian assessment of deconstruction, see David H. Hirsch, *The Deconstruction of Literature: Criticism after Auschwitz* (1991); see also Paul Morrison, *The Poetics of Fascism: Ezra Pound, T. S. Eliot, Paul de Man* (1996). Culler's *On Deconstruction* (1982) offers a clear assessment of the theory and its history. For a brief but informative survey of contemporary criticism, see Christopher Butler, *Postmodernism: A Very Short Introduction* (2002). An obituary is in the *New York Times*, 31 Dec. 1983.

ANN T. KEENE

DENFIELD, Louis Emil (13 Apr. 1891–28 Mar. 1972), admiral and chief of naval operations, was born in Westborough, Massachusetts, the son of Louis Denfield, an attorney, and Etta May Kelley Denfield. He graduated from Duluth (Minn.) High School in 1908, was admitted to the U.S. Naval Academy that year, and graduated as an ensign four years later. Following routine assignments aboard the battleships *Virginia* and *Arkansas*, he served on a destroyer. During World War I he was stationed at Queensland, Ireland, as executive officer of the *Ammen*, and in 1918 he advanced to temporary lieutenant commander. After the war Denfield reported to Boston, served several years as inspector of the navy's New England division, and fulfilled additional service aboard destroyers and submarines. In 1924 he began his long association with staff service by joining the ship movements division at the Office of the Chief of Naval Operations, residing there two years. In 1929 he returned to Washington, D.C., as aide to the chief of navigation. In 1933 he was promoted to commander while serving as secretary to Admiral Richard Henry Leigh. Four years later he joined the staff of influential Chief of Naval Operations William D. Leahy, who took a keen interest in his advancement. Having risen to captain in 1939, Denfield assumed command of Destroyer Squadron One the following year, just prior to performing detached service as a special naval observer in London. Returning in April 1941, Denfield took his post as chief of staff to the commander of the Atlantic fleet. In this capacity, he was charged with developing a task force organization to safely escort convoys across the Atlantic. His planning proved so sagacious that he received the Legion of Merit.

The December 1941 attack on Pearl Harbor accelerated Denfield's rise up the chain of command and enhanced his reputation for efficiency. Commencing in April 1942, he became a rear admiral and was appointed assistant chief of the Bureau of Navigation, subsequently redesignated the Bureau of Personnel. There he remained until the spring of 1945, when he was given command of Battleship Division Nine. In this capacity Denfield directed the fire of the three ultramodern battleships—*Wisconsin*, *New Jersey*, and *Missouri*—throughout the Okinawa campaign. By war's end, his ships were bombarding the Japanese coastline. Soon afterward he returned to Washington, D.C., as head of the Bureau of Personnel with the rank of vice admiral. Denfield next became charged with postwar demobilization, which he handled with characteristic energy and dispatch. By 1947 he was at sea again as commander in chief, Pacific, with the rank of full admiral. That fall Admiral Chester Nimitz announced his intention to resign as chief of naval operations (CNO), and Denfield, assisted by his former mentor Admiral Leahy (now chairman of the Joint Chiefs of Staff) succeeded him, edging out Admirals William H. P. Blandy and Arthur W. Radfield.

Denfield was widely regarded as a gifted administrator; however, his tenure as CNO proved unsatisfactory. The U.S. defense establishment was then experiencing postwar fiscal retrenchment, further exacerbated by the onset of the Cold War with the Soviet Union. The traditional rivalry between military and naval concerns was also complicated by the creation of an independent U.S. Air Force in September 1947. The development of jet aircraft and atomic weapons had convinced many in defense circles that the traditional role of the U.S. Navy was obsolete. Denfield and Navy Secretary John L. Sullivan resisted all attempts to reduce navy expenditures or curtail its strategic mission. Both were also determined to preserve naval aviation and prevent the U.S. Marine Corps from being absorbed by the air force and army under the scheme of defense unification. To this end, Denfield became a vocal proponent of the *United States*, the nation's first super carrier, expressly de-

signed to operate jet aircraft. Moreover, because many of these aircraft were nuclear-capable, he intended such ships to break the air force monopoly on atomic weapons delivery. Denfield and Sullivan were initially successful, and in 1948 both Congress and President Harry S. Truman approved funding for the new carrier over strenuous objections from air force officials. But, in view of stringent funding caps, Denfield had to scrap thirteen other vessels under construction to fund the *United States*.

By 1949 the Berlin airlift and the creation of the North Atlantic Treaty Organization (NATO) had enhanced air force arguments against the funding of super carriers. Because air force bombers could now operate off European airfields well within range of Soviet targets, carrier aviation was increasingly viewed as superfluous. Critics of an independent navy were supported by a new secretary of defense, Louis A. Johnson, who had a personal dislike for the navy and its officers. Accordingly, Johnson managed to cancel the *United States*, even though its keel had been laid. This action triggered an internecine struggle within the War Department. The resulting "revolt of the admirals" comprised a wholesale attack by the navy upon air force procurement of the massive Convair B-36 bomber, which had become the centerpiece of Johnson's policies. In the midst of the turmoil, Denfield left Washington to visit Europe in connection with ongoing NATO affairs. His presence was missed during intense deliberations before the House Armed Services Committee, and the navy failed to have its super carrier reinstated. Worse, in September 1949 Denfield unofficially endorsed a letter, penned by a subordinate, which maintained that navy morale was at its lowest since 1916. When the letter was leaked to the press, Johnson, already angry at Denfield for testifying against the B-36, agitated for his removal. Truman had already agreed to appoint him for another two-year stint as CNO but eventually demanded his resignation, which was received on 28 October 1949. As a sop to the discredited admiral, Johnson offered Denfield a high-ranking naval post in Europe, but he declined and retired from active service in March 1950. He was succeeded by Admiral Forrest P. Sherman.

Denfield's views on the flexibility of naval aviation, when contrasted with the military inflexibility of strategic bombing, was vindicated during the Korean War, 1950–1953. In an age of limited war, strategic air power and atomic weapons became irrelevant to the tactical situation at hand, while jet-powered carrier aircraft demonstrated both utility and effectiveness for battlefield strikes and supply-line interdiction.

Back in civilian life, Denfield served as an advisor to Sunoco (Sun Oil Company) from 1950 to 1971. He died at his home in Westborough, Massachusetts, and was interred at Arlington National Cemetery. Denfield married Rachel Metcalf in June 1915; they had no children.

• No personal letters exist by Denfield, but much of his official correspondence is in Record Group 80, Records of the

Secretary of the Navy, National Archives, Washington, D.C. A small file of clippings is also kept on him at the Naval Historical Foundation, Washington Navy Yard. The only biographical sketch is Robert W. Love, ed., *The Chiefs of Naval Operations* (1980). Details of the controversies surrounding defense unification are found in Jeffrey G. Barlow, *Revolt of the Admirals: The Fight for Naval Aviation, 1945–1950* (1998); Paolo E. Coletta, *The United States Navy and Defense Unification, 1947–1953* (1981); and Michael A. Palmer, *Origins of the Maritime Strategy: American Naval Strategy in the First Postwar Decade* (1988). Shorter accounts from a variety of perspectives include Andrew L. Lewis, "A Revolting Development," *U.S. Naval Institute Proceedings* 125 (Sept. 1999): 76–83; Warren A. Trest, "View from the Gallery: Laying to Rest the Admirals' Revolt of 1949," *Airpower History* 42 (Spring 1995): 16–29; and Herman S. Wolk, "Battle of the B-36," *Air Force Magazine* 79 (July 1996): 60–65. A useful obituary is in the *New York Times*, 30 Mar. 1972.

JOHN C. FREDRIKSEN

DEROSE, Peter (10 Mar. 1900–23 Apr. 1953), composer of popular music and radio personality, was born in New York City, the son of Anthony DeRose, an Italian immigrant zither player, and Armelina Agresti DeRose, an Italian immigrant. Educated at DeWitt Clinton High School and tutored in music by one of his sisters, DeRose was working as a stock boy for the G. Schirmer music publishers in New York when, one day during his lunch hour, he turned out his first composition, "When You're Gone I Won't Forget You." Fired for this transgression against the work rules, he sold the song for $25. During the next two years it sold two and a half million copies. DeRose then crossed the street to the G. Ricordi music publishing company, where he was hired as a junior salesman. He promised Ricordi he would write no songs on their time, but within four months the company was displaying six of his newly published songs. Flush with success, DeRose quit his job and in 1923 formed an orchestra with several of his siblings. In 1922 he became an early member of the American Society of Composers, Authors and Publishers.

In 1923 DeRose met May Singhi Breen, a popular ukulele player, and the pair formed a partnership. That same year, as "The Sweethearts of the Air," they made their debut on the local NBC station and for the next 16 years were a regular feature. The program aired at 10:30 in the evening; Breen played ukulele and DeRose, the piano. They sang in harmony and engaged in sentimental conversation. In later years DeRose is said to have presented Breen with an orchid at every broadcast. They made their network debut (the Blue Network, later ABC) in 1927. DeRose and Breen married in 1929; they had no children, but adopted Breen's daughter by a former marriage. On their first wedding anniversary, DeRose wrote "When Your Hair Has Turned to Silver (I Will Love You Just the Same)," a throwback to the sentimental songs of pre–World War I Tin Pan Alley.

Although DeRose contributed to Broadway shows such as *Burlesque* (1927), *Yes, Yes, Yvette* (1927), and

the 1928 edition of *Earl Carroll Vanities*, his work did not achieve popularity until 1934. That year orchestra leader Paul Whiteman commissioned DeRose to create a piano work; five years later, dissected and fitted with words by Mitchell Parish suitable to a reverie of lost love, this became "Deep Purple" and "Lilacs in the Rain." "Deep Purple" was popularized by the dance orchestra of Larry Clinton but soon escaped into the era's popular repertoire, where it remained throughout the century. "Deep Purple" showed its roots as a piano piece particularly in its octave-plus leaps, controlled cascades, muted passages, and poignant climax. In 1934 DeRose collaborated with Billy Hill on "Wagon Wheels," a tumbling, jingly faux-Western work, which remained a permanent part of that subgroup's repertoire. It was DeRose's second most popular composition and was interpolated in the 1934 edition of the Ziegfeld Follies.

For the balance of the decade, DeRose continued to produce music in various veins. Among the more popular and long-lasting were another "purple" work, "The Lamp is Low," with its classical borrowings from Ravel's *Pavane for a Dead Princess*; the dramatic "On a Little Street in Singapore," popularized by the young Frank Sinatra with the Harry James Orchestra; the lilting "All I Need Is You"; and "A Marketplace in Old Monterey," with aspirations to tone poetry.

At the same time, DeRose continued to write successfully for the Western market, including "Somewhere in Old Wyoming," "Muddy Waters," and "The Oregon Trail." But in 1933 he and Hill had varied the approach with "Have You Ever Been Lonely?" This slightly mournful, highly sentimental lament lay dormant for a while, only to erupt into major popularity when "Western" metamorphosed into "Country/Western" during the 1950s and 1960s. Recorded by many, the song passed into the standard repertoire of that subgenre.

By the 1940s DeRose was writing music for ice shows, and at the outbreak of World War II he collaborated with Sam Lee on "The Song of the Seabees," a stirring march. The Seabees were the U.S. Navy's construction battalion, and in an era when all the services were acquiring new anthems DeRose was ready and able. He also wrote patriotic and semireligious songs, including "I Hear America Singing" and "God Is Ever Beside Me" (1944). During the escapist years following World War II he proved equal to the task of writing jingly tunes including "(It's a) Marshmallow World (in the Winter)" and "24 Hours of Sunshine." In 1949 Breen joined in with her own feel-good "Forever and Ever," a Hit Parade regular.

Throughout his life DeRose continued to turn out piano compositions. The titles convey the content: "Maytime in Vienna," "American Waltz," "The Starlit Hour." In the last year of his life he collaborated on an unfinished operetta, "Counter Melody," with veteran lyricist Otto Harbach, who said, "Peter had a knack of finding words to which he could give wings." His contributions to cinema were limited to "Song of Love" and "About Face" (1952).

DeRose lived in Asbury Park, New Jersey, for many years. He died in New York City. Among his monuments is one in the Kensico Cemetery, White Plains, New York, shared with Breen, who was admitted to the Ukulele Hall of Fame in 2000.

DeRose was perhaps the most versatile popular composer of the first half of the twentieth century, mastering an astonishing variety of genres, apparently in harmony with his eclectic lyricists. His longevity largely rests with the highly melodic work he turned out during the 1930s, particularly in collaboration with wordsmith Parish, a master of lush and almost overripe verse. DeRose almost inadvertently created one haunting standard song, "Deep Purple," that lured singers of every persuasion and outlived the rise and fall of fickle taste.

• DeRose's archive remains with family members. May Singhi Breen's biography *Peter DeRose* was published in 1954. DeRose's work is mentioned on various web sites. Bill Owen and Frank Buxton, *The Big Broadcast: 1920–1950* (1972), contains detail on the DeRoses' radio careers. An obituary is in the *New York Times*, 24 Apr. 1953.

JAMES ROSS MOORE

DIAMOND, Louis K. (11 May 1902–14 June 1999), pediatrician, was born in the Ukraine, Russian Empire, the son of Eleazor Diamond, occupation unknown, and Lena Klein Diamond. After emigrating to the United States with his parents at age two, he grew up in Manhattan. He entered Harvard University in 1919 and worked his way through school, always holding at least two jobs. Although he was initially interested in chemistry, the summers he spent working as a camp counselor in New England helped to foster an interest in the field of pediatrics. On graduating in 1923, he entered Harvard's medical school, receiving his M.D. in 1927.

Shortly after finishing medical school, Diamond studied briefly with Florence Sabin at the Rockefeller Institute before returning to New England, where he spent the next several years studying pediatrics at Children's Hospital under the guidance of Dr. Kenneth Blackfan. On 2 July 1929 he married Flora Kaplan; they had two children.

Although just out of medical school, Diamond set up one of the first pediatric hematology research centers in the United States at Children's. Focusing on anemias, by 1930 he had succeeded in identifying thalassemia, a hereditary anemia that affected children of Italian and Greek ancestry.

His most important discovery, however, came when he and Dr. Blackfan found that what seemed to be four separate infant diseases were actually variations on a single syndrome, erythroblastosis fetalis, otherwise known as Rh disease (because it was originally identified in Rhesus monkeys). Diamond and Blackfan, along with Dr. J. M. Baty, presented their findings in a landmark paper published in the *Journal of Pediatrics* in 1932. Several years later Dr. Philip Levine identified the source of infant mortality as being the mother's Rh-negative blood adversely reacting with the Rh-positive blood of her newborn infant. Although doctors experimented with complete blood transfusions to save the lives of newborn infants, the process was both difficult and dangerous. In response to the new information, Diamond prevailed on a group of Boston area hospitals to collaborate and found the Blood Grouping Laboratory in 1942, where pregnant women could receive blood screenings that would alert their physicians to possible postpartum complications.

Diamond continued to work on the problem of blood transfusions in newborns with a variety of colleagues until 1946, when he and Dr. F. H. Allen, Jr., developed a technique that allowed the transference to take place through the infant's umbilical cord vein. Regular transfusions were difficult owing to the small size of blood vessels in newborns, and there was a further complication due to the use of steel needles and rubber catheters. Diamond used plastic tubing on the umbilical vein, which was larger than average and remained open for several days after birth. For his work Diamond received the Mead Johnson Award from the American Academy of Pediatrics in 1946; the results were published in the *New England Journal of Medicine* in 1951.

Diamond had remained on the staff of Children's Hospital following the completion of his residency and remained there until retiring in 1968, eventually rising to the rank of associate physician-in-chief of the Hematology Division. He concurrently served on the faculty of the Harvard University Medical School, where he became a full professor in 1963. His most important outside assignment came between 1948 and 1950, when he was picked to head the American Red Cross's transfusion services. Despite having to deal with issues such as postwar apathy, resentment on the part of local blood banks against an American organization, and difficulties in southern states over the use of racially nonsegregated blood, Diamond by all accounts made a major contribution toward establishing the Red Cross as a permanent medical entity in a number of communities nationwide.

Despite his position on the cutting edge of medical technology, Diamond often deplored the trend toward what he perceived to be an overreliance on technology among medical students; while conducting rounds, he often startled residents who had just recited a litany of patient test results by asking them about the color of the child's cheeks. In addition to his role in training many future leading pediatricians, Diamond also participated in a number of medical associations, including the American Pediatric Society, which he served as president.

In his later years Diamond continued to be an active researcher; for his work in preventing kernicterus (a condition associated with rhesus incompatibility and leading to brain damage) he received the Award for Scientific Research in Mental Retardation from the Joseph P. Kennedy, Jr., International Foundation in 1966. During his long career Diamond also received the Carlos J. Finlay Gold Medal, Cuba (1951), the Award of Merit from the Netherlands Red Cross (1959), and the Theodore Roosevelt Medal for Distinguished Public Service in Science (1964). He also participated in producing treatments for kwashiorkor, a disease caused by protein deprivation that ravaged Third World children, and was among the first to use chemotherapy in treating childhood leukemia. During his career he published some 200 scholarly articles, the most widely cited of which was *Atlas of the Blood of Children* (with Kenneth Blackfan, 1944).

After retiring from Harvard in 1968, Diamond moved to the University of California at San Francisco, where he served as an adjunct professor of pediatrics and had a chair named in his honor. He again retired in 1987 and moved to UCLA, where he remained active into his nineties. He died at his home in Los Angeles.

Although his field of research encompassed many areas and his techniques for overcoming Rh blood rejection were later supplanted by advancing technology, Louis Diamond earned the title "father of pediatric hematology" for his ground-breaking work that greatly reduced mortality rates among newborn infants.

• No collection of Diamond's papers has been located, but his reminiscences can be found within the Oral History Collection at Columbia University in New York. Diamond's career receives its most thorough overview in Charles A. Janeway, "Presentation of the Howland Award to Louis K. Diamond," *Pediatrics Research* 7 (1973): 853–57, while his role within the national Red Cross receives attention in Douglas Starr, *Blood: An Epic History of Medicine and Commerce* (1998). Obituaries are in the *Los Angeles Times* and the *New York Times*, 25 June 1999.

EDWARD L. LACH, JR.

DICK, A. B. (16 Apr. 1856–15 Aug. 1934), office machine and supplies entrepreneur, was born Albert Blake Dick in rural Bureau County, Illinois, the son of Adam Dick and Rebecca Wible. In 1863 the family moved to nearby Galesburg, where Adam Dick rose from a sash maker to plant manager at George W. Brown & Company, a corn picker manufacturer. In 1872, after receiving a public school education, Albert Dick joined the Brown Company. By 1879 he had become an assistant bookkeeper; he then moved to nearby Moline, Illinois, where he worked for what later became the John Deere Company, manufacturers of agricultural implements. He also became a partner in the Moline Lumber Company. At that time he married Alice Sheldon Mathews, the daughter of a Galesburg merchant and banker. The couple had one child, Mabel Eleanor Dick, who married Thomas W. Swan, dean of the law school at Yale University and a federal judge in New York City.

In 1883 the Dicks moved to Chicago, where Albert Dick opened a wholesale hardwood lumber dealership near the mouth of the Chicago River. He incorporated the firm in 1884 as the A. B. Dick Company and served as president and treasurer. Among the four stockholders, Dick held 60 percent, and Thomas W. Dunn of Moline held 20 percent. By 1887 the company had a branch office in Memphis, Tennessee. Alice Dick died in Chicago in 1885.

Albert Dick sought to run an efficient business, minimizing his inventory of stock. To achieve this he circulated daily inventory sheets to area mills and lumberyards, and he used the stock of other firms when necessary to complete orders for his own customers. Reportedly the repetitive daily task of writing up to fifty forms inspired him to develop a duplicating machine more economical than movable-type printing. By 1887 he developed a handwritten stencil with perforations that, when pressed by a hand roller, squeezed ink, producing many copies. When he sought to patent his "mimeograph" (mime-o-graph) process, he discovered that the famed inventor Thomas Edison had already done so. Edison's stencil was part of a motorized "electric pen" system that was marketed in the late 1870s in the United States and western Europe.

In the mid-1880s Dick approached Edison about obtaining a license under his electric pen patents and soon attracted Edison's interest in this new business. Edison's patent #224,665 was the governing one among stencil processes of several innovators from the 1870s. In the late winter and spring of 1887 Edison regained licensing rights he had granted to other promoters. Dick then signed contracts with him and agreed to pay per unit royalties and an annual minimum for production under the patents. Traveling to New York frequently, Dick made personal contact with Edison, Edison's associates, and potential sales agents. Dick also enlisted Edison's research efforts in improving the stencil process.

Dick marketed early versions of the machine as the "Edison Mimeograph," utilizing the commercial power of the inventor's name. Such promotion worked to the advantage of both men. Edison gained royalty on every sale, and the fledgling A. B. Dick firm obtained profit on each unit. Both also gained on the sale of the needed stencil supplies, and the Edison group shared with Dick the names of possible domestic and foreign agents. As the sales of both machines and supplies grew, Dick sold his lumber business late in 1887 and changed the corporate charter to focus on the sale and improvement of the mimeograph and related supplies. The company's capitalization increased from $25,000 to $150,000.

Ever appreciative of the alliance, Dick maintained a warm working relationship with Edison. As sales expanded, the need for capital also grew; Edison purchased shares in the company, and both men participated in numerous patent litigation cases. At the end of 1889 Dick obtained from Edison the rights for foreign sales of domestic production and concluded exclusive sales agreements for Great Britain and Ireland. Being in Chicago, the rail center of the United States, Dick approached the railroad companies, some of the pioneers in big businesses in America. They were among the first to adopt the mimeograph, using it to make many copies of messages for distribution across their rail networks. Developing not only a sizable domestic market but a foreign one as well, the Dick Company earned a profit of more than $60,000 in 1892. That year, Dick married Mary Henrietta Mathews, a sister of his first wife, in Geneva, Switzerland. They had four sons.

Dick and his associates continued to improve the stencils and the machines. Late in the century, with the increased popularity of the typewriter, Dick introduced a new, waxed-cloth stencil for making typed copies. This expensive cloth stencil was later replaced with a cheaper Japanese hazel paper stencil. Early in the twentieth century he introduced the rotary mimeograph, which sharply increased the rate at which copies could be made.

Signaling his growing financial success, Dick in 1902 completed an elegant home in Lake Forest, Illinois, a prestigious community thirty miles north of Chicago. The entrepreneur took an active part in local business and community affairs, notably joining the Lake Forest College Board of Trustees as treasurer in 1904. He also served on the boards of various Chicago corporations and banks.

By the end of the first decade of the twentieth century, the A. B. Dick Company had sold more than 180,000 mimeographs valued at $3.5 million. Annually the company produced nine thousand machines and sold stencils and related supplies valued at triple the machine sales. Dick oversaw continued product improvements, such as applying electric motors to large machines and introducing in 1912 the "Dermatype" stencil, from which 100,000 copies could be made.

Dick's business profited significantly by supplying the ink, paper, and related materials for his patented machines and stencils. His sales policy of linking ("tying in") the supplies to patented items was financially beneficial, though it resulted in antitrust litigation. In 1912 the U.S. Supreme Court upheld the tactic in a widely publicized case. In 1914 the U.S. Congress passed the Clayton Act, which among other things limited such sales practices. While managing a worldwide business, Dick established the Mimeograph Chemical Research Laboratory that developed the "Mimeotype," a dry process that in 1924 replaced the former wet stencils. As he reached his sixtieth year, Dick brought his oldest son Albert Blake Dick, Jr., into the family business as a clerk and salesperson. In 1919 Dick appointed this son vice president and treasurer. Dick's other sons, Edison Dick and Charles Mathews Dick, also joined the firm. In 1913 A. B. Dick became vice president of the Lake Forest College Board of Trustees, a position he retained until 1920. He retired from the board the following year, when he reached age sixty-five. He continued as the president of the A. B. Dick Company until his death in Lake Forest, at which time the Chicago company employed 1,700 people and had branches and agents in major cities at home and abroad.

Dick entered the copying business with the emergence of the American national market and the accompanying rise of big business. Witnessing the rapid expansion of offices with new efficiency-driven office equipment, such as the typewriter and the telephone, he exploited patented technical improvements, trademarks, national advertising, and a reputation for reliable modest-cost products to pilot his fledgling company to a position of market dominance. The firm maintained that position until the 1960s, when the Xerox Corporation introduced rivaling electrostatic copying techniques.

• A large collection of Dick's correspondence and financial and legal papers is at the Edison National Historic Site, West Orange, N.J. Much of this material is published in Thomas E. Jeffrey et al., eds., *Thomas A. Edison Papers: A Selective Microfilm Edition*, pt. 2 (1987–). A small collection of machines and related advertising materials is at the Henry Ford Museum and Greenfield Village in Dearborn, Mich. Papers relating to the college board of trustees are at Lake Forest College, Lake Forest, Ill.

The A. B. Dick Company privately printed Glen Buck, *Fifty Years: 1884–1934, A. B. Dick Company,*(1934), a promotional volume dedicated to Dick issued months before his death. It includes a sketch of company developments and his portrait. Books referring to Dick and the history of duplicating processes include Barbara Rhodes and William Wells Streeter, *Before Photocopying: The Art and History of Mechanical Copying, 1780–1938* (1999); and W. B. Proudfoot, *The Origin of Stencil Duplicating* (1972). Frank Lewis Dyer and Thomas Commerford Martin, *Edison: His Life and Inventions* (1910), and Alfred O. Tate, *Edison's Open Door* (1938), detail the Dick-Edison relationship, however, the recollections of Tate, Edison's secretary at the time, are not consistent with the surviving correspondence. Studies reliably discussing Edison's electric pen duplicating process include Jill Cooper, "Intermediaries and Invention: Business Agents and the Edison Electric Pen and Duplicating Press," *Business and Economic History* (Fall 1996): 130–42; JoAnne Yates, *Control through Communication: The Rise of System in American Management* (1989); and Paul Israel, *Edison: A Life of Invention* (1998). References to Dick's activities at Lake Forest College are in Franz Schulze, Rosemary Cowler, and Arthur H. Miller, *30 Miles North, A History of Lake Forest College: Its Town and Its City of Chicago* (2000). Obituaries are in the *New York Times*, 16 Aug. 1934, and the *Galesburg, Ill., Daily Register-Mail*, 16 Aug. 1934.

REESE V. JENKINS

DICKEY, James (2 Feb. 1923–19 Jan. 1997), writer, was born in Atlanta, Georgia, the son of Eugene Dickey, a lawyer, and Maibelle Swift Dickey. Because Maibelle Swift had inherited a small fortune from her father's tonic company, Swift's Southern Specific, Eugene rarely practiced the law. Instead, he indulged his passion for cockfighting, raising prize-winning roosters on a farm on the outskirts of Atlanta. While Eugene had little patience for the niceties of Atlanta's aristocratic society (his people hailed from the North Georgia mountains), Maibelle was more of a city girl. She was educated at Washington Seminary, the same school *Gone with the Wind* author Margaret Mitchell had attended, and she did her best to resuscitate the traditions of the Old South in her large home on mansion-lined West Wesley Road. From an early age, Dickey felt the tension between his rough-and-tumble father and his refined, sickly mother. At first he sided with his mother, deploring the bloodiness of his father's cockfighting. As he got older, he gradually adopted his father's persona, renouncing everything that smacked of excessive civility and embracing what seemed most primitive in human experience.

When Dickey graduated from E. Rivers Grammar School in 1936, the yearbook characterized him as "a good old scout." None of his friends found anything extraordinary about his behavior. He enjoyed playing football and marbles, wore handsome clothes, and, because school bullies beat up rich boys, he made half-hearted attempts to disguise his family's affluence. Around the age of six he had expressed his literary interests to his mother by stitching together a few pages into a book titled *The Life of James Dickey*, in which he imagined a career for himself as a combat pilot. At North Fulton High School between 1936 and 1941, he continued to blend in with the crowd, playing football, running track, and maintaining a C average. In order to better prepare himself for the academic and athletic rigors of college, he attended the private Darlington School in Rome, Georgia, for an extra year. Then in 1942 he entered Clemson Athletic and Military College as a cadet with the intention of studying engineering and becoming a football star. After a disappointing record in the classroom and on the freshman football team, he enlisted in the Army Air Corps to achieve his childhood dream of flying planes.

In 1943 Dickey's military ambitions suffered a crucial blow when he nearly crashed a PT-17 Stearman airplane during flight training in Camden, South Carolina. After the mishap, he was reclassified as a radar observer and went to Hammer Field in Fresno, California, for further training. On the train to the West Coast, Dickey met an attractive, wealthy Bryn Mawr student, Gwendolyn Leege, who lived in California. This was the first of many tumultuous affairs. Although he wanted to marry her, in late 1944 he reluctantly boarded a troopship for the war-torn Pacific islands. For the next year, he and his pilot, Earl Bradley, flew thirty-eight missions in P-61 Black Widows for the 418th Night Fighter Squadron. Between missions, he discovered his true passion—literature— and even wrote his first pamphlet of poems, *Poetical Remains*, which was heavily influenced by the nineteenth-century "decadent" poet Ernest Dowson (his most famous phrase was "gone with the wind"). Although Dickey was never involved in any of the heroic dogfights or firebombing raids he bragged about, the war transformed him. It convinced him that many of the civilized ways of his aristocratic upbringing were a sham and that the world was essentially a Darwinian struggle for survival and dominance.

Returning to the United States in 1946, Dickey was determined to triumph in academic pursuits. To begin his formal literary education, he transferred to Vanderbilt University, which had been a hotbed of the Southern Renaissance. Robert Penn Warren, Allen Tate, John Crowe Ransom, and Donald Davidson had all been associated with the university as students or professors. During the next four years, Dickey earned a reputation as the best poet on campus, a superb student, an aggressive womanizer, and a sometimes hilarious poseur who often lied about his accomplishments. Dickey himself traced his penchant for "creative lying" to his English professor, Monroe Spears, who encouraged him to cast free of realism in his poems. Dickey, however, exercised his imagination at all times, regularly boasting of his one hundred missions as a combat pilot, his heroic escape from his plane after being shot down off the Philippines, and his stellar football play at Clemson that had attracted NFL scouts. For the rest of his life he deliberately created a mythic image of himself as an all-American hero.

In 1948, after marrying Maxine Syerson and graduating near the top of his class with Phi Beta Kappa honors, Dickey earned a master's degree at Vanderbilt for a thesis on Herman Melville's poetry. He taught at Rice Institute in Texas, but the Air Force recalled him during the Korean War to teach radar operation. In 1951, Maxine gave birth to Christopher, the first of their two sons. (Christopher later became a *Newsweek* journalist and also a memoirist who wrote a scathing account of growing up with his difficult father in *Summer of Deliverance*.) Bored and frustrated by his second stint in the military, Dickey returned to Rice in 1952, where he found teaching English as depressing as teaching radar. The main problem was that he wanted time to write poetry, and the English Department chairman wanted him to spend his time teaching, doing research, and writing scholarly essays. Realizing that he could not advance at Rice without a doctorate, Dickey welcomed a *Sewanee Review* fellowship that allowed him to spend a year traveling and writing in Europe with his family. The Southern writer Andrew Lytle, who had become a mentor to Dickey, helped him secure a teaching position at the University of Florida. Dickey's second academic job was as dismal as his first. He lasted only a semester and a half in Gainesville, Florida. Reprimanded by the administration for reading "The Father's Body" to a group of women writers, who deemed his poem obscene, he abruptly quit and took a job as a copywriter for the McCann-Erickson advertising company in Atlanta. While he appreciated his new salary, Dickey found the business world even more deadening and time-consuming than academia. He often complained that he was selling his soul to the devil during the day and trying to buy it back at night by writing poetry.

Despite his many disappointing jobs, in the late 1950s Dickey wrote some of his best poetry. In 1958 and 1959 he won prestigious awards from *Poetry* magazine and the Longview Foundation, and he also began publishing in the *New Yorker*. On the strength of his first book, *Into the Stone and Other Poems* (1960), the Guggenheim Foundation awarded him a fellowship to return to Europe for another year of writing. In 1962, with his family in tow, he began writing his best-selling novel *Deliverance* and worked on his poetry in various hotels and rented houses in Europe. Books appeared in rapid succession. He published *Drowning with Others* in 1962, *Helmets* in 1964, and *Buckdancer's Choice* in 1965. Reviewers praised his adept combination of surreal and natural images and the way he created highly imaginative narratives by mythologizing his experiences as a soldier, hunter, athlete, and family man. Nineteen sixty-six was his annus mirabilis: he won the National Book Award for *Buckdancer's Choice*, the Poetry Society of America's Melville Cane Award, and an award from the National Institute of Arts and Letters. He served as poet-in-residence at Reed College, San Fernando Valley State College, and the University of Wisconsin, and then earned the top position for a poet in the United States when he became poetry consultant at the Library of Congress. In 1967, influential critic and editor Peter Davison argued in the *Atlantic Monthly* that of all the contemporary American writers only Dickey and Robert Lowell deserved the title "major."

Dickey finished his best-known book, the novel *Deliverance* (1970), in the late 1960s as poet-in-residence and English professor at the University of South Carolina, a position he held until his death. In *Deliverance* he returned to one of his favorite themes: the conflict between civilization and savagery in the modern world. He drew on his experiences in the Philippines during World War II, but also those in his native Georgia. As Dickey once admitted, the four main characters who leave their homes in Atlanta for the wilderness of North Georgia embody aspects of his own personality. As in many of his poems (the novel actually began as a poem), he dramatizes a rite of passage that "delivers" his personae from civilization into a savage environment, where they have to kill to survive, and that later delivers them back to civilization. He told an interviewer that the plot derived from Arnold Van Gennep's theories concerning rites of passage and Joseph Campbell's theory that myths of heroic journeys typically involve "a separation from the world, a penetration to some source of power, and a life-enhancing return." Recalling his boyhood journeys to his father's ancestral ground in North Georgia, his "separation" from civilized life in America when he went overseas as a soldier, and his canoe trips in the mountains when he was an Atlanta ad man, Dickey altered the classical paradigm of the mythical journey so that the penetration to a source of power actually became crippling and haunting rather than "life-enhancing." Savagery in the form of homosexual rape and murder transform the Atlanta men on their canoe trip, but the horrendous experiences leave permanent scars.

Most of the reviews of *Deliverance* were positive. Stefan Kanfer in *Time* praised the novel as a compelling adventure story, even though some of the events seemed unbelievable. Evan Connell in the *New York Times* found the book to be a dramatic tour-de-force, but thought the story would have been even better without a first-person narrator. The rape scene and violent murders, however, offended some reviewers. Benjamin DeMott complained in the *Saturday Review* about the book's adolescent "shoot-em-up" melodrama. Some feminist critics thought the novel was yet another indulgence in Hemingwayesque machismo. Natives of North Georgia alleged that Dickey had stereotyped the mountain men as subhuman rapists. High schools in North Dakota and elsewhere banned the book from courses and libraries. As if predicting these negative responses, Dickey has his narrator Ed Gentry discuss the problem of communicating savage experiences to normal, civilized folk. At the end of the novel, Ed decides that most people simply cannot accept the truth about human barbarism; they would rather live in "civilized" denial. That's one of the reasons he decides to lie about his horrendous experiences on the canoe trip to his family and friends when he returns to Atlanta. Despite its detractors, *Deliverance* remains a powerful testament to the horror that frequently erupts in our modern world and our various ways of coping with it.

After the novel's appearance in print, he quickly transformed it into a screenplay for Warner Brothers and later played a role (as the portly Southern sheriff) in the blockbuster film made by John Boorman, which was nominated for several Academy Awards, including best picture. After the financial and critical success of *Deliverance*, Dickey became one of the most highly paid writers on the reading circuit. He also began to follow the tragic path of many other famous American writers. His alcoholism and womanizing out of control, he offended the large crowds who came to see him as often as he entertained them. His wife periodically threatened to leave him, took to drink to dull the pain of her marriage, and died from esophageal hemorrhaging brought on by alcoholism in 1976. Two months after her funeral, Dickey married one of his students, Deborah Dodson, whose drug problems were exacerbated by his erratic behavior. They had a daughter, Bronwen, in 1981. Incensed by their father's loyalty to Dodson, especially after finding out about her threats on his life and her heroin and cocaine use, Dickey's two sons virtually abandoned him.

Dickey's drinking and chaotic marriage affected the quality but not the quantity of his writings. In the 1970s he wrote two coffee table books, including the popular *Jericho: The South Beheld* (1974); a screenplay of Jack London's *Call of the Wild* for television; the idiosyncratic memoir *Self-Interviews* (1970); the collection of journal entries and essays *Sorties: Journals and New Essays* (1971); and three new poetry books, including *The Strength of Fields* (1979), whose title poem he composed for President Jimmy Carter's inauguration. He remained prolific in the 1980s and 1990s, publishing two more novels as well as more coffee table books, poetry books, and collections of essays. His fiction continued to draw on his military experiences. Like *Deliverance*, which allegorizes his journey from Atlanta to the brutality of war in the form of a journey into the savage wilderness of North Georgia, his massive novel *Alnilam* (1987) charts the journey of an older man resembling Dickey to an Army Air Corps base where a man resembling the younger Dickey had crashed his plane. The novel *To the White Sea* (1993) also recounts a military journey, this time by a homicidal tail gunner, Muldrow, from firebombed Tokyo to a snowy island in the northern Japanese archipelago. Tired of Dickey's bombastic and often politically offensive comments in public, critics from the 1970s on tended to focus on the same overbearing traits in his novels and poems. While much of the criticism of Dickey's writing was unfair, the consensus was that his books after *Deliverance* promised much and delivered little. Even Dickey sometimes talked about his efforts as ambitious failures. Although he tried to rehabilitate his image by renouncing many of the macho stereotypes he had cultivated for himself, he was his own worst advocate, blustering drunkenly in public and sometimes on the page as well. His effort to go beyond his early mythic and narrative poetry and write in a more fragmentary, modernist way was noble. Unfortunately, his chaotic lifestyle interfered with his ability to realize his high goals. With his wife often in trouble with the police, he continued to drink relentlessly until 1994, when his liver gave out and he suffered a near-fatal case of jaundice. He quit drinking and began divorce proceedings, but he never recovered his health. He died from fibrosis of the lungs in Columbia, South Carolina.

• Dickey was one of the most prolific post–World War II writers. During the four decades that comprised his career he published over twenty books of poetry, including *Poems, 1957–1967* (1968), *The Eye-Beaters, Blood, Victory, Madness, Buckhead, and Mercy* (1970), *The Zodiac* (1976), *Tucky the Hunter* (1978), *The Early Motion* (1981), *Falling, May Day Sermon, and Other Poems* (1981), *Puella* (1982), *The Central Motion* (1983), *Bronwen, the Traw, and the Shape Shifter* (1986), *The Eagle's Mile* (1990), and *The Whole Motion: Collected Poems, 1945–1992* (1992). Although Dickey maintained that poetry was always at the center of his creative wheel, his prose works were almost as numerous. They include: *Symbol and Image in the Shorter Poems of Herman Melville* (1950), *The Suspect in Poetry* (1964), *Babel to Byzantium: Poets and Poetry Now* (1968), *Night Hurdling: Poems, Essays, Conversations, Commencements, and Afterwords* (1983), *Wayfarer: A Voice from the Southern Mountains* (1988), and *Southern Light* (1991).

Many critical books have been written about Dickey. The most comprehensive is the 800-page biography by Henry Hart, *James Dickey: The World as a Lie* (2000), which makes use of the voluminous Dickey archive at Emory University and the smaller archives at Washington University, the Library of Congress, and other U.S. libraries. Christopher Dickey's *Summer of Deliverance* (1998) is a much shorter account and, as a memoir by an angry son who shared many of the ambitions and personality traits of his father, is less objective. Harold Bloom's *James Dickey* (1987) and Robert Kirschten's *Struggling for Wings: The Art of James Dickey* (1997) are representative collections of essays about Dickey's career. For a sharply critical assessment of the way Dickey deliberately promoted himself, see Neal Bowers, *James Dickey: The Poet as Pitchman* (1985). Matthew Bruccoli and Judith Baughman, *James Dickey, A Descriptive Bibliography* (1990), is an extremely valuable record of publications by and about Dickey, and their *Crux* (1999) is a large

and judicious collection of Dickey's letters. For a useful introduction to Dickey's poetry, consult Robert Kirschten, *James Dickey and the Gentle Ecstasy of Earth* (1988). Ernest Suarez, *James Dickey and the Politics of Canon* (1993), provides an astute assessment of the sociopolitical reasons for the rise and fall of Dickey's reputation. Also helpful for gaining a better understanding of the critical reactions to Dickey's many books is Gordon Van Ness, *Outbelieving Existence* (1992). An obituary is in the *New York Times*, 31 Jan. 1997.

HENRY HART

DIXON, Jeremiah. *See under* Mason, Charles

DMYTRYK, Edward (4 Sept. 1908–1 July 1999), motion picture director and one of the "Hollywood Ten," was born in Grand Forks, British Columbia, the son of Michael Dmytryk, a Ukrainian immigrant; his mother's name is not known. Edward's mother died of a burst appendix when he was eight. By that time, his father, after hearing that the Canadian government was interning all immigrants who had once been citizens of the Austro-Hungarian Empire, had smuggled the family across the border to Northport, Washington.

Dmytryk remembered his father as a "superb survivor" but a "cruel" man who administered discipline through frequent beatings. In 1917 he moved the family to San Francisco where he eked out a living as a truck driver and motorman. There he remarried, and the family then moved to Sherman, a Los Angeles suburb that was later renamed West Hollywood.

When he was six Dmytryk peddled newspapers on street corners and later caddied at the Los Angeles Country Club. By fourteen he was on his own, working as a messenger for $6 a week at Famous Players-Lasky studios while attending Hollywood High School. Dmytryk enrolled at the California Institute of Technology in 1926 at studio expense but quit after his first year, deciding that film would be his work from then on. He was "broke, busy and bashful" and tried to make himself "indispensable." In the process, he learned the film business, becoming a projectionist at Paramount when he was nineteen "only after the boss got tired of chasing me out of the projection booth," he recalled.

When he was twenty-one Dmytryk became an assistant editor at Paramount for $40 a week. His first job as editor was on *The Royal Family of Broadway* in 1930. During Dmytryk's decade as editor he developed a great respect for the position's power to "mold, improve and even recreate a motion picture," seeing it as "the art of the cinema" even though it was practiced "in the relative obscurity of the cutter's cubicle." Dmytryk worked with some of the best directors in Hollywood, including Ernst Lubitsch, George Cukor, Leo McCarey, Henry Hathaway, and Norman Taurog, usually sitting on the set as they filmed their scenes. It was there that Dmytryk learned to trust his very first reaction to what he had seen.

In 1932 Dmytryk married Madeleine Robinson "out of sheer loneliness" but later confessed that he failed to remember "one truly happy moment" in the union that ended in divorce in 1948. They had one child. Dmytryk found the "intensity" of his commitment to moviemaking "far greater than that in my real life."

Dmytryk directed his first film in 1935, an independent "B" western called *The Hawk*; it was shot in five days for $5,000, with Dmytryk running through 130 camera and lighting setups in a single day. In 1939 he was brought in to finish directing a Paramount "B" called *Million Dollar Legs* when the studio fired the first director. Dmytryk's efficiency was rewarded. He was signed to direct "B" pictures at Paramount for $250 a week. Four films quickly followed, each shot with limited budgets and nonstar casts.

Between 1940 and early 1942 Dmytryk made seven low-budget films for Columbia Pictures. He worried that he was becoming "just another hack." In 1943 RKO fired the director of *Hitler's Children* and hired Dmytryk for $500 to finish the picture. Dmytryk played it as "a simple exploitation B" involving young people forced to live in horror in Nazi Germany. The picture cost $205,000 and made more than $3 million at the box office. Dmytryk was given a $5,000 bonus and, through a new agent, Famous Artists, negotiated a "fat contract." At thirty-four "I was on my way," he recalled.

In 1943 Dmytryk made two more films for RKO, each a hit. *Behind the Rising Sun* would be his last "B" at RKO. *Tender Comrade*, starring Ginger Rogers, was later labeled by the House Un-American Activities Committee as Communist propaganda because of its depiction of war factory wives who lived communally to cut costs. The film's screenwriter Dalton Trumbo was later cited by the committee for his Communist Party connections. Dmytryk defended the film as simply showing how the home front coped with the realities of war.

Dmytryk's next film at RKO, *Murder, My Sweet* (1944), became a classic. The private eye genre had seen *The Maltese Falcon* two years before, but Dmytryk's telling of the Raymond Chandler tale of murder and blackmail led to a new realism in movies. Former singing star Dick Powell plays world-weary private detective Philip Marlowe, whose "feet hurt" and mind feels "like a plumber's handkerchief." He is a creature of the night whose disillusionment needs "the office bottle to spark me up." Marlowe is a loner with little love in his life. He goes "grouse-hunting" but finds women do little "to improve my morale." Dmytryk's spare lighting, point of view camera, and direct address narration evoke a bleak subterranean world where nothing is as it seems and the audience shares the protagonist's perilous predicament. All this anticipated the postwar film noir movement.

In late 1944 or early 1945 Dmytryk joined the Communist Party, believing this was a way of fighting for the underclass while "mobilizing America against fascism." The affiliation lasted only a few months.

When party officials demanded changes in *Back to Bataan*, a film Dmytryk directed in 1945, Dmytryk balked and quit the party. His producer Adrian Scott was also a party member and appears to have faced the same party pressure.

The next two years were the "happiest" of Dmytryk's life. The critical and financial success of *Cornered* (1945) confirmed his growing reputation as "Hollywood's hottest young director." Dmytryk separated from his wife in 1946 and began seeing Jean Porter, an M-G-M contract player he met on the set of *Till the End of Time* (1946). *So Well Remembered* (1947), a British-American coproduction, continued the winning streak. *Crossfire* (1947), the first serious screen treatment of anti-Semitism, became a widely praised message film leading to Dmytryk's Academy Award Best Director nomination. His path-breaking work in high-contrast lighting and wide-angle photography using multiple lenses added a shadowy texture to the tale of a racially motivated murder.

In the fall of 1947 Dmytryk was one of nineteen filmmakers subpoenaed to testify before the House Un-American Activities Committee investigating communist infiltration in Hollywood. He became one of the "Unfriendly Ten" who refused to testify on constitutional grounds of freedom of speech. He was cited for contempt of Congress, a ruling upheld in the courts. Fired by RKO, Dmytryk moved with Jean Porter to England, where he made three films. The couple married in 1948; they had two children.

When Dmytryk's British visa expired in 1951, he returned to the United States and was arrested. He served four and a half months of a six-month sentence at a federal prison in Mill Point, West Virginia. After his release, he testified before HUAC, naming names of fellow communists, the only member of the Hollywood Ten ever to do so. Dmytryk testified that John Howard Lawson, Adrian Scott, and Albert Maltz had pressured him to express the views of the Communist Party in his films. He later justified his action by claiming the names he gave the committee were already known to HUAC investigators. Also, he had no desire "to sacrifice my family and career in defense of the Communist Party, from which I had long been separated and which I had grown to dislike and distrust."

Dmytryk's testimony made him a pariah among Hollywood liberals but ended his blacklist. He made three "B" pictures with Columbia before a series of successful "A" pictures with some of Hollywood's leading actors and actresses: *The Caine Mutiny* (1954) and *The Left Hand of God* (1955), with Humphrey Bogart; *Broken Lance* (1954) and *The Mountain* (1956), starring Spencer Tracy; *Soldier of Fortune* (1955), starring Clark Gable and Susan Hayward; *Raintree County* (1957), featuring Elizabeth Taylor and Montgomery Clift; *The Young Lions* (1958), with Marlon Brando and Clift; *Warlock* (1959), with Henry Fonda and Richard Widmark; *A Walk on the Wild Side* (1962), with Barbara Stanwyck; *The Carpetbaggers* (1963), with Alan Ladd; *Where Love Has Gone* (1964), starring Bette Davis and Hayward; *Mirage*

(1965), featuring Gregory Peck; and *Alvarez Kelly* (1966), with William Holden and Widmark. Dmytryk's reputation for working well with high-priced talent was based on his conviction that "a film crew should be highly organized" with the director at its head. "The hand on the tiller can be gentle," he believed, "but it should always be firm."

Bluebeard (1972), starring Richard Burton, was Dmytryk's last major theatrical release. Critics complained that that film and many made since the blacklist period failed to show the heart and style of Dymtryk's earlier work. Dmytryk turned to teaching and writing about film first at the University of Texas in the late seventies and the University of Southern California in the 1980s. By that time his books on screen editing and directing were in wide use.

Shortly before his death Dmytryk told reporters he had no real regrets about being swept up in the anti-Communist hysteria of the postwar period nor in having to name names before a Congressional committee, but he did regret that the controversy would always overshadow his work as a director. "When I die," he explained to an interviewer, "I know the obits will first read, 'one of Hollywood's Unfriendly Ten,' not 'director of *The Caine Mutiny, The Young Lions, Raintree County* and other films.'" To many students of film, that work across five decades established Dmytryk as one of the most innovative and influential directors of cinema's first century.

• Dmytryk's autobiography *It's a Hell of a Life but Not a Bad Living* appeared in 1978. A second autobiographical work, *Odd Man Out: A Memoir of the Hollywood Ten*, was published in 1996. Dmytryk's books on filmmaking include *On Screen Directing* (1984); *On Film Editing: An Introduction to the Art of Film Construction* (1984); *On Screen Acting: An Introduction to the Art of Acting for the Screen* (1984), which he co-authored with his wife; *On Screen Writing* (1985); *On Filmmaking* (1986), a compendium of his previous books on motion picture making; and *Cinema: Concept and Practice* (1988). Dmytryk's career in the context of the Hollywood blacklist period is the subject of Bernard F. Dick, *Radical Innocence: A Critical Study of the Hollywood Ten* (1989), pp. 135–65. A filmography appears on pp. 235–36. Dmytryk's reflections on his long career appear in the British Broadcasting Company Production "Hollywood: The Golden Years," episode five, focusing on the period 1942–1952 at RKO Studios. It was produced in 1987 and broadcast on Anglo-American television networks that same year. Another major interview was given to James Bawden, author of "Edward Dmytryk Remembers: An Interview," *Films in Review* (Dec. 1985), pp. 583–89. Robert Fischer's German-language biography *Edward Dmytryk, Film Director* appeared in 1990. A critical biographical piece was written by David Thomson for *A Biographical Dictionary of Film* (1976), pp. 140–41. His obituary is in the 3 July 1999 editions of the *New York Times* and the *Los Angeles Times*.

BRUCE J. EVENSEN

DODGE, David Low (14 June 1774–23 Apr. 1852), merchant and peace reformer, was born in Brooklyn, Connecticut, the son of David Dodge and Mary Stuart (widow of the late William Earl), farmers. Dodge was raised in a strict Calvinist family and remained involved in religious matters all his life. He spent much of his formative years working on the farm. He received a limited common school education. Although he was largely self-taught, Dodge became a schoolteacher at age nineteen. He taught school for several years, first at community schools and then in private ventures.

On 7 June 1798 he married Sarah Cleveland, daughter of the Reverend Aaron Cleveland. They had one son. In 1802 Dodge became a dry goods dealer in Hartford, Connecticut. Later, as owner, he headed the first cotton factory, near Norwich, built in his native state. His growing prosperity also enabled him to start a jobbing business in New York City, where he moved with his family in 1807.

Financially secure, Dodge began taking a more active role in religious and philanthropic endeavors. One of his most important enterprises was a deepening commitment to the abolishment of war. His two half brothers had been killed in the American Revolution.

In 1805, while carrying a large sum of money, he nearly shot an innkeeper who had mistakenly wandered into his room late at night. In 1808, having survived an attack of spotted fever, he remarked: "At this solemn moment the word of God appeared a reality; a sure foundation on which to rest my eternal hopes. From this period, my war spirit appeared to be crucified and slain; and I felt regret that I had not borne some more public testimony against it" (quoted in Charles DeBenedetti, *The Peace Reform in American History*, p. 35).

In 1809 Dodge wrote a pamphlet titled *The Mediator's Kingdom Not of This World*. Published anonymously, the first edition of 1,000 copies sold out quickly. He now established himself as one of the earliest nonsectarian peace advocates in America. In the pamphlet, Dodge resorted to biblical injunctions in his condemnation of personal self-defense as well as defensive wars: "That all kinds of war, revenge, and fighting were utterly prohibited under the gospel of dispensation we think it appears evident not only from the life of our glorious Mediator but from his expressed precepts" (quoted in Peter Brock, *Pacifism in the United States*, p. 451). Although the pamphlet was well received, it did little in the way of providing concrete alternatives to the violent method of resisting evil except for a somewhat naive invocation of God's protection. A number of critics, including Noah Worcester, William Ladd, and Sylvanus Haynes, also questioned his stance on defensive warfare.

After publication of his pamphlet Dodge began gathering around himself a small circle of like-minded peace reformers. It marked a movement away from the earlier sectarian religious antiwar groups such as the Quakers, the Mennonites, and the Church of the Brethren. Dodge's new nonsectarian peace movement consisted mainly of middle-class citizens. Historian Merle Curti described them as "Congregationalist and Unitarian gentlemen accustomed to social deference and committed to moral improvement through gradual enlightenment" (Curti, *Peace or War*, pp. 34–37). In early 1812, Dodge and his followers discussed organizing a group to enlist the evangelical churches in waging a campaign against war. The outbreak of war with England that year postponed the budding venture. Dodge and his colleagues feared that their actions would be misinterpreted.

In 1812 Dodge also wrote his most famous peace work, *War Inconsistent with the Religion of Jesus Christ*. However, publication was delayed until after the War of 1812. Dodge's book marked the beginning of nonsectarian organized peace work. In *War Inconsistent with the Religion of Jesus Christ* Dodge adopted a radical Christian perspective, one also laced with economic interpretations. He condemned war as an oppressor of the poor: "The calamities of war necessarily fall more on the poor than on the rich, because the poor of a country are generally a large majority of its inhabitants" (pp. 8–11). Most important, he denounced defensive war as contrary to the Gospel—"the pretended distinction between offensive and defensive war is but a name"—and called upon all Christians to renounce both Satan and war (pp. 36–42). "Christ taught his disciples the doctrines of peace," Dodge proclaimed, "and commanded them to take up the cross and follow him to live in peace with all men" (pp. 73–74). His pamphlet was one of the most effective statements of Christian pacifism in the early part of the nineteenth century, articulating a number of theological views that future nonresistant radicals would utilize in their efforts to abolish all forms of violence.

The well-to-do New York City merchant not only "tucked peace tracts into the boxes of goods sent out from his store rooms" but fulfilled his earlier hopes of creating a society devoted to the cause of peace (Curti, *Peace or War*, p. 37). On 16 August 1815, Dodge organized the New York Peace Society and became its first president. The society, numbering between thirty and forty, consisted of members who were respectable and bourgeois. It was probably the first peace society in the world. Its program was largely directed by Dodge: "Our articles of association were of the strict kind, against all carnal warfare, whether offensive or defensive, as being wholly opposed to the example of Christ, and the spirit and precepts of the gospel" (Dodge, "Autobiography," printed in the *Memorial of Mr. David L. Dodge*, p. 99). Dodge later distributed a thousand copies of *Observations on the Kingdom of Peace, under the Benign Reign of Messiah* (1816), another peace tract; this small piece prophesied the second coming of the Prince of Peace and highlighted the society's main goals. Circulation of its antiwar message, not growth, was the New York Peace Society's primary mission.

After reaching a membership of about sixty, Dodge's society began to decline. In 1827, he retired from business. A year later he played a significant role in merging the New York Peace Society with several other groups to form the first national peace organization, the American Peace Society. At his own home,

Dodge presided over its first organizational meeting. He remained associated with the society for many years, as a member of its board of directors and later as a life director. Although he refused to hold public office or even to vote, Dodge did believe in participating in noteworthy causes. Many were of a religious nature, including establishing the New York Bible Society and the New York Tract Society, to which he had a strong commitment as primary benefactor.

In later years, as the organized peace movement gained momentum under the leadership of Noah Worcester, William Ladd, and Elihu Burritt, Dodge played a much less active role. He became disappointed with peace leaders like Worcester and Ladd who refused to condemn defensive war. Dodge died in New York City. He had set the tone for radical peace reform in antebellum America.

In denouncing all acts of violence, Dodge insisted that "Christians were a people redeemed from the sinful world," a temperament that distinguished his nonresistance from all other peace reformers of his generation (Ziegler, *The Advocates of Peace in Antebellum America*, p. 35).

• There is no full-length biography of Dodge. His speeches and tracts are located in the American Peace Society Papers, Swarthmore College Peace Collection, Swarthmore College. Dodge's most important writings include *The Mediator's Kingdom, Not of This World* (1809); *Observations on the Kingdom of Peace, under the Benign Reign of Messiah* (1816); and his classic position on Christian nonresistance, *War Inconsistent with the Religion of Jesus Christ* (1815), also reprinted in Peter Brock, ed., *The First American Peace Movement* (1972). Dodge's autobiography is *Memorial of Mr. David L. Dodge, Consisting of an Autobiography Prepared at the Request and for the Use of His Children, with a Few Selections from His Writings* (published only for the family by S. K. Whipple & Co., 1854). A useful account of Dodge's life is Edwin D. Mead, "David Low Dodge: Founder of the First Peace Society," *World Unity* 11, no. 6 (1933): 365–72, and 12, no. 1: 29–36. Scholarly works discussing Dodge's role in the pre–Civil War peace movement are Merle Curti, *The American Peace Crusade, 1815–1860* (1929) and *Peace or War: The American Struggle, 1636–1936* (1936); Peter Brock, *Pacifism in the United States: From the Colonial Era to the First World War* (1968); Charles Chatfield, *The American Peace Movement: Ideals and Activism* (1992); Valerie H. Ziegler, *The Advocates of Peace in Antebellum America* (1992); and David C. Lawson, "Swords into Plowshares, Spears into Pruninghooks: The Intellectual Foundations of the First American Peace Movement, 1815–1865," Ph.D. diss., University of New Mexico (1975).

CHARLES F. HOWLETT

DOHNÁNYI, Ernst von (27 July 1877–9 Feb. 1960), composer, concert pianist, teacher, and conductor, also known as Ernó and baptized Dohnányi Erno Jeno Frigyes, was born in Pozsony, Hungary—later known as Pressberg, then Bratislava, Slovakia. (The population of Pozsony was approximately half Hungarian and half German, so Dohnányi was comfortable with the language and heritage of both.) He was the son of Frederick von Dohnányi (Dohnányi

Frigyes), professor of mathematics and physics at the Royal Catholic Chief Gymnasium (Királyi Katolikus Főgimnásium) and an accomplished cellist and composer. Dohnányi's mother, Ottilia Szlabey, was tiny; she was sometimes referred to as fiercely determined and willing to sacrifice her comfort for others. Dohnányi embodied these characteristics as an adult helping family and friends survive the vicissitudes of wartime Europe. His sister, Mitzi, was a year younger. A brother died in infancy. When traveling outside of Hungary, he called himself Ernst von Dohnányi.

When Dohnányi was six, his father taught him to play the piano. A year later he added violin lessons. The piano student soon surpassed the teacher. He had the ability to memorize easily, sight-read flawlessly, and perform well with minimal practice. Like Mozart as a child, his head was filled with musical images that demanded expression. At seven, Dohnányi composed his first piece. At eight, he began to study with Károly Forstner (Forstner Károly), organist at Pozsony Cathedral. In Dohnányi's first public performance, on 3 November 1886, the nine-year-old played in Mozart's G Minor Piano Quartet. On 28 December 1890, twelve-year-old Dohnányi's first solo recital included Chopin's Nocturne op. 31, no. 1; Mendelssohn's Scherzo in B Minor; Liszt's Eighth Hungarian Rhapsody; and two of his own compositions.

During the summers, Dohnányi played organ at the Pozsony Cathedral and the Evangelical Church of Breznóbánya. Although music was his major focus, he enjoyed art, nature, mountain climbing, and tennis. He loved to walk, often composing en route. In September 1894, at the age of seventeen, he went to Budapest to study at the National Hungarian Royal Academy of Music (Liszt Ferenc Zeneakadémia), now the Franz Liszt Academy of Music (Liszt Ferenc Zeneművészeti Főiskola). There, he met and courted Elsa Kunwald. He also met Johannes Brahms, who arranged for him to perform in Vienna before the Tonkünstler Verein (composers' association). During the Hungarian Millennium celebration in 1896, Dohnányi won a prize for his first symphony, Symphony in F Major. He received his artist's diplomas in piano and composition in June 1897.

After graduating, Dohnányi moved to Berlin, where during two piano recitals in October 1897 he premiered his compositions. On 17 November 1897, he performed Beethoven's G Major Piano Concerto with the Budapest Philharmonic. With youthful self-confidence, Dohnányi habitually improvised cadenzas with panache and often programmed his unfinished compositions, devising endings as he played.

In 1898 he went to England to work with conductor Hans Richter. Although he never studied English formally, he picked it up quickly through everyday use. In March 1899, in Vienna, Austria, Dohnányi played his Piano Concerto, op. 5, in a competition to commemorate the seventieth anniversary of the Bösendorfer piano factory; he won the grand prize. The same year, he became engaged to Elsa Kunwald. His first performance in the United States was with the Boston Symphony Orchestra in March 1900. In April he gave concerts in Liverpool and London. He spent the summer in Hungary with the Kunwald family and married Elsa on 11 October 1900. They had three children.

In 1900 in Troy, New York, Dohnányi was asked to perform Beethoven's Kreutzer Sonata with renowned violinist Fritz Kreisler. In October 1905, Dohnányi joined the faculty at the Königliche Preussische Hochschule für Musik in Berlin, Germany. He taught piano only six hours a week, was given a lengthy vacation, and had plenty of time to compose. Although he was the youngest teacher, he received the highest salary. At first he disliked teaching but eventually grew to love it. As a state employee, he automatically became a Prussian citizen while retaining his Hungarian citizenship. He became a full professor in 1908, while continuing his concerts throughout Europe. His music was usually dedicated to family and friends. For instance, in a set of ten bagatelles for piano, Sphären Musik (Music of the Spheres) memorialized a hot air balloon flight he shared with the Commander of the Austrian Air Force. On 22 January 1910 Dohnányi premiered an operatic ballet, Der Schleier der Pierrette, at the Royal Opera in Dresden. Three major roles were assigned to opera singers; minor roles were performed by ballet dancers. His comic opera, Tante Simona, with libretto by Victor Heindl, premiered in Dresden in January 1913.

Controversy arose when Dohnányi, who was full of fun, used humor in his music. Variationen über ein Kinderlied, op. 25 (Variations on a Nursery Tune), premiered in February 1916. The introduction and eleven variations incorporate "Ah, vous dirai-je, Maman"; the twelfth variation includes a serious passacaglia but returns to humor. Dohnányi's dedication read, "Freunden des Humors zur Freude, den Anderen zum Ärger" (to the enjoyment of friends of humor, to the annoyance of the others). If the dedication stated his goal, he achieved it. Upon publication, Dohnányi omitted the inscription but regretted that when some critics complained about his so-called lack of musical decorum. For some time thereafter, discussion about the propriety of humor in music continued in the print media.

During World War I there were few concerts and Dohnányi composed little. He disagreed with German politics and renounced his German citizenship. Prior to World War I, he had met Elza Glafrés, who was also married. On 1 December 1914 Dohnányi returned to Budapest to join Elza and become professor of piano at the Franz Liszt Academy of Music. They planned to marry, but their respective spouses refused to divorce them. In January 1917 their son was born. They were each finally divorced and able to marry in a civil ceremony on 2 June 1919, followed by a religious ceremony in a Catholic chapel on 5 June 1919. Dohnányi opposed the Communist regime then in power, so the family moved to Norway. When the dictatorship ended, they returned to Budapest, where he resumed teaching and concertizing. In 1920, Dohnányi first heard jazz during a boat crossing to the United States and thought it was a musical joke. On learning that it was considered a serious musical idiom, he ridiculed it as a "caricature of music" that "lacked style."

In 1922 the Hungarian University of Szeged awarded him an honorary doctorate. Beginning in January 1924, he made annual concert tours to the United States. In 1925 he served as conductor of the New York State Symphony Orchestra for five months. To celebrate his fiftieth birthday in 1926, the Hungarian State honored him with a gift of 50,000 pengős. Now middle-aged, Dohnányi dreamed of a quieter, more peaceful life. He built a house on a mountain slope complete with a tennis court and swimming pool. In 1931 the Hungarian government awarded him the Corwin Chain, its highest decoration in the field of arts and sciences. He was also the general music director of Hungarian radio. During the winter of 1932-1933 Dohnányi organized the First International Liszt Competition for the academy. In July 1934, he developed a thrombosis and was bedridden for several months but continued composing.

In 1937, Dohnányi was appointed an honorary member of the upper house of the Hungarian Senate. In the spring he was hospitalized for three months with nicotine poisoning. He also suffered a thrombosis for the second time in his right arm. That winter he met 27-year-old Ilona [Helen] Zachár. She was married and had two children; Dohnányi was still married to Elza. Nevertheless, their mutual attraction grew. Ilona, who spoke five languages fluently, became a respected translator and writer. Dohnányi's thrombosis returned in 1939, leaving him bedridden for three months, and in 1943 a bout with thrombophlebitis kept him in bed for six weeks. Meanwhile, Hungary had allied with Germany, and in March 1941 new laws had been passed that required Jewish musicians to be fired. Dohnányi opposed this and in August 1943 he resigned from the Academy of Music. On 11 May 1944 he disbanded the Budapest Philharmonic rather than dismiss Jewish players. He felt that musicians should not participate in politics and should not be persecuted for their beliefs.

To avoid possible bombing raids, Dohnányi and Ilona, her children, and her chambermaid moved to the country. On 24 November 1944, they left Hungary permanently, traveling to Vienna. Once there, their mornings were often spent in the cellar due to air raids. When Vienna was invaded by the Russians, they abandoned most of their belongings and money. A Hungarian colonel drove them to Linz, Austria. Settled there, Dohnányi played the organ at church, gratis, and organized a choir of refugees.

Earlier, as a member of the Hungarian senate, Dohnányi had signed legislation founding an anti-Russian national association. Because of this, the now Communist-controlled Hungarian government listed him as a war criminal. When the war ended, the Hungarians were considered enemies by the American military government, so they were supplied no food rations and were not allowed to earn money. One Sunday, American officers heard Dohnányi at the church organ. Soon after, he was invited to play for American soldiers and to conduct the Philharmonic Broadcasting Orchestra. Unfortunately, Dohnányi became the victim of rumors perpetrated by jealous colleagues, some of whom, ironically, he had helped anonymously. Dohnányi was officially cleared of being a war criminal in December 1945, but the false accusations continued to beleaguer him for the rest of his life. To compound his grief, Dohnányi lost both of his sons. Hans, who served in the Hungarian military, was executed for his part in a conspiracy to kill Hitler. Matthew, also a Hungarian soldier, died in a prison camp.

After the war, Ilona obtained papers from the British consul that allowed her, Dohnányi, and his secretary to travel. Dohnányi gave a concert in Edinburgh, Scotland, in October 1946, then they returned to Vienna for more concerts. Postwar conditions were terrible, so Dohnányi sought permission from several countries to emigrate. A major problem was that he and Ilona were still unmarried and some countries would not consider admitting them as a family.

On 26 July 1947, the day before his seventieth birthday, Dohnányi was honored at a banquet at Innsbruck, Austria. Meanwhile, the Hungarian government still wanted to extradite him for his supposed war crimes. He felt his life was in danger. He gave concerts in England that autumn, then, in December, he and Ilona went to Beaulieu-sur-Mer, France. Food was expensive and scarce. He signed a contract for concerts in Buenos Aires, Argentina, and, on 10 March 1948, Dohnányi and Ilona, with her children, left Europe forever. They arrived in Buenos Aires on 4 April 1948. The concerts were successful, but the false rumors resurfaced, making it difficult to book more. Furthermore, the humidity affected Dohnányi both mentally and physically. His arm swelled for several days after performances.

In August Dohnányi was asked to be general director of the Universidad Nacional de Tucumán's new music school. On 8 September 1948 he arrived in Tucumán. He established a faculty and orchestra. However, all plans had to be approved by the dean of the Faculty of Culture and Art, who proved slow to respond. In November Dohnányi gave concerts in New York, and on 17 February 1949 he and Ilona were married there. They returned to Buenos Aires to find that construction had not started, salaries were unpaid, housing was unsatisfactory, and there were constant disagreements with the dean. When Karl Kuersteiner, dean of the School of Music at Florida State University in Tallahassee, asked Dohnányi to become a professor of piano and composition starting in the fall of 1949, he accepted. There he had a spacious house with a nice garden, and only had to teach six hours a week. However, again he was falsely accused of being a Nazi sympathizer. Concerts were canceled and he was blacklisted in the musical community. He received help from the American Civil Liberties Union, but the case dragged on for months. For diplomatic reasons, on 1 June 1950 Dohnányi went to the United States Consulate in Havana, Cuba, to apply for a nonquota visa. Later, each family member had to endure the same time-consuming and expensive process.

Well into his seventies, Dohnányi traveled throughout the United States teaching, conducting, and giving concerts. Critics were awed by his masterful undiminished technique. Each summer he taught classes at Ohio University, where he received an honorary doctorate in 1954. He also taught and performed in other venues throughout the United States. In 1955 Dohnányi and Ilona became American citizens. During May 1957 Dohnányi and Edward Kilenyi went to Pittsburgh, where they made a series of four television tapes for the "Heritage" series produced by Fred Rogers. Dohnányi was awarded an honorary doctor of Music degree on 1 June 1957 by Florida State University.

In January 1960, Dohnányi and Ilona went to New York for recording sessions. He finished on 5 February, but while there he contracted influenza, suffered two heart attacks, and died. He was buried on 13 February in Tallahassee's Roselawn Cemetery. In 1968, Dohnányi's name was finally removed from the Eastern European blacklist. In 1990, he was posthumously awarded the Kossuth Prize, the highest award a Hungarian citizen can receive. A performing arts high school in Hungary and a street adjacent to the Liszt Academy have been named in his honor.

Throughout his life, he was known as a creative and somewhat unique teacher with definite opinions. For instance, when teaching piano, Dohnányi maintained that how one practiced was more important than how much—that too much technical practice was a waste of time. Sight-reading, however, was essential; so were transposition, improvisation, and scales. He also advised practicing in the dark to gain a thorough knowledge of the keyboard. When ready to perform, one should sit a few moments at the piano, wait for silence, then play.

Dohnányi was regarded as a "last Romantic" because his birth dovetailed with the end of this musical era, while his schooling and compositional style expressed it. His compositions explored many genres including purely symphonic music, choral works, opera, and ballet and nationalistic music—primarily Hungarian.

• More information about Dohnányi can be found in his own *Message to Posterity from Ernst von Dohnányi*, translated from Hungarian by Ilona von Dohnányi, Mary F. Parmenter, ed., (1960). According to the introduction, "This book is made up of a series of meditations uttered by . . . Ernst von Dohnányi during the final period of his life. . . ." His wife, Ilona, expressed her perspective on his life in *Ernst von Dohnányi: A Song of Life* (2002). The most prolific biographer of Dohnányi is James A. Grymes. His most notable book, *Ernst von Dohnányi: A Bio-Bibliography* (2001), includes four sections: a brief biography, a list of works, a discography, and an annotated bibliography. See also Marion Ursula Rueth, "The Tallahassee Years of Ernst von Doh-

nányi" (master's thesis, Florida State University, 1962). An obituary appears in the *New York Times*, 11 Feb. 1960.

JEAN SANDERS

DORRIS, Michael (30 Jan. 1945–11 Apr. 1997), writer and academician, was born Michael Anthony Dorris in Louisville, Kentucky, the son of Jim Leonard Dorris, a soldier, and Mary Burkhardt Dorris. Jim Dorris was killed in the late stages of World War II or shortly after the war, depending on the source consulted. As a result, Dorris was raised by his mother, aunt, and two grandmothers. As a youngster, Dorris read voraciously, borrowing books from adults and spending time in libraries. Following high school, he enrolled at Georgetown University, the first member of his family to attend college. He earned a B.A. degree (cum laude) in 1967 and an M.Phil. from Yale University in 1970. He was a successful academician, holding faculty appointments at the University of Redlands (1970–1971), Franconia College (1971–1972), and Dartmouth College (1972–1989, adjunct 1989–1997). While at Dartmouth, he founded and taught in the Native American Studies Program. Dorris's ancestry has been described as mixed Irish, French, and Native American, with the latter more specifically identified as "Modoc on his father's side."

He was a prolific writer, producing works in a variety of genres for audiences ranging from young adults to literary scholars, historians, educators, and physicians. Over the course of his writing career, Dorris contributed to what Kenneth Lincoln, noted poet and scholar of American Indian literatures and cultures on the faculty of the UCLA English department, termed the "Native American Renaissance," an outpouring of literary work by contemporary American-Indian authors, starting with N. Scott Momaday's Pulitzer Prize–winning novel *House Made of Dawn* (1968).

In 1971, acting on a desire "as clear and basic to [him] as instinct, and as undeniable and undissectable" (*The Broken Cord*, p. 6), Dorris adopted a Sioux infant, becoming possibly one of the first single males in the United States to adopt a child. He adopted two more American-Indian children in the mid-1970s.

In 1981, Dorris married Louise Erdrich, acclaimed poet, novelist, and former student of his in the Dartmouth Native American Studies Program. Together, the couple raised a blended family of Dorris's adopted children and three biological daughters. Their marriage was storied in literary circles. Erdrich dedicated her first novel, *Love Medicine* (1984), to Dorris, stating, "[To] Michael Dorris, who gave his own ideas, experiences, and devoted attention to the writing. This book is dedicated to him because he is so much a part of it." Dorris, in turn, dedicated his first novel, *A Yellow Raft in Blue Water* (1987), to Erdrich: "FOR LOUISE / Companion through every page, Through every day / Compeer." Dorris and Erdrich edited each other's work and in 1991 cowrote a novel, *The Crown of Columbus*, and a work of nonfiction, *Route Two and*

Back. The couple worked together on all their literary projects. In a 1990 interview with Laura Coltelli, they described their collaborative approach to composition: "We edit it together. We go over every word and achieve consensus on every word; basically, we agree on every word when it's finally finished (Coltelli, p. 50).

A Yellow Raft in Blue Water achieved critical notoriety. Set in Seattle and on a western Montana Indian reservation and focusing on a range of issues from family to spirituality, heritage to concealed paternity, the novel portrays the complex interrelationship of three characters—fifteen-year-old Rayona, her mother Christine, and Aunt Ida (believed to be Christine's mother and Rayona's grandmother). Told through the interwoven perspectives (braiding is a recurring motif) of these three characters, the novel established characteristics of Dorris's subsequent work. It featured nonlinear plot lines, incremental revelation of character through external points of view, and a credible female voice, which he attributed to the influence of the women who raised him. Thematically, the novel focused on issues of identity, specifically evidenced in characters of mixed-race heritage. Dorris's work broached the issue through mixed-blood American-Indian characters as well as characters of mixed African-American and American-Indian ancestry, particularly Rayona, the protagonist of *A Yellow Raft in Blue Water*, who reappeared in his posthumously published young adult novel *The Window* (1997).

Dorris's most widely acclaimed work, earning for him the National Book Award, was *The Broken Cord* (1989), a nonfictional, scholarly, and (at times) painfully personal examination of fetal alcohol syndrome (FAS). In it Dorris described the devastating impact of FAS by revealing its effects on his own adopted son, detailing the developmental, social, emotional, and academic difficulties the child faced. The book is honest; its language blunt, but vivid, as in this passage describing his son's birth:

> From what I've learned from the sum of gathered profiles divided by the tragedy of each case, the delivery of my premature son was unlikely to have been a joyous occasion. Most fetal alcohol babies emerge not in a tide, the facsimile of saline, primordial, life-granting sea, but instead enter this world tainted with stale wine. Their amniotic fluid literally reeks of Thunderbird or Ripple, and the whole operating theater stinks like the scene of a three-day party. Delivery room staff who have been witness time and again tell of undernourished babies thrown into delirium tremens when the cord that brought sustenance poison is severed. Nurses close their eyes at the memory. An infant with the shakes, as cold turkey as a raving derelict deprived of the next fix, is hard to forget. (p. 261)

The work's impact was far-reaching. In addition to its adaptation on film for television, the work sparked congressional hearings on FAS which eventually led to new alcoholic beverage labeling laws.

A less noted aspect of Dorris's work is his writing for young adults. Dorris published three young adult novels—*Morning Girl* (1992), *Guests* (1994), and *Sees Behind Trees* (1996), in addition to *The Window*. Dorris's young adult works, like his adult novels, deal with the theme of identity, but they also delve into family issues such as sibling rivalry and intergenerational understanding, as well as contrasting world views of American Indians and non-Indians. By setting the first three works in the historical past, Dorris helped young readers formulate nonstereotypical views of American-Indian life in the "pre-contact" and colonial periods, while *The Window* addresses the theme of mixed-race identity in contemporary times.

In 1995 a life that on the surface appeared wonderful began to unravel. Dorris's storied marriage was in trouble, and the two separated; in 1996, they divorced. Isolated from his children and estranged from the woman he was, as Ruth Coughlin described, "addicted to" (Streitfeld, F4), Dorris suffered from sleep deprivation and deep depression. In addition to the demise of his marriage and separation from his children, charges of child abuse impended. Two of his adopted children accused Dorris of physical and sexual abuse. Though he vehemently denied the charges, Dorris seemed resigned to the notion that the accusations and resulting trials would destroy him. As he emailed a friend, "My only possibility for a life is to win a vicious trial—by demolishing my wife and children. It is worse than I imagined" (Streitfeld, F5). Dorris first attempted suicide in March 1997. On 11 April 1997, he succeeded in taking his own life in a Concord, New Hampshire, hotel room. News of his death shocked the literary and academic worlds. Those who read his work and marveled at its range were unaware of his inner torment, impending humiliation, and the depths of despair brought on by the dissolution of his marriage and family. Erdrich's response to Dorris's death and to the charges of sexual abuse calmed a frenzied press. "It was always intended to be a private, family matter. I don't believe in trying a man in the press after he is dead and judging him guilty or innocent" (Walker, p. 6). Further, she added, "He deserves, in his death, some self-respect and dignity" (Lyman, A14).

Through his work, which included essays directed toward improving the presentation of the American-Indian experience by teachers in P-12 school curricula, Dorris sought to inform the public and eradicate stereotypes of American Indians by conveying the fundamental humanity and spirituality of supposed godless savages, the humor of supposed stoic peoples, and the great civilizations of the supposed uncivilized "pre-Columbian" peoples of North America.

• Interviews are especially helpful sources of information on Dorris, including those he did with Allan Chavkin and Nancy Feyl Chavkin (*Conversations with Louise Erdrich and Michael Dorris* [1994]), with Bill Moyers as part of his *World of Ideas Anthology Collection* video recording (1994), and with Laura Coltelli (*Winged Words: Interviews with American Indian Writers* [1990]). Dorris's major works, besides those mentioned in the text, include *Working Men* (1993), *Rooms in the House of Stone* (1993), *Paper Trail: Essays* (1994), and *Cloud Chamber: A Novel* (1997). An explication of Dorris's young adult novels appears in Jim Charles, "The Young Adult Novels of Michael Dorris," *The ALAN Review* 25:3 (Spring 1993). Detailed accounts of the circumstances surrounding Dorris's death include Rick Lyman, "Writer's Death Brings Plea for Respect, Not Sensation," *New York Times*, 18 Apr. 1997; David Streitfeld, "Sad Story: Novelist Michael Dorris Couldn't Come Up with a More Compelling Plot," *Washington Post*, 13 July 1997, and Martin Walker, "Inside Story: Broken Cords," *Guardian*, 22 Apr. 1997. Obituaries are in the *New York Times*, 15 and 16 Apr. 1997.

JIM CHARLES

DRUCKMAN, Jacob (26 June 1928–24 May 1996), composer, was born Jacob Raphael Druckman in Philadelphia, the son of Samuel Druckman, a manufacturer and amateur musician, and Miriam Golder Druckman. He began piano lessons at age three, violin at six, and later also played trumpet in jazz ensembles. At ten, he began studying harmony and counterpoint with Louis Gesensway, a local composer and concertmaster of the Philadelphia Orchestra; he also studied with Renée Longy of the Curtis Institute. He began composing at twelve.

In 1949 Aaron Copland invited Druckman to join his summer composition class at Tanglewood. (Copland would prove a helpful mentor to Druckman in later years.) Druckman entered the Juilliard School that year and studied with Bernard Wagenaar, Vincent Persichetti, and Peter Mennin. In 1954 he married Muriel Helen Topaz, a dancer and dance educator. They had a daughter and a son, Daniel, who became a musician and performed with the New York Philharmonic as associate principal percussionist.

In 1954–1955 Druckman studied with Tony Aubin at the École Normale de Musique in Paris; in 1956 he graduated from Juilliard with a master's degree. The following year, he joined the faculty of Juilliard, where he taught for fifteen years.

Druckman's works of the 1950s bear the stamp of his admiration for the music of Claude Debussy and Igor Stravinsky in particular. As time went on, he turned toward the newer compositional procedures of his day. *Dark upon the Harp* (1962), a setting of psalm texts for soprano and brass quintet, exemplifies Druckman's skill in wresting expressive power from an atonal musical language. Later in the 1960s, he investigated the electronic medium, which he found compelling for what it revealed by contrast about the qualities of human performance. He created notable pieces such as *Animus I–IV* (1966–1977), in which live soloists interact dramatically with synthesized and electronically manipulated sounds on prerecorded tape. From 1961 to 1967 he taught at Bard College as well as Juilliard.

Well known by 1970 as a composer of chamber music, Druckman made a breakthrough with *Windows*, his first work for large orchestra, commissioned by the Serge Koussevitzky Music Foundation. Its score allowed the conductor and the ensemble some freedom in determining the content of the performance. "The conductor has the capability of casting off groups of instruments—or individual instruments—doing repetitive phrases and of changing some or all of these with a given signal," Druckman explained. "This procedure is rather like a bunch of geese being driven down a road. . . . you know approximately what they're going to do, but you don't know which goose is going to be honking at which given point" (Gagne and Caras, p. 157). *Windows* also incorporated brief passages suggesting fragments of older musical forms such as chorales and waltzes; Druckman described these episodes as "memories of memories."

Windows won a Pulitzer Prize in 1972, and Druckman went on to write a number of well-received pieces for orchestra, always distinguished by a focus on instrumental color, which he said was as "intrinsic and structural" to his music as the sonata allegro form was to Mozart. Not all listeners agreed that the quality of sound itself could hold substantial compositions together; one critic characterized his music as "heavy in short-breathed utterances" (James R. Oestreich, "A Drummer Joins a Tribute to His Composer Father," *New York Times*, 26 May 1997). Indeed, Druckman often seemed determined to forgo not only an obvious large-scale structure but also the local cohesion that a continuous melody might provide. Still, his music was most often described as "exciting," "entertaining," or even "springy with vitality and passion" (Paul Griffiths, "From Druckman's Scores, a Celebratory Sampling," *New York Times*, 14 Apr. 2000).

Besides *Windows*, noteworthy compositions from this phase of Druckman's career included his viola concerto (1978), a gripping work in which, he wrote, "the beautiful but slightly veiled voice of the viola is surrounded by the terrible power of the full orchestra." *Aureole* (1979), commissioned by Leonard Bernstein and the New York Philharmonic, paid homage to Bernstein by incorporating a melody from the older composer's third symphony and also evoked Stravinsky's *Rite of Spring*, both in particular phrases and in the skillful buildup and release of tension over time. *Brangle* (1989) was a brilliant elaboration of dance rhythms in three movements, its title referring to the Renaissance dance called *branle* in French. *Counterpoise* (1994) for soprano and orchestra set contrasting texts by Emily Dickinson and Guillaume Apollinaire, who inhabited worlds so different that Druckman imagined them as "airborne" and "almost subterranean," respectively. In parallel with these major orchestral works, Druckman continued to produce significant music for chamber ensembles.

From 1972 to 1976, Druckman taught at Brooklyn College. In 1976, he became professor of composition, chair of the composition department, and director of the electronic music studio at the Yale University School of Music, positions he retained for the rest of his life.

Druckman was appointed conductor in residence by the New York Philharmonic in 1982 and in that role organized a series of new-music festivals titled "Horizons." The festivals in 1983 and 1984 were devoted to the concept of a "New Romanticism," by which Druckman meant to acknowledge, and endorse, what he perceived as a widespread change in composers' attitudes toward music. He wrote of this movement as being directed toward the "sensual, mysterious, ecstatic," and away from the "feeling that it was necessary . . . to start from scratch and have absolutely nothing to do with the past." The highly influential programs included works by composers such as David Del Tredici and John Adams, who explicitly rejected "classic" modernism and instead embraced tonality and rhythmic simplicity. However, Druckman's vision of "New Romanticism" also included less easily accessible music by figures such as Toru Takemitsu and Iannis Xenakis.

The leadership Druckman exercised through the Horizons Festivals was of a piece with his influence as a teacher and as a director of musical philanthropy (he was named president of the Koussevitzky Foundation in 1980 and the Aaron Copland Fund for Music in 1991). Druckman's students who went on to become distinguished composers included Aaron Jay Kernis, Michael Torke, and Anthony Davis. Of his mentor, Davis said, "He had a lofty spirit, and because of this, I believe he provided a clear path, not only for me, but for so many other composers to flourish." Druckman died in New Haven.

• Druckman's music manuscripts and other papers are held by the New York Public Library for the Performing Arts. Issued by Druckman's principal publisher, Boosey & Hawkes, *Jacob Druckman: A Complete Catalogue of His Works* (1981), is a helpful guide to the first three decades of his output and includes a biographical sketch. A 1975 interview with Druckman is in Cole Gagne and Tracy Caras, *Soundpieces: Interviews with American Composers* (1982), pp. 154–62; additional interview material is held at the Yale University Music Oral History Archive. Austin Clarkson's article "Druckman, Jacob Raphael" in the *New Grove Dictionary of Music*, 2d ed. (2000), is a useful overview. Several of Druckman's works are described in Andrew Porter, *Music of Three Seasons* (1978). An informative obituary by Anthony Tommasini is in the *New York Times*, 27 May 1996.

JONATHAN WIENER

DUMM, Edwina (21 July 1893–28 Apr. 1990), cartoonist, known as "Edwina," was born Frances Edwina Dumm in Upper Sandusky, Ohio, the daughter of Frank Edwin Dumm, an actor, playwright, and newspaperman who had left a career in the theater in New York to look after his father's newspaper business. Her mother's name is unknown. When Edwina was about eleven, her father sold the newspaper and went to Marion, Ohio, where he worked on Warren G. Harding's *Star* for a year before moving to Columbus, Ohio. Edwina had decided upon a career in art while still in grade school and chose newspaper cartooning, she once said, "because there were a lot more newspapers in Ohio than art galleries." She sought to improve her drawing skill with the Landon correspondence course but also took business classes in high school; after graduation she worked as a stenographer for the board of education.

In 1915, Dumm became the staff artist for a fledgling weekly newspaper, the *Columbus Monitor* (sometimes termed the *Saturday Monitor*). Beginning with the first issue on 7 August, she drew illustrations, political portraits, a full page of cartoon reportage and comment called "Spot-Light Sketches," and an editorial cartoon (although she didn't start signing her editorial cartoons until 27 November). When the *Monitor* went to daily publication in July 1916, she did likewise with her editorial cartoon, becoming, before women could vote, the only woman in the nation employed as a graphic political commentator on a daily basis. She did cartoons on the usual array of topics—from local, national, and international events to the weather and suffrage. Throughout her *Monitor* tenure, she also sometimes did a comic strip about a young tomboy and her dog, *The Meanderings of Minnie*.

The *Monitor* ceased publication on 5 July 1917, and Edwina left Columbus that fall. She had realized long before that the most substantial careers in cartooning were launched from New York, and she had diligently saved enough money to stake herself to a year's trial there. She had also regularly sent samples of her work to the George Matthew Adams syndicate and had been encouraged by Adams, who liked her dogs. On arrival in New York, Edwina went to see Adams, who invited her to do a comic strip about a boy and his dog. By 1918, *Cap Stubbs* was being distributed nationally, six days a week (no Sunday), and within six months its circulation was enough to give Edwina a living.

One of the longest-running and truest-to-life of the comic strips about boyhood, Edwina's strip was based upon her recollections of her own childhood as a shy tomboy in Upper Sandusky, a small town where everybody knew everything about everybody, and all the kids (including Edwina and her brother) played together, trooping jubilantly through streets and yards and across the surrounding countryside in their play, daydreaming wistfully at their desks while in school. *Cap Stubbs* offered a joke every day but sometimes told a continuing story for a few weeks at a time—no punch lines, no cliff-hangers, only gentle "down home" humor about such boyish pursuits as playing baseball or make-believe army, splashing around in the old swimming hole, sharing a bag of candy from the corner grocery store, building a raft or tree house, running a lemonade stand, and so on. But mostly there was no plot—just a boy being a boy, a dog a dog, and a grandmother Gran'ma. Cap was a regular backyard boy, persistent in his pleas for parental permission, creative in concocting excuses for his mistakes, thoughtful after the fact, eager to avoid the company of the neighborhood girl he secretly admired, everlastingly and irrepressibly energetic and imaginative.

Tippie was an authentic dog, Cap's constant cohort, all over the place always, tongue sticking out, tail wagging, ears cocked, his wet, cold nose into everything. And Gran'ma—Sally Bailey, who lived with her daughter Mary and son-in-law Milton Stubbs—was perhaps the most acute characterization in Edwina's gallery of penetrating portraits, the untitled star of the strip. A dumpy, dimply old lady with her hair in a bun and her apron tied high over a rotund tummy, Gran'ma looked as comfortable as a well-sat-in and therefore somewhat shapeless sofa. Perpetually astonished at the latest outrage Cap perpetrated in the absent-mindedness of some boyish activity (getting dirty while playing baseball, for instance), Gran'ma was always at the boy, scolding, nagging, fussing—and then passing out cookies or a slice of fresh-baked pie.

Shortly after settling in New York, Edwina continued her art education by enrolling in the Art Students League, where she studied for a time under George Bridgman. Edwina's New York sojourn, however, was interrupted when she contracted tuberculosis and to recover moved to New Canaan, Connecticut, where she maintained a summer home until World War II. She continued throughout her recuperation to produce her comic strip, sitting up in bed. Her mother came to help and moved permanently to New York when her husband died, while Edwina was in her twenties.

In addition to doing the strip, the cartoonist also did some freelance illustrating, and in 1928 her work attracted the attention of critic Alexander Woollcott, who asked her to illustrate his book about three dogs, *Two Gentlemen and a Lady.* Edwina's drawings were noted by some of Woollcott's cronies at the humor magazine *Life,* then in one of its final spasms of readjusting its editorial sights in order to survive. Edwina was asked to produce a weekly full-page comic strip about a frisky woolly-haired terrier, whom a readers' contest subsequently christened Sinbad. The dog was so lively and cute that Adams asked Edwina to replace the short-haired Tippie (who had been modeled on Buster Brown's dog, Tige) with a version of Sinbad, creating thereby a problem of pesky delicacy. The dog's change in appearance was a change in breed and could be accomplished only by writing Tippie out of the strip, not a development to be approached casually. Boys love their dogs, and vice versa, and the strip's readers valued that relationship in the strip. Edwina solved the daunting assignment ingeniously: Tippie got lost and then found by a crippled boy, who became so fond of the dog that when Cap at last discovered where his pet was and came to reclaim him, not even he could bear to part the bonded pair. And so, Cap acquired a new dog, a woolly-haired Tippie.

Throughout her long life (even after the strip ceased), Edwina drew for magazine articles and books as well as her strip. She also illustrated *Alec the Great,* a syndicated verse feature about a dog written by her brother, Robert Dennis Dumm (1931 to 1939 and again from 1947 to 1969). In the mid-1930s, in an unusual cross-syndicate maneuver, King Features persuaded Edwina to do a Sunday version of the strip; focusing on the dog, it was titled *Tippie,* and in 1935 the daily strip was retitled *Cap Stubbs and Tippie* in order to signal the relationship between the two. In the 1940s she illustrated several sheet music publications of songs written about Tippie by her roommate, Helen Thomas. The two also collaborated on an unpublished book, *Tippie's Circus Fantasy.* In 1951, Edwina was one of the first three female cartoonists admitted to membership in the National Cartoonists Society, until then a defiantly all-male organization. Edwina never married, maintaining that she had neither the domestic skills nor the interest for it. She died in her home in Manhattan.

Edwina's mature drawing style—relaxed and loose pen work, open and airy without being sketchy—was ideal for catching in mid-flight the energetic antics of boys and dogs (particularly a woolly-haired dog) who were constantly on the run, careening headlong down streets and alleys and across vacant lots in fevered pursuit of their latest fancy. The strip ceased as of 3 September 1966, but by then Edwina's fond evocation of her own turn-of-the-century tomboy childhood in small-town America had been stitched securely into the quiltwork of the national memory.

• Very little has been written about Edwina Dumm. In twenty annual editions of *Who's Who in America,* her name never appears; there is no public archive of her papers. The only extensive interview with her, "Edwina at 93," in *Nemo,* no. 25 (Apr. 1987), bubbles with her feisty personality. Her career as a political cartoonist is outlined and analyzed in "Edwina Dumm: Pioneer Woman Editorial Cartoonist, 1915–1917," by Lucy Shelton Caswell in *Journalism History,* 15, no. 1 (Spring 1988), and a short appreciation of her career and her own advice to beginning cartoonists appear in *Cartoonist PROfiles,* no. 38 (June 1978). Entries about Edwina appear in *The World Encyclopedia of Comics* (1999) and *The Encyclopedia of American Comics* (1990). The *New York Times* published a not very informative obituary, 2 May 1990.

ROBERT C. HARVEY

DUNN, Robert Ellis (28 Dec. 1928–5 July 1996), dance composition instructor and innovator, was born in Clinton, Oklahoma, to parents whose names are not known. From age six to nine, he studied tap dancing and toured his state with a tap-dancing troupe. At nine, he took piano lessons, and in high school he played in the band and the orchestra and sang in the glee club. He left home to pursue music composition and theory at the New England Conservatory in Boston. While earning his bachelor of music degree (which took him twelve years to complete), he indulged his passion for dance by attending ballet and later modern dance performances. Meanwhile, he became a repertory coach for singers at the Conservatory. One of his singers encouraged him to take a dance class at the Boston Conservatory of Music with a former student of Mary Wigman (founder of the German Expressionist school of dance). To help make a living, Dunn expanded his studies there to include choreography, ballet, modern dance, and other dance forms; he accompanied dance classes; and he taught percussion to dancers.

In 1958 Dunn began to play piano for Merce Cunningham's dance company, first in Boston, then at the American Dance Festival in New London, Connecticut, that summer. He married Judith Goldsmith, a Cunningham dancer, in 1958; they had no children and later divorced. At the festival, Martha Graham discovered Dunn and asked him to move to New York City to become her personal pianist. He agreed, though he continued to play for Cunningham. In addition, he played for many other important modern dance choreographers, such as José Limón, Helen Tamiris, and Pearl Lang. He met John Cage while working with Cunningham, eventually studying experimental composition with him at the New School for Social Research in New York. Cage, whose approach to sound, time, and performance greatly influenced Dunn, encouraged him to teach a choreography class, because, as Dunn put it, "things were really rather dull and monolithic in the field of modern dance, a lot of people were itching to do something much more experimental" (the *Post*, p.7). This class attracted choreographers, composers, and visual artists of all types; the group came to be known as the Judson Dance Theater. The avant-garde blending of artistic and philosophical voices of New York City at the time was clearly represented in his workshops. Encouraged by Dunn's drive for breaking boundaries in theater/dance production and stimulated by the growing rebellious fervor of the early 1960s, Dunn's choreographers challenged conventional dance aesthetics through their highly unique explorations of formalism, space, lighting, and sound. What resulted was the first postmodern dance concert, "A Concert of Dance #1," presented on 6 July 1962 at the Judson Memorial Church in New York City's Greenwich Village. As the audience entered the church, they were met with a film projection, which they were forced to cross. As the film ended, the lights came up to reveal six dancers already in motion. Twenty-three pieces were presented in an evening which evoked the charged, experimental concepts practiced in class. Dunn sought to generate an "anxiety [between] . . . dancer and choreographer, and later for the audience, without automatic and unconscious retreat to safer formulae" (Dunn quoted by Banes, p. 31).

Dunn taught almost passively but with a strong and inspiring force. In reaction to the strictness of most dance at the time, he suspended judgment in teaching in order to encourage simplicity and clarity of thought and concept. He wanted to move away from "technique" as it was understood. In a typical workshop, Dunn presented several structural assignments, mostly consisting of short sentences with two or three guidelines. There were no absolute rules. He thought that any and all movement, including nonmovement (stillness) and basic pedestrian positioning, was dance. He brought his interests in Zen Buddhism, the Bauhaus movement, and Taoism to make "a 'clearing,' a sort of 'space of nothing,' in which things could appear and grow in their own nature" (Dunn, *Contact Quarterly*, p. 1). He encouraged everyone to keep their perspectives open and to suspend judgment while trying new ideas, such as starting in darkness or finishing after the lights came on.

Although Dunn stopped teaching the course in 1962, the class, the concepts and the members' devotion continued. His students included Steve Paxton, Yvonne Rainer, Simone Forti, and Meredith Monk. He taught the workshop one last time in the summer of 1964. After ending the Judson workshops, Dunn moved on to teach choreography, improvisation, and movement analysis at a variety of institutions including Columbia University Teachers College, the University of Maryland at College Park, and the University of Wisconsin at Milwaukee. From 1965 to 1972 he was a member of the Congress on Research in Dance and first assistant curator at the Dance Collection at the New York Public Library for Performing Arts at Lincoln Center. In 1974 he married Gretchen Frentzel Benedict and became a stepfather to her two children; he and Gretchen had no children of their own. In 1985 he received a "Bessie" New York Dance and Performance Award. In 1988 he received the American Dance Guild Award. In 1993 the Laban/Bartaneiff Institute of Movement Studies in New York created a scholarship in his name. He died at his home in New Carrollton, Maryland.

• For an excellent in-depth account of the Judson Dance Theater, including many interviews with firsthand participants and observers, see Sally Banes, *Democracy's Body: Judson Dance Theater 1962–1964* (1983). For a beautiful collection of personal responses to those who studied or created with Dunn, see "The Legacy of Robert Dunn," *Movement Research Performance Journal* 14, ed. Wendy Perron. Dunn's excerpted journal entries can be found in *Contact Quarterly 14, no. 1* (Winter 1989): 10–13. For an interview with Dunn about his working methods and ideas, see Don McDonagh, *The Rise and Fall and Rise of Modern Dance* (1990), pp. 46–63. For a technical run-through of how Dunn created and taught his course, directions for his piece "Pivot/Delay," and an excerpted master's thesis on Dunn's pedagogy, see Danielle Bélec, "Improvisation and Choreography—the Teachings of Robert Ellis Dunn," in *Contact Quarterly* 22, no. 1 (Winter/Spring 1997): 42–51. To read about Dunn's thoughts and feelings in regard to teaching choreography, see Dunn's "Can Choreography Be Taught? (Apologies to Louis Horst)," in *Ballet Review* 4, no. 2 (1972): 15–18. For a thorough personal account of being Dunn's student, see Bernice Fisher, "Master Teacher Robert Ellis Dunn: Cultivating Creative Impulse," *Dance* magazine, Jan. 1984, pp. 84–86. Other articles include "Navigator on the Sea of Movement," *UWM Post* (University of Wisconsin Milwaukee) 27, no. 52, and Tom Strini, "Modern Dance's Real Father," *Milwaukee Journal*, 27 Nov. 1983. See also Jennifer Dunning's obituary, *New York Times*, 7 July 1996.

JADA SHAPIRO

DYER, Mary Marshall (7 Aug. 1780–13 Jan. 1867), anti-Shaker author, was born Mary Marshall in

Northumberland, New Hampshire, the daughter of Caleb Marshall, a farmer, and Zeruiah Harriman Marshall. Raised on the northern New England frontier, she had no formal schooling, though later in life she recalled proudly that she and nine of her eleven siblings became teachers.

In 1799 Mary married widower Joseph Dyer and settled in Stratford, New Hampshire, where their children Caleb, Betsey, and Orville were born, joining a son, Mancer, from Joseph's first marriage. In 1805, the Dyers moved north to Stewartstown, New Hampshire, where Jerrub and Joseph were born. Around 1809 the Dyers became Freewill Baptists. Two years later, they learned of the Shaker religion when an itinerant preacher shared a copy of the Shaker book *The Testimony of Christ's Second Appearing* (1810). Intrigued by Shaker philosophy, the Dyers visited the Enfield, New Hampshire, Shaker community. There they found a Protestant sectarian faith that espoused communal living, celibacy, and confession of sin. The Dyers learned that Shakers believed the Second Coming of Christ was at hand, not as a physical person but as a spirit dwelling within each individual believer. Joseph approved of the large, productive farms and Mary was attracted to the Shaker espousal of gender equality, the Shaker view of a god with both masculine and feminine elements, and especially the possibility of women becoming preachers. Believing they had found the path to salvation, the Dyers in 1813 converted and moved their entire family to the Enfield Shaker community.

At first the Dyers were quite satisfied. In 1814, they indentured their children to the Shakers. But while Joseph became even more attached to the Shaker life, Mary became disenchanted and in January 1815 announced her decision to leave the sect. The Shaker elders and Joseph consented to Mary's departure. But when Mary requested the return of her children, she was refused. Convinced that her children were in danger, Mary Dyer fled from the Shakers, hoping to find help in retrieving her children.

Mary built a network of family, friends and supporters to provide for her daily needs, help her obtain her children, and force her estranged husband to provide for her. But over the next two years numerous confrontations with Joseph failed to gain Mary her children or substantial financial support. She then turned to the New Hampshire legislature for help. In 1817 and 1818 she placed petitions before the legislature seeking a resolution to her unusual situation. Although there was much public sympathy for this distraught mother, the legislature refused to intervene in what they saw as private Shaker and family affairs. A savvy self-promoter, Dyer then turned to the printed word to argue her case, publishing five books between 1818 and 1852. Her first publication, *A Brief Statement of the Sufferings of Mary Dyer* (1818), gained enormous public attention. She argued that Shakerism broke families apart, forcing children to be raised without a mother's love and leaving nonbelieving wives without financial support. Stung by Mary's accusations, Joseph Dyer defended the Shakers and himself in *A Compendious Narrative* (1818). Mary Dyer's complaints traveled across the country. Ohio Shaker Richard McNemar responded to Dyer and anti-Shaker authors Eunice Chapman and James Smith in *The Other Side of the Question* (1819), in which he dismissed Dyer's problems as mere "domestic broils." In 1823 Dyer published her largest anti-Shaker work, *A Portraiture of Shakerism*, to which the Shakers responded with *A Review of Mary Dyer's Publication* (1824), to which Dyer then responded with *Reply to the Shakers' Statements* (1824). Dyer went on an extended speaking tour across New England, sold her books, appeared in court, and led a mob attack against the Enfield Shakers, arguing for what she called "the just rights of women." The response of the general public was mixed. Some agreed that Dyer's depiction of Shakerism was accurate; others called Dyer's accusations "horrid lies." While many former Shakers agreed with Dyer's claims, others did not. Shaker seceder and author C. C. Hodgdon included an anti-Dyer poem in his memoirs of life among the Shakers (1838).

Prompted by Dyer's situation of being married to, yet estranged from, a Shaker, the New Hampshire legislature amended that state's divorce law, allowing Dyer to file for divorce. In 1830, after a contentious battle, the Dyers divorced. Mary Dyer returned to her maiden name, bought a house in the town of Enfield, and watched her Shaker children grow to adulthood from a distance.

Dyer was pulled back into anti-Shaker activity when her youngest son, Joseph, died from unknown causes in 1840. Dyer blamed the Shakers' worship practices, which had been reinvigorated in an ecstatic revival known as the Era of Mother's Work (1837–1850). In 1847 Dyer published *The Rise and Progress of the Serpent*, restating her accusations against Shaker belief and practice. Dyer helped organize a legislative petition, signed by 498 people, against the New Hampshire Shakers. The legislature heard the complaints in late 1849 but took no action against the sect. In 1852 Dyer published her final work, *Shakerism Exposed*, and continued to travel across New England lecturing on the dangers of Shakerism.

Dyer remained in the town of Enfield until her death. Her former husband and four of her five children remained Shakers for life. Mary Dyer was the most persistent anti-Shaker author, the most publicly visible, and the one to whom the Shakers responded most vigorously. Dyer did not destroy Shakerism, but she forced the Shakers to articulate their beliefs and practices in public and in print. Dyer's books demonstrated the power of print to give underrepresented persons a voice in the nation. She gained enormous public attention because her complaints about her disrupted family touched a nerve in a period of rapid cultural and social change. She raised questions still relevant today about the rights and obligations of husbands and wives, the structure of the family, and the limits of religious freedom.

• Mary Marshall Dyer's major publications include *A Brief Statement of the Sufferings of Mary Dyer* (1818), *A Portraiture of Shakerism* (1822), *Reply to the Shakers' Statements* (1824), *The Rise and Progress of the Serpent* (1847), and *Shakerism Exposed* (1852). Joseph Dyer's response is found in *A Compendious Narrative* (1819 and 1826). Richard McNemar's *The Other Side of the Question* (1819) provides a Shaker response to the activities of several anti-Shakers, Dyer among them. Hodgdon's anti-Dyer poem is found in Charles C. Hodgdon, *Just Published, Hodgdon's Life and Manner of Living among the Shakers* (1838). Complete bibliographic information on Dyer's publications, including books and broadsides, can be found in Mary Richmond's *Shaker Literature* (1977), pp. 74–77. Shaker commentary on Dyer's life and activities runs throughout the correspondence in the Western Reserve Historical Society Shaker Collection (Cleveland, Ohio; on microfilm in many major research libraries). The Dyers' precedent-setting divorce case is recorded in *Dyer v. Dyer*, 5 N.H. 271 (1830). A scholarly study of Dyer's life is found in Elizabeth A. De Wolfe, *Shaking the Faith: Women, Family, and Mary Marshall Dyer's Anti-Shaker Campaign, 1815–1867* (2002). See also Jean M. Humez, "'A Woman Mighty to Pull You Down': Married Women's Rights and Female Anger in the Anti-Shaker Narratives of Eunice Chapman and Mary Marshall Dyer," *Journal of Women's History* 6 (Summer 1994): 90–110, and the discussion of Dyer's life as a "career apostate" in Lawrence Foster, *Religion and Sexuality: The Shakers, the Mormons, and the Oneida Community* (1984), pp. 51–54. Dyer's obituary is in the *Granite State Free Press*, 18 Jan. 1867.

ELIZABETH A. DE WOLFE

E

ECKBO, Garrett (28 Nov. 1910–14 May 2000), landscape architect, was born in Cooperstown, New York, the son of Axel Eckbo, a businessman, and Theodora Munn Eckbo. In 1912 the Eckbos moved to Chicago. Eckbo's parents divorced, and Garrett and his mother settled in Alameda, California, where the small family struggled financially. After completing high school in 1928, Eckbo spent six months living in Norway with a wealthy uncle, Eivind Eckbo, whose sumptuous lifestyle inspired the young man to return to the United States and seek a paying job. Eckbo worked half a year as a bank messenger for the American Trust Company in San Francisco, diligently saving his money for college. In 1932, after a year in Marin Junior College in Kentfield, California, he enrolled at the University of California, Berkeley. He thumbed through the course catalog and decided to pursue its landscape design curriculum mostly because he had always liked drawing and playing with plants in his home garden.

The Berkeley landscape program, which was part of the School of Agriculture, was then already four decades old. The university's grounds had been originally designed by Frederick Law Olmsted, one of the founders of landscape architecture, as a distinct discipline in the nineteenth century. At Berkeley, Eckbo was influenced by two recently hired faculty members, H. Leland Vaughan and Thomas Church, both of whom helped the young landscape designer move beyond the formalized beaux-arts style currently in vogue in the design world and characterized by careful planning and rich decoration stemming from classical architectural and artistic influences. Eckbo received his B.S. in landscape architecture in 1935 and landed his first job as a garden designer for the Armstrong Nurseries in Los Angeles. After a year, however, he became restless to expand his intellectual and artistic horizons and, through a competition, won a scholarship in 1936 to begin study at the Graduate School of Design at Harvard University.

At Harvard the former Bauhaus director Walter Gropius and his colleague Marcel Breuer exposed Eckbo to the ideas of the social role of architecture. The link between society and spatial design became the guiding principle for Eckbo throughout his lengthy career. His approach to design recognized the subtle interplay of space, human activity, the geometry of design, climate, and, of course, vegetation. In addition to the influence of European architects like Gropius, Eckbo was also receptive to the new compositional techniques of abstract painters, such as Wassily Kandinsky and László Moholy-Nagy, and in-

corporated some of their ideas into his landscape projects, for example, through the massing and layering of plants to convey a sense of movement similar to that shown by these abstract artists. While at Harvard, Eckbo also became close friends with two of his classmates, Dan Kiley and James Rose, who played prominent parts in the evolution of landscape architectural practice in the twentieth century. In a series of articles published in *Architectural Record* in 1939 and 1940, Eckbo, Kiley, and Rose called for a reconceptualization of landscape architecture as an artistic enterprise, which laid the theoretical groundwork for future design concepts. In 1937 Eckbo married Arline Williams, the sister of Edward Williams, a Berkeley classmate and future business partner. They had two daughters. The next year Eckbo earned his master of landscape architecture degree, and he and Arline headed back to California.

In 1939 Eckbo worked for the Farm Security Administration to improve the living environments of hundreds of migrant agricultural workers in California's Central Valley. With U.S. entry into World War II in 1941, Eckbo's focus shifted from housing farm workers to housing the thousands defense employees pouring into California to work in the munitions and aircraft manufacturing plants.

The end of World War II signaled a new era for architectural design in California as well as the rest of the country. The growth of suburbia required a different type of architectural design that reflected the need for low-maintenance gardens suited to a more leisure-oriented lifestyle. In 1945 Eckbo joined his brother-in-law and Robert Royston to create a landscape design firm, which soon became famous for designs that took advantage of the state's mild climate in creating an informal outdoor room reflecting the increasingly social role of the garden. Eckbo and his wife in 1946 moved to Los Angeles to establish a southern branch of the company. Eckbo's projects—which numbered in the hundreds—ranged from small gardens to college campuses, from urban plazas to subdivisions and town centers.

By the end of the decade Eckbo had produced an extensive body of work, and although he had already written a number of journal articles over the years, he was ready now to share his ideas and experiences with a larger audience. *Landscape for Living* (1950) was the distillation of more than a decade and a half of thought and work in landscape architecture and is considered a seminal book in the profession. Eckbo synthesized his reading in a number of disciplines, including psychology, sociology, architecture, what later became ecology, and even political philosophy, and presented a cogent argument that abstract concepts could find realization in innovative landscapes. Other books followed—*The Art of Home Landscaping* (1956), *Urban Landscape Design* (1964), *The Landscape We See* (1969), *Public Landscape* (1976), and *People in a Landscape* (1998)—but none equaled the sophistication and brilliance of the first.

In 1956 ALCOA Aluminum approached Eckbo to create a design using aluminum as its major feature. The Forecast Garden in ALCOA's Wonderland Park, which Eckbo completed in 1959, is often considered one of the most significant post–World War II landscape gardens. It makes creative use of aluminum, a rustproof and noncorrosive material, as an expandable mesh to provide shade and opaque dividers throughout the garden. Another well-known Eckbo contribution was the Open Spaces Master Plan for the University of New Mexico at Albuquerque, which occupied him between 1962 and 1978. For this project Eckbo designed a plan that closed many campus streets, providing peripheral parking and a comfortable and safe space for pedestrians.

In the early 1950s Eckbo began teaching occasionally in the landscape architecture programs at Berkeley and at the University of Southern California. In 1965 he left his private practice and became chair of the Department of Landscape Architecture at Berkeley, a position he held until 1969. In 1964 his design firm reorganized to include Francis Dean, Donald Austin, and Williams and was referred to as EDAW. In 1978 Eckbo became professor emeritus, and the next year he left EDAW to form a new firm, called Eckbo Kay Associates, with Kenneth Kay. In 1983 Eckbo scaled down his workload and established a smaller practice called Garrett Eckbo and Associates. He spent the remainder of his life writing, presenting lectures, and working as a consultant on various projects, focusing especially on environmental design. He died at his home in Oakland, California.

Eckbo's career spanned more than a half century, but throughout the decades he remained true to his vision of melding art and science to create an environment that was both functional and comfortable. His goal was to craft a landscape design that successfully balanced social, ecological, and qualitative standards to create an inviting place for contemporary urban life as it developed in the second half of the twentieth century. More than anyone else, Eckbo freed landscape design from the strict symmetry of Beaux-Arts formalism and replaced it with the functionalist freedom associated with twentieth-century art and architecture.

• Eckbo's papers are in the College of Environmental Design Archives, University of California, Berkeley. A collection of Eckbo's writings is in Mary A. Vance, *Garrett Eckbo: A Bibliography* (1980). Biographical accounts include Marc Treib and Dorothée Imbert, *Garrett Eckbo: Modern Landscapes for Living* (1997); Treib, "Looking Forward to Nature: An Appreciation of Garrett Eckbo, 1910–2000," *Landscape Architecture* 90 (Dec. 2000): 60–67, 88–90; and J. William Thompson, "Standard-Bearer of Modernism," *Landscape Architecture* 80 (Feb. 1990): 89–95. Two useful published interviews are Laurie Michael, Garrett Eckbo, and Karen Madsen, *An Interview with Garrett Eckbo: January 1981* (1981); and Eckbo and Suzanne B. Riess, *Landscape Architecture: The Profession in California, 1935–1940, and Telesis* (1993). An obituary is in the *New York Times*, 18 June 2000.

EDWARD A. GOEDEKEN

EDISON, Harry "Sweets" (10 Oct. 1915–27 July 1999), was born in Beaver Dam, Kentucky, to Wayne Edison and Katherine Meryl Borah Edison, whose occupations are not known. (There is some uncertainty regarding his birthplace; several published sources state he was born in Columbus, Ohio, but documentary evidence indicates otherwise.) Before Edison was old enough to attend school, his father, who is said to have been a Hopi or Zuni, left the family. Edison then moved with his mother to Columbus, where he went to school and learned to play the trumpet. When Edison was twelve he first heard his idol, Louis Armstrong, in person. At that point he decided to become a bandsman, and, while still a schoolboy, he was accepted into several local bands, culminating in stints with the St. Louis Jeter-Pillars band and, most importantly, Lucky Millinder's blues-oriented aggregation, which toured nationally. During a Millinder stand in New York, one of William "Count" Basie's trumpeters fell ill, and Edison stepped in. He stayed on for twelve years as a major component of that swinging outfit, which reached the top echelon of American dance bands.

The original Count Basie band, arising from Kansas City, was unique in its reliance on soloists and "head arrangements"—instrumental numbers evolved by the whole band but never written down. The band's specialties, which were hardly ever copied by other organizations, allowed soloists such as Edison to explore new ideas within a sympathetic context: the whole band listened, made necessary adjustments, and resumed the basic riffs when the soloist, having made his statement, sat down and the next one got up.

Edison had been with the Basie band for two or three months when its most illustrious soloist, tenor saxophone innovator Lester Young, started calling him "Sweetie Pie," largely for his ability to sound sweet and fresh while swinging outrageously. Basie shortened it to "Sweets" and the name stuck for the rest of Edison's life.

Although the Basie band, with its driving rhythm section (in later years generally regarded as the swing era's best), still toured until Basie's death in 1984, there was a break in 1950 when the Count abruptly decided to go small, briefly forming a sextet. Edison was on his own, but not for long. Now possessed of a style that had veered from the flamboyance of Armstrong toward a more clipped and often humorous one, Edison worked successively with the bands of tenor saxophonist Coleman Hawkins, drummer Buddy Rich, and the aggregation of soloists touring the nation under impresario Norman Granz's Jazz at the Philharmonic banner. (Edison played in the first

JATP concert in Los Angeles in 1944.) Later in the 1950s he turned up once more in Hollywood, where he lived most of the rest of his life.

A fair number of former big bandsmen and arrangers had already found refuge in the ad hoc groups formed to back star vocalists on recording sessions. These included Billy May (Glenn Miller) and Nelson Riddle (Tommy Dorsey), both at Capitol Records. Capitol signed up Edison, and when Frank Sinatra, then in his early years at Capitol, heard of it, he insisted that Riddle include Edison on Sinatra sessions. According to Peter Vacher's obituary of Edison in the (London) *Guardian*, Sinatra told Edison, "When you hear a hole, fill it." Edison later commented, "When a crack appeared, I just put in one of my twiddly bits." Edison's contributions, typically with a mute and usually only a few bars apiece, added to the richness of Sinatra albums such as "In the Wee Small Hours of the Morning" and "Songs for Swinging Lovers." The latter set is often the only album from the prerock era to be included in critics' and listeners' choices of the century's best.

Edison stayed with Sinatra for fourteen years and, because of Sinatra's interest in Warner Bros. films, worked regularly in the studio's orchestra. Like many other session musicians, Edison found congenial work in Los Angeles's small but innovative jazz clubs. He even managed one for a time. In 1963 he married Margaret Christine Rose Wylie, a Canadian. They had a daughter and divorced in 1981. From the mid-1960s Edison returned to his jazz roots, forming his own small groups and regularly reuniting with Basie, especially when the Count took his band to Europe. Recording regularly with European groups, Edison also cut some historic sides for Granz's Verve label, including a set with two of his idols, trumpeter Roy Eldridge and Lester Young, then seriously ill and making his last statement on record.

By the 1970s Edison had become an elder statesman of jazz. He liked to play in person or at recording sessions wearing a full-length mink coat and a velour hat. In 1983 Edison received a tribute from the Los Angeles Jazz Society, the first it had ever produced; the LAJS gave him another in 1992. In the midst of the 1990s revival of interest in the big band era, Edison received a Duke Ellington fellowship to Yale University, where he taught young musicians. In 1991 Edison received the title "Master Musician" at that year's Lincoln Center awards. Edison featured prominently in Ken Burns's Public Broadcasting System 1999 television series, "Jazz."

In 1998 Edison, in poor health, returned to Columbus, where he died. A symbol of his era in American popular music, Edison carved a unique presence within big bands of many types. He also showed other musicians from the big band era how to survive its demise.

• The best obituary of Edison is Peter Vacher, the *Guardian* (London), 29 July 1999. A letter to the author by Vacher was helpful. Two pieces by Max Jones, a chapter on Edison in *Talking Jazz* (1988) and an article in *Melody Maker* (British publication), 18 Apr. 1981, are useful. Edison's daughter contributed family details for this essay. There are various short obituaries and appreciations available on the Internet.

JAMES ROSS MOORE

EDWARDS, Leo (2 Sept. 1884–28 Sept. 1944), writer, was born Edward Edson Lee in Meriden, Illinois, the son of Eugene Henry Lee and Mary Emilia Cannon Lee. He reported that he never knew his father, who had evidently left home soon after Edwards's birth, and was brought up by his mother, who took in washing to support the family. He went to school in Utica, Illinois, until he was thirteen. Then he moved with his mother to Beloit, Wisconsin, where he went to work as an errand boy in a machine shop at fifty cents a day. A serious, diligent student, he earned high grades, especially in his English classes, and nurtured a dream of being a writer. As he advanced from "chaser" to toolmaker, he saved up to buy a typewriter and tried his hand at fiction, sometimes written on the back of wallpaper because he couldn't afford writing paper. For years, none of his efforts were accepted. In 1908 his first publication, "Only a Dog," a brief bathetic tale recounting the death of a stray dog, appeared in the *Beloit Daily News* and won a third prize of two dollars in a Christmas story contest. The same year he published the words and music of a romantic song, probably at his own expense. In 1909 he married Gladys Eveline Tuttle; the couple had one child.

In 1913, after more failed attempts to sell his stories, Edwards gave up hopes of a literary career and wrote advertising copy. He took a six-month correspondence course in the subject, talked his boss into transferring him to the advertising department of the machine shop, and soon rose to the position of assistant manager of the department, at a salary of $65 a month. In 1915 he took a job with the Burroughs Adding Machine Company in Detroit, where he became head of national advertising. During his two years with Burroughs, Edwards resumed his efforts at fiction, contributing numerous pieces to the company's house organ. By then he had discovered his vocation as a writer of stories for boys. He left Detroit for an advertising job in Shelby, Ohio, to renew his sense of small-town America, made friends with young people, and became active with the Boy Scouts. In 1920 he published "The Cruise of the Sally Ann" in the local newspaper, the *Daily Globe*. Combining mystery, action, and humor, the story featured four teenaged pals based on youthful friends in Shelby. The *Globe* promoted it and its author enthusiastically, and later that year Edwards expanded the story into a serial for *Boys Magazine*. Encouraged by his success, in 1921 he quit his job and returned to Beloit to become a full-time writer.

His stories sold well, and he became a regular contributor, still writing as Edward Edson Lee, to several juvenile publications. *Boys Magazine* paid him $275 for a five-part serial, "The Rose Colored Cat," in 1921. That same year he turned to his own experience in advertising and created a series for *The American Boy* about a seventeen-year-old who rises, as its author had done, from errand boy to advertising manager. Published in 1922 by D. Appleton as *Andy Blake in Advertising*, it had modest sales—only 1,467 copies were bound, and it was soon taken out of print—but it enabled him to approach Grosset & Dunlap with a proposal for a boys' series. In 1923 he received a contract and began reworking the serials he had published in *The American Boy* and *Boys Magazine* for book publication. It was at this point that he assumed the pen name Leo Edwards.

Thriftily making use of the stories, characters, and settings he had already created, Edwards began churning out novels with the same cast. From 1924 to 1940 he produced sixteen novels featuring the high-spirited, adventurous teenager Jerry Todd, and eleven focusing on Jerry's slightly more rustic chum Poppy Ott. In 1928 Grosset bought the rights to *Andy Blake in Advertising* and republished it as *Andy Blake* to begin a new series for older readers. Edwards varied his output from 1930 to 1933 with a series starring Trigger Berg, a nine-year-old who is barely distinguishable from Jerry and Poppy except that he lives in another town and has a different set of pals. Narrated like the others in the first person, the series identifies Trigger as younger only by such stylistic features as recurrent exclamations of "Whoopee!" in his diary. In 1931 and 1932 he reverted to the subject of his first publication with the adventures of a puppy named Tuffy Bean, targeting a still younger audience. The last three series all floundered after four books each, but the Jerry Todd and Poppy Ott books continued to sell well. The first, *Jerry Todd and the Whispering Mummy* (1924), sold more than 300,000 copies in its first six years, and in 1929 his *Jerry Todd and the Bob-Tailed Elephant* was Grosset & Dunlap's bestselling title. In the early 1930s he reportedly received more than 10,000 fan letters a year, and the fan club he initiated, the Secret and Mysterious Order of the Freckled Goldfish, claimed a membership of nearly 27,000 in 1935.

In *Poppy Ott and the Tittering Totem* (1929), Edwards introduced a column that he called "Our Chatter-Box," printing letters from his readers and replying with personal anecdotes about his life and work. The authenticity of this correspondence has been questioned—Arthur Prager, in his critical reappraisal of children's series *Rascals at Large* (1971), noted wryly that most of the fan letters "were written in a style very similar to the author's own, and read for all the world like jacket blurbs" (p. 252)—but there is no doubt that he had a warm personal relationship with his young readers. His home in Cambridge, Wisconsin, was open to fans of all ages, and his many visitors included fellow writers of boys' books Edgar Rice Burroughs and Edward Stratemeyer.

By the end of the 1930s, Edwards's simple, wholesome stories seemed dated, and his sales fell off. As his finances deteriorated, so did his personal life; he separated from his wife around 1940, and he ceased

writing. At the beginning of World War II, he was forced to look for work in a factory. He discovered that he had cancer in 1944 and moved to his son's home in Rockford, Illinois, where he died. The nostalgic appeal of his sunny tales long survived him, however. At the end of the century, his books were avidly collected, and aging fans maintained a flourishing Web page devoted to his life and work.

Edwards's characters were like neither Horatio Alger's ragged city urchins nor Stratemeyer's prosperous suburban adolescents; they were just average gullible children, and their popularity was due in large part to the modesty of their gifts and achievements. Their adventures, as narrated in both the Poppy Ott and the Jerry Todd series by Jerry, were almost plausible, and their language caught the cadence of real kids' speech. Clean-minded, honorable, but far from heroic, they were an only slightly idealized version of typical American boys of the early twentieth century.

Often stiff and awkward in his prose and with little claim to narrative skill—particularly in his last three or four books his plots tend to fall apart—Edwards had a gift for believable characterization and a boisterous sense of fun. Children of his time found his lively stories a refreshing change from the romanticized and sententious fiction that then dominated the field, and his rollicking adventures retain their freshness and vitality in spite of their naiveté.

• Much autobiographical information is included in the "Chatter-Box" feature appearing in Edwards's novels from *Poppy Ott and the Tittering Totem* (1929). Contemporary articles about Edwards include "'The Cruise of the Sally Ann,'" the [Shelby, Ohio] *Daily Globe*, 27 Mar. 1920; Trevor Taylor, "'Never Be Satisfied,' Says Edward E. Lee," *The Star Reporter* 1, May 1922; and Ted S. Holstein, "Ten Thousand Letters a Year from Youthful Admirers All Over the Nation," *Wisconsin Magazine*, Mar. 1931. Recollections by his son Eugene can be found in "Leo Edwards as Remembered by His Son Eugene 'Beanie' Lee," *Yellowback Library*, Nov./Dec. 1982; and Jim Sames, "Son of Children's Author Recalls 'Golden Days' of Father's Life," *Hernando* [Florida] *Times*, 11 Aug. 1985.

Little critical examination of Edwards's work has been published, but a somewhat ironic discussion of his novels is included in Arthur Prager, *Rascals at Large; or, The Clue in the Old Nostalgia* (1971), pp. 251–64. The man and his work are affectionately discussed in R. H. Gardner, "Catching Up with a Childhood Dream," *Milwaukee Journal*, 13 Oct. 1974, reprinted in *Authors in the News*, vol. 1 (1976), pp. 298–300. Extensive bibliographic data and biographical minutiae on Edwards, along with some of his early fiction, painstakingly culled from magazines and newspapers, are reprinted in Robert L. Johnson and Julius Robert Chenu, *The Tutter Bugle: The Book* (1988) from their bimonthly fan magazine *The Tutter Bugle* (1967–1971 and 1975–1976). Gary LaCom's introductory note "Our Chatter-Box" in his *Jerry Todd's Troubles in Doubles* (1996) contains some useful material about Edwards's working methods.

DENNIS WEPMAN

ENGEN, Donald Davenport (28 May 1924–13 July 1999), naval officer, test pilot, public servant, was born in Pomona, California, the son of Sydney M.

Engen, a stockbroker and later an Internal Revenue Service employee, and Dorothy Davenport Engen. Engen spent his childhood years in southern California, principally in Pasadena. When he was in fourth grade, he decided that he wanted to attend the U.S. Naval Academy in Annapolis, Maryland, and become a naval officer.

Graduating from high school at the age of sixteen, Engen for one year attended Pasadena Junior College to prepare for the Naval Academy entrance examinations. However, when the navy lowered the minimum age for pilots to eighteen, Engen seized the opportunity and on 9 June 1942 signed up as a seaman second class in the navy's V-5 program. He subsequently progressed rapidly through the pilot training program and was designated a naval aviator and commissioned ensign one year later, on 9 June 1943. On 23 September 1943, Engen married Mary Baker, whom he had met at Pasadena Junior College the previous year. They had four children.

Engen spent much of the remainder of World War II flying combat missions from aircraft carriers in the Pacific. On 25 October 1944, while flying an SB2C-3 dive bomber from the USS *Lexington* during the Battle of Leyte Gulf, Engen scored a direct hit on the Japanese carrier *Zuikaku*, an action for which he was awarded the Navy Cross.

Following the war, Engen left the navy for a brief period and flew with the Naval Air Reserve while exploring a number of career alternatives. However, his love for naval aviation was strong and he returned to active duty on 30 August 1946 as a lieutenant (j.g.). He continued a distinguished career that saw him rise to the grade of vice admiral and serve in three wars—World War II, Korea, and Vietnam. In Korea, Engen flew F9F-3 Panther jet fighters on strikes against enemy targets from June to November 1950. He attended the prestigious Empire Test Pilots School at Farnborough, England, in 1953, and became a nationally known test pilot, respected by designers, engineers, and pilots alike. Engen held five sea commands: Fighter Squadron 21 (1960–1961), Carrier Air Group 11 (1962–1963), ammunition ship USS *Mount Katmai* (rearming U.S. navy ships engaged in combat operations against North Vietnam, 1964–1965), aircraft carrier USS *America* (1966–1967), and Carrier Division 4 (1971–1973). Meanwhile, he earned a Bachelor of Science degree in business administration from George Washington University in 1968. At the time of his retirement in 1978 as a vice admiral, he was deputy commander-in-chief, U.S. Atlantic Command and U.S. Atlantic Fleet.

In retirement, Engen became general manager of Piper Aircraft Corporation plant in Lakeland, Florida, in charge of manufacturing cabin-class general aviation airplanes. He resigned on 1 April 1980 and moved with his wife to Alexandria, Virginia, where they lived for the rest of his life.

In June 1982, following a year with Ketron, Inc. selling war gaming services to the military, Engen was appointed by President Ronald Reagan to the National Transportation Safety Board, an independent agency responsible for investigating major national transportation disasters, including aviation. From April 1984 until July 1987, again at President Reagan's request, Engen served as administrator of the Federal Aviation Agency. His service was marked by his efforts to improve safety in civil aviation. He established the Office of Aviation Safety, ordered special inspections of airline safety practices, and issued a series of rules upgrading the safety of airline cabin interiors and combating the risk of in-flight fire. He was a strong advocate of airport development and pushed to advance the efficiency of the National Aerospace System by expanding the nation's Air Route Traffic Control Centers.

In 1987, Engen was appointed president and CEO of the Aircraft Owners and Pilots Association's Air Safety Foundation, a private, nonprofit organization dedicated to improving general aviation safety in the United States. During his tenure, Engen aggressively and successfully pursued a course designed to advance the cause of aviation safety and make the Air Safety Foundation financially independent.

After leaving the Air Safety Foundation in 1992, Engen did aviation consulting and teaching until 1995, when he was selected by the National Air and Space Museum (NASM) to be the Admiral DeWitt C. Ramsey Fellow of Naval Aviation History. In July 1996 he was selected to be the Director of NASM, in the aftermath of the controversy about the exhibition of the *Enola Gay*, the B-29 bomber that dropped the atomic bomb on Hiroshima in 1945. Engen devoted considerable time and effort to strengthening ties with civil and military aviation communities, as well as continuing the museum's extensive educational programs and exhibitions. His principal legacy to the museum was his deep personal commitment to the Udvar-Hazy Center, an exhibition and restoration facility built at the Washington Dulles International Airport.

Before his plans for the Dulles Center could come to fruition, in July 1999 Engen was killed in a tragic accident. While on vacation he was flying with his friend and longtime glider pilot William S. Ivans when the glider crashed near Minden, Nevada. Engen had been a pilot for fifty-seven years and had flown more than 7,500 hours in more than 260 types of aircraft. He was interred in Arlington National Cemetery with full military honors.

Engen's distinguished career spanned over fifty years in the military, the government, private industry, and nonprofit organizations. During his 36 years of naval service, he received 29 military decorations and awards, including the Navy Cross, the U.S. Navy's highest award for valor. Among his many civil and military awards were the Society of Experimental Test Pilots' Doolittle Award for Technical Management (1984); the National Achievement in Aviation Award from the Aero Club of Washington (1988); the National Aeronautics Association Elder Statesman of Aviation Award (1989); the Yuri Gagarin Gold Air and Space Medal (1992); and the Aero Club of New

England Godfrey Cabot Trophy (1997). He was also inducted into the Test Pilot Hall of Fame.

• Many details of Engen's personal and professional life can be found in his oral history, on file at the U.S. Naval Institute Oral History Collection, Annapolis, Maryland. Other oral histories in the collection provide rare insights into flight testing U.S. Navy aircraft, including those of Vice Admiral William P. Lawrence and Rear Admiral Edward L. Feightner. For a fascinating overview of the development of the navy's aviation capabilities during the latter half of the twentieth century, as well as the details of his first twenty-five years as a naval aviator, see his memoir *Wings and Warriors: My Life as a Naval Aviator* (1997). Works that address the Battle of Leyte Gulf and other major naval battles of the Pacific War include Samuel Eliot Morison, *The Two-Ocean War: A Short History of the United States Navy in the Second World War* (1963); Clark G. Reynolds, *The Fast Carriers: The Forging of an Air Navy* (1978); and E. T. Wooldridge, ed., *Carrier Warfare in the Pacific* (1993). Engen's obituary appeared in most major newspapers, including the *New York Times*, 15 July 1999.

E. T. WOOLDRIDGE

EWBANK, Weeb (6 May 1907–17 Nov. 1998), college and professional football coach, was born Wilbur Charles Ewbank in Richmond, Indiana, the son of Charles Ewbank, owner of a small chain of grocery stores, and Stella Dickerson Ewbank. As a youth, Ewbank made deliveries from a horse-drawn wagon for his father. At Richmond's Morton High School, Ewbank was a star player in football, basketball, and baseball and was named captain in all three sports his senior year. Ewbank acquired his nickname—Weeb—because his younger brother could not pronounce Wilbur. In 1924 Ewbank entered Miami University (Ohio), where he played quarterback and was captain of the baseball team. After graduating from Miami with a B.S. in physical education in 1928, Ewbank taught at Van Wert (Ohio) High School, where he was athletic director and coached all sports. In 1926 he married Lucy Massey, his high school sweetheart; they had three daughters.

In 1930, Ewbank returned to Miami University as a teacher in the college of education. He also coached several sports, including football, at McGuffey High School, a demonstration school run by the university. Ewbank received an M.A. degree in education from Columbia University in 1932. He enlisted in the navy in 1943 and became an assistant football coach under Paul Brown at the Great Lakes Naval Training Station. In 1946, Ewbank accepted a position as assistant football coach and head basketball coach at Brown University. The following year he was appointed head football coach at Washington University (St. Louis). In two seasons he led the Maroons to their best record in thirty years with fourteen wins and four losses, including a 9–1 record in 1948. Ewbank entered professional football in 1949 when he rejoined Paul Brown of the Cleveland Browns as a line coach. Like Brown, Ewbank believed in thorough organization, careful preparation, and an outstanding quarterback. During Ewbank's tenure with Cleveland (1949–

1953), the team won both an All-America Conference and a National Football League (NFL) championship.

In 1954 Ewbank became head coach of the NFL Baltimore Colts, a team that had won only three games the previous season. Although the Colts struggled for several seasons under his direction, Ewbank gradually built a first-rate organization and acquired talented players, including Alan Ameche, Raymond Berry, Lenny Moore, Art Donovan, Gino Marchetti, and Gene Lipscomb. The most important acquisition was quarterback Johnny Unitas, whom he recruited from a Pittsburgh sandlot team. In 1958, Unitas led the Colts to an NFL western division title. The 1958 NFL championship game between Baltimore and the New York Giants is often called "the greatest game ever played." Before a sellout crowd at Yankee Stadium and a national television audience (including millions who had never seen an NFL game before), the Colts defeated the Giants 23–17 in the first ever sudden-death overtime game. Many associate the game with the spectacular rise of pro football during the second half of the twentieth century. The following year the Colts repeated as NFL champions by again defeating the Giants 31–16.

Over the next three seasons, the Colts, aging and plagued by injuries, barely managed a .500 record. Baltimore owner Carroll Rosenbloom, who once called Ewbank "my crewcut IBM machine," fired him after the 1962 season (quoted in "Friends Honor Late Coach"). In 1963, David "Sonny" Werblin, who rescued the Titans, the New York American Football League (AFL) franchise, from bankruptcy, hired Ewbank as head coach and general manager at the suggestion of Rosenbloom. "I thought it was bad when I took over Baltimore," Ewbank recalled, "but we [New York] were no better than an expansion team that first year" (quoted in the Houston *Post*). Ewbank built a solid organization around the team, renamed the Jets, and acquired talented players through the college draft and free agency. The key addition was quarterback Joe Namath who was drafted in 1966 and signed a contract with the Jets for the then unheard of sum of $400,000. Ewbank, a conservative midwesterner, had numerous clashes with Namath, whose playboy lifestyle and carefree attitude earned him the nickname "Broadway Joe," but the two managed to coexist as the team became a contender in the AFL. In 1968, the Jets, led by Namath, won the AFL championship and faced the heavily favored NFL Baltimore Colts in Super Bowl III, one of the most memorable games in pro football history.

The NFL dominated the first two play-off games with the AFL (known later as the Super Bowl), and few people gave the upstart Jets much of a chance against the Colts. Interest in the game increased when a cocky Joe Namath boldly guaranteed a Jet victory in a statement to the media. "I really wished that Joe hadn't said that," Ewbank remembered. "Actually we all thought we would win—we just didn't want the Colts to know" (quoted in Pro Football Hall of Fame news release, 5 May 1978). In January 1969, Ewbank guided Namath and the Jets to a 16–7 victory over Baltimore in one of the greatest upsets in football history. Ewbank became the only coach to win championships in both the NFL and the AFL. He continued as coach and general manager of the Jets until his retirement in 1973. As a professional coach, Ewbank's record was 130–129–7.

Only 5 feet, 8 inches tall and heavyset, Ewbank did not look athletic, but he was an innovative coach in the tradition of Paul Brown. Ewbank maintained and utilized voluminous records on all aspects of the game, graded players on every play, and used classroom lectures. He was not a strict coach, but he earned a reputation for his thorough preparation and the understanding and realistic way he handled players. More than a dozen of Ewbank's former players and assistant coaches became head coaches in the NFL, including Raymond Berry, Don Shula, Chuck Knox, Walt Michaels, and Buddy Ryan. Ewbank was awarded an honorary doctorate degree by Miami University in 1960 and became a charter member of the Miami University Athletic Hall of Fame in 1969. He was inducted into the Pro Football Hall of Fame in 1978. Ewbank died in Oxford, Ohio.

• Materials relating to Ewbank's career are in the Pro Football Hall of Fame, Canton, Ohio. He wrote three books: *Weeb Ewbank's Pro Football Way to Physical Fitness* (1967); *Goal to Go* (1972); and *Football Greats* (1977). *Goal to Go* is helpful on his early coaching career. The following sources provide an overview of Ewbank's professional coaching career: "Pro Football Hall of Fame News Release," 5 May 1978; "Weeb Ewbank: The Man Who Propels," Houston *Post*, 23 Feb. 1969; "A Coach Looks Back on 20 Years," *New York Times*, 16 Dec. 1973; Larry Fox, "Ewbank Will Quit Coaching After '73," New York *Daily News*, 19 Dec. 1972. An obituary is in the Cincinnati *Post*, 18 Nov. 1998.

JOHN M. CARROLL

EXLEY, Frederick (28 Mar. 1929–17 June 1992), novelist, was born in Watertown, New York, the son of Earl Exley, a telephone lineman, and Charlotte Merkley Exley. His father, a local sports hero and a man of legendary toughness, figures crucially in the early pages of *A Fan's Notes: A Fictional Memoir* (1968), Exley's first and best book. It was from him, the son wrote in *A Fan's Notes*, that "I acquired this need to have my name whispered in reverential tones." For young Fred Exley, growing up in a city where every friendship started with the question "Earl Exley your father?" was emotionally wounding. Pride in his father competed with humiliation. His father died of cancer when Fred was sixteen, but a half century of bitter memories remained ahead of Fred.

Exley attended Watertown public schools but required a postgraduate year at John Jay High School in Katonah, New York, to qualify for college. At John Jay, which Exley called "the most productive year of my life," he briefly lived up to his father as an interscholastic all-star in basketball and a starter on the football team. He attended Hobart College for a year

as a predental student but transferred to the University of Southern California (USC), where he majored in English. He graduated in 1953. After his graduation and his father's death, Exley transferred his hero worship from Earl Exley to Frank Gifford, an All-American halfback at USC during Fred Exley's time there and the superstar running back of the New York Giants. Football and Gifford provided motifs for the one book on which Exley's reputation rests. Football gave Exley a feeling of being alive, "an island of directness in a world of circumspection."

To describe his subject in *Misfit: The Strange Life of Frederick Exley* (1997), Jonathan Yardley invented the term "Fredness." Among its characteristics were small-town insularity and an unmet mandate to succeed on its—Watertown's—terms, madness leading to three confinements in mental wards, dipsomania and a need to be onstage that could be fulfilled only in bars, a likely misogyny that was ratified by violent failures in two marriages, and above all a deep-seated sense of entitlement.

His litany of failures gave Exley a drifter's appeal (in both senses of the word). For a time Exley appeared to alternate brief confinements in places like Stony Lodge, a private mental institution in Westchester County, and Harlem Valley, a state hospital in Dutchess County (both in New York), with brief attempts to be a high school English teacher. Exley claimed, according to Yardley, that he taught high school English for a total of seven years in the Watertown area, but did not last long at any particular school. He regarded classrooms as asylums for the sane. One account in *Notes* is as unsparing of himself as of his students: "I knew then that I'd never be a teacher. [They] despised me, I loathed them, and we moved warily about each other, snarling."

Although he failed as a teacher, Exley often retreated to the world of books in the early 1950s and during the decade leading up to the publication of *A Fan's Notes* in 1968. In an unintentional parody of Jack Kerouac's *On the Road* (1957), Exley barely survived a drunken itinerancy that took him from Watertown to Chicago and back. Chicago in the 1950s, with its bar hopping and cocktail parties, proved his city of choice. Besides it was the free-style arena of his favorite fictive hero, Saul Bellow's Augie March. Other stopgap jobs, each lasting about three months, led to bibulous stays in Phoenix, Denver, and Miami. Finally his brother William Exley and family, who lived in Baltimore, took him in until they could take Fredness no more. Exley's mother, who had married again, rescued him in 1957 with a plane ticket to Watertown.

Exley's personal life destructed in tandem with his job performances. Less than a year after he returned to Watertown and the familiar stone house where his mother still lived, he entered Stony Lodge. There he met Francena Fritz, a social worker. By the fall of 1958 he had been discharged from Stony Lodge but signed himself back in at Harlem Valley. Harlem Valley, with its "chateau-like houses," pleased Exley. He was diagnosed paranoid schizophrenic and was subjected to electroshock therapy.

Fritz, "an attractive girl [who drove] a steel-gray Mercedes 190 SL convertible" according to *A Fan's Notes*, often visited Exley. Shortly after his discharge they were married on Halloween 1959. Francena was already three months pregnant when they married, and she soon gave birth to a daughter. The marriage, doomed from the start, ended in 1962 with a Mexican divorce, though Francena remained devoted to Exley to the end.

In 1967 Exley met Nancy Glenn, who was twenty years old and married. Exley was thirty-six. Working the switchboard of the yacht club her husband owned just north of Miami, Glenn could hear from the bar a stream of profanity issuing from a man everyone called "Ex." In Yardley's account, Glenn learned that this "obnoxious guy" had just been hired as a bookkeeper and that "he's writing a book." Yardley believes that it was because of this unfinished book, which became *A Fan's Notes*, that she fell in love. She left her husband and took a flat in Palm Beach Shores, where she and Exley became lovers. Glenn, ill and pregnant, followed Exley to Watertown, where they were married on 13 September 1967. Their daughter was born four months later. "She doesn't look a thing like me," Exley remarked. He showed little interest in mother or daughter. On 8 January 1971 a divorce order required the now-published author to pay $100 weekly for support. He never paid a cent, and within a year Glenn married again. Nevertheless a bond developed between the father and daughter that ended only with his death.

Neither Yardley nor anyone else can say how *Notes* came to be written. "The best source for the origins of *A Fan's Notes* is *A Fan's Notes*," Yardley avers. During his first stay in Harlem Valley in the early 1960s Exley came under the care of "Dr. K.," who arranged a private room where Exley could write. Glenn believed "he was sitting up in his room on a finished manuscript." In 1964 Lynn Nesbit, just out of college but already Donald Barthelme's agent, agreed to represent Exley. Harper and Row brought out *A Fan's Notes* in September 1968. Initially the book attracted no reviews, then in December 1968 Christopher Lehmann-Haupt of the *New York Times* lavishly praised it as "a singularly moving, entertaining, funny book," and Jack Kroll of *Newsweek* called it a "beautiful attempt to tell the truth whose authenticity is the measure of its truth-telling."

Though a critical triumph, the book was a modest seller. It won the William Faulkner Award for best first novel of 1968 and the Richard and Hilda Rosenthal Award from the National Institute of Arts and Letters. The novel was among the five finalists for the National Book Award for Fiction. By late 1969 Exley had received only $2,800 in royalties.

As Yardley accurately notes, Exley's second and third books were "afterthoughts, or footnotes, to his first." *Pages from a Cold Island* (1975) honors Edmund Wilson, who died at nearby Talcottville in 1972. The homage, the work's centerpiece, pales beside the tribute to Gifford in his first book. *Last Notes from Home* (1988), the final leg of Exley's autobiographical triangle, focuses on the death in Hawaii of Exley's older brother Colonel William Exley, a hero in three wars yet a casualty of cancer at age forty-six.

Despite being published by Random House with the imprimatur of Bob Loomis, its top editor, Exley's last two books were quickly remaindered. After his one great statement, Exley's art followed his life in swift decline. "No one was ever harder on Fred Exley than Fred Exley," wrote Yardley, and it is this terrifying honesty that gives *A Fan's Notes* the staying power the life lacked. D. H. Lawrence declared that writers shed their illnesses in books. This was surely true of Exley. *A Fan's Notes* makes Fredness interesting for all its perversity. For Yardley, Exley is "Huck Finn gone alcoholic, but still lighting out for the territory, putting as much distance as possible between himself and civilization." Exley died at Alexandria Bay, just outside Watertown, after a stroke.

• Exley's papers and manuscripts are at the University of Rochester. With an author whose three books draw so heavily on his own life, it is not surprising that biographical sources are scarce. Jonathan Yardley's *Misfit: The Strange Life of Frederick Exley* is a brilliant cultural inquiry but not a full-fledged biography. Despite errors in the dates of Exley's two marriages and divorces, Thomas Deegan's long entry in *Dictionary of Literary Biography*, vol. 143 (1981), provides a substantive critical account of the life. An obituary is in the *New York Times*, 18 June 1992.

RICHARD HAUER COSTA

F

FAHEY, John (28 Feb. 1939–22 Feb. 2001), solo acoustic guitar player, composer, and arranger, was born John Aloysius Fahey in Takoma Park, Maryland, the son of Aloysius Fahey and Jane Fahey, both federal bureaucrats. Fahey lived in a household where both parents played piano, and he was encouraged to take up an instrument. He chose the guitar.

Fahey graduated from high school and entered the University of Maryland as a philosophy major in 1956, then he transferred to American University in Washington, D.C., where he earned a B.A. degree. His activities centered on a growing interest in what he later termed "American primitive guitar" and described in a radio interview as "unschooled technique" (meaning improvisational technique of folk or ethnic rather than classical origin). It was a new fusion of folk, blues, and classical solo guitar.

In 1958 Fahey recorded a tape under the pseudonym of "Blind Joe Death," paid for with money he saved from a job as a gas station attendant (or by some accounts, borrowed from an Episcopal priest). He made a deal with RCA to press 100 copies of *Blind Joe Death*, which became the prototype of a new solo American guitar style, based in syncopated rhythm but with a classical guitar approach. One of the most critically successful debuts in folk history, it caused a stir owing to its then-radical departure from the guitar's traditional role as accompaniment to vocals. The album remained in print for decades after its release.

Fahey enrolled in the master's program at the University of California at Los Angeles (UCLA) in 1965 and completed his master's degree in 1967. His thesis was about Charlie Patton, a then-obscure artist who had been the prime source and inspiration for the Delta blues style that peaked with Robert Johnson. One of the earliest detailed studies of Patton, Fahey's thesis became widely known and was later included with a boxed set of Patton's recordings issued by Revenant Records. Fahey also was instrumental in the formation of the 1960s blues group Canned Heat, with whom he played until they moved on to an electric sound. During the mid-1960s Fahey and two friends, Henry Vestine (of Canned Heat) and Bill Barth, sought out and rediscovered the legendary bluesman Skip James, considered one of the great natural geniuses in American music. James had created a guitar and piano style that was radically different from the barrelhouse of the time, replacing its strong syncopated beat with a supple rhythm that was more implied than obvious, much like a modern jazz pianist. When his music surfaced in the discovery of old 78-rpm records, folk scholars were eager to find him. Af-

ter Fahey and his friends tracked him down, James made a sensational comeback at the Newport Folk Festival, though he never achieved lasting financial success.

In 1964 Fahey recorded *Death Chants, Breakdowns, and Military Waltzes*, the signal release of a new label he formed with Ed Denson called Takoma Records. Denson handled the business and promotional end, while Fahey recorded albums and handled the search for new talent. Among his discoveries were Robbie Basho and Leo Kottke, whose first record gave the fledgling label its first bona fide hit. Also Fahey produced a session by a young pianist named George Winston, who later became a popular New Age pianist.

In 1969 Fahey married Jan Lenbow; they had no children. That year he contributed a version of his composition "Dance of Death" to the soundtrack of *Zabriskie Point*. He cut short a budding career as a sound track composer by getting into near fisticuffs with the director, Michelangelo Antonioni. In the early 1970s Fahey recorded two albums for Reprise Records, *Rivers and Religion* and *After the Ball*. Critical reaction at the time was mixed, and the relationship ended when the records failed to sell well. By the end of the decade he had divorced his first wife, married and divorced a second, and sold his label to Chrysalis Records.

Fahey and his third wife Melody moved to Salem, Oregon, in 1981. He contracted Epstein Barr virus, which resulted in chronic fatigue. To make matters worse, he unknowingly had diabetes, exacerbated by heavy drinking. The records kept coming but were heard by a shrinking audience. In 1994 Rhino released *Return of the Repressed*, a retrospective compiled and annotated by Barry Hansen. The double CD set received considerable critical attention, and Fahey was the focus of renewed appreciation.

The success of the anthology encouraged a reissue program that featured remastered versions of his earliest work. This put Fahey in the frustrating situation of competing with his past, which most of his fans preferred to the more adventurous work of the late 1990s. Fahey reacted to the revival of his older music by recording a series of albums that sometimes puzzled or alienated his cult. In *City of Refuge, Womblife,* and *The Epiphany of Glen Jones* he explored fusions of abstract guitar work with found sounds or postindustrial noise and punk. Critical reaction was generally good, although audience reaction was mixed and sales were modest. In 1998 Fahey reconciled the divergent visions of his work in *Georgia Stomps, Atlanta Struts and Other Contemporary Dance Favorites*, a collection of improvisations in the old style but with a different sonic palette made possible by the electronic experiments.

Fahey died in Salem from complications following what was supposed to be a minor operation. His final work was the 2001 release *Hitomi*, a progressive work with an Asian feel. His final output included a volume of writings on a Chicago label, an involvement with another label, Revenant, which reissued classic works by Dock Boggs, and the previously unreleased fourth volume of Harry Smith's *Folk Anthology*. Fahey's death ended a life of achievements that put him on a par with other fingerpicking masters, such as Chet Atkins and Merle Travis.

• Ben Ratliff, "A 60's Original with a New Life on the Fringe," *New York Times*, 19 Jan. 1997, is an informative article. Much useful material on Fahey is available on various websites, including "Fare Forward Voyager," a "casually annotated" Fahey discography, at http://www.deltasnake. com/fahey/voyager1.htm; the "Folk Library Index for John Fahey," a compilation of links to all known Fahey resources, at http://www.folklib.net/index/f/fahey_john. shtml; and RollingStone.com's biography at http://www. rollingstone.com/artists/default.asp?oid 812. An obituary is in the *New York Times*, 25 Feb. 2001.

AL HANDA

FARKAS, Alexander S. (1930–28 July 1999), department store executive, was born Alexander Spencer Farkas in New York City, the son of George Farkas, department store owner, and Ruth Lewis Farkas, a sociologist and ambassador to Luxembourg.

Known as "Sandy" Farkas, he attended Choate and the Bronx High School of Science. He graduated in 1949 from the University of Chicago in three years with an A.B., then studied business at Cornell University. He loaded freight and worked in advertising, with a dream of becoming a college sociology professor. But in 1951 his father brought him into the family business.

George Farkas had founded Alexander's department store in 1928, naming it and his son after his own father. George's business strategy included offering housewares and fashions at cut-rate prices by eliminating free custom alterations and fancy décor, and by purchasing, rather than leasing, the land on which he built his stores. George Farkas's rigorous training program required that Sandy work in all departments except the cafeteria. Starting as head of stock in the women's coat department, Sandy joked that his main responsibility was carrying merchandise from rack to rack. He learned the business well and progressed quickly. In 1959 he was promoted to president and general merchandising manager, although his father remained chairman.

Sandy Farkas tried to make the store more fashionable and attractive by installing crystal chandeliers and arranging to be the exclusive outlet for the excess inventories of European fashion houses. While continuing his father's policies of "no credit, no charge accounts, no deliveries, and no alterations," Sandy sought to expand the business by opening new stores and moving the flagship store from Fordham Road and the Grand Concourse in the Bronx to Fifty-eighth Street and Lexington Avenue in Manhattan in 1963. In the mid-1960s, following an unseasonably warm winter that brought decreased sales, and chafing under his father's control as well as questioning his business decisions, Sandy Farkas quit Alexander's and went to work for a men's clothing manufacturer. Within a week, his father offered Sandy a written contract giving him control over the merchandise, and Sandy agreed to return. He once commented, "I'm probably the only son working in a family business who has a written contract, but it has made for harmony." By the 1960s, under Sandy Farkas's leadership, Alexander's had expanded to sixteen stores and generated annual sales of more than $500 million. One strategy he employed was to import merchandise of good quality from Eastern Europe and mainland China at considerably lower wholesale prices.

In 1968, to avoid a possible takeover by rival discounter Korvettes, George Farkas made Alexander's a public corporation and then retired at age sixty-six; he, his wife, and one of their sons soon sold their shares, while Sandy remained with the family store. The company faced stiff competition from discount retailer K-Mart and outlet centers. The stock attracted the attention of real estate developers who recognized the increasing value of the land for development that did not include the retail stores. A bad acquisition led to losses in 1980, and Sandy's two remaining stockholder brothers joined with the real estate development company to take control of Alexander's. Sandy Farkas once described the Alexander's buildings as "monuments to the family," and development schemes that would tear down the retail stores and replace them with high-rise office buildings affronted his sensibilities. A change in the makeup of the board of directors left Sandy as president and chief executive officer, but his younger brother Robin assumed control as chairman of the board. Sandy resigned in 1984. Under outside management, Alexander's spiraled into bankruptcy in 1992 when the last eleven stores were sold. Only by selling stores had the company earned any profits after 1987. Ironically, the stock prices increased significantly when investors realized the value of the real estate, and Alexander's continued to exist as a real estate company.

Farkas had one child with his first wife. After divorces from his first and second wives, whose names do not appear in readily available sources of information, Farkas, in 1963, married Francine Moss Glansrach, with whom he had three children. In 1977 he married Joan Foxwell. After their divorce, he married Linda Saltzman. Farkas died of cancer in Highland Park, Florida.

• Steven Levy, "Farkas vs. Farkas," *New York* magazine, 9 Feb. 1981, covers the decline of Alexander's. *New York Times* articles (27 May 1962, 22 July 1965, 11 June 1977) reveal limited information about his multiple marriages and divorces. An obituary is in the *New York Times*, 29 July 1999.

SUSAN HAMBURGER

FECHNER, Robert (22 Mar. 1876–31 Dec. 1939), labor union and New Deal official, was born in Chattanooga, Tennessee, the son of Charles Robert Fechner, a carriage trimmer, and Virginia Roberts Fechner. Fechner grew up in the Georgia towns of Macon and Griffin. He briefly attended the Georgia Institute of Technology in Atlanta, but he left school at the age of sixteen and apprenticed himself in the Augusta shops of the Georgia Railroad as a machinist. His training as a machinist lasted until 1896.

At the start of the Spanish-American War in the spring of 1898, Fechner enlisted as a private in Company E of the Second Georgia Volunteer Infantry. The Second Georgia trained for an invasion of Havana. However, with the capture of Santiago in July 1898 and the end of the war in August, Fechner's division never left the United States. Instead, it spent time in Huntsville, Alabama, before returning to Atlanta for deactivation that November. During 1898 Fechner also joined the International Association of Machinists (IAM).

Aside from serving in the Georgia State Guard, Fechner spent much of his early twenties working in Central and South America on coffee plantations, in mines, and at metal smelters as a journeyman, or boomer, machinist. Young machinists commonly traveled between employers to gain experience with the machining requirements of different industries.

In 1902 Fechner married Clare L. Dickey, the daughter of the railroad executive John Franklin Dickey. The Fechners had no children.

After his travels as a boomer machinist, Fechner returned to the United States in 1905 and took a job as a machinist for the Central of Georgia Railroad in Savannah. An active member of the International Association of Machinists in Georgia, he was elected general chairman of IAM District 49 in 1908. He also served as the secretary treasurer of the Georgia Federation of Labor from 1910 to 1916. Fechner became prominent within the IAM and in 1914 was elected to its executive board. He and his wife subsequently moved to Wollaston, Massachusetts, near Boston. Fechner became an IAM general vice president in 1925 and retained this position until his death, taking a leave of absence from 1933 to 1939. During his years as a union officer, Fechner became an adept negotiator, working to settle disputes across North America, including a machinists' strike against the Boston and Maine Railroad in 1917.

In March 1933 the newly inaugurated president Franklin Roosevelt announced that a conservation work program would be an important aspect of the poverty relief programs of his New Deal. This proposal aroused the ire of organized labor. President William Green of the American Federation of Labor asserted that the projected pay of $1 per day for conservation workers would depress the pay of workers in general. Green also opposed the program's proposed quasi-military camp structure. To placate labor,

Roosevelt nominated Fechner as the new agency's director. Roosevelt, while assistant secretary of the navy from 1913 to 1921, had negotiated with Fechner and the IAM during World War I and knew of Fechner's work to end the Boston and Maine strike. Fechner had also been instrumental in obtaining the IAM's endorsement of Roosevelt during the 1932 presidential campaign.

Fechner's blue-collar background set him apart from Harry Hopkins, Rexford Tugwell, Harold Ickes, and other prominent New Deal officials. Fechner, though he lectured on labor relations at several northeastern universities in the 1920s and 1930s, had much less formal education than most other New Deal leaders. Called a "potato bug among dragonflies" by *Time* magazine in 1939, Fechner agreed, stating that "most of my clerks are better educated than I am" ("National Affairs," *Time*, 6 Feb. 1936, p. 12). Fechner worked long hours and eschewed the social limelight. Studying the effects of industry on human relations and labor-management relations were among his favorite leisure activities. Fechner, a Democrat, was a member of several fraternal societies, including the Masons, Eagles, and Elks.

As director of Emergency Conservation Work (renamed the Civilian Conservation Corps in 1937), Fechner gained a reputation for ably administering an independent agency in which Roosevelt had great personal interest. That agency worked closely with an advisory council representing four departments: War, which operated most camps; Labor, which selected enrollees; and Agriculture and Interior, which administered projects. Under Fechner's leadership, the people who served in the Civilian Conservation Corps (CCC)—nearly 2.5 million—built national, state, and local parks, fought soil erosion, and battled insects and fires in national parks and forests. All the workers were men; most were between the ages of eighteen and twenty-four, and most earned $30 per month. They were required to send $22 to $25 of their monthly earnings to dependents at home. Approximately two hundred volunteers lived in a typical camp; enrollees served for renewable six-month terms.

Although the CCC was one of the most popular New Deal agencies (the 1936 Republican presidential candidate, Alfred Landon, endorsed making the CCC a permanent government bureau), its director was not immune to controversy. Civil rights leaders criticized the limited enrollment and leadership opportunities available to blacks in an officially color-blind agency. Fechner's union informally excluded nonwhites until 1948. Fechner, citing a lack of support among local residents for the establishment of camps of African-American CCC enrollees in rural areas, was reluctant to enroll blacks in the CCC, to pressure state and local relief officials to accept the placement of African-American CCC camps, or to allow black officers to command African-American camps. As a result the CCC placed many of its African-American camps on military bases; only two camps ever received black officers.

Fechner also aroused the umbrage of educators, who wanted CCC camps to provide enrollees, many of whom had never graduated from high school, with greater educational opportunities. While Fechner allowed camps to provide educational programs and ensured that the staff of each camp included an education coordinator, he insisted that the CCC was a relief program where educational opportunities were incidental to its main purpose. Though many CCC enrollees took advantage of the classes offered in camps and earned high school diplomas or learned new skills, they did so voluntarily and on their own time after a day's work. Meanwhile military leaders disliked Fechner's opposition to providing enrollees with military training. After Fechner's death, the CCC provided its enrollees some noncombatant training.

Fechner died in Washington, D.C. He was succeeded as CCC director by his assistant, James J. McEntee. Fechner was buried in Arlington National Cemetery.

Fechner's hard work and leadership were key to creating and maintaining the public image of one of the most popular and geographically dispersed New Deal programs. A *Washington Post* editorial on Fechner's death further noted that the CCC had "become a symbol of human reclamation," "rescuing . . . young men from blind alleys and giving them opportunities they could not have otherwise enjoyed" (1 Jan. 1940). From state parks in West Virginia and shelterbelts in the Midwest to forests in Alaska, the works of Fechner and the CCC became important parts of the landscape of the United States.

• Fechner left no collection of personal papers. Official papers from his service as CCC director are in Record Group 35 at the National Archives and Records Administration in Washington, D.C. Several letters are in the Franklin D. Roosevelt Presidential Library in Hyde Park, N.Y. The papers of the International Association of Machinists and Aerospace Workers (IAMAW) are in the Pullen Library of Georgia State University in Atlanta, though most of the collection's materials postdate 1935. The State Historical Society of Wisconsin has an extensive collection, mostly on microfilm, of IAMAW records from 1920 to 1974.

John Salmond, *The Civilian Conservation Corps, 1933–1942: A New Deal Case Study* (1967), examines Fechner's administration of the agency. John Saalberg, "Roosevelt, Fechner and the CCC—A Study in Executive Leadership" (Ph.D. diss., Cornell Univ., 1962), is similar to Salmond's study. Mark Perlman, *The Machinists: A New Study in American Trade Unionism* (1961), is a history of the IAM to the 1950s. David Montgomery, *The Fall of the House of Labor: The Workplace, the State, and American Labor Activism, 1865–1925* (1987), provides a history of organized labor and develops the role of the IAM in the labor movement of the late nineteenth century and early twentieth century. Period issues of the IAM's *Machinist's Monthly Journal* provide context for Fechner's years as a union official, including Arthur E. Holder, "Summary Record of 63d Congress: Measures of Interest to Labor Enacted," 27, no. 4 (Apr. 1915): 329–30; Robert Hunter, "The Perils Confronting Labor," 22, no. 3 (Mar. 1910): 228–33; and Fechner's own short columns in the journal's "On the Firing Line" section (see, e.g., pages 1124–5 of the Dec. 1915 issue). Obituaries are in the *New York Times*, 1 Jan. 1940, and the *Washington Post*, 1 Jan. 1940.

EDWARD J. ROACH

FENWICK, Millicent (25 Feb. 1910–16 Sept. 1992), politician, was born Millicent Vernon Hammond in New York City, the daughter of financier Ogden Haggerty Hammond and Mary Picton Stevens. She was the great-granddaughter of Edwin Augustus Stevens, founder of the Stevens Institute of Technology in Hoboken, New Jersey. In 1915 Fenwick's mother perished on the *Lusitania* when it was torpedoed and sunk by the Germans. Her father survived and two years later married Marguerite "Daisy" McClure Howland, a widow. Having a son of her own, Daisy did not nurture Millicent or her two siblings. Millicent's happiest childhood years were spent at Foxcroft, an all-girl boarding school in Middleburg, Virginia. In 1925, President Calvin Coolidge appointed her father ambassador to Spain. Daisy pulled her two stepdaughters out of Foxcroft to move to Madrid; the two boys remained in boarding school in the United States. As a result, Millicent, who had a hunger for knowledge, never received a high school diploma. She was primarily self-educated and spoke fluent Italian, French, and Spanish.

In 1929, after spending four years abroad socializing with royalty and diplomats, the Hammonds returned to the states just as the stock market crashed. The family's wealth, derived primarily from a trust fund created by Mary Picton Stevens on the day the *Lusitania* set sail from New York, insulated them from the economic woes many others suffered. The Hammonds spent most winters in New York City and summers in Bernardsville, New Jersey. It was here that Millicent Hammond fell in love with aviator Hugh McLeod Fenwick, who at the time was married to Dorothy Ledyard, the daughter of the president of the New York Stock Exchange. Millicent professed her love for Fenwick to his wife and, soon after, Fenwick and Ledyard divorced. On 11 June 1932 Millicent Hammond married Hugh Fenwick, much to the chagrin of her parents, who did not approve of her marrying a divorced man. The couple had two children. After six years of marriage they separated when Fenwick went to Europe to sell planes. Their divorce was finalized in 1945.

In 1938, Millicent Fenwick was a single mother with two young children to support and a trail of debt left by her husband. Although she had an income generated by the trust fund her mother had established, it was not enough to cover expenses. She applied for a job in New York at Bonwit Teller, an upscale department store. Ultimately, she was rejected because she lacked a high school diploma. Disappointed, Fenwick asked if she could sell stockings or be a message runner between departments. Again, she was rebuffed. At twenty-eight, she was too old.

Eventually she landed a job as a caption writer at *Vogue*—the beginning of her fourteen-year career at the magazine, during which time she worked her way up to associate editor and wrote *Vogue's Book of Etiquette* in 1948. One of her earlier assignments was a 1939 trip to South America with fashion photographer Toni Frissell. The two women, both tall and lean, traveled 15,000 miles over forty days to four countries and reported on the lifestyles and fashions of women in Brazil, Argentina, Chile, and Peru.

Around the same time, on another continent, Adolf Hitler was amassing power and the Germans were invading Poland. Fenwick had difficulty comprehending how Germany, one of the most literate countries in the world, had elected Hitler. "It was like a bad dream. With the Depression still having its effects here in the United States, nobody knew what was going to happen. The world was in a state of flux. There across the Atlantic was this madman. You couldn't help but be interested in politics," said Fenwick (quoted in Osowski, p. 25). Hitler's power prompted Fenwick to distrust government. She identified her skepticism as the reason why she became a Republican. She believed "a good Republican is as sensitive to the suffering of others as anyone else, but a first reaction will be 'Let's get together and do something,' not 'The government must take charge of this'" (quoted in Fenwick, *Speaking Up*, p. 33).

In 1958, Fenwick, who had been elected to the Bernardsville Board of Education twenty years earlier, won a seat on the Bernardsville Borough Council, the first woman to do so. Active in local politics and civil rights, she served as a vice-chair of the New Jersey Republican Committee in 1961 and as vice-chair of the New Jersey Committee of the U.S. Commission on Civil Rights from 1958 to 1972.

In 1969, Fenwick ran for the New Jersey Assembly and won. She is often quoted for her reported retort during a debate about the Equal Rights Amendment in which a male colleague said he thought of women as "kissable, cuddly, and smelling good." Millicent responded in her aristocratic voice, "That's the way I feel about men. I only hope for your sake that you haven't been as disappointed as often as I have" (as quoted in Walker, p. 7). Known for her quick wit, candidness, and passion for consumer rights and civil rights, Fenwick was reelected in 1971. She did not finish her second term in the New Jersey Assembly because Gov. William Cahill appointed her the Director of Consumer Affairs, making Fenwick the highest-ranking and highest-paid woman ($26,500) in his administration.

In spring 1974, Fenwick resigned from her Consumer Affairs post to run for Congress. Her primary opponent was Thomas H. Kean, then speaker of the assembly. Fenwick squeaked out a victory by 76 votes to face Democrat Frederick Bohen in the general election. Both were interested in filling the seat vacated by the retirement of Rep. Peter H. B. Frelinghuysen.

On 5 November 1974, at the age of 64, Fenwick won her first congressional election and the press hailed her victory as a geriatric triumph. She was the oldest member of the freshman class and was often referred to as the pipe-smoking grandmother. As she said, she would have preferred being referred to as the "hard-working grandmother, after all it has the same number of syllables."

In August 1975, shortly after the passage of the Helsinki Final Act—an international agreement signed by the United States, the Soviet Union, and thirty-three other countries to protect human rights—Fenwick was a member of a congressional delegation to the Soviet Union. On that trip she met with numerous dissidents about human rights violations. On her return, Fenwick introduced legislation, which President Gerald Ford signed into law, that created the U.S. Commission on Security and Cooperation in Europe, better known as the Helsinki Commission. It established a congressional commission to monitor the compliance by signatory countries of the third "basket" or set of provisions of the Helsinki Accords dealing with the rights of individuals, freedom of movement, and family reunification. The bipartisan congressional commission included a member of the Commerce, Defense, and State Departments much to the dismay of Henry Kissinger, then secretary of state. Fenwick believed the inclusion of the executive branch representatives was vital, as those agencies, along with Congress, shared responsibility for monitoring the Helsinki Accords.

In 1982, after four terms in the House of Representatives, Fenwick decided to run for the U.S. Senate. Because of the 1980 U.S. Census, much of Fenwick's Fifth District was incorporated into the redrawn Twelfth District. The gerrymandering coupled with the resignation of Sen. Harrison Williams (due to the Abscam scandal, in which members of Congress accepted bribes from an undercover FBI agent) prompted her decision to seek a seat in the Senate. Her Democratic challenger was political newcomer Frank Lautenberg. In a surprise upset, Lautenberg won with 52 percent of the vote to Fenwick's 48 percent. The difference was less than 66,000 votes out of nearly 2 million cast.

After Fenwick's defeat, President Ronald Reagan appointed her as the first U.S. Ambassador to the United Nations Food and Agriculture Organization in Rome. Fenwick, fluent in Italian, served there from 1983 until her retirement in 1987 when she returned to Bernardsville. She remained active in local and state politics. Her daughter, Mary Reckford, had succumbed to leukemia in 1987.

During Fenwick's public service career she earned a reputation for integrity and moral values. Her principled positions, including her opposition to congressional raises and PAC money, prompted Walter Cronkite to call her the "conscience of Congress." She served as the basis of Garry Trudeau's *Doonesbury* character Congresswoman Lacey Davenport. As former New Jersey Governor Thomas H. Kean said, "She was the only really ambitious seventy-year-old I've ever met. She loved serving in office, and whether in the state assembly or the United States Congress, she never ceased marveling that she had actually been chosen to represent the people. In legislative bodies she remained a maverick . . . she hated hypocrisy and those who abused the public trust. Stubborn to a fault, she never betrayed her ideals or paid much attention to the polls. In the end, that was probably why she lost her last election, but the example she set and the way she conducted her life continue to stand as a model for all those who might want to pursue public life" (quoted in Schapiro, pp. ix–x).

• Millicent Fenwick's congressional papers can be found at Rutgers University in the Special Collections & University Archives at the Alexander Library in New Brunswick, New Jersey. While Rutgers University has an extensive collection, the University of Oklahoma at Norman also houses some of Fenwick's congressional material in the Carl Albert Center. Books by Millicent Fenwick include *Vogue's Book of Etiquette* (1948) and *Speaking Up* (1982), a compilation of her congressional newsletters, editorials, and other articles she wrote. A comprehensive biography by Amy Schapiro, *Millicent Fenwick: Her Way* (2003), spans Fenwick's life before, during, and after her congressional years. Another useful source is Peggy Lamson, *In the Vanguard: Six American Women in Public Life* (1979). Informative articles include Stanley Osowski, "Thoroughly Marvelous Millicent," *Newark!: The Magazine of Metropolitan New Jersey* (Jan. 1973): 25; Connecticut Walker, "Rep. Millicent Fenwick: A Star in the New Congress," *Parade* (4 May 1975); Judy Bachrach, "Six from the Class of '75 . . . Millicent Fenwick," *Washington Post*, 23 Feb. 1975; and Elisabeth Bumiller, "The Wit & Grit of Millicent Fenwick," *Washington Post*, 20 Jan. 1982. Also of value is the *Almanac of American Politics*, 1976, 1978, 1980, 1982, and *Current Biography*, 1977. Oral histories of Millicent Fenwick are in the Columbia University Oral History Project and as part of the Foreign Affairs Oral History Collection at the National Foreign Affairs Training Center for the Department of State. An obituary is in the *New York Times*, 17 Sept. 1992.

AMY SCHAPIRO

FERRIS, George Washington Gale, Jr. (14 Feb. 1859–22 Nov. 1896), civil engineer and builder of the Ferris Wheel, was born in Galesburg, Illinois, the son of George Washington Gale Ferris and Martha Edgerton Hyde Ferris, farmers. Ferris's grandfather Silvanus Ferris, along with Reverend George W. Gale, founded the village of Galesburg in central Illinois. In 1864 the Ferrises moved to Carson City, Nevada, where they established a ranch. George's father planted the many trees around the state capitol grounds in Carson City, including American elms and spruces. In 1873 George entered the California Military Academy in Oakland, graduating in 1876. That fall he enrolled at Rensselaer Polytechnic Institute in Troy, New York. There he studied civil engineering and engaged in extracurricular activities, including the football, baseball, and rifle teams and the Glee Club. Although required to be reexamined in some courses before passing, he received his engineering degree in February 1881, with a senior thesis titled, "Review of Wrought Iron Deck Bridge on the Boston Hoosac Tunnel & Western Railway at Schaghticoke, N.Y."

Ferris quickly became an accomplished and active engineer engaged in significant railroad and bridge projects. Following graduation, he worked for General J. H. Ledlie, a railroad contractor in New York City. During his first year, he was sent to Charlestown, West Virginia, as a transitman locating a proposed route of the Baltimore, Cincinnati & Western railway through the valley of the Elk River. He also planned the route of a narrow-gauge track in Putnam County, New York. In 1882 he became an engineer and then general manager for the Queen City Coal Mining Company in West Virginia, where he designed and built a coal trestle over the Kanawha River. He also built three 1,800-foot tunnels. In 1883, on the closing of the Queen City Company, he became assistant engineer of the Louisville Bridge & Iron Company in Louisville, Kentucky. He supervised the concrete work of the pneumatic caissons for the Henderson Bridge across the Ohio River. This work was so dangerous and taxing on his health that he was reassigned to supervise construction of the bridge's superstructure. By the mid-1880s he had become a recognized expert on the properties of structural steel use in bridges and large structures and was also establishing a reputation as an astute businessman. In 1885 he joined the Kentucky and Indiana Bridge Company of Louisville and was placed in charge of testing iron and steel from Pittsburgh steel mills.

In 1886 Ferris married Margaret Ann Beatty of Canton, Ohio, and they moved to Pittsburgh. In partnership with James C. Hallsted, he established the firm of G. W. G. Ferris & Company, Inspecting Engineers. Soon they opened branch offices in New York and Chicago. The company conducted mill and factory work inspections and testing throughout the United States. While primarily occupied with the organization and administration of this company, he also turned his attention to the promotion and financing of large-scale engineering projects. In 1890, while retaining his ties to G. W. G. Ferris & Company, he founded a second firm, Ferris, Kaufman and Company, which engineered major bridges across the Ohio River at Wheeling and Cincinnati.

Although engaged in many notable civil engineering projects early in his career, Ferris achieved national celebrity and enduring fame for his conception, design, and building of the Great Ferris Wheel that became the signature attraction of the World's Columbian Exposition in Chicago in 1893. Daniel H. Burnham, director of works of the exposition, in early 1892 challenged U.S. civil engineers to design a "novel" and "daring" structure that would surpass the Eiffel Tower, engage the public spirit, and symbolize the exposition's emphasis on new technology. Ferris was immediately inspired and reportedly sketched the idea and plan for the Great Wheel in a Chicago restaurant. He assigned design detail and construction responsibility to his partner, William F. Gronau, also a graduate of Rensselaer Polytechnic Institute. Ferris himself used his genius as a businessman to secure the concession in late 1892 after a lengthy negotiation with the board of directors of the exposition, to raise the financing during a period of general national depression in 1893, and to organize the manufacture of parts by numerous companies in the East and Midwest. Despite a brutally cold winter, quicksand, and a spring of ceaseless rain, the Wheel was finished on 21 June 1893. Rising 264 feet above the Midway and 825 feet in circumference, it weighed more than 2.6 million pounds, had thirty-six cars, each with a capacity to hold sixty passengers, was powered by two 1,000-horsepower steam engines, and was illuminated by more than 3,000 electric lights. The Wheel proved completely safe, as documented in *Scientific American* in 1893, withstanding gale-force winds and storms, absorbing lightning, and running flawlessly through the duration of the exposition. Ferris's magnificent wheel dominated the exposition by its size and popularity, carrying 1.4 million riders. It is the first example of technology being harnessed purely as a pleasure machine, and it captured the imagination of a nation.

Ferris soon faced patent infringement suits from creators of smaller pleasure wheels, from which he eventually emerged victorious but at great personal and financial cost. Ferris rejected offers from Coney Island, London, and elsewhere to purchase the Wheel and instead relocated and reassembled it in a small park in Chicago. This venture was a miserable failure. Ferris's Wheel would delight fairgoers once more at the Louisiana Purchase Exposition in St. Louis in 1904. It came to a most ignominious end when the Great Wheel succumbed to a wrecking dynamite charge on 11 May 1906.

Despite such evident early promise, the disastrous financial aftermath of the Wheel appears to have broken Ferris. His health may have been somewhat precarious since his early bridge-building projects, and his childless marriage apparently failed when his wife returned to her Canton, Ohio, hometown prior to 1896. In an attempt to meet his financial obligations, Ferris sold most of his interest in G. W. G. Ferris & Company to his partners. He died in Pittsburgh. Typhoid fever was identified on his death certificate as the cause of death, though kidney disease may also have contributed to his decline.

Ferris exemplified the daring entrepreneurship, optimism, and building acumen of the nineteenth-century engineer in the United States. In their published eulogy of Ferris, partners Gustave Kaufman and D. W. McNaugher praised his spirit: "He was always bright, hopeful and full of anticipation of good results from all the ventures he had on hand. These feelings he could always impart to whomever he addressed in a most wonderful degree, and therein lay the key note of his success. In most darkened and troubled times . . . he was ever looking for the sunshine soon to come. . . . He died a martyr to his ambition for fame and prominence" (quoted in Anderson, p. 75). Ferris contributed significantly to forging the future of steel in large-scale building construction. His leadership was not only technical in nature, through the development of testing and the application of steel in project design, but also cultural, erecting a steel structure in the American imagination. The Ferris Wheel's merger of technology and entertainment led the way for social acceptance of powerful new technologies and for the dominance of technology-driven amusement in the century to follow. The feverish pace of his engineering projects and businesses mirrored the accomplishments of U.S. engineers who created a civilization for a new century. Writing in November 1893 about the amazing technology and skill evident in the Ferris Wheel, civil engineer Wm. H. Searles found the young Ferris to represent "a good promise for America in the twentieth century" (p. 623).

• Ferris family archival papers are at the College Archives, Seymour Library, Knox College, Galesburg, Ill. Ferris family genealogical research papers, including significant records on the Ferris Wheel and patent litigation, have been assembled by Lora C. Little and are held at the New York Genealogical and Biographical Society Library in New York City. The most important patent infringement case is *The Garden City Observation Wheel Company vs. the Ferris Wheel Company*; more than 400 pages of court documents are available at the Chicago Branch of the National Archives. A detailed account of Ferris's life and work is in Norman Anderson, *Ferris Wheels: An Illustrated History* (1993). Anderson includes coverage of the building of the Ferris Wheel, the patent cases, and references to primary sources such as legal decisions, company records, and family papers. Articles on the Ferris Wheel at the World's Columbian Exposition include Jack Fincher, "George Ferris Jr. and the Great Wheel of Fortune," *Smithsonian* 14 (July 1983): 109–18; Sisley Barnes, "George Ferris' Wheel: The Great Attraction of the Midway Plaisance," *Chicago History* 6, no. 3 (1977): 177–82; Jack Klasey, "Who Invented the Ferris Wheel?" *American History Illustrated* 28 (Sept.–Oct. 1993): 60–63; Carl Snyder, "Engineer Ferris and His Wheel," *Review of Reviews* (U.S. ed.), 8 Sept. 1893, pp. 269–70. For technical information on the 1893 Ferris Wheel see "The Great Wheel at Chicago," *Scientific American* 69 (July 1893): 8–9; Wm. H. Searles, "The Ferris Wheel," *Association of Engineering Societies Journal* 12 (Dec. 1893): 614–23; and F. G. Coggin, "The Ferris and Other Big Wheels," *Cassier's Magazine* 6 (July 1894): 215–22. See also Joseph Dimuro, "The 1893 Ferris Wheel and the Cultural Politics of National Identity" (Ph.D. diss., University of Chicago, 2000). Obituaries are in the *Pittsburgh Post*, 23 Nov. 1896; *Engineering Record* 34 (1896): 479; and *Iron Age* 58 (1896): 1019. Ferris's final resting place is unknown; see "Ashes of George W. G. Ferris," *New York Times*, 8 Mar. 1898, p. 5.

JUDITH ADAMS-VOLPE

FIELDS, James Thomas (31 Dec. 1817–24 Apr. 1881), publisher, editor, writer, and lecturer, was born in Portsmouth, New Hampshire, the son of Michael Fields, a sea captain, and Margaret Beck Fields. His father died at sea before James's fourth birthday, leaving his devoted mother little more than the modest house where she raised her two sons. A gregarious and book-loving boy, James completed high school at the age of thirteen, then headed for Boston. Although college was never an option, a family friend arranged what turned out to be the next best thing: an apprenticeship with the booksellers Carter and Hendee at what is still known as the Old Corner Bookstore. Remaining at that workplace after Carter and Hendee sold out to Allen and Ticknor in 1832, and after William D. Ticknor became sole owner in 1834, the ambitious young clerk learned all about retail bookselling and brought home stacks of books to read every night. During the next few years he joined the Boston Mercantile Library Association and participated in its literary debates; he often attended plays and brought friends home to discuss them; and he regularly wrote and published poems.

Like most of his Boston counterparts, Ticknor was a bookseller who was also—if incidentally—a publisher. But in 1840 Fields began taking initiatives that would change the Old Corner's identity and his own. Conjoining his love of literature and his sound business sense, he persuaded Ticknor to publish Thomas De Quincey's *Confessions of an English Opium-Eater* and two other books by English authors requiring no royalty payments, then edited and wrote prefaces for all three. All sold well. In 1842 Fields persuaded Ticknor to publish the first authorized American edition of poems by the rising young English poet Alfred Tennyson, an authorization he secured by promising the 10 percent royalty that Tennyson wanted and a rival American publisher had refused. That volume also sold well. Another consequential initiative came in 1843. At a time when a distinctive American literature was still in its infancy and publishers were reluctant to gamble on its success, Fields persuaded Ticknor to publish John Greenleaf Whittier's *Lays of My Home, and Other Poems*. Again, Fields boosted a writer's income and reputation as well as the firm's.

Also in 1843, at the age of twenty-six, Fields became a junior partner in the new firm of William D. Ticknor & Company. Another man also became a partner that year—John Reed, Jr., who invested $8,000 in the firm. But "in consideration of his knowledge of the business" (to quote the articles of incorporation), Fields was required to invest only himself. Genially and shrewdly, he handled negotiations with authors and book reviewers as well as printers and bookbinders, responding to tastes that he also helped shape.

Fields broadened his participation in the world of letters in 1847 when he took his first trip abroad. To his great delight, he was welcomed into friendship by dozens of England's most eminent writers and publishers. By the time he returned to Boston, he had contracted for scores of new publications (as he would again do during all three of his subsequent trips abroad).

In 1849 Fields published his own *Poems*, a collection of competent verse studded with the kind of purple passages favored by period taste; it was the first of five such volumes. He also began to prepare the first collected edition of all De Quincey's work (which eventuated in twenty-three volumes). That same year Fields called on the renowned short story writer Nathaniel Hawthorne, who had just been fired from his job as surveyor of the Salem Custom House following the Whigs' presidential victory. That visit would have a major effect on Hawthorne's career and on subsequent American literary history.

Fields offered the cash-strapped Hawthorne immediate publication of anything he had ready for the press. Though Hawthorne initially protested that he had nothing to show, Fields took home an unfinished narrative that Hawthorne had expected to include in what would be his third collection of short stories. But, aware that publishing Hawthorne's first novel would be a marketing coup and that novels sold better than short stories, the publisher persuaded the author to expand his dark story of Puritan Boston into the powerful novel that is still ranked among the best that America has ever produced, *The Scarlet Letter* (1850). From then on, Fields was Hawthorne's devoted friend as well as his exclusive publisher, shrewdly promoting and marketing all his work and steadily encouraging him to produce more of it. And, like many other eminent American writers, including Ralph Waldo Emerson and Oliver Wendell Holmes, Hawthorne later said that he owed his "literary success, whatever it has been or may be," to his connection with Fields.

Two major changes in Fields's life occurred in 1854. When Reed withdrew from the business, Fields became a partner in the new firm of Ticknor & Fields. That same year, at the age of thirty-seven, he entered into a remarkably happy marriage with the twenty-year-old Ann West Adams (Annie Adams Fields). Fields's marriage to Adams was in fact his second marriage. In 1844 Fields had become engaged to Mary Willard, who died of tuberculosis; six years later he married Mary's sister Eliza, who soon died of the same disease. But after a brief courtship, he married Adams, a first cousin of the Willards', whose distinguished relatives included two U.S. presidents, and who would become one of the country's most celebrated literary hostesses as well as a poet, biographer, and social reformer. They were married until his death and had no children.

During the next sixteen years, Ticknor & Fields solidified its reputation as America's most important literary publisher. The firm's list of eminent American authors included Henry Wadsworth Longfellow, Holmes, Emerson, James Russell Lowell, Whittier, Hawthorne, and Harriet Beecher Stowe, and its English eminences included Tennyson, Robert Browning, William Makepeace Thackeray, Charles Dickens, and George Eliot. As they all knew, Fields hired Boston's best printers and bookbinders and maintained high production standards, and no publisher was a more skillful marketer. Even writers who could command higher fees from other publishers contracted with Ticknor & Fields. For reader and writer alike, the firm's imprint was a mark of quality.

Predictably, the Old Corner Bookstore became a favorite meeting place for cultured Bostonians. Writers stopped by to see new books (their own and others') and to converse with friends (Fields among them). Fields was "the literary partner of the house," as the New York editor and critic George William Curtis wrote years later, "the friend of the celebrated circle who have made . . . Boston . . . justly renowned" ("Editor's Easy Chair," *Harper's* 63 [July 1881]: 305). Friends who stepped into Fields's office for a chat might be invited to dine with him at a nearby restaurant, and his hospitality dramatically increased after 1856, when he and his wife moved into the new house on Charles Street that they would occupy for as long as they lived. During a single week, the Fieldses might give a dinner party for twelve and a reception for twenty while also entertaining several houseguests.

One of the happiest years of the Fieldses' life began when they sailed for England in June 1859, a year during which they began new intimacies (with Dickens and Stowe, among others) and solidified old ones. A particularly important event of that year was Ticknor's acquisition of the *Atlantic Monthly*, a two-year-old "Magazine of Literature, Art, and Politics," then edited by Lowell, which had gone bankrupt. Fields immediately undertook to increase the magazine's circulation by soliciting lively manuscripts from established writers (like Hawthorne) as well as from neophytes. By the time he became editor in the summer of 1861, the *Atlantic* had become the country's most prestigious and influential literary periodical. Its sphere of influence extended well beyond New England, with submissions and subscriptions flowing in from New York, Ohio, California, and even London.

As editor, Fields assumed responsibility for the entire magazine, deciding what to accept or reject, what to commission or cajole, what revisions to require, and how much to pay the author. And for both author and publisher, earnings multiplied when a series of *Atlantic* essays or a serialized novel appeared in book form.

Major changes in the firm followed Ticknor's unexpected death in the spring of 1864. Abandoning retail bookselling, Fields sold the Old Corner Bookstore and moved into larger quarters overlooking the Boston Common. And the *Atlantic* editor also acquired three additional magazines—the *North American Review*, *Our Young Folks*, and *Every Saturday*.

Another triumph was persuading Dickens to make his second U.S. reading tour. The five-month tour that began in the fall of 1867 was enormously profitable for both the author and the publisher, as was Dickens's authorization of Fields as his exclusive American publisher. Both of the Fieldses rejoiced in their intimacy with him, an intimacy that deepened when they visited him in 1869. They were both stunned by his death the following year.

By then the Fieldses had endured another kind of grief. In 1868 the popular essayist Gail Hamilton concluded that her old friend Fields had bilked her by switching her royalty payments from a percentage basis to a unit rate, and she convinced Hawthorne's widow Sophia Hawthorne that Fields had also cheated her. Though arbiters found no legal wrongdoing, Fields's reputation was stained, a stain Hamilton spread by publishing the thinly disguised attack on him entitled *The Battle of the Books* (1870). Presum-

ably that attack, his burdensome business responsibilities, and his grief at Dickens's death figured in Fields's decision to retire from publishing at the end of 1870.

During his final decade, Fields continued to write essays and poems for the *Atlantic* and other periodicals—most notably essays on writers he had known that appeared first in the *Atlantic* and then as a volume entitled *Yesterdays with Authors*. He also began an enormously successful career as a lecturer. Whether he was booked into a village lyceum or a college auditorium, in Boston or the Midwest, and whether he spoke under an umbrella topic such as "Masters of the Situation" or "Cheerfulness" or focused on one of the many writers he had known and loved, Fields could be depended upon to entertain, instruct, and inspire. In 1875 his earnings enabled the Fieldses to build the summer cottage that still stands on the shores of Manchester, where they continued their long-established tradition of dispensing hospitality to their large circles of friends.

James T. Fields—the foremost publisher of good literature in mid-nineteenth-century America and one of the period's greatest magazine editors—died at Charles Street; he is buried at Mount Auburn Cemetery.

• The Fields Collection at the Huntington Library includes thousands of letters as well as notebooks, lecture notes, and other manuscripts. Other important holdings are at the Houghton Library of Harvard University, the Massachusetts Historical Society, the Boston Public Library, and the Berg Collection of the New York Public Library. Fields's most important publication is *Yesterdays with Authors* (1872; expanded ed., 1877); *Underbrush* (1877) collects essays initially published in the *Atlantic* and other periodicals; and *Ballads and Other Verses* (1881) is his final collection of poems. He also produced a wide assortment of anthologies with such self-defining titles as *Good Company for Every Day of the Year* (1866). The three main biographies are Annie Fields, *James T. Fields: Biographical Notes and Personal Sketches with Unpublished Fragments and Tributes from Men and Women of Letters* (1881), W. S. Tryon, *Parnassus Corner: A Life of James T. Fields, Publisher to the Victorians* (1968), and James C. Austin, *Fields of the* Atlantic Monthly: *Letters to an Editor, 1861–1870* (1953). Useful supplements include William Charvat's "James T. Fields and the Beginnings of Book Promotion, 1840–1855," included in *The Profession of Authorship in America: 1800–1870*, ed. Matthew Bruccoli (1968); Rosemary Fisk's unpublished 1985 doctoral dissertation, "The Profession of Authorship: Nathaniel Hawthorne and His Publisher, James T. Fields" (Rice Univ., 1984); John William Pye's *James T. Fields: Literary Publisher* (1987); and biographies of Annie Fields, including Rita K. Gollin's *Annie Adams Fields: Woman of Letters* (2002). Obituaries of Fields appeared in the *Boston Transcript* on 25 April 1881 and in the *New York Times* the following day; and "Recollections of James T. Fields" by his old friend Edwin P. Whipple appeared in the *Atlantic Monthly* 48 (Aug. 1881): 253–60.

RITA K. GOLLIN

FILLMORE, Abigail Powers (17? Mar. 1798–30 Mar. 1853), wife of Millard Fillmore, thirteenth president of the United States, was born in the Adirondacks town of Stillwater, New York, the daughter of Lemuel Powers, a Baptist minister, and Abigail Newland Powers. Abigail left Stillwater as a young child when her father died and her mother moved the family to Sempronius, New York, where she had relatives.

Both her parents valued education highly and passed on their appreciation of books to her. Lemuel Powers, although never wealthy, left a substantial library, and his wife helped educate their children herself. By the time she was sixteen, Abigail was teaching at the New Hope Academy in Sempronius, and it was there, three years later, that Millard Fillmore, who was two years younger than she, became one of her students. When Fillmore, whose family was also enduring reduced circumstances, tried his hand at teaching, he and Abigail Powers found that they shared a strong intellectual curiosity; he later wrote that he had been "stimulated" by her "companionship" (quoted in Hoganson, p. 155).

Although they became engaged in 1819, the couple did not marry until 5 February 1826, and during much of that interval they lived so far apart that they saw each other infrequently. Even after their marriage Abigail continued to teach for two years in Aurora, New York, where the couple lived; she would thus become the first U.S. president's wife to work outside the home following marriage. With the birth of her first child, Millard Powers Fillmore, in April 1828, and the election of her husband to the New York State Assembly in November that same year, she quit teaching and devoted herself to homemaking.

In 1830, when her husband opened a law office in Buffalo, the family moved there and Abigail became active in efforts to improve the schools and establish a lending library. She also began collecting books for a family library that eventually numbered four thousand volumes. A second child, Mary Abigail, was born there in 1832, the same year that Millard Fillmore was elected to the House of Representatives as part of the coalition that would become the Whig party. After serving two years, then resuming his law practice in Buffalo for two years, he returned to Washington in 1837 as a Whig congressman. This time Abigail accompanied him, leaving their two children in Buffalo with relatives. Since the legislative session lasted only a few months each winter and most representatives chose to stay in boarding houses rather than maintain a second home in the nation's capital, it was not unusual for them to decide against uprooting young children. The Fillmores followed this pattern during the six years he served in Congress, but Abigail wrote frequently to the children, and she closely monitored their education and upbringing.

As a Washington wife, Abigail Fillmore kept herself informed on political topics and attended Senate and House debates, although she preferred the solitude of literature and music in her own quarters. She read widely, delving into history, politics, religion, and literature, but her favorite authors were William Makepeace Thackeray and Charles Dickens. In 1842, after her husband's term had ended and they had returned to live full time in Buffalo, Abigail fell and injured her foot, an injury that would cause her suffering for the rest of her life. Walking or standing for long periods became very painful, and she retreated more and more to the solace of a good book. When her husband was elected comptroller of New York State in 1847 and worked out of an office in the state capital, Albany, she moved with him to a boarding house, and they occasionally took part in the city's social life.

By the time her husband was inaugurated as vice president in 1849, Abigail was nearly fifty-one years old and suffering from multiple health problems. Plagued by frequent headaches and back pain, she decided to remain in Buffalo rather than move to Washington, D.C., but the letters she and her husband exchanged testify to their continued closeness and mutual devotion. "How lonesome this [hotel] room is in your absence," he wrote her in April 1850. "You have scarcely been out of my mind since you left. . . . How I wish I could be with you" (quoted in Caroli, p. 48).

That summer, when Zachary Taylor died suddenly and Millard Fillmore became president, Abigail agreed to move to Washington. As First Lady, she preferred smaller gatherings to large balls and sometimes sent her teenage daughter to host the more glittering events. A lively conversationalist in small groups, Abigail felt most comfortable at Saturday dinners attended by twenty or so guests, but she also appeared occasionally at receptions and larger parties. She is remembered most for establishing the first White House library—in the oval room on the second floor—and for selecting the books, which were paid for by a congressional appropriation of $2,000. Her guests included noted authors, such as Charles Dickens and Washington Irving, and performers, including singer Jenny Lind.

In early March 1853, Abigail, who had been ill, attended the inauguration of her husband's successor and then developed pneumonia. The family moved to the Willard Hotel, near the White House, so that she could convalesce before they began a long-planned trip through the southern states. Her condition worsened, however, and she soon died. The Senate adjourned in a mourning tribute, and her family began its sad journey back to Buffalo with her remains. She was buried there at Forest Lawn Cemetery, where her husband and his second wife, Caroline McIntosh Fillmore, were later buried.

Like most presidents' wives of the nineteenth century, Abigail Fillmore left unclear the extent of her influence on her husband's career. She reportedly counseled him against signing the Fugitive Slave Act, an important component of the Compromise of 1850, but was unsuccessful. An avid reader of newspapers and books, she sometimes conveyed her ideas to her husband by letter. His biographers have singled her out as one of his most important counselors. Although First Lady for less than three years, Abigail Fillmore earned the respect of official Washington; at her death, newspapers praised her blending of "good sense with high principle" (quoted in Hoganson, p. 164).

• Letters written by the young Abigail Powers were destroyed or lost; correspondence with her husband has, however, been deposited with his papers at various libraries, principally the State University of New York at Oswego, and, to a lesser extent, the Buffalo and Erie County Historical Society. See Lester W. Smith, ed., *Guide to the Microfilm Edition of the Millard Fillmore Papers* (1975).

Abigail Fillmore has not had a full-length biography. For a short but very thorough account of her life, see Kristin Hoganson, "Abigail (Powers) Fillmore," in Lewis L. Gould, ed., *American First Ladies: Their Lives and Their Legacy* (2001). Biographies of Millard Fillmore that contain useful information on her include Benson Lee Grayson, *The Unknown President: The Administration of President Millard Fillmore* (1981); Robert J. Rayback, *Millard Fillmore* (1959); Robert J. Scarry, *Millard Fillmore* (2001); and Elbert B. Smith, *The Presidencies of Zachary Taylor and Millard Fillmore* (1988).

On Abigail Fillmore's role in establishing the White House library, see William Seale, *The President's House* (1986). For a comparison of her with other presidents' wives, see Betty Boyd Caroli, *First Ladies* (1995). An obituary is in the *New York Daily Tribune*, 31 Mar. 1853.

BETTY BOYD CAROLI

FINCKE, William M. (1 Jan. 1878–31 May 1927), pacifist minister and educator, was born William Mann Fincke in New York City, the son of William H. Fincke, a wealthy businessman, and Julia Murrid Clark Fincke. In 1897 he graduated from the Hill School and in the fall entered Yale University, "where he played halfback on the varsity eleven" (*New York Times*, 1 June 1927). Fincke graduated from Yale's Sheffield Scientific School in 1901. In 1902 he married Helen Hamlin in Buffalo, New York; they had two boys.

In 1902, Fincke became general manager of his father's car ferry service on Lake Erie, where he oversaw the shipping of coal to industrial plants along the Great Lakes. But he lost interest in industrial management and was troubled by capitalism's exploitation of the laboring class. In 1908, he abandoned the business world in order to study at Union Theological Seminary. There he read the works of social gospel theologians Walter Rauschenbush and Washington Gladden. Critical of the church's traditionally conservative role in relationship to wealth, labor, and social reform, Fincke adopted the doctrines of radical pacifism and socialism as part of his religious calling. In 1911, he received a bachelor's degree in divinity.

In May 1911, he was ordained a Presbyterian minister and appointed pastor of the Greenwich Presbyterian Church in lower Manhattan. When the United States entered World War I in April 1917, Fincke delivered a pacifist sermon titled "A Ministry of Reconciliation." He rejected the notion that "this war is . . . expedient as a fight for liberty and democracy" and one "true to her [America's] ideal of international brotherhood" (quoted in "A Minister and His Church

in War"). His congregation promptly voted him out of his pulpit, 210 to 124.

In the fall of 1917, Fincke volunteered his services in Europe as a stretcher-bearer and served in France with the Presbyterian Hospital Unit. On his way overseas, a German U-boat sank his ship, and he was rescued. His close encounter with death, along with the pain and suffering he witnessed on the battlefield, strengthened his pacifist convictions. Ideologically, he clung to a liberal pacifism that was world-affirming, social, and not individualistic. The conversion of whole societies, not simply personal salvation, became his primary consideration. In his mind, peace was no longer the absence of war but also a process of change toward greater social justice.

When Fincke returned from the war in 1918, he became director of the Presbyterian Labor Temple in New York City. Located on Second Avenue and East Fourteenth Street, the Temple offered social programs, religious services for "the unchurched masses of the city," and education classes for the city's ethnically diverse working-class community (Howlett, *Brookwood Labor College*, p. 5). In 1919, during the epic steel strike, Fincke traveled to Duquesne, Pennsylvania, with a group of Fellowship of Reconciliation pacifists. He led the free-speech fight supporting the striking workers. He was imprisoned for one evening on a charge of disturbing the peace.

The crushing of the steel strike of 1919 by local authorities and business leaders convinced Fincke to carry out his new mission: an innovative educational program encouraging "a nonviolent way of life, [a] program of political change, and [a] technique of social action" (Howlett, "John Nevin Sayre and the American Fellowship of Reconciliation," p. 405). His goal was to establish a progressive labor school ministering to young adults from working-class and peace-minded families. Previously, on 19 March 1914, Fincke and his wife, who later ran for comptroller of New York in 1920 on the first Farmer-Labor Party ticket, had purchased the old Brookwood Estate in Katonah, New York, for $3,700. In late 1919, he and his family moved to the Westchester County estate. The main house, where they also lived, was converted into an experimental school building and dormitory.

Relying on John Dewey's philosophy of progressive education, Fincke and his wife focused on training working-class teenagers who, after reaching adulthood, "would play an important role in bringing about social and political reforms within their own particular labor organization as well as in the industrial sector of American society as a whole" (quoted in Altenbaugh, *Education for Struggle*, p. 70). Pedagogically, he organized subject matter in radically different ways by incorporating the life of the surrounding community into the business of instruction and enlisting students more directly in the daily management and operation of school affairs.

Aided by Fellowship activists like John Nevin Sayre, Norman Thomas, and Robert Williams Dunn, the

Brookwood School officially opened in the fall of 1919. A promotional brochure noted that the school constituted "a laboratory for the testing of real democracy in organization" (Howlett, *Brookwood Labor College*, pp. 14–15). The school encouraged workers' control and a curriculum designed to prepare students for future social service through college as well as assist those who wish "directly to study economic and social problems with the background of history necessary to make themselves effective leaders" (Howlett, *Brookwood Labor College*, pp. 15–16). There was no fixed charge for tuition, and students were accepted on the basis of personal merit. Fincke's own personal wealth, along with contributions from sympathetic activists, was used to cover operating costs, including faculty salaries.

Students who attended the Brookwood School were mainly sixteen- to nineteen-year-old workers from the needle trades in New York City and farms in the lower Hudson Valley. Led by Fincke, Brookwood taught not only traditional subjects such as math and English but also such courses as "The Literature of Revolt," "The History of Workers in America," and "Social and Economic Problems of Today." Alice Edgerton, a Quaker student, praised Fincke's goal of "educating boys and girls in the interests and service of a world to be governed by love and brotherhood" (Edgerton, "Brookwood Methods," pp. 3–4).

The constant need for more students and additional costs forced Fincke to turn over the Brookwood Estate to the growing postwar workers' education movement. The groundwork for the transformation took place during a conference at the school on 31 March to 1 April 1921. In adhering to Fincke's original purpose of social improvement through the laboring masses, the board of directors of the new school established Brookwood Labor College, an adult residential labor college.

In 1922, Fincke and his wife decided to establish a new educational enterprise, a laborers' peace school for young children. They relocated to a farm in nearby Pawling. On this Dutchess County farm, the Finckes set up the Manumit School with a focus on teaching younger children from working-class families. Manumit symbolized "an alliance of progressive labor and progressive education" (Altenbaugh, *Education for Struggle*, p. 166). Boys and girls between the ages of nine and fourteen were encouraged to attend in order to receive "the knowledge, inspiration, and power necessary to establish a social order based on a proper appreciation of labor, to interpret the new educational movement to the American labor movement, and to interest it in a reevaluation of child education" (Howlett, *Brookwood Labor College*, p. 34). Manumit's primary focus was promoting industrial democracy. "The community life of our school," Fincke's founding statement proclaimed, "is the socialized incarnation of our belief in industrial democracy" ("A New Community School," *Survey* 53, Oct. 1924, pp. 91–92).

Fincke's school was an experiment in cooperative living. A vital part of school life was the daily farm routine involving the cultivation of crops, tending to the gardens, and raising stock on the rolling acres of farm land. Much like his earlier Brookwood School, Manumit followed the progressive educational philosophy of John Dewey. A. J. Muste, noted pacifist minister and dean of Brookwood Labor College, served on Manumit's Board of Directors. One Manumit student was Jean Rosenthal, a noted pioneer of theatrical lighting design who later attended Yale.

Fincke died at St. Luke's Hospital in New York City after a prolonged illness. He was only forty-nine. The Manumit School remained in operation for some time after his death as a testimony to his genuine friendship for children and his belief that social movements for human improvement were an essential aspect of education. His conversion from the world of corporate leadership to promoting peace and social justice through the laboring masses highlighted his contribution to the postwar workers' education movement. Throughout his adult life, Fincke envisioned a form of education that would "develop the individual so that he can meet the many labor problems of today" (quoted in *New York Times*, 1 June 1927, p. 27).

• Primary sources containing references to Fincke's role with Brookwood and Manumit are the John Nevin Sayre Papers, Swarthmore College Peace Collection; the American Civil Liberties Union Papers, Seeley Mudd Library, Princeton University; and the Brookwood Labor College Papers, Walter P. Reuther Library, Wayne State University. There is no full-length biography. Fincke's role in workers' education and promoting peace and fellowship is recounted primarily in two works: Richard Altenbaugh, *Education for Struggle: The Labor Colleges of the 1920s and 1930s* (1990), and Charles F. Howlett, *Brookwood Labor College and the Struggle for Peace and Social Justice in America* (1993). Other works that mention Fincke are Jo Ann O. Robinson, *Abraham Went Out: A Biography of A. J. Muste* (1981); Sarah N. Cleghorn, *Threescore: The Life of Sarah N. Cleghorn* (1936); Alice Edgerton, "Brookwood Methods," *The Friend* 38 (Jan. 1920) 3–4; Richard Altenbaugh, ed., *Historical Dictionary of American Education* (1999). The role of progressive education is recounted in the standard work by Lawrence Cremin, *The Transformation of the School: Progressivism in American Education, 1876–1957* (1961). See also Charles F. Howlett, "John Nevin Sayre and the American Fellowship of Reconciliation," *Pennsylvania Magazine of History and Biography* 114 (July 1990). A useful unpublished paper relating to Manumit is Scott Walter, "Labor's Democratic School: The Manumit School for Workers' Children, 1924–1934," presented at the History of Education Society, 1 Nov. 1998. A brief testimonial to Fincke is Nellie M. Seeds, "William M. Fincke: The Founder of Brookwood and Manumit," *Labor Age*, Aug. 1927, pp. 10–11. The origins of Manumit are discussed in "A New Community School," *Survey*, Oct. 1924, pp. 91–92. Commentary on Fincke's pacifism is found in an unsigned editorial, "A Minister and His Church in War," *Survey*, 2 June 1917, pp. 228–29. Two memorials are the *Nation*, 15 June 1927, pp. 228–29, and the *Survey*, 5 July 1927, p. 410. An obituary is in the *New York Times*, 1 June 1927.

CHARLES F. HOWLETT

FITZSIMMONS, Frank (7 Apr. 1908–6 May 1981), trade union official, was born Francis Edward

Fitzsimmons in Jeannette, Pennsylvania, the son of Francis Fitzsimmons, a brewery worker, and Ida May Stahley, a housewife. At the age of seventeen, after his father died, Fitzsimmons left school and worked as a bus driver. From 1926 to 1934, he worked for transit lines in Detroit, except for a brief stint with the Brooklyn-Manhattan Transit Company, finally becoming a truck driver for Detroit's National Transit Corporation. In 1934 he joined local 299 of the International Brotherhood of Teamsters (IBT), becoming a supporter of the local's young president, James R. Hoffa. In 1937 Hoffa appointed Fitzsimmons business manager, in 1940 supported his election as local vice president, and in 1943 endorsed his election as secretary-treasurer of the Michigan Conference of Teamsters (which Hoffa largely controlled). Known in union circles derisively as Hoffa's "gopher," Fitzsimmons lacked the complexity and rebelliousness of his controversial mentor. A conservative business unionist and loyal supporter of the Republican party, Fitzsimmons was considered by many unionists to be an inarticulate "yes" man more interested in playing golf and discussing baseball than in developing policies to advance the rights of workers. In 1953 Fitzsimmons was indicted for extorting kickbacks from construction companies in Michigan. The charges were subsequently dropped.

When Hoffa became president of the IBT following the imprisonment of Dave Beck and the union's expulsion from the AFL-CIO, he arranged for Fitzsimmons to become vice president in 1961. In 1964 Hoffa was convicted of jury tampering and conspiracy and fraud in the disposition of Teamster pension funds, and he had Fitzsimmons declared general vice president to manage the union in his absence. That year Fitzsimmons negotiated a renewal of the national labor contract that Hoffa had first negotiated with truck companies and, at Hoffa's behest, in 1969 he joined with United Auto Workers president Walter Reuther to form the Alliance for Labor Action. A long-time labor militant, Reuther had taken his union out of the AFL-CIO in 1968 and saw the alliance as a vehicle to attract unorganized white and blue collar workers and revive the trade union movement. Many saw the alliance as the beginning of a liberal alternative to the AFL-CIO. Fitzsimmons said of the alliance, "We are formulating our commitment to the total welfare of the community." Following Reuther's death in 1970, Fitzsimmons emerged from Hoffa's shadow.

In 1971 Hoffa was released from prison by a White House pardon, under the condition that he refrain from union activity for 13 years, and Frank Fitzsimmons became president of the Teamster Union.

Fitzsimmons and his union strongly supported the Nixon administration and Richard Nixon personally, serving on a federal board managing wage and price controls after George Meany and other trade union leaders had repudiated the board. Fitzsimmons continued to praise Nixon even after revelations in the Watergate conspiracy had cost the president much of his support in Republican ranks.

Fitzsimmons also aided the administration and his own brand of conservative business unionism by using the Teamsters to raid the membership of César Chávez's United Farm Workers (UFW), a union strongly supported by liberals and the AFL-CIO and actively opposed by California business and national conservative Republicans. In December 1972, in a speech before the American Farm Bureau Federation, Fitzsimmons called for an alliance between the Teamsters and the employers of farm labor. In the spring of 1973, as the UFW contracts in California came up for renewal, the Teamsters, with the support of most California growers, launched the raid. The Teamsters offered the growers lower wages, no benefits, and most of all, an end to UFW labor hiring halls with protected workers. The UFW launched strikes against the Teamster-grower alliance, which the Teamsters fought by importing "guards" (goon squads) to use against the UFW. In the following months UFW pickets suffered two deaths and over three hundred injuries, sixty from gunshot wounds, from the teamster attacks. Also, with the active support of Governor Ronald Reagan's administration, over 3,000 UFW pickets were arrested by local and California state police. The UFW in the process lost most of its contracts and membership.

Although UFW fortunes revived with the election of Edmund "Jerry" Brown as governor in 1974 and the creation of a state farm labor board, and Teamster farm locals came to support higher wages and benefits in conflict with the UFW, the affair was a textbook case of employer-union collaboration against the interests of workers—in this case, some of the poorest workers in the country. Under Fitzsimmons's leadership, the Teamsters clearly acted against AFL-CIO policy and labor's interest to assist conservative California agribusiness close to the Nixon administration.

Jimmy Hoffa's attempt to abrogate his pardon agreement and run for president against Fitzsimmons in 1976, many analysts believe, was a major factor in his disappearance in 1975. There is a general consensus that Hoffa was removed by the underworld, and some writers contend that crime figures saw their interest in Teamster corruption and racketeering better served by Fitzsimmons than Hoffa. The disappearance of Hoffa eliminated opposition to Fitzsimmons, except among union dissidents and reformers. The involvement with organized crime and misuse of pension funds that had characterized the administrations of Dave Beck and James R. Hoffa continued with Fitzsimmons. His son Richard Francis was convicted of taking bribes from trucking company executives in exchange for sweetheart contracts. Another son, Donald, was charged (but not tried and convicted) with pension fund fraud, i.e., charging teamster pension funds millions of dollars in bogus commissions. Union dissidents strongly criticized Fitzsimmons for putting relatives in high-paying union jobs, drawing a $150,000 salary, and living in a luxurious Washington suburban home, with an executive jet and chauffeur-driven limousine, all paid for by the union.

Fitzsimmons was helped in 1979 when Lane Kirkland, George Meany's successor as president of the AFL-CIO, let the Teamsters rejoin the federation. Fitzsimmons also storngly supported Ronald Reagan's presidential bid in 1980, but he was apparently disappointed when the new administration passed over the Teamsters' choice for secretary of labor. Scholars often see conservative business unionism (cooperation with employers against the interest of workers) and labor racketeering as the worst aspects of the American trade union tradition. Frank Fitzsimmons clearly embodied both.

Fitzsimmons died of cancer on 6 May 1981 at his home near the La Costa golfing resort in the San Diego area. . He was survived by two children from his first marriage and two children from his second marriage, to Mary Patricia, in 1952. (The name of his first wife and the date of this marriage do not appear in readily available sources of information.)

• See Steven Brill, *The Teamsters* (1978), for a decent overview of the Teamsters' corrupt practices and Fitzsimmons's relationship with Hoffa. See also Arthur Sloan, *Hoffa* (1991). The *New York Times*, 7 May 1981, contains an obituary of Fitzsimmons.

NORMAN MARKOWITZ

FORSYTHE, Albert Edward (25 Feb. 1897–4 May 1986), aviator and physician, was born in Nassau, the Bahamas, the son of Horatio Alexander Forsythe, a civil engineer, and Lillian Maud Byndloss Forsythe. When he was three, the family moved to Jamaica. His mother died of pneumonia while Forsythe was a child. His father soon remarried, eventually fathering thirteen children. The family was comfortably middle class, employing several servants. A gifted student, Forsythe attended the Titchfield School, where he excelled in mathematics. When he was fourteen, the headmaster of the school recommended that he be sent to England to complete his education. His father preferred to send him to Tuskegee Institute in Tuskegee, Alabama, an institution founded by Booker T. Washington to educate African Americans.

Arriving in the United States, Forsythe was met in Miami by relatives, who cautioned him about segregation in the South. Blacks could not use the same eating facilities, bathrooms, or water fountains as whites. They were expected to act deferentially toward whites. At Tuskegee Forsythe studied architecture. But he became interested in medicine, and because Tuskegee did not provide medical training, he decided to go elsewhere. For ten years Forsythe, who, according to his nephew, had "never had to polish his own shoes," supported himself with menial jobs while attending school part time. In 1923, he received his Bachelor of Science degree from the University of Toledo, Ohio.

He next attended McGill University, in Montreal, Canada. The onset of diabetes caused him to drop out of school for a time, but a stringent diet controlled the symptoms and allowed him to resume his studies.

On receiving his degree in 1930, he joined the Atlantic City, New Jersey, practice of a Dr. Lucas. Although he encountered some professional barriers because of his race, he prospered, enjoying a thriving practice.

While in Atlantic City, Forsythe became interested in flying. Although he could afford to purchase a plane, he could find no one to teach him to fly. At this point, he met C. Alfred Anderson, an African-American pilot who flew newspapers from Philadelphia to Atlantic City. Anderson introduced him to Ernest Buehl, a former German World War I pilot who had tutored Anderson. Buehl taught Forsythe to fly. Forsythe and Anderson became fast friends; both desired to use their aviation skills to "open doors" for young African Americans. Aviation was a field for pioneers, where skill counted for more than race. The two believed that if they could encourage young African Americans to enter aviation, it would eventually lead to advancement in other areas.

Forsythe and Anderson determined to show the world that black pilots could do anything that white pilots could do. To prove their point, they planned three daring long-distance flights, designed to garner a maximum of publicity. After fundraising activities in black churches and civic and civil rights organizations, they planned their first flight, a round trip to California. They were sponsored by the Atlantic City Board of Trade, in whose honor they christened their plane, a Fairchild monoplane, *The Pride of Atlantic City*. On 17 July 1933, the aviators started this journey, which, according to Forsythe, "was purposely made to be hazardous and rough, because if it had been an ordinary flight, we wouldn't have attracted attention." The plane was equipped only with a compass and an altimeter; it had no radio, lights, or parachutes. They used a Rand McNally road map to chart their course—until it blew out of Forsythe's hands. Despite heavy rain and strong winds, they made it to Los Angeles and back, making stops in towns with large African-American populations and becoming the first black men to complete a round-trip transcontinental flight. On their return to New Jersey, they were fêted by a gala reception in Atlantic City. In Newark, a parade in their honor on 23 September 1933 was attended by 15,000 and followed by a private audience with the governor.

Their second trip, from Atlantic City to Montreal, took place in November 1933. It was equally successful and set another record, making the crew the first black pilots to fly over an international border. Their third and most ambitious flight was a so-called goodwill trip with stops in twenty-five Caribbean and Latin American countries. At Tuskegee Institute their new Lambert Monocoupe plane was christened *The Spirit of Booker T. Washington*, in honor of Forsythe's mentor. Nettie H. Washington, Booker T. Washington's granddaughter, attended the ceremony, as did hundreds of faculty, students, and members of the public. The aviators began their journey on 8 November 1934.

Their first port of call was Nassau, the Bahamas. No plane had landed there before. A makeshift landing site had been prepared for them by cutting brush and lowering telephone poles, and friends had sent them detailed directions. Despite delays, the pair made a triumphant landing and were greeted by tumultuous crowds, including several members of Forsythe's family. During the next leg of their flight the tropical rain was so hard that "it peeled the paint off their struts," according to a 1988 interview of Anderson by *People*. Nevertheless, they successfully reached Cuba, went on to Kingston, Jamaica, and from there to Haiti, the Dominican Republic, and Puerto Rico. They were about to embark on a trip to British Guiana when a downdraft caused the plane to crash. Fortunately, both pilots were unhurt, but the plane was wrecked. Their trip was over.

Forsythe returned to New Jersey. He became interested in the prevention and treatment of tuberculosis and, to expand his knowledge in this area, returned to McGill, where he received a degree in public health in 1939. As an expert in public health, he trained visiting nurses who treated tubercular patients in their homes. On 27 April 1945 he married one of these nurses, Frances Chew Turner; they had no children. In 1951 he relocated his medical practice to Newark and moved to Montclair, New Jersey. In 1976 the couple moved to a high-rise in Newark. While still involved in his practice, civil rights, and public health, Forsythe developed a new interest, painting, and began taking art courses at a local museum. In 1977, at the age of eighty-one, he gave up his medical practice.

With old age came recognition. On 22 September 1979, Anderson and Forsythe were honored as Pioneers in Aviation by the Smithsonian Institution. In 1984 the Newark Library held a reception in Forsythe's honor. The mayor of Newark spoke of his many accomplishments and lauded his ongoing efforts to recruit minority students into aviation careers. He was also inducted into the New Jersey Aviation Hall of Fame, the first black man to be so honored.

Forsythe continued to speak at black churches and schools, encouraging young people to become aviators. While traveling to Atlantic City to give a lecture, he fell ill; he died in Atlantic City. His old friend Anderson gave the eulogy and the mayor of Atlantic City lamented his death as a loss to "the people . . . making history for black people throughout the world." On 6 February 1999, the U.S. Postal Service issued a cachet in honor of Anderson and Forsythe and their contributions to aviation and civil rights.

• A biography, *Black Flight: Breaking Barriers to Blacks in Aviation* (2002), written by his nephew Roger Albert Forsyth (who spelled his name without the final "e"), gives helpful information on Forsythe's early years and his personal life. For information on his aviation career, Lawrence P. Scott and William Womack, Sr., *Double V: the Civil Rights Struggle of the Tuskegee Airmen* (1994), and Von Hardesty and Dominick Pisano, *Black Wings: The American Black in Aviation* (1983), are helpful. Contemporary accounts of Forsythe's Caribbean trip are in "Negro Fliers in Havana," *New York Times*, 11 Nov. 1934, and "The Goodwill Flyers Call on Governor," *Daily Gleaner* (Jamaica), 14 Nov. 1934. Accounts of the issuance of a postage stamp, "US Postage Stamp to Honor 'Chief' Anderson and Dr. Forsythe," are in the *Negro Airmen International News*, Dec. 1988, p. 1. An interview with Anderson, in which he discusses his friendship with Forsythe, is in "Chief Anderson," *People*, 28 Nov. 1988, p. 149. Obituaries are in the *New York Times*, 6 May 1986, the *Newark Star-Ledger*, 7 May 1986, and the *Afro-American*, 7 May 1986.

MIRIAM SAWYER

FOX, Roy (25 Oct. 1901–20 Mar. 1982), popular bandleader, was born in Denver, Colorado. His parents (names unknown) were itinerant musicians who often worked in Salvation Army bands. When he was two, Fox's family moved to Los Angeles, where he completed his education at Polytechnic High School.

By eleven Fox was playing cornet in kids' bands. Soon he was playing with professional dance bands. In 1912 Abe Lyman formed a dance band that included major talents such as trombonist Miff Mole, future bandleader Gus Arnheim, and Fox, now also proficient on violin.

The engagement with Lyman led to other jobs in Los Angeles and nearby beach towns, and by the time he was twenty Fox was leading his own band at a nightclub in Culver City, a locus for film production. After the club burned down a year later, Fox formed a band for the new Los Angeles Biltmore Hotel. Briefly in partnership with the cabaret singer Marion Harris, by the middle 1920s Fox had left her and was freelancing in New York, where he married a Ziegfeld Follies dancer named Dorothea (family name unknown). They had no children and were divorced by 1943. In 1927 Fox was summoned by Gus Arnheim, then forming a band at the new Cocoanut Grove of the Ambassador Hotel in Los Angeles.

With Arnheim's band Fox became noted for his subtle violin sounds. In his autobiography he credits the violinist Jascha Heifetz with telling him that he, Fox, played "like a whisper." Fox then formed a band for the new Montmartre club in Hollywood. Soon it was in demand at film studios as sound came to the movies, and Fox found himself conducting background music. At the William Fox (no apparent relation) studios, Roy Fox became its executive in charge of music production, having been promised large-scale budgets. During Fox's tenure, the studios released a number of notable musicals. These included in 1929 the *William Fox Movietone Follies of 1929*, whose backstage story prefigured *Forty-Second Street*, *Hearts of Dixie*, which daringly used American spirituals and starred Stepin Fetchit, and perhaps the best musical of its time, *Sunny Side Up*, whose original score by Ray Henderson, Lew Brown, and Buddy DeSylva included "If I Had a Talking Picture of You," a national hit.

The musical unit was hitting its stride in 1930 when Fox received an invitation to form a small American group for a limited engagement at the Cafe de Paris, an exclusive night spot in London's West End. Encouraged by Abe Lyman, Fox accepted. He didn't return to America until the second World War.

American sidemen and leaders had been flocking to Britain since the Original Dixieland Jazz Band opened it to jazz dance music in 1921. Leaders such as the Massachusetts-born Carroll Gibbons (in residence at the top-line Savoy Hotel since 1924) had combined with local talent to open what became known as the golden age of British dance bands.

After characteristic bureaucratic struggles over the makeup of his band (it eventually became almost entirely British), Fox settled at London's new Monseigneur restaurant, where he became the most elegant of leaders, soft-spoken and immaculately dinner-jacketed. During these years, while Britain never recovered from the damage caused by World War I, it seemed that radio could save the entertainment industry. Like other bands, Fox's profited when the British Broadcasting Company (later Corporation) decided to dedicate much of its late-night programming to on-location dance music.

By 1931, Fox's band, featuring the crooning guitarist Al Bowlly (later with the Ray Noble orchestra) and trumpeter Nat Gonella, was among the most entertaining in Britain. Then followed one of the sporadic interruptions that characterized Fox's life: he became seriously ill, spent a year recovering in Switzerland, and upon his return found that pianist-arranger Lew Stone had conducted so well that the band had become his.

The band Fox formed in 1933 proved to be his best-loved aggregation, featuring its male vocalist Denny Dennis, a "British Bing Crosby." An American listener would never have mistaken it for a swing band; it lacked the pyrotechnics, the general freedom of American bands like Benny Goodman's or Tommy Dorsey's. But Fox's would also have ranked well beyond the American "hotel bands," too often characterized by an excessive "sweetness" or arbitrary tempi. Achieving a genuinely warm sound by playing in a straightforward manner not particularly reliant upon strings (a hazard of many British bands), it specialized in contemporarily popular music, often from American sources such as film and visiting musical theatrical productions. Its heyday lasted until 1938, when ill health again forced Fox into temporary retirement.

Fox then took a band to Australia, where he was stranded when war broke out in 1939. Existing law made it impossible to return to Britain and so he returned to the United States, where by 1943 he was leading a New York band broadcasting weekly from La Martinique to Britain. Fox's contributions alternated with those of Glenn Miller's Army Air Force Band "sending" to the United States. In the same year Fox married vocalist Kay Kimber. They had no children and were divorced in 1947.

When the war ended, Fox returned to Great Britain, where his new band, opting for a more contemporary sound, was markedly unsuccessful. In 1947 he married actress Eileen O'Donnell. They had a son and were divorced in 1966. In 1952 Fox began running his own theatrical booking agency, which also failed. He ran afoul of British bankruptcy laws and was unable to discharge his debts until 1966.

Fox died in a home for retired variety artists in Middlesex, England. He is now recalled as a partial pioneer in many areas of twentieth-century music, significant in the early development of California (i.e., largely white) jazz and dance music, and an early developer of the Hollywood musical film. A man whose instincts for the "big trend" were often excellent, as well as a man who indulged them too often for his own personal good, Fox ranked high in the early histories of American dance bands, American musical films, and transatlantic popular music in general.

• Fox's autobiography is *Hollywood, Mayfair and All That Jazz* (1975). Among many British publications covering Fox are Chris Hayes, *Signature Tunes* (1989) and *Leader of the Band* (1994). Detail regarding the William Fox film musicals is found in Clive Hirschhorn, *The Hollywood Musical* (1991). Most useful obituaries are English, including the *Times* (London), 23 Mar. 1982. This essay stems in large measure from listening to Fox's music, from English radio programs, and from album notes.

JAMES ROSS MOORE

FRANKS, David Salisbury (27 Mar. 1742–7 Oct. 1793), revolutionary officer and diplomat, was born in Philadelphia, the son of Abraham Franks, a Jewish merchant. His mother's name is unknown. In 1760 Franks enrolled in Franklin's Academy of Philadelphia, where he studied for several years. After the British victory during the French and Indian War, his family went to Canada to seek new business opportunities. They first settled in Quebec during the late 1760s. In 1774 the family moved to Montreal. David Franks and his father became two of the earliest Jews engaged in mercantile activities in this city. In 1775 David Franks became the *parnas* or president of the Montreal Shearith Israel Congregation.

Franks, ambitious and domineering, opposed the 1774 Quebec Act, which did not recognize the civic and religious status of Canadian Jews. In 1775 he denounced King George III as a fool and upbraided him for failing to establish representative government in the province of Quebec. Franks was arrested for making treasonable statements about the king and was detained for sixteen days. As a result of the influence of Governor Sir Guy Carleton, Franks was released on 19 May 1775 by Judge John Fraser. After the army of General Richard Montgomery captured Montreal on 13 November 1775, Franks expressed sympathy for the ideas of the American revolutionaries. In 1776 General David Wooster appointed him paymaster of the American garrison in this city. Franks also extended loans to the Americans and sold them military supplies. He denounced his father for his loyalty to England, and in 1776 David Franks retreated from Montreal with the Continental soldiers.

Perceived as "a friend of the American cause," Franks became involved in important activities during the War of Independence. During the summer of 1776 he spent time first in Albany, where he joined the Continental army, and then in Philadelphia. While in Philadelphia, 19 July, he asked members of the Continental Congress to repay him for monies, amounting to $6,648.84, he had loaned during the Canadian expedition, of which he received $4,600. In October 1777 he returned to upstate New York, where he served as a volunteer in a Massachusetts regiment during the Battle of Saratoga. As a result of his knowledge of the French language, Franks in 1778 secured another appointment. With recommendations from the French ambassador, Count Alexandre Gérard, and from Silas Deane, one of the American commissioners in Paris, Franks went to Sandy Hook to serve as a liaison officer for Count Charles-Henri d'Estaing, the head of the French naval contingent in America.

In July 1778 Franks was made a major in the Continental army and went to Philadelphia to serve as an aide to General Benedict Arnold, whom Franks had met during the Canadian expedition. When in May 1779 Arnold was accused of seeking personal profits in administering affairs in Philadelphia, Franks testified in his defense and helped in his being exonerated of those charges. Later that year Franks went to Charleston, South Carolina, to work under General Benjamin Lincoln. In July 1780 he was transferred to West Point and again became one of Arnold's aides. In September 1780 Arnold betrayed the American cause. However, on 25 September of that year, in a letter to General George Washington from the British ship *Vulture*, Arnold explained that Major David Franks was not aware of any of his actions and did nothing "injurious to the public."

His past connections to Arnold, however, aroused suspicion regarding Franks's loyalty. On 2 October 1780 he was arrested in Philadelphia; the next day a court-martial acquitted him of treason. In October he served under Washington at West Point and still encountered insidious allegations concerning his activities with Arnold. On 20 October he asked Washington to summon a court of inquiry to review his case. Five days later Washington established the court at West Point, and on 2 November it rendered the verdict that Franks was innocent of all charges of treasonable activities. Immediately thereafter Washington publicly proclaimed him an officer of "the highest honor" and assigned him the responsibility of delivering several significant messages to the Marquis de Lafayette. In 1781 Franks was promoted to lieutenant colonel, and that year he decided to end his military career.

From 1781 to 1787 Franks was actively involved in American diplomatic activities. Because of his friendship with Robert Morris and his knowledge of French, he was appointed a diplomatic courier, and between 1781 and 1783 he delivered confidential dispatches, reports, and letters from John Jay and William Carmichael in Madrid to Benjamin Franklin and William Temple Franklin in Paris. In 1783 Franks returned to America. On the recommendation of Robert R. Livingston, secretary for foreign affairs, Franks in early 1784 was commissioned by Congress to take the treaty ending the American Revolution to Franklin in Paris. After the completion of this mission, in September 1784, Thomas Barclay, the special agent, named Franks, who had complained to Franklin and Thomas Jefferson about being sick and short of money, the American vice consul at Marseilles.

In 1786 Franks was appointed a member of the Morocco Trade Commission, which was headed by Barclay. Franks assumed an active role in drafting significant commercial provisions of this pioneering document between American and Moroccan statesmen. Moreover in 1787 he presented copies of this proposed treaty to Jefferson in Paris and to John Adams in London. In April of that year Franks arrived in New York City. He completed his important mission and submitted this document and related dispatches to Jay, who had succeeded Livingston as the Confederation's foreign affairs secretary. Thereafter Franks's career as a diplomat came to an end.

Franks spent his last years in Philadelphia. In 1789 he received for his service in the War of Independence four hundred acres of western lands. Moreover his friendship with Robert Morris enabled Franks's appointment in 1791 as an assistant cashier of the Bank of North America. A member of the Society of Cincinnati, Franks, who never married and who did not abandon Judaism, died in Philadelphia during the yellow fever plague that swept the city in 1793. His remains were interred in Christ Church Cemetery.

Franks's career, which has been frequently overlooked as a result of his association with Arnold, was important to American history during the last half of the eighteenth century. His active and diverse life reveals his success in developing friendships with Washington, Morris, Franklin, and other prominent American revolutionaries. Honest, energetic, highly emotional, and constantly in debt, Franks became the highest-ranking Jewish military officer during the War of Independence. He also was the only Jew to occupy diplomatic positions during the American Revolution and the significant decade of the 1780s. In sum, the life of Franks vividly illustrates the gradual acceptance of Jews into positions of leadership in late eighteenth-century America.

• Some of Franks's letters are in collections in the American Philosophical Society and in the Library of Congress. Primary sources concerning Franks's military and diplomatic activities are in W. C. Ford, ed., *Journals of the Continental Congress*, vols. 5, 6, 13, 20, 23, and 32 (1904–1937); John C. Fitzpatrick, ed., *Writings of Washington*, vols. 12 and 20 (1931–1944); Francis Wharton, ed., *The Revolutionary Diplomatic Correspondence of the United States*, vols. 4–5 (1889); Mary A. Giunta and J. Dane Hargrove, eds., *The Emerging Nation: A Documentary History of the Foreign Relations of the United States under the Articles of Confederation, 1780–1789*, vol. 1 (1996); Elizabeth Nuxoll and Mary A. Gallagher, eds., *The Papers of Robert Morris, 1781–1784: May 5–December 31, 1783*, vol. 1 (1995); Leonard Labaree, Barbara Oberg, and Ellen R. Cohn, eds., *The Papers of Benjamin Franklin,* vols. 36–37 (2001–2004); and Julian P. Boyd, ed., *Papers of Thomas Jefferson,* vol. 6 (1951). Three incisive biographical accounts of Franks are Samuel Rezneck, *Unrecognized Patriots: The Jews in the American Revolution* (1975); Jacob R. Marcus, *United States Jewry, 1775–1985,* vol. 1 (1989); and Hersch L. Zitt, "David Salisbury Franks: Revolutionary Patriot (c. 1740–1793)," *Pennsylvania History* 16 (Apr. 1949): 77–95. For Franks's life in Canada, see Jacob R. Marcus, *Early American Jewry: The Jews of New York, New England, and Canada, 1694–1794,* vol. 1 (1951). His connections to Benedict Arnold are described in Willard S. Randall, *Benedict Arnold: Patriot and Traitor* (1990); James T. Flexner, *The Traitor and the Spy: Benedict Arnold and John André* (1953); and Carl Van Doren, *Secret History of the American Revolution* (1941). Significant developments concerning Franks's diplomatic career and later life are examined in Edwin Wolf II and Maxwell Whiteman, *History of the Jews of Philadelphia from Colonial Times to the Age of Jackson* (1956); and Oscar S. Straus, "New Light on the Career of Colonel David S. Franks," *Publications of the American Jewish Historical Society* 10 (1902): 101–8.

WILLIAM WEISBERGER

FROMAN, Jane (10 Nov. 1907–22 Apr. 1980), singer, was born Ellen Jane Froman in University City, Missouri, a suburb of St. Louis, the daughter of Elmer Ellsworth Froman, a traveling salesman, and Anna Barcafer Froman, a musician who taught piano and voice and also performed. When Ellen Jane was five, her parents separated, and she never saw her father again; the couple subsequently divorced. Mother and daughter returned to the mother's hometown, Clinton, Missouri, where Anna Froman taught in local schools and directed church choirs. Ellen was placed in a local convent school, despite the fact that the family was Protestant. She began studying piano with her mother at an early age and quickly became proficient, but she was unhappy at school and developed a pronounced stutter that remained with her for the rest of her life.

Encouraged by her mother to sing, Ellen discovered that whenever she did so her stuttering vanished. In 1920 she and her mother moved to Christian College in Columbia, Missouri. Her mother became the director of vocal studies at the school (now Columbia College), and Ellen entered its high school division, where she appeared in numerous musical productions. She went on to matriculate at Christian, where she performed in school musicals, and received an associate's degree in liberal arts in 1926. That fall she enrolled at the University of Missouri's School of Journalism in Columbia—not to become a newspaper professional but to perform in the school's annual musical comedy revue. A talent scout in the audience hired her for an annual children's Christmas show in St. Louis, and, billed as "Ellen Jane Froman, the Blues Singing Co-Ed of Missouri University," she received rave reviews.

An indifferent journalism student and confirmed partygoer, Froman, to her mother's chagrin, soon flunked out of the university. Her mother then enrolled her at the Cincinnati Conservatory of Music in the fall of 1928 to begin a rigorous program of vocal studies. There Froman excelled, and to pay her own way she obtained scholarships and secured singing jobs at area teas and parties, accompanying herself on the piano; she also earned money singing in a church choir. Froman was a hit wherever she appeared. In 1930 she sang at a party for Powel Crosley, Jr., owner of the Cincinnati Reds baseball team and radio station WLW. Crosley hired her to sing on his station; she performed both popular songs and singing commercials.

As the largest independent radio station in the country, WLW claimed a wide audience, and Froman quickly became a favorite of its listeners. Her distinctive contralto caught the attention of celebrated orchestra leader Paul Whiteman, who tried to interview her during a trip to Cincinnati, but the station, eager to hold onto the singer who had become its star attraction, thwarted Whiteman's attempt to meet her. At work Froman became friendly with a fellow performer, Don Ross, part of a vaudeville duo called Brooks and Ross. Ross seized an opportunity to market Froman's talent and in 1931 persuaded her to move with the team to Chicago, where he believed she could get a better radio job.

Froman was invited to audition at NBC Radio, and despite the fact that she had broken her ankle minutes before the appointment and was in great pain, she sang effortlessly for the station's music director—Paul Whiteman. Froman was hired and soon had a contract for a regular weekly music show. She quickly graduated to her own daily fifteen-minute show, with her own orchestra. She followed the popular "Amos 'n' Andy," which virtually guaranteed her a huge audience, and her show was broadcast on NBC stations throughout the country. In less than a year she was known nationwide as a singing star.

By late 1932 Don Ross had moved on to New York as a solo act, and with his encouragement Froman, who had also been singing in Chicago theaters as part of the elaborate stage shows then offered in tandem with screen presentations, followed him in January 1933. She was hired to sing two days a week on one of the nation's top radio shows, "The Chesterfield Hour," whose lineup included Bing Crosby and other major stars of the day. Her popularity on the show led to simultaneous engagements at major movie theaters in New York, including the Paramount and Radio City Music Hall, and an invitation to appear in the 1933 Ziegfeld Follies, which opened at Christmastime after tryouts in Boston; she joined a cast that included comedians Fred Allen and Fanny Brice. Brice took Froman under her wing, helping the younger woman over initial stage fright and awkwardness and passing along "her own great fund of priceless experience," as Froman later recalled in an unpublished autobiography. The show and Froman were huge hits, and Froman and Brice remained lifelong friends.

Froman, who had married Don Ross in September 1933, stayed with the Follies for a year while continuing to perform on radio. A regular on seven shows, and making records as well, Froman had emerged as a major popular singing star, with a repertory of hit songs by George Gershwin, Richard Rodgers and Lorenz Hart, and other major songwriters of the day. She and Ross, continuing to act as her manager, bought a penthouse on the Upper East Side of Manhattan and led the glamorous life of show business celebrities. In 1934, a year after arriving in the city, she was named in a nationwide listener poll as the number-one female singer on the radio. That same year she was asked by George Gershwin to introduce on the radio the aria "Summertime" from his opera *Porgy and Bess*, and he gave her exclusive radio performance rights for an entire year.

Though her stuttering continued to plague her—to such an extent that when she was called on to speak during radio programs, another female voice would do the talking—this handicap did not prevent her from emerging as the nation's favorite female vocalist by the end of the decade. In addition to her radio performances and her recordings, she appeared in Broadway musicals, was heard in chic nightclubs in Manhattan, Chicago, and Miami, and sang in several otherwise forgettable Hollywood movies. Always elegantly gowned, and projecting an image of refined sophistication, the beautiful brunette was now billed as "Park Avenue's Favorite Entertainer." One indication of her success was the widely quoted assessment of prominent showman Billy Rose: asked to name the ten best female singers of the day, he replied, "There's Jane Froman and nine others." When her picture appeared on the cover of *Life* magazine in March 1938, Froman had reached the height of fame. She was now also able to speak during performances without stuttering, though the affliction continued to plague her when she was not behind a microphone.

Tensions had developed in Froman's personal life as her husband's career stalled. The William Morris Agency took over Froman's management, and anxious to keep her marriage going, she took several breaks from her own career to spend more time at home. But her popularity remained high as World War II began in Europe in September 1939. By 1941 she was actively involved in the war effort, traveling to Canada with Richard Rodgers to perform in person and on the radio for Canadian troops. When the U.S. entered the war in December, she and comedian Ed Wynn were the first to respond to President Franklin D. Roosevelt's call for leading performers to entertain American troops. She sang at training camps, bond drives, and special Victory Concerts for war relief across the country throughout 1942. When she appeared in her adopted hometown of Columbia, Missouri, to do a concert series, she scheduled a special performance for a black audience after learning that only whites were allowed into the segregated concert halls.

When President Roosevelt called on American entertainers in December 1942 to perform for troops overseas, Froman was again the first to respond, and while she waited for an assignment she continued to perform at military camps, hospitals, and bond drives, always keeping a packed suitcase nearby. Finally, on 21 February 1943, Froman departed for London with half a dozen other entertainers on the Pan-American seaplane Yankee Clipper. Several stops were scheduled for refueling, and as the plane was coming in for a landing in Lisbon on the evening of 22 February, it crashed into the icy Tagus River. Twenty-four passengers were killed, but fifteen survived—among them Jane Froman.

The critically injured Froman clung to part of the floating wreckage for nearly an hour before being rescued, held up by one of the plane's officers, John Burn. She remained in Lisbon hospitals for two months, as doctors tended to multiple fractures and a nearly severed right leg and placed virtually her entire body in a cast. Though she received permission from President Roosevelt to fly back to New York by military plane for more extensive medical care, her condition forced her to make the return trip by Portuguese freighter, narrowly dodging German torpedoes during the two-week journey through rough seas. At Doctors Hospital in Manhattan, Froman was told that her leg needed amputation. Thus began a saga of poor health that kept Froman in and out of hospitals for more than a decade and in pain for the rest of her life. Over the years she endured thirty-nine major operations to keep her leg and to heal the rest of her massive injuries. She resolved that one day she would again walk.

Friends in the entertainment world rallied around her, and through the intervention of President Roosevelt she was given penicillin, a drug then reserved for military use, to treat several life-threatening infections. In the face of mounting medical and other crash-related expenses that ultimately totaled hundreds of thousands of dollars—Froman even had to pay $2,000 for her freighter passage home—she was determined to return to work as soon as possible. Don Ross and producer Lou Walters put together a musical revue for her called "Artists and Models" that allowed her to sit while onstage, and after rehearsals from a wheelchair in her hospital room, the show opened in October 1943, first in Boston and then in New York. The five-foot six-inch Froman was now a frail eighty-five pounds, her right leg and right arm encased in casts that weighed another thirty-five. Carried on and off the stage for twenty-two times at each performance—and painfully dropped on several occasions—she still managed to give a riveting performance and receive standing ovations from weeping fans. The show soon closed, largely dismissed by the critics, but Froman scored a huge personal victory.

Buoyed by that success as proof of her continuing popularity—newspaper coverage of her accident and her struggle to recover had made her a national heroine—Froman sang on the radio and in nightclubs over the next two years. Still unable to stand alone without support, though she could get about awkwardly on crutches, Froman performed in clubs on a motorized platform that also carried a piano, as well as her accompanist; she was often joined on the rolling platform by major singing stars, including Frank Sinatra. By late spring of 1945, shortly after the war ended in Europe, she felt well enough to return overseas to carry out the tour that had ended abruptly two years earlier. In three and a half months she performed ninety-five shows in six countries, traveling more than thirty thousand miles, attracting huge, adoring crowds of servicemen and civilians alike, and she became a heroine to millions of wounded GIs.

Following the tour, Froman was in and out of hospitals for the next two years, working whenever she could to pay her mounting expenses. Other major stars, including singer Sophie Tucker and comedian Joe E. Brown, canceled dates so that Froman could have their engagements. In 1947 she remained in bed for eight months following a grueling series of bone graft operations to save her leg yet again, but this time the surgery seemed to work, and she was now able to walk with the aid of a leg brace and a cane.

During Froman's long recuperation, she kept in touch with John Burn, the flight officer who had helped rescue her, and they drew closer as her marriage to Don Ross disintegrated. Ross and Froman were divorced in February 1948, and a month later she and Burn were married. Froman continued to perform and record, and in 1952 her career received a further boost when a movie was made of her life. Titled *With a Song in My Heart*—and featuring the eponymous Rodgers and Hart title song that Froman had made famous—it starred Susan Hayward; Froman dubbed all the songs. As a consequence of the film's popularity, Froman was given her own weekly television show in the fall of 1952 and the following year on the show introduced the song "I Believe," which became a hit recording. The show was canceled in 1955, and a year later Froman and Burn were divorced, but despite these setbacks she continued to perform in nightclubs until her retirement in 1961, when she moved back to Columbia, Missouri.

In the early 1950s, Froman had sued Pan American for $2.5 million in damages, but after a protracted court battle she received a settlement of less than $10,000. In 1962 the U.S. House of Representatives awarded Froman and two other crash survivors $20,000 each—a token acknowledgment that her injuries occurred while performing at the request of the U.S. government. That same year Froman married a college classmate, Rowland Smith. They lived quietly together in Columbia while Froman devoted herself to raising money for educational and charitable organizations, among them the Jane Froman Foundation for Emotionally Disturbed Children. Froman, who never had children of her own, had established the foundation as part of the Menninger Clinic in 1951, following her lengthy stay at the clinic for treatment of depression; as part of her own therapy she had worked extensively with disturbed young patients there. At the time of her death she was a trustee of the Menninger Foundation and several other organizations.

On Christmas Eve 1979 Froman, already in frail health, was seriously injured in a car accident in Columbia. She never completely recovered and was largely confined to her home until her death four months later.

• Biographical information can be found in Jane Froman's unpublished autobiography, included in a large collection of Froman memorabilia housed at Columbia College, as well as the Jane Froman Papers and the Jane Froman Collection, which includes recordings and taped interviews; both are part of the Western Historical Manuscript Collection at the University of Missouri, Columbia. Additional Froman memorabilia is archived at the Boone County Historical Society and Museum, also in Columbia. In addition, see Ilene Stone, *Jane Froman: Missouri's First Lady of Song* (2003), which includes a partial list of magazine articles about Froman that appeared during her career, as well as a list of Froman's recordings currently available. A detailed account of Froman's suit against PanAm is found in Stuart M. Speiser, *Lawyers and the American Dream* (1993); Speiser was one of her attorneys. An obituary is in the *New York Times*, 23 Apr. 1980.

ANN T. KEENE

FRY, Varian (15 Oct. 1907–13 Sept. 1967), editor, journalist, and teacher, was born on West 150th Street in Manhattan, the only child of Arthur Fry, a partner in a small Wall Street brokerage firm, and Lillian Mackey Fry, a Hunter College graduate who taught school until her mental condition forced her into early retirement.

Two years after their son's birth the couple moved to Ridgewood, New Jersey, and set up a household with two of Lilian's maiden sisters. At age fourteen, Varian was sent to the prestigious Hotchkiss Prep School in Lakeville, Connecticut, where he remained for two very unhappy years. Bright but unruly and rebellious, he continuously got into trouble with the school authorities and by mutual consent left Hotchkiss in 1924 for the Taft Prep School in Watertown, Connecticut, where he lasted all of six months. Enrolled in 1925 at the Riverdale Country School but living at home, he commuted to classes in a brand-new four-door Packard given to him by his doting father. By the end of that year, the headmaster suspended Varian for "loss of control and unpardonable impertinence." Urged and supported by his father, he applied to Harvard University in the spring of 1926 and despite conflicting recommendations was accepted. His freshman year was spent in a frenzy of intellectual and social activity. Together with a classmate, Lincoln Kirstein, Fry launched the *Hound & Horn*, a magazine intended to introduce Harvard students to such artists as James Joyce, T. S. Eliot, Pablo Picasso, Gertrude Stein, and Igor Stravinsky.

The two young publishers/editors fell out with each other in early 1926, and Varian was forced to give up his position at the magazine to which he had devoted much time and energy. Disappointed, he plunged into a social life that consisted mostly of drinking and rowdy behavior and eventually led to his being placed on probation for his sophomore year. Thanks to his father's intervention, he was reinstated and allowed to enter his junior year in good standing. He spent the summer of 1928 in Greece at the American School of Classical Studies, but after his return in the fall of that year he again got into trouble and was expelled from Harvard with the understanding that he could apply for readmission if he could prove that he had "developed a proper sense of responsibility" and not "disgrace" the institution.

Shortly before his expulsion, he had met and befriended a woman editor at the Atlantic Monthly, Eileen Avery Hughes, who was six years his senior. She successfully pleaded Varian's case for readmission by pledging to keep him under control. He was allowed to rejoin his original class in the fall of 1930 and graduated in May of the following year with a B.A. in Classical Studies.

Fry and Hughes were married in June 1931. For a time they lived in Boston, Massachusetts, and Grafton, New York. By the end of that year they moved to Manhattan, where Fry had gotten a job as a part-time writer for *Consumers' Research* and as a substitute teacher of English and Latin.

From 1932 to 1935 he held editorial posts at various magazines, among them *The Living Age*, which specialized in foreign affairs and on whose behalf he traveled to Germany in May 1935. His observations about Hitler's Germany appeared in the *New York Times* on 17 July 1935. Two years later, Fry became editor-in-chief of the Foreign Policy Association's Headline Books while working part-time for the Committee on Aid to Spanish Democracy, where he alienated most of its members because of his uncompromising positions that ultimately forced him to resign. He withdrew from contact with almost all his friends and, living in virtual isolation but keeping his job at the Foreign Policy Association, wrote articles and positional papers, a brief history of the United States' relationship with Latin America, and a study on international cooperation.

In the summer of 1939 he had met Karl Frank, alias Paul Hagen, the organizer in the United States of a German social democratic group under the name "Neubeginnen" that opposed Hitler. On 16 May 1940 Hagen alerted Fry to the great danger to European antifascist artists and writers as a result of Germany's imminent occupation of France. The two, joined by Harold Oram, met soon thereafter and decided to come to the aid of the endangered intellectuals. On 25 June 1940 at the Commodore Hotel in Manhattan they formed an Emergency Rescue Committee, collected $3,500, and established a list of names of those thought to be particularly threatened. The decision was also made to send someone immediately to occupied France, preferably an American with a good command of French and some experience in dealing with artists and political exiles. After two weeks of fruitless searching, the Committee, with some reluctance, asked Fry, who had volunteered earlier, whether he would go. Armed with a statement from the YMCA certifying him as one of their social workers, a letter of introduction by Sumner Welles from the State Department, $3,000, and the list of names taped to his leg, Fry arrived in Marseilles on 15 August 1940. As specified by the Emergency Rescue Committee, he was to stay for three weeks, write a report on the conditions of the refugees, find someone to act as a permanent agent of the Committee, track down as many people on the list as possible, and assist those people in reaching neutral Portugal. Instead, Fry, realizing the magnitude of the problem, took it upon himself to remain in Marseilles, at great personal risk, for a whole year, during which he managed to facilitate the departure from Nazi-occupied France of some of the most famous artists and writers of the twentieth century, among them Marc Chagall, André Breton, Max Ernst, André Masson, Franz Werfel, and Heinrich Mann. With no experience in underground work, he quickly assembled a group of dedicated and trustworthy people to help him carry out his rescue work, which ranged from dispensing financial aid and moral support to such covert operations as forging documents, transferring money secretly, and creating a clandestine network to smuggle refugees out of France by sea or across the Pyrenees. Though apprised of the content of a cable sent on 26 September 1940 by the State Department to all its consulates in France, stating that the U.S. government would not countenance any activities by American citizens desiring to evade the laws of the governments with which it maintained friendly relations, Fry not only continued but expanded his dangerous work on behalf of the refugees.

On 29 August 1941, accused by the collaborationist French government of being an "undesirable alien" for protecting Jews and anti-Nazis, he was escorted by Vichy police to the Spanish border and expelled from France. He arrived in the United States on 2 November 1941, but, because of his independent posture in Marseilles, he was considered a *persona non-grata* by his own Emergency Rescue Committee and given no official acknowledgement for his remarkable accomplishment, that of saving some 2,000 people from eventual extermination. His book about his experience in France, *Surrender on Demand*, published in April 1945, by Random House, received scant notice. The lack of recognition affected his mood and caused him to become alienated from erstwhile friends and his wife. They separated in 1942 but remained very close. Her death in 1948 only deepened his feeling of abandonment and rejection. His spirits revived during the winter of 1948/1949, shortly after he had made the acquaintance of Annette Riley, sixteen years his junior. They were married in November 1950 and settled in Ridgefield, Connecticut; they had three children. None of the activities he engaged in after his return—journalism, editing, teaching—brought him the fulfillment, excitement, and sense of power he had felt during that one year in France. He became more and more estranged from friends and family. In August 1967 he and Annette obtained a Mexican divorce. Two weeks later, he was found dead in bed, probably from an excess of medication to control his bouts with depression.

The only official recognition he had received until then had come from the French government, which on 26 April 1962 awarded him the *Croix de Chevalier de la Légion d'Honneur*. It took fourteen more years before his own country honored him with the Eisenhower Liberation Medal and in 1993 an exhibition at the United States Holocaust Memorial Museum in Washington. In a ceremony attended by Secretary of State Warren Christopher he was declared in 1996 by the Yad Va Shem in Jerusalem as "Righteous among the Nations," while the Marseilles municipality in 1999 named the square in front of the American Consulate Place Varian Fry.

• Many of Fry's notes, letters, and photographs can be found at the Rare Book and Manuscript Library, Columbia University. His book about his Marseilles venture, *Surrender on Demand* (1945), is also available in a special version for high school students entitled *Assignment Rescue* (1968). Informative memoirs are Lincoln Kirstein, *Mosaic* (1994); Hans Sahl, *In Search of Myself* (1994); and Mary Jayne Gold, *Crossroad Marseilles, 1940* (1980). A revealing biography by Andy Marino, *A Quiet American* (1999), exists also in a British edition under the title *The American Pimpernel*. Sheila Isenberg, *A Hero of Our Own* (2001), contains a useful bibliography. Two noteworthy documentaries are *Varian Fry: The Artists' Schindler* (BBC, 1992) and *Villa Air-Bel: Varian Fry in Marseilles, 1940/41* (TV Munich, 1987). Tributes to Fry by Max Frankel and Alfred Kazin appeared in the *New York Times Magazine*, 23 Nov. 1992, and the *New Republic*, 9 Feb. 1998, respectively. A substantial obituary is in the *New York Times*, 14 Sept. 1967.

JUSTUS ROSENBERG

FULLERTON, William Morton (18 Sept. 1865–26 Aug. 1952), journalist and writer, was born in Norwich, Connecticut, the son of Bradford Morton Fullerton, a divinity student, and Julia Ball Fullerton. His father had temporarily dropped out of Andover Theological Seminary in Massachusetts, but after the boy was born, he returned to complete the course, then went to serve a congregation in Palmer as minister. "Will" or "Morton" attended the village school and, briefly, Phillips Academy in Andover. Handsome, bright, and even as a child strangely magnetic, he was idolized by his parents, his younger brother, and his half-cousin Katharine (later Katharine Fullerton Gerould), who was taken into the family as a baby when he was 14 and whom he taught to read and inspired to write. When he entered Harvard in the class of 1886, the family moved to a parish in Waltham, near Cambridge, so that he could commute. He was still living in a parsonage during his first job (1886–1888), as literary editor of the *Boston Record Advertiser*.

In 1885, with George Santayana and other classmates, Fullerton started *Harvard Magazine*, in which Bernard Berenson was also active. Fullerton received prizes, and a magna, but his failure to win a fellowship

for study abroad darkened his Harvard memories. At the *Advertiser* he paid homage to the venerable John Greenleaf Whittier but boldly defended the presence of the *Decameron* on college reading lists. He was interviewed by *The Literary World*. Santayana mocked his self-promotional reports of professional honors but was uneasily curious about his success with women and sent him, uncharacteristically, a "Rabelaisian" analysis of "amatory attitudes"—whoring, masturbation, pederasty, etc. (pp. 74–75). Fullerton had already had many girl friends; he also had homosexual relationships with the poet Bliss Carman and others.

In 1888 Samuel Longfellow, the poet's brother, took Fullerton to Europe. The following year Hamilton Aïdé, the English artist and writer, took him to Egypt and Greece. He then settled in London among Aïdé's aristocratic homosexual set. He had an affair with the sculptor Lord Ronald Gower, Oscar Wilde's "Lord Henry Wotton" in *The Picture of Dorian Gray*. Wilde himself he knew only casually. He published in the *Yellow Book* a sonnet on George Meredith, whom he ranked next to Shakespeare for both genius and ideas, especially his opposition to marriage. In the more conventional literary world, he became a friend of Meredith and his son (later Fullerton's editor at Constable). Fullerton was close to Henry James. (The evidence indicates that their friendship was not sexual.) James introduced Fullerton to the Ranee of Sarawak, with whom he had a passionate liaison, but whom he dropped when he left London.

In 1890 he wrote a witty and telling essay, "English and Americans," in which he came down eloquently on the side of America. When, American and unqualified, he was taken on by the *Times*, people said it was through his connections. In 1891 he was sent to work as a reporter under the famous, flamboyant chief correspondent Henri von Blowitz in Paris, where he spent the rest of his life.

Fullerton found lodgings with a Mme. Mirecourt, stage name of a captivating ex-singer and actress who became his mistress. Her apartment was elegant enough for him to entertain Ronald Gower and the Marquess of Lorne, a son-in-law of Queen Victoria.

Reporting speeches in the Chamber of Deputies, he was struck by fragments of a bomb thrown by terrorists. He reasoned away any residue of supernatural religion; in a time of bloody social protest, he declared for human rights, freedom, science, and the "modern spirit" (p. 92). He reached the peak of his journalistic career covering the second court-martial of Alfred Dreyfus, the French army captain who had been found guilty of treason mainly because he was a Jew. For weeks, Fullerton's compelling minute-by-minute narration of the trial dominated the *Times*'s main page, with picturesque description and analysis of lawyers, witnesses, and the prisoner. The judges were "a standing warning of the danger which individual liberty and social justice run from the untrammeled development in our modern society of military institutions" (p. 102). Despite his elaborate syntax, Fullerton's reports were intense and suspenseful. Openly partisan, anonymous as were all *Times* articles, they aroused sympathy and indignation on behalf of Dreyfus in England. He also published signed magazine articles, e.g., "Impressions in Cairo" (1891), "Monsieur de Blowitz" (1893), and the humorous and atypically self-deprecatory "At Arcachon" (1897), about philology and oysters. Such pieces kept his name before editors and readers and allowed him to eke out a salary.

Fullerton worked hard, but spent idyllic holidays with Mirecourt. He bought old books, dined with Paul Verlaine, and refused a loan to Oscar Wilde when Wilde came to Paris after release from jail. With his talents and achievements, he was confident of succeeding Blowitz. When Blowitz retired in 1902 and Fullerton learned that the Vienna correspondent, William Lavino, would be the next chief, it was the greatest shock of his life. London told him that, not knowing what else to do with him, they were sending him to Madrid, a minor post, with a small raise. He must go to Portugal first, to cover a royal visit by Edward VII to Carlos II.

In Lisbon, euphoric at being wafted from humiliation to moonlight fêtes, Fullerton had a love letter from a young Frenchwoman, Camille Chabbert, who was living at court with a small child fathered by King Carlos and studying for grand opera. Against his principles Fullerton married her, and they lived in Madrid for nine months, quarreling violently.

He filed verbose copy, submitted confusing expense accounts, and wrote indiscreetly of the Vatican's hold on Spain. In early 1904 he was abruptly recalled to Paris and demoted to second assistant, at his old salary. Neither he nor Camille (still in Spain) could possibly economize. Mirecourt, furious about his marriage demanded money before she would take him back. Fullerton told his parents that he needed money for her. They replied that they had been tolerant of his youthful "love episodes" (p. 61) but that now he had a sacred obligation to his wife. They agreed to send money on the condition that he would swear not to give it to Mme. Mirecourt. By then, however, he was divorcing Camille—illegally, with her collusion, and in her absence—and Mirecourt took him back.

In the Paris office Fullerton was helpful to Lavino in routine work and reviewed French books in the Times's literary supplement. On his own, he published some travel essays as *Terres Françaises* (1905), a pleasant, unobtrusively scholarly book that was "crowned" by the Académie Française. He sent a copy to Professor Charles Eliot Norton at Harvard, saying it would show the people who had thought him unworthy of a fellowship 20 years ago what he had done by himself.

In 1907 he took his first home leave in years. His cousin Katharine had learned that her adoption was only informal and out of loyalty to her foster parents had taken steps, herself, to make it legal. A Radcliffe graduate now, teaching at Bryn Mawr, she hero-worshipped Fullerton, who, seeing her grown up,

pretty, and romantic, persuaded her to promise to marry him. In Lenox, he stayed overnight with Edward and Edith Wharton, and Edith fell in love with him. On his return to Paris, he wrote to Henry James in panic: Mirecourt threatened to show his employers compromising letters from Ronald Gower and others unless he paid her a huge amount of money or married her. James grandly denounced the "mad, vindictive, and obscene old woman" (p. 28).

In 1908, in France, Fullerton and Edith Wharton became lovers. When she left, he ignored her letters; on her return in 1909 he easily won her forgiveness, and the affair resumed its uneven course. Katharine, wretched at not hearing from Fullerton, came to France to ask if they were engaged. Giving her Delphic answers ("without marriage there is no life for you nor for me" [p. 53]), he joked with other women about his "amours" with his sister (p. 59).

In 1909, to enable Fullerton to redeem his letters without offending his pride, Wharton (who was ignorant of their contents) had the publisher Macmillan ask him to write a book on Paris; when Fullerton agreed, she gave Henry James money that James asked Macmillan to give Fullerton as if it were an advance on royalties. (Advances were normally paid only on submission of manuscript.) He told Macmillan that Fullerton could use the money, as he was responsible for his old, ill father. Fullerton, unaware of the subterfuge, repaid a portion of the sum demanded by Mirecourt and signed a legal agreement to pay the balance in installments. She returned his letters. Fullerton's friends called it blackmail, but he had lived at Mirecourt's expense for years.

Meanwhile, Fullerton remained engaged to Katharine. Fullerton had a sociopathic inability to love, a lack of affect, and a need for power. When Katharine begged him to tell her how they stood, he promised that they would talk about it next summer. Katharine at once married another man and, as Katharine Fullerton Gerould, became a popular writer.

In 1910 Fullerton faced a crisis at the *Times*. He had lost hope of promotion. He and the current chief hated each other. He was ordered to stop publishing anywhere except in the paper. Forbidden to use his name and threatened with dismissal, he accepted a loan from Wharton and resigned. In 1912, he went to Luxembourg to work on a book. With him was Hélène Pouget, a sculptor's model. They lived together till he died, though her Huguenot mother disowned her.

Fullerton had not been dismissed by the *Times*, as he had feared he would be, because of incriminating letters from the 1890s, but the experience of fear may have made him more prudent in his homosexual involvements. From this time, his bisexuality was evidently known to very few people. After his death, Camille Chabbert called him a pederast: whether she meant during their marriage sixty years earlier, or in the more recent past, is not clear. He distanced himself from Oscar Wilde's circle and privately expressed abhorrence for Wilde himself. His air of mystery may have resulted from concealment of an important aspect of his character—as well as from the weight of state secrets that he let it be known he carried.

Fullerton's "America Revisited" (1911) and "The Unmarried Woman in France" (1913) were amiable footnotes to social history, but his major work, *Problems of Power*, also published in 1913, was an ambitious, hard-boiled, anti-idealistic survey of the world on the brink of the First World War, densely documented, with classical allusions. Fullerton argued that democratic government was only a façade for multinational companies and banks and public opinion. "The populace or the mob, armed by the humanitarianism of our special form of Christian civilization, possesses, in the devices of universal suffrage and parliamentary government, sure instruments for the immediate and frequently selfish utilization of the wealth of the community, and for the satisfaction of party interests and class appetites in injudicious and often anti-national ways" (quoted in Mainwaring, p. 210). The book was a marked success. "[I]t would be a good thing," wrote Theodore Roosevelt, "for all our people to read Mr. Fullerton's book" (p. 210).

Fullerton had once upheld human rights. Now he believed that national security should prevail over civil liberties. When the United States entered the war, Fullerton joined army intelligence. Pentagon records show him analyzing and advising. After the war he was disgusted with Woodrow Wilson's "self-determination": small nations should be used as weapons, like "gas shells, grenades, avions" (p. 220); Germany should be a "'Boche Reserve' like the American 'Indian Reserves'" (p. 219). He talked with the heads and would-be heads of state, exiles, leaders of ethnic minorities, refugees, conspirators, who thronged to Paris as the Treaty of Versailles was hammered out.

G-2 service continued for two years after the peace, overlapping the most brilliant period of Fullerton's life. In the 1920s and 1930s, he was U.S. secretary-general in the League of Nations Intellectual and Artistic Cooperation Commission. He remained notorious as a womanizer and prominent as a columnist. For five years he edited a Franco-American section in *Le Figaro*; after which long articles by W. Morton-Fullerton appeared bimonthly on page one, usually inveighing against Germany. In Franco-American disputes, he sided with France: an argument that America should forgive France her war debts occupied five columns of a six-column front page and brought him promotion in the Legion of Honor to commander. A greater honor, Fullerton was one of Les Quarante-Cinq, a group of forty-five eminent intellectuals and artists. He revised his past, intimating that he had been chief *Times* correspondent. His ignominious stint in Madrid became "a prolonged and urgent mission" (p. 12)

In 1936, Fullerton quarreled with the *Figaro* management and went to the *Journal des Débats*. When France fell in 1940, he quit. He was in a dangerous position. He did not object to dictatorships, but—as everyone knew—loathed Germany. When the United States entered the war, he was interned as an enemy alien but soon released. His postwar allusions to life during the Occupation were guarded and equivocal. After his death his executor found and burned a correspondence with Jacques Doriot, Hitler's appointee as Governor of Paris, which may have saved him. In any case, he and Mme. Pouget lacked food and fuel. In 1944, Leon Edel, entering Paris as a soldier, found him sorting letters, shabby, "those fine mustaches now ragged and unkempt . . . [but] the charm was always there" (p. 264).

Fullerton's charm sometimes glints in articles written before he left the *Times*, in perceptive, graceful passages far from his turgid French journalese. Impressive and seductive in person, on paper Fullerton seems empty, with no commitment except to himself. He was thought to be enigmatic, mysterious. James drew on him for the character of his London journalist, Merton Densher, in *The Wings of the Dove*. Today Fullerton is interesting mostly for his interaction with fascinating people and for his part in public and private events, comic and tragic, too complicated to summarize. Strangely, little would be known about him if he had not kept and annotated letters that he surely knew would discredit him.

Some of the papers he was sorting were already subjects of dispute. He suavely declined to surrender letters from Edith Wharton (deceased) which he was wrongly told were not his property. He and Santayana quarreled vindictively over his refusal to return the "Rabelaisian" letters Santayana had written in 1887 (p. 267). When Fullerton died, Mme Pouget, by then his common-law wife, had hundreds of his papers; Camille Chabbert, claiming to be his illegally divorced wife, took them at revolver point.

• The papers Camille Chabbert had commandeered became available to scholars in the 1970s and 1980s. Like hundreds of other mostly unpublished documents concerning Fullerton, they are lodged in some 250 archives and in private hands. *The History of the Times*, vol. 3 (1947), was published during Fullerton's lifetime, but because he had left the paper in 1910, references to him are not always reliable. Leon Edel, who met Fullerton in 1930 and 1944, discussed him in *Henry James* (1953–1972) and *Henry James Letters* (4 volumes in one, 1974). From 1975 on, Fullerton appears in books on Edith Wharton, but the accounts of his life, including his relations with Wharton, are based on inaccurate documentation. Above, page numbers in parentheses refer to Marion Mainwaring, *Mysteries of Paris: The Quest for Morton Fullerton* (2001), which contains lists of Fullerton's writings and of archival sources. Obituaries by James Coquet and H. Warner Allen are in *Le Figaro* and the *Times* (London), respectively, both 29 Aug. 1952.

MARION MAINWARING

G

GAINES, William M. (1 Mar. 1922–3 June 1992), publisher, was born William Maxwell Gaines in the Bronx, New York, the son of Maxwell Charles Gaines, a printer's representative, and Jessie Postlewaite Gaines. In 1933 his father thought of reprinting newspaper comic strips in pamphlet form, which became the first comic books. By 1939, in association with National Comics' Harry Donenfeld and Jack S. Liebowitz, Max Gaines formed All-American Comics, publishers of *Wonder Woman* and other titles.

Perceiving his son as lacking direction, Max Gaines brought him to work at All-American after school, with disappointing results. Young Bill Gaines seemed psychologically incapable of taking anything seriously. Intending to become a chemist, he flunked out of the Polytechnic Institute of Brooklyn after three years. In 1942, he joined the Army Air Corps, serving as base photographer. A failed return to Brooklyn Poly led to Gaines's enrolling at New York University with the firm goal of a teaching career.

In 1947 Max Gaines, now head of Entertaining Comics, was killed in a boating accident, leaving EC in the hands of Bill and his mother. In his final year of college, Bill Gaines reluctantly took control of the company. He graduated from NYU in 1948 with a B.S. in education. The renamed Educational Comics floundered until 1950 when Gaines and editor Al Feldstein decided to inaugurate a line of literate horror comic books, beginning with *Crypt of Terror*. Renamed *Tales from the Crypt*, the title was quickly followed by *The Vault of Horror* and *The Haunt of Fear*. Their combined success inspired a flood of copycat titles from other publishers, which fed a growing anti–comic book hysteria. In 1954 a subcommittee of the U.S. Senate Committee on the Judiciary to Investigate Juvenile Delinquency ordered Gaines to testify. During the televised session, Gaines attempted to justify the graphic mayhem and gore his staff had served up with tongues safely in cheek. But the publicity nearly ruined EC and resulted in strict new guidelines set forth by the new Comics Code Authority of America. For decades the comic book industry avoided horror and excessively realistic crime themes.

In 1952 Gaines published *Mad*, the brainchild of artist Harvey Kurtzman. Originally, *Mad* was a comic book that parodied other comic books, but Kurtzman in 1955 persuaded Gaines to convert it to a full-blown satirical magazine aimed at a wider audience. *Mad* now became an iconoclastic hodgepodge of low satire and high hilarity overseen by a gap-toothed mascot named Alfred E. Neuman, written and drawn by what

Gaines gleefully promoted as "the usual gang of idiots."

Nothing like it had been published since the days of the cartoon humor magazine *Judge*. By 1956 *Mad's* circulation had soared to half a million copies per issue, numbers not seen since World War II. Gaines ran his fiefdom with the aplomb of a benevolent potentate drunk on a cocktail of unchecked paternalistic power and self-absorbed absurdity. When future *Mad* artist Mort Drucker was first escorted into his office, Gaines was watching the 1956 World Series. "If the Dodgers win," Gaines told Drucker, "you're hired."

A distribution crisis nearly sank *Mad* that year when First Leader News went out of business. Months later, replacement distributor American News likewise folded. Gaines salvaged the magazine by going to his father's old nemesis, Jack Liebowitz, who ran the powerful Independent News Distributing Company, which carried Liebowitz's popular line of *Superman* comic books, as well as magazines like *Playboy*. Liebowitz agreed to distribute *Mad* and the magazine was saved.

Having seen his fortunes rise and fall so often, Gaines captained a tight business ship, which as much as anything explained why, despite ferocious competition and changing tastes in humor, *Mad* flourished in the decades that followed. He steadfastly refused to take advertising for his magazine, or compromise it in any other way. "Don't let your business expand to the point that you can't control it," he expounded in Frank Jacobs's semibiographical book, *The Mad World of William M. Gaines*. "Keep your staff intact and don't hire unneccesary people just because you're successful. Insist the people who work for you are efficient. Provide incentives, such as bonuses and trips. Increase salaries regularly, but not capriciously. Provide a quality product for your customers at a price they can afford. Do not gouge them with spin-off merchandise. Make everything—your people, your office, your operation—just big enough for success."

Gaines never lost focus on *Mad's* madcap mix of poking fun at sacred cows, Madison Avenue, and celebrities alike, adhering to its zany formula without inhibiting staff creativity. Even after selling the magazine for undisclosed millions in 1961, he stayed on with the magazine as publisher, explaining, "My staff and contributors create the magazine. What I create is the atmosphere." In 1962, *Mad* was absorbed into National Comics. A decade later, circulation peaked at over 2.4 million copies. The magazine ultimately became a component of the AOL Time Warner publishing empire.

Aimed at adolescents and adults alike, *Mad* straddled the generational fence, touching an irreverent nerve in the conservative 1950s, inspiring the underground comics movement of the 1960s as well as the future creators of *The National Lampoon* and *Saturday Night Live*. Gaines married three times. His 1944 marriage to Hazel Grieb was dissolved in 1947. He married Nancy Siegel in 1955, divorcing her in 1971; they had three children. In 1987 he married Anne Griffiths. He died in Manhattan.

A Rabelaisian anti-establishment figure who wore long hair and a full beard before either became fashionable, Bill Gaines combined an innate if not intuitive sense of what appealed to adolescent readers with the forthright fearlessness to lead in an industry of followers, seasoned with a hard-earned business acumen that would have both astounded and gratified Maxwell C. Gaines.

• For an insider's account of Gaines and his *Mad* empire, see Frank Jacobs's 1972 book *The Mad World of William M. Gaines*. Maria Reidenbach's *Completely Mad: A History of the Comic Book and Magazine* (1991), provides an overview of the magazine's first forty years. A comprehensive interview conducted by Gary Groth appeared in *The Comics Journal* 81 (May 1983): 53–84. A final interview was published in *Comics Scene Spectacular* 7 (Sept. 1992). An obituary is in the *New York Times*, 5 June 1992.

WILL MURRAY

GENNARO, Peter (23 Nov. 1919–28 Sept. 2000), dancer and choreographer, was born in Metairie, Louisiana, the son of Charles Gennaro, a grocery store owner, and Conchetta Sabella Gennaro. As a toddler, Gennaro delighted in dancing and exhibited natural rhythmic talent. By age four, he was winning prizes in local dance contests. As a youngster he used money from odd jobs to take tap and acrobatic lessons. After enlisting in the U.S. Army during World War II, Gennaro danced with an army entertainment troupe touring India, Burma, and China. When the war ended, he worked six months in the bar and restaurant his family owned then moved to New York to pursue a professional dance career. Funded by the GI Bill, Gennaro studied ballet and modern and ethnic dance forms at the American Theatre Wing and at the Katherine Dunham School. He performed in student recitals and experimental dance concerts at the 92nd Street Y. In 1947 Gennaro was hired to dance with the corps de ballet of Chicago's San Carlo Opera Company. There he met dancer Margaret Jean Kinsella whom he married in 1948; they had two children.

Later that year Gennaro danced in the touring company of the Broadway revue *Make Mine Manhattan*. During the early 1950s, he performed in the Broadway musicals *Arms and the Girl*, *Kiss Me Kate*, *Guys and Dolls*, and *By the Beautiful Sea*. With his sinuous hip movements, high kicks, and rapid-fire tapping skills, Gennaro soon became one of the era's leading Broadway specialty dancers. He received critical accolades for his performance in "Steam Heat," the show-stopping trio from the 1954 musical *The Pajama Game*, which introduced Broadway audiences to Bob Fosse's choreography. His next featured dance role

was performing the comic "Mu-cha-cha" duet with Judy Holliday in the 1956 musical *Bells Are Ringing*, cochoreographed by Fosse and Jerome Robbins.

In 1957 Robbins recruited Gennaro to be his cochoreographer for the landmark Broadway musical *West Side Story*. Gennaro created the fiery Latin dance movements in the satiric "America" number. He went on to choreograph the Broadway musicals *Fiorello!* (1959), *The Unsinkable Molly Brown* (1960, film version 1964), *Mr. President* (1962), *Bajour* (1964), *Jimmy* (1969), *Irene* (1973), *Annie* (1977), for which he won a Tony Award, and *Carmelina* (1979).

By the late 1950s Gennaro had also begun to dance and choreograph for television variety shows, and he worked on numerous programs, including *Your Hit Parade*, *The Entertainers*, *The Judy Garland Show*, *The Andy Williams Show*, the *Bell Telephone Hour*, *The Bing Crosby Show*, *The Steve Allen Show*, *The Polly Bergen Show*, *Hollywood Palace*, and *The Red Skelton Show*, among others. He and his troupe, the Peter Gennaro Dancers, became best known for their regular appearances on Perry Como's *Kraft Music Hall* and *The Ed Sullivan Show* during the 1960s. Gennaro thus became one of the most recognized and admired dancers of his generation. His television work also included "The Colddiggers of 1969," an award-winning commercial for Contac cold medicine, as well as the Tony Award–winning "I Love New York" commercial in the 1970s.

From 1971 to 1978 Gennaro produced and choreographed spectacular stage shows at Radio City Music Hall. He also choreographed several Miss America pageants, a pas de deux for ballerina Natalia Makarova and Gary Chryst, a novelty disco dance commissioned to celebrate the 1978 debut of Agree shampoo, the 1982 Broadway revival of the musical *Little Me*, and the London production of *Singin' in the Rain* (1985).

Having started to teach dance to augment his income during the early years of his performing career, Gennaro had become one of the country's most popular dance instructors. He taught jazz dance to professional performers and to high school and college dance teachers. He received the Dance Educators Award in 1957 and 1963 and *Dance Magazine*'s award in 1964. As a result of childhood ear infections, Gennaro was hearing-impaired and in 1974 was given the Eleanor Roosevelt Humanitarian Award by the New York League for the Hard of Hearing for overcoming his hearing loss in a field concerned with sound and movement.

A slight, dark-haired man (five feet six inches tall), with a perpetually upbeat personality, Gennaro was commonly described as a softhearted "family man." Throughout his career, he avoided accepting jobs that would require him to spend too much time away from his wife and children. Gennaro died in New York City.

Gennaro's flashy dancing contributed to the popularity of American jazz dance during the golden ages of both the Broadway musical and the television variety show. Considered a first-rate show business choreographer, he was praised by critics for his ability to manipulate space adroitly in dance sequences for the television screen. In musical theater Gennaro carried forth the tradition of the integrated musical, creating notable dances that supported the shows' dramatic fabrics by evoking moods, historical periods, or characterizations. His choreography for *Fiorello!* convincingly conjured the ambience of the ethnic neighborhoods of New York's Lower East Side, while the rambunctious backwoods dancing and an uppity ballroom sequence he devised for *The Unsinkable Molly Brown* entertainingly portrayed contrasting turn-of-the-century societies. Gennaro will probably be best remembered, however, for his contributions to *West Side Story* and the sparkling dances he created for the plucky orphans and slippery villains in *Annie*. In January 2002, Gennaro was inducted posthumously into the Theatre Hall of Fame.

• Photographs, reviews, films, and videotapes of Gennaro's dancing and choreography can be viewed at the Library of Congress, the New York Public Library for the Performing Arts, and the Museum of Television and Radio in New York. "Introduction to Modern Jazz," a Labanotation score of a technique class Gennaro devised, is housed in the New York Public Library's Dance Collection. The Library of Congress has an audio recording of music and an illustrated manual for "A Dance Class with Peter Gennaro."
Biographical information and insights into Gennaro's ideas about choreography are in Walter Terry, "The Choreographer's Job," *New York Herald Tribune*, 8 Jan. 1961; Lydia Joel, "Conversation with Peter Gennaro," *Dance Magazine* 38 (Aug. 1964): 18–19; Harold Stern, "The Master of the Jazz Forms Turns to TV," *Dance Magazine* 44 (June 1970): 44–47; and Sidney Fields, "*Annie*'s Dance Master," *New York Daily News*, 1 Dec. 1977. An obituary is in the *New York Times*, 30 Sept. 2000.

LISA JO SAGOLLA

GEORGE, Walter (29 Jan. 1878–4 Aug. 1957), judge and U.S. Senator from Georgia, was born Walter Franklin George on a farm near Preston, Georgia, the son of sharecroppers Robert Theodoric George and Sarah Stapleton George. George's formative years in hardscrabble South Georgia imbued him with an understanding of the struggles of the common man. His father subscribed to the *Congressional Record*, and young George studied it intently, often memorizing speeches. This oratorical bent germinated while he attended the Houston Institute, a public school near Cordele. At sixteen, when selected as a last-minute substitute speaker before a large Confederate Memorial Day crowd, he extemporaneously embellished a speech he had memorized on Robert E. Lee, which the audience responded to enthusiastically. The experience made him decide on the law as a career. In 1900, he graduated Phi Beta Kappa from Mercer University, a Baptist institution in Macon. He taught grade school to finance his way through Mercer's law school, which today bears his name. He graduated in 1901. That year he was admitted to the bar, purchased the practice of a young lawyer in Vi-

enna, Georgia, and immediately embarked on a winning streak so formidable that colleagues in the area sought other work to supplement their income.

In 1903, he married Lucy Heard of Vienna. They had two sons. George's manner in personal relationships was so reserved, low-key, and Victorian that he even called his wife "Miss Lucy." She called him "Mr. George."

In 1906, George ran for solicitor of the Vienna city court as a Democrat in the functionally one-party South and established his career-long precedent of winning every election. In the next eleven years he attained increasingly responsible prosecuting and judicial positions, highlighted by his service on the Georgia Supreme Court as associate justice from 1917 to 1922. In 1922, he resigned to handle the estate of his father-in-law, Joseph Heard; but when Senator Thomas E. Watson died on 26 September 1922, George won the seven-candidate race for his seat. He deftly appealed to Watson's old South Georgia political base and the state's business interests in the campaign. By then, the intense patriotic fever that had characterized the nation's entry into World War I had already receded into often bitter disillusionment. George's platform repudiated further foreign alliances, immigration, foreign loans, and involvement with the League of Nations. He advocated strengthening the Volstead Act and opposed a bonus for veterans—a stance he would reverse in the 1930s.

In 1932 George, though initially unimpressed with Franklin D. Roosevelt, acquired a deep respect for his political acumen and determination to ameliorate the effects of the Great Depression. Despite initial misgivings about creation of the Tennessee Valley Authority, George finally supported the measure. He more emphatically supported New Deal initiatives such as the Social Security Act, the Agricultural Adjustment Act, and legislation that established such landmark institutions as the Securities and Exchange Commission and the Rural Electric Administration.

George opposed the president on other important measures, however, including the "death sentence" for utility holding companies, the Wages and Hours Act, and the Wagner housing measure. Like many other Democrats in the Senate, George also opposed the Judicial Reorganization Act of 1937 (known as the Supreme Court packing scheme). It perhaps grated more tellingly on the president, however, when in the wake of that sustained public humiliation George frequently joined fellow Southern senators in opposing the administration on a number of other issues.

By the summer of 1938, Roosevelt's attempts to liberalize the party had only been marginally successful. Although liberals such as Alben Barkley had been renominated in Kentucky, and Lyndon Johnson, among others, had secured nominations in Texas, conservatives such as Guy Gillette in Iowa and Alvin Adams in Colorado had more than offset those liberal gains in the Senate. FDR therefore worked to defeat the renomination of George, a major part of a southern strategy that also targeted Senators Ellison Du-

Rant "Cotton Ed" Smith, of South Carolina, and Millard Tydings, of Maryland.

In August 1938 Georgia was almost frantic with anticipation when FDR accepted an invitation to appear at the Gordon Institute Stadium at Barnesville, ostensibly to throw a switch to provide electricity for the first time to 357 rural families. On 11 August, before a crowd of 50,000 spectators, FDR endorsed Federal District Attorney Lawrence S. Camp, attacked George, and comically forgot all about the switch in the process. Though he projected a tone of personal respect and friendship to George, his speech otherwise was a clear and determined effort to portray him as a reactionary obstacle to the progress of the common man in Georgia. The tumultuous reaction of the crowd made George's humble retort inaudible to all but a few around the platform. After shaking hands with the president, George replied, "Mr. President, I regret that you have taken this occasion to question my democracy and to attack my public record. I want you to know that I accept that challenge."

Though Woodrow Wilson had written a single letter in an attempt to defeat isolationist Tom Hardwick in 1918, this level of presidential intervention in Georgia politics was unprecedented. Many newspaper editors complained of FDR's interference, and George exploited this resentment. George, who had not even made a speech on his own behalf since 1926, now embarked on a brilliant campaign against Camp and Eugene Talmadge.

By stressing his humble tenant farmer roots and awakening the deep resentment that much of white Georgia still felt over the Civil War and Reconstruction, he switched the focus of the campaign from social and economic issues. In their place, he coaxed an empathy from Georgians for one of their own, and exploited their deep resentment toward the federal government. After many of his speeches, George and much of his audience were in tears. The band played "Dixie" at the end of each rally. George also fully exploited the archaic county unit system in place at the time, initially implemented as one tool to end Reconstruction. It maximized the influence of the least densely populated rural areas and minimized the relative strength of urban areas and the more heavily populated rural counties. George won only a plurality of the popular vote, but swept to victory with 59 percent of the unit vote. His success rendered FDR's 1938 purge an exercise in futility in the South. Smith in South Carolina and Tydings in Maryland were also elected.

The outbreak of the war in Europe reunited FDR and the southern Democrats, including the previously isolationist George. George's conversion was neither instantaneous nor total. He opposed, for instance, cash-and-carry arms sales to the European democracies. By 1940, however, when Key Pittman (D-Nev.) died and George ascended to the helm of Foreign Relations, George successfully argued that Great Britain was our first line of defense, that by making her defenses stronger we would strengthen our own, and that a viable Great Britain would improve U.S. industries and make the nation more self-reliant. He stressed that if Great Britain fell—as appeared chillingly possible at the time—the target was America. The bill was reported favorably out of Foreign Relations 15–8 on 13 February 1941. Before it passed the Senate about three weeks later, nerve-wracking amendments had to be voted down or molded into something that would not dilute what George termed its "moral effect" on the world. The House of Representatives passed the bill as amended by the Senate on 11 March 1941.

Little more than three months later, on Pat Harrison's death, George gave up the chairmanship of Foreign Relations to become chairman of the Senate Finance Committee. The changes that transpired during his leadership were complex and essential to the successful prosecution of the war. Some indication of their magnitude can be gleaned from the fact that the number of Americans who had to file income tax returns increased from seven million in 1941 to forty-two million in 1942. The fact that George marched overwhelmingly in tandem with the administration during the war did not wholly mitigate his independent streak nor erase all old enmities. A day or so after Finance unanimously rejected a proposal advanced by Henry Morgenthau, secretary of the Treasury and close personal friend of the president, George proposed his own flat Five Percent Victory Tax. It was implemented into law despite Treasury's well-founded conviction that it bore unjustly on low-income families, was only half as productive as the rejected scheme, and did not have comparable inflationary brakes.

In 1943, George's son, a navy flier, went down over the Atlantic while searching for a downed plane. Two years later, George made an eloquent speech in the Senate endorsing the charter of the United Nations. He portrayed it as the best hope for the fulfillment of the peace promised to those who had died in the war.

George waged many battles with both the Harry Truman and Dwight D. Eisenhower administrations against what he considered excessive spending and high taxes. When the Democrats regained majority status in Congress in 1955, George began his second, lengthier tenure as chairman of Foreign Relations, leaving the stewardship of Finance to Harry F. Byrd (D-Va.). George's relationship with Secretary of State John Foster Dulles, nurtured through weekly breakfast meetings, was mutually respectful. George helped steer Eisenhower's controversial Formosa Resolution through the Senate. This authorized the president to use military force to defend Formosa and the Pescadores Islands against armed attack, along with any other territories necessary to defend those islands. Later George urged the administration to seek a Far Eastern Conference with Peking without National Chinese representation, a bold stance at the time that drew the ire of Senator Joseph McCarthy (R-Wisc.) and other hard-line Cold Warriors. Though negotiations on that basis were eventually held, the administration entered them with rigidly fixed positions that ensured failure.

George's last accomplishment concerned his sponsorship of a law that allowed totally disabled workers to collect Social Security benefits at the age of 50 and enabled working women to retire earlier. His Senate colleague from Georgia, Richard Russell, said that George was prouder of that law than any other single piece of legislation in his long career. At 78, George somewhat bitterly decided not to run for reelection in 1956. Though the reason given was health, he knew that defeating 42-year-old Governor Herman Talmadge, son of Eugene, would be difficult. Though George had been a consistent, if sometimes understated by deep South standards, white supremacist throughout his career, Talmadge's more caustically articulated stands made him a formidable potential opponent, particularly in the wake of Brown v. Board of Education. President Eishenhower appointed George special ambassador to NATO after he retired from the Senate in January 1957. George died in Vienna, Georgia.

George was a leader who demonstrated an ability to grow in terms of outlook throughout his career. Though his national reputation never matched his influence in the Senate, that influence grew formidably in his more than thirty-four years in that body. Presidents, fellow legislators, and other actors in the political arena ignored his toughness, shrewdness, and deliberate nature at their own expense. Time and again he demonstrated a propensity to go against the grain at key points in his career, but his innate caution usually made him do so only when there was enough political cover to make success likely. On matters of race, though never as hateful as contemporaries Theodore G. Bilbo (D-Miss.) or fellow Georgians Eugene and Herman Talmadge, George consistently conformed with the political status quo of the Jim Crow South; his poor record was typical of the time and place. The best that might be said in that area was that he usually supported New Deal endeavors that economically aided his African-American constituents. Though he contributed to and supported many initiatives that aided the common man and woman, he was careful not to alienate the business interests that constituted such an important part of his political base. Always mindful of frugality, he possessed the flexible intelligence to recognize when greater goals necessitated its temporary abandonment. His influence on foreign affairs was even more notable. If Lend-Lease had not been passed, Great Britain and the Soviet Union might not have endured the German onslaught.

George's longevity allowed him to reap the full benefits of the seniority system: he served on twelve Senate committees (was chairman of five, including Foreign Affairs twice and Finance) and one joint committee. His deepest imprints were felt in matters of finance—particularly taxation—and foreign affairs, though his expertise was also eventually recognized on many agricultural and educational issues. Neither a visionary nor a demagogue, George was a man of clear talent and ambition who took on the world as it was and usually succeeded in making his imprint felt.

• There are a number of research collections around the country with useful primary sources dealing with George. Three of the most bountiful are located in Hyde Park, N.Y., at the Franklin D. Roosevelt Library; in Savannah, Ga., at the Georgia Historical Society; and in Atlanta, Ga., at Emory University's Robert W. Woodruff Library. The Library of Congress in Washington is a repository for many reports and prints of the various committees that George sat on during his Senate career. It also houses such all but disappeared gems as a radio address with Speaker of the House Sam Rayburn given on 16 March 1954 that gave the nation the Democratic side of a pending tax cut. Though George's import is certainly deserving of major biographical treatment, it has not happened yet. In the meantime, the younger reader may gain a good idea of his life and times by investigating Josephine Mellichamp's *Senators from Georgia* (1976). Those interested in his domestic prewar relations with the New Deal administrative machinery will find Michael S. Holmes's *The New Deal in Georgia* (1975) insightful. A well-written, hugely entertaining—though occasionally inaccurate—partisan critique of George's Senate career through his pivotal 1938 campaign is contained in Allan A. Michie and Frank Ryhlick's *Dixie Demagogues* (1939). The best known, though somewhat reverential and otherwise less-than-evenhanded treatment of George's 1938 campaign was Luther H. Zeigler, Jr.'s contribution to vol.33, no.4 of the *Georgia Historical Quarterly* (Dec. 1959). Kenneth S. Davis puts George's accomplishments during a crucial point of his service to the country in wonderful perspective just before he died in *FDR, the War President, 1940–1943* (2000). Many facets of George's second term as chairman of the Senate Foreign Relations Committee are adroitly addressed by Richard A. Melanson and David Mayers in *Reevaluating Eisenhower* (1987). A front-page obituary is in the *New York Times*, 5 Aug. 1957.

PAUL T. SAYERS

GILBERT, A. C. (15 Feb. 1884–25 Jan. 1961), toy manufacturer, marketer, and lobbyist, was born Alfred Carlton Gilbert, the son of Frank Gilbert, a banker, and Charlotte Ann Hovenden Gilbert, in Salem, Oregon. A sickly boy, according to some (although he himself later denied that story), he built himself up into a muscular physical specimen after his family relocated to the frontier town of Moscow, Idaho. The 5-foot 7-inch, 135-pound dynamo was a college football player, during his one year (1902–1903) at Pacific University in Forest Grove, Oregon, and a pole-vaulter and coach while in college and medical school at Yale from 1904–1909. Gilbert perfected a vaulting device—a bamboo pole that used a vaulting box instead of a spike to anchor the pole. He took home a gold medal in the sport from the 1908 London Olympics, where he tied for first place. (After his own gold medal triumph, Gilbert was long involved in the games, serving from 1924 to 1948 as a member of the American Olympic Committee and helping to manage the American Olympic Team in 1928, 1932, and 1936. His authorship of an article on pole-vaulting in the *Encyclopaedia Britannica* also attested to his knowledge of that activity.)

In 1909 Gilbert received his M.D. from Yale, although he never practiced medicine. He believed instead that a medical degree would improve his knowledge of physical education. In 1910 his training as a magician inspired him and his friend John Petrie to found the Mysto Manufacturing Company in Westville and New Haven, Connecticut. He also served as president of the firm. Gilbert was the first to advertise toys extensively. He began with the launching of his erector sets in 1913, promoting them to fathers and sons in national magazines such as *Popular Mechanics* and the *Saturday Evening Post* with the come-on phrase "Hello Boys! Make Lots of Toys." Later he made specific pitches to boys in their own publications such as *Youth's Companion, St. Nicolas,* and *American Boy.* Gilbert claimed that he thought of the idea of erector kits in the fall of either 1911 or 1912 while passing under steel girders designed to carry electric lines on the commuter train from Connecticut to New York. But there were competing manufacturers of similar products. His version was different in that it provided motion propelled by small motors, had gears and pinions, and featured steel beams that were flat rather than bent at a 90-degree angle. In 1918 he acquired the U.S. patent for steel-beamed construction sets from the Structo Manufacturing Co. of Freeport, Illinois (the British rights went to the Meccano Company).

In 1916 he bought out Petrie, renamed the firm the A. C. Gilbert Company, and built toy construction kits and chemistry sets. That same year Gilbert became the founder and first president of the Toy Manufacturers Association of the U.S.A. In this role, he became the toy industry's first successful lobbyist. In 1917 after the U.S. Council for National Defense proposed to save wood and metal for wartime use by banning gift-giving (suggesting that parents buy war bonds rather than toys), Gilbert led a group of toy manufacturers who visited the council in Washington, D.C., with toys in hand. He argued their case, appealing to the boy in each of its members, and persuaded the council to reverse its decision.

During the 1920s, a steep postwar tariff was placed on imported toys, aimed in particular at the German industry that had been so successful before the war. Gilbert manufactured radio kits, maintained his own radio station, and was a radio sports commentator, even interviewing Babe Ruth. His company later went beyond chemistry and erector sets (with its designs for building bridges, windmills, airplanes, carousels, trucks, parachute jumps, and zeppelins) to include marketing microscopes, telescopes, and even glass-blowing kits. In 1950, Gilbert offered a somewhat unpopular atomic energy lab with a Geiger counter and in 1958 a chemistry kit specifically for girls. But boys (and their fathers) were always his primary customers.

Gilbert often spoke about the importance of toys in building "solid American character," and he emphasized "good clean fun." A perpetual boy at heart, with an energetic and optimistic personality very much like Theodore Roosevelt's (whom he met after his Olympic success), Gilbert was an avid outdoor man and hunter. But the Olympic champion often came out in him. Gilbert once said that "everything in life is a game but the important thing is to win." When he did not do well in golf, he gave it up. He wrote several books for boys on chemistry, mineralogy, carpentry, and meteorology, ensuring that his science kits were accurate by hiring experts from Yale, Columbia University, and General Electric. He maintained his corporate office at Erector Square, New Haven, and his woodsy 600-acre combination game preserve and estate, which he named Paradise, in nearby Hamden, Connecticut.

In 1913 Gilbert had made an astute purchase: the American rights to the revered German firm of Richter Building Bricks (the manufacturer of Anchor Stone Bricks). In 1930, he took over the Meccano Company of America, producers of construction kits and toy trains. Ironically, Meccano of Britain in 1990 brought back erector sets under the Gilbert name to the American market after the A. C. Gilbert Company had gone out of business. Gilbert purchased the Chicago-based American Flyer line of electric toy trains (established in 1907) in 1938. In 1942, his company temporarily ceased making all erector sets and trains that used critically needed materials and made use of wooden girders instead. However, the federal government encouraged Gilbert to continue to manufacture chemistry sets in order to foster interest in America's chemical industry for national defense purposes and because they used very few, if any, vital materials.

Gilbert ran a welfare-minded, nonunion company, paying higher than average wages. He offered free medical and legal help. A man with a common touch, he walked the factory floor and punched the clock morning and night along with his employees. A. C. Gilbert married Mary Thompson on 19 September 1908; they had met at Pacific University. The couple had two daughters and one son, A. C. Gilbert, Jr., who followed in his father's footsteps as president and chairman of the company after the elder Gilbert retired in 1954. Unfortunately, the son did not long outlive the father, who died from a heart ailment in Boston at New England Baptist Hospital. The company as a separate entity folded in 1967 before its later revival.

In the 1940s and 1950s, Gilbert Halls of Science opened in Washington, D.C., Miami, and Chicago to serve as both museums and places to market products. The Gilbert Institute of Erector Engineering gave boys recognition through honorary degrees of accomplishment. Gilbert often conducted erector design contests with prizes such as cash awards and scientific trips. A. C. Gilbert's Discovery Village in his home town of Salem, Oregon, strives to promote many of his values, such as provoking curiosity, fostering enjoyment, and facilitating understanding in youths, just as he had initiated boys into the professional mysteries of engineering and science. Since

1991, the A. C. Gilbert Heritage Society has served to exchange information among enthusiasts of Gilbert collectibles.

• For an autobiography (written with the assistance of Marshall McClintock), see *The Man Who Lives in Paradise* (1954). Helpful sections on Gilbert are found in Gary Cross, *Kids' Stuff: Toys and the Changing World of American Childhood* (1997), and Sydney Stern and Ted Schoenhaus, *Toyland: The High-Stakes Game of the Toy Industry* (1990). The entry on erector sets in David Hoffman, *Kid Stuff: Great Toys from Our Childhood* (1996) is useful, as is the colorfully illustrated article by Bruce Watson, "Hello Boys! Become an Erector Master Engineer!" in *Smithsonian* (May 1999): 120–34. A brief synopsis of Gilbert's career is in Frederick J. Augustyn, Jr., "The American Switzerland: New England as a Toy-Making Center," *Journal of Popular Culture* (Summer 2002): 1–13. Obituaries of Gilbert are in the *New York Times* and the *Boston Globe*, both on 25 Jan. 1961; in *Time*, 3 Feb. 1961; and in *Newsweek* on 6 Feb. 1961.

FREDERICK J. AUGUSTYN, JR.

GILBERT, John (10 July 1899–9 Jan. 1936), actor, was born John Cecil Pringle in Logan, Utah, the son of John Pringle, a theatrical producer, and Ida Adair Apperly, an actress. His parents divorced when he was a small child. His mother, a minor star of the provincial stage, regarded him as an impediment to her career. "Sometimes I think she hated me," he later wrote. "Children have a curious sense of honesty of emotions. . . . She could catch me up with dramatic tears and love words. I knew it wouldn't last, that in a moment she would push me impatiently aside or throw a chair at my head" (quoted in Fountain, p. 10). He accompanied her as she traveled with various stock companies, living in a succession of boarding houses. He reportedly taught himself to read by picking out words from her scripts while he watched her act. Around 1910, his mother married Walter Gilbert, a stage comedian, from whom John took his last name. They settled in San Francisco for a few years, and during this period he attended the Hitchcock Military Academy in San Rafael, California—his only sustained formal education. When his mother died of tuberculosis in 1913, he was forced to drop out of school. He later recalled that after her funeral, his stepfather gave him ten dollars and informed him that he would have to take care of himself.

After working as a rubber goods salesman in San Francisco, Gilbert in 1914 became the assistant stage manager for a theatrical stock company in Spokane, Washington. One of his stepfather's friends, Herschell Mayall, was a leading actor at director Thomas Ince's film studio in Santa Monica, California, and through this connection Gilbert decided to attempt a film career. His first screen appearance may have been as an extra in a William S. Hart western, *Hell's Hinges* (1916), although some film historians believe that he worked as an extra in a few earlier pictures. His first leading role was as a hunchback who falls in love with a pretty blind girl in *Princess of the Dark* (1917). In 1917 he jumped from Ince-Triangle to Paralta Pic-

tures, where he was employed primarily as a screenwriter. The following year he married Olivia Burwell; they had no children and divorced in 1923.

In 1919 Gilbert won his first significant part, playing opposite Mary Pickford in *The Heart o' the Hills*. Despite this success, he was often insecure about his performances and found that he preferred working behind the camera. That year he joined the production team of the prominent director Maurice Tourneur, for whom, as he later recalled, he worked "18 hours a day—writing, co-directing, titling, cutting, and, least of all—acting" (quoted in Higgins, p. 266). He was lured away from this promising situation by Jules Brulatour, a producer who wanted him to direct films starring his wife, Hope Hampton. Gilbert directed one film with Hampton, *Love's Penalty* (1919); although magazines such as *Variety* and *Photoplay* praised his work, he himself characterized the film as "ghastly . . . It was inconceivable that it could have been so bad," and he impetuously walked out on his directing contract (quoted in Fountain, p. 63).

In 1923 Gilbert married Leatrice Joy, an actress; they had one child and divorced in 1924. During the early 1920s he returned to acting, appearing in nineteen films for Fox Studios, including John Ford's well-directed melodrama *Cameo Kirby* (1923), in which he had a prominent role as a handsome riverboat gambler. In 1924 he moved to Metro-Goldwyn-Mayer, where he quickly became a star. That year he appeared in two noteworthy films: King Vidor's *His Hour*, in which he played a dashing Russian prince, and Victor Seastrom's *He Who Gets Slapped*, in which he was cast as a daredevil circus performer. In 1925 he starred in two silent film masterpieces, Erich von Stroheim's *The Merry Widow* and Vidor's *The Big Parade*. As the film historian Steven Higgins has suggested, in these films Gilbert, unlike other romantic leading men of the period, proved willing "to use his popularity with audiences as a bargaining chip, testing his craft and thereby stretching the limits of his fans' loyalty" (p. 266). In *The Merry Widow*, a black comedy that examined male sexual decadence, he gave a subtle performance as a virile, womanizing Viennese prince who falls in love with an American widow (played by Mae Murray). Although he played the most sympathetic male character in the film, his role as a wolfish, untrustworthy lover represented a significant departure from the conventional romantic heroes he had typically portrayed. In *The Big Parade*, Hollywood's first great war film, he gave a sensitive, deliberately unglamorous performance as an infantryman in World War I. Critics hailed the film's realistic war scenes, and Gilbert's love scenes with costar Renée Adorée, in which he tries to woo a French girl in spite of language and cultural differences, are considered to be among the most charming in silent film. *The Big Parade* was a nationwide phenomenon, grossing $15 million, a huge sum for the era, and playing for a record ninety-six consecutive weeks at the Astor Theater in New York City.

With the death of Rudolph Valentino in 1926, Gilbert became Hollywood's reigning matinee idol. MGM cast him in a string of "great lover" roles; at the same time, his performances became more mannered and less interesting. He appeared in two additional films directed by Vidor: *La Bohème* (1926), in which he played opposite Lillian Gish as a love-struck poet, and *Bardelys the Magnificent* (1926), a swashbuckling costume epic. During the late 1920s he reached the peak of his popularity when he appeared in three smash-hit pictures with Greta Garbo—*Flesh and the Devil* (1927), *Love* (1927), and *A Woman of Affairs* (1928). Although the films were essentially soap operas, they were also unabashedly erotic, featuring languorous scenes of lovemaking, exquisitely photographed in close-up by cinematographer William Daniels. The two actors carried on a widely publicized love affair while making the films, which contributed to their appeal. The film historian Jeanine Basinger has described a typical scene from *Flesh and the Devil*, noting its impact on audiences in the 1920s:

> She places a cigarette between her lips, which are wet and open. Then she puts it in his mouth instead. He starts to light it and the light from the match illuminates their beautiful faces. She slowly blows it out, then remarks that blowing out a match is an "invitation to kiss." They come together. . . . (p. 385)

Off screen, Gilbert led a tempestuous private life. His contemporaries found him to be bright and often full of fun, but he was also emotionally callow, self-pitying, and given to making drunken scenes. The actress Eleanor Boardman remembered that if he "had good reviews, he hit the ceiling, and he was the happiest man in the world. But if he had a bad review, he got in the dumps and you couldn't get him out" (quoted in Eyman, pp. 298–99). King Vidor believed that he was "not too well established in a role of his own in life," so that "whatever role he was playing, he literally continued to live it off screen" (p. 134). His relationship with Garbo was especially tortured. He proposed marriage to her repeatedly and was turned down; after finally agreeing to marry him, in 1926, she jilted him on their wedding day. She continued to live with him in an on-again, off-again relationship until 1929. Gilbert also had difficulties with MGM's vice-president, Louis B. Mayer, who despised his flamboyance. According to Hollywood lore, on the day of Gilbert's failed wedding to Garbo, Mayer reportedly made a crude comment about the couple's sexual relationship, and the distraught actor knocked him down. Mayer then allegedly shouted that he would "destroy" Gilbert.

Beginning in 1929, Gilbert's career declined precipitously. One of the enduring myths of Hollywood is that he was a victim of the transition from silent to sound films, because his voice was high-pitched and effeminate. But Gilbert had an adequate light baritone speaking voice and starred in ten "talkies." Other explanations have been given for the actor's downfall.

Film historians note that audiences' tastes changed quickly with the introduction of sound. In an era of wisecracking comedies and terse gangster films, the grandiose romances in which Gilbert specialized came to be seen as hammy and old-fashioned; a reviewer of Gilbert's first sound film, *His Glorious Night* (1929), observed that "his prowess at lovemaking, which has held [audiences] breathless, takes on a comedy aspect. . . . The love lines, about pulsating blood, hearts and dandelions, read far better than they sound from under the dainty Gilbertian moustache" (quoted in Basinger, p. 394). But Gilbert adapted to new audience expectations and gave fine, "modern" performances in a few movies: *The Phantom of Paris* (1931), *Downstairs* (1932), and *The Captain Hates the Sea* (1934). Film critics particularly note his excellent work in *Downstairs*, an audacious black comedy for which he wrote the original story, in which he played a charismatic, immoral chauffeur who sexually manipulates his female employers at several wealthy households.

Many of Gilbert's contemporaries believed that his career was sabotaged by Louis B. Mayer. At first glance, this seems improbable: Mayer, a hardheaded businessman, was due ten percent of the profits from the actor's movies, and he was unlikely to undermine his own earnings. Nevertheless, there is little doubt that MGM mismanaged Gilbert's transition to sound films. Following the disastrous reception of *His Glorious Night*, the studio chose to release *Redemption* (1930), a film made prior to *His Glorious Night* that had been initially shelved because it was judged so bad as to be unreleasable. These two consecutive flops harmed Gilbert's popularity and gave rise to the notion that he was an inadequate actor for the "talkies." Afterward, Mayer refused to give him choice roles. For example, the director Howard Hawks recalled that he had intended to cast Gilbert in the lead role in *The Dawn Patrol* (1933), a major hit about British aviators. Mayer seemed amenable to the idea and invited the actor and director to his office to discuss the film; at the meeting, however, he proceeded to spew obscenities at Gilbert, and Hawks realized that Mayer "had called [them] to the studio for the sole purpose of humiliating Jack" (Fountain, p. 159). Many roles initially intended for Gilbert, including one opposite Jean Harlow in *Red Dust* (1932), another hit film, were given to Clark Gable, who, as a rising star at the studio, was much cheaper to employ. In 1933 Garbo forced the studio to cast Gilbert opposite her in *Queen Christina*; rather than highlight their reunion, studio advertising emphasized her starring role and presented Gilbert's name in tiny type. In 1934 he took out an advertisement in the *Hollywood Reporter* complaining that "Metro-Goldwyn-Mayer will neither offer me work nor release me from my contract."

Gilbert's downfall was exacerbated by his own behavior. Drinking heavily, his self-confidence shattered, he suffered from bleeding ulcers, chronic insomnia, and bouts of paranoia. He had two unsuccessful marriages in his later years: to the actress

Ina Claire from 1929 to 1931, and to the actress Virginia Bruce (with whom he had one child) from 1932 to 1934. At the time of his death, his companion was the actress Marlene Dietrich. He died at his home in Beverly Hills when a nurse gave him an injection to help him sleep and he had an adverse reaction to the drug, causing him to choke to death on his tongue.

• For information on Gilbert's life, see the biography *Dark Star* (1985), written by his daughter Leatrice Gilbert Fountain. Jeanine Basinger, *Silent Stars* (1999), includes a valuable scholarly examination of his career. See also Steven Higgins's entry on Gilbert in James Vinson, ed., *The International Dictionary of Films and Filmmakers: Volume III Actors and Actresses* (1986). Kevin Brownlow's excellent documentary film series *Hollywood: A Celebration of the American Silent Film* (1980) includes an episode, "Star Treatment," devoted to Gilbert; the film includes insightful interviews with his second wife, Leatrice Joy, and directors King Vidor and Clarence Brown. See also Brownlow's companion book, *Hollywood: The Pioneers* (1979). For Gilbert's transition to sound films, see Scott Eyman, *The Speed of Sound: Hollywood and the Talkie Revolution, 1926–1930* (1997). For his relationship with Greta Garbo, see Barry Paris, *Garbo: A Biography* (1995). Other useful discussions of Gilbert are in King Vidor's autobiography, *A Tree Is a Tree* (1953), and Bosley Crowther's history of MGM, *The Lion's Share: The Story of an Entertainment Empire* (1957). An obituary is in the *New York Times*, 10 Jan. 1936.

THOMAS W. COLLINS, JR.

GILBRETH, Frank B., Jr. (17 Mar. 1911–18 Feb. 2001), author and newspaper columnist, was born Frank Bunker Gilbreth, Jr., in Plainfield, New Jersey, the son of Frank Bunker Gilbreth, an efficiency expert, and Lillian Moller Gilbreth, who worked with her husband on time and motion study. At a time when better-educated parents had fewer children, and politicians such as Theodore Roosevelt were worried about "race suicide," Lillian M. Gilbreth, who had graduated from the University of California, Berkeley, in 1900, and her husband wanted to demonstrate that women could have a career as well as raise a family. Therefore the Gilbreth children were brought up along "business efficiency" lines. Older children supervised younger ones, household jobs were shared, and bigger tasks, such as painting a fence, were put out to tender among the children.

Frank, Jr., was the Gilbreths' fifth child and first boy. Eight more children were born over the next eleven years to make a total of six boys and seven girls. (This number includes a stillborn child whom the Gilbreths omitted from their own accounts of their family, so that the number of children they had is usually stated as twelve.) They lived in Providence, Rhode Island, in 1912–1919, then returned to Montclair, New Jersey. After Frank Gilbreth, Sr., died in 1924, Lillian Gilbreth continued to work as an industrial engineer. She put all eleven surviving children through college, but her work necessarily meant repeated absences from home, and the children brought themselves up with the supervision of elder sisters or relatives.

Graduating from Montclair High School, Gilbreth then spent a year at St. John's College in Annapolis, Maryland, before attending the University of Michigan, where he was editor of the *Daily*, the college newspaper. He graduated at the depth of the depression in 1933, but, partly through his mother's contacts, he secured a job at the New York *Herald Tribune*. He moved briefly to the Charleston, South Carolina, *News and Courier* and then to the Associated Press. He returned to the *News and Courier* in 1947 and stayed there for the rest of his career, except for the period when he served as a naval officer in World War II. He took part in three invasions in the Pacific theater and was decorated with two air medals and a bronze star.

Gilbreth married Elizabeth Cauthen of Charleston in 1934; they had one daughter, Elizabeth G. Cantler, who became the features editor of the *News and Courier* (renamed the *Post and Courier*). Elizabeth Gilbreth died in 1954, and the following year he married Mary Pringle Manigault; they had two children.

When Gilbreth returned from his service in World War II, he discovered that his sister Ernestine had written a family history—a detailed account of growing up in a large family in a rather run-down house in New Jersey. When she could not find a publisher, Gilbreth reworked the manuscript, making it lighter and more amusing. Titled *Cheaper by the Dozen*, the book was published in 1948 by Thomas Y. Crowell, in time for the Christmas trade, and became a bestseller the following year. It has been in print ever since. *Cheaper by the Dozen* is largely autobiographical, though some events were telescoped or changed to make them more entertaining. It describes Frank B. Gilbreth's efficiency ideas and how he tried, not always successfully, to apply them to his family. Frank, Jr., once wrote that the regimentation of his childhood "may sound as gay and informal as a concentration camp, but it really seemed more like a game at the time" (*Time Out for Happiness*, p. 147). A movie starring Clifton Webb and Myrna Loy was made in 1950, the year Frank, Jr., and Ernestine Gilbreth Carey published a sequel, *Belles on Their Toes*, which was also made into a movie.

Gilbreth published a total of twelve books and numerous articles in publications ranging from the *New York Times* to *Family Circle*. Four of his books were on the *New York Times* bestsellers list, and three were condensed by *Readers' Digest*. His first solo book, *I'm a Lucky Guy* (1951), was followed by *Held's Angels*, illustrated by cartoonist John Held, Jr. (1952), which poked fun at the flappers of the Roaring Twenties. Later books include *Innside Nantucket* (1954), about an inn run by his brother Bob and sister-in-law; *Of Whales and Women: One Man's View of Nantucket History* (1957); *How to Be a Father* (1958); *Loblolly* (1959); *He's My Boy* (1962); and *Time Out for Happiness* (1970), about his mother and father.

Despite being born in New Jersey, raised in Providence, Rhode Island, and summering in Nantucket, Massachusetts, for much of his life, Gilbreth became a devoted resident of Charleston; he even wrote a *Dictionary of Charlestonese*, a pamphlet that gently mocked the local accent. More than 200,000 copies were sold, with the royalties going to the newspaper's Good Cheer fund. He was deeply involved with the Charleston *Post and Courier*. For more than four decades, using the pseudonym Ashley Cooper, after the two rivers that converge in Charleston, he wrote "Doing the Charleston," one of the longest-running columns in American newspaper history. In 1993 he published a collection of these columns titled *Ashley Cooper's Doing the Charleston*, and in 1994 he published another family memoir, *Ancestors of the Dozen*.

Gilbreth retired as assistant publisher and vice president of the Evening Post Publishing Company. In 1998 he was named to the South Carolina Academy of Authors. His national reputation rests on *Cheaper by the Dozen*, but to residents of Charleston, his adopted home, he will be remembered as Ashley Cooper. He died in Charleston.

• There is no known biography of Frank B. Gilbreth, Jr.; the best sources for his early life are his own books, notably *Cheaper by the Dozen* (1948) and *Time Out for Happiness* (1970). Details of his early life also appear in a biography of his mother by Jane Lancaster, *Lillian Moller Gilbreth: A Dozen Lives*, which will be published in 2002 by Northeastern University Press. Obituaries are in the *New York Times*, 20 Feb. 2001, and the Charleston *Post and Courier*, 19 Feb. 2001.

JANE LANCASTER

GILL, Brendan (4 Oct. 1914–27 Dec. 1997), writer and preservationist, was born in Hartford, Connecticut, the son of Michael Gill, a physician, and Elizabeth Duffy Gill. (His parents did not give him a middle name, but he later took the middle name "Michael" in honor of his father.) Although his mother died when he was seven years old, he later recalled that he had a happy childhood in a prosperous Irish-Catholic household: "My father . . . had not the slightest idea what to do with us children, except to supply us with houses, servants, money, trips to Europe, extravagant gifts, admiration, and love" (*Here at the New Yorker*, p. 50). In high school he was named chairman of his school's literary magazine and won a prize for literary excellence. Thereafter he attended Yale University, where he became editor of the *Yale Literary Magazine* during his junior year. In 1935 he won a cash prize from the university for his poem "Death in April"; he used the money to self-publish a book of poetry, *Death in April and Other Poems* (1935). He graduated *magna cum laude* from Yale in 1936 and was elected to Phi Beta Kappa. That year he married Anne Barnard; they had seven children.

Following his graduation, Gill began submitting poems and stories to the *New Yorker* magazine; one of his submissions—a comical piece about a chance encounter with the novelist Sinclair Lewis—was accepted by the magazine in 1936. Over the next two years he published a few short stories in the *New Yorker* dealing with Catholicism. "It became evident that the editors . . . knew little about Catholics and especially about Catholics in religious orders, and that they were eager to read about them," he later wrote. "This was lucky for me, because although I knew almost as little about nuns and priests as they did, I was feverishly eager to oblige them and was therefore ready to make up anything that I didn't know or was unable to discover" (*Here at the New Yorker*, p. 93). In 1938 the magazine hired him as a staff writer, but he quit the following year to devote himself to writing fiction full time. During the early 1940s he published several short stories in mass-circulation magazines such as the *Saturday Evening Post* and *Good Housekeeping*. He also continued to explore Catholicism in short stories for the *New Yorker*, including the widely anthologized "The Knife," which portrays the relationship between a widowed father and his young son, who believes that he will bring his dead mother back to life by saying a "Hail Mary." Reflecting Gill's own standing as a lapsed Catholic, his stories typically satirized institutional Catholicism while showing compassion for individual Catholics.

In 1942 Gill returned to the *New Yorker* as a staff writer, a position that he would hold for the rest of his life. One of his primary duties was anonymous, serving as a reporter and "rewrite man" for one of the magazine's most popular sections, "The Talk of the Town." In this capacity, he often wrote brief factual articles—always with a wry, understated tone—on peculiar individuals, objects, or procedures; topics included such ephemera as the child's toy Silly Putty and a man who had carved the world's tallest wooden statue, "totem poles included." Commenting on such work, he later noted that while other *New Yorker* writers handled "the guns of big events," much of his journalistic career was "devoted to sedulously setting off firecrackers" (*Here at the New Yorker*, p. 140). He also contributed short stories, profiles of noteworthy people, and book reviews to the magazine during the 1940s and 1950s. Regarded by his colleague the novelist John Updike as a book reviewer of "real ardor and verve" ("Citizen Gill," p. 70), Gill was particularly clear-eyed in his criticisms of popular, overpraised works by major writers. For example, in a review of John O'Hara's *A Rage to Live* (1949), he correctly foresaw that O'Hara's abandonment of short fiction to write sprawling, self-important novels would ultimately prove a "catastrophe" for his literary reputation.

In 1951 Gill won the National Book Award for his first novel, *The Trouble of One House* (1950). The book deals with the death of a young mother and the impact of her death on her upper-middle-class Irish Catholic family. Typical of Gill's best fiction, the book is critical of its characters but also compassionate about their flaws; the only character dealt with sentimentally—the mother—is also the novel's weakest, leaving a problematic center in an otherwise strong work. Critics especially praised *House*'s exploration of the interrelationship between past and present, how "the nuances of the characters' previous relationships with each other not only explain their responses to [the mother]'s death, but actually seem forced into life for the first time by that death" (Kendle, p. 361). Much less effective was Gill's second novel, *The Day the Money Stopped* (1957), a story about a spoiled playboy who fights with his siblings over his dead father's will. Told almost entirely through dialogue, the novel was adapted by Gill and playwright Maxwell Anderson for Broadway; it closed after four performances.

Gill was noted for being the only gregarious writer on the *New Yorker* staff; according to his colleague Nancy Franklin, "if you happened to be of the melancholic . . . persuasion, Brendan's cock's-crow energy and torrential exuberance were galling" ("Citizen Gill," p. 73). Calling himself "a confident believer in Jane Austen's dictum that everything happens at parties," Gill estimated that he typically attended five or six public or private functions a week (*Here at the New Yorker*, p. 213). He made many of his friendships through his membership in the Century Association, a club for artists, writers, and "amateurs of arts and letters" who were also prominent members of the city's Establishment. Much of his writing reflected his fascination with the lives of wealthy urban sophisticates. He wrote a short, entertaining biography of actress Tallulah Bankhead (*Tallulah*, 1972); a biographical essay on songwriter Cole Porter (the introduction to *Cole: A Book of Cole Porter Lyrics and Memorabilia*, by Robert Kimball, 1971); the captions for a book of photographs by society photographer Jerome Zerbe (*Happy Times*, 1973); the text for two photographic studies on the homes of the very rich (*Summer Places*, 1977; *The Dream Come True: Great Houses of Los Angeles*, 1980); and dozens of profiles of his friends and acquaintances in New York City (*A New York Life: Of Friends and Others*, 1990). Gill's writings on the city's social elite often had an ambiguous tone; while typically elegant and erudite, he could also be gossipy and malicious. In reviewing *A New York Life*, author Caroline Seebohm noted that "the insertion of . . . gratuitous slights, combined with Mr. Gill's obsession with his subjects' social and financial position, the clubs they belong to and their sexual proclivities," indicated the author's status as an outsider, which was evidently "an unhealed wound" (*New York Times*, 21 Oct. 1990).

Gill served as a film critic for the *New Yorker* between 1960 and 1967 and as a drama critic specializing in Broadway plays between 1968 and 1987. A lifelong student of architecture—with a particular interest in Beaux-Arts Classicism—during the 1960s he became one of the leaders of New York City's landmarks preservation movement. Outraged over the destruction of Pennsylvania Station, in 1966 he co-founded the Victorian Society in America, which sought to preserve the city's nineteenth-century architectural heritage. In the late 1960s Gill and former first lady Jacqueline Kennedy Onassis spearheaded a successful, widely publicized campaign by the city's Municipal Art Society to save Grand Central Terminal from demolition. He later served as chairperson of the New York Landmarks Conservancy. Among his other prominent civic positions, he served as chairperson of the Andy Warhol Foundation for Visual Arts; as a vice-president of the American Academy of Arts and Letters; as a member of the board of directors of the Whitney Museum of American Art; and as a founder of the P.S. 1 Center for Contemporary Art in Queens, New York. As a spokesperson for these organizations, he championed a vision of the city that was neither traditional nor elitist; for example, he fought to save commonplace buildings in Harlem, praised Raimund Abraham's postmodern design for the Austrian Culture Institute, and condemned the "Disneyfication" of Times Square during the early 1990s, when the area's porn shops were eliminated. In 1985 he was named secretary of the jury for the Pritzker Architecture Prize, the highest international award for architecture. In 1987 he became the *New Yorker*'s architecture critic, writing for a section titled "The Skyline." He also wrote more than 100 articles for *Architectural Digest* during the 1980s and 1990s. In 1988 the Municipal Art Society established an award, the Brendan Gill Prize, given annually to an artist whose work celebrated urban life.

Gill published his two most significant books in the 1970s. *Ways of Loving* (1974) collected several first-rate short stories from the *New Yorker*, including the O. Henry Award–winning "Fat Girl," a disturbing story about an indolent, sexually promiscuous office worker. The book also included two fine novellas: "The Malcontents," which dealt with the members of a dysfunctional, nomadic rich family; and "Last Things," a deeply affecting story about an elderly man trying to set his life in order. In 1975 he published an excellent memoir, the bestselling *Here at the New Yorker*. Beautifully written, consistently entertaining, and often acerbic, the book presents vivid anecdotes about many of his well-known colleagues on the magazine, including editors Harold Ross and William Shawn and writers Edmund Wilson, James Thurber, and Wolcott Gibbs. Historians of the magazine find that *Here at the New Yorker*, together with Thurber's *The Years with Ross*, provides an indelible portrait of the magazine during its heyday in the 1930s and 1940s.

In 1987 Gill published a biography of Frank Lloyd Wright, *Many Masks: A Life of Frank Lloyd Wright*, which many critics and scholars dismissed as a sensationalistic exploration of the architect's personality flaws. During the late 1980s Gill became the center of a literary controversy when he published an article attacking mythology scholar Joseph Campbell, "The Faces of Joseph Campbell," in the *New York Review of Books* (28 Sept. 1989). Gill, who had known Campbell when they were both members of the Century Association in New York City, insisted that he was an anti-Semite and dismissed his "follow your bliss" philosophy, popularized on the PBS series "Joseph Campbell and the Power of Myth with Bill Moyers," for sanctioning materialism and selfishness. Late in his life, when asked to describe his eclectic writing career,

Gill responded: "Fiction is my chief interest, followed by architectural history, followed by literary and dramatic criticism. If these fields were to be closed to me, I would write copy for a bird-seed catalogue. In any event, I would write." He died in New York City.

• Gill's other works include a short biography of Charles Lindbergh, *Lindbergh Alone* (1977); a book of poetry, *Wooings: Five Poems* (1980); and *Late Bloomers* (1996), a collection of profiles about people who achieved great success late in life. Gill is interviewed in the documentary film *Frank Lloyd Wright* (1998), by Ken Burns and Lynn Novick. The best source of information on Gill's life is his memoir *Here at the New Yorker* (1975). Also valuable is the article on Gill in *Contemporary Authors Online*. A good, brief critical discussion of his fiction is "Brendan Gill: An Overview," by Burton Kendle, in *Contemporary Novelists* (6th ed., 1996). *New Yorker* writers such as John Updike, Philip Hamburger, and Roger Angell offer their reminiscences about Gill in "Citizen Gill: Remembering the Quintessential New Yorker," in the *New Yorker* (12 Jan. 1998, pp. 70–74). "Celebrating Brendan Gill: A Prodigal Legacy of Wit, Erudition, and Passion," *Architectural Digest* (July 1998, pp. 26–45), includes extensive excerpts from Gill's writings about architecture. An obituary is in the *New York Times*, 29 Dec. 1997.

THOMAS W. COLLINS, JR.

GOH, Choo San (14 Sept. 1948–28 Nov. 1987), choreographer, was born in Singapore, the son of Kim Lok Goh, a merchant, and Siew Han Ch'ng. He was the youngest of ten children born to the couple. Goh followed in the path of three of his older siblings to train as a dancer. Watching performances by touring overseas ballet companies stimulated his interest in dance. His older sister Soonee Goh trained at the Royal Ballet School in London and returned to Singapore to cofound the Singapore Ballet Academy. His brother Choo Chiat Goh also trained at the Royal Ballet, later becoming a principal dancer in the Beijing Ballet. Soo Khim Goh, another sister, trained at the Australian Ballet and cofounded the Singapore Dance Theatre in 1988. Goh went to school at the Nanyang Primary and proceeded to Raffles Institution and the University of Singapore, where he received a B.S. in 1970. His Chinese parents spoke Mandarin, and the children were brought up with very traditional values. Goh's earliest desire was to become an airline pilot, but his studies in ballet, taught by Soonee Goh, led him toward his eventual career path as a dancer. At his father's insistence, he first completed his university education and graduated with a degree in biochemistry.

In 1970 he traveled to Europe hoping to find a position in a ballet company and was offered a place with the Dutch National Ballet in Amsterdam. The company had a rich blend of classical and contemporary choreography. Goh joined as a corps de ballet member and was eventually elevated to soloist. He excelled in works by the company's resident choreographers, Toer van Schaik and Rudi van Dantzig, as well as in works by George Balanchine and Petipa. This environment was a fertile training ground for his growing interest in choreography: while still a dancer with the company Goh created his first ballets.

These small ballets brought Goh to the attention of Mary Day, the director of the Washington School of Ballet in Washington, D.C. In 1976 she offered him a position with her newly founded Washington Ballet. Goh saw this as a chance to grow along with the new company and took on the responsibilities of company teacher and resident choreographer. Over the next few years his pieces for the company became increasingly sophisticated and definitive, and works such as *Fives* (1978), using Ernest Bloch's Concerto Grosso, began to emerge.

Goh came to the attention of several important artistic directors of dance companies as word of his talent spread. Many noted that his work was filled with a usage of classical ballet vocabulary that seemed influenced by his Asian heritage. His vision was more "symphonic" in that he utilized numerous soloists in a ballet rather than the traditional principal dancer/corps de ballet arrangement typical in classical choreography. For the Houston Ballet he created two new works (1979 and 1980), and for the Alvin Ailey Dance Company he created *Spectrum* (1981). American Ballet Theatre commissioned *Configurations* to be created for Mikhail Baryshnikov soon after. His only full-length work, *Romeo and Juliet*, to Prokofiev's famous score, was created for the Boston Ballet (1984). Goh's primary commitment was with the Washington Ballet, for which he created one or two new works each year in addition to restaging for them some of the successful ballets he was now creating for other companies. In 1984 he was named associate director of the company while retaining his title as resident choreographer. He also taught each summer at the American Ballet Center in New York.

The city of Washington presented Goh with the Mayor's Award for Excellence in the Arts in 1986. Alan M. Kriegsman, dance critic for the *Washington Post*, wrote that Goh "has propelled the Washington Ballet to international status on the jetstream of his talent . . ." (21 Feb. 1985). The company did its first large-scale overseas tour in 1984 and over the next few years performed in Europe, South America, and the Far East repeatedly, featuring programs of Goh's choreography. In addition to *Fives*, some of the most well-known works he created for the Washington Ballet include *Variations Sérieuses*, *Birds of Paradise*, *In the Glow of the Night*, *Unknown Territory*, and *Schubert Symphony*. All of these ballets were performed by other companies throughout the world. Goh's demanding schedule in the 1980s included ballets with the Bat Dor Dance Company, the Paris Opera Ballet, the Royal Danish Ballet, the Joffrey Ballet, and the Royal Swedish Ballet. Singapore recognized his talent as a choreographer by presenting him with the Cultural Medallion in 1987, the country's highest award for artistic achievement.

In 1987 Goh became seriously ill and after a very brief illness died at his home in New York City; news reports stated that he died of viral colitis. Before his death he had decided that a foundation to further choreographic endeavors would be part of his legacy. The Choo San Goh & H. Robert Magee Foundation was formed in 1992. Its most visible function is to present the annual Choo San Goh Award for Choreography. The foundation also oversees the licensing of Goh's ballets in performances by dance companies throughout the world. Singapore Dance Theatre has added to their repertoire ten of Goh's works.

• In 1997 Singapore Dance Theatre commissioned a monograph on Goh by Janek Schergen entitled *Goh Choo San, Master Craftsman in Dance*. It contains a detailed overview of his life in text and photos of his ballets. Obituaries are in the *New York Times* and the *Washington Post*, 30 Nov. 1987.

JANEK SCHERGEN

GOLDENSON, Leonard H. (7 Dec. 1905–27 Dec. 1999), entertainment industry executive, was born Leonard Harry Goldenson in Scottdale, Pennsylvania, the son of Lee Goldenson, a haberdasher whose business interests included several local movie theaters, and Ester Broude Goldenson, a Russian immigrant. He attended public schools in the rural coal- and steel-producing region southwest of Pittsburgh, excelling in academics and athletics and winning admission to Harvard College, an extraordinary accomplishment in 1923 for a boy from a provincial middle-class Jewish family. After completing his B.S. degree in business administration in 1927, he attended Harvard Law School, receiving his LL.B during the Depression year of 1930. He was admitted to the New York state bar that year.

The young attorney found his way into show business after favorably impressing a client who was a trustee in the bankruptcy reorganization of Paramount Pictures. Though only twenty-eight, he was appointed head of the film studio's New England theater division and rose swiftly through the management ranks of the Paramount chain, which consisted then of more than 1,700 theaters. In 1944 he was named president of Paramount Theatres Services Corporation and elected to the board of directors of the parent company, Paramount Pictures, Inc.

A combination of government regulatory initiatives and new developments in communication technology reshaped the structure of the American entertainment industry after World War II. Goldenson, perhaps more than any other film executive, showed a consistent ability to understand the implications of these changes and to act in ways that turned new conditions to advantage.

In 1948 the U.S. Supreme Court upheld a Federal antitrust action that effectively barred film studios from owning movie theaters, forcing Paramount to divest the division that Goldenson headed. United Paramount Theaters, Inc. (UPT) was launched as an independent company in 1950, with Goldenson as its president. During this same period, commercial television service was gradually being introduced to the American public. Film executives—and especially

theater owners—generally shunned television, regarding it as a dangerous threat to the movies. Goldenson, however, had seen potential in the new medium from its very beginnings. As early as 1939 he had championed the cause of a short-lived experimental station that Paramount had operated in Chicago. By his own account, he was convinced by 1950 that television was an "irresistible tide" in popular entertainment and was "hell bent" to get into the business. Accordingly, he sold off 875 of UPT's 1,424 movies theaters, many of them massive "palaces" located on prime downtown real estate. While his competitors were devising ways to defend the movies from the dreaded onslaught of television, Goldenson was building a war chest for his own corporate invasion of the broadcasting industry.

This was no mean task. In 1950, only 108 licensed television stations operated in the United States. The great majority were either owned by or affiliated with the National Broadcasting Company (NBC) and the Columbia Broadcasting System (CBS), the two companies that dominated radio. A third radio network, the American Broadcasting Company (ABC), had also begun television service. Unlike its rivals, NBC and CBS, which had amassed great fortunes in radio advertising since the 1920s, ABC came into being in 1943 as the result of a Federal Communications Commission (FCC) ruling that forced the Radio Corporation of America to divest one of its two NBC networks, known as the "Red" and the "Blue." The Blue network was sold to Edward J. Noble, head of the Life Savers candy company, and renamed the American Broadcasting Company. But it had fewer affiliates than its rivals and lacked the prestige to sign major stars. By 1950 it was teetering near bankruptcy. Goldenson set his sights on a takeover of ABC, courting Noble with terms more favorable than might be expected for a failing enterprise.

In 1951 plans to combine UPT and ABC were announced and, after almost two years of debate, won the required approval of the FCC. Goldenson, who headed the merged corporation, had become an unwelcome member of a very exclusive club. David Sarnoff of NBC and William Paley of CBS regarded television as a natural extension of the radio industry they had founded and had thus far resisted the efforts of movie interests to share in it. Unwilling to pay Hollywood studios for programming, they had committed their networks to live broadcast genres, such as "talking heads," drama, and music hall vaudeville—forms that were theatrical rather than cinematic.

In 1953 ABC's biggest problem was a lack of stations in the many markets around the country that still had fewer than three TV stations. "We could only reach about 20% of viewers. NBC and CBS had the best television stations locked up," Goldenson told an interviewer. "I felt that the only way to do it was to get programs that stations would take instead of theirs." The strategy that Goldenson devised not only saved ABC but also ended the war between the television and movie industries by marrying them. Believing that filmed action series and nature shows would prove more popular than visually static live programming, he endeavored to make filmed entertainment the distinguishing feature of ABC.

Walt Disney, who was seeking capital to construct a proposed theme park in southern California, was a willing partner. "The banks and the other networks had already turned Disney down," Goldenson recalled. "They thought it would be another Coney Island." Within months of assuming control of ABC, Goldenson signed Disney to a seven-year deal for a weekly prime-time series bearing the title of the theme park, *Disneyland*, and allowing Disney to appear on camera as its host, free to promote the park and his other projects "At $40 million, it was then the biggest programming package in history," according to Goldenson. The agreement also gave ABC a 35 percent interest in Disneyland, which Goldenson sold in 1961 for $17 million. Other filmed Disney programs soon came to ABC, including *The Mickey Mouse Club* and *Zorro*.

Goldenson's next production deal, made with Warner Brothers, had an even more powerful impact in the transformation of television into a film-based medium. Studio head Jack Warner agreed to deliver three hour-long action series to ABC. *Cheyenne*, which premiered in 1955, was the first Western with outdoor shooting to appear on prime-time network television. It led its time period in the ratings in many of the cities where ABC was carried, persuading some station managers to drop existing programming to air it and convincing owners of new stations to affiliate with ABC. The success of ABC's film series persuaded Sarnoff and Paley to abandon their anti-Hollywood strategies and make deals of their own with the studios.

Unfortunately for Goldenson, his wealthier rivals became only too willing to follow his lead. By 1958, the three television networks were collectively airing more than twenty filmed Westerns on prime-time schedules, and when Disney's ABC contract expired in 1961, NBC promptly wooed the show away. All told, it would take Goldenson more than twenty years to bring the ABC television network to full parity with NBC and CBS. However, he pursued that goal relentlessly in every way possible. After finishing behind CBS and NBC every season since television ratings had first been measured, ABC moved up to second place in 1977–1978 and won the season a year later.

During the 1960s, Goldenson kept ABC alive and healthy by building it into what was arguably a prototype for contemporary multimedia entertainment companies, bringing recording, publishing, and electronics companies under his corporate umbrella. ABC radio was reorganized from a conventional network into a collection of demographically oriented mininetworks, turning it into a highly profitable division. By contrast, NBC failed repeatedly in a series of reformatting schemes before exiting the radio business in 1981.

As a corporate leader in an industry not known for personal loyalty, Goldenson demonstrated a remarkable ability to cultivate a cadre of long-serving executives who were bold enough to institute innovations yet mindful enough of convention so as not to violate viewer expectations. Some noteworthy Goldenson protégés included Michael Eisner in top management, Barry Diller in entertainment programming, and Roone Arledge in sports and news. Arledge was so successful in building ABC Sports from a nominal operation to an industry leader that Goldenson appointed him head of the news division, taking considerable criticism for Arledge's lack of journalistic credentials. ABC News nevertheless rose to parity in the ratings under Arledge's direction while improving its news coverage with innovative programs such as *Nightline* and *20/20*. Newsman Ted Koppel praised Goldenson as "a man who gave his executives the leeway to be as good as they possibly could be."

Goldenson remained at the helm of ABC for more than three decades, before retiring gradually in the late 1980s to his vacation home on Longboat Key in Tampa Bay, Florida. Having spent approximately $8 million dollars to buy a failing company in 1953, he presided over the sale of ABC to Capital Cities Broadcasting for $3.5 billion in 1985, the largest price to that date of an entertainment company.

Goldenson married Isabelle Weinstein in 1939. They had three daughters and made their home for many years in Mamaroneck, north of New York City. Following the death of their first child from cerebral palsy, they dedicated themselves to battling the disease and were among the founders of the United Cerebral Palsy Society (later Foundation) in 1946. Their personal philanthropy included a $60 million gift to the Harvard Medical School in 1994, which was earmarked for research on neurological diseases.

Goldenson enjoyed playing tennis and spending time with his family, an unprepossessing and plainspoken figure in the glitzy world of mass entertainment. At a memorial service at Temple Emanuel of New York, friends and colleagues eulogized him with memories of his preference for driving an older car rather than being chauffeured in a late-model limousine; of spotting him in a coach seat on an airplane, while lesser executives in his own company sat in first class; and of his appearance at a social gathering in blue jeans, as others, dressed in expensive evening clothes, jockeyed for his ear. He died on Longboat Key.

• Goldenson's autobiography, *Beating the Odds*, written with Marvin J. Wolf, was published in 1991. A comprehensive account of his early career appears in *Current Biography* 1957. Commentary on Goldenson's later years, especially his positioning of ABC for the cable era, appears in Ken Auletta's *Three Blind Mice* (1991). A transcription of a taped interview conducted by Jack Kuney shortly before Goldenson's death in 1999 is held by the Center for the Study of Popular Television in its oral history collection at the Syracuse University Library. Obituaries appeared in major newspapers, including the *New York Times*; the most comprehensive of these is in the *Los Angeles Times* of 28 Dec. 1999.

DAVID MARC

GOLDKETTE, Jean (18 May 1893–24 Mar. 1962), dance bandleader, businessman, and classical pianist, was born in Patras, Greece, the son of Angelina Goldkette, an actress. It is not known who Jean's father was. The Goldkette family was a troupe of entertainers that traveled throughout Europe and the Ottoman Empire. Angelina met and married John Poliakoff, a journalist, in Moscow in 1903. Raised in Greece and Russia, Jean studied classical piano from an early age, and he attended the Moscow Conservatory of Music. He moved to Chicago in 1910, when he was 17, to live with George Goldkette, an uncle. His mother and stepfather moved to the United States in 1919.

In Chicago, Goldkette continued his piano training, first at the Lewis Institute and later at the American Conservatory of Music. His first major exposure to jazz was when, in his early twenties and playing with Charlie Horvath at Lamb's Café in Chicago, he heard Tom Brown's Band from Dixieland. Goldkette's fellow band members stormed out of the club, angered by the new music, but Goldkette was intrigued. He later contended that his entire career was determined by this event.

Shortly afterward Goldkette went to work for Edgar Benson, who managed several white bandleaders. In 1918 Goldkette joined the U.S. Army for a short military tour and was honorably discharged in December of that year. He then moved to Detroit, where he played with Andrew Raymonds' Band. From 1918 to 1921 he played with the Detroit Athletic Club (DAC) orchestra, and made several recordings with Duane Sawyer, a saxophone player with the DAC band, on the Gennett label. In 1921 he became musical director of the DAC, a position he held until 1938.

In 1922 Goldkette became a partner with Charlie Horvath and purchased the palatial Chinese Gardens ballroom and restaurant in Detroit, which he quickly remodeled into the Graystone Ballroom. Beginning in 1923, Goldkette formed several corporations: his own musical booking agency, the National Amusement Corporation; Graystone, Inc.; the Detroit College of Music, and the Jean Goldkette Orchestra and Attractions, Inc. With the National Amusement Corporation, he organized and served as manager (called "booking agent") for a variety of dance bands that played in midwestern dance halls. His flagship band, the Victor Recording Orchestra (also known as the Graystone Orchestra), maintained a long-standing engagement at the Graystone Ballroom.

With the Graystone Ballroom band Goldkette gained a reputation as one of the most prominent white bandleaders of the 1920s and one of the most effective recruiters of hot young jazz artists. For the rest of the decade Goldkette organized and managed more than twenty sweet dance bands throughout the Midwest and East, rivaling in popularity Paul Whiteman in New York City.

Of the artists who played for Goldkette, one of the most famous was the cornet titan Bix Beiderbecke (1924, 1925–1927). Beiderbecke had a checkered work history with Goldkette. Tradition has it that the bandleader fired Beiderbecke for not being able to read music well enough, but rehired him a year later. Other prominent band members included the C-melody saxophone player and musical partner of Beiderbecke, Frankie Trumbauer, who was the musical director of Goldkette's orchestra at the Arcadia Ballroom in St. Louis (1925–1926) and was in Goldkette's Victor Orchestra (1927); the reedman Jimmy Dorsey (1925); the trombonist Tommy Dorsey (1925); the violinist Joe Venuti (1924–1925); and the guitarist Eddie Lang (1926). Other prominent band members at one time or another were the clarinetists Don Murray, Danny Polo, and Pee Wee Russell; the banjoist and guitarist Howdy Quicksell; the trombonists Spiegle Willcox and Bill Rank; the drummer Chauncey Morehouse; and the New Orleans double bass master Steve Brown. Brown was the closest thing to a star member of the band (having been a member of the seminal white jazz group in Chicago, the New Orleans Rhythm Kings) and was often featured up front as soloist. According to the alto saxophonist Stanley "Doc" Ryker, Brown was an important figure in the transition from tuba to bass, and no bass player of the era "could equal Steve slapping the bass. He had a really distinctive style and an uncanny sense of rhythm" (Kline, p. 1).

Goldkette rarely played in his orchestras, and he seldom even fronted them. His contribution was that of organizer and manager. He was instrumental in helping Hank Biagini form the Orange Blossoms (later called the Casa Loma Orchestra), perhaps the finest late-1920s white swing band. In addition, he helped organize one of the most swinging black bands of the preswing era, McKinney's Cotton Pickers. Beginning in 1926, this band was associated with the Graystone Ballroom, where many battles of the bands were held.

In the 1920s, Goldkette's bands—in particular his Graystone band—were regarded as among the greatest and most legendary of the era, rivaling those of Paul Whiteman, Ben Pollack, Coon-Sanders, Hal Kemp, Roger Wolfe Kahn, and Isham Jones. In September 1927, Goldkette's Graystone Victor Orchestra even beat Fletcher Henderson's in New York's Roseland Ballroom in a famous band battle. A modern-day listener, however, is apt to be puzzled by Goldkette's historical reputation, since most of his recorded legacy is not noteworthy. Of the records issued in 1924, many were cornball, mushy, halting, and completely forgettable. With the addition of Beiderbecke as chief soloist (though solos in those days were more breaks than extended stretches) and with the arranging prowess of Bill Challis (who later was a major contributor to Whiteman), some excellent sides were cut. The trombonist Russ Morgan was musical director and arranger for several of Goldkette's bands, including the Book-Cadillac Hotel Orchestra; he later freelanced as an arranger for such prominent bands as that of Fletcher Henderson, led his own band, and became a recording executive.

Goldkette's records are basically of the sweet (in contrast to hot) variety, and these RCA Victor sides reflect this all too well. On the other hand, his live performances reportedly had more vitality and swing than his recordings. A well-known piece of jazz lore has it that Eddie King, the Victor executive in charge of the Goldkette projects, did not allow the band to cut loose in the studios and confined the sessions to pat, commercially safe arrangements. Also the records are blemished with indifferent vocalists, who were not part of the band. However, because of Goldkette's knack for hiring good musicians, many of whom were among the hottest white Chicago and New York jazzmen, his records contain some truly haunting hot licks and genuinely swinging moments. *My Pretty Girl* (1 Feb. 1927) and *Clementine* (15 Sept. 1927) are generally considered his most jazz-oriented records. Both feature Beiderbecke, and the latter contains his longest solo on a Goldkette recording. There are also superb Beiderbecke solos on *Proud of a Baby* (28 Jan. 1927) and *In My Merry Oldsmobile* (23 May 1927). Critics have traditionally praised the opening ensemble of *Sunday* (15 Oct. 1926), ascribed to Challis as arranger.

Goldkette supported this all-star band from 1923 to 1929, playing for dances—most regularly at the Ivy Ballroom in Philadelphia, the Pla-Mor Ballroom in Kansas City, and the home-base Graystone Ballroom in Detroit—and touring the Midwest and East Coast. Continual financial woes and quarrels with difficult band members finally took their toll on this bespectacled, serious-minded band manager. Whiteman had been trying to recruit Goldkette's best players, and others had gone to work for Roger Wolfe Kahn or had taken on freelance work in New York City. On 18 September 1927, Goldkette organized a farewell engagement for his lead orchestra in New York's Roseland Ballroom. He then reorganized the orchestra and continued to record as the Victor Recording Orchestra into 1929.

By the mid-1930s, Goldkette had dropped out of most of his jazz associations and was working primarily as a booking agent and a classical pianist. In 1940 he became the music director of NBC Radio. He played from time to time with the Detroit Symphony Orchestra and in the 1940s and 1950s formed short-lived and commercially unsuccessful ensembles. In 1959 Goldkette revived some of the arrangements from the 1920s and added some new arrangements by Sy Oliver for a Camden "reunion" LP issued as *Dance Hits of the 1920s in Stereo*. Also in the 1950s he was president of the National Actors Foundation, a nonprofit organization dedicated to developing new talent.

Goldkette was a phenomenal band organizer and a popularizer of jazz. He was among the first to bridge the New Orleans style of jazz and that of the swing era. In 1939 he married Lee Allaire. They had no children and were divorced in 1940. In 1961 Goldkette

moved to Los Angeles, where he had close friends in the music industry such as Frankie Laine and Johnny Green. He died in nearby Santa Barbara.

• Substantial corrections to prevailing misinformation were provided by Jean Goldkette's grandnephew, Alann Krivor (Jean Goldkette Foundation, 2916 Fernan Hill Rd., Coeur d'Alene, ID 83814). For summaries of Goldkette's life, see "Goldkette, Jean," in John Chilton, *Who's Who in Jazz* (1972), p. 122; "Goldkette, Jean," in Leonard Feather and Ira Gitler, *The Biographical Encyclopedia of Jazz* (1999), p. 260; and Richard M. Sudhalter, "Goldkette, Jean," in *The New Grove Dictionary of Jazz*, ed. Barry Kernfeld (1994), p. 436. There are helpful though sketchy sections on Goldkette in George T. Simon, *The Big Bands* (1967); and Albert MacCarthy, *Big Band Jazz* (1974). A more accurate biography by Stan Kuwik, "From Prince to Pauper," appears in the International Association of Jazz Record Collectors' *IAJRC Journal* 22, no. 1 (Jan. 1989): 1–9, and no. 2 (Apr. 1989): 46–56. A useful article is Jerry Kline, "Goldkette's Doc," *Mississippi Rag*, Sept. 1978, p. 1. Additional useful information is in Jeff Hopkins's liner notes to *Jean Goldkette and His Orchestra: Victor Recordings (1924–1928)* (Trans-Atlantic Radio 011) and Ate van Delden's liner notes to *Jean Goldkette Bands 1924–1929* (Timeless Historical 1084).

STEPHEN C. GALLEHER

GOLDMAN, Richard Franko (7 Dec. 1910–19 Jan. 1980), composer, conductor, and author, was born Richard Henry Maibrunn Goldman in New York City, the son of the famed bandmaster Edwin Franko Goldman and Adelaide Maibrunn Goldman. Richard grew up in a stimulating musical and intellectual environment. He attended Townsend Harris High School, affiliated with the City College of New York for exceptionally gifted children, from which he graduated at age sixteen. He then decided to study music. Clarence Adler taught him piano and composition, and Pietro Floridia, an opera composer, taught him compositional technique by having him copy, note for note, operatic scores of the masters.

Goldman enrolled in 1927 at Columbia University, where he specialized in philosophy, Romance languages, and English. He began to write criticism for the *Columbia Spectator*, and he also contributed articles on music to the *Columbia Varsity*, the school's literary journal. He graduated in 1930, Phi Beta Kappa.

Goldman was awarded a special fellowship in art and archaeology and returned to Columbia for one year of graduate study. During that time he also studied Greek, wrote an article for the *Musical Courier*, and taught art history at a private summer school on Long Island. He did not return to Columbia the following year. Instead, he studied composition with Nadia Boulanger in Paris. But he found her excessively rigid and remained only a few months. Goldman met a young American art student, Alexandra Rienzi, whom he married in 1934. They had one child. In 1933 he made an extensive trip through Portugal. He loved the country, its language, art, architecture, landscape, and ambiance.

Later that year he returned to the United States and wrote "pulp" fiction. On the strength of his income, he and Rienzi married and moved into the Goldman country house at Mount Tremper, New York, where they lived in a summer house. Both wrote pulp fiction, under the respective pseudonyms Captain Jonathan Sanders and Susan Ramsey.

During this period Richard Goldman continued his serious literary activities as well. He worked on a novel, wrote articles for the *Etude* and the *School Musician*, and did a series of book reviews for the *Brooklyn Daily Eagle*. The articles for the *School Musician* set forth some of his ideas on education that later became a personal crusade. In Goldman's words, what was important in education was "the cultivation of discrimination and perception, and the selection, from the accumulated record of the past, of what retains meaning and what is useful for our present needs, esthetic, intellectual, and moral."

During the summers of 1934–1937 Goldman taught music appreciation and conducting at the Ernest Williams School in Saugerties, New York. There Edwin Goldman heard his son conduct and offered him the position of associate conductor of the Goldman Band. It was then that Richard Goldman decided to replace his middle names—Henry Maibrunn—with Franko.

In 1937 Goldman wrote his first book, *The Band's Music*, for which Percy Grainger wrote the foreword. The reviews were extremely favorable, and Grainger thought it "flawless."

Goldman received invitations to guest conduct bands elsewhere. From 1938 to 1942 he conducted at several high schools, colleges, and universities, including Pennsylvania State Teacher's College, Oberlin College, and Susquehanna University. For at least one year he was the conductor of the International Ladies Garment Workers Union Band.

The years 1937 to 1942 marked the greatest concentration of Goldman's composing activity, when he produced *Monochromes* for solo flute; *Divertimento* for flute and piano; *Nine Bagatelles* for piano; *Hymn for Brass Choir, A Curtain-Raiser and Country Dance*, and *A Sentimental Journey* for band; *The Lee Rigg* for orchestra; and *Sonatina* for piano. Goldman's music falls into two categories, serious and more popular. His serious music is like the mainstream music of the day, similar in style to that of Igor Stravinsky, Aaron Copland, and Sergei Prokofiev. The works for band belong to the latter category. He also made numerous transcriptions and arrangements for band, mostly of contemporary composers.

In 1940 the Goldmans moved to New York City. Goldman was admitted to the American Society of Composers, Authors, and Publishers (ASCAP) as a composer in 1946. Also that year he wrote his second book, *The Concert Band*, resumed his membership in the League of Composers, and returned to his position with the Goldman Band. In the summer of 1946 he conducted the premiere of Arnold Schoenberg's *Theme and Variations for Wind Band*. In 1947 he led the band in the first American performance of Hector Berlioz's *Funeral and Triumphal Symphony*, which he had reconstructed for modern instruments. At the invitation of William Schuman, president of the Juilliard School, Goldman became the chairman of the new Department of Literature and Materials of Music.

During the late 1940s Goldman continued to compose, arrange, and edit music. In addition to continuing with Juilliard and the Goldman Band, he joined the editorial board of Henry Cowell's publication series New Music, began a twenty-year tenure as New York critic for the *Musical Quarterly*, and was actively involved in the League of Composers, of which he was executive director from 1946 to 1950. In 1949 the Goldmans moved to Katonah, New York.

After the death of his father in 1956, Goldman took over full responsibilities for the Goldman Band. In the fall of 1959 he resigned his position at Juilliard to do more traveling and writing.

In 1967 Goldman accepted the positions of director of the Peabody Conservatory and president of the Peabody Institute of the City of Baltimore. He was praised for the academic excellence he brought to the school and for the lasting impression he made on students. He retired from Peabody in 1977. In addition to three honorary doctorates (among them Lehigh University in 1964), he received numerous awards, including the Juilliard Music Foundation Award (1955) and the Alice M. Ditson Award (1961).

Goldman died in Baltimore. There were many public and private tributes to Goldman's life. R. P. Harriss of the *News American* said, "He was a very civilized man, simple and warm in manner," and went on to comment on "his vast erudition and notable accomplishments." Virgil Thomson said in an interview with Noel K. Lester, "Goldman was a distinguished composer, writer, conductor, and educator. He worked carefully and well; everything he touched bore the mark of distinction and all qualities of excellence."

• Goldman donated his library of band music to the School of Music, University of Iowa, in 1967. Myron D. Welch, "The Goldman Band Library, Part 1," *Journal of Band Research* 19 (1984): 26–30, describes the Goldman collection. Goldman's publications include Richard Franko Goldman, *Selected Essays and Reviews, 1948–1968* (1980). See also Noel K. Lester, "Richard Franko Goldman: His Life and Works" (Ph.D. diss., Peabody Conservatory of Music, 1984); and Dorothy Klotzman, "Goldman, Richard Franko," in *The New Grove Dictionary of American Music* (1986), vol. 11, p. 239. An obituary is in the *New York Times*, 22 Jan. 1980.

DOROTHY A. KLOTZMAN

GONZÁLEZ, Henry B. (3 May 1916–28 Nov. 2000), U.S. congressman, was born Enrique Barbosa González in San Antonio, Texas, the son of Leonides González Cigarroa, a politician and newspaper editor, and Genoveva Barbosa Prince de González. Leonides, a former mayor of Mapimi, Durango, in Mexico, fled the turmoil of the Mexican Revolution in 1911 and settled his family in San Antonio.

After graduating from Thomas Jefferson High School in San Antonio in 1935, Henry attended San

Antonio Junior College, from which he received an associate's degree in 1937. For the next two years González studied engineering and law at the University of Texas at Austin. Lack of funds forced him to return to San Antonio, where he enrolled in the St. Mary's University School of Law. In 1940 he married Bertha Cuellar; they had eight children. González received his LL.B. degree in 1943.

During World War II González served as a civilian cable censor for military intelligence. He also worked as an assistant juvenile probation officer for Bexar County from 1943 to 1946, when he became chief probation officer. He soon resigned, frustrated with the incompetence and racism of his superiors. González then worked for a language translation service and served briefly as deputy director of the Bexar County Housing Authority.

González began his political career in 1950 with an unsuccessful bid for a seat in the Texas House of Representatives. Three years later he was elected to the San Antonio City Council, serving part of his term as mayor pro tempore. In 1956 he won a seat in the Texas senate, becoming the first Hispanic elected to that body in more than a century. As a senator, González earned a reputation as a liberal opposed to racial discrimination and the regressive state sales tax. He garnered national attention when he and a fellow senator filibustered for thirty-six hours in an effort to kill a bill promoting racial segregation.

González developed considerable political ambitions during this period. He ran for Texas governor in 1958 but lost in the Democratic party primary by a 3-to-1 margin. During the 1960 presidential campaign, González and U.S. Senator Dennis Chavez of New Mexico served as national cochairmen of the Viva Kennedy clubs, Hispanic organizations that promoted Democratic candidate John F. Kennedy. In 1961 he ran in the special election for the U.S. senate seat of Lyndon Johnson, who had resigned from the senate to become vice president. González won only 9 percent of the vote. Later that year he ran in a special election for a vacated seat in the U.S. House of Representatives. González won the election, a victory that made him the first Hispanic Texan to serve in the U.S. House of Representatives. He remained the representative for Texas's Twentieth Congressional District for the next thirty-seven years, never facing a serious challenge for his seat.

In 1961 House leaders assigned González to the Committee on Banking and Currency, which held responsibility for issues ranging from international finance to public housing. The Texas congressman quickly established himself as a liberal who supported Kennedy's New Frontier and, later, Lyndon Johnson's Great Society programs, especially measures relating to civil rights. The first bill González introduced as a member of Congress called for a constitutional amendment to abolish poll taxes. He was one of only eleven southern Democrats who voted for the Civil Rights Act of 1964.

González's colleagues came to know him as a man of fierce independence and uncompromising integrity. Although he maintained widespread support within the Hispanic community, he never styled himself as an ethnic candidate. In the late 1960s, Chicano militants derided him for his unwillingness to associate with their cause. González was unrepentant, condemning from the House floor groups such as the Mexican-American Youth Organization as hateful and divisive. González also could be prickly and sensitive about his reputation. In 1963 he shoved a Texas Republican who charged that he had communist sympathies. In 1986 at a San Antonio diner, the seventy-year-old González assaulted a customer who called him a communist. Such accusations reveal the difficulties that González and other liberal politicians faced in the conservative Texas political environment.

In 1977 González received national attention as chairman of the House Assassinations Committee, a body established to investigate the John Kennedy and Martin Luther King, Jr. assassinations. González charged that the committee's lead counsel, Richard Sprague, was mismanaging the investigation. He fired Sprague and then announced that he was resigning from the committee, alleging that powerful forces, including organized crime figures, were preventing the committee from achieving its goal. While the incident did not affect his popularity among his constituents, his reputation suffered among colleagues in the House. González became known as a quixotic crusader whom many of his peers ignored.

His outsider status did not slow González, who became an increasingly vocal critic of many U.S. government policies during the 1980s. Twice he called for the impeachment of Ronald Reagan, first in 1983 after the invasion of Grenada and again in 1987 in response to the Iran-Contra scandal. He initiated a public feud with Samuel Pierce, Jr., Reagan's Secretary of Housing and Urban Development, over the administration's decision to cut federal low-cost housing programs. He was not merely a foe of Republicans, however. In 1989 González became chairman of the House Banking, Finance, and Urban Affairs Committee. He used that position to investigate the savings-and-loan industry, an effort that embarrassed several Democratic senators who had close ties to industry leaders. González helped to draft the savings-and-loan bailout legislation that became law in 1989.

During the 1990s González used his chairmanship to investigate allegations that the administration of George H. W. Bush had provided assistance to Iraqi leader Saddam Hussein, including access to military technology. González later called for Bush's impeachment, charging that the president had gone to war in Iraq without congressional approval. He also worked to assist impoverished Americans, helping secure the passage of the Affordable Housing Act in 1990. For his efforts on behalf of the poor and disadvantaged, González received numerous awards, including the John F. Kennedy Profile in Courage. Citing poor health, he declined to run for reelection in 1998. He died in San Antonio.

González's 1956 election to the Texas Senate marked a turning point in Texas politics in that it created opportunities for Hispanics in the state to exercise political power. However, at the national level González remained a marginal political figure, despite his many years of service in the U.S. Congress. His willingness to champion unpopular causes and his confrontational personal style prevented him from building the support within Congress that would have furthered his career. As a result, González garnered national attention only when his actions seemed eccentric or, in the case of the 1986 assault, outrageous. However, his constituents remember him as a man of integrity and forthrightness who unfailingly represented their interests.

• González's papers are maintained in the Sarita Kenedy East Law Library, St. Mary's University, San Antonio, Texas. The only studies of Gonzalez's career are the Ralph Nader Congress Project, *Henry B. Gonzalez: Democrat from Texas* (1972), and Eugene Rodriguez, Jr., *Henry B. Gonzalez: A Political Profile* (1976). An unsigned article in *Current Biography* yearbook (1993), pp. 214–217, is useful, as are Julie Leininger Pycior, *LBJ & Mexican Americans* (1997), and Ignacio M. García, *Viva Kennedy* (2000). See also Christopher Hitchens, "No Fool on the Hill," *Harper's Magazine* (Oct. 1992): 84–94. Obituaries are in the *New York Times* and the *Washington Post*, both 29 Nov. 2000.

THOMAS CLARKIN

GORDONE, Charles (12 Oct. 1925–16 Nov. 1995), playwright and actor-director, was born Charles Edward Fleming in Cleveland, Ohio, the son of Charles Fleming and Camille Morgan Fleming. His stepfather was William Gordon. The boy never knew his biological father and often referred to himself as "part Indian, part Irish, part French, and part Nigger." With the birth of Charles, the family moved to the mother's hometown, Elkhart, Indiana, where young Charles went to school. Shirley Gordon Jackson, the older of his two sisters, recalled that the family then moved out of the "colored" part of town and crossed the railroad tracks to the white side of Elkhart's "Mason-Dixon line." All of Charles's school friends were white. He was a straight-A student, "doing everything right," winning honors in dramatics, music, writing, and debate. He also received sixteen letters in sports and set a school record in the high jump.

"Run outa town because I dated a black girl," Charles left for Los Angeles after graduating from high school. There, he joined the Army Air Corps Special Services and helped organize entertainment programs. "Everything was segregated," he remembered. "We even had separate chow halls."

The day after his discharge Gordon returned to Elkhart, became involved with a local girl, Juanita Burton, and married her after she became pregnant; they had two children, but the marriage failed. After that, a period of itinerancy led to promiscuity, wantonness, and alcoholism.

In 1945 he returned to Los Angeles and worked as a cop ("the army had put that gung-ho thing in me") but judged himself to be a "miserable failure." Taking advantage of the G.I. Bill, he studied music and later drama at Los Angeles City College. Charles and a fellow actor, Tony Carbone, drove the southern route to New York City in 1952, ignoring the warning from his teachers that there would be no work there for blacks. Three weeks after they arrived in Manhattan, Gordone landed a role as an eccentric half-caste in Moss Hart's *Climate of Eden* on Broadway. Upon joining Actors' Equity, he saw another Charles Gordon on the Equity membership list. He renamed himself by adding his middle initial, E, to "Gordon."

After *Eden* closed, he endured the angst of the improvident actor in New York with the occasional role and the frequent binge, won an Obie (off-Broadway award) for his performance as George in an all-black production of John Steinbeck's *Of Mice and Men*, and then experienced encounters that changed his fortunes. Although Gordone did no serious writing during the 1950s—for a time he worked as a waiter—he turned to directing in 1958 and made his debut with an ambitious production of Goethe's *Faust* for the Village's offbeat Judson Memorial Church players. He also met Jeanne Warner, a blonde nurse from Columbus, Ohio. They lived together as husband and wife, though the legality of the marriage was open to question because of inconclusive evidence of the dissolution of the first marriage. They had one child.

In 1961 Gordone landed a small role as a queen's valet in the historic off-Broadway production of Jean Genet's *The Blacks*. He called the experience lifechanging: "Living with Genet's words night after night for four years—traveling to Europe—forced me to confront the hatred and fear I had inside me about being black. It set my head straight." At various times the cast included almost every substantial black name in live theater. Godfrey Cambridge, Lou Gossett, and Cicely Tyson became friends for life. Cambridge and Gordone formed CORE's (Congress of Racial Equality) Committee for the Employment of Negro Performers, and they picketed *Subways Are for Sleeping*. "All we wanted," he said, "was to get black performers an equal chance to audition for jobs."

During the long run of *The Blacks*, Gordone began setting down some of the vignettes for a play that would become *No Place to Be Somebody*. The play nearly died in manuscript. The Gordones at first failed to find backers. After an experimental production directed by Gordone, in November 1967, which nobody in show business attended, two years of desperation ensued. Finally, following a showcase of three weekends at director Ted Cornell's tiny Other Stage in South Manhattan, the much-shortened play was launched on 4 May 1969 by Joseph Papp on a 248-performance run at the New York Shakespeare Festival's Public Theatre, followed by an acclaimed limited engagement at Broadway's ANTA Theatre.

No Place's power lies in the stunning interplay between Johnny Williams, angry and bitter, trying to make it as a small-time hustler, and Gabe Gabriel, angry but hopeful, a young playwright trying to find another way to be somebody. Gabe sees the futility of Johnny's course but can't find an acceptable alternative. They perform a tragic duet that Gordone laced together with flashes of what he called "black-black comedy." *New York Times* drama critic Walter Kerr proclaimed Gordone "the most astonishing new American playwright to come along since Edward Albee." *No Place to Be Somebody* won the 1970 Pulitzer Prize. In January it started a run of nearly two years at the Promenade Theatre, Broadway at Seventysixth, and was presented by two national touring companies in Los Angeles, San Francisco, Chicago, and Boston, all directed by Gordone. He was also presented at Carnegie Recital Hall in May 1970, performing his poems and short sketches in an evening entitled "Gordone Is a Muthah."

With so much success crowded into one year of his life, Gordone set a standard never again approximated. The Pulitzer accomplishment, rooted in the 1960s upsurge in militant black theater in New York, was also a kind of disaster for so politically conservative a playwright. "There can be no black experience without the white experience," Gordone once observed. "I believe there never has been such a thing as 'black theater.' What is called black theater has, as it should, come out of the civil rights movement [but] Broadway theater has depicted blacks in sensational and stereotypical ways [without] showing any interest in the black experience" ("Yes, I Am a Black Playwright, But. . . ," *New York Times*, 25 Jan. 1970).

Gordone's apostasy from any constricted ethnic identity—his alienation from most African-American political organizations that dealt exclusively with black urban problems—only partially explains why his playwriting career lacked a second act. His fall was inseparable from his alcoholism. In 1982 Gordone headed west.

The 1980s found Gordone in Berkeley and San Francisco where once again he entered into a companionate symbiosis. Susan Kouyomjian, a young and innovative producer, invited him to direct Tennessee Williams's *Night of the Iguana* at her community theater in Berkeley. He stayed, and they did fifteen plays together—from Strindberg to Eugene O'Neill—cast untraditionally with minority actors while at once acknowledging their ethnicity and the plays' historical contexts. And he stopped drinking.

Kouyomjian remained with him for the rest of his life. They married in 1987. In summer 1987 he completed a D. H. Lawrence Fellowship at Taos, New Mexico, and that fall accepted an invitation to lecture at Texas A and M, where he stayed until his death, directing plays and teaching playwriting and acting in the drama and English departments. His fascination with the American West was reflected in his last play, *Roan Browne and Cherry*, which received a workshop production at the university. Gordone also wrote a series pilot for CBS television, "Heart and Soul," but

the writers' strike of 1987 prevented the project from going forward.

No Place to Be Somebody, as reviewer Stanley Eichelbaum wrote after its Bay Area opening, "isn't just another piece that lashes out at Whitey. It's a powerful, funny, searingly theatrical and fascinating human tragi-comedy about the black man's hate-love relationship with whites and with his own race as well. For there's lots of harsh comment on black paranoia and intra-racial hatred, along with the more familiar hang-ups of black rage" ("A Powerfully Affecting Black Play," *San Francisco Examiner*, 12 Nov. 1970). Written with more coherence than the early plays of LeRoi Jones and with none of the ethnic stereotypes of Lonne Elder III, *No Place* crosses the barroom drama of William Saroyan's *The Time of Your Life* and O'Neill's *The Iceman Cometh* with the social outrage of John Osborne's *Look Back in Anger*.

• Bobbs-Merrill published *No Place to Be Somebody* in 1970. Most theater critics agree that the play, whose most recent national tour—Detroit, Chicago, Philadelphia, Atlanta, and Miami—was during the fall of 1993, is best appreciated in performance. A revealing essay, "From Nowhere to No Place," largely a self-interview, appeared in the *New York Times*, 8 June 1969, one month after *No Place. . .* opened on Broadway. The entry on Gordone in *Contemporary Authors*, vol. 180 (2000), pp. 166–176, includes an autobiographical essay. An obituary is in the *New York Times*, 19 Nov. 1995.

RICHARD HAUER COSTA

GOREY, Edward (22 Feb. 1925–15 Apr. 2000), author and artist, was born Edward St. John Gorey in Chicago, Illinois, the son of Edward Leo Gorey, a newspaperman, and Helen Dunham Garvey Gorey, a government clerk. The couple divorced when their son was eleven and remarried when he was twenty-seven. By the age of three, young Edward had taught himself to read, revealing the precocity that would enable him to skip both first and fifth grades. By the time he was five, he had read *Dracula* and *Alice in Wonderland*, works that would have a lasting effect upon his artistic sensibility. He attended the progressive Francis W. Parker high school and after graduating studied at the Chicago Art Institute for a semester before being inducted into the U.S. Army in 1943. He spent the rest of World War II stationed at Dugway Proving Ground, Utah, a testing site for mortars and poison gas, where he served as a company clerk.

Discharged in 1946, Gorey entered Harvard College. There he majored in French, acquiring an enduring interest in French Surrealism and Symbolism as well as Chinese and Japanese literature. He roomed with poet Frank O'Hara and, with several other young poets and actors, formed the Poets Theatre, a forerunner of the New York Artists' Theatre. Graduating in 1950, Gorey worked in Boston bookstores part time, tried to write novels but failed, and "starved, more or less," as he put it ("my family was helping to support me").

In 1953 he moved to Manhattan to take a job in the art department of Doubleday's new Anchor Books division, where he drew many of the covers for the early editions. Staying late at the office, he began work on his first book, *The Unstrung Harp*. Published later in the year, this slender volume depicts (in prose on one page facing an illustration on the next) the impermeably mundane life of a professional writer, who begins a new novel every other year on 18 November exactly. Gorey also met Frances Steloff, founder of the Gotham Book Mart and champion of such unconventional authors as James Joyce; she became one of the first to carry his books.

In 1957 Gorey began attending performances of the New York City Ballet, achieving a perfect attendance for twenty-five years, always attired in a floor-length fur coat, long scarf, blue jeans, and white sneakers, which, in combination with his full-bearded visage, created an appearance "half bongo-drum beatnik, half fin-de-siècle dandy," according to Stephen Schiff (p. 84).

By 1959 four of Gorey's books had been published and attracted the attention of critic Edmund Wilson, who provided the first important notice in a review in the *New Yorker*, calling Gorey's work "surrealistic and macabre, amusing and somber, nostalgic and claustrophobic, poetic and poisoned." The same year, Gorey, joining Jason Epstein and Clelia Carroll, founded and worked for Looking Glass Library, a division of Random House that published classical children's books in hardcover, with Wilson as one of the consulting editors. In 1961 Gorey illustrated *The Man Who Sang the Sillies*, the first of a half-dozen John Ciardi works that he would illuminate, and he employed the first of his numerous pen names (all loose anagrams of his name) in *The Curious Sofa* by "Ogdred Weary." He launched the Fantod Press in 1962 to publish those of his works that failed to enlist support elsewhere. A year later, Looking Glass Library collapsed, and Gorey, with fourteen of his books published, went to work for Bobbs Merrill. After an unsatisfactory year, he quit the job and the workaday world; henceforth, he would earn a living solely as a freelance author and illustrator, eventually producing over ninety of his own works and illustrating another sixty by others (Edward Lear and Samuel Beckett among them).

The first of several exhibitions of his work was mounted in 1965 at California College of Arts and Crafts in Oakland. In 1967 Steloff sold the Gotham Book Mart to Andreas Brown, who entered into an unusual relationship with Gorey: in 1970 Gorey's *The Sopping Thursday* became the first of his books to be published by the bookstore, which also mounted an exhibition of his works that year and began serving as an archive for his art. *Amphigorey*, his 1972 anthology reprinting the first fifteen of his books, won an American Institute of Graphic Arts award as one of the year's fifty best-designed books.

In 1964, Gorey began spending more and more time at Cape Cod, where he became involved in theatrical enterprises. He designed sets and costumes for the Nantucket summer theater production of *Dracula*

in 1973 and again in 1977 for the Broadway production, winning a Tony Award for costume design. In 1978, *Gorey Stories*, a musical revue based on his published works, debuted off Broadway in January and on Broadway in October. Gorey's oeuvre reached television in 1980 when he designed the first version of the swooning lady animated titles for Public Broadcasting System's *Mystery!* In 1983 Gorey moved permanently to Cape Cod, first to Barnstable and then to Yarmouthport, remaining there for the rest of his life. In 1985 he wrote the first of his ten musical revues (for which he also designed the sets and costumes), *Tinned Lettuce*, which opened at New York University. All of Gorey's subsequent theatrical works were produced on or near Cape Cod, where he died.

Except for three outsized anthologies, his books are all small in dimension and liberally illustrated with a picture on every page in the manner of children's books. Although Gorey believed children could readily appreciate the unaccountable horrors and fiendishly comic gruesomeness of his tales, he did not write for youngsters. The humor in his tales can be properly grasped only by adults who can savor the comedy created by the unexpected juxtaposition of Gorey's somber albeit caricatural renderings and his deadpan prose. The world he evoked is ostensibly a genteel one, an elegant past now gone to seed, usually populated by bored crypto-Edwardians, whom he depicts with spindly figures and spherical or egg-shaped heads. The pictures in some of his books are as unembellished as Japanese prints, but Gorey's characteristic manner is to garnish his drawings with meticulous hachuring and pointillist cross-hatching, so intensely applied as to be almost painful in its exquisite punctiliousness. This technique plunges his fictional milieu into deep fustian shadow, giving the stories a vaguely sinister, melancholy menace.

Contributing to the ambiance is Gorey's parallel text of hand-lettered laconic declarative sentences (sometimes in rhyme) that relate the most disturbing events in an almost elliptical fashion. In *The Loathesome Couple* (1977), the titular pair kidnap a young girl and spend the better part of a night "murdering the child in various ways." *The Curious Sofa* (subtitled "A Pornographic Work") includes the immortal line, "Still later Gerald did a terrible thing to Elsie with a saucepan." In *The Admonitory Hippopotamus* (unpublished at the time of Gorey's death), a five-year-old girl playing in a gazebo suddenly sees a spectral hippopotamus "rising from the ha-ha." "Fly at once," commands the hippo; "all is discovered." Ghastly events are described in a bland, unemotional style "as though the narrator hadn't quite grasped the gravity of the situation" (Schiff, p. 87). Millicent Frastley is sacrificed to the Insect God; Charlotte Sophia is run over by her own father who fails to recognize her. In the infanticidal ABC book, *The Gashlycrumb Tinies* (1963), all the children die in alphabetical order: "O is for Olive run through with an awl / P is for Prue trampled flat in a brawl."

As disasters overtake them, the principals themselves seem as oblivious as the indifferent gods. *The Doubtful Guest* (1958) is vintage Gorey. In it, a furry sort of penguin, wearing a long scarf and tennis shoes, shows up uninvited at a dreary mansion and, without the slightest resistance from the resident Edwardian family, makes itself at home, peering up flues in fireplaces, tearing up books, sleepwalking, dropping favorite objects into the pond, and eating the china for breakfast. "Every Sunday it brooded and lay on the floor, / Inconveniently close to the drawing-room door" where its prone form blocks entrance and egress. Nothing is ever resolved; day after day, the household watches the creature numbly until at last the narrative concludes inconclusively: "It came seventeen years ago—and to this day / It has shown no intention of going away."

Gorey's books "are like the remnants of a once proud civilization whose decline and fall have resulted not from dwindling armies or crumbling economies but from an invasion of the inexplicable—random brutality, spates of angst and ennui, odd words and odder weapons, and the kind of skittering beasties you catch only out of the corner of your eye" (Schiff, p. 84). Taking his work seriously, Gorey cautioned, would be "the height of folly." Still, when a publisher rejected one of his books on the grounds that it wasn't funny, Gorey professed astonishment: "It wasn't supposed to be," he said; "what a peculiar reaction." Mel Gussow, writing the *New York Times* obituary, delivered perhaps the best assessment: "He was one of the most aptly named figures in American art and literature. In creating a large body of small work, he made an indelible imprint on noir fiction and on the psyche of his admirers."

• Among the pen names Gorey adopted for many of his nearly 100 titles are Ogdred Weary, Dogear Wryde, D. Awdrey-Gore, E. G. Deadworry, Drew Dogyear, Regera Dowdy, Raddory Gewe, Aedwyrd Gore, and Garrod Weedy; Eduard Blutig and O. Mude are translations into German of Edward Gorey and Ogdred Weary, respectively. In addition to books mentioned above, the titles of some of his most popular works suggest the ornately perverse turn of the author's mind: *The Listing Attic* (1954), *The Fatal Lozenge: An Alphabet* (1960), *The Hapless Child* (1961), *The Willowdale Handcar or the Return of the Black Doll* (1979), *The West Wing* (1963), *The Gilded Bat* (1967), *The Blue Aspic* (1968), *The Osbick Bird* (1970), *The Abandoned Sock* (1972), *The Lavender Leotard; or, Going a Lot to the New York City Ballet* (1973), *The Glorious Nosebleed* (1975), *The Tunnel Calamity* (1984), *The Improvable Landscape* (1986), *The Hapless Doorknob/A Shuffled Story* (1989), *The Floating Elephant* (1993), and *The Retrieved Locket* (1994).

The two best sources of information about Gorey's life and work are Stephen Schiff, "Edward Gorey and the Tao of Nonsense," the *New Yorker*, 9 Nov. 1992, and Clifford Ross and Karen Wilkin, *The World of Edward Gorey* (1996), containing samples of his drawings, an interview, an extensive critical examination, and a chronology and complete bibliography. Additional insights and information can be found in Amy Benfer, "Edward Gorey," on the Internet at salon.com under "Brilliant Careers"; in Edmund Wilson, "The Albums of Edward Gorey," the *New Yorker*, 26 Dec.

1959; and in *Contemporary Authors*, New Revision Series vol. 78 (1999), which includes a reprinted interview with Gorey. Brad Gooch, *City Poet: The Life and Times of Frank O'Hara*, a biography of O'Hara (1995), tells of Gorey's college life with his friend. Three anthologies collect over fifty of Gorey's books: *Amphigorey* (1972), *Amphigorey Too* (1975), and *Amphigorey Also* (1983). An obituary is in the *New York Times*, 17 Apr. 2000, and a useful remembrance is Alison Lurie (to whom *The Doubtful Guest* is dedicated), "On Edward Gorey," *New York Review*, 25 May 2000.

ROBERT C. HARVEY

GOTTLIEB, Sidney (3 Aug. 1918–6 Mar. 1999), biochemist and government official, was born in the Bronx, New York, the son of Louis Gottlieb, occupation unknown, and Fanny Beusler Gottlieb. The son of Orthodox Jewish immigrants from Hungary, he grew up without embracing Judaism but briefly dabbled in socialism. After beginning his college education at City College of New York, he attended Arkansas Polytechnic Institute (later Arkansas Tech University) in 1937–1938 before finally graduating magna cum laude from the University of Wisconsin with a degree in chemistry in 1940. Gottlieb struggled with a stuttering habit throughout his life and also had to overcome a clubfoot, which kept him out of military service during World War II. He began graduate study in biology at California Institute of Technology in Pasadena, where in 1942 he met and married Margaret Moore, the daughter of Presbyterian missionaries; the couple would have four children.

After receiving his Ph.D. in 1943, Gottlieb's whereabouts for the next several years are not known. He joined the newly formed (1949) Central Intelligence Agency (CIA) in 1951 and would spend the balance of his professional career there. As a protégé of Richard Helms—who later served as the agency's director—Gottlieb moved steadily up the ranks until he was appointed head of the Chemical Division of the CIA's Technical Support Staff (TSS) in 1953. In April of that year, Gottlieb was placed at the head of an umbrella project titled MKULTRA. The CIA, reacting to the tensions of the early Cold War years and reports filtering out of Korea about American POWs being "brainwashed," became obsessed with finding alternative means of controlling human behavior (and preventing the Russians and Red Chinese from doing likewise). Gottlieb and his associates experimented with a wide variety of drugs but focused most of their attention on a recently discovered drug called LSD. In addition to experimenting with the drug himself and administering it to his staff, Gottlieb supervised research on the subject—occasionally conducted with money funneled through private foundations—at a number of drug companies and academic institutions, including Columbia Presbyterian Medical Center and the University of Illinois medical school.

Gottlieb also oversaw cooperative efforts with the U.S. Army Chemical Corps Special Operations Division (SOD) at Ft. Detrick in Frederick, Maryland. At a meeting between CIA and SOD officials at Deep

Creek Lake in Maryland in November, 1953, Gottlieb spiked with LSD the drinks of several of the officials, including Dr. Frank Olson, a former military officer then working on the deployment of chemical and biological weapons for the Army. Most of the men quickly recovered from their "trip," but Olson fell into depression and while being treated committed suicide by jumping out of a New York City hotel room window.

Despite the setback that Olson's death caused—Gottlieb escaped with a mild reprimand—the drug experiments continued throughout the 1950s under Gottlieb's supervision. The CIA operated safe houses in New York and later San Francisco where civilians, most of whom were prostitutes or others involved in minor crime, were without their knowledge dosed with LSD and other drugs and their reactions observed. Perhaps the greatest abuses occurred at the National Institute of Mental Health–sponsored Addiction Research Center in Lexington, Kentucky, where a host of subjects (nearly all of them African-American drug addicts) were kept on LSD for extended periods of time and were rewarded with the drug of their choice following the experiment; in one instance seven men were kept "high" for a period of seventy-seven consecutive days.

In addition to working with mind-controlling substances, Gottlieb also devoted considerable time to researching toxins that might be put to use in assassination attempts. One such case involved African nationalist leader Patrice Lumumba, who was suspected by Washington of having Marxist leanings. In late 1960 Gottlieb actually journeyed to Africa and delivered to a local field agent a toxin that caused symptoms similar to those of diseases common to that area. However, Lumumba was captured and killed by a rival for the control of the former Belgian Congo before the CIA could act. Earlier that same year, an Iraqi colonel, Abdul Kassam, who was thought to be promoting Soviet interests, was killed by a firing squad before a poisoned handkerchief could be delivered to him. The highest-profile target of CIA covert operations, however, was Cuban dictator Fidel Castro. Over a period of time Castro was the target or potential target of many CIA plots, including a plan that sought his death by means of poisoned cigars. None of the plans came to fruition, owing either to their impracticality or to a loss of resolve to carry them out.

Despite his failure to produce much in the way of concrete results, Gottlieb continued to rise through the organizational ranks of the CIA and eventually became head of the TSS division. On retiring in 1973, he was awarded the Distinguished Intelligence Medal, and most of the MKULTRA files were deliberately destroyed.

Early in his retirement years Gottlieb and his wife journeyed to India, where he ran a hospital for lepers. During the 1970s he pursued a master's degree in speech therapy from San Jose State University in California. He also faced some unpleasant scrutiny at the hands of U.S. Senator Frank Church's committee that investigated CIA misdeeds. Gottlieb ultimately acknowledged that the techniques he had worked with produced "unpredictable" results and were open to question on ethical grounds (Marks, p. 219). After moving to Virginia, Gottlieb spent his final years working in a hospice and attempting to run a commune while remaining engaged in his favorite hobbies, which included goat herding, folk dancing, and raising Christmas trees. He died in Washington, Virginia, of undisclosed causes.

While both friends and critics lauded Gottlieb's intelligence and patriotism in performing his duties with the CIA, his methodology was questioned, and the subsequent years only added to the depth of criticism among his detractors. His career stands as a stark example of the age-old question of whether ends are universally justified by means.

• No collection of Gottlieb's papers has been located, and his professional files were largely destroyed at the time of his retirement. The best secondary source of information on his life and career is John Marks, *The Search for "The Manchurian Candidate": The CIA and Mind Control* (1979). The CIA has been the subject of numerous (mostly critical) published reviews in recent years, and Gottlieb is mentioned in several of them; among the best are Brian Freemantle, *CIA* (1984), and John Ranelagh, *The Agency: The Rise and Decline of the CIA* (1986). An obituary is in the *New York Times*, 10 Mar. 1999.

EDWARD L. LACH, JR.

GRAHAM, Katharine Meyer (16 June 1917–17 July 2001), newspaper publisher, was born Katharine Meyer in New York, the fourth child of Eugene Meyer, a wealthy investor, and Agnes Ernst Meyer, a prominent social critic with artistic interests. By the time Eugene Meyer met his wife, he had already earned a fortune on Wall Street, and in 1917, shortly after Katharine's birth, he began a second career in public service. Relocating from New York City to Washington, D.C., Meyer and his wife left their children in New York in the care of a nanny and governess. It was not until Katharine was four years old that the Meyer children were reunited with their parents in Washington. But even sharing the family home was no guarantee of emotional closeness to their parents; one of Katharine's early memories was of having to make an appointment to see her mother.

Eugene Meyer was Jewish, but his wife had been raised in the Lutheran faith, and religion did not play a large role in the Meyer household. Graham later wrote in her autobiography, "Remarkably, the fact that we were half Jewish was never mentioned any more than money was discussed. I was totally—incredibly—unaware of anti-Semitism, let alone of my father's being Jewish" (Graham, *Personal History*, p. 52).

After serving seven presidents in a variety of government jobs, Eugene Meyer retired from public service in 1933 and purchased the financially troubled *Washington Post* newspaper. Katharine was at the time a junior in high school at the elite Madeira School in

Virginia. Seeing a chance to draw closer to her detached father, she took a job as a copygirl at the *Post* the following summer.

In the fall of 1934 Graham enrolled at Vassar College planning to study German and economics. At the beginning of her junior year, however, she transferred to the more intellectually charged University of Chicago, from which she graduated with a B.A. in history in 1938. In 1939, following a stint as a cub reporter for the *San Francisco News*, she returned to Washington to take a $25-per-week job handling the Letters to the Editor Department at the *Washington Post*. *Time* magazine quoted her father as saying, "If it doesn't work out, we'll get rid of her" (Graham, *Personal History*, p. 102).

Within a year of joining the *Post*, Graham met her future husband Philip Graham. Two years older than Katharine, Phil Graham had risen from relatively humble beginnings in rural Florida to attend Harvard Law School and then served as a law clerk for the Supreme Court justice Felix Frankfurter. The couple married in 1940 in a ceremony photographed by Edward Steichen, a family friend. The Grahams had four children.

In 1948 Eugene Meyer left the *Post* in the hands of 33-year-old Phil Graham. In explaining his decision to hand over the paper to his son-in-law, Meyer said that no man should have to work for his wife. But by the early 1950s Phil Graham had worked himself to exhaustion and suffered from a variety of illnesses. He also began drinking excessively, which led to quarrels with his wife. Meanwhile Katharine Graham was becoming shyer and less confident. More than ever she found herself standing in the shadow of her husband.

In 1957 Phil Graham's life began to spin out of control. Although he had a long history of heavy drinking bouts, he now fell into deep depression. Diagnosed with manic depression, he entered treatment with a psychiatrist at a time when lithium carbonate—the standard treatment for the illness a few decades later—was unavailable in the United States.

On Christmas Eve 1962 Katharine discovered that her husband was having an affair with a young *Newsweek* reporter. Phil initially promised to terminate the relationship, but within weeks he asked for a divorce. Given Phil Graham's unstable emotional state, his family arranged to have him admitted to a private mental hospital. After his release he began drifting in and out of rationality—threatening to take total control of the *Post*—while he continued his affair with the *Newsweek* reporter. But in June 1963, suffering from extreme depression, he returned home. Katharine, unsure that she could help her husband through another severe depression, saw no choice but to have him returned to the hospital. That August, after he had been given a temporary pass to leave the hospital, Phil joined his wife at the couple's country home in Virginia. There, while Katharine was taking a nap, he killed himself.

Katharine Graham suddenly was thrust into the role of president of the Washington Post Company.

Insecure in her new role, she at first simply went through the motions of being a newspaper executive. Finally in 1965, with her hands full with the paper's business, political, and newsroom problems, she named Ben Bradlee, a former *Post* reporter, managing editor.

Although Graham had supported the war in Vietnam during the Lyndon B. Johnson administration, Bradlee and Graham made a decision in 1971 that transformed the *Washington Post* into a symbol of moral opposition to the war. That year, after a federal judge stopped the *New York Times* from publishing the Pentagon Papers—a secret government history of the U.S. involvement in Vietnam—the *Post* obtained its own copy of the documents and printed them.

An even more important milestone was reached in 1972, when the paper reported a break-in at the offices of the Democratic National Committee, a news story that marked the beginning of the Watergate scandal, which the *Post* continued to unravel. With the Richard Nixon White House threatening to financially ruin her company, Graham left the Watergate investigation largely in the hands of Bradlee. (Attorney General Richard Kleindienst was threatening to prosecute the *Post* and the *Times* with regard to the Pentagon Papers, and to enforce regulations that would bar ownership of radio and television properties after conviction for certain criminal offenses.) But it was Graham who eventually gave the go-ahead to reporters to follow up some of the more elusive leads in the Watergate affair.

In 1973 the paper won a Pulitzer Prize for its coverage of Watergate, and a year later Richard Nixon resigned the presidency. In her autobiography Graham wrote of Nixon's resignation, "A miracle of sorts had taken place—this country was about to change presidents in an utterly democratic way, with the processes that had been put into place two centuries before working in this unprecedented situation" (Graham, *Personal History*, p. 496). But what she did not say was that the resignation might never have occurred had it not been for her newspaper. Following Watergate, Graham emerged, in the words of the *Times* of London, as "one of the world's most powerful women" (21 July 2001).

In the post-Nixon years Graham's home in Georgetown became both a salon and a site of political summitry. Her seventieth birthday party in 1987, for example, was attended by President Ronald Reagan, Henry Kissinger, and Secretary of State George Shultz. It was therefore hardly surprising when, shortly after arriving in Washington in 2001 as the nation's forty-third president, George W. Bush arranged to have himself invited to one of Graham's dinners.

Graham died in Boise, Idaho. During her life—eight decades of which were spent in the nation's capital—Graham knew sixteen U.S. presidents, more than a third of all those who had served in the nation's highest office.

• Graham won a Pulitzer Prize in 1998 for her memoirs, *Personal History* (1997). *Katharine Graham's Washington* (2002), published posthumously, is a collection of essays annotated by Graham. Unauthorized biographies are Deborah Davis, *Katharine the Great: Katharine Graham and the "Washington Post"* (1979); Carol Felsenthal, *Power, Privilege, and the "Post": The Katharine Graham Story* (1993); and Sandy Asirvatham, *Katharine Graham* (2002). Norma Jean Lutz, *Business & Industry* (1999), includes a readable portrait of Graham. Surprisingly Carl Bernstein and Bob Woodward, *All the President's Men* (1974), which chronicles the *Washington Post* investigation of Watergate, contains only eleven page references to Graham. Tom Shales, "Mrs. Graham," *Electronic Media,* 23 July 2001, p. 4, is an unusual glimpse of the personal side of Graham by a veteran *Washington Post* reporter. Obituaries are in the *Washington Post* and the *New York Times,* 18 July 2001, and the *Times* of London, 18 July 2001 and 21 July 2001.

RANDALL FROST

GREEN, Chuck (6 Nov. 1918–7 Mar. 1997), African-American jazz tap dancer, was born Charles Green in Fitzgerald, Georgia (his parents' names and occupations are unknown). As a young boy, he stuck bottle caps to the bottoms of his bare feet and danced on the sidewalk for coins. At the age of six, he won third place in an amateur dance contest in which Noble Sissle was the bandleader and soon thereafter toured the South as a child tap dancer. At the age of nine, he was spotted by a talent agent and taken to New York to study tap dance.

Nat Nazzaro, known as the "monster agent" by those who knew of his practice of signing vulnerable young performers to ironclad contracts, signed Green to his own contract when he was twelve years old. A few years later, Green formed the team of Shorty and Slim with childhood friend James Walker, a talented comic and dancer. They studied the great comedians of the day, picking up lines of patter from such shows on the black vaudeville circuit as Pigmeat Crack Shot and Hunter Pete and Repeate. "Their act was hilarious. Chuck was a natural—so cute," tap dancer Leonard Reed remembered, adding that Walker at the time was tall and skinny and Green was small as a chair. They did what was called "dumb talk comedy," a rapid rhythmic banter that was interspersed between the songs and dances. As Walker played a broken-down vibraphone that looked as if it were failing apart, Green sang, "Some people was born to be doctors. . . some people were born to be kings . . . I fortunately was born to swing." Then they tap-danced, with Green making graceful turns and Walker excelling in "legomania" (highly individual and unusual leg movements in jazz dancing, such as rubber-legging).

Nazaro at the time also managed Buck and Bubbles (Ford Lee "Buck" Washington and John Sublett Bubbles). He suggested that Green and Walker study the singing-dancing-comedy team that had bypassed the black vaudeville Theater Owners Booking Association (TOBA) circuit to become headliners on the white vaudeville circuit; by 1922 they had played New York's prestigious Palace Theatre. Changing the name of their act to Chuck and Chuckles, Green and Walker were groomed as a "juvenile act" to Buck and Bubbles. Bubbles soon took Green under his wing, calling him "the son I never had," and offered to teach him what he knew, though it came in the form of a challenge. "Bubbles would do a step just once," Green explained, "and then say, 'you got one chance.' He was a creator. They called him the 'father of rhythm.'" Bubbles's style of rhythm tapping—in which he "loaded the bar" (put many extra beats into a bar of music) and dropped his heels, hitting unusual accents and syncopations—was revolutionary. He prepared for the new sound of bebop in the 1940s and anticipated the prolonged melodic lines of "cool jazz" in the 1950s. "If you dropped your heels, you could get a more floating quality, like a leaf coming off the top of a tree," said Green, who became a protégé of Bubbles. "It changed the quality of the sound, gave it tonation."

Through the 1930s and early 1940s, Chuck and Chuckles toured Europe, Australia, and the United States, performing in such venues as Radio City Music Hall and the Paramount, Apollo, and Capital theaters. Jobs were plentiful and their manager had the team doubling up on performances. They averaged five stage shows a day, played nightclubs until early morning, and toured nonstop with big bands across the country and abroad. By 1944, the strain and wear of performing had taken its toll. The team of Chuck and Chuckles broke up, and Green was committed to a mental institution. When he was released some fifteen years later, he was changed—extremely introverted and seemingly in a world of his own. His friends thought it a miracle he could still dance. By experimenting with the new harmonies, rhythmic patterns, and melodic approaches of the bop musicians, Green created his own bop-influenced style of rhythm tapping that was ad-libbed, up-tempo, and ultracool. In the sixties, Green began to perform again on stage and television. He appeared with the Copasetics (a tap fraternity dedicated to the memory of Bill "Bojangles" Robinson) on a show hosted by Dick Cavett on the popular educational channel WNET. On 6 July 1963 he performed at the Newport Jazz Festival as a member of the "Old Time Hoofers" with Honi Coles, Charles "Cooky" Cook, Ernest Brown, Pete Nugent, Cholly Atkins, and Baby Laurence. The show was introduced by jazz historian Marshall Stearns and marked the resurgence of tap dance in popular culture.

At New York's Village Vanguard in 1964, the legendary tap dancer Groundhog faced Green in a tap challenge. "I've been waiting to battle Chuck Green for twenty years," Groundhog told Stearns. "Dancing is like gang war and tonight I'm up against one of the best." Groundhog's rapid and syncopated staccato tapping was foiled by Green's relaxed and fluid style of jazz tapping and almost dreamlike grace. In 1969 Green appeared with members of Harlem's Hoofers Club for a series of "Tap Happenings" that were produced in New York City by Letitia Jay.

Through the seventies and eighties, Green continued to perform with the Copasetics. Host Honi Coles introduced him as "Chuck Green, the greatest tap dancer in the world." When asked why that special title was bestowed on Green, Coles answered, "His slow dance is genius. Most dancers would fall on their face. His timing is like a musician's."

In the late eighties, Green toured Europe with The Original Hoofers, appeared as a guest soloist at the Kennedy Center Honors, and was awarded an honorary professorship at Washington University. In New York in 1987, he began teaching a weekly two-hour tap class to a dedicated cross section of New York's top professional jazz dancers. With great clarity and precision, he led his students into the complexity of his material with warmth and ease, allowing the dancer to hear and feel the weight of the rhythm and movement.

In the late eighties and early nineties, Green was twice honored with a New York Dance and Performance Award (the Bessies) for his innovative achievements and technical skill in dance, and for his work in *Black and Blue* (1989) on Broadway. Tall and big-footed, Green was a surprisingly light, graceful, and melodious rhythm dancer who was known for his specialty "strut" when he came on stage and for his tick-tock tap sounds. Whether dancing to such favorite tunes as "A Train" or "Caravan," Green's smooth and graceful rhythm tapping was uncluttered, even, and beautifully phrased. He has been called the "Poet of Tap."

In the "Green, Chaney, Buster, Slyde" number from the 1996 Broadway musical *Bring in 'Da Noise, Bring in 'Da Funk,* Savion Glover celebrates Green as a master teacher who "was educatin' people, not entertainin'." "Chuck's dancin'," rapped Glover as he danced before a multipaneled mirror, "was like, kind of slow. Every tap was clean, you know what I'm sayin'. You hear every tap. He was, just like, on the slow type, smooth type."

Chuck Green died in Oakland, California.

• The fluency of Green's tap dancing is captured in George Niremberg's documentary film *No Maps on My Taps* (1979) with "Sandman" Sims and Bunny Briggs. His free-association poetry of speech is beautifully rendered in the film *About Tap* (1987). His gentleness of spirit is immortalized in *Masters of Tap* (1983), a documentary film that also includes Honi Coles and Will Gaines. The sheer musicality of Green's solo dancing is seen in the film *Dance Black America* (1984). Guy Trebay reports on the Groundhog-Green tap challenge at the Village Gate in "Hoofing It," *Village Voice,* 21 Jan. 1984. A rare interview with Green was conducted by Jane Goldberg and is included in the article "Sharing the Train with Chuck Green: A Glimpse of the Journey," *International Tap Association Newsletter* 7, no. 5 (Jan.–Feb. 1997): 3–5. Delilah Jackson shares a moving personal memoir of Green in her article "Gentle Giant of Dance Remembered," *International Tap Association Newsletter,* 8, no. 2 (July–Aug. 1997): 17–18. Obituaries are in the *New York Times,* 14 Mar. 1997, and the *New York Post,* 15 Mar. 1997.

CONSTANCE VALIS HILL

GREEN, Seth (19 Mar. 1817–20 Aug. 1888), fish culturist, was born near Rochester in Monroe County, New York, the son of Adonijah Green and Betsy Bronson, farmers. The Greens had arrived in Monroe County in 1811, built a log cabin, and cleared land for crops. While Seth was young, they moved to the village of Carthage near the lower falls of the Genesee River, where Adonijah became a tavern keeper. As a youth, Green roamed the woods, fields, and streams near Rochester, often with Seneca Indian youths, learning woodlore from them and becoming a skilled and avid hunter and fisherman. After completing a local grammar school education, he turned to his love of fishing as a career. By the age of eighteen he was a commercial fisherman on Lake Ontario and nearby streams, learning the habits and habitats of different species of fish and how to catch them.

In 1837, while fishing for brook trout in Canada, Green observed salmon as they prepared nest sites and laid eggs. He noted that males ate many of the eggs and that females buried those that survived in gravel. He perceived an opportunity to produce far more fish than occur naturally; if he could control fertilization of the eggs, he could protect all of the eggs from being eaten. He nursed the idea for many years, intent on pursuing his goal of artificially propagating fish.

In 1848 Green married Helen Cooke of Rochester; they had four children. In partnership with his brother, Monroe, he opened a fish market in Rochester; by 1857 they employed nearly a hundred men. But Green could see that fish resources were declining and his interest in renewing those resources grew. Meanwhile, in 1848 Milne Edwards had reported the successful propagation of trout in France, and in 1850 a fish hatchery was established in France. Word of these successes stimulated American interests. In 1853 Theodatus Garlick and H. A. Ackley of Cleveland, Ohio, succeeded in cultivating trout.

Following these leads, in 1864 Green purchased a portion of Caledonia Creek, a tributary of the Genesee River, and began efforts to artificially propagate brook trout. According to G. Brown Goode of Wesleyan University, Green thus became the first American to carry on fish culture on a commercially profitable basis. In 1865 Green applied to the French government for salmon eggs, beginning an exchange that facilitated the international growth in fish culture and Green's international reputation.

In 1867 the New England Fish Commission asked him to go to the Connecticut River and try artificial propagation of American shad. Local fishermen were dubious, fearing that if Green were successful, the market value of their catch would plummet. They tried repeatedly to sabotage his efforts. Green seemed oblivious to the opposition and doggedly pursued his goal through trial and error. Techniques used for trout did not work for shad. Instead of placing the eggs on a gravel bottom with cold water flowing over them, as he had done with trout eggs, the shad eggs required warm water. He developed a floating hatching box with a wire bottom that tilted into the current. Nearly all eggs placed in these boxes hatched. Green's careful observations of fish behavior paid off; he succeeded beyond all expectations. An unprecedented abundance of shad in the Connecticut River in 1870 was attributed to his efforts, although later scientists suggested perhaps wrongly so.

In 1868, Green was appointed as one of three commissioners of the newly formed New York Fishery Commission. The commissioners' charge was to increase fish production in New York waters. Two years later he resigned to become superintendent of the Commission, which owned fish hatcheries at Caledonia and Cold Spring Harbor. He remained as superintendent at Caledonia until his death.

Over the years Green successfully bred large numbers of shad, trout, and salmon for introduction into lakes and streams throughout North America. He successfully transported 10,000 young shad by train from the Hudson River on the Atlantic coast to the Sacramento River in California—a difficult feat in 1871. The major problems were getting adequate water and maintaining water quality and temperature. In the West, shad became more abundant than in their native eastern habitats, quickly becoming established in other western river systems. Also in 1871, in collaboration with W. Clift, Green introduced shad to tributaries of the Ohio and Mississippi rivers. In 1874, he visited Michigan's Au Sable River to capture grayling prior to their spawning. He arrived too late, but rather than give up, he searched for, found, and successfully returned with fertilized eggs. In addition to successfully propagating native species on a commercial scale, Green artificially produced hybrids between some species in efforts to combine the positive qualities of the parent species.

Green was among the earliest members of the American Fish Culturists' Association (later to become the American Fisheries Society). He rarely missed one of their meetings. When the American Fish Culturists' Association held its first annual meeting in 1872, Green was selected as chairman of the Executive Committee. In 1872 and again in 1875 he was awarded a gold medal for his fish culture efforts by the Société Impériale d'Acclimation of France. In 1876 Green received a certificate from the United States Centennial Commission at the International Exhibition in Philadelphia, where he had been selected as a judge. In 1880, the German Fishermen's Club of Berlin awarded him a gold medal for his work.

In addition to his fish culture work, Green served as editor of the sports department of the magazine *The First American Angler*. He wrote three books: *Trout Culture* (1871), *Fish Hatching and Fish Catching* (with R. B. Roosevelt, who wrote the latter half, 1879), and *Home Fishing and Home Waters* (1888).

Green's prowess as a fisherman is remembered nearly as well as his scientific accomplishments. He was a master at trout fishing and famous as a fly caster for his long-distance casts. He is also credited with the invention of a fishing reel and a complex deep trolling rig known as the Seth Green Rig. Green is also memorialized by the Seth Green Fish Hatchery in Caledonia, New York.

Although Green's innovative hatching boxes have long been replaced by more efficient technology and the trolling rig that bears his name is rarely used, Green was a pioneer and driving force in American fish culture. He readily shared his knowledge and never wavered in pursuit of goals that others viewed with skepticism or hostility. Modern fish culture grew rapidly and prospered as a result of his efforts. Along with artificially propagating fish came an increasing awareness of the fragility of aquatic ecosystems and the problems brought on by pollution, dams, and overfishing. While fish conservation grew from Green's efforts, we are also left with a negative legacy—the presence of fish such as American shad in waters far outside their normal range. Such exotic fish compete with and often displace native species, creating conservation problems that were not considered in the 1800s.

• Biographical sketches of Seth Green are included in *American Naturalist* 22 (1888): 759–60; *Dictionary of American Biography* (1931), and *American Biographies* (1940). A lengthy, romantic biography of Green by Sylvia Black appears in *Rochester History* 6, no. 3 (1944): 1–24. An obituary is in the *New York Times*, 20 Aug. 1888.

JEROME A. JACKSON

GREENFIELD, Elizabeth Taylor (c. 1817–31 Mar. 1876), singer and teacher, was born a slave in or near Natchez, Mississippi. Her father may have been born in Africa, and her mother, Anna, was of mixed ancestry. Various sources offer no less than seven different birthdates between 1807 and 1824. Greenfield's use of "Taylor" rather than "Greenfield" in certain documents suggests that her parents used this surname, but little record of them survives.

When their owner, wealthy widow Elizabeth Holliday Greenfield, joined the Society of Friends and moved to Philadelphia in the 1820s, Greenfield's parents were manumitted and emigrated to Liberia. Though records suggest her mother planned to return, Greenfield never saw her parents again. She lived with her mistress until she was about eight years old and then rejoined her as a nurse/companion in about 1836; she seems to have lived with relatives in the interim. Several sources assert that Greenfield's mistress cared for her, and probate records show that her will called for an annuity to be paid to Greenfield. When her mistress died in 1845, though, her will was fiercely contested, and Greenfield received only a token sum.

Biographer Arthur LaBrew speculates that Greenfield began singing in church in the early 1830s. Though Quaker, her mistress seems to have approved of Greenfield's musical aspirations, and a family friend (probably one of physician Philip Price's daughters) gave her some rudimentary instruction. Greenfield was singing at private parties by at least the mid-1840s, and LaBrew notes a performance in Baltimore around 1849 with black musician William Appo. By 1850, one Philadelphia directory listed her as a "music teacher."

In October 1851, Greenfield traveled to Buffalo, New York, supposedly to hear the "Swedish Nightingale" Jenny Lind. She impressed Electa Potter, wife of prominent Buffalo attorney Heman B. Potter, with both her voice and her carriage, and the Potters became her patrons. Their support and introductions to Buffalo's leading citizens led to a public performance on 22 October. Greenfield's "debut," which featured works by Bellini and Donizetti, was praised by Buffalo newspapers, and Greenfield, whom several reviewers compared favorably with Lind, was quickly dubbed the "African Nightingale." A comparison with another singer, "Irish Swan" Catherine Hayes, won out, though, and Greenfield became forever known as the "Black Swan."

The favorable press and promotion by Buffalo merchant Hiram Howard led to additional performances in Rochester and Lockport and an agreement with Colonel J. H. Wood, a promoter of mixed repute and sometime-associate of P. T. Barnum. Wood set up a tour in 1852 that took Greenfield across the North; she performed in over thirty cities, ranging from Boston and Providence to Chicago and Milwaukee. She also traveled to Ontario and to smaller abolitionist strongholds like Niles, Michigan. Her repertoire was similar to Lind's, and the press regularly compared the two. She also began to include popular American works like Stephen Foster's "Old Folks at Home." Praise for—and even amazement at—her vocal range (claimed to encompass over three octaves) was consistently tempered with comments emphasizing her lack of formal training; racist newspapers referred to her as the "African crow." Nonetheless, Greenfield filled theaters, and the tour was quite successful. After a brief rest, Greenfield made arrangements for a performance in New York City and a tour of Great Britain, during which she would further her training. Buffalo citizens held a benefit concert on 7 March 1853 to help support her travel to Britain.

After the outpouring of cross-racial support in Buffalo, Greenfield's time in New York City was both frightening and frustrating. The theater, Metropolitan Hall, was threatened with arson for featuring a black performer, its management barred blacks from attending, and Greenfield herself was refused entry to another theater to see Italian contralto Marietta Alboni. Still, her performance on 31 March attracted over 2000 and cemented her celebrity. Soon after, in apology to New York City's African Americans, Greenfield gave a second concert to an integrated audience specifically to benefit black charities.

Trouble followed her to Britain, though. Her British manager refused to advance her funds against future performances, and Greenfield struggled to meet basic expenses before finally withdrawing from her contract. She contacted well-known abolitionists Lord Shaftesbury and Harriet Beecher Stowe for aid, and they introduced her to Britain's abolitionist elite. The Duchess of Sutherland became Greenfield's patron, and Sir George Smart, composer to the Chapel Royal, began tutoring her. Greenfield's May 1853 performance at Stafford House, Sutherland's London home, led to several other performances. Sutherland and Smart eventually engineered a command performance for Queen Victoria on 10 May 1854. Victoria's praise—and her £20 gift—did much to help Greenfield's spirits; however, she returned to the United States in July 1854.

Greenfield began touring the North soon after her return; in this second U.S. tour and in her third in 1856 Greenfield returned to several of the cities from her first tour but also sought new venues—traveling as far south as Baltimore and performing more widely in Canada. Her 1854 tour included performances by black tenor Thomas J. Bowers, a Philadelphian known as the "colored Mario." The 1856 tour was complemented by the 1855 publication of *The Black Swan at Home and Abroad*, a 64-page promotional biography that heavily emphasized her early successes and her British tour. Greenfield's final extended tour in 1863 included mainly cities in the upper North.

After 1863, she gave occasional concerts, often to benefit African American causes, and regularly sang at events sponsored by the Civil and Statistical Association of the Colored People of Pennsylvania, including lectures by Frances E. W. Harper and General O. O. Howard. LaBrew has also found evidence that she founded a "Black Swan Opera Troupe," which gave performances in Washington in 1862 and Philadelphia in 1866.

Between tours and after 1863, Greenfield lived in Philadelphia near her extended family (she never married). She achieved local note as a music teacher and is intermittently listed in city directories as a musician and a teacher (though one simply lists her occupation as "black swan"). Among her students, she counted Carrie Thomas, the leading soprano of the original Hampton Institute Singers, and Lucy Adger, whose family achieved local prominence for their talents. A devout Baptist, she also directed the choir and sang at Shiloh Baptist Church. When she died in Philadelphia, she was eulogized in newspapers across the country.

Harriet Beecher Stowe said that had Greenfield received the education given her white peers "*no* singer of any country could have surpassed her" (*Sunny Memories*, vol. 2, p. 139). Given such talent, as well as her unprecedented international fame, her successes as a teacher, and her pioneering efforts to promote other black musicians, Greenfield was undoubtedly, as the author and activist Martin Delany noted, among the most extraordinary persons" of the nineteenth century (p. 102). Even years after her death, Greenfield's memory was so important to African-American music that when a new generation of Americans listened to the early work of Fletcher Henderson and Ethel Waters in the 1920s the records—from the Pace Phonograph Company, one of the first black-owned recording companies—bore a stylized black swan, the symbol for the "Black Swan Records" label.

• Greenfield received extensive coverage in contemporary newspapers; a sampling can be found in the microfilm collection *The Black Abolitionist Papers*, ed. C. Peter Ripley et al. (1981). *The Black Swan at Home and Abroad* (1855), an anonymous biography that greatly expands the British pamphlet *A Brief Memoir of "The Black Swan," Miss E. T. Greenfield* (1853), provides a rich account of Greenfield's life and early career, though it was clearly written for promotional purposes and thus omits, deemphasizes, and/or reenvisions some details. Other early discussions of Greenfield can be found in Martin Delany, *The Condition, Elevation, Emigration, and Destiny of the Colored People of the U.S.* (1852), and Harriet Beecher Stowe, *Sunny Memories of Foreign Lands* (1854). James Monroe Trotter's account in *Music and Some Highly Musical People* (1878), pp. 66–87, borrows heavily from *The Black Swan at Home and Abroad* and makes errors in some of its original material, but it does discuss Greenfield's life after 1855. The vast majority of accounts of Greenfield written after 1880 rely heavily on *The Black Swan at Home and Abroad* and/or Trotter.

Among twentieth-century scholars, Arthur LaBrew has added most to our knowledge through his privately printed two-volume biography *The Black Swan: Elizabeth Taylor Greenfield* (1969–1984), and *Studies in Nineteenth Century Afro-American Music* (1983). These hard-to-find texts are summarized in LaBrew's entry on Greenfield in *Notable Black American Women*, ed. Jessie Carney Smith (1992), pp. 412–16. Recent scholarship, including Rosalyn Story, *And So I Sing: African American Divas of Concert and Opera* (1990), and Thomas L. Riis, "Concert Singers, Prima Donnas, and Entertainers: The Changing Status of Black Women Vocalists in Nineteenth Century America," in *Music and Culture in America, 1861–1918*, ed. Michael Saffle and James R. Heintze (1998), pp. 53–78, has begun to consider Greenfield's impact on American music and culture. Obituaries appear in several major newspapers of the time, including the *New York Times*, 2 Apr. 1876.

ERIC GARDNER

GUILLEDO, Francisco. *See* Villa, Pancho.

GUNTHER, Charles Frederick (6 Mar. 1837–10 Feb. 1920), Chicago confectioner, politician, and antiquarian, collector, was born Carl Friedrich Guenther in Wildberg, Wurttemberg, Germany, the son of Marie and Johann Martin Guenther, a candle and soap maker. The family immigrated to Pennsylvania in 1842, and at age ten Gunther began work as a government mail carrier, traveling forty miles daily by horseback. In 1850 they resettled in Peru, Illinois, an important ice harvesting center on the canal linking Chicago with the Mississippi watershed. Gunther found work as a cashier in a bank, where he came in contact with many of the merchants who shipped 100,000 tons of ice down the southern rivers during prosperous years.

In December 1860 Gunther headed south to seek his fortune along the waterways, securing a position in Memphis with the ice merchants Bohlen, Wilson & Company. The following April, South Carolina fired on Fort Sumter and it surrendered. As northerners fled the city, Gunther wrote that he was "bound to stick by Memphis and defend her . . . a start is all I am wishing for and I am going to have it." War soon choked the river trade, and Gunther spent his days watching a bumper crop of sugar fill the levee, observing Union prisoners in the city's slave market, and reading *Plutarch's Lives* and the *Eclectic Magazine of Foreign Literature, Science, and Art*. He drilled with the local militia, voted for Jefferson Davis, and shipped as purchasing steward on the *Rose Douglass*, a commercial steam vessel consigned by the Confederates. He also helped transport soldiers and supplies along the Mississippi tributaries. In December 1862 his ship was captured and burned at Van Buren, Arkansas, by General James Blunt's army. Gunther, a civilian, was released and made his way back to Illinois.

Gunther's navigating savvy served him well during the final years of the war when he was employed as the first traveling salesman for Chicago wholesale confectioner C. W. Sanford, covering the South and other states. After the war he returned to Europe and observed candy manufacturers. In 1868 he started his own Chicago confectionery, introducing caramels to the trade. In April 1870 the up-and-coming entrepreneur married Jennie Burnell of Lima, Indiana; the couple had two sons.

Following the 1871 Chicago fire, which destroyed his business, Gunther opened a soda parlor in the McVicker's Theatre building and then a six-story wholesale candy factory and retail store at 212 South State Street in 1886. His slogan, "Not How Cheap but How Good," reflected Gunther's interest in the upscale candy trade during a period when large quantities of adulterated or "short count" goods flooded the market. Demonstrating sophisticated advertising acumen, Gunther offered retail dealers preprinted "fancy signs," display designs, electrotype newspaper advertisements, and illustrated catalogs of such packaged delights as "La Flor de Gunther Cigars' de chocolate." Gunther catered to Chicago's elite—society doyen Bertha Honoré Palmer maintained an account at his store—as well as the city's burgeoning popular entertainment and tourist trade. Customers at his lavishly decorated candy emporium were invited upstairs to view Civil War uniforms, guns, and flags, an Egyptian mummy whose label read "Pharaoh's daughter who discovered Moses in the bulrushes," and the "Skin of the Serpent that Tempted Eve in the Garden of Eden."

Gunther realized an opportunity to merge his historical, commercial, and political interests in Libby Prison, a notorious Richmond prisoner-of-war facility. In 1886 Chicago insurance executive William Gray hoped to annex the prison to the city's exposition facility in time for the 1888 Republican national convention. The project floundered until Gray persuaded Gunther to head a consortium of investors following the convention. They hired the architectural firm of Burnham and Root, dismantled the prison, shipped it to Chicago on 132 railroad cars, and rebuilt it as a Civil War museum on South Wabash Avenue. The massive reconstruction opened one month prior to Chicago's better-known 1889 Auditorium complex and attracted hundreds of thousands of visitors before the city secured the influential 1893 World's Columbian Exposition.

The four-story Libby Prison War Museum, featuring Gunther's growing collection of Americana, was an immediate success. In contrast with the Smithsonian Institution's 1881 United States National Museum, which emphasized scientific analysis and economic development of natural resources, the Libby Prison War Museum chronicled U.S. history. Popular exhibits included a kitchen escape tunnel dug by Union prisoners and a hospital room "chamber of horrors" showcasing Gunther's collection of Abraham Lincoln assassination relics, reportedly the country's largest, amid battlefield surgical instruments and shrunken "Inca" heads. Museum catalogs promoted Gunther's candy, Libby Prison cigars, the Libby Prison Hotel and Restaurant, silver Lincoln souvenir spoons, and buttons carved from the original prison flooring. Gunther became an international celebrity and traveled extensively to add to his collection. The press avidly followed his buying sprees and the public deluged him with offers of documents and artifacts that greatly enriched his holdings.

The Libby Prison War Museum profited from and helped galvanize growing veterans' organizations such as the Grand Army of the Republic, becoming a national center for former soldiers who managed its day-to-day operations, published a monthly newspaper, guided tours, and hosted reunions. Over one-third of all elderly men in the northern states were receiving Civil War pensions at the end of the nineteenth century, an open-ended system of disability, old-age, and survivors' benefits that peaked after Republicans captured both houses of Congress on the strength of the "old soldiers" vote in 1888. Gunther, a Democrat who campaigned as a former Lincoln Republican, undoubtedly benefited from veterans' votes when he launched his own political career. Yet he was markedly ambivalent toward his Civil War patrons. In 1896, when attendance waned, the museum's manager, noting Gunther's distaste for veterans, feared that he would raze the prison. Gunther was also an outspoken critic of the Republican-supported tariffs that financed the generous system of veterans' benefits, particularly the sugar tariff that inflated the price of refined sugar, the staple of the confectionery industry.

The demise of the Libby Prison War Museum closely followed Gunther's political debut. Elected to two consecutive terms as a Second Ward alderman on the Chicago City Council (1896–1900) and a single term as city treasurer (1901–1903), Gunther was one of the first candidates endorsed by the Municipal Voter's League, a civic reform organization mobilized in the wake of William T. Stead's exposé If Christ Came to Chicago. Chicago Democrats played an active role in national party politics and were deeply involved in the 1896 convention at the city's Coliseum, where tariffs and "free silver" coinage were hotly contested issues. Following William Jennings Bryan's electrifying nomination, Gunther and Chicago's "gold" Democrats formed a third party and held a convention in Indianapolis, nominating John McAuley Palmer for the presidency to break Bryan's campaign. Gunther invested in the politically and commercially lucrative national convention trade following the destruction of the Coliseum by fire in 1897, demolishing Libby Prison and constructing a new Coliseum in its place. The prison's wooden doors and a selection of bricks were donated to the Chicago Historical Society. Gunther offered his collection to the city if it would build a new Garfield Park museum, but state law stipulated that park buildings could only be erected to house natural history, art, or science collections.

Gunther's political career had few highlights. He waged war with South Water Street merchants, authoring a fruit ordinance to check the use of "tarlatan" or colored netting that obscured short weight sales. He was petitioned to run for mayor and actively sought the 1908 gubernatorial nomination, losing to former Vice President Adlai Stevenson. Gunther's popularity took another hit the same year when reformers attempted to shut down the First Ward Ball, a notorious annual Coliseum fundraiser for the unsavory political bosses "Bathhouse" John Coughlin and Michael "Hinky Dink" Kenna, who controlled the city's vice district. Gunther was targeted in the campaign as president of the Chicago Coliseum Company but refused to cancel the contract for the ball despite a powerful bomb detonated in a Coliseum annex and the Chicago Tribune's threat to publish a list of attendees.

Gunther's legacy as a civic-minded business leader and collector has stood the test of time. He helped establish Chicago as the center of the American confectionery industry and was on the cusp of the initiative to develop Chicago as a world-class city. At a time when monumental postwar museums were dedicated to the arts and sciences, Gunther amassed the most substantial nineteenth-century collection of American historical artifacts. The Chicago Historical Society purchased the major portion of Gunther's holdings following his death in Chicago, securing the museum's international reputation with authenticated treasures that included the 1507 Cosmographiae Introductio suggesting the continental name America; rare manuscripts documenting the Northwest Territory and Revolutionary, Indian, and Civil Wars; the table on which Robert E. Lee composed his Appomattox Court House surrender; and Abraham Lincoln's Petersen house death bed.

• Relevant archival resources at the Chicago Historical Society include the Papers of Charles F. Gunther, the Libby Prison War Museum Association, the Chicago Historical Society, and Otto Schmidt, as well as correspondence in artifact authority files. An excellent article detailing Gunther's collection is Clement M. Silvestro, "The Candy Man's Mixed

Bag," *Chicago History* 2, no. 2 (Fall 1972): 86–99. A report on the Chicago Coliseum by the Commission on Chicago Historical and Architectural Landmarks (1981) is helpful. Gunther's political career can be traced through numerous *Chicago Tribune* articles in Apr. 1896, 1898, and 1901, Sept. 1897, and Aug. 1908. The Chicago Historical Society also maintains a newspaper clipping file. Gunther is briefly mentioned in Henry G. Abbott, [George H. A. Hazlitt] *Historical Sketch of the Confectionery Trade of Chicago* (1905); Carter Henry Harrison, Jr., *Stormy Years* (1935); and Lloyd Wendt and Herman Kogan, *Lords of the Levee* (1943). An obituary is in the *Chicago Tribune*, 11 Feb. 1920.

NANCY BUENGER

GWATHMEY, Robert (3 Jan. 1903–21 Sept. 1988), artist and activist, was born near Richmond, Virginia, an eighth-generation native of Welsh descent, to Robert Gwathmey, a railroad engineer, and Eva Harrison Gwathmey. Following brief stints at North Carolina State College (1922–1923) and Maryland Institute of Design (1925–1926) and at sea on a commercial freighter, he attended the prestigious Pennsylvania Academy of the Fine Arts (PAFA, 1926–1930), where he was awarded several prize fellowships and met his future wife, also an aspiring artist, Rosalie Hook of Charlotte, North Carolina. They married in 1935 and had one son, Charles Gwathmey, who became one of the most prominent architects of his generation. When Charles was born, Rosalie Gwathmey took up photography, acquired professional skills, and later earned public recognition for her work. Beginning in the 1940s Robert Gwathmey often asked Rosalie to photograph rural scenes in their native South and used those images as the basis for some of his most striking paintings. Despite that collaboration Gwathmey was typical of his generation in regarding photography as an inferior art form.

A gifted draftsman, Gwathmey taught art at Beaver College near Philadelphia (1930–1937) and the Carnegie Institute in Pittsburgh (1939–1942) and then drawing at Cooper Union in New York City on a part-time basis (1942–1968). He was determined to "make it" as an independent painter and protected his time carefully, which was essential because he worked deliberately and often destroyed completed pieces that did not satisfy him. In 1938 he trashed virtually all of his previous art because it seemed too derivative from work by his teachers at the PAFA. At that point he found both the subject matter and the style that became distinctively his own: African-American sharecroppers painted in a vividly colorful and flat style (no chiaroscuro), often using geometric patterns outlined in black, reminiscent of medieval stained glass. Although he did not romanticize the labor and leisure of his subjects, he followed the French artist Jean-François Millet in boldly making the American counterpart to peasant life his dominant motif.

In Philadelphia Gwathmey joined several radical groups sympathetic to the working class and maintained that commitment to social justice throughout his life. During the 1940s a Marxist reading group met monthly at the Gwathmey apartment, and his name appeared frequently in the Communist *Daily Worker* on petitions in support of humanitarian causes. Beginning in 1942 Gwathmey was under Federal Bureau of Investigation (FBI) surveillance for twenty-seven years. He was later active in the civil rights movement and opposed the U.S. war in Vietnam. He greatly admired the Mexican muralists José Clemente Orozco, David Alfaro Siqueiros, and Rufino Tamayo and made a trip to Mexico City in an effort to get Siqueiros released from prison.

In 1940 Gwathmey found a dealer sympathetic to his politics, Herman Baron of the ACA Gallery in Manhattan, and his work quickly gained visibility and won a series of awards that led to such prestigious collections as the Museum of Fine Arts in Boston and the Carnegie Museum in Pittsburgh purchasing his paintings. As part of his commitment to a democratic art, Gwathmey pioneered the new technique of serigraphy, a form of silk-screening that made colorful works of art available at prices that ordinary people could afford.

Gwathmey greatly admired the social satire of Honoré Daumier, and some of his best-known works are obvious critiques of racist politicians, the poll tax, lynching, and other attempts to keep black tenant farmers socially and politically impotent. His favorite symbols for segregation and the South's traditional means of repression were barbed wire and an omnipresent black crow. He also liked to incorporate the lively circus signs and ads for patent medicines commonly pasted on the sides of such rural structures as tobacco barns. Most prominent were the numerals 666, the label of a useless medication quite popular in the South prior to 1950. It delighted Gwathmey that 666 was also the biblical symbol for the devil. During the 1940s, when he produced many of his finest paintings, Gwathmey was most likely to paint blacks working in fields or gathering for church, in community activities, and singing, often with a guitar visible. He loved the antilynching dirge "Strange Fruit" made famous by Billie Holiday in 1939 and played it frequently.

As part of the generation of social realists, Gwathmey's close contemporaries were Philip Evergood (his best friend), Jacob Lawrence, Ben Shahn, and Antonio Frasconi. In 1945, when Gwathmey had begun to achieve wide recognition among modern artists, he defined his sense of mission with these words: "A social artist is a man who is going to integrate the life of his times. Since the moving picture camera exposes the ills of contemporary life so convincingly and authentically, what style is the painter to use? Social painting is not, to the mind, limited to the obviously pictorial. You can transcend the literary . . . if your imagery is strong and inventive enough" (Kammen, p. 214). His was.

By the 1950s Gwathmey had also mastered the art of still life painting, preferring to paint wildflowers in stunning displays. During the 1960s he sought to present the ideal of a "color-blind" society by depicting figures with tawny skin color but Caucasian features (such as *The Observer* [1960]), often done as a modified self-portrait. Within a decade, however, he ceased that practice out of respect for the rise of black nationalism and the creed that "black is beautiful." During his later years Gwathmey began painting white people, though often with satirical intent. During his last years, when Parkinson's disease began to impair his hand, his simplified work often emphasized objects in a multidimensional manner, perhaps to demonstrate that he could go beyond his customary flat style if he chose to. He died in East Hampton, New York.

Gwathmey's last completed painting, *Man Drinking* (1984), reveals much about his temperament and candor. He had a strong penchant for wine (whiskey actually), women, and song. He was also a great raconteur with a strong Tidewater drawl, and he loved movies and playing horseshoes. Gwathmey openly conducted an intimate relationship with his dealer, Terry Dintenfass, for almost a decade, ending in 1967 though she remained his dealer for the rest of his life. With her and through her he strongly encouraged younger artists with diverse styles, ranging from the modernist Sidney Goodman to the "folk artist" Ralph Fasanella. The success of abstract expressionism and pop art during the third quarter of the twentieth century meant Gwathmey's figural emphasis was unfashionable and eclipsed, yet he never wavered in his commitment to representational art with a powerful message, such as *Homo Sapiens* (1973), a grim yet stunning image of mortal combat—man's inhumanity to man.

Gwathmey was elected to the American Academy and Institute of Arts and Letters in 1971 and to the National Academy of Design two years later. The Cooper Union mounted a major exhibition of his work in 1985, and an even larger retrospective traveled to five venues in 1999–2000. People familiar with his oil paintings and serigraphs tend to assume that he must have been African American. He balanced his passion for social justice with equally strong aesthetic ideals. As he wrote in the later 1960s: "Art is the conceptual solution of complicated forms, plus the perceptual fusion of personality. . . . Never does beauty come from decorative effects, but from structural coherence. . . . The artist desires to find and to separate truth from the complex of lies and evasions in which he lives" ("A Midsummer Night's Dream," n.d., Gwathmey Papers, microfilm roll D245, Archives of American Art, Smithsonian Institution, Washington, D.C.).

• Gwathmey wrote "Art for Art's Sake?," *American Art* 7, no. 1 (Winter 1993): 99–103. See also Michael Kammen's biography *Robert Gwathmey: The Life and Art of a Passionate Observer* (1999); Charles K. Piehl, "The Southern Social Art of Robert Gwathmey," *Transactions of the Wisconsin Academy of Sciences, Arts and Letters* 73 (1985): 54–62; and Piehl, "A Southern Artist at Home in the North: Robert Gwathmey's Acceptance of His Identity," *Southern Quarterly* 26 (Fall 1987): 1–17. An obituary is in the *New York Times*, 22 Sept. 1998.

MICHAEL KAMMEN

H

HAMMING, Richard Wesley (11 Feb. 1915–7 Jan. 1998), mathematician and computer scientist, was born in Chicago, Illinois, the son of Richard James Hamming, a credit manager, and Mabel Grace Redfield Hamming. His father, a native of Holland, ran away from home to fight in the Boer War and was left for dead on the battlefield with a saber wound in his neck. He spent some time in Texas as a cowboy before settling into an office job in Chicago.

Hamming attended Crane Technical High School and Crane Junior College in Chicago. He became interested in mathematics in high school when, as he related, "I realized that I was a better mathematician than the teacher" (quoted in Perry, p. 80). He had intended to study engineering, but Crane closed during the Depression and his only scholarship offer was from the University of Chicago, which did not have an engineering school. In 1937 he took a B.S. in mathematics from Chicago, in 1939 an M.A. from the University of Nebraska, and in 1942 a Ph.D. in mathematics from the University of Illinois. He married Wanda Little at Illinois on 5 September 1942, after she received her M.A. in English literature. They had no children.

In April 1945, after brief teaching positions at the University of Louisville and the University of Illinois, Hamming was recruited to work at Los Alamos, to run the IBM machines that were doing atomic bomb calculations for the Manhattan Project. Wanda Hamming followed him to Los Alamos a few weeks later, where she was hired to use a desk calculator, working eventually for Enrico Fermi and Edward Teller. Although Hamming jokingly described his position at Los Alamos as "computer janitor," the work gave him a vision of the role that numerical computation was destined to play in science and technology in the future. He saw that computers could do simulations of some experiments that were not possible in the laboratory. He stayed at Los Alamos for six months after most of the other scientists had left, "to figure out what had happened there, and why it had happened that way" (quoted in Perry, p. 80). (Hamming enjoyed telling how he had turned down an invitation to witness the Trinity atomic bomb test because "If my calculations are wrong, you fellows are not coming back, and I don't want to be there." When the Hammings left Los Alamos, they bought a used car that had once belonged to Klaus Fuchs, and sold the car two weeks before Fuchs was arrested as a Soviet spy. The timing of the sale attracted the attention of the FBI. According to Wanda Hamming, "they charged in and interviewed Dick aggressively until he observed

that it had been the FBI who had originally given Fuchs a security clearance.")

In 1946 Hamming went to Bell Laboratories, where he joined a group of applied mathematicians that included communication theorist Claude Shannon and statistician John Tukey. The group regarded itself as chartered to "do unconventional things in unconventional ways and still get valuable results" (quoted in Perry, p. 82). Hamming was hired to do elasticity theory, but the presence of computers required him to spend more and more time on them, and his career became centered on bringing large-scale scientific computation into Bell Labs. Most of his research between 1946 and 1960 dealt with numerical methods for a broad range of scientific and engineering problems, although his most significant work was on error-correcting codes and digital filters. He was from time to time promoted to head a group of researchers, but since he explicitly did not want management responsibilities, these assignments always came to an end.

Hamming is most famous for the Hamming error-correcting codes and for the concept of Hamming distance, which is central to coding theory. Data in digital systems are typically stored, transmitted, and processed in binary form as blocks of 0's and 1's ("bits"). If a single bit is in error, that is, a 1 is misread as a 0 or vice versa, the message is garbled or the computation spoiled. In large computers, an enormous number of computations must be performed without a single error in the end result. Hamming set himself the task of making the computer itself detect and correct isolated errors, so that the computation could proceed in a way that would be more efficient than simply doing everything multiple times and accepting the majority result.

His approach was based on a generalization of parity checking. A simple parity check works as follows. Suppose we have a block of 0's and 1's and we add an extra check bit, which is chosen so that the whole message has an even number of 1's in it. This is called an even parity check. At the receiving end, if there are not an even number of 1's in the message, then there must be an odd number of errors in the message. If errors occur independently and if the message is short and the bit error rate is small, then the message most probably contains a single error, but we do not know which bit is incorrect.

Hamming found a way of constructing a set of messages containing multiple check bits that refer to different, interlaced sets of message bits, so that it is possible to reconstruct the original message if there is only one bit in error. There is a more general, geometric way of interpreting his ideas. Suppose we have two messages, say 1101010 and 1001110. The Hamming distance between these messages is the number of positions in which they differ. In this example the messages differ in the second and fifth positions, so the Hamming distance is 2. Hamming pointed out that each additional error in a message increases the Hamming distance between the erroneous message and the correct message by one unit. Therefore if a communication system is designed to use only a set of messages that are separated by large Hamming distances, it is possible to detect and correct many errors by simply replacing the received message with the nearest legal message. This concept, in the hands of others, has led to families of codes that permit the correction of an arbitrary number of errors by the use of appropriate redundancy. Heavy-duty codes are used, for example, on noisy deep-space communication channels and to correct burst errors on compact discs.

Hamming's work on digital filters for signal processing began during his first years at Bell Laboratories and continued through most of his career. In analog signal processing, a signal is usually a varying electrical voltage, and the function of a filter is to remove unwanted parts of the signal, such as random noise, or to extract useful parts, such as the components lying in a certain frequency range. In digital signal processing, a signal is a sequence of numbers, which may be thought of as the values of an analog signal at uniform time intervals. A digital filter is embodied by a computer, often a specialized processor, that generates the successive values of the filtered signal by multiplying a set of values of the original signal by a set of coefficients ("weights") and adding them together to produce the filtered value. Hamming found a simple set of weights, subsequently called the Hamming window, that is particularly effective in isolating a selected frequency. Different windows have been designed to meet different requirements, but the Hamming window is still widely used because of its simplicity and effectiveness.

After 1960 Hamming became increasingly interested in teaching and writing. He wrote nine books, some of which went through multiple editions and were translated into various languages, and published some seventy-five technical articles. Between 1960 and 1976, while retaining his base at Bell Laboratories, he held visiting or adjunct professorships at Stanford University, the City College of New York, the University of California at Irvine, and Princeton University. In 1976 he retired from Bell Laboratories to become an adjunct professor (later senior lecturer) of computer science at the Naval Postgraduate School in Monterey, California. He became Distinguished Professor Emeritus in 1997 and taught his last class in December 1997, a few weeks before his death.

Among his major professional honors were the Turing Award (1968) of the Association for Computing Machinery (ACM) and the Emanuel R. Piore Award (1979) of the Institute of Electrical and Electronics Engineers (IEEE). In 1988 the IEEE Richard W. Hamming medal was named after him, and he was its first recipient. In Munich in 1996 he received the $130,000 Eduard Rhein Award for his work on error-correcting codes. He was president of the ACM (1958–1960), a member of the National Academy of Engineering, and a Fellow of IEEE.

Hamming came into the world of computing just as it was shifting from the desk calculator to electronic computers. From his days at Los Alamos he saw, much sooner and more clearly than most people, the significance that computers would have in the postwar world, and he undertook to educate his colleagues for that world. He was a showman, especially during his later years, but his focus was practical; his most celebrated maxim was, "The purpose of computing is insight, not numbers." To a very large extent, he took the same advice that he gave to generations of young researchers: "It's better to do the right problem the wrong way than to do the wrong problem the right way"; "Let's not raise the falutin' index [an injunction against high-falutin' or pretentious terminology]"; and "If you don't work on important problems, it's not likely you'll do important work."

• The first paper on error-correcting codes, still regarded as a classic in its field, was R. W. Hamming, "Error-detecting and error-correcting codes," *Bell System Technical Journal* 29 (1950): 147–60. Hamming's approach to numerical mathematics, which stressed his "insight, not numbers" philosophy and was highly effective in its day, is described in R. W. Hamming, *Numerical Methods for Scientists and Engineers*, 2d ed. (1973). His approach to digital filters is set forth in his monograph *Digital Filters* (3d ed., 1989). Hamming's personal style—and his "trademark" plaid jacket—were highlighted in a profile by Tekla S. Perry, *IEEE Spectrum* 30, No. 5 (May 1993): 80–82. The *New York Times* obituary, with a less than flattering photograph, appeared on 11 Jan. 1998. A memorial article by Samuel P. Morgan described Hamming's technical contributions in *Notices of the American Mathematical Society* 45 (Sept. 1998): 972–77.

SAMUEL P. MORGAN

HAMPTON, Lionel Leo (20 Apr. 1908–31 Aug. 2002), jazz vibraphonist and bandleader, was born in Louisville, Kentucky, the son of Charles Edward Hampton, a railroad worker and musician, and Gertrude Morgan. For a substantial portion of his career Hampton made himself out to be younger, giving his year of birth as 1913 or 1914. But in 1989, when he published his autobiography, he was proud of his age. Then he gave the correct birth year, 1908, which is confirmed by the Department of Public Records in Louisville. A further confusion emerged in the early 1990s, when citizens of Birmingham, Alabama, forged documents to convince Hampton that he was born there rather than in Louisville. This deception subsequently made its way into jazz literature as well.

According to Hampton's autobiography, his father was drafted into the army immediately after Lionel's birth, and Gertrude Hampton returned to live with her family in Birmingham. Hampton added that he did not again see his father, who was blinded in France, until 1939, when they met at a Veterans Administration hospital in Dayton, Ohio. But Hampton was born in 1908, and the draft was not instituted until World War I. Thus at least six years are unaccounted for, suggesting that Charles Hampton may have abandoned the family.

Hampton grew up in a black middle-class neighborhood in Birmingham. Although he was raised by his mother, he was largely under the authority of his grandparents, Richard Morgan, a railroad fireman, and Louvenia Morgan, a healer who was deeply involved in the African-American Holiness Church. There Hampton had his first substantial musical experiences as a child drummer. Around 1919 the family migrated to Chicago, following the lead of Hampton's uncle, Richard Morgan, Jr., whose bootlegging successes in association with Al Capone provided the family with a moderately affluent lifestyle. His uncle also introduced Hampton to an emerging musical style, jazz, which came to be associated with illicit activities in Chicago. Fearing these influences, Louvenia Morgan sent Hampton to the Holy Rosary Academy in Kenosha, Wisconsin, where he received strict instruction in the rudiments of drumming. He also had opportunities to experiment with pitched percussion instruments, such as xylophones, orchestral bells, and tympani. When the school failed fourteen months later, he continued his education at St. Monica's School in Chicago.Under these circumstances, Hampton converted to Catholicism. From his grandmother's teachings he maintained a steadfast belief in healing by prayer. Later in life he became a Christian Scientist.

Hampton joined the *Chicago Defender* newsboys' band under the direction of the renowned African-American music educator Major Nathaniel Clark Smith. Gradually working his way toward the most coveted position in the percussion section, Hampton successively played cymbals, bass drum, snare drum, tympani, and xylophone, and on this last instrument, independent of the newsboys' band, he began to learn melodic jazz solos, copying famous recordings by Louis Armstrong and Coleman Hawkins.

Hampton then became the drummer in a band led by the alto saxophonist Les Hite. In 1927, after Hite had gone west to try to establish a career in Los Angeles, he sent for Hampton to join him. Initially they struggled to find work under various leaders.

During this period Hampton met Gladys Riddle, who took charge of his business affairs. Hampton was and remained always an exuberant performer, devoted to entertaining his audiences and willing to try outrageous stunts. Off the stage he was notoriously irresponsible, devoted to partying, admittedly incapable of saving money, and consequently willing to tolerate Riddle's unending efforts to supervise his behavior and finances.

In 1930 Hite and Hampton joined the house band at Frank Sebastian's Cotton Club, and Hampton's career took off. The orchestra broadcast radio shows from the club that promoted Hampton as the world's fastest drummer. From July 1930 to March 1931 Frank Sebastian's Cotton Club Orchestra recorded under the leadership of the guest soloist Louis Armstrong, and "Memories of You," from October 1930, included Hampton's first solo on vibraphone. Under Hite's leadership the band made film soundtracks, with Hampton performing as drummer in the movie *Sing, Sinner, Sing* (1933). Later, again under Armstrong's leadership, Hampton appeared as the masked drummer in Bing Crosby's musical comedy *Pennies from Heaven* (1936).

By August 1936, when Benny Goodman sat in on clarinet at the Paradise Club in Los Angeles, Hampton was leading his own group, principally as a vibraphonist. Goodman brought along the pianist Teddy Wilson and the drummer Gene Krupa the next night and invited Hampton to a recording session in Hollywood the following day. The renowned Goodman trio thus became a quartet, with Hampton contributing two classic solos as a vibraphonist on "Moonglow" and five days later on "Dinah." In November 1936 Goodman hired Hampton. From this moment the most popular swing combo in the United States, now composed of two whites and two blacks, provided an unusually high-profile model of racial equality in an era when musical groups, like so much else, were rigidly segregated.

Hampton and Riddle headed for New York and stopped momentarily in Arizona, where they married in November of 1936; they had no children. The couple settled in Harlem, and Hampton toured nationwide with Goodman. The Goodman quartet performed in the film *Hollywood Hotel* (1937) and made an extraordinary succession of recordings featuring Hampton's tastefully melodic and energetic vibraphone playing. From an artistic standpoint, this body of music constitutes the zenith of Hampton's legacy. The best tracks include "Stompin' at the Savoy" and "Sweet Sue—Just You" (both recorded in 1936); "Ida, Sweet as Apple Cider," "Runnin' Wild," "Avalon," "The Man I Love," and "I'm a Ding Dong Daddy" (all 1937); and "The Blues in Your Flat," "Sugar," and "Dizzy Spells" (all 1938). In March 1938, after Krupa left to go on his own, Hampton sometimes played drums with Goodman's big band and small group, and he recorded with the latter as both its drummer and its vibraphonist. Further outstanding titles are "Sweet Georgia Brown" and "'S Wonderful," both recorded in 1938, as well as "Till Tom Special" and "Six Appeal" from sessions in 1940 in Goodman's sextet with the guitarist Charlie Christian.

Concurrently Goodman's label Victor hired Hampton to organize ad hoc small-group swing recordings. These ninety-four tracks are not on the level of Goodman's own small-group recordings or those made by Teddy Wilson with Billy Holiday, but there are fine moments, most notably a rendition of "When Lights Are Low," recorded in 1939. While showcasing Hampton's vibraphone playing, these small-group recordings also display his talents as a rapid-fire novelty pianist, playing in a percussive, two-fingered, perpetual-motion style ("Piano Stomp," 1937); as a drummer; and as a pleasant though undistinguished singer. In October 1939 Hampton also recorded as a drummer in a studio band accompanying the blues singer Ida Cox.

In July 1940 Goodman disbanded his orchestra. Thereafter, for more than sixty years, Hampton led his own groups. The earliest of these helped to pioneer an extroverted rhythm-and-blues style, above all in its renditions of Hampton's tune "Flying Home." "Hey-ba-ba-re-bop," featuring Hampton's singing and recorded in 1945, was another prominent title of this ilk. The band was renowned for its circus antics in performance—a saxophone hurtling through the air, Hampton dancing on a drum, and other stunts. These are captured in the acclaimed film short *Lionel Hampton and His Orchestra* (1949). Otherwise the band's significance resided in the large number of young jazz musicians who passed through en route to becoming stars. In the 1940s these included the tenor saxophonists Illinois Jacquet (whose solo on the first recording of "Flying Home" in May 1942 launched his career), Arnett Cobb, Dexter Gordon, and Johnny Griffin; the trumpeters Joe Newman and Clark Terry; the singers Dinah Washington, Joe Williams, and Betty Carter; the guitarist Wes Montgomery; and the bassist Charles Mingus. Betty Carter recalled, "I learned how to travel with men, how to be independent, how to look out for yourself, how to be in control, how to get on the stage, how to get *off* the stage, how to be disciplined, how to sit in a bus for hours and hours. I learned a lot from Gladys and Hamp both, not always realizing then that I was getting it" (Michael Bourne, "Betty Carter: It's Not About Teaching. It's About Doing," *Down Beat* 61, Dec. 1994: 17). In the early 1950s the trumpeters Clifford Brown, Art Farmer, and Quincy Jones were members. Jones doubled as an arranger for Hampton and appeared with him as a soloist in the film *Harlem Jazz Festival* (1955).

From the perspective of mainstream jazz rather than incipient rhythm and blues, Hampton's most important recording of this era is a rendition of "Stardust" presented in August 1947 at a Just Jazz concert in Pasadena, California, by a group of veteran swing musicians as the Lionel Hampton All Stars. On this lengthy track Hampton's vibraphone provides a restrained, tasteful, sparkling accompaniment to a succession of gorgeous instrumental ballad solos. He then follows with his own solo, characteristically energizing the proceedings by playing at four times the speed of the underlying ballad tempo and yet managing to convey a sense of logical tunefulness, not frenzy.

In Hampton's own band the policies of the notoriously tightfisted Gladys Hampton made the hiring of unknown youngsters a practical necessity, but apart from her extravagant forays into furs and jewelry, she salted away huge sums of money. By the 1960s the Hamptons owned twenty-two houses in Los Angeles, property in Las Vegas, and a stake in a Texas oil field. As a wealthy man Hampton became involved in diverse philanthropic endeavors. The most prominent of these were low-income housing projects in Harlem and in Newark, New Jersey, established after Gladys's death in 1971, at which time Hampton moved to a hotel downtown before settling permanently into an apartment on West Sixty-fourth Street near Lincoln Center. In 1985 he permanently endowed the Lionel Hampton Jazz Festival and in 1987 the Lionel Hampton School of Music, both at the University of Idaho. He intended to donate a huge collection of memorabilia to the school, but nearly everything was lost in 1997, when a faulty lamp started a fire that destroyed that apartment.

Hampton loved performing and for decades toured internationally and incessantly. In 1965, when interest in big bands had declined severely, he established an octet, the Jazz Inner Circle, but he continued to lead a big band whenever circumstances allowed. His group is seen and heard in *No Maps on My Taps* (1978), perhaps the finest documentary film on African-American tap dancing. Eventually the Jazz Inner Circle grew back into a big band. Apart from that group, Hampton also led an all-star swing group, the Golden Men of Jazz, in 1991–1992. An active political supporter, switching from Democrat to Republican and back to Democrat, he played at the presidential inaugurations of Truman, Eisenhower, Nixon, George H. W. Bush, and, in 1996 at the age of eighty-eight, Clinton.

Hampton suffered stokes in 1992, in 1995, and in 1996. Ultimately obliged to lead his band from a wheelchair, he nevertheless persevered and continued to appear with the band into the twenty-first century, providing irrepressible inspiration even when he could scarcely play any longer. He died in New York City.

• The only significant materials that survived Hampton's apartment fire were assorted arrangements for big bands, which are at the University of Idaho. An immense annotated archive of photos, videos, broadcasts, recordings, and published items compiled by "Hans Bebop" is available at http://www.lionelhampton.nl. Hampton's *Hamp: An Autobiography* (1989), written with James Haskins, is a careless and unquestioning authorized biography, heavily padded with dull name-dropping, yet its first chapters provide considerable insight into middle-class African-American life in the South and in Chicago in the early twentieth century. The substantial appendix by Vincent Pelote in *Hamp* provides a comprehensive catalog of Hampton's recordings except for those made with Goodman, which are in D. Russell Connor, *Benny Goodman: Listen to His Legacy,* 4th ed. (1988). This body of recordings is surveyed and celebrated by Gerry E. Lambert, "Lionel Hampton: Jazz Giant," *Jazz Journal* 14 (Nov. 1961): 2–4, 14 (Dec. 1961): 7, 9, 44, and 15 (Jan. 1962): 5–7; Joe H. Klee, "Good Vibes," *Mississippi Rag* 4 (Jan. 1977): 1–3; and Bruce Crowther and Victor Schonfield, "Hamp the Champ," *Jazz Journal International* 31 (July 1978): 6–9, 18.

Marshall Royal with Claire P. Gordon, *Marshall Royal: Jazz Survivor* (1996), supplies ambivalent reminiscenses from an outspoken alto saxophonist who was Hampton's sideman for a number of years. For other details, see Bill Coss, "Lionel Hampton: Bothered and Bewildered," *Down Beat* 29 (10 May 1962): 19–21; Stanley Dance, *The World of Swing* (1974), pp. 265–78; Arnold Jay Smith, "Lionel

Hampton: Half a Century Strong," *Down Beat* 15 (10 Aug. 1978): 20–21, 53–54, 56, 62; Les Tomkins, "Lionel Hampton Recalls When Swing Began," *Crescendo International* 20 (Aug. 1983): 20–22; Stan Woolley, "Flyin' Hamp," *Jazz Journal International* 36 (July 1983): 6–8; Burt Korall, "Lionel Hampton," *Modern Drummer* 12 (Dec. 1988): 30–33, 68, 70, 72, 74, 76; Sid Gribetz, "Lionel Hampton: More Glory Days," *Jazz Times* 23 (Feb. 1993), 40–41; and "Lionel Hampton—A Biography," *Crescendo and Jazz Music* 35 (Apr.–May 1998): 18–19. An obituary by Peter Watrous is in the *New York Times*, 1 Sept. 2002.

BARRY KERNFELD

HANGER, James Edward (25 Feb. 1843–9 June 1919), soldier and businessman, was born at his father's plantation, "Mt. Hope," near Churchville, Augusta County, Virginia, the son of William Alexander Hanger, planter, and Eliza Hogshead Hanger. After receiving his early education in local schools, in 1859 he enrolled at Washington College (now Washington & Lee University) in Lexington, Virginia, where he studied engineering.

At the onset of the Civil War, Hanger, as a native of Virginia and the son of a slave owner, sympathized with the South. In the spring of 1861 he left college and joined the Churchville Cavalry, a newly formed unit made up of men from his hometown including two of his brothers. Learning that the unit had been stationed in what was then the western portion of Virginia, Hanger headed west and arrived in Philippi on 1 June. There he found that his unit had been temporarily relocated south to Buchanan. Hanger remained with the small group of untrained and poorly equipped Confederates under the overall command of Col. G. A. Porterfield.

Early on the morning of 3 June, Hanger was on guard duty when he heard the opening shots of what would prove to be the first land battle of the American Civil War. He ran into a barn to find his horse, only to suffer a serious wound when a Union cannonball ricocheted off the barn's rafter and struck him below his left knee. Hanger then hid in the barn while the rest of his comrades fled; the battle, which otherwise produced slight casualties, became known in the Northern press as the "Philippi races." Found by Union soldiers later that afternoon, Hanger was taken captive and shortly thereafter had his left leg amputated above the knee by an Ohio army surgeon, Dr. James D. Robinson.

After remaining in Philippi for several weeks (where he convalesced in the homes of nearby residents), Hanger was sent to Camp Chase in Ohio. In August 1861 he was exchanged in Norfolk, Virginia. Unhappy with the wooden leg that he had been given, Hanger returned home to Churchville and vowed to produce a better one. Using whittled barrel staves and metal components, Hanger made a limb that used rubber bumpers instead of the then-standard catgut tendons and featured hinges on both the knee and the foot. Determined to help other war veterans, Hanger then moved to Richmond and founded J. E. Hanger,

Inc. with a view toward mass-producing his innovative artificial limbs. The Confederate government provided financial support, and soon "Hanger limbs" became the replacement device of choice for numerous servicemen.

In 1871 Hanger moved to Staunton, Virginia. That same year, he obtained a patent on his invention. In 1873 he married Nora McCarthy in Richmond; the couple had eight children. In 1888 Hanger moved the firm again, this time to Washington, D.C., and obtained additional patents on improvements to his original design. Although he retired from active management of his business around 1905, he retained the title of president and in 1915 traveled to Europe, where he observed firsthand the latest techniques for dealing with wounded soldiers. His efforts resulted in his firm's receiving special contracts with both the French and British governments during and after World War I.

Hanger was active in the Presbyterian Church and was credited with numerous other inventions, including a horseless carriage (used as a toy by his children), an adjustable reclining chair, and a lathe that could produce his prosthetic devices. At the time of his death in Washington, D.C., his firm had offices in Philadelphia, Atlanta, St. Louis, Pittsburgh, Paris, and London.

Hanger is regarded as the "father of modern prosthetics." With his youthful dreams of battlefield glory shattered as one of the very first casualties in what would prove to be a long and bloody war, he turned his misfortune into an industry that benefited countless thousands of individuals. His firm continued as Hanger Orthopedic Group, Inc.

• No collection of Hanger's papers has been located, and secondary material on his life and career is scarce. He was the subject of an extensive article, "He Lost His Leg and Gave It to Thousands," in the *West Virginia Hillbilly* (Summersville, W. Va.) on 27 May 1961, and was also mentioned in Eva Margaret Carnes, *The Tygarts Valley Line: June–July, 1861* (1961).

EDWARD L. LACH, JR.

HANNA, William (14 July 1910–22 Mar. 2001), animated-cartoon director and producer, was born William Denby Hanna in Melrose, New Mexico, the son of William John Hanna, a construction superintendent for water and sewer systems, and Avice Joyce Denby. During Hanna's childhood, his father's work took the family—which included six daughters in addition to Hanna, the only son—to points throughout the West, including Baker, Oregon, Logan, Utah, and San Pedro, California, and other towns in the Los Angeles area. Hanna graduated from Compton High School in 1928 and entered Compton Junior College as a journalism major. He dropped out when the onset of the Great Depression left his family in difficult circumstances.

The Hannas moved to Hollywood, California, when the father was involved in the construction of the Pantages theater. Hanna worked alongside his father on that project, as he had on earlier jobs, but he had no desire to spend his life in construction. Looking for work in Hollywood in 1930 after the Pantages was completed, he was hired as a janitor by the new Harman-Ising cartoon studio. Hugh N. Harman and Rudolf C. Ising had begun producing sound cartoons called "Looney Tunes"—rowdy slapstick exercises starring a stereotypical black, Bosko—for Warner Bros. earlier that year.

Hanna's most important duty was washing the sheets of celluloid on which the animators' drawings were traced and painted before they were photographed. "Cels," as they were called, were used repeatedly, to save money. "I used to get there early and empty wastebaskets and sweep and wash cels," Hanna said. "That didn't keep me busy, so I painted [cels]" (quoted in Barrier, *Hollywood Cartoons*, p. 289). Hanna was "an enthusiastic kid," Ising remembered, and within a year or two he had become head of the studio's inking and painting department, supervising the young women who traced and painted the cels.

Hanna recalled that "the combined artistic endeavors" of his mother and his sisters—they were (mostly) unpublished poets and essayists—"did produce a singular impression on me. They imparted to me a great appreciation of rhythm, timing, and imagery" (Hanna, *A Cast of Friends*, p. 14). Although Hanna later concluded that he was not cut out to be a writer or a musician, his knowledge of music led to his composing what he called "songs and lyrics" for the Harman-Ising cartoons. Those cartoons, like other early sound cartoons, were organized musically—the animation was governed by a musical beat—and Hanna was soon deeply involved in determining the timing of the comic action on the screen. Such control of timing was one of the basic tools of a cartoon director in the 1930s.

In 1934, Harman-Ising began releasing its cartoons through Metro-Goldwyn-Mayer and making Technicolor musical fantasies, called "Happy Harmonies," that invited comparisons with Walt Disney's contemporaneous "Silly Symphonies." Hanna worked on stories with Hugh Harman, and in 1936 he codirected his first cartoon, a Happy Harmony called *To Spring*. His codirector was an animator who made the character layouts—drawings that showed the animators how to stage the scenes that Hanna timed. That year Hanna married Violet Wogatzke; they were to have two children.

In 1937, Harman and Ising broke with MGM. Hanna was one of four key Harman-Ising staff members whom MGM hired away to set up a new cartoon studio near the MGM lot in Culver City, California. Hanna and Robert Allen, a former Harman-Ising animator, were the new studio's first directors. Other staff members were hired from the Terrytoons studio in New York. Among them was an animator, Joseph Barbera, whose name would later be inextricably associated with Hanna's.

The new MGM studio's cartoons, based on the "Captain and the Kids" comic strip, were not successful, and in 1938 MGM hired Harman and Ising to produce cartoons that were, like the Happy Harmonies, animal fables and fairy tales in the Disney vein. Hanna was demoted, writing for Ising's cartoons alongside Barbera. The two men hit it off, Hanna seeing in Barbera's drawing ability a remedy for his own shortcomings as a draftsman. In 1939, they began codirecting their first cartoon, *Puss Gets the Boot*, while still members of Rudolph Ising's unit. Fred Quimby, the MGM cartoons' producer, gave Hanna and Barbera their own unit in September of that year.

Puss Gets the Boot starred a gray cat named Jasper and a mouse that MGM's publicity identified as Pee-Wee. The cartoon was well received by theater audiences when it was released in 1940, and MGM, in a break with its usual practice at the time, let Hanna and Barbera make a second cartoon, *The Midnight Snack* (1941), with the same characters. They were renamed Tom and Jerry for that cartoon. Hanna and Barbera made almost nothing but Tom and Jerry cartoons—114 in all—after that, for the next sixteen years. They won seven Academy Awards for best cartoon. They also produced animated inserts for several live-action MGM features, most notably *Anchors Aweigh* (1945), in which an animated Jerry danced with a live-action Gene Kelly.

As they worked, Hanna and Barbera sat at desks facing each other, talking out the stories of their cartoons in detail. Barbera then made the sketches that guided the animators in how to draw the action, and Hanna prescribed the timing. The Tom and Jerry cartoons reflected the two directors' differing backgrounds in another way: the cat-and-mouse comedy was violent like that in the Terrytoons, but the cartoons had the smooth surfaces of the Disney and Harman-Ising cartoons.

Hanna and Barbera succeeded Quimby as the MGM cartoons' producers in 1956, but by then the end of the cartoon studio, and of theatrical short cartoons generally, was in sight. "We were on payroll there for a year," Hanna said, "knowing that at the end of that year, if we did not do something more with MGM, we would be out on our own" (quoted in Barrier, p. 547). Hanna and Barbera could not interest MGM in an animated television series, but with the help of George Sidney, who had directed *Anchors Aweigh* and other MGM musicals, they sold the idea to Screen Gems, Columbia Pictures' television subsidiary. They gave up ownership of about 20 percent of their new company, H-B Enterprises, in return for Sidney's and Columbia's backing. Hanna and Barbera opened a studio in Hollywood on 7 July 1957, and their first television cartoon, "Ruff and Reddy," was broadcast on NBC on 14 December 1957.

The success of H-B's syndicated cartoon series "Huckleberry Hound" in 1958 fueled the rapid rise of what was soon called Hanna-Barbera Productions, and by 1960 Hanna-Barbera had two more syndicated series on the air, "Quick Draw McGraw" and

"Yogi Bear." It was also that year that its prime-time series "The Flintstones" made its debut, on 30 September 1960. An animated situation comedy set in prehistoric times, with more than a passing resemblance to the Jackie Gleason television series "The Honeymooners," "The Flintstones" ran on ABC for six years.

"I undertook the production end of the business," Hanna wrote, "which involved timing the scenes and working with the artists and animators to turn out the cartoons. Joe developed into the salesman of our unit, an undertaking that complemented his natural powers of persuasion to perfection. He developed a phenomenal flair for marketing our shows that netted us a bounty of network sales almost from the onset" (Hanna, p. 99).

As effectively as Hanna and Barbera worked together for more than a half century, they could hardly be described as friends. As Barbera wrote, "We have almost nothing in common" (Barbera, *My Life in 'Toons*, p. 120). Hanna was a devoted family man, deeply involved with the Boy Scouts since childhood, and a lover of the outdoors. Barbera, on the other hand, craved night life and Hollywood glamour. At work, Barbera said, "we were always less of a 'team' than we were opposite, but equal, ends of a remarkably smooth production continuum. Bill's job began precisely where mine left off" (Barbera, p. 121).

In 1966, Hanna, Barbera, and Sidney sold their company to Taft Broadcasting Company for a reported $12 million, but the terms of the sale provided that the two founders would remain in charge. Hanna-Barbera Productions enjoyed its greatest success in the late 1960s and early 1970s, when its animated series dominated the Saturday-morning schedules of the three major networks and it was, measured by the number of employees (as many as 600), the world's largest animation studio.

Hanna-Barbera passed through several changes of corporate ownership over the next three decades, ultimately winding up as part of AOL Time Warner. Despite the cartoon studio's gradually declining fortunes as other cartoon producers chipped away at its Saturday-morning franchise and networks assumed greater sway over program choices, Hanna and Barbera did not relinquish significant control until 1989. Even then, they both continued to come to work every day for years. Hanna died in North Hollywood, California.

In one sense, Hanna and Barbera saved Hollywood animation when they opened their television cartoon studio in 1957. Other studios, like Disney and Warner Bros., were closing or cutting back, and many of the most distinguished veterans of Disney's animated features and of popular short cartoons like the Bugs Bunny series joined the Hanna-Barbera staff as directors, animators, and writers. Hollywood animation paid a heavy price for being saved, however. In the words of one analysis, "Hanna and Barbera were eager to comply with television's harsh demands for quantity and predictability. They reduced the animation, the stories, the dialogue, and the characters to increasingly rigid and predictable patterns, the better to facilitate production" (Barrier, p. 561). Hanna, who acknowledged his "managerial intensity [that] could well have won me election as tyrant of the week, month, or, more precisely, production season by a landslide of votes" (Hanna, p. 185), played a crucial and probably indispensable role both in animation's survival and in its transformation from art and craft into factory-made product.

• Hanna's autobiography, *A Cast of Friends* (1996), is generally trustworthy, as is Joseph Barbera's *My Life in 'Toons: From Flatbush to Bedrock in under a Century* (1994), although both suffer from the careless minor lapses that almost invariably mar even the best show-business autobiographies. Both books devote many more pages to Hanna-Barbera Productions than to the MGM cartoons. For extended discussion of the latter, as well as material on the earliest days of Hanna-Barbera, see Michael Barrier, *Hollywood Cartoons: American Animation in Its Golden Age* (1999). Hanna and Barbera and their company were subjects of a number of skeptical journalistic assessments in Hanna-Barbera's heyday; one of the best is John Culhane, "The Men Behind Dastardly & Muttley," *New York Times Magazine*, 23 Nov. 1969. An obituary is in the *New York Times*, 23 Mar. 2001.

MICHAEL BARRIER

HARMAN, Fred (9 Feb. 1902–2 Jan. 1982), cartoonist and painter, was born Fred Charles Harman, Jr., in St. Joseph, Missouri, the son of Fred Charles Harman, a lawyer and rancher, and Birdie Olive Walker Harman. At the time of his birth his parents were visiting relatives in St. Joseph while vacationing away from their homestead near Pagosa Springs, Colorado. The family returned to Colorado when young Fred was two months old, and he grew to adolescence on the ranch, learning how to ride horseback and herd cattle and teaching himself to draw by copying pictures in mail-order catalogs. Harman's first published drawing appeared in a Saturday youth section of the *St. Joseph News-Press* when he was six, but he did not begin to make a living with his graphic skill until he was eighteen.

In 1916 the Harman family, now including two more sons, moved to Kansas City. In the spring of 1917, when the United States entered the European conflict, young Fred quit school to join the Missouri National Guard, and he spent the next several months guarding Kansas City's reservoir. He was released from duty a year later and returned to the Harman homestead in Colorado, where he spent the summer and fall working as a cowhand at ranches in the vicinity. By Christmas 1918 he was back in Kansas City, a pressman's helper on the *Kansas City Star*, but he never lost his affection for the West and the outdoor life on a ranch and returned to Colorado often during the next several years. In 1920 he found a job with the Kansas City Film Ad Company and worked with two other cartoonists destined for future fame—Walt Disney and Ub Iwerks. Disney left for Hollywood in the summer of 1923. Harman freelanced at commercial art for the next year, went back to Colorado briefly, then in the fall of 1924 joined the art department of Artcrafts Engraving Company in St. Joseph, where he specialized in boots and saddles. On 25 June 1926 he married Lola May Andrews, and when their only child, a son, was born the next May, Harman went to California in search of better prospects. He visited his brothers, both of whom were working in animation for Disney, but decided against an animation career and returned to St. Joseph.

By early 1929 Harman was in St. Paul, Minnesota, doing freelance illustrations for the Midwest's largest art department at Buckbee-Mears and operating an art agency with an advertising friend. In 1932, soon after the Great Depression hit Minnesota, Harman sold out to his partner and prepared for Sunday rotogravure sections of newspapers a series of short stories and illustrative paintings titled *On the Range* that he offered, without success, to the *Des Moines Register-Tribune* for syndication. When the newspaper declined, Harman went to Hollywood again in the summer of 1933, and, financed by loans from his brothers and their friends, he self-syndicated a daily comic strip, *Bronc Peeler*, about the Old West. Bronc is a gangly two-fisted, fast-riding redheaded young cowpoke whose adventures Harman rendered in a confident, sinewy pen line that resonated authenticity, evoking the artist's own early life on horseback in Colorado's Blanco Basin. The panels of the strip brandish high-speed horseflesh and gnarly, bowlegged hombres as Bronc chases after tinhorn gamblers, town bullies, horse thieves and rustlers, stagecoach robbers, and owlhoots of every stripe. The genuine appearance of the strip is so authoritative that its B-movie plots and hoked-up lingo are very nearly overwhelmed by the ambiance. In harness with his Hollywood tradition, Bronc is accompanied on his early adventures by a grizzled old desert rat named Coyote Pete. But when Harman's wife suggested that a younger sidekick might attract a larger juvenile readership for the strip, the cartoonist replaced Pete with a Navajo youngster named Little Beaver, whose pidgin locutions were an affront to his ethnicity. Having shot a trout with bow and arrow, Little Beaver chases it downstream, saying, "Me killum fish—now to ketchum before him float away." Intended perhaps as comic relief, a plucky smart-mouthed sidekick, Little Beaver became much more. Ingenious and courageous, he often rescued his mentor, and the boy quickly proved more popular than the old-timer he displaced. On 7 October 1934, when Harman added a Sunday strip to his workload, he also produced a linear newsprint-suitable version of his earlier *On the Range* paintings for the bottom half of the page, accompanying it with a rustic Will Jamesian patois describing life in the Old West.

The work of self-syndication was daunting. Harman wrote his continuities, drew the strip, arranged for the engravings to be made and mats to be shipped to client newspapers, and drove around the country trying to sell the feature to newspaper editors. He also freelanced artwork to various publications, hobnobbed with cowboys real and reel, and teamed with Curley Fletcher, the "Cowboy Poet" and author of the song "The Strawberry Roan," to produce three issues of *Ride*, a slick magazine about the West. Harman's break came in 1938, shortly after he had illustrated a Big Little Book, *Cowboy Lingo*, for Whitman Publishing Company, whose president liked Harman's work and recommended an agent in New York, Stephen Slesinger. Slesinger offered Harman an illustration assignment in New York, and the artist promptly moved there and joined Slesinger's art staff, leaving *Bronc Peeler* in the dust. But not for long. That summer, as Harman told it: "Fred Ferguson, president of Scripps Howard's NEA newspaper syndicate, came into the office inquiring about a Fred Harman he had heard about who drew a Little Beaver cartoon. When I stuck out my eager paw and said, 'Howdy—I'm Fred Harman,' he dang near lost his voice in surprise" (Harman, *True West*, 60). At Ferguson's instigation, Harman created a sample Sunday comic strip in which Bronc Peeler was transformed into Red Ryder, and Slesinger negotiated a ten-year contract with the Newspaper Enterprise Association syndicate (NEA). *Red Ryder* debuted on 6 November 1938, its rawboned, redheaded hero in his signature red shirt, white wide-brimmed low-crown hat, and chaps; a daily strip started 27 March 1939.

Red Ryder is older and broader of shoulder than his antecedent, but Little Beaver is exactly the same: spunky and outspoken, the human chorus to Red's granite-faced struggle against rascality, grunting a supportive "You betchum, Red Ryder" with such regularity that the expression became a catch phrase. The stories had the same sort of fast-breaking action-packed plots and central-casting villains as before. Harman now used a juicy brush, splashing drawings through the panels in a fluid, sketchy manner, accenting them with realistic black shadow. Fittingly in a western, Red is on horseback much of the time, astride a big black horse named Thunder (Little Beaver rides a paint pony called Papoose), and Harman could make his hero sit a horse convincingly. The bandy-legged mannerisms of *Bronc Peeler* continue, as do Harman's characteristic treatment of everything wooden, imparting a knotty reality to the environs—fence posts tilt askew in the parched earth, the planks of boardwalks and buildings are weathered and warped in the sun and therefore uneven, the wheels on wagons almost certainly wobble. Every landscape has towering buttes in the distance, and shaggy pine trees and tufts of scraggly juniper bushes dot the hillside trails near the little Colorado town of Rimrock. In the first year or so of the strip's run, Red meets his lifelong paramour, the dark-haired beauty Beth Wilder, and his arch enemy, Ace Hanlon, the cardsharp scoundrel who for the next twenty-five years would pester the townspeople with one swindle after another. Completing the cast of regulars are Rimrock's cantankerous Sheriff Newt and Red's aunt, the Duchess, a doughty matriarchal old scout whose rough edges never quite conceal the warmth of her heart.

But Little Beaver was undoubtedly the most popular of the strip's cast (so much so that much subsequent publicity referred to the strip as "Red Ryder and Little Beaver," suggesting Harman's attachment to the character that rescued him from illustrating children's books for Slesinger). The affectionate and respectful relationship between the resourceful wise-cracking kid and the big sobersided redhead was arguably what gave the otherwise headlong action strip its heart and endeared it to readers. During World War II, the Indian youth's name was also deployed with several combat units that effectively adopted him as a mascot.

Red Ryder was among the most successful westerns in comic strip history, appearing eventually in 750 newspapers. Republic Pictures produced a twelve-chapter serial in 1940, followed by twenty-seven feature-length motion pictures (1944–1949), and a radio program that started in February 1942 ran three half-hour programs a week until 1951. The *Red Ryder* comic book appeared sporadically beginning in September 1940 and became bimonthly in December 1943 and monthly in January 1946 until the last issue, number 151, in April 1957. Red Ryder's name was used on an array of merchandise, the most celebrated of which was the Daisy 111 Model 40 Red Ryder Western Carbine, known popularly as the Red Ryder BB gun, which was first offered in 1939 to the purchasing public for $2.95. Ubiquitously advertised on the back covers of comic books through the 1950s, the rifle continued to be a popular item for the rest of the century.

By 1940, his financial success assured, Harman returned to his roots, buying land near Pagosa Springs and building on the slope of Square Top Mountain a cabin with a majestic view of the rugged San Juan Mountains of Archuleta County. Although he envisioned his domicile as a hideaway, the promotional press dubbed it "Red Ryder Ranch," and it was soon the destination of touring fans. The red-haired Harman participated enthusiastically in publicity campaigns, appearing around the country at rodeos as "Red Ryder," and he always had a "Little Beaver" imitator with him, a succession of youths recruited from the nearby Jicarilla Reservation. Harman continued to control his creations, but he acquired assistant artists over the years so he would have time to paint. When the strip ceased on 26 December 1964, it was being produced almost entirely by Bob MacLeod. Harman, meanwhile, resumed full-time a painting career that had been interrupted for thirty years.

Harman began wintering in Albuquerque and finally bought a year-round home and studio in Phoenix, where he died of complications from a stroke suffered on December 27. He produced over 350 oil paintings, scores of pen-and-ink drawings, and numerous bronze sculptures on western themes. He was inducted into the Society of Illustrators early in his comic strip career and was a charter member of the National Cartoonists Society in 1947. In 1958 he received the Sertoma Club's American Way of Life Award for Colorado's Outstanding Citizen. In 1963 he joined four other artists (Joe Beeler, Charlie Dye, Jon Hampton, and George Phippen) to found the Cowboy Artists of America. Among the honors Harman valued most was his official adoption into the Navajo Nation, a distinction enjoyed by only seventy-five other non–Native Americans. His name and comic strip creation are perpetuated in the annual Pagosa Springs Red Ryder Rodeo, a suitable legacy of cartooning's most accomplished representation of the American West.

• Harman's papers and many of his artworks are at the Fred Harman Western Art Museum, once the cartoonist's home near Pagosa Springs, Colorado. A detailed account of Harman's life until the syndication of *Red Ryder* is the autobiographical article "New Tracks in Old Trails," *True West*, Sept.–Oct. 1968, 6–11, 57–61. Dean Krakel's introduction to a book of Harman's paintings, *The Great West in Paintings* (1969), also supplies a few details of Harman's life. Other accounts include Paul Friggens, "He's at Home on the Range and Quick on the Draw," *Quill* (Society of Professional Journalists), Feb. 1939; James Poling, "Ryder of the Comic Page," *Collier's*, Aug. 1948, 16–17, 77; and Mark Yost, "Red Ryder's Eternal Home on the Range," *Wall Street Journal*, 23 Dec. 2003, D8 (all somewhat inflated with promotional mythology). See also entries in Maurice Horn, *Comics of the American West* (1977); Ron Goulart, *The Adventurous Decade* (1975); and Goulart, ed., *The Encyclopedia of American Comics* (1990). Red Ryder's celluloid career began with the Republic serial *The Adventures of Red Ryder*, starring Don "Red" Barry (1940). Subsequent Republic films with "Wild" Bill Elliott, George "Gabby" Hayes (first two), and Bobby Blake as Little Beaver include *Tucson Raiders* (1944), *Marshal of Reno* (1944), *The San Antonio Kid* (1944), *Cheyenne Wildcat* (1944), *Vigilantes of Dodge City* (1944), *Sheriff of Las Vegas* (1944), *Great Stagecoach Robbery* (1945), *Lone Texas Ranger* (1945), *Phantom of the Plains* (1945), *Marshal of Laredo* (1945), *Colorado Pioneers* (1945), *Wagon Wheels Westward* (1945), *California Gold Rush* (1946), *Sun Valley Cyclone* (1946), *Conquest of Cheyenne* (1946), *Sheriff of Redwood Valley* (1946), *Santa Fe Uprising* (1946) with Allan "Rocky" Lane as Red Ryder; *Stagecoach to Denver* (1946), *Vigilantes of Boomtown* (1947), *Homesteaders of Paradise Valley* (1947), *Oregon Trail Scouts* (1947), *Rustlers of Devil's Canyon* (1947), and *Marshal of Cripple Creek* (1947). Equity/Eagle Lion films with Jim Bannon as Red Ryder and Don Kay Reynolds as Little Beaver include *Ride, Ryder, Ride* (1949), *Roll, Thunder, Roll* (1949), *The Fighting Redhead* (1949), and *Cowboy and the Prizefighter* (1949). An obituary is in the *New York Times*, 5 Jan. 1982.

ROBERT C. HARVEY

HARMAN, Hugh N. (31 Aug. 1903–25 Nov. 1982), and **Rudolf C. Ising** (7 Aug. 1903–18 July 1992), animated cartoon producers and directors, were born, respectively, in Pagosa Springs, Colorado, and Kansas City, Missouri. Harman's parents were Fred Harman, Sr., a lawyer and rancher, and Birdie Walker Harman; information on Ising's parents does not appear in readily available sources. Harman and Ising both began their careers with studios in the Kansas City, Missouri, area, the most notable of which were predecessors of the Walt Disney studio. Hugh Harman's elder brother Fred, Jr., a prominent Western artist who would later go on to create the comic strip character "Red Ryder," worked with Walt Disney at the Kansas City Film Advertising Company in 1920 and 1921, and presumably it was he who introduced his younger brothers Hugh and Walker to Disney. Ising answered Disney's newspaper advertisement for an artist in 1921 and started to assist Harman and Disney with the production of cartoons for a local Kansas City exhibitor. When Laugh-O-Gram Films, Inc., was formed by Walt Disney in May 1922, Hugh Harman animated alongside Disney, while Ising both drew and operated the filming equipment. When Laugh-O-Gram Films failed in October 1923, Harman and Ising, along with C. Griffin Maxwell, formed Arabian Nights Cartoons; they produced during 1924 a trial film in a proposed "Arabian Nights" series, which was not successfully marketed, and a notable experimental illustrated sing-along film, which apparently was not completed.

In mid-1925 Harman and Ising moved to Los Angeles to join the nascent Disney Bros. Studio, where Harman continued to animate and Ising both animated and operated the cameras. During this time, the principal product of the Disney studio was the so-called "Alice in Cartoonland" series, which, by the use of matte effects, mixed live action with animation. The last of this series was animated in April 1927 and was followed by the "Oswald the Lucky Rabbit" series; both of these were produced by Margaret Winkler and her husband Charles Mintz. After some initial production troubles in 1927, the "Oswald" series was successfully marketed by Mintz through Universal Pictures. Harman continued to work on the series, but Ising left the studio in March 1927, in part because, allegedly, the camera work caused him to fall asleep, triggering some expensive mistakes. (Ising was said to have had a very sleepy demeanor, and some have theorized that he was the inspiration for the desperately sleepy Barney Bear in the 1939 Metro-Goldwyn-Mayer [MGM] cartoon "The Bear That Couldn't Sleep," which Ising himself directed.) In early 1928 negotiations between Charles Mintz and Walt Disney resulted in Mintz's taking control of the production of the "Oswald" series, and he hired away a number of Disney's artists, including Harman. Ising, after a brief stint that included working on educational films regarding plastic surgery, was reunited with Harman at the Mintz studio. Mintz, however, subsequently lost the rights to the "Oswald" series to Walter Lantz in the spring of 1929, resulting in Harman and Ising's being temporarily unemployed.

Harman and Ising worked in the summer of 1929 to produce a pilot film titled "Bosko the Talk-Ink Kid," which was one of the first animated cartoons to use a lip-synchronized sound track; it is a very simple cartoon, with "Bosko," a fairly recognizable black boy at this juncture, interacting with a live-action Rudy Ising. While the cartoon was never commercially released, Harman and Ising were able to use it to persuade Leon Schlesinger, a producer of main title artwork and silent-film intertitles (who, more importantly, had connections to the Warner Bros. studio), to back a series of synchronized sound cartoons. In January 1930 Schlesinger entered into a contract with Harman and Ising for one cartoon and options for three yearly series, which would become the series called "Looney Tunes" and would utilize music from the Warner Bros. music library. The first cartoon in the series, "Sinkin' in the Bathtub," was released in May 1930.

The series proved to be a commercial success, and in 1931 Schlesinger commissioned a second series of cartoons with the title "Merrie Melodies." In time, "Looney Tunes" featured continuing characters (principally Bosko, who had devolved into a creature of indeterminate species, and his girlfriend, Honey), while "Merrie Melodies" were one-shot cartoons, without continuing characters but specifically featuring various Warner Bros.–owned songs. For the most part, Harman was responsible for directing the "Looney Tunes," while Ising directed the "Merrie Melodies." The "Merrie Melodies" proved to be as successful as the "Looney Tunes," and both series were produced in quantity through the early part of 1933.

Harman aggressively tried to push Schlesinger into increasing the budgets for the cartoons and moving into color, especially in the wake of the Disney studio's success in 1932 with "Flowers and Trees," the first cartoon to use the sophisticated three-strip Technicolor system. Schlesinger refused, however, to take any actions to increase the budgets for the cartoons, with the result that Harman and Ising left the studio when the last of the three-year options expired. (Schlesinger would relent the following year, and the "Merrie Melodies" began to be produced in color in 1934.) Harman and Ising produced a pair of "Cubby Bear" cartoons for the Van Beuren Studio in the latter part of 1933, while they were negotiating for a permanent position.

Harman and Ising took the Bosko and Honey characters to MGM, at that time the premier movie studio in Hollywood, and started a brief series with the characters (eventually redesigned to be recognizable as black children), as well as a more sophisticated series, "Happy Harmonies," which were similar to the "Silly Symphonies" series produced by Disney in that they made lavish use of color and animation, set to music, to tell a story. Harman stated in later years that at this time he had been influenced by the work of the Russian filmmakers Sergei Eisenstein and V. I. Pudovkin. Backed by the substantial financial resources of MGM (budgets for the cartoons were more than double the budgets for the Warner Bros. cartoons), the series achieved some commercial and artistic success, with many of the cartoons being compared to the Disney studio's output, at that time viewed as the industry standard.

Starting in 1937, however, the management of MGM began to be concerned about the cost overruns on the Harman-Ising cartoons and took more active control over the production of the cartoons, bringing production in house and installing Fred Quimby (an allegedly humorless executive) as the chief producer. Harman and Ising continued to produce MGM's color cartoons, while other directors—most notably Isadore "Friz" Freleng, during a brief period when he was away from Warner Bros.—produced the studio's black-and-white cartoons. (Remarkably, Harman and Ising subcontracted to produce one cartoon for the Disney studio at that time, "Merbabies," which was released in 1938 in the "Silly Symphonies" series.)

In the late 1930s the studio did produce a number of notable cartoons. In 1939 Hugh Harman produced "Peace on Earth," a remarkable antiwar cartoon told from the point of view of animals that had survived a world war. Released during the early months of World War II, the cartoon had a significant impact (it was even cited by the Nobel Peace Prize jury), and even today it has a powerful effect. Ising in turn produced a cartoon with a cute little mouse, Cheezer, titled "The Milky Way," that became in 1940 the first non-Disney cartoon to win an Academy Award. Ising also produced the first Tom and Jerry cartoon in 1940, which was directed by (though not credited to) William Hanna and Joseph Barbera.

Harman and Ising continued to produce cartoons for MGM through 1942, but they were gradually eased out by MGM management, to be replaced by Hanna and Barbera, who took over Ising's unit, and Fred "Tex" Avery, the legendary animator who moved from Warner Bros. at that time to take over the Harman unit.

Harman teamed with former Disney staffer Mel Shaw to produce films for the military during the war and did some preliminary work with Orson Welles to produce an adaptation of Antoine de Saint-Exupéry's *The Little Prince*, which did not proceed to production, suffering the same fate that befell a proposed feature-length film based on the legend of King Arthur. Ising joined the U.S. Army Air Forces, becoming part of its 18th Air Force Base Unit, also known as the First Motion Picture Unit (FMPU), and taking charge of its animation unit, which produced numerous training films for the armed forces during World War II.

Neither Harman nor Ising was involved in the production or direction of theatrical cartoons again. Harman, though, is known to have produced industrial films for Stokeley Van Camp and the American Dental Association in the 1940s and is credited with writing one "Woody Woodpecker" cartoon for Walter Lantz in 1954 as well as some unsold pilots for television. Ising worked in the production of commercials and television programs during the same period and was honored by the International Animation Society in 1976.

Harman and Ising have a unique distinction in animation history. They were involved, at an early stage, in the creation of three studios that played a major role in animation: Disney, Warner Bros., and MGM. Some animation historians have criticized the work of Harman and Ising. Leonard Maltin has noted, with respect to the MGM cartoons, that "[w]hen one examines the body of Harman-Ising's work, the same-

ness is stultifying, and the cartoons' virtues diminish in importance"; with respect to the Warner Bros. cartoons, Maltin's judgment is that "it [is] hard to distinguish one H-I cartoon from another." This is, perhaps, a little harsh. As Maltin himself acknowledges, the individual cartoons remain bright and entertaining today, as they surely were when audiences first saw them. Many otherwise forgettable songs of the early 1930s survive, in part, because of the cheerful treatment given them by Harman and Ising in the early "Looney Tunes" and "Merrie Melodies." The MGM cartoons, with their lush, rich colors, can still impress, especially when paired with a moving story, such as "Peace on Earth," or a vigorously funny script, such as "Abdul the Bulbul Ameer." More importantly, Harman and Ising, while at Disney, Warner Bros., and MGM, nurtured a number of animators, including Friz Freleng, Bob Clampett, Bob McKimson, William Hanna, and Joe Barbera, who would go on to become some of the most significant animation directors of the 1930s, '40s and '50s. Harman and Ising, in a little over a decade, produced a body of work that had a quiet but significant impact on the Hollywood cartoon.

• Harman and Ising have not been made the subject of full-length biographies. However, much information about them can be found in two general animation history surveys: Leonard Maltin, *Of Mice and Magic: A History of American Animated Films* (rev. ed., 1987), and Charles Solomon, *Enchanted Drawings: The History of Animation* (rev. ed., 1994). Harman and Ising are featured prominently in Russell Merritt and J. B. Kaufman's survey of the silent-era Disney work, *Walt in Wonderland: The Silent Films of Walt Disney* (1993), which contains many interesting photographs of Harman and Ising during their formative period. Steve Schneider touches on the work of Harman and Ising in his survey of Warner Bros. cartoons, *That's All, Folks!* (1988). Jerry Beck and Will Friedwald's *Looney Tunes and Merrie Melodies: A Complete Illustrated Guide to the Warner Bros. Cartoons* contains detailed synopses of all of Harman and Ising's Warner Bros. cartoons, with commentary by the authors. (Jerry Beck extended the courtesy of reviewing a draft of this entry.) Harman's and Ising's respective obituaries are in the 30 Nov. 1982 and 23 July 1992 editions of rhe *New York Times*.

E. O. COSTELLO

HARRINGTON, Oliver W. (14 Feb. 1912–2 Nov. 1995), cartoonist, was born Oliver Wendell Harrington in New York City, the son of Herbert Harrington, a porter, and Euzenie Turat Harrington. His father came to New York from North Carolina in the early 1900s when many African Americans were seeking greater opportunities in the North. His mother had immigrated to America, arriving from Austria-Hungary in 1907, to join her half sister. Ollie Harrington grew up in a multiethnic neighborhood in the south Bronx and attended public schools. He recalled a home life burdened by the stresses of his parents' interracial marriage and the financial struggles of raising five children. From an early age, he drew cartoons to ease those tensions.

In 1927, Harrington enrolled at Textile High School in Manhattan. He was voted best artist in his class and started a club whose members studied popular newspaper cartoonists. Exposure to the work of Art Young, Denys Wortman, and Daniel Fitzpatrick later influenced his style and technique. About that time, toward the end of the Harlem Renaissance, he began to spend considerable time in Harlem and became active in social groups there. Following his graduation from Textile in 1931, he attended the National Academy of Design school. There he met such renowned artists and teachers as Charles L. Hinton, Leon Kroll, and Gifford Beal. During his years at the Academy, Harrington supported himself by drawing cartoons and working as a set designer, actor, and puppeteer.

In 1932 he published political cartoons and "Razzberry Salad," a comic panel satirizing Harlem society. They appeared in the *National News*, a newspaper established by the Democratic party organization in Harlem, which folded after only four months. He then joined the Harlem Newspaper Club and was introduced to reporters such as Ted Poston, Henry Lee Moon, and Roi Ottley of the *Amsterdam News*, as well as Bessye Bearden of the *Chicago Defender* and her son Romare Bearden. In 1933, Harrington submitted cartoons to the *Amsterdam News* on a freelance basis. During the next two years, he also attended art classes at New York University with his friend Romare Bearden. In May 1935, he joined the staff of the *News* and created "Dark Laughter," soon renamed "Bootsie" after its main character, a comic panel that he would draw for more than thirty-five years. Harrington remarked that "I simply recorded the almost unbelievable but hilarious chaos around me and came up with a character" (quoted in *Freedomways* 3, p. 519).

When the Newspaper Guild struck the *News* in October 1935, Harrington, while not a guild member, supported the strike and would not publish his cartoons until it was settled. During the strike, he became friends with journalists Benjamin J. Davis (later a New York City councilman) and Marvel Cooke, who were members of the Communist party. While probably not a party member, he maintained active ties to the left from that time. Harrington soon returned to freelance work and taught art in a WPA program. Edward Morrow, a Harlem reporter and graduate of Yale University, and Bessye Bearden encouraged him to apply to the School of the Fine Arts at Yale, which accepted him in 1936. Supporting himself with his "Bootsie" cartoons (which he transferred to the larger-circulation *Pittsburgh Courier* in 1938), scholarship assistance, and waiting on tables at fraternities, Harrington received a Bachelor of Fine Arts degree in 1940. He won several prizes for his paintings, although not a prestigious traveling fellowship at graduation, which he believed was denied him because of his race.

In 1942, after working for the National Youth Administration for a year, Harrington became art editor for a new Harlem newspaper, the *People's Voice*, edited by Adam Clayton Powell, Jr. He also created a new comic strip, "Jive Gray." In 1943 and 1944 he took a leave from the *Voice* to serve as a war correspondent for the *Pittsburgh Courier*. While covering African-American troops, including the Tuskegee Airmen, in Italy and France, he witnessed racism in the military to a degree he had not experienced before. In Italy he met Walter White, executive secretary of the National Association for the Advancement of Colored People (NAACP).

In 1946 White, who was attempting to strengthen the NAACP's public relations department following racial violence against returning veterans, hired Harrington as director of public relations. But by late 1947 the two had become estranged and Harrington resigned to become more active politically. With the "Bootsie" cartoons and book illustration work again his principal source of income, and after ending a brief wartime marriage, he joined a number of political committees in support of the American Labor party and Communists arrested in violation of the Smith Act. In 1950 he became art editor of *Freedom*, a monthly newspaper founded by Louis Burnham and Paul Robeson. He also taught art at the Jefferson School for Social Sciences, a school that appeared on the Attorney General's list of subversive organizations. Informed of his ties to the school, the FBI opened a file on Harrington.

By early 1952, with some of his friends under indictment and others facing revocation of their passports, Harrington left the United States for France. Whether he had knowledge of the FBI investigation is unclear, but by the time he reached Paris, the Passport Office there had been instructed to seize his passport if the opportunity arose. Meanwhile, Harrington settled into a life centered around the Café Tournon with a group of expatriate artists and writers that included Richard Wright and Chester Himes. Himes called Harrington the "best raconteur I'd ever known" (quoted in Himes, p. 35). His "Bootsie" cartoons and illustration work continued to provide income and he traveled throughout Europe. For a short time, following a brief second marriage in 1955, he settled in England, but he returned to Paris in 1956 as the Algerian War was worsening. The war divided the African-American community, and Harrington became embroiled in a series of disputes with other expatriates. His visit to the Soviet Union in 1959 as a guest of the humor magazine *Krokodil* again attracted intelligence officials.

Saddened by the death of his close friend Richard Wright, and his income dwindling due to financial difficulties at the *Courier*, in 1961 Harrington traveled to East Berlin for a book illustration project and soon settled there for the remainder of his life. He submitted cartoons to *Das Magasin* and *Eulenspiegl* and in 1968 became an editorial cartoonist for the *Daily Worker*, later *People's Weekly World*. His press credentials enabled him to travel to the West, and many of his old friends, including Paul Robeson and Langston Hughes, visited him in East Germany. In 1972 Harrington returned for a brief visit to the United States; in the 1990s he visited more regularly. In 1994, after the publication of two books of his cartoons and articles raised interest in his work, he was appointed journalist-in-residence for a semester at Michigan State University. He died in East Berlin. He was survived by his third wife, Helma Richter, and four children: a daughter from his second marriage, a son from his third, and two daughters from relationships with women to whom he was not married. Harrington's complex personal life, as well as his politics, was sometimes a motive for his travels.

Harrington was often referred to as a "self-exile," but he never described himself that way. "I'm fairly well convinced that one is an exile only when one is not allowed to live in reasonable peace and dignity as a human being among other human beings" (quoted in *Why I Left America*, p. 66). Remembered as the premier cartoonist of the African-American press for three decades and a central figure in the expatriate community in Paris in the 1950s, he battled racism through his art, his writings, and an alter ego named "Bootsie."

• Useful sources on Harrington's life include his two books edited by M. Thomas Inge, *Dark Laughter: The Satiric Art of Oliver W. Harrington* (1993) and *Why I Left America and Other Essays* (1993). An earlier collection of his cartoons, *Bootsie and Others*, with an introduction by Langston Hughes, was published in 1958. Several reminiscences by Harrington were published in the journal *Freedomways*, including "How Bootsie was Born," 3 (1963): 519–24; "Our Beloved Pauli," 11 (1971): 58–63; and "Look Homeward Baby," 13 (1973) 135–43, 200–215. For more on Harrington's Yale years, see James V. Hatch's biography of his friend Owen Dodson, *Sorrow Is the Only Faithful One: The Life of Owen Dodson* (1993). For additional information on the expatriate community in Paris, see Michel Fabre, *From Harlem to Paris* (1991); James Campbell, *Exiled in Paris* (1995); Tyler Stovall, *Paris Noir: African Americans in the City of Light* (1996); Hazel Rowley, *Richard Wright: The Life and Times* (2001); and the memoirs of Chester Himes, *My Life of Absurdity* (1976). An obituary is in the *New York Times*, 7 Nov. 1995. It contains some factual errors, as have other accounts of Harrington's life. These may stem from Harrington's own stories, his perception of what he wanted his image to be, or perhaps simply from his sense of mischief.

CHRISTINE G. MCKAY

HARRIS, Bill (28 Oct. 1916–21 Aug. 1973), trombonist, guitarist, and composer, was born Willard Palmer Harris in Philadelphia, Pennsylvania, the son of Willard Massey Harris, an attorney for the U.S. Marine Corps, and Mabel Palmer Harris. Bill's older half brother Robert was a professional bassist who performed with the Ted Weems Orchestra.

As a child, Harris studied piano for six months before contracting scarlet fever. Immediately following convalescence, he abandoned the piano and tried the tenor saxophone, trumpet, and drums before concentrating exclusively on the trombone. Although his father wanted him to study law, Harris spent much of his late adolescence employed in a number of occupations, including truck driver, electric meter reader, warehouse laborer, and semiprofessional musician. In 1935, partly in deference to his parents, Harris joined the Merchant Marines. Two years later he returned to

Philadelphia, where in 1938 he married Elizabeth "Bette" Alexander. They had three children. He resumed truck driving and performed part time at country clubs and wedding receptions with childhood contemporaries Buddy DeFranco and Charlie Ventura.

Harris did not pursue music full time until he was twenty-four. With the exception of sporadic lessons with Philadelphia brass instructor Donald Reinhart, he was completely self-taught and a poor sight reader. In 1941, on Ventura's recommendation, Harris was deputized a sideman for Gene Krupa's band; he was released after one week due to poor sight-reading. Similar results occurred two months later with the Ray McKinley band. An interim period with bandleader Buddy Williams of Dayton, Ohio, followed. In 1942, during Harris's temporary stint with Bob Chester, Benny Goodman heard Harris perform on a Chester radio broadcast and in 1943 invited him to join his group. He was with Goodman for nine months. When the band relocated to California for the filming of the movie *Sweet and Lowdown*, Harris purchased a home in Santa Monica and remained there when Goodman disbanded in early spring 1944. Engagements with Charlie Barnet and Freddy Slack followed before he was chosen by Goodman to lead a band at New York's Café Society with saxophonist Zoot Sims. In 1944, after another brief period with Chester, he joined Woody Herman's band at Detroit's Eastwood Gardens.

Harris's rambunctious and widely emulated trombone improvisations accelerated the popularity of Herman's first nationally recognized ensemble, known retrospectively as the "First Herd." His eccentric personality and reputation for outrageous practical jokes meshed well with other Herman band members such as tenor saxophonist Flip Phillips and bassist Chubby Jackson. The band's much-heralded recordings of Harris features, for example, "Bijou" and his own composition "Everywhere," led to victories in a number of music polls, including the *Down Beat* Reader's Poll (1945–1954), the *Down Beat* Critic's Poll (1953–1954) and the *Metronome* Reader's Poll (1946–1955). When Herman disbanded the "First Herd" in 1946, Harris led his own groups around New York and played intermittently with Charlie Ventura. In 1948 he rejoined Herman's new band.

When Herman disbanded this "Second Herd," Harris began a four-year association with Norman Granz's *Jazz at the Philharmonic*. Between JATP tours, he performed with Oscar Pettiford, Benny Carter, and the Sauter-Finnegan Orchestra. In 1956 he joined Herman's "Third Herd." After two years he departed over salary issues. Harris then moved his family to the Miami, Florida, area and lived in semi-retirement as a part-time disc jockey. In 1959 Herman coaxed him back for one more enlistment as part of the English-based Anglo-American Herd. A short time later, Harris accepted a second much shorter tenure with Goodman, performing in Europe and New York with a nine-piece band that included xylophonist Red Norvo, trumpeter Jack Sheldon, and Phillips.

Throughout the 1950s, in addition to his numerous JATP recordings, he was heard on a handful of albums, including *New Jazz Sounds* (1954) with Carter, *Bill Harris Herd* (1956), and *Bill Harris and Friends* (1957).

During the 1960s, Harris alternated between his Florida and Las Vegas residences, working regularly with Norvo and trumpeter Charlie Teagarden while fronting lounge bands on both trombone and guitar. His permanent exile from Las Vegas was sealed when a popular entertainer released him from his backup orchestra for (in his words) "looking too old." He was later dispatched from the employ of Miami's Tropicana Hotel, as part of a management-led initiative to downsize their brass section. With the exception of occasional performances with Phillips, his final days were spent in relative obscurity and his last means of support was as a security guard. His last notable performance was a JATP reunion at the Monterey Jazz Festival in 1971. Harris died in Coral Gables, Florida, of heart failure caused by his deteriorating physical condition after years of neglecting what had been a treatable form of cancer.

Contemporary disinterest in the Harris legacy is difficult to explain. Although strongly influenced by J. C. Higginbotham, he was an innovator of the first rank and arguably one of the most important transitional jazz stylists. His signature approach to jazz trombone playing served as an evolutionary bridge between progressive traditionalist Jack Teagarden and post-swing modernist J. J. Johnson. Harris's extroverted style, which included a trademark "burry" sound (wide tones with vibrato in each note), influenced an entire generation of musicians and helped to establish the trombone as a popular jazz solo instrument.

• Regrettably, there are few written examinations of Bill Harris, with the exception of anecdotal vignettes in Woody Herman biographies, most notably in Woody Herman and Stuart Troup, *The Woodchopper's Ball: The Autobiography of Woody Herman* (1990). See also William D. Clancy with Audree Coke Kenton, *Woody Herman: Chronicles of the Herds* (1995); Robert C. Kriebel, *Blue Flame: Woody Herman's Life in Music* (1995); and Gene Lees, *Leader of the Band: The Life of Woody Herman* (1995). Shorter observations include Leonard Feather, "Bill Harrasses His Horn," *Metronome* 41, no. 12 (1945): 27,45, and B. Lamb, "The Big Sound of Bill Harris," *Melody Maker* 15 (Sept.1973): 48. At present, the most comprehensive Harris research materials exist in private collections and are difficult to obtain.

TOM SMITH

HARRISON, Anna (25 July 1775–25 Feb. 1864), first lady to President William Henry Harrison, was born Anna Tuthill Symmes near Morristown, New Jersey, the daughter of John Cleves Symmes, a New Jersey Supreme Court justice and Revolutionary War soldier, and Anna Tuthill Symmes. After her mother died in 1776, she was reared by her father and her maternal grandparents. Her grandmother made sure that she received a proper education, and Anna took classes, both in classical languages and in English, first at the Clinton Academy in Easthampton and then at a New York City boarding school operated by Isabella Graham. After the Revolutionary War, Judge Symmes became a land speculator and judge in the Northwest Territory, settling near present-day Cincinnati. In 1795 he arranged for his daughter to move west with him. By then he had married Susanna Livingston. (A previous union with Mary Henry Halsey, about which there are few records, proved short-lived.)

Anna was small in stature with dark hair and eyes. She and her new stepmother visited with her older sister and brother-in-law, Maria and Peyton Short, in Kentucky, where in 1795 Anna met and fell in love with William Henry Harrison, an army lieutenant who was on leave from his post in the Ohio Territory. Judge Symmes, however, did not approve of his daughter's chosen mate or his occupation: Symmes viewed soldiers as being no better than criminals. The couple nevertheless wed on 25 November 1795 in the Symmeses' home while Judge Symmes was away on business. By 1813, Judge Symmes had come to accept and respect Harrison, naming him an executor of his estate.

Anna and William Henry Harrison developed a deep and loving relationship in which she provided the spiritual fortifications for the family, and he expanded his military and political career in Ohio and Indiana. Between 1796 and 1814 Anna Harrison gave birth to ten children. As was becoming acceptable for middle-class women in the nineteenth century, Anna Harrison was attended by a male physician, who had served in the army with her husband, for several of her deliveries.

The family lived first in the military garrison Fort Washington until Harrison resigned from the army in 1798 and purchased a large farm of more than 150 acres. The following year, the family journeyed to Philadelphia, where Harrison was serving as territorial delegate in the U.S. House of Representatives. In 1800 Anna Harrison gladly returned to Indiana with her husband when he was named territorial governor; she much preferred the frontier life to the social demands of the East Coast.

By 1804 the Harrisons were living in a thirteen-room mansion named "Grouseland" built especially for Anna Harrison. Harrison oversaw her husband's land holdings and her children's education and religious training. She also functioned as the social and cultural hostess of the territory. Her only demand while entertaining guests in the Indiana Territory was that there be no official functions on the Sabbath. The family's accounts were seldom balanced, in part because William Henry Harrison engaged in land speculation on relatively meager earnings and in part because Anna Harrison was a poor money manager.

During and after the War of 1812, Harrison faced challenges keeping her family together. She had to assume sole responsibility for parenting her children, since William Henry Harrison had rejoined the military. In addition, she and her children relocated to

Cincinnati in order to assure their safety. Also, she and her husband assumed responsibility for her father's physical and financial care when his home burned during the war and, after his death in 1814, rebuilt his home and managed his holdings.

Since William Henry Harrison's political career grew in importance after the war, Anna Harrison faced even more financial responsibilities as hostess to numerous public events in Ohio and as mother to a large family. Besides entertaining the many guests who passed through her home, Anna Harrison conducted a school for North Bend children in her twenty-two-room log cabin home.

When William Henry Harrison campaigned for the presidency in 1836 on the Anti-Masonic ticket and in 1840 on the Whig ticket, his wife was not pleased. Since she would have preferred that they remain in Ohio, his loss in 1836 did not disappoint her. When the results were different in 1840, Anna Harrison avoided making the journey to Washington, D.C., to take over her new responsibilities as first lady and instead asked that her daughter-in-law, Jane Irwin Harrison, act as the nation's hostess in her stead. Such a move was common among nineteenth-century first ladies, and her husband's premature death on 4 April 1841 meant that she never needed to leave her Ohio home.

As a widow, Harrison, her sole surviving son, John Scott Harrison, and her son-in-law, John Cleves Short, worked together to settle William Henry Harrison's estate. She became even more committed to her religious faith during her twilight years, proselytizing among her living children and grandchildren. However, she did not forego all things secular and kept abreast of national politics. She opposed slavery and supported her grandsons' military careers with the Union Army during the Civil War, telling one of her grandsons: "I do not feel as much concerned for you as I should: I have parted so often with your grandfather under similar circumstances, and he was always returned to me in safety, that I feel it will be the same with you."

While her life was typical for a woman of her economic and social stature, Harrison achieved several firsts for presidential spouses. Besides being the oldest first lady, she was the first first lady to receive a formal education, to never assume her official duties, to be widowed while her husband was still president, to receive a government pension, and to be the grandmother of a president (Benjamin Harrison). When she died she was buried next to her husband in North Bend on the Ohio River.

• Primary source materials on Anna Harrison's life are William Henry Harrison's papers and the Short Family Papers, both in the Library of Congress, Manuscripts Division. See also Beverley W. Bond, Jr., ed., *The Correspondence of John Cleves Symmes: Founder of the Miami Purchase* (1926), and Bond, ed., *The Intimate Letters of John Cleves Symmes and His Family Including Those of His Daughter, Mrs. William Henry Harrison, Wife of the Ninth President of the United States* (1956). For secondary source materials, see Laura C. Hol-

loway, *Ladies of the White House* (1870); Kathleen Prindiville, *First Ladies* (1941); Mary Ormsbee Whitton, *First First Ladies, 1789–1865: A Study of the Wives of the Early Presidents* (1948); Sol Barzman, *The First Ladies* (1970); Paul F. Boller, Jr., *Presidential Wives* (1988); Diana Dixon Healy, *America's First Ladies: Private Lives of the Presidential Wives* (1988); and Lewis L. Gould, ed., *American First Ladies: Their Lives and Legacy*, 2d ed. (2001). The information in Holloway, Whitton, and Gould is the most reliable.

NANCY BECK YOUNG

HARTSHORNE, Charles (5 June 1897–9 Oct. 2000), philosopher, was born in Kittanning, Pennsylvania, the son of Marguerite Haughton Hartshorne and Francis Cope Hartshorne, a clergyman. He entered Haverford College in 1915, leaving to join the Army Medical Corps for two years. He completed his college work at Harvard and in 1923 took the Ph.D. in philosophy there. Among his teachers were Ralph Barton Perry, William Ernest Hocking, Clarence Irving Lewis, H. M. Sheffer, and J. H. Woods. His dissertation was on "The Unity of All Things," a statement of the metaphysical system that he had developed at that time. He later described the position it presented, somewhat disparagingly, as "a qualified spiritual monism." Awarded a Sheldon fellowship, Hartshorne studied for two years in Europe, attending lectures by Edmund Husserl and Martin Heidegger.

Back at Harvard, he spent three years as an instructor and research fellow. He and Paul Weiss edited the papers of Charles Sanders Peirce, which were published in six volumes by Harvard University Press from 1931 to 1935. He found in Peirce a congenial spirit and appropriated many of his concepts. One year he was assistant to Alfred North Whitehead, whose thought, also, was congenial to the vision he had been shaping on his own and influenced his future formulations. Throughout his career he introduced students to Whitehead and expounded his ideas.

In 1928 Hartshorne joined the philosophy department at the University of Chicago, where, except for a Fulbright appointment in Australia, he taught until 1955. Also in 1928 he married Dorothy Cooper, who played an important role as editor and bibliographer of his writings. They had one child.

During his years at Chicago Hartshorne published a series of books that established him as a leading metaphysician. *Beyond Humanism* (1937) argued that human beings cannot understand themselves apart from the wider natural world and the divine. *Man's Vision of God* (1941) showed that when properly reformulated, and with a coherent idea of God, the traditional arguments for God are convincing. *The Divine Relativity* (1949) was a sustained argument that treating God only as absolute is both religiously and philosophically wrong. *Reality as a Social Process* (1953) developed the ideas that becoming, or process, is fundamental throughout reality, and that all the things that become are interrelated. These books established Hartshorne as a major challenge to dominant currents in both philosophy and theology.

Hartshorne's influence was as much on theologians as on philosophers, and, in due course, he received a joint appointment in the Divinity School. His commitment to constructing a new metaphysics and philosophy of religion was out of step with the climate of the time, including that of the Chicago philosophy department. He left Chicago in 1955 partly to find more congenial colleagues at Emory University. In 1962, approaching the mandatory retirement age at Emory, he moved to the University of Texas, which allowed him to teach until he was eighty. He continued to be a productive author during this period. He gave intensive attention to the ontological argument for the reality of God. (See *The Logic of Perfection and Other Essays in Neoclassical Metaphysics*, 1962, and *Anselm's Discovery*, 1965.) He was convinced that Anselm's second (modal) formulation of the argument was not vulnerable to the objections traditionally brought against the ontological argument in general. He insisted that the existence of God cannot be contingent. Either God necessarily exists, or it is necessarily true that God does not exist.

Hartshorne was a key figure in a wider movement of process thought, a naturalistic philosophy emphasizing that the "nature" of which human beings are a part is far richer than that depicted by materialists and determinists. It consists of events that have some existence and value in themselves and for themselves as well as influence on others. He did much to promote this movement, especially in its Whiteheadian form, and his own distinctive views have stamped it significantly. Among his most influential contributions to process thought, and especially to process theology and philosophy of religion, was his sustained critique of classical theism.

Hartshorne insisted that the traditional formulations of the doctrine of God were neither coherent nor religiously satisfactory. They affirmed only one side of what is embodied in real perfection, that is, the element of immutability and absoluteness. True perfection includes perfect relatedness and, thus, change. What remains changeless is God's perfect responsiveness to all that is changing. He opposed the classical doctrine of omnipotence. In its clearest form, this implies that God determines all events, just as they occur. It denies creaturely freedom and cannot avoid depicting God as directly responsible for all sin and evil. Hartshorne taught, in contrast, that God creates the conditions that provide the optimum balance of order and freedom. Within the limits set by God, creatures determine the details of what happens. Much takes place by chance interactions of decision-making creatures.

Another influential contribution was his defense of reason. Hartshorne argued against the widespread loss of confidence in reason, which expressed itself in the dominant philosophical community as the abandonment of metaphysics and of constructive philosophy generally. In theology, it led to fideism, the belief that teachings derived from revelation are not subject to rational evaluation. Hartshorne was convinced that much of the suspicion of reason came from particular intellectual mistakes that reason could itself correct rather than from an inherent weakness in reason.

Organizations promoting process thought in a form influenced by Hartshorne are active not only in the United States and Canada but also in such countries as Belgium, France, Hungary, Japan, Korea, China, and Australia. They are loosely connected through the International Process Network headquartered in Brisbane, Australia.

Although Hartshorne's fame rests chiefly on his philosophy, he also brought his philosophical views to bear in two scientific fields. His first book was an original development of the theory that all the senses constitute a single affective continuum (*The Philosophy and Psychology of Sensation*, 1934). He maintained from his youth an interest in birds, and on his extensive travels he recorded birdsongs. He taught that birds have a subjective life and are motivated by enjoyment of singing, and he compiled extensive data supporting this theory in *Born to Sing* (1973). At the age of one hundred he published *The Zero Fallacy and Other Essays in Neoclassical Philosophy* (1997)! Much of the content consisted of earlier essays; Mohammad Valady did the editing. Nevertheless, the book included new material by Hartshorne.

His wife died in 1995. He died at home in Austin five years later.

• The repository for Hartshorne's philosophical and theological writings is the Center for Process Studies, Claremont School of Theology, Claremont, California. His autobiography is *The Darkness and the Light* (1990). The best overview of his philosophy is *Creative Synthesis and Philosophic Method* (1970). Volume 20 of The Library of Living Philosophers is devoted to his thought: *The Philosophy of Charles Hartshorne* (1991); this contains a bibliography of his writings to that point. An obituary is in the *New York Times*, 13 Oct. 2000.

JOHN B. COBB, JR.

HARTZ, Louis (7 Apr. 1919–20 Jan. 1986), political scientist and historian, was born in Youngstown, Ohio, the son of Russian Jewish immigrants Max Hartz and Fannie Plotkin Hartz. Shortly after his birth, the family, which included two older boys, moved to Omaha, Nebraska, where his father ran a grocery. In 1936 with the help of a scholarship from a local newspaper, Louis entered Harvard. After compiling a brilliant record as an undergraduate and graduate student, earning an S.B. in 1940 and a Ph.D. in 1946, he joined the Harvard faculty, winning tenure at the early age of thirty-one, and rapidly made a name for himself as an enormously popular and effective teacher and an outstanding scholar with a national and international reputation. On 3 July 1943 he married Stella Feinberg; they had a son.

Three major books comprise the essence of Hartz's contribution to political science, while a fourth volume, although so obscure as to seem to lack scholarly value, shows such remarkable foresight that it cannot be neglected. The New Deal, which dominated the climate of political opinion during Hartz's student days, provided the impetus for his first book, published in 1948 and titled *Economic Policy and Democratic Thought: Pennsylvania, 1776–1860*. A common charge of the opponents of the New Deal was that government intervention in the economy violated the principles of free enterprise to which the country had been committed since its earliest days. But Hartz, like historians of the Progressive school, found evidence in early Pennsylvania of substantial government intervention in a political context of sharp conflict between certain business interests and a vigorous popular opposition. Both sides, he noted, appealed to principles, but the principles of each reflected the same capitalist ethos. What moved them was not principle but expediency. Louis Hartz's quarrel with American history had begun.

His next and most celebrated book, *The Liberal Tradition in America* (1955), gave to this disillusionment a keener intellectual edge by widening its focus from America alone to comparison with Europe. Despite America's boasted pluralism, Hartz argued, political conflict has always been confined by a parochial outlook, which he termed "liberalism." By that he meant a commitment in economic matters to capitalism and in politics to democracy. His device to bring out these limitations was the contrast with the far wider possibilities of politics revealed by comparison with Europe. There liberalism also flourished, but also in interaction and competition with socialism on its Left and a true conservatism on its Right.

Although Hartz is often classified with the consensus school of historians and political scientists, he was by no means complacent. Some critics have concluded that he wanted to see a greater role for Marxist socialism. But Hartz was never a Marxist in method or belief. His demonstration of how the liberal tradition dominated American society testifies to the power not of economic circumstances but of an idea.

Crucial to the power of liberalism, however, was a great void in American history, namely, the absence of a true social revolution. The French Revolution, conceived as the transition from a feudal to a bourgeois-liberal society, was the model, showing how class conflict, leading not only to political transformation but also and especially to economic transformation, could be an instrument of progress. America escaped that experience, since its settlers did not overthrow a feudal regime but fled from it to a new world. Lacking a feudal past, the historical memory of Americans had no foundation for a true Tory conservatism on European lines. More important, Americans were deprived of the conception of class and class conflict necessary to convert the economic presence of a proletariat into a socialist movement. On this fundamental level, Hartz rejected Marxism, indeed turned it upside down, finding in the power of an idea the explanation of that inexplicable nonevent for Marxists, "the absence of socialism " in this most capitalist of countries.

Hartz's third book, *The Founding of New Societies* (1964), transformed the specific thesis about America into a general hypothesis about new nations. Just as the first American settlers had founded their new nation on a liberal fragment of European political culture, so also, Hartz contended, other colonists from European countries had founded new nations on this and other fragments of the original cultural whole: bourgeois-liberal fragments in English Canada and Dutch South Africa, feudal fragments in Latin America and French Canada, and proletarian fragments in Australia and British South Africa. The Hartzian fragment theory had considerable influence on the field of comparative politics, especially the developing countries of the Third World. Its greatest impact, however, was in Canada, where for more than two decades the issues raised by Hartzian theory invigorated the study of Canadian political culture.

Already in the mid-1960s in one of his seminars, Hartz was struggling toward even more ambitious goals. Reflecting his continuous search for transcendence of current thinking about politics, his fourth book, grandly titled *A Synthesis of World History* (1983), attempted to construct a comprehensive view of the past that would open a vision of the future no less encompassing. The book attracted virtually no attention. Yet when one reviews its predictive outline of the high politics of the concluding decades of the twentieth century, it displayed remarkable prescience. Considering the years when this vision was being conceived—the preface is dated 1979—it is surely striking that Hartz made no reference to the conflicts of the Cold War, which then had another decade to run. On the contrary, he foresaw a radically different division of mankind, fundamentally the same as that spectrum of clashing civilizations that later became the focus of much scholarly analysis and journalistic observation.

In his sketch, Hartz identified five great "culture areas," each with its colonial fragments. Paralleling Europe's Christianity, these not surprisingly turn out to have a religious core: Islam, Hinduism, Confucianism, and African totemism. While in previous centuries each great culture could survive and develop intact, thanks to its geographical isolation, the recent increase in worldwide interaction had thrown them into "instant contiguity." Today we call this "globalization." Hartz did not, however, think that this confrontation would lead to intercultural conflict and war. He anticipated rather a new and comprehensive cultural integration as modernity, a European concept, would sweep over the world, perhaps subject to modification by the less rationalistic and more affectual values of other peoples. From his intense study of the local politics of early America, Hartz had expanded his focus to ever wider horizons, culminating in this intellectually stimulating, ethically provoking, and factually not entirely implausible vision of the politics of the whole world.

In the early 1970s, Hartz's highly successful professional career and quite normal personal and family life was brought to an end by the sudden onset of a severe emotional disturbance. No exact medical diagnosis could be made since one symptom of his illness was a resolute denial that anything was so wrong as to require medical attention. This breakdown led to estrangement from his family, including divorce in 1972, alienation from old friends, and finally a senseless conflict with the students, administration, and faculty. In 1974 he resigned from Harvard. Still mentally keen, however, he continued his scholarly work until his death from an epileptic seizure in Istanbul in 1986.

One of the most original and influential political scientists of his generation, Hartz made a wide and deep impact not only in his discipline but also in historical and humane studies. His work still shows no sign of fading as a baseline for critiques of American political culture.

• A comprehensive list of books and articles by and about Hartz is in Patricia Eugenia de los Rios Lozano, "Louis Hartz: Political Theorist," unpublished Ph.D. dissertation, Graduate School of the University of Maryland, 1994. The complete citations for the three major works are *Economic Policy and Democratic Thought: Pennsylvania, 1776–1860* (1948, repr. 1968); *The Liberal Tradition in America* (1955); and *The Founding of New Societies: Studies in the History of the United States, Latin America, South Africa, Canada and Australia* (1964). The citation for his last book, which was published by a "vanity press," is *A Synthesis of World History* (1983). Another volume published under his name and titled *The Necessity of Choice: Nineteenth Century Political Thought* (1990) is actually an attempt by some of his former students to reconstruct his lectures on that subject from notes they had taken in the course.

Deserving special emphasis are two articles, John Patrick Diggins, "Knowledge and Sorrow: Louis Hartz's Quarrel with American History," and Patrick Riley, "Louis Hartz: The Final Years, The Unknown Work," both of which appeared in *Political Theory*, vol. 16, no.3 (1988). These two essays were originally presented as papers at a conference on Hartz that took place at Harvard on 23 Jan. 1987 and was attended by a number of scholars from the United States and Canada. A recording of their discussion can be found in the Harvard Archives. A recording of the debate (on 9 Apr. 1974, in the Faculty of Arts and Sciences) regarding the issues raised by Hartz and leading to his resignation is available subject to the consent of the dean of that faculty.

As for his personal life, there is more detail in the de los Rios dissertation and, with regard to the events leading to his resignation from Harvard, in the present author's Memorial Minute published in the *Harvard Gazette*, vol. 89, no. 36 (27 May 1994). The Harvard Archives also have a substantial collection of his papers, including notes on seminars and lectures. Until 2006, however, access will require the consent of Hartz's son Steven, an attorney practicing in Miami, Florida. Obituaries are in the *New York Times* and the *Boston Globe*, 24 Jan.1986.

SAMUEL H. BEER

HASKELL, Charles Nathaniel (13 Mar. 1860–5 July 1933), first governor of Oklahoma, was born in Leipsic, Putnam County, Ohio, the son of George Haskell, a cooper, and Jane Reeves Haskell. Haskell was only three when his father died, and several years later he went to live with Thomas J. Miller, a school-

teacher in the community. Although only able to obtain a sporadic education in local common schools, by age seventeen Haskell had earned a teaching certificate. He spent several years teaching school while simultaneously studying law. Haskell was admitted to the state bar in 1880 and the following year moved to nearby Ottawa, where he set up his own practice. On 11 October 1881 he married Lucie Pomeroy, with whom he had three children before her death in 1888. In September 1889 he married Lillie Elizabeth Gallup; they had three children.

In 1887 Haskell expanded his horizons from law to business and enjoyed success as a railroad promoter. He incorporated and built the Finley, Fort Wayne & Western and later obtained the Ohio Southern line, which he then extended north to Detroit and south to Ironton, Ohio. He likewise extended the Columbus & Northwestern from Columbus to St. Mary's and around the end of the century was responsible for completing the Detroit & Toledo Shore Line. Also interested in telephone line construction, Haskell first ventured into the southwest in 1900 while engaged in projects in Texas. Attracted by possibilities within Indian Territory, he relocated to Muskogee (now in Oklahoma) in 1901 and quickly became one of the leading businesspeople of the area. In addition to building all or part of several rail lines (including the Frisco & Midland Valley Railroad and the Kansas, Oklahoma & Gulf), he set up a bank (the Territorial Trust & Banking Company), a hotel (the Turner), and a newspaper (the *New State Tribune*). Haskell also played a leading role in establishing the local streetcar company.

Haskell first became active in politics as a member of the so-called Sequoyah Convention of 1905, which met at Muskogee and drafted a constitution for the proposed new state of Sequoyah, which was to be created from the old Indian Territory. Part of the modern state of Oklahoma, the area had been originally settled by members of the Five Civilized Tribes (Cherokee, Chickasaw, Choctaw, Seminole, and Creek), who had been forcibly relocated there during the nineteen century. The Indian Territory was bordered by Oklahoma Territory to its west. The Native American population of the Indian Territory, while willing to consider statehood, had no desire to be dominated by the white settlers of Oklahoma Territory. Hence one of the great issues of the day in the area was whether the two territories were to be admitted to the Union as one or two states and under what conditions.

As one of the vice presidents of the convention, Haskell worked to assuage the concerns of the various constituencies within the convention and helped produce a remarkable constitution that was considered a model of progressivism for its day. Among its provisions were regulations for child and female labor and for purity levels in food and drugs. Although the convention's efforts came to naught when Congress rejected the proposed admission, Haskell gained valuable experience and as such was a natural choice for floor leader of the Democrats (the majority party) when another convention met the following year. With political sentiments clearly favoring the admission of the Twin Territories as the state of Oklahoma, Haskell played a leading role as a member of the so-called Constitutional Cabal, along with Robert L. Williams and William "Alfalfa Bill" Murray, in drafting the constitution that was ultimately accepted when Oklahoma gained admission to the Union in 1907. That year Haskell won an overwhelming victory as the Democratic nominee for governor and was inaugurated on 16 November 1907.

In addition to setting up the new state government, Haskell signed into law considerable progressive legislation, including child labor statutes and a graduated income tax. Perhaps the most innovative development was a measure that guaranteed bank depositors against losses from bank failures. The law later served as a model for the Federal Deposit Insurance Corporation legislation of the 1930s. Less progressive, however, was legislation that made Jim Crow racial segregation the law of the land, as was the so-called "grandfather clause" law that attempted to disenfranchise African Americans. Haskell served as the treasurer of the Democratic National Committee in 1908 and played a key role in helping the party presidential nominee William Jennings Bryan carry Oklahoma that fall. Haskell was forced to resign his post, however, when allegations arose during the campaign that he had accepted bribes from Standard Oil Company.

Haskell's most controversial moment as governor concerned the location of the state capital, then at Guthrie. Voters on 11 June 1910 decided in favor of abrogating a portion of the Enabling Act (which granted statehood) that mandated the capital remain at Guthrie until 1913. On the night of the election, Haskell moved the state seal to the Lee-Huckins Hotel in Oklahoma City and declared it the state capital. While controversial, his decision was later upheld by both the state and federal Supreme Courts.

Broken in health and finances and unable to succeed himself, Haskell left office in 1911. After failing to gain the nomination to the U.S. Senate in 1912, he helped organize the Middle States Oil Corporation and spent the 1920s engaged in a variety of business ventures, including the Louisiana & Northwestern Railroad Company (1922), a Mexican toll road (1927), the Municipal Gas Company of Muskogee (1929), and the Sapulpa Gas Company. Although he lived in New York during the later portion of his life, he died in Oklahoma City.

Haskell's place in history is secure by virtue of his status as the first governor of Oklahoma. Perhaps more importantly, he belongs among the ranks of countless self-made businesspeople of the late nineteenth century who later made solid contributions to the public lives of their respective communities.

• Haskell's papers are at the Oklahoma Historical Society in Oklahoma City. He is the subject of Oscar Presley Fowler, *The Haskell Regime: The Intimate Life of Charles Nathaniel Haskell* (1933). A good modern treatment of his life and career is in H. Wayne and Anne Hodges Morgan, *Oklahoma: A Bicentennial History* (1977). Obituaries are in the *Oklahoma City Daily Oklahoman*, 6 July 1933, and the *New York Times*, 6 July 1933.

EDWARD L. LACH, JR.

HASSENFELD, Merrill (19 Feb. 1918–21 Mar. 1979), toy manufacturer, was born in Providence, Rhode Island, the son of Henry Hassenfeld, a Polish Jewish immigrant toy maker, and Marion Frank Hassenfeld. In 1923 Henry Hassenfeld and his brothers, Harold, Hillel, and Herman, founded what became Hasbro Industries. The firm, then called Hassenfeld Brothers, initially made pencil boxes and other school supplies. Merrill graduated from the University of Pennsylvania in 1938. That same year he joined the Providence-based company. During World War II, he manufactured play doctor and nurse kits and air raid warden sets.

From 1943 through 1944, Hassenfeld was president of Hasbro (as the company was called by 1952). In 1952 he introduced Mr. Potato Head (acquired from the Brooklyn toy inventor George Lerner). In 1964 he promoted the male action figure G.I. Joe, which had been originated in 1963 by Don Levine (the director of marketing and development whom Hassenfeld had astutely hired in 1956). Hassenfeld also presided over some failures, most notably the bouncing compound Flubber (purportedly "flying rubber"), modeled after the mythical substance in the Disney movie *Son of Flubber* (sequel to *The Absent-Minded Professor*) released in 1963. But when the Silly Putty–like substance made of rubber and mineral oil was accused of causing rashes, Hassenfeld dutifully recalled it at tremendous expense. He buried it behind his company's new warehouse (and also, reportedly, in his own backyard) and paved it over with a parking lot when local dumps would not take it and the Coast Guard would not allow him to dispose of it in Narragansett Bay.

Hassenfeld was an important bridge between the founding generation of Hassenfelds in America and the succeeding group, represented by his late son (and immediate heir), Stephen, and his younger son (and later chairman and CEO of Hasbro), Alan. The middle child of his wife, the former Sylvia Kaye, whom he had married in 1940, was their daughter Ellen Hassenfeld Block. She did not actively enter the toy-making industry. Thus, Hasbro remained true to the derivation of its name, the Hassenfeld Brothers Company.

A good negotiator, Hassenfeld was honored and well liked in the toy industry. He was also active in community life, serving as 1968 United Way chairman, president of the Jewish Federation of Rhode Island, honorary national chairman of the United Jewish Appeal, and a trustee of Brandeis University. The latter institution, which he helped to found, made Hassenfeld a fellow in 1963. With his death from a heart attack during a Hasbro committee meeting in Providence, the two branches of his family split the business. His brother Harold's family took over the Empire Pencil Company in Tennessee, while Merrill's family kept the toy business. The Toy Hall of Fame inducted Hassenfeld into its ranks in 1985.

• Good accounts of Hasbro, Inc.'s competitive relationships with other toy manufacturers and its ultimate success are found in G. Wayne Miller, *Toy Wars: The Epic Struggle between G.I. Joe, Barbie, and the Companies That Make Them* (1998), and Sydney Stern and Ted Schoenhaus, *Toyland: The High-Stakes Game of the Toy Industry* (1990). A good overview of the G.I. Joe action figure is Ed Liebovitz, "Macho in Toyland," *Smithsonian*, Aug. 2002, pp. 26–27. For comparative stories of the New England family-based firms of Milton Bradley, A. C. Gilbert, Hasbro, and Parker Brothers, see Frederick J. Augustyn, Jr., "The American Switzerland: New England as a Toy-Making Center," *Journal of Popular Culture* (Summer 2002): 1–13. Obituaries of Hassenfeld are in the 22 Mar. 1979 issues of the *New York Times*, the *Boston Globe*, the Providence *Journal*, and the Pawtucket *Evening Times*.

FREDERICK J. AUGUSTYN, JR.

HAWKINS, Erskine (26 July 1914–11 or 12 Nov. 1993), trumpet player, swing bandleader, was born Erskine Ramsay Hawkins in Birmingham, Alabama, the son of Edward Hawkins, a soldier, and Carey Hawkins (maiden name unknown), a teacher. Hawkins's father was killed in World War I while serving in France. His mother exposed Erskine and his four siblings to music. Hawkins began his musical education at five, initially playing drums and later moving on to alto saxophone, baritone saxophone, and trombone throughout his youth. From the time he was eight till he was twelve, he played in four- and five-piece bands during the summer. These performances took place at Tuxedo Park, just outside of Birmingham, where local musicians often gathered. Hawkins would later make the location famous with his hit "Tuxedo Junction." It was Hawkins's music teacher, S. B. Foster, a trumpet player (referred to affectionately as "High-C" Foster), who persuaded Hawkins to take up the trumpet.

In 1930 Hawkins earned an athletic scholarship to the Alabama State Teachers College in Montgomery, where, intending to follow in his mother's footsteps, he pursued a bachelor of science degree. Within a few weeks, Hawkins discontinued his athletic endeavors and turned his attention to the school's jazz band. Initially, he was accepted into the school's second tier band, the 'Bama State Revelers. There, he joined several childhood friends from Birmingham. They included Haywood Henry (clarinet and saxophone), Wilbur "Dud" Bascomb (trumpet) and his brother Paul (saxophone), Avery Parrish (piano), and Bob Range (trombone), many of whom later joined the Erskine Hawkins Orchestra. At college, Hawkins also took private music lessons.

After several weeks, Hawkins was moved up to the school's top-tier band, the 'Bama State Collegians. Shortly thereafter, several of his bandmates were also promoted. At the time, J. B. Sims was the leader of the 'Bama State Collegians, who played several nights a week. The experience proved helpful to their development, and soon they earned some professional gigs and gained local popularity. The profits went directly to the school, which allocated to the band members, many of them scholarship students, a small portion of the revenue for spending money.

The Collegians attracted the attention of booking agent Joe Glaser, who got the group a gig at the Grand Terrace Ballroom in Chicago. In 1934, the band did a tour of one-night stands, traveling as far as Asbury Park, New Jersey. The Asbury Park show proved very important. Several New York luminaries, including John Hammond, Benny Carter, and Frank Schiffman, the owner of the Apollo Theatre and the Harlem Opera House, came especially to hear Hawkins.

In 1935, Schiffman offered the Collegians an extended engagement at the Harlem Opera House, where they were well received. The same year, Hawkins married Florence Browning. Due to their success at the Harlem Opera House, and to Hawkins's spectacular trumpet playing, the band garnered immediate bookings, although they were not as polished as some of New York's top dance bands.

The band signed with their first manager, known only as "Feet" Edson, who had convinced them to remain in New York rather than return to school. The band recorded their first album that year for the U.S. Vocalion label; they recorded several subsequent sessions for Vocalion from 1936 through 1938, billed as Erskine Hawkins and His 'Bama State Collegians. However, now signed to formal management, and with all the members of the Collegians no longer attending school, the group had to relinquish use of that name. They also did shows at the Apollo Theatre and eventually got a steady gig at the Ubangi Club in Harlem that lasted two years.

In 1936, the group did a stint at the Savoy Ballroom, alternating with Chick Webb's orchestra. At the Savoy, Hawkins became acquainted with the club's owner, Moe Gale, who was a well-connected booking agent, and in 1937 Hawkins signed a management contract with him. Gale engineered a recording contract for the band with RCA Victor's Bluebird label and established the band as a main attraction at the Savoy, where it became a fixture until the club's closing in the 1950s. Under new management, and with a new record contract, the band would now be billed as "Erskine Hawkins (the 20th-Century Gabriel) and His Orchestra." During its prime, the group did long stints at the Copacabana and the Blue Room and toured extensively through the South, the Midwest, and California.

In 1939, the band recorded arguably its greatest hit, "Tuxedo Junction." Initially, the tune was never intended for recording. As legend has it, the band was in the studio and needed to record one more track to complete the session. They decided to expand the short riff they used at the club to signal the alternating band to the bandstand (the Savoy had two bands that would rotate, each doing forty-minute sets), haphazardly naming it "Tuxedo Junction," in honor of the trolley stop near Tuxedo Park where Hawkins had played when he was young. The tune became an instant hit, selling over a million copies. Soon thereafter, Glenn Miller recorded "Tuxedo Junction," selling even more records than Hawkins; later, Gene Krupa recorded it as well.

In 1940 Hawkins scored another major hit with "After Hours," a tune that came about when another song, "Fine and Mellow," which featured vocals, proved to be too long. Several choruses of solo piano were cut. Later, the choruses were used as the basis for an instrumental and given the name "After Hours" by RCA Victor's producers. The bluesy track, which prominently featured Avery Parrish, the band's pianist, influenced many pianists of that generation. In 1945, the band scored another hit with "Tippin' In."

In 1947 Hawkins was awarded an honorary doctorate of music from the Alabama State Teachers College. In 1950, he was granted a legal separation from his first wife. Later he married Gloria Dumas (the date of their marriage is unknown). He had no children in either of his marriages. That same year, Hawkins's contract with RCA Victor was terminated; he then took part in three recording sessions with the Coral label. He signed with Decca in 1954. His band, however, continued to dwindle. By the time the band recorded an album for the label in 1961, there were only six members. Hawkins continued leading small bands, and in 1967 was contracted by the Concord Hotel at Kiamesha Lake, New York. This engagement lasted over twenty years, keeping Hawkins playing into his seventies; he also continued making frequent festival appearances.

A reunion was arranged and recorded by Platinum Records, for which Sam Lowe (former Hawkins band member and arranger) now worked as an A&R man; those present included "Dud" and Paul Bascomb and Haywood Henry from the original band. In 1989 Hawkins was awarded a Lifetime Work Award for Performing Achievement from the Alabama Hall of Fame. He died in his home in Willingboro, New Jersey; the date appears variously as 11 or 12 November.

"Erskine Hawkins and His Band" never enjoyed the success with white audiences of groups such as the Jimmie Lunceford band. The Hawkins band, however, is remembered best for providing impeccable swing for dancers, tasteful arrangements, and a sense of camaraderie and teamwork. Undoubtedly, this tone was set by Hawkins, who often allowed his soloists, especially his first-chair trumpeter Wilbur "Dud" Bascomb, to solo as much as he did.

• For biographical information on Hawkins, see Gene Fernett's *Swing Out* (1970), which features an entire chapter on Hawkins, including an interview with Hawkins band member Haywood Henry and several early photographs. Albert McCarthy devotes three pages to Hawkins in *Big Band Jazz* (1977), which offers biographical information mixed with musical criticism. Chip Deffaa's "Erskine Hawkins—Twentieth-Century Gabriel" in *The Mississippi Rag* (May 1990) offers an extensive interview with Hawkins recounting the height of his success in Harlem. Gerald Gold's "Erskine

Hawkins Blows," featured in the *New York Times*, 10 Apr. 1988, is mainly a retrospective piece, with Hawkins interviewed, and helpful information on his later years. For a comprehensive Erskine Hawkins discography, check the *All Music Guide to Jazz* (1998). An obituary is in New Jersey's *Sunday Star Ledger*, 14 Nov. 1993.

BRIAN FORÉS

HENDERSON, Joe (24 Apr. 1937–30 June 2001), jazz tenor saxophonist, was born Joseph Arthur Henderson in Lima, Ohio, the son of Dennis Lloyd Henderson, a steel-mill worker, and Irene Farley. Henderson was one of fifteen children, and his interest in jazz was sparked by an older brother's collection of recordings. He took up clarinet in elementary school and briefly played the now-obscure C-melody saxophone before settling on the larger tenor sax. When Henderson was getting started, that same brother helped him imitate a simple blues solo recorded by the tenor saxophonist Lester Young. Henderson progressed rapidly. While in high school he began performing professionally, wrote his first composition, "Recordame," and gained a working knowledge of the piano from two local professional pianists who had been classmates of his siblings.

In his late teens Henderson married and had a son; further details of this relationship are unknown. After he graduated from high school, Henderson left Lima to study music at Kentucky State College in Frankfort. One year later he moved to Detroit and continued his education, studying flute and double bass at Wayne State University and saxophone and music theory from the head of the Teal School of Music, Larry Teal. Henderson played locally in jazz and rhythm-and-blues groups and by 1960 was leading his own band.

Inducted into the army in 1960, Henderson gained a place in an army band at Fort Benning, Georgia. He reached the finals of an army talent show as a member of a jazz quartet and as a consequence of this exposure was invited to tour worldwide as a bassist in a combo entertaining troops. He doubled on saxophone as circumstances allowed. Discharged in August 1962, Henderson soon thereafter went to New York City. There he met the trumpeter Kenny Dorham and, through Dorham's introduction, made an impressive debut sitting in on a tune for the saxophonist Dexter Gordon at the club Birdland at Gordon's invitation. After working with the organist Brother Jack McDuff and spending a brief period in Las Vegas as a member of the band accompanying the Four Tops, Henderson returned to New York and established a jazz quintet as coleader with Dorham.

In April 1963 Henderson found himself in a studio for the first time, recording Dorham's album *Una Mas* for the Blue Note label as a member of a small group including Herbie Hancock on piano and Tony Williams on drums. The strength of Henderson's playing led to an invitation to participate in numerous Blue Note sessions through the remainder of the decade. Under his own name Henderson mainly recorded albums of his own and Dorham's compositions. Some of Henderson's themes became jazz "standards," a part of the music's permanent repertory. By far the best known of these is "Recordame," his composition from high school, recorded in a version modified from the original to reflect the rhythms of the then-current bossa nova style (and perhaps also acquiring its Brazilian-ish title at this time) on Henderson's initial album as a leader, *Page One* (June 1963). Other notable compositions include the title tracks of his albums *In 'n Out* and *Inner Urge* (both recorded in 1964), presenting fast, twisting, harmonically challenging themes that continued to serve as vehicles for saxophone virtuosity for younger generations of players, with Henderson's own recorded tenor saxophone solos showing the way. In "Punjab" and "Serenity," from *In 'n Out*, he situated his penchant for long melodic phrases and elusive harmony into relaxed, swinging contexts, and in "Isotope," from *Inner Urge*, he crafted a clever blues melody that stretched across nearly the whole twelve-bar form in a single grand phrase. His Blue Note albums from later in the decade presented further compositions, including "A Shade of Jade" on the album *Mode for Joe* (recorded in 1966) and the title tracks of *The Kicker* (1967), *Tetragon* (1967–1968), and *Black Narcissus* (1969), the last a pretty jazz waltz.

As a sideman for Blue Note, Henderson recorded notable tenor saxophone solos at sessions led by the guitarist Grant Green, the trumpeters Lee Morgan and Dorham, and the pianists Andrew Hill and Horace Silver. In the title track of Green's LP *Idle Moments* (made in Nov. 1963) Henderson improvised with exactly the same sort of delicate perfection that figured prominently on his CD *Lush Life* nearly three decades later. On Hill's album *Point of Departure* (recorded in Apr. 1964) Henderson played a sort of avant-garde bebop alongside Dorham, the reed player and flutist Eric Dolphy, the bassist Richard Davis, and Williams. Though never as radical a soloist as Dolphy, Henderson improvised in a manner that at moments approached free jazz. The other dates displayed Henderson at his earthiest, playing with a solid awareness of rhythm-and-blues tenor saxophone styles on the title track of Morgan's LP *The Sidewinder* (recorded in Dec. 1963) and improvising a memorable, tuneful Latin-jazz melody of ever-increasing intensity on Silver's album *Song for My Father* (Oct. 1964). Dorham's *Trumpet Toccata*, from September 1964, includes Henderson's most dance-oriented composition, the Latin blues "Mamacita."

In the spring of 1964 Henderson replaced Junior Cook in Silver's quintet, with which he toured and recorded for two years. After leaving Silver in 1966, he put together a rehearsal big band with Dorham in New York City. This was a no-budget gathering of dedicated musicians who rehearsed in the afternoon at The Dom, a nightclub in Greenwich Village. Dorham dropped out of the band the following year, but Henderson kept it going until he moved to the West Coast in 1972. Henderson played occasionally in

Miles Davis's band early in 1967, and he co-led the Jazz Communicators with the trumpeter Freddie Hubbard around 1968. Henderson performed and recorded as a soloist with the pianist Wynton Kelly's trio at the Left Bank Jazz Society in Baltimore in mid-April 1968, and from 1969 to 1970 he was a member of Hancock's sextet, with which he made two albums. In 1971 Henderson joined the group Blood, Sweat, and Tears, but he found this affiliation boring and quit after only four months despite the offer of a six-figure salary. Henderson repeatedly placed artistic concerns over finance, and as it turned out major financial success came to him anyway, later in life, on his own terms. Around this time Henderson married Linda. They had no children. Other details are unknown.

In 1972 Henderson settled in San Francisco. He worked whenever he wanted, both locally and in the Northwest and regularly in Japan and Europe, but he returned to New York for performances only rarely during the 1970s and 1980s. His friends nicknamed him "the Phantom" for his propensity to drop out of sight after stressful periods of work. When his schedule allowed, he also taught saxophone in San Francisco. He was deeply devoted to his students, one of whom, Karlton Hester, described Henderson as a "modern-day Griot," explaining that a single lesson from Henderson would be several hours long, "rich in Zen-like musical content," and "unrelenting in its attention to detail."

In the early 1980s Henderson appeared in Europe with such accompanists as the pianists George Gruntz and Tete Montoliu, and he performed and recorded with Hubbard and the pianist Chick Corea in small groups in New York and California. An excerpt from an Italian tour with Corea in 1982 was captured on the video *Chick Corea and Band: A Very Special Concert*, released in 1985. In mid-November 1985 Henderson recorded a two-volume album, *The State of the Tenor*, in a series of trio performances with the bassist Ron Carter and the drummer Al Foster at the Village Vanguard in New York. Henderson made another trio album while on tour with the bassist Charlie Haden and Foster in Italy in 1987, and in 1988 he recorded *The Countdown* in Berkeley, California, in a quartet led by the pianist Mulgrew Miller.

For many years Henderson enjoyed interpreting Thelonious Monk's composition "Ask Me Now." A version revealing his playing at its best is on the album *Tenor Tribute*, recorded in Germany in 1988 under the leadership of the saxophonist Arnett Cobb (but without Cobb on this track). In the late 1980s and early 1990s, perhaps with an eye toward encouraging women in jazz, Henderson made a number of tours as the principal soloist with a band of women accompanists, most notably providing the first major exposure for the Canadian pianist Renee Rosnes. He also made yet another trio album, this time with the bassist Rufus Reid and Foster, in New York in 1991.

In 1992, ironically during an era when the recording industry was brutally rushing young musicians into the limelight, the veteran Henderson catapulted to fame with *Lush Life*, an album of compositions by Billy Strayhorn recorded the previous autumn. In 1993 Henderson released an album of pieces associated with Miles Davis, *So Near, So Far (Musings for Miles)*. These discs won Grammy Awards, each as instrumental jazz album of the year, and Henderson's playing throughout them is masterful. On *Lush Life*, Henderson's thematic statements and improvisations range from tender, gorgeous melodies to abstract, cerebral lines to sustained passages of hard-driving swing and bebop. *So Near, So Far* places Henderson in partnership with the guitarist John Scofield, accompanied by Dave Holland on bass and Foster on drums, and focuses on the more forthright elements of his musical personality.

By the late 1980s Henderson had reestablished his big band in San Francisco, and he occasionally presented it in public in the Bay Area beginning around 1990. Following the success of *Lush Life*, he was invited to present a big band at Lincoln Center in New York in 1992, and at that time he recorded portions of his last great album, *Joe Henderson Big Band*. Thereafter he maintained a version of the group in both San Francisco and New York. Henderson completed the big band disc in New York in 1996, after he had issued another acclaimed small-group date, *Double Rainbow: The Music of Antonio Carlos Jobim* (recorded in 1994), although this bossa nova album, which brought him yet another Grammy Award, was not quite at the level of the previous Strayhorn and Davis projects.

Henderson's last major endeavor in 1997 was a less-successful recording of pieces from *Porgy and Bess*. He had emphysema for many years and was obliged to stop playing in public after suffering a stroke in 1998. He died in San Francisco.

• Four meticulously prepared books of musical transcriptions of Henderson's compositions and improvisations, two drawing from the Blue Note years and two from the Grammy Award–winning albums, are Don Sickler, *The Artistry of Joe Henderson*, ed. Bobby Porcelli (c. 1978); [Anonymous], *Joe Henderson: Artist Transcriptions, Saxophone: Selections from "Lush Life" & "So Near, So Far"* (1995); Jim Roberts, *The Best of Joe Henderson* (c. 1996); and James Farrell Vernon, *Joe Henderson's Transcribed Solos for Tenor Sax* (c. 1996). The earliest essay on Henderson is by Kenny Dorham in the trumpeter's liner notes to the album *Page One* (1963). Henderson was not the subject of an interview in a major jazz magazine until the appearance of Ray Townley's essay "The Herculean Tenor of Joe Henderson," *Down Beat* 42 (16 Jan. 1975): 18–20, 40–41, and that piece is useful for little more than revealing the depth of Henderson's irritable reaction to being compared to Sonny Rollins and John Coltrane. Substantial later essays are George Goodman, Jr., "Jazz: Joe Henderson Pays a Rare Visit," *New York Times*, 27 Oct. 1977; David Woods, "Joe Henderson," *Jazz Journal International* 44 (Dec. 1991): 6–8; Howard Reich, "Sax Appeal: Uncovering the Lush Elegance of Joe Henderson," *Chicago Tribune*, 16 Aug. 1992; Mel Martin, "Joe Henderson," *Saxophone Journal*, Vol. 15 (Mar.–Apr. 1991): 12–14, 16–20; Zan Stewart, "Joe Henderson's Years at the Top," *Down Beat* 60 (May 1993): 17–20; and Don Heckman, "Joe Henderson: Paying Homage to Jobim," *Jazz Times* 25 (June 1995): 34–36, 38–39. An obituary by Ben Ratliff is in the *New York Times*, 3 July 2001.

BARRY KERNFELD

HENRY, Ernie (3 Sept. 1926–29 Dec. 1957), jazz saxophonist, was born Ernest Albert Henry in Brooklyn, New York. His parents' names and occupations are not presently known, but his father played piano and his sister was a piano teacher and church organist. Henry studied piano at age eight, violin at age ten. At age twelve he picked up the alto saxophone, which was to be his primary instrument for the rest of his life. Brooklyn at the time was home to a number of young jazz musicians, including drummer Max Roach, baritone saxophonist Cecil Payne, and pianist Randy Weston. This community of young musicians helped foster Henry's development, and he would work with Payne throughout his professional career.

After serving in the army, Henry began his professional career and joined the musician's union (local 802) in 1947. On 27 August 1947 he made his recording debut, recording four tunes with vocalist Kenny Hagood for Savoy records. That same year, Henry worked at the Onyx Club on 52nd Street in Manhattan with pianist, composer, and arranger Tadd Dameron. At the time, 52nd Street was the center of bebop, the new movement in jazz. Dameron's band also featured the outstanding bebop trumpeter Theodore "Fats" Navarro. On 26 September 1947, Dameron recorded four of his compositions (two takes of each) with Henry and Navarro for Blue Note records. Henry's performances that day were uneven. On both takes of "The Squirrel," a medium-tempo twelve-bar blues, his phrasing was awkward and his saxophone technique uncertain. However, on both takes of "Our Delight," a moderately fast bebop tune, his solo exhibited mastery of the difficult chord progression. The influence of saxophonist Charlie Parker was unmistakable; however, this did not diminish the talent that Henry showed, as every young saxophonist of the time was highly influenced by Parker.

By the summer of 1948, Henry joined the big band of trumpeter John Birks "Dizzy" Gillespie, perhaps the greatest star of bebop. Henry sat next to Cecil Payne, his acquaintance from Brooklyn, in the reed section. During a July 1948 concert at the Pasadena Civic Auditorium, Gillespie featured Henry for the first sixteen bars of Thelonious Monk's composition "'Round Midnight" (recorded and released on GNP records). Henry's intensely personal and soulful interpretation of the melody received a tremendous ovation from the capacity crowd. In October 1948, Henry recorded with Navarro and trumpeter Howard McGhee for Blue Note records. Henry's solo on McGhee's blues "The Skunk" was masterful. His earlier awkwardness was gone and his unique bluesy style was emerging. Henry left Gillespie in 1949. From 1950 to 1952 he worked with saxophonist Illinois Jacquet, recording with Jacquet for Verve. Henry did not have a featured solo. He then sank into obscurity.

Many bebop jazz musicians became addicted to narcotics, and Henry was no exception. To complicate matters, he was battling with high blood pressure.

Orrin Keepnews, a record producer for Riverside, believes that Henry lacked self-confidence. On the recommendation of pianist Randy Weston, one of Henry's old Brooklyn acquaintances, Keepnews in 1956 went to hear Henry at a jam session in Brooklyn. Henry had also been endorsed by pianist Thelonious Monk, Riverside's newest and biggest star. Keepnews signed Henry immediately. On 23 August 1956, after nearly ten years of sideman roles and obscurity, Henry made his recording debut as leader. For the date, which included trumpeter Kenny Dorham, pianist Kenny Drew, and drummer Arthur Taylor, Henry wrote three original compositions and chose one standard, "Gone With the Wind." A week later, Henry returned to the studio with the same ensemble to record two more original compositions and another standard, "I Should Care."

By now, Henry's unique personal style had fully emerged. He was never a technically sophisticated player, and thus he avoided doubling the time on slower tempos and rarely played long phrases on fast tempos. The strident quality of Henry's tone, along with a penchant for sustained bent notes, gave his playing an emotional, urgent quality. This approach was most effective when playing the blues, as can be heard on Henry's minor key composition "Cleo's Chant" from the 30 August date. Henry's recording of "I Should Care," from the same day, displayed his remarkable sensitivity when playing ballads.

By December 1956 Henry was back to steady work with Dizzy Gillespie's big band, which at the time was packed with young talent including Lee Morgan, Benny Golson, and Wynton Kelly. On 23 September 1957, Henry recorded four tunes for Riverside with an eight-piece group. The personnel included four of his band mates from the Gillespie band: Morgan, Golson, Kelly, and Melba Liston. The date also reunited him with Cecil Payne. A week later, Henry recorded with Kelly, bassist Wilbur Ware, and drummer "Philly Joe" Jones. The resulting album, titled *Seven Standards and a Blues*, would be his masterpiece. In this recording, the quartet format allowed him to explore fully the personal voice he had created.

But the blood pressure condition that Henry had been battling worsened. After a performance with Gillespie, Henry died in his sleep at his parents' home in Brooklyn. Although Henry had been off drugs the previous year, Cecil Payne believed that he died of a drug overdose: He recalled that Henry had bought "a bag" of heroin on a subway and consumed a third of it, an overdose (*Jazz Monthly*, May 1964).

Henry was a tragic figure in jazz. Though not a major innovator, he developed a unique and personal musical voice at a time when few of his contemporaries had done so. His Riverside recordings are among the very best of the years immediately following Charlie Parker's death, and they bore promise of still greater things to come.

• There are a few articles written on Henry: the most informative are Derek Ansell, "The Forgotten Ones: Ernie Henry," *Jazz Journal International*, Sept. 1987, p. 21, and Jack Cooke, "Fading Flowers—A Note on Ernie Henry," *Jazz Monthly*, July 1961, pp. 9–10. Also helpful are Orrin Keepnews's liner notes for Henry's albums *Presenting Ernie Henry* (Riverside LP 12–222, OJC CD 1920) and *Last Chorus* (Riverside LP 12–266, OJC CD 1906). An obituary is in *Down Beat*, 2 Feb. 1958.

SAM MILLER

HEPBURN, Katharine (12 May 1907–29 June 2003), actress, was born in Hartford, Connecticut, the daughter of Thomas Hepburn, a surgeon who pioneered research on venereal disease, and Katharine Houghton, an influential suffragist and proponent of birth control. Hepburn grew up in a well-to-do, free-thinking household. Her mother's associates in the suffragist movement were frequent guests in the family parlor, where the Hepburn children were permitted to listen in on conversations about prostitution and contraceptives. Her father subscribed to a philosophy of stern self-reliance, encouraging his children to be intensely competitive and requiring them to take cold baths to build fortitude (a practice Katharine continued throughout her life). Katharine Hepburn was educated by tutors at home and, beginning in 1918, at a local private school. Demonstrating her natural athleticism, as a teenager she won a junior ice-skating championship and took second prize in a state women's golf tournament. The family suffered a tragedy in 1921, when her older brother died in a probable suicide.

In 1924 Hepburn enrolled at her mother's alma mater, Bryn Mawr, a prestigious women's college in Pennsylvania. She received poor marks until her junior year, when she worked hard to improve her grades so she could participate in campus theatricals. Her performance in a campus May Day play earned her a letter of introduction to Edwin Knopf, a theater producer in Baltimore. After graduating in 1928 with a degree in English, she acted in bit parts for Knopf's summer stock company. She was subsequently hired for a small role in his Broadway production *The Big Pond*, written by George Middleton and A. E. Thomas. A week before the play opened, the lead actress was dismissed, and the novice Hepburn was elevated to the role. On opening night she suffered from stage fright and rushed through her lines, and she was fired the next day. She thereafter understudied for the popular comedian Hope Williams in Philip Barry's *Holiday*.

In December 1928 Hepburn married Ludlow Ogden Smith, an insurance broker from a wealthy Pennsylvania family. Before consenting to marry, she insisted that he change his name to S. Ogden Ludlow, because she did not want to be known as the plain-sounding "Mrs. Smith." They lived together as a couple only briefly, as Hepburn preferred to pursue her career. They had no children and divorced in 1934.

At first Hepburn failed to establish herself as a Broadway actress. She appeared in supporting parts in an adaptation of Ivan Turgenev's *A Month in the Country* and in Benn Levy's *Art and Mrs. Bottle*. She won the lead role in an adaptation of Alfredo Casella's *Death Takes a Holiday* but was fired during out-of-town tryouts after a clash with the director over her interpretation of the character. Similarly she was fired during rehearsals for Philip Barry's *The Animal Kingdom*, in which she had a featured role opposite the British star Leslie Howard, who could not abide her "insufferable bossiness" (quoted in Edwards, p. 74). Hepburn later recalled that during this period of her career she benefited from being wealthy, which enabled her to stand up for herself: "I don't know what I would have done if I'd had to come to New York and get a job as a waiter or something like that. I think I'm a success, but I had every advantage; I should have been [a success]" (*New York Times*, 30 June 2003). In 1932 she got her first noteworthy part as an athletic Amazon queen in Julian Thompson's *The Warrior's Husband*, based on the Greek comedy *Lysistrata*. The play ran for eighty-three performances, and Hepburn received good critical notices.

Following this sole stage success, Hepburn abruptly became a Hollywood star. She took a screen test for RKO Studios and came to the attention of the film director George Cukor. He cast her in his movie *A Bill of Divorcement* (1932), in a costarring role as the daughter of a shell-shocked World War I veteran, played by John Barrymore. The following year Hepburn appeared in two significant films, as the tomboyish Jo March in Cukor's memorable adaptation of Louisa May Alcott's *Little Women* and as a naive, stagestruck actress relentlessly pursuing her career in *Morning Glory*. *Little Women* was a blockbuster, and Hepburn won the Academy Award for Best Actress for *Morning Glory*. Cukor believed audiences were drawn to her on the screen because of her "oddness." With her angular, somewhat androgynous face, she was considered unconventionally beautiful. She spoke with a distinctive New England Brahmin accent, which quickly became fodder for nightclub impressionists. Her acting blended occasional "high theater" mannerisms—"such flutterings and jitterings and twitchings, such hand-wringings and mouth-quiverings," the *New York Times* lamented in a review of *Quality Street* (1937)—with a modern sense of female self-possession and purposefulness.

Between 1935 and 1938 Hepburn appeared in several films that became classics. She was brilliant in *Alice Adams* (1935), director George Stevens's exploration of the tensions in a family verging on genteel poverty in a small American city. As a bright, imaginative young woman who channels her energies into pretentious social climbing, Hepburn was both comical and touchingly vulnerable. In 1937 she costarred with Ginger Rogers in Gregory La Cava's *Stage Door*, a unique ensemble film that portrays the sense of community among women at a boardinghouse for aspiring Broadway actresses. In 1938 Hepburn demonstrated her gifts as a comedian when she appeared in two of Hollywood's finest comedies, Cukor's *Holiday* and Howard Hawks's *Bringing Up Baby*. Both films teamed her with Cary Grant. *Holiday* (which she had understudied on Broadway) is a sophisticated drawing room comedy in which she played the nonconformist daughter of a millionaire banker. The anarchic *Bringing Up Baby*, considered by many film historians to be the pinnacle of the screwball comedy genre, features her as a ditzy, imperturbable heiress who pesters Grant, a fussy paleontologist, into helping her find her aunt's pet leopard, Baby.

During the decade, however, several of Hepburn's projects were well-publicized flops. In 1934, following the success of *Little Women*, she planned to make a triumphant return to Broadway in *The Lake*, by Dorothy Massingham and Murray McDonald. But she struggled with her character, inspiring Dorothy Parker to make her famous jibe, "Go to the Martin Beck Theatre and see Katharine Hepburn run the gamut of emotion from A to B" (*New York Journal-American*, 27 Dec. 1933). The play closed after fifty-five performances. In 1936 Hepburn starred in an expensive failure at RKO, Cukor's *Sylvia Scarlett*. The oddball movie features her as a girl who disguises herself as a boy in order to work as a con artist; she thereupon becomes romantically entangled with a male painter. The film eventually gained cult status, admired as a daring portrayal of ambivalent sexuality. But the producer Pandro Berman remembered it as "the greatest catastrophe of Kate's Thirties career" (quoted in Bergan, p. 60). This was followed by other box-office disappointments, including *Bringing Up Baby*. After that film failed, RKO deliberately assigned Hepburn to an inferior project, *Mother Carey's Chickens*, knowing she would refuse the movie in violation of her contract. She refused, and her contract was voided.

During these years an influential trade publication labeled her "box-office poison." Film scholars suggest that her typical screen persona, as a strong-minded patrician woman, was unpopular with Great Depression–era audiences, who preferred the "ordinary" female characters portrayed by actresses such as Jean Arthur and the escapist fare provided by Shirley Temple and Deanna Durbin. Hepburn's own behavior contributed to the public perception that she was aloof and unconventional. She often dressed in men's shirts and dungarees, refused to sign autographs for fans, and was on poor terms with the press. For example, in an early interview with a fan magazine, she was asked if she had any children. "Yes, two white and three colored," she shot back. She resented reporters who tried to dig into her private life, particularly when they reported on her alleged engagements to her agent Leland Hayward and to the aviator and producer Howard Hughes.

Hepburn returned to her family home in Connecticut in 1938 and then skillfully reestablished her career in a series of moves unprecedented among the female stars of her era. She spent two months collaborating with the playwright Philip Barry on the script for his romantic comedy *The Philadelphia Story*. She convinced her sometime suitor Hughes to put up financial backing for a Broadway production. She then secured for herself one-quarter ownership in the play and the film rights and waived her acting fee in exchange for 10 percent of the play's gross profits. *The Philadelphia Story* opened in New York in 1939 and became a smash hit, running for 415 performances. Hepburn sold the screen rights to Metro-Goldwyn-Mayer and at the same time won a guarantee that she could star and choose her director and costars. The 1940 film version, directed by Cukor and costarring Grant and James Stewart, was another hit, assuring Hepburn's Hollywood comeback. Interestingly her character, a rich socialite, displays many of the same personality flaws—arrogance, impatience, self-absorption—often publicly attributed to Hepburn. The plot involves her coming to see the error of her ways and learning to have "an understanding heart." In this manner, the film scholar James Harvey has written, *The Philadelphia Story* provided "an inspired solution . . . to the problem of Hepburn's career," chastising and rehabilitating the actress through her character (Harvey, p. 409).

During the 1940s Hepburn began one of the most famous partnerships in Hollywood history, both on and off the screen, with the actor Spencer Tracy. The pair appeared together in nine films over a period of twenty-five years. They were particularly admired for their deft interplay in three romantic comedies, Stevens's *Woman of the Year* (1942) and Cukor's *Adam's Rib* (1949) and *Pat and Mike* (1952). In these films Hepburn played accomplished career women, brilliant but high-strung, and Tracy played gruff, sensible, solidly masculine men. They came together, said Hepburn, like a "fancy French dessert" meeting "meat and potatoes" (*New York Times*, 30 June 2003). The films portray them as equals in their clash of the sexes, each learning to make accommodations to the other—although Hepburn's are inevitably the larger accommodations. Their dramas together, including Elia Kazan's *The Sea of Grass* (1947) and Frank Capra's *State of the Union* (1948), were less well received. Offscreen they carried on a lengthy affair, from around 1940 until Tracy's death in 1967, during which time Tracy, a devout Catholic, refused to leave his wife. Hepburn spent many years attempting to nurse him through his severe alcoholism. She later acknowledged her atypical behavior in their relationship, in which she always tried to place his interests and demands first: "This was not easy for me because I was definitely a *me me me* person" (Hepburn, 2001, p. 389). Their affair was an open secret in Hollywood but was not publicly reported until 1971, when the screenwriter Garson Kanin published the best seller *Tracy and Hepburn: An Intimate Memoir*. After Tracy's wife died in 1984, Hepburn spoke about the relationship openly and often.

While she was involved with Tracy, Hepburn appeared in only a handful of films without him. Among her notable efforts was John Huston's *The African Queen* (1951), a rousing comedy adventure in which she played a spinster missionary who falls in love with a dissolute riverboat pilot, played by Humphrey Bogart. She subsequently played a spinster who briefly finds love in Venice in David Lean's *Summertime* (1955). In 1959 she appeared as a domineering southern matriarch in *Suddenly Last Summer*, based on a garish Tennessee Williams one-act play. Hepburn battled repeatedly with the director Joseph L. Mankiewicz and spit in his face on the last day of filming. During the 1950s she returned to the stage in New York, London, Australia, and Connecticut, appearing in plays by Shakespeare and George Bernard Shaw. In 1962 she gave one of her finest screen performances as the tragic, drug-addicted mother in *Long Day's Journey into Night*, the director Sidney Lumet's faithful three-hour version of the Eugene O'Neill play. Between 1962 and 1967 Hepburn took no work, devoting herself full-time to caring for the ailing Tracy. In 1967 the pair starred in their final film together, Stanley Kramer's *Guess Who's Coming to Dinner*, giving effective performances in an otherwise unsatisfactory exploration of interracial marriage. Hepburn won the Academy Award for Best Actress for her role. Two weeks after the filming, Tracy died of a heart attack.

Following Tracy's death, Hepburn engaged in a flurry of ambitious activity. She won her third Best Actress Academy Award as Eleanor of Aquitaine in *The Lion in Winter* (1968), a fine historical drama, opposite Peter O'Toole. She challenged herself by starring in a Broadway musical, *Coco* (1969), based on the life of the designer Coco Chanel; the play received negative reviews but ran for more than seven months, bolstered by her drawing power. The film *The Madwoman of Chaillot* (1969) was a grandiose disappointment. In 1973 she acted in television movies of two plays, Edward Albee's *A Delicate Balance* and Tennessee Williams's *The Glass Menagerie*. She then reunited with Cukor for *Love among the Ruins* (1975), giving a spirited performance in an Edwardian love story opposite Laurence Olivier. In 1981 Hepburn won an unprecedented fourth Best Actress Academy Award for *On Golden Pond*, which costarred Henry Fonda. During her career she was nominated for a dozen Oscars, a record broken by Meryl Streep in 2003. In 1991 Hepburn published *Me: Stories of My Life*, a sketchy memoir that nevertheless conveys her frank, self-assured voice. In 1993 she appeared on cable television in a documentary, *Katharine Hepburn: All about Me*. Her final film appearance was in *Love Affair* (1994). She died in Old Saybrook, Connecticut.

• Hepburn's papers are in the Margaret Herrick Library at the Academy of Motion Pictures Arts and Sciences. Along with her memoir *Me: Stories of My Life* (1991), Hepburn published *The Making of the African Queen; or, How I Went to Africa with Bogart, Bacall, and Huston and Almost Lost My Mind* (1987). A good biography is Anne Edwards, *A Remarkable Woman: A Biography of Katharine Hepburn* (1985). Ronald Bergan, *Katharine Hepburn: An Independent Woman* (1996), draws heavily from Edwards but is also useful. Barbara Leaming's *Katharine Hepburn* (1995) offers a wealth of research into Hepburn's family background; however, the book pays little attention to her career and has been criticized for its speculative approach to her relationships with Tracy and the director John Ford. For Hepburn's relationship with Cukor, see Patrick McGilligan, *George Cukor: A Double Life* (1991). For her relationship with Tracy, see Garson Kanin, *Tracy and Hepburn: An Intimate Memoir* (1971). For an excellent scholarly discussion of *Alice Adams* and *Stage Door*, see Elizabeth Kendall, *The Runaway Bride: Hollywood Romantic Comedy of the 1930s* (1990). James Harvey, *Romantic Comedy in Hollywood from Lubitsch to Sturges* (1987), considers *Bringing Up Baby*, *The Philadelphia Story*, and *Adam's Rib*. For an important analysis of Hepburn's career from the perspective of feminist film criticism, see Andrew Britton, *Katharine Hepburn: Star as Feminist* (2003). Also worthwhile is Molly Haskell, *From Reverence to Rape: The Treatment of Women in the Movies* (1987). For views of Hepburn by her friends, see Kanin, *Hepburn and Tracy*, and A. Scott Berg, *Kate Remembered* (2003). An obituary is in the *New York Times*, 30 June 2003.

THOMAS W. COLLINS JR.

HERBLOCK (13 Oct. 1909–8 Oct. 2001), political cartoonist, was born Herbert Lawrence Block in Chicago, Illinois, the son of David Julian Block, a chemist and electrical engineer, and Theresa Lupe Block. Young Herbert drew from a very early age, and his father enrolled him in the Art Institute of Chicago's Saturday classes when he was eleven; the next year, he was awarded a part-time scholarship. While in high school, he drew cartoons for the school's weekly newspaper and for the suburban *Evanston News-Index*. He also regularly contributed paragraphs of witticism to a popular *Chicago Tribune* column of reader submissions, "Line o' Type or Two," for which, following his father's suggestion, he used a portmanteau pen name created by combining his first name and his last, hinging it at the common consonant. Upon graduation from high school in 1927, he worked briefly as a reporter for the Chicago City News Bureau and then freelanced artwork before entering Lake Forest College that fall. For the next two years, he commuted daily from the family home, then in Winnetka; but when a summer job temporarily replacing the editorial page cartoonist for the *Chicago Daily News* turned into a permanent position, Herblock abandoned his college career to second the paper's front page political cartoonist, Vaughn Shoemaker.

The cartoons of both cartoonists were distributed nationally by the newspaper, and Herblock's work attracted the attention of editors at the Newspaper Enterprise Association, a newspaper feature syndicate headquartered in Cleveland, Ohio, to which he relocated in early 1933 when N.E.A. offered him a job as staff editorial cartoonist. In the spring of 1942, Herblock won his first Pulitzer Prize, but within a year, he was no longer at N.E.A. From early 1943 until late 1945, he was, as he put it, "associated with the U.S. Army." After basic training at Camp Robinson, Arkansas, Herblock went into public relations at the Army Air Force Tactical Center near Orlando, Flor-

ida, where he drew cartoons and wrote press releases. He was eventually transferred to New York where he continued drawing and writing and helped edit a "clip sheet" of information, safety tips, cartoons, and photographs for the Camp Newspaper Service, the military version of a feature syndicate that distributed its products to military units all over the world. Upon discharge from the army, Herblock began doing editorial cartoons for the *Washington Post* and continued until he died, over 55 years later.

For most of that time, Herblock regarded the *Washington Post* as his home, and he ate most of his meals in the paper's second-floor cafeteria. Unmarried, his personal habits teetered into slovenliness. Sartorially, he was permanently rumpled. His office was a chaotic warren of stacks of old newspapers and magazines, clippings and discarded pieces of clothing, and coffee cans filled with soft-lead pencils and used brushes. His daily routine was unvarying. He arrived at the paper after noon, and by five o'clock or so, he had concocted four or five ideas for a cartoon. Then he walked around the office, showing them to various reporters and editors whose assignments gave them intimate knowledge of the subject Herblock was tackling that day. And after getting responses to his day's crop of ideas, Herblock picked one and drew the final version of it. Inked with pen and brush, his cartoons of the early 1930s were linear productions in the manner of J. N. ("Ding") Darling of the *Des Moines Register*. But within a few years, Herblock was embellishing his drawings with a grease crayon, rubbing it across the pebble-finish drawing paper to give the pictures a variety of gray tones. By the mid-1950s, Herblock's drawing style was the most imitated in the field.

Herblock published his first book in 1952 and was firmly established as a journalistic power in Washington as well as in the nation. He wrote eleven more books, including one autobiography and one about a stray cat who took up residence with him for a time. The other nine were collections of his cartoons accompanied by Herblock's text, which supplied historical and political background. And his prose was as forthright and unaffected as his artwork. His first book is called *The Herblock Book*, and its first chapter is titled "Begin Here."

No other cartoonist has matched Herblock in career longevity: his first editorial cartoon was published 24 April 1929; his last, 72 years later, on 26 August 2001. He cartooned through thirteen presidents, none of whom, regardless of political affiliation, escaped the cartoonist's scrutiny and ridicule. Dwight Eisenhower and Richard Nixon repeatedly canceled their subscriptions to the *Post* because of Herblock's cartoons. Herblock portrayed Ike as a friendly, simple-minded buffoon, and he always gave Nixon a sinister-looking five o'clock shadow and once drew him crawling out of a sewer. When Nixon was elected president, Herblock drew his own cluttered office as a barber shop with a sign on the wall: "This shop gives to every new President of the U.S. a free shave." The Democrats fared no better: Herblock once drew Jimmy Carter with a blurred face like an out-of-focus television image, and he gave Lyndon Johnson the imperious air of a monarch who ruled by divine right. Herblock believed it was the role of the political cartoonist to criticize the government, and he did it, guided by "the small-L liberal trinity of freedom, equality and brotherhood," which, wrote the *Post*'s David Von Drehle, "endowed his vast body of work with awesome consistency." He was a lifelong advocate for civil rights and for the environment. His first cartoon for the *Chicago Daily News* showed a clear-cut forest of tree stumps over the caption, "This is the forest primeval—."

Herblock is one of only five cartoonists to win three Pulitzer Prizes (1942, 1954, 1979), and he shared a fourth with the *Washington Post* for its coverage of the Watergate scandal. In 1994, he was awarded the Presidential Medal of Freedom, the nation's highest civilian award. He received awards from virtually every journalist organization, and in 1957 he was named "cartoonist of the year," receiving the National Cartoonists Society's Reuben Award. But it is not the length of Herblock's career or the number of awards he won that gave him the stature that inspired unqualified admiration and envy among his colleagues. They admired him for his principled stand on public policy and social issues; and they envied him his unprecedented independence—his absolute freedom to express his opinions without editorial interference.

Celebrating Herblock's fiftieth anniversary at the *Post*, Katharine Graham, then the publisher, wrote: "He fought for and earned a unique position at the paper: one of complete independence of anybody and anything. Since he arrived at the *Post*, five editors and five publishers all have learned a cardinal rule: Don't mess with Herb." He won his independence as a crusading spirit whose tenacious will could not be denied, whose passions had a logic so persuasive that they repeatedly earned their way into print. Effectively the liberal conscience of the paper, Herblock's steely incorruptibility and his trenchant and unrelenting assault on hypocrisy in a newspaper published in the seat of government (where there is plenty of political hypocrisy to assault) contributed, as Graham acknowledged, to the elevation of the *Washington Post* from a fourth-rate paper in the city to a first-rate paper in the nation. For his first half-dozen years at the *Post*, he showed preliminary sketches of cartoon ideas to an editor. But after the presidential election in 1952, Herblock's cartoons went into print at the *Post* without let or hindrance. By this time, he had coined the term "McCarthyism" in a cartoon published 29 March 1950, less than two months after Wisconsin's Senator Joseph R. McCarthy first attracted attention by making the dubious assertion that 205 communists worked in the State Department. The cartoon depicted several Republican Party leaders trying to get the G.O.P. elephant to stand atop a shaky stack of paint-smeared buckets labeled "McCarthyism"; the reluctant elephant says, "You Mean I'm Supposed to Stand on That?" In one of his most powerful cartoons

of this era (one of the most effective visual metaphors made meaningful and potent by the accompanying wording), a man is dashing up a ladder toward the torch in the Statue of Liberty's hand; labeled "Hysteria," the man shouts "Fire!" as he carries aloft a bucket to extinguish freedom's flame. From the same period, Herblock's emblem of the menace of nuclear weapons was a huge anthropomorphic bomb wearing an antique Greek helmet and labeled "Mr. Atom."

When he died, Herblock left an estate of over $50 million ($49 million of it in *Washington Post* stock) with which he endowed a foundation in his name to foster education, to improve the Washington community, and to encourage young editorial cartoonists. As a measure of his stature in American journalism, Herblock was one of only two newspaper cartoonists recognized by *Editor & Publisher* as belonging among the fifty "most influential" newspaper people of the twentieth century.

• The original art of Herblock's cartoons (he never gave any away to admirers) is archived at the Library of Congress. Herblock's autobiography, *Herblock: A Cartoonist's Life* (1993), supplies most of the biographical information, supplemented by many articles written about him during his long career and at the time of his death. He was a member of Sigma Delta Chi, Professional Journalist Society, an honorary member of Phi Beta Kappa, and a Fellow of the American Academy of Arts and Sciences. Herblock's books are *The Herblock Book*, 1952; *Herblock's Here and Now*, 1955; *Herblock's Special for Today*, 1958; *Straight Herblock*, 1964; *The Herblock Gallery*, 1968; *Herblock's State of the Union*, 1972; *Herblock Special Report*, 1974; *Herblock on All Fronts*, 1980; *Herblock Through the Looking Glass*, 1984; *Herblock at Large*, 1987; *Bella and Me: Life in the Service of a Cat*, 1995. Obituaries are in the *Washington Post* and the *New York Times*, both 8 Oct. 2001.

ROBERT C. HARVEY

HERMAN, Michael (c. 1911–3 May 1996), and **Mary Ann Herman** (1912–24 Mar. 1992), folk music and folk dance teachers, were born into urban immigrant communities in Cleveland, Ohio, and New York City, respectively. Little is known about Michael's early life, except that he was of Ukrainian descent. Mary Ann Bodnar, the daughter of Matwey and Anna Bodnar, grew up in a New York City ghetto that reflected a melding of many different cultures. She attended a Ukrainian neighborhood school. After graduating from James Monroe High School, she attended several colleges in the New York area but never received a degree. She became a dancing performer in her neighborhood Ukrainian folk group and launched her folk dance teaching career at the YMCA.

In 1930 Michael Herman, who had attended Western Reserve University in Cleveland, came to New York City to study concert violin at the Juilliard School of Music. Then, few people who were not of a particular Old Country ethnic group took part in folk dancing and folk music. Physical education teachers in public schools taught some folk dancing, but most of the dances were of Anglo-Saxon origin. Michael became acquainted with local ethnic groups and was asked to play at their dances, and sometimes he assisted in teaching them.

In 1931, Michael met Mary Ann Bodnar, and in 1932 they were married. They performed in Vasil Avramenko's Ukrainian group and helped to found the Folk Festival Council of the Foreign Language Information Service. With a growing reputation and knowledge of the many styles of folk music and dance, Michael in 1933 took a job teaching folk dance at the New School for Social Research. With Mary Ann joining Michael to teach, attendance at the folk dance sessions increased. Next came more requests in New York City to teach at Columbia University's International House and the International Institute. This growing appreciation of different folk cultures and the Hermans' popular reputation culminated in their being asked to direct a folk dancing program on the American Commons exhibit at the 1939–1940 New York World's Fair.

They took full advantage of the opportunity. "Everyone that wandered by would want to dance because this wonderful music was pouring out! Before they knew it, someone had them dashing around in a Russian Troika, or an American Shoo Fly, or something else," Mary Ann recalled. "That is how we could see the idea of a folk dance house way back in 1940" (quoted in *Pioneer Folk Dance Leaders*, p. 23). Armed with a list of over 1,500 names and addresses of people from the Fair who had expressed an interest in international folk dancing, the Hermans made it their mission to establish a place to teach it.

With the help of friends, the Hermans found a building, bought records, and hired musicians. On 15 October 1940, the Hermans opened a Folk Dance Center in the Ukrainian National Home on East 6th Street. They moved to the Polish Dom (National Home), then to the German National Home. The Hermans offered more and more evening dance classes, all the while dreaming of a permanent home for their classes, folk costumes, records, and reference library. Getting proper music was also very difficult in the earlier years. "Since there were no records for most of the dances," Michael recalled, "I played the violin, Mary Ann was on the piano, Walter Erikkson and Sven Tollefson were on the accordion, Walter Andreasen on bass, and Frances Witowski on the clarinet" (quoted in *Pioneer Folk Dance Leaders*, p. 23). They moved to their permanent location, the Folk Dance House, in 1950 or 1951.

They appealed to many age groups, offering evening sessions for adults and Saturday afternoon programs for teenagers. They designed programs for schoolteachers as well as special arts and crafts and dancing programs for children. Although dancing was the primary activity, the Hermans immersed participants in the music, language, costumes, food, history and customs of the folk groups. They brought in specialists from other countries and sponsored teacher-training workshops to foster good techniques in breaking down complicated dance steps into "teach-able" elements.

Folk Dance House became the epicenter for the spread of international folk dancing throughout the United States and beyond. The Hermans attracted many well-known personalities: Burl Ives danced and sang during intermissions, encircled by attentive folk dancers; Gene Kelly, Peter Lorre, Damon Runyon, Mike Todd, and Jerome Robbins also visited Folk Dance House. During the World War II years, Mary Ann continued running the teaching sessions while Michael served in the Armed Forces. Once Michael returned to Folk Dance House, he resumed teaching and making records. He also wrote *Folk Dances for All* (1947) and *Folk Dance Syllabus Number One* (1953).

At the encouragement of Jane Farwell, who had established a Recreation Laboratory Camp in 1938, the Hermans began looking in Maine for a suitable location for a folk dance camp. They settled in Bridgton and in 1951 opened the Maine Folk Dance Camp. The camp became a local fixture. During the summer, Mary Ann held dance programs at the Town Hall in Bridgton to benefit local schools and hospitals. Every Fourth of July she had dancers from camp decorate a float and participated in the Bridgton Fourth of July Parade. Her offerings brought the outside world to Bridgton.

To ensure the quality of folk music, the Michael Herman Orchestra recorded under the Folk Dancer label. Michael discovered the Banat Tamburitzans, a native orchestra that played the *kolos* of Yugoslavia. This orchestra recorded many dances from the Balkans and performed at festivals and workshops. The Folk Dancer label also recorded music of Ralph Page's Orchestra, Kostya Polyansky's Balalaika Orchestra, The Duquesne Tamburitzans, French Canadian fiddler Jean Carrignan, and others. Mary Ann, concerned with the quality of folk teaching, gave workshops all over the country on teaching techniques, using her comical "shouldn't do" demonstrations to prove a point. Teaching people something as simple as how to hold hands in a circle was as important as teaching an intricate series of steps. She always stressed that the object was to teach people how to *dance* a dance, and not to just *do* a dance.

In 1956 the U.S. State Department sent the Hermans, as part of an international group, to Japan. For six weeks they taught 46 dances of 16 different countries to more than 21,000 Japanese in 21 cities. This visit resulted in the founding of the Japanese Folk Dance Federation.

In the early 1970s the building on Sixteenth Street that housed Folk Dance House was demolished. The Hermans moved to the Armenian Cathedral in New York City and St. Margaret's Church in Flushing, New York. The Hermans divided their time between the Maine Folk Dance Camp, in the summer, and New York, for the other nine months. Mary Ann supervised the camp, while Michael focused on the New York dance sessions and the Folk Dancer record business.

After Mary Ann's death at the age of eighty at their home in Long Island, Michael continued to run the camp for another two years. Then suddenly he closed it and put it up for sale; he died soon after in a Long Island hospital. (The Maine Folk Dance Camp ceased to exist; it was later reincarnated in the Mainewoods Dance Camp).

The Hermans changed the way folk dance and folk cultures were regarded in the United States. During the 1930s and 1940s, American-born children of immigrants were losing their heritage and folk identity, while their parents were hoarding the particular culture. "In the early days no one went out of their neighborhood to dance with another nationality group. People felt that their dances should only be for themselves," Michael recalled (quoted in *Pioneer Folk Dance Leaders*, p. 22). "Everyone can join the circle," Mary Ann declared. She danced the Sardana for Pablo Casals, after which he kissed her hand; instructed the great Igor Moiseyev and his famous dance troupe on how to do the Virginia Reel; and coaxed Prince Akihito to do the Virginia Reel with her at the 1964–1965 New York World's Fair.

Over the years, visitors from Switzerland, Sweden, Denmark, Germany, France, Australia, Great Britain, Canada, Japan, and other countries carried the Hermans' philosophy abroad. Teachers from many cultures shared their heritage with dancers from all walks of life and of all ages. Most international folk dancers in recent decades either learned to dance at Maine Folk Dance Camp or learned from someone who learned to dance from the Hermans. The Hermans were instrumental in preserving many of the international folk dances that would have otherwise died, even in their own lands.

• An article in which Mary Ann Herman was extensively quoted was published in *Quo Vadimus*, vols. 14 and 15 (1980). This folk magazine, published by David Henry, is now called *Quo*. An interview by Mutti Ehrlich for *Ethnic News* 1, no. 11 (Nov. 1967), contained invaluable information about the Hermans' role in the spread of international folk dancing as a form of recreation. Carole Howard, an associate professor at Central Michigan University (CMU), published an extensive article about Mary Ann and Michael Herman in the book titled *International Folk Dancing U.S.A.*, ed. Betty Casey (1981). The article appears in the section called "Pioneer Folk Dance Leaders" on pages 22–26. Howard places a lot of emphasis on Mary Ann's teaching workshops and her ability to make dancing fun for all ages. Obituaries for Mary Ann and Michael Herman are in the *New York Times*, 27 Mar. 1992, and 13 May 1996, respectively.

KATHRYN N. DEMOS

HERRESHOFF, L. Francis (11 Nov. 1890–4 Dec. 1972), yacht designer, was born Lewis Francis Herreshoff in Bristol, Rhode Island, the son of the renowned steam engineer and yacht designer Nathanael Greene Herreshoff and Clara DeWolf Herreshoff. L. Francis's early education in his chosen profession was provided at the Herreshoff Manufacturing Company, the yacht-building firm that his father and uncle, John Brown Herreshoff, started in 1878. During L. Francis's youth, it was arguably the leading such enterprise in the world. Much of his boyhood was spent in the Herreshoff shops and on board the boats they produced. He was privileged to observe the design, building, and racing of dozens of sailing yachts, including America's Cup defenders.

Nathanael Herreshoff, however, neither trained nor encouraged his son to enter the field of yacht design. In 1908 L. Francis attended the College of Agriculture and Mechanic Arts at Kingston, Rhode Island. In 1910 his father assigned him the role of running the family dairy farm in Bristol. In 1917 he left the farm to serve in the U.S. Naval Reserve. He commanded patrol boats on the Rhode Island coast and later designed shapes for underwater devices. The navy released him in 1919.

L. Francis did not return to the farm. In 1920 he left Bristol to work for W. Starling Burgess, a brilliant, self-trained yacht designer, in Provincetown, Massachusetts, and later Boston. In 1923 L. Francis invented the modern tang method of attaching wire rigging to the mast, which allowed higher tensioning of the wire and thus stiffer and faster sailing rigs. He was the first to use longitudinal construction in a wooden hull with supporting members running lengthwise (invented in 1924 and patented after further use in 1929) in his design for the highly successful R-class sailing racer the *Yankee*.

When Burgess closed his office in 1926, L. Francis set up his own yacht design business in Marblehead, Massachusetts, where he would live the rest of his life. In his first five years designing under his own name, he tried, with mixed results, to build on his success with the *Yankee*. His sequel, the *Live Yankee* (1927), with streamlined hull and rig and flexible rudder, was the most innovative racing design of the time, though it was not as successful as the *Yankee*. For the R-boat *Gypsy* (1927, not his design), he devised an overlapping jib, the forerunner of the modern Genoa jib. The 87-foot M-boat *Istalena*, a double-ender that he designed in 1928, had a poor first season but then went to the top of her class. He helped introduce the 30-square-meter class to the United States and produced four successful designs for the class (1929–1932). His biggest racer, at 130 feet, was the J-boat *Whirlwind*, one of four contenders for the defense of the America's Cup in 1930. She was also his biggest disappointment. The most advanced and certainly the most beautiful of the four, with great potential for speed, she was never properly tuned up for racing and was poorly sailed, winning only a single trial race, and that thanks to a lucky wind shift. After the 1930 races, she was offered for sale on condition she never be sailed again. She was broken up for junk in 1935. The *Whirlwind* debacle effectively ended L. Francis's quest to be at the forefront in the design of racing sailboats.

L. Francis had a complicated relationship with his father. He was of artistic temperament, while his father was a hard-driving engineer. From 1920 to 1925 the two had little contact, but then a newspaper article about L. Francis prompted his father to write to him. L. Francis sent blueprints of some of his designs to his father, who provided comment. His father died in 1938.

In the 1930s Herreshoff turned primarily to the design of cruising sailboats. He had designed a handsome and able clipper-bowed schooner in 1923 while working for Burgess. In 1930, her owner wanted a larger boat, and Herreshoff drew the plans for the 57-foot ketch *Tioga*, a hauntingly beautiful vessel inspired by the schooner *America*. There followed a series of six more clipper-bowed ketches and a schooner (1934–1960), all with well-raked masts; these designs became his hallmark. They varied in length from 33 feet up to the *Tioga II*'s 72 feet (1935). The *Tioga II*, later named *Ticonderoga*, was a fabulous yacht whose speed matched her beauty. Though her original intended use was day-sailing and short-range cruising, she held more ocean racing course records than any other yacht.

In 1942 Boris Lauer-Leonardi became editor of *The Rudder* magazine and courted Herreshoff as a major contributor. He began to design boats for *The Rudder*'s "How to Build" series. His first, the H-28, a ketch, is the epitome of what a small cruising boat should be and became his most popular design; scores of them have been built in several countries. His designs in the series continued into 1950 and included the unique world cruiser Marco Polo, a 55-foot three-masted lifeboat that could make long, fast passages under power and sail, and the Meadow Lark, a 33-foot sharpie cruiser that could float in a foot of water.

In a series of forty-six articles that ran in *The Rudder* from 1944 through 1947, Herreshoff laid out the fundamentals of his profession as he saw them. Under the title "The Common Sense of Yacht Design," the articles (published with the same title in book form, two volumes, 1946 and 1948) presented what expert critics have judged to be the best treatise written on the subject. Additional series that Herreshoff wrote for *The Rudder* from 1949 through 1960 were "Capt. Nat Herreshoff," an admiring biography of his father; "The Compleat Cruiser," a lengthy cruising yarn designed to teach neophytes how to enjoy life afloat; and "An Introduction to Yachting," an account of the sport that emphasized its traditions. (These three series were also published as books with the same titles as the articles in 1953, 1956, and 1963, respectively.) In all, Herreshoff wrote 234 articles for *The Rudder*, the last one appearing in 1965. His designs and articles in the How to Build series were published posthumously in book form as *Sensible Cruising Designs* (1973). Writing for *The Rudder* opened a window onto the world for Herreshoff. Readers wrote to him from every continent with their questions about yacht design. He answered each letter promptly, courteously, and knowledgeably.

In later life, Herreshoff designed few boats for clients. But in 1956 he designed a slim, 28-foot, double-ended canoe yawl that he named Rozinante, inspired

by a boat of that name in "The Compleat Cruiser." It was the perfect day-sailer and overnighter, exquisite in every way, docile, comfortable, and fast. The boat became one of his most admired designs.

In 1945, Herreshoff bought and moved into "The Castle," a well-known Marblehead house with a view of the harbor from its crenellated parapet. It made a perfect residence for him for the rest of his life, providing a large drafting room and shop for his lathes, a great hall to house his collections of art and antiques, and a generous fireplace around which to gather his many friends and disciples, young and old. He never married. He was an exquisite craftsman in wood and metal and particularly enjoyed lathe work. He made hundreds of beautiful objects from wooden dishes to tables to brass saluting cannon, most of which he gave to his friends. He designed his last boat in 1963. He died in Boston.

Herreshoff was the consummate artist—in his values, his personality, his lifestyle, and, above all, in his creation of beautiful yacht designs. He was also, in his published writings, his letters, and his conversations, a great teacher of artistic, sensible yacht design. He completed only 131 designs to the point where yachts could be built from his drawings, and only 73 of the designs were built. Perhaps 500 vessels have been built to these designs. Herreshoff sought artistic perfection and complete, practical detail in each design; he came remarkably close to achieving his goal.

• Mystic Seaport Museum, Mystic, Connecticut, has a collection of Herreshoff's plans of yacht designs and a collection of his manuscripts and letters, including much incoming correspondence. The most valuable and interesting letters are those exchanged with his father (1925–1938). The Museum also has a few boats designed by Herreshoff, as well as some of his personal possessions, including drafting instruments. Herreshoff's knowledgeable, opinionated, sometimes whimsical writings repay study. In addition to his books mentioned in the text above are *An L. Francis Herreshoff Reader* (1978) and the text portion of *Yachts, Designs, and Much Miscellaneous Information* (1967), which collect the remainder of his articles from *The Rudder*. For an outstanding appraisal of Herreshoff's achievements as a yacht designer, see Phillip C. Bolger's article on him in *Nautical Quarterly*, no. 9. An exhaustive, well-illustrated history of the *Ticonderoga* is Jack Sommers's book of that name (1997). An obituary is in the *New York Times*, 4 Dec. 1972.

ROGER C. TAYLOR

HEUDUCK, Paul Johannes (21 May 1882–8 Sept. 1972), and **Arno Paul Heuduck** (28 July 1917–12 Nov. 1988), mosaicists, were both born in Berlin, Germany. Paul Heuduck was the son of Louise Dressler Heuduck and Johannes Heuduck, a cabinetmaker. Little is known about Paul Heuduck's youth in Germany aside from the fact that he was the youngest of seven children and that at the age of fourteen he began work as an apprentice at the Berlin stained glass and mosaic firm Puhl-Wagner. As an apprentice mosaicist, Paul lost a finger after cutting himself on a shard of glass. He married Martha Untze (b. 1887), the daughter of one of his coworkers at Puhl-Wagner, and the couple had three children.

Paul joined the German army during World War I and served in Africa, but he returned to Puhl-Wagner after the war. In 1923, his employer established in the United States what would come to be known as the Ravenna Mosaic Company, a joint venture with the Emil Frei Glass Studio, a St. Louis art and stained glass company. At this time, while Paul was setting mosaics in a 1,100-year-old chapel in Aachen, Germany, his employers offered him the choice of working either on a new project in America, the decoration of the St. Louis Cathedral (now the Cathedral Basilica of St. Louis), or on Stockholm's City Hall (the "Golden Hall"). Paul elected to take his family to America.

In 1923, Paul emigrated to the United States through Ellis Island, his family following him a few months later. His wife, however, died only two years later of complications from an abscessed tooth. A few years later, Paul married another German immigrant, Elsa Massmeier. Details of this marriage are unavailable, but it is known that she died several years later. Paul's third marriage (date unknown) was to Berthe Weber (1890–1953), a French immigrant.

The record of the Ravenna Mosaic Company's early years is incomplete at best. From 1923 until 1937, the company operated a studio in St. Louis, Missouri, and had offices in New York City under the direction of Gerdt Wagner, the principal shareholder and owner. During the company's early period, much of the labor of fabricating mosaics in reverse on paper was done in Berlin by the Puhl-Wagner studio. The mosaics were then shipped to America to be patched and set in concrete at the job site by Ravenna. Paul initially lived and worked in St. Louis, but as he rose in the company, he spent increasing amounts of time at the New York City studio. In about 1926, Paul's family moved with him to Englewood, New Jersey. The family had returned to Missouri by 1935, when Arno graduated from Webster High School in St. Louis and began working in the St. Louis studio. At about this time, Arno took art classes at the Washington University School of Fine Arts.

In 1936, Ravenna reincorporated in New York, and for the first time Paul Heuduck appears as one of the principal stockholders of the company. In September of 1937, Paul bought all of Ravenna's assets and the company was subsequently operated by the Heuduck family out of the St. Louis studio. In 1938, Ravenna apparently collaborated with the artist Bancel La Farge on large mosaics for a chapel in St. Matthew's Cathedral in Washington, D.C. Despite these commissions, however, the Depression brought to a halt all work on Ravenna's greatest project and the largest mosaic project in the world, the decoration of the St. Louis Cathedral. In truth, Ravenna barely survived the Second World War, since mosaic craftsmanship had little to offer the American war effort. At war's onset, Arno worked in a St. Louis ammunitions factory. He was later inducted into the Army Air Force, where he spent the last years of the war.

The prosperity following World War II brought expanded prospects for work to the Ravenna Company, with Paul as president and Arno as vice president. In 1943, work resumed on the St. Louis Cathedral when Ravenna began work with Hildreth Meière, executing the murals "The Sacrifice of Isaac" and "Malchizedeck" for the Cathedral's east and west sanctuary walls, respectively. The same year Arno married Delpha Deterding; they had three children. From 1946 to 1948, Arno took business classes at Saint Louis University's School of Commerce and Finance, preparing himself to run the family business, even though his professional interests lay elsewhere.

The 1950s saw renewed construction in both the St. Louis Cathedral and the National Shrine of the Immaculate Conception in Washington, D.C. In 1951, Ravenna returned to the National Shrine to install mosaics in the Resurrection Chapel. Two years later, Berthe, Paul's third wife, died. The following year Ravenna installed mosaic panels designed by artist Richard Haines on the exterior of UCLA's music building.

In 1955, Ravenna executed Lumen Winter's impressive marble mural "Labor is Life" at the new AFL-CIO headquarters building in Washington, D.C. That year also marked the beginning of nearly ten years of uninterrupted construction in the St. Louis Cathedral. During this period, Hildreth Meière designed and Ravenna executed mosaics for the eight domes on the main floor of the Cathedral (1955), the ambulatory dome, the sanctuary dome and the soffit (underside) of the northern arch (1956), the north wall (1957), the south dome, four pendentives under the dome, the soffit arch between the south and main domes (1959), the Historical Arch, three bulnoses and another soffit arch (1960), the Social Workers Arch, the educational arch, south ceiling arch, southern wall, and the marble and mosaic border for the south rose window (1961). Ravenna also installed the windows in the sanctuary dome (1957) and south dome (1959), both sets of which were manufactured in Germany by the heirs of the Puhl-Wagner Company. Following Meière's death, artist John de Rosen continued work in the Cathedral, designing the Last Judgment Arch and two pendentives beneath the central dome (1963). Ravenna also installed the windows in the central dome (1964) and mosaics beneath the east and west balcony areas according to forty-year-old designs by Otto Oetken.

In 1960, the Ravenna Company returned to New York City to install mosaics on the twenty-second, twenty-third, and twenty-fourth floors of the Time Building. The following year, Ravenna embarked on a long period of construction in the National Shrine of the Immaculate Conception, beginning with the Miraculous Medal Chapel and the Our Lady of Perpetual Help Chapel. In 1962, Ravenna executed another series of panels designed by Richard Haines for UCLA's Physics Building. These commissions were followed by jobs at the National Shrine, including the Our Lady of Mt. Carmel Chapel and Our Lady Queen of All Hearts Chapel (1933) and Our Lady of Good Counsel Chapel and Our Lady of Guadalupe Chapel (1964). Ravenna also executed Millard Sheets's designs for the Shrine's sanctuary dome, Joseph Young's cartoons for the west apse, and John de Rosen's designs for the Immaculate Heart of Mary Chapel (1965). In 1967, Ravenna installed Max Ingrand's mosaics in the Shrine's chancel dome and Ernoe Koch's mosaics for two barrel vault ceilings. Elsewhere in Washington, D.C., Ravenna installed John de Rosen's *Pool of Bethsaida* and *St. Matthew Baptizing* in the baptistery at St. Matthew's Cathedral. In 1968, Ravenna executed mosaics in the Shrine's Our Lady of the Rosary Chapel, a job requiring 1,250,000 individually fractured and set tesserae in 2,500 colors. The following year, Ravenna installed Millard Sheets's designs for the Shrine's Blessed Sacrament Chapel as well as additional mosaics by John de Rosen in St. Matthew's Cathedral's Blessed Sacrament Chapel.

While the 1970s was a comparatively slow time for architectural mosaic, Ravenna nonetheless oversaw the completion of Mary Reardon's designs for the east and west nave ceilings of the National Shrine and John de Rosen's exterior mosaics at St. Matthew's Cathedral in 1970. In the last decade of his life, Paul Heuduck no longer installed mosaics, but he continued setting them in the studio. He died in St. Louis. His headstone, in St. Michael's Cemetery in St. Louis, is decorated in mosaic.

With Arno as president, Ravenna installed mosaics in two barrel vault ceilings in the National Shrine. In August of 1974, Arno moved the studio to a farm in Fredericktown, Missouri. Although the move ostensibly signaled Arno's retirement, he reportedly continued to wake up at an early hour every day to set mosaics in the barn that housed the new workshop. He also kept horses on the farm, and it is known that they often poked their heads through the windows of the studio while Arno worked. From Fredericktown, Arno executed the only mosaics installed in the St. Louis Cathedral during the 1970s, a small panel for the Our Lady of Perpetual Help Chapel. In 1978, Ravenna completed its final installation in the National Shrine, the mosaics in the Irish Oratory Chapel, adapted by artist Joseph Murphy from representations of the evangelists' symbols found in the Book of Kells.

In the 1980s Ravenna returned to the St. Louis Cathedral to install a final series of murals designed by Mary Reardon. The first of these was *The Resurrection* (1984), which decorated the Cathedral's east transept dome. In 1986, *Pentecost*, thought to be the world's largest artistic representation of the Holy Spirit, was installed in the west transept dome. In 1987, the final mosaics were installed along the east and west walls of the nave. On 8 November 1988, Arno Heuduck was awarded the Order of St. Louis the King by the Archdiocese of St. Louis, a remarkable honor consid-

ering that Arno was a lifelong practicing Methodist. Arno died three days later.

• The complete Ravenna Company records can be found at the Special Collections and Archives at Pius XII Memorial Library, Saint Louis University. The Puhl-Wagner company records are housed at the Archives of Stained Glass and Mosaic Institutions (the Puhl & Wagner and Gottfried Heinersdorff collection) at the Berlinische Galerie, Landesmuseum für Moderne Kunst, Fotografie und Architektur in Berlin, Germany. The Missouri Historical Society Archives house the Emil Frei Papers (1860–1959), some of which were apparently reproduced on microfiche for the Smithsonian Institution's Archives and Manuscript Collection. A good overview of the Ravenna Mosaic Company's work is provided in James F. Scott's documentary *Worlds of Bright Glass* (1992), which features a number of Ravenna's major projects and an interview with Arno Heuduck. A number of the Heuducks' mosaic panels, tools, and designs can be found on display in the Mosaic Museum on the lower floor of the St. Louis Cathedral Basilica, and the parish archives of the Cathedral house a large number of photographs and full-scale cartoons of the Cathedral's mosaics. Paul Heuduck's obituary is in the *New York Times*, 10 Sept. 1972, and his son's death was announced in the *St. Louis Post-Dispatch*, 13 Nov. 1988.

ROBERT BLASKIEWICZ

HIGGINBOTHAM, A. Leon, Jr. (25 Feb. 1928–14 Dec. 1998), jurist and civil rights leader, was born Aloysius Leon Higginbotham in Trenton, New Jersey, the son of Aloysius Leon Higginbotham, Sr., a laborer, and Emma Lee Douglass Higginbotham, a domestic worker. While he was attending a racially segregated elementary school, his mother insisted that he receive tutoring in Latin, a required subject denied to black students; he then became the first African American to enroll at Trenton's Central High School. Initially interested in engineering, he enrolled at Purdue University only to leave in disgust after the school's president denied his request to move on-campus with his fellow African-American students. He completed his undergraduate education at Antioch College in Yellow Springs, Ohio, where he received a B.A. in sociology in 1949. In August 1948 he married Jeanne L. Foster; the couple had three children. Angered by his experiences at Purdue and inspired by the example of Supreme Court Justice Thurgood Marshall, Higginbotham decided to pursue a legal career. He attended law school at Yale and graduated with an LL.B. in 1952.

Although Higginbotham was an honors student at Yale, he encountered racial prejudice when he tried to find employment at leading Philadelphia law firms. After switching his sights to the public sector, he began his career as a clerk for Court of Common Pleas judge Curtis Bok in 1952. Higginbotham then served for a year as an assistant district attorney under future Philadelphia mayor and fellow Yale graduate Richardson Dilworth. In 1954 he became a principal in the new African-American law firm of Norris, Green, Harris, and Higginbotham and remained with the firm until 1962. During the same period he became active in the civil rights movement, serving as president of the local chapter of the National Association for the Advancement of Colored People (NAACP); he was also a member of the Pennsylvania Human Relations Commission.

Between 1960 and 1962 Higginbotham served as a special hearing officer for conscientious objectors for the United States Department of Justice. In 1962 President John F. Kennedy appointed him to the Federal Trade Commission, making him the first African-American member of a federal administrative agency. Two years later President Lyndon Johnson appointed him as U.S. District Court Judge for the Eastern District of Pennsylvania; at age thirty-six, he was the youngest person to be so named in thirty years. In 1977 President Jimmy Carter appointed him to the U.S. Federal Court of Appeals for the Third Circuit in Philadelphia. He became chief judge in 1989 and remained in the position until his retirement in 1993.

As a member of the federal bench, Higginbotham authored over 650 opinions. A staunch liberal and tireless defender of programs such as affirmative action, he became equally well known for his legal scholarship, with more than 100 published articles to his credit. He also published two (out of a planned series of four) highly regarded books that outlined the American struggle toward racial justice and equality through the lens of the legal profession: *In the Matter of Color: Race and the American Legal Process, The Colonial Period* (1978), in which he castigated the founding fathers for their hypocrisy in racial matters, and *Shades of Freedom: Racial Politics and Presumptions of the American Legal Process* (1996).

Higginbotham also taught both law and sociology at a number of schools, including the University of Michigan, Yale, Stanford, and New York University. He enjoyed a long relationship with the University of Pennsylvania, where he was considered for the position of president in 1980 before deciding to remain on the bench. Following his retirement in 1993, Higginbotham taught at Harvard Law School and also served as public service professor of jurisprudence at Harvard's John F. Kennedy School of Government. In addition, he served on several corporate boards and worked for the law firm of Paul, Weiss, Rifkind, Wharton, and Garrison in both New York and Washington.

Although most of his career was spent outside the public limelight, Higginbotham came to the forefront of public attention in 1991 when he published an open letter to Supreme Court nominee Clarence Thomas in the *University of Pennsylvania Law Review*. Castigating Thomas for what he viewed as a betrayal of all that he, Higginbotham, had worked for, Higginbotham stated, "I could not find one shred of evidence suggesting an insightful understanding on your part of how the evolutionary movement of the Constitution and the work of civil rights organizations have benefited you." Although widely criticized for his stance, Higginbotham remained a critic of Thomas's after he joined the Supreme Court and later attempted

to have a speaking invitation to Thomas rescinded by the National Bar Association in 1998.

In his later years Higginbotham filled a variety of additional roles. He served as an international mediator at the first postapartheid elections in South Africa in 1994, lent his counsel to the Congressional Black Caucus during a series of voting rights cases before the Supreme Court, and advised Texaco, Inc., on diversity and personnel issues when the firm came under fire for alleged racial discrimination in 1996. In failing health, Higginbotham's last public service came during the impeachment of President Bill Clinton in 1998, when he argued before the House Judiciary Committee that there were degrees of perjury and that President Clinton's did not qualify as "an impeachable high crime." The recipient of several honorary degrees, Higginbotham also received the Wallenburg Humanitarian Award (1994), the Presidential Medal of Freedom (1995), and the NAACP's Spingarn Medal (1996). After he and his first wife divorced in 1988, Higginbotham married Evelyn Brooks, a professor at Harvard, and adopted her daughter. He died in a Boston hospital after suffering a series of strokes.

Although he never served on the Supreme Court, Higginbotham's impact on the legal community seems certain to continue. A pioneer among African-American jurists, he also made solid contributions in the areas of legal scholarship, training, and civil rights.

• The Harvard University School of Law in Cambridge, Massachusetts, maintains a file on Higginbotham. He never completed a planned autobiography, but his career on the bench can be traced in issues 223 through 429 in the *Federal Supplement* (for his decisions on the district court) and in issues 560 through 983 in the *Federal Reporter*. His controversial criticism of Clarence Thomas appeared in "An Open Letter to Justice Clarence Thomas from a Federal Judicial Colleague," 140 *University of Pennsylvania Law Review* 1005 (1992). He was the subject of an extensive tribute by Charles J. Ogletree, Jr., Edward R. Becker, and Nathaniel R. Jones, Elaine R. Jones, and Eleanor Holmes Norton: "In Memoriam: A. Leon Higginbotham, Jr.," in *Harvard Law Review*, vol. 112, no. 8, (June 1999): 1801–33. Obituaries appeared in the *New York Times*, the *Philadelphia Inquirer*, and the *Boston Globe*, all on 15 Dec. 1998.

EDWARD L. LACH, JR.

HIGGINS, Billy (11 Oct. 1936–3 Mar. 2001), jazz drummer, was born in Los Angeles, California, the son of Samuel Higgins and Ann Blackstone. His parents' occupations are unknown. In October 1952, on his application for a social security account number, he gave his full name as Billy Higgins (that is, not William and without a middle name). Higgins's life reversed the jazz stereotype, whereby an innocent and promising young musician destroys himself prematurely through overindulgence in alcohol or drugs. For Higgins, by contrast, strength of character, musical talent, and an innate sweetness eventually won out against a difficult path into adulthood. Higgins played drums from childhood and began playing professionally at the age of twelve. He attended the Forty-Ninth Street and George Washington Carver Schools in east Los Angeles before moving to the Watts area, and at Jacob Reece, a detention school for high school students, he met the cornetist Don Cherry.

Higgins credited the local drummer Johnny Kirkwood with informally teaching him crucial fundamentals of musicianship. Before he was ready to break into the immensely competitive jazz scene in Los Angeles in the early 1950s, Higgins began working in rhythm and blues bands while also holding a job as a stock clerk at the University of California, Los Angeles (UCLA) Medical Center. His experiences with the guitarist Slim Gaillard, the pianist Amos Millburn, the guitarist Bo Diddley, the singer Jimmy Witherspoon, and other, lesser-known rhythm and blues artists helped him learn to interact with bandsmen in any setting.

During the 1950s Higgins played jazz with Teddy Edwards and Dexter Gordon, saxophonists; Carl Perkins, pianist; and Leroy Vinnegar, bassist; among others. Around 1956 Higgins became a member of the Jazz Messiahs, a quartet including Cherry and George Newman, alto saxophonist. They performed in Vancouver, British Columbia, that year. In March 1957 Higgins made his first recordings in a quartet led by the bassist Red Mitchell, with James Clay on tenor saxophone and flute and Lorraine Geller on piano. That same year Clay, Newman, and Cherry rehearsed with Ornette Coleman, a revolutionary free-jazz alto saxophonist.

In August 1957 the Jazz Messiahs returned to Vancouver. Around this time Ed Blackwell, Coleman's drummer, returned to his hometown, New Orleans, and Higgins replaced him. Later in 1957 Higgins once again traveled to Vancouver for a two-week engagement with Coleman, Cherry, and the bassist Don Payne. In February 1958 he recorded in a group led by Stan Getz, tenor saxophonist, and Cal Tjader, vibraphonist, in San Francisco. Later that month he appeared in Los Angeles on Coleman's first album, *Something Else! The Music of Ornette Coleman*.

In October and November 1958 Coleman, Cherry, and Higgins were members of the pianist Paul Bley's quintet at the Hillcrest Club in Los Angeles, with Charlie Haden on bass. Haden then joined Coleman's piano-less quartet. In Hollywood, California, the group recorded the historic free-jazz album *The Shape of Jazz to Come* in May 1959 and a second album, *Change of the Century*, in October. Higgins's role in this setting was to maintain a sense of swing rhythm in a loose-limbed, unpatterned manner that supported Coleman's unconventional compositions and improvisations.

Higgins had become addicted to heroin at the age of eighteen, and in the 1950s he was arrested several times on narcotics-related charges and once for assault. Consequently he had to receive permission from his parole officer to travel to New York for Coleman's controversial and highly publicized two-and-a-half month debut at the Five Spot, beginning in November 1959. The quartet toured nationally in the winter of 1960 and then returned to the Five Spot early in April 1960. But in mid-April, because of his past convictions, Higgins was denied a "cabaret card," a license permitting musicians to appear in New York venues serving alcohol. Consequently Higgins was obliged to quit Coleman's quartet at the height of its fame, and Blackwell took his place.

Higgins played with the pianist Thelonious Monk for an engagement at the Blackhawk in San Francisco and then returned to Los Angeles, where he joined the saxophonist John Coltrane's quartet. This affiliation began late in August 1960 and ended one month later, when Coltrane's first choice on drums, Elvin Jones, became available. Higgins's period of probation had ended, so he left for New York again and there participated in Coleman's historic recording of a double-quartet improvisation on the album *Free Jazz* on 21 December 1960, for which he and Blackwell served together as the drummers. In January 1961 Higgins made an album with the other pioneering figure in free jazz, the pianist Cecil Taylor.

While Higgins was playing in a Manhattan coffeehouse, where a cabaret card was not required, the tenor saxophonist Ike Quebec, who scouted talent for the Blue Note label, heard his performance. Higgins began to work extensively as a house drummer for Blue Note, recording dozens of small-group albums over the course of the decade under the leadership of, among others, the pianists Sonny Clark (*Leapin' and Lopin'*, 1961) and Herbie Hancock (*Takin' Off*, 1961); the saxophonist Gordon (*Go!* 1962); the trumpeter Lee Morgan (*The Sidewinder*, 1963); the saxophonists Jackie McLean (*Action*, 1964) and Hank Mobley (*Dippin'*, 1965); and the vibraphonist Bobby Hutcherson (*Stick Up!* 1966). During this period Higgins also appeared on another leading jazz label, Prestige, and with Cherry he made the album *Our Man in Jazz* for RCA Victor in July 1962 as a member of the tenor saxophonist Sonny Rollins's quartet. Higgins and Cherry then performed with Rollins. Early in 1963 Higgins and Cherry left New York to tour in Europe with Rollins, traveling from Scandinavia to Italy. Back in New York, Higgins resumed his busy schedule as a freelance drummer in the recording studios. On some sessions he worked with the pianist Cedar Walton, and from 1966 Higgins often performed in public with groups involving Walton. In autumn 1966 Higgins was a member of a quintet led by the trumpeter Lonnie Hillyer and the alto saxophonist Charles McPherson, and he briefly rejoined Coleman late in summer 1967. At some point he played in the quintet led by the tenor saxophonist Harold Land and Hutcherson.

Higgins's musical ability was never in question. He became one of those magical drummers for whom the drum kit was, in effect, an extension of his body and from which he drew an infinite constellation of percussive timbres, whether with sticks, brushes, mallets, or fingers and hands, creating sounds that left fellow jazz drummers in awe. But in the late 1960s Higgins's ongoing addiction to heroin brought his personal life to its lowest ebb. He entered the Addiction Research and Treatment Corporation in Brooklyn and in 1971 became one of the program's most successful graduates, recovering his health and never looking back. Subsequent accounts of Higgins paint a portrait of a sprightly, joyous man.

Higgins's affiliation with Walton continued into the 1990s and included Higgins's membership in Walton's trio and their cooperative group Eastern Rebellion. The two men appeared in bands led by Mobley (c. 1970–1972) and by the tenor saxophonist Clifford Jordan, the latter association involving the groups the Magic Triangle and Glass Bead Games in the 1970s. With Land, Hutcherson, and others, Walton and Higgins were members of the sextet the Timeless All Stars from around 1981 to 1992. Walton in turn appeared under Higgins's leadership, including five small-group recording dates in Italy, Los Angeles, and New York, producing most notably *The Soldier* (1979) and *Billy Higgins Quintet* (1993). Higgins appeared in the video *Ron Carter and Art Farmer: Live at Sweet Basil with Billy Higgins and Cedar Walton*, filmed in New York in 1990.

Apart from these diverse groups with Walton, Higgins co-led the Brass Company with the trumpeter Bill Hardman and the bassist Bill Lee (1972–1973), and he played again with Cherry (1975) and with Coleman (1977). In 1977 Higgins moved from New York back to Los Angeles. In 1979 he recorded with the alto saxophonist Art Pepper and then toured Japan with Pepper, and he went to London in a group led by the tenor saxophonist George Coleman. In Paris, Higgins briefly acted in the film *Round Midnight* (1986), and he played with Gordon, Hancock, and Hutcherson on its soundtrack. In 1987 Ornette Coleman's now-classic quartet with Cherry and Haden reunited for performances and recordings.

Throughout these two decades and extending into the 1990s Higgins continued his freelance recording activities with prominent jazz artists, the details of which are far too numerous to mention. Among the highlights are the quartet portions of Ornette Coleman's album *In All Languages* (1987); Haden's album *Silence*, including the trumpeter Chet Baker and the Italian pianist Enrico Pieranunzi (1987); and the cooperative trio albums *First Song* with Haden and Pieranunzi and *The Essence* with the pianist Hank Jones and the bassist Ray Drummond (both 1990). Higgins revealed an entirely different aspect of his talents on the bassist Anthony Cox's album *Dark Metals* (1991), playing the *gambare*, a plucked lute from Mali, rather than drums, in a duo with Cox on the track "Gambre" and presenting himself as an exceptional bossa nova singer and guitarist in duos with Cox on the tracks "Molly" and "Samba je hed."

In 1989 Higgins established the World Stage, a jazz club in Los Angeles, and in 1994, for its fifth anniversary, he performed there with McLean and Walton. Higgins was forced to retire in October 1995 owing to ill health. In March 1996 he underwent two liver transplants. He resumed his career in 1997, reactivat-

ing his involvement with the World Stage and performing with Ornette Coleman in New York in July and with the tenor saxophonist Charles Lloyd in San Francisco in October. That year Higgins received an American Jazz Master Fellowship from the National Endowment for the Arts. In 1998 he played with Walton at the Village Vanguard in New York and with Coleman, Haden, and the alto saxophonist Lee Konitz at the Umbria festival in Italy. He led a quartet on the West Coast through the year 2000, when the transplanted liver began to fail. He last performed on 22 January 2001 at another benefit concert given by his students and colleagues. Higgins died in Inglewood, California.

Despite his importance in jazz, the literature on Higgins is sparse, and mention of his family is virtually nonexistent. An article on a benefit concert to help underwrite his liver transplant notes that he was then living with his wife Gina (her maiden name unknown) and a son, Benjamin (Hamlin). One obituary lists four sons, a daughter, and a stepson (Ratliff). Another lists four sons and two daughters (Thurber). Other information is unavailable. Whether Higgins had a previous marriage is also unknown.

• Identified as "Billy," Higgins discusses his recovery from drug addiction in part 2 of Kenneth Brodney, "Does Methadone Have to Be for Life?" *Village Voice*, 10 June 1971, pp. 18–20, 17 June 1971, pp. 42, 44, 48. For brief essays on Higgins's career, see Valerie Wilmer, "Billy Higgins: Drum Love," *Down Beat* 35 (21 Mar. 1968): 27, 30, and "Billy Is Born Again," *Melody Maker*, 4 Sept. 1971, p. 18; Charles M. Bernstein, "The Traditional Roots of Billy Higgins," *Modern Drummer* 7 (Feb. 1983): 20–23, 74–75; Lee Hildebrand, "Jazzman Billy Higgins: He's Had Time for Everyone but Himself," *San Francisco Chronicle Datebook*, 5 Oct. 1986, p. 48; and Bill Milkowski, "Transcendent Soul: Billy Higgins," *Jazz Times* 38 (Nov. 1998): 38–41, 130–31. The best accounts of Higgins's affiliations with Ornette Coleman and John Coltrane respectively are in the biographical appendix to David Wild and Michael Cuscuna, *Ornette Coleman, 1958–1979: A Discography* (1980), pp. 58–61, and in Lewis Porter, *John Coltrane: His Life and Music* (1998), pp. 178–79. Jesse Hamlin, "Drumming up Support for Billy," *San Francisco Chronicle*, 29 July 1996, discusses a benefit concert. Obituaries are by Ben Ratliff, *New York Times*, 4 May 2001, and Jon Thurber, *Los Angeles Times*, 4 May 2001.

BARRY KERNFELD

HIGGINS, George V. (13 Nov. 1939–6 Nov. 1999), lawyer and writer, was born George Vincent Higgins in Brockton, Massachusetts, the son of John Thompson Higgins and Doris Montgomery Higgins, schoolteachers. Theirs was an Irish Catholic household in a working-class neighborhood. He read Ernest Hemingway, Arthur Conan Doyle, and John O'Hara and wrote his first unpublished novel, *Operation Cincinnatus*, when he was fifteen. In 1957 he graduated from Rockland High School. He attended Boston College, graduating in 1961. Beginning in 1962 he worked as a journalist for the *Providence Journal and Evening Bulletin* and the Associated Press, covering mafia battles and the statehouse. In 1965 he married Elizabeth

Mulkerin, with whom he had two children. In 1965 he received an M.A. from Stanford and in 1967 received a law degree from Boston College. In 1967 he worked as deputy assistant and in 1969 as assistant attorney general of Massachusetts. From 1970 to 1973 he was assistant U.S. attorney and prosecuted several underworld murders. He cited the deadline pressure of his AP job and the narrative organization of trial law as major influences on his fiction.

Higgins claimed to have drafted a dozen novels before the critical and commercial success of *The Friends of Eddie Coyle* (1972). Coyle is a midlevel dealer in Boston's illegal gun trade. Hardly glamorous, Coyle's world requires him to oscillate between the acute vigilance needed for self-preservation and the same money and family pressures that afflict all middle-class citizens. Higgins told the story in dialogue, which reveals plot, motive, and theme. He showed an ear for underworld slang, which he polished until it echoed Damon Runyon and Raymond Chandler. Critics raved about this novel, several comparing it to Hemingway's short story "The Killers."

His second novel, *The Digger's Game* (1973), follows a small-time hood who gambles away $18,000 in Las Vegas, putting himself in debt to a loan shark, whom he tries to pay off without getting himself killed. This novel "confirms that Higgins writes about the world of crime with an authenticity that is unmatched," wrote Jonathan Yardley in the *Washington Post Book World* (1 Apr. 1973). Higgins entered private practice in 1974, giving himself time to write and to teach at Northeastern University and Boston University. Among his clients were Watergate conspirator G. Gordon Liddy and Black Panther Eldridge Cleaver.

Cogan's Trade (1974), Higgins's third and most ambitious early work, explored the morality of a mob hit man. In this more difficult novel, the plot was delineated through bits of dialogue. "Like Joyce," wrote Roderick MacLeish in the *Times Literary Supplement*, "Higgins uses language in torrents, beautifully crafted, ultimately intending to create a panoramic impression" (16 Aug. 1974). The three early novels cemented a reputation for Higgins as the most literary and experimental of contemporary crime writers.

He turned to Washington, D.C., in the era of Watergate for *A City on a Hill* (1975), which focused on scandal as seen from the staff level: unfulfilled dreams, excessive ambition, and compromised idealism. He also published a nonfiction work about this milieu, *The Friends of Richard Nixon* (1975).

Committing himself to the "book a year" life of a professional writer, Higgins reviewed books and wrote magazine articles and newspaper columns. His outlook was conservative and debunking, finding favor in the *Wall Street Journal*, which offered him a television column, and *National Review*. In this period Higgins published *The Judgment of Deke Hunter* (1976) and *Dreamland* (1977), novels mostly overlooked by critics. In 1978 he took a partner in his law firm. In 1979, after fourteen years of marriage, he divorced; seven

months later he married Loretta Lucas Cubberley. *A Year or So with Edgar* (1979) was his only work of fiction in the late 1970s.

In the early 1980s Higgins was again prolific. He created a series character, Boston criminal lawyer Jerry Kennedy. In *Kennedy for the Defense* (1980), he switched to character-driven plotting. Feeling the same job pressures and materialistic values as Higgins's earlier criminals, Kennedy seldom gets to trial: his clients are guilty, and he advises them to plead so or to plea bargain, demonstrating the moral complexities of the justice system. Here, as in *Penance for Jerry Kennedy* (1985) and *Defending Billy Ryan* (1992), Higgins's implicit argument is that lesser charges, reduced sentences, and early probation are vital to both "justice" and the functioning of the penal system. Some critics also saw an argument that criminal lawyers, seemingly cynical and avaricious, served "justice" better than a formal but inflexible structure. The trio of Kennedy novels was uniformly praised, reviewers finding that they were novels about the law by a writer, rather than "lawyer novels."

Between the Kennedy novels, Higgins wrote *The Rat on Fire* (1981), about an arsonist who, for insurance money, burns scarce tenement housing. After *The Patriot Game* (1982), Higgins returned to the political milieu in *A Choice of Enemies* (1984) and to his technique of total dialogue. Critics found the story of the fall from power of Bernie Morgan, speaker of the Massachusetts state house, told from the perspective of hallways and cloakrooms, interesting and authentic; but many thought the technique had hit a wall. In 1984 Higgins also published *Style versus Substance: Boston, Kevin White, and the Politics of Illusion*, about Boston's celebrated mayor, and *Old Earl Died Pulling Traps: A Story*.

Over the next fifteen years, Higgins wrote thirteen novels and three more nonfiction books. But apart from the final Kennedy novel, there was no common denominator beside tone and technique in his work. Of *Imposters* (1986), *Outlaws* (1987), and *Trust* (1989), reviewers found the last the most interesting. Protagonist Earle Beale was a corrupt basketball player and then a corrupt car dealer. He is jailed on a technicality, and his early release raises suspicions that he is a jailhouse snitch; complications, often funny, that began in prison extend upward through society and out of sight.

In his nonfiction, Higgins examined marriage (*Wonderful Years, Wonderful Years*, 1988) and baseball (*The Progress of the Seasons: Forty Years of Baseball in Our Town*, 1989). After *Victories* (1990), Higgins wrote a prototypical lawyer novel, *The Mandeville Talent* (1991), about a young Manhattan lawyer who moves to Goshen, Massachusetts, and solves the murder of his wife's grandfather 23 years earlier. In 1992 Jerry Kennedy reappeared in *Defending Billy Ryan*. Higgins also wrote *Bomber's Law* (1993), in which the cops end up chasing each other, and the highly praised *The Agent* (1999), which follows detective Francis Clay as he investigates the death of a bisexual sports agent. His most interesting later novel was *A Change of Gravity* (1997), in which Higgins tracks the political career of Danny Hilliard, who rises through Massachusetts politics with the aid of a young working-class Machiavelli. By the time Danny becomes chair of the state's Ways and Means Committee, he has contracted the hubris of power—while his well-greased manager wheels and deals to keep their careers afloat.

Higgins died of natural causes, at 59, as *At End of Day* (2000) went to press. Reviewers found no falling off in talent. Higgins was "one of the finest creators of dialogue in the twentieth century," wrote Bill Ott in *Booklist*: "if praising Higgins's knack for putting talk on the page became a knee-jerk reaction, the talk itself never lost its vitality. Nor did it lose its uniqueness" (p. 1144).

• While there are no books on Higgins's life or work, there is much periodical literature on both. *Contemporary Authors*, NRS 17, pp. 205–11, contains a good interview, and *Contemporary Authors*, NRS 96, pp. 162–67 a useful career overview. The *New York Times* and *New York Times Book Review* reviewed almost all of his books between 1972 and 1999, often including sidelights on the author. Jonathan Yardley of the *Washington Post Book World* also reviewed seven of the novels between 1973 and 1997. The *Times Literary Supplement* published three reviews, including Roderick MacLeish's. *Booklist* published three pieces in addition to Bill Ott's review of Higgins's career ("Remembering George Higgins," 15 Feb. 2000). Retrospective obituaries appeared on 8 Nov. 1999 in both the *New York Times* and the *Washington Post*.

WILLIAM MARLING

HIGHSMITH, Patricia (19 Jan. 1921–4 Feb. 1995), writer, was born Mary Patricia Plangman in Fort Worth, Texas, the daughter of Jay Bernard Plangman and Mary Coates Plangman, commercial artists. Her parents divorced nine days before her birth. When Highsmith was three, her mother married Stanley Highsmith, another commercial artist. The family moved to New York City when Patricia Highsmith was six, then back to Texas when she was eight. A year later they returned to New York. Highsmith grew up an unhappy child with a self-involved and critical mother and a stepfather she did not like. In 1933 her mother took her back to Fort Worth, saying she and Stanley intended to divorce, but the couple reconciled in New York and left Patricia in Texas with her grandmother. The twelve-year-old felt betrayed and abandoned. She sought solace and information in books that probed emotional and psychological extremes, including Karl Menninger's *The Human Mind* (1930) and the tales of Edgar Allan Poe (with whom she shared a birth date).

In 1934 Highsmith rejoined her mother and stepfather in New York City. A year later she made her first writing sale when *Woman's World* paid the fourteen-year-old $25 to publish her letters from summer camp. In high school she wrote short-form fiction, some of which was published in her school's literary magazine. One reason she began shaping experience into prose, Highsmith said, was that "I longed for order and security" (Wilson, p. 55). Those qualities were easier for Highsmith to find on the page than in real life. Alienated from her family, confused and guilty over homosexual leanings, Highsmith displayed symptoms of anorexia throughout her teens.

In 1938 Highsmith entered Barnard College, where she experienced further intellectual, creative, and social awakening. "Here was the taste of freedom I craved," she wrote (Wilson, p. 63). She became an enthusiastic participant in the lesbian subculture of nearby Greenwich Village. In 1939, in sympathy with Spanish civil war antifascists, Highsmith joined the Young Communist League (YCL). But in 1941, put off by the rigid nature of the Communist Party's aesthetic dictates demanding that an author's plots demonstrate a predetermined universal message—and more appreciative now of the appeal of money—she quit the YCL.

For the *Barnard Quarterly*, Highsmith wrote more short stories, clever but unsettling tales of alienation and anxiety. One 1941 story, "The Heroine," rejected by the *Quarterly* as too disturbing, was later bought by *Harper's Bazaar* and became an O. Henry Memorial Award Prize winner in 1946. Highsmith was determined to become a professional writer. Among her favorite authors, during and after World War II, were Kafka, Sartre, Camus, Dostoevsky, Nietzsche, and Kierkegaard—all concerned with matters of personal identity, guilt and innocence, reality and illusion, good and evil, love and hate, which characterized her own work. Highsmith also read the Bible. After she graduated from Barnard in 1942, Highsmith got a job concocting plots for comic books. At night she worked on her own stories. She had several homosexual and a few heterosexual affairs.

In 1947 Highsmith began writing what would be her first published novel, *Strangers on a Train*. She finished the book the next year during two months at the artists colony Yaddo, which she attended with the help of Truman Capote. *Strangers on a Train* (1950), which turns on two chance acquaintances agreeing to "exchange" murders, became one of Highsmith's best-known works, thanks in part to a 1951 film version by Alfred Hitchcock.

In 1948 Highsmith began seeing a psychoanalyst, partly in an attempt to "cure" her homosexuality. During her months of therapy she wrote *The Price of Salt* (reissued as *Carol*), a novel of lesbian love published in 1952 under the pseudonym Claire Morgan. This was Highsmith's most successful book in terms of sales, with over a million copies sold in paperback. *The Price of Salt* was a pioneering work of lesbian fiction in that it had a happy ending. Happiness eluded or was avoided by Highsmith in her own personal relationships. The writer seemed to require emotional turmoil and frustration to fuel her literary work. She often used real-life experience and actual people to seed her fiction. "Specifically, she used the women in her life—a quite dizzying parade of lovers—as muses," wrote her biographer, "drawing upon her ambiguous responses to them and reworking these feelings into fiction" (Wilson, p. 3). An artist and illustrator named Mary Jane Ronin influenced the writing of Highsmith's 1960 novel *This Sweet Sickness*; without Ronin, the author noted in a journal, "it would have been quite a different book" (Wilson, p. 215). The character of Carol in *The Price of Salt* was based in part on Highsmith's experiences with a couple of other lovers (one of them the daughter of radio manufacturer Atwater Kent) but was inspired primarily by an elegant woman whom Highsmith served while working at the toy department in Bloomingdale's in December 1948, and whose house she later spied on.

In 1954 Highsmith wrote *The Talented Mr. Ripley*, the first of five novels involving the antihero Tom Ripley, an art forger, con man, and murderer with whom the author felt a close sense of identification. "I often had the feeling Ripley was writing it and I was merely typing," Highsmith said of the initial Ripley book (Wilson, p. 199). Briskly paced, the Ripley novels are Highsmith's most accessible and in a sense most likable books though no less disturbing for the moral vertigo induced in readers forced to identify with an amoral protagonist. "You're sort of at sea in her books," said the publisher Otto Penzler, "you don't know who are the good guys and the bad guys because there are no nice people. Nobody's nice, nobody's good" (Wilson, p. 223).

The French director René Clément adapted *The Talented Mr. Ripley* for his 1960 film *Plein soleil* (*Purple Noon*), with Alain Delon as the lead character. The German director Wim Wenders in 1977 cast Dennis Hopper as Ripley in *The American Friend*, an adaptation of *Ripley's Game* (published in 1974). Matt Damon played the title role in Anthony Minghella's 1999 movie *The Talented Mr. Ripley*. In 1982 Jonathan Kent portrayed Ripley in scenes from *Ripley under Ground* (published in 1970), filmed for the English television program *The South Bank Show*.

Highsmith always had greater recognition and sales in Europe than in the United States, where she was roughly pigeonholed as a detective-story writer. In Europe she was taken more seriously as a novelist of psychological fiction. In 1992 Julian Symons described her books as "finely subtle character studies," saying the best were "as interesting as anything being done in the novel today" (Symons, pp. 196–98). Graham Greene called Highsmith "the poet of apprehension" (Wilson, p. 7). In 1963 Highsmith moved to Europe for good, after having traveled there often, and lived in England and France before settling in Switzerland. She died in Locarno, Switzerland.

Highsmith's work—more than thirty novels and books of short stories—has arguably enjoyed more popularity after her death than before it, as twenty-first-century events have made her ethically ambiguous fiction, with its semisurrealistic logic, seem less postmodern than simply contemporary. "In the wake of September 11," wrote Ed Siegel in the *Boston* *Globe*, "Highsmith's world is not only more like ours, where crime and punishment or cause and effect don't necessarily go hand in hand, she seems a more important writer than ever" (Wilson, p. 464).

• Highsmith's papers are in the Swiss Literary Archives in Berne, Switzerland. Highsmith analyzed her own working methods in *Plotting and Writing Suspense Fiction* (1966). A biography of the author (who discouraged biographers during her lifetime) is Andrew Wilson's empathic *Beautiful Shadow: A Life of Patricia Highsmith* (2003), written with access to her private journals. Marijane Meaker, *Highsmith: A Romance of the 1950s* (2003), is a candid memoir by one of Highsmith's lovers (also known by the pseudonyms Vin Packer, Ann Aldrich, and M. E. Kerr). For a brief but incisive discussion of Highsmith's crime-related fiction, see Julian Symons, *Bloody Murder: From the Detective Story to the Crime Novel* (1992). An obituary is in the *New York Times*, 5 Feb. 1995.

Tom Nolan

HILDRETH, Richard (28 June 1807–11 July 1865), journalist, antislavery activist, philosopher, and historian, was born in Deerfield, Massachusetts, the son of Hosea Hildreth, a Congregational (later Unitarian) minister and educator, and Sarah McLeod Hildreth. He attended Phillips Exeter Academy, where his father was professor of mathematics and natural philosophy. After graduating from Harvard in 1826, he spent a year teaching school in Concord, Massachusetts. This experience inspired his earliest historical writing, *An Abridged History of the United States* (1831), a school textbook.

Hildreth studied with attorneys in Newburyport and Boston and was admitted to the bar in 1830, but he never practiced law. Instead, he turned to politics and journalism: first as a National Republican, then as a Whig. He believed that a strong national government was needed to mediate competing interests, protect the vulnerable, and carry out ambitious works of public utility. As co-founder, reporter, editor, and part owner of the *Boston Atlas*, he supported Henry Clay's American System and vehemently opposed the limited-government, individualistic rhetoric of Andrew Jackson, whom he called a "contemptible demagogue" (Emerson, p. 47).

In 1834 Hildreth sold his share in the *Atlas* and traveled south in search of a more healthful climate. For eighteen months he stayed on a plantation in Florida, where he wrote an antislavery treatise, *Despotism in America* (1840), and America's first antislavery novel, *The Slave; or, Memoirs of Archy Moore* (1836). *The Slave* follows the fortunes of the slave Archy Moore through slavery, escape, capture, love, fatherhood, separation from his family, and finally to a life of freedom in Britain. In the course of the story Archy is sold, inherited, and seized in payment of debt. Some of his owners are cruel, others indifferent, others merely weak. Most striking is the kind woman who sets out to treat her slaves well. The slaves, having learned to take full advantage of any relaxation of the master's vigilance, produce so little that the plantation fails, and with it the experiment in benevolent slave owning. This episode illustrates Hildreth's belief that the slave system was intrinsically corrupting to master and slave alike.

Though *The Slave* never achieved the popularity of later antislavery fiction, *Despotism in America* became an important source book for economic arguments against slavery. In it Hildreth argued that slavery enslaved masters too; they did not have liberty to be benevolent (a point made vividly in *The Slave*). It emphasized the negative effects of slavery on the South: dependency on agricultural practices that depleted the land, neglect of commerce and manufacture, constant fear of slave rebellion and the resulting siege mentality. He elucidated the relationship between slavery and racism: contempt, antipathy, and disgust toward slaves was "artfully, though imperceptibly, transferred from condition to race" and used, in a circular argument, as a justification for slavery. According to Donald Emerson the work was "a bible for countless preached or printed attacks on slavery" (p. 84). Wendell Phillips called it "the profoundest philosophical investigation" of slavery and its effects.

Returning to Massachusetts in 1836, Hildreth drew on his experiences in Florida to write on slavery and the dispossession of the southeastern Indians for the *Atlas*, which was becoming the premier Whig newspaper in New England. Within a few months, despite chronic physical illness (probably tuberculosis) and intermittently disabling periods of depression, he returned to full-time journalism as an editor, court reporter, and Washington correspondent. In addition, he wrote speeches, pamphlets, two books on the banking crisis, and a campaign biography of William Henry Harrison, of whom he was an early and ardent supporter. Hildreth's biographer credits the *Atlas*'s endorsement of Harrison with undermining the presidential aspirations of Daniel Webster.

As Massachusetts debated the liquor license law of 1838, Hildreth became increasingly active in the temperance cause. He served as corresponding secretary of the Moral Suasion Temperance Society, organized demonstrations in favor of the license law, and founded a short-lived temperance paper, the *Boston Spy*. In 1838 and again in 1839, the Massachusetts Whig party split into "regular" and "temperance" factions. In 1838, each faction nominated its own slate of candidates; the temperance Whigs were triumphant. In 1839, the Whigs nominated a mixed slate (with Hildreth as candidate for state House of Representatives), but when pro-liquor Whigs threatened to vote Democratic, the Whigs replaced all the temperance candidates a few days before the election. The temperance Whigs then nominated their own slate. Hildreth took a leading role in urging temperance Whigs not to vote for anyone, Whig or Democrat, who did not support the liquor licensing law. The Democratic candidate was elected governor, and the licensing law repealed. Richard Haughton, then editor of the *Atlas*, blamed the temperance faction for the Whigs' poor showing in the election. In the ensuing

spate or recriminations, Hildreth resigned from the *Atlas*.

From 1839 to 1843 Hildreth lived in British Guiana. He supported himself by editing two newspapers and a local guidebook, light work that left him time for study and reflection. He translated Jeremy Bentham's *Theory of Legislation*, which had only been published in French, and began work on an ambitious philosophical work, "The Science of Man," "an attempt to apply the inductive method to the moral sciences" (preface to *Theory of Morals*). He completed the first two of a projected six or more volumes, *Theory of Morals* (1844) and *Theory of Politics* (1853).

In *Theory of Morals* Hildreth rejected the idea that virtue is that which is pleasing to God, arguing that morality is rooted in an instinctive human desire to avoid giving pain to others. Though virtue "grows . . . out of man's very constitution," he wrote, it cannot operate properly in people who are suffering from hunger, fear, and hopelessness. He concluded, "To render mankind more virtuous, it is essentially necessary . . . to relieve their pains" (p. 269). For these ideas the book was denounced, even by Hildreth's fellow Unitarians, as licentious, blasphemous, and atheistic. Shaken by this response, he refrained for ten years from publishing *Theory of Politics*.

In 1844 Hildreth married the portrait painter Caroline Gould Negus. They had two sons, one of whom died in childhood. For eight years Caroline supported the family while Richard researched and wrote his *History of the United States of America* (1849–1852). Influenced by German ideas of "scientific" history, he rejected the fashion for "centennial sermons and Fourth-of-July orations . . . in the guise of history" and set about "bursting the thin, shining bubble . . . of a colonial golden age of fabulous purity and virtue" (preface to *History*). The *History* won Hildreth considerable respect. Even those who disliked its plain style and irreverent treatment of the Founders praised its detail, accuracy, and "impartiality." Though considered for a professorship of history at Harvard in 1849 and again in 1851, he was turned down.

Failure to obtain an academic position, and disappointing sales of the *History*, led Hildreth to abandon plans for a final installment covering the period after 1821. Instead, he revised *Theory of Politics*, adding reflections on revolution and on the relationship between capitalism and democracy written in response to the revolutions of 1848. Hildreth's sympathetic presentation of socialism reflected his reading of French utopian socialists and may have been influenced by his wife, who had once been a director of a utopian socialist society in Boston. He asked, "Is there never to be an Age of the People—of the working class?" and warned, "This socialist question of the distribution of wealth, once raised, is not to be blinked out of sight" (*Theory of Politics*, p. 267, 273–74).

A central concern of *Theory of Politics* is the morality of rebellion against an unjust government. The question was of more than academic interest to Hildreth, for this was the period of his greatest activity as an abolitionist. He counseled submitting to unjust laws "when forcible resistance would be productive of more evil than good," but not "aiding in their enforcement." However, "unarmed or passive resistance to bad laws is always morally right" (*Theory of Politics*, p. 255). In accordance with these principles he joined the Vigilance Committee formed to prevent the Fugitive Slave Law from being put into operation in Boston and donated legal services to fugitive slaves and those charged with helping them.

Hildreth returned to newspaper work in 1854 as editor of the *Boston Telegraph* and a regular contributor to the *New York Tribune*. In 1856 the Hildreths moved to New York, where Richard had been offered a position as a "principal editor" of the *Tribune*. A fellow journalist recalled, "I think he did very much toward giving the newspaper an anti-slavery tone; perhaps at one time he was in advance of its editor [Horace Greeley], not in his detestation of the institution, but in his eagerness for its speedy overthrow" (quoted in Emerson, p. 156). The *Tribune*'s large circulation made this the period of Hildreth's life in which he reached the largest audience and had the greatest influence.

Hildreth's health worsened during his time at the *Tribune*, and by 1860 it broke down completely. Hoping that a warmer climate would help him again, Caroline used all her influence to get him appointed consul to Trieste in 1861. He resigned this position in 1864 and was supported during his last months by contributions from friends. He died in Florence. After her husband's death Caroline remained in Italy, where she died of cholera two years later.

Hildreth was best known in the decades following his death as a historian of the United States. His reputation, along with the idea of "objective" history, declined during the twentieth century. His antislavery novel, remarkably free from the patronizing tone that characterized most antislavery works by whites, now appears to be his greatest work. Drawing on his own observations and his deep sympathy with the enslaved, he was able to write convincingly in the voice of a slave at a time when few authentic slave narratives had been published.

• The major biography of Hildreth is Donald E. Emerson, *Richard Hildreth* (1946). Biographical sketches appear in many nineteenth-century biographical dictionaries; the most substantial is by William S. Thayer in *Cyclopaedia of American Literature* (1856). A biographical sketch and a detailed bibliography of Hildreth's magazine articles, poetry, fiction, pamphlets, speeches, and contributions to reference books are in Louis S. Friedland, "Richard Hildreth's Minor Works," *Papers of the Bibliographical Society of America* (1946) 40: 127–50. Martha M. Pingel, *An American Utilitarian: Richard Hildreth as a Philosopher* (1948), considers Hildreth's philosophy and includes otherwise unpublished fragments of two unfinished volumes of his "Science of Man" series and a selection of short works. These include letters to Andrews Norton and Francis Bowen, which contain Hildreth's clearest statement of his personal philosophy and religious beliefs. Two classic mid-twentieth-century evaluations of Hildreth's importance as a historian, Alfred H. Kelly, "Richard Hildreth," in William T. Hutchinson, ed., *The Marcus W. Jernegan Essays in American Historiography* (1937), and Arthur M. Schlesinger, Jr., "The Problem of Richard Hildreth," *New England Quarterly* 13 (1940): 223–45, initiated a revival of interest in Hildreth and his work that lasted for some twenty years. For a more recent view, see Michael Kraus and Davis D. Joyce, *The Writing of American History* (1985). Hildreth is identified as America's first antislavery novelist in Lorenzo Dow Turner, *Anti-Slavery Sentiment in American Literature Prior to 1865* (1929). Nancy Bentley, "White Slaves: The Mulatto Hero in Antebellum Fiction," *American Literature* 65, no. 3 (1993): 501–22, compares *The Slave* with Harriet Beecher Stowe's *Uncle Tom's Cabin*, William Wells Brown's *Clotel*, and works by Frederick Douglass. An obituary is in the *New York Tribune*, 2 Aug. 1865.

Lynn Gordon Hughes

HILL, Martha (1 Dec. 1900–17 Nov. 1995), dance educator, was born Grace Martha Hill in East Palestine, Ohio, the daughter of Grant Hill, a mining engineer, and Grace Todd Hill. The eldest of four children, Martha Hill described herself as a "Bible Belt" child who was expected to exhibit proper demeanor. Charity, fortitude, honesty, and good faith were key to her Presbyterian upbringing, characteristics that she kept throughout her life. From age six, she took piano and voice lessons, following in her father's footsteps as an amateur musician. A family outing at a Pittsburgh exposition introduced her to the art of Terpsichore in the form of a "skirt" dancer performing in the style of Loie Fuller.

An excellent student, Hill was also a patriotic one: as valedictorian of her senior class she delivered an essay on "Americanism." Her "secret idol" was her step-aunt, who performed on a steamboat that toured up and down the Missouri River. "I adored her from afar!" Martha explained, "She was my inspiration about dance." Drawn to movement as a means of expression, in 1918 Hill enrolled in a two-year program at the Battle Creek Normal School of Physical Education, where she studied folk, aesthetic, and interpretative dancing with Marietta J. Lane. In 1921 she took over Lane's position as "Assistant in Dancing and Athletics." From 1923 to 1926 she was director of dance at Kansas State Teachers College. In the summer of 1926 she went to New York City to study ballet with Louis Chalif and "free" expression with Anna Duncan. After seeing Martha Graham dance, Hill immediately sought her out for lessons. Then, her savings spent, she accepted another faculty position, this time at the University of Oregon. She returned to study with Graham during the summers of 1928 and 1929. Graham then invited Hill to join her group, and for the next two years she performed in Graham's early experimental works, as well as in *Heretic* and *Primitive Mysteries*, using the stage name Martha Todd. Beginning in 1929 Hill taught at the experimental Lincoln School operated by Teachers College, Columbia University, while completing degree work there.

In 1930 Hill moved to Greenwich Village after accepting a position as director of dance within the School of Education at New York University, where she developed a graduate program in dance. Bennington College president Robert Devore Leigh hired Hill to create a program with a dance major when the school opened its doors in October 1932. She split her teaching week between the two colleges until 1951.

In 1934 Hill founded and codirected with Mary Josephine Shelly Bennington's Summer School of the Dance (held at Mills College in 1939, and renamed Bennington School of the Arts 1940–1943). Hill championed dance artists and their companies in residence as the educational "experts," and the school soon became a stronghold for modern dance. Hill became the symbolic "bridge" connecting students with master teachers such as Martha Graham, Louis Horst, and Doris Humphrey and was responsible for bringing new choreographic works to fruition at Bennington, including such masterpieces as Graham's *Letter to the World*, Humphrey's *Passacaglia in C minor*, and Hanya Holm's *Trend*. In 1948 she recreated the Bennington model with the Connecticut College–New York University Summer School of Dance at Connecticut College in New London. That summer, the school established the American Dance Festival, which produced Graham's landmark work *Diversion of Angels* (first titled *Wilderness Stair*) during its inaugural season and José Limón's *Moor's Pavane* in the summer of 1949. The school became the Connecticut College Summer School of Dance for its fourth season, in 1951. Merce Cunningham and Paul Taylor were among those who joined Graham, Humphrey, and Limón in successive years.

In 1951 Hill became the founding director of the Juilliard School's dance division, a position she held until 1985 when she became artistic director emerita. At Juilliard she developed a dance curriculum that would be replicated in conservatories and dance departments throughout the world. Believing that the field now demanded dancers with equal training in both ballet and modern dance, she recruited choreographer Antony Tudor as the head of the ballet department, along with such modern leaders as Graham, Humphrey, Horst, Limón, and Anna Sokolow.

In 1952 Hill married Thurston Jynkins Davies, former president of Colorado College. After his death in 1961, Hill continued to live in her apartment in Brooklyn Heights, New York, until her death thirty-four years later.

Hill was a pivotal figure in the development of dance in the twentieth century and helping to make it a part of higher education in the United States. She was responsible for creating major centers in dance education where generations of dance leaders prospered and emerging dance artists trained. She continued to be active until the end of her life, maintaining a position of prestige and spreading her influence to Australia, Hong Kong, and Israel. She served on a number of panels and advisory commissions, receiving a stream of accolades throughout her lifetime.

Among her awards were honorary doctorates from Adelphi University (1965), Mt. Holyoke College (1966), Bennington College (1969), Towson State University (1981), the Juilliard School (1987), and Purchase College of New York State (1992).

• Hill is the subject of an archival video collection, the Martha Hill Oral History Project, produced at Hong Kong Academy for the Arts, July 1990, and figures prominently in *The Early Years: The Bennington Years*, produced at Purchase College. Both can be viewed at the New York Public Library for the Performing Arts. For further reading on Hill at Bennington, see Sali Ann Kriegsman's *Modern Dance in America: The Bennington Years* (1981) and Janet Mansfield Soares, "Martha Hill: The Early Years," Ballet Review 28, 4 (Winter 2000). On her work with Graham, see the chapter on Hill in Robert Tracy, *Goddess* (1996). See also Anna Kisselgoff, "The Innovations of Martha Hill" in the *New York Times* (28 Mar. 1982). An obituary is in the *New York Times*, 21 Nov. 1995.

JANET MANSFIELD SOARES

HIRSCHFELD, Albert (21 June 1903–20 Jan. 2003), caricaturist, was born in St. Louis, Missouri, the third son of Isaac Hirschfeld, an occasionally employed salesman, and Rebecca Rothberg, the driving force of the family and, as a sales clerk in a department store, its chief support. Albert proved a prodigy of an artist, and when he was eleven his mother, advised to take her son to New York City for better education in art, packed up the family and moved there. Albert attended public school, then the Art Students League and at night the National Academy of Design. He was soon fascinated by vaudeville and theater, and at age seventeen he began his lifelong association with the entertainment industry as an errand boy for Goldwyn Pictures Publicity Department in New York. A year later he was briefly art director at Selznick Pictures before he opened his own art agency to service the studio on a contract basis. When the producer went bankrupt, Hirschfeld was left in debt, and in 1923 he went to work for Warner Brothers. He retired his debts in a year.

Aspiring to be a painter and sculptor, Hirschfeld went to Paris in 1924 and, by his own account, spent most of the rest of the decade there and in Spain, North Africa, and Italy, periodically returning to New York to replenish his purse. The Left-Bank bungalow he rented with two others had no hot water, so Hirschfeld stopped shaving and henceforth wore a full beard. At various times he received training under the Academie Julien and the London County Council, and his paintings were exhibited in Paris, Chicago, New York, and St. Louis. In December 1926, during one of his visits to New York, his first theatrical drawing was published in the *New York Herald Tribune*, to which he contributed for the next twenty years. His work began appearing in other newspapers in the city, and in 1927 he signed a contract with Metro Goldwyn Mayer (MGM) to do promotional drawings at $15,000 a year, an arrangement that lasted for thirty years. On 13 July 1927 he married Florence Ruth

Hobby, an actress, and promptly convinced the *Tribune* to send him with his wife to Moscow to report on Russian theater. They stayed for a year. On 29 January 1928 Hirschfeld began his lifelong relationship with the *New York Times* with the publication of a drawing of the vaudevillian Harry Lauder.

In 1932 Hirschfeld joined the journalist and author Alexander King in publishing a short-lived avantgarde satirical magazine, *Americana*, but most of his published work in the 1930s appeared in the theater sections of New York newspapers. During the Great Depression years Hirschfeld, like many creative personalities of his generation, set out to save the world with his art and produced, without pay, political cartoons for *New Masses*, a crusading magazine with socialist (even communist) leanings. But by the end of the decade Hirschfeld had become disenchanted with "the infallibility of political doctrine," adding, "I have ever since been closer to Groucho Marx than Karl" (Hirschfeld, 1970, pp. 14, 15). In 1943 Hirschfeld agreed to do his theatrical drawings exclusively for the *New York Times*, and did so for the rest of his life. His nontheatrical efforts—renditions of personalities in motion pictures, television shows, politics, and other cultural venues—were increasingly published in magazines as well as newspapers, eventually in virtually every periodical of any significance. On 8 May 1943 Hirschfeld married another actress, the Hamburgborn Dorothy "Dolly" Louise Clara Haas, following a last-minute divorce from his first wife, from whom he had been separated for several years and with whom he had no children. To celebrate the birth of their only child in 1945, Hirschfeld started hiding her name, Nina, in his drawings, thereby inaugurating what he called the "national insanity" of readers trying to count the number of times the name appears, sometimes as strands of hair, sometimes as folds in a shirt, sometimes in the filigree of a piece of jewelry, sometimes all the above and more in a single drawing.

In 1946 Hirschfeld's passion for the theater persuaded him to join his writer friend S. J. Perelman in writing a musical, *Sweet Bye and Bye*, which closed immediately after opening in Philadelphia on 21 September 1946. But Hirschfeld and Perelman continued their collaboration the next year, traveling from Shanghai to Singapore and recording their adventures in a series of articles for *Holiday* magazine. By the early 1950s Hirschfeld's fence-post signature predominated in American theatrical caricature. He was the last of a breed that had proliferated with the burgeoning of magazine journalism in the twenties and thirties.

The emerging American film industry during the 1920s broadened the function of caricature. Eschewing caricature as a weapon of ridicule in the political arena, caricaturists working for motion picture studios and theatrical ventures used their skills to venerate celebrity—even sometimes to create it. Hirschfeld's 1935 caricatures of the Marx Brothers, for example, defined their look. Thenceforth MGM makeup crews strived to make the zany trio look like Hirschfeld's drawings, enacting in microcosm the reciprocating phenomenon of celebrity caricature. Explained Hirschfeld, "The caricatures became the image the public figure had been striving to become" (Hirschfeld, 1970, p. 21). In describing his approach, Hirschfeld said: "The art of caricature . . . is not necessarily one of malice. It is never my aim to destroy the play or the actor by ridicule. . . . My contribution is to take the character—created by the playwright and acted out by the actor—and reinvent it for the reader" (Hirschfeld, 1970, p. 30). Perhaps for this reason Hirschfeld called himself a "characterist" rather than a "caricaturist." Upon the expiration of the MGM arrangement in 1956, he began an association with United Artists that lasted for twenty-five years.

Hirschfeld's early inspirations were Al Frueh and Miguel Covarrubias. From the latter, with whom he shared a studio in the early days, Hirschfeld learned that caricatures could be designs, abstract shapes arranged in telling configurations. But Hirschfeld did not begin with the buoyant line for which he was ultimately so celebrated. It was in evidence within a year of his newspaper debut, but it was not until he visited the South Pacific island of Bali for nine months in 1931 that his love affair with line began in earnest. On the island the sun bleached out all color, he said, "leaving everything in pure line" (Hirschfeld, 1970, p. 19). When he left the island, Hirschfeld left painting and sculpture too.

Typically in his portrayal of the cast and ambiance of a stage production, a movie, or a television show, Hirschfeld created arabesques of line, mass, texture, and shape, masterpieces in black and white; and in rendering movement particularly, his effortless lighter-than-air line achieves its ultimate expressiveness, where single lines coil and spring in imitation of the performers' action. His sweeping, undulating line is matchless in supple grace and telling simplicity, his likenesses of show business personalities and even the stray politician are eerily accurate, and his compositions are playful interpretations of plays as well as personages. Barbra Steisand is birdlike in Hirschfeld's drawing—"all points, with a wide-open mouth and lidded eyes," according to Richard F. Shepard and Mel Gussow (*New York Times*, 20 Jan. 2003). The rotund Zero Mostel, drawn as Tevye in *Fiddler on the Roof*, is "a circle of black beard and hair," they said, with fierce eyes glowering up at an uncomprehending heaven. The comedian Phil Silvers is all high forehead and enormous eyeglasses, just a tiny curve for a mouth. Carol Channing is a happily gaping mouth and spangled eyes. In drawings of Ray Bolger, the dancing figure never touches the floor. Hirschfeld created his interpretations from life. In Broadway's theaters he was a fixture on opening nights, sitting on the aisle in the dark, famously making cryptic sketches unseen on a notepad concealed in his pocket. After the play he returned to his brownstone in the East Nineties and, sitting at his drawing board in a barber's chair, converted his pocket notes into the elegant drawing that appeared on Sunday.

In 1975 Hirschfeld received a special Tony, the Antoinette Perry Award, signaling that the theater world welcomed him not only as an observer but also as one of its own. In 1991 the U.S. Postal Service issued a series of stamps bearing Hirschfeld's caricatures of comedians, and in 1994 he did another series of stamps with caricatures of silent film stars. His second Tony Award in 1994 was the Brooks Atkinson Award, of which he was the first recipient. The National Cartoonists Society gave him the Milton Caniff Lifetime Achievement Award in 1996, and that year New York City's Landmarks Conservancy pronounced him a Living Landmark. On 23 October 1996, two years after Dolly Haas died, Hirschfeld married Louise Kerz, an arts historian. There were no children from this marriage. In late 2002 it was announced that on his one hundredth birthday the Martin Beck Theater on West Forty-fifth would be renamed the Al Hirschfeld Theater, the first time a Broadway theater was named after a visual artist. He was elected to the American Academy of Arts and Letters in 2003. According to his wife, on the Friday before Hirschfeld died in Manhattan, the White House told him he would receive the National Medal of the Arts. But his greatest honor resides in the tradition he came to represent. Arthur Gelb, once managing editor of the *New York Times*, observed that it was widely accepted in show business that "you haven't arrived until you've been drawn by Al" (quoted in Graybow, 20 Jan. 2003). For seventy years Hirschfeld's pen-and-ink players—some with stars twinkling for eyes, others with whirling pinwheels, blind squints, or starkly staring dots—gesticulated extravagantly with tentacle fingers at the end of elastic arms and loped or swirled joyfully across the front page of the *New York Times* theater section or just loitered there. Either way they created a visual chronicle of American show business in the twentieth century, both catalog and history. After a play closes, often all that is left of it for the record is a handful of newspaper reviews—and Hirschfeld's drawing.

• Small permanent collections of the estimated seven thousand drawings Hirschfeld produced are in the St. Louis Art Museum, the Cleveland Art Museum, the Museum of the City of New York, the Smithsonian Institution National Portrait Gallery, the Metropolitan Museum of Art, the Whitney Museum, and the New York Public Library. The Margo Feiden Galleries in New York City have offered his work for sale for twenty-five years. Most of the biographical information about Hirschfeld is in his autobiographical essays in book collections of his drawings, but many of those essays repeat in the contents of his *The World of Hirschfeld* (1970). The artist's comments on individual drawings in his *Hirschfeld on Line* (1998), with Mel Gussow's biographical introduction, add substantially to the account. Some of Hirschfeld's nontheatrical work is collected in his *Manhattan Oases* (1932; repr., *Speakeasies of 1932*, 2003) and *Harlem as Seen by Hirschfeld* (1941; repr. with some additional material, *Hirschfeld's Harlem*, 2004). Hirschfeld wrote and illustrated with imaginary showbiz denizens a lighthearted primer of the entertainment world, *Show Business Is No Business* (1951). Other compilations of Hirschfeld's work are Hirsch-feld, *The American Theatre as Seen by Hirschfeld* (1961), *Hirschfeld* (1979), and *Hirschfeld: Art and Recollections from Eight Decades* (1991); Clare Bell, *Hirschfeld's New York* (2001); and David Leopold, *Hirschfeld's Hollywood* (2001). Hirschfeld's presence in Brooks Atkinson and Al Hirschfeld, *The Lively Years: 1920–1973* (1973), is extensive. Fifty volumes of the annual book series *The Best Plays of [the Year]*, ranging from 1952–1953 to 2001–2002, include a section of Hirschfeld's drawings. Hirschfeld's caricatures illustrate John Fisher, *Call Them Irreplaceable* (1976). Hirschfeld illustrated several books by S. J. Perelman, including *Westward Ha?* (1948), which reprinted the 1947 *Holiday* magazine series; *Listen to the Mocking Bird* (1949), and *The Swiss Family Perelman* (1950). Max Wilk, *And Did You Once See Sidney Plain? A Random Memoir of S. J. Perelman* (1986), includes Hirschfeld's drawings, most reprinted from Perelman's books. Another cast of imaginary Hirschfeld characters illustrates Garson Kanin's Runyonesque *Do Re Mi* (1955), a fictional exposé of what the dust jacket calls the "jukebox gangland world." All of the members of the famed Algonquin Roundtable appear under Hirschfeld's pen in Margaret Case Harriman, *The Vicious Circle* (1951). In 1995 his work was preserved on a CD-ROM, *Hirschfeld: The Great Entertainers*, and in 1996 Susan Dryfoos produced a videotape, *The Line King: The Al Hirschfeld Story*, which shows him at work, stroking that impeccable line into being. An obituary by Richard F. Shepard with Mel Gussow is in the *New York Times* online, 20 Jan. 2003, and in print, 21 Jan. 2003. The Associated Press and Reuters produced articles, the latter by Martha Graybow, online, 20 Jan. 2003; and Richard Corliss wrote an appreciative obituary for Time.com, the online *Time* magazine, 29 Jan. 2003.

ROBERT C. HARVEY

HITCHINGS, George H. (18 Apr. 1905–27 Feb. 1998), chemist, was born George Herbert Hitchings in Hoquiam, Grays Harbor County, Washington, the son of George Herbert Hitchings, a shipbuilder, and Lillian Matthews Hitchings. After attending grade school in Berkeley and San Diego, California, and Bellingham, Washington, Hitchings completed his secondary education in Seattle, where he was class salutatorian. He attended the nearby University of Washington and was initially interested in medicine before settling on chemistry as a major. Elected to Phi Beta Kappa his junior year, he earned a B.S. (1927) and an M.S. (1928). Hitchings then completed his education at Harvard University, where he earned a Ph.D. in biological chemistry in 1933. In May of that same year, he married Beverly Reimer. They had two children.

After serving at Harvard as a tutor, instructor, and finally (1936) associate in biochemistry, Hitchings became a senior instructor in the subject at Western Reserve University (later Case Western Reserve) in 1939. He joined the Burroughs Wellcome Company in 1942 and remained with the firm for the balance of his career. On joining the firm at the Tuckahoe, New York, location, Hitchings became the sole member of the Department of Biochemistry. Although financial support was limited and his staff would remain relatively small for years, he was free to develop his own lines of inquiry.

Hitchings made a critical addition to his staff in 1944 when he hired Gertrude Elion. Despite the fact that she was female and did not possess a doctorate—two factors that generally worked against researchers seeking employment in that era—Hitchings was impressed with her intelligence and the two worked together for decades. They focused their efforts on understanding how cells within the human body metabolize nucleic acid, one of the building blocks of protein. They also worked extensively with bacteria, viruses, and protozoa in an attempt to alter the way these entities reproduced. They attempted to introduce compounds into the cellular structures to "fool" the cells into thinking they were reproducing when in fact their growth had been halted.

Their first big breakthrough came in 1945, when they created their first "false building block," a substance closely related to thiamine, one of the four chemical bases of DNA. In 1947 the team also received financial assistance from the Sloan-Kettering Institute in exchange for submitting certain compounds that were tested for their effectiveness in treating cancer. One of the first such compounds, 2,6-diaminopurine, eventually led to the production in 1951 of 6-mercaptopurine, which proved extremely effective in treating leukemia in children. Hitchings continued to work with 6MP and in 1959 discovered that it decreased the ability of rabbits to produce antibodies against foreign substances in their bodies. When a less toxic form of the drug—called azathioprine, or Imuran—was developed, surgeon Roy Calne successfully used it to control tissue rejection in humans after kidney transplants. Hitchings also discovered that 6MP was broken down in the body by xanthine oxydase, an enzyme that converts purine into uric acid. Since gout is caused by an excess of uric acid in the body, Hitchings developed allopurinol, which helped to block the production of uric acid by competing with xanthine oxydase.

As Hitchings moved up through the corporate ranks, serving successively as chief biochemist, associate research director, research director, and finally vice-president in charge of research in 1967, Elion often followed him on the promotion ladder. The two continued to enjoy success even as Burroughs relocated its research facilities to the Research Triangle Park in North Carolina in 1970. During the 1970s their work led to the development of cycloid, which was one of the first effective antiviral drugs brought to market that featured acceptable levels of side effects and which quickly played a major role in the treatment of genital herpes. Having successfully introduced drugs that combated bacterial infections (cottrimoxazole or trimethoprim A) as well as malaria (pyrimethamine), the two researchers went on to develop zidovudine, which led directly to the development of AZT, one of the first medications to prove effective against AIDS.

Although Hitchings officially retired in 1975, he remained professionally active well into his nineties. Although he held eighty-nine U.S. patents, authored or coauthored over 300 published papers, and served as president of the American Association for Cancer Research in 1983 and 1984, he was largely unrecognized outside of his profession, at least partly because he labored in an industrial setting. All that changed in 1988 when he and Elion, along with British scientist Sir James Black, shared the Nobel Prize for Physiology or Medicine, an honor that many felt was overdue. In his later years Hitchings became deeply involved in philanthropy, serving as director (1968) and later president (1971) of the Burroughs Wellcome Fund, a small nonprofit foundation dedicated to assisting underfunded areas of biomedical research. He also founded what later became the Greater Triangle Community Foundation and was active in the American Red Cross and the United Way. After his first wife died in 1985, Hitchings married Dr. Joyce Shaver in 1989. In his last years he suffered from Alzheimer's disease and died at his home in Chapel Hill, North Carolina.

Although he labored in relative obscurity for years, George Hitchings finally received recognition for his lifesaving contributions to the field of pharmacology.

• Hitchings's papers have not been located, although his firm (now known as Glaxo Wellcome) holds some material relating to his life and career. The best source of information on Hitchings is his autobiography written after his 1988 award, which can be found on the web at http://www.nobel.se/medicine/laureates/1988/hitchings-autobio.html. Obituaries are in the *Washington Post*, 1 Mar. 1998, and the *New York Times*, 2 Mar. 1998.

EDWARD L. LACH, JR.

HOCKETT, Charles F. (17 Jan. 1916–3 Nov. 2000), linguist, anthropologist, and composer, was born Charles Francis Hockett in Columbus, Ohio, the son of Homer Carey Hockett, a historian, and Amy Francisco Hockett. At the age of sixteen, he entered Ohio State University, where his father served on the faculty. The university offered neither a linguistics nor an anthropology major to meet Hockett's interests in languages and cultures, so he began the study of Greek as part of a combined undergraduate/graduate program in ancient history. His first Greek instructor was the linguist George M. Bolling, who encouraged him to enroll in an introductory linguistics course that Bolling was teaching. As a textbook for the class Bolling used Leonard Bloomfield's *Language* (1933), published just weeks earlier. Hockett became Bloomfield's chief intellectual heir. Not only did his own work frequently develop ideas introduced by Bloomfield, but he also worked with Bloomfield's fieldnotes, editing volumes on Eastern Ojibwa and Menomini that appeared posthumously under Bloomfield's name.

Following simultaneous receipt of the bachelor and master of arts degrees in 1936, Hockett began graduate study in anthropology at Yale University. His area of focus was linguistics, and his language of specialization was Potawatomi, an Algonquian language in which he conducted fieldwork in northern Wisconsin in the summer of 1937. In the summers of 1938 and 1939 he attended the Linguistic Institute of the Linguistic Society of America, held in those years at the University of Michigan. There he met Bloomfield, a specialist in the Algonquian languages and a faculty member at the Institute. After receiving the doctoral degree in 1939 with a dissertation on Potawatomi, Hockett went to the University of Chicago to study briefly with Bloomfield, then to the University of Michigan, where he met Shirley Orlinoff, a mathematician. They married in 1942 and together had five children.

Drafted into the U.S. Army in 1942, Hockett was assigned to a program developing teaching materials in foreign languages, and became a specialist in Chinese. Through this work, in both Washington, D.C., and New York City, and in his earlier studies at Yale, Chicago, and Michigan, he was at the center of the entire generation of linguists who followed Bloomfield, many of whom were later known as "Bloomfieldians" or, more accurately, "post-Bloomfieldians." Hockett became an acknowledged leader of this group and his publications would later be cited widely as codifications of the theories and practices of American structural linguistics of the late 1930s, the 1940s, and much of the 1950s. Especially widely read and frequently cited were his articles "A System of Descriptive Phonology" (*Language* 18 [1942]: 3–21) and "Problems of Morphemic Analysis" (*Language* 23 [1947]: 321–43) and his book *A Manual of Phonology* (1955). The linguistics program at Cornell University, where he joined the faculty in linguistics and anthropology in 1946, remained a center for structural work throughout most of Hockett's career.

Hockett's theoretical linguistic work was always connected to his findings in descriptive work, and it sometimes challenged the precepts of his post-Bloomfieldian colleagues. For example, in 1947 he published two important articles on simultaneous phonological features, one drawing on an American Indian language ("Componential Analysis of Sierra Popoluca," *International Journal of American Linguistics* 13: 258–67), the other on Chinese ("Peiping Phonology," *Journal of the American Oriental Society* 67: 253–67). In both he rejected the "principle of linearity," which held that phones representing adjacent phonemes must occur in the same linear order in both phonetic and phonemic notation. Hockett saw this assumption as largely derived from orthographic tradition and noted that phonological features could be simultaneous or successive.

"Two Models of Grammatical Description" (*Word* 10 [1954]: 210–34) is perhaps Hockett's most widely cited article. Here he discussed criteria for the evaluation of competing models. Although Hockett himself claimed that his intention was to suggest that the item-and-process model deserved serious consideration, many readers took the article as "a defense of item-and-arrangement and an attack on item-and-process" (*The State of the Art*, 1968, p. 29). Item-and-arrangement grammars state forms and the arrangements, or

distributions, in which they occur; item-and-process grammars take a single form as basic and derive related forms from that basic form. In the mid to late 1950s, this was seen as a debate between established American structural linguistics and the emerging generative theory of Noam Chomsky.

In 1958 Hockett published *A Course in Modern Linguistics*, a textbook that "reflects the great achievements of structural linguistics: the broad compass of languages described, the self-confident treatment of systems of great diversity" (Uriel Weinreich, "Mid-Century Linguistics: Attainments and Frustrations," *Romance Philology* 13 [1960]: 320). Appearing within a year of Chomsky's *Syntactic Structures* (1957), Hockett's text became a bastion of American structuralism but was soon overshadowed by the growth of generative theory. Although he continued to explore a wide range of linguistic subjects (including animal communication, language and psychiatry, universals of language, linguistics and mathematics, slips of the tongue), he also devoted much of his writing in the 1960s and 1970s to critical analyses of, and alternatives to, the views of Chomsky, beginning with his 1964 presidential address to the Linguistic Society of America. Published as "Sound Change" (*Language* 41 [1965]: 185–204), the title was ambiguous, referring primarily to historical phonological change in human languages, but also, on a more subtle level, to the nature of then on-going changes in linguistic theory.

Hockett became perturbed by what some termed "the eclipsing stance" of linguists who had "become so enamored of their particular approach that they incline to scoff at any other" (quoted from his *Refurbishing our Foundations*, 1987, p. 1), seeing this especially in the writings of some followers of Chomsky. But he also acknowledged a similar stance on the part of his own group of post-Bloomfieldians in the 1940s. To address this, Hockett increasingly incorporated into his own writing accounts of the historical background of concepts and movements in linguistics. "Sound Change" proposed four major breakthroughs in the history of linguistics: the early nineteenth-century genetic hypothesis on the relatedness of languages, the late-nineteenth-century hypothesis on the regularity of sound change, the phonemic hypothesis of the early twentieth century, and what Hockett termed the "accountability hypothesis," primarily found in the work of Chomsky, establishing requirements for a formal theory of language. Soon, however, Hockett concluded that Chomsky's views were "largely in error" but "too powerful merely to be shrugged aside," and he responded with *The State of the Art*. From that point on, much of his work was historiographically oriented, including the very important collection of Bloomfield's work that he edited, *A Leonard Bloomfield Anthology* (1970).

Hockett remained on the Cornell faculty until his retirement in 1982. He served as president of the Linguistic Society of America (1964) and the Linguistic Association of Canada and the United States (1982). In the 1990s he spent time as adjunct professor of linguistics at Rice University but increasingly turned his attention to his greatest and lifelong pleasure, musical composition, with works for voice and works for instruments (ranging from piano to oboe to cello) in forms from opera to sonata to song. Several of his pieces were performed as part of the 75th anniversary celebration of the Linguistic Society of America in 1999. He died in Ithaca, New York, his home for more than fifty years.

• A brief autobiographical essay is "Preserving the Heritage," in *First Person Singular*, ed. Boyd H. Davis and Raymond K. O'Cain (1980), pp. 98–107. Hockett included commentary on his own contributions to linguistic theory in two articles written in the 1990s: "The Birth and Deaths of the Phoneme," *Idéologies dans le Monde Anglo-Saxon* 8 (1995): 5–50, and "Approaches to Syntax," *Lingua* 100 (1997): 151–70. *The View from Language: Selected Essays 1948–1974* (1977) contains fourteen essays by Hockett from anthropological and ethnolinguistic perspectives, with introductory notes; also from this perspective is his book *Man's Place in Nature* (1973). Hockett's contributions to American linguistics are discussed throughout *American Structuralism*, by Dell Hymes and John Fought (1981), and in *A Short History of Structural Linguistics*, by Peter Matthews (2001), especially pp. 83–103. A bibliography of his work 1939–1979 appears in *Essays in Honor of Charles F. Hockett*, ed. Frederick B. Agard, Gerald Kelley, Adam Makkai, and Valerie Becker Makkai (1983). An obituary is in the *New York Times*, 13 Nov. 2000.

JULIA S. FALK

HOLMES, Hamilton (8 July 1941–24 Oct. 1995), orthopedic surgeon and one of the first two black students to desegregate the University of Georgia, was born Hamilton Earl Holmes in Atlanta, Georgia, the son of Alfred "Tup" Holmes, a businessman, and Isabella Holmes, a grade school teacher. His influences in civil rights were strong; his father, grandfather Hamilton Mayo Holmes, and uncle Oliver Wendell Holmes filed suit to desegregate Atlanta's public golf courses in 1955. (The 1956 Supreme Court decision on their cases made the golf courses the first integrated public facilities in Atlanta.) His mother had been part of a program that integrated blind or partially sighted children into mainstream classrooms.

Holmes, nicknamed "Hamp," was a successful student at Henry McNeal Turner High School in Atlanta. Though shy, occasionally stuttering when he spoke (see Hunter-Gault, p. 111), he was president of his junior and senior class, co-captain of the football team, captain of the basketball team, and valedictorian of his senior class. When the Turner Wolves football team won the homecoming game, Holmes presented the game ball to Charlayne Hunter, Turner's Homecoming Queen of 1958–1959, who would later integrate the University of Georgia with Holmes and become noted journalist Charlayne Hunter-Gault.

In 1958, Jesse Hill, Jr., an Atlanta civil rights leader, began compiling a list of accomplished high school seniors in Atlanta's black high schools as potential college integrators. He found Holmes and Hunter in 1959. Holmes suggested that they apply for admission

to the University of Georgia. While readying his application papers, Holmes attended Morehouse College in Atlanta. For a year and a half, UGA's registrar office denied admission to Holmes and Hunter for a variety of reasons, including that the dormitories were full. During admissions interviews, Holmes was asked if he had ever visited a house of prostitution, a "tea parlor," or "beatnik places" (quoted in Trillin, p. 23).

On 2 Sept. 1960, attorney Donald Hollowell filed suit with the federal district court in Athens, claiming that they had been denied admission to UGA on account of their race, in violation of the 1954 U.S. Supreme Court decision that declared racial segregation unconstitutional. Just before the December 1960 trial, UGA registrar Walter Danner wrote that Hunter would be admitted the following fall, while Holmes had been rejected for being "evasive" during the interview, and that there had been "some doubt as to his truthfulness" (quoted in Trillin, p. 37). (A similar reason had been given eight years before in Horace Ward's rejection from UGA's law school. Ward assisted in Holmes's and Hunter's trial, as did Donald Hollowell, Vernon Jordan, Gerald Taylor, and Constance Baker Motley.)

On 6 January 1961, while Georgia's then-governor Ernest Vandiver was promising that "no, not one" black student would attend UGA under his authority, federal judge William A. Bootle declared that Holmes and Hunter were "fully qualified for immediate admission."

On 7 January 1961, escorted by Ward, Holmes registered at UGA. At the entrance to campus some students burned crosses and hanged a black effigy named "Hamilton Holmes." Hunter also enrolled. During their first week tension culminated in a riot on campus, which had been so well planned that students vied for dates to the event. Following the riot, Holmes and Hunter were temporarily suspended. Yet no subsequent acts of violence ensued. Once, when Holmes had parked his car near the Kappa Alpha fraternity house, he returned to find it blocked by another car and by a crowd of fraternity brothers. Holmes found a flashlight in his car and held it in his pocket, pretending it was a gun. The students moved the blocking car.

While Hunter received considerable media attention, Holmes retreated into solitude, studying, playing basketball at an all-black YMCA, eating his meals at Killian's Four Seasons—the small restaurant operated by the family with whom he boarded in Athens—and faithfully returning to Atlanta every weekend to visit a steady girlfriend, his friends, and his family. "I haven't actually cultivated any close friendships," Holmes told Calvin Trillin (see p. 85). Holmes excelled scholastically at UGA, making the Phi Kappa Phi honor society. Yet his morale reached a particularly low point his junior year. "I'm just counting the days" until graduation, he told Trillin his senior year (quoted in Trillin, p. 89).

In 1963, Holmes graduated with a bachelor of science degree cum laude and became the first black medical student at Emory University in Atlanta. In 1967 he received his medical degree. That same year he married Marilyn Elaine Vincent; they had two children. In 1969 he became a major in the U.S. Army, serving in Germany. After his discharge from the army in 1973, he became assistant professor of orthopedics and associate dean at Emory University School of Medicine. At Grady Memorial Hospital in Atlanta, he served as senior vice president of medical affairs, medical director, and head of orthopedic surgery for the Grady Health System. Though his years at UGA seem dismal, he later became a supporter of his alma mater. In 1981, he helped plan UGA's bicentennial celebration, and two years later he became the first black trustee to the University of Georgia Foundation. In 1985, as part of UGA's bicentennial, the Holmes-Hunter lectureship was established, and Holmes attended each year, joined by Hunter-Gault in 1992. He died in his sleep in Atlanta, two weeks after having quadruple bypass surgery.

• A comprehensive study of the desegregation at the University of Georgia, complete with candid, thorough interviews with Holmes, Hunter, and their families, is Calvin Trillin, *An Education in Georgia: Charlayne Hunter, Hamilton Holmes, and the Integration of the University of Georgia* (1964; repr. with new introduction, 1991). A particularly intimate view of the experience and her friend "Hamp" is Charlayne Hunter-Gault, *In My Place* (1992). An obituary appears in the *New York Times*, 28 Oct. 1995.

MARY JESSICA HAMMES

HOPKINS, Mark (1 Sept. 1813–29 Mar. 1878), railroad builder, was born in Henderson, Jefferson County, on Lake Ontario's eastern shore in upstate New York, the son of Mark Hopkins, Sr., a storekeeper in Great Barrington, Massachusetts, and Anastasia Lukins Kellogg Hopkins. In 1825 the Hopkins family moved to St. Clair, Michigan Territory, north of Detroit, where Mark Hopkins continued his schooling. When Hopkins was fifteen or sixteen his father died, and Hopkins left home for Reynolds Basin, Niagara County, New York, to become a junior clerk in the mercantile house of Hayward and Rawson. When Rawson dissolved the firm, he took the industrious youth to a similar job in Lockport, on the Erie Canal. After a few years Hopkins left to form the partnership of Hopkins and Hughes, and he also began to study law in the Lockport office of his brother Henry Hopkins, an attorney. By 1839 Mark Hopkins decided against becoming a lawyer, but he put his legal training to good use in business. Though never much of a joiner, he was briefly interested in the military life and served as a major and brigade inspector in the militia.

Hopkins then joined a Mr. Williams, who had invented an improved plow. He and Williams both manufactured and sold the newfangled farm implement, with Hopkins selling all over New York and Ohio. After terminating his business with Williams, Hopkins became bookkeeper for the New York commission house of James Rowland & Company. As partners re-

tired, Rowland entrusted the dependable Hopkins with virtual control of the firm's business.

In 1848 Hopkins became infected with California gold fever and joined an ad hoc New England Trading and Mining Company, investing $500 in equipment and supplies. Sometimes described as skinny as a rail, Hopkins was actually 5 feet, 10 inches, 160 pounds, and in good health. Leaving New York on 22 January 1849 on the ship *Pacific*, he found the first leg of the voyage unexciting, just "a comfortless three weeks existence." He wrote his brother Moses Hopkins that, to keep fit and avoid "ship fever," he exercised regularly and took saltwater baths every morning. But Captain Hall J. Tibbits began to abuse passengers as well as crew. While the captain and his family dined well, the travelers had to make do with the crew's fare—salt junk (salt pork), beans, and ship's biscuit, hardtack. The rebelling passengers successfully appealed to the U.S. consul at Rio de Janeiro and the U.S. minister to Brazil to remove the tyrant. The passage to San Francisco was uneventful, and Hopkins signed a testimonial to the new captain, George T. Eastabrook, that was published in the leading San Francisco paper, the *Daily Alta California*.

The New England company soon broke up, but its members put up tents in San Francisco's Happy Valley to sell surplus stores. They transported lighter cargo ashore in small boats, then hauled it inland in carts. Hopkins and the others also bought building materials for $300 and constructed a house that they sold for $2,250. Hopkins wrote to Moses that now he could try his luck in the mines. With other ex-passengers of the *Pacific*, he made a longboat expedition up the Sacramento River to Cottonwood Creek, where no boat had gone before. But there was no gold, so the partners traded their craft for two wagons and three yoke of oxen for a trip to Sacramento. On the trip they were forced to crack the bones of a dead ox for marrow to keep from starving.

Hopkins put a wagon and oxen to work hauling supplies from Sacramento to Hangtown (later Placerville) before he became a partner with a friend, Edward H. Miller, in a Sacramento wholesale and retail grocery store, Hopkins and Miller. The store was so profitable that the men bought real estate and, by never borrowing, survived the disastrous fire of 1852. In 1851 and 1854 Hopkins returned to the East on business. In 1854 he married his cousin, Mary Frances Sherwood; they had one adopted child. The next year he and Edwards parted amicably, and Hopkins joined Collis P. Huntington in a hardware firm, Huntington and Hopkins, that soon dominated the trade on the Pacific Coast.

Hopkins next dabbled briefly in politics. A nominal Whig, he joined the bigoted American Party, or Know-Nothings, and was elected to the Sacramento City Council. Always a Free Soiler or abolitionist, the alderman soon moved to the new, more creditable Republican Party, but he declined opportunities to become prominent in it. However, this political experience, like his legal training, stood him in good stead in business affairs, which now turned to the railroads.

Theodore Dehone Judah was jeered at as "Crazy Judah" because of his grandiose idea of a transcontinental railroad. After his plan for the western half of the line was rejected by San Francisco capitalists, he turned to the well-off merchants of Sacramento, including Hopkins, Huntington, Leland Stanford, and Charles Crocker. They subscribed to pay Judah to survey a route through the Sierra Nevada via Dutch Flat and Donner Summit. In 1861 they organized the Central Pacific Railroad (CP) with Stanford as president, Hopkins as treasurer, Huntington as vice president, and Crocker in charge of actual construction. The quartet, soon known as the "Big Four," broke ground in 1863 and joined rails with those of the Union Pacific in Utah in 1869. From the incorporation of the great railroad until his death, the canny Hopkins was the CP's trusted financial expert.

Hopkins was not only the oldest but the oddest of the Big Four. Where the others, especially Huntington, epitomized the robber barons of the Gilded Age, Hopkins was an unlikely railroad mogul. Compared to his flamboyant, aggressive, and arrogant colleagues, the modest, closemouthed treasurer seemed almost a silent partner. When noted by the press at all, he was seen as "Uncle Mark," a genial, even kindly man, different from his ruthless partners. Hopkins, however, had a genius for painstaking and prudent management of funds. Absolutely essential to the success of the railroad because of his firm, conservative control of finances, Hopkins also acted as a counterweight against the excesses of his partners, particularly Huntington, whom the Populist mayor Adolph Sutro of San Francisco accused of being capable of stealing everything short of a red-hot stove. The long-term compatibility of such opposites as Hopkins and Huntington is inexplicable, but the latter trusted the former more than anyone else. Hopkins, though reticent, admitted to being "the balance wheel" that kept the Big Four functioning. He was also its main communicator, keeping the other parties informed and drumming up government (and other) money and political support. Hopkins was also the peacemaker. Huntington, for example, derided the pompous, ponderous Stanford as unfit to be president.

Hopkins disliked oratory and was handicapped by shyness, a soft voice, and a lisp. Yet his rare public speaking was convincing because of his obvious sincerity and his tight command of facts. Contemporaries called Hopkins the Nestor and Mentor of the Big Four. He took his mentoring seriously. Frugal almost to the point of miserliness, he picked up spikes left behind by railway workers and fished used carbon paper from office wastebaskets to set an example for workers. His only "hobby" was business, though he did a little gardening. But even gardening was vegetables for his thrifty table, not flowers. Typically, he was too busy to attend either the groundbreaking of the railroad or the driving of the ceremonial Last Spike. He lived in a modest rented cottage in San Francisco until his wife, jealous of the other partners' wives, developed a taste for ostentation. She finally persuaded him to build an enormous mansion atop Nob Hill, similar to those of Stanford, Huntington, and Crocker. Unfinished at his death, it became the Hopkins Art Institute, later the San Francisco Art Institute. Today his Nob Hill memorial is the posh and world-famous Hotel Mark Hopkins.

By 1877 Hopkins was hobbled by arthritis and sciatica and could work only intermittently, sometimes at his log cabin retreat at Soda Springs in California's Sierra Nevada mountains. Hoping for relief from Arizona sunshine, he was in a CP private car (unlike his colleagues, he never had his own "varnish," or palace car) when he died in his sleep on a siding in Yuma, Arizona. Only after his death did Hopkins become controversial. His widow became estranged from their adopted son, Timothy Hopkins, when she married again. Then came a flood of lawsuits, with litigants claiming the estate and accusing the widow of participating in a complicated swindle.

• Hopkins's letters home in 1849–1850 are in the Huntington Library, San Marino, Calif., and were published by John Pomfret in the *Huntington Library Quarterly* 26, no. 1 (Nov. 1962): 59–70. The C. P. Huntington Collected Letters file in the Library of Congress includes some of Hopkins's letters. The biography by Benjamin B. Redding, *A Sketch of the Life of Mark Hopkins of California* (1881), is brief but informative. It was reprinted in Stuart Bruchey, *Memoirs of Three Railroad Pioneers* (1981). Hopkins figures in Oscar Lewis, *The Big Four* (1959), and David Lavender, *The Great Persuader* (1970, repr. 1998), which refers to Huntington. Most histories of the Central Pacific and its successor the Southern Pacific dwell on construction, but those with good information on the talented treasurer include Robert West Howard, *The Great Iron Trail* (1962); John Hoyt Williams, *A Great and Shining Road* (1988); David Haward Bain, *Empire Express* (1999); and Stephen E. Ambrose, *Nothing Like It in the World* (2000). The story of litigation over Hopkins's fortune is in Estelle Latta, *Controversial Mark Hopkins* (1953). Obituaries are in the *Sacramento Bee*, 29 Mar. 1878; the *Sacramento Union*, 29 Mar. 1878; the *San Francisco Chronicle*, 30 Mar. 1878; the *San Francisco Examiner*, 30 Mar. 1878; and the *Daily Alta California*, 30 Mar. 1878.

RICHARD H. DILLON

HORGAN, Paul (1 Aug. 1903–8 Mar. 1995), writer, was born Paul George Vincent O'Shaughnessy Horgan in Buffalo, New York, the son of Edward Daniel Horgan, a printing company owner of English-Irish descent, and Rose Marie Rohr Horgan, the daughter of an émigré German poet. The family was Roman Catholic, and Paul Horgan professed that faith throughout his life. In 1915 Edward Horgan, suffering from tuberculosis and seeking a better climate, moved his wife and three children to Albuquerque, New Mexico. Young Paul was immediately captivated by the vast, sparsely settled landscape of his new frontier home, and its historic associations fired his romantic imagination. Legends of the conquistadors, the original Spanish settlers, abounded, as did tales of Apache warfare and the ways and wiles of local denizen Billy the Kid.

Steeping himself in the lore of the Southwest, Horgan continued his education locally and attended Albuquerque High School before completing his formal education at the New Mexico Military Institute in Roswell. There he excelled in the arts—music, theater, painting—and developed a talent for writing, and while at the institute he also worked as a reporter and music critic for the Albuquerque *Morning Journal*. Horgan's father died in 1921, and two years later, following his mother's recovery from a severe illness, the family returned east. Horgan enrolled at the Eastman School of Music in Rochester, New York, to study voice and prepare for a career in theater. But after several years, he decided to concentrate on his first love, writing, and returned to the Southwest to more fully explore the creative potential inherent in its landscape and history.

In 1924 Horgan published several poems in *Poetry* magazine. In 1926 he became the librarian at his alma mater, the New Mexico Military Institute, and used that job to support himself as he established a literary career. Over the next few years he wrote several adult novels but failed to find a publisher. In 1931 he published *Men of Arms*, an account of soldiering throughout history, written for boys; he also provided illustrations for the book. That same year one of his short stories was selected for inclusion in the *O. Henry Memorial Prize Stories*, an annual anthology. In 1933 Horgan experienced even greater success when his book *The Fault of Angels*, a fictionalized account of his experience at the Eastman Theatre, won that year's Harper Prize Novel contest.

Henceforth, Horgan turned almost exclusively to the Southwest for his subject matter, beginning with *No Quarter Given* (1935), a lengthy novel detailing the life of a composer from the East Coast who settles in New Mexico. The book received mixed reviews at the time, though later critics, in retrospective appraisals of Horgan's career, praised it as well crafted. Over the next seven years Horgan published a series of fictional works set in the historical Southwest, including the novels *Main Line West* (1936), *A Lamp on the Plains* (1937), *Far from Cibola* (1938), *Figures in a Landscape* (1940), and *The Common Heart* (1942). During this time he also published *From the Royal City* (1936), a nonfictional compilation of early accounts of life in Santa Fe; *The Return of the Weed* (1936), a collection of short stories; and the historical play *Yours, A. Lincoln* (1942). In addition, he wrote the libretto for *A Tree on the Plains* (1942), Ernst Bacon's musical play about the American frontier.

Horgan's short novel *The Habit of Empire* (1939) was his first work to receive wide critical attention. Retelling the story of the conquistador Juan de Oñate and his 1599 conquest of the lands that later became New Mexico, the book also featured lithographs by Horgan's friend Peter Hurd, a former classmate at the New Mexico Military Institute who became a noted painter. The work drew praise for its psychological perceptiveness in portraying the confrontation between Native Americans and their Spanish Catholic conquerors. Peter Hurd's marriage to Henriette Wyeth, the daughter of noted illustrator N. C. Wyeth, had drawn Horgan into the Wyeth family circle, and over the years Horgan made many visits to the family compound in Chadds Ford, Pennsylvania. All the Wyeths, in particular N. C., the patriarch, were strong supporters of Horgan's work and encouraged both his writing and his artistic talents.

Horgan's writing career was interrupted by World War II, during which he served as chief of army information for the Department of War in Washington, D.C. He eventually rose to the rank of lieutenant colonel and was awarded the Legion of Merit. During his tenure at the war department he wrote a pamphlet on venereal disease for distribution to American soldiers; he later noted wryly that the pamphlet, several million copies of which were published, was his biggest seller. Following Horgan's discharge early in 1946, he lectured at the University of Iowa Writers Workshop for one semester, then returned to Roswell as assistant to the president of the military institute. Under contract from *Look* magazine, Horgan composed the text for *Southwest*, a volume in the magazine's *Look at America* series, published in 1947. That same year a Guggenheim fellowship enabled him to resign from the institute and devote himself full time to writing.

In 1952 Horgan published two novels with southwestern themes: *Devil in the Desert* and *One Red Rose for Christmas*. The Guggenheim grant also enabled him to complete a work begun in 1940: an exhaustive history of the Rio Grande River and its people. Appearing in 1954 in two volumes, *Great River: The Rio Grande in North American History* was praised by reviewers, in particular for its vivid portrayal in both factually accurate and compelling prose of the three cultures—Native American, Spanish, and Anglo—that figured in the river's long history. *Great River* established Horgan's reputation as an eminent historian of the American Southwest, and it received not only the 1954 Pulitzer Prize in history but also the Bancroft Prize, an award usually reserved for academic historians.

Great River was followed by a series of books with specifically Catholic themes: the novels *The Saintmaker's Christmas Eve* (1955), which included illustrations by Horgan, and *Give Me Possession* (1957); *The Centuries of Santa Fe* (1956), a history of missionaries in the Southwest; and *Rome Eternal* (1959), a travel book heavily illustrated with photographs by Joseph Vadala that received an award from the Catholic Book Club. A second Guggenheim grant in 1958 supported his work during this period.

During the 1960s Horgan published a series of fiction and nonfiction works, beginning with the novel *A Distant Trumpet* (1960), which centers on the exploits of the U.S. Cavalry in Arizona during the late nineteenth century; it was subsequently made into a Hollywood movie. This was followed by *Citizen of New Salem* (1961), a biography of the young Abraham

Lincoln; *Mountain Standard Time* (1962), comprising his three previously published novels *Main Line West, Far from Cibola*, and *The Common Heart*; *Toby and the Nighttime* (1963), a children's tale; and the nonfictional *Conquistadors in North American History* (1963). By this time Horgan had settled back east in Connecticut, moving to Middletown in 1960 to become a fellow of the Center for Advanced Studies at Wesleyan University. Two years later he became director of the center, a post he held until 1967. For several years he served as professor of English at Wesleyan and was named emeritus professor and writer-in-residence in 1971, holding both positions until his death. He continued his close ties with the Southwest, however, returning for visits and research.

The prolific Horgan did not stay his creative pace at Wesleyan, where he taught courses in southwestern history and literature. In 1964 he published *Things as They Are*, the first in a series of novels that became known as "the Richard trilogy," after their protagonist, an artist identified only as Richard. The Richard trilogy, which also includes *Everything to Live For* (1968) and *The Thin Mountain Air* (1977), follows its central character from early childhood to adulthood and echoes Horgan's own life story. *Peter Hurd: A Portrait Sketch from Life*, Horgan's biographical tribute to his longtime friend, was published in 1965. Two years later his short-story collection *The Peach Stone* appeared.

For the most part, critics continued to be respectful of Horgan's fiction, but he remained a solid mid-list author in this genre. He never emerged as a major novelist, though he enjoyed a brief episode of literary stardom in 1970 following the publication of *Whitewater*. This novel about adolescence in a small town in the Southwest enjoyed modest critical praise and became a bestseller, earning Horgan substantial royalties. That same year he published *The Heroic Triad: Essays in the Social Energies of Three Southwestern Cultures*, a kind of coda to *Great River* that received strongly positive reviews; he also edited *Maurice Baring Restored*, a collection of essays by the early-twentieth-century English writer whom Horgan considered a major influence on his own work. In 1972 he published *Encounters with Stravinsky: A Personal Record*, an account of a friendship formed during Igor Stravinsky's visits to Santa Fe. A year later his handbook *Approaches to Writing* was published by Wesleyan; a second edition appeared in 1988.

For nearly five decades Horgan had been fascinated by a major historical figure of the American Southwest: nineteenth-century bishop John Baptist Lamy, who came from France to what is now New Mexico as a Roman Catholic missionary and whose contributions to the colonization of the region are considered substantial by most historians. Lamy had been the inspiration for novelist Willa Cather's masterpiece, *Death Comes for the Archbishop* (1927), and Horgan, a long-standing admirer of Cather's fiction, was himself inspired by her novel to write the first substantial biography of the cleric. Upon publication, *Lamy of Santa Fe: His Life and Times* (1975) was proclaimed as Horgan's greatest achievement, even among a minority of naysaying academicians who had previously dismissed his work because he lacked a college degree, and it earned Horgan a second Pulitzer Prize in history.

Now in his seventies, Horgan continued to write both fiction and nonfiction, though at a slower pace. *Josiah Gregg and His Vision of the Early West*, a biography of a nineteenth-century Southwest trader, was published in 1979. This was followed by the monograph *Henriette Wyeth* (1980) and an essay collection, *On the Climate of Books* (1981). Horgan's final novel, *Mexico Bay*, which recounts the life and experiences of a Southwest historian not unlike Horgan himself, appeared in 1982. In the remaining years of his life Horgan published five more works of nonfiction (*Of America: East and West*, 1984; *Under the Sangre de Cristo*, 1985; *A Certain Climate: Essays in History, Arts, and Letters*, 1988; *A Writer's Eye*, 1988; and *Tracings: A Book of Partial Portraits*, 1993), as well as a collection of light verse, *The Clerihews of Paul Horgan* (1985).

In private life, Horgan, who never married, was an avid fan of classical music; a founder of the Santa Fe Opera Company, he served on its board of directors. Drawing and painting also remained favorite pastimes. He died in Middletown, Connecticut.

Dismissed by some critics as an old-fashioned regional Catholic writer who spread his talents too widely, Horgan has been vastly praised by others, including historian David McCullough, who paid tribute to "his luminous imagination." Horgan has been compared favorably by McCullough and others to fellow westerner Wallace Stegner. Although Stegner undeniably outdistanced Horgan as a novelist, Horgan's achievements as a chronicler of regional American history cannot be denied.

• For biographical information on Paul Horgan, see Robert Gish, *Paul Horgan* (1983), and *Nueva Granada: Paul Horgan and the Southwest* (1995); see also James M. Day, *Paul Horgan* (1967). In addition, see entries by Gish under "Paul Horgan" in *Fifty Western Writers: A Bio-Bibliographical Sourcebook* (1982), pp. 194–204, and in *A Literary History of the American West* (1987), pp. 574–86. See also David McCullough, "Historian, Novelist, and Much, Much More," *New York Times Book Review*, 8 Apr. 1984, pp. 3, 22. For a critical overview of Horgan's work, see "Horgan, Paul," *Contemporary Literary Criticism*, vol. 53 (1989), pp. 168–76. An obituary appears in the *New York Times*, 9 Mar. 1995.

ANN T. KEENE

HORSE, John (01 Jan. 1812?–1882), Seminole Maroon leader and Mexican army officer, also known as Juan Caballo, John (or Juan) Cavallo, John Cowaya, John Coheia, Gopher John (beginning in 1826), and Juan de Dios Vidaurri (during and after 1856), was born in the Florida Alachua savanna west of Saint Augustine. His father is believed to have been of mixed American Indian and Spanish heritage, and his mother of African and American Indian descent. Until his early thirties, he was considered a Seminole slave. His surname is a translation of that of Charles Cavallo, his Indian owner. Cavallo might also have owned Horse's mother and been his father.

The Seminole Maroons were mostly runaways from South Carolina and Georgia plantations, together with slaves captured by Seminoles from Florida plantations and some free blacks. Some were considered Seminole slaves, but servitude among the Seminoles was based upon tribute and deference. Typically, Seminole slaves gave their owners a small annual tribute of crops or livestock in exchange for protection against reenslavement by whites. The Maroons lived apart from the Seminoles in communities headed by their own principal men, and they controlled most aspects of their daily lives. Little is known of Horse's early years, but during that period the Seminole Maroons experienced the traumas of the East Florida annexation plot (1812–1813), the destruction of the Negro Fort at Prospect Bluff on the Apalachicola River (1816), the First Seminole War (1818), the annexation of Florida by the United States (1821), and forced removal to a reservation south of Tampa under the terms of the Treaty of Moultrie Creek (1823).

By 1826, Horse was living in his owner's village on Thonotosassa Lake, twelve miles from Fort Brooke, near Tampa Bay. He took to visiting the military post, and the wily teenager played a prank on one of the officers there, tricking him into paying for two gophers (edible terrapins) multiple times. The officer gave Horse the nickname Gopher John, by which he became known to U.S. Army officers on the frontier for the next fifty years. Horse continued to frequent Fort Brooke for several years, interacting with the officers there by running errands and serving as a guide on hunting trips. He also raised livestock and came to own ninety head of cattle and other property.

Horse's life soon would change dramatically as Indian and Maroon resistance to the removal policies of Andrew Jackson culminated in the Second Seminole War, 1835–1842. As leader of the Oklawaha Maroons, Horse actively opposed the U.S. forces in Florida at the beginning of the war. But offered the promise of freedom, he agreed to surrender and remove west with the Seminoles in March 1837. The American commander reneged on his promises, however, and in early June Horse and the Seminole leaders Osceola and Coacoochee (Wild Cat) carried off the hostages they had surrendered under the terms of the truce. Horse and Coacoochee were captured in October and imprisoned at Fort Marion in Saint Augustine, but the two led a daring and successful escape during the night of 29–30 November.

On 25 December 1837, Horse led the Maroons, and Coacoochee, Alligator, and Sam Jones the Seminoles, in the battle of Okeechobee, the most important engagement in the most serious and protracted of all "Indian" wars. But Okeechobee proved to be the pinnacle of Seminole and Maroon resistance to removal. Again promised freedom, Horse surrendered with Alligator and his band in April 1838 and immediately boarded transports at Tampa bound for the West. He returned to Florida the following year in the new role of U.S. government agent. Between 1839 and 1842, Horse served as a paid guide, interpreter, and intermediary who persuaded 535 Indians to sue for peace and remove west.

By 1840, Horse had married Susan July, the daughter of July, a Seminole Maroon guide and interpreter killed in Florida, and Teena, who removed to the Indian Territory. The couple remained together until his death more than forty years later. They had one son who grew to adulthood, Joe Coon. Susan and Joe Coon both died soon after John Horse.

In 1842, Horse was described as "a fine looking fellow of six feet, as straight as an Indian" (Porter, *Black Seminoles*, p. 37). He was powerfully built and sported silver armlets, sashes, leggings, and the plumed turban favored by the Seminoles. His long, dark hair always was groomed. He became known on the frontier as an excellent marksman and horseman, with a liking for strong liquor. He came to speak at least five languages: Afro-Seminole (an English-based creole spoken by the Maroons), Hitchiti and Muskogee (spoken by the Seminoles), Spanish, and, later in Mexico, Kickapoo.

Horse left Florida for good in the summer of 1842, sailing to the Indian Territory via New Orleans. He and his family made their home on the Deep Fork of the North Canadian River. Upon the death of Charles Cavallo in Florida, Horse had become the property of the Seminole chiefs. In February 1843, for services rendered to the Seminoles during removal, the chiefs declared him to be free. As a free black in the Indian Territory, Horse was in grave danger of being kidnapped by Creeks or whites and returned to slavery. Some of the Seminoles also resented his serving as a government agent in Florida and his growing influence within the tribe. Consequently, he spent much of his time at Fort Gibson serving as an interpreter for those Seminoles residing around the post.

In April 1844, Horse accompanied a Seminole delegation, headed by Coacoochee, to Washington. He had been back at Fort Gibson only a few days when a Seminole shot at him with a rifle, wounding him slightly and killing the horse he was riding. He and his family were forced to move from the Deep Fork to Fort Gibson and reside there for the next three and a half years. Besides the horse shot under him, Horse already had acquired over fifty head of stock, a wagon, tools, and farming implements on the Deep Fork. These, too, were lost.

In January 1845, the Seminoles, the Creeks, and the United States signed a treaty aimed at uniting the two tribes. Because of their minority status, Seminole interests would be buried beneath those of the Creeks, creating a source of contention in the future. For now, though, the Seminoles agreed to settle on their assigned lands. For sixty days, from February until early April, Horse drove his wagon pulled by three yoke of oxen in the train that removed the Seminoles and their belongings from their camps near Fort Gibson to the Little River country. But his position remained precarious. During the removal, Seminoles made a second attempt on his life, and again he was forced to seek refuge at the post. In April, he traveled to Washington, seeking permission to resettle in Florida. He spent the next year in the nation's capital working on behalf of his people. Horse succeeded in securing the protection of the Maroons by the military at Fort Gibson and the referral of their case to the president. He then returned to the Indian Territory.

In June 1848, attorney general John Mason decided that the Maroons should be returned to the Seminoles. Ordered to leave the post, in early January 1849, Horse led his family and followers from Fort Gibson to Wewoka Creek, where they established a community some distance from the Seminoles. The settlement was situated just north of the present-day town of Wewoka, Seminole County, Oklahoma.

Horse's sister, Juana, already had suffered two of her children being sold to a Creek by her Seminole owner. Fearing that he, his family, and his fellow Maroons would be kidnapped and sold or reenslaved and subjected to Creek slave codes, Horse entered into an alliance with the disaffected Coacoochee that resulted in bands of Maroons and Seminoles quitting the Indian Territory in November 1849. They traveled through Texas to Coahuila in northern Mexico, where legal servitude had been abolished in 1829.

Naming Horse's followers Mascogos, the Mexicans in 1852 gave the Maroons, the Seminoles, and a band of Southern Kickapoos separate land grants at Nacimiento, near Múzquiz, to establish military colonies. In exchange for land, tools, and livestock, the immigrants agreed to protect the Mexican interior by engaging in campaigns against Apache and Comanche raiders. The Mexican authorities viewed John Horse as the undisputed head of the Mascogos and referred to him as El Capitán Juan Caballo.

During the early 1850s, Horse became extremely unpopular with Texas settlers on the border, being regarded as impudent and boastful of having killed many whites in Florida. To the delight of local residents and the border press, he was expelled from Fort Duncan while laying claim to a horse that had been taken from him and sold. Then, while attending a dance in Piedras Negras, he became involved in a brawl and was shot and wounded by a Texan. The slave catcher Warren Adams rushed across the border with his henchmen and took Horse back to Eagle Pass in handcuffs. Coacoochee crossed over from Mexico and paid $500 in twenty-dollar gold pieces for the return of his friend and ally. As a warning to Adams, the coins were stained with human blood.

Beginning in 1856, John Horse sometimes was referred to as Juan de Dios Vidaurri. This name may have derived from a godfather, following Horse's Catholic baptism. That same year, smallpox claimed the life of Coacoochee and many other Seminoles. Disillusioned with Mexico, the remaining Seminoles returned to the Indian Territory between 1859 and 1861. To prevent attacks by Texas filibusters, in 1861 Horse and most of the 350 Mascogos moved to the Laguna de Parras in southwestern Coahuila.

In 1864, the Maroons experienced conflict resulting from the French invasion of Mexico under Emperor Maximilian. The group retained a tradition that Horse persuaded the invaders not to burn their dwellings. It has been said that he joined the Mexican army to fight against the French and that his exploits were so successful that he was commissioned a colonel. He did become known on the border as El Coronel Juan Caballo, but more likely the title derived from service against Indian raiders. As further reward, the Mexican government gave him a silver-mounted saddle with a gold-plated pummel in the shape of a horse's head. He used that saddle when riding his favorite horse, a white with blue eyes named American.

In 1865, John Kibbetts and a large number of Maroons felt it safe to return to Nacimiento. In the late 1860s American officials suggested that they return to the United States as part of a policy aimed at relocating border Indian bands hostile to white settlers. During the summer of 1870, the Nacimiento Maroons crossed the border and made camp on Elm Creek at Fort Duncan. In August, the able-bodied men enrolled in the U.S. Army as a new unit that came to be known as the Seminole Negro Indian Scouts. Horse crossed over to Fort Duncan from Parras in December, but he never served with the scouts. Some of his supporters followed in late 1872 and early 1873, but most chose instead to return to Nacimiento.

After Horse returned to Texas, there was contention among the Maroons as to who should be considered their leader. In December 1873, the 130 Maroons at Fort Duncan elected Kibbetts headman over Horse by a majority of seventeen. Kibbetts's success may be explained by most of Horse's supporters having returned to Nacimiento. The aging but knowledgeable and experienced Horse thereafter assumed a patriarchal role and offered counsel on important issues affecting the Maroons in Texas. The Kibbetts-Horse group removed to Fort Clark in early 1876 and built a settlement on Las Moras Creek, which became the scouts' home base. Horse and his family made their home just above the fort's graveyard, on the west side of the creek.

Local whites feared that the Maroons would acquire land outside Fort Clark, and also accused them of stealing cattle and other property. During the evening of Friday, 19 May 1876, Horse was attacked while returning to the Maroon village from a saloon in neighboring Brackettville. Hired assassins ambushed Horse and Titus Payne just south of the post hospital. Horse was on horseback, while Payne walked alongside. Payne was killed instantly and four bullets tore through Horse's leg and body, but his mount American, although wounded in the neck, carried him to safety.

That incident, and subsequent attacks on other group members, caused Horse and other leading Maroons to rejoin their kinsmen at Nacimiento. In the late 1870s and early 1880s, the Mascogos and Mexican Kickapoos faced a grave crisis when their title to land at Nacimiento was contested, and they faced eviction. They determined to send a representative to state their views before Mexican president Porfirio Diaz. Consequently, Horse, possibly accompanied by one or two other Maroons, set out for Mexico City during the first week of August 1882. The outcome is unknown as Horse died before he could reveal the details of his mission. Accounts vary as to the circumstances of his death. Some say that he was murdered in a cantinaon the return journey, but more likely he died of a sudden bout of pneumonia in a military hospital in Mexico City in the early afternoon of 9 August.

John Horse was the dominant personality in Seminole Maroon affairs for half a century. He was a counselor of Seminole leaders, an agent of the U.S. government, and a Mexican army officer. He served the Seminole Maroons as warrior, diplomat, and patriarch and represented their interests from Washington, D.C., to Mexico City. He took up arms against the United States, the French, and hostile Indians. He survived three wars and at least four attempts on his life and had escaped from the grasp of renowned slave hunters. A truly remarkable frontier character, this multilingual, mixed-heritage Maroon leader dressed in Indian fashion and rode the Rio Grande border country on a white horse astride a saddle embellished with silver and gold. Apparently, his final mission to Mexico City had succeeded, for Diaz subsequently protected the Mascogos from efforts to evict them from the hacienda. A decade after Horse's death, the Mexican government reaffirmed the Mascogos' and Mexican Kickapoos' title to land at Nacimiento, land upon which descendants of the Seminole Maroons still reside today.

• Manuscripts relating to John Horse's exploits in Mexico are contained in General Luis Alberto Guajardo, comp., "Apuntes Datos y Noticias para la Historia de Coahuila," c. 1613–1911, and Múzquiz, Coahuila, Records, Western Americana Collections, Beinecke Rare Book and Manuscript Library, Yale University. Other documents relating to Horse's later years in Texas and Coahuila are in the National Archives Microfilm Publications, Microcopy M619, File 488–70, "Papers Relating to the Return of the Kickapoo and the Seminole (Negro) Indians from Mexico to the United States, 1870–1885," Rolls 799, 800. The Kenneth Wiggins Porter Papers at the Schomburg Center for Research in Black Culture, New York Public Library, include manuscript biographies of Horse and Coacoochee as well as research files containing oral testimony of group descendants in Texas and Mexico relating to the Maroon leader. A revised version of the John Horse biography, with additional information gathered by the editors, is Kenneth W. Porter, *The Black Seminoles: History of a Freedom-Seeking People,* ed. Alcione M. Amos and Thomas P. Senter (1996). Horse's gopher prank is documented in George A. McCall, *Letters from the Frontiers* (1868), and is explored in Kenneth W. Porter, "Davy Crockett and John Horse: A Possible Origin of the Coonskin Story," *American Literature* 15 (Mar. 1943): 10–15. Other Porter articles focusing on the Maroon leader include "Farewell to John Horse: An Episode of Seminole Ne-

gro Folk History," *Phylon* 8 (1947): 265–73; "Lament for Wild Cat," *Phylon* 4 (1943): 39–48; "Seminole Flight from Fort Marion," *Florida Historical Quarterly* 22 (1944): 112–33; "Seminole in Mexico, 1850–1861," *Chronicles of Oklahoma* 29 (1951): 153–68; and "Wild Cat's Death and Burial," *Chronicles of Oklahoma* 21 (1943): 41–43. Still other Porter articles containing information on Horse have been compiled in Porter, *The Negro on the American Frontier* (1971). Laurence Foster, *Negro-Indian Relationships in the Southeast* (1935; repr. 1978), also contains oral testimony by Maroon descendants. The standard histories of Horse and his people are Daniel F. Littlefield, Jr., *Africans and Seminoles: From Removal to Emancipation* (1977; repr. 2001), and Kevin Mulroy, *Freedom on the Border: The Seminole Maroons in Florida, the Indian Territory, Coahuila, and Texas* (1993; repr. 2003).

KEVIN MULROY

HOVHANESS, Alan (8 Mar. 1911–21 June 2000), composer, was born Alan Vaness Chakmakjian in Somerville, Massachusetts, the only child of Haroutiun Chakmakjian, an immigrant Armenian chemistry professor, and Madeline Scott Chakmakjian, a woman of Scottish ancestry. She insisted her son use the simpler Vaness as his surname. When Hovhaness was five, the family moved to Boston's Arlington suburb, where he attended the public schools. As a boy he was drawn to music, painting, writing, and astronomy. Parental disapproval of his composing forced him to hide his scores and compose nocturnally, a habit he maintained for life. Despite a conventional American upbringing, young Alan developed an inclination for meditation and spiritual matters. With his father, he climbed the mountains of New England, where he claimed to have had his earliest metaphysical experiences. Mountains and nature were forever his main sources of inspiration. Following his high school graduation in 1929, Hovhaness spent two years at Tufts University. Soon after his mother's death in 1931, he augmented his middle name to Hovhaness (an Armenian form of "Johannes"), which had been his paternal grandfather's name. He later officially changed his surname to Hovhaness.

Hovhaness decided on a musical career by his mid-teens, already having penned some operas. His earliest composition lessons were with Frederick Converse at the New England Conservatory in the early 1930s, a decade during which Hovhaness made a meager living playing piano for concerts in the Boston area and social gatherings of Arabs, Armenians, and Greeks. Hovhaness married Martha Mott Davis, an artist, in 1931. The marriage produced Hovhaness's only child, a daughter named Jean Christina in honor of her godfather and family friend, the Finnish composer Jean Sibelius. The marriage ended in divorce in 1938. Hovhaness married four more times between 1938 and 1977, but the dates of the marriages and the names of his second, third, and fourth wives are not known. His fifth wife was Elizabeth Whittington.

In 1935 Hovhaness and his wife visited Finland to meet Sibelius. The following year Hovhaness saw the dancer Uday Shankar (brother of sitarist Ravi Shankar) and the Indian musician Vishnu Shirali perform in Boston, a revelatory experience for him. In 1940 he rediscovered the music of his paternal ancestors on becoming organist at the Armenian church in Watertown, Massachusetts, where he remained until 1950.

A decisive artistic shift came in 1943, following an unsympathetic reception to Hovhaness's music at Tanglewood's summer music school. Encouraged by his artist friend Hyman Bloom and the mystic Hermon di Giovanno, Hovhaness discarded much of his already considerable output and rethought his musical identity. He drew upon the rich legacy of Armenian church music, fascinated particularly by the possibilities of what he termed "giant melody." Sharply at odds with mainstream trends, this Armenian creative phase saw melody assuming paramount importance to the point where harmony was often completely static. Beginning in February 1944 Hovhaness trained an amateur ensemble to play his new pieces, many of which had Armenian titles. The ensemble's New York debut, performing the piano concerto *Lousadzak* (Coming of light), received a rave review in the *New York Herald Tribune*. The composers Lou Harrison (who wrote the review) and John Cage forged lifelong friendships with Hovhaness at this point. Cage may even have been influenced by the imprecise textures of *Lousadzak*, which predated Cage's own hugely influential ideas of chance elements in music. In a February 1947 *Herald Tribune* article, the composer Virgil Thomson noted, "Among all our American contributions to musical art . . . [Hovhaness's] is one of the most curious and original." From 1948 to 1951 Hovhaness was on the faculty of the Boston Conservatory of Music. He then moved to New York to compose full-time.

In the 1950s Hovhaness achieved considerable recognition and repute. The Armenian influences receded, giving way to a more Western style. Commissions came for orchestras, radio, television (NBC), dance (Martha Graham), and stage. In 1954–1955 he experienced success on Broadway with his score for Clifford Odets's play *The Flowering Peach*. MGM Records released several Hovhaness recordings, and a longtime champion, the conductor Leopold Stokowski, commissioned Symphony No. 2 (subtitled *Mysterious Mountain*) for his debut with the Houston Symphony in 1955, bringing the composer national exposure. This work's subsequent recording by the Chicago Symphony under the legendary conductor Fritz Reiner earned Hovhaness international attention.

In the early 1960s Hovhaness won research scholarships to travel in India, Japan, and Korea that enabled him to study with native musicians. He was the first Westerner to participate at the Madras Music Festival with an all-Hovhaness concert on New Year's Day 1960. In India he collected over three hundred ragas (musical scales) into a book. In Japan he transcribed thirteen pieces of the centuries-old gagaku court music, a feat he considered his greatest contribution to music. In 1962 Hovhaness spent six months as composer in residence at the East-West Center of the University of Hawaii. Such extensive and exotic travels satisfied his yearning for spiritual and philosophical nourishment and inevitably brought new colorations and aesthetic impulses to his music. This Indo-Oriental phase of the 1960s placed Hovhaness's music at its most tangential from Western models. From the mid-1960s, almost uniquely for an American classicist, Hovhaness financed his own record label to promote his works. Named Poseidon Society, the label's twenty-odd releases were either conducted or supervised by the composer. Some pressings of these discs ran to two thousand copies at a time to meet national and international demand.

In 1972 Hovhaness settled permanently in Seattle, attracted by the Cascade Mountains. There he married his sixth wife in 1977, the Japanese soprano and former actress Hinako Fujihara, with whom he found a lasting happiness. Perhaps this happiness contributed to the continued prolificacy of his twilight years, which included a marked retreat from earlier musical exoticisms.

From the 1970s Hovhaness lived entirely off the proceeds of his work, through commissions and performances. He was lauded in other ways too, accumulating five honorary doctorates and in 1977 election to the American Academy of Arts and Letters. In his final years the composer witnessed the widespread availability of his music and a younger generation of conductors and performers taking up his works, keeping him one of America's best-recorded composers. He died in Seattle.

Hovhaness's legacy is twofold. First, his unfashionable ideas about a healing or spiritual role for classical music predated such New Age trends of the late twentieth century. Second, like the American composers Henry Cowell and Lou Harrison, Hovhaness was a pivotal figure in introducing Eastern musical techniques and aesthetics into Western concert music, thus spearheading their subsequent absorption into classical as well as mainstream musical culture.

Despite an output exceeding 450 works in all genres, Hovhaness's music has been unfairly neglected in academic circles, mainly because it was obstinately tuneful in a modernist age and somewhat indifferent to the intellectualism of the postwar musical climate. However, regular performances of the evocative mood pieces in which he excelled—like *Mysterious Mountain* and *Lousadzak*—ensure partial survival of a largely unexplored output.

• A good all-round article is Richard Kostelanetz, "The Transcendental Contemporary: A Profile of Alan Hovhaness," *Michigan Quarterly Review* 18, no. 3 (Summer 1979): 365–78. A discography, a detailed biography, and a discussion of some works are at http://www.hovhaness.com. For in-depth analysis of his music up to 1972, see Arnold Rosner, "An Analytical Survey of the Music of Alan Hovhaness" (Ph.D. diss., State Univ. of New York, Buffalo, 1972). For a classified list of most of his works, see Richard Howard, *The Works of Alan Hovhaness, a Catalogue: Opus 1–Opus 360* (1983), which is also available at http://www.musicweb.

uk.net/classrev/2000/feb00/hovanessworks.htm. An obituary is in the *Seattle Times*, 22 June 2000 (http://archives. seattletimes.nwsource.com/cgi-bin/texis/web/vortex/display? slug = alan22&date = 20000622&query = hovhaness).

MARCO SHIRODKAR

HOYTE, Lenon (4 July 1905–1 Aug. 1999), doll collector and art teacher, was born Lenon Holder in New York City, the oldest child of Moses Holder, a carpenter, and Rose Holder, who sewed hats for infants for a Manhattan department store. The family owned a house on 128th Street in Harlem, and Hoyte attended public schools there. It was a comfortable childhood, but ironically the doll collector to be and her sister were forbidden to play with dolls when the younger girl, after chewing on the hands of their dolls, contracted lead poisoning. Hoyte studied both art and education at the City College of New York, earning a B.S. degree in 1937, and at Teacher's College of Columbia University. She had private art teachers as well, and she painted in media such as oil, casein, and watercolor. In 1930 Hoyte was hired to teach in New York City elementary and junior high schools, which she did for 40 years. She began teaching art and added puppetry and doll making.

In 1938 she married Lewis Hoyte, a pharmacist; they had no children. The couple bought a fourteen-room house at 6 Hamilton Terrace, becoming the second black occupants of the small enclave of three-story brownstones in Harlem built at the beginning of the twentieth century. Hoyte was always a collector, and she began filling her home with antiques, "cutting her teeth" with 1,500 china pitchers. The collection grew when her family home was razed in 1949 to make way for a housing project. A large crystal chandelier was the prize among the many objects she added. She also collected china, cut glass, samplers, and richly carved furniture. Hoyte continued to teach and to participate in church and sorority activities. On two occasions she organized exhibitions of her antique pitchers as fundraisers to purchase a new organ for St. Philip's, her church. Deeply involved in church activities, Hoyte at various times taught Sunday school, directed a girls' club, and served on the church's board for housing for the elderly.

Hoyte chaired several committees for her sorority, Phi Delta Kappa. In 1962 the sorority asked her to arrange an exhibition of dolls to benefit the mental health clinic at Harlem Hospital. The exhibition was a success financially, and it changed Hoyte's life. For the next three decades she collected dolls and their paraphernalia so earnestly that her collection became internationally known. At first Hoyte acquired her dolls at flea markets and garage sales. As her search became more passionate, she visited antique stores throughout the United States, Europe, and the Caribbean. She chose dolls, she said, "when they speak to me; I know right away, just like people." She believed, "It's important to save old dolls and toys because they show us what life once looked like" (*New York Amsterdam News*, 16 Apr. 1983). Hoyte delved into the

history of each doll, and as a teacher she saw that the dolls stimulated children's curiosity about the past and provided a genuine interest in history (*Encore*, 6 Dec. 1976).

Besides the dolls, Hoyte collected dollhouses, doll carriages, tea sets, stoves, toy schoolrooms, books, toy pianos, and other musical instruments. She retired from teaching in 1970. That year, using the name her students gave her, she incorporated her collection as Aunt Len's Doll and Toy Museum, on display in the basement of her home. Visitors came by appointment only, and the entrance fees remained low for maximum accessibility. With about 2,000 dolls, museum space was tight. But collectors find room, and twenty years later the dolls possibly numbered 6,000 (*New York Times*, 9 Sept. 1999).

The museum was divided into five sections. The Americana Room contained handmade cloth black dolls of the antebellum South, numerous Shirley Temples, and others of American manufacture. The Schoenhut Room was devoted to the works of the renowned nineteenth-century doll maker and his Humpty-Dumpty Circus of forty animals and figures. The Collector's Room housed the rarest dolls by master doll makers, such as Léon Casimir Bru, Émile Jumeau, and Jules Nicholas Steiner, that ranged in size from miniature to over three feet. The Dollhouse Pavilion, with an electrified dollhouse, and International Dolls completed the museum.

Hoyte regarded cloth dolls as her specialty, and at one time she planned to write a book about them but never did. Highlights of the collection included wax-molded Nicholas and Alexandra of Russia in ermine and vermilion robes, an Edison talking doll, a doll of the Queen Anne period, an 1880 black Bru bisque head bebe in pink silk, and two "crying babies" of papier-mâché made by Leo Moss, a black doll maker from Georgia. The large number of black dolls was remarkable for its range over time, place, and medium. The doll dressed in silk tells one story, while the doll fashioned out of a small whisk broom and a nut tell another. Collecting works of beauty, rarity, and craftsmanship, Hoyte also tried to keep the collection current and included Barbie, Ken, and Muhammad Ali. A double doll of Flip Wilson and Geraldine was on the shelves along with the Three Stooges and W. C. Fields.

Dolls from the collection won many awards in annual competitions. During Black History Week in 1975 (changed to a month-long celebration in 1976), Hoyte showed twenty-four dolls at the American Museum of Natural History. The exhibition, *Historical Black Dolls*, remained on display for six months.

As the collection quickly grew in objects and popularity, Hoyte realized her one-woman operation would have to change. She began to envision a much larger and permanent space so it could be a tool for education, a place where both children and adults could develop their ideas of the past. She also wanted her home to remain as well, saying: "I want the house to stay as it is, to be used to foster love. There have been so many beautiful antique homes in Harlem, and so many collections, broken up. It ought to be left" (*Encore*, 6 Dec. 1976). But for museum accreditation she needed to catalog her holdings. In the mid-1970s the New York State Council on the Arts awarded Hoyte a small grant that enabled her to hire a part-time assistant. With help from the Community Service Society, Hoyte received a matching grant of $9,000 from the National Endowment for the Arts in the early 1980s.

In 1990 New York City mayor Edward Koch presented the Mayoral Award of Honor for Art and Culture to Hoyte. Her home was burglarized soon after, and nine dolls were stolen. Later four of them, George Washington, Martha Washington, Abraham Lincoln, and Benjamin Franklin, reappeared in the front parlor. She asked no questions, but some few years later she closed the museum because she was no longer able to run it. Hoyte sold thousands of her dolls before she put the rest up for auction at Sotheby's in New York. The auction on 16 December 1994 realized $742,854.

• Sotheby's catalogue, *The Collection of Lenon Holder Hoyte Exhibited as "Aunt Len's Doll and Toy Museum"* (1994), contains an article from *Dolls*, Sept.–Oct. 1985 (Joseph Kelleher, "Her Home Is Her Museum"), and two autobiographical sketches by Hoyte, although they are short on dates. Copious photographs and detailed descriptions reveal the scope of the collection. Other articles with helpful information include Ernest Swiggett, "Aunt Len's Doll and Toy Museum," *Unique NY,* Sept. 1975, pp. 19 ff.; Sandy Satterwhite, "Aunt Len's Fabulous Children," *Encore*, 6 Dec. 1976, p. 36; Frank Hercules, "To Live in Harlem," *National Geographic,* Feb. 1977, pp. 178–207; Anna Quindlen, "About New York," *New York Times,* 13 May 1981; Carol Schatz, "Hoyte, Lady with Love for Dolls," *New York Amsterdam News,* 16 Apr. 1983; and Jane Lusaka, "Aunt Len's Doll and Toy Museum: Collector Lenon H. Hoyte Creates a Lasting Legacy," *Orator,* Winter 1993, pp. 3–4. An obituary is in the *New York Times,* 9 Sept. 1999.

BETTY KAPLAN GUBERT

HUGGINS, Charles Brenton (22 Sept. 1901–12 Jan. 1997), surgeon and Nobel laureate, was born in Halifax, Nova Scotia, Canada, the son of Charles Edward Huggins, a pharmacist, and Bessie Marie Huggins. Huggins graduated from Acadia University at the age of nineteen and received his medical degree from Harvard in 1924. He did his residency at the University of Michigan, where he met Margaret Wellman, a surgery nurse. They married in 1927 and had two children. Margaret Huggins died in 1983.

Huggins joined the University of Chicago Department of Surgery in 1927 as one of the new medical school's eight original faculty members. Although he had no training in urology, he taught himself in this field and delivered lectures with clarity and intuitiveness. He was named chief urologist in 1930. He attained the rank of full professor of surgery in 1936.

In 1940, using an ingenious surgical occlusion of the urinary duct to isolate the prostate gland from the urinary duct in dogs, Huggins studied the effects of hormones on prostate secretion and growth. In 1941 he reported that deprivation of male hormone led to regression of metastatic prostate cancer in men. In the 1950s he showed that removal of female hormones by ovariectomy and adrenalectomy led to repression of advanced breast cancer in many women. Through these studies Huggins demonstrated that many cancer cells are not autonomous but are controlled by external chemical signals. He was one of the first to bring science at the molecular level into urology and cancer research. For these contributions many consider Huggins the founder of the endocrinology of cancer. In 1966 Huggins was awarded the Nobel Prize in medicine and physiology. When he received the Nobel Prize in Sweden, Huggins noted, "First in my thoughts on this happy occasion is gratitude to my wife who has endured much as a science widow."

Huggins also made fundamental discoveries in other fields. In the 1930s he showed that the epithelium lining of the rat urinary tract or bladder transplanted under the abdominal wall induced bone formation. This suggested that specific cellular factors are involved in cell transformation. Huggins wrote, "It was the first discovery of induced change of one cell to another kind of cell." In 1939, after eighteen publications on this subject, Huggins ceased this line of research. However, he returned to this research in 1968 and described the use of dried powders of acid demineralized bones and teeth as the sources of osteogenic stimuli. His studies yielded nineteen additional publications on the subject and stimulated others to isolate a family of morphogenetic factors that induce bone formation.

During the 1940s methods for measuring blood enzymes were cumbersome. To simplify such assays, Huggins synthesized enzymatic substrates that were colorless but gave rise to colored products upon enzyme cleavage. He termed these substrates "chromogenic." The colorimetric methods became common in many research and clinical laboratories. Even in the early twenty-first century molecular or genetic cloning technologies routinely utilized a colorimetric method to identify bacterial clones. In the late 1940s Huggins also demonstrated that sulfhydryl groups are involved in serum protein coagulation, and he envisioned the chemical process involved in structural alteration of proteins leading to coagulation. Another well-known contribution was his development of a method for reproducible induction of mammary tumors with 7,12-dimethylbenz[a]anthracene (DMBA) in rats. This animal model, often called "Huggins's mammary tumor machine," was used to show hormonal dependency of mammary cancer. The method has been widely used by cancer researchers.

During his long research carrier, Huggins published 280 papers based on his own bench work and written by himself. His last formal research paper, published in the *Proceedings of the U.S. National Academy of Sciences* in January 1984, is entitled "Regression of Myelocytic Leukemia in Rat after Hypophysectomy." He was a self-admitted workaholic, working seventy hours a week until he was near eighty years old. Huggins was a superb animal caretaker. He insisted on keeping experimental animals in his own laboratory for close observation and never hesitated to use mouth-to-mouth resuscitation to save animals. At the age of ninety-two he still worked many hours a day in the laboratory and operated on animals himself. He continued to look for new methods for treatment of leukemia. Notebook recording of his experiments continued into 1993.

Besides a Nobel Prize, Huggins received numerous awards, including gold medals from the American Medical Association in 1936 and 1940, the Charles L. Meyer Award in cancer research from the National Academy of Sciences in 1943, and the Albert Lasker Award for Clinical Research in 1963. He was awarded the Order of Merit from Germany and the Order of the Sun from Peru. He was an honorary fellow of the Royal College of Surgeons in both Edinburgh and London and was the recipient of many honorary degrees. Huggins served as the chancellor of his alma mater Acadia University from 1972 to 1979 to express the gratitude he felt for his excellent undergraduate education.

In 1951, with a generous contribution from Ben May, an Alabama businessman, Huggins established the Ben May Laboratory for Cancer Research at the University of Chicago. He chose "Discovery Is Our Business" as its motto. Huggins proclaimed, "Cancer research is basic science—honestly done with simplicity, elegance and proof." As the director of Ben May Laboratory, he often restricted his administrative work to Sunday mornings. To avoid faculty members taking time from bench work, he never requested an annual report or held a formal faculty meeting. He avoided committee meetings and warned his disciples to stay clear of administrative matters, which, he claimed, "often attract mediocre minds."

A proponent of "small is better" and declaring "creative things do not emerge with too many pigeons flying about the room," Huggins invited only a dozen scientists to serve as faculty members during the nineteen years he was the director of the Ben May Laboratory. These he selected for creativity rather than background or publication records. Transformation of young scholars into creative scientists was Huggins's hobby. He allowed none to continue working on what he or she had done previously. Huggins's disciples made many landmark discoveries in biomedical sciences. "Do not go to meetings, write books, or go to the library to find what to work on. They are a waste of time," he advised them. Other maxims included: "Work on new and important problems that are not in books;" "Discover in your brain first, do experiments to prove it, and then you may want to go to library afterward to find out whether you can connect your new discovery to what is known already, and then publish a concise paper." If Huggins felt a faculty member stayed in the office too long, he slipped under the door a piece of paper on which he had written:

"With blood on the hands I have a chance, seated at the desk I have no chance" or "Confucius said: The true science is that done with own hands." He said, "Head, heart and hand are three H's of experimentation—all are involved in creativity in the medical sciences."

Huggins loved the University of Chicago, which he believed was built for "discovery of truth." In 1946 he accepted the chairmanship of urology at the Johns Hopkins Medical School, sold his summer house, and moved to Baltimore. However, he relinquished the position within days and returned to Chicago, where he remained. As a replacement at Johns Hopkins he sent his student William Wallace Scott, who eventually built the Hopkins Department of Urology into one of the best programs of its kind.

Huggins lived within walking distance of his laboratory during his seventy years at the university. He was famously frugal and carried a homemade lunch in a brown paper bag. He locked his door and ate lunch promptly at noon, took a nap, and started afternoon work precisely at 1:00 p.m. His desk was a flat board on two cabinets, and he sat on a small laboratory chair. His office was always a part of a laboratory with working benches. He painted animal cages, stools, garbage cans, electric outlets, file holders, chemical containers, and even cylinder carts in red or green, noting that these colors stimulated him and kept him young. At home Huggins read classics, listened to Mozart and Bach, and went to bed at 9:00 p.m.

Huggins was rarely involved in lengthy discussions of religious or political issues. One clear exception was his concern for democracy and human rights in Taiwan. During the 1980s he met many democracy movement leaders from Taiwan, often in lunch meetings in the conference room in the Ben May Laboratory. When he visited Taiwan in 1985 at the invitation of the National Academy of Sciences (Academia Sinica), Huggins surprised dictatorial government officials by meeting with many leaders of the democratic movement, including church leaders, professors, and lawyers. By the twenty-first century many of these leaders, after coming to power, acknowledged Huggins's support. Huggins died at his home in Chicago.

• A collection of Huggins's papers is held by the University of Chicago Library. His 1966 Nobel Lecture is available at http://www.nobel.se/medicine/laureates/1966/Huggins-lecture.html. Huggins is discussed in Clifford Welsh, "Host Factors Affecting the Growth of Carcinogen-Induced Rat Mammary Carcinomas: A Review and Tribute to Charles Brenton Huggins," *Cancer Research* 45 (1985): 3415–43; Paul Talalay, "Charles Brenton Huggins," in *Remembering the University of Chicago*, ed. Edward Shils (1991); and "Tales from the Forefront: A Tribute to the Life and Times of Charles Brenton Huggins, MD," *Medicine on the Midway,* Summer 1997, pp. 19–35. Obituaries are by Shutsung Liao, *Journal of the American Medical Association* 278 (12 Nov. 1997), p. 1545; Paul Talalay, *Cancer Research* 57 (1 Sept. 1997); and in the *Washington Post,* 16 Jan. 1997.

SHUTSUNG LIAO

HUNCKE, Herbert (9 Jan. 1915–8 Aug. 1996), writer, was born Herbert Edwin Huncke in Greenfield, Massachusetts, the son of Herbert Spencer Huncke, a manufacturer, and Marguerite Bell Huncke. His father manufactured precision tools, and his mother was the daughter of a wealthy rancher from Laramie, Wyoming. An inheritance helped Huncke's father to open H. S. Huncke & Company, makers of precision tools, in Chicago. In 1919 the family moved there.

Huncke showed an early interest in urban street life, and as a preteen he took to wandering the streets of Chicago, staying out all night with friends. At twelve he ran away, hitchhiking as far as Geneva, New York, where he was picked up by the police and returned to his family. He later remembered the experience as his first real taste of freedom, a welcome respite from the familial tensions that led to his parents' divorce the same year (1927). He hung out in speakeasies among Chicago's bohemian crowd, smoking marijuana, using heroin, and meeting older characters such as a carnival hermaphrodite and a heroin dealer named Elsie John. In 1929 Huncke and John were arrested in a heroin bust; Huncke, a minor, was released. That same year he was molested by a stranger in Chicago's lakefront. He also began dating older men he met along the lakefront who kept him in money and elegant clothes.

Huncke dropped out of high school his sophomore year and began making drug deliveries with his friend Johnnie, who was shot to death in a hotel hallway by police. Estranged from his family and having had enough of Chicago, Huncke hit the road at the beginning of the Great Depression, hitchhiking to California and riding the railroads, carrying his meager possessions (clean socks, a razor) in a cigar box. After a brief return to Chicago, he spent most of the 1930s drifting around the country, getting by on his wits and working odd jobs in New Orleans, Texas, East St. Louis, Idaho, and California.

In 1939 Huncke settled in New York City. By then, he was broke and headed straight to Times Square. A quick study, well spoken and charming, he soon became acquainted with the hustling scene and began hanging out with the grifters, petty criminals, and drug dealers who frequented all-night cafeterias such as Bickford's and the Automat; here he met many of the striking characters, such as Russian Blackie and Detroit Redhead, who would populate his memoirs. Homeless and ultimately alone, he robbed cars and sold drugs (and himself) to get enough money for a room at the YMCA or an SRO (single room occupancy hotel). Huncke now began writing in earnest, although he had written intermittently earlier. He recorded his impressions and memories in notebooks, often locking himself in a men's rest room stall in Grand Central Station because it was the only place he could write in peace. He was also addicted to drugs—primarily heroin, but he would use anything he could get his hands on, especially benzedrine (a powerful amphetamine), marijuana, and alcohol—a condition that continued throughout his life.

In 1940 or thereabout, Huncke was arrested for burglarizing a car and spent six months in prison on Hart's Island. After his release and with World War II raging, he and a friend named Phil White joined the merchant marine and shipped out, ostensibly to give themselves a break from drugs and the rigors of street life on Forty-second Street. Their vessel was shelled near England, and he arrived on the beach at Normandy three days after the invasion. Hardly managing to curb their drug use, White and Huncke stole morphine syrettes from the lifeboats and scored drugs in whatever port city they found themselves. In 1944, back in New York, Huncke was introduced to a friend of White's named William S. Burroughs, who stopped by their apartment to sell them a sawed-off shotgun (some accounts call it a machine gun) as well as morphine syrettes such as they had been using at sea. Huncke was initially suspicious that the Harvard-educated Burroughs, conservatively dressed in a snap-brim hat and overcoat, was an FBI agent, but eventually warmed up enough to treat Burroughs to his first shot of morphine. Burroughs described the episode in his debut novel, *Junky* (1953), where Huncke appeared as Herman.

At that time, Burroughs was living in an apartment with Joan Adams, whom he married and later shot to death in a misguided game of William Tell. It was there that Huncke associated with Columbia University students who congregated around Burroughs and Adams: Allen Ginsberg, Jack Kerouac, and Lucien Carr among them. They were awed by Huncke's regal manners, street savvy, and mesmerizing storytelling abilities. "Talk is my stock in trade," Huncke would often say, and Kerouac wrote in a letter to his friend Neal Cassady (fictionalized as Dean Moriarty in Kerouac's *On the Road*; Huncke was called Elmo Hassell): "He is the greatest storyteller I know, an actual genius at it, in my mind." Burroughs, Ginsberg, and Kerouac began forays into Times Square to observe Huncke holding court at the cafeteria tables and to soak up the atmosphere and characters of Bickford's and the Automat. It was from Huncke that Kerouac first heard the term "beat," meaning exhausted to one's core, which Kerouac applied to the Beat Generation.

In 1946 Huncke was approached in a bar by an associate of Dr. Alfred Kinsey, who was in New York gathering data for what would become his groundbreaking study of sexuality, *Sexual Behavior in the Human Male* (1948). Dr. Kinsey paid Huncke ten dollars for an interview about his sexual life—from early experiences to his current life as a hustler—and also paid him an additional two dollars for every interviewee he'd bring by, which eventually included Ginsberg, Burroughs, and Kerouac. That same year, Burroughs invited Huncke to join him in Texas near New Waverly, where he had moved to become a citrus farmer. In January 1947, Huncke rode a Greyhound bus to Texas but forgot to bring the marijuana seeds he intended to cultivate. Undaunted, Huncke soon found seeds in Houston, as well as a drug store that provided the group with cases of benzedrine and paregoric, a tincture of laudanum—an opiate—all sold over the counter. The Burroughs farm was isolated, and Huncke helped out around the house and periodically ventured to the city for supplies and drugs. They remained at the farm until October, returning to New York with mason jars full of a marijuana crop to sell (though it turned out to be worthless because it was improperly cured).

In New York, Huncke lived in Allen Ginsberg's apartment and participated in a string of burglaries with Vickie Russell (AKA Detroit Redhead) and Little Jack Melody. Together they formed a thieves' ring and stored their booty—including an enormous cigarette machine—in Ginsberg's apartment. Ginsberg, who would not participate in the burglaries but was nonetheless interested enough to come along and watch, found himself in over his head when one night, driving with Russell and Melody, they were chased by police and the car full of stolen goods flipped over a median. Melody, Russell, and Ginsberg were arrested. Ginsberg avoided prison with the help of testimonies from Columbia luminaries such as Mark Van Doren and Lionel Trilling, but Huncke, with a previous record and no such connections, was convicted in a string of fifty-two burglaries and sentenced to five years in Sing Sing prison. He served three years and was paroled. But in 1954 he was again convicted of burglary and remained incarcerated until 1959. By then, Burroughs, Ginsberg, and Kerouac were internationally known writers and the "Beat Generation" was in full swing.

Huncke was surprised to learn that he had become a semi-legendary figure through the writings of his friends (although they had failed to contact him while he was in prison). He took a Lower East Side apartment in the same building as Ginsberg and soon found himself back in their orbit. He read his memoirs in public for the first time, stories such as "Elsie John," the vivid chronicle of his hermaphrodite friend, and "In the Park," a harrowingly objective account of his being molested in Chicago. He began using drugs again, this time preferring amphetamine, taken intravenously, which was becoming increasingly popular among the bohemian crowd of the Lower East Side. He became close with writers and artists such as Janine Vega, John Wieners, Irving Rosenthal, Bill Heine, and Alexander Trocchi. He moved from one apartment to another, writing extensively, telling stories and charming acquaintances out of their money, and also, from time to time, stealing. In 1965 the Poets Press published his first book, *Huncke's Journal*.

In the late 1960s he met Louis Cartwright, a young photographer who would become his companion. They lived together, off and on, for the next twenty-five years, until 1994, when Cartwright was stabbed to death, a murder that remains unsolved. Huncke spent his last two years living in New York City's Chelsea Hotel, his rent subsidized by the Rex Foundation,

Jerry Garcia's charitable arm of the Grateful Dead. Huncke continued to hold court to a rapt audience of younger friends and admirers and maintained stormy relationships with fellow "beats" Ginsberg and Burroughs (Kerouac had died in 1969). His first mainstream publication, the only one during his lifetime, occurred in 1968, when *Playboy* published his short story "Alvarez." In 1980 a collection of stories, *The Evening Sun Turned Crimson*, was published, and an autobiography, *Guilty of Everything*, was published in 1990. A mixed collection of his writings, *The Herbert Huncke Reader*, was published in 1997.

Though never as well known as his famous friends, Huncke was a notable writer whose autobiographical stories are detailed, authentic, nonjudgmental descriptions of a life lived without apology. He is known among counterculture aficionados as the original hipster. Huncke has been called the *Ur*-beat, the model for the hip, streetwise sensibility celebrated in the popular culture by Ginsberg, Kerouac, and Burroughs.

• Helpful biographical detail and critical analysis can be found in John Tytell, *Naked Angels: The Lives and Literature of the Beat Generation* (1976), Steven Watson, *The Birth of the Beat Generation: Visionaries, Rebels and Hipsters, 1944–1960* (1995), and the *Dictionary of Literary Biography*, Vol. 16: *The Beats: Literary Bohemians in Postwar America*, ed. Ann Charters (1983). Irving Rosenthal wrote a memorable account of Huncke, capturing the man's charisma and charm, in his novel *Sheeper: "The Poet! The Crooked! The Extra-Fingered!"* (1967). Filmmaker Laki Vazakas produced *Huncke and Louie* (1998), a candid video documentary of Huncke's twilight years and his relationship with Cartwright. An obituary is in the *New York Times*, 9 Aug. 1996.

BEN SCHAFER

HUNLEY, Horace L. (29 Dec. 1823–15 Oct. 1863), promoter and financier of three Confederate submarines, was born Horace Lawson Hunley in Sumner County, Tennessee, just north of Nashville, the son of John Hunley, a cotton broker, and Louise Lawson Hunley. In 1830, with his family, Horace moved, by way of Mississippi, to New Orleans, where his father had served during the War of 1812 at the Battle of New Orleans under General Andrew Jackson. In 1834 his father died after a long illness, leaving the family too poor to return to Tennessee. Horace's mother then married a wealthy New Jersey planter. The stepfather's business and society connections put Horace on the road to success.

In 1849 Hunley earned a law degree from the University of Louisiana (present-day Tulane University) and practiced briefly in St. Tammany Parish before settling in New Orleans in 1852. He served a brief session in the state legislature as a representative from Orleans Parish. The New Orleans Directory for 1855 lists Horace L. Hunley as having a law office at 21 Commercial Place and a home at 44 Apollo Street. In 1857 his residence was 42 Carondelet Street and from 1859 to 1861, the New Orleans Custom House. Also in 1857 Hunley was appointed corresponding clerk to the Customs House at New Orleans and in 1860 Special Deputy Collector of Customs, to act in the absence of Francis H. Hatch, Collector of Customs for the Port and City of New Orleans. Hatch, a close family friend, endorsed Hunley wholeheartedly.

Hunley was determined to find a place in history. He read the biographies of famous men, made notations in his notebook on their attributes, and aspired to join their ranks. Secession and war afforded him this opportunity and he became an avid patriot for the Confederacy. At the outset of hostilities, Hunley was placed in charge of a former lighthouse schooner, *William R. King*, which he prepared for a voyage under the Confederate War Department. The schooner's name was altered to *Adela*. On 10 June 1861 it sailed from Berwick Bay bound for the Yucatan to search for the ships *Windsor Forest* and *Bamberg* and collect arms and munitions for the southern cause. Although Hunley could not find either ship, he did gather intelligence useful to the blockade-running efforts of the Confederacy. His report to Hatch stated: "I am confident that any quantity of arms could be safely introduced into Louisiana over this course in a small light draft steamer with very little danger." Motivated by his dedication to the southern cause, he refused compensation for his part in *Adela's* cruise.

Hunley's official employment with the Customs House ended with *Adela's* blockade-running mission, but his connections led him to more adventurous plans. On 12 March 1862 Francis Hatch granted a privateering commission to James R. McClintock and Baxter Watson, local steam gauge manufacturers and the inventors of a two-man submersible named *Pioneer*. In 1862, Hatch sent an application for a letter of marque to Confederate Secretary of State J. P. Benjamin in Richmond, Virginia. The applicants were listed as John K. Scott, Robert R. Barron, Baxter Watson, and James R. McClintock of New Orleans. Horace Hunley and his friend Henry Jefferson Leovy, an attorney with the New Orleans firm Ogden and Leovy, provided a surety bond of five thousand dollars. In their application, he and his partners requested "authority to cruise the high seas, bay, rivers, estuaries, etc., in the name of the Government, and aid said Government by the destruction or capture of any and all vessels opposed to or at war with the said Confederate States, and to aid in repelling its enemies."

The ambitions of the *Pioneer's* builders were never realized, although the vessel was put through successful trials on Lake Pontchartrain. She was scuttled when New Orleans surrendered to Union forces on 25 April 1862. Hunley immediately moved his business to Jackson, Mississippi, and in May 1863 he contemplated joining the Confederate forces at Vicksburg; he left instructions to his friend and partner Leovy for the disposition of his wealth if he should die. During the latter half of 1863, he traveled to Mobile, Alabama. There he rejoined his partners in the development of a second submarine. William A. Alexander and Lt. George E. Dixon, both engineers of the Twenty-first Alabama Regiment, were detailed to do government work at the machine shop where the

submarine was being constructed. The second boat, named either *Pioneer II* or *American Diver*, also never saw combat. Hunley may have paid for its construction himself. McClintock attempted to build an electromagnetic engine for the submarine, but this failed to provide sufficient power. Consequently, McClintock replaced it with a hand crank turned by four men. The submarine sank in heavy seas while being towed near the mouth of Mobile Bay. There was no loss of life.

Hunley then sold shares to finance another submarine. He retained a one-third share for himself and sold the remaining $10,000 interest to four men— E. C. Singer, R. W. Dunn, B. A. Whitney, and J. D. Breaman—engaged in manufacturing and deploying mines for the Confederacy. They were to receive 50 percent of the value of each ship destroyed as a reward for their efforts. The *H. L. Hunley* had a hull 40 feet long, 3.5 feet wide, and 4.2 feet high. It carried a crew of eight men, seven of whom turned a hand crank while the commander steered with a rudder and controlled the depth with diving planes. Ballast tanks, fore and aft, could be flooded and the water expelled by pumps. The ship's only weapon was a torpedo that was at first towed but later mounted on a long spar. A spear at the end of the torpedo was driven into the side of the enemy ship. The *Hunley* then backed away from the enemy ship and detonated the torpedo with a lanyard.

The *Hunley* was put through a series of trials in Mobile Bay but was transferred to Charleston, South Carolina, for active duty. Hunley believed the submarine would break the Union blockade of Charleston and facilitate the repulsion of Union forces at nearby Morris Island. Initially, McClintock was given charge of the submarine after its arrival at Charleston but failed to conduct a successful attack. Shortly thereafter, the Confederate Army seized the *Hunley* and put it under the command of the Confederate Navy. In the following weeks, the vessel sank in shallow water and five of the crew drowned. The submarine was repaired, and Hunley assumed command with an experienced crew summoned from Mobile.

On 15 October 1863, during a routine diving exercise, the the *Hunley* failed to resurface. All eight crewmen, including Hunley, were lost. Divers recovered the vessel a few weeks later. Sources familiar with the operation of the submarine reported that Hunley had failed to ignite the candle that provided the single source of light for viewing the vessel's dive planes, compass, and depth gauge. Hunley had apparently failed to close a valve that allowed water into the forward ballast tank. Additionally, the 35-degree angle of the dive was too steep and the sub plowed into the muddy bottom. The crew attempted to release the iron keel ballast but did not turn the release mechanism far enough before water filled the vessel. The bodies of Hunley and second officer Parks were found in their respective conning towers, each with his right arm upraised against the hatches. Hunley still grasped the unlit candle in his left hand.

Hunley was correct in his belief that his submarine would be successful and attain a place in history. On 17 February 1864 Lt. George E. Dixon refitted the ship, and attacked and sank the sloop of war USS *Housatonic*. Consequently, the *H . L. Hunley* became the first successful combat submarine and accomplished a feat that would not be repeated until World War I. Although successful, the *Hunley* did not return from this voyage and claimed the lives of a third crew. The wreck of the submarine was found in 1995, recovered in 2000, and the bodies of Dixon and his crew exhumed in 2001.

• Horace L. Hunley's correspondence can be found in the War Department Collection of Confederate Records in the National Archives. His birth and family information are recorded in the family bible. Copies of these records are archived at the Warren Lasch Conservation Center in North Charleston, South Carolina. Also see these books: Brian Hicks and Schuyler Kropf, *Raising the* Hunley (2002); Mark Ragan, *The* Hunley: *Submarines, Sacrifice, & Success in the Civil War* (1999); James E. Kloeppel, *Danger Beneath the Waves* (1987); and Ruth H. Duncan, *The Captain and Submarine CSS* H. L. Hunley (1965).

ROBERT S. NEYLAND

HUNTER, Robert M. T. (21 Apr. 1809–18 July 1887), congressman and statesman, was born Robert Mercer Taliaferro Hunter at "Mount Pleasant," his father's estate in Essex County, Virginia, the son of James Hunter, a planter, and Maria Garnett Hunter. Born into a family that had achieved local prominence, he grew up in comfortable surroundings. After receiving his early education through home tutoring, he entered the University of Virginia and graduated in July 1828. Interested in government and history, he decided to become a lawyer and studied under Judge Henry St. George Tucker of Winchester, Virginia, a leading advocate of the emerging doctrine of states' rights. Admitted to the bar in 1830, he returned to Essex County and began his own legal practice.

In 1834 Hunter was elected to the Virginia House of Delegates. Although elected as an independent, he soon formed an alliance with anti-Jackson states' rights Whigs. In his first political office, he soon displayed the contradictory series of positions that would mark his entire political career; while he rejected local legislative efforts to support Missouri Senator Thomas Hart Benton's expunging resolution and also opposed Virginia's support of the specie circular, he angered fellow Whigs by refusing to support statewide internal improvements. On 4 October 1836 he married Mary Evelina Dandridge, with whom he had eight children.

Hunter joined the U.S. House of Representatives in 1837, after running for office as a "Sub-Treasury, Anti-Clay, states' rights Whig." While in Congress he continued to antagonize his fellow Whigs with his support of President Martin Van Buren's subtreasury plan. In December 1839 Hunter became the popular compromise candidate of a deadlocked House and was elected to the Speakership of the House; at age thirty, he was the youngest man ever to hold the post. His attempts at nonpartisanship pleased no one, and Hunter further offended the Whigs when he declined to endorse William Henry Harrison for president in 1840. Increasingly influenced by John C. Calhoun, Hunter aligned with states' rights Democrats, and in 1841 the Whigs completely rejected Hunter. Although reelected with the support of the Democrats in 1840, Hunter lost his 1842 bid due to continued Whig hostility and redistricting.

During his two years out of office Hunter promoted Calhoun's unsuccessful presidential bid, lending his name to a campaign biography (1843). He also corresponded widely with northern Democrats concerning Calhoun's prospects. Although unsuccessful in elevating Calhoun to the presidency, Hunter returned to the House in 1845 and helped lead a successful effort to return Alexandria County (later Arlington County) to Virginia from the District of Columbia. In December 1847 the Virginia legislature elected Hunter to the U.S. Senate, where he continued to pursue an independent course. Frustrated by Calhoun's failure to reach the White House and by continued northern intransigence on the slavery issue, Hunter attended the Nashville Convention of 1850 and emerged as a leading exponent of states' rights; following the death of Calhoun that same year, he became known, along with Jefferson Davis and Robert Toombs, as a member of the so-called "Southern Triumvirate." Still capable of conciliation, he worked as chairman of the Senate Committee on Finance to pass the tariff bill of 1857, a move that won him many friends in the North.

Although he held favorite son status with Virginia Democrats, Hunter eventually threw his support to John C. Breckinridge in the 1860 presidential campaign. Following the election of Abraham Lincoln, Hunter still held out hope for sectional rapprochement and served with the group of senators that produced the Crittenden Compromise. He finally left the Senate in March 1861 shortly before the state of Virginia seceded.

In July 1861 Hunter succeeded Robert Toombs as secretary of state for the Confederacy. As secretary he urged the European powers to ignore Union threats regarding the Southern blockade, arguing that its ineffectiveness rendered it irrelevant. Unhappy with the diplomatic efforts of Confederate commissioners in England, he recalled William Lowndes Yancey and reassigned A. Dudley Mann and Pierre A. Rost to other posts. His dispatch of John Slidell and James M. Slidell to Europe helped precipitate the infamous *Trent* affair, in which a Union sloop forcibly removed the two from the British vessel *Trent* while engaged in a diplomatic mission. This incident almost led to war between the Union and Great Britain.

Hunter left office in February 1862 and served in the Confederate senate for the balance of the war, where he was elected president pro tem and sat on a number of committees, including conference, finance, and foreign relations. Generally supportive of President Jefferson Davis, Hunter parted ways with Davis over the arming of slaves, which he strongly opposed. He served as a member of the ill-fated peace conference in early 1865 at Virginia's Hampton Roads, where (with Vice President Alexander Stephens and Assistant Secretary of War John A. Campbell) he unsuccessfully attempted to negotiate a peace treaty favorable to Southern interests with President Lincoln and Secretary of State William Seward.

After the war, Hunter was accused of complicity in Lincoln's assassination and was jailed at Fort Pulaski, Georgia. Following his release, he returned to "Foothill," his estate in Essex County, Virginia, which had suffered heavy damage at the hands of Union general Benjamin Butler, and resumed his law practice. As a member of the Underwood convention in 1867 and 1868, he helped draft a new state constitution. He served as state treasurer from 1874 until 1880, when he was defeated for reelection by a Readjuster candidate associated with William Mahone. Hunter was appointed as collector of the port of Tappahannock by President Grover Cleveland in 1885 and held this post until his death at his estate two years later.

Throughout his career, Hunter remained difficult to categorize by ideology; he thus developed neither a political school of thought nor a cult of personality. Nevertheless, his place in history is secure due to his actions and policies in a variety of high positions in both the U.S. and Confederate governments.

• Hunter's papers are scattered, with the largest collections being found at the Virginia Historical Society and the Virginia State Library and Archives, both in Richmond, Virginia. He was the subject of *A Memoir of Robert M. T. Hunter* (1903), written by his daughter Martha T. Hunter, and Henry H. Sims's *Life of Robert M. T. Hunter: A Study in Sectionalism and Secession* (1935). Recent scholarship on his life and career includes John E. Fisher, "Statesman of a Lost Cause: The Career of R. M. T. Hunter, 1859–1887," Ph.D. diss., University of Virginia, 1968; Jeffrey J. Crow, "R. M. T. Hunter and the Secession Crisis, 1860–1861: A Southern Plan for Reconstruction," *West Virginia History* 34 (1972–1973): 273–90; Fisher, "The Dilemma of a States' Rights Whig: The Congressional Career of R. M. T. Hunter, 1837–1841," *Virginia Magazine of History and Biography* 81 (1973): 387–404; William S. Hitchcock, "Southern Moderates and Secession: Senator Robert M. T. Hunter's Call for Union," *Journal of American History* 59 (1972–1973): 871–84; and Richard Randall Moore, "Robert M. T. Hunter and the Crisis of the Union, 1860–1861," *Southern Historian* 13 (Spring 1992): 25–35. An obituary is in the *Richmond Dispatch*, 20 July 1887.

EDWARD L. LACH, JR.

HUTCHINSON FAMILY SINGERS, musicians and reformers, comprised Adoniram Judson Joseph (14 Mar. 1817–11 Jan. 1859), John Wallace (4 Jan. 1821–29 Oct. 1908), Asa Burnham (14 Mar. 1823–25 Nov. 1884), Abigail Jemima (29 Aug. 1829–23 Nov. 1892), and sometimes Jesse, Jr. (29 Sept. 1813–15 May 1853) (who composed several of their most notable songs and occasionally performed alongside his siblings), the children of Jesse Hutchinson and Mary "Polly" Leavitt Hutchinson, farmers in Milford, New Hampshire. The Hutchinson children were educated in public schools and took part in the choir sponsored by the Baptist Church. The church and, to a lesser extent, itinerant music teachers were the main sources of their musical training, outside of what they taught themselves.

In 1841, after a well-received Milford concert by the entire Hutchinson family, John, Judson, and Asa set out to make it as professional musicians, despite the fact that few Americans then made a living as musicians, and their parents—along with many others—regarded music making as morally suspect. The brothers called themselves the Aeolian Vocalists and toured rural New England, accompanying their singing with two violins (played by John and Judson) and a basslike instrument more akin to a violoncello (played by Asa). This endeavor brought them some critical acclaim but little financial reward. As a result, the three spent much of the year working in grocery and hardware stores operated by their older brothers in Lynn, Massachusetts.

In 1842, following a performance by a family from Switzerland called the Rainers, who dressed in native costume and sang Tyrolean melodies, the three Hutchinson brothers adopted songs from the Rainers' repertoire, and added their twelve-year-old sister "Abby," dressed in Tyrolean garb, to the quartet. Some early reviewers dubbed the Hutchinsons "The New Hampshire Rainers." The Hutchinson Family Singers became more successful.

That same year they celebrated their own identity by supporting the temperance movement. The popularity of temperance reform, which was closely associated with the church, provided the Hutchinsons a chance to be heard at mass gatherings such as temperance-sponsored picnics and parades. By singing anti-alcohol tunes such as "King Alcohol," moreover, the Hutchinson Family Singers gained the backing of ministers and other religious officials. The Philadelphia *Christian Observer* endorsed their concerts as "a place where a Christian may be, and not feel that he is doing wrong."

In 1843 the Hutchinson Family Singers were at the forefront of the antislavery movement. Sponsored by Nathaniel P. Rogers, a well-known New Hampshire newspaper editor, the singers electrified antislavery conventions with their improvisational skills, incorporating the dialog of the debates immediately into their lyrics and turning songs into chronicles of the meetings' proceedings. Soon they were in demand by organizers of antislavery gatherings, who understood that if the New Hampshire singers performed, large crowds were virtually guaranteed. Even abolitionist leader William Lloyd Garrison felt that it was a "disappointment of us all" when the Hutchinsons were not present.

Antislavery, though not as popular as temperance, employed a much more active and extensive media network. Both vilified and praised for espousing antislavery, the Hutchinson Family Singers gained considerable publicity. Often their performances generated controversy, and sometimes the singers faced proslavery mobs. One notable debate exploded over the Hutchinsons' publication of "Get Off the Track!" their antislavery anthem. Unable to secure a more established publisher to print their work, the Hutchinsons issued the song. The sheet music irked both the proslavery public and moderate antislavery advocates with its cover lithograph depicting a series of railroad cars named "Liberator" and "Immediate Emancipation" pulling "Liberty Votes and Ballot Boxes," while a train in the background identified as "Clay [Henry Clay]" fell into a ravine. Their support for William Lloyd Garrison and immediate emancipation sparked a firestorm among Boston's major newspapers. "The Hutchinsons Doomed," ran the headline in the *Morning Chronicle*, 20 April 1844, and the *Atlas* of the same date warned the public "to regard the aforesaid tribe as from henceforth utterly extinct."

The Hutchinson Family Singers overcame adversity to link themselves to a burgeoning middle class through a variety of tunes—from Jesse, Jr.'s "The Old Granite State" (their signature song) and "The Bereaved Slave Mother" (an antislavery piece) to sentimental ballads such as "My Mother's Bible." The Hutchinsons netted over $1,000 per night (a sum that exceeded the annual wages of many workers) during their New York concerts. From August of 1845 through July of 1846 they toured Great Britain, a trip that proved to be enormously successful. News of their British accomplishments was eagerly scooped up by the American press while Hutchinson Family Singer imitators in the United States (including a group of their own relatives) tried to fill the void in their absence.

The overwhelming success of the Singers was diminished by the marriage of Abby Hutchinson to wealthy New York financier Ludlow Patton on 28 February 1849. They had no children. Because this was a time when many still disapproved of women working in the public eye, Abby Hutchinson immediately retired from the group. She and her husband traveled throughout the world, although she occasionally appeared on stage with her brothers.

The Hutchinson brothers also married: John to Fanny Burnham Patch, 21 February 1843; Judson to his cousin Jerusha Peabody Hutchinson, July 1844; and Asa to Elizabeth B. Chase, 26 April 1847. John and Fanny had two children, Judson and Jerusha had two, and Asa and Elizabeth had four. The Hutchinson brothers performed on their own, and each brother toured the nation, but their popularity declined. The Family Singers did not take lightly their loss of popularity. Judson committed suicide in his brother John's home in Lynn, Massachusetts, in 1859. Later, John was sued for breach of promise when he ended engagements to women more than fifty years younger than he.

The Hutchinson Family Singers were one of the nation's first popular musical groups and the first to combine tremendous celebrity with socially active entertainment. They also helped confer respectability on professional musicians and establish the legitimacy of American performers in a field formerly dominated by European-born artists.

• The largest collection of documents about the Hutchinson Family Singers (including sheet music, photographs, and newspaper clippings) is located at the Wadleigh Memorial Public Library in Milford, New Hampshire. Dale Cockrell, ed., *Excelsior: Journals of the Hutchinson Family Singers, 1842–1846* (1989) consists of a common diary kept by the performers and valuable annotations provided by the editor. A younger brother of the Hutchinson Family Singers, Joshua, published short, but intimate vignettes of his siblings and the rest of their family in *A Brief Narrative of the Hutchinson Family* (1874). For a less accurate but entertaining reconstruction of the group, see John Hutchinson's two-volume memoir *The Story of the Hutchinsons*, published in 1896.. Philip Jordan, *Singin' Yankees* (1947), and Carol Ryrie Brink, *Harps in the Wind: The Story of the Singing Hutchinsons* (1947), are the only modern biographies of the New Hampshire entertainers and both rely heavily on John Hutchinson's memoir. A two-CD compilation titled *Homespun America* (1993) includes performances of nine songs from the Hutchinson Family Singers' repertoire. Obituaries for Judson, Asa, Abby, and John Hutchinson are in the *New York Times*, respectively, 13 Jan. 1859, 1 Dec. 1884, 26 Nov. 1892, and 30 Oct. 1908.

SCOTT E. GAC

I–J

ISING, Rudolf. *See under* Harman, Hugh N.

JACKSON, Milt (1 Jan. 1923–9 Oct. 1999), musician, was born in Detroit, Michigan, the son of Manley Jackson and Lillie Beaty Jackson. (His parents' occupations are unknown). Jackson was surrounded by music from an early age, and his strongest influence came from the music he heard during weekly religious meetings: "Everyone wants to know where I got that funky style. Well, it came from church. The music I heard was open, relaxed, impromptu soul music" (quoted in Nat Hentoff's liner notes to *Plenty, Plenty Soul*). Inspired by the music he heard in church, Jackson began playing the guitar when he was seven years old. Four years later he began studying the piano and, while attending Miller High School, focused on the drums in addition to playing tympani and violin and singing in the school's choir (at sixteen he sang in a local gospel quartet called the Evangelist Singers). Jackson eventually took up the vibraharp, or vibraphone, after hearing Lionel Hampton play the instrument in Benny Goodman's band.

In 1941 Jackson began his professional career, playing the vibraharp in two local groups, led by Clarence Ringo and George E. Lee. His career was interrupted by a two-year stint in the U.S. Army (1942–1944). In 1944 he started the Four Sharps, his first group. There would always remain a special place in Jackson's heart for the Detroit music scene that nurtured him: "[Detroit] was a beautiful environment then. I wish they could have kept that environment and enhanced it. The environment of the 40's in Detroit was very similar to the environment of 52nd Street when I first came to New York. . . . In Detroit we had Al McKibbon, Howard McGhee, Teddy Edwards, who actually moved to the West Coast, the Jones brothers" (quoted in Rusch, p. 4).

In 1945 visiting jazz giant trumpeter Dizzy Gillespie discovered Jackson and asked him to come to New York. While working in Gillespie's band, Jackson was introduced to Charlie "Yardbird" Parker, who was chiefly responsible for forging the musical revolution known as "bebop." Jackson was overwhelmed by the experience of playing with Parker: "I remember one night we were playing 'Hot House' and Bird was playing so fantastic that I came in four bars late in my solo" (quoted in DeMicheal, p. 19).

Playing with Gillespie proved to be a springboard for Jackson's career, and within his first few years in New York he played with a veritable who's who of jazz. On 2 July 1948 he recorded with the pianist and composer Thelonious Monk for the seminal Blue Note label. Jackson also worked with the clarinetist

Woody Herman and his orchestra in 1949. Upon returning to the Gillespie band in 1950, Jackson played alongside the tenor saxophonist John Coltrane. In addition to playing the vibraharp, he doubled as pianist and, on occasion, as vocalist for the Gillespie band. While playing with Gillespie, Jackson met pianist John Lewis, with whom he would be associated musically for the next forty years. Lewis had served as the pianist in Gillespie's big band between the years of 1946 and 1948, and it was in that band that the nucleus of the Modern Jazz Quartet was born.

Around 1951–1952 Jackson made his first album under his own name, *The Milt Jackson Quartet* (reissued on compact disc in 1991 on the Savoy label SV-0111). Rounding out the group were Lewis on piano; bassists Ray Brown, who became a mainstay in pianist Oscar Peterson's group, and Percy Heath; the father of bebop drumming, Kenny Clarke; and drummer Al Johns. The group made public appearances as the Milt Jackson Quartet, but between 1953 and 1954 Heath became the MJQ's full-time bassist and the initials of the group came to stand for the Modern Jazz Quartet. The Modern Jazz Quartet became one of the longest running small groups in jazz, and with the exception of Clarke being replaced by Connie Kay in 1955, the lineup of the group remained intact until Kay's death.

Mixing blues with Lewis's more classically aimed compositions and wearing tuxedos at all of their live appearances, the MJQ took jazz music to places normally not associated with jazz, including concert halls and theaters. Critics were favorable, and the term "chamber jazz" was used to describe their music. Some musicians, however, felt that the group was "pretentious," but that did not hinder its popularity. Milt Jackson's vibes provided the perfect foil for Lewis's stoic compositions.

Jackson married Sandra Kaye Whittington in 1959; they had one daughter.

In the 1960s Jackson recorded albums with John Coltrane and Ray Charles. In 1974 the MJQ disbanded, leaving Jackson free to pursue a solo career, although the quartet reunited in 1981 and performed on a few tours. He recorded albums for Pablo and for producer Creed Taylor's CTI label and remained a vital and active jazz musician until his death in Manhattan. His improvisational skill and unique sound made him a true original in jazz, and he has influenced countless other musicians.

• Recordings by Jackson include *Pyramid* (with MJQ; Atlantic), *Django* (OJC), and *Sunflower* (CTI). Biographical information on Jackson can be found in Nat Hentoff's liner notes to *Plenty, Plenty Soul* (Atlantic 1269-2), and in *Con-*

temporary Musicians, vol. 15 (1996). See also Bob Rusch, Milt Jackson Interview," *Cadence*, May 1977, pp. 3–6; and Don De Michael, "Jackson of the MJQ," *Down Beat*, 6 July 1961, pp. 18–21. An obituary is in the *New York Times*, 11 Oct. 1999.

P. J. COTRONEO

JACOBS, Bernard (13 June 1916–27 Aug. 1996), theatrical businessperson, was born in Harlem, New York, the son of Harry Jacobs, a dealer in wool waste, and May Jacobs (maiden name unknown), an immigrant from what Jacobs called "that huge area somewhere in Russia or Poland." Jacobs's sister later recalled an incident when, at age three, Jacobs, fascinated by cows being milked, reported, "And they mixed the milk with water."

Jacobs was educated at DeWitt Clinton High School, New York University (graduating in 1937), and the Columbia University School of Law (graduating in 1940). In 1944, after spending four years in the South Pacific with the U.S. Army, he married Betty Shulman. They had two children. Also in 1944 Jacobs entered law practice with one of his brothers and specialized in matters involving jewelry. In 1958 Gerald Schoenfeld, who had recently become the legal counsel for the theater magnate Jake J. Shubert (brother of Lee Shubert), persuaded Jacobs to work for Shubert also.

The Shubert Brothers chain once numbered over 100 theaters, but in his declining years Jake Shubert sold many theaters and was forced to give up his stranglehold on bookings. When he died in 1963, Shubert left his estate to the tax-free charitable arm of his enterprises. In 1973, after considerable struggle within the organization, Jacobs and Schoenfeld became president and chair respectively of the Shubert Foundation, hence of the whole Shubert empire. Though Jacobs lacked the flamboyance of previous power brokers, Jacobs and Schoenfeld, who became popularly known as "the Shuberts," dominated Broadway for the rest of the century.

Their ascendancy began in 1974, after Jacobs and Schoenfeld decided, as apparently all Shubert decisions were made jointly, to expand beyond theater ownership into investing in shows, a practice the company had abandoned during its decades in decline. In 1974 they imported the English drama *Equus* and underwrote the musicals *Pippin* and *Grease*, all moneymaking hits.

Unlike other kings of Broadway, such as David Merrick, Jacobs and Schoenfeld were not interested in producing or directing. They preferred to exercise their generally conservative, commercially driven taste in encouraging the directorial careers of others, including Harold Prince, Bob Fosse, Jerome Robbins, and Michael Bennett. They were said to have "put business back into show business." Jacobs fully computerized Shubert's ticketing operation and cooperated with Broadway's new half-price ticket booth, thus leading the modernization of theatrical ticket selling.

Bennett proved their most important investment. Jacobs was credited with encouraging the off-Broadway (Public Theater) producer Joseph Papp to try Bennett's highly original musical *A Chorus Line* in one of his theaters. *A Chorus Line* eventually gave 6,137 performances at the Shubert, shattering every long-run record and opening an era of blockbuster musicals

The two lawyers were excellent guardians of their company's fortunes and particularly worked to maintain control throughout litigious times. The company's accelerating prosperity was boosted in 1979 by a federal tax ruling that held that a private charity such as Shubert's could, after all, hold shares in profit-making companies. After the payment of normal taxes, the foundation could invest profits in tax-free ventures. As property values dived and soared, the pair's achievement and power base was to hold onto the 16½ remaining Shubert theaters in New York. (The organization owned half of the Music Box Theatre, the other half remaining with the Irving Berlin Trust. A half-dozen other Shubert houses were scattered across the country.) In shrunken years, when openings might number fewer than a score, "the Shuberts" held a true stranglehold on Broadway.

Because many Shubert productions were imported shows that carried success with them, "the Shuberts" were criticized for not boosting native playwrights. But if Jacobs was not a creative force, he was an enthusiastic theatergoer who reported a "seismic emotional jolt" at *Dreamgirls*, their long-running 1981 African-American musical.

Schoenfeld and Jacobs, together and privately, decided what to show in their theaters, what to invest in, and whom to hire. One company executive said: "It's a little like the Kremlin in here. Who knows what goes on behind those [literally golden] doors?" Nevertheless Jacobs specialized in labor relations. Beginning in 1961 he was the New York management's chief negotiator in all dealings with theatrical trade unions. His settlements sometimes seemed soft, but Jacobs is said to have remarked, "Why shouldn't the unions make a living too?" He reportedly cherished his gold lifetime membership card from Stagehands Union Local Number One, the only card given to a theatrical executive.

Jacobs was for many years vice president of the League of American Theaters and Producers, management's "trade union." As the "inside man" of "the Shuberts," he was also charged with real estate management, advertising policy, and theater maintenance. Jacobs innovated a long-lived program involving the New York City Board of Education that awarded fifty free tickets to a Shubert show each week to deserving students. The program began in 1982 with the imported British musical *Cats*. Jacobs was not otherwise liberal with freebies. Notably turning down a request by the Baron de Rothschild for a benefit performance that meant an entire house's seats, Jacobs commented: "Who is he? Just a man with a 'de' in front of his name."

Although often visible in "Shubert Alley" between the Shubert and Booth theaters, Jacobs was happiest out of the news but involved with theater. He was a visiting professor at the Yale School of Drama, and he was adjunct professor in the Columbia School of Dramatic Arts. He was a long-time trustee of the Actors' Fund. In 1986 his health began to decline, and he was diagnosed with global amnesia, an in-and-out loss of memory. He thereafter collected many awards and honors, including the medal of the Actors' Fund (1992), election to the Theater Hall of Fame (1994), and a Distinguished Achievement award from Columbia Law School (1995). Jacob was posthumously awarded a special Antoinette Perry (Tony) Award for lifetime achievement in 1997, when the awards ceremony was dedicated to him.

Jacobs died in New York. Often described in his dealings as "soft-spoken but steely," Jacobs helped steady Broadway in the decades following the departure of some of its most creative lights. If in the American theater show business came to emphasize business, no one was more responsible than Jacobs.

• All papers pertaining to "the Shuberts" remain in the Shubert Archive, New York City. Jacobs was so successful at remaining unpublicized that he does not figure in most theater histories or standard reference works. Greg Evans, "B'way after Bernie: Biz Ponders Act Two" (*Variety*, 2–8 Sept. 1996), reviews Jacobs's career and speculates on Broadway after "the Shuberts." Peter Marks, "Who Will Fill the Void on Shubert Alley?" (*New York Times*, 30 Aug. 1996), is along similar lines. Nancy Coyne's lively and useful article "Bernie Jacobs: Now and Forever" appears in the program for the Actors' Fund Tribute to Bernard B. Jacobs (1992), pp. 8–11 (a copy is at the Shubert Archive). An obituary by Mel Gussow is in the *New York Times*, 28 Aug. 1996.

JAMES ROSS MOORE

JOHNSON, Francis (16 June 1792–6 Apr. 1844), musician, bandleader, and composer also known as Frank Johnson, was born in Philadelphia, Pennsylvania. Little is known of his youth and parentage. Most sources cite Martinique as his birthplace, but Stephen Charpié's (1999) work with baptismal records establishes his birth date, birthplace, and status as a free African American. Though skilled at a number of instruments, Johnson seems to have first attained local prominence as a fiddler at dances, parties, and the like; there is some evidence that he played with Matthew "Matt" Black's band in the late 1810s. Johnson also seems to have received some limited instruction during this period from Richard Willis, an Irish immigrant who later directed the West Point military band and who introduced the keyed bugle (also known as a Kent bugle) to the United States.

Johnson's prowess with this new instrument, along with his skills as a bandleader and a showman, made him known throughout the city—so much so that Robert Waln's satiric *The Hermit in America on a Visit to Philadelphia* (1819) included him in a description of a cotillion party as the "inventor-general of cotil-

lions" (quoted in Southern, *Readings*, p. 124). In 1815 the music publisher George Willig began circulating Johnson's works and in November 1818 published Johnson's *A Collection of New Cotillions*.

The 1820s saw a series of successes. Johnson published several more compositions—mainly dances and marches—and tightened his relationship with Willig. In 1822 Johnson and his band spent the summer in the Saratoga Springs resort area, and their successes led to a long-standing engagement. Eventually Johnson also performed at other resort areas, including Cape May, New Jersey, and White Sulphur Springs, Virginia. He also developed associations with several Philadelphia militia units, including the First Troop Philadelphia City Calvary, the elite State Fencibles, and most importantly the Washington Guards Third Company (later called the Washington Grays). These events cemented Johnson's reputation in Philadelphia and won him growing national acclaim. In 1824 he received two major commissions—one for much of the music for the Marquis de Lafayette's triumphant return to Philadelphia and another to score a revival of Joseph Cowell's "grand spectacle" of musical theater *The Cataract of the Ganges*, which ran at Philadelphia's Walnut Street Theatre in late 1824 and early 1825.

During the late 1820s and early 1830s Johnson fell into a regular—though still richly creative—pattern. He wintered in Philadelphia, where he taught both black and white students (though in a segregated environment), gave concerts, composed, and continued publishing. He spent summers performing at various resort areas and the rest of the year touring the Northeast. Perhaps his most notable achievement during this period was his work for the centennial of George Washington's birth, for which he performed as part of the Washington Grays' 1832 visit to Mount Vernon.

Johnson attracted some of the best black musicians of his time to his band, and in November 1837 he handpicked four—William Appo, Aaron J. R. Connor, Edward Roland, and Francis Seymour—to travel with him on a British tour. Their repertoire was wide and varied, ranging from Mozart and Gioacchino Antonio Rossini to American popular songs; the band switched seamlessly from brass to strings and even sang occasionally. When they returned to the United States the next year, Johnson had both international fame and a silver bugle, presented to him by the young Queen Victoria after a command performance. Perhaps more importantly Johnson had grown as a musician. His time in England exposed him to the work of Johann Strauss (especially his waltzes) and to the promenade concert begun by Philippe Musard. The former led Johnson to compose several of his own waltzes, which were popular throughout the late 1830s and early 1840s. The latter led to the first American promenade concert in Philadelphia during the 1838 Christmas season, thus beginning a musical tradition that continued into the twenty-first century.

Between 1838 and his death, Johnson toured the Northeast, going as far as Toronto. He also traveled to St. Louis on a commission from the St. Louis Fire Company. In off months, he contined to compose, publish, and teach from his home in Philadelphia. In March 1841 he conducted a 50-piece orchestra and a 150-voice chorus led by Morris Brown, Jr., in a performance of Haydn's *Creation*. His 1843–1844 promenade concerts offered the first integrated concerts in the United States. Johnson fell ill, though, in March 1844 and died in Philadelphia. During the funeral march hundreds of mourners, including his brass band, followed his casket, on which his silver bugle was placed. Over a century later, in 1980, the Washington Grays named Johnson an honorary member.

Though scholars have begun to document Johnson's public career, little is known of his personal life. He married Helen Appo (sister of his band mate William Appo), but the date is unknown. Charpié suggests that this was not his first marriage. Little is known about the ways Johnson dealt with racial discrimination, though records of several instances of such discrimination survive. Throughout Johnson's life his main focus seems to have been his music. One white student, Isaac Mickle, described Johnson's music room as filled with instruments and "thousands of musical compositions" in "admirable confusion" (Mickle, p. 196).

While Johnson's simple presence on the stage—to say nothing of his extensive conducting and composing—was a radical statement about race and politics, his music generally fit with the styles and topics of the day (though pieces like his "Recognition March on the Independence of Haiti" and "The Grave of the Slave," based on a Sarah Forten poem published in the *Liberator*, emphasized questions of race). His dance music centered on entertainment; his martial music was heavily nationalistic. Though not especially innovative in composition, Johnson was consistently adept at playing to audiences. For example, his "Philadelphia Firemen's Cotillion," dedicated to the city's fire association, supposedly included fire bells, a field bugle, and the band shouting "Fire! Fire!" Such work often included improvisation, leading some critics to suggest that Johnson was a distant forefather of ragtime and jazz. A savvy businessperson as well as a respected musician, he regularly adapted his band to various functions—from a four-piece group (with Johnson on bugle) for marching, to a larger military band (including woodwinds and French horns), to Johnson's Quadrille Band and Johnson's Celebrated Cotillion Band (in which some of the wind players switched to strings). As American tastes shifted toward early brass bands, Johnson was at the forefront.

Johnson's importance in American music generally has been greatly underestimated. One of the most prolific early American composers (with well over two hundred published pieces), Johnson was the first African American to publish sheet music, the first black musician and arguably the first American musician to tour Europe with a band, and one of the first musicians to participate in integrated public concerts. He mentored a number of successful black musicians, and scholars credit him as the leader the Philadelphia School of composers—arguably the first such group in the United States. His compositions remained in print until late in the nineteenth century and enjoyed some reemergence in the late twentieth century.

• Several of Johnson's published compositions survive. Notable collections of his sheet music are at the Keffner Collection of Sheet Music, University of Pennsylvania, and the American Music Research Center, University of Colorado; several Johnson compositions are indexed in the database *Early American Secular Music and Its European Sources* (http://www.colonialdancing.org/Easmes). Charles K. Jones and Lorenzo K. Greenwich's two-volume compilation *A Choice Collection of the Works of Francis Johnson* (1983–1987) offers a number of facsimile reprints. Arthur LaBrew's privately printed *Studies in Nineteenth-Century Afro-American Music: Captain Francis Johnson* (1994) offers additional facsimiles as well as biographical information. Among recordings that include Johnson's work, BMG/Musicmasters, *Music of Francis Johnson & His Contemporaries* (1990), is a good introduction. Robert Waln's [Peter Atall, pseud.] description of Johnson in *The Hermit in America on a Visit to Philadelphia* (1819) is reprinted in Eileen Southern, *Readings in Black American Music*, 2d ed. (1983). Isaac Mickle's description is in *A Gentleman of Much Promise: The Diary of Isaac Mickle, 1837–1845*, ed. Philip English Mackey (1977). Johnson is mentioned in several nineteenth-century biographical dictionaries of African Americans. The best early source is John Cromwell, "Frank Johnson's Military Band," *Southern Worker* 29 (1900): 532–35; reprinted in *Black Perspective in Music* 4, no. 2 (1976): 208–212.

Modern consideration of Johnson was effectively begun by Eileen Southern, who wrote, among other pieces on Johnson, "A Portfolio of Music: The Philadelphia Afro-American School," *Black Perspective in Music* 4, no. 2 (1976): 238–59; "Frank Johnson and His Promenade Concerts," *Black Perspective in Music* 5, no. 1 (1977): 3–29; an entry in her *Biographical Dictionary of Afro-American and African Musicians* (1982), pp. 205–207; and a discussion in her *Music of Black Americans*, 3d ed. (1997), pp. 105–106 and passim. Stephen Charpié's work is summarized in his entry on Johnson in Samuel A. Floyd, ed., *International Dictionary of Black Composers*, vol. 2 (1999), pp. 615–620, which also includes an extensive list of Johnson's work. An obituary is in the *Philadelphia Public Ledger*, 6 Apr. 1844.

ERIC GARDNER

JOHNSON, Gerald W. (6 Aug. 1890–22 Mar. 1980), journalist and writer, was born Gerald White Johnson in Riverton, North Carolina, the only son and second of five children of Archibald Johnson, a schoolteacher and editor, and Flora McNeill Johnson, a schoolteacher. In 1895, Archibald Johnson was appointed editor of *Charity and Children*, the house paper of the Thomasville Baptist Orphanage; the family joined him in Thomasville the following year. After attending the orphanage school for the first seven grades, Johnson went to the Thomasville Public School for one year; he then spent the 1907–1908 academic year at Mars Hill College, a two-year Baptist institution near Asheville. In the fall of 1908, Johnson matriculated to Wake Forest College, became editor of the student newspaper, and earned his B.A. degree in 1911.

Following graduation, he served briefly as editor of the *Thomasville Davidsonian,* and then as a reporter for the *Lexington* (N.C.) *Dispatch* (1911–1913), before joining the *Greensboro Daily News* in 1913. In 1917, Johnson enlisted for military service in World War I and had a brief tour of combat in France in 1918; following a period of study at the University of Toulouse in 1919, he returned to the *Daily News.* In 1922, Johnson married Kathryn Hayward; they had two daughters. In 1924, Johnson was appointed professor and head of the new journalism department at the University of North Carolina in Chapel Hill; in the next two years he would also contribute essays to two important new journals, the *Virginia Quarterly Review* (1925) and H. L. Mencken's *American Mercury* (1924). Johnson had already drawn Mencken's attention in 1923 with his essay "The Congo, Mr. Mencken" in response to the latter's dismissal of Southern culture in "The Sahara of the Bozart" (1920/1922); this and other critical essays on Southern issues (e.g., the Ku Klux Klan, religious fundamentalism, New South boosterism) published in Emily Clark's *Reviewer* (1923) and Howard W. Odum's *Journal of Social Forces* (1923) led to Johnson's receiving an invitation in 1926 to join Mencken and the staff of the *Baltimore Evening Sun.*

Johnson continued to criticize Southerners for their romantic notions of the Old South and for not facing the realities and embracing the potential of the New South, most fiercely in his dismissal of the Southern Agrarians (John Crowe Ransom, Robert Penn Warren, Allen Tate, Donald Davidson, et al.) and their manifesto *I'll Take My Stand* (1930) in his essay "No More Excuses: A Southerner to Southerners" (1931). At the same time, however, he honored Confederate soldiers and Southerners who had attempted to rebuild (from 1870 to 1900) the civilization they had lost in the Civil War ("The Cadets of New Market: A Reminder to the Critics of the South" [1929]). In the 1930s, Johnson turned from "South-Watching" (although he would never cease writing about the South) to "America-Watching," but his passionate defense of the New Deal, endorsement of Franklin Delano Roosevelt in 1936 and 1940, and support for America's aid to England and entry into World War II would increasingly place him at odds with Mencken and the editorial opinion of the Sun papers. In 1943 he resigned and set out on his own.

As a freelance writer and critic, Johnson wrote or contributed to seven books between 1944 and 1950 alone, and sold articles to such large-market magazines as *Vogue,* *Life,* and *Look,* but he also continued to publish articles in the Sun papers, book reviews in the *New York Herald Tribune* (1937–1965), and essays in such journals as the *VQR, New Republic, American Scholar, Atlantic Monthly,* and *Saturday Review of Literature.* In the 1950s, Johnson gained fame as a fierce critic of Joseph McCarthy, supported Adlai Stevenson in his two unsuccessful presidential campaigns (1952, 1956), and expanded his role as a voice for the "plain people" of America in his television commentary "How Things Look from Bolton Street" (1952–1954). Although Johnson supported Stevenson over John F. Kennedy for the Democratic presidential nomination in 1960, he grew to admire JFK in his brief presidency. With the increasing expansion of the Vietnam War, however, Johnson scorned President Lyndon Johnson for misleading the country, supported Eugene McCarthy in 1968, but voted for Hubert Humphrey over Richard Nixon. He dismissed Nixon as "The Nothing King" (as he titled an essay in 1974) after his resignation following the Watergate scandal, called President Gerald Ford's pardon of Nixon "grossly immoral" (in a letter to his sister Katherine Johnson Parham, 3 Jan. 1975, quoted in Fitzpatrick, p. 259), and voted in 1976 for Jimmy Carter, about whose patient handling of the Iranian crisis he wrote his last piece, a letter to the editor of the *Baltimore Sun* for 19 November 1979. Johnson died four months later in Baltimore.

Johnson voted for every Democratic Party nominee from Woodrow Wilson (1912) to Carter. As a Southern liberal, Johnson defended free speech, endorsed separation of church and state, supported woman suffrage, and despised racial prejudice and violence, but believed that race relations could be improved without weakening social segregation. As a liberal, he supported the New Deal and the role of the federal government versus states' rights, promoted "The Liberal of 1946" (1946) as "a man unterrified" by the challenges of the postwar world, criticized Southern Democrats, particularly the Dixiecrats of 1948 who obstructed civil rights, and wrote the liberal manifesto for Stevenson's campaigns in 1952 and 1956. As a realist, Johnson relentlessly criticized failings in American society, but as an optimist, he "believed that democracy, for all its flaws, was the most humane form of government" (Fitzpatrick, p. xii). Johnson "saw the American experience as a morality play and believed unashamedly in heroes" (Fitzpatrick, p. xii), such as George Washington, Andrew Jackson, Abraham Lincoln, Robert E. Lee, Wilson, and FDR (*American Heroes and Hero-Worship* [1943]). However, Johnson also celebrated the "average American" who had endured the upheavals of the twentieth century, while both heroes (Wilson and FDR) and villains (Lenin and Hitler) had passed from the scene (*Incredible Tale: The Odyssey of the Average American in the Last Half Century* [1950]).

Johnson wrote forty-four books, including nine biographies, ten books for juveniles on American history and government, three novels, and many historical studies and commentaries. His true forte, however, was the essay, and two anthologies, *South-Watching* (1983) and *America-Watching* (1976), provide easy access to many of his most memorable pieces. Mencken called Johnson "the best editorial writer in the South" (quoted in Clark, pp. 120–21) and "one of the most competent newspaper men in America" (quoted in Fitzpatrick, p. 125). Outliving Mencken by twenty-four years, Johnson came to be regarded as "The Second-Ranking Sage of Baltimore" (Hoopes).

• Johnson's papers are held in the university archives at Wake Forest University, Winston-Salem, N.C. An excellent biography is Vincent Fitzpatrick, *Gerald W. Johnson: From Southern Liberal to National Conscience* (2002), which also contains a comprehensive bibliography of Johnson's publications (excluding newspaper columns and articles). *America-Watching: Perspectives in the Course of an Incredible Century* (1976) reprints sixty-six essays from 1923 to 1975 and excerpts from five books, with a brief introduction by Henry Steele Commager. *South-Watching* (1983, 2d ed., 2002) reprints twenty-two essays from 1923 to 1965, with a substantial introduction by Fred Hobson. Johnson's unpublished manuscript from the late 1970s, "To Be Living at This Time: An Assessment of Values," appears in the *Virginia Quarterly Review* (1992), edited, with preface and postscript, by Vincent Fitzpatrick. Cited also in this article are Emily Clark, *Innocence Abroad* (1931), and Roy Hoopes, "Gerald Johnson: 'The Second-Ranking Sage of Baltimore,'" *Maryland Magazine*, summer 1990, pp. 14–17. Hoopes's title alludes to William Manchester, *The Sage of Baltimore: The Life and Riotous Times of H. L. Mencken* (1952), the title of the British edition of Manchester's *Disturber of the Peace: The Life of H. L. Mencken* (1950), with an introduction by Gerald W. Johnson. Obituaries appear in the *Baltimore Sun*, 23 Mar. 1980, the *Baltimore Evening Sun*, and the *New York Times*, both 24 Mar. 1980.

FREDERICK BETZ

JONES, Casey (14 Mar. 1863–30 Apr. 1900), railroad engineer and folk hero, was born John Luther Jones in southwest Missouri, the son of Frank Jones, a schoolteacher, and Ann Nolen Jones. He was the oldest of five children. In 1876 the family moved to Cayce, Kentucky, the town that would be the origin of his nickname and where he was first exposed to railroading. Jones married Jane Brady on 25 November 1886; they had three children.

Jones's initial railroad experience was as a "cub" (beginner) telegraph operator with the M & O Railroad at Columbus, Kentucky, in 1878 when he was only fifteen. A few months later he began working as a brakeman on the line between Columbus and Jackson, Tennessee. In order to achieve his long-range goal of becoming an engineer, Jones transferred again, this time becoming a fireman on the M & O line between Jackson, Tennessee, and Mobile, Alabama.

In March 1888 Jones moved to the Illinois Central as fireman on the Water Valley and Jackson (Tennessee) Districts of the Mississippi Division. Records of the Brotherhood of Locomotive Firemen's lodge in Water Valley, Mississippi, show that Jones joined on 21 July 1890. He was promoted to engineer in February 1891, and his name first appears on the register book of the Brotherhood of Locomotive Engineers lodge at Water Valley on 10 March 1891. Jones maintained memberships in both labor organizations.

In the summer of 1893, the Chicago World's Fair was attracting huge crowds. When a call went out for engineers, Jones spent that summer in suburban service in Chicago. It was here that he first saw the 638, the Illinois Central freight engine on display at the fair. At the closing of the fair, the 638 was to be sent to the Mississippi Division. Jones asked for and received permission to run the engine back to Water Valley. It was the beginning of a long association.

Over the years Jones had his share of extra passenger runs, and he liked the work and the pay. Passenger runs offered a much shorter working day, better pay, and considerable prestige, all of which appealed to the young engineer. His first opportunity at a regular passenger job came in February 1900 when W. W. "Bill" Hatfield transferred from Memphis, Tennessee, back to a run out of Water Valley, Mississippi. Jones applied for Hatfield's old job, even though it meant moving his family to Memphis and leaving the 638.

The new position was a test of Jones's ability as an engineer. The Illinois Central had been regularly shortening the running time of its passenger trains between Chicago and New Orleans. The new schedules posed an increasingly daunting challenge for the engineer. On the night of 29 April 1900, Jones and his fireman, Sim Webb, left Memphis one hour and thirty-five minutes late because the train had not come in on time. When he stopped for water at Grenada, Mississippi, Jones had already made up fifty minutes. By the time he reached Goodman, Mississippi, he was only five minutes late.

As Jones headed south, the stage was being set for his tragic wreck. A freight train with a broken air hose was sidetracked at Vaughan, Mississippi, and several of its cars were out on the main line. When Jones saw the cars, he slowed the engine to about 30 miles per hour. His fireman, Sim Webb, jumped to safety. Seconds later, Jones's engine, the 382, crashed into the caboose and several of the cars and finally stopped. Jones was mortally wounded in the throat by a bolt or piece of splintered wood.

Like the names of many other railroad engineers who lost their lives during this period, Casey Jones's name might have faded into obscurity were it not for Wallace Saunders, a laborer at the railroad shop in Canton, Mississippi, who made up a song about the accident. An Illinois Central engineer, William Leighton, heard it and mentioned it to his brothers, vaudeville performers Frank and Bert Leighton. The Leighton brothers sang a version of "Casey Jones" in various theaters around the country. By the time the song spread across the country, America had a new folk hero.

Why Jones did not jump is a question that has been discussed by railroad enthusiasts for many years. Railroad historian Bruce Gurner's explanation is as good as any. "You have to understand that Casey loved his job, his engine and the railroad," Gurner notes. "If there was one chance in a million he could do something, he wanted to be there to do it."

• Jones's personal papers, railroad documents, and related materials are in the Casey Jones Village, Jackson, Tenn., the Water Valley Casey Jones Railroad Museum, Water Valley, Miss., and the Casey Jones Railroad Museum State Park, Vaughan, Miss. Fred Lee, *Casey Jones* (1940), is a full-length biography. Bruce Gurner, *Casey Jones and the Wreck at Vaughan* (1973), is a monograph on the accident. See also Peter A. Hansen, "The Brave Engineer," *Trains*, Apr. 2000, pp. 34–43. Reports of the wreck appeared in the Memphis *Commercial Appeal*, 30 Apr. 1900, and in the New Orleans *Times-Democrat*, 30 Apr. 1900. An obituary is in the Jackson (Tenn.) *Sun*, 1 May 1900.

JACK GURNER

JONES, Claudia (21 Feb. 1915–25 Dec. 1964), Communist, journalist, and feminist, was born Claudia Vera Cumberbatch in Trinidad, the daughter of Sybil Cumberbatch and Charles Bertram Cumberbatch. Jones's mother came from a family of landowners, while her father's family owned hotels. Claudia spent her first eight years in Trinidad while the colony experienced major political, social, and economic upheavals.

In 1922 Claudia's parents migrated to New York, and she and her sisters arrived in February 1924. They came, Claudia explained three decades later in a letter to American Communist Party head William Z. Foster, "to find their fortunes in America where 'gold was to be found on the street' and they dreamed of rearing their children in a 'free America.'" Instead, she wrote, her family "suffered not only the impoverished lot of working class native families" but also from racism (Jones to Foster, 1955, p. 1). The chronic respiratory ailments from which she suffered throughout her life stemmed in part from living in poverty as a child in Harlem. In the late 1920s, Charles Cumberbatch edited the *West Indian-American*, a Harlem-based community newspaper. She credited him with instilling in her racial pride. In 1928 Sybil Cumberbatch died at the age of thirty-seven of spinal meningitis aggravated by being overworked in a New York textile factory. In 1930 Claudia graduated from high school and was forced to work to support her family.

Mass protests in Harlem led by the Communist Party, USA (CPUSA), in defense of the Scottsboro boys (nine African-American teenagers who were falsely accused and sentenced to death for raping two white women in Alabama in 1931), and large rallies to protest the 1935 Italian invasion of Ethiopia acquainted Claudia with struggles against racism, the threat of fascism, and imperialism. In 1935 she joined the African Patriotic League, a Harlem-based black nationalist organization, and she wrote about the Italo-Ethiopian War (1935–1936) for the group's newspaper, the *Harlem Bulletin*. In 1936 she joined the Young Communist League (YCL) and the CPUSA soon after. It was also at this time that she adopted "Jones" as her last name. She may have done so both to protect her family from authorities and to adopt a new political identity. By the end of the decade, she was appointed editor of the YCL's national newspaper, the *Weekly Review.*

During World War II, she wrote prolifically about the importance of defeating fascism abroad and ending Jim Crow segregation at home. Between 1943 and 1945, she edited *Spotlight*, the national publication of the American Youth for Democracy, formerly the YCL. In addition to her political activism, in 1940 she married rank-and-file CPUSA member Abraham Skolnick, a factory worker of Russian Jewish descent. The couple had no children, and they divorced in 1947. She never remarried.

Jones emerged as the highest-profile black woman in the American Left during the late 1940s and early 1950s. In 1945 she was elected to the CPUSA's National Committee. In 1946 she helped found the Congress of American Women, a short-lived group. Her 1949 article, "An End to the Neglect of the Problems of the Negro Woman!" published in the CPUSA's theoretical journal, *Political Affairs*, stands as her most famous piece of writing. In it she sharply criticized racism and sexism within the party, popularized the concept of "triple oppression"—the racial, class, and gender exploitation experienced by black women—within the Left, and helped launch aggressive campaigns against "white chauvinism" within the CPUSA.

No black woman faced as much political persecution during the McCarthy period as did Jones. Her alien status and Communist affiliation opened the door to government repression beginning with her first arrest in January 1948. In June 1951, she—along with seventeen other CPUSA national officials—was arrested under the Smith Act (1940), a law that made it a crime to teach or advocate the violent overthrow of the U.S. government. In October 1951, she was rearrested, this time under the 1950 Internal Security Act (better known as the McCarran-Walter Act) requiring Communists to register with the Justice Department. The law also allowed for the deportation of aliens who participated in subversive activities. In November 1953, she and twelve Communist defendants were found guilty of violating the Smith Act. After losing a series of appeals, she entered the Federal Reformatory for Women at Alderson, West Virginia, to serve a one-year sentence in January 1955. On 23 October 1955, she was paroled and deported to Great Britain on 9 December 1955. She never returned to the United States.

After her arrival in England, she remained actively involved in radical politics. She enlisted in the Communist Party of Great Britain, and she mentored a younger generation of African, Asian, and Caribbean militants who resided in London. Founding and coediting the *West Indian Gazette and Afro-Asian Caribbean News* with veteran Pan-Africanist Amy Ashwood Garvey in 1958 was Jones's crowning achievement of her final years. In the same year, she cocoordinated the first West Indian Carnival in Britain, which has become a major annual event. In the early 1960s, she also took part in antiapartheid campaigns and in efforts to eliminate nuclear weapons. Her chronically poor health contributed to her untimely death on Christmas day in 1964. Her associates buried her next to Karl Marx in London's Highgate Cemetery.

In recent years, Jones has been discovered by a new generation of radical black feminists who see her as a foremother for using Marxism to formulate a black socialist feminist perspective. Several books about her have been published, and a number of conferences, including a 1998 tribute at the Schomburg Center for Research in Black Culture (New York), have been held to honor her life and work.

• Primary materials about Jones can be found in several archival collections. Diaries and correspondence mostly from the last ten years of her life can be found in the Claudia Jones Memorial Collection, Schomburg Center for Research in Black Culture, Harlem, New York. Her detailed six-page autobiographical letter written to American Communist Party head William Z. Foster in 1955 is located in the Howard "Stretch" Johnson Papers, Tamiment Library, New York University. Jones's FBI files contain nearly 1,000 pages. However, information in government surveillance documents, especially about her personal life, is sometimes inaccurate.
For major works by Jones, see *Jim-Crow in Uniform* (1940); *Lift Every Voice—For Victory!* (1942); "On the Right to Self-Determination for the Negro People in the Black Belt," *Political Affairs* 25, no. 1 (Jan. 1946): 67–77; "For New Approaches to Our Work Among Women," *Political Affairs* 27, no. 8 (Aug. 1948): 738–43; "An End to the Neglect of the Problems of the Negro Woman!" *Political Affairs* 28, no. 6 (June 1949): 51–67; "For the Unity of Women in the Cause of Peace," *Political Affairs* 30, no. 2 (Feb. 1951): 151–68; *Ben Davis, Fighter for Freedom* (1954); "The Caribbean in Britain," *Freedomways* 4, no. 3 (Summer 1964): 341–57.
A growing body of secondary literature discusses Jones's life, thought, and journalism. See Erik S. McDuffie, "Long Journeys: Four Black Women and the Communist Party, USA, 1930–1956" (2003); Dayo F. Gore, "To Light a Candle in a Gale Wind: Black Women Radicals and Post–World War II Radicals in U.S. Politics." (Ph.D. diss., New York University, 2003); Kate Weigand, *Red Feminism: American Communism and the Making of Women's Liberation* (2001); Carole Boyce Davies, "Deportable Subjects: U.S. Immigration Laws and the Criminalizing of Communism," *The South Atlantic Quarterly* 100, no. 4 (Fall 2001): 949–66; Rebecca Hill, "Fosterites and Feminists: or 1950s Ultra-Leftism and the Invention of AmeriKKKa," *New Left Review* 228 (March/April 1998): 67–90; Linn Shapiro, "Red Feminism: American Communism and the Women's Rights Tradition, 1919–1956" (Ph.D. diss., American University, 1996); Claudia Rosemary May, "Nuances of un-American Literature(s): In Search of Claudia Jones; a Literary Retrospective of the Life, Times, and Works of an Activist/Writer (Ph.D. diss., University of California, Berkeley, 1996); Beverly Guy-Sheftall, ed., *Words of Fire: An Anthology of African-American Feminist Thought* (1995); Elean Thomas, "Remembering Claudia Jones," *World Marxist Review* 30 (Mar. 1987): 67–69; Angela Y. Davis, *Women, Race, and Class* (1981). Biographies such as Buzz Johnson's *"I Think of My Mother"—Notes on the Life of Claudia Jones* (1985), Marika Sherwood's *Claudia Jones: A Life in Exile* (1999), and Jennifer Tyson's *Claudia Jones, 1915–1964: A Woman of Our Times* (1988) provide useful sketches of Jones's life.
ERIK S. McDUFFIE

JONES, John Winston (22 Nov. 1791–29 Jan. 1848), congressman, was born near Amelia Court House, Amelia County, Virginia, the son of Alexander Jones, occupation unknown, and Mary Ann Winston Jones. Following his father's death in 1802, Jones came under the care of his uncle, Reverend David C. Jones, who tutored him. To help pay for his younger brother's education, Jones taught school for several years in Amelia and Lynchburg and continued his own formal education at the College of William and Mary in Williamsburg. On graduating in 1813, he gained admittance to the bar and began practicing law in Chesterfield County. Around 1815, he married Harriet Boisseau, with whom he had two or more children and settled on an estate, "Dellwood," near Petersburg, Virginia.

Jones advanced rapidly within the legal community and was appointed prosecuting attorney for the Fifth Judicial Circuit of Virginia in 1818. In 1829 he began serving as a trustee of the newly established Chesterfield Academy; he was also, despite not seeking the post, the leading vote getter in his district for delegate slots for the proposed state constitutional convention. Jones served on the convention's judiciary committee, but was generally overshadowed in an assembly whose membership included John Randolph and John Marshall as well as former presidents James Madison and James Monroe.

In 1834 Jones was elected to the U.S. House of Representatives. He served as a Democrat from 1834 to 1844 and was the administration's choice for Speaker in 1840 before ultimately losing out to Robert Hunter. In 1841 Jones assumed the chairmanship of the Ways and Means Committee, where he found himself at odds with former President John Quincy Adams (then serving in the House) over his treatment of fellow representative and committee member Richard Fletcher of Massachusetts. After Fletcher had denied certain portions of a newspaper report that quoted him as stating that the Ways and Means Committee was under control of the White House, Jones (who was otherwise generally noted by his contemporaries as mild mannered) had rebuked Fletcher on the House floor so severely that Adams later characterized Jones as a "ruffian" (*Memoirs*, vol. 10, p.163).

In 1844 Jones won a closely contested race with fellow Virginian John M. Botts for the Speakership. Although his single term in office later led to his being described as "a clever politician who made but an indifferent presiding officer," not one of his decisions was overturned; he also established the precedent of naming a speaker pro tempore (in this case, John B. Weller) to function in his place while his own disputed election was being resolved, thus creating a standard procedure that would help future Speakers avoid conflict of interest charges. While Speaker, Jones continued to clash with Adams over issues as mundane as pay appropriations for tradesmen engaged in work on government facilities, and resentment on the part of Adams appears to have lingered, for upon relinquishing his post, he denied Jones the customary thanks due him on the basis that the testimony to his impartiality "was too broad a lie for me to swallow."

Declining to stand for reelection in 1844, Jones returned to Virginia and resumed his agricultural and legal pursuits. He was involved in a sensational murder trial in which he and a former fellow former House Speaker Andrew Stevenson successfully defended Thomas Ritchie, Jr., a Richmond newspaper editor charged with killing another editor in a duel in 1846. That same year, again against his wishes, he was elected to the Virginia House of Delegates and soon succeeded W. O. Goode as Speaker. Although he was reelected the following year, Jones's health collapsed and he was unable to take his seat. He died shortly thereafter at his home near Petersburg. After remaining in the family for several years, Dellwood was purchased by what is now Virginia State University and became part of that institution's Agricultural Experiment Station.

The life and career of Jones remain a paradox. Nearly forgotten today, he managed to achieve prominence almost in spite of his efforts. While his only lasting contribution to the American political scene was his establishment of procedural actions within the House of Representatives during cases of conflict of interest, he continues to be at least a footnote in history because of his brief service in the House as both Speaker and Chairman of the powerful Ways and Means Committee.

• No collection of Jones's papers appears to have survived, and secondary information on his life and career is scarce. Some information is available in Francis Earle Lutz, *Chesterfield: An Old Virginia County* (1954), and W. H. Smith, *Speakers of the House of Representatives of the United States* (1928). For his relations with John Quincy Adams, see vols. 10, 11, and 12 of Adams's *Memoirs* (1874–77; repr. 1969) as well as Leonard Falkner, *The President Who Wouldn't Retire* (1967). An obituary appeared in the *Richmond Enquirer*, 4 Feb. 1848.

EDWARD L. LACH, JR.

JONES, Robert Trent, Sr. (20 June 1906–14 June 2000), golf course architect, was born in Ince, England, the son of William Rees Jones, a construction engineer, and Jane Southern Jones. The family immigrated to the United States in 1909, taking up residence in East Rochester, New York, where the father worked in a railroad car shop. As a teenager Robert Jones caddied at the Country Club of Rochester, occasionally for Walter Hagen, a rising young professional golfer, and learned to play at a nine-hole course, Genundawal, in East Rochester. Jones became one of the more promising golfers in the area. In an open tournament in Rochester, he was the low amateur, finishing one stroke behind the winning professional. He aspired to a career as a professional golfer, but a duodenal ulcer temporarily forced him out of play.

Jones dropped out of high school and worked as a draftsman for a company maintaining refrigerator cars for the New York Central Railroad. He disliked his job and was "still in love" with golf. Having watched Donald Ross, an immigrant Scot who was then the leading golf course architect in the nation, build the Oak Hill course in Rochester, Jones resolved to become an architect of golf courses. No specific qualifications for the profession existed—landscape architects, golfers, and greenskeepers often designed courses—so Jones took a position as manager of the Sodus Country Club in Sodus Bay, New York. A wealthy member of the club, Paul Bashford, encouraged him to go to Cornell University for specialized education as an architect.

With some financial support from Bashford, Jones entered Cornell in 1926 as a special student, taking courses in landscape architecture, horticulture, agronomy, and economics. He created, as it were, a curriculum for his vocation. Between terms in the summer of 1927, he played in the Canadian Open, finishing as the low amateur. He met Ione Tefft Davis at Cornell. They married in 1934 and subsequently had two children. Leaving Cornell in 1930 without a degree, Jones became a junior partner with Stanley Thompson, the gifted Canadian architect known for the beauty and "naturalness" of his courses. Thompson, Jones and Company, which had offices in New York City and in Toronto, Canada, had to work in the face of the Great Depression, which ravaged their profession. Architects built fewer than 200 courses in the 1930s, and about 600 golf clubs went bankrupt. The partners remodeled a few courses, but on at least three occasions they lost fees because clubs for which they were working went broke. Jones, who was responsible for seeking jobs in the United States, did manage to secure contracts to build six courses for the Works Progress Administration.

Parting amicably from Thompson as economic conditions improved, Jones opened his own business in New York City in 1938, with his wife running the office. He obtained a few contracts for remodeling courses, nearly all in New York, but after the United States entered World War II, few courses were built. He worked on a course for the U.S. Military Academy at West Point, completing twelve holes before the money for it ran out, and one for the International Business Machine Company near its headquarters at Poughkeepsie, New York.

At the war's end American golf course architects entered an era of expanding opportunities. In the next few decades the American population grew rapidly, moved increasingly into the suburbs, became more prosperous, had more leisure time, and wanted to play golf. Through the 1950s about a hundred new courses opened annually, and in the 1960s 400 opened annually.

With his experience, education, zeal, and personality, Jones was ready to build and rebuild courses. He advertised his services in magazines and gathered a staff of landscape architects, turf experts, and draftsmen. Now his ascent to preeminence in golf course architecture began. He proved to be adept at selling himself and his ideas to his clients. According to Jack Nicklaus, Jones was the world's best salesperson, a man who might meet a group of developers at an airport in Spain, sketch out on a paper napkin a course that met their approval, and then take the next flight home. He had many celebrities as clients, among them

Lowell Thomas, King Hassan II of Morocco, and Laurance Rockefeller. Jones was the first architect in the nation whose name became a selling point in marketing a course.

In 1946 Jones remodeled five holes of the Augusta National Club. His design of the sixteenth hole, with its kidney-shaped green, received considerable praise. In 1948, collaborating with Bobby Jones, he built the Peachtree course north of Atlanta. More than in any other course bearing his name, he incorporated in Peachtree the essence of his design philosophy. Believing that average and low-handicap golfers alike should enjoy play on the same course, he built tees as long as eighty yards; by adjustments of tee markers, the course thus could be shortened or lengthened from 6,000 yards to 7,400 yards. He crafted huge greens averaging 8,000 square feet, whereas typical greens were about 4,000 square feet. Hence he provided four or five pin positions, some difficult, some easy. From tee to green he introduced bunkers and ponds that permitted a variety of shots. He described Peachtree as a model of "modern golf architecture" (Jones, p. 88; Cornish, p. 114).

Peachtree, Augusta, and many of Jones's other courses exemplified what he called the "heroic school" of design, a blending of the "penal school" and the "strategic school." In the penal design that characterized many courses of the 1920s, a golfer had to negotiate a profusion of hazards—bunkers and ponds, for instance—with no alternate routes to the green. Such "cruel architecture," as Jones saw it, unduly punished a player for a slightly missed shot. In the strategic design a player had to "think" his or her way around the course to avoid hazards and had to position the ball for a safe route to the green. Rather than using one design in preference to the other, Jones adopted the "heroic" design, one that demanded that "better players" effect a "heroic carry or gamble . . . to get into position for a birdie" but one that also gave "lesser players" an option for a safer route (Jones, pp. 46–47; Cornish, p. 118). The concept illustrated Jones's view that there should be difficult pars and easy bogeys.

If Jones gave balm to average golfers, he often incurred the wrath of touring professionals. He had no animus against the improved equipment—steel shafts, soled wedges, and high-compression balls—coming into use in the 1930s. But he feared that tournament promoters, catering to the American infatuation with new records, softened courses by watering greens and cutting roughs short. Moreover, professional golfers, he complained, wanted "dead flat greens and dead flat fairways, very little rough and very few traps. That kind of course wouldn't require an architect; you could order it from a Sears Roebuck catalog." His duty as an architect was to protect the integrity of the game. The player, he said, "is the attacker and the architect is the defender" (Jones, p. 42; Grimsley, p. 247).

Surely Jones was the "defender" at the courses hosting the U.S. Open in the 1950s. From 1951 to 1956 he revamped four of the six courses, rendering all of them more difficult. His remodeling of Oakland Hills near Detroit especially distressed professionals. He rebunkered holes and shaped undulating greens in a penal mode. He leveled the bunkers 200 yards from the tee and built new, punitive ones 250 yards out. The results were dramatic. The professionals recorded just two subpar rounds, and the winner, Ben Hogan, finished seven over par. (Hogan was hardly pleased by the experience.) At Baltusrol near Newark, New Jersey, Jones's redesign of the lower course for the open in 1954 led to a remarkable incident. Hearing complaints that he had unduly lengthened the par-three fourth hole to 194 yards over water, he led the tournament chairman and club professional to the tee at 165 yards and hit a mashie shot for a hole-in-one. "Gentlemen," he declared, "I think the hole is eminently fair" (Jones, p. 91).

Querulous professionals, though, did not diminish Jones in the world of golf. Already well known before he redesigned Oakland, he became renowned in the following years. In 1951, soon after the open at Oakland, Herbert Warren Wind, the foremost American writer on golf, wrote a lengthy and laudatory essay on Jones for the *New Yorker* that substantially enhanced Jones's reputation. Only Louis "Dick" Wilson, who was noted for his on-site supervision of construction, could rival the quality of his courses. But Jones was the dominant architect from 1945 through the 1960s. In that period, with his sons Robert Jones, Jr., and Rees Jones joining him in the 1960s, he built over 200 courses.

During the 1970s and 1980s Jones saw a diminution of his empire, particularly in the United States. High interest rates and soaring inflation reduced the demand for his services. Additionally, professional golfers, like Nicklaus, Arnold Palmer, and Hale Irvin, and nonarchitects, notably Pete Dye, appropriated a share of the market for the design of golf courses. In the United States, Jones designed sixty-five courses. Earlier he had built some courses abroad, about twenty-one, but they were hardly the staple of business. Now he began to reach out to clients in the four corners of the globe. His travel by air, which he disliked, amounted to 300,000 miles some years and took him to Europe, South America, Africa, Asia, the South Pacific, and the Caribbean, where he often landed contracts from wealthy people, such as the Aga Khan in Sardinia. Jones built sixty courses abroad in the two decades. Truly, he could boast, as he did, that the "sun never sets on a Robert Trent Jones golf course" (Anderson, 16 June 2000). Several of the courses were stunning, particularly Ballybunion in Ireland and Sotogrande in Spain, but a few observers feared that his courses were becoming "excessively flowery" (Dobereiner, p. 133).

During the 1990s Jones acquired just eight contracts. One, though, was the largest in the history of golf. In 1990 Sunbelt Golf, Inc., and the state of Alabama, seeking to make the state a tourist attraction, commissioned Jones's firm to build eighteen courses, eleven championship and seven short courses, in seven localities. Shouldering much of the workload, Roger Rulewich, Jones's principal associate, had the courses built by 1993. Named the Robert Trent Jones Golf Trail, they were a tribute to his reputation.

The sources vary considerably on the number of courses Jones and his firm designed and redesigned. At his death Jones had built, said Dave Anderson, "over" 500 courses. A press release from Rees Jones's office fixed the number at 450. Jones had built them in forty-five states and twenty-nine foreign countries. Whatever the number credited to Jones, certainly he was the most prolific course architect of the twentieth century and, as one commentator stated, the "most significant" (Jones, p. 24). *Golf Digest* rated twenty Jones courses among the nation's best 100. Of the 100 "most outstanding courses" in the world, *The World Atlas of Golf* listed seventeen designed by Jones. They had served as a venue for seventy-nine national tournaments in the United States, including twenty for the U.S. Open and twelve for the Professional Golfers Association championship. Always self-confident, Jones asserted, "All 400 of my golf courses should be in the top 100" (McMillan, p. 52). Listing the favorite courses of his design and redesign, Jones chose five in "alphabetical" order: Ballybunion, Firestone South in Akron, Mauna Kea in Hawaii, Sotogrande, and Spyglass in California.

Honored with numerous awards, Jones was the first golf architect inducted into the World Golf Hall of Fame and the first recipient of the Donald Ross Award from the American Society of Golf Course Architects. He was an articulate spokesman for golf and his profession. His book *Golf's Magnificent Challenge* (1989), a tour de force on golf course architecture, was rated by the U.S. Golf Association as the best golf book of 1990. Jones died in Fort Lauderdale, Florida.

• Two typescripts in the office of Rees Jones, Inc., in Montclair, N.J., are important documents regarding Jones's life: "Robert Trent Jones, Sr., 1906–2000," a press release written by Robert Trent Jones, Jr., on his death; and "Geographical Listing of Golf Courses Designed by Robert Trent Jones, Sr." Jones's *Golf's Magnificent Challenge* (1989), in part an autobiography, at points is chronologically vague and contradicts other sources on the facts, but it is especially interesting in Jones's extended exegesis on the pain and pleasure of building golf courses. Jones wrote on his theory of architecture and his choice of the "Top Ten" courses in the world in Will Grimsley, *Golf: Its History, People, and Events* (1966). The evolution of golf course architecture and Jones's place in it is surveyed in Geoffrey S. Cornish and Ronald E. Whitten, *The Architects of Golf: A Survey of Golf Course Design from Its Beginnings to the Present* (1993). An abbreviated but good treatment of the same subjects is in George Peper, *Golf in America: The First One Hundred Years* (1944). A witty and eloquent view of various aspects of golf, including the design of courses, is in Peter Dobereiner, *The Glorious World of Golf* (1973). See also Gerald Astor, *The PGA World Golf Hall of Fame Book* (1991). All of these sources praise Jones's work in one way or another. But Curt Sampson, *Hogan* (1996), scorns Jones's design at Oakland Hills.

Of the numerous articles that have looked at Jones and his courses, especially noteworthy is Herbert Warren Wind, "Profiles, Linksland, and Meadowland," *New Yorker,* 4 Aug. 1951, pp. 28–42. For an interesting retrospective, see Robin McMillan, "A Life Remembered," *Met Golfer,* Oct.–Nov. 2000, pp. 31–35, 49–55, which includes an interview with Rees Jones. Dave Anderson wrote the obituary in the *New York Times,* 16 June 2000, and a memorial commentary, "Trent Jones' Legacy: Make Them Think," *New York Times,* 17 June 2000.

CARL M. BECKER

JONES, Sissieretta (5 Jan. 1868–24 June 1933), singer, was born Matilda Sissieretta Joyner in Portsmouth, Virginia, the daughter of Jeremiah Malachi Joyner and Henrietta Beale Joyner, former slaves, church activists, and amateur musicians. Jones attended a school for freedmen's children in Portsmouth and showed great vocal talent. A probably apocryphal story says that a couple from Providence, Rhode Island, upon hearing Jones, offered her father a job. Regardless of the truth of this story, in 1876 the Joyner family did move to Providence, where Jones continued to attend school and sing in area churches.

At age fifteen Jones studied at the Providence Academy of Music under Ada Baroness Lacomb. During her late teen years, Jones further cultivated her talent and heard a number of important musicians of the day (including the African-American Marie Selika Williams). She also fell in love with David Richard Jones, who was originally from Baltimore and was working as a bellman at a Providence hotel. The couple married in Providence on 4 September 1883. No children seem to have been born to this union, though occasional rumors of a child who died in infancy surfaced later in Jones's career.

There is some speculation that Jones furthered her musical education at a conservatory in Boston, but no records of this exist beyond interviews with Jones and oral history. Some scholars speculate that she actually studied privately with a conservatory professor. Between 1886 and 1888 Jones gave performances, including one with Blind Tom Bethune (Blind Tom). Dubbed "New England's Rising Soprano Star," Jones gave concerts in New York in July and early August 1888. A review of one such event by the *New York Clipper* tagged her with the sobriquet that followed her for the rest of her career, the "Black Patti," which drew a comparison to the diva Adelina Patti and, like the dubbing of the earlier black singer Elizabeth Greenfield as the "Black Swan," called attention to the separation of races inherent in American society.

These concerts led to an extensive tour of the West Indies in 1888 with the Tennessee Jubilee Singers, one of the many all-black singing groups spawned by the earlier success of Fisk University's Jubilee Singers. Jones was well received; dignitaries attending her concerts began striking medals to commemorate the performances. (Many later publicity photographs show her wearing the medals.) She returned to the United States in late 1888, studied briefly with the singer Luisa Cappiani, and sang in several major U.S. cities.

She returned to the West Indies for a second tour in 1890.

To this point Jones had been managed under a succession of fairly informal arrangements or by her husband, who was quickly developing a reputation as an alcoholic and a spendthrift. Jones's accomplishments, though, attracted the interest of the well-known promoter Major James B. Pond (who managed, among others, Mark Twain and Henry Ward Beecher). Jones signed a one-year contract with Pond, only to later realize that it allowed Pond to reengage her for two more years without any increase in compensation.

Jones's American career was reaching its peak. At what her biographer Willia Daughtry called the "apex of the fair-exposition era," Jones performed at important fairs in Toronto and Pittsburgh in October 1892, although she did not, as some sources report, perform at the World's Columbian Exposition in Chicago in 1893. Her triumphs of this period included the massively attended April 1892 Madison Square Garden African Jubilee, a White House performance in September 1892 for President Benjamin Harrison (whose wife was especially taken with Jones's voice), and a concert with Antonín Dvořák in 1894. Jones received consistently strong reviews but ran into repeated trouble when she or her husband tried to book concerts without Pond's involvement. In a protracted set of legal battles, the courts generally sided with Pond, but Jones's successes on stage continued.

Jones launched an extensive European tour, which included performances before the Prince of Wales and the German kaiser. In the end, though, her European tour was bittersweet. Free from the tensions of America's particular brand of racism, she moved easily through more liberal circles. But her mother's illness forced Jones to return to the United States, and her marriage was rapidly deteriorating. Jones and her husband divorced in late 1898.

Back in Providence, it became painfully clear that Jones needed to adapt her talents to support herself and her family. However, even though her voice was internationally acclaimed, it was also clear that she would never perform in mainstream opera. Thus in 1896 she formed a company called Black Patti's Troubadours and began touring the nation, mainly in a series of one-night stops.

The Troubadours' brand of variety show—music, comedy, skits, and so forth—proved popular. From August to May each year between 1896 and 1913, the group (with numerous personnel changes) performed in major cities, like New York and Philadelphia, as well as in smaller venues across the country, ranging from Peru, Illinois, Wallace, Idaho, and Lynchburg, Virginia, to Valdosta, Georgia. Though much of the troupe's show directly invoked the minstrelsy that dominated black entertainers throughout the period, Jones attempted to hold herself aloof—initially singing only her "operatic kaleidoscope" (a collection of material from such composers as Verdi, Haydn, Wagner, and Handel). Only later did she incorporate the more popular songs (including works by Stephen Foster)

that she had previously included in her solo performances. She also added selections from musical theater, like William Gilbert and Arthur Sullivan's *H.M.S. Pinafore*. Jones became quite famous for her rendition of Foster's "Swanee River" ("Old Folks at Home").

During this period Jones became noted for her management of the troupe and her encouragement of budding performers. Many members of the troupe (including Bob Cole and Abbie Mitchell) went on to successful careers in the black theater. Acclaim for Jones's voice remained steady, even if white journalists consistently viewed her as a racial curiosity rather than a serious artist. In the early years of the twentieth century, the black press fought more actively against minstrelsy, which was already in decline, and Jones's troupe created new material—full-length shows like *A Trip to Africa* (1909–1910) and *In the Jungle* (1911–1912)—to satisfy audiences. Aging, overworked, and often worried about her mother, Jones fell ill in 1913, and the 1913–1914 season was canceled.

Jones's performances in Will A. Cook and Harrison Stewart's *Lucky Sam from Alabam'* at the opening of the Troubadours' 1914–1915 season began as a triumphant comeback but ended in a canceled show in Memphis and the abrupt dissolution of the troupe. Jones performed at only two other large concerts—one in New York and one in Chicago—in her lifetime. Various trade papers carried reports of the causes of these events, ranging from financial mismanagement to drunken troupe members and a crooked theater manager, but just why her career ended at this moment remains cloudy.

Jones continued to care for her ailing mother, who died in 1924, and was active in her church, but without any means of support, she gradually sank into poverty. She first sold off the small rental properties she owned in Providence, then many of the gifts—medals, gowns, and jewelry—from her touring years before she was placed on state relief. The local NAACP president, William Freeman, aided her, and the state placed two foster children in her home. But most of her friends deserted her. Her years of work and frustration, coupled with cancer, led to her death, nearly destitute, in Providence.

In many ways Jones embodies both the heights and the tragic limits black women artists faced in the late nineteenth century and early twentieth century. One of the earliest black biographical dictionaries called her "one of the marvels of the nineteenth century" (Scruggs, p. 325). She sang for kings, presidents, and adoring fans across the globe, but she also faced consistent discrimination. Recognized as one of the greatest sopranos of her time, Jones never performed on the operatic stage. The fortune made in her early career was squandered by a series of bad managers (almost all men, most white). Her stage name forever reminded her that she was not the original Patti, nonetheless she understood that such name recognition was one of the few ways to ensure her career. Similarly, though she aspired to Verdi, she was best known later in life for songs common to minstrel shows. An important precursor to twentieth-century figures like Marian Anderson, she remains obscure even in contemporary scholarship.

• A valuable collection of material on Jones is in the Carl R. Gross Collection in Howard University's Moorland-Spingarn Research Center. Gross, a Providence historian who knew Jones, gathered several of her clippings, photographs, medals, and other memorabilia. Willia Estelle Daughtry, *Vision and Reality: The Story of "Black Patti" Matilda Sissieretta Joyner Jones* (2002), offers the most extensive secondary work on Jones and includes material from family members and friends. John Graziano, "The Early Life and Career of the 'Black Patti': The Odyssey of an African American Singer in the Late-Nineteenth Century," *Journal of the American Musicological Society* 53, no. 3 (Fall 2000): 543–96, is a valuable counterpoint to Daughtry. Jones is noted in most of the biographical dictionaries of African Americans published in the late nineteenth century and early twentieth century; among the most valuable is L. A. Scruggs, *Women of Distinction* (1893), which quotes extensively from a biography of Jones prepared for advertising purposes. William Lichtenwanger, "Sissieretta Jones," *Notable American Women*, vol. 2, ed. Edward T. Jones (1971), and Daughtry, "Sissieretta Jones," *Black Women in America,* ed. Darlene Clark Hine (1993), are also useful. Jones remains only a footnote in most histories of American music; treatments in Eileen Southern, *The Music of Black Americans*, 3d ed. (1997); Rosalyn Story, *And So I Sing: African American Divas of Concert and Opera* (1990); and Thomas L. Riis, "Concert Singers, Prima Donnas, and Entertainers: The Changing Status of Black Women Vocalists in Nineteenth Century America," in *Music and Culture in America, 1861–1918,* ed. Michael Saffle (1998), are exceptions. An obituary is in the *Providence Sunday Journal,* 16 July 1933.

ERIC GARDNER

JOVANOVICH, William (6 Feb. 1920–4 Dec. 2001), publisher and author, was born Vladimir Jovanovich in Louisville, Colorado, the youngest child of immigrant parents, Iliya M. Jovanovich, a coal miner of Montenegrin descent, and Hedviga Garbatz Jovanovich, a textile worker of Polish descent. Born in a mining camp tent, he learned Serbian and Polish from his parents and entered elementary school in Denver unable to speak English. Although he had a lifelong attachment to his parents' backgrounds, he embraced English energetically enough that upon completion of high school he was awarded a four-year scholarship to the University of Colorado. There he earned his A.B. degree in 1941, and then received a two-year fellowship to pursue graduate studies at Harvard in English and American literature.

In 1942, during World War II, Jovanovich joined the navy. The following year, while stationed in Mobile, Alabama, he married Martha Evelyn Davis; they were to have three children. He served in the navy until 1946, earning the rank of lieutenant. That year he entered Columbia University planning a dissertation about Ralph Waldo Emerson. The following year, however, Jovanovich found himself in need of employment because of a lack of funds. He signed on at Harcourt Brace, which had become since its founding

in 1919 a first-rate literary house, with authors such as Sinclair Lewis and Carl Sandburg. He sold and edited college and high school books in the firm's textbook division, making $50 per week. He also created in the early 1950s two widely used textbook series, *Adventures in Literature* and *Warrinter's English Composition and Grammar*. Jovanovich was so successful after six years that he became head of the school division. In 1954 he became president of the company.

Still meeting personally with school superintendents for suggestions, he initiated innovations such as complementing schoolbook text with attractive color illustrations and printing separate teachers' editions. His focus on educational, medical, and scientific areas made Harcourt Brace one of the largest publishers of such works and by the mid-1980s the top publisher of textbooks. Jovanovich did not ignore the literary part of his business, continuing to publish top-quality authors, for example, T. S. Eliot, C. S. Lewis, and Alice Walker (he published her blockbuster *The Color Purple*). He himself edited T. S. Eliot's letters and George Orwell's collected essays, and he was also instrumental in editing and publishing Charles Lindbergh's *Autobiography of Values* posthumously.

Jovanovich attracted renowned authors in Europe by allowing their editors to publish under their own names. Helen and Kurt Wolff, for instance, joined Harcourt in 1961 and published their authors using their own imprint. This practice brought to Jovanovich's list authors like Italo Calvino, Umberto Eco, and Günter Grass. In recognition of his successes, shareholders voted to change the company's name to Harcourt Brace Jovanovich in 1970. That same year Jovanovich was named chairman and chief executive officer.

Aggressively innovative, Jovanovich expanded his company in unexpected ways, acquiring in 1976, for example, three Sea World parks, in Orlando, San Diego, and Aurora, Ohio, and later adding another in San Antonio. Other acquisitions under Jovanovich included insurance companies, television stations, the Cypress Gardens Park in Winter Haven, Florida, the History Book Club, farming periodicals, and even a San Diego chain of fish-and-chips restaurants. Jovanovich was independent-minded in other ways, rebelling against the high costs of New York City by moving his headquarters to Orlando in 1984 and adding offices in San Diego. Jovanovich also refused on principle to publish exercise and diet books, believing that they would diminish the company's prestige. Because of differences over copyright issues, he was the only major publisher to refuse membership in the Association of American Publishers.

Paradoxically, Jovanovich's successes caused him trouble as the firm became more attractive for takeover bids. In 1981, for example, he blocked an aggressive takeover attempt by the Warner entertainments conglomerate. A $2 billion bid by British publishing tycoon Robert Maxwell in 1987, however, was so expensive to repel that the company fell deeply into debt. Though Jovanovich had wanted never to resort to such tactics, he borrowed $3 billion for a leveraged buyout to gain controlling interest of his own company. Maxwell backed away, but Harcourt could never pull from under the crushing interest payments. In an effort to reduce debt, the Sea World businesses were sold to Anheuser-Busch in 1989. That same year, Jovanovich felt it wise to step down as chief executive; and, several months later, in May of 1990, he gave up the chairmanship of the company. In 1991, Peter Jovanovich, his son and successor, sold the company to General Cinema Company. The business was divided into pieces following a subsequent sale.

While running Harcourt, Jovanovich began writing. His published works include *Now, Barabbas* (1964), a collection of essays discussing book publishing, education, and literature; *The World's Last Night* (1990), a novel with autobiographical details; and three other novels. Remembering his own humble beginnings, Jovanovich also took an interest in minority and underprivileged people. He established a Division of Urban Education at his firm to focus on the educational needs of inner-city children. Concerned about the small number of minorities in publishing, he headed COPE, the Committee for Opportunity in Publishing Employment, which met regularly with minority high school and college students to attract them to the profession.

Jovanovich continued writing in retirement but suffered poor health near the end of his life. He died at his home in San Diego.

Jovanovich pioneered the use of color illustrations in textbooks and teachers' editions. Also, the practice of allowing editors to publish their authors under their own imprints at a major house has become widely used since Jovanovich developed the concept. Two series created by him in the early 1950s, *Adventures in Literature* and *Warriner's English Composition and Grammar*, were still in use fifty years later. When Jovanovich took the reins of Harcourt Brace in 1954, the company had 125 employees and $8 million in annual sales. By the end of his tenure in 1990, the firm had 12,000 employees and annual sales of $1.7 billion. In 1988 he was among the top nine highest paid media executives in the nation, with salary and bonuses in excess of $1.2 million. Although not able to retain control of his dramatically enlarged company, Jovanovich will be remembered for his many accomplishments and innovative thinking that left their mark on the entire publishing industry.

• Jovanovich was a very private man who seldom spoke with reporters. He did grant a long interview in 1972 to *Publishers' Weekly* for its centenary issue. His collection of essays titled *Now, Barabbas* (1964) includes his ideas about the publishing business and the importance of literature and education. He penned the introduction to *The Wartime Journals of Charles A. Lindbergh* (1970). He is also the author of several other works, including *Of the Making of Books* (1957), *Stations of Our Life* (1965), *Madmen Must* (1978), *The World's Last Night* (1990), *A Slow Suicide* (1991), and *Serbdom* (1998). There is not yet a biography; however, there is a good deal of biographical information in several lengthy obit-

uaries: *New York Times*, 6 Dec. 2001; *Washington Post*, 8 Dec. 2001; *Chicago Tribune*, 7 Dec. 2001; and *Times* (London), 20 Dec. 2001.

ALAN KELLY

JULIA, Raul (9 Mar. 1940–24 Oct. 1994), actor, was born Raul Rafael Carlos Julia y Arcelay in San Juan, Puerto Rico, the son of Raul Julia, a restaurateur, and Olga Arcelay Julia. Brought up in financially comfortable circumstances in the suburbs of San Juan, Julia attended a Roman Catholic grammar school run by American nuns, giving him early exposure to English. As an adult his English pronunciation retained only a trace of his Puerto Rican origins. Julia's introduction to acting came in the first grade when he played the devil in a school play. He continued to be active in student dramatics at San Ignacio de Loyola High School and at the University of Puerto Rico, where he received a bachelor's degree in liberal arts.

After graduation Julia disregarded his parents' wishes that he attend law school and began to pursue a career in the theater. He participated in several productions at the Tapia Theater in San Juan and appeared in a local nightclub review. There he was noticed by the American actor Orson Bean, who suggested that he study acting in New York with noted drama coach Wynn Handman. In 1964 Julia arrived in New York and enrolled in Handman's classes at the American Place Theater. Soon thereafter he made his New York acting debut in a Spanish-language production of Calderon's *Life Is a Dream*. He then worked with Phoebe Brand's Theater in the Street, performing plays in English and Spanish in low-income neighborhoods.

In 1966, Julia began his association with producer Joseph Papp's New York Shakespeare Festival when he was cast as Macduff in a Spanish-language version of *Macbeth* for the festival's mobile theater unit. The following summer he played Demetrius in an outdoor production of *Titus Andronicus* at the festival's Delacorte Theater in Central Park. In 1968, Julia appeared as a clerk in a festival production of Vaclav Havel's *The Memorandum*. His other stage appearances during the late 1960s included parts at the O'Neill Theater in Connecticut and the Arena Stage in Washington, D.C.

Between acting assignments Julia supported himself with various jobs, including a stint as house manager at the Public Theater, the New York Shakespeare Festival's flagship theater in Lower Manhattan. In 1968 he made his Broadway debut in *The Cuban Thing*, a drama by Jack Gelber that closed after a single performance. His film debut came in a brief scene in *Stiletto*, a 1969 crime drama, and his television debut in an episode of the detective series *McCloud* in 1970. In the early 1970s he had a recurring role as Rafael the Fix-It Man on the children's television program *Sesame Street* and appeared for a time on the television daytime drama *Love of Life*.

Tall, slender, and dark haired, with a wide face and large, almost bulging green eyes, Julia was an impressive and energetic presence both on stage and off. His broad, highly animated acting style and deep voice were well suited to the demands of the theater. Julia's breakthrough came when he was cast as the strutting, womanizing Proteus in a musical adaptation of *Two Gentlemen of Verona* produced by the New York Shakespeare Festival. Initially staged at the outdoor Delacorte Theater in the summer of 1971, the well-received production was remounted at Broadway's St. James Theater, opening in December 1971. In his review of the summer production, Peter Schjeldahl of the *New York Times* described Julia as "a breathtaking actor . . . making one hang with awed attention on each syllable of soliloquy" (8 Aug. 1971, pt. 2, p. 1). *Two Gentlemen of Verona* earned Julia a Tony Award nomination for best actor in a musical. For his lead role in a 1975 revival of Frank Loesser's musical *Where's Charley?* at the Circle in the Square he received a second Tony Award nomination for best actor in a musical. His role in *Where's Charley?*, that of an Oxford student who impersonates his aunt, exemplifies Julia's success at avoiding typecasting as Latin characters. Other notable New York stage roles included Macheath in Kurt Weill's *The Threepenny Opera* (1976), which gave him another Tony nomination for best actor in a musical; Lopakhin in Anton Chekhov's *The Cherry Orchard* (1977); Petruchio, opposite Meryl Streep's Kate in *The Taming of the Shrew* (1978); and the title role in *Othello* (1979). In 1978, Julia played the title role in the national tour of *Dracula* and took over the role from Frank Langella in the play's Broadway production in 1979. Maury Yeston's popular musical *Nine*, based on Federico Fellini's film *8 1/2*, provided Julia with one of his greatest theatrical triumphs. In the lavish 1982 musical Julia played an Italian film director examining his relationships with women. *Nine* earned Julia a fourth Tony Award nomination.

In 1976 Julia married Merel Poloway, a dancer he had met in the national tour of the musical *Ilya Darling* in 1968; they had two children. An earlier marriage, which produced no children, ended in divorce around 1970.

Julia's flamboyant performing style lost some of its potency when toned down for films; when not toned down it seemed excessive. Julia's film career was further complicated by the narrow casting practices of the film and television industries, which generally limited him to Hispanic and other "ethnic" roles. In films, as in theater, Julia moved easily between comedy and drama. One of his most notable screen performances came in the 1985 film version of Manuel Puig's novel *The Kiss of the Spider Woman*, directed by Hector Babenco, in which he played a fiery political activist sharing a prison cell with a gay window dresser played by William Hurt. Director Barry Sonnenfeld's popular comedies *The Addams Family* and its sequel *Addams Family Values*, released in 1991 and 1993, respectively, provided Julia with a larger-than-life film role that made good use of his exuberant, theatrical manner. As Gomez Addams, one of a cast of characters based on Charles Addams's macabre magazine cartoons, Julia chomped cigars and popped his eyes in grand style. Julia's other films include *The Panic in Needle Park* (1971), with Al Pacino, a gritty drama about heroin addiction; director Francis Ford Coppola's romantic fantasy *One from the Heart* (1982); and *Moon over Parador* (1988), a satiric comedy with Richard Dreyfuss, about an actor impersonating a Latin American dictator. On television, Julia played the title role in *Romero* (1989), an autobiographical film about martyred El Salvadorean bishop Oscar Romero; he also portrayed Brazilian social reformer Chico Mendes in *The Burning Season* (1994), for which he was awarded a posthumous Emmy Award as best actor in a television movie or miniseries. Julia, who made his home in Manhattan, was active in hunger relief programs and served for several years as the spokesman for the Hunger Project, a foundation devoted to the elimination of world hunger. He died at North Shore University Hospital in Manhasset, New York, from complications of a stroke.

• For lengthy interviews with Julia, see Guy Flatley, "Raul Julia—The Man You Love to Hiss," *New York Times* (26 Dec. 1971), and Phoebe Hoban, "Meeting Raul," *New York* magazine (25 Nov. 1991), pp. 52–56. An obituary is in the *New York Times*, 25 Oct. 1994.

MARY C. KALFATOVIC

JULIAN, Hubert F. (20 Sept. 1897–19 Feb. 1983), aviator, was born Hubert Fauntleroy Julian in Port of Spain, Trinidad, the son of Henry Julian, a cocoa plantation manager, and Silvina "Lily" Hilaire Julian. He was educated at the Eastern Boys' School, an excellent private school in Port of Spain. In 1909 he saw his first airplane; minutes later, he witnessed its pilot's fatal crash. Nevertheless, Julian was instilled with a passion for both the exotic and the mechanical aspects of aviation. In 1912 his parents, who wanted their only child to be a doctor, sent him to England for further education. When World War I broke out, Julian went to Canada and attended high school in Montreal. Late in the war he took flying lessons with Canadian ace Billy Bishop. One of the earliest black aviators, he earned his Canadian pilot's license at the age of nineteen. In 1921 he was awarded Canadian and American patents for an airplane safety device he called a *parachuttagravepreresistra*. Although it was never produced commercially, the invention operated on principles that later propelled helicopters and deployed the parachute system that returned space capsules to earth. When activated by the pilot of a plane in distress, a parachutelike umbrella would blow open and lower the disabled plane to the ground by a system of rotating blades.

In July 1921, Julian settled in jazz-age Harlem, already cultivating the flamboyant elegance that would be his lifelong hallmark. He became active in Marcus Garvey's Universal Negro Improvement Association and an officer in its paramilitary unit. Under Garvey's influence, Julian became absorbed in African history, an interest that later led to an active role in the history of Ethiopia. He broke into the African-American aviation scene as a parachutist, appearing at an August 1922 air show on Long Island headlined by African-American aviator Bessie Coleman. Two highly publicized parachute jumps over Manhattan in 1923 inspired a New York journalist to dub him "the Black Eagle," a sobriquet which delighted Julian and which he retained for life.

Invitations to lecture and perform air stunts poured in. Although many of Julian's exploits were greeted with skepticism and charges of self-promotion, he maintained that his activities were all intended to demonstrate that African Americans were as capable of extraordinary achievement as anyone else. Early in 1924, he announced plans for a solo flight from New York to Liberia and Ethiopia. On 4 July 1924 his overhauled World War I–era hydroplane the *Ethiopia I* lifted off from the Harlem River. Within minutes a pontoon broke off. The plane plummeted 2,000 feet into Flushing Bay. A solo transatlantic crossing would not be achieved until Charles Lindbergh's successful flight in 1927.

Over the next five years, Julian barnstormed all over the United States. In 1927 he married Essie Marie Gittens, a childhood friend from Port of Spain. She remained Julian's "constant advisor and companion" until her death in 1975; one daughter survived her (*New York Amsterdam News*, 11 Jan. 1975, p. A3). Julian subsequently married Doreen Thompson, with whom he had a son.

In 1930 Julian was recruited by the prince regent of Ethiopia, Ras Tafari Makonnen, to train the nascent Ethiopian air force. Soon after his arrival in Ethiopia, Julian's aerobatic prowess so impressed the prince regent that he awarded him Ethiopian citizenship and an air force colonelcy. The Ethiopian cadets and their entire air power—two German-made monoplanes and a British Gypsy Moth recently given to the future emperor—were to perform at the prince regent's November 1930 coronation as Emperor Haile Selassie I. During an air show rehearsal, Julian took up the untried Gypsy Moth. The engine failed and the prized plane crashed. Whether or not the plane had been sabotaged, the Imperial Air Force had only two planes remaining; Julian was asked to leave the country.

On 30 July 1931 Julian received a U. S. Department of Commerce private pilot's license. On 6 December 1931 he took part in the Los Angeles air show, organized by African-American aviator William Powell, headlined "the Black Eagle and the Five Blackbirds." For the first time, six African-American pilots appeared together. Throughout the early 1930s, Julian flew in capacities as varied as barnstormer, rum runner, and private pilot for evangelist Father Divine. When the Italo-Ethiopian war became imminent in 1935, Julian returned to Ethiopia as a volunteer. He briefly commanded the air force, but a violent dispute with Chicago aviator John C. Robinson led to Robinson's appointment as air force commander in Julian's stead.

After the Italians overran Ethiopia in 1936, Julian publicly disavowed the Ethiopian cause—for which he was reviled in America. He traveled to Italy, ostensibly to offer his services to Benito Mussolini. He later wrote that his intent in fact was to assassinate Il Duce, but that his loyalties became known and their meeting never took place. During the summer of 1939 he was the war correspondent of the *New York Amsterdam News* in France. Back in New York, Julian announced that he would prove African Americans were as capable in the film industry as, he claimed, he had proved them in aviation. He assisted in producing two Oscar Micheaux films, *Lying Lips* (1939) and *The Notorious Elinor Lee* (1940).

In Europe the war was escalating. In 1940 Julian served briefly with a Finnish air regiment, then publicly challenged Reichsmarschall Hermann Goering to an air duel over the English Channel to defend the honor of the black race, which Adolf Hitler and Goering had defamed. The challenge was not accepted. Volunteering to join the Royal Canadian Air Force, Julian found he could no longer pass the flying test. In July 1942 he enlisted in the U.S. Army as an alien infantryman and became an American citizen on 28 September 1942. In May 1943 he was honorably discharged at the age of 45. After the war he parlayed his international contacts into global businesses, founding first a short-lived air freight charter, Black Eagle Airlines. In 1949 Black Eagle Enterprises, Ltd., was registered as a munitions dealer with the U.S. Department of State. Over the next two decades, Julian supplied arms and materiel to clients in developing nations and diplomatic crisis spots around the globe.

A resident of the Bronx, New York, since the 1950s, Julian died there in the Veterans Administration Hospital. Although for fifty years he carried the honorific "Colonel" from his Ethiopian days, he was buried in Calverton National Cemetery, Long Island, courtesy of his service as a private in the U.S. infantry.

• Contemporary accounts include a *New Yorker* profile by Morris Markey (11 July 1931, pp. 22–25, and 18 July 1931, pp. 20–23); passages in memoirs by two early aviators, Clarence Chamberlin, *Record Flights* (1928), pp. 232–46, and William A. Powell, *Black Wings* (1934), reprinted as *Black Aviator* (1994), pp. 22–28, 98–104; and journalist H. Allen Smith, *Low Man on a Totem Pole* (1941), pp. 72–81. Also included are newspaper articles, notably in the *New York Amsterdam News*, the *New York Times*, and the *Herald Tribune*. The only monographs are Julian's autobiography, *Black Eagle*, as told to John Bulloch (1964), and a biography by John Peer Nugent, *The Black Eagle* (1971). An informative although critical chapter in William R. Scott, *The Sons of Sheba's Race: African Americans and the Italo-Ethiopian War, 1935–1941* (1993), pp. 81–95, discusses Julian's involvement in Ethiopia. There is no known obituary. Six months after his death, the *New York Amsterdam News*, 1 Oct. 1983, noted that the lack of publicity was due to his second wife's dislike of his reputation as the "Black Eagle."

CAROLINE M. FANNIN

K

KAHLES, Charles William (12 Jan. 1878–12 Jan. 1931), cartoonist, was born in Lengfurt, Bavaria, in Germany, the son of Peter Kahles, a butcher, and Elizabeth Herberick Kahles. With his mother, his sister, and his brother, Kahles came to the United States in 1883 to join his father and an older brother, who had preceded the family to Brooklyn, New York, where they established a business and a home in Windsor Terrace, then a rural neighborhood. Kahles filled sketchbooks with scenes of the countryside and the animals he saw there and, with his siblings, attended Windsor Terrace District No. 3 School. He also apprenticed in the stained glass shop of a neighbor and, later, studied art at Pratt Institute and at the Brooklyn Art School.

Although Kahles intended to become a fine artist, his first employment, at the age of sixteen, was as a newspaper sketch artist, supplying pen-and-ink drawings of news events and local dignitaries for the *New York Recorder*. In 1895, he went to Williamsport, Pennsylvania, to work on *Grit*, a weekend "family reading" newspaper, but after a few months he left for the *New York Journal*, which he joined shortly after William Randolph Hearst bought it in the fall of that year. Kahles remained there for several years and produced his first cartoons for Hearst's Sunday supplement, *American Humorist*. But in 1898 he was working chiefly as an assignment news artist at the *New York World*. He subsequently became a cartoonist, he would later say, entirely by accident: the paper's editorial cartoonist was absent one day, and Kahles volunteered to produce that day's cartoon. It was well received, and "from that moment," he told his daughter years later, "my doom was sealed. Never since that fateful day has anyone taken me seriously."

By 1900, Kahles was producing two regular weekly comic strips for the *World*: *Butch the Butcher's Boy*, about a tough kid whose bullying is always punished; and *Clarence the Cop*, about an Irish policeman whose well-meaning maladroitness results in his being transferred to beats that grow increasingly remote with every succeeding week, prompting him to say each time, "Now, Oi wonder what they sint me way out here fer?" In 1901, Kahles began the first of several weekly comic strips that he would do for the *Philadelphia Press* for the next couple years: *Mr. Suburb*, whose whiskered title character experiences both triumphs and travails in the remote residential regions of the city. Like most newspaper cartoonists of the time, Kahles produced a variety of comic strips, each one reprising in successive appearances the theme that initiated it. Most of them were quite short-lived,

exhausting the humorous possibilities inherent in their concepts within a few weeks or months. Kahles, however, was unlike most of his colleagues in working for more than one newspaper or feature syndicate simultaneously. In 1902, while doing several strips for the *World*, he drew others for papers in Philadelphia. Notable among these were *Sandy Highflier the Airship Man*, chronicling the aerial mishaps of a balloon-borne aviator, and *Billy Bounce*, about a messenger boy whose rubber suit enables him to bound around town as if flying. In the annals of newspaper cartooning, no one equaled Kahles's prolific endeavors during the years 1905–1906, when he was simultaneously writing and drawing seven or eight weekly comic strips for the *World* and his Philadelphia clients. At the end of this productive period, he invented his most enduring comic turn, *Hairbreadth Harry*.

"Harry (Harold) Hollingsworth" debuted 21 October 1906 in the *Philadelphia Press* under the title *Our Hero's Hairbreath* [*sic*] *Escapes*. A spoof of boys' adventure stories and dime novel western thrillers, the strip stars a boyish youth with a propensity for getting into and out of the most dire predicaments. In one of his initial death-defying adventures, Harry, wearing a campaign hat like Teddy Roosevelt, is chased up a tree by a ferocious bear but is rescued by a passing airship, dangling a hook that conveniently comes within Our Hero's grasp. Many of Harry's earliest escapes were effected by such a deus ex machina or freak occurrence, like a suddenly erupting waterspout that jet-propels him to safety. On another occasion, Harry saves the crew of a foundering ship: he slings himself to the ship by bending a tree to serve as a catapult, then catapults the sailors ashore by similarly deploying the ship's mast. On 23 December 1906, *Our Hero* inaugurated the cliffhanger "ending" for which the series is justly and fondly remembered: carried off by a ravenous eagle at the end of one week's installment, Harry engineers his escape the next week by feeding the eagle morphine tablets that he claims are appetizers.

On 20 January 1907, the strip took its familiar title, *Hairbreadth Harry, the Boy Hero*, and Kahles continued to threaten his protagonist's life and limbs with shattering explodings and to rescue him with miraculous hurtlings. That spring, the strip began to assemble the cast that would animate the action for three decades. First to arrive, on 3 March, was the hook-nosed Relentless Rudolph Rassendale, twirling his black moustache, baring his teeth in an evil grin, and trying to steal Harry's remarkably large diamond. That summer, Rudolph's appearance gelled as he donned the funereal top hat and black hammer-claw coat that provided the world with a durable caricature of villainy. Then, on 22 September, the strip's eternal triangle was completed when Belinda Blinks the Beautiful Boilermaker joined the villain who pursued her to supply our Boy Hero with a damsel in distress to rescue. In her first appearance, she is about to be ripped to shreds by a lumber-mill buzz saw into the teeth of which the fiendish Rudolph is conveying her bound firmly to a log, but Harry, displaying superhuman strength, stops the blade by prying the mill wheel from its axle and then flings the grimacing Rudolph into the mill race. Carrying the swooning Belinda, Harry watches his dastardly foe being swept away and utters the memorable axiom, "He who laughs last has a smile on his face."

The strip's burlesques soon settled into a parody of the overwrought melodrama of theatrical tradition. The leering Rudolph, whose amorous advances Belinda invariably rejects, seeks satisfaction by tying her to railroad tracks. "So, me proud beauty," he intones, "since you refuse to marry me, prepare to be bound by other ties!" "You vermin!" she cries. Or, as her landlord, Rudolph throws her out into the cold winter's night for failing to pay her rent (or to return his affections). Kahles's sense of humor was expressed not only in the exaggerated action and farcical dilemmas of the strip but in the juxtaposition of pictures that contradict the narrative text that appears beneath. Belinda, for instance, is at first described as "a ravishing creature of dazzling loveliness," but Kahles drew her as a plain-faced, scrawny fright. The overblown prose of the captions, in their very extravagance, further heightens the sense of absurdity that animates the strip. Belinda was older than the youthful Harry when they met, but as the strip's plots grew more complex, Harry aged. And as his jaw became prominently squarer and his bearing more manly, Belinda became prettier. By 1916, the two were sweethearts in the usual Hollywood manner. Harry followed many occupations and took many expeditions to exotic destinations, and everywhere he found himself perpetually pitted against the heartless Rudolph, who pursued Belinda (or sought simple revenge upon ever victorious Harry) with indefatigable zest.

In addition to his newspaper work, Kahles produced advertising art and cartoons and comic illustrations for magazines, contributing to *Judge*, *Life*, *Puck*, and *Brownings' Magazine*. His drawing style for these was more realistically detailed, illustrational rather than caricatural, as it was in *Harry*. In about 1908, perhaps overworked, Kahles contracted inflammatory rheumatism and, recuperating in the Adirondacks, stopped doing most of his strips, continuing only *Clarence the Cop*, *Pretending Percy*, and *Hairbreadth Harry*. On 22 June 1910, he married Julie Estelle Phelps, a convent-educated schoolteacher whom he had been courting for several years. They lived separately and divorced in 1917, having only one child, Jesse, who lived with her mother until the age of ten, when she joined her father, who had married again, on 4 June 1918, this time to Helen Harrison Sturtevant, a widow twice-wed.

Since about 1916, Kahles had concentrated his efforts on the weekly *Hairbreadth Harry*, and in 1923 he began a daily version. He also painted landscapes, portraits, and still lifes. He played the piano and chess, once becoming champion of the Brooklyn Chess Club. After his daughter joined his household in 1921, Kahles worked far enough ahead on his strips to take summers off for vacations in Europe in 1924, 1926, and 1928. In 1926, West Brothers Happiness Comedies produced five Hairbreadth Harry movies. During the decade, Kahles moved to Queens Village and then to Great Neck, where he died of a heart attack, leaving a three months' supply of *Hairbreadth Harry*, then the second-longest running comic strip still being published (outstripped only by 1897's *Katzenjammer Kids*). *Harry* was continued for some years by F. O. Alexander. The daily version ceased on 17 January 1940, and the Sunday on 2 August 1939.

Kahles's prodigious output as a young cartoonist was emblematic of the sort of work a newspaper cartoonist did in the first decade of the twentieth century, and during those years Kahles ventured onto new ground several times. *Clarence the Cop* was the first policeman comic strip and the first to continue a storyline from week to week. *Sandy Highflier* was the first strip about aviation, and the hero of *Billy Bounce* was the first comic strip character to fly without a machine. But it was with *Hairbreadth Harry* that Kahles achieved his landmark work. It was the first serial adventure strip, and it was so successful for so long that its starring trio have become embedded in American popular culture, readily conjured up by Harry's oft-recited epithet, "Rassendale, you hound!"

• The titles and running dates of Kahles's comic strips, all Sunday strips, in order of their introductions, are *Little Red Schoolhouse* (1898, 1901), *Butch the Butcher's Boy* (1900; also appeared as *Butch the Bully*, 1903), *Clarence the Cop* (1900–1909), *Mr. Suburb* (1901–1902), *Charlie Harduppe* (1902), *A Fairy Tail* (1902), *Sandy Highflier the Airship Man* (May 1902–1903), *Burglar Bill* (12 Jan.–23 Feb. 1902), *Mrs. Biggerhalf and Her Smaller Half* (18 May–10 Oct. 1902), *Billy Bounce* (originated by W. W. Denslow in 1901; continued by Kahles, 1902–1908), *The Teasers* (1902–1908), *Pretending Percy* (1903–1909), *Mr. Buttin* (18 Oct. 1903–24 Dec. 1905), *The Terrible Twins* (2 Apr. 1905–18 Feb. 1906), *Fun in the Zoo* (originated by Gus Hutaf 13 Nov. 1904; continued by Kahles 16 Feb.–23 July 1905), *Doubting Thomas* (1905–1906), *The Funny Side Gang* (4 Feb. 1906–4 Apr. 1907), *The Merry Nobles Three: They Never Can Agree* (1906), *Hairbreadth Harry* (Sundays, 21 Oct. 1906–2 Aug. 1939; dailies, 1923–17 Jan. 1940), *Tatters and Turk* (originated by Robert Carter in 1902; continued by Kahles in 1907), *Billy Bragg* (4 Mar. 1906–16 Aug. 1908), *The Yarns of Captain Fib* (for *Judge Magazine*, c. 1908–1910), *Clumsy Claude* (1909–1915), *Optimistic Oswald* (1912), and *The Kelly Kids* (1919–1923). The most complete account of Kahles's career and life is in the unpublished biography "Curses! Foiled Again" written by his daughter, Jesse Kahles Straut. She produced several shorter versions, one of which appeared in *Cartoonews*, no. 15 (1977): "More on C. W. Kahles." An essay of appreciation by Mark Johnson was published in *Nemo: The Classic Comics Library*, no. 14 (Aug. 1985). An exhibition of *Hairbreadth Harry* strips, *"The Battle for Belinda,"* was mounted in the City College Museum in Philadelphia in 1987, resulting in a tabloid-size catalog with text by Mark Johnson, Art Wood, and F. O. Alexander. An obituary is in the *New York Times*, 22 Jan. 1931.

ROBERT C. HARVEY

KANE, Bob (24 Oct. 1916–3 Nov. 1998), comic-book artist, was born Robert Kahn, the son of Herman Kahn, an engraver in the New York *Daily News* printing department in New York City, and Augusta Kahn (maiden name unknown). Growing up in a depressed neighborhood in the Bronx, Robert Kahn showed an early interest in drawing. His father encouraged him to pursue what he thought was a lucrative profession. Majoring in art at DeWitt Clinton High School in the Bronx, Kahn on graduation received a scholarship to take a two-year course of study at the Commercial Art Studio located in the Flatiron Building in Manhattan. While in school, he found work with Eisner-Iger Studios, drawing one-panel gag cartoons and a comic strip. At the age of eighteen, he changed his name to Bob Kane for professional reasons.

Compelled to abandon his art lessons after only one year of study to help support his family, Kane worked for his uncle in a garment factory. Later, he went to work for the Max Fleischer Animated Film Studio doing Betty Boop cartoons. He left that position to find a more compatible job with National Publications (later known as DC Comics). There he penciled a comic strip titled "Rusty and His Pals." His boss, Vince Sullivan, delighted with the public acceptance of Jerry Siegel and Joe Shuster's Superman, invited Kane in spring 1939 to create National's second costumed superhero. Collaborating with Bill Finger, a writer, Kane created Batman. "I made Batman a superhero-vigilante," Kane notes. "Bill turned him into a scientific-detective." Kane's square-jawed Batman had a modus operandi similar to Chester Gould's Dick Tracy.

Batman and his alter ego, Bruce Wayne, playboy-millionaire resident of Gotham City, made his debut with Commissioner James Gordon in *Detective Comics* #27 for May 1939. Robin followed as Batman's young sidekick in *Detective Comics* #38 for April 1940. Like Batman, Robin had a secret identity: Dick Grayson, orphaned (as Bruce Wayne had been) after his parents were murdered by robbers. "I was the first to create a boy wonder in costume," Kane observes. With Robin's appearance, sales of *Detective Comics* increased significantly.

The most important supervillains created by Kane, Finger, and their assistants were Clayface, Catwoman, the Penguin, and the Joker. Batman and his adversaries were violent. The Joker was a murderer with an insatiable appetite for jewelry. When in 1940 Batman unleashes a mighty punch that sends the pathetically deranged criminal Adam Lamb plummeting down a flight of stairs to his death, Batman comments grimly, "This is the only time I was ever sorry to see a criminal die!" Kane's drawings created a somber environment.

According to Jim Steranko, a comic-book artist, Gotham City was represented by Kane as a "nocturnal chiaroscuro" of New York City. Steranko points out that Kane's art had "structural deficiencies" and Kane's drawings of persons were "stiff" and "unrealistic." Nevertheless, "the inadvertent betrayal of realism seemed to add rather than detract from the grim romanticism of the Batman formula."

From 1939 to 1943 Kane penciled and inked many of the Batman stories appearing in *Detective Comics*, *Batman Comics*, and *World's Finest Comics*. When Dick Sprang, one of National Publications' ghost artists for Batman stories, turned down editor Jack Schiff's invitation to pencil the Batman newspaper dailies in 1943, Schiff offered the position to Kane. The strip lasted only three years with Kane drawing most of the dailies and a handful of Sundays.

Kane married his first wife, Beverly, in the 1940s; the couple had a daughter before their divorce in the late 1950s.

Although Kane retained his byline on every Batman title, after 1943 he was replaced as the top artist for Batman stories in the comics. His most talented replacement, Dick Sprang, transformed Batman and Robin into sympathetic heroes with a deep commitment to bringing justice to the victims of crime. Dennis O'Neil, a comic-book writer, observes that by the mid-1940s, Batman and Robin resembled heroes who had "just stepped out of a Norman Rockwell painting rather than refugees from an urban nightmare." This trend to soften Batman's appearance and personality continued through the early 1960s when Julie Schwartz replaced Jack Schiff as editor of DC Comics. Nonetheless, comics featuring Batman declined in popularity and DC management considered the possibility of ending the career of the Caped Crusader.

ABC saved Batman and Robin in 1966 with their successful television show starring the Dynamic Duo. With Adam West as Batman and Burt Ward as Robin, the show featured a talented cast of actors playing supervillains with a sense of humor. William Dozier, the producer of the series, had renewed interest in the Dynamic Duo by poking fun at them. Batmania swept the country. Kane took advantage of this craze by holding one-man shows of his paintings of Batman and Robin throughout the United States. By 1969 Batmania had run out of steam. Julie Schwartz at DC Comics listened sympathetically to freelancers intent on restoring Batman to the shadowy figure Kane had originally brought to his character. Dennis O'Neil and artist Neal Adams collaborated for a five-year period, reestablishing Batman as a grim avenger stalking the streets of Gotham City at night in his relentless pursuit of vicious and demented supervillains.

Kane capitalized on this turn of events and agreed to serve as consultant for the film noir released in 1989 starring Michael Keaton as Batman and Jack Nicholson as the Joker. However, Kane expressed disappointment that his second wife, actress Elizabeth Sanders Kane, was denied a small role in the movie because of union restrictions and agreements involving British Equity and Actors' Equity Association. (Kane had married Elizabeth in 1986; there were no children from this marriage.)

Kane believed that Bruce Wayne, the Batman, was "the epitome of every fantasy I ever had as a youngster." If so, it was a horrific tale of an avenger preying upon the fears of his readers. While Kane's byline appears on every Batman comic book, the Batman saga evolved over an extended period of time and incorporated the artistic and literary talents of many comic-book professionals who saw in Batman an urban American with a complex and often contradictory personality.

• Bob Kane's career is examined in his autobiography (written with Tom Andrae), *Batman and Me*, Forestville, California, 1989. Kane's art is evaluated in Jim Steranko, *The Steranko History of Comics*, vol. 1 (1970). For information on the characters created by Batman artists and writers, see Michael L. Fleisher, "Batman," in *The Encyclopedia of Comic Book Heroes*, vol. 1 (1976). A more up-to-date treatment is Scott Beatty, *Batman: The Ultimate Guide to the Dark Knight* (2001).

SALVATORE MONDELLO

KAPELL, William (20 Sept. 1922–9 Oct. 1953), pianist, was born in New York City, the son of Harry Kapell, a bookstore owner, and Edith Wolfson Kapell. His father was of Spanish and Russian Jewish descent; his mother was born in Poland. Young Kapell grew up in the Yorkville section of Manhattan, on the Upper East Side, and developed an early fondness for music. At the age of ten, he was given a formal lesson and proved to be so proficient that six weeks later his teacher, Dorothea Anderson LaFollette, entered him in a local children's competition. He won first prize— a turkey dinner with the then-popular classical and movie pianist José Iturbi.

Kapell continued his studies with LaFollette and, encouraged by her, gave small recitals in private homes. On graduating from his local public school, he was granted a full scholarship to the private Columbia Grammar School as a secondary student. As a youth Kapell was athletic and especially enjoyed playing football and baseball, but when it became clear that he was going to become a professional pianist, he had to forgo such activities for fear of injury to his hands. In his senior year he was admitted to the Philadelphia Conservatory of Music, where he became the pupil of Olga Samaroff, and in 1939, at age seventeen, he won the annual Youth Contest for pianists sponsored by the Philadelphia Orchestra. The prize was an appearance as soloist with the orchestra in February 1940, where he played the Saint-Saëns Concerto in G minor. That summer Kapell appeared again with the orchestra, playing the Beethoven Concerto in C minor. Soon afterward he followed Madame Samaroff to the Juilliard School of Music in New York to continue studying with her on a full scholarship.

Kapell was one of several musicians to win the annual Walter W. Naumburg Musical Foundation competition in March 1940, and his prize was a debut recital in New York City's Town Hall in October 1941. The following February he won the Town Hall Endowment Series Award, presented to the young artist under thirty who had given the outstanding performance at the hall in the previous year; at nineteen, he was then the youngest person ever to receive the award. In the summer of 1942 Kapell was invited by the New York Philharmonic to play a new concerto by the contemporary Armenian composer Aram Khachaturian. His performance, at the symphony's summer concert series at Lewisohn Stadium in the Bronx, was a sensation and launched Kapell's career as a professional pianist. He went on to play the Khachaturian concerto dozens of times in performance over the next decade, and it became one of the works most closely identified with him. Although the concerto itself was then and continues to be considered a relatively lightweight piece of music, Kapell's artistry seemed to bring to it an extra dimension that enhanced its appeal.

In the fall of 1942 Kapell began touring the country, both giving recitals and performing as a soloist with major orchestras. By 1943 he was appearing in series with such acclaimed musicians as the pianist Arthur Rubinstein, the violinist Mischa Elman, and the contralto Marian Anderson, a testament to his esteem. In 1944 the Philadelphia Orchestra signed him to an unprecedented three-year contract as a soloist. Confined to playing on the North American continent during World War II, he began to make appearances overseas soon after the war ended, beginning with a tour of Australia in 1945. The following year, after replacing an ailing Vladimir Horowitz in concert with the Boston Symphony, Kapell toured South America, and in 1947 he began to perform throughout Europe as well.

Kapell's repertoire encompassed a long list of works, classical, romantic, and modern, by composers that included Bach, Scarlatti, Mozart, Beethoven, Chopin, Mendelssohn, Schubert, Brahms, Schumann, Liszt, and Debussy as well as Sergei Rachmaninoff, Prokofiev, and Shostakovich. His performances attracted enthusiastic responses from audiences and critics alike, who praised his extraordinary combination of technical brilliance, dramatic flair, and introspective sensitivity, qualities rarely found together in a single musician. A certain pugnaciousness—what would later be called "attitude"— exhibited in personal interviews only enhanced his public appeal in a postwar world hungering for fresh new faces and can-do dispositions, and in the popular press he was often compared with the on-screen persona of his contemporary, the movie actor John Garfield, whom he also physically resembled. That image softened somewhat after Kapell's marriage in 1948 to Rebecca Anna Lou Melson and the subsequent births of their two children; thereafter friends and music critics alike sensed a growing maturity in both his personality and his playing.

By the early 1950s Kapell was being hailed both at home and abroad as the first internationally recognized American-born pianist, and many critics believed him destined to join the likes of Horowitz, Rubinstein, and Artur Schnabel in the pantheon of keyboard immortals. Reaching out to other musicians, Kapell began studying with Schnabel, and he also made a point of setting aside time to play with the cellist Pablo Casals and his fellow pianist Rudolf Serkin. In the late summer and early fall of 1953, Kapell toured Australia, playing thirty-seven concerts in fourteen weeks. He not only appeared in large cities like Sydney and Melbourne but also in remote areas of the country, including inland bush settlements. The tour was a triumph, and in early October a weary but elated Kapell, who had turned thirty-one only a few weeks earlier, boarded an airplane for the return flight to the United States. On the morning of 29 October 1953, as the plane was preparing to land in San Francisco, it crashed on nearby King's Mountain on Half Moon Bay. No one on board survived.

Kapell's sudden and shocking death was devastating, and he was mourned throughout the world as a musical giant. Fellow musicians paid tribute to him in performance, and the American composer Aaron Copland dedicated his longest work for keyboard, the "Piano Fantasy" (1957), in his memory. Yet over the following decade Kapell was gradually forgotten in the public mind as his numerous 78-rpm recordings went out of print: long-playing records (LPs) were displacing 78s, and oddly only a handful of Kapell's were reissued as LPs. By 1960 no music catalogs listed any Kapell recordings for sale. All those extant were now in the hands of collectors, and secondhand stores were charging as much as $250 for a single Kapell recording. In the following decades, limited reissues appeared from time to time, thanks to the perseverance of Kapell's widow, but did not remain in print. But the memory of Kapell was kept alive among a new generation of pianists, including Gary Graffman, Leon Fleisher, and Van Cliburn, who publicly acknowledged their indebtedness to him and who shared with others bootlegged tapes of his performances. In addition the University of Maryland's biannual piano competition was named after him.

Kapell's widow subsequently remarried and, as Anna Lou Dehavenon, became a noted social anthropologist. Long praised for her tireless efforts to keep her husband's reputation alive—even to the point of forgoing recording royalties—she is given major credit for the issuance in 1998 of a set of nine compact discs (CDs) from BMG Classics that offer virtually every recorded performance Kapell made for RCA Victor, BMG's predecessor, as well as a transcription of an interview conducted the year of his death. The event was hailed as a milestone, and in the ensuing years a number of single CDs appeared featuring performances by Kapell as well as a two-CD set presented in the Philips series "Great Pianists of the Twentieth Century" (1999). Especially prized are his recordings of the second and third Rachmaninoff piano concertos and the *Rhapsody on a Theme of Paganini* as well as concertos and other works by Beethoven, Brahms, Prokofiev, and Shostakovich.

• For a biography of Kapell, see the noted music critic Tim Page's *William Kapell: A Documentary Life History of the American Pianist* (1992). See also Harold C. Schonberg, *The Great Pianists* (1987), by the longtime music critic of the *New York Times*. For late-twentieth-century assessments of Kapell, see Page, "William Kapell's Piano Benchmark," *Washington Post*, 27 Sept. 1998; and Michael Kimmelman, "William Kapell: A Larger, Truer Vision of a Passionate Modern," *New York Times*, 11 Oct. 1998. An obituary is in the *New York Times*, 29 Oct. 1953.

ANN T. KEENE

KAUFMANN, Gordon (19 Mar. 1888–1 Mar. 1949), architect, was born Gordon Beni Kaufmann in Lewisham, south London, the elder son of Gustav Kaufmann, a merchant, and his wife, whose name is unrecorded. Kaufmann was educated at the Hausa school in Bergedorf, Germany, and in 1903–1904 at the Whitgift School in England. He may have attended the (British) Royal College of Art and London Polytechnic.

From 1908 to 1910 Kaufmann served an architectural apprenticeship with A. W. S. Cross in London. He married Elsie Bryant in 1911. They had two daughters. In 1914 Kaufmann moved, in the hope of improving his wife's health, to Los Angeles, where, after several years of working at odd jobs, he finally took up his profession with great distinction.

Kaufmann soon revealed himself as not so much a theorist as a pragmatic, imaginative architect. In 1925 he designed the 46,000-square-foot, faux-medieval English Greystone Mansion in Beverly Hills for the oil developer Edward L. Doheny. A man of personal charm who carried with him an air of mystery, Kaufmann soon established himself with Los Angeles's downtown power brokers. Scripps College, the second of the Associated Colleges of Claremont, was about to be built, and its president, Ernest Jacqua, supported Kaufmann's bid to design it. Beginning in 1926, Kaufmann created an attractively Mediterranean environment characterized by arcades and intimate courtyards. He designed each new building in accordance with its function and introduced the use of reinforced concrete. He was responsible for several similar buildings on the adjacent Pomona College campus. These led him in 1928 to the new California Institute of Technology in Pasadena. Kaufmann designed its dormitories and Atheneum (mainly in Italian Renaissance style). In 1933 these buildings brought a certificate of honor from the American Institute of Architects. In 1930 Kaufmann helped design the earliest buildings on the new Westwood Village campus of the University of California, Los Angeles. All these buildings helped create a distinctive southern California style characterized by terra cotta tiled roofs and white stuccoed walls, which became popularly known as "Californian." Kaufmann's style, perhaps better called "tastefully eclectic," perfectly suited a region whose fantasies were regularly realized.

One of the most remarkable events of his wholly unpredictable life originated in 1930. Kaufmann, mentioned as the prospective designer of a new home for the powerful *Los Angeles Times*, learned of the proposed Hoover dam in Nevada. He was subsequently hired (without open competition) by the U.S. Bureau of Reclamation to design its administration building in Boulder City, where the dam workers would also be housed. When asked, Kaufmann proposed that he design the dam itself. California state historian Kevin Starr remarked that Kaufmann, without background in industrial design, had been awarded "the single greatest industrial project in the history of the United States."

For Hoover dam, Kaufmann abandoned "Californian" and created a definitive image of the American 1930s. (He also made for himself a second area of expertise, subsequently designing the Shasta and Parker dams in California.) The Hoover dam's design included intake towers like skyscrapers and a coloration that made it appear to have grown naturally from the reddish soil beneath it. The Hoover dam, the only product of America's dam-building years to rank as a work of art, is a masterpiece of Art Deco wedded to the machine age, and it achieves an appearance suggestive of fascistic power. Starr suggests that its impact derives partly from Kaufmann's cinematic enthusiasms, in particular the futuristic German film *Metropolis* (1927).

In 1933 Kaufmann and Edwin Bergstrom were named supervising architects for all WPA (Works Progress Administration) buildings in the Los Angeles area. Kaufmann's designs for the *Times* led to its award-winning building (1935), hotels, churches and other creations in the general Los Angeles area, such as the late-Thirties Parklabrea Towers, a highly modernistic cooperative apartment complex that introduced to Los Angeles high-rise living (carefully gauged for a city prone to earthquakes). Others included the Georgian-style grandstand and clubhouse at Santa Anita racetrack in Arcadia and the Hollywood Palladium, a low-slung triumph of concrete and swooping lines, the most modernistic of ballrooms. These were followed by several streamlined buildings for the Vultee aircraft corporation in Pomona.

Among the architectural honors garnered by Kaufmann were the Home Beautiful award (1931), Legion of Merit (United States), the gold medal in commercial and industrial design at the Paris International Exposition (1937), and a bronze medal from Argentina. He was made a fellow of the American Institute of Architects and became the official architect for Greater Los Angeles Plans, Inc., whose future projects included an opera house. He was negotiating with Scripps College to update its campus when World War II intervened and yet another previously unforeseen side of the man was revealed. The Kaufmanns moved to Washington, D.C., where Kaufmann was commissioned a colonel in the U.S. Army's Chemical Warfare Service. He served until November 1945.

Living in the affluent Flintridge area in the foothills near Pasadena, Kaufmann resumed his career. He capped twenty years of support for the Boy Scouts of America by becoming the president of its local area council in 1948. A man of imagination wedded to practical and sometimes unpredictable action, Gordon Kaufmann died in Los Angeles.

• Kaufmann's early life is inferred from the archives of the Whitgift School, Croydon, England. A good overall view of Kaufmann's Los Angeles architecture is Charles Moore, Peter Becker, and Regula Campbell, *The City Observed: Los Angeles, a Guide to its Architecture and Landscapes* (1984). Also useful is Alson Clark, "The Californian Architecture of Gordon B. Kaufmann," *Review of Society of Architectural Historians*, So. Calif. chapter (1982). Two books by Kevin Starr, *Endangered Dreams: The Great Depression in California* (1996) and *Material Dreams: California Through the 1920s* (1996), provide important background information. Kaufmann's dam-designing is treated in Richard Guy Wilson, "Massive Deco Monument," *Architecture* (Dec. 1983): 45–47, and "Machine Age Iconography in the American West: The Design of Hoover Dam," *Pacific Historical Review* 54, no. 4 (Nov. 1985): 463–93, and Julian Rhinehart, "The Great Dam," *The Nevada Magazine*, Oct. 1995. A fascinating tale of college political intrigue is part of Stefanos Polyzoides, "Gordon B. Kaufmann, Edward Huntsman-Trout and the Design of the Scripps College Campus," in Alson Clark et al., *Johnson, Kaufmann, and Coate: Partners in the California Style* (1992). Obituaries are in the *New York Times* and the *Los Angeles Times*, both 2 Mar. 1949.

JAMES ROSS MOORE

KELLER, Fred S. (2 Jan. 1899–2 Feb. 1996), psychologist and educator, was born Fred Simmons Keller on a farm in Rural Grove, New York, the son of Vrooman Barney Keller, a salesman, and Minnie Vanderveer Simmons Keller. Keller's early education was disrupted by his family's frequent relocations, prompting him to drop out of high school. He then worked as a messenger boy and telegraph operator for the Western Union Telegraph Company in Saranac Lake, New York. In 1918 he enlisted in the U.S. Army, where he served in the field artillery at Camp Jackson, South Carolina. During World War I he was first stationed in France, where he experienced combat, then he was sent to Germany with the Army of Occupation. In 1919 Keller left the army with the rank of sergeant, and in September of that year he returned to high school at Goddard Seminary in Barre, Vermont, on an athletic scholarship for football. In the fall of 1920 he gained admittance to Tufts College (now University), where under the tutelage of Robert C. Givler he became interested in psychology and philosophy. In response to his poor performance, Keller left and worked a year for the Andover Press in Andover, Massachusetts. He then returned to Tufts and majored in psychology, graduating with a bachelors degree in 1926.

After graduation Keller entered graduate study in the Harvard University Psychology Department (M.A. 1928, Ph.D. 1931), which was chaired by Edwin G. Boring. During his first two years at Harvard, Keller taught undergraduate courses at Tufts, tutored Harvard undergraduates, and worked with M. H. Eliot as a graduate assistant, helping with the undergraduate laboratory. While at Harvard, Keller met B. F. Skinner and entered a lifelong friendship with him. Solidifying this friendship was their outspoken endorsement of behaviorist principles, which often put them at odds with the Harvard faculty.

After graduating from Harvard, Keller obtained a teaching position at Colgate University, where he taught from 1931 through 1938. In 1936 he married Frances Scholl; they had two children. The following year his first book, *The Definition of Psychology* (1937), was published, which enabled him to obtain an instructorship at Columbia University in 1938. *The Definition of Psychology* was an introductory text that provided students with a historical overview of psychology from its philosophical beginnings to its status as a science in the mid-1930s. Keller taught at Columbia for twenty-six years, until his retirement in 1964, and attained the rank of full professor in 1950. During his time at Columbia, Keller first read Skinner's *The Behavior of Organisms* (1938), which influenced profoundly Keller's research and teaching. The book inspired Keller to introduce the faculty and students of the Columbia psychology department to reinforcement theory, which asserts that the frequency of a behavior is contingent upon the type of responses to that particular behavior.

When World War II began, Keller used his experiences as a telegraph operator and his knowledge of reinforcement theory to carry out experiments to improve Morse code training for radio operators. Keller and his colleagues at Columbia developed the "Code-Voice" training method, which provided trainees with instant feedback on their responses to single bits of code rather than the traditional method of having trainees decipher long bits of code. Code-Voice proved more effective than previous methods of instruction and was adopted by the Army Signal Corps in 1943. Keller also used Code-Voice to train Columbia undergraduates who were preparing for military service. In 1948 President Harry S. Truman awarded Keller the Certificate of Merit for his work on Code-Voice.

In 1946 Keller and his colleague William N. Schoenfeld introduced the first laboratory course in introductory psychology, in which undergraduates learned reinforcement principles through work with white rats as experimental subjects. In subsequent years the success of laboratory-based instruction inspired many other colleges and universities to adopt this method of instruction. To accompany the laboratory course, Keller and Schoenfeld wrote *Principles of Psychology* (1950), which was essentially the first introductory psychology textbook, based on Skinner's reinforcement theory.

Nearing retirement in 1961, Keller accepted a Fulbright-Hays invitation to teach reinforcement theory at the University of São Paulo, Brazil, where he and his assistant, Rodolfo Azzi, developed a laboratory based on Keller's Columbia model. Following his success in São Paulo, Keller was invited back to the newly founded University of Brazilia in 1963. During the Christmas break of that year, he began an experiment in classroom instruction for introductory psychology students based upon Skinner's method of programmed instruction. Subsequently Keller developed his Personalized System of Instruction, also known as the Keller Plan, a self-paced method of instruction focusing on student mastery of specific course objectives utilizing reinforcement theory. Keller planned to introduce this method to the Brazilian psychology students. After retiring from Columbia, he returned to the University of Brazilia with three collaborators, Azzi, Carolina Martuscelli Bori, and J. Gilmour Sherman, but a government coup caused Keller and Sherman to leave Brazil, while Azzi and Bori introduced the Keller Plan to sixty undergraduates.

Upon returning to the United States, Keller held visiting, adjunct, and honorary positions at numerous institutions, including Arizona State University (1964–1967), Western Michigan University (1968–1970), the Cecil H. and Ida Green Honors Chair at Texas Christian University (fall 1973), Georgetown University (spring 1973), and the University of North Carolina at Chapel Hill (1980s and early 1990s). Keller died at his home in Chapel Hill, North Carolina..

Keller was a warm and caring educator who was eager to apply reinforcement principles to everyday human activities. He was rewarded with numerous accolades for his excellence in educational reform. Keller introduced students in the United States and Brazil to the experimental methods of reinforcement through laboratory experiences and its effect on pedagogy through the Keller Plan. Because of the success of Keller's excursion in Brazil, many Brazilian students pursued advanced degrees in psychology in the United States, and several American professors continued his work in Brazil. In 1986 a preschool was named for him in Yonkers, New York, where some of his former graduate students used his personalized instruction methods.

Throughout his life Keller had few critics. His self-effacing manner during speeches, his rapport with students, and his emphasis on education rather than experimentation made him a difficult target to critique. However, many educators have used the Keller Plan less frequently over the years because of its emphasis on memorization rather than the deep processing of information.

• Keller's papers are in the Dimond Library, University of New Hampshire. Other major works by Keller include *Learning: Reinforcement Theory* (1954, 1969); *Behavior Modification: Applications to Education* (1974); *The Keller Plan Handbook*, with J. G. Sherman (1974); *Summers and Sabbaticals* (1977); and *Pedagogue's Progress* (1982). Keller wrote a series of five articles on Code-Voice for the *Journal of Applied Psychology* 27–30 (1943–1946). A description of the laboratory course at Columbia is in Keller and William N. Schoenfeld, "The Psychology Curriculum at Columbia College," *American Psychologist* 4 (1949): 165–72. For articles by Keller on personalized instruction, see *The Control of Behavior*, eds. Roger Ulrich, Thomas Stachnik, and John Mabry (1966); "Good-bye, Teacher . . . ," *Journal of Applied*

Behavior Analysis 1 (1968): 79–89; "Ten Years of Personalized Instruction," *Teaching of Psychology* 1 (1974): 4–9; and "Lightning Strikes Twice," *Teaching of Psychology* 12 (1985): 4–8. Biographical material is in Murray Sidman, "Fred S. Keller: Rememberings," *Journal of the Experimental Analysis of Behavior* 66 (1996): 1–6; and James A. Dinsmoor, "Studies in the History of Psychology: CVI. An Appreciation of Fred S. Keller, 1899–1996," *Psychological Reports* 79 (1996): 891–98. An obituary is in the *New York Times*, 11 Feb. 1996.

MICHAEL J. ROOT

KELLOGG, Charles Edwin (2 Aug. 1902–9 Mar. 1980), soil scientist, was born near Ionia in Ionia County, Michigan, the son of Herbert Francis Kellogg, a farmer, and Eunice Irene Stocken Kellogg. Following graduation from Palo High School, Kellogg enrolled at Michigan State College, where he pursued studies in science and mathematics, and eventually specialized in the new field of soil science. At that time, Americans had begun to view soils as natural bodies, the creations of unique combinations of soil-forming factors.

As a student, Kellogg participated in two major events in the utilization of soil data for planning. During the summers from 1923 through 1926, he did research and mapped soils for the land economic survey, an interdisciplinary project of the Michigan Department of Conservation. One objective of the survey was to help solve the problem of the cut-over lands, which had been logged by timber companies. The inefficient use of land vexed failing farmers and taxed the local economy and the state. Very early, Kellogg had learned to view soil properties in the context of their meaning to and interaction with the local society. He earned his bachelor of science degree in 1925 and remained at Michigan State College on a fellowship in soils, April 1926–April 1928, sponsored by the Michigan State Highway Department. Later he made a second contribution to the utilization of soils data. New concrete highways in some portions of Michigan had buckled. Kellogg made a study of the relationship between soil characteristics and the appropriate design for cement-concrete highways. The work led to definite procedures for highway construction in accordance with the soil conditions as assessed by detailed soil surveys. On December 25, 1925, Kellogg married Lucille Jeanette Reasoner; they had two children.

From April 1928 until December 1929, Kellogg directed soil surveys and carried out research on soil genesis for the Wisconsin Geological and Natural History Survey. In 1930 Michigan State College of Agriculture and Applied Science awarded him a Ph.D. for his dissertation "Preliminary Study of the Profiles of the Principal Soil Types of Wisconsin." The study was in the new field of "pedology."

In January 1930 Kellogg took an assistant professorship at the North Dakota Agricultural College, where he also was in charge of the soil survey program and land classification. He advised on the design of the soil survey of McKenzie County, North Dakota,

so that it could be used in land classification for rural tax assessment. Once again, Kellogg made innovations in the area of what soil scientists would come to call "interpretations" of soil survey data for utilitarian purposes. His work in North Dakota brought him to the attention of the U.S. Department of Agriculture, whose soil scientists had responsibility for the soil survey, an activity that had started in 1899. In February 1934, Kellogg accepted a position specializing in land classification in the Bureau of Chemistry and Soils. On 1 July 1934 he became acting chief, Division of Soil Survey, and then chief of the division on 1 July 1935.

For nearly thirty-seven years Kellogg directed the work of the soil survey division. He sought to make the published soil survey a more useful document for farmers and other users. Curtis F. Marbut, Kellogg's predecessor, had worked to establish the soil survey as a scientific document, but he generally eschewed including "interpretations." Interpretations assessed the suitability of soils for particular uses such as for crops, forests, grazing, or a host of nonagricultural uses. Kellogg believed that the soil scientists themselves should work with other technical specialties to develop the interpretations of the soil survey.

The early years of Kellogg's leadership focused on tools to improve and advance the soil survey. He wrote the first edition of the *Soil Survey Manual* (1937) to give soil scientists more precise instructions, definitions, and procedures. In 1936 he had issued a USDA publication *Development and Significance of the Great Soil Groups of the United States*. That publication was used widely in college classes and gave a rather full discussion, in qualitative terms, of the five factors of soil formation. Kellogg wrote extensively in a clear lucid style. His most popular book, *The Soils That Support Us* (1941), examined the relationship of soil properties to historical developments. Many of his writings concerned public policy in soils and agriculture, but others ranged more widely, such as the *Scientific Monthly* series "The Scientist and Social Policy in the Democratic State." (1942)

After World War II, Kellogg traveled, studied, wrote, and spoke on world soil resources. He made tropical soils something of a specialty. His was one of only a few voices advising caution during the headlong exportation of Western agricultural technology. In Kellogg's opinion, Western agriculturalists should not recommend abandonment of traditional systems such as shifting cultivation, or slash and burn, until the supporting systems for a higher level of technology gradually developed.

The merger of the soil survey division into the Soil Conservation Service on 19 November 1952 brought additional resources. Kellogg greatly accelerated the field mapping and publication of soil surveys. To accelerate the mapping and provide a more useful document, he took several initiatives. Intense soil survey institutes at cooperating universities informed soil scientists of the latest developments in soil science. He ordered the development of a new soil classification system. *Soil Taxonomy* (1975) made greater use of laboratory analysis and quantification in definitions. Quantifiable boundaries and parameters defined the various categories in the system. Greater precision in description enhanced interpretations. Kellogg hoped that the new classification system would aid transfer of both empirical experience and research results internationally. He initiated a soil geomorphology research program that not only achieved its immediate objective of aiding the soil survey but also gained international renown for its contributions to the discipline. Kellogg was also an avid reader and student of literature. James Joyce was his favorite writer; he also liked D. H. Lawrence, Marcel Proust, and the diarist John Evelyn. Kellogg encouraged students and his charges to become general readers so that reading became a habit. Beginning with mimeographed lists for students, he prepared several versions of the *Reading for Soil Scientists, Together with a Library.*

On 31 May 1971 Kellogg retired from the U.S. Department of Agriculture. He died in Hyattsville, Maryland, and was buried in Palo, Michigan. Kellogg achieved one of the most distinguished careers in the history of soil science, a career marked by a dedication to assist land users through knowledge of soils. He attended college during the formative years of the young discipline termed soil science. As a student and young professor he made landmark contributions in "interpretations" of soil surveys. In his later career he advised, domestically and internationally, on soils and sustainable agricultural development.

• Charles Edwin Kellogg's correspondence and other papers are among Record Group 54, Records of the Bureau of Plant Industry, Soils, and Agricultural Engineering and Record Group 114, Records of the Natural Resources Conservation Service, National Archives, College Park, Md., and the Special Collections, National Agricultural Library, Beltsville, Md. Also, consult David Rice Gardner, *The National Cooperative Soil Survey of the United States,* Historical Notes No. 7 (Washington, D. C.: Natural Resources Conservation Service, U.S. Department of Agriculture, 1998); Roy W. Simonson, *Historical Highlights of Soil Survey and Soil Classification with Emphasis on the United States, 1899–1970.* Technical Paper No. 18 (Wageningen, The Netherlands: International Soil Reference and Information Centre, 1989); and Douglas Helms, Anne B. W. Effland, and Patricia J. Durana, eds., *Profiles in the History of the U. S. Soil Survey* (2002). An obituary is in the *Washington Post,* 20 Mar. 1980.

DOUGLAS HELMS

KERR, Michael (15 Mar. 1827–19 Aug. 1876), politician, was born Michael Crawford Kerr in Titusville in Crawford County, Pennsylvania, one of the eight children of Samuel Kerr, a surveyor, and Catherine Coover Kerr. He had a twin brother named Marshall. After studying in local schools, Kerr finished a primary education that he called "not of the highest order" (Kerr to Charles Lanman, Mar. 13, 1875, Indiana Historical Society) at the Erie Academy in 1845. Kerr was married to a Miss Coover (her first name is unknown) when he was eighteen; they had one son.

He taught school for several years and entered law school at Louisville University in Kentucky, graduating in 1851. Kerr then moved to New Albany, Indiana, where he served as city attorney for a year and then as prosecuting attorney for the county. Elected to the Indiana legislature as a Democrat in 1862 and named reporter of the Indiana Supreme Court that same year, he was known as "an extreme States' rights man before the war" (N.Y. *Tribune,* 20 Aug. 1876).

Kerr was elected to the House of Representatives in 1864 from a Democratic district. Two years later he faced Walter Quintin Gresham, the Unionist-Republican nominee, who charged him with not being a strong supporter of the Union cause. Kerr pulled out a victory by a 1,250-vote margin and was reelected with more secure majorities in 1868 and 1870. In Congress, he accused the Republican party of failure "to submit to the just restraint of law or to respect the Constitution" in its economic policy and its interpretation of Reconstruction (*National Education–Speech*). He championed hard money, favored lenient policies toward the South, and resisted expansion of federal powers. He also opposed adoption of the Fourteenth Amendment.

Kerr had contracted tuberculosis in 1870 and often was too weak to perform his legislative duties. He traveled around the United States and to Europe seeking a cure for his affliction without success. A small frame and a quiet voice made him seem an unlikely man to gain influence in the House of Representatives. Nonetheless, a Texas newspaper said that he "was regarded with unbridled admiration by Democrats and almost universal dread and hatred by the more illiberal and unscrupulous class of Republicans" (*Galveston Daily News,* 20 Aug. 1876). Kerr served as floor leader of his party in the House during the Forty-second Congress (1871–1873). After some personal indecision, he gave back the salary increase he received as a result of the Salary Grab Act passed in February 1873 before he left office.

In 1872 Kerr ran for reelection from Indiana's at-large seat but was defeated by a margin of 162 votes. Two years later when the Democrats regained control of the House in a sweeping victory as a result of the hard times arising from the Panic of 1873 he won his old district by a landslide. Although maintaining that "Politics is not my trade" (Kerr to Lanman), Kerr was moving to the front of his party in Congress. With the Democrats ready to organize the House in December 1875, he became a leading candidate for the Speakership. His campaign rested on his reputation as a staunch defender of hard money, his "pronounced and uncompromising advocacy of free trade" (N.Y. *Tribune,* 20 Aug. 1876), and his opposition to subsidies and land grants. Most of all, his sympathy for the South and its racial policies enhanced his appeal to an incoming Democratic majority that contained almost fifty veterans of the Confederacy.

Kerr's major rival for the Speaker's post was Samuel J. Randall of Pennsylvania, an exponent of the protective tariff. Helping the Kerr effort was Manton

Marble, owner and editor of the New York *World*. Marble and his eastern allies saw Kerr as a man who could be managed in the interests of the economic policies that conservative Democrats favored. Using Kerr's friendliness to the South as the basis of their appeal, Marble and others like him wanted to persuade Kerr to assist the efforts of the Texas and Pacific Railroad to receive government aid. These considerations were kept under wraps, and Kerr's friend suggested publicly that Randall might be closer to the Texas and Pacific than his rival. Kerr himself was moving around the country for much of 1875 in a futile quest to find relief from his disease. His absence from the political scene did not hurt his chances; while he was away, the men behind his candidacy were able to focus attention on Randall's perceived weaknesses as a supporter of tariffs and subsidies.

As the voting for Speaker neared, Kerr sought to quiet fears about his health. He informed Marble in September 1875 that "if it become rationally apparent that I will be physically incompetent to undergo its labors, I will retire from the contest" (House, pp. 258–59, n. 23). By October 1875 his health had improved, and he became more involved in the campaign. The defeats of Democratic candidates in state elections in Ohio and Pennsylvania in the autumn of 1875 hurt the chances of a Speakership hopeful with inflationary views and made Kerr look more attractive to a majority of his Democratic colleagues.

The Democrats caucused on 9 December 1875, and Kerr emerged victorious on the third ballot with 90 votes to 63 for Randall. His tenure as the speaker was not very successful because his party made political mistakes and the Republican minority rallied around its leader, James G. Blaine. A House committee in June 1876 cleared Kerr of the false charge that he had taken money from a lobbyist. By that time, his health had once again deteriorated and he sought relief at a sanitarium in Rockbridge Alum Springs, West Virginia, where he died. Kerr was a talented legislator who reflected the internal contradictions and problems of the Democrats in the post–Civil War era. His brief tenure as Speaker left very little imprint on the office.

• There is no known collection of papers. The Indiana Historical Society has two Kerr letters with considerable biographical data, and the Crawford County Historical Society in Pennsylvania is helpful on his family background. The Manton Marble Papers at the Library of Congress shed light on the campaign for the speakership. Biographical sources are Patricia Foster Heinen, *The Kerr Families of Early Oil Creek Township, Crawford County Pa* (1993), and William Wesley Woolen, *Biographical and Historical Sketches of Early Indiana* (1883). His legislative style is evident in *National Education–Speech of Hon. Michael C. Kerr of Indiana, Delivered in the House of Representatives, February 18, 1871* (1871) and discussed in more detail in *Memorial Addresses on the Life and Character of Michael Crawford Kerr (Speaker of the House of Representatives) Delivered in the House of Representatives December 16, 1875, and in the Senate February 27, 1877* (1877). Albert V. House, "The Speakership Contest of 1875: Democratic Response to Power," *Journal of American History* 52 (1965): 252–74, and Margaret Thompson, *The "Spider Web": Congress and Lobbying in the Age of Grant* (1985), evaluate how Kerr became Speaker. Newspaper accounts of Kerr's life are in the *Galveston Daily News* and the *New York Times*, both August 20, 1876. The best obituary is in the New York *Tribune* on that same date.

LEWIS L. GOULD

KERR, Walter (8 July 1913–9 Oct. 1996), theater critic, was born Walter Francis Kerr in Evanston, Illinois, the son of Walter Kerr, a construction foreman, and Esther Daugherty Kerr. He became a critic at the precocious age of thirteen, when he came up with the idea of writing "a movie column *by* a kid *for* kids" for the *Evanston Review*, a weekly suburban newsmagazine. During his late teens he wrote film reviews aimed at an adult readership for the *Evanston News-Index*. He won a scholarship to attend DePaul University in 1931, but financial difficulties forced him to drop out after two years. In 1935 he returned to school at Northwestern University's School of Speech, where he earned a bachelor's degree in 1937 and a master's degree in 1938. In 1943 he married Jean Collins, who became a successful comic playwright and memoirist, best known for *Please Don't Eat the Daisies*; they had six children.

In 1938 Kerr had joined the newly formed drama department at the Catholic University of America in Washington, D.C., where he taught speech and in 1945 was appointed associate professor of drama. At Catholic University he typically directed five or six plays each year, including a few written by himself or in collaboration with his wife. Some of his own plays were successful enough in amateur productions to attract the interest of Broadway producers. *Count Me In*, a musical comedy revue, was brought to Broadway in 1942, where it received poor reviews and closed after 61 performances. *Sing Out, Sweet Land: A Musical Biography of American Song* (1944), which featured folk music performed by Burl Ives, ran for 102 Broadway performances. An adaptation of Franz Werfel's novel *The Song of Bernadette* was a dismal failure, closing in 1946 after only three performances. In 1949 Kerr enjoyed a modest Broadway success, in collaboration with his wife, with the musical comedy revue *Touch and Go*, which he also directed. The play lightly satirized theatrical trends of the day, featuring, for example, scenes from the story of Cinderella as they might have been directed by "method acting" advocate Elia Kazan. The play received good critical notices, played for 176 performances in New York City, and ran for an additional six months in London.

In 1950 Kerr wrote an article on the theater for the *New York Times*, receiving dozens of letters in response. He later recalled that this prompted him to reconsider his lukewarm Broadway career: "I said, '. . . I do one lousy piece and I've got a stack of mail this high. Maybe I'm barking up the wrong tree. It looks to me as though whatever equipment I have isn't basically creative at all. Maybe it's analytical'" (quoted in *Contemporary Authors*, p. 281). In October 1950 he resigned from Catholic University to become the drama critic for *Commonweal*, a prestigious Catholic magazine. The following year he was hired on a temporary basis as the drama critic for the *New York Herald Tribune*; after two months on the job, his position was made permanent. Although he continued to pursue a Broadway career as a director and playwright during the 1950s, he met with mixed responses. In 1954 he directed *King of Hearts*, cowritten by Jean Kerr and Eleanor Brooke, which enjoyed a run of 279 performances. But *Goldilocks* (1958), a lavish musical comedy cowritten by the Kerrs and starring Don Ameche, was judged by critics to be "an uninteresting bore"; the play lost most of its $360,000 investment.

With his academic background, Kerr quickly established himself as the most erudite of the "big seven" Broadway critics who wrote for New York City daily newspapers during the 1950s. He wrote three books in which he described his theories about art: *How Not to Write a Play* (1955), *Criticism and Censorship* (1956), and *The Decline of Pleasure* (1962). He was influenced by the aesthetic principles of Thomas Aquinas, which he had taught about extensively at Catholic University. Kerr subscribed to the Thomist notion that art is a "spiritual food" essential to human life: "if we are to take Saint Thomas's words seriously, we are bound to acknowledge that a lively, cheerful, open-hearted interest in art is a clear prerequisite for personal and social health" (*Criticism and Censorship*, p. 85). He agreed with the Thomist emphasis on integrity, proportion, and clarity. He also believed strongly that art should not serve an abstract purpose but rather should intuitively explore human experience. Thus, he argued against judging art based on moral grounds: "When the pietist counsels us to draw men not as they are but as they ought to be . . . he is asking us to alter the proportions, to omit something, to falsify the universe." Similarly, he was hostile to the didacticism of playwrights such as Henrik Ibsen and Bertolt Brecht. He believed that absurdist playwrights such as Samuel Beckett and Eugene Ionesco were too coldly symbolic in their work; at the same time, he considered Tennessee Williams to be the greatest American playwright of the 1950s, because he privileged "life" over "form." Throughout his career as a critic, he praised plays that he felt offered rich character studies within a traditional structure: Eugene O'Neill's *A Moon for the Misbegotten*, William Inge's *Bus Stop*, Albert Hackett and Frances Goodrich's *The Diary of Anne Frank*, Robert Bolt's *A Man for All Seasons*, and Jason Miller's *That Championship Season*, among others.

Between 1951 and 1966, Kerr wrote more than a thousand reviews of Broadway and off-Broadway plays for the *Herald Tribune*. Most of these were written under tight deadlines; he later recalled that he usually rushed directly from a theatrical production to his newspaper office, where he had "about an hour to write the review, sometimes less" (quoted in *Contemporary Authors*, p. 281). Despite this stricture, he produced impressively thoughtful criticism. The British

theater critic Kenneth Tynan called him "the cogent best" of the mainstream theater reviewers, possessing a "nimble, flexible, and informed" style that targeted "the sort of reader who has reached a good median level of sophistication" (*Curtains*, p. 283). Kerr was especially good at conveying the texture of a theatrical experience, so that "you visualize a play you haven't seen and care about it—positively or negatively" (*Los Angeles Times Book Review*, 9 Sept. 1979). Drawing from his firsthand knowledge of playwrighting and directing, he offered constructive reviews, pointing out successes and lapses in craftsmanship. He was often praised for his reasonable, unpretentious tone, which sprang from his belief that the audience was the final arbiter of a play's quality. As he wrote in his collection *Pieces at Eight* (1957): "The critic who attempts to reverse the judgment of an audience, to 'instruct' it in taste, is the critic who deals in lost causes . . . a bore and a fool."

In 1966 the *Herald Tribune* went out of business. Kerr received job offers from numerous publications, eventually choosing to join the *New York Times*. Initially hired as their sole theater critic, he was uncomfortable with this position: "I knew in advance that the power of the *Times*, with one man writing both daily and Sunday [reviews], would be absolute. I wanted the vote split" (quoted in Bladel, p. 1). In 1967 the newspaper hired an additional critic, Clive Barnes, to write daily reviews and made Kerr their critic for Sunday editions. Nevertheless, he became a dominant force in the American theater, hailed by *Newsweek* magazine as a "Supercritic" whose opinions could make or break plays. He also became increasingly controversial. The theater world's avant-garde viewed him as a conservative, one who upheld the status quo on Broadway. During the mid-1960s the *Village Voice* gave him a mock award for "outstanding disservice to the modern theater," claiming that he had used his talents to promote a "commodity theater without relevance to dramatic art, the imagination, or our age." Robert Brustein, the dean of the Yale School of Drama, insisted that Kerr was consistently opposed to every experimental play: "The fact that Walter Kerr will be the only drama critic of importance and will determine the success or failure of every production dooms the theater to 25 years of mediocrity" (quoted in Bladel, p. 2).

Kerr's critics exaggerated his dedication to the conventional Broadway play, but they were correct that he was essentially conservative about the theater. He recognized that, in the cultural ferment of the 1960s, the theater was moving from "a logical theater into a phenomenological one": traditional plays such as Lillian Hellman's *The Little Foxes* were too "beautifully sealed," with "no loose ends left lying about, no moral ambiguities. . . . In our new state of mind we distrust what is orderly because we are now sharply aware that in everything ordered there is something extremely arbitrary" (*Thirty Plays Hath November*, p. 31). But he also believed that the experimental theater, with its distrust of all logic, quickly exhausted itself. He decried the rash of absurdist plays during the 1960s, many of them patterned after Samuel Beckett's *Waiting for Godot*, in which "the message was that there was no message." "The form was simply too easy to fake," he later wrote. "It didn't require talent to put random nonsense on paper and call it Absurdism" (*Journey to the Center of the Theater*, p. 75). Citing the grotesque spectacles staged by the Living Theater and directors Peter Brook and Charles Ludlum—"Puck getting about on stilts . . . nude bodies in glass cases . . . dances with thalidomide victims"—he pointed out that "the avant-garde normally rejects conventional theater because it is too tainted with show business, but our avant-garde has become show biz incarnate" (*Journey to the Center of the Theater*, p. 73). He praised playwrights who he believed successfully dramatized existentialist concerns, particularly Harold Pinter. At the same time, he was generally dismissive of several talented young playwrights of the 1960s and 1970s. He believed that Sam Shepard and John Guare were "not quite full-bodied enough to assert themselves as literary forces capable of commanding a large audience, of sustaining an entire evening" (*Journey to the Center of the Theater*, p. 76). He accused David Mamet's *American Buffalo* of "logorrhea" and criticized Tom Stoppard's *Travesties* and David Rabe's *Streamers* for being inaccessible or unappealing to audiences. His insistence that the audience must be won over—that "a talented playwright cannot really wish to court disenchantment and narrow his base"—was perhaps his greatest weakness as a critic.

In 1967 Kerr published *Tragedy and Comedy*, an ambitious study of the historical development of the tragic and comic forms, with an emphasis on the Greek theater. *Thirty Plays Hath November* (1969), a collection of essays and criticism, included an extensive discussion of the character and origin of Shylock in William Shakespeare's *The Merchant of Venice*. Kerr found links between Shylock and a *commedia dell'arte* figure, Pantalone, and suggested that Shylock was a brilliantly complex comic character, not a melodramatic villain or a tragic victim as often portrayed on the stage. His essay received high praise from many academics. A lifelong admirer of silent films, which he had watched avidly as a boy, Kerr also wrote *The Silent Clowns* (1975), an insightful, gracefully written study of Charles Chaplin, Buster Keaton, and Harold Lloyd. In 1978 he was awarded the Pulitzer Prize for criticism—the first given to a theater critic—for "the whole body of his critical work." He retired from the *New York Times* in 1983, but he occasionally wrote for the paper in the years that followed. In 1990 the Ritz Theater in New York City was renovated and renamed the Walter Kerr Theater. When he died in Dobbs Ferry, New York, Broadway marquees were dimmed in his honor.

• Kerr's other books, all of which collect his drama criticism for the *New York Herald Tribune* and the *New York Times*, are *The Theater in Spite of Itself* (1963), *God on the Gymnasium Floor and Other Theatrical Adventures* (1971), and *Journey to the Center of the Theater* (1979). There is no known biography on Kerr. For information on his life, see the opening chapter in Roderick Bladel, *Walter Kerr: An Analysis of His Criticism* (1976), which also includes a helpful examination of Kerr's aesthetic principles. For positive assessments of Kerr as a critic, see Kenneth Tynan, *Curtains* (1961), and Lehman Engel, *The Critics* (1976). For a negative assessment, see Stuart Byron and Terry Curtis Fox, "Changing 'Times,'" in *New York* magazine (23 July 1979). The article on Kerr in *Contemporary Authors, New Revision Series* (vol. 7) offers a summary of the views of his defenders and detractors; the article also includes an interview with Kerr. An obituary is in the *New York Times*, 10 Oct. 1996.

THOMAS W. COLLINS, JR.

KESEY, Ken (17 Sept. 1935–10 Nov. 2001), author, was born Ken Elton Kesey in La Junta, Colorado, the son of Fred Kesey, a dairy farmer, and Geneva Smith Kesey. He was brought up as a strict Baptist. In his early childhood Kesey moved with his family to Springfield, Oregon, where his father and maternal grandparents ran a creamery. As a youth Kesey spent much of his time hunting, fishing, swimming, and working on his family's farm, which helped form the strong sense of the natural environment that runs through Kesey's fiction. An excellent student and athlete at local public schools, Kesey as a teenager was also an accomplished magician and performed at various Oregon venues, including local television stations. In 1953 Kesey entered the University of Oregon, where he majored in speech and communications and played on the football and wrestling teams. Of medium height, with a muscular, athletic build, curly red hair, and blue eyes, Kesey spent summers during college in Los Angeles trying his hand at movie acting. In 1956 he married Faye Haxby, a fellow student. The couple had three children.

After he graduated from college in 1957, Kesey spent a year working at his family's creamery. During this time he decided to become a writer. In 1958 he enrolled in the creative writing graduate program at Stanford University, which he attended intermittently over the next three years. His instructors at Stanford included the novelist Wallace Stegner and the editor Malcolm Cowley, and the future writers Larry McMurtry, Wendell Berry, and Robert Stone were among his fellow students. While at Stanford, Kesey wrote three unpublished novels and became active in the local bohemian community. Inspired by the beat literature of the 1950s, especially the work of Jack Kerouac and William Burroughs, Kesey and his cohorts were interested in exploring the use of hallucinogenic drugs as a way of liberating creativity and enhancing spiritual awareness. In 1959 Kesey enthusiastically served as a paid volunteer in a government-funded study of the effects of hallucinogenic drugs that was conducted at a Veterans Administration hospital in Menlo Park, California. He later got a job as an attendant in the hospital's psychiatric ward.

Kesey's experiences with drugs and as a hospital employee inspired him to write the novel *One Flew over the Cuckoo's Nest* (1962) about Randle Mc-

Murphy, a minor offender who feigns mental illness to gain transfer from a prison farm to what he thinks are the softer conditions of a mental hospital. Once in the hospital McMurphy is appalled at the docility of the other patients and urges them to revolt against the authoritarian rule of their overseer, Big Nurse Ratched. The story is told from the point of view of one of the patients, Chief Bromden, a Native American who escapes from the hospital after McMurphy is lobotomized. Critics praised *One Flew over the Cuckoo's Nest* as a brilliant parable of the individual fighting against an oppressive, conformist society and placed it in the American literary tradition of Ralph Waldo Emerson, Henry David Thoreau, and Walt Whitman in advocating self-reliance and personal sovereignty. *Time* (16 Feb. 1962) called it "a strong, warm story about the nature of human good and evil . . . a roar of protest against middlebrow society's Rules and the invisible Rulers who enforce them" (p. 90). Though it fell short of being a best seller at the time of its publication, the novel struck a chord with readers in the 1960s, especially young people, and its popularity continued in subsequent decades. It stands alongside J. D. Salinger's *The Catcher in the Rye* (1951) and John Knowles's *A Separate Peace* (1960) as a favorite of American adolescents and is sometimes included in high school and college literature courses.

In 1962 Kesey sold the rights to *One Flew over the Cuckoo's Nest* to the actor Kirk Douglas for $28,000. A stage version of the novel, adapted by Dale Wasserman and starring Douglas as McMurphy, opened at Broadway's Cort Theatre in November 1963. Receiving mixed reviews, the production closed after three months. In 1975 a film version of the novel coproduced by Douglas's son, the actor Michael Douglas, was released to critical acclaim. A huge box office success, the film won the Academy Award for best picture and earned Jack Nicholson and Louise Fletcher Academy Awards for their performances as McMurphy and Nurse Ratched. Kesey was initially involved with writing the film's screenplay but withdrew from the project because of creative differences with the filmmakers. He later sued the film's producers and won a settlement. Kesey claimed to have never seen the completed film, and he frequently disparaged what he knew of its contents. He especially objected to the film telling the story from the viewpoint of McMurphy, rather than indirectly through the eyes of Chief Bromden, and the casting of the diminutive and dark-haired Nicholson as McMurphy, who is described in the novel as a tall and brawny redhead.

Kesey's second published novel, *Sometimes a Great Notion*, a lengthy saga about feuding brothers in an Oregon logging family, appeared in 1964. Strongly influenced by Kesey's admiration for the work of William Faulkner, the novel's narrative complexity and sprawling storyline bears little resemblance to *One Flew over the Cuckoo's Nest*. Critical notices were generally negative, but many reviewers were impressed by the book's ambitious scope. Kesey considered

Sometimes a Great Notion his best work. A lackluster movie version of the novel, directed by and starring Paul Newman, was released in 1971.

Kesey remained a fervent advocate of the beneficial use of LSD, marijuana, peyote, and other hallucinogens. To promulgate these beliefs, Kesey, whose ebullient personality and well-developed verbal skills made him a natural leader, gathered a number of his Bay Area counterculture friends into a group called the Merry Pranksters. In 1964 the Pranksters set off for New York City in an old school bus, dubbed "Furthur" and painted in psychedelic colors, and stopped along the way to explain their ideas and to perform shows incorporating light, color, and rock music. Kesey and the Pranksters continued these performances, which became known as "acid tests," around the Bay Area in the mid-1960s. The journalist Tom Wolfe detailed their exploits in a series of articles for the *New York World Journal Tribune* (Jan.–Feb. 1967) that was later expanded into the best-selling book *The Electric Kool-Aid Acid Test* (1968). Kesey had a child with one of the female Pranksters, Carolyn Adams, known as "Mountain Girl."

In 1968, after serving an eight-month sentence in the San Mateo, California, county jail for marijuana possession, Kesey settled with his family on a farm in Pleasant Hill, Oregon, near where he had grown up. He devoted much of his attention to local community affairs, bringing up his children, and raising cattle, but he remained a prominent counterculture personality and gave frequent interviews.

He continued to write, but publication of his work became sporadic. He published two more novels, *Sailor Song* (1992), a science fiction story set in an Alaskan fishing community, and *Last Go Round* (1994), written with Ken Babbs, about an aging rodeo rider. Both novels were poorly received. His other writings include *Kesey's Garage Sale* (1973), a miscellany of essays and interviews; *Demon Box* (1986), a collection of short stories and poems; *Furthur Inquiry* (1990), a recollection of the Pranksters bus trip; and two highly regarded children's books, *Little Tricker the Squirrel Meets Big Double the Bear* (1990) and *The Sea Lion* (1991). For several years in the 1970s and the early 1980s he published a literary magazine, *Spit in the Ocean*. While in the San Mateo jail, Kesey had kept a journal, to which he added illustrations after his release in 1968; the manuscript was posthumously published as *Kesey's Jail Journal* in 2003.

Kesey came to believe that an immediate sensory experience was more powerful than literature and that the printed word was a limited form of storytelling soon to be made obsolete by advances in computer, recording, and video technology. To exemplify these ideas, he participated in multimedia performances of his children's books. Kesey died at Sacred Heart Medical Center in Eugene, Oregon.

• The papers of Ken Kesey are at the University of Oregon in Eugene. Of Kesey's countless press interviews, two notable ones are Henry Allen, "A 60's Superhero after the Acid Test," *Washington Post*, 9 June 1974, p. L1; and Chip Brown,

"Ken Kesey Kisses No Ass," *Esquire*, Sept. 1992, pp. 160–64, 208–10. Scholarly examinations of Kesey's work include Bruce Carnes, *Ken Kesey* (1974); Barry H. Leeds, *Ken Kesey* (1981); M. Gilbert Porter, *The Art of Grit: Ken Kesey's Fiction* (1982); and Stephen L. Tanner, *Ken Kesey* (1983). Paul Perry, *On the Bus: The Complete Guide to the Legendary Trip of Ken Kesey and the Merry Pranksters and the Birth of the Counterculture* (1990), is chiefly a collection of photographs but includes interviews with Kesey and some of the Pranksters. A chapter on Kesey is in Peter O. Whitmer, *Aquarius Revisited: Seven Who Created the Sixties Counterculture That Changed America* (1987). *Spit in the Ocean: All about Kesey* (2003), edited by Ed McClanahan, is a tribute that includes essays and interviews. An obituary is in the *New York Times*, 11 Nov. 2001.

MARY C. KALFATOVIC

KETCHAM, Hank (14 Mar. 1920–1 June 2001), cartoonist, was born Henry King Ketcham in Seattle, Washington, the son of Weaver Vinson Ketcham and Virginia Emma King Ketcham. His mother died when he was twelve. His father, who had served in the U.S. Navy during World War I, was employed irregularly, particularly during the Great Depression, but the family lived in the Queen Ann Hill district of Seattle not far from the paternal grandparents' home in the university district, and Hank knew no great deprivations growing up. In Queen Ann High School, he was a cheerleader, participated avidly in school theatricals, drew cartoons for the school newspaper, and became enamored of animated cartooning. After graduating in 1937, he entered the University of Washington and planned to major in art and drama, but he left just before the end of his freshman year to find a job in animation in Los Angeles.

Following a short interval with an art service, Ketcham was hired at Universal Studios by Walter Lantz Productions as an in-betweener, drawing the scores of pictures that connected and continued the action between key poses. After fourteen months and a promotion to assistant animator, he left Lantz for the Walt Disney Studios in the fall of 1939. At Disney, Ketcham worked on *Pinocchio, Bambi, Fantasia, The Adventures of Ichabod and Mr. Toad,* and many Donald Duck shorts. In late 1941, he joined the navy, which rated him a photographic specialist and assigned him to their war bond division in Washington, D.C. There he met Alice Louise Mahar. They married in 1942. With the navy Ketcham produced sales and training material. Using his free time in the evenings and on weekends, he freelanced in advertising art and sold cartoons by mail to major magazines. By the end of World War II, he was doing a weekly pantomime cartoon about a diminutive sailor called Half Hitch for the *Saturday Evening Post*. On discharge in 1946 Ketcham moved to Westport, Connecticut, and continued doing freelance work for *Collier's, Saturday Evening Post, Look, True,* the *New Yorker*, and others. That fall, his son Dennis Lloyd Ketcham was born.

In 1948, Ketcham moved back to California and settled in Monterey, selling his cartoons and fulfilling advertising commissions by mail. One October day in 1950, his wife, reporting to him in his bedroom studio, explained the commotion elsewhere in the house: "Your son is a menace." To which Ketcham muttered, "Dennis? A menace?" The euphony proved irresistible: Ketcham assembled a dozen little kid gags and sent them off to his agent; within a month, he had a syndicate contract to produce "Dennis the Menace" as a single-panel newspaper cartoon; it debuted on 12 March 1951.

The mischievous tow-headed, freckle-faced eponymous "five-ana-half"-year-old kid with a prominent cowlick captured readers' affection by being both annoying and endearing. As he and a playmate dismember books and magazines with scissors, Dennis says, "Once I start a book, I can't lay it down until I finish it." The same duo are depicted playing with toy boats in a bathtub that is overflowing, and a scowling Dennis says, "Listen! There go the sirens! It's getting so I can't lock the door fifteen minutes before she calls the fire department!" In the toy department of a store, the sales clerk looks alarmed as Dennis, holding a squirt gun in his hand, asks, "What kind of ink works best in this thing?" To a young friend, Dennis, frowning fiendishly, says, "Sure wish I was three years old again—knowing the things I know now." Showing up at the neighbor's front door with an empty bowl in his hand, Dennis says to the lady of the house, "My mother would like to borrow a dish of ice cream, Mrs. Wilson." Dennis's father and mother, Henry and Alice Mitchell, are visual echoes of the cartoonist and his wife, as Dennis is of the real-life Dennis, albeit drawn at so diminutive a dimension as to exaggerate by contrast his destructive effect upon the world around him. Within a few months, the population of the cartoon expanded to include a large pet dog, male and female playmates, and an elderly couple next door, Mr. Wilson, who was plagued by Dennis, and Mrs. Wilson, who was charmed by the child and amused by the reactions of her husband to the persecutions Dennis so innocently perpetrates.

Before the end of the year, over a hundred newspapers had subscribed. It was undoubtedly the rhyming name that cracked the legendary industry resistance to cartoons about little kids. Ketcham had earlier experimented with a kid comic strip, dubbed "Little Joe," that had not sold. But "Dennis the menace" sang like a national anthem, and the feature continued its rapid increase in circulation for the next several years, impressing his peers in the National Cartoonists Society to such an extent that they awarded him the Reuben as Cartoonist of the Year for 1952.

In January 1952 Ketcham began producing a Sunday version of "Dennis," which appeared in comic strip, not single panel, form. To assist in this effort, he hired a cartoonist and a writer, Al Wiseman and Fred Toole. Shortly thereafter, a comic book debuted and others joined Ketcham's staff. By the end of the decade, "Dennis" was a full-fledged cottage industry, but the Ketcham family was falling apart. Dennis's mother could not endure the strain of raising her son, who was afflicted with learning disabilities, in the environment of a national franchise; in the winter of 1959, she sought a divorce but in the midst of the proceedings died of an overdose of barbiturates.

Ketcham married Jo Anne Stevens on 1 July 1959, and the following winter, under the auspices of the U.S. State Department, the couple went to the Soviet Union, ostensibly to establish a "humor exchange" as part of the U.S. People to People Program. Stopping before and after their forty-day visit in Russia at most of the European capitals, Ketcham produced "Dennis" from hotel rooms and, for three months, from a villa on Spain's Costa del Sol. In the spring, the Ketchams decided to stay abroad indefinitely and settled in Geneva, Switzerland.

Ketcham's second marriage ended during the Swiss sojourn. In June 1970 he married an Austrian, Rolande Praeprost; they had two children. Ketcham made yet another beginning in 1970, launching a second newspaper cartoon feature. Intending to provide the navy with a "Beetle Bailey" equivalent, he revived his wartime "Half Hitch," but this time as a comic strip. In this version, Hitch talks. Dick Hodgins, Jr., drew the strip in the Ketcham manner over scripts by Bob Saylor, but despite enthusiastic support from the navy, the strip did not win an audience among civilians and was discontinued in 1975.

The Ketchams returned in early 1978 to Monterey, where Ketcham indulged a lifelong passion for golf at nearby Pebble Beach while managing the licensing of Dennis characters to such entities as Dairy Queen. The Sunday strip was turned over to Ron Ferdinand in the mid-1980s, and when Marcus Hamilton took over the daily cartoon in the mid-1990s, Ketcham took up watercolor painting. But if he no longer drew every line on the daily cartoon, he exercised extraordinary control over the product of his art staff, requiring them to submit pencil roughs for approval and even after that sometimes rejecting final inked artwork. Debilitated slowly over his last years by bouts with cancer, Ketcham died at home in Monterey one week after a 50th-anniversary exhibit of his work opened at the International Museum of Comic Art at Boca Raton, Florida.

After fifty years, "Dennis" appeared in over 1,000 papers in 48 countries and 19 languages. The enduring success of the feature is undoubtedly due to the universality of its star's personality. An appealing if aggravating combination of impishness and innocence, Dennis is the kid everyone recognizes as his or her own offspring. "Dennis" was reprinted in scores of books and inspired a live-action television series (1959–1963), animated cartoons (1988–1989), a musical (1990), a 1993 motion picture (with Walter Matthau playing Mr. Wilson), and a playground in Monterey. In addition to the Reuben, the National Cartoonist Society awarded Ketcham its Silver T-Square in 1976 for outstanding service to the profession. He was a member of several distinguished golf clubs, including Cypress Point (Pebble Beach) and the Royal and Ancient (St. Andrews, Scotland).

Ketcham steadfastly avoided the topical realism of contemporary life, the morality of which he found "dreadful." He explained, "I make it a point of staying away from the ugly side of life. It's just my nature. I'd rather have upbeat things around me. Lord knows, there are enough things dragging you down. The newspaper headlines can be murderous and bloody, but in my world, the birds are singing." With this determination underpinning his work, it is understandable that he could produce the quintessential American suburban family life cartoon from the shores of Lake Geneva in Switzerland for seventeen years—1960–1977, a tumultuous era. Relying on Sears catalogs and his memory, he simply went on reproducing a picture of American life that he had lived as a young father during the long sunny "summer" of the Dwight D. Eisenhower years. As Judith Weinraub observed in the *Washington Post* in May 1990, in the "essential world" of the cartoon, "women are ladies, and profanity doesn't get stronger than 'heckuva.' Mom is at home with the kids, and the closest the cartoon gets to touching on world events is acknowledging such holidays as Christmas and Easter."

Ketcham's artwork made "Dennis" a monument to stylistic achievement. His drawings are decorative in design, masterfully a blend of contrasting patterns and textures—fat lines and thin ones, mass and shape, hearty blacks and parched white. At this sort of thing, Ketcham had no equal. He was a master technician, and his graphic invention seems inexhaustible. Within the limited confines of a single panel cartoon he constantly found different ways to present his stock situations. Ketcham's drawings are full of telling details that add dimensions of reality to the pictures. And each such detail is rendered in his unique manner, each a stylistic triumph, no matter how seemingly inconsequential in the context of the cartoon's gag. He was tireless in maintaining an exacting standard for himself and his assistants, and with a half-century of daily cartooning on the record, Ketcham joins the longevity ranks of a very few of his colleagues. With "Dennis" he created a classic in American popular literature.

• Ketcham's papers and memorabilia are archived in the Special Collections of the Mugar Memorial Library at Boston University. The most detailed treatment of Ketcham's life is his autobiography, *The Merchant of Dennis* (1990). In *I Wanna Go Home* (1965), Ketcham relates his adventures in the Soviet Union and European capitals, 1959–1960. *Dennis the Menace* has been reprinted in a score of paperback books beginning in 1952 with *Dennis the Menace*, and a retrospective of the cartoon reprints Ketcham's selection in *Dennis the Menace: His First Forty Years* (1991). Obituaries are in the *New York Times* and the *Los Angeles Times*, 2 June 2001.

ROBERT C. HARVEY

KEYSER, Louisa (c. 1850–6 Dec. 1925), Washoe basket weaver, also known as Dat So La Lee, was likely born in Carson Valley (Nevada) or Antelope Valley (California and Nevada), the daughter of Da da uongala and a woman whose name she did not remember, who perhaps died in childbirth. Conflicting reports suggest that Keyser married three times, but only her marriage to Charlie Keyser is well documented. Louisa Keyser had no surviving children, so she is considered an ancestor to the descendants of Charlie Keyser's two previous wives, Delia Aleck and Maggie Miles Merrill. By the late 1890s Keyser was working in Carson City, Nevada, as a laundress and housekeeper for Abram "Abe" and Amy Cohn. Abe Cohn owned the Emporium Company clothing store, and Amy Cohn was transforming a portion of that store into a curio shop for Native American basket weaving. Recognizing Keyser's unusual talent for basket weaving, the Cohns soon relieved her of household chores, hiring other Washoe women in her place, and patronized Keyser as a full-time artist specialist. In return for her products, they provided Keyser and her husband with food, lodging, and medical attention until their deaths.

By 1898 Keyser had innovated a new curio style of coiled Washoe basket weaving that has endured for over a century. Inspired by California Native basketry on display in the Emporium, Keyser added redbud as a design material to the bracken fern root (black) already in use, doubled the fineness of the stitching technique, and placed scattered patterns of flamelike motifs on an incurving basket shape, which she called *degikup*. Spared from the necessity of obtaining food, Keyser had the time to elaborate the *degikup*, increasing its size and fineness to the point that a single basket took a year or more to weave. She laid aside such major works to complete other baskets that required less time, including various twined utensils, and miniature versions of both the coiling and twining types. These sold well, but many of the latter were gathered into the private Amy Cohn Miniature Collection. The major baskets, in contrast, became too expensive to sell, and by the time of Abe Cohn's death in 1934, three-fourths of these major works remained unsold. Abe Cohn never equaled the price of $1,400 paid by the Pittsburgh collector Gottlieb A. Steiner in 1914. In 1915–1916 Cohn tried to convince Steiner to buy more baskets in the hope of building a museum for the remainder on the property he purchased next to his house on Proctor Street. When Steiner declined because of ill health, Cohn used the property to build a small house for Keyser and her husband.

Although she lived in Carson City with the Cohns, Keyser frequently visited her brother Jim Bryant (d. 1908), a resident of Carson Valley to the south. Bryant's wife Scees became Keyser's close friend and her major imitator in basket weaving. After Scees's death in 1918, Keyser adopted Scees and Jim Bryant's son Hugh.

Keyser's life before the patronage relationship with the Cohns was obscured primarily through Amy Cohn's active program of falsification. Cohn contended that Keyser's baskets were part of an unchanging Washoe tradition. Her biographical sketch of Keyser, republished canonically by several authors, is filled with inaccuracies. Thus Keyser was not born in the 1830s as Cohn proposed but more likely around 1850. She was not a Washoe "princess," as such inherited hierarchy was not known in Washoe society. She did not work in Monitor, California, for Abe Cohn's parents and help raise him. Rather, Abe Cohn grew up in Virginia City, and the housekeeper was Irish. Keyser's preferred *degikup* shape was not an ancient ceremonial form but her innovative adaptation of California basketry. The designs she wove were not family crests and were not symbolic. Because of Amy Cohn's promotion of her as a "traditionalist" weaver, Keyser became known primarily by the Washoe name Dat So La Lee, which may be translated as "wide hips." The theory that this name was taken from the eminent Carson City physician S. L. Lee was proposed by him, but not until Keyser was on her deathbed.

Keyser was central to all of Amy Cohn's attempts to promote Washoe basketry to the curio market. Cohn took Keyser to the California and Nevada state fairs in 1900 to demonstrate basket weaving and likewise to the Industrial Arts Exposition in St. Louis in 1919. In winter Keyser was often expected to weave in the front window of the Emporium Company to attract customers, and in summer she stayed at the curio shop on Lake Tahoe, called the Bicose, that Cohn operated from 1903 until her death in 1919. This continual public display led many locals to focus on Keyser as an example of both positive (noble) and negative (savage) stereotypes of Washoe people and of Native Americans in general.

On the positive side, Amy Cohn promoted Keyser as an artist. Cohn published pamphlets that explained Keyser's work, sent information to two experts (George Wharton James and Otis Tufton Mason) who were compiling major works on Native basketry, and by 1900 kept accurate records on each basket in the form of certificates, copies of which were issued to purchasers. Less than two years before her death, Amy Cohn compiled these certificate records into ledgers, one for the Emporium Company in Carson City and the other for the Bicose in Tahoe City. Abe Cohn and his second wife Margaret maintained the Carson City ledger after Amy Cohn's death, completing a uniquely detailed documentation. Abe Cohn also commissioned a short documentary film of Keyser, made in 1922, and in 1925 entertained Edward Sheriff Curtis, who photographed Keyser and several of her baskets.

On the negative side, Keyser was frequently the butt of jokes related by Abe Cohn to tourists, friends, and the local press and designed to exemplify the presumed childishness, ignorance, and unevolved nature of Native Americans bewildered by technological progress. For example, Keyser supposedly discarded a specially ordered corset because it failed to transform her into the svelte model in the advertisement, and she supposedly became bored with the train ride to St. Louis and set off walking home to Carson City from Kansas City. In these popular tales the relationship between Abe Cohn as the rational, male non-Native and Keyser as the childish, ignorant female Native are rendered as the caricature of a Victorian marriage to reaffirm and legitimate an asymmetric political and economic relationship between these two peoples in early twentieth-century Nevada.

Keyser died in Carson City. Abe Cohn had a nearly finished major *degikup* buried with Keyser, claiming that this would continue Washoe tradition, even though the baskets left unfinished by Scees were not buried but were in fact finished by Keyser. Keyser was buried in the Washoe cemetery adjoining the Stewart Indian School south of Carson City. Newspaper reports claimed that the grave was left unmarked at the time to prevent theft of this valuable work.

After Keyser's death Abe Cohn increasingly focused on the curio trade, giving up the clothing business altogether in 1928. The storefront of his new shop, called the Kit Carson Curio Store, was covered with an enlarged version of Curtis's portrait of Keyser. Abe Cohn managed this curio store until his death, and Margaret Cohn sold off the remaining inventory in the mid-1940s. At that time the state of Nevada purchased twenty of Keyser's major works to display in the Nevada State Museum in Carson City and the Nevada Historical Society in Reno.

• The complete Carson City version of the ledger of Keyser's baskets is in the Nevada State Museum, and the incomplete Tahoe City version is in the Nevada Historical Society. Pamphlets containing Amy Cohn's fabrications of Keyser's life and achievements are in the archives at the Nevada State Museum and the Southwest Museum in Los Angeles. See also the publication of Cohn's 1909 lecture "Arts and Crafts of the Nevada Indians," *Nevada Historical Society Biannual Report* 1 (1909): 75–79. Information supplied by Amy Cohn was included in the two major compilations of Native American basketry, George Wharton James, *Indian Basketry* (1901), and Otis Tufton Mason, *Aboriginal American Basketry* (1904). Other publications that drew on Cohn's material include Herbert Alden French, "Dat-so-la-lee, A Washoe Basket Maker," *Saturday Wave,* 25 August 1900, pp. 13 ff.; Clara McNaughton, "Nevada Indian Baskets and Their Makers," *Out West* 18 (1903): 433–39, 579–84, "Native Indian Basketry," *New West,* Oct. 1912, pp. 17–20, and "Dat-so-la-lee," *General Federation of Women's Clubs Magazine* 14, no. 2 (1915): 14–15; and Jane Green Gigli, "Dat So La Lee, Queen of the Washoe Basket Makers," *Nevada State Museum Popular Series* 3 (1974): 1–27.
Articles refuting Cohn's mythic history for Keyser and speculating on its rationale include Marvin Cohodas, "Dat so la lee and the Degikup," *Halcyon* 4 (1982): 119–40, "Washoe Innovators and their Patrons," in *The Arts of the North American Indian,* ed. Edwin Wade and Carol Haralson (1986), "Washoe Basketweaving: A Historical Outline," in *The Art of Native American Basketry: A Living Legacy,* ed. Frank W. Porter III (1990), and "Louisa Keyser and the Cohns: Mythmaking and Basket Making in the American West," in *The Early Years of Native American Art History,* ed. Janet C. Berlo (1992). These articles draw on a manuscript history of the Cohn family prepared by Jerry and Carlene Cohn that is in the author's possession. Obituaries are in the Carson City *Nevada Appeal,* 7 Dec. 1925, and the Reno *Nevada State Journal,* 13 Dec. 1925.

MARVIN COHODAS

KILEY, Richard (31 Mar. 1922–5 Mar. 1999), actor, was born Richard Paul Kiley in Chicago, Illinois, the son of Leo Joseph Kiley, a chiropractor turned railroad statistician, and Leonore McKenna Kiley. Kiley first attended a progressive school and thrived in the atmosphere of creativity. However, he was then enrolled in a parochial school, St. Thomas the Apostle, where self-expression and creativity were replaced by unquestioning obedience to authority and an overly rigid discipline. Kiley's first experience on stage was in his high school's production of *The Mikado,* in which he played the title role.

Kiley attended Loyola University in Chicago in 1939 and 1940 and then the Barnum Dramatic School, also in Chicago, in 1941 and 1942 on scholarship. There he studied acting and worked professionally in radio, which was perfectly suited to his rich, unmistakable baritone. In 1943 he joined the U.S. Navy, and he served for the next three years as a gunnery instructor, although this meant putting his dreams of an acting career on hold for the duration of World War II.

Chicago was a long way from Broadway to an aspiring young actor like Kiley. "All my life I wanted to act," he later recalled, "and I knew that New York was the place to go." He went to New York but was friendless and so impoverished that he "couldn't even afford to get drunk." In 1947 Kiley played Poseidon in an Equity Library production of *The Trojan Women* in New York. His big break came the following year, when Anthony Quinn left for Hollywood. Kiley took over the part of Stanley Kowalski in the national touring company production of *A Streetcar Named Desire,* Tennessee Williams's most haunting and lyrical play.

Television was in its infancy in the late 1940s. Kiley was one of the intrepid young actors who braved the rigors of performing live before a huge audience, gaining invaluable experience and wide exposure. He appeared in dozens of roles on television in the late 1940s, and by the early 1950s the prolific actor was in great demand. He appeared in episodes of "The U.S. Steel Hour," "Kraft Television Theatre," "The Alcoa Hour," "Alfred Hitchcock Presents," "You Are There," "Goodyear Television Playhouse," and others. In 1948 Kiley married Mary Bell Wood. They had six children but divorced in 1967.

Kiley next appeared in a revival of George Bernard Shaw's *Misalliance,* which opened at City Center on 18 February 1953. In the *New York Herald-Tribune* the next day Walter Kerr called Kiley's performance as Percival "hilariously mannered" in this "engaging improvisation on the thousand themes dearest to Shaw's heart" (*New York Theatre Critics' Reviews,* p. 355). Richard Watts, Jr., of the *New York Post* called *Misalliance* a "theatrical treat" ("Shaw's 'Misalliance': A Joy at City Center," 19 Feb. 1953).

The City Center revival was such a success that the play moved to the Music Box Theatre on Broadway. It was uniformly praised by the New York critics, and

Kiley won a Theater World Award for his performance. Later that year he appeared on Broadway in the smash musical hit *Kismet* and sang the lovely *Stranger in Paradise*, based on the music of Aleksandr Borodin. In 1954 Kiley was Ben in *Sing Me No Lullaby*, and he appeared in *Time Limit!* in 1956. Three years later he won his first Antoinette Perry Award for Best Actor in a Musical for his performance in *Redhead*, a Victorian murder mystery that starred Gwen Verdon and was directed by Bob Fosse, both of whom became his personal friends.

In 1951 Kiley launched into film work in addition to his stage and television appearances. He played Thomas Clancy in *The Mob* for Columbia Pictures, and in the following year he played Dr. James G. Kent in *The Sniper* (1952), also for Columbia. In *Pickup on South Street* (1953), a nightmarish tale of underworld brutality that starred Richard Widmark and Jean Peters and was directed by Samuel Fuller, Kiley played the confused and menacing Joey. A handsome man, Kiley was nevertheless sometimes cast as a villain because he lacked the artificial, standard good looks of the stereotypical lantern-jawed Hollywood leading man of the 1950s, such as Rock Hudson and Stephen Boyd. In 1955 Kiley appeared in *The Phoenix City Story* (Allied Artists) and gave a heartrending performance in *The Blackboard Jungle* for MGM as the well-meaning but unfortunate teacher Joshua Edwards. "Basically, I've always been a character man," Kiley told Mike Wallace in a 1977 radio interview.

Throughout his life Kiley tirelessly divided his time between the theater, films, and television. In 1958 he went to Italy to star as the woeful James Tyrone in Eugene O'Neill's *A Moon for the Misbegotten*, which also starred Colleen Dewhurst, at the Spoleto Festival. Returning to Broadway in *Advise and Consent* in 1960, he played Brig Anderson, who was, in critic Howard Taubman's words, "a gifted young senator, . . . haunted by an accusation of homosexuality who takes his life rather than compromise" (*New York Times*, 18 Nov. 1960). In 1962 he costarred with Diahann Carroll in Richard Rodgers's first solo effort with both music and lyrics, *No Strings*.

Kiley's familiar face and distinctive voice were never far from America's television sets. In the 1960s he made numerous guest appearances in episodes of "The Nurses," "The Defenders," "Coronet Blue," "The F.B.I.," "The New People," and "The Name of the Game." Kiley in 1965 became the recognizable voice narrating the "National Geographic" television series that continued for thirty years. In 1968 Kiley married the actress and dancer Patricia Ferrier, whom he had met during the run of *Redhead*. They had no children. In the 1970s he was seen in such television classics as "Gunsmoke," "Bonanza," "Night Gallery," "Columbo," and "Medical Center."

The part of a lifetime came to Kiley in 1965, when he was cast in the difficult dual role of Miguel de Cervantes and Don Quixote in *Man of La Mancha*, costarring Joan Diener, book by Dale Wasserman, music by Mitch Leigh, and lyrics by Joe Darion. It opened on 22 November 1965 at the American National Theatre and Academy (ANTA) Washington Square Theater and ran for five years. Kiley jumped at the part, although he admitted to the *San Francisco Chronicle* later, "It is the toughest part a lot of people will ever play." The show opened to rave reviews by the New York critics and was a hit with audiences, who, judging by the number of tours and revivals it spawned, could never get enough of the errant knight who tilted with windmills. For this portrayal Kiley won his second Tony Award for Best Actor in a Musical as well as the Drama Critic's Poll and Drama League Award, all in 1966.

La Mancha turned into a smash musical, not least because of Kiley's powerful performance and his rendition of "The Quest," known popularly as "The Impossible Dream." The song became a big money-maker for nearly every popular singer, and it was said to have been Robert F. Kennedy's favorite song. (Kennedy came backstage once to congratulate Kiley on his performance.) *Man of La Mancha*, with its message of unyielding optimism amid changing perceptions and fresh questions regarding the true nature of illusion and reality, was timely in the turbulent America of the 1960s.

Energetic as ever, Kiley appeared on the New York stage in *The Incomparable Max* (1971), *Voices* (1972), *Absurd Person Singular* (1974), and a revival of *The Heiress* with Jane Alexander in 1976. He also read poetry with Princess Grace at the Edinburgh Festival in 1979 and toured in *Mass Appeal* and *Ah! Wilderness*, among many other plays. Describing Kiley in a revival of Arthur Miller's tragedy *All My Sons*, Frank Rich, writing in the *New York Times*, 23 April 1987, called him "an owlish figure these days, with that resonant voice as finely shaded as ever." Rich described Kiley's portrait of Joe Keller as "a once pompous Babbitt whose pathetic, last-ditch realization of his greed rises like bile from deep within."

Kiley's remaining films include *The Little Prince* (1974), music and lyrics by Alan Jay Lerner and Frederick Loewe; *Looking for Mr. Goodbar* (1977); *Jurassic Park* (1993); *Phenomenon* (1996); and *Patch Adams* (1998). In 1982 and 1983 Kiley received an Emmy for Best Supporting Actor and a Golden Globe Award for Best Supporting Actor in Television for his work as Paddy Cleary in the acclaimed television miniseries "The Thorn Birds." Kiley won two more Emmys for "A Year in the Life" (1987–1988) and "Picket Fences" (1993—1994).

Kiley lived quietly in the country of upstate New York with his family and the animals he loved. He liked to hike for miles. He became active on behalf of the National Endowment for the Arts and many other causes, including the environment. On 1 February 1999 Kiley was inducted into the Broadway Hall of Fame.

Kiley succeeded in every medium he explored in the realm of entertainment. Enormously versatile, he played hundreds of roles in thousands of performances and was always well liked by his peers. To mark his death, all the lights on Broadway were dimmed in his honor, Broadway's highest award.

• Kiley's *Man of La Mancha* costume and other artifacts and memorabilia are in the New-York Historical Society. He left his letters, photocopies, and working scripts to the Lincoln Center Theatrical Library. Two radio interviews with Kiley are "Mike Wallace at Large," CBS Radio, Oct. 1977; and "Salute to Richard Kiley," National Public Radio, Mar. 1999. Reviews include Frank Rich, *New York Times*, 23 Apr. 1987; and *New York Theatre Critic's Reviews*, vol. 14 (1953). See also Myrna Katz Frommer and Harvey Frommer, comps., *It Happened on Broadway: An Oral History of the Great White Way* (1998). Obituaries are in the *New York Times*, 6 Mar. 1999, and *Variety*, 9 Mar. 1999.

ANDREA WEEVER

KING, Albert Freeman Africanus (18 Jan. 1841–13 Dec. 1914), physician, was born in Oxfordshire, England, the son of Edward King, a physician, and Louisa Freeman King. His father had long been active in efforts to improve the lot of the poor in England and recolonize Africa with former slaves through the Tropical Emigration Society; he named his son "Africanus" in recognition of these interests. After completing his early schooling in nearby Bicester, King immigrated with his father and siblings to the United States in 1851. Following a brief period in Alexandria, Virginia, the family settled on a plantation near Warrenton. King studied medicine at the National Medical College (now the Medical School at George Washington University) in Washington, D.C., and completed his studies in 1861. He had barely established his practice at Haymarket, Virginia, when the Civil War erupted nearly on his doorstep. He gained valuable experience treating the Confederate wounded after the First Battle of Bull Run. He later served as acting assistant surgeon at Lincoln Hospital (located on the site of present-day Lincoln Park) in Washington, D.C., where he treated wounded Union soldiers.

King spent the balance of the war in Philadelphia, where he earned a medical degree from the University of Pennsylvania in 1865. That year he returned to Washington and was present at the Good Friday performance of "Our American Cousin" at Ford's Theater when President Abraham Lincoln was fatally shot by John Wilkes Booth. The young physician was one of the first persons to reach the stricken president, and he worked alongside Dr. Charles Leale and Dr. Charles Taft as they attempted to assist Lincoln. Although it soon became clear that the president would not recover, they moved him across the street to a boarding house where they continued to labor over him until he died early the following morning.

When the Civil War ended, King returned to the National Medical College as a lecturer in toxicology. In 1870 he became an assistant in obstetrics and in the following year was named professor of obstetrics and diseases of women and children. He held the latter position until 1904—when instruction in pediatrics and gynecology was separated from obstetrics—and

remained in that chair until his death. In addition to his teaching duties, he served as dean of the school from 1879 until 1894. King also gave an intensive "short" course in obstetrics each year at the University of Vermont in Burlington following the close of the school year before spending his vacation in York Harbor, Maine. On October 17, 1894, he married Ellen A. Dexter; the couple had three children.

Although he apparently did little clinical teaching, King was widely regarded as an excellent classroom lecturer. He also served as a visiting or consulting physician at a number of hospitals, including George Washington University, Children's, and Episcopal Eye, Ear, and Throat. He also produced a textbook—the *Manual of Obstetrics* (1882)—that proved to be so popular that King was in the process of preparing its twelfth edition at the time of his death. King also wrote a number of papers (eighty-two in all) on a wide range of subjects, including "The Prevention of Malarial Diseases, Illustrating *inter alia* the Conservative Function of Ague," which he first read before the Philosophical Society of Washington on 10 February 1882. Despite its distinguished audience, its conclusions that the disease was transmitted by mosquitoes, and that a means of combating it existed, King's paper—for reasons that were unclear to his eulogizers and that remain so to this day—attracted little attention and was published only in a truncated form by *Popular Science Monthly* in September 1883. Although not the first to suggest the relationship between mosquitoes and malaria—Sir Henry Holland and later Josiah Nott had previously advanced similar theories earlier in the century—King's was the most complete and lucid explanation of the problem, citing nineteen specific instances in which malaria and mosquitoes were both present. The idea finally gained acceptance after the turn of the century, following the work of U.S. army doctors in Cuba.

King was an active member of several professional societies, including the Medical Society of the District of Columbia, which he served as vice president (1877, 1880) and president (1883), and the Washington Obstetrical and Gynecological Society (president, 1885–1887). He was awarded two honorary degrees and was elected a Fellow of the American College of Surgeons (1913). He died at his home in Washington two days after becoming ill while teaching.

Dr. King's career was a textbook example of the vagaries of history: a man of unquestionable talent and intelligence, he received footnote status for his role in the assassination of President Lincoln while later suffering inexplicable silence after releasing groundbreaking medical research results. Nevertheless, his contemporaries appreciated his writings within his chosen specialty as well as his solid contributions within the classroom.

• Dr. King's papers do not appear to have survived. His efforts regarding President Lincoln are documented in James A. Bishop, *The Day Lincoln Was Shot* (1955), and Dorothy Meserve Kunhardt and Philip B. Kunhardt, Jr., *Twenty Days: A Narrative in Text and Pictures of the Assassination of*

Abraham Lincoln and the Twenty Days and Nights that Followed—The Nation in Mourning, the Long Trip Home to Springfield (1965). The best secondary sources regarding his life and career remain "In Memoriam: Albert Freeman Africanus King, A.M., M.D., LL.D." by J. Wesley Bovee, in *Transactions of the American Gynecological Society* 40 (1915): 533–39; "Memorial Meeting, January 20, 1915, in Honor of the Late Dr. A. F. A. King," *Washington Medical Annals* 14, no. 2 (Mar. 1915); and Floyd Elwood Keene, ed., *Album of the Fellows of the American Gynecological Society, 1876–1930* (1930). Obituaries are in the *Washington Post* and the *Evening Star* (Washington), 15 Dec. 1914.

EDWARD L. LACH, JR.

KIRBY, Jack (28 Aug. 1917–6 Feb. 1994), comic-book artist and writer, was born Jacob Kurtzberg in New York City, the son of Benjamin Kurtzberg, a tailor, and Rose Kurtzberg (maiden name unknown), Jewish immigrants from Austria. The family moved from a predominantly Jewish neighborhood on the Lower East Side to a Suffolk Street tenement house. Jacob was an avid reader of science fiction books and pulp magazines. Every Saturday he and his brother went to the movies, where they were fascinated by the fast-paced action featured in the low-budget films. At the same time Jacob learned Jewish folk tales from his mother.

Soon drawing became his passion, and his parents encouraged him to pursue a career in art. "They had a deep faith in me," Kirby noted. "I loved them for it." He stopped attending public school at the beginning of the twelfth grade, changed his name to Jack Kirby for professional reasons, and enrolled for formal art training at Pratt Institute. Unfortunately, on Kirby's first day of classes his father lost his job, and Kirby withdrew from Pratt to help support his family. Kirby honed his drawing and writing skills while earning a living, developing early in his career a reputation for completing assignments promptly. He worked for the Max Fleischer Studio doing Popeye animated films. Later in the 1930s he joined the Lincoln News Syndicate doing various comic strips. For Associated Features Syndicate, in 1937, Kirby did his first solo comic strip, "The Lone Rider," inspired by the Lone Ranger, a popular radio western hero played by Brace Beemer. At the end of the decade, he found employment with the Fox Feature Syndicate, where he met his first major collaborator, Joe Simon, a freelance writer with a reputation as a skillful businessman.

World War II ushered in the "Golden Age" of American comic books and established the team of Simon and Kirby as the most prominent collaboration in the field. Freelancing for Timely Publications under Martin Goodman, Simon and Kirby did the first ten issues of *Captain America Comics*, introducing Captain America, the most famous patriotic superhero ever to appear in comic books. Steve Rogers, once a weakling rejected by the army, is transformed by Dr. Reinstein's serum into America's mightiest defender. The first issue featured his first encounter with the Red Skull, a Nazi feared even by Hitler himself. An

immediate commercial and artistic triumph, *Captain America Comics* joined *Action Comics*, featuring Superman, and *Detective Comics*, starring Batman, as the preeminent titles in the burgeoning field. Unlike Jerry Siegel and Joe Shuster's *Action Comics* and Bob Kane's *Detective Comics*, Jack Kirby's *Captain America Comics* introduced a dynamic comic-book art style that was widely imitated by other artists. Jim Steranko, an American comic-book artist, notes that Kirby's Captain America "stories became pure orchestrations of motion." Steranko argues that "the Kirby formula" was "a maximum of excitement in a minimum of time and space." Kirby believed that he had "evolved a storytelling style that came close to motion pictures" (quoted in *History of Comics*, 1970). He should have been especially influenced by the fast-paced chapter serials of the 1930s shown on Saturday matinees throughout New York City.

In May 1942, Jack Kirby married Rosalind Goldstein, whose father was a tailor. The couple had a son and three daughters. Like Simon, Kirby was drafted into the army and saw action in northern France. Frostbitten in combat, Kirby was hospitalized and discharged in 1945. Before Simon and Kirby were inducted into the army, Jack Liebowitz, their boss at National Comics, kept the team and their assistants busy building up an inventory of comic-book stories. In one of their most interesting Boy Commandos stories in *Detective Comics* for December 1943, a Flying Fortress named Rosalind K completes a bombing mission in northern Italy after the Boy Commandos and their adult leader Rip Carter bail out and the pilots are killed by enemy fire.

When Simon and Kirby resumed their careers after the war, they found a declining market for comics. Comic-book superheroes had fallen into disfavor and many boys, representing the largest audience for comics, had stopped reading comics in favor of television viewing. A congressional investigation into the alleged harmful influences of comic books on boys, buttressed by the noted psychiatrist Fredric Wertham's book *Seduction of the Innocent* in 1954, appeared to suggest the end of the comics industry.

Simon and Kirby responded to this unfavorable environment for comic books by creating *Headline Comics* and *Justice Traps the Guilty*, a clear message to parents and congressional leaders that comics taught boys that crime does not pay. More popular were their romance comics. Intended for adult women, they created *Young Romance* and struck a deal with Maurice Rosenfeld, general manager of Crestwood Publications, whereby Simon and Kirby would share the profits with Crestwood, an uncommon arrangement at the time. An instant success, *Young Romance* paved the way for other romance comics, convincing comic-book publishers that their magazines had appeal beyond the teenage male market. Although Simon and Kirby remained prominent in the comic-book business, their own company, Mainline Publishing, folded in 1955, and Simon decided to abandon the field to pursue a career in advertising. Kirby, continuing the practice of working from his home in Mineola, New York, created many of the key fictional characters that would usher in the "Silver Age" of comic books, beginning in the late 1950s and ending by the late 1960s. For National Comics, he introduced Challengers of the Unknown in *Showcase 6*. Considered the first "Silver Age" hero team, it consisted of four males—a mountain climber, an Olympic wrestling champion, an astronaut, and a scientist. A female physicist joined the team later on.

Challengers of the Unknown were the forerunners of the Fantastic Four, illustrated by Kirby and written by Stan Lee of Marvel Comics. The first superhero team introduced by Marvel Comics since the "Golden Age," it consisted of Reed Richards as Mr. Fantastic, Sue Storm as the Invisible Girl, Johnny Storm, Sue's brother, as the Human Torch, and Ben Grimm as The Thing, a grotesque. Mr. Fantastic possessed the ability to reshape his body like Plastic Man had done in the 1940s. Lee writes, "I had only to give Jack an outline of a story and he would draw the entire strip, breaking down the outline into exactly the right number of panels replete with action and drama." Lee would then add the captions and dialogue. Introduced in 1961, the Fantastic Four became superheroes as a result of an accident and frequently exhibited human failings. With Lee's dialogue featuring bantering and jabbering exchanges between the heroes and the villains while engaged in the serious business of fighting for some significant end, Kirby's dynamic action sequences were transformed into burlesque. This rather odd collaboration between Lee and Kirby spawned the antiheroes of the 1960s and became the favorite fictional characters of a generation of young boys.

The team of Lee and Kirby created Hulk, the X-Men, Iron Man, and the Silver Surfer to name only the most popular. Kirby was so busy in 1964 and 1965 that he was penciling more than one hundred comic books each year. Asked by his wife, "How do you think up these things?" Kirby replied, "I don't know, I just do." Kirby may have established the record for the greatest number of consecutive comics penciled by an artist in a series—one hundred two issues of *Fantastic Four*. Indeed, in the 1960s Kirby was such a dominant artist in comic-book illustration that many collectors believe the "Silver Age" ended with his last issue of *Fantastic Four*. He became known as "The King."

In 1970, when Kirby left Marvel Comics to join rival DC Comics, he received carte blanche to develop a plot he had long considered—a cosmic war between the gods and the demons, with Earth as the prize. In the 1960s, Kirby had introduced a more limited version of this theme: Galactus, the devourer of worlds, was prevented by his rebellious sentinel, the Silver Surfer, and the Fantastic Four from eating energy-rich Earth to replenish his cosmic powers. For two years at DC Comics, Kirby labored to develop what he called the "Fourth World." New Genesis under High-Father challenged Apokolips under Darkseid. The latter sought the antilife equation in order to control human thought and action. This conflict presented in *The New Gods*, *The Forever People*, and *Mr. Miracle* lacked coordination, confused readers, and failed commercially.

His last comic-book titles of the 1970s were *Kamandi*, *OMAC* (One Man Army Corps), *The Demon*, and *Devil Dinosaur*, in which Kirby told his action-filled stories in a clear, concise style appropriate to the word-picture limitations of comic books. Near the end of his life, Kirby's early comic books became expensive collectibles. In 2000, a copy of *Captain America Comics* #1 sold for a record-breaking $265,000.

During his long career as a comic-book writer and artist, Jack Kirby created or co-created more than four hundred characters. This prodigious output was perhaps the most significant contribution made by anyone to comic books. Within this massive body of work, there was a common thread—incorruptible common people and superheroes, committed to honesty and fair play, could overcome evil and personal adversity, provided they made the effort and believed in themselves.

• The best book on the career of Jack Kirby is Ray Wyman, Jr., et al., *The Art of Jack Kirby* (1992). Also see Stan Lee, *Origins of Marvel Comics* (1974), and Jim Steranko, *The Steranko History of Comics*, vol. 1 (1970). For listings of Kirby's comics and their prices, see *The Overstreet Comic Book Price Guide* (2001). Obituaries are in the *Los Angeles Times* and the *New York Times*, 8 Feb. 1994. (Wonderland Comics of Rochester, New York, assisted in locating comic books needed for the preparation of this article.)

SALVATORE MONDELLO

KLEIN, Edmund (22 Oct. 1922–23 July 1999), dermatologist, was born in Vienna, Austria, the son of David Klein, a scholar and cantor, and Helen Bibelman Klein. As a student in secondary school, Klein barely escaped from Austria in 1938, during the Anschluss. Although he managed to convince his sister that she should leave as well, he was unable to persuade his parents to accompany him. He landed in England with no funds, job, or place of residence, moving soon afterward to Canada. Still penniless, he nevertheless entered the University of Toronto and received a bachelor's degree in 1947. He remained at Toronto to attend medical school and earned his M.D. under the direction of Dr. Charles H. Best (the co-discoverer of insulin) in 1951. On 25 October 1952 he married Martha Alice Doble, with whom he had five children.

On finishing medical school, Klein first served as a research fellow at Harvard (1951–1952) and then as a research associate at the Children's Medical Center in Boston (1952–1958). He also completed a residency in dermatology at Massachusetts General Hospital (1956–1959). It was during this period that—in cooperation with Dr. Isaac Djerassi—Klein made his first important contribution to medical technology. By developing a technique that allowed the separation of whole human blood into its component parts of plasma, platelets, white blood cells, and red blood cells, Klein greatly increased the efficiency of the entire transfusion process; now three people could benefit from a single donor instead of one, with red blood cells used for anemic individuals, platelets for cancer patients, and plasma for those with decreased blood volume. Klein's results were published in both the *New England Journal of Medicine* and the *Journal of Pediatrics* and earned him the first prize for originality of research from the International Society for Hematology in 1956.

Klein moved to the Tufts University School of Medicine in 1959, where he served for two years as assistant professor of dermatology and medicine. In 1961 he moved to Buffalo, New York, where he joined the Roswell Park Memorial Institute as chief of dermatology. The institution was a great fit for Klein; the first center in the United States devoted specifically to cancer research, it was to remain his professional home for the next twenty years. Chief among Klein's accomplishments at Roswell was a topical treatment for skin cancer with 5-fluorouracil, for which he won the Lasker Award in 1972. A dogged believer in the potential of immunotherapy—which helps the body "learn" to fight diseases and infections on its own—Klein was among the first to clinically explore the use of lymphocytes to help cancer patients produce their own white blood cells.

Concerned about the sun-worshipping tendencies of Americans leading to the potential for a massive increase in the number of skin cancer cases in an aging American population, Klein wasted few opportunities to raise public awareness of the problem. He served as a member of the National Advisory Council on Health Care Technology at the federal Department of Health and Human Services and testified numerous times before Congress in support of increased funding for cancer research.

Despite his contributions to medical research, Klein achieved his greatest notoriety when, in a July 1977 article in *Reader's Digest* he stated "authoritatively" that former President Lyndon Johnson, who had died four years earlier, had had skin cancer. Klein described a consultative phone call made by the president's physicians in which he had argued successfully for a surgical treatment of the problem. In the post-Watergate era in which the story appeared, the allegations of a secret medical cover-up in the White House proved irresistible to the media. Although Klein claimed to have been authorized by a member of Johnson's family to disclose the facts, he declined to name his source, and both the Johnson family and the former physicians flatly denied the story, admitting only that Johnson had been treated for a skin condition of lesser severity.

Despite the flap over presidential medicine, Klein continued to develop new treatments and therapies at Roswell. One of the most important of his later innovations was his creation of an intravenous therapy for Kaposi's sarcoma that featured low dosages of vinblastine. This proved to be one of the first effective treatments of a cancer that gained increasing prominence as the AIDS epidemic unfolded. Klein remained as head of dermatology at Roswell until 1982, although he continued to conduct research at the facility for several years thereafter. He received an award from the American Society for Laser Medicine and Surgery in 1986 that honored his earlier work (dating from the mid-1960s) using laser techniques on animal subjects that preceded eventual test trials on humans. Klein died in Buffalo.

One of a host of talented Jewish emigrants fleeing from Hitler's tyranny in the 1930s, Klein made solid contributions to the medical profession. He is still recognized among his professional peers for his pioneering work in immunology, which earned for him the title of "father of cancer immunotherapy."

• Klein's papers have not been located. The two best sources of secondary information on his life and career are J. L. Ambrus and Robert A. Schwartz, "Edmund Klein, M.D. (1921–1999)," *Journal of Medicine* 30, no. 5–6 (1999): 291–98, and Schwartz, "Edmund Klein (1921–1999)," *Journal of the American Academy of Dermatology* 44, no. 4 (Apr. 2001): 716–18. The article that proved so controversial was "Skin Cancer: The Avoidable Killer," by Donald Robinson, *Reader's Digest* 3, no. 663 (July 1977), pp. 123–126. An obituary is in the *New York Times*, 30 July 1999.

EDWARD L. LACH, JR.

KNOWLES, John (16 Sept. 1926–29 Nov. 2001), author, was born in Fairmont, West Virginia, the son of James Myron Knowles, a coal company executive, and Mary Beatrice Shea Knowles. He attended local Fairmont public schools until age fifteen, when his well-to-do family sent him to Phillips Exeter Academy in New Hampshire. His experiences at this exclusive all-male boarding school strongly influenced his fiction. After graduating from Phillips Exeter in 1944, Knowles spent several months in the U.S. Army Air Corps Aviation Cadet program. Released from military service at the end of World War II, he enrolled at Yale University, where he was a member of the swimming team, was on the staff of the *Yale Daily News*, and published some short stories in student literary magazines. At Yale he became acquainted with the author Thornton Wilder, who encouraged his literary ambitions and gave him advice on crafting fiction.

After receiving a bachelor's degree in English from Yale in 1949, Knowles worked for two years as a reporter and drama critic for the *Hartford Courant*. He then spent four years as a freelance journalist, living in France, Italy, Greece, and New York City, and wrote a novel, influenced by the work of French metaphysical novelists, about life on an Italian island, *Descent to Proselito*; he withdrew the manuscript from publication after Wilder criticized it as artificial and lacking in genuine emotion. Some of Knowles's short stories appeared in commercial magazines, most notably "Phineas" in *Cosmopolitan* (May 1956). From 1957 to 1960 he lived in Philadelphia, where he was employed as an associate editor and features writer for *Holiday*, a travel magazine. The strong sense of place and sensitivity to the physical environment in

Knowles's fiction has been attributed to his experience as a travel writer. While on assignment for *Holiday*, Knowles met the novelist Truman Capote, who became a lifelong friend.

Following Wilder's advice to write a novel close to his own life experience, Knowles in the mid-1950s began work on *A Separate Peace*, an expansion of the short story "Phineas" loosely based on his own prep school experiences. In 1959, after it was rejected by American publishers, *A Separate Peace* was accepted for publication in Britain by Secker and Warburg. Impressed by the enthusiastic reception given the novel in Britain, Macmillan acquired the book for publication in the United States, where it appeared in early 1960. The brief novel examines the ultimately tragic friendship between two students—Gene, a sensitive introvert (from whose viewpoint the story is told), and Phineas, a gregarious and athletic free spirit—at a New England boarding school during World War II. The title reflects the heightened sense of isolation and privilege felt by the students at their elite school while war rages elsewhere; it also refers to the integration of the wild and cautious sides of Gene's personality brought about by the events portrayed, and his newfound self-control enables him to better face the turbulent adult world into which he and his fellow students will be immediately thrust upon graduation. *A Separate Peace* garnered excellent reviews. Jonathan Yardley, writing in the *New Republic*, called it "a minor but very nearly perfect piece of work; a tight, cohesive account of the corruption of innocence that is not merely the finest 'prep school novel' but a genuine work of art" (Yardley, pp. 27–28). *A Separate Peace* won the William Faulkner Foundation Award for best first novel, won the Rosenthal Award of the National Institute of Arts and Letters, and was nominated for the National Book Award.

Not a bestseller upon publication, *A Separate Peace* eventually gained a strong and enduring following in part through the efforts of literary scholars, who were drawn to the book's effective use of symbolism (though Knowles claimed he employed no deliberate symbolism) and its well-delineated theme of redemption. Articles about *A Separate Peace* appeared frequently in academic journals in the 1960s. The book found its most enthusiastic readership among adolescents, and it stands alongside J. D. Salinger's *Catcher in the Rye* (1951) as a favorite of high-school-age readers. In some schools *A Separate Peace* is included in the English literature curriculum. A poorly received film version of *A Separate Peace*, directed by Larry Peerce and starring Parker Stevenson and John Heyl, was released by Paramount Pictures in 1973.

None of Knowles's subsequent novels came close to matching the acclaim accorded *A Separate Peace*. His writing was praised for its clear, polished style but was faulted for being mechanical and offering unconvincing characters. His other novels include *Morning in Antibes* (1962), about a troubled young American living on the French Riviera in the 1950s; *Indian Summer* (1966), contrasting a young man's search for personal freedom and emotional contentment with his childhood friend's accumulation of power and wealth; *The Paragon* (1971), about a young man grappling with his family history; *Spreading Fires* (1974), concerning a sexually ambivalent American diplomat posted in the south of France; *A Vein of Riches* (1978), a family saga set in the West Virginia coal-mining country where Knowles spent his early years; and *Peace Breaks Out* (1981), a companion novel to *A Separate Peace* about a young man returning from combat in World War II to teach at the private school from which he had graduated a decade earlier.

Failure to follow up, either critically or commercially, on the success of *A Separate Peace* prevented Knowles from joining the ranks of leading authors of his generation. By the 1980s he was generally viewed as a minor figure whose reputation rested upon one short novel. His last two novels, *A Stolen Past* (1983), about an American writer's friendship with a Russian nobleman, and *The Private Life of Axie Reed* (1986), a look at the personal affairs of a successful female politician, received little attention and were not reviewed by major publications. Knowles considered this critical dismissal unfair and claimed that his work was judged in comparison to *A Separate Peace* rather than on its own merit. Knowles is also the author of a collection of short stories, *Phineas* (1968), and a nonfiction book about his travels in Europe, *Double Vision: American Thoughts Abroad* (1964).

A trim man with a long face, large pale eyes, and a high forehead, Knowles never married and was probably homosexually oriented. Dealing with one's sexuality and other basic instincts while functioning in a constricting society was a theme that ran through Knowles's work. He was a writer in residence at the University of North Carolina at Chapel Hill (1963–1964) and at Princeton University (1968–1969). He lived in New York City for most of the 1960s before taking up permanent residence at his seaside home in Southampton, Long Island, in 1970. In the mid-1980s he moved to Florida, where he taught creative writing at Florida Atlantic University. He died in Fort Lauderdale, Florida.

• Knowles wrote the following essays about his writing career: "Where Does the Young Writer Find His Real Friends?" *New York Times Book Review*, 8 Apr. 1962, p. 2; "The Writer-in-Residence," *New York Times Book Review*, 7 Feb. 1965, p. 2; and "My Separate Peace," *Esquire*, Mar. 1985, pp. 106–9. Hallman Bell Bryant, *"A Separate Peace": The War Within* (1990), offers a detailed examination of Knowles's work, focusing on *A Separate Peace*. Jonathan Yardley, *New Republic*, 13 Feb. 1971, pp. 29–30, is a review of *A Separate Peace*. An obituary is in the *New York Times*, 1 Dec. 2001.

MARY C. KALFATOVIC

KONER, Pauline (26 June 1912–8 Feb. 2001), dancer and choreographer, was born Pauline Koner in New York City, the daughter of Samuel Koner and Ida Ginsberg Koner, who immigrated in 1905 from Odessa and Byelorussia, respectively. Her father, a lawyer, created a plan for Workman's Circle, a Jewish socialist and benevolent association that pioneered group medical coverage. Her mother helped to create Pauline's costumes. The family's friends were primarily Russian intellectuals, singers, and painters. Koner grew up in the Bronx, Coney Island, and Bensonhurst, Brooklyn, a landscaped residential neighborhood at the time.

Koner made an impromptu dance debut when she was four. Entranced by an organ-grinder's tarantella, she improvised a solo and drew an appreciative crowd. At age eleven, she was taken to see Anna Pavlova dance Michel Fokine's *The Dying Swan*. The following year she took ballet classes at Fokine's studio on Riverside Drive and appeared in the children's corps of the great choreographer's company. Koner's father provided legal services to the Fokines in exchange for his daughter's training.

From the outset Pauline Koner was determined to develop an individual movement style. She studied with Japanese experimentalist Michio Ito and toured for two years with his company. She learned Spanish dancing from Angel Cansino and also performed with Yeichi Nimura. Her first solo concert on 7 December 1930 at the Guild Theatre was favorably reviewed by John Martin in the *New York Times*, the headline announcing "The Dance: A New Talent" (14 Dec. 1930). Her second solo concert occurred a year later on 6 December 1931, also at the Guild Theatre. That same year Koner starred in Edwin Strawbridge's *Le Pas d'Acier* with the Metropolitan Opera Ballet.

Strongly individualistic in private as well as on stage, Koner in 1932 set off alone to tour Egypt and Palestine. She studied ethnic dances of the region and gave public performances, along with one memorable shipboard improvisation. Writing in her autobiography, Koner revealed, "I allow heartbeat, pulse, breath to take over. These feed rhythm and motion and mind. Time, space, and energy synthesize and I dance. Afterward, it takes time to re-enter the world" (*Solitary Song*, p. 62). Experiences in the Middle East entered her repertory with *Yemenite Prayer* and *Debka*. Requisite annual New York appearances took place at the Shubert Theatre on 5 November 1933 and at the Little Theatre on 29 April 1934. She also performed *La Maja Maldita* as a soloist at Radio City Music Hall. On 10 November 1934, Koner set sail to spend the next twenty months in the Soviet Union.

Russian was spoken in the Koner home, and Pauline had studied the language at Columbia University. Still, it could not have been easy to arrive at her destination on the day when Sergei Kirov, president of the Leningrad Soviet and temporary namesake for the Maryinsky Theatre, was assassinated. Her contract was with the Soviet Concert Bureau and included appearances in Moscow and St. Petersburg (Leningrad) as well as in remote factory villages. The basic structure of her program was to open with *Rondo* to a score by Mozart and *Waltz Momentum*, by Harvey Brown. *Bird of Prey* and *Three Funeral Marches*, purely modern dances, were presented before a fiery Spanish fi-nale. Besides performing in St. Petersburg, Koner gave classes for teachers at the House for Artistic Training of Children, taught, and gave lecture demonstrations at the Maryinsky School, now the Vaganova Choreographic Institute.

When Koner returned to New York in 1936, she found the modern dance scene much more active, with the American Dance Association and the Federal Dance Project of the Works Progress Administration underway. Themes of social consciousness were on view in both theater and dance productions. She completed a brief West Coast tour in 1937 and acquired a loft on lower Fifth Avenue. The following year, a concert at the Humphrey-Weidman Studio Theatre showed new influences on Koner. Among her pieces were *Song of the Slums* and *Suite of Soviet Impressions*. She had met conductor Fritz Mahler, a second cousin of the composer, at a holiday party. They were married on 23 May 1939 in a ceremony performed by Mayor Fiorello La Guardia in the summer City Hall at New York's 1939 World's Fair; the couple remained together until his death in 1973.

In the early 1940s, besides solo recitals and touring, Koner choreographed and performed for the Roxy Theater and created works for Holiday on Ice. With Kitty Doner in 1945, she created *Choreotones* for CBS Television. The series was one of the earliest and most successful attempts to present modern dance on television. Among Koner's other television productions was "Alice," part of Ford's 1949 television ballet series *Through the Crystal Ball*.

A letter from modern dance pioneer Doris Humphrey following a Koner performance in 1945 led to Humphrey's becoming Koner's mentor. Humphrey invited Koner to be the permanent guest artist with the José Limón Dance Company (1946–1960). With José Limón, Koner created important roles in *Moor's Pavane* and *La Malinche*, as well as in Humphrey's *Ruins and Visions*. She continued to make solos and work for her own performance group. Among these were *Cassandra* (1953), *Concertino* (1955), *The Shining Dark* (1956), *Solitary Song* (1963), *Cantigas* (1973), and her best known, *The Farewell (1962)*, which was made to commemorate Humphrey's untimely demise. In 1973 Koner, following the death of her husband, headed the Pauline Koner Consort (1976–1982). Her dances have been performed by the companies of Limón, Alvin Ailey, and Batsheva, among others.

Koner was a master teacher; her course "Elements of Performing" was regularly given at the American Dance Festival (in both New London and Durham), Jacob's Pillow Dance Festival, and many universities. She was among the founding faculty at the North Carolina School of the Arts (1965–1976), served as an adjunct professor at Brooklyn College (1975–1979), and taught at the Juilliard School. Under auspices of the Fulbright Commission, she gave lecture demonstrations and courses in Japan and also was invited to Italy, the Philippines, India, Holland, Chile, and Brazil. Koner died in New York City.

Koner believed compassion to be the root of all art and that creative people should be catalysts in society. Using her extraordinary gifts as a performer, choreographer, and teacher, she fulfilled what she held was an artist's chief responsibility: to illuminate, transcend, and reveal a given moment in time. In a filmed presentation of *The Farewell*, Koner makes use of her extraordinary dramatic presence, precise technique and surprising lyricism. She transmits a palpable sense of loss with an emotional dynamic that reverberates among viewers. Ultimately, as is the case with all human mourning, she must let go, and the episode is ended. The beauty of choreographic composition and mesmerizing power of Koner's dancing leave audiences with a sense of true catharsis.

• A valuable repository of photographs, films and videotapes is housed in the Jerome Robbins Dance Division at the New York Public Library, Lincoln Center (NYPL/LC). Additional visual and textual materials related to her dances are at the Dance Library of Israel. Koner's autobiography, *Solitary Song* (1989), is informative. Her *Elements of Performance: A Guide for Performers in Dance, Theatre, and Opera* (1993) was used as a text for her course. In Selma Jeanne Cohen's *The Modern Dance: Seven Statements of Belief* (1966), Koner's "Intrinsic Dance" is interestingly compared to views from six other choreographers. Jack Anderson, "Pauline Koner, An American Original," *Dance Magazine*, Jan. 1998, pp. 82–84, provides details on the latter part of her long career. Other *Dance Magazine* articles of note are Marcia Marks, "Pauline Koner Speaking," parts 1–3, Sept.–Nov. 1961); "The American Way," June 1964, pp. 36–41, 75–77; Olga Maynard, "Pauline Koner: A Cyclic Force," Apr. 1973, pp. 56–69; and Joan Pikula, "Communication and Compassion: Pauline Koner," Mar. 1978), pp. 64–69. David Sears, "Pauline Koner," appears in *International Encyclopedia of Dance*, vol. 4, pp. 38–39. The Dance Magazine Award presentation by John Martin of the *New York Times* and Koner's acceptance speech on 16 Apr. 1964 are preserved on two audio cassettes in the Oral History Archives (NYPL/LC). Anna Kisselgoff's "Pauline Koner's Golden Anniversary," *New York Times*, 2 July 1978, is well paired with Jack Anderson's *Times* obituary, 9 Feb. 2001.

CAMILLE HARDY

KRAMER, Stanley (29 Sept. 1913–19 Feb. 2001), motion picture producer and director, was born Stanley Earl Kramer in New York City's Hell's Kitchen, the only child of Mildred Kramer, a secretary in the New York office of Paramount Pictures; his father is not named in Kramer's autobiography or any other published source of information. His parents separated shortly after his birth, and he was raised by his mother in a "dark and airless hole in the wall" (Kramer and Coffey, p. 10) that she shared with her immigrant parents, Polish Jews who labored in the city's garment district. He ran with West Side gangs that "ruled the streets," forming alliances with blacks "as an instrument of protection," and sometimes menace, against the neighborhood Irish, Italians, and Hispanics.

Under his mother's "constant" urging, Kramer dutifully got good grades and graduated from DeWitt Clinton High School at fifteen, realizing a dream by becoming the first in his family to go to college. He wanted to be a writer or ballplayer but obeyed his mother's practical advice and received an undergraduate degree in business administration from New York University in 1933. Satirical pieces he wrote for *Medley*, the university's humor magazine, won him a $70-a-week job as a junior writer for Twentieth-Century Fox in Hollywood. Six months later he was out of a job but determined to learn more about filmmaking. Kramer became a stagehand on the "swing gang" but lost the job two weeks later because of his inability to swing a hammer. His back lot work at $18 a week with friend and future collaborator Mark Robson included moving furniture, shifting scenes, and unloading animals for location work.

For the next eight years Kramer kicked around the fringes of the movie industry, as an office boy, apprentice writer, and assistant film editor at Metro-Goldwyn-Mayer and as a staff writer for Columbia and then Republic Pictures. "The pay was low, the glory small," he remembered, "but each was a good place to learn" (Spoto, p. 23). Kramer kept writing between studio assignments, selling scripts to "Lux Radio Theatre," "The Rudy Vallee Show," and the Edward G. Robinson radio series "The Big Town." In 1941 Kramer worked as an executive assistant to independent producer David L. Loew on two films— *So Ends Our Night* and *The Moon and Sixpence*. By 1942 Kramer thought he was ready to produce his own pictures. He hired George Glass, a veteran publicity agent, but couldn't find financing. Kramer entered the U.S. Army and made training films for the Signal Corps at Astoria, New York, where he met heir to the Sears Roebuck fortune Armand Deutsch and writer Carl Foreman, two men who would help him launch his career as an independent filmmaker.

With Deutsch's money Kramer bought two Ring Lardner stories set in New York that Foreman converted into screenplays. Kramer's Screen Plays, Inc., begun in May 1947, brought *So This Is New York* to the screen in 1948 and *Champion* in 1949. The first film failed to turn a profit and quickly disappeared from view; the second, made in twenty-four days at a half-million dollars, grossed $18 million. The movie helped jumpstart the career of actor Kirk Douglas and director Mark Robson and made the 36-year-old Kramer "a boy wonder," according to *New York Times* film critic Bosley Crowther.

Kramer refused overtures from the major studios, explaining, "I was an independent and determined to stay that way." He moved in with his uncle Earl Kramer, a distributor for Universal Pictures and publicity agent, and brought his mother to Hollywood to live with them. Kramer produced four more films as an independent in the next three years. Kramer had encountered anti-Semitism in the army and was eager to depict the military's racism toward blacks in *Home of the Brave* (1949). Foreman's script and Robson's direction brought the film high critical praise. Kramer skillfully produced the film for a modest $365,000, proving even a message movie could make money. *The Men* (1950), also scripted by Foreman and starring Marlon Brando in his screen debut as a paraplegic war veteran, was a hit with critics but a bust at the box office. *Cyrano de Bergerac* (1950) won José Ferrer an Oscar but lost Kramer and United Artists money. *High Noon*, written by Foreman and released in 1952, won Gary Cooper the Best Actor Oscar. Cooper's portrayal of a small-town sheriff left to fight an outlaw gang alone helped make the film, under Fred Zinnemann's taut direction, a Western classic.

In March 1951 Kramer, tiring of his role as "shill" in financing his films, made "the most dangerous and foolhardy move of my entire career" (Kramer and Coffey, p. 74) by agreeing to join Columbia Pictures as an independent producer. The studio's "malevolent chief," Harry Cohn, offered Kramer the secure financing he sought to expand his production schedule. The Stanley Kramer Co. was given complete control over subject matter, treatment, casting, and production on four films a year over five years. The alliance, however, lasted two and a half years and produced eleven films. Of these, only *The Caine Mutiny* (1954) was a commercial success, although *Death of a Salesman* (1951) and *The Member of the Wedding* (1952) were warmly received by critics. *The Wild One*, savagely attacked as antisocial when it was released in 1954 because of its depiction of teen violence, later became a cult classic.

Kramer left the "dubious shelter" of studio productions in 1954 and made his debut as director in *Not as a Stranger* (1955), seen by some as an indictment of the medical profession. The film cost $2 million to make and grossed $50 million. Kramer's startling success heartened independent producers at a time in which the Hollywood studio system was disintegrating. The Paramount Consent Decree had stripped theaters from the vertically integrated studios that owned them. Even worse for the studios, half of American moviegoers now stayed home and watched television. Independent producers who worked economically on popular projects began to work vigorously in this new cinematic terrain.

Kramer considered the motion picture industry "the most frightened and easily intimidated of any major industry in the United States." That was why he found himself drawn to material that could entertain while provoking its audience to think. He failed to achieve this outcome with his next film as producer-director. *The Pride and the Passion* (1957), depicting Spain's War of Independence, went $1 million over budget and lacked, in Kramer's view, "a really human dimension." Kramer's next four films, however, solidified his growing stature among critics as one of the few filmmakers prepared to examine serious social issues. Kramer explored race relations in *The Defiant Ones* (1958); nuclear annihilation in *On the Beach* (1959); the struggle between faith and science in *Inherit the Wind* (1960); and Nazi war crimes in *Judgment at Nuremberg* (1961).

Spencer Tracy received Oscar nominations for his portrayals of defense attorney Clarence Darrow in *Inherit the Wind* and an earnest American judge in *Judgment at Nuremberg*. It was the beginning of the most satisfying collaboration of Kramer's career. He considered Tracy the greatest actor with whom he had ever worked, and they became close personal friends. Kramer sought properties that could star Tracy and found two more. The veteran actor was the straight man in Kramer's wildly manic and highly profitable *It's a Mad, Mad, Mad, Mad World!* (1963) and the self-doubting liberal father of a daughter who wants to marry a black man in *Guess Who's Coming to Dinner?* (1967). Tracy was posthumously nominated for an Oscar in his final film, and co-star Katharine Hepburn won an Academy Award for her performance.

The films that Kramer produced without Tracy, *Pressure Point* (1962), *A Child Is Waiting* (1963), and *Invitation to a Gunfighter* (1964) seemed to lack his characteristic substance and moral force. Only *Ship of Fools* (1965), which Kramer produced and directed, was a critical success. None of Kramer's six remaining films were particularly memorable. *The Secret of Santa Vittoria* (1969); *R.P.M.* (1970); *Bless the Beasts and Children* (1971), a film celebrated by animal rights activists; *Oklahoma Crude* (1973); *The Domino Principle* (1977); and *The Runner Stumbles* (1979) triumphed neither at the box office nor among critics. His television work in the 1970s, particularly *The Trial of Julius and Ethel Rosenberg* (1974) and *The Court-Martial of Lt. William Calley* (1975), fared somewhat better.

Kramer's thirty-five films received sixteen Oscars and eighty-five Academy Award nominations, including six for best producer and three for best director. In 1962 Kramer received the Irving G. Thalberg Memorial Award for outstanding work in film. He also received the Producers Guild of America's David O. Selznick Lifetime Achievement Award. *High Noon*, *Guess Who's Coming to Dinner?*, and *It's a Mad, Mad, Mad, Mad World!* made the American Film Institute list of one hundred best movies of all time.

Kramer married actress Ann Pearce in 1950; their twelve-year marriage ended in divorce. They had two children. In 1966 he married actress Karen Sharpe. They had two daughters, one of whom was named after his friend Katharine Hepburn. Kramer retired from movie making in the early 1980s and moved his family to Seattle, where he had his own radio show and taught filmmaking at Bellevue Community College. In the late 1990s Kramer wrote his autobiography and lived in the Motion Picture Home, a retirement community for those who had worked in the film industry. He died in Woodland Hills, a suburb of Los Angeles.

In 1960 Kramer told interviewers, "I don't make films to stir the world," but by the mid-1990s he hoped he would be remembered as a provocateur who "knew how to use a film as a real weapon against discrimination, hatred, prejudice and excessive power." The actor Sidney Poitier thought Kramer's work "a testament to courage, to integrity, honesty, and determination." The director Steven Spielberg believed that Kramer had inspired a generation of independent filmmakers "with an art and passion" that transcended movies and stirred "the conscience of the world."

• Kramer's papers are in the Department of Special Collections, Young Research Library, University of California at Los Angeles. His autobiography, *A Mad, Mad, Mad, Mad World: A Life in Hollywood* (1997), was written with Thomas M. Coffey. It says little of his personal life and focuses almost exclusively on the making of his films. Donald Spoto's *Stanley Kramer: Film Maker* (1978; repr. 1990) takes a similar approach. Kramer discusses his craft and work with Spencer Tracy in Roy Newquist et al., *A Special Kind of Magic* (1967). Alvin H. Marrill compiled Kramer's filmography for Herbert G. Luft, "Stanley Kramer," a historical summary of Kramer's work in Hollywood that appeared in *Films in Review* (Mar. 1985), pp. 131–47. Kramer's early life and career are chronicled in *Current Biography 1951* (1952), pp. 356–58. Early appreciations include Ezra Goodman, "Champion Producer," *New York Times*, 10 Apr. 1949, p. 4, and Bosley Crowther, "'A' Movies on 'B' Budgets," *New York Times Magazine*, 12 Nov. 1950, pp. 24, 38–40. An obituary is in the *New York Times*, 21 Feb. 2001, and a career appreciation is in the *Chicago Tribune*, 23 Feb. 2001.

BRUCE J. EVENSEN

KRENEK, Ernst (23 Aug. 1900–22 Dec. 1991), composer and librettist, was born Ernst Heinrich Křenek in Vienna, Austria, the son of Ernst Josef Křenek, an officer in the Quartermaster Corps of the Austro-Hungarian army, and Emanuela Josefa Auguste Cizek. At the age of six he began piano lessons with his mother, which continued with one of the teachers when he entered a private school run by the Christian Brothers. By 1908 he had begun writing short piano pieces that his mother notated for him and in 1910 began studying with a teacher at the Kaiser's Music School. By 1916 Krenek had decided to become a composer. Because Arnold Schoenberg was in the Austrian army, Krenek studied with Franz Schreker, a popular composer of romantic operas. Schreker's emphasis on counterpoint prepared Krenek for his encounter with a book on counterpoint by Ernst Kurth, who stressed that music comprised precisely planned streams of energy represented in carefully controlled tonal patterns and that each note had to serve a purpose. Krenek's works of this time (1917–1919) are mostly sketches for songs and piano pieces, and they reflect these principles.

In the spring of 1918 Krenek was drafted into the Austrian army despite his father's efforts to keep him out. When his training was completed he was posted to Vienna, where he continued his music studies. In 1920 Schreker was appointed director of the National Academy of Music in Berlin, and Krenek followed him to continue his studies. His two years in Berlin were an important period of maturing: he attended the salon of pianist and composer Ferruccio Busoni, met the young conductor Hermann Scherchen, and befriended pianists Eduard Erdmann and Artur Schnabel; all had significant effects on his life.

In 1921 Krenek's First String Quartet, Opus 6, was performed at a music festival in Nuremberg, Germany. The piece made Krenek instantly famous and was reviewed in more than fifty publications. Its stark dissonances and vigorous rhythms show the influence of Krenek's study of Béla Bartók's quartets. The celebrity resulted in a contract with Universal Edition, which published all of Krenek's music until the Nazis took control of Austria in 1937. During the early 1920s he composed four string quartets; three symphonies; a piano concerto; the operas *Zwingburg* (about social upheaval and freedom), *Der Sprung über den Schatten* (he wrote his own text, about a psychologist who liberates his patients), and *Orpheus und Eurydike* (text by Oscar Kokoschka); and several songs, piano pieces, and smaller orchestral works.

In 1922 Krenek met Anna Mahler, a painter and daughter of composer Gustav Mahler. Anna's mother Alma, asked Krenek to prepare Gustav's incomplete Tenth Symphony for performance and introduced him to composer Alban Berg. That same year Krenek was invited to join the board of the newly formed International Society for Contemporary Music (ISCM), and throughout his life he remained an active member. In 1923 the Second Symphony, Opus 12, his most ambitious symphony, was performed at a music festival in Kassel. In December he received a stipend from arts patron Werner Reinhart to spend a year in Switzerland writing music, and in 1924 he met the poet Rainer Maria Rilke and the music philosopher Theodor Adorno. In mid-January 1924 he married Anna Mahler; they divorced less than a year later.

In early 1925 Krenek traveled to Paris, where he met the group of composers known as "Les Six" and as a result decided that his musical style should become more accessible. At the 1925 Congress for Aesthetics Krenek made satirical comments about twelve-tone music, which angered Schoenberg and served to estrange them until they met again in Los Angeles as exiles. In 1924, in spite of great fame as an "advanced" composer of atonal music with many performances of his music, Krenek, who needed money, worked as assistant to Paul Bekker, director of the State Opera.

Krenek returned to tonality with his opera *Jonny spielt auf* (1927); this marked the beginning of his self-called "Neoromantic" period, which was influenced by his study of Franz Schubert. *Jonny spielt auf* (about the contrast between "serious" and popular music and the adventures of a black American violinist) was an immediate success and was quickly produced in more than 100 cities. He immediately began composing three one-act operas to capitalize on his success: *Der Diktator* (loosely based on Benito Mussolini), the fairy tale *Das geheime Königreich*, and the satire on sports hero-worship *Schwergewicht, oder Die Ehre der Nation*.

In 1928 Krenek settled in Vienna and completed his grand opera *Leben des Orest* to his own text and *Reisebuch aus den österreichischen Alpen*, a cycle of twenty songs extolling the Austrian countryside in the style of Franz Schubert's *Winterreise*. In August 1928 he married an actress, Berta Haas (or Hermann, as she was known on the stage). At the end of 1928 Krenek and Adorno began a published debate, Krenek defending the creator's responsibility to be true to his personal standards of artistic merit and Adorno arguing that the composer was responsible to the conditions of the times.

From 1930 through 1933 Krenek contributed to the arts page of the newspaper *Frankfurter Zeitung*. He also composed his Romantic Fifth String Quartet, Opus 65, and a satiric opera on the 1918 collapse of the Austrian regime, *Kehraus um St. Stephan*.

On his return to Vienna in 1929, Krenek became good friends with composers Alban Berg and Anton Webern. His discussions with them, Adorno, and his friend Willi Reich led him to adopt the twelve-tone system. He received a commission from the Vienna State Opera to write an opera based on the life of the Holy Roman Emperor Karl V (1500–1558), reflecting the disintegration of society and the Austrian condition. Believing that he had exhausted tonality, he composed *Karl V*, the first completed twelve-tone opera. Owing to political events, the opera's production was cancelled and did not take place until 1938 in Prague.

In 1932 Krenek, with Berg, Rudolph Ploderer, and Reich, founded *23 (Dreiundzwanzig)*, a satirical magazine; it was published until 1937. With the ascent of the Nazis in Germany in 1933, Krenek was branded as a radical artist; his music was banned as "degenerate," and he was no longer allowed to write for the *Frankfurter Zeitung*. In 1936 Krenek was asked to prepare an edition of Monteverdi's *L'incoronazione di Poppea* for the Salzburg Opera Guild's trip to the United States the following year. He traveled with the company to America, presented lecture recitals, and wrote his impressions and experiences for the *Wiener Zeitung*. On his visit to Los Angeles, he became enamored of the American West.

Soon after his return to Europe, the Nazis annexed Austria, and Krenek immigrated to the United States. By 1938 he was teaching at the Malkin Conservatory in Boston and, in 1939, the University of Michigan Summer School, where his students included George Perle and Robert Erickson; from 1939 to 1942 he taught at Vassar College. In Vassar's library he studied the music of Johannes Ockeghem (1430–1495), which influenced his masterful a cappella work on biblical texts, *Lamentatio Jeremiae prophetae*, Opus 93, an experiment in row rotations that anticipated the serialism of Pierre Boulez and Karlheinz Stockhausen.

In 1942 Krenek was appointed dean of music at Hamline University in St. Paul, Minnesota, where he taught until 1947. His students included Wilbur Ogdon, Glenn Glasow, Gladys Nordenstrom, and Robert Erickson. He soon formed close friendships with Dimitri Mitropoulos, the conductor of the Minneapolis Symphony Orchestra, and violinist Louis Krasner. Together the three founded the Minneapolis chapter of the ISCM.

In 1945 Krenek became a U.S. citizen, and he dropped the hachek above the "r" in his name. The Hamline years were very productive; major works included the impassioned *Cantata for Wartime*, Opus 95; Seventh String Quartet, Opus 96; *Santa Fe Time Table*, Opus 102; *Symphonic Elegy*, Opus 105, dedicated to Anton Webern; the chamber opera *What Price Confidence?*; and the Fourth Symphony, Opus 113.

In 1947 Krenek went to Hollywood at the encouragement of George Antheil, whom he had met in 1927, hoping to support himself by composing for films. Instead he was obliged to take teaching positions in obscure Los Angeles schools. Other than guest lectureships, of which there were many, his last academic appointment was at the Chicago Musical College in 1949; but he left by December because of the weather.

In 1950 Krenek determined to live permanently in the Los Angeles area. He divorced his wife and married composer Gladys Nordenstrom on 8 August. He returned to Europe for the first time since World War II and taught in the Darmstadt Summer School for New Music, which invigorated him.

During the 1950s Krenek's most important works were written to commission and included the chamber operas *Dark Waters* and *The Bell Tower*; Fifth and Sixth Piano Sonatas, Opus 121 and Opus 128; several concertos; *Medea*, Opus 129, a dramatic monologue commissioned by soprano Blanche Thebom for soprano with orchestra; and *Eleven Transparencies* for orchestra. The major work of this period, the opera *Pallas Athene weint*, was commissioned by the Hamburg State Opera; a parable on the downfall of democracy dedicated to Adlai Stevenson, it premiered in 1955.

The pivotal event in Krenek's postwar compositional style was an invitation by composer Herbert Eimert to work in his Cologne electronic music studio in 1955; it resulted in *Spiritus Intelligentiae Sanctus*, Opus 152, premiered in an electronic music concert in 1956. Working in the electronic medium provided an impetus for him to develop a serial style when its instigators were mostly abandoning it. He became interested in the dialectic of predetermination and chance, as well as the significance of time. It was as Christian Gauss lecturer at Princeton University in spring 1957 that Krenek learned of the sestina, a medieval poetic form that seemed to him to be compatible with serialism. His *Sestina*, Opus 161, for soprano and ensemble to his own text, combined row rotations with the medieval form. He used serialism for many works in the ensuing nine years. In 1958 Krenek renewed his friendship with Igor Stravinsky, whom he had met in the 1920s, and helped him learn twelve-tone and serial techniques. In 1959 Krenek returned to Princeton to lecture at the Seminars in Advanced Musical Studies.

In 1960 Krenek received several honors, including the Silver Medal of Austria, the Gold Medal of Vienna, and memberships in the Berlin Academy of

Arts, Austrian State Academy of Music in Vienna, and National Institute of Arts and Letters in New York. In 1966 he moved to Palm Springs, and on his advice Robert Erickson and Wilbur Ogdon were recruited to found the music department at the University of California, San Diego (UCSD).

During this time Krenek composed eight significant orchestral works, five major works for soprano and ensemble, two electronic works (along with several other works that included electronic music), and two television operas, *Ausgerechnet und verspielt* and *Der Zauberspiegel* (on the clash between chance and order.) He also received commissions from the Hamburg State Opera for the operas *Der goldene Bock*, premiered in 1964, and *Sardakai, oder Das kommt davon*, premiered in 1970. His interest in serialism and time was often reflected in the titles of his ensemble and orchestral music of this period, such as *Quaestio temporis*, Opus 170, *From Three Make Seven*, Opus 177, and *Instant Remembered*, Opus 201 (with soprano). These works used timbres structurally, and some left parameters open to free manipulation or offered performers various possibilities for combining composed elements.

For approximately the last twenty years of his life, Krenek's compositional style became more relaxed, although he continued to use twelve-tone and serial techniques. He became more introspective and autobiographical in both his writings and his compositions, such as the song cycle *Spätlese*, Opus 218, written for Dietrich Fischer-Dieskau. His last works are a true "late harvest," consisting of three major orchestral works, including the autobiographical *Arc of Life*, Opus 234, and major vocal works, including the humorous television opera *Flaschenpost vom Paradies*, the satirical, funny chamber opera *They Knew What They Wanted*, and the autobiographical *Dissembler*, Opus 229 (for baritone and piano). He summarized his life in the Eighth String Quartet, Opus 233, which quoted from his other quartets, and in the monumental oratorio *Opus sine nomine*, Opus 238, which was his last large work.

Krenek continued to receive honors, though few came from the United States. There were Krenek Festivals in Europe and America and an appointment as Regent's Lecturer at UCSD in 1970, which resulted in four lectures published as *Horizons Circled* in 1974. In 1978 his Archive was established at UCSD, and another in 1980 at the Vienna City Library. The annual Krenek Prize for composition was established by Vienna in 1986. He died in Palm Springs and was buried in a state funeral in the composer's section of the great Vienna cemetery.

Despite the Nazis' ban, Krenek's music has survived and is often played. Stravinsky was convinced that Krenek's stature would be recognized, which has been true in Europe. However, his music has been neglected in the United States, partly because he lived in Palm Springs, which was outside the main American musical current, and he held no steady academic appointment. Although he lived in America for the majority of his life and wrote some two-thirds of his 242 opus numbers there, he is not viewed as an American composer. In addition, he is accused of writing in too many idioms and not having a unified "voice" in his music. Yet Krenek's sound is uniquely his own.

• Krenek's music and literary manuscripts are in the Vienna Stadt- und Landesbibliothek, the Library of Congress, and the Geisel Library at the University of California, San Diego. His autobiography was published in part as "Self analysis," *New Mexico Quarterly* 23 (1953): 5–57, and in its entirety in German as *Im Atem der Zeit* (1998). His diaries in German and English are published as *Die amerikanischen Tagebücher, 1937–1942; Dokumente aus dem Exil*, ed. Claudia Maurer Zenck (1992). Collections of essays by Krenek in English are *Exploring Music* (1966) and *Music Here and Now* (1939); a compilation of his lectures on twentieth-century music is *Horizons Circled: Reflections on My Music* (1974). For the German reader his collection of travel essays *Gedanken unterwegs: Dokumente einer Reise* (1959) shows a different side of him. His important treatise on twelve-tone music is *Studies in Counterpoint: Based on the Twelve-tone Technique* (1940).

An excellent biography is John L. Stewart, *Ernst Krenek: The Man and His Music* (1991). An extensive bibliography is Garrett Bowles, *Ernst Krenek: A Bio-bibliography* (1989). The importance of Krenek's opera *Jonny spielt auf* is discussed in Susan C. Cook, *Opera for a New Republic: The Zeitopern of Krenek, Weill, and Hindemith* (1988), and the reception of *Karl V* is discussed in Claudia Maurer Zenck, "The Ship Loaded with Faith and Hope: Krenek's *Karl V* and the Viennese Politics of the Thirties," *Musical Quarterly* 71 (1985): 116–34. The Ernst Krenek Society in San Diego publishes the biannual *Ernst Krenek Newsletter*. An obituary is in the *New York Times*, 24 Dec. 1991.

GARRETT H. BOWLES

KURTZ, Frank (1911–31 Oct. 1996), athlete, military aviator, was born Frank Allen Kurtz in Davenport, Iowa, the son of Frank Kurtz, Sr., an insurance salesman, and Dora Kurtz (maiden name unknown). His parents divorced shortly after he was born. Kurtz ran away from home at the age of twelve to hawk newspapers in Kansas City, Missouri. Possessed of youthful dynamism, he was soon featured in the *Kansas City Star* as one of its best newsboys. Around this time Kurtz took an interest in swimming and exhibited great potential as a diver. At the behest of Olympic champion swimmer Johnny Weissmuller (the future *Tarzan* movie actor), he moved to Los Angeles to train under noted diving coach Clyde Swendsen of the Hollywood Athletic Club. Kurtz flourished under his tutelage and took the bronze medal at the 1932 Olympic Games in Los Angeles. Around this time he attended the University of Southern California, where he met Margo Rogers, also a student there. In 1938 they married.

Kurtz had also expressed an interest in aviation and received flight instruction at the age of sixteen under the auspices of Frank Birely, an orange drink magnate. By 1935 Kurtz had established several aerial speed and distance records. Two years later he joined the U.S. Army Air Corps. In December 1941 Kurtz was flying Boeing B-17D heavy bombers with the 19th

Bombardment Group while stationed at Clark Field in the Philippines. This plane was an early version of the soon-to-be-famous strategic weapon, lacking both self-sealing fuel tanks and a defensive tail turret. He survived the surprise Japanese air attack on 8 December 1941, which destroyed most American air power in the Far East, and subsequently conducted bombing and rescue missions in the Philippines and Java. In the spring of 1942 Kurtz was based in Australia, where his career became indelibly associated with a famous B-17, serial number 40–3097. This hybrid craft was rebuilt with parts cannibalized from damaged B-17s. It was christened the "Swoose" (a name that originated with a song recorded by the Kay Kyser band about an unhappy bird that was half swan and half goose).

Kurtz established himself as one of the most daring B-17 pilots of the Pacific War by ferrying General George H. Brett, Commander of Allied Air Forces in Australia, and various congressional dignitaries in and out of combat zones around Port Moresby, New Guinea. It was during one of these flights, while transporting Congressman Lyndon Baines Johnson (the future president), that the Swoose suffered from navigational malfunctions and had to make an emergency landing in the Australian outback. The plane was repaired and in May 1942 Kurtz used it to establish a speed record by flying between Sydney, Australia, and Wellington, New Zealand, in 5 hours and 10 minutes. There the Swoose was stripped entirely of armament to save weight, and Kurtz established another nonstop record by reaching Honolulu, Hawaii, in 23 hours and 7 minutes. A passenger on these flights was English Air Chief Marshal Sir Charles Burnett, Royal Air Force, whose return to England from a tour of the Pacific was greatly expedited. On 4 August 1942, Kurtz took the Swoose out of the Pacific theater completely by landing in the United States, rendering it the first four-engine bomber to return home from the war front. He also set another Pacific speed record of 36 hours and 10 minutes to Hamilton Field, California, from Australia.

While home on leave in 1943, Kurtz basked in his wartime celebrity and toured the country selling war bonds. The following year he became the father of Swoosie Kurtz, named after his famous aircraft. (She became an award-winning actress.) He subsequently volunteered for duty in Italy and was assigned to the 463rd Bomb Group, soon popularly regarded as the "Swoose Group." Kurtz completed an additional sixty missions before transferring stateside as commander of Kirtland Air Force Base in Albuquerque, New Mexico. There he was responsible for providing aerial support for the Manhattan Project, which ultimately devised the first atomic bomb. By war's end, Kurtz was among the U.S. Army Air Forces' most highly decorated pilots, having received five presidential citations, three Air Medals, three Silver Stars, three Distinguished Flying Crosses, and the French Croix de Guerre.

After the war Kurtz settled in Los Angeles, where he was a long-time employee of the General Electric Corporation. In 1946, on learning that the Swoose was about to be decommissioned and sent to the smelter, he arranged for the city government to purchase the craft as a war memorial at March Field in Riverside, California. He was also active in Olympic affairs for many years and finally retired from the air force in 1960 with a rank of colonel. He died at his home in Toluca Lake. The Swoose, the oldest B-17 bomber extant, has since been transferred to the Paul E. Garber preservation, restoration, and storage facility of the Smithsonian Institution at Silver Hills, Maryland.

• There are no known collections of Kurtz's personal papers or records. The Archives, National Air and Space Museum, Smithsonian Institution, however, maintains a file of clippings, letters, and other materials about him. Among his published writings are "Randolph Prepares Young Men for Kelly, Dream Field of all Flying Cadets," *U.S. Air Services* 23 (Apr. 1938): 12–14; "Captain Frank Kurtz on the Job in Australia," *U.S. Air Services* 27 (Aug. 1942): 14, 46; and "Operation 30," *Boeing* magazine 19 (Apr. 1949): 8–9, 14. The best published accounts of his wartime exploits are W. L. White, *Queens Die Proudly* (1943), and Herbert S. Brownstein, *The Swoose: Odyssey of a B-17* (1993). For greater historical context, see Gene E. Salecker, *Fortress against the Sun: The B-17 Flying Fortress in the Pacific* (2000). A personal perspective of events by his wife is in Margo Kurtz, *My Rival, the Sky* (1945). Useful obituaries are in the *New York Times*, 9 Nov. 1996, and *People* magazine, 25 Nov. 1996.

JOHN C. FREDRIKSEN

L

LAKE, Margaret Maiki Souza Aiu (28 May 1925–20 June 1984), master of Hawaiian hula (dance), was born Margaret Maiki Souza in Honolulu, Hawaii, the daughter of Peter Charles Souza and Cecilia Paiʻohe Gilman Souza. Lake was raised in Palolo Valley, Honolulu, in a traditional Hawaiian manner of hanai or "adoption," by a maternal grandaunt, Cecilia Rose Mahoe, and her husband, John William Kealoha, whose children had died. Lake considered them her "grandparents," but upon their deaths she returned to her biological mother. She was educated at St. Francis Convent School, a Catholic school for girls, and lived there with the sisters for three and a half years. She later lived in the care of another grandaunt, Helen Pamaieulu Haʻo Correa, a keeper of the Blessed Sacrament Church (Catholic) in Pauoa Valley, Honolulu. Lake called her aunt "Tutu," an affectionate and familial Hawaiian term for a grandparent.

Lake was fourteen or fifteen years old when two events directed her toward the hula. First, World War II brought a demand for entertainment hula for the visiting and recuperating servicemen. She and her cousins danced "professionally" at the Club Pago Pago in Honolulu. Second, one of these cousins, Nellie Wong, met Roselie Lokalia Montgomery, a master hula instructor of the ancient or traditional form of hula. Lake, who studied with Montgomery, recalled: "Hula of the day of the kings was just a memory to some of the old timers then. The old hula lived only in the talent of a few masters. Fortunately, these were training a small number in spite of the odds against their ever putting their learning to good use" (*Honolulu Advertiser*, 3 Aug. 1973).

Lake was trained in a full range of the ancient and traditional hula. In 1943, at the age of eighteen, she graduated (ʻuniki) as an ʻolapa or dancer. She entertained at the Club Pago Pago for eight years, while she continued to study, learn dances, and seek mentorship from several masters of the time.

Lake had married, but she kept this first marriage private. The name of her first husband is not known. On 21 February 1947 she married Rodney P. Boniface Aiu, a communications chief and later fire chief of the city and county of Honolulu. They adopted two boys and had five children of their own.

During her training as a dancer of ancient hula, Lake, a devoted Christian, encountered difficulty in practicing the traditional rituals and prayers to the goddess of hula, Laka. She brought this problem to "Tutu" Helen, who helped her reconcile the Christian and Hawaiian beliefs and traditions. "I was determined from that night forward to study and search further for information relating to my studies of the hula, to try to understand the teaching of my kumu, and to please her," Lake recalled (Ariyoshi, p. 37). She had been studying to become a nurse, but with the encouragement of Helen Correa, Lake began to teach the hula to members of the Hawaiian Club at the Blessed Sacrament Church, and they gave public performances at the church and other locations in Honolulu. Soon individuals requested private hula instruction. In 1946 Margaret Aiu's Hula Studio was established at the church.

Lake was an innovator in the performance and teaching of hula. With the help and encouragement of Tutu Helen, Lake adopted the hula *kuʻi* that combined old and new steps with the "mannerisms of 1800's" (Ariyoshi, p. 63). She employed a new teaching style that departed from the traditional recital and memorization. Her students learned Hawaiian genealogies, culture, mannerisms, legends, poetry, and the "beauties of our own Hawaii" (Ariyoshi, p. 73). Lake instituted written instructions because she had been advised by Mary Kawena Pukui, a Hawaiian cultural authority and her mentor, that, since the Hawaiian language was no longer spoken, it would be better to have things written down. Lake put up a blackboard in the studio, which was unheard of, and required that her students conduct individual research, on which they were tested once a month. If they failed, they were obliged to leave.

The demand for instruction increased. In 1948 Lake raised tuition from $5 to $8 and moved the studio to a larger room over a neighborhood supermarket in Makiki, Honolulu. Continuing her involvement in professional entertainment, she spent the weekends on the island of Kauai, where she danced at the Hawaiian Town Club. In 1952 she received permission from her teachers to change the name of her dance studio to Halau Hula o Maiki. However, a sign painter reversed the wording to read "Hula Halau o Maiki," and out of aloha (courtesy) for him, she kept it as he had painted it.

Lake's creativity and innovation in hula were demonstrated when her dancers gave a first-time performance adapted to the song "Kaulana Nâ Pua" at Kapiʻolani Park near Waikiki. This song had been composed in the nineteenth century as a protest of the overthrow of the Hawaiian kingdom. This sober song, though nearly forgotten, was given to Lake by Vickie Ii Rodrigues, a mentor. Rodrigues "urged her to choreograph it and costume the production in the style of 1880s." She recalled that it "was received with biting criticism." The next day, they performed a dance in honor of King Kalakaua, "Iâ ʻoe e ka Lâ," for a Lei Day program at city hall, using "white gowns of the missionary period." The audience ridiculed the "nightgowns," and Lake "ducked behind the shrubbery and wept" (*Honolulu Advertiser*, 3 Aug. 1973).

In 1953, using the experience in staging tableaus and pageants she had gained at church, Lake worked with Kamokila Campbell, a well-respected authority on Hawaiian traditions, to choreograph a dance production entitled "The Polynesian Ballet of Hawaii." The Hula Halau moved again, this time to a room over a live poultry shop.

Lake was active in the staging of the annual Aloha Week parade and in 1957 played the role of Queen Kapiolani during the Aloha Week pageant at 'Iolani Palace. She considered the 1962 Aloha Week pageant produced by John Kneubuhl, a respected Hollywood screen playwright of Hawaiian-Samoan ancestry, as her "greatest work." She directed the choreography, trained the chanters, and even designed the queen's wardrobe (*Honolulu Star-Bulletin*, 20 Apr. 1963).

On 16 November 1967 Lake and her husband divorced. She met Haywood Kahauanu Lake, a well-known entertainer, and they married on 15 June 1972, the same year her first student graduated as a *kumuhula* (teacher) from the Hula Halau. In 1974 the dance school moved to a room above a radiator shop, and the sign was corrected to Halau Hula o Maiki. During this year she was employed by Paradise Park, a theme park in Mânoa Valley, Honolulu, to supervise all their Hawaiian cultural activities.

In August 1978 Lake's dream of creating a cultural center dedicated to hula was realized when she opened Hâlau Hawaii in Waikiki. She combined a standard halau operation with exhibits of Hawaiian arts and crafts, a research library, the Maiki Hall for hula performances, rooms for different types of hula, and a store (Ariyoshi, p. 64). Unfortunately the market for cultural tourism was limited at that time, and Hâlau Hawaii closed in 1979. The sisters at St. Francis High School remembered their former student in her distress and extended their facilities for the Hâlau to continue. The "dance academy" was reestablished on 15 April 1979. It moved again in May 1982 to Puck's Alley in Mô'ili'ili, Honolulu. Lake died of a heart attack just before the staging of what was to have been her "last" public concert.

The list of graduates of Halau Hula o Maiki includes many of Hawaii's prominent entertainers. Lake also has been recognized by many as the "Mother of Hawaiian Renaissance" for her leadership in the revival and transmission of ancient traditions and culture. Her innovation in hula shifted the focus to the dancer and the dance movement, as in ballet and modern dance, thereby enlivening it and making it popular among a new generation. This innovation became a standard for modern hula. However, she maintained that she was a traditionalist. "What I am trying to do is to preserve and maintain the old way of dancing, which our elders taught us. I want to share my knowledge and my pupils with the public," she said (*Honolulu Advertiser*, 21 June 1984).

• For further information on Lake see Rita Ariyoshi, *Hula Is Life: The Story of Hâlau Hula o Maiki* (1998); Silva Wendell and Ailen Suemori, *Nana I Na Loea Hula* (1984); Ka'upena Wong and Kahuanu Lake, *Maiki, Chants and Mele of Hawaii* (1992); Adrienne L. Kaeppler, *Hula Pahu: Hawaiian Drum Dances*, vol. 1, *Ha'a and Hula Pahu Sacred Movements* (1993); the *Honolulu Advertiser*, 3 Aug. 1973; and the *Honolulu Star-Bulletin*, 20 Apr. 1963. An obituary is in the *Honolulu Advertiser*, 21 June 1984.

MALCOLM N. CHUN

LAME DEER, John Fire (1903–15 Dec. 1976), coauthor of a popular account of American Indian life, was born with the Lakota name Tahca Ushte (Lame Deer) and the English name John Fire on the Lakota reservation in southwestern South Dakota, the son of Silas Let-Them-Have-Enough and Sally Red Blanket. He was one of twelve children, but many of his siblings did not reach maturity and others died in early adulthood. He was raised in large part by his maternal grandparents, Good Fox and Plenty White Buffalo, in a small log cabin located on or near the border between the Pine Ridge and Rosebud reservations. Around the age of eight, he was forced by an agent of the Bureau of Indian Affairs to go to a school where the main focus was on discipline and where no teacher was capable of teaching at any level higher than the third grade. After six years in this school, he was sent to a white boarding school, where he became increasingly rebellious. Apparently he stayed only two years.

In 1920 his mother died of tuberculosis, leaving him with his grandparents, his father, and a sister. His father, a Hunkpapa Lakota (his mother was a Minneconjou Lakota), went north to his relatives in the Standing Rock reservation, splitting his land and livestock between his two children. These possessions were not especially significant to Lame Deer. Before the 1887 passage of the Dawes Allotment Act, which checkerboarded reservations into individually owned lots, the Lakota, like most other Indians, had no privately owned and saleable land. The land they were allotted was not in fact saleable until twenty-five years after the passage of the act, a measure intended to prevent white speculators from buying up the reservations. But that measure expired shortly after the departure of Lame Deer's father, and Lame Deer, with little or no attachment to the concept underlying the deed to the land, quickly sold it. He had a much deeper attachment to cattle-raising, but as more and more whites took possession of Indian land, barbedwire fences crisscrossed the formerly open range, and the recently established tradition of the collective roundup became impossible to maintain. He sold the livestock too.

His experience of forced confinement in highly regimented government-run schools had already led him to associate free movement with Indianness, and the fencing of the range confirmed that association. What followed was an explosive twenty-year period of roaming and experimentation that frequently took him away from Lakota territory and tradition but provided him with what he thought of as a crucial expression of his Indianness. Over this period, he was a cross-dressing rodeo clown, a member of the peyote church, a tribal policeman, a bootlegger, a sign painter, and a sheepherder, among other things. Around 1930, he was dragged back into the world of white confinement when he was convicted of car theft and jailed for nine months in Chillicothe, Ohio. But after one more experience of this kind—a brief conscription in the army in 1942—the institutions of the white world no longer confined him in such literal, physical ways. From this point on, the freedom of his body from such enclosures would be less an issue than the freedom of his spirit from subtler enclosures, such as consumerism, domesticity, and racial prejudice.

At sixteen, he had gone on a vision quest and experienced a spiritual visitation that made him, at least potentially, a *wicasa wakan*, or holy man. At intervals during his period of roaming, he had received more specific instruction in Lakota spirituality, much of it in *yuwipi* healing, which centers around the power of stones. After leaving the army, he began to take these practices more seriously; in his as-told-to autobiography, *Lame Deer: Seeker of Visions* (1972), he says that this was the moment in his life when he finally "settled down to [his] only full-time job—being an Indian" (p. 59). But rather than associating Indianness with the freedom of "a common, wild, natural human being" (p. 38), as he had during the heyday of his "find-out," he now tended to associate it with "clinging to our old Sioux ways—singing the ancient songs correctly, conducting a sweat-lodge ceremony as it should be, making our old beliefs as pure, as clear and true as I possibly can, making them stay alive, saving them from extinction" (pp. 205–06).

Lame Deer had one child, Archie Fire Lame Deer, born out of wedlock in 1935 to Josephine Quick Bear.

In 1967, while in New York to participate in Martin Luther King's peace march, Lame Deer met the 55-year-old Viennese artist Richard Erdoes. A friendship quickly sprang up between the two men, and around 1969, after a series of visits, Lame Deer convinced Erdoes to help him write a book about his life and about Lakota culture. That book, *Lame Deer: Seeker of Visions*, became a high-water mark of the association between the American-Indian civil rights movement and the white counterculture. In it, Lame Deer and Erdoes combine an entertaining account of Lame Deer's life, emphasizing wildness, pleasure, and freedom, with a quasi-anthropological account of Lakota customs, emphasizing sacred recurrence and tribal values. This mixture made it attractive to general readers, and before his death in Winner, South Dakota, Lame Deer had achieved a measure of national fame.

The book's popularity grew steadily after his death and has survived the critic Julian Rice's demonstration that Lame Deer and Erdoes's treatment of Lakota customs is heavily indebted to earlier anthropological literature. Despite its questionable origins, the book continues to be both a good read and a revealing account of the tension between freedom and belonging in twentieth-century American-Indian life.

• For representative reviews of the book, see the *New York Times Book Review*, 18 Mar. 1973, p. 37, and the *Times Literary Supplement*, 6 July 1973, p. 780. Scholarly accounts include Julian Rice, "A Ventriloquy of Anthros: Densmore, Dorsey, Lame Deer, and Erdoes," *American Indian Quarterly* 18 (1994): 169–96, and Timothy Sweet, "Ghost Dance?: Photography, Agency, and Authenticity in *Lame Deer: Seeker of Visions*," *Modern Fiction Studies* 40 (1994): 493–508. A personal account of Lame Deer may be found in Richard Erdoes and Archie Fire Lame Deer, *Gift of Power: The Life and Teachings of a Lakota Medicine Man* (1992). An obituary is in the *New York Times*, 16 Dec. 1976.

GEOFF SANBORN

LARDNER, Ring, Jr. (19 Aug. 1915–31 Oct. 2000), screenwriter, was born Ringgold Wilmer Lardner, Jr., in Chicago, Illinois, the son of Ringgold Wilmer Lardner, a writer and journalist, and Ellis Abbott Lardner. He and his three brothers grew up in a privileged environment of live-in servants and a nanny. Family friends included Heywood Broun, Zelda Fitzgerald and F. Scott Fitzgerald, Dorothy Parker, and H. L. Mencken. In 1919, the family moved to Greenwich, Connecticut, where they lived for two years before moving to a three-story house on two acres in Great Neck, Long Island. There they remained until 1928, when they began spending summers in East Hampton and living the rest of the year in Manhattan.

All four boys could read and write by the age of four, and all were voracious readers by six. Lardner differed from his brothers in being overweight and poorly coordinated. Naturally left-handed, he was made to write and eat with his right hand. He developed a stutter, which he minimized by taking public speaking at Phillips Academy in Andover, Massachusetts. At fourteen, he frequently slipped away from school to drink bootleg beer in a nearby town. While trying to enter a classmate's room through a window to steal treats, Lardner fell four stories, breaking his pelvis and shoulder. After graduating from high school, he entered Princeton, where he wrote for the literary and humor magazines. On the strength of that work, Alexander Woollcott recommended that the seventeen-year-old be assigned to write on college life for the 1933 inaugural issue of *Esquire*. Lardner was paid $100 for "Princeton Panorama," his first professional writing assignment.

At the end of his sophomore year, Lardner dropped out and spent the summer in Europe, witnessing anti-Semitism under Hitler in Germany and unbridled hope under communism in the Soviet Union. He enrolled at the University of Moscow's new Anglo-American Institute, where he studied crime and punishment, admiring the Soviet emphasis on reeducation and rehabilitation. In 1935, he was a reporter for the *New York Daily Mirror*, covering suicides, accidents, crime, and labor strikes. Seeing great numbers of unemployed, homeless, and hungry Americans convinced Lardner that capitalism should be replaced with a more equitable system.

Lardner went to work for movie producer David O. Selznick in California, beginning his screenwriting career in 1936 when Selznick asked Lardner and Budd Schulberg to rewrite some scenes in *A Star Is Born.* Schulberg, who was a member of the Communist party, soon recruited Lardner, and both became active, along with other Communists, in the Screen Writers Guild. Lardner's first vote in a presidential campaign was cast in 1936 for Earl Browder, the Communist party candidate. In February 1937 Lardner married Silvia Schulman, Selznick's secretary. They had two children and were divorced in 1945. In mid-1937 Lardner left Selznick for Warner Brothers, where he worked for about a year then freelanced on various projects. With Michael Kanin, Lardner co-wrote the screenplay for *Woman of the Year,* which won an Academy Award for Best Writing, Original Screenplay for 1942. Lardner missed the ceremony because he was in Virginia, writing training films for the Army. Now an award-winning screenwriter, Lardner signed a lucrative contract with Metro Goldwyn Mayer and had no trouble getting work until 1947.

In 1946, Lardner married Frances Chaney, the widow of his younger brother David, who was killed in World War II. Frances had two children; she and Lardner had one child together. In September 1947, Lardner was subpoenaed by the House Un-American Activities Committee (HUAC), chaired by J. Parnell Thomas, to answer questions about his involvement with the Communist party. Forty-one witnesses were subpoenaed; Lardner was among nineteen who indicated they would not answer questions about their political affiliations. Eleven of those nineteen were asked HUAC's famous question: "Are you now or have you ever been a member of the Communist Party?" Acting on legal advice, Lardner attempted to answer the question fully but in his own way. He was interrupted repeatedly and told that any American would be proud to answer the question. Finally he managed to give his famous response: "I could answer it, but if I did, I would hate myself in the morning" (Lardner, *I'd,* p. 9). Playwright Bertolt Brecht, who was not a citizen, left the country after giving testimony. The others, known as the Hollywood Ten, remained and were found in contempt of Congress. All ten served prison sentences and were blacklisted from the movie business for nearly twenty years. When appeals were exhausted nearly three years after his testimony, Lardner entered federal prison in Danbury, Connecticut, where he worked as a clerk. He received sixty days off his one-year sentence for good behavior and an additional fifteen-day reduction for improvements he made in rewriting prison documents. He was released in April 1951.

Although novels were not supposed to be included in the blacklisting, which Hollywood producers denied ever existed, the novel Lardner wrote in prison, *The Ecstasy of Owen Muir,* was rejected by major American publishers. Lardner wrote scripts for mov-

ies and television under pseudonyms for greatly reduced fees, but he was not hired to write in his own name until *The Cincinnati Kid,* released in 1965. His greatest success was the screenplay for the 1970 movie *M*A*S*H,* which he adapted from the novel and which won him another Oscar. Lardner was the last surviving member of the Hollywood Ten when in August 2000 the Writers Guild of America restored his writing credits and those of the seven other blacklisted writers. Lardner died at his Manhattan apartment.

• In addition to more than twenty screenplays, Lardner wrote *The Lardners: My Family Remembered* (1976); the novels *The Ecstasy of Owen Muir* (1954; 1997) and *All for Love* (1985); and *I'd Hate Myself in the Morning: A Memoir* (2000). Informative interviews are Barry Strugatz and Pat McGilligan, "Ring Lardner, Jr.: American Skeptic" in *Backstory 3: Interviews with Screenwriters of the 1960s* (1997), and Matthew J. Bruccoli, *Conversations with Writers* (1977). Notable obituaries are in the *New York Times,* 2 Nov. 2000, and *Variety,* 6 Nov. 2000).

CLAUDIA MILSTEAD

LASSWELL, Fred, Jr. (25 July 1916–4 Mar. 2001), cartoonist, was born in Kennett, Missouri, son of Fred Lasswell, a movie theater owner and farmer, and Nellie Florence Waldridge Lasswell. In 1918 the family moved to Gainesville, Florida, to a ten-acre chicken farm not yet equipped with electricity or indoor plumbing. They moved again in 1926 to Tampa, Florida, where Fred attended Seminole Heights Elementary School. Starting at age twelve, he drew cartoons and comic strips for his school newspapers. Through high school, he earned money by hawking the *Tampa Morning Tribune* on the streets in Ybor City, which, at the time, was the venue of much of Tampa's nightlife, including saloons, gambling halls, and brothels. Quitting school two weeks before his high school graduation, Lasswell worked part time in the art and engraving department of the *Tampa Daily Times* and for an advertising agency, which was so short of office space that he worked in the men's restroom, seated on a toilet with the lid down and balancing a drawing board on his lap. And that's where he was, Lasswell was fond of recounting, when Billy DeBeck found him in the late spring of 1934.

DeBeck had launched his comic strip *Barney Google* on 17 June 1919 on the sports page of the *Chicago Herald and Examiner,* but it just limped along until 1922 when Barney acquired a racehorse named Spark Plug. With suspense about the outcomes of Spark Plug's races, the strip increased in readership and circulation. In 1923, songwriter Billy Rose contributed to the celebrity of the strip with "Barney Google," a song that became a smash hit due, doubtless, to an irresistible refrain that referred to a conspicuous feature of Barney's appearance—"Barney Google with the goo goo googly eyes." Although he lived in New York, DeBeck wintered at St. Petersburg, and he was golfing near Tampa when he saw a poster that Lasswell had lettered. DeBeck hired him to letter *Barney Google*.

Lasswell became a member of the DeBeck household, and DeBeck undertook Lasswell's education, recommending books and directing him to copy accomplished pen-and-ink artists—Charles Dana Gibson, Phil May, and others—including his own work in the comic strip, which he made Lasswell copy line for line. Lasswell also enrolled in the Art Students' League in New York and the Phoenix Art Institute.

The circulation of *Barney Google* had begun to slip by 1934, so the resourceful DeBeck shifted its locale from the city and the racetrack to the backwoods of Appalachia, joining numerous other popular entertainments of the thirties in acquainting a mainstream American audience with hill country culture. In the early fall of 1934, Barney Google inherited property in the mountains of North Carolina, and when he journeyed there to inspect his estate, he encountered on November 17 a cantankerous hillbilly named Snuffy Smith and his wife Loweezy and an ensemble of picturesque characters. After Snuffy's debut, most of DeBeck's stories were set in an imaginary mountain community called Hootin' Holler. It could have been Lasswell Land: Lasswell was country. And he undoubtedly helped DeBeck to conjure up the aura of the new hillbilly locale.

Lasswell scoured used bookshops in lower Manhattan for books on hill folklore. DeBeck went through these volumes and marked words and phrases; then Lasswell entered all of these into a log book, which DeBeck later consulted for ideas and vocabulary, deploying such dialect spellings as "hit" (for "it"), "hyar" ("here"), "mought" ("might"), "orter" ("ought to"), "propitty" ("property"), and so on. Aided by his country-boy assistant, DeBeck also concocted entirely new expressions that had the ring of Appalachian argot—"daider'n a door-knob," "time's a-wastin,'" "a leetle tetched in the haid," "shif'less skonk," "bodacious idjit," "ef that don't take th' rag off'n th' bush," and others. And many of these (like "balls o'fire" and "jughaid") joined other, earlier DeBeck coinages in the popular lingo of the day ("heebie jeebies," "horsefeathers," "hotsy totsy," "osky wow wow," and "sweet mama," to cite a few). Lasswell started contributing gags and other ideas to the strip almost at once but did not solo on the strip until 1941. At that time he wrote and drew a six-week sequence (Feb.–Mar.) in which 30,000 soldiers go to Hootin' Holler for practice maneuvers and encounter hostile hillbillies who have mistaken the uniformed legions for "revenooers" bent on destroying the local distilling business.

Despite the authenticity of the strip's language, the stories and situations partook of the stereotypical portrayals of mountain men and women. Mountain men carried rifles wherever they went, and Snuffy was always willing and able to "bounce a passel of rifle balls off'n punkin haids" of miscreants in his path. Laziness, chicken thievery, stills of corn whiskey, ignorance, illiteracy, belief in ghosts and wood goblins and other supernatural creatures, feuding families, weddings of the offspring of feuding families, and stubborn individuality are frequent motifs in DeBeck's Snuffy Smith tales. Snuffy himself is the epitome of self-centered, opinionated indolence, but he became so popular with readers that by the end of the 1930s he was given equal billing with the eponymous star when the strip was retitled *Barney Google and Snuffy Smith*.

Shortly after hostilities broke out in Europe, Snuffy enlisted in the army (13 Nov. 1940); Barney joined the navy a year later (in September), and on the day after Pearl Harbor, Lasswell tried to enlist but failed the physical because of poor eyesight. By the following summer, he had joined the war effort, wrangling a job as a radio operator in Africa with Pan American Airways. In November, DeBeck died of cancer, and King Features Syndicate wired Lasswell, DeBeck's longtime assistant, to ask him to take over the strip. Lasswell promptly returned stateside where he soon managed to sign up with the Marines in order to work on *Leatherneck* magazine in Washington, D.C. (for which he created a special strip, *Hashmark*) while producing *Barney Google and Snuffy Smith* during evenings in his apartment. The first strip to carry his signature appeared on 8 March 1943. After the War, Lasswell, acting on the advice of syndicate officials, gradually eased Barney out of the strip to concentrate on the eccentric Snuffy, thereby stimulating faltering circulation. The subscription list climbed steadily, reaching more than 500 newspapers by 1964, and by its 70th anniversary in 1989, the strip (now known as *Snuffy Smith)* was in nearly 900 papers worldwide, having inspired two motion pictures and numerous animated cartoons.

Drawing upon memories of his youth and his sympathy for rural America to maintain the country folksiness of the strip, Lasswell felt at home with the hillbillies of Hootin' Holler. As Brian Walker said (in the 75th anniversary reprint volume, *Barney Google and Snuffy Smith*): "This sensibility is what makes Fred Lasswell's contribution to the legacy of *Barney Google and Snuffy Smith* uniquely his own. The beautifully rendered backgrounds of Fred's Hootin' Holler evoke a rural ambience that is distinct from DeBeck and Barney's urban milieu. Fred has also established a loving relationship between Snuffy and Loweezy that gives the strip a feeling of warmth and tenderness."

Lasswell first drew in DeBeck's style and then slowly adopted a bolder line. Lasswell also introduced a host of intriguing characters for his postwar stories, but in the mid-fifties he gave up the long continuities that had characterized the strip and converted to gag-a-day in keeping with the industry trend. Lasswell married twice; there were three sons from the first marriage, which ended in divorce. In 1964 he married Shirley Ann Slesinger. At his death from a heart attack at home in Tampa, Florida, Lasswell had been meeting the syndicate deadline for 58 years almost to the day. In longevity, he joins a very tiny band of his peers—Edwina Dumm, Paul Robinson, Chester

Gould, Charles Schulz, Hank Ketcham, Mort Walker, Milton Caniff, to name a few of the few.

To his colleagues in the National Cartoonist Society, Lasswell was "Uncle Fred," an active contributor to the convivialities of the group since its birth in 1946, and he was honored as well as beloved by his peers. In 1964 he was awarded both the Reuben statuette as "cartoonist of the year" and the category plaque for "best humor strip." And he is the only cartoonist to have twice (1984 and 1994) received NCS's Elzie Segar Award "for unique and outstanding contributions to the profession of cartooning."

Lasswell, despite his carefully cultivated hayseed demeanor, was quite at home in the high tech era, maintaining a state-of-the-electronic-art studio. He established a web page very early in the cyberspace age and produced a video disc series on "how to draw" cartoons (one in Spanish) and a bilingual laser disc with a bar-coded workbook and a hypercard stack for computers. He was always innovating. In the 1940s, he produced a comic book for the blind using a Braille-inspired system. And in 1962, he obtained a patent for a citrus harvesting machine he'd designed in 1958 and licensed the idea to International Harvester.

Lasswell's success with his strip establishes him as one of the few cartoonists to take over an existing feature and sustain and even improve upon the original concept. Much of the difference between the two incarnations lies in the difference between telling stories and telling jokes. DeBeck was expert at milking comedy out of suspense with a seemingly unending string of cliff-hangers and tantalizers. But Lasswell gave the strip personality and heart as well as humor.

• The best source of information about Fred Lasswell's life is his autobiographical chapter in Brian Walker's *Barney Google and Snuffy Smith: 75 Years of an American Legend* (1994). A few additional details are supplied in the 1972 and 1996 editions of the *National Cartoonists Society Album* (membership directory). An obituary appeared in the *New York Times*, 6 Mar. 2001.

ROBERT C. HARVEY

LAWRENCE, Jacob (7 Sept. 1917–9 June 2000), painter, was born Jacob Armstead Lawrence in Atlantic City, New Jersey, the son of Jacob Lawrence, a railroad cook, and Rosalee Armstead Lawrence, a domestic servant. Later recognized as the first artist to document through his art the African-American experience as an important chapter of American history, Lawrence himself experienced racism, poverty and instability, alienation, a broken home, and the exuberant street life of the black community. At age two, he moved with his family to Easton, Pennsylvania. In 1924 his father deserted the family and eventually bought a shop in the Harlem section of New York City; his mother took the children to Philadelphia, where they lived for six years before moving to Harlem. There Jacob occasionally encountered his father,

but they did not become close, and the father never contributed financially to his family.

In 1930, the Harlem Renaissance—a period of literary, artistic, and musical blossoming in the black community—was in its waning days, but there was still an excitement in the air. That year, however, Lawrence engaged in petty vandalism and theft with kids he met on the street, and his mother enrolled him in an after-school program at the Utopia Children's Center, an arts and crafts settlement house. There he met the noted painter and educator Charles Henry Alston (1907–1977), who quickly recognized his talent and encouraged him to pursue art. "It would [have been] a mistake to try to teach Jake," Alston was later quoted as saying. "He was teaching himself, finding his own way. All he needed was encouragement and technical information" (in Wheat, 1968).

At age sixteen, Lawrence dropped out of high school to support his mother and siblings, taking jobs at a laundry and a printing plant. But he continued to paint, taking classes taught by Alston at the Harlem Community Center. He also developed an appreciation of art history, especially Italian Renaissance masters, at the Metropolitan Museum of Art, a sixty-block walk from his home. By the mid-1930s, he rented a small studio space within Alston's studio, a gathering point for a variety of Harlem cultural limelights. There Lawrence became acquainted with an older generation of prominent black artists, writers, and performers, such as poet Langston Hughes, novelists Ralph Ellison and Richard Wright, and painter Aaron Douglas (1899–1979).

Lawrence's mature style developed early, combining the patchwork elements of synthetic Cubism and the use of bold, solid colors and flat forms in the manner of Henri Matisse with a clear sense of black identity. It is not at all clear where he developed his style—neither Alston nor Douglas were particularly influenced by European modernism, and the Metropolitan Museum did not then collect or exhibit contemporary art—but he may have seen pictures in magazines or just picked up ideas at Alston's studio.

Lawrence's first significant paintings, such as *Street Scene—Restaurant*, *Interior Scene*, and *Street Orator*, were produced in 1936 and 1937. His first one-man exhibition took place in 1936 at the Harlem Artists Guild. In 1937 he won a two-year scholarship to the American Artists School and, the following year was accepted into the Federal Arts Project of the federal government's WPA. Being around other artists introduced him to new ideas and gave him confidence that he could pursue art seriously. That confidence was strengthened in 1940 when a fellowship from the Julius Rosenwald Fund enabled him to move into his own studio.

Lawrence's greatest artistic strengths were his use of vibrant color and his ability to tell stories. (The main criticism of his body of work is that he was more of an illustrator than a fine artist.) In the late 1930s, he created a series of forty-one paintings on the life of Toussaint L'Ouverture, who led a slave rebellion that eventually drove the French out of Haiti in the first years of the nineteenth century. This series was first exhibited at the Baltimore Museum of Art in 1939. He kept busy, producing a suite of thirty-two paintings depicting the life of black orator Frederick Douglass in 1938 and another thirty-one works recounting the life of Harriet Tubman, the underground railroad leader, in 1939.

The Rosenwald fellowship enabled Lawrence to create his most heralded body of work, a sixty-painting series on "The Migration of the Negro" (1940–1941), which examined the movement of millions of African Americans from the sharecropping fields of the American South to tenements in the cities of the industrial North between the two world wars. This series drew heavily from memory and observation: his mother had been born in Virginia, while his father had moved up from South Carolina. "I remember that people in the neighborhood were always talking about a new family arriving," Lawrence recalled in 1984. "To me, it was a dramatic event my parents and I were part of, just as we were part of Harriet Tubman's escape. I saw the same drama when I looked at [Honoré] Daumier's *Third Class Carriage* or thought about the Jews crossing the Red Sea."

This series was first shown at the Downtown Gallery in 1941, which showed work by some of the most prominent artists, and it brought the twenty-four-year-old artist to national prominence. Critics raved, and the Museum of Modern Art in New York City and the Phillips Memorial Gallery (now the Phillips Collection) in Washington, D.C., bought every painting in the show, thirty apiece—the Modern took the even-numbered pictures while the Phillips received the odd-numbered.

After that 1941 show, Lawrence never lacked for exhibitions and sales. However, he remained involved in the great events of his time. Joining the Coast Guard in 1943, he was assigned to a troop carrier. He also took an active role in the Civil Rights movement of the 1960s. He received commissions to create a poster for the Summer Olympic Games in Munich (1972), a print for the United States Bicentennial celebration (1976), a mural for Howard University (1980), and a fourteen-year-long mosaic installation in a subway station in New York's Times Square, which was completed in the year after his death. He also taught at Pratt Institute in Brooklyn and the University of Washington in Seattle, where he retired in 1986. In addition, he illustrated books by Langston Hughes and John Hersey, as well as several children's books: *Aesop's Fables*, *Genesis*, and the story of Harriet Tubman.

Lawrence continued to work in series for the remainder of his career: on the abolitionist John Brown (1942); the soldiers' experience of the Second World War (1946–1947); struggles for freedom in American history (1955), and desegregation in the American South (1960s). In 1949, he suffered a nervous breakdown and committed himself to Hillside Hospital in Queens, New York, where he remained for nine months. During that stay, Lawarence continued to paint, completing a series of eleven works entitled "Sanitarium" that was exhibited at the Downtown Gallery in 1950. These paintings focus on other patients rather than himself and were his first to feature white people in prominent, nonthreatening roles. In 1968 he began a series on buildings, in which he depicted racial harmony, as blacks and whites worked together on construction projects—perhaps metaphorically building a color-blind society.

In 1941, Lawrence married Gwendolyn Clarine Knight, a West Indian-born painter whom he met at the Harlem Art Workshop in the 1930s and who survived him. He died at his home in Seattle.

• A variety of publications tell the story of Jacob Lawrence's life and artistic achievement, including *Jacob Lawrence, American Painter* by Ellen Harkins Wheat (1968) and *Jacob Lawrence* by Richard J. Powell (1992). *Jacob Lawrence: Thirty Years of Prints (1963–1993): A Catalogue Raisonné*, ed. Peter T. Nesbett, with an essay by Patricia Hills (1994), and *The Complete Jacob Lawrence* by Peter T. Nesbett and Michelle DuBois (2000), on the other hand, provide information on what the artist created and when and how he created it, as well as its history of ownership. An obituary appeared in the *New York Times*, 14 Feb. 2000.

DANIEL GRANT

LAWRENCE, Joshua (10 Sept. 1778–23 Jan. 1843), Baptist minister, was born in Deep Creek, North Carolina, the son of John Lawrence, a plantation owner, and Absilla Bell Lawrence. When Lawrence was ten years old, nightmares of the world's destruction haunted his sleep, while worries about his wickedness consumed his waking hours. These trials persisted throughout Lawrence's adolescence. Nevertheless, the young man filled his days with gambling, drinking, dancing, swearing, and—according to his autobiography—"adultery." Just before Lawrence's seventeenth birthday, his father died, leaving Lawrence the farm in Edgecombe County, where he lived the rest of his life.

From 1798 to 1800 Lawrence's spiritual struggles intensified. He often prayed three times a day but occasionally lapsed into sin and doubt. During this period Lawrence married Mary Knight; the couple had thirteen children. Shortly after his marriage, Lawrence, working alone in his fields, had a vision of Jesus Christ hovering in the air. Minutes later a smoldering image of hell appeared. The next day Lawrence experienced the change of heart that marked his conversion, but the polarized tenor of the previous day's visions punctuated a life engaged in what Lawrence described as spiritual warfare. After his conversion, Lawrence was baptized and joined the Baptist church at Fishing Creek near his home. By 1801 he had started preaching, and he was quickly ordained by two of North Carolina's leading Baptist ministers, Jesse Read and Lemuel Burkitt. Lawrence's early ministry coincided with a series of spectacular revivals sweeping the South, and his preaching met with similar success. Within two years his efforts added more than one hundred names to the rolls at the Baptist church near the falls of the Tar River.

The issue that defined much of Lawrence's ministerial career first surfaced in 1803. At that year's annual meeting of the Kehukee Baptist Association, Lawrence voted with the majority of other delegates to back the nascent missionary movement. Support for missionary endeavors within the Kehukee Association fluctuated for the next two decades, and no record exists of Lawrence's activities during these years. But by 1825 Lawrence had become one of the South's fiercest antimissionary preachers. Writing that year as a self-described "clodhopper," Lawrence published *The American Telescope*, a pamphlet that skewered missionaries as money-hunting hirelings who ignored the needy, feted the wealthy, pocketed charitable donations, and schemed to establish a national church. A year later Lawrence circulated a petition, "The Declaration of the Reformed Baptist Churches of North Carolina," that asked all the churches of the Kehukee Association to declare "nonfellowship" with missionary societies, theological seminaries, tract societies, and various other institutions of evangelical Protestantism. Within a year Kehukee became the first multichurch body in the United States to declare its formal opposition to the missionary enterprise.

Lawrence and his fellow antimissionaries began calling themselves Primitive or Old School Baptists, a name that signaled their belief that they upheld the same doctrines proffered by Jesus and his disciples nearly two thousand years earlier. Lawrence and the Primitives were in fact Calvinists who were distressed by what they perceived as their fellow Baptists' increased faith in human effort, rather than God's grace, to bring about salvation. Lawrence's opposition to missions earned him the ire of evangelicals across the South. Unsubstantiated rumors circulated about Lawrence's drunkenness and his penchant for preaching while surrounded by armed guards. He received death threats in the mail. Lawrence found missionaries and their backers in the very churches where he preached. In 1829 Lawrence, who had cofounded the Baptist church in Tarboro, North Carolina, a decade earlier, spearheaded a split in the church after some of its members invited P. W. Dowd, a formally trained minister and an advocate of missions, to pastor the church. In response Lawrence seized the church books, and his followers excommunicated anyone who had declared his or her support for missionary societies. In the 1830s and the early 1840s Lawrence continued publishing his antimissionary polemics, many of which were serialized in the Tarboro-based biweekly, the *Primitive Baptist*. In works such as *A Basket of Fragments for the Children* (1833) and *The North Carolina Whig's Apology for the Kehukee Association* (1830), Lawrence argued that missionaries' "man-made" religion attempted to usurp God's unique ability to dispense saving grace. He also began to worry that young male missionaries preyed on naive daughters and wives. But Lawrence returned time

and again to missionaries' avarice. In "Teeth to Teeth: Tom Thumb Tugging with the Wolves for the Sheepskin" (1837), Lawrence lambasted missionaries whose endless search for funds had transformed the "church of God" into "a house of church traffic, a den for wolves, and a lodging for spiritual dogs, and a place of rendezvous for thieves and robbers to divide their spoil" (2). Similar themes streaked his nonreligious writing. A Jacksonian Democrat, Lawrence railed against banks and the circulation of paper money.

Despite the antiwealth rhetoric that marked his writings, Lawrence proved a successful southern planter. As a young farmer in 1800 he owned four slaves and the fields he had inherited from his father. By 1841 Lawrence held land in three North Carolina counties, oversaw a workforce of at least twenty slaves, and supplemented his plantation's profits from cotton, corn, and pork with large catches of shad from the nearby creek. Despite several years of poor health late in his life, Lawrence continued preaching. In his last days a revival swept one of the churches he pastored, and more than two dozen new members filled the pews. Shortly thereafter Lawrence died at his Edgecombe County plantation. He was one of the most prolific and eloquent spokespersons of the Primitive Baptists.

• The 1812 manuscript of Lawrence's autobiography, *Victorious Grace*, is at the Southern Historical Collection at the University of North Carolina at Chapel Hill. The university's North Carolina Collection also holds several other rare Lawrence publications. Many of Lawrence's religious writings appeared in the *Primitive Baptist*. His autobiography was finally published in four installments during 1841. And "Teeth to Teeth: Tom Thumb Tugging with the Wolves for the Sheepskin," a book-length work, was serialized during 1837. His observations on more worldly matters often graced the pages of the *Tarboro Press*; in letters to the editor and a semiregular column titled "The Opossum Fighter's Thoughts," Lawrence offered his observations on matters ranging from the banking crisis to musketry. R. D. Hart's "Biography of Elder Joshua Lawrence" is in the *Primitive Baptist*, 28 Oct. 1843. Sandra Hayslette, "Missions, Markets, and Men: A Baptist Contest of Values in Tarboro, North Carolina, 1800–1835" (M.A. thesis, University of North Carolina at Chapel Hill, 1995), argues that Lawrence defended a masculinized Calvinism against what he saw as an onslaught of feminized missionaries. For more on Lawrence and the Primitive Baptists, see Bertram Wyatt-Brown, *The Shaping of Southern Culture* (2001), and Cushing Biggs Hassell and Sylvester Hassell, *History of the Church of God* (1886).

JOSHUA GUTHMAN

LAWRENCE, Robert Henry, Jr. (2 Oct. 1935–8 Dec. 1967), aviator and astronaut, was born in Chicago, Illinois, the son of Gwendolyn Annette Williams Lawrence, a civil servant, and Robert Henry Lawrence, Sr., a disabled veteran. While Lawrence and his sister were quite young, their parents divorced. Their mother married Charles Duncan, who worked as a Veterans Administration underwriter and in periodicals circulation. Robert H. Lawrence, Sr., remained a strong influence in his children's lives.

Lawrence, a bright and self-disciplined youngster, attended Haines Elementary School in inner-city Chicago. The family was far from affluent, but the Duncans provided support and intellectual stimulation, nurturing Lawrence's interests in chess, model airplanes, and chemistry. Summers spent at the home of family friends near St. Louis, Missouri, allowed the children to enjoy country surroundings and trips to baseball games and nearby Lambert Airfield. During the school year in Chicago, visits to museums, concerts, or the zoo were regular weekend events.

At the age of twelve Lawrence entered Englewood High School. He excelled in chemistry and as a long-distance runner, winning city championships in mile and half-mile races. He graduated in 1952, aged sixteen, in the top 10 percent of his class. He then enrolled in Bradley University, Peoria, Illinois. There he earned a B.S. in chemistry and distinguished himself as a cadet lieutenant colonel in the university's Air Force Reserve Officer Training Corps. Upon graduation in 1956, at the age of twenty, he was commissioned as a second lieutenant in the U.S. Air Force.

Following completion of his flight and flight instructor training, Lawrence was assigned to Fürstenfeldbruck Air Base near Munich, Germany. There he served as a fighter pilot and as a flight instructor for pilots in the German air force. After a fatality occurred during training, Lawrence recommended that the language of instruction be changed from English to German. He reasoned that the pilot trainees could react more rapidly in emergencies if instructed in their native language. The change proved successful, impressing both the student pilots and the German government with Lawrence's acumen.

On 1 July 1958 Lawrence married Barbara Cress, also of Chicago, whom he had first met six years before. They had one son. Lawrence returned to the United States in 1961 and enrolled in a joint program of Ohio State University and the Air Force Institute of Technology at Wright-Patterson Air Force Base (AFB). He earned a Ph.D. in nuclear chemistry from Ohio State in August 1965. His dissertation explored the conversion of tritium beta rays to methane and ethane gas.

During the 1960s national attention focused on the American space program and on civil rights issues. In 1963 the U.S. Air Force captain Edward J. Dwight, Jr., enrolled in the Aerospace Research Pilot School (ARPS) at Edwards AFB, California, amid much fanfare. Many assumed that Dwight would be selected for astronaut training and eventually would be the first African American in space. However, Dwight was not selected for aerospace projects either by the National Aeronautics and Space Administration (NASA) or the air force. Lengthy eligibility disputes and charges of discrimination blighted Dwight's career, and he resigned from the air force in 1966.

After he received his doctorate, Lawrence was assigned to Kirtland AFB, New Mexico, as a research scientist at the Air Force Weapons Laboratory. He accumulated more than 2,500 flight hours, of which 2,000 were in jet aircraft. He applied twice to join NASA's astronaut training program without success. He then was accepted by the U.S. Air Force Aerospace Research Pilot School at Edwards AFB. In June 1967, upon his successful completion of ARPS training, Lawrence was named to the air force's Manned Orbiting Laboratory (MOL) program.

The air force's space flight program complemented but was not coordinated with NASA's Mercury and Gemini programs. A precursor to the International Space Station program, the MOL program was to equip two astronauts for a thirty-day Earth orbit. MOL pilots and NASA astronauts also conducted extensive test flights in various high-performance jet aircraft. Lawrence's research investigated the gliding flight of unpowered aircraft landing from a high orbit. The unpowered steep-descent glide became the landing technique later used by NASA's space shuttle orbiters.

On 8 December 1967, only six months after he joined the MOL program, Lawrence was copilot of a Lockheed F-104 Starfighter during a proficiency flight consisting of a set pattern of steep-descent approaches. The plane crashed on landing. Both officers ejected from the aircraft. The pilot, Major Harvey Royer, sustained serious injuries but survived; Lawrence was killed.

Lawrence was the only MOL pilot killed in the line of duty, but he was the ninth to die in America's combined aerospace programs. Five NASA astronauts were killed in earlier experimental flight tests, and on 27 January 1967 Lieutenant Commander Roger B. Chaffee, Lieutenant Colonel Virgil I. "Gus" Grissom, and Lieutenant Colonel Edward H. White were killed in a flash fire during a test of the *Apollo I* rocket on the launch pad at Cape Kennedy (Cape Canaveral), Florida.

In June 1969 the MOL program merged with NASA's space program, and the seven MOL astronauts who were under thirty-six years of age were transferred to NASA. Had Lawrence lived, he would also have been eligible for transfer to the NASA program.

After Lawrence's death, no minority astronaut candidates were announced until 1978, when an astronaut class of thirty-five included three African Americans, Colonel Guion S. Bluford, Jr., Dr. Ronald E. McNair, and Colonel Frederick D. Gregory; the first Asian American, Colonel Ellison S. Onizuka; and six women, among them Dr. Shannon W. Lucid, Dr. Judith A. Resnick, and Dr. Sally K. Ride. Bluford became the first African American to go into space in 1983. Also in 1983 Ride was the first woman in space. Four members of that 1978 group, McNair, Onizuka, Resnick, and Major Francis R. "Dick" Scobee, perished in the *Challenger* shuttle disaster in 1986.

Although informally recognized as the nation's first African-American astronaut from the time of his selection for the MOL program, Lawrence was not officially designated an astronaut by the air force until January 1997. On the thirtieth anniversary of his death, in December 1997, Lawrence's name was added to the Astronauts Memorial Foundation Space Mirror at the Kennedy Space Center, Cape Canaveral, Florida. Dedicated in 1991, the Space Mirror Memorial honors astronauts who died on American space missions or during mission training.

• Biographical information on Lawrence is in Khephra Burns and William Miles, *Black Stars in Orbit* (1995), a juvenile work based on numerous interviews with African American astronauts and members of their families; Betty Kaplan Gubert et al., *Distinguished African Americans in Aviation and Space Science* (2001); and J. Alfred Phelps, *They Had a Dream: The Story of African-American Astronauts* (1994). Information on NASA's astronaut recruitment program is in Joseph D. Atkinson, Jr., and Jay M. Shafritz, *The Real Stuff* (1985). Obituaries appeared on 9 Dec. 1967 in the *New York Times,* the *Chicago Tribune,* and the *Washington Evening Star.*

CAROLINE M. FANNIN

LAX, Anneli (23 Feb. 1922–24 Sept. 1999), mathematician and educator, was born Anneli Cahn in Kattowitz, then in Germany but soon part of Poland following a plebiscite, the daughter of Alfred Cahn, a Jewish urological surgeon, and Margarete Kramer. In 1929, to escape discrimination against Germans, the family moved to Berlin. It was a move from the frying pan into the fire; in 1933 Adolf Hitler came to power, and the Cahn family fled, first to Paris, where Anneli learned French. Love of the French language stayed with her the rest of her life. Unable to settle permanently in France, the family moved to Palestine and in 1935 to the United States.

Anneli Cahn finished high school in New York in two years, graduating at the age of sixteen. Her father had a hard time establishing a medical practice, so Anneli was on her own. She won a four-year scholarship to study mathematics at Adelphi College. Unfortunately at that time Adelphi had a minuscule mathematics department; it took some effort for Anneli to overcome the gaps in her undergraduate education.

After her graduation in 1942 Anneli was hired as an assistant researcher in the aeronautics department of New York University. Her work with James Stoker on elasticity demonstrated that she was an extremely conscientious investigator. Richard Courant invited her in 1943 to join his mathematics institute as a graduate student. She remained a part of Courant's institute and his extended family for the rest of her life.

In 1948 Anneli Cahn married Peter Lax, a fellow graduate student in mathematics. Between the births of their two sons, Anneli Lax began work on her dissertation under the direction of Courant. The topic grew out of the work of E. E. Levi on hyperbolic equations with multiple characteristics. Levi had shown that, in a linear partial differential equation in two variables with constant coefficients and real charac-

teristics, if the highest order term has c as a characteristic of multiplicity k and if the term of order less by j has c as a characteristic of multiplicity k-j, then the initial value problem can be solved. Lax showed that the conditions imposed by Levi are necessary as well. This deep result, called the Levi-Lax condition, was extended by Swensson to hyperbolic equations in any number of variables. Lax received her Ph.D. in 1955. In 1961 she was appointed to the faculty of the Department of Mathematics at New York University, where she rose through the ranks to full professorship. She retired in 1992.

The launching of *Sputnik* by the Soviet Union in 1957 shocked America out of its complacent assumption of superiority in science and mathematics and brought about a revolution in support of science and science education. The National Science Foundation established the School Mathematics Study Group (SMSG) to write high school texts embodying the famous—or infamous—New Math. In addition to writing texts, the SMSG sponsored a series of monographs for high school students called the New Mathematical Library. Lax accepted the editorship of this series, a post she held for nearly forty years, until the end of her life. By 1999 a total of forty-one volumes had been published under the aegis of the Mathematical Association of America. In the year 2000 the series was renamed the Anneli Lax New Mathematical Library.

Many of the authors of these forty-one volumes were well-known research mathematicians, including Edwin Beckenbach, Richard Bellman, H. S. M. Coxeter, K. O. Friedrichs, Wilhelm Magnus, Ivan Niven, Oysten Ore, George Pólya, M. M. Schiffer, Norman Steenrod, and Leo Zippin. Most were not accustomed to writing for high school students, so Lax scrutinized the manuscripts and supplied, where necessary, background material that the majority of high school students would not be familiar with. In one volume coauthored by two mathematicians, Lax inserted an entire new chapter; each author thought it was written by the other. Lax devoted untold hours to polishing and supplementing each manuscript, designing covers, preparing page dummies, and proofreading with a Germanic devotion. In the editing of some of the later volumes, she was assisted by the brilliant and equally perfectionist Peter Ungar.

In 1980 the mathematics department of New York University assigned Lax to design a remedial course in mathematics for freshmen. What to do about ill-prepared students who feared or hated mathematics has been a persistent and formidable problem for colleges. Lax found that often math-anxious students could understand simple sentences but were baffled by nuanced, complex sentences, as mathematical statements frequently are. The course she devised and called "Mathematical Thinking" presented mathematics not as a body of facts but as a set of problems to be analyzed and resolved. Its novelty was that the students were not only required to find answers but also to write about their thinking, their strategies, and even their mistakes. She found it helpful to team up with Erica Ducan, an instructor in a freshman composition class.

Lax opposed standardized tests, especially in mathematics. She thought they neither set nor upheld standards but standardized the acquisition of skills, and the wrong skills at that. They inevitably resulted in teaching to the test, bad in any subject and fatal in mathematics.

In 1986 Lax received a grant from the Ford Foundation to introduce her teaching technique to the faculties of some high schools in New York. In this task she was ably assisted by the distinguished educator John Devine and three graduate students, the mathematician Giuliana Davidoff, the educator Eileen Fernandez, and the psychologist Janet Mindes. In 1995 the Mathematical Association of America awarded Lax its highest recognition, the Gung-Hu Award for Distinguished Service, for her contributions to mathematical publishing and education in a broad sense.

In 1997 Lax was diagnosed with cancer of the pancreas. She underwent an operation and treatment and lived two more years filled with incessant activity. Six weeks before she died, she embarked on a strenuous trip to Europe, visiting Jürgen Moser, attending the eightieth birthday conference of Lars Garding in Lund, and traveling to Germany to view a total eclipse of the sun. Upon her return from Europe she spent a week at her beloved Loon Lake in the Adirondacks. She died at her home on Manhattan's Upper West Side.

Lax was an exceptionally beautiful woman; she wore her beauty lightly. The love of her family and of numerous close friends was a great source of happiness to her. She was without peer as a mathematical editor, and her ideas for fighting "math anxiety" remain relevant in the twenty-first century.

• Works by Lax include "Cauchy's Problem for Partial Differential Equations with Multiple Characteristics," *Communications on Pure and Applied Mathematics* 9 (1956): 615–33, and, with G. Groat, "Learning Mathematics," in *Mathematics Tomorrow*, ed. Lynn Steen (1981). For an extension of her mathematical theory, see L. Swensson, "Necessary and Sufficient Conditions for the Hyperbolicity of Polynomials with Hyperbolic Principal Parts," *Arkiv för Matematik* 8 (1968): 145–62. Ivan Niven, "Yueh-Giu Gung and Charles Y Hu Award for Distinguished Service to Anneli Lax," *American Mathematical Monthly* 102 (1995): 99–100, discusses her award. Remembrances are E. Fernandez and A. B. Powell, "Remembering Anneli Cahn Lax," *Journal of Mathematical Behavior* 19 (2000): 1–7, and Mark Saul, "Anneli Cahn Lax," *Notices of the American Mathematical Society* 47 (2000): 766–69.

PETER D. LAX

LE CLERCQ, Tanaquil (2 Oct. 1929–31 Dec. 2000), ballerina, teacher, author, and photographer, was born in Paris, France, the daughter of Edith Whittemore Le Clercq, a socialite from St. Louis, Missouri, and the American writer Jacques Georges Clemenceau Le Clercq, a poet and a prolific translator, principally from the French. Le Clercq's father named her after "Paul Tanaquil"—his own occasional pseudonym, which referred to the Etruscan queen and prophetess of ancient Rome. From Le Clercq's childhood on, however, she was known as "Tanny" to family and friends.

When Le Clercq was three and a half, her family moved to New York City, where she attended the Lycée Français. At four, she began to study dancing at the King-Coit School of Theatre and Design. Reviewing one of King-Coit's inventive public performances in 1935, John Anderson wrote in the *New York Evening Journal*, "Mistress Tanaquil LeClercq reduces my critical vocabulary to dust and ashes." Le Clercq was not yet six years old. At seven, she became a pupil of Mikhail Mordkin, a partner of Anna Pavlova. In 1941, at age eleven, she auditioned at the School of American Ballet (S.A.B.) and was awarded a scholarship. The chief judge, George Balanchine, remarked that "she looks like a real ballerina already, only very small, as if you were looking at her through the wrong end of a telescope" (Taper, p. 205).

Le Clercq—to her father's regret, yet with her mother's support—concluded her full-time academic schooling at the age of twelve to concentrate on ballet. At S.A.B. she proved herself to be outstanding, and, by the time she was in her late teens, Balanchine was ready to utilize her astonishing gift for classical dancing, her elegantly attenuated figure (5 feet six and a half inches, 108 pounds—the word "coltish" was applied to her almost universally throughout her career), and her spirited, even impatient, personality. In 1946, when she was seventeen, he featured her spectacularly in the fourth, "Choleric," section of his new ballet *The Four Temperaments*, which he was preparing for the first concert of Ballet Society, the direct precursor of the New York City Ballet (NYCB), which would make its debut two years later. During 1946, Balanchine also employed Le Clercq in several other ballet projects, among them two of his rare Mozart works: *Symphonie Concertante*, a ballet of high classicism that was given its première for a student audience, and *Resurgence*, an occasional piece made for a luncheon to benefit the March of Dimes, in which Le Clercq played a child who fell victim to poliomyelitis, and Balanchine himself played a figure called Threat of Polio.

Le Clercq—the first NYCB ballerina to have been trained primarily at S.A.B.—never danced in the corps de ballet. For the ten years with Ballet Society and NYCB that constituted her career, she was cast in a host of starring and featured parts in both repertory and new works, most prominently by Balanchine but also by Jerome Robbins (*Age of Anxiety, Afternoon of a Faun, The Cage, The Concert*), Frederick Ashton (*Illuminations*), Antony Tudor (*Lilac Garden*), Merce Cunningham (*The Seasons*), and Ruthanna Boris (*A Candle for St. Jude; Cakewalk*), many of which she performed to critical acclaim.

Still, her most intense devotion was reserved for Balanchine, whom she married on 31 December

1952, when she was 23 and he was 48 and already thrice divorced. As a dancer, she had the range, fluency, and intuitive musicality to flourish in his older repertory, and she was also a creative inspiration. The new ballets in which Balanchine showcased her were characterized by surprise, beauty, firecracker intensity, and often an odd, even spooky, wit. She was a dancer's dancer. The ballerina Maria Tallchief wrote: "Watching her you could see all of George's training in the precision of her feet and legs, her beautiful port de bras, her response to the music" (Tallchief and Kaplan, p. 190). The ballerina Allegra Kent wrote: "With her poetic face, she had a new and different ballet look. Like a lean Giacometti, she reflected modern art. . . She could show poetic and mysterious depth with her exquisite acting ability, or she could be an elegant clown" (Kent, p. 46).

It is still possible to glimpse the Le Clercq who captivated Balanchine in the sparkling Dewdrop of *The Nutcracker*; in the New Yorker who dismisses love with a handshake in *Ivesiana*; in the soignée flirt of *Bourrée fantasque*; and in the glamorous dance hall girl whose whipping virtuosity brings down the curtain in the finale of *Western Symphony*. Even though *Concerto Barocco* and *Symphony in C* were not originally made for her, her dancing in them remains a standard a half century later. Probably the Balanchine role for which Le Clercq is most celebrated is that of the doom-eager ball goer in white in his 1951 *La Valse*. Happily, a film of this nuclear-age masterpiece made close to its première reveals her with all of her feverish brilliance intact.

In late October 1956, after a matinee performance at the Royal Theatre in Copenhagen, where NYCB was on tour, Le Clercq suddenly ran an actual high fever and, within hours, succumbed to poliomyelitis, which paralyzed both of her legs and one arm.

At the age of twenty-seven, she embarked on the rest of her life, a journey that would be marked by confinement in an iron lung and some forty-four years in a wheelchair. For a full year, Balanchine—devastated and guilt-ridden that he had somehow brought on her illness through his polio ballet when she was a teenager—attended to her constantly, hoping that she might regain the ability to walk, and for nearly a decade he maintained the marriage. Eventually, his work in the studio refocused his feelings, and in 1969, hoping to marry the ballerina Suzanne Farrell, he obtained a Mexican divorce.

Le Clercq, who was so independent in spirit that she learned to travel to Europe entirely by herself, exhibited unimaginable courage and grace after she was forced to leave the stage. During the 1960s, she became a remarkable photographer and authored two books: *Mourka*, a charming portfolio of photographs about her and Balanchine's beloved cat (the couple had no children), and *The Ballet Cook Book*, a kind of indirect autobiography. Like Balanchine, she was a fanatic solver of crossword puzzles, and she also created some of them for the *New York Times*. During the 1970s, she taught ballet at the Dance Theatre of Har-

lem. (She had started teaching young: in 1950, at the King-Coit School, where her mother was the receptionist, she was the first teacher of Nancy Reynolds, who as an adult became the leading scholar of Balanchine in the world and the director of research at the George Balanchine Foundation.) Accounts by friends chronicle a woman who could still passionately enjoy such natural events as the sighting of a deer, who could still exercise a sharp wit, and who could both laugh herself and entertain others.

When Balanchine died in 1983, he provided amply in his will for Le Clercq: her inheritance included the American performance royalty rights to 85 of his 425 works, of which Balanchine's biographer Bernard Taper estimates that perhaps 60 are still performable. Although she was one of the few Balanchine legatees who did not join in the Balanchine Trust, the organization formed in 1987 to manage the welter of performance and media rights he passed on to his dancers and close colleagues, Le Clercq permitted the trust to represent her. With small or struggling ballet companies, she could be generous, giving them performance rights for free (and sometimes adding a personal donation toward their production), yet she didn't hesitate to stand up against potentially corrupting powers. At one point in the late 1980s, when a member of the NYCB board—then distraught by the prospect that Balanchine left no works to the company he had founded—offered Le Clercq one million dollars for her rights, she answered that her ballets were not for sale. She died of pneumonia on the forty-eighth anniversary of her wedding to Balanchine.

• There is no book-length biography of, or overt memoir by, Le Clercq. The most informative chapter-length interview with her is by Barbara Newman in *Striking a Balance: Dancers Talk about Dancing* (1982); also helpful is the 1996 paperback edition of Bernard Taper's *Balanchine*, which includes a chapter on the choreographer's legacy not found in previous editions. Authoritative portraits of Le Clercq as an artist can be found in Nancy Reynolds's *Repertory in Review: 40 Years of the New York City Ballet* (1977); in Maria Tallchief's *Maria Tallchief* (1997, written with Larry Kaplan); in Allegra Kent's *Once a Dancer . . .* (1997); in Edwin Denby's *Dance Writings* (1986); in the collection of memoirs, edited by Francis Mason, *I Remember Balanchine* (1991); and in Newman's interview with Bruce Marks in *Striking a Balance* (p. 219). *Tanaquil Le Clercq: 1929–2000*, the souvenir book from NYCB's memorial tribute, gives an affecting and specific idea of her as a dancer and a person through rare photographs and a word portrait by Holly Brubach. An excellent newspaper profile published in Le Clercq's lifetime is Angela Taylor's in the 28 Feb. 1969 edition of the *New York Times*. A vivid and detailed history of Le Clercq's relationship with Jerome Robbins is contained in Amanda Vaill's "Swan Song," which appeared in the May 2001 issue of *Talk* magazine and is an excerpt from Vaill's forthcoming Robbins biography. Some films and many photographs of Le Clercq, as well as clippings about her, can be found at the Dance Division of the New York Public Library for the Performing Arts. Several films with footage of her also can be purchased, among them Anne Belle's *Dancing for Mr. B.: Six Balanchine Ballerinas* (1989)

MINDY ALOFF

LEE, William Andrew (12 Nov. 1900–27 Dec. 1998), distinguished U.S. Marine Corps officer, was born at Ward Hill, Massachusetts; his parents' names are unknown. In May 1918 he enlisted in the marines as a private and was briefly engaged against German forces along the western front. Afterward he commenced routine tours of duty on land and sea, including a stint with the marine complement aboard the battleship *Arkansas*. U.S. foreign policy at that time was increasingly prone to intervene in Central America, and the marine corps functioned as an instrument of "gunboat diplomacy." In 1927 Lee accompanied an expeditionary force to Nicaragua to protect American lives and property against a group of rebel guerrillas under Augusto Cesar Sandino. Lee established himself as one of the foremost marksmen in a service renowned for accurate shooting..

While fighting under legendary marine corps officer Lewis B. "Chesty" Puller, Lee was continually engaged in numerous small unit actions, twice winning the Navy Cross for fighting, in March and December 1930. On 20 September 1932, he participated in his most celebrated action. While accompanying Puller and a patrol of forty Nicaraguan Guardia Nacional troops, Lee was attacked by an estimated 150 rebels. Suffering from two severe wounds and under intense fire, Lee unstrapped a Lewis machine gun from a mule and held the enemy at bay. Their patrol endured four more days of intense skirmishing, having covered 150 miles in ten days before it reached safety. For his heroism under fire, Lee received his third Navy Cross, becoming the most highly decorated marine of his day. Puller, an officer of sparse praise, allegedly declared: "In the days of wooden ships, Lee would have been an Iron man." The nickname stuck throughout Lee's career.

In 1932, following several tours in Nicaragua, Lee shipped back to the United States. That year he was twice winner of the Elliott Trophy Cup for marksmanship and also outshot 5,000 competitors to receive the Wimbolden Cup. In 1935 he was named warrant officer and appointed as marine gunner. For many years, he commanded both howitzer and special weapons platoons at Quantico, Virginia. In 1939 he shipped overseas to Beijing, China, and was subsequently reassigned to the marine barracks at Qinhuangdao near Tientsing. In August 1941 he was chief marine gunner and officer in charge of the small bore gallery.

When Pearl Harbor was attacked, Lee and his 20-man detachment were preparing to defend the rifle range at Camp Holcomb in Tientsing against superior Japanese forces. On 8 December 1941 superiors ordered the unit to surrender. Lee remained captive in Japan for 44 months, where he endured hunger, deprivation, and torture with his legendary stoicism. In October 1943, while a prisoner, he advanced in rank to commissioned warrant officer. In the fall of 1945 he was repatriated and returned to Quantico to serve as executive officer, plans and training officer, and chief range officer. In May 1946 he rose to lieutenant colonel, capping his career the following September by becoming commanding officer of the Rifle Range Detachment at Quantico. In 1950 he retired with the rank of colonel.

In November 1992, the Marine Corps paid tribute by naming a $5.5 million remotely engaged target system range at Quantico in his honor. He died at Fredericksburg, Virginia, and was interred at Arlington National Cemetery.

During his thirty-two-year career, "Ironman" Lee was one of the most exemplary and legendary marines of the "Old Corps" (pre–World War II). His final tally of decorations included three Navy Crosses, three Purple Hearts, and two Medals of Valor from the Nicaraguan government. He was married twice: to Helen Lloyd in 1937 and, following her death, to Anne Bradbury in 1964. There were three children from the first marriage, one from the second.

• No collection of personal or official papers is extant, but the Marine Corps Historical Center, Washington Navy Yard, D.C., maintains a small file on Lee. For background information on various theaters of operation throughout his tenure in service, consult George B. Clark, *Devil Dogs: Fighting Marines of World War I* (1999); Frederick B. Rowe, *Marines in China: From T'ai-Pings to Mao* (1965); Clark, *Treading Softly: U. S. Marines in China, 1819–1949* (2001); Clark, *With the Old Corps in Nicaragua* (2001); and Jon T. Hoffman, *Chesty: The Story of Lieutenant General Lewis B. Puller* (2001). Obituaries are in the *Free Lance-Star* (Fredericksburg, Va.), 1 Jan. 1999, the *New York Times*, 2 Jan. 1999, and *Leatherneck* magazine 62 (Mar. 1999).

JOHN C. FREDRIKSEN

LEMMON, Jack (8 Feb. 1925–27 June 2001), Oscar- and Emmy-winning actor, was born John Uhler Lemmon, III, in Newton, Massachusetts, the only child of John Uhler Lemmon, Jr., a baker turned doughnut company executive, and Mildred LaRue Noel Lemmon. Jack was a shy and sickly child who had missed a year of schooling by the age of eight. He won laughs and acceptance by appearing in a school play wearing a hat and cape "two sizes too big" (1988 AFI tribute). It was the beginning of a lifelong love of acting.

At thirteen, he was sent to Phillips Academy in Andover, where he ran track, studied little, taught himself to play the piano, and wrote a score for the graduation play. His mother was a "frustrated singer" who encouraged his performing (1993 interview). He dreamed of studying drama at Yale, but at his father's urging he took business classes at Harvard, beginning in 1943. Lemmon loved performing in the Hasty Pudding Theater Club but cut so many classes that he was put on academic probation. In 1945 he was commissioned an ensign in the navy and appeared in a training film. In 1947 he graduated from Harvard, borrowed $300 from his father, and moved to New York City.

For seven months Lemmon was a piano player and bouncer along Second Avenue and 54th Street. His break came in radio soap operas. During 1948 he appeared as Bruce in "Brighter Day" and Dr. Butch Brent in "The Road of Life." Other parts followed. Lemmon was a physical actor who became "petrified" in radio acting because "you couldn't use your face or body" (1993 C. Rose interview). Roles from "ten lines to the lead" in comedies and dramas on live television changed that, including appearances on *Playhouse 90, Studio One*, and the *Kraft Television Theater*. Lemmon costarred with Cynthia Stone in four separate series, including "Heaven for Betsy." They married on 7 May 1950. Their son Christopher was born within a year.

Lemmon studied under Uta Hagen, who found the young actor "enormously enthusiastic" and "joyously hard-working." A wide range of Broadway roles followed, including the lead in a 1953 revival of *Room Service* that won him a contract at Columbia Pictures. Teamed with Judy Holliday, the always energetic Lemmon received "the best piece of advice on acting I ever got" on the set of his first film, *It Should Happen to You!* (1954). Veteran director George Cukor urged him "to act less" and "let it happen, without letting the acting show" (1992 interview). *Phffft!* (1954) with Holliday continued their successful manic pace. Lemmon supported Betty Grable in *Three for the Show* (1955). The actor's performance as the lazy and lecherous Ensign Pulver in *Mister Roberts* (1955) won him an Oscar for best supporting actor and typed him as Hollywood's hottest new funny man.

He enjoyed singing in *My Sister Eileen* (1955), but *You Can't Run Away from It* (1956) and two films with friend Ernie Kovacs, *Operation Mad Ball* (1957) and *Bell, Book and Candle* (1958), confined him to comedy roles. He and Cynthia divorced in 1956, and his determination to "get ahead" in his career left little time for his son Chris. Lemmon's riotous work in drag in *Some Like It Hot* (1959) was nominated for an Oscar and seemed to seal his unhappy fate as an actor in screen comedy. The film's director, Billy Wilder, knew Lemmon was "no clown," but simply "had mastered the art of comedy." Wilder remarked that "most actors can show you one or two things, and they've emptied their shelves. Jack Lemmon is Macys and Tiffanys and the Sears and Roebuck catalog" (1988 AFI tribute).

His range was seen in his portrayal of C. C. Baxter in *The Apartment* (1960), also directed by Wilder. Baxter is an American male struggling to make it in the postwar corporate world. A junior executive with a can-do attitude, he lends his apartment to supervisors for their extramarital affairs. Lemmon liked "characters who are faulted, who have weaknesses and have to make a choice" (1992 interview). Baxter, however, is "blind to any sense of morality" until he falls for his boss's girlfriend. Wilder's film was voted Best Picture of the Year and Lemmon was again an Oscar nominee. He was "always on the same wave length" when working with Wilder. "I knew what he wanted even before he said it" (1998 C. Rose interview).

Lemmon badly wanted a drama "for my own satisfaction as an actor" (1992 interview). His star power persuaded Warner Brothers to produce *Days of Wine and Roses* (1962), the disturbing story of a public relations man and his wife who descend into alcoholism. Lemmon's stereotype-shattering portrayal of Joe Clay, a straight-jacketed drunk who battles delirium, was a revelation to reviewers and led to Lemmon's fourth Oscar nomination. Producer/director Garson Kanin considered Lemmon "the most fearless actor in Hollywood." Lemmon told an interviewer, "If the part scares me, I've got to do it" (1993 interview).

In 1952, while filming *Irma La Douce* (1963) for Wilder in Paris, Lemmon married actress Felicia Farr; the couple had one child, a daughter. Lemmon's co-star Shirley MacLaine called the actor "the great landscape painter of the screen." The *Saturday Review* spoke for many when it declared Lemmon had established himself as "one of the screen's finest all-around performers." Gregory Peck observed that Lemmon was "the closest thing to an American Olivier that we have" (1988 AFI tribute).

Under the Yum Yum Tree (1963) and *Good Neighbor Sam* (1964) were popular hits that concluded Lemmon's Columbia contract but did little to advance his critical reputation. *The Fortune Cookie* (1966), deftly directed by Wilder, united Lemmon with Walter Matthau in a rich collaboration that would yield some of the screen's funniest moments. As claims attorney "Whiplash Willie," Matthau has Lemmon feign a neck injury to collect a large settlement. In Neil Simon's *The Odd Couple* (1968) Lemmon is the overly fastidious Felix Unger who makes life miserable for Matthau's character, slovenly sportswriter Oscar Madison. Matthau appreciated Lemmon's "marvelous grasp of reality. He allows us to see the comedy and tragedy of the world through the eyes of someone he hints we may even be." Lemmon explained the team's success, "We're three stars—me, Walter and the two of us together" (1998 C. Rose interview).

Lemmon won the Academy Award for his performance in *Save the Tiger* (1973) as Harry Stoner, a dress manufacturer who burns down his business to collect insurance money. This was followed by memorable work in Simon's *The Prisoner of Second Avenue* (1975) and in a television version of Olivier's *The Entertainer* (1976). Lemmon received critical acclaim as a whistle-blowing nuclear scientist in *The China Syndrome* (1979); as a distressed father seeking his son in the Costa-Gavras political thriller *Missing* (1982); and as an overly complacent parish priest in *Mass Appeal* (1984). Lemmon triumphed as James Tyrone in the Broadway revival of *Long Day's Journey into Night* (1986) and as the office loser in *Glengarry Glen Ross* (1992). *Grumpy Old Men* (1993) with Matthau was an unexpected box office hit and led to their reteaming in *Grumpier Old Men* (1995), *Out to Sea* (1995), and *The Odd Couple II* (1998). His winning performance as a dying university professor in *Tuesdays with Morrie* (1999) won him an Emmy.

Whenever he was working on a movie, Lemmon would whisper "magic time" just before his scene began. "I love acting," he said, when accepting the Life Achievement Award from the American Film Institute in 1988. "If once or twice in your life you can get a part with some depth you can go beyond entertaining and touch people and move them." The actor captured through a range of roles the predicament of the postmodern man in the aspirin age and became, as a result, a seminal figure in the second half-century of American cinema.

• Lemmon spoke of his long career in 1988 when he received a Life Achievement Award from the American Film Institute. He was interviewed in a Library of Congress series called "Reflections on the Silver Screen" in 1992. He analyzed his acting on "The Charlie Rose Show" on 1 Oct. 1993 and 9 Feb. 1998. Lemmon's interview with the Bravo Network and their "Inside the Actors Studio" series appeared on 29 Jan. 1998. Also in 1998, Lemmon did an interview with Walter Matthau that was broadcast over the Turner Classic Movies network. Lemmon's biographers include Don Widener, *Lemmon: A Biography* (1975); Joe Baltake, *The Films of Jack Lemmon* (1977); Will Holtzman, *Jack Lemmon* (1977); and Michael Freedland, *Jack Lemmon* (1985). Major articles are in *Current Biography,* 1961 and 1988, and Michael Buckley, *Films in Review,* Dec. 1984, pp. 578–85, and Jan. 1985, pp. 19–26. His obituary is in the *New York Times* and the *Los Angeles Times,* both 29 June 2001. Major appreciations are in the *Washington Post,* 1 July 2001, the *Christian Science Monitor,* 2 July 2001, and a broadcast on National Public Radio's "Weekend Edition," 30 June 2001.

BRUCE J. EVENSEN

LEVERTON, Ruth M. (23 Mar. 1908–14 Sept. 1982), scientist and dietitian, was born Ruth Mandeville Leverton in Minneapolis, Minnesota, the daughter of Ernest Richard Leverton, an engineer, and Helen Ruth Mandeville Leverton. The family moved often because of her father's career. After her high school senior year in Deadwood, South Dakota, they moved to Lincoln, Nebraska, where she began studying at the University of Nebraska.

Leverton earned her bachelor of science degree in home economics in 1928 and began teaching in public schools in Nebraska. She taught high school home economics for two years in small Nebraska towns and discovered that she needed more intellectual challenges. After exploring her options, she moved to Tucson, Arizona, to study at the University of Arizona. Leverton began working with Dr. Margaret Cammack Smith, who was studying the causes of fluorosis (tooth mottling). Leverton's master's research took her to rural St. David, Arizona (63 miles southeast of Tucson), where she lived for three weeks to collect data from nineteen children. Her results showed that the children's diets were not deficient in calcium, phosphorus, or protein, thus providing evidence that the high intakes of fluorine in St. David were responsible for mottled teeth.

In 1932 Leverton earned her M.S. in nutrition. Committed to research, she moved to Illinois, where she enrolled in a doctoral program in nutrition at the University of Chicago. Lydia J. Roberts, her mentor, directed her into iron research. She earned her Ph.D. in 1937 with a dissertation on iron levels in women, and the University of Nebraska, her alma mater, recruited her to become an assistant professor.

The university was seeking someone with leadership skills to promote human nutrition research. Space, however, was limited, and Leverton was given a laboratory in the meat science building. At that time, most nutrition research utilized animal models. As a dietitian, Leverton knew that involving humans in nutrition research had great potential, and she struggled to convince the university to construct a building specifically for human nutrition research. (The university eventually did build such a facility, and in May 1978 formally named it Ruth Leverton Hall.)

At the University of Nebraska, Leverton continued to study iron and women's health. In one study, she assessed hemoglobin levels of women who had donated blood to determine that dietary protein—and not just iron—was needed to normalize iron status. As a dietitian, Leverton advocated beef as a source of iron and protein, and in another study she actually provided daily servings of meat to pregnant women to document its effectiveness in maintaining iron levels. Leverton's research focus slowly evolved from iron to protein, for which she probably is best known. At that time, little research had been done with amino acid requirements, and the studies that had been done had used only males as subjects.

Leverton was responsible for determining women's requirements for five of the essential amino acids. To do this, she fed her subjects a semipurified diet that provided all of the essential amino acids. Gradually, the amino acid of interest was reduced from the diet until the subjects began breaking down their own protein tissue for metabolism. The smallest amount of the amino acid needed to maintain protein balance was recorded as that woman's amino acid requirement.

After seventeen years at the University of Nebraska, Leverton was promoted to full professor of human nutrition, and she was named director of human nutrition research at the Nebraska Agricultural Experimentation Station. She longed for change, though, and in 1954 she moved to Stillwater, Oklahoma, where she became assistant director of the Agricultural Experimental Station and assistant dean of home economics at Oklahoma Agricultural and Mechanical College, which later became Oklahoma State University.

In 1957 Leverton joined the United States Department of Agriculture (USDA) in Washington, D.C., as assistant director of the Human Nutrition Research Division, making her the highest ranked woman in the agency. One year later, Leverton became the associate director of the USDA's Institute of Home Economics, where she worked until 1970; from 1970 to 1974 Leverton was also the science adviser in USDA's Agricultural Research Service.

Throughout her career, Leverton had been quite interested in international nutrition issues. She firmly believed that world peace was dependent on sufficient access to healthy food. Leverton traveled as a Fulbright scholar to the Philippines in 1949–1950; before returning to Nebraska, she traveled throughout Africa, Asia, and Europe. From 1965 to 1973, she represented the United States at the biennial Food and Agriculture Organization conference meetings in Rome and also participated in the Ninth International Congress of Nutrition in Mexico City in 1972. To promote international health and participate in nutrition workshops, Leverton also traveled to Burma (now Myanmar), the Netherlands, Australia, England, Israel, India, Taiwan, Hong Kong, Japan, Korea, Spain, and Guatemala.

Leverton received many awards in her lifetime, but the most prestigious ones were awarded late in her career. The USDA awarded her the Distinguished Service Award in 1972, and in 1973 the American Institute of Nutrition awarded her the Conrad A. Elvehjem Award for public service. In 1977 the American Dietetic Association awarded Leverton its Medallion Award for exemplary service to the field of dietetics.

After many years of research, teaching, and administration, Leverton retired in 1974. For many years she remained close to Washington, D.C., where she worked part-time as a consultant and also as an adjunct faculty member at Howard University. Later, Leverton moved to Champaign, Illinois, where she owned a farm. She died in Champaign.

Leverton's career spanned five decades. During all of the nutritional science and dietetics events of the twentieth century—development of the recommended dietary allowances (RDAs), food rationing, and organization of federal food assistance programs—Leverton was there, at the forefront, leading the way.

• During her life, Leverton wrote over 200 articles, chapters, monographs, and books. Some of her key papers can be found in the *Journal of Home Economics* 27 (1935): 236–39; *Journal of the American Medical Association* 130 (1946): 134–36; *Journal of the American Dietetic Association* 24 (1948): 480–84; and *Journal of Nutrition* 58 (1955): 59–81. A brief biography of Leverton can be found in Martha J. Bailey, *American Women in Science: A Biographical Dictionary* (1994), pp. 208–09; see also the *Journal of Nutrition* 129 (Oct. 1999): 1769–72. An obituary is in the *Lincoln Evening Journal*, 16 Sept. 1982.

JEFFREY S HAMPL

LEVY, David (2 Jan. 1913–25 Jan. 2000), advertising and broadcasting executive, television producer, and writer, was one of twin sons born to Benjamin Levy, an accountant, and Lillian Potash Levy of Philadelphia. He excelled as a student, especially in mathematics and writing, both of which would remain lifelong pursuits. An economics major at the University of Pennsylvania's Wharton School of Business, he received a B.S. degree in 1934 and an M.B.A. in 1935.

After completing his education, Levy hoped to sustain himself teaching economics while he worked at writing. But a three-year job search during the bleakest years of the Great Depression yielded only one offer, from a school in Istanbul, which Levy could not consider because relocation expenses were not included. "In my free time, I was always writing radio scripts," he said in recounting his life for Syracuse University's oral history archives. "Very often they'd be ideas for game shows. I'd write the answers, the questions, the dialogue, and so on. I kept sending these ideas to the New York ad agencies hoping I'd sell a show. Advertising agencies dominated big-time radio. Many of the programs were created by advertising agency executives in those days."

In 1938 he received a response from a radio production unit of the Young & Rubicam (Y&R) agency inviting him to apply for a staff writing position with *We, the People*, a human-interest series in which everyday people were interviewed about their personal triumphs over adversity. Levy got the job and moved to New York City. He rose quickly through the ranks at Y&R radio production, advancing to director and then to program supervisor in less than two years.

Though he enjoyed working in radio production, Levy felt that his training at Wharton qualified him for a more lucrative position as an account executive. However, like many Madison Avenue agencies at this time, Y&R had an informal policy of restricting Jewish employees to positions in broadcasting or film production, effectively barring them from management. According to Levy, the policy had been broken at Y&R only once in the firm's history, and that had been in 1923, when founder Raymond Rubicam had hired merchandising expert Samuel Cher. However, Sigurd S. Larmon, who would eventually succeed Rubicam as head of the agency, had taken a keen interest in Levy, believing that the creativity he had demonstrated in his radio work, coupled with his academic background in business theory, constituted an ideal credential for a broadcast advertising executive.

Larmon saw an opportunity to advance Levy in 1940, when Y&R took charge of the Republican party presidential campaign of Wendell Willkie. He assigned Levy to write radio spots for Willkie and to produce a special election eve program for the candidate, believing that a job well done would mollify bigoted colleagues who objected to the hiring of "left-wing Jews." Though Willkie lost the election to Franklin Roosevelt, Levy was promoted and subsequently became a lifelong Republican activist, producing ads and serving as a media consultant for many candidates. As senior radio and television advisor to the Dwight Eisenhower campaigns in 1952 and 1956, he helped craft television spots that put primary emphasis on slogans and made use of visual devices, such as animated characters, as attention-getters. In one of these, for example, an elephant is depicted carrying a sign saying, "We like Ike," while the slogan is chanted on the soundtrack. The Eisenhower commercials are often cited by admirers and critics as a watershed in the use of television for political advertising. Levy also produced the film *Four More Years* for the Committee to Re-elect the President (i.e., Richard Nixon) in 1968, and headed a committee to nominate General Alexander Haig for president in 1988.

Levy married Lucile Alva, a secretary, in 1941, and they had a son and a daughter. The couple was divorced in 1970. A second marriage, to Victoria Robertson, a singer and actress, took place in 1987. A member of the Naval Reserve during World War II, he received a commission as a lieutenant in 1944 and was assigned to the U.S. Treasury Department as chief of the radio section of the War Finance Division. Levy was awarded the Treasury Medal and a Distinguished Service Citation for his radio advertising campaign to sell U.S. War Bonds.

After the war, Levy became a well-known figure at Y&R, managing the accounts of such blue-chip clients as Time, Inc., and General Foods. He was quick to grasp the advertising potentials of television and gained a reputation as a savvy strategist in the formative days of the new medium. With advertising agencies extending their dominion over broadcast production from radio to television, he emerged as an important deal maker in early television, matching clients with appropriate programming concepts and stars. He was, in this way, responsible for dozens of hits, including such series as *Arthur Godfrey's Talent Scouts*, *Robert Montgomery Presents*, *The People's Choice* (starring Jackie Cooper), and *Bat Masterson* (starring Gene Barry).

Levy's years at the Y&R television shop coincided with the implementation of the television "blacklist." During much of the 1950s, performers, writers and production personnel who had histories of left-wing political activism—or who, in some cases, were merely accused of "red" sympathies by self-appointed citizens' groups—were barred from working in television. Though there are varying accounts as to how the blacklist was enforced, most agree that advertising agencies, wary of threats of boycotts against their clients' products, were instrumental in the process of denying individuals the right to work.

Levy always insisted that he was not personally involved in the practice, despite his pivotal position at a leading agency. "It was taken out of our hands at Young & Rubicam, and handed to David Miller, our attorney. So, everything went through him. We never got involved," he said. He refused to discuss the subject in greater detail. When challenged on this by an interviewer during a 1996 videotaping for an oral history archive, he walked off the set.

In 1959, Levy left Y&R to become vice president in charge of network programs and talent at NBC Television. An outspoken opponent of violence on television, he helped to develop several successful dramatic series for the network, including *Dr. Kildare* and *Bonanza*, which were praised for avoiding violent storylines during a period otherwise dominated by shoot-'em-up westerns and crime dramas. In 1961, however, he resigned from the NBC position and moved to the Los Angeles area to create and produce his own television programs and to pursue other types of writing, including fiction, drama, and poetry.

Levy's first program to reach the air was *The Addams Family* (ABC, 1964–1966), a sitcom he adapted from the Charles Addams cartoons that had appeared in the *New Yorker* for many years. He went on to create, write, and produce several other sitcoms and game shows, none of which were major hits. But his contacts and business know-how were much sought after by other producers, and for the balance of his career he held executive and consulting positions with major production companies, including Filmways, Paramount Television, Goodson-Todman and Four Star International. He was a founding member and long-time executive director of the Caucus of Producers-Writers-Directors, a conservative organization that supported stricter standards on expressions of violence, sexuality, and profanity on television and opposed the power of labor unions in the industry.

Throughout his career as an advertising and broadcast executive, Levy always maintained an identity as a literary artist, writing or editing dozens of scripts for the radio and television series sponsored by his clients. He also tried his hand at musical theater, collaborating on three stage shows, including *Hey Ma . . .* starring Kaye Ballard, which opened to a brief run at the Promenade Theatre in New York in 1984. He published a considerable body of fiction, including short stories for *Collier's*, *Good Housekeeping*, and other magazines, as well as four novels, mostly concerned with corruption in the halls of media power: *The Chameleons* (1964), *The Gods of Foxcroft* (1970), *The Network Jungle* (1976), and *Potomac Jungle* (1990). A book of poetry, *Against the Stream*, appeared in 1970. He expressed disappointment toward the end of his life that his successes as a writer paled in contrast to his accomplishments as a businessman.

Levy's attempt to harmonize a career in business with the vocation of a writer is an often-told American story, recalling the lives of such major literary figures as Wallace Stevens (an insurance executive and poet), William Carlos Williams (a pediatrician and poet), and William Gaddis (a securities analyst and novelist). But as an advertising man, Levy walked a thin line between the art of writing and the craft of using writing to mass-market products. At times the differences may have become obscure to him. "In *Who's Who*, they list writing as my 'avocation,'" he told an interviewer, with some anger. "How many books do I have to publish until it becomes my vocation?" His disappointment in failing to achieve his goals as an artist may serve as a cautionary tale to the thousands of young writers, filmmakers, and designers who take "day jobs" in the American advertising industry each year.

• Biographical articles can be found in *Contemporary Theatre, Film, and Television* and *Les Brown's Encyclopedia of Tele-*

vision. Two extensive interviews, one on audiotape, the other on videotape, as well as transcripts of both, are held by the Syracuse University Library in the Steven H. Scheuer Collection of the Center for the Study of Popular Television. Obituaries are in the *Los Angeles Times*, 31 Jan. 2000, and the *New York Times*, 6 Feb. 2000.

DAVID MARC

LEWIS, John (3 May 1920–29 Mar. 2001), pianist, composer, and educator, was born John Aaron Lewis in La Grange, Illinois. His parents' names do not appear in readily available sources of information; reportedly, his father was an interior decorator (or, according to some sources, an optometrist), his mother a classically trained singer. After the death of his father, Lewis moved with his mother to Albuquerque, New Mexico, as a young child. By the time he was four, his mother had also passed away. Being raised mostly by relatives in a large musical family, Lewis at the age of seven began studying piano with his aunt. As a teenager he performed locally with his cousins and several older musicians. In 1938 he enrolled at the University of New Mexico, where he first majored in anthropology, then switched to music.

After graduating in 1942, Lewis served overseas in the U.S. Army Special Services Musical Branch. While in the army he met drummer Kenny Clarke, who had already established himself in New York as a prominent bebop musician. On receiving his discharge in November 1945, Lewis moved to New York and began studying at the Manhattan School of Music. At Kenny Clarke's suggestion, he began writing arrangements for the innovative Dizzy Gillespie big band and in 1946 became the band's pianist, contributing popular arrangements on songs such as "Emanon" and "Two Bass Hits." Two years later he left Gillespie and became a freelance musician. During this period Lewis worked and recorded regularly with jazz legends Charlie Parker, Illinois Jacquet, Lester Young, and Ella Fitzgerald. In 1949 and 1950, he worked as both arranger and pianist on a series of recordings with a nine-piece band headed by trumpeter Miles Davis. The music included on these recordings helped to inspire a middle- and late-1950s musical movement known as "cool jazz."

In 1952 Lewis began working with the Modern Jazz Quartet, a group that included members of Dizzy Gillespie's rhythm section and the Milt Jackson Quartet. With Lewis's leadership and the talents of vibraphonist Milt Jackson, bassist Percy Heath, and drummer Kenny Clarke, the Modern Jazz Quartet soon became one of the most successful small groups in jazz history. Lewis believed that by strengthening the music through structure, jazz could reach a wider audience. Percy Heath told critic Gary Giddins that "John's vision for the group was to change the music from just a jam session, or rhythm section and soloist idea, to something more . . . to change the whole attitude about the music." In 1955, percussionist Connie Kay replaced Kenny Clarke, and the group's personnel remained unchanged for nearly forty years. The quartet became known for its understated interplay, sophisticated arrangements, and its ability to present music as serious as Bach or as swinging as Duke Ellington; at the same time, Lewis found a perfect vehicle to showcase his personalized piano style, which favored polyphonic counterlines, subtle embellishments, and a sparseness rare to jazz pianists of the day. In search of a more respectable image, the quartet members performed in tuxedos, and they favored bookings at concert halls and classical music festivals. The group consistently sold albums and filled theaters until their seven-year hiatus that began in 1974 with the departure of Milt Jackson. On Jackson's return in 1981, the quartet reunited and continued to record and perform on a limited level.

Although the Modern Jazz Quartet enjoyed commercial success and longevity, the group had many critics. Some jazz purists and writers found their music to be pretentious, limiting to Milt Jackson's soloing talents, and untrue to the improvisational nature of jazz. In 1963, a concert review in Time magazine suggested that Mr. Lewis had "gone perilously far in his quest to make jazz more respectable without making it more substantial." Despite their critics, however, the group retained a large loyal fan base, and many of Lewis's compositions with the quartet, such as "Django," "Afternoon in Paris," and "Three Windows," became jazz classics.

Lewis's fame and talents also provided opportunities for him to take on various projects. In the late 1950s he became one of the first modern jazz composers to write for popular films. His 1957 score for the French film *No Sun in Venice* won a Cannes Film Award, and his 1959 score for the film *Odds against Tomorrow* is considered by many to be one of his most successful film efforts. From 1958 to 1983, Lewis became the musical director of the Monterey Jazz Festival. From 1962 to 1965, he was the leader and cofounder of Orchestra U.S.A., which combined a jazz ensemble with strings, and from 1985 to 1992 he held the position of musical director and conductor of the American Jazz Orchestra. Lewis also wrote for musical theater, ballet, and television. Having obtained a master's degree from the Manhattan School of Music in 1953, he believed strongly in the benefits of music education. From 1957 till 1960, Lewis was head of faculty for the Lennox School of Jazz in Massachusetts. He also taught improvisation at Harvard University and City College of New York from 1975 till 1982. He received honorary doctorates from the University of New Mexico, Columbia College in Chicago, the New England Conservatory of Music, and Berklee College of Music.

Lewis married a woman named Mirjana, whose maiden name is unknown, in 1962; they had two children and stayed together until his death. Often described as soft spoken, modest, and sophisticated, Lewis kept his professional life separate from his private life. He was a disciplined and talented man who had a clear understanding of his musical goals despite various criticisms. Despite a long battle with prostate cancer he continued to pursue his musical activities till the end of his life. He died in New York.

• While there is not yet a large-scale biography of Lewis, many magazine articles deal with different aspects of the composers career. For a quality career overview, see Andrew Lepley, "Farewell to the Quartet," *Down Beat*, Apr. 2000, pp. 38–41. Nat Hentoff, "John Lewis: The Modern Jazz Quartet's Music Director Answers Complaints about the Group and Also Delivers His Music Philosophy," *Down Beat*, 20. Feb. 1957, p. 15, has many interesting quotes from Lewis about current criticism. Books such as Len Lyons, *The Great Jazz Pianists Speaking of Their Lives and Music* (1983), and Martin Williams, *The Jazz Tradition* (1983), devote entire chapters to Lewis. Textbooks such as Lewis Porter, *Jazz from Its Origins to the Present* (1993), and Gunther Schuller, *The Swing Era: The Development of Jazz 1930–1945* (1989), further discuss Lewis's contributions. An obituary is in the *New York Times*, 2 Apr. 2001.

JAY SWEET

LIBERMAN, Alexander (4 Sept. 1912–19 Nov. 1999), sculptor and painter, was born Alexander Semeonovitch Liberman in Kiev, Russia, the son of Semeon Liberman, a well-regarded timber industry analyst for both the czarist and Bolshevik governments, and Henriette Pascar, a half-gypsy who directed the first state-run children's theater in Moscow. During the early years of the Russian Revolution, chaotic conditions in St. Petersburg and Moscow, where Liberman spent his early childhood, were reflected in an unruly temperament, which forced his parents to school him at home. In 1921 Semeon Liberman received permission from Lenin to take his son abroad, where Alexander was sent to boarding schools in England and France. His mother accompanied him to England, while his father continued to work in Moscow before finally and permanently leaving for France, where the family was reunited in 1926.

In 1921 Liberman became the first Jew ever enrolled at St. Pirans School in Maidenhead, England, a source of ostracism that led him to downplay his Jewishness then and throughout his life. In 1930 he earned a bachelor of arts degree in philosophy and mathematics from the Sorbonne in Paris, although his dominating mother pushed him to be a painter. Between 1930 and 1932 he studied painting with André Lhote, a Cubist-inspired artist whose writings and teaching proved more influential than his art and whom Liberman found overbearing and dogmatic. Liberman also attended classes in the architecture section of the École des Beaux-Arts. However, his father suffered financial reversals during the first years of the Great Depression, and Liberman worked first as an assistant to the renowned poster designer Cassandre and from 1933 to 1936 as an assistant art director at the Paris-based magazine *Vu*, a photojournalist publication that was the model for *Life* magazine in the United States. At *Vu* Liberman designed photomontage covers and in 1937 won the gold medal for magazine design at the International Exhibition in Paris.

Changes were afoot for the Liberman family, as Semeon's financial situation improved. In 1936 Alexander married German ski champion Hilda Sturm. He quit his job, and the newlyweds went to live in a house that his father bought for them on the French Riviera. Liberman devoted himself to painting and living a quiet life, which did not please his wife, and the couple divorced the following year, having had no children.

Liberman returned to Paris at the outbreak of the Second World War, seeking unsuccessfully to enlist in the French army (he was denied owing to a chronic ulcer condition), and escaped the onrushing German forces by sailing to the United States by way of Portugal in 1941, joining his parents, who had left Europe earlier. Liberman brought with him a childhood friend, Tatiana du Plessix, and her daughter Francine, who became an accomplished writer. Tatiana was the niece of painter Alexander Iacovleff, who had been Liberman's mother's lover for a time. Iacovleff's primary patron was Lucien Vogel, the founder of *Vu* who was by 1941 working at Condé Nast in New York City, primarily for *Glamour* magazine. Vogel introduced Liberman to Condé Nast, recommending him for the job of art director at *Vogue* magazine (one of the Condé Nast publications). Liberman stayed with *Vogue* for twenty-one years and was later promoted to editorial director for all of the Condé Nast magazines, a title he held for decades. He married Tatiana du Plessix in 1942; they had no children.

It was at this point that Liberman's career appeared to divide into two, unrelated paths—his work as an increasingly powerful, sometimes highly autocratic, art director and his growing presence in the fine art realm. In fact, the two paths were strongly intertwined. As art director, Liberman occasionally commissioned notable artists, such as Man Ray and Joseph Cornell, to create illustrations for *Vogue*, and he regularly used modernist paintings as backgrounds at fashion shoots. He also wrote articles on contemporary artists for the magazine and hired major art critics to write essays and reviews, all of which contributed to making *Vogue* a tastemaker in the worlds of art and couture. (The hiring of art critics also brought charges that he used his position self-servingly to win the allegiance of these critics.)

Liberman did little painting during the war but afterward resumed this pursuit. While accomplished in their own right, his paintings never coalesced into a single, definable style: Sometimes he painted postimpressionist landscapes and other expressionist portraits; he experimented with Jackson Pollock–style drip painting, then shifted to a hard-edged style and even heavily impastoed colors. Critics and art historians questioned Liberman's commitment to painting, seeing him as drifting through the fashionable styles of his lifetime. Perhaps his ongoing connection with Condé Nast reinforced the sense among critics that Liberman was more a commercial than a fine artist. "What is *Vogue* but a silly fashion magazine?" he himself once said (quoted in Kazanjian and Tomkins,

Alex, p. 327), and all his efforts to elevate its tone and look could not make him or others forget the ephemeral character of fashion magazines.

While on vacation in France in 1959, Liberman began his first serious exploration of sculpture, learning how to cut and weld large sections of steel. From the start Liberman's sculptures were monumental—sometimes twenty or thirty feet high—and often constructed from discarded tank drums, boiler heads, giant pipes, and I-beams. In 1970 August Heckscher, philanthropist, former New York City parks commissioner, and founder of the Heckscher Museum of Art in Huntington, New York, related that Liberman "told me it was through printing that he first became interested in sculpture. He said that handling the types, feeling of the solid thing and the spaces between words and letters and so on had trained his eye" (oral history interview by Paul Cummings, on file at the Smithsonian Archives of American Art).

Although Liberman continued to paint, his sculptures solidified his reputation as a serious artist and have been exhibited and collected (along with his paintings) by the Albright-Knox Art Gallery in Buffalo, New York; the Art Institute of Chicago; the DeCordova Museum and Sculpture Park in Lincoln, Massachusetts; the Guggenheim Museum in New York; the Los Angeles County Museum of Art; the Metropolitan Museum of Art and the Museum of Modern Art in New York City; the Houston Museum of Fine Arts; the Phoenix Art Museum; the Storm King Art Center in Mountainville, New York; and the Whitney Museum of American Art in Manhattan. Perhaps as good an indicator of Liberman's artistic daring as anything else, his sculpture *Adam* (1970), which stood outside the Corcoran Gallery in Washington, D.C., was denounced in 1972 by President Richard M. Nixon, who ordered "this horror" removed. *Adam*, a 28-foot-tall steel sculpture painted orange and red that extends outwards 29 feet one way and 24 feet another, resembles a huge fire hydrant. In 1978 it was relocated to the front of the east wing of the National Gallery.

Liberman was also an accomplished photographer—his photographs have been exhibited at the Museum of Modern Art and elsewhere—and writer. He wrote and photographed *The Artist in His Studio* (1955), recording the work spaces of Georges Braque, Paul Cézanne, Henri Matisse, Pablo Picasso, and a number of other School of Paris artists; *Marlene Dietrich: An Intimate Photographic Memoir* (1992); and a personal memoir, *Then* (1995). *Prayers in Stone* (1997) examined the relation between architecture and religion.

Liberman worked at Condé Nast until 1995. His demanding wife, Tatiana, died in 1991, and he married Tatiana's nurse, Melinda Pechango, shortly thereafter; they had no children. He died in Miami Beach.

• For information on Liberman, see Dodie Kazanjian and Calvin Tomkins, *Alex: The Life of Alexander Liberman* (1993), a chatty blend of biography, insights, and artistic overview; and Barbara Rose, *Alexander Liberman* (1981), a more for-

mal reading of an artist's development and place in the art world. An obituary is in the *New York Times*, 20 Nov. 1999.

DANIEL GRANT

LIEBOWITZ, Jack S. (10 Oct. 1900–11 Dec. 2000), publisher, was born Jacob in Proskurov, Russia, the son of a father whose name is unknown and his wife, Minnie. Soon after his birth, Liebowitz's natural father vanished from Jacob's life under circumstances that are unclear. Grandparents raised Jacob until his mother wed Julius Liebowitz, who gave the boy his last name.

In 1910 the couple and their six children emigrated to New York's Lower East Side. As a union organizer for the International Ladies Garment Workers Union, Julius Liebowitz was a poor breadwinner, and young Jacob's childhood was difficult. Yet he managed to graduate from New York University with a degree in accountancy in 1925.

Going into business for himself with only one client, Jack Liebowitz was soon managing millions of dollars in strike funds for the ILGWU. But the 1929 stock market crash left him destitute. Through his stepfather, Liebowitz met Harry Donenfeld, a printer of leaflets for the union. In 1932 Donenfeld found himself stuck with stacks of magazines printed by his Donny Press for an insolvent publisher, Ramer Reviews. In order to recoup his losses, Donenfeld took over Ramer's assets for debt, then went into business with former distributor Paul Sampliner, forming the Independent News Company to distribute the unsold magazines and other unsold products. Donenfeld hired Liebowitz as his accountant.

From this modest start was launched Merwil Publications, publisher of risque pamphlets such as *Pep* and *Spicy Stories*, Donenfeld and Liebowitz kicked off a genuine phenomenon in 1934 with *Spicy Detective Stories*, a daring new formula fiction magazine comprising hard-boiled private eye fiction spiced with sex and violence. By 1936, as Culture Publications, the partners were issuing a burgeoning *Spicy* line of magazines, which sold briskly. The support of Independent News was crucial to their success, as most distributors would not have handled them.

In 1937 Donenfeld entered into an alliance with another Donny Press client, comic book publisher Major Malcolm Wheeler-Nicholson. Their new venture was called Detective Comics, Inc., with Liebowitz as treasurer and part owner. Wheeler-Nicholson soon became insolvent, and Liebowitz purchased his share of the company in a November 1937 bankruptcy auction. Under Liebowitz and Donenfeld, Detective Comics expanded rapidly.

In 1938, Liebowitz created *Action Comics*, wherein debuted the oft-rejected original superhero Superman. Although accounts vary as to Liebowitz's exact role in purchasing the property, Liebowitz gave the all-important final approval to accept and cover-feature the "Man of Steel." Superman became an overnight sensation, leading to Batman (who first appeared in *Detective Comics* in 1939) and a wave of superheroes that dominate popular culture to this day.

The stunning success of Superman and Batman led Liebowitz and Donenfeld to disassociate themselves from their Spicy pulp magazine line, which had come under intense scrutiny from public censors, and to concentrate on their safer and more profitable comic books, whose characters Liebowitz astutely exploited by licensing them to radio, films, and toy and novelty manufacturers.

During the late 1930s and through the Second World War, comic book sales boomed, often reaching unheard-of million-copy monthly circulations. Competition became ferocious. In 1939, Donenfeld and Liebowitz entered into a partnership with comic book pioneer Maxwell Charles Gaines to create All-American Comics. The new enterprise produced seminal characters like Wonder Woman, Green Lantern, the Flash, and the Justice Society of America. Independent News distributed the group.

"Some people viewed comics as a passing fad," Liebowitz recalled in *Fifty Who Made DC Great*. "Not me. From the beginning, I felt that comics could be a vital part of the publishing field. They had a broad appeal and a great potential for telling stories. I thought that children, in particular, would love the colorful fantasies they presented."

By 1944, Gaines wanted to strike out on his own. Liebowitz and Donenfeld purchased his interest, merging the two companies into National Comics, Inc., the largest comic book publisher then in existence, and for decades the longest continually operating. Liebowitz became a full partner in the company.

Over time, much of the daily operation of National Comics and Independent News fell into business manager Liebowitz's capable hands. He developed Independent News into the largest magazine and paperback book distributor in the United States, in part because he took on the distribution of *Playboy* during its formative years, building up its circulation base through Independent's superior clout and market penetration.

An important National Comics offshoot was inaugurated during this time when Liebowitz installed his nephew, Jay Emmett, as head of Licensing Corporation of America. LCA's aggressive licensing elevated National Comics's many characters from mere popular entertainment vehicles to lucrative and universally recognizable cultural icons.

Liebowitz married twice. His first wife's maiden name was Rose Sherman, and they had two children together; the date of their marriage is unknown. Rose died in 1956. Two years later, Liebowitz married Shirley Schwartz; their marriage produced no children. From 1956 to 1968, Liebowitz served as the president of New York's Long Island Jewish Hospital—now North Shore–Long Island Jewish Health System—for which he was a founding trustee. He donated a wing, the Rose M. Liebowitz Pavilion. A separate special surgical unit was named for his second wife.

Propelled by the unremitting popularity of Superman and Batman and the powerhouse clout of Independent News, National Comics outgrew its closely held origins. Liebowitz took the company public in 1961 under the name National Periodical Publications. Donenfeld retired, and Liebowitz became company president.

In 1967, Liebowitz engineered the sale of NPP to Kinney National Services, which acquired Warner Bros. studios the following year, and an important new alliance was forged. It produced a major motion picture series featuring Superman and Batman, as well as spin-off television shows. The company became Warner Communications, later Time-Warner. Independent News was renamed Warner Publishers Services. NPP was renamed DC Comics. Although he retired in 1970, Liebowitz was given a seat on the board of directors, which he held well into his 90s, throughout the expanding media company's phenomenal growth. He died in Great Neck, New York.

Liebowitz is an example of an immigrant who through sheer vision and business acumen became a key figure in developing twentieth-century popular culture, especially comic books. He was also a paradox, a socialist-turned-capitalist, as much remembered for his generous philanthropy as for his sharp business practices, which most notoriously deprived originators Jerry Siegel and Joe Shuster of any but the most meagre fruits of their billion-dollar creation, Superman.

• For the official corporate view of Liebowitz, see the 1985 promotional pamphlet *Fifty Who Made DC Great* and Les Daniels's 1995 book *DC Comics: Sixty Years of the World's Favorite Comic Book Heroes*. A less sanitized account can be found in Will Murray's "DC's Tangled Roots," *Comic Book Marketplace* 53 (Nov. 1997). Mike Catron gives perhaps the fullest account of Liebowitz's life in *The Comics Journal* 230 (Feb. 2001). An obituary is in the *New York Times*, 13 Dec. 2000.

WILL MURRAY

LILIENFELD, Julius Edgar (18 Apr. 1882–28 Aug. 1963), scientist and inventor, was born in Lemberg, Galicia, part of the Austro-Hungarian Empire (now Lviv, Ukraine), the son of Siegmund Lilienfeld, a Jewish lawyer, and Sarah Jampoler Lilienfeld. After attending the Oberrealschule in Lemberg, Julius Lilienfeld entered the Polytechnic University of Berlin-Charlottenburg in 1899 to study mechanical engineering. He soon switched to the Friedrich Wilhelm University in Berlin to study physics, chemistry, and philosophy with special emphasis on experimental physics. He completed requirements for a Ph.D. degree in February 1905. His dissertation research was on the use of light spectra for quantitative analysis of gas mixtures.

Lilienfeld joined Otto Wiener's Physics Institute at the University of Leipzig in 1905. There he undertook research on various electrical discharge phenomena. His research on the properties of electrical conductivity in a high vacuum culminated in defense and publication of his *Habilitation* thesis in 1910. During this period he also undertook the installation at the institute of apparatus for liquefying gases. Cryogenic pumping using liquid hydrogen enabled him to attain extremely high vacuums. His results later proved controversial, however, and it is possible that unrecognized effects may have confounded his conductivity measurements.

Following acceptance of his thesis in 1910, Lilienfeld took a position as Privatdozent in the institute, an unsalaried lecturer position dependent on fees from students who signed up for his lectures. He extended his earlier work on conductivity and fashioned X-ray tubes that operated at a high vacuum with a heated filament as a source of electrons, obtaining a series of German patents beginning in 1911. Earlier X-ray tubes required a poor vacuum, that is, the presence of some residual gas. In these earlier tubes the electrons that were the source of the X rays when they struck the target of the tube were produced by collision with the cathode of positive ions from residual gas. Lilienfeld also patented his heated-filament X-ray tubes in the United States. The U.S. patent for one of his designs, submitted in April 1914 and approved in November 1914, was not issued until March 1917 for want of payment of a $20 fee, presumably delayed by problems of communication across the Atlantic Ocean during World War I. This design anticipated the famous X-ray tube design using a hot tungsten filament and a high vacuum independently invented and patented by W. D. Coolidge of General Electric Corporation in October 1916.

In 1916 Lilienfeld was promoted to professor extraordinary (similar to an untenured associate professor position in the United States) at Leipzig. He continued his work on electrical discharges, extended his investigations to field emission of electrons, and applied this to the development of cold-cathode high-vacuum X-ray tubes. He is credited with the discovery and explanation in 1919 of what became known as Lilienfeld transition radiation, which is polarized light coming from the vicinity of the target of an X-ray tube due to the time rate of change of the virtual dipole between the electrons and their image charges formed as electrons near the surface of the tube's target.

In 1921 Lilienfeld traveled to the United States to lecture and to pursue his patent claims, particularly those relating to General Electric's X-ray tubes, and to attempt to regain rights to his U.S. patents, which had been seized by the Alien Property Custodian in 1919. By 1922 he was spending a large portion of his time in the United States. In 1926 he resigned his faculty position at Leipzig to stay in the United States. He married Beatrice Ginsburg on 2 May 1926 in New York City. Lilienfeld held a series of temporary appointments during this period, including one at New York University. He also experimented with solid-state electronic devices. On 8 October 1926 he applied for the first of three patents that were the forerunners of modern field-effect transistors. These patents were granted between 1928 and 1933. They correctly il-

lustrated field-effect principles but did not lead to commercial devices because of the crude semiconductor materials then available. The word *transistor* had its beginning in 1946 in work at Bell Telephone Laboratories that used high-purity germanium to create a solid-state amplifying device. Practical field-effect transistors date from applications of single-crystal silicon in 1960.

In 1928 Lilienfeld took a research and development position with Amrad, Inc., a manufacturer of radios and radio parts, in Malden, Massachusetts. He began work on the electrochemistry of anodic aluminum oxide films and their application in the manufacture of electrolytic capacitors, essential components in much electronic equipment. His detailed studies between 1928 and 1932 of the anodization process and of the structure of the resulting films have received subsequent confirmation. His 1931 patent describing a method for producing stable crystalline anodic films remained the basis for the manufacture of electrolytic capacitors into the twenty-first century. He developed and patented other improvements even after his Malden laboratory, then known as Ergon Research Laboratories of Magnavox Corporation, closed its doors in 1935.

Lilienfeld became a U.S. citizen in 1934. In 1935 he and his wife built a house in St. Thomas in the U.S. Virgin Islands in the hope of escaping an allergy associated with wheat fields from which Lilienfeld had suffered for most of his life. Lilienfeld frequently traveled between St. Thomas and various mainland locations and continued to test new ideas and patent the resulting products. In his lifetime he obtained fifteen German patents and sixty U.S. patents. He died in St. Thomas.

Although Lilienfeld's work on high-vacuum X-ray tubes and on field-effect transistors came at the wrong times to bring him fame and although his leading role in capacitor technology is barely known, he deserves recognition as a talented if eclectic scientist and as a prolific inventor. In 1988 the annual Julius Edgar Lilienfeld Prize of the American Physical Society was established through a bequest by Beatrice Lilienfeld to recognize "outstanding contributions to physics by an individual who has exceptional skills in lecturing to audiences of non-specialists."

• Lists of Lilienfeld's publications and patents and many details of his early work in Germany are in Christian Kleint, "Julius Edgar Lilienfeld: Life and Profession," *Progress in Surface Science* 57, no. 4 (April 1998): 253–327. Lilienfeld's early work on X-ray tubes is described in Robert G. Arns, "The High-Vacuum X-ray Tube: Technological Change in Social Context," *Technology and Culture* 38, no. 4 (October 1997): 852–90. His transistor work is summarized in Arns, "The Other Transistor: Early History of the Metal-Oxide-Semiconductor Field-Effect Transistor," *Engineering Science and Education Journal* 7, no. 5 (October 1998): 233–40. Obituaries are in the *New York Times*, 30 Aug. 1963, and *Physics Today* 16, no. 11 (November 1963): 104.

ROBERT G. ARNS

LINDBERGH, Anne Morrow (22 June 1906–7 Feb. 2001), author and aviator, was born Anne Spencer Morrow in Englewood, New Jersey, the second of the four children of Dwight W. Morrow, an investment banker, senator, and diplomat, and Elizabeth Reeve Cutter, a civic leader and advocate for women's education. Dwight Morrow's work took him to many European capitals, and his children often traveled with him. Anne's formal education was at Miss Chapin's School in Manhattan and Smith College, where she received awards for her poetry and essays. Intelligent and extremely observant, Anne was also shy, emotional, and self-critical. She began keeping a diary in her early teens and later characterized herself as someone for whom "an experience was not finished until it was written or shared in conversation" (*Hours of Lead, Hours of Gold*, p. 4).

In December 1927 Dwight Morrow, then U.S. ambassador to Mexico, invited Charles A. Lindbergh to make a goodwill visit. The shy Midwesterner's recent solo flight across the Atlantic had made him one of the most famous people in the world. To thank his hosts, Lindbergh took the Morrow girls up in his plane, and Anne, terrified at the start, found the experience "liberating." Lindbergh, a man of action, science, and machines, was quite different from the artists and intellectuals she knew. She was dazzled. Since the hero was mobbed everywhere he went, their courtship involved disguises and changes of vehicles. They found privacy only in the air. A few days before her wedding, Anne wrote to a friend: "Wish me courage and strength and a sense of humor. I will need them all." They were married on 27 May 1929 in a secret ceremony at her parents' Englewood manor and were harassed by the press throughout their honeymoon. They had six children.

Charles Lindbergh did not intend to give up aviation for conventional married life, and he trained Anne Lindbergh to be his copilot. Determined to measure up as "crew," she earned a pilot's license and studied radio theory, Morse code, and navigation. Flight in the days of open cockpits was dangerous; her father rewrote his will to allow for her premature death. Despite her occasional terror, she loved the freedom and beauty of flying, the chance to work closely with her husband, and the feeling of doing something "real." Together they surveyed air routes from Canada to China via the Arctic Circle (July–Oct. 1931) and crisscrossed the Atlantic in the Northern and Southern Hemispheres (July–Dec. 1933). It is difficult to separate Anne Lindbergh's work as a flier from that of her husband. She always deferred to him in public but was secretly proud of her prowess in radio communications. In 1934, the National Geographic Society recognized her forty thousand miles of exploration with its prestigious Hubbard Award. She described the Arctic and Atlantic journeys in two bestselling books, *North to the Orient* (1935) and *Listen! The Wind* (1938). Her lyrical writing style, intimate tone, and precise observations were praised by the likes of Sinclair Lewis and Alexander Woollcott.

On 1 March 1932 the Lindberghs' first child, Charles Jr., was kidnapped from their remote New Jersey home. The state police and the national press devoted all resources to what was dubbed "the crime of the century." After ten weeks of false leads, fraudulent and well-meaning intercessions, and a ransom payment, the toddler's body was found in nearby woods. Emotional by nature, Anne Lindbergh did her best to match her husband's stoic control of his grief. Bruno Richard Hauptmann was later linked to the ransom money and tried, and he was executed in April 1936. In 1935, uncomfortable with the press and the public's oppressive interest in their lives and worried for the safety of their second son, born five months after the kidnapping, the Lindberghs moved to England. In 1936 an American attaché in Munich invited the Lindberghs to visit. They made several trips to Germany and even considered moving to Berlin. Charles and Anne Lindbergh also traveled in the Middle East, India, and the Soviet Union, always piloting their own plane. They returned to the United States in the spring of 1939.

Charles Lindbergh had been shown Germany's planes and factories and found them far ahead of his own country's flying power. This and, perhaps, a belief that communism was a worse enemy than nazism led him to publish articles and give radio addresses opposing America's involvement in Europe's affairs. His opinion that the Jews, the British, and the media were acting against America's welfare in urging war on Adolf Hitler caused substantial tension with members of the Morrow family and Anne Lindbergh's former social circle. The former hero was widely denounced as a traitor and anti-Semite. Subsequently, historians, biographers, Anne Lindbergh herself, and the Lindberghs' daughter Reeve have tried to explain what he was thinking. At the time Anne Lindbergh felt her duty was to support her husband. In *The Wave of the Future* (1940), a book-length essay, she tried to interpret his isolationist position for the public. It was not well received, and although she wrote magazine articles, she did not publish another book for fifteen years. In the 1950s she largely devoted her time to family life in suburban Connecticut.

Charles Lindbergh was rigid in domestic matters, strict with his children and also with Anne. He had high expectations for her as a writer and was annoyed when housekeeping, child care, or letter and diary writing took her away from publishable work. Her expectations of perfect harmony in married life were also unrealistic, and consequently she was often depressed. Anne Lindbergh wrote about balancing personal needs, social expectations, and obligations to family and community in her most popular and enduring work, *Gift from the Sea* (1955). This book and Charles Lindbergh's Pulitzer Prize–winning memoir *The Spirit of St. Louis* (1953) rehabilitated their reputations. In the 1960s and 1970s they were both advocates for ecological conservation, which she wrote about in *Earth Shine* (1969). After her husband's death in 1974, Anne Lindbergh published five volumes of her diaries and letters but no new work. In 1975 the readers of *Good Housekeeping* voted her one of their ten most-admired women. She served as guardian of her husband's legacy until strokes left her disoriented. She died at her home in Passumpsic, Vermont.

As a celebrity and as a writer of nonfiction, magazine articles, fiction, poetry, and the diaries that chronicle her response to personal tragedy, war, and the ups and downs of married life, Anne Lindbergh was a presence in American culture for more than half a century. *Saturday Review* critic John Ciardi's sneering review of her *The Unicorn and Other Poems* (1956) provoked what the editor Norman Cousins called "the biggest storm of reader protest" in the magazine's history. *Gift from the Sea,* which spent eighty weeks on the *New York Times* bestseller list, is considered a classic of prefeminism, and her thoughts on staying "whole in the midst of the distractions of life" continue to find new readers. With her accomplishments as an aviation pioneer largely unknown to the general public, only time will tell if she will be remembered for her books or for unhappy events in her life as Mrs. Charles A. Lindbergh.

• The Anne Morrow Lindbergh Papers and the Charles A. Lindbergh Papers are in the Manuscripts and Archives in Sterling Memorial Library at Yale University. Other books by Anne Lindbergh include *The Steep Ascent* (1944), *Dearly Beloved* (1962), and five volumes of diaries and letters, *Bring Me a Unicorn: Diaries and Letters, 1922–1928* (1972), *Hour of Gold, Hour of Lead: Diaries and Letters, 1929–1932* (1973), *Locked Rooms and Open Doors: Diaries and Letters, 1933–1935* (1974), *The Flower and the Nettle: Diaries and Letters, 1936–1939* (1976), and *War within and Without: Diaries and Letters, 1939–1944* (1980). Full-length biographies include Dorothy Herrmann, *Anne Morrow Lindbergh, A Gift for Life* (1992); Susan Hertog, *Anne Morrow Lindbergh: A Biography* (1999); and Joyce Milton, *Loss of Eden: A Biography of Charles and Anne Morrow Lindbergh* (1993). A. Scott Berg's excellent biography of Charles Lindbergh, *Lindbergh* (1988), draws on many conversations with Anne Lindbergh and other family members. Reeve Lindbergh, *Under a Wing* (1998) and *No More Words* (2001), provide an intimate view of her parents' lives and her mother's enfeebled last years. Roxane Chadwick, *Anne Morrow Lindbergh: Pilot and Poet* (1987), is intended for children but serves as an excellent, concise introduction to her life and sensibility. Lindbergh's writings are studied in Elsie F. Mayer, *My Window on the World: The Works of Anne Morrow Lindbergh* (1988); W. Donald Thomas, *Anne Morrow Lindbergh: The Literary Reputation, a Primary and Annotated Secondary Bibliography* (1988); and David Kirk Vaughan, *Anne Morrow Lindbergh* (1988). The 8 Feb. 2001 issue of the *New York Times* has an obituary.

AMY ASCH

LINDSAY, John Vliet (24 Nov. 1921–19 Dec. 2000), U.S. representative and mayor of New York City, was born in Manhattan, the son of George Nelson Lindsay, an investment banker, and Florence Eleanor Vliet. Lindsay's father, the son of an immigrant English brick manufacturer, rose to the chairmanship of American Suisse Corporation (a subsidiary of Credit Suisse). His mother was a Wellesley graduate. Lindsay attended the Buckley School for boys in Manhattan and went to prep school at Saint Paul's in Concord, New Hampshire. He graduated in 1940 and entered Yale University that same year. He graduated from Yale with a B.A. in history in 1943. During World War II, Lindsay served in the U.S. Navy in Sicily and the Pacific, leaving with the rank of lieutenant in 1946. He then attended Yale Law School. After graduating in 1948, Lindsay joined the New York law firm of Webster, Sheffield, Fleischmann, Hitchcock, and Chrystie. In 1949 he married Mary Harrison; the couple had four children. Like many other northeastern, white, Anglo-Saxon Protestants (WASPs), Lindsay gravitated toward progressive Republican, reformist politics. In 1951 he helped found Youth for Eisenhower, and in 1955 he joined the Justice Department as Attorney General Herbert Brownell's executive assistant. With Brownell's encouragement, Lindsay decided to return to New York City and run for U.S. representative in Manhattan's well-to-do "silk-stocking" Seventeenth Congressional District. The incumbent Republican Frederick R. Coudert, Jr., decided to retire, and Lindsay narrowly defeated the Democrat Anthony B. Akers in the general election. Lindsay was easily reelected for three further terms.

Once in Congress, Lindsay proved to be a progressive and liberal Republican. More often than not he sided with liberal northern Democrats on civil rights, civil liberties, immigration, and urban issues. In 1962 Lindsay particularly infuriated the House Republican leaders when he led a band of northeastern liberal Republicans that provided the margin of victory for President John F. Kennedy's proposal to expand the House Rules Committee. He also successfully cultivated a reputation as a political reformer who endorsed high ethical standards on Capitol Hill.

These positions left Lindsay increasingly isolated within the House Republican conference, and in 1965 he decided to run for mayor of New York City. Initially this appeared to be a quixotic venture given the 3-to-1 Democratic registration advantage. But the Democratic incumbent Robert F. Wagner decided to retire, Lindsay was an attractive and energetic campaigner, and the Democratic nominee, Comptroller Abraham D. Beame, was uninspiring. On election day Lindsay won a narrow 43-percent to 40-percent victory over Beame with the Conservative William F. Buckley, Jr., taking 13 percent. Lindsay's upset victory and his relative youth and charisma immediately made him a significant national political figure, but his first term as mayor was bedeviled by labor issues and racial-ethnic conflict in New York. Lindsay had to deal with series of challenges from the city's powerful labor unions, beginning with a transit strike on the day he took office and in 1968 a fifty-five-day teacher's strike in response to the transfer of white schoolteachers from the mostly black Ocean Hill–Brownsville section of Brooklyn. The decentralization plan was a response to minority demands for more control over minority neighborhood schools. In Ocean Hill–Brownsville the local board used this power to "transfer" nineteen white teachers and administrators, which provoked a backlash from the largely Jewish teachers' union who feared for their members' tenure and job security.

In the fall of 1968 further labor disputes raised doubts about Lindsay's effectiveness as a leader. In February 1969, after a major blizzard had nearly crippled the city, homeowners in Queens jeered Lindsay. Later that year Lindsay's unpopularity among middle-class, white ethnic voters in the outer boroughs caused him to lose the Republican primary for mayor to Republican state senator John Marchi, a conservative. But Lindsay ran for the general election as a Liberal-Fusion candidate. The loyalty of minority voters and Manhattan liberals was sufficient to secure his election in November, with 42 percent of the vote, over Marchi and the Democrat Mario A. Procaccino.

Lindsay's second term was no happier than his first. Racial tensions continued, especially when Lindsay proposed a low-income housing project in the white, middle-class, Forest Hills section of Queens in 1971. The crime rate and welfare rolls rose, as did the costs of labor settlements. By the time Lindsay left office the city's overall debt had almost quadrupled from $2.5 billion to $9 billion. Meanwhile Lindsay, having switched parties to become a Democrat in 1971 and espousing an anti-Vietnam War and pro-cities platform, embarked on a disastrous campaign for the 1972 Democratic presidential nomination that ended after he finished sixth in the Wisconsin presidential primary.

After leaving office in 1973, Lindsay resumed his legal career at Webster, Sheffield and continued writing and commenting on politics. In 1980 he mounted a final political campaign for the Democratic nomination for the U.S. Senate, losing to Elizabeth Holtzman. From 1984 to 1992 he served as chair of the Lincoln Center Theater. Lindsay's final years were difficult as Webster, Sheffield and the law firm he subsequently joined both folded in the 1990s. In addition he was plagued by health problems. He died in Hilton Head, South Carolina.

Lindsay's singular achievement was to demonstrate concern for the grievances of minority voters in New York City and to bring blacks and Hispanics fully into the city's political system while avoiding the devastating racial riots that wracked other major American cities in the mid- and late 1960s. His conciliatory approach to racial tensions was largely absent in the governments of other major cities at the time. Lindsay also adhered to the highest ethical standards as mayor and appointed an investigative commission in 1972 to address police corruption following the revelations of Frank Serpico and others about officers accepting bribes from gamblers and drug dealers. Yet Lindsay lacked the political skills to accommodate minority grievances without alienating the city's white middle class. He was never able to get the upper hand over New York's recalcitrant labor unions, and expensive strike settlements and heavy borrowing during his administration contributed to the city's bankruptcy in 1975. Lindsay was one of the last of the truly progressive Republican reformers descended from the Mugwumps of the late nineteenth century. Unfortunately he came to political power in New York at a time when "good government" was inadequate to deal with the multifarious economic, social, and ethnic conflicts facing the modern metropolis.

• Lindsay's papers are at Yale University and the New York City municipal archives. Lindsay wrote two autobiographical accounts of his administration and campaigns, *Journey in Politics: Some Informal Observations* (1967) and *The City* (1969). A comprehensive work on Lindsay as mayor of New York is Vincent J. Cannato's *The Ungovernable City: John V. Lindsay and the Struggle to Save New York* (2001). Contemporary works for Lindsay's 1965 campaign and his first term as mayor include Barbara Carter's *The Road to City Hall: How John V. Lindsay Became Mayor* (1967); Oliver Pilat's *Lindsay's Campaign: A Behind-the-Scenes Diary* (1968); and Nat Hentoff's *A Political Life: The Education of John V. Lindsay* (1969). On liberal Republicanism and its decline see Nicol C. Rae, *The Decline and Fall of the Liberal Republicans* (1989). An obituary is in the *New York Times*, 21 Dec. 2000.

NICOL C. RAE

LITWACK, Harry (20 Sept. 1907–7 Aug. 1999), college basketball coach, was born in Galicia, then part of the Austro-Hungarian empire, the son of Jacob Litwack, a cobbler, and Rachel Rech Litwack. At the age of five he immigrated with his parents to the United States; he grew up in Philadelphia. Raised in a home in which only Yiddish was spoken, he developed a lasting love for the game of basketball. "When I was a kid, every phone pole had a peach basket on it," he recalled. "Every Jewish boy played basketball."

Litwack attended Southern High School (1921–1925), where he played guard on the basketball team and earned all-scholastic honors while his team won the public high school league championship during his senior year. On graduating he attended nearby Temple University and captained the basketball team for two years. Receiving his diploma from Temple in 1930, Litwack spent the next six years playing for the Philadelphia Sphas, a professional team with origins in the South Philadelphia Hebrew Association. While playing for the Sphas, Litwack helped the team win championships in both the Eastern and the American Basketball Leagues and also formed a connection—one that proved critical to his career—with team owner Eddie Gottlieb, a legendary figure in local basketball circles. Concurrent with his professional career, Litwack coached at nearby Simon Gratz High School (leading the team to a 15–2 record in 1930) and in 1931 returned to his alma mater where he served as freshman coach and assistant varsity coach. On 7 June 1943 he married Estelle Cabot, with whom he had two daughters.

During Litwack's twenty-year stint as an assistant coach at Temple, he helped the Owls earn an overall record of 151–32, including a victory over the University of Colorado in the first championship game of the National Invitation Tournament (NIT) in 1938. In 1950–1951 he also served as assistant coach of the Philadelphia Warriors in the fledgling National Basketball Association (NBA) under his old mentor Gottlieb, who was the owner-coach of the franchise.

In 1952 Litwack became the head basketball coach at Temple. Having earned the nickname "Chief" and usually sporting a cigar, he presided over teams that were known for their solid zone defense—he is credited with developing the box and one formation—and compiled an overall record of 373 wins and 193 losses. During his tenure, Temple suffered only one losing season and made a total of thirteen postseason appearances, including third-place finishes at the 1956 and 1958 National Collegiate Athletic Association (NCAA) tournaments and the championship of the NIT Tournament in 1969.

Litwack's success was a major factor in the development of the so-called "Big Five" rivalry, which consisted of five Philadelphia-area schools (Temple, LaSalle, Villanova, St. Joseph's, and the University of Pennsylvania) and which provided basketball fans in the Northeast with many memorable moments in the years before college basketball became driven by television ratings. Known as a low-key recruiter in a profession that was increasingly caught up in a high-stakes win-at-all costs mentality, Litwack specialized in getting the most from his players, many of whom were local boys who had been overlooked by larger, more prestigious schools. At a school where much of the student body came from blue-collar backgrounds and were the first in their family to attend college, his approach worked to perfection. Perhaps his greatest player was guard Guy Rodgers, who had been dismissed by other coaches as being too small to be effective. Rodgers responded to Litwack's guidance by leading the Owls to a three-year record of 67 and 16, which included the school's two appearances in the NCAA Final Four.

Following a long and colorful career, which included writing numerous articles on the sport, sponsoring clinics, and even doing yeoman duty as an official, Litwack retired following the 1972–1973 season. He remained active in the sport, serving as co-owner (with fellow basketball coach Bill Foster of the University of Miami) of the Pocono All-Star Sports Resort in East Stroudsburg, Pennsylvania. Recognition for his achievements came in the form of admission to a number of halls of fame, including the Temple University, Big Five, Pennsylvania State, and Naismith Memorial Basketball Hall of Fame in Springfield, Massachusetts (1975). He died at his home in Huntingdon Valley, Pennsylvania.

Admission to the Basketball Hall of Fame was a fitting tribute. As was readily recognized by his peers, during an era when his sport was becoming increasingly commercialized and beset by scandals that included point-shaving allegations, he epitomized the best of his profession, obtaining the most from his players while conducting a program that was both successful and scandal-free.

• The Naismith Memorial Basketball Hall of Fame in Springfield, Massachusetts, maintains a file on Litwack. The best secondary source of information on his life and career is Zander Hollander, ed., *The Modern Encyclopedia of Basketball* (1979); his teams at Temple also received extensive coverage in local newspapers such as the *Inquirer*, the *Daily News*, and the *Bulletin*. An obituary is in the *New York Times*, 9 Aug. 1999.

EDWARD L. LACH, JR.

LLOYD, Margaret (1887–29 Feb. 1960), dance critic, was born in South Braintree, Massachusetts, to parents whose names and occupations are unknown. She manifested an early interest in writing, although not about dance. She also entered into an early marriage with a football player and had a daughter with him. The marriage ended in divorce.

Lloyd was a Christian Scientist and by 1931 had begun to write film reviews for the *Christian Science Monitor*. However, Leslie A. Sloper, the paper's music and theater editor, noticed her keen interest in dance. Since this was when American modern dancers, notably Martha Graham and Doris Humphrey, were carving out independent careers and when European and Russian ballet artists were emigrating to the United States, Sloper asked Lloyd in 1936 to become the *Monitor's* first dance critic. Lloyd and Sloper married (it is not known exactly when); they had three children. In 1949 Sloper died while they were attending the opera. During the same year, her only book, *The Borzoi Book of Modern Dance*, was published. In this era when writings about dancers tended to treat them as exotic creatures, Lloyd's pragmatic view of her subjects as social beings was a major contribution to the field.

Lloyd was a spirited woman with a keen sense of humor. As a critic, she ignored her assigned press seats and constantly moved about as though she were a museum-goer circling a piece of sculpture. In addition to being a passionate critic, she was a perceptive, sharp-tongued interviewer. Of a performance of Michel Fokine's *Bluebeard* (1942), she commented, "The plot thickens transparently." Of an interview with the irascible Anglo-Irish dancer Anton Dolin, she said, "The twinkle was in the words, rather than in the eyes." And of the rising American modern dancer Sybil Shearer, "She is a perfectionist who likes to believe that perfection is humanly attainable . . . The altitudinal (*sic*) dances come from love of Nature, love of God, whom she is not afraid to speak of out loud as a friend of hers."

In her reviews, Lloyd was unremittingly honest, even if this honesty revealed certain weaknesses in perception. It took time to attune herself to the nonnarrative works of George Balanchine, who was just beginning to establish himself in the United States. She dismissed his masterpiece *Serenade* (1934) with the curt observation, "The effect is artificial." And in

1946 she confessed, "Balanchine's works, like certain processed cereals, may be full of 'locked-in goodness,' but the goodness, in the sense of spiritual richness, remains locked-in and well out of sight for this writer."

Although Martha Graham was at her zenith, Lloyd had not yet become entirely comfortable with Graham's use of abstraction, any more than she was with Balanchine's. She was far more at ease with Doris Humphrey's nature-motivated narrative style. She went so far as to call Graham's *Deaths and Entrances* (1943) a "morbid dissection of the darker reaches of the mind" and went on to say, "a new feature was the introduction of small, portable objects . . . the sight or touch of which summons remembrances so vivid they blot out the present moment. This allusion to the intensification of memory experience through sensory contact . . . affords considerable aid to our uneasy progress through the fantasy."

Of Humphrey's *Day on Earth* (1947) she commented comfortably, "*Day on Earth* is an exquisite pastoral. The theme is the blessedness and sustaining power of work . . . This is a work that should not be analyzed in words, for words are crass and paltry in comparison with its delicacy of mood. It is enough that it shimmers and sings and enmeshes the spectator in its reverie."

After the Second World War, a veritable wave of impressive ethnic dance companies began to appear in the United States. The most important ones came from Russia, Spain, Japan, and Bali. Margaret Lloyd embraced them with enthusiasm and, more important, understanding. She finished her review of one of these, the Roberto Iglesias Company, in leap year 1960; filed the piece, and then sat down in her armchair to take a nap. She never woke up.

• Margaret Lloyd's *Borzoi Book of Modern Dance* (1949), while no longer current, is still highly informative. "Margaret Lloyd: A Search for Human Values" and "Margaret Lloyd: A Rapture of Approach," both written by Doris Hering in *Dance Magazine*, Sept. and Oct. 1960, were drawn from her personal scrapbooks. An obituary appeared in the *New York Times*, 2 Mar. 1960.

DORIS HERING

LONE WOLF (c. 1820–1879), Kiowa warrior and chief, was born Guipagho. The names of his parents may have been Bo-hone-Kaw-ghi and Kaw-Say, but this is not known with certainty. He grew to manhood during the height of the buffalo and horse era when Kiowa parties ranged freely across the open plains hunting game and raiding settlements in Texas and Mexico. In Kiowa society prestige depended on success in raiding and warfare; Lone Wolf became proficient at both. He apparently had two wives and two children.

In 1863 Lone Wolf was escorted to Washington in a government effort to forge peaceful Indian-white relations. Instead, he returned home convinced that the whites would kill each other off in their civil war and allow the Indians to reclaim their lands. In 1865 Lone Wolf was pressured into signing the Treaty of Little Arkansas, which restricted the tribe's hunting territory to parts of the Panhandle of Texas and all of Indian Territory west of the 98th meridian. The agreement did little to deter raiding activity. Upon the death of Dohason in 1866, Lone Wolf became head chief. However, Kiowa unity was soon fractured as tribal members became divided over what policy to follow toward whites. Lone Wolf had the support of the more militant faction, while Kicking Bird emerged as the spokesman for the peace party.

Lone Wolf attended the council at Medicine Lodge in October 1867 but was not among the chiefs who signed the treaty that forced the Kiowas to accept a reservation in Oklahoma. When military action ensued against the Cheyennes and Arapahos, Lone Wolf moved his people to a safe haven at Fort Cobb, Indian Territory. Following the Washita Massacre, 27 November 1868, Lieutenant Colonel George A. Custer and General Philip Sheridan charged that Lone Wolf and Satanta had participated in the fighting . However, Colonel William Hazen, commander at Fort Cobb, refuted their claim. He also intervened to prevent Sheridan from attacking the Kiowas near Fort Cobb. Nevertheless, Sheridan had Lone Wolf and Satanta arrested and threatened to hang both unless all the Kiowas reported to the fort immediately.

The chiefs were not released until mid-February 1869, after Sheridan denounced Lone Wolf as a liar and murderer and declared that he would hold the chiefs responsible for any misconduct by their people. Lone Wolf promised that "after this you will not see any more blood. We have thrown everything bad away from us." But the chief had little control over his tribesmen. Suffering from food shortages, Indian bands began sneaking off the reservation. Even Kicking Bird, a proponent of accommodation with the government, yielded to pressure and led a raid into Texas in July 1870. Lone Wolf participated in this foray in which three soldiers were killed. When castigated for his latest transgressions, the chief angrily asked the agent why he was so mad that a few Texans had been killed when several Indians had also been killed.

In May 1871 General William Sherman arrested Satanta, Set-angya, and Big Tree for attacking the Warren wagon train. In an apparent attempt to intimidate Sherman, Lone Wolf strode into the meeting, heavily armed, and handed out weapons to his tribesmen. When guards and Indians raised their guns, a battle appeared imminent. Fortunately, bloodshed was averted when Satanta and other unarmed Indians shouted "No, no, no," and Sherman ordered the soldiers not to fire.

The following spring Lone Wolf's son Tau-ankia (Sitting-in-the-Saddle) was shot in the knee while on a raiding trip. His life was saved by his friend Mammedaty. In September Lone Wolf traveled to Washington, where he skillfully negotiated the release from prison of Satanta and Big Tree. This made him a hero on the reservation. In turn he promised to keep his people near Fort Sill. This promise was broken when Lone Wolf received news on 13 January 1874 that Tau-ankia and his nephew Gui-tain had been killed by Fort Clark troopers while returning from a raid in Mexico. The death of his only son, recorded in the Kiowa calendar, sent the chief and his village into deep mourning. In May his warriors recovered the men's bodies but were forced to rebury them when pursued by troops.

Brooding over the death of Tau-ankia, and thinking only of revenge, Lone Wolf led his militant faction into the Red River War. In June 1874 he joined in the attack on Adobe Walls in the Texas Panhandle. On July 12 he and Maman-ti mounted a spectacular attack against a force of Texas Rangers in Lost Valley, a few miles northwest of Jacksboro, Texas. Mammedaty counted the first coup and turned over the body of a ranger to Lone Wolf who, after decapitating the victim, declared his son avenged. During the victory dance the grateful Lone Wolf passed his name, his medicine, and his shield to Mammedaty, who became Lone Wolf the Younger. Later in 1874 the chief's village was destroyed in Palo Duro Canyon. On 26 February 1875 he surrendered at Fort Sill with his band of over 250 followers.

Lone Wolf was among the leaders sentenced to prison in Fort Marion, Florida. In May 1878, suffering from malaria, he was permitted to return to Fort Sill but died the following year. He was secretly buried in an unmarked grave on Mount Scott. The town of Lone Wolf, Oklahoma, bears his name.

No Kiowa leader surpassed Lone Wolf in his determination to preserve his people's lands and their traditional way of life. Deeply steeped in the Kiowa warrior tradition, he found it impossible to adapt to the realities of the new order imposed by the white invaders. The passing of Lone Wolf and his generation marked the end of the ancient Kiowa way of life. Lone Wolf the Younger inherited the mantle of leadership. Like his predecessor, he led Kiowa resistance to government influence on the reservation, but he preferred to fight in the courts, not on the open plains. N. Scott Momaday, a well-known Kiowa author, is his great-grandson. According to Parker McKenzie, Kiowa informant, there was no blood relationship between the two Lone Wolfs.

• An essential primary source on the Kiowas is James Mooney, *Calendar History of the Kiowa Indians* (1898). Lone Wolf's relations with the army and reservation agents are discussed in Wilbur S. Nye, *Carbine and Lance: The Story of Old Fort Sill* (1942); William H. Leckie, *The Military Conquest of the Southern Plains* (1963); and Lawrie Tatum, *Our Red Brothers and the Peace Policy of President Ulysses S. Grant* (1899; repr. 1970). Genealogical information on Lone Wolf and Mammedaty is found in N. Scott Momaday, *The Names: A Memoir* (1976) and in Parker McKenzie, *Letter to William Welge,* Archives Division, Oklahoma Historical Society, 9 Nov 1996.

MARVIN E. KROEKER

LORDE, Audre (18 Feb. 1934–17 Nov. 1992), poet, essayist, and feminist, was born Audrey Geraldine Lorde in New York City, the daughter of Frederic Byron Lorde, a laborer, and Linda Gertrude Belmar Lorde, both West Indian immigrants from Grenada. As a child, when someone asked about her thoughts, she replied by quoting poetry, and at the age of twelve she wrote poems. Lorde attended Hunter High School, where she met other girls who wrote poetry. She edited the school's literary magazine, but when an English teacher rejected a love poem Lorde had written about a boy, she sent it to *Seventeen* magazine, and it became her first professional publication. After working at a variety of jobs in New York and Stamford, Connecticut, Lorde spent the year 1954 in Cuernavaca, Mexico, taking courses at the National University of Mexico. There, she accepted and firmly established her sense of identity as a lesbian and a poet.

In 1955, Lorde returned to New York, took classes at Hunter College, and immersed herself in the city's lesbian community. At work and school, she kept her sexual preference a secret, while at the same time keeping her college attendance private as she socialized at downtown working-class lesbian bars. She felt further marginalized by her unwillingness to take on the butch or femme—exaggeratedly masculine or feminine—roles that defined the 1950s lesbian bar culture. Despite her alienation even within the lesbian community, she found among its members a desire to create across color lines a mutually supporting community of women. In 1959, Lorde graduated from Hunter; in 1961 she earned a master's degree in library science from Columbia University. She worked at Mount Vernon Public Library until 1963 and later worked as head librarian at Town School Library in New York City from 1966 to 1968. In 1962 she married a white attorney, Edward Ashley Rollins. They had two children and divorced in 1970.

In the 1960s, Lorde's poetry was published regularly in magazines and anthologies, and she became active in the civil rights, antiwar, and women's movements. Her first book of poetry, *The First Cities* (1968), was published by her high school friend Diane Di Prima's small Poet's Press. The poet Dudley Randall praised the book as a strong expression of African-American identity and experience that refrained from political confrontation. That same year, Lorde received a grant from the National Endowment for the Arts. She also spent a term as poet in residence at historically black Tougaloo College in Mississippi, where she relished the chance to work with black students and familiarize herself with southern black culture. With the time away from her children and the financial freedom of the NEA grant, she was able to commit herself to her writing as she had not been able to before, and that spring she wrote most of the poems in *Cables to Rage* (1970), her second book. More political than her first book, this one responded to racism, sexism, violence, and the silences that permitted oppression. The book also included "Martha," a poem that acknowledges her lesbianism. While working at Tougaloo, she met Frances Louise Clayton, with whom she would live for nineteen years, primarily on Staten Island. Clayton helped Lorde raise her children and later helped her cope with breast cancer.

Later in 1968, when she returned to New York, Lorde began teaching part time in the City University of New York system. In 1978, she became a professor at John Jay College of Criminal Justice and in 1981 at Hunter College. Lorde's third collection of poetry, *From a Land Where Other People Live* (1973), was nominated for a National Book Award. She explored her complex identity within a global political context in which other blacks, women, mothers, and lesbians also faced oppression. *New York Head Shop and Museum* (1974), her fourth book, narrowed her focus specifically to New York, offering a tour of a decaying city. Up to this point, Lorde had worked only with small presses, but in 1976 a large publisher, W. W. Norton, published *Coal*. Through their now mutual publisher, she befriended widely admired lesbian feminist poet Adrienne Rich, who helped introduce Lorde's work to white readers. Inspired by a trip with her children to Benin in 1974 and now fully confident in her literary power, Lorde lay claim, in *The Black Unicorn* (1978), to the spirituality and strong goddesses of African mythology, introducing them to her American readers and calling upon them for strength to survive in the African diaspora. *Our Dead Behind Us* (1986) likewise drew on African myth, including the strength of the Dahomean Amazons and the Rainbow Serpent Aido Hwedo in the face of American racism and sexism as well as South African apartheid.

A biopsy in 1977 showed evidence of breast cancer, and Lorde underwent a modified radical mastectomy, losing her right breast. The first of her prose books, *The Cancer Journals* (1980), included three essays about the process of discovering, coping with, and reflecting upon her cancer. She felt isolated because the models for coping available to her were primarily white and heterosexual, so one of her goals was to provide a precedent for women like her, a sign for some other black lesbian with breast cancer that she was not alone. *The Cancer Journals* received the American Library Association Gay Caucus Book of the Year Award in 1981. A similar feeling that as a young black lesbian she had no precedent, model, or myth she could use to understand her identity, inspired *Zami: A New Spelling of My Name* (1982), which she called a "biomythography." In a somewhat fictionalized memoir of childhood through young adulthood, Lorde offered an account of her own confusion, pain, errors, and delights on the road toward accepting and understanding herself as a black lesbian. Her prose collection *Sister Outsider: Essays and Speeches* (1984) aired the divisions across the various elements of Lorde's own identity—black, lesbian, feminist, activist, woman, lover, mother, poet, friend—and particularly those divisions between African-American women that prevent their collaboration. The title of another prose collection, *A Burst of Light* (1988), is a journal of her cancer's recurrence,

this time in her liver, and it recounted her insistence on taking control of her medical treatment.

The awards she received include, among others, the 1975 Broadside Press Poet's Award, the 1988 Manhattan Borough President's Award for Excellence in the Arts, the 1990 Bill Whitehead Memorial Award, and in 1991 the Walt Whitman Citation of Merit. She was appointed Poet Laureate of the State of New York in 1991, and she held honorary doctorates from Hunter College, Oberlin College, and Haverford College. She died on St. Croix, in the U.S. Virgin Islands, where she had been living with feminist scholar Gloria I. Joseph.

Though much of Lorde's writing focused on identity, she never regarded identity as stable. Identity involved, instead, the tensions between the various aspects of life. She acknowledged that while American culture offered models and myths with which many can feel comfortable, she found few that applied comfortably to her particular combination of identities. The title of one of her essays, "The Transformation of Silence into Language and Action," was therefore practically a motto for her whole career. Her poetry and prose transformed a silence about difference that colluded with its oppression into the power of articulated identity. Feeling excluded from the Western mythic traditions, she advanced instead an African mythic tradition, a "black unicorn" as opposed to the pallid European one. And for those "others" who have felt excluded by social and cultural norms, she offered a concrete example of a real woman who laboriously negotiated cultural and social exclusion. As a child, she rewrote her name according to her own taste, dropping the "y," and she subtitled her "biomythography" *A New Spelling of My Name*. Continuing in that practice of naming herself, of declaring her own identity, Lorde took on in an African naming ceremony yet another name, Gambda Adisa—Warrior: She Who Makes Her Meaning Known.

• Lorde's papers are housed at Spelman College. *The Collected Poems of Audre Lorde* (1997) includes all the poems from her books. Lorde discussed her work, life, and politics in several published interviews, including two with Karla Hammond: *American Poetry Review* (March/April 1980), pp. 18–21, and *Denver Quarterly* (Spring 1981), pp. 10–27, and one with Claudia Tate, *Black Women Writers at Work* (1983). A special issue of *Callaloo* includes some of Lorde's uncollected prose as well as an interview with Charles H. Rowell (14, no. 1 [1991], pp. 83–95). Illuminating studies of her poetry include, among others, Gloria T. Hull, "Living on the Line: Audre Lorde and *Our Dead Behind Us*" in *Changing Our Words: Essays on Criticism, Theory, and Writing by Black Women*, ed. Cheryl A. Wall (1989), pp. 150–72; Sagri Dhairyam, "'Artifacts for Survival': Remapping the Contours of Poetry with Audre Lorde," *Feminist Studies* (Summer 1992), pp. 229–56; Brenda Carr, "'A Woman Speaks . . . I am Woman and Not White': Politics of Voice, Tactical Essentialism, and Cultural Intervention in Audre Lorde's Activist Poetics and Practice," *College Literature* 20, no. 2 (1993), pp. 133–53; and Kara Provost, "Becoming Afrekete: The Trickster in the Work of Audre Lorde," *MELUS* 20, no. 4 (Winter 1995), pp. 45–59. Ada Gay Griffin and Michelle Parkerson directed a film documentary, *A Litany for Sur-*

vival: The Life and Work of Audre Lorde (1995). An obituary is in the *New York Times*, 20 Nov. 1992.

JAMES D. SULLIVAN

LUDLOW, Louis Leon (24 June 1873–28 Nov. 1950), congressman and journalist, was born in a log cabin on a Fayette County farm, seven miles from Connersville in southeastern Indiana, one of eight children of Henry Ludlow, a farmer, and Isabelle Smiley. He grew up in a hardscrabble rural environment and attended grade school and high school in Connorsville. After his high school graduation in 1892, he began his journalism career as a reporter with the *Indianapolis Sun*, the smallest of that city's newspapers. Ludlow had correctly gauged that he stood a good chance of being hired even without training or experience. He enrolled at Indiana University but left after contracting a severe case of typhoid fever in 1894 that aborted his college career.

From 1895 to 1899 Ludlow worked as a reporter for the *Indianapolis Sentinel* and from 1899 to 1901 as a political writer for the *Indianapolis Press*. On 17 September 1896 Ludlow married Katherine Huber, the *Sentinel's* society editor. They had four children. In 1901 Ludlow began his career as a Washington correspondent with the *Sentinel*, subsequently moving to the *Indianapolis Star* in 1903 and the *Columbus (Ohio) Dispatch* in 1913. He served at various times as a correspondent for other Indiana newspapers, such as the *Terre Haute Tribune* and the *Muncie Star* as well as the *Tacoma Ledger*, the *Denver Post*, the *Milwaukee News*, and the *Savannah Press*. Well liked and highly regarded, Ludlow was elected in 1927 to a term as president of the National Press Club.

In 1928 Ludlow was elected to Congress as a Democrat, defeating the Republican incumbent by some 6,000 votes in a district the Republican presidential candidate carried by over 30,000. Ludlow became the first person to move from the Capitol's press gallery to the floor of Congress. He served from 4 March 1929 to 3 January 1949, when he retired to newspaper work because he felt that heart trouble diminished his ability to serve his constituents. Because of redistricting, he represented various districts (the Seventh District from 1929 to 1933, the Twelfth District from 1933 to 1943, and the Eleventh District from 1943 to 1949), but his constituency always included Indianapolis.

Although Ludlow called himself a "Jeffersonian Democrat," his political philosophy has been described as a "unique blend of Christianity, Jeffersonianism, and isolationism" (Griffin, p. 269). He was an outspoken opponent of executive power, but he supported President Franklin D. Roosevelt and many New Deal measures. Ludlow also spoke out strongly for antilynching legislation and championed an equal rights amendment for women. He is, however, best remembered for his unsuccessful campaign to enact a constitutional amendment requiring a national referendum before the country could go to war except in the case of attack.

Such an amendment did not originate with Ludlow. Some had called for such a measure before the United States entered World War I in 1917, and a war referendum plank appeared in the 1924 Democratic and Progressive party presidential platforms. By the 1930s, as war loomed in Europe and Asia, isolationist sentiment grew in the United States. In 1934 congressional investigations asserted that munitions makers and bankers had promoted American entry into World War I. Disillusionment about the outcome of that war led to renewed popular interest in such a referendum. In January 1935 Ludlow introduced a resolution for an amendment that called not only for a referendum but also for a limit on any possible war profits. But the resolution remained bottled up in the House Judiciary Committee as isolationists concentrated on legislation circumscribing Americans' activity in case of a war outside the United States. Ludlow's attempts to move the resolution out of committee were boosted in December 1937, when Japanese forces sank an American gunboat during their invasion of China and fear of war mounted in the United States. Unusual coalitions arose both for and against congressional action to discharge the resolution from the Judiciary Committee. Supporters ranged from the liberal Texas Democrat Maury Maverick to the conservative Illinois Republican Everett Dirksen. Most of the nation's press fulminated against Ludlow, as did the nation's foreign policy establishment (for example, Secretary of State Cordell Hull and the former secretary of state Henry Stimson). However, the Gallup Poll—as it had found year after year since 1935—measured support at better than two-thirds of those polled.

Ludlow got the necessary signatures for a petition forcing a House vote on discharging the resolution from the Judiciary Committee. The Roosevelt administration actively lobbied against the discharge. Roosevelt sent a letter to the House, read by its Speaker, expressing fears that such an amendment was "impractical" and would cripple a president's ability to conduct the nation's foreign affairs. The discharge resolution was defeated on 10 January 1938, with 188 favoring consideration and 209 opposed. A larger percentage of Republicans than Democrats voted in favor of discharging the resolution.

The vote's closeness—a shift by just eleven representatives would have changed the outcome—prompted the historian William Leuchtenburg to observe that it demonstrates Roosevelt's "tenuous control of foreign policy, and as late as 1938 . . . the hardrock strength of isolationist sentiment" (Leuchtenburg, p. 230). By 1945 Ludlow, who never again achieved such fame, had come to support American participation in the United Nations but did hope that the UN charter would include a clause on war referenda.

The prolific Ludlow, who apart from his journalism wrote dozens of articles and corresponded with hundreds (estimates are that he received more mail per day than any other representative), authored five books, including the autobiographical *From Cornfield to Press Gallery* (1924); a popular history about Indiana pioneers (1925); the satirical novel *Senator Solomon Spiffledink* (1927); an attack on bureaucracy's "wasteful and evil tendencies," *America Go Bust* (1933); and a plea for his proposed amendment, *Hell or Heaven* (1937). In 1940 he received an honorary LL.D. from Butler University, and in 1980 he was inducted into the Indiana Journalism Hall of Fame. He died in Washington, D.C.

Ludlow's years as a journalist prepared him well for the House of Representatives, and he was an effective and well-regarded journeyman congressman who conscientiously served his constituents. His dedication to a contemporary popular belief that a national referendum should restrain the U.S. government's ability to wage war brought him out of obscurity in the mid-1930s, and for a moment he became an important touchstone in the ongoing debate about restraints on the government's ability to wage war.

• Ludlow's papers, more than 8,000 items, including correspondence, petitions, scrapbooks, and newspaper clippings, are at the Lilly Library, Indiana University. See Ray Boomhower's article in *Encyclopedia of Indianapolis* (1994); Walter R. Griffin, "Louis Ludlow and the War Referendum Crusade, 1935–1941," *Indiana Magazine of History* 64 (1968): 267–88; and William Leuchtenburg, *Franklin D. Roosevelt and the New Deal: 1932–1940* (1963). An obituary is in the *New York Times*, 29 Nov. 1950.

DANIEL J. LEAB

M

MARSHALL, E. G. (18 June 1910–24 Aug. 1998), actor, was born Edda Gunnar Marshall in Owatonna, Minnesota, the only child of Charles Gunnar Marshall, an executive of the Northwestern Bell Telephone Company, and Hazel Irene Cobb Marshall. (In 1997 Marshall told the Associated Press that he was born in 1914, but in its obituary the *New York Times* (26 Aug. 1998) noted that "published records listed his birth date as 18 June 1910.") As a boy Marshall was a self-described loner, enjoying solitary walks in the woods more than the company of schoolmates, who teased him mercilessly for his Norwegian name, calling him "Edna" rather than "Everett," the anglicized name he tried to adopt. His hobbies included collecting Native American artifacts, an interest that developed into a lifelong passion for archaeology. An excellent student, he won admission to elite Carleton College in nearby Northfield, but wanting a taste of city life in Minneapolis, he transferred to the University of Minnesota, where he studied English literature.

Marshall developed an interest in public speaking while in college and briefly contemplated studying for the Lutheran clergy. But the growing sense of self-confidence he found in eliciting the responses of an audience, coupled with a love for dramatic literature, led him to pursue a career in acting. In 1933 he successfully auditioned for the Oxford Players, a touring company that mounted contemporary and classical theater productions. He remained with the troupe for five years, learning the basics of stagecraft while playing minor roles and gaining a reputation as a remarkably quick study with a photographic memory.

Marshall first appeared on the New York stage in 1938, when he was summoned by the Federal Theatre Project to take over a role in its Broadway production of *Prologue to Glory*, a politically charged depression-era work on the early life of Abraham Lincoln. Relocating permanently to New York, he immersed himself in the city's theater scene.

"I was among the charter members of the Actors Studio," Marshall recalled in an interview. "Robert Lewis, Elia Kazan and Cheryl Crawford conceived it, and invited me and others to join. We did a lot of original, fresh things. Herbert Berghof and I did scenes from Kafka—things like that. It was exciting, because where else could you have colleagues and contemporaries—people like Marlon Brando and Monty Clift [Montgomery Clift]—there to watch and to make comments? It was a great time" (Marc and Scheuer).

By the 1950s Marshall had become a familiar figure to theater-goers, both on and off Broadway, as well as in summer stock and in touring productions. Admired by directors for his hard work and intelligent handling of difficult roles, he gained parts in some of the memorable theater productions of the twentieth century, including the world premieres of Eugene O'Neill's *The Iceman Cometh* (1946) and Arthur Miller's *The Crucible* (1953) and in the American premiere of Samuel Beckett's *Waiting for Godot* (1956).

In a characteristically modest self-appraisal, Marshall described himself to the *London Times* (11 June 1977) as a theatrical "utility man." In fact he demonstrated remarkable versatility in fifty years on the American stage, proving as much equal to the task of playing the lead in a Shakespearean tragedy (for example, *Macbeth*, 1973) as a straight man in a Neil Simon comedy (for example, *Plaza Suite*, 1969). Other stage roles of note include Oscar Hubbard in the Lincoln Center revival of Lillian Hellman's *The Little Foxes* (1967) and Weller Martin in D. L. Coburn's *The Gin Game* (1978). Effecting a mature, distinguished countenance even in his youth, he was rarely offered romantic or glamorous roles.

While some actors with stage credentials of this caliber were reluctant to perform in the electronic media during the mid–twentieth century, Marshall aggressively pursued roles in radio, movie, and television drama. His crisp elocution also put him in demand as a narrator of documentary and educational films. While remaining committed to live theater throughout his career, Marshall achieved especially great success in television. During the 1950s (the so-called "golden age of television drama") he appeared in scores of live and prerecorded "teleplays," including productions aired on such highly regarded anthology series as *Studio One*, *Armstrong Circle Theatre*, and *Playhouse 90*.

In a rare show business feat, the actor achieved both popular and critical acclaim as the star of a weekly television series. In *The Defenders* (CBS, 1961–1965) he played the attorney Lawrence Preston, head of a New York father-and-son law partnership. The series vigorously explored social issues that were otherwise taboo on television. Preston defended a doctor who had performed an abortion at a patient's request (this at a time when the procedure was illegal throughout the United States), a blacklisted actor who was blocked from taking a small role in a film, and a traveler who violated State Department visa restrictions. Marshall conveyed a discreet sense of moral outrage over social iniquity, managing to temper Preston's indignation with an abiding faith in the American legal system.

"We knew we were 'pushing the envelope,'" Marshall said with some pride in recalling his work on *The Defenders* (Marc and Scheuer). A social activist in his own right, he gave both time and money to organizations supporting universal health care, environmental quality, and other causes. The actor contributed several suggestions to the series, such as the inclusion of African-American judges in courtroom scenes, and he created a number of story ideas. During the show's first two seasons, Marshall won successive Best Actor Emmy Awards, and his diligence in the portrayal of a crusading defense attorney, which included his taking a course in jurisprudence, was recognized by the American Bar Association (ABA) with his appointment as an ABA fellow.

Later in the decade Marshall took his only other starring role in a television series as Dr. David Craig in *The New Doctors* (NBC, 1969–1973). He felt, however, that the opportunities for meaningful work on weekly television series were in decline and subsequently turned down many offers of starring roles in such series. He did, however, frequently appear in made-for-television movies, including *Ike* (1986), in which he portrayed President Dwight Eisenhower.

Marshall's film career suffered to some extent from a frank disdain for Hollywood as a place to live and work, but he performed character roles in a number of noteworthy pictures, including *Call Northside 777* (1948), *The Caine Mutiny* (1954), and *Town without Pity* (1961). In 1957 he won featured roles in two films adapted from television plays, Paddy Chayefsky's *The Bachelor Party* and Reginald Rose's *Twelve Angry Men*. Rose was particularly impressed by Marshall's performance as a self-righteous juror in a murder case and was instrumental in casting him in *The Defenders*. One of Marshall's finest screen efforts was in Woody Allen's *Interiors* (1978). The actor showed his range once again, playing an aging man who, inviting the scorn of his children, leaves a chronically depressed wife for a gregarious companion. He often played politicians, such as the president of the United States in *Superman II* (1981) and John Mitchell in *Nixon* (1995).

Marshall married Helen Wolf in 1939, and the couple had two children. They were divorced in 1953. In 1955 Marshall married Judith Coy, a painter, and they had three children. Late in his life Marshall lived in suburban Bedford, New York. He continued to work, full schedule, into his seventies, taking a recurring role as a doctor in the television series *Chicago Hope* in 1994 and, after an absence of thirty years, the character of Lawrence Preston in two *Defenders* revival films for television. He completed the second of these just months before his death at his home in Bedford.

Marshall was a consummately professional actor who consistently showed more interest in developing his craft and participating in worthwhile projects than in the glitz, glamour, or multimillion-dollar fees that tend to shape many American show business careers. His appearances in hundreds of television programs and films kept his face in the public eye, but his name never became a "household word." An "actor's actor," he is more apt to be remembered by those who worked with him.

• An oral history interview with Marshall, conducted by David Marc and Steven H. Scheuer, is held in the collections of the Center for the Study of Popular Television at the Syracuse University library (videotape with transcription, 16 Oct. 1997), and a print interview appeared in the *London Times* (11 June 1997). Marshall's complete film and television credits can be found in the Internet Movie Database (http://www.imdb.com). Obituaries are in the *New York Times* and the *Los Angeles Times*, both 26 Aug. 1998.

DAVID MARC

MARTIN, Dean (7 June 1917–25 Dec. 1995), singer and actor, was born Dino Paul Crocetti in Steubenville, Ohio, the son of Gaetano Crocetti, a barber, and Angela Barra Crocetti. From an early age, he was interested in music and loved to sing. One of his cousins later remembered that he would walk around his home in an old slouch hat, "sort of croon[ing] all the time" (quoted in Schoell, p. 6). A poor student, he dropped out of high school during his sophomore year. He worked for a time as a filling-station attendant and at a steel mill, but the work bored him, and he became more interested in pursuing Steubenville's nightlife than in holding down a steady job. Known as "Little Chicago," the town teemed with big-city vices; Martin later joked that "there was everything there a boy could want. Women. Music. Nightclubs. Liquor" (quoted in Schoell, p. 6). By the age of seventeen, he had run bootleg whiskey from Ohio to Pennsylvania, fought a few bouts as an amateur welterweight boxer, and worked as a clerk at a Steubenville cigar store that served as a front for a notorious gambling den. In 1936 he worked as a croupier in the store's back rooms, where he became expert at stealing silver dollars from the gaming tables by dropping them into his shoes.

Martin first sang publicly in 1934, when his friends dared him to take the stage at a resort near Youngstown, Ohio. Over the next few years he sang regularly at clubs and community centers in Steubenville and Youngstown. Possessing a sleepy-sounding baritone, he deliberately patterned his relaxed, intimate style after Bing Crosby. "When a Bing Crosby movie came to Steubenville, I would stay there all day and watch," he later recalled. "And that's where I learned to sing, 'cause it's true I don't read a note. I learned from Crosby, and so did Sinatra [Frank Sinatra], and Perry Como. We all started imitatin' him. He was the teacher for all of us" (quoted in Tosches, p. 74). His first professional work as a singer, in 1939, was for a band led by Ernie McKay, who billed him as "Dino Martini" (after Nino Martini, a popular romantic singer of the day). In the summer of 1940 he joined a regionally popular big band headed by Sammy Watkins, which played at Cleveland's top supper club; at this time "Dino Martini" Americanized his name, becoming "Dean Martin."

In 1941 Martin married Elizabeth MacDonald; they had four children but divorced in 1949. In 1942 he had his first real taste of success, singing on NBC's nationally broadcast "Fitch Bandwagon" radio program with Watkins's orchestra. The following year he broke his contract with Watkins to sign with the powerful MCA talent agency. He made his New York City debut in September 1943 at the Riobamba club, as a last-minute replacement for Frank Sinatra. Over the next few years he established himself as a minor singing star on the city's nightclub circuit, billed as "the boy with the tall dark and handsome voice." He also proved to be incredibly irresponsible with money, spending almost everything he earned on liquor, crap games, and women. He reportedly borrowed money from more than a dozen people to have plastic surgery on his nose, but each time he squandered the money on something else; finally, one of his managers paid a doctor directly to perform the surgery. In exchange for cash advances, he signed contracts with several different managers and other backers, including the comedian Lou Costello, agreeing to give them a percentage of his future earnings; eventually he signed away more than 100 percent of his income, which precipitated several lawsuits (and out-of-court settlements) after he became a major star.

In 1946 Martin rocketed to fame when he teamed with the comedian Jerry Lewis. Their partnership began by accident: they were booked as separate acts at the same club, the Havana-Madrid in New York City, and in order to enliven an apathetic audience one evening, they began heckling each other. Soon they developed a slapstick routine that featured Lewis playing a bumbling, nerdy busboy who interrupted Martin while he tried to sing; the act culminated with them chasing each other through the audience, playfully poking and grabbing each other, yanking tablecloths onto the floor, spraying each other with seltzer, and spilling customers' drinks and eating their food. Audiences loved the childish mayhem, and the pair received an enthusiastic notice in *Billboard* magazine: "Lewis's double-takes, throwaways, mugging and deliberate over-acting are sensational. Martin's slow takes, ad-libs, and under-acting make him an ideal fall guy" (quoted in Tosches, p. 126). They were subsequently booked at the 500 Club in Atlantic City, where they became a phenomenon. People lined up for blocks trying to get into their sold-out shows, and soon Martin and Lewis were elevated to headliners earning $1,200 a week. By late 1948 they were commanding as much as $12,000 a week for playing at premiere clubs across the nation, including the Copacabana in New York City, where they set an attendance record; the Chez Paree in Chicago; the Beachcomber in Miami; and Slapsy Maxie's Cafe in Los Angeles, where Hollywood royalty such as James Cagney, Joan Crawford, Humphrey Bogart, and Gary Cooper reportedly jockeyed for tables on their opening night.

In 1948 producer Hal Wallis signed Martin and Lewis to star in films for Paramount Pictures. The following year Martin married Jeanne Biegger, a model; they had three children and divorced in 1973. Beginning with *My Friend Irma* (1949), the team of Martin and Lewis made sixteen pictures for Para-

mount, all of them commercial successes. Their highest-grossing film, *Sailor Beware* (1952), made $27,000,000 worldwide at a time when most theater tickets cost a quarter; that year they finished first in the annual *Motion Picture Herald* listing of the top ten stars. The team's comic schtick in their films varied little from their nightclub routines, with Martin typically playing a suave singer and Lewis playing a puerile nerd. Critics tended to dismiss the comedies, pointing out that they lacked wit and relied too heavily on Lewis's incessant mugging. Among their films, *Artists and Models* (1955) and *Hollywood or Bust* (1956), both directed with a fanciful style by Frank Tashlin, are generally considered to be their best. Martin and Lewis's comedy routines were also featured on television, where the pair served as intermittent hosts of the popular *Colgate Comedy Hour* on NBC from 1950 to 1955.

Simultaneously with his comedy career with Lewis, Martin pursued a solo singing career. He recorded several singles for Diamond, Apollo, and Embassy Records during 1946 and 1947, but none of them proved to be hits. In 1948 he signed a contract with Capitol Records, where he and Lewis had a minor hit with "That Certain Party" (1948), a novelty number. In 1949 Martin had his first top-ten hit, "Powder Your Face with Sunshine." Although he recorded more than eighty sides over the next four years, including duets with Peggy Lee, Margaret Whiting, and Helen O'Connell, he reached the top ten only once, with the ersatz Italian love song "That's Amore" (1953). In 1954 he recorded duets with Nat King Cole, and the following year he released his first two long-play albums, *Dean Martin Sings* and *Swingin' Down Yonder*. In 1955 he also enjoyed a major hit with "Memories Are Made of This," a pleasant if not particularly memorable pop love song, which sold over a million copies and stayed on the hit charts for six months. Later in the decade he had a top-ten hit with "Return to Me/Ritorna a Me" (1958). Although he was never considered to be an important song interpreter, Elvis Presley cited him as his favorite singer; Presley's hit ballad "Love Me Tender" was sung in Martin's lover-in-a-bedroom style.

Amid considerable negative publicity, in 1956 the team of Martin and Lewis broke up, primarily because of personal conflicts and Martin's weariness at playing the straight man to Lewis's clown. Martin later remarked that the two pivotal moments in his career were "meeting Jerry Lewis" and "leaving Jerry Lewis" (quoted in *New York Times*, 26 Dec. 1995). Many show business observers predicted that he would not fare well as a solo act, and his appearance in a failed romantic comedy, *Ten Thousand Bedrooms* (1957), heightened the sense that his Hollywood career was in jeopardy. Reviewing the film, *New York Times* critic Bosley Crowther commented that Martin was "just another nice-looking crooner without his comical pal. Together, the two made a mutually complementary team. Apart, Mr. Martin is a fellow with little humor and a modicum of charm." But he surprised such critics the following year when he gave a good dramatic performance opposite acting heavyweights Montgomery Clift and Marlon Brando in *The Young Lions*, a critical and box-office success. In the film he played a Broadway star who uses his connections to avoid combat during World War II; goaded by a sense of guilt, he finally becomes a reluctant battlefield hero. Over the next few years Martin established himself as a solid dramatic actor, specializing in charismatic but morally ambiguous characters. Among his noteworthy roles were that of a dying gambler in Vincente Minnelli's excellent melodrama *Some Came Running* (1958); a playboy songwriter in Minnelli's charming musical *Bells Are Ringing* (1960), costarring Judy Holliday; and a ne'er-do-well brother in a decadent southern family in *Toys in the Attic* (1963), an adaptation of Lillian Hellman's stage play. He gave his best performance in Howard Hawks's classic western *Rio Bravo* (1959), an unusual genre picture that concentrated on the interrelationships of the main characters rather than on action. Martin played an alcoholic deputy who struggles to regain his sobriety and a sense of dignity when the town's sheriff (played by John Wayne) is threatened by a band of hired thugs.

In the late 1950s Martin became a fixture in Las Vegas, often performing at the Sands nightclub and casino, where he was a part owner. Through his friendship with Frank Sinatra, with whom he had starred in *Some Came Running*, he became a member of the "Rat Pack," a group of Las Vegas entertainers—including singer/dancer Sammy Davis, Jr., actor Peter Lawford, and comedian Joey Bishop—who partied, womanized, and sometimes performed together. Although Martin was apolitical, at Sinatra's behest he helped the Rat Pack barnstorm for John F. Kennedy during his presidential campaign in 1960; some historians have suggested that the group's association with Kennedy contributed to the blurring of the line between politics and entertainment in the United States. The Rat Pack also made several slapdash movies together, including *Ocean's Eleven* (1960) and *Robin and the Seven Hoods* (1964). In Las Vegas Martin adopted the comic persona that would come to dominate the rest of his career—that of a supremely casual, smut-minded, half-inebriated entertainer who couldn't care less about his performance. (Many of his colleagues attested that his ever-present martini glass was usually filled with apple juice.) In 1964 he starred in Billy Wilder's controversial black comedy *Kiss Me, Stupid*, playing a hedonistic Las Vegas singer named "Dino"; some film critics view his performance as a fascinating, somewhat self-lacerating mockery of his public image. Beginning in 1965 he brought his nightclub persona to television on *The Dean Martin Show* on NBC, a variety program that ran for nine seasons and was syndicated worldwide.

In 1964 Martin had the biggest hit of his recording career, the Nashville Sound–influenced "Everybody Loves Somebody," which had the distinction of knocking the Beatles' "A Hard Day's Night" off the top of the *Billboard* pop chart. Between 1964 and 1969 he released eleven albums for Reprise Records that sold at least 500,000 copies apiece.

In 1967 NBC signed Martin to the richest contract in television history to that time, agreeing to pay him 34 million dollars over the next three years. Combined with the millions of dollars that he earned annually from his films, recordings, and Las Vegas appearances; his extensive real-estate holdings, which included several apartment buildings, ranches, a country club, a restaurant, and his part-ownership in the Sands; and several hundred thousand shares of stock in NBC's parent company, RCA, he had become one of the wealthiest performers in show business.

Around this time Martin seemed to lose all interest in his career. Always viewed by others as amiable and funny but somewhat disengaged, even from his family and friends, he became increasingly withdrawn, preferring to spend his time alone playing golf or watching westerns on television. His second wife, Jeanne, once explained to an interviewer, "He'd come home. I'd say, 'What happened today?' He'd say, 'Nothing.' I'd look at the news, and there would be the king and queen of England visiting the set and meeting Dean Martin. It just simply didn't faze him. No one, nothing impressed him deeply" (quoted in Tosches, p. 257). During the late 1960s he churned out a number of uninspired comedies and westerns, including the popular spy-movie spoof *The Silencers* (1966). In 1970 he starred as an arrogant pilot in the blockbuster disaster movie *Airport*. In 1973 he married Catherine Mae Hawn, a model; they had no children and divorced in 1976.

By the early 1980s Martin was in semi-retirement from show business. In 1987 he suffered a personal tragedy when his son Dean-Paul Martin, an actor and Air Force Reserve pilot, died in a training accident. A Rat Pack reunion tour the following year ended disastrously when Sinatra, failing to lure him into a night on the town, became angry and dumped a plate of spaghetti over his head; he quit the tour immediately and rarely spoke to Sinatra again. Devastated by the death of his son, he spent his final years living as a virtual recluse. He died in Beverly Hills, California.

• The best sources for information on Martin's life are two biographies: Nick Tosches, *Dino: Living High in the Dirty Business of Dreams* (1992), an overwritten but compelling book that is especially valuable for its descriptions of his early life and his Las Vegas career, and William Schoell, *Martini Man: The Life of Dean Martin* (1999), which concentrates on his Hollywood films. For information on the comedy team of Martin and Lewis, see James L. Neibaur and Ted Okuda's *The Jerry Lewis Films: An Analytical Filmography of the Innovative Comic* (1995), and Lewis's often self-serving and unreliable memoir, *Jerry Lewis in Person* (1982). For information on the Rat Pack, see Schoell and Lawrence J. Quirk, *The Rat Pack: The Hey Hey Days of Frank and the Boys* (1998). An obituary is in the *New York Times*, 26 Dec. 1995.

THOMAS W. COLLINS, JR.

MARTIN, John Bartlow (4 Aug. 1915–3 Jan. 1987), author, political consultant, and speechwriter, was born in Hamilton, Ohio, the son of John Williamson Martin, a carpenter, and Laura Bartlow Martin. When Martin was three years old, his father moved the family to Indianapolis, Indiana, to a home on Brookside Avenue. It was "a mean street in a mean city," Martin noted in his autobiography (1986). A lifelong Democrat, a party affiliation his son later shared, the elder Martin nevertheless refused to join the Ku Klux Klan, which was a significant social and political force in Indiana during the 1920s. The boy's childhood was unsettled. His brothers both died, and his father's business as a general contractor failed during the Great Depression. His parents divorced but later remarried. Encouraged by his teachers at Arsenal Technical High School in Indianapolis, Martin found comfort in books and devoured the works of Ernest Hemingway, Sherwood Anderson, Sinclair Lewis, Thomas Wolfe, and H. L. Mencken. Although his father hoped Martin would work as an engineer, the youngster, as early as grade school, wanted to be a writer.

Upon his graduation from high school at age sixteen, Martin attended DePauw University, a Methodist liberal arts institution in Greencastle, Indiana. He later admitted that he "behaved like a fool" during his freshman year in college, drinking and playing cards instead of attending class and studying. Expelled by university authorities for drinking, he returned to Indianapolis and joined his father in the search for employment. Martin eventually found a job pasting stock market quotations onto sheets of paper with the names of stocks for the Indianapolis office of the Associated Press (AP). Promoted to night copyboy, Martin yearned for a full-time reporter's job. Sam Ochiltree, the Indianapolis AP bureau chief and the father of one of Martin's high school friends, refused to hire Martin as a reporter unless he finished his degree at DePauw. Readmitted to the university in early 1935, Martin majored in political science, edited the school's newspaper, and worked as a stringer for the *Indianapolis Times*, part of the Scripps-Howard newspaper chain. He married his college sweetheart, Barbara Bruce, in 1937, but they divorced two years later; they had no children.

While completing his courses at DePauw, Martin in 1937 accepted a job as a reporter with the *Times*. He graduated from the university with a B.A. later that year. His first assignment was to replace Heze Clarke, a veteran reporter, on the 4:00-a.m.-to-noon shift at police headquarters. Rising up through the ranks, Martin covered numerous beats for the newspaper, including city government. Upon the urging of Norman Isaacs, the *Times* managing editor, Martin wrote freelance articles for magazines.

In 1938 Martin moved to Chicago, where he produced stories for a number of true crime magazines. In August 1940 he married Frances Smethurst; they had three children. Martin published articles in *Harper's* on such Indiana-related subjects as the downfall of the Klan leader D. C. Stephenson. In 1944 Knopf published the first of Martin's numerous

books, *They Call It North Country*, which explores the history of Michigan's Upper Peninsula. Following a short stretch in the army (1944–1946), Martin resumed his writing career and traveled the Midwest to research a story for *Life* on the postwar mood. In 1947 he wrote a history of the Hoosier State, *Indiana: An Interpretation*, for Knopf.

In the 1940s and 1950s Martin's writing appeared frequently in the "big slicks," mass circulation magazines such as the *Saturday Evening Post*, *Collier's*, *Look*, *Life*, and the *Atlantic Monthly*. He several times won the magazine publishing industry's highest honor, the Benjamin Franklin Award. Martin's reputation as one of the country's ablest reporters was cemented in 1948 with the appearance in *Harper's* of his article examining a coal mine explosion in Centralia, Illinois, that resulted in the deaths of approximately 100 men. While other journalists interviewed famous people, Martin, in his words, talked to "the humble—what the Spaniards call *los de abajo*, those from below." Throughout his career he attempted in his writing to highlight the importance and worth of individuals in an increasingly complex world. He wrote his stories in his home in the Chicago suburb of Highland Park and in a cabin on Smith Lake in Upper Michigan. When he was not traveling to research his articles, Martin treated his freelance work as a regular job, starting at nine in the morning, breaking for a half-hour lunch, and continuing until five at night, five days a week.

Martin's career changed in the early 1950s, when a friend asked him to serve as an editor of a book of speeches by Illinois governor Adlai Stevenson. When Stevenson won the 1952 Democratic presidential nomination, Martin joined the campaign team and became a member of a group of speechwriters called the "Elks Club," so named because the speechwriters worked in an Elks Club building in Springfield, Illinois. Other "Elks Club" members included David Bell, W. Willard Wirtz, Arthur M. Schlesinger, Jr., John Kenneth Galbraith, and Archibald MacLeish. In Stevenson's 1952 and 1956 presidential campaigns, Martin worked as both a speechwriter and an editorial advance person, uncovering information from a particular region in advance of the candidate's visit. He also served in this capacity with John F. Kennedy's successful 1960 presidential campaign. Kennedy appointed Martin ambassador to the Dominican Republic, a post he held until 15 February 1964.

Martin returned to Indiana in 1968 to serve as an adviser to Robert Kennedy's successful campaign in the state's Democratic presidential primary. Robert Kennedy's assassination following the California presidential primary, according to Martin's son John Frederick Martin, "broke the back of my father's spirit." Martin worked for the eventual Democrat presidential nominee, Hubert Humphrey, but gradually moved away from his political work to write again. He produced an account of his days in the Dominican Republic, a two-volume Stevenson biography, and his memoirs. In 1969 he began teaching journalism at the

Northwestern University Medill School of Journalism, a position he held for ten years. In 1988 the school established the John Bartlow Martin Award for Public Interest Magazine Journalism. Martin died in Highland Park, Illinois. In 1999 he was inducted into the Indiana Journalism Hall of Fame.

• Martin's papers are in the Library of Congress in Washington, D.C. He explored his time in the Dominican Republic in *Overtaken by Events: The Dominican Crisis from the Fall of Trujillo to the Civil War* (1966) and his entire career in *It Seems Like Only Yesterday: Memoirs of Writing, Presidential Politics, and the Diplomatic Life* (1986). Other valuable overviews of his career are John Frederick Martin, "John Bartlow Martin," *American Scholar* 59 (Winter 1990): 95–100; John Kuenster, "John Bartlow Martin: The Responsible Reporter," *Voice of St. Jude*, Apr. 1960, pp. 34–39; Allen Borden, "John Bartlow Martin," *Wilson Library Bulletin* 30 (Jan. 1956): 364; and Ray E. Boomhower, "A Voice for Those from Below: John Bartlow Martin, Reporter," *Traces of Indiana and Midwestern History* 9 (Spring 1997): 4–13. An obituary is in the *New York Times*, 5 Jan. 1987.

RAY E. BOOMHOWER

MARTINEZ, Maria Montoya (1885–20 July 1980), potter, was born Maria Montoya on the San Ildefonso Pueblo in the Rio Grande Valley of New Mexico (approximately twenty-five miles northwest of Santa Fe), the third of five daughters of Tomas Montoya, a farmer, and Reyes Pena Montoya. No birth certificate exists for any of the Montoya daughters, and accounts of Maria's life list her birth variously from 1881 to 1887. The first official record of her life is that of an 1887 baptism. Maria might have been an infant at the time, but in an interview in the 1970s (Peterson, p. 73) she recalled the baptism, which if true would suggest that she was older. She chose 5 April as the day on which to celebrate her birthday. She is often referred to by her first name alone, occasionally Maria Poveka, which means Pond Lily in the Tewa language. Life in the pueblo revolved around subsistence farming and pottery, which was in decline as less expensive, mass-produced ceramic ware gained popularity. The population of the San Ildefonso Pueblo declined by about half during Maria's childhood, from 150 to 80, as many of the young people in this Tewa Indian tribe left their ancestral homes for jobs in the cities.

Later Maria spoke of trying to find a way out of the endemic poverty of the pueblo (Marriott, p. xix), but the options were few, especially for women. She spent two years at St. Catherine's Indian School in Santa Fe and considered becoming a teacher. She spoke English, Spanish, and Tewa, although she never learned to read in any language. Otherwise she helped her father around the farm.

Maria's interest in pottery developed in an unplanned way. Nicolasa Montoya, a potter and Maria's aunt by marriage, had a workroom filled with large polychrome cooking pots, and when she was eleven or twelve years old, Maria watched her aunt work for hours on end. Maria's mother, who worried that Maria was distracting or tiring out Nicolasa, was much annoyed. Maria never received any formal instruction and learned pottery technique only by watching her aunt and other potters on the pueblo, a practice she followed years later when others came to learn from her. Nicolasa did not use a potter's wheel, a rotating device that enables potters to rapidly produce perfectly round ceramic vases and bowls. Instead she painstakingly arranged hand-coiled ribbons of clay in a circular fashion to build up the pot shapes. Hand coiling was a centuries-old tradition among Native Americans of the Southwest, and Maria, who primarily spoke Tewa and was ever mindful of long-established tribal custom, never adopted the potter's wheel. Maria's pots are perfectly rounded, and she meticulously burnished them to eliminate any traces of tool marks.

In 1904 Maria married Julian Martinez (1885?–1943), another resident of the pueblo and the son of a farmer and saddle maker. Julian Martinez performed odd-job labor on farms, at St. Catherine's Indian School, where he met Maria, and for white archaeologists excavating ancient pueblos at Frijoles and Pajarito, near San Ildefonso. The couple spent their honeymoon at the 1904 World's Fair in St. Louis, Missouri, where Maria had been invited to exhibit her pots. She was invited to every subsequent world's fair until the outbreak of World War II.

The pueblo areas attracted, in addition to the archaeologists, a colony of white artists and writers, including the novelist D. H. Lawrence. Some of the artists encouraged pueblo Indians to take up painting. Julian Martinez, one of those, produced watercolors and tempera drawings on paper and later painted designs on Maria's pots. Julian also acquired from the whites a taste for alcohol, which shortened his life.

While working for the archaeologists after 1907, Julian Martinez found a shard of shiny, jet-black pottery, which he brought to Maria. The two experimented with techniques that would replicate that deep, rich ebony. In 1908 Edgar Lee Hewett, director of the Museum of New Mexico, asked Maria to duplicate these ancient pots.

For years Maria and Julian experimented while producing the traditional polychrome pots that she formed and he decorated. Most of their pots were small, eighteen inches in height or less, which made them appealing to white purchasers, their primary customers. In 1915 they created their first large (four and five feet tall) storage vessels, which had been traditional in the pueblos since before recorded time. In 1919 Julian finally discovered the method of creating the shiny black-all-the-way-through pottery—by firing the red clay with dried horse manure. The carbon in the black smoke permeated the clay completely. Julian continued to paint designs in black on the pots before the final firing. These designs formed a matte area within the glossy ceramic, and the final result was referred to as black-on-black.

The new pots enticed collectors from all over the United States. In addition Maria's work was exhibited at a number of museums in the United States, inspiring many people to visit her at the San Ildefonso Pueblo. Among her visitors were President Franklin D. Roosevelt, the philanthropist John D. Rockefeller, who bought nine of her earliest black pots, the actors Greer Garson and Joseph Cotten, and the first ladies Eleanor Roosevelt and Lady Bird Johnson. Maria was inspired by Eleanor Roosevelt's words: "Keep on the Indian Way. Send your children to school, but keep your own way" (Peterson, pp. 110–11). She died at home on the pueblo.

Maria and Julian had four sons, but only one, Adam, outlived his mother. Adam's wife Santana and Maria's son Anthony took on the job of decorating Maria's pots after Julian's death. Maria and Julian taught others in the San Ildefonso Pueblo how to produce black pottery, which became the main source of employment there. Succeeding generations of the Martinez family have continued the work.

Over the years Maria signed her work differently. Early on she thought white collectors would prefer a more Anglo-sounding name and used "Marie." Other signatures include "Marie & Julian," "Marie & Santana," "Maria Poveka," "Maria/Popovi," "Poh ve ka" and of course "Maria."

• A number of the works about Martinez are actually museum exhibition catalogs that include biographical information, some varying widely in the facts. Among the most reliable works are Richard L. Spivey, *Maria* (1970); Susan Peterson, *The Living Tradition of Maria Martinez* (1977); Alice Marriott, *Maria: The Potter of San Ildefonso* (1948); and the Smithsonian Institution exhibit catalog *Maria Martinez: Five Generations of Potters* (1978), ed. Susan Peterson. Maria's longtime friend Elsie Karr Kreischer, with Roberta Sinnock, wrote a children's book, *Maria Montoya Martinez: Master Potter* (1995). An obituary is in the *New York Times*, 22 July 1980.

DANIEL GRANT

MASON, Charles (Apr. 1728–25 Oct. 1786), and **Jeremiah Dixon** (27 July 1733–22 Jan. 1779), British astronomers and surveyors, were responsible for establishing the Mason-Dixon Line. Charles Mason was born at Wherr (now Weir) Farm, Oakridge Lynch, Gloucestershire, England, the son of Charles Mason, a baker and miller, and Anne Damsel Mason. He attended Tetbury Grammar School and received additional tutoring from mathematician Robert Stratford. He lived near the astronomer royal, Dr. James Bradley, and Reverend Nathaniel Bliss, Savilian Professor at Oxford. It was through these local connections that Mason's prowess as a mathematician came to the attention of Bradley, who in 1756 offered him the position of assistant (or "labourer") at the Royal Observatory, Greenwich, with a salary of £26. At about this time Mason married Rebekah (maiden name unknown), with whom he had two sons.

At the observatory Mason compiled tables of lunar distances for deriving longitude, based on the work of Tobias Mayer. A congenial person and a meticulous observer of nature and geography, Mason was elected a corresponding member of the American Philosophical Society in 1767.

Dixon was born at Bishop Auckland, County Durham, the son of George Dixon, a Quaker colliery owner of Cockfield, and Mary Hunter Dixon. He and his elder brother George were educated at a school in Barnard Castle run by John Kipling. Dixon became friends with Hurworth mathematician William Emerson and the famous London instrument maker John Bird of Bishop Auckland. Of his early career as a land surveyor little is known. He may have learned the profession from his brother George. In 1760 he was expelled from the Quaker meeting house for excessive drinking. As a Quaker, albeit ethically weak but physically strong, slavery offended Dixon. The proposal for electing Jeremiah Dixon a corresponding member of the American Philosophical Society went forward with Mason's but for unknown reasons he was not elected until 1768.

In 1760, the Royal Society of London was preparing to observe the first transit of Venus for a hundred years. Dixon was recommended to the society, probably by John Bird, as one of the observers. Charles Mason was teamed with the Cambridge astronomer Reverend Nevil Maskelyne, FRS, to observe the Transit from the island of Saint Helena. However, the society also required observers at the East India Company's trading post at Bencoolen (Bengkulu, Sumatra). On 11 September 1760, Mason was offered the job with Dixon as his assistant; Dixon agreed "to accompany Mr. Mason, and be under his directions." Their contract with the society (each was to receive £200) was signed on 25 October, and thus was born the famous Mason-Dixon partnership.

They sailed from Portsmouth on 8 January 1761 aboard HMS *Seahorse*. In the late morning of 10 January the *Seahorse* was attacked by the French *L'Grand*. During the battle, the *Seahorse* was damaged, and it returned to Plymouth for repairs. It sailed on 3 February 1761 and arrived in Cape Town on 27 April. There a temporary observatory was erected where the astronomers successfully observed the transit of Venus; they remained in Cape Town until 3 October then joined Nevil Maskelyne on Saint Helena. Dixon returned briefly to South Africa to make gravity observations while Mason assisted Maskelyne with astronomical and tidal measurements. It was Mason and Dixon's observations in Africa that established their reputations for excellence and won them the praise of the scientific community and, especially, that of the future astronomer royal, Nevil Maskelyne.

In 1763, Mason and Dixon were chosen to complete a survey to define the borders of two colonies in the Americas: Pennsylvania and Maryland. Pennsylvania's charter of 1681 had triggered a dispute between William Penn and the Calverts (Lords Baltimore) of neighboring Maryland. After many attempts at negotiation, the matter was referred to the English court of chancery. Mason and Dixon arrived in Philadelphia on 15 November 1763, where they received instructions from the commissioners for Pennsylvania and Maryland. Their first task was to find the latitude of Philadelphia. On 7 January 1764, they headed west to find a point having the same latitude as Philadelphia, arriving at the farm of John Harlan (Stargazers' Farm, Embreeville), which became their headquarters. They made observations and took measurements, then measured fifteen miles due south to establish "the Post mark'd West," establishing a point on the Pennsylvania-Maryland border. On 12 June they reported to the commissioners that "the Post mark'd West" lay in the latitude of 39 degrees 43 minutes 18.2 seconds north. From this spot, the famous Mason-Dixon Line would extend due west and east. The work of laying out the line remained to be done.

They then set out to ascertain Lord Baltimore's eastern border (modern Delaware). It was this so-called Tangent Line, running for over eighty miles from the Delaware Middle Point (established 1751) to where it grazed the curious 12-mile circular border line centered on New Castle, Delaware, that had perplexed the proprietors' American surveyors. Mason devised a strategy to run a perfectly straight line from the Middle Point to the Tangent Point, using as his guide a star in the tail of the Great Bear (Ursa Major) constellation. The results of their work were astonishingly accurate and the line deviates only a few feet at the midway point.

On 5 April 1765 they began surveying the Maryland-Pennsylvania border (Mason-Dixon Line). The first section of the West Line was completed on 28 May as far as the Susquehanna River, after which they completed Lord Baltimore's eastern boundary from the Tangent Point due north to the West Line. Returning to the Susquehanna on 21 June, Mason and Dixon with their large team of laborers and assistants, including American surveyors, began the second part of the West Line. By 21 October, they had reached the foot of North Mountain, which point marked the limit of their work for 1765. Work resumed on 1 April 1766 and by 18 June had reached as far as Savage Mountain. The Savage Mountain point marked the line of the 1763 royal proclamation that forbade settlement beyond the Alleghenies (the so-called dividing mountains). At this point work had to stop until the Native American chiefs of the Six Nations agreed to its continuance. General Sir William Johnson, the government's agent for Indian affairs, had the task of negotiating terms.

While Mason and Dixon awaited the outcome, they began on another task, unrelated but historically important: the first measurement in North America of a degree of latitude. This measurement, for the Royal Society, would add to the work of the French Académie Royale des Sciences in defining the size and shape of the Earth. The 1766 season concluded with Mason and Dixon extending the West Line eastward to the Delaware River. They spent the winter months at Harlan's farm making the first gravity observations in America, using a pendulum clock made by Jackson of Philadelphia and the same John Shelton clock used by Maskelyne at Saint Helena.

Finally, the Six Nations consented to the work's proceeding and provided "deputies" to act as supervisors and provide protection. In addition, the commissioners sent Captain Hugh Crawford, a war veteran and renowned trader and explorer, as the survey's guide. Work recommenced on 7 July 1767 and proceeded as far as the Cheat River, which some deputies believed marked the end of their commission. Shortly after, the survey team had the first of several encounters with unfriendly Native American bands. A few miles west of the Monongahela River in October 1767, a warpath was reached which the deputies refused to pass. This marked the end of Mason and Dixon's famous line. (U.S. surveyors including David Rittenhouse and Andrew Ellicott completed the work in 1785.) Mason and Dixon's final task for the commissioners was to draw maps of all the borderlines and have them officially printed. In the intervening period, they were able to complete their measurements of a degree of latitude. The commissioners, entirely satisfied, discharged Mason and Dixon on 27 August 1768. In 1769 the two were again employed by the Royal Society to observe the 1769 transit of Venus. Mason went to Cavan, in Ireland, while Dixon went to Norway with William Bayly, who later sailed with James Cook.

In 1770 Dixon retired to his home in Cockfield, a "gentleman." He continued to practice as a land surveyor, making maps of the estates of Lanchester Common and Auckland Castle. He died unmarried at Cockfield on 22 January 1779, leaving his personal fortune to Margaret Bland and her two daughters. He was buried in an unmarked grave in Friends' ground (the Quaker cemetery) at Staindrop.

Mason continued to work for the Royal Observatory, the Board of Longitude, and the Royal Society. In 1770 he married Mary Williams, daughter or sister of his friend Robert Williams of Tetbury (who may have acted as guardian to Mason's sons while Mason was in America); the couple had five sons and one daughter. Three years later, Mason traveled in Scotland to locate a suitable mountain for Maskelyne's gravity experiment, identifying the peak of Schiehallion. He was offered the chance to conduct the experiment himself, but the offer was derisory and he declined. From his home at Bisley, Mason continued to refine the lunar tables and made substantial improvements to the Nautical Almanac, which continued to appear many years after his death. He applied unsuccessfully to the Board of Longitude for the £5,000 longitude prize under the terms of the 1774 Act of Parliament but received only £1,317, which, according to the French astronomer Jérôme Lalande, fell well short of his expectations.

In July 1786, Mason returned with his family to America, writing on 27 September from the Sign of the George on Second Street, Philadelphia, to his friend Benjamin Franklin. He was by then very ill and passed his scientific papers to his friend Reverend John Ewing, provost of the University of Pennsylvania, asking him to publish an American version of the

Nautical Almanac; sadly, Ewing did not pursue the opportunity. Mason died in Philadelphia and is buried in Christ Church burying ground.

Mason and Dixon's partnership was a perfect merging of scientific astronomy with land surveying, laying the foundations of modern geodetic field survey. While the Mason-Dixon Line is their lasting memorial, all their scientific accomplishments were of the highest caliber. Neither man was honored with a memorial, nor did they receive any public recognition for their contributions to science and peace.

• The libraries of the National Maritime Museum and the Royal Society in London are the principal sources for what little exists. The library of the Religious Society of Friends in Britain has a copy of Penny's book (noted below) and much other supportive information about early Quakers. The Sackler Archive Resource at the Royal Society provides reliable (but short) sketches of fellows, and the web site of the Harlan family in America (http://www.harlanfamily.org) is full of interesting snippets and worth a visit. This researcher has relied much upon interviews and correspondence with, among others, Jeremiah Dixon's descendent George Dixon; Eugene Smith of Pennsylvania; artist David H. Naylor, owner of Mason's birthplace; and John Loosley, who collected details about the Mason family.

The main body of information on Mason and Dixon's work in America is in A. Hughlett Mason's transcription "Journal of Charles Mason and Jeremiah Dixon," *Memoirs of the American Philosophical Society* 76 (1969) (whole volume). Thomas D. Cope was an authority and wrote several papers, including "The Stargazers' Stone," *Pennsylvania History* 6, no 4 (Oct. 1939); "Charles Mason and Jeremiah Dixon," *Scientific Monthly* 62 (June 1946); "Collecting Source Material about Charles Mason and Jeremiah Dixon," *Proceedings of the American Philosophical Society* 92, no. 2 (1948): 111–14; "Charles Mason, Jeremiah Dixon and the Royal Society," *Notes and Records of the Royal Society of London* 9 (Oct. 1951): 56–78; and "Some Contacts of Benjamin Franklin with Mason and Dixon and Their Work," *Proceedings of the American Philosophical Society* 95 (June 1951): 232–38. For a source of short biographic sketches (including many early American scientists), recommended is Whitfield J. Bell, Jr., "Patriot-Improvers: Biographical Sketches of Members of the American Philosophical Society, 1743–1768," *Memoirs of the American Philosophical Society* 226 (1997). The *Dictionary of National Biography* and its *Missing Persons* supplement provide some useful details but also include some errors. An authoritative source for Jeremiah Dixon is Norman Penny, *My Ancestors* (1920), while Derek Howes's excellent *Nevil Maskelyne: The Seaman's Astronomer* (1989) contains some details about Charles Mason's later life. A complete treatment of the men and their work is found in Edwin Danson's *Drawing the Line: How Mason and Dixon Surveyed the Most Famous Border in America* (2000).

EDWIN DANSON

MASON, John Landis (1832–26 Feb. 1902), tinsmith and inventor of glass jars, was born in Vineland, New Jersey, the son of a Scottish farmer whose name is not known. While still a young man, he moved to New York City where he worked as a tinsmith in his own shop on Canal Street. It was in the rented room where he lived, at 154 West Nineteenth Street, that he had the idea of a glass jar to preserve fresh fruits and vegetables.

As early as 1810, Nicolas Appert, a Frenchman, published his principles of food preservation through sterilization. Appert's theory was that heating would preserve foods by arresting the natural tendency to spoil. The problem was how to seal in the harvesttime freshness of the goods, because, as Louis Pasteur was later to explain, bacteria could lead to spoilage. Tin cans met this need but were not widely used because soldering the tops made the process too complicated and costly. Any glassblower could produce a canning jar, and any tinsmith could produce lids, but the difficulty was in making a jar that had threads at the top to allow a metal (zinc) cap with porcelain lining to be screwed down on a rubber gasket to form an airtight seal. Mason endeavored to keep foods airtight by a process that could be implemented in any home. His invention was a mold to make jars with threaded tops.

On 30 November 1858, Mason received a patent on a mold that would produce a glass canning jar with a threaded top. The invention was called "Improvement in Screw-Neck Bottles," or sometimes "Improved Jar." The date of that patent appeared on canning jars for the next three-quarters of a century.

Following issuance of the patent, Mason formed a partnership with T. W. Frazier, Henry Mitchell, and B. W. Payne; the four of them started a business at 257 Pearl Street in New York to manufacture lids for Mason jars. The jars were purchased from various glassblowers who used Mason's patented mold to blow jars with threaded tops. The first glassblower to produce the new jars was Clayton Parker of Bridgeton, New Jersey, who worked in Samuel Crowley's glass factory on the Mullica River. The jars were affordable and reusable, allowing every farm family to preserve summer produce for winter eating. Such was the quality of the Mason jars that some jars were handed down from one generation to the next. One woman claimed she had used the same set of jars annually for fifty-eight years.

Little is known of Mason's activities during the Civil War years, as his name does not appear in the New York City directories for 1863 and 1864. Following the war, his business moved to Spring Street. Later, in 1873, he moved to New Brunswick, New Jersey, where he married a woman by the name of Jennie (surname unknown); they had eight daughters, four of them twins.

While living in New Brunswick, Mason produced more inventions and received eight patents on Mason jars, two on lids, and one on a baby bottle designed after his original "Improved Jar." In 1876 he received patents on a folding life raft, a soap dish, and a brush holder. His original Mason jar patent expired in 1875, after a legal life of seventeen years. Prior to that, Mason had sold his rights to the original patent and the later jar patents to the Consolidated Fruit Jar Company. He also had some affiliation with the Hero Fruit Jar Company of Philadelphia. Consolidated and Hero were quite successful for about a decade, but by 1888 other companies had entered the field—notably the Ball Brothers Corporation, led by Frank Clayton Ball and George Alexander Ball—and Consolidated and Hero lost their joint monopoly. Although patent suits were threatened against the Ball Brothers and their customers, none were filed. Ball had advantages over the Consolidated and Hero Fruit Jar Companies in that Ball could make both the jars and the lids. By the early 1900s, Consolidated and Hero were out of business.

In 1903, the first fully automatic machine for making jars was invented at the Ball Brothers' factory and the container industry no longer had to rely on individual glassblowers. Mason did not live to see the automatic machine. He and his family had moved to Brooklyn, New York, in the early 1890s. His wife died in 1898. With his daughters married and his wife gone, Mason returned to New York, where he lived in a tenement on West 168th Street. He died as a charity patient in the House of Relief on Hudson Street in lower Manhattan, having earned nothing from his inventions since the 1880s.

Prior to Mason's invention, winter meals in America were dreary; the only available fruits and vegetables were dried. But the Mason jar allowed gardeners to seal in the harvest-time freshness of fruits and vegetables. Mason's invention has stood the test of time and has been little improved on since its origination in 1858. To this day, his name appears on the "Mason" jars produced by various manufacturers. Mason never got particularly rich from his invention, but to him goes the credit for conceiving and producing America's first hermetically sealed glass jars. Today, the majority of jars are still manufactured by Alltrista Corporation (a corporation spun off by Ball Corporation)—with Mason's name on them—in sizes ranging from a half-pint to several gallons. Mason's name is synonymous with quality in home canning.

• There is very little biographical data available on John Mason, but *Mason Jar Centennial, 1858–1958* (1958) is the most complete. Frank Ball's *Memoirs of Frank Clayton Ball* (1937) offers a competitor's analysis of Mason and his invention. Similarly, Frederic Alexander Birmingham, *Ball Corporation: The First Century* (1980), offers an outsider's view of Mason. A newspaper article by Meade Landis, "1st Mason Jar Blown by Local Man: Invention Is Credited to Ex-Resident of Vineland," *Bridgeton Evening News*, 15 Nov. 1954, includes interviews with people who either knew Mason or worked in glass factories that made his jars.

DALE L. FLESHER

MATTHAU, Walter (1 Oct. 1920–1 July 2000), actor, was born Walter Jake Matthow in New York City, the son of Milton Matthow, an electrician and legal process server, and Rose Berolsky Matthow, a garment worker. Both of his parents were eastern European–born Jews. Matthau, who often gave false information to interviewers, claimed that his real surname was Matuschanskayasky. Although Milton Matthow's father probably Americanized his name after coming

to the United States, Matthau never bore the original family name, and its exact spelling is not known. When Matthau was three years old, his father abandoned the family, and the boy was brought up in poverty by his mother on Manhattan's Lower East Side. Matthau attended New York City Public School 25 and Junior High School 64.

Matthau discovered early on that he enjoyed performing in public. As a child he appeared in amateur stage productions at local settlement houses and gave recitations at school assemblies. Harboring an ambition to be a radio announcer, he imitated the speech of radio personalities and deliberately softened his New York accent. As a teenager Matthau sold refreshments at the Second Avenue Theater and played a bit part in the theater's Yiddish-language production of *The Dish Washer* in 1936. In 1939 Matthau graduated from Seward Park High School and subsequently worked at a series of jobs, including file clerk and boxing coach. He also did a brief stint as a logger with the Civilian Conservation Corps in Montana. In 1942 he joined the U.S. Army Air Corps and rose to the rank of staff sergeant as a radio operator.

Matthau left the military in late 1945 and returned to New York, where he enrolled in the drama workshop at the New School for Social Research. His classmates at the workshop, which was run by the noted stage director Erwin Piscator, included Rod Steiger, Tony Curtis, Beatrice Arthur, and Elaine Stritch. From 1946 to 1948, while continuing his studies at the New School, Matthau appeared in summer stock productions at the Erie County Playhouse in Pennsylvania, the Orange County Playhouse in Westtown, New York, and the Southwold Playhouse on Long Island. At the start of his professional acting career he changed the spelling of his last name to Matthau, which he considered more elegant. In 1948 he married Geraldine Grace Johnson, a drama student. The couple had two children.

In December 1948 Matthau made his Broadway debut in a walk-on part in Maxwell Anderson's *Anne of the Thousand Days*, starring Rex Harrison as Henry VIII and Joyce Redman as Anne Boleyn. Tall, thin, and dark-haired with prominent jowls, a deep voice, and a stooped posture that made him seem older than he was, Matthau understudied an elderly actor in the role of a bishop and performed the role several times during the play's Broadway run. In 1949 he took over the role entirely for the play's national tour. Matthau had parts in numerous Broadway plays in the early 1950s, most notably *Season in the Sun*, a comedy by Wolcott Gibbs, in 1951; *In Any Language*, a farce directed by George Abbott and starring Uta Hagen, in 1952; and *The Ladies of the Corridor*, a comedy by Dorothy Parker and Arnaud d'Usseau, in 1953. He also acted in many television productions, including *Philco Television Playhouse*, *The U.S. Steel Hour*, and *Robert Montgomery Presents*.

In 1955 Matthau made his screen debut as a villain in *The Kentuckian*, an adventure film starring and directed by Burt Lancaster. Later that year he returned to Broadway in a principal supporting role in George Axelrod's satire of the business world *Will Success Spoil Rock Hunter?* starring Jayne Mansfield and Orson Bean. Established as a versatile and reliable character actor adept at both comedy and drama, Matthau for the next decade divided his attention among stage, film, and television. His Broadway roles included in 1958 a frenzied orchestra manager in Harry Kurnitz's music world comedy *Once More with Feeling*, starring Joseph Cotten, and in 1961 a French aristocrat in Marcel Achard's farce *A Shot in the Dark*, starring Julie Harris, for which Matthau won a Tony Award for best featured or supporting actor in a play. His notable screen roles during this period included a disillusioned television writer in *A Face in the Crowd* (1957), directed by Elia Kazan; a gangster in *King Creole* (1958), an Elvis Presley vehicle; a criminal posing as a Central Intelligence Agency (CIA) officer in *Charade* (1963), a stylish thriller directed by Stanley Donen and starring Cary Grant and Audrey Hepburn; and an unscrupulous adviser to the president, played by Henry Fonda, in *Fail Safe* (1964), a Cold War suspense directed by Sidney Lumet. On television Matthau appeared on episodes of dramatic series such as *Dr. Kildare*, *Route 66*, and *Alfred Hitchcock Presents*. In 1961 he starred in the short-lived syndicated drama series *Tallahassee 7000* playing a special investigator for the Florida state police.

Matthau divorced Johnson in 1958. The next year he married Carol Grace Marcus, an actress and socialite and the former wife of the playwright William Saroyan. They had one child. Matthau made his lone foray into directing with the low-budget crime drama *Gangster Story* (1960), in which he costarred with Marcus.

Matthau moved from supporting actor to star with Neil Simon's comedy *The Odd Couple*, directed by Mike Nichols. The play about two divorced men with contrasting personalities who share an apartment opened at Broadway's Plymouth Theatre in March 1965 with Matthau as the sloppy, laconic, cigar-chewing Oscar Madison and Art Carney as the fastidious and excitable Felix Unger. *Newsweek* wrote that Matthau played Madison "with immense, shambling, bearish vitality, rising continually from a crouch, like a neurotic ape, to issue hoarse comments on the state of his nerves and of civilization, suffering splendidly, a perfect embodiment of urban and domestic despair" (22 Mar. 1965, p. 91). *The Odd Couple* became one of Broadway's longest-running plays and earned Matthau a Tony Award for best actor. He left *The Odd Couple* in November 1965 to take the role of an ambulance-chasing lawyer in the film *The Fortune Cookie* (1966), a sardonic comedy directed by Billy Wilder. Matthau won an Academy Award for best supporting actor for *The Fortune Cookie* although he actually costarred in the film with Jack Lemmon. In 1966 Matthau suffered a major heart attack. He was plagued by serious health problems, including cancer and continuing heart disease, for the rest of his life. His colleagues marveled at his ability to bounce back quickly from life-threatening illnesses.

After achieving film stardom, Matthau made no further significant stage or television appearances, though he continued to consider himself primarily a stage actor. From the mid-1960s onward he resided in southern California and grew to dislike even visiting New York. As a star he was pegged as primarily a comedic performer, and his lead roles exhibited a narrower range than his supporting roles. In 1968 Matthau was reteamed with Lemmon, who had become his close friend, in the popular film version of *The Odd Couple*, directed by Gene Saks, in which Matthau repeated the role of Oscar Madison. Matthau and Lemmon costarred in six more films, all comedies, *The Front Page* (1974), *Buddy, Buddy* (1981), *Grumpy Old Men* (1993), *Grumpier Old Men* (1995), *Out to Sea* (1997), and *The Odd Couple II* (1998). Matthau also starred in *Kotch* (1971), a drama directed by Lemmon, for which Matthau earned an Academy Award nomination for best actor. He received another best actor Academy Award nomination for *The Sunshine Boys* (1975), directed by Herbert Ross, the story of two aging vaudevillians based on a Neil Simon play. Notable among Matthau's other films are *Cactus Flower* (1969), with Ingrid Bergman and Goldie Hawn, based on Abe Burrows's long-running Broadway comedy about a philandering dentist; *Hello, Dolly!* (1970), a screen version of the hit Broadway musical, with Barbra Streisand in the title role; *Plaza Suite* (1971), three comedy vignettes by Simon in which Matthau played three different characters; *Charley Varrick* (1973), a bank heist suspense film; *The Bad News Bears* (1976), about a scruffy Little League baseball team coached by Matthau; and two films with Glenda Jackson, *House Calls* (1978), a romantic comedy set in a hospital, and *Hopscotch* (1980), a takeoff on espionage films. Matthau's final film was *Hanging Up* (2000), a comedy in which he portrayed the ailing father of battling sisters played by Diane Keaton, Meg Ryan, and Lisa Kudrow.

In his private life Matthau exhibited much of the same acerbic, deadpan humor that he specialized in on screen. His chief avocation was gambling, especially betting on sporting events, and before gaining the wealth that came with movie stardom, he was often deeply in debt to bookmakers. Matthau died in Santa Monica, California.

• Detailed interviews with Matthau are Lillian Ross, "Profiles—The Player III," *New Yorker*, 4 Nov. 1961, pp. 98–101; C. Robert Jennings, "Matthau in Full Flower," *Esquire*, Dec. 1968, pp. 193–94, 262–63; and Thomas Meehan, "What the OTB Bettor Can Learn from Walter Matthau," *New York Times Magazine*, 4 July 1971, pp. 7, 12–14. Rob Edelman and Audrey Kupferberg, *Matthau: A Life* (2002), is a complete biography of Matthau; a shorter, less-thorough biography is Allan Hunter, *Walter Matthau* (1984). Carol Matthau, *Among the Porcupines* (1992), a memoir by Matthau's second wife, offers insight into his personal life. An obituary is in the *New York Times*, 2 July 2000.

MARY C. KALFATOVIC

MAULDIN, William Henry (29 Oct. 1921–22 Jan. 2003), cartoonist, was born in Mountain Park, New Mexico, the son of Sidney Albert Mauldin, a farmer and jack-of-all-trades, and Edith Katrina Bemis, a farmer. Growing up in a somewhat haphazard fashion as his family moved from New Mexico to Arizona and back while his father pursued a variety of occupations, "Bill," the second of two sons, displayed artistic ability early. At the age of fifteen he enrolled in the Charles N. Landon correspondence school of cartooning. While in high school in Alamogordo, New Mexico, Mauldin earned money doing posters and advertising illustrations. After his parents divorced in 1937, he and his brother Sidney Mauldin struck out on their own and moved to Phoenix, Arizona, where they lived in a family friend's boardinghouse and attended Phoenix Union High School. Bill concentrated on journalism and art classes and gained practical experience by drawing cartoons for the school paper, but he failed to accumulate enough credits to graduate with his class in June 1938. Instead, borrowing money from his maternal grandmother, he entered the Chicago Academy of Fine Arts, taking courses in life drawing and cartooning while drawing restaurant posters in exchange for meals. After a year he returned to Phoenix, where he did posters and political cartoons for various politicians, working simultaneously for both candidates in the gubernatorial race.

Mauldin's hand-to-mouth existence ended in September 1940, when he joined the Arizona National Guard, which was almost immediately "federalized" into the regular U.S. Army's Forty-fifth Infantry Division. One afternoon a week Mauldin drew cartoons for the unit's weekly newspaper. In early 1941 the Forty-fifth moved to Camp Barkeley near Abilene, Texas, where Mauldin met Norma Jean Humphries. They married on 28 February 1942, on the eve of the Forty-fifth's departure to Fort Devens, Massachusetts, for amphibious landing training in preparation for the U.S. entry into World War II. The Mauldins had three sons.

The Forty-fifth invaded Sicily on 10 July 1943, and the appearance of Mauldin's drawings, at first embellished with the graduated gray tones of grease-crayon shading, quickly changed as he mastered the more linear graphic mannerisms that the indigenous war-torn printing equipment could not erode. Mauldin depicted the life of the "dogface" (foot soldier) the way it was. Rained on, shot at, and kept awake in trenches day and night, the combat soldier was wet, scared, dirty, and tired all the time; and Mauldin's spokesmen—the scruffy, bristle-chinned, listlessly dull-eyed, stoop-shouldered Willie and Joe in their wrinkled and torn uniforms—were taciturn but eloquent witnesses on behalf of the persecuted. Through simple combat-weary inertia, they defied pointless army regulations and rituals: they would fight the war, but they would not keep their shoes polished. Slouching along a muddy road, they philosophize: "Hell. When they

run, we try to ketch 'em. When we ketch 'em, we try to make 'em run." In another cartoon the two are hugging the ground under enemy fire, and Joe says: "I can't git no lower, Willie. Me buttons is in th' way." A weary Willie, standing in front of a medic's table, says: "Just gimme a coupla aspirin. I already got a Purple Heart." (All cartoons quoted appear in the post-war book, *Up Front*.)

Although Mauldin was assigned to division headquarters and worked full-time as a cartoonist, he spent much of his time out in the field, sitting in dugouts and listening to GIs' stories about jeeps, foxholes, K rations, and their other primitive living conditions. Soon after the Allied campaign reached Naples in December 1943, Mauldin left the weekly *45th Division News* to join the staff of the daily *Stars and Stripes*. Because Mauldin's cartoons so faithfully represented the average foot soldier's plight and proclivities, they were immensely popular with the men in the trenches. But Mauldin earned the enmity of the Third Army's legendary general George S. Patton, who pressured the cartoonist to clean up Willie and Joe and give them shaves because otherwise they were bad for morale. Mauldin, however, persisted. Willie and Joe remained bedraggled in the extreme and unshaven in perpetuity, while the cartoonist continued poking fun at army brass and exposing regulations as pointless whenever they meet reality. In one of Mauldin's classics, in the *Up Front* compilation, Willie and Joe are in town celebrating their recent victory in liberating the environs. They have been accosted by an officious MP, who admonishes them about the unkempt state of their uniforms, to which Willie says, "I lost them buttons capturing this town." The famed war correspondent Ernie Pyle wrote about the soldier cartoonist, and Mauldin's cartoons, entitled *Up Front*, were soon syndicated to stateside newspapers nationwide.

Mauldin's drawing style for the wartime cartoons was aptly evocative of the ambiance of the dogface's life. He drew with a brush, and his lines are bold and fluid but clotted with heavy black areas. Clothing and background detail disappear into deep trap-shadow darkness that give the pictures a grungy aspect approximating visually the damp and dirt of a soldier's life on front lines everywhere. The images of Mauldin's reportage of the raw ironies of the battlefield, relieved by the sardonic sense of humor that found a common humanity alive and well amid the tedium and hazards of combat life, won Mauldin the first of his two Pulitzer Prizes in 1945. A collection of his battlefield cartoons, *Up Front*, was published that year. In the book's extensive prose, Mauldin discussed the inspiration for his cartoons and life in the military—his life and the lives of the soldiers he knew. As a personal account of his adventures as an observer on the front lines during war and, hence, as a record of the things most soldiers thought about when not keeping their heads down, *Up Front* is one of the best books about war.

Mauldin was a celebrity when he was discharged, and his syndicated cartoons now featured soldiers returning to civilian life. Under a succession of titles (*Sweatin' It Out*, *Willie and Joe*, and *Bill Mauldin's Cartoon*), Willie and Joe shed their shabby uniforms and dressed in mufti. Initially the circulation of his feature doubled, but Mauldin's cynical comedy did not work in everyday life. He started by reflecting the experiences of returning GIs, their anger at shortages, including no housing for themselves and their new families and few goods and fewer jobs, and at unthinking yahoos who failed, apparently, to appreciate sufficiently the sacrifices the veterans had made. His ire up, Mauldin went on to assault segregation, racism, and the Ku Klux Klan and then right-wing veterans' organizations and politicians. While taking essentially the same satirical stance they had taken in the service, his cartoons were now seen as "political" rather than "entertaining," and newspapers began to drop his feature, saying they had their own political cartoonists. Mauldin's marriage also failed, ending in a divorce in 1946. On 27 June 1947 he married Natalie Sarah Evans; they had four children before they divorced in December 1971. Mauldin and his syndicate soon severed their relationship, and he stopped cartooning for about a decade. During this time Mauldin wrote books and acted in two 1951 movies, *Teresa* and *The Red Badge of Courage*. Willie and Joe went to Hollywood too in the movies *Up Front* (1951) and *Back at the Front* (1952). A passionate Democrat, Mauldin also ran unsuccessfully for Congress in 1956 in a densely Republican district in Rockland County, New York.

Mauldin returned to cartooning in 1958, when he replaced the retiring Daniel Fitzpatrick as the political cartoonist at the *St. Louis Post-Dispatch*. Mauldin's liberal voice again had a home where he could continue the battle he had begun in the army. In 1962 he joined the *Chicago Sun-Times*, where he cartooned for the next thirty years. Mauldin was awarded a Purple Heart and the Legion of Merit during World War II. The National Cartoonists Society presented him with the Category Award for Editorial Cartooning in 1959 and the Reuben as Cartoonist of the Year in 1961. Mauldin received his second Pulitzer Prize in 1959, but he achieved greater notice with the cartoon he produced after the assassination of John F. Kennedy—the picture of the statue of Abraham Lincoln in the Lincoln Memorial in Washington, D.C., bent forward in his seat, head in his hands, a perfect posture of grief, an emblem of national mourning.

On 29 July 1972 Mauldin married Christine Ruth Lund; they had two children. Mauldin settled in Santa Fe, New Mexico, sending his cartoons to Chicago electronically until retirement was forced upon him in 1991. Pursuing his avocation as an auto mechanic, he dropped a large car part on his drawing hand. By the spring of 2002 he was in a nursing home in Orange County, California, where he would die with Alzheimer's disease. When other World War II veterans learned of his condition, they wrote letters and came to visit and reminisce about the war and about Willie and Joe and what those cartoon characters had meant to them.

Mauldin easily ranks among the top ten American political cartoonists of the twentieth century. He belongs in that pantheon because he hit his subjects hard, pulling no punches in presenting his opinion, and because he yoked words to pictures for emphatic, memorable statements that were often powerful visual metaphors. But with Willie and Joe, Mauldin did something more, he created myth. At least a score of the cartoon images of Willie and Joe are iconographic, imprinted with every wrinkle and whisker intact into the cultural consciousness of American popular arts.

• Over two hundred of Mauldin's World War II cartoons in original art are archived and displayed at the Forty-fifth Infantry Division Museum in Oklahoma City. Extensive biographical information is in Mauldin's own account, *The Brass Ring: A Sort of a Memoir* (1971), but the book covers his life only through World War II. Most of his other books, beginning with *Up Front*, include commentary as well as cartoons but little biographical data. They are *Star Spangled Banter* (1941; reissued with different content in 1944), a collection of cartoons about life in an army training camp; *Sicily Sketchbook* (1943); *Mud, Mules, and Mountains* (1944); *Bill Mauldin's Army* (1944; repr. 1983); *This Damn Tree Leaks* (1945); *Back Home* (1947); *A Sort of a Saga* (1949); *Bill Mauldin in Korea* (1952); *What's Got Your Back Up?* (1961); *I've Decided I Want My Seat Back* (1965); *Mud and Guts: A Look at the Common Soldier of the American Revolution* (1978); and *Let's Declare Ourselves Winners . . . and Get the Hell Out* (1985). The cover story in *Time*, 18 June 1945, "Bill, Willie and Joe" (pp. 16–18), focuses on the soldier cartoonist; a second cover story in *Time*, 21 July 1961, "Hit It If It's Big" (pp. 50–54), includes some postwar information about Mauldin. His wartime career was also the subject of Frederick C. Painton, "Up Front with Bill Mauldin," *Saturday Evening Post*, 17 Mar. 1945, pp. 22–23, 69, 71. Mauldin retired Willie and Joe with the failure of his postwar syndication, but he brought them back in a series of cartoons for a special issue of *Collier's*, "Preview of the War We Do Not Want (World War III)," 27 Oct. 1951. Obituaries are in the *Los Angeles Times*, 23 Jan. 2003; the *New York Times*, 23 Jan. 2003; and the *Chicago Tribune*, 23 Jan. 2003.

ROBERT C. HARVEY

MAYFIELD, Curtis (3 June 1942–26 Dec. 1999), rhythm and blues performer and composer, was born Curtis Lee Mayfield, Jr., in Chicago, Illinois, the first child of Curtis Lee Mayfield (born Curtis Lee Cooper) and Marion Washington. He was raised in impoverished circumstances by his mother and his grandmother, Sadie Riley, and rarely saw his father, who deserted the family after the fifth child was born. By the time Mayfield attended Wells High School, the family had settled on Chicago's North Side in the Cabrini-Green housing project. His paternal grandmother, Anna Belle Mayfield, was a minister, and Mayfield sang in her church's gospel group, the Northern Jubilee Singers, which included his three cousins and future rhythm and blues star Jerry Butler.

Mayfield in his sophomore year dropped out of school to become the guitarist/tenor vocalist in a vocal harmony group, the Impressions, which included

Jerry Butler, Sam Gooden, and brothers Arthur and Richard Brooks. In 1958 the group, with Butler's baritone lead, achieved a national hit with the moving ballad "For Your Precious Love." This was one of the first songs in the soul music style, a gospelized type of rhythm and blues that dominated black music for the next two decades. When Butler quit the group, the Impressions regrouped by featuring Mayfield, with his soft high tenor lead, and adding Fred Cash; in 1959, however, the Impressions temporarily disbanded.

In 1960 Mayfield started touring, writing, and recording with Jerry Butler, providing songs that made the singer a major recording artist of hit records, notably "He Will Break Your Heart" (1960) and "Need To Belong" (1963). In 1960 Mayfield established his own publishing company, Curtom, for his songs. At the time this was a virtually unprecedented move for an African-American songwriter.

In 1961 Mayfield married Helen Williams, but the union lasted no more than two years. They separated when Mayfield was around twenty-one (but the divorce did not come until years later). The couple had one son. About a year after his split with Williams, Mayfield began a relationship with Altheida Sims; they had six children and eventually married. Mayfield also had two other children with another woman, Diane Fitzgerald.

Mayfield reunited the Impressions in 1961, and immediately they got a major hit record with the much-copied Mayfield composition "Gypsy Woman," a strongly melodious song with a cha cha–inflected beat that typified his early output. Mayfield sustained the Impressions' popularity with similarly styled songs for the next two years. With "It's All Right," a hit record in 1963, however, he developed a more intense gospelized approach, with dramatic switching off of leads from the remaining three members—Mayfield, Fred Cash, and Sam Gooden (the Brooks brothers having dropped out). The energy level was likewise raised in the musical arrangements, with blaring horns and a stronger backbeat.

In 1962, Mayfield was hired as a composer by Carl Davis, head of A&R for Columbia's rhythm and blues subsidiary OKeh. For the label Mayfield provided a remarkable number of memorable hit songs, particularly "Monkey Time" (1963) for Major Lance, "It's All Over" (1964) for Walter Jackson, and "I Can't Work No Longer" (1965) for Billy Butler. Mayfield also provided songs to Chicago artists on other labels, particularly to Gene Chandler, who built a successful recording career with the songwriter's ballads (notably "Rainbow," 1963, and "Just Be True," 1964), and to Jan Bradley, who got a hit record with Mayfield's "Mama Didn't Lie" (1963). During the same period, Mayfield kept the Impressions high on the record charts with such hits as the stirring ballad "I'm So Proud" (1964), the rousing anthemlike number "Keep On Pushing," and the sublime secular gospel classic "People Get Ready" (1965). The latter was the

centerpiece of the Impressions' most outstanding LP, *People Get Ready.*

In 1965, to better concentrate on the Impressions and his own entrepreneurial endeavors, Mayfield left the employ of OKeh and substantially reduced the number of songs he gave to other artists to record. The large catalog of hit songs he had composed during the previous five years was unrivaled by any single rhythm and blues composer of the time. He entered the record label business in 1966, forming Mayfield Records (on which he produced the girl group the Fascinations) and the Windy C label (on which he produced the vocal group the Five Stairsteps). Failing to sustain these small operations, in 1968 he founded Curtom Records, which became a $10 million-a-year business by the mid-1970s, primarily with Mayfield-composed and -produced film soundtrack albums featuring such artists as Aretha Franklin, Gladys Knight and the Pips, and the Staple Singers.

During the late 1960s, Mayfield helped pioneer the use of social commentary and political messages in black music, reflecting the greater militancy of the civil rights movement and the general social unrest in the country. His first message song with the Impressions, "We're a Winner" (1967), was banned by many stations as too militant; and after the summer of 1968, when the Impressions moved to Curtom, Mayfield made the social messages ever more overt with such hits as "This Is My Country" (1968) and "Choice Of Colors" (1969). These were the first of his many humanistic songs in which he preached love, peace, understanding, and harmony among all racial and religious groups.

Mayfield left the Impressions in 1970 to begin a solo career. His *Superfly* album (1972) was a multi-million-selling soundtrack LP for a movie about a Harlem drug dealer; it yielded two million-selling singles, "Freddie's Dead" and "Superfly." Featuring conga-led and bass-heavy songs, *Superfly* put Mayfield in the forefront of the new funk music (a highly rhythmic bass-heavy style of r&b), which was pushing traditional soul music off the charts in the early 1970s. For the first time in his career, Mayfield reached a substantial white audience. Curtom, like many independent labels, succumbed to the competition from the major labels in the late 1970s, and Mayfield was forced to close his operation in 1980. He moved to Atlanta, Georgia, and continued his career there. In 1990 he was permanently paralyzed from the neck down when stage scaffolding fell on him. This accident essentially ended Mayfield's career as a musician and composer. He died in Roswell, Georgia.

Mayfield was inducted into the Rock and Roll Hall of Fame twice, as a member of the Impressions in 1991 and as a solo artist in 1999. He received the Grammy Legends Award in 1994. He is recognized as one of the principal architects of the Chicago soul music industry, from the many hats he wore working as a recording artist, songwriter, producer, and record company entrepreneur. As a member of the Impressions and later as a solo artist, he forged distinctive musical styles out of his gospel roots that contributed significantly to the shaping of black popular music. As a composer, first with his traditional rhythm and blues love songs and later with his inspirational songs, he created an enduring legacy of African-American songs.

• Robert Pruter's interviews with Curtis Mayfield (1986), Altheida Sims Mayfield (2001), and Marion Washington Jackson (2001) provided family history information. *Chicago Soul* (1991) by Robert Pruter gives the most extensive coverage on Mayfield's life and career. An African-American perspective on Mayfield's career in terms of the black civil rights movement can be found in Earl Ofari's interview "Curtis Mayfield: A Man for All People," *Soul Illustrated* (Summer 1973): 19–20. Of the many published interviews conducted with Mayfield the following was most insightful: Paolo Hewitt, "So Proud: The Moral Standard of Soul," *New Musical Express* (9 July 1983): 24–26, 43. An invaluable musicological explanation of Mayfield's guitar style and compositional method is in Chuck Phillips and Andy Widders-Ellis, "The Soul of an R&B Genius," *Guitar Player* (August 1991): 52–56. The best newspaper obituary is by Dave Hoekstra, "A Lasting Impression," *Chicago Sun-Times*, 27 December 1999.

ROBERT PRUTER

MCCAIN, John Sidney (9 Aug. 1884–6 Sept. 1945), naval officer, was born in Teoc, Mississippi, the son of John S. McCain and Elizabeth Young McCain. He graduated from high school in Carrolton, Mississippi, and in 1901 attended the University of Mississippi for one year. In 1902 he entered the U.S. Naval Academy at Annapolis, Maryland, graduating in February 1906 in a class that included other distinguished World War II flag officers such as Aubrey W. Fitch, Frank Jack Fletcher, and John H. Towers. As a passed midshipman, McCain served in the Asiatic Station on the battleship USS *Ohio* (BB-12), cruiser USS *Baltimore* (C-3), gunboat USS *Panay* (PG-45), and destroyer USS *Chauncey* (DD-3). In 1908, after the two years then required by law before commissioning, McCain was commissioned ensign. In 1909 he married Katherine Davey Vaulx, with whom he was to have three children, including John S. McCain, Jr. (USNA 1931), who also reached the rank of admiral. (His grandson, John S. McCain III, also a graduate of the U.S. Naval Academy, won fame as a POW in North Vietnam and became a U.S. senator, representing Arizona.)

Between 1908 and 1935, McCain served in a number of surface warships: the battleship USS *Connecticut* (BB-18) (1908–1909), armored cruisers USS *Pennsylvania* (ACR-4) (1909), USS *Washington* (ACR-11) (1909–1912), USS *Colorado* (ACR-7) (1914–1915), and USS *San Diego* (ACR-6) (1915–1918), and battleships USS *Maryland* (BB-46) (1921–1923) and USS *New Mexico* (BB-40) (1926–1928). McCain's commands at sea during those years were the cargo ship USS *Sirius* (AK-15) (1926) and the ammunition ship USS *Nitro* (AE-2) (1931–1933). Shore duty during this period included assistant to the captain of the yard, Naval Station, Cavite, the Philippines; officer-in-charge, Machinists Mates' School, Charleston Navy Yard, Charleston, South Carolina; and four tours in the Bureau of Navigation (Navy Department).

In June 1935, McCain reported for flight training at the Naval Air Station, Pensacola, Florida, for training as an "aviation observer." Due to a lack of qualified aviators with the prerequisite experience and seniority to command ships and stations, as required by congressional legislation, senior officers were put through a course in aviation involving most of the normal flight training syllabus, except solo flight. Then-Captain McCain completed flight training in August 1936, at the age of fifty-two, and was assigned as commander, Aircraft Squadrons and Attending Craft at the Fleet Air Base, Coco Solo, Canal Zone, with additional duty as commanding officer of the base. He remained there until May 1937, then took command of the carrier USS *Ranger* (CV-4) in the Pacific and Caribbean until July 1939, after which he commanded the Naval Air Station, San Diego, California.

On 23 January 1941, McCain was promoted to rear admiral and assumed command of Aircraft, Scouting Force, with the responsibility for coordinating the services of the Army Air Forces units with naval units in conducting antisubmarine patrols along the West Coast of the United States during the early months of World War II. In May 1942, he was designated commander, Aircraft, South Pacific and Southern Pacific Force, in command of all U.S. Navy land- and tender-based aircraft before and during the Solomon Islands campaign, for which service he was awarded the Distinguished Service Medal. The commendation noted his "tireless energy and extraordinary skill" in contributing to the occupation of the Guadalcanal-Tuagi area and to the damaging and destruction of Japanese vessels and aircraft.

Rear Admiral McCain returned from the Pacific to the Navy Department in Washington, D.C., to serve as chief of the Bureau of Aeronautics from 2 October 1942 until August 1943, at which time he became the first deputy chief of Naval Operations (Air), with the rank of vice admiral. In August 1944 McCain returned to combat in the Pacific, first as commander, Task Group 38.1, then as commander, Second Carrier Task Force (Task Force 38). Under Admiral McCain's leadership, Task Force 38 was in almost continuous action during the remainder of the war. It spearheaded the drive into the Philippines, supported the capture of Okinawa, and drove through the Western Pacific from the Indochina coast to the Japanese home islands. For heroism and great achievement in the Pacific during the latter part of the war, Admiral McCain received the Navy Cross, and Gold Stars in lieu of second and third Distinguished Service Medals.

McCain was unorthodox in habit and tactics, according to Theodore Taylor in *The Magnificent Mitscher* (1954). He sported a dilapidated green cap attached to a standard officer's cap frame with an admiral's gold-braided brim, rolled his own cigarettes, and habitually left a trail of ashes as he moved about the bridge of his flagship. McCain emerged from World War II with the reputation as a leader with the common touch, according to his operations officer, Captain John S. "Jimmie" Thach. McCain believed in "talking to the people who are actually doing it." He was a fighter, who enjoyed a wonderful rapport and friendship with his immediate boss, Admiral William F. "Bull" Halsey, commander, Third Fleet.

Vice Admiral McCain died of a heart attack on 6 September 1945, shortly after returning to Coronado, California, from the surrender ceremony on board the battleship USS *Missouri* (BB-63) in Tokyo Bay. He was en route to Washington, D.C., for assignment as deputy director of the Veterans Administration. He was buried in Arlington National Cemetery and promoted posthumously to the rank of admiral by a joint resolution of Congress. The destroyer USS *John S. McCain* (DL-3), named in his honor, was commissioned on 12 October 1953. Later converted to a guided missile destroyer (DDG-36), the vessel was recommissioned on 6 September 1969 and eventually decommissioned on 29 April 1978.

• Critical assessments of McCain's performance in the Pacific War can be found in a number of oral histories in the U.S. Naval Institute's Oral History Collection, Annapolis, Maryland, including those of Vice Adm. Gerald F. Bogan, Adm. Arleigh A. Burke, and Adm. John S. Thach. Thach is particularly supportive of McCain's performance and gives rare insights into McCain's character and leadership abilities. Other viewpoints can be found in E. T. Wooldridge, ed., *Carrier Warfare in the Pacific* (1993), a collection of excerpts from oral histories of notable naval aviation leaders in the Pacific War. McCain is frequently mentioned in any work dealing with the Pacific War. Representative of these are works of naval aviation historian Clark G. Reynolds, among them *Admiral John H. Towers: The Struggle for Naval Air Supremacy* (1991), and *The Fast Carriers: The Forging of an Air Navy* (1968). Other works that address the major carrier air battles in the Pacific include Samuel Eliot Morison, *The Two Ocean War; A Short History of the United States Navy in the Second World War* (1962); J. J. Clark, with Clark G. Reynolds, *Carrier Admiral* (1967); William F. Halsey and J. Bryant III, *Admiral Halsey's Story* (1947); and E. B. Potter's *Bull Halsey* (1985) and *Nimitz* (1976).

E. T. WOOLDRIDGE

MCCRORY, John Graham (11 Oct. 1860–20 Nov. 1943), retail store chain founder, was born John Graham McCrorey in East Wheatfield Township, Indiana County, Pennsylvania, the son of James E. McCrorey and Mary A. Murphy, farmers. His paternal grandfather, a Presbyterian immigrant from Ulster, had settled in East Wheatfield in 1814. When McCrory was two years old, his father enlisted in the Union army and four months later, on 5 March 1863, died from an illness. A few years after her husband's death, Mary McCrorey moved with her family to Mechanicsburg, near where she had been born, to be closer to her family's church and to provide better schools for her two children. John McCrory spent his youth in and

around Mechanicsburg, attending local schools and during vacations working for farmers and as a country store clerk. At the age of eighteen he left home to work in the mills of the Cambria Iron Company in Johnstown and soon got a job in the company's store, known as Wood, Morrell & Company.

Using his own savings and money borrowed mainly from his sister Jennie, McCrory in 1882 opened in Scottdale a five- and ten-cent store that also stocked some higher priced merchandise. Over the next ten years he opened and closed many more stores, often operating as many as a dozen at the same time. His first store limited to items selling for no more than a dime opened in Lawrence, Massachusetts, in 1891, and the second opened in Jamestown, New York, shortly after. In 1893 McCrory married Lillie Peters, the daughter of a minister; they had two sons, one of whom survived childhood. Lillie McCrory died in 1902, and in 1904 he married Carrie McGill, also a minister's daughter; they had three daughters.

In 1897 McCrory took a bold step toward expansion. His chain consisted of dime stores in Johnstown and Jamestown and six "bazaar" stores, mainly in small towns of 3,000 to 5,000 near Johnstown. Like many of the other founders of retail chains, he filled key staff positions with relatives and friends: John H. McCullough, his sister's husband, was vice president, and his cousin George Clinton "Clint" Murphy managed the Jamestown store. But then an ambitious tinware and hardware salesman from Wilkes-Barre, Sebastian S. Kresge, persuaded McCrory to train him and take him on as an equal partner in return for an investment of $8,000. Together they opened one store in Memphis managed by Kresge and another in Detroit, where Clint Murphy moved in as manager. In early 1899 Kresge took over as manager of the Detroit store, and in the fall of that year he ended their partnership by paying McCrory $3,000 and giving up his share of the Memphis store. From sole ownership of the Detroit store, Kresge built one of the country's largest and most successful variety store chains.

After his partnership with Kresge dissolved, McCrory conservatively expanded his own firm by reinvesting profits. In 1906 he moved the general offices and purchasing department to New York City to be near suppliers. Murphy then resigned as a buyer at the Johnstown office and opened his own store in McKeesport; over the next few years the G. C. Murphy Company operated about a dozen additional stores in other small towns near Pittsburgh but by 1911 teetered on the brink of financial collapse. Then another cousin, John S. Mack, resigned from his position as the general manager for McCrory Stores in Johnstown, bought the controlling share of G. C. Murphy, and successfully managed its further growth. The departure of Murphy, Mack, and later other key executives did not, however, impede McCrory. In 1912 J. G. McCrory Company incorporated in Delaware with the founder and president as almost the sole owner of $7 million of common stock. By then he and the firm had dropped the "e" from the original spelling of the name. Other branches of the family had long spelled the name "McCrory," but the company also claimed that the shorter name allowed it to save money on the cost of gilt lettering for store signs. Within a year of incorporation it had about 3,000 employees in about 110 stores, many in rapidly growing small towns, and gross sales exceeded $8 million, making it the fourth largest variety store chain in the country. Soon, the brokerage firm Merrill, Lynch became the principal underwriter of its stock, with Charles Merrill a significant shareholder as well as a personal friend of McCrory.

The firm continued to expand throughout the East and South until the Depression. At its peak in 1929 it was the fifth largest variety store chain, operating about 240 locations—including some in the largest cities—with gross sales of more than $44 million. But the combination of declining sales, shrinking credit, and costly long-term rental leases dangerously complicated finances. After his son, Van, the firm's vice president, died in a hunting accident in 1929, McCrory sold the controlling share to Merrill, Lynch. McCrory, who remained as president until he became chairman in 1931, announced his intention to operate the business more aggressively and profitably. Nevertheless, the price of McCrory stock fell from its high of $65 to only $2, and on 14 January 1933, though assets still exceeded liabilities, the firm declared bankruptcy. Eight months later McCrory and Charles Merrill, by then a court-appointed receiver, parted on bad terms as a result of the bankruptcy proceedings. McCrory retired to his summer home in Brush Valley, Pennsylvania, where he died.

In addition to his retail business, McCrory had extensive real estate investments in several locations, most notably with his brother-in-law, McCullough, in Florida's Orange and Osceola counties. Deeply religious, McCrory contributed generously to many churches and branches of the YMCA. In 1936 McCrory Stores reorganized from bankruptcy and, through a series of mergers, by 1990 had become the parent company of several other variety store chains, including S. S. Kresge, G. C. Murphy, and W. W. McLellan, all of which had started through connections with John McCrory. However, in 2002 the McCrory Corporation liquidated its entire business.

• Valuable profiles of McCrory appear in Joshua Thompson Stewart, *Indiana County, Pennsylvania: Her People, Past and Present, Embracing a History of the County* (1913), and Clarence D. Stephenson, *Indiana County 175th Anniversary History* (1989). Additional information is in Edwin J. Perkins, *Wall Street to Main Street: Charles Merrill and Middle-class Investors* (1999). Additional materials are available at the Historical and Genealogical Society of Indiana County. Obituaries are in the *New York Times* and the *Indiana Evening Gazette*, both 21 Nov. 1943.

ALAN R. RAUCHER

MCCUTCHEON, John T. (6 May 1870–10 June 1949), cartoonist, was born John Tinney McCutcheon on a farm in Tippecanoe County, Indiana, a few miles south of Lafayette, the son of John Barr McCutcheon, a drover with literary aspirations and, later, sheriff of the county and city treasurer of Lafayette, and Clara Glick McCutcheon. The family moved to a suburb of Lafayette when John was ten, by which time his older brother, George Barr McCutcheon, the future novelist, had taught him to draw. On 15 November 1884, John's first cartoon was published in the *Elston News*. At sixteen, John entered Purdue University, where he wrote articles and drew cartoons and other illustrations for campus publications and met George Ade, future humorist and playwright, who pledged him to Sigma Chi fraternity. Graduating with a B.S. degree in 1889, McCutcheon went to Chicago where he doubled the one-man art department at the *Chicago Daily News* (successively renamed the *News-Record*, then *Chicago Record*, then *Record-Herald*). Working as a news sketch artist, McCutcheon illustrated trials, sporting events, crime scenes, art show openings, and such catastrophes as fire and flood. He also drew portraits of politicians and dignitaries as well as border decorations and other visual trimmings. In 1892, he sketched the construction and then the ensuing activity of the World's Columbian Exposition.

Within a year of McCutcheon's arrival in Chicago, Ade joined him at the newspaper, and they became inseparable companions for nearly eight years. Ade reported their urban adventures in a popular long-running series in the *News*, "Stories of the Streets and the Town," which McCutcheon illustrated, the collaboration collected later in book form (1894). In 1895, the pair journeyed together to Europe, twice weekly sending reports to the *News* in words and pictures that were subsequently published in a pamphlet, *What a Man Sees Who Goes Away from Home*. About this time, McCutcheon was directed to draw for the newspaper's front page a humorous commentary picture, an editorial cartoon rather than a news sketch. McCutcheon, who thought of himself as a reporter, was assisted in his transition to commentator by Ade, who, the cartoonist later said, "helped materially: he provided the excellent suggestions that gave my early cartoons whatever distinction they had" (*Drawn from Memory*). McCutcheon continued to cover news events, attending and sketching the 1896 national conventions of both the Republicans and the Democrats. During the ensuing campaign, the cartoonist produced a memorable visual device when he casually filled an unoccupied space in the corner of a cartoon with a drawing of a little dog. When readers commented favorably, he responded by inserting the "flop-eared, dough-faced hound" into his cartoons regularly for months thereafter.

In 1898, McCutcheon took a six-month leave from the newspaper to make an around-the-world shakedown cruise aboard a new Coast Guard cutter, the *McCulloch*. When the Spanish American War broke out, the *McCulloch* was transferred to the U.S. Navy and accompanied the Pacific fleet to the Philippines, where McCutcheon witnessed the successful U.S. assault on Spanish colonial might at Manila Bay. Mc-

Cutcheon cabled his newspaper with a news report of the event and was immediately famous nationwide. Ordered to sign up cable correspondents in the region, McCutcheon spent the next two and a half years visiting places whose names ring with exotic romance—from Borneo and Bombay to Samarkand and Zanzibar and South Africa, where he looked in on the Boer War. When in 1900 he returned at last to Chicago, McCutcheon repaid Ade by supplying him with material for his first operetta, *The Sultan of Sulu.*

In the spring of 1902, seeking to repeat the crowd-pleasing success of his little dog, McCutcheon drew a front-page cartoon of a boy in a straw hat and patched pants, carrying a fishing pole, accompanied by an assortment of gamboling dogs. Captioned "A Boy in Springtime," the drawing was neither topical nor political: it was, as McCutcheon said, "purely human interest." It provoked comment among readers, and over the years McCutcheon supplied encores in a series of "Boy" cartoons displaying youthful activities by season. In another popular series of cartoons that year, McCutcheon reported on the American tour of Prince Henry of Prussia, depicting in elaborate and recognizable detail the landmarks and incidents of the dignitary's progress through several cities. In a third series launched in 1902, the cartoonist secured his place in the affections of his Midwestern readers: in the Bird Center cartoons, he drew the local population of this imaginary hamlet at various civic activities—church social, county fair, Fourth of July parade—accompanying the drawing with notes and comments as if it were a society news item in a small-town newspaper. "The purpose of the series," he explained, "was to show how very cheerful and optimistic life may be in a small town [where] no one feels himself to be better than his neighbor, and the impulse of generosity and kindness is common to all." The Bird Center cartoons, like the Prince Henry cartoons, were later collected in a book.

In June 1903, McCutcheon was lured onto the staff of the region's most widely circulated paper, the *Chicago Tribune*, where he remained, doing front-page cartoons, for the next 43 years. His most memorable efforts included the "Mysterious Stranger" cartoon of 1904, in which Missouri joined the Republican ranks in voting for Theodore Roosevelt, and "The Colors," published at the outbreak of World War I on 7 August 1914, a somber reminder of the cost of war: evoking the pastoral vistas of his youth in Indiana, the four horizontal panels of the cartoon showed, first, a field of corn stalks, then the same field strewn with bodies, then with mourners, then with tombstones, under which McCutcheon's poem ran in four parallel stanzas: Gold and green are the fields in peace,/Red are the fields in war;/Black are the fields when the cannons cease/And white forevermore. McCutcheon had used the same four-stage method in his most popular cartoon, "Injun Summer." First published 30 September 1907, it portrayed a field of corn stalks transforming slowly into a village of tepees in the imagination of a young observer; beginning in 1912, it was reprinted

by request annually for decades. The last of his widely reprinted sentimental favorites was a World War II effort: captioned "Mail Call," it focused on a soldier who, in a crowd of others, was the only one who failed to receive a letter from home. This cartoon inspired one reader to write over 11,000 letters to men in the service during the war.

Even on political subjects, McCutcheon's cartoons were more good-natured in their satire than savage. Explaining his credo as a cartoonist, he wrote: "I always enjoyed drawing a type of cartoon which might be considered a sort of pictorial breakfast food. It had the cardinal asset of making the beginning of the day sunnier . . . a happy man [being] capable of a more constructive day's work than a glum one. . . . However, some subjects demand more stinging rebukes than can be administered with ridicule or good-natured satire." Although he drew such cartoons, he did them "with a feeling of regret . . . [because] it would seem better to reach out a friendly pictorial hand to the delinquent than to assail him with criticism and denunciation." During the New Deal of Franklin D. Roosevelt, which the *Tribune* opposed, the paper hired another cartoonist, Carey Orr, to produce merciless broadside salvos. McCutcheon's cartoons continued, in the words of one observer, "a gentle mixture of corn shucks, bombazine, bent-pin fishhooks, and 'slippery ellum' whistles." Although he spent his career in the nation's second-largest city, his work was more expressive of rural than urban America, but his acceptance by the *Tribune's* readers, as historian Gerald Johnson noted, was doubtless due to these readers' having nostalgic recollections of their own origins in small towns *(The Lines Are Drawn)*. Even the 1931 cartoon that earned him the Pulitzer Prize was, while sharply bitter, infused with the traditional Midwestern country aura of homespun virtue. Captioned "A Wise Economist Asks a Question," the drawing shows a man on a park bench being asked by a squirrel, "Why didn't you save some money for the future when times were good?" "I did," says the man, who is identified as the "victim of bank failure."

Throughout his time at the *Tribune*, McCutcheon continued to write as well as to draw, and he traveled extensively. In 1906, he spent six months in Central Asia, reporting in word and picture for the newspaper; in 1909–1910, he was in Africa for four and a half months, covering a big game hunt; in 1912, he took a pirate cruise in the Bahamas and Haiti; in 1914, he was in Mexico with Pancho Villa. By happenstance, he was with the German army when it invaded Lorraine in 1914; he returned to Europe in 1915 as a war correspondent. And he attended and reported on the Paris peace conference in 1919. In later years, McCutcheon's passion for travel led him to finagle an unusual contract with the *Tribune*: he was permitted four months' leave every year. He went around the world several times, often flying when airplane travel was still primitive, and he once traversed 13,000 miles over four continents by Zeppelin. He was the first newspaperman to cross the Gobi Desert in an open automobile. After his marriage on 20 January 1917 to Evelyn Shaw, twenty-five years younger, whom he had known since her birth, most of his travel was to a tropical island he purchased that year just north of Nassau in the Bahamas. They had four children, including Shaw McCutcheon, a cartoonist. In 1925, he and his wife journeyed to the South Sea Islands and then around the world together.

McCutcheon died in his Lake Forest home. For decades he had been called the "dean of American cartoonists," but he was also a war corespondent, combat artist, news photographer, and world traveler. His place in the history of American journalism, however, is secured by his having introduced and perfected the "human interest" editorial cartoon. The *Chicago Tribune*'s editorial at McCutcheon's death recognized that "his special excellence lay in a combination of a highly developed sense of irony, a delight in the ridiculous, a small boy's curiosity, a big boy's delight in excitement and adventure, and an all-pervading warmth of personality." As his colleague Carey Orr wrote, "He was the first to throw the slow ball in cartooning, to draw the human interest picture that was not produced to change votes or to amend morals but solely to amuse or to sympathize. The reader said to himself, 'This man understands me.'"

• McCutcheon's personal papers are housed at the Syracuse University Library. Most of the details of his life, particularly his adventures as a young man, are rehearsed in his autobiography, *Drawn from Memory* (1950), which was completed by his wife after his death, working from material he had dictated to her. In addition to titles of his collaborations with George Ade mentioned above, his books include illustrated stories as well as cartoon collections: *Stories of Filipino Warfare* (1900), *Cartoons by McCutcheon* (1903), *Bird Center Cartoons* (1904), *Cartoons That Made Prince Henry Famous* (1902), *Mysterious Stranger and Other Cartoons* (1905), *Congressman Pumphrey* (1907), *In Africa* (1910), *T. R. in Cartoons* (1910), *Dawson '11, Fortune Hunter* (1912), *The Restless Age* (1921), *An Heir at Large* (1922), *Clifford & John's Almanack* (1921, with text by Clifford Raymond), *Crossed Wires* (1928), and *The Master of the World* (1928). McCutcheon's Pulitzer Prize–winning cartoon is discussed by Gerald W. Johnson in his history of the cartoon awards, *The Lines Are Drawn* (1958). The *New York Times* obituary is in the 10 June 1949 edition, but a much more extensive one was published in the *Chicago Tribune*, 11 June 1949.

ROBERT C. HARVEY

MCDONALD, William C. (25 July 1858–11 Apr. 1918), first governor of New Mexico, was born in Jordanville, Saratoga County, New York, the son of John McDonald and Lydia Marshall Biggs McDonald, farmers. After obtaining his early education in the public schools of Herkimer County, he completed his formal academic training at Cazenovia Academy in Cazenovia, New York, during which time he also taught school and studied law. In 1880, sensing greater opportunities in the West, he moved to Fort Scott, Kansas, and was admitted to the local bar. That same year he moved again, this time to White Oak, New Mexico, where he briefly worked as a clerk in a

dry goods store. In 1881 he received an appointment as U.S. deputy mineral surveyor for New Mexico.

McDonald retained his federal appointment until 1890 and also acquired a working knowledge of civil and mining engineering during the same period. In 1885 he entered public life as the assessor of Lincoln County; he held that position until 1887. In 1890 McDonald entered the cattle business as the manager of the Carrizozo Cattle Ranch Company. He eventually bought the Carrizozo Company from his employers, gained control of the El Capitan Live Stock Company, and ranked among the leading cattlemen of the Southwest. On 31 August 1891 he married Frances Jane McCourt at Las Vegas, New Mexico; the couple had one child, a daughter.

While establishing his cattle empire, McDonald held a variety of public posts: he served a term in the territorial house of representatives (1891), chaired the Lincoln County Board of Commissioners (1895–1897), and between 1905 and 1911 served as a member of the New Mexico Cattle Sanitary Board. Always a student of public affairs, McDonald also chaired the central committee of the territorial Democratic party in 1910. With the territory long held in the grip of the Republican party, Democratic leaders coalesced behind McDonald to enable the party to gain a foothold within New Mexico, which in 1911 was admitted to statehood. Although reluctant to seek higher office, McDonald finally succumbed to repeated pleas from his party and served as its first candidate for governor. Elected with 31,036 votes over Republican nominee Holm O. Bursum (who received 28,019 votes) in November 1911, McDonald was sworn into office in January 1912.

But McDonald faced a hostile legislature that had a two-thirds Republican majority. While the legislature never succeeded in overriding a single McDonald veto, his five years in office were marred by government gridlock. A strong advocate of public schools, McDonald also took a zealous approach to rooting out corruption in government, and his papers include documentation of investigations of several individual employees as well as allegations against the Sante Fe County Commission. McDonald was equally interested in seeing that investors did not fall prey to organized scams, and projects such as a dam across the Rio Grande River and passageways for the El Paso and Southwestern Railroad (as well as other irrigation and land development schemes) received his careful scrutiny.

Perhaps the most significant event to occur during McDonald's term was the raid of the Mexican bandit Pancho Villa on Columbus, New Mexico, on 9 March 1916. Although Villa was soon pursued across the Mexican border by American troops under the command of General John "Black Jack" Pershing, the new state remained in an uproar for the remainder of the year.

After leaving office on 1 January 1917, McDonald returned to his ranch at Carrizozo. When the United States entered World War I in April 1917, he agreed to serve as the state's fuel administrator. He died in El Paso, Texas, and was buried in Carrizozo. Although unable to accomplish much during his term in office, McDonald will always have a place in history by virtue of his being the first man to serve as governor of the state of New Mexico. Owing to constitutional restrictions, he also held the distinction of holding office for a longer period of time—five years—than any of his successors until the latter half of the twentieth century.

• McDonald's papers are held at the New Mexico State Records Center and Archives in Santa Fe, New Mexico. His career is discussed in Warren A. Beck, *New Mexico: A History of Four Centuries* (1962). Still useful as well is Charles F. Coan, *History of New Mexico*, 3 vols. (1925).

EDWARD L. LACH, JR.

MCGHEE, Brownie (30 Nov. 1915–23 Feb. 1996), blues musician, was born Walter Brown McGhee in Knoxville, Tennessee, the son of George "Duff" McGhee, a farmer and itinerant mill worker, and Zella Henley McGhee. Even as a child, he was called "Brownie." His family was musically active. Brownie's father was a guitarist and singer. One of Brownie's uncles, John Evans, was a fiddler and gave him his first instrument—a homemade banjo fashioned from an empty can of marshmallows. Through his mother, Brownie was exposed to the music of Jimmie Rodgers, a white country singer, as well as Bessie Smith and Lonnie Johnson, the great African-American blues recording artists. As a child, Brownie contracted polio, which stunted the growth of his right leg and left him physically deformed. He therefore devoted much time to music. He played in church, acquiring some skill on the piano and organ, and with his father sang in a gospel quartet called The Golden Voices. He also toured with carnivals, medicine shows, and a group known as the Rabbit Foot Minstrels. His brother, Granville "Stick" (or "Sticks") McGhee, played guitar as well, and the two of them played together on occasion. (Granville received his nickname because he was often seen pushing Brownie around town in a homemade cart that had a tree branch for a handle.) Brownie left high school to play his guitar and work and busk around various towns in the South. In 1937 he underwent an operation to help correct his limp. Taking advantage of his increased mobility, he spent even more time traveling and playing music.

Sometime around 1939 Brownie was traveling in North Carolina with the harmonica player Jordan Webb, busking for small change and trying to avoid the police. In Durham, McGhee and Webb were introduced to J. B. Long, a white record store manager who managed blues singer Blind Boy Fuller. Long arranged for Brownie to record in Chicago, and in August of 1940 McGhee recorded his first sides for Okeh records with Jordan Webb on harmonica. Fuller's health was failing, and Long was perhaps grooming Brownie, among others, to fill his shoes. Fuller died

in February 1941, leaving Long without a "star" recording act. Long procured Fuller's steel-bodied National guitar for Brownie's next recordings, made under the pseudonym "Blind Boy Fuller #2." Despite this deceit and exploitation, Brownie continued his association with Long and Okeh records and in the fall of 1941 recorded with the harmonica player Sonny Terry.

In 1942 McGhee and Terry made their way to New York City and participated in that city's burgeoning folk music revival, working mostly as a duo. Brownie, young and handsome, provided a contrast with his older partner, who was noticeably blind and wore spectacles. Their earthy and exuberant country blues struck a chord with the middle- and working-class patrons of the folk clubs. McGhee and Terry befriended the more popular blues singer Huddie Ledbetter, known as Lead Belly, and often shared the bill with him. Fewer records were made during the war, so these concerts helped Brownie and the other musical transplants from the South earn at least a meager living. Beginning around 1945 Brownie ran the House of Blues, a school in Harlem for aspiring blues singers and guitarists. McGhee also worked for a seller of voodoo charms sometime during this period, though what exactly he did is unknown.

After World War Two the recording industry picked up, and Brownie's career took off. His ongoing collaboration with Sonny Terry in the acoustic blues format was becoming popular with the mostly white, educated, and liberal (in those days "leftist") fans of American roots music. In 1948 he recorded with a rhythm and blues combo and scored a hit with "Robbie Doby Boogie." The following year he wrote the sequel to this tune, "New Baseball Boogie." These tunes were tributes to the great African-American ball players Robbie Doby and Jackie Robinson. His work in this vein was popular, especially with African Americans. Consequently, McGhee was one of the few black artists of the pre-civil rights era to reach both a white and a black audience.

In 1950 McGhee married Ruth Dantzler; they had six children. Having to provide for a large family may have been some of the incentive that kept McGhee so busy during the 1950s. Fortunately, his versatility extended beyond the role of music performer. In 1955 he and Terry appeared in Tennessee Williams's Broadway musical *Cat on a Hot Tin Roof*. His associations with this landmark play continued through 1958, as he was part of the touring company that went on the road that year. He also appeared in Langston Hughes's *Simply Heavenly*, an off-Broadway musical revue that ran for several months at the Playhouse Theater during the summer of 1957.

During the 1950s the winds of change were beginning to affect the buying trends of music fans. McGhee continued to perform with his rhythm and blues combo as well as with Sonny Terry in a more or less traditional blues setting. However, their records for the Old Town label in 1956–1957 did poorly. In 1958 Terry and McGhee signed with the Folkways record label, which promoted them as authentic representatives of the Piedmont style of country blues.

McGhee and Terry worked steadily through the 1960s. Ironically, they played for mostly white audiences at folk festivals and coffeehouses throughout North America and Europe. An accurate description of their sound was offered by the noted Philadelphia folk music disc jockey Gene Shay in his liner notes to *Brownie McGhee and Sonny Terry at the Second Fret* (1962). Shay wrote of "Sonny's falsetto squeals and vocalized harmonica" and noted that "Brownie's guitar supplies strong rhythmic chording and single line improvisation." A few of McGhee's best recordings from this period are *Hometown Blues*, with Terry, and the 1976 release *Blues Is Truth* with Sugar Blue on harmonica and his brother Stick on guitar. Although McGhee pursued a few projects without Terry, the bulk of his work from the early sixties until their split in 1976 was as a member of the duo.

McGhee was one of the few blues musicians successful enough to retire somewhat comfortably. He made his home in Oakland, California. During the 1980s he made an appearance on the television sitcom "Family Ties" and started the Blues Is Truth Foundation. He passed away after succumbing to cancer in Oakland, California.

McGhee sang in a warm and articulate vocal style not typical of blues singers in general. His guitar playing was clean and inventive. He worked tirelessly for decades, leaving behind an extraordinary recorded legacy. The foundation he started is testament to his dedication to the African-American art form known as the blues.

• Helpful biographical information is available in Samuel B. Charters's book *The Country Blues* (1959; rev. ed., 1975). A brief biographical entry and a selected discography are in Austin Sonnier, Jr., *A Guide to the Blues* (1994). Many interesting photos and an in-depth discussion on the blues in general can be found in Lawrence Cohn, *Nothing But the Blues* (1993). Noted blues scholar Paul Oliver, in *The Story of the Blues* (1969), tells of McGhee's childhood years. Liner notes by Gene Shay and Bill Dahl for *Sonny Terry and Brownie McGhee at the Second Fret* (1962) and *Absolutely the Best Sonny Terry and Brownie McGhee* (2000), respectively, describe McGhee's playing and singing style. Obituaries are in the *San Francisco Chronicle*, 19 Feb. 1996, and the Philadelphia *Inquirer*, 20 Feb. 1996.

CHARLES MESSINGER

MCMAHON, Thomas A. (21 Apr. 1943–14 Feb. 1999), writer and educator, was born in Dayton, Ohio, the son of Howard Oldford McMahon, a physical chemist, and Lucille Nelson McMahon, a scientist. He grew up in Lexington, Massachusetts, in a house his parents designed and built. After earning a B.S. from Cornell University in 1965, he entered the Massachusetts Institute of Technology (MIT), where he earned an M.S. in 1967 and completed his Ph.D. (with a focus on fluid mechanics) in 1970. He married Carol Ehlers on 20 June 1965; the couple had two children.

After joining the faculty of Harvard University as a postdoctoral fellow in 1969, McMahon spent his entire career there, as assistant professor (1971), associate professor (1974), and finally the Gordon McKay Professor of Applied Mechanics and professor of biology (1977). An effective teacher and adviser, McMahon was also skillful at securing grant funds for research. The author of numerous articles in publications such as *Scientific American* and *Science*, he also produced two books: *On Size and Life* (with John Tyler Bonner, 1983) and *Muscles, Reflexes, and Locomotion* (1984), which *Science* magazine later named a classic in the field.

McMahon combined a long-standing interest in physiology with a knack for applied physics to help create biomechanics, a science that utilized the principles of mechanics in studying locomotion in animal species, including humans. Always interested in practical applications of his work, McMahon produced some notable innovations during his career. In the 1970s, in collaboration with faculty colleague Peter R. Greene, he developed a new type of indoor track—made largely of plywood and known as a tuned track—that gave track and field competitors the sensation of sailing through the air. More important, the new track enabled runners to reduce their times by an average of 3 percent while cutting in half the number of related injuries. First used at Harvard's Gordon Indoor Track and Tennis Facility, similar tracks were later installed at Yale University, Madison Square Garden in New York City, and the Brendan Byrne Meadowlands Arena in East Rutherford, New Jersey. In the 1980s he produced a paper, later published by the American Physiological Society and replete with computerized projections, that outlined a type of jogging that was both safer and more effective than conventional techniques. McMahon dubbed his find "Groucho running" because the bowlegged stance was similar in form to the antics of noted comedian Groucho Marx. Never one to hide from the more whimsical side of science, McMahon and a graduate student, James Glasheen, demonstrated in 1996 how the basilisk, a lizard species native to Central and South America, was able to sprint across water and hence earn the nickname "Jesus Christ lizard."

While accomplished in the fields of pure and applied science, McMahon also nurtured a second career—that of a novelist. Although he claimed that he tried to keep that part of his life "under wraps . . . It's an invisible part of me," McMahon found the process of invention fascinating. He later explained, "People turn on lights, use the telephone, and other inventions every day. But they know little about the inventors or the circumstances that gave birth to these conveniences. I enjoy weaving such elements into fictional stories that inform people and divert them from everyday cares." His first novel, *Principles of American Nuclear Chemistry: A Novel* (1970), concerned the lives of scientists working on the development of the atomic bomb. His second novel, *McKay's Bees* (1979), was a fictional account of Gordon McKay, who gave his name to McMahon's faculty chair. McMahon's last novel, *Loving Little Egypt* (1987), featured a visually handicapped technician, Mourly Vold, who creates a toll-free network for the blind at the expense of the phone company. The latter two novels developed a cult following and were later adapted for the stage, and *Loving* won the Rosenthal Foundation Award of the American Academy of Arts and Letters.

McMahon's last major innovation came with the help of Toby Hayes and Steve Robinovitch: a pelvic-padding system that helped prevent osteopathic fractures in elderly medical patients. He was contemplating an investigation into the ability of ants to walk on glass ceilings when he unexpectedly died in Wellesley, Massachusetts, following abdominal surgery.

Although reluctant to claim the spotlight as a novelist, McMahon seems certain to be remembered for his quirky works of literature as much as for his solid contributions in the area of applied science. As one whose career belied the belief that there was no longer room for achievement in multiple areas of endeavor in an era of increasing specialization, McMahon set an example for other iconoclasts.

• No collection of McMahon's papers has been located, and secondary material concerning his life and career is scarce. Reviews of his works appeared in the *New York Times*, 31 July 1979, the *New York Times Book Review*, 19 Aug. 1979, and the (London) *Times Literary Supplement*, 1 Feb. 1980. Obituaries are in the Boston Globe, 18 Feb. 1999, the *New York Times*, 19 Feb. 1999, and the *Los Angeles Times*, 20 Feb. 1999.

EDWARD L. LACH, JR.

MEEUSE, Bastiaan Jacob Dirk (9 May 1916–27 July 1999), botanist and naturalist, was born in the small town of Sukabumi on the island of Java, the son of Adrianus Meeuse and Jannigje Kruithof Meeuse. His father taught mathematics and natural science in an agricultural college, and his mother taught in a Dutch-language primary school for Chinese children. Both parents were in the Dutch East Indian colonial service. Bastiaan and his brother Adriaan, who was two years older than Bastiaan, were taught by their mother at home, and they also went to the Chinese school with her and sat in the back of the class. During free time the boys enjoyed the tropical environment, and started collecting and raising butterflies and moths.

The family spent 1922 and 1923 in the Netherlands on a European leave. There the boys became familiar with European plants and animals (including catching mating sticklebacks), but they were happy to return the next year to Java and a life of greater freedom. In 1926 the family moved to Buitenzorg (Bogor), where both parents resumed teaching. The boys took advantage of the tropical environment and famous botanical garden and zoological museum.

In 1931 the family repatriated to the Hague, Netherlands, where Bastiaan Meeuse finished secondary school and took examinations for entry into the University of Leiden. There he studied general botanical subjects, plant physiology, animal physiology, economic botany, and animal behavior. He also studied biochemistry for a year at the University of Delft with Professor Gerrit van Iterson. After receiving the B.Sc. at Leiden in 1936, Meeuse continued his studies there and in 1939 passed the *doctoraal examen* (similar to the master's degree in the United States). His father died that year, and Meeuse moved to the University of Delft to work in van Iterson's laboratory. During the next three years Meeuse taught part-time at the Horticultural School at Boskoop and simultaneously worked on a doctoral thesis with van Iterson. In 1942 Meeuse became van Iterson's assistant. Also in 1942 he married the biology student and artist Johanne J. ten Have. They would have two children. During the summers Meeuse assisted Niko Tinbergen, the animal behaviorist with whom he had taken courses at Leiden and who was a Nobel laureate at Oxford University, in studies of courtship behavior of certain butterflies.

In 1943 Meeuse submitted his lengthy thesis on the conversion of starch in potatoes to sucrose at low temperatures and was awarded the degree of doctor of technical science with honors at Delft. He finished this work just before the German occupation officials started demanding "declarations of loyalty" from prospective doctors. Soon afterward he discontinued his work in van Iterson's laboratory because the situation had become too dangerous. Meeuse spent almost two years away from the laboratory and did not return until May 1945, after serving with the underground forces as a radio operator. Early in 1946 Meeuse, as van Iterson's chief assistant, spent two months visiting laboratories in England to study scientific advancements made during the war years.

In 1947 Meeuse was awarded a two-year Rockefeller Foundation Fellowship to work in the laboratory of David Goddard at the University of Pennsylvania on respiration and fermentation of pea seedlings. Upon his return to the Netherlands in 1949, he was appointed *lector* (similar to assistant professor) in general biology at Delft. In June 1950 Meeuse became acting head of the biochemical laboratory. During this period he researched the enzymatic hydrolysis of starch in maple and birch in the spring and used paper chromatography to identify the sugars in the exuding saps.

In 1951 Meeuse accepted an assistant professorship at the University of Washington–Seattle. He taught general botany and elementary and advanced plant physiology and was recognized as a stimulating teacher and lecturer. He supervised his first doctoral student, Prasanta Datta, and together they identified the heat resistant moss oxalic acid oxidase as a flavoprotein. In the summers of 1953 and 1954 Meeuse taught algal physiology at the Friday Harbor Marine Laboratory, where he learned much about the marine plants and animals of the region and identified the nature of reserve polysaccharides of *Euglena* and *Laminaria* in collaboration with his Dutch colleague

D. R. Kreger. Meeuse wrote two reviews for the prestigious *Handbuch der Pflanzenphysiologie*, published some fifteen other papers in scientific journals, and wrote the semipopular book *The Story of Pollination* (1961). At the same time the Meeuses bought a house and settled into life in the new country.

As a freshman at Leiden, Meeuse had heard lectures by Professor A. W. H. van Herk on the voodoo lily, *Sauromatum guttatum*, not a true lily but an aroid from whose dry tubers single flowers emerge. Each of these flowers has a long appendix that at the time of pollination warms to some 10 degrees Celsius above the air temperature because of intense cellular oxidation and emits a carrion-like odor that attracts pollinating carrion beetles. Van Herk believed this behavior was stimulated by an activating hormone, which he called calorigen, but he was unable to isolate or prove the existence of such a substance. In 1956 van Herk sent some 200 tubers of *S. guttatum* to Meeuse and urged him to finish the voodoo lily work. After two or three years of growing the tubers, Meeuse started to study this plant in earnest. For about ten years Meeuse and his laboratory, with National Science Foundation funding, pursued this research. His paper in *Scientific American* (1966) and his review in *Annual Review of Plant Physiology* (1975) gave details of the principal results of the studies, but calorigen was still elusive.

As the intensity of work on *Sauromatum* declined, Meeuse wrote a number of papers and reviews on *Sauromatum* and thermogenic respiration, then he devoted more time to flowers and pollination in general. He provided scientific guidance for the successful color film *Sexual Encounters of the Floral Kind* (1983), produced by Oxford Scientific Films. With Sean Morris, Meeuse wrote *The Sex Life of Flowers* (1984), which also appeared in a German edition, *Blumen-Liebe* (1984). Meeuse composed some fifteen articles for the *University of Washington–Washington Park Arboretum Bulletin* on butterflies, bees, and ants and their influences on pollination, wrote a widely used reader on pollination in the Carolina Biological Supply Company series, and contributed two articles to the fifteenth edition of *Encyclopedia Britannica*. In this period he also was a course director in a number of Chautauqua-type courses in various locations in the United States, instructed in the Organization for Tropical Studies field course in Costa Rica in the summer of 1980, and in the summer of 1985 was a visiting professor at the University of Nijmegen (Netherlands). His ability to give stimulating lectures in English, Dutch, or German brought many invitations to visit and lecture both in the United States and abroad. In addition to these specialized lectures, he often gave popular lectures on insects, flowers, and pollination to various groups. His amazingly broad knowledge of biology, his elephant-like memory of details, and his enthusiasm for imparting interesting facts to the audience always came out in his lecturing.

After retiring in 1986, Meeuse was still interested in *Sauromatum*, but he passed on the active work with this plant to Hanna Skubatz, an experienced biochemist and postdoctoral associate in the department. Along with Ilya Raskin, Skubatz, and others, Meeuse took satisfaction in the work that finally identified salicylic acid, related to aspirin, as the florigen that induces thermogenic respiration in *Sauromatum*. Another subject of his earlier research, oxalic acid oxidase, had seemed esoteric but in the 1980s provided a useful clinical tool in diagnosing excess oxalate in the blood of persons subject to calcium oxalate gall stones. Altogether Meeuse authored some 180 scientific publications on a wide variety of subjects, and 39 of those publications were on some aspect of heat production in *Sauromatum* or other aroids. He died in Kirkland, Washington, a suburb of Seattle.

• The files of the Department of Botany, University of Washington–Seattle, include a full list of Meeuse's publications, all in scientific journals, and two curriculum vitae, one written by Meeuse in 1951 and the other written by his brother Adriaan D. J. Meeuse in 1986. Among his publications see Meeuse, "The Voodoo Lily," *Scientific American* 215 (1966): 80–88; and I. Raskin, A. Ehman, W. R. Melander, and B. J. D. Meeuse, "Salicycle Acid: A Natural Inducer of Heat Production in *Arum* Lilies," *Science* 237 (1987): 1601–2, which has a voodoo lily photograph on the front cover. An obituary is in the *New York Times*, 9 Aug. 1999.

RICHARD B. WALKER

MEIÈRE, Hildreth (3 Sept. 1892–1 May 1961), artist, was born in New York City, the daughter of Marie Hildreth and Ernest Meière. Meière's mother had forsaken an artistic career in order to raise a family, but she raised her daughters in a home that Hildreth Meière later described as one in which "art was known and loved" (Meière, "Life and Times," p. 1). Meière lived in Flushing, New York, until 1901, when she was sent to study at Manhattanville, a prestigious and rigorous convent school run by the Religious of the Sacred Heart in New York City. Meière boarded there until her graduation in 1911.

In the 1880s Marie had studied art in Paris, where she befriended the American Impressionist Mary Cassatt. Upon Marie's return to New York she studied at the new Art Students League, where, according to Meière's biographer, she became a member of the Board of Control (Sharer, p. 29). Marie fully supported her daughter's decision to study art after graduation. According to family lore, Marie told her daughter that if she wanted to be a writer, she would send her to Smith; if she wanted to be a painter, she would take her to Italy" (Dunn, "From Pavlova to the Cathedral Basilica," p. 1), which she did. Meière received her first formal art training in the Florentine studio of the British painter Gordon Carmichael. In Italy, too, Meière discovered the architectural mural, the form to which she would devote most of her professional life. "We went to Italy and the glories of the Renaissance and all that proceeded it opened my eyes, and I fell in love, once and for all, with mural painting and great beautiful walls," Meière recalled in 1946.

After about a year, Meière returned to study in New York at the Art Students League, where, unusual for its time, men and women were allowed to study art together (Sharer, pp. 71–74). In 1913 Meière's family moved to San Francisco; there she spent over three years studying at the California School of Fine Arts (now the San Francisco Art Institute) and producing character studies from theatrical performances. The first pieces she exhibited and sold were from this period, sketches from Pavlova's ballet performances, and, next, of Margaret Anglin's Greek plays. In 1915 Anglin introduced Meière to her set and costume designer, Livingston Platt, who felt she might find work in New York. In January of 1916, Meière struck out on her own to start her career in New York City.

For the next few years, Meière earned her living designing costumes and lobby sketches for the theater. She was well positioned through her theater and family connections. In 1916 she was introduced to Louise Benedict Harmon, the wife of the playboy and well-known aviator Clifford Harmon. Louise Harmon quickly became Meière's greatest friend and patron and introduced her to New York's social elite. During the autumn of 1916, Platt placed increasing numbers of orders with Meière; she also received a large order for costume designs for a Metropolitan Opera production of Reginald de Koven's *Canterbury Pilgrims* (letter to Marie Meière dated 28 Aug. 1916).

Meière was relatively unproductive the following year, due in part to physical and possible psychological ailments; following a tonsillectomy, she worked only sporadically. "I know you don't believe in nerves, Mama, but [I'm] wrestling with them for the first time. [. . .] Every now and then I keep wanting to burst into tears, everything seems wrong, hopeless or useless," she wrote to her mother (letter to Marie Meière dated 3 Mar. 1917). In 1917 Meière sublet her studio and moved in with Louise Harmon, decisions that her family did not support. Meière took classes at the Art Students League, where she met Ernest Piexotto, who later became her advisor.

Early in 1918 Meière took an interest in war work. Unable to secure work designing recruiting posters, in November she joined the navy. She served in the Yeomanettes, who she later described as "the little ripples that preceded the WAVES of the Second World War" (Meière, "Dossier," p. 2). She remained in New York and studied as a mapmaker but was assigned as an architectural draftsman for the navy. She hoped to use her architectural training to secure some work in the reconstruction of Europe after the war, but no opportunities materialized. Following her honorable discharge in 1919, she spent three years studying with Ernest Piexotto at the School of Applied Design for Women, where she workedon Beaux-Arts Institute projects. At the School of Applied Design, she could take courses at the Beaux-Arts Institute, where women were not allowed to enroll.

In February of 1920, Meière read in an article in the *New York Times* that the American Academy in Rome was initiating a fundraising campaign so that it could admit women. Meière immediately assembled a portfolio and secured letters of recommendation from Frank Dumond and Ian Sloan of the Art Students' League, architect Thomas Hastings, H. Parkhurst of the School of Applied Design, and Byron Burroughs of the Metropolitan Museum of Art (Sharer, pp. 74–75). She was also interviewed by Edwin Blashfield and Brock Towbridge of the academy. By mid-March, however, the academy advised Meière that she was ineligible. Meière applied for admission again the next year but was never admitted to the academy (Sharer, p. 81).

In March 1921, while working on Beaux-Arts projects, Meière met architect Bertram Grosvenor Goodhue, who hired her to paint the high altar at St. Mark's Church in Mt. Kisco, New York. Thereafter she worked frequently with Goodhue's office as his principal muralist. In 1922 and 1923, while Meière was studying at the Art Institute of Chicago, Goodhue commissioned her to do the dome of the National Academy of Sciences Building in Washington, D.C., and the interior design of the Nebraska State Capitol Building, which included the rotunda dome, a tapestry for the Senate chamber, and the building's 200-foot-long marble floor. The National Academy of Sciences Building was dedicated just days after Goodhue's death in the spring of 1924. Meière continued to collaborate with Bertram Grosvenor Goodhue Associates, the successor to Goodhue's firm (quoted in Dunn, "Her Words," p. 11).

In the summer of 1925, Meière traveled to Italy to secure a price from an Italian firm for the glass mosaics of Temple Emanu-El. There she met Hartley Burr Alexander, who had planned the symbology of the Nebraska Capitol interior. During a trip to the Cathedral of Siena in Tuscany they conceived of a new design for the capitol's floor. Having failed to receive a quote from the Italians, Meière traveled to Berlin and within a week had a quote from the mosaic studios of Puhl-Wagner-Heinersdorf, whose subsidiary in the United States was the Ravenna Mosaic Company. Meière frequently collaborated with the Ravenna Company over the next thirty years (quoted in Dunn, "Her Words," p. 2).

In 1928 Meière was awarded the Architectural League of New York's Medal of Honor in decorative painting for her work in the Nebraska State Capitol. It was the first time this honor had been bestowed on a woman; it was not until 1934 that women were even allowed to join the League. Later that same year, Meière returned to Berlin to work on the Temple Emanu-El mosaics and a commission for mosaics in the apse of St. Bartholomew's Episcopal Church in New York City. In January 1929 Meière was elected first vice president of the Mural Painter's Society. That same year, she was selected to design mosaics in the narthex of St. Bartholomew's.

That summer, Meière traveled to Europe and fell in love with an Austrian, Richard von Goebel. They were married in a civil ceremony in New Jersey on 29

May 1929. Louise Harmon, though suspicious of Goebel's motives, gave them their reception, and she was present at their church wedding in Austria on 26 June. When Meière returned alone to New York to work in late September, she was pregnant with her daughter Louise (named for Louise Harmon). Meière learned that von Goebel's previous marriage had not been annulled by the Catholic Church and initiated annulment proceedings of her own. She retook her maiden name. In 1930, when her daughter was born, Meière was completing the magnificent abstract mosaic designs for the "Red Room," the banking room of the Irving Trust Building at One Wall Street, a stunning example of art deco architectural design and one of two commissions she had in the building.

In 1932 Meière received her most widely recognized commission, the three plaques adorning the exterior of Radio City Music Hall: *Dance Drama*, and *Song*, which she made in collaboration with metalworker Oscar B. Bach. She designed another plaque for Rockefeller Center, *Radio and Television Encompassing the Earth*, which was installed at the now razed R.K.O. Theater. (A replica of this plaque recently has been installed in the subway entrance across from the McGraw Hill Building.)

In 1933 Meière participated in Chicago's World's Fair. Her works there included a sixty-foot mural for the National Council of Women and a terra-cotta pool for the American Telephone and Telegraph Building. That same year, she traveled to Istanbul and Greece to study medieval and ancient mosaics. For the next several years, Meière continued to work on religious commissions and to travel. Frequent travel replenished Meière's enthusiasm and inspiration for her enormous murals. Her trips abroad doubled as opportunities to study her craft and as sources for lectures and slide shows. During a trip with young Louise to Oberammergau in 1934 to see the city's famed passion play, Meière saw Hitler. In the summer of 1936, on her return from a trip to Russia to see eleventh-century mosaics, she stopped in Berlin to attend the Olympic Games. She took an interest in Hitler and fascism, though her attitudes toward Nazi propaganda and art were unclear. During the Spanish Civil War, her sympathies seem to have been with Franco's Catholic Nationalists. In 1938, Meière traveled to France and then on to Spain to see the Civil War on an arranged visa through the American Spanish Relief Fund. Her job was to report on how funds were being distributed. She also filmed the destruction of churches in Toledo and other Spanish cities.

With the outbreak of the second World War, Meière's interest in fascism ended. She was unable to join the WAVES because her daughter was under eighteen, but as vice president of the Citizens Committee for the Army, Navy, and Air Corps, she used her connections in the art world to organize artists to design portable triptychs for military chaplains. Meière personally designed over seventy of the more than 700 triptychs these artists produced.

Meière had faired quite well during the Great Depression and designed a number of large murals. Since the mid-1930s she had been planning for the 1939 New York World's Fair. She worked on eleven commissions for four buildings there (Medicine and Public Health, Telephone, Johns-Manville, and the Temple of Religion). She received a number of religious and profane commissions, including the altar of the Lady Chapel at St. Patrick's Cathedral in New York City (1940), commissions on the ships *America*, *African Queen*, and *Brazil* (1940), and the *President Monroe* (1941), an exterior frieze at the Municipal Center in Washington, D.C. (1941), and several commissions for reredos in churches and chapels throughout the east.

In 1945 Meière was tapped for the first of many commissions in the Cathedral of St. Louis (now the Basilica Cathedral of St. Louis) in St. Louis, Missouri. This was in collaboration with Paul and Arno Heuduck of the Ravenna Mosaic Company, with whom she had worked in the Temple Emanu-El, St. Bartholomew's Episcopal Church, and at One Wall Street. The Cathedral in St. Louis was designed to house the largest collection of mosaics in the world, and Meière eventually became the most widely represented artist on its walls. Her first commission there was *The Sacrifice of Isaac*, which adorned the east sanctuary wall.

In 1948 Meière was approached by the Vestry of St. Bartholomew's Church to design a stained glass window for the church's south clerestory. She accepted the commission eagerly since she had never worked in stained glass. By this point in her career, Meière had designed for ceramic tile, marble and glass mosaic (including silhouette mosaic), terra-cotta, tapestry, metal and enamel, leather, and gesso. She seems to have delighted in experimenting with new media, and she attributed part of her success to the fact that a versatile artist was "useful" to architects (Dunn, "Dossier," p. 2). Over the next ten years, Meière designed four stained glass windows for St. Bartholomew's Church.

In 1951 Meière designed the mosaics in the Resurrection Chapel in the National Episcopal Cathedral in Washington, D.C., and a gesso and metal-leaf map for the U.S.S. *United States* the following year. She also received commissions for lobby mosaics in the Travelers Insurance Building (1956) and the Prudential Life Insurance Building (1960). In 1953 Meière's alma mater, Manhattanville College of the Sacred Heart, presented her with an honorary Doctorate of Humane Letters. Three years later, Meière became the first woman ever to receive the Fine Arts Medal, the highest honor given by the American Institute of Architects.

In the late 1950s and early 1960s, Meière was again at work in the Cathedral of St. Louis. She designed massive mosaic murals throughout the nave, including domes, arches, pendentives, and north and south walls. In 1957, Meière persuaded the cathedral's pastor to allow her to raise a section of her full-scale tempera cartoon into the dome so that she could see her design in place before submitting it. The large section, which bore an 18-foot-tall likeness of St. Matthew, had to be raised over 100 feet in the air twice before she was satisfied with the cartoon. Meière died of leukemia before her work in the Cathedral was completed. Nina Wheeler Blake, her assistant, completed the project.

Meière was one of the most productive mural artists of the twentieth century, and perhaps the most prolific mosaic muralist ever. Her mammoth designs in concrete, mosaic, tile, and stone embodied permanence, undissipated power, perpetual motion, and strength that ran counter to the pessimism and fragmentation pervasive in the arts during the years between the wars. This was, in part, due to the influence of her sponsors—generally corporate, religious, and state institutions—but her suitability to execute her sponsors' artistic visions was enabled by the privileged class that she moved in throughout her life. That Meière was ultimately devoted to the permanence of beauty may be seen in her reflection on the significance of her design for the lobby ceiling at One Wall Street: "Considering Wall Street as a narrow canyon through which rushes the concentrated energies of the financial world, a great wave sucking up humanity in a struggle for money, the question arises, 'Why this great effort? What is Money?' And the answer was felt to be 'Money is what it buys, and unless it buys Beauty in some form, it has no lasting form. . . .'" (quoted in Dunn, "Her Words," p. 16).

• Meière's daughter, Louise Meière Dunn, has preserved Meière's designs and papers at her family home in Stamford, Conn., including Meière's unpublished autobiographical essays "Dossier" (c. 1946), "Ramblings of a Mural Painter" (c. 1953), "Hildreth Meière—Her Life and Times (Not Hard)" (c. 1955), and Meière's letters to her family in San Francisco between 1916 and 1924. Mrs. Dunn's collection is gradually being donated in its entirety to the Smithsonian's Archives of American Art. Meière's correspondence with Paul and Arno Heuduck, as well as images of some of their project together, can be found in the business records of the Ravenna Mosaic Company, which are housed in the archives of Pius XII Memorial Library at Saint Louis University. Also available at Saint Louis University is a transcript of Mrs. Dunn's lecture "From Pavlova to the Cathedral Basilica of St. Louis: A Woman before Her Time in a Man's World," delivered at Pius Library on 22 Apr. 2003. The most complete account of Meière's life is Jean Sharer's unpublished 2001 dissertation, "Hildreth Meière, 1892–1961." Louise Meière Dunn's unpublished manuscript "Her Words and Mine" highlights a number of her mother's most important works. The Cathedral Basilica of St. Louis maintains an archive of many of Meière's full-scale cartoons for her commissions in the Cathedral.

ROBERT J. BLASKIEWICZ

MELLETTE, Arthur Calvin (23 June 1842–25 May 1896), first governor of South Dakota, was born in Henry County, Indiana, the son of Charles Mellette and Mary Moore Mellette, farmers. After obtaining an early education at nearby Marion Academy that was supplemented by considerable independent study, he entered the sophomore class at Indiana University and received his A.B. in 1864. On graduating, he joined the Union army (as a substitute for an invalid brother) and served as a private in Company H of the 9th Indiana Infantry until the end of the Civil War.

After gaining his discharge, Mellette returned to his alma mater and studied law. In 1866, graduating with an LL.B., he was admitted to the bar. On 29 May of that year he married Margaret Wylie; the couple had four sons. Mellette set up a law partnership and began practicing in Muncie, Indiana. His horizons soon expanded, however, to journalism, where he enjoyed success as editor of the *Muncie Times* and held public office. He served as county prosecuting attorney (1868–1870) and in 1870 also served as county superintendent of schools. In 1871 Mellette began a four-year stint representing Delaware County in the Indiana House of Representatives. While a member of the legislature, Mellette was best known for his role in creating the Indiana township school system, which served as a model for school systems in other states.

In the late 1870 Mellette's wife's health began to decline. Thinking that a drier climate might benefit her, he briefly considered Colorado before finally moving to the Dakota Territory, where, through the influence of friends, he was appointed register for the U.S. land office. Originally settling in Springfield, he soon moved to Watertown, where he remained for many years. On retiring from office in 1882, he resumed his legal practice but had achieved sufficient financial success that he was able to devote a large portion of his time to personal matters. Still interested in public affairs, Mellette served as a member of the first territorial constitutional convention in Sioux Falls in 1883. While a member of the convention he took a leading role in limiting state debt and state officer salaries and also saw to it that the state took little responsibility for internal improvements.

During the long struggle for statehood (and the controversy over whether the Dakota territory should be admitted as one state or two), Mellette was a firm supporter of the creation of two separate states. Although elected as provisional governor of the "State of Dakota" in 1885, he could not assume the post when congressional Democrats in Washington balked at admitting additional Republican states. A longtime supporter of Benjamin Harrison's presidential ambitions, Mellette managed to control the fractious Republican party in the territory and secured its support for his fellow Hoosier. In 1888 Mellette became the national Republican committeeman for the territory and the following year officially became territorial governor after Harrison gained the White House. After North and South Dakota were formally admitted to the Union in 1889, Mellette won election as the state's first governor over Democrat P. F. McClure, receiving 53,964 votes to McClure's 23,840.

In addition to the challenges of setting up a new state government, Mellette also had to deal with the effects of a severe drought in 1889, which affected farmers in the territory and forced him to walk a public relations tightrope. Although sympathetic to the plight of the farmers, Mellette was also deeply conscious of the possible effects of negative publicity on attempts to induce settlers into the region; hence, he spent a great deal of time trying to keep news of the drought out of the Eastern newspapers while working behind the scenes to aid constituents. Mellette also had to address public concerns over the rise of the so-called Ghost Dance, a quasi-religious movement among Native Americans that encouraged the belief in a return to the "good old days" through supernatural intervention. However, the issue became moot in the wake of the brutal massacre at Wounded Knee in 1890. In an era when agrarian populism was on the rise, resentment by farmers of small-town businessmen and railroad monopolies resulted in the formation of a number of political organizations, including the Dakota Alliance, whose president, Henry L. Loucks, challenged Mellette during his 1890 bid for reelection. Despite having to run against two candidates, Mellette was reelected with 44.5 percent of the vote.

On leaving office in 1893, Mellette returned to Watertown and his law practice. Plans to spend his final years in a leisurely study of physics soon came to naught, and his retirement was not a happy one. Dogged by the loss of a son as well as a decline in his own health following a buggy accident, Mellette suffered a further indignity in 1895 when his close friend, and retiring state treasurer W. W. Taylor embezzled $367,000 and emigrated to South America. Having pledged Taylor's security bond, Mellette felt honorbound to make up the lost funds and turned over his financial assets to the state. In a last ditch attempt to rebuild his life, Mellette moved his family to Pittsburg, Kansas, where he briefly reestablished his law practice before dying. In 1911 the South Dakota state legislature honored Mellette with the creation of a county bearing his name.

Mellette's place in history is secure by virtue of his status as the first governor of South Dakota. Although not as well known as other major builders of the West, he was one of the many self-educated and self-made individuals who helped forge the American form of civilization on the frontier.

• Mellette's papers are held at the South Dakota State Historical Society in Pierre, South Dakota. His life and career can be traced in a number of publications, including Howard R. Lamar, *Dakota Territory, 1861–1889: A Study of Frontier Politics* (1956), J. Leonard Jennewein and Jane Boorman, eds. *Dakota Panorama* (1961; 4th ed., 1988), and John Milton, *South Dakota, A Bicentennial History* (1977).

EDWARD L. LACH, JR.

MENUHIN, Yehudi (22 Apr. 1916–12 Mar. 1999), violinist and conductor, was born Yehudi Mnuchin in New York City, the son of Moshe Mnuchin and Marutha Sher Mnuchin, both Hebrew teachers and immigrants from Russia by way of Palestine. The family moved to San Francisco in 1918 and in 1919 changed the spelling of the name to "Menuhin" in hopes this would be easier for Americans to pronounce. Menuhin started violin lessons at age four and made his first public appearance in 1922 at the San Francisco Civic Auditorium. His first important teacher was Louis Persinger, concertmaster of the San Francisco Symphony. In 1925 Persinger moved to New York to concentrate on chamber music. With support from the San Francisco attorney and philanthropist Sidney Ehrman, Menuhin went along to continue his studies, accompanied by his mother and two sisters.

Menuhin gave his first New York concert in 1926. That year Ehrman offered to sponsor musical training in Europe for Menuhin, who then embarked on studies in Paris with the Romanian violinist and composer Georges Enesco. In 1927 Menuhin's performance of the Beethoven Violin Concerto in Carnegie Hall attracted national attention, and in 1928 he began recording and touring the United States. In 1929 he performed concertos by Bach, Beethoven, and Brahms in a single program with Bruno Walter and the Berlin Philharmonic, which was received as a triumph. The audience included Albert Einstein, who embraced Menuhin after the performance with words to the effect that "now I know there is a God in heaven." In 1931 the Menuhins took up residence in Paris, where the novelist Willa Cather became a family friend. The following year Menuhin made the premiere recording of Edward Elgar's Violin Concerto.

Menuhin undertook a world tour in 1935, performing in thirteen countries and sixty-three cities. When he returned to California in 1936, he set aside eighteen months for a deeper consideration of the music he was performing. He returned to the concert stage in 1937 and in 1938 met Nola Nicholas, the daughter of a rich Australian businessman, while performing in London. They married that year and had two children; the marriage ended in divorce nine years later.

During World War II, Menuhin gave hundreds of free concerts for American and Allied troops all over the world. In 1943 he discovered the music of Béla Bartók, performed his Violin Concerto No. 2, and recorded it with Antal Doráti; later that year Menuhin met Bartók and commissioned from him a sonata for solo violin. In 1944 he met Diana Gould, a British ballerina and actress, whom he married in 1947. They had two children. Immediately after the war, Menuhin made a tour of Nazi concentration camps, playing for the survivors with accompaniment by the composer Benjamin Britten. However, his solidarity with fellow Jews came into question soon afterward, when he spoke out in favor of Wilhelm Furtwängler, the distinguished conductor who was widely viewed as a Nazi collaborator and ostracized.

In 1950 Menuhin provoked controversy on a tour of South Africa by giving impromptu free concerts in black townships as a protest against apartheid. Later that year, he toured Israel and made friends with many prominent Israelis, but his popularity there fluctuated in later years as he became a frequent critic of Israel's role in the Middle East.

Although Menuhin never lost his status as a super-star of the violin, technique became an issue for him as he matured. Ironically, while he gained intellectual and emotional perspective on his art, he lost the ef-fortless control of his bowing arm that characterized his early performances and recordings. Some critics detect a decline in his playing as early as 1938, while others place it later. He is said to have had trouble maintaining a steady pressure on the strings, which would result at times in a wobbling or unstable tone. Menuhin did not acknowledge technical problems un-til much later, but a concern with excessive muscle tension may explain his fascination with yoga, which he practiced daily starting in 1951. The following year, while on a tour of India, he met a gifted teacher, B. K. S. Iyengar, who took charge of his yoga studies for years thereafter. On this tour Menuhin also met the sitarist Ravi Shankar, whom he later helped intro-duce to Western audiences.

From 1955 onward Menuhin made his home in Eu-rope, first in Gstaad, Switzerland, then near Florence, and finally in London. In 1957 the director of tourism in Gstaad asked Menuhin if he would arrange a cou-ple of summer concerts there; the concerts developed into an annual festival under Menuhin's artistic direc-tion. Starting in 1957, Menuhin also directed the an-nual music festival in Bath, using this opportunity to develop his skills as a conductor.

While touring Russia in 1945 and 1962, Menuhin visited the Central School for Young Musicians in Moscow, which offered gifted children an integrated program of music study and general education, thus helping to create a steady flow of world-class perform-ers. He resolved to create an institution that would pursue the same goals while avoiding the regimented and anonymous character of the Russian model. In 1963 he launched the Yehudi Menuhin International School in London, offering instruction in stringed in-struments and piano to fifteen pupils. A year later the school moved to a mansion Menuhin had purchased in nearby Stoke d'Abernon. The school grew to ac-commodate more than fifty students; its most promi-nent alumnus during Menuhin's lifetime was the vi-olinist Nigel Kennedy. In 1977 Menuhin established another school, the International Menuhin Academy in Gstaad for young professional string players.

Menuhin pursued a busy schedule of tours and re-cording throughout his life. In later years he placed increasing emphasis on conducting and phased out his activity as a violinist, giving his last public perfor-mance on the violin in 1996. He died in Berlin while on tour with the Sinfonia Varsovia, a Polish orchestra he often conducted.

The British government recognized Menuhin's multiple achievements in 1965 with an honorary knighthood, which took full effect in 1985, when he became a British citizen. In 1994 he was made Baron Menuhin of Stoke d'Abernon.

Menuhin's career as a child prodigy established him as one of the century's greatest musical celebrities worldwide, a position he maintained for an astonish-ing seventy years and more. Apart from his contri-butions to education, he is remembered for his bril-liant musicianship, preserved in abundant recordings, and a personal magnetism that survives in his ap-pearances on film. The violinist Itzhak Perlman said of him: "Menuhin was the most natural player. . . . He was always so human, he would go right to your heart whatever he played. It had a humbleness."

• An archive of Menuhin's papers exists but is closed to the public pending its placement in a permanent home. Menu-hin published an autobiography, *Unfinished Journey*, in 1977 and an expanded edition in 1996. His other writings include a book of advice to violinists, *Life Class* (1986), published in the United States as *The Compleat Violinist*. Humphrey Bur-ton, *Yehudi Menuhin* (2000), is a comprehensive biography drawing on extensive interviews with Menuhin by the au-thor. Diana Menuhin's memoir *Fiddler's Moll* (1984) helps to convey the texture of Menuhin's life. David Dubal, *Con-versations with Menuhin* (1991), is a useful compilation of interviews. Menuhin's career is documented in several films; among them, Bruno Monsaingeon's *The Art of Violin* (2000) captures Menuhin's impressions of other great violinists and observations on Menuhin's playing by his contemporaries. An obituary is in the *New York Times*, 13 Mar. 1999.

JONATHAN WIENER

MILLER, Lewis (24 July 1829–17 Feb. 1899), ed-ucator, religious leader, and industrialist, was born in Greentown, Ohio, the third son of John Miller and Mary Elizabeth York Miller, farmers. Miller's mother died soon after his birth. In 1830 his father married Elizabeth Tawney Aultman, a widow with two chil-dren, who bore six more children and brought a fer-vent Methodism to the household. An enthusiastic reader, Lewis Miller relished his little time spent in the local school. The demands of farming frustrated his desire for extensive formal education. By age sixteen Miller occasionally taught school but perceived little opportunity for advancement in the profession with-out additional schooling. He learned the plaster trade, which offered shorter hours than farming, and de-voted the extra time to personal studies.

Beginning in 1849 a series of professional and per-sonal changes afforded Miller the means to pursue his educational ambitions. With his stepbrother Corne-lius Aultman, Miller moved to Plainfield, Illinois, to work in agricultural manufacturing. Miller quickly mastered the machining trade. Although the pair re-turned to Ohio one year later, Miller's stay was sig-nificant. He briefly attended Plainfield Academy, and he met Mary Valinda Alexander, the daughter of a prominent farmer. They married in 1852, settled in Canton, Ohio, and had eleven children.

Miller thrived as manufacturing head of Ball, Ault-man & Company. His ingenuity produced numerous design improvements, foreshadowing the more than ninety U.S. patents he earned in his lifetime. Competitors, it seemed, offered little motivation to Miller, whose own motto was: "Let's see how we can beat ourselves!" (Hendrick, p. 64). His most famous design, the Buckeye mower and reaper (1855), earned top prize from the U.S. Agricultural Society. The key feature was a floating cutter blade, which negotiated uneven terrain and pioneered safety concerns in agricultural machinery. Still unqualified for many teaching jobs, Miller found that his faith provided an outlet. Serving as superintendent of Canton's Sunday school program, he recruited secular teachers and introduced acclaimed reforms mirroring secular school practices, such as dividing students into age-specific grades.

A majority owner of C. Aultman & Company by 1858, Miller relocated to Akron, Ohio, to open a second facility, Aultman, Miller & Company, in 1863. Production of the Buckeye mower had increased over 500 percent, and Miller was already wealthy. As Sunday school superintendent at Akron's First Methodist Church, he erected the first building intended specifically as a Sunday school after contributing a substantial portion of the required funding. Miller's design, aided by the architect Jacob Snyder and known as the "Akron Plan," was the structural complement to his adaptation of secular practices in church school. Two stories of classrooms were arranged in a horseshoe format around a central stage. Folding partitions provided privacy for grade-appropriate instruction but easily opened to the stage for communal exercises at the beginning and end of services. Congregations worldwide copied Miller's design and methodological reforms, and local entities capitalized on his talents. In 1869 Miller joined the Akron Board of Education, soon becoming its president. Orville Hartshorn, the president and founder of Mount Union College (Alliance, Ohio), invited Miller to join his young Methodist institution's board of directors. Miller served as board president from 1868 until his death. Hartshorn's college had already exhibited liberal tendencies, championing women's equal access to education, and Miller's ideas made that education practical. Miller's broad elective curriculum, especially in sciences, encouraged students to explore beyond the classics, and a four-term system allowed students in the farming region to work during harvest season. Miller also funded the construction of a dormitory that bears his name.

In 1874, with John Heyl Vincent, Miller cofounded the Chautauqua Institution, and he served as president until his death. Miller and Vincent designed the initial two-week summer program as a training summit for Sunday school teachers, aiming for "an enlarged recognition of the Word" (Vincent, p. v). In 1875 Miller's friend Ulysses S. Grant was the first of many notable visitors to lend support. Chautauqua flourished in an atmosphere Miller described as "not undenominational, but all-denominational" (Vincent, p. v). Recalling his early vision of Chautauqua, Miller reflected, "What more appropriate than . . . some beautiful plateau of nature's own building for its rostrum, with the sky for its frescoed ceiling, the continents for its floor, the camp-meeting spirit of prayer and praise for its rostrum exercises, the church-school for thought and development?" (Vincent, p. v). Vincent credited Miller with expanding the curriculum, bringing "science and literature . . . to the support of Christianity" (Vincent, p. 20). Under Miller's guidance, Chautauqua became a hub of popular education, adding more pragmatic nuances, such as correspondence courses in literature, allowing broad access to common people. Still a businessman, Miller in 1880 built the Athenaeum Hotel, his own profit-seeking venture in Chautauquan accommodations.

National financial panic and failing health plagued Miller throughout the 1890s. He spent these years continuing his involvement in his various business and educational offices. In early 1899 acute abdominal problems necessitated surgery in New York City. En route his train was stranded overnight without heat. Miller survived in a weakened state and underwent the operation, but he failed to recover. He died in New York City.

Historians have largely overlooked Miller. Some have wondered about his seeming anonymity in the Chautauqua project, citing that he was "so constantly taken up with secular details . . . that he was able to take part in but few of its exercises" (Hurlbut, p. 141). This is explained by his humility and pragmatic idealism. Education and Christian faith were his ideals. Ingenuity and business were his skills, the means to the ideal ends. Knowing he was not a gifted orator, he left the public affairs and addresses of Chautauqua to his more eloquent partner and worked behind the scenes. Those close to him understood this. Thomas Edison, Miller's son-in-law, argued that although "inventing and manufacturing were his vocation, education was his avocation, and he surely accomplished as much, if not more, in the . . . latter as he did at the former." Miller was "eternally making money in his factory in order to . . . better carry on his schemes for education" (Hendrick, pp. iv, v). Not a mere "money man" and far more important than the phrase "silent partner" would suggest, Miller was thus the rare self-contained philanthropist, involved at every stage of his good works: conceptualization, finance, and labor.

• A collection of the Miller family papers is maintained at the Smith Library of the Chautauqua Institution, Chautauqua, N.Y. A biography of Miller is Ellwood Hendrick, *Lewis Miller: A Biographical Essay* (1925), which includes an introduction by Thomas Edison. Invaluable accounts of the Chautauqua Institution are John Heyl Vincent's *The Chautauqua Movement* (1886), with an introduction by Miller; and Jesse Lyman Hurlbut, *The Story of Chautauqua* (1921). See also Theodore Morrison, *Chautauqua: A Center for Education, Religion, and the Arts in America* (1974). An obituary is in the *New York Times*, 18 Feb. 1899.

DAVID J. MCCOWIN

MOORE, Alfred (21 May 1755–15 Oct. 1810), Revolutionary officer, attorney general of North

Carolina, and associate justice of the U.S. Supreme Court, was born in New Hanover County, North Carolina, the son of Maurice Moore, a judge, and Anne Grange Moore. In 1764 Judge Maurice Moore, who was among the principal leaders of the Cape Fear River country, sent his son to Boston for his education. Prior to the outbreak of the Revolution, Alfred returned home and read law with his father. He won his license to practice law in April 1775 and on 1 September married Susanna Elizabeth Eagles of Brunswick County; they had two children.

Full grown, Moore stood four feet five inches tall and, at about ninety pounds, seemed almost boyish in appearance, with a head rather large for his small body. Nevertheless, he developed into a splendid horseman and was noted for his grace and physical coordination. He charmed those he met by his fine features, clear and sonorous voice, and witty and animated speaking.

In September 1775, Moore was elected captain of Company B of the First North Carolina Regiment, which was led by his uncle James Moore. Soon recognized for his exceptional ability at handling horses and arms, Alfred took part in the rousing Patriot victory over Tory forces at Moore's Creek Bridge in February 1776. He was then sent south with his unit to the defense of Charleston, South Carolina, where he acquitted himself bravely.

Moore's military service was interrupted by a series of family calamities. His older brother was killed at the head of his troops in early 1776, and in January 1777 his father died. In September of that year his sister Sarah lost her husband, General Francis Nash, at the Battle of Germantown, New Jersey. This left Alfred, at twenty-two, the oldest surviving male in the family and responsible not only for his wife and their two children but for his mother and for his sister's fatherless children. He resigned from the army in March 1777 and returned to Buchoi, his Brunswick County rice plantation.

Moore concentrated on running the plantation and his family's business ventures and was able to put these affairs in good order. In 1781, however, with the British invading North Carolina and capturing nearby Wilmington as a supply base for Charles Cornwallis, he recruited and trained a company of militia and fought Cornwallis in March at the Battle of Guilford Court House, a Pyrrhic victory for the British. Afterward, with the British still occupying Wilmington, the state's largest town, Moore transformed his company into raiders and for a time lay low around Wilmington, seizing opportunities for quick strikes.

General James Craig, British commander in the area, found himself harassed and exasperated by Moore's tactics and resolved to deal him a setback. He sent cavalry to sack and burn Moore's plantation and crops, carry away his slaves and stock, and leave his family in straitened circumstances. When this effort failed to achieve its goal, Craig offered to restore Moore's property and arrange an amnesty if he would lay down his arms. Rejecting the offer, Moore fought

his way into Virginia behind Cornwallis and was present at the British surrender at Yorktown in October 1781. Four years later, Moore County, North Carolina, was created in recognition of his wartime services.

In his law practice, Moore was admired for his legal acumen, his professional success, and his winning courtroom persona. With William R. Davie of Halifax, he came to be recognized as one of the two finest lawyers in the state. "The clearness and energy of his mind enabled him," says a political foe, "to disentangle the most intricate subject and expose it in all its parts to the simplest understanding." A federalist, Moore entered politics in 1782 and won election as Brunswick County's state senator in 1792. From 1782 to 1791, he served in exemplary fashion as state attorney general. He lost his final campaign, in the General Assembly for the U. S. Senate in 1795, by one vote. He was a strong advocate of a state university, chartered in 1789 in Chapel Hill as the first such institution in the country, and served for eighteen years on the school's board of trustees.

An acknowledgment of his ability at the zenith of his career was the appointments he received from the state and national governments. His first, as delegate to the Annapolis Convention in 1786, was negated when the North Carolina delegation, informed that only trade would be discussed, refused to serve. In 1798 he was appointed by President John Adams to a commission to arrange a treaty with the Cherokee Indians. He was also named judge of the superior court during 1798 and 1799 and enjoyed a high reputation there for his masterful judgment and refusal to be bound by precedent.

In 1799, after Supreme Court Justice James Iredell's death, Adams appointed Moore to the vacancy. During his brief tenure on the court, he delivered an opinion in only one case, endorsing the federalist view that "a limited partial war" existed with France (*Bas v. Tingey*, 4 Dallas, 37). By and large, he supported Chief Justice John Marshall's decisions, such as the right of the courts to determine the constitutionality of statutes. He was the second and, so far, last person from his state to sit on the high court. It is alleged that "the conviviality that characterized . . . politicians of that era, induced [in him] an indolent habit," leading to his resignation in 1804. Some sources attribute his departure to ill health. Moore's final six years were devoted to maintaining and enlarging his estate, which was considerable by the time of his death.

• The best primary source for Moore's life and career is Walter Clark, ed., *The State Records of North Carolina* (1895–1914), vols. 13–21. The principal secondary sources are Griffith J. McRee, ed., *Life and Correspondence of James Iredell, One of the Associate Justices of the Supreme Court of the United States* (1858); William S. Powell, *Dictionary of North Carolina Biography* (1991); *Raleigh News and Observer*, 3 June 1951; Dumas Malone, ed., *Dictionary of American Biography* (1934); W. H. Hoyt, ed., *The Papers of Archibald D. Murphey*, 2 vols. (1914); J. L. Taylor, *A Sketch of the Life and Public Services of the Late Hon. Alfred Moore* (1844); and

American State Papers, Indian Affairs, vol. 1 (1832). The only known obituary for Moore is in the *Raleigh Times*, 1 Nov. 1810.

THOMAS C. PARRAMORE

MOORE, Audley "Queen Mother" (27 July 1898–2 May 1997), radical black cultural nationalist, was born Audley Moore, the daughter of St. Cyr Moore and Ella Hunter Moore, in New Iberia, Louisiana, a small town near New Orleans. As a young child, she heard stories about her maternal grandfather being lynched, her paternal grandmother being raped by a slave master, and her father being forcibly removed from his position as deputy sheriff by whites. Yet her family instilled in her a strong sense of racial pride and resistance.

By 1914, with only a fourth-grade education, Moore was obliged to take care of her younger sisters, Eloise and Lorita. They moved to New Orleans, where she worked as a domestic and hairdresser, and learned firsthand the drudgery of the black urban, working-class life. Moore and her sisters moved to Anniston, Alabama, a highly segregated town, during World War I. Eloise Moore established a recreation center for black soldiers from the nearby Fort McClellan, since they were barred from military recreation halls and white-owned establishments in town.

They returned to New Orleans, where in 1919 Moore heard Jamaican black nationalist Marcus Garvey speak for the first time. She was instantly attracted to his message of racial pride, self-determination, Pan African unity, and the glories of ancient Africa. As she recalled years later, ". . . it was Garvey who brought the consciousness to me" (quoted in Gilkes, p.123). She enthusiastically joined Garvey's Universal Negro Improvement Association. At the same time, she married Frank Warner, a working-class Haitian immigrant and Garveyite who had come to New Orleans in search of better opportunities. By 1923, the couple moved to New York City to work for the Garvey movement.

By the end of the decade, she organized Harlem tenants and campaigned for the Republican party. In 1930, she had a son. In late 1933, she took part in an exciting, massive Communist-led protest in Harlem demanding the freedom of the Scottsboro boys, nine black adolescents falsely accused of and sentenced to death for raping two white women in Alabama. Impressed with the Communist party's commitment to fighting for racial justice, she joined the Communist-affiliated International Labor Defense and became a party member. Later in life, she credited the party, noting, "I really learned to struggle in the Communist party" (Prago, p.9).

A powerful speaker and tireless organizer, she became a leading Communist in Harlem during the 1930s and 1940s, organizing efforts around Scottsboro, the Italian invasion of Ethiopia, housing, unemployment, and unions. In 1943 she served as the campaign manager for Benjamin J. Davis, Jr., a black Communist who was elected to the New York City council. She also joined the National Association of Colored Women and Mary McLeod Bethune's National Council of Negro Women. In the late 1940s, she worked on the legal defense committee for Claudia Jones, a high-ranking black woman Communist indicted by the government for subversion. Moore left the party in 1950, claiming it was no longer committed to fighting for racial equality.

After her resignation from the party, she gradually emerged as a radical black cultural nationalist, embracing all things African (real and imagined). She espoused the premise that black people themselves had to lead their own movements and that African Americans needed to, as she often put it, "denegroize" their minds of internalized racism (Gilkes, p. 116). She also began wearing African clothes, which became her trademark

With her sister Eloise, Moore founded the Universal Association of Ethiopian Women, an organization dedicated to welfare rights, antilynching, and prisoners' rights. Moore claimed that she and Eloise in the late 1950s schooled Malcolm X on the importance of Africa to the black American struggle. In 1962, she founded the Reparations Committee of Descendants of U.S. Slaves, Inc., after discovering an obscure clause in a Methodist encyclopedia that stated "international law considers an enslaved people satisfied with their condition if the people do not demand recompense after 100 years have passed" (Gilkes, p. 115). Decades before the movement gained momentum, Moore vocally called for reparations from the federal government as compensation for slavery and discriminatory Jim Crow laws in the South. Moving to Philadelphia in the early 1960s, she served as an elder mentor to the Revolutionary Action Movement, a black radical organization. She also became a follower of Robert Williams, a black militant who advocated armed self-defense. Later in the decade, she and Lorita started the Ethiopian Coptic Church of North and South America. In 1968, she was a co-founder of the Republic of New Afrika, an organization that called for the establishment of an independent black state in the American South.

In 1972, she took an extensive trip to Africa to attend the funeral of Kwame Nkrumah, the exiled Pan Africanist founder of Ghana, in Guinea. She was invited to Ghana, where according to her own report the title "Queen Mother" was bestowed on her by Otumfuo Opoku Ware II, spiritual and cultural leader of the Asante people. She also traveled to Dar es Salaam, Tanzania, where she addressed the All-African Women's Conference. She traveled to Africa several more times in later years. Inspired by her travels, she founded the Queen Mother Moore Research Institute and the Eloise Moore College of African Studies and Vocational and Industrial School on a mountain in upstate New York they named Mount Addis Ababa. The two institutions, however, burned down in 1978. Though critical of the white feminist movement for racism, she nevertheless remained an advocate of black women's organizations.

During the 1980s Moore was a recipient of several awards, and she was one of fifty prominent African American women featured in Brian Lanker's critically acclaimed *I Dream a World: Portraits of Black Women Who Changed America* (1989). In 1994, she addressed a Detroit conference of the National Coalition of Blacks for Reparations, where she declared "Reparations. Reparations. Keep on. Keep on. We've got to win" (*New York Times*, 7 May 1997). She was of one of four revered elder black women activists invited to address the 1995 Million Man March in Washington, D.C. Beloved by many for her passionate commitment to reparations and fighting against racism, her death marked the end of a long, extraordinary career of political activism merging black nationalism, Pan Africanism, and Communism.

• Audley Moore's 1963 pamphlet *Why Reparations? Reparations is the Battle Cry for the Economic and Social Freedom of More Than 25 Million Descendants of African Slaves* makes a powerful case for federal compensation for slavery and racial discrimination (Schomburg Center for Research in Black Culture, New York City). The bulk of her personal papers are not contained in any repository. News about Moore in the 1940s often appeared in the *Amsterdam News* and the Communist party's *Daily Worker*. And articles during the 1970s can be found in *Muhammad Speaks* and the *Amsterdam News*. A lengthy oral history interview by Cheryl Gilkes can be found in *The Black Women Oral History Project*, vol. 8 (1991), edited by Ruth Edmonds Hill. See also interviews by Mark Naison and Ruth Prago for *Oral History of the American Left* (OHAL) in Tamiment Library, New York University. Although often containing incorrect information, her FBI files are also useful. Muhammad Ahmad, "Queen Mother Moore," in Mari Jo Buhle, Paul Buhle, and Dan Georgakas, eds., *Encyclopedia of the American Left*, 2d. ed. (1998), pp. 512–13, and Barbara Bair, "Audley 'Queen Mother' Moore," in Darlene Clark Hine, ed., *Black Women in America: A Historical Encyclopedia*, vol. 2 (1994), pp. 812–13 are valuable overviews of her life and activism. Two dissertations contain extensive discussion of Moore: see Kai Jackson-Issa, "Her Own Book: Autobiographical Practice in the Oral Narratives of Queen Mother Audley Moore" (1999), and Erik S. McDuffie, "Long Journeys: Four Black Women and the Communist Party, USA, 1930–1956" (forthcoming). Moore is also briefly discussed in Robin Kelley, *Freedom Dreams: The Black Radical Imagination* (2002); Mark Solomon, *The Cry Was Unity: Communists and African Americans, 1917–1936* (1998); and Irma Watkins-Owens, *Blood Relations: Caribbean Immigrants and the Harlem Community, 1900–1930* (1996). A stunning photograph and good synopsis of her life appears in Brian Lanker, *I Dream a World: Portraits of Black Women Who Changed America* (1989). Earlier scholarship also contains useful information about Moore's activism: see Mark Naison, *Communists in Harlem during the Depression* (1983), and "The Black Scholar Interviews: Queen Mother Moore," *The Black Scholar* (Mar.–Apr. 1973). An obituary is in the *New York Times*, 7 May 1997.

ERIK S. McDUFFIE

MOORE, Charles (22 May 1928–23 Jan. 1986), choreographer and dance teacher, was born in Cleveland, Ohio, to parents whose names and occupations are unknown. As a child he was a popular soprano soloist in churches and studied voice at the Karamu House, a local arts center near his home devoted to celebrating the African-American experience through the arts in a racially integrated environment. As he grew older he studied modern dance with Eleanor Frampton at the cultural center. He had the opportunity to see Asadata Dafora, the famed West African choreographer and dancer, perform the Ostrich Dance at Severance Hall. This event so moved Moore toward his future work in recreating African dance that he "never forgot that first glimpse of Africa" (Hegedus and Pennebaker).

In 1948 Moore received a Charles Weidman dance scholarship and moved to New York City. There he learned ballet and modern and African dance from Weidman, Pearl Primus, Dafora, and Katherine Dunham. He also studied with the Nigerian dancers M. Olatunji and S. Ilori and the Ghanaian dancers Kobla Ladzekpo and A. Opoku. From 1952 to 1960 Moore was a member of Dunham's dance company. At the Dunham School of Dance and Theater he also met his future wife, the dancer and performer Ella Thompson. They married in 1960 and had one son. In 1959 Moore began teaching Dunham's technique in New York City at the Clark Center, at the New Dance Group Studio, and for Harlem Youth Activities (Har-You-Act). He later taught her technique at his own school. He also taught dance at Hunter College, Medgar Evers College, City College, and the Hanson Place Methodist Church in Brooklyn.

Working with this group of celebrated instructors, performers, and choreographers of African and African-inspired dance fostered his passion to create, preserve, and perform the traditional dances of Africa. "There is a pride in these dances and every one of them has something in it that makes you feel gorgeous. And they're so important historically. Before Dafora, about all we knew of Africa was what we saw in the Tarzan movies," Moore explained (Jennifer Dunning, "Protecting a Harvest, Choosing a Wife," *New York Times*, 29 Feb. 1996). He became a well-respected performer and was featured in many dance companies, including those of Dunham, Geoffrey Holder, Donald McKayle, Pearl Primus, Talley Beatty, Jean Leon Destiné, and Alvin Ailey. He was known for fully embodying the roles given to him. He said of performing with Dunham, "When I danced her dance, *Shango*, I wasn't Charles Moore anymore, I was possessed. You had to be in order to do the dance" (Hegedus and Pennebaker). In addition he performed on Broadway in several productions, including the revivals of *House of Flowers* (1954–1955) and *Carmen Jones* (1956), *Jamaica* (1957–1959), *Kwamina* (1961), *The Zulu and the Zayda* (1965–1966), *Trumpets of the Lord* (1969), and *Les Blancs* (1970), and he was in the New York City Opera production of *Bomarzo* (1968–1969). He also appeared on television with Harry Belafonte, Sammy Davis, Jr., Anne Bancroft, and Lauren Bacall.

In 1974 Moore and his wife founded the Charles Moore Center for Ethnic Studies in New York City under the parent company Dances and Drums of Africa, one of the oldest nonprofit African-American arts organizations in Brooklyn. At that time he also established the Charles Moore Dance Theatre and the Charles Moore Youth Ensemble "to demonstrate the beauty and variety of African, Caribbean, and African American culture" (Charles Moore Dance Theatre advertisement postcard, New York Library for the Performing Arts). The center educated children and adults in full programs of modern and African dance and percussion. Through diligent study and research, Moore used his company to carefully and respectfully reconstruct many African dances that were considered lost. He creatively blended the techniques of his teachers with his own interpretations. His company specialized in authentic recreations of African and Caribbean dances, revivals of works by great African choreographers, and original pieces created out of the spirit of African and Caribbean traditional dances "with respect for heritage and a boldness and jubilation that make tradition come alive" (advertisement poster, New York Library for the Performing Arts). His company included master drummers, such as Chief Bey, as well as dancers. He often brought renowned African musicians and dancers to the United States to teach and perform. From 1974 to 1985 his company performed nationally and internationally.

One of Moore's most celebrated pieces was his interpretation and performance of Dafora's *Ostrich Dance* or *Awassa Astrige* (1932). Wearing a skirt of ostrich feathers, Moore strutted about the stage, torso undulating, the wide expanse of his arms rippling as his head jutted forward rhythmically. Each bit of arm was distinctly articulated. He held his head proudly, his eyes were alert, and his movement was constant, repetitive, and focused. Moore became an ostrich. "It's a tribute to Moore that his choreography has kept so close to some of the first African dances to be seen in this country" (Robertson, p. 32).

Though Moore never went to Africa, his reconstructions of traditional African dances, such as *Bundao*, *Spear Dance*, *Sacred Forest*, and *African Congo*, were well respected and inspired a wealth of related dances in the repertoires of other African dance companies in the United States. At the time of his death in New York, Moore was working on *Traces: An American Suite*, an overview of American black dance encompassing slavery to the early 1940s. The well-known dance critic Jennifer Dunning wrote that *Traces* "ought to be required viewing for anyone who believes that multiculturalism and traditional black American arts are inseparable concepts" (Dunning, p. 17). It was completed under the care of his wife with additional choreography by Eleanor Harris and Pepsi Bethel.

After Moore's death, Louis Johnson created *Spirit, A Dance for Charles* to celebrate Moore's devotion to the power of African music and dance. Johnson's tribute is a testament to Moore's influential role in popularizing African dance with the American public.

• Many programs, reviews, advertisements, posters, and interviews are in the Charles Moore and Charles Moore Dance Theatre Collections in the Dance Collection at the New York Library for the Performing Arts. Chris Hegedus and D. A. Pennebaker with David Dawkins, *Dance Black America* (1984), a video, includes Moore's performance of *The Ostrich Dance*, his company's performance of Dunham's *Shango*, and an interview with Moore. The video *Free to Dance* (2000), a documentary about the African-American presence in modern dance, contains segments about Moore, many of the choreographers he studied with, and his drummer Chief Bey. Reviews include Jennifer Dunning, "Moore Troupe Makes a Point on Popular Black Culture," *New York Times*, 6 Mar. 1993; and Michael Robertson, "From Soho to Africa," *Dance Magazine*, Oct. 1976, p. 32. See also Lynne Fauley Emery, *Black Dance from 1619 to Today* (1988); and Derry Swan, "Charles Moore," in Jack Salzman et al., eds., *Encyclopedia of African-American Culture and History* (1996). An obituary is in the *New York Times*, 25 Jan. 1986.

JADA SHAPIRO

MOORE, Clayton (14 Sept. 1914–28 Dec. 1999), actor, was born Jack Carlton Moore in Chicago, Illinois, the son of Sprague C. Moore, a prosperous real estate broker, and Theresa Violet Fisher Moore, the daughter of a wealthy investor. The family lived in Chicago in a spacious Victorian home and had a summer residence at Loon Lake in Canada. Jack's father was an avid sportsman and taught his sons how to fish and use firearms. Jack excelled in athletics; when he was fifteen he won the Illinois Athletic Club Championship for swimming in the 100-yard dash. He did not complete his high school education; instead, he joined the Flying Behrs, a professional trapeze act.

Moore worked as a model in Chicago and New York City. In 1937 he moved to Los Angeles to pursue a career in motion pictures. He studied acting, changed his name to Clayton Moore for professional reasons, and found minor acting roles in Hollywood. Gossip columnists paid attention to Moore when he began dating actress Lupe Velez. In 1940, he married Mary Francis, a dancer, but the marriage lasted less than a year.

With *The Perils of Nyoka* (1942), made by Republic Pictures, Moore gained a secure foothold in motion picture chapter serials intended for young audiences. Working regularly in these action films, he came under the influence of stuntman Tom Steele, who taught him how to stage a fist fight, take a fall, twirl a gun, and leap over the back end of a horse.

Drafted into the army air force in 1942, Moore was stationed in Kingman, Arizona, where he entertained the servicemen. In 1943 he married Sally Allen; they had no children, but adopted a daughter in 1958.

Following the war, Moore did more chapter serials for Republic Pictures. His performance as the grandson of Zorro in *The Ghost of Zorro* (1949) came to the attention of George W. Trendle. With writer Fran Striker, in 1933 Trendle had created "The Lone Ranger" radio show, a popular children's program known for its action-filled stories and its impeccable moral teachings. For radio, Brace Beemer played the role of the Masked Rider of the Plains, while the Shakespearian actor John Todd played his faithful Indian companion Tonto. But Trendle, who needed younger actors for a television version of the Lone Ranger, hired Moore to play the Lone Ranger and Jay Silverheels to play Tonto. Moore had to practice Beemer's "special way of saying things." Aired on ABC-TV beginning 15 September 1949, the series quickly became an unqualified commercial success, and Moore, an overnight American hero.

The first three Saturday morning episodes of "The Lone Ranger" set the standard for the series. Led by "Captain Dan Reid," five Texas Rangers, including Dan's brother "John" (Clayton Moore), pursued the notorious Butch Cavendish Gang. Double-crossed by their scout, they were gunned down by outlaws. Badly wounded, "John," the sole survivor, is rescued by Tonto, recovers from his injury, dons a mask, and swears to maintain law and order in the Old West. He will never shoot to kill. His silver bullets are symbols of justice.

In 1951 Trendle fired Moore after the show's second season for reasons known only to Trendle himself. John Hart, his replacement, never attained Moore's popularity. In 1953 Trendle sold all rights to the show and the Lone Ranger character to Jack Wrather. Moore and Silverheels starred in two feature films made by Wrather, *The Lone Ranger* (1956) and *The Lone Ranger and the Lost City of Gold* (1958). Saving children who had been taken captive or become lost was one of the major themes in Lone Ranger stories.

Following the cancelation of the television show in 1957, Moore earned his living primarily by making public appearances dressed as the Lone Ranger.

In 1979, the Wrather Corporation won a lawsuit preventing Moore from wearing the mask of the Lone Ranger or from representing himself as the Lone Ranger in public appearances. "It was like a slap in the face," Moore recalled. The Wrather Corporation was planning to release a new movie of the Lone Ranger with a young actor in the title role and did not wish to confuse the public with two men wearing the same outfit. In 1981, *The Legend of the Lone Ranger*, starring Klinton Spilsbury, was released. It flopped at the box office and the Wrather Corporation in 1984 gave Moore permission to put on his Lone Ranger costume in public appearances. In his autobiography, Moore noted that he would "continue to wear the mask proudly and to try my best to live up to the standards of honesty, decency, respect, and patriotism that have defined the Lone Ranger since 1933."

Following the death of his wife in 1986, Moore married her nurse; this marriage, his third, produced no children and ended in divorce. In 1992 he married Clarita Petrone.

Moore's Lone Ranger was popular in the Cold War era when American patriotism needed fictional heroes who stood for traditional American values and who were resolute in the defense of such values against totally evil foes. He died in West Hills, California.

• See Clayton Moore with Frank Thompson, *I Was That Masked Man* (1996). For the motion picture serials, see Ken Weiss and Ed Goodgold, *To Be Continued* (1972). Also helpful are Phil Hardy, *The Western* (1983), and Harry Castleman and Walter J. Podrazik, *Watching TV: Four Decades of American Television* (1982). An obituary is in the *New York Times*, 29 Dec. 1999.

SALVATORE MONDELLO

MORON, Alonzo Graseano (12 Apr. 1909–31 Oct. 1971), educator and public servant, was born Alonzo Brown in Charlotte Amalie, St. Thomas, Danish Virgin Islands, the son of Caroline Louisa Brown, a seamstress, and Joseph Metzante Moron, about whom little is known. No father was listed on Alonzo Moron's birth certificate, and Joseph Moron played no significant role in his son's life. Alonzo Moron's mother, who worked out of her house, reared her two children as a single parent in a working-class neighborhood. Moron spent his first eight years as a Danish colonial subject in poverty and changed his surname from Brown to Moron in his early teens.

In 1917 the United States bought the islands and administered them through the U.S. Navy. Educational opportunities on St. Thomas remained limited, however, and Moron, an exceptional student, left St. Thomas at the age of fourteen to obtain his high school education. In 1923 he arrived at Hampton Institute, Hampton, Virginia, virtually penniless and enrolled in Hampton's academy (high school), where he learned the trade of upholstery. He accumulated an outstanding academic and personal record and graduated in 1927 fourth in a class of 131 students. Moron experienced racial segregation in the mainland United States from the very day he landed in Norfolk, Virginia, aboard a navy ship and was refused service at a restaurant. This incident, Moron recalled, made him determined to fight for democracy. While at Hampton he witnessed the consolidation of the ideology of racial segregation with the passage of the Massenburg Law in 1926. This law segregated all public functions in Virginia, including those at private institutions such as Hampton.

After Hampton, Moron entered Brown University and graduated in 1932 with a degree in sociology. That year he married Leola Rowena Churchill from Franham, Virginia. They had no children. Moron entered the University of Pittsburgh on a scholarship provided by the National Urban League and received a master's degree in social work in 1933. Upon graduating, he worked briefly with the Baltimore Emergency Relief Commission as a caseworker, the first black permitted to do so. He returned to the U.S. Virgin Islands to work on the staff of its first civilian governor, Governor Paul Martin Pearson. During the Franklin D. Roosevelt administration, Moron was appointed commissioner of public welfare, a federal appointment. In this capacity he determined who was eligible to receive relief and how it was to be distributed.

In 1935 Moron returned to the mainland at the urging of John Hope, the president of Atlanta University, who groomed Moron for a position of responsibility in the new, first-of-its-kind, federal housing development in Atlanta. In 1936 Moron became the assistant manager of University Homes, where he remained for eight years. He also taught as an adjunct at Atlanta University's School of Social Work, which brought him into contact with the leading sociologists, social workers, and activists of the time. In 1944 he applied to Harvard Law School, believing race relations in the South could be improved by using the law to effect change. After studying law at Harvard on a Rosenwald fellowship for two years, he accepted the position of business manager of Hampton Institute. He received an LL.B. degree from Harvard Law School in 1947.

In 1949 Moron was chosen by the Hampton Institute Board of Trustees to be Hampton's first black and first alumnus president. He served as Hampton's president until 1959, during which time the college developed a liberal arts curriculum and disbanded some of its historic programs, such as its agriculture program.

Moron's commitment to certain ideals shaped his presidency and his national leadership in the movement for racial equality. He was committed to integration in every venue, and he maintained that integration had to be conjoined with equality. He took actions to ensure that Hampton Institute remained an interracial oasis in the South, and he declined to support any project that perpetuated segregation. Moron recognized that the 1954 *Brown v. Board of Education* decision was of immense significance to black higher education and black youth, and he positioned Hampton Institute accordingly. While he called for the integration of all educational institutions, Moron felt that private black colleges would continue to educate black youth and leaders and would be of immense significance to black progress.

In 1955 Moron attempted to desegregate the local Dixie Hospital in Hampton, Virginia. The hospital merely offered a diploma for black nurses, while Hampton Institute offered a bachelor of science degree in nursing education. Discussions took place for the two institutions to share in the education and accommodation of nurses training at Dixie Hospital. President Moron offered to help the hospital train its black nurses if it would drop its segregationist policies. The hospital's administration refused, and at Moron's recommendation, the Board of Trustees of Hampton Institute voted to discontinue negotiations with the hospital.

In 1956 some state legislators tried to evade court-ordered desegregation by amending Virginia's constitution to allow parents to receive tuition vouchers to send their children to private schools. Moron spoke forcefully against the Gray Amendment, as it was known, saying that it represented a threat to the ex-

istence of public education. In so doing he became a spokesperson for blacks in Virginia at a time when they were disenfranchised. Nationally Moron's activities at the 1957 anniversary celebration of the Highlander Folk School, where Martin Luther King, Jr., and other leaders and activists gathered to discuss the South's major problems, led to his being red-baited by the Georgia Commission on Education. This public body had been created by the Georgia legislature to preserve segregation in the public schools. The Commission published a report attacking the conference attendees, charging the leaders of the Highlander Folk School with training communists who would foment racial strife across the country. A quarter of a million copies were distributed nationally and the major daily newspaper of Newport News and Hampton joined in the attack. Moron fought these allegations by describing the tactics of the Georgia Commission as resembling those used by communist parties. He sent an open letter to Georgia's Governor Marvin Griffin offering to meet the Commission. Moron regarded the activities of the Georgia Commission as linked to those of the massive resisters, and continued to give national addresses on the need for a more complete democracy.

Although Hampton's faculty and students supported Moron for his civil rights activities, he encountered difficulties from some trustees, alumni, and faculty for the college's changed orientation, including the elimination of the agriculture program. Events came to a head in 1959, when he was forced to resign. Moron spent the rest of his life in the West Indies as a public servant, working in housing and urban development. Between 1960 and 1961 he was acting commissioner of education and was appointed the regional director of the Housing and Home Finance Agency for the U.S. Virgin Islands. He maintained his commitment to adequate housing for the poor. He was working in San Juan, Puerto Rico, as a deputy regional director for the Department of Housing and Urban Affairs when he died.

Moron held a number of national appointments. He was on the Caribbean Commission during the Harry S. Truman administration and the National Manpower Council during the Dwight D. Eisenhower administration. He was appointed to the boards of governors of the American Red Cross, the Southern Regional Council, and the United Negro College Fund. He received an honorary degree from Wilberforce University in 1950 and another from Brown University in 1955. He was inducted into the Alpha Phi Alpha Fraternity in 1922 and into Phi Beta Kappa in 1950.

Although he is remembered primarily as the first black president of Hampton Institute, the larger significance of Moron's work was that he was an activist president who used his position as the leader of a premier private black college to support the civil rights movement. His adversarial style of leadership was unique for Hampton Institute, which has been identified primarily as the school that educated Booker T.

Washington and promoted a conciliatory approach to segregation.

• Most of the primary information about Moron's life is in the Hampton University Archives, Hampton, Va. Some of Moron's correspondence is in the Library of Congress in the papers of Margaret Mead, who was a trustee of Hampton Institute during the Moron administration and a personal friend. Moron published a number of book reviews, including reviews of *Negro Youth at the Crossways* by E. Franklin Frazier in *Phylon II* (1941, pp. 193–194) and *Riots and Ruins*, by Adam Clayton Powell, Sr., and Richard R. Smith, *Phylon VI* (1945, pp. 383–386.) His articles include "Public Housing from a Community Point of View," *Social Forces* 19 (Oct. 1940): 72–78; "Where Shall They Live? The Accommodation of Minority Groups in Urban Areas," *American City*, Apr. 1942, pp. 68–70; "Community Responsibilities of the Practicing Physician," *Journal of the National Medical Association* 42 (Nov. 1950): 371–77; and "Maintaining the Solvency of the Private College through Efficient Management," *Journal of Negro Education* 27 (Spring 1958): 141–44. An obituary is in the *New York Times*, 1 Nov. 1971.

HODA M. ZAKI

MOSES, Isaac (1742?–16 Apr. 1818), Jewish merchant and revolutionary, was born in Giessen, Germany, the only child of Rischa Levy Moses and David Moses, whose occupations are not known. Isaac as a child was reared and educated in this small German town. In 1764 he went to New York City in search of business opportunities. He was probably brought there by his uncle Hayman Levy, a prosperous New York merchant. Four years later Moses became a naturalized citizen of the colony of New York. Between 1764 and 1775, he developed numerous business skills, working in Levy's lucrative Bayard Street mercantile firm that especially became known for its predominant role in the fur trade. During these years, the ambitious Moses sold deerskins, bearskins, Indian blankets, spermaceti oil, and logwood to European merchants. He also was a distributor of English woolens, Irish linens, French wines, and West Indian rum in domestic markets. On 8 August 1770 Moses married Reyna Levy, the daughter of Sloe and Hayman Levy. The couple had ten children.

Moses actively supported the American patriots, thinking that war against England would increase profits in his business and that leaders in an independent America would extend political and religious liberties to Jews. In 1775, along with New Yorkers Samuel Myers and Moses Myers, who were not related, he established the mercantile firm of Isaac Moses & Company. Moses became the senior partner in this business, headed in 1775 its New York branch office, and immediately tried to further the American military cause. With the consent of his partners, Moses that same year provided the Continental Congress with $20,000 in hard currency, in exchange for an equivalent amount in Continental paper dollars, to finance American armies involved with the Canadian Expedition. As a result of the British occupation of New York City, Moses and his family in 1776 left that city and moved to Philadelphia. During the remaining years of the revolution, Moses directed in Philadelphia the affairs of the American branch of this international commercial house.

Moses through this firm attempted in various ways to assist the American revolutionaries. The trading operations of the firm enabled it to prosper between approximately 1776 and 1780 and involved Philadelphia, Amsterdam, and St. Eustatius: Moses sent flour, grain, furs, indigo, lumber products, and hardware to his two partners in Amsterdam and to his agents on St. Eustatius, a Dutch island in the Caribbean. Moreover, he received guns, ammunition, military clothing, and blankets from the Myerses and from his Caribbean associates. Moses sold these greatly needed products, thus helping the American patriots. He also derived sizable profits from these business activities. By 1780, Moses's property was estimated to be worth 115,200 pounds, and he was the fifth wealthiest resident of revolutionary Philadelphia.

Moses was also involved with privateering. His feelings of patriotism, his quest for large and quick profits, and his intimate connections to the circle of Robert Morris might explain why Moses was willing to engage in such risky ventures. In 1779 he and his partners acquired the *Chance*, a small ship with six guns that unsuccessfully attacked British ships in Caribbean waters. In July of 1780, he and Morris purchased two ships. A year later Morris was named Agent of the Marine and consequently served as head of the American Navy for the next three years. Moses and Morris owned the *Havannah*, a schooner with six guns that was headed by Captain Peter Young, and the *Black Prince*, a brigantine with twelve guns that was under the direction of John Robertson. Both of these vessels captured several British ships in the vicinity of the Delaware Bay and provided some profits to their owners and their crews. In late August 1781 Moses bought for his firm the *Fox*, a ship with ten guns. This vessel primarily transported the firm's merchandise to Philadelphia. It also provided some assistance to the Pennsylvania Navy during the last months of the War of Independence and proved to be of minimal significance to privateering activities. It appeared that the privateering ventures of Moses during the last year of the Revolutionary War were unsuccessful. After Admiral Sir George Rodney captured St. Eustatius in early 1781, Moses, who also owned shares in four other ships, was unable to trade with his agents on this island and thus experienced a sharp decline in profits.

Moses engaged in other important activities during the decade. In 1780 he enlisted in the Pennsylvania Militia and was made a private in Captain Andrew Burkhard's Company of Colonel William Will's 3rd Philadelphia Battalion. The participation of Moses in this company was minimal. However, he became actively involved in financial matters. In 1780 he purchased stock valued at $400 in the Bank of North America, a financial institution created by Robert Morris that year to assist in reducing debts incurred during the War of Independence. Moreover, Moses, "with cash in hand," acquired in 1781 from Morris bills of credit to help restore confidence in the treasury. In August 1783 Moses, with accrued profits from his European currency transactions, bought from the superintendent of finance fifty thousand Dutch guilders and ten thousand French livres.

During the early 1780s, Moses also played a prominent role in Jewish activities in Philadelphia. He served in 1782 as *parnas* or president of the Mikveh Israel congregation. He made a large donation to the congregation for the building of a new synagogue on Cherry Street. Under his leadership, the construction of this edifice was completed in 1782. However, Moses and other members of Mikveh Israel in 1783 experienced disappointment. A petition, which they signed and which urged the Pennsylvania Council of Censors to abrogate a Christian test oath in the state constitution that prevented Jews from holding political offices, was rejected by that body. Soon thereafter, Moses and his family prepared to go back to New York, where Jews since 1777 had enjoyed religious and political liberties.

In late 1783 Moses returned to New York City; he spent the rest of his life there and primarily became concerned with business matters. In 1784, the New York Legislature heard addresses from Moses and other merchants about selling the properties of Loyalists. After members of this body enacted in 1784 a bill to permit the selling of these lands to individuals who had supported the revolutionary cause, Moses purchased that year in New York City several valuable land parcels that had been owned by the Tory James De Lancey. However, Moses in 1785 encountered severe financial problems that resulted from acutely falling prices and from the many claims of his creditors. Under these circumstances, the firm of Isaac Moses & Company was dissolved on 7 January 1786. That year Moses obtained the legal services of Alexander Hamilton, who assured Moses's creditors that he was worth ninety-eight thousand pounds. Nevertheless, in 1786 Moses declared bankruptcy.

During the late 1780s, Moses engaged in various kinds of businesses in New York City and became financially successful. He became an auctioneer especially known for selling prints, paintings, and antique furniture. He also established Isaac Moses & Sons, an international trading company that imported textiles, jewelry, wines, and china from Asia and Europe. This firm also exported furs, cotton, and foods and became a very lucrative operation by the first decade of the nineteenth century. By 1815 Moses was a major stockholder in the Bank of New York. He also had large holdings in New York City real estate; he owned choice properties on Wall, Greenwich, and Pearl streets.

Moses was affiliated with several important institutions. In 1767 he was made a Mason in New York City's Union Lodge. His affiliation with Freemasonry might explain in part why he supported the American revolutionary cause; the connections of Moses to this order also permitted him to make friends in the business world. Furthermore, he belonged to the New York City Chamber of Commerce and to the Marine Society of the City of New York. Moses also served as *parnas* of New York's Shearith Israel synagogue in 1775, 1789, 1790, and 1792. He died of cancer in New York City and was buried in the cemetery of this congregation.

Moses was resourceful, dignified, and cultured. Known for his success as a merchant capitalist, he developed the largest transatlantic Jewish merchant-shipping firm during the American Revolution and became the wealthiest Jew at this time. With cordial ties to Robert Morris and to other prominent patriots, Moses was recognized as "a true Whig and a friend of the liberties of the country," as he described himself in a memorial to Congress, for he expended both considerable monies and energy to promote the American Revolution. Moses, who had the distinction of heading both the New York and Philadelphia Jewish congregations during the last quarter of the eighteenth century, helped to foster the cause of Jewish civil liberties in the newly created nation.

• There are some primary materials and secondary sources relating to Moses's career. Some of his letters and business records are housed in the Library of the American Jewish Historical Society in New York and in the collections of the American Jewish Archives in Cincinnati. Brief biographical accounts of Moses appear in David De Sola Pool, *Portraits Etched in Stone: Early Jewish Settlers, 1682–1831* (1952), and in Jacob R. Marcus, *Early American Jewry: The Jews of Pennsylvania and the South, 1655–1790*, vol. 2 (1955). His business achievements during the American Revolution are assessed in Samuel Rezneck, *Unrecognized Patriots: The Jews in the American Revolution* (1975), and in Jacob R. Marcus, *United States Jewry, 1776–1985*, vol. 1 (1989). Ships of Moses involved in privateering are mentioned in Leon Huhner, "Jews Interested in Privateering in America during the Eighteenth Century," *Publications of the American Jewish Historical Society* 23 (1915): 163–76; in John W. Jackson, *The Pennsylvania Navy, 1775–1781: The Defense of the Delaware* (1974); in Nathan Miller, *Sea of Glory: A Naval History of the American Revolution* (1974); and in William W. Fowler, Jr., *Rebels Under Sail: The American Navy during the Revolution* (1976). His connections to Morris are described in Lauren R. Schwartz, *Jews and the American Revolution: Haym Salomon and Others* (1987), and in Elizabeth M. Nuxoll and Mary A. Gallagher, eds., *The Papers of Robert Morris, 1781–1784: May 5–December 31, 1783*, vol. 1 (1995). For his role in Philadelphia Jewry and in the Jewish civic rights movement, consult Edwin Wolf II and Maxwell Whiteman, *History of the Jews of Philadelphia from Colonial Times to the Age of Jackson* (1956), and William Weisberger, "Freemasonry as a Source of Jewish Civic Rights in Late Eighteenth-Century Vienna and Philadelphia: A Study in Atlantic History," *East European Quarterly* 34 (Winter, 2000): 419–45.

WILLIAM WEISBERGER

MOYER, Andrew Jackson (30 Nov. 1899–17 Feb. 1959), mycologist, was born in the northern Indiana farming community of Van Buren Township (Star City Post Office), the son of Edward Reuben Moyer and Minnie McCloud Moyer, farmers. Andrew was two years old when his mother died, and he went to live with neighbors, the Osborn family, who raised him through grammar school. In 1914 Andrew moved with his father and new stepmother to Logansport, Indiana, where he stayed until he joined the U.S. Army's Student Training Corps at Wabash College in October 1918. World War I ended the next month, and he was discharged with the rank of private that December, but the service financed his A.B. degree, which he completed in 1922. Following Wabash College, he spent a year at the University of Wisconsin before earning his M.S. degree at North Dakota Agricultural College (1925) and a doctorate in plant pathology at the University of Maryland (1929).

Although he attended the University of Wisconsin for only one year (1922–1923), he found there the interest that guided his career, microbial nutrition. Wisconsin professors Elmer V. McCollum and Harry Steenbock were leaders in vitamin research, while Edwin B. Fred and William H. Peterson carried out studies that paved the way for industrial production of acetic acid, fermented from corncobs and used in making solvents and smokeless gunpowder. At the North Dakota Agricultural College, Moyer wrote his master's thesis on the metabolism of *Fusarium*, a mold that causes flax disease, and he focused again on molds for his dissertation at the University of Maryland, "Studies in the Growth Response of Fungi to Boron, Manganese, and Zinc." Until then, molds were mostly of interest as plant pathogens that caused problems such as potato blight, corn smut, and wheat rust; but almost simultaneous with Moyer's graduation in 1929, English physician Alexander Fleming reported a new antibacterial property of a substance isolated from one particular mold, which he termed "penicillin."

For about a decade, Fleming's discovery remained a curiosity, while investigators learned about how to isolate and freeze-dry it to a stable yellow powder; its susceptibility to being destroyed in an acid medium or the presence of copper and zinc; its resilience in the presence of pus (unlike sulfonamides); and that it worked well against the bacilli of streptococcus and staphylococcus diseases, pneumonia, anthrax, gas gangrene, diphtheria and gonorrhea but not as well against typhoid and not at all against tuberculosis, plague, or cholera. By 1940, Ernst Chain, Howard Florey, Norman Heatley, and other colleagues at Oxford University were able to assemble convincing evidence on penicillin as a chemotherapeutic agent, even though they were unable to produce enough to treat successfully even a single patient.

Meanwhile, in 1931 Moyer married Dorothy Randall Phillips, whom he met at the University of Maryland; they had no children. That same year he took a research position with the U.S. Department of Agriculture's Bureau of Plant Industry, under Orville E. May, at the Arlington Experiment Farm in Virginia (where the Pentagon is located today). When May became director of the USDA's newly created Northern Research Laboratory in Peoria, Illinois, in December 1940, he invited Moyer to join him. There investigators were preparing to study molds of corn and wheat using large-scale fermentation equipment. Those investigations had hardly begun when, in July 1941, Howard Florey and Norman Heatley arrived in Peoria to see if penicillin could be produced in sufficient quantities for the wartime military.

May assigned Moyer the task, and in four months he achieved a tenfold increase in yield by growing *Penicillium notatum* in corn steep liquor (a mildly acidic by-product of corn wet-milling). Later he added the milk sugar lactose and neutralizing agents to double yields again, while growing the organism in large fermentation vats. A laboratory volunteer found the more productive *Penicillium chrysogenum*, growing on a cantaloupe from a Peoria market, which X-ray mutations further enhanced. By March 1944, Moyer and his colleagues had completed their work—showing how to produce penicillin in industrial fermentation— when Pfizer opened the first commercial plant for penicillin production in Brooklyn, New York, in time to supply the antibiotic for the Normandy invasion.

In 1945 wartime secrecy and the Allies' cooperation over penicillin's development ended: Moyer was permitted to publish his research; commercial rivalries surfaced across the Atlantic; and controversy arose over patent rights. Neither Fleming nor Florey's group, who unquestionably discovered and isolated penicillin, took out patents—British law at the time granted patents only for processes in making drugs, not the products. Perhaps they too, like many British and American chemists, expected a synthesis process to supersede fermentation in manufacturing, but by 1947 synthesized penicillin proceeded slower than the projections. No longer constrained, Moyer, acting for the USDA, submitted and received patents on the fermentation method: US#2423873, 15 July 1947 (with Robert D. Coghill; for using phenylacetic acid as an assay); US#2442141, 25 May 1948 (for a nutrient medium of corn-steep liquor, glucose and sodium nitrate); US#2443989, 22 June 1948 (for submerged cultures); and US#2476107, 12 July 1949 (for lactose, as a slowly assimilating energy source). Immediately English politicians and newspapers asserted that British scientists had discovered penicillin and that the Americans had "stolen" it. Although the prices of penicillin dropped dramatically and British pharmaceutical companies paid no royalties on Moyer's patents, political sniping over the Atlantic continued, even after Parliament revised its patent law in 1948 to stop, as one London paper put it, "foreigners filching our ideas." By 1950, however, the Allies were again at war, in Korea, and the matter dissolved.

In 1957 Moyer retired from the U.S. Department of Agriculture. He died after a month-long illness at the Veterans Administration Hospital in Bay Pines, St. Petersburg, Florida. He was buried at Parklawn Memorial Cemetery in Rockville, Maryland. In 1987 the National Inventors Hall of Fame posthumously inducted Moyer—the first government scientist to be so honored—for his work that advanced penicillin from a laboratory curiosity to the most widely used antibiotic.

• After her husband's death, Dorothy Moyer compiled three volumes of his papers and patents, which she presented, bound or on microfilm, to the National Agricultural Library (Beltsville, Md.), the University of Maryland (College Park, Md.), Wabash College (Crawfordsville, Ind.), and Oxford University (Oxford, England). His own account (with Robert D. Coghill), "Penicillin: The Laboratory Scale Production of Penicillin I Submerged Cultures by *Penicillium notatum* Westling (NRRL 832)," appeared in the *Journal of Bacteriology* 51:1 (1946): 79–93. Howard Florey and Ernst Chain (who shared the 1945 Nobel Prize with Alexander Fleming) published "The Development of Penicillin in Medicine," in *The Smithsonian Report for 1944* (Washington: Smithsonian Institution, 1945), pp. 461–66; and Robert Bud explains the Anglo-American postwar patent rivalry in "Penicillin and the New Elizabethans," *British Journal for the History of Science* 31 (1998): 305–33. An obituary is in the *New York Times*, 19 Feb. 1959.

G. TERRY SHARRER

MURPHY, William Parry (6 Feb. 1892–9 Oct. 1987), medical researcher, was born in Stoughton, Wisconsin, the son of Thomas Francis Murphy, a Congregational minister, and Rose Anna Parry Murphy. In 1914, after finishing his secondary education in the public schools of Stoughton, Murphy received his B.A. from the University of Oregon. He remained in Oregon for two years, teaching physics and mathematics in the high schools of Portland. Then he entered the University of Oregon Medical School, where in addition to studying medicine he worked as a laboratory assistant in the Anatomy Department. After finishing his freshman year at the University of Oregon Medical School, he spent the summer working at the Rush Medical School in Chicago. In 1919 Murphy was awarded the William Stanislaus Murphy Fellowship, which enabled him to transfer to the Harvard Medical School, where he completed his medical studies and received an M.D. in 1922. Murphy married Pearl Harriet Adams in 1919; they had a son, who became a physician, and a daughter, who died in 1936. After an internship at the Rhode Island Hospital in Providence, he became an assistant resident physician in the service of Henry A. Christian at the Peter Bent Brigham Hospital in Boston. Murphy held this position for eighteen months, then he was appointed junior associate in medicine at the Brigham Hospital. At about this time he met George R. Minot, and through this association Murphy was invited to join the 311 Beacon Street Group, a medical practice originally comprised of the three doctors Gerald Blake, Edwin A. Lock, and Minot. While practicing with this group, Murphy was introduced to the pernicious anemia work Minot had begun at Johns Hopkins.

In the early 1920s, at about the time insulin was discovered, Minot developed diabetes. By 1923–1924 Eli Lilly was producing enough insulin for Minot to receive eighteen units of insulin before breakfast and twelve units before dinner in the evening. Because of his association with Minot, Murphy played a role in Minot's treatment and thus became one of the first to report the results of the use of insulin in the treatment of diabetes.

While working in the laboratory of William H. Howell at Johns Hopkins, Minot learned about the hyperplastic state of the bone marrow in pernicious anemia (first described in 1875 by William Pepper in Philadelphia), learned how to distinguish newly formed red blood cells (RBCs) from the old cells already in circulation, and wrote his first paper on this subject. Upon his return to Boston, Minot extended his ability to investigate the blood by learning a new staining technique for RBCs from J. Homer Wright (the Wright stain). Minot, Wright, and Murphy observed in the mid-1920s that the blood of pernicious anemia patients contained RBCs of widely varying sizes, some nucleated RBCs, and RBCs with dark spots—Howell-Jolly bodies. Reflecting on these abnormalities, the three physicians hypothesized that they represented different stages in the development of RBCs and most likely were caused by some defect in RBC formation by the bone marrow.

Minot and Murphy further suspected that the bone marrow's failure to form RBCs resulted from a lack of some nutritional factor in the diet. The idea that a dietary deficiency was the cause of pernicious anemia was strengthened by the work of George H. Whipple, who had demonstrated that feeding liver to dogs, made anemic by repeated bleeding, stimulated RBC production. Minot and Murphy began feeding a liver-rich diet to their patients. Within a short period they observed that the RBC counts of their patients dramatically increased and the general conditions of their patients improved. Based on these findings, Murphy and Minot recommended that pernicious anemia patients be fed a diet rich in liver. This recommendation was not well received by their colleagues in Boston, who could not believe that this deadly anemia was caused by a simple dietary deficiency. Another factor that delayed the acceptance of Murphy and Minot's treatment of pernicious anemia was the reluctance of their patients to eat the huge amounts of raw liver prescribed.

By 1926 Murphy and Minot had successfully treated forty-five anemia patients. Reginald Fitz, a colleague of theirs at the Brigham Hospital, persuaded them to present their findings at the 1926 annual meeting of the American Association of Physicians in Atlantic City in a theater on Steel Pier. Fitz suggested that Minot present the clinical aspects of the pernicious anemia treatment and that Murphy and Robert Monroe discuss the physiology. Minot and Murphy agreed to this arrangement, and the work was presented in two parts, part A, "Clinical Aspects, George R. Minot (by invitation)," and part B, "Physiological Aspects, William P. Murphy (by invitation), Fitz, Reginald, and Monroe, Robert (by invitation)." Fitz read part B. The paper describing the work was published in the *Journal of the American Medical Association* in August 1926.

The therapy proposed by Murphy and Minot had severe drawbacks, the principal one being that patients had to eat from one-half pound to a pound of raw liver each day. In some severe cases it was necessary to homogenize the livers and feed them with a stomach tube to insure enough liver was administered. Minot and Murphy realized that if the active factor could be extracted from liver and concentrated, pernicious anemia treatment would be greatly simplified. To obtain such a preparation Murphy and Minot sought the aid of Edwin Cohn, a physical biochemist at Harvard. In a short time Cohn prepared a liver extract fifty to one hundred times more potent than raw liver. This active liver preparation became known as Fraction G and was subsequently manufactured by Eli Lilly under a patent assigned to Harvard University. In the early 1930s, Murphy demonstrated that a single intramuscular injection of liver extract containing active ingredients equivalent to eleven pounds of liver was effective when administered at intervals of several weeks.

William Castle's discovery in 1928 of the requirement of an "intrinsic" factor in addition to the "extrinsic" factor (found in liver and red meat, later isolated and named vitamin B_{12}) significantly advanced knowledge of the pathogenesis and improved treatment of pernicious anemia. The liver Murphy and Minot fed their pernicious anemia patients was effective because it contained enough of the extrinsic factor not to require the intrinsic factor for absorption. Subsequent investigations found that the intrinsic factor is produced in certain stomach cells and promotes the absorption of the vitamin B_{12} required by the bone marrow for RBC formation. More recently it has been found that, in addition to a lack of the extrinsic factor and intrinsic factor, low amounts or absences of gastric acid and folic acid are involved in the development of pernicious anemia.

Minot, Murphy, and Whipple were awarded the 1934 Nobel Prize for physiology and medicine "for their discoveries concerning liver therapy in cases of anemia." From 1928 until 1935 Murphy was an associate in medicine at Brigham Hospital, and in 1935 he became a associate in medicine and consultant in hematology, in which capacity he served until his retirement. From 1935 to 1948, while overseeing the developments of his discovery, Murphy was an associate in medicine at Harvard and then a lecturer in medicine until his retirement. In 1958 he was granted emeritus status at both Harvard and the Peter Bent Brigham Hospital.

While serving in these positions, Murphy became interested in the management of chronic leukemia. In 1940 he presented a paper before the pharmacology section of the American Medical Association (AMA) in which he stated that he believed chronic leukemia was caused by the absence of some factor that controlled normal white blood cells. Murphy also criticized the use of large doses of X rays in treating chronic lymphatic leukemia, pointing out that intense irradiation debilitated the patient and aggravated the disease. To avoid these undesirable effects, he recommended small doses of X rays spread out over the body, applied by the spray technique, when the leukemia relapsed. By using this therapeutic regimen, Murphy thought the patient could be maintained in a state of well-being and avoid long, debilitating periods of illness.

Murphy's important contributions to medical science were rewarded by numerous honors, including the Cameron Prize and Lectureship at the University of Edinburgh (1930), the Bronze Medal of the American Medical Association (1934), and the Gold Medal of the Massachusetts Humane Society (1937). He was a member of numerous prestigious medical societies. Murphy died at his home in Brookline, Massachusetts.

• A brief biography of Murphy is in *The National Cyclopedia of American Biography*, vol. G (1946). Information about the development of the use of liver in the treatment of pernicious anemia is in F. M. Rackemann, *The Inquisitive Physician: The Life and Times of George Richards Minot, A.B., M.D., D.Sc.* (1956); Paul DeKruif, *Men against Death* (1932); and "Medicine's Living History, Recollections of Liver Therapy," *Medical World News*, 8 Sept. 1972. An obituary is in the *Boston Sunday Globe*, 11 Oct. 1987.

DAVID Y. COOPER

NASH, N. Richard (7 June 1913–11 Dec. 2000), playwright and novelist, was born Nathan Richard Nusbaum on the gritty south side of Philadelphia, the son of S. L. Nusbaum, a bookbinder, and Jenny Singer Nusbaum. A scrapper from his early years on, Nash grew up on rough streets and first worked as a ten-dollar-a-match boxer. But he was also a good student, attracted to ideas. After graduating from South Philadelphia high school in 1930, he attended the University of Pennsylvania, where his studies in English and a budding impulse to write vied with his penchant for philosophy. He combined both when he graduated with a bachelor of science degree in 1934, publishing two books on philosophy, *The Athenian Spirit* and *The Wounds of Sparta*. A year later he married Helena Taylor. The couple had a son.

Nash soon left philosophy to write plays. His new calling brought him success almost immediately when in 1940 his first play, *Parting at Imsdorf*, was recognized with the Maxwell Anderson Verse Drama Award. He then accepted a post teaching drama at Bryn Mawr College (where the girls' school setting would feed a later work), and at the outbreak of World War II, he, like many others from the literary and journalistic communities, served in the Office of War Information.

In June 1946 Nash's play *The Second Best Bed* opened at the Ethel Barrymore Theatre on Broadway. A comedy about William Shakespeare's relationship with Anne Hathaway, it focused critical attention on Nash as a notable new voice of the American theater. During this time he penned several screenplays for Hollywood, including *Welcome Stranger*, for Paramount, and *Nora Prentiss*, for Warner Brothers (both released in 1947). In November 1948 Nash was again on Broadway at the Fulton Theatre with *The Young and the Fair*, a drama about a Boston girls' school, starring Frances Starr and Julie Harris. Although it received good reviews, it closed before long. His next play, *See the Jaguar*, which opened at the Cort Theatre on 3 December 1952, was judged less exceptional than *The Young and the Fair* by New York reviewers, although it won the International Drama Award in Cannes and the Prague Award.

Nash's fortune, as well as his lasting fame, was made two years later with *The Rainmaker*, which opened on Broadway on 28 October 1954, starring Geraldine Page in the lead role of Lizzie Curry. The play became his signature piece and ensured his place in American popular culture. The story is about a spinster farm girl in drought-stricken Kansas whose life is transformed by a fast-talking charmer of a con man named Starbuck, who promises rain. The play's humanity and universal message of hope and faith struck an instant chord with the public. In the *New York Times*, critic Brooks Atkinson called the play "warm, simple and friendly."

In 1956 *The Rainmaker* was made into a film starring Katharine Hepburn, Burt Lancaster, and Lloyd Bridges, that became a classic. Another version starring Tommy Lee Jones as Starbuck was filmed for television in 1982. Onstage, *The Rainmaker*, like such beloved American icons as *Oklahoma!* and *A Streetcar Named Desire*, has remained a staple of stock and amateur theaters. Performed worldwide, it has been translated into forty languages.

After the success of *The Rainmaker*, Nash prolifically continued to turn out screenplays, teleplays, and librettos. During the 1950s he regularly wrote scripts for NBC's Philco Playhouse, including *House in Athens*, *The Brownstone*, *The Happy Rest*, and an adaptation of *The Rainmaker*. He also wrote for ABC's Theatre Guild of the Air. In 1959, Nash's screenplay was featured in Samuel Goldwyn's all-star Technicolor version of *Porgy and Bess*.

Divorced from his first wife in 1954, in 1956 Nash married actress Janice Rule; the marriage lasted only a few months, and by November of that year he was married again, to Katherine Copeland. They had two daughters, and, with a new family, Nash divided his time between New York and his main home, a farm in Pipersville, Pennsylvania.

Nash's next two plays on Broadway, *Girls of Summer* (1956) and *Handful of Fire* (1958), failed to capture the public in a way even remotely approaching *The Rainmaker*. Neither did the 1960 musical *Wildcat*—despite Nash's libretto, a score by Cy Coleman and Carolyn Leigh, and the star presence of Lucille Ball, who financed the project. *Wildcat* was one of musical theater's more celebrated flops. Nash and *Wildcat*'s director-choreographer, Michael Kidd, served as the show's producers. But public and press were disappointed by Lucy as a spunky oil prospector; reviewers wrote that it was "cumbersome"and "unhumorous." (One number from the show would go on to musical theater immortality: the Coleman-Leigh march "Hey Look Me Over.") *Wildcat* closed in less than six months.

In 1963, however, *The Rainmaker* changed Nash's fortunes again—this time as a musical, with Nash adapting his play, and music and lyrics by Harvey Schmidt and Tom Jones, fresh from their success with *The Fantasticks*. Impresario David Merrick, who produced it, spared little expense: choreography was by Agnes de Mille and the scenery by venerable designer Oliver Smith. Opening to rave reviews on 24 October at the Broadhurst Theatre, *110 in the Shade*, as it was now called, was a moderate Broadway hit, although it was revived by the New York City Opera in the 1990s.

During the 1960s and 1970s, Nash penned the librettos for two more Broadway musicals, *The Happy Time*, an ill-fated Robert Goulet vehicle, and *Sarava*, another Broadway failure based on the Brazilian film *Dona Flor and Her Two Husbands*. But Nash was a dogged worker with a personal tenacity that bespoke his origins as a south Philly street fighter. In 1977 he had another hit—this one on neither stage nor screen, but with a novel, *East Wind, Rain*. The yarn, set in Hawaii on the eve of Pearl Harbor, ran the gamut from revenge and lust (it begins with a castration) to a desperate race to untangle coded clues revealing an imminent Japanese attack on the United States. The book was not only well reviewed, it became a best-seller. At his death, Nash had just finished another novel, *The Wildwood*.

In 1999, the year before Nash's death, *The Rainmaker* was revived on Broadway starring Woody Harrelson and Jayne Atkinson. The story of the clash between the realists and the dreamers still resonated almost half a century after the play's premiere. As Nash once put it, "I tried to tell a simple story about droughts that happen to people, and about faith."

In the pantheon of American playwrights, N. Richard Nash never achieved a rank alongside groundbreaking giants like Arthur Miller or Tennessee Williams. Rather, Nash represents the quintessential (and financially successful) professional—with a touch of the poet—whose prolific contributions to the American theater and film worlds helped those mediums thrive in the mid-twentieth century. However, if Nash lacks household name recognition as an author, his creations stand in for him: *The Rainmaker*'s pair of dreamers, Starbuck and Lizzy, have transcended into the cultural consciousness, in an exclusive club whose members include Miller's Willy Loman and Williams's Blanche DuBois.

• A source on the life of Nash is the clipping file held by the New York Public Library for the Performing Arts at Lincoln Center. There is an entry on Nash in *Who's Who in the Theatre*, 17th ed. (1981). Obituaries are in the *New York Times*, 19 Dec. 2000, *Variety*, 1–7 Jan. 2001, and the *Los Angeles Times*, 23 Dec. 2000.

DEBORAH GRACE WINER

NATHANS, Daniel (30 Oct. 1928–16 Nov. 1999), Nobel Prize–winning virologist, was born in Wilmington, Delaware, the son of Samuel Nathans and Sarah Levitan Nathans, Russian-Jewish immigrants whose occupation is unknown. Although his early childhood during the Great Depression was poor in material things, his family placed great value in education. He graduated with a degree in chemistry from the University of Delaware in 1950 and then entered medical school at Washington University in St. Louis. Nathans intended to return to Wilmington as a general practitioner, but a summer in Oliver Lowry's laboratory

at Washington University convinced him that his vocation was basic research. Following graduation from the Washington University School of Medicine in 1954, Nathans did a medical internship at the Columbia-Presbyterian Hospital in New York City. He then spent two years as a clinical associate at the National Cancer Institute. In 1956 he married Joanne Gomberg, who was for many years a lawyer for the city of Baltimore. They had three sons. After returning to Presbyterian Hospital for two more years as a medical resident, Nathans left the clinic for a lifetime in the laboratory.

In 1959 Nathans began his basic research career at the Rockefeller Institute with the famed biochemist and Nobel laureate Fritz Lippman. After developing a bacterial cell-free system that supported protein synthesis, Nathans discovered the existence of soluble factors required for this process. In collaboration with Norton Zinder, he also showed that bacteriophage RNA supported the synthesis of viral coat protein in a cell-free system, the first example of a purified mRNA that directed the synthesis of a specific protein. These initial observations and breakthroughs led to fundamental insights into the mechanism of protein synthesis.

In 1962 Nathans joined the faculty of the Johns Hopkins University School of Medicine. During his early years in Baltimore, Nathans carried out important studies on the regulation of bacteriophage translation by the viral coat protein, and he determined the mechanism of action of puromycin, an inhibitor of protein synthesis. In the late 1960s Nathans was assigned to teach medical students about animal viruses, and he soon realized that the study of simple animal viruses that caused tumors would provide important insights into the biology of animal cells and carcinogenesis.

While he was in Israel on sabbatical in 1969, Nathans received an epochal letter from Hamilton Smith, a faculty colleague from Johns Hopkins. In the letter Smith described a new enzymatic activity from the bacterium *Hemophilus influenzae*, called a restriction enzyme, that degraded DNA from foreign cells but did not degrade its own DNA. Smith soon showed that the *H. influenzae* restriction enzyme cut DNA at specific sites consisting of short defined nucleotide sequences. Nathans immediately recognized the implications of this discovery. "That set me off thinking, that we could use restriction enzymes to dissect the genome of a small papovavirus and learn something about how the virus works . . . and perhaps learn something about what genes are required for transformation," he recalled in 1996. Here were the tools to reduce an apparently monotonous DNA molecule into homogeneous, manageable pieces derived from specific regions of the viral genome, which then could be analyzed one at a time.

For his studies, Nathans selected a simple tumor virus, SV40, which was able to grow lytically in monkey cells and to cause permanent tumorigenic transformation of rodent cells. With his student Kathleen

Danna, Nathans showed that Smith's enzyme cleaved SV40 DNA into eleven specific pieces that could be separated by polyacrylamide gel electrophoresis. These results ushered in a new era of genetics. In the 1971 paper published in the *Proceedings of the National Academy of Sciences*, Nathans outlined his vision: "When the order of fragments in the genome is known, it should be possible to map 'early' and 'late' genes and those genes that function in all transformed cells. It may also be possible to localize specific genes by testing for biological activity, e.g. T-antigen production or abortive transformation.... It should [also] be possible to . . . obtain quite small, specific fragments useful for the determination of nucleotide sequence" (Danna and Nathans, p. 2917).

This vision soon became reality. Together with Danna and George Sack, a medical fellow, Nathans constructed the first "cleavage map" of a viral genome by determining the specific order of each fragment relative to the others. This map served as a framework for localizing functional elements of SV40 DNA, including the origin of SV40 DNA replication, the first genetic signal physically mapped on an animal virus genome. In the next few years, Nathans and his students and collaborators dissected the genome of SV40 by exploiting the ability of the restriction endonucleases to cleave DNA at specific sites. Restriction enzymes were used to identify different strains of SV40 DNA and to follow the genetic changes that occurred during virus evolution. Methods to map the locations of mutations on the viral genome were developed, as were methods to map the regions of the genomes that were expressed in cells and encoded specific viral proteins. The small fragments of DNA were also suitable for determining the sequence of bases along the polynucleotide strand, culminating in the determination of the complete nucleotide sequence of SV40 DNA by Walter Fiers and Sherman Weissman and their coworkers in the late 1970s.

Nathans also developed novel techniques to construct mutations at predetermined sites in the viral genome. These mutants were then reintroduced into cells and assayed for biological activity to determine the activities of individual viral proteins and regulatory signals. These studies led to the identification of individual nucleotides that controlled the rate of viral DNA replication and to the characterization of the SV40 large T-antigen as a multifunctional regulatory protein. No longer were geneticists forced to subject genomes to random mutagenesis and then undertake the laborious task of identifying the interesting mutants. In the new genetics made possible by restriction endonucleases, the genome was deliberately manipulated to generate the desired mutant. Nathans had replaced the haphazard methods of genetic analysis with a more directed, rational approach.

Many of the techniques developed by the Nathans laboratory helped form the foundation of genetic engineering, which was being developed by Paul Berg, Stanley Cohen, Herbert Boyer, and others. Now cellular genes were accessible to the molecular, restriction enzyme-based techniques pioneered by Nathans. Indeed the use of restriction enzymes to analyze and manipulate genes forms the core of genetic engineering, the biotechnology industry, and much of modern genetics.

Nathans received many honors for his research. He was elected to the National Academy of Sciences, and he received numerous awards, including the National Medal of Science. In 1978 he shared the Nobel Prize for Physiology or Medicine with Hamilton Smith and Werner Arber, a Swiss geneticist who carried out important studies on restriction-modification systems in bacteria. The Nobel citation recognized the role this work played in the birth of modern genetics.

As well as being a superb scientist, Nathans was also widely regarded as thoughtful and fair, and his counsel was valued. During the administration of President George H. W. Bush, Nathans was a member of the Presidential Council of Advisors on Science and Technology. Nathans was also a senior investigator of the Howard Hughes Medical Institute and was for many years the chairman of the Department of Microbiology at John Hopkins, where he built one of the strongest basic science departments in the country. Nathans also served as interim president of the Johns Hopkins University in 1995–1996 and led the university through a challenging time of upheaval in academic medicine. He compared the presidency to the year he spent as a medical intern, which also forced him to make quick decisions based on limited data. This comparison reflected Nathans's modest and soft-spoken personality, one that never sought self-aggrandizement.

The year after he completed his term as university president, Nathans was diagnosed with acute myelogenous leukemia. He died in Baltimore.

Nathans changed how viruses and genes are studied. Beginning with the insight that restriction endonucleases could be "trypsins and chymotrypsins for DNA" (as he stated in his Nobel lecture), he focused on developing new approaches for subjecting genes to increasingly detailed and sophisticated molecular analysis. He was fond of repeating the advice that scientists should not be satisfied with the surface nuggets along the streambed but should dig a mine and find the mother lode. He found his "mother lode" in developing a new set of tools to analyze the genes of a small virus, and the result transformed virology and genetics.

• In a taped interview, 1 July 1996, with Daniel DiMaio, Nathans reflected at length on his background, scientific career, and administrative duties. The interview is available from Alpha Omega Alpha as part of its Leaders of American Medicine series. Kathleen Danna and Nathans published the groundbreaking paper "Specific Cleavage of Simian Virus 40 DNA by Restriction Endonuclease of *Hemophilus Influenzae* in *Proceedings of the National Academy of Sciences (USA)* 68, no. 12 (1971): 2913–17. Nathans's Nobel lecture, "Restriction Endonucleases, Simian Virus 40, and the New Genetics," appeared in *Science* 206 (1979): 403–409. An obituary is in the *New York Times*, 18 Nov. 1999.

DANIEL DiMAIO

NELSON, Gene (24 Mar. 1920–16 Sept. 1996), tap dancer, was born Eugene Leander Berg in Seattle, Washington, the son of Leander Berg, a machinist, and Lenore Nelson Berg, a baker and singer. The family later moved to Los Angeles. Nelson became inspired to tap dance at age twelve, when he saw Fred Astaire in *Flying Down to Rio* (1933). "I had to learn to do that! He made it look so easy," Nelson recalled. He enrolled at the Miramar Hotel with Roy Randolph for Saturday classes in tap dancing. These classes were short-lived, though, as Nelson failed to practice every day. After seeing several more Astaire films, Nelson told his parents he wanted to resume tap lessons. His first "big-time" tap teacher was a seasoned professional New York dancer named Steve Granger from the Albright School of Dance. Nelson studied privately, and the first routine he learned was Bill "Bojangles" Robinson's "Doin' the New Lowdown."

When Nelson entered Santa Monica High School he quickly learned that boys who took dancing lessons were automatically "sissies." Like other male dancers of the twentieth century, such as Gene Kelly and James Cagney, Nelson spent a lot of time defending himself. But when the "macho boys" discovered that Nelson could be useful performing at school functions, he was accepted.

After his first year in high school, Nelson left Albright and went to the biggest professional school in Hollywood, Fanchon & Marco, where he trained intensely in acrobatics, advanced tap, and adagio work. Fanchon & Marco were tied in with the Paramount Theatre in downtown Los Angeles, where they had a big chorus line called the Fanchonettes, similar to the Rockettes at Radio City Music Hall. The Paramount offered a movie and four shows a day, including vaudeville acts and a full orchestra. This schedule was interrupted three times a year for *The Fanchon & Marco Juvenile Revue*, which played for two weeks. Nelson's first professional job was in their revue. He earned $15 a week.

Nelson's school work began to suffer, so his parents pulled him out of dance classes. Though he quit the dancing lessons, he became head cheerleader and put together the largest cheerleading team the school ever had. In 1938 he graduated, but barely.

In his late teens Nelson became obsessed with ice-skating. With his dance and acrobatic background, he appeared to be a natural. In August 1938, just three months after his high school graduation, he was asked to audition for Sonja Henie's *Hollywood Ice Revue* at the Polar Palace in Hollywood. He got the job at $75 a week. Nelson toured with Henie for two years and performed as a chorus skater and dancer in two of her films at Fox Studios. During this time Nelson abandoned tap and began taking ballet to improve his skating. He studied with Bert Prival, who was then teaching for Nico Charisse.

In late 1940 Nelson costarred in an ice show, *It Happens on Ice*, that Henie produced at the Center Theatre in New York. On Sunday, 7 December 1941, Nelson was about to make his entrance for the matinee performance when the news of Pearl Harbor arrived. Knowing that he would be called for the draft, he instead enlisted in the Signal Corps at Fort Monmouth, New Jersey. With a report date in March 1942, Nelson promptly married his fiancée Miriam Franklin on 22 December. They had one child. Franklin, one of the great Broadway tap dancers, was then appearing in the Ethel Merman show *Panama Hattie* and was assistant to Robert Alton, who choreographed the show. Nelson credited Franklin as the one who got him back on track with tap dancing at that time.

A buck private in the Signal Corps, Nelson was assigned to Company L of the Fifteenth Regiment Officers Candidate School as a company clerk. Hating his assignment, he eased the boredom by tap dancing to whatever music he could find on his portable Philco radio. In a true "Hollywood" moment, one afternoon a short, bald soldier named Irving Lazar stuck his head through the door, watched Nelson for a while, then invited him to be in the post show the following week. Nelson accepted without hesitation. Lazar later became one of Hollywood's most powerful agents.

The audience for the show included Irving Berlin and his army staff, Sergeant Josh Logan, Sergeant Ezra Stone, and Sergeant Robert Sidney, all Broadway luminaries. They were scouting talent for Berlin's all-army show *This Is the Army*. The next day Nelson received transfer orders to Camp Upton, Long Island, on special duty with "This Is the Army Company." There he joined a company of 365 talented actors, dancers, singers, musicians, and technical crew members.

This Is the Army appeared on Broadway standing room only (SRO) for six months and then went on a national tour that ended in Hollywood, where a filmed version of the show was made in 1943 starring Ronald Reagan, George Murphy, Joe Louis, and the original cast. Then followed a world tour with a downsized cast for 1,238 total performances from 4 July 1942 to September 1945. The grand total attendance was 2,468,005 armed forces and civilians. Nelson regarded these the most grueling and rewarding years of his life.

After the war Nelson returned to Hollywood, California, where his wife had been working at Paramount Studios. She had met John Darrow, a major agent who handled Gene Kelly, June Allyson, Van Johnson, and the directors Chuck Walters and Robert Alton, all of whom were at MGM. Nelson was invited to audition for Alton and was signed to a stock contract at Fox Studios. The Hollywood executives (Jewish themselves) decided that his Swedish name Berg sounded "too Jewish" and ordered it changed to something more mainstream. Nelson submitted a few suggestions, including Nelson, his mother's maiden name. Eugene Leander Berg became Gene Nelson.

Nelson was given some bit movie parts but never quite broke through. Then came *Lend an Ear* (1948), a neat little stage revue directed and choreographed by Gower Champion. It opened at Las Palmas Theatre in Hollywood and played for six months, then it went to Broadway and became a hit at the Broadhurst Theatre. After eight months in the show Nelson was beckoned back to Hollywood, and this time he made his mark.

Warner Bros. had just signed Doris Day and Virginia Mayo, and the studio was resuming production of musical films. Nelson made ten musicals in three years for them. He choreographed all of his numbers with the help of his wife and Al White, a fine dancer who assisted Leroy Prinz, the dance director at Warner. Nelson choreographed his dances so each dance movement surpassed the last with a seeming effortlessness. His films included *Tea for Two* (1950), *West Point Story* (1950), *Lullaby of Broadway* (1951), *She's Working Her Way through College* (1952), and *So This Is Paris* (1955). Nelson was immortalized in one top grade Hollywood movie, *Oklahoma!* (1955), in which his tap enhanced the character of "dumb ol'" Will Parker.

Nelson's marriage to Miriam Franklin ended in divorce. He married Marilyn Morgan in 1958; they had two children and later divorced. Little information is available on his third, childless marriage, to Jean Martin, which also ended in divorce.

After the demise of movie musicals, Nelson pursued a highly successful career in television. He starred in many specials and then worked as a prolific director in both film and television, with credits such as two Elvis Presley features, *Kissin' Cousins* (1963) and *Harum Scarum* (1965). In 1971 he made a sensational comeback on Broadway in the smash show *Follies*, in which he stopped the show nearly every night with "The God-Why-Don't-You-Love-Me Blues (Buddy's Blues)."

In his later years Nelson stayed active in tap dancing, often making appearances in tap shows and celebrations. He produced a set of instructional tap dance videos entitled *Come Tap with Me* based on his choreography. He died in Los Angeles.

Nelson was the last of the great screen tap dancers during the golden age of musicals. He made all of his major musical films in the 1950s. Had he appeared just ten years earlier, he would have hit the production peak of the movie musical rather than the tail end of it. Nonetheless his ingenuity, grace, and talent resulted in scores of classic tap dance numbers recorded for posterity on film. Nelson's style was smooth, rhythmic, and romantic. His work incorporated the best of tap woven together with jazz, ballet, acrobatics, and gymnastics.

• Rusty E. Frank, *TAP! The Greatest Tap Dance Stars and Their Stories, 1900–1955* (1990, 1995), includes a chapter about Nelson based on extensive interviews. Tony Thomas, *That's Dancing* (1984), also includes a chapter on Nelson. An obituary is in the *New York Times*, 18 Sept. 1996.

RUSTY E. FRANK

NESBITT, Robert (11 Jan. 1906–3 Jan. 1995), theatrical producer, was born in London, the son of Robert Nesbitt and Ada Isobel Nesbitt. After education at the private Repton School and some time at Exeter College, Oxford, Nesbitt entered the world of London journalism and theatrical advertising.

Nesbitt had been writing moderately successful theatrical lyrics and libretti when opportunity came his way during the Great Depression year of 1932. The director of a new revue, *Ballyhoo*, for which Nesbitt had collaborated on songs and was handling promotion, dropped out, and Nesbitt asked if he could take over. Nesbitt and his partner William Walker then rewrote most of the show. The *London Observer* praised the show for capturing the "lackadaisical, which is the dominant quality of British youth today."

Ballyhoo brought Nesbitt to the attention of André Charlot, the acknowledged master of intimate revue, who was undertaking a comeback from several years of failure and a bankruptcy. From 1934 to 1937, when Charlot left Britain, Nesbitt was Charlot's right-hand man. From Charlot he particularly learned the economic and aesthetic value of using stage lighting to help create the illusion of splendor.

When World War II broke out, and after London theaters recovered from initial panic to get back into business, Nesbitt's great years began. Largely working for the impresario George Black, Nesbitt created a series of revues that proved to be the most spectacular entertainment available to Britons during these austere years. These were only nominally "revue"; they contained little in the way of topicality or indeed of commentary at all, and they tended to feature the era's outstanding variety artists, usually the silliest or most notorious. Nesbitt gained one of his nicknames—*Prince of Darkness*—for his ability to create dramatic, often chiaroscuric mood amidst the mayhem.

In 1943 Nesbitt married Iris Lockwood, formerly one of "Mr. Cochran's Young Ladies," impresario C. B. Cochran's classy chorus. They had no children and remained married until Nesbitt's death.

Nesbitt's London success as director continued after the war. One of his 1947 shows introduced a twelve-year-old singer, Julie Andrews. During those years, London legislation came to allow the occasional statuesque (and statuelike, because they could not move) nude in certain kinds of shows, and Nesbitt produced a few of these. In 1954 he received his first summons to Broadway. There, the revue *Catch a Star* brought him to the attention of Joe Sullivan, Al Gottesman, and Bob Rice, who were developing hotels and casinos in Las Vegas, then in its first major postwar building spree. In 1955 these entrepreneurs, inspired by hotels such as the Sands, which played on the vaguely Middle Eastern (and certainly movie-inspired) concept and image evoked by the term *desert*, built the Dunes, a sprawling hotel featuring a 30-foot-tall statue of an arms-folded "Sultan."

At the time, most Las Vegas hotels featured swimming pools, an ongoing "lounge show," frequently alternating small musical groups, and a lavish twice-nightly "floor show" featuring a star entertainer.

Under Nesbitt's theatrical direction, however, the Dunes sought a different kind of floor show reminiscent of his London revue. In 1955 Nesbitt created the first *Magic Carpet* revue, duly advertised on a huge electric sign atop New York's Capitol Theater. Settings and lighting were opulent, state of the art—everything that Nesbitt could not afford in wartime London. Beautiful girls were indeed lavishly promoted and featured, but during the shows they remained no more undraped than Nesbitt's statuesque London females, a testament to Nesbitt's enduring notion of taste.

The Dunes did not do well during its first year, and the ownership panicked, bringing in a new manager and briefly closing most of its operations. After its reopening, Nesbitt departed, making no more contributions, and the new managers brought in *Minsky's Follies* as the main evening entertainment. The barebreasted allure of the *Follies* (by now, hotels all over Vegas were advertising and presenting *Folies Bergère*–type shows) and other such skin-displaying productions seemed more to the liking of tired businessmen and hopeful gamblers. Nesbitt had a look at Hollywood, found that a projected revival of the *Ziegfeld Follies* on Broadway had been scuttled, and left for Britain, never to return to the United States. The Dunes continued through highs and lows, eventually being demolished in 1994 to make way for the huge Treasure Island, one of the symbols of Las Vegas's reincarnation as home to the "family vacation."

Nesbitt's greatest British years lay before him. In cooperation with impresario Sir Bernard Delfont he converted an old variety venue to the Talk of the Town, a theater-restaurant for 800 guests, which presented London's most reliable and star-studded entertainment for the next quarter-century. During these years, Nesbitt also was generally the director for the Royal Variety Performances, often at the London Palladium, and therefore in charge of most of the top-of-the-line international entertainment. Nesbitt, who estimated that he had seen 90 percent of all British revues since his childhood, was involved with collaborators on several unfinished histories of revue at the time of his death.

Nesbitt died in Paris, where the Nesbitts had gone for an anniversary celebration. His last words were "I'm not feeling very well, but it's probably nothing that another glass of champagne won't put right."

A man of meticulous planning and impeccable dress, he was equipped with a mild but firm way of suggesting, "Do you think . . .?" to ensure that his vision of a performance would be endorsed. Nesbitt's claim to American fame lasted only a very short time, but during it he helped define the course and reputation of entertainment in what proved to be an icon of the late twentieth century—Las Vegas, Nevada. He was responsible for the first spectacular Las Vegas revues.

• Nesbitt's role in the development of Las Vegas entertainment is the focus of Eugene P. Moehring, *Resort City in the Sunbelt: Las Vegas 1930–1970* (1989). Nesbitt's post–Las Vegas years are covered in Bernard Delfont with Barry Turner, *East End, West End* (1990). A great deal of this essay stems from personal interviews with Robert Nesbitt. All the major London newspapers carried extensive obituaries of Nesbitt; particularly useful are those in the *Times* and the *Daily Telegraph*, both 6 Jan. 1995, and the *Guardian*, 11 Feb. 1995.

JAMES ROSS MOORE

NEWELL, Robert Henry (13 Dec. 1836–early July 1901), writer, was born in New York City, the son of Robert Newell and Ann Lawrence Newell. The father, a prospering manufacturer, won substantial awards as an inventor, but his death in 1854 ended his son's plan to enter college after education in private schools. As early as 1858 Newell had published short pieces that led to his joining the staff of the *New York Sunday Mercury*, a thriving and respected weekly newspaper that carried much imaginative writing.

Newell, like most belletrists of his era, considered poetry the supreme genre. His popular breakthrough came with the topical *Papers* signed as "Orpheus C. Kerr (office seeker)." The first, in the letter format that "Kerr" would always use, was dated 20 March 1861, soon after President Abraham Lincoln's inauguration. Though the datelines consistently placed the writer in Washington, D.C., Newell stayed in New York, seldom if ever traveling to the capital. Later sources that list him as a "war correspondent" may overread "Kerr's" fictional soldiers and burlesque skirmishes.

The many reprintings of the first three volumes of the *Papers* prove their popularity during the Civil War. Abraham Lincoln, a connoisseur of humor, even reread the *Papers*, sometimes recapping a favorite passage for his Cabinet and other politicians. He judged almost impersonally; the earlier *Papers* belittled Lincoln's performance also. Though "Kerr" posed fitfully as a New England Yankee, Newell had links with the New York Democrats; the *Papers* started out with ridicule of federal incompetence. They highlighted the graft-ridden and inefficient procurement by the War Department, the inept leadership of the Army of the Potomac, and the feckless cynicism of middle-rank officers. Increasingly, they derided both the timid military strategy and bold political ambitions of General George B. McClellan. Yet they also grew in hostility toward the Confederates, typified by wealthy slave owners, and the Peace Democrats, typified by a Kentuckian. While at first ambivalent and condescending toward fugitive slaves, the *Papers* supported emancipation and satirized the proposals to colonize them outside the United States. More staunchly, they grew in respect toward Lincoln. As casualties mounted they also began to express the tragedies of the common soldier.

Newell kept aiming higher than newspaper humor. "Kerr," superior to the gross misspellings of Artemus Ward (Charles Farrar Browne) and well-read in world (that is, European) literature, often overreaches with puns that depend on an elite vocabulary. His allusions invoke classical sources, and he inserts poetry and fiction for which Newell probably anticipated a dignifying response. Only gradually did the *Papers* stick much closer to topicality and to consistency of persona. After pausing for Newell's trip to California, the *Papers* became less frequent while more pointed and more tightly ironic. They ended at number CIX, dated 11 April 1865, with reverent praise of Lincoln and support of the freed persons. Nevertheless, their appeal would fade far more quickly than the blunt, jeering, laboriously illiterate letters of Petroleum V. Nasby (David Ross Locke).

Newell's weaker source of fame was his marriage to the actress Adah Isaacs Menken (born Ada McCord in 1835). Both his assistant editing of the *Sunday Mercury* and his duties as a drama critic acquainted him with Menken, who was already notorious as a free spirit. They married in September 1862; she divorced him, unopposed, in August 1865, technically alleging desertion; but they had separated quickly, reconciling just briefly for her tour in the Far West. She could have had plausible motives for accepting Newell, but his sedate personality could not mesh with her impulsiveness and self-promotion. She may have hoped that he would help her settle into one of the more literary identities she aspired to; he could have hoped to nurture an erratic yet creative mind. He later avoided sourness about her, and his try at an autobiographical novel stopped inconclusively. Though she heightened her notoriety before dying in 1868, the *New York Times* (13 July, p. 7) closed his obituary with "He was a bachelor."

With nine-tenths of the *Papers* finished by July 1863 and earning royalties in hard covers, Newell, who had left the *Sunday Mercury*, doubtless composed more of the pieces collected in his first book of poetry. Because such volumes seldom sold well, the publishers had to hope for the "Kerr" appeal to carry over, even if E. P. Hingston, in his preface for a British edition of the *Papers*, claimed that Newell's "poems are almost as well known in the States as are his burlesque letters." Personally, Hingston had observed, he was "very retiring in his manners" and "very literary in his tastes." The neo-Romantic ode that headed *The Palace Beautiful and Other Poems* (1865) rose through Love and a "God within" toward esthetic ideality. However, only Newell's pseudo-dialect poems would strike a chord, at least while "elocution" flourished. *Mark Twain's Library of Humor* (1888) used Kerr/Newell's "A Great Fit," a thin string of quatrains about a brutal fight between Arkansawyers. Still, William Cullen Bryant reprinted five of the *Papers'* (ten) "Poems Received in Response to an Advertised Call for a National Anthem"—skillful, discerning parodies of well-known contemporaries.

Newell probably longed to emerge as a poet-oracle. However, *Versatilities* (1871) hedged with "Illiteraria," a section of stereotyped, ethnic versifying. *Studies in Stanzas* (1882) sounded a last, weak hurrah for his ambitions as poet. Earlier, he had fallen back on commentary about Reconstruction, gathered into *Smoked Glass* (1868), to close out the *Orpheus C. Kerr Papers*. The headnote in *Mark Twain's Library of Humor* would further identify Newell as "a veteran editor and prolific author." For steady income he worked on the *New York World* from 1869 to 1874, responsible especially for an adaptable column of "Social Studies." As his last job, he edited the weekly *Hearth and Home* until it folded in December 1875. He inspired no anecdotes for the annals of journalism and never got to the inner circle of the rising monthly magazines.

Deservedly, his four novels have sunk yet further out of sight. While *Avery Glibun, or Between Two Fires: A Romance* (1867) professed to combine the old and a new school of fiction, it ranged from melodrama to urban realism confusingly and dully. *The Cloven Foot* (1870), which explicitly adapted *The Mystery of Edwin Drood* to American scenes, also baffled and bored even those who speculated about how Charles Dickens had meant to finish up. Newell was groping toward a major issue. *Appleton's Journal* (2 July 1870) acknowledged his call in "Social Studies" for developing native themes rather than imitating the Victorian novelists. His *Walking Doll; or, the Asters and Disasters of Society* (1872) tried to interweave upper and lower layers of contemporary Manhattan, but historians of the "rise" of realism dismiss it. If *There Was Once a Man* (1884) fell still further short of William Dean Howells' "fidelity to experience and probability of motive," it might interest historians of Darwinism. The *Brooklyn Eagle* would class Newell as a "veteran newspaperman."

In the mid-1880s Newell went silent as a writer, perhaps from an eye ailment or psychosomatic fatigue. He dwindled toward obscurity in Brooklyn, though the very first edition of *Who's Who in America 1899–1900* did include him. He died from a heat stroke at home, unnoticed for several days.

• No library has reported a sizable holding of Newell's personal papers. The most accurate basic facts were in *Who's Who in America 1901–1902*. Stephen Leacock cogently evaluated his humor in *Dictionary of American Biography*, vol. 13 (1934). In *Abraham Lincoln: The War Years* (1939) Carl Sandburg revitalized the *Papers* to show their appeal for the president. For *Dictionary of Literary Biography*, vol. 11, *American Humorists 1800–1950* (1982), Michael Butler patiently and penetratingly covered all of Newell's books. The *Brooklyn Eagle*, 12 and 13 July 1901, gives the best-informed obituary.

LOUIS J. BUDD

NIEBAUM, Gustave Ferdinand (30 Aug. 1842–5 Aug. 1908), fur trader and wine maker, was born Gustav or Gustave Nybom in Helsingfors (now Helsinki), the son of a police official of Swedish and Baltic-German stock; his parents' names do not appear in currently accessible records. Finland at the time was a semiautonomous grand duchy of Russia. Niebaum became a sailor, but not just an ordinary seaman. Intelligent and a graduate of a gymnasium, Europe's equivalent of an American high school, he enrolled in Helsinki's Nautical Institute. Graduating at nineteen, he soon secured his master's papers and was in command of his own ship by 1864, in the service of the Russian American Company, sailing to Alaska.

In 1867 the United States took possession of Russian America, or Alaska. Its purchase by Secretary of State William Seward was derided as "Seward's Folly" and "Seward's Icebox," but Niebaum helped make critics swallow their words in 1868 when he sailed to San Francisco with a $600,000 cargo of furs in his ship's hold. In San Francisco the young man was welcomed as a partner into Hutchinson, Kohl & Co., shipping merchants and fur dealers. By 1869, that company had developed into the Alaska Commercial Company. John F. Miller of Napa Valley, an ex-Civil War general, was its president, with Lewis Gerstle, Louis Sloss, and Niebaum as partners. (In 1902, Niebaum was chosen president, a post he held until his death.)

With his knowledge of five languages, the young partner was a natural envoy for the Alaska Commercial Company, and he sold furs from London to St. Petersburg. By 1891 he was acting consul general of Russia in San Francisco. On business trips to Europe he developed an interest in wine. Other interests included translating documents of the Norsemen for publication and collecting Alaskan Indian and Eskimo artifacts, including totem poles.

In 1873 Niebaum married a San Franciscan, a Miss Shingleberger. References to her first name are conflicting: she was either Suzanne (Susan) or Louise. One thing is certain: Gustave's bride strongly disliked the sea. To please his wife, Niebaum abandoned plans to build and sail an ocean-going yacht. Instead, he converted his wine appreciation hobby into an avocation that quickly metamorphosed into a second career. He then determined to make his own wine, which would equal that made in Europe.

More familiar with schnapps, aquavit, and vodka than wine, Niebaum embarked on a crash course of study. He first placed standing orders with booksellers such as Joseph Baer of Frankfort for all volumes, old or new, on grape growing and wine making. He hired a copyist to transcribe the texts of books that he was unable to buy. His original personal library of 600 volumes, partly reassembled in recent years at Inglenook Winery, can be considered to be the direct ancestor of today's Napa Valley Wine Library, which is housed in the St. Helena Public Library.

Niebaum did not leave either trading firm, nor did he abandon the last of several homes in San Francisco. But in 1879 he paid $20,000 to buy a Napa Valley estate that included 54 acres of Black Malvoisie (Malvasia) and Zinfandel vines. He also built a summer home that became a regional showplace. In 1880 Niebaum paid $48,000 to buy the adjacent Rohlwing Ranch and Hastings's Nook Farm. He fell in love with the beautiful Napa Valley site, even its Celtic name, Inglenook, which meant a cozy fireplace corner, a Scots hearthside seat. In 1880 he supervised the clearing of 60 acres for better-grade vines. This eventually became a 300-acre model vineyard; it was the heart of his 1,100-acre estate extending from the valley floor to the foothills of the Mayacamas Mountains. The range sheltered Inglenook from cold winds and sea fogs and watered his property with a picturesque stream. Niebaum built a distillery, outbuildings, and a stable that the local press described as palatial. With a strong esthetic sense, he forbade the needless cutting of oaks in order to preserve the estate's natural setting.

In 1881 Niebaum bought 900 choice Sauvignon Blanc cuttings to graft onto native American *Riparia* rootstock, supposedly (but not quite) resistant to the phylloxera, the plant louse that was beginning to devastate California vineyards. A rare combination of pragmatist and visionary, he had his men plant new varietals—Sauvignon Blanc, Riesling, Semillon, Cabernet Sauvignon, and Pinot Noir (all superior to Malvoisie, Zinfandel, and, especially, Mission vines)—in rows only three and a half feet apart instead of the usual seven or eight feet. This was for quality of fruit as well as higher yield per acre. By the fall of 1881 he had 64 bearing acres and 90 more planted. He then hired Hamden Wallace McIntyre, the Alaska Commercial Company's agent in Alaska's Pribilof Islands, to be Inglenook's resident manager. He knew that the Scots-American from Vermont had worked for New York's Pleasant Valley Wine Company. Probably he suspected McIntyre's great skill as a cellarman, particularly as a blender of wine. Still, he was surprised by his colleague's ability as an architect. Trained only as an engineer and draftsman, McIntyre was a natural genius. He went on to become the West's first, and greatest, winery architect.

Niebaum and McIntyre in 1881 replaced the inadequate Nook Farm winery with a temporary (55 x 120 feet) wooden one at Inglenook. The practical millionaire was also thrifty. He carefully dismantled the old structure to salvage building materials for the new one. Later, instead of buying straw to cushion cased bottles, he used tules, Napa River bulrushes, because they were free. The first vintage and crush (1882) was a success at 80,000 gallons. With Inglenook in McIntyre's capable hands, Niebaum began his "postgraduate" study by touring France, Germany, Spain, Italy, Portugal, and Hungary during grape harvests, examining climates, soils, planting techniques, and pest controls. He also collected more cuttings of the Continent's "noble" varieties of vines.

Meanwhile, McIntyre, with the help of San Francisco professional architect William Mooser, designed and began building (1883) a grand (220 by 72 feet) three-story chateau of a cellar. Although the last nail was not driven till 1890, the 300,000-to-500,000-gallon winery was ready for its first crush in 1887. Dominating the heart of Napa Valley, it remains Niebaum's great (physical) monument. Its odd architectural mix of Eastlake and semi-Gothic, long softened by vines, is perfect for its setting, and has become the star of the Valley's ensemble of wineries. More important was a less tangible "monument," Niebaum's successful efforts to restore California's good name after mediocre wines had tarnished its reputation. He did so by not only planting superior vines but also by "inventing" quality control in wine making. He stationed men at his conveyor belt to remove not just leaves and stems but unripe or spoiled grapes as well. Less-than-absolutely-perfect fruit was destined for his distillery, not his winery. And his still accepted only pure juice, no pomace, so his brandy did not pick up the fusel oil that imparted a disagreeable odor and flavor to much "California cognac." A zealot for cleanliness, he had his winery arteried with water and steam pipes and its concrete floor channeled to drain off water before it could stagnate. He wore white gloves to inspect the cellar's interior for dust. Outside, paths and driveways were carefully raked each day.

To ensure that customers would receive a premium-quality beverage, Niebaum aged his wine more than his competitors, and he pioneered estate bottling. Instead of selling his wine to wholesalers in bulk (casks), as was the custom, he sold only "in glass." Every bottle bore his distinctive label and logo, plus a branded cork secured with wire. (Dealers were accused not only of bottling Napa wine with fake French labels but of adulterating it with preservatives and coloring agents such as fuchsin.) Publicity-shy himself, he nevertheless pioneered modern wine advertising by hiring Ferdinand Haber as his representative. Haber made Inglenook wines popular in the East. During the 1890s, a time of depression in the wine industry, Niebaum's products not only continued to sell well but won awards at exhibitions in Melbourne, Paris, Dublin, Bordeaux, Berlin, and Atlanta. The early wine writer Frona Wait compared the quality of Inglenook wine to that of France's legendary Chateau Lafite and Chateau d'Yquem and Germany's Schloss Johannisberg.

Niebaum died in San Francisco. In 1908 the *St. Helena Star* observed that the late "Captain Niebaum was an enterprising and public-spirited citizen whose commanding presence will be missed both in the metropolis [San Francisco] and in Napa County." As for the Finn himself, he would have been more delighted to read, in 1939, thirty-one years after his death, that the San Francisco Wine and Food Society, sampling two of his 1890s red wines, found them frail with age, to be sure, but still "exquisitely perfumed, smooth and delicately rich."

• There is no biography of Captain Niebaum nor archive of his papers. His life must be pieced together from such books as Tom Parker's *Inglenook Vineyards* (1979); Charles L. Sullivan's *Napa Wine* (1994); William F. Heintz's *California's Napa Valley* (1999); and Frona Wait's *Wines and Vines of California* (1973). There is a front-page but brief obituary in the St. Helena Star, 7 August 1908.

RICHARD H. DILLON

NORTON, Joshua Abraham (fl. 1818 or 1819–8 Jan. 1880), merchant and self-proclaimed emperor of the United States and protector of Mexico, was born in London, England, the son of John Norton, a farmer and merchant, and Sarah Simmonds Norton. In 1820 the Nortons immigrated to Algoa Bay, Cape of Good Hope (now South Africa).

The Nortons were among the first influx of British colonists to South Africa, known to local history as the "1820 settlers." Only eighteen, including the Nortons, were Jewish. Little is known of Joshua Norton's early years. His father farmed near Graham's Town before establishing a business in Algoa Bay, now Port Elizabeth. As a young man, Norton operated a ship's chandlery in Port Elizabeth, which failed in the early 1840s. He may also have served briefly in the Cape Mounted Riflemen.

Following his father's death in 1848, the family business was sold. In 1849 Norton arrived in San Francisco, California, with approximately $40,000, a significant sum at the time. He invested in real estate and commodities, supplying the thousands attracted by the gold rush, and amassed a fortune of a quarter of a million dollars within four years.

Respected in the community for his acumen and integrity, Norton was a member of San Francisco's Vigilance Committee, albeit perhaps reluctantly: this powerful group of citizens exacted their own brand of justice in the somewhat lawless young city in the early 1850s. Norton protested that the accused ought to be allowed due process of law, not lynched outright. He was a charter member of Occidental Masonic Lodge No. 22 in 1852, and was also among the prominent businesspeople of San Francisco who petitioned Congress for the establishment of a local branch of the U.S. Mint.

In 1852 Norton built the first rice mill on the Pacific Coast. He then attempted to corner the 1852–1853 rice market, buying up the available South American rice. However, the market was glutted by the arrival of several delayed shipments of rice from Asia. Norton then lost a series of lawsuits involving former partners and importers. His real estate went to satisfy creditors, including the banker William Tecumseh Sherman, later a general in the Union army. Norton declared bankruptcy in 1856. He continued to advertise goods on commission in a small way, and his lodgings became less prestigious over time.

Norton later claimed that an act of the California legislature in 1853 had conferred on him the title of emperor of California, although no such legislation is on record. Norton's dissatisfaction with the republic form of government and a humorous advocation of himself as absolute monarch apparently evolved from irony to chronic delusion. Biographers and others differ on the diagnosis and origin of Norton's mental state, from eccentricity to paranoid schizophrenia, from seeds sown in his parents' partisanship for the Bourbon line of French royalty to the societal madness and subsequent financial collapses of gold rush era California.

On 17 September 1859, in a proclamation published in the *San Francisco Bulletin*, Norton declared himself emperor of the United States and ordered an assembly of states' representatives "to make such alterations in the existing laws of the Union as may ame-liorate the evils under which the country is laboring, and thereby cause confidence to exist, both at home and abroad, in our stability and integrity." No such assembly took place; however, the self-styled Norton I continued to issue edicts for more than twenty years. Objecting to the "abuse" of "universal suffrage," he abolished Congress (12 October 1859). Concerned over the rebellion at Harpers Ferry, he gave notice that "order and the rights of property" should be maintained. Upon John Brown's execution, he discharged Governor Henry Wise of Virginia, appointing John C. Breckinridge of Kentucky in his place (28 December 1859).

On 26 July 1860, in response to the turmoil caused by Abraham Lincoln's presidential nomination and the southern states' threats of secession, the emperor dissolved the Republic of the United States and established an absolute monarchy, believing that this might better advance the "Peace, Prosperity and Happiness" of the people. However, he further directed that order be maintained by "persons in authority" through the enforcement of existing laws and regulations. In 1862 Norton assumed the additional title protector of Mexico upon that country's invasion by Louis Napoleon.

The empire was financed from an early stage in part by the issuance of scrip, usually fifty-cent bonds, to mature in 1880. San Francisco at this period abounded with eccentric characters, whom the citizenry tolerated and appreciated. In addition, completion of the transcontinental railroad in 1869 opened the area to easy access from the East, and the emperor became a noted attraction to the newly arrived tourists. Proclamations purporting to be those of Emperor Norton, but more slapdash in style and less visionary in subject, appeared in rival newspapers.

Temperate and gentlemanly, Norton I patrolled the city streets to ensure that sidewalks were clear, that the police were on duty, and in general that all city ordinances were enforced. He attended church regularly, visiting all denominations so as not to show favoritism. He was a member of the Mechanics Institute and proposed safety modifications for a railroad switch, although he could not afford the model required for a patent application.

Several of Norton's proclamations evidenced his shrewd business sense and a far-reaching vision, as when he advocated support for Frederick Marriott's powered airship (25 July 1869), which achieved a successful unmanned test flight but was destroyed before a planned manned flight could take place. On 23 March 1872 Norton decreed that a suspension bridge be built "as soon as convenient" between Oakland Point and Goat Island (now Yerba Buena Island), then on to San Francisco. The Bay Bridge was completed in 1936.

Norton's character figured in several contemporary plays and light operas popular as early as 1861 as well as in later novels by authors cognizant of his life and times. Notable among the novels were Robert Louis Stevenson's *The Wrecker* (1892), in which Emperor Norton appears as himself, and Mark Twain's *The Adventures of Huckleberry Finn* (1885), which metamorphosed Emperor Norton into the "King."

Norton died of apoplexy on a San Francisco street while on his way to a scientific lecture in the year his promissory notes came due. More than 10,000 mourners paid their respects when he was buried in the Masonic Cemetery.

• A few of Norton's letters are at the Bancroft Library, University of California, Berkeley, along with additional contemporary material. Other papers are at the Museum of the City of San Francisco, the San Francisco Public Library, and the California State Library. William Drury, *Norton I: Emperor of the United States* (1986), posits Norton as schizophrenic. Allen Stanley Lane, *Emperor Norton: Mad Monarch of America* (1939), includes text for many Norton proclamations, both real and putative, not included in Drury. Robert Ernest Cowan, Anne Bancroft, and Addie L. Ballou, *The Forgotten Characters of Old San Francisco, Including the Famous Bummer & Lazarus and Emperor Norton* (1964), collects several contemporary recollections and a gallery of portraits. A short discussion of Norton's probable sanity is in David Weeks and Jamie James, *Eccentrics: A Study of Sanity and Strangeness* (1995). Obituaries are in the *San Francisco Chronicle*, 9 Jan. 1880; the *San Francisco Morning Call*, 9 Jan. 1880; and the *New York Times*, 10 Jan. 1880.

CAROLINE M. FANNIN

NUGENT, Richard Bruce (2 July 1906–27 May 1987), artist and writer, was born in Washington, D.C., the son of Richard Henry Nugent, Jr., a Pullman porter and Capitol elevator operator, and Pauline Minerva Bruce Nugent. Although his mother's family was prominent among Washington's African-American elite, the Nugents were of modest means. A precocious child, Nugent read widely in his father's larger-than-average library. He was only thirteen years old and already attending Washington's renowned Dunbar High School when his father died of "galloping consumption." Shortly thereafter his mother moved to New York City, where she secured employment as a waitress and maid. Nugent and his brother Gary Lambert "Pete" Nugent remained with relatives in Washington for a few months, then joined their mother in New York. Bruce Nugent secured employment as a delivery boy and later as a bellhop. His job as an errand boy and art apprentice at the catalog house of Stone, Van Dresser and Company was the beginning of his career in the arts. His brother Pete, who learned tap dancing on the streets, dropped out of school to dance professionally. During the 1930s Pete Nugent's group "Pete, Peaches and Duke" was America's top "class act," performing in a characteristically elegant, precise, and graceful style.

Bruce Nugent pursued both art and artists. He took classes at the New York School of Industrial Arts and at Traphagen School of Fashion and insinuated himself into the most outrageously bohemian circles of Greenwich Village. When he announced to his mother that he would now devote himself to art rather than gainful employment, she responded by refusing to support him and sent him back to Washington to stay with his grandmother. There Nugent attended the weekly salon of Georgia Douglas Johnson, a poet whose "evenings" were the center of African-American Washington's intellectual life. At Johnson's he met Langston Hughes and became reacquainted with the Howard University philosophy professor Alain Locke, whose mother had been a close friend of Nugent's grandmother. The first African-American Rhodes Scholar and a Harvard Ph.D., Locke was a leading sponsor of the New Negro movement. He took a personal interest in young Nugent and published Nugent's "Sahdji," a short, ironic tale of male bonding and jungle lust, in his landmark anthology *The New Negro* (1925).

In August 1925 Nugent accompanied Hughes to a National Association for the Advancement of Colored People (NAACP) banquet in New York, where Hughes was to receive an award. Hughes introduced Nugent to the central figures of what came to be known as the Harlem Renaissance, an upsurge of African-American cultural activity centered in Harlem that began after World War I and lasted well into the 1930s. Late in 1925 Nugent moved to New York and plunged enthusiastically into the Harlem scene, joining Jean Toomer's Gurdjieff group and moving in with Wallace Thurman, a writer and an editor of the *Messenger*. Soon Nugent's art was published in *Opportunity*, the monthly magazine of the National Urban League, and in March 1926 an art deco Nugent drawing graced the cover. Other appearances in *Opportunity* followed. Nugent's art was highly stylized, oftern reflecting the influences of Aubrey Beardsley and Erté. Dance was one of his favorite themes. Silhouettes in brush and ink and line drawings executed in pen and ink or pencil were important segments of his oeuvre.

In the summer of 1926 Nugent joined with Hughes, Thurman, Aaron Douglas, Zora Neale Hurston, Gwendolyn Bennett, and John P. Davis to plan and publish *FIRE!!*, destined to become one of the most significant achievements of the Harlem Renaissance. Intended as the first issue of a "Negro arts quarterly," *FIRE!!* was a collective effort by the younger generation of Harlem intellectuals to break free of the restraints on style and content imposed by established (white) publishers and older race leaders. The first and only issue appeared in November 1926. Nugent's contributions to *FIRE!!* under the pseudonym Richard Bruce were two drawings and the modernist prose composition "Smoke, Lilies and Jade," discreetly characterized by Langston Hughes as "a green and purple story . . . in the Oscar Wilde tradition" (*The Big Sea*, 1940). Although *FIRE!!* contained some superb material, financial difficulties derailed the periodical.

A quintessential bohemian, often without a permanent residence, Nugent was a brilliant conversationalist who unabashedly acknowledged his erotic interest in men. He delighted in the consternation his appearance and demeanor created, as reflected in a comment by Carl Van Vechten in a letter to Hughes: "As I went out William Pickens [field secretary of the NAACP] caught my arm to ask me who 'the young man in evening clothes' was. It was Bruce Nugent, of course, with his usual open chest and uncovered ankles. I suppose soon he will be going without trousers" (*Letters of Carl Van Vechten*, 1987, pp. 95–96).

In 1927 Nugent and several of his Harlem contemporaries made their stage debuts in DuBose Heyward and Dorothy Heyward's *Porgy*, the precursor to the opera *Porgy and Bess*. Nugent remained in the production throughout its Broadway run and subsequent three years on tour through dozens of cities, including a six-week run in London. In 1933 Nugent appeared again on Broadway, this time as a dancer, in *Run Little Chillun,* a pageant play about the conflict between Christianity and Vodun ("voodoo") in a small southern town. In the late 1930s Nugent worked for the Federal Writers' Project composing vignettes of Harlem Renaissance personalities and researching the lives of New Yorkers of the Dutch colonial period. In the early 1940s he joined Wilson Williams's short-lived Negro Ballet Company.

Despite his unconcealed homosexuality, Nugent married Grace Marr, the sister of one of his associates in the Williams company, in 1952. Marr, a nurse educator, was for a time assistant executive secretary of the American Nurses Association with responsibility for intergroup relations in an era when the profession was still segregated. Her marriage to Nugent lasted until her death in 1969. They had no children.

In his middle and later years Nugent continued to write, draw, and paint, producing several unpublished novels and many artworks on paper and canvas. He supported himself with part-time jobs, occasional portrait commissions, and the kindness of friends. He remained involved in Harlem cultural affairs, serving on the board of the Harlem Cultural Council from the late 1960s through the 1970s. However, he did not pursue a conventional career as an artist or a writer partly because of his temperament and partly because the commercial potential of his unconventional subject matter was limited. He died in Hoboken, New Jersey, having outlived most of his Harlem Renaissance contemporaries.

To those contemporaries, encountering Nugent was one of the excitements of Harlem in the 1920s. For thirty years after the 1926 publication of "Smoke, Lilies, and Jade," Nugent remained the only African-American writer who expressed his homoerotic interests unambiguously both in conversation and in print. For example, in "Geisha Man," a novelette first published in *Gay Rebel of the Harlem Renaissance* but written in the 1920s, Nugent wrote: "I am a song: I would be sung on the tones of many bodies. On the graceful curve of that lad, his contours showing through his trousers as he sits on the bench, beauty rippling his sleeve as he moves his art. On that man—on the calves of his leg and the warm movement of his thigh suggested beneath his clothing. . . ."

Nugent refused to accept his "place" and, in defiance of cultural arbiters both black and white, insisted on participating in the avant-garde discourses of his time. When serious historical scholarship of the Harlem Renaissance began in the 1970s, Nugent, whose memory was astonishingly accurate and whose viewpoint was remarkably objective, became an increasingly important source of first-hand information about the era.

• Nugent's papers are held in the private collection of Thomas H. Wirth. The best single source of information about Nugent is *Gay Rebel of the Harlem Renaissance: Selections from the Work of Richard Bruce Nugent*, ed. Thomas H. Wirth, which contains Nugent's most important writings and visual art, including previously unpublished material, and an extended biographical introduction. Of Nugent's previously published writings, the most important are "Shadow," a poem in Countee Cullen's anthology *Caroling Dusk* (1927); the story "Sahdji," which was rewritten as a ballet and published in *Plays of Negro Life*, ed. Alain Locke and Montgomery Gregory (1927); "Smoke, Lilies and Jade," reprinted in David Levering Lewis, ed., *The Portable Harlem Renaissance Reader* (1995); and the story "Pope Pius the Only," *Challenge*, Spring 1937, pp. 15–18. Also significant are his "Bible stories." "Beyond Where the Star Stood Still" was published in *Crisis*, Dec. 1970, pp. 405–8; "The Now Discordant Song of Bells" was published in *Wooster Review*, Spring 1989, pp. 32–42. These and two other Bible stories are included in *Gay Rebel of the Harlem Renaissance*. Examples of Nugent's art in print include drawings on the endpapers of Steven Watson, *The Harlem Renaissance* (1995); "Drawings for Mulattoes" in *Ebony and Topaz*, ed. Charles S. Johnson (1927); a lynch victim in *Opportunity*, Jan. 1928, p. 13; several charming Harlem dancers in *Dance Magazine*, May 1928, pp. 23, 54; "Frankincense," the cover of *Crisis*, Dec. 1971; a striking illustration for "Smoke, Lilies and Jade" in *To Conserve a Legacy: American Art from Historically Black Colleges and Universities*, ed. Richard J. Powell and Jock Reynolds (1999); and twelve images in *Transition #89* (2001). In addition three articles about Nugent and his work are illustrated with examples of his art, Thomas H. Wirth, "Richard Bruce Nugent," *Black American Literature Forum*, Spring 1985, pp. 16–17; Michelle Y. Washington, "Souls on Fire," *Print*, May–June 1998, pp. 56–65; and Ellen McBreen, "Biblical Gender Bending in Harlem: The Queer Performance of Nugent's Salome," *Art Journal*, Fall 1998, pp. 22–28.

Published interviews with Nugent are in Camille Billops and James V. Hatch, *Artists and Influences* (1982); and Jeff Kisseloff, *You Must Remember This: An Oral History of Manhattan from the 1890s to World War II* (1989). Other articles about Nugent and his work include Eric Garber, "Richard Bruce Nugent," in *Dictionary of Literary Biography*, vol. 51, *Afro-American Writers of the Harlem Renaissance to 1940* (1987); Joseph Allen Boone, "Bruce Nugent, 'Smoke, Lilies and Jade': Harlem as a Homo State of Mind," in *Libidinal Currents: Sexuality and the Shaping of Modernism* (1998); Charles Michael Smith, "Bruce Nugent: Bohemian of the Harlem Renaissance," in *In the Life: A Black Gay Anthology*, ed. Joseph Beam (1986); and Seth Clark Silberman, "Lighting the Harlem Renaissance Afire!!: Embodying Richard Bruce Nugent's Bohemian Politic," in *The Greatest Taboo: Homosexuality in Black Communities*, ed. Delroy Constantine Simms (2001). An obituary is in the *Washington Post*, 3 June 1987.

THOMAS H. WIRTH

O

OCHOA, Severo (24 Sept. 1905–1 Nov. 1993), biochemist, was born in Luarca, a small village on the north coast of Spain, the son of Severo Manuel Ochoa, a lawyer and a businessman, and Carmen de Albornoz. When Ochoa was seven years old, his father died, but the family import-export business in Puerto Rico preserved income. The family moved to Málaga, a city on the south coast. There he attended primary, secondary, and high schools. In 1923 he entered the University of Madrid Medical School, where he hoped to study with Spanish neurohistologist and Nobel awardee Santiago Ramón y Cajal, but Cajal retired. During his second year, Ochoa met Juan Negrín, the chairman of the department of physiology and one of Spain's most distinguished physiologists. From his third year onward he became involved in research at Negrín's laboratory.

Ochoa made the transition from physiology to biochemistry when performing experiments on muscular contraction. In 1927 he went to the University of Glasgow to study with Noel Patton, in 1929 to Germany to the laboratory of the Nobelist physiologist Otto Meyerhof, and in 1932 to the National Institute for Medical Research in London. In 1931 he defended his Ph.D. thesis on the role of adrenal glands in muscular contraction. In 1931 he married Carmen García Cobián; they had no children.

In 1935 Ochoa was appointed head of the physiology section of the newly created Instituto de Investigaciones Médicas in Madrid. At the outbreak of the Spanish Civil War the following year, he left Spain to develop his scientific career. With the help of Negrín, at that time minister of the Republican government, he and his wife departed for Paris in September and then moved in October to Heidelberg, where Ochoa rejoined Meyerhof's laboratory. The physiological research carried out there was becoming biochemical: entire muscles had been replaced as subjects of study by muscle extracts and partial reactions of fermentation and metabolism of carbohydrates (sugars). In 1937 Meyerhof, a Jew, left Germany because of the Nazi regime. He helped Ochoa move to the Marine Biological Laboratory at Plymouth, England, the same year. Ochoa soon moved again to Oxford University, to work with Rudolf A. Peters, a distinguished British biochemist.

In 1940, at the beginning of World War II, Ochoa crossed the Atlantic to Mexico. With the support of the Rockefeller Foundation Refugees Program, he then went to Carl and Gerty Cori's laboratory at Washington University in St. Louis. In 1942 he moved to New York University as a research associate in medicine. Ochoa's work with distinguished physiologists and physiologist-biochemists, many of them Nobel prize awardees, and his own well-regarded work on oxidation of products of carbohydrate metabolism (the process through which the products of digestion are degraded to small molecules to produce energy for the organism) led him to be regarded as a promising biochemist in the United States. In 1946 he was appointed chair of the NYU department of pharmacology and ten years later chair of the department of biochemistry of the university's medical school. By this time he was already doing research on the enzymes of the cycle of citric acid, proposed by Hans Krebs, and on oxidative phosphorylation (the production of energy coupled with metabolic degradation of carbohydrates).

In 1959 Ochoa was awarded the Nobel Prize for Physiology or Medicine for his work on the synthesis of RNA (ribonucleic acid), based on research undertaken with his French postdoctoral student Marianne Grunberg-Manago. (The prize was shared with Arthur Kornberg in recognition of Kornberg's work on DNA synthesis.) In extracts of the oxidative bacteria *Azotobacter vinelandii*, Grunberg-Manago found a new enzyme, the polynucleotide phosphorylase (PNPase), which produces polymers very similar to RNA. In 1945 Oswald Avery's group at the Rockefeller Institute of Medical Research in New York established that nucleic acids were responsible for genetic heredity. In 1955, when Ochoa first published a paper on PNPase, it attracted the attention of the biological community because it suggested the possibility of synthesizing nucleic acids in the test tube. Although it soon turned out that polynucleotide phosphorylase was not involved in the biological synthesis of RNA, it became a useful tool in elucidating the genetic code (the triplets of DNA that codify the incorporation of each of the twenty amino acids to yield proteins).

In 1961 Marshall Nirenberg and Heinrich Mattaei at the National Institutes of Health in Bethesda, Maryland, presented their earliest results on this research on the genetic code at an International Congress of Biochemistry held in Moscow. Ochoa, using this enzyme and many other techniques available at that time, took part in the research on genetic decoding soon after. By the mid-1960s the work of the groups headed by Nirenberg, Ochoa, and the chemist H. Gabind Korana led to a complete list of the triplets that codify all the amino acids. From then on, Ochoa led his laboratory in research on protein synthesis and on the mechanisms of initiation and termination of the synthesis (how the composition of DNA includes in its structure "instructions" for initiating and finishing the synthesis of a given protein). Thus, by this time,

Ochoa was using the knowledge, techniques, and tools of molecular biology (a subfield of biology dedicated to the study of nucleic acids, DNA and RNA, and their mechanisms in life production and reproduction).

In the early 1970s plans for a new research center in Madrid were drawn up, to be named after Ochoa and with the hope that Ochoa would head it, but shifts in the makeup of Francisco Franco's cabinet and resulting changes in science policy delayed the center's development and reduced its budget. Ochoa never became its head, though he supported its work in other ways. In 1974 Ochoa retired from NYU and accepted a position at the Roche Institute of Molecular Biology in Nutley, New Jersey, where he continued his research on protein synthesis and replication of RNA viruses until 1985, when he returned to Spain. There Ochoa became very influential in the promotion of both biochemistry and molecular biology. He gave advice to Spanish science policy authorities and scientists, some of them trained as postdoctoral students in his own laboratory in New York and at the Roche Institute. Ochoa died in Madrid.

• Ochoa wrote a short autobiography, "The Pursuit of a Hobby," *Annual Review of Biochemistry* 49 (1980): 1–30. A *festschrift* volume in his honor was edited for his seventieth birthday by A. Kornberg, B. L. Horecker, L. Cornudella, and J. Oró, *Reflections on Biochemistry* (1976), to which many former fellows, colleagues, and friends contributed and which includes a biography by his Spanish colleagues F. Grande and C. Asensio. Ochoa's influence in Spain is detailed in M. J. Santesmases, "Severo Ochoa and the Biomedical Sciences under Franco," *Isis* 91 (2000): 706–34. Reminiscences by Marianne Grunberg-Manago in *Biographical Memoirs of the Fellows of the Royal Society, London* 43 (1997): 349–65 and by Arthur Kornberg in *Proceedings of the American Philosophical Society* 141 (1997): 478–92 are useful recollections of his life and research. An obituary is in the *New York Times,* 3 Nov. 1993.

MARíA JESúS SANTESMASES

O'CONNOR, Carroll (2 Aug. 1924–21 June 2001), actor, was born John Carroll O'Connor in New York City, the son of Edward Joseph O'Connor, a lawyer and businessman, and Elise Patricia O'Connor (maiden name also O'Connor), a teacher and real estate agent. O'Connor's family was prominent in the New York Irish-American community; his maternal grandfather was owner and editor of the *Irish Advocate*, a weekly newspaper. O'Connor spent his first four years in the Bronx, then the family moved to Queens, first to the Elmhurst section and later to the then-affluent Forest Hills area. Though he exhibited superior verbal skills as a child and grew up in a family that exposed him to high culture, O'Connor, who was known by his middle name, was a mediocre and unmotivated student at local public schools.

After graduating from high school in 1941, O'Connor attended Wake Forest University in Winston-Salem, North Carolina, for a year, then worked for a short time as a copyboy for the *New York Times.*

In 1942 he enrolled at the U.S. Merchant Marine Academy at King's Point, Long Island, but he was expelled after a few months for poor performance. For the next three years he worked as a merchant seaman on cargo ships, including some in armored convoys carrying wartime military supplies across the Atlantic. In the autumn of 1946 he returned to New York, where he took a job at his grandfather's newspaper and eventually served a short stint as its editor.

In 1948, after visiting a friend in Montana, O'Connor enrolled at the University of Montana, majoring in journalism. He gave his first performances as a actor with the university's drama club, the Masquers. In 1950, after visiting relatives in Dublin, he transferred to University College, Dublin. In 1951 he married Nancy Fields, who had been a fellow student at the University of Montana. The couple adopted one child.

O'Connor's appearance in a University College student production of T. S. Eliot's *The Cocktail Party* attracted the notice of the producer Shelagh Richards, who offered him a small part in a professional production of Kate O'Brien's *That Lady* at Dublin's Gaiety Theatre. In the summer of 1951 O'Connor was a member of an acting company organized by Richards that performed several plays at the Edinburgh Festival. Soon afterward he participated in a live television production of one of those plays, Lennox Robinson's *The Whiteheaded Boy*, for the BBC in London. In 1952 O'Connor received a bachelor's degree in history from University College, and he stayed in Dublin for two more years. He appeared in productions at the Gate Theatre and toured Ireland with a theater troupe organized by the actor Cyril Cusack.

In 1954 O'Connor returned to New York and looked for work in the theater while supporting himself as a substitute English teacher in the New York City public schools. Unable to find any significant acting jobs, he began to question the wisdom of pursuing an acting career. He spent the 1955–1956 academic year at the University of Montana, earning a master's degree in English and working as a faculty teaching assistant.

O'Connor returned to New York to teach in the public schools while he attempted to establish himself in the theater. His big break came in 1958, when he was cast as Buck Mulligan in an off-Broadway staging of *Ulysses in Nighttown*, a dramatization of a section of James Joyce's novel *Ulysses*. Directed by Burgess Meredith and starring Zero Mostel as Leopold Bloom, the well-received production ran for five months at the Rooftop Theatre. In 1959 O'Connor, who was of medium height with a stout frame and prematurely gray hair that made him seem older than he was, again played Buck Mulligan when the play toured several European cities. Later in 1959 O'Connor appeared as an oafish Hollywood producer in an off-Broadway production of Clifford Odets's drama *The Big Knife*. O'Connor's off-Broadway work led to his signing with a talent agency. In 1960 he made his first major American television appearance as a prosecutor in *The Sacco-Vanzetti Story*, a New York–produced NBC dramatic special directed by Sidney Lumet. O'Connor made his screen debut in the small role of a fire department chief in *Parrish* (1961), a poorly received melodrama about love affairs on a tobacco farm. Filmed in Connecticut, it starred Claudette Colbert and Troy Donahue.

In the early 1960s O'Connor moved to Los Angeles and spent the next decade as a steadily employed character actor in television and films. His film roles included a truck driver in *Lonely Are the Brave* (1962), a psychologically oriented western starring Kirk Douglas; the assassin Casca in *Cleopatra* (1963), a big-budget spectacle with Elizabeth Taylor in the title role and Richard Burton as Mark Antony; a blustering naval commander in *In Harm's Way* (1965), a World War II drama directed by Otto Preminger with Henry Fonda and John Wayne heading an all-star cast; a hard-nosed army general in *What Did You Do in the War, Daddy?* (1966), a World War II comedy directed by Blake Edwards and starring James Coburn; a gangster in *Point Blank* (1967), a murder mystery starring Lee Marvin and Angie Dickinson directed by John Boorman; a suburban father in *For Love of Ivy* (1968), a romantic comedy directed by Daniel Mann with Sidney Poitier and Abbey Lincoln; and a police detective in *Marlowe* (1969), a mystery directed by Paul Bogart and starring James Garner. On television O'Connor made frequent guest appearances on various series, including *The Outer Limits*, *The Time Tunnel*, *Voyage to the Bottom of the Sea*, *The Untouchables*, and *The Man from U.N.C.L.E.*

O'Connor moved from relatively obscure character actor to household name with his portrayal of the loudmouthed working-class bigot Archie Bunker in the television comedy series *All in the Family*. Modeled on the successful British series *Till Death Do Us Part*, the program's frank treatment of controversial subjects, such as racism, sexuality, death, and women's rights, went far beyond anything previously seen on American television. O'Connor's fellow cast members included Jean Stapleton as Archie's dim-witted yet lovable wife, Sally Struthers as his defiant daughter, and Rob Reiner as his politically liberal son-in-law and chief nemesis. The characters lived together in a cramped house in a blue-collar New York neighborhood.

Debuting with little ballyhoo as a midseason replacement program on CBS in January 1971, *All in the Family* immediately drew the attention of television viewers and critics. By the fall of 1971 it was the most-watched television show in the United States, and it remained at the top of the ratings for the next five years. O'Connor's portrayal of Archie Bunker was often cited as a reason for the success of the controversial program. "There have been scenes on *All in the Family* equal to the best that commercial television has had to offer, most of them due to the skill of Carroll O'Connor. . . . [W]ith his mastery of every inflection, every lift of the eyebrow, of a certain lower-middle-class type, O'Connor succeeds [in making] details

prevail over stereotype and caricature," wrote Dorothy Rabinowitz in *Commentary* (Rabinowitz, p. 70). The popularity of *All in the Family* ushered in a new era of television comedy that permitted more adult-oriented subject matter.

In the autumn of 1979, in response to declining popularity and the resignations of cast members, the program was revamped into *Archie Bunker's Place*, with O'Connor portraying Archie as a widower operating a local tavern. The show ceased production in 1983. O'Connor's portrayal of Archie Bunker earned him the Emmy Award for Outstanding Lead Actor in a Comedy Series in 1972, 1977, 1978, and 1979.

Acclaim as Archie Bunker led to O'Connor starring in special television productions, including an adaptation of George Gershwin and Ira Gershwin's political satire musical *Of Thee I Sing* in 1972 and a 1977 small-screen version of the Edwin O'Connor novel *The Last Hurrah*, about a politician in the twilight of his career. He costarred with Ernest Borgnine in the feature film *Law and Disorder* (1974), directed by Ivan Passer, a lackluster comedic drama about frustrated citizens who form their own police force.

In 1983, with his run as Archie Bunker over, O'Connor made his Broadway debut as the patriarch of a troubled family in *Brothers*, a drama by George Sibbald. O'Connor also directed the play, which closed after a single performance. In 1985 O'Connor made another Broadway appearance, playing the father of a Vietnam veteran struggling to readjust to civilian life in James Duff's drama *Home Front*. The play ran for thirteen performances.

In 1988 O'Connor returned to series television in the drama *In the Heat of the Night*, playing Sheriff Bill Gillespie, a gruff, middle-aged, white police chief reluctantly joining forces with a young black chief of detectives, played by Howard Rollins, to fight crime in a Mississippi town. The program was based on a popular 1967 film of the same name starring Rod Steiger and Sidney Poitier. The hour-long show ran for four seasons on NBC, then moved to CBS for two more seasons. In 1989 O'Connor won the Emmy Award for Outstanding Lead Actor in a Drama Series for *In the Heat of the Night*.

Soft-spoken, erudite, and serious-minded, O'Connor was well versed in literature and history. He enjoyed reading, traveling, and visiting friends in the international film and theater worlds. The 1995 suicide of his son, who had for years battled drug addiction and alcoholism, led O'Connor to become a passionate antidrug spokesman. He advocated for the passage of California state laws to make suppliers of illicit drugs liable in drug-related deaths.

Suffering from diabetes, heart disease, and other ailments, O'Connor worked only sporadically during the last few years of his life. He made guest appearances on various television series, including *Mad about You* and *Party of Five*, and delivered his final screen performance in the romantic comedy *Return to Me* (2000), playing the Irish grandfather of the film's star, Minnie Driver. O'Connor died in Los Angeles.

• O'Connor's autobiography, *I Think I'm Outta Here* (1998), is a relatively frank and detailed life story that displays his wide-ranging knowledge and thoughtful if somewhat humorless personality. Interviews with O'Connor are Richard Warren Lewis, "A Candid Conversation with Archbigot Archie Bunker's Better Half," *Playboy*, Jan. 1973, pp. 61–74, 205; Mike Wallace, "Carroll O'Connor Answers the Tough Questions about Archie Bunker," *Good Housekeeping*, Oct. 1974, pp. 86, 200–207; and Leslie Bennetts, "Can Carroll O'Connor Shake Off Archie Bunker?," *New York Times*, 6 Nov. 1983, sec. 2, pp. 1, 4. Dorothy Rabinowitz, "Watching the Sit-Coms," *Commentary*, Oct. 1975, pp. 69–71, is a detailed critique of O'Connor's portrayal of Archie Bunker. Richard Adler, ed., *"All in the Family": A Critical Appraisal* (1979), and Donna McCrohan, *Archie & Edith, Mike & Gloria* (1987), discuss O'Connor's work on *All in the Family*. An obituary is in the *New York Times*, 22 June 2001, p. B8.

MARY C. KALFATOVIC

O'CONOR, John F. X. (1 Aug. 1852–31 Jan. 1920), clergyman, writer, and educator, was born John Francis Xavier O'Conor in New York City, the son of Daniel O'Conor, a builder, and Jane Lake O'Conor. Educated in New York City, he excelled in philosophy and in 1872 won the medal for the natural sciences at St. Francis Xavier College. He graduated with a B.A. that year. On 9 October 1872 he entered the Society of Jesus at Sault au Récollet, Canada. He continued his literary studies at the Jesuit house of studies in Roehampton, England (1874–1876), and pursued philosophy in the Jesuit College at the University of Louvain, Belgium (1876–1879). He began his academic career teaching classical and modern rhetoric and oratory at Manresa, West Park, New York (1879–1881), classical and Anglo-American poetry at Georgetown University, Washington, D.C. (1881–1883), and French at Boston College, Boston, Massachusetts (1883–1884). During his theological studies at Woodstock College, Woodstock, Maryland, he was ordained a Roman Catholic priest by Archbishop (later Cardinal) James Gibbons on 29 August 1885. O'Conor returned to Xavier College in 1888 as a professor and administrator, and with an inheritance he received, he initiated the construction of the college auditorium. He spent a year concentrating on ascetical theology in Frederick, Maryland, then professed his solemn Jesuit vows on 2 February 1891.

O'Conor learned Latin, Greek, French, and Flemish during his early studies and subsequently acquired a knowledge of German, Italian, Portuguese, and some Slavic languages. A protégé of Johann N. Strassmaier, S.J. (1846–1920), the eminent scholar of ancient Middle Eastern antiquities, who introduced him to the ancient inscriptions in the British Museum, O'Conor became interested in Hebrew, Sanskrit, Arabic, Syrian, and Ethopic. Classes he took at Harvard University and Johns Hopkins University in the cuneiform alphabet and ancient languages enabled him to decipher the Cylinder of Nebuchadnezzar II (d. 562 B.C.). In 1885 his translation was exhibited with the cylinder and published in the *New York Herald* and

in a triple-text edition. The *Cuneiform Text of a Recently Discovered Cylinder of Nebuchadnezzar King of Babylon from the Original in the Metropolitan Museum of Art* praises God for Nebuchadnezzar's construction and preservation of temples, especially his restoration of the Temple of the Sun at Sippara. The inscriptions presented in O'Conor's "An Arabic Coin" (*Hebraica* 5 [Jan.–Apr. 1889]: 200–202) are the familiar call to prayer, praise of Mohammed, and notations that the coin was struck in A.D. 827 in the caliphate (A.D. 813–33) of Abdalla, the son of Haround al Rachid of *Arabian Nights* fame; Abdalla also built and preserved temples. In 1900 some of the faculty of Xavier College collaborated with O'Conor on the first English translation of the Latin *Autobiography of St. Ignatius Loyola*, reflections on the interior life of the Spanish courtier, soldier, and mystic who founded the Society of Jesus.

An effective teacher, lecturer, and preacher, O'Conor spent fourteen years intermittently at Xavier College between 1888 and 1918. He also became headmaster at Gonzaga College in Washington, D.C. (1902–1903), and taught at St. Joseph's College (later University) in Philadelphia (1903–1906). As founding president of Brooklyn College in New York (1908–1911), he was responsible for fundraising, construction, building the library collection, and recruiting students. The collegiate divisions of Xavier and Brooklyn Colleges were consolidated into Fordham University's program, and Brooklyn College was later renamed Brooklyn Preparatory School; the institution closed in 1972. O'Conor lectured on art, theater, music, and education. Several of his lectures appeared in print, among them *Education in the City Schools of New York,* delivered before the Quid Nunc Club on 16 March 1900 and stressing the value of moral and religious instruction. He was an assistant pastor at the churches of St. Francis Xavier (1898–1802, 1913–1914) and St. Ignatius Loyola (1907–1908, 1914–1915, 1918–1920) in New York City and at Old St. Joseph's Church in Philadelphia (1906–1907), and he served as chaplain at the Georgetown University Hospital (1915–1917).

O'Conor's contributions to St. Joseph's College (later University) during his three years as professor of philosophy and literature (1903–1906) give a sense of his energy and determination. The institution had focused on secondary education since its founding in 1851 but was developing its college curriculum, and O'Conor was instrumental in improving the library. While there he published the sixth edition of his *Reading and the Mind: With Something to Read* (1903), which reflects the emerging place of contemporary English and American authors in the Latin school curriculum weighted toward the Greek and Roman classics. The appended lists propose a wide selection of British and American authors and titles for primary, secondary, and college classes. In 1903 O'Conor designed the college shield and founded the professional men's sodality of Philadelphia. Within a year the membership numbered over 120 graduates of area colleges and members of the learned professions. His

Dante, a Drama (1904) involved some 150 members of the Dramatic Society and was "written in collaboration with the Dante class." O'Conor told a reporter from the *New York Herald* (3 May 1904) that it was produced "with the object of counteracting the impression" made by Sir Henry Irving's presentation of Dante as profligate and irreverent in the play by Victorien Sardou (1831–1908). The *North American* and three Philadelphia papers, the *Inquirer*, the *Public Ledger*, and the *Record*, reviewed O'Conor's production on 2 May 1904. He facilitated the publication of *The Tragedy That Wins, and Other Short Stories* (1905) by "juniors and seniors of the English class," the forerunner of the college literary magazine.

In addition to his steady stream of scholarly and popular articles, O'Conor's numerous books and pamphlets include translations from cuneiform, Latin, and Italian as well as books concerned with travel, biography, education, religion, and literary criticism. His most admired literary work, *Facts about Bookworms* (1898), published in London and then in New York in a limited, numbered edition, was well received by critics at home and abroad and explains his passion for libraries. His "Cardinal Newman as a Literary Study" in *Donahue's Magazine* (June 1882) initiated a brief correspondence with the cardinal. *A Study of Francis Thompson's Hound of Heaven*, an explication of one of the most popular religious poems of the day, was repeatedly reprinted between 1912 and 1929. O'Conor directed productions of his plays and operettas, for which he composed the music. His most popular mystery play, *Everysoul* (*"Everysoul" and the Land of the Sunrise Sea*, 1913) was staged throughout the United States, and *The Mystery of Life* (1919), his last musical, was produced in New York and starred his friends and acquaintances, "well-known Broadway favorites" (*Catholic News*, Feb. 1920).

O'Conor put into practice the conviction that faculty and students should be colleagues in research and publication. He was known for his ability to recognize opportunities and for his expeditious completion of projects that improved the resources, enriched the curricula, and extended the influence of several colleges and universities. Drawing on his familiarity with the holdings of some of the best libraries in the United States and abroad and consulting with a number of librarians, he improved the collections at Boston College, Georgetown University, Xavier College, and St. Joseph's University. His authority as a scholar in ancient Middle Eastern languages and history is attested by the fact that his publication of the Nebuchadnezzar inscription, the first of its kind in the United States, remains normative.

• The surviving documents concerning O'Conor are in the archives of the institutions he served and in the records of the New York Province and the Maryland Province of the Society of Jesus at Georgetown University (see "Special Collections at Georgetown: A Brief History" at http://gu-lib.lausun.georgetown.edu/dept/speccoll/libhist.htm). *The Letters and Diaries of John Henry Newman*, vol. 30 (1976),

Stephen Dessain and Thomas Gornall, eds., contains two letters from O'Conor. A partial bibliography fills a page and a half in *The National Union Catalog Pre-1956 Imprints* (1976), vol. 426. O'Conor's articles in *Woodstock Letters* include "Three Letters from Cardinal Newman" (20, no. 1 [1891]: 3–5) and "The Jesuit Missions in the United States" (23, no. 1 [1894]: 1–22). Obituaries are in the *New York Times*, 1 Feb. 1920; the *Catholic News*, Feb. 1920; and *Woodstock Letters* 49, no. 3 (Oct. 1920): 351–53.

FRANCIS F. BURCH

O'DWYER, Paul (29 June 1907–23 June 1998), attorney and politician, was born Peter Paul O'Dwyer in Bohola, County Mayo, Ireland, the son of Patrick O'Dwyer and Bridget McNicholas O'Dwyer. Both parents were schoolteachers. Greatly influenced by the struggles of Irish Republicans for independence from Great Britain during his childhood, O'Dwyer graduated from nearby St. Nathys College in 1924 and then attended Dublin University for six months before immigrating to the United States.

On arriving in New York in 1925, O'Dwyer dropped his first name and also met his brother William O'Dwyer—seventeen years his senior and later mayor of New York City—who had come to the United States to study for the priesthood and had instead turned to the law. Inspired by his example, the younger O'Dwyer enrolled in night school at Fordham University and worked as a laborer during the day. After transferring to St. John's University he graduated in 1929 with an LL.D. and received special permission to take the bar exam (he was not yet a U.S. citizen) from Benjamin Nathan Cardozo, then the chief judge of the New York Court of Appeals.

After obtaining both his citizenship and state bar membership in March 1931, O'Dwyer was unable to gain employment as an attorney. Following a brief stint in the merchant marine, he became a clerk in the office of Oscar Bernstien, who introduced him to luminaries such as John L. Lewis, Dorothy Parker, and Lillian Hellman. O'Dwyer eventually became a partner in the firm, known as O'Dwyer & Bernstien, while representing a variety of clients, including a number of labor unions. He married Kathleen Rohan on 19 August 1935; the couple had four children.

In 1946 O'Dwyer—ever sympathetic to the plight of the underdog—became involved in the Zionist movement. He served as chairman of the Lawyers Committee for Justice in Palestine until 1947 and also argued before the United Nations for the establishment of the state of Israel. He also raised funds for the Irgun Zvai Leumi (a militant Jewish organization then operating against the British in Palestine), traveled to Europe to facilitate illegal emigration to the Holy Land, and on at least one occasion took part in a gun-running operation himself. This experience undoubtedly proved helpful in 1948, when O'Dwyer successfully obtained the dismissal of a case against Joseph Untermeyer and a coconspirator when the two were charged with violating New York's Sullivan law while attempting to ship arms to Israel.

Convinced that "politics is the only machinery around on which you can really straighten things out," O'Dwyer ran for Congress as a Democrat in 1948 and suffered the first of what would prove to be a string of electoral defeats, this time against incumbent congressman Jacob Javits. During the 1950s he continued to build his legal practice—adding show business personalities such as Suzy Parker and Ethel Merman to his client list—and remained politically active, joining with Eleanor Roosevelt and former governor Herbert Lehman in 1958 to form the Committee for Democratic Voters, a Democratic Party reform group. In 1960 he cochaired the New York Citizens Committee for Kennedy and Johnson and then was rebuffed in his attempt to become the Democrats' Senate candidate in 1962. In 1963 O'Dwyer won a seat (representing Manhattan at large) on the New York City Council, where he pushed through an increase in city workers' minimum wage to $1.50 an hour in the face of strong opposition.

O'Dwyer added civil rights to his agenda in the 1960s, often serving as a volunteer defense attorney for little or no compensation on behalf of civil rights workers in the South. In 1964 he served as a delegate to the Democratic National Convention, where he was a leader in the fight to obtain credentials for the predominantly African-American Freedom Democratic Party from Mississippi. In 1965 he resigned from the City Council only to suffer a crushing defeat in the Democratic mayoral primary. Undaunted, in 1966 he managed Percy Sutton's winning campaign for the borough presidency of Manhattan and also argued successfully before the United States Supreme Court that Puerto Rican citizens should be allowed to take voting literacy tests in Spanish. In 1968 O'Dwyer formed the Coalition for a Democratic Alternative, a group of maverick antiwar Democrats that supported Senator Eugene McCarthy in his attempts to oust incumbent President Lyndon Johnson. O'Dwyer also won an upset victory in that year's Democratic Senatorial primary, only to lose badly in the fall election to incumbent Javits.

In 1972 O'Dwyer defended Father Philip Berrigan and the Harrisburg Eight, who faced charges of an antigovernment plot during the Richard Nixon administration. After a mistrial, the charges were dismissed. In 1973 he won his final elective office—president of the New York City Council—and during his four-year term successfully changed the official date of New York City's founding from 1664 (the date the English took over) to 1625 (when the Dutch founded the settlement). He also took a leading role in establishing the city's Department of Archives. Defeated by Carol Bellamy in his reelection attempt in 1977, O'Dwyer remained active in politics. After the death of his first wife in 1980, O'Dwyer married Patricia Hanrahan in 1984. In addition to working as the national coordinator for the American League for an Undivided Ireland, he served as the city's commissioner for the United Nations under Mayor David Dinkins (who credited O'Dwyer with salvaging Dink-

ins's political career). He resigned his post in order to criticize several member nations for their human rights violations. O'Dwyer died at his home in Goshen, New York.

Although less well known than his older brother, Paul O'Dwyer avoided the ethical challenges that ultimately destroyed his sibling's career. Although his belief that "the ideals should always come first" often placed him outside mainstream politics and cost him elections, he lived to see many of the ideals that he fought for come to fruition.

• O'Dwyer's papers have not been located. His autobiography, *Counsel for the Defense*, was published in 1979, and he is also the subject of a lengthy entry in *Current Biography* (1969) that covers his career through the end of the 1960s. An obituary is in the *New York Times*, 25 June 1998, and he was also the subject of a retrospective article in *Newsday* (New York), 30 June 1998.

EDWARD L. LACH, JR.

ORMANDY, Eugene (18 Nov. 1899–12 Mar. 1985), conductor, was born Jenö Blau in Budapest, Hungary, the son of Jewish parents. His father was Benjamin Blau, a dentist and amateur violinist; his mother was Rosalie Blau (her maiden name is not known with certainty, but in several accounts she is referred to as Rosalie Ormandy Blau). Named after the Hungarian violin virtuoso Jenö Hubay, the young prodigy showed musical talent at age two and seemed predestined to become a concert violinist. At the age of three, he received his first violin, which his father made sure he practiced. By age five, he was enrolled in the Royal State Academy of Music in Budapest; he studied the violin under Hubay from the age of nine. His other professors included composers Béla Bartók and Zoltán Kodály. When he was almost fourteen, he received his diploma as the youngest graduate ever of the Royal Academy. At seventeen, he accepted a teaching position at the Academy while studying at the University of Budapest. He graduated at age twenty with a degree in philosophy.

In 1917 Jenö toured Hungary and Germany as a soloist with the Blüthner Orchestra and in 1920 toured France and Austria playing solo recitals. Setting his sights on concertizing in America, he arrived in New York in 1921 only to find that the series of concerts promised him never materialized. It was at this time that he Americanized his first name to Eugene, having changed his last name to Ormandy while touring Europe. With only about $20 in his pocket, Ormandy auditioned for a violinist's chair with an orchestra that played for silent movies at the Capitol Theater in New York. Within a week, he went from last chair to concertmaster.

In 1922 Ormandy married harpist Stephanie Goldner; they divorced in 1947. In 1926 he became an American citizen—exactly five years and ninety days after his arrival, the minimum waiting time. His love for America was instant and lasting; he once remarked in an interview that he "was born in New York City at the age of twenty-two."

It was at the Capitol Theatre that Ormandy revealed a talent for conducting when he filled in at the last minute for the regular conductor who was ill. Finding himself a better conductor than violinist, and desiring the additional $25 that came with the job, Ormandy chose to become the orchestra's conductor. This decision would change the course of his life. His conducting career took off after famed impresario Arthur Judson attended a dance recital at the Capitol and became enthralled with Ormandy's vigorous conducting. Under Judson's management, Ormandy became a conductor with the CBS radio network. In 1931 he began his association with the Philadelphia Orchestra after Judson booked him as a last-minute replacement for Arturo Toscanini, who was incapacitated by bursitis. To the audience's surprise, the unknown conductor more than filled the legendary Italian's shoes. This exposure led to an invitation to conduct the Minneapolis Symphony Orchestra in 1931, replacing the ailing Henri Verbrugghen.

After five years of making the Minneapolis into an orchestra of international repute, and numerous recordings for RCA Victor, in 1936 Ormandy left Minneapolis to become the Philadelphia Orchestra's associate conductor. In 1938 he succeeded Leopold Stokowski as musical director of the Philadelphia Orchestra. Stokowski and Ormandy were polar opposites. Flamboyant, good looking, and fervently partisan toward "new music," Stokowski would chide audiences, as some walked out in the middle of a concert, on the importance of being open-minded. Ormandy, on the other hand, was short of stature and quiet-tempered, approaching the role of music director as an accommodating "organization" man. In an era when conductors such as Stokowski, the brooding Serge Koussevitzky, and the fiery Arturo Toscanini were promoted as almost godlike "maestros," Ormandy must have seemed an anachronism.

The transition from Stokowski to Ormandy, however, which ended in 1941 after the last of Stokowski's guest appearances, was uncharacteristically smooth and amicable. Under Stokowski, the orchestra was famed for its "Philadelphia sound," which was characterized by clarity of phrasing, skillful execution, and warm sonorities. Ormandy, who was actually quite honored to have such an unrivaled ensemble placed in his hands, sought to preserve Stokowski's unique sound. The changes he made were implemented gradually, placing tonal emphasis on the orchestra's peerless string section. He also reintroduced uniform bowing and conventional seating arrangements—in contrast to Stokowski's free bowing and experimental instrument placement—to bring a consistent sound to the orchestra. Another change he made was in programming less modern or experimental music. Stokowski had been a fervent champion of "new music" and often scheduled his programs along the lines of 50 percent established classical repertoire and 50 percent music by contemporary composers. Ever eager

to please the conservative Philadelphia audiences, Ormandy selected 75 percent of his programs from the established repertoire and only 25 percent from relatively new compositions.

Over the next four decades, Ormandy's name became synonymous with the Philadelphia Orchestra. He possessed perfect pitch and was able to memorize an orchestral score overnight. The orchestra became his musical voice, characterized by a Romantic conception of sound, emphasizing tonal color and instrumental balance rather than interpretation of the score. He readily admitted his debt to Toscanini in his quest for perfect sound: at the Capitol Theater, he had sneaked into the Italian maestro's rehearsals with the New York Philharmonic and studied his methods. Yet Ormandy's sound was uniquely his own. He commented, "My conducting is what it is because I was a violinist. Toscanini was always playing the cello, Koussevitzky the double-bass, Stokowski the organ. The conductors who were pianists nearly always have a sharper, more percussive beat, and it can be heard in their orchestras."

Like Toscanini, Ormandy put himself and the Philadelphia in the service of remaining true to the letter and spirit of the score. Composers such as Bartók, Dmitri Shostakovich, Jean Sibelius and Sergei Rachmaninoff regarded Ormandy's performances of their works as unparalled. In 1941 Rachmaninoff—whose association with the Philadelphia Orchestra began when Stokowski was musical director and who recorded his complete works for piano and orchestra with both Stokowski and Ormandy—made an announcement to Ormandy and the orchestra on the first day's rehearsal of his valedictory work, the *Symphonic Dances*: "Today when I think of composing, my thoughts turn to you, the greatest orchestra in the world. For that reason, I dedicated this, my newest composition, to the members of the Philadelphia Orchestra and to your conductor, Eugene Ormandy."

Carrying on Stokowski's tradition of broadcasting and recording, in 1948 the Ormandy/Philadelphia team performed the first televised symphonic concert on the CBS network, the American premiere of Rachmaninoff's rediscovered *First Symphony*, beating out Toscanini and the NBC Symphony's broadcast by ninety minutes. In 1950, Ormandy married his second wife, Margaret Frances "Gretel" Hitsch of Vienna, who remained with him until his death. They had no children.

Ormandy's accompaniment was regarded as without equal by virtuoso soloists who performed with the orchestra. Pianists such as Arthur Rubinstein, Vladimir Horowitz, and Robert Casadesus and violinists such as Isaac Stern, Joseph Szigeti, and David Oistrakh were put at ease by his sympathetic approach. On his ability to intuitively communicate with musicians, violinist Dylana Jenson remarked, "He was incredibly supportive. . . . The Philadelphia Orchestra had built up such a rapport with him after so many years, so he didn't have to do very much with his conducting to get the orchestra to totally respond to what he wanted—he got an immediate response."

Taking full advantage of the recording medium, Ormandy and the Philadelphia's most lasting legacy is the recordings they made for RCA Victor, from 1936 to 1942 and 1968 through 1980, and for Columbia Records, from 1944 through 1968. When Columbia introduced the inexpensive, long-playing record in 1948, the records introduced their performances to listeners around the world and brought them invitations to appear abroad, beginning with a tour of Great Britain in 1949.

Soon the Philadelphia became the world's most traveled orchestra. Yet, despite his self-assumed role as musical diplomat on behalf of the United States, he never forgot his European Jewish roots: in 1955, when the Vienna Philharmonic visited Philadelphia, Ormandy pointedly refused to shake the hand of conductor Herbert von Karajan, who had been a member of the Nazi party, apparently as a means of furthering his career in Hitler's Germany.

In 1960 Ormandy was instrumental in the return of Leopold Stokowski as guest conductor. If, as earlier, many critics claimed that the "Philadelphia sound" was entirely Stokowski's doing, by now Ormandy was secure enough in his own predominance to exclaim "The Philadelphia Sound—it's me." The 1960s also saw some discontent within the orchestra: labor strife over recording royalties and grueling recording and touring schedules had been building up since the late 1950s, and in 1966 the musicians' union put the orchestra on strike. Ormandy, as deferential as ever, stayed out of the way and went on a conducting tour of Europe. Stokowski, however, jumped into the fray and led a benefit concert at Carnegie Hall on behalf of the striking musicians. Once the grievances were resolved, Ormandy returned and in 1967 took the orchestra on their first tour of Japan. In 1970, President Richard Nixon presented the Presidential Medal of Freedom to Ormandy for his efforts in using music to spread American goodwill, and in 1973 Secretary of State Henry Kissinger arranged for Ormandy and the orchestra to tour Communist China in conjunction with Nixon's policy of openness with the Mao regime.

During the late 1970s, after hundreds of recordings and hundreds of thousands of miles on tour, Ormandy realized that he was slowing down. Suffering from a heart ailment, he cut back the number of concerts he performed and in 1980 named Italian conductor Riccardo Muti as his successor for music director. By the mid-1970s both Columbia's and RCA's classical catalogues were dominated by Ormandy's recordings. Ormandy continued to perform as Conductor Laureate, a position he held until his death, marking the longest unbroken association between a conductor and a major orchestra. His last concert was with the Philadelphia Orchestra at Carnegie Hall on 10 January 1984. He died in Philadelphia.

In his own lifetime, Eugene Ormandy was dismissed by some critics as "conservative," by others as "unimaginative" (Igor Stravinsky once quipped that Ormandy was an ideal interpreter of Strauss waltzes). Since his death, however, a reappraisal of his work has begun. In 1998, San Francisco music critic Stuart Canin rhetorically pondered, "The large question in Philadelphia these days is how to resurrect the Ormandy years without Eugene Ormandy. The Philadelphians, bellwether orchestra of the U.S. music scene for so many years and a non-stop recording machine which supplied turntables with music as far as the ear could hear, have lost their recording contracts, had bitter labor disputes, and had short-term conductorships. The Sterns, [Rudolf] Serkins, and everyone else used to want to record under the Philadelphia umbrella, and their records sold. Now, no longer do the top-name soloists record every concerto in sight with the Philadelphians." In 1999, the centenary of his birth, Ormandy was the subject of a BBC World Service radio tribute and biography. Ormandy's reputation in the Far East has never needed rehabilitating: while 1999 saw no special rereleases of his recordings by either RCA or Columbia in the United States, RCA Records Japan issued a 15-CD set in commemoration of the centenary, which was so well received that they issued a 20-disc follow-up issue in April 2001.

• The Eugene Ormandy Archive, which includes the conductor's letters, professional papers, music scores, and sound recordings, is housed in the Annenberg Rare Book & Manuscript Library of the University of Pennsylvania in Philadelphia. Most of Ormandy's stereophonic recordings have been rereleased by Sony and RCA Victor, and a great number of his historical mono and 78-r.p.m. recordings have been issued by Biddulph, an independent British label. There have been no biographical books devoted solely to Ormandy, though music critic Herbert Kupferberg, clearly an Ormandy and Philadelphia partisan, has provided a thorough biography in *Those Fabulous Philadelphians—The Life and Times of a Great Orchestra* (1969). His writings on Ormandy can be found also in a condensed, though updated, form in his essay "The Ormandy Era" in John Ardoin, ed., *The Philadelphia Orchestra: A Century of Music*, pp. 73–91 (1999). A retrospective interview with Ormandy, conducted by editor Robert Chesterman in 1971, is in *Conductors in Conversation*, pp. 103–24 (1990). Edward Arian's case study *Bach, Beethoven and Bureaucracy: The Case of the Philadelphia Orchestra* (1971), documents labor grievances; this volume is as acrimonious as Kupferberg's profiles are laudatory. An obituary and critical appreciation are in the *New York Times*, 13 Mar. 1985.

ROBERT L. JONES

OSTROFF, Eugene (6 July 1928–26 Aug. 1999), historian of photography, was born in Brooklyn, New York, the son of John Ostroff and Beatrice Weiss Ostroff. After attending the University of California at Los Angeles in 1946, he transferred to Los Angeles City College to study photography, graduating as an Associate in Arts in 1948. He attended New York University from 1948 to 1950 and Columbia University from 1955 to 1958. At Columbia he studied the emerging field of photographic engineering with Professor Lloyd E. Varden and decided to pursue this as his career.

During the years he attended NYU and Columbia, Ostroff gained practical experience as a photographer at the Rockefeller Institute of Medical Research in New York (1950–1957) and as supervisor of technical services at the photographic manufacturer Ilford (1957–1960). In 1960 he was engaged by the Smithsonian Institution as curator of photography of the National Museum of History and Technology, then located in the Smithsonian's Arts and Industries Building. One of his responsibilities was the planning of a Hall of Photography for the new building of the Museum of History and Technology (now called the National Museum of American History), which was about to be built on the north side of the Mall. The Hall of Photography opened to the public in 1972, and Ostroff was named supervisor of a newly established Division of Photographic History.

In 1962 he married Caroline Lindt, and they had three children. The marriage ended in divorce in 1977. In 1995 he married Elise Rutgers deVries; they had no children.

From the beginning of his tenure at the Smithsonian, Ostroff continued the acquisition and exhibition programs initiated by his predecessors, and he used his contacts to bring the work of younger photographers to public view. He also began to collect equipment and photographic examples reflecting new developments in technology, and to fill in gaps in early photography. The field of photographic history was then in its infancy, and Ostroff became one of the small number of specialists exploring in depth the early methods of photographic image-making. The enlarged premises he managed in the new Museum of History and Technology allowed him to expand the collection and mount a lively new series of special exhibitions to supplement the permanent installation.

Among the photographers shown were Robert Capa, Richard Avedon, Irving Penn, Elliott Erwitt, Eikoe Hosoe, Barbara Morgan, Berenice Abbott, Imogen Cunningham, Arthur Rothstein, Russell Lee, and many others, providing visitors with an opportunity—unmatched in most American museums at the time—to see the work of contemporary artists in depth. Earlier work, drawn from the vast holdings of the national museum, was shown as well. Ostroff was particularly interested in showing the remarkable images of the Western landscape made by such photographers as Timothy O'Sullivan, Carleton Watkins, and William Henry Jackson.

The new Hall of Photography included a working daguerreotype studio, complete with posing chair and head clamp (so the subject did not move during the long exposure) as well as an operating darkroom that allowed visitors to see one of the first photographic processes. Albumen prints from the 1850s, examples of ambrotypes, tintypes, early silver-gelatin film negatives and silver prints, and pioneering examples of color photography, all were shown. He placed on display collodion negatives (large glass plates coated with

photosensitive emulsion and exposed in a camera while the emulsion is still wet), and he showed the heavy equipment that had to be transported into the wilderness by the photographers who recorded the American West on these plates. Ostroff even persuaded the Navy Air Force to send an aerial reconnaissance plane across the country to make a photograph from coast to coast at high speed; the result was shown along with the camera used to make it, as an example of the latest in photographic technology.

With such a diverse and extensive collection in his care, and given his background in photographic chemistry and technology, it is not surprising that Ostroff should have turned his attention to the conservation of early images. This is still an evolving area of professional concern, and in the 1950s and 1960s it was in an even more rudimentary stage. Ostroff's earliest published suggestions for cleaning and handling daguerreotypes involved solutions that sometimes caused further deterioration in the image, and later, in *Caring for Photographs* (1982), he revised the guidelines for conserving these fragile and unique early images. He experimented with a variety of chemical and optical strategies for recovering badly deteriorated negative and positive images made in different photographic processes, and he published significant papers that brought him to the attention of curators and other colleagues around the world.

Among the early photographers whose work Ostroff collected, none was more significant than William Henry Fox Talbot, inventor of the "calotype," the first practical positive/negative photographic process. A number of Talbot's early experimental images had faded almost to invisibility. Around 1965, Ostroff conducted experiments on a few of the most deteriorated examples with the nuclear scientists at the Brookhaven National Laboratory on Long Island. He proved that it was possible to recover at least some visual information from these objects through neutron activation, bombarding the almost blank paper with charged particles in the Brookhaven nuclear accelerator and taking a photographic image from the newly activated metallic particles left on the faded sheets of paper. He published the results of these experiments in two of his most important articles, "Early Fox Talbot Photographs and Restoration by Neutron Irradiation" (*Journal of Photographic Science* 13 [1965]: 213–27), and "Restoration of Photographs by Neutron Activation" (*Science* 154, No. 3745 [1966]: 119–23).Ostroff traveled widely, consulting with museums in Brazil, Israel, and Great Britain, as well as in America. In 1982, under the auspices of UNESCO, he was invited to Burma to assist the Department of Archaeology in Rangoon in housing and conserving its photographic collections, and in 1989, at the opening of the Museum of Imaging and Technology in Bangkok, Thailand, he was the keynote speaker on the evolution and trends in photography. In 1994 Ostroff retired from the Smithsonian Institution, intending to publish a book on the cultural and industrial history of photography. Five years later he was in the process of revising the text for submission to a publisher when he died in Washington, D.C.

Ostroff was an active member of professional societies in his field. He published widely, both in professional journals and for a general audience. From 1960 onward he served on an American National Standards Institute committee concerned with the preservation, storage, and display of photographs. In 1969 he was named a Fellow of the Royal Photographic Society. He was also an honorary member of the Photographic Society of New York and the Photographic Historical Society of New England. He received several awards and fellowships from the Society of Photographic Scientists and Engineers.

When Ostroff joined the Smithsonian Institution, only a few institutions in America, and a handful elsewhere in the world, devoted themselves to photography. He quickly became a leader in his field, showing how the earliest techniques of photography—which had been largely forgotten by the 1960s—could be explained to the public, and made available to professionals. Irving Penn has made platinum prints, and Chuck Close recently has produced daguerreotypes—processes that Ostroff helped to recover from the past and make available for new creative uses. Ostroff's publications on photographic technology explored the intricacies of this ubiquitous graphic medium and provided the basis for the sound curatorial practices that are now in place.

• The results of Ostroff's research can be found in his many articles in such publications as *Journal of Photographic Science*, *Photographic Science and Engineering*, *Science*, and *Museum News*. Two of these have been cited above. Others include "Talbot's Earliest Extant Print, June 20, 1835, Rediscovered." *Photographic Science and Engineering* 10, no. 6 (Nov.–Dec. 1966): 350–54; "Photographic Enlarging: A History," *Photographica Journal* (Nov.–Dec. 1984): 1–39; chapters in *Caring for Photographs* (1982), *Processing for Permanence* (1972), *The Inventors of Photography* (1970); and exhibition catalogs such as *Western Views and Eastern Visions*, Washington, D.C.: Smithsonian Institution Traveling Exhibition Service, 1981, and *Photographing the Frontier*, Washington, D.C.: Smithsonian Institution Traveling Exhibition Service, 1976. Accounts of the history of the Smithsonian's photographic holdings can be found in Helena E. Wright's article "Developing a Photographic Collection, National Museum of American History," *History of Photography* 24, no. 1 (Spring 2000): 1–6, and Larry J. Schaaf, "The Talbot Collection, National Museum of American History," *History of Photography* 24, no. 1 (Spring 2000): 7–15. Obituaries are in the *New York Times*, 2 Sept. 1999, and the *Washington Post*, 29 Aug. 1999.

ALAN M. FERN

OTHMER, Donald F. (11 May 1904–1 Nov. 1995), chemical engineer, was born Donald Frederick Othmer in Omaha, Nebraska, the son of Frederick Othmer, a sheet metal worker, and Fredericka Darling Othmer. The family's finances were modest and Othmer claimed he earned every penny he spent, since he worked a paper route for 35 cents a week at age ten. He developed his engineering skills working with wood and metal in his father's shop. His inspiration for chemistry came from his Omaha Central High School teacher, Dr. H. A. Senter, a German chemist who modeled his classroom after Robert Bunsen's 1850 lab at Heidelberg University, complete with a continuous flame in the middle of the lab bench.

From 1921 to 1923, Othmer attended the Armour Institute (now the Illinois Institute of Technology). Although he enrolled as a chemical engineer, the program emphasized analytical chemistry because it was a common starting point for chemists in the work force. Othmer, who enjoyed working with his hands, disliked analytical chemistry intensely and left the Institute for the University of Nebraska in Lincoln. A year later he received his B.S. degree in chemical engineering. His first job after receiving his degree, however, was as an analytical chemist at a meat packing company.

Othmer then earned his M.S. (1925) and Ph.D. (1927) in chemical engineering at the University of Michigan. There he worked in the evaporator laboratory as an assistant to Walter L. Badger, who specialized in heat transfer and process design. Othmer expected to work for a related industry, such as sugar or chemical equipment, but was instead wooed by the Eastman Kodak Company in Rochester in 1927, where he took a position for $3,000 a year. Kodak wanted to develop an affordable process for cellulose acetate "safety film," particularly for X-ray film and home movies, to replace the extremely flammable cellulose nitrate film then on the market. In order to create a distillation process for the concentration of acetic acid (needed for the production of cellulose acetate), Othmer taught himself glass blowing to make his own distillation columns. Soon the equilibrium or "Othmer" still was developed and became, with future modifications, a staple in chemistry labs for studying distillation. Othmer created nearly forty patents for Kodak and was paid $10 for each. Estimating how much more money Kodak gained as a result of these patents, Othmer quit in 1931 to seek his own fortune.

Unfortunately, the Great Depression was not an ideal time for entrepreneurship. He found little investment interest in the stills and processes he developed in the basement lab of a small chemical products company. In September 1932, Othmer accepted an instructor position at the Brooklyn Polytechnic Institute (now Polytechnic University). The next year he took a pay cut due to the depression but was promoted to assistant professor. In 1937 he was made professor and head of the Chemical Engineering Department.

During the thirties, Othmer obtained patents for various distilling processes, especially in azeotropic distillation, where a substance is added to create different boiling points to separate chemicals. Academic surroundings afforded Othmer the opportunity to research and the freedom to work independently as a consultant for Eastman Kodak, Gray Chemical Company, Standard Oil of New Jersey (later Exxon), Hercules Powder Company, and others. He helped Tennessee Eastman in developing cyclonite (RDX), a high explosive used in World War II. During World War II, the Defense Department put Othmer in charge of the defense of Brooklyn in case of a gas attack, the State Department sent him to Central America to explain how to convert rotting banana stems into alcohol, and Army intelligence recruited him into spy school with the intention of having him inspect the chemical plants left behind by the retreating Germans in France (the war ended too quickly to implement this mission).

With the war over, Othmer and Dr. Raymond Kirk, the Chemistry Department Head at Polytechnic, created the *Kirk-Othmer Encyclopedia of Chemical Technology* as an English equivalent to Fritz Ullmann's *Enzyklopädie der technischen Chemie*. The first edition of fifteen volumes was published between 1947 and 1957. Kirk died in 1957 at the time the fifteenth volume was published. Othmer continued editorial duties on the second, third, and fourth editions of what is commonly known as the *Kirk-Othmer Encyclopedia*. A Spanish edition was also published.

In 1950 Othmer married Mildred Topp, who was also from Omaha, Nebraska; she had been living in New York City as a buyer for Topps, the Omaha department store started by her mother. The couple had no children. Though they never moved from their Brooklyn brownstone overlooking New York Harbor, the Othmers traveled frequently as Donald consulted with companies throughout Europe, Asia, and South America. He was hired in 1951 to blueprint plans for the entirety of Burma's chemical industry, whose plants had been blown up by the British, including one Othmer designed, before the Japanese seized them. Othmer later suspected his finished report, three years and thousands of pages of work funded largely by the U.S. government to stem Communist influence, "rotted away in files in that awful climate" (*Oral History*, p. 92).

As he grew older, Othmer engaged in a wide variety of research, including patents on processes for the desalination of ocean water, harnessing energy from varying ocean temperatures, solar power, sewage treatment, and methanol as a replacement fuel for gasoline—an issue he was also a strong advocate for. Othmer obtained over 150 American and foreign patents. A prolific writer, he published over 350 journal articles. In 1978, he received the distinguished Perkin Award for his contributions to chemical engineering. The Othmers amassed a fortune of several hundred million dollars from long-term investments in the stock market, most of which they left to scientific, academic, and social institutions, including the Chemical Heritage Foundation in Philadelphia, where he established the Othmer Library to promote the study of the history of chemistry. He died at the Long Island College Hospital in Brooklyn, which was another beneficiary of his philanthropy.

Othmer never retired from Polytechnic, even though he had been a professor emeritus since 1976. While he had a long career creating chemical pro-

cesses, writing articles and developing the *Kirk-Othmer Encyclopedia*, his proudest achievements were those of a teacher. To an interviewer in 1987, he said, "I had dozens, no scores, no hundreds of brilliant students with the motivation and ability to succeed in our profession, and [they] have done so" (*The Chemical Engineer*, Oct. 1987, p.15).

• The most extensive history of Donald Othmer is his *Oral History* conducted by James J. Boehing in 1994 and housed at the Chemical Heritage Foundation, Philadelphia. *Donald Frederick and Mildred Topp Othmer: A Commemorative of Their Lives and Legacies* (1999), edited by Arnold Thackray and Amy Beth Crow, contains a short biography and various essays and remembrances as well as a helpful listing of honors, patents, and published work. Career overviews can be found in Mary Ellen Bowden, *Chemical Achievers* (1997), p. 149; Claudia M. Caruana, "Donald F. Othmer: Chemical Engineer and Entrepreneur," *Chemical Engineering Progress* (Feb. 1988): 70–73; and Larry Resen, "A Venerable Chemical Engineer," *The Chemical Engineer* (Oct. 1987): 14–15. For an in-depth study of his scientific achievements, one would need to research the many articles Othmer wrote in such journals as *Industrial and Engineering Chemistry* and *Mechanical Engineering*. The Othmer Library at the Chemical Heritage Foundation houses his archives and the most complete selection of his writings. An obituary is in the *New York Times*, 3 Nov. 1995.

JOSH MCILVAIN

OUTLAW, Wyatt (1820–26 Feb. 1870), African-American leader, probably was born in Alamance County, North Carolina. His mother gave her name as Jemima Phillips; she may have been a member of a free African-American Phillips family who lived in Caswell County, North Carolina, in the early nineteenth century. His father is unknown. Some of Outlaw's contemporaries thought he was the son of Chesley Farrar Faucett (1792–1872), a merchant with agricultural and tanning operations in northern Alamance County who served in the state legislature during 1844–1847 and 1864–1865. Faucett, whose white sons were killed in Confederate service, acknowledged his own Unionist sympathies early in 1864, coincidental with Outlaw's move to Union-occupied eastern North Carolina, where he joined Union forces.

The judge and writer Albion Tourgée knew both Outlaw and Faucett and characterized them fictionally in *Bricks without Straw* (1880). Tourgée depicted Faucett sympathetically as an aged justice of the peace known for kindness as a slaveholder, quiet wartime Unionism, and cooperation with the Union League during Reconstruction. Outlaw is glimpsed in two composite characters, both of whom were slaves owned by the Faucett figure. One was an educated and frail preacher of African and European ancestry, a pensive strategist who supported himself as a shoemaker. By contrast, the other man was a strong, dark-skinned, assertive, and successful tobacco farmer.

Young Wyatt Outlaw lived much of his prewar life on the farm of George Outlaw and Nancy Outlaw, neighbors of Faucett. George Outlaw's 1854 will indicated a special status for "my man Wyatt": he was not to be sold, and it appears that Wyatt should receive the money from his annual hire. Likely Wyatt Outlaw was a cabinetmaker or furniture maker, the occupation he pursued following the Civil War. The 1860 census suggests he also grew tobacco with or for Nancy Outlaw and her daughter. The farm produced 3,500 pounds of tobacco that year. Nancy Outlaw was sixty-nine, and the only other adults on the farm were her thirty-five-year-old daughter and a forty-year-old enslaved man of mixed ancestry, presumably Wyatt Outlaw.

Outlaw served in Company B of the Second Regiment U.S. Colored Cavalry in Virginia and Texas from 1864 until February 1866. He was back in Alamance County by April. He bought a lot with a four-room house on Main Street in Graham, the county seat, where he opened a woodworking shop. He also repaired wagons and sold liquor at the shop, which became a gathering place for blacks and for white and black working people. A black Baptist church and an African Methodist Episcopal church organized in the shop. Outlaw served as marriage bondsman for at least six men during 1866 and 1867. William A. Albright, a white magistrate and a Republican, did the paperwork for most of Outlaw's bonds. Albright's courthouse office as clerk of superior court was convenient to Outlaw's shop, and they were friends.

In 1866 Outlaw attended the Freedman's Convention in Raleigh and was elected to the five-man board. With seven other officers, they were to coordinate statewide "agents" and "lecturers." Delegates were urged to promote the organization of "auxiliary leagues" of "colored people" throughout their counties for the purpose of reporting "cruelties" and "outrages" to the state organization and the newspapers. At the convention Outlaw probably met William Woods Holden (1818–1892), provisional governor of North Carolina, who would be elected governor in 1868. Holden was one of a handful of white dignitaries who accepted the convention's invitation to attend. The governor urged education for black children and stressed his view that "The colored people were entitled to all their civil rights, and would have them. The common government would see to that, if necessary" (*Minutes of the Freedmen's Convention*, p. 26).

Soon Outlaw organized the Alamance County Loyal Republican League, which consisted of black and white workingmen. Later a member recalled that "Mr. Outlaw" had organized the league with the purpose of building a church and a school in Graham. Another member described the organization as helping voters resist intimidation. In July 1867 Outlaw accepted a Union League commission from Holden, who encouraged various Republican forces in North Carolina to unite. Outlaw was to organize local councils of the league and supervise them. A year later, as the newly elected Republican governor, Holden appointed Outlaw as a town commissioner for Graham, and later Outlaw was elected town commissioner. This body organized an armed night patrol of five men, black and white, in response to Ku Klux Klan attacks in the town. Outlaw was part of a police patrol that dispersed a party of night riders.

Outlaw's success as a leader and spokesperson for full political rights for black men and for previously powerless white men was an obstacle to any return to the social, political, and economic status quo ante bellum of his county. In addition local features heightened the tensions and lent credibility to challenges to the old order. The area had not presented a proslavery front prior to the Civil War, and prewar leaders enforced the appearance of a pro-Confederate consensus with difficulty during the war. After the war their key concern was cheap labor: blacks for agriculture and whites for textiles. The North Carolina Railroad crossed Alamance County and had established its Company Shops near the center. Cooperation and conflict among black and white railway workers focused some of the tension and connected it with state and regional railway and political interests.

Testimonies gathered in the wake of Outlaw's death and also for the Holden impeachment indicate that The Company Shops camp of the Ku Klux Klan made the decision to kill Outlaw and assigned the execution to a camp in the Hawfield community east of Graham, where slavery and the pro-Confederate consensus had been stronger than in most other sections of the county. Seizing Outlaw in his home-shop, the attackers bludgeoned him down Main Street to the center of Graham and hanged him from an elm limb facing the courthouse. The following morning, a Sunday, the body was taken into the courthouse. Eighteen men were indicted for Outlaw's murder. By the time the cases came to trial in March 1874, the state legislature had followed a federal precedent in indemnifying persons accused of crimes as members of "secret societies," so the charges were dropped.

The murders of Outlaw and John Walter Stephens, a white political ally in Caswell County, attracted national notoriety to Ku Klux Klan violence in the area. Holden ordered the state militia to put down insurrection in the two counties. Soon the governor's political enemies demanded his impeachment, charging that his militia had used unlawful and cruel methods in rounding up persons suspected of Ku Klux Klan activity. Further, Holden's attackers secured the influence of the newspaperman Josiah Turner, Jr. (1821–1901). Turner blamed black-white political alliances typified by Outlaw and Holden for alleged black-on-white crime. Turner's accounts of Reconstruction events later formed the basis for Joseph Grégoire de Roulhac Hamilton's seminal *Reconstruction in North Carolina* (1914), originally a 1904 dissertation written under William A. Dunning (1857–1922). Thus Outlaw's life and death came to transcend his locale.

Cohabitation bonds for Alamance County did not survive Reconstruction, and the name of Outlaw's wife is not known. The lack of a postwar reference to her suggests that she died or moved prior to his 1866 return. Apparently they had three sons. Two months after Outlaw's death, his mother moved the children from Graham. The 1870 census listed Julius Outlaw, 10; Wyatt Outlaw, 8; and Oscar Outlaw, 6, living with her a few miles west of Chesley Faucett's store. By 1880, both Outlaw's mother and Faucett had died, and two of the boys were living in Graham. Young Wyatt lived with a white merchant who had served with his father on the Graham town council. Julius lived nearby with a veteran of the Second Regiment U.S. Colored Cavalry and his family.

• Collections with information on Outlaw include Ku Klux Klan Papers, Special Collections Department, Duke University Library, Durham, N.C.; Alamance County Board of Commissioners, State Archives, Division of Archives and History, Raleigh, N.C.; William W. Holden, Governor's Papers, State Archives, Division of Archives and History, Raleigh, N.C.; "Recollections of Jacob Alston Long, 1918," Southern Historical Collection, University of North Carolina, Chapel Hill, N.C.; and Albion Tourgée Papers, Chautauqua County Historical Society, Westfield, N.Y. Other important sources are *Trial of William W. Holden, Governor of North Carolina, before the Senate of North Carolina, on Impeachment by the House of Representatives for High Crimes and Misdemeanors*, 3 vols. (1871); Horace Raper and Thornton W. Mitchell, eds., *The Papers of William Woods Holden, 1841–1868* (2000); and *Minutes of the Freedmen's Convention Held in the City of Raleigh* (1866). Josiah Turner, Jr., in the *Raleigh Weekly Sentinel*, 14 Mar. 1870 and 1 Sept. 1870, was the only contemporary source to so much as imply that Outlaw personally used violence or sanctioned its use in response to Ku Klux Klan attacks. The records of the U.S. Colored Troops are available at www.itd.nps.gov/cwss/. Outlaw's life is explored in Carole Watterson Troxler, "'To look more closely at the man': Wyatt Outlaw, a Nexus of National, Local, and Personal History," *North Carolina Historical Review* 77 (Oct. 2000): 403–33, which also gives documentation for various facets of Outlaw's experiences. Other essential works include Roberta Sue Alexander, *North Carolina Faces the Freedmen: Race Relations during Presidential Reconstruction, 1865–67* (1985); Allen W. Trelease, *White Terror: The Ku Klux Klan Conspiracy and Southern Reconstruction* (1971) and "Review Essay: On Making Sense of William W. Holden," *North Carolina Historical Review* 65 (1988): 355–58; and George C. Rable, *But There Was No Peace: The Role of Violence in the Politics of Reconstruction* (1984). For an analysis of Outlaw and the Union League in the context of railway labor issues and railroad "redemption," see Scott R. Nelson, "Alamance: A Trenchant Blade," in *Iron Confederacies: Southern Railways, Klan Violence, and Reconstruction* (1999).

CAROLE WATTERSON TROXLER

P

PAKULA, Alan J. (7 Apr. 1928–19 Nov. 1998), film director, was born Alan Jay Pakula in New York City, the son of Paul Pakula, the co-owner of a printing business, and Jeannette Goldstein Pakula. Even as a young boy Pakula was interested in movies, and he became an avid reader of *Variety*, the trade magazine for the film industry. He attended the Bronx High School of Science and later recalled, "[I] kept wondering what I was doing there when my interests were in music and art" (*New York Post*, 15 Apr. 1976). During his senior year Pakula switched to the Hill School in Pottstown, Pennsylvania, from which he graduated in 1944. In early 1945 he spent two months working as an office boy for the Leland Hayward Theatrical Agency, which cemented his interest in the performing arts. He enrolled at Yale University, where he majored in drama and graduated in 1948. He later described his first experience as a director at Yale: "I remember . . . the feeling that [actors] were finding things in themselves they could not have found without me. I was a sort of catalytic agent. . . . I used to leave rehearsals and go down the street with great goat-like leaps, like something from a Thomas Wolfe novel" (Milne, p. 89).

In 1948 Pakula moved to Hollywood, where he worked at Warner Brothers as an assistant in the cartoon department. In 1949 he directed a stage production of Jean Anouilh's *Antigone* for the Los Angeles Circle Theater. The following year he became an apprentice to the screenwriter, producer, and director Don Hartman at Metro-Goldwyn-Mayer, and he moved with Hartman to Paramount Pictures in 1951. In 1957 Pakula produced his first film, *Fear Strikes Out*, an acclaimed drama starring Anthony Perkins as the major league baseball player Jimmy Piersall, who struggled with mental illness. Pakula and the film's director Robert Mulligan formed their own production company, Pakula-Mulligan Productions. Taking time off from his film duties, Pakula in 1960 returned to the stage to direct *Laurette*, which was based on the life of the Broadway star Laurette Taylor. Although he hoped to bring the play to Broadway, it failed in a preliminary run in New Haven, Connecticut.

In 1962 Pakula produced *To Kill a Mockingbird*, the best of the Pakula-Mulligan films, a sensitive adaptation of Harper Lee's novel about children growing up in a racist southern town. The film won two Academy Awards and was nominated for three others, including best picture. Pakula collaborated with Mulligan on five more films, including the relationship comedy *Love with the Proper Stranger* (1963), which received three Academy Award nominations, and *Up the Down*

Staircase (1967), an insightful drama about a beginning teacher at an inner-city school. Despite his successes, he later admitted he felt stymied. "I never wanted to be a producer," he told an interviewer. "It was sheer accident, and I was passive about it for so long it bewilders me. . . . I've always wanted to direct, ever since I was seventeen" (Milne, p. 89). In 1963 he married Hope Lange, an actress. They had no children and divorced in 1969.

In 1969 Pakula ended his partnership with Mulligan and finally turned to directing. His first film, *The Sterile Cuckoo* (1969), examines a romance between two college-age misfits played by Liza Minnelli and Wendell Burton. Although sentimental and often plodding, the movie demonstrated Pakula's talent for working with actors. Minnelli, making her screen debut, was nominated for an Academy Award. The director's next film was the superior psychological thriller *Klute* (1971), starring Jane Fonda as a New York City call girl who is stalked by a sadistic former customer. In an effort to elevate his lurid story, Pakula concentrated on the psychology of Fonda's character, an intelligent, emotionally aloof would-be actress who wants to go "straight" but compulsively continues to work as a prostitute. "It was the story of a girl who's obsessed with seducing," he later explained. "She's a girl who feels impotent herself; the only time she feels any sense of power is when she's sexually in control, and knows a man wants her in a way she doesn't want him" (*American Film*, pp. 76–77). Fonda won the Academy Award for Best Actress for her performance, which was largely developed through improvisations. The film is also noteworthy for its claustrophobic visuals, devised by Pakula and his frequent collaborator, the cinematographer Gordon Willis. In 1973 Pakula married Hannah Boorstin, a writer and historian; they had no children.

In 1974 Pakula directed *The Parallax View*, which stars Warren Beatty as a journalist who stumbles onto a shadowy conspiracy to carry out political assassinations. The film's story is deliberately oblique, offering characters and situations that are consistently misread by the hero, Beatty's character, who becomes a pawn in the game of the conspirators and is eventually murdered. Although largely ignored at the time of its release, *The Parallax View*, with its chilling vision of a society manipulated and controlled by unknown powers, was later seen as an astute reflection of the American zeitgeist of the late 1960s and early 1970s, a period marred by assassinations, the Watergate scandal, and the disclosure of Central Intelligence Agency plots. Pakula's most acclaimed film, *All the President's Men* (1976), stars Robert Redford and Dustin Hoffman as Bob Woodward and Carl Bernstein, the *Wash-*

ington Post reporters who exposed the Watergate cover-up. The movie succeeds on many levels, as a dramatization of historic events, as a suspenseful mystery even though viewers are already aware of the outcome, and as a documentarylike examination of investigative journalism. Pakula's effective visual design called for deep-focus photography and intense lighting for scenes in the newsroom, which he described as "a world without shadows, . . . somewhere where nothing gets away," contrasted with murky scenes of the Watergate burglars and a White House informant (*American Film*, p. 76). *All the President's Men* was a critical and popular success, becoming the top-grossing picture of 1976 and garnering four Academy Awards. Pakula was nominated for best director but did not win. Commenting on *The Parallax View* and *All the President's Men*, both of which deal with the theme of political conspiracy although their endings are vastly different, he explained that the first film represented "my fear about what's happening" and the second film represented "my hope. Like most of us I'm balanced between the two" (Thompson, p. 13).

Given the excellence of Pakula's "paranoid trilogy"—*Klute*, *The Parallax View*, and *All the President's Men*—his subsequent films were generally disappointing. Most critics judged *Comes a Horseman* (1978), a western starring Fonda and Jason Robards, Jr., beautifully shot but dull. *Starting Over* (1979), a relationship comedy, features Burt Reynolds as a newly divorced man. Although charmingly low-key, the movie is not as interesting as two other divorce-themed films released around the same time, the Academy Award–winning *Kramer vs. Kramer* (1979) and Paul Mazursky's excellent *An Unmarried Woman* (1978). *Rollover* (1981), an expensive box-office flop starring Fonda and Kris Kristofferson in an incomprehensible mystery set in the world of high finance, marked the nadir of Pakula's career. He regained his stature with critics with *Sophie's Choice* (1982), a powerful drama about the relationship between a young writer and a guilt-ridden Auschwitz survivor brilliantly played by Meryl Streep. Pakula was nominated for an Academy Award for his faithful screenplay adaptation of William Styron's lengthy novel, which, the *New York Times* noted, he compressed with "amazing comprehensiveness" into a two-and-a-half-hour film.

Following *Sophie's Choice*, Pakula turned out several unremarkable movies, including the semiautobiographical love story *See You in the Morning* (1989), based on his own screenplay. During the 1990s he helmed two popular legal thrillers, *Presumed Innocent* (1990) and *The Pelican Brief* (1993). Although intelligently directed, they displayed none of the depth and eccentricity of his thrillers from the 1970s. Commenting on the impersonality of Pakula's later films, the critic Janet Maslin pointed out that his work had suffered because of changes in the movie industry, as Hollywood in the 1980s and 1990s increasingly focused on making marketable "products": "The atmosphere that fostered his [early thrillers] allowed for quiet moments, subtle plotting and an air of profound anxiety that have all but vanished from today's more breathless thrillers" (*New York Times*, 23 Nov. 1998).

During the late 1990s Pakula became a spokesperson for the National Alliance for the Mentally Ill, relating the struggles of his stepson Robert Boorstin, a senior adviser in the U.S. Treasury Department who suffered from manic depression. Pakula's interest in mental illness also stemmed from his lifelong fascination with psychology. In an interview he explained that he routinely told strangers on airplanes that he was a psychiatrist: "If you say you're a filmmaker, they say, 'What's Jane Fonda like?' If you say you're a psychiatrist, it's amazing how people tell you the story of their lives" (*New York Times*, 13 May 1998). Pakula was killed outside New York City in an automobile accident on the Long Island Expressway.

Throughout his career Pakula was regarded as one of Hollywood's finest directors of actors. Although he never won an Academy Award, three of the most significant actors of his era won Academy Awards under his guidance, Fonda for *Klute*, Robards for his portrayal of the *Washington Post* editor Ben Bradlee in *All the President's Men*, and Meryl Streep for *Sophie's Choice*. While the majority of his films were unexceptional, his "paranoid trilogy" stands as one of the highlights of American cinema during the 1970s.

• For information on Pakula's life, see the short biographies in *Contemporary Biography* (1980) and *Contemporary Authors Online* (2000). Insightful interviews are Tom Milne, "Not a Garbo or a Gilbert in the Bunch," *Sight and Sound*, Spring 1972, pp. 89–93; Richard Thompson, "Mr. Pakula Goes to Washington: Alan J. Pakula on *All the President's Men*," *Film Comment*, Sept.–Oct. 1976, pp. 12–19; and "Alan J. Pakula," by an unidentified interviewer, *American Film* 11, no. 2 (1985): 13, 76–77. A useful critical assessment of his career is Janet Maslin, "Finding Depth in Society's Shallow End," *New York Times*, 23 Nov. 1998. For an excellent scholarly reading of *The Parallax View*, see James W. Palmer and Michael M. Riley, "America's Conspiracy Syndrome: From Capra to Pakula," *Studies in the Humanities* 8, no. 2 (Mar. 1981): 21–27. An obituary is in the *New York Times*, 20 Nov. 1998.

THOMAS W. COLLINS, JR.

PAREDES, Américo (3 Sept. 1915–5 May 1999), folklorist, was born in Brownsville, Texas, the son of Justos Paredes, a rancher, and Clotilde Manzano de Paredes. Growing up bilingual, conversant in English and Spanish, Paredes attended grammar school, high school, and junior college in Brownsville. Intent on pursuing a literary career, he began writing poetry at an early age, publishing a number of pieces in *La Prensa*, a San Antonio–based Spanish language daily newspaper. In 1937 he published his first collection of poetry, *Cantos de adolescencia*. He also began working as a journalist for the *Brownsville Herald*, writing a notable series of articles on the traditions and folklore of the lower Rio Grande Valley.

On 13 August 1939 he married Consuelo "Chelo" Silva, a well-known singer in Mexico and south Texas with whom he often performed traditional songs at parties and gatherings. The marriage, however, soon ended in divorce and did not result in any children. With the outbreak of World War II, Paredes took a defense-related job with Pan American Airways, until he was drafted into the army in 1944. He served as a correspondent for *Stars and Stripes*, covering the war crimes trials in Japan. Discharged in 1946, he remained in Asia, taking a job as public relations officer for China with the international branch of the American Red Cross. At this time he also contributed a weekly column about daily life in Korea, Japan, and China to *El Universal*, a Mexico City daily. On 28 May 1948 he married Amelia Sidzu Nagamine, daughter of a Japanese diplomat and his Uruguayan wife; they had four children.

Utilizing the GI Bill, Paredes returned to college, graduating *summa cum laude* in 1951 with a degree in English from the University of Texas at Austin. Pursuing graduate studies in English and Spanish at the same institution, he received his M.A. in 1953 and his Ph.D. in 1956. After teaching for a year at Texas Western College (now the University of Texas at El Paso), in 1957 he joined the English faculty at the University of Texas at Austin. From his institutional base in English, later combined with a joint appointment in anthropology, Paredes began to solidify his reputation as a folklorist.

In many ways, Paredes's childhood on the border, raised in a family steeped in Mexican traditions, and his early career as poet, performer, and journalist had prepared him for this pursuit. As an academic, Paredes delved more deeply into the folklore and culture of the Texas-Mexico border. His first major work, *"With His Pistol in His Hand": A Border Ballad and Its Hero* (1958), for instance, grew out of an early interest in *corridos* (folk songs or ballads). A study of the legend of Gregorio Cortez, who challenged the Anglo-dominated society of the Lower Rio Grande Valley, and the various *corridos* composed to celebrate his feats, *"With His Pistol in His Hand"* demonstrated several defining characteristics of Paredes's work: a masterful control of both oral and archival sources, an intimate familiarity with the social, economic, cultural, and historical contexts, and a sophisticated understanding of the flexibility of folklore genres and conventions. It also elaborated on topics that became important in Paredes's later work, particularly the connection between folklore and cultural conflict and the cultural productions and contributions of Mexican Americans. This body of writings proved inspirational to a later generation of scholars and activists, participants in the Chicano movement, who found in Paredes's writings a record of resistance and struggle in which to ground their activism.

The 1960s and 1970s proved particularly fruitful as Paredes published articles on the relation between folklore and history, folk etymology, *machismo*, and jests. His edited works in this period included *Folktales of Mexico* (1972) and *A Texas-Mexican Cancionero: Folksongs of the Lower Border* (1976). He also made important theoretical contributions to the study of folklore, anticipating in his essay "Some Aspects of Folk Poetry" (1964) the "new folkloristics" with its emphasis on the study of folklore as performance. In an important 1978 article, "On Ethnographic Work among Minority Groups," Paredes was one of the first scholars to initiate a critique of ethnographic methods and assumptions. He specifically faulted anthropologists for their failure to consider the social contexts in which speech events and fieldwork take place, pointing out, for instance, how an ethnographer's unfamiliarity with the performative and figurative uses of an informant's language could distort the process of ethnographic interpretation, as could the relative ethnic, class, and power positions occupied by researcher and informant in a fieldwork situation. Always interested in the international aspects of folklore scholarship, Paredes also wrote about the theoretical bases of folklore in Latin America and the United States.

Paredes also promoted folklore and the burgeoning field of Chicano studies from a number of editorial and administrative positions. From 1969 to 1973 he served as editor of the *Journal of American Folklore*, where he encouraged the exploration of new theoretical perspectives. *Towards New Perspectives in Folklore* (1972), a collection he co-edited with Richard Bauman, highlighted some of these trends. In 1967 he played a key role in the founding of the University of Texas Center for Intercultural Studies in Folklore and Ethnomusicology (later renamed the Américo Paredes Center for Cultural Studies) and served as its director. In 1970 he founded the university's Center for Mexican American Studies, creating an important institutional and supportive base for Chicano scholarship; he served as its director until 1978.

After his retirement from active teaching in 1984, Paredes contributed to the literary explosion of the Chicano movement, publishing fiction and poetry dealing with the Mexican-American experience. His novel *George Washington Gómez*, for instance, written in the late 1930s but published in 1990, explored the theme of Mexican-American identity. His poetry, particularly some of the poems in his collection *Between Two Worlds* (1991), continued this theme but also featured a number of lyrical pieces. In 1994 he published *The Hammon and the Beans and other Stories*, again largely composed of stories written in the 1930s and 1940s. Like his novel, a number of the stories in *The Hammon and the Beans* depict Mexican-American efforts to cope with social, economic, and cultural transformations in the Lower Rio Grande Valley. A year before his death, Paredes published his last novel, *The Shadow*. A finalist in the Austin Writers' League 1998 Violet Crown Award for Fiction, the work, revised from a 1950s manuscript, examined class prejudice among Mexican Americans.

Paredes received a number of honors, including a Guggenheim fellowship, an endowed professorship, and a Charles Frankel award from the National Endowment for the Humanities. In 1990 the Mexican government inducted him into the Order of the Aztec Eagle, the highest honor Mexico bestows on noncitizens. In 1997, his colleagues in the American Folklore Society's Section on Latino, Latin American, and Caribbean Folklore named him the most important and influential scholar in the field of Mexican-American and borderlands folklore.

Paredes died in Austin, Texas.

• Biographical information can be gathered from a number of sources. An interview conducted with Paredes by Héctor Calderón and José Rósbel López-Morín and published in the journal *Nepantla: Views from South* (2000): 197–228, provides valuable information on Paredes's early life, his education, and his work in literature, folklore, and Mexican-American studies. One of the most complete sources on Paredes's life and writings is María Herrera-Sobek's "Américo Paredes: A Tribute," *Mexican Studies/Estudios Mexicanos* (Summer 2000): 239–66. Herrera-Sobek's article also contains a complete listing of Paredes's principal works. *Folklore and Culture on the Texas-Mexican Border* (1993), edited by Richard Bauman, reprints eleven of Paredes's significant articles. Ramón Saldívar critically assesses Paredes's literary output and describes the social, political, and economic situation of the South Texas border country in his introduction to Paredes's collection of stories *The Hammon and the Beans and Other Stories* (1994). Manuel Peña and Richard Bauman critically assess the role of Paredes in folklore and Chicano studies in their obituary written for the *Journal of American Folklore* (Spring 2000): 195–98. An obituary also appears in the *New York Times*, 7 May 1999.

JOSEPH C. JASTRZEMBSKI

PARK, Lawrence (16 Dec. 1873–28 Sept. 1924), art historian, was born in Worcester, Massachusetts, the son of John Gray Park and Elizabeth Bigelow Lawrence. He was educated at a private school in Worcester and at Harvard University, from which he graduated in 1896. He then took classes in the School of Drawing and Painting at the Museum of Fine Arts in Boston and from 1897 to 1901 worked as an architectural draftsman. In 1901 he established himself as an architect in Boston. In 1905 Park married Maria Davis Motley, a grandniece of the historian John Lothrop Motley; they had one son.

Park was interested in genealogy and family portraits, and this developed into a desire to learn more about the art and artists of colonial America and the early federal period of the United States. He collected data on early American portrait painters, traveling widely to view original paintings, and made detailed notes and pencil sketches. His first publication in the field of art history was a monograph on the colonial Massachusetts painter Joseph Badger, which appeared in the *Proceedings of the Massachusetts Historical Society* in December 1917 (reprinted as a separate publication in 1918). This was followed by *Joseph Blackburn, A Colonial Portrait Painter*, published in the October 1922 *Proceedings of the American Antiquarian Society* (reprinted as a separate publication in 1923). Badger and Joseph Blackburn, well-known painters in their day, had been all but forgotten when Park became interested in them, and his thoroughly researched publications, each containing a biograph-

ical sketch of the artist and a catalog of his paintings, are the definitive studies of both painters.

Park's expertise in early American art was soon widely recognized. In 1917 he became a member of the corporation of the Worcester Art Museum, and in 1919 he was appointed curator of colonial art at the Cleveland Museum of Art. (He accepted after being assured he did not have to relocate to Ohio.) In 1921 he joined Helen Frick on the pioneering expedition to survey and record portraits in Virginia for the newly established Frick Art Reference Library, and he traveled to South Carolina on a similar mission for the library the following year. By this time Park had begun the research for what would be his best-known publication, a catalog of the work of the prominent American artist Gilbert Stuart. (His interest in Stuart was prompted in part by his wife's ownership of three portraits by that artist.) Despite declining health, Park collected information on most of Stuart's portraits. Park died in Groton, Massachusetts. His notes were edited for publication by William Sawitzky and were published in four volumes as *Gilbert Stuart: An Illustrated Descriptive List of His Works* (1926).

Park "was a man of fine personality and character, of dignity and charm," according to his friend Sawitzky (Park, *Gilbert Stuart*, vol. 1, p. 8). He was not a true art historian in the modern sense of that term. He always approached the artists he studied from the point of view of his early interest in genealogy. However, his monographs on Blackburn and Badger are useful studies of the lives and works of those two artists and continue to be consulted by scholars in the twenty-first century. His catalog of the work of Stuart, though now dated, was the first useful listing of that artist's extensive oeuvre and is still used today.

• A collection of Park's papers is in the library of the Henry Francis du Pont Winterthur Museum, Winterthur, Del. His research notes on Gilbert Stuart and the notes and drawings he made in Virginia and South Carolina in 1921 and 1922 belong to the Frick Art Reference Library in New York City. A tribute by William Sawitzky that contains much biographical information is in Park's *Gilbert Stuart: An Illustrated Descriptive List of His Works*, vol. 1 (1926).

DAVID MESCHUTT

PARKER, H. T. (29 Apr. 1867–30 Mar. 1934), dance, music, and theater critic, was born Henry Taylor Parker in Boston, the son of William Fisk Parker and Susan Sophia Taylor Parker, whose occupations are unknown. He entered Harvard University in 1886 but apparently left in 1889 without graduating. He was immediately attracted to the writing of criticism and acquired the dual position of New York correspondent of the *Boston Evening Transcript* and drama critic of the *Commercial Advertiser* (subsequently the *New York Globe*). By 1905, he had settled into the *Transcript* and into Boston. He wrote all of his extensive copy in longhand, thereby becoming the bane of the paper's typesetters.

Parker was the quintessential New England gentleman. He carried a bamboo cane, wore pince-nez eyeglasses, and never dressed casually. Like the composer Louis Horst, whom he admired, he smoked incessantly, allowing the cigarette's glowing ember to accumulate precariously. Although he was phenomenally prolific, writing the measurable equivalent of a novel a month, Parker, or H. T. P., as he signed columns, was especially known for his writings about dance. Perhaps that is because he traveled regularly to New York and, in the summers, to England and the Continent, to catch the newest trends in this fast-growing art.

He never married and always went alone to theater and concert hall. He also scrupulously maintained objectivity by avoiding friendships with artists, even when he felt as close as he did to dance-mime Angna Enters. (She was so appreciative of his observations that she dedicated her autobiography, *First Person Plural*, to him and wrote, "No one could possibly have been more sensitive to figures of the dance than H. T. Parker. His awareness, his perceptions and discoveries helped to keep Boston abreast of all the movements in the theater and music arts. His page in the *Boston Evening Transcript* was a Platonic grove.")

Knowing that dance was a young art in this country, he did not hesitate to chastise Boston audiences for insensitivity to or a lack of sophistication. At the end of a Diaghilev Ballets-Russes season, for example, he noted, "As the way is with the Boston public, it was slow to discover the novel artistry flowering into as novel sensation, illusion, and beauty that the Russians were bearing into our theatre. It spent nearly a week . . . in reconnoitering them." This somewhat moralistic tone helped to create a supportive environment for the arts.

Parker was totally receptive to artistic innovation. Of the controversial Isadora Duncan, he wrote: "Out from a corner of the hangings came Miss Duncan. Perhaps flowers decked her hair and tunic. Oftener she was unadorned. The dance began. There was no impression of physical beauty or of physical charm. Eye and fancy saw only beautiful motion, exquisitely adjusted to the line of the music, animated to its rhythm, attuned to its harmonies. The music ran in arabesques of sound. The dancer moved likewise in as lovely arabesques of motion. Came a point of rest, and the lines of her body flowed into soft, clear pose."

Sometimes his prose had a turn-of-the-century prolixity, as in this 1922 impression of Michel Fokine: "Most, however, he is Fokine, when before these dun curtains, orchestra-less, upon a stage in a hall, before none too well attuned spectators, he summons eighteenth-century air, aspect, atmosphere, like some Watteau of the dance, some Pope of the precise and polished poetry of pose and motion." Later in the review, he added, "Give Mr. Fokine time and opportunity and we shall yet have an American ballet, Russian crossed." (Parker had the right idea but the wrong man. It remained for George Balanchine to evolve an "American ballet, Russian crossed.")

In 1934 he welcomed Martha Graham: "Miss Graham is not a dancer who plays upon her audience with comeliness or with charm. The fine, full muscling of her body implies a latent energy to transmit more than it suggests smooth and gracious surfaces, reflects, then wills and accomplishes.. . . Her presence is remote, rather than sympathetic, less ingratiating than impressive."

Later that year he awaited the Boston arrival of the new Ballet Russe de Monte Carlo. He described the repertory, printed pictures of the dancers, in short, whetted the appetite of his readers. Before the company arrived, he died, in Boston.

• Parker's dance criticism is generously represented in *Motion Arrested: Dance Reviews of H. T. Parker*, ed. Olive Holmes (1982). An early collection of his writings, *Eighth Notes*, was published in 1922 and reprinted in 1968 as *Eighth Notes, Voices and Figures of Music and the Dance*. Obituaries are in the *Boston Evening Transcript* and the *Boston Herald*, both 31 Mar. 1934.

DORIS HERING

PATTERSON, Louise (9 Sept. 1901–27 Aug. 1999), cultural and political radical, activist, and feminist, was born Louise Alone Toles in Chicago, the daughter of William Toles, a bartender, and Lula Brown Toles. In 1904, her parents separated, and in the next ten years she lived throughout the Northwest with her mother and her stepfather, William Thompson. Often the only black child in town, she was the target of vicious racial insults. In an effort to maintain her self-respect, she strove to excel in school. In 1919, she enrolled at the University of California at Berkeley. There she attended a lecture by W. E. B. Du Bois, the founder of the National Association for the Advancement of Colored People. "For the first time in my life," she recalled, "I was proud to be black" (quoted in Lewis, 103). His talk prompted her to dream of traveling to New York City and becoming involved in racial politics. In 1923, one of only a handful of black students, she graduated cum laude in Economics.

With the encouragement of Du Bois, in 1925 Thompson took a position at a dilapidated black college in Pine Bluff, Arkansas, and in 1927 at the Hampton Institute. But her support for a student strike against the school's racially conservative administration cost Thompson her job. In 1928, she took a position as a social worker with the National Urban League in New York City. But she soon became disillusioned with the profession's paternalism. She also became immersed in the Harlem Renaissance, working as the secretary to Zora Neale Hurston and Langston Hughes. Hughes remained a lifelong friend. In 1928, she was married to novelist Wallace Thurman, but they separated after less than six months.

With the onset of the Depression, Thompson gravitated toward the Left. In 1931, she founded the Harlem branch of the Friends of the Soviet Union, and Harlem intellectuals congregated at her apartment to discuss Marxism and the Soviet Union. In 1932, she was asked to organize a group of African Americans to travel to the Soviet Union and make a film about racial conditions in the United States. She pulled together twenty-two black artists and writers, including Langston Hughes. The film was canceled after they arrived, making international headlines. Yet she was deeply impressed with the Soviet Union, viewing it as a striking model for building a society committed to social equality. "Because of what I had seen in the Soviet Union," she recalled, "I . . . was ready to make a change" (LTP Papers, 14 May 1987 interview, p. 22).

After she returned to Harlem, she became widely known as "Madame Moscow" for her vocal support of the Soviet Union. Her critics included African-American journalist Henry Lee Moon, who had been one of the cast members for the film. She was also attracted to the Communist movement due to its efforts to free the Scottsboro boys, nine black adolescents who had been falsely accused and sentenced to death for raping two white women in Alabama. In 1933, she organized a successful Scottsboro march in Washington, D.C., and joined the Communist party; in 1934 she joined the International Workers Order (IWO), a Communist-affiliated fraternal organization. By the end of the decade, she was elected IWO national secretary. In 1937 she attended the World Congress against Racism and Fascism in Paris, and observed the Spanish Civil War. In 1938, she co-founded with Hughes the short-lived Harlem Suitcase Theater, which produced the wildly popular "Don't You Want to Be Free?"

In 1940, she married Communist leader William Patterson, and they moved to Chicago. Three years later, she gave birth to a daughter. In the late 1940s, she and Patterson, W. E. B. Du Bois, Alpheus Hunton, and Paul Robeson formed the Council of African Affairs, an organization dedicated to ending colonialism. By 1950, the Pattersons had returned to New York.

In 1951, Thompson Patterson with actor Beulah Richardson and journalist Charlotta Bass founded the Sojourners for Truth and Justice, an all-black women's progressive civil rights organization. The group issued a call for African American women to join in a demonstration "to call upon our government to prove its loyalty to its fifteen million Negro citizens" (LTP Papers, Box 15, Folder 26). The stifling anti-Communist political atmosphere of the era partially contributed to the Sojourners' demise.

Louise and William Patterson fell victim to McCarthyism during the early 1950s. On 6 April 1951 she was called to testify in *People of New York v. International Workers Order*, a New York State court case, because of her involvement with the IWO, which had been deemed a "subversive" organization. She invoked the Fifth Amendment but was not jailed. William Patterson, however, was incarcerated and lost his passport due to his political activities. She organized national campaigns to free him and for the return of his passport as well as those of Du Bois and Robeson.

Although some African-American activists broke their ties with the Left, Thompson Patterson continued agitating for progressive causes. In the early 1960s, she helped noted historian Herbert Aptheker found the American Institute for Marxist Studies. In 1969, she returned to the Soviet Union, marveling at the tremendous changes that had taken place in the nation. The Pattersons' New York apartment served as a place where many young black militants came to gain valuable political insight.

In the early 1970s, she headed the New York Committee to Free Angela Davis, the African-American Communist who had been accused of involvement in the shooting death of a California judge in August 1970. After her husband's death in 1980, she founded the William L. Patterson Foundation. In the late 1980s, with the assistance of scholar Margaret Wilkerson, Thompson Patterson began writing her memoirs. She was discussed in numerous critically acclaimed studies of W. E. B. Du Bois, Langston Hughes, the Harlem Renaissance, and the black Left, and she appeared in several documentaries. She also received many awards. By the mid-1990s her health declined; consequently her memoir was never completed. It would have been a fascinating account of an extraordinary African-American woman who took part in many of the most significant social, political, and cultural movements in the United States and abroad during the twentieth century.

• There are many primary sources on Louise Thompson Patterson. Her rich personal papers, including several transcribed interviews and her unfinished memoir, are available at the Special Collections Department, Robert W. Woodruff Library, Emory University, Atlanta, Ga. Information can also be found about her in the Matt N. and Evelyn Graves Crawford Papers, Special Collections, Emory University; Langston Hughes Papers, Beinecke Rare Book and Manuscript Library, Yale University, New Haven, Conn.; and in the Communist Party, USA Files, Library of Congress, Washington, D.C. Although often containing inaccurate information about her activities, the FBI files of Thompson Patterson, William Patterson, and the Sojourners for Truth and Justice are also useful. News about Thompson Patterson often appeared in *The Crisis*, *Amsterdam News*, *Chicago Defender*, and *Baltimore Afro-American*, as well as in the Communist party's *Daily Worker*, especially during the 1930s. The Tamiment Library at New York University contains audiotapes of her lengthy 1981 interview with Ruth Prago, which was part of the Oral History of the American Left (OHAL) project.

For brief biographies and short essays about Thompson Patterson see Margaret Wilkerson, "Excavating Our History: The Importance of Biographies of Women of Color," *Black American Literature Forum* 24, no. 1 (Spring, 1990): 73–84; Robin Kelley, "The Left," in Darlene Clark Hine, *Black Women in America: A Historical Encyclopedia* (1994), pp. 708–14; and Kelley, "Louise Thompson Patterson" in Mari Jo Buhle, Paul Buhle, and Den Georgakas, *Encyclopedia of the American Left* (1990), pp. 564–65. Insightful discussions of Thompson Patterson's involvement in the Harlem Renaissance and American Communist movement can be found in Erik S. McDuffie's forthcoming dissertation "Long Journeys: Four Black Women and the Communist Party, USA, 1930–1956" (New York University); David L. Lewis,

W. E. B. Du Bois: The Fight for Equality and the American Century, 1919–1963 (2000); Arnold Rampersad, *The Life of Langston Hughes*, vols. 1, 2. (1986–1988); Faith Berry, *Langston Hughes: Before and Beyond Harlem* (1983; repr. 1995); Mark Naison, *Communists in Harlem during the Depression* (1983; repr. 1985); and Robert Hemenway, *Zora Neale Hurston: A Literary Biography* (1977; repr. 1980). See also Arthur J. Sabin, *Red Scare in Court: New York versus the International Workers Union* (1993). For documentaries, see Louis Massiah, *Louise Alone Thompson Patterson* (2002); Massiah, *W. E. B. Du Bois—A Biography in Four Voices* (1995), and St. Clair Bourne, *Langston Hughes: The Dream Keeper* (1988). An obituary is in the *Los Angeles Times*, 19 Sept. 1997.

ERIK S. McDUFFIE

PATTERSON, Robert (23 Mar. 1753–9 Nov. 1827), Kentucky and Ohio pioneer, was born near Bedford Springs, Pennsylvania, the son of Jane Patterson and Francis Patterson, a Scotch-Irish Presbyterian cattle raiser, tanner, and miller. When he was three, his mother died, and young Robert was raised by his stepmother, Catherine Perry. From an early age, Patterson was eager to join the hunters, scouts, and militiamen he saw on their way west from nearby Fort Bedford. He made his first venture into the Ohio Valley in 1772 as a volunteer in the Lancaster Rifles and then served in the Pennsylvania Rangers during Lord Dunmore's War two years later, during which he scouted as far as the Pickaway Plains in present-day southern Ohio.

Patterson first heard about Kentucky at this time and probably met Daniel Boone, James Harrod, Simon Kenton, George Rogers Clark, Benjamin Logan, and others who later became his associates. After his company disbanded in 1776, Patterson set off down the Ohio River with six companions. He initially settled at McClelland's Station (later Georgetown) that fall but entered land claims for himself and various family members at Cane Run, where he built a crude cabin and planted corn. During a daring effort to obtain supplies from Fort Pitt the following year, he and five other young men were attacked by Indians as they made their way along the Ohio River. Patterson was severely wounded in the arm and shoulder and spent the winter and spring of 1776–1777 recuperating at his family's home in Pennsylvania.

That fall Patterson returned to Kentucky and lived at Harrodsburg through the following year. In May 1778, he joined Clark's expedition against the British-held towns in the Illinois country as a sergeant. Promoted to lieutenant by the following April, Patterson led twenty-five men to his Cane Run claim to clear land and to build a blockhouse and stockade, naming the site Lexington in commemoration of the Revolutionary War battle. Later that year, he joined Col. John Bowman's expedition against the Shawnee towns on the Little Miami River, north of the Ohio. Patterson returned to Pennsylvania in early 1780 to marry Elizabeth Lindsay, the sister of a boyhood companion. The newlyweds lived in Patterson's cabin in Lexington, but in times of danger they were forced into the crowded stockade, where their first two children died. The nine children that followed all survived to adulthood.

For the next dozen years, Patterson defended the Kentucky settlements. Captain Patterson commanded a company in Clark's 1780 expedition into the Miami Valley and helped build a blockhouse at the future site of Cincinnati before attacking the Shawnee villages at Old Chillicothe and Piqua. During 1782, Patterson led the Lexington militia in relief of Bryan's Station, barely survived a dreadful ambush at the Battle of Blue Licks, and served as a colonel under Clark during the fall campaign into the Miami country. He led a regiment of militia in Clark's third expedition north of the Ohio in 1786, during which his hand was badly smashed and his old shoulder wound reopened, never to reheal. Patterson participated in his sixth and last expedition north of the Ohio in October 1791 as commander of a regiment in General Arthur St. Clair's disastrous march deep into the Miami Valley. Nearly a third of the 3,000 regulars and militia were lost, but Patterson distinguished himself by keeping his men engaged as a rear guard defense during the retreat southward.

Patterson simultaneously pursued a variety of political and civic activities. In 1780 he was elected town trustee when Lexington was organized and served more than a dozen terms until 1803. He was county sheriff (1780) and justice of the peace (1783), and he held several lesser public offices. Patterson pushed for Kentucky statehood as representative to the second and third constitutional conventions at Danville (1785) and as representative to the Virginia House of Burgesses (1790). He was then elected to two terms in the Kentucky Assembly (1792 and 1798). Patterson was one of the original trustees of the Lexington Presbyterian Church (1783), Transylvania University (1783), and Lexington Library (1789). In 1788, he joined Mathias Denman and John Filson to promote a town site on the north side of the Ohio River. That December, Patterson led the first party of settlers to what became Cincinnati and laid out the streets and lots. In 1794, when Patterson sold his interest, Cincinnati was already the most important town in the Northwest Territory.

Despite owning half a dozen slaves, Patterson became committed to the cause of emancipation. In a report commissioned by the Presbyterian General Assembly in 1794, he and two ministers advocated a plan of gradual freedom with preparation. In pursuit of that goal, Patterson in 1798 advertised a Sunday school for slaves and took a leading role in promoting antislavery candidates to revise Kentucky's constitution. Perhaps as a result of the defeat of the emancipationists and a new constitution that made the abolition of slavery nearly impossible, Patterson decided to find a new home in Ohio. He purchased a 1,000-acre farm on the Miami River just south of Dayton and in 1804 moved his entire household. Most of Patterson's former slaves remained with him on Rubicon farm, as the Ohio homestead was called, but at least two had to sue for their freedom. The ill will this episode created among his Dayton neighbors made it nearly impossible for him to maintain the same status he had in Kentucky. He was hounded out of the Presbyterian Church and lost four consecutive elections to the Ohio Senate (1808–1814). Patterson's public services were limited to a brief term as trustee of the Dayton Academy (1808), appointment as quartermaster in the U.S. Army during the War of 1812 with the rank of colonel, and leadership of Bible and hymnbook associations. Patterson built lumber, grain, and cotton mills at Rubicon farm before he died quietly at home. Dayton newspapers took no notice of his passing.

Patterson's contributions to the settlement of Kentucky and Ohio have been largely overlooked, perhaps because the lives of romanticized frontiersmen, like Patterson's contemporaries Boone, Clark, and Logan, have been portrayed as more exciting and decisive than the sedentary lives of permanent settlers and town founders. Yet both aspects of frontier development were necessary for the successful planting of American society in the wilderness, and Patterson was among those rare men who made notable contributions to both. Patterson patrolled the frontier and led men into battle, but he also left enduring legacies by founding Lexington and Cincinnati and helping to establish Dayton as a commercial and manufacturing center. Two descendants, grandsons John Patterson and Frank Patterson, formed the National Cash Register Company in that city in 1884.

• The largest collection of Patterson manuscript materials is the Patterson Family Papers housed in the Special Collections and Archives, Wright State University Library, Dayton, Ohio. Selected Patterson manuscripts relevant to frontier Kentucky comprise the Robert Patterson Papers in the Draper Manuscripts at the State Historical Society of Wisconsin, Madison. Charlotte Reeve Conover wrote the only Patterson biographies, based primarily on extensive family reminiscences collected in the mid- and late nineteenth century, but they have since disappeared. They are *Concerning the Forefathers: Being a Memoir, with Personal Narrative and Letters of Two Pioneers, Col. Robert Patterson and Col. John Johnston* (1902) and the derivative *Builders in New Fields* (1939). Additional glimpses of Patterson's life can be found in George W. Ranck, *History of Lexington Kentucky: Its Early Annals and Recent Progress* (1872), and Charles R. Staples, *History of Pioneer Lexington, Kentucky, 1779–1806* (1939). See also the Patterson Homestead Museum at www.daytonhistory.org/patt_home.htm.

EMIL POCOCK

PECK, James (19 Dec. 1914–12 July 1993), activist, was born in Manhattan, New York, the son of Samuel Peck, a wealthy clothing wholesaler. Heir to the Peck and Peck fortune, James Peck grew up in Manhattan and attended the Choate School in Wallingford, Connecticut. In 1932 he enrolled at Harvard University, but he dropped out after his freshman year, largely because he felt that life in Cambridge, Massachusetts, was too disconnected from the radical social causes, including racial equality and workers' rights, that mattered to him. Peck had created something of a scandal in 1933 when he brought a black date to the Harvard freshman dance.

Restless and unsure of what to do next, Peck went to Paris in 1933, remaining there for a couple of years. After his return to the United States in the mid-1930s he worked as a seaman. During these years Peck first engaged in union activities, helping to organize what became the National Maritime Union. During a 1936 strike he was brutally beaten. It was during this period when, at the behest of Roger Baldwin of the American Civil Liberties Union, Peck began working as a reporter on union activities for Federated Press.

In 1940, with World War II looming ever more ominously, Peck, always a pacifist, declared himself a conscientious objector (CO), and he began working for the War Resisters League and writing a column for the *Conscientious Objector*. As a result of his CO status and his peace activism, he was interned in Danbury, Connecticut, from 1943 to 1945. While in prison he organized a protest against racial segregation in the mess hall. After a month of protest, during which time prison authorities placed Peck and his fellow organizers in solitary confinement, the prison warden announced the end of segregation in the prison's dining facilities.

After the war Peck continued to work with the War Resisters League, but he also began a long relationship with the Congress of Racial Equality (CORE). He was an ardent advocate of introducing Gandhi's principles of nonviolent confrontation to the struggle for racial justice. In 1947 he was among a group of demonstrators who burned their draft cards outside the White House. That year he participated in one of the first major civil rights challenges of the postwar era. The Supreme Court had ruled in *Morgan v. Virginia* (1946), that "Jim Crow" racial segregation of public conveyances contravened the commerce clause of the Constitution. Peck was among a group of sixteen men, half black and half white, who sought to publicize the *Morgan* ruling and test whether bus companies were complying with it. Peck was the first victim of violence on what was called the Journey of Reconciliation. In Durham, North Carolina Peck was arrested with the civil rights activist Bayard Rustin and Andrew Johnson, a law student from Cincinnati, for challenging state segregation laws. Officials dropped the charges once the NAACP sent a lawyer to defend the men.

From 1949 to 1965 Peck served as the editor for CORE's newsletter, the *CORElator*, for sixteen years, the periodical's entire run. In 1950 he married Paula Zweier; they had two children. But Peck ascended to his greatest level of fame on the Freedom Rides in May 1961. Peck was the only person to participate in both the Journey of Reconciliation and the Freedom Rides. After minor incidents in Virginia and the Carolinas, including Peck's spending a night in a rural South Carolina jail, the Freedom Riders entered Alabama prepared for violence, having previously been warned by Martin Luther King, Jr., and others. On

Mother's Day, May 14, Peck was on the second of two Trailways buses carrying Freedom Riders through Alabama. The first bus was besieged by a mob and eventually firebombed a few miles from Anniston. A group of white thugs took over the second Trailways bus and beat the passengers, delivering such savage blows to the white Freedom Rider Walter Bergman that he suffered permanent brain damage. Upon the Riders' arrival in Birmingham, a white mob set upon them when they debarked. The Ku Klux Klan had been given assurances by the city's commissioner of public safety, Bull Connor, that they would have fifteen minutes to do their worst to the bus passengers before the police would intervene. Peck was one of several riders to receive a vicious beating that day. In 1983 Peck won a $25,000 lawsuit against the Federal Bureau of Investigation, which had previous knowledge that there would be violence in Alabama but did nothing to prevent it.

In June 1965 Peck was forced out of CORE when that organization took a radical turn and expelled all of its white officials. He continued to organize for civil rights and against the Vietnam War and nuclear tests. He was arrested for protesting during the May 1971 May Day demonstration against the Vietnam War in Washington, D.C. He also published numerous articles and wrote three books, *We Who Would Not Kill* (1958), *Freedom Ride* (1962), and *Upper Dogs versus Underdog* (1969).

For most of his life Peck was committed to racial and economic justice and peace. He was long respected for putting his life on the line for the causes he felt were most important. With the Freedom Rides he spent several weeks as a national figure, though within the peace and civil rights communities he was both known and respected for more than five decades.

Peck died in Minneapolis, where he lived for his last eight years. Ten years before his death he suffered a stroke that paralyzed him on one side.

• James Mosby's interview with Peck is in the Civil Rights Documentation Project of the Ralph Bunche Oral History Project at Howard University. The best sources on Peck are his own writings and books about the events in which he participated. An especially apt starting point is his book *Freedom Ride*, which explains his participation in the Civil Rights movement from the 1940s through the early 1960s. His work on the *CORElator* is also invaluable. An obituary is in the *New York Times*, 13 July 1993.

DEREK CHARLES CATSAM

PETTINGILL, Olin Sewall, Jr. (30 Oct. 1907–11 Dec. 2001), ornithologist and educator, was born in Belgrade, Maine, the only child of Olin Sewall Pettingill, a physician, and Marion Bradbury Groves Pettingill. The boy was called Sewall within the family to distinguish him from his father, who shortly after receiving his M.D. degree in 1909 was diagnosed with tuberculosis. In the four years following his father's recovery in 1911, Sewall and his mother accompanied him as he successively held medical positions at three sanitariums, in New York, Massachusetts, and Rhode

Island. In 1915, Dr. Pettingill became superintendent at the Western Maine Sanitarium in Hebron, and there the family remained for six years. Sewall was taught at home by his mother until 1916, when he was permitted to attend a school set up on the sanitarium grounds for youngsters who had been exposed to tuberculosis and were under observation. His interest in birds began in boyhood, stimulated in part by the writings of the naturalist Thornton W. Burgess, whom he subsequently met while in college.

In 1921, when the father took up the superintendency of a newly opened sanitarium in Middleton, Massachusetts, young Pettingill attended Holten High School in nearby Danvers, graduating in 1925. After failing several of the examinations for entrance to Bowdoin College, he studied at Kents Hill School for a year preparing for another attempt. In 1926, though earning only "conditioned" status in Roman History, he entered Bowdoin. Sewall decided to make his career in ornithology, and, while still a student, participated in the first of many ornithological expeditions. At Bowdoin, he met and later assisted Thornton W. Burgess in filming the nearly extinct heath hen on Martha's Vineyard.

In 1930, Pettingill began doctoral studies at Cornell, which had the only graduate program in the nation focusing solely on ornithology. There he studied under Arthur A. Allen. As a graduate student in 1931, he served as the photographer on the Carnegie Museum of Pittsburgh's expedition to Hudson Bay, returning with some of the earliest photos of subarctic bird species. On New Year's Eve 1932, Pettingill married his childhood sweetheart Eleanor Rice, with whom he had two daughters.

Pettingill received his Ph.D. in 1933. A revision of his dissertation on the American Woodcock was published in the *Memoirs of the Boston Society of Natural History* in 1936. He took a temporary teaching position at the Ithaca (N.Y.) Night School in 1933 and became a teaching fellow at Bowdoin during 1933–1934. In academic year 1935–1936 he was an instructor at Westbrook Junior College for Women in Portland, Maine. The next year, he obtained an appointment as assistant professor at Carleton College in Minnesota, where he remained until 1954, rising over the years to full professor. Former students often recalled his preference for wearing items of red clothing. In 1945, he took a year off to study whooping crane distribution and migration for the U.S. Fish and Wildlife Service in Texas and Canada. During most summers from 1938 to 1967, Pettingill taught at the University of Michigan Biological Station near Cheboygan, Michigan, where he himself had first studied in the summer of 1928. His research interests focused on the behavior, breeding, ecology, and geographical distribution of birds.

Pettingill's book *Laboratory and Field Manual of Ornithology*, published in 1939, subsequently underwent two revisions, the last in 1956. This book and its successor, *Ornithology in Laboratory and Field* (1970, 1985), were used in at least 150 American colleges and universities for nearly half a century. Pettingill also wrote the first books to encourage American birders to take advantage of post–World War II highway expansion and prosperity. The idea for these books came to him in late 1945 when he, his wife, and some friends visited the so-called "Hawk Mountain" (Blue Mountain) in Drehersville, Pennsylvania, where hawks congregated every autumn during their annual migration. Some fifty persons were there, mostly from the immediate area. Pettingill began to wonder whether people other than locals knew the best times to go birding at places like Hawk Mountain, what birds to look for, and, most important, how to get there. As he later reminisced, "Why not write a guide to places of birds, a guide to sites for birds, or simply a guide to bird-finding?" (Pettingill, 1980). His *Guide to Bird-Finding East of the Mississippi* (1951) and *Guide to Bird-Finding West of the Mississippi* (1953) were revised in 1977 and 1981.

Beginning in 1941, he created a number of both instructional and popular films about birds for Coronet Films and Walt Disney Productions. In 1953–1954, he led a Disney-sponsored expedition to the Falkland Islands. Over the next twenty years, he returned there on five occasions to film and study penguins. His short films for Disney included the widely viewed *Nature's Half Acre*, *Water Birds*, *Vanishing Prairie*, and *Islands of the Sea*. Other expeditions took him to Mexico (1941), Iceland (1958), Midway Atoll (1963), and New Zealand (1965–1966). From 1943 until 1978, he lectured for the National Audubon Society's screen tour program, which entailed much travel in North America, the Caribbean, and England. During these trips he spoke to some half-million persons. On four occasions in the 1970s, he served as naturalist-lecturer for Lindblad tours of Antarctic waters.

In 1960, he was appointed director of development for the Cornell Laboratory of Ornithology, and within months he was named the Laboratory's director, succeeding his former mentor A. A. Allen. There, Pettingill began publication of the periodical *Living Bird*, and in 1972, a year before his retirement, he published the first edition of the laboratory's home study course in bird biology. Two years later, he received the laboratory's Arthur A. Allen award, for broadening popular interest in ornithology. Pettingill spent his early retirement years in Wayne, Maine, where generations of Pettingills had lived since 1819. In 1978, he became visiting professor of biology at Virginia Polytechnic Institute and State University.

Throughout his career, Pettingill found time for professional and amateur organizations in his field. President of the Maine Audubon Society in 1959 and 1960, he served as secretary of the National Audubon Society from 1957 to 1959 and again from 1963 to 1966. He was also a member of the society's national board for nineteen years (1955–1974) and from 1957 to 1968 wrote a column for *Audubon Magazine*, "Bird-Finding with Olin Sewall Pettingill." A Life Fellow and a secretary of the American Ornithologists Union,

Pettingill also served the Wilson Ornithological Society as secretary, vice president, and president. He was also a life member of the British Ornithologist's Union and the Ornithological Society of New Zealand. He edited *Enjoying Maine Birds* (1960) and was coauthor of *Enjoying Birds in Upstate New York* (with Sally F. Hoyt, 1963) and *Birds of the Black Hills* (with N. R. Whitney, Jr., 1965). In 1966, he coauthored, with Robert S. Arbib, Jr., and Sally Hoyt Spofford, *Enjoying Birds around New York City*. In 1968, he served as editor-in-chief of *The Audubon Illustrated Handbook of American Birds*. His other books include *Bird Life of the Grand Manan Archipelago* (1939), *The Bird Watcher's America* (1965), and *Another Penguin Summer* (1975). He also contributed articles on birds to various dictionaries and encyclopedias. An autobiography covering Pettingill's early years appeared in 1992. Pettingill received honorary doctorates of science from Bowdoin (1956) and Colby (1975) Colleges and from the University of Maine (1982).

His wife Eleanor died in 1977, and in 1985 Pettingill married Josephine Stott Dawson, a widow. In 1987 they moved to a retirement community in Bedford, a suburb of Fort Worth, Texas, near the home of one of his daughters. Nine days after his second wife's death, in 2001, he died there.

• Personal communications from Joyce Cooper, Vermont Institute of Natural Science, 17 Feb. 2003, and from Pettingill's daughter Polly-Ann Pettingill Losito, 22 Feb. 2003, supply valuable information. In June 1988 Pettingill presented his collection of some 1,500 ornithological books and 4,000 volumes of bound journals to the Vermont Institute of Natural Science, Woodstock, Vermont, where they constitute the Olin Sewall Pettingill Jr. Ornithological Library. He donated his library of 300 motion picture films and color slides to the Roger Tory Peterson Institute in Jamestown, New York. His autobiography *My Way to Ornithology* (1992) provides an account of his first twenty-nine years until his appointment to the Carleton faculty in 1936. Pettingill wrote about his travels in the South Atlantic in "People and Penguins of the Faraway Falklands," *National Geographic*, Mar. 1956, and his wife Eleanor Rice Pettingill offered her account of their adventures there in *A Penguin Summer* (1960). There is no biography of Pettingill. Artist-ornithologist George Miksch Sutton, a friend and longtime colleague of Pettingill's who was a fellow doctoral student at Cornell, sheds light on their student experiences in *Bird Student: An Autobiography* (1980). A description of how Pettingill developed his bird-finding concept can be found in his "Valedictory to Bird Finding," *Birding*, Oct. 1980. The history of the Hawk Mountain Sanctuary is in Maurice Broun, *Hawks Aloft: The Story of Hawk Mountain* (1949). Pettingill's work with the Audubon Society is mentioned in Graham's *The Audubon Ark: A History of the National Audubon Society* (1990). Some discussion of his contributions as director of the Cornell Laboratory of Ornithology can be found in Gregory S. Butcher and Kevin McGowan, "History of Ornithology at Cornell," in W. E. Davis, Jr., and J. A. Jackson, eds., *Contributions to the History of North American Ornithology* (1995). Sketches of Pettingill's life and work include Frank Graham, "The Man from Wayne: Sewall Pettingill: An American Ornithologist," *Audubon*, Mar. 1981, and Lola Oberman, "Olin Sewall Pettingill, Jr.," *Bird Watcher's* Digest, Jan.–Feb. 1995. An obituary is in the *Citizen* (Auburn, N.Y.)

on 13 Dec. 2001. Appreciations of Pettingill's life and career were published in *Birdchat*, 20 Dec. 2001; *Birding*, Feb. 2002; *Living Bird*, Spring 2002; *International Hawkwatcher*, Aug. 2002; and the *AUK*, Oct. 2002.

KEIR B. STERLING

PHILLIPS, Duncan (26 June 1886–9 May 1966), art collector, writer, and museum founder, was born in Pittsburgh, Pennsylvania, the son of Duncan Clinch Phillips, a business executive, and Eliza Laughlin Phillips, the daughter of James Laughlin, a banker and cofounder of the Jones and Laughlin Steel Company. In 1896 the family moved to Washington, D.C., where Phillips attended private schools. In 1908 he received a B.A. in English literature from Yale University. There he had published essays and reviews on esthetic matters. After graduation, he made his home in Washington while continuing to educate himself in the visual arts through reading, collecting, extended sojourns in New York, and travel to Asia and Europe. In 1912 he published his first article in a professional art magazine, and two years later a group of essays appeared as his first book, *The Enchantment of Art* (rev. ed., 1927). In these personal reflections on art and literature, he proposed that appreciation of art enhances life more generally.

Following the closely spaced deaths of his father and only sibling, a brother, Phillips conceived the idea of an art gallery in their memory. With the concurrence of his mother, in 1918 he created the Phillips Memorial Art Gallery in rooms of the family home at Twenty-first and Q Streets, Northwest. It was incorporated as a foundation in 1920 and regularly opened, on a part-time basis, to the public the following year. Phillips envisioned its character as a welcoming, domestically scaled venue for unhurried appreciation and study of art. Establishing the museum focused Phillips's energies on expanding and refining his collection. Quickly, he methodically set about purchasing representative works by artists he admired, motivated largely by the desire to share widely his love of art. Like his evenhanded internationalism, his devotion to public education was unusual among private collectors of his generation. To further this aim, the museum from its inception presented frequent rearrangements of the collection to illuminate a single artist or tendency. In addition to accompanying essays, Phillips also took the initiative to publish catalogues and other informative materials, and for a time the museum offered art instruction.

When the museum opened, the general nature of the collection had already been established, with one important exception. Phillips had yet to develop an appreciation for the more radical forms of modern art. He had, in fact, written vehemently in opposition to such art displayed at the 1913 Armory Show, which he found "quite stupefying in its vulgarity," and had continued to react with distaste to abstraction and formal distortion. Instead, the original collection emphasized less controversial European and American Realists, Impressionists, and Symbolists. Among others, these included Daumier, Monet, and Fantin-Latour, as well as James McNeill Whistler, George Inness, Childe Hassam, Maurice Prendergast, John Twachtman, Arthur B. Davies, Robert Henri, Ernest Lawson, and John Sloan. He also owned a fine Chardin.

In 1921 Phillips married artist Marjorie Acker; they had two children. While continuing to paint in an Impressionistic realist style, Mrs. Phillips became a full partner in every aspect of the gallery's management, particularly in the acquisition of additional works of art. Her trained eye and familiarity with studio practice encouraged Phillips to explore avenues of artistic expression he had earlier rejected. Additions to the collection during the 1920s demonstrate her husband's evolution into an enthusiast for modern art. His significant purchases during the early part of the decade included works by El Greco, Delacroix, Courbet, Constable, Alfred Sisley, and Redon. In 1923 he signaled his ambitions for the museum and consolidated the strength of his nineteenth-century holdings by purchasing Renoir's *Luncheon of the Boating Party*. One of the artist's finest and most appealing works, it has remained the collection's single most renowned and popular item. However, before the end of the 1920s Phillips had made his first purchases of work by Cézanne, Bonnard, Matisse, Picasso, Braque, Arthur Dove, John Marin, Georgia O'Keeffe, and Charles Demuth.

In 1930 the family moved, making available the entirety of the residence to museum uses. Despite retrenchments during the Depression, Phillips never ceased augmenting the collection. Indicating his continuing growth in personal taste, in the 1940s he bought work by Soutine, Kandinsky, Mondrian, Morris Graves, and Jacob Lawrence. Later he purchased works by Miró, Nicolas de Staël, Richard Diebenkorn, Kenneth Noland, and Morris Louis, as well as Mark Rothko, Adolph Gottlieb, Willem de Kooning, and other abstract expressionists. Over the years he also created notable "units" that represent in depth such favorites as Daumier, Degas, Bonnard, Vuillard, Rouault, Albert Pinkham Ryder, J. Alden Weir, Prendergast, Sloan, Braque, Klee, Ben Nicholson, Dove, Marin, Karl Knaths, and Milton Avery. In 1960 he oversaw construction of an annex (later enlarged) to the museum, which the following year was renamed the Phillips Collection. Building on its strengths, the museum after Phillips's death continued, in accordance with the founder's wishes, to acquire works that supplement Phillips's vision.

Along with many articles, exhibition catalogues, and gallery brochures, Phillips published several books, including *A Collection in the Making* (1926), *The Artist Sees Differently* (1931), and *The Leadership of Giorgione* (1937), a scholarly meditation on the Renaissance artist, an early love, with attention to his relevance for modern art. Phillips was not an original esthetician, and his old-fashioned prose style cannot be described as forceful or entertaining. However, his writings exhibit a deeply felt and sincere desire to articulate with honesty and precision the reasons for his pleasurable response to individual works of art. Over time he worked out a mature philosophy of value in art, based on principles of individualism, expressiveness, craftsmanship, and continuity with tradition. Intuitively he was drawn to sensuous color and a poetic or lyric response to life. He disliked extremism, vulgarity, and art beholden to any intellectually, politically, or socially defined program. Despite these clearcut tastes, he prized tolerance and approached new forms of art on the basis of personal attraction, independent of fashion, theory, or nationalism. The quality of the collection confirms the strength of his judgments. Although he for the most part bypassed expressionism, surrealism, geometric painting, and pop art, his legacy otherwise recapitulates progressive European and American art of the century or so before his death, with emphasis on the painterly tradition. Underscoring his belief in the universality of great works of art, the collection's relatively few earlier works confirm the values he sought in contemporary art, an individualistic point of view and a love of art for its own sake.

• Phillips's papers are housed at The Phillips Collection and the Archives of American Art. Among his own extensive writings, the two collection catalogues he prepared are particularly useful for insights into his philosophy and purposes. These are *A Collection in the Making* (1926) and *The Phillips Collection Catalogue: A Museum of Modern Art and Its Sources* (1952). The most extensive and reliable published source of information about Phillips and his collection is Erika D. Passantino, ed., *The Eye of Duncan Phillips: A Collection in the Making* (1999). The best source of biographical material is Marjorie Phillips, *Duncan Phillips and His Collection* (1970). Also useful are Sasha M. Newman, *Arthur Dove and Duncan Phillips: Artist and Patron* (1981), Benjamin Forgey, "The Odyssey of Duncan Phillips," *Portfolio* (Nov./Dec. 1981): 66–71, and Elizabeth Hutton Turner, *In the American Grain: The Stieglitz Circle at the Phillips Collection* (1995). Obituaries are in *Time*, 20 May 1966; *Newsweek*, 23 May 1966; *Arts Magazine*, June 1966; and the *Burlington Magazine*, Aug. 1966.

ANN LEE MORGAN

PIKE, Kenneth Lee (9 June 1912–31 Dec. 2000), linguist and field consultant, was born in Woodstock, Connecticut, the son of Ernest R. Pike, a physician, and Hattie May Granniss Pike. He was the seventh of eight children in a strongly religious family where Scripture readings, hymns, and prayers were part of daily life. Following graduation from Woodstock Academy in 1928, he went to work as a supermarket clerk in Providence, Rhode Island. Shortly thereafter, Pike vowed to enter the ministry if his father recovered from an illness. In 1929 he enrolled at Gordon College of Theology and Missions in Boston. His parents had spent two years as missionaries in Alaska, and Pike decided to apply for a position as a Christian missionary to China after earning a bachelor's degree in theology at Gordon in 1933. His application was rejected because of his "nervous" disposition, and instead, following a postgraduate year at Gordon, he

went in the summer of 1935 to Camp Wycliffe, a training program for Bible translators in Arkansas.

The summer course at Camp Wycliffe included some lectures on anthropology, a demonstration of grammatical analysis, and ten days' instruction in phonetics, the linguistic specialization that became the focus of Pike's academic writing for the following decade. When the summer ended, Pike and several other students went to Mexico City with Cameron Townsend, director of the camp. Pike was soon on his own in the countryside studying the Mixtec Indian language. Much of his later work and his ideas about a holistic approach to language, behavior, and knowledge grew out of this early experience.

He spent most of the next several years in Mexico, returning to the United States each summer to teach phonetics at Camp Wycliffe. In 1938 he married Evelyn Griset, Townsend's niece. They built a cabin in San Miguel where Pike gathered data, developed an alphabet, wrote phonological and grammatical descriptions of Mixtec, and translated the New Testament; material from his study of Mixtec tones became the basis a decade later for his book *Tone Languages* (1948). Evelyn Pike had studied at Camp Wycliffe and later taught phonetics and grammar, coauthoring several textbooks and linguistic studies of Mexican languages. The couple had three children.

Reading Leonard Bloomfield's *Language* (1933) on his own, Pike learned more linguistics, and beginning in 1937 he attended the Linguistic Institute of the Linguistic Society of America, held each summer at the University of Michigan. Here he studied with Edward Sapir, discussed linguistics with Bloomfield, and became a doctoral candidate at Michigan under Charles C. Fries. His dissertation, completed in 1941, was published as *Phonetics: A Critical Analysis of Phonetic Theory and a Technic for the Practical Description of Sounds* (1943). His major contribution in this work was a systematic classification of a wide variety of language sounds, drawing on data from the Americas, Asia, and Africa. Townsend had suggested that he write such a book as a text for the missionary students whose ultimate goal was translation of the gospels into the native languages of the peoples they were evangelizing. In the many cases of languages that did not have writing systems, the first step in developing an appropriate alphabet was the determination of their sounds.

Throughout his career, Pike emphasized the utility of linguistics to the work of the missionary linguists of the Summer Institute of Linguistics, the formal name of the Camp Wycliffe program after it was incorporated in 1942. His textbook *Phonemics: A Technique for Reducing Languages to Writing* (1947) was a practical guide to the creation of alphabets, but it was also a contribution to the development of American descriptive linguistics. Here and in a classic article, "Grammatical Prerequisites to Phonemic Analysis," in *Word* 3 (1947): 155–72, Pike argued for the use of grammatical information in arriving at the phonemic analysis of a language. This position was not adopted by

American linguists of the time, but it was later a key concept in generative phonology.

Pike became president of SIL when it was founded; he continued in that role until 1979 and then assumed the title of president emeritus. Throughout his service, he acted as a field consultant in linguistic analysis to thousands of missionary linguists, conducting SIL workshops around the world. To these SIL members, students of linguistics at academic institutions, and sometimes church groups Pike became famous for his monolingual demonstrations. A stranger speaking a language unknown to Pike would come onto a stage, and Pike—using a handful of simple props (some leaves, a stone, a piece of fruit) without an interpreter or the English language—would in less than an hour elicit examples of the language, write them down in phonetic transcription on blackboards, analyze aspects of the phonological and grammatical systems represented in the data, and even speak a few phrases of the language.

In 1948 Pike was appointed to the linguistics faculty at the University of Michigan, a position he held concurrently with the presidency of SIL until he retired from both positions in 1979. An interest in grammar, first apparent in the article "Taxemes and Immediate Constituents," in *Language* 19 (1943): 65–82, became the focus of his work in the 1940s and 1950s, resulting in the development of tagmemics, an extension of concepts and methods used in phonology to the analysis of grammar. Like all his work, Pike's tagmemics was a practical approach, a tool in the work of SIL. It was not widely adopted elsewhere.

Pike expanded tagmemics to encompass language in society and social behavior, a holistic theory with origins in his immersion experience in Mixtec language and culture in Mexico. *Language in Relation to a Unified Theory of the Structure of Human Behavior* (3 vols., 1954–1960; 2d. rev. ed., 1967) was his definitive statement of this approach, and it was here that he coined the terms *etic* and *emic*. These terms refer to two perspectives in the observation and analysis of data. *Etic* describes the details observed by a trained outsider who is unaware of the structural significance of the elements that are perceived. *Emic* is the perspective of an insider who knows the system and whether the differences between details are significant or not. Pike drew the etic/emic distinction from the linguistic terms "phonetic" (the unanalyzed sounds used in a language) and "phonemic" (the structural units of the sound system), but he extended it to other areas of behavior, and it has spread to the social sciences. When he turned to philosophical considerations in his later years, Pike employed the terms in his book *Talk, Thought, and Thing: The Emic Road toward Conscious Knowledge* (1993).

Pike's influence within academic linguistics in the United States diminished as generative theory gained a commanding position in the 1960s, but he was widely respected for his methods and practical applications in the descriptions of languages. He was elected to the presidency of the Linguistic Society of America (1961) and the Linguistic Association of Canada and the United States (1977–1978), held membership in the National Academy of Sciences, and lectured in more than forty countries during his life. Within his religious community, he was admired not only for the training of missionaries in linguistic analysis, but also for his Bible lessons and Christian poetry. He died in Dallas, Texas, headquarters of SIL International.

• An autobiographical essay is "A Linguistic Pilgrimage," in *First Person Singular III*, ed. E. F. K. Koerner (1998), pp. 143–58. On tagmemics, see Kenneth L. Pike and Evelyn G. Pike, *Grammatical Analysis*, 2d. ed. (1982), and Kenneth L. Pike, *Linguistic Concepts: An Introduction to Tagmemics*, (1982); see also *Emics and Etics: The Insider/Outsider Debate*, ed. Thomas N. Headland, Kenneth L. Pike, and Marvin Harris (1990). Twenty-five of Pike's religious talks appear in his book *With Heart and Mind: A Personal Synthesis of Scholarship and Devotion* (1962). *Selected Writings to Commemorate the 60th Birthday of Kenneth Lee Pike*, ed. Ruth M. Brend (1972), contains many of Pike's major articles, a few of his religious essays and poems, a biographical sketch by his sister Eunice V. Pike, and a bibliography of his writings. More inclusive are the biography *Ken Pike: Scholar and Christian* (1981) by Eunice V. Pike, and *Kenneth Lee Pike Bibliography*, comp. Ruth M. Brend (1987).

JULIA S. FALK

PIÑERO, Miguel (19 Dec. 1946–17 June 1988), playwright and poet, was born Miguel Antonio Gomez Piñero in Gurabo, in east central Puerto Rico, the oldest child of Adelina Piñero and Miguel Angel Gomez Ramos, whose occupations are unknown. The family was poor and, with the couple's four additional children, large (later Adelina Piñero had two more out of wedlock, then three more with her second husband). In 1950 the family moved to New York City and settled on Manhattan's Lower East Side. Four years later Adelina Piñero, who was pregnant at the time, was forced out onto the streets when her husband left her, and she and her children subsisted there for several months until welfare payments came through.

In school Miguel Piñero was often unruly and truant, and he was transferred to three different schools on the Lower East Side. His education was an amalgam of survival tactics for streets ridden with crime and drugs and a love of language learned from both parents, who were natural storytellers. His mother wrote verse and rudimentary novels, which she read regularly to her children. Miguel Piñero read comic books, newspapers, and magazines and wrote some verse as a child and a teenager, though his struggles in school and forays into petty crime and drugs eclipsed everything else. From the time he was eleven or twelve he was in and out of juvenile detention centers. At fifteen he was sentenced to a year in reform school at the Otisville (New York) Training School for Boys. Two years later he was caught burglarizing a jewelry store and was sentenced to three years in the New York City correctional facility on Rikers Island.

Known to his friends as Mikey, Piñero, wiry and slight at five feet, six inches, with large brown eyes, carried on conversations with a throwaway cool street rap style. Though he would not write in earnest for some time, his prison experiences defined Piñero as a writer. Paroled at nineteen, he emerged a heroin addict, having learned, as he said later, "how to jump cables, how to break into a house easier, how to have no feelings at all when you stick somebody" (*Current Biography*).

Piñero joined a number of programs for education and drug rehabilitation (including Phoenix House). He also became interested in ethnic pride, joining an antidrug Puerto Rican gang, the Young Lords. But unable to beat his addiction, he found himself back on the street, pushing drugs and committing robberies to support his habit. He was again sentenced to Rikers Island for possession of drugs. On his release his mother committed him to the Manhattan State Hospital. There he earned his high school equivalency certificate. But his addiction again led him back to drug deals and robberies. He usually targeted pimps and pushers, who, as he later explained to one interviewer, though armed and dangerous, would not call the police. In 1971 he was caught in an armed burglary of a Lower East Side apartment. Two witnesses at his trial agreed that he was "the nicest burglar" they had ever met. Piñero was sentenced to five years in the New York State penitentiary at Ossining—Sing Sing.

During this incarceration Piñero began to write seriously. First he wrote love letters for fellow inmates for pay. Then a theatrical workshop organized by directors Clay Stevenson and Marvin Felix Camillo came to Sing Sing. Piñero showed Camillo some of his poetry, and Camillo became his mentor, entering one of his poems, "Black Woman with a Blonde Wig On," in a contest. It won Piñero a $50 second prize. Under Camillo's guidance, Piñero acted in the workshop and then adapted his poetry to a theatrical format, with skits and short plays, including *All Junkies* and the revue *Straight from the Ghetto* (with Neil Harris). Piñero began the play *Short Eyes*, using the prison term for a child molester, the most reviled of offenders among other prisoners. Piñero finished the first act in a week, typing it in the four hours a day permitted him on the prison typewriter. Subtitled *The Killing of a Sex Offender by the Inmates of the House of Detention Awaiting Trial*, the play told the story of prisoners in a holding room into whose midst is deposited an accused child molester. Against the backdrop of social hierarchy, tension, and inner morality that defines prison life, the inmates sadistically torment and kill the confessed sex offender; they later learn that he was innocent.

The *New York Times* theater critic Mel Gussow attended a program of short works presented by the Sing Sing theatre workshop, including twelve pieces by Piñero. Gussow wrote an article about the performance and the hooting, hollering appreciation from the inmate audience and guards ("Sing Sing Audi-

ence: Captivated, Not Captive," 27 May 1972). As a result of the article and under Camillo's tutelage, Piñero began his parole by joining the street theater group known as the Family at the Theatre of Riverside Church. The Family was made up of ex-inmates and ex-drug addicts under the stewardship of the actress Colleen Dewhurst. In January 1974 *Short Eyes* debuted before the public at the Theatre of Riverside Church.

Immediately the play caught the attention of New York critics and the theater elite, who recognized Piñero as a uniquely powerful new voice (if somewhat lacking in theatrical skill). Jack Kroll wrote in *Newsweek* (8 Apr. 1974) that the play "needed no apology—it isn't occupational therapy and it isn't a freak show; it's an authentic, powerful theatrical piece." Piñero was compared, in his depiction of prison life, to the French dramatist Jean Genet. Other critics cited the play's eye for dark humor. Harold Clurman wrote in the *Nation*, "The picture is one of people restricted by poverty, ignorance, disease and social corruption, through which one perceives traces of the originally healthy fiber" (20 Apr. 1974, p. 20).

Joseph Papp, the impresario behind the Public Theatre, moved *Short Eyes* in March 1974 to an off-Broadway run at the Public, followed by a run at Lincoln Center's Vivian Beaumont Theatre. It garnered honors for best play from the New York Drama Critics Circle Award as well as an Obie and a Tony nomination in 1974. Piñero's mother, who had always encouraged him in his writing, lived to see *Short Eyes* reach the stage but died before the height of its success.

With Papp and the Public Theatre behind him, Piñero continued to write, but his sudden success did little to soothe him. "Here I was with $60 one day," he told *People* magazine, "and all of a sudden somebody was giving me $15,000. I was being asked to lecture at Princeton, at Rutgers, at Pratt Institute. Here I have no education whatsoever and I am working as a mentor to the top students at Pratt Institute. What the hell am I doin' here?"

In 1974 Piñero turned his downtown apartment into a poetry and theater space to nurture other writers—many of them troubled teens—from his own ethnic background, which he dubbed "Nuyorican." "That's what we could do for them," Piñero told the *New York Times* (5 May 1974), "instill pride, and confidence in their own intelligence so that they can feel there are things they can do instead of hustling." With his friend Miguel Algarin, Piñero opened the Nuyorican Poets Café on East Third Street. He and Algarin then edited *Nuyorican Poetry: An Anthology of Puerto Rican Words and Feelings* (1975). He also gathered fifteen young hustlers from Times Square in 1974 and fashioned them into a theater group to perform his one-act play *Subculture*. But Piñero continued to have brushes with the law. In 1974 he was arrested for cursing at a subway attendant whom he saw shouting racial epithets at two Puerto Rican turnstile jumpers; the case was thrown out of court. Three years later he was arrested for allegedly robbing passengers in a taxi and then stealing the cab. He fought the charge—a luxury, he said, because now he had the money to do so—and after a year he was cleared.

In 1975 Piñero went to Philadelphia to play God in Bruce Jay Friedman's play *Steambath* and decided to stay there, using the city as a setting for his next play, *Eulogy for a Small Time Thief*. In 1977 the play was given its premiere off-off-Broadway at New York's Ensemble Studio Theatre. Also that year *Short Eyes* was released as a film, for which Piñero wrote the screenplay, adding an additional part for himself, that of Go Go, a drug-dealing child molester. The film was generally well received. In 1977 he married Juanita Lovette Rameize. They adopted a son. Piñero and Rameize divorced two years later.

Writing again for the stage, Piñero continued to explore the underside of life, with convicts, drug dealers, pimps, and whores, which he featured again in his play *The Sun Always Shines for the Cool*. This play debuted in 1978 at New York's 78th Street Theatre Lab, and was less well received than his earlier work. Moving from Philadelphia to Los Angeles, he founded the One Act Theatre Festival, where he premiered his play *Guntower* along with his comedies *Paper Toilet* and *Cold Beer*. In Los Angeles, Piñero turned his hand to television, writing two episodes of *Baretta* and appearing as an undercover narcotics officer in one. He also appeared in an episode of *Kojak*. He played a drug dealer in the movie *Fort Apache, the Bronx* (1980) with Paul Newman, and later in the 1980s he appeared in the movies *Breathless*, *Exposed*, and *Deal of the Century* (all 1983), and *The Pick-Up Artist* (1987), usually playing cons and hustlers.

In 1980 Piñero published a volume of his collected poetry, *La Bodega Sold Dreams*. When Papp told him to "get off the street thing and do something different," Piñero wrote *A Midnight Moon at the Greasy Spoon*, a play about growing old that premiered at New York's Theatre for the New City in 1981. Gussow wrote in the *New York Daily News* (27 Apr. 1981) that the play suffered from "restless disarray" but remarked on its "flavorful atmosphere and characters." Others view it as his most fully realized play.

Known for his generosity to friends as well as his personal disorganization, Piñero achieved recognition as the premier theatrical and literary voice of urban Hispanic culture in America while failing to extricate himself from the street life from which virtually all his writing continued to spring. He died in New York. Over a decade later, in December 2001, the filmmaker Leon Ichaso released a movie about his life, *Piñero*, starring Benjamin Bratt, with Rita Moreno as Piñero's mother and Mandy Patinkin as Papp. Though critics noted that the movie refrained from moralizing, they saw it as a portrait of a damned artist whose self-destruction was, as the *New York Times* called it, "an appalling waste" (13 Dec. 2001). John Leguizamo, the initial force behind the making of the film, withdrew from playing the role of Piñero, reportedly unable to confront Piñero's insinuated bisexuality and encounters with male prostitution. However, the real Joseph Papp called Piñero "an extraordinarily original talent . . . the first Puerto Rican playwright to really break through and be accepted as a major writer for the stage."

• A clippings file on Piñero is in the New York Public Library for the Performing Arts at Lincoln Center. Piñero is covered in *Current Biography* (1983); *Contemporary Authors Online* (2002); *The Scribner Encyclopedia of American Lives*, vol. 2, *1986–1990* (1999); and *Dictionary of Hispanic Biography* (1996). See also Leroy Aarons, *People*, 14 Nov. 1977; and Mel Gussow, "From the Streets, a Poet of the Stage," *New York Times*, 3 July 1988. Stephen Holden reviewed the film *Piñero* in "Playing Piñero as Just Enough of a Mess," *New York Times*, 13 Dec. 2001. Obituaries are in the *New York Times*, 18 June 1988; the *Los Angeles Times*, 18 June 1988; and the *Washington Post*, 19 June 1988.

DEBORAH GRACE WINER

PITKIN, Walter Boughton (6 Feb. 1878–25 Jan. 1953), philosopher and pundit, was born in Ypsilanti, Michigan, the son of Caleb Seymour Pitkin, a printer, and Lucy Tryphene Boughton Pitkin. In 1880 the family moved to Detroit, where Caleb Pitkin worked as a printer for the Detroit *Journal*; he later worked for the *Detroit Evening News*.

In 1896 Walter Pitkin graduated from Detroit High School and then enrolled at the University of Michigan. Though he was a talented student of languages and philosophy, he became ill and failed to complete his degree. In 1900 he obtained a position as an attaché to the U.S. commission for the Paris Exposition. Following the closure of the exposition, Pitkin sold the abandoned exhibits to fund further travel and study at the Sorbonne and the University of Berlin. In 1901 he returned to the United States to enter the doctoral program at the Hartford Seminary in Connecticut. During that time he met Mary Bartholomew Gray, daughter of a Hartford banker. He married her in 1903; they had five sons.

In 1903 the Hartford Seminary awarded Pitkin a two-year fellowship to study at the University of Berlin, where he read Arabic, psychology, and philosophy. Among his tutors were Edmund Husserl and Georg Simmel, philosophers who were unknown in America at the time but who were to become influential in the development of modern philosophy and sociology. In 1905 Pitkin attended the International Congress of Psychology in Rome, where he met William James. Pitkin's engagement with pragmatist philosophy led to published exchanges with James that brought Pitkin to the attention of the faculty at Columbia University. Pitkin later claimed that James's recommendation led to his initial appointment as lecturer in psychology and philosophy at Columbia University, where he taught between 1905 and 1909. At Columbia, Pitkin's work with the "New Realist" group of philosophers in 1910 culminated with the publication of *The New Realism: Cooperative Studies in Philosophy* (1912), a manifesto for philosophical understanding based on the methodologies of the physical sciences.

Academia was never Pitkin's sole occupation, however, and his ideas reached a popular audience through his work in journalism. He wrote for and edited a number of journals and newspapers throughout his life. In 1907 he was associate editor for the *New York Tribune*, and between 1909 and 1910 he worked for the *New York Evening Post*. At Columbia he taught story writing aimed at mass-market publication and wrote popular fiction under sundry pseudonyms. Only one of these pseudonyms, Leavitt Ashley Knight, is known. In 1912 Pitkin was appointed as professor of journalism in the newly created School of Journalism at Columbia University, a position he kept until his retirement in 1943.

During World War I, Pitkin worked for the New Republic News Service, based in Washington, D.C., an information syndicate that aimed to pool knowledge and information generated by social and cultural leaders. Pitkin believed that information provision and distribution was the key to social improvement. After the war he worked with the publisher E. W. Scripps and the director of La Jolla Institute, William E. Ritter, to set up a science news syndicate, the Science News Service. Fearing Japanese expansionism at this time, Scripps sponsored a conference on the problems of the Pacific Coast, which highlighted to Pitkin the centrality of population control as an organizing principle. The conference led to his authorship of *Must We Fight Japan?* (1921). The book argued that Japanese expansion and militarism posed a threat to world peace, and it was written in the hope of increasing understanding of the "Asian problem" on the Pacific Coast. To prevent the threat of war, Pitkin advocated multilateral disarmament and increased restriction of Asian immigration and imports to America. Later, in his memoirs he claimed the book delayed military action between Japan and the United States until Pearl Harbor.

During the 1920s Pitkin rose to public acclaim through his teaching, publishing, and entrepreneurship. As well as teaching journalism, philosophy, and psychology at Columbia, he marketed a correspondence course in short fiction (*New York Times Book Review and Magazine*, 22 May 1921, p. 32), worked as the American editor of the *Encyclopaedia Britannica* in 1927–1928, and wrote for *Parents' Magazine* between 1927 and 1930. He also wrote a book on sound cinema and for a short time became a story supervisor for Universal Pictures. His importance at the time was described by Luigi Barzini, who wrote that Pitkin was "a famous, almost legendary figure" who revolutionized the writing profession (Barzini, 1985, pp. 151–62). Pitkin's scientific and psychologically based theories of successful writing "filtered into the actual writings of scores of authors," remarked the author Thomas Uzzell, whose own book, he claimed, could be subtitled "Pitkin Applied" (Uzzell, 1923, p. ii).

Pitkin published prolifically during the late 1920s and the 1930s, writing textbooks, short stories, popular psychology, and numerous magazine editorials. His concerns over human intelligence and social decline emerged in textbooks on rapid reading and treatises on the psychology of success and achievement. He became most well known in 1932, however, for his authorship of the best-selling nonfiction *Life Begins at Forty*, a self-help book that counseled all those who needed to learn "to live more abundantly" on less. *Life Begins at Forty* promised a new age of machine-made leisure and civilization, less work and more time to cultivate intellect, intelligence, and happiness. By cultivating new attitudes and interests and by dismissing "cheap pleasures," which "are designed and planned chiefly for our untutored and vulgarized young Americans who spend billions yearly in shoddy activities miscalled amusement and leisure-time entertainment," the overforties were promised that they would be "the truly civilized and happy of the land" (Pitkin, 1932, p. 143).

Pitkin published two other books that year (*A Short Introduction to the History of Human Stupidity* and *The Consumer: His Nature and His Changing Habits*), and he also founded the Institute of Life Planning. The mix of utopian energy and despair in much of his writing came from his belief that human culture and intelligence lagged behind technological advances. While most people were "stupid," they could be improved through the rational application of scientific principals of living. Pitkin found his depression-weary audience receptive for advice, and his books offered a course for success. "Life begins at forty" was a catchphrase within a year of the book's publication, and the work became a publishing phenomenon. Popular songs and films with the same title soon appeared. Pitkin's books also spawned an industry of self-help imitators in the popular publishing market. His appearances on popular radio shows confirmed him as a household name of the thirties.

Along with his interest in "life planning," Pitkin believed in scientific improvements on a wider scale. He conducted experiments with scientific farming methods on his own land, hoping to improve large-scale agricultural production, and he wrote for the *Farm Journal* between 1935 and 1938. Pitkin's belief that life was a problem of human engineering, alongside his concern with intelligence, stupidity, and civilization, led him to support population control as a form of scientific planning. In 1947 Pitkin wrote the foreword and postscript to *Human Breeding and Survival* by Guy Irving Burch, who held office in the American Eugenics Society.

In the 1930s Pitkin's writing increasingly turned to the industrial and political organization of society. He dedicated books to the "survival and prosperity" of the middle classes, and his initial enthusiasm for the scientific organization of the New Deal turned to disenchantment. In 1939 Pitkin launched an organization called the American Majority, a conservative "league of the middle class against the predatory rich and the predatory poor" (letter to the editor, *Literary Review*, 12 Aug. 1922). Always believing that the free flow of scientific knowledge and information would result in a successful democracy, at the start of World War II he switched his attention to a multilingual world news service that would fight the war of communications against the Nazi fifth column.

In 1943 Pitkin retired from Columbia, but he continued to write and publish. His wife died in October 1943, and in 1948 he married Katherine B. Johnson, his personal assistant and secretary since 1925.

As a journalist and a writer of popular self-improvement titles, Pitkin produced provocative writing that digested philosophical and scientific theories for a mass market. His works appealed strongly to middle-class, middle-aged readers. Writing presciently in 1922 that "we forget nearly all the facts which determine the survival of cabbages, and kings, and best-sellers," Pitkin knew that his self-help formula would outlive his memory (Pitkin, 1922). He died in Palo Alto, California.

• Some of Pitkin's letters are in the correspondence collections of Harold Prell Breitenbach, Burton Historical Collection, Detroit Public Library and Bentley Historical Library, Michigan; Lawrence Dennis, Stanford University, California; Horace Kallen Papers, American Jewish Archives, Ohio; Verne Marshall, Herbert Hoover Presidential Library, Iowa; William E. Ritter, Bancroft Library, California; Evelyn Scott Collection, University of Texas at Austin; and Oswald Garrison Villard, Houghton Library, Harvard University. The Hartford Seminary holds a file on Pitkin; James Boylan, historian of the Columbia School of Journalism, has recorded references to Pitkin from the collection at the Columbia University archives. Pitkin's publications include *The Art and Business of Story Writing* (1912); *The Political and Economic Expansion of Japan* (1921); *As We Are* (1922); *How to Write Short Stories* (1922); *The Twilight of the American Mind* (1928); *The Art of Rapid Reading* (1929); *The Secret of Happiness* (1929); *The Psychology of Achievement* (1930); *The Secret of Achievement* (1930); *The Art of Sound Pictures* (1930); *The Art of Learning* (1931); *More Power to You* (1933); *Take It Easy: The Art of Relaxation* (1935); *Let's Get What We Want: A Primer in a Sadly Neglected Art* (1935); *Capitalism Carries On* (1935); *Escape from Fear* (1940); *The Art of Useful Writing* (1940); *Road to a Richer Life* (1949). The only full-length account of Pitkin's life is his florid autobiography, *On My Own* (1944). He is briefly mentioned in Garth Jowett, *Film: The Democratic Art* (1985); Stephen L. Recken, "Fitting-In: The Redefinition of Success in the 1930s," *Journal of Popular Culture* 27, no. 3 (1993): 205–22; Joseph F. Kett, *The Pursuit of Knowledge under Difficulties* (1994); Lawrence Chenoweth, *The American Dream of Success: The Search for the Self in the Twentieth Century* (1974); and Lawrence Levine, *The Unpredictable Past* (1993). On Pitkin's work, see Luigi Barzini, *O America, When You and I Were Young* (1977; repr., 1985), and Thomas Uzzell, *Narrative Technique* (1923). An obituary is in the *New York Times*, 26 Jan. 1953.

SUSAN CURRELL

PLATO, Ann (c. 1820–?), writer and teacher, was probably born in Hartford, Connecticut. Her parentage and birth date are unknown, though it is likely that she was related to the Plato family prominent in Hartford's nineteenth-century black community. Little is known of her childhood; she was probably educated at home, at church, and in some of the schools sporadically set up by and for Hartford's African Americans in the 1830s. She was a member of the Talcott Street Congregational Church, and through church activities, she was exposed to the uplift thinking of the Reverend Amos Beeman, the Reverend Hosea Easton, the Hartford activist James Mars, and later the Reverend James Pennington. She would also have watched the Amistad case unfold.

Plato published *Essays* in 1841. Prefaced by Pennington, the small volume contains sixteen short essays, four biographical sketches, and twenty poems. The essays are quite didactic and focus—either directly (as in "Religion") or indirectly (as in "Education," "Benevolence," and "Obedience")—on encouraging readers to embrace Protestant Christianity. The essays show that Plato was fairly well read; she cites, among others, Benjamin Franklin, John Milton, and several classical authors. The essays also show a consistent concern for mental and spiritual uplift, noting, for example, that "the human mind was made for action" but that "no person can be considered as possessing a good education without religion" (Plato, 1988, pp. 50, 28). The biographical sketches focus on pious women Plato knew who died young but virtuous, and they offer similar calls to Christianity. The poems treat such subjects too but are a bit more varied. Some, like "Lines, Written upon Being Examined in School Studies for the Preparation of a Teacher" and "The Infant Class," seem clearly autobiographical; others, like "I Have No Brother" and "Daughter's Inquiry," may be. Most echo the romantic sentimentalism of the time. The book was cheaply produced, probably in a small run, and the audience was likely highly localized.

Several comments in Plato's *Essays* suggest that she was already teaching in 1841. She may have been aiding the Penningtons in a black school in the Talcott Street Church. But the first records to document her work as a teacher show that she taught at the Elm Street School (also known as the South African School), one of two schools operated by the black community, between 1844 and 1847. The schools were ill equipped, and attendance varied widely. According to Thomas Robbins, a member of the Hartford School Society who visited all of the city schools in 1844 and 1845, at times there was "quite a deficiency of Books," and the physical classroom was "in much need of improvement" (quoted in White, 1974, pp. 52–53). Still, though Robbins found what happened in her classroom uneven, he noted that Plato "takes pains, & is pretty well qualified. She has taught some time" and that "the scholars appeared fond of their school" (White, 1974, p. 52). Robbins's reports noted work in reading, writing, spelling, history, geography, and math as well as regular prayer. Plato also asked her students to recite for the community on some occasions. She invited Robbins to such an exhibition in September 1845, and the local abolitionist paper, the *Charter Oak*, reported another in May 1846. Two prominent African Americans, the photographer Augustus Washington and the abolitionist Selah Africanus, also taught in Hartford's black schools during this period. It seems safe to assume that there was dialogue on pedagogy and perhaps on politics, abolition, and colonization.

Nothing is known of what happened to Plato after 1847. She may have married (though Hartford marriage records do not list her) or left Hartford.

Plato's significance to African-American literature and culture rests on her status as the first woman to publish a collection of essays (as opposed to speeches, which Maria Stewart published a few years before) and one of the first to publish a selection of poetry. Her work is uneven and, though there are some sparks, not especially strong. Still it exemplifies one strand of a philosophy of religious uplift in antebellum African-American thought and shows an active young mind coming to terms with a complex world. Pennington—and several modern critics—compare her to Phillis Wheatley, though, in both content and approach, a more useful comparison could be made to Hartford's most famous white poet of the time, Lydia Sigourney. Critical work on Plato has been relatively limited, in part because Plato says little about race and the web of issues surrounding it. Some twentieth-century scholars have criticized her harshly for this absence and especially for the relative absence of comments on slavery.

• Two of Plato's letters to Thomas Robbins and Robbins's report on his school visits are in the Thomas Robbins School Papers at the Connecticut Historical Society. A modern edition of Plato's *Essays* (1988) includes an introduction and critical reading by Kenny J. Williams. Plato is not listed in any of the key nineteenth-century biographical dictionaries of African Americans, and most listings in reference sources rely almost solely on Plato's book for biographical details. Though it does not focus on Plato, David O. White, "Hartford's African Schools, 1830–1868," Connecticut Historical Society Bulletin 39 (Apr. 1974): 47–53, which relies heavily on the Robbins papers, is useful for Plato's biography. The discussion of the May 1846 exhibition is in the Charter Oak, 21 May 1846. Another useful critical reading of Plato's work is Katherine Clay Bassard, Spiritual Interrogations (1999).

ERIC GARDNER

POMEROY, Theodore Medad (31 Dec. 1824–23 Mar. 1905), politician, was born in Cayuga, New York, the son of Reverend Medad Pomeroy, a Presbyterian clergyman, and Lilly Maxwell Pomeroy. He attended local common schools and the Munroe Collegiate Institute in Elbridge, New York. In 1840 he entered Hamilton College and graduated two years later, delivering the classical oration at commencement. His college friends later remembered his modest means and his intense belief that "all his capital lay between his ears" (*Hamilton Literary Monthly* 27: 163). In 1843 he moved to Auburn, New York, where he studied law in the office of William H. Seward. After admission to the bar in 1846, he practiced law with several partners. On 4 September 1855 he married Elizabeth Leitch Watson; the couple had five children.

Pomeroy was elected to the post of village clerk of Auburn in 1847 and then reelected three times. The Whig party nominated him for district attorney of Cayuga County in 1850 and he won a narrow victory. His success as a prosecutor, especially in the 1851 case of a murdered peddler, led to his reelection in 1853. Like many former Whigs, Pomeroy became a Republican after 1854 and was elected to the New York Assembly in 1856. In the 1857 session he served on the Committee on Cities and helped frame the Metropolitan Police Bill. In 1858 he was a strong opponent of Republican fusion with the Know-Nothing Party and was instrumental in defeating an attempt to create a joint ticket for the two parties at the Republican state convention. Pomeroy "was a decidedly sturdy and consistent Republican and he could be earnest to the point of bitterness on occasion" (the Auburn *Bulletin*).

Pomeroy was a delegate to the Republican National Convention in Chicago in 1860 and favored William Seward for the presidency. Later in the same year the Republicans in the Twenty-fifth Congressional District nominated him for the vacant House seat, and he was elected by a wide majority. In 1862 he was a successful candidate from the Twenty-sixth Congressional District and won the seat again in 1864 and 1866. During his last two terms, he chaired the Committee on Banking and Currency. He was conservative on fiscal measures but otherwise a supporter of the Abraham Lincoln administration. When he sat in Congress, Pomeroy had a full head of hair, a well-trimmed mustache, and a goatee.

Although Pomeroy was a loyal Republican, his exact position on the Reconstruction controversies of his era is not clear. One of William Seward's biographers calls him "a violent Radical" (Van Deusen, p. 492). Modern scholars place him more on the conservative side of the congressional party based on his voting record. His views on financial questions favored reduction of the war debt and a currency backed by the gold standard. He rarely spoke on the floor about the issues of voting rights for the freed slaves or the constitutional issues involving the treatment of the defeated South. He was an effective legislator in the cloakrooms and gained a popularity among members of both parties.

Pomeroy decided that he would not run for Congress again in 1869, and as the final session of the Fortieth Congress drew to a close it seemed that he would retire to private life and a lucrative career with the American Express Company. That firm had asked him to become its first vice president in charge of political relations. Since the Speaker of the House, Schuyler Colfax, was to be inaugurated as vice president with the new President Ulysses S. Grant on 4 March 1869, he resigned on 3 March. That left the House in need of a Speaker for the single busy day at the end of the session. Pomeroy was chosen unanimously to succeed Colfax for the largely ceremonial post but one that did involve the management of some legislation in the waning hours of the session. A contemporary newspaper said of the new presiding officer, "In the combination of characteristics needed in a Speaker, no man in the House is his superior" (*Hamilton Literary Monthly* 27: 252). Pomeroy told his colleagues, "The unanimity with which I have been chosen to preside for this brief period is evidence of itself that your choice carries with it no political significance" (*Congressional Globe*, 4 Mar. 1869, p. 1868). He carried out the duties of the office with efficiency and speed. Later in life he maintained that had he chosen to run for reelection he would have been elected Speaker in the Forty-first Congress. Since one of his rivals would have been the popular James G. Blaine of Maine, Pomeroy's retrospective confidence was probably misplaced.

Departure from Congress did not end Pomeroy's political career. He served as mayor of Auburn, New York, in 1875–1876 and was nominated to the New York Senate in 1877. He spent two years in that body as chairman of the Committee on Cities. Chosen a delegate to the 1876 Republican National Convention, he was selected as the temporary chairman of the gathering. In 1878 Pomeroy was considered a possible gubernatorial candidate for the Republicans but did not secure the nomination.

In business Pomeroy continued his connection with the American Express Company for many years; he also was a partner in the banking firm of William H. Seward & Co. after 1869. Investments in the local water company and the Oswego Starch factory rounded out his business interests. Pomeroy participated in charitable activities in his community. He died in Auburn.

Pomeroy became the Speaker of the House for one legislative day because of the unique historical circumstances arising from Schuyler Colfax's elevation to the vice presidency in 1869. If Pomeroy's brief moment of fame soon faded, he did nothing to embarrass the Speakership during the hours he occupied the post. His one-day term remains the shortest for any Speaker in the annals of the House of Representatives.

• Pomeroy's papers for the 1860s are at the University of Rochester. The University of North Carolina at Chapel Hill has a small collection of five letters written to him during the Civil War. The archives of Hamilton College contain good biographical information, including an extensive obituary, one letter to a sister, and some recollections by college friends in the *Hamilton Literary Monthly* 27 (Jan. and Feb. 1893). The Alonzo G. Beardsley records at Duke University have information on Pomeroy's legal practice. Robert W. Pomeroy, *A Sketch of the Life of Theodore Medad Pomeroy, 1824–1905* (1910), a memoir by his son, is the only known biography. The *Congressional Globe* is important for its focus on Pomeroy's legislative career. The *New York Tribune*, 4 Mar. 1869, has good coverage of Pomeroy's day as the Speaker. Glyndon G. Van Deusen, *William Henry Seward* (1967), describes Pomeroy as a Radical Republican in one brief reference. Michael Les Benedict, *A Compromise of Principle: Congressional Republicans and Reconstruction 1863–1869* (1974), pp. 28, 49, 55, lists Pomeroy as conservative on

monetary issues and aid to railroads and labels him a "consistent conservative." The obituary in the Auburn *Bulletin*, 24 Mar. 1905, is an excellent treatment of his life from a contemporary perspective.

LEWIS L. GOULD

PORTER, H. Boone (10 Jan. 1923–5 June 1999), religious educator, was born Harry Boone Porter, Jr., in Louisville, Kentucky, the son of Harry Boone Porter, Sr., a businessman and founder of the Porter Paint Company, and Charlotte Wiseman Porter. Porter attended St. Paul's School in Concord, New Hampshire and after graduating entered Yale University, where he studied philosophy and art. In 1943 he served with an intelligence unit of the U.S. Army in the Pacific theater. After the war he returned to Yale and graduated in 1947. On 28 June of that same year he married Violet Monser, with whom he would have six children.

Porter remained in New Haven, Connecticut, following graduation and entered the Berkley Divinity School, graduating in 1950. It was there, under the direction of Dr. Edward Hardy, that Porter first focused on church liturgy and worship, two subjects that continued to hold his interest through his career. Having received ordination as an Episcopal deacon in the Diocese of Kentucky (1950), Porter spent the next two years at the General Theological Seminary in New York City, where as a fellow and tutor he taught and completed the requirements for a Master of Sacred Theology degree in 1952. By now an ordained priest, he then traveled to England where he spent two years completing the requirements for his doctorate.

On returning to the United States in 1954, Porter served at the Nashotah House Seminary in Wisconsin, where he began teaching church history and eventually rose to the rank of associate professor. While in Wisconsin he also officiated at several local churches and completed his first books, *William Augustus Muhlenberg: Pioneer of Christian Action* (1959) and *The Day of Light: The Biblical and Liturgical Meaning of Sunday* (1960). In that same year Porter returned to the General Theological Seminary, where he served as the first tenured professor of liturgy. Although Porter retained an active interest in church history—producing *Sister Anne: Pioneer in Women's Work* (1960), *Truman Hemingway: Priest–Farmer* (1961), and *Samuel Seabury: Bishop in a New Nation* (1962)—his focus increasingly fell on the field of liturgy. In the late 1960s he wrote *Ordination Prayers of the Ancient Western Churches* (1967) and *Growth and Life in the Local Church* (1968); he also edited *A Prayer Book for the Armed Forces* (1967). In 1962 Porter joined the Standing Liturgical Committee and served in the Home Department of the executive council of the Episcopal Church, in whose service he visited a variety of missionary locations, including Native American and African-American congregations. As the decade wore on, Porter became increasingly interested in the marginalized elements of American society and their relation to Episcopalianism, and he became an active participant in several civil rights marches during the mid-1960s.

Porter left General Theological in 1970, when he became director of the National Town and Country Church Institute (Roanridge) near Kansas City, Missouri. During his seven years at Roanridge, Porter increasingly worked for internal change within the Episcopalian church, including a revival of the traditional deaconate within the church, the legitimization of priests who happened to be serving in secular occupations—a subject he had addressed in *Hemingway*, and an increased emphasis on nontraditional theological education, including instruction via extension. In 1977 the Institute folded. Porter then moved to Milwaukee, where he served for the next thirteen years as the editor of *The Living Church*, a weekly magazine in which his own column, titled "The First Article," provided him with a pulpit from which to expound his views.

Among Porter's efforts to revitalize the Episcopal Church, none was more far reaching (or more controversial) than his leadership in revising the wording of the Book of Common Prayer in 1979. Most notable was his work on the Eucharistic Prayers, which altered language that had been essentially unchanged since 1662 into a more modern vernacular. Language that once read

> All Glory be to thee, Almighty God, our heavenly Father, for that thou, of thy tender mercy, didst give thine only Son Jesus Christ to suffer death upon the cross for our redemption; who made there, by his one oblation of himself once offered, a full perfect, and sufficient sacrifice, oblation, and satisfaction, for the sins of the whole world.

was changed to the more modern

> Holy and gracious Father: In your infinite love you made us for yourself; and, when we had fallen into sin and become subject to evil and death, you, in your mercy, sent Jesus Christ, your only and eternal Son, to share our human nature, to live and die as one of us, to reconcile us to yourself, the God and Father of all . . . He stretched his arms upon the cross, and offered himself, in obedience to your will, a perfect sacrifice for the whole world.

On retiring from his duties at *The Living Church*, Porter returned to Connecticut and continued to write and study. Among his later publications were *Jeremy Taylor: Liturgist* (1979) and a collection of his columns titled *A Song of Creation* (1986). Porter also attended Yale on a part-time basis, earning a master's degree in environmental studies in 1995. A resident of Southport, Connecticut, he died in Bridgeport.

Although not well known outside of his denomination, Boone Porter (as he preferred to be called) was one of the leading voices of mainstream Protestantism in the late twentieth century. While his efforts to increase the range and scope of church outreach to rural and minority residents resulted in solid accomplishments, he will always be best known for his liturgical reforms that resulted in a more accessible Book of Common Prayer.

• No collection of Porter's papers has been located. The best secondary source of information on his life and career (which includes an autobiographical sketch) is Ralph N. McMichael, Jr., ed., *Creation and Liturgy: In Honor of H. Boone Porter* (1993). Obituaries are in the *Milwaukee Journal-Sentinel*, 9 June 1999, and the *New York Times*, 11 June 1999.

EDWARD L. LACH, JR.

POWERS, J. F. (8 July 1917–12 June 1999), short-story writer and novelist, was born James Farl Powers in Jacksonville, Illinois, the son of James Ansbury Powers, a musician and an employee of Swift and Co., and Zella Routzong Powers. The family moved to Rockford and then to Quincy, where Powers was educated by Franciscan friars at Quincy Academy College before settling in Chicago when he was eighteen.

The Great Depression, more than any other single factor, made him a writer. He studied English for two years in the night program of the Chicago branch of Northwestern University; he did not receive a degree because he could not afford to continue. After visiting employment agencies in the morning, he spent afternoons reading in the Chicago Public Library. Working as an editor on the Historical Records Survey, a WPA project, and as a clerk at Brentano's, he became aware of Richard Wright and Nelson Algren and thought about writing himself.

In 1943, his first short story, "He Don't Plant Cotton," about African-American musicians in a Chicago bar, was published in *Accent*, a little magazine of great distinction. His literary career as a Catholic writer was formally launched with "Lions, Harts, Leaping Does," about two aging Franciscan friars, also published in *Accent* and chosen as a best American short story of 1944. His short stories, mostly about Roman Catholic priests, appeared regularly in the *New Yorker* but also in the *Partisan Review, Commonweal, Kenyon Review*, and other literary journals. His first collection, *The Prince of Darkness and Other Stories*, was published in 1947; *The Presence of Grace*, another collection, appeared in 1956. Characteristically, Powers's titles suggest a larger, more illuminating context for his fiction. *Morte D'Urban*, his long-awaited first novel, won the National Book Award in 1963. His third collection of short stories, *Look How the Fish Live*, was published in 1975, but his second novel, *Wheat That Springeth Green*, did not appear until 1988.

Powers met his wife, Elizabeth Alice "Betty" Wahl from St. Cloud, Minnesota, in 1945 when he was on parole after serving thirteen months in the Sandstone Prison in Minnesota for refusing to be inducted into the Army during World War II. They married on 22 April 1946, had five children, and remained together until her death in 1988. She also wrote for the *New*

Yorker and was the author of *Rafferty & Company* (1969).

Beginning in 1951, the family lived in Ireland for short periods of time; they lived permanently in Greystone, County Wicklow, between 1963 and 1965 and between 1966 and 1975. They returned to St. Cloud for the summer of 1968 to watch the Democratic and Republican national conventions and support their friend Senator Eugene McCarthy (D.-Minn.). Despite his memories of the Depression and having a large family to support, Powers shied away from teaching. Still, out of exigency, he taught as a visiting professor at Marquette University, the University of Michigan, and Smith College. He became regents professor of English at St. John's University, a Benedictine institution, in Collegeville, Minnesota, in 1975 and continued there until 1993.

In 1943, the year of his signature story "Lions, Harts, Leaping Does," Powers published three little-known didactic narratives in *The Catholic Worker*. In one of them, "Night in the County Jail," he makes a blatant statement: "The upholstery of Christianity has held up better than the idea and practice." Powers never wavers from this belief, but he expresses it with more nuance and irony in his mature fiction, which concentrates mainly on Roman Catholic priests living banal lives in Midwestern parish rectories. Powers once said that priests were his focus because "they officially are committed to both worlds in the way that most people officially are not. This makes for stronger beer. . . . I want to deal with things that I regard as important, like life and death."

The comic tension of Powers's stories exists in the distance between a priest's commitment to his ideal of a religious vocation and how he lives it on a daily basis, especially when he reduces the mystery of salvation to easy answers or, without soul-searching, sells out to false gods. The Catholic landscape provides the images, symbols, tone, and atmosphere that are Powers's special style, but religious certitudes—namely the essential Christian mysteries of Incarnation, Redemption, and Resurrection—provide the core of his vision. Powers commented in an interview that he "would not fly blind and write without regard to a body of philosophy. . . . [There] are laws, moral laws as real as gravity. This does not mean that in this world the hand of the good man will be raised, the crowd will roar, and the new champ will be the saint and not the devil. But the last round is not here. The decision will not be rendered in this ring."

Although Powers's characters make their own choices, he clearly believes that grace is available to them. In "Defection of a Favorite," the last story in a trilogy about Father Ernest Burner, Powers offers a pun on "grace" as a style of living: "In the past [Father Burner] had lacked the will to accept his setbacks with grace and had derived no meaning from them." When *Morte D'Urban* (1963) appeared, many chapters were known to readers because they were published as short stories in the *New Yorker*. His Father Urban Roche of the Order of Saint Clement is a rich and subtle blending of every priest Powers has created. He is a complex man of many guises: a posturing knight, a Midwestern Rotarian, an American dreamer on his way to spiritual misadventure and a "fortunate fall" brought about by a blow to his head by a golf ball. At the end of the novel, when Urban is a shell of his former self, we see the depth and complexity of Powers's vision—the loser as winner and the winner as loser. "Keystone" (1963), published during the Second Vatican Council, shows the Church in an identity crisis: a bishop runs his diocese like an American corporation, "second only to Standard Oil," but builds a medieval cathedral in the heart of the city. Members of the Catholic hierarchy have adjusted, or pandered, so much to the secular world that they lack imagination for articulating a contemporary, authentic spirituality. The newly ordained but shallow clergy in *Look How the Fish Live* (1975) respond to the profound challenges of Vatican II by scheduling masses with folk music and hanging homemade banners, proclaiming "Joy," in the sacristy. It is the unnamed father of a large family in the title story who ponders quietly about "putting a few questions to God." *Wheat That Springeth Green*, a National Book Award nominee, follows the life of Father Joe Hackett, who as a seminarian wanted to "grow in holiness" but for years dissipates his days, attentive only to the "upholstery of Christianity" and his own appetites, before renewing himself in service of the poor.

To read Powers is to rekindle the debate between faith and fiction. A belief in the operative power of grace can lead to a failure in artistic technique if the habits of a character's lifetime suddenly change. But Powers maintains psychological credibility and deepens the miracle of grace by showing its action through the very ordinary world of human activity. The question is whether his fiction will continue to be read and appreciated when his characters are mainly priests living in mid-twentieth-century America. His stakes are beyond the parochial, however. He blurs the distinctions between saint and sinner, the religious and the secular. The rectory is a place for him to lament the loss of mystery and point out the need for a salvation greater than ourselves. As a comic realist, he paints a universal world: human beings are fallen and wounded, essentially alienated and alone, susceptible to the Demon without and the demon within themselves. Much like Chaucer, he observes the spectacle of the human comedy, exposing the unique unremarkability of people no longer concerned with trying to understand great things. His closest literary affinities are with Sinclair Lewis, Flannery O'Connor, Edwin O'Connor, Evelyn Waugh, Leon Bloy, and the dying words of Georges Bernanos's country priest—"Does it matter? Grace is everywhere."

Powers was buried from St. John's Abbey in Collegeville, Minnesota, where he lived.

• J. F. Powers's papers are extensive; they are held privately by the Powers Family Literary Property Trust, Katherine A. Powers, Trustee, 438 Windsor Street, Cambridge, MA 02141. Three interviews with Powers are very helpful: Bob

Lundegaard, "Author: 'Writing Is a Sweaty Job,'" Minneapolis *Sunday Tribune*, 7 Apr. 1963; also see Sister Kristin Malloy, O.S.B., "The Catholic and Creativity," *American Benedictine Review* 15 (Mar. 1964): 63–80, and Donald McDonald, *Catholics in Conversation* (1960). Recommended critical studies include John V. Hagopian, *J. F. Powers* (1968); Leo J. Hertzel, "Brother Juniper, Father Urban, and the Unworldly Tradition," *Renascence* 17 (Summer 1965): 207–10; John J. Kirvan, C.S.P., "Ostergothenburg Revisited," *Catholic World* 158 (Feb. 1964): 308–13; Naomi Lebovitz, "The Stories of J. F. Powers: The Sign of the Contradiction," *Kenyon Review* 20 (Summer 1958): 494–99; Flannery O'Connor, "The Church and the Fiction Writer," *America* 96 (31 Mar. 1957): 733–35; George Scouffas, "J. F. Powers: On the Vitality of Disorder," *Critique: Studies in Modern Fiction* 2 (Fall 1959): 41–58; John P. Sisk, "The Complex Moral Vision of J. F. Powers," *Critique: Studies in Modern Fiction* 2 (Fall 1958): 28–40; Walter Sullivan, "J. F. Powers and His Priestly Company," *Sewanee Review* 98 (Fall 1990): 712–15; Ellie Wymard, *J. F. Powers: His Christian Comic Vision* (Ph.D. dissertation, University of Pittsburgh, 1968); and Wymard, "The Church of J. F. Powers," *Commonweal* 103 (12 Mar. 1976): 182–185.

Several reflective essays written around the time of his death and subsequently offer insight into Powers's life and convictions: Andrew M. Greeley, "J. F. Powers: R.I.P.," *Commonweal* 126 (16 July 1999): 10; J. V. Long, "Clerical Characters: Rereading J. F. Powers," *Commonweal* 125 (8 May 1998): 11–15; Katherine A. Powers, "Reflections on J. F. Powers: Author, Father, Clear-Eyed Observer," *Boston Globe*, 18 July 1999; Michael True, "J. F. Powers' Plain, Elegant Art," *National Catholic Reporter* 35 (16 July 1999): 11; and James Wood, "Church Mice," *New Yorker*, 11 Dec. 2000. An obituary is in the *New York Times*, 17 July 1999.

ELLIE WYMARD

PROSKOURIAKOFF, Tatiana (23 Jan. 1909–30 Aug. 1985), artist, architect, and archaeologist, was born in Tomsk, Siberia, the daughter of Avenir Proskouriakoff, an engineer and chemist, and Alla Nekrassova, a physician who graduated with the first class of women from a Russian medical school. The parents were aristocrats. The family traveled to the United States in late 1915, when Avenir Proskouriakoff was sent to supervise the manufacture and sale of weapons to Russia. When Tatiana and her older sister Ksenia contracted diphtheria and scarlet fever, they and their mother returned to Russia. The following spring they joined their father in Philadelphia, Pennsylvania. When the Russian Revolution broke out, the family elected to remain in their adoptive country. Tatiana Proskouriakoff attended Pennsylvania State University and graduated in 1930 with a bachelor of science degree in architecture. Though she never pursued architecture as a profession, her training and artist talents came into play later.

Proskouriakoff failed to find a job in architecture during the Great Depression. She worked as a clerk at Wanamaker's department store, while designing patterns for needlework with her aunt. Attaining access to the Pennsylvania State University Museum, she volunteered to draw for one of the curators there and later earned very low wages or a stipend for her efforts. This busy work impressed the archaeologist

Linton Satterthwaite, who invited Proskouriakoff to join his 1936 expedition to Piedras Negras in northwestern Guatemala. Piedras Negras was a classical site of Mayan ruins that Satterthwaite had been excavating for some time. Over the next few years Proskouriakoff produced a series of reconstructive drawings depicting ancient Mayan cities. Further expeditions and in-the-field drawings allowed her to study the diversity of the architectural styles in Honduras, Mexico, and Guatemala. Her famous sketches were first published as *An Album of Maya Architecture* (1946).

Proskouriakoff's second book, *A Study of Classic Maya Sculpture* (1950), offered a formal analysis of the motifs of Mayan art. She developed the method of style dating stelae (freestanding carved stone monuments) that permitted the placement in time of all monuments with or without decipherable dates. She charted changes in art styles during a 600-year span.

Prior to her work with Mayan writings, the only texts that had been deciphered consisted of astronomical and calendrical information. Mayan epigraphy (the study of inscriptions) was stagnant; dates had been deciphered for sixty years, but their significance remained unknown. Proskouriakoff's *Historical Implication of a Pattern of Dates at Piedras Negras, Guatemala* (1960) is regarded as her most important work. She showed that the inscriptions of Stela 14 from Piedras Negras described historical and biographical items from the lives of the Mayan people and their rulers. She identified the glyph that represented birth—an "upended" frog. This led to the recognition of birth and death glyphs, the name glyphs of the rulers, parentage information, the capture of enemies, and other aspects of Mayan lives. Modern scholars credit Proskouriakoff's tireless, pioneering research in Mayan culture with deciphering age-old Mayan hieroglyphic writing.

Proskouriakoff devoted her life to research and scholarship. Her work was well respected, yet she struggled with self-doubt and depression. Her personal diaries reveal that she established important relationships with her archaeological peers Gustav Stromsvik and Harry Pollock. However, she confided that she had "escaped personal happiness" (personal papers, Peabody Library). She never married.

Proskouriakoff was the honorary curator of Mayan art at the Peabody Museum of Harvard University. In 1962 she was awarded the fifth Alfred V. Kidder Medal for her discovery that the Classic Maya recorded their own dynastic histories. The Alfred V. Kidder Medal, which Proskouriakoff designed in 1950, is awarded for eminence in the field. Proskouriakoff also was nominated for the 1947 Woman of the Year by Pennsylvania State University. She died from a long illness in Cambridge, Massachusetts.

• Proskouriakoff's personal papers, including many diaries, are in the Harvard University Peabody Library. For more information see Char Solomon, *Tatiana Proskouriakoff: Interpreting the Ancient Maya* (2002). The National Geographic Society documentary film *Code of the Maya Kings*

(2001) chronicles the life and work of Proskouriakoff. She is featured in Ute Gacs et al., eds., *Women Anthropologists: A Biographical Dictionary* (1988). An obituary appears in the *New York Times*, 11 Sept. 1985; a memorial notice by Ian Graham is in *American Antiquity*, Jan. 1990.

CATHERINE DYER KLEIN
KAREN BACHMAN BARNETT

PUENTE, Tito (20 Apr. 1923?–1 June 2000), musician, bandleader, and all-around showman, was born Ernesto Anthony Puente, Jr., in Harlem, New York, the son of Ernesto Puente, a foreman at a razor blade factory, and Ercilia Ortíz de Puente. (Most sources give his birth date as 1923, but in a questionnaire Puente himself filled out for Leonard Feather's 1955 *Encyclopedia of Jazz*, he wrote "1925.") Both of Puente's parents were immigrants from Puerto Rico. He earned his nickname from his mother, who called him Ernestito, which means "Little Ernest." It was later shortened to "Tito." Puente grew up on 110th Street, off of Madison Avenue, in the neighborhood known as Spanish Harlem or El Barrio.

Puente showed a musical sense early, banging on pots and pans on the kitchen table as a child. His neighbors implored his mother to get her son music lessons, which she did when Tito was seven. Puente initially played the piano but as a youngster also learned to play alto saxophone, clarinet, marimba, and drums. Eventually, he ended up playing timbales. Later, Puente also played vibes, the metallic cousin of the marimba. By Puente's early teens he had already gained a reputation as a musical prodigy around El Barrio, and in 1937 he joined a group called the Happy Boys, playing at Manhattan's Park Palace Hotel. He also performed locally as a Fred Astaire–style dancer with his sister, but a serious ankle injury from a bicycle accident strengthened his focus on music. In 1939 he toured the United States with the band of José Curbelo.

Puente's first big break came in 1940 when he joined Machito and His Afro-Cubans, playing timbales. Machito's band was one of the first to fuse Afro-Cuban rhythms with jazz. The fit was natural for Puente. "I grew up in East Harlem where I was exposed to good jazz and good Latin music," he told Peter Kohan. Puente convinced Machito to move him to the front of the stage—drums were traditionally kept in the back—and Puente's inherent showmanship quickly made him the center of attention. In Machito's band, Puente also met Cuban-born trumpeter and arranger Mario Bauzá, who was a catalyst of the early fusion of Latin music and jazz and an influence on Puente's musical philosophy later in his career. During this time Puente also played with one of the original "kings" of Latin music, Puerto Rican pianist and bandleader Noro Morales.

In 1942 Puente was drafted into the U.S. Navy, where he served until 1945. While in the navy, he married Mirta Sanchez. They had one son; the marriage ended in divorce. After his tour of duty, he received presidential honors for participating in nine battles. After the war he took advantage of the GI Bill and studied composition, arranging, and conducting at the Juilliard School of Music in Manhattan. At night Puente continued his involvement in the Latin music scene, playing again with Curbelo, Pupi Campos, and Fernando Alvarez and his Copacabana Group, where he earned his initial reputation as an arranger. In 1948, at the urging of promoter Federico Pagani, Puente formed his own group, the Picadilly Boys. Puente disliked the name, which referred to "picadillo" (beef and pork hash), and soon changed it to "Tito Puente and His Orchestra." That same year he won his legendary "Battle of the Bands" with the Damaso Perez Prado orchestra at the Manhattan Center. Puente was subsequently crowned "King of Latin Music" or "El Rey" by journalist Bobby Quintero. His first hit, "Abaniquito," came in 1949 for Tico Records. It was the first of 117 albums he recorded over the next fifty years.

The late 1940s saw the advent of Latin jazz, pioneered by legendary trumpeter Dizzy Gillespie and recordings by alto saxophonist Charlie Parker with the Machito Orchestra. "Naturally, one of my original influences was Dizzy, while he led his band that included [the late Cuban percussionist] Chano Pozo," Puente recalled in an interview with Kohan. As the years went by, Puente recorded Latin jazz, but his emphasis was on keeping the music danceable. He would record well-known tunes and rearrange them into the rhythm (mambo, cha-cha-cha, merengue, etc.) that he felt best suited the tune. Puente himself contributed two well-known tunes to the repertory, "Oye Como Va" and "Pa' Los Rumberos." "Oye Como Va" has been recorded numerous times by various artists, most notably by guitarist Carlos Santana in 1970.

Puente and his orchestra were at the forefront of the mambo craze of the 1950s, playing regularly at New York's Palladium opposite his former employer, Machito. By 1952 the Palladium had become the major spot for Latin music and dance in the United States. Puente's future as an ambassador of Latin music was foreshadowed by the crowds at the Palladium. He recalled in an interview with Fernando González, "What I remember most about the Palladium is the people. Every night there were Irish, Jews, Chinese, blacks, Puerto Ricans, you name it, everybody was there and there was never a problem" (*Newark Star Ledger*, 3 May 1997).

Puente's numerous records from the 1950s reflected his view of Latin music and jazz, adding a Latin rhythm section to a straight jazz arrangement. Puente himself noted his admiration for the orchestras of Woody Herman, Stan Kenton, and Count Basie. Their influence can be heard on his big band record from 1956, *Puente Goes Jazz* (RCA). Puente recorded with the Herman orchestra on *New Cha-Cha-Cha/ Mambo Herd* (1958). Puente's growing fame in the 1950s attracted some of the finest talent in Latin music, and his orchestra employed percussionists Mongo Santamaria, Ray Barretto, and Willie "Bobo" Correa, all of whom became notable bandleaders. Puente also helped propel the careers of singers La Lupe and Celia Cruz in the 1960s and 1970s. Around this time, he had a son and a daughter with Margie Asencion, whom he later married.

Puente maintained his nickname "El Rey" through the changing currents of Latin music in the 1960s and afterward. Puente's own longevity gave him a sense of pride and the music a sense of continuity. He told Fernando González in 1997, "The longevity is important to me, especially because I did it staying the same, true to the music." Puente eschewed the term "salsa," which was applied to Latin music in the 1990s. "The word salsa combines all kinds of music into one, like the mambo, the cha-cha, the merengue, all music with Caribbean origins. When they call it salsa, you don't actually define what [the] rhythm is. That's why I don't particularly care for the word," he declared to Kohan.

Puente earned his status as an icon through constant touring, by his own account consistently playing nearly 300 dates per year, all over the world. He played in places ranging from Castro's Cuba to Singapore. He performed with various symphony orchestras and played for three U.S. presidents. In 1997 he received the National Medal of Arts from President Bill Clinton. Puente won five Grammy Awards and played himself in the 1992 film *The Mambo Kings*. His many achievements made him a source for Puerto Rican pride. Graphic artist Nestor Otero said that Puente gave Puerto Ricans living in the mainland United States and around the world a sense of community. Through it all, "El Rey" still held court from time to time at his restaurant on City Island, New York, and continued to give concerts.

Puente's final concert was in Puerto Rico. He was hospitalized in Puerto Rico in May 2000 before returning to New York City, where he died. He was survived by his wife and three children. One of his sons, Tito Puente, Jr. (actually III), keeps his family's musical legacy alive as a performing musician.

• Steven Joseph Loza, *Tito Puente and the Making of Latin Music* (1999), is a comprehensive biography. It includes interviews with managers, friends, family, and numerous important Latin jazz musicians such as Poncho Sanchez, Hilton Ruiz, and Jerry González. The book also offers musical transcriptions and analysis. Puente gave numerous interviews to reporters in the New York metropolitan area, and many of these articles are collected in the press clippings file at the Institute of Jazz Studies at Rutgers University, Newark, New Jersey. Details about Puente's career and involvement in other bands can be found in virtually any book on Latin music, such as John Storm Roberts, *Latin Jazz* (1999); Roberts, *The Latin Tinge: The Impact of Latin American Music on the United States* (2d ed., 1999); and Vernon Boggs, *Salsiology: Afro-Cuban Music and the Evolution of Salsa in New York City* (1992). The entire transcript of Peter Kohan's interview with Puente can be found at jazzradio.org. An obituary is in the *New York Times*, 2 June 2000.

JAVIER GONZALEZ

PULLER, Lewis Burwell, Jr. (18 Aug. 1945–11 May 1994), marine corps officer and winner of the 1992 Pulitzer Prize, was born at Camp Lejeune, North Carolina, the son of General Lewis B. "Chesty" Puller, one of the most highly decorated marines in American history, and Virginia Montague Evans Puller, a schoolteacher. He had two sisters. The Puller family could trace their military tradition back to Major John Puller, a confederate cavalryman, who died while fighting in 1863. Lewis Puller, Sr., spent thirty-seven years in the marines, retiring in 1955, and there was never any doubt that his only son would follow in his footsteps. While young Puller was growing up in rural Virginia, his family would be visited at any time of the day or evening by former marines stopping by to pay homage to the decorated three-star general. Lewis, Jr., completed his secondary education at Christchurch School in 1962 and then attended William and Mary College, graduating in 1967. He promptly joined the marines, receiving his basic training at Quantico, Virginia, followed by a stint at the Marine's Officer Candidate School, from which he emerged as a second lieutenant in July 1968. The next month he married Linda Ford Todd, with whom he had two children. Later that same month, Puller was sent to Vietnam as a platoon commander in the Second Battalion of the First Marine Regiment of the First Marine Division.

Assigned to the coastal plain near Danang, dubbed "the Riviera," Puller led his platoon on patrols into the jungle, sometimes engaging in firefights with the North Vietnamese forces. On 11 October 1968, during a routine skirmish, Puller stepped on a booby-trapped 105mm howitzer round. Along with the loss of his legs, he also lost the thumb and little finger from his right hand and all but half of the forefinger and thumb on his left hand. His torso was riddled with shrapnel, and he suffered a dislocated shoulder and punctured eardrum as well. Triage physicians in Danang stabilized the severely wounded Puller, who was promptly returned to the U.S. Naval Hospital in Philadelphia; there he spent nearly twenty-two months in the Sick Officers Quarters enduring several surgeries and hundreds of hours of physical and occupational therapy. He was never able to accommodate prosthetic legs and spent the rest of his life in a wheelchair. For his abbreviated tour in Vietnam he earned two Purple Hearts, the Navy Commendation Medal, the Silver Star, the Vietnam Cross of Gallantry—and a future vastly different from the one he had foreseen before joining the service.

Released from the hospital in August 1970, Lewis, his wife Toddy, and his son Lewis B. Puller, III, settled in Williamsburg, Virginia. In September 1971 Lewis enrolled in the Marshall Wythe School of Law at William and Mary. On graduation from law school in 1974, Puller worked for the Veteran's Administration in the general counsel's office. As the Vietnam War wound down amid growing antiwar sentiment, Puller's own views about the war began to shift, and by the middle of the 1970s he had become convinced that the war had been a mistake and publicly declared that, if given the choice a second time, he would not have gone to Vietnam. In April 1975 he sought appointment to the newly created Presidential Clemency Board, established by President Gerald Ford to evaluate the cases of military deserters and draft evaders. In August 1976 Puller left the Veterans Administration to work for the Paralyzed Veterans of America.

He had become increasingly interested in politics and in 1977 volunteered to help Charles Robb's campaign for lieutenant governor of Virginia. This experience whetted his political appetite, and in 1978 he ran for the U.S. House of Representatives seat in Virginia's First Congressional District against the incumbent, Paul Trible. Puller's campaign did not go well, and his strident antiwar sentiments, which he readily voiced, were not popular among the staunchly promilitary citizens in that part of Virginia. Puller lost badly, garnering only 28 percent of the vote, and he slipped into depression. He had often abused alcohol during his years of recovery, and the recent drubbing at the polls pushed him over the edge. His suicide attempt was unsuccessful, however, because he was too drunk to start his car in his garage to asphyxiate himself. This traumatic event led him to join Alcoholics Anonymous in September 1981, after which he led a sober life for more than a decade.

In 1979, after his electoral defeat, Puller had joined the Office of the General Counsel at the Department of Defense. Upon achieving sobriety, Puller established a happy routine of work and family. After seeing the movie *An Officer and a Gentleman* in the early 1980s, Puller decided his own story might be worth telling. He went home, picked up a Bic pen and a yellow legal pad, and started writing. In 1991 the book appeared as *Fortunate Son: The Autobiography of Lewis B. Puller, Jr.* Puller explained in interviews that after he and his fellow veterans returned from Vietnam, no one was interested in hearing from them. The book gave him a chance to tell his story. He declared that the book was an affirmation of his love for his wife, his father, and his country. In 1992 his book won the Pulitzer Prize for biography or autobiography.

Upon the completion of his book, Puller took a leave of absence from his Department of Defense job and became a writer in residence at George Mason University. He expressed an interest in writing a biography of Senator Bob Kerrey, whom he had met while both were recuperating at the U.S. Naval Hospital. In 1992 Puller was a featured speaker at the Memorial Day services at the newly constructed Vietnam Veterans Memorial in Washington, D.C. The next year he journeyed to Vietnam to dedicate a new school in the Quang Tri province, for which he had helped raise money. Meanwhile in 1991 Puller's wife, Toddy, had been elected to the Virginia legislature. Three years later, in 1994, they separated, and Puller's chronically delicate emotional state deteriorated as he fell once again under the influence of alcohol. He died at home from a self-inflicted gunshot wound.

To the names of those etched on the black marble of the Vietnam Veterans Memorial should be added that of Lewis B. Puller, Jr., whose death was as much a result of the war as were the deaths of those who died on the battlefield. For, although he survived the war, he carried forever his battle wounds in his heart and in his head. As a young man, his only desire had been to emulate the military experiences of his distinguished father, and despite the horrible results of his own brief military career, Lewis Puller, Jr., remained steadfast in his love for his father, family, and country.

• The College of William and Mary archives maintains a small collection a materials on Puller. The chief source of information about his life is his autobiography. For an insightful review of the book and of Puller's life, see William Styron, "The Wreckage of an American War," *New York Times Book Review*, 16 June 1991. A brief interview appears in Brian Lamb, comp., *Booknotes: America's Finest Authors on Reading, Writing, and the Power of Ideas* (1997), pp. 356–58. An obituary is in the *New York Times*, 12 May 1994.

EDWARD A. GOEDEKEN

PURCELL, Edward M. (30 Aug. 1912–7 Mar. 1997), physicist, was born in Taylorville, Illinois, the son of Edward A. Purcell, manager of the Illinois Southeastern Telephone Company in Taylorville, and Elizabeth Mills Purcell, a high school Latin teacher. As a youngster, Purcell had access to various electronic devices that had been discarded by the telephone company; he also studied the *Bell System Technical Journal*. As he later acknowledged, in this journal he glimpsed a "wonderful world where electricity and mathematics and engineering and nice diagrams all came together." He entered Purdue University in the fall of 1929 as a student of electrical engineering. As a junior, he signed up for an independent-study course in the physics department. For his junior-year project he refurbished a spectrometer based on a Rowland grating, and he built an electrometer to measure nuclear half-lives. As a senior, he worked on electron diffraction. In the spring of 1933, Purcell graduated with a B.S.E.E. degree, and during the following summer he wrote his first two papers growing out of his undergraduate research. (Both were later published.) Purcell was headed toward a career in physics.

An influential physicist from Europe, Karl Lark-Horovitz, arrived at Purdue during Purcell's undergraduate years. With the support of Lark-Horovitz, Purcell was awarded an exchange fellowship and assigned to the Technische Hochschule in Karlsruhe, where he studied physics. On his trip to Europe, aboard ship he met his future wife, Beth C. Busser, also an exchange student. They married in 1937 and had two sons. From Europe, Purcell went to Harvard in 1934 as a graduate student. His dissertation research, under the direction of Kenneth T. Bainbridge, a pioneer in mass spectroscopy, was on focusing particles in a mass spectrometer. When he obtained his doctorate in 1938, he joined the Harvard physics faculty as a faculty instructor.

In 1940, after the outbreak of war in Europe, Purcell moved from Harvard to the Massachusetts Institute of Technology, where the Radiation Laboratory was being organized. He spent the duration of the war at the Rad Lab, as it was called, developing microwave radar systems. Early he became leader of the Fundamental Development Group. This wartime experience had a defining influence on Purcell's subsequent professional career.

When the war ended, Purcell and others remained at the Rad Lab into the fall of 1945 chronicling the technical achievements of the radar project in a series of books. At the Rad Lab, Purcell reported to I. I. Rabi, who, in 1938, discovered the magnetic resonance method, a powerful technique for measuring properties of the atomic nucleus. Rabi's discovery focused on individual atoms moving through an evacuated chamber. Purcell extended this method when he and his coworkers Robert V. Pound and Henry C. Torrey discovered magnetic resonance in a solid. By so doing, Purcell opened the way for nuclear magnetic resonance (NMR) and later magnetic resonance imaging (MRI), a powerful diagnostic tool for physicians. This work led to his 1952 Nobel Prize in physics. (Purcell shared the prize with Felix Bloch who independently made the same discovery at Stanford University by a quite different method.)

When his responsibilities at the Rad Lab ended, Purcell returned to Harvard, where he remained for the rest of his career. In 1951 Purcell and his graduate student Harold "Doc" Ewen made another great discovery. The spectrum of the hydrogen atom has been studied intensely. The radiation of one particular spectral transition of hydrogen occurs at radio frequencies with a wavelength of 21 centimeters. It is referred to as the hydrogen 21-cm line. Purcell and Ewen pondered whether this transition could be observed emanating from hydrogen atoms in interstellar space. Purcell encouraged Ewen to look for this line, and this became Ewen's thesis topic. The 21-cm radiation emanating from hydrogen atoms located in deep space was first observed on 25 March 1951. This discovery opened the way to mapping the spiral arms of the Milky Way galaxy and provided radio astronomy the stimulus to use atomic and molecular spectroscopy as a research method. Purcell's work in radio astronomy brought him into astrophysics. During the 1960s, he sought to understand the interactions of interstellar dust grains and the propagation of light through the galaxy.

Later, Purcell became interested in biophysics. He was fascinated by the ability of a tiny organism, like the *E. coli* bacterium, to carry on its complicated life in its difficult environment. As Purcell pointed out, locomotion for the *E. coli* would be analogous to humans swimming in thick molasses. In 1984 he and Howard Berg, his collaborator, were awarded the Biological Physics Prize from the American Physical Society. In recognition for his broad contributions to science, Purcell was elected to membership in the National Academy of Sciences and was a foreign member of the Royal Society.

Throughout his professional life, Purcell had a deep interest in teaching. He taught and developed courses, mainly undergraduate, at Harvard. He was a coau-

thor, with W. H. Furry and J. C. Street, of *Physics*, an introductory textbook, and he was the sole author of a classic textbook, *Electricity and Magnetism*, which was developed as a part of the Berkeley Physics Course series. For his contributions to physics education, in 1968 the American Association of Physics Teachers awarded Purcell its highest honor, the Oersted Medal. He was particularly proud of this recognition.

Besides being a research physicist and a teacher, Edward Purcell was a public servant. After World War II, Purcell's advice was sought by the nation's leaders. He was a member of advisory groups for various agencies, including the U.S. State Department, the U.S. Air Force, and NASA. From its inception in 1957 until he resigned in 1965, he served on the President's Science Advisory Committee during the administrations of Dwight D. Eisenhower, John F. Kennedy, and Lyndon B. Johnson. In 1980 he was awarded the National Medal of Science. Although he was famous and won many honors, Purcell lived his life with a rare gentleness, kindness, consideration, and humility.

• An account of two independent discoveries of NMR is given by John S. Rigden, "Quantum States and Precession: The Two Discoveries of NMR," *Reviews of Modern Physics* 58, 433–48 (1986). A 1977 interview conducted by Katherine R. Sopka is on file at the Center for History of Physics at the American Institute of Physics. Robert V. Pound is the author of the a biographical article in Vol. 78 of *Biographical Memoirs* published by the National Academy of Sciences. Obituaries appeared in the *New York Times* on 10 March 1997 and in *Nature*, 17 April 1997.

JOHN RIGDEN

PUSEY, Nathan Marsh (4 Apr. 1907–14 Nov. 2001), twenty-fourth president of Harvard University, was born in Council Bluffs, Iowa, the son of John Marsh Pusey, a wholesale grocer, and Rosa Drake, a schoolteacher. Pusey's father died when he was a year old, leaving his mother to raise three children on the $65 per week that she earned as a school principal. After graduating from Abraham Lincoln High School in Council Bluffs in 1924, Pusey entered Harvard College on a Charles Elliott Perkins Scholarship. The Perkins scholarship was conditional on a student's making the dean's list every year; Pusey held onto it all four years, in the process acquiring a reputation as something of a grind—albeit a likable one—in the midst of the Yard's Roaring Twenties revelry. He did find the time to play on the basketball team his freshman year, and as a senior he won the esteem of his classmates by placing first in a Harvard-Yale literary "brain test." After graduation Pusey toured France and Italy and then got a job teaching at Riverdale Country Day School, in the Bronx borough of New York City. He spent the summer of 1931 studying Greek and that fall became a graduate student in Harvard's classics department. The following year, with a master's degree in ancient history, he traveled to Athens for a fellowship at the American School of Classical Study. In 1935, Lawrence College, in Appleton, Wisconsin, invited him to lead a "great books" program on its campus.

In 1936 Pusey married Anne Woodward, a Bryn Mawr graduate from Council Bluffs whom he had once tutored in algebra; they had three children. After completing his doctorate in Greek history at Harvard in 1937, Pusey taught at Scripps College, in Claremont, California, and later at Wesleyan University, in Middletown, Connecticut. During the war years he remained at Wesleyan as a physics instructor to naval V-5 students.

Summoned back to Lawrence College as its president in 1944, Pusey spent nine productive years increasing the endowment, improving faculty benefits, and introducing curricular changes. After Joseph R. McCarthy was elected U.S. senator from the district in 1946—Pusey first met him on the smoking car of the Appleton-Madison train—an adversarial relationship developed between the two. During McCarthy's 1952 reelection bid, Pusey published a broadside outlining the senator's public record and casting doubt on McCarthy's claim that the federal government was awash in Communist infiltrators. The senator excoriated Pusey in turn. When Pusey resigned his post at Lawrence College to head to Cambridge, McCarthy sniped, "Harvard's loss is Wisconsin's gain."

Pusey took office as Harvard president in October 1953, and within weeks Senator McCarthy publicly challenged him. McCarthy pressed for the dismissal of four faculty members he accused of Communist activities, calling Harvard "a privileged sanctuary for Fifth Amendment Communists" and "a smelly mess." Pusey was praised in the academic community for his response, which argued, essentially, that no Harvard faculty member could possibly be a Communist, as Communists lacked the independence of mind required of first-rate scholars. "Americanism," he said, in a widely reported statement, "does not mean enforced and circumscribed belief; it cannot mean this. Our job is to educate free, independent and vigorous minds capable of analyzing events, of exercising judgment, of distinguishing facts from propaganda, and truth from half-truths and lies." The four faculty members stayed.

Pusey was appalled at the overcrowded and dilapidated condition of Harvard's labs and libraries, dormitories, offices, and athletic facilities. Bidden by the Harvard Corporation to focus his attentions on invigorating undergraduate education and the liberal arts at the university, Pusey in 1957 launched the Program for Harvard; with a stated goal of $82.5 million, it was far and away the most ambitious fundraising effort ever attempted by an institution of higher learning. (The previous ceiling had been $15 million.) The campaign ended up raising about $100 million, pouring fresh funds into faculty salaries and professorships, financial aid, and construction. Pusey's bold vision, and his single-minded commitment to realizing it, raised the bar on fundraising. In total, during the Pusey years, Harvard's endowment grew from $304

million to more than $1 billion; the number of faculty and administrators grew from 3,000 to 8,500; student enrollment rose from 10,000 to 15,000; the construction of more than 30 buildings nearly doubled its floor space; and the budget quadrupled. The investment in new professorships and facilities materially advanced Harvard's status as a research university. Moreover, thanks to a new "need-blind" admissions policy enacted in the early 1960s—Pusey was a passionate believer in meritocracy—the expanded student body reflected a new and dynamic diversity of backgrounds. He began negotiations for a merger between Harvard and its nearby sister school, Radcliffe College, and approved an initial experiment in co-residence.

A devout Episcopalian, Pusey made one of his earliest priorities the strengthening of Harvard's moribund Divinity School, citing the urgent need for religious education and decrying modern society's "almost idolatrous preoccupation with the secular order." He was an ardent supporter of the Memorial Church and of its role in the life of the university.

The student protest movement of the late 1960s surprised Pusey, who held the old-fashioned assumption that most young people were apolitical by nature. He objected to the coercive methods used by the protesters, which he viewed as incompatible with the modes of thought and discourse integral to a university. As passions mounted in opposition to the Vietnam War, the students developed a list of demands, including the barring of ROTC from the campus, a halt to Harvard's expansionism within Cambridge, and an end to its complicity in the "military-industrial complex." Pusey's immovability in the face of these demands, which reminded him of Senator McCarthy's anti-intellectual assaults more than a decade earlier, was seen by many students and faculty as infuriatingly inadequate. In April 1969, several hundred protesters, led by Students for a Democratic Society, took over University Hall, the main administrative building, and forcibly ejected nine deans. Late that night, Pusey called in the state and city police, who, suited in full riot gear, advanced on the building at dawn, driving out the protesters with tear gas and batons; 45 students were injured and 197 arrested. It was a watershed event in the life and career of the earnest Pusey, whose stoic reserve and dogged adherence to principle were now disparaged by students and faculty alike. The loyal booster who once rarely missed a Crimson football game, sometimes even accompanying teams on trips, and for whom reasoned persuasion and respect for differences of opinion were the foundation stones of academic culture, now found himself cursed and spat on as he walked through the Yard. Still, he had no regrets. His moral compass was rock-steady: the civilizing mission and independence of the university must be preserved at any cost. For Pusey, the decision had been a simple one.

Pusey took early retirement in 1971. He served for the next four years as head of the Andrew F. Mellon Foundation, in New York. After leaving Mellon he devoted himself to writing a book, *American Higher Education, 1945–1970: A Personal Account,* which was published in 1978. He remained active in the Episcopal Church, serving on the central committee of the World Council of Churches and, in 1979–1980, as president of the United Board for Christian Higher Education in Asia. He also continued on the boards of several charities, including Fountain House, a mental health program. He died in New York City.

Pusey was an important transitional figure in the history of one of the world's great universities. He was the first non–New Englander to head Harvard. He arrived at a Harvard still dominated by the prep school scions of old Brahmin families and left behind a complex, modern community where minorities and women played an increasingly visible role. He was a cautious and courtly traditionalist who nonetheless enabled Harvard to step firmly into the future, by his expansion of the faculty and physical plant, his meritocratic reforms in admissions and hiring, his reinvention of the art of university fundraising, and his resolute defense of academic freedom.

• Pusey's papers are located in the Harvard University Archives. Besides *American Higher Education, 1945–1970,* he was also the author of an earlier book, *The Age of the Scholar* (1963). For an excellent treatment of Pusey and his era at Harvard, see John T. Bethell, *Harvard Observed* (1998). Other perspectives on Pusey's place in Harvard history can be found in Richard Norton Smith, *The Harvard Century: The Making of a University to a Nation* (1998), and in Morton and Phyllis Keller, *Making Harvard Modern: The Rise of America's University* (2001). For an official retrospective of his years as president, see *The Pusey Years at Harvard,* published by the Harvard University News Office (1971). An obituary is in the *New York Times,* 15 Nov. 2001.

DEBORAH SMULLYAN

Q

QUESTEL, Mae (13 Sept. 1908–4 Jan. 1998), actress, was born in the Bronx, New York, the daughter of Simon Kwestel, a Russian immigrant of unrecorded occupation, and Frieda Glauberman Kwestel. Questel is reported to have shown a precocious ability to recite at the age of two and a half, and she gave public performances in school and at charity benefits at the age of five. By 1916 she had performed at Carnegie Hall and Town Hall and had played a small role in David Belasco's Broadway production of *Daddy*. At the recommendation of the violinist Mischa Elman, a family friend, she took lessons with Joseph G. Geiger, a famous elocution teacher who counted the radio announcer Ben Grauer and the actress Sylvia Sidney among his students. In 1923 Questel briefly attended the Theater Guild school, where she studied dramatics, dancing, and singing, but her Orthodox Jewish grandparents opposed a career in the theater and forced her to leave. After graduating from Morris High School in the Bronx, Questel gave private elocution lessons while living with her parents.

In 1925, then spelling her name "Questelle," Questel surrendered to the persuasion of high-school sorority friends and entered an impersonation contest at the RKO Fordham Theater in the Bronx. She won $150 for her imitation of the singer Helen Kane, then appearing at the theater. Her mimicry so impressed the RKO management that they offered the pert 5-foot, 2-inch redhead a contract to go on the vaudeville circuit. Much against her parents' and grandparents' wills, she signed with the William Morris Agency. Changing the spelling of her name a second time, she nevertheless always insisted on the original pronunciation. "Accent the second syllable, rhymes with 'compel,'" she explained (Collins, p. 15). She billed herself "Mae Questel—Personality Singer of Personality Songs." Performing sometimes solo and sometimes with partners, she appeared often at the Palace on Broadway and presented novelty numbers and impersonations of such celebrities as Maurice Chevalier, Eddie Cantor, Marlene Dietrich, Mae West, and Fanny Brice as well as Helen Kane. Kane had become famous for her song "I Wanna Be Loved by You," introduced with its interpolated scat lyrics "boop oop a doop" in 1928, and Questel was so expert at imitating the childlike voice with which Kane rendered it that, when the popular singer had to cancel a performance at RKO Proctor's Fifty-eighth Street Theater in 1929, Questel was called on to pinch-hit for her. The following year Questel married Leo Balkin, with whom she had two children. The couple later divorced, and Questel married Jack E. Shelby in 1970. No children were born of her second marriage.

In 1930 the animator Max Fleischer created the cartoon character Betty Boop, a French poodle who within two years evolved into a coyly sexy human vamp clearly based on Helen Kane, complete with seductive manner and "boop-oop-a-doop" signature. Questel was hired to do the voice in 1931, and she played the character until the series was discontinued in 1939, performing in more than 150 cartoon shorts. Her recording of the song "On the Good Ship Lollipop," made for Decca in Betty Boop's saucy style and with her familiar tag line, sold more than two million copies. In 1932 Questel starred in the NBC radio show *Betty Boop's Frolics* and played flirtatious Boop-like roles in several Hollywood movies, including a series of short features with Rudy Vallee. Paramount offered her a film contract, but she chose to remain in New York with her family.

Questel's talents were not limited to the high-pitched voice of Betty Boop. In 1933 Fleischer called on her for his *Popeye the Sailor* series to dub the hero's relatively sexless girlfriend Olive Oyl, whom she rendered in a manner based on that of the actress ZaSu Pitts. She also assumed the role of the tot left on Olive's doorstep, Swee'pea. Questel voiced both of these characters in 454 cartoons for Fleischer until the series was discontinued in 1967, and she played them for the run of the radio show from 1935 to 1938. Her vocal range was impressive. At one point when the actor playing Popeye on radio was unable to perform, she filled in for him, lowering her voice to match his rasping tones. In addition to her regular work in the *Betty Boop* and *Popeye* series, she provided the cartoon voices of Little Lulu, Little Audrey, and Casper the Friendly Ghost as well as those of various dogs, parrots, ducks, owls, monkeys, lions, witches, and babies on radio and in animated films. The dialects she commanded included French, Polish, German, and Spanish, all languages she spoke with some fluency.

Questel had a notable career in radio apart from her work as a cartoon voice. During the 1940s she performed frequently in *Duffy's Tavern* and *The Henry Morgan Show*, as the Dragon Lady in *Terry and the Pirates*, as herself in *Tom, Timmy & Mae with Tom Glazer*, and in various roles, serious and comic, on *True Story*, *The Green Hornet*, *Mr. and Mrs. North*, and *Perry Mason*. In the following decade she appeared on television in soap operas such as *Somerset* and *All My Children*, comedies such as *The Goldbergs*, and dramatic shows such as *The U.S. Steel Hour* and *Martin Kane, Private Eye*. In her television roles, as in those she played on radio, Questel created a wide variety of characters, from flirtatious flappers to tough city girls. Between 1953 and 1957 she participated in the interactive animated show *Winky Dink and You* both before the camera as a comedienne and behind it as the voice of the elf Winky Dink. She appeared in many commercials, where she became well known as the talking Fizzies tablet, Nabisco's Buffalo Bee, and most memorably Scott paper towels' folksy Aunt Bluebell from 1971 to 1978. She also recorded humorous and popular songs on the Golden, Jubilee, and Columbia labels and performed in such classics as *Everyman* and *Faustus* for Caedmon Records.

In 1948 Questel made her first major appearance on Broadway in *Dr. Social*. On Broadway, as on radio and television, the versatile actress played various roles but was best known for such comic portrayals as that of a Jewish housewife in *A Majority of One* (1959–1961). Later New York stage performances included *Come Blow Your Horn* and *Enter Laughing* (1963), and *Where Have You Been, Billy Boy?* (1969). Her film credits include *A Majority of One* (1961), *Funny Girl* (1968), *Move* (1969), and Woody Allen's "OedipusWrecks" segment of *New York Stories* (1989). In 1988 she was called on to dub the voice of the animated character Betty Boop once again in the film *Who Framed Roger Rabbit?*

Questel parleyed a talent for mimicry and a vivacious personality into a long and honored career in every phase of the theater, working uninterruptedly until she began to show signs of Alzheimer's disease in the early 1990s. She died in her apartment on Madison Avenue in Manhattan.

• Newspaper accounts of Questel's career include "Bronx Girl Winner of Kane Concert," *New York Telegraph*, 31 Dec. 1929; Evelyn Seeley, "Busy Little Betty Boop Squeaks Way to Fame for Mae Questel, Her Voice," *New York World-Telegram*, 12 July 1932; Sidney Skolsky, "Tintypes," *New York Daily News*, 16 Jan. 1932; Liza Wilson, "The Voice Is Familiar, But—," *American Weekly* (*New York Journal-American*), 10 Dec. 1961; "Mae's Voice Her Fortune," *Newark* (N.J.) *Evening News*, 17 Mar. 1963; Robert Wahls, "Footlight," *New York Sunday News*, 8 Dec. 1963; "A Star of 1900 Films Known Only by Voice," *New York Post*, 25 May 1964; and Glenn Collins, "When Mia Meets Mama, It's Mae Questel," *New York Times*, 26 Feb. 1989. For her contribution to animated films, see Andrew J. Lederer, "Mae Questel: A Reminiscence, History and Perspective," *Animation World Magazine*, 2, no. 12 Mar. 1998: 32–34. Questel's association with the Fleischer studios is detailed in Leslie Cabarga, *The Fleischer Story*, rev. ed. (1988). Obituaries are in the *New York Times*, 8 Jan. 1998, and the *Washington Post*, 9 Jan. 1998.

DENNIS WEPMAN

QUIMBY, Harriet N. (11 May 1875–1 July 1912), aviator and journalist, was born in Arcadia Township, Manistee County, Michigan, the daughter of William Quimby and Ursula Cook Quimby, farmers. Her full middle name is unknown. The youngest known child of a disabled Civil War veteran and a medicinal herbalist, in adulthood Quimby let it be thought that she had been born in 1885 in California and educated in Europe by wealthy parents. It has also been reported

that Quimby was born in Coldwater, Branch County, Michigan, the younger of two daughters. However, Quimby's parents moved from Branch to Manistee County in 1867 with older children, two of whom died before Harriet's birth and one shortly thereafter. By 1880 only Harriet and one older sister survived. No education records have been found, although residents' recollections indicated that Quimby attended the local public school in Arcadia.

In the late 1880s the Quimbys moved to Arroyo Grande, California, north of Los Angeles, where William Quimby was in the grocery business. In the mid-1890s they moved to the San Francisco and Oakland area; Harriet Quimby's occupation is listed in the 1900 census as "actress."

Quimby evidenced determination, intelligence, a facility for language, and a dramatic beauty. With these assets, she reinvented herself. While making the rounds of San Francisco theaters, Quimby met a fellow actress, Linda Arvidson, who later married the filmmaker D. W. Griffith. Together Quimby and Arvidson held a recital to attract critical attention. Quimby had more success as a journalist, however, and her theater reviews and feature articles appeared in several San Francisco newspapers.

In 1902 or 1903 Quimby moved to New York City, where she worked as a freelance writer. By early 1905 she had joined the staff of *Leslie's Illustrated Weekly* as a feature writer and drama critic. Over the next few years Quimby became so prolific that her articles, which frequently covered the theater and cultural life in New York City, were published under several pseudonyms as well as her own name. By 1906 she was dramatic editor of *Leslie's*. She purchased and drove her own automobile and reported on the attractions and cuisine of Italy, Egypt, and Cuba among other locales. In 1911 her investigative reporting spotlighted an official inquiry into police corruption and prostitution in New York City. In addition hundreds of photos credited to Quimby accompanied both her own articles and those of others.

In October 1910 Quimby was assigned to cover the Belmont Park Aviation Meet. She met John Moisant, winner of the main event, and asked him to teach her to fly. Moisant agreed, but on 31 December 1910 he was killed at an air meet in New Orleans. About this time Quimby also became a tangential participant in the fledgling movie industry. Of the more than sixty one-reel films Griffith produced for the Biograph studio in 1911, Quimby is credited with seven screenplays.

In the spring of 1911 Quimby persuaded *Leslie's* to pay her tuition at the Moisant School of Aviation in Mineola, New York, run by John Moisant's brother Alfred Moisant. In return she wrote a series of articles on the experience, "How a Woman Learns to Fly." Despite arriving at the field before dawn, heavily veiled, her identity was soon discovered and reported in the *New York Times* under the headline "Woman in Trousers Daring Aviator" (11 May 1911). Quimby received her license on 1 August 1911, becoming the first licensed woman pilot in the United States. Two earlier American women pilots, Blanche Stuart Scott and Bessica Raiche, remained unlicensed. Raymonde de la Roche, the first licensed woman pilot in the world, had received her license in France on 8 March 1910. With her typical blend of flair and practicality, Quimby commissioned her signature flying suit, a hooded, plum-colored garment of wool-backed satin, which converted readily from walking skirt to knickerbocker trousers, combining flexibility, warmth, and style without adding bulk.

Flying monoplanes at a time when biplanes were still more common, Quimby and Mathilde Moisant, who became the second licensed woman pilot in the United States within weeks of Quimby's achievement, began to take part in air meets by September 1911. In November both women joined the Moisants' aerial demonstration team, the Moisant International Aviators, Inc., and flew in exhibitions in Mexico City. Quimby soon left the Moisants' troupe and hired her own manager, A. Leo Stevens. By now she had achieved national celebrity status as "America's first female aviator." Recognizing the economic potential of aviation, she encouraged other women to participate in the field as professionals.

While she was in Mexico City, Quimby began to consider a flight across the English Channel. Early in 1912 she took a leave from *Leslie's* and sailed for England. Sponsored by the *London Daily Mirror* and filmed by the Gaumont newsreel company, Quimby took off from Dover in fog at 5:30 a.m. on 16 April 1912, flying a borrowed fifty-horsepower Bleriot monoplane equipped with a compass. Although Quimby was unfamiliar both with the plane and with instrument flying, she landed one hour and nine minutes later on the beach between Hardelot and Equihen, France, about twenty-five miles south of Calais, the first woman to pilot an airplane across the English Channel. However, Quimby's achievement received little notice in the general press. On 15 April the RMS *Titanic* sank in the North Atlantic with great loss of life.

Quimby returned to the United States with a new 2-passenger, 75-horsepower Bleriot monoplane, which proved to have a highly sensitive balance. She planned to fly it in exhibition at the Harvard-Boston air meet at Squantum, Massachusetts, at the end of June. Arrangements were also made for Quimby to fly an official shipment of U.S. mail from Squantum to New York City on 7 July, the last day of the meet.

On the evening of 1 July 1912 Quimby was killed while returning from a test flight to Boston Light, a round trip of about twenty miles from the airfield. Quimby's passenger, the air meet manager William A. P. Willard, was seen to make a movement in his seat before he was thrown from the open cockpit, then Quimby was thrown out. They plummeted into Dorchester Bay. It has been suggested that Willard shifted his weight and the plane became unbalanced. The aircraft righted itself and descended with little damage. Newspaper reports and eyewitnesses suggested that

Quimby had been wearing her seatbelt on takeoff; it was not known how she could have fallen without first unfastening it. The accident was one of the first air crashes subjected to significant investigation. On her death certificate, the year and place of Quimby's birth are 1885, California.

• Archival collections include files at the National Air and Space Museum of the Smithsonian Institution, Washington, D.C., and the National Harriet Quimby Collection in the Converse College archives, Spartanburg, S.C. An eponymous research conference met annually from 1995 to 2000; its journal is in the National Air and Space Museum. Quimby's principal aviation articles are reprinted in Phil Scott, *The Pioneers of Flight: A Documentary History* (1999). Early mentions of Quimby are in Amelia Earhart, *The Fun of It: Random Records of My Own Flying and of Women in Aviation* (1932, repr. 1991), which assesses Quimby's flight achievements in light of twenty years' development in aviation, and Mrs. D. W. Griffith (Linda Arvidson), *When the Movies Were Young* (1928, repr. 1977), which provides vignettes of Quimby's life in San Francisco and New York. Ed Y. Hall, *Harriet Quimby: America's First Lady of the Air* (1993), quotes extensively from her writings and includes a bibliography of Quimby's articles in *Leslie's*; an appendix in the 3d ed. (1997) discusses findings regarding Quimby genealogy. Henry M. Holden, *Her Mentor Was an Albatross: The Autobiography of Harriet Quimby* (1993), focuses on Quimby's aviation years. Among aviation histories, Eileen F. LeBow, *Before Amelia: Women Pilots in the Early Days of Aviation* (2002), places Quimby in context with other early women aviators, and Doris L. Rich, *The Magnificent Moisants: Champions of Early Flight* (1998), details Quimby's experience with the Moisants and the Channel crossing. Articles about Quimby's death are in the *New York Times*, 2 and 3 July 1912, and the *Boston Globe*, 2 and 3 July 1912.

CAROLINE M. FANNIN

QUINE, W. V. (25 June 1908–25 Dec. 2000), philosopher, was born Willard Van Orman Quine in Akron, Ohio, the son of Cloyd Robert Quine, an office worker who in 1917 founded the Akron Equipment Company, and Harriet Ellis Van Orman Quine, a teacher. His parents were of Manx-German and British-Dutch ancestry, respectively. Quine's happy and active boyhood in Akron is engagingly described in his autobiography, *The Time of My Life* (1985). Quine received a B.A. from Oberlin College in 1930, majoring in mathematics. His diverse talents and interests, in mathematics, science, and psychology but also in language, literature, and poetry, attracted him to philosophy. At the end of his junior year at Oberlin his mother bought him Bertrand Russell and Alfred North Whitehead's three-volume *Principia Mathematica* (1910–13), and he applied to Harvard to work with Whitehead for a Ph.D.

Quine was only twenty-three when he received his Ph.D. in 1932, after just two years at Harvard. His dissertation simplified and clarified various aspects of Russell and Whitehead's work. It exemplifies many of Quine's characteristic features as a philosopher: his acute awareness of obscurity and confusions, his constructive ability to find new viewpoints that make things fall into place, and his concern with ontological issues. That year Quine was given Harvard's Sheldon Travelling Fellowship, which brought him to Vienna, Prague, and Warsaw and put him in contact with Moritz Schlick and the Vienna Circle, Rudolf Carnap in Prague, and Jan Lukasiewicz, Stanislaw Leśniewski, and Alfred Tarski in Warsaw. Quine later described his meeting with Carnap as his "first experience of sustained intellectual engagement with anyone of an older generation, let alone a great man . . . [the] most notable experience of being intellectually fired by a living teacher rather than a book" (*The Time of my Life*, p. 98).

Quine's year in Europe was followed by three years in Harvard's first group of six junior fellows. From 1936 to 1941 he was a faculty instructor at Harvard, and in 1940 he was appointed an associate professor with tenure effective one year later. After the United States entered World War II, Quine served from 1942 to 1946 in naval intelligence, mostly in Washington; in 1945 he was made a lieutenant commander. He became a full professor at Harvard in 1948, and in 1956 he succeeded C. I. Lewis as Edgar Pierce Professor of Philosophy, a position he held until his retirement in 1978.

The war years brought an end to Quine's marriage to his college sweetheart, Naomi Clayton, whom he had married in 1930. The couple, who divorced in 1947, had two children together. In 1948 Quine married Marjorie Boynton; their union lasted until Marjorie's death in 1998 and produced two children.

Early encyclopedias classified Quine as a logician, but he soon came to be regarded as a general philosopher: initially, as a philosopher of logic and language, but eventually as a metaphysician, whose radical thoughts about ontology, epistemology, and communication had repercussions within all major areas of philosophy. His early work, from his dissertation until World War II, was largely in logic, with the article "New Foundations for Mathematical Logic" (*American Mathematical Monthly* 44 [1937]: 70–80) regarded as his most important contribution. This eleven-page presentation of a new system of set theory inspired many further contributions and is today still the subject of intensive research and discussion by logicians who are studying the properties of the system and trying to find out whether it is consistent

After World War II, Quine returned to the issue that was a central concern in his dissertation: "to know or decide what there is or are" (*The Time of my Life*, p. 98). He insisted on the need to make clear what the entities are that one talks about: "no entity without identity." He also sought clarity concerning what entities are assumed by a theory. In "On What There Is" (*Review of Metaphysics* 2 [1948]: 21–38), one of his most-quoted essays, he argued that a theory is committed to all those entities that belong to the universe of discourse of the theory: "to be is to be the value of a variable." In Quine's later work, this realism took an intriguing new turn, not yet fully explored in the secondary literature, toward indeterminacy of reference.

In 1941 Quine turned to the modalities, the notions of necessity and possibility, and argued that they are hopelessly unclear. That a statement is necessary is sometimes "explained" by saying that it is true in all possible worlds. But, Quine objected, what is such a "possible world," and how can we tell which worlds are possible? We are just moving in a circle here. Gradually, Quine strengthened his arguments against the modalities, until in *Word and Object* (1960) he showed that, when modality is combined with quantification, modal distinctions collapse. That is, everything that is possible is true, and everything that is true is necessary. His argument presupposes a view on reference that to that point had gone unquestioned. The so-called "new theory of reference" arose as a response to Quine's critical objections and owes much to his acute analysis of the underlying problems.

Quine's main contributions were to the theory of meaning. In "Two Dogmas of Empiricism" (*Philosophical Review* 60 [1951]: 20–43), which was included in his first collection of essays, the widely read *From a Logical Point of View* (1953; rev. ed., 1961), Quine criticized the traditional view on meaning and related notions, like synonymy and analyticity. He sketched an alternative view on meaning, which was worked out in *Word and Object*. This skepticism grew into a major revamping of previous philosophical views on communication and the relation of language to the world. The central idea is one that Quine shares with most other philosophers and linguists, namely, the public nature of language. Quine's major contribution was to develop the idea with great persistence, to extreme consequences that many philosophers find problematic. One of these consequences, indeterminacy of translation, is the thesis of Quine's that has been most widely discussed. According to this thesis there can be many different manuals (grammars and dictionaries) for translation between two languages. Translations done with the help of one manual can be incompatible with translations done by another. Yet each manual is compatible with all the evidence available to the translator. The evidence here includes all publicly accessible evidence connected with the use of language, in speech as well as in writing. Unless one assumes evidence that is not publicly accessible, for example, grasping of Fregean senses or other intensional entities, there is no reason to regard one of these translation manuals as the right one, the others as wrong. This is not merely an epistemic matter, of our not being able to tell which manual is right; there is nothing to be right or wrong about. Translation is not merely underdetermined by the evidence, translation is indeterminate.

The indeterminacy thesis is a consequence of more fundamental ideas concerning the public nature of language that Quine refined in his later writings. This later work involves the whole range of Quine's philosophical insights: his views on epistemology, ontology, causality, natural kinds, time, space, and individuation. Quine created a new way of looking at these eternal questions of philosophy and their interconnections. He leaves a transformed philosophical landscape for new generations of philosophers to explore.

Quine was a member of a large number of academies and received many prizes, including the first Rolf Schock Prize in Stockholm in 1993 and the Kyoto Prize in Tokyo in 1996. He died in Boston.

Quine's writing style is lively, often playful, and always sparklingly clear. More than sixty years separate his first book, *A System of Logistic* (1934), from his twenty-third, *From Stimulus to Science* (1995). Many of his books were published in several editions and they have appeared in more than fifty translations, ranging over sixteen languages. Quine's articles have been even more widely translated and reprinted. His "Two Dogmas of Empiricism" (1951) has been included in more than twenty anthologies, and several other of his articles are nearly as widespread. With Ludwig Wittgenstein, Martin Heidegger, and John Rawls, Quine is among the most often quoted philosophers of the twentieth century.

• Numerous books and more than 2,000 articles, many of which appear in volumes devoted to his work, have been written on Quine. The main biographical source is Quine's autobiography, *The Time of My Life* (1985). Lewis Hahn and Paul Schlipp, *The Philosophy of W. V. Quine* (Library of Living Philosophers, vol. 18) (1986; 2d expanded ed., 1998) contains a complete bibliography of his work. Among other books assessing Quine's work are the following: Donald Davidson and Jaakko Hintikka, eds., *Words and Objections: Essays on the Work of W. V. Quine* (1969), with replies by Quine; Robert W. Shahan and Chris Swoyer, eds., *Essays on the Philosophy of W. V. Quine* (1979; replies by Quine in the journal *Philosophical Topics* 12 [1981], 227–43); Robert B. Barrett and Roger F. Gibson, eds., *Perspectives on Quine* (1990), with comments by Quine; Paolo Leonardi and Marco Santambrogio, eds., *On Quine: New Essays* (1995), with responses by Quine; Alex Orenstein and Petr Kotatko, eds., *Knowledge, Language and Logic: Questions for Quine* (1999), with replies by Quine; and Dagfinn Føllesdal, ed., *The Philosophy of Quine* (2001), a five-volume collection of selected articles on Quine. Obituaries appeared in major newspapers and journals all over the world, including the *New York Times* (27 Dec. 2000), the *Wall Street Journal* (4 Jan. 2001), the *Times* (London) and the *Guardian* (both 30 Dec. 2000), the *Economist* (11/12 Jan. 2001), *Le Monde* (1 Jan. 2001), *Die Zeit* (3 Jan. 2001), *Neue Zürcher Zeitung*, *Il Corriere della Sera*, *Il Manifesto* (all 4 Jan. 2001), and the *Chronicle of Higher Education* (2 Feb. 2001).

DAGFINN FØLLESDAL

QUISENBERRY, Dan (7 Feb. 1953–30 Sept. 1998), baseball player, was born Daniel Raymond Quisenberry in Santa Monica, California, the son of John Quisenberry, an automobile dealer, and Roberta Burmood Quisenberry. His parents divorced when Quisenberry was seven, and he grew up with his mother and his stepfather, Art Meola, in Costa Mesa, California. He attended Costa Mesa High School, where, he maintained, "I was average in everything I did," including baseball.

After graduation in 1971 Quisenberry attended the local Orange Coast (junior) College and put in two more undistinguished years as a ballplayer. Then he transferred to LaVerne College, a small school affiliated with the National Association of Intercollegiate Athletics, where he blossomed as a pitcher. In 1974 he compiled a 12–2 record with a 2.02 earned run average (ERA), and he followed that up with a national best 19-win season in 1975. That year he reverted from overhand pitching to his high school submarine style, which became his trademark. Despite his impressive record, he was not drafted. Ben Hines, his coach, landed him a $500-per-month contract with the Kansas City Royals.

Quisenberry spent the next four and a half seasons toiling in the minor leagues, mostly with Jacksonville in the AA Southern League, and he pitched consistently well. In 1976 he married his college sweetheart Janie Howard; they had two children. Following the 1978 season, Quisenberry enrolled at Fresno Pacific College to work on a physical education degree with the thought of teaching and coaching. He never finished his degree there, but he did become a devout Christian at the Mennonite college. His faith provided him a deep inner peace and an emotional even keel. Sportswriter Dick Kaegel quoted him as follows: "Fresno Pacific is a Mennonite school and just being around the brethren—the way they gave of themselves, shared what they had with each other, their level of commitment—all made me feel, 'That's the way I want to be'" ("Against Odds: Quiz Made Royals Special," *Kansas City Star*, 1 Oct. 1998). A "madman" in college, Quisenberry became calm and even-keeled. Though he continued to be an intense competitor, he always kept his cool, never blamed anyone for mistakes, and became a team player.

In 1979, after Quisenberry spent half a season at Triple A Omaha, the Kansas City Royals called him up to the major leagues for good. He compiled a 3–2 record with a 3.15 ERA that half season, and his sinker ball proved the secret of his success. The first batter he faced grounded into a 4–6–3 double play, and with Gold Glove second baseman Frank White leading a fine Royal defense, Quisenberry relied on his sure fielders for his success. He struck out only about one batter per three innings in his career. "Grass is a wonderful thing for little bugs and sinker ball pitchers," he explained. His self-deprecating sense of humor and friendly personality made him friends with almost everyone, and his witticisms became legendary. After his first visit to the Metrodome in Minneapolis, an unpopular stadium that one sportswriter described as "soulless," Quisenberry said, "I don't think there are any good uses for nuclear weapons, but this might be one."

The 6-foot, 2-inch, 185-pound right-handed hurler did not intimidate batters. A pale, skinny, mustachioed redhead with a modest 85-mile-per-hour fastball, he admitted: "I'm not a Mercedes at all. I'm more like a Volkswagen. They get a lot of mileage out of me, but it's not going to look pretty." Though his sinker lacked a sharp break (he called it "Peggy Lee" after the singer's recording of "Is That All There Is?"), it proved extremely effective. In 1980 he had a 12–7 record, a 3.09 ERA (his last over 3.00 until 1988), and tied for the American League (AL) lead with 75 relief appearances. He struck out the New York Yankee Willie Randolph for the last out of the AL Championship Series, sending the Royals to their first World Series and avenging losses in 1976, 1977, and 1978 to their Yankee nemeses. Philadelphia beat Kansas City in 6 games in the series, though, with "Quiz," as he was nicknamed, pitching in each game and recording a win, a save, and two losses.

The next five years constituted the apex of Quisenberry's career. In 1982 his 35 saves led the league, and the following season he set a new American League record with 45 saves, one more than his 44 in 1984. Those last two seasons he was runner-up in voting for the Cy Young Award. He saved another 37 in 1985 and won his fourth straight *Sporting News* Fireman of the Year Award as the top relief pitcher. From 1980 to 1985 he won 41 and saved 212, playing a role in 52 percent of Kansas City's wins. In 1985 Kansas City won its only World Series of the twentieth century, beating St. Louis in the I-70, all-Missouri showdown, with Quisenberry winning the pivotal sixth game.

In 1986 the manager Dick Howser moved to a committee of closers instead of his ace. The famed Quisenberry sinker seemed not to be sinking, and batters started hitting it in the air, spelling trouble for the idiosyncratic submariner. In 1988, used sparingly and with his ERA up to 3.55, Quiz asked for and got his release, enabling him to sign with his old manager Whitey Herzog of the St. Louis Cardinals. Quisenberry pitched for the Cards for a year and a half with modest success, then announced his retirement on 30 April 1990 after a month with the San Francisco Giants. His career statistics included 674 games, 244 saves, a 56–46 won-lost record, a 2.69 ERA, and only 1.38 walks per 9 innings.

Reporters (and fans) loved Quiz because he was always good for a quotation. Sometimes he told tall tales to credulous sportswriters while his teammates muffled their laughter. He was appreciated during his career and afterward for his wonderful wit and his sweet, joyful personality. Early in his Royal career he became active in Harvesters, a community food network to aid the poor, and he stuck with this ministry. Once he retired from baseball, he took writing courses and settled on poetry as a creative way to use his love of words. While he was invariably funny in person, through poetry he pondered issues like doubt and fear, the sorts of things athletes are supposed to repress. He published a book of poetry, *On Days Like This* (1998), and gave readings at libraries and churches in the Kansas City area.

In January 1998 Quisenberry was diagnosed with a brain tumor. The man who had never been on the disabled list in his career underwent radiation treatment, chemotherapy, and two surgeries. On 30 May 1998 he was inducted into the Royals Hall of Fame, but in the fall he succumbed to the tumor at his home in Leawood, Kansas.

• Roger Angell, *Season Ticket: A Baseball Companion* (1988), a collection of articles reprinted from the *New Yorker*, includes two pieces on Quisenberry written in late summer 1985. Obituaries are in the *New York Times*, the *Kansas City Star*, the *Los Angeles Times*, and the *American Reporter*, all 1 Oct. 1998.

JOHN R. M. WILSON

R

RAY, James Earl (10 Mar. 1928–23 Apr. 1998), assassin of the Rev. Martin Luther King, Jr., was born in the blue-collar town of Alton, Illinois, the son of George Ray, a sometime railroad brakeman, mechanic, and farmer, and Lucille Ray, a steam presser at a dry cleaning business. His father's family had a long history of violence and run-ins with the law; his great-grandfather was hanged, his grandfather was an alcoholic bootlegger, and his own father was convicted on a charge of breaking and entering. His mother worked tirelessly to support Ray and his eight siblings. The family endured severe poverty, despite several moves in Illinois. Ray started school in 1935 and was teased by other children for his torn pants and filthy shirt. Shy and withdrawn, he hated school and flunked the first grade. Given to occasional outbursts of anger and fistfights, he had few friends.

By fifteen, Ray began regularly visiting his recently paroled uncle Earl in nearby Quincy, Illinois, accompanying him on trips to illegal gambling halls, barrooms that mixed heavy drinking and brawling, and a seedy whorehouse. He also picked up a right-wing political philosophy that was anti–Franklin Roosevelt and pro-German. In 1944, when he was in eighth grade, he dropped out of school. He was increasingly impressed by Adolf Hitler and the Nazi philosophy that could lead to an all-white country without any blacks or Jews. After trying his hand at a few blue-collar jobs, in 1946 he impulsively joined the army, asking to be assigned to Germany. Ray's army service was disastrous: he quickly got involved in the black market, frequented local houses of prostitution, caught syphilis once and acute gonorrhea twice, and started using alcohol and amphetamines. Charged with being drunk in his quarters, he briefly went AWOL. At his November 1948 court martial, he was demoted to a buck private and sent to hard labor for three months, which was truncated when he was given a general discharge two days before Christmas "for ineptness and lack of adaptability for military service."

After his return to the states, he took low-paying menial jobs. He had trouble holding them and moved frequently, from Alton, Illinois, to Chicago, Colorado, and California, all within a year. In October 1949, he had his first run-in with the police—an arrest for burglary at a downtown Los Angeles office building. Convicted of second-degree robbery, he received a short prison sentence and was given an early release in December. While traveling back east, he was arrested in Marion, Iowa, for vagrancy and suspicion of robbery. After serving a three-week jail sentence, he returned to Quincy, Illinois. There, he reunited with his family and landed an assembly line job at a local plastics plant, a position he held for ten months before suddenly quitting. A month later he was arrested for vagrancy and received a ninety-day sentence.

Ray then moved to Chicago and took another assembly-line manufacturing job. He lasted eight months before he quit. On 6 May 1952, the twenty-four-year-old Ray was arrested for robbing a taxi driver at gunpoint. Pleading guilty, he served most of his term in the Pontiac prison, where he was solitary and unhappy. Two days after his twenty-sixth birthday, in 1954, he was finally released, with the probation report noting that Ray's "prognosis seems to be problematic to doubtful."

Ray again tried his hand at legitimate blue-collar jobs in Alton, but by August he was back to crime, arrested for robbing a local dry cleaner. Posting bail, he left town and returned to Quincy. The following March, Ray and a friend went on a cross-country spree with money orders they had stolen from a post office. After his arrest and a guilty plea, Ray received a 45-month sentence at the famous Kansas Leavenworth Penitentiary. His nearly three years there were uneventful except for one occasion when he refused to be transferred to the prison's honor farm, which was integrated. Ray preferred his racially segregated cell block.

After his release in April 1958, Ray almost immediately got involved in burglaries and robberies. In July, his luck ran out after an armed holdup of a supermarket. Convicted by a jury, he drew a twenty-year sentence at the Missouri State Penitentiary, one of the nation's toughest. There, Ray, who was described by his brother Jerry as "a natural hustler" got involved in selling and using drugs, primarily amphetamines. He also continued to express his distaste for blacks to many of his fellow prisoners, even boasting to some that when he got out, he would collect $10,000 for killing Dr. King. The House Select Committee on Assassinations in the 1970s discovered that people connected to a racist St. Louis attorney who was offering a $50,000 bounty for King's death visited or were incarcerated at the same prison with Ray.

Ray unsuccessfully tried to break out of prison in 1961 and again in 1966. He finally succeeded on 23 April 1967, almost a year before Dr. King's assassination. During that time, Ray managed to stay free by moving around frequently; he dabbled in petty crimes ranging from burglaries to marijuana dealing. He reunited with his ex-felon brothers John and Jerry and then headed to Canada. In August 1967, Ray lived in Birmingham, Alabama, until he left in early October for Mexico. Then in mid-November he crossed the border again, booking into a flophouse in Los Angeles. In December of 1967 Ray drove to New Orleans in what appears to have been a rendezvous with his brother Jerry (the latter has denied it).

In Los Angeles, Ray had plastic surgery on his nose (he said he thought it too sharp), ran a personal ad in hopes of meeting a woman, took ballroom dancing lessons, joined a correspondence school for locksmiths, and enrolled in a bartending school. Then suddenly, in mid-March, less than a month before Dr. King was killed, Ray left Los Angeles and headed east. He arrived in Selma, Alabama, on 22 March, the same day Dr. King visited the city. When King left the next day, Ray did as well, driving to King's hometown of Atlanta. On 29 March, Ray paid cash for a powerful .30–06 rifle with a telescopic sight. Ray left Atlanta for Memphis on 3 April, the day the press reported that Dr. King was going there to lead striking sanitation workers in a march.

Ray spent the night of 3 April at a local hotel. On 4 April, in mid-morning, he checked into a flophouse on South Main Street that provided an unobstructed view of Dr. King's hotel. The press had reported King's location—and even broadcast his room number. Ray set himself up in a locked bathroom, and while King relaxed later in the afternoon on the hotel's balcony, Ray made one shot that struck and killed the civil rights leader. After the shooting, Ray fled from the flophouse carrying the murder weapon, but before he could make it to his Mustang, he spotted a parked police car and ditched the rifle in the foyer of a store front. Although he managed to drive to Atlanta and then board a bus for Canada within a day, the abandoned rifle was key in putting the FBI on his trail. Ray stayed in Canada for a month. He wanted to get to Rhodesia or South Africa, where he thought that because of his racial views he might be received as a hero; however, he did not have enough money for the air tickets. Instead, on 6 May, he flew to England. There he ran low on funds, robbed a jewelry store, and on 8 June, sixty-five days after the assassination, he was arrested at Heathrow airport while attempting to board a flight to Germany.

Ray pled guilty to Dr. King's assassination and was sentenced to life in prison. Shortly after, he recanted, but the court refused to act. From then on, Ray continued trying to get a new trial. He gave dozens of interviews and wrote two books, with increasingly elaborate stories about his claim of innocence. All of his stories revolved around a mysterious figure he called Raoul, who, he said, directed his conduct from the time of his 1967 prison break to the murder of Dr. King. Ray admitted buying the murder weapon and renting the room at the flophouse where the fatal shot was fired, but he insisted he had merely dropped the gun off for Raoul and had left before the assassination.

Ray's claims about the mysterious Raoul have been thoroughly investigated by several Memphis district attorneys, Tennessee attorneys general, divisions of the U.S. Justice Department, and the House Select Committee on Assassinations (1976 to 1979). All concluded that Raoul was a figment of Ray's imagination. Ray, however, managed to convince members of Dr. King's family that he was innocent and that somehow he had only been a patsy in the assassination. He died in prison of kidney failure.

• A comprehensive reinvestigation is the Select Committee on Assassination's *Final Report* (1979). Brief overviews of the case, both published only a year after the assassination, are Clay Blair's *The Strange Case of James Earl Ray* and Gerald Sparrow's *The Great Assassins*. William Bradford Huie obtained Ray's cooperation, and George McMillan had help from most of Ray's family, in two fascinating biographies, *He Slew the Dreamer* (Huie, 1970) and *The Making of an Assassin* (McMillan, 1976). The present author's *Killing the Dream* (1998) answers the major conspiracy theories that developed in the thirty years after the assassination. An obituary appears in the *New York Times*, 24 Apr. 1997.

GERALD POSNER

REAGAN, Ronald Wilson (6 Feb. 1911–5 June 2004), governor of California and fortieth president of the United States, was born in Tampico, Illinois, the second son of John Edward "Jack" Reagan, a shoe salesman, and Nelle Wilson. The future president lived in a series of rural Illinois towns before his family settled in Dixon in 1920. Jack Reagan struggled with alcoholism most of his life, forcing the family to relocate frequently, often just ahead of the bill collector. Nelle Reagan, a fervently religious member of the Protestant evangelical Disciples of Christ, held the family together and encouraged her son, nicknamed "Dutch," to stay in school and participate in drama and sports. As a teenager and a young adult Reagan worked seven summers as a local lifeguard and was credited with saving over seventy swimmers from drowning. From 1928 until 1932 Reagan attended nearby Eureka College, a small, religiously affiliated institution, where he majored in economics and sociology. As he had in high school, he served as student body president at Eureka and acted in campus plays.

Reagan attributed his lifelong optimism to his childhood, which he later described as "one of those rare Huck Finn–Tom Sawyer idylls." In fact Mark Twain's account of life along the Mississippi River is a harrowing chronicle of racism, violence, slavery, and superstition in which Huck's drunken father tries to kill him. As one chronicler of Reagan's life observed, he subtly distorted his memory "toward small perfections, like the buildings of Disneyland." Reagan's favorite White House speechwriter, Peggy Noonan, "had the feeling he came from a sad house" and for the rest of his life "thought it was his job to cheer everyone up."

During the Great Depression, Jack Reagan supported his family by working for a New Deal work-relief program. In appreciation Ronald became a fervent supporter of Democratic president Franklin D. Roosevelt and memorized many of Roosevelt's best-known speeches. Even after he rejected liberalism and Roosevelt's efforts to create a welfare state, Reagan admired Roosevelt as an inspirational leader and used many of the president's phrases to advance his own conservative agenda.

After graduating from college in 1932, Reagan worked as a radio announcer, first with station WOC in Davenport, Iowa , and then as a sports broadcaster with WHO in Des Moines. His voice projected warmth and sincerity, and he mixed his narration of baseball games with colorful and folksy anecdotes that audiences appreciated.

Reagan's life often seemed to resemble the novels of Horatio Alger he read in childhood in which a plucky young hero finds success. In 1937, while in California to cover the Chicago Cubs spring training, he took a screen test for the Warner Brothers Studio and won a film contract. During the next four years he thrived as a player in so-called B films produced by the studio on a steady basis. Reagan took direction well, learned lines easily, and was well liked by fellow actors and film executives. On-screen his character often responded to adversity with a wisecrack, and his offscreen personality mimicked his casting. In his later career this characteristic both charmed audiences and deflected any serious introspection.

Although many of his films were forgettable, in 1940 Reagan played the Notre Dame football star George Gipp. *Knute Rockne—All American* became Reagan's most acclaimed role, and he often used his character's dialogue ("win one for the Gipper") in his later political career. Also in 1940 Reagan married the actress Jane Wyman. The couple had a daughter, Maureen, in 1941 and adopted a son, Michael, in 1945.

Soon after the United States entered World War II, the U.S. Army Air Corps called Reagan (who had already joined the Army Reserves) to active duty. Ineligible for combat due to poor eyesight, he served from 1942 through 1945 in an Air Corps film unit based in Hollywood. Several of his wartime pictures depicted the global conflict as a form of entertainment, as did *This Is the Army*, in which Reagan played a corporal staging a variety show. As the film ends, the recruits march off to battle singing in harmony.

This and other wartime films imprinted themselves in Reagan's memory. During the 1980 presidential campaign, Reagan brought himself and audiences to tears recalling, in a quivering voice, the story of a pilot who sacrificed his life cradling a wounded comrade rather than bailing out from a crippled plane. "Never mind son," the pilot tells the terrified young airman, "we'll ride this one down together." Reagan seemed puzzled when journalists later questioned how he could possibly know what two dead men said to each other moments before their plane crashed in the middle of the Pacific Ocean. In fact he had described a montage of scenes from beloved wartime movies.

Although he served his country honorably, Reagan seemed self-conscious about his lack of combat experience. Reflecting on this in his 1965 memoir *Where's the Rest of Me?* Reagan explained that, when peace came in 1945, he wanted the same thing as millions of other citizen-soldiers, to return home, rest, make love to his wife, "and come up refreshed to do a better job in an ideal world." This artful phrasing obscured the fact that Reagan had left neither home nor his wife, as he was stationed in Hollywood.

Several times as president Reagan embellished his military record, such as in 1983, when he claimed firsthand experience of the Holocaust by having filmed the liberation of Nazi death camps. When journalists pointed out that he had not left U.S. soil during the war, an aide explained that Reagan meant to say that he had been moved by seeing a wartime film about the liberation of the camps.

These inaccuracies were probably not intended consciously to deceive, but they suggest the depth of Reagan's belief in myths of individual heroism and his desire to be part of the larger shared experience of what later became known as the "greatest generation." They also reveal his tenacity in holding onto an idea once he believed it. Throughout his public career, Reagan told stories of Pilgrims, patriots, cowboys, Indians, and other icons of "rugged individualism" who often seemed to have emerged from film scripts. Even the Strategic Defense Initiative antimissile program he proposed in 1983 bore a striking resemblance to the plot of the 1940 film *Murder in the Air* in which Reagan appeared. In evoking these symbols, he sounded sincere and persuasive in large part because he believed in what he said.

Between 1945 and 1965 Reagan made over fifty additional films, but he never commanded "star" power. In the late 1940s he became active in the Screen Actors Guild, an actors' union, serving first as a board member and then as president from 1947 to 1952. Although he campaigned for Democratic political candidates in 1948, Reagan, like many Americans, became increasingly fearful of communist influence at home and abroad. He joined efforts by the film studios and the House Committee on Un-American Activities to purge from Hollywood left-leaning actors, writers, and directors, whom he compared to renegade Indians in western movies, sent by the Soviet dictator Joseph Stalin to brainwash Americans.

In 1949 Reagan's marriage to Jane Wyman ended in divorce. (Reagan was in fact the first divorced man elected president.) Three years later, in 1952, he married another actress, Nancy Davis. They remained devoted to each other throughout Reagan's life. This second marriage produced two children, Patricia, born in 1952, and Ronald, born in 1958. His children from both marriages reported that Reagan's relations with them were often cold and distant.

Reagan's political allegiance to the Democratic party ended in 1952, when he endorsed the Republican presidential nominee Dwight D. Eisenhower. That same year Reagan began an eight-year career working as an "ambassador of goodwill" for the General Electric Corporation. He appeared on the weekly television series *General Electric Theater* and traveled around the country for the consumer products giant, delivering thousands of after-dinner speeches. Year in and year out he warned audiences about the perils of big government, creeping regulation, and communism. Corporate leaders, he argued, defended American freedom despite the burdens of high taxes, impediments to the free market, and other antibusiness measures imposed by Democrats. In spite of the serious nature of his talks, Reagan's self-depreciating style, replete with anecdotes and humor, conveyed an upbeat rather than gloomy message. These speeches closely resembled his later presidential language.

Even as the Republican party in the 1950s, led by President Eisenhower, accepted many New Deal tenets, such as Social Security, minimum wage laws, and farm subsidies, Reagan's politics moved in a more conservative direction. Like many residents of the so-called Sunbelt, Reagan saw threats coming from "big government collectivism." Although government programs like the GI Bill, veterans' home loans, highway construction, and defense spending had sparked dynamic economic growth in the Sunbelt, conservatives remained wary. In their view government collectivism eroded traditional values by foisting liberal curricula on public schools, undermining church authority, imposing federal rules (like desegregation) on local institutions, and interfering with the free market though welfare programs and income redistribution schemes. These produced rising levels of crime, promiscuity, and divorce.

Many Sunbelt conservatives spoke the language of militant evangelical Christianity. They envisioned an imminent battle between the forces of good and evil, followed by the return of Jesus, who would gather believers in Heaven and consign non believers to oblivion. National leaders, they held, should not negotiate or compromise with an evil such as communism but must destroy it. In 1961 Reagan argued this point at a rally in California, where he forecast a final battle with godless communism. By 1970, he predicted, "the world will be all slave or all free."

Conservatism burst onto the national scene in 1964, when Arizona senator Barry Goldwater, who had broken in 1958 with moderate members of his party, secured the Republican presidential nomination. Despite his supporters' hopes, Goldwater proved a divisive candidate. The incumbent, Lyndon B. Johnson, depicted him as a grouchy extremist prepared to roll back the New Deal and unleash a nuclear war. For Reagan, however, Goldwater's candidacy provided a national forum.

Late in the senator's faltering campaign, Reagan delivered a televised fund-raising speech titled "A Time for Choosing." Derived from talks he had delivered over the previous decade, Reagan's speech was by turn humorous and indignant as he spoke of bloated bureaucracies and the government's threat to personal freedom. Brazenly lifting phrases made famous by Franklin Roosevelt, Abraham Lincoln, and Winston Churchill, Reagan declared: "You and I have a rendezvous with destiny. We can preserve for our children this, the last best hope of man on earth, or we can sentence them to take the first step into a thousand years of darkness. If we fail, at least let our children

and our children's children, say of us we justified our brief moment here. We did all that could be done." He laced the speech with criticism of taxes and the national debt, asserting that the "Founding Fathers" knew that "government does nothing as well or as economically as the private sector of the economy."

Despite making major inroads in the formerly solid Democratic South, Goldwater lost to Johnson in a landslide. But Reagan, in a real sense, won. Where the senator grimaced and scowled, Reagan smiled and cajoled. Although his core ideas resembled Goldwater's, Reagan communicated them with an almost inspirational quality. Within a few months of Johnson's triumph, a group of wealthy California businessmen, including Holmes Tuttle and Henry Salvatori, organized a Friends of Ronald Reagan committee to promote his candidacy for governor of California in 1966.

In the ensuing campaign Democrats disparaged Reagan as an amateur and an extremist. Neither label fit. As in his later campaign for the White House, Reagan promised a few simple things: to reduce the size and scope of government and to throw the rascals out. "I am not a politician . . . I am an ordinary citizen" opposed to high taxes, government regulations, big spending, waste, and fraud, he declared in 1966. For six years as governor and for eight more as president, Reagan stayed on message. He used dramatic if sometimes fanciful anecdotes—many sent to him by admirers—to point out the excesses or absurdities of government regulation. Whe n speaking of liberalism, his voice oozed with contempt. If the topic was communism, he sounded resilient and impervious. Describing the plight of hard-pressed taxpayers or small business owners, he radiated empathy and recalled his own humble origins.

Reagan worked closely with campaign consultants, who recognized his "mastery of the electronic media." As much as possible Reagan waged the campaign on television, where his ability to deliver a well-rehearsed script in an off-the-cuff manner excelled. Reagan coasted to a primary victory over a weak rival and went on to challenge the two-term Democratic incumbent Pat Brown in the general election.

A centrist politician, Brown had presided over one of California's fastest growth spurts. To cope with a surging population and demand for public services, Brown pushed such things as the expansion of higher education, more aid to public schools, and freeway construction. This investment in infrastructure promoted California's economic success and made it an attractive place to live but required major tax hikes to pay for it all. The public services were popular, but the taxes were resented. Many middle-class Californians also felt uneasy about social changes. Events such as the Watts ghetto riot of 1965 and racial conflicts elsewhere in the state, the raucous Free Speech movement at the University of California's Berkeley campus, rising crime rates, and growing agitation against the Vietnam War troubled them. Even though the moderate Brown actually supported the war in

Vietnam, Reagan hung all these resentments on his Democratic opponent.

Reagan spoke mostly in symbolic terms, raising issues like freedom, personal autonomy, and traditional values. He linked the incumbent to riots, welfare cheats, criminals and the judges who "coddled" them, the "mess at Berkeley," and the spoiled "bums" who protested the Vietnam War and indulged in "sexual orgies so vile I cannot describe them to you." "Hippies," he quipped, "act like Tarzan, look like Jane and smell like Cheetah." But relying as much on inspiration as denigration, Reagan told audiences, "We can start a prairie fire that will sweep the nation and prove we are number one in more than crime and taxes . . . this is a dream, as big and golden as California itself" (Pemberton, p. 69). His sincerity and willingness to tell jokes on himself (when asked what kind of governor he might be, he quipped, "I don't know, I've never played a governor") undercut Brown's effort to portray him as a dangerous extremist. Most voters viewed Reagan as a pleasant man aroused by grievances they shared. In November 1966 they swept him into office by a margin of nearly a million votes.

Reagan took his oath as governor in January 1967 at a midnight inauguration, an hour recommended by Nancy Reagan's astrologer. "For many years now," he told Californians, "you and I have been hushed like children and told there are no simple answers to the complex problems which are beyond our comprehension." In truth, he countered, "there are simple answers—there just are not easy ones" (Pemberton, p. 70). But Reagan seemed unsure of what they were. Shortly after taking office, he could not answer a question put to him by a journalist who asked about his priorities. Turning to an aide, the new governor remarked, "I could take some coaching from the sidelines, if anyone can recall my legislative program." For a while, he limited himself to ordering an across-the-board budget cut for state agencies, imposing a hiring freeze, and asking state employees to work without pay on holidays.

After a while, however, Reagan settled into a comfortable governing style that blended conservative rhetoric with flexible policies. He denounced student protestors, forced out several liberal college administrators, and sent state police to quell disturbances at Berkeley. But he abandoned plans to slash education spending or to probe "Communism and blatant sexual misbehavior" in the state university system. Reagan blamed Brown for an inherited budget deficit, then approved the largest tax increase in state history. He praised budget cutting and reduced a few programs, but during his two terms state spending doubled from $5 to $10 billion. Although he criticized a casual attitude toward sex, in 1967 Reagan signed one of the nation's most liberal abortion statutes, easing access to the procedure. Later, when abortion became an especially sensitive litmus test among conservatives, Reagan explained he had never read the law's provisions and blamed a loophole that permitted doctors to perform more procedures than intended.

Reagan's bold rhetoric and cautious governance came to be known as "populist conservatism." His favorite targets were "liberal elitists" whose social agenda might be well intentioned but whose policies hurt working people, encouraged dependence, and stifled initiative. Reagan's style disarmed Democratic critics and encouraged conservative supporters. He easily won reelection in 1970. During his second term, the governor promoted a modest reform designed to help the "tax payer" and punish the "tax taker." He denounced "welfare cheats," then struck a deal with the Democratic legislature that modestly tightened eligibility standards while substantially increasing benefits.

Declining to run for a third term, Reagan decided to leave office on a high note. He devoted much time in the 1970s to writing opinion columns and radio commentaries that made him and his ideas more familiar to the nation. Reagan continued to criticize public programs as inferior to private business and insisted that independent ranchers and private entrepreneurs had carved an empire from a wilderness, obscuring the fact that California, like the entire West, had thrived on public water, power, roads, and defense contracts.

Reagan's two terms as governor coincided roughly with the presidency of Richard Nixon. Although both claimed to be conservatives, they had little respect for each other. Nixon had a visceral skill in appealing to voters' resentments, especially those relating to racial issues, such as school busing. His so-called southern strategy sought to attract disenchanted southern white Democrats and northern Catholics and ethnic blue-collar voters to the GOP fold. Yet, rhetoric aside, Nixon was not a "small government" or foreign policy conservative. He supported creation of the Environmental Protection Agency, the Consumer Products Safety Commission, the Occupational Health and Safety Administration, clean air and water laws, price and wage controls, minority set-asides in federal contracts, not to mention détente with the Soviet Union and a historic opening to China. All of these initiatives made conservatives bristle. Nixon reached a compromise settlement in Vietnam in 1973, to the displeasure of Reagan, who had earlier proposed "turning it into a parking lot." Thus many conservatives like Reagan took a certain glee in Nixon's resignation in 1974 as a result of the Watergate scandal. The power vacuum in the GOP after Nixon's fall cleared the path for a conservative takeover of the party.

Vice President Gerald Ford, who succeeded Nixon in August 1974, disappointed conservatives by his selection of the liberal Republican Nelson Rockefeller as vice president, his continued pursuit of arms control agreements with the Soviet Union, and his willingness to work with the Democratic majority in Congress. Reagan challenged Ford for the GOP nomination in 1976. The Californian won a handful of mostly southern primaries but lacked the national following needed to win his party's support. However, his challenge resulted in Rockefeller being dropped from the ticket and the adoption of a party platform that repudiated the détente policies of Nixon, Ford, and Henry Kissinger. Ford went on to lose the election to a little-known former Georgia governor, Jimmy Carter.

Carter's perceived failures from 1977 to 1980 paved the way for Reagan's emergence as a credible national leader. By 1980 the collapse of détente with the Soviet Union, rampant inflation, slow economic growth, gasoline price hikes and rationing, and the unresolved fate of fifty-two Americans held captive in Iran doomed the Carter administration and energized the candidacy of Ronald Reagan. Calling this combination of troubles the "misery index," Reagan asked voters if they were better or worse off in 1980 than four years earlier. Downplaying his conservative economic and social ideas and even tapping the moderate George H. W. Bush, his principal rival, as his running mate, Reagan won the GOP nomination. His campaign focused on a promise to restore national strength and pride. "This is the greatest country in the world," he declared. "We have the talent, we have the drive, we have the imagination. Now all we need is the leadership" (Pemberton, p. 89). Promising to bring the public "a little good news," Reagan ridiculed those who suggested "that the United States had had its day in the sun."

A rising clamor against taxes and the mobilization of religious conservatives also helped Reagan's candidacy. In 1978 California voters approved Proposition 13, a rollback of property taxes. Although Reagan had not initiated the antitax drive, he quickly embraced it, recognizing its dual appeal—voters liked lower taxes, and lower taxes meant less money for the kinds of programs conservatives disliked.

The increasingly active role of the so-called religious right, organized in groups like the Moral Majority and the Christian Coalition, also benefited Reagan. Jimmy Carter had mobilized evangelical Christians in 1976 with professions of his born-again conversion. In 1980 Reagan convinced many of these voters, especially in the South, to switch to the GOP by stressing his opposition to abortion and gay rights and support for school prayer, teaching "creationism" as an alternative to evolution, and giving tax breaks to all-white "Christian academies."

Reagan won election in 1980 in a three-person contest, which pitted him against Carter and a liberal independent, Illinois representative John Anderson. Carter's failure, despite heroic efforts, to win the release of the Iran hostages doomed his candidacy. Reagan won about 52 percent of the popular vote to Carter's 41 percent and Anderson's 7 percent. In the electoral vote count, Reagan trounced Carter 489 to 49.

When polled about their choices, only 11 percent of voters said they selected Reagan because he was a "real conservative." Most simply felt "it's time for a change" and preferred almost anyone to Carter. Choosing Reagan represented more a rejection of a failed incumbent and the disaffiliation of southern white and northern ethnic voters from the Democratic party than the formation of a new conservative consensus.

In his inaugural addre ss on 20 January 1981, President Reagan scoffed at those who described the United States as suffering from a national "malaise." It was time, he declared, "for us to realize that we are too great a nation to limit ourselves to small dreams." Reagan spoke of past American heroes and stressed a few easily understood economic grievances, such as inflation and a burdensome tax system. Breaking with the past, he asserted that "in this present crisis, government is not the solution to our problem, government is the problem."

Over the next eight years, through recession and economic recovery, Cold War and renewed détente, Reagan forged a powerful bond with the public. Even when most Americans opposed specific administration programs, such as efforts to ban abortion, cut school aid, or fund anticommunist guerrillas in Central America, they continued to voice confidence in the president. Ultimately Reagan's popularity appeared so unrelated to success and so undiminished by policy failure or a series of scandals that critics like Colorado Democratic representative Pat Schroeder dubbed him the "Teflon President." Reagan's supporters attributed his popularity both to the success of his programs and to his skill as what they called the "Great Communicator." Many Democratic leaders and journalists expressed wonder that presidential gaffes and fanciful anecdotes (like his assertion that redwood trees produced air pollution or that nuclear missiles could be recalled after firing) had so little negative impact. Some even called him an "amiable dunce." But the television commentator Bill Moyers hit nearer the mark in a televised interview in 1981 when he observed that "we didn't elect this guy because he knows how many barrels of oil are in Alaska. We elected him because we want to feel good."

Reagan effortlessly upheld his part of the bargain. Just three months after Reagan took office, on 30 March 1981, a crazed gunman nearly killed the president and wounded several bystanders. In the hospital emergency room Reagan grasped his wife's hand and told her, "Honey, I forgot to duck." As he went into surgery, he quipped to the medical staff, "I hope you are all Republicans." This spunk and optimism evoked appreciation among ordinary Americans.

Reagan appeared decisive in other situations as well. In August 1981, seven months into his first term, nearly twelve thousand unionized air traffic controllers ignored a no-strike clause in their contract and walked off the job. The Professional Air Traffic Controllers Organization (PATCO) had endorsed Reagan's candidacy. This fact as well as their legitimate complaints over staffing issues made union leaders assume the president would tolerate their job action. They guessed wrong. Reagan had long abandoned his sympathy toward organized labor and relished the opportunity to flex his muscles. When the strikers defied his back to work order, the president fired them and sent military personnel into aircraft control towers to keep commercial flights aloft. Reagan's tough stance impressed the public, intimidated the labor movement, and convinced business interests that he was firmly on their side.

As president Reagan challenged many of the liberal programs that had dominated the federal government since the New Deal. He and his administration labored to roll back the network of social welfare programs; limit the role of federal courts in promoting civil rights and liberties; eliminate regulation of business, banking, and the environment; reduce federal income tax rates; and encourage a conservative social ethic regarding the role of religion in public life, reproductive rights, and drug use. Reagan placed particular stress on removing what he saw as the dead hand of government regulation from the private sector, believing this would unleash market forces, create new wealth, and foster greater equality. Finally, by "rearming America" he would challenge Soviet advances in the Third World and ultimately defeat what he called "the evil empire."

Although Reagan won election twice, and by an especially wide margin in 1984 against former vice president Walter Mondale, his average popularity over eight years was just about the same as the two other post-1945 two-term presidents, Eisenhower and Bill Clinton. Reagan's approval numbers spiked just before the 1984 election and again as he left office in 1989. But on average his approval rating stood at 54 percent, compared to Bill Clinton's average of 55 percent.

As a candidate and upon taking office, Reagan criticized the nearly $1 trillion national debt as "mortgaging our future and our children's future." The nation must stop living beyond its means, he explained, and concentrate on essentials. He pledged to cut the "bloated" federal bureaucracy and tax burden that stifled individual and business initiative. Reagan embraced a controversial theory known as "supply-side economics," the notion that reduced tax rates and other aid to business would generate increased economic growth to make up for lost revenue.

The president unveiled his economic package of tax and program cuts to Congress in February 1981. It contained substantial reductions on income and business taxes; lowered capital gains, estate, and gift taxes; permitted faster depreciation on business investments; shifted some social service expenditures to the states; and cut back on parts of the federal bureaucracy that regulated business, the environment, and public health. Although critics sometimes accused Reagan of being lazy, he pressed hard for passage of his economic and related defense programs. During his first four months in office he met with members of Congress seventy times to lobby for his budget proposals. He appealed to the public to bring pressure on their representatives and enlisted the support of about three dozen conservative southern Democrats, the so-called Boll Weevils, who held the balance of power in the nominally Democratic House of Representatives.

The Omnibus Budget Reconciliation Act of 1981 passed the House and Senate on 31 July. It cut expenditures for fiscal year 1982 by nearly $35 billion and over the 1982–1984 period by about $140 billion. Defense spending was the big winner, while social programs were hit hard. Although middle-class entitlements like Social Security and Medicare survived more or less intact, food stamps, school lunch programs, public housing subsidies, and job training took major hits.

Two weeks later Reagan signed into law the Economic Recovery Tax Act, which contained the largest tax cut in U.S. history. Over five years the revenue loss to the Treasury totaled $750 billion. The bill reduced personal income taxes by 25 percent, cut capital gains and estate taxes, and reduced business taxes. The oil industry received numerous benefits.

"Reaganomics," as pundits dubbed his policy, produced mixed results. Federal income taxes declined, most significantly for the wealthiest 20 percent of taxpayers. For most other Americans, increased payroll, Social Security, and state taxes meant that they paid nearly the same total tax bill in 1989 as in 1981. After a steep recession in 1981–1982, the economy resumed growth for the remainder of Reagan's presidency. But it did not perform especially well. Growth, employment, and inflation looked good compared to the dismal late 1970s and early 1980s. However, the economy actually produced more jobs and grew faster during the 1960s, the early 1970s, and the 1990s than it did under Reagan. Reagan had condemned the annual budget deficits and the cumulative national debt accumulated by Democratic presidents. But their alleged profligacy paled in comparison to his own. The annual federal budget deficit grew to record levels under Reagan, while the cumulative national debt doubled to $2 trillion. Despite pledges to reduce the size, scope, and cost of government, federal employment and expenditures increased from 1981 to 1989. To stanch the flow of red ink, Reagan quietly approved tax increases in 1982 and 1983.

Business benefited from both tax and regulatory reductions during the Reagan years. For example, the Justice Department adopted a more relaxed attitude toward monopoly, dropping antitrust suits against corporate giants like IBM and AT&T. The Interior Department, led by James Watt, lifted restrictions on oil drilling, logging, and mining in national forests and coastal areas. A combination of regulatory and legislative changes permitted savings and loan institutions to vastly expand their lending practices from single-family homes to risky commercial real estate. Automobile manufacturers were permitted to reduce the safety margins on items like bumpers. All of these actions increased profitability, often at a cost to the environment, consumers, and worker safety.

The president generally avoided discussing the specifics of his budget or the nation's economy. Even when the United States went from being the world's largest creditor nation to the largest debtor and as its foreign trade imbalance grew worse, Reagan maintained a sunny disposition. When asked about this by a journalist, he simply denied that it was so.

No president before Reagan used television so effectively to communicate his ideas and to mobilize voters. He was also exceptionally persuasive in one-on-one encounters with members of Congress. Yet offscreen or off script Reagan often lacked focus, clarity, and direction. Unscripted news conferences were painful to watch and were kept to a minimum. More than most presidents, he relied on skilled White House staff to promote his programs. During Reagan's first administration, Chief of Staff James Baker, Baker's deputy Michael Deaver, and Counselor Edwin Meese carefully monitored Reagan's legislative agenda and his public appearances. All three left the White House for other jobs during the second administration. Many of Reagan's most controversial actions, such as trading arms for hostages and visiting a Nazi cemetery, took place when his second-term team gave him bad advice. In fact during Reagan's second term Congress passed only one piece of major legislation promoted by Reagan, a tax reform supported by many Democrats. Mostly at Congress's initiative, the president signed a modest immigration reform bill.

Even his closest aides found Reagan exceptionally detached from details and often had to guess at what he wanted them to do. At cabinet meetings Reagan frequently read from letters and inspirational stories sent him by admirers. But after a few minutes he displayed what aides called a "glassy-eyed look," and they continued without his input. Reagan's friend and economic adviser Martin Anderson recalled that the president's aides "compensated for the fact that he made decisions like an ancient king or a Turkish pasha, passively letting his subjects serve him" (Anderson, pp. 289–91). Reagan told his spokesperson Larry Speakes that he was happiest when "each morning I get a piece of paper that tells me what I do all day long." As he put it, being president was "something like shooting a script," in which characters appeared and departed and the plot advanced.

Much of the praise lavished on Reagan centered on his foreign policy achievements. To many Americans his unapologetic celebration of patriotism and military fortitude not only made the nation safer but, in the words the British prime minister Margaret Thatcher, won the Cold War "without firing a shot." Upon Reagan's death in June 2004, Republican leaders like Texas congressman Tom DeLay praised him as an "intellectual warrior" who "marshaled ideas like troops" and freed the world from the threat of communism. Another funeral orator asserted that when Reagan became president in 1981, the Soviets and their proxies were winning the Cold War. But by the time he left office, the Soviets had been tamed and by 1991 had ceased to exist.

Shortly before Reagan left office in 1989 Robert MacFarlane, the third of Reagan's six national security advisers, wrote his former boss that the transformation of the Soviet system represented a "vindication of your seven year strategy." Confronted by the "renewal" of American economic, military, and spiritual power, Soviet leaders understood that "they simply had to change their system or face inevitable decline" (Pemberton, p. 154). Unlike presidents before him, Reagan made the defeat of communism a primary goal. Eisenhower and Nixon talked a tough game but valued stability over confrontation and sought to make deals with the Kremlin. Reagan considered communism both a moral evil and an inherent threat to peace. Some have claimed that, by not only talking but acting tough, by rearming America, Reagan "won the Cold War."

Without question, Reagan expanded U.S. military power and restored public confidence in presidential leadership. His inspiring rhetoric uplifted the spirits of Americans—and many foreigners—who had considered themselves victims in an unfriendly world of hostage taking, nuclear threats, rising oil prices, and Third World insurgencies. Yet as in his domestic policy, a gulf often existed between the idealism, self-assurance, and occasional bluster of Reagan's calls to action and his administration's actual accomplishments.

Reagan oversaw the largest military buildup in peacetime history and played a critical role, especially in his final years in office, in transforming the Soviet-American relationship. But whether doubling arms spending and talking tough had a direct impact on Soviet policy remains uncertain. Many of Reagan's other initiatives, such as using covert force in Central America, the Middle East, and Africa, had unintended, sometimes dire consequences. Armed intervention did not cause the violence endemic to these regions, but it did little to alleviate it or to further American interests. For example, the Central Intelligence Agency (CIA)'s extensive program from 1982 to 1988 of arming Islamic fighters resisting Soviet forces in Afghanistan ultimately promoted the rise of a fundamentalist terror network that included Osama bin Laden. Reagan's occasional support for dictatorships along with a willingness to negotiate secretly with terrorists marked some of his administration's worst failures. In light of two wars later fought against Iraq, it is startling to recall how strongly Reagan supported Saddam Hussein in Iraq's decade-long war with Iran, despite the Iraqi dictator's use of poison gas against both his own population and Iranian troops.

As both a candidate and as president, Reagan spoke forcefully about the division he saw between the peaceful democratic world led by the United States and the aggressive web of communist dictatorships controlled by Moscow. In 1980 and often thereafter he remarked that the Soviet Union "underlies all the unrest that is going on" in the world. If "they weren't engaged in this game of dominos, there wouldn't be any hotspots in the world" (New York Times, 17 Jul. 1980). Reagan stressed his religious antipathy for communism in an address to the National Association of Evangelicals on 8 March 1983. The Soviet Union, he declared, was "the focus of evil in the modern world," truly an "evil empire."

Reagan held what he saw as a simple truth: the Soviet Union was doomed to fall. In addressing the British Parliament on 8 June 1982, the president dismissed the Soviet Union as a force that "runs against the tide of history." With communism's economic, political, and social system all "astounding" failures, Reagan consigned communism to the "ash heap of history." Although Reagan's perception of the Soviet Union might be "primitive," as CIA deputy director Robert Gates described it, his clarity of vision allowed him to see the future in ways that eluded more sophisticated thinkers.

Reagan attributed the United States' vulnerability to its failure to win the Vietnam War. The resulting "Vietnam syndrome," an unwillingness to use force to resist Soviet pressure or to defend foreign friends and interests, explained why American diplomats in 1979 had been seized and held as hostages in Iran while Soviet troops occupied Afghanistan and Moscow-backed insurgents made a play for power in Central America and Africa. "It's time," he told cheering Vietnam-era veterans in 1980, "we recognize that ours, in truth, was a noble cause." Alexander Haig, whom the newly elected Reagan named secretary of state in 1981, echoed this theme, proclaiming that the American people would "shed their sackcloth and ashes." Taking a cue from the president's call in his inaugural address to "dream heroic dreams," the new administration pledged to restore the nation's military superiority, defend allies, and in what was later informally called the "Reagan doctrine," assist anticommunist movements throughout the world. Not by chance, the president's aides explained, did Iran release its long-held American captives just as Reagan took the presidential oath on 20 January 1981.

From 1981 to 1985 Reagan utilized tough rhetoric, a big boost in arms spending, trade sanctions, and covert interventions to challenge Soviet power. Yet in most cases, including Lebanon, Nicaragua, Angola, and Mozambique, U.S.–supported forces failed to achieve their goals. In Afghanistan, CIA support for the Islamic-based mujahideen helped drive out Soviet invaders but at a terrible, unanticipated cost. Many of the militants in Afghanistan and Pakistan formed the core of what later became both the Taliban and Osama bin Laden's al-Qaeda movements. Reagan's personal determination to fund the anticommunist contra rebels in Nicaragua, despite Congress's ban on aid, prompted his illegal arms sales to Iran as well as the arms-for-hostage debacle known as Iran-contra, which became public late in 1986.

Reagan inherited an unstable, violent Middle East and left the region in pretty much the same condition. Conflicts between Israelis and Palestinians, among Lebanese factions, within Afghanistan, and between Iraq and Iran continued during the 1980s and set the stage for future problems, some involving terrorism aimed at the United States.

In the early 1980s Lebanese religious and political factions resumed their periodic civil slaughter, with Israel and Syria backing armed groups. When the White House criticized Secretary of State Haig's June 1982 support for an Israeli invasion of Lebanon, Haig quit in a huff. George Shultz, named as Haig's successor, had no more success in stabilizing the area.

As chaos engulfed Lebanon, the United States dispatched Marines to join French and Italian troops as peacekeepers. Once there, the Marines assisted Christian militias fighting Muslim forces backed by Syria. In response on 18 April 1983 a suicide squad blew up the U.S. embassy in Beirut, killing sixty-three people. U.S. Navy ships off the Lebanese coast then bombarded several Islamic strongholds. On 23 October Muslim fighters retaliated by driving a truck filled with explosives into a U.S. Marine barracks near the Beirut airport, killing 241 uniformed Americans.

Reagan offered a stirring tribute to the fallen Marines but no credible explanation of their mission or the reason for their deaths. In his 1984 State of the Union message, he described the Marine presence as "central to our credibility on a global scale." Two weeks later, without explanation, he withdrew American forces from Beirut.

Public reaction to the disaster was muted in part because of lavish media attention focused on a simultaneous crisis in Grenada, a tiny Caribbean island. Although Grenada had been ruled by Marxists since 1979, neither the Carter nor the Reagan administration had paid much attention to it. The only American presence consisted of five hundred students enrolled in a private medical college. A contingent of armed Cuban construction workers labored on an airport designed to boost tourism (as Grenada claimed) or to serve as a Soviet-Cuban air base (as Washington asserted).

A more militant Marxist faction seized control of Grenada on 12 October 1983. Immediately after the 23 October catastrophe in Beirut, Reagan declared that the American students on Grenada might become hostages, although none had been threatened. On 25 October he ordered thousands of Marines and army troops to liberate Grenada and the American students from a "brutal gang of thugs."

In more of a comic opera than a war, the invaders quickly secured the island. The students flew home, and a photograph of one kissing American soil became a staple in the president's reelection commercials. As if to compensate for the Beirut debacle, the Pentagon awarded an unprecedented eight thousand medals to members of the assault force. Free elections restored representative government to the island. Most Americans approved the operation, telling pollsters they were pleased that the United States had "won one for a change." Ironically news coverage of the invasion alerted many Americans to Grenada's lovely beaches and eventually sparked a tourist boom, facilitated by the Cuban-built airport.

Despite the muddle in places like Beirut, many conservatives argue that Reagan had a "secret" plan to spend the Soviets into bankruptcy through a new arms race and especially his Strategic Defense Initiative ("Star Wars") antimissile plan revealed in 1983.

This high-tech military competition would supposedly break the back of the creaky Soviet economy. In fact the Soviets never competed in the Reagan arms race and correctly considered Star Wars a pipe dream.

The critical variable in ending the Cold War was the assumption of power by the 54-year-old Mikhail Gorbachev in 1985. As the best-educated, best-traveled, and most personable Soviet chief since Vladimir Lenin, Gorbachev charmed foreign leaders and recognized the inherent, long-term weakness of the Soviet system. He sought to save it through a combination of democratic political and market reforms. The Soviets did not so much "lose" the arms race and Cold War as call it off. Moreover they did so exactly at the moment when Reagan desperately needed a lift to recover from the Iran- contra scandal.

From the beginning of his presidency, Reagan and his closest aides had appeared obsessed by a perceived Soviet and Cuban threat to the Western Hemisphere. Administration rhetoric often sounded like a replay of the early Cold War. State Department and CIA spokespeople described a "Moscow-Havana" axis whose Soviet-armed Cuban agents conspired to spread revolution in both Africa and Latin America.

As a candidate in 1980 Reagan had bitterly criticized the Carter administration for abandoning the Nicaraguan dictator Anatasio Somoza, whose family had ruled the country as a fiefdom since the 1920s. Once elected, Reagan warned that the leftist Sandinista movement, which had toppled Somoza, had turned Nicaragua into a Soviet outpost and a "safe house and command post for international terror."

In spite of Reagan's passion, the public had responded apathetically. When it came to Latin America, pollsters found that most Americans did not care who dominated, say, Tegucigalpa or Managua. At the same time they deferred to Reagan as long as Americans were not killed in combat. As a result the administration had focused on supplying military aid to friendly governments in the region and supporting covert warfare that placed few American lives at risk. For example, during the 1980s, Reagan authorized spending nearly $5 billion to shore up the government of tiny El Salvador, a nominal democracy dominated by hard-line militarists that had been battling a left-wing rebellion since 1979. Congress placed a cap on the number of U.S. military advisers in El Salvador but otherwise asked few questions.

Reagan's actions toward Nicaragua proved more controversial. Nothing he did in his eight years as president tarnished his reputation or called into question his judgment so seriously as his decision to sell weapons to Iran as part of a scheme to ransom U.S. hostages in Beirut and fund anticommunist fighters in Central America. Nicaragua's Sandinista leaders were, as Reagan asserted, Marxists who disliked the United States, received aid from Cuba and the Soviet Union, and blocked free elections. But Sandinista abuses hardly matched the brutality inflicted on civilians by pro–U.S. regimes in nearby El Salvador, Guatemala, and

Honduras. In any case Nicaragua was a tiny nation with fewer inhabitants than many American cities. To portray it as a major hemispheric threat distorted reality.

In 1981 Reagan had ordered CIA director William Casey to organize an anti-Sandinista force called the *contrarevolucionarios*, or contras. The president praised them as "freedom fighters" and "the moral equal of our Founding Fathers." Over the next few years contra ranks swelled to over ten thousand men. Most contra leaders were veterans of the old Somoza dictatorship, not incipient Thomas Jeffersons.

In December 1981 Reagan had signed a secret order authorizing contra aid for the purpose of deposing the Sandinistas. As reports surfaced linking contra attacks to thousands of civilian deaths in Nicaragua, Congress in 1982 passed a resolution named for Representative Edward P. Boland that capped CIA assistance to the rebels at $24 million and ordered that none of the funds be used to topple the Nicaraguan government. In October 1984, after learning that the CIA and contras had illegally mined Nicaraguan harbors, Congress passed a stricter version of the Boland law that barred any U.S. government funds going to the contras for any purpose.

These restrictions infuriated Reagan, who disparaged Congress as a committee of busybodies. He told National Security Adviser Robert McFarlane and his deputy Admiral John Poindexter as well as the National Security Council (NSC) staffer Lieutenant Colonel Oliver North "to do whatever you have to do to help these people keep body and soul together" (McFarlane and Smardz, p. 68). For a president who seldom issued clear instructions to subordinates, this was a definitive order.

McFarlane, Poindexter, and North devised a scheme to "privatize" contra aid by soliciting funds from friendly foreign governments, like Brunei, and wealthy American conservatives, such as Adolph Coors, which they used to buy weapons and provide support to the guerrillas. The president did not know all the details, but McFarlane and his successor as national security adviser, John Poindexter, kept him closely informed of their activities and received his blessing.

During 1985 contra aid merged with ongoing secret and illegal contacts with Iran. Reagan had several times publicly condemned the Iranian regime as an "outlaw state." U.S. law barred providing Iran any military equipment unless the president informed Congress in writing of a compelling reason to do so. Reagan found a reason but declined to notify anyone.

For some time Reagan had been moved by the plight of seven Americans who had been kidnapped in Beirut and held hostage by Islamic militias linked to Iran. With the exception of one hostage, CIA agent William Buckley, all were private citizens who had remained in Lebanon despite official warnings. Recalling public disgust with Carter's handling of the Iranian hostages, Reagan acted boldly. In mid-1985 an Iranian businessman contacted McFarlane and claimed that he could secure the hostages' release in return for U.S. arms sales to "moderate" elements in Iran who might take power following the death of Ayatollah Khomeini.

Despite his public pledge "never to negotiate with terrorists," Reagan told McFarlane, "Gee, that sounds pretty good." In a diary entry the president indicated he liked the idea of making a deal to get "our seven kidnap victims back." He said nothing about building a new relationship with Iran. Over the next year Reagan authorized several secret arms sales to Iran. Although three hostages were eventually released, three more were taken as replacements.

This harebrained scheme took an even more bizarre turn when North conceived what he called a "neat idea": overcharging the Iranians for American weapons and using the profits to support the Nicaraguan contras. As North joked, the Iranians would unknowingly make a "Contra-bution." This violated federal law, since profits from any sale of U.S. government property had to be returned to the Treasury, not given to the president's pet guerrilla charity in defiance of Congress.

The tangled scheme began to unravel in October 1986, when Sandinista gunners shot down a CIA chartered plane carrying weapons to the contras. A surviving American crew member told his interrogators about the secret U.S. aid program. In early November the other shoe dropped when Iran publicly disclosed the illegal arms sales and revealed the weapons had not gone to "moderates" but to anti–U.S. Khomeini loyalists who had hoodwinked the Reagan administration.

Reagan, CIA director Casey, North, and other participants tried to cover up the scandal by shredding documents and lying about their actions to the press, to Congress, to a special prosecutor, and to the American public. Despite compelling evidence of his active role, Reagan insisted he knew nothing about any arms-for-hostages deal or illegal funding of the contras. The public did not believe him, and in early 1987 Regan's approval rating plummeted to 47 percent. The president appointed a blue-ribbon inquiry panel chaired by former senator John Tower. After hearing misleading and confused testimony from Reagan and others, the Tower commission concluded in its February 1987 report that the Iran arms sales had devolved into a sordid ransom scheme designed to illegally fund the contras. Reagan's actions ran "directly counter" to his public promise to punish terrorists. The report portrayed the president as disengaged, uninformed, and easily manipulated. Reagan sidestepped the criticism by firing several of his aides linked to the scandal and by giving a speech on 4 March 1987 in which he appeared to accept responsibility without actually doing so. The "facts" might suggest he permitted ransom payments and other illegal acts, Reagan asserted, but in his "heart" he never meant to break the law. Congressional probes and criminal trials over the next few years added many details to the Iran-contra episode. After Reagan left

office, several participants confirmed that the president had approved their actions and had blocked a full investigation.

Despite talk among Democrats of impeachment, Reagan survived the scandal. The competing investigations into Iran-contra often lacked focus. Despite public disappointment in his actions, the president retained an important quotient of goodwill. But perhaps the most important reason why the scandal faded was the striking improvement in Soviet-American relations. Since 1985 a thaw had begun between Moscow and Washington. By 1987 fundamental changes had occurred inside the Soviet Union, and Reagan rushed to embrace them. Ironically, improved relations with the "evil empire" salvaged Reagan's presidency.

To his credit Reagan exhibited the skill, flexibility, and good sense to respond positively to Gorbachev's reforms in the Soviet Union and calls for arms cuts and international cooperation. After Reagan fired many of his own hard-line advisers linked to Iran-contra, in December 1987 Reagan and Gorbachev signed a landmark intermediate-range missile reduction agreement. Six months later, on 31 May 1988, Reagan visited the Soviet Union. Speaking to a crowd in Red Square, Reagan answered a question about how he felt visiting the "evil empire." "I was talking about another time, another era," he responded (Oberdorfer, p. 299). In an aside Gorbachev sardonically asked the president's sixth national security adviser, Colin Powell, "What are you going to do now that you've lost your best enemy?" (Powell, p. 438). Powell, like Reagan, had no answer. Nevertheless as the promise of cooperation replaced the anxieties of the Cold War, Reagan left office one of the most popular presidents in post–World War II America, with an approval rating of about 70 percent.

Reagan achieved a mixed political legacy. Although a foe of abortion, a promoter of school prayer, and a critic of deficit spending, he declined to use his political capital in getting Congress to address these issues. He did, however, shift the center of gravity of American politics to the right. Reagan had promoted a "war on drugs" beginning in 1986, all but ignored the growing AIDS epidemic, and cooperated closely with religious conservatives. Big government and taxes became political epithets after 1981, with both major parties committed to the principles of smaller government and tax reduction. Some have called antitax rhetoric "Reagan's revenge," since the loss of revenue tied the hands of his successors who might want to initiate new federal programs. Reagan's four Supreme Court appointments (William Rehnquist promoted to chief justice and associate justices Sandra Day O'Connor, Antonin Scalia, and Anthony Kennedy) also had a long-term impact on moving the judiciary in a more conservative direction.

After Reagan left the presidency and returned to California in 1989, the warm glow around him began to fade. The massive failure of the savings and loan industry in the early 1990s, due in large part to deregulation and tax changes pushed by Reagan, cost taxpayers hundreds of billions of dollars in bailouts. Reagan's successor, President George H. W. Bush, bore the brunt of criticism for the problem. Bush also presided over growing budget deficits caused in large part by Reagan's and his own antitax pledges. Many Americans were offended by Reagan collecting multimillion-dollar speaking fees from Japanese corporations at the same time that Japanese exports were contributing to big job losses in the U.S. manufacturing sector.

When Clinton recaptured the White House for the Democrats in 1992, Reagan's legacy seemed further diminished. The former president made fewer public appearances and in November 1994 revealed to the public, in a moving letter he composed himself, that he had been diagnosed with Alzheimer's disease. During the next decade, sheltered by his wife and family, Reagan withdrew from sight and descended into the fog of his illness. Some historians and journalists who covered Reagan have speculated whether his occasional lapses of lucidity, some dating from his first administration, might have been early symptoms of dementia.

Reagan's impact on American politics revived with the election of George W. Bush as president in 2000. A more direct political heir to Reagan than his own politically moderate father, the younger Bush resurrected many of Reagan's conservative initiatives, ranging from tax cuts to antimissile defense. By 2000, largely because of Reagan's influence, the Republican party had become far more conservative than it had been even in 1980. Reagan's death in June 2004 elicited an outpouring of national emotion, as politicians from both parties claimed parts of his mantle. If nothing else, Americans recalled fondly Reagan's ability to sell a policy with a smile rather than the sour fury of many of his conservative successors.

• Reagan's papers are deposited at the Ronald Reagan Presidential Library, a branch of the National Archives and Record Service's presidential library system, located in Simi Valley, California. Reagan's pre- and postpresidential ghostwritten memoirs, Reagan with Richard Gipson Hubler, *Where's the Rest of Me?* (1965; repr. 1981), and Reagan, *An American Life* (1990; repr. 1992), are neither reliable nor informative. However, two edited collections of Reagan's personal letters and radio commentaries, Kiron Skinner, Annelise Anderson, and Martin Anderson, eds., *Reagan in His Own Hand: The Writings of Ronald Reagan That Reveal His Revolutionary Vision for America* (2001), and Kiron Skinner, Annelise Anderson, and Martin Anderson, eds., *Reagan: A Life in Letters* (2003), provide valuable insight into his thinking. Reagan's authorized biography by Edmund Morris, *Dutch: A Memoir of Ronald Reagan* (1999), disappointed nearly everyone with its odd mix of fictional and factual characters. Among the most reliable general accounts of Reagan's life and political career are Lou Cannon, *President Reagan: The Role of a Lifetime* (1991; repr. 2000) and *Governor Reagan: His Rise to Power* (2003); Haynes Bonner Johnson, *Sleepwalking through History: America in the Reagan Years* (1992); William E. Pemberton, *Exit with Honor: The Life and Presidency of Ronald Reagan* (1997; repr. 1998); John W. Sloan, *The Reagan Effect: Economics and Presidential Leadership* (1999); Garry Wills, *Reagan's America: Innocents at Home* (1987; repr. 2000); Michael Schaller, *Reckoning with Reagan: America and Its President in the 1980s* (1992); Don Oberdorfer, *From the Cold War to a New Era: The United States and the Soviet Union, 1983–1991* (1998); Jack F. Matlock, *Reagan and Gorbachev: How the Cold War Ended* (2004); Martin Anderson, *Revolution: The Reagan Legacy* (1990); Robert C. McFarlane (with Zofia Smardz), *Special Trust* (1994); Colin Powell with Joseph E. Persico, *My American Journey* (1995); and Jane Mayer and Doyle McManus, *Landslide: The Unmaking of the President, 1984–1988* (1988). A substantive obituary of Reagan can be found in the *New York Times*, 6 June 2004.

MICHAEL SCHALLER

REDENBACHER, Orville (16 July 1907–20 Sept. 1995), food industry entrepreneur, was born Orville Clarence Redenbacher near Brazil, Clay County, Indiana, the son of William Joseph Redenbacher and Julia Dierdorff Redenbacher. While growing up on his family's farm, Redenbacher was active in the local 4-H club and earned national recognition for his achievements in the form of a medal presented by the governor of New York, Al Smith. He also developed an early fascination with popcorn, which his family grew for cash sales on the farm and which his father reportedly ate every night. After graduating from high school, Redenbacher entered Purdue University, where he majored in agriculture and took careful note of the university's ongoing experiments with genetic crop hybrids. In addition to serving as the president of his fraternity—Alpha Gamma Rho—he also played sousaphone in the famed Purdue Marching Band, later noting, "That's where I learned to toot my own horn."

Redenbacher graduated in 1928 and on 26 December of that year married Corinne Rosemond Strate, with whom he later had three daughters. After briefly serving as a teacher of vocational agriculture at a high school in Fontanet, Indiana, Redenbacher became a county agent, which, as he later explained, was his ideal job: when he was a boy, "the county agent was a kind of hero to me." He made innovative use of his position, becoming one of the first agents to make live radio farm report broadcasts from his office as well as using mobile units in order to report from farm locations. In 1940 Redenbacher left the extension service after receiving a job offer from Henry and Hy Smith to manage Princeton Farms, a huge operation that sprawled over parts of three counties and at 12,000 acres was the largest farm in Indiana. Although now charged with a large range of responsibilities, Redenbacher continued to experiment with hybrid popcorn varieties and also became interested in the potential farm uses of liquid fertilizer. In 1950 he purchased the George F. Chester and Son Seed Company, an established firm, and in partnership with Charles Bowman successfully transformed the firm—later renamed Chester Hybrids, Inc.—into a successful vendor of liquid fertilizer as well as seeds.

Although the two partners enjoyed substantial profits as liquid fertilizer became increasingly popular, Redenbacher retained his interest in popcorn. He had successfully produced a commercial variety as early as 1943, but he was determined to improve the yield of existing popcorn whose kernels would pop (at best) to twenty times their original size. In 1965 Redenbacher finally achieved his long-sought breakthrough: his new "snowflake" variety was light, fluffy, and tasty and expanded to forty times its original size after popping.

Whether there would even be a market for his innovation, however, remained in question. Redenbacher's new discovery was expensive to produce, and skeptics wondered aloud whether anyone would pay more than twice the going rate for what many viewed as a snack food. Dubbing his product "Redbow" (from both partners' names) Redenbacher took to the road and often peddled his creation out of the back of a station wagon. In a foreshadowing of his future publicity efforts, he employed a grandson, Gary, to personally deliver autographed jars of popcorn to radio broadcasters at Chicago Cubs baseball games. When Redenbacher decided to attempt a nationwide sales campaign, he hired a Chicago-based marketing firm that advised him to name the product after himself and to place his picture on the label. Although he was chagrined at having paid $13,000 for a name which, as he pointed out, his mother had suggested for free, a breakthrough occurred in 1970 when Marshall Field's department store, a leading Midwestern retail chain, agreed to carry his product. Sales took off, and within five years Redenbacher's brand was the best-selling variety of popcorn in the country. After the death of his wife in 1971, Redenbacher married Nina Reder.

Although his success was considered modest by food industry standards (given the fragmented nature of the retail popcorn industry), his product soon drew corporate attention. After several years of working with Hunt-Wesson, Inc. (later a subsidiary of ConAgra), the partners sold their interest in the product to the firm outright in 1976. Redenbacher then began a new career, serving as the media spokesperson for his popcorn. At hundreds of personal appearances he made every year, he would hand out cards that read "I met Orville Redenbacher, the Popcorn King" as a way of answering skeptics who viewed him as a mere media creation. But he became most widely known for his television commercials, in which he often appeared with his grandson Gary. Wearing his trademark bow tie and sporting thick glasses and wavy white hair, Redenbacher soon became an instantly recognizable media star.

Redenbacher remained active until his death, which occurred at his home in Coronado, California. His signature product remained immensely popular and accounted for some 45 percent of the microwave popcorn market; ironically, Redenbacher preferred to prepare his own popcorn on a stove top. A self-proclaimed "funny looking farmer with a funny sounding name," Redenbacher was actually a hard-working businessman and innovator who achieved success as an entrepreneur and within the corporate world as well.

• There is no known collection of Redenbacher's papers. Although laudatory in nature, the best secondary source of information on his life and career is Robert Topping and Len Sherman, *Popcorn King: How Orville Redenbacher Created One of America's Most Popular Brands* (1996). Obituaries are in the *Chicago Tribune* and the *New York Times*, both 20 Sept. 1995.

EDWARD L. LACH, JR.

REED, Janet (15 Sept. 1916–28 Feb. 2000), dancer, was born in Tolo, a village near Medford, Oregon, the daughter of Charles Lindsay Reed, a rancher and amateur artist, and Esther Smith Reed, a beautician. The marriage ended when Reed was very young, and she spent her early years with her maternal grandparents on their farm and in Medford, where she was first exposed to dancing at a local school. Although she initially "balked like a steer" at the prospect of dancing, she was chosen for a pageant and fell in love with performing onstage.

In 1924 she joined her mother in Portland, beginning serious ballet studies with Isa Dora Moldovan and Alta Easton Davis. In 1932 Willam Christensen, who had established a ballet program at his uncle's dancing school, spotted the petite (just over five feet tall) redhead in a recital and invited her to study with him. Money was scarce. In exchange for dancing lessons, Reed's mother became the Christensen women's hairdresser. Briefly, until she became anemic, Reed, still in high school, danced nights in a speakeasy.

Also in 1932, she was a supernumerary in Léonide Massine's *La Boutique Fantasque* in a touring performance by the Ballet Russe de Monte Carlo, which featured Alexandra Danilova, the first ballerina Reed had seen. Danilova became a role model for the talented teenager, as she did for many American ballet students of the time. In 1934 Reed was the first American Sugarplum Fairy when Christensen staged excerpts from *The Nutcracker* for his Portland Ballet, accompanied by the Portland Junior Symphony.

In 1937 Christensen became the director of the Oakland branch of the San Francisco Opera Ballet School, taking along Reed and eight other Portland dancers. The following year, having successfully toured the west coast with the fledgling opera ballet company, he replaced Serge Oukrainsky as artistic director, and Reed became the company's principal ballerina. From 1937 to 1941, she originated roles in thirteen of the seventeen ballets that constituted the company's repertoire. Despite never having seen *Coppelia*, she danced Swanhilda in the first staging of the ballet in America, developing the role from performance photographs. Wrote critic Alfred Frankenstein, "she not only charmed with her dancing but turned in a dramatic performance that realized to the full the peppery resourceful character of Delibes's heroine" (*San Francisco Chronicle*, 1 Nov. 1939). Reed recalled that because she was the only dancer in the company who could perform the necessary thirty-two fouettes in the Black Swan pas de deux, she was Odile in this country's first full-length evening performance of *Swan Lake*, with Jacqueline Martin dancing Odette.

With the company, Reed toured the country, taking *Coppelia*, *Swan Lake*, and mixed bills of Christensen's choreography as far east as Chicago, where a critic judged her "an artist of the top rank" (in *San Francisco Ballet: The First Fifty Years*, 1983). On tour in Seattle in 1938 the dancers crossed paths with dancers from Ballet Caravan, also on tour, including Eugene Loring, who saw Reed perform at the Moore Theatre. Impressed with her acting skills as well as her dancing, he invited her to join Dance Players, the short-lived company he formed in 1941. Eager to work with a variety of choreographers, Reed borrowed the train fare to New York from her landlady. Reed danced in Loring's *Billy the Kid*, *City Portrait*, and *Prairie*, and Lew Christensen's *Jinx*, for which she created the role of the lead girl.

Dance Players folded in 1942, and Reed was hired by Ballet Theater initially as a guest artist performing the roles of Anabelle Lyons, who had left the company, in Antony Tudor's ballets and originating roles in his *Dim Lustre* and *Undertow*. It was, however, in Jerome Robbins's groundbreaking first ballet, *Fancy Free*, with Leonard Bernstein's first score for the stage, that Reed came into her own. The work, about three sailors on leave and their competition for the attentions of two girls, struck a real nerve at its premiere on 18 April 1944 during World War II. Reed's glamorous looks, sparkling stage presence, and gift for comic timing made her ideal for the role of the Second Girl, and reviews indicate that audiences as well as critics adored her.

In 1946 Reed married Branson Erskine and left Ballet Theatre to start a family. In 1947 her son Reed was born. Later that year she starred in *Look Ma I'm Dancing*, a musical with choreography by Robbins, which had a six-month run on Broadway. In 1949 George Balanchine, in whose work she had performed at Ballet Theatre, invited her to join the fledgling New York City Ballet. There she danced for nine years, creating roles in his *Bourree Fantasque*, *Jeu de Cartes*, *Western Symphony*, *À la Francaix*, *Ivesiana*, and *The Nutcracker* as well as Ruthanna Boris's *Cakewalk* and Robbins' *Ballade* and *Pied Piper*. In 1953 she gave a sidesplittingly funny performance as the drunken debutante in a revival of Lew Christensen's *Filling Station*, on stage and later on film for television's "Show of Shows." "As the female inebriate," wrote critic Walter Terry, "[she] added another irresistible characterization to her long list of achievements. . . . The diminutive and ever-beautiful ballerina filled each action with delicious humor. Not a gesture evaded the touch of her perfect timing. Nothing was overdone, nothing left unfinished in a comedy portrayal as perfect as I have ever seen in ballet" (*New York Herald Tribune*, 13 May 1953).

In 1958 Reed's daughter was born and Reed became company ballet mistress, working directly with Balanchine to rehearse his ballets and helping to audition and develop dancers. In 1961 she left the position and taught at Bard and Vassar Colleges as well as her own Kingston School of Ballet. In the 1960s she acted as a consultant for the U.S. Department of State Cultural Exchange Programs and the Ford Foundation.

In 1974 Reed returned to the Pacific Northwest as founding director of Seattle's Pacific Northwest Ballet School and Company until 1976, remaining in the area until her death. Reed, a descendant of pioneers, was herself a pioneer; as dancer, teacher, and artistic director, playing a vital role in the development of ballet as an American art form in the twentieth century—not only as a founding member of the New York City Ballet but particularly in her native West where she helped establish two first-class companies, the San Francisco Ballet at the beginning of her career and the Pacific Northwest Ballet at the end.

• There are no book-length accounts of Reed's life; however, Cobett Steinberg, Laura Leivick, and Russell Hartley, *San Francisco Ballet: The First Fifty Years* (1983), contains a good summary up to that point. An interview conducted by Tobi Tobias for the New York Public Library Dance Collection's Oral History Project (1978) is also valuable. The Dance Collection is also the repository of Reed's scrapbooks. Extensive references to Reed are also to be found in Debra Hickenlooper Sowell, *The Christensen Brothers: An American Dance Epic* (1998), and in Anatole Chujoy, *The New York City Ballet* (1953). Anna Kisselgoff's obituary in the *New York Times* is dated 6 March 2000.

MARTHA ULLMAN WEST

RESOR, Helen Lansdowne (20 Feb. 1886–2 Jan. 1964), advertising executive, was born Helen Lansdowne in Grayson in the mountains of Northwest Kentucky, the youngest of nine children of George Lansdowne, occupation unknown, and Helen Baylett Lansdowne. When Resor was four years old, her mother left her father and took the children to Covington, Kentucky, where she obtained work as a clerk. "You're never going to get caught the way I was. You're going to learn how to work," Resor's mother told her (Fox, p. 94).

Resor graduated as high school valedictorian in 1903, then took on several short-term jobs in business and advertising in Cincinnati, Ohio. After roughly a year each at the World Manufacturing Company, the *Commercial Tribune*, Procter and Collier, and the Street Railways Advertising Company, she accepted an offer to return to Procter and Collier as an advertising copywriter. In 1908, when Stanley Resor and his brother Walter Resor opened a Cincinnati branch office of the J. Walter Thompson advertising agency, Helen Resor joined them as the office's sole copywriter.

Resor's success as a copywriter was immediate. That year she took over the Woodbury's Soap account, and with her line "A Skin You Love to Touch," the company's sales increased tenfold within eight years. She also created the advertisements that introduced Crisco, Yuban Coffee, Lux Flakes, and Cutex. Resor was the first woman to present her ideas to the board of directors of Procter and Gamble and was, by her own account, the first woman to be successful in national advertising.

In January 1911 Stanley Resor and Helen Lansdowne Resor moved to the New York office of J. Walter Thompson. In March 1916 Stanley Resor obtained control of the J. Walter Thompson Company, and in March 1917 Helen and Stanley married. They had three children. Although Helen Resor never took on an official executive title and only became a member of the board in 1924, she quickly became "one of the main architects of J. Walter Thompson's growth" (*News Bulletin*, 10 Jan. 1964). By World War I, Resor, like her husband, had established a national reputation. With their leadership the J. Walter Thompson agency became the largest advertising agency in the world.

In New York, Resor directed the Women's Editorial Department, a branch of the agency run by women primarily for women consumers. Under her direction a whole generation of women entered the profession and, arguably, transformed it. She hired an exceptionally talented and well-educated group of women, less than half of whom had previous experience in advertising. Several had worked as teachers, suffrage workers, or social workers. For many of these highly educated women, Resor was a primary role model. One employee, Nancy Stephenson, put it this way: "Women in advertising, and particularly in the Thompson offices around the world, owe Mrs. Resor a great deal—not only for the opportunities she opened up for women, but for the inspiring standards she set for us to follow" (*News Bulletin*, 10 Jan. 1964). Many Women's Editorial Department employees in fact specifically applied to J. Walter Thompson because of the agency's reputation for hiring women and treating them "justly" (Scanlon, p. 182).

Because women consumers reputedly accounted for 85 percent of the nation's spending, the Women's Editorial Department workers played a significant role in the evolution of advertising. They provided advertisements for products aimed at women, such as household and cleaning items, food and beauty products, and clothing and accessories. Resor recognized that female consumers had been looked down upon, and her goal was to change that. A private person, she refused invitations for interviews and left little in the way of personal information. In a stockholder's affidavit, however, she claimed that the success of the J. Walter Thompson Company was largely owed to its focus on women consumers: "The advertising appeal which seeks to increase the sales of products bought by women must be made with knowledge of the habits of women, their methods of reasoning, and their prejudices. My work for the Company has been based on these conditions and principles, and I believe that it is conceded in the advertising industry that our agency is pre-eminent when it comes to advertising articles for women" ("Stockholder's Affidavit," p. 69).

Resor retired from J. Walter Thompson in the late 1950s, and although her own work was often overshadowed by the successes of her husband and of the agency, some astute observers of the industry recognized her contributions. An article in *Advertising Age*, the industry newspaper, put it clearly: "Those who have studied the history of the Thompson agency believe that Helen Resor's contribution to its growth has been in every way as great as her husband's" (5 Nov. 1962).

Resor supported woman suffrage, Planned Parenthood, and Radcliffe College. An anonymous backer of many artists, she also gave special commissions to artists in England to help them reestablish their work after World War II. In addition she served as chair of the Babies Ward of the New York Post-Graduate Hospital.

Resor's husband died in 1962. Resor died in New York City, survived by her three children. A *New York Herald Tribune* obituary called her the greatest copywriter of her generation. She essentially invented sex appeal in advertising. "Using muted sexuality and what may now appear to be tame physical contact between a man and a woman, Lansdowne created a sensation, and sales of Woodbury's Soap increased 1000 percent in eight years" (Scanlon, 175–76).

• The archives of the J. Walter Thompson Company, housed at the Duke University Library, Durham, N.C., contain the available company records, including newsletters and stockholder's affidavits, and published information about Resor's life and career. Biographical profiles include Harriet Abbott, "Doctor? Lawyer? Merchant? Chief? Which Shall It Be? Women's New Leadership in Business," *Ladies' Home Journal*, July 1920, pp. 43 ff.; Helen Lansdowne Resor, "Stockholder's Affidavit," J. Walter Thompson Company Archives, Duke University Library; "Advertising Loses a Titan as Resor Dies," *Advertising Age*, 5 Nov. 1962. See also Stephen Fox, *The Mirror Makers* (1984); and Jennifer Scanlon, *Inarticulate Longings: The Ladies' Home Journal, Gender, and the Promises of Consumer Culture* (1995). An obituary is in the *New York Herald Tribune*, 3 Jan. 1964.

JENNIFER SCANLON

REYNOLDS, Quentin (11 Apr. 1902–17 Mar. 1968), journalist and author, was born in the Bronx, New York, the son of James J. Reynolds, principal and assistant superintendent of schools, and Katherine Mahoney Reynolds. His family moved to Brooklyn, where he attended the local schools and the Manual Training High School. He entered Brown University in 1919, graduating in 1924. At Brown he boxed (he was the campus heavyweight boxing champ), swam, and played varsity football. After leaving Brown and serving a stint as a pool lifeguard, Reynolds worked as a reporter for the Providence *Journal*, reporter and editor for the Brooklyn *Times*, and in 1932 sportswriter and reporter for the New York *Evening World* and the *World Telegram*. He also managed to secure an LL.B. from Brooklyn Law School in 1931. In 1932, a victim of an economy drive, he was released by the *World Telegram*. Through Damon Runyon, Reynolds found employment as a news reporter, sportswriter, and rewrite man for the Hearst organization's International News Service (INS).

In 1932, the INS sent Reynolds to Germany. In Heidelberg, his articles on a student duel and on a speech by Joseph Goebbels, which set off a frenzy of nationalistic and anti-Semitic sentiment, attracted the attention of a Collier's editor, who asked Reynolds to do an article on how the Nazi government was conditioning German youth for war. On the strength of the article, *Collier's* offered Reynolds a position as a correspondent. He accepted, leaving the INS in 1933.

Collier's was a weekly magazine and expected Reynolds to deliver articles on a regular basis. Between 1933 and 1939, Reynolds wrote 383 articles, on many subjects, especially Broadway personalities, football players, prize fighters (including the young Joe Louis), and golfers. He also crafted an article on Colonel Fulgencio Batista, the Cuban dictator, and another (that attracted the attention of the State Department) concerning the massacre of Haitian immigrants by the Dominican dictator Rafael Trujillo's soldiers.

In 1939, war erupted in Europe, and the following year Reynolds was assigned to Paris, before the German attack on France in 1940. He managed to obtain permission to circulate in the French army zone, where he witnessed warfare first hand, including a dogfight between French and German fighters, and the bombing of Beauvais. Reynolds barely escaped to England before the German army took Paris.

Impressed by the British people's confidence in their ability to resist the coming German onslaught, Reynolds wrote an article titled "England Can't Lose." He also wrote a series of articles about the Battle of Britain. At the suggestion of a literary agent, he fashioned his articles on the fall of France and the Battle of Britain into a book, *The Wounded Don't Cry* (1941). He employed the same formula, turning articles he had written about his experiences in Moscow and Cairo into *Only the Stars Are Neutral* (1942).

Reynolds married Virginia Peine, an actress, in New York on 30 March 1942, and after a two-week honeymoon he was sent back to England. Having secured a place on the British command ship for the raid on Dieppe, Reynolds vividly described the debacle (*Rehearsal for Conflict*, published in 1943), in which half the commandos were casualties and the command ship was shelled by German shore batteries and attacked by the Luftwaffe.

Reynolds's subsequent peregrinations took him to Moscow, North Africa, and Italy. In Palermo, he and several correspondents learned that General George Patton had slapped a hospitalized soldier. At Eisenhower's request, Reynolds and the other correspondents suppressed the story, since they considered themselves patriots first and then correspondents, a view that a subsequent generation of journalists would condemn.

In a series of articles for *Collier's* in 1947, and in a book, *Leave It to the People* (1949), Reynolds pronounced his firm belief that the people of Europe would reject communism by means of the ballot. He maintained that of the twenty-four books he wrote or edited, *Leave It to the People* (1949) was the one "most deserving of attention" (*By Quentin Reynolds*, p. 320). Indeed, this book received generally favorable reviews; critics were especially impressed with the section on Israel, where Reynolds achieved a series of private interviews with the secret leaders of the Irgun and the Stern group.

The same year that *Leave It to the People* appeared, Reynolds reviewed a biography of Heywood Broun for the *New York Times* Sunday Book Review. In the review, Reynolds quoted a passage in which the author took exception to Westbrook Pegler's dim view of Broun's liberalism. Enraged, Pegler in his nationally syndicated column charged Reynolds with being an "absentee war correspondent," raised doubts about his bravery under fire, and alluded to Reynolds's "communism and war profiteering" (Louis Nizer, *My Life in Court*, p. 17).

Reynolds, bewildered by the accusations, was determined to defend his integrity as a journalist. He hired Louis Nizer, an outstanding trial lawyer, to handle his libel suit against Pegler. Nizer hunted down witnesses to challenge Pegler's charges and to testify to Reynolds's character and journalist veracity. After Reynolds survived unscathed aggressive questioning by Pegler's lawyer, Pegler took the stand. Nizer conducted his questioning brilliantly, trapping Pegler into admitting careless errors, the use of hearsay, and even to having lied in the column. In 1954, five years after the libel suit was filed, the jury awarded Reynolds the unprecedented sum of $175,000. Even the embarrassment stemming from the publication of his book *The Man Who Wouldn't Talk* (1953) could not dim Reynolds's satisfaction at the outcome of the trial. (The subject of the book, George DuPre, convinced Reynolds and many others that he had been a daring British spy in World War II, but his story was exposed as a fabrication soon after the book appeared.) Reynolds continued his career after the trial. In 1960 he and Virginia Peine divorced. His last book, *With Fire and Sword*, which he coedited, was published in 1963. He died at Travis Air Force Base, in California.

Contemporary reviewers found his books lively and colorful but also overly personal and all too often unreflective. On the other hand, Reynolds wrote on the run, and this kind of deadline journalism inhibited the deliberation and incisive criticism that would have satisfied his critics. Still, Reynolds, one of the most popular and widely read of America's roughly five hundred overseas correspondents, gave his readers a convincing sense of the sliver of the war he had witnessed in France, Britain, Russia, Italy, and North Africa.

• Brown University has the original copies of Reynolds's books, as well as a clipping file on him. The most complete account of his life is found in his autobiography, *By Quentin Reynolds* (1963). On the Westbrook Pegler libel trial, consult Louis Nizer's *My Life in Court* (1961). The argument over World War II government censorship and journalists' self-censorship can be followed in Philip Knightly, *The First Casualty* (1975), and Robert W. Desmond, *Tides of War: World News Reporting 1931–1945* (1984). An obituary is in the *New York Times*, 18 Mar. 1965.

RICHARD HARMOND

RIGGS, Bobby (25 Feb. 1918–25 Oct. 1995), tennis player, was born Robert Larimore Riggs in Los Angeles, California, the son of Gideon Wright Riggs, a minister of the Church of Christ, and Agnes Jones Riggs. During his childhood, Riggs's older brothers pushed him into various sports competitions. He began playing tennis at age twelve. Esther Bartosh, a leading local tournament player and an anatomy instructor at the University of Southern California, impressed by Riggs's potential, taught him stroke mechanics and guided him through boys' tournaments, most of which he won. Before he graduated from Franklin High School in 1935, Riggs captured the California Interscholastic singles title in three consecutive years. Earlier he reached the semifinal round of the 1932 U.S. Boys (under age fifteen) championship and ranked third nationally in that classification. In 1933 he won his first national title, the U.S. Junior (under age eighteen) doubles, with Bob Harman. In 1934 Riggs lost the U.S. Junior singles final to the New Englander Gilbert Hunt, but in 1935 he defeated Gil Hunt in the final and secured the doubles crown with his fellow Californian Joe Hunt.

By spring 1936 Riggs's game had matured under Bartosh's guidance. A slim right-hander, slightly under five feet, eight inches tall, Riggs lacked power but hit all his strokes with textbook efficiency and exhibited no weaknesses. Essentially a baseliner and a tireless retriever, he covered the court with amazing speed, possibly the fastest player of his time, running down and returning balls that seemed impossible to reach. He possessed good tactical judgment; a cool, even temperament; and a strong, constant will to win, the latter especially when wagering on himself, which he did constantly. Riggs was unpopular with tennis officials, however, particularly with Perry T. Jones, secretary of the Southern California Tennis Association (SCTA), who directed the area's junior tennis activity. They disliked Riggs's cocky, jaunty court manners and regarded his incessant gambling as a bad influence on other juniors.

In 1936 Jones and the SCTA furnished the directors of major tournaments in the East with negative critiques of Riggs's play. Riggs persuaded his friend Jack Del Valle to become both driver and financial backer for him and Wayne Sabin, another talented youngster, on a tour of the eastern tournaments. Surprising tennis results followed. Riggs immediately won the Missouri Valley and U.S. Clay Court singles and, with Sabin, both doubles events. These victories assured invitations to all the important eastern tournaments. Subsequently Riggs reached nine more finals and won six, including the prestigious Newport Invitation. His record earned him a fourth-place national ranking behind Don Budge, Frank Parker, and Bitsy Grant. In October Riggs entered the University of Miami in Florida, but he soon withdrew.

The brown-haired youth's successes continued through 1937, as he won fourteen singles tournaments and ranked second nationally behind Budge. In the U.S. championships at Forest Hills, New York, Riggs lost in a semifinal to Baron Gottfried von Cramm of Germany after leading two sets to love. Later Riggs beat von Cramm in the Pacific Coast championship. His biggest disappointment was failure to be selected for the U.S. Davis Cup team. Again in 1938 Riggs won fourteen tournaments and ranked second after Budge. The climax of his season was his defeat of Adrian Quist in the Davis Cup challenge round, which, coupled with Budge's two singles victories, enabled the United States to conquer Australia, 3–2, and retain the cup.

Riggs, a small 140-pounder, had his finest year in 1939. With Budge now a professional, Riggs was America's top amateur. Sent abroad by the U.S. Lawn Tennis Association, Riggs lost to Don McNeill at the French championship and suffered a 6–0, 6–1 shellacking by von Cramm at Queen's Club, London. Supremely confident, however, Riggs bet on himself to win the championship singles at Wimbledon and did so, vanquishing his American teammate Elwood Cooke in the final. With Cooke, Riggs won the doubles, and with Alice Marble he won the mixed doubles. Years later Riggs claimed he bet on all three events and amassed winnings at 216 to 1 odds. Back home he captured his first U.S. singles title, but in 1940 he lost his crown to McNeill, a bitter disappointment that cost Riggs the opportunity to accept a lucrative offer to turn professional. Riggs remained an amateur in 1941, when he regained his U.S. title, prevailing through a five-set final with Ted Schroeder, then he turned professional.

In a 1942 professional tour Riggs finished second behind Budge and ahead of Frank Kovacs, Fred Perry, and Lester Stoefen. During World War II he served in the U.S. Navy, assigned to special service, mostly playing tennis exhibitions in the Pacific theater. Discharged in November 1945, he edged Budge in a 1946 tour, twenty-three matches to twenty-one. In 1947 tours he registered a victory margin over Budge, Kovacs, and Perry, but in 1948, his last year as a major tour competitor, Jack Kramer overwhelmed him, sixty-nine matches to twenty. During the next few years Riggs worked as a tour promoter. His several U.S. professional singles titles include Grass Court 1946, 1947, 1949; Hard Court 1945, 1946; Indoors 1947; and Clay Court 1954.

Riggs married Catherine Ann Fischer in 1939; they had two children. After they divorced, Riggs in 1953 married the wealthy New York socialite Priscilla Wheelan and moved to New York, where he took up golf and "hardly touched a racket for the next sixteen years, except for occasional friendly betting matches" (Riggs, 1973, p. 86). He constantly bet on himself in private golf matches, sometimes assuming bizarre handicaps, and gained a reputation as a "hustler." He denied cheating and insisted that he relied on his judgment about handicaps and his competitive juices. Riggs and Wheelan had four children.

As the open tennis era commenced, Riggs resumed tournament play. From 1970 to 1988 he won many U.S. older age bracket championships and continued to bet on handicap "friendlies." He and Priscilla divorced in 1973. That year Riggs challenged Billie Jean King to a "Battle of the Sexes." When King refused, he played and defeated Margaret Smith Court, 6–2, 6–1. Subsequently King accepted his challenge and on 20 September 1973 defeated him at the Houston (Texas) Astrodome, 6–4, 6–3, 6–3. Watched by perhaps 50 million television viewers, it was the most publicized tennis match of the twentieth century. Some regarded it as a signal victory for the woman's liberation movement. King, who played an effective serve-and-volley style, called her victory "the culmination of nineteen years of tennis." Riggs denied he threw the match for money and admitted, simply, "She outplayed me. There are no secrets."

Riggs died in Leucadia, California, typically upbeat to the end. In 1967 he was enshrined in the International Tennis Hall of Fame. He ranks perhaps as the most underrated of U.S. champions because, despite his accomplishments, he lacked the spectacular, aggressive game of other great champions. It is indeed ironic that his excellent record should be overshadowed in popular recall by the result, the ballyhoo, and the surrounding circumstances of the Riggs-King exhibition match, staged like a circus act with the players carried to the court on gold-wheeled vehicles, and played on a court laid on top of a baseball infield.

• Riggs wrote two full-length autobiographies, *Tennis Is My Racket* (1949) and, with George McGann, *Court Hustler* (1973); and a shorter one, "Now I'll Talk," as told to Ed Fitzgerald, *Sport Magazine*, November 1946, pp. 59–65. Good biographical treatments are in Bud Collins and Zander Hollander, eds., *Bud Collins' Tennis Encyclopedia* (1997); and Stan Hart, *Once a Champion* (1985). A description of Riggs's type of tennis game is Julius D. Heldman, "The Style of Bobby Riggs," in *The Fireside Book of Tennis*, ed. Allison Danzig and Peter Schwed (1972). The so-called "Battle of the Sexes," the Bobby Riggs–Billie Jean King exhibition match, is reported in the *New York Times*, 21 Sept. 1973. Obituaries are in the *New York Times*, 27 Oct. 1995, and *Tennis Week*, 30 Nov. 1995.

FRANK V. PHELPS

RIGGS, Lynn (31 Aug. 1899–30 June 1954), playwright and poet, was born Rollie Lynn Riggs near Claremore, Indian Territory (Oklahoma), the son of William Grant Riggs, a rancher and banker, and Rose Ella Duncan Gillis Riggs, who was one-eighth Cherokee. His mother died of typhoid fever two years later, and his father married Juliette Scrimsher Chambers,

one-fourth Cherokee, who was lacking in motherly tendencies.

At Eastern University Preparatory School in Claremore, young Riggs sang folk songs, played guitar, and playacted in Friday night "speakings." An expert horseman, he herded cattle, plowed fields, and drove a delivery wagon, but his dream was to become an actor. After graduation in 1917, he made his way to New York and acted as an extra in cowboy movies being produced in the Bronx. Between jobs, he worked in Macy's and read proof for the *Wall Street Journal*.

Next he tried his luck in Hollywood, working as an extra in movies, from dusty cowboy characters to tuxedo-clad sophisticates toasting Rudolph Valentino. He earned enough to enroll in the University of Oklahoma in 1920. While working his way through school, he participated in campus literary and musical organizations. He published poems in *Poetry* magazine and in *Smart Set*. He sang in "The Sooner Quartet," which toured the Midwest with a summer Chautauqua ensemble.

During his senior year, struck by physical and emotional illness—symptoms of tuberculosis, plus unresolved personal conflicts—Riggs fled to Santa Fe. There in Sunmount Sanitarium, a place of scenic beauty, healthy living, and literary companions, Riggs recuperated within a few months. He took up residence within the lively writers' colony of Santa Fe.

Among his new friends was Ida Rauh Eastman, a founder of the Provincetown Players. She became Riggs's chief fan and mentor. She organized the Santa Fe Players and produced his one-act play "Knives from Syria." In 1925, Riggs returned to New York with his first full-length play, *Big Lake*, and another in process, resolved on a career in playwrighting.

In April 1927 the American Laboratory Theatre staged *Big Lake*, a story of young love and innocence. Called "poetic," the play received mixed reviews. In 1926, Otto Kahn optioned Riggs's next play, *Sump'n Like Wings*, but he dropped it and the play was never produced in New York. This and Riggs's next play, *A Lantern to See By*, became typical of Riggs's Oklahoma plays, taking place in the early 1900s and depicting the hard but courageous lives of young adults in Indian Territory—a time and place unique in American history.

Riggs completed two more Oklahoma plays in 1927, *The Lonesome West* and *Rancor*, about a dysfunctional marriage. These were produced by the renowned Hedgerow Theater repertory company near Philadelphia. His romantic cowboy comedy, *Roadside* (also called *Borned in Texas*) played in New York and at Hedgerow in 1930. He continued to publish poems, many in *Poetry* and three in *Bookman* ("Epitaph," "Slight Monument," and "The High Words"), and his "Spring Morning—Santa Fe" was accepted for an anthology.

In 1928 Lee Shubert and J. J. Shubert produced *The Domino Parlor*, about gambling, drinking, and heartbreak in an Oklahoma saloon. Riggs felt they misunderstood the intention of his play, and critic Barrett Clark said in *An Hour of American Drama* (p. 153) that it was badly miscast. It resurfaced more successfully in 1946 as *Hang on to Love*.

In July 1928, Riggs sailed for France, supported by a Guggenheim Fellowship for a year. In Cannes-sur-Mer, he wrote his best-known play, *Green Grow the Lilacs*, a comedy about love, struggle, and hope in a new land. He included many old songs, which he later published in the 1932 anthology, *Cowboy Songs, Folk Songs and Ballads from Green Grow the Lilacs*. In 1931, the Theatre Guild tried out *Green Grow the Lilacs* for seven weeks before opening in New York on 26 January 1931. It ran for sixty-four performances then toured the Midwest and was nominated for a Pulitzer prize. Ironically, Riggs is best known for the 1943 adaptation of *Green Grow the Lilacs* by Richard Rodgers and Oscar Hammerstein called *Oklahoma!* The pair's brilliant music replaced the old folk songs, but the script closely follows Riggs's play. *Oklahoma!* set new Broadway records and has continued to play internationally.

Riggs spent much of the 1930s writing screenplays in Hollywood, while continuing work on his own plays and poems. His realistic depiction of the American cowboy in such films as *The Plainsman* "changed the American Western," said Mary Hunter Wolf, a noted Broadway theater director and arts educator (*Haunted by Home*, jacket). In his only play about Indian people, *The Cherokee Night*, Riggs explored the disorderly lives of mixed-breed young adults, born of Native people and Caucasian settlers in a time of transition. Playing at Hedgerow Theater in 1932 and Federal Theater, New York City, in 1936, this experimental, nonchronological play in six scenes was met with confusion. Interest in this unique example of Native-American literature renewed with recent interest in ethnic strains in modern American literature. For example, Scene Six from *The Cherokee Night* is used to illustrate alienation and literary experimentation in the *Heath Anthology of American Literature* (1990).

Many of Riggs's published poems from Santa Fe were compiled in *The Iron Dish* by Doubleday-Doran (1930). Although Riggs's playactors spoke in the "poetic" Oklahoma dialect he loved, his poems were in his own contemporary voice. He created unique metaphors from the Cherokee's organic view of nature. In 1982, this contributor found a lost manuscript of his later poems and published it, with commentary, as *This Book, This Hill, These People: Poems by Lynn Riggs*.

He continued to write in various formats to the end of his life: short stories, including "Eben, the Hound and the Hare," *Gentry* (Summer 1953); a comedy for the new medium of television, *Some Sweet Day* (Philco-Goodyear Playhouse, 1953); a pageant for Western Reserve University's 125th anniversary, *Toward the Western Sky* (1951); and an unfinished novel. Riggs died of cancer in Memorial Hospital in New York City.

Although widespread fame and fortune eluded him, Riggs left a legacy of literary slices of a manner of life that, as he said, was "rapidly fading away." His characters, settings, and plot lines came out of his childhood milieu, an evolving society hidden away within a country well into the industrial and urban revolution. He wondered at what he saw, and he believed it was worth remembering. To him, however, his writings were not a "history"—only true tales of people of courage and small triumphs.

• The Western History Collections in the University of Oklahoma Library have most of Riggs's manuscripts and published works, plus letters and reminiscences in the Betty Kirk Boyer and Walter S. Campbell files. Beinecke Library of Yale University has manuscripts from agent Lucy Kroll and extensive correspondence in the Barrett H. Clark papers. Additional materials are in the University of Tulsa McFarlin Library; in the Billy Rose Collection, New York Library at Lincoln Center; and at Harvard Houghton Library in the Witter Bynner papers.

Samuel French, Inc. published many Riggs plays in book form, including *The Cherokee Night and Russet Mantle* (1936) and *Four Plays* (1947): *A World Elsewhere, The Year of Pilar, The Cream in the Well*, and *The Dark Encounter*. French published as manuscripts *Big Lake, Green Grow the Lilacs, Hang On to Love, Roadside*, and *Russet Mantle*. For poems, see *The Iron Dish* (1930) and *This Book, This Hill, These People: Poems by Lynn Riggs*, ed. Phyllis Braunlich (1982).

A biography by Phyllis Cole Braunlich, *Haunted by Home: The Life and Letters of Lynn Riggs*, was published in 1988. See also Braunlich in *The Dictionary of Literary Biography*, vol. 175, *Native American Writers*, pp. 249–58. For criticism of the plays, see Braunlich, "The Cherokee Night of R. Lynn Riggs," *Midwest Quarterly* 30 (Autumn 1988): 45–59, and "The Oklahoma Plays of R. Lynn Riggs," *World Literature Today* (Summer 1990): 390–94. Two dissertations are Charles Aughtry, "Lynn Riggs, Dramatist: A Critical Biography" (Brown University, 1959), and Eloise Wilson, "Lynn Riggs, Oklahoma Dramatist," (University of Pennsylvania, 1957). An obituary is in the *New York Times*, 1 July 1954.

PHYLLIS COLE BRAUNLICH

RODBELL, Martin (1 Dec. 1925–7 Dec. 1999), Nobel Prize–winning cell biologist, was born in Baltimore, Maryland, the son of Milton Rodbell, a grocer, and Shirley Abrams Rodbell. Although his parents never attended college, they stressed the importance of education to their son. Rodbell's initial impulses toward science did not come from school but rather from two of his childhood friends. His father did not allow him to have a chemistry set in the basement, which served as the grocery storeroom, so instead the boys used his friend's basement to "try to blow up things and watch mixtures change colors." The three boys attended Baltimore City College, a highly selective all-boys public high school. The school was patterned after European preparatory schools, which placed a strong emphasis on the liberal arts and offered only a few science courses.

Rodbell entered Johns Hopkins University in the fall of 1943. He was torn between his high school love of languages, especially French, and his grade school love of science. His initial studies at Johns Hopkins, however, were interrupted by World War II. In 1944 Rodbell joined the U.S. Navy and served as a radio operator. Despite his desire as a Jew to fight Adolf Hitler, he spent the majority of his time stationed in the South Pacific. He contracted malaria in the Philippines, then served for the remainder of the war as a radio operator in the Pacific fleet.

In 1946 Rodbell resumed his studies at Johns Hopkins and was attracted to French literature and philosophy. His father, however, wanted him to become a doctor, so he took premed courses. Although put off by the competitive premed atmosphere, he was inspired by the enthusiasm of Bentley Glass, a biology professor. Glass encouraged Rodbell to take chemistry to make up for his deficiency in the subject, and consequently Rodbell stayed an extra year and graduated with a B.A. in 1949.

That year Rodbell met Barbara Ledermann, who came to the United States after surviving the war in the Dutch underground. A photographer and trained ballet dancer, Ledermann performed in a production of a Johns Hopkins drama group. They married in 1950, the day before Rodbell left for the University of Washington to begin his graduate training in biochemistry. The couple had four children.

Rodbell flourished in the youthful Biochemistry Department. He selected Donald Hanahan as his thesis adviser and worked tirelessly in the lab for the next four years. His thesis research focused on how the liver makes lecithin (a complex mixture of lipids), part of the cell membrane. Unfortunately for Rodbell, another researcher working on the same problem disproved the conclusions of his thesis. Rodbell quickly determined that his errors were caused by impurities in some of his chemicals. He learned never rely on the purity of biological chemicals.

After completing his Ph.D. in biochemistry in 1954, Rodbell took a postdoctoral fellowship at the University of Illinois in the Chemistry Department under Herbert E. Carter. His work at Illinois concerned the biosynthesis of the antibiotic chloramphenicol. After two years at the University of Illinois, he decided to pursue laboratory research. The Rodbell family moved to Maryland, where Martin Rodbell had taken a position with the National Institutes of Health (NIH), the organization he remained with for the rest of his life.

Initially his research at the NIH dealt with lipids, but in 1960 he returned to his initial interest in cell biology at the Free University of Brussels and Leiden University, where he received fellowships. Upon returning to the NIH, Rodbell attracted attention when he developed methods to separate and purify fat cells and to remove the fat from cells while not altering the cell structure, which resulted in cells he called "ghosts."

In 1969 Rodbell formulated a theory about how cells communicate, called "signal transduction." He proposed that communication among cells was made up of three distinct components: the discriminator, the transducer, and the amplifier. The discriminator, the receptors on the cell membrane, receive the information from outside the cell; the transducer moves the information through the cell membrane; and the amplifier intensifies the signals to begin reactions inside the cell or transmits the information to other cells. The discriminator and amplifier were largely understood, but in 1970 Rodbell discovered that the principal component of the transducer was guanosine triphosphate (GTP), and over the next decade he demonstrated that it activates a protein, the G-protein, in the cell membrane. With his theory and experiments, he discovered the key step in how the cells in the body communicate. This marked the origin of the field of signal transduction.

In late 1970s Alfred Gilman confirmed the existence of the G-protein, and for their discovery of "G-proteins and the role of these proteins in signal transduction in cells," Rodbell and Gilman were awarded the Nobel Prize in physiology or medicine in 1994. Subsequent research has confirmed the importance of signal transduction by linking malfunctioning G-proteins with the effects of cholera, alcoholism, diabetes, and some cancers among other diseases. Work focuses on developing drugs to target these malfunctioning G-proteins.

In 1985 Rodbell became the scientific director of the National Institute of Environmental Health Sciences (NIEHS). He retired in 1994. Rodbell delivered the inaugural NIEHS Rodbell Lecture on 16 November 1998, the day before he went into the hospital for treatment of cardiovascular problems. In his speech, after reflecting on his career and discoveries, he stated, "Nature doesn't always do things the way we expect it to, and we need to have humility about that." He died in Chapel Hill, North Carolina.

• The Martin Rodbell Papers are at the National Library of Medicine (NLM), which offers a selection along with biographical information at http://profiles.nlm.nih.gov/GG/Views/Exhibit/. Rodbell's Nobel autobiography, his Nobel lecture, and the 1994 Nobel Prize press release are available at http://www.nobel.se. The University of Washington site on Rodbell at http://www.washington.edu/alumni/columns/june96/rodbell1.html includes a biography and excerpts from a 1996 university interview with him. Personal accounts of Rodbell by a wide range of people are available at the NIEHS site "In Memory of Dr. Martin Rodbell," http://www.niehs.nih.gov/external/mrmry.htm. A brief biography of Rodbell is Brigham Narins, *Notable Scientists from 1900 to the Present* (2001). An obituary is in the *New York Times*, 11 Dec. 1998.

JOHN S. EMRICH

ROERICH, Nicholas (9 Oct. 1874–13 Dec. 1947), artist, author, humanitarian, was born Nicholas Konstantinovich Roerich in St. Petersburg, Russia, the son of Konstantin Roerich, a lawyer and notary, and Maria Kalashnikova Roerich. He was raised in the comfortable environment of an upper-middle-class Russian family and enjoyed contact with the writers, artists, and scientists who often came to visit. At an early age he showed a curiosity and talent for archeology, paleontology, botany, and geology. The young Roerich also showed a particular aptitude for drawing, and at the age of sixteen he began to think about pursuing a career as an artist. In 1893, to satisfy his father, who did not consider painting to be a fit vocation for a responsible member of society, Nicholas enrolled in both the Academy of Art and St. Petersburg University, where he studied law.

In 1895 Roerich met the prominent writer, critic, and historian Vladimir Stasov, who introduced the young painter to many artists and composers of the time, such as Modest Moussorgsky, Nikolai Rimsky-Korsakov, Igor Stravinsky, and the great basso Fyodor Chaliapin. At concerts at the Court Conservatory Roerich heard the works of Glazunov, Liadov, Arensky, Wagner, and Scriabin and developed an enthusiasm for music. The late 1890s saw a blossoming in Russian arts, led by Sergei Diaghilev, who was a year or two ahead of Roerich at law school and was among the first to appreciate his talents as a painter and student of the Russian past. With Princess Maria Tenisheva and others Diaghilev founded the trend-setting magazine *The World of Art*. Roerich contributed and sat on its editorial board.

Soon after leaving the university, Roerich met Helena Shaposhnikova, daughter of the architect Shaposhnikov and niece of Moussorgsky. They were soon engaged, and on Roerich's return from a European tour in 1901 they were married. They had two children. Helena Roerich was an unusually gifted woman: a talented pianist, author of many books, and Russian translator of Helena Blavatsky's *Secret Doctrine*. At this time Roerich won the position of secretary of the School of the Society for the Encouragement of Art in St. Petersburg, later becoming its head, the first of many positions that Roerich would occupy as a teacher and spokesman for the arts. In the summers of 1903 and 1904 the family set off on an extended journey throughout Russia that resulted in a collection of seventy-five oil paintings that recorded remnants of the Russian past—ancient monuments, churches, city walls and castles. On his return to St. Petersburg in 1904, he promulgated a plan to protect such cultural monuments throughout the world, a plan consummated thirty-one years later in the Roerich Pact and Banner of Peace.

Returning to St. Petersburg, Roerich began painting the first of his works based on religious themes. In such early paintings as *Message to Tiron, Fiery Furnace*, and *The Last Angel*, he dealt mostly with Russian saints and legends, rendered in a style strongly reminiscent of early Italian Renaissance frescoes and Russian ikon painting. In 1906 Diaghilev arranged an exhibition of Russian paintings in Paris, including sixteen works by Roerich. The following year Roerich did the costumes and sets for Rimsky-Korsakov's *Ivan the Terrible* in Paris. In the "Polovtsian Dances" from *Prince Igor*, also designed by Roerich, Diaghilev introduced a corps of Russian dancers that became famous as the Ballets Russes, which included Anna Pavlova, Michel Fokine, and Vaslav Nijinsky. Roerich's designs furthered his reputation for depicting ancient cultures and their practices. Roerich was the prime mover and, with Igor Stravinsky, the cocreator of the ballet *Le Sacre du Printemps* (*The Rite of Spring*). The motif for the ballet grew out of Roerich's absorption with antiquity and, as he wrote in a letter to Diaghilev, "the beautiful cosmogony of earth and sky." In the ballet Roerich sought to express the primitive rites of ancient man as he welcomed spring, the life-giver, and made sacrifice to Yarilo, the Sun God. The ballet provoked an explosion of controversy that was to continue for many years.

War clouds were gathering in Europe, and in paintings of the period, such as *Battle in the Heavens*, Roerich used the stark contrast of light and darkness to suggest the awful scale of the conflict he felt was descending upon the world. In 1915 he was recuperating from pneumonia in Finland with his family when, with the advent of the revolution, it became impossible to return to Russia. In 1918, however, he was invited to exhibit his work in Stockholm, and from there the family proceeded to London, where Sir Thomas Beecham arranged for him to design a new production of *Prince Igor* for the Covent Garden Opera. In 1920 he was invited to exhibit a collection of over 200 paintings at the Kingore Gallery in New York. The critic Olin Downes wrote about the exhibition, "In the midst of our modern society, so positive and yet so limited, Roerich gives to his fellow artists a prophetic example of the goal they must reach—the expression of the inner life." Mary Siegrist of the New York *Sun* typified the general critical approval when she wrote, "From these canvasses there speaks an arresting and formidable genius."

There followed a busy and productive two years in America for Roerich, resulting in his designing *The Snow Maiden* and *Tristan and Isolde* for the Chicago Opera Company, and tours of the American West and Monhegan Island on the coast of Maine. During this time the Roerichs founded the Agni Yoga Society, which espoused a living ethic encompassing and synthesizing the philosophies and religious teachings of all ages. Plans were laid for the founding of the Master Institute of United Arts in New York, in which he was to realize the educational concepts he had successfully developed in St. Petersburg and establish a museum of his paintings. Neither the Institute nor the museum survived beyond 1937, but the Museum was reborn in 1949 as the Nicholas Roerich Museum in New York, where it now remains with a permanent exhibition of 150 of the artist's finest and most representative works.

In 1923 the Roerichs traveled to India, whose Eastern traditions and philosophy had attracted them for years. They set out for the slopes of the Himalayas and initiated a five-year journey that took them to Chinese Turkestan, Altai, Mongolia, and Tibet, where they studied the religions, languages, customs, and culture of the inhabitants. In his book *Heart of Asia*, Roerich created an account of the land and its people and vividly portrayed them in five hundred or so paintings.

In 1928, at the end of this first major expedition, the family settled in the Kullu Valley, in Northern India. Here they built a home and established the Urusvati Himalayan Research Institute. The research included botanical, ethnological-linguistic, Tibetan, and Chinese pharmacopeia and the exploration of archeological sites. In the early 1930s Roerich returned to New York for the dedication of the Master Institute. The country was in the throes of the Great Depression, and large sections of the farm belt were stricken with drought and soil erosion. On his return to Kullu, Roerich organized an expedition under the sponsorship of the United States Department of Agriculture to search for drought-resistant grasses. Except for infrequent trips abroad, Roerich remained in Kullu for the remainder of his life.

In spite of his accomplishments, and the high esteem in which he was held by contemporary world figures such as Franklin Roosevelt and Eleanor Roosevelt, Mohandas Gandhi, Jawaharlal Nehru, Rabindranath Tagore, and many others—he was honored by forty countries—Roerich remained an enigma. He was idolized by his followers, but the high moral tone of his humanitarianism drew the scorn and ridicule of those who misunderstood his goals and motives. He was even suspected of spying for several of the major world powers then maneuvering for dominion in Central Asia.

• Comprehensive archives can be found at the Roerich Center in Moscow, and at the Nicholas Roerich Museum in New York, where an archive including photographs, reproductions, diaries, and books and articles by and about Roerich is maintained. The museum also houses a large collection of his paintings and displays artifacts and memorabilia from the artist's expeditions into Central Asia. Roerich's explorations, philosophical thinking, and commentaries on art and culture are well documented in his books, including *Adamant* (1924), *Heart of Asia* (1930), *Shambhala* (1930), *Fiery Stronghold* (1933), *Himavat* (1946), and *The Invincible* (1947). The most complete biographies are those by Jacqueline Decter, *Nicholas Roerich: The Life and Art of a Russian Master* (1989), and Kenneth Archer, *Roerich East and West: Paintings from the Nicholas Roerich Museum* (1999). An obituary is in the *New York Times*, 16 Dec. 1947.

EDGAR LANSBURY

ROGERS, William Pierce (23 June 1913–2 Jan. 2001), secretary of state and attorney general, was born in Norfolk, New York, the only child of Harrison Alexander Rogers, a paper mill executive and banker, and Myra Beswick Rogers. At an early age Rogers took odd jobs to earn spending money. His mother died when he was thirteen, and he moved to Canton, New York, to live with his maternal grandparents. In 1930 he graduated at the head of his Canton High School class and then attended Colgate University on a tuition scholarship. He worked at various jobs throughout his college years to help meet living expenses and in 1934 graduated with a B.A. degree.

More scholarships enabled him to enter Cornell Law School, from which he graduated fifth in his class in 1937. At Cornell, Rogers met Adele Langston, a classmate, whom he married on 27 June 1936. They had four children.

Rogers's first law position was with the Wall Street firm of Cadwalader, Wickersham and Taft, which he joined soon after passing the New York bar examination in 1937. In the late 1930s the New York district attorney Thomas Dewey was becoming famous for his crime-busting efforts, and in 1938 Rogers was selected as one of Dewey's young assistant district attorneys. Between 1938 and 1942 Rogers argued over one thousand cases in court. In early 1942 he joined the U.S. Naval Reserve and served as a lieutenant junior grade on the USS *Intrepid*. His ship participated in raids on Japan and, in April 1945, the invasion of Okinawa. After his discharge in 1946, Rogers returned to New York and resumed work in the district attorney's office.

In April 1947 Rogers was appointed counsel to the Senate's Special Committee to Investigate the National Defense Program. During this time his life intersected with Congressman Richard M. Nixon of California, who was six months his senior. Rogers advised Nixon to pursue the Alger Hiss case, which helped launch Nixon's political career and cemented a long-lasting friendship. In 1950 Rogers returned to private law practice in the Washington office of the New York law firm of Dwight, Royall, Harris, Koegel and Caskey. Two years later, however, he was back in the political limelight, this time at the 1952 Republican National Convention, where he worked to convince the credentials committee to seat the delegates for Dwight Eisenhower instead of those who favored Robert A. Taft. Rogers traveled with Nixon, the vice presidential candidate, during the campaign. When Nixon came under fire for being the recipient of a secret campaign fund, Rogers advised him to defend himself on national television. Nixon's speech, in which he used sentimental references to his dog Checkers, invoked sympathy and support from the public and helped to save his career. Upon Eisenhower's victory, Nixon recommended that Rogers be appointed deputy attorney general in the new administration.

During the Eisenhower years Rogers continued to serve as a counselor for Nixon. In 1955, when Eisenhower had a heart attack, and in 1957, when Eisenhower suffered a small stroke, Rogers was at Nixon's side, offering levelheaded advice. In November 1957 Eisenhower chose the 44-year-old Rogers to succeed Herbert Brownell, Jr., as attorney general. As deputy attorney general, Rogers had worked to pass the 1957 Civil Rights Act, and as attorney general he made enforcement of its provisions one of his major goals. He established the Civil Rights Division in the Justice Department and actively prosecuted cases that involved the denial of voting rights. In 1957 he also promoted the enforcement of the Supreme Court's 1954 desegregation decision at Central High School in Little

Rock, Arkansas, arguing that delaying integration was not acceptable. (Although Eisenhower was known not to be enthusiastic about the Court's *Brown v. Board of Education* decision, he did back up his Justice Department when action was called for.)

After Nixon lost the 1960 presidential election, Rogers in 1961 rejoined his old law firm as a senior partner. During the 1960s Rogers served on the defense counsel for two significant libel cases before the Supreme Court, *New York Times v. Sullivan* (1964) and *Associated Press v. Walker* (1967). In addition to his legal work, Rogers also gained experience in international law and in 1965 served as a member of the United States delegation to the United Nations.

Although Nixon ran for president in 1968, Rogers remained immersed in his private legal practice and participated little in the campaign. Nevertheless, upon his election, Nixon insisted that Rogers become secretary of state. Although Rogers's diplomatic experience was limited, his supporters touted this as a positive attribute since he would be less doctrinaire than some of his predecessors. Nixon also believed Rogers's negotiating skills would help improve the State Department's relations with Congress. Moreover, since Nixon would conduct his presidency's most important diplomacy himself, he had no need for a strong secretary of state who might compete for the diplomatic spotlight.

During the early months of his tenure Rogers concentrated on upgrading the State Department's computer system and communicating often with members of Congress on foreign policy. He also promoted American interests in Europe and the Far East. As secretary of state Rogers preferred to maintain a low profile and serve as a top-level confidant to Nixon. His style did not mesh well with the energetic and forceful Henry Kissinger, who occupied the post of national security adviser. From the outset the two men clashed over foreign policy formulation and implementation. Added to this volatile mixture was the strong personality of Secretary of Defense Melvin Laird. For the most part during his first term Nixon carried out American foreign policy in consultation with Kissinger, often bypassing Rogers and the State Department. Thus Rogers was kept in the dark about American negotiations with the Soviet Union that resulted in the Strategic Arms Limitation Talks (SALT 1) and with the Chinese that led to the establishment of diplomatic relations. Nor was Rogers aware of Kissinger's diplomatic efforts to reduce American involvement in the Vietnam War. The Middle East was the only area where Rogers was given some latitude to initiate policy. In 1969 Rogers proposed the "Rogers Plan," which called for Israel to withdraw its forces from Arab territories occupied since the 1967 war in exchange for Arab promises to support a binding commitment to peace. Although both sides rejected his plan, Rogers persevered, and during 1970 he succeeded in obtaining a cease-fire agreement among Egypt, Jordan, and Israel and the resumption of negotiations under the auspices of the United Nations.

After his reelection in 1972, Nixon requested Rogers's resignation, which Rogers gave in September 1973; Kissinger was appointed his successor as secretary of state. The next month Nixon presented his retired colleague with the Medal of Freedom, the nation's highest civilian honor. Rogers then returned to his law firm and retired from politics. In 1986 he was called out of retirement by President Ronald Reagan to head the investigation into the January 1986 *Challenger* space shuttle disaster, which killed seven astronauts; Rogers's final report was sharply critical of NASA's attention to flight safety and led to extensive changes in the space program's operations. He continued working in private law practice until shortly before his death in Bethesda, Maryland.

From humble circumstances, Rogers rose to become a leading public figure in the years after World War II. His close personal relationship with Nixon benefited both men professionally. Rogers contributed to his country in important ways as a lawyer, especially in the areas of civil rights and libel laws. As secretary of state he improved the inner workings of the State Department and its relations with Congress during President Nixon's first term and then capped his career with a successful investigation of the *Challenger* disaster. A private man, content to work in the background, Rogers quietly and steadfastly served his country as a public official for forty years.

• Rogers's papers are in the Eisenhower Presidential Library and are part of the Nixon Presidential Materials Project in the National Archives in Washington, D.C. Useful sources on Rogers's public career are Stephen E. Ambrose, *Nixon*, 3 vols. (1987–91); Henry Kissinger, *The White House Years* (1979); and Richard M. Nixon, *RN: The Memoirs of Richard Nixon* (1978). The *New York Times* of 4 Jan. 2001 has an obituary.

EDWARD A. GOEDEKEN

ROMERO, Cesar (15 Feb. 1907–1 Jan. 1994), actor and dancer of film, television, and stage, was born in New York City, the son of Cesar Juelin Romero, a sugar exporter, and Maria Marti Romero, a concert pianist. The family's privileged Cuban ancestry included the celebrated revolutionary patriot and poet José Marti, who was Romero's maternal grandfather. Romero attended the Collegiate School in Manhattan and a boarding school, where he became stage struck while appearing in four roles in *The Merchant of Venice*.

When the sugar market collapsed, Romero's father lost a fortune, but he found a position for his son on Wall Street. Romero, however, had no interest in banking. Show business was his goal. Debonair, six feet two inches, and darkly handsome with his signature trim mustache, Romero was the prototype of the Latin lover, a species that enjoyed huge popularity in the 1920s, personified by silent screen stars like Rudolph Valentino. In New York, Romero was a popular bachelor-about-town, escorting debutantes to swank parties. One particular heiress suggested they form a dance team. "It was the only way I knew how to get into show business," Romero later said.

A gifted ballroom dancer, Romero began dancing professionally in Manhattan nightclubs and theaters. He turned to acting, appearing on Broadway in the musical *Lady Do* (1927), among other plays, and touring in a production of Preston Sturges's *Strictly Dishonorable* (1929). He was performing in the original Broadway production of George S. Kaufman and Edna Ferber's play *Dinner at Eight* (1932–1933) when scouts from MGM spotted him and signed him to a contract with the studio. Romero moved to Hollywood, and his film debut came in 1934, when he was cast as a gigolo opposite William Powell and Myrna Loy in *The Thin Man*.

During the 1930s Romero bounced around a number of studios, including Warner Brothers, to whom he was loaned by MGM just before the latter canceled his contract; Paramount, where he appeared as one of Marlene Dietrich's lovers in *The Devil Is a Woman* (1935); and Universal, where he was under contract for three years, cast in movies such as *The Good Fairy* and *Diamond Jim* (both 1935). Universal loaned him several times to the Hollywood mogul Darryl F. Zanuck, head of the newly formed Twentieth Century studios. Zanuck snapped up Romero's contract in 1937, when Universal failed to raise the actor's salary. Romero became a fixture in Zanuck's empire, known after a merger as Twentieth Century Fox.

The next fifteen years at Fox brought Romero many of the movie roles for which he became famous. He averaged about five or six movies a year, often musicals, appearing with Shirley Temple in *Wee Willie Winkie* (1937), in which he played an Afghan leader, and *The Little Princess* (1939) and with the Norwegian skating star turned movie star Sonja Henie in *Happy Landing* (1938) and *Wintertime* (1943). Beginning in the late 1930s Romero played the Cisco Kid in a series of B movies that included *The Return of the Cisco Kid* (1939), and in the 1940s he shared the screen with Fox's popular musical leading ladies, such as Betty Grable (with whom he danced in *Springtime in the Rockies* [1942]), Alice Faye, and Carmen Miranda. In 1947 he appeared as Hernando Cortéz (one of his favorite roles) in *Captain from Castile*, with Tyrone Power.

Romero made over one hundred films. Though at the beginning of his career he was hailed as "the next Valentino," he was not so much a leading man as the second lead or character part who rarely got the girl. Affable and low-key, without a trace of the temperament popularly ascribed to his Latin origins (his nickname was "Butch"), Romero was well-liked by his colleagues and was known as a consummate professional. He looked on his typecasting with humor, observing later: "I was saddled with the label because I had a Latin name. My background is Cuban, but I'm from New York City. I'm a Latin from Manhattan."

As did many other young men of his generation, Romero interrupted his career during World War II. He joined the U.S. Coast Guard in 1943 and re-

mained with it for three years. In 1946 the government sent him, along with his fellow matinee idol Power, on a goodwill tour of South America on which they were mobbed at every turn by hoards of fans, particularly women.

In the 1950s and 1960s, after he left Fox, Romero continued to appear in movies, like the all-star *Around the World in 80 Days* (1956), *Donovan's Reef* with John Wayne (1963), *Ocean's Eleven* (1960) with Frank Sinatra and Dean Martin, in which he played a Las Vegas gangster, and *Marriage on the Rocks* (1965), again with Sinatra and Martin. Like many of his peers, when the studio system disintegrated and advancing age did not afford many roles, Romero did not ignore his work ethic but appeared in regional and dinner theaters.

Romero also made frequent appearances on television from its earliest days, with the series *The Cisco Kid* and as a guest star on the *Milton Berle Show*, the *Dinah Shore Show*, *Buck Rogers*, *Bonanza*, and *Wagon Train*. The role for which he is most remembered, however, was a spin-off from the 1966 movie *Batman*, a farcical depiction of the comic book adventures in which Romero was uncharacteristically cast as the clown-faced, punch-line-flinging villain the Joker. On the ensuing *Batman* television series, which ran from 1966 to 1968, Romero's flagging career revived, and the Joker's attempts to foil the caped crusaders while inflicting harm on the citizens of Gotham City ensured Romero cult status with new generations of fans. Perhaps the most contentious moment of Romero's *Batman* turn was when the producers requested he shave off his signature mustache, and Romero refused. The producers compromised by agreeing that the clown-white makeup could simply be applied over the mustache, which is why any close inspection of Romero's *Batman* appearances reveals a clearly visible mustache beneath the greasepaint.

After *Batman*, with his fame renewed, Romero played character roles and comic villains in a series of Disney movies, including *The Strongest Man in the World*, and made guest appearances in a number of television movies and on series such as *Ironside*, *Fantasy Island*, *Charlie's Angels*, and *The Love Boat*. In the 1980s, at the age of seventy-eight, he was again featured as a series regular on the long-running nighttime soap opera *Falcon Crest*, playing Jane Wyman's love interest.

Toward the end of his sixty-year career Romero reflected: "I can't really complain. I was never a superstar in this business, I've always had a good steady position, and that's a damn sight more than a lot of them have had that have come and gone." Romero never married, preserving into his late years his image as the suave man-about-town, a frequent fixture at Hollywood and New York social affairs. He died in Santa Monica, California. At the time the actress Anne Jeffreys, a longtime friend, remarked: "He was elegant and eloquent. His manners, his dress were impeccable. He was the last of an era."

• The clippings file in the New York Public Library for the Performing Arts at Lincoln Center is a source for Romero's life. Entries on Romero are in Leonard Maltin, *Leonard Maltin's Movie Encyclopedia* (1995); *Who's Who Among Hispanic Americans*, 2d ed. (1992–1993); and *Contemporary Theatre, Film and Television*, vol. 12 (1994), reproduced in Biography Resource Center at http://www.galenet.com. Obituaries are in the *New York Times*, 3 Jan. 1994; the *Chicago Tribune*, 3 Jan. 1994 and 9 Jan. 1994; the *London Times*, 5 Jan. 1994; and *People Weekly*, 17 Jan. 1994.

DEBORAH GRACE WINER

ROU, Louis (c. 1683–25 Dec. 1750), French Reformed (Huguenot) minister, was born in Holland, the eldest son of Jean Rou, a former *conseiller* at the Parlement of Paris. His mother's name is not known. In 1683, as Louis XIV escalated persecution of Huguenots, the Rou family fled from France to Holland, where Jean became an interpreter at the States-General. The Rous formed close ties to other Huguenot refugees in Holland, including the apocalyptical theologian Pierre Jurieu. Louis studied Latin, Greek, and Hebrew, as well as theology, at the University of Leyden. After completing a ministerial apprenticeship with the Huguenot refugee congregation in Copenhagen, Rou was ordained by the Walloon Synod at Tertholen on 31 August 1709.

In July 1710, Rou began his career at the French Reformed Church in New York, one of the city's oldest and largest congregations. Around this time, he married fellow refugee Marie Le Bouteaux, who gave birth to a son, Louis, on 25 December 1712. She, and perhaps the child, died soon afterward. On 3 November 1713, Rou married fourteen-year-old Renée Marie Gougeon of New Rochelle. Because of her tender age, the Huguenot-turned-Anglican pastor in New Rochelle, Daniel Bondet, refused to marry them. However, a Dutch Reformed minister, Gualtherus Du Bois, agreed to perform the ceremony. Rou's remarriage to someone so young shortly after his first wife's death angered and embarrassed his congregation. The couple eventually had fourteen children, which was above the norm for Huguenots in New York and, consequently, further alienated some of Rou's congregants. Five of these children passed away before Rou himself died.

In 1718, perhaps because of their disapproval of Rou's personal life, the church elders hired an assistant minister, Jean Joseph Brumeau de Moulinars, who assumed many of Rou's duties. One responsibility that Rou had refused to accept was to visit the independent Huguenot congregation in New Rochelle four times a year to perform baptisms and communion. He insisted that they attend the French-speaking Anglican church in New Rochelle whose Huguenot ministers (the aforementioned Daniel Bondet and his successor, Pierre Stouppe) had conformed and received Anglican ordination. Moulinars, however, eagerly visited the nonconformists in New Rochelle. An intense rivalry between Rou and Moulinars developed, and by 1724 Rou did not have the support of newly elected church elders. These elders declared Moulinars to be the only minister and refused to pay

Rou. In response, Rou claimed that the election had been rigged, and he initiated legal proceedings to reclaim his position. Meanwhile, his wife circulated a petition in his favor. Rou used his connections with prominent Anglican politicians, including his chess partner Governor William Burnet, to press his case. In 1725, Rou turned his dispute into a public debate by publishing his responses to the accusations leveled against him in a pamphlet titled "Collection of Papers Concerning Mr. Lewis Rou's Affair." As a naturalized English citizen, Rou proudly cloaked himself in the protection of English law. He addressed Moulinars's contention that he was an Anglican sympathizer by insisting that his "esteem and respect" for the Church of England was not a crime. Rou further argued that the twenty or thirty people who had deposed him were "depriving at least eighty families of his ministry and spiritual comforts" and that the elders had thrown the church into "confusion and disorder." Moreover, he tried to bypass the elders' authority by asserting that only the synod of the Walloon Churches, which had ordained him, could remove him from his position. On 24 February 1726, the case was decided in Rou's favor. He was reinstated as pastor of the New York Church and Moulinars became the full-time minister to the nonconforming Huguenot congregation in New Rochelle. Most of Rou's major opponents, including the prominent De Lanceys, left the French Church to attend Anglican Trinity Church.

Rou's ninety-five manuscript sermons, written between 1704 and 1750, comprise one of only two collections of French Reformed sermons in North America. His sermons offer illuminating insights into eighteenth-century Huguenot beliefs. They are written in French, well prepared, and frequently showcase Rou's erudition, with references to obscure biblical passages, the early church fathers, and classical sources. Occasionally he noted that it took forty-five to fifty minutes to deliver a particular sermon. Some were preached several times throughout his lengthy career. Sermon content demonstrates that Rou was a theological Calvinist, who had not strayed from his Huguenot roots. He frequently discussed predestination, unconditional Election (God selects people for salvation, regardless of individual merit), the perseverance of the Elect (salvation cannot be revoked), and the total depravity of man. He repeatedly attacked the "Church of Rome" for its "errors and abuses," particularly the doctrine of transubstantiation. Following his controversy with the elders, Rou's sermons assumed an arrogant and sarcastic tone, which undoubtedly prompted others to defect to Anglican or Dutch Reformed Churches.

Rou was a man of diverse interests and talents. His responses to the 1725 charges demonstrate a keen, legalistic mind. He was also widely recognized as a chess aficionado. Unfortunately, his "Critical Remarks upon the Letter to the Craftsman on the Game of Chess," written in 1734, was lost. Summaries of this manuscript, which was dedicated to Rou's current chess partner, Governor William Cosby, suggest his mastery of the game and its history and vocabulary. His Latin poem on chess is extant, as are numerous verses on both secular and religious topics.

Rou served as minister of the French Church until he died in New York after a lingering illness. His obituary in the *New-York Gazette, or Weekly Post Boy* described him as "a gentleman of great learning and unaffected piety" who left "a sorrowful widow with a numerous hopeful issue." Since he left no inheritance, the French Church of New York gave his widow an annual pension of twelve pounds. Rou's forty-year tenure, although sometimes contentious, provided his church with greater stability and longevity than most Huguenot congregations in North America. Moreover, his erudition and his literary and linguistic abilities made him a leading member of eighteenth-century New York society.

• Originals and microfilm copies of "Sermons and Other Writings of Louis (Lewis) Rou (1704–1750)," 3 vols., are in the Theodorus Bailey Myers Collection, Manuscript and Archives Section, New York Public Library (NYPL). Transcriptions and translations of two sermons are in the Nigel Massey Collection, Huguenot Historical Society Library and Archives, New Paltz, N.Y. "Collection of Papers Concerning Mr. Lewis Rou's Affair" (1725) is in the Rare Book Collection, NYPL. Originals are Lewis Rou, "Eighteen Pieces of Manuscript," Manuscript Collection, New-York Historical Society (NYHS). Several references to Rou's controversy with the elders may be found in French Church of St. Esprit, N.Y.C., "Consistory Minutes, 1723–66" (photostat copies), Manuscript Collection, NYHS. Other pertinent church records have been published in Alfred V. Wittmeyer, ed., *Registers of the Births, Marriages, and Deaths of the "Église Française à la Nouvelle York," from 1688 to 1804* (1968); and Samuel S. Purple, ed., *Records of the Reformed Dutch Church in New Amsterdam and New York: Marriages from 1639 to 1801* (1890). Rou's obituary appeared in the *New-York Gazette, or Weekly Post Boy* on 31 Dec. 1750.

Jon Butler, *The Huguenots in America: A Refugee People in New World Society* (1983), contains numerous references to Rou. Somewhat dated, but still useful, are John A. F. Maynard, *The Huguenot Church of New York: A History of the French Church of Saint Esprit* (1938), and Alfred V. Wittmeyer, *An Historical Sketch of the "Église française à la Nouvelle York," from 1688 to 1804* (1886). For further discussion of Rou's relationship to Anglicanism, see Paula Wheeler Carlo, "Anglican Conformity and Nonconformity among the Huguenots of Colonial New York," in *From Strangers to Citizens: The Integration of Immigrant Communities in Britain, Ireland and Colonial America*, ed. R. Vigne and C. Littleton (2001). Regarding the chess manuscript, see Daniel Willard Fiske, "The Lost Manuscript of the Reverend Lewis Rou's 'Critical Remarks upon the letter to the Craftsman on the Game of Chess,' written in 1734 and dedicated to His Excellency William Cosby, Governor of New York" (1902); also, Fiske, "The Reverend Lewis Rou, Pastor of the French Protestant Church, New York City, and the Missing Manuscript of his Tract Relating to Chess, entitled . . ." (1902).

PAULA WHEELER CARLO

ROUTT, John Long (25 Apr. 1826–13 Aug. 1907), governor of Colorado, was born in Eddyville, Caldwell County, Kentucky, the son of John Routt and Martha Haggard Routt, farmers. His father died when he was still an infant, and his mother moved the family to Illinois, first to Hancock County then to McDonough County before finally settling in Bloomington in 1836. There Routt attended public schools before becoming apprenticed to a builder and machinist. He married Esther A. Woodson on 1 August 1845; the couple had four children.

Routt worked as a tradesman until 1851, when he began dealing in both public lands and town properties with varying degrees of success. He entered public life when he was elected alderman in Bloomington; in 1860 he became sheriff of McLean County. He resigned that post in 1862 when he raised Company E of the 94th Illinois Infantry. Routt served as captain of his unit and narrowly escaped death at the Battle of Prairie Grove in Arkansas, during which three bullets passed through his clothing. He later undertook a perilous mission during the Vicksburg campaign, which brought him to the attention of Union general Ulysses S. Grant. In the spring of 1863 Routt was named an army quartermaster and later served as chief quartermaster of the Army of the Frontier on the Rio Grande and rose to the rank of colonel.

On mustering out in September 1865 Routt returned home and found that he had been elected treasurer of McLean County in absentia. He served two terms and declined renomination for a third. In 1869 Grant, now president, appointed Routt U.S. Marshall for the southern district of Illinois; Routt served in that position until 1871, when Grant appointed him second assistant postmaster general. In February 1875 Grant, having unleashed a political firestorm through his attempts to reappoint Edward Moody McCook as governor of the Colorado Territory, sought to heal the bitter feud within the local Republican party by appointing Routt as the new territorial governor. Routt's first wife died in 1872, and in 1874 he married Eliza Pickrell, with whom he had one daughter.

Routt arrived in Colorado on 21 March 1875 and was inaugurated nine days later. Grant's expectation that Routt—as an outsider—might be able to unite the Republican party proved correct. During the state's constitutional convention of 1875–1876 Routt, although conservative on most issues, proved to be a strong advocate of woman suffrage, a view that was also shared by his new wife. His performance at the convention so impressed voters that he was elected as the new state's first chief executive despite not having even declared his candidacy for the position. While governor, Routt served as president of the state land board and managed, with the help of Congressional grants, to secure for the state some of the best land then available. His personal trip to the town of Creede helped prevent threatened violence by squatters who were contesting the state's land claims. He also took an active role in establishing the new state's credit, and he was successful enough that previously issued state warrants that had been selling at 75 percent of par showed continual appreciation; by the time Routt left office they were selling at 12 percent above par.

Despite his efforts on the part of the state, Routt, like many politicians of that era, had trouble distinguishing between public and private interests. He spent considerable time while in office operating his silver mine, the "Morning Star," to the detriment of his official duties. Perhaps realizing that his interests lay elsewhere, Routt declined renomination at the end of his term and turned to full-time mining and ranching. He reentered public life briefly during the mid-1880s when he served a single two-year term as mayor of Denver (1883–1885). Despite his lack of interest in the position, Colorado voters returned Routt to the governor's mansion for another two-year term in 1891. During his second stint in office Routt—who served on the Board of Capitol Managers from 1883 until 1898—oversaw the construction of the long-delayed state capitol building.

After leaving office in 1893, Routt—having been frustrated in his attempts to legalize woman suffrage as part of the state's constitution—lent his support to the Colorado Non-Partisan Equal Suffrage Association, a small group that succeeded in convincing state voters to approve passage of the issue in a referendum held that same year; his wife became the first registered female voter in the state. In his later years Routt traveled extensively in an attempt to shore up his declining health; he died in Denver. Routt County in Colorado is named in his honor.

Despite accomplishing little during his stints in public office, Routt is significant chiefly for his supporting role in the 1893 passage of woman suffrage that made the state the second in the Union to allow women to vote.

• Routt's papers are held at the Colorado State Archives in Denver, Colorado. Secondary information on his life and career is scarce. The best source is Albert B. Sanford, "J. L. Routt, First State Governor of Colorado," in *Colorado Magazine* 3 (1926), pp. 81–86. Additional information can be found in Carl Abbott, Stephen J. Leonard, and David G. McComb, *Colorado: A History of the Centennial State* (1982), and in Stephen J. Leonard and Thomas J. Noel, *Denver: Mining Camp to Metropolis* (1990). An obituary is in the *Denver Post*, 13 and 14 Aug. 1907.

EDWARD L. LACH, JR.

ROWAN, Carl T. (11 Aug. 1925–23 Sept. 2000), was born Carl Thomas Rowan in Ravenscroft, Tennessee, the son of Thomas David Rowan, a laborer, and Johnnie Bradford Rowan. The family moved to McMinnville, Tennessee, while Carl was still an infant. Carl and his four siblings grew up in a house lacking electricity and running water. His father often stacked lumber, earning twenty-five cents an hour, but the Rowans, like most black families in McMinnville, were poor.

Hunger was something Rowan faced on a daily basis. Often he took a box of salt, sat among the tomato plants that grew on the side of their house, and ate one hot tomato after another. The family also was plagued by rats, roaches, and other vermin. In 1933, as the children lay asleep on a pallet, Carl's sister was

bitten by a rat, a traumatic experience for young Carl. For fuel during the winter, Carl collected bark from the lumber mill and coal that had fallen off the trains.

Although his childhood was shadowed by the Great Depression, Rowan profited from his relationship with his English teacher, Bessie Taylor Gwynn, who advised him not to lower his standards to those of the crowd and to concentrate on improving his grammar. She also encouraged him to keep up with what was going on in the world. Rowan, who had no radio at home and could not afford a newspaper subscription, became a newsboy for the *Chattanooga Times*. The position gave him the opportunity to read the newspaper every day.

Rowan tripled his subscription list and turned out to be one of the star newsboys in his hometown. As a reward for their hard work, the circulation manager took the local newsboys for an outing in Chattanooga. But at dinner the manager of the restaurant insisted that Rowan eat in the kitchen because he was black. In 1942 Rowan graduated from Bernard High School as class president and valedictorian.

In the summer of 1942 Rowan enrolled in Tennessee State University (TSU) and also worked at a nearby tuberculosis hospital. At the end of his freshman year at TSU he joined the officer training program of the U.S. Navy and in 1944 became one of the first fifteen African Americans commissioned in the navy. After two years of training, he was assigned to the USS *Mattole*, then transferred to the USS *Chemung*, where he was given deputy command of the communications division. In 1946 he received an honorable discharge and returned to Tennessee. But when two highway patrol officers harassed him and called him "boy," Rowan resolved to leave Tennessee. In autumn 1946 he enrolled in Oberlin College in Ohio, and in 1947 he received his bachelor's degree in mathematics. He then attended the University of Minnesota, where he completed a master's degree in journalism in 1948.

Later that year, Rowan worked briefly for the *Baltimore Afro-American*. Then Gideon Seymour, executive editor of the *Minneapolis Tribune*, hired Rowan as a general reporter—not a reporter specializing in African-American news. On 2 August 1950 Rowan married Vivien Louise Murphy. They had three children. Approximately a year later Rowan felt compelled to write about what it felt like to be an African American in the South, and he persuaded his editor to send him on assignment there. His journey led him first to his home town of McMinnville, where distressingly little had changed. He traveled six thousand miles in six weeks, often putting his life on the line. Once he had to flee a bus station after he challenged a stationmaster in a "whites only" waiting area for refusing to accept his nickel for a newspaper. Rowan kept his camera hidden as much as possible, especially when interviewing those who remembered lynchings.

Rowan's visits to Tennessee, Georgia, Texas, Alabama, and Oklahoma led to eighteen articles in the *Minneapolis Tribune* in February and March 1951.

The articles became a journalistic sensation. *Time* magazine called them a "perceptive, well-written series on segregation and prejudice in the south as only a Negro could know them." *Editor and Publisher* proclaimed them "a significant, readable glimpse into the American race problem as only a Negro sees it." The Sydney Hillman Foundation awarded Rowan a $500 prize for the "best newspaper reporting in the nation."

Rowan proceeded to write on other aspects of race relations. In 1954 he won the Sigma Delta Chi Award for best national reporting for a series of articles on school desegregation. That year, the U.S. State Department sent him to India as a combination goodwill ambassador and educational lecturer. While in India, he wrote a series of articles that earned him Sigma Delta Chi's award for best foreign correspondent in 1955. Rowan received a third Sigma Chi Delta Award in 1956 for his reports on Asia and the Bandung Conference of 1955.

In 1955 Rowan again journeyed into the land of Jim Crow. This time he visited Montgomery, Alabama, the birthplace of the nonviolent philosophy of the civil rights movement. Blacks in Montgomery had organized a boycott of the city's bus system to encourage courteous treatment of blacks. Rowan interviewed Martin Luther King, Jr., Rosa Parks, and others and provided detailed coverage of the long boycott. Of Parks, Rowan wrote, "She said later that her action was spontaneous. Perhaps it was from tiredness, perhaps the resentment that is welling up high inside the new Negro was manifesting itself." Of King, he wrote, "A wave of anger and indignation rolled over the Negro community like a giant mushroom from a hydrogen bomb. But young Dr. King's philosophy of nonviolence did not waver." Because the boycott was costing the bus companies a great deal of money, the white establishment resorted to trickery to end it. Rowan's editor told him the Associated Press was reporting that the Montgomery bus boycott had ended. Suspicious, Rowan telephoned King and Fred Gray, the attorney involved, and discovered that the boycott leaders had not agreed to end the boycott. The report was part of a plot by bus officials to make blacks believe the boycott was over so they would start riding the city buses again. Rowan's hotline between Montgomery and Minneapolis had foiled the plot. The boycott went on for more than a year.

The Montgomery bus boycott led to Rowan's third book, *Go South to Sorrow* (1957). He dedicated the book to his children with the words: "May they never have to journey into this sadness."

In 1961 President John F. Kennedy appointed Rowan deputy assistant to the secretary of state. In 1963 Rowan became U.S. ambassador to Finland. President Kennedy told Rowan his job was to "help the Finns keep the faith and to cling to independence and freedom until that certain day came when the Kremlin would realize that it could not oppress its neighbors."

In 1964 President Lyndon B. Johnson summoned Rowan from Finland and appointed him director of the U.S. Information Agency to succeed the former CBS newsperson Edward R. Murrow. In that position Rowan directed Voice of America, which broadcast news and information about the United States to foreigners.

In 1965 Rowan returned to print journalism, writing three columns a week for the *Chicago Daily News*. His columns appeared in more than one hundred newspapers. In addition Westinghouse paid him $30,000 a year for television commentary. He wrote for *Readers Digest*, did a daily radio commentary, and became the first regular black panelist on a television talk show, *Agronsky and Company* (later *Inside Washington* with Gordon Peterson).

In 1997 Rowan received the National Association for the Advancement of Colored People (NAACP) Spingarn Medal, the organization's highest honor. He wrote his final column a week before his death in Washington, D.C. "Even though he was feeling sick, he said he had to go in and do the column," his son recalled.

• Rowan's papers are archived at Oberlin College. Rowan wrote an autobiography, *Breaking Barriers* (1991). Gladys Zehnpfennig, *Carl T. Rowan: Spokesman for Sanity* (1971), tells the story of his early years, to 1968. Barbara Matusow, "Visible Man," *Washingtonian* 30 (Fall 1995): 44–49, traces Rowan's career. J. Mendelsohn and Carl Rowan, "Second Start," *People Weekly*, Feb. 1998, pp. 117–18, chronicles the events leading to the amputation of Rowan's leg, which saved his life. An obituary is in the *New York Times*, 24 Sept. 2000.

LORRAINE FULLER

ROZELLE, Pete (1 Mar. 1926–6 Dec. 1996), professional football executive, was born Alvin Ray Rozelle in South Gate, California, a suburb of Los Angeles, the son of Raymond Foster Rozelle, a grocery store proprietor, and Hazel Viola Healey Rozelle. Nicknamed "Pete" at age five by an uncle, Rozelle showed an early interest in sports. He played basketball and tennis for Compton High School and took pride in noting that during a basketball practice his two front teeth were knocked out by Duke Snider, a high school teammate and later a Hall of Fame baseball player. Rozelle served in the U.S. Navy at the end of World War II. In 1946 he enrolled in Compton Junior College, where he became the college's athletic news director. That same year the Cleveland Rams of the National Football League (NFL) moved the team's franchise to Los Angeles and chose Compton College as the site of its training camp. Rozelle briefly worked for the Rams as assistant to the public relations director but soon left to complete his college education at the University of San Francisco. He graduated in 1950 and was hired as the university's athletic news director.

In 1952 Tex Schramm, general manager of the Rams, chose Rozelle as the team's public relations director. For three years the ambitious Rozelle gained valuable executive experience and made important contacts on the business side of professional sports. He then spent a year with the public relations firm of

P. K. Macker in San Francisco, where he represented Australian athletes during the 1956 Olympic Games. While he was in San Francisco, Rozelle married Jane Coupe; they had one child. In 1957, at the urging of NFL commissioner Bert Bell, Rozelle returned to Los Angeles and accepted the post of general manager of the strife-ridden Rams. Rozelle quickly displayed his natural talent for public relations by ending the turmoil within the Rams organization and greatly impressed its principal owner, Dan Reeves.

When the owners of the twelve NFL franchises gathered in Miami Beach for their annual meeting in January 1960, they faced serious challenges. Bell had died three months earlier, and the newly formed American Football League (AFL) was embarking on a destructive rivalry with the NFL for players and markets. The NFL's first order of business was to elect a new commissioner, but after acrimonious debates for more than a week, no one was chosen. Reeves suggested his unknown general manager as a risky compromise candidate, and on the twenty-third ballot Rozelle, at the age of thirty-three, was elected the NFL's sixth commissioner. During the long balloting, Rozelle, waiting in a hotel washroom, kept washing his hands to pass the time. He had to confess that he was "totally shocked because I was so young and because they'd considered so many other people who had so much more experience than I." And he later quipped to the owners, "I can honestly say I come to you with clean hands" (Kindred).

Rozelle moved NFL headquarters from Philadelphia to New York City and immediately began to revolutionize the central management of professional sports. He first convinced all NFL teams to pool revenues from television and advertising and to distribute them equally to all franchises. While large-market cities complained, the owners quickly saw this strategy as essential to the well-being of the league. It created parity, so even small-market teams had a real chance of winning. Rozelle, who called this collective approach "League Think," was the first sports commissioner to realize that a united sports league would be able to secure lucrative national television contracts. To exempt the NFL from antitrust laws, Rozelle successfully argued before Congress for the legalization of single-network national television, and in 1961 he negotiated a $4.65 million contract with CBS. Under Rozelle's bold leadership, NFL television revenues tripled to $14 million per year by 1964, and the popularity of professional football increased exponentially. He initiated Sunday doubleheader games, enforced television blackouts of local teams whose stadiums did not sell out, and created ancillary streams of income by selling a variety of merchandise with team logos through NFL Properties. He also established NFL Films and the NFL Hall of Fame, and he created valuable goodwill through NFL Charities. To solidify the commissioner's authority and to maintain the integrity of the league, Rozelle fined the venerable George Halas, owner coach of the Chicago Bears, for abusing officials in 1962, and the next year he suspended Paul

Hornung and Alex Karras, two of the NFL's brightest stars, for gambling. His League Think policy succeeded beyond the owners' wildest dreams, and professional football became big business, with Rozelle serving as the CEO.

By 1966 the AFL had become a viable league and posed a serious threat to the NFL's growing prosperity, forcing Rozelle to engineer another triumph that vaulted professional football into the forefront of American sports, in effect surpassing baseball as the national pastime. With Madison Avenue–slick precision, Rozelle managed the rival leagues into an amicable merger, resulting in immense profits for both factions. Of even more lasting significance was Rozelle's 1967 creation of the end-of-season game between the champions of the two leagues, soon named the Super Bowl. This game became the most popular single-day sporting event in the United States, eventually approaching the status of a national holiday.

Another Rozelle marketing masterstroke came in 1970, when he persuaded ABC to televise football on Monday evenings. The resulting *Monday Night Football* program changed America's prime-time viewing habits. Additional Rozelle innovations were instant replay, the expansion of the play-offs, and the sale of luxury boxes to wealthy corporate clients. The NFL became so popular by the late 1970s that cities desperate for a franchise pledged to build grand stadiums at public expense and made outrageously generous offers to induce teams to leave older venues. By 1980 the NFL had swelled to twenty-eight teams, professional football had become a billion-dollar brand-name industry of international proportions, and Rozelle seemingly could do no wrong.

Despite its huge revenue and influence, professional football encountered many problems. When Rozelle blocked the Oakland Raiders' move to Los Angeles, Al Davis, the Raiders' maverick owner, successfully sued the NFL, and the unpopular "franchise free agency" was born. Furthermore it was widely believed that Rozelle favored owners over players, who grew militant as salaries stagnated. The commissioner was forced to institute the "Rozelle Rule," which required teams signing a free agent to compensate the player's former team with high draft choices to be determined after the signing by the commissioner. This policy in effect ended free agency. Consequently, the players struck in 1982 and 1987, a salary cap was installed, and the Rozelle Rule was declared illegal in a suit brought by a group of players, which cost the league $13.65 million in damages. In addition to legal and labor troubles, the NFL was embarrassed by widespread steroid and recreational drug use among players. Two more new leagues formed, which further troubled the NFL in the courts and in the boardrooms.

The decision Rozelle most regretted allowed NFL games to be played on Sunday, 24 November 1963, two days after President John F. Kennedy was assassinated. Rozelle reluctantly made this decision after Pierre Salinger, the president's press secretary and

Rozelle's college friend, advised him to proceed with the schedule. The commissioner's office received a firestorm of criticism. Rozelle later admitted: "I was more than depressed over the assassination. I had lost someone whom I'd respected as the leader of the country, but I was also a close friend of the Kennedy family" (*Los Angeles Times*, 7 Dec. 1996).

On balance, during his nearly three decades as commissioner, Rozelle made many more good decisions than bad. He is best remembered as the father of the Super Bowl and *Monday Night Football*. But he considered his greatest achievements to be his skill in lobbying Congress to pass the Sports Broadcasting Act of 1961, which legalized the sale of television rights by the league rather than by individual franchises, and the Football Merger Act of 1966, which allowed the AFL to join the NFL, creating one of the most stable, competitive, and profitable leagues in the history of American sports. Rozelle brought football from the sports page to the business page, from daytime to prime time. Dave Kindred of *Sporting News* placed Rozelle's tenure as commissioner on his list of the five most significant developments of twentieth-century sports. Rozelle was elected to the Hall of Fame in 1985, while he was still in office. Despite this honor, he was growing increasingly weary of the constant lawsuits, strikes, unsanctioned franchise moves, bitter rivalries of upstart leagues, and difficulties of mollifying twenty-eight diverse egos as ownership became more independent and combative. In 1989 he resigned and was universally praised as the premier commissioner of all of professional sports. The award for the most valuable player in the Super Bowl was named in his honor, and another Pete Rozelle award was created to recognize exceptional contributions to professional football on radio and television. In an in- credible coincidence, both Rozelle and his second wife, Carrie Cooke, developed brain tumors in 1993. When Rozelle died of brain cancer in Rancho Santa Fe, California, Wellington Mara, the owner of the New York Giants, said, "He'll be forever remembered as the standard by which all sports executives are judged" (*Los Angeles Times*, 7 Dec. 1996).

• Rozelle wrote the foreword to *My Sunday Best* (1972) by George Herbert Allen and the introductions to *The Encyclopedia of Football* (1977) and *The Super Bowl* (1991). A candid interview with Rozelle is in *Playboy*, Oct. 1973. David Harris, *The League: The Rise and Decline of the NFL* (1986), is a fascinating exposé of business, legal, and labor issues in the NFL that heavily details Rozelle's role on the nonfootball side of the league's management. See also Jerry Green, *The Super Bowl Chronicles* (1992), and Dave Kindred, "Most Significant Developments This Century," *Sporting News*, 21 Apr. 1999. Rozelle was named Sportsman of the Year in a cover story by Kenneth Rudeen in *Sports Illustrated*, 6 Jan. 1964. *Time* named Rozelle one of the most important people of the twentieth century in its "TIME 100" edition, 7 Dec. 1998; see the article by Michael Lewis. Paul Attner, "The Power of Persuasion (Pete Rozelle)," *Sporting News*, 20 Dec. 1999, also ranks Rozelle as one of the twentieth century's most powerful persons in sports. Other articles of note include Paul Zimmerman, "He Quit, For Pete's Sake," *Sports Illustrated*, 3 Apr. 1989, and Peter King, "Pete Rozelle Had It All Figured Out," *Sports Illustrated*, 19 Sept. 1994. Rozelle is featured in the ESPN Classic Sports Century Biography series "Rozelle Made the NFL What It Is Today" by Bob Carter. Rozelle is also mentioned in many business-related publications. See David Lidsky, "This Is NFL Films," *Fortune*, 4 Aug. 1986; Brendan Koerner, "When the Super Bowl Wasn't So Super," *US News and World Report*, 27 Dec. 1999; and "CBS, NBC Share First Super Bowl," *Advertising Age*, 13 Dec. 1999. Obituaries are in the *Los Angeles Times*, 7 Dec. 1996; the *New York Times*, 7 Dec. 1996; and *Sporting News*, 16 Dec. 1996.

Bruce L. Janoff

S

SALVEMINI, Gaetano (8 Sept. 1873–6 Sept. 1957), historian and anti-Fascist activist, was born in the southern Italian town of Molfetta (Apulia, Bari province) in an extended family of small farmers and fishermen. He was the son of Ilarione Salvemini, a member of the *carabinieri* (national police force) and part-time teacher; and Emanuela Turtur Salvemini, who read to her son extensively. Both parents nurtured Gaetano in the politics of the Italian left; Ilarione had fought as a volunteer with Giuseppe Garibaldi's Red Shirts in their campaign to liberate the Italian South from the Spanish Bourbons as part of the Risorgimento (unification movement). Acutely aware of the poverty of his family and friends, the young Salvemini came to attribute the "Southern Problem" (the vast regional inequality) to conscious exploitation of the region by the Piedmontese dynasty and the ruling class of northern politicians and businessmen with whom they had allied. Consequently he embraced the prosouthern (*meridionalista*) views of local radical parliamentarian Matteo Imbriani and would later emerge as a major voice for the Italian South (Mezzogiorno).

Despite the stifling constraints of a childhood spent in this small southern town, Salvemini found intellectual stimulation in books, particularly the romantic novels of Jules Verne, the clarity of Euclidian geometry, and the tutelage of a liberal priest who taught the young student history and critical analysis and introduced him to the works of the literary historian Francesco De Sanctis.

A scholarship to the University of Florence thrust the seventeen-year-old into a milieu that afforded him both a profession and a refuge from life's perils. His professors immersed him in a wider, secular world whose influences ranged from classical philosophy through nineteenth-century economic liberalism to the contemporary currents of positivism and scientific objectivism. His fellow students, most from the northern and central Italian middle and upper classes, engaged him in extensive dialogues on political and social theory. Among the most popular sources for discussion were writers who shaped his ideas: the democratic federalist Carlo Cattaneo, the Marxist Antonio Labriola, and contributors to Filippo Turati's journal, *Critica Sociale*. It was also in Florence—in the "Little Apulia" neighborhood—that he met his future wife, Maria Minervini.

In 1894, after completing his degree, Salvemini began the pursuit of what would become a long and distinguished career in teaching, historical scholarship, and political commentary in both Italy and the United States. After a frustrating few years in secondary schools, he published a version of his thesis, *Magnati e popolani a Firenze dal 1280 al 1295*, a social-economic examination of thirteenth-century Florence. He was then hired in 1901 as professor of medieval and modern history at the University of Messina. While on the faculty at the university, Salvemini suffered a terrible tragedy from which he never fully recovered. The devastating earthquake of 1908 buried his wife and five children before his eyes while he clung desperately to a window support that saved his life. He managed to endure by plunging relentlessly into his work; eight years later, he married again (Fernande Dauriac Luchaire of Brest, France) and accepted a position at the University of Florence, where he taught for a decade.

In the years before World War I, Salvemini's political thought evolved from socialism to a unique construct of pragmatic inquiry that he called *concretismo*, forged from a fusion of secular values derived from the Enlightenment, liberalism, and socialism and tempered by his own political experience as a poor southerner. He thus aligned himself with Luigi Einaudi—in opposition to both Benedetto Croce and Antonio Gramsci—among influential twentieth-century Italian empiricist thinkers who rejected abstract philosophy in favor of inductive analysis.

A member of the Socialist party for seventeen years, Salvemini resigned in 1910 in protest against the party's refusal to endorse universal suffrage and to oppose the Libyan War. Thereafter, he followed a path of resolute independence that rejected all formal party structures. In 1911, Salvemini founded the important radical journal *L'Unità* in which he regularly assailed the government of five-time prime minister Giovanni Giolitti, whom he labeled "il ministro della malavita" ("minister of the underworld"). Later, in light of the severity of Fascist repression, he would reach a more favorable assessment of Giolitti, parallel to that of A. William Salomone's *Italian Democracy in the Making* (1946).

During the divisive debate over Italian neutrality in World War I, Salvemini led the democratic interventionist campaign—along with Leonida Bissolati and others—in support of democratic principles and national self-determination. At the war's end, Salvemini won election to the Chamber of Deputies as an independent candidate on the veterans' ticket. In his only term in parliament, he supported the internationalist program of Woodrow Wilson, while continuing his rhetorical barrage against the Italian nationalists and the foreign policies of Sidney Sonnino.

While visiting Paris in the fall of 1922, Salvemini was stunned by the news of the Fascist March on

Rome. Already an opponent of Mussolini, Salvemini did not initiate his anti-Fascist campaign until 1924, when Socialist deputy Giacomo Matteotti was murdered by Fascist thugs. With faculty and students at the University of Florence, Salvemini founded the Circolo di Cultura, which quickly established itself as the nucleus of Florentine anti-Fascism. When Fascist police raided the Circolo office, Salvemini—with Piero Calamandrei, Carlo and Nello Rosselli, and Ernesto Rossi—launched *Non Mollare*, an anti-Fascist underground publication, which led to his arrest. In August 1925, Salvemini, after being released from prison on a technicality, escaped across the border to France to begin two decades of political exile.

Salvemini spent the early years of exile in England and France, lecturing, writing, and organizing, most significantly the anti-Fascist group *Giustizia e Libertà* (Justice and Liberty). In the process, he came to view the United States as a crucial player in any effort to counter Mussolini and to shape a post-Fascist state. In 1934, Harvard University awarded Salvemini the Lauro de Bosis chair in the history of Italian civilization, a position that enabled him to teach at Harvard through the end of 1948. While in exile, Salvemini published countless articles and a series of books that focused on the Fascist regime: *The Fascist Dictatorship in Italy* (1927); *Mussolini diplomate* (1932), in French (published in Italian as *Mussolini diplomatico*); *Under the Axe of Fascism* (1936); and (with Giorgio La Piana) *What to Do with Italy* (1943), in which Salvemini vehemently opposed any role of the Church or the monarchy in postwar Italy. In exposing the Fascist regime to intense scrutiny, these books have been viewed as a fusion of history and polemic; in response, he readily admitted that, like all writing, his work was "carpeted with biases." While teaching and writing, Salvemini led the American anti-Fascist movement, launching the Mazzini Society in New York in 1939 and working tirelessly to convince U.S. authorities to investigate American Fascist organizations. (He became a naturalized U.S. citizen in 1940.)

In 1949 Salvemini responded to pleas from numerous friends to resume his Italian career and join them in molding the new Italian republic. He returned to Italy to spend his final years, first at the University of Florence, then among friends at a villa in Capo di Sorrento, where he died. Salvemini remains a major anti-Fascist figure and a historian whose work influenced the study of Italy both in the United States and in Europe.

• Among the most important manuscript collections are those housed at the Istituto Storico per la Resistenza in Toscana (Florence). There are several indispensable sources for any study of Salvemini, including his own published works and correspondence. Most important are his *Opere*, 19 vols. (Milan, 1961–1974), and his many books. Several biographical studies exist: Massimo L. Salvadori, *Gaetano Salvemini* (Turin, 1963); Enzo Tagliacozzo, *Gaetano Salvemini: Un profilo biografico* (Rome, 1963); and Charles Killinger, *Gaetano Salvemini, A Biography* (Praeger, 2002). The definitive catalogue of works by and about Salvemini is Michele Can-

tarella, ed., *Bibliografia salveminiana, 1892–1984* (Rome, 1986). An obituary appeared in the *New York Times*, 7 Sept. 1957.

CHARLES KILLINGER

SAPIRO, Aaron (5 Feb. 1884–23 Nov. 1959), lawyer, was born in San Francisco, the son of Jacob Sapiro, a peddler, and Selina Wasserwitz Sapiro. When Aaron was nine years old, his father was killed in a streetcar accident, leaving Aaron's mother to care for seven young children. After wealthy relatives refused to help, Sapiro's mother placed four of the children in San Francisco's Pacific Hebrew Asylum, where Aaron lived until he graduated from Lowell High School in 1900. Recognizing his intellectual and oratorical gifts, the orphanage sent him to Hebrew Union College in Cincinnati to study for the rabbinate. Simultaneously Sapiro attended the University of Cincinnati, graduating Phi Beta Kappa in 1904 and earning an M.A. in history the following year. While he was teaching a children's Bible class in a Stockton, California, synagogue one summer, Sapiro met Michael Arndt, a prominent clothing store owner, and his wife Rose Arndt. The Arndts took more than a passing interest in the serious seminarian. After hearing him preach, Rose Arndt decided that Sapiro should become a lawyer. She bailed him out of the seminary with a substantial contribution and sent him to the University of California in San Francisco (Hastings College of the Law), from which he graduated in 1911. Two years later Sapiro married the Arndts' younger child (and his former Bible school pupil) Janet Arndt. They had four children.

In 1911 Sapiro began his legal career with the California Bureau of Industrial Relations, where he rewrote the state's workers' compensation statute. His interests in social welfare and economics brought him to the attention of David Lubin and Harris Weinstock, half brothers, wealthy Sacramento merchants, and farmers who began careers in public service after 1900. Lubin and Weinstock took on Sapiro as their protégé and instilled in him their belief that world peace and national prosperity could only be secured through agricultural prosperity. Under their tutelage Sapiro studied the history and philosophy of agricultural cooperation, particularly the nineteenth-century European and American innovations that had begun to change the way California fruit growers marketed crops. These new organizations combined the legal powers of industrial trusts and the economic powers of monopolies to enable growers to control processing, brand names, and advertising. In 1915, when Weinstock became chair of the California State Bureau of Markets, Sapiro joined him as legal counsel. Weinstock and Sapiro thought that government should not merely funnel information to producers; instead, government should actively participate in markets to make them not only efficient but also fair. Sapiro organized more than two dozen cooperatives all over the state, following the models established by the organizations selling Sunkist citrus, Sun-Maid raisins, and Blue Diamond almonds.

Sapiro's fame as a cooperative organizer spread across the country. After trying in vain to join the army officers' corps in 1918, he left state employment and moved his law office to Chicago. From there he launched an impressive bid to lead the national cooperative movement, giving long orations to cotton and tobacco growers in the South and providing consultation and advice to the American Farm Bureau Federation, several secretaries of agriculture, and the U.S. Department of Agriculture. He oversaw the organization of dozens of cooperatives in the major staple crops, which required the coordination of thousands of farmers across many states under long-term contracts. Of more lasting significance, Sapiro wrote a model law granting cooperatives immunity from antitrust prosecution, and by 1926 thirty-eight states had enacted the law. When it was challenged in the courts, Sapiro personally argued the case before the U.S. Supreme Court, which in 1928 upheld the law unanimously. Thus Sapiro could boldly claim monopoly to be the farmers' right: "Only the farmer can have a complete [and] unlimited monopoly and still be in any measure within the law" (Woeste, 1998, p. 198). Stunning as these achievements were, they could not change the economic facts of agricultural life during the 1920s: overproduction and low prices. When some of the crown jewels of Sapiro's cooperative movement collapsed under the pressure of the continued postwar recession, he came under attack. His unyielding insistence on his model in all its particulars, some traditionalists complained, caused the cooperative movement's spectacular failures.

That sort of critique became widespread by about mid-decade, but Henry Ford's anti-Semitic newspaper gave an aura of legitimacy to it that went beyond rational debate. In 1924 Ford's *Dearborn Independent* ran a series of articles attacking every cooperative Sapiro had organized—and some with which he had no connection whatever—as a fraudulent scheme. Ford's editor insisted that the automaker's aim was merely to assist the nation's farmers by pointing out the flaws in Sapiro's approach, but the newspaper's anti-Semitic bias was plain to its readers. The paper accused Sapiro of standing at the head of a worldwide conspiracy of Jews whose aim was to enslave American farmers and redirect their profits to Jewish speculators, financiers, and Bolshevists. The paper also accused Sapiro of legal malpractice and misrepresentation. Sapiro promptly filed a $1 million libel lawsuit in Detroit's federal court, a lawsuit Ford first invited and then ignored. In March 1927 the case finally came to trial. By then it had become a David versus Goliath marquee event. The drama climaxed when Ford was reportedly involved in a car accident and thus was unable to testify. Ford settled the case out of court with an apology that neglected to mention Sapiro's name and a settlement check that did not fully reimburse Sapiro for his expenses. The halfhearted apology— Ford claimed to have no knowledge of what appeared in his newspaper—inspired widespread ridicule. Nonetheless Sapiro proclaimed his satisfaction with the outcome: "I begin again in ruins but confident that I have vindicated the faith of my wife and my mother in me as a Jew" (Sapiro, 1982, p. 84).

The hero's status that the resolution to the Ford libel case conferred did not last long. In 1928 Sapiro moved to New York and began the next phase of his legal career. Convinced that individual entrepreneurs were increasingly disadvantaged in a marketplace fraught with intense competition, fluctuating prices, and monopolistic combinations, he began to represent labor and small trade groups. He formed associations of taxicab drivers, dry cleaners, milkmen, and motion-picture exhibitors, serving a variety of similar clients in major cities, simultaneously or in quick succession, a pattern that characterized the rest of his career. But mistakes in judgment led to disastrous outcomes. His association with the launderers' and dyers' industries in Chicago led to his 1933 indictment with Al Capone and twenty-two others on charges of racketeering. Though all defendants were acquitted, the episode tarred Sapiro's name. A second ignominy followed the conviction of a client on mail fraud charges in New York in 1934; the disgruntled client accused Sapiro and an associate of jury tampering. Certain he had done nothing wrong, Sapiro successfully fought his criminal prosecution, but he could not fend off the enmity of the state bar association, which disbarred him in 1937. Federal disbarment followed in 1941. During the disbarment proceeding, Sapiro's wife underwent surgery for breast cancer and died in 1936.

After his wife's death, Sapiro moved back to California, where he continued to serve clients in maritime labor unions and the movie industry among others. For a time he worked with Harry Bridges, an alleged Communist and rising star within the Congress of Industrial Organizations (CIO). Bridges's covert Communism and high-handed and dismissive attitude toward other labor leaders angered and alienated Sapiro. In 1939, when the federal government sought to deport Bridges, Sapiro testified against him. The government lost its case; moreover, James M. Landis, the federal trial examiner, citing Sapiro's New York disbarment, pronounced his testimony uncredible. The end of Sapiro's work in the maritime labor movement also marked the end of his career as a lawyer in public service. For the next two decades he practiced law quietly in Los Angeles, representing John Barrymore and Igor Stravinsky in domestic and contractual matters. In his last years Sapiro suffered horribly from arthritis and was unable to write with anything other than an enormous pencil. He was briefly married to Dixie Saper, a nurse who cared for him in his last years; they divorced shortly before his death in Los Angeles. At his request, his body was donated to the University of California–Los Angeles for arthritis research.

• Some of Sapiro's letters are in the collections of prominent Americans from the period, including Herbert Hoover, Hoover Presidential Library; Lewis Lichtenstein Strauss, American Jewish Historical Society, New York City; Louis Marshall, American Jewish Archives, Cincinnati; James R. Howard, Iowa State University; Herman Bernstein, YIVO Institute for Jewish Research, New York City; and the U.S. Department of Agriculture, National Archives, College Park, Md. A sample of his writing on agricultural cooperation is Aaron Sapiro, "The Law of Cooperative Marketing Associations," *Kentucky Law Journal* 15 (1926): 1–21. For his perspective on the Ford lawsuit, see Sapiro, "An Experience with American Justice," *Free Synagogue Pulpit* 8, no. 5 (1927–1928): 3–40; and Sapiro, "A Retrospective View of the Aaron Sapiro–Henry Ford Case," *Western States Jewish Historical Quarterly* 15, no. 1 (1982): 79–84. A good historical overview of Sapiro's work is Grace Larsen and Henry E. Erdman, "Aaron Sapiro: Genius of Farm Co-operative Promotion," *Mississippi Valley Historical Review* 49, no. 2 (Sept. 1962): 242–68. A reassessment of his work in the law of agricultural cooperation is in Victoria Saker Woeste, *The Farmer's Benevolent Trust: Law and Agricultural Cooperation in Industrial America* (1998). Obituaries are in the *New York Times*, 25 Nov. 1959, and the *Los Angeles Times*, 25 Nov. 1959.

VICTORIA SAKER WOESTE

SAPOSS, David J. (22 Feb. 1886–13 Nov. 1968), labor historian and economist, was born in Kiev, Russia, the son of Isaac Saposnik, a peddler of goods, and Shima Erevsky Saposnik. In 1895, the Saposnik family moved to the United States and shortened its name to Saposs. In 1900, after completion of the fifth grade, Saposs left school and held a variety of jobs in the Milwaukee area, including newsboy and worker at the Blatz and Schlitz breweries. In 1906, he was elected shop steward for the Brewery Workers' Union.

Although lacking a high school diploma, Saposs in 1907 gained admission to the University of Wisconsin. He helped pay his way through college by working as a stenographer in night court in Madison. He majored in economics and in 1911 received his degree. In 1913, as a graduate student at Wisconsin, he became a research assistant to famed labor historian John R. Commons and published a chapter, "Colonial and Federal Beginnings to 1827," in Commons's classic four-volume work *A History of Labour in the United States* (1918).

On 3 July 1917, at age thirty-one, Saposs married the University of Chicago-educated social worker Bertha Tigay. They had two daughters.

From 1917 to 1922, he served in numerous investigative and educational capacities: expert in charge of accident prevention and industrial service for the New York Department of Labor; investigator of immigrant workers and trade unions for the Americanization Study for the Carnegie Corporation; investigator for the Inquiry into the Steel Strike of 1919, sponsored by the Inter-church World Movement Commission; and educational director of the Amalgamated Clothing Workers. For two years, Saposs also worked as codirector of the Labor Bureau, Inc., providing pertinent economic information to various labor organizations. He was both a student and an ardent supporter of the American labor movement.

In 1922, Saposs accepted a position as instructor at the newly established Brookwood Labor College in Katonah, New York. Brookwood, the nation's most noted residential labor college for union workers, was part of the post–World War I workers' education movement. The college sought to train union organizers. Saposs's examination of the strategies employed by radicals in their labor union activities resulted in the publication of *Left-Wing Unionism* (1926)—a popular work that provided "insight into the sophisticated means of radical political warfare that had been developed in the American labor movement" (biographical sketch of David Saposs prepared by the State Historical Society of Wisconsin, Saposs Papers, Box 1, Fl 1)—as well as *Readings in Trade Unionism* (1926; repr. 1969). A reviewer for the *New York Times Book Review* commented that *Left-Wing Unionism* "has wielded a scalpel on an intricate tangle of economic tissues and psychological cells" (quoted in *New York Times* obituary, 16 Nov. 1968).

While at Brookwood, Saposs taught classes in labor history, trade union organization, and economics. He considered industrial unionism as the key issue between radicals and nonradicals in the labor movement. In his teachings and publications, Saposs noted the effectiveness of prewar socialist-led unions in organizing workers from the noncraft trades. The establishment of rival organizations—those that challenged the traditional hierarchy of craft unionism—grew out of the socialist and anarchist activities of the nineteenth century. He examined closely the issues of dual unionism. He insisted that the intense activity of insurgency can spur conservative labor elements into organizing more workers, which would bode well for the entire labor movement. He respected both radical and conservative viewpoints but consistently maintained a nonpartisan, factual position.

During his early tenure at the labor college, Saposs took graduate courses in history and economics at Columbia University. He studied under the noted European historian Carlton J. H. Hayes. Between 1926 and 1928, he took a sabbatical from Brookwood and resided in France, where he headed the Labor Division of Columbia's Social and Economic Study of Post-War France. This led to his scholarly study titled *Labor Movement in Post-War France* (1931). The work noted how the postwar growth of labor's political power enabled it to champion social reform while throwing in its lot with middle-class liberals and other democratic groups in support of democracy and republicanism. Upon his return to Brookwood, Saposs assumed the editorship of the Brookwood Labor College Pamphlets. The pamphlets were an attempt to provide a means for more prolabor literature in a decade marked by intolerance and xenophobia. Saposs contributed to the series with *American Labor History* and coauthored with Katherine H. Pollak *How Should Labor Vote?* (1932).

When Saposs was about to resume his teaching duties, Brookwood's long-standing feud with the AFL reached epidemic proportions. Although Saposs maintained a scholarly, nonpartisan approach to labor issues, Brookwood's support for the organization of unskilled workers in the mass production industries and flirtation with socialist theories aroused the ire of AFL leaders. AFL president William Green expressed dismay at the college's public criticisms of craft unionism. Green ordered his vice president, Matthew Woll, to investigate Brookwood's teachings. One particular incident was quickly used to discredit the college. On 17 April 1928, Brookwood students decorated the college with Samuel Gompers's picture draped in red and placed in a group consisting of Karl Marx, V. I. Lenin, Eugene Debs, Leon Trotsky, and Rosa Luxemburg. Woll reported to the AFL Executive Council that Brookwood's curriculum was propagandistic, communistic, and represented a basic threat to the principles of the AFL. At its annual meeting, the Executive Council suspended Brookwood's charter and ordered its affiliates to withdraw students and financial support. Ironically, Brookwood gained greater prominence within progressive labor circles as a result of the condemnation.

In 1933, however, a serious split took place among the faculty. A minority faction, led by famous pacifist minister and Dean of the College A. J. Muste, favored Brookwood's association with the Conference for Progressive Labor Action. CPLA advanced the idea of a labor party promoting a planned economy under workers' control and social ownership of national resources. Saposs, along with the majority faction, fought to maintain Brookwood's nonpartisan position in labor struggles and to concentrate only on union issues. The split was so bitter that in February Muste resigned. At the end of the academic year, Saposs accepted a one-year position as senior research associate at the Twentieth Century Fund. In 1936 he published *Labor and Government*, and in 1938 *Collective Bargaining, Today and Tomorrow*.

Saposs served as chief economist and head of the research division of the National Labor Relations Board from 1935 to 1940. By the end of the decade, he spent considerable time fending off challenges that he was a Communist. In March 1940, charges were made that a majority of members on the board "continue brazenly and openly to foster Communists and kindred radicals as they have done in the past" (quoted in *Current Biography*, 1940). Members of the House Un-American Activities Committee investigated Saposs's writings and past affiliation at Brookwood. The committee recommended the abolition of appropriations for the research division. Saposs's defenders argued, "What the NLRB foes really sought was abolition of Economist Saposs," who "though often denounced as a Communist, is neither Red nor useless, but a zealous watchdog of labor rights" (quoted in *Current Biography*, 1940). The bureau was abolished on 11 October 1940. His work on the board had served as "an integral part of the New Deal's efforts to better the status of the American workers" (biographical sketch of David Saposs, prepared by the State Historical Society of Wisconsin, Saposs Papers, Box 1, Fl 1).

During and after World War II, Saposs worked in a number of government positions. Between 1940 and 1946, he served as labor consultant to Nelson A. Rockefeller in his position as U.S. coordinator of inter-American affairs and chief, Reports and Statistics Office, Manpower Division, U.S. Office of Military Government for Germany. Until his retirement from government service in 1954, Saposs also served as special assistant to the commissioner of labor statistics for the Department of Labor and special advisor to the director of the European Labor Division of the U.S. Economic Cooperation Administration. Known internationally "as a walking encyclopedia of labor-related information," his career in government service was devoted to economic issues and labor activities. His primary objective had always been to support the rights of workers and advance their economic opportunities. Ideologically, he insisted that a strong union movement depended upon government support.

After 1954, Saposs confined his efforts to scholarly publishing and teaching. Despite his own unpleasant encounter with HUAC, he was a consistent critic of Communist attempts to infiltrate American society. He published two widely read works critical of communism: *Communism in American Unions* (1959) and *Communism in American Politics* (1960). His fifty years as a thoughtful observer of Communist attempts to attain political power through trade unions, united fronts, and various radical and liberal elements led to his warning that although the Communist movement may have changed its tactics, its basic philosophy remained the same: domination of the world. Communism, Saposs observed, "continues to operate as a vassal of a foreign power and is part of an international conspiratorial movement" (quoted in Saposs, *Communism in American Politics*, p. 229). Within the labor movement, moreover, Communists had consistently concentrated "on siding with dissident elements in the unions, instigating discontent, subtly planting and circulating rumors, and even resorting to other means of discrediting the current leadership. In this manner they hope to rise to leadership and power" (quoted in Saposs, *Communism in American Unions*, p. 268). He also wrote *National Labor Movements in the Post-War World* (1963), based largely on his work in the European Labor Division and as lecturer on American and international labor for the U.S. Department of State, and *Case Studies in Labor Ideology* (3 vols., 1964–1971). From 1954 to 1956, Saposs was a Senior Research Associate at Harvard's Littauer Center; in 1957–1958, he was visiting professor, Institute of Labor and Industrial Relations, University of Illinois; in 1962 and 1964, he served as senior specialist, East-West Center, University of Hawaii; and from 1959 to 1965, he was professor of American and international labor at American University. His teachings, free of ideological partisanship, reflected the practical application of his own involvement and support for labor unionism throughout the first half of the twentieth century.

From 1913 to 1968, Saposs published fourteen books and numerous articles, pamphlets, and reports concerning U.S. and international labor, socialism, and communism. Known throughout the scholarly world as "Mr. Labor History," Saposs died of a stroke in his home in Washington, D.C.

• The David J. Saposs Papers in the State Historical Society of Wisconsin comprises the richest repository of information. The collection houses thirty-four boxes of biographical materials, general correspondence, writings and speeches, drafts of published manuscripts, and teaching curriculums. Saposs's most important publications detailing his views on labor radicalism, industrial movements at home and abroad, and Communist activities in labor and politics include *Left-Wing Unionism* (1926; repr. 1967); *The Labor Movement in Post-War France* (1931; repr. 1972); *Communism in American Unions* (1959; repr. 1976), and *Communism in American Politics* (1960). Sketches of Saposs's career, particularly his role in the interwar workers' education movement, can be gleaned from the following sources: James O. Morris, *Conflict within the AFL: A Study of Craft versus Industrial Unionism* (1958); Richard J. Altenbaugh, *Education for Struggle: The American Labor Colleges of the 1920s and 1930s* (1990); Charles F. Howlett, *Brookwood Labor College and the Struggle for Peace and Social Justice in America* (1993); and Jo Ann O. Robinson, *Abraham Went Out: A Biography of A. J. Muste* (1981). A conference honoring Saposs was held at the University of Wisconsin, Jan. 14–15, 1966. It was sponsored by the Industrial Relations Research Institute, Department of Economics, and the Wisconsin State Historical Society. Papers from this conference were edited by Jack Barbash, *The Labor Movement: A Re-examination* (1967). An obituary appears in the *New York Times*, 16 Nov. 1968.

CHARLES F. HOWLETT

SARAZEN, Gene (27 Feb. 1902–13 May 1999), professional golfer, was born Eugene Saracini in Harrison, New York, the son of Italian immigrants Federico Saracini, a carpenter, and Adela Saracini. At age eight, Sarazen began working as a golf caddy at the Larchmont Country Club in Harrison. At eleven he was carrying clubs at the Apawamis Golf Club about four miles from Harrison; there occasionally he had the opportunity to play the course. As the United States entered World War I, he left school to hammer nails for his father and other carpenters building barracks at nearby Fort Slocum. Later he attributed his wrist strength to the hammering. At completion of the construction, his father moved the family to Bridgeport, Connecticut, where Federico worked in an artillery factory and his son worked in the Remington Arms plant. Sarazen soon contracted pneumonia. When his physician recommended that he find employment outdoors, Sarazen resolved to take up a career in golf. Recuperating, he began to practice and play at Beardsley Park, the local public course. Incredibly, he and the local professional, playing together, each holed their tee shots on the same par-three hole. He was pleased to read about the feat in the local newspaper but disliked the appearance of his

name in print; Saracini was too long, and Eugene was more suitable for a violinist. He wanted a "crisp" name coming off the tongue like Chick Evans or Jim Barnes, two luminaries in golf, and reduced his name simply and firmly to Gene Sarazen.

Late in 1919 Sarazen began his career in an earnest but lowly way, attending to members' clubs and sweeping the pro shop at the Brooklawn Golf Club near Bridgeport. He honed his game there and won some "money matches" and $50 in a pro-amateur tourney at the Metacomet Golf Club in Providence. Then he joined the tail end of the winter tour, winning $75 in a tournament at Augusta, Georgia. Through a friendship made on the tour, he obtained a position as the assistant pro at the Fort Wayne (Indiana) Country Club; from there he moved to the Titusville (Pennsylvania) Golf Club as the head pro. While at the clubs, he played twice in the National Open, finishing thirtieth in 1920, and twenty-two strokes behind the winner in 1921. In 1921, for the first time he played with Bobby Jones, soon to become the nation's leading golfer.

Sarazen first gained some national repute in the winter tour of 1922. He won the Southern Open at New Orleans—the purse was $1,000—and finished in the top ten in ten of the thirteen tournaments. A fellow pro asserted that he was the "most promising player I have ever seen." Standing but five feet, five inches tall, with an olive-complexion, often sporting a red sweater and colorful tie and always wearing knickers, he cut a striking figure striding down a fairway. With the side of his left wrist and left hand in an interlocking grip leading his compact swing, he shoved his left side firmly forward, his drives consistently straight and long at 240 and 250 yards when he was on his game. Congenial and optimistic, he quickly caught on with galleries.

Sarazen realized the promise of his winter tour the following summer. Moving as head pro to the Highland Country Club in Pittsburgh after the tour, he practiced intensively, his contract with the club exempting him from giving lessons. He played at the Skokie Country Club in Glenview, Illinois, a month before the National Open. Practice did not make perfect, but it did suffice. Though he fell four strokes behind the leader after the third round, he rallied and won by two strokes. A few weeks later, he played in the PGA tournament at the Oakmont Country Club near Pittsburgh, a course he knew well. He detected an "anti-Sarazen attitude" there. It derived, he believed, from the "older British school" that resented his "unblushing" remarks about his abilities; he also arrived late for his first match, which some observers mistakenly took as the act of a prima donna when actually his train had been delayed. But he won the championship, defeating in one match Jock Hutchinson, the fine Scottish golfer who had become an American citizen, and winning the final match 4 and 3 against Emmett French, a burly homegrown pro.

Now Sarazen had emerged as a serious rival to Walter Hagen. At the clamoring of their supporters, the golfers agreed to play a seventy-two-hole match for the "World's Golf Championship." In a match played on two courses, Sarazen prevailed. In the ensuing years, they sustained a spirited but friendly rivalry. Hagen believed that he could "rattle" Sarazen by showing up late for matches; Sarazen thought that he was able to deflect manipulation by Hagen, notably his persistent attempts to mislead opponents into the use of the wrong club. In 1923 Sarazen defeated Hagen in the PGA tournament at the Pelham Country Club in New York, edging him one up in thirty-eight holes. Hagen gained a measure of revenge in 1927, defeating Sarazen in a seventy-two hole match in Coral Gables.

After his victories in the National Open and PGA tournaments, Sarazen had a fistful of endorsements for balls and clubs, among them one with the Wilson Sporting Goods Company that lasted seventy-six years. He played in numerous exhibition matches and organized a correspondence school in golf. Capitalizing on his new reputation and a smiling personality, he went to Hollywood to make a short film with comedian Buster Keaton. In 1924 he married Mary Catherine Henry, whom he had met in Hollywood in 1923; they soon had two children. Their marriage lasted until her death in 1986.

For a few years after 1923 Sarazen acknowledged that his golf game "deteriorated enormously." No longer a contender for the major titles, he could not even claim a minor victory. He attributed his decline to his grip, which caused him to hook his balls out-of-bounds. Herbert Warren Wind, the noted golf writer, claimed that Sarazen's obsession to improve his swing sabotaged his excellent "natural" swing. Sarazen gradually corrected his grip, and at Ty Cobb's suggestion he began using a driver twice as heavy as his usual one. Using it, he strengthened his grip, which he insisted had to control the club at the top of the swing, and grooved his arc. By 1928 he had recovered his stroke. From 1928 through 1931 he won fourteen titles, among them the Western Open. He was also a runner-up in the British Open (1928) and the PGA tournament (1931). But in the major championships, the ones that "really count," he said, he was "always behind the winner."

As the season of 1932 approached, Sarazen sought to strengthen his sand trap play. To that end he worked in a small machine shop and fashioned out of a niblick a new club with a heavy-soled flange that permitted him to strike down on the ball and drive it up. With his sand wedge, which became a standard club for all players, he was soon an excellent trap player.

At the 1932 British Open, Sarazen led almost from the first hole and won, his 283 the lowest score since the British had initiated the seventy-two hole tourney in 1892. After the second round, the golf correspondent for the *London Times* declared that Sarazen "made the game and the course look childishly easy. Every hole was the same—a vast drive, an iron shot of sorts to within seven or eight yards of the flag, and

a putt that shivered past the hole to finish one foot beyond the hole."

Returning to the United States, he went to the Fresh Meadows County Club in Flushing, New York, where he had been the head pro from 1925 to 1930, to play in the National Open. After thirty-six holes, he was five strokes behind the leader, Phil Perkins; but then he used only 100 strokes in the last twenty-eight holes—eight under par —and won by three strokes. Bobby Jones called his play in the run "the finest competitive exhibition on record" (quoted in Sarazen, p. 164). In 1933 he challenged for the lead much of the way in the British Open at St. Andrews, but two poor bunker shots cost him the championship. He took some solace in capturing the PGA title again, this time at the Blue Mound Club at Milwaukee; he crafted out of the victory, too, a defiant answer to Tommy Armour, a leading player of the 1920s, who had proclaimed on the eve of the tourney that he, Hagen, and Sarazen were all washed up. The following year, his short game betraying him in the National Open, he finished one stroke behind the winner, Olin Dutra.

In 1935 Sarazen won the Masters with a memorable shot. He came to the fifteenth hole, a par five at 485 yards, needing three birdies and a par to tie the leader in the clubhouse, Craig Wood. He hit a long drive leaving him 220 yards from the green but not in a good lie. Conferring with his caddy, "Stovepipe," he decided to use his four wood. He rode into the shot using all his strength. Rising in a low trajectory, with Sarazen running to watch it, the ball landed on the green, bounced for the cup and went in for a double-eagle. With one shot he had tied Wood. He completed the round in par and then defeated Wood in a thirty-six hole playoff, 144 to 149. It became the most celebrated shot in the history of golf.

Sarazen never again won a major title. He won five minor titles from 1936 to 1940 but did not fare well in any of the major tournaments until 1940 when he tied Lawson Little in the National Open at the Canterbury Country Club in Cleveland. Little then won in a playoff. When the United States entered World War II, with the PGA tour virtually shut down, he became a representative of the Vinco Corporation, a manufacturer of precision tools. After the war, he played in major tournaments for several years. Occasionally, he showed something of his old brilliance. He reached the quarter finals of the PGA championship in 1947 and finished tenth in the Masters in 1950 and twelfth in 1951, and he finished sixteenth in the British Open in 1958. He captured the PGA Senior Championship in 1958. At the Masters in 1963, paired with Arnold Palmer, he played the defending champion to a tie after the first thirty-six holes. Soon retiring from competitive play, Sarazen became the host for "Shell's Wonderful World of Golf," a series of international matches created for television. For years he returned to Augusta to make a ceremonial tee shot to open the Masters.

Altogether, Sarazen won thirty-eight PGA titles, including seven major victories. He was the first to win all four of what became known as the Grand Slam titles—the Masters, the National Open, the British Open, and the PGA championship. He was a member of six Ryder Cup teams, compiling a record of seven wins in matches, two losses, and three ties. He became a charter member of the PGA Hall of Fame in 1940 and of the PGA World Golf Hall of Fame in 1974.

Sarazen was a popularizer of golf. Through his dramatic play and personality, he appealed to thousands of Americans as a "compensatory hero," one of many sports figures in the 1920s and 1930s—Babe Ruth, Bill Tilden, and Jack Dempsey were others—who gave thousands of Americans laboring in bureaucratic routine or the drudgery of the assembly line a vicarious release from the anonymity of everyday life. During these years he played innumerable exhibitions in the United States with Hagen and Babe Didrikson, and he also gave exhibitions overseas, often with the trick shot artist Joe Kirkwood.

Sarazen sought to protect the integrity of golf. In 1923, on the eve of the British Open at Troon, he joined Hagen in denouncing the St. Andrew's golf committee for its use of "autocratic power" in banning punched irons. He refused to play the Agua Caliente Open in 1935 because Mexican authorities permitted pari-mutuel betting on the players. In the 1950s he urged the PGA to admit blacks to the tour.

Sarazen was ever looking for ways to make golf more pleasurable. Believing that putting, which accounted for nearly half of the strokes of a score, was excessively important, he proposed that the cup be enlarged from 4 1/4 inches in diameter to 8 inches. He ridiculed players, including Jack Nicklaus and Ben Hogan, for contemplating short putts minute after minute, all the while distracting other players and deadening the gallery. His own play was brisk. He quickly surveyed the ball on the green and struck it virtually on the run. For ordinary golfers with little time to play after their workday, he called for much shorter courses. All of his measures for reform came to naught.

Sarazen found time to be a gentleman farmer. He and his wife purchased a 125-acre farm near Danbury, Connecticut, in 1933 and then bought an adjoining seventy-five acre farm. After operating the farm as a dairy and barely turning a profit for ten years, they sold it in 1943 and then purchased another one near Germantown, New York. Sarazen found a kind of security in his farms and relished his image and nickname of "Squire" Sarazen.

As Sarazen grew older, he often met fans asking him about Jones and Hagen. He developed a standard response. Casting his eyes to the heavens, he would say "They're waiting for me now on the first tee." He died in Naples, Florida.

• For golf in the context of American sports, see Benjamin G. Rader, *American Sports: From the Age of Folk Games to the Age of Spectators* (1983). Sarazen's autobiography (written with Herbert Warren Wind) is *Thirty Years of Championship Golf: The Life and Times of Gene Sarazen* (1950). Though derived largely from the autobiography, useful chapters on Sarazen appear in Gerald Astor, *The PGA World Golf Hall of Fame* (1991); Will Grimsely, *Golf: Its History, People & Events* (1966); and Herbert Warren Wind, *The Story of American Golf: Its Champions and Its Championships* (1948). Brief accounts of Sarazen's competitive record are in Peter Alliss, *The Who's Who of Golf* (1983); and *Golf Magazine's Encyclopedia of Golf* (1993). Among newspaper and periodical articles, see "Southern Season Honors to Sarazen," *New York Times* (hereafter abbreviated as *NYT*), 16 Apr. 1922; "Sarazen Wins Open Golf Championship," *NYT*, 16 July 1922; "Sarazen Is Victor Over Emmett French," *NYT*, 19 Aug. 1922; "How Gene Sarazen, New Open Champ Arrived," *Literary Digest*, 19 Sept.1922, pp. 54–56; "Denounces Golf Officials," *NYT*, 18 June 1923; Sol Metzger, "Sarazen's Golf Instinct," *Country Life*, 23 June 1923, pp. 42–43; "The Open Golf Championship," *London Times*, 11 June 1932; "After Ten Years Another Championship," *Literary Digest*, 25 June 1932, pp. 32–33; "Gene as a Tinker," *Literary Digest*, 10 Sept. 1932, p. 34; "Sarazen, Assailing Mutual Betting in Golf, Refuses to Compete in Agua Caliente Open," *NYT*, 3 Feb. 1935; "Spectacular Finish Enables Sarazen to Gain Tie with Wood in August Golf," *NYT*, 8 Apr. 1933; Dave Anderson, "Sarazen's Century of Perspectives," *NYT*, 16 May 1999; Brian Hewitt, "Gene Sarazen," *Golfweek*, 22 May 1999; "Gene Sarazen (1902–1999)," *Golf Magazine*, July 1999, pp. 18 + . An obituary of Sarazen appears in the *New York Times*, 14 May 1999.

CARL M. BECKER

SATANTA (01 Jan. 1815?–11 Oct. 1878), Kiowa war chief and diplomat, was born on the Great Plains, probably somewhere between the North Platte and Canadian Rivers, the son of Red Tipi (To-quodole-kaip-tau), a leading Kiowa priest. His maternity is uncertain, but in later years he said his mother was Arapaho. Soon after birth, he received the baby name of Big Ribs (Gauton-bain) due to his large size. As he grew up, he assumed his permanent warrior name, Set-t'ainte (White Bear). Whites, unable to pronounce it, called him Satanta, the name by which he is commonly known.

Tribal lore indicates that Red Tipi recognized Satanta's potential early in life and kept him under close supervision into his late twenties, until he was satisfied that his son was fully prepared for the leadership role Red Tipi intended for him. Consequently, Satanta did not marry until he was in his late twenties or early thirties. In 1850 his first wife, Zone-ty, gave birth to a son, Gray Goose (Tsau-lau-te), who became his favorite child. Kiowas practiced polygamy; the exact number of Satanta's wives is uncertain, but modern descendents believe he had only two. Likewise, estimates of the actual number of his children vary, the confusion arising from the Kiowa custom of considering nephews and nieces as sons and daughters.

Satanta had several emblems of authority. The most important were his sun shield and his lance. His most famous emblem, however, was a bugle, and sometimes he is represented in Kiowa calendar histories by the glyph for a bugle. He supposedly acquired the bugle in a fight with soldiers, in which he killed the bugler and took his instrument. Although many plains Indians had bugles, and even learned army calls to signal each other, it most often was associated with Satanta.

Satanta's position as a prominent leader among the Kiowas appears to have been established by the 1850s. He distinguished himself in battle against Pawnees, Cheyennes, and their allies, and in raids into Texas and Mexico. He also participated in a treaty council with the federal government at Fort Atkinson, Kansas, in 1853, which eased the fighting over the remainder of the decade.

With the secession of Texas in 1861, federal troops were withdrawn, and many Texans enlisted in the Confederate forces. The plains were left largely unprotected, and Indian raids into Texas became chronic. Satanta was involved in many of these depredations, including the Elm Creek or Young County raid of 1864, considered the worst in Texas history. Some six hundred Kiowas and Comanches in two groups swept through Young County, about seventy-five miles west of Fort Worth. Several ranches were burned, eleven citizens were killed, and seven women and children were carried into captivity.

The end of the Civil War meant the reestablishment of federal authority, and in October 1865 government officials met with Satanta and other Kiowa leaders on the Little Arkansas River near the present site of Wichita, Kansas, in an effort to negotiate an end to the raids. Although the Kiowas agreed to the treaty, Satanta continued raiding.

Satanta achieved national prominence in October 1867, when he spoke for the Kiowas and Comanches at a treaty conference at Medicine Lodge, Kansas. His speeches were reported in the *New York Times* and other national newspapers. In his most important oration, he said, "A long time ago this land belonged to our fathers; but when I go up to the [Arkansas] river I see camps of soldiers on its banks. These soldiers cut down my timber, they kill my buffalo; and when I see that my heart feels like bursting."

As before, the treaty did little to end the fighting. To resolve the issue, Maj. Gen. Philip H. Sheridan led a winter campaign on the Southern Plains. On 28 November 1868, Sheridan's cavalry, commanded by Lt. Col. George Armstrong Custer, attacked a string of villages along the Washita River in southwestern Oklahoma. Although evidence almost conclusively establishes that Satanta was at the Fort Cobb Agency at the time, Sheridan and Custer accused him of murdering two white captives during the fight and interned him for several weeks.

Satanta settled on the Kiowa-Comanche Reservation near Fort Sill, Oklahoma. In May 1871, however, he joined a party of more than a hundred Kiowas and Comanches, led by the medicine man Maman-ti (Sky Walker), for a raid into Texas. Other participants were Satank (Set-angya; Sitting Bear), a septuagenarian but a ruthless senior war chief, and the teenage sub-chief Big Tree. On 18 May they attacked a wagon train west of Jacksboro, Texas, killing seven teamsters and driving forty mules back to Oklahoma.

The raiders' arrival back at their agency coincided with the arrival of W. T. Sherman, commanding general of the army, at nearby Fort Sill. Sherman personally arrested Satanta, Big Tree, and Satank for their parts in the raid and ordered them to Texas for trial. Satank later jumped a guard and was killed, but Satanta and Big Tree were taken back to Texas for trial.

On 5 July 1871, Satanta and Big Tree were convicted in Jacksboro on seven counts of murder and sentenced to death. On the advice of federal officials, Gov. Edmund J. Davis commuted their sentences to life in prison, as hostages against Kiowa good behavior. Two years later, on 8 October 1873, Davis paroled the two, on assurance by the federal government that future raiders would be punished.

Satanta ceased raiding, and tended to keep to himself. With the outbreak of the Red River War of 1874, he resigned his position as war chief, apparently hoping to remain neutral. Nevertheless, he was absent from the mandatory roll call at Fort Sill and was present when fighting broke out at the Cheyenne-Arapaho Agency at Darlington, Oklahoma. These were considered parole violations, and on 3 October 1874 he was taken into custody. Satanta survived in prison in Huntsville, Texas, for four years. On 10 October 1878, he learned he would never be released. The following day, he committed suicide by jumping from a second-floor landing.

Satanta's place in history is contradictory. His oratory and diplomacy gained him national prominence, but this fame was later eclipsed by chiefs like Sitting Bull, Crazy Horse, and Joseph. The 1871 wagon train massacre and Sherman's decisive response created a permanent rift within the already fractious Kiowas and heralded their end as a free people. Today, he remains as a symbol of Kiowa freedom and defiance.

• The most recent biography of Satanta is Charles M. Robinson III, *Satanta: The Life and Death of a War Chief* (1997). An analysis of the 1871 wagon train massacre and its aftermath, also by Robinson, is in *The Indian Trial: The Complete Story of the Warren Wagon Train Massacre and the Fall of the Kiowa Nation* (1997). Classic works include Lawrie Tatum, *Our Red Brothers and the Peace Police of President Ulysses S. Grant* (1899; reprint, 1970); James M. Mooney, *Calendar History of the Kiowa Indians* (1898; reprint, 1979); and Clarence Wharton, *Satanta, the Great Chief of the Kiowas and His People* (1935). Wilbur S. Nye interviewed many of Satanta's contemporaries as old men when he was posted to Fort Sill, Oklahoma, in the late 1920s and early 1930s. Their accounts are published in *Carbine and Lance: The Story of Old Fort Sill* (1937; reprint, 1969). An excellent study of the Kiowa factions of the 1860s and 1870s, as well as an appraisal of Nye's work, is Stan Hoig, *The Kiowas and the Legend of Kicking Bird, with Three Kiowa Tales by Col. W. S. Nye* (2000).

CHARLES M. ROBINSON III

SAYLOR, John Phillips (23 July 1908–28 Oct. 1973), conservationist, was born on a farm near Johnstown, Pennsylvania, the son of Tillman Saylor, an attorney, and Minerva Phillips Saylor, a former schoolteacher. After graduating from Johnstown High

School at age sixteen Saylor attended Mercersburg Academy in south central Pennsylvania, a college preparatory school for boys. He struggled academically but nonetheless was accepted at Franklin and Marshall College in Lancaster, Pennsylvania. After graduating in 1928, he went on to law school at the University of Michigan but left that program to attend Dickinson School of Law in Carlisle, Pennsylvania, from 1930 to 1933. On graduation, he joined his father's law firm and in 1937 married Johnstown schoolteacher Grace Doerstler. They had two children. In 1942 Saylor joined the navy. He served as a communications officer aboard the U.S.S. *Missoula* and participated in the invasion of Iwo Jima. After the war he returned to Johnstown and resumed his law practice. But in 1949, after the district's newly elected congressman had died in a plane crash, Saylor won a special election to succeed him. He would win twelve more congressional contests, serving until 1973.

A hulking man who wore black-rimmed glasses, Saylor stood 6'4" and weighed 240 pounds. He was affable, outgoing, and hardworking, with a flair for humor and showmanship. He also could be blustery, cantankerous, intimidating, and vindictive. "He was a large man, with a large voice, and he liked to use it," recalled one staff member (Smith, p. 556). A Republican, he represented Armstrong, Cambria, and Indiana counties in western Pennsylvania. Because the district was heavily dependent on coal mining, he was assigned to the House Interior and Insular Affairs Committee. On that committee, he rose to ranking minority member and made his mark as the leading conservationist in the House of Representatives.

Saylor's conservation perspective, which stressed the preservation of wilderness and the inviolability of the national park system, was shaped by several forces. Growing up in western Pennsylvania, he hunted, fished, hiked, camped, and developed a love for the outdoors. At a young age he accompanied his family to Yellowstone and became a lifelong champion of the national parks. A religious man, he believed that preserving resplendent landscapes brought individuals closer to the Creator. He also was influenced by the emerging ecological outlook following World War II that emphasized wilderness preservation, environmental protection, and the interconnectedness between humans and the natural world. Moreover, the economic interests of his congressional district prompted his opposition to public power projects such as atomic generators and massive federal hydroelectric dams on western rivers because they competed with coal as a source of electricity. His antipathy toward public power brought him into conflict with the Interior Department's Bureau of Reclamation, the government agency mainly responsible for federal dam building in the West, and western legislators who favored multipurpose dams because they provided water to irrigate arid lands and cheap electricity to attract industry.

Saylor first made an impact as a conservationist in the mid-1950s during the battle over the Colorado River Storage Project (CRSP) bill. That measure proposed a series of federally constructed multipurpose dams in the Colorado River watershed to provide water storage, irrigation, and hydroelectric power to Colorado, Utah, Wyoming, and New Mexico. A large hydroelectric dam located at Echo Park near the confluence of the Green and Yampa Rivers would have flooded part of Dinosaur National Monument on the Utah-Colorado border. Conservation organizations such as the Sierra Club, Wilderness Society, and National Parks Association denounced the project because Echo Park dam would set an alarming precedent by intruding upon a nationally protected area. With Saylor spearheading the opposition in the House, saying that the project would violate a "beauteous stretch of wilderness in a cherished national monument," preservationists managed to delete Echo Park dam from the bill. Saylor's dogged defense of Dinosaur Monument earned the gratitude and respect of leading conservationists across the nation.

During the debate over the Pacific Southwest Water plan, one of the most heated conservation battles of the 1960s, Saylor successfully led House opposition to the proposed construction of two mammoth federal power dams at Bridge and Marble Canyons on the lower Colorado River because the impounded water would have encroached upon Grand Canyon National Monument. Closer to home, Saylor unsuccessfully opposed federal construction of Kinzua Dam on the Allegheny River in western Pennsylvania. He was the only member of Pennsylvania's congressional delegation to denounce Kinzua Dam because it would flood lands of the Seneca Nation, thus violating a federal treaty that had stood since 1794.

Saylor is best known as the architect of two landmark pieces of conservation legislation. In 1964 after a nine-year battle, the Wilderness Act, which set aside nine million acres of pristine land in the American West, was approved by Congress and signed into law. Four years later, the Wild and Scenic Rivers Act protected eight free-flowing rivers from future dams and commercial development. Both measures provided for future additions to the program. By the turn of the century, the wilderness system encompassed more than 100 million acres and the wild and scenic rivers program numbered more than a hundred streams.

Besides protecting wild places and national preserves from economic development, Saylor worked during the 1960s to protect the environment (the Clean Air and Clean Water Acts) and to add scenic and remote lands to the national park system—national seashores at Cape Cod (Mass.), Padre Island (Tex.), and Point Reyes (Calif.), and national parks at Canyonlands (Utah), Redwoods (Calif.), and North Cascades (Wash.). He helped push through Congress the Land and Water Conservation Fund that created revenue to purchase additional wild lands through user fees at federal recreational areas. He also coauthored legislation granting statehood to Alaska and Hawaii.

Known affectionately as "St. John" by many conservationists, Saylor won awards and acclaim for his work from the Sierra Club, Wilderness Society, Izaak Walton League, National Parks Association, and National Wildlife Federation. Arguably the most forceful and influential preservationist in Congress in the twentieth century, Saylor died in Houston, Texas, following heart surgery in late October 1973.

• Saylor wrote an essay on his conservation hero, Theodore Roosevelt, titled "The Conservation Legacy of Theodore Roosevelt," *National Parks Magazine* 32 (July–Sept. 1958), pp. 114–16. And he championed the preservation of wilderness and scenic rivers in "Saving America's Wilderness," *The Living Wilderness* 21 (Winter–Spring 1956–1957), pp. 1–12, and "Once Along a Scenic River," *Parks & Recreation* 3 (Aug. 1968), pp. 20–21, 57–58. For an overview of Saylor's career and his efforts to preserve wild rivers, see Thomas G. Smith, "Voice for Wild and Scenic Rivers," *Pennsylvania History* 66 (Autumn 1999): 554–79. His congressional papers are housed at the Indiana University of Pennsylvania. An obituary is in the *Washington Post*, 29 Oct. 1973.

THOMAS G. SMITH

SCHAEFER, George Louis (16 Dec. 1920–10 Sept. 1997), producer and director for television, stage, and screen, was born in Wallingford, Connecticut, the son of Elsie Otterbein Schaefer and Louis Schaefer, a silver salesman. Schaefer grew up mostly in Oak Park, Illinois, and attended Lafayette College in Easton, Pennsylvania, where he directed several student drama productions and served as president of the debating club and editor of the campus newspaper. During summer recesses he returned to Oak Park to direct productions of the Pastime Players, a semiprofessional troupe that he had helped start while he was in high school. In 1941 Schaefer received a B.A. in English and psychology, graduating magna cum laude and Phi Beta Kappa. Lafayette College awarded him an honorary degree in 1964.

"I've always disliked acting myself," Schaefer stated in an interview with the *New York Journal-American* years later (18 Oct. 1965). "The idea of doing something over and over appalls me. . . . So . . . I *had* to be a director." With that aim in mind, he in 1941 began graduate work at the Yale Drama School, but he joined the U.S. Army following the Japanese attack on Pearl Harbor. Assigned to a Special Services drama unit based in Honolulu, Schaefer served under the command of Maurice Evans, the famed actor. Evans quickly recognized Schaefer's talents and became a mentor and collaborator.

Among the scores of plays that Schaefer directed for the army was *G.I. Hamlet*, an adaptation of Shakespeare's tragedy especially intended for American servicepeople. The production was a great success, and following the war's end, it was mounted on Broadway, with Evans repeating in the title role. In 1946 the drama critic George Jean Nathan hailed the little-known Schaefer as "best director of the year." In 1948 Schaefer and Evans codirected a Broadway production of George Bernard Shaw's *Man and Superman*.

Schaefer's ability to make "high-brow" dramas available for commercial audiences—without drawing the usual critical catcalls for "vulgarizing" them—became a source of pride for the young director as well as his professional trademark. In 1949 he began a four-year stint with the New York City Center as executive producer and artistic director, staging Shakespeare's *Richard II* and *The Taming of the Shrew*, Henrik Ibsen's *The Wild Duck*, and other classical plays. After leaving the company, Schaefer coproduced (with Evans) his first contemporary drama for the New York stage, *Teahouse of the August Moon* by John Patrick, which won the Tony Award for best play of 1953 and ran on Broadway for three years. Schaefer went on to direct a string of major productions, including John Cecil Holm's *The Southwest Corner* (1955), George Bernard Shaw's *The Apple Cart* (1956), and *The Body Beautiful* (1958), a musical by Jerry Bock and Sheldon Harnick. A tireless worker, he spent summers directing musical comedies at the Texas State Fair in Dallas, where he met his wife, Mildred Trares, an actress and singer. The couple married in 1954; they had no children.

The nascent television industry took notice of Schaefer's capacity for pleasing large audiences with plays usually thought of as "difficult." In 1953 Schaefer was asked to become producer director of *The Hallmark Hall of Fame*, a ninety-minute anthology drama showcase presented on NBC at various times of the year in conjunction with the sponsor's holiday greeting card campaigns. Schaefer recounted events leading to the creation of the program, which became the longest-running drama series of the twentieth century: "I remember, we had a lunch: Maurice Evans, Joyce C. Hall [founder and head of Hallmark] and Pat Weaver [first head of the NBC television network]. Pat was behind the idea . . . he outlined what it would cost. Joyce said he would have to think about it. Apparently he was going back to Kansas City that day and on the taxi trip to the airport, he decided, 'We're going to do this! Let's go for it!' That was really the beginning of that incredible series. We put on six a year and then cut it down to about five a year and did occasional repeats, once we had [video] tape" (interview with Marc).

Wary of the extraordinary sponsor control over artistic material that was often exerted in the broadcasting industry, Schaefer made a personal agreement with Hall. Hallmark could exercise consultation and approval rights over a script presented by Schaefer. Once script approval was secured, however, Schaefer would be free to mount the production without interference. The contract was extraordinary, giving Schaefer a degree of artistic freedom that some contemporary television producers might envy.

The Hallmark Hall of Fame was among the most ambitious and most honored anthology drama series in television. Its premiere season, 1953–1954, included three live Shakespeare productions, *Hamlet*, *Macbeth*, and *Richard II*, all starring Evans. A 1960–1961 Hallmark production of *Macbeth*, costarring

Evans and Judith Anderson, was filmed in Scotland and cost more than $1 million, a huge sum for the times. Schaefer's theater credentials, augmented by his growing reputation for television drama, convinced many actors who otherwise shunned the medium to appear on *The Hallmark Hall of Fame.*

In all, Schaefer produced and directed seventy-two *Hallmark Hall of Fame* dramas, garnering four of his five career Emmy Awards as well as four Directors Guild of America Awards, a Peabody, a Sylvania, and most of the other honors available for television drama. Just a few of the memorable *Hallmark* productions include Lillian Hellman's *The Little Foxes,* starring Greer Garson (1956–1957); James Costigan's *The Little Moon of Alban* (1957–1958), one of the few original dramas done for the series; Ibsen's *A Doll's House,* starring Julie Harris (1959–1960); and Shakespeare's *The Tempest,* starring Richard Burton (1959–1960). Schaefer, perhaps more than any of his contemporaries, used television's close-up shot to develop a stage-based video aesthetic that was friendly to classic works of theater and to the actors who were experienced in performing them. The opportunity that Schaefer was creating for disseminating difficult works for a mass audience was, however, lost during the 1960s as the networks abandoned the television "play" in favor of a cinema-based technique that emphasized outdoor shooting and action sequences at the expense of character and plot development.

While just about every other prime-time anthology drama program was canceled by the television networks during the late 1950s, Schaefer's *Hallmark* continued to flourish, and the show made a graceful transition from live to prerecorded performances in the 1960s. Like most directors, Schaefer regretted the passing of live television. He emphasized, however, that viewing live television drama, despite the nostalgia with which it is remembered, should not be mistaken as an experience equal to that of attending live theater. He made the point in this anecdote in a 1995 interview: "When Lynn [Lynn Fontanne] and Alfred [Alfred Lunt] did *The Magnificent Yankee,* . . . Joyce Hall was in New York at the time and I invited him to a final run-through. . . . Joyce was absolutely knocked out. He kept saying, 'Can't we let the people at home see this? Can't we do the shows without scenery, and catch this kind of excitement?' I had to explain to him that there is no way to do that [on television]" (interview with Marc).

In 1959, in recognition of his achievements, Schaefer was made executive producer of the program. He formed his own company, Compass Productions, to supply the *Hallmark* series and to carry out other ventures. The following year he was appointed founding director of the Hallmark Fund for Television Drama, a nonprofit foundation awarding cash grants to promising writers for work on original television plays.

Schaefer's versatility and his seemingly limitless energy extended to film direction as well. His theatrical screen releases included John Christopher's *Pendulum* (1969), a well-regarded crime drama; *Doctors' Wives* (1971), a farce by Paddy Chayefsky, the most heralded playwright of the live television era; and an extraordinary adaptation of Ibsen's *An Enemy of the People* (1978), scripted by Arthur Miller and starring Steve McQueen. Schaefer's movies made for television include *A War of Children* (CBS, 1972), concerning the sectarian violence in Northern Ireland; and *Right of Way* (HBO, 1983), which paired veteran stars Bette Davis and Jimmy Stewart as an aging couple who make a suicide pact.

Schaefer was elected president of the Directors' Guild of America (1979–1981) and was appointed by President Ronald Reagan to the National Council on the Arts (1982–1986). In 1984 Schaefer joined the theater department of the University of California, Los Angeles (UCLA), and soon after he was named associate dean of the School of Theater, Film, and Television, a position he occupied until 1991. In his later years he continued to work, directing Harold Stanley's *The Man Upstairs* (CBS, 1992), which featured Katharine Hepburn in her final television appearance; and the Mary Chase comedy *Harvey* (CBS, 1997), which he had first mounted for television in a 1958 production starring Art Carney.

Schaefer defied the odds for a successful life as an artist in the twentieth century. Maintaining high personal standards, he managed to win the respect and loyalty of three constituencies that rarely are pleased at once: corporate executives, the general public, and the finest artists in his profession. He is likely to be remembered for his pursuit of an American popular drama that was somehow greater in value than crass amusement, elitist pretense, or the sum of both. Schaefer died in Los Angeles.

• Schaefer's videotaped, transcribed interview with the television critic Steven H. Scheuer is in the collections of the Center for the Study of Popular Television at Syracuse University's Bird Library. Copies of *The Academy of Television Arts and Sciences Tribute to George Schaefer* (2 Dec. 1986), originally presented as a television program, are in the UCLA Film and Television Archive and the Academy of Television Arts and Sciences in Los Angeles. Schaefer's autobiography is *From Live Tape to Film* (1995). In-depth interviews include a conversation—focused on the phenomenon of live television just as it was going into decline—with J. P. Hanley, "Schaefer—Problems in Directing," *New York Times,* 13 Oct. 1957; an interview in the*New York Journal-American,* 18 Oct. 1965; and an interview by David Marc, Los Angeles, 30 Oct. 1995, available in the Steven H. Scheuer Collection in Television History, Center for the Study of Popular Television, Syracuse University Library. An obituary appears in the *New York Times,* 12 Sept. 1997.

DAVID MARC

SCHARRER, Berta Vogel (1 Dec. 1906–23 July 1995), cell biologist and pioneering neuroendocrinologist, was born Berta Vogel in Munich, Germany, the daughter of Karl Phillip Vogel, a prominent judge in the Bavarian state court, and Johanna Weiss. Berta grew up in happy circumstances at home and in school, and she showed an early interest in biology and in becoming a scientist. But after 1914 her life was shadowed by World War I, by Germany's defeat and economic chaos, and ultimately by the rise of Nazism, which gained an early foothold in Munich. Scharrer entered the University of Munich in the swale of Adolf Hitler's conspiracy to overthrow of the Bavarian government, and she graduated with a Ph.D. in 1930, as the Nazis came to national prominence.

At the University of Munich, Scharrer met two men who powerfully influenced the rest of her life. The first was Karl von Frisch, her principal doctoral studies professor, who had shown that both fish and honeybees can see colors and that bees can discriminate among dozens of floral scents. Over decades he described the complex ways insects communicate and won the 1973 Nobel Prize in physiology or medicine for that research. Von Frisch directed Scharrer's dissertation on the comparative taste and nutritional quality of various nectars for honeybees. Her second male inspiration was Ernst Scharrer, another of von Frisch's graduate students, who studied fish neurons and came to the conclusion that nerve cells were capable of secreting chemicals much as endocrine cells released hormones. In 1934 Berta Vogel and Ernst Scharrer married. They also pursued parallel lines of research, starting at the Research Institute of Psychiatry in Munich—Berta with invertebrates, Ernst with vertebrates.

From 1934 to 1937 the couple worked at the University of Frankfurt, where Ernst was director of the Edinger Institute for Brain Research and Berta researched without title or salary. At the time most biologists held that nerve impulse transmission was strictly an electrical process. Thus the Scharrers' hypothesis that neurons—at least in fish and insects—secreted chemical signals that acted upon distant organs encountered considerable resistance. But while they worked to bolster the "nerve-gland cell" (Ernst's term) argument, Hitler's dictatorship became insufferable. Though the Scharrers were not Jews, they felt the hostility projected against all Nazi opponents, so they decided to flee Germany. In 1937 Ernst Scharrer accepted a year-long Rockefeller Fellowship at the University of Chicago. The Scharrers promised German authorities they would return to Frankfurt, though they has no intention of doing so. They became U.S. citizens in 1945.

After a year at the University of Chicago, the Scharrers moved to the Rockefeller Institute for Medical Research in New York in 1938, then to Western Reserve University in Cleveland in 1940, and to the University of Colorado in Denver in 1946. At these institutions Ernst held salaried positions and Berta did not, though she published studies on the brain anatomy and neurosecretions of her favorite model organism, the South American woodroach. She hypothesized that nerve-gland cells in the human brain functioned similarly. (Indeed other researchers showed that neuroendocrine cells in the human hypothalamus have axons that extend to the posterior pituitary, where antidiuretic hormone and oxytocin

are released into the blood to effect kidney and uterus functions respectively.) She also noted that severing nerve-gland brain cells in the woodroach produced stomach tumors in the insect—a phenomenon with an odd parallel in human lung cancer, where tumor cells produce antidiuretic hormone.

Between 1934 and 1955 Berta Scharrer never held a faculty position at any of the universities where she carried on her research. In 1955 an offer arrived from Yeshiva University in New York City for Ernst to become chair and Berta full professor of anatomy at the newly forming Albert Einstein College of Medicine. They both accepted and moved from Denver to the Bronx. By this time other scientists had come to accept the chemical transmission of nerve impulses, and research began to focus on identifying the chemicals known as "neurotransmitters." Over 300 were eventually identified. The Scharrers' textbook Neuroendocrinology (1963) provided the field with a strong foundation in clinical research.

The Scharrers seldom attended professional meetings apart, and in April 1965 they traveled to the annual anatomy meeting in Florida. During a vacation afterward, they went swimming and got caught in an undertow. Ernst drowned. For the first time in her life, Berta was alone. Returning to Einstein College, she took over Ernst's administrative duties in the Department of Anatomy for two years while continuing research into the fine structure of insect neurons and the pathways secretory granules traveled in tissue.

Gradually Scharrer's attention turned to two other questions about nerve-gland cells: when did they evolve, and what role do they play in regulating the immune system? Realizing that highly specialized tissues tended to evolve from common origins, she proposed that nerve-gland cells were ancestors of both the endocrine and the nervous systems. In the gastrointestinal tract, where the enteric nervous system both excites and inhibits digestive activity, and also regulates the mucosal tissues' response to pathogens, she could see, on the one hand, how the woodroach processed food and, on the other, why diarrheal illnesses are the leading cause of human mortality. Researchers around the world continue investigations the Scharrers pioneered for secrets neuroendocrinology may hold for understanding autoimmune diseases and inflammation responses.

Scharrer received honorary degrees from eleven universities, and her many awards included the U.S. National Medal of Science in 1985. Her last professional paper about recent progress in comparative neuroimmunology appeared in 1992, when she was eighty-six. She died at her home in the Bronx. Not surprisingly the leading award for achievement in neuroendocrinology, endowed by Lilly Deutschland GmbH in 1999, is the Ernst and Berta Scharrer Prize.

TERRY SHARRER

SCHLESINGER, Leon (20 May 1884–25 Dec. 1949), film producer, was born in Philadelphia, the youngest of ten children of Leopold Schlesinger, a teacher, and Bertha Schlesinger (maiden name unknown). When he was 14, Schlesinger took a job as an usher at Blaney's Arch Street Theater, graduating to theater cashier, manager, and songbook agent. His theater jobs put him in contact with various celebrities and inspired him to try acting. He landed bit roles and became a press agent, vaudeville and road show manager, and movie salesman. For a time he worked in the box office of a Chicago theater, where he became treasurer. In 1909 he married Berenice Katz. They had no children.

In 1922 Schlesinger moved to Hollywood; he became a salesman for Agfa Films and later the Metro Corporation, where he specialized in the importation and exportation of movies. He then established and eventually sold his interest in the Pacific Title and Art Studio, which became the leading manufacturer of high-quality dialogue titles for silent films. In 1926, the Pacific Title and Art Studio contracted with the Walt Disney Studio to produce titles for animated films. Schlesinger also worked with Warner Bros. mogul Jack Warner, and the two became friends. Legend has it that he won Warner's praise for being one of the backers of *The Jazz Singer*, the industry's first talking film, released by the studio in 1927. Schlesinger later produced a number of B Westerns, including some featuring the rising young actor John Wayne.

By 1930 Schlesinger, fearing a diminished market for his title cards as silent films were being phased out, sought new ventures. Spurred by the success of the first talking cartoon, Walt Disney's *Steamboat Willie* (1928), he began producing animated shorts for Warner, teaming with ex-Disney animators Rudolf Ising and Hugh Harman. Dubbed the Looney Tunes, these cartoons were based loosely on Disney's well-known Silly Symphonies series and employed music as an integral element. The first release, *Singing in the Bathtub* (1930), a surreal eight-minute short introducing characters Bosko and Honey, proved so popular that Schlesinger's animation division soon embarked on a second series, Merrie Melodies, which featured more cartoons in Technicolor. With his brother-in-law Ray Katz as his business manager, Schlesinger demanded that his animators work quickly, churning out at least one cartoon a month for maximum profit. He also recognized that he could make money by promoting the popular songs and sheet music from the films.

Approximately three years after their first Warner Bros. cartoon, Ising and Harman became tired of the relentless pace, low production budget, and mediocre product. They left Schlesinger, taking the studio's only star, Bosko, and began making films for MGM. All that Schlesinger retained was the studio's famous tag line: "That's all [sic] folks." Schlesinger, however, jumped at the chance to be solely in charge and continued to build his new studio, dubbed "Termite Terrace," by luring away animators from Disney and other studios with promises of big salaries and great opportunities. He launched the careers of artists such

as Friz Freleng, Bob Clampett, Tex Avery, Chuck Jones, Frank Tashlin, Robert McKimson, and composer Carl Stalling, who became legends in the field of animation and established the fast-paced, irreverent Warner Bros. style that was just as engaging to adult audiences as it was to children. Schlesinger also discovered the vocal talent of Mel Blanc, the former radio personality, who lent his voice to over 400 characters in over 3,000 different shorts, or roughly 90 percent of all Warner Bros. cartoon productions. Schlesinger's studio grew to more than 200 employees.

A tight-fisted money man and entrepreneur, Schlesinger was not concerned with art but rather with keeping production up and costs down. While Disney might spend $100,000 for an animated short, Schlesinger limited his studio's budget to about $9,000 each, including his profit skimmed from the top (Kanfer, p. 95). He once observed of himself and rival animation studio head Max Fleischer, "We're businessmen. Walt Disney's an artist. With us, the idea with shorts is to hit 'em and run. With us, Disney is more of a Rembrandt" (quoted in *Time*, 27 Dec. 1937, p. 19). Unlike Disney, Schlesinger refused to consider producing feature-length animated films.

Schlesinger's lack of interest in cartoon production and his hands-off approach did not always win him the admiration of his staff but yielded one distinct advantage: the freedom for gifted animators to create and experiment, resulting in a stable of cartoon characters that have become some of the most zany and enduring in animation history: Porky Pig, Bugs Bunny, Daffy Duck, and Elmer Fudd. Speaking with a lisp, Schlesinger gave his animators just one order: "Put in more joketh, fellaths" (quoted in Kanfer, p. 94). He grew to trust his staff and appreciate its sense of humor, prompting Tex Avery to comment, "Schlesinger laughed at everything . . . He was the best boss I guess I ever had in the business . . . I could sell him anything I wanted to do" (quoted in Barrier, p. 358). Schlesinger's studio also oversaw the development of many innovations in animation production, including the introduction of human characters in cartoons and the use of oils instead of water for backgrounds, and produced animated sequences for feature films, such as *The Big Broadcast* and *Love Thy Neighbor*.

Schlesinger's greatest claim to fame, however, was providing the inspiration for Daffy Duck. His animators claimed that Schlesinger's lisp plus his belief that the world owed him a living made him a "perfect prototype" for the cartoon character. The cartoonists, however, feared the consequences of lampooning their boss. Animator Chuck Jones recounted the nervousness of the staff when Schlesinger first previewed Daffy.

> To save ourselves the embarrassment of being fired, all of us were careful to write our resignations before that fateful day when Leon strode into our production room and sprawled on the gilt throne he had snatched from some

early Warner pseudo-De Mille film or other. The rest of us, of course, still sat on beat-up splintery church pews from an early family film. The new Daffy Duck lit up on the screen at Leon's courteous command: "Roll the garbage!" The cartoon played to the studio audience, accompanied mainly by crickets, prayers and silence. Then the lights went on, and Leon leaped to his feet, glared around: 'Jeethus Christh, that's a funny voithe! Where'd you get that voithe?' (Jones, pp. 89–91)

Schlesinger appeared as himself in the 1940 film *You Ought to Be in Pictures*, a combined animation and live-action effort directed by Friz Freleng. Set at the Schlesinger Studio, the cartoon featured Daffy Duck convincing Porky Pig to march into Schlesinger's office and demand to be released from his meager cartoon contract so that he can go on to make great films. Porky does, and Schlesinger rips up the contract, mouthing to the audience, "He'll be back." While Porky is off seeking his fortune, Daffy denigrates him to Schlesinger in an attempt to get his job. When Porky returns, he realizes that he has been double-crossed, and Schlesinger hires him back. According to Friz Freleng, although Schlesinger initially did not understand the point of the film, "he trusted me quite a bit, and he let me do what I wanted to do, as long as it didn't cost him a lot of money" (quoted in Maltin, p. 242).

At 5 feet 7 1/2 inches, Schlesinger cut a portly profile. He lived in Beverly Hills and cultivated a brash style, dressing like a dapper vaudeville hoofer with spats and a yellow carnation in his lapel, wearing heavy cologne, and adopting expensive pastimes. He maintained a yacht, *Merrie Melody*, at Newport Harbor, where he reportedly declined to entertain his own animators, who he said did not earn enough money. He also followed deep sea angling. An avid fan of the harness races, Schlesinger continued to show up at the track and place bets from his wheelchair even after he became ill.

In 1944, Schlesinger retired, selling his interests to Warner Bros. for approximately $700,000, and was replaced by Edward Selzer, who proved to be humorless, even less popular, and substantially more interfering than his predecessor. He continued to work with the licensing and merchandising of Warner Bros. characters until six months before his death. Schlesinger's estate was valued at $904,700.

Even though Schlesinger contributed little of the creative spark that characterized the Warner Bros. cartoons, his name appeared most prominently at the beginning of each film and on the comic books. In all, he produced nearly 450 animated films, solidifying his role in the Warner Bros. animation legacy.

• Although no book-length biography of Schlesinger is available, information on him is in the following animation histories: Leonard Maltin, *Of Mice and Magic: A History of American Animated Cartoons* (1990); Norman M. Klein, *7 Minutes: The Life and Death of the American Animated Cartoon* (1993); Stefan Kanfer, *Serious Business: The Art and Commerce of Animation from Betty Boop to Toy Story* (1997); and Michael Barrier, *Hollywood Cartoons: American Animation in Its Golden Age* (1999). See also Steve Schneider, *That's All Folks: The Art of Warner Brothers Animation* (1988). Animator Chuck Jones's autobiography, *Chuck Amuck: The Life and Times of an Animated Cartoonist* (1989), contains an insider's account of Schlesinger's studio. Obituaries are in the *New York Times*, 26 Dec. 1949; the *Philadelphia Inquirer*, 26 Dec. 1949; and *Daily Variety*, 28 Dec. 1949.

KATHY MERLOCK JACKSON

SCHMITT, Arthur J. (14 June 1893–29 Mar. 1971), inventor, CEO, and philanthropist, was born Arthur John Schmitt in Austin, Illinois (later annexed by Chicago), the son of Henry W. Schmitt and Barbara Elizabeth Schneider Schmitt, owners of a leather-tanning business. Schmitt read *Popular Mechanics* and *Scientific American* and worked in machine shops. He dropped out of high school, bored with a system that catered to average students. Within a year, he was piloting his own airplane, but after a crash his father forbade him to fly. Schmitt fitted the salvaged engine to a chassis and produced a propeller-driven car that did not qualify for competition but was demonstrated at Metronome Company of America's auto races. In conventional cars, he raced against Victor Carlstrom, Eddie Rickenbacker, Bertram (Bert) Acosta, and Barney Oldfield. His negotiations with Metronome showed shrewd business sense: according to their contract, Schmitt's percentage was figured on the gross, not the net, and his travel expenses were guaranteed. At nineteen, after his father's death, Schmitt purchased a French Bleriot monoplane, the same model that first flew the English Channel. Soon afterward, he built his own conventionally powered automobile.

At eighteen, Schmitt worked with the chief engineer at the Rambler auto plant in Kenosha, Wisconsin, and attended evening drafting classes. He held jobs with the Thomas B. Jeffrey Company, Bucyrus Erie, and the Sterling Milling Company in Memphis, Tennessee, becoming plant manager, a position exempting him from the World War I draft. He nevertheless enlisted, hoping that Victor Carlstrom would use his influence as a Marine flyer of some fame to get him into Marine Corps Aviation. While an artilleryman at Camp Jackson, South Carolina, he studied and built radios.

In 1918 he became a journeyman electrician in Chicago and began to make individual radio components. In 1923 he and Walter Horn started Walnart Manufacturing Co. to make radio tube sockets. Schmitt bought out his partner and in 1928 merged with the Continental-Diamond Fiber Company, becoming manager of the Cleveland, Ohio, Division. The merger did not survive the depression.

In 1932 he formed the American Phenolic Corporation. Later that year he submitted his first patent, a phenolic resin (bakelite) radio tube socket. A single piece of plastic both insulated the metal parts and supported them mechanically. Ingenious combinations of metal and plastic became the mark of Schmitt's products. A later blue plastic with outstanding insulating and manufacturing properties was used in the company's "blue line connectors." Schmitt foresaw the post-depression demand for radio parts. Additional patents were submitted in 1936 and 1938. RCA contracted for a million tube sockets. The product line expanded to include a microphone connector that became the industry standard. Eventually, seventy patents were granted to Schmitt or his researchers.

Schmitt's company and the Army Air Corps developed standard military electrical connectors. American Phenolic made about 62 percent of all the electrical connectors used in U.S. planes during World War II. Amphenol AN/MS connectors made generators, radios, guns, and aircraft components (such as wings) more easily interchangeable. Schmitt's company also developed a family of coaxial cables, a center metallic conductor insulated with plastic and shielded electrically and mechanically by a braided metal sleeve. From 1942 to 1944 only American Phenolic manufactured this cable in the United States. Coaxial cables were used in high-flying airplanes, radar applications, and the atomic bomb program. The company also developed Thiokol to protect airplane connectors from leaking hydraulic fluid and contaminants that cause short circuits. Schmitt's company developed the microribbon connector and collaborated with RCA in developing television twin-lead. Dependent companies and foreign subsidiaries were formed.

In 1956 the company changed its name to Amphenol Electronics Corporation and, on 17 May 1957, it went public on the New York Stock Exchange. The same year, it purchased Danbury-Knudsen, Inc. of Danbury, Connecticut. In 1958, it merged with the G. W. Borg Corporation to form Amphenol-Borg Electronics. In 1964, Schmitt stepped down as chairman and CEO, positions he had held for thirty-two years. In 1968, Amphenol-Borg joined Bunker Ramo Corporation becoming the Amphenol Components Group.

Schmitt was active in philanthropy and education. By the late 1930s, he had learned to value formal education. Competition in electrical engineering required education, and leadership in the coming age of science and technology would require a sense of justice, morality, and wisdom. He maintained that engineers were too narrowly educated, and that industrial leadership required a broad education. After a three-year study of the strengths and weaknesses of engineering education, and discussions with educators and business leaders, he formed the Arthur J. Schmitt Foundation on 15 December 1941 to operate a school and research institute. On 12 June 1942 he founded the Fournier Institute in Lamont, Illinois, near the Argonne National Laboratory. He assembled an exceptional faculty and recruited students who already showed leadership and an ability to get things done and had maintained an 85 average. Tuition, room, and board were free, and the curriculum of 192 credits included electrical engineering, business, humanities, music, and realistic research experiences. With a student/faculty ratio of 1 to 6, the cost of educating students at Fournier was double that of larger engineering schools.

The foundation's research, begun in 1942, focused on code transmission, antennas, and insulation projects. By 1954, the IRS had ruled that the foundation's tax-exempt status was inconsistent with ownership of companies and development of patents. Schmitt and his advisors intended that the patents he donated and the patents later developed would provide both royalties and launch businesses to provide the longevity lacking in royalties alone. The Alpine Plastic Bag and the Acme Resin companies, formed to support Fournier, were sold. Fournier Institute closed in June 1955. Fournier students relocated to the Notre Dame, Marquette, and Illinois universities, where they received full tuition, room, and board. The Foundation's more recent fellowships for graduate work have aided over 1,000 students.

Although largely self-educated, Schmitt was awarded three honorary doctorates, was a trustee of DePaul University, the College of St. Francis, Joliet, Illinois, and the Illinois Institute of Technology. He was a member (1948–1951) of the University of Notre Dame's Advisory Council for Science and Engineering, president of the Illinois Manufacturers Association, and Director of Catholic Charities of Chicago. Schmitt never married; he regularly celebrated holidays and Sunday breakfasts with his mother, his brothers and sisters, and their children. He lived on the forefront of technology, clearly saw its possibilities, and moved aggressively to shape its future. He died in Lamont, Illinois.

• The archives of the Arthur J. Schmitt foundation contain many of the papers and other materials relating to its founder. The papers of the Fournier Institute, with many of Schmitt's addresses, are in the DePaul University Archives, and issues of the *Amphenol Engineering News* 1948–1960 are in the University of Chicago Library. Schmitt's biography is Arthur J. Schaefer, *Quest for Leadership: The Arthur J. Schmitt Story*, printed by Cathedral Pub., for the Arthur J. Schmitt Foundation, 1985. Schmitt's first and probably only formal publication, *Application of Impregnated Fabric Bearings to Roll Necks*, appeared in *Transactions of A.S.M.E.* (American Society of Mechanical Engineers), LIV, no. 8 (1 April 1932): 25–27. News coverage included stockholders' approval of the merger of Amphenol with G. W. Borg Corporation in the *New York Times*, 4 Nov., 1958, and Schmitt's selection as president and chairman of Amphenol-Borg Electronics Corporation in the *New York Times*, 31 Dec. 1958. An obituary is in the *Chicago Tribune*, 30 Mar. 1971; he is listed in *Who Was Who in America*, vol. 5, 1969–1973.

THADDEUS J. BURCH

SCHOOP, Trudi (9 Oct. 1903–14 July 1999), mime and dance and movement therapist, was born Gertrude Schoop in Zurich, Switzerland, the daughter of Friedrich Maximilian Schoop, a newspaper editor and president of Dolder Hotels, and Emma Olga Böppli

Schoop, a freethinker who was uninterested in the conventions of the time. All three of Schoop's siblings were artistic. Max became a painter, Paul later wrote the scores for Trudi's dances, and Hedi was a dancer, actress, ceramist, and painter. Their home was always open to artists and intellectuals. Trudi, brought up in this free-wheeling environment, suffered mightily the rigidity of school in Zurich.

Schoop spoke of her formal schooling as a time when her spirit and body separated. She developed many secret fears and compulsions, and doctors sent her for a cure to a sanitarium in the Swiss mountains. Yet she retained her love for what she defined as the elements of life: energy, rhythm, melody, and space. When she danced she was both courageous and happy. Through dance she expressed her own ideas and feelings. She locked herself in a room and improvised dances that metaphorically became structured expressions of her anxieties. These dances enabled her to externalize her fears, and the experience became a strong underpinning to her later work as a dance therapist.

With no training, Schoop created dances. At the age of sixteen she rented a big room, hired a pianist, and enveloped herself in choreography. About six months later she gave her first public performance. In *The Slave*, a dance she found especially meaningful, the ending represents the final breaking of chains. At this time dancers in Europe, such as Mary Wigman, Rudolf von Laban, and Emile Jaques-Dalcroze, searched for new forms and moved away from the limitations of ballet. Schoop left for Germany to study. She attended the school of Ellen Tells, a disciple of Isadora Duncan, while continuing to perform throughout Switzerland and Germany to great acclaim. In 1924, after the unexpected death of her father, Schoop returned to Zurich and opened a school for "artistic dancing."

The studio was successful, and Schoop enjoyed teaching. Soon after she opened her studio, a physician sent a schizophrenic man to her class, and for weeks he did not move. Schoop subsequently became an intense observer of movements when people danced and when they performed tasks. She became fascinated with gesture, posture, and facial expression and the conflicts expressed in individual bodies and in their movements.

When she returned to choreography, Schoop found a stylized way of storytelling about human foibles, the comic mime form for which she became famous. Her brother Paul composed the music for her pieces. In the late 1920s she performed solo works in Berlin, in an avant-garde café called Die Katakombe, with a group of artists seeking to respond to the emergence of Nazism. This became an important part of Schoop's artistic life.

In 1932 Schoop was invited to participate in the International Dance Congress in Paris. She took a group of her best students to perform in a new piece, her first for an ensemble. It was then that she created her character Fridolin, an awkward young person in conflict with the world. The judges awarded her work a prize, citing hers as "the message of humanity in our time."

Schoop met Hans Wickihalder, who owned Corso, a musical comedy theater, and who also was in the import-export business, and they married in 1929; they had no children. Wickihalder was greatly supportive of Trudi's art and enabled her to form a troupe that consisted of acrobats, ballet dancers, and musical comedians. The troupe included many nationalities and personalities, but Schoop eventually molded a company that performed her pantomimes, humorous statements about human fragilities. Known as Trudi Schoop and Her Comic Ballet, they traveled throughout Europe, and Sol Hurok, the impresario, eventually saw them. He arranged a tour in the United States from 1937 to 1939. They were well received in every city. Some of the better-known pieces were *Fridolin*, *Want Ads*, *The Blonde Marie*, and *Hurray for Love*. Schoop became known as "the female Charlie Chaplin." Thomas Mann wrote of her, "This woman is a phenomenon in her talent for humorously affective expression," and the dance critic John Martin hailed *The Blonde Marie* for its "great gusto and good humor."

When war broke out in Europe, the company disbanded. Schoop returned to Switzerland and her husband. She was fondly remembered by the Swiss decades later for her dances in the political café Cornichon. It was dangerous to make political statements, even in neutral Switzerland, and the performers developed a sign language that defied censorship. Friends let them know if German officials were coming so they could alter material. Schoop performed a burlesque of *The Dying Swan* in which she portrayed Adolf Hitler, complete with black tutu and a mustache, ending with the equivalent of frenzied salutes before Hitler fell moribund. The German consul was outraged, and the Swiss government never allowed her to repeat the performance.

After World War II, Schoop re-formed her group and again toured Europe and America. In 1947, tired of traveling and dispirited, she disbanded her troupe. She was in the United States when her husband suddenly died in 1951. She put down new roots in Van Nuys, California, a home filled with dogs and cats and open to friends. Eventually her energy needed a new outlet.

In 1957 Schoop decided she wanted to dance with psychotic patients. In her book *Won't You Join the Dance?* (1974) she described, with her humorous sensibility, how she began, erred, and came back to try again. Her experience with observation of gesture and posture and her understanding that people either expressed or were conflicted about expressing feelings enabled her to develop a technique for working with psychotic patients. She recognized that the mind and body are reciprocal in their interactions and that the body becomes "a blabbermouth." She later developed her theories by speaking of the *Ur* experience, a German word that encompasses endless and boundless energy, time, and space. She believed dance enabled humans to deal with the reality of their finite world and simultaneously with the transcendent experience of all humans in time and space.

Schoop worked for many years in psychiatric hospitals, including Camarillo State Hospital, where research confirmed the success of her work. She taught many who wished to become dance therapists through classes and workshops in the United States and Europe, and she wrote a seminal book describing her work and her beliefs that has been translated into several languages. Schoop is recognized as one of the pioneers in the field of dance and movement therapy by the American Dance Therapy Association. Above all she lived life as the essence of humanity. She was a woman who showed kindness, humor, empathy, and willingness to give of herself.

• Schoop wrote *Won't You Join the Dance? A Dancer's Essay into the Treatment of Psychosis* (1974) with the help of Peggy Mitchell, and her sister Hedi Schoop illustrated it. Schoop's 1978 lecture in Los Angeles about her theories of *Ur* and her early demons is "Motion and Emotion," *American Journal of Dance Therapy* 22, no. 2 (Fall–Winter 2000). Joan Chodorow wrote of her experiences in Schoop's classes, *Dance Therapy and Depth Psychology: The Moving Imagination* (1991). The University of California Extension Center for Media and Independent Learning has two films about Schoop, *Come Dance with Me* (1992), which shows her work with long-term patients at a psychiatric clinic in Switzerland, and *The Conquest of Emptiness* (1993), a portrait of Schoop speaking about herself and her work, interweaving interviews, archival footage of her dancing, and scenes of her interactions with patients. Obituaries are in the *Los Angeles Times*, 21 July 1999, the *San Francisco Chronicle*, 22 July 1999, and the *New York Times*, 23 July 1999.

SHARON CHAIKLIN

SCOTT, James Brown (3 June 1886–25 June 1943), international relations lawyer and head of the Division of International Law of the Carnegie Endowment for International Peace, was born in Kincardine, Ontario, Canada, the youngest of the five children of John Scott, a stonecutter, and Jeannette Brown. Both parents emigrated from Scotland to New York in the 1840s. In 1854, shortly after their marriage, his parents relocated to Canada. Scott's father was a devout Presbyterian, and his mother nurtured Scott's strong spirit of independent thinking.

In 1876 the Scott family finally settled in Philadelphia, Pennsylvania. Scott graduated from Central High School in 1887 and then enrolled at Harvard. He graduated summa cum laude in 1890, and a year later he obtained his master's degree in international law. He then studied in Europe, where he earned the degree of Doctor of Civil and Cannon Laws from the University of Heidelberg in 1894.

When he returned from Europe, Scott began his own law practice in Los Angeles. He helped organize the Los Angeles Law School, now part of the University of Southern California, and worked as dean until 1899. He took a leave of absence to serve in the military during the Spanish-American War. A member of Company C of the Seventh Regiment of the California Volunteer Infantry, he was deployed to the Philippines. His military service reflected the attitude of many "practical-minded" members of the pre–World War I peace movement. His participation in the movement was part of the trend from noninstitutional pacifism to institutional internationalism. Scott upheld the concept of legal equality of sovereign states while also tolerating the inequality of power among them until international conferences could formulate a set code of laws that all nations would accept. While he was in the Philippines he helped draft the text for governing the islands after the Spanish surrendered.

In 1899, upon his return from the Far East, Scott left southern California and to accept the position of dean of the University of Illinois College of Law. In 1901, while teaching at the law school, he married Adele Cooper Reed in Champaign. They had no children. Two years later, after the publication of *Cases on International Law* (1902) solidified his reputation in the field, he was appointed professor of law at Columbia University.

Scott's expertise in the field of international law and the theories he developed were largely influenced by the theological and moralistic views of Francisco de Vitoria and the Dutch jurist Hugo Grotius. Grotius in particular argued that nations can be governed by natural law and that it is possible to formulate a general code acceptable to most governments. Scott, following Grotius's lead, insisted that "we must be aware that obedience to law is enforced at times not by the threat of physical or corporal punishment, but from the feeling amounting to a certainty that the breach of the law in question would expose us to the reprobation of all good men and women" (Scott, 1906, p. 147). International law would enable nations to function effectively in a civilized world, the same way citizens obey the laws in their respective countries.

In 1906 Secretary of State Elihu Root hired Scott as solicitor of the Department of State. The following year Scott accompanied the American delegation to the Second Hague Peace Conference, and he subsequently published a two-volume text with accompanying documents, *The Hague Peace Conferences of 1899 and 1907* (1909). His work reflected his view that the 1907 conference was a "distinct success." The conference had "substituted arbitration for the use of force in the collection of contract debts"; it regulated "the rights and duties of neutrals and neutral states in land warfare"; it "forbade the opening of hostilities without a declaration"; it "sought to define the status of enemy merchant ships at the outbreak of war"; it "regulated the laying of mines"; and most significantly it "organized an international prize court" (Scott, 1908, p. 21). Reaffirming the 1899 declaration concerning the necessity of a limitation of armaments and providing for the broad foundations for a court of arbitral justice were the principal themes enunciated in his massive study of the two peace conferences.

Scott's advocacy of world peace reflected the new direction the American peace movement took at the beginning of the twentieth century. The peace movement became a prestigious calling devoted to the legal settlement of disputes, the maintenance of government contracts, the development of an "international mind," and the encouragement of the scientific study of war and its alternatives. Between 1901 and 1914 forty-five new peace organizations were established as specialized agencies whose purpose was to transmit the peace leadership's knowledge to the populace and to encourage conciliatory gestures among governments. Among the leaders in the movement were Root, Theodore Marburg, John Bassett Moore, Nicholas Murray Butler, and Scott.

In 1906 Scott became one of the principle founders of the American Society of International Law. Committed to establishing an international legal system, Scott served as the society's secretary from 1906 to 1924, and he also served as president from 1929 to 1939. Founder and editor of the society's *American Journal of International Law* (1907–1924), he was the moving force behind the journal's publication. He reasoned: "Such a publication would . . . disseminate instruction regarding the great principles of international law and those questions that lead to differences between nations. [It] would be most useful in stimulating the scholars who are devoting themselves to that subject" (Scott, 1905, pp. 140–41).

In 1910, along with Root and Butler, Scott became associated with the steel magnate Andrew Carnegie's new foundation devoted to the study of world peace. Scott resigned his State Department position in early 1911 to become director of the Carnegie Endowment's Division of International Law, a position he held until 1940. Under his leadership the division produced an enormous program of publications, including collections of documents and opinions of early legal scholars. Scott edited many of the works and also encouraged the endowment to sponsor grants to societies promoting the cause of world peace. Additionally Scott's commitment to education and to the principle of international conferences enabled him to serve as a delegate or technical adviser at the Paris Peace Conference of 1919, the Washington Naval Conference of 1921–1922, and the Sixth Pan-American Conference of 1928. He also participated in adjudication settlements involving conflicts between Denmark and Brazil, Poland and Brazil, and Belgium and Switzerland. Scott was a firm believer in the future greatness of South America.

Scott's leadership in the Carnegie Foundation coincided with his service in the Judge Advocate General's Office after U.S. entry into World War I. Scott's work with the judge advocate general was directly related to his continuing desire to promote international law. Like other internationalists in the American Society of International Law, Scott was dismayed at the German government's flagrant violations of the Hague conventions. He argued that Germany had violated the treaty guaranteeing Belgium's neutrality and had upset the existing rules of international law governing naval warfare and freedom of the seas. The prosecution of this war on the part of the Allies was necessary to develop more precise definitions of nations' rights and responsibilities within the structure of a world community.

As a strong supporter of arbitration and conciliation, Scott's most noteworthy project was the creation of an international court of justice: "What we want in international law is a court of justice, permanent in nature . . . composed of judges acting under a sense of judicial responsibility, always in session at The Hague, ready and willing, desirous to take the jurisdiction of cases presented to it" (Scott, 1909, p. 56). His idea of a permanent court was based upon the U.S. Supreme Court's ability to rule over the states. Prior to the Great War, Scott praised the establishment of the International Court of Prize, a court of appeals involving neutral ships captured in wartime, as "the first really important world judiciary" (Scott, 2001, pp. 465–66). Disillusioned by the world war and its results, however, Scott criticized the Covenant of the League of Nations, believing that such an organization actually accepted the reality of war instead of abolishing it. Yet he did respond favorably to the creation by the Treaty of Versailles of a Permanent Court of International Justice and participated in its development.

In the interwar years Scott, the organizational leader, worked with the European-based Institute of International Law, serving as president in 1925–1927 and 1928–1929. He was also cofounder of the Academy of International Law at The Hague. His thoughts and views concerning the roles of courts and international law as well as his own involvement in the cause of peace were later summarized in his two-volume *Law, the State, and the International Community* (1939). This work in particular surveyed the major currents of political and judicial thought from Greek and Roman times to the end of the sixteenth century. Although he wrote a number of scholarly works, his writings were never popularly received. Their technical nature limited his audience.

Scott had little to say about Adolf Hitler's acts of aggression and the onset of World War II. Political events in the 1930s were complicated, in his view, by the weakness of the League of Nations and the U.S. Senate's refusal to have the United States join the World Court in 1935. Like Japanese military expansionism in the Far East, Hitler's actions represented, Scott thought, a breakdown in the role of law in civilized society. He wanted to see Hitler and others of his ilk brought before the World Court and tried as criminals for transgressing the code of international law.

A publicist for international law, Scott lectured in Europe, the United States, and Latin America. He was fluent in three European languages. Throughout his career he held academic posts as lecturer and professor of law and international law at George Washington University (1900–1911), Johns Hopkins University

(1909–1916), Georgetown University of Foreign Service (1921–1940), and Georgetown University Law School (1933–1940). Scott was a refined and sensitive person. Many contemporaries, however, considered him "cold" and "impersonal." In 1940 Scott retired to Anne Arundel County, Maryland. The former Spanish-American War veteran and holder of seventeen honorary degrees died at his home in Wardour, Maryland, in the middle of World War II.

• Scott's personal papers are at Georgetown University. A considerable amount of his correspondence is in the papers of the Carnegie Endowment for International Peace, Butler Library, Columbia University. His speeches and reports on international law and peace are compiled in the *Annual Reports of the Lake Mohonk Conferences on International Arbitration* (1895–1916). Among those see in particular his articles in the *Annual Report of the Eleventh Meeting of the Lake Mohonk Conference on International Arbitration, 1905* (1905); "The Law of Nations and the American Society of International Law," *Annual Report of the Lake Mohonk Conference on International Arbitration, 1906* (1906); "The Second Hague Conference," *Annual Report of the Lake Mohonk Conference on International Arbitration, 1908* (1908); and "The Proposed International Court of Arbitral Justice," *Annual Report of the Lake Mohonk Conference on International Arbitration, 1909* (1909). Scott's other notable works include *Peace through Justice: Three Papers on International Justice and the Means of Attaining It* (1917); *The Spanish Origin of International Law: Francisco de Vitoria and His Law of Nations* (1934); *The Hague Peace Conferences of 1899 and 1907*, 2 vols., edited by Shabtai Rosenne (2001); and as editor, *The Classics of International Law* (1964). A scholarly biography is Christopher Rossi, *Broken Chain of Being: James Brown Scott and the Origins of Modern International Law* (1998). A contemporary observation on Scott's role in the Carnegie Foundation and the American Society for International Law is George Finch, "James Brown Scott, 1866–1943," *American Journal of International Law* 38 (Apr. 1944): 183–217. Some scholarly works on Scott and the peace movement are Warren F. Kuehl, *Seeking World Order: The United States and International Organization to 1920* (1969); C. Roland Marchand, *The American Peace Movement and Social Reform, 1898–1918* (1972); David S. Patterson, *Toward a Warless World: The Travail of the American Peace Movement, 1887–1914* (1976); and Charles DeBenedetti, *Origins of the Modern American Peace Movement, 1915–1929* (1978). An obituary is the *New York Times*, 27 June 1943.

CHARLES F. HOWLETT

SEGAL, George (26 Nov. 1924–9 June 2000), sculptor, was born in the Bronx (New York), the son of Jacob Segal and Sophie Gershenfeild Segal. He attended Stuyvesant High School before moving with his family to a chicken farm in South Brunswick, New Jersey, when he was fifteen. Between 1941 and 1949 he studied art, architecture, and art education at a series of schools (Cooper Union, Rutgers University, Pratt Institute and New York University) while working on his parents' farm; he earned a B.S. at New York University and an M.A. at Rutgers. In 1946, he married Helen Steinberg and bought his own farm, in North Brunswick, New Jersey, putting aside his artistic ambitions for a number of years; the couple would have two children.

In 1953, Segal met Allan Kaprow, a painter and installation artist heavily influenced by the composer and performer John Cage, who renewed Segal's interest in the art world and in creating art. Segal began teaching art in 1955 (he continued to teach until 1967) and, within three years, converted his chicken coops into a series of studios, giving up farming and devoting himself to art full time.

Actually, George Segal had started his art career as a painter, but, as he later explained, "it was the ideas about what painting should and shouldn't be that were being taught at the time that gave me trouble. There were all these rules and regulations that had to be followed: the surface of the canvas had to remain intact; there could be no illusion of depth; the complete rejection of figuration. I was asked to shut out the validity of what I could see and what I could touch. After a while, the only space I understood was the space between my own body and the canvas" (interview with Daniel Grant, 1993).

By the late 1950s, Segal was working in sculptural forms, creating life-size human figures using chicken wire, burlap, and plaster. In 1961, while teaching a night school art class, one of his students who was married to a Johnson & Johnson chemist brought in some newly created plaster-impregnated bandages that were designed to set fractures. Recognizing their potential, Segal began bandaging models, relieved of the need to sculpt out the details of their shape.

It was at Segal's farm that the first "Happening" (an art installation complete with an artistic performance) took place in 1958, organized by Kaprow, and Segal was to participate in other Kaprow-sponsored events in years to come. A new era in art was taking shape: pop art began as a movement in England in the late 1950s and blossomed in the United States in the early 1960s. Segal, along with other pop artists of the era—including Jim Dine, Red Grooms, Robert Indiana, Roy Lichtenstein, Marisol, Claes Oldenburg, James Rosenquist, Andy Warhol, and Tom Wesselmann—rejected the dominant abstract expressionism of the 1950s to focus on recognizable, everyday objects from mass culture (advertising signs, celebrities, clothing, Coke bottles, comic books).

Segal's plaster cast figure installations received favorable attention early on and were shown in galleries and, eventually, museums all over the world. In the mid-1970s Segal began to use his plaster casts as molds for bronzes that were displayed as outdoor public artworks, for which he began to receive a growing number of commissions. In 1964 the Moderna Museet in Stockholm, Sweden, was the first museum to purchase one of his works. Thereafter Segal's sculptures were acquired by the Cleveland Museum of Art, the Dallas Museum of Art, the Guggenheim Museum (New York City), the National Gallery of Art and the Hirshhorn Museum and Sculpture Garden (Washington, D.C.), the Nelson-Atkins Museum of Art (Kansas City, Missouri), the San Francisco

Museum of Modern Art and the Whitney Museum of American Art (New York City), among other collections.

Segal's work consists of life-size human figures that are placed in an actual environment, such as an elevator or lunch counter or the interior of a bus, with props that were often retrieved from junkyards. His technique was to wrap live models (sometimes family members and friends, dressed or nude) in long medical bandages, then cover them in plaster. After the plaster had dried, it was carefully cut open, freeing the model; the individual's shape remained as well as the rough texture of the bandages. After that, the plaster cast was resealed. In Segal's work of the 1960s and '70s, he generally left the plaster cast shapes white and unadorned, which gave them the appearance of ghostly figures inhabiting the real world; by the 1980s he began to paint many of his plaster casts.

His work does not glorify the mundane, nor does it parody the figures who appear to be suspended in motion, allowing them to be studied at one's leisure. The stillness creates an often somber psychological mood, comparable to the work of painter Edward Hopper. The figures, who appear to be in deep contemplation, may seem trapped in environments or situations over which they have no control; the colorful soft drink poster advertisement or the blinking traffic lights next to them adds an intrusive element to their lives. "In becoming Pop Art," critic Harold Rosenberg wrote, "objects separate themselves from their functional reality and are changed into artlike equivalents of themselves—a condition best symbolized by George Segal's solid white plaster ghosts." Segal's work also has been compared to European artists Honoré Daumier and Käthe Kollwitz, who similarly focused sympathetic attention on ordinary working people.

In 1978 a retrospective of the artist's sculpture was organized by the Walker Art Center in Minneapolis, Minnesota; the exhibition traveled to the San Francisco Museum of Modern Art and the Whitney Museum. Twenty years later, the Montreal Museum of Fine Arts organized a retrospective of Segal's drawings, paintings, and sculpture, which traveled to the Hirshhorn Museum and Sculpture Garden, the Jewish Museum, and the Miami Art Museum. In 1997, Segal received Japan's Praemium Imperiale award, that nation's top prize for literary, performing, or visual artists anywhere in the world. Two years later, President Bill Clinton presented Segal with the National Medal of Honor, this country's highest award for lifetime cultural achievement.

The artist died at his home in North Brunswick.

Segal's work is properly identified with pop art. While other pop artists focused, however, on the effluvia of consumer society in a "cool," detached, and witty manner, Segal's art retains a feeling of compassion. That pathos is evident in his bronze-plated plaster cast figures of five desperate men, called *The Breadline*, which he created for the Franklin D. Roosevelt Memorial in Washington, D.C., and in the figures of Abraham and Isaac that he made for the campus of Kent State University in Ohio in commemoration of the shooting of four students by National Guardsmen on 4 May 1970.

The Pop Art 1960s created a number of art-world stars, who relished their celebrity status and the personas they created for public consumption. Segal, on the other hand, did not court publicity, instead concentrating on his art and using his renown to advance the cause of artists' rights.

• Useful sources for further reading about George Segal include Dore Ashton, *American Art Since 1945* (1982); Edward Lucie-Smith, *American Realism* (1994); Steven Henry Madoff, ed., *Pop Art: A Critical History* (1997); Sam Hunter, *George Segal* (1989); Phyllis Tuchman, *George Segal* (1983); and Harold Rosenberg, "Marilyn Mondrian: Roy Lichtenstein and Claes Oldenburg," in *The De-Definition of Art* (1979). "George Segal: American Still Life," a documentary produced by New Jersey Public Television, aired nationally on PBS in 2001. An obituary is in the *New York Times*, 10 June 2000.

DANIEL GRANT

SELLERS, Charles Coleman (16 Mar. 1903–31 Jan. 1980), biographer and librarian, was born in the Philadelphia suburb of Overbrook, Pennsylvania, the son of Horace Wells Sellers, an engineer and architect who worked on the restoration of Independence Hall in the 1920s, and Cora Wells, Horace Sellers's first cousin. Charles Sellers earned a B.A. from Haverford College in 1925 and an M.A. in American history from Harvard in 1926. Sellers's early biographical writings focused on atypical subjects, such as the eloquent, idiosyncratic nineteenth-century American evangelist Lorenzo Dow, *Lorenzo Dow: The Bearer of the Word* (1928), and the self-proclaimed evangelist and advocate of free love Theophilus Ransom Gates, *Theophilus the Battle-Axe* (1930). In 1930 Sellers also authored a sympathetic portrait of Benedict Arnold, *Benedict Arnold: The Proud Warrior*. During his early years Sellers, who loved the theater, participated in amateur dramatic performances and playwriting. In the 1930s and 1940s three of his plays were produced. In 1932 he married Helen Earle Gilbert of Hebron, Connecticut, an actress, poet, and author of children's stories, whose work was published in *Poetry Magazine* and *Sewanee Review*. They had two children. Between 1932 and 1938 Charles and Helen Sellers presided over Tracey's Book Store in Hebron. In 1937 Charles Sellers became bibliographic librarian at Wesleyan University in Connecticut. The Sellers sold the bookstore the following year.

Charles's father inspired his son's lifelong love of books and book collecting. Horace Sellers began documenting the life and work of Charles Willson Peale (1741–1827), his great great grandfather, and in 1914 he published "Charles Willson Peale: Artist-Soldier" in the *Pennsylvania Magazine of History and Biography*. On Horace Sellers's death in 1933, Charles Sellers became heir to his father's preparatory work and embarked on a more substantial study of Peale. He also studied the extensive family papers, which included some 3,000 letters, diaries, documents, books, and miscellaneous items. These papers, filled with personal and professional details of the lives of the artistically talented Peale family, were also a rich resource for the study of early American history, science, and culture. Peale and his extended family became the centerpiece of Sellers's research and writing. In 1939 Sellers privately published his first volume on Peale, *The Artist of the Revolution: The Early Life of Charles Willson Peale.*

In 1945 the American Philosophical Society (APS), America's oldest scholarly organization for the advancement of science and art, where Peale once served as curator, purchased Sellers's family papers (the Peale-Sellers collection). When Charles Sellers completed his second volume on Peale in 1947, the society published volumes one and two under their imprint as *Charles Willson Peale*. In 1949 Sellers left Wesleyan to become curator of Dickinsonia at Dickinson College in Carlisle, Pennsylvania, a post he held until 1956. Initially this was a part-time position that enabled him to become a library research associate at APS in Philadelphia (1947–1951), which provided him with easy access to the Peale-Sellers collection as he compiled his catalogue raisonné of the art of Charles Willson Peale, a major endeavor that showcased his industrious and highly organized scholarship. This work, *Portraits and Miniatures of Charles Willson Peale*, published as part of the APS Transactions for 1952, became a valuable resource for historians interested in the art of Peale and a convenient source of information on individuals from many walks of eighteenth-century and early-nineteenth-century American life who were painted by Peale. In 1952, the year after the death of his first wife, Sellers married Barbara S. Roberts; the couple had no children.

In 1956 Sellers became librarian of the Waldron Phoenix Belknap, Jr., Research Library of American Painting at Winterthur, Delaware, and in 1959 he edited Belknap's *American Colonial Painting*. Concurrently Sellers began his tenure as librarian of Dickinson College (1956–1968). During this period he expanded the college's manuscript holdings, planned the new library, enlisted benefactors, and authored numerous pamphlets and brochures on the growing collections. In 1965 he acquired the important Joseph Priestly Family Collection. Sellers's interest in the historical role played by portraits of famous men led him to publish *Benjamin Franklin in Portraiture* (1962). While the first third of the book describes the circumstances of the creation of the Franklin life portraits, the remainder is a descriptive catalog of these images and works related to them. In 1968 Sellers returned to his earlier position of historian and curator of Dickinsonia, but he remained active in the library's functions. The 1969 publication by APS of *Charles Willson Peale with Patron and Populace*, a supplement to Sellers's 1952 *Portraits and Miniatures*, added discussions of portraits not included in the previous work as well as Peale's prints, drawings, history paintings, landscapes, and decorations for public events and other miscellaneous productions of his artistic and scientific imagination. Also that year Sellers completed a one-volume biography, *Charles Willson Peale* (1969), an empathetic and imaginative historical recreation of the life of his protagonist, deftly articulated with primary source materials. A refinement and enrichment of his earlier two-volume work, it introduced Sellers to a broader readership and in 1970 earned him the Bancroft Prize for History.

In 1973, in conjunction with Dickinson's bicentennial, Sellers published *Dickinson College: A History*. At this time an endowment fund was established in his honor to develop the library's Special Collections of Manuscripts and Rare Books. In 1976 Sellers published *Patience Wright: American Artist and Spy in George III's London*. A vivid narrative of the talented, eccentric, and dynamic New Jersey–born wax modeler Patience Lovell Wright (1725–1786), this publication evolved out of Sellers's earlier research on Wright's friend Franklin. Sellers's home was filled with some of the finest examples of the Peale family's art, and although he was not an art historian by training, many of the numerous articles, book reviews, and catalog essays he authored between the 1940s and the 1970s made significant contributions to the then-nascent study of American art. Sellers was described by family and friends as studious, shy, kind, and self-effacing but also intensely focused, highly observant, articulate, and witty. His work and his life were inseparable.

Aside from membership in the Society of the Cincinnati, a hereditary honor based on family military affiliation with George Washington during the American Revolution, Sellers was awarded an honorary doctorate of letters from Temple University in 1957 and was named Historian of the Year by the Cumberland County (Pennsylvania) Historical Society in 1972. In April 1979 he became the eighth member of his family to be elected a member of the intellectually prestigious American Philosophical Society, and in May 1979 he was awarded an honorary doctorate of letters by Dickinson. Sellers's second wife died in 1979. That year he began plans for a history of the American theater with his fiancée, Peggy Barnes. Sellers's twelfth and final book, *Mr. Peale's Museum: Charles Willson Peale and the First Popular Museum of Science and Art*, was his contribution to the study of the development and display of the natural sciences in the United States and the role of "rational amusement" in the context of an American museum. Sellers did not live to see its release in February 1980. He died of a heart attack while on a visit with his daughter and grandson in Sydney, Australia.

• Sellers's personal library, including significant American and European historical and literary imprints as well as works of religious biography, iconography, and magic lore, was distributed between Dickinson College and the American Philosophical Society. Sellers's research notes for his publications as well as his personal correspondence, lecture manuscripts, and literary papers, which include poems, plays, novels, and short stories, most of them unpublished, were given to Dickinson (Sellers papers). Works by his first wife, Helen Earle Gilbert, are also in this collection, as is correspondence with and publications by one of his closest friends since their days at Haverford, the novelist and poet Frederic Prokosch (1908–1989). Sellers's files on paintings, visual materials, and correspondence related to the art of the Peales as well as a number of other American artists were bequeathed to APS along with Sellers's working files for *Benjamin Franklin in Portraiture* and *Mr. Peale's Museum* (Charles Coleman Sellers Papers). For a full listing of Sellers's publications see "A Bibliography of the Published Works of Charles Coleman Sellers," Dickinson College, 1981. The Peale-Sellers papers as well as other materials on the Peale and Sellers families that Sellers donated or bequeathed to APS are available to researchers through the microform publication *The Collected Papers of Charles Willson Peale and His Family*, ed. Lillian B. Miller (1980). This publication and its related historically annotated letterpress volumes, *The Selected Papers of Charles Willson Peale and His Family* (1983–), also reproduce numerous items from other public and private collections across the country that directly document the endeavors and lives of the Peale family members and their contributions to American history, science, and culture. These publications have been generated by the Papers of Charles Willson Peale and His Family, a project established at the National Portrait Gallery of the Smithsonian Institution in 1974. Arguably Sellers's labors brought the value of the Peale materials to the attention of his fellow historians, who chose to make them readily accessible. It was fitting therefore that the first volume of *The Selected Papers*, edited by Lillian B. Miller et al, which was published in 1983, was dedicated to Sellers's memory. An obituary by Whitfield J. Bell, Jr., is in *The American Philosophical Society Yearbook, 1980* (pp. 622–625).

CAROL EATON SOLTIS

SENGSTACKE, John H. H. (25 Nov. 1912–28 May 1997), newspaper publisher and civil rights advocate, was born John Hermann Henry Sengstacke in Savannah, Georgia, the son of Herman Alexander Sengstacke, a Protestant minister, and Rosa Mae Davis, a missionary worker. Sengstacke was close to his uncle, Robert Sengstacke Abbott, the founding publisher of the *Chicago Defender.* The weekly newspaper had quickly established itself as one of the nation's premier black newspapers in the early twentieth century. Abbott, who did not have children, decided to make his nephew his heir. Abbott sent Sengstacke to his own alma mater, Hampton Institute (now Hampton University) in Hampton, Virginia, so Sengstacke would be prepared to take over the family business. Upon his graduation in 1933 at the age of twenty-one, Sengstacke immediately became president, vice president, and general manager of the Chicago publishing company. In 1936 Sengstacke founded the *Michigan Chronicle*, another prominent black newspaper in the Jim Crow era. On 9 July 1939 he married Myrtle Elizabeth Picou, with whom he had three sons; they were divorced.

After Abbott's death in 1940, Sengstacke inherited the *Chicago Defender.* Also that year he established and became the first president of the Negro Newspaper Publishers Association (NNPA). This organization sought to give the black newspaper, the most powerful

local forum for African Americans outside the black church, a national collective voice. The purpose of the NNPA, he explained in 1942, was to help "consolidate its energy, unify its aims, and concentrate on a practical strategy for a sustained frontal attack on the issues, institutions, and personalities which are blocking the progress of the race" (quoted in Perry, p. 18). He served three terms as president of the association during his lifetime. Sengstacke remained connected with his fellow black newspaper publishers throughout his long career.

Sengstacke was a discreet man but a tough advocate for African Americans. In June 1942, when Attorney General Francis Biddle considered prosecuting black newspapers for their blistering criticisms of the treatment of black soldiers, Sengstacke would not relent. "If you want to close us, go ahead and attempt it," he declared (quoted in Staples, p. 27). Biddle hesitated. With some help from the National Association for the Advancement of Colored People (NAACP), the administration and the NNPA brokered a deal that would give black press reporters greater access to Washington. No sedition charges were filed. In 1944 Sengstacke was instrumental in getting Harry McAlpin, a black reporter, to desegregate the White House press corps.

Sengstacke's past prodding of the White House to desegregate the nation's military forces did not escape the notice of President Harry Truman. In 1948 the president appointed Sengstacke to the Committee on Equality of Treatment and Opportunity in the Armed Forces. The committee's findings led to the desegregation of the nation's military by 1949.

Yet Sengstacke remained primarily a newspaper publisher. Under his leadership the *Defender*—which became the first African-American daily in 1956—produced hard-hitting editorials against Jim Crow laws and ran opinion pieces by writers such as Langston Hughes, who created his "Simple" stories first as *Defender* columns. In the 1960s Sengstacke worked with some other black newspaper publishers to provide financial support for sit-in protesters trying to desegregate southern public facilities. In addition to publishing the *Defender* and the *Chronicle*, Sengstacke by 1970 had also purchased the *Memphis Tri-State Defender* and the *Pittsburgh Courier,* the latter another national black newspaper voice against segregation.

Although he was in the high-profile media business, Sengstacke was most comfortable away from the spotlight. He spent his political capital as a behind-the-scenes power broker. Sengstacke and his friend Congressman William L. Dawson, another African American, encouraged Richard J. Daley to run for mayor of Chicago in 1955. In return Daley used the city's patronage power to secure city government jobs for African Americans. Sengstacke remained loyal to the Daley machine during its twenty-one-year reign, even breaking ranks with some black political leaders when the *Defender* endorsed Daley's son Richard Daley to follow in his father's footsteps in 1989. Until his death Sengstacke continued to write the paper's political endorsements.

Sengstacke died in Chicago, suffering complications from a stroke. Sengstacke was perhaps the most prominent figure in America's black press during the middle of the twentieth century. He led the African-American print media from its height in the 1940s through the civil rights movement of the 1960s to the changes in black America in the 1990s. His legacy is the continued existence of both the *Chronicle* and the *Defender* as well as of the NNPA, which has been renamed the National Newspaper Publishers Association and is based in Washington, D.C.

• Sengstacke's leadership of the *Chicago Defender* is briefly, if sporadically, discussed in Roi Ottley, *The Lonely Warrior: The Life and Times of Robert S. Abbott* (1955); Enoch Waters, *American Diary: A Personal History of the Black Press* (1987); and Ben Burns, *Nitty Gritty: A White Editor in Black Journalism* (1996). Details about early NNPA history under Sengstacke's leadership are in Armistead S. Pride and Clint C. Wilson II, *A History of the Black Press* (1997); and Earnest L. Perry, Jr., "Voice of Consciousness: The Negro Newspaper Publishers Association during World War II" (Ph.D. diss., University of Missouri–Columbia, 1998). See also Jerry Thomas, "Who's Who Remembers Trailblazing Publisher of *Defender*: Sengstacke Hailed for Civil Rights Work and Business Savvy," *Chicago Tribune*, 8 June 1997; and Brent Staples, "Citizen Sengstacke," *New York Times Magazine*, The Lives They Lived sec., 4 Jan. 1998. An obituary is Ron Grossman and Jerry Thomas, "Defender Publisher Dies at 84: Sengstacke Blazed Civil Rights Trail," *Chicago Tribune*, 29 May 1997.

TODD STEVEN BURROUGHS

SIMAK, Clifford D. (3 Aug. 1904–25 Apr. 1988), science-fiction writer, was born Clifford Donald Simak in Millville, Wisconsin, the son of John Lewis Simak, a farmer, and Margaret Wiseman Simak. He attended local schools and spent a short time at the University of Wisconsin but left to become a high school teacher. In 1929, after a few years of teaching, he took a job as a staff reporter on a small local paper. That same year he married Agnes Kuchenberg; the couple had two children. During the following decade, Simak worked for several small papers in the Midwest, and in 1939 he joined the staff of the *Minneapolis Star and Tribune*, for which he wrote a column called "Science in the News." He became the news editor of the *Star* in 1949, and in 1961 he assumed the post of coordinator of the *Tribune*'s Science Reading Series, written for schools, which won an Award for the Advancement of Science from the Westinghouse-American Association. He wrote the column "Medical News" for the *Tribune* until his retirement in 1976.

Simak's daily involvement with both the news and science led naturally to an interest in the rapidly emerging field of science fiction, and from the early 1930s he occasionally submitted stories to pulp magazines of the genre, publishing his first piece, "The World of the Red Sun," in December 1931 in *Wonder Stories*. It was not until the end of the decade, however, after publishing no more than half a dozen stories, that he began to apply himself seriously to fiction. A facile writer, he quickly became a regular contributor to such magazines as *Astounding Science-Fiction*, whose new editor John W. Campbell came to dominate the field and who encouraged him in his work.

Simak maintained his dual career as a journalist and science-fiction writer for most of his working life, presenting complex scientific information with clarity and grace in his newspaper writing and creating fantastic extrapolations of the impact of science on society in his fiction. From the beginning, Simak had a distinctive angle of vision; avoiding the clichés of space wars and superheroes, he emphasized the responsibilities of technology and the importance of preserving human values. His characters—at least, the human beings among them—were common people with normal failings, and he tried, as quoted in his *New York Times* obituary, "to place humans in perspective against the vastness of universal time and space." His rural upbringing was reflected in his frequent pastoral settings and in the moral values he espoused. His human heroes tend to be countrymen, close to the Earth and sensitive to its needs. When he dealt with alien life, it is usually superior in intelligence and compassion to that of Earth, as in his 1961 story "Green Thumb," in which an agricultural agent encounters an extraterrestrial plant with telepathic powers and profoundly sympathetic feelings. Animals and robots, also generally superior to humans in most regards, complete the *dramatis personae* of Simak's fiction and reflect his recurring theme of the equality of all sentient beings and the Earth as one day becoming a member of a harmonious community of worlds.

The best-known novel from Simak's pen began as a series of stories in *Astounding* published between 1944 and 1957 and gathered together as *City* in 1952. Described in the author's (London) *Times* obituary (29 Apr. 1988) as "a science fiction classic," it comprises eight loosely connected tales spanning 10,000 years of the Webster family, tracing the history of mankind from the supercity of the near future to an idyllic nontechnological society on Jupiter occupied by the remnant of humanity following the collapse of urban society. Earth has been left to a race of intelligent, surgically altered dogs who narrate the tales as fables from a forgotten past. In the last story, technologically sophisticated ants develop a complex civilization of their own, complete with air-polluting factories, and drive the peaceful canine society to follow the human example and abandon Earth. In a ninth story, "Epilog," written in 1973, Simak revealed that the ants had recapitulated the human experience by destroying their cities and disappearing. *City* earned Simak the International Fantasy Award in 1953, the first of many honors the science-fiction community was to pay him. At a time when science-fiction writers generally celebrated technology, *City*'s bleak vision of its dangers was a striking innovation, and the novel greatly influenced the medium.

Although the theme that the author summarized as "the confrontation of machines and man" (*Skirmish*, "Foreword," p. 8) was to remain central to his work, Simak frequently dealt with religious questions and man's preoccupation with immortality. In *Why Call Them Back from Heaven?* (1967), science has displaced religion by providing a means of resurrection at the cost of all human values. *A Choice of Gods* (1972) asserts the need to recognize a guiding intelligence in the management of the universe, and *Project Pope* (1981) describes a society in which religion has died out among humans but been taken up by robots, who are creating an ultimate computer as a spiritual leader. From the late 1960s, Simak was occasionally to enter the field of fantasy, although without abandoning the pastoral nostalgia that informs his science fiction. His 1968 novel *The Goblin Reservation* includes trolls, goblins, and banshees among its characters, and the whimsical satire *Out of Their Minds* (1970) includes such fictional characters as Don Quixote, Superman, and Br'er Fox. *Enchanted Pilgrimage* (1975) and *The Fellowship of the Talisman* (1978) deal with Christian mythology in a medieval setting, drawing on Arthurian legend.

At his death in Minneapolis, Minnesota, Simak left a legacy of some thirty novels and over a hundred short stories, as well as four popular science texts, mostly drawn from his newspaper columns. His work was widely anthologized and translated into a dozen languages and earned him Hugo awards, the science fiction equivalent of the Oscar, in 1959, 1964, and 1980, and a Grand Master Award from the Science Fiction Writers of America for lifetime achievement in 1977. Among the most respected practitioners of his craft, he was also one of the best loved, noted for his modesty, friendliness, and generosity to new authors. Isaac Asimov, in an obituary in *Locus*, described him as "the man who, in the kindliest way possible, revolutionized my life"(June 1988, p. 77). In prose that was remarkable for its directness and lucidity, Simak did much to transform the early "space operas" into serious novels with a substantial moral dimension and to broaden the market for the genre.

• Simak provides a clear statement of his literary principles and goals in the introduction to *Skirmish: The Great Short Fiction of Clifford D. Simak* (1977). Reviews of his work are in the science-fiction magazines *Galaxy, Analog, Magazine of Science Fiction and Fantasy*, and *Amazing Stories* from the 1950s to the 1980s. More general examination of his fiction appears in Samuel Moskowitz, *Seekers of Tomorrow* (1966); Donald A. Wollheim, *The Universe Makers* (1971); Thomas D. Clareson, ed., *Voices for the Future: Essays on Major Science Fiction Writers*, vol. 1 (1976); Paul Walker, *Speaking of Science Fiction* (1978); and Brian W. Aldiss, *Trillion Year Spree: The History of Science Fiction* (1986; rev. ed., 2001). His anti-utopian themes are examined in Kingsley Amis, *New Maps of Hell* (1960), and Harold L. Berger, *Science Fiction and the New Dark Age* (1976). A detailed bibliography of Simak's work to the time of its publication is Muriel R. Becker, *Clifford D. Simak: A Primary and Secondary Bibliography* (1980). Obituaries are in the *New York Times*, 28 Apr. 1988, and *Locus*, June and July 1988.

DENNIS WEPMAN

SIMJIAN, Luther (28 Jan. 1905–23 Oct. 1997), inventor, was born Luther George Simjian in Aintab (now Gaziantep), Turkey, the son of George Simjian, a representative with an Austrian insurance company for the Turkish territory, and Josephine Zaharian Simjian; both parents were Armenian. Josephine Simjian died when Luther was a few months old. When Luther was two, his father remarried. Until age nine Luther lived in Aintab with his father, stepmother Mary, and two younger half sisters. Most of his relatives lived nearby. His parents were college educated and well off financially. His father traveled frequently for business and enjoyed bringing back items that were new to his family and friends.

Even as a young child Luther had a very creative mind and was interested in optics and photography. A toy he built when he was seven years old illustrates this. After a trip to Paris, an uncle returned to Aintab with a "magic lantern," a device popular in Europe that could project images through decorated glass slides. Luther was so intrigued by this device that he decided to make one of his own, since the original was for adult use only. He had observed how the bottoms of glass bottles built into the ceiling of the local Turkish baths refracted light. He made his own magic lantern from a glass bottle bottom with the right curvature to form a lens, a kerosene lantern for the light source, and cartoon slides that he made by drawing with matches onto smoked glass; he then gave "shows" to the neighborhood children.

During World War I Armenians were considered enemies of the Ottoman Empire. In 1915 the Simjian family escaped to Aleppo (now called Halab) in Syria. They spent the next four years in Aleppo, in semi-hiding. Luther, still a boy, was allowed to wander in the city and provided most of the contact between his family and the outside world. He helped support the family with odd jobs, continuing his education with tutoring from his stepmother. After the war the family returned to Aintab. In 1920, when Simjian was 15 years old, his family traveled to visit relatives, leaving him behind so that he could continue attending school. During their trip his sisters and stepmother were killed in the Armenian Massacre at Marash, and his father was unable to return to Aintab. Simjian then decided to leave the Turkish Empire. Alone, he fled to Beirut and then to Marseilles. He wanted to go to America, so he wrote to his father's brothers to ask for help. While he was waiting for them to arrange passage, he worked at odd jobs to support himself. His artistic talents and an interest in photography attracted him to a photographer who taught him how to tint photographs. After he had been in France for six months, his uncles in the United States completed his immigration forms.

Before the end of 1920 Simjian arrived at Ellis Island and went to New Haven, Connecticut, where his relatives lived. Within a week he found a job coloring photographs using the painting skills he had learned in France, moved into a furnished room, and, still only fifteen years old, became self-sufficient. He soon found another job in the medical department of Yale University. As a medical photographer he took pictures of specimens, made lantern slides for doctors, and showed the slides for class lectures. He learned as much as possible during the lectures he could attend and went to school at night to prepare for medical school. He introduced new techniques into the existing art of photographing medical specimens, and soon he was regarded as an expert.

In 1928 Simjian was asked to design and head a newly established photographic department at Yale Medical School. Presented with this opportunity, he decided to set aside, or at least to postpone, plans to attend medical school. During the next few years he developed and patented photographic techniques, including methods for projecting microscope images, photographing specimens under water, and taking colored X rays.

After the photographic department was well established, Simjian turned his interests toward artistic and portrait photography. To avoid the stiff poses common in yearbook portraits, he experimented with a self-photographing camera that allowed a subject to look into a mirror and see the framed pose the camera would take. He obtained several U.S. and European patents for a "pose-reflecting apparatus for photographic use." After inventing and patenting the new camera, Simjian decided to license and manufacture it. Because the process was a threat to established photography studios, he looked outside the camera and film industries for support. With the financial and administrative backing of Sperry Gyroscope, he set up a company, PhotoReflex, named after the camera. In 1931 a portrait cabinet containing the camera and posing apparatus was introduced at Wanamaker's department store in New York City. The invention of the "PhotoReflex Studio" led to invention of the autofocus camera, because he needed a way for the camera to automatically focus as the sitter looked around and changed positions. The basic and very original patent on this in 1932 changed the whole photography industry. He did not receive much money for his autofocusing invention, but he did get publicity. He eventually sold the rights to the PhotoReflex camera and name but reserved the rights to use the technology for nonphotographic applications.

By 1933 Simjian's reputation as an inventor was established. He resigned from Yale in 1934 and moved to New York. He took courses at Columbia that he felt would be useful in the promotion of his inventions, focusing on business education, writing, and international banking. In 1934 he finished another major invention, the colored X-ray machine. He had conceived the idea at Yale while trying to improve the quality of lecture slides. He decided to apply the new technology of television to X-ray images. Scanning was done in three separate colors, each of which could be enhanced as necessary, and the three scans could then be recombined to form a colored image.

The separate scans could also be sent through a wire to another location for analysis. This transformed the field of X-ray technology.

After a short time in New York, Simjian traveled in Europe, looking at options and promoting his camera. He set up a laboratory in London and started a company called Miroflex to market the PhotoReflex camera. But war had begun in Europe and manufacturing efforts turned away from commercial products. On his return to New York, he met Gladys Cannon from Illinois. After a short courtship they were married on 15 April 1936; they had two children. The Simjians lived for about two years in New York then moved to Connecticut. Simjian sold the PhotoReflex name but kept his company and renamed it Reflectone Corporation. The name was derived as a combination of "reflection," since mirrors and optics were the basis of much of his early work, and "tone," which evoked the new technologies of acoustics, communication, and electronics.

About this time he came up with the idea of using the optical system of his PhotoReflex camera for a rotating boudoir chair with an attached, movable mirror that reflected the user's image from every angle, making it easier for women to apply makeup. The user could sit in front of a vanity mirror, rotate on this chair and continue to see the back of her head while keeping both hands free. After several years of development, this chair, promoted under the name Reflectone Mirror Chair, also became a small commercial success, and he continued to improve on the idea for many years.

Simjian continued to come up with new ideas. He patented a system in which a picture could be developed immediately while still preserving the negative. He invented a flight speed indicator for airplanes. As World War II approached Simjian realized that the United States would be pulled into an aerial war; recognizing the importance of training and the need for airmen to quickly identify enemy aircraft, he invented the Aircraft Range Estimation Trainer, which was widely used for training Allied pilots and tail gunners. This trainer was "a mechanism used for training aviators in identifying aircraft and determining their distance, their speed of movement, their direction of movement and other related factors that are important in combat flying" (Patent 2,392,871). He designed the three-dimensional device using synchronized mirrors similar to those on his PhotoReflex camera and mirror chair, an airplane model, and controlled lighting. By remotely changing the speed and angles of the model plane while the pilot or gunner watched through a sight, the instructor could produce the effect of flight, thus training the student to identify an enemy aircraft and judge its motion. The U.S. Navy approved the design and placed orders for approximately 2,000 devices. Reflectone grew from three employees to more than a hundred in order to fill orders for this trainer. The device was credited by the War Department with having contributed to the success of the air war. Simjian considered this his most significant invention of the era because of the many lives it saved.

After this, Simjian was considered a specialist in the visual aspects of flight training. Through the 1940s and 1950s, Reflectone developed and manufactured training devices for night vision, radar, missile control, radar fire control, weapons systems, cockpit procedures, and many other functions. Simjian changed his company's name from Reflectone Corporation to Reflectone Electronics, Inc., because most of the products were electronic in nature. Eventually the company became a manufacturer of flight simulators, with 250 employees by 1950.

Simjian invented the TelePrompTer, which allowed a speaker to read text from directly in front of the television camera, by synchronizing the camera with the text projector so the projector light would not interfere with the lighting required for the filming. He saw the need for a machine that would allow a worker to deposit his weekly pay into a bank and receive a receipt for the transaction, and therefore developed the Automatic Bank Deposit and Cashing Machine. The machine used microfilm to record whatever cash or checks were deposited, along with a deposit slip, plus a picture of the person making the deposit. He obtained more than twenty patents for this. The machine was originally installed in select companies for use by employees. He then envisioned having machines in banks to replace tellers so that customers could pay bills, cash checks, and make deposits automatically. In 1961 Reflectone Electronics, Inc., introduced the Bankograph. A few banks in New York tried out these automatic teller machines, but after a few months they decided to discontinue their use. For security reasons the machines had to be kept in bank lobbies, and most customers preferred to deal directly with tellers. Simjian's models were operated completely by mechanical means, before the application of electronic computing to the process made depositing and cashing cost-effective. He is sometimes referred to as the "father of the ATM" because he introduced the idea behind these now-ubiquitous machines.

Simjian remained president and chairman of Reflectone for twenty-two years. He was a successful businessman whose company became a significant commercial success. He felt great responsibility for his employees and was involved in their lives. However, he realized that he would rather focus on new problems and challenges instead of being involved in business. He sold the company to Universal Match Corporation in 1961. Later Reflectone was spun off as an independent public company. The company moved its operations to Tampa, Florida, in 1980. In 1999 British Aerospace bought out Reflectone as a wholly owned subsidiary, and the name was changed to BAE Systems. In 2000 the division was sold to CAE of Montreal, Canada, and again changed names.

After selling Reflectone, Simjian built Command Automation, a small research and development lab of his own in Fort Lauderdale, Florida. The breadth of his interests is reflected in the variety of patents he received. In the 1960s he developed an indoor, computerized golf practice range; when a golf ball was struck, an analog computer calculated and projected its flight on a screen. He developed a remotely accessed automatic postage-metering machine; Pitney Bowes bought the rights for further development but ultimately used another design instead. He invented an exercise bike, a method for tenderizing meat, medical applications using ultrasound, golf balls, cooking devices, the use of ultrasound as an anticounterfeiting device, an athletic shoe, and a bandage. He also made improvements to many earlier inventions.

In 1978, the Connecticut Patent Law Association awarded Simjian the Eli Whitney award for his work. This award is given annually to "an outstanding individual in recognition of significant contributions made to law or science."

Simjian continued inventing until his death. His last patent, a method of improving the sonority of a musical instrument, was awarded in 1997 just months before his death. He died in Fort Lauderdale, Florida. A pioneer in photographic and optical inventions, with more than 200 U.S. patents and several hundred foreign patents, his favorites were the electronic transmission of X rays and the range estimation trainer, because they contributed to saving lives. He considered himself a "real inventor, not a product developer" and preferred to sell his inventions to other producers and manufacturers. He saw his inventions as a means to finance his ideas. Once he finished an invention, he would turn to something else. A coworker said of him: "Simjian looked at things a different way. Most people see something as it is. He would see it as it could be."

• Simjian wrote and self-published *Portions of an Autobiography* in 1997, shortly before his death; no biography has been commercially published. He described some of his early inventions in "Photography at the School of Medicine," *Yale Scientific Magazine* (May 1929), pp. 19–20. Other published articles about Simjian's work include "Self-Photography," *Literary Digest* (4 July 1931), p. 19; "Colored X-Rays," *Time Magazine* (9 July 1934), pp. 42–43; "New X-Ray Device Shows Color and Transmits Image by Wire," *New York Herald Tribune* (27 June 1934), p. 1; "Machine Accepts Bank Deposits," *New York Times* (12 Apr. 1961); "Inventor Will Receive Eli Whitney Award," *Greenwich Time* (15 May 1978); Marguerite A. Cushing, "Connecticut Spotlight on Luther Simjian," *Spotlight* (Sept. 1987), pp. 66–67; and Alexandra Bandon, "Make it New—Luther Simjian A.T.M.," *New York Times Magazine* (4 Jan. 1998). Obituaries are in the *New York Times* (2 Nov. 1997, correction 4 Nov. 1997) and the *Tampa Tribune* (4 Nov. 1997).

ELIZABETH H. KING

SLAYTON, Deke (1 Mar. 1924–13 June 1993), astronaut, was born Donald Kent Slayton in Sparta, Wisconsin, the son of Charles Sherman Slayton and Victoria Adelia Larson Slayton, dairy farmers. Young Slayton was educated in the Sparta public schools. Thrilled from an early age with airplanes, he entered the U.S. Army Air Corps as a private unassigned during World War II and received his wings in April 1943 after completing flight training at Vernon and Waco, Texas. He flew B-25s with the 340th Bombardment Group and completed fifty-six combat missions in Europe. After this combat tour, Slayton returned to Columbia, South Carolina, where he became a B-25 instructor pilot. With the war virtually over in Europe, Slayton went to the Pacific in April 1945 and flew seven combat missions in B-26 bombers with the 319th Bombardment Group.

After World War II Slayton enrolled at the University of Minnesota in Minneapolis on the GI Bill. In 1949 he received a bachelor of science degree in aeronautical engineering. He then went to work for the Boeing Aircraft Company in Seattle, Washington, before being recalled to military service in 1951, serving with the Minnesota Air National Guard. At that point Slayton decided to make the air force his career; he served in several assignments before attending the USAF Test Pilot School at Edwards Air Force Base, California, in June 1955. He then worked as a military test pilot.

In 1955 Slayton married Marjory Lunney of Los Angeles; they had a son. The marriage ended in divorce. In 1983 he married Bobbie Osborn. They had no children; however, he helped raise Bobbie's two children.

In April 1959 NASA selected Slayton as one of the first seven astronauts for Project Mercury. Slayton and his fellow astronauts participated in a press conference at NASA Headquarters in Washington, D.C., in which the media characterized them as the best the nation had to offer. Certainly they carried on their shoulders hopes and dreams of the nation, now engaged in a "cold war" with Soviet communism. Slayton was irritable at the press conference. He nudged Alan Shepard and whispered, "They're applauding us like we've already done something, like we were heroes or something."

Slayton was scheduled to pilot the Mercury-Atlas 7 mission, but in August 1959 flight surgeons determined that he had a mild, occasional irregular heart palpitation. They grounded him. He now became the de facto head of the astronauts, and in September 1962 NASA named him coordinator of astronaut activities, making him responsible for the operation of the astronaut office. In November 1963, he resigned his commission as an air force major to assume the role of director of flight crew operations.

For a decade he oversaw the astronauts, making crew assignments and managing the full range of astronaut activities. Slayton personally chose all of the crews, determining among other things that Neil Armstrong would be the first person to walk on the Moon in July 1969. In March 1972, following a comprehensive review of his medical status, Slayton was restored to full flight status and certified eligible for space flights.

In the summer of 1975 (15–24 July) Slayton made his only space flight as Apollo docking module pilot of the Apollo-Soyuz Test Project (ASTP) mission, which culminated in the first meeting in space between American astronauts and Soviet cosmonauts. Completing the U.S. flight crew for this nine-day Earth-orbiting mission were Thomas P. Stafford (Apollo commander) and Vance D. Brand (Apollo command module pilot). In the Soviet spacecraft were cosmonauts Alexey Leonov (Soyuz commander) and Valeriy Kubasov (Soyuz flight engineer). The rendezvous and docking of the two nations' spacecrafts was symbolic of the political détente between the United States and the Soviet Union. During the mission Slayton told a worldwide audience, "It feels great. The only thing that upsets me is to have missed this fun for the last 16 years. I never believed it was quite as great as it really is."

After completing ASTP, Slayton stayed with NASA in various positions until his formal retirement on 27 February 1982. He then founded Space Services Inc., of Houston, a company that developed rockets for small commercial payloads. At the time of his death in League City, Texas, he was director of EER System's Space Services Division in Houston.

His remains were cremated and scattered on his family farm near Sparta, Wisconsin.

• There is no formal collection of Slayton's papers. Sizable biographical files on him are located in the NASA Historical Reference Collection, NASA Headquarters, Washington, D.C.; at the National Air and Space Museum, Smithsonian Institution, Washington, D.C.; and in the official records of NASA, Record Group 255 of the National Archives and Records Administration. Slayton published with Alan Shepard a memoir of the race to the Moon, *Moonshot: The Inside Story of America's Race to the Moon* (1994), and a formal autobiography, *Deke! U.S. Manned Space, From Mercury to the Shuttle* (1994), written with Michael Cassutt. Excellent biographical accounts are in Courtney G. Brooks, James M. Grimwood, and Loyd S. Swenson, Jr., *Chariots for Apollo: A History of Manned Lunar Spacecraft* (Washington, DC: NASA Special Publication–4205, 1979); Edward Clinton Ezell and Linda Neuman Ezell, *The Partnership: A History of the Apollo-Soyuz Test Project* (Washington, DC: NASA Special Publication–4209, 1978); Andrew Chaikin, *A Man on the Moon: The Voyages of the Apollo Astronauts* (1994); and Barton C. Hacker and James M. Grimwood, *On the Shoulders of Titans: A History of Project Gemini* (Washington, DC: NASA SP–4203, 1977). Obituaries are in the *New York Times, Los Angeles Times, Aviation Week & Space Technology, Space News,* and *Washington Post,* all 14 June 1993.

ROGER D. LAUNIUS

SMITH, Courtney C. (20 Dec. 1916–16 Jan. 1969), educator and college president, was born Courtney Craig Smith in Winterset, Iowa, the son of Samuel Craig Smith, a lawyer and banker, and Myrtle Dabney Smith. In 1929 his father died, and two years later the family moved to Des Moines. Smith was active on the debate team, won public-speaking prizes, and was president of both the National Honor Society and the Latin Club at Roosevelt High School .

In 1934 Smith was awarded a scholarship to attend Harvard University, where he earned his way by waiting on tables in the Harvard Freshman Union and working in the Harvard Freshman Union library, Widener Library, and Leverett House library. He studied English literature and set his sights on becoming an educator. During his Harvard years he spent summers traveling with his older sister, Florence Smith, who organized and led European tours for young adults. On the last of those trips he met Elizabeth Bowden Proctor, whom he married on 12 October 1939. They had three children.

In 1938 Smith graduated from Harvard magna cum laude and was elected to Phi Beta Kappa. He won a Rhodes Scholarship and in the fall of 1938 went to Merton College, Oxford, England, to study English literature. A year later he returned to Harvard for graduate studies, where he became a tutor and a teaching fellow. He worked under professors Hyder E. Rollins and James B. Munn and in 1944 was awarded a Ph.D. His dissertation, "The Seventeenth-Century Drolleries," was a study of collections of witty stories and songs that flourished in seventeenth-century England.

Near the end of his studies Smith was accepted into the U.S. Naval Reserve, and by January 1944 he was in active service as an ensign (j.g.). He trained at Quonset Point, Rhode Island, and Hampton Institute, Virginia, and was then deployed to Pensacola Naval Air Station, Florida. In Pensacola, a racially segregated city, he served as the "liaison officer for Negro personnel" for 2,500 African Americans serving the navy at the base. In that capacity Smith negotiated to maintain African Americans' rights, coached them about safe travel within the community, supervised remedial education, increased "colored recreation," and established links with community welfare agencies, attempting to bridge the gap between the official naval policy of nondiscrimination and the reality of racist laws and customs. Smith's liaison work led him to begin reading African-American and contemporary American literature.

Released from the navy, Smith in 1946 accepted an appointment to teach English literature at Princeton University. He became an advocate for the integration of American literature into the traditional curriculum of the English department and was made the head of a new undergraduate seminar in modern literature. In 1950 he served as the acting director of the American Civilization program.

While teaching at Princeton, Smith also reengaged with the Rhodes Scholars program. He served as secretary of the New Jersey selection committee, then became assistant to Frank Aydelotte, American secretary of the Rhodes Scholar Program. Smith succeeded Aydelotte as American secretary in January 1953, when Aydelotte retired. After serving a year as codirector of the Woodrow Wilson Fellowship Program, he was appointed director in July 1952. In the next twelve months Smith obtained funding from the Carnegie and Rockefeller philanthropies and oversaw the program's transformation from a regional to a national scale.

Smith in the meantime became a leading candidate for the vacant presidency at Swarthmore College in Pennsylvania. With the support of Aydelotte, who was on Swarthmore's board of managers, Smith was appointed president of the college in April 1953, at the age of thirty-six. Taking office in September, he was immediately active in improving alumni relationships and fundraising, sustaining and developing the campus, appointing new faculty, and raising faculty salaries. Ultimately he obtained funds for a new state-of-the-art library, a much-needed science building, an award-winning dining hall for students, three dormitories, and a modern infirmary. During Smith's sixteen-year presidency Swarthmore regularly was ranked the leading small liberal arts college in the United States.

While he significantly increased financial support from the alumni, Smith also drew new resources to the college through his extensive contacts in education, philanthropy, and government, including an ever-growing network of well-placed Rhodes Scholars. From 1953 to 1969 Smith was a trustee of the Markle Foundation, and in 1955 he was elected to a six-year term on the Harvard University Board of Overseers. He chaired the overseers' visiting committees for philosophy and the divinity school and assisted in the latter's adoption of a more contemporary curriculum that trained ministers in pastoral care as well as theology.

Smith effectively tapped the resources of philanthropic foundations and individual donors. He drew on the college's wealthy Philadelphia alumni and received two major endowment grants from the Ford Foundation. In 1964 Swarthmore won a Rockefeller Foundation grant to promote increased enrollment of African-American students.

Smith also exploited his substantial contacts in government. He lobbied locally and with state and federal agencies to thwart plans for an interstate beltway that would have encroached on the Swarthmore College campus. He argued vehemently against the disclaimer provisions for student loans within the National Defense Education Act of 1958, organizing a coalition to oppose the disclaimer that included the American Civil Liberties Union, the American Association of Colleges, and Senators Joseph Clark of Pennsylvania and John F. Kennedy of Massachusetts. An advocate for higher education in general and the liberal arts specifically, Smith frequently spoke at a variety of forums throughout the United States.

Smith was a strong president at Swarthmore. The college's board of managers invariably accepted his advice and recommendations. He personally interviewed, and essentially selected, candidates for faculty positions and chaired all faculty meetings. But by the mid-1960s Smith's administrative style seemed out of step with the trend toward increased faculty power.

In the spring of 1966, at the urging of a group of faculty, Smith appointed the Commission on Educational Policy to review the Swarthmore College curriculum and administrative structures. The commission's report, published in 1967, proposed a less-centralized administration, recommending that the college appoint a provost to lead the faculty and remove that responsibility from the president. It also proposed extensive changes in the college's honors program, regarded as a keystone of its reputation for distinction in undergraduate education, and argued for improving research opportunities for faculty while continuing the college's liberal arts focus. Smith led the faculty in a systematic review of the commission's 165 recommendations, most of which they adopted in the spring of 1968.

In the summer of 1968 Smith announced that he would leave Swarthmore the next year to become the president of the Markle Foundation, which he had led through a two-year reevaluation. But in the fall of 1968 he encountered an increasingly contentious disagreement over the role of African-American students at Swarthmore. In the first week of January 1969 a group of students occupied the college admissions office. Although intense negotiations followed, their demands could not be accommodated through the rational dialogue that Smith favored. In a speech to the college community on 13 January 1969 he publicly lamented that "we have lost something precious at Swarthmore." On the morning of 16 January, without having reached a resolution of the college's crisis, Smith collapsed and died of a heart attack in his office. The *New York Times* editorialized a few days later that Smith's death "appallingly underscores the price extorted" by confrontational actions. Comments at Swarthmore were more restrained: at the college's memorial service Smith was described as "a man who hungered after righteousness," yet "never knew bitterness or hatred."

• The Courtney C. Smith Presidential Papers are at the Friends Historical Library, Swarthmore, Pa. Smith's personal papers are in the custody of Elizabeth Smith Ingram, Chevy Chase, Md. Other important documents are in the Rockefeller Foundation Archives and Markle Foundation Archives at the Rockefeller Archive Center, Sleepy Hollow, N.Y. A contemporary sketch of Smith's career is in *Current Biography* 20 (Dec. 1959): 26–27. A sympathetic summary of Smith's accomplishments by his successor at Swarthmore, Robert D. Cross, is in *Dictionary of American Biography*, supp. 8 (1988). An obituary is in the *New York Times*, 17 Jan. 1969.

DARWIN H. STAPLETON
DONNA H. STAPLETON

SMITHSON, James (c. 1765–27 June 1829), scientist and philanthropist, was born James Lewis Macie, probably in France, the illegitimate son of Hugh Smithson, later the first Duke of Northumberland, and Elizabeth Hungerford Keate Macie, a wealthy widow from Weston, England. Little is known of Macie's childhood in France. In 1782 he enrolled in Pembroke College, Oxford, where he excelled in chemistry and mineralogy. Two years later, he embarked on his first geological collecting tour, in Scotland and the Hebrides, with a group of distinguished scientists. In

1786 he received an M.A. from Pembroke College and a year later was elected a fellow of the Royal Society, London, its youngest member. He presented his first paper to the society on 7 July 1791, "An Account of Some Chemical Experiments on Tabasheer," recounting his chemical analyses of this substance found in the hollow of bamboo canes. Thus began a career of scientific research, exacting experimentation, and specimen collecting. In 1800 he was elected to the new Royal Institution of Great Britain, an organization devoted to "diffusing the knowledge and . . . the application of science to the common purposes of life."

In 1766, his mother, Elizabeth Macie, inherited the Hungerfords of Studley fortune. When she died in 1800, she left her considerable estate to Macie and his half brother, Henry Louis Dickinson. Macie is not known to have had any contact with his father, who died in 1786. However, in 1794, one of Hugh Smithson's legitimate daughters, Dorothy Percy, bequeathed £3000 to her half-brother. At the turn of the century, after both his parents had died, Macie changed his surname to Smithson.

Smithson went on the Grand Tour of Europe from 1792 to 1794 and spent most of his adult life traveling on the Continent. The sciences he studied—chemistry, geology, and mineralogy—were exciting new fields. Indeed, Smithson wrote that chemistry was "yet so new a science . . . our knowledge . . . of it is so incomplete, consisting entirely of isolated points, thinly scattered, like lurid specks on a vast field of darkness, that no researches can be undertaken without producing some facts leading to consequences which extend beyond the boundaries of their immediate object." Smithson lived for many years in France and was a member of the French Academy. He was inspired by the French Revolution but disillusioned by its bloody aftermath. He traveled throughout Europe, including Germany, Scandinavia, Switzerland, and Italy, in order to add to his mineral collection. He studied the eruption of Mount Vesuvius and a 1794 meteor shower near Siena, Italy. He counted among his correspondents Dominique François Arago, Jons Jakob Berzelius, Henry Cavendish, Antoine Lavoisier, and Hans-Christian Oersted. His twenty-seven published papers span a wide range of topics, from "On the Composition of Zeolite" to "Some Observations on Mr. Penn's Theory concerning the formation of the Kirkdale Cave" to "An Improved Method of Making Coffee." Notable among these is "A Chemical Analysis of Some Calamines," (1802) based upon which the eminent chemist L'Abbé Haüy named a carbonate of zinc "smithsonite" in his honor.

Colleagues remarked upon his poor health throughout his adult life. His only other passion than science was gambling, but, educated in the mathematical theory of odds, he limited his gaming to a predetermined amount. During the Napoleonic Wars, when England and Denmark declared war in August of 1807, Smithson was trapped in the port of Tonningen, then in Denmark. He spent two years under house arrest in Denmark and Germany. His colleague, Sir Joseph

Banks, president of the Royal Society, eventually secured his release in 1808. His health further deteriorated due to the poor conditions in which he was held.

On 23 October 1826, while living in London, Smithson wrote his will. In 1819 Henry Louis Dickinson left his portion of the Hungerford estate to his half brother, Smithson, to be held in trust for his son, Henry James Hungerford. Smithson in his will left the entire Hungerford estate to his nephew, then a young man. But Smithson added a peculiar last clause, noting that if his nephew died without heirs, legitimate or illegitimate, his estate was to go to the United States, "to found at Washington, under the name of the Smithsonian Institution, an Establishment for the increase and diffusion of knowledge among men." Smithson died while living in Genoa, Italy. His will was considered so extraordinary that it was published in the (London) *Times* and reprinted in the *New York American*. Hungerford, his nephew and heir, was young, and so it was considered unlikely that this clause would ever go into effect. Six years later, however, on 5 June 1835, Hungerford died of unknown causes in Pisa, Italy, leaving no heirs. Since the peculiar last clause now went into effect, Smithson's solicitor, Charles Drummond, notified American officials of the bequest. President Andrew Jackson did not believe he had the constitutional authority to accept Smithson's bequest, so he referred the issue to the U.S. Congress. After heated debate as to whether the federal government had the authority to accept the gift, on 1 July 1836 Congress authorized Jackson to pursue the bequest. A claim was filed in the British Court of Chancery, and the estate, valued at $508,318.46, was awarded to the United States on 9 May 1838. For the next eight years, the U.S. Congress debated what to do with the estate—establish a university, astronomical observatory, scientific research laboratory, museum, or library? On 10 August 1846, President James K. Polk signed compromise legislation establishing the Smithsonian Institution, which included most of these ideas. In the years since its founding, the Smithsonian has become the world's largest museum/research complex, with some sixteen museums and numerous research centers.

In 1904, when the Protestant Cemetery near Genoa where Smithson was buried was closed, Alexander Graham Bell, a member of the Smithsonian's Board of Regents, brought Smithson's remains from Italy, and he was laid to rest at the institution he endowed. The questions remain what Smithson meant by the "increase and diffusion of knowledge" and why he chose to bequeath his estate to a country he had never visited. Some speculate it was because he was denied his father's titles and estate, due to his illegitimacy; thus, his name lives on through his Institution. Others argue that he was inspired by the American revolution and the United States' experiment with democracy. Some also attribute his philanthropy to ideals inspired by such organizations as the Royal Institution, which was dedicated to using scientific knowledge to improve the human condition. Smithson never wrote about or discussed his bequest with friends or colleagues, so we are left to speculate on the ideals and motivations of a gift that has had such significant impact on the arts, humanities, and sciences in the United States.

• Little evidence is left of Smithson's life since his papers were destroyed in a fire in the Smithsonian Castle in 1865. A small collection remains in the Smithsonian Institution Archives. There is no modern biography of Smithson, but older published sources include Leonard Carmichael and J. C. Long, *James Smithson and the Smithsonian Story* (1965), and Samuel P. Langley, "A Biographical Sketch of James Smithson," in George Brown Goode, *The Smithsonion Institution, 1846–1896, The History of Its First Half-Century* (1897), pp. 1–24. J. R. McD. Irby, "On the Works and Character of James Smithson," *Smithsonian Miscellaneous Collections* 21 (1881): 143–155; Walter Johnson, "A Memoir on the Scientific Character and Researches of James Smithson, Esq., F.R.S.," *Smithsonian Miscellaneous Collections* 21 (1881): 123–141; and William J. Rhees, *James Smithson and his Bequest* (1880), were the first attempts to analyze Smithson's life and scientific contributions.

PAMELA M. HENSON

SNOW, Hank (9 May 1914–20 Dec. 1999), country musician, was born Clarence Eugene Snow in Brooklyn, Nova Scotia, Canada, the son of George Snow, a sawmill worker, and Marie Boutlier Snow. His parents' marriage soured when he was a small child. He later recalled that he and his siblings feared being taken away to an orphanage by a government organization, the Overseers of the Poor, because of their family's unhappy home life. When his parents divorced around 1922, he became the ward of his paternal grandmother; two of his sisters were placed in foster homes. He despised his grandmother, who beat him with a leather strap because he was a chronic bedwetter. He often ran away in attempts to visit his mother, who lived in a nearby town, Liverpool. Around 1925 a judge ordered that he be returned to his mother, who soon thereafter married a fisherman named Charles Tanner. A heavy drinker with a violent temper, Tanner physically and emotionally abused his stepson. "I was constantly called 'little bastard,' 'son of a bitch,' and other names too filthy to put in print," Snow later wrote. "[He] was extremely jealous of Mother whenever I was near. . . . For no good reason he would twist my frail arms and hit me with his fists. Many times he knocked me on my back onto a bare floor" (pp. 27–28). Snow dropped out of school during the fifth grade. At the age of twelve, seeking to escape the turmoil of his home, he took a job as a cabin boy on a fishing schooner that operated out of Lunenburg, Nova Scotia.

Snow was taught to play the guitar by his mother, who also introduced him to the music of Vernon Dalhart, the first recording star in country music. While at sea, Snow occasionally entertained the fishermen on his boat by singing and playing the harmonica in exchange for nickels and pieces of fudge. He worked on various schooners for four years, quitting in 1930 after surviving a terrifying storm that drowned more than 130 Nova Scotian fishermen.

Snow first became seriously interested in music at the age of sixteen, when he heard his mother playing a Jimmie Rodgers record, "Moonlight and Skies." Within a few weeks, he purchased a mail-order guitar and found himself "picking it up just about every free moment I had, and I experimented with guitar runs and chord progressions that sounded like Jimmie Rodgers. [He] had become my idol" (p. 83). Over the next few years he led a peripatetic existence, sleeping on broken sofas in the homes of relatives, often surviving on meals of molasses and bread, and working as a stevedore, lumberjack, lobsterman, and Fuller Brush salesman. Determined to become a music star like Rodgers, he hitchhiked in 1933 to Halifax, Nova Scotia, where he successfully auditioned at radio station CHNS. Given a weekly, unpaid radio show, Snow, billed as "The Cowboy Blue Yodeler" (in imitation of Rodgers's moniker, "America's Blue Yodeler"), proved to be locally popular and in 1935 became a paid performer with a daily show sponsored by Crazy Water Crystals, a laxative manufacturer. However, he continued to live a hand-to-mouth existence; in the winter of 1935 he was forced to go on city relief, shoveling ice from the street in front of the hotel that housed the CHNS radio station. That year he married Minnie Aalders, who worked as a chocolate dipper at a candy factory. Their only child, whom they named after Jimmie Rodgers, was born in the charity ward at a Salvation Army hospital.

While performing on CHNS, Snow began billing himself as "Hank, the Yodeling Ranger," having learned that Rodgers had been made an honorary Texas Ranger. A radio announcer advised him to take the name "Hank" because it sounded more "country" than his given name, Clarence. In 1936 he signed a recording contract with Canadian Bluebird, a subsidiary of RCA Victor. His early recordings were usually ballads and story songs, many of which included excellent, Rodgers-inspired yodeling. But as his voice deepened over the next few years, he was forced to give up yodeling and change his moniker to "Hank, the Singing Ranger." During the late 1930s he toured extensively through eastern Canada, often playing at movie theaters during the intermissions between films and supplementing his income by teaching guitar lessons. In 1942 he became a featured performer on radio station CKNB in Campbellton, New Brunswick, which was powerful enough to broadcast into border towns in the United States. After receiving fan letters from as far away as Kentucky, he determined to make the jump from Canada into the U.S. country music market. "I just liked the sound—America," he later told an interviewer. "Texas was always big in my mind. Because I wrote a lot of songs about Texas, you know, I'd read about these places, seen them in the movies" (quoted in Guralnick, p. 41). Between 1936 and 1949 he recorded approximately ninety sides for Bluebird, several of which proved to be major hits in Canada, including "The Blue Velvet Band," "Galves-

ton Rose," "My Blue River Rose," and "I'll Not Forget My Mother's Prayers." None of his records, however, was released by RCA Victor in the United States.

Snow first performed in the United States in 1944, playing a few shows in Philadelphia. That year he met country singer Big Slim Aliff, who in 1945 got him a regular slot on the popular "Wheeling Jamboree" program, broadcast from radio station WWVA in Wheeling, West Virginia. Aliff, a former cowboy, also taught Snow how to perform riding tricks on horseback; these stunts became an important component of Snow's live shows. During the late 1940s, in an attempt to become a singing cowboy in the movies, he made two extended trips to Hollywood. He later characterized this experience as a "shell game," in which various promoters advised him to buy expensive advertisements in trade magazines, then sent him to loan companies that charged exorbitant rates to borrow money to pay for the advertisements. He was booked into only a few shows on the West Coast, made no headway at the studios, and eventually spent more than $13,000 trying to start a Hollywood career. In 1948 he moved to Dallas, where he appeared on the "Big D Jamboree." A group of local disc jockeys played one of his Canadian records, "Brand on My Heart," until it became a grassroots hit in Texas and other southwestern states, despite having never been released or distributed outside of Canada. This success finally convinced RCA Victor to sign him to an American recording contract in 1949.

In Dallas, Snow became friends with country star (and fellow Jimmie Rodgers enthusiast) Ernest Tubb, who used his influence in Nashville to get Snow a spot on the Grand Ole Opry. He debuted on the show in January 1950, but the audience initially gave him a cool reception. After several frustrating weeks, he expected to be fired and made plans to return to Canada, but in March 1950 his record "I'm Movin' On" was released. The song, which celebrated the freedom to travel provided by the railroad, featured Snow's strong baritone voice, his "hot" flat-picking guitar style, and his propulsive rhythm section of fiddler Tommy Vaden, bassist Ernie Newton, and steel guitarist Joe Talbot. Snow later described the song's electric effect on his career: the Opry audiences "were completely indifferent one week, and the next week they were wildly enthusiastic" (p. 324). "I'm Movin' On" was a nationwide number-one hit that stayed on the charts for forty-four weeks. "The Golden Rocket," another train song, became his second number-one hit in late 1950.

Between 1951 and 1954 every Snow release reached the top ten on the country charts. These included "Rhumba Boogie," "Bluebird Island" (a duet with Anita Carter), "The Gold Rush Is Over," "Married by the Bible, Divorced by the Law," and "Spanish Fireball." In 1954 Snow had two number-one hits, "I Don't Hurt Anymore" and "Let Me Go, Lover." A somewhat nasal singer with remarkably crisp enunciation, he proved adept at performing songs in a variety of styles: slow honky-tonk ballads about love gone wrong; Jimmie Rodgers-influenced traveling songs and story songs; novelty numbers that he sang with a comical, rapid-fire delivery; driving, boogie-oriented numbers; and songs with a Latin or Hawaiian flavor. During the 1950s he became the first country artist to release "concept albums," which were built around a specific theme or style of music. These included *Old Doc Brown* (1955), a set of talking blues and recitations; *When Tragedy Struck* (1958), a collection of sentimental standards; and tributes to Rodgers. In 1953 he and Tubb established a memorial and museum dedicated to Rodgers in Rodgers's hometown of Meridian, Mississippi. In the mid-1950s Snow played an important role in Elvis Presley's fledgling career, helping to book him on the Grand Ole Opry and the Louisiana Hayride and touring with him extensively in 1955.

During the 1960s Snow was a vocal critic of the "Nashville Sound," a pop-oriented style that dominated country music during the decade, typically featuring crooning backup singers and string sections. Although he occasionally capitulated and recorded in this style, for the most part he remained a staunch country traditionalist. Perhaps for this reason, he enjoyed less chart success during the 1960s, with only three top-five hits: "Beggar to a King," "I've Been Everywhere," and "Ninety Miles an Hour (Down a Dead-End Street)." He continued to busily record, however, often releasing three LP albums per year. His most popular album of the decade was *Souvenirs* (1961), which featured new recordings of many of his biggest hits from the 1950s. One of the few major country singers who was also an excellent musician, he recorded two albums of instrumental duets with Nashville guitar virtuoso Chet Atkins. His discography from the 1960s also includes several gospel albums, an album of train songs, and a tribute album to the Sons of the Pioneers. He toured in Europe and Southeast Asia, spending eighteen days in Vietnam in 1966; the tour was intended not only to entertain U.S. troops but also to defy the antiwar sentiments of demonstrators in the United States.

During the 1970s Snow served briefly as president of the Association of Country Entertainers, a group that opposed Nashville's growing pop orientation. His last number-one hit, "Hello, Love," was released in 1974. In 1977 he founded the Hank Snow Foundation for the Prevention of Child Abuse in Nashville. The following year he was inducted into the Nashville Songwriters International Hall of Fame, and in 1979 he was elected to the Country Music Hall of Fame. During his career he released approximately 140 albums; eighty-five of his songs reached the country charts, including twenty-seven top-five singles. In 1981 RCA Records unceremoniously dropped him from his contract, ending a forty-five-year affiliation. He continued to appear regularly on the Grand Ole Opry into the early 1990s. His contemporaries noted his steely, "all-business" demeanor both on- and off-stage; "you get an unmistakable impression," wrote music journalist Peter Guralnick, "of the fierce combativeness which must have carried him through a loveless childhood and a thoroughly improbable career" (p. 37). Respiratory illness prevented him from playing at the Opry during the mid-1990s, but he managed to return in 1996, receiving standing ovations. He spent his last years at his modest home on three acres in suburban Nashville, which he had grandly named "Rainbow Ranch." He died in Nashville.

• The best source of information on Snow's life is his lengthy, detailed autobiography, *The Hank Snow Story* (1994), cowritten with Jack Ownbey and Bob Burris. An excellent profile of Snow appears in Peter Guralnick, *Lost Highway: Journeys and Arrivals of American Musicians* (1979). For his career within the context of country music history, see Bill C. Malone, *Country Music USA: A Fifty-Year History* (1968); Malone and Judith McCulloh, eds., *Stars of Country Music: Uncle Dave Macon to Johnny Rodriguez* (1975); and Barry McCloud, *Definitive Country* (1995). Bear Family Records has extensively documented Snow's career on compact disc, including *The Yodeling Ranger (1936–1947)* (1993), a five-CD collection of his Canadian recordings; *The Singing Ranger (1949–1953)* (1994), a four-CD set that includes his early U.S. hits; and *The Thesaurus Transcriptions* (1994), five CDs of transcriptions from the early 1950s made for radio airplay. The best single-disc retrospective of his career is RCA's *The Essential Hank Snow* (1997). An obituary is in the *New York Times*, 21 Dec. 1999.

THOMAS W. COLLINS, JR.

SNYDER, John P. (12 Apr. 1926–28 Apr. 1997), cartographer, was born John Parr Snyder in Indianapolis, Indiana, the son of Ralph Snyder, an accountant, and Freda Snyder. He attended elementary and high school in Indianapolis, where he was an excellent student and was president of the honor society in his senior year. As a youth he developed a strong curiosity about maps, a hobby that was to become his vocation.

In 1943 he began the study of chemical engineering at Purdue University. In 1944, as he was about to be drafted, he took a radio and radar training test after which he was inducted into the navy. He remained in the navy until 1946, serving in the Chicago and Corpus Christi areas. Returning to Purdue, in 1948 he received a Bachelor of Science degree in chemical engineering. The following year he earned a master's degree in the same field from the Massachusetts Institute of Technology.

Snyder's first employment was with the Proctor and Gamble Company in Cincinnati. There he joined an interracial choral group at Fellowship House where he met Jeanne Kallmeyer. In 1952 they were married. In 1953 they moved to Bloomfield in northern New Jersey so that he could work in nearby Kearney at Congoleum-Nairn, manufacturers of floor coverings. Their two children were born in Bloomfield. In 1956 he worked in Summit, New Jersey, as a chemical engineer for Ciba Pharmaceutical Products, later a division of the Ciba-Geigy Corporation. He remained with this company until 1980. In Bloomfield his principal civic activity was the Better Human Relations Council, serving as president in 1958. He led the formation of a speaking trio composed of a Jew, a black, and a white Christian (the individuals varied) who lectured to PTA and similar groups about the meaning of discrimination. It was an uphill battle. In 1958 the family joined the Quakers after attending the nearby Montclair Friends Meeting.

To be closer to his position at Ciba-Geigy, the Snyders moved to Madison, New Jersey, where he became interested in politics. In 1956 he ran for councilman as a Democrat in the Republican borough and lost by 5 votes out of 6,000; he ran again the following year and lost by 300. In 1968 he was elected a delegate from the congressional district, supporting Senator Eugene McCarthy, and he attended the National Democratic Convention in Chicago. In 1969 he ran for mayor of Madison on the Democratic ticket. His defeat ended his political career. Meanwhile he had kept up his interest in maps, publishing in 1969 *The Story of New Jersey's Civil Boundaries, 1606–1968* and in 1973 *The Mapping of New Jersey: The Men and the Art.*

In 1976, while on vacation, he attended a symposium on geodesy and cartography at Ohio State University. He was especially interested in a paper by Dr. Alden Colvocoresses, a senior member of the National Mapping Division of the U.S. Geological Survey, who described the need for a new map projection on which to map the ground track of the LANDSAT satellite launched in 1972 by NASA. This was a particularly complex problem because both the earth and the satellite were moving. Colvocoresses explained that specialists in government had been unable to solve the problem. Snyder set to work with his hand-held calculator and some months later sent the Survey his solution, the Space Oblique Mercator Projection. It provided true scale along the ground track of the satellite with minimum distortion elsewhere. The Survey gave him the John Wesley Powell Award in 1978 and offered him an appointment. In 1978 he went on half-time at Ciba-Geigy and part-time at the Survey. In 1980 he resigned from Ciba-Geigy, moved the family to Reston, Virginia, the headquarters of the Survey, and began full-time employment with the Survey. In 1984 he was promoted to Research Physical Scientist, the agency's expert on map projections. In 1988 he officially retired from the Survey, although he continued to do part-time work there.

Snyder and his wife transferred their membership in the Friends organization to the Reston Friends Meeting, in which he served as clerk. He also served the Baltimore Yearly Meeting on the publication and nominatimg committees. In 1992 they moved to the Friends House Retirement Community in Sandy Spring, Maryland.

In 1985 Snyder joined the American Cartographic Association and in 1990 was elected president; he served for eight years as chairman of its committee on map projections, which published four widely used booklets. He served on the editorial board of *The American Cartographer* for eight years and was a member of the U.S. National Committee for the International Cartographic Association. From 1986 to 1991 he was a lecturer on map projections at George Mason University.

Snyder was a world authority on map projection. He devised a number of new map projections including several satellite tracking projections, the Oblique Equal-Area and the "Magnifying Glass" Azimuthal Projection. He developed his own computer program to produce hard-copy world maps with graticule and coastlines centered anywhere for more than 120 projections, which he used to prepare the many hundreds of illustrations in his publications. He did not publish it but allowed his friends to use it.

He died in the hospital in Olney, Maryland.

• Snyder's library and papers are in the Geography and Map Division of the Library of Congress. His first publication, while he was a student (1949), was a short article on a map projection and appeared in *Navigation*. Thereafter his works can be divided into two categories: those he published while a chemical engineer, up to about the late 1970s, and those he published after that period. He was a prolific writer in both periods but less so while active as a chemical engineer.

His publications in the first period include three technical papers which he coauthored and one book to which he contributed: *Plant Engineer's Manual and Guide*; *The Story of New Jersey's Civil Boundaries, 1606–1968*, published by the New Jersey Geological Survey in 1969, followed in 1988 by a supplement; in 1973 *The Mapping of New Jersey: The Men and the Art*, published by Rutgers University Press; and *The Mapping of New Jersey in the American Revolution*, published by the New Jersey Historical Commission (1975). His second career, in cartography, produced a much longer list of publications. In the period from 1977 to 1996, in addition to numerous book reviews and papers at meetings, he published more than thirty articles in the following professional journals: *The American Cartographer* (and its later title, *Cartography and Geographic Information Systems*); *Annals of the Association of American Geographers*; *Surveying and Mapping*; *Photogrammetric Engineering and Remote Sensing*; *Cartographica*; *The Cartographic Journal*; and *Mercator's World*. He also authored several Bulletins of the U.S. Geological Survey, including *Space Oblique Mercator Projection—Mathematical Development* (No. 1518), *Map Projections Used by the U. S. Geological Survey* (No. 1532), and *Bibliography of Map Projections* (No. 1856, with Harry Steward), as well as *An Album of Map Projections* (Prof. Paper 1453, with Philip M. Voxland).

In addition, he published two books: *Flattening the Earth—Two Thousand Years of Map Projections* (1993) and, with Lev M. Bugayevskiy, *Map Projections—A Reference Manual* (1995). At the time of his death he was working with Qihe Yang, a Chinese scholar, on a third book, *Map Projection Transformations*. It was completed by Waldo R. Tobler and published in 2000.

ARTHUR H. ROBINSON

SOHAPPY, David (25 Apr. 1925–6 May 1991), Indian fishing rights advocate, was born on the Yakama Indian Reservation in Washington State, the son of Jim Sohappy, a Wanapum Indian fisherman and rancher, and Eliza Wahpennoyah. (The name of the Yakama Nation was spelled "Yakima" in David Sohappy's lifetime but was officially changed to "Yakama" in 1992.) In the Sahaptin language his Indian name, Tucknashut, means provider. Sohappy is the anglicized spelling of souihappie, meaning "shoving something under a ledge." Although the Wanapum were among the fourteen tribes and bands covered by the Yakama Treaty of 1855, no Wanapum leader signed the treaty, and the tiny band remained on the Columbia River about fifty miles northeast of the Yakama Reservation's eastern edge. There they continued to follow their traditional lifestyle centered on fishing and gathering roots and berries. By the time of Sohappy's birth, his grandmother had an allotment of land on the Yakama Reservation, and it was there that Sohappy spent much of his childhood. From April to October the family lived on the bank of the Columbia catching and drying the fish that would sustain them through the winter. The remainder of the year they lived on the reservation, supplementing the salmon with game, roots, and huckleberries. Sohappy left school after the fourth grade because his family believed that "white" education would deprive him of his Indian cultural and spiritual heritage.

Later, he worked as a mechanic in a government garage, but when fishing season began each year Sohappy went to the river for a few days or a few weeks. In 1945 he married Myra Sam, a childhood playmate. They had eight children. Drafted in 1946, he served eleven months in the army air force, reaching the rank of sergeant. After the army discharged all fathers, Sohappy returned to the Yakama Reservation, where he operated the family's farm, worked for another farmer, and held a series of jobs, including carpenter, electrician, plumber, and heavy equipment operator. He continued to follow the traditional ways, fishing for several weeks each year. In the mid-1960s he was laid off from his job in a sawmill and moved his family to Cook's Landing, a tiny windswept point of land jutting into the Columbia River. There he began to fish most of the year, setting in motion events that would place him in the center of three far-reaching legal battles.

The federal treaties of the 1850s guaranteed Northwest Indian tribes the right to fish at their "usual and accustomed places" outside their reservations. The states of Oregon and Washington, however, tried in the 1960s to control the Indians' fishing with regulations that generally left tribal fishers with a minuscule share of the salmon that were central to their religion, culture, and diet. Intensified state enforcement coincided with the Sohappys' move to the river. David Sohappy believed that the Creator had placed the fish in the rivers for the Indians and that as long as they took only what they needed to survive, the Creator would continue to send the fish. Sohappy paid no attention to federal, state, or tribal rules. He fed an extended family of forty, provided the salmon that are central to Washat religious ceremonies, and conducted ceremonies in his own longhouse. In the early 1960s state officials seized his nets. He got more nets and kept fishing. In 1968 the state of Washington arrested him. Sohappy went to federal court. The case

he filed, *Sohappy v. Smith*, evolved into *U.S. v. Oregon* in which U.S. District Judge Robert C. Belloni ruled in 1969 that states must manage the fisheries so that Indians would get a fair share of the salmon. He did not define "fair," but five years later in another case Judge George Boldt defined fair as comprising half the fish.

Those rulings led to a vicious backlash against tribal fishing, in which Indian fishermen were taunted and in some cases physically threatened, tribal fishing gear was damaged, editorials denounced the rulings and the judges, and bumper stickers and signs proclaimed "Can an Indian, not a salmon" and other anti-Indian phrases. However, the rulings also resulted in the tribes gaining a voice in establishing fishing seasons and regulations. Sohappy continued to fish when he needed food or cash, often in violation of the new rules. "You can't slap a salmon down on the counter to pay for gas," Myra Sohappy once explained (interview with the author, 1966). In 1982 a massive federal–state sting operation culminated in a raid by armed officers on Cook's Landing and other Indian villages. After an extended legal battle through federal and tribal courts, Sohappy was sentenced to five years in prison for selling 178 fish for $4,675 and was given five years' probation for selling an additional 139 fish. The case brought national and international attention, including congressional hearings, to the issue of Indian fishing rights. Myra Sohappy took her husband's plight to the United Nations Human Rights panel in Geneva, Switzerland. The case also focused the attention of Senators Daniel K. Inouye of Hawaii and Daniel J. Evans of Washington on the Army Corps of Engineers' unfulfilled 1939 promise to provide 400 acres of fishing sites to replace traditional sites covered by the backwater of the Bonneville Dam. By 1982, the corps had provided only 41 acres, including Cook's Landing where the Sohappys lived. With appeals exhausted, in 1986 Sohappy and one of his sons went to federal prisons, along with three others. In twenty months in prison, Sohappy suffered a stroke, the worsening of his diabetes, and vision problems. He was released on parole in May 1988.

While the criminal case was in process in 1984, the government began action to evict the Sohappy family and others from Cook's Landing and other fishing sites. David Sohappy won that case in 1991, but the final ruling came five months after his death in a nursing home in Hood River, Oregon. These cases established specific legal recognition of Indian fishing rights, gave Indian tribes a voice in managing Northwest fisheries, and led the government finally to keep a 1939 promise to Indians of the Columbia River.

David Sohappy's insistence on adhering to the ways of his ancestors brought him into conflict with his own tribal government as well as with state and federal governments. Even those who opposed him recognized that his defiant actions were key to the recognition of Indians' fishing rights and to pushing the government into fulfilling its long-ignored promise of designated fishing sites. Daniel Inouye, then chairman of the Senate Select Committee on Indian Affairs, wrote after Sohappy's death, "David's inspiration to all Indian people, his courage, his vision and his gentle spirit will live on in Indian country" (quoted in *Oregonian* obituary).

Sohappy rejected any form of violence, did not drink alcohol, and was a leader in the Seven Drum religion founded by an ancestor in the 1800s. A dignified, almost regal, figure, Sohappy exhibited a natural eloquence that made him a favorite of reporters. His apparent solemnity masked a wry sense of humor, but he was serious about his religion and rights. In a statement from prison to the Senate Select Committee on Indian Affairs in 1988, Sohappy said, "All these years of arguing with the state, and sometimes with my own tribe, don't mean much if I have to be remembered as a criminal and a dangerous poacher. My struggle has been for all the Indian people who have rights along the Columbia River, for our children and for the natural salmon in the river" (quoted in Ulrich, 1999).

• The most extensive discussions of David Sohappy are in three books: Roberta Ulrich, *Empty Nets: Indians, Dams and the Columbia River* (1999), William Dietrich, *Northwest Passage: The Great Columbia River* (1996), and Robert Clark, *River of the West: Stories from the Columbia* (1995). Newspaper coverage of the various court cases was substantial, particularly in the *Oregonian* of Portland. There also is extensive documentation in files of the Army Corps of Engineers and Bureau of Indian Affairs in the National Archives and Records Administration repository in Seattle. Obituaries are in the *New York Times*, 9 May 1991, and the *Oregonian*, 14 June 1991.

ROBERTA ULRICH

SOLTI, Georg (21 Oct. 1912–5 Sept. 1997), conductor, was born György Stern in Budapest, Hungary, the son of Móricz Stern, a struggling businessman, and Teréz Rosenbaum Stern. He started piano lessons at the age of six, and was admitted at twelve to the Franz Liszt Academy of Music, where he studied piano for six years; Béla Bartók was briefly his instructor. At fourteen or so, he attended a performance of Beethoven's Fifth Symphony conducted by Erich Kleiber, was profoundly moved, and decided he wanted to be a conductor.

Upon graduating from the conservatory in 1930, György Stern pursued his goal by working as a coach and rehearsal pianist at the National Opera in Budapest. About this time, he changed his surname from Stern to Solti, after a randomly chosen town in Hungary. His Jewish background nevertheless precluded further advancement in Budapest, so he went in 1932 to Karlsruhe, Germany, as an assistant to the conductor Josef Krips, only to be dismissed a few months later owing to pressure from a Nazi newspaper. In 1936 and 1937 he assisted Arturo Toscanini at the Salzburg Festival in Austria, and this credential gained him the chance to conduct one performance of Mozart's *Marriage of Figaro* at the Budapest Opera, 11 March 1938. His debut was eclipsed by the news in that evening's papers that Germany was invading Austria.

Solti left for Zurich in 1939 to escape the persecution of Jews by the Nazi-aligned Hungarian dictatorship. His plan was to emigrate to the United States, and he managed to get an offer of employment in Cincinnati but failed to convince the American consulate that it was genuine. In Switzerland, he could not get a work permit and lived from hand to mouth until 1942, when he won the piano division of the Swiss Music Competition in Geneva; this entitled him to a permit for teaching up to five voice students. He also received engagements to perform as a pianist and managed to conduct a few concerts.

In 1946, the shortage of German conductors free of Nazi associations led to an opportunity for Solti to conduct Beethoven's *Fidelio* in Munich, and his performance earned him the music directorship of the Bavarian State Opera. That year Solti signed a recording contract with Maurice Rosengarten of European Decca, who later recalled, "He discussed conditions as if he had been a star conductor for years! He was so sure of himself that I decided he must have the makings of a great conductor" (Culshaw, p. 18). Around this time he adopted the German form of his given name, Georg. Also in 1946 Solti married Hedi Oechsli; they had no children and divorced in 1966.

Solti was generally well received in Munich but received discouraging signals from the Bavarian minister of culture, who wanted to replace him with a German. In 1952 he moved to Frankfurt as musical director of the opera there. He first visited the United States in 1953 to conduct the San Francisco Opera; guest engagements followed with the Chicago Symphony Orchestra (CSO) in 1954 and the New York Philharmonic in 1957. Between 1958 and 1965, he conducted the Vienna Philharmonic for Decca in the first complete studio recording of Wagner's opera cycle *Der Ring des Nibelungen*. While based in Frankfurt, Solti became friends with the philosopher Theodor Adorno, who persuaded him to perform the works of Gustav Mahler and Anton Bruckner; these composers became a special focus of Solti's repertoire.

Solti was hired in 1960 as music director of the Los Angeles Philharmonic but withdrew when the chairman of the board, Dorothy Chandler, engaged Zubin Mehta as chief guest conductor without consulting Solti. Meanwhile, Solti had been invited to direct the Royal Opera House, Covent Garden, a post he would occupy from 1961 through 1971. (During his first year at Covent Garden, he also served as senior conductor of the Dallas Symphony Orchestra.) Solti achieved a notable improvement of performance standards at Covent Garden, in part by imposing a level of discipline that caused the balding conductor to become known as the "Screaming Skull." In 1964, he was interviewed for television by Valerie Pitts, a BBC reporter; they married in 1967 and had two daughters.

Solti became music director of the CSO in 1969, taking over from the French conductor Jean Martinon, whose tenure had been marked by a disabling lack of rapport with the players. In working with the Chicago musicians, Solti adopted a more relaxed approach than at Covent Garden, though stopping short of informality. (He faulted Leonard Bernstein for encouraging his musicians to call him "Lenny" rather than "Maestro.") Solti quickly earned the respect of the Chicago personnel, and his ideas of orchestral tone were well suited to the orchestra's strengths. He drew from them a big sound marked by strongly present brass and lower strings and solid precision of rhythm. Within a few years, the orchestra's seasons were selling out on a regular basis. Solti took the orchestra on its first European tour in 1971, a successful venture that he often repeated; they also toured widely in the United States.

Under Solti's baton, the CSO acquired the reputation of a world-class ensemble. Surprisingly, he carried out his work with the CSO without ever taking up residence in the United States. Instead, he organized his appearances in three "mini-seasons" of four weeks each within the orchestra's schedule, during which he stayed in a hotel. In between, the CSO was led by guest conductors and Solti returned home to London, where he now had roots. (He became a British citizen and was knighted in 1972.) Solti's other commitments during his Chicago years included the music directorship of the Orchestre de Paris from 1972 to 1975 and the artistic directorship of the London Philharmonic from 1979 to 1983.

In 1991 Solti stepped down as Chicago's music director, assuming the title of laureate conductor. From 1992 to 1994 he served as music director of the Salzburg Easter Festival. He pursued a full schedule of conducting engagements until his death while he was on vacation in Antibes, France.

Solti set a record by winning thirty-two Grammy awards for his recordings. Many considered him the world's greatest conductor, especially after the death of Herbert von Karajan in 1989. With Fritz Reiner, George Szell, Antal Doráti, and Eugene Ormandy, he was one of a handful of Hungarian conductors who contributed greatly to American musical life in the twentieth century.

• Solti's *Memoirs* (1997; with Harvey Sachs), completed just before his death, is a rich source of information. John Culshaw, *Ring Resounding* (1967), tells how Decca recorded Wagner's complete *Ring* cycle with Solti as conductor. William Furlong, *Season with Solti: A Year in the Life of the Chicago Symphony* (1974) aptly conveys Solti's manner and presence. The video edition of the television series *Orchestra!* (1991) offers extended views of Solti rehearsing an orchestra and discussing music history. An obituary is in the *New York Times*, 6 Sept. 1997.

JONATHAN WIENER

SOWERBY, Leo (1 May 1895–7 July 1968), composer, organist, and teacher, was born in Grand Rapids, Michigan, the son of John Sowerby, a postal supervisor, and Florence Gertrude Salkeld Sowerby. His mother died when he was four, and three years later his father married Mary Wiersma. His step-

mother provided his earliest musical instruction and arranged for Leo to study piano with Mrs. Frederick Burton. Sowerby proved to be a phenomenal prodigy and was performing Liszt's *"Don Juan" Fantasy* in public recital at age ten. Shortly after this, he taught himself harmony from a text borrowed from the library and wrote his first compositions, *Dawn of Day* and *Prelude*, both for piano. By 1909, he had written eighteen works and had exhausted the musical resources of Grand Rapids. He was sent to Chicago, where he studied piano and composition with Carl Lampert, who then sent him to Arthur Olaf Andersen, a former pupil of Vincent d'Indy, at the American Conservatory of Music, where he received an M.M. degree in 1918. Although Sowerby had numerous influences and was associated with a number of composers during his life, Andersen was his only formal teacher.

In 1910 Sowerby, inspired by César Franck's *Trois chorales*, began teaching himself to play the organ. Without an organ to practice on, he used a piano, with a butcher-paper sketch of foot pedals on the floor beneath his feet. The first concert appearance of Sowerby's orchestral music was a performance of his violin concerto in Chicago on 18 November 1913 conducted by Glenn Dillard Dunn. This received favorable public notice, although one critic declared "he displays no musical ability" (cited by Burnet Tuthill). Eric DeLamarter thought highly enough of his musicality to program an all-Sowerby concert with members of the Chicago Symphony in January 1917, which again sharply divided public from critical opinion. On this program was the première of Sowerby's orchestration of his organ piece *Comes Autumn Time*. The Chicago Symphony's conductor Frederick Stock then commissioned *A Set of Four* and performed it with his orchestra.

By this time, Sowerby had met Percy Grainger, and a few informal study sessions with him were significant in his musical and professional development. Grainger had his greatest impact on his colleague by imparting his enthusiasms, particularly for Frederick Delius, and for introducing Sowerby to patron of the arts Elizabeth Sprague Coolidge. Delius was one of the composers that Sowerby admired, along with Franck and d'Indy, although the imprint of these and other models were never to be overly strong in his works.

Following the entry of the United States into World War I, Sowerby served in the army, where he played the clarinet in the 86th Division Army Band and became bandmaster of the 332nd Field Artillery. In March 1919, his unit was demobilized and he returned to Chicago to resume concertizing and composing full time. He also joined the faculty of the American Conservatory and deputized for DeLamarter at the Fourth Presbyterian Church. These affiliations were to last, in one form or another, until the last decade of his life. That same year, he composed the anthem *I Will Lift Up Mine Eyes unto the Hills*, which was destined to become his most enduring and most widely performed work. Unfortunately, he did not reap his due monetarily, having sold the rights to the song to the publisher for $10. By 1920 Sowerby had already written several of the works that were to establish him on the orchestral scene, including *Comes Autumn Time* (1916) and his Piano Concerto no. 1 (1916; rev. ed., 1919).

In 1921, the American Academy in Rome wished to inaugurate a competition modeled on the Prix de Rome that would provide a residency there with no responsibilities other than to compose. After surveying the landscape of existing musical talent, the committee offered the prize to Sowerby. He spent three fruitful years in Rome and composed a dozen major scores, including *King Estmere, From the Northland,* his first string quartet, violin and cello sonatas, and his monumental and as yet unperformed *Psalm Symphony.* The official first competition gave its prize to Howard Hanson, and these two midcentury symphonists began a relationship while in Rome that lasted to the end of Sowerby's life. Sowerby returned to Chicago in 1924 and was appointed to the composition faculty of the American Conservatory the following year. In 1927 he became organist and choirmaster at St. James Episcopal Church, a position once held by Dudley Buck. He served in these two capacities for the next three and a half decades and counted Norman Luboff, Ned Rorem, William Ferris, Edwin Fissinger, Gail Kubik, Florence Price, and Robert Whitney among his students.

Before the decade was out, Sowerby contributed significantly to music beyond the classical area. In 1924 and 1925 he often traveled with Paul Whiteman's jazz orchestra. He composed two works drawing on his familiarity with this group's style: *Synconata* and *Monotony,* the first of which was based on motives inspired by Sinclair Lewis's novel *Babbitt.* Not long after this, Carl Sandburg sought Sowerby's contribution to his American Songbag project, and in 1927 Sowerby arranged sixteen folk songs for this collection. The Sandburg connection also proved to be the impetus for the tone poem *Prairie,* one of his most popular orchestral works. Sowerby wrote that his aim in composing *Prairie* was to have "the listener . . . imagine being alone in an Illinois cornfield, far enough away from railways, motor cars, telephones and radios to feel at peace and one with the beauty that is about." This period marked the end of Sowerby's concert career as a pianist and organist; henceforth he devoted his energies to composing and teaching.

During the 1930s Sowerby's works were being conducted by Serge Koussevitzky in Boston and Eugene Ormandy in Philadelphia, in addition to Stock's continuing advocacy in Chicago. In this decade he composed the Symphony in G for organ (1930–1931), the Passacaglia, Interlude, and Fugue for orchestra (1931–1932), and the choral work *Forsaken of Man* (1939). Within a span of little more than two years, the Eastman School of Music conferred an honorary doctorate on him, he was elected to the American Academy of Arts and Letters, and *Time* magazine ran

a full-scale profile of him. Another important event dating from this time was the start of his long association with organist E. Power Biggs, who in 1938 premiered Sowerby's Organ Concerto in C with Koussevitzky and the Boston Symphony Orchestra. Biggs was the recipient of another half-dozen works from him and played a large part in keeping Sowerby's name in the public eye through the post–World War II years, performing and recording his organ masterpiece, the Symphony in G, along with a number of his smaller-scale works. The Symphony in G opens with a massive sonata-allegro movement that is followed by an interlude in 5/4 meter of striking originality. In the finale, Sowerby turns to one of his most favored forms, the passacaglia, and takes it through a series of 33 variations that counterbalances the first movement both in mood and in monumental scale. This work is a summation of the organ symphony tradition passed down from the French school of Louis Vierne and Charles-Marie Widor and avoids the multiple implicit risks of sounding archaic, derivative, or overblown.

In 1940 Sowerby was appointed a lay member of the Joint Committee on the Revision of the Hymnal for the Episcopal Church. By then, he was able to draw on years of experience at St. James to synthesize a philosophy of church musicianship that demanded commitment and preparation on the part of the organist, choirmaster, and choir on a much higher level than he considered to be the current standard.

During the 1940s Sowerby completed his third and fourth symphonies. Serge Koussevitzky considered commissioning his third symphony, although the eventual dedicatee proved to be Stock and the Chicago Symphony on its fiftieth anniversary. Honors accumulated; the Society for Publication of American Music presented its award to him four times, and a Pulitzer music committee gave its 1946 Award to his *Canticle of the Sun.* The fourth symphony was premiered by Koussevitzky in 1949, although it was the last time one of his symphonies was played for forty years.

Chicago was Sowerby's home and professional base of operations for more than fifty years, but in 1962 he was invited by Rector Dean Francis Sayre to found and direct a College of Church Musicians affiliated with the National Cathedral in Washington, D.C. His final years were spent working with the college's small group of students and composing for several hours a day. In 1963 he was presented to Queen Elizabeth II and became the first American ever elected to the Royal School of Church Musicians. Dedicated to composing and teaching to the end, he died at Wa-Li-Ro Choir Camp in Port Clinton, Ohio.

Sowerby's music remains a staple of the organ repertoire; his choral works frequently appear on concert and church service programs. Nevertheless, there are few parallels to the precipitous and total eclipse of his orchestral music. From the 1920s through the mid-1940s, its prominence was such that Oscar Sonneck, the noted American musicologist, delivered his notorious "fourth B" comment ("Bach, Beethoven, Brahms and Sower-B"), but it fell so far out of public favor for the rest of the composer's life that an assessment of his legacy is problematic. Sowerby's style speaks a language that communicates directly with, most prominently, symphony orchestra audiences, the Episcopal Church, and organists. This is its greatest strength and also its Achilles's heel. That the majority of his music goes unperformed is perhaps due to a sound that can be overly assertive for some ears while striking others as too tied to its time and sources. Ironically, his longtime status of de facto composer-in-residence for the Chicago Symphony may have worked against his reputation by allowing him to be pigeonholed as such. His 550 compositions, comprising every genre except opera, remain as testaments to his considerable talents. The subsequent obscurity of a large portion of them is much less a reflection of their musical value than a comment on the evanescence of fame and the vagaries of the public's tastes.

• The Leo Sowerby Archive is located at the Northwestern University Music Library, and other substantial collections of Sowerby materials are at the Newberry Library of Chicago, Syracuse University, and the Library of Congress. A talk detailing his philosophy of church musicianship appeared in the Dec. 1958 issue of *Diapason*, pp. 8, 40–41. See also Burnet C. Tuthill's perceptive and thorough appraisal of Sowerby at the height of his popularity in *Musical Quarterly* (1938): 249–64. A personal remembrance by Lester H. Groom in *American Organist* (May 1995): 54–55 gives a glimpse of Sowerby's personality and its effect on others. This same issue contains an excellent biographical article by Francis J. Crociata, president of the Leo Sowerby Foundation. Crociata has written essays on Sowerby and his music that accompany recordings of his tone poems (Cedille CDR 90000 033) and Second Symphony (Cedille CDR 90000 039). Other recordings of his less frequently encountered works have notes by the late Sowerby authority Ron Huntington and Robert Osborne, and a program of chamber and chamber orchestra pieces has biographical and analytical material by Crociata based on essays by Huntington. An obituary is in the *New York Times*, 8 July 1968.

PETER HIRSCH

SPALDING, Albert (15 Aug. 1888–26 May 1953), concert violinist, was born in Chicago, Illinois, the son of J. W. Spalding, a merchant, and Marie Boardman Spalding, a gifted contralto and pianist who had performed with the Chicago Symphony under Theodore Thomas. In 1876 J. W. Spalding and his brother A. G. Spalding, the Hall of Fame sporting pitcher, founded the A. G. Spalding and Brother sporting goods company. In his memoirs, *Rise to Follow*, Albert wrote that as a small boy he was fascinated by his family's Steinway piano in their New York apartment. The family wintered at their villa in Florence, Italy. On both continents they entertained the leading musicians of the day, so Albert was surrounded by music from his earliest days. For Christmas 1895 he asked for and received a violin from his parents. He immediately began violin lessons in Florence from a local violinist, Ulpiano Chiti. "He was a hunchback," Spalding wrote, "which, in super-

stitious Italy, is a good omen." Indeed, it was. Albert progressed rapidly. When the family returned to their summer home at the shore in Monmouth Beach, New Jersey, he continued lessons with Jean Buitrago.

In 1903, Chiti suggested that Albert go to Bologna, Italy, and play for the examining board of the historic music conservatory for a diploma. To obtain a diploma one did not need to enroll in the conservatory; outsiders could compete for a diploma by taking a rigorous set of examinations. This included performing one of the thirty-six studies of Fiorillo and one of the twenty-four caprices of Rodé (the numbers drawn by lot), as well as a complete concerto (Spalding played the Mendelssohn), a sonata (Spalding chose Tartini's "Devil's Trill"), one of Bach's six unaccompanied sonatas and partitas (again drawn by lot), and a sight-reading of a manuscript from the school's library. To gain the diploma, one also had to pass an examination on the piano and complete exercises in theory, harmony, and counterpoint. Officials at the conservatory originally objected to Spalding's taking the exam because he was so young. They relented, however, and Spalding scored an amazing 48 out of 50 points, becoming the youngest person since Wolfgang Amadeus Mozart to win the diploma. His piano accompanist for the examination was the young composer Ottorino Respighi. In 1924 the two were reunited and Spalding gave the French premiere of Respighi's *Concerto Gregoriano* with Serge Koussevitzky and the Paris Symphony. In 1925 he gave the U.S. premiere.

On 6 June 1905, after further studies with Narcisse-Augustin Lefort, Spalding made his Paris debut playing Camille Saint-Saëns's B minor concerto, the Bach *Chaconne*, and a group of violin solos. Shortly thereafter, the seventeen-year-old Spalding met Saint-Saëns, who spent over two hours accompanying him at the piano. The composer was so impressed that he asked the boy to play the B minor concerto at a concert in Florence with him conducting. When Spalding made his London debut with the famed German conductor Hans Richter and the London Symphony Orchestra in 1906, Richter asked him to play the same concerto. Spalding later learned that Saint-Saëns himself had written to Richter to suggest that Spalding play his concerto.

On 8 November 1908 Spalding made his official U.S. debut at Carnegie Hall with Walter Damrosch conducting the New York Symphony. Spalding signed a contract with Edison Records that same year and recorded for the company for some twenty years. In 1910 he toured Russia, and he returned there in the 1912–1913 and 1913–1914 seasons. Spalding had met the famed accompanist André Benoist during his first American tour. By 1911, Benoist was his full-time accompanist—a musical partnership that lasted nearly forty years.

World War II interrupted Spalding's career. He enlisted in the Air Service of the Signal Corps and, given his language skills, found himself stationed in Foggia, Italy, where he was adjutant to Fiorello H. La Guardia, who later became mayor of New York. For his service, Spalding was awarded the Cross of the Crown of Italy and made Chevalier of the French Legion of Honor.

In the spring of 1919 Spalding resumed his concert career with a tour of Italy. He returned to the United States that summer; on 19 July he married Mary Vanderhoef Pyle in Ridgefield, Connecticut. They had no children. Spalding toured the United States in the 1919–1920 season. By the 1930s, he was firmly established as one of the world's leading concert violinists. He recorded for Brunswick Records in the 1920s and for RCA Red Seal Records in the 1930s and 1940s. Among his many recordings were the Mendelssohn and the Spohr "Gesangsszene" concertos, with Eugene Ormandy conducting the Philadelphia Orchestra; Mozart's *Sinfonia Concertante*, with the legendary violist William Primrose; and sonatas by Franck, Mozart, and Handel, with André Benoist. He performed frequently on the radio, appearing on Coca-Cola's "The Pause that Refreshes" every Sunday afternoon for over two years with conductor André Kostelanetz. He was also a prolific composer, writing some 60 works for the violin, 30 songs, more than 20 piano pieces, 4 string quartets, and a number of orchestral works. None rose to the level of greatness. They are now virtually forgotten, but leading musicians in Spalding's day performed them (including the Flonzaley String Quartet and violinists Mischa Elman, Jacques Thibaud, and Mischa Mischakoff). Spalding recorded several of his own works for the violin, including the evocative and lyrical *Etchings* (a set of short descriptive pieces for violin and piano with names like "Desert Twilight," "Hurdy-Gurdy," and "Fireflies"), a virtuosic arpeggio study for unaccompanied violin called *Dragonfly*, and the technically difficult and dense Sonata in E minor for solo violin—a twentieth-century homage to the solo sonatas of Bach. He even wrote and recorded his impression of a southern plantation melody, *Alabama*, probably inspired by Mary Jackson, the African-American nanny from Alabama who cared for Spalding and his brother when they were children. In his memoirs, Spalding wrote that the "majestic," "imperious," and "tender" Jackson would "croon us to sleep in a husky voice, mixing strange African words with more intelligible ones in her improvised cradle songs" (p. 11).

On 7 February 1941 Spalding premiered the violin concerto of Samuel Barber with Eugene Ormandy and the Philadelphia Orchestra. Barber had composed the concerto in 1939 for the young violinist Iso Briselli, who rejected the work because he said the last movement was "unplayable." In 1940 Barber took the concerto to Spalding, who immediately agreed to perform it. Although Spalding never commercially recorded the concerto, which has become an American classic, an acetate recording of the premiere is said to exist.

With the outbreak of World War II, Spalding again enlisted—serving in London, North Africa, and Italy as a member of the Office of Strategic Services (OSS). As a result of his wartime service, France promoted him to "Officier" in the Legion of Honor. He gave fewer concerts after the war, although he performed frequently with the great Hungarian pianist and composer Ernst von Dohnányi. The two recorded the complete Brahms sonatas, as well as Dohnányi's own violin sonata on the Remington label, for which Spalding continued to record after retiring from the concert stage in 1950. Spalding wrote a volume of memoirs in 1943 and a novel based on the life of the eighteenth-century Italian violinist Giuseppe Tartini titled *A Fiddle, A Sword, and a Lady: The Romance of Giuseppe Tartini* (Holt, 1953). A volume of Spalding's courtship letters to Mary Pyle, written while he served in World War I, has also been published. Toward the end of his life, he taught at Boston University and the University of Florida at Tallahassee. True to his lineage, he was an avid tennis player.

Spalding was a refined violinist whose playing reflected his cultivated background. It lacked broad mannerisms and was, thus, distinctively modern. One of Spalding's most immediately recognizable traits was a rapid vibrato that, as Henry Roth has written, contributed "to a tone of striking beauty" (p. 164). His playing may have lacked the innate charm of Fritz Kreisler and the brilliant technique and sheer passion of the influx of Russian violinists of the likes of Jascha Heifetz and Mischa Elman, but Boris Schwarz notes that Spalding's "straightforward" and "honest" playing was "refreshingly different" (*Great Masters of the Violin*, p. 499). And, at a time when Americans found it difficult to be taken seriously as leading concert artists, Spalding became a star. Along with Maud Powell and Eddy Brown, he became part of the first great triumvirate of American-born concert violinists.

• Spalding's papers, along with those of André Benoist, are housed at Boston University. His memoirs, *Rise to Follow: An Autobiography* (1943; repr. 1977), details the early part of his life, and *Ton Albert qui t'adore: The Courtship Letters of Albert Spalding to Mary V. Pyle*, ed. Suzanne Spalding Winston (1988), provides glimpses into his service in World War I. The memoir of Spalding's longtime accompanist, André Benoist, *The Accompanist . . . and Friends: An Autobiography of André Benoist*, ed. John Anthony Maltese (1978), also provides much information about Spalding, along with many photographs. Interviews with Spalding appear in Frederick H. Martens, *Violin Mastery: Talks with Master Violinists and Teachers* (1919), and Samuel and Sada Applebaum, *The Way They Play, Book I* (1972). A lengthy biographical sketch appears in David Ewen, *Living Musicians* (1940). Recordings of 96 radio broadcasts of Spalding, including his weekly appearances on Coca-Cola's "The Pause That Refreshes," are housed at the Library of Congress. Additional radio broadcasts of Spalding can be found at the Rodgers & Hammerstein Archives of Recorded Sound at the New York Public Library for the Performing Arts. Spalding's commercial recordings have been reissued on compact disc by Biddulph, Pearl, Symposium, and other companies.

JOHN ANTHONY MALTESE

SPALDING, Henry Stanislaus (10 Jan. 1865–27 Dec. 1934), educator, author, and clergyman, was born in Bardstown, Kentucky, one of eleven children of William Thomas Spalding and Isabella Ann Livers Spalding, founders and operators of a clothing business. The Spaldings were descendants of Thomas Spalding, who landed in St. Mary's County, Maryland, in 1657/58 and the family had migrated to Nelson County, Kentucky, after the Revolutionary War. Two of Henry Spalding's cousins, Martin John Spalding and John Lancaster Spalding, were noted Catholic bishops, and five of his siblings also entered religious orders. A brother was a Dominican priest, and four sisters were St. Catherine of Kentucky Dominican nuns. Spalding often referred to himself as the black sheep of the family because the others wore the white habit of St. Dominic and he had the black Jesuit cassock. A brother, W. Thomas Spalding, became postmaster of Bardstown.

In 1881 Spalding enrolled at St. Joseph's College in Bardstown and in 1883 at St. Mary's College in St. Mary's, Kansas. Both were Jesuit colleges. On 7 August 1884 he entered the Society of Jesus at Florissant, Missouri, where he continued his studies in the humanities.

From 1888 to 1893 Spalding taught English and Latin grammar and literature at Marquette College in Milwaukee, Wisconsin. He was joined by Francis James Finn, another young Jesuit educator and prolific writer, who published *Percy Wynn*, a book for boys, in 1891. Spalding was doubtless influenced by Finn, and in 1901 he published his first boys' adventure story, *The Cave by the Beech Fork*. Fifteen more boys' books followed, some translated into German, Spanish, and Polish. Most were tributes to his heritage, depicting the lives and deeds of young heroes in the setting of the Catholic families around Bardstown, Kentucky. Although he wrote fiction, Spalding accurately described the culture, legends, and beliefs of the families, the crafts that enabled them to live and farm successfully, and the flora and fauna of the region. The heroes were paragons of ethical lives and the practice of their religion.

From 1893 to 1896 Spalding studied philosophy at St. Louis University in St. Louis, Missouri, and from 1896 to 1899 he studied theology at Woodstock College in Woodstock, Maryland. In 1899 he was ordained a Roman Catholic priest by Cardinal James Gibbons. Spalding also studied theology at St. Louis University (1899–1900), taught for a year at Creighton University in Omaha, Nebraska (1900), and then took a concentration in liturgical and aesthetical theology at St. Stanislaus in Florissant, Missouri (1901–1902). While he was at Creighton, he made the introductions and recommendations that brought the St. Catherine Dominican sisters to Spalding Academy of Spalding, Nebraska.

In 1902 Spalding returned to Marquette. There he held the offices of vice president, prefect of studies and discipline, and regent of the schools of medicine, dentistry, and pharmacy. At the turn of the century, the investigations of the Carnegie Foundation for the Advancement of Teaching and the conditions that motivated its report on *Medical Education in the United States and Canada* (1910), commissioned by Henry Smith Pritchett and written by Abraham Flexner, were putting pressure on proprietary medical schools to improve the quality of what they taught and to introduce standard curricula through mergers or by joining universities. Spalding worked with Alexander J. Burrowes, the university president, and Louis Francis Jermain, a medical doctor, to establish a medical school at Marquette University and then to raise its standards. As vice president (1902–1909), he initiated negotiations with Dr. William H. Earles, owner of the Milwaukee Medical College, and then with the medical doctor owners of the Milwaukee College of Physicians and Surgeons. In 1906 an affiliation was negotiated with the former. It was not until January 1913 (and after Spalding's transfer to Chicago in 1909) that Marquette was able to assume full ownership of and responsibility for both schools. The investigations and the report of the Carnegie Foundation and the Council of Medical Education of the American Medical Association's threat of a poor rating were major motivations during the final negotiations. In 1967 Marquette University and the Medical College separated; the latter reincorporated as the Medical College of Wisconsin. Spalding helped Marquette College obtain university status in 1907 and also helped lay the groundwork for absorption of the Milwaukee Law School and the Milwaukee University Law School to form the Marquette University Law School as a part of Marquette University.

In 1909 Spalding was transferred to St. Ignatius College in Chicago, Illinois, where he and Burrowes worked to organize Loyola University, partly by transferring programs from St. Ignatius College. Spalding also established schools of medicine and law. Working with the physicians John Dill Robertson, Francis E. Thornton, William F. Waugh, and Maximilian Herzog among others, Spalding facilitated agreements with Illinois Medical School in 1909, Bennett Medical School and Reliance Medical School in 1910, and the College of Medicine and Surgery of Chicago in 1911 to form what became the Chicago Stritch School of Medicine of Loyola University. The assimilations were not complete until 1917. From 1913 to 1919 Spalding was regent of the schools of medicine, law, pharmacy, engineering, and sociology.

From 1919 to 1922 Spalding taught English and logic at Xavier College in Cincinnati, Ohio. In 1922, charged with increasing its readership, he became editor of the *Queen's Work* magazine. In 1927 Father Daniel Aloysius Lord replaced him, and Spalding returned to his alma mater, St. Mary's College in Kansas, as professor of sociology. In 1930 he was diagnosed with pernicious anemia. During periods of recuperation, he taught sociology at various colleges and in 1933 instructed Jesuit seminarians at West Baden College in West Baden, Indiana.

Since 1912, as a medical school regent, Spalding had been interested in and taught ethics and sociology. He wrote textbooks on these subjects, including *Talks to Nurses: The Ethics of Nursing* (1902), and revised others, including *Moral Principles and Medical Practice, the Basis of Medical Jurisprudence* by Charles Coppens (1921). Spalding also popularized history, particularly about Father Jacques Marquette, and advocated the erection of the statue in Marquette's honor in the Capitol in Washington, D.C. Spalding's last two books, *Catholic Colonial Maryland* (1931) and *Arrows of Iron* (1934), sought to prepare young people and others for the Maryland tricentenary celebration in March 1934. In the last trip of his life, Spalding attended this celebration at St. Mary's City, Maryland. He died at St. Mary's Hospital in Cincinnati, Ohio.

• For more information, see Raphael N. Hamilton, *The Story of Marquette University* (1953); Richard A. Matré, with Marilu Matré, *Loyola University and Its Medical Center: A Century of Courage and Turmoil* (1995); and "The Medical School Situation in Milwaukee," *Wisconsin Medical Journal,* January 1913, pp. 9–15, an editorial reprinted in its entirety in the *Marquette Bulletin* for 1913–1914. On his appointment to Loyola in Chicago, see "The Rev. H. S. Spalding to Head Loyola College," *Milwaukee Sentinel,* 9 June 1912. Obituaries are in the *Cincinnati Times Star,* 27 Dec. 1934, and the *Cincinnati Enquirer,* 28 Dec. 1934.

THADDEUS J. BURCH

SPITZER, Lyman, Jr. (26 June 1914–31 Mar. 1997), theoretical astrophysicist and director of the Princeton University Observatory, was born in Toledo, Ohio, the son of Lyman Spitzer, a well-to-do businessman, and Blanche Brumback Spitzer. Young Lyman was educated in Toledo until he was fifteen, and then entered Phillips Academy, Andover, Massachusetts. Under the tutelage of a kindly teacher, he developed a strong interest in physics. Reading the popular books of English theorists Arthur Eddington and James Jeans inspired Spitzer's enthusiasm for research in the grandest topic in astrophysics, the evolution of the universe. In 1932 he entered Yale, earning his B.A. in theoretical physics under Leigh Page, and in 1935 went to Cambridge, England, for graduate work with Eddington. This did not work out; Eddington was notorious for not paying attention to his students, and after one year Spitzer returned to the United States as a graduate student at Princeton under Henry Norris Russell, the dean of American astrophysics. He was an inspiring teacher, and Spitzer learned much from him. After receiving his Ph.D. in 1938, he became a postdoctoral fellow at Harvard and then in 1939 was appointed an instructor in physics and astronomy at Yale. In 1940 he married Doreen Damaris Canaday of Toledo, a graduate of Bryn Mawr; they had a son and three daughters.

During Spitzer's postdoctoral year at Yale, physicist Hans Bethe showed that the source of the energy radiated by stars was the conversion of hydrogen into helium by thermonuclear reactions (fusion) in their interiors. Spitzer, realizing that the high-luminosity stars could not be as old as the Galaxy because they would have exhausted their hydrogen long ago, reasoned that they must have formed more recently within the Galaxy, from "interstellar matter." Based on observational data combined with his own keen physical insight and knowledge of atomic physics, he began a long series of theoretical investigations of the properties of interstellar matter. Even before he began this study, Spitzer had disproved the then-accepted theory that the planets in our solar system formed as a result of a tidal interaction from the condensation of gas thrown out from the sun and another (hypothetical) star passing near it. Spitzer showed that any such gas would dissipate into interstellar space. He became the leading theorist of interstellar gas and dust, all of his work closely linked to observational results.

Spitzer's research career was interrupted by World War II, during which he worked on the transmission of sound in water, as a member of a group developing methods for the detection and location of enemy submarines. In 1947 he was appointed professor of astronomy at Princeton University and director of its observatory, succeeding Russell, who had reached retirement age. Spitzer brought Martin Schwarzschild, whom he had come to know and respect at Harvard, along with him under a package arrangement. It included frequent working visits to Mount Wilson Observatory by each of them. Spitzer and his students made many advances in understanding interstellar matter.

Spitzer had long been aware that the Earth's atmosphere absorbs all incoming ultraviolet light from stars, thus obscuring some of the most important features in their spectra, many of which are crucial for analyzing interstellar matter. In an early study for an air force "think tank," published only as a classified document in 1946, Spitzer listed and discussed in detail the scientific advantages of a remotely operated observatory mounted in an artificial satellite above the atmosphere. This study, widely known to scientists inside the government, established Spitzer as a leader in the field, which the United States entered fully in 1957 after the Soviet Union launched Sputnik. He led the planning for an orbiting astronomical observatory, which was sent into space in 1972. Called Copernicus, it was built around a 32-inch reflecting telescope and a spectrograph that worked in the ultraviolet. It enabled astronomers to measure absorption lines of many interstellar atoms, ions, and molecules in this spectral region. The group of young astronomers and astrophysicists Spitzer assembled at Princeton were among the most productive users of the satellite observatory, adding greatly to our knowledge of many elements in interstellar space.

During the years of preparation for the much larger, more powerful instrument that became the Hubble space telescope, Spitzer chaired many committees and provided new ideas that went into its development. When this costly project was nearly cut from the federal budget in the mid-1970s, he and John N. Bahcall lobbied incessantly in Washington to keep it alive. They were successful, and after the HST was launched in 1990 Spitzer returned to full-time astrophysical research with it. His many papers, the last published only the year before his death, attested to his continued scientific curiosity and drive.

Spitzer also did important theoretical work on stellar dynamics, particularly on stars in globular clusters. The evolution of the cluster depended on the gravitational interaction between stars, which typically numbered in the millions. Spitzer isolated the important aspects of such problems and then worked out their consequences mathematically and numerically. He published many papers in this field, from his postdoctoral days at Harvard through his years at Princeton, several of them with collaborators, including Schwarzschild and the Mount Wilson astronomer Walter Baade, a visiting lecturer at Princeton in 1950.

After World War II, Spitzer made considerable efforts to harness thermonuclear reactions, the fusion of light elements as used in the "hydrogen bomb," under controlled conditions for the peaceful generation of energy. He and other scientists knew that fossil chemical fuels such as coal, gas, and oil would ultimately be exhausted and civilization would have to depend on nuclear sources of energy. Beginning in 1953 Spitzer directed this Project Matterhorn, basically an advanced development program in plasma physics, involving gas suddenly heated to temperatures similar to those deep in the interior of the Sun. Confinement by magnetic fields was the only viable method of holding the superheated gas together long enough to ignite it. Over the years much has been learned about basic atomic and radiation physics and magnetohydrodynamics, but to date no useful amounts of power have been generated. Spitzer gave up the directorship of Matterhorn in 1961, but he continued an active interest in it for many years, on a diminishing part-time basis.

Throughout his career Spitzer combined theoretical insight, mathematical powers, physical knowledge, and an outstanding ability to work with others, doing creative research himself at the same time he directed their efforts along productive lines. He wrote several important research monographs on interstellar matter and stellar dynamics. After his formal retirement in 1982 he continued active research as an emeritus professor. He died at his home in Princeton.

• Spitzer's scientific correspondence is preserved in the Department of Rare Books and Special Collections of Firestone Library, Princeton University. He published an excellent short account of his scientific career, "Dreams, Stars and Electrons," in *Annual Review of Astronomy and Astrophysics* 27 (1989): 1–17. He also published insights into his own life and research in the form of brief "commentaries" preceding each of his papers, popular articles, and letters republished in Lyman Spitzer, Jr., and Jeremiah P. Ostriker, eds., *Dreams, Stars, and Electrons: Selected Writings of Lyman Spitzer, Jr.* (1997). This book also contains a complete bibliography of all his published books, papers, and articles. An obituary is in the *New York Times*, 2 April 1997, and a technically oriented one is in *Physics Today* (Oct. 1997): 123–24.

DONALD E. OSTERBROCK

STAMOS, Theodoros (31 Dec. 1922–2 Feb. 1997), artist, was born in New York City, the son of Theo-

doros Stamatelos and Stamatina Apostolakos, Greek immigrants who had come from Sparta, where the father had worked as a fisherman. The family name was shortened not long after their arrival in lower Manhattan, where the parents had a hat-cleaning and shoe-shine shop. At age eight Stamos ruptured his spleen in a fall, and it was removed in an operation that required five blood transfusions. As part of his recuperation, Stamos was sent to a camp, where he made his first drawings on a small, portable blackboard. In the next few years he also created clay sculptures.

In 1927 Stamos took a number of drawings to the American Artists School, where he was accepted to attend night classes in sculpture with instructors Simon Kennedy and Joseph Kinzal while continuing his regular education at Stuyvesant High School. In time the American Artists School, recognizing his precocious talent, gave Stamos a scholarship.

In 1939 Stamos left high school three months short of graduation, and not long after he was expelled from art school for "political activities," according to a profile of the artist published in 1947 in *ARTnews*. His ruptured spleen kept him out of the army during World War II.

The expense of producing sculpture led Stamos to switch to painting (he was completely self-taught in this medium). He supported himself through a variety of jobs over the next number of years, including teletype operator, book salesman, enamel polisher, stock clerk in a beauty supply house, tourist guide, prism grinder, hat blocker, and printer. His longest-held jobs were as a florist and a picture frame maker. Through making frames he met a number of noted artists, including Arshile Gorky and Fernand Léger.

Stamos's paintings, at first in a semi-primitive style and later in a more abstract, patterned style that owed a debt to Milton Avery, were exhibited at various galleries. His first one-person show was in November 1943 at the Wakefield Gallery, which was located in a Manhattan bookshop and was run by Betty Parsons. Within a few years Parsons opened her own prominent gallery featuring the leading New York School artists. A reviewer for the *New York Times* (5 Dec. 1943) lauded the "strength and originality" of Stamos's paintings.

Perhaps as important as his artistic talents were Stamos's knack for meeting the right people and getting along with them. The artists who became known as the New York School—Jackson Pollock, Willem de Kooning, Franz Kline, Adolph Gottlieb, and Barnett Newman, among others—were a notoriously quarrelsome bunch, battling (verbally and occasionally physically) each other and the dealers and critics around them. Younger than these more acclaimed artists by between ten and twenty years, Stamos was accepted by them and managed to maintain their affection.

During the 1940s Parsons collected artists for her gallery, and through her Stamos met Gottlieb, Newman, Mark Tobey, the collector Peggy Guggenheim, and the painter Mark Rothko. Stamos's reputation would be intertwined inextricably with Rothko. Possibly the most famous photograph of this period in the art world is a portrait of all the artists represented by Parsons at her gallery in 1951 taken by Nina Leen. Parsons stands on a table in the background, while Stamos is seated up front with a severe expression that reflects the alienation and defiance of a new group of artists soon to leave their mark on the world.

Stamos was never completely an abstract artist—there were always references to the landscape or seascape as well as Greek myths—but he distorted and arranged recognizable shapes into whimsical patterns, gaining plaudits from critics and collectors. A critic for *ARTnews* (Apr. 1946) praised the "quiet poetic quality" of his work, and a critic for *ART Digest* lauded a painting's "low-keyed beauty of a subtle, sensuous nature" at a show in 1947. The art critic Clement Greenberg, writing in the *Nation* (11 Dec. 1948), sounded a more sour note, writing, "Stamos, as it happens, has borrowed most of his style from the lower registers of William Baziotes, a serious and vastly superior artist."

Stamos gave solo shows at the Duncan Phillips Gallery (later the Phillips Collection) in Washington, D.C., in 1950 and 1954, the Corcoran Gallery of Art in 1958, and the Andre Emmerich Gallery in 1966, among others. His work was included in a variety of group exhibitions, and a growing number of museums began to collect Stamos's work, including the Albright-Knox Gallery in Buffalo, New York; the Detroit Institute of Art in Michigan; the Tel Aviv Museum in Israel; the Art Gallery of Ontario in Toronto; the Hirshhorn Museum and Sculpture Garden in Washington, D.C.; and the Guggenheim Museum, Metropolitan Museum, Museum of Modern Art, and Whitney Museum of American Art in New York City. In 1951 he received a Tiffany Fellowship and five years later a fellowship from the American Academy of Arts and Letters. Sales were not brisk, but they were sufficient to allow Stamos in 1948 to close the frame shop after seven years. Periodically he taught at art schools and art colonies, including Black Mountain College in North Carolina, Brandeis University in Massachusetts, and the Art Students League and Columbia University in New York City.

In February 1970 Stamos's good friend Rothko committed suicide (Rothko's wife died of heart failure six months later). Stamos offered the Rothko family a part of the Stamos family burial plot in East Marion, Long Island, and was asked to take over the installation of the Rothko Ecumenical Chapel in Houston, Texas. Two years before taking his life, Rothko had drawn up a will, naming three executors who would create a foundation that would receive the bulk of his paintings: Bernard Reis, an art collector and accountant; Morton Levine, an anthropology professor at Fordham University who was also named guardian of the artist's younger child, Christopher Rothko; and Stamos. One of the executors' first actions was to sell 798 of Rothko's paintings to New York's Marlborough Gallery for $1.8 million and consign to the same gallery 698 more at a 50 percent commission. Frank Lloyd, the owner of Marlborough Gallery, quickly sold many of these paintings, realizing profits of 800 percent. Additionally payments by Lloyd to the Rothko estate were to be made over thirteen years without interest.

In 1971 Herbert Faber, the guardian of Rothko's older child, Kate Rothko, filed a lawsuit accusing the three executors of conspiracy to defraud the estate and waste its assets. Reis was charged with self-dealing for being the accountant to both the Rothko family and the Marlborough Gallery, while Stamos was accused of going along with the deal in order to be taken on as a Marlborough artist. (In fact in 1971 Stamos became part of Marlborough's stable, and his first exhibition at the gallery was held the following year.) Levine was accused of acting in bad faith.

In 1975 a judge removed Stamos and the other two executors from the Rothko estate and canceled the contracts they made selling and consigning the 798 paintings to Marlborough. In Stamos's case, conflict of interest was not proved, but the judge found a "self-serving breach of loyalty" and that he acted "improvidently and negligently in view of his own knowledge of Reis' self-serving and the entire case of events." As a result Stamos and Reis jointly with Frank Lloyd were deemed liable for the present value of the paintings sold by Lloyd, or $9.3 million. Stamos appealed enforcement of the decision, claiming hardship—his only assets were his house and paintings—but he was denied in 1977. However, since only Lloyd actually profited from the sale of Rothko's paintings, he was required to pay all $9.3 million in fees and fines, and he returned some of the paintings to the estate for credit. The court awarded Stamos's Manhattan residence to the Rothko estate in lieu of legal fees, but Kate Rothko relented and gave the likable Stamos a life tenancy.

However, Stamos's reputation was blackened, and he did not have another New York exhibition until 1977. He was represented by a number of dealers, one of whom, Louis K. Meisel, who handled the artist's work from 1976 to 1982, claimed that the Rothko trial "put Stamos on the radar scope for a lot of collectors. A lot of people had heard of him, but now they decided to look at his work, and many of them became buyers" (interview with the author, Sept. 2002). In 1983 Stamos filed a $5 million libel suit, which he later dropped, against the BBC for the production and broadcast of a docudrama based on the Rothko case, called "The Rothko Conspiracy," which aired first in England and later in the United States. Also in 1983 a small number of mainly European collectors of Stamos's work formed a group called the Circle of Friends of Theodoros Stamos that aimed to promote Stamos's work primarily in Europe and in the United States.

In 1970 Stamos visited Greece—only the second time he had done so—and began to return there regularly, spending summers on the island of Lefkada. In 1975 he cemented this relationship to his parents' homeland with a gift of forty-five of his own works to the National Gallery of Athens. There he was celebrated as one of Greece's great artists. In 1997 the exhibition "Theodoros Stamos: 1922–1997, a Retrospective" went up at the National Gallery Alexandros Soutzios Museum, Athens, Greece.

Stamos died in Yiannina, Greece. He had never married or had any children.

• Dore Ashton, *The New York School* (1972), offers a strong sense of the world in which the abstract expressionists developed. Lee Hall, *Betty Parsons: Artist, Dealer, Collector* (1991), describes how the art world discovered Stamos. A highly readable account of the Rothko trial is Laurie Adams, *Art on Trial: From Whistler to Rothko* (1976), which reveals the defining missteps this ambitious artist took after his friend died. An obituary is in the *New York Times*, 4 Feb. 1997.

DANIEL GRANT

STEPHENS, John Lloyd (28 Nov. 1805–13 Oct. 1852), writer and archaeologist, was born in Shrewsbury, New Jersey, the son of Benjamin Stephens, a merchant, and Clemence Lloyd Stephens. When Stephens was thirteen months old, the family moved to New York City. He began his education in public school at age six and in 1815 entered the Classical School. He entered Columbia College at age thirteen, the year his mother died. After his graduation in 1822, Stephens studied law with Daniel Lord in New York and at Tapping Reeve's Litchfield Law School in Litchfield, Connecticut, where he received a degree in 1824.

Stephens then traveled to the newly settled Illinois Territory with his cousin Charles Hendrickson. Stephens wanted to go further west, but Hendrickson refused. They traveled down the Mississippi to New Orleans and returned to New York by boat.

Stephens entered the bar in 1827 and worked for his father. Active in politics, he campaigned for President Andrew Jackson in 1828. Stephens's campaigning ended in 1834, when he caught a streptococcic throat infection. His doctor recommended a vacation in Europe.

Stephens traveled from France to Rome, Greece, and Turkey. At Constantinople he took a Russian ship to Odessa, and he was the first American in Kiev. He toured Moscow, St. Petersburg, Minsk, Warsaw, and Vienna and returned to Paris in November 1835. While waiting for a ship to the United States, he read Leon de Laborde's *Voyage de l'Arabie Petrée*, published in 1830, which depicted the ruined cliff city of Petra in what is now Jordan. Inspired, Stephens changed his plans and journeyed up the Nile to Cairo and the pyramids, an established tourist route. However, Stephens left this beaten path to cross the Arabian Desert under the guidance of bedouins to Petraea and on to the Holy Land. In 1836 Stephens returned to New York via London, where he met the English architectural illustrator Frederick Catherwood.

The *American Monthly Magazine* published four of Stephens's travel letters in 1835 and 1836. On his return to the United States, Stephens wrote his first book, *Incidents of Travel in Egypt, Arabia Petraea, and the Holy Land*, published in 1837. This book was an instant bestseller, and it established his reputation as the greatest travel writer of his day. Edgar Allan Poe wrote a long, enthusiastic review in the *New York Review*: "Mr. Stephens writes like a man of good sense and sound feeling." Herman Melville mentioned Stephens in his novel *Redburn* (1849): "I very well remembered staring at a man . . . who was pointed out to me by my aunt one Sunday in Church, as the person who had been in Stony Arabia, and passed through strange adventures there all of which with my own eyes I had read in the book which he wrote. . . ." Stephens's popularity is attributed to his mix of erudition and a lively, personal style as well as the great public interest in travel writing. He published *Incidents of Travel in Greece, Turkey, Russia, and Poland* in 1838.

Catherwood moved to New York in 1837. Stephens read several partial accounts of ancient ruins in the Yucatán Peninsula of Mexico and proposed that Catherwood accompany him as an artist on a trip to furnish material for another book. Archeology was not an established discipline at the time, and nothing was known about Mayan culture. Through his political connections Stephens obtained a diplomatic appointment to Central America, which he hoped would smooth his travels. In 1839 Stephens and Catherwood sailed to Belize, continued down the coast to Livingston, Guatemala, and crossed the Sierra Madre mountain range with mules and porters. They found the region in a civil war, and local officials refused to recognize Stephens's diplomatic credentials. After a brief imprisonment by militia, Stephens and Catherwood reached the ruined Mayan city of Copán, which Stephens purchased from the owner for fifty American dollars. He hired local Indians to clear away the underbrush and was astounded at the quality and size of the buildings and sculptures. Stephens knew he had discovered an important lost civilization, a New World equivalent to the ruins of the Middle East. "Of the moral effects of the monuments themselves," he wrote,

> standing as they do in the depths of the tropical forest, silent and solemn, strange in design, excellent in sculpture, rich in ornament, different from the works of any other people, their uses and purposes in history so entirely unknown . . . I shall not pretend to convey any idea. (*Incidents of Travel in Central America*, pp. 123–124)

Catherwood stayed to sketch the site, while Stephens continued to Guatemala City to close the American legation there, then on to investigate a route across the Isthmus of Panama. He and Catherwood reunited in Guatemala City, and they proceeded to the ruins of Palenque in Chiapas, then up the Pacific Coast to Uxmal. They returned to New York from Sisal, Mexico, in 1840.

The size and quality of the ancient cities exceeded Stephens's expectations. His third book, *Incidents of Travel in Central America, Chiapas, and Yucatán*, illustrated by Catherwood and published in 1841, sold 20,000 copies in the first three months and continued through many editions. In 1841 Stephens returned to the Yucatán with Catherwood and Samuel Cabot, a physician and paleontologist. Beginning in Merida, they traveled to Uxmal and on to sites in the Yucatán, including Chichen Itza and Tulum. In 1842 Stephens returned to New York and wrote his fourth and last book, *Incidents of Travel in Yucatán*, published in 1843. These two books on the ruins made a sensation at the time and remained important into the twenty-first century because they established the field of Mayan archaeology. Stephens provided accurate, detailed descriptions of the ruins, and he was the first to establish that the many Mayan sites were part of a single civilization that existed up to the time of the Spanish conquest and that the Indians were the direct descendants of that civilization.

Stephens returned to business and politics. In 1848 he undertook to build a railway line over the Isthmus of Panama on the route of the present-day canal. The forty-mile stretch of railroad took five years to complete, and the mortality rate among the laborers was enormous. Nevertheless the 1851 California gold rush made the railway profitable. Stephens had contracted malaria during his previous travels in the area, and his health declined. He collapsed in February 1852 and returned to New York, where he died in October of hepatitis from malaria plasmodia.

Regarding the value of Stephens's work, the modern archaeologist Jeremy A. Sabloff wrote:

> What is significant and modern-sounding about Stephens' books, especially in contrast to most other discussions of Mayan sites, are his careful descriptions of the archeological materials, his eye for detail, and the relative lack of speculation amid his observations. He saw the cultural similarities among lowland Maya sites and inferred that the lowlands had been occupied by a single cultural group who had built their cities before the Spanish conquest (but not too much earlier) and whose descendants still lived in the same area. Moreover he viewed the Maya as an indigenous people and did not attribute their achievements to long-distance diffusion from Asia, Africa or some mythical land. (quoted in Ziff, pp. 60–61)

Stephens engaged local workers to chop back jungle foliage to uncover the sites, and along with the artist Frederick Catherwood prepared detailed accounts of the building and carvings. He lamented the destruction of old sites by local people seeking a ready source of building material, and negotiated to buy several sites from landholders, a project complicated by the fact that only Mexican nationals could purchase property.

Stephens hoped to export a significant sample of Mayan works to New York as the foundation of a projected Museum of American Antiquities. However, most of these objects were destroyed in a fire in 1842 that consumed Catherwood's Panorama of Jerusalem, where they were on temporary display. Several 500-pound carved stone slabs, which arrived after the fire, ended up on the estate of John Church Cruger, on Crugers Island in the Hudson near Barrytown. They remained there until 1918, when they were purchased by the American Museum of Natural History.

• No papers of Stephens's are known to have survived. A thorough biography is Wolfgang Von Hagen, *Maya Explorer: John Lloyd Stephens and the Lost Cities of Central America and Yucatán* (1948). Von Hagen also edited a two-volume edition of *Incidents of Travel in Yucatán* in 1962. A more compact account of Stephens's life and writing is in Larzer Ziff, *Return Passages: Great American Travel Writing 1780–1910* (2000). The Smithsonian Institution Press published abbreviated, scholarly editions of *Incidents of Travel in Central America, Chiapas, and Yucatán*, in 1993, and *Incidents of Travel in Yucatán*, in 1996. An informative editorial is in the *New York Tribune*, 14 Oct. 1852. An obituary is in the *New York Times*, 14 Oct. 1852.

HELENE LITTMANN

STOCKBRIDGE, Levi (13 Mar. 1820–2 May 1904), educator and agricultural leader, was born in Hadley, Massachusetts, the son of Deacon Jason Stockbridge, a farmer and state legislator, and Abigail Montague. After attending local schools he entered Hopkins Academy. Upon graduation he began farming and spent his winters teaching in district schools. Determined to bring scientifically based improvements into agriculture, Stockbridge studied all the available literature in the embryonic discipline of scientific farming and also trained himself in forensics at the local lyceum. He married Syrena Lamson on 20 January 1841; they had three children. Following his first wife's death in 1850, he married Joanna Smith on 4 November 1853. This marriage also produced three children.

With a growing reputation as a progressive leader within the community, Stockbridge found it a natural step to enter politics. First elected to the Massachusetts state legislature as a representative in 1855, he also became active in the emerging movement to provide academic instruction in agriculture. While serving on the state Board of Agriculture, he was named to a committee charged with cooperating with other interested advocacy groups in founding an agricultural school, and in 1861 he introduced at the board's annual meeting a resolution stating that the time for creating such an institution had arrived. After President Abraham Lincoln signed the Morrill Land Grant Act into law in July 1862, thus providing federal financial assistance to each state toward the establishment of academic training in agriculture, the movement gained new momentum. The flexibility of the Morrill Act, which allowed the use of funds either to create a new, separate agricultural college or to establish agricultural instruction at an existing institution, ensured the emergence of both political controversy and competing interests. In 1865–1866 Stockbridge served in the state senate. A long-time advocate of establishing an agricultural school in the western portion of the state, he moved to Amherst in 1867 in order to become the first instructor in agriculture and farm superintendent at the newly established Massachusetts Agricultural College.

As was true of most of the new "land grant" colleges, conditions at the school were primitive. Many hours of field work were demanded of the students in addition to their attendance at classes, and Stockbridge had few resources aside from a rundown farm, which served as the institution's first practical laboratory. Despite student resentment at the required amount of labor, Stockbridge proved to be a popular teacher and exemplar. His seemingly endless capacity for physical work impressed his charges, and his occasional financial assistance to needy students earned their gratitude as well. In addition to his dual positions at the college, Stockbridge continued to be active in politics, winning terms in the state house (1870 and 1883) and on the Amherst board of selectmen (1870, 1883–1887, and 1889–1890) and serving as moderator of the town meeting. An advocate of cooperative movements, he was instrumental in founding the local chapter of the Grange in 1873. Perhaps more important than his political activities, however, were his ventures into scientific research. As state cattle commissioner from 1869 until 1891, Stockbridge won praise for his efforts to control contagious diseases. Besides experimenting with tobacco growing, he investigated the leaching of nutrients from plants, the formation of dew, and the value of soil mulch, among other agricultural questions. His greatest success came in the study of fertilizer, with his research into the proper proportion of nitrogen, phosphoric acid, and potash for each individual type of plant crop resulting in patents for the so-called Stockbridge Formulas, about which he wrote important papers.

Stockbridge's work with the now-familiar N-P-K ratios brought him recognition, but it had practical consequences as well. In its first few years, the Massachusetts Agricultural College struggled mightily with finances and faced a possible merger with nearby Amherst College. Stockbridge's donation of $1,000 (the first proceeds of his fertilizer work) to the land grant school in 1878 helped establish the Massachusetts Agricultural Experiment Station, which deflected the enmity of farmers who had felt that their tax dollars were being wasted in support of useless "book learning" at the MAC. Although advancing age and the college's budget crisis had prompted Stockbridge to resign as farm superintendent in 1880, he was persuaded to assume the presidency of the school in an attempt to keep it from going under. Despite the lack of support from the local press (which took a dim view of his 1880 campaign for a seat in the U.S. House as a candidate of the Greenback party), Stockbridge succeeded in balancing the budget—at the cost of re-duced faculty salaries—as well as gaining badly needed state financial support for both the college and the experiment station.

Stockbridge resigned as president of the Massachusetts Agricultural College in 1882 and was named honorary professor of agriculture. Following the death of his second wife that year, on 23 October 1883 he married Elizabeth Ashcroft Strong, who survived him; they had no children. He died at his winter home in Florida. His son Horace Edward Stockbridge (by his second wife) also achieved distinction as an agricultural leader in the postbellum American South.

• Stockbridge's papers are held at the University of Massachusetts in Amherst. His research results were published in the *Thirteenth Annual Report of the Massachusetts Agricultural College* (1876) and the *Sixteenth Annual Report . . .* (1879). The best secondary source of information on his life and career is Harold Whiting Cary, *The University of Massachusetts: A History of One Hundred Years* (1962), while W. H. Bowker, *Levi Stockbridge and the Stockbridge Principle of Plant Feeding* (1911) and F. P. Rand, *Yesterdays at Massachusetts Agricultural College* (1933) also remain useful. Obituaries appear in the *Springfield Republican*, 4 May 1904, and the *Amherst Record*, 11 May 1904.

EDWARD L. LACH, JR.

STODDARD, Seneca Ray (13 May 1843–26 Apr. 1917), landscape photographer and conservationist, was born in Wilton, New York, the son of Charles Stoddard, a part-time farmer who also did craft work and/or lumbering, and Julia Ray Stoddard. Stoddard's childhood home, the Wilton hamlet of Dimick's Corners, was located in the shadow of Mount McGregor, the highest peak of the Adirondacks' Palmer Range.

Following the deaths of Julia Stoddard and her infant daughter in 1854, Charles Stoddard married Laura Cook and two years later moved his family north. By the close of the decade they were living in Burke, Franklin County, in Hawk's Hollow, a hamlet on the northern edge of the Adirondacks, just out of sight of the mountains' peaks. Seneca Ray Stoddard attended common school in Burke through the age of seventeen. He probably commenced some training as a carriage painter in Burke as well. In 1861 his family moved to the Albany-Troy area. The following year Stoddard began work as a journeyman carriage painter for the Gilbert Car Company on Green Island in Watervliet (Albany County). Gilbert, a manufacturer of railway cars, employed "ornamental painters" to decorate its finished coaches with painted panels of landscapes and other scenes.

Stoddard's sojourn on Green Island, then known as West Troy and closely linked to Troy proper on the Hudson River's east bank, affected him in two distinct ways. First, he experienced the last blooming of Troy's vibrant midcentury art world, centered in fine coach painting but also nourished by wealthy manufacturers' patronage of independent artists and citywide art exhibitions. Second, he confronted the smoky, noisy, disordered world of the new industrial city. Iron-making Troy was then a place of strikes, riots—a mid–

Civil War draft riot swept over Green Island in 1863—fires, and crowds of alien newcomers, including the desperately poor, potato-famine Irish.

In 1864 Stoddard left Troy to establish his own painting business in the Adirondack lumber-processing community of Glens Falls, New York, a village on the way to becoming a city located less than ten miles northeast of Stoddard's Wilton birthplace. By 1867 Stoddard had ceased advertising as a "Carriage, House, Sign, Banner, and Ornamental" painter, and in October of that year a local newspaper praised stereographs of Glens Falls's scenes executed by "Mr. Stoddard, Photographer." In May 1868 Stoddard married Helen Augusta Potter, the daughter of a wealthy Glens Falls insurance agent and merchant; the couple had two sons. By the summer of 1868 Stoddard was making many small 2.5-inch by 3-inch stereo images of nearby Lake George as well as larger views of 4 inches by 7 inches or greater. He used the wet-plate technology of the day, which required that a photographer of outdoor scenes transport not only a camera weighing fifty pounds or more but also an array of chemicals to "fix" the glass plate negatives after exposure.

In 1870 Stoddard lived on Elm Street in Glens Falls, the site of his home and studio for the remainder of his career, and claimed the profession of "landscape painter." Over the next few years he painted and photographed Lake George views, increasingly using the larger, four-inch by seven-inch plates in his photographic work. His photographs of these years resemble the landscapes painted by the noted Hudson River School artist John Kensett on Lake George at about the same time. Since the 1950s art historians have pointed to these late Kensett works—as well as to the 1850–1875 works of Sanford Gifford, Martin Heade, FitzHugh Lane, Frederic Church, and others—as expressing a native American style called luminism. Such paintings feature deep vistas with expanses of water and sky and almost always a small human figure, who contemplates the far horizon. Typically a rising or setting sun beams light from the center of the horizontal compositions, with the light the focus of the austere, often slightly melancholy views. Luminist painting shows the influence of photography, both in its treatment of perspective space and in its minimal use of color. In 1971 the curator and scholar John Wilmerding labeled Stoddard a luminist photographer. Wilmerding's *American Light* (1971) also explores luminism's intellectual roots in Ralph Waldo Emerson's writings on the divinity of Nature.

In 1873 Stoddard photographed and painted in the Adirondacks and published the first of a long-running series of guidebooks to the region, *Adirondacks Illustrated*, in which he expressed Emersonian beliefs about the goodness, beauty, and healing properties of unspoiled wilderness. From this same year he began widespread marketing of his images to tourists via sales in area hotels, ceasing most painting activity by 1875.

During the 1870s Stoddard also wrote for the Glens Falls and Troy newspapers—mainly accounts of Adirondack trips and humorous sketches—and took an active role in the New York State Temperance movement, becoming "Grand Worthy Patriarch" of the state organization's "Eastern Division" in 1875. Raised a Methodist, Stoddard hinted at spiritualist beliefs in his earliest writings. Toward the close of his life he turned away from traditional religious forms, preferring to worship only in "Nature's Temple." From his early writings through the later ones, he also revealed an antipathy toward urban living that carried over into antipathies toward both large industrial concerns and immigrant groups.

Through the 1870s and into the mid-1880s Stoddard made hundreds of landscape images on Lake George and in the Adirondacks, also working to some extent in New Hampshire's White Mountains, on the Maine seacoast, in the lower Hudson Valley, and along the Saint Lawrence River. Though Stoddard used the more rapid dry-plate photographic method from the early 1880s, his body of work from the fifteen-year period forms a stylistic whole of serene, light-filled, predominantly horizontal views, with people and buildings—when they appear—treated as sharply defined, often dramatically highlighted forms that are frequently appreciated as abstract, geometric shapes. His views of the Adirondacks in particular preserve its social and architectural history at a time when wealthy tourists and elaborate "camps" and hotels were first making their appearance in a region of bark huts, hermits, Native American hunters, logging camps, and hardscrabble farms.

In 1878 Stoddard served as a photographer on the New York State Survey of the Adirondacks, where he gained sufficient knowledge to publish, two years later, his own popular *Map of the Adirondacks*. In 1881 he published another successful map of Lake George. His interest in technology led him to invent in 1882 a camera attachment for use in dry-plate photography—manufactured without success by an Auburn, New York, firm—and to perfect the "magnesium flash" for taking night photographs. In 1890 he successfully tested this flash in New York City, capturing striking night views of the Statue of Liberty and the Washington Square Arch.

From the mid-1880s through the 1890s Stoddard made a series of photographic trips to Europe, the Near East, the American West and South, and Alaska, achieving financial success by presenting "illustrated" lectures of his travels to audiences throughout the northeastern United States. During this era he lectured on the Adirondacks as well, showing lantern slides of the exquisite early images. In 1891 he helped win a significant political victory with these images; he delivered his illustrated lecture on the Adirondacks to the sitting New York State Legislature and swayed the body to pass the Adirondack Park Bill.

After his wife's death in 1906, Stoddard launched a Glens Falls–based magazine, *Stoddard's Northern Monthly* (later *Stoddard's Adirondack Monthly*) of articles and short stories advocating wilderness conservation. In 1908 he married Emily Doty, the family's longtime housekeeper; they had no children. After the magazine failed the same year, Stoddard completed a hydrographic chart of Lake George and his *Auto-Road Map* of the Adirondacks and the Champlain and Hudson Valleys. He died in Glens Falls. His photographs of the Adirondack region powerfully fixed the image of the Adirondacks as an earthly paradise in the public mind.

• Many of Stoddard's photographs are in the Chapman Historical Museum in Glens Falls and the Adirondack Museum in Blue Mountain Lake, N.Y. Collections of his papers are also held at both museums. Informative works include Maitland C. De Sormo, *Seneca Ray Stoddard: Versatile Camera-Artist* (1972); Jeanne Winston Adler, *Early Days in the Adirondacks: The Photographs of Seneca Ray Stoddard* (1997); and Jeffery L. Horrell, *Seneca Ray Stoddard: Transforming the Adirondack Wilderness in Text and Image* (1999). An obituary is in *Proceedings of the New York State Historical Association* 17 (1919): 266.

JEANNE WINSTON ADLER

STOUPPE, Pierre (1690–6 Jan. 1760), Huguenot minister, Anglican priest, missionary, and educator, was born into a Reformed Protestant family in Switzerland. Many details of his early life are unavailable and the remainder are sketchy, but he was almost certainly related to Jean-Baptiste Stouppe, a minister of the French Reformed (Huguenot) Church of London in the 1650s. J.-B. Stouppe's surname was originally Stoppa, and his family came from the Italian-speaking area north of Lake Como. In 1620, as persecuted Protestants, the Stoppas fled from this predominantly Catholic area to Zurich. Both Pierre and Jean-Baptiste were educated for the ministry at the Calvinist Genevan Academy.

In 1716 the Huguenot Church in Orange Quarter, South Carolina, asked the elders of the Huguenot Church of London to help them find a minister. The elders recommended Pierre Stouppe. His preaching ability, religious orthodoxy, and good character impressed the London elders, but they noted that his spoken French was poor, which suggests that French was not his primary language. Nevertheless, they felt he was intelligible and would soon overcome this deficiency. Although Stouppe accepted the call, he did not serve contentious Orange Quarter for long. From 1719 to 1723, he pastored the Huguenot church in Charleston until he conformed to Anglicanism and returned to London to receive episcopal ordination.

Numerous Huguenot churches and ministers in England and the colonies had conformed. The Anglican hierarchy offered a stabilizing influence for the sometimes disorderly Huguenot churches. Moreover, the Society for the Propagation of the Gospel (SPG), the Church's missionary arm, provided salary supplements for Anglican pastors and missionaries. In December 1723 Stouppe was ordained as a deacon, and as a priest three months later, by Bishop Edmund Gibson. The testimonial for Stouppe presented to the SPG before his ordinations described him as "affable and courteous in disposition, prudent and circumspect in affairs, sober and pious in his life and conversation, and zealous for the propagation of the Christian faith." Stouppe was quickly appointed missionary to the French-speaking Anglican congregation in New Rochelle, New York. But he asked the SPG to delay his departure since his wife and child were ill.

Stouppe arrived in New Rochelle in July 1724. The town had been founded in 1689 by Huguenots who left France in 1685 when the Edict of Nantes, which had given them limited religious liberty, was revoked. They quickly established a French Reformed church, but in 1709 church members voted to conform to Anglicanism. In a 1727 letter to the SPG Secretary, Stouppe described New Rochelle as a poor, overwhelmingly French farming community. Out of a population of about 400, seventy-eight were slaves. There was no schoolmaster, but Stouppe noted that mothers and fathers educated their children. In a 1742 letter, he described his congregation as "a sober, industrious, religious people."

Between 1724 and 1740, Stouppe wrote more than seventy-five highly literate manuscript sermons in French, which may be the only extant collection of Anglican-Huguenot sermons in America. Hence, they are a rich source for insights into this creolized denomination. Most are based on a section of the French translation of the Anglican catechism and underscore the basics of faith. The sermons demonstrate that Stouppe's conformity did not result in a major doctrinal shift. He emphasized characteristically Calvinist doctrines such as predestination, Election (salvation) regardless of good works, perseverance of the Elect (once a person has received God's grace, it cannot be forfeited), and criticized as unscriptural the signing of the cross practiced by Anglicans and Roman Catholics. He offered occasional English language services to accommodate the small group of non-French persons in New Rochelle and to familiarize French speakers with English.

Education was of particular importance to Stouppe. He proudly reported to the SPG secretary the numbers of young people who had been admitted to communion after undergoing intense instruction and examination in the fundamentals of faith. Stouppe also cared about secular education and served as schoolmaster; prominent Huguenots sent their sons to Stouppe's boarding school. One of his better-known pupils in the 1750s was John Jay, the future Chief Justice of the Supreme Court. William Jay's biography of his father, John, described Stouppe as "a native of Switzerland and of odd habits. Ignorant of the world, regardless of money, and remarkable for absence of mind, he devoted every minute of his leisure to his studies, and particularly to the mathematics." Jay also noted that the parsonage was in poor condition, food was limited, and that French was spoken by the inhabitants of the village as well as in the parsonage. (The total immersion in French that Jay encountered in New Rochelle must have been useful to him as a member of the peace delegation in Paris after the American Revolution.) The boys and girls of New Rochelle were also well served by Stouppe's efforts. Midcentury documents for the town suggest that virtually all males could sign their names and that most females had mastered this skill. Since reading was typically taught before writing in the colonial period, it appears that reading ability was nearly universal.

One of Stouppe's SPG-missionary duties was to Christianize slaves. Stouppe's involvement in these activities is mentioned throughout his correspondence with the SPG Secretary. Slaves were baptized by request as young people or adults, unless presented as babies by Christian parents. They attended services with free persons, but sat in a separate area. Some were admitted to communion after undergoing the same rigorous process as whites. Christianization, however, did not mean emancipation.

In 1759 Stouppe was unable to leave the parsonage because of paralysis. He still performed baptisms and marriages at home until he died in New Rochelle. His congregation wrote that they had "great reason to lament his loss." He was survived by his wife, Madeleine, whose modest 1768 will does not mention any children. (Her maiden name and the date of their marriage are not known.) Nevertheless, Stouppe's legacy was a rich one for the many young people he had educated, some of whom became distinguished leaders, and for the refugee descendants who were edified by his lengthy, productive, and dedicated ministry. Moreover, he forged a hybrid Anglican-Huguenot faith, and his French and English services facilitated the acculturation of New Rochelle residents.

• Originals of SPG correspondence to and from Stouppe are at Lambeth Palace Library in London. Microfilm copies are available at large research libraries in the United States. Society for the Propagation of the Gospel in Foreign Parts, "Records," (Yorkshire, England: Microform Academic Publishers, 1964), Series A, vols. 18–26, Series B, vols. 1, 3, 10, 11, 13, 15–19, Series C, vol. 1. Specific citations are too numerous to list but can be located in the indexes for each volume. Pierre Stouppe appears on the ordination lists located at Guildhall Library in London. The only version of Stouppe's sermons is in manuscript form, in French, at the Library of the Huguenot Society of America, New York City. William Jay's *The Life of John Jay* (1833) contains a brief profile of Stouppe and his school in the 1750s. The will of "Magdalen Stouffe" is in William S. Pelletreau, ed., *Early Wills of Westchester County, New York, from 1664 to 1784* (1898).

Jon Butler, *The Huguenots in America: A Refugee People in New World Society* (1983), is the most essential overview of that topic. For Stouppe family origins, see Giorgio Vola, "The Revd. J. B. Stouppe's Travels in France in 1654 as Cromwell's Secret Agent," *Proceedings of the Huguenot Society of Great Britain and Ireland* 27, no. 4 (Summer 2001): 509–26. A forthcoming book by Bertrand Van Ruymbeke, *From Babylon to Eden: A Social and Religious History of the Huguenots in Pre-Revocation France and Proprietary South Carolina*, discusses Stouppe's career in that colony. Paula Wheeler Carlo, "'Playing Fast and Loose with the Canons and Rubrick': French Anglicanism in Colonial New Rochelle," *Journal of the Canadian Church Historical Society* (July 2002), explores Stouppe's theology and its relationship to mainstream Anglicanism. For a more in-depth discussion of Stouppe's activities in New Rochelle, see Carlo, "The Huguenots of Colonial New Paltz and New Rochelle: A Social and Religious History" (Ph. D. diss., City University of New York, 2001).

PAULA WHEELER CARLO

STRASBERG, Susan (22 May 1938–21 Jan. 1999), actress, was born Susan Elizabeth Strasberg in New York City, the daughter of Lee Strasberg, an acting coach and director, and Paula Miller, an actress and acting coach. Strasberg's parents were both involved with the politically conscious Group Theater in the 1930s, and her father became one of the most influential figures in the American theater in the 1950s through his teaching of Method acting at New York's Actors' Studio. Strasberg grew up immersed in an atmosphere that blended intellectualism and bohemian ideas with middle-class stability. Prominent theater personalities, such as the actress Tallulah Bankhead, the actor John Garfield, and the playwright Clifford Odets, were regular visitors to her family's Manhattan apartment. Strasberg attended New York City Public School #9 and the High School of Music and Art. A petite brunette with large brown eyes, she at age fourteen worked briefly for the John Robert Powers modeling agency.

In 1953 Strasberg made her professional acting debut when the actress Jo Van Fleet, an associate of her father at the Actors' Studio, arranged for her to take a small part in *Maya*, a symbolic drama by Simon Gantillon produced at the off-Broadway Theatre de Lys. Soon after this Strasberg signed with a talent agency, and her career advanced rapidly. She had major parts on television, including in *Omnibus* and *Kraft Television Theatre* productions, and had a regular role on *The Marriage*, a domestic comedy series starring Jessica Tandy and Hume Cronyn that aired on NBC in the summer of 1954. Strasberg transferred to the High School of Performing Arts and was later given private tutoring. She occasionally sat in on classes at her father's celebrated Actors' Studio, but to retain her independence she never studied there formally.

Strasberg's first film role was that of a mentally ill adolescent in the director Vincente Minnelli's *The Cobweb* (1955), starring Lauren Bacall and Charles Boyer. She then played the tomboyish younger sister of Kim Novak in the screen version of William Inge's hit Broadway drama *Picnic* (1955) about sexual frustration in small town Kansas. Directed by Joshua Logan and also starring William Holden and Rosalind Russell, *Picnic* was a critical and box office smash. It was, however, Strasberg's work on Broadway in the title role in *The Diary of Anne Frank* that brought her real fame. Adapted by Frances Goodrich and Albert Hackett, directed by Garson Kanin, and costarring Joseph Schildkraut as Anne Frank's father Otto Frank, *The Diary of Anne Frank* opened on 5 October 1955 to excellent critical notices for both the play and its young leading lady. Richard Watts, Jr., of the *New York Post* (6 Oct. 1955) called Strasberg's portrayal of the teenage diarist who perished in a Nazi death camp "lovely and sensitive . . . a beautiful performance, warm, rich, at times with comedy overtones but always moving and real." The superlative reviews prompted the producer Kermit Bloomgarden to put Strasberg's name above the title on the Cort Theater's marquee, making her one of the youngest performers in Broadway history to be given such billing. Strasberg's work in *The Diary of Anne Frank* earned her a Tony Award nomination for best dramatic actress.

In 1957 Strasberg enjoyed another Broadway success when she costarred with Helen Hayes and Richard Burton in Jean Anouilh's romantic comedy *Time Remembered*, directed by Albert Marre, in which she played a young milliner who impersonates the dead lover of a grieving prince. During the run of the play the still teenage Strasberg had an affair with the significantly older and married Burton that left her emotionally devastated. Returning to screen acting, Strasberg costarred with Henry Fonda and Christopher Plummer in *Stage Struck* (1958). Directed by Sidney Lumet and made entirely in New York, the film was a handsomely photographed but uninspired remake of the 1933 Katharine Hepburn vehicle *Morning Glory* about a young actress who must choose between love and stardom.

In 1958 Strasberg played Minnie Powell in an off-Broadway production of Sean O'Casey's *Shadow of a Gunman*, and also that year she played the young prostitute Kitty in a production of William Saroyan's *The Time of Your Life* at the world's fair in Brussels. She stayed in Europe to star in the Italian-Yugoslavian film *Kapo* (1960) about a young Nazi concentration camp prisoner who is saved from death by claiming to be held for criminal rather than religious reasons and who eventually becomes a camp guard. Directed by Gillo Pontecorvo, *Kapo* received an Oscar nomination for best foreign film of 1960 but did not receive general release in the United States until 1964. Strasberg's other films of this period include *Hemingway's Adventures of a Young Man* (1962), a glossy but poorly received Hollywood production based on short stories by Ernest Hemingway, and the British-produced thriller *Scream of Fear* (1961), in which she played a wheelchair-bound young woman who suspects her father has been murdered by her stepmother. Also starring Christopher Lee and Ann Todd, *Scream of Fear* was not a success at the time of its release but later gained a following among aficionados of the suspense genre. In 1963 Strasberg returned to the Broadway stage, playing the lead role of Marguerite Gautier in a lavishly mounted production of *The Lady of the Camellias*. Directed by Franco Zeffirelli and with a text adapted by Terrence McNally from the Alexandre Dumas fils novel, the production garnered mostly unfavorable reviews and closed after a few performances. It was Strasberg's last significant stage appearance.

Settling in California in the mid-1960s, Strasberg devoted the remainder of her acting career to film and television work. She had roles in *The High Bright Sun* (1965) with Dirk Bogarde, *The Trip* (1967) with Peter Fonda, and *The Brotherhood* (1968) with Kirk Douglas. In 1965 Strasberg married the actor Christopher Jones. The couple had one child before divorcing in about 1967. During their marriage Strasberg and Jones costarred in the drama *Chubasco* (1968) about a fishing boat captain's daughter who marries one of her father's crewmen.

Though an attractive and competent screen performer, Strasberg lacked charisma. Her delicate and wistful qualities, which had served her well as a young actress on stage, were not as effective on screen in adult roles. Strasberg continued to work steadily but failed to land major roles in first-rank films. By the late 1960s she was surpassed professionally by more dynamic actresses, such as Jane Fonda and Faye Dunaway. She supported herself with television work, including guest appearances on episodes of *The Virginian*; *Marcus Welby, M.D.*; *McCloud*; *Night Gallery*; and other programs. In 1973–1974 she had a recurring role on the detective series *Toma* on ABC.

Talkative, emotional, and inquisitive, Strasberg devoted much of her spare time to various forms of mental therapy. In the 1980s she moved back to New York, published a candid, name-dropping autobiography, *Bittersweet* (1980), which covered her first thirty-five years, and briefly toured in a one-woman show, *A Woman's Rites*. Her later films include *Rollercoaster* (1977), *In Praise of Older Women* (1979), *Sweet Sixteen* (1981), *The Delta Force* (1986), and *Light in the Jungle* (1990). Strasberg died at her home in Manhattan.

• In addition to her autobiography, Strasberg wrote *Marilyn and Me: Sisters, Rivals, Friends* (1992), which recounts her relationship with the actress Marilyn Monroe, who came to study with her parents at the Actors' Studio in the mid-1950s and became an integral part of her family's life. Strasberg is profiled in *Current Biography* (1958). Lengthy interviews with Strasberg are Judy Klemesrud, "Susan Strasberg Looks Back: Scenes from a Bittersweet Life," *New York Times*, 27 Apr. 1980; and Sally Quinn, "The Strasberg Confessions," *Washington Post*, 6 June 1980. An obituary is in the *New York Times*, 23 Jan. 1999.

MARY C. KALFATOVIC

STRAX, Philip (1 Jan. 1909–9 Mar. 1999), radiologist, was born in Brooklyn, New York, the son of Jacob Strax, a garment worker, and Molly Pelchow Strax. He received his B.S. degree from New York University in 1928 and remained there to attend medical school, earning his M.D. in 1931. He married Bertha Goldberg in 1932; they would have four children. On completing his internship and residencies at Jewish Hospital of Brooklyn (1931–1933) and New York Postgraduate Medical School (1933–1936), respectively, Strax opened a general family practice in Manhattan and also served as a roentgenologist at Bellevue Hospital.

Strax might have remained an obscure member of the medical community were it not for his wife's untimely death in 1947 from breast cancer at the age of thirty-nine. Devastated by his wife's death, he decided to devote the remainder of his professional career to fighting the disease. Although surgeons and radiologists had attempted to apply radiological technology to the detection of breast cancer as early as 1913, the general consensus within the medical profession was that the technology was of limited usefulness; many physicians felt that mortality from the disease was largely a function of the strength of each individual occurrence, and placed little importance on early detection. Also, the diagnostic equipment at that time was better suited to examining hard tissues such as bones because it produced unclear images when used on soft tissue.

On 28 January 1949, Strax married Gertrude Jacobsen; they would have two children. In 1950 he went to New York's City Hospital, where he served as director of radiology until 1966 (concurrently holding the same post at Elmhurst General Hospital between 1962 and 1966). Heartened by improvements in radiology that allowed better imaging of soft tissues, Strax, working with colleagues Sam Shapiro and Louis Venet, undertook a massive controlled study between 1963 and 1966 among more that 62,000 women in the New York area. Sponsored by the Health Insurance Plan (HIP) of Greater New York, the study was the first attempt to determine the effectiveness of mammograms in reducing mortality from breast cancer. During the study, half of the women involved were given mammograms as well as manual breast examinations, while the control group received no treatment at all. When the first results of the study were released several years later, it was determined that the group receiving mammograms had suffered one-third fewer deaths than the control group. Follow-up evaluations confirmed the original findings of the study and also confirmed a continued significant reduction in mortality among participants.

After assuming the position of director of radiology at New York's LaGuardia Hospital in 1966, Strax literally took his act on the road, becoming the first person to organize mobile breast examination vans that visited area neighborhoods. Sponsored by the Guttman Institute, each van was capable of providing up to seventy mammograms a day at little or no cost to local women. In addition to serving as the director of the Guttman Institute, Strax also organized Park Avenue Radiology in New York as well as the Strax Institute in Fort Lauderdale, Florida. He served at LaGuardia until 1979 and in 1980 received the National Annual Award of the American Cancer Society for his contributions to breast cancer detection. In 1988 he was the recipient, along with Sam Shapiro, of a $100,000 award from the General Motors Cancer Research Foundation for his work on the HIP study, which, according to the foundation, "almost unilaterally changed medical thinking about early detection." A fellow of the American College of Radiology,

Strax was also the author of several books on cancer, most notably *Early Detection: Breast Cancer Is Curable* (1974), and was the editor of *Control of Breast Cancer* (1988).

Strax also had a lifelong interest in poetry and wrote three books on the subject. He retired to Hollywood, Florida, and died at the home of his daughter in Bethesda, Maryland.

Although debate continues about mammograms (particularly for women under 50), there is no doubt that many lives have been saved by the pioneering work of Philip Strax. His career was a classic example of a professional who, through dogged persistence in the face of collegial doubt, turned personal tragedy into a solid advance in medical diagnostic procedures.

• No collection of Strax's papers has been located. The results of his groundbreaking study with HIP can be found in P. Strax, L. Venet, and S. Shapiro, "Value of Mammography in Reduction of Mortality from Breast Cancer in Mass Screenings," *American Journal of Roentgenology* 117 (1973): 686–89. His work is placed in historical context in Richard H. Gold, "The Evolution of Mammography," *Radiologic Clinics of North America* 30, no. 1 (1992): 1–19. An obituary is in the *New York Times*, 11 Mar. 1999.

EDWARD L. LACH, JR.

STURTEVANT, Edgar H. (7 Mar. 1875–1 July 1952), linguist, was born Edgar Howard Sturtevant in Jacksonville, Illinois, the son of Alfred Henry Sturtevant, a teacher and farmer, and Harriet Morse Sturtevant. His grandfather, Julian Monson Sturtevant (1805–1886), was president of Illinois College, and his father taught mathematics there before turning to farming. Edgar shared his grandfather's academic interests and as a boy reportedly taught himself Sanskrit while milking his father's cows. He graduated from Whipple Academy in 1893 and spent two years at Illinois College before following his Latin teacher, Harold W. Johnston, to Indiana University, where in 1898 he earned the bachelor of arts degree.

Studying at the University of Chicago under Carl Darling Buck, Sturtevant received the doctoral degree in 1901 with a dissertation on Latin case forms. While in Chicago he met Bessie Fitch Skinner. They married in 1903, during a period in which Sturtevant held a series of short appointments teaching Latin and sometimes Greek at various colleges. They had three children. In 1907 he was appointed to an instructorship in classical philology at Columbia University in New York, and he was promoted to assistant professor in 1913. During these years at Columbia he authored numerous articles and reviews on Latin, Greek, and comparative linguistics, culminating in 1917 with his textbook *Linguistic Change: An Introduction to the Historical Study of Language* and in 1920 with the classic research monograph *The Pronunciation of Greek and Latin: The Sounds and Accents*, of which the second edition (1940) remained in print into the twenty-first century. In 1920, despite his growing reputation in the field of classical linguistics, he was dismissed by Columbia University, which was experiencing low enrollments in Greek and Latin as the post–World War I generation of students turned to modernism in language studies as well as in art and music. Sturtevant found employment as a bank clerk but continued his research.

In 1923 Sturtevant was appointed assistant professor of Greek and Latin at Yale University with promotion to associate professor of linguistics in 1926 and to professor the following year. As Yale added several more linguists to its faculty, Sturtevant became director of graduate studies, and the university acquired a well-deserved reputation as the premier linguistics program in the United States.

Always open to new ideas and interests, Sturtevant became engrossed in the study of Hittite soon after it became apparent that the language, deciphered in the late 1910s, was related to the Indo-European language family. Indo-European is the name commonly given to a large group of languages spoken in Europe, Iran, and India, all of which are assumed to have developed from a common source, a hypothesized language that no longer exists. When Hittite was discovered and then deciphered, many scholars considered it just another branch of Indo-European. A few, however, including the German Emil Forrer, proposed that Hittite was not a continuation of Indo-European but rather a branch coordinate with it. Sturtevant adopted the latter position and published in *Language*, the journal of the Linguistic Society of America, his first important paper on the subject, "On the Position of Hittite among the Indo-European Languages" (1926). He argued that Hittite contained more archaic phenomena than could be reconstructed for Indo-European and therefore Hittite and Indo-European were both developments from an earlier common stage, for which he introduced the term Indo-Hittite.

For the rest of his life Sturtevant investigated the phonology and the morphology of the Hittite language. He published a remarkable number of papers on these subjects, more than forty in *Language* alone, as well as four monographs, *A Hittite Glossary* (1931, 2d ed. 1936), *A Comparative Grammar of the Hittite Language* (1933, 2d ed. 1951), *A Hittite Chrestomathy* with George Bechtel (1935, corrected reissue 1952), and *The Indo-Hittite Laryngeals* (1942). Sturtevant was a leading figure in the search for the proper place of Hittite in relation to Indo-European and through his research produced considerable evidence that Hittite and the other closely related Anatolian languages were the earliest to separate from the Indo-European parent. The Indo-Hittite theory remained under consideration by modern scholars and was still the subject of debate in the early twenty-first century.

A prolific scholar, Sturtevant was also an excellent academic administrator. In 1924 he, along with Leonard Bloomfield and George M. Bolling, constituted the organizing committee for the founding of the Linguistic Society of America (LSA), which met for the first time in December of that year. Shortly thereafter Sturtevant took up an idea proposed by another LSA member for a linguistic institute, at which scholars could gather during the summer months to discuss their research and to teach their specializations to one another. By resolution of the LSA executive committee, of which he was a member, Sturtevant in 1927 was named director and ex officio chair of the Committee of Administration for the LSA Linguistic Institutes. Over the next four years and even beyond, when he served as associate director of later institutes on many occasions, Sturtevant worked tirelessly on the curriculum, staffing, and funding of these summer programs, which attracted both senior scholars and students at all levels.

The first two Linguistic Institutes were held at Yale University in the summers of 1928 and 1929; the next two took place at the College of the City of New York in 1930 and 1931. Although the majority of LSA members at the time were interested primarily in historical linguistics, as was Sturtevant, from the beginning he sought to include at the institutes courses that were not historically oriented, courses in phonetics, courses in Native American languages and field methods, and courses in the study of modern American English dialects. The common theme in these new nonhistorical topics was an emphasis on the spoken forms of language, a point Sturtevant had made in his first book, *Linguistic Change*: "Linguistic science is . . . primarily concerned with spoken language" (*Linguistic Change*, p. 10). This for Sturtevant was the key distinction between the new linguistics and the older philology. Linguists studied speech, using written material only as clues to what speech must have been like in older languages; philologists dealt with written documents, influenced by the goals and methods of literature, archaeology, history, and culture.

Sturtevant's contributions to historical linguistics were recognized by his election as LSA president for 1931. He was also president of the American Oriental Society, 1936–1937, and was the first holder of the Hermann and Klara H. Collitz Professorship in comparative Indo-European linguistics at the 1948 Linguistic Institute. In 1946 an issue of the journal *Language* was dedicated to him. In 1951 he had agreed to teach Hittite at the Linguistic Institute at the University of California, Berkeley, but the trip aggravated his heart disease. He was forced to return home, and he died the next year in New Haven, Connecticut. His last public talk, at the Linguistic Institute, was on Hittite and the prehistory of Indo-European. It was published in *Language* the year he died.

Sturtevant is mentioned only briefly in most histories of American linguistics. He was not a member of the post-Bloomfieldian descriptivist group that dominated the discipline in the United States in the 1940s and 1950s, but he was instrumental in the shift from historical to nonhistorical linguistics that took place in the 1930s. His decisions about courses and teaching faculty for the Linguistic Institutes as well as his own teaching of the introductory linguistics course there contributed to a change that continued to characterize American linguistics, which emphasized synchronic over diachronic study. After a four-year hiatus during the Great Depression years, the LSA Linguistic Institutes began again in 1936. Subsequently they were held every year on a different university campus, then every other year starting in the late twentieth century. They remain a major activity of the society Sturtevant helped found.

• Sturtevant's papers are at Yale University (Edgar Howard Sturtevant Papers) and at the Western Historical Manuscript Collection, Columbia, Mo. (Linguistic Society of America Records, Series FFFF: Edgar H. Sturtevant Correspondence). "The Indo-Hittite Hypothesis," text of a 1938 lecture at the Linguistic Institute and his most concise statement of his position, was published posthumously in *Language* 38 (1962): 105–10. His last institute address was published as "The Prehistory of Indo-European: A Summary," *Language* 28 (1952): 177–81. Sturtevant, *An Introduction to Linguistic Science* (1947), is based on Sturtevant's introductory courses at Yale and the Linguistic Institutes. A bibliography of Sturtevant's major works, compiled by Bernard Bloch, is in *Language* 28 (1952): 428–34. For an account of his contributions as director of the Linguistic Institutes, see Julia S. Falk, "The American Shift from Historical to Non-Historical Linguistics: E. H. Sturtevant and the First Linguistic Institutes," *Language & Communication* 18 (1998): 171–80. Obituaries are E. Adelaide Hahn, *Language* 28 (1952): 417–28; and Murray B. Emeneau, *American Philosophical Society Yearbook*, 1952, pp. 339–43. The obituaries are reprinted in Thomas A. Sebeok, ed., *Portraits of Linguists*, vol. 2 (1966).

JULIA S. FALK

T

TALBERT, Billy (4 Sept. 1918–28 Feb. 1999), tennis player, was born William Franklin Talbert in Cincinnati, Ohio, the son of Rezin C. Talbert, operator of a livestock business and a former minor league baseball pitcher, and Clara Talbert. As a child, Talbert enjoyed sports, especially baseball. His hope of becoming a big league player was shattered at age ten when he contracted diabetes and faced a lifetime of insulin injections, diet restrictions, and limited exercise. In 1932, when Talbert was fourteen, his physician, noting the youngster's extreme unhappiness with his inactivity, recommended that he play tennis, a sport he had rejected earlier as a sissy's game.

Talbert began playing tennis on asphalt courts at Coy Field and soon discovered that he liked the sport. Quickly learning the fundamental strokes and strategy from Roy Fitzgerald, a college student in charge of the courts, he competed in team matches against boys from other Cincinnati public parks. Thoroughly obsessed by the game, Talbert progressed swiftly and soon dominated local junior boys' competition. He became the number-one player on the Hughes High School team and in 1936, his graduation year, won the Ohio state interscholastic singles title. In 1934 the Ohio Valley Tennis Association had sent him to the national boys' championship at Culver Military Academy in Indiana, where his performance earned him a number-ten ranking among boys under age fifteen in the United States. The following two years he ranked sixteenth and eighth, respectively, among junior boys (under age eighteen).

In 1936 Talbert enrolled at the nearby University of Cincinnati. An excellent student, he supported himself with various part-time jobs for the next three years and participated in tennis tournaments during vacations and other opportunities, with steadily improving results. In 1938 he was chosen as a member of the U.S. Junior Davis Cup Squad. When he was chosen again in 1939, Talbert decided to leave college and devote himself full-time to tennis. He performed creditably in midwestern clay and eastern grass court tournaments, earning U.S. singles rankings of twenty-first in 1939 and sixteenth in 1940. Thereafter, as an established player, he ranked among the top eleven Americans for each of the next fourteen years, and second in 1944 and 1945.

The right-handed Talbert stood five feet, eleven inches tall and weighed 155 pounds. Because sugar imbalances sometimes caused him to lose stamina, he developed an energy conserving style: groundstrokes with short backswings, serves without any backswings, and crisp volleys and sure overheads intended to end rallies decisively. Talbert compensated for a lack of power with consistency and excellent court generalship. He proved even more successful in doubles than in singles, earning first-place U.S. doubles rankings eight times from 1942 to 1952, seven with Gardnar Mulloy and once with Tony Trabert, a fellow Cincinnatian who became an outstanding champion, largely on account of Talbert's coaching.

Off the courts, "Talb," as Talbert was called by his peers, fit comfortably into the social scene surrounding competitive tennis. A slim, urbane, and debonair figure surmounted by a closely cropped haircut, he readily mixed with tennis folk and seldom missed tournament parties or postmatch celebrations, yet he strictly adhered to his medical needs. Deferred from military service during World War II because of diabetes, Talbert worked in a defense plant and later at an electronics laboratory during the war but still managed to enter some tournaments. In 1942 he married Dorothy Keane, of St. Louis, Missouri, but the childless marriage ended quickly.

In 1944 Talbert reached the final of the U.S. championships at Forest Hills, New York, but lost to Frank Parker. The following year he won eight successive tournaments and again faced Parker in the U.S. title final but, hobbled by an injured knee suffered the day before when vanquishing "Pancho" Segura in the semifinal, lost in straight sets.

Talbert's greatest victories occurred in doubles matches when he was paired with Mulloy. Talbert supplied the finesse, Mulloy, the power. On return-of-serve Talbert played the right-hand ("deuce") court, Mulloy the left-hand ("ad") court. They won U.S. doubles crowns in 1942, 1945, 1946, and 1948 and were runners-up in 1950 and 1953. Overall, they captured about forty doubles titles. Talbert also was a runner-up in three other nationals, with Dave Freeman, Segura, and Billy Sidwell.

A member of the U.S. Davis Cup teams of 1946, 1948, 1949, 1951, 1952, and 1953, Talbert won nine matches and lost one. He was 2–0 in singles and 7–1 in doubles (5–1 with Mulloy and 2–0 with Trabert). He became team captain in 1952 and served as nonplaying captain through 1957. Under Talbert's astute direction, the U.S. team won the cup from Australia in 1954 but lost the next three challenge rounds, principally because the best American players had turned professional and became ineligible for amateur events.

Although he ceased playing on the tournament circuit after 1954, Talbert remained active in the tennis world. He was tournament director of the U.S. Open championships at the West Side Tennis Club in Forest Hills from 1971 through 1975 and at the U.S. Tennis Association (USTA) Tennis Center in Flushing

Meadows, New York, from 1978 through 1987. He was instrumental in securing adoption of the sudden-death tiebreak scoring system by the USTA. As a tennis authority, Talbert wrote his autobiography in 1959; *Tennis Observed*, a history of the U.S. men's singles championships, in 1967; and several excellent texts on tennis from 1956 to 1963, all in partnership with an experienced writer.

In 1948 Talbert married Nancy Pike, an editor for the fashion magazine *Vogue*. They had two sons. Also in 1948, through a tennis connection, Talbert obtained a sales position with the U.S. Banknote Corporation, which produced financial document forms and certain foreign currencies. In 1954 he became a vice president, a post he held until his death in New York City.

In 1967 the International Tennis Hall of Fame enshrined Talbert as one of America's great doubles champions, a winner of many singles titles, and, with Margaret Osborne du Pont, a record setter who captured four consecutive U.S. mixed doubles finals from 1943 through 1946. During his career he won more than 160 tournament events, including 27 U.S. championships in various categories. A talented athlete despite his illness, Talbert helped vast numbers of diabetics, especially children, cope with the disease. Through lectures, group sessions, personal interviews, and correspondence, he tirelessly encouraged and furnished practical advice developed from his own experience to others, synchronizing his efforts with those of the American and New York diabetes associations.

• The prime source on Talbert is his autobiography, written with John Sharnik, *Playing for Life: Billy Talbert's Story* (1959). A suitable supplement is an interview chapter in Stan Hart, *Once a Champion: Legendary Tennis Stars Revisited* (1985), pp. 115–35. Concise biographies are in *Current Biography 1957*, pp. 545–47; by Jerry Jaye Wright in *Biographical Dictionary of American Sports: Outdoor Sports*, ed. David L. Porter (1988), pp. 400–401; and by Bud Collins in *Bud Collins' Tennis Encyclopedia*, ed. Collins and Zander Hollander (1997), pp. 500–501. Talbert's efforts to raise funds for diabetes treatment and research are detailed in David Hulburd, "The Man Who Beat Diabetes," *Life*, 7 Sept. 1953, pp. 107–15. Obituaries are in the *New York Times*, 2 Mar. 1999, and *Tennis Week*, 25 Mar. 1999.

FRANK V. PHELPS

TARLOFF, Frank (4 Feb. 1916–25 June 1999), screen and television writer, was born in Brooklyn, New York, the son of Samuel Tarlovski and Rachel Yelin Tarlovski, Polish-Jewish immigrants who operated a small newspaper and penny candy store. (The family name was mistakenly recorded as Tarloff by an immigration officer at Ellis Island and was retained by the couple.) They made a modest living until Samuel Tarloff's death in 1928, when the business faltered. "We were poverty-stricken a year before everyone else," Tarloff quipped, making reference to the Great Depression, which began after the stock market crash of 1929.

Despite difficult circumstances, Tarloff became an avid reader and excelled in his studies, graduating from Abraham Lincoln High School at age sixteen and winning admission to Brooklyn College, which charged no tuition fees. College was an ambiguous experience, Tarloff later recalled: "I felt like I was entering another world. In terms of exposure to art and thought, I gained some sophistication, which had value for me. But I was miserable. Those were terrible times and I could see no bright future ahead. I hated the idea of the poverty, of struggling for everything—and of missing out on so much. I majored in math, because it seemed like it might be possible to become a teacher or an accountant, neither of which I wanted to be. I didn't even think of writing. I was a 'C+' English student."

Tarloff had gravitated toward the social circles of political radicals while still in high school, and his attachments intensified at Brooklyn College. "Most of my friends were communists, many of them members of the Young Communist League. I didn't join, but was more of a 'fellow traveler.' I sold *The New Masses* [a radical magazine] around the college and hung around with political people. They seemed to appreciate my sense of humor."

After he graduated with a B.A. in 1936, Tarloff was influenced to try his hand at writing by his neighborhood friends Irwin Shaw and David Shaw, brothers who were budding writers. "I was in their house more than my own, because I liked it better there. I saw what was happening to Irwin, even before he wrote *Bury the Dead* [his first successful novel]. He was writing for comic strips and for radio shows, making $350 a week, which in those days meant he was rich. This opened up the sense in both David and me that there was another kind of life to be had—through writing."

Tarloff and David Shaw began collaborating on comedy sketches for left-wing political rallies, which organizers solicited to help bring in crowds. Late in 1936 they were asked to help prepare entertainment for an event sponsored by the Communist Party at Vassar College. "We ended up writing 'Academic Epidemic,' which was practically a full-length musical comedy," he recalled in a 1997 interview for the oral history collections of Syracuse University. "It was very funny and very wild, full of wonderful songs. We all acted in it as well."

Academic Epidemic was so successful that the cast was asked to mount a second production at the New School for Social Research in New York City, where all three performances played to sold-out houses. An attempt was made to bring the show to Broadway, but it ended in a fiasco when a handful of writers made claims on the play, though for the most part they were acquaintances who had dropped by while Tarloff and Shaw were working on the script. Tarloff's disappointment was offset by a newfound confidence that he could entertain people with his writing.

With Irwin Shaw's help, Tarloff got his first professional job writing radio scripts for "Bringing Up Father," an NBC comedy; the series, however, was canceled in a matter of months. Tarloff's play, *They Should Have Stood in Bed*, opened on Broadway on 13 February 1942, but the (nonmusical) comedy closed after eleven performances. Later that year Tarloff traveled to California with a friend and decided to stay when he was offered a job writing extra dialogue at Metro-Goldwyn-Mayer (MGM). "I could hardly believe it," he said. "I was making money by writing, something I enjoyed. I could hardly believe I was making money! For the first time in my life, every little need that came up was *not* a tragedy."

At MGM, as elsewhere, Tarloff was socially inclined toward politically involved people. "I became friendly with Dalton Trumbo, who was a top writer in Hollywood, making $5,000 a week, and with Howard Lawson [John Howard Lawson] and Paul Jarrico. I was accepted as one of them. We used to have lunch together at what was called the 'Red table' at the MGM commissary. I joined the Communist Party soon after." In addition to working on films, such as *Campus Rhythm* (1943) and *Behave Yourself* (1951), he wrote scripts for a number of successful radio comedies, including "Baby Snooks" (starring Fanny Brice), "A Date with Judy," and "Meet Corliss Archer." Tarloff married Lee Barrie (née Wurtzburger), a singer, on 5 January 1942. They had two children.

The unexpectedly pleasant life Tarloff had created for himself came crashing down during the "Red scare" of the early 1950s. Though his membership in the Communist Party USA had been brief and he had not attended a meeting in years, he was summoned in 1951 to testify at hearings of the House of Representatives Un-American Activities Committee (HUAC). "Five minutes after I was served with the subpoena, I got a telegram from the William Morris Agency telling me that I was no longer their client. No explanation was given," Tarloff said. He appeared before HUAC as an "unfriendly witness," taking the Fifth Amendment and refusing to name others as party members. He lost his job writing for "I Married Joan," a television sitcom, and could find neither work nor representation in Hollywood.

Blacklisted, Tarloff moved with his family to London in 1952. He hoped to find work in the British film industry but encountered a swelling population of exiled American writers pursuing the same plan. However, with the help of the writer Artie Stander, a longtime friend, Tarloff made a living by writing scripts under pseudonyms (most often "David Adler") for U.S. television programs. Tarloff credited Sheldon Leonard and Danny Thomas, the producers of such comedy hits as "Make Room for Daddy," "The Andy Griffith Show," and "The Dick Van Dyke Show," for knowingly accepting his work despite the consequences that exposure might have brought them. Tarloff also made uncredited contributions to a number of feature films, including *School for Scoundrels* (1960), a British comedy starring Terry-Thomas. "I did okay. In some ways those London years were the best years of my life," he said.

The blacklist, which neither began nor ended in any "official" way, faded from cultural memory during the 1960s. Tarloff decided that, after a dozen years undercover, he would risk using his real name in the credits of *Father Goose*, a 1964 feature film starring Cary Grant that he had written with S. H. Barnett and Peter Stone. The screenplay won an Oscar, and the sudden adulation signaled an end to Tarloff's exile.

Returning to Hollywood, Tarloff adapted his own novel, *A Guide for the Married Man* (1967), into the script for a film that starred Walter Matthau as a husband taking lessons from a friend on how to cheat on his wife. Other notable screen credits include *The Double Man* (1967), an espionage thriller starring Yul Brynner, and *The Secret War of Harry Frigg* (1968), a war comedy starring Paul Newman. Tarloff's television work during the 1970s included scripting for popular sitcoms, such as "Maude" and "The Jeffersons."

An active member of the Writers Guild of America (WGA) after his return to the United States, Tarloff served several terms as a member of the WGA board of directors and on its arbitration and negotiation committee. He fought to have the names of blacklisted writers, actors, and other contributors placed in the credits of restored prints of the films they had worked on. He was also critical of the prejudice against older writers that he encountered in the television industry. "When I hit 70, I found myself unhirable—again. No matter that I had an Academy Award or anything else," he said. "When Sheldon Leonard asked for me, specifically, to work on a reunion movie of *I Spy*, the network said, 'Forget it! Here's a *list* of the people who we will accept.' Well, I'd heard that before." Tarloff died of lung cancer at his home in Beverly Hills.

• Direct quotations in this article are from an oral history interview that David Marc conducted with Tarloff in 1997. The interview, audiotaped and transcribed, is part of the Television History Archive of the Center for the Study of Popular Television at Syracuse University. Tarloff is among the subjects examined in Patrick McGilligan and Paul Buhle, *Tender Comrades: A History of the Hollywood Blacklist* (1997), which includes an excerpt of an interview with Tarloff by Buhle. Obituaries are in the *Las Vegas Review-Journal*, 28 June 1999, and the *New York Times*, 5 July 1999.

DAVID MARC

TAYLOR, John W. (26 Mar. 1784–18 Sept. 1854), congressman, was born in Charlton, Saratoga County, New York, the son of John Taylor, a farmer who later became a judge, and Chloe Cox Taylor. After receiving his early education at home, Taylor entered Union College in Schenectady, New York, in 1799. Although he had originally planned a career in the ministry, he became interested in the legal profession and graduated in 1803. Upon completing his formal education, Taylor briefly taught school at the Ballston Centre Academy and studied law with Samuel Cook. In 1807, upon gaining admittance to the bar, he entered into a law partnership with Cook in Ballston Spa and also ran a lumber mill in Hadley. On 10 July 1806 he married Jane Hodge in Albany, New York. They had eight children.

Taylor entered his life's calling, public office, on the local level as a justice of the peace in Ballston Spa in March 1808. A month later he added the duties of state loan commissioner. These offices were rewards for supporting the faction of the Republican Party led by De Witt Clinton. In the spring of 1811, Taylor won a seat in the state legislature, and he took office in January of the following year. Although the Republicans controlled the lower house, their Federalist opponents composed most of the talent within the body, and Taylor quickly rose to a position of leadership. He headed committees on expiring laws and one concerned with the possible abolition of slavery. He took a leading role in unsuccessfully opposing the creation of a local substitute for the Bank of the United States, fearing that too many banks issuing too much currency would lead to general depreciation. Taylor also headed a bipartisan committee that investigated scandals involving a lottery to benefit his alma mater, Union College.

In December 1812 Taylor won election to the U.S. House of Representatives. He remained in that body for the next twenty years and eventually chaired the Committee on Elections (twice) and the Committee on Revisal and Unfinished Business. Initially appointed a member of the Committee of Military Affairs by House Speaker Henry Clay, Taylor defended President James Madison against Federalist attacks regarding the conduct of the War of 1812 and rendered valuable assistance on a special committee charged with overhauling the nation's militia. As a member of the Committee of Ways and Means, he supported the reestablishment of a national bank and the implementation of a protective trade tariff.

Taylor entered the national limelight in February 1819, when he seconded an amendment by fellow New York representative James Tallmadge to the Missouri enabling act that would have prohibited slavery in the new state. While unwilling to disturb slavery in the states where it already existed, Taylor opposed its extension beyond the Mississippi River, fearing that free market labor could not successfully compete in a slaveholding environment. "Our vote this day will determine whether the high destinies of this region, and, of those generations, shall be fulfilled or whether we shall defeat them by permitting slavery, with all its baleful consequences, to inherit the land," he warned (Spann, p. 190). His antislavery speeches were among the first in Congress. Although initial reaction to his speeches on the subject was muted, the issue made Taylor the de facto leader of the so-called "restrictionists," and with Clay's backing he won election as Speaker of the House in 1820.

As Speaker, Taylor won approval throughout the political spectrum for his parliamentary skill, yet his attempts to remain above the partisan fray failed to overcome suspicions from a faction of the New York Republican party, led by Martin Van Buren and known as the "Bucktails," that Taylor remained a stalwart supporter of their arch nemesis Clinton. A longtime advocate of economy in government, Taylor also offended Secretary of War John C. Calhoun and Secretary of the Navy Smith Thompson with his support of military budget cuts in response to the declining tax revenues in the aftermath of the panic of 1819. The combined opposition from New York and the Madison administration resulted in replacement of Taylor as Speaker after one term.

Though despondent about losing the Speakership, Taylor bided his time in Congress, taking few leadership roles. He became close to John Quincy Adams, who had supported his bid for reelection as Speaker, and backed Adams's successful bid for the presidency in 1824. With Adams's endorsement, Taylor regained the Speakership in 1825, and he generally supported administration policies. The Adams administration's difficulties, however, gave hope to Taylor's rivals. Van Buren, whose faction was emerging as the Democratic Party, again worked to dump Taylor. In 1826 Taylor was again ousted from the Speakership. He remained in Congress until 1832, when he was defeated for reelection largely because of an unsubstantiated rumor of marital infidelity spread by his enemies, a coalition of Jacksonians, Van Burenites, Masons, and opponents of the Second National Bank.

Taylor returned to Saratoga County and practiced law for a number of years. In 1840 he resumed elective politics and was elected to the New York State Senate. He resigned in 1842 after becoming incapacitated by a stroke. In 1843 he relocated to Cleveland, Ohio, where he resided with one of his daughters until he died.

Although his place in history is secure by virtue of his two stints as Speaker of the House of Representatives, Taylor was at best a minor figure in the political scene of his day. His speeches during the initial controversy over the admission of Missouri to the Union provide valuable insights into the issues surrounding that debate. Reluctant to abandon the idea of statesmanship over partisan politics, he was largely unable to navigate the political currents that swirled through the American landscape of his day.

• Taylor's papers are divided among the New-York Historical Society and the New York Public Library in New York City and the New York State Library in Albany. Edward Kenneth Spann, "John W. Taylor, the Reluctant Partisan, 1784–1854" (Ph.D. diss., New York Univ., 1957), is informative on his life and career. Obituaries are in the *New York Tribune*, 22 Sept. 1854, and the *Ballston Journal*, 27 Sept. 1854.

EDWARD L. LACH, JR.

TAYLOR, Paul Schuster (9 June 1895–14 Mar. 1984), economist, was born in Sioux City, Iowa, the son of Henry James Taylor, a lawyer, and Rose Schuster Taylor. The couple met at the University of Wisconsin. Henry Taylor had been elected superintendent of schools in Dane County, Wisconsin, and Rose Taylor taught school before her marriage. Paul Taylor grew up in Sioux City, and in 1913 he entered the University of Wisconsin, where he majored in economics and law. From Professors John R. Commons, E. A. Ross, and Richard Ely he learned Progressive reform commitments and a broad-minded, almost humanistic approach to social science.

After receiving a B.A. in 1917, Taylor entered the U.S. Marines as a captain. In France in 1918 he was exposed to gas that severely damaged his lungs and was sent home to recuperate; his voice and larynx never completely recovered. He enrolled in graduate school in economics at the University of California, where he also studied with historians, and in 1922 received a Ph.D. His dissertation, a study of the West Coast seamen's union, revealed a sympathy with workers that he was to display all his life. In 1920 he married Katharine Page Whiteside; they had three children before they divorced in 1935.

In 1922 Taylor joined the Berkeley economics faculty, but his true career was launched by the Progressive sociologist Edith Abbott. As head of a Social Science Research Council project, she was looking for someone to undertake a study of the rapidly increasing Mexican migration into the United States. Taylor took up this task with enthusiasm and, taking a leave from the university, headed immediately into the field to study migrant workers. From 1927 to 1930 he was on the road much of the time, driving through the San Joaquin and Imperial Valleys in California, into Colorado and Texas, and as far east as Pennsylvania. He not only sought quantitative data on Mexican employment patterns but also learned Spanish and interviewed workers and employers. He even documented what he learned with photographs. His approach integrated Commons-school economics with cultural and ethnographic matters—collecting Mexican *corridos* (popular ballads), for example. He published thirteen monographs on Mexicans and Mexican-Americans, one of only a tiny handful of Anglo scholars concerned with them.

Although Taylor had earned tenure, the Berkeley economics department responded to his unconventional work by denying him promotions and salary increases for nearly two decades. When the Great Depression hit, migrant farmworkers resumed their earlier labor struggles for decent wages and unionization, and the state of California hired Taylor to research the biggest strike, in the cotton fields. His exhaustive report showed that the strike arose from legitimate worker grievances, not from outside communist agitation as the large farm owners and local press claimed. Appointed field research director for rural rehabilitation for the California State Relief Administration, he conducted investigations designed to demonstrate the need to improve conditions for migrant farmworkers.

In 1934 Taylor saw the work of the documentary photographer Dorothea Lange and recruited her to his project. They were married in December 1935. Theirs was a living and working partnership that continued until Lange's death in 1965. They had no children together but were parents to Lange's two sons from her first marriage as well as Taylor's three children. In 1935 they produced five reports on the conditions of migrant agricultural workers, and Taylor used their data to get state and federal relief funding for housing for farmworkers. In the process of these investigations Taylor and Lange discovered the "Dust Bowl" westward migration of ruined tenant farmers. Lange was hired as a photographer by the federal Farm Security Administration, and throughout the 1930s the two often traveled together, Taylor collecting quantitative and qualitative information as Lange made photographs. Taylor risked his colleagues' further disapproval by publishing, with Lange, a popular book of text and photographs on the Dust Bowl, *American Exodus*, in 1939.

Taylor's research formed a basis for the 1939 hearings conducted by the La Follette committee of the U.S. Senate on civil liberties violations against farmworkers. This work antagonized powerful people at the University of California, Berkeley, where agribusiness was well represented among the university's regents and where university agricultural research provided direct support to the big growers (for example, creating hybrids, designing farm machinery, training in agricultural management). Taylor's research, combined with the values of his Iowa upbringing, brought him to the conclusion that the power of the big growers in California agriculture was incompatible with democracy. Despite Robert La Follette's exposé of violence against farmworkers by sheriffs and deputies recruited by the Associated Farmers (the organization of big industrial farm owners), farmworker unionization struggles were not successful until the 1960s, when Taylor, then retired, supported the United Farm Workers.

During World War II, Taylor was one of a tiny handful of prominent whites to protest the mass incarceration of Japanese-Americans.

In 1943 Taylor became involved with protests against federal provision of vast quantities of water to agribusiness at taxpayer expense. After 1950 this became his major focus. The federal Reclamation Act of 1902, which provided funding for dams and canals to bring water to parched southwestern farms, had limited the amount of subsidized water for irrigation to 160 acres per person. But this restriction was systematically violated, so the reclamation programs constituted huge subsidies to the biggest growers and enabled them to squeeze out small farmers. In 1944 Taylor led opposition to the insertion of an exemption from the 160-acre limitation into the U.S. Senate bill authorizing the Central Valley Project to bring water into the San Joaquin Valley. For the rest of his life Taylor fought a losing battle against this policy.

The growers' tactic of branding their opponents as communists contributed to extreme McCarthyism in California, and the university regents installed a loyalty oath in 1949. The administration fired two tenured professors who acknowledged membership in the Communist Party. The faculty first proposed a compromise oath, but the regents rejected it. The faculty then divided, and Taylor was among several hundred who protested, receiving support from some 1,200 academics around the country. After 157 university employees, mostly nonfaculty and thus untenured, were fired, Taylor and the majority of protesters capitulated and signed. Taylor reasoned that he could contribute more from within than from outside the university. Thirty-one faculty members continued to refuse and were dismissed.

From 1952 to 1956 Taylor served as chair of his department; he then headed the university's Institute of International Studies until his retirement in 1964. Beginning in the late 1950s Taylor served as a consultant for the U.S. State Department and the Ford Foundation, investigating land tenure and advocating land reform in Vietnam, Egypt, Colombia, Korea, and Ecuador. He applied to the Third World the principles and knowledge he had developed from decades of work on U.S. agriculture and rural poverty. Always strongly anticommunist, Taylor argued for land reform and community development in the conviction that the concentration of vast landholdings in a few hands and the severe exploitation of farm labor made the development of democracy impossible and made communist popularity grow.

Paul Taylor died in Berkeley, California.

• Taylor's papers are in the Bancroft Library at the University of California, Berkeley. His books include *A Spanish-Mexican Peasant Community: Arandas in Jalisco, Mexico* (1933), *An American Mexican Frontier: Nueces County, Texas* (1934), *Mexican Labor in the United States*, 3 vols. (1928–1934), and *The Sailors' Union of the Pacific* (1923). He wrote dozens of articles, some of which are collected in Paul Taylor, *On the Ground in the Thirties* (1983). Articles about Taylor include Richard Steven Street, "The Economist as Humanist: The Career of Paul S. Taylor," *California History* 58, no. 4 (1979–1980): 350–61, and "Paul S. Taylor and the Origins of Documentary Photography in California, 1927–1934," *History of Photography* 7, no. 4 (1983): 293–304; and Joyce Eli, "Dorothea Lange and Paul Taylor: Chroniclers and Conscience of a Decade," *Californians*, Mar.–Apr. 1985, pp. 10–22. An obituary is in the *San Francisco Chronicle*, 15 Mar. 1984.

LINDA GORDON

TESCHEMACHER, Frank (13 Mar. 1906–1 Mar. 1932), musician, was born Frank M. Teschemacher in Kansas City, Missouri, the son of Charles M. Teschemacher (pronounced *tesh*-maker), an executive of the Alton Railroad Company, and Charlotte McCorkell Teschemacher. ("M." was Frank's middle name in full, though it may have been meant to stand for McCorkell.) When Frank was six, his father was transferred to Chicago, where the family settled into an upper-middle-class neighborhood in the suburb of Austin. Starting with the usual childhood piano lessons, Teschemacher soon abandoned them to teach himself popular music on the banjo. After a few years of amused parental tolerance, it was decided when he was ten that he would continue his eclectic musical education by studying the violin. He became a competent violinist and an excellent sight reader.

Born with severely crossed eyes (a condition that improved in later years) and plagued by teenage acne, Teschemacher was withdrawn and self-conscious. At Austin High School he substituted musical study for the more common rituals of adolescent socialization. His social life revolved around a musical clique of young neighborhood musicians, informally known as the Austin High Gang. The assemblage included, at one time or another, brothers Jimmy McPartland and Dick McPartland, Bud Freeman, Jim Lanigan (a future bassist with the Chicago Symphony), pianist Dave North, and drummer Dave Tough. In 1922, the boys were exposed to the recordings of the New Orleans Rhythm Kings and formed a band with the express purpose of emulating them. Teschemacher organized most of the band's rehearsals, which sometimes took place in the Teschemacher home. From these efforts came the Blue Friars, a band named for the Loop area speakeasy where the Rhythm Kings often played. It was not long before the group was performing at tea dances and organizing their own engagements, with Teschemacher providing most of the band's arrangements.

Frank took up the clarinet at the relatively advanced age of eighteen, during a summertime engagement with Bud Freeman in 1924. He soon mastered it and made it his primary instrument. During that time, the young Benny Goodman was often seen listening to Teschemacher while attempting to hide his presence from other musicians. When spotted, he would be asked to sit in by Teschemacher or other band members. The influence of Teschemacher's frenetic style was recognizable in Goodman's playing through the 1920s.

In the fall of 1924, Teschemacher played under the leadership of trumpeter Wingy Manone at the Merry Gardens ballroom with Freeman and a fast-talking guitarist named Eddie Condon. Later the Blue Friars came under the management of promoter Husk O'Hare, who changed their name to the Red Dragons and arranged for them to be studio musicians at radio station WHT. Eventually O'Hare found freelance work and an engagement at the White City amusement park, where the band was dubbed Husk O'Hare's Wolverines. Witnessing the pull that jazz had on their son, Teschemacher's parents tried to steer him toward a college education in classical music. Their efforts proved fruitless when he dropped out of high school in his senior year.

As Wolverine activities wound down, Teschemacher spent the latter part of 1924 and much of 1925 expanding his musical associations to include trumpeter Muggsy Spanier, pianist Joe Sullivan, and drummer Gene Krupa, all of whom had fallen under the spell of cornetist Bix Beiderbecke. From 1926 until the spring of 1928, he worked with bands led by Floyd Towne, Art Kassell, and Charlie Straight and was enlisted for a plethora of recording dates. In December 1927 he joined Jimmy McPartland, Freeman,

Sullivan, Lannigan and Krupa for two groundbreaking sessions led by Condon and singer Red McKenzie called the McKenzie-Condon Chicagoeans. Teschemacher arranged all four of the recorded tracks, and his raucous, trumpet-influenced clarinet solo on "Nobody's Sweetheart Now" became an anthem for a style of extroverted jazz that came to be known as the Chicago School. This idiom demonstrated little regard for the tried and tested contrapuntal devices associated with New Orleans jazz, and dared to expand the parameters of linear solo construction. The December 1927 recordings led to a string of similar efforts in the spring of 1928, with Teschemacher alternating between clarinet and alto saxophone, and he was called to arrange music for many of the sessions.

On 15 February 1928 Teschemacher married Helen Berglund, a young Swedish immigrant. The Teschemacher family did not approve of the union, and Teschemacher's numerous engagements out of town strained the marriage. Two years later they divorced after a period of estrangement.

On 28 April 1928, Teschemacher led his only known recording session, producing two sides, with only a test pressing of "Jazz Me Blues" surviving the destruction of the original masters. He then ventured to New York to join the old Chicagoans in an ill-fated scheme to back singer Bea Palmer. After the group disbanded, Teschemacher remained in New York to record sides with trumpeter Red Nichols and trombonist Miff Mole, before traveling to Atlantic City to join society bandleader Sam Lanin and later Ben Pollack. He then returned to New York where he made recordings with Don Redman and Jimmy and Tommy Dorsey. Suffering from homesickness, he left New York and returned to Chicago in the fall of 1928.

For the next three years, Teschemacher often performed in society orchestras, including those led by Ted Lewis and Jan Garber. While in Garber's employ, in addition to his woodwind responsibilities he played violin and occasionally sang. He supplemented his society work with jazz projects coordinated by Jess Stacy, Elmer Schoebel, the Melrose brothers, and Manone. In 1931 he struck up an association with cornetist Bill Davison, and the two immediately made plans to form a big band.

The group had secured a coveted engagement at Guyon's Paradise Ballroom when tragedy struck. On the morning of 1 March 1932, Teschemacher was traveling as a passenger in Davison's topless Packard convertible when the vehicle was struck broadside by a taxicab. Teschemacher was thrown from the car and died. Some eyewitnesses suggested that among the cab's occupants was a Guyon's bouncer who wanted to stop the convertible to resume a fight he had initiated with Teschemacher at a speakeasy several hours before. In the subsequent coroner's inquest, both Davison and the taxi driver were cleared of any wrongdoing.

The significance of Teschemacher's music is difficult to discern. His image was to many that of a martyr following his death and was later diminished by many of his own contemporaries. He was probably more talented than his detractors have asserted and less talented than his admirers have claimed. His recorded output of thirty-four tracks (and a handful of other "mystery recordings" reputed to have been identified by a computer matching system called the Smith/Westbrook Method) does little to justify his vaunted reputation. His earlier recordings were mostly derivative, though some innovation and refinement characterized his later efforts. He was perhaps the most versatile of the Beiderbecke disciples—and their most ardent cheerleader.

• A thorough study of the Teschemacher legacy is Vladamir Simosko, "Frank Teschemacher: A Reappraisal," *Journal of Jazz Studies* 3, 1 (Fall 1975): 28–53. The text is supplemented by a detailed and lengthy bibliography. Further biographical treatment can be found in the Eddie Condon (with Thomas Sugrue) autobiography *We Called It Music: A Generation of Jazz* (1947; rev. ed., 1970); Nat Shapiro and Nat Hentoff, *Hear Me Talkin' to Ya: The Story of Jazz by the Men Who Made It*, (1955; rev. ed., 1966), p. 118; and the notes attributed to Marty Grosz that accompany the Time-Life booklet in the *Giants of Jazz* series, *Frank Teschemacher* (1982), which features an intriguing test to determine the identity of six reputed Teschemacher "mystery recordings." Recent findings regarding the accident that caused Teschemacher's death can be found in T. Smith, "An Investigation of the Death of Frank Teschemacher," *International Association of Jazz Educators Research Proceedings Yearbook* (Jan. 1998): 56–62.

TOM SMITH

THOMPSON, Jim (27 Sept. 1906–7 Apr. 1977), writer, was born James Myers Thompson in Anadarko, Oklahoma Territory, the son of James S. Thompson, a county sheriff, and Birdie Myers Thompson. Jim Thompson grew up in rural poverty in Nebraska and Texas. He began drinking as a teenager, a prelude to a life of alcoholism.

Thompson's unsettled childhood gave way to an itinerant adulthood. He moved every few years, not stopping in one place until he was in his fifties. He began full-time work as a hotel bellboy during high school; in 1926 he moved to West Texas and worked in the oil fields. In 1929 Thompson enrolled briefly at the University of Nebraska, where he wrote sketches, poems, and stories, some of them crime stories, which he published in the pulp magazines. Thompson married Alberta Hesse in 1931. They had three children.

In 1936 Thompson joined the Oklahoma Federal Writers project, a formative tie that fostered in the young writer an idealism firmly based in the New Deal. So powerful was Thompson's identification with this form of state-sponsored artistic support, argues Sean McCann in *Gumshoe America* (2000), that his later crime fiction may be read as "a lament for the state leadership and civic purpose that [he] associated with the WPA" (McCann, p. 218). Thompson rose to the directorship of the Oklahoma Federal Writers Project in 1938, but he quit the next year in a dispute over his far left–leaning politics. At that point he turned to writing full-time with the support of a Rockefeller Foundation Fellowship, beginning an oral history of the labor movement in the southwestern building trade. Unable to produce a manuscript acceptable to his publisher, Thompson in 1940 moved to San Diego, California, and worked in the aeronautics industry, which provided the setting of his first published novel, *Now and on Earth* (1942). In 1946 Thompson published an autobiographically based proletarian novel, *Heed the Thunder*. Neither book sold well. Thompson became a journalist in 1947, working for the San Diego *Journal*.

In 1949 Thompson turned to the crime fiction for which he is remembered. His first crime novel, *Nothing More Than Murder*, challenges conventional notions of guilt and innocence while showcasing a scabrous commentary on the cutthroat rural film distribution industry, where large corporate combines overwhelm smaller, more personal operations. The story is narrated by the criminal, a device that became a virtual Thompson signature. He wrote no detective stories, preferring to inhabit the twisted minds of the transgressors rather than those of the straight-and-narrow thinkers who try to bring them to justice. Though publication of this novel was followed by a period during which Thompson worked as an editor at *Saga* magazine in New York City, this foray into crime writing eventually led Thompson to one of the most productive periods enjoyed by any American writer.

Between 1952 and 1954 Thompson blazed through a series of eleven brilliant crime novels (plus two autobiographies), writing them so fast that he created a backlog at his publisher. (So rapidly did Thompson produce these books that it is impossible to determine the order in which he composed them.) Thompson's books were issued as paperback originals, mostly by Lion Books. They regularly sold in excess of 200,000 copies, but they brought Thompson little glory and little money. Despite receiving respectful reviews, Thompson was unable to consolidate a reputation as a serious writer in a literary marketplace that was dividing itself between high-toned literary works of deliberately limited appeal and paperbacks aimed at the mass market.

Ironically, Thompson found himself slotted in the mass-market category on the strength of some of the most demanding books in the annals of crime fiction. Though the genre is guided by a highly restrictive set of conventions, Thompson stretched crime fiction to its formal limits. His narrators are notoriously unreliable—sometimes insane, sometimes dead, sometimes both—and his endings usually raise more questions than they answer. Perhaps because of his fondness for dead and doomed storytellers, Thompson never fell back on the staple of popular crime writing, the series character. Each of his books stands alone.

Thompson wrote against the grain of a largely formulaic genre. Crime fiction generally features endings that tie everything up neatly and restore order to a perturbed world, but Thompson's stories often fall apart along with their tellers. In *A Hell of a Woman* (1954), for example, he juxtaposes two endings, shuffling the pieces together so that, while the narrator is apparently mutilated and left to die, one cannot be completely sure. Such ambiguity is total Thompson and is central to his innovative approach. More consistently than any other writer in the genre, Thompson brought the themes and techniques of literary modernism under the crime story umbrella.

This experimentation has a clear 1950s context. Thompson's stories of people coming unglued registered the fears and concerns boiling beneath the prosperity of postwar America. For example, in 1952 Thompson published one of the first serial-killer novels, *The Killer inside Me*. Instead of focusing on the police working to catch the criminal, Thompson places the reader inside the murderer's head for a wild and uncomfortable ride to an apocalyptic ending. The conflagration that consumes the killer and his pursuers at the end of the novel invokes the anxieties of the Cold War and the atomic age. Of course Thompson was also rendering his own agitation as a perpetually poor, binge-drinking alcoholic writer with a hardscrabble past, a financially insecure present, and a perpetually uncertain future. Throughout his career, Thompson borrowed liberally from the details of his own life for both setting and personal histories of his shaky characters.

Thompson's creative heyday abruptly ended when his longtime publisher, Lion Books, announced in 1954 that it would stop publishing paperback originals. His longtime editor, Arnold Hano, moved to California the next year. After this upheaval, says Thompson's biographer Robert Polito, "he would never write so consistently again" (Polito, p. 387). Thompson still wrote a lot though—crime stories, true crime stories, adventure stories, novels—and he even turned again to journalism briefly.

One of Thompson's fans, the film director Stanley Kubrick, rescued the author from premature obscurity. Still a relative unknown in 1955, Kubrick invited Thompson to collaborate with him on the screenplay for *The Killing* (1956), which became a lively heist movie. This led to another collaboration on the script for *Paths of Glory* (1957), one of the most compelling antiwar films ever made. A courtroom drama set during World War I, *Paths of Glory* depicts the court martial of three French soldiers for retreating against orders from certain death in an attack demanded by a glory-seeking commanding general. Despite an eloquent defense by their advocate (played by Kirk Douglas), they are executed so that the general can save face. The movie raised the stars of both Douglas and Kubrick (who would collaborate again on *Spartacus* [1960]), but Thompson's career remained earthbound.

Thompson received no acclaim for his work on these movies. In fact he had to fight Kubrick for his rightful place in the credits. Meanwhile he continued to write. Thompson's last notable novel was the fine

Pop. 1280 (1964), which examines topical racial issues through the warped narrative prism of Nick Corey, a priapic and psychotic rural sheriff who builds his murders into a huge Rube Goldberg–like self-preservation scheme. By the mid-1960s Thompson was largely played out; his career ran down through a series of forgettable novels, novelizations, and teleplays. He died in Los Angeles after a series of strokes had left him unable to write.

"Just you wait," Thompson once said to his wife, "I'll be famous after I'm dead about ten years" (Polito, p. 508). He was right. In the late twentieth century Thompson became the subject of sustained critical attention and two biographies. During his lifetime Thompson wrote twenty-four novels, two autobiographies, three novelizations, two screenplays, and scores of articles and stories. His novels have been reissued in handsome editions, and respected, high-profile Hollywood films have been made from his books. In death Thompson gained the recognition and remuneration that eluded him in life. His posthumous success is an irony worthy of one of his own books.

• Thompson's papers are at the New York University Library. Thompson's novelizations are *Ironside* (1967), *The Undefeated* (1969), and *Nothing but a Man* (1970). In addition to the works mentioned above, Thompson's novels include *After Dark, My Sweet* (1955), *The Alcoholics* (1953), *Child of Rage* (1972), *The Criminal* (1953), *Cropper's Cabin* (1952), *The Getaway* (1959), *The Golden Gizmo* (1954), *The Grifters* (1963), *The Kill-Off* (1957), *King Blood* (1973), *The Nothing Man* (1954), *Recoil* (1953), *Savage Night* (1953), *South of Heaven* (1967), *A Swell-Looking Babe* (1954), *Texas by the Tail* (1965), *The Transgressors* (1961), and *Wild Town* (1957). His autobiographies are *Bad Boy* (1953) and *Roughneck* (1954). Biographies are Michael J. McCauley, *Jim Thompson: Sleep with the Devil* (1991), and Robert Polito, *Savage Art: A Biography of Jim Thompson* (1995), which is the definitive life. For critical work on Thompson see Sean McCann, *Gumshoe America* (2000), and Greg Forter, *Murdering Masculinities* (2000), each of which devotes a chapter to Thompson.

LEONARD CASSUTO

THOMPSON, John D. (6 Aug. 1917–13 Aug. 1992), nurse, was born John Devereaux Thompson in Franklin, Pennsylvania, the oldest son of William McKinley Thompson, a traveling salesman, and Margaret Devereaux Thompson, a mathematics teacher. Thompson was raised in Canton, Ohio. His mother, who was Irish-Catholic, interested him in religion and mathematics. When he was twelve, she died in childbirth.

At nineteen, Thompson studied nursing at Bellevue Hospital's Mills School of Nursing for Men in New York City. At Bellevue, Thompson developed splendid social skills, especially conversation, dancing, and a love for music. In 1939 he completed the Mills program. "What I didn't realize was that the experience would mark me forever. It is impossible to become a nurse in a place like Bellevue and not have the imprint remain with you the rest of your life" (Weeks, p. 2).

After a short stint as a nurse, Thompson enrolled in the U.S. Navy. He served throughout World War II as a pharmacist's mate on the aircraft carrier *Ranger*. After the war he returned to New York and enrolled at City College of New York, working nights on the Bellevue Prison Ward, and received his bachelor's degree with distinction in business in 1948.

Thompson, having decided to become a hospital administrator, enrolled in a new one-year program at Yale University, which required a second year of residency. He completed his training at Montefiore Hospital in 1950 and stayed on for the next six years, working first for E. M. Bluestone and later for Martin Cherkasky, both Montefiore Hospital directors. In 1952 Thompson married Andriana Natale, a surgeon he met at Montefiore. They had seven children.

In 1956 Thompson returned to Yale to study hospital function and design with support from the Hill-Burton Hospital Construction Act. He and Bob Fetter of Yale's Administrative Science Department produced an array of statistics on hospital operations. Thompson's data led to the concept of diagnosis-related groups or DRGs. This concept changed the system of hospital payment from one based on hospital cost per patient to a flat rate based on the diagnosis and treatments as set by physicians.

While professor and director of the program in hospital administration, Thompson also served as associate dean for planning at Yale's medical school with deans Fritz Redlich and Lewis Thomas. Thompson was a confidant of Yale president Kingman Brewster, for whom he reorganized the hospital bylaws to accommodate the merging of Grace and New Haven Hospitals into Yale–New Haven Hospital.

A student of history, Thompson wrote on the history of hospitals, nursing, and medicine. With Grace Goldin, he published *The Hospital: A Social and Architectural History* (1975). He repeatedly returned to the reading room of the British Library at the British Museum, where he pored over nineteenth-century letters, books, and documents in an effort to understand the genesis of Florence Nightingale's work on mortality differences among London hospitals, and to expand on that work.

In 1981, the Ronald Reagan administration and Congress, seeking to end hospital cost inflation, started using Thompson and Fetter's DRGs-based prospective payment system for hospitals under the Medicare program. The new system paid hospitals a flat amount per case, depending on the diagnosis and treatment, rather than a proportion of total hospital costs. Reimbursement incentives went from "spend as much as you can" to "reduce the costs per case," a revolutionary change that transformed hospital behavior. The most immediate impact was a reduction in the length of patients' hospital stays, with a corresponding reduction in the number of hospital beds. Hospitals closed, hospital buildings were closed, hospital wards were closed, and nurses were laid off. More than two decades after their introduction, DRGs remained the basis for Medicare hospital reimbursements and were also being used to establish managed care contracts, a source of continuing financial uncertainty for hospitals.

Thompson was a colorful teacher, sporting a distinctive moustache, a Muniemaker cigar, and in later years a sportsman's vest that, after the DRG was adopted for Medicare, he referred to as his flak jacket. He used earthy language to emphasize important points, sometimes causing concern to the members of religious communities who were students in his program. He inculcated his students with the need for evidence to buttress any professional argument. At the same time he never let anyone forget that the patient came first.

Thompson had a long and productive professional association with the Yale School of Nursing and the professional nursing community in New Haven. His joint appointment to the faculty there began with Dean Florence Wald and developed with the clinical programs of scholarship and care that flourished under the leadership of Dean Donna Diers.

Thompson loved vocal music, especially opera and the Yale singing group the Whiffenpoofs. In 1988, he retired from Yale, though he never stopped working there. He died in New Haven.

Thompson is remembered for his DRG work. He was also, however, a unique nurse, teacher, scientist, and historian. An authority on every aspect of hospitals and their history, construction, management, and financing, he remained a part of the hospital institution he had walked into as a nineteen-year-old nursing student. He derived his interest from a wide array of texts, heroes, and heroines, especially Nightingale. Joyce Clifford, an eminent American nurse, said Thompson humanized the hospital administration field.

• The first paper describing diagnosis related groups is Thompson, R. B. Fetter, and C. D. Mross, "Case-Mix and Resource Use," *Inquiry* 12 (1975): 300–12. Thompson presented the Leuven Lectures, published later as *Applied Health Services Research* (1977). His work is discussed in Rosemary Stevens, *In Sickness and in Wealth: American Hospitals in the Twentieth Century* (1989; rev. ed., 1999), and in W. White, ed., *Compelled by Data: John D. Thompson, Nurse, Health Services Researcher and Health Administration Educator* (2003). An oral history resource is L. E. Weeks, *John D. Thompson in First Person* (1989). An obituary is in the *New York Times*, 15 Aug. 1992.

EDWARD HALLORAN

TOUSARD, Anne-Louis (12 Mar. 1749–10 Apr. 1817), soldier, engineer, and diplomat, was born in Paris, the son of Charles Germain de Tousard, a French general, and Antoinette de Poitevin de la Croix. In 1765 he graduated from the French Artillery School in Strasbourg, and he then served in Bayonne, Douay, Bapaume, and Mézières. The French government permitted him to volunteer for service in America, and he arrived in Portsmouth, New Hampshire, on 20 April 1777 as part of a group of French officers under Philippe Tronson du Coudray. Du Coudray

had been recruited by the American agent Silas Deane with the promise of a general's commission and command of artillery in the Continental army. His seeming arrogance in taking charge when Henry Knox, an American, had just been given command of American artillery caused several American generals to threaten to resign. Officers who accompanied him were not initially commissioned and had to serve as volunteers at first.

On 28 October 1777, after the accidental death of du Coudray resolved the controversy over his rank, Tousard received his captaincy. Part of the coterie of French officers associated with the Marquis de Lafayette, Tousard served at the battles of Germantown and Brandywine Creek and during the winter encampment at Valley Forge. In late March and April 1778 he acted as an adviser on fortifications to a band of Oneida Indians, working in their New York territory, in exchange for their joining the Continental army in Pennsylvania. He remained with this group at the Battle of Barren Hill, 20–21 May 1778, along the Schuylkill River, where a force of 2,200 Continental troops under Lafayette was forced to retreat in the face of a British force approximately four times larger. Though some contemporary accounts differ, recent research credits the Oneidas with covering the American retreat, ensuring its success.

Later in 1778 Tousard was assigned to Brigadier General John Sullivan in his joint French-American campaign to take Newport, Rhode Island, from the British. At the battle on Quaker Hill, 28 August 1778, Tousard lost his right arm to a cannonball while capturing a cannon from the British. This brought him brevet promotion to lieutenant colonel (date of rank 29 October 1778) and a lifetime pension of $30 per month (paid in a lump sum in 1794 at Tousard's request).

Tousard returned to France to recover from his wound, and on 3 July 1779 he was made a member of the Royal Order of St. Louis in recognition of his service in America. He was commissioned a major in the provincial artillery regiment of Toul on 5 April 1780. On 8 July 1784 he accepted a commission as lieutenant colonel of the Regiment du Cap, a regular French unit assigned to the colony of Saint-Domingue (now Haiti), where he came to own a plantation. On 19 February 1788 he married Marie-Reine Joubert, the widow of a planter, in Limbe, Saint-Domingue. They had two daughters, one of whom, Martine, married the Philadelphia merchant John Dutilh.

In August 1791 a slave revolt led by Toussaint L'Ouverture plunged the colony into civil war. Tousard's troops participated in engagements at Port-Margot in September 1791 and at Fort-Dauphin in November 1791. In October 1791, to broaden the colonial government's support, he proposed that the colonial assembly arm mulattoes and "free men of color." The failure of this initiative led to these groups allying with the slaves and forcing a truce of sorts on their terms. Between 1789 and 1792 political divisions in revolutionary France, reflected in the colony, led to changes in policy over the issue of citizenship for people of color. In September 1792 the French government sent three commissioners to the colony to enforce the decree of full citizenship for mulattoes and free blacks and to take charge of the largely royalist Regiment du Cap. Accused of "counterrevolutionary" actions by the commissioners, Tousard and the other officers of the regiment were arrested and sent to France in October 1792. Imprisoned on 15 December 1792, Tousard was released in February 1793 through American diplomatic intervention and in part because of his vigorous written defense of his actions in Haiti, published that year in the United States under the title *Justification of Lewis Tousard.*

In April 1793 Tousard returned to his farm near Wilmington, Delaware, where his wife died in July 1794. In 1795 he married Anna Maria Geddes; they had two daughters. In April 1795 Tousard was appointed a major in the Corps of Artillerists and Engineers and took up duties building fortifications at Fort Mifflin, Pennsylvania; Fort Adams, Rhode Island; Fort McHenry, Maryland; and West Point, New York. He provided the technical and organizational basis for American artillery and fortification practice, an influence that lasted to the Civil War. A student of the French artillery master practitioner Jean-Baptiste Vaquette de Gribeauval (1715–1789), Tousard converted the American artillery from the British to the French system, a process that rationalized the types and numbers of cannon. He also assisted Eleuthère Irénée du Pont in establishing the Delaware gunpowder mill.

In 1798 Tousard submitted a comprehensive program for a military academy that profoundly shaped the early U.S. Military Academy, formally established in March 1802. He became inspector of artillery in May 1800 (though not formally appointed until 14 April 1801) and took command of the Second Regiment of Artillerists and Engineers in January 1801. Joseph Gardner Swift, destined to be the first graduate of the U.S. Military Academy, reported to Tousard for instruction at Fort Adams in July 1801.

Ironically, the military academy Tousard proposed proved to be the end of his American military service. Diplomatic tensions with the French were high, and not wanting a French or a Federalist officer to oversee the academy, the Thomas Jefferson administration, heavily influenced by Secretary of War Henry Dearborn's bias against both, selected Jonathan Williams, a grandnephew of Benjamin Franklin, as the first superintendent. This was coupled with an army reorganization, and Tousard resigned in March 1802. He rejoined the French army in July 1802 and was appointed a battalion commander in the army of General Victor Leclerc, Napoleon's brother-in-law, who attempted to restore Haiti to French rule. Decimated by yellow fever, this force withdrew from the island in December 1803, and Tousard returned to France. In 1805 he was appointed French vice consul at New Orleans, and he was posted to Baltimore, Maryland, in the same capacity in 1809. In Baltimore he oversaw

the business affairs of Elizabeth Patterson Bonaparte, the American wife of Jerome Bonaparte, brother of Napoleon. In 1811 Tousard returned to New Orleans as consul, and he remained there until 1816, when he returned to France. He died in Paris.

Tousard published *American Artillerists Companion* (1810), a three-volume textbook on the history, use, and manufacture of cannon and shot based on standard French works and his own experience in war. Adopted as a textbook at West Point in 1816, the work advocated standardization and interchangeability of weapons and their components and became an early influence on American manufacturing.

• Tousard's papers are in the Maryland Historical Society, the Library of Congress, the Historical Society of Pennsylvania, the Hagley Museum and Library (Delaware), and the University of Michigan. A comprehensive treatment of Tousard's contributions to the U.S. Army is Norman B. Wilkinson, "The Forgotten 'Founder' of West Point," *Military Affairs* 24 (Winter 1960): 177–188.

MICHAEL A. BURKE

TOUSSAINT, Pierre (1766–30 June 1853), businessman and philanthropist, was born a slave in the French colony of Saint Domingue (Haiti). Little is known of his early life except that, like his mother and maternal grandmother, he spent his youth as a house slave on a plantation in the Artibonite Valley in central Haiti near the port of Saint Marc. In the library of the plantation owner, Pierre Bérard, young Toussaint discovered the works of classical French preachers such as Bossuet and Massillon. Apparently it was from his reading of these sermons, rather than from any contact with the notoriously corrupt local clergy, that Toussaint developed his deep devotion to the Catholic faith.

In 1787, as political conditions on the island deteriorated, Jean-Jacques Bérard, who had inherited his father's estate, left Saint Domingue for New York, accompanied by his wife, Pierre Toussaint, and four other slaves. The following year Bérard died suddenly in Saint Domingue on a fruitless visit to recover his property. His death left his widow, Marie Elizabeth Bérard, penniless in New York City. However, Toussaint supported her as well as himself from his earnings as a hairdresser, one of the few occupations that were open to African Americans. Shortly before her death, on 2 July 1807, she and her second husband formally emancipated Toussaint in a ceremony at the French consulate in New York City.

Thereafter Toussaint established a lucrative business as a hairdresser for upper-class women. His customers included the Hamiltons, Schuylers, and Livingstons, the cream of New York society. "As a hairdresser for ladies he was unrivalled," wrote one prominent socialite, Hannah Lee Sawyer. "He was the fashionable coiffeur of the day." Thanks to his income from this occupation, as well as a frugal lifestyle and wise investments, Toussaint prospered and was able to buy his own house at 144 Franklin Street. In 1811 he purchased the freedom of his sister Rosalie as well as that of another refugee from Saint Domingue, Mary Rose Juliette, whom he married in St. Peter's Church on 5 August 1811.

Although Toussaint's occupation as a hairdresser was financially rewarding, it was physically demanding. He regularly spent sixteen hours each day traveling throughout the city to the homes of his wealthy customers. The most convenient form of transportation would have been the extensive network of horsecars, but African Americans were barred from using them, one example of the widespread racial discrimination that he had to endure in antebellum New York. Moreover, as an African American in the largely Irish Catholic community, and as a Haitian Catholic in the largely Protestant black community, Toussaint belonged to a minuscule minority within each of these minority groups and was thus doubly disadvantaged. Culturally he remained a Frenchman throughout his life, using French in his prayers, correspondence, and reading of Scripture.

Within the Catholic community, even during his lifetime, Toussaint enjoyed the reputation of an exceptionally devout and charitable person. Every day he attended the 6:00 a.m. Mass in St. Peter's Church, where he was a pewholder for many years. He was also a benefactor of the Church of St. Vincent de Paul, New York's first French Catholic church, established in 1840. Perhaps his favorite charity was St. Patrick's Orphan Asylum, an institution that he often visited. Although his marriage was childless, Toussaint and his wife made it a practice to take into their home destitute black children and to care for them until they were able to fend for themselves.

Toussaint played no role in the abolitionist movement, which is not surprising in view of the anti-Catholic sentiments of many abolitionists. Although he was one of the few African Americans in New York City who could meet the property qualifications to vote, there is no indication that he ever cast a ballot. He was essentially a private peace-loving person who eschewed any political activity that might lead to violence, a legacy of his own personal experience of revolution in Saint Domingue. When someone asked him why he was not an abolitionist, he replied: "They have not seen blood flow as I have." He sought to bring relief to blacks and whites alike, but through personal charitable efforts and generous financial contributions. He died in New York City, and a funeral Mass was celebrated for him in St. Peter's Church. The pastor, Father William Quinn, eulogized him as a faithful parishioner for sixty-six years "who always had wise counsel for the rich [and] words of encouragement for the poor."

In 1990 Cardinal John O'Connor of New York introduced in Rome the cause of Pierre Toussaint's canonization. In 1997 the Holy See declared him "Venerable," the first step in the lengthy process of securing official church recognition of him as a saint. His body was placed in the crypt beneath St. Patrick's Cathedral.

• The Papers of Pierre Toussaint, containing some 1,200 items (but only five letters written by him), are in the Manuscript Division of the New York Public Library. The main source for his life is *Memoir of Pierre Toussaint, Born a Slave in Saint Domingo* (1854; repr. 1992), published anonymously by Hannah Lee Sawyer, a contemporary admirer. Arthur and Elizabeth Sheehan, *Pierre Toussaint: A Citizen of Old New York* (1955), and Ellen Tarry, *The Other Toussaint: A Modern Biography of Pierre Toussaint: A Post-Revolutionary Black* (1981), both are uncritical popular biographies. Two informative articles, Henry Binsse, "Pierre Toussaint: A Catholic Uncle Tom," *Historical Records and Studies* 12 (1918): 90–101, and Leo R. Ryan, "Pierre Toussaint: God's Image Carved in Ebony," *Historical Records and Studies* 25 (1935): 39–58, suffer from an unintentional condescension that emphasizes Toussaint's deference to white society. Thomas J. Shelley, "Black and Catholic in Nineteenth-Century New York: The Case of Pierre Toussaint," *Records of the American Catholic Historical Society of Philadelphia* 102 (1991): 1–18, attempts to place Toussaint in the context of his time.

THOMAS J. SHELLEY

TOWER, John G. (29 Sept. 1925–5 Apr. 1991), U.S. senator, was born John Goodwin Tower in Houston, Texas, the son of Joe Z. Tower, a Methodist minister, and Beryl Goodwin Tower. After graduating from high school in Beaumont, Texas, in 1942, Tower enrolled at Southwestern University in Georgetown, Texas. His education there was interrupted by service in the U.S. Navy during World War II. He saw combat in the Pacific aboard a gunboat. Tower returned to Southwestern after the war and received his bachelor's degree in 1948. He then pursued graduate work in political science at Southern Methodist University (SMU). To support his studies he worked as a radio announcer in Taylor, Texas, and subsequently as an insurance agent in Dallas. In 1951 Tower was hired as an assistant professor of political science at Midwestern University (later Midwestern State University) in Wichita Falls, Texas, where he remained until his election to the U.S. Senate. However, he was allowed to spend a year abroad studying at the London School of Economics and Political Science, and he finally received his master's degree from SMU in 1953. Tower married Lou Bullington in 1952. The couple had three daughters before they divorced in 1976. Tower wed Lilla Burt Cummings the following year, but this second marriage ended in 1987.

While he was in his twenties, Tower joined the Texas Republican party, and he quickly made a name for himself as a party spokesperson and supporter of the conservative Robert Taft. Not surprisingly he held no elective office before going to the Senate. White Texans by the 1950s were beginning to shed their reflexive Democratic affiliation (the state went for the Republican Dwight Eisenhower in 1952 and 1956), but it was a top-down process, slow to reach the local and legislative arenas. By 1960, though, that process had proceeded far enough to benefit Tower. Assigned the unenviable task of running as the Republican candidate for senator against the formidable Lyndon

Johnson, Tower under the circumstances did amazingly well, garnering over 900,000 votes, more than 40 percent of the total. Many Texans it seems objected to Johnson running simultaneously for reelection to the Senate and for the vice presidency. In a special election held the following spring to fill Johnson's vacated Senate seat, Tower ran again and this time won against the conservative Democrat William Blakely. Tower thus became the first Republican sent to the U.S. Senate from Texas since Reconstruction.

Texas Democrats like Johnson and Sam Rayburn continued to wield extraordinary influence on the national scene, but in many respects Tower was the shape of things to come in state politics. Reelected to the Senate in 1966, 1972, and 1978, Tower never won by huge margins, and his early victories can be attributed in part to many liberal Democrats' refusal to support the conservatives their party nominated to oppose him. But increasing numbers of conservative Democrats were growing disenchanted with a party they saw as led by northern liberals, and many whites in Texas's burgeoning cities were voting Republican. Consequently others replicated Tower's successes. Republicans in Texas by the 1990s were almost routinely winning gubernatorial and senatorial elections.

Tower also rode point for the GOP in national politics. The first Republican from a former Confederate state to serve in the Senate since the popular election of senators had been mandated in 1913, Tower helped his party stake out its new power base in the South and the West. He embodied the hard-edged conservatism of this rising Sun Belt wing of the GOP as an early supporter of Barry Goldwater's presidential candidacy and an opponent of the Civil Rights Act of 1964, the Voting Rights Act, and Medicare. Named to the Labor and Public Welfare Committee and the Banking and Currency Committee upon entering the Senate, Tower found his métier with his appointment to the Armed Services Committee in 1965. For all of his devotion to states' rights and leeriness of federal authority, Tower supported a strong national defense and an aggressively anticommunist foreign policy, and he developed a reputation for expertise on security issues. His politics surely served certain of his constituents well. Many in the Texas business community resented federal intrusion when it came to promoting civil rights, union representation, environmental protection, or social welfare, but at the same time they profited off federal dollars in the form of defense and construction contracts.

A member of the minority through his first three terms, Tower saw his influence ripen in the early 1980s, after Ronald Reagan was elected president and the Republicans took control of the Senate. Now chair of the Armed Services Committee, Tower played a key role in the military buildup of the Reagan years, which included enlarging the navy and modernizing nuclear forces. He and his staff helped order the administration's defense priorities, helped sculpt the Pentagon's expanded budgets, and helped shepherd them through Congress. But sensing that the political tide was beginning to shift, Tower chose not to run for reelection in 1984 and left the Senate in January of the following year.

Shortly after Tower's retirement, Reagan named him to lead negotiations with the Soviets at the Strategic Arms Reduction Talks in Geneva, Switzerland. Tower resigned from this post in the spring of 1986 and subsequently headed a consulting firm whose clients included large defense contractors. Late in 1986 Reagan tapped Tower to head the President's Special Review Board appointed to investigate the Iran-Contra affair. The board, which came to be known as the Tower Commission, had to work quickly and without the cooperation of central figures in the scandal. The commission report, issued in February 1987, focused blame on National Security Council staffers and Reagan's lax management style.

Tower's expertise in security issues and his hard work during the 1988 campaign led President-elect George H. W. Bush to select him as secretary of defense. The nomination quickly ran aground. The *Atlanta Constitution* aired rumors (which Tower attributed to his recently divorced second wife) that the nominee was a hard-drinking philanderer, while Democratic senators expressed concern that as a consultant he had grown too close to defense industries he would have to do business with as secretary. The Democratic-controlled Senate rejected him by a 53–47 vote. This "first" was less happy than the firsts that had attended Tower's initial election to the U.S. Senate. He was the first cabinet nominee of a newly elected president ever to be voted down by the Senate.

In 1990 President Bush appointed Tower to chair the President's Foreign Intelligence Advisory Board. The following year Tower died in a plane crash near Brunswick, Georgia.

• Southwestern University in Georgetown, Texas, has a large archive of John Tower Papers. Tower's own publications include *A Program for Conservatives* (1962) and *Consequences: A Personal and Political Memoir* (1991), which focuses on the controversy surrounding his nomination as secretary of defense. John R. Knaggs, *Two-Party Texas: The John Tower Era 1961–1984* (1986), is a sympathetic account by a Republican party activist. See also Roger Olien, *From Token to Triumph: The Texas Republicans since 1920* (1982). Obituaries are in the *Washington Post*, 6 Apr. 1991, and the *New York Times*, 6 Apr. 1991.

PATRICK G. WILLIAMS

TREUTLEN, John Adam (16 Jan. 1734–1782), first constitutional governor of Georgia, was born Hans Adam Treuttlen in Kürnbach, Germany, the son of Hans Michel Treuttlen, a cooper, and Clara Job. The village of his birth, governed by the states of Hesse, Baden, and Württemberg as a condominate, was bitterly divided confessionally between Protestants and Catholics and disapproved of the marriage of Treutlen's Lutheran father to Clara Job, his servant, who had converted to Catholicism. Their marriage on 18 April 1731 required special permission by the sovereign of Württemberg and her readmission to the Lutheran faith. These and other adverse circumstances favored the family's emigration and subsequently became a carefully guarded secret that kept the date and place of John Treutlen's birth a matter of speculation and error for 265 years.

In April 1744 the family left for America. No credible particulars are known about Treutlen immediately after his departure from Kürnbach, but Clara and the four boys were in Gosport, England, the following year, where Treutlen likely acquired his reputedly accent-free command of English. In November 1745 Treutlen, his mother, and two of his brothers obtained passage with the so-called Fourth Palatine Transport of Salzburgers that arrived in Georgia on 22 January 1746 after an arduous journey. The village of Ebenezer on the Savannah River, refuge for Protestant Salzburgers expelled by their Catholic ruler, later became Treutlen's political power base.

The Salzburgers' pastor, Johann Martin Boltzius, brought Treutlen to Ebenezer, entered him in the Salzburgers' excellent school, apprenticed him to a shopkeeper, and nurtured his Christian instruction, hoping to train the intelligent, well-spoken boy as a teacher. Treutlen was confirmed at Ebenezer on 7 June 1747 and entered the close-knit congregation that became a powerful factor in Georgia's struggle for independence.

Boltzius's relationship with Treutlen did not remain unmarred. The pastor agonized over the youth's independent spirit and his preference for mercantilism over teaching. Boltzius's disapproval of Treutlen's marriage in 1756 to Margarethe Dupuis of Purrysburg, South Carolina, caused further bitterness between the two men. Treutlen and his wife had eight children.

Treutlen taught reading and writing at the Ebenezer school, but he declined a renewal of his contract in April 1759 to devote himself fully to the sale of Savannah merchandise in his Ebenezer shop. He purchased town lot number nine with a two-acre garden and became a successful rival of the respected local merchant John C. Wertsch, who proved a powerful adversary. During Georgia's prohibition of slavery, Treutlen prospered, but when the act of 1735 barring slavery was repealed, he acquired slaves and became truly wealthy. After Pastor Boltzius's death in November 1765, a leadership crisis erupted at Ebenezer with repercussions far beyond the town's parameters. Treutlen emerged as one of the political leaders, joining forces with Pastor Christian Rabenhorst. His chief adversaries were Wertsch and the followers of Pastor Christoph Friedrich Triebner. In 1766, 1768, and 1773 Treutlen served as road commissioner in Georgia. About the same time he acquired thousands of acres of land in Georgia's St. Matthew's and St. Philip's Parishes along with several large tracts in South Carolina's St. Peter's Parish and Granville County and on Cowpen Branch. His wife's family also held land in South Carolina's Granville and Orangeburg areas.

In the summer of 1774 the rift in Ebenezer's congregation, which had also split along political lines, erupted in armed conflict, and Henry Melchior Muhlenberg, the "Father of Lutheranism in America," was summoned from Philadelphia to calm the parishioners. He consulted with the congregation in Charleston and the Reverend John Joachim Zubly of Savannah's Independent Church and brokered a short-lived peace. From widely advertised elections for new church leadership, Treutlen—now justice of the peace—emerged as one of the new deacons and the leader of the Rabenhorst party, which was aligned with the radical faction among American revolutionaries, with Wertsch and Triebner in opposition.

When the Provincial Congress assembled at Savannah on 4 July 1775, the Salzburger community in St. Matthew's Parish elected Treutlen and, among others, Jacob Waldhauer and Jenkin Davis of the republican faction and John Flerl and Christoph Cramer of the Loyalists. St. Andrews Parish, which had formulated a resolution for manumission of slaves in Georgia, elected Lachlan McIntosh, his brothers George McIntosh and William McIntosh, and several other family members. Zubly—elected from Savannah—preached the sermon "So Speak Ye and So Do as They That Shall Be Judged by the Law of Liberty." He was selected a delegate to the Continental Congress amid fears of the enemy within. Zubly was accused of traitorous conduct, a charge that he denied and that extant records do not support. Returning to Georgia, he found his home vandalized. Zubly was taken into custody by the Council of Safety in July 1776 and banished. His estate confiscated, he went to South Carolina.

Treutlen advanced to the Council of Safety and was one of only thirty-six men to serve Georgia in both the royal and the revolutionary legislatures. In the fall of 1776 and the spring of 1777 a succession of foiled power plays cost Button Gwinnett, a signer of the Declaration of Independence, the coveted appointment as general of the Georgia brigade, which went to Lachlan McIntosh. Gwinnett's botched invasion of Florida under executive power, which he briefly held after Governor Archibald Bulloch's death in February 1777, infuriated McIntosh and deprived Gwinnett of reelection as governor. Gwinnett died after a duel with McIntosh on 16 May 1777.

On 8 May 1777 Treutlen was elected Georgia's first governor by a handsome majority under the new constitution, which required that elected officials be Protestant. During his brief term, which ended with the election of John Houstoun in January 1778, Treutlen fought prominent members of the conservative revolutionaries. The best-known document is his *Proclamation* of 15 July 1777 offering a reward of £100 for the capture of William Henry Drayton, who promoted a union between South Carolina and Georgia. Drayton, born in South Carolina and educated at Oxford, England, was a "radical conservative." Active in the prerevolutionary movement in South Carolina, Drayton was president of the state's Council of Safety in 1775 and was chief justice in 1776. He was a member of the Continental Congress in 1778 and served until his death in 1779. In his scathing reply of 1 August 1777, Drayton referred to the case of George McIntosh and called Treutlen a traitor who deserved to be hanged for the "enormities" of abuse to life and liberty of individuals under his management.

Treutlen's letter of 19 June 1777 to John Hancock, then president of the Continental Congress, defends his action against McIntosh, the brother of General Lachlan McIntosh, and states that several council members, including George Bailie, Sir Patrick Houstoun, and George McIntosh, were indebted for £20,000 to the merchant William Panton and gave him bills of exchange that he used to illegally divert a consignment of rice to enemy ports. Legal proceedings against Georgia's council members, although begun during Gwinnett's term, carried over into Treutlen's tenure. George McIntosh was imprisoned, and his considerable property was confiscated. Treutlen's letter to Hancock is of importance because it documents his personal initiative in rearresting McIntosh, who was out on bail, to deliver him to the Continental Congress as a prisoner. There he was released for insufficient cause.

Treutlen's patriotic zeal is evident in his appeal for Hancock's assistance: "True it is that we are surrounded with Enemies on every side, and our small friends the Tories, within our Bowels, are so very numerous and have such ties of Consanguinity, that all our Efforts against these Enemies of American Freedom have hitherto been languid and ineffectual." As the Revolutionary War entered its most passionate phase, the English seized Ebenezer on 2 January 1779, erecting redoubts and recruiting sufficient Loyalists to form a company for reconnaissance. While in British hands, Ebenezer became a thoroughfare for British troops and their prisoners, and Jerusalem Church was a stable for their horses. Pastor Triebner and his followers were guaranteed royal protection of person and property. Many joined the British in marauding parties that pilfered and burned the property of Whigs in the settlement. During the sieges and captures of Savannah and Augusta, Ebenezer was briefly the capital of Georgia in 1782.

After his wife's death in 1777, Treutlen in 1778 married Anne Unselt, a widow. His Georgia home destroyed, Treutlen moved to South Carolina with his family. He was elected to both the Georgia and South Carolina Assemblies and took his seat at Jacksonborough, South Carolina, in January 1782. He failed to appear at the Georgia Assembly in April 1782. A letter dated 5 May 1783 to the Reverend Henry Melchior Muhlenberg in Philadelphia, signed by seven Ebenezer citizens, states that Treutlen had been married but eight days to a third wife when he was "cut to pieces with the sword" by "Tories or refugees." A letter from the Ebenezer pastor Johann Ernst Bergmann to Europe, dated 27 August 1787, also states that Treutlen had been "hacked to pieces by the English because he was an avid rebel." A marker erected by the Daugh-

ters of the American Revolution at Metts' Cross Road in present-day Calhoun County, South Carolina, claims to indicate the spot where Treutlen was murdered. A county in Georgia is named for him.

• Treutlen's original birth and family records are at the Evangelical Church in Kürnbach, Germany. The Library of Congress has a copy of Treutlen's frequently reprinted *Proclamation*, and the Georgia Historical Society has a copy of his letter to John Hancock in collection 807. Sources from Treutlen's contemporaries about his career and death are chiefly letters by the Salzburgers' various pastors in the archive of the Franckesche Stiftungen in Halle, Germany. The South Carolina Department of Archives and History has several records of Treutlen's property and judgment roll transactions in that state. Of the printed sources, the most important are A. G. Voigt, trans., *Ebenezer Record Book* (1929); Samuel Urlsperger, *Ausfuehrliche Nachricht von den saltzburgischen Emigranten, die sich in America niedergelassen haben* [Detailed reports on the Salzburger emigrants who settled in America], trans. and ed. George Fenwick Jones (1968); and T. G. Tappert and J. W. Doberstein, trans., *The Journals of Henry Melchior Muhlenberg* (1982). Numerous articles, including those in the Georgia and South Carolina biographical directories of their houses of representatives, contain inaccurate information about Treutlen. A richly illustrated and detailed treatment of the Ebenezer settlement and its political, religious, and cultural significance in Georgia's frontier environment is Ulrike Huber and Helene M. Kastinger Riley, "'Gottes Brünnlein hat Wassers die Fülle,'" *Salzburg Archiv 26* (1999): 111–62, which contains extensive bibliographical references and recently discovered information on Treutlen. See also http://hubcap.clemson.edu/german/TreutlenMonth.html; http://www.gasalzburgers.org/index.html; http://www.spck.org.uk/about-us/history.html; http://www.franckesche-stiftungen.de; and http://www.kuernbacher.de.

HELENE M. KASTINGER RILEY

TRIPP, Charles B. (6 July 1855–26 Jan. 1930), sideshow performer known as "the Armless Wonder," was born armless from the shoulders down in Woodstock, Canada. (No information about his parents is available, and it is not known what his middle initial stands for.) There are no verified descriptions of Tripp's early years, but the account given in his publicity literature states that he was a handsome, well-adjusted child who easily learned to use his legs and feet to do the mundane tasks other people accomplished with their arms and hands. He came from a modest background. Carpentry was his early occupation, and he supplemented his performance income with carpentry work all of his life. His father either died when Tripp was an adolescent or left the family, because from an early age Charles Tripp supported his mother and sister. He wrote by holding a pen between his toes. His penmanship was elegant, a skill he capitalized on when in later life he signed the photographs he sold in conjunction with his exhibition in the most famous sideshow venues of the world.

In 1872, at the age of seventeen, Tripp traveled to New York City with his mother in search of P. T. Barnum, the great showman and originator of the American freak shows. As the story goes, Barnum hired the boy on the spot. After years of success popularizing museums and sponsoring performers, Barnum was becoming an entrepreneur of traveling extravaganzas. Tripp joined the Great Traveling World's Fair, in which Barnum first used the phrase "the Greatest Show on Earth." Tripp was affiliated with the Barnum and Bailey circus for twenty-three years and was featured in their famous four-year turn-of-the-century tour of Europe. For twelve years after that Tripp was a regular with Ringling Brothers. A widely circulated photograph of Tripp and Eli Bowen, a famous legless wonder, riding a bicycle built for two hailed them as the original odd couple, but there is no clear evidence that they were an exhibition team. In the early part of the twentieth century Tripp resided in the off-season at his home in Olney, Illinois.

By 1915 Tripp had been on exhibit for close to forty-five years and was no longer a big draw for the major circuses. A bachelor up until then, he married around this time (the exact date is not known) and moved down to the second rung of the sideshow business, the carnival circuit. Mae, his wife, traveled with him for the next fourteen years, selling tickets for midway ride concessions while Charles Tripp exhibited himself. Tripp had been in show business for fifty-seven years when he died of pneumonia in Salisbury, North Carolina, their permanent residence. He is buried in Olney, Illinois. Apparently the Tripps were struggling financially at the time. Soon after Charles Tripp's death, Mae Tripp, then seventy-five years old, wrote a friend seeking employment as a ticket seller in a carnival because she did not have enough money to pay the rent.

Tripp is the best-known "armless wonder" to have appeared in the American freak show in its hundred years of popularity (1840–1940). His persona was that of a dignified gentleman, competent in many mundane tasks of life. On stage he showed patrons what he could do with his feet: carpentry, penmanship, paper cutting, and the like. Being born without limbs is not common, but developing skills with other parts of the body to compensate for a deficit is. In other words, although he was cast as a special person, "an armless wonder," and is legendary in the history of the freak show, in another way of thinking, he was rather ordinary.

Tripp's contribution to disability enlightenment is difficult to assess. On the one hand he and exhibits like him made visible the competence of people who might be thought of as inherently deficient. On the other hand his presentation as an "armless wonder" suggested that his accomplishments were beyond the expectations of the regular person with a disability.

• The best primary sources can be found at the Circus World Museum, State Historical Society of Wisconsin, Baraboo, Wis.; the Hertzberg Collection, San Antonio Public Library, San Antonio, Tex.; and the Ringling Museum of the Circus, Sarasota, Fla. For more on Tripp's presentation, see Robert Bogdan, *Freak Show: Presenting Human Oddities for Amusement and Profit* (1988). For obituaries, see "A Real Hero," *Salisbury Evening Post*, 27 Jan. 1930, and "Tripp," *Billboard*, 1 Feb. 1930, p. 89.

ROBERT BOGDAN

TROUT, Robert (15 Oct. 1909–14 Nov. 2000), broadcast journalist, was born Robert Albert Blondheim in Wake County, North Carolina, near Raleigh, the only child of Louis Blondheim and Juliette Mabee Blondheim, farmers. When Trout was nine the family moved to Washington, D.C., where his father opened a shoe store. He attended public schools and was, by his own account, not much interested in his studies. He had no aspirations of becoming a journalist. He did develop an early passion for radio and later recalled, "When I was supposed to be asleep at night, I was often in bed with the light out listening to my little [homemade] crystal set" (interview by Ron Simon, Scheuer Collection). Trout credited radio with awakening a desire in him to know more of the world. He made several attempts to run away from home and spent a summer as a cabin boy on a transatlantic passenger ship.

Trout graduated from Washington Central High School in 1927. He worked at odd jobs, including stints as a soda jerk, a gas station attendant, and a cab driver. Hoping to gain experience that might help him become a novelist, he agreed to write scripts without pay for WJVS, a radio station in suburban Virginia. His career as a broadcaster began in 1931 as the result of a proverbial show business "big break":

> A chap used to come over from the *Alexandria Gazette*, at six o'clock in the evening to do a news program. It was for no fee, just to get publicity for the paper. That was the nearest thing that we or anybody had to a news program, really. One day he didn't appear, and with about one minute to air, I was propelled into a chair and handed that day's copy of the *Gazette*. So for fifteen minutes I sat there and read the newspaper into the microphone. (Interview by Ron Simon, Scheuer Collection)

Satisfied with his performance, the station manager gave Trout a regular job reading the news. His duties soon included writing and hosting the station's hunting and fishing and satire programs as well.

In 1932 the Columbia Broadcasting System (CBS) radio network, then in its fourth year of operation, bought WJSV, changed the station's call letters to WTOP, and moved operations to downtown Washington. The twenty-three-year-old Trout was retained by the new management and thus became part of the embryonic organization that grew into CBS News. Trout seized the opportunity and in effect transformed himself into a world-class professional journalist. He changed his name from Blondheim to Trout (the family name of a boyhood friend) and grew a moustache to affect greater maturity and dignity. "I hadn't gone to college," he said. "It was a sore subject with me for a long time. In fact, I was sort of worried about it and I used to conceal the fact if somebody asked me" (interview by Ron Simon, Scheuer Collection).

In short order Trout was in daily contact with the rich, famous, and powerful of the world, interviewing them on the air and socializing with them for news tips. As CBS's de facto "Washington correspondent," he was the voice of the network at live presidential events, beginning with Herbert Hoover's 1932 lighting of the White House Christmas tree. He covered all four of Franklin D. Roosevelt's inaugurations and hosted national coverage of each of Roosevelt's "fireside chats." Trout's slim, six-foot, one-inch frame, his pencil moustache, and his crisp elocution led British and other European dignitaries to invite him to private clubs, an irony that Trout both appreciated and exploited professionally.

At the same time Trout retained a common touch as master of what were known in early radio as "stunt broadcasts." Examples include "man-in-the-street" interviews conducted during the middle of a snowstorm, reports delivered from behind the wheel of a moving car, and a conversation with a sideshow midget while riding a Ferris wheel. He covered both major party political conventions in 1936, and a year later he went to London as the sole American radio correspondent on hand at the coronation of King George VI. In 1938 Trout became perhaps the first true "news anchor" as host of CBS's *World News Roundup*, a daily dinnertime half-hour news show presented live from New York. In 1938 Trout married Catherine "Kit" Cranes. The couple took a small apartment on the West Side of Manhattan, which remained their principal residence for the rest of their lives. They had no children.

Seamlessly applying his suave erudition to a plainspoken vocabulary and delivering the mixture in his signature baritone, Trout created one of the first effective personas for American broadcast journalism: an insider making things understandable to common people. He credited something akin to an actor's device as crucial to his success. "[Radio is] like talking on the telephone," he said. "I'd pretend there's one person at the other end, instead of two million" (interview by Ron Simon, Scheuer Collection). Trout's colleagues marveled at his ability to effortlessly "chat" with radio listeners during the dreaded long pauses that often occur in live event coverage, a talent also appreciated by Franklin Roosevelt, whose public appearances were sometimes delayed by problems related to his need to use a wheel chair.

During World War II the CBS radio network established itself as the nation's premier broadcast news source. Though Trout did reporting stints in Europe, including some live coverage of the London blitzkrieg, his principal role was as the voice of CBS to the American people. He reported the war news, battle by battle, on his daily programs, *The World Today* and *Headlines and Bylines*. On D day he remained at the microphone for more than seven hours straight, an indication of why he was known as "the iron man of broadcasting." Trout was the first to deliver the news to the American public of both the German and the Japanese surrenders, the latter with these well-remembered lines: "The Japanese have accepted our terms fully. This is the end of the Second World War!"

As the radio networks reorganized for peacetime, Edward R. Murrow, who had become CBS's "star" correspondent during the war, hoped to relinquish his on-air duties in favor of an editorial and administrative role, and Trout continued anchoring the network's flagship evening news program. However, Frank Stanton, the head of the CBS radio network, believed Murrow's public name was too great an asset to squander, especially with the company gearing up to launch television service. In 1947 Stanton demanded that Murrow take over the program from Trout. "I was suddenly fired for the first and only time in my career," said Trout.

Trout was hired almost immediately by the rival NBC network, where he spent the next five years doing many of the same radio chores he had done at CBS and doing his first television work. He also hosted a television game show, *Who Said That?* from 1948 to 1951, which he said helped him become accustomed to the new medium. In 1952, however, he returned to CBS at the behest of his long-time colleagues.

Trout claimed to have understood that television would usurp radio's role as the nation's primary news source. However, he preferred radio. "Radio news is really a writer's medium," he said. "Though I could ad-lib when I needed to, what I really enjoyed was writing my radio broadcasts and polishing them up, like formal essays, and then performing them over the air. On television I always got the feeling my words were playing second-fiddle to the picture, even if the picture was me." Nevertheless Trout successfully made the transition, covering major events, hard news, and whimsical feature stories.

Given Trout's lifelong project of self-gentrification, it is not surprising that he took up sailing and horseback riding as hobbies. A confirmed New Yorker since soon after his arrival, Trout particularly enjoyed long daily walks around the city, often covering one hundred blocks (five miles) or more, walking stick in hand.

In 1957 Trout was offered the job of anchoring local newscasts for WCBS-TV in New York. While some correspondents of his experience might have resisted the idea of moving to local news, Trout jumped at the chance to get to know the city more intimately. He especially enjoyed working on local documentaries for the station's *Eye on New York* series, examining issues such as political corruption and the state of the subway system. During this period he was also called upon to take occasional national or international assignments for CBS, among them the first American space flight by Alan Shepard in 1961, floor coverage of the 1964 political conventions, and the funeral of Winston Churchill in 1965. He also narrated documentaries for *CBS Reports* on such subjects as questionable practices in the funeral industry and gun control.

In 1965, wishing to spend more time at a house he owned in Madrid, Trout softened his work schedule to become what he described as a "roving European correspondent" for the network, mainly contributing features on events such as the running of the bulls at Pamplona and Christmas from St. Peter's Square. Management changes at CBS News during the 1970s, however, brought his career with the company to a gradual, sputtering end. "Finally, I was getting paid just for the pieces I did, treated like a freelance. Then I was told I was going to get $25 for a piece, and I couldn't do that. So I called my agent and he got me a job at ABC" (interview by Ron Simon, Scheuer Collection). Trout continued as an active reporter for ABC News, covering the political conventions and contributing stories from Europe. He was presented a 1979 Peabody Award for "nearly fifty years of service as a thoroughly knowledgeable and articulate commentator on national and international affairs." His wife died in 1994.

At the age of eighty-six Trout did a series of pieces for *All Things Considered*, the daily news program of National Public Radio (NPR). In the series he reexamined some of the signature events of the twentieth century that he had covered, giving special attention to the role and technique of radio reporting in World War II. "He was the last remaining link to the beginning of broadcast journalism," said John McDonough, the NPR producer who worked with Trout on the last piece just three weeks before the reporter died in New York City.

Jim Wooten, an ABC colleague, said of Trout, "His voice was quite mellifluous, his pronunciation and enunciation were impeccable and perfect. But I think what really set him apart was that throughout all his life he maintained . . . an incredible level of energy and curiosity. These strike me as the two underpinnings of good reporting and good journalism." Trout's life and career paralleled the development of American broadcast journalism from the early days of commercial radio to the age of satellite-delivered television, and his contributions to the form, content, and style of the art are among the fundamentals of modern news media. Beyond that, he was an American original, a self-made man from a modest background who reinvented himself across the boundaries of traditional social class lines to seize a once-in-a-lifetime opportunity.

• Trout's papers are in the Media History Archives of the University of Texas at Austin. Extensive oral history interviews conducted in 1998, including tapes and transcriptions, are in the Steven H. Scheuer Collection at the Center for the Study of Popular Television, Syracuse University, and are available at http://newhouse.syr.edu/research/POPTV/mission.htm. Stanley Cloud, *The Murrow Boys: Pioneers on the Front Lines of Broadcast Journalism* (1996), offers material on Trout and a context for his career. An obituary is in the *New York Times*, 15 Nov. 2000.

DAVID MARC

TRUEBLOOD, Benjamin Franklin (25 Nov. 1847–26 Oct. 1916), college president and peace activist, was born in Salem, Indiana, the son of Joshua Trueblood and Esther Parker Trueblood, farmers. They were Quakers. After graduating in 1868 from a Quaker school, Earlham College, where he majored in Greek and Roman literature, Trueblood served as a professor of classics at Penn College in Oskaloosa, Iowa. His commitment to moral principles was a benchmark of his character and stood him in good stead throughout his professional career. On 12 July 1872 he married Sarah Hough Terrell of New Vienna, Ohio; they were to have three children. From 1872 to 1879 he was president of Wilmington College, another Quaker school, in Wilmington, Ohio. From 1879 to 1890 he continued his administrative career as president of Penn College.

In 1890 Trueblood left the presidency of Penn and spent a year in Europe as an agent for the Christian Arbitration Society. For the remainder of his life he was an instrumental figure in European peace councils. His fluency in a number of modern languages facilitated his reputation among European peace groups. In 1892 he was selected as secretary of the American Peace Society, a position he held until 1915. For most of that period he was the only full-time salaried peace worker in the United States. According to the historian Roland Marchand, Trueblood "combined the genteel style and moralistic temper of the American Peace Society's background with a more practical interest in the details of programs for international arbitration and world federation" (Marchand, p. 15). Under his leadership the society's membership grew from 400 to close to 8,000, and subscriptions to its journal, the *Advocate of Peace*, climbed from 1,500 to more than 11,000. He also played a major role in relocating the society's headquarters from Boston to the U.S. capital.

Trueblood made the crusade for peace national in scope. He was instrumental in the peace movement's dramatic growth at the end of the nineteenth century. Between 1865 and 1901 the peace movement, adjusting to industrialization, became a cosmopolitan endeavor. Linked at home to a worldly-minded elite of lawyers, business leaders, educators, and politicians, Trueblood's peace movement valued arbitration and a mechanistic means of organizing an industrial world of great power interdependence.

Aside from organizing branch societies and writing about peace, Trueblood popularized the efforts for international arbitration. He was partly responsible for establishing the Lake Mohonk (New York) Conference on International Arbitration, "a series of single annual meetings begun in 1895 for the discussion and promotion of 'arbitration'" (qtd. in Marchand, p. 18). He also was a participant in the International Law Association and the American Society of International Law. He consistently brushed aside elitism within the arbitration movement in favor of widespread public support: "We have looked too much, possibly, at the heads of government rather than to the cultivation of public sentiment among the people" (qtd. in Patterson, p. 46). In keeping with the cosmopolitan nature of the movement, he insisted that an interdependent world economy brought about by the Industrial Revolution could hasten the movement toward world federation: "Commerce has woven an economic web which binds all the nations closely to each other" (Trueblood, "War a Thing of the Past," pp. 49–50).

Trueblood was opposed to all forms of militarism and violence. In the 1890s he kept a close eye on events in Latin America. Regarding the Venezuelan boundary dispute and Andrew Carnegie's own paradoxical peace sentiments, Trueblood sarcastically commented, "So great and enthusiastic has our attachment to it [arbitration] become, that our government, inspired by the extraordinary virtue of some of its citizens, has already decided that in certain eventualities it will go to war" (Trueblood, "The United States, Great Britain, and International Arbitration," p. 22). Additionally, when the yellow journalistic tones grew louder in response to the de Lome letter and the *Maine* explosion, Trueblood advised peace advocates to oppose intervention in Cuba. (In communication with a friend in Havana, the Spanish ambassador to the United States, Enrique de Lome, had characterized President William McKinley as a "cheap politician." The sinking of the *Maine* with the loss of more than 250 lives so incited American opinion against Spain that McKinley was forced into war.) But the American Peace Society chose to keep silent about the Spanish-American War of 1898 because the jingoistic press encouraged ultrapatriotic Americans to view peace organizations as disloyal. Trueblood had this advice for his followers: "Refusing to give ear to floating rumors, they should keep themselves in a calm, self-possessed attitude, which will have a direct restraining effect on others" (qtd. in Patterson, p. 53). Nevertheless, he was to denounce in the strongest possible terms the actions of American forces in the Philippines during the insurrection led by Emilio Aguinaldo. At a meeting of religious leaders at the Tremont Temple in Boston in May 1902, Trueblood said, "We have allowed a false notion of patriotism to smother criticism, and to persuade us that the nation can do no wrong. . . . We have spoken of the Philippine inhabitants in a manner to create contempt for them and to induce a treatment of them scarcely fit for wild beasts. It is we who are guilty, as well as the men who have done the burning and the torture" (see Online Resources).

One of Trueblood's most important peace activities was editing the *Advocate of Peace*. Although a skillful writer, he added few ideas to pacifist thought and was never fully capable of grasping the interconnections between industrial capitalism and war. Because of his devotion to conscientious objection, Trueblood never put himself in a position to comprehend the realities of power politics and the expanding nature of American corporatism. Still he wrote most of the journal's editorials and many of its articles. He campaigned tirelessly for arbitration and the limitation of armaments. In 1899, inspired by Immanuel Kant's notion of an international state, Trueblood published a modest book, *The Federation of the World*, based on two lectures he gave at the Meadville Theological School in Pennsylvania. He "portrayed federation as a slowly accelerating development leading inevitably to the unity of the human race" (qtd. in Patterson, p. 112). *Federation* praised the forthcoming Hague Peace Conference and insisted that an internationalist state based on a federation model was "necessary and inevitable" (qtd. in Howlett, p. 119). A second work, published posthumously and compiled by Edwin D. Mead, *The Development of the Peace Idea and Other Essays* (1932), highlighted Trueblood's optimism regarding the Hague Peace Conferences and prospects for a Permanent Court of International Arbitration.

Prior to the outbreak of war in Europe in 1914, Trueblood was stricken by a severe stroke. In ill health he continued editing the society's journal. The growth of war expenditures in Europe led him to predict that war was almost a certainty: "If . . . the long-talked-of general war in Europe does not occur it will be next to a miracle" (qtd. in Patterson, p. 226). Prompted by his deteriorating condition, Trueblood in 1915 resigned as secretary. He died in Newton Highlands, Massachusetts. His longtime friend and peace colleague Mead remarked, "It is right to say that he was the only professional peace worker in the United States, the only man who made service of the peace cause his vocation" (qtd. in Patterson, p. 28).

• The Benjamin F. Trueblood Correspondence is in the American Peace Society Papers, Swarthmore College Peace Collection, Swarthmore College. Many of Trueblood's articles are in the *Advocate of Peace*. His *The Federation of the World* (1899) discusses the importance of arbitration, while *The Development of the Peace Idea and Other Essays* (1932) is a collection of his major addresses, essays, and lectures with an introduction by Mead. Two important articles by Trueblood are "War a Thing of the Past," *Cosmopolitan Student* I (Apr. 1910): 49–50; and "The United States, Great Britain, and International Arbitration," *New England Magazine* 14 (Mar. 1896): 21–26. Charles Beals, *Benjamin Franklin Trueblood: Prophet of Peace, 1847–1916* (1916), is a twenty-page homily. Scholarly works examining Trueblood's activities include Merle Curti, *Peace or War: The American Struggle, 1636–1936* (1936); Calvin D. Davis, *The United States and the First Hague Peace Conference* (1962) and *The United States and the Second Hague Peace Conference: American Diplomacy and International Organization, 1899–1914* (1976); Warren F. Kuehl, *Seeking World Order: The United States and World Organization to 1920* (1969); and Charles DeBenedetti, *The Peace Reform in American History* (1980). An essential bibliographic reference is Charles F. Howlett, *The American Peace Movement: References and Resources* (1991). David S. Patterson, *Toward a Warless World: The Travail of the American Peace Movement, 1887–1914* (1976), includes a detailed analysis of Trueblood's role in the pre–World War I peace movement. See also C. Roland Marchand, *The American Peace Movement and Social Reform, 1898–1918* (1973). An obituary appears in the *New York Times*, 27 Oct. 1916.

See also Charles M. Woodman, "Benjamin F. Trueblood: An Appreciation," *American Friend*, o.s., 23 (1916): 948–50.

CHARLES F. HOWLETT

TSONGAS, Paul Efthemios (14 Feb. 1941–18 Jan. 1997), politician and U.S. senator, was born in Lowell, Massachusetts, the son of Efthemios George Tsongas, a dry-cleaner, and Katina Tsongas, who died of tuberculosis when Paul was six. After attending public schools in Lowell and graduating from Lowell High School in 1958, Paul worked his way through Dartmouth College where he earned a B.A. degree with a major in history in 1962. Inspired by President John F. Kennedy's call for America's youth to perform public service, Tsongas joined the Peace Corps and from 1962 to 1964 volunteered as a teacher in Ethiopia.

Upon his return to the United States he enrolled in the law school at Yale University. During the summers of 1966 and 1967 he was an intern for Republican Congressman F. Bradford Morse, who represented his home district. In 1967 he completed the requirements for his LL.B. degree and was admitted to the Massachusetts bar. Instead of seeking a legal position, the newly minted lawyer rejoined the Peace Corps and spent the next year working as a training coordinator in the West Indies. His appetite for public service had been whetted by his Peace Corps years—an experience that transformed his political inclinations from conservative Republican to liberal Democrat—and within months after his return to Lowell he sought a seat on the Lowell City Council, a position he held from 1969 until 1972. From 1968 to 1969, he served on the Governor's Committee on Law Enforcement for the Commonwealth of Massachusetts; from 1969 to 1971 he also worked as the state's deputy assistant attorney general. To provide a stable family income, Tsongas then established a private law practice, but he remained active in local politics. While on the Lowell City Council he was instrumental in crafting that city's Lowell Plan, which created a national park to preserve the community's historical factory buildings while at the same time spurring private investment in new businesses to revive Lowell's depressed economy. He also found time to further his education by attending Harvard University's John F. Kennedy School of Government and completing a Master of Public Administration degree in 1973. He married Nicola Sauvage in 1969; they had three children.

Tsongas's political ambitions grew beyond his hometown, and in 1974 he ran for his district's Congressional seat, which had safely been in Republican hands for most of the twentieth century. Fortunately for Tsongas, F. Bradford Morse, for whom the young Tsongas had worked as an intern, had retired in 1972 and the one-term Republican incumbent, Paul W. Cronin, was harmed by the Watergate scandal. Tsongas won by a margin of almost 35,000 votes out of some 164,000 cast. He reflected the new breed of Democratic officeholder in the post-Watergate era committed to political reform, responsible engagement with foreign nations, and a more prudent fiscal policy, while at the same time adhering firmly to his liberal principles concerning, for example, affirmative action and women's rights. His voting record earned him a nearly 90 percent rating from the Americans for Democratic Action and a rating of nearly zero percent from the American Conservative Union.

During his two terms in the House of Representatives, Tsongas served on the Banking, Currency and Housing Committee and the Interior and Insular Affairs Committee. He was especially interested in issues relating to international lending, human rights, and the environment. Adamantly opposed to increasing the defense budget, Tsongas voted against construction of the B-1 bomber. The high cost of heating in his home state spurred him to oppose deregulation of natural gas, although he did support increasing the gasoline tax to encourage conservation. As a member of the House Subcommittee on Energy and Environment, Tsongas energetically championed research on solar power and throughout his political career he supported efforts to harness both solar and nuclear power.

After four years in the House of Representatives, Tsongas decided he was ready for a try at the Senate. His opponent, Senator Edward W. Brooke, was seeking his third term and had the distinction of being the first African American ever to be elected to the Senate by popular vote. But Brooke's image was harmed by a messy divorce. Tsongas survived a competitive primary, besting four other candidates, and received the endorsement of Senator Edward M. Kennedy. Tsongas emphasized his commitment to improving the Massachusetts economy, establishing a national health insurance program, and obtaining more federal assistance to the old industrial cities of New England. He won 55 percent of the vote and remained undefeated in politics.

Tsongas brought to his new job his usual liberal credentials, but with a twist: he became increasingly critical of the 1960s liberal Democratic approach of solving problems by creating more federal programs. In 1980 he startled his audience at the Americans for Democratic Action convention by advocating more flexible liberalism and less antibusiness rhetoric. Ronald Reagan's election later that year proved conclusively Tsongas's contention that the Democrats were going to have to change to survive. In 1981 Tsongas outlined his thoughts in more detail in *The Road from Here: Liberalism and Realities in the 1980s*, wherein he urged liberal colleagues to embrace "compassionate realism," paying greater attention to economic, energy, and environmental issues. Tsongas actively opposed Reagan's use of military solutions for the political problems of Central America—his faction was dubbed the "Tsonganistas"—and he vigorously denounced the 1982 Israeli invasion of Lebanon. He consistently voted against increased defense spending. On domestic issues he supported affirmative action and the Equal Rights Amendment.

Tsongas's rising political fortunes were dealt a severe setback in 1983 when he was diagnosed with lymphoma. He resigned from the Senate at the end of his term and returned to Lowell to receive treatment for his illness. He became a partner in Foley, Hoag & Eliot, a Boston law firm, and wrote about his cancer experience in *Heading Home*. For the next several years he was content to practice law and help his wife raise their three daughters.

By the end of the 1980s, however, Tsongas's health had improved and his cancer was in remission. He became increasingly disenchanted with George H. W. Bush's policies and began to think about reentering the political arena. In 1991 he published a small pamphlet entitled *A Call to Economic Arms: Forging a New American Mandate*, which crystalized his current thinking about America's role as an active and positive force in economic globalization. Tossing caution to the winds, he announced his candidacy for president in April 1991, long before anyone else. His somber—and sometimes preachy—demeanor on the campaign trail led him to be dubbed "St. Paul" by the media, but his message of fiscal responsibility sold well in New England. He came in first in the New Hampshire primary. After that, however, the Bill Clinton campaign steadily moved ahead and Tsongas withdrew in mid-March.

Tsongas resumed his law practice but remained politically active by joining in 1992 with retired Senator Warren B. Rudman to establish a new group called the Concord Coalition, whose primary goal was to advocate a balanced federal budget. He also found time in 1995 to write *Journey of Purpose: Reflections on the Presidency, Multiculturalism, and Third Parties*, which summarized his experiences running for president. Soon after the 1992 election, however, Tsongas was hospitalized with a recurrence of his cancer and he underwent a bone-marrow transplant in 1996. In January 1997, he was hospitalized in Boston, where he died.

Tsongas's political career on the national stage was relatively brief—only ten years—but his quiet, self-deprecatory demeanor did not deter him from forcefully speaking out against what he considered the excesses of the Reagan and Bush administrations. As a leader of the neoliberal or "New" Democrats of the post-Watergate era, Tsongas advanced the shift in the Democratic liberal philosophy from big government of the 1960s to the smaller government with its concomitant balanced budgets that would become the norm in the late 1990s. Tsongas's fervent attention to environmental, energy, and fiscal responsibility issues also revealed a man seeking to lead his party out of the political wilderness as the century waned.

• Tsongas's papers are maintained in the Special Collections Department of the University of Massachusetts–Lowell Center for Lowell History. Congress published a memorial volume titled *Paul Efthemios Tsongas: Late Senator from Massachusetts* (1997) as well as an earlier book upon his retirement, *Tributes to the Honorable Paul E. Tsongas of Massachusetts in the United States Senate, upon the Occasion of His Retirement from the Senate* (1984). Tsongas's published works include *The Road from Here: Liberalism and Realities in the 1980s* (1981); *Heading Home* (1984); *A Call to Economic Arms: Forging a New American Mandate* (1991); and *Journey of Purpose: Reflections on the Presidency, Multiculturalism, and Third Parties* (1995). An obituary is in the *New York Times*, 20 Jan. 1997.

EDWARD A. GOEDEKEN

TURPIN, Ben (17 Sept. 1869–1 July 1940), film and vaudeville comedian, was born Bernard Turpin in New Orleans, Louisiana, the son of a confectioner. His father's name does not appear in readily available sources of information; his mother's maiden surname was Buckley. Both his parents were of French extraction. As a child, Turpin entertained customers by pulling taffy in the window of the family candy store. Turpin was seven years old when his family moved to New York City's Lower East Side. When he reached his late teens, his father reportedly presented him with $100 and sent him forth to find his fortune. Turpin promptly lost all of his money in a game of craps in New Jersey. Too embarrassed to return home, he hopped a freight train to Chicago, where he survived several months by begging at the back doors of wealthy homes.

In his early twenties, Turpin entered show business as half of a vaudeville comedy duo that booked for $20 a week. He gained popularity on his own when he developed a stage version of the popular comic strip character The Happy Hooligan. Turpin's Hooligan routine involved a brutal acrobatic move known as the "108." This was a standard backward summersault from a standing position that Turpin modified by landing on the back of his head or, often, his face. In the 1890s and early 1900s Turpin toured with Sam T. Jack's Chicago-based vaudeville companies and performed in circuses, at fairs, and in burlesque houses. During his tenure on the vaudeville circuit, the comedian developed his trademark crossed eyes (strabismus). The cause of Turpin's disorder is usually attributed to optic nerve damaged sustained from performing the "108s" or, less likely, to his comically crossing his eyes during the routine.

In 1907 Turpin joined the Essanay film company, formed in Chicago by George K. Spoor and Broncho Billy Anderson. Turpin's screen debut was in *Ben Gets a Duck and is Ducked* (1907), a one-reel comedy in which he is arrested after chasing a duck into a city fountain. Turpin told Harry Carr of *Photoplay* magazine that, during these early years at Essanay, "I was the chief comedian and the shipping clerk and the property boy, the scenery shifter and janitor, not to mention being the telephone girl and scenario writer" (Carr, p. 61). For all of this, Turpin was paid $25 a week. Also in 1907, Turpin married Carrie Lemieux, an actress from Quebec; they had no children. In 1909, he left Essanay to tour in vaudeville, and his wife traveled with him, helping out with the Happy Hooligan routine. The Turpins returned to Essanay in 1914 and resumed performing in one-reelers. Ben found steady work in Wallace Beery's *Sweedie* series, in which Beery appeared in drag as a catastrophe-prone maid, and in the *Snakeville* western-comedy series. Turpin started to gain notice, but he remained in secondary roles.

Charlie Chaplin moved to Essanay in 1915 and began to mentor Turpin, casting him as a fellow job applicant at a movie company in his first picture for the studio, *His New Job*. Later that year, Turpin moved with Chaplin to Essanay's new facilities in Niles, California, where they continued to film shorts. The best known of these are *A Night Out* (1915), in which Turpin plays Charlie's drinking buddy, and *A Burlesque of Carmen* (1916). Though Chaplin was largely responsible for nudging Turpin's career in the right direction, the two comedians had an ambivalent relationship. Turpin resented the more famous comedian and disliked his meticulous style of directing. Chaplin's cinematographer, Rollie Tothero, recalled that "Ben wanted 'equal time' with Charlie and a salary to match. When Charlie saw Ben getting as much of the show and publicity as himself, he let Ben go . . ." (Lahue and Gill, p. 377). In April of 1916 Turpin broke his Essanay contract and followed Chaplin to Mutual Studios, where he made more than thirty comedies under the Vogue production label. In his 13 months at Vogue, Turpin earned $100 a week as a featured player in shorts that starred Paddy McQuire and Rube Miller. By now, the key elements of Turpin's screen persona were in place. They included an inordinately bushy false mustache, the crossed eyes, an expressively bobbing Adam's apple, the willingness to undertake punishing spills, and a wildly incongruous posture of self-confidence.

Turpin's popularity encouraged Mack Sennett to lure the star to his stock company in 1917. Under Sennett, he enjoyed his greatest success, earning $3,000 a week by the early 1920s. Turpin continued to make mostly two-reelers, though he carried occasional features. The Sennett films include a number of parodies, among them *East Lynne with Variations* (1919), *Uncle Tom without the Cabin* (1919), and *The Reel Virginian* (1924). In *Three Foolish Weeks* (1924), a parody of *Foolish Wives* (1922), Turpin introduced the character Rodney St. Clair, a spoof of Erich von Stroheim that he would reprise several times. In 1921, Sennett starred Turpin in *A Small Town Idol*, the seven-reel feature widely considered to be Turpin's masterpiece. Turpin played Sam Smith, a poor villager who becomes a Hollywood western star and returns home to seek love. The National Board of Review rated *Idol* as one of the best films of the year, and *Variety*'s critic praised it for "revealing amazing resource for amusing nonsense . . . done in a screamingly funny vein of seriousness which gives the travesty the keenest edge" (15 April 1921, p. 40). Sennett followed this success with a five-reel spoof of Rudolph Valentino's *The Sheik* (1921) titled *The Shriek of Araby* (1923). Though praised by fans, the film was less successful than *Idol*. *Variety*'s review opened with "Five reels of Ben Turpin looking two ways at one time

proves tiresome" (14 June 1923, p. 26). Still, Turpin proved to be one of Sennett's most bankable players of the 1920s. As a publicity stunt in 1921, Sennett insured Turpin's eyes for $25,000 with Lloyd's of London. The policy would pay if the comedian's vision suddenly straightened.

A series of strokes left Carrie Turpin an invalid in 1924, and in July of 1925 Turpin retired to care for her. She died on October 1, 1925. A month later, Turpin was hospitalized for appendicitis, and during his recovery he fell in love with his nurse, Babbette E. Dietz, a native of North Dakota. They married in July 1926; there were no children from this marriage. Turpin returned to the screen that year, and, after fulfilling his contract with Sennett, he concentrated on freelancing. Work was infrequent, partly because Turpin demanded a minimum of $1,000 per week. He made cameo appearances in *The College Hero* (1927), *The Love Parade* (1929), and *The Show of Shows* (1929). In the 1930s Turpin made brief appearances in six features and played a cross-eyed stable boy in Mascot's twelve-part serial *The Law of the Wild* (1934). He also worked in several shorts, including Laurel and Hardy's *Our Wife* (1931), and in *Keystone Hotel* (1935), Warner Bros.' attempt to recreate the Keystone Kops comedies.

Turpin, however, hardly needed the work. During the 1920s he had shrewdly invested in real estate. He was quite eccentric with regard to his wealth. At the height of his career Turpin would reportedly ride the public bus to work and proudly announce to his fellow riders, "I'm Ben Turpin. $3,000 a week!" (Horton, p. 16). He routinely did janitorial chores around the apartment buildings he owned, and he kept the furniture in his own house covered in white sheets. In the late 1930s Turpin squelched rumors that he was penniless by buying two office buildings for $50,000 in cash.

Turpin's final appearance was in the 1940 Laurel and Hardy feature *Saps at Sea*, released three months before his death. He played an electrician whose crossed vision leads him to cross wires with ridiculous results. Of this last role, *Variety* simply noted, "lessers include some oldtimers, among them . . . Ben Turpin" (8 Mar. 1940, p. 20). He died in Santa Monica, California.

Though Turpin was a lesser member of the slapstick pantheon, he is an enduring icon. James Agee classed Turpin as a "gifted comedian" who "had an immense vocabulary of . . . cliches and . . . never tried to break away from them" (Agee, p. 70). Turpin spent most of his career working in shorts, the bread and butter of slapstick. He was a craftsman, not a genius, playing in an estimated 161 pictures. When the staff of *Life* magazine selected the cover for the 1949 issue that featured Agee's article "Comedy's Greatest Era," they chose to feature not Chaplin or Buster Keaton but Ben Turpin, his bushy mustache, Adam's apple, and crossed eyes, once again, on prominent display.

• A variety of promotional material and press articles from Turpin's career are held in the "Ben Turpin Clippings File" of the Daniel Blum Collection at the Wisconsin Center for Film and Theater Research, State Historical Society, Madison, Wisconsin. For Turpin's reflections on his career at Essanay see Harry Carr, "Looking Backward with Ben," *Photoplay* (Dec. 1918), pp. 60–61, 104. The most thorough career overview and filmography is provided by Barry Brown, "Ben Turpin, 1869–1940," *Films in Review* (Oct. 1977), pp. 467–83. Other worthwhile biographical essays are Kalton Lahue and Sam Gill, "Ben Turpin," *Clown Princes and Court Jesters* (1970), pp. 377–85; Kalton Lahue, "Turpin," *8mm Film Collector* (Sept. 1964), pp. 3, 11, 22–23; and Daniel Horton, "Looking for Laughs, Ben Turpin," *Classic Images* (Dec. 1982), pp. 16–17. For an influential appraisal of slapstick, see James Agee, "Comedy's Greatest Era," *Life* magazine (5 Sept. 1949), pp. 70–88. Obituaries are in the *New York Times*, 2 July 1940, and *Variety*, 3 July 1940.

SCOTT HIGGINS

TURRENTINE, Stanley William (5 Apr. 1934–12 Sept. 2000), jazz tenor saxophonist, was born in Pittsburgh, Pennsylvania, the son of Thomas Turrentine, Sr., a construction worker who earlier had played tenor saxophone and clarinet in the Savoy Sultans. His mother, Rosetta, maiden name unknown, was a pianist. As a child Turrentine played piano by ear. At thirteen he took up cello but secretly learned to play his father's tenor sax when he was supposed to be practicing cello. Turrentine's love for the instrument and his potential talent were immediately apparent, and his father bought him a tenor sax and gave him strict instructions. He was to stand in a corner, projecting the saxophone's sound back toward himself, and play nothing but sustained tones, gradually working his way through the instrument's highest and lowest registers, until he was satisfied with the tone quality of every note. This foundation yielded a gorgeous overall instrumental timbre, top to bottom, and on some notes a distinctive and immediately identifiable whooping sound that became in effect Turrentine's musical signature. Over the next few years he practiced with his father and went with his father to hear renowned jazz musicians at the jam sessions then flourishing in Pittsburgh.

Music at the family's church was of little interest to Turrentine, but their home was situated next to a Sanctified church, with instruments blaring through open doors. Late in life he recalled that this raw form of African-American gospel music was another strong influence on the development of his soulful playing.

Having begun to help support the family by playing locally, Turrentine at sixteen quit Pittsburgh's Schenley High School to join the guitarist Lowell Fulson's rhythm-and-blues band, which for a time included Ray Charles on piano. Around 1952 Turrentine spent a period in Cleveland, where he played with the jazz pianist and arranger Tadd Dameron. Early in 1953 Turrentine replaced John Coltrane in the rhythm-and-blues band led by the alto saxophonist Earl Bostic, working alongside his brother, the trumpeter Tommy Turrentine (22 Apr. 1928–13 May 1997). Serving in the U.S. Army from 1956 to 1958, Stanley Turrentine was a member of the 158th Army Band. In March

1959, a few months after his discharge, he rejoined Tommy as a member of the drummer Max Roach's group, with which he recorded several albums and in March 1960 toured Europe. In the 1950s Turrentine married, and his first daughter was born. The relationship ended when, while they were living in Philadelphia, his wife suggested that he give up playing and apply for a job at the post office. Further details are unknown.

On 25 April 1960 Turrentine first made his mark in jazz as a soloist on the Blue Note label with a lengthy session under the leadership of the organist Jimmy Smith, issued on the albums *Midnight Blue* and *Back at the Chicken Shack*. In June of that year Turrentine began recording for Blue Note as a leader. There followed numerous such dates under his own name, including the albums *Up at Minton's* and *Z. T.'s Blues* (both from 1961); further sessions with Smith, including *Prayer Meetin'* (1963); a similar affiliation with the organist Shirley Scott that yielded, among others, the albums *Dearly Beloved* (1961) and *A Chip off the Old Block* (1963); and various LPs as a sideman under the leadership of such jazz musicians as the trumpeter Dizzy Reece; the pianists Duke Jordan, Horace Parlan, Duke Pearson, and Horace Silver; the drummer Art Taylor; the saxophonist Ike Quebec; and the guitarist Kenny Burrell. Turrentine's solo on Ma Rainey's classic tune "See See Rider," from Quebec's album *Easy Living*, recorded in January 1962, exemplifies the blues roots of his style.

The emergence of the Hammond organ as a popular jazz instrument in the 1950s opened up the possibility of achieving a full-voiced sound with only three instruments, saxophone, organ, and drums, when the organist was of Smith's or Scott's stature and able to supply not only chords and melody but also bass lines in lieu of a bassist. In this economical manner, as a member of a soul-jazz trio with Scott, Turrentine toured African-American nightclubs in the South, the so-called "chitlin' circuit." Many such clubs had their own Hammond organs, thus relieving the musicians of the need to cart around these cumbersome, heavy instruments.

"Mr. T," as he was affectionately known, began playing with Scott in 1960, and the following year they married. They had three daughters. The oldest, Lisa, recalled the happiness of their home. The family lived, she said, the Cosby life before there was a *Cosby Show*. In summers they toured together, everyone packing into the car and heading to the parents' jobs. But in 1971, perhaps owing to the pull of successful individual careers, Turrentine and Scott separated. If their separation was owed to personal animosity, they certainly kept a tight lid on it. Both were remembered time and again as among the most gracious, humble, and approachable people in the world of jazz. They subsequently divorced, and by 1975 Turrentine had married Rhita. Her maiden name and other details of this third marriage are unknown.

Like so many of his colleagues, Turrentine had no knowledge of the intricacies of recording contracts, licensing, royalties, and song publishing, and he entered into disadvantageous agreements with Blue Note. Unlike so many others, he was given a second chance when in the 1970s he taught himself the rudiments of musical finance while scoring huge successes with several recordings, beginning with the title track of his album *Sugar* (1970) and a version of Coltrane's tune "Impressions" from that same album. Each rendition anticipated a widely accessible blend of jazz and rhythm and blues that came to be known a quarter-century later as "smooth jazz." In 1974, on the title track of his album *Pieces of Dreams*, Turrentine's bluesy rendering of the melody was accompanied by a jazz group playing in a restrained bossa nova style and was fleshed out by an orchestra featuring French horns, strings, and harp. In this manner and in other ways, including the placement of his characteristic playing into a disco setting, Turrentine reached into the realm of "easy-listening" music.

In the mid-1980s, when the Blue Note label was reactivated, Turrentine resumed a soul-jazz style. He recorded the album *Straight Ahead* in November 1984 and toured in small groups of his own or in reunions with Smith and Burrell.

Turrentine suffered from high blood pressure, and in the late 1980s he experienced a pulmonary edema that sent him into a coma for twenty-eight hours. Since the mid-1960s Turrentine had been living in New Jersey, just across the river from Manhattan. In an effort to lessen the stress in his life, he moved to a quieter place, Kensington, Maryland, and then settled in Fort Washington, Maryland. In the early 1990s he made two new soul-jazz albums, including *More Than a Mood* (1992). Turrentine toured extensively throughout the decade.

On 10 September 2000, before the last night of a week-long engagement at the Blue Note club, Turrentine suffered a stroke at a Manhattan hotel. Hospitalized in New York City, he died two days later. He was survived by his fourth wife Judith. Her maiden name and the marriage date are unknown. Turrentine was the stepfather to her son, but they had no children together.

• The video *Stanley Turrentine in Concert* (1990), featuring a quintet he led at the Village Gate in Greenwich Village, affords an opportunity to see and hear Turrentine playing some of his best-known tunes. It also includes segments in which he reminisces about life in Pittsburgh and his early experiences in rhythm and blues. Excerpts from Turrentine's recorded improvisations have been transcribed into musical notation by Gregory Jay Balfany in "A Motivic Study of Twenty Selected Improvised Solos of David Sanborn and Stanley Turrentine" (D.M.A. diss., University of Wisconsin–Madison, 1988) and by Hunt Butler as *The Stanley Turrentine Collection* (1997). The central sources on Turrentine are brief essays and interviews in jazz periodicals, including Michael James, "Introducing Stanley Turrentine," *Jazz Monthly* 7 (July 1961): 7–8; Herb Nolan, "Dues on Top of Dues: Stanley Turrentine," *Down Beat* 5 (1975): 12–13, 39; Bret Primack, "Stanley Turrentine: We're in the Marketplace Now!" *Down Beat* 45 (19 Oct. 1978): 13–14, 53; Les Tomkins, "Tenor Integrity for the People: Stanley Turrentine,"

Crescendo International 19 (Apr. 1981): 6–7, continued as "I'd Like to Do a Blowing Date Again, Says Stanley Turrentine" (May 1981): 12–13; Gene Kalbacher, "The Blue Notes of Mr. T.," *Down Beat* 52 (May 1985): 16–19; Roland E. Bush, "Straight Ahead with Mr. T," *Coda* no. 210 (Oct.–Nov. 1986): 16–17; Eugene Holley, Jr., "Stanley Turrentine: The Timeless Tenor," *Jazz Times* 22 (Oct. 1992): 61; James T. Jones IV, "Stanley Turrentine: Mr. T's Mood Swings," *Down Beat* 59 (Oct. 1992): 27–29; Herb Boyd, "From the Hill: Ray Brown and Stanley Turrentine Share Their Pittsburgh Connection," *Down Beat* 67 (Dec. 2000): 58–61, 63; and Larry Fisher, "A Conversation with Stanley Turrentine," *Jazz Research Proceedings Yearbook* 20 (2000): 53–56. An obituary by Ben Ratliff is in the *New York Times*, 14 Sept. 2000.

BARRY KERNFELD

TYLER, Letitia Christian (12 Nov. 1790–10 Sept. 1842), first lady of the United States, wife of President John Tyler, was born at Cedar Grove Plantation about twenty miles east of Richmond, Virginia, the daughter of Robert Christian, a well-to-do planter, and Mary Browne Christian. Letitia grew up on the family estate. Her father was a Federalist. Letitia's portrait indicates that she was beautiful, but little is known definitively about her early life. It is likely she had no more than the minimal education of most upper-class women of her day. By all accounts she was rather quiet and shy and very religious, preferring simple pursuits with family and close friends to public life.

As a young woman she met John Tyler, who was studying law after graduating from the College of William and Mary in Williamsburg, Virginia. John Tyler's family plantation was located about fourteen miles from Cedar Grove, which was on the road between Greenway and Richmond. This made it convenient for the suitor to stop there on his way to the capital after his father became governor in 1809. Only one of his love letters to Letitia survives. In it he promised never to cease loving her, and he wrote a few sonnets celebrating their relationship. However, the five-year courtship appears to have been rather sedate, as Tyler mentioned numerous times that he had never dared even to kiss Letitia's hand until three weeks before the wedding.

On John Tyler's twenty-third birthday, 29 March 1813, the couple was married at Cedar Grove. On the eve of the wedding, the groom told a friend that he experienced no fear at the approaching nuptials.

Shortly after the marriage Robert and Mary Christian both died. Letitia Tyler's inheritance eased the financial situation for the newlyweds as they settled at Mons-Sacer, a five-hundred-acre portion of Greenway that John had inherited from his father. About four months later, John Tyler joined a militia group called the Charles City Rifles that had been raised to defend Richmond during the War of 1812. He was appointed captain of the group and was dispatched to Williamsburg as part of the Fifty-Second Regiment of the Virginia Militia. The unit was soon transferred to the Second Elite Corps of Virginia. A few weeks later the British withdrew from the area, the unit disbanded, and the men returned home without ever engaging in combat.

The Tylers lived at Mons-Sacer for two years, then sold it and moved to a nearby property, where they built a home called Woodburn. In 1821 they bought Greenway and moved back to John Tyler's boyhood home. In 1815 their first child, Mary, was born, followed by Robert Tyler, John, Jr., Letitia, Elizabeth, Anne Contesse, Alice, and Tazewell. Anne Contesse lived only three months, and a ninth child was either born dead or died shortly after birth. The other children all survived their mother.

In 1816 Tyler was elected to the U.S. House of Representatives and in 1827 to the U.S. Senate. Except for one season, 1828–1829, Letitia Tyler remained at home with the children. She apparently had little interest in politics or social life and usually found it necessary to economize because the family was large, and the plantation's assets were tied up in land and slaves. She apparently performed the duties of plantation mistress extremely well and was completely devoted to her children.

When John Tyler served as governor of Virginia from 1825 to 1827, Letitia Tyler was forced into a more public life. Faced with a constant money shortage, she entertained at the governor's mansion with charm but simplicity. Nevertheless, the governorship proved costly, and the family was in serious financial difficulty by the time her husband moved on to the U.S. Senate in 1827, where the salary helped somewhat to ease the family's economic problems.

After John Tyler resigned from the Senate, the family moved to Williamsburg in 1837. By this time the children were getting married and leaving home. Mary had married Henry Lightfoot Jones; in 1838 John, Jr., married Mattie Rochelle in what proved to be an unhappy union. Letitia wed James A. Semple in 1838, forming another unhappy alliance that eventually resulted in separation. In 1839 Robert married Priscilla Cooper, daughter of the tragedian actor Thomas A. Cooper, and this proved to be a successful union that delighted the Tylers.

Priscilla and her mother-in-law developed a deep love for each other, despite the fact that shortly before the wedding Mrs. Tyler had suffered a stroke that left her partially paralyzed. Still, she managed to supervise the household from her bedchamber and became an even more devout Episcopalian, spending much time in Bible reading.

When John Tyler became vice president of the United States in 1841, he planned to continue living in Williamsburg for his wife's comfort. President William Henry Harrison died a month later, however, and Tyler suddenly became the nation's tenth president. The family moved into the White House, and Priscilla assumed the role of hostess, since Letitia Tyler was unable to perform the duties. Priscilla proved more than equal to the task, maintaining a heavy schedule of public events at the White House.

Labeled "His Accidency" by his detractors, John Tyler experienced anything but a placid administration. Crises such as the resignation of Harrison's cabinet (with the exception of Secretary of State Daniel Webster) and demonstrations at the White House in which the president was burned in effigy surely had a negative effect on the first lady, whose health continued to decline. Her one and only appearance downstairs at the White House was for the marriage of her daughter Elizabeth to William N. Waller on 31 January 1842. Letitia Tyler died within the year, and her funeral service was conducted in the East Room of the White House by the rector of St. John's Episcopal Church. Her health and disposition had unfortunately prevented her from making an impact on the role of first lady.

• No personal papers or letters written by Letitia Tyler have been found. Most of what is known about her comes from letters and papers of her husband, including the John Tyler Papers at the Library of Congress, Duke University, the University of Virginia, and the College of William and Mary. The most accessible source is the three-volume set of family letters, *Letters and Times of the Tylers* (1884), published by Lyon Gardiner Tyler, one of John Tyler's children by his second wife, Julia Gardiner Tyler. Letitia's role as first lady is discussed in Laura C. Holloway, *Ladies of the White House* (1881), but the account is unreliable. Margaret Brown Klapthor, *First Ladies* (1981), and Lewis L. Gould's edited work, *American First Ladies, Their Lives and Their Legacy* (1996), both contain analyses of Letitia Tyler's role as first lady. The most complete consideration of Letitia Tyler in the context of her husband's career can be found in Oliver P. Chitwood, *John Tyler: Champion of the Old South* (1939), and Robert Seager II, *And Tyler Too: A Biography of John and Julia Gardiner Tyler* (1963).

MELBA PORTER HAY

V

VALENS, Ritchie (13 May 1941–3 Feb. 1959), pioneer rock and roll singer and musician, was born Richard Steve Valenzuela, the son of Joseph Steve Valenzuela, a tree surgeon who also worked at a variety of jobs such as mining and training horses, and Concepcion Reyes Valenzuela, in Los Angeles, California. Both parents lived in San Fernando, a suburb in Los Angeles County, and worked in a munitions factory in Saugus, just north of San Fernando. At the time of Ritchie's birth Concepcion, or Connie, as she preferred to be called, had a four-year-old son from a previous marriage. Before Ritchie was three, his parents separated; Ritchie stayed with his father, who had recently bought some property in nearby Pacoima. His parents, however, continued to see each other until his father's death in 1951.

Ritchie became interested in music at an early age. One of his cousins helped him make a toy guitar from a cigar box when he was five. His father loved blues, Latin, and flamenco music, and at the age of nine Ritchie received a guitar from his father. His cousins John Lozano and Dickie Cota taught him how to play. His favorites were the cowboy songs of Gene Autry and Roy Rogers.

In 1951, after Ritchie's father died from complications related to diabetes, the family moved into his father's house in Pacoima. For about a year Ritchie stayed with two uncles, one in Norwalk, the other in Santa Monica, California, because, according to some sources, he was "running wild." But most remembered him as shy and unnoticeable—except when he played music. The Valenzuela household was small and overcrowded, and Ritchie spent a great deal of time with his maternal uncle and aunt, Lelo and Ernestine Reyes, who also lived in Pacoima. From the time he was eleven, they were an integral part of his life and career. To this day, they have kept his music and memory alive.

Ritchie had attended elementary schools in several communities, including Pacoima, Norwalk, and Santa Monica. When he was thirteen, he entered Pacoima Junior High School. An average student, he often brought his guitar to school and practiced or played for his friends during recess and lunch time. He was learning rhythm and blues and rock and roll, singing the songs of Elvis Presley, Chuck Berry, Jerry Lee Lewis, and especially Little Richard, whom Ritchie imitated with such fervor that he was often called "the 'Little Richard' of the [San Fernando] Valley." In January 1957, a mid-air collision between a US Air Force F-89 fighter and a civilian airliner on test flights occurred over the junior high school's athletic field, killing five in the airplanes, three students on the ground and injuring ninety people. The tragedy left Ritchie, who was not at school that day, with a lifelong fear of airplanes.

At sixteen, Ritchie entered San Fernando High School. There he joined some classmates in forming a musical group that eventually became a professional local band called the Silhouettes. Headed by then twenty-one-year-old vibe player Gil Rocha, the group included musicians of Mexican, Hispanic, Italian, Japanese, and African-American descent. Ritchie, as the featured vocalist, created a stage presence that he retained throughout his professional career, combining the passionate, frenetic rhythms of Little Richard and Bo Diddley on vocals and guitar with a humility and reserve that reflected his true personality.

Bob Keane, who was starting up Del-Fi Records, saw Ritchie perform and recognized that he "had a lot of vitality, a lot of drive and this Latin rock" (Mendheim, p. 43). Keane soon after invited Ritchie to his basement studio and recorded several songs with a few veteran musicians such as guitarist/arranger Rene Hall, drummer Earl Palmer (who also recorded with Ricky Nelson), and stand-up bassist Buddy Clarke. Keane then recorded Ritchie at Gold Star Studios in Hollywood, adding the talents of veteran musicians Bill Pitman, Carol Kaye, and Irvin Ashby (guitarists, formerly of the Nat King Cole trio), bass player Red Collender, and Ernie Freeman on piano. Most of the songs were recorded at Gold Star. Most of the musicians remembered Ritchie as a likeable person who was very serious about his musical performances. "He had no ego whatsoever," Palmer recalled. "He was always asking questions about whether his performance was okay" (Mendheim, p. 49). Bob Keane shortened Ritchie's last name—from Valenzuela to "Valens."

In August 1958, Valens's "Come On, Let's Go" was released, getting much air play on KFWB and other radio stations in the Los Angeles area. By October, this song, based on a phrase commonly used by Valens, reached no. 42 on the Billboard charts. He toured eleven cities on the East Coast, including New York, Philadelphia, and Washington, D.C., and appeared on teen television shows such as the Alan Freed show in New York and Dick Clark's American Bandstand. In November, Valens released "Donna," written for Donna Ludwig, a San Fernando high school friend. "Donna" made it to no. 2 on the Billboard charts. "La Bamba," the flip side of "Donna," was a traditional Mexican wedding song; originally from Vera Cruz, it was a *huapango*, a song consisting of nonsense verses. Although Valens had previously played the song solo and with the Silhouettes, he was reluctant to record it because he had difficulty pronouncing the Spanish words and, according to Bob Keane, he felt it might "demean his culture" (Mendheim, p. 63). It ranked no. 22 on the Billboard charts in 1959. ("La Bamba" has since been recorded by Trini Lopez, the Kingston Trio, Joan Baez, and Harry Belafonte, among many others.)

In January 1959, Valens returned to California to star in Alan Freed's final film, *Go Johnny Go* (Freed had produced a series of rock and roll films to promote the music), which starred Jimmy Clanton, Sandy Stewart, Chuck Berry, Jackie Wilson, Eddie Cochran, and other performers. Valens sang "Ooh, My Head" (in later years the song was made popular again under the title "Boogie with Stu" by Led Zeppelin). Valens made more recordings and demos at Keane's basement studio and at Gold Star Studios, gave performances around the southern California area, and appeared in Buddy Bregman's television special *The Music Shop*, one of the first variety shows done in color.

In late January, Valens left on the Winter Dance Party tour, which gave performances throughout the Midwest. This show had only five featured acts: Valens, Buddy Holly and the Crickets, the Big Bopper (J. P. Richardson), Dion and the Belmonts, and Frankie Sardo. One of Holly's Crickets was Waylon Jennings. Beginning in Milwaukee, the tour was beset with problems. The buses broke down or their heaters failed, and the performers did not have the luxury of staying in hotels. Holly chartered a private plane to take him, Waylon Jennings, and Tommy Allsup to the next stop in Minnesota. The Big Bopper, who had a cold, persuaded Jennings to give up his seat. Valens and Allsup flipped a coin over who would take the last seat. Valens won the toss.

After their Clear Lake venue, the plane was scheduled to fly from the nearby Mason City airport to Moorehead, Minnesota. The performance at the Surf Ballroom in Clear Lake was the last for Ritchie Valens, the Big Bopper, and Buddy Holly. Shortly after midnight, the three performers got into a Beechcraft Bonanza piloted by Roger Peterson. The plane crashed, killing all aboard.

More than a thousand people from all over the West attended Valens's funeral in San Fernando. He was buried at Mission San Fernando cemetery.

Del-Fi Records continued to release both single and LP recordings of Valens. Memorial concerts continued throughout the southern California area into early 1961, the most famous being the Long Beach Civic Auditorium concert on New Year's Eve 1961, the first appearance of the Beach Boys. Both national and international memorial fan clubs formed and continued into the mid-1960s. However, with the demise of Del-Fi Records, Ritchie Valens's legacy waned until the release in 1978 of the movie *The Buddy Holly Story*, when a Chicano/Latino rock group, Los Lobos, began to sing some of Valens's songs, including "La Bamba."

From 1962, attempts had been made to do a film on Ritchie Valens's life. In 1987, *La Bamba* was released, directed by Luis Valdez and produced by Taylor Hackford and Bill Borden. In response to the popularity of the movie, Del-Fi Records was revived, and a star for Valens was put on the Hollywood Walk of Fame. A recreation center in Pacoima was named after him, and in 2001 he was admitted into the Rock and Roll Hall of Fame.

The first successful Latino rock performer, Valens was the "father" of Latino/Chicano rock. An initiator of the "garage band" sound, which contributed to what later became known as "surf music," he combined elements of rock and jazz (along with Duane Eddy, Eddie Cochran, and ultimately Bo Diddley). He was one of the first rockers to use the idea of a medley of melodies called "through-composed" in traditional music circles, and one of the first to use asymmetrical rhythms and pentatonic melodies previously confined to black urban blues. Amazingly, this making of music history was accomplished by a 17-year-old through a few songs and fragments that barely filled three albums in a period of less than eight months.

• Mendheim, Beverly, *Ritchie Valens: The First Latino Rocker* (1987; rev. ed., 1996) is a concise biography that emphasizes Valens's contributions to the history of rock and roll. Liner notes to the CD compilation *Ritchie Valens: The Lost Tapes* (1990) and the boxed CD set *Ritchie Valens: Come On, Let's Go* (1992) contain useful information on Valens's life and music.

BEVERLY MENDHEIM

VILLA, Pancho (1 Aug. 1901–14 July 1925), world flyweight boxing champion, was born Francisco Guilledo in Ilog, Negros Occidental, Philippines, the son of Rafael Guilledo and Maria Villaruel Guilledo, workers on a hacienda in La Carlota. When Villa was only six months old, his father left the family to join the U.S. Navy. Without schooling, Villa worked from an early age, driving bullock carts through the cane fields. He left home at age eleven, going to Iloilo, Panay, where he worked as a bootblack. Later, with another boy, he went to Manila, where he became one of the numerous bootblacks in the business district.

Eventually Villa began attending amateur boxing events, and he decided to enter an "amateur night" program at Olympic Stadium. As F. P. Finch wrote in the *Manila Times* (14 July 1925), Villa "soon distinguished himself, more by the ferocity with which he fought than by any particular skills. Starting with nothing but a savage attack, he soon developed a satisfactory defense." Paquito Villa, the referee at the stadium, saw promise in the youngster and became his mentor. Villa legally adopted Guilledo and renamed him "Pancho Villa."

Beginning in 1919 Pancho Villa fought four- and six-round bouts, winning nearly all of them. He was just 5 feet 1 inch and weighed only about 100 pounds when he began his career, but he eventually grew heavier (110 to 115 pounds), which became his usual fighting weight. He first attracted attention through a series of fights with Mike Ballerino, a soldier in the American army who outweighed him by a dozen pounds. The two met eight times in 1920 and 1921, and Villa won all but two, which were draws. However, Ballerino always gave Villa stiff competition, and two of their later fights were for the recently established Orient bantamweight title, which Villa won.

In 1922, after a few more victories, Villa accepted the invitation of Frank Churchill, a promoter and manager of Filipino boxers, to accompany him to the United States and box there. Because there have been few American boxers small enough to compete in Villa's flyweight class (limit 112 pounds) and the division has never been popular in the United States, Villa's presence seemed mainly intended to provide companionship to another boxer, the lightweight Elino Flores, a highly regarded prospect. As it turned out Villa was far more successful than Flores and was the first of a long line of Filipinos who became popular in U.S. rings.

Villa lost close unofficial decisions to his first opponents in the United States, the future bantamweight champion Abe Goldstein and the future flyweight champion Frankie Genaro. After four consecutive victories over minor opposition, Villa lost again to Genaro in Brooklyn in a disputed decision. He was then matched with the former bantamweight champion Johnny Buff in a fight, also in Brooklyn, billed for the American flyweight title and scored an eleven-round knockout. This victory seems to have given Villa confidence. Henceforth he was almost unbeatable.

Villa won his next eight fights in 1922 and 1923, defending his American flyweight title successfully three times, against Goldstein, Terry Martin, and Frankie Mason. He was again matched with Genaro for the title in New York on 1 March 1923 and lost in fifteen rounds after a thrilling, action-filled battle. Many viewers believed Villa deserved the decision, but Genaro fought coolly and won most of the late rounds.

It had been expected that the winner of the Genaro-Villa fight would box Jimmy Wilde for the world flyweight title, but because of the closeness of the fight and Villa's popularity, he got the match instead of Genaro. Villa and Wilde met on 18 June 1923 before forty thousand fans in the Polo Grounds, New York City. Wilde, a Welshman, had held the title since 1916 and was nicknamed "the Mighty Atom" because of his terrific punching ability. However, he was thirty-one years old and no longer had the stamina to withstand Villa's persistent attacks. It was a one-sided fight in which Wilde bravely lasted into the seventh round before he was knocked out.

Villa then won ten consecutive fights in the last six months of 1923. He defended his title successively once, against Benny Schwartz, and numbered among his other victims the former bantamweight champion Kid Williams and the future bantamweight champion

Bud Taylor. In 1924 he successfully defended his title against Frankie Ash of England and scored another win over Taylor. In the summer of 1925 Villa was scheduled to defend his title against Genaro but claimed an injury. Villa would not go through with the fight, resulting in a suspension by the New York State Athletic Commission. He then returned to the Philippines for the first time since 1922 and was reunited with his wife, Gliceria Concepcion, whom he had married only a few days before leaving for the United States.

Villa stayed in the Philippines until May 1925. There he successfully defended his title against his fellow countryman Clever Sencio (Inocencio Moldez). Villa then returned to the United States and on 4 July 1925 fought the future welterweight champion Jimmy McLarnin in Oakland, California, losing a ten-round decision. A few days before this fight, Villa had undergone extraction of a painful wisdom tooth. After the McLarnin fight, he had three more teeth extracted. Villa neglected to use the prescribed antiseptics and, although in pain, spent his time in revelry, celebrating the birth of a son (his only child). A massive infection spread to glands in the throat. Ignoring an order to go to the hospital, Villa collapsed and died soon afterward. He was regarded as a national hero in the Philippines, and his success in the ring inspired many other Filipinos to enter professional boxing, a number with considerable success.

Villa was extremely popular with New York–area boxing fans because of his aggressive style and outgoing personality. The sportswriter Francis Albertanti said Villa was "the best of all the flyweights. He could do everything [in the ring]. What a colorful fellow he was! Every fight he ever made was a great one. I never saw a better all around fighter" (quoted in Carroll, 1947). He was flamboyant in the ring and outside, and money flowed through his fingers. Another sportswriter, Bill Miller, wrote, "He was just a free-handed, liberal spender, fond of giving happiness to people he liked, and he liked almost everyone" ("Boxing's Mosquito Fleet," pt. 2). He was one of the greatest and best-loved athletes of the Philippines.

• A biographical article on Villa by F. P. Finch is in the *Manila Times*, 14 July 1925. Villa's record is in H. G. Goldman, ed., *The Ring 1986–87 Record Book and Boxing Encyclopedia* (1987). Articles on Villa are Bill Miller, "Boxing's Mosquito Fleet," pt. 2, *Ring*, May 1932, pp. 22–23, 42, pt. 3, *Ring*, June 1932, pp. 22–23, 44; Miller, "The Fighting Filipinos," *Ring*, July 1942, pp. 16–18, 45; and Ted Carroll, "The Fighting Filipinos," *Ring*, Nov. 1947, pp. 32, 46. An obituary is in the *New York Times*, 15 July 1925.

LUCKETT V. DAVIS

VINING, Elizabeth Gray (6 Oct. 1902–27 Nov. 1999), writer, was born Elizabeth Janet Gray in Philadelphia, Pennsylvania, the daughter of John Gordon Gray, a manufacturer of scientific instruments, and Anne Moore Gray. She was known as Elizabeth Janet Gray throughout much of her professional career, publishing most of her books under that name.

Though her family's roots in the Quaker community of Philadelphia went back to colonial times, she was raised as an Episcopalian and grew up with her older sister in comfortable surroundings in the Germantown section of that city. Educated at Quaker institutions, she graduated from the Germantown Friends School in 1919 and Bryn Mawr College in 1923. She earned a degree in library science from the Drexel Institute in 1926 and that fall became an assistant cataloger at the library of the University of North Carolina at Chapel Hill.

As a teenager Gray had submitted stories to children's religious publications, and several were published. Thus encouraged, she had decided while still an undergraduate to pursue a career as a writer of children's books. While working as a librarian to support herself, she completed her first children's novel, *Merediths' Ann*, which was published in 1929. That same year she married Morgan Vining, associate director of the extension division of the University of North Carolina at Chapel Hill. Over the next three years Gray published three more children's books featuring young heroes and heroines in contemporary settings, *Tilly-Tod* (1929), *Meggy MacIntosh* (1930), and *Tangle Garden* (1932), all of which met with favorable reviews.

In September 1932, as the Great Depression tightened its hold on the nation, the couple moved to New York City so Morgan Vining could pursue a doctorate in university administration at Teachers College of Columbia University. Working as a librarian at Columbia University to support herself and her husband, Gray continued to write children's fiction. By all accounts the Vinings had an idyllic marriage, but their happy life together ended abruptly in October 1933, just as Gray's fifth novel, *Jane Hope*, was published, when Morgan Vining was killed in a car accident in New York State. Gray was seriously injured in the accident and took some time to recuperate, both physically and emotionally. They had no children, and Gray never remarried.

During her long recovery, aided by family and friends and extensive reading in reflective literature—the essays and poems of Ralph Waldo Emerson, the Old Testament, and the writings of John Donne and William Butler Yeats, among others—Gray began attending Quaker meeting and found herself rediscovering the inner peace she had known through attendance at Friends services during her school days. Gradually she learned, as she wrote many years later in her autobiography, *Quiet Pilgrimage* (1970), that "grief is something not to overcome or to escape but to live with." In 1934 she formally joined the Society of Friends, embarking on a spiritual journey that became the center point of both her personal and professional lives.

In the summer of 1934 Gray felt well enough to resume her writing career, and she traveled to Scotland to gather material for a children's biography of Sir Walter Scott. While working on the biography, she completed another novel for children, *Beppy Marlowe of Charles Town* (1936), a work of historical fiction set in London and South Carolina in the eighteenth century. By now settled in an apartment in Philadelphia with her mother and her sister, Gray devoted the next few years to both her writing and the study of Quakerism. These interests converged in her biography of William Penn, the Quaker founder of Pennsylvania, which she wrote for children as well as older readers seeking an introduction to his life and beliefs. Both *Penn* and *Young Walter Scott* were published in 1938, and like Gray's earlier works, they received favorable reviews.

During the next seven years, which comprised World War II, Gray wrote children's fiction and adult nonfiction and also spent time at Pendle Hill, a Quaker community and retreat in suburban Philadelphia. *Contributions of the Quakers*, which combines biography and history, appeared in 1939. A year later her contemporary children's novel *The Fair Adventure* was published. In 1942 she edited a book about Pendle Hill, *Anthology with Comments*, and that same year published *Adam of the Road*, a children's book of historical fiction set in thirteenth-century England. Like most of Gray's writing for children, *Adam of the Road* embodies the theme of finding one's true calling, reflecting her own oft-quoted belief in Emerson's line from "Spiritual Laws," "Each man has his own vocation." *Adam of the Road* won the prestigious Newbery Medal in 1943 as the best children's book published during the previous year and is considered Gray's masterpiece.

Over the next few years, as the war continued, Gray continued to spend time at Pendle Hill, probing ever more deeply into Quaker thought. She also offered her writing skills to the American Friends Service Committee (AFSC), a Quaker organization that promoted international peace and human understanding, and as a staff member wrote pamphlets on racism and other topics relating to social justice. She also wrote another contemporary children's novel, *Sandy*, published in 1945 as the war finally came to an end with the Allied defeat of both Germany and Japan.

In early 1946 Gray was preparing to begin a new children's book on colonial Virginia and had already made plans to spend the following summer at the McDowell Colony, a writers' retreat in New Hampshire. One day in March she read a front-page story in the *New York Times* about a search for an American tutor for the twelve-year-old crown prince Akihito of Japan. The crown prince's father, the defeated emperor Hirohito, had made the surprising request to a group of American educators who were touring what was now known as Occupied Japan; the educators had been invited to Japan by U.S. government officials to make recommendations for the modernization and westernization of the Japanese educational system. The emperor, whose life had been spared in the aftermath of defeat and the subsequent war crimes trials, was eager to show his willingness to cooperate with the Occupation government, and by inviting an American teacher to teach English to his son, the heir to the throne, he was making perhaps the most significant gesture possible in that direction.

There were several reasons why Hirohito's request and the subsequent search were widely publicized and caught the American public's attention, but the most important was probably the appearance only four years earlier of *Anna and the King of Siam*, a best-selling novel based on the diaries and letters of Anna Leonowens, a young English widow who tutored the children of the Siamese king in the 1860s and who is credited with bringing about democratic reforms in that nation. (The novel of course became the basis for a play of the same name and subsequently for the hit musical *The King and I*.) If a teacher's efforts had led to reform in Siam, then perhaps, so the public fancy had it, the same worthy by-product could be accomplished in Japan.

Gray read the story with passing interest and dismissed it from her mind as the search continued for a woman "around fifty" who was religious but not, in the emperor's words, "a Christian fanatic." On a day late in May, as Gray was preparing to leave the staff of the Friends Service Committee, a committee official in charge of Quaker relief efforts in Japan called her into his office and asked her if she would mind being suggested by the AFSC for the tutoring appointment. At first she dismissed the idea as out of the question: she was largely unfamiliar with Japan, she had no teaching experience, and she was content with her present life. But the counsel of Friends prevailed, and she agreed to be interviewed. In the wake of a successful interview and warm recommendations from such prominent Quaker educators as Rufus Jones, Howard Brinton, and Stanley Yarnall, Gray was offered the job, and she accepted.

Gray arrived in Japan in mid-October and took up her duties immediately as "Mrs. Vining." She quickly realized that more would be called for than teaching English. She found her pupil a shy, reclusive boy, virtually suffocated by court chamberlains and courtiers, with few interpersonal skills; his only enjoyment apparently came from learning about fish. Over the next four years, however, she was able to transform the unhappy prince into a mature and poised young man as she helped him discover both joy and self-direction in his life. (She also encouraged his interest in fish, and Akihito became an internationally known specialist in ichthyology.)

Gray's own account of her experiences in Japan, which also included teaching English to Akihito's mother and his sisters and personal interaction with the entire royal family, is modestly related in her memoir *Windows for the Crown Prince*, which was published in 1952, two years after her return to Philadelphia, under her married name, Elizabeth Gray Vining. The book became an enormous best seller and made Gray known to millions of Americans heretofore unfamiliar with her writing. Akihito, who became emperor of Japan in 1989, remained a lifelong friend and correspondent, visited her several times over the years, and sent her flowers each year on her birthday for the rest of her life.

After her years in Japan, Gray wrote twenty more books, including children's fiction as well as biographies for both children (among them *Mr. Whittier*, 1974) and adults (*Friend of Life: The Biography of Rufus M. Jones*, 1958). She also wrote two additional memoirs, *Return to Japan* (1960), an account of her return visit to the crown prince and his family in 1959 for Akihito's wedding, and *Being Seventy: The Measure of a Year* (1978). Her memoirs; her autobiography, *Quiet Pilgrimage*; and her last book, *A Quest There Is* (1982), a meditation on Quaker beliefs, were published under the name Elizabeth Gray Vining. She lived for many years prior to her death at a Quaker retirement community in Kennett Square, Pennsylvania.

• Many of Gray's papers are housed, under the name Elizabeth Gray Vining, in the de Grummond collection in the McCain Library and Archives at the University of Southern Mississippi. The most reliable source of biographical information is her autobiography, *Quiet Pilgrimage*. In addition, see Chuck Fager, "An Appreciation of Elizabeth Gray Vining," in *Types & Shadows: Journal of the Fellowship of Quakers in the Arts*, no. 16 (Winter 1999–2000). An obituary is in the *New York Times*, 1 Dec. 1999.

ANN T. KEENE

VON MISES, Ludwig (29 Sept. 1881–10 Oct. 1973), economist and social philosopher, was born Ludwig Heinrich Edler von Mises in Lemberg, Austria-Hungary (today, Lviv, Ukraine), the son of Arthur von Mises, a railroad engineer and civil servant, and Adele von Mises, born Adele Landau. Von Mises was still a small boy when his family moved to Vienna. In 1892 he entered the *Akademisches Gymnasium*, where he received a humanistic education and befriended Hans Kelsen. Early on, von Mises was particularly interested in history and politics. After graduation, in 1900, he therefore began to study at the department of law and government science of the University of Vienna.

Studying under Carl Grünberg, von Mises started off as an exponent of the so-called Historical School of government science, which stressed fact-finding and despised theoretical analysis. But in the fall of 1903 he read Carl Menger's *Principles of Economics*, the foundational text of the Austrian School of economics. The book turned him away from the historicist approach, and in the following years he deepened his studies of economic theory, especially in the seminar of Eugen von Böhm-Bawerk, a former finance minister and champion of the Austrian School.

Von Mises graduated in February 1906 (Juris Doctor). He started a career as a civil servant in Austria's financial administration, but after a few months he quit in disgust with bureaucracy. For the next two years he worked as a trainee in a Vienna law firm and also started lecturing on economics. In early 1909, he joined the Vienna Chamber of Commerce and Industry, where he worked for the next twenty-five years.

The chamber was at the time a semi-governmental organization and through its publications exercised a considerable influence on Austrian politics.

Parallel to his pecuniary activities, von Mises pursued ambitious scholarly interests and wrote a treatise on money and banking. In his *Theorie des Geldes und der Umlaufsmittel* (1912), translated into English in 1934 as *Theory of Money and Credit*, he made two lasting contributions to economics: he demonstrated how Menger's value theory applied to money, and he presented a new business-cycle theory in the light of which economic crises appeared as resulting from inflation-induced misallocations of resources. He also showed that money could not possibly be neutral, and that increases of the quantity of money always had redistribution effects.

During World War I von Mises served as a front officer in the Austro-Hungarian artillery and as an economic adviser to the War Department. He gained firsthand experience of the realities of war socialism, which he would later digest in his theory of socialism, and of the dynamics of interventionism. In the last year of the war, he received a prestigious but unpaid appointment as *professor extraordinarius* at the University of Vienna.

After the war, von Mises briefly became an adjunct member of the new republican government of German Austria (the name carried by the Austrian state until September 1919). He was the authority on financial matters pertaining to foreign affairs. But his main practical achievement in this period was to persuade socialist leader Otto Bauer, a former friend and fellow student, not to attempt a Bolshevik coup. He also published a book explaining the collapse of multicultural Austria-Hungary. In *Nation, Staat und Wirtschaft* (1919; translated as *Nation, State, and Economy* [1983]), he argued that German imperialism had resulted from applying the power of the State to solve the problems of the multicultural communities that prevailed in the eastern provinces of Germany and Austria.

In the fall of 1919, von Mises wrote his most famous essay, on "economic calculation in the socialist commonwealth." He argued that a socialist leadership lacked the essential tool for the rational allocation of resources—economic calculation—and that only the money prices of a capitalist economy make it possible to compare alternative investment projects in terms of a common unit. Two years later he published a treatise on socialism (*Die Gemeinwirtschaft*, 1922), which had a decisive impact on a whole generation of rising intellectual leaders—men such as F. A. Hayek and Wilhelm Röpke, who after World War II would lead the nascent neoliberal movement.

During the early 1920s, von Mises successfully fought inflation in Austria and had a decisive impact on the monetary and financial reforms of 1922. But he could not prevent the steady increase of government regulations and the deterioration of Austria's public finances. He developed an entire new theory of interventionism showing that government intervention is inherently counterproductive. Practically this ruled out all variants of third-way policies and left *laissez-faire* capitalism as the only meaningful option on the political menu. In 1927, he published a concise presentation of his utilitarian political philosophy in *Liberalismus*.

In the late 1920s he started publishing papers on the epistemological character of economics. Von Mises argued that economic science could not be verified or refuted through the analysis of observable data. Economics was an *a priori* science like mathematics or logic or geometry. Moreover, economics was just a part of a larger social science, which he would later call "praxeology"—the logic of human action.

Von Mises eventually found the time to synthesize the various strands of his work into a praxeological treatise when, in 1934, he was called to a chair in international economic relations at the Graduate Institute for International Studies in Geneva. He would hold the chair until 1940, the same year in which his treatise was finally published under the title *Nationalökonomie*. While in Geneva, in 1938, he married Margit Serény (née Herzfeld), whose daughter Gitta Serény later became a well-known author. They had no children from the marriage.

In July 1940, von Mises left Geneva to avoid being captured by the German armies or being delivered to them by the Swiss government. He moved to New York City and started a new life, receiving U.S. citizenship in 1946. Von Mises first found employment with the National Bureau of Economic Research, then worked as an advisor for the National Association of Manufacturers, and eventually became a visiting professor at New York University in 1945. He would "visit" with NYU for the next twenty-four years.

In the U.S. he became the *spiritus rector* of the renascent libertarian movement, to which he gave a distinct Austrian School flavor. Close ties to the Foundation for Economic Education, the William Volker Fund, and the Earhart Foundation gave him the necessary organizational and financial backing. Von Mises's influence reached a peak in the years following the publication of the English version of his praxeological treatise under the title *Human Action* (1949). In the 1950s, his NYU seminar produced many important intellectual leaders of postwar libertarianism, such as Murray Rothbard, Hans Sennholz, George Reisman, Ralph Raico, Leonard Liggio, and Israel Kirzner.

In the 1960s, von Mises's vigor and productivity declined very considerably. He taught at NYU until 1969 and died in New York City. For almost four decades, he had been the uncontested dean of the Austrian School of economics. His legacy as a social philosopher inspired a thriving movement.

• Von Mises's post-1938 personal papers are collected in the archive of Grove City College in western Pennsylvania. Copies of both the Moscow Archive papers and the Grove City Archive papers are held at the Mises Institute in Auburn, Alabama. Smaller notable collections of correspondence and other materials can be found at the Vienna Chamber of Commerce, at the Graduate Institute for International Studies in Geneva, Switzerland, and at the Hoover Institution of Stanford University. An essential source on von Mises's life and work is his autobiographical *Notes and Recollections* (1978), but this work only covers the time until 1940 and it only deals with his intellectual development in the context of the times. Another important source, dealing more with von Mises the man, is Margit von Mises's *My Years with Ludwig von Mises* (1984). Von Mises's pre-1938 personal papers are collected in the Special Archive for Historico-Documentary Collections, in Moscow, Russia. In 1938, these papers were stolen from von Mises's Vienna apartment. At the end of World War II, the Red Army found them, together with many other collections, in an abandoned train in Bohemia and brought them to Moscow. There is not yet any comprehensive biography of von Mises in print. Good intellectual biographies are Murray Rothbard's *Ludwig von Mises: Scholar, Creator, Hero* (1988) and Israel M. Kirzner's *Ludwig von Mises: The Man and His Economics* (2001). Rothbard also wrote *The Essential von Mises* (1973). An obituary is in *Human Events*, 20 Oct. 1973, p. 7.

JÖRG GUIDO HÜLSMANN

W

WAGNER, Gorgeous George (24 Mar. 1915–26 Dec. 1963), professional wrestler, was born George Raymond Wagner in Butte, Nebraska, the son of Howard James Wagner and Bessie May Francis. His family moved to Waterloo and Sioux City, Iowa, before settling in Houston, Texas, when Wagner was seven years old. In 1929 he dropped out of school, did odd jobs to help support his family, and began wrestling at the Houston YMCA. In 1932 Wagner received thirty-five cents for winning a seven-minute bout at a local carnival. His YMCA wrestling coach, however, disapproved of Wagner's participation in the match, reminding him afterward that he was no longer an amateur but a professional. The coach's sentiment reflected the disdain many in the amateur wrestling community held toward professional wrestling, which by then was more popular entertainment than skilled and competitive sport.

Wagner, however, preferred earning a living as a professional wrestler to menial work. In 1938 he captured his first championship, defeating Buck Lipscomb for the Northwest middleweight crown in Eugene, Oregon. That year, and again in 1941 and 1943, he won the Pacific Coast Light Heavyweight Championship. On 26 May 1950 Wagner defeated Don Eagle and claimed the American Wrestling Association (AWA) world heavyweight title. On 27 July 1950, in a bout to unify the AWA and the National Wrestling Association (NWA) and to decide a single world heavyweight champion, Wagner lost to Lou Thesz, the NWA world heavyweight champion, in Chicago, Illinois.

Standing 5 feet, 9 inches and weighing 215 pounds, Wagner was an average, physically unimposing wrestler. In 1943 he made radical changes to his appearance, wardrobe, and style to improve his popular appeal. He grew his dark hair long, died it platinum blond, and permed it into tight waves, which he pinned back with gold-plated bobby pins. He entered the ring to the tune of "Pomp and Circumstance," wearing brightly colored satin robes with fur collars, and accompanied by a valet, who removed the robe, spread a rug at Wagner's feet, and sprayed the wrestling area with a perfumed disinfectant. Although he coined the nickname "the Human Orchid," Wagner became known by the moniker "Gorgeous George" after a ring announcer overhead a woman in the audience exclaim, "Isn't he gorgeous?" In 1950 Wagner officially changed his name to "Gorgeous George."

The use of the perfumed disinfectant evolved more out of hygienic necessity than theatrical display. After learning from his physician that an infected mat burn resulted from wrestling on a dirty mat, Wagner instructed his valet, "Jeffries" (a role played by several individuals over time), to arrive at the arena before the fans and other competitors and spray the wrestling mat and ring with a disinfectant. In 1944 he and Jeffries arrived for a tournament in Klamath Falls, Oregon, after several bouts had taken place. Insisting upon wrestling on a clean mat, Wagner had Jeffries enter the ring before him and spray the area. The crowd responded in a variety of ways, as some were amused and others repulsed by the act. Wagner adopted it as part of his prematch repertoire, eventually requiring Jeffries to disinfect his opponent with the spray. Another gimmick was to remove his gold-plated bobby pins and toss them to his adoring female fans. Wagner adopted this ploy after his opponents demanded the removal of the pointed pins from his hair before matches.

Wagner's popularity coincided with the rise of television in the late 1940s and early 1950s. He made his first television appearance on 11 November 1947, an event ranked forty-fifth in the top one hundred television acts of the twentieth century by *Entertainment Weekly*. His theatrical style suited the new medium, and he was an instant national celebrity. The sportswriter Arthur Daley of the *New York Times* described one of Wagner's televised bouts as "insufferable" and "obnoxious," noting that "if Gorgeous George has not killed wrestling in New York for good and all, the sport is hardy enough to survive a hit by an atomic bomb" (quoted in Roberts and Olsen, p. 100). Hardy indeed, professional wrestling not only survived Wagner's histrionics but flourished, in part owing to the proliferation of television.

During his years as a wrestler, Wagner had a wife and two children, whose names he kept from being publicly known. Divorced from his first wife, he married Cheri Dupre, and they had one son. This marriage also ended in divorce.

In 1959, before his last major match, Wagner vowed to shave his head if he lost to Whipper Watson of Canada. After losing to the Canadian, he cut off his golden locks before sixteen thousand fans in Toronto. In 1962 Wagner retired from professional wrestling. At the peak of his career in the early 1950s, he earned as much as $160,000 a year. Wagner owned over one hundred elaborate robes, one trimmed in ermine fur, which cost $1,900. Owner of a 195-acre turkey ranch in Beaumont, California, he earned as much as $128,000 a year from that enterprise. Wagner had known since 1962 that he had liver disease, for which he was hospitalized after his retirement. He died in Los Angeles.

Wagner's appearance, wardrobe, and style were mimicked by other professional wrestlers. For example, in the 1980s Randy "Macho Man" Savage adopted "Pomp and Circumstance" to signal his entrance into the ring. Indeed professional sports in general began to incorporate recorded music during interludes in play and halftimes. Like Wagner, subsequent wrestlers such as Savage and Hulk Hogan grew their hair long and sported ponytails. The appearance and style of these wrestlers blurred the lines between masculinity and femininity, introducing an androgynous figure who evoked conflicting feelings in audiences.

• Profiles of Wagner include Daryle Feldmeir, "Gorgeous Moneybags," Minneapolis Tribune, 8 May 1955. His historic television debut is chronicled in "Gorgeous George Steps into the TV Ring," Entertainment Weekly Television Top 100: The 1950s, http://www.ew.com/ew/fab400/tv100/50sp1.html. For historical examination of the impact of television upon sports, especially professional wrestling and the contributions of Wagner, see Randy Roberts and James Olsen, Winning Is the Only Thing: Sports in America since 1945 (1989). Benjamin G. Rader, In Its Own Image: How Television Has Transformed Sports (1984), and Elliot J. Gorn and Warren Goldstein, A Brief History of American Sports (1993), also consider the impact of television on sports. The history of professional wrestling has been overlooked by historians, but for a short account see Mike Chapman, Encyclopedia of American Wrestling (1990). In contrast, the sociology of the sport has received wide attention, and a good analysis is Sharon Mazer, Professional Wrestling: Sport and Spectacle (1998). Obituaries are in the New York Times and the Los Angeles Times, both 27 Dec. 1963.

ADAM R. HORNBUCKLE

WALKER, Maggie L. (15 July 1867–15 Dec. 1934), educator, social activist, and bank president, was born Maggie Lena Draper in Richmond, Virginia, the daughter of Elizabeth Draper, a former slave, and Eccles Cuthbert, an Irish-American journalist. Her natural parents could not marry. (The Virginia law prohibiting the marriage of mixed-race couples was overturned in 1967, a century after Maggie's birth.) In 1868 Elizabeth Draper married William Mitchell, a mulatto butler who, like herself, was employed by the wealthy abolitionist and Union spy Elizabeth Van Lew. Several years later Elizabeth and William Mitchell found jobs independent of the Van Lews, and moved their family to a rented house on a short street (alley) near the Medical College of Virginia. William Mitchell became headwaiter at the St. Charles Hotel, and Elizabeth Mitchell's work as a laundress was highly regarded. Their combined wages provided the family a tenuous financial security. That security quickly vanished in 1876, when William Mitchell's body was found in the James River, the apparent victim of robbery and murder, though the coroner's report indicated suicide by drowning. The widowed Elizabeth was left to provide for herself and her two small children on the meager income from her laundry business. Years later Maggie Walker described that difficult time in her life. "I was not born with a

silver spoon in my mouth, but with a laundry basket practically on my head," she said (Maggie Walker Papers, "Stumbling Blocks Speech," 1904).

Elizabeth Mitchell's illiteracy probably accounted for her determination to see that Maggie and Johnnie, her other child, received the best education available to African Americans in Richmond in the 1870s and 1880s. They attended the Lancaster School operated by Quakers. Maggie Walker excelled at Lancaster and at the Richmond Colored Normal School. On the eve of her graduation from the normal school in 1883, Walker joined with her classmates in one of the first recorded school strikes by African Americans in the United States. The class of 1883 successfully protested the Richmond Public Schools' discriminatory policy of holding separate graduation ceremonies for white and black students. "Our parents pay taxes just the same as you white folks, and you've got no business spending big money out of those taxes to pay for the theater for white children unless you do the same for black children," they challenged (Branch and Rice).

In the fall of 1883, Walker's former teacher Lizzie Knowles offered her a teaching position at Valley School. Walker accepted and taught there for three years. During that time, she also took business classes at night. In 1886 she married Armstead Walker, Jr., the son of a prominent black contractor. Because married women were not allowed to teach in Virginia, Walker gave up her teaching job. The Walkers had three sons.

At a time when most married women were expected to be contented homemakers, Walker volunteered at the Independent Order of St. Luke (IOSL), the benevolent organization founded by the former slave Mary Prout in Baltimore, Maryland, in 1867. Walker imagined that the Order could become much more than a benevolent burial society. Armed with a respected normal school education and business acumen gained through the successful completion of business classes, she sought ways to strengthen and expand the Order, especially in the areas of education and employment for women. She later was responsible for the establishment of an educational loan fund for needy children and the employment of more women in the Order. She was also the chief architect of the Juvenile Branch, established in 1895 as a training ground for young people.

Walker's rise through the ranks of the Order was swift. With her election as Right Worthy Grand Secretary of the Order in Hinton, West Virginia, in the fall of 1899 Walker became its top executive. She quickly breathed new life and vitality into the Order by expanding the number of councils and recruiting new members. By the 1920s the Order had 100,000 members in twenty-eight states.

Walker is best known as the founder of the St. Luke Penny Savings Bank, which opened for business on 2 November 1903. As its first president, Walker gained the distinction of being the first woman to charter a bank in the United States. In a rousing speech delivered at the 1901 meeting of the Right Worthy Grand Council (IOSL), she exhorted her colleagues to establish the bank. "What do we need to further develop and prosper us, numerically and financially? First we need a savings bank, chartered, officered and run by the men and women of this Order. Let us put our money's together; let us use our money's. . . . Let us have a bank that will take the nickels and turn them into dollars," she urged (*Fiftieth Anniversary-Golden Jubilee Historical Report of the R.W.G. Council, I. O. St. Luke 1867–1917*, pp. 23–24). In 1930 Walker led a successful merger that resulted in the present-day Consolidated Bank and Trust Company, the oldest continuously existing black-owned and black-run bank in the United States.

During her tenure as its leader (1899–1934), Maggie Lena Walker enlarged the operations of the Order to include enterprises of importance to the African-American community, including a weekly newspaper, the *St. Luke Herald* (first published in 1902 to serve as the mouthpiece of the Order) and the Emporium department store (with a bank inside) that opened on Broad Street in Richmond on 10 April 1905. Walker's idea of one-stop shopping was far ahead of its time; however, the overriding purpose was to provide an alternative to the white-owned department stores that routinely discriminated against African Americans.

Walker was an outspoken opponent of lynching and of discrimination against African Americans and women. As such she fought vigorously to eradicate all forms of discrimination. She was among the four black bank presidents who organized and led a nine-month boycott of Richmond's newly segregated streetcars in 1904. She spearheaded the 1920 voter registration drives after the passage of the Nineteenth Amendment, which gave women the right to vote. Walker ran on the Lily Black Republican ticket in Virginia in 1921 as a candidate for superintendent of public instruction. Another prominent name on the ticket was the firebrand editor of the *Richmond Planet*, John Mitchell, Jr., who ran as a candidate for governor. (No candidate on the Lily Black Republican ticket was elected.) In November 1917 she cofounded the Richmond chapter of the National Association of Colored People (NAACP) and became its first vice president. She was elected in 1924 as a member of the national board of directors. She also served on the boards of the National Association of Colored Women, the Virginia Interracial Commission, and the Negro Organization Society of Virginia.

Believing that education was the best means of leveling the economic and social playing field for African Americans, Walker worked tirelessly with Mary McLeod Bethune, Janie Porter Barrett, Nannie Burroughs, Charlotte Hawkins Brown, and other nationally known educators to ensure quality education for black children. She contributed generously to the schools founded by each of these women.

Walker's health gradually declined, and by 1928 she was using a wheelchair. She equipped her home with an elevator and altered her Packard car to accommodate her wheelchair so she could continue to work. She died at her home on East Leigh Street in Richmond. Her home was designated a National Historic Site on 15 July 1979, the anniversary of her birth. Never giving up or allowing society or circumstances to "circumscribe" her sphere, Walker widened the arena of opportunity for all people in education, business, and politics.

• The Walker Papers, which include speeches, diaries, and letters, are in the Archives, Maggie L. Walker National Historic Site, Richmond, Va. These primary sources provide the best and most complete information. They include Gertrude Marlow, "Ransom for Many: Life of Maggie Lena Walker," an unpublished comprehensive study of Walker's life conducted for the National Park Service, and Walker's "Stumbling Blocks Speech" (1904). In 1927, Walker's former classmate and co-leader of the 1883 school strike, Wendell P. Dabney, wrote *Maggie L. Walker: Her Life and Deeds* as part tribute and part biography. A useful biography of Maggie Walker written for young readers is Muriel M. Branch and Dorothy M. Rice, *Pennies to Dollars: The Story of Maggie Lena Walker* (1997). *Our Inspiration: The Story of Maggie Lena Walker* (1998), a television documentary written by William H. Sydnor, Jr., and produced by PBS station WCVE, is also a valuable source of information.

MURIEL MILLER BRANCH

WALTON, Lester A. (20 Apr. 1882–16 Oct. 1965), diplomat, journalist, civil rights activist, and theater producer, was born Lester Aglar Walton in St. Louis, Missouri, the son of Benjamin A. Walton, Sr., and Olive May Camphor Walton. After graduation from Sumner High School, Walton began his career as a journalist at the *Globe-Democrat*. He worked as a court reporter, covered general stories, and wrote a column on golf for the *St. Louis Star Sayings*, later the *St. Louis Star-Time*, from 1902 to 1906. Walton was thus the first African American to write for a white daily, and he was an active member of the St. Louis Press Club. For a time he also wrote for the *St. Louis Post-Dispatch*, under Herbert Bayard Swope.

During these years Walton and Ernest Hogan, a well-known entertainer, were copyrighting the words and music, respectively, to songs such as "Time Will Tell," "You Ain't Nothin' and You Never Will Be," and "My Mind Is Rolling." By 1906 Hogan had persuaded him to come to New York as his personal assistant. It was an avocation Walton enjoyed. He was still writing songs in 1926 ("When a Woman Will She Will" and "All for One, One for All") and during the 1950s, when he wrote the lyrics and music for "Welcome to New York," dedicated to Mayor Robert F. Wagner, and "Jim Crow Has Got to Go," a popular song at civil rights demonstrations.

In New York Walton continued reporting, and in 1908 he was named managing editor and drama critic for the *New York Age*, an important black newspaper founded in 1880. He held these positions until 1914, and again from 1917 to 1919. Walton and Gladys Moore, daughter of Fred A. Moore, who published the *Age*, married in June 1912 in Brooklyn; they had two daughters. In 1913 Walton launched a campaign to persuade newspapers and magazines of the need for "typographical emancipation" by capitalizing the word "Negro."

During his two years away from journalism Walton turned his abilities to developing Harlem theater. With a Mr. Morganstern he coleased and comanaged the Lafayette Theater, which opened in 1912. In this position until 1916, he expanded the range of opportunities for black theater professionals, especially playwrights and actors. Dancers and singers, although they too had a dearth of venues to display their talents, were in greater demand. The company came to be known as the Lafayette Players, enjoying critical acclaim into the 1930s and training actors who later achieved wider recognition. From 1916 to 1919 Walton again pursued his two interests, working with the Military Entertainment Service, a World War I forerunner of the United Service Organizations (USO), to provide shows for black servicemen, and as a correspondent at the Versailles Peace Conference in 1919 for the *New York Age*. Later in the year he returned to the Lafayette as sole manager, remaining until 1921 but keeping his interest for many years after.

In 1922 Walton joined the staff of the *New York World*, where his former colleague Swope was managing editor. He wrote for both the daily and Sunday editions, covering general news stories as well as subjects of particular interest to the Harlem community. The *World* was one of the first papers to capitalize "Negro." When it ceased publication in March 1931, just weeks after Walton's father died, black papers mourned Walton's personal and professional losses and noted the effect on the black population of the demise of the sympathetic newspaper. The *Pittsburgh Courier* described Walton as "the only Negro who rubbed shoulders with the best newspaper men of the city on even terms." In May Walton moved to another white paper, the *New York Herald Tribune*, resigning after a short time because he was refused a byline. Returning to the *New York Age* as associate editor in 1932, he was able to pursue another of his interests, Liberia, the nation founded in 1822 by the American Colonization Society as a homeland for freed slaves. Walton was an authority on Liberia, having traveled there in 1933 as an observer during the controversy that resulted in severed relations between Liberia and the United States. He wrote several articles on the small African nation, including one on its industrial development for *Current History* in April 1929. As international correspondent for his newspaper and for the Associated Negro Press, Walton developed further his interest in the country.

When the United States resumed relations with Liberia, President Franklin D. Roosevelt in 1935 appointed Walton envoy extraordinary and minister plenipotentiary, a position he held until 1946, longer than any other minister to that country. The *New Yorker* briefly interviewed him and commented, "He was chosen, of course, because Liberia is populated in part by American Negroes and their descendants"

(31 Oct. 1942). During his tenure Walton successfully negotiated treaties with the United States dealing with extradition, commerce, navigation, and aviation. A port was constructed in Monrovia, the capital, as was Robertsfield air base. Later known as Roberts International Airport, it was a valuable supply link during World War II.

Walton wrote the entry on Liberia for the 1947 edition of the *Encyclopedia Britannica*, and he acted as advisor to the Liberian delegation to the United Nations General Assembly during 1948–1949. When the New York City Commission on Human Rights was formed in 1955, he was one of its original members. Walton remained on the commission until 1964, when crippling arthritis forced him to retire, with emeritus status. In 1957 he helped settle the dispute between the *New York Amsterdam News* and the New York Newspaper Guild. Walton was a founder of the Negro Actors Guild and served on its board, as well as on the board of the Coordinating Council of Negro Performers. During his six decades of professional life Walton belonged to many theatrical, political, and journalism groups, and he received numerous honors. In 1927 Lincoln University in Pennsylvania awarded him an honorary master of arts and Wilberforce University in Ohio a doctor of laws. Liberia conferred upon him its highest award, the Grand Band, Humane Order of African Redemption, in 1947, the same year he was elected a fellow of the American Geographic Society. Walton died in Harlem.

Walton made historic contributions in the three careers he followed, seemingly all at the same time. The common denominator in all his activities was his desire for full integration of African Americans into U.S. society. He played a pioneering role in developing dramatic roles for black actors at a time when minstrel shows were common fare. He was a prolific writer for both black and white newspapers when society was strictly segregated. His diplomatic skills resulted in friendly relations between the United States and Liberia, and his civic work in New York advanced equality in housing and other civil rights.

• The Lester A. Walton Papers, 1903–1977, at the Schomburg Center for Research in Black Culture, New York Public Library, comprise twenty-three boxes or eleven and a half linear feet. His several careers in entertainment, diplomacy, journalism, and politics are documented, as are personal matters. The center also holds a microfiche clipping file with articles written from 1927 to 1965 by and about Walton from both black and white sources. G. James Fleming and Christian E. Burckel, eds., *Who's Who in Colored America* (7th ed., 1950), provides useful information. See also Marguerite Cartwright, "Lester A. Walton—Distinguished Diplomat," *Negro History Bulletin*, Oct. 1955, pp. 12–13. Obituaries are in the *New York Times*, 19 Oct. 1965, and the *New York Amsterdam News*, 23 Oct. 1965.

BETTY KAPLAN GUBERT

WASHINGTON, Augustus (1820 or 1821–7 June 1875), abolitionist, photographer, and Liberian statesman, was born in Trenton, New Jersey, the son of Christian Washington, a former slave from Virginia who operated an oyster saloon, and a woman who is identified only as a native of South Asia. She apparently died soon after his birth, for his father remarried in October 1821. Washington was raised in Trenton and until early adolescence attended school with white students. When access to such schooling ended in the face of growing racism, he was left to continue his education on his own. He worked for his father for several years, studied intermittently, and became an avid reader of Benjamin Lundy's *Genius of Universal Emancipation* and William Lloyd Garrison's *Liberator*. These papers aroused Washington's hatred of slavery and racial prejudice and inspired him to become an activist. Eager to contribute to the uplift of his community, he organized a debating society and, at the age of sixteen, briefly conducted a small school for black children. In 1837 Washington heeded the advice of a prominent abolitionist, most likely Lewis Tappan, and enrolled in the Oneida Institute, a progressive academy and college in Whitesboro, New York, that combined academics with a program of manual labor. He remained there for nearly a year and a half and completed both the preparatory course and his freshman year. When a lack of funds forced him to leave school and seek employment in 1838, he secured a teaching post at the African Public School in Brooklyn and also served as a subscription agent and correspondent for the influential *Colored American* newspaper.

An advocate for unrestricted black suffrage, Washington was a delegate to the Convention of the Colored Inhabitants of the State of New York held in Albany in 1840, and he afterward organized mass meetings in support of a petition drive to secure the franchise. Like other abolitionists he opposed the American Colonization Society's campaign to send free blacks and manumitted slaves to Africa. "I abhor with intense hatred the motives, the scheme, and spirit of colonization," he declared in the *Colored American* (31 July 1841).

With assistance from friends in the abolitionist movement, Washington resumed his formal education. In 1841 he was admitted to the Kimball Union Academy in Meridan, New Hampshire, and in 1843 entered Dartmouth College as its sole African-American student. To support himself, Washington turned to the fledgling field of photography and became one of its earliest African-American practitioners when he learned to make daguerreotypes during the winter of his freshman year. He parlayed his new skill into a profitable enterprise by daguerreotyping members of the Dartmouth faculty and residents of the town of Hanover, but he put his camera aside when his portrait business interfered with his studies. As a consequence, he was unable to keep pace with debts incurred at Dartmouth and left the college in the autumn of 1844.

Settling in Hartford, Connecticut, Augustus Washington took charge of that city's North African School. He taught classes in the basement of the Talcott Street Congregational Church—pastored by the Reverend James W. C. Pennington—until sometime in 1846 when he returned to the practice of photography and opened one of Hartford's first daguerrean galleries. Advertising his services in antislavery newspapers, including Connecticut's *Charter Oak* and New York's *Ram's Horn*, Washington initially sought the patronage of those sympathetic to the abolitionist cause. His success is reflected by the fact that soon after opening his gallery, he made the earliest known daguerreotype portrait of radical abolitionist John Brown. At a time when black businessmen faced enormous obstacles, Washington competed effectively against Hartford's white-owned daguerrean galleries and bested his early rivals. By offering quality portraits at attractive prices and astutely marketing his services, he attracted a large clientele that included citizens of all classes from Hartford and its environs.

In 1850 Washington married Cordelia (maiden surname unknown), who was ten years younger than he. The couple had four children. With the passage of the Fugitive Slave Act of 1850, Washington grew increasingly pessimistic about the long-term prospects for African Americans in the United States. Despite his success as a daguerreotypist, he could no longer reconcile his aspirations for the future with the harsh reality of racism in antebellum America. In 1851, after rejecting various emigration options within the Americas, he withdrew his opposition to the American Colonization Society and argued in favor of African colonization in a letter published in the *New-York Daily Tribune*. He announced his intention to emigrate in 1853, and, armed with sufficient photographic supplies to enable him to continue his career as a daguerreotypist, he sailed for Liberia with his wife and two young children.

Washington became one of the first resident photographers in West Africa. His surviving portraits constitute a unique visual record of the republic's early statesmen and business leaders. He later expanded his enterprise by visiting Sierra Leone, the Gambia, and Senegal, where he operated portrait studios on a short-term basis. Although he had planned to earn his livelihood as a daguerreotypist and by running a small store, Washington soon concluded that his future lay in agriculture. He acquired and developed substantial property along the St. Paul River to become one of Liberia's leading sugarcane growers. He also assumed a significant role in that nation's political affairs. First elected to the House of Representatives in 1863 and later chosen as its Speaker, Washington won election to the Liberian Senate in 1871. Two years later he became the founding editor of the *New Era* newspaper. When he died in Monrovia, his passing was noted by the *African Repository* as "a severe loss to Western Africa."

As a pioneering African-American daguerreotypist in the United States and later in West Africa, Washington occupies a singular place in the history of photography. Beyond his achievements in that field, his decision to break ranks with his fellow abolitionists and emigrate to Liberia makes him one of the more intriguing figures of the antebellum period.

• Several of Washington's letters to officials of the American Colonization Society are housed in the American Colonization Society Collection in the Manuscript Division of the Library of Congress and are available on microfilm. For additional letters by Washington, excerpts from his articles for the *New Era* (Monrovia) newspaper, and reports from contemporaries detailing his activities in Liberia, see those issues of the American Colonization Society's *African Repository* published between 1851 and 1875. Washington offers revealing accounts of his early life and his struggles to obtain an education in two letters written to Reverend Theodore Sedgwick Wright on 1 Jan. 1846 and 15 Jan. 1846 and published in the *Charter Oak* (Hartford), n.s., 5 Feb. 1846 and 12 Feb. 1846, respectively.

Wilson Jeremiah Moses, ed., *Liberian Dreams: Back to Africa Narratives from the 1850s* (1998) includes four letters written by Washington between 1851 and 1863 and prefaces them with a concise history of the African colonization movement. David O. White, "Augustus Washington, Black Daguerreotypist of Hartford," *Connecticut Historical Society Bulletin* 39, no. 1 (Jan. 1974): pp. 14–19 and "Hartford's African Schools, 1830–1868," *Connecticut Historical Society Bulletin* 39, no. 2 (Apr. 1974): pp. 47–53, provide valuable information about Washington's years in Hartford. Carol Johnson, "Faces of Freedom: Portraits from the American Colonization Society Collection," *The Daguerreian Society Annual, 1996* (1997): 264–78, focuses on Washington's career in Liberia. Washington is discussed in Deborah Willis, *Reflections in Black: A History of Black Photographers, 1840 to the Present* (2000); however, the entry contains several factual errors. The most detailed account of Washington's life and career is found in Ann M. Shumard's *A Durable Memento: Portraits by Augustus Washington, African American Daguerreotypist* (1999), the exhibition booklet published by National Portrait Gallery, Smithsonian Institution. A brief obituary of Washington is in the *African Repository* 50, no. 8 (Oct. 1875).

ANN M. SHUMARD

WASHINGTON, Grover, Jr. (12 Dec. 1943–17 Dec. 1999), jazz saxophonist, was born in Buffalo, New York, the son of Grover Washington, Sr., a steelworker, and Lillian Washington (maiden name unknown), a beautician. He was exposed to music early in a household where there always seemed to be music, including a steady stream of gut bucket blues, classical, rhythm and blues, and gospel, as well popular jazz of the day. His mother sang in the church choir and encouraged her young son to practice. Grover Washington chose the instrument his father was most fond of, the saxophone. Grover's two younger brothers, who also became musicians, selected other instruments—Michael the piano and Darryl the drums.

At his initial lesson with private instructor Elvin Shepard, Washington meticulously prepared his horn for the tutoring session but was led instead to the piano. There, Shepard explained that the piano was a means of visualizing and understanding both melody and harmony and also an indispensable aid in transcribing the intricate solos and chord progressions of bebop jazz. Washington also learned jazz by listening

to adult musicians: "When I was a kid, we used to sneak into clubs because that was the only way we would get to hear any kind of live jazz," he recalled (quoted in Randolph, p. 8). Eventually, the owner of Buffalo's Pine Grille allowed Washington to quietly sit in the back of the club to observe and learn while sipping iced tea.

Washington played his first professional gig at the age of twelve, for which he was paid in pizza. In high school, he attended summer classes so he could finish early and pursue his music. In 1959, with his parents' blessings, he took to the road with his own band, the Four Clefs. Inexperience took its toll, and the group disbanded soon after. Washington then settled in Mansfield, Ohio, where he roomed above a funeral home and played the organ and worked at odd jobs. Performing at a ski resort with Keith McAllister's organ trio, he recorded on an album, *Let's Ska at the Ski*, an outing that featured Washington on bass and saxophone. McAllister reportedly formed the Down Hill label to produce the recording.

In 1965 Washington was drafted into the army. He was scheduled to go to Fort Gordon, Georgia, and then ship out to Vietnam, but he convinced a company clerk to arrange a music audition for him. He passed the audition and became a member of the nineteenth Army band stationed at Fort Dix, New Jersey. He played mainly saxophone for Uncle Sam but also played the bass as well or other instruments as the need arose.

Washington began moonlighting in Philadelphia and surrounding areas during his off hours to earn extra money and gain exposure, contacts, and experience. He was a less than exemplary soldier and often found himself in a desperate scramble to make it back to the base on time. In November 1966, while playing at the Roadside Grill in Sharon Hill, he met his future wife and partner for life, Christine Jane Bitner. They married in 1967 and had two children. After his discharge from the army in May 1967 the couple settled in Philadelphia, the city that would become his home and launch his stellar career.

Serving as a sideman at recording sessions for the Prestige label gave him his first professional arranging credits and brought him in contact with producers Bob Porter and Creed Taylor. His horn work on Johnny "Hammond" Smith's *Breakout* album (1970) brought him into the company of Stanley Turrentine and the master of "funky" blues Hank Crawford. Washington was gigging steadily in the Philly and New York area when he was called for a sideman session on a Hank Crawford date at the studios of legendary engineer Rudy Van Gelder. As the session progressed, and it became clear that Crawford was going to be detained in Memphis, producer Creed Taylor casually asked Washington if he played alto, offering him the opportunity to put the lead lines and solo work on the recording. Primarily a tenor player, Washington didn't own an alto sax at the time, and a horn was rented for him to complete the record. That session became *Inner City Blues* (1971), Washington's first recording for the Kudu label, a subsidiary of CTI records. With his recording debut behind him, the releases *All the Kings' Horses* (1972), *Soul Box* (1973), *Mister Magic* (1975), and *Feels So Good* (1975) followed. All are characterized by large ensembles, complete with string sections and a core of musicians such as keyboardist Bob James, guitarist Eric Gales, and percussionist Ralph McDonald, who were identified with the CTI sound. *A Secret Place* (1976) *and Live at the Bijou* (1977), also released on the Kudu label, marked a departure from the big orchestrated sound.

Motown records acquired Washington's catalog in the late seventies through a distribution deal gone sour. The relationship with Motown produced the albums *Reed Seed* (1978) and *Skylarking (1980)* before Washington sought greener pastures with Joe Smith and Electra Records. While with Elektra, Washington enrolled in the Esther Boyer College of Music on the campus of Temple University to pursue a Ph.D. in music theory and composition. He submitted a composition assignment for which he earned a "C" grade. The song was *Make a Memory*, a selection that would become one of his most popular tunes on his critically acclaimed album *Winelight* (1980). The record included the monumental single "Just the Two of Us," featuring Bill Withers on vocals, and made Washington a household name. The pressures of maintaining his professional career and his dissatisfaction with some of the attitudes toward jazz he encountered at the college caused him to abandon this scholastic endeavor. Washington did, however, help launch the career of Pieces of a Dream, a young talented instrumental trio from Philadelphia. He recorded for Elektra from 1979 through 1984 and produced seven titles as a leader. He later signed on with Columbia and released six full-length recordings between 1987 and 1999. *Aria* was released posthumously on the Sony Classics label in 2000.

As a bandleader, Washington (although very meticulous in what he wanted as far as his overall sound) understandably afforded his band members the freedom to add their true uninhibited, artistic creativity to the recording project or concert performance. Also, according to his wife, Christine, "He was a great reader and could remember even the most obscure tunes even if only played once many years ago" (interview with Gig B. Brown, 2001). Washington was often dubbed the "Father of Smooth Jazz." While his sound has been characterized as sultry, mellow, and songlike, his setup always incorporated a variety of large-bore (very open) hard rubber mouthpieces and hard reeds, often a Rico Royal 4 or 5, depending on the horn. He was known for his lyrical melodies and earthy blues-drenched solos that evoke even the most remote and guarded emotions.

Washington died in New York City, following the taping of a segment for the "Saturday Early Show" for CBS.

• There is no book-length biography. Useful articles include H. Mandel, "Grover Washington, Jr.: No Tricks To Mister Magic's Music," *Down Beat* 42, no. 13 (1975), pp. 14 ff.; S. Bloom, "Grover Washington, Jr.: Class Act of Commercial Jazz," *Down Beat* 46, no. 8 (1979), pp. 12 ff.; "Grover Washington, Jr.: Evolution of an Artist," *Radio Free Jazz* 20, no. 7 (1979), pp. 10 ff.; A. J. Liska, "Grover Washington, Jr.: The Midas Touch," *Down Beat* 50, no. 4 (1983), pp. 14 ff.; and Linda Randolph, "As Silk," *Temple University Public Radio Tempo*, Spring 2001, p. 8. An obituary is in the *New York Times*, 19 Dec. 1999.

GIG B. BROWN

WASHINGTON, Margaret Murray (9 Mar. 1861–4 June 1925), educator and activist, was born Margaret James Murray in Macon, Mississippi, the daughter of Lucy Murray, a washerwoman and possibly an ex-slave, and an Irish immigrant whose name is unknown. The year of her birth is also uncertain. The 1870 census lists it as 1861, but on her tombstone the date is 1865. It is known that Margaret's father died when she was seven. The next day she moved in with a Quaker brother and sister named Sanders. Although she remained close to her mother and four siblings, Margaret's adoptive parents greatly influenced her life.

The Quakers persuaded Margaret to become a teacher, one of the few professions open to women and one that offered an opportunity to help the African-American community. In 1879 Margaret began her career in the classrooms of local Mississippi schools. In 1880 she entered Fisk Preparatory School in Nashville, Tennessee, to improve her teaching abilities. She apparently claimed to be younger than she was, perhaps to improve her chances for admission. She spent the next eight years working her way through Fisk University as a half-rater, a student who worked half-time and studied half-time. Professors praised her for her intellect. In 1889 she graduated with honors.

Prairie View State College in Texas immediately offered Margaret a position, but she instead taught English at Tuskegee Institute in Alabama. In 1890 she became lady principal at the school, one of the most powerful positions at Tuskegee, previously held by Booker T. Washington's revered late wife Olivia Davidson Washington. Within a year Booker T. Washington began courting Margaret, but she initially resisted his offers of marriage. She quarreled with his favorite brother, reciprocated the hostility of his daughter, and feared taking on the responsibility for his three young children. On 10 October 1892 Booker and Margaret married in Tuskegee.

Marriage meant that Margaret Washington took over the tasks traditionally assigned to a school president's wife, such as the reception and entertainment of guests. Booker T. Washington, who traveled widely to raise funds for his school and to serve as a spokesperson for the race, typically spent six months of every year away from home. Much of the responsibility for conducting the day-to-day activities of the institute as well as for guiding the young Washington children fell upon Margaret's shoulders. Margaret Washington eventually formed a close bond with the boys, but the daughter, Portia Washington, kept her distance.

Margaret Washington fully subscribed to the conservative mission of Tuskegee. In common with her husband, she believed that blacks should better themselves through industrial education with the hope of one day becoming worthy of equality with whites. According to the theory espoused by Booker T. Washington, whites judged blacks according to the lowest elements of the race. For blacks to acquire rights, the race had to be uplifted. Because women bore responsibility for the maintenance of the home and the care of children, they were in the best position to elevate the masses. Unlike her friend and Fisk classmate W. E. B. Du Bois, Margaret Washington never pushed for political rights and never advocated any conduct that could be deemed threatening to whites.

At Tuskegee Institute, Margaret Washington served on the fifteen-person executive board that ran the school in her husband's absence. As lady principal and founder of the Women's Industries Division, she monitored the progress of the female pupils and supervised the female faculty. She also taught every aspect of domestic life, including cooking, cleaning, canning, gardening, sewing, needlework, decorating, crafting, shopping, childcare, and moral values. Many of the institution's female graduates became teachers, thereby upholding Margaret's dictum that educated African Americans had an obligation to serve the race.

Although best known as the wife of Booker T. Washington, Margaret Washington is significant in her own right for helping found the black women's movement. In 1895 she participated in the formation of the National Federation of Afro-American Women. A year later, as president of this organization, she helped merge the group with the Colored Women's League to create the National Association of Colored Women (NACW). The largest black women's organization of the early twentieth century, the NACW copied Tuskegee's "Lifting as We Climb" motto while it called on a united black womanhood to better the race. Margaret Washington edited and published the NACW journal, much to the anger of the antilynching and prosuffrage activist Ida B. Wells-Barnett, who staged a 1912 revolt that nearly overthrew Washington's conservative regime. Washington sought slow and incremental change, but Wells-Barnett refused to submit to injustice and promoted a confrontational style in the manner of Frederick Douglass and W. E. B. Du Bois. While Washington made few public demands on whites, Wells-Barnett used protest and direct action to challenge instances of racism. A badly split NACW elected Washington president for the next four years but adopted a platform in favor of the political activities she had long eschewed. The era of accommodation to racism was waning.

Widowed in 1915, Washington suffered from ill health. Decades filled with an extraordinarily heavy workload had taken a toll, but she refused to retire. Always a much-requested speaker, she in 1919 launched an attack on those blacks who had abandoned their obligations to the southern community by joining the Great Migration to the better racial and economic climate of the North. In 1921 Washington founded and served as the first president of the short-lived International Council of Women of the Darker Races. The association, part of the Pan-African movement, collected and disseminated information about the conditions facing women and children of color around the world. Washington also remained the first lady of Tuskegee after Booker's death, continuing to help run the institute. Vibrant right to the end, she surprised both family and friends by dying in her Tuskegee home.

Washington dedicated her life to social change but refused to attempt to alter the political landscape that made it possible to suppress African Americans. Her brand of conservative activism obligated blacks to better the lives of others without placing a similar burden upon whites. Despite its flaws, this message of accommodation proved enormously popular within black circles in the violence-torn years after Reconstruction. By espousing a strategy for survival and promoting the hope of a better future, Washington became one of the most widely admired black women in the world.

• Washington's papers are in the Tuskegee University Archives in Alabama. Additional information is in the Booker T. Washington Papers, also at Tuskegee. A full-length biography of Washington is Linda Rochell Lane, *A Documentary of Mrs. Booker T. Washington* (2001) Much information about Washington is in works focusing on her husband, including Louis Harlan and Raymond Smock, *The Booker T. Washington Papers* (1974–1981), a thirteen-volume publication. An obituary is in the *Tuskegee Messenger*, 27 June 1925.

CARYN E. NEUMANN

WAUD, Alfred R. (2 Oct. 1828–6 Apr. 1891), artist and illustrator, was born Alfred Rudolph Waud in London. He was descended from an old Yorkshire family, but the names of his parents are not known. (His surname rhymes with *road*.) In 1849 he entered the Government School of Design at Somerset House in London with the intention of becoming a marine painter. Although he did not realize this ambition, he drew nautical subjects throughout his career. While still a student, he also worked as a painter of theatrical scenery. Waud emigrated to the United States in 1850, planning to seek employment with the actor and playwright John Brougham, who was then building a theater in New York City. The theater was still under construction when Waud arrived, however, and he was forced to turn to other artistic endeavors. From 1851 to 1852 he worked as an illustrator for the *Carpet-Bag*, a periodical in Boston, and he divided his time between Boston and New York for the rest of the decade. Around 1855 he married Mary Gertrude Jewett, with whom he had four children. He provided illustrations for a book by W. S. Hunter, Jr., *Hunter's Panoramic Guide from Niagara to Quebec* (1857), and in 1860 joined the *New York Illustrated News* as a staff illustrator.

Waud's work as an artist-journalist covering the Civil War is his most important achievement. In April 1861 the *News* named him a "special artist" and assigned him to cover the Army of the Potomac, the primary Union army in Virginia. At first based in Washington, D.C., Waud met and drew the commander-in-chief, General Winfield Scott, of whom he reported, "I had the honor of shaking hands with him and can safely say that his lion eye is still as imposing as ever, although he occasionally uses his spectacles" (Ray, p. 15). He then moved into the field, where he sketched the First Battle of Manassas in Virginia (21 July 1861) and the resulting Union retreat back to Washington, D.C. This was his baptism of fire. The following month Waud covered a Union expedition to Cape Hatteras, North Carolina, that resulted in the capture of two Confederate forts, and he spent the autumn making sketches of Union military activity in Virginia's Tidewater region. He also contributed occasional articles to the *News*.

At the end of 1861 Waud joined *Harper's Weekly*, the leading illustrated weekly periodical in the United States, as a special artist and continued to cover the war in Virginia. He made quick rough but accurate drawings in the field, which were then rushed by courier or by mail to the *Harper's Weekly* home office in New York. A staff of engravers transcribed the rough drawings into finished engravings that were then printed in each edition. This was the only way Waud's drawings and those of the other special artists could be published; photoreproduction was not invented for another generation.

Waud covered every battle fought by the Army of the Potomac from First Manassas in 1861 to Petersburg, Virginia, in 1865. Unlike the war photographers, whose cumbersome equipment prevented them from getting too close to any military engagement, Waud and his fellow special artists got into the thick of combat. Waud also depicted aspects of life in camp, such as the sutler's store and, on one occasion, the wedding of a Union officer. As Waud reported in *Harper's Weekly* on 3 October 1863, the life of a special artist was exciting but involved much discomfort and danger: "Your artist was the only person connected with newspapers permitted to go upon the recent advance to the Rapidan. . . . It was a very wet and uncomfortable trip part of the time. I did not get dry for two days; and was shot at into the bargain, at Raccoon Ford, where I unconsciously left the cover and became a target for about twenty sharpshooters. Luckily I was not touched; but I did some tall riding to get out of the way" (Ray, p. 29). In September 1862 Waud was detained behind Confederate lines, which presented him with a rare opportunity to sketch the enemy's troops. He was one of only two special artists present at the Battle of Gettysburg (the other was Edwin Forbes of *Frank Leslie's Illustrated Newspaper*) and was the only one to get close to the fighting. His drawing of Pickett's Charge is thought to be the only contemporary depiction by an eyewitness.

Apart from temporary assignments in Washington, D.C., and Virginia's Shenandoah Valley in 1864 and 1865, Waud remained with the Army of the Potomac until the war's end. He was at Appomattox, Virginia, on 9 April 1865, when General Robert E. Lee surrendered to General Ulysses S. Grant. No artist or correspondent was permitted to observe the actual surrender ceremony, but Waud made two drawings of General Lee riding away afterward.

Waud handled a number of assignments for *Harper's Weekly* in the years immediately following the war, the most significant of which was a series of illustrations depicting life in the postbellum South. He also covered the inauguration of President Grant on 4 March 1869 and even designed the invitation to the inaugural ball. His illustrations continued to appear in *Harper's Weekly* through 1870, but by 1871 he had joined a new illustrated weekly, *Every Saturday*. He teamed with the writer Ralph Keeler for a series on New Orleans and the Mississippi Delta. While on this assignment they learned of the Great Chicago Fire (9 October 1871) and hurried to that city to cover the fire and its aftermath. *Every Saturday* ceased publication soon afterward, and Waud subsequently worked as a freelance artist and illustrator. He was one of several artists commissioned by the publisher D. Appleton and Company to illustrate William Cullen Bryant's monumental *Picturesque America* (1872–1874). Waud's subjects included views of Pittsburgh, Cincinnati, New Orleans, Milwaukee, Chicago, Minneapolis, and St. Louis.

Following a brief residence in Bethlehem, Pennsylvania (1873–1874), Waud and his family returned to New York City, where they resided in a twenty-two-room mansion with a staff of servants. Waud earned a good living freelancing and exhibited his work at the National Academy of Design. He specialized in historical illustration and maritime subjects and depicted scenes from the American Revolution—including the Battle of Harlem Heights and the capture of Major John André—and the War of 1812. Although he was no longer employed by *Harper's Weekly*, his illustrations continued to appear there from time to time. His most important work during this period was as one of the contributing illustrators for the series of articles on the Civil War published in *Century Magazine* between 1883 and 1887, subsequently published in book form in 1888 as *Battles and Leaders of the Civil War*. For this Waud redrew in a more finished fashion many of his original wartime sketches. He continued to travel throughout the United States in search of new subjects, and he died in Marietta, Georgia, while on a sketching tour of Southern battlefields.

In the years immediately following his death, Waud's work was all but forgotten. But beginning in the mid–twentieth century his original drawings (rather than the wood engravings after them) were reproduced in books and articles on the Civil War, and this widespread dissemination of his work has restored the reputation he enjoyed during his lifetime as one of the best combat artists of his day. Supreme Court

Justice Oliver Wendell Holmes, then a young Union army lieutenant, wrote to his parents during the war, "Waud is quite a truthful draughtsman." Waud's fellow special artist Theodore R. Davis stated in 1868 that Waud "made for himself a reputation, and became recognized as the best special artist in the field. His collection of sketches is by far the most complete and valuable made during the war" (Ray, pp. 31–32).

Waud's younger brother William Waud (c. 1830–1878) emigrated from London to New York in the mid-1850s and worked as an illustrator with his brother there and in Boston. In 1861 William Waud joined *Frank Leslie's Illustrated Newspaper* as a special artist and traveled widely in the different theaters of war. In 1864 he joined *Harper's Weekly*, where he worked with his brother in covering the Petersburg campaign. He subsequently covered General William Tecumseh Sherman's march through the Carolinas and the Abraham Lincoln funeral train on its journey to Springfield, Illinois. Much less is known about him than about Alfred Waud, and his post–Civil War career is obscure. William Waud died in Jersey City, New Jersey.

• The largest collection of Alfred R. Waud's drawings is in the Library of Congress, Washington, D.C., which owns 1,150 sketches by Alfred Waud and William Waud. A second, smaller collection of drawings by Alfred Waud is in the Historic New Orleans Collection, and the thirty-one sketches Alfred Waud made of the Chicago fire and its aftermath are with the Chicago Historical Society. Other drawings by Alfred Waud are in the Museum of Fine Arts, Boston; the Missouri Historical Society, St. Louis; and the Franklin D. Roosevelt Library, Hyde Park, N.Y. Alfred Waud included himself in many of his drawings, and photographs of him by Alexander Gardner, James Gardner, and Timothy O'Sullivan are in the Library of Congress. The only known likeness of William Waud is a wood engraving showing him sketching, published in *Frank Leslie's Illustrated Newspaper*, 31 May 1862, after a drawing by himself. Frederic E. Ray, *Alfred R. Waud, Civil War Artist* (1974), and Stephen W. Sears, *The American Heritage Century Collection of Civil War Art* (1974), provide good overviews of Alfred Waud's life and career and also contain useful information on William Waud. A short account of Alfred Waud's life and career is in *American Artists and Their Work* (1889). An obituary for Alfred Waud is in the *New York Times*, 10 Apr. 1891.

DAVID MESCHUTT

WAY, Mary (1769– Nov. 1833), artist, was born in New London, Connecticut, the elder daughter of Ebenezer Way, a storekeeper, and Mary Taber Way. Until 1811 Mary Way lived at home. She never married. Her family, though well connected locally, was not rich.

Her earliest artistic production, starting in her teens, took the form of so-called dressed miniatures. These were profiles rendered in watercolor on paper for the sitter's face, hair, and hands (if shown), while the hat or headdress and clothing were rendered in fine fabrics cut out, folded as needed, and pasted on— the effect, a two-dimensional doll. Her sitters were her kinfolk and Connecticut neighbors. The style is unique and readily identifiable. About forty examples are known, three with her name on the back. They measure roughly two and a half inches in height. She also did slightly larger portraits, not "dressed," on paper.

While still in New London, however, she experimented with the miniaturist's best medium, watercolor on ivory. In 1811, her success emboldened her to try her luck in New York, where she moved and advertised. Generally very poor, she gradually established herself, gaining in reputation. In New York she had access to exemplars to copy and to the loan of manuals of instruction as well as tips from fellow painters. She visited others' studios and public auctions. By all these means she continued to advance in difficult techniques that normally required a teacher (which she could never afford). Established practitioners of both miniature portraiture and conventional painting thought her rooms worth visiting; a market grew, slowly, for her portraits as well as her decorative little paintings of didactic scenes popular at the time, with symbolic figures: "Friendship," for example, or "Christ Healing the Blind." The 1818 exhibition put on by the young American Academy of Fine Arts accepted two portraits by her hand. Of one of these, or perhaps some other one created by Way during the same period, her niece says, "It is without exception the most superb piece of painting I ever beheld . . . so much softness and harmony I never saw in any painting. I won't even except Dickinson's *Cupid and the Graces*." Comparison through the half-dozen surviving and identified works on ivory by Way does indeed raise her almost to the level of the best known of her countrymen, Anson Dickinson or Edward Malbone. She is the first woman known to have practiced art as a profession in the United States.

In Way's family correspondence (some 350,000 words!), the great majority consists of letters exchanged among herself, her sister, Betsy Way Champlain, and her niece, Eliza Champlain—the latter two, also painters. A sample is enough to indicate the interest of this collection to students of art history, as well as the qualities of Mary Way herself: her sense of the absurd in herself as well as others, her intelligence and literacy, her curiosity and ambition, her eagerness to learn and teach. She writes to her sister in 1813,

The evils I apprehended when I came to New York was debt and a prison, poverty and disgrace its inseparable attendant. The dread of connoisseurs never once enter'd my imagination. This was in some measure owing to vanity, or that self-conceit which you know is a family disorder, as well as to my ignorance of the art, having had no opportunity to study the work of other painters. I had seen but few equal, and none superior to my own—concluding therefore I had nearly arrived at perfection, I very modestly set myself down a first rate genius. . . . [But in New York, Joseph] Wood has show'd and told me his stile and manner and lent me a book of rules [by John Payne] which he approves and practises. From this I shall make a few extracts. . . .

"The harmony of nature in the colours arises from objects participating of one another by reflection, for there is no light which does not strike some body, nor is there any enlighten'd body which does not reflect its light and colour at the same time. . . ."

Now if all this is Greek and Latin to you as it was to me at first, you must not only cry over it, but study it out as I did. "And where's the profit of this dry study," says I to [William] Williams, as he was endeavoring to expound the matter to my comprehension. "Is not the effect sufficient, without bothering ourselves about the cause?" "The reason is because we do not see them. Without a true knowledge of colours it is impossible for us to discern the beauty and harmony of nature."

And she continues with her exposition. Woods and Williams were painters known in other contexts, while Payne's book was popular in many editions.

Mary Way's efforts and artistic development were cut short in 1818 by the onset of glaucoma; within a year, her niece was obliged to finish her commissions for her. In the summer of 1820, word of her blindness reached the directors of the academy, who put on a benefit exhibition for her relief. The yield of $141.35 was delivered to her with ceremonious compassion by the president, Colonel John Trumbull. By the close of the year she was back in New London, there to live with her sister. While many letters from her were still to be written, through dictation, she leaves no further mark on the record.

Way's work went mostly unnoticed until 1992. Then William Lamson Warren, long an enthusiast and expert in early Americana and connected with the resurrected eighteenth-century site Sturbridge Village in Massachusetts, published an article on her "dressed miniatures," giving them their name. With the publication of her family's correspondence in 1997, she very rapidly became a focus of interest among those seeking to put a personality behind the ordinarily unsigned, nameless surviving American miniatures (they number in the thousands). Overenthusiastic attributions have accordingly cropped up, touching also her sister's work. But Way's place in American art history, albeit a modest one, seems assured.

• William Lamson Warren, "Mary Way's Dressed Miniatures," *The Magazine Antiques* 142 (1992), pp. 540–49, is amply illustrated in color, including a magnification of the most dramatic of Way's "dressed" portraits, that of her younger relative and initial host in New York, Charles Holt, a publisher. For her letters and a treatment of her world in general, see Ramsay MacMullen, *Sisters of the Brush, Their Family, Art, Life, and Letters 1797–1833* (1997).

RAMSAY MACMULLEN

WEAVER, Robert C. (29 Dec. 1907–17 July 1997), economist, political administrator, and educator, was born Robert Clifton Weaver in Washington, D.C., the son of Mortimer Grover Weaver, a postal clerk, and Florence Freeman Weaver. Weaver grew up in a middle-class and educated family, one of seven African-American families in a Washington suburb. His father worked for the post office. (One grandfather, Robert Freeman, graduated with the first class from Harvard's dental school and was the first African American to earn a degree as a dentist.) Weaver attended segregated schools in Washington, graduating from the elite Dunbar High School, where he earned a scholarship to Harvard. In 1925 he entered Harvard, one of only two African Americans in his class. Four years later he graduated cum laude with a B.S. in economics, then he received his M.S. (1931) and his Ph.D. (1934). In pursuing his Ph.D. at Harvard he had to overcome the bias of the eminent Frank William Taussig, a professor who argued that blacks "had no aptitude for graduate work in economics" (Bardolph, p. 363).

At Harvard, Weaver connected with the small core of black students, including John Preston Davis and William Hastie, fellow Dunbar High School alumni who were already attending the law school, and Ralph Bunche in the graduate school of arts and sciences. These friends remained important throughout his career. During their student years they discussed race and politics, especially the inadequacy of the black Republican leadership. When the Great Depression intensified the social and economic problems confronting black America, Weaver and his colleagues looked to the example of Reconstruction, the use of federal power to redress the plight of the slaves. They called on the federal government to ensure black civil and political rights. The New Deal seemed to offer the possibility of similar federal intervention for economic justice.

In the summer of 1933 Weaver and Davis organized the Negro Industrial League to pressure New Deal agencies to address the needs of blacks. They monitored the hearings of the National Recovery Administration to insure that blacks benefited from the program. In the fall of 1933 Weaver was invited to join the New Deal as assistant to Clark Foreman, who had just been named special adviser on the economic status of Negroes for the Interior Department. A year later Weaver assumed Foreman's position as Secretary Harold Ickes's adviser for African-American affairs. In July 1935 Weaver married Ella V. Haith. They adopted one child.

Weaver spent ten years with the Franklin D. Roosevelt administration, first in the Interior Department (1933–1937), then as special assistant to the administrator of the U.S. Housing Commission (1937–1940), and finally during the war with the National Defense Advisory Commission (1940–1942), the Office of Production Management (1942–1943), and the War Production Board (1943–1944). As an economist Weaver believed the key to racial equality was economic opportunity, especially jobs and housing. Weaver focused his administration's efforts on these areas. In 1938 he produced a landmark study, *Urban Negro Workers in the United States, 1925–1936*, which provided the statistical data for his arguments. For example, in his 1946 study, *Negro Labor: A National Problem*, Weaver used employment data from this study as the basis for his argument that African Americans had been excluded from manufacturing jobs in the 1920s and that this exclusion worsened in the 1930s and had a significant impact on their economic status. Furthermore, he argued that discrimination in jobs and segregation in housing both reflected and fed racial prejudice, and required the intervention of the federal government to provide a physical and economic setting in which blacks could achieve their potential. He also expressed his views in analytical articles on economic issues—mostly in the *Crisis* and *Opportunity* but also in publications like the *Journal of Political Economy* and *Atlantic Monthly*. Weaver functioned as a liaison between the New Deal and African Americans, presenting New Deal programs to the black community and communicating African-American interests and concerns to the administration. His approach relied on logical argument supported by reams of data, rather than an emotional appeal to social justice.

During the 1930s Weaver was one of the core members of Roosevelt's "Black Cabinet." While the presence of this group in the administration was unprecedented, its effectiveness was limited. One member, Mary McLeod Bethune, had access to Eleanor Roosevelt and through her to the president, but on the whole black members of the administration had little input into policy development. Weaver's efforts to attain equal treatment for blacks in New Deal programs met with only occasional success, as political concerns made the New Deal administrators reluctant to challenge discriminatory wage and hiring practices in the South. Occasionally opportunity arose. In 1940, near the end of the reelection campaign, an incident at a campaign rally threatened to embarrass the administration among black voters. Weaver used the incident to leverage the promotion of Benjamin O. Davis, Sr., to the rank of general and to arrange for high-level positions in the war preparedness effort for two other blacks, including his old friend Hastie.

Weaver left federal service in 1944. During the next fifteen years he held a variety of positions. He served as the director of the Mayor's Committee on Race Relations in Chicago (1945–1946), on the National Council on Housing, and with the United Nations Relief and Rehabilitation Administration (1946); he served as director of the John Hay Whitney Foundation's Opportunity Fellowship Program (1948–1955) and held positions with the Fulbright Fellowship program, the Julius Rosenwald Fund, and the Ford Foundation (1959–1960); he was involved with the NAACP, the American Council on Race Relations (1945–1948), and the United Negro College Fund; he served on the faculty at Northwestern University, New York University, and the New School for Social Research; and he authored two books on race, housing, and employment opportunity. In 1955 Weaver became the first African American to serve in the governor's cabinet in New York State. During these years in the private sector, Weaver remained involved in housing, employment issues, and race relations, and he strengthened his reputation as a scholar with his publications and university work.

Weaver published four books. *Negro Labor: A National Problem* (1946) discusses the difficulty African American workers face in their efforts to gain access to higher-paying skilled jobs. *The Negro Ghetto* (1948) examines residential segregation and housing policy in the North, and the economic factors related to housing segregation. *The Urban Complex* (1964) is a collection of Weaver's writings and addresses from the 1950s and early 1960s on the social, economic, and political problems related to urbanization, while *Dilemmas of Urban America* (1965) is based on the series of Godkin Lectures Weaver presented at Harvard University in March 1965, and examines urban development, urban renewal, and the complexities of race in formulating and implementing urban policy.

In 1961 President John F. Kennedy appointed Weaver head of the federal Housing and Home Finance Agency. Five years later, when President Lyndon B. Johnson organized the cabinet-level Department of Housing and Urban Development (HUD), he named Weaver its first secretary. On 18 January 1966 Weaver became the first African American to serve in the cabinet.

Weaver still believed the solution to racial problems required significant intervention by the federal government. He rejected the more radical and militant elements of black leadership. As the administrator of HUD he broadened his views beyond jobs and housing and was credited with developing many innovative solutions to urban redevelopment, including long-range planning for urban needs, economic incentives to expand home ownership and encourage private investment in blighted areas, and partnerships among the federal government, state and local agencies, and the private sector. During this period he wrote two books on urban problems and urban renewal.

When Richard Nixon assumed the presidency in 1969, Weaver again returned to the private sector. He spent the remaining years of his career in academia as president of Baruch College and then as distinguished professor of urban affairs at Hunter College. His wife of over fifty years died in 1991. Weaver died in New York City.

Weaver's contributions were recognized by a series of awards and honors, including the Spingarn Medal of the NAACP and the Albert Einstein Commemorative Award. On 11 July 2001 the Housing and Urban Affairs headquarters building in Washington was renamed the Robert C. Weaver Federal Building.

Weaver represented a new type of African-American leadership based on appointed government office rather than on prominence in the civil rights movement. He worked within the system rather than outside it. His approach was analytical and academic, and he most often delivered his message in print or in private argument rather than through public oratory. Deeply influenced by the Great Depression, Weaver maintained that racism and the economic plight of African Americans could only be overcome through federal action. He spent his life working to that end.

• The largest collection of Weaver's paper is in the Schomburg Center for Research in Black Culture, New York Public Library. Insight into Weaver's political and social views can best be found in his own writings. The most extensive overview of Weaver's life is the entry by Darius L. Thieme in *Black Heroes of the 20th Century*, ed. Jessie Carney Smith (1998). Much of the scholarly writing about Weaver focuses on his experiences in the New Deal. John B. Kirby, *Black Americans in the Roosevelt Era: Liberalism and Race* (1980), provides the most extensive discussion of Weaver's involvement in the New Deal and the "Black Cabinet." Patricia Sullivan, *Days of Hope: Race and Democracy in the New Deal Era* (1996), relies on three interviews with Weaver to provide an insightful discussion of his youth and his relation to other black members of the New Deal. Other books with material on Weaver's role in the New Deal include Harvard Sitkoff, *A New Deal for Blacks: The Emergence of Civil Rights as a National Issue* (1978), and Raymond Wolters, *Negroes and the Great Depression: The Problem of Economic Recovery* (1970). Weaver is covered in several studies of twentieth-century black politics, including Richard Bardolph, *The Negro Vanguard* (1959), which discusses Weaver's role in the Averell Harriman administration in New York during the late 1950s; and John Egerton, *Speak Now against the Day: The Generation before the Civil Rights Movement in the South* (1994), which provides some coverage of Weaver's work against job discrimination during World War II. Kenneth Robert Janken, *Rayford W. Logan and the Dilemma of the African American Intellectual* (1993), comments briefly and critically on Weaver's efforts to place a friend in a government position. An obituary is in the *New York Times* (20 July 1997).

CARY D. WINTZ

WEBB, Frank J. (21 Mar. 1828–7 May 1894), writer and educator, was born Frank Johnson Webb in Philadelphia. He may have been the son of Frank Webb, a china packer and community activist; his mother's name is unknown. Little is known of Webb's life prior to his marriage to Mary (Mary Webb; maiden name unknown) in 1845. Webb apparently lived on the fringes of Philadelphia's black elite, and he seems to have been related to the Forten family by marriage.

Webb and his wife worked in clothing-related trades, and he participated in the Banneker Institute, an African-American literary and debating society. When their business failed around 1854, the Webbs attempted to move to Rio de Janeiro. Webb was denied passage because of his race, and this event was reported in several abolitionist newspapers.

In the meantime, Mary Webb began giving dramatic readings. Harriet Beecher Stowe noticed her and wrote a dramatization of *Uncle Tom's Cabin* titled *The Christian Slave* "expressly" for her readings. This led to tours of the North, in late 1855 and early 1856, and England, in late 1856. Webb seems to have managed both tours, and he wrote a biographical account of Mary that prefaced the British edition of *The Christian Slave*. Through Mary's readings, Webb built connections with several abolitionists among the British aristocracy.

In 1857 George Routledge and Company published Webb's novel *The Garies and Their Friends*. Prefaced by Stowe and Lord Brougham and dedicated to Lady Byron, *The Garies* was one of the first novels written by an African American. Though akin to the sentimentalism of *Uncle Tom's Cabin*, Webb's novel may well have perplexed Stowe's readers. *The Garies* focuses on free black life in the North, treats Northern white mob violence in depth, considers issues like "passing" and black entrepreneurship, depicts a James Forten–like wealthy black character, and, arguably, begins to assert an emergent black nationalist ethos. Phillip Lapsansky, a modern scholar, characterizes it not as "an antislavery novel" but as an antiracist work, "the first American novel to deal with race relations and colorphobia in the urban north" (Lapsansky, p. 29). It received positive notices from the British press but was all but ignored in the U.S.; it fell into obscurity until the late 1960s.

When his wife's health forced her to seek a better climate, friends among the British aristocracy secured a position for Webb in the post office of Kingston, Jamaica, and the couple moved there in 1858. Though her health briefly improved, she died in Kingston on 17 June 1859. Webb continued at the post office and eventually married a Jamaican native, Mary Rodgers; the couple had four children between 1865 and 1869. Webb returned to the United States without his family sometime in 1869.

Settling in Washington, D.C., Webb tried to revive his literary career while clerking for the Freedmen's Bureau and attending law school at Howard University. He published two serialized novellas and a handful of poems and articles in an African-American newspaper, the *New Era*, between January and April of 1870. While his articles considered racial issues (e.g., school integration), the novellas both focused on white characters in European settings. In his letters to journalist Mary Wager Fisher, he also mentioned completing a second novel titled *Paul Sumner*, which he claimed was superior to *The Garies*. Webb hoped a major house like Harpers would accept it, but the novel was never published.

The failure of the Freedmen's Bureau and of his attempts to make a living through writing led Webb to leave Howard before completing his degree and move to Galveston, Texas, probably near the end of 1870. He secured work at the post office, became active in city and state politics, and edited a short-lived newspaper, *The Galveston Republican*. Webb actively supported radical Louis Stevenson against incumbent congressman William T. Clark, who was a close ally of Texas governor Edmund J. Davis, claiming that, though Republicans, Clark and Davis had not sufficiently supported the black community. Webb's stand offended not only Davis, but also Galveston's powerful black political boss, George T. Ruby; at a public meeting in August 1871, Ruby actually called for Webb's arrest. Davis retained power in the Republican party even though Clark eventually lost to Democrat Dewitt Giddings, and Webb's career as an editor ended. Ruby, though, left the state in 1873, and Webb's relationship with his successor Norris Wright Cuney seems to have been better: Webb attended the 1875 Republican state convention.. His family joined him in Galveston in early 1873, and the Webbs had two more children. For unknown reasons, Webb and his family moved to nearby Colorado County in the late 1870s.

Webb returned to Galveston in 1881 to become the principal of the Barnes Institute, one of the first public schools for blacks in Galveston. He continued as principal and teacher for the next thirteen years, during which the school grew significantly, was renamed the West District Colored School, and sent graduates on to the newly formed Central High School (one of the first black high schools in the state). Two of his children taught in the Galveston public schools. Webb was also active in St. Augustine's Protestant Episcopal Church, which was founded in 1884. When he died in Galveston, his colleagues placed a notice in the Galveston *Daily News* eulogizing him as "a teacher who was ever ready to proffer the hand of aid and the voice of sympathy to the needy. . . ."

Webb remains an enigma in many ways—arguably a "renaissance man" without a renaissance. Prior to the 1960s, his first novel was often dismissed (sometimes as a ruse by a white author), and the manuscript he considered his strongest work has never been found. Intimate with prominent abolitionists on both sides of the Atlantic, he never became an anti-slavery activist. Smart and talented—Stowe described him as "a gentleman of superior cultivation and refinement"—he nonetheless bounced from place to place until the last decades of his life. Generally neglected by scholars, his contributions to literature and education in the face of discrimination mark him as a significant figure among nineteenth-century Americans.

• Two of Webb's letters are housed in the Mary Wager Fisher papers at Duke University. Webb's biographical sketch of his first wife appears in the British edition of Harriet Beecher Stowe's *The Christian Slave* (1856). Records of Webb's educational career are housed at the Rosenfeld Library in Galveston. Biographical studies on Webb include Phillip Lapsansky, "Afro-Americana: Frank J. Webb and His Friends," *Annual Report of the Library Company of Philadelphia for the Year 1990* (1991), pp. 27–43; Rosemary Crockett, "Frank J. Webb: The Shift to Color Discrimination," in *The Black Columbiad*, ed. Werner Sollors and Maria Diedrich (1994), pp. 112–22; Allan Austin's entry on Webb in the *Encyclopedia of African American Culture and History*, vol. 5 (1996), p. 2796; and Eric Gardner, "'A Gentleman of Superior Cultivation and Refinement': Recovering the Biography of Frank J. Webb," *African American Review* 35, no. 2 (Summer 2001): 297–308. Arthur P. Davis "rediscovered" *The Garies* and edited a reprint in 1969. Both the introduction to this volume and Robert Reid-Pharr's introduction to the 1997 edition provide useful critical insight into the novel,

though they contain significant biographical errors. A brief obituary of Webb appears in the 8 May 1894 Galveston *Daily News*.

ERIC GARDNER

WEBB, Mary (1828–17 June 1859), dramatic reader, was born in New Bedford, Massachusetts. Her parents' names and specific details of her youth remain unknown, though nineteenth-century accounts spin rich tales of her parentage and childhood. According to her husband Frank Webb, her father was "a Spanish gentleman of wealth" and her mother "a woman of full African blood" who escaped from slavery while pregnant with Mary and later died from anxiety produced by the Fugitive Slave Act (Webb, p. i). Other sources claim she was the child of a Cuban official, and a letter of introduction written by Harriet Beecher Stowe claims she was sent to Cuba as a child and was educated in a convent. There was even speculation that she was the daughter of the Spanish general and statesman Baldomero Espartero.

In 1845 Mary Webb married Frank Johnson Webb, and the couple settled in Philadelphia, where they worked in the clothing trades until their business failed in 1854. The couple's financial need led Mary Webb to consider "turning her marked elocutionary powers to some practical account" (Webb, p. ii). She studied briefly with H. O. Apthorp, who ran a "vocal institute" in Philadelphia, and gave a private reading in early April 1855. This reading led to her public debut on 19 April 1855 in the Assembly Building in Philadelphia. Billed as the "Black Siddons," after the British actress Sarah Siddons, Webb attracted a racially diverse audience of several hundred, including Lucretia Mott. Her success in Philadelphia led to engagements in Boston and Worcester in May 1855. She read selections from Shakespeare, Richard Brinsley Sheridan, John Greenleaf Whittier, and "the favorite Irish, Negro, and French eccentricities."

While reviews were not uniformly positive and attendance was mixed, events surrounding the readings introduced Webb to a number of abolitionists, including Thomas Wentworth Higginson and Harriet Beecher Stowe. Stowe took the role of patron and apparently provided both lodging and a voice teacher for Webb during the summer of 1855. More important, though Stowe had resisted all requests to dramatize her blockbuster *Uncle Tom's Cabin* (1852), she compiled a selection of slightly revised scenes from her novel under the title *The Christian Slave* "expressly" for Webb's readings. Stowe's selection heavily emphasized black characters and especially black women; of the most interest, Cassy, whose role in the novel is relatively brief (albeit pivotal), has the longest soliloquy in the play and is arguably the center of its final act.

Webb gave the first public reading of *The Christian Slave* on 6 December 1855 in Boston's Tremont Temple as part of an antislavery lecture series set up by Samuel Gridley Howe that included such notables as Wendell Phillips. The event drew over a thousand—

ranging from the black abolitionist William Cooper Nell to the poet Henry Wadsworth Longfellow. Attendees were encouraged to purchase an inexpensive edition of *The Christian Slave* published a few days before. By all accounts, though the text offers stage directions, Webb gave this reading and all subsequent readings standing behind a podium; she relied mainly on vocal variation for characterization and made few gestures. Reviewers from both the mainstream and abolitionist presses agreed that the large audience regularly offered "marked applause" and that Webb had a "sweet voice" and "perfect self-possession."

The Boston reading was quickly followed by performances for large audiences in Worcester and Plymouth and smaller groups in New York City (where she appeared with the abolitionist Oliver Johnson) and Brooklyn. The Webbs' friendship with Nell and Mary Webb's early successes led Nell to introduce them to Amy Post and Isaac Post, who helped secure subsequent engagements in Rochester and Buffalo. During the spring of 1856 Webb embarked on a "western tour" (including a reading in Cleveland), but few details of this trip are known. She gave another performance in Rochester on 5 May 1856 and a week later read at Touro Hall in Hartford, Connecticut. In these later performances Webb still read from *The Christian Slave*, but she also included extensive excerpts from Longfellow's *Hiawatha*, which she reportedly read in "full Indian dress." It seems likely that, as with the singer Elizabeth Greenfield, part of Webb's appeal to audiences was as a curiosity; newspaper coverage consistently discussed her connection to Stowe and her race (often spending significant time commenting on her color). Like Greenfield, Webb both engaged in occasional spectacle (like the Native American costume) and struggled to prove her talent went beyond curiosity.

Soon after the Hartford reading, the Webbs traveled to Great Britain, armed with letters of introduction from Stowe and others. As she had three years earlier for Greenfield, Stowe's friend the Duchess of Sutherland became Mary Webb's patron and opened her home (London's Stafford House) for Webb's first British reading on 28 July 1856. The event attracted several members of Britain's abolitionist aristocracy and was covered extensively by the London press; the *Illustrated London News* even carried a striking illustration of Webb giving the reading. The success of this reading (and the stamp of approval from luminaries like Sutherland) led to other engagements, and when Stowe's sister Mary Beecher Perkins visited London in July 1857, she reported that the Webbs were intimate with several British nobles.

Webb's health declined though, and after a brief stay in the south of France, the Webbs returned to the United States in early 1858 before traveling on to Jamaica, where the Webbs' aristocratic friends had secured a position for Frank. The Webbs clearly had intentions of continuing Mary's career; she gave a semiprivate reading attended by Charlotte Forten and other abolitionists in March 1858 and a public reading in Kingston in May 1858, soon after her arrival in Jamaica. However, her health continued to decline, and she died in Kingston a year later.

Webb has generally been neglected by both historians and critics, perhaps in part because both her fame and her life were quite brief and because she left no personal narrative. Still, along with Elizabeth Greenfield, she is one of the few African-American women who gained international fame before the Civil War. As one of the first African-American women to take the public platform in both the United States and Britain, she paved the way for important events like Sarah Parker Remond's tour of Britain (1859–1861) and for a reconsideration of how black voices are represented in Stowe's work and the larger debates over slavery and race.

• Mary Beecher Perkins's letters mentioning the Webbs are at the Harriet Beecher Stowe Center, Hartford, Conn. Frank Webb's introduction to the British edition of *The Christian Slave* (1856) provides the most detailed contemporary account of Mary Webb's life, though it was clearly written for promotional purposes. Webb's readings were covered in several newspapers; a sampling of these accounts and letters from William Cooper Nell mentioning the Webbs are in the microfilm collection C. Peter Ripley et al., eds., *The Black Abolitionist Papers, 1830–1865* (1981). Phillip Lapsansky, "Afro-Americana: Frank J. Webb and His Friends," *Annual Report of the Library Company of Philadelphia for the Year 1990* (1991), marked the beginning of modern consideration of Mary Webb's life. Susan F. Clark, "Solo Black Performance before the Civil War: Mrs. Stowe, Mrs. Webb, and 'The Christian Slave,'" *New Theatre Quarterly* 13 (Nov. 1997): 339–48; and Eric Gardner, "Stowe Takes the Stage: Harriet Beecher Stowe's *The Christian Slave*," *Legacy, A Journal of American Women Writers* 15, no. 1 (Spring 1998): 78–84, offer further biographical information and analyze Webb's performances and reception. Gardner's "'A Nobler End': Mary Webb and the Victorian Platform," *Nineteenth-Century Prose* 29, no. 1 (Spring 2002): 103–16, studies the Webbs' time in England; and Rosemary Crockett, "Frank J. Webb: The Shift to Color Discrimination," in *The Black Columbiad*, eds. Werner Sollers and Maria Diedrich (1994), includes information on her readings in Britain and Jamaica. An obituary is in the *National Anti-Slavery Standard*, 3 Sept. 1859.

ERIC GARDNER

WEDEMEYER, Albert C. (9 July 1897–17 Dec. 1989), soldier, was born Albert Coady Wedemeyer in Omaha, Nebraska, the son of Albert Anthony Wedemeyer, a civilian employee with the Army Quartermaster Department, and Margaret Elizabeth Coady Wedemeyer. In 1916 Wedemeyer entered the U.S. Military Academy at West Point, New York. His class graduated two years early, in 1918, because of the need for officers during World War I, although the graduates returned to West Point in 1919 for six months of "polishing." Wedemeyer was commissioned a second lieutenant in the infantry, and after attending the infantry school at Fort Benning, Georgia, he was promoted to first lieutenant in 1920, a rank he held until he was elevated to captain in 1935. During these years he served with infantry regiments in the United States, the Philippines, and China and as an aide to generals in the United States and the Philippines. On 25 February 1925 Wedemeyer married Elizabeth Dade Embick, the daughter of Colonel Stanley Embick. They had two sons.

A tall, handsome man and an ambitious and talented officer, Wedemeyer in the interwar period prepared himself for a significant role in a future conflict. Encouraged by his father-in-law, one of the Army's most important strategic thinkers, Wedemeyer began to read widely on the strategic and economic aspects of warfare. From 1934 to 1936 he was a student at the Army Command and General Staff School at Fort Leavenworth, Kansas, which trained promising officers for staff work and command at the division and corps level. From 1936 to 1938 he attended the Kriegsakademie, the German Army's general staff school in Berlin. There Wedemeyer studied German battle doctrine, the place of raw materials, productive capacity, and industrial manpower in modern war, and the relationship between military power and national policy.

Following troop assignments at Fort Benning from 1938 to 1940, Wedemeyer, recently promoted to major, was transferred to the Office of the Chief of Infantry, and in 1941 he was assigned to the War Plans Division of the War Department General Staff. Impressed with Wedemeyer's reports about his Kriegsakademie experiences, General George C. Marshall, army chief of staff, assigned him to a group of officers that was charged with preparing a mobilization plan for the United States in case it entered World War II. Largely drafted by Wedemeyer and known as the Victory Plan, the final report spelled out the manpower and material resources the nation would need to defeat the Axis and, with some modifications, served as the basis for America's wartime mobilization.

During the war Wedemeyer rose in rank from lieutenant colonel to lieutenant general while holding posts in the United States and Asia. Initially, he was one of the principal planners in the Operations Division of the General Staff. There he urged a strategy of direct confrontation with Germany through an early cross-Channel invasion of Western Europe, a view that often placed him at odds with British strategists who favored an emphasis on operations in the Mediterranean Theater. In the fall of 1943 Wedemeyer was appointed deputy chief of staff of the Southeast Asia Command. Serving under Lord Louis Mountbatten, he worked on plans for offensives in Sumatra and Malaya and tried to mediate the personal and policy differences between Generalissimo Chiang Kai-shek, leader of Nationalist China, and General Joseph W. Stilwell, commander of U.S. Army forces in the China-Burma-India Theater and Chiang's chief of staff.

When Stilwell was relieved in October 1944, Wedemeyer was named commander of army forces in China and Chiang's chief of staff. At the time, the Nationalist war effort, plagued by corruption, poor leadership, and low morale, was flagging, and Sino-American relations were strained. Wedemeyer worked hard to strengthen Nationalist military capabilities through increased training of Chiang's troops, pressed for more supplies for China, and drew up plans for offensives to reclaim Chinese territory from the Japanese. These steps notably improved Chinese combat effectiveness by the summer of 1945. Equally important, Wedemeyer was more tactful than Stilwell, and while not blind to the political and military weaknesses of the Nationalists, he came to like and even admire Chiang, leading to a definite improvement in relations between the United States and the Nationalist government. After Japan surrendered in August 1945, Wedemeyer remained in China, helping to disarm and repatriate Japanese troops and transport Chiang's troops to areas that had been occupied by the Japanese. When fighting broke out between Chiang's Nationalists and the Chinese Communists in the fall of 1945, Wedemeyer, a strong anti-Communist, urged support for the Nationalists and warned that the attempts of President Harry Truman to bring peace to China through a coalition government would ultimately lead to a Communist triumph.

Upon his return to the United States in April 1946, Wedemeyer was appointed commander of the Second Army, headquartered at Fort Meade, Maryland. In the summer of 1947 Secretary of State George Marshall sent him on a fact-finding mission to assess conditions in China and Korea. Meeting with Chinese Nationalist leaders, he criticized their lethargy and predicted they would be defeated by the Communists unless they instituted far-reaching military and political reforms. Even though Nationalist leaders were not receptive to his urgings, Wedemeyer called for large-scale American aid to bolster Chiang's army and government and proposed that the United States attempt to undercut the growing Communist grip on Manchuria through a United Nations trusteeship. The Truman administration, unwilling to make a major commitment on the Chinese mainland in 1947, rejected many of Wedemeyer's recommendations and suppressed parts of his report for several years on the grounds that they were inconsistent with American policy. This action provided ammunition for critics of Truman who later charged that his administration had "lost" China to communism.

The final years of Wedemeyer's military career were anticlimactic. From 1947 to 1949 he was head of the Plans and Operations Division of the General Staff, and from 1949 until his retirement in 1951 he commanded the Sixth Army at the Presidio in San Francisco, California. In retirement Wedemeyer served as an executive with the Avco Manufacturing Corporation and the Rheems Manufacturing Company and was active in the conservative wing of the Republican Party.

Wedemeyer stands out as one of the Army's premier planners and strategists during World War II and for his efforts to improve Nationalist Chinese fighting ability and Sino-American relations in the final year of the war against Japan. He died at Fort Belvoir, Virginia.

• Wedemeyer's papers are located in the Hoover Institution on War, Peace and Revolution at Stanford University, Palo Alto, California. In *Wedemeyer Reports!* (1958) Wedemeyer is critical of Allied strategy against Germany and argues that the United States could have done more to prevent the Communist victory in China. Additional insights into his thinking can be found in Keith E. Eiler, "The Man Who Planned Victory: An Interview with Gen. Albert C. Wedemeyer," *American Heritage* 34 (Oct.–Nov. 1983): 36–47, and Keith E. Eiler, ed., *Wedemeyer on War and Peace* (1987). His work as a planner and strategist during World War II can be followed in Charles E. Kirkpatrick, *An Unknown Future and a Doubtful Present: Writing the Victory Plan of 1941* (1990); Ray Cline, *Washington Command Post* (1951); and Mark A. Stoler, *Allies and Adversaries: The Joint Chiefs of Staff, the Grand Alliance, and U.S. Strategy in World War II* (2000). His service in China during and after World War II is described in Charles F. Romanus and Riley Sunderland, *Time Runs Out in CBI* (1959); Tang Tsou, *America's Failure in China, 1941–50* (1963); William Stueck, *The Wedemeyer Mission: American Politics and Foreign Policy during the Cold War* (1984); and Forrest C. Pogue, *George C. Marshall: Statesman, 1945–1959* (1987). Obituaries are in the *New York Times* and the *Washington Post*, both 20 Dec. 1989.

JOHN KENNEDY OHL

WELLS, Junior (9 Dec. 1934–15 Jan. 1998), blues harmonica player and vocalist, was born Amos Blackmore in Memphis, Tennessee; his parents' names are not known. He was raised on a farm just outside of nearby Marion, Arkansas, and attended school through grade school but did not pursue a high school education. Wells, as he was known by the late 1940s, began playing harmonica on the streets of West Memphis, Arkansas, where his family had relocated during World War II. Largely a self-taught musician, Wells was influenced by the recordings of John Lee "Sonny Boy" Williamson as well as a local resident, Herman "Little Junior" Parker, who later recorded for RPM and Duke records.

In 1946 Wells moved with his mother to Chicago, where he became attracted to the blues clubs, most of which were located in the city's predominantly African-American West Side and South Side neighborhoods. Within two years Wells was sitting in with well-known local musicians, such as Tampa Red, who enjoyed a protracted engagement at the C & T Tavern in the late 1940s. Wells, now using an electric amplifier to project the sound of his harmonica within the noisy clubs, impressed the more experienced musicians and in 1950 joined guitarist-vocalists Arthur "Big Boy" Spires and Louis Myers to form the Little Chicago Devils, later known as the Three Aces. When drummer Freddy Below joined the group in 1951 they became known as the Four Aces and regularly played the local blues club circuit.

Wells's first major break came in 1952, when Muddy Waters's harmonica player, "Little Walter" Jacobs, left the band to lead his own ensemble, and the departing musician recommended Wells for the band. Although Wells began performing regularly with one of the genre's biggest names, he continued to play "side gigs" in Chicago. In 1953 he made his recording

debut for the local States label. Accompanied by the Aces, who were augmented by pianist Johnnie Jones and slide guitarist Elmore James, Wells made a handful of superb recordings, including "Eagle Rock," "Cut That Out," "Junior's Wail," and "Hoodoo Blues."

Shortly thereafter the nineteen-year-old Wells was drafted into the U.S. Army, an event that slowed down but did not entirely stop his musical career. In April 1954 he went AWOL and recorded a second, equally artistically successful session for States. This time he was accompanied by Waters on guitar, pianist Otis Spann, and bass player and producer Willie Dixon. Forced to serve the rest of his two-year term in the army, Wells could not tour and perform regularly with Waters, and his tenure with the band ended.

Wells returned to the Chicago blues scene after leaving the army in late 1955, briefly rejoining Waters's band before re-forming the Aces—this time with guitarist Syl Johnson joining Below and Dave Myers. The group played for an extended period at the Du Drop Inn on Wentworth Avenue, which helped to solidify his place as a respected and popular blues musician in Chicago. Early in 1957 Wells returned to the studio, signing a recording contract with Mel London's Chief Records. The resulting recordings are not as compelling as the States sides, but they also feature Dixon.

In 1958 Wells began a lifelong affiliation with guitarist Buddy Guy, with whom he performed at Pepper's Lounge and Theresa's, a South Side basement club. Wells recorded a handful of successful selections for London's newly formed Profile label in 1959, including the bestselling release "Little by Little." Four months later Wells recorded his initial (and perhaps strongest) version of what became his signature song, "Messin' with the Kid." The song's swagger and bravado appealed to Wells and his audiences. It is distinctive for its alternating rhumba rhythm and 4/4 sections, which give the song a somewhat unusual rhythmic character. His association with London continued for two more years until the company closed.

In the mid-1960s Wells's career shifted in three important ways. First, he began recording albums for Bob Koester's small but important Delmark label. Wells's 1966 *Hoodoo Man*, which owes an artistic debt to both John Lee Williamson and James Brown, won the *Down Beat* award for the year's best R & B recording and remains a classic. Second, Wells's audience began to expand beyond its core of urban black listeners to encompass younger white listeners; by decade's end, the majority of his public appearances were on college campuses and in clubs. Third, he cemented his relationship with Guy (who appears on *Hoodoo Man*), and the two remained closely associated until Wells's death.

The period between 1966 and 1970 was one of Wells's strongest. He worked on a series of albums for Vanguard; the first was *It's My Life*, some of which was recorded live at Pepper's Lounge. His crowning achievement was *South Side Blues Jam*, recorded for

Delmark, which is arguably Wells's best long-play recording. It included Spann and Guy. In 1970 the Junior Wells–Buddy Guy band also toured with the Rolling Stones, marking Wells's transition to a blues icon in the world of rock and pop music.

Wells spent the rest of his career touring and recording albums in the United States and Europe. The recordings, whose quality was wildly uneven, ranged from a lackluster *Buddy Guy and Jr. Wells: Alone and Acoustic* (1989) to a much stronger band effort in *Better Off with the Blues* (Telarc, 1993). When the band was not touring, Wells continued to perform at Theresa's, his Chicago home base, and at Guy's Checkerboard Lounge. Guy and Wells were often hailed as the "Original Blues Brothers."

Wells contracted cancer in the mid-1990s but continued to perform for two more years. One of his final recordings, *Come On in This House*, received a 1996 Grammy nomination for Best Traditional Blues Album. He died in Chicago.

• There is no book-length study of Wells's life. The notes that accompany recordings provide some of the best information on his life and music. Additional printed resources include Mike Rowe, *Chicago Blues: The City and the Music* (1975); Donald E. Wilcock with Buddy Guy, *Damn Right I've Got the Blues* (1993); and John Cohassey, "Junior Wells," in *Contemporary Musicians*, vol. 17 (1996). An obituary is in the *New York Times*, 17 Jan. 1998.

KIP LORNELL

WELTY, Eudora (13 Apr. 1909–23 July 2001), fiction writer, was born Eudora Alice Welty in Jackson, Mississippi, the daughter of Christian Welty, an executive with an insurance company, and Chestina Andrews Welty. She grew up in a household well stocked with books: "I learned from the age of two or three that any room in our house, at any time of day, was there to be read in, or to be read to" (Welty, *One Writer's Beginnings*, 1984, p. 5). As a child she loved to listen for stories in the conversations between her parents and their friends. "Listening *for* [stories] is something more acute than listening *to* them," she later wrote. "I suppose it's an early form of participation in what goes on. Listening children know stories are *there*" (*One Writer's Beginnings*, p. 14). During grade school she read extensively at the town library, where her mother insisted that she be allowed to check out adult books. In high school she became involved with an artistic-minded group of friends, many of whom went on to successful careers in the arts, including Broadway conductor Lehman Engel and novelist Hubert Creekmore. Welty excelled at Latin, painted and wrote short stories, and was voted "Best All Round Girl" and "Most Dependable" by her senior classmates.

Following her graduation from Central High School in 1925, Welty attended the Mississippi State College for Women. At the school she participated in numerous extracurricular activities, including acting in several plays and helping to found a humor magazine, *Oh, Lady!* The school newspaper published her cartoons and prose, primarily comical detective stories set in Paris and satirical playlets aimed at campus figures. She recalled of her college writing: "I became a wit and humorist of the parochial kind, and the amount I was able to show off in print must have been a great comfort to me" (*One Writer's Beginnings*, p. 79). In 1927 she transferred to the University of Wisconsin in Madison, where she majored in English and minored in art history. While there she decided that she would become a writer. Her parents backed her in this decision, but her father advised that she should also prepare for an alternate career so that she could support herself. After earning her B.A. in 1929, she spent two years taking courses in advertising and typing at the Columbia University School of Business in New York City. Engaged more by the city's cultural life than by her studies, she spent as much time as possible going to the Metropolitan Museum of Art and attending Broadway shows and jazz performances in Harlem.

In 1931 Welty returned to Jackson when her father became ill and died. During the early 1930s she worked as an editor and writer for a radio station and as the Jackson society reporter for the *Memphis Commercial Appeal*. In 1935 she became a junior publicity agent for the Works Progress Administration in Mississippi. In this capacity she traveled throughout the state's eighty-two counties, writing articles about various WPA projects for local newspapers. She said that her experiences forced her to recognize the "complete innocence" of her upper-middle-class life, seeing "at close hand and really for the first time the nature of the place I'd been born into" (*Eye of the Story*, p. 349). With an inexpensive camera, she took hundreds of photographs of what she encountered—African-American children on their way to Sunday school, tomato pickers on a work break, a female bootlegger. Her unposed pictures typically showed Mississippians going about their daily lives with good humor and steadfastness, even amid the conditions of the nation's poorest state in the depths of the Great Depression. Welty made at least two trips to New York City in an attempt to have her photographs published, with some success: one appeared in the book *Eyes on the World: A Photographic Record of History-in-the-Making* (1935), and in 1936 *Life* magazine published six others. That year an exhibition of her work was held at an optician's store on Madison Avenue.

Welty's WPA travels also spurred her to write short stories, with the idea that she might assemble her photographs and fiction in a book. She wrote them spontaneously, sometimes in a single sitting, with little or no revision. Several have become among the most widely anthologized short stories in American literature. "Why I Live at the P.O." displayed her droll sense of humor and her keen ear for idiomatic speech. The story's self-righteous narrator, Sister, recounts her grievances against her younger sister, Stella-Rondo, the spoiled family favorite, which culminates in her removing her belongings from the family home—including a thermometer, a Hawaiian ukulele, and "all my watermelon-rind preserves and every fruit and vegetable I'd put up, every jar"—and setting up quarters in the local post office, where she works as postmistress. (She exults: "They could of all bit a nail in two, especially Stella-Rondo. . . . I says, 'You 'tend to your house, and I'll 'tend to mine.'") Welty was inspired to write the story when she saw an open ironing board in a rural post office. The blackly comic "Petrified Man" portrayed the cruelties and jealousies of women in a beauty parlor gossiping about a side-show freak, who turns out to be a wanted rapist. Some stories focused on African-American experience: "Powerhouse," written immediately after Welty attended a Fats Waller concert, celebrated the imaginative power of jazz musicians; "A Worn Path" portrayed the mettle of an elderly woman on a long trip to a doctor's office. Other stories, such as "The Whistle" and "A Piece of News," dealt with the isolated, circumscribed lives of poor white Mississippians.

Welty offered her photos-and-fiction manuscript, titled "Black Sunday," to a few New York publishers, who expressed their admiration but turned her down. Her first published short story, "Death of a Traveling Salesman," appeared in a small literary magazine, *Manuscript*, in 1936. The *Southern Review*, edited by Robert Penn Warren, published six of her stories between 1937 and 1939. But she had difficulty finding acceptance for other works: "Why I Live at the P.O." was rejected by Warren, *Story*, the *New Yorker*, *Collier's*, *Good Housekeeping*, *Mademoiselle*, and *Harper's*, and at one point she burned the manuscript for "Petrified Man," then rewrote it from memory. In 1939 she met the author Katherine Anne Porter, who became an influential advocate for her literary career. The following year she was accepted as a fellow in the prestigious Bread Loaf summer creative writing program at Middlebury College. In 1941 the *Atlantic Monthly* introduced her to a national readership, publishing "Powerhouse," "A Worn Path," and "Why I Live at the P.O." That year she won an O. Henry Award for "A Worn Path," and her first short story collection, *A Curtain of Green and Other Stories*, was published, with an introduction by Porter. The book was greeted with qualified praise. *Publisher's Weekly* called her a "new and important American writer"; some critics categorized her as a talented regionalist who wrote too much about the grotesque.

During the early 1940s Welty wrote fiction that drew from local lore about the Natchez Trace, an ancient trail through Mississippi that had been traveled by Indians and frontier settlers. Her novella *The Robber Bridegroom* (1942) was a whimsical fantasy pastiche that combined figures from legend (keelboatman Mike Fink) and history (the Harpe brothers, notorious Trace highwaymen) with many elements from European fairy tales. *The Wide Net and Other Stories* (1942) was a collection of stories set in the region around the Trace. In this fiction she abandoned the relatively straightforward storytelling of her earlier work. Her narrative technique was impressionistic, as-

sociational, and ambiguous, "as though the author cannot be quite sure what did happen, cannot quite undertake to resolve the meaning of the recorded event" (*Robert Penn Warren Reader*, p. 197). "First Love" was a disturbing story about a young deaf-mute and his infatuation with Aaron Burr, who had fled to the Mississippi territory in 1807 to plot a conspiracy against the federal government. The folksy, bizarrely comic "The Wide Net" concerned a group of men dragging a river for a (presumably) drowned woman; excited by their task and the fish that they catch instead, they celebrate with a vigorous feast. Several stories explored issues of female identity: "Livvy," about a young African-American woman married to an elderly man; "The Winds," which included many details from Welty's childhood; and the bleak "At the Landing," about a naively romantic woman who becomes the victim of a gang rape. "The Wide Net" and "Livvy" won O. Henry Awards, but critics were sometimes perplexed by Welty's work. Lionel Trilling compared her to the modernist writer Virginia Woolf, intending this to be negative; he felt that both writers were guilty of "coy mystifications." *The Nation* accused her of being obscure but admitted that her fiction had "tremendous emotional impact."

Some Welty scholars have speculated that she was involved during the 1940s in a serious romantic relationship with John Robinson, a teacher and short-story writer from Jackson to whom she dedicated "The Wide Net" and her novel *Delta Wedding*. Robinson, who was homosexual, eventually settled in Italy. Welty never married, telling an interviewer in 1996 that "various things caused me to stay single. . . . I'm sure I would have been very happy had I married and had children. . . . But on the other hand I've had many compensations. Your personal life is something you work out as you can" (quoted in Waldron, *Eudora Welty: A Writer's Life*, p. 225).

During World War II she moved for almost a year to New York City, where she worked as a book reviewer for the *New York Times*. In 1946 she published *Delta Wedding*, a novel about the plantation life of a wealthy Mississippi Delta family during the 1920s. Beautifully written and outwardly idyllic, the novel received—and continues to receive—some negative criticism for its perceived failure to address racial issues. In 1946 *The Nation* dismissed it as "a narcissistic Southern fantasy"; in 1996 *New Yorker* writer Claudia Roth Pierpont called it a "tour de force of distraction —food, flowers, dotty old aunts" that "spread[s] fairy dust over the cotton fields." Other readers have reached the opposite conclusion, that the book is a subtle examination of the penchant of human beings for self-delusion. The novelist Reynolds Price considers *Delta Wedding* to be the "single most illuminating book we have about the fantastic complexity of race relations in the Deep South." The novel addressed what would become central subjects of Welty's later fiction: family life and community life and their attendant traditions, prejudices, and expectations, which nurtured individuals but also pressured them to conform.

In 1949 Welty published *The Golden Apples*, a collection of interconnected stories that has been hailed as one of the masterpieces of American literary modernism, on a par with works such as William Faulkner's *The Sound and the Fury* and T. S. Eliot's *The Waste Land*. The book featured her most far-reaching consideration of gender issues. While exploring misogyny in Southern society and the roles that men and women were impelled to play, her stories also offered possibilities for surmounting gender boundaries. "June Recital" and "The Wanderers" deal with the fates of two unconventional women, an imperious German piano teacher and her rebellious star pupil, in a small Southern town. "Moon Lake" examines the murkiness of preadolescent sexuality by telling the story of an orphan girl, a Boy Scout, and a near-drowning at a summer camp. In "Music from Spain," set in San Francisco, a man strikes his wife for no evident reason and then takes to the city's streets; there he meets a Spanish guitarist, and the two men form a brief but emotionally charged bond. Scholars have often focused on the intertextuality of *The Golden Apples*. Welty alluded to various literary sources—classical mythology, *Paradise Lost*, the poems of William Butler Yeats—taking their tropes and reimagining them in bold new ways. As Rebecca Mark points out, by transforming masculinist texts Welty "liberates our fixed notions of gender and sexuality."

During the early 1950s Welty spent a good deal of time in Europe. She traveled on a Guggenheim Fellowship and stayed in Dublin for extended visits with the novelist Elizabeth Bowen, a close personal friend. Bowen described Welty as "quiet, self-contained, easy, outwardly old-fashioned, very funny indeed when she starts talking" (quoted in Waldron, p. 210). In 1954 she published *The Ponder Heart*, an extended comic monologue in which a spinster details the romantic tangles of her randy but unworldly uncle. A successful Broadway adaptation was staged in 1956. *The Bride of the Innisfallen and Other Stories* (1955) featured a few stories set in Europe, reflecting Welty's travels. Many scholars find this collection to be her least interesting because it reiterated ideas from earlier stories. The years between 1956 and 1966 were a difficult time during which she largely remained in Jackson and tended to ailing family members. In 1960 she turned down a Ford Fellowship grant that would have allowed her to study playwriting at the Actors Studio in New York City. She completed only one book during this period, the children's tale *The Shoe Bird* (1964).

Welty was sometimes criticized for not making public pronouncements about the struggle for African-American civil rights in the South during the 1960s. She later recalled that she "was one of the writers who received dead-of-night telephone calls, when I was harangued by strangers saying, 'Why are you sitting down there writing your stories instead of out condemning your society?'" (quoted in the *New York Times*, 24 July 2001). She responded in an essay, "Must the Novelist Crusade?" initially delivered as a lecture at Millsaps College in Jackson and published in 1965 in the *Atlantic*. Arguing that "morality as shown through human relationships is the whole heart of fiction," she insisted that the novelist's responsibility is to explore human experience rather than to polemicize: "there is absolutely everything in great fiction but a clear answer." Elsewhere she stated that "a fiction writer should let writing speak for itself" (quoted in Waldron, p. 276). She wrote two stories for the *New Yorker* dealing with the racial situation in Mississippi, the O. Henry Award–winning "The Demonstrators" (1966) and "Where Is the Voice Coming From?" (1963). Written on the night of the murder of NAACP organizer Medgar Evers in Jackson, the latter story is a first-person account by Evers's assassin, who says about his victim: "There was one way left, for me to be ahead of you and stay ahead of you, by Dad, and I just taken it. . . . We ain't never now, never going to be equals and you know why? One of us is dead."

Welty's mother and her only living brother died four days apart in 1966, after which the author entered into an intense period of writing. In 1970 she completed *Losing Battles*, a lengthy novel that she had worked on intermittently since the mid-1950s. Set in the poverty-stricken hill country of northeastern Mississippi, the book was simultaneously a rowdy family comedy and an elegy for the passing rural folklife of the South. The novel was presented primarily through dialogue, as the family members swap favorite stories. Welty later said that this presented her with the challenge of having to "reveal what the character said but also what he thought he said, what he hid, what others were going to think he meant, and what they misunderstood, and so forth—all in his single speech" (quoted in Prenshaw, *Conversations with Eudora Welty*, p. 77). Critics have been divided on whether she was entirely successful; some have praised the novel's unique chorale-like form, while others have noted the "endless talk" and the lack of interiority of the characters. In 1971 many of Welty's photographs from her WPA days were collected in *One Time, One Place: Mississippi in the Depression; A Snapshot Album*. (An expanded collection, *Photographs*, was published in 1989.) In 1972 she published her finest novel, the emotionally wrenching *The Optimist's Daughter*, which won the Pulitzer Prize for fiction. The book tells the story of a middle-aged woman, the only surviving member of her family, who returns to her Southern hometown to attend her father's funeral. Initially nostalgic about her past, she gradually becomes more honest about her parents and herself, finding both pain and solace in her memories. Welty said that she wrote the book in order to comprehend her guilty feelings following the deaths of her family members.

During the 1970s and 1980s Welty traveled to scores of colleges and universities, giving readings of her stories and speaking about favorite writers such as Anton Chekhov and Jane Austen. She received numerous awards, among them the Gold Medal for the Novel from the National Institute of Arts and Letters, the Chevalier de l'Ordre des Arts et Lettres from the government of France, and the Presidential Medal of Freedom. She was reportedly passed over for the Nobel Prize for Literature because the committee deemed her to be insufficiently political. During these years she experienced "the most rewarding love of her life," but nothing is known publicly about the relationship (*New York Times*, 27 July 2001). She was noted for her generosity toward aspiring writers and admirers, often inviting them into her family home in Jackson when they showed up on her doorstep. In 1980 *The Collected Stories of Eudora Welty* was published to great acclaim. In 1983 she delivered a series of lectures at Harvard University, which were published the following year as *One Writer's Beginnings*. The memoir offered fond recollections about her early life and discussed how she "learned to see" and "found a voice" as a writer. The book was embraced by the public, becoming a surprise best-seller. At the same time, some critics complained that she was too reticent about personal matters; others wondered about the undercurrent of anger in her depiction of her mother, who could be controlling. Welty's refusal to discuss her private life became a bugaboo for some scholars. She declined to make her letters public and discouraged would-be biographers, in all instances insisting that her writing should speak for her life.

In her later years Welty continued to work on fiction, including a projected novel about a community of single women, but published nothing. Her efforts were eventually hampered by problems with arthritis and osteoporosis. As Reynolds Price has suggested, her public image as "the genial and polite Honorary Maiden Aunt of American letters" (*New York Times*, 27 July 2001) and the stories for which she was most celebrated, endearing works such as "Why I Live at the P.O." and "A Worn Path," gave a misleading sense of her contribution to literature. She was a profound explorer of the inner lives of women and one of the preeminent short-story writers of the twentieth century. She died in Jackson.

• Welty's papers are in the Eudora Welty Collection at the Mississippi Department of Archives and History. Suzanne Marrs, ed., *The Welty Collection* (1988), details these holdings. The most useful bibliography is Noel Polk, *Eudora Welty: A Bibliography of Her Work* (1994). Her interviews are collected in two volumes edited by Peggy Whitman Prenshaw, *Conversations with Eudora Welty* (1984) and *More Conversations with Eudora Welty* (1996). Her nonfiction pieces are collected in *The Eye of the Story* (1978). The only book-length biography is Ann Waldron, *Eudora: A Writer's Life* (1998). Michael Kreyling's excellent *Author and Agent: Eudora Welty and Diarmuid Russell* (1991) provides insight into the development of her literary career; the book also reproduces a few of her letters. Nicholas Dawidoff, "Only the Typewriter Is Silent," in the *New York Times* (10 Aug. 1995), is a short profile of Welty in her old age. For views of Welty by her friends, see Reynolds Price, "One Writer's Place in Fiction," in the *New York Times* (27 July 2001), and Lehman Engel, *This Bright Day: An Autobiography* (1974).

An important early critical essay on Welty is Robert Penn Warren, "The Love and Separateness in Miss Welty," *Kenyon Review* 6 (1944): 246–59, repr. in *A Robert Penn Warren Reader* (1987). Among the many scholarly studies on her work, useful overviews are Kreyling, *Understanding Eudora Welty* (1999), and Ruth M. Vande Kieft, *Eudora Welty* (1962; rev. ed. 1987). For important feminist interpretations, see Rebecca Mark, *The Dragon's Blood: Feminist Intertextuality in Eudora Welty's* The Golden Apples (1994), and Patricia S. Yaeger, "'Because a Fire Was in My Head': Eudora Welty and the Dialogic Imagination," *PMLA* 99 (Oct. 1984): 955–73. Peter Schmidt, *The Heart of the Story: Eudora Welty's Short Fiction* (1991), is a fine study of her stories. For a negative assessment of Welty, see Claudia Roth Pierpont, "A Perfect Lady," *New Yorker* (5 Oct. 1998): 94–104. For the political aspects of her writing, see Marrs, *One Writer's Imagination: The Fiction of Eudora Welty* (2002), and Marrs and Harriet Pollack, eds., *Eudora Welty and Politics: Did the Writer Crusade?* (2001). An obituary is in the *New York Times*, 24 July 2001.

THOMAS W. COLLINS, JR.

WHITEAKER, John (4 May 1820–2 Oct. 1902), first governor of Oregon, was born in Dearborn County, Indiana, the son of John Whiteaker and Nancy Smales Whiteaker, farmers. Largely self-educated (with less than six months' worth of formal education in his lifetime), Whiteaker assisted his father on the family farm and later worked as both a carpenter and a cabinetmaker. He also volunteered for military duty during the Mexican-American War, but his company remained on inactive status. On 22 August 1847, he married Nancy Jane Hargrave; the couple had six children.

Like many of his contemporaries, Whiteaker succumbed to "gold fever" when news of the strike at Sutter's Mill arrived in 1849. Leaving his family behind in Indiana, he journeyed to California, where he acquired sufficient savings to return for his family in 1851. Intrigued by the possibilities of the newly formed Oregon Territory, Whiteaker and his family traveled westward over the Oregon Trail, arriving in 1852. After settling in Lane County, Oregon, Whiteaker established himself in farming.

Noted by his contemporaries for his intelligence and character, Whiteaker soon became active in local public affairs and in 1855 was elected county judge of probate. He won election to the territorial legislature in 1857, the same year that the adoption of a state constitution mandated the selection of a governor. Nominated for the post by one of two factions of the new state's Democratic party, Whiteaker ended up running against the other faction's candidate—E. M. Barnum—when the Republican nominee withdrew from the race prior to the June 1858 election. Whiteaker won the election by 1,138 votes and was inaugurated on 8 July of that year. When Congress formally admitted Oregon to the United States in February 1859, Whiteaker formally assumed his duties on 3 March.

Known among his constituents by the nicknames "Honest John" and "Old Soap, Socks, and Pickles" (for his persistent encouragement of those home industries), Whiteaker's one four-year term was shadowed by the Civil War. Although personally favoring slavery—as did the state's two U.S. Senators—Whiteaker presided over a state whose population (52,465 according to the 1860 Census) had overwhelmingly rejected slavery during the ratification of its constitution (in any event, slavery had been banned under the Organic Act of 1848 that formally created the Oregon Territory). Despite being vilified as an alleged traitor, Whiteaker remained loyal to the Union and, apart from an occasional uprising from Southern sympathizers, Oregon was spared from hostilities during the Civil War. Whiteaker's administration presided over such developments as the establishment of the state's first bank, in Portland (1859), the first state fair (in Oregon City), the founding of the Oregon Steam Navigation Company, and the implementation of daily stage travel between Portland and Sacramento, California.

Although not renominated in 1862, Whiteaker remained in politics after leaving office in September 1862. Elected to three consecutive terms in the lower house of the legislature (1866, 1868, and 1870), he served as that body's presiding officer in his last term. He served as a member of the commission to examine, report upon, and receive the locks and canal at the falls of the Willamette River, and in 1872 he became chairman of the state's board of equalization. In 1876 Whitaker was elected to the state senate, where he also served as the presiding officer before being elected to the U.S. House of Representatives in 1878. While a member of Congress Whiteaker served as chairman of the Revolutionary Pensions Committee and attracted national attention when the Democrats chartered a train to take him to Washington in time to cast a vote for a Democrat as Speaker of the House. He also introduced a bill that would have authorized federal negations with several Northwestern Native American tribes—including the Umatilla and the Warm Springs—with a view to negating the title to their reservation lands and removing them beyond the borders of Oregon. Although defeated for reelection in 1880, Whiteaker was appointed a Collector of Internal Revenue in Oregon in 1885 and held the post until 1889. A thirty-second-degree Mason and a member of the Grange as well as the Oregon Historical Society, Whiteaker retired to Eugene, Oregon, where he died.

Although his career lacked the prominence achieved by many of his peers, Whiteaker's place in history will remain secure by virtue of his service as the first governor of Oregon. One of the thousands lured westward by the promises of gold and a better life, he made a solid contribution to his adopted home state during its formative years.

• Whiteaker's papers are held at the Lane County Historical Society in Eugene, Oregon. His life and career are the subjects of Nellie Banfield, "The Public Career of John Whiteaker," B.A. thesis, University of Oregon (1912), and Lucia Wilkins Moore, "John Whiteaker, First Governor of Oregon," in *Lane County Historian*, vol. 6, no. 1 (Feb. 1959). He was also the subject of an entry in George S. Turnbull, *Governors of Oregon* (1959).

EDWARD L. LACH, JR.

WILLIAMS, Joe (12 Dec. 1918–29 Mar. 1999), blues and popular singer, was born Joseph Goreed in Cordele, Georgia, the son of Willie Goreed and Anne Beatrice Gilbert, whose occupations are unknown. At the age of "about three" Goreed, his mother, and grandmother moved to Chicago, where he was educated at Austin Otis Sexton Elementary School. From age ten Goreed funded his own education, which concluded at Englewood High School, by singing locally. At age twelve he founded the Jubilee Boys, who sang in Chicago churches, while earning $20–30 singing at late-night clubs. At age sixteen family members decided he would be professionally known as Williams. That year he dropped out of school and was soon singing four nights a week with the Johnny Long band. His repertoire was primarily the mainstream popular songs of the day, usually written by whites for those with a "white" point of view. "Moonlight and Shadows," a tune from *The Jungle Princess* (1936), a Dorothy Lamour film introducing the sarong, is an example. But by 1938 Williams had also been "opened up to the blues," a genre singularly African American in origin and appeal.

During the next twelve years Williams sang mostly mainstream ballads in many cities and with many groups; he also worked as a janitor, a door-to-door salesman, and a doorman. His personal life was chaotic. In 1943 he married Wilma Cole; they had no children and were divorced in 1946. Williams suffered a nervous breakdown, which lasted most of 1947. That year he married Ann Kirksey; they had no children and were divorced in 1950. By the end of the decade his singing career had virtually ended.

Things began to change in 1950. Williams was in a nightclub audience listening to the Count Basie band when someone recognized him and called on him to sing a few numbers. He responded with several standards, all written by African Americans: Duke Ellington's "Solitude" and Fats Waller's "Honeysuckle Rose" and "Ain't Misbehavin'." He received $50 for his efforts and decided to pursue a singing career again. In 1951 he married Lemma Reid; they had two children and were divorced in 1964.

In 1955, after receiving what he later called a "vague offer" the year before from the Basie band, Williams got a clear one and accepted. By then Basie was already a phenomenon. Although most of America's memorable bands—excepting Ellington—had collapsed after World War II, when the public seemed more interested in new sounds and television, Basie's ensemble had become one of the most innovative.

The first Basie recording session (in 1955) featuring Williams proved historical. It included "Every Day (I Have the Blues)," previously identified with its creator, Peter Chatman. Williams's eight-minute tour de force showed his uncanny flexibility, vocal range, and control. That same year Williams created major hits with "In the Evening," "The Comeback," and "All Right, Okay (You Win)." The 1955 *Down Beat* magazine poll named Williams America's top male vocalist.

Williams stayed with Basie, touring and recording more blues classics, until 1960. Then he struck out on his own with a wider repertoire, though in subsequent years there were frequent reunions with the legendary bandleader. Williams often gave Basie credit for his own renascence, but it is demonstrable that the Basie band achieved wider popularity after Williams joined it. Both were national treasures.

In 1965 Williams married Jillean Hughes d'Eath, an Englishwoman whom he had met in New York. They had no children and remained married until Williams's death. In 1967 they moved to Las Vegas, where Williams's particular mixture of mainstream and blues singing to a big band accompaniment commanded a year-round market. There he remained for the rest of his life, though he regularly undertook national and international tours and made recordings. He appeared as a soloist with the Boston Pops and the symphony orchestras of Cincinnati and Detroit. Williams appeared in two films, *Jamboree* (1957) and *Cinderfella* (1960). During the 1980s he appeared regularly on television on comedian Bill Cosby's "The Cosby Show" as "Grandpa Al." In 1988 Williams founded a scholarship fund for music students at the Community College of Southern Nevada in Las Vegas.

Referring to his straightforward versions of mainstream music, Williams once said, "There's nothing wrong with singing a song the way it was written, with making a song say 'Please like me'" (*New York Times*, 31 Mar. 1999). He died in Las Vegas a day after collapsing on the sidewalk, having left (without permission) a hospital where he had been confined for a week with respiratory problems related to chronic emphysema.

Williams was the most popular blues singer of his era, rivaled only by Ray Charles, enveloping multiethnic audiences with the richness and flexibility of his baritone voice. Mixing the sound and phrasing of jazz with the blues, Williams began the creation of "urban blues." "Joe definitely dressed the blues up," singer Kevin Mahogany recalled. "He made it okay to listen to the blues for those who misperceived what they were all about. You didn't have to be downtrodden, sitting out in a field, and moaning about your life" (liner notes to *The Ultimate Joe Williams*).

The awards and honors Williams accumulated during the last half of his life included selection as best male vocalist by the International Critics Poll in 1955, 1974–1978, 1980, 1981, 1983, 1984, and 1989–1991; best male vocalist, Billboard disc jockey poll 1959; and best male vocalist, Grammys, 1985 and 1992. Popularizing mainstream music to an essentially blues audience, Williams was one of the most honored entertainers of the late twentieth century.

• Material relating to Williams is stored in the Hamilton College archives in Clinton, New York. His biography is Leslie Gourse, *Every Day: The Story of Joe Williams* (1985). Gourse's *Louis' Children: American Jazz Singers* (1984) also covers Williams's life to the time of its writing. Ondine Leblanc, *Contemporary Musicians: Profiles of the People in Music*, vol. 11 (1994), contains valuable information on Williams's years in Georgia. Kevin Mahogany's notes for the CD *The Ultimate Joe Williams* (Verve 559 700 2) are illuminating. Obituaries are in the *Las Vegas Review-Journal*, 30 Mar. 1999, and the *New York Times*, 31 Mar. 1999.

JAMES ROSS MOORE

WILLIAMS, Tony (12 Dec. 1945–23 Feb. 1997), jazz drummer, was born Tillmon Anthony Williams, Jr., in Chicago, Illinois, the son of Tillmon Williams, a postal worker and jazz saxophonist. In his application for a social security account number in June 1969, Williams gave his mother's name as Alyce Duart. In his obituary the *New York Times* spelled her forename differently, giving what was evidently a later married name, Alyse Janez. California Death Records spell her maiden name as Duarte.

Williams was raised in Boston. In childhood he routinely listened to his father play on weekends, and at around the age of eight he took up jazz drumming, demonstrating an immediate affinity for it. At the age of eleven Williams began taking lessons from Alan Dawson, a drummer who worked in groups with his father. Williams meticulously studied the recordings of the best bebop drummers, including Max Roach, Art Blakey, Philly Joe Jones, and Roy Haynes, imitating each man's approach to drum tuning and stick technique. More broadly Williams's foremost inspiration was the trumpeter Miles Davis.

In 1960 Williams began playing jazz professionally, often with the tenor saxophonist Sam Rivers. In December 1962 Williams accompanied the alto saxophonist Jackie McLean while serving as the house drummer at the nightclub Connelly's in Boston. McLean invited Williams to join his group in New York for performances in the play *The Connection* and other jobs. Davis heard Williams play with McLean and in May 1963 hired him to record portions of the album *Seven Steps to Heaven*, the title track featuring Williams's drumming. Williams then joined Davis's group.

Williams already knew the band's repertory, and he propelled it with a bubbling energy that had been missing since Philly Joe Jones left Davis in 1958. Williams also introduced, in collaboration with Davis's pianist Herbie Hancock and double bass player Ron Carter, an uncanny spontaneous interaction and rhythmic elasticity by endlessly varying explicit expressions of the beat while maintaining its abstract constancy. In doing so he managed to convey the sense of a rhythmic "groove" while avoiding repetitive patterns.

Magnificent examples abound throughout Davis's recordings from 1963 to 1967, all made for the Columbia label. Among these the album *"Four" and*

More, recorded in concert at Lincoln Center in New York in 1964, offers a catalog of his talents. Throughout most of the album, Williams continuously changes rhythms at blistering tempos. On "Joshua," he utilizes silence for contrast, stopping his drumming altogether during moments of the saxophone and piano solos. He takes a coloristic solo on "Walkin'," suspending the steady beat. He plays rhythmic solos during the theme of "Seven Steps to Heaven," and this track also features passages in which he cleverly halves the tempo in a manner that superimposes relaxed swing on top of fast bebop. The title track of Hancock's album for the Blue Note label, *Maiden Voyage,* recorded in 1965, provides the finest recorded example of Hancock, Carter, and Williams collectively toying with implicit beat and meter. On "Fall" and "Nefertiti" from Davis's album *Nefertiti,* recorded in 1967, traditional instrumental roles are reversed, with the trumpet and saxophone playing repeated lines while the drums roam freely.

During these years with Davis, Williams appeared on other historic albums for Blue Note in addition to *Maiden Voyage.* These included McLean's *One Step Beyond,* recorded in 1963, the pianist Andrew Hill's *Point of Departure,* the reed player and flutist Eric Dolphy's *Out to Lunch,* Rivers's *Fuchsia Swing Song,* all recorded in 1964, and *The Soothsayer,* from 1965, under the leadership of Davis's saxophonist Wayne Shorter.

In the late 1960s Davis gradually expanded his group and moved from an esoteric brand of jazz toward a fusion of jazz, rock, and funk. After several years of stability, the personnel in his group began to turn over quickly, and Williams left early in 1969, just after recording the album *In a Silent Way.* Williams formed his own fusion group, Lifetime, placing jazz improvisation in an extremely loud, rock-based context. The group, which struggled unsuccessfully, began as a trio with John McLaughlin on guitar and Larry Young on organ. Later, Jack Bruce joined on bass. Early in 1972 Williams was briefly a member of the tenor saxophonist Stan Getz's Latin jazz quintet. He then stopped performing for nearly three years.

From late 1975 into 1976 Williams led a new version of Lifetime, featuring the guitarist Alan Holdsworth. Resuming his activities in straightforward jazz settings, Williams formed the Great Jazz Trio, led by the pianist Hank Jones, with whom he toured and recorded from 1976 to 1978. Concurrently, for concerts, tours, and recordings in 1976, 1977, and 1979, Hancock led Shorter, Carter, and Williams in a quintet, V.S.O.P., with Freddie Hubbard rather than Davis on trumpet. Williams left New York for the San Francisco Bay Area in 1977, initially living in a country home near San Anselmo in Marin County. He studied composition at the University of California, Berkeley.

A quartet comprising Hancock, Carter, Williams, and the trumpeter Wynton Marsalis toured in 1982, and the following year this group became a quintet, V.S.O.P. II, with Branford Marsalis joining on saxophone. In April 1986 Williams formed his own quintet with the Miles Davis disciple Wallace Roney on trumpet, Billy Pierce on saxophone, and Mulgrew Miller on piano; the bass chair passed from Charnett Moffett to Robert Hurst to Ira Coleman. The quintet toured and recorded, and it appeared in the video *New York Live,* filmed in 1989. Williams wrote many original compositions for the group, and his drumming routinely took the foreground role in performances. A representative sample of both his compositions and his performance style may be heard on the album *Tokyo Live,* recorded in concert in March 1992.

In the early 1990s Williams settled on the San Francisco peninsula near Pacifica. Davis died in 1991, and in 1992 Roney, Shorter, Hancock, Carter, and Williams toured for six months as the Miles Davis Tribute Band. Williams then resumed leading his quintet, but it disbanded not long thereafter, in February 1993.

Williams married Colleen (her maiden name unknown) around 1994. In mid-December 1996 he performed in the club Birdland in New York in a trio with Miller and Carter. He died in Daly City, California, suffering a heart attack two days after an ostensibly routine gall bladder operation.

• The finest account of Williams's years with Davis is by Jack Chambers, *Milestones 2: The Music and Times of Miles Davis since 1960* (1985). Michael Cuscuna summarizes the troubled history of the jazz-fusion trio Lifetime in his liner notes to *The Complete Blue Note Recordings of Larry Young* on the Mosaic label (1991). Among many published interviews providing additional details of Williams's career and insights into his personality, the best include Don DeMicheal, "Tony Williams: Miles' Man," *Down Beat* 32 (25 Mar. 1965): 19, 36–37; Pat Cox, "Tony Williams: An Interview Scenario," *Down Beat* 37 (28 May 1970): 14–15, 33; Vernon Gibbs, "Tony Williams: Report on a Musical Lifetime," *Down Beat* 43 (29 Jan. 1976): 16–18; Lee Underwood, "Tony Williams: Aspiring to a Lifetime of Leadership," *Down Beat* 46 (21 June 1979): 20–21, 54, 60; Paul de Barros, "Tony Williams: Two Decades of Drum Innovation," *Down Beat* 50 (Nov. 1983): 14–16, 61; Rick Mattingly, "Tony Williams," *Modern Drummer* 8 (June 1984): 8–13, 44–48; Herb Wong, "World Class Drummer: Tony Williams," *Jazz Times,* Sept. 1988, pp. 18–19; and Bill Milkowski, "Tony Williams: A Master's Perspective," *Modern Drummer* 16 (July 1992):, 20–25, 68–70, 72, 74–75, 78. An obituary by Peter Watrous is in the *New York Times,* 26 Feb. 1997.

BARRY KERNFELD

WINDSOR, Marie (11 Dec. 1922–10 Dec. 2000), actress, was born Emily Marie Bertelsen in Marysvale, Utah, the only biological child of Lane Joseph Bertelsen and Etta Marie Long Bertelsen (she had two adopted siblings). Once a silver-mining boom town, Marysvale then had a population of only five hundred, and Windsor lived with her family in the town's once-grand hotel. Obsessed with movies, especially the actress Clara Bow, Windsor declared at age eight that acting would be her life's work.

As Windsor blossomed into a statuesque young woman, she became the pride of her hometown. She towered over her competition in statewide beauty pageants and earned a scholarship to Brigham Young

University, where she studied for two years, majoring in art and drama. Winnings from pageants and talent shows paid her way to Hollywood, where she enrolled in Maria Ouspenskaya's renowned acting class. Initial interviews at the studios taught her to deal with rejection. "I was told my eyes were too big and too far apart," she recalled. "Or else that I was too tall. Or too *something.*"

Another obstacle was her name, which agents found unwieldy. While being squired by an agent to a party in the Hollywood Hills, she was rechristened Marie Windsor. With few acting parts coming her way, Windsor worked as a cigarette girl at the Sunset Strip's popular Mocambo nightclub. The indignity of the job finally squeezed tears from her—witnessed by the producer Arthur Hornblow, Jr. Taking pity, he offered her a small part in a film, *The All-American Co-Ed* (1941), being made at Hal Roach Studios.

Windsor's debut was inauspicious. "We wore vegetable costumes, in a kind of 4-H Club revue," Windsor related. "I was the Carrot Girl." Spotty roles in a variety of "B" pictures followed, her meager earnings augmented by modeling assignments for pinup artists, including the legendary Alberto Vargas. Disillusioned with her progress at the studios, Windsor moved to New York to season herself with theater and radio work. Her determination to be a movie actress was unwavering. "I'd decided that I would just claw my way up the mountain," she declared.

In New York in 1944, appearing opposite Jackie Gleason in the sketch comedy *Follow the Girls*, Windsor was "discovered" by an MGM talent scout. The offer of a six-month contract (with options) from the "Tiffany" of studios pulled Windsor back to the West Coast. Because of her dark hair, Amazonian figure, and husky voice, she was quickly pigeonholed as a dark and sultry vamp in films such as *Song of the Thin Man* (1947) and *The Three Musketeers* (1948). In 1946 she married the musician Ted Steele, but the union was short-lived. On a surprise visit to San Francisco, she caught her husband with another woman. Divorce came after only eight months of marriage. They had no children.

In 1948, although MGM once billed Windsor as "the next Joan Crawford," it dropped her contract, a devastating disappointment. She was "rescued" by a pair of maverick talents, Abraham Polonsky, a writer and director, and John Garfield, an actor who had formed his own production company, Enterprise Studios. Garfield cast Windsor as a femme fatale in an adaptation of the journalist Ira Wolfert's novel *Tucker's People*, an exposé of the New York numbers rackets. Windsor's portrayal of Edna Tucker, a slinky, sinful temptress, established the mold for virtually all subsequent roles during her prime. The film, titled *Force of Evil*, eventually was lauded as a classic film noir.

At the time, however, it was a box office flop, and for a time Windsor received few new offers. Her frustration was acute. "I took an aptitude test at UCLA, to see what kind of work I was really suited for," Windsor recalled. "It was determined I should be a painter—or a service station mechanic."

Instead, Windsor caught on at Republic Pictures, roping and riding her way through a series of westerns, *Hellfire* (1949), *The Fighting Kentuckian* (1949), and *Dakota Lil* (1950) among others. But the studio boss Herbert Yates did little to promote her. "He was too busy chasing Communists," Windsor suggested dryly, noting that he invested virtually all the studio's 1949 marketing budget in *The Red Menace*, one of a wave of anti-Communist films sparked by the House Committee on Un-American Activities purge of Hollywood "Reds."

Finally, freelancing for RKO Radio Pictures, Windsor landed a plum starring role in a modest suspense picture, *The Narrow Margin*. It was essentially a reprise of Edna Tucker, only splashier. The film, a "sleeper," became RKO's biggest hit of 1952. Not long after, Windsor went on a United Service Organizations (USO) tour for the troops in Korea. The misery she encountered on hospital ships convinced her never to complain again about her lot in Hollywood. "My credo was, work is work—even if you're wearing a cat suit and zipping around on roller chairs in some rickety clapboard spaceship"—a reference to her 1953 sci-fi abomination *Cat Women of the Moon* (later regarded as a cult classic).

During the 1950s Windsor made desirable, duplicitous dames her stock-in-trade in films such as *Japanese War Bride* (1952), *City That Never Sleeps* (1953), *Hell's Half Acre* (1954), *No Man's Woman* (1955), and a slew of early television dramas. In 1954 she married Jack Hupp, a real estate broker, a former All-American basketball star at the University of Southern California, and the grandson of the silent screen cowboy Earl Rodney. They had one son.

The pinnacle of Windsor's career was the 1956 release *The Killing*, an audacious crime thriller, the first Hollywood-financed film to be directed by Stanley Kubrick. Her portrayal of greedy, two-timing Sherry Peatty (opposite the equally typecast Elisha Cook, Jr.) earned Windsor the best notices of her career. United Artists disliked the film and refused to promote it. Ads touting her for a best supporting actress nomination were paid for by Windsor herself.

During the 1960s Windsor became a television mainstay, still cast as the "other" woman as she reached middle age. She became a voluble presence in the Screen Actor's Guild, principally as an outspoken member of the union's conservative faction.

In the 1970s Windsor's big screen appearances diminished. In *Hearts of the West* (1975), she had a bawdy turn with young Jeff Bridges—twenty-two years after being romanced by his father Lloyd Bridges in *The Tall Texan*. In 1983 her onscreen longevity—as well as her nonstop charity work—earned her a star on Hollywood's Walk of Fame. But the crowning glory of her later career was finding at age sixty-five the "perfect" role, as a one-time "B" movie actress venturing into legitimate theater in the stage play *The Bar off Melrose*. The playwright Terry

Kingsley-Smith based the character of Frances Carson on Windsor, who had known his mother, the writer Dorothy Kingsley, at MGM in the 1940s. Windsor won the 1987 Los Angeles Drama Critics Award for Best Actress.

Both Windsor and her husband were eventually beset with physical traumas. Windsor suffered through a series of torturous back operations in the 1990s, and Hupp was stricken with Parkinson's disease. But the actress was bolstered by inclusion on the American Film Institute's ballot for Hollywood's Greatest Screen Legends, which cited *The Killing* as her "signature" performance.

Windsor died in Beverly Hills, California. She is remembered as a hardworking actress who, through her uniqueness, perseverance, and finely honed craft, left her legacy on Hollywood as "the Queen of the B's."

• This article draws on the author's interviews with Marie Windsor. Useful sources include Eddie Muller, *Dark City Dames: The Wicked Women of Film Noir* (2001); and Karen Burroughs Hannsberry, *Femme Noir: Bad Girls of Film* (1998), which discusses Windsor on pages 556–68. An obituary is in the *New York Times*, 14 Dec. 2000.

EDDIE MULLER

WITHERSPOON, James "Jimmy," "Spoon" (18 Aug. 1922–18 Sept. 1997), blues and jazz singer, was born in Gurdon, Clark County, Arkansas, the son of Leonard Witherspoon, a railroad brakeman, and Eva Tatum, a laundress. References to 8 August as his birthday result from a typographical error. The year of birth quoted was given by the singer himself in some late interviews and is consistent with his age as recorded in the 1930 U.S. census.

His father died when Witherspoon was about six. As a child Witherspoon sang in the First Baptist Church choir in Gurdon. At sixteen he moved to Los Angeles, where he earned his living by washing dishes, but he began singing after hours at Lovejoy's on Central Avenue. From 1941 to 1943 he served in the merchant marine as chief steward and cook. During his tour of duty he sang at the Grand Hotel, Calcutta, with the band of the expatriate African-American pianist Teddy Weatherford and also appeared on a forces radio program.

In 1944 Witherspoon settled in Vallejo, California, where his professional career began at the Waterfront Cafe. Later that year he replaced the singer Walter Brown with the band of the pianist Jay McShann, with which he made his first records in mid-1945. Witherspoon toured and recorded with McShann until 1948, establishing himself as a leading practitioner of the style of blues singing, called blues shouting, characteristic of the southwestern states. In 1947 his recording of "Ain't Nobody's Business" enjoyed major success in the rhythm-and-blues charts, launching a solo career that involved a long series of recordings for the Down Beat (1948), Modern (1948–1952), Federal (1952–1953), and Checker (1954–1956) la-

bels. He also toured nationwide with bands led by the saxophonist Big Jim Wynn.

By the mid-1950s the recording business was shifting toward music for teenage audiences. Witherspoon was fortunately able to find a new audience in the wider jazz market. In 1956 he recorded the album *Callin' the Blues* with the traditional jazz band of Wilbur De Paris. In 1957 he was reunited with Jay McShann to rerecord some of his best-known numbers. Following the well-regarded 1958 album *Singin' the Blues*, Witherspoon was recruited as a last-minute addition to the October 1959 Monterey Jazz Festival, where he made a late-night appearance with a band that included Coleman Hawkins, Ben Webster, and Earl Hines. This appearance and the resulting album established Witherspoon's new commercial direction. He subsequently appeared with jazz musicians of established reputation, especially Ben Webster. In 1961 Witherspoon made a European tour with the Buck Clayton All Stars and recorded a live album at the Paris Olympia.

In 1961 Witherspoon appeared twice at Carnegie Hall in New York City, the second time in a Jon Hendricks presentation, *Evolution of the Blues*, which had also been presented at the Newport Jazz Festival. Albums for the Prestige label in 1962–1965 further established Witherspoon's reputation. In 1963 he toured Japan with the Count Basie Orchestra, and he followed with European tours later in the decade, recording in Stockholm in 1964 and in London in 1965 and 1966. Television appearances in the sixties included Ralph Gleason's "Jazz Casual" and "Jazz Scene USA." Witherspoon appeared at prestigious jazz clubs, such as the Half Note, Village Gate, and Village Vanguard in New York City and the Jazz Workshop in San Francisco. Witherspoon rarely discussed his first marriage, about which little is known; he married his second wife, Diane Atkins, in 1962. They had three children.

In the late 1960s a wider market for blues emerged, and Witherspoon hoped to take advantage of it with recordings for ABC. In 1971 he toured and recorded with the English rock artist Eric Burdon. Witherspoon's 1974 album recorded in England, *Love Is a Five Letter Word*, on which his accompanists included Pete Wingfield, made a modest showing in the charts. These associations are of limited musical significance. Witherspoon later said: "I had to survive . . . . I went along with it but I wasn't contented or happy" (Deffaa, 1996, p. 235). In 1972 he was the disc jockey in his own radio series, *Jimmy Witherspoon Show*, in Los Angeles, and in 1974 he appeared in the film *The Black Godfather*.

By the late 1970s Witherspoon had resumed a heavy touring schedule with jazz groups. He appeared and recorded in both Europe and Australia and in 1980 recorded in Paris a seminal album with Panama Francis and His Savoy Sultans.

In 1982 Witherspoon's career was brought to an abrupt halt by the discovery that he had throat cancer A course of radiotherapy at the Christie Hospital in

Manchester eradicated the tumor. It was not at first certain that he would be able to resume singing, but he made a full recovery. He returned to Britain in December 1982, partly to perform in a benefit for the hospital. In 1985 he recorded duets with the blues singer Joe Turner, once identified by Witherspoon as his earliest musical influence. He continued a punishing schedule of national and international touring, often working with the pianist Bross Townsend, into mid-1997. Witherspoon died at his home in Los Angeles.

Though he is normally classed as a blues shouter, the term is a strange one for an artist conspicuous for his command of dynamics. His sure sense of timing allowed him to generate a fluent swing that was capable of uplifting his accompanists, a useful accomplishment, especially with some of the bands he worked with outside the United States. He straddled blues and jazz not only in his marketing but in his music, giving the impression of singing sounds while never losing his grip on the meanings of his lyrics, which were generally drawn from the blues repertoire. After his cancer treatment, his range was diminished, but his voice was deeper and more hoarse with perhaps even greater emotional expressiveness as a result.

• Interviews with Witherspoon by Anthony Navarro, Frank Joseph, and Norbert Hess, *Living Blues*, no. 33, July–Aug. 1977, pp. 15–24; Arnold Shaw, *Honkers and Shouters: The Golden Years of Rhythm and Blues* (1978), pp. 211–16; Chip Deffaa, *Living Blues*, no. 93, Sept.–Oct. 1990, pp. 17–22, reworked in his *Blue Rhythms: Six Lives in Rhythm and Blues* (1996), pp. 217–42; and André Hobus, *Blues Gazette* 3 (Summer 1996): 5, contain biographical information. Sheldon Harris, *Blues Who's Who* (1979), covers his career to 1979. Assessments are in Deffaa's works and most listeners' guides to both blues and jazz. A comprehensive discography of his work to 1970 is in Mike Leadbitter, Leslie Fancourt, and Paul Pelletier, *Blues Records 1943–1970*, vol. 2, *L–Z* (1994). Later recordings are listed in Walter Bruyninckx and Domi Truffandier, *85 Years of Recorded Jazz* (2004). The obituary by Dave Penny, *Blues and Rhythm* 124 (Nov. 1997): 19, includes interview material relating to Witherspoon's true birth date.

HOWARD RYE

WOLF, Eric R. (1 Feb. 1923–6 Mar. 1999), anthropologist, was born Erich Robert Wolf in Vienna, Austria, the son of Arthur Wolf, a textile factory manager, and Maria Ossinovsky Wolf, a Russian whom he met while a prisoner of war in Siberia. Growing up in a secular Jewish household, Wolf absorbed the cultural riches of Vienna but also the spreading turmoil of the interwar years. At ten, he moved with his family to a factory town near the German-Czech border, where he encountered textile workers ravaged by the economic depression and the growing Nazi menace. The solace that Wolf took from family stories of faraway places (his father as a business traveler in Latin America, his mother's father living in Harbin, China) presaged his passion for anthropology. Following the *Anschluss*, Arthur Wolf sent his son to school in England,

where a year later he was classified as an enemy alien and placed in an internment camp. Among his camp mates was sociologist Norbert Elias, whose informal seminars drew Wolf to social science. In the summer of 1940, Eric (his name now Anglicized) emigrated with his parents to New York City, where he enrolled in then free Queens College.

Wolf interrupted his college education to volunteer for the Tenth Mountain Division of the U.S. Army. When his unit retook German-held territory in Italy, he was wounded. He later received the Silver Star for exceptional bravery. In 1943, he married Kathleen Bakeman, a social worker, and adopted two sons. The marriage ended in divorce in 1972.

Wolf completed his B.A. at Queens College in 1946 and, taking advantage of the GI Bill, enrolled in Ph.D. studies at Columbia University. There, he was one of a cohort of students, most of them veterans, who challenged anthropology's reigning paradigm that each group of people has "a" culture—coherent, bounded, and outside of history. Forming what they called the Mundial Upheaval Society, they discussed historical texts influenced by Marxism, and they welcomed the arrival in 1947 of Julian Steward, an anthropologist who stressed material and ecological factors. Steward organized a team of students to conduct ethnographic research in Puerto Rico. Living among the coffee growers of the Central Highlands, Wolf described their way of life and vulnerability to world coffee prices in his doctoral dissertation (1951), which formed part of Steward's book, *The People of Puerto Rico* (1956).

Wolf next focused on nation states and peasantries, new subjects for anthropology. *Sons of the Shaking Earth* (1959), his first and still widely read book, integrated archaeological, ethnological, and historical knowledge on the development of indigenous polities in Mexico, their subjugation to Spanish colonizers, and the regionally varied conditions leading to the Mexican Revolution. During 1960s fieldwork in the South Tyrol in Northern Italy, Wolf explored the long-term effects of different states on the ethnic identities of two similar villages, one German-speaking, the other speaking a Romance dialect. Coauthored with his student John W. Cole, *The Hidden Frontier: Ecology and Ethnicity in an Alpine Valley* (1974) helped dissolve anthropologists' disinterest in western Europe.

Several classic essays on the role of sociocultural groups and networks in national integration and on peasants belong to this period. *Peasants* (1966) mapped a new field of study: "rural cultivators whose surpluses are transferred to a dominant group of rulers." Offering a worldwide comparison of peasants' economic, social, and cultural circumstances, Wolf pointed toward a general understanding of their participation in anticolonial struggles. Whereas much social science writing of the time viewed these restive populations as "underdeveloped" and in need of outsiders' technical expertise, he saw them as "the party of humanity."

In 1961 Wolf accepted a professorship at the University of Michigan, after teaching at the Universities of Illinois (1952–1954), Virginia (1955–1958), Yale (1958–1959), and Chicago (1959–1961) and winning a Guggenheim Fellowship in 1960. The first teach-in against the Vietnam War was held on the Michigan campus in March 1965; he helped originate the idea and was a leading participant. Supported by a National Institutes of Health (NIH) Career Award (1964–1969), he researched six cases of peasant revolution, among them Vietnam, for a comparative study, *Peasant Wars of the Twentieth Century* (1969). With his colleague Joseph C. Jorgensen, Wolf also led the American Anthropological Association's Ethics Committee in an investigation of charges that ethnographic data were being employed in counterinsurgency in Southeast Asia. Although a majority in the Association applauded this action, it was controversial, leading to Wolf's later reflection that for him anthropology had lost its innocence as a harmonious "church of marginals" (see Ghani 1987: 353; Wakin 1992; Wolf and Jorgensen 1970).

In 1971 Wolf left Michigan to become a Distinguished Professor at the Herbert H. Lehman College and Graduate School of the City University of New York, an institution still devoted to educating minority and immigrant students. He married the anthropologist Sydel Silverman in 1972; they had no children. With her encouragement, he researched the historical development and spread of capitalism. *Europe and the People Without History* (1982), the book that emerged from this effort, explores the implications of European capitalist expansion for selected non-Europeans: Native Americans on the "commodity frontier" of the fur trade; slaves and indentured servants; peasants and proletarians; migrants whose children he was teaching (often in Spanish) at Lehman. The book sealed Wolf's reputation as a scholar of world historical processes who eschewed the triumphalist celebration of western civilization.

It was Wolf's lifelong project to analyze Nazism, which had so marked his early years in Austria. His last book, *Envisioning Power: Ideologies of Dominance and Crisis* (1999), takes the daring step of juxtaposing the Third Reich with other societies confronting severe economic, demographic-ecological, and military dislocations. Resultant anxieties about the future caused people to succumb to cosmic and frenzied ideologies. In addition to German National Socialism, he applied this framework to Aztec human sacrifice, to Kwakiutl potlatching (in its most extreme form), and, more broadly, to nativist movements like Cargo Cults and Ghost Dances. Wolf's aversion to Eurocentric categories is here coupled with a parallel critique of a romanticized cultural relativism; in his view, no form of society is immune to ideological extremism.

Wolf was a leader in opening post–World War II anthropology to the study of peasants, nation states, capitalism, and colonial expansion. Relating the anthropological concept of culture to power, he transformed the discipline's engagement with the other social sciences and with history, whose practitioners also acknowledge him as a leader. He received a MacArthur Foundation "Genius Award" in 1990 and honorary doctorates from several universities. In 1995, he was elected to the National Academy of Sciences. Principled and politically engaged, he was seen by many as a moral compass, charting a role for scholar-activists in a turbulent and unjust world. Although tough-minded and a giant repository of knowledge, he was generous and unpretentious. Students, friends, and colleagues have commemorated him as a magnanimous humanist and teacher. Shortly before his death in Irvington, New York, he reported dreaming of an encounter with the Aztec god Tlaloc in a "cave that looked like the Ford Foundation." Although unimpressed by Wolf's Silver Star and love of baroque music, the ferocious Tlaloc told him that if he so desired he could do anthropology—that "impossible but necessary" endeavor—for eternity.

• Eric Wolf's papers have been collected and archived by the University of Michigan. Wolf wrote about his intellectual development in *Pathways of Power: Building an Anthropology of the Modern World* (2001), a collection that includes his best-known essays and several never before published. The intersection of private biography and public scholarship comes through in Ashraf Ghani's "A Conversation with Eric Wolf," in the *American Ethnologist* 14 (1987): 314–67, also available on film through the Wenner-Gren Foundation for Anthropological Research. Wolf's and Jorgensen's role in the ethics debate in the Anthropological Association is covered in their essay "Anthropology on the Warpath, an Exchange" in *New York Review of Books*, 8 April and 22 July 1971. This subject is also presented in Eric Wakin, *Anthropology Goes to War; Professional Ethics and Counterinsurgency in Thailand* (1992).

Alongside his landmark books, Wolf wrote over 100 articles and essays, produced a seminal short text, *Anthropology* (1964), and edited or coedited four collections. Much of his opus has been translated into several languages. A festschrift volume, *Articulating Hidden Histories: Exploring the Influence of Eric R. Wolf* (1995), edited by Jane Schneider and Rayna Rapp, presents an overview of Wolf's pioneering concepts and demonstrates his enduring influence over two generations of students. It also includes a comprehensive bibliography of Wolf's writings from 1950 to 1995. An obituary is in the *New York Times*, 10 Mar. 1999.

JANE SCHNEIDER

Y–Z

YAROSZ, Teddy (24 June 1910–29 Mar. 1974), middleweight boxer, was born Thaddeus Joseph Yarosz in Pittsburgh, Pennsylvania, the son of Joseph Yarosz, a railroad laborer and later a worker in steel mills, and Victoria Kot Yarosz. Both of his parents were Polish immigrants. The family left Pittsburgh and lived briefly in Salem, in eastern Ohio, then in Monaca, twenty-five miles northwest of Pittsburgh, where Teddy lived for the rest of his life. His father died when he was sixteen, causing him to leave Monaca High School, where he was a very good student, and work to help support himself, his mother, seven siblings, and three cousins who lived with the family. He put aside plans to go to college, but when he started making some money from boxing, he hired a local teacher to tutor him and did eventually obtain a high school diploma.

Yarosz began boxing in a local gymnasium at age fifteen, much to his father's displeasure. On one occasion, his father chopped up his boxing gloves with a hatchet and whipped him when he came home showing signs of battle. His older brother, Eddie, was also a boxer, and in 1929 they both reached the welterweight finals of the Allegheny Mountain Association tournament and would have fought each other if Eddie had not withdrawn. Teddy became champion and earned a trip to a tournament in Boston. Soon afterward, in the summer of 1929, he became a professional. He caught the eye of Ray Foutts, a boxing manager and promoter based in East Liverpool, Ohio. The honest and hard-working Foutts guided Yarosz throughout his career.

From 1929 to 1932 Yarosz fought sixty times and won all except for a draw with lefthander Eddie Wolfe in 1932. By 1931 he was fighting main events in Pittsburgh, generally outpointing his opponents by a wide margin. His boxing style was mostly orthodox, with extensive use of an excellent left jab and a quick right hand, fast movement afoot, and a busy, two-fisted style that usually overwhelmed his opponents. Taller and with longer reach than most of his opponents, Yarosz often led successfully with his right, avoiding counterpunches with his quick reflexes.

In 1933 Yarosz lost to Wolfe and then fought another draw with him, but he made rapid progress, defeating former welterweight champion Tommy Freeman and leading middleweight contender Vince Dundee. Yarosz had grown into the middleweight division, and in early 1934 he won a claim to the world title in that division by outpointing Jimmy Smith and ex-champion Ben Jeby. Unfortunately, the middleweight division was confused by several conflicting claims to the championship, and this confusion persisted for years.

Next, Yarosz knocked out ex-welterweight champion Pete Latzo and then met Dundee, another title claimant, for the U.S. championship. On 11 September 1934 in Pittsburgh Yarosz won a close decision over the much more experienced Dundee. As a result, Yarosz and Frenchman Marcel Thil had the strongest claims to the middleweight title.

Having enjoyed an almost unbroken run of successes, Yarosz appeared destined to become the undisputed middleweight champion. But in his first fight of 1935, a nontitle affair with Babe Risko in Scranton, Pennsylvania, he sustained a broken kneecap in the first round and had to surrender in the seventh. After a layoff, he defended his title claim against Risko in Pittsburgh on 15 September and was in complete command of the fight until the fourth round, when his knee gave way with a torn ligament. Although he somehow completed the fight despite the severe pain, he was badly beaten and lost the U.S. championship.

In May 1936, after a long rest, Yarosz returned to action and never again had a problem with his knee. He defeated Risko, who was no longer the middleweight champion, in a rematch and then beat three other fighters who had held, or would hold, the middleweight title. Then Yarosz engaged in an exciting three-fight series with Pittsburgh native Billy Conn, the future light-heavyweight champion, losing the first two meetings on extremely close decisions but winning the third. These three fights were among the major ethnic events in Pittsburgh sports history, in which a popular Polish American was pitted against an equally popular Irish American.

Yarosz continued to box until 1942, beating many difficult opponents but tending to lose decisions more frequently. One of his best victories came in 1939 at the expense of Archie Moore, who later held the light-heavyweight title. He lost to Ezzard Charles, a future heavyweight champion, in his penultimate fight. Yarosz retired with only 18 losses in 128 fights, despite having met most of the best middleweights and some of the best light-heavyweights of the 1930s. He was knocked out only once, by Risko, in the fight in which he suffered the broken kneecap. He fought twelve world champions, some of them two or three times. Arguably, Yarosz was the best middleweight of the 1930s.

Yarosz epitomizes the U.S. athlete of the first half of the twentieth century, a time when professional boxers were far more numerous than in later years. Like most athletes of the time, he was white, the son of immigrants, and from a large family. His schooling ended early due to adverse circumstances. In 1940 he had married Eugenia Lesniak, and all of their five children attended college. Although more successful than many who tried boxing and other professional athletics, Yarosz did not become wealthy and had to work for a living after leaving the ring. Rejected for military service in World War II because of his damaged knee, he operated a tavern and restaurant but eventually sold the business in 1955. He thereafter worked as a caster in a steel factory.

Yarosz was handsome, quiet-spoken, modest, and well liked. He played the violin expertly and later took up the accordion and wind instruments. He received many local, regional, and state honors, including membership in the Pennsylvania and Pittsburgh Sports Halls of Fame. Yarosz died in Rochester, Pennsyvlania, never having retired from his job in the steel industry.

• Yarosz's record is in H. G. Goldman, ed., *1986–87 Ring Record Book and Boxing Encyclopedia*. Articles about Yarosz in *The Ring* magazine are W. Wood, "Teddy Yarosz, Uncrowned Champion," Jan. 1934, pp. 6–7, 46, and N. Fleischer, "Yarosz, Crowned Champion," Nov. 1934, pp. 8–9. Yarosz's career is described in J. D. McCallum, *The Encyclopedia of World Boxing Champions since 1882* (1975), p. 149. Obituaries are in the *Pittsburgh Press*, 30 Mar. 1974, and *The Ring*, July 1974. A kinsman of Yarosz, Ralph Brown of St. Paul, Minnesota, provided copies of useful documents and family information.

LUCKETT V. DAVIS

YELLOW ROBE, Rosebud (26 Feb. 1907–5 Oct. 1992), educator, was born near Rapid City, South Dakota, the daughter of Lily, a nurse, and Chief Chauncey Yellow Robe, a Native American activist and educator. Rosebud, a great-grandniece of Sitting Bull and Iron Plume, was educated in a one-room schoolhouse near her home until she attended public high school in Rapid City, South Dakota. In the late 1920s she was one of the first Native American students to attend the University of South Dakota. Her life's work was greatly influenced by her parents.

Rosebud, the eldest of three daughters, followed in the footsteps of her father, who spent his lifetime teaching about Native American life. Although he was one of the first students to attend Carlisle Indian School, a boarding school in Carlisle, Pennsylvania, designed to enable Native Americans to become assimilated into Anglo society by effectively removing all traces of their cultural heritage, Chauncey Yellow Robe used his education to further the cause of Native Americans. He was later chosen to represent the North American Indians at the Congress of Nations at the opening of the World's Columbian Exposition in Chicago, was active in the Society of American Indians, and worked for years at the United States Indian School in Rapid City, South Dakota. In 1922, Rosebud's mother died, and Rosebud was left to help care for her two younger sisters.

While attending the University of South Dakota, Rosebud won acclaim for her performances of American Indian dances for "Strollers," a yearly student production. At the university, with a student body of about 1,000, she was considered attractive and popular. A sorority rushed her, but she was eventualy disallowed when it was discovered that by its constitution only Caucasians were accepted as members. A few years later President Calvin Coolidge and his wife visited the Black Hills of South Dakota during the summer of 1927. On 4 August, President Coolidge was named an honorary member of the Sioux tribe, and Rosebud presented him with the full feather headdress. This ceremony and other performances at the university resulted in many offers to Rosebud, including one from Cecil B. De Mille, who encouraged her to come to Hollywood to appear in the title role of *Ramona*. She declined. In 1930 her father had taken part in the motion picture *The Silent Enemy*. Chief Yellow Robe wrote and narrated the prologue to the film, which had an authentic Native American cast.

Shortly before her father's death in 1930, Rosebud married A. E. Seymour, a newspaper reporter who had covered President Coolidge's visit. They moved to New York, where their daughter Tahcawin de Cinq-Mars ("Buddy") was born. After her father's death, Rosebud's youngest sister, Evelyn Yellow Robe, moved to New York to live with Rosebud and her family.

In New York Rosebud was involved in theater and lectures at the Museum of Natural History. For two years during the 1930s she appeared on CBS National Radio Network in her own scripts. In 1930 Rosebud got the job of setting up the Indian Village at Jones Beach, Long Island, with teepees, a craft center, and a lawn for storytelling. For the next twenty years, Rosebud Yellow Robe was director of the educational/recreational project under the supervision of the State Park Commission, with the schools of Long Island and New York City participating. She wore the clothing of her culture, working mostly with children, teaching them about Native Americans through handicraft, games, songs, and stories. Through this work, tens of thousands of children were provided with a new and realistic depiction of American Indians. Like her father, she tried to neutralize the negative impact of western films and misconceptions of Indians, "I can't stand to see my people portrayed as such villains," she said. "Even tiny children when they hear I am an Indian retreat from me." Rosebud, her sister Evelyn, and her daughter Buddy worked at Jones Beach every summer until World War II. At that time, Rosebud began a wartime job working for Sperry Gyroscope as a speaker.

In 1949 her husband died. In 1951 she married Alfred Frantz; there were no children from this marriage. Six months later, her granddaughter Karen Winona Moy was born, the daughter of Buddy and Kenneth Moy.

During the 1950s Rosebud appeared regularly on an NBC-TV program for children and on the *Robert Montgomery Presents* series. She also participated with Twentieth Century–Fox in a publicity tour for the film *Broken Arrow* (1950), which was notable for its sympathetic depiction of Native American culture told from the Indian viewpoint. In 1969 she published *An Album of the American Indian*, which summarized the life of seven different Native American tribes before the Europeans came, describing how the arrival of whites changed the life of the Indians through war and isolation on reservations. Ten years later, in 1979, she published *Tonweya and the Eagles, and Other Lakota Tales*, a collection of animal tales told to her by her father, handed down through the Native American oral tradition.

Rosebud's lifetime contributions and commitment to education was honored in May 1989. The W. H. Over State Museum—in conjunction with the South Dakota State Historical Society—held a three-day celebration for her, including Rosebud Yellow Robe Day and University of South Dakota Commencement Day. She was awarded the Doctor of Humane Letters degree and was recognized as an outstanding example of the numerous Native Americans who have attended the University of South Dakota. She died in New York City. In 1993–1994 the University of South Dakota established the Rosebud Yellow Robe Society to honor philanthropists whose lifetime cumulative donations to the university exceeded $500,000, and a scholarship for Native Americans was established in her name.

Rosebud Yellow Robe dedicated a lifetime to communicating the values of her people to others. She continued her father's fight against intolerance, discrimination, and ignorance.

• Personal papers including letters written by and about Rosebud Yellow Robe are located in the Archives & Special Collections Library at the University of South Dakota. Collections of her family artifacts are also displayed at the university, at the W. H. Over State Museum. A brief biographical article by Bill Bleyer, "Special Honor, Special Women," appears in *Newsday*, 31 Aug. 1998. Longtime family friend Marjorie Weinberg-Berman is the author of a forthcoming book titled *The Real Rosebud*. Obituaries are in the *New York Times*, 7 Oct. 1992, and *People* magazine, 26 Oct. 1992.

KAREN BACHMAN BARNETT
CATHERINE DYER KLEIN

YOUNG, Loretta (6 Jan. 1913–12 Aug. 2000), actress, was born Gretchen Michaela Young in Salt Lake City, Utah, the daughter of John Earle Young, an auditor for the Denver, Rio Grande, and Western Railroad, and Gladys Royal Young. When Young was three years old, her father abandoned the family. Soon thereafter she moved with her family to Los Angeles, where her mother opened a boardinghouse catering to film industry personnel. In 1917, at age four, Young made her film debut as an extra in *The Only Way* for the Famous Players–Lasky studio. That year she also appeared as an extra in *The Primrose Ring*, starring Mae Murray, who took a liking to the attractive child and informally adopted her.

Young returned to her family after living for eighteen months with Murray and was an extra in *The Sheik* (1921) with Rudolph Valentino. She then attended local Catholic schools, including the Ramona Convent in Alhambra, California. In 1927 Young abandoned formal education to return to films by accepting a small part in *Naughty but Nice*, starring Colleen Moore, for the First National studio. Young's part had originally been offered to one of her older sisters, Polly Ann and Elizabeth, the latter acting under the name of Sally Blane. Impressed with the teenage Young's preternaturally mature beauty and willingness to work hard, First National signed her to a contract and changed her first name to Loretta. After she played a small part in *The Whip Woman* (1927), she was loaned by First National to Metro-Goldwyn-Mayer for a supporting role in *Laugh, Clown, Laugh* (1928), starring Lon Chaney. Dark-haired and of medium height, with a slender, lithe figure, porcelain skin, high cheekbones, and pale gray eyes, Young appeared in minor roles in five more silent films in 1928. In 1929 she successfully made the transition to sound movies with *The Squall*, directed by Alexander Korda. Established as a promising "starlet," she was teamed with another young First National contract player, Douglas Fairbanks, Jr., in a series of low-budget films aimed at the youth market. In 1930, just after her seventeenth birthday, Young eloped to Arizona with the actor Grant Withers, with whom she had costarred in *The Second-Floor Mystery* (1929). The childless union was annulled after nine months.

During the early 1930s Young appeared in dozens of films. Many were quickly produced and quickly forgotten low-budget fare or "programmers," but some were top-notch projects that allowed her to develop into a major star. Her more significant films of this period include *Platinum Blonde* (1931), a comedy directed by Frank Capra and costarring Jean Harlow; *Zoo in Budapest* (1933), an off-beat romance with Gene Raymond; *A Man's Castle* (1933), a drama set in a shantytown and costarring Spencer Tracy, with whom Young had a serious off-screen romance; *The House of Rothschild* (1934), a historical drama with George Arliss; and *Bulldog Drummond Strikes Back* (1934), a comedic adventure with Ronald Colman. In early 1935 Young, now under contract to Twentieth Century–Fox, was paired with Clark Gable in the screen version of Jack London's Alaskan adventure novel *The Call of the Wild*. Young and Gable had an affair during the film's location shooting in the Pacific Northwest, and in late 1935 Young gave birth to a daughter fathered by Gable. After leaving the girl in an orphanage for a period, Young took the child back, pretending to adopt her. Although rumors about the child's true origins were whispered in Hollywood, the elaborate hoax was successful and enabled Young to avoid what was then the career-destroying stigma of having an illegitimate child.

Although she was unquestionably in the top tier of Hollywood stars, Young never reached the level of stardom where she was called upon to carry a picture by herself. She was almost always paired with a male star of equal or greater fame. In the late 1930s she made five films with Tyrone Power, who was also under contract to Twentieth Century–Fox, most notably *Suez* (1938), directed by Allan Dwan, a fictionalized account of the creation of the Suez Canal, with Young as the French empress Eugénie and Power as the canal engineer Ferdinand de Lesseps. Young also appeared in three films with another Twentieth Century–Fox star, Don Ameche, including *The Story of Alexander Graham Bell* (1939). Her other films of this period include *Kentucky* (1938), a romance set in horse-breeding country with Richard Greene; and *Eternally Yours* (1939), a comedy about a magician and his wife, with David Niven. In 1940 Young married Thomas Lewis, an advertising executive in charge of accounts with radio program sponsorship. The couple, who separated in 1956 and divorced in 1969, had two children.

Leaving Twentieth Century–Fox in 1940, Young freelanced for the remainder of her screen career. Making up for the lack of studio support, she hired a personal publicist to keep her name before the public and control her public image. Young unashamedly considered herself more of a "movie star" than an actress and rarely appeared in public without carefully arranged clothes, hairstyle, and makeup. A devout Roman Catholic, she was highly conscious of the potential influence of Hollywood on American morals. Her piety and her assertiveness with business associates earned her the moniker "Attila the Nun." Without a studio contract, she appeared in far fewer films, but they were of a generally high quality and enabled her to display a wider range as an actress. Her films of the 1940s include *Bedtime Story* (1941) with Fredric March; *China* (1943) with Alan Ladd; *Along Came Jones* (1945) with Gary Cooper; *The Stranger* (1946) with Orson Welles; *The Bishop's Wife* (1947) with Cary Grant and David Niven; and *Rachel and the Stranger* (1948) with William Holden and Robert Mitchum. In 1947 she won the Academy Award for best actress for her portrayal of a Swedish maid who becomes a member of the U.S. Congress in the comedy *The Farmer's Daughter*. After dozens of films over almost two decades of stardom, it was the first time she had even been nominated for an Oscar. She earned a second best actress Oscar nomination for *Come to the Stable* (1949), a sentimental tale about French nuns setting up a children's hospital in Connecticut. Based on a short story by Clare Boothe Luce, *Come to the Stable*, which costarred Celeste Holm, was Young's favorite among her own films.

In the early 1950s, as her film career finally began to peter out (her final screen appearance came in the 1953 comedy *It Happens Every Thursday* with John Forsythe), the tenacious and indefatigable Young quickly turned to television and became one of the first major film performers to star in a television series. Premiering in September 1953 on NBC, *The Loretta Young Show* (originally titled *Letter to Loretta*) was a half-hour dramatic anthology series offering morally elevating stories that reflected Young's personal taste. Young introduced each episode (and acted in about half of them) and closed the program with a quotation or lines of verse that reinforced the meaning of the story. She brought her movie star glamour and personal chic to the series by making her initial appearances emerging from a doorway in a different designer gown each week. Young also served as executive producer of the series and maintained tight control over its contents. Though never near the top of the ratings, the show ran for eight seasons, keeping to the same Sunday nighttime slot, and earned Young the Emmy award for best actress in a dramatic series in 1955, 1957, and 1959. She was the first performer to win both an Oscar and an Emmy. NBC rebroadcast episodes of the series in the afternoon from 1960 to 1964. In 1962 Young returned to prime-time television in *The New Loretta Young Show*, a family comedy-drama in which she played a widowed magazine writer with seven children. The new program, which ran on CBS, lasted for only one season.

With the demise of her second television series, Young's acting career essentially ended. Remaining slender and elegant into her old age, she spent the last decades of her life socializing with friends in the film industry, traveling, and participating in Catholic devotional activities and charity work. She returned to acting in two made-for-television movies, *Christmas Eve* (1986) and *Lady in the Corner* (1989). In 1993 she married Jean Louis, a clothing designer she had been friends with for decades. Young died of colon cancer in Los Angeles and is buried beside her mother in Holy Cross Cemetery, Culver City, California.

• Young's unrevealing memoir, cowritten with her publicist Helen Ferguson, is *The Things I Had to Learn* (1961). An interview with the elderly Young is Stewart Wiener, "Miss Loretta Young in the Desert," *Palm Springs Life*, Dec. 1995, pp. 58–64, 80. Joan Wester Anderson, *Forever Young: The Life, Loves, and Enduring Faith of a Hollywood Legend* (2000), is an authorized biography (Young instigated the project and supplied information and photographs) that emphasizes Young's religious beliefs. An additional biography is Joe Morella and Edward Z. Epstein, *Loretta Young: An Extraordinary Life* (1986). Judy Lewis, *Uncommon Knowledge* (1994), is a memoir by Young's daughter by Clark Gable that offers much insight into Young's personal life. Ronald L. Bowers, "Loretta Young: Began as a Child-Extra and Exuded Glamour for Forty Years," *Films in Review*, Apr. 1969, pp. 192–217, is a comprehensive examination of Young's film career. An obituary is in the *New York Times*, 13 Aug. 2000.

MARY C. KALFATOVIC

YOUNGS, Ross (10 Apr. 1897–22 Oct. 1927), member of the National Baseball Hall of Fame, was born in Shiner, Texas, the son of Stonewall Jackson Youngs, a section boss for the San Antonio and Arkansas Pass Railway, and Henrie Middlebrook Youngs. Ross was the second of three sons. In the early 1900s Jack Youngs's leg was crushed in an accident. He received a generous settlement from the railroad and a pension. He moved his family to San Antonio and bought a cattle ranch in the nearby hamlet of Christine. In 1907 the New York Stock Exchange crashed, and Youngs's cattle business suffered.

Abandoning his family, he moved to Houston. Henrie Youngs was forced to turn her home into a boarding house.

Ross, though one of the smallest boys in his elementary school class, was an exceptional athlete. At a San Antonio grade-school track meet, Ross won the 50-yard, 100-yard, and 200-yard dashes as well as the running broad jump. He also finished second in the pole vault. At San Antonio High School he quickly gained attention as a football player. On 27 October 1913, reporting a victory over Saint Edwards College, the *San Antonio Express News* noted that the sixteen-year-old "Young [news accounts throughout his career misspelled his last name] at right half played through three quarters and a part of the last, and one of the touchdowns was his after he obtained possession of a forward pass and ran thirty-five yards. . . . Time after time during the contest he brushed by the left end for gains of ten, fifteen and twenty yards" (King, 7 Mar. 2001, pp. 1c, 3c).

In 1914, just weeks before his seventeenth birthday, Ross signed a professional baseball contract for $75 a month. That summer he played for the Austin Senators of the Texas League. His first experience at professional baseball was a failure. He compiled a .103 batting average. In September 1914 Youngs enrolled at West Texas Military Academy. He turned his attention to the gridiron and was an instant success. In the summer of 1915, still under contract, he played third base for the Senators. In the fall he returned to West Texas Military, where he became the best football player in the city of San Antonio. In nine games West Texas scored 149 points; Youngs accounted for 63 of them. Many colleges, including the University of Pennsylvania, offered him football scholarships. He turned them down to play baseball.

In 1916 the nineteen-year-old Youngs, now physically matured, tore through the Western Association League. In 139 games, at 5 feet, eight inches and 162 pounds, the left-handed batter led the league in batting average (.362), hits (195), and runs scored (103). He also stole 42 bases. Youngs's manager on the Sherman, Texas, team wrote to the famous New York Giants manager John McGraw about his star player. McGraw dispatched the legendary scout Dick Kinsella to watch Youngs play. Kinsella immediately sent a telegram to McGraw stating, "Grab Him!" The Giants paid the Sherman, Texas, team $2,000 for Youngs's contract. McGraw, skeptical about tips regarding prospects, later reflected: "Even shrewd judges of baseball talent go astray in sizing up a youngster. But I was impressed enough by what I heard to give Youngs a trial at training camp. He was a smart, aggressive kid, full of life and pep" (King, Mar. 7, 2001, p. 3c). Upon witnessing Youngs play, McGraw dubbed him "Pep," a nickname that stuck with Youngs throughout his major league career.

Although Youngs played third base for Sherman, McGraw was convinced that he was not an infielder: "I told him that he would have to play the outfield, that he did not have the hands for an infielder. . . . I

sent him to Rochester with orders to convert him into an outfielder" (King, 8 Mar. 2001, p. 1c). Under the guidance of the Rochester manager Mickey Dolan, a member of McGraw's 1916 Giants, Youngs hit .356 and stole 34 bases. He also learned how to play the outfield. The Rochester fans loved Youngs's hustle. At the conclusion of the 1917 season he was brought up to the Giants.

In 1918, his first full year in the majors, the powerful right-handed thrower was positioned in the outfield. He quickly learned how to handle the Polo Grounds' right field wall. "The ball coming to right field curves a good deal," Youngs proclaimed. "You have to learn to judge that curve and on many ball fields, especially the Polo Grounds, there's a right field wall that you must get acquainted with. A mistake in judging the ball hot off that wall might well mean a game" ("The Right Fielder's Side of the Case: An Interview with Ross Youngs," Ross Youngs File, National Baseball Hall of Fame). That year he also excelled at the plate. He batted .302, with 143 hits and 10 stolen bases. By his second full year with the Giants his aggressive style of play earned him the label "Ty Cobb, Jr." His Hall of Fame teammate Frankie Frisch observed years later: "Ross was the hardest-running, devil-may-care guy I ever saw coming into an opposing infielder" (Broeg, p. 1c).

Youngs's superb throwing arm and above-average speed compensated for his often overly enthusiastic style of defensive play. What set him apart from other ballplayers, however, was his aggressive style of baserunning. "Base stealing," Youngs remarked, "is one thing you have to learn. . . . [It] is by no means a thing of speed alone. Some fairly slow men are good base runners. Some fast men are notoriously poor. . . . You have to study the pitchers to be a good base stealer and that takes time" (Lane, pp. 377–78). Fresco Thompson, an infielder for the Pittsburgh Pirates, recalled an encounter with Youngs during the 1925 season. Playing second base, Thompson "hustled over to second to make the double-play. But as I caught the ball and started to pivot something HIT me. . . . I came about five feet back of second and in a most undignified position. I brushed myself off . . . saying in a hurt manner to Ross: 'That's a pretty tough way to treat a youngster, isn't it?' 'Well, kid,' he replied, in his slow Texas drawl, 'you know we're not playing for marbles around here'" ("Mr. Thompson Meets Mr. Youngs," Ross Youngs File, National Baseball Hall of Fame).

During his eight seasons with the Giants, Youngs compiled a .322 batting average and became the first player in World Series history to connect for two hits in a single inning—a double and triple against the New York Yankees in the seventh inning of the third game in the 1921 series. In four consecutive World Series, 1921–1924, the Giants won the first two, and Youngs played in every game and batted .286. During his major league career, spanning 10 years, Youngs topped the .300 mark 9 times. Twice he had 200 or more hits in a season. In 1919 he led the league in doubles, and in 1923 he led in runs scored. Youngs's greatest season was in 1924. He compiled a .356 batting average and hit 10 home runs with 74 runs batted in. "Youngs was a real hitter," one veteran sports commentator wrote. "He was a left-handed hitter and gripped his bat with his hands about six inches apart and he not only crowded the plate, but he crowded the pitcher, too. He would run up on the pitcher to beat the break on a curve" (Frank Graham, "The Saga of Ross Youngs," Ross Youngs File, National Baseball Hall of Fame).

Despite his remarkable season in 1924, Youngs was implicated in a scandal just before the regular season ended. On the eve of the first World Series game against the Washington Senators, an allegation charged that the Giants rookie Jimmy O'Connell offered the Philadelphia Phillies shortstop Heine Sands $500 near the end of the season to "take it easy" on the Giants so they could win the pennant. O'Connell said he made the offer under the direction of the Giants coach Cozy Dolan with the backing of Youngs, Frankie Frisch, and George Kelly. Baseball Commissioner Kenesaw Mountain Landis investigated the charges. Dolan and O'Connell were banned from baseball. The other players, including Youngs, vigorously denied the charges, and Landis cleared them to play in the World Series.

At the pinnacle of his playing career, Youngs married Dorothy Peinecke, who was from Brooklyn. The marriage, which had been delayed because the World Series went seven games, took place on 12 October 1924. They had a daughter. At the time of Youngs's death divorce proceedings were underway. Youngs's celebrity status and his desire to spend his off-seasons in San Antonio created a strain in their marriage. A skilled dancer, Youngs was frequently seen at hotel ballrooms around the city. He spent considerable time playing golf and won amateur trophies in San Antonio and New York. He also carried with him a collection of pearls befitting his reported $12,000-a-year contract. But Youngs's mother was most instrumental in causing the marital breakup. Henrie Youngs apparently did not approve of Dorothy, and the couple separated when their daughter, Caroline, was born in December 1925.

In 1925 Youngs's batting average fell below .300 for the first time in his career. During spring training in 1926 he was diagnosed with Bright's disease; medically referred to as nephritis, it is an illness diagnosed by a sudden appearance of blood in the urine. The Giants hired a full-time nurse to travel with him. In 95 games Youngs managed to hit .306. He also spent time tutoring the future Hall of Famer Mel Ott. In 1927 Youngs remained in San Antonio, where he succumbed to the disease. In Youngs's memory, McGraw hung a picture of Youngs behind his office desk at the Polo Grounds, next to a photograph of the legendary pitcher Christy Mathewson. A bronze tablet honoring Youngs was placed on the right field wall of the Polo Grounds.

In 1,211 career games Youngs compiled 1,491 hits, 236 doubles, 93 triples, 812 runs scored, 592 runs batted in, 153 stolen bases, and a .441 slugging percentage. In the early twenty-first century he still held the third-best batting average in franchise history, behind Bill Terry's .341 and George Davis's .332. A shortened career and nagging accusations stemming from the 1924 scandal delayed his entry into the Baseball Hall of Fame. At the urging of Baseball Commissioner Ford Frick, the Veterans Committee selected Youngs on 7 August 1972. It finally validated McGraw's observation at the time of his player's death: "He was the greatest outfielder I ever saw on a baseball field. The game was never over with Young[s] until the last man was out. He could do everything a baseball player should do and do it better than most players. As an outfielder he had no superiors. . . . In all his years with the Giants, he never caused one minute's trouble for myself or the club. On top of all this, a gamer ball player than Young[s] never played ball" (*New York Times*, 23 Oct. 1927).

• A slim collection of news clippings and information related to Youngs's playing days is at the National Baseball Hall of Fame, Cooperstown, N.Y. An excellent five-part series on Youngs's life and career is David King, "Giant in His Field," *San Antonio Express News*, 6 Mar.–10 Mar. 2001. Another news account is Tim Griffin, "Fame, Forever Fleeting," *San Antonio Express News*, 27 July 1997. A useful contemporary article is F. C. Lane, "How Ross Young Was Christened 'Pep,'" *Baseball Magazine*, July 1923, pp. 377–78. Youngs's selection into the Hall of Fame is the subject of Bob Broeg, "Pep Youngs Flashy as Frisch on Basepaths," *St. Louis Post-Dispatch*, 1 Feb. 1972. A number of works, some scholarly in nature, discuss the history of the New York Giants and Youngs's career, including Andrew Goldblatt, *The Giants and the Dodgers: Four Cities, Two Teams, One Rivalry* (2003); Frank Graham, *The New York Giants: An Informal History of a Great Baseball Club* (2001); Noel Hynd, *The Giants of the Polo Grounds: The Glorious Times of Baseball's New York Giants* (1988); Peter Williams, *When the Giants Were Giants: Bill Terry and the Golden Age of New York Baseball* (1994); Lawrence S. Ritter, *The Glory of Their Times: The Story of the Early Days of Baseball Told by the Men Who Played It* (1966); Stew Thornley, *New York's Polo Grounds: Land of the Giants* (2000). Obituaries are in the *New York Times*, 23 Oct. 1927; the *Boston Sunday Globe*, 23 Oct. 1927; the *Herald Tribune*, 23 Oct. 1927; and the *Sporting News*, 27 Oct. 1927.

CHARLES F. HOWLETT

YOUSKEVITCH, Igor (13 Mar. 1912–13 June 1994), ballet dancer and choreographer, was born Igor' Ivanovich Iuskevich in Piryatin, a small Ukrainian community southeast of Kiev; the son of Ivan Iuskevich, a judge, and Sophia Lipsky Iuskevich. His first memory of dance was the Russian opera *Tsar Saltan*. While his earliest years were grounded in a comfortable, middle-class household, the tumultuous changes wrought by World War I and the spread of the Bolshevik revolution soon overwhelmed this stability. After Ukrainian nationalists joined with the Poles to march as far east as Kiev, the Red Army pushed the Polish-Ukrainian forces back into Poland.

In 1920 Youskevitch's father fled with his family to Belgrade, Yugoslavia.

Adapting to his new surroundings, Igor was a natural athlete who from the age of ten excelled at swimming, calisthenics, and gymnastics. His innate strength, agility, and sense of timing made him a successful member of the Yugoslav Sokol gymnastic group. He graduated from the Russian–Serbian high school in 1930 and attended Belgrade Royal University briefly.

Traveling with the Sokol group to competitions, he gained recognition for his gymnastic prowess; his skill at a tournament in Prague in 1932 drew the attention of Yugoslav ballerina Xenia Grunt. Grunt, who needed "a young man with strong muscles" (Youskevitch, in Newman, p. 46) for an acrobatic dance number, offered the job to Youskevitch. After two short months of training, he debuted in concert as Grunt's partner and went on to perform with her in Paris. While Grunt's productions met with little success, the critics saw that her relatively untrained partner had genuine potential. When she returned to Yugoslavia, Youskevitch stayed on in Paris to study dance and launch his life's vocation.

At the relatively late age of twenty, Youskevitch began his ballet training in earnest with Olga Preobrajenska at her school in the Studio Wacker. Preobrajenska had been trained by the famed ballet masters Enrico Cecchetti, Lev Ivanov, and Marius Petipa at the St. Petersburg school and was principal soloist with the Maryinsky Theater. She introduced Youskevitch to the classical style with which he came to be identified throughout his long international career. Preobrajenska, described by critics as a "poetess of dance" with a penchant for improvisation, became a pivotal figure for Youskevitch, and he claimed her as a singular mentor.

By 1934 Youskevitch was prepared to join Bronislava Nijinska's Les Ballets de Paris and soon after became a member of Les Ballets de Leon Woizikowski. Working with Woizikowski offered him entry into the second company of the Ballets Russes de Colonel Wassily de Basil. Throughout his career, he continued to move in and out of the various companies that claimed lineage in the splintered genealogy of the Ballets Russes following the death of founder Serge Diaghilev. With Basil's company, Youskevitch quickly became principal dancer and from 13 October 1936 to 14 July 1937 undertook an extended tour of Australia and New Zealand. While with Woizikowski, Youskevitch met dancer Anna Scarpova, whom he would later call "the best critic I ever had" (Youskevitch, in Newman, p. 56). They were married in 1938 and in 1944 had a daughter. In 1938 he and Scarpova both joined Serge Denham's Ballets Russes de Monte Carlo. As principal dancer, Youskevitch explored a broad range of works; he was reunited with choreographer Bronislawa Nijinska in *The Snow Maiden* and created roles in Léonide Massine's *Gaité Parisienne* and *Rouge et Noir*.

Youskevitch stayed with the Ballets Russes de Monte Carlo until 1944 when he volunteered to serve in the U.S. Navy. He went from premier danseur noble to seaman second class and an American citizen. On the last night of Youskevitch's shore leave critic Edwin Denby wrote that he was at the peak of his classic style. "His style is calm, rich and elastic. It is completely correct. . . . The changing shape of the dancing body is vigorously defined. . . . The distribution of energy is intelligent and complex. . . . His stage presence has none of that hard insistence on attention that breaks the illusion and flow of a classic ballet" (Denby, p. 129). Youskevitch did not strive for an empty virtuosity; he believed that the classical dancer should not show effort, preparation, or any movement that detracts from the expression of the movement "so as to emphasize, not the dancing, but more the expression of the step, what it's supposed to convey" (Youskevitch, in Newman, p. 51).

By the time Youskevitch left the dance world for the military, he had accomplished much. He provided a strong role model whose romantically masculine presence promoted ballet as an acceptable profession for men at a crucial moment in the developing American ballet. After serving in the military for two years, however, he had returned overweight and out of shape, far from his prewar dancing condition. His wife urged him to return to ballet class. He was 34 years old, but, prevailing against all odds, he quickly returned to the concert stage, joining Massine's Ballets Russes Highlights to dance with many of his former cohorts: Alexandra Danilova, Tamara Toumanova, Dame Alicia Markova, Mia Slavenska, and André Eglevsky. The fall of that same year, Youskevitch became premier danseur at (American) Ballet Theater, marking his triumphant reentry into the American ballet world.

Ballet Theater provided a venue for Youskevitch's talent in a wide range of roles including Antony Tudor's *Romeo and Juliet*, Nijinska's *Schumann Concerto*, and *A Streetcar Named Desire*, choreographed by modern dancer Valerie Bettis, in which he played an uncharacteristically brutal Stanley to Nora Kaye's Blanche. In 1947 George Balanchine choreographed his first major classical work for the Ballet Theater repertory. Balanchine constructed *Theme and Variations* for Youskevitch as a veritable syllabus of classic dance ideas from the great days of Russian ballet. The dance underscored Youskevitch's unique stage persona and impressive technical skill. Set to Tchaikovsky's Suite no. 3 in G Major, *Theme and Variations* also featured the pairing of Yousekevitch with Alicia Alonso, a young ballerina who had come up from the corps de ballet.

Onstage, Youskevitch was recognized for his sensitivity and gallant attention to his partner. He described the danseur's relationship with the ballerina as "a kind of refined love affair" (Youskevitch, in Newman, p. 58). He had accompanied many of his generation's great ballerinas—Markova, Danilova, Kaye, and Slavenska—but his partnership with Alonso was to become legendary. Alonso's classical lyricism was enhanced by what critic Walter Terry described as "a very real femininity," which provided the ideal counterpoint to Youskevitch's elegant virility. Their onstage pairing lasted until 1960 and included many works such as their renowned *Giselle* and the *Black Swan* pas de deux.

Alonso divided her time between Ballet Theater and Ballet de Cuba in her homeland; Youskevitch frequently accompanied her in Cuba. Following the Cuban revolution in 1959, Alonso's company became Ballet Nacional de Cuba. Youskevitch, along with Danilova and dance critic Ann Barzel, helped to select that company's members. By 1955, Youskevitch and Alonso were back touring extensively with the Ballet Russes de Monte Carlo, with Yousekevitch serving as artistic director for that company until 1957. On leaving the Monte Carlo group, he continued to choreograph and restage classic ballets. In 1960 he rejoined Ballet Theater as a guest artist on that company's first visit to the Soviet Union. This tour brought Youskevitch full circle, returning to the country of his birth and to the historic stronghold of classic ballet as a member of an established American ballet company.

Youskevich and contemporaries such as Danilova and Eglevsky were from a unique generation of dancers whose work bridged Russian dance tradition and the emerging American strain. In a genuinely American variation, Youskevitch extended his performance life beyond the concert stage and into the movie theater. MGM films released *Invitation to the Dance* on 1 January 1956. Directed by Gene Kelly, the film was the first commercial feature devoted to dance as the sole means of artistic expression and communication. The film is perhaps best remembered for Kelly's combination of live dancing with cartoon animation in the Hanna-Barbera sequence "Sinbad the Sailor." But Youskevitch was featured in two sections, "Ring Around the Rosy" and the opening ballet "Circus" with Kelly and French ballerina Claire Sombert. While a commercial disappointment, *Invitation to the Dance* provides an excellent record of Youskevitch's dancing and a testament to the vitality that he brought to American ballet.

Ending his nearly thirty-year touring career in 1962, Youskevitch opened a ballet school with Scarpova and founded a small semiprofessional ballet company, Youth Ballet Romantique, featuring their daughter Maria. He continued as a guest teacher and ballet master with many schools around the country. He joined the faculty of the University of Texas at Austin in 1971. Adopting western shirts, jeans, and cowboy boots, he claimed that the Texas panorama reminded him of his childhood home. Youskevitch wrote numerous articles that shed light on his personality, career and performance philosophy. His critical review of Soviet defectors Mikhail Baryshnikov, Rudolf Nureyev, and Alexander Godonov in "Former Soviet Stars as Seen by a Colleague," (*New York Times*, 21 Feb. 1982), underscores the attributes that he found most valuable to the danseur. "The Male Image," *Dance Perspectives* 40 (Winter 1969): 13–23,

provides revelatory insight into the era and Youskevitch's philosophy as he writes regarding the contrasting qualities he perceived in the motivation and performance of the male and female dancer.

His retirement in 1982 inspired a tribute that expanded to become a four-day conference titled "Dance Celebration: Fifty Years of Ballet in America." The climax of the conference was a performance that celebrated his retirement, his fifty-year career in dance, and his seventieth birthday. As a stunning finale to that performance, an immense movie screen was lowered onto the stage on which was projected a historic film of Youskevitch and Alonso dancing their signature pas de deux from *Giselle*. Slowly the screen lifted to unveil Youskevitch and Alonso in the flesh. As the audience sat transfixed, the venerable couple completed their legendary duet one final time. Watching from the wings, famed choreographer Agnes de Mille was heard to whisper, "There will never be another *Giselle* to equal this" (de Mille in Barker, p. 29).

Professor Emeritus Youskevitch was the recipient of many awards including the Dance Magazine Award in 1958 and the Capezio Award in 1990. For his long association with the Cuban ballet, in 1993 he was awarded the Premio del Gran Teatro de La Habana by the Cuban government. Through the dance, Youskevitch became an international star whose work came to define the strong danseur noble and ushered in a new appreciation for and acceptance of the male role in American ballet. Even after retirement, Youskevitch continued to share his insight and passion for dance, establishing the New York International Ballet Competition. As the competition's artistic director he taught and inspired dancers from all over the world until his death in New York.

• In addition to his articles and interviews, Yousekevitch contributed an autobiographical section to Barbara Newman's *Striking a Balance: Dancers Talk about Dancing* (1982), pp. 45–59. "Busing Les Ballets," *Ballet Review* 11 (Fall 1983): 30–31, provides a humorous remembrance of touring Europe with Léon Woizikowski's ballet company in 1935. Selma Jeanne Cohen provides a fond and very personal account in "Prince Igor: The Story of Youskevitch," *Dance Magazine* (May 1953): 14–17. Dance critics Edwin Denby, *Looking at the Dance* (1949), and Walter Terry, *The Dance in America* (1956) and *Great Male Dancers of the Ballet* (1978), offer archival review material of Youskevitch in performance. Vital to untangling the twisted history of his associations with the many permutations of the Ballets Russes is Jack Anderson, *The One and Only: The Ballet Russes de Monte Carlo* (1981), and Lynn Garafola, *Diaghilev's Ballets Russes* (1989). Youskevitch's retirement concert is recounted by Barbara Barker in "Celebrating Youskevitch," *Ballet Review* no. 11 (Fall 1983): 27–29. Marilyn Hunt has provided the bulk of biographical writing on Youskevitch. Her articles include "Danseur Noble," *Ballet News* 3 (Mar. 1982): 16–18, and "Igor Youskevitch Dancing,"*Ballet Review* 11 (Fall 1983): 32–63, which contains a chronology of his work and many photos that remain as mute testimony to his striking presence. An obituary is in the *New York Times*, 14 June 1994.

MARY ANNE SANTOS NEWHALL

ZUMWALT, Elmo Russell, Jr. (29 Nov. 1920–2 Jan. 2000), admiral, was born in San Francisco, California, the son of Elmo R. Zumwalt, Sr., and Frances Frank Zumwalt, both physicians. He grew up in Tulare, California, where both parents practiced medicine. An Eagle Scout and class valedictorian, he graduated from Tulare Union High School in 1939. He then spent a year at the Rutherford Preparatory School in Long Beach, California, while waiting for an appointment to the U.S. Naval Academy, which he duly received upon the recommendation of Senator Hiram Johnson.

At the Naval Academy, Zumwalt performed well. He served as company commander, was a regimental three-striper, and also twice won the academy's public speaking contest. In 1942, graduating 24th out of his class of 615 academically, he also showed his inherent disdain for what he considered fussy and meaningless regulations, finishing 275th in conduct. He was immediately commissioned as an ensign and assigned to the destroyer *Phelps* in June 1942. Zumwalt later served on the destroyer *Robinson*. In 1944, during the Battle of Leyte Gulf, he received the Bronze Star for gallant service as an evaluator in the ship's combat information center, where he furnished information crucial to American success, and was promoted to lieutenant. In 1945 Zumwalt captured a Japanese gunboat, charged up the Huangpu River, and occupied Shanghai. During the six weeks he spent in Shanghai he met Mouza Coutelais du Roche. They married in October 1945 and had four children.

After the war Zumwalt was accepted to both medical schools and law schools and also was a finalist for a Rhodes Scholarship. He decided to stay in the U.S. Navy. He was posted as executive officer on two destroyers, the USS *Saufley* and the USS *Zellars*. In January 1948 he returned to the United States and spent a year and half as an assistant professor in the Navy ROTC program at the University of North Carolina–Chapel Hill. In April 1950 he was promoted to lieutenant commander and again returned to sea as captain of the USS *Tills*. During the Korean War he served as navigator for the battleship *Wisconsin* and received a Letter of Commendation with Ribbon and Combat V.

In June 1952 Zumwalt returned to school and spent a year at the Naval War College in Newport, Rhode Island. In June 1953 he began to hone his political and administrative skills within the naval bureaucracy with his appointment as the Navy Department's Head of Shore and Overseas Bases Section, Bureau of Naval Personnel, in Washington, D.C. In 1957 he was transferred to the Office of Assistant Secretary of the Navy (Personnel and Reserve Forces) and for the next two years served as special assistant for naval personnel and then as special assistant and naval aide.

In December 1959 Zumwalt returned to sea as commander of one of the first guided missile frigates, the USS *Dewey*. Promoted to captain, he spent ten

months in mid-1961 at the National War College in Washington, D.C. While he was at the War College, his reputation as an upcoming expert on the vagaries of the Soviet leadership brought him to the attention of Paul Nitze, who was assistant secretary of defense for international affairs. In June 1962 Nitze assigned Zumwalt to his staff. When Nitze became secretary of the navy in 1963, he brought Zumwalt along as his executive assistant and senior aide. For his work with Nitze, Zumwalt earned the Legion of Merit and was promoted to rear admiral at age forty-four, the youngest in history to that date. In July 1965 he was once again at sea, this time as commander of Cruiser-Destroyer Flotilla Seven. It was not long, however, before he was back in Washington, this time for a two-year stint as director of the Systems Analysis Group in the Office of the Chief of Naval Operations (CNO). In this capacity he represented the CNO within the Defense Department and on Capitol Hill.

Zumwalt had opposed American involvement in Vietnam, arguing that this action would needlessly deflect American naval and military forces from the larger task of confronting what he perceived to be the growing Soviet threat. Nevertheless in August 1968 Zumwalt was ordered to Vietnam as commander of the U.S. Naval Forces and chief of the Naval Advisory Group, and the next month he was promoted to vice admiral ahead of 130 more senior officers. While in Vietnam, Zumwalt sought to impede the movement of North Vietnamese troops along that nation's numerous waterways. As part of Operation Sealord (Southeast Asia Lake, Ocean, and Delta Strategy), Zumwalt conceived of a "brown water navy," consisting of patrol boats and hovercraft, and sent it to the Mekong Delta and other estuaries to cut off Viet Cong supply routes. Zumwalt also authorized the use of Agent Orange, a powerful chemical defoliant, which stripped away the dense jungle growth crowding the waterways and concealing enemy snipers. Agent Orange reduced American naval causalities, but it also had horrendous aftereffects on the environment and those who were exposed to it.

In July 1970 Zumwalt was promoted to admiral, again the youngest to date and ahead of thirty-one men his seniors in the Navy Register. He succeeded Admiral Thomas H. Moorer as chief of naval operations (CNO). Zumwalt confronted the dual challenge of declining enlistment rates and rebuilding an aging naval fleet in the face of a parsimonious and warweary Congress. In typically direct fashion, he reformed traditional naval discipline through a series of 121 memos that were called "Z-grams." In addition to allowing neatly trimmed beards and more relaxed clothing standards, Zumwalt insisted on the abolition of all discrimination against minorities. He also allowed women to go to sea. Though these new regulations were bitterly opposed by traditionalists, Zumwalt held firmly to his new policies, and both enlistment and retention rates increased.

Zumwalt's other major task was to cope with the refurbished Soviet navy without spending much money or ruffling the culture of détente being crafted by President Richard Nixon and Secretary of State Henry Kissinger. Zumwalt mothballed older ships and used his limited resources to construct smaller and faster craft. Again traditionalists howled that his mothballing proposals would ruin America's naval forces. He also pressed for more nuclear-powered aircraft carriers and for the prompt development of the Trident nuclear submarine and missile system.

In July 1974 Zumwalt retired, and in 1976 he ran unsuccessfully as a Democrat for a Senate seat from Virginia. That same year he published his memoirs, *On Watch*. In 1986 he wrote a joint memoir with his son Elmo Zumwalt III, who suffered, like many other Vietnam veterans, from exposure to Agent Orange. Zumwalt expressed profound sorrow for his son's debilitating illness, but both men remained convinced that the use of Agent Orange had been militarily appropriate. The younger Zumwalt died in 1988, and out of his grief the admiral established the first national bone marrow donor program to help other cancer patients. During retirement Zumwalt served on various corporate boards. He died at the Duke University Medical Center in Durham, North Carolina, from complications of surgery for a chest tumor.

Zumwalt earned over three dozen medals and decorations, culminating in 1998, when President Bill Clinton bestowed upon him the Medal of Freedom, the nation's highest civilian award. As chief of naval operations, Zumwalt enacted reforms that dramatically and permanently reshaped the navy into a more humane and just institution for all who served. Although he spent his career working to improve the U.S. Navy's ability to effectively respond to the Soviet naval threat, he is best remembered for his courageous willingness to challenge the naval traditionalists and unflinchingly seek to modernize his branch of the nation's armed forces in the last third of the twentieth century. He will also, however, be remembered for his decision to use Agent Orange in Vietnam, a choice that would have long-lasting effects on the soldiers of that war.

• Zumwalt's papers are in Texas Tech University's Vietnam Archive. With his son Elmo Zumwalt III he wrote *My Father, My Son* (1986). Also useful is Leslie Julian Cullen, "Brown Water Admiral: Elmo R. Zumwalt, Jr., and United States Naval Forces, Vietnam, 1968–1970" (Ph.D. Diss., Texas Tech Univ., 1998). For Zumwalt's Vietnam tour, see Norman Friedman, "Elmo Russell Zumwalt, Jr.," in *The Chiefs of Naval Operations*, ed. Robert William Love, Jr. (1980). An obituary is in the *New York Times*, 3 Jan. 2000.

EDWARD A. GOEDEKEN

A

Adams, Alice
Agronsky, Martin
Albert, Carl
Allen, Steve
Anfinsen, Christian B.
Atanasoff, John Vincent
Avery, R. Stanton

B

Bad Heart Bull, Amos
Barboncito
Barnett, Jackson
Bates, Peg Leg
Becker, Abraham Jacob
Becker, Magdalena
  Hergert
Belanger, Mark
Bell, Alfred H.
Berne, Eric
Berry, Ananias "Nyas"
Berry, James
Berry, Warren
Blasdel, Henry Goode
Bloch, Bernard
Bloch, Konrad E.
Blunden, Jeraldyne
Boorda, Jeremy Michael
Boudreau, Lou
Bowerman, Bill
Bradley, Wilmot Hyde
Bragg, Janet
Brannan, Charles F.
Breger, Dave
Briggs, Ansel
Brooks, Gwendolyn
Brower, David
Brown, Eddy
Brown, George E., Jr.
Brown, Les
Brown, Willa
Browning, John M.
Brugger, Kenneth C.
Budge, Don
Buell, Marjorie Henderson
Bullard, Eugène Jacques
Bulloch, James
Burke, Arleigh
Burke, Billie
Burnett, Peter Hardeman
Burnham, Louis E.

Burris, Samuel D.
Burroughs, Stephen
Burton, Richard
Butler, David
Butler, William Allen

C

Cadmus, Paul
Calderón, Alberto P.
Campbell, John
Capezio, Salvatore
Cardozo, Michael H.
Carey, James Francis
Carlebach, Shlomo
Carnahan, Melvin Eugene
Carnera, Primo
Casey, Robert
Cashin, Bonnie
Chafee, John H.
Chamberlain, John
Charles, Ray
Cherry, Don
Childs, Marquis
Childs, Morris
Chiles, Lawton
Cinqué
Claiborne, Craig
Clampett, Bob
Cole, Jack
Colley, Russell
Colón, Jesús
Como, Perry
Conkwright, P. J.
Conover, Willis Clark, Jr.
Coors, Adolph
Corso, Gregory
Cotter, John L.
Coverdell, Paul
Craighead, Frank Cooper,
  Jr.
Cram, Donald J.
Crumit, Frank
Currie, Lauchlin
Curtis, William
  Buckingham

D

Dalitz, Morris B. "Moe"
Dangerfield, Rodney
Daniel, Clifton
Danielian, Leon

DeBenedetti, Charles
  Louis
Dederich, Charles
de Latour, Georges
del Río, Dolores
de Man, Paul
Denfield, Louis Emil
DeRose, Peter
Diamond, Louis K.
Dick, A. B.
Dickey, James
Dixon, Jeremiah. See under
  Mason, Charles
Dmytryk, Edward
Dodge, David Low
Dohnányi, Ernst von
Dorris, Michael
Druckman, Jacob
Dumm, Edwina
Dunn, Robert Ellis
Dyer, Mary Marshall

E

Eckbo, Garrett
Edison, Harry "Sweets"
Edwards, Leo
Engen, Donald Davenport
Ewbank, Weeb
Exley, Frederick

F

Fahey, John
Farkas, Alexander S.
Fechner, Robert
Fenwick, Millicent
Ferris, George
  Washington Gale, Jr.
Fields, James Thomas
Fillmore, Abigail Powers
Fincke, William M.
Fitzsimmons, Frank
Forsythe, Albert Edward
Fox, Roy
Franks, David Salisbury
Froman, Jane
Fry, Varian
Fullerton, William Morton

G

Gaines, William M.
Gennaro, Peter

George, Walter
Gilbert, A. C.
Gilbert, John
Gilbreth, Frank B., Jr.
Gill, Brendan
Goh, Choo San
Goldenson, Leonard H.
Goldkette, Jean
Goldman, Richard Franko
González, Henry B.
Gordone, Charles
Gorey, Edward
Gottlieb, Sidney
Graham, Katharine Meyer
Green, Chuck
Green, Seth
Greenfield, Elizabeth
  Taylor
Gunther, Charles
  Frederick
Gwathmey, Robert

H

Hamming, Richard
  Wesley
Hampton, Lionel
Hanger, James Edward
Hanna, William
Harman, Fred
Harman, Hugh N.
Harrington, Oliver W.
Harris, Bill
Harrison, Anna
Hartshorne, Charles
Hartz, Louis
Haskell, Charles Nathaniel
Hassenfeld, Merrill
Hawkins, Erskine
Henderson, Joe
Henry, Ernie
Hepburn, Katherine
Herblock
Herman, Mary Ann
Herman, Michael
Herreshoff, L. Francis
Heuduck, Arno Paul
Heuduck, Paul Johannes
Higginbotham, A. Leon,
  Jr.
Higgins, Billy
Higgins, George V.
Highsmith, Patricia

Hildreth, Richard
Hill, Martha
Hirschfeld, Al
Hitchings, George H.
Hockett, Charles F.
Holmes, Hamilton
Hopkins, Mark
Horgan, Paul
Horse, John
Hovhaness, Alan
Hoyte, Lenon
Huggins, Charles Brenton
Huncke, Herbert
Hunley, Horace L.
Hunter, Robert M. T.
Hutchinson, Abigail Jemima
Hutchinson, Adoniram Judson Joseph
Hutchinson, Asa Burnham
Hutchinson, Jesse, Jr.
Hutchinson, John Wallace

I

Ising, Rudolf C. *See under* Harman, Hugh N.

J

Jackson, Milt
Jacobs, Bernard
Johnson, Francis
Johnson, Gerald W.
Jones, Casey
Jones, Claudia
Jones, John Winston
Jones, Robert Trent, Sr.
Jones, Sissieretta
Jovanovich, William
Julia, Raul
Julian, Hubert F.

K

Kahles, Charles William
Kane, Bob
Kapell, William
Kaufmann, Gordon
Keller, Fred S.
Kellogg, Charles Edwin
Kerr, Michael
Kerr, Walter
Kesey, Ken
Ketcham, Hank
Keyser, Louisa
Kiley, Richard
King, Albert Freeman Africanus
Kirby, Jack

Klein, Edmund
Knowles, John
Koner, Pauline
Kramer, Stanley
Krenek, Ernst
Kurtz, Frank

L

Lake, Margaret Maiki Souza Aiu
Lame Deer, John Fire
Lardner, Ring, Jr.
Lasswell, Fred, Jr.
Lawrence, Jacob
Lawrence, Joshua
Lawrence, Robert Henry, Jr.
Lax, Anneli
Le Clercq, Tanaquil
Lee, William Andrew
Lemmon, Jack
Leverton, Ruth M.
Levy, David
Lewis, John
Liberman, Alexander
Liebowitz, Jack S.
Lilienfeld, Julius Edgar
Lindbergh, Anne Morrow
Lindsay, John Vliet
Litwack, Harry
Lloyd, Margaret
Lone Wolf
Lorde, Audre
Ludlow, Louis Leon

M

Marshall, E. G.
Martin, Dean
Martin, John Bartlow
Martinez, Maria Montoya
Mason, Charles
Mason, John Landis
Matthau, Walter
Mauldin, Bill
Mayfield, Curtis
McCain, John Sidney
McCrory, John Graham
McCutcheon, John T.
McDonald, William C.
McGhee, Brownie
McMahon, Thomas A.
Meeuse, Bastiaan Jacob Dirk
Meière, Marie Hildreth
Mellette, Arthur Calvin
Menuhin, Yehudi
Miller, Lewis
Moore, Alfred

Moore, Audley "Queen Mother"
Moore, Charles
Moore, Clayton
Moron, Alonzo Graseano
Moses, Isaac
Moyer, Andrew Jackson
Murphy, William Parry

N

Nash, N. Richard
Nathans, Daniel
Nelson, Gene
Nesbitt, Robert
Newell, Robert Henry
Niebaum, Gustave Ferdinand
Norton, Joshua Abraham
Nugent, Richard Bruce

O

Ochoa, Severo
O'Connor, Carroll
O'Conor, John F. X.
O'Dwyer, Paul
Ormandy, Eugene
Ostroff, Eugene
Othmer, Donald F.
Outlaw, Wyatt

P

Pakula, Alan J.
Paredes, Américo
Park, Lawrence
Parker, H. T.
Patterson, Robert
Peck, James
Pettingill, Olin Sewall, Jr.
Phillips, Duncan
Pike, Kenneth Lee
Piñero, Miguel
Pitkin, Walter Boughton
Plato, Ann
Pomeroy, Theodore Medad
Porter, H. Boone
Powers, J. F.
Proskouriakoff, Tatiana
Puente, Tito
Puller, Lewis Burwell, Jr.
Purcell, Edward M.
Pusey, Nathan

Q

Questel, Mae
Quimby, Harriet N.

Quine, W. V.
Quisenberry, Dan

R

Ray, James Earl
Reagan, Ronald Wilson
Redenbacher, Orville
Reed, Janet
Resor, Helen Lansdowne
Reynolds, Quentin
Riggs, Bobby
Riggs, Lynn
Rodbell, Martin
Roerich, Nicholas
Rogers, William Pierce
Romero, Cesar
Rou, Louis
Routt, John Long
Rowan, Carl T.
Rozelle, Pete

S

Salvemini, Gaetano
Sapiro, Aaron
Saposs, David J.
Sarazen, Gene
Satanta
Saylor, John Phillips
Schaefer, George Louis
Scharrer, Berta
Schlesinger, Leon
Schmitt, Arthur J.
Schoop, Trudi
Scott, James Brown
Segal, George
Sellers, Charles Coleman
Sengstacke, John H.
Simak, Clifford D.
Simjian, Luther
Slayton, Deke
Smith, Courtney C.
Smithson, James
Snow, Hank
Snyder, John P.
Sohappy, David
Solti, Georg
Sowerby, Leo
Spalding, Albert
Spalding, Henry Stanislaus
Spitzer, Lyman, Jr.
Stamos, Theodoros
Stephens, John Lloyd
Stockbridge, Levi
Stoddard, Seneca Ray
Stouppe, Pierre
Strasberg, Susan

Strax, Philip
Sturtevant, Edgar H.

T

Talbert, Billy
Tarloff, Frank
Taylor, John W.
Taylor, Paul Schuster
Teschemacher, Frank
Thompson Patterson,
  Louise
Thompson, Jim
Thompson, John D.
Tousard, Anne-Louis
Tower, John G.
Treutlen, John Adam

Tripp, Charles B.
Trout, Robert
Trueblood, Benjamin
  Franklin
Tsongas, Paul Efthemios
Turpin, Ben
Turrentine, Stanley
  William
Tyler, Letitia Christian

V

Valens, Ritchie
Villa, Pancho
Villa, Pancho
Vining, Elizabeth Gray
von Mises, Ludwig

W

Wagner, Gorgeous
  George
Walker, Maggie L.
Walton, Lester A.
Washington, Augustus
Washington, Grover, Jr.
Washington, Margaret
  Murray
Waud, Alfred R.
Way, Mary
Weaver, Robert C.
Webb, Frank J.
Webb, Mary
Wedemeyer, Albert C.
Wells, Junior
Welty, Eudora

Whiteaker, John
Williams, Joe
Williams, Tony
Windsor, Marie
Witherspoon, Jimmy
Wolf, Eric R.

Y

Yarosz, Teddy
Yellow Robe, Rosebud
Young, Loretta
Youngs, Ross
Youskevitch, Igor

Z

Zumwalt, Elmo Russell, Jr.

ADAMS-VOLPE, JUDITH
Ferris, George Washington
Gale, Jr.

ADLER, JEANNE
WINSTON
Stoddard, Seneca Ray

ALOFF, MINDY
Le Clercq, Tanaquil

ARIEL, YAAKOV
Carlebach, Shlomo

ARNS, ROBERT G.
Lilienfeld, Julius Edgar

ASCH, AMY
Lindbergh, Anne Morrow

AUGUSTYN, FREDERICK
J., JR.
Gilbert, A. C.
Hassenfeld, Merrill

BARNETT, KAREN
BACHMAN
Proskouriakoff, Tatiana
Yellow Robe, Rosebud

BARRIER, MICHAEL
Hanna, William

BECKER, CARL M.
Jones, Robert Trent, Sr.
Sarazen, Gene

BEER, SAMUEL H.
Hartz, Louis

BERMAN, MILTON
Claiborne, Craig

BETZ, FREDERICK
Johnson, Gerald W.

BLASKIEWICZ, ROBERT
Heuduck, Arno Paul
Heuduck, Paul Johannes
Meière, Marie Hildreth

BOCKRIS, VICTOR
Corso, Gregory

BOGDAN, ROBERT
Tripp, Charles B.

BOHNING, JAMES J.
Bloch, Konrad E.

BOOMHOWER, RAY E.
Chamberlain, John
Childs, Marquis
Martin, John Bartlow

BOWLES, GARRETT H.
Krenek, Ernst

BRANCH, MURIEL
MILLER
Walker, Maggie L.

BRAUNLICH, PHYLLIS
COLE
Riggs, Lynn

BROWN, GIG B.
Washington, Grover, Jr.

BRUGGE, DAVID M.
Barboncito

BUDD, LOUIS J.
Newell, Robert Henry

BUENGER, NANCY
Gunther, Charles Frederick

BURCH, FRANCIS F.
O'Conor, John F. X.
Schmitt, Arthur J.
Spalding, Henry Stanislaus

BURKE, MICHAEL A.
Tousard, Anne-Louis

BURROUGHS, TODD
STEVEN
Sengstacke, John H. H.

CARLO, PAULA WHEELER
Rou, Louis
Stouppe, Pierre

CAROLI, BETTY BOYD
Fillmore, Abigail Powers

CARROLL, JOHN M.
Ewbank, Weeb

CASSUTO, LEONARD
Thompson, Jim

CATSAM, DEREK
CHARLES
Peck, James

CHAIKLIN, SHARON
Schoop, Trudi

CHARLES, JIM
Dorris, Michael

CHUN, MALCOLM N.
Lake, Margaret Maiki Souza
Aiu

CLARKIN, THOMAS
González, Henry B.

COBB,, JOHN B., JR.
Hartshorne, Charles

COHODAS, MARVIN
Keyser, Louisa

COLLINS, THOMAS W.,
JR.
Gilbert, John
Gill, Brendan
Kerr, Walter
Martin, Dean
Pakula, Alan J.
Snow, Hank
Welty, Eudora

COOPER, DAVID Y.
Murphy, William Parry

COSTA, RICHARD HAUER
Exley, Frederick
Gordone, Charles

COSTELLO, E. O.
Harman, Hugh N.
Ising, Rudolf C.

COTRONEO, P. J.
Jackson, Milt

CURRELL, SUSAN
Pitkin, Walter Boughton

DANSKY, ELI
Coors, Adolph

DANSON, EDWIN
Mason, Charles
Dixon, Jeremiah

DAVIS, LUCKETT V.
Bowerman, Bill
Carnera, Primo
Villa, Pancho
Yarosz, Teddy

DeLOCA, PAUL
Curtis, William Buckingham

DEMOS, KATHRYN N.
Herman, Michael
Herman, Mary Ann

DE WOLFE, ELIZABETH
A.
Dyer, Mary Marshall

DILLON, RICHARD H.
Hopkins, Mark
Niebaum, Gustave
Ferdinand
de Latour, Georges

DiMAIO, DANIEL
Nathans, Daniel

ELLIOTT, CLARK A.
Brugger, Kenneth C.

EMRICH, JOHN S.
Rodbell, Martin

EVENSEN, BRUCE J.
Dmytryk, Edward
Kramer, Stanley
Lemmon, Jack

FAHEY, DAVID M.
Bulloch, James

FØLLESDAL, DAGFINN
Quine, W. V.

FALK, JULIA S.
Bloch, Bernard
Hockett, Charles F.
Pike, Kenneth Lee
Sturtevant, Edgar H.

FANNIN, CAROLINE M.
Bullard, Eugène Jacques
Julian, Hubert F.

FANNIN, CAROLINE M.
(cont.)
Lawrence, Robert Henry, Jr.
Norton, Joshua Abraham
Quimby, Harriet N.

FERN, ALAN M.
Ostroff, Eugene

FLESHER, DALE L.
Mason, John Landis

FORÉS, BRIAN
Hawkins, Erskine

FRANK, RUSTY E.
Berry, Ananias "Nyas"
Berry, James
Berry, Warren
Nelson, Gene

FREDRIKSEN, JOHN C.
Boorda, Jeremy Michael
Burke, Arleigh
Denfield, Louis Emil
Kurtz, Frank
Lee, William Andrew

FROST, RANDALL
Graham, Katharine Meyer

FULLER, LORRAINE
Rowan, Carl T.

GAC, SCOTT E.
Hutchinson, Abigail Jemima
Hutchinson, Adoniram
Judson Joseph
Hutchinson, Asa Burnham
Hutchinson, Jesse, Jr.
Hutchinson, John Wallace

GALLEHER, STEPHEN C.
Goldkette, Jean

GARDNER, ERIC
Greenfield, Elizabeth Taylor
Johnson, Francis
Jones, Sissieretta
Plato, Ann
Webb, Frank J.
Webb, Mary

GOEDEKEN, EDWARD A.
Carnahan, Melvin Eugene
Chafee, John H.
Eckbo, Garrett
Puller, Lewis Burwell, Jr.
Rogers, William Pierce
Tsongas, Paul Efthemios
Zumwalt, Elmo Russell, Jr.

GOLLIN, RITA K.
Fields, James Thomas

GONZALEZ, JAVIER
Puente, Tito

GORDON, LINDA
Taylor, Paul Schuster

GOULD, LEWIS L.
Coverdell, Paul
Daniel, Clifton
Kerr, Michael
Pomeroy, Theodore Medad

GRANT, DANIEL
Bad Heart Bull, Amos
Lawrence, Jacob
Liberman, Alexander
Martinez, Maria Montoya
Segal, George
Stamos, Theodoros

GREEN, MICHAEL
Blasdel, Henry Goode
Dalitz, Morris B. "Moe"

GRUENDLER, SHELLEY
Conkwright, P. J.

GUBERT, BETTY KAPLAN
Brown, Willa
Capezio, Salvatore
Hoyte, Lenon
Walton, Lester A.

GURNER, JACK
Jones, Casey

GUSTAFSON, JOHN L.
Atanasoff, John Vincent

GUTHMAN, JOSHUA
Lawrence, Joshua

HALLORAN, EDWARD
Thompson, John D.

HAMBURGER, SUSAN
Farkas, Alexander S.

HAMMES, MARY JESSICA
Holmes, Hamilton

HAMPL, JEFFREY S
Leverton, Ruth M.

HANDA, AL
Fahey, John

HARDY, CAMILLE
Koner, Pauline

HARMOND, RICHARD
Craighead, Frank Cooper,
Jr.
Reynolds, Quentin

HART, HENRY
Dickey, James

HARVEY, ROBERT C.
Breger, Dave
Buell, Marjorie Henderson
Cole, Jack
Dumm, Edwina
Gorey, Edward
Harman, Fred
Herblock
Hirschfeld, Al
Kahles, Charles William
Ketcham, Hank
Lasswell, Fred, Jr.
Mauldin, Bill
McCutcheon, John T.

HAY, MELBA PORTER
Tyler, Letitia Christian

HELMS, DOUGLAS
Kellogg, Charles Edwin

HELPERN, ALICE
Danielian, Leon

HENSON, PAMELA M.
Smithson, James

HERING, DORIS
Lloyd, Margaret
Parker, H. T.

HERSHFIELD, JOANNE
del Río, Dolores

HIGGINS, SCOTT
Turpin, Ben

HILL, CONSTANCE VALIS
Bates, Peg Leg
Green, Chuck

HIRSCH, PETER
Sowerby, Leo

HORNBUCKLE, ADAM R.
Wagner, Gorgeous George

HOWLETT, CHARLES F.
DeBenedetti, Charles Louis
Dodge, David Low
Fincke, William M.
Saposs, David J.
Scott, James Brown
Trueblood, Benjamin
Franklin
Youngs, Ross

HUGHES, LYNN GORDON
Hildreth, Richard

HÜLSMANN, JÖRG GUIDO
von Mises, Ludwig

JACKSON, JEROME A.
Green, Seth

JACKSON, KATHY
MERLOCK
Schlesinger, Leon

JANOFF, BRUCE L.
Allen, Steve
Rozelle, Pete

JASTRZEMBSKI, JOSEPH C.
Paredes, Américo

JELKS, EDWARD B.
Cotter, John L.

JENKINS, REESE V.
Dick, A. B.

JONES, ROBERT L.
Ormandy, Eugene

JOYCE, WILLIAM L.
Campbell, John

KALFATOVIC, MARY C.
Burton, Richard
Julia, Raul
Kesey, Ken
Knowles, John
Matthau, Walter
O'Connor, Carroll
Strasberg, Susan
Young, Loretta

KAMMEN, MICHAEL
Gwathmey, Robert

KEENE, ANN T.
Cadmus, Paul
Calderón, Alberto P.
de Man, Paul
Froman, Jane
Horgan, Paul
Kapell, William
Vining, Elizabeth Gray

KELLY, ALAN
Conover, Willis Clark, Jr.
Henderson, Joe
Jovanovich, William
Turrentine, Stanley William

KERNFELD, BARRY
Cherry, Don
Hampton, Lionel
Williams, Tony

KILLINGER, CHARLES
Salvemini, Gaetano

KING, ELIZABETH H.
Simjian, Luther

KLEHR, HARVEY
Childs, Morris

KLEIN, CATHERINE DYER
Proskouriakoff, Tatiana
Yellow Robe, Rosebud

KLOTZMAN, DOROTHY A.
Goldman, Richard Franko

KOKEN, KATHRYN LORIMER
Briggs, Ansel

KOTLOWSKI, DEAN J.
Albert, Carl

KOZLOSKI, LILLIAN D.
Colley, Russell

KROEKER, MARVIN E.
Becker, Abraham Jacob
Becker, Magdalena Hergert
Lone Wolf

LACH, EDWARD L., JR.
Belanger, Mark
Brannan, Charles F.
Brown, George E., Jr.
Burnett, Peter Hardeman
Butler, David
Casey, Robert
Cram, Donald J.
Diamond, Louis K.
Gottlieb, Sidney
Hanger, James Edward
Haskell, Charles Nathaniel
Higginbotham, A. Leon, Jr.
Hitchings, George H.
Hunter, Robert M. T.
Jones, John Winston
King, Albert Freeman Africanus
Klein, Edmund
Litwack, Harry
McDonald, William C.
McMahon, Thomas A.
Mellette, Arthur Calvin
O'Dwyer, Paul
Porter, H. Boone
Redenbacher, Orville
Routt, John Long
Stockbridge, Levi
Strax, Philip
Taylor, John W.
Whiteaker, John

LANCASTER, JANE
Gilbreth, Frank B., Jr.

LANSBURY, EDGAR
Roerich, Nicholas

LAUNIUS, ROGER D.
Slayton, Deke

LAX, PETER D.
Lax, Anneli

LEAB, DANIEL J.
Ludlow, Louis Leon

LIAO, SHUTSUNG
Huggins, Charles Brenton

LILLE, DAWN
Blunden, Jeraldyne

LITTMANN, HELENE
Stephens, John Lloyd

LORNELL, KIP
Wells, Junior

MacMULLEN, RAMSAY
Way, Mary

MAINWARING, MARION
Fullerton, William Morton

MALTESE, JOHN ANTHONY
Brown, Eddy
Spalding, Albert

MARC, DAVID
Agronsky, Martin
Goldenson, Leonard H.
Levy, David
Marshall, E. G.
Schaefer, George Louis
Tarloff, Frank
Trout, Robert

MARKOWITZ, NORMAN
Fitzsimmons, Frank

MARLING, WILLIAM
Higgins, George V.

McCOWIN, DAVID J.
Miller, Lewis

McDUFFIE, ERIK S.
Burnham, Louis Everett
Jones, Claudia
Moore, Audley "Queen Mother"
Patterson, Louise

McILVAIN, JOSH
Anfinsen, Christian B.
Othmer, Donald F.

McKAY, CHRISTINE G.
Harrington, Oliver W.

MENDHEIM, BEVERLY
Valens, Ritchie

MESCHUTT, DAVID
Park, Lawrence
Waud, Alfred R.

MESSINGER, CHARLES
McGhee, Brownie

MIHM, STEPHEN ANDERSON
Burroughs, Stephen

MILLER, KEITH L.
Bell, Alfred H.

MILLER, SAM
Henry, Ernie

MILSTEAD, CLAUDIA
Lardner, Ring, Jr.

MONDELLO, SALVATORE
Como, Perry
Kane, Bob
Kirby, Jack
Moore, Clayton

MOORE, JAMES ROSS
Clampett, Bob
Crumit, Frank
DeRose, Peter
Edison, Harry "Sweets"
Fox, Roy
Jacobs, Bernard
Kaufmann, Gordon
Nesbitt, Robert
Williams, Joe

MORGAN, ANN LEE
Phillips, Duncan

MORGAN, SAMUEL P.
Hamming, Richard Wesley

MULLER, EDDIE
Windsor, Marie

MULROY, KEVIN
Horse, John

MURRAY, WILL
Gaines, William M.
Liebowitz, Jack S.

NELSON, CLIFFORD M.
Bradley, Wilmot Hyde

NELSON, DANIEL
Avery, R. Stanton

NEUMANN, CARYN E.
Washington, Margaret Murray

NEWHALL, MARY ANNE SANTOS
Youskevitch, Igor

NEYLAND, ROBERT S.
Hunley, Horace L.

NOLAN, TOM
Highsmith, Patricia

OCASIO, RAFAEL
Colón, Jesús

OHL, JOHN KENNEDY
Wedemeyer, Albert C.

O'MALLEY, PATRICIA TRAINOR
Carey, James Francis

OSTERBROCK, DONALD E.
Spitzer, Lyman, Jr.

PARRAMORE, THOMAS C.
Moore, Alfred

PETERSON, SAMANTHA
Cashin, Bonnie

PHELPS, FRANK V.
Budge, Don
Riggs, Bobby
Talbert, Billy

PLEASANTS, JULIAN M.
Chiles, Lawton

POCOCK, EMIL
Patterson, Robert

POSNER, GERALD
Ray, James Earl

PRUTER, ROBERT
Mayfield, Curtis

RAE, NICOL C.
Lindsay, John Vliet

RAUCHER, ALAN R.
McCrory, John Graham

RIGDEN, JOHN
Purcell, Edward M.

RILEY, HELENE M. KASTINGER
Treutlen, John Adam

ROACH, EDWARD J.
Fechner, Robert

ROBINSON, CHARLES M.,
III
Satanta

ROBINSON, ARTHUR H.
Snyder, John P.

ROOT, MICHAEL J.
Keller, Fred S.

ROSENBERG, JUSTUS
Fry, Varian

ROSNER, RACHAEL I.
Berne, Eric

RYE, HOWARD
Witherspoon, Jimmy

SAGOLLA, LISA JO
Gennaro, Peter

SANBORN, GEOFF
Lame Deer, John Fire

SANDERS, JEAN
Dohnányi, Ernst von

SANDILANDS, ROGER J.
Currie, Lauchlin

SANTESMASES, MARÍA
JESÚS
Ochoa, Severo

SAWYER, MIRIAM
Bragg, Janet
Forsythe, Albert Edward

SAYERS, PAUL T.
George, Walter

SCANLON, JENNIFER
Resor, Helen Lansdowne

SCHAFER, BEN
Huncke, Herbert

SCHALLER, MICHAEL
Reagan, Ronald Wilson

SCHAPIRO, AMY
Fenwick, Millicent

SCHARRER, TERRY
Scharrer, Berta

SCHERGEN, JANEK
Goh, Choo San

SCHNEIDER, JANE
Wolf, Eric R.

SCHWENINGER, LOREN
Burris, Samuel D.

SCOTT, MELINDA
Brown, Les

SHAPIRO, JADA
Dunn, Robert Ellis
Moore, Charles

SHARRER, G. TERRY
Moyer, Andrew Jackson

SHELLEY, THOMAS J.
Toussaint, Pierre

SHERWIN, ELISABETH
Adams, Alice

SHIRODKAR, MARCO
Hovhaness, Alan

SHUMARD, ANN M.
Washington, Augustus

SLADE, JOSEPH W.
Browning, John M.

SMITH, THOMAS G.
Saylor, John Phillips

SMITH, TOM
Harris, Bill
Teschemacher, Frank

SMULLYAN, DEBORAH
Pusey, Nathan

SOARES, JANET
MANSFIELD
Hill, Martha

SOLTIS, CAROL EATON
Sellers, Charles Coleman

STAPLETON, DARWIN H.
Smith, Courtney C.

STAPLETON, DONNA H.
Smith, Courtney C.

STERLING, KEIR B.
Pettingill, Olin Sewall, Jr.

SULLIVAN, JAMES D.
Brooks, Gwendolyn
Lorde, Audre

SWEET, JAY
Lewis, John

TAYLOR, ROGER C.
Herreshoff, L. Francis

THORNE, TANIS C.
Barnett, Jackson

TOBIAS, MARILYN
Cardozo, Michael H.

TRACY, SARAH
Dederich, Charles

TROXLER, CAROLE
WATTERSON
Outlaw, Wyatt

ULRICH, ROBERTA
Sohappy, David

VAN NUYS, FRANK
Brower, David

WALKER, RICHARD B.
Meeuse, Bastiaan Jacob
Dirk

WEEVER, ANDREA
Burke, Billie
Kiley, Richard

WEISBERGER, WILLIAM
Franks, David Salisbury
Moses, Isaac

WEPMAN, DENNIS
Butler, William Allen
Edwards, Leo
Questel, Mae
Simak, Clifford D.
Cinqué

WEST, MARTHA ULLMAN
Reed, Janet

WIENER, JONATHAN
Druckman, Jacob
Menuhin, Yehudi
Solti, Georg

WILLIAMS, PATRICK G.
Tower, John G.

WILSON, JOHN R. M.
Boudreau, Lou
Quisenberry, Dan

WINER, DEBORAH GRACE
Nash, N. Richard
Piñero, Miguel
Romero, Cesar

WINTZ, CARY D.
Weaver, Robert C.

WIRTH, THOMAS H.
Nugent, Richard Bruce

WOESTE, VICTORIA
SAKER
Sapiro, Aaron

WOOLDRIDGE, E. T.
Engen, Donald Davenport
McCain, John Sidney

WYMARD, ELLIE
Powers, J. F.

YOUNG, NANCY BECK
Harrison, Anna

ZAKI, HODA M.
Moron, Alonzo Graseano

For indexing purposes, places of birth have been indicated by names of the fifty states and the District of Columbia rather than by historical names of colonies and territories.

ALABAMA
Hawkins, Erskine

ARKANSAS
Witherspoon, Jimmy

ARIZONA
Barboncito

CALIFORNIA
Brower, David
Brown, George E., Jr.
Budge, Don
Cashin, Bonnie
Clampett, Bob
Engen, Donald
Davenport
Higgins, Billy
Quisenberry, Dan
Riggs, Bobby
Rozelle, Pete
Sapiro, Aaron
Valens, Ritchie
Zumwalt, Elmo Russell,
Jr.

COLORADO
Berry, Warren
Brannan, Charles F.
Burke, Arleigh
Cotter, John L.
Fox, Roy
Harman, Hugh N.
Jovanovich, William
Kesey, Ken

CONNECTICUT
Bradley, Wilmot Hyde
Chamberlain, John
Dodge, David Low
Fullerton, William
Morton
Gill, Brendan
Pike, Kenneth Lee
Plato, Ann
Schaefer, George Louis
Way, Mary

DELAWARE
Burris, Samuel D.
Nathans, Daniel

DISTRICT OF COLUMBIA
Burke, Billie
Craighead, Frank
Cooper, Jr.
Nugent, Richard Bruce
Weaver, Robert C.

FLORIDA
Chiles, Lawton
Horse, John

GEORGIA
Bragg, Janet
Bullard, Eugène Jacques
Bulloch, James
Dickey, James
George, Walter
Green, Chuck
Holmes, Hamilton
Sengstacke, John H. H.
Williams, Joe

HAWAII
Lake, Margaret Maiki
Souza Aiu

ILLINOIS
Boudreau, Lou
Breger, Dave
Brown, Eddy
DeBenedetti, Charles
Louis
Dick, A. B.
Edwards, Leo
Ferris, George
Washington Gale, Jr.
Gorey, Edward
Hamming, Richard
Wesley
Herblock
Kerr, Walter
Kiley, Richard
Lardner, Ring, Jr.
Lawrence, Robert
Henry, Jr.
Lewis, John
Mayfield, Curtis
Moore, Clayton
Powers, J. F.
Purcell, Edward M.

ILLINOIS *(cont.)*
Ray, James Earl
Reagan, Ronald Wilson
Schmitt, Arthur J.
Spalding, Albert
Sturtevant, Edgar H.
Thompson Patterson,
Louise
Williams, Tony

INDIANA
Blasdel, Henry Goode
Boorda, Jeremy Michael
Butler, David
Ewbank, Weeb
Ludlow, Louis Leon
McCutcheon, John T.
Mellette, Arthur Calvin
Moyer, Andrew Jackson
Redenbacher, Orville
Snyder, John P.
Trueblood, Benjamin
Franklin
Whiteaker, John

IOWA
Childs, Marquis
Coverdell, Paul
Kurtz, Frank
Pusey, Nathan
Smith, Courtney C.
Taylor, Paul Schuster

KANSAS
Becker, Magdalena
Hergert
Brooks, Gwendolyn

KENTUCKY
Brown, Willa
Dorris, Michael
Edison, Harry "Sweets"
Hampton, Lionel
Porter, H. Boone
Resor, Helen Lansdowne
Routt, John Long
Spalding, Henry
Stanislaus

LOUISIANA
Berry, Ananias "Nyas"
Berry, James

LOUISIANA *(cont.)*
Gennaro, Peter
Moore, Audley "Queen
Mother"
Turpin, Ben

MAINE
Pettingill, Olin Sewall, Jr.

MARYLAND
Fahey, John
Rodbell, Martin

MASSACHUSETTS
Belanger, Mark
Carey, James Francis
Colley, Russell
Dalitz, Morris B. "Moe"
Denfield, Louis Emil
Higgins, George V.
Hildreth, Richard
Hovhaness, Alan
Huncke, Herbert
Lee, William Andrew
Lemmon, Jack
Lloyd, Margaret
Park, Lawrence
Parker, H. T.
Stockbridge, Levi
Tsongas, Paul Efthemios
Webb, Mary

MICHIGAN
Jackson, Milt
Kellogg, Charles Edwin
Pitkin, Walter Boughton
Quimby, Harriet N.
Sowerby, Leo

MINNESOTA
Leverton, Ruth M.
Marshall, E. G.

MISSISSIPPI
Claiborne, Craig
Greenfield, Elizabeth
Taylor
McCain, John Sidney

MISSISSIPPI *(cont.)*
Washington, Margaret
Murray
Welty, Eudora

MISSOURI
Carnahan, Melvin
Eugene
Froman, Jane
Harman, Fred
Hirschfeld, Al
Ising, Rudolf C.
Jones, Casey
Lasswell, Fred, Jr.
Teschemacher, Frank
Walton, Lester A.

NEBRASKA
Othmer, Donald F.
Wagner, Gorgeous
George
Wedemeyer, Albert C.

NEVADA
Keyser, Louisa

NEW HAMPSHIRE
Burroughs, Stephen
Dyer, Mary Marshall
Fields, James Thomas
Hutchinson, Abigail
Jemima
Hutchinson, Adoniram
Judson Joseph
Hutchinson, Asa
Burnham
Hutchinson, Jesse, Jr.
Hutchinson, John
Wallace

NEW JERSEY
Gilbreth, Frank B., Jr.
Harrison, Anna
Higginbotham, A. Leon,
Jr.
Lawrence, Jacob
Lindbergh, Anne
Morrow
Mason, John Landis
Stephens, John Lloyd
Washington, Augustus

NEW MEXICO
Hanna, William
Martinez, Maria
Montoya
Mauldin, Bill

NEW YORK
Allen, Steve
Atanasoff, John Vincent

NEW YORK *(cont.)*
Bloch, Bernard
Burnham, Louis Everett
Butler, William Allen
Cadmus, Paul
Cardozo, Michael H.
Casey, Robert
Conover, Willis Clark,
Jr.
Corso, Gregory
Danielian, Leon
DeRose, Peter
Eckbo, Garrett
Exley, Frederick
Farkas, Alexander S.
Fenwick, Millicent
Fillmore, Abigail Powers
Fincke, William M.
Fry, Varian
Gaines, William M.
Goldman, Richard
Franko
Gottlieb, Sidney
Graham, Katharine
Meyer
Green, Seth
Harrington, Oliver W.
Henry, Ernie
Herman, Mary Ann
Hopkins, Mark
Horgan, Paul
Hoyte, Lenon
Jacobs, Bernard
Kane, Bob
Kapell, William
Keller, Fred S.
Kirby, Jack
Koner, Pauline
Kramer, Stanley
Lindsay, John Vliet
Lorde, Audre
Matthau, Walter
McDonald, William C.
Menuhin, Yehudi
Meière, Marie Hildreth
Newell, Robert Henry
O'Connor, Carroll
O'Conor, John F. X.
Ostroff, Eugene
Pakula, Alan J.
Peck, James
Pomeroy, Theodore
Medad
Puente, Tito
Questel, Mae
Reynolds, Quentin
Rogers, William Pierce
Romero, Cesar
Sarazen, Gene
Segal, George

NEW YORK *(cont.)*
Stamos, Theodoros
Stoddard, Seneca Ray
Strasberg, Susan
Strax, Philip
Tarloff, Frank
Taylor, John W.
Washington, Grover, Jr.

NORTH CAROLINA
Daniel, Clifton
Johnson, Gerald W.
Lawrence, Joshua
Moore, Alfred
Outlaw, Wyatt
Puller, Lewis Burwell, Jr.
Trout, Robert

OHIO
Blunden, Jeraldyne
Crumit, Frank
Dederich, Charles
Dumm, Edwina
Gordone, Charles
Hartz, Louis
Haskell, Charles
Nathaniel
Henderson, Joe
Herman, Michael
Hill, Martha
Hockett, Charles F.
Martin, Dean
Martin, John Bartlow
McMahon, Thomas A.
Miller, Lewis
Moore, Charles
Quine, W. V.
Spitzer, Lyman, Jr.
Talbert, Billy

OKLAHOMA
Albert, Carl
Avery, R. Stanton
Barnett, Jackson
Cherry, Don
Conkwright, P. J.
Dunn, Robert Ellis
Riggs, Lynn
Thompson, Jim

OREGON
Bowerman, Bill
Gilbert, A. C.
Reed, Janet

PENNSYLVANIA
Agronsky, Martin
Anfinsen, Christian B.
Brown, Les
Buell, Marjorie
Henderson

PENNSYLVANIA *(cont.)*
Cole, Jack
Como, Perry
Druckman, Jacob
Fitzsimmons, Frank
Franks, David Salisbury
Goldenson, Leonard H.
Harris, Bill
Hartshorne, Charles
Johnson, Francis
Kerr, Michael
Levy, David
McCrory, John Graham
Nash, N. Richard
Patterson, Robert
Phillips, Duncan
Saylor, John Phillips
Schlesinger, Leon
Sellers, Charles Coleman
Thompson, John D.
Turrentine, Stanley
William
Vining, Elizabeth Gray
Webb, Frank J.
Yarosz, Teddy

RHODE ISLAND
Chafee, John H.
Hassenfeld, Merrill
Herreshoff, L. Francis

SOUTH CAROLINA
Bates, Peg Leg

SOUTH DAKOTA
Lame Deer, John Fire
Yellow Robe, Rosebud

TENNESSEE
Burnett, Peter
Hardeman
Fechner, Robert
Hunley, Horace L.
McGhee, Brownie
Rowan, Carl T.
Wells, Junior

TEXAS
González, Henry B.
Highsmith, Patricia
Paredes, Américo
Tower, John G.
Youngs, Ross

UNKNOWN
Lone Wolf
Satanta

UTAH
Browning, John M.
Gilbert, John

UTAH *(cont.)*
Windsor, Marie
Young, Loretta

VERMONT
Briggs, Ansel
Cram, Donald J.
Curtis, William
 Buckingham

VIRGINIA
Adams, Alice
Gwathmey, Robert
Hanger, James Edward
Hunter, Robert M. T.
Jones, John Winston
Jones, Sissieretta
Knowles, John

VIRGINIA *(cont.)*
Tyler, Letitia Christian
Walker, Maggie L.

WASHINGTON
Hitchings, George H.
Ketcham, Hank
Nelson, Gene
Sohappy, David

WISCONSIN
Brugger, Kenneth C.
Murphy, William Parry
Simak, Clifford D.
Slayton, Deke

WYOMING
Bad Heart Bull, Amos

ARGENTINA
Calderón, Alberto P.

AUSTRIA
Klein, Edmund
Krenek, Ernst
von Mises, Ludwig
Wolf, Eric R.

BAHAMAS
Forsythe, Albert Edward

BELGIUM
de Man, Paul

CANADA
Bell, Alfred H.
Berne, Eric
Currie, Lauchlin
Dmytryk, Edward
Huggins, Charles
   Brenton
Scott, James Brown
Snow, Hank
Tripp, Charles B.

ENGLAND
Dixon, Jeremiah
Jones, Robert Trent, Sr.
Kaufmann, Gordon
King, Albert Freeman
   Africanus
Mason, Charles
Nesbitt, Robert
Norton, Joshua Abraham
Waud, Alfred R.

FINLAND
Niebaum, Gustave
   Ferdinand

FRANCE
de Latour, Georges
Le Clercq, Tanaquil
Smithson, James
Tousard, Anne-Louis

GALICIA
Lilienfeld, Julius Edgar
Litwack, Harry

GERMANY
Bloch, Konrad E.
Carlebach, Shlomo
Coors, Adolph
Gunther, Charles
   Frederick
Heuduck, Arno Paul
Heuduck, Paul Johannes
Kahles, Charles William
Lax, Anneli
Moses, Isaac
Scharrer, Berta
Treutlen, John Adam

GREECE
Goldkette, Jean

HAITI
Toussaint, Pierre

HUNGARY
Dohnányi, Ernst von
Ormandy, Eugene
Solti, Georg

IRELAND
O'Dwyer, Paul

ITALY
Capezio, Salvatore
Carnera, Primo
Salvemini, Gaetano

JAVA
Meeuse, Bastiaan Jacob
   Dirk

MEXICO
del Río, Dolores

NETHERLANDS
Rou, Louis

PHILIPPINES
Villa, Pancho

PUERTO RICO
Colón, Jesús
Julia, Raul
Piñero, Miguel

RUSSIA
Becker, Abraham Jacob
Childs, Morris
Diamond, Louis K.
Liberman, Alexander

RUSSIA *(cont.)*
Liebowitz, Jack S.
Proskouriakoff, Tatiana
Roerich, Nicholas
Saposs, David J.
Youskevitch, Igor

SCOTLAND
Campbell, John

SIERRA LEONE
Cinqué

SINGAPORE
Goh, Choo San

SPAIN
Ochoa, Severo

SWITZERLAND
Schoop, Trudi
Stouppe, Pierre

TRINIDAD
Jones, Claudia
Julian, Hubert F.

TURKEY
Simjian, Luther

VIRGIN ISLANDS
Moron, Alonzo
   Graseano

WALES
Burton, Richard

CUMULATIVE INDEX BY OCCUPATIONS
AND REALMS OF RENOWN:
Introduction and Synoptic Outline

This index includes all subjects found in the original edition of the *American National Biography* (*ANB*) as well as those found in *ANB Supplement 1* and *ANB Supplement 2*. The abbreviation "*Suppl. 1*" or "*Suppl. 2*" following a subject's name indicates that the subject is to be found in *ANB Supplement 1* or *ANB Supplement 2*. All other subjects will be found in the original edition of the *ANB*.

The Cumulative Index presents occupations and realms of renown in a different order than the alphabetical Index by Occupations printed in the original edition of the *ANB*. The Cumulative Index arranges the headings for occupations and realms of renown according to one or more broad topical areas so that related occupations can be viewed together. There are seventeen topics at the broadest level, as follows:

Archives, Collections, and Libraries

Art and Architecture

Business and Industry

Education

Exploration, Pioneering, and Native Peoples

Government and Politics

Health and Medicine

Humanities and Social Sciences

Law and Criminology

Military and Intelligence Operations

Miscellaneous Occupations and Realms of Renown

Performing Arts

Religion and Spirituality

Science and Technology

Society and Social Change

Sports and Games

Writing and Publishing

Many subjects of biographies pursued more than one occupation or achieved fame in several realms of renown. Their names will thus be found under multiple headings in this index. In addition, some of those headings are included in more than one broad topical area. For example, the heading Stage / Screen Actors appears under the broader topics of Film and also Theater and Live Entertainment, both of which are related to the broadest area of Performing Arts.

The best way to use this index is to start with the Synoptic Outline printed on pages 630–636, which will show the user where to look in the main body of the index for the occupational category of interest.

SYNOPTIC OUTLINE

ARCHIVES, COLLECTIONS, AND LIBRARIES

American Indian Artifacts
  Collectors
Antiquarian Book
  Collectors
Antiquarians
Antique Collectors
Archivists
Archivists of the United
  States
Arms and Armor
  Collectors
Art Collectors
Art Museum Curators /
  Administrators
Autograph Collectors
Automobile Collectors
Bibliographers
Book Collectors
Discographers
Encyclopedists
Genealogists
Indexers
Librarians
Librarians of Congress
Manuscript Collectors
Museum Curators /
  Administrators
Numismatists
Zoo Curators /
  Administrators

ART AND ARCHITECTURE

Applied Arts
Blacksmiths
Book Designers
Bookbinders
Cabinetmakers
Calligraphers
Ceramists / Potters
Clockmakers
Engravers
Fashion Designers
Flatware Designers
Furniture Designers /
  Manufacturers
Glass Artists
Goldsmiths
Graphic Designers
Hatters
Industrial Designers
Interior Designers
Jewelers
Medal / Coin Designers

Mosaicists
Musical Instrument
  Makers
Papermakers
Pewterers
Printers
Silversmiths
Tanners
Taxidermists
Textile Designers
Tilemakers
Type Designers
Typographers
Watchmakers
Weavers
Woodcarvers

Architecture
Architects
Golf Course Architects
Landscape Architects
Marine Architects

Art
Art Connoisseurs
Artist's Models
Cartoonists / Comic Strip
  Creators
Children's Book Writers /
  Illustrators
Folk Artists
Illustrators
Painters
Photographers
Printmakers
Scientific Illustrators
Sculptors

BUSINESS AND INDUSTRY

Agriculture
Agriculturists
Apiarists
Cattle Raisers / Traders
Cowboys
Farmer Organization
  Leaders
Farmers
Foresters
Horticulturists
Plantation Managers /
  Overseers
Plantation Owners
Ranchers
Seedsmen
Soil Scientists
Winegrowers / Vintners

Clothing, Fashion, and Textiles
Clothing Industry Leaders
Cosmetics Industry
  Leaders
Cotton Brokers /
  Merchants
Modeling Agency
  Executives
Seamstresses
Textile Industry Leaders
Wool Industry Leaders

Communication
Computer Industry
  Leaders
News Agency Owners /
  Managers
Telegraph Industry
  Leaders
Telephone Industry
  Leaders

Construction
Building Materials
  Industry Leaders
Carpenters
Construction Industry
  Leaders
Copper Industry Leaders
Lumber Industry Leaders

Entertainment and Recreation
Amusement Park
  Owners / Managers
Brothelkeepers
Casino Owners /
  Managers
Circus Owners / Managers
Game and Toy
  Manufacturers
Greeting Card
  Manufacturers
Hotel Owners / Managers
Impresarios
Motion Picture
  Distributors
Motion Picture Studio
  Executives
Music Promoters
Nightclub Owners /
  Operators
Radio / Television
  Industry Leaders
Recording Industry
  Leaders
Resort Owners

Sporting Goods Industry
  Leaders
Sports Organization
  Executives
Sports Promoters
Tent Show Owners
Theater Owners /
  Managers
Theatrical Agents

Finance, Management, Insurance, and Real Estate
Accountants
Advertising Industry
  Leaders
Bankers / Financial
  Industry Leaders
Business Consultants
Business Machine
  Industry Leaders
Capitalists / Financiers
Computer Industry
  Leaders
Entrepreneurs
Financial Managers
Franchise Industry
  Leaders
Insurance Industry
  Leaders
Land Agents
Land Promoters
Real Estate Business
  Leaders
Speculators
Talent Scouts

Food and Beverage
Bakers
Bar Owners /
  Saloonkeepers
Brewers
Chefs
Chewing Gum Industry
  Leaders
Confectioners
Distillers
Fast-Food Business
  Leaders
Flour Milling Industry
  Leaders
Food Business Leaders
Grain Dealers
Grocery Store Owners
Meatpackers
Restaurateurs
Soft Drink Industry
  Leaders

Sugar Refining Industry
    Leaders
Wine Merchants

Household Goods and Appliances
Air Conditioning Industry
    Leaders
Cabinetmakers
Ceramists / Potters
Cleaning Aids
    Manufacturers
Furniture Designers /
    Manufacturers
Housewares / Household
    Appliance
    Manufacturers
Sewing Machine
    Manufacturers

Labor
Factory Workers
Labor Organizers /
    Leaders
Labor Relations Experts
Miners
Slaves

Manufacturing and Mining
Aluminum Industry
    Leaders
Barbed Wire
    Manufacturers
Blacksmiths
Chemical Industry
    Leaders
Clockmakers
Computer Industry
    Leaders
Coopers
Cork Industry Leaders
Electronics Industry
    Leaders
Explosives Manufacturers
Firearms Manufacturers
Glass Industry Leaders
Gunsmiths
Hatters
Hemp / Cordage Industry
    Leaders
Industrialists
Iron and Steel Industry
    Leaders
Machinery Manufacturers
Medical Equipment
    Manufacturers
Mining Industry Leaders
Musical Instrument
    Makers
Ordnance Manufacturers
Paper Industry Leaders
Pencil Industry Leaders

Petroleum Industry
    Leaders
Pharmaceutical Industry
    Leaders
Photographic Industry
    Leaders
Plastics Industry Leaders
Prospectors
Rubber Industry Leaders
Sailmakers
Salt Industry Leaders
Scientific Instrument
    Makers
Silversmiths
Smelting / Refining
    Industry Leaders
Tilemakers
Tobacco Industry Leaders
Tool Manufacturers
Watchmakers
Weavers
Woodcarvers

Public Utilities
Electricity Industry
    Leaders
Gas Industry Leaders
Public Utilities Executives

Retail / Wholesale Goods and Services
Animal Trainers
Antique Dealers
Art Dealers
Boardinghouse Operators
Booksellers
Department Store Owners
Dog Breeders
Drugstore Owners
Dry Cleaning Business
    Executives
Fur Traders
Horse Traders
Ice Merchants
Locksmiths
Mail-Order Business
    Leaders
Merchants
Patent Medicine Makers
Press-Clipping Service
    Owners
Public Relations Business
    Leaders
Scribes
Shoemakers
Stenographers
Taxidermists
Traders with Indians /
    Pioneers
Trappers
Undertakers

Variety Store Owners
Whaling Industry Leaders

Transportation
Aerospace Industry
    Leaders
Airline Industry Leaders
Automobile Industry
    Leaders
Bicycle Makers
Canal Builders /
    Promoters
Car Rental Company
    Owners
Elevated Railway
    Operators
Horse-Drawn Vehicle
    Manufacturers
Keelboatmen
Railroad Industry Leaders
Rubber Industry Leaders
Sailors
Ship Captains
Shipbuilders
Shipping Industry Leaders
Stagecoach Company
    Owners
Steamboat Captains /
    Pilots
Steamboat Owners /
    Operators
Streetcar Company
    Owners
Taxicab Company Owners
Tramway Company
    Owners

EDUCATION
Acting Teachers
Art Teachers
Arts Organization
    Administrators
Dance Teachers
Early Childhood
    Educators
Educational Institution
    Officials
Educators
Lecturers
Legal Scholars
Medical Educators
Music Educators
Orators
Penmanship Experts
Physical Culturists
Physical Education
    Teachers / Leaders
Reading Teachers
Religious Educators
Science Educators

Scientific Organization
    Administrators
Singing Teachers
Special Educators
Speech Teachers

EXPLORATION, PIONEERING, AND NATIVE PEOPLES
Adventurers
American Indian Cultural
    Intermediaries
American Indian Leaders
American Indian
    Religious Leaders
Captives of American
    Indians
Captivity Narrativists
Conquistadors
Explorers
Frontiersmen / Pioneers
Guides / Scouts
Hawaiian Leaders
Indian Agents
Navigators
Traders with Indians /
    Pioneers

GOVERNMENT AND POLITICS

Colonial Government and Revolutionary Politics
British Legislators
Colonial Agents
Colonial Founders /
    Officials
Colonial Governors
    General
Colonial Governors /
    Proprietors
Colonial Militiamen
Colonists
Landowners / Patroons
Loyalists (American
    Revolution)
Patriots (American
    Revolution)
Revolutionary Leaders
    (American Revolution)
Signers of the Declaration
    of Independence

Government (Federal)
Attorneys General
    (Federal)
Civil Servants
Commissioners of
    Agriculture

GOVERNMENT AND POLITICS *(cont.)*
Commissioners of Education
Commissioners / Superintendents of Indian Affairs
Congressional Officers / Staff
Diplomats
Federal Government Officials
First Ladies of the United States
Foreign Advisers
National Park Officials
Postal Officials
Postmasters General
Presidential Advisers
Presidential Press Secretaries
Secret Service Agents
Secretaries of Agriculture
Secretaries of Commerce
Secretaries of Commerce and Labor
Secretaries of Defense
Secretaries of Health and Human Services
Secretaries of Health, Education, and Welfare
Secretaries of Housing and Urban Development
Secretaries of Labor
Secretaries of State
Secretaries of War
Secretaries of the Air Force
Secretaries of the Army
Secretaries of the Interior
Secretaries of the Navy
Secretaries of the Treasury
Solicitors General
Speakers of the U.S. House of Representatives
State Department Officials
Territorial Delegates
Treasurers of the United States
U.S. Presidents
U.S. Representatives
U.S. Senators
U.S. Supreme Court Chief Justices
U.S. Supreme Court Justices
U.S. Vice Presidents
White House Staff

Government (Non-Federal)
Attorneys General (State)
County Officials
Mayors
Military Governors
Municipal Government Officials
Resident Commissioners
State Government Officials
State Governors
State Legislators
Territorial Delegates
Territorial Governors

Government of the Confederacy
Confederate Agents
Confederate Legislators / Government Officials
First Lady of the Confederacy
President of the Confederacy
Vice President of the Confederacy

Politics
Abolitionists
Anticommunists
Antisuffragists
Black Nationalists
Civil Rights Activists
Communists
Environmentalists
Fenians
Lobbyists
Nationalists
Nazi Leaders
Political Consultants
Political Figures
Powerbrokers
Presidential Candidates
Socialists
Suffragists
Vice Presidential Candidates
Zionists

HEALTH AND MEDICINE

Abortionists
Allergists
Anesthesiologists
Artificial Heart Recipients
Cardiologists
Chiropractors
Dance Therapists
Dentists
Dermatologists
Eclectic Physicians
Gastroenterologists
Gynecologists
Homeopathic Physicians
Hydropathists
Hypnotherapists
Midwives
Music Therapists
Naturopaths
Neonatologists
Neurologists
Neurosurgeons
Nurses
Nutritionists
Obstetricians
Oncologists
Ophthalmologists
Orthopedic Surgeons
Osteopaths
Otolaryngologists
Parapsychologists
Pathologists
Pediatricians
Pharmacists
Phrenologists
Physicians
Psychiatrists
Psychoanalysts
Psychobiologists
Psychologists
Public Health Officials
Radiologists
Siamese Twins
Speech Therapists
Surgeons
Surgeons General
Syphilologists
Teratologists
Transsexuals
Urologists
Veterinarians
Veterinary Pathologists

HUMANITIES AND SOCIAL SCIENCES

Criticism
Architectural Critics
Art Critics
Dance Critics
Film Critics
Literary Critics
Music Critics
Television Critics
Theater Critics

History and Related Scholarship
Archaeologists
Architectural Historians
Art Historians
Buddhist Studies Scholars
Church Historians
Comparatists
Dance Historians
Documentary / Historical Editors
East Asian Studies Scholars
Ethnomusicologists
Film Historians
Historians
Historians of Science
History of Religions Scholars
Hymnologists
Legal Historians
Legal Scholars
Literary Scholars
Music Historians
Music Theorists
Musicologists
Mythologists
Natural Historians
Orientalists
Religious Studies Scholars
Social Historians &bsp;/n Commentators
Theater Historians
Theologians

Linguistics and Philology
Assyriologists
Classicists
Cryptanalysts
Egyptologists
Epigraphists
Grammarians
Hebraists
Interpreters
Language Theorists
Lexicographers
Linguists
Papyrologists
Philologists
Phoneticists
Phonographers
Sanskritists
Semitists
Slavists
Sumerologists
Translators

Philosophy
Ethicists
Logicians
Philosophers
Transcendentalists

Social Sciences
Anthropologists
Child Development Experts
Criminologists
Demographers

Economists
Epidemiologists
Ethnographers
Ethnologists
Ethnomusicologists
Folklorists
Home Economists
Industrial Relations
  Experts
Learning Theorists
Market Researchers
Organization and
  Management Theorists
Parliamentarians
Policy Analysts
Political Scientists
Pollsters
Sex Researchers
Sexual and Marital
  Counselors
Sociologists
Statisticians

LAW AND
CRIMINOLOGY

Crime and Law
Enforcement
  Alleged Assassins
  Alleged Murderers
  Assassination Conspirators
  Assassins
  Bootleggers
  Detectives
  Forgers
  Gangsters
  Informants
  Kidnappers
  Law Enforcers
  Murder Victims
  Murderers
  Outlaws
  Perjurers
  Pirates
  Regicides
  Smugglers
  Swindlers
  Thieves
  Vigilantes

Legal Practice
  Attorneys General
    (Federal)
  Attorneys General (State)
  Court Clerks
  Court Reporters
  Judge Advocates
  Jurists / Judges
  Justices of the Peace
  Law Reporters
  Lawyers

Litigants
Patent Experts
Public Prosecutors
Solicitors General
U.S. Supreme Court Chief
  Justices
U.S. Supreme Court
  Justices

MILITARY AND
INTELLIGENCE
OPERATIONS

American Revolution
  Revolutionary Army
    Officers
  Revolutionary Naval
    Officers

Civil War
  Confederate Army Officers
  Confederate Naval
    Officers
  Union Army Officers
  Union Naval Officers

Intelligence
  Alleged Traitors
  Informants
  Intelligence Operatives /
    Officials
  Spies
  Traitors

Military (General U.S.
and Foreign)
  Blockade Runners
  British Army / Navy
    Officers
  Colonial Militiamen
  Congressional Medal of
    Honor Recipients
  Filibusters
  French Army / Navy
    Officers
  Guerrillas
  Guides / Scouts
  Inspectors General
  Judge Advocates
  Mercenaries
  Military Chaplains
  Military Deserters
  Military Engineers
  Military Governors
  Privateers
  Soldiers
  Spanish Army / Navy
    Officers
  War Heroes

U.S. Military Services
  Air Force Chiefs of Staff
  Air Force Officers
  Army Air Corps / Army
    Air Forces Officers
  Army Air Service Officers
  Army Chiefs of Staff
  Army Officers (1784–
    1860)
  Army Officers (1866–
    1995)
  Army Signal Corps
    Aviators
  Chiefs of Naval
    Operations
  Coast Guard Officers
  Joint Chiefs of Staff
    Chairmen
  Marine Corps Aviators
  Marine Corps
    Commandants
  Marine Corps Officers
  Naval Aviators
  Naval Officers (1784–
    1860)
  Naval Officers (1866–
    1995)
  Women's Airforce Service
    Pilots
  Women's Army Corps
    Officers

MISCELLANEOUS
OCCUPATIONS AND
REALMS OF RENOWN

  Confidantes
  "Daughter of the
    Confederacy"
  Duelists
  Eccentrics
  Eponyms
  Family Members
  Feudists
  Folk Heroes
  Gamblers
  Holocaust Survivors
  Legendary Figures
  Lighthouse Keepers
  Nobel Prize Winners
  Press Agents
  Psychics
  Salon Hostesses
  Slave Traders
  Socialites
  Travelers
  Witchcraft Hysteria
    Victims

PERFORMING ARTS

Dance
  Choreographers / Dance
    Directors
  Dance Company Directors
  Dance Therapists
  Dancers

Film
  Cinematographers
  Costume Designers
  Documentary Filmmakers
  Film Animators
  Motion Picture Censors
  Motion Picture Editors
  Motion Picture Producers /
    Directors
  Screenwriters
  Special Effects Experts
  Stage / Screen Actors

Music
COMPOSING AND
CONDUCTING
  Bandleaders
  Choral Directors
  Composers / Arrangers
  Librettists
  Lyricists
  Opera Company
    Managers
  Orchestral Conductors
  Songwriters

INSTRUMENTAL
PERFORMANCE
  Accordionists
  Banjoists
  Bassists
  Buglers
  Calliope Players
  Cellists
  Clarinetists
  Comb Players
  Cornetists
  Fiddlers
  Flugelhorn Players
  Flutists
  Guitarists
  Harmonica Players
  Harpsichordists
  Horn Players
  Keyboard Players
  Oboists
  Organists
  Percussionists
  Pianists
  Saxophonists
  Sitar Players
  Trombonists

**PERFORMING ARTS:
MUSIC** *(cont.)*
  Trumpeters
  Vibraharpists
  Violinists
  Violists

TYPES OF MUSIC AND
SINGING
  Blues Musicians / Singers
  Cantors
  Chanters
  Concert Singers
  *Country Musicians /
    Singers*
  Folk Musicians / Singers
  *Gospel Musicians /
    Singers*
  Jazz Musicians
  Jazz Singers
  Opera Singers
  Popular Singers
  Ragtime Musicians
  Reggae Musicians
  *Rhythm and Blues
    Musicians / Singers*
  Rock Musicians / Singers
  Soul Musicians / Singers
  Western Swing Musicians

Radio and Television
  Disc Jockeys
  *Radio / Television
    Engineers*
  *Radio / Television
    Personalities*
  *Radio / Television
    Producers / Directors*
  Radio / Television Writers
  Religious Broadcasters

Theater and Live
Entertainment
  Acrobats
  Burlesque Performers
  Circus Performers
  Clowns
  Comedians
  Costume Designers
  Cowboys
  Daredevils
  Impersonators
  Magicians
  Midgets
  Mimes
  Minstrel Show Performers
  Monologuists
  Orators
  Puppeteers
  Rodeo Performers
  Sharpshooters
  Siamese Twins

  Stage / Screen Actors
  Theatrical Designers
  *Theatrical Producers /
    Directors*
  Toastmasters
  Vaudeville Performers
  Ventriloquists

**RELIGION AND
SPIRITUALITY**

Denominations
  Adventist Leaders
  *African Methodist
    Episcopal Bishops*
  *African Methodist
    Episcopal Clergy*
  *African Methodist
    Episcopal Lay Leaders*
  *African Methodist
    Episcopal Zion Bishops*
  African Orthodox Bishops
  Anglican Activists
  Anglican Bishops
  Anglican Clergy
  Baptist Clergy
  Baptist Lay Leaders
  *Christian Connection
    Leaders*
  Christian Science Leaders
  *Colored Methodist
    Episcopal Church
    Bishops*
  Congregational Clergy
  Disciples of Christ Clergy
  Dutch Reformed Clergy
  Episcopalian Bishops
  Episcopalian Clergy
  Episcopalian Lay Leaders
  Evangelical Clergy
  *Evangelical and Reformed
    Clergy*
  Free Methodist Clergy
  French Reformed Clergy
  German Reformed Clergy
  Greek Orthodox Clergy
  Islamic Leaders
  *Jehovah's Witnesses
    Leaders*
  Jewish Clergy
  Jewish Lay Leaders
  Lutheran Clergy
  Lutheran Lay Leaders
  Mennonite Bishops
  *Methodist Episcopal
    Bishops*
  *Methodist Episcopal
    Church, South, Bishops*
  *Methodist Episcopal
    Church, South, Clergy*
  *Methodist Episcopal
    Clergy*

  *Methodist Episcopal Lay
    Leaders*
  *Methodist Pioneers / Lay
    Leaders*
  *Methodist Protestant
    Clergy*
  Moravian Bishops
  Moravian Clergy
  Moravian Lay Leaders
  Mormon Leaders
  *Polish National Catholic
    Bishops*
  Presbyterian Clergy
  Presbyterian Lay Leaders
  Puritan Clergy
  Puritans
  Quaker Clergy
  Quakers
  *Reformed Church in
    America Clergy*
  Roman Catholic Bishops
  *Roman Catholic
    Cardinals*
  Roman Catholic Clergy
  *Roman Catholic Lay
    Leaders*
  *Romanian Orthodox
    Bishops*
  Russian Orthodox Clergy
  Shakers
  Southern Baptist Clergy
  *Southern Baptist Lay
    Leaders*
  Swedenborgian Clergy
  *Swedenborgian Lay
    Leaders*
  Unitarian Clergy
  Unitarian Lay Leaders
  *Unitarian Universalist
    Clergy*
  Universalist Clergy
  Universalist Lay Leaders
  *Wesleyan Methodist
    Clergy*

Spiritual Communities
and Movements
  Alleged Heretics
  *American Indian
    Religious Leaders*
  Antinomian Leaders
  Buddhist Leaders
  Christian Converts
  *Christian Fellowship
    Members*
  Cult Leaders
  Ethical Culture Leaders
  Evangelists
  Freethinkers
  Gurus
  Humanists

  Inspirationist Leaders
  Military Chaplains
  Millennialists
  Missionaries
  Monks
  Mystics
  Nuns
  Occultists
  Pentecostals
  Religious Broadcasters
  Religious Martyrs
  Saints
  Sectarian Leaders
  Separatist Leaders
  Spiritual Healers
  Spiritualists
  Theologians
  Theosophists
  *Witchcraft Hysteria
    Victims*
  Zionists

**SCIENCE AND
TECHNOLOGY**

Earth Sciences
  Cartographers
  Gemologists
  Geochemists
  Geodesists
  Geographers
  Geologists
  Geomorphologists
  Geophysicists
  Hydrographers
  Hydrologists
  Limnologists
  Meteorologists
  Mineralogists
  Oceanographers
  Paleontologists
  Petroleum Geologists
  Petrologists
  Seismologists
  Soil Scientists
  Volcanologists

Life Sciences
  Anatomists
  Bacteriologists
  Biochemists
  Biologists
  Biometricians
  Biophysicists
  Botanists
  Conchologists
  Cytologists
  Dendrochronologists
  Ecologists
  Embryologists
  Endocrinologists

Entomologists
Evolutionists
Geneticists
Gerontologists
Hematologists
Herpetologists
Immunologists
Insect Pathologists
Malacologists
Mammalogists
Marine Biologists
Medical Scientists
Microbiologists
Molecular Biologists
Morphologists
Mycologists
Naturalists
Neuroanatomists
Neurobiologists
Neuroscientists
Ornithologists
Paleobotanists
Paleoecologists
Parasitologists
Pharmacognosists
Pharmacologists
Physiologists
Plant Collectors
Plant Geneticists
Plant Pathologists
Plant Physiologists
Psychobiologists
Toxicologists
Virologists
Zoologists

Mathematical Sciences
Computer Scientists
Mathematicians
Statisticians

Physical Sciences
Astronomers
Astrophysicists
Biochemists
Biophysicists
Chemists
Crystallographers
Geophysicists
Physical Scientists /
    Natural Philosophers
Physicists
Phytochemists
Planetary Scientists
Space Scientists
Spectroscopists

**Technological and
Applied Sciences**
AGRICULTURE
Agriculturists

Apiarists
Cattle Raisers / Traders
Cowboys
Farmer Organization
    Leaders
Farmers
Foresters
Horticulturists
Plantation Managers /
    Overseers
Plantation Owners
Ranchers
Seedsmen
Soil Scientists
Winegrowers / Vintners

AVIATION
Astronauts
Aviators
Balloonists
Test Pilots

COMPUTER SCIENCE
Computer Industry
    Leaders
Computer Scientists

ENGINEERING
Acoustical Engineers
Aerospace Engineers
Automotive Engineers
Chemical Engineers
Civil Engineers
Communications
    Engineers
Construction Engineers
Consulting Engineers
Electrical Engineers
Industrial Engineers
Mechanical Engineers
Military Engineers
Mining Engineers
Nuclear Engineers
Radio / Television
    Engineers
Steam Propulsion
    Engineers
Structural Engineers

GENERAL
Ballisticians
Inventors
Machinists
Mechanics
Metallurgists
Microscopists
Millwrights
Scientific Instrument
    Makers
Surveyors
Telegraphers

**SOCIETY AND SOCIAL
CHANGE**

Civics and Philanthropy
City and Regional
    Planners
City and Town Founders /
    Benefactors
Civic Leaders
Clubwomen
Foundation Officials
Freemasons
Institutional Founders /
    Benefactors
Organization Founders /
    Officials
Patrons of Science
Patrons of the Arts
Philanthropists

**Political Activism and
Reform Movements**
AIDS Activists
Abolitionists
Agricultural Reformers
Alleged Slave Revolt
    Leaders
Alleged Traitors
Anarchists
Animal Welfare Activists
Antiabortion Rights
    Activists
Anticommunists
Antimasonic Movement
    Leaders
Antinuclear Activists
Antisuffragists
Birth Control Advocates
Black Nationalists
Civil Liberties Activists
Civil Rights Activists
Civil Service Reformers
Communists
Conscientious Objectors
Conservationists
Consumer Rights
    Advocates
Dress Reformers
Ecologists
Economic Reformers
Educational Reform
    Advocates
Environmentalists
Eugenicists
Evolutionists
Fenians
Futurologists
Gay Rights Activists
Historic Preservationists
Human Rights Activists
Humanitarians

Immigration Reform
    Advocates
Insurgents
Internationalists
Ku Klux Klan Leaders
Labor Organizers /
    Leaders
Land Reformers
Nationalists
Nazi Leaders
Pacifists
Peace Activists
Political Activists
Remonstrants
Revolutionaries
Slave Revolt Leaders
Social Reformers
Socialists
Suffragists
Temperance Movement
    Leaders
Traffic Regulation
    Reformers
Traitors
Ufologists
Utopian Community
    Leaders
White Supremacists
Women's Rights Advocates
Zionists

Social Welfare
Charity Workers
Health and Safety
    Reformers
Housing Reformers
Penologists
Prison Officials
Prison Reformers
Public Health Officials
Relief Workers
Sanitarians
Social Reformers
Social Workers

SPORTS AND GAMES

Athletic Coaches /
    Managers
Baseball Players
Basketball Players
Billiards Champions
Bobsledders
Bowlers
Boxers
Bridge Champions
Chess Champions
Cyclists
Figure Skaters
Football Players
Golf Teachers

SPORTS AND GAMES
(cont.)
 Golfers
 Harness Racers
 Ice Hockey Players
 Jockeys
 Long-Distance Walkers
 Mountaineers
 Olympic Medalists
 Polo Players
 Race Car Drivers
 Racehorse Breeders /
  Trainers
 Rodeo Performers
 Rowers
 Speed Skaters
 Sports Inventors
 Sports Officials
 Sports Organization
  Executives
 Surfers
 Swimmers / Divers
 Tennis Players

 Track and Field Athletes
 Wrestlers
 Yachtsmen

WRITING AND PUBLISHING

Editing and Publishing
 Anthologists
 Bible Editors
 Book Designers
 Book Editors / Publishers
 Bookbinders
 Crossword Puzzle Editors
 Documentary / Historical
  Editors
 Engravers
 Fashion Magazine Editors
 Literary Agents
 Literary Executors
 Magazine and Journal
  Editors / Publishers
 Music Editors / Publishers

 News Agency Owners /
  Managers
 Newspaper Editors /
  Publishers
 Printers
 Typographers

Literature and Journalism
 Almanac Makers
 Autobiographers /
  Memoirists
 Biographers
 Broadcast Journalists
 Captivity Narrativists
 Cartoonists / Comic Strip
  Creators
 Children's Book Writers /
  Illustrators
 Cookbook / Food Writers
 Diarists
 Dramatists
 Essayists

 Etiquette Writers
 Fiction Writers
 Humorists
 Letter Writers
 Literary Inspirations
 Medical Writers
 Nature Writers
 Pamphleteers
 Photojournalists
 Poets
 Poets Laureate of the
  United States
 Print Journalists
 Radio / Television Writers
 Science Writers
 Screenwriters
 Slave Narrative Authors
 Speechwriters
 Sportswriters
 Tract Writers
 Travel Writers

CUMULATIVE INDEX BY OCCUPATIONS
AND REALMS OF RENOWN

Readers are encouraged to consult the Introduction and Synoptic Outline,
pp. 629–636, for guidance in using this index.

ARCHIVES, COLLECTIONS, AND LIBRARIES

American Indian Artifacts Collectors
Lawson, Roberta Campbell
Mercer, Henry Chapman
Rindge, Frederick Hastings

Antiquarian Book Collectors
Deinard, Ephraim
Rich, Obadiah
Rosenbach, Abraham Simon Wolf
Weeks, Stephen Beauregard

Antiquarians
Deane, Charles
Dow, George Francis
Drake, Francis Samuel
Earle, Alice Morse
Farmer, John
Grim, David
Gunther, Charles Frederick *Suppl. 2*
Hazard, Caroline
Hazard, Samuel
Jordan, John Woolf
Sachse, Julius Friedrich
Whitmore, William Henry

Antique Collectors
Garvan, Francis Patrick
Hogg, Ima
Hoyte, Lenon *Suppl. 2*
Lyon, Irving Whitall
Nutting, Wallace

Archivists
Bettmann, Otto *Suppl. 1*
Candler, Allen Daniel
Fitzpatrick, John Clement
Knight, Lucian Lamar
Leland, Waldo Gifford

McAvoy, Thomas Timothy
Rhees, William Jones
Schellenberg, Theodore Roosevelt

Archivists of the United States
Connor, Robert Digges Wimberly

Arms and Armor Collectors
Dean, Bashford
Riggs, William Henry

Art Collectors
Abrams, Harry Nathan
Altman, Benjamin
Arensberg, Walter Conrad
Avery, Samuel Putnam
Bache, Jules Semon
Barnes, Albert Coombs
Bliss, Lillie P.
Chrysler, Walter Percy, Jr.
Clarke, Thomas Benedict
Cone, Claribel
Cone, Etta
Dale, Chester
Daniel, Charles
du Pont, Henry Francis
Evans, William Thomas
Fenollosa, Ernest Francisco
Freer, Charles Lang
Gellatly, John
Gilcrease, Thomas
Guggenheim, Solomon Robert
Havemeyer, Louisine Waldron
Hirshhorn, Joseph H.
Huntington, Henry Edwards
Janis, Sidney
Jarves, James Jackson
Karolik, Maxim
Mather, Frank Jewett, Jr.

Mellon, Andrew William
Morgan, Mary Jane
Olsen, Fred
Phillips, Duncan *Suppl. 2*
Powers, Daniel William
Price, Vincent
Quinn, John
Reed, Luman
Robinson, Edward G.
Rosenwald, Lessing Julius
Ross, Denman Waldo
Sachs, Paul Joseph
Sackler, Arthur Mitchell
Schomburg, Arthur Alfonso
Scull, Robert Cooper
Simon, Norton Winfred
Spreckels, Alma
Stanford, Jane Eliza
Stokes, Isaac Newton Phelps
Sullivan, Mary Quinn
Van Braam Houckgeest, Andreas Everardus
Vincent, Frank
Webb, Electra Havemeyer
Wolfe, Catharine Lorillard

Art Museum Curators / Administrators
Barr, Alfred Hamilton, Jr.
Baur, John I. H.
Breeskin, Adelyn Dohme
Cahill, Holger
Force, Juliana Rieser
Goodrich, Lloyd
Mather, Frank Jewett, Jr.
Moore, Charles Herbert
Rebay, Hilla
Rich, Daniel Catton
Sachs, Paul Joseph
Speyer, A. James
Steichen, Edward
Taylor, Francis Henry

Autograph Collectors
Gardiner, Leon
Sprague, William Buell

Automobile Collectors
Harrah, William Fisk

Bibliographers
Bolton, Henry Carrington
Cole, George Watson
Darton, Nelson Horatio
Deinard, Ephraim
Eames, Wilberforce
Evans, Charles
Ford, Worthington Chauncey
Garrison, Fielding Hudson
Goff, Frederick Richmond
Goldstein, Fanny
Greene, Belle da Costa
Griffin, Appleton Prentiss Clark
Griswold, William McCrillis
Howe, James Lewis
Jackson, William Alexander
Jewett, Charles Coffin
Morgan, Dale Lowell
Oko, Adolph S.
Perkins, Frederic Beecher
Sabin, Joseph
Sonneck, Oscar George Theodore
Swem, Earl Gregg
Weeks, Stephen Beauregard
Wheeler, William Adolphus
Wilson, Halsey William
Winship, George Parker

Book Collectors
Avery, Samuel Putnam
Brown, John Carter

Cushing, Harvey
  Williams
Day, F. Holland
Deinard, Ephraim
Dowse, Thomas
Draper, Lyman
  Copeland
Duyckinck, Evert
  Augustus
Fiske, Daniel Willard
Folger, Emily Jordan
Folger, Henry Clay
Gardiner, Leon
Hoe, Robert
Huntington, Henry
  Edwards
Livermore, George
Logan, James
  (1674–1751)
Mackenzie, William
Moorland, Jesse Edward
Nash, John Henry
Ray, Gordon Norton
Rollins, Philip Ashton
Rosenwald, Lessing
  Julius
Schomburg, Arthur
  Alfonso
Shaw, William Smith
Sprague, William Buell
Warden, David Bailie
Weeks, Stephen
  Beauregard
Widener, Harry Elkins

Discographers
Allen, Walter Carl

Encyclopedists
Deane, Samuel
Deutsch, Gotthard
Duyckinck, George
  Long
Heilprin, Michael
Neumark, David

Genealogists
Farmer, John
Whitmore, William
  Henry

Indexers
Edmands, John
Griswold, William
  McCrillis
Weeks, Stephen
  Beauregard

Librarians
Ahern, Mary Eileen
Allibone, Samuel Austin

Anderson, Edwin
  Hatfield
Bancroft, Frederic A.
Beach, Harlan Page
Beer, William
Bellini, Carlo
Billings, John Shaw
Bjerregaard, Carl Henrik
  Andreas
Bogle, Sarah Comly
  Norris
Bostwick, Arthur Elmore
Brett, William Howard
Burr, George Lincoln
Butler, Lee Pierce
Chadwick, James Read
Coggeshall, William
  Turner
Cole, George Watson
Cutter, Charles Ammi
Dana, John Cotton
Davis, Raymond Cazallis
Dewey, Melvil
Dexter, Franklin
  Bowditch
Durrie, Daniel Steele
Eames, Wilberforce
Eastman, William Reed
Edmands, John
Engel, Carl
Evans, Charles
Fairchild, Mary Salome
  Cutler
Farrand, Max
Fiske, Daniel Willard
Flexner, Jennie Maas
Flint, Weston
Folsom, Charles
Foss, Sam Walter
Freedley, George
Galbreath, Charles
  Burleigh
Garrison, Fielding
  Hudson
Goff, Frederick
  Richmond
Golder, Frank Alfred
Goldstein, Fanny
Green, Samuel Swett
Greene, Belle da Costa
Griffin, Appleton
  Prentiss Clark
Griswold, William
  McCrillis
Guild, Reuben Aldridge
Hamlin, Talbot Faulkner
Hanson, James Christian
  Meinich
Harris, Thaddeus
  William

Holden, Edward
  Singleton
Homes, Henry Augustus
Hutchins, Margaret
Isom, Mary Frances
Jackson, William
  Alexander
Jewett, Charles Coffin
Johnson, Theodore
  Elliott
Klingelsmith, Margaret
  Center
Kroeger, Alice Bertha
Larned, Josephus Nelson
Legler, Henry Eduard
Lydenberg, Harry Miller
Martel, Charles
Marvin, Cornelia
Marx, Alexander
Meigs, Return Jonathan
  (1801–1891)
Miner, Dorothy Eugenia
Moore, Anne Carroll
Mudge, Isadore Gilbert
Oko, Adolph S.
Perkins, Frederic
  Beecher
Plummer, Mary Wright
Root, Azariah Smith
Schomburg, Arthur
  Alfonso
Sellers, Charles Coleman
  Suppl. 2
Sharp, Katharine
  Lucinda
Shera, Jesse Hauk
Sibley, John Langdon
Smith, Lloyd Pearsall
Sonneck, Oscar George
  Theodore
Spencer, Anne
Stearns, Lutie Eugenia
Steiner, Lewis Henry
Swem, Earl Gregg
Thwaites, Reuben Gold
Timothy, Lewis
Turner, William
  Wadden
Tyler, Alice Sarah
Uhler, Philip Reese
Utley, George Burwell
Van Name, Addison
Vaughan, John
Ward, James Warner
Wheeler, William
  Adolphus
Whitehill, Walter Muir,
  Jr.
Whitney, James Lyman
Winser, Beatrice
Winship, George Parker

Winsor, Justin *Suppl. 1*
Wolfe, Linnie Marsh
Wood, Mary Elizabeth
Wroth, Lawrence
  Counselman

Librarians of Congress
Beckley, John James
Evans, Luther Harris
MacLeish, Archibald
Mumford, Lawrence
  Quincy
Putnam, Herbert
Spofford, Ainsworth
  Rand
Watterston, George

Manuscript Collectors
Gardiner, Leon
Isham, Ralph Heyward
Quinn, John
Rollins, Philip Ashton
Schomburg, Arthur
  Alfonso

*Museum Curators /
Administrators*
Allen, Joel Asaph
Angle, Paul McClelland
Anthony, Harold Elmer
Barbour, Thomas
Barnum, P. T.
Bickmore, Albert Smith
Chapman, Frank
  Michler
Dana, John Cotton
Dow, George Francis
Du Simitière, Pierre
  Eugène
Friedmann, Herbert
Goode, George Brown
Gordon, George Byron
Hodge, Frederick Webb
Hough, Walter
Kimball, Fiske
Lucas, Frederic
  Augustus
Mason, Otis Tufton
Montgomery, Charles
  Franklin
Ostroff, Eugene *Suppl. 2*
Otis, George Alexander
Phillips, Duncan
  Suppl. 2
Putnam, Frederic Ward
Richmond, Charles
  Wallace
Ridgway, Robert
Saint-Mémin, Charles
  Balthazar Julien Févret
  de

Savage, Edward
Stejneger, Leonhard
   Hess
Stimpson, William
Stout, Gardner
   Dominick
True, Frederick William
Vaillant, George Clapp
Wetmore, Alexander
Winser, Beatrice
Wissler, Clark

Numismatists
Brand, Virgil Michael
Clapp, George Hubbard
Cogan, Edward
Crosby, Sylvester Sage
Du Bois, William Ewing
Mickley, Joseph Jacob
Newell, Edward
   Theodore
Phillips, Henry, Jr.
Saltus, J. Sanford

Zoo Curators /
Administrators
Ditmars, Raymond Lee
Perkins, Marlin

ART AND
ARCHITECTURE

Applied Arts
Blacksmiths
Davenport, Thomas
Deere, John
Jefferson, Isaac
Yellin, Samuel

Book Designers
Armitage, Merle
Conkwright, P. J.
   Suppl. 2
Rogers, Bruce
Updike, Daniel Berkeley
Whitman, Sarah de St.
   Prix Wyman

Bookbinders
Fortune, Amos

Cabinetmakers
Buckland, William
Goddard, John
Gostelowe, Jonathan
Herter, Gustave, and
   Christian Herter
Hitchcock, Lambert
Lannuier, Charles-
   Honoré

Marcotte, Léon
   Alexandre
Phyfe, Duncan
Quervelle, Anthony
Savery, William
Seymour, John
Seymour, Thomas
Stickley, Gustav
Townsend, John

Calligraphers
Dwiggins, William
   Addison

Ceramists / Potters
Grueby, William Henry
Martinez, Maria
   Montoya *Suppl. 2*
Nampeyo
Ohr, George E.
Overbeck, Margaret,
   Hannah Borger
   Overbeck, Elizabeth
   Grey Overbeck, and
   Mary Frances
   Overbeck
Wood, Beatrice *Suppl. 1*

Clockmakers
Bond, William Cranch
Thomas, Seth

Engravers
Ames, Ezra
Johnston, Thomas

Fashion Designers
Carnegie, Hattie
Cashin, Bonnie *Suppl. 2*
Daché, Lilly
Demorest, Ellen Curtis
Ellis, Perry
Halston
Hawes, Elizabeth
Klein, Anne
Miller, Elizabeth Smith
Potter, Clare *Suppl. 1*
Rosenstein, Nettie

Flatware Designers
Codman, William
   Christmas

Furniture Designers /
Manufacturers
Bertoia, Harry
Eames, Charles
   (1907–1978)
Hunzinger, George
   Jakob
Jelliff, John

Lloyd, Marshall Burns
Stickley, Gustav
Sypher, Obadiah Lum

Glass Artists
Albers, Josef
Carder, Frederick
La Farge, John Frederick
   Lewis Joseph
Lathrop, Francis
   Augustus
Tiffany, Louis Comfort
Tillinghast, Mary
   Elizabeth
Whitman, Sarah de St.
   Prix Wyman

Goldsmiths
Ramage, John

Graphic Designers
Bass, Saul *Suppl. 1*
Bell, Mary A.
Feininger, Lyonel
   Charles Adrian
Penfield, Edward
Rand, Paul *Suppl. 1*
Steinberg, Saul *Suppl. 1*

Hatters
Daché, Lilly
Stetson, John Batterson
Swan, Timothy

Industrial Designers
Bayer, Herbert
Deskey, Donald
Dreyfuss, Henry
Eames, Charles
   (1907–1978)
Eames, Ray
Geddes, Norman Bel
Loewy, Raymond
   Fernand
Noyes, Eliot Fette
Stevens, Brooks *Suppl. 1*
Tupper, Earl Silas
Wright, Russel

Interior Designers
Baldwin, Billy
Buckland, William
Colman, Samuel
Deskey, Donald
de Wolfe, Elsie
Draper, Dorothy
Herter, Gustave, and
   Christian Herter
La Farge, John Frederick
   Lewis Joseph

Lathrop, Francis
   Augustus
Marcotte, Léon
   Alexandre
Reiss, Winold Fritz
Tiffany, Louis Comfort
Tillinghast, Mary
   Elizabeth
Wheeler, Candace
   Thurber

Jewelers
Bulova, Arde
Cartier, Pierre *Suppl. 1*
Tiffany, Charles Lewis

Medal / Coin Designers
Brenner, Victor David
Fraser, Laura Gardin
Weinman, Adolph
   Alexander

Mosaicists
Heuduck, Arno Paul
   Suppl. 2
Heuduck, Paul Johannes
   Suppl. 2

Musical Instrument Makers
Babcock, Alpheus
Chickering, Jonas
Gemunder Family
Johnston, Thomas
Steinway, Christian
   Friedrich Theodore
Steinway, Henry
   Engelhard
Steinway, William

Papermakers
Hunter, Dard

Pewterers
Will, William

Printers
Aitken, Robert
Bailey, Francis
Bailey, Lydia R.
Bradford, Andrew
Bradford, John
Bradford, William
   (1663–1752)
Bradford, William
   (1722–1791)
Carter, John
Cassin, John
Collins, Isaac
Currier, Nathaniel
Dawkins, Henry
Day, Stephen

Applied Arts *(cont.)*
Dobson, Thomas
Donahoe, Patrick
Doolittle, Amos
Draper, John
Draper, Margaret Green
Draper, Richard
Duane, Margaret
  Hartman Markoe
  Bache
Dunlap, John
Edes, Benjamin
Fleet, Thomas
Foster, John
Fowle, Daniel
Franklin, Ann Smith
Franklin, James
Gaine, Hugh
Gales, Joseph
Gill, John
Goddard, Mary
  Katherine
Goddard, Sarah Updike
Goddard, William
Goudy, Frederic William
Green, Anne Catharine
Green, Bartholomew
Green, Jonas
Green, Samuel
Greenleaf, Thomas
Hall, Samuel
  (1740–1807)
Hamlin, William
Hoen, August
Holt, John
Houghton, Henry Oscar
Hugo, E. Harold
Humphreys, James
Hunter, Dard
Ives, James Merritt
Jansen, Reinier
Johnson, Marmaduke
Johnston, Thomas
Keimer, Samuel
Kneeland, Samuel
Loudon, Samuel
Maxwell, William
  (1766?–1801)
McFarland, J. Horace
Mecom, Benjamin
Mein, John
Miller, Henry
  (1702–1782)
Munsell, Joel
Nash, John Henry
Nicholson, Timothy
Nuthead, William
Parker, James
Parks, William
Prang, Louis
Revere, Paul

Rind, Clementina
Rives, John Cook
Rivington, James
Robertson, James
  (1747–1816)
Rudge, William Edwin
Russell, Benjamin
Seaton, William Winston
Sholes, Christopher
  Latham
Sower, Christopher, II
Stevens, Alzina Ann
  Parsons
Tanner, Benjamin
Thomas, Isaiah
Timothy, Ann
Timothy, Elizabeth
Timothy, Lewis
Towne, Benjamin
Updike, Daniel Berkeley
White, Thomas Willis
Zenger, John Peter

Silversmiths
Atsidi, Sani
Dummer, Jeremiah
  (1645–1718)
Fitch, John
Hull, John
Hurd, Jacob
Hurd, Nathaniel
Kirk, Samuel Child
Le Roux, Bartholomew
Moore, Edward
  Chandler
Myers, Myer
Revere, Paul
Richardson, Joseph
Stone, Arthur John
Syng, Philip, Jr.
Welles, Clara

Tanners
Fortune, Amos

Taxidermists
Akeley, Carl Ethan

Textile Designers
Cornell, Joseph *Suppl. 1*
Wheeler, Candace
  Thurber

Tilemakers
Mercer, Henry
  Chapman

Type Designers
Bayer, Herbert
Dwiggins, William
  Addison

Typographers
Goudy, Frederic William
Nash, John Henry
Ruzicka, Rudolph

Watchmakers
Bulova, Arde
Crosby, Sylvester Sage

Weavers
Bresci, Gaetano
Keyser, Louisa *Suppl. 2*

Woodcarvers
López, José Dolores
Skillin, John
Skillin, Simeon, Jr.

Architecture
Architects
Adler, Dankmar
Adler, David
Ain, Gregory *Suppl. 1*
Albers, Josef
Aldrich, Chester Holmes
Ariss, John
Atwood, Charles Bowler
Austin, Henry
Bacon, Henry, Jr.
Banner, Peter
Barber, Donn
Baum, Dwight James
Bayer, Herbert
Benjamin, Asher
Bennett, Edward Herbert
Bethune, Louise
  Blanchard
Billings, Charles
  Howland Hammatt
Blodget, Samuel, Jr.
Bosworth, Welles
Bottomley, William
  Lawrence
Boyington, William W.
Brattle, Thomas
Breuer, Marcel Lajos
Brown, Glenn
Browne, Herbert
  Wheildon Cotton
Bryant, Charles
  Grandison
Buckland, William
Bulfinch, Charles
Bunshaft, Gordon
Burnham, Daniel
  Hudson
Button, Stephen Decatur
Carrère, John Merven
Cluskey, Charles Blaney
Coit, Elisabeth

Colter, Mary Elizabeth
  Jane
Cook, Abner Hugh
Cope, Walter
Corbett, Harvey Wiley
Coxhead, Ernest Albert
Cram, Ralph Adams
Cret, Paul Philippe
Dakin, James Harrison
Davis, Alexander
  Jackson
Day, Frank Miles
Delano, William Adams
Dinkeloo, John Gerard
Dow, Alden Ball
Eames, Charles
  (1907–1978)
Edbrooke, Willoughby J.
Eidlitz, Leopold
Elmslie, George Grant
Emerson, William Ralph
Ferriss, Hugh
Flagg, Ernest
Ford, O'Neil
Fuller, R. Buckminster
Furness, Frank
Gallier, James, Sr.
Gilbert, Cass
Gill, Irving
Gilman, Arthur Delavan
Godefroy, Maximilian
Goff, Bruce Alonzo
Goodhue, Bertram
  Grosvenor
Graham, Ernest Robert
Greene, Charles
  Sumner, and Henry
  Mather Greene
Griffin, Marion Lucy
  Mahony
Griffin, Walter Burley
Gropius, Walter
Gruen, Victor David
Hadfield, George
Hallet, Etienne Sulpice
Hamlin, Talbot Faulkner
Hardenbergh, Henry
  Janeway
Harrison, Peter
Harrison, Wallace
  Kirkman
Hastings, Thomas
Haviland, John
Hayden, Sophia
  Gregoria
Herts, Henry Beaumont,
  II
Hoadley, David
Hoban, James
Holabird, William
Hooker, Philip

Architecture *(cont.)*
Hornbostel, Henry
Howe, George (1886–1955)
Howe, Lois Lilley, Eleanor Manning, and Mary Almy
Hunt, Richard Morris
Jay, William
Jenney, William Le Baron
Kahn, Albert
Kahn, Louis I.
Kaufmann, Gordon *Suppl. 2*
Keck, George Fred
Keely, Patrick Charles
Kimball, Fiske
Kocher, A. Lawrence
Lafever, Minard
Lamb, Thomas White
Lamb, William Frederick
Latrobe, Benjamin Henry (1764–1820)
Le Brun, Napoleon
L'Enfant, Pierre Charles
Lescaze, William Edmond
Lienau, Detlef
Lindeberg, Harrie Thomas
Little, Arthur
Long, Robert Cary
Longfellow, William Pitt Preble
Maginnis, Charles Donagh
Magonigle, Harold Van Buren
Mangin, Joseph François
Manigault, Gabriel (1758–1809)
Marshall, Benjamin Howard
Maybeck, Bernard Ralph
McArthur, John, Jr.
McComb, John, Jr.
McIntire, Samuel
McKim, Charles Follen
Mead, William Rutherford
Meem, John Gaw
Meigs, Montgomery Cunningham
Mendelsohn, Erich
Merrill, John Ogden
Meštrović, Ivan
Mies van der Rohe, Ludwig
Mills, Robert
Mix, Edward Townsend

Mizner, Addison Cairns
Morgan, Julia
Mullett, Alfred Bult
Munday, Richard
Neutra, Richard Joseph
Nichols, Minerva Parker
Nichols, William
Notman, John
Noyes, Eliot Fette
Owings, Nathaniel Alexander
Parris, Alexander
Parsons, Samuel, Jr.
Peabody, Robert Swain
Pelz, Paul Johannes
Pereira, William Leonard
Perkins, Dwight Heald
Pittman, William Sidney
Platt, Charles Adams
Polk, Willis Jefferson
Pond, Irving Kane
Pope, John Russell
Post, George Browne
Potter, Edward Tuckerman
Potter, William Appleton
Price, Bruce
Proskouriakoff, Tatiana *Suppl. 2*
Ramée, Joseph
Reid, Neel
Renwick, James, Jr.
Richardson, H. H.
Riggs, Lutah Maria
Roche, Martin
Rogers, Isaiah
Rogers, James Gamble
Root, John Wellborn
Saarinen, Eero
Saarinen, Eliel
Schindler, Rudolph Michael
Schwarzmann, Hermann Joseph
Shaw, Howard Van Doren
Shutze, Philip Trammell, II
Skidmore, Louis
Sloan, Samuel T.
Smith, Chloethiel Woodard
Smith, Robert (1722–1777)
Spencer, Robert Clossen, Jr.
Speyer, A. James
Stein, Clarence Samuel
Stewart, John George
Stokes, Isaac Newton Phelps

Stone, Edward Durell
Stonorov, Oskar Gregory
Strickland, William
Sturgis, John Hubbard
Sturgis, Russell
Sullivan, Louis Henri
Sully, Thomas (1855–1939)
Tallmadge, Thomas Eddy
Tefft, Thomas Alexander
Thompson, Martin Euclid
Thornton, William
Toombs, Henry Johnston
Town, Ithiel
Trumbauer, Horace
Upjohn, Richard
Upjohn, Richard Michell
Urban, Joseph
Van Brunt, Henry
Van Osdel, John Mills
Vaux, Calvert
Walker, Ralph Thomas
Walter, Thomas Ustick
Warren, Herbert Langford
Warren, Russell
White, Stanford
Wight, Peter Bonnett
Willard, Solomon
Williams, Paul Revere
Withers, Frederick Clarke
Wright, Frank Lloyd
Wright, Henry
Yamasaki, Minoru
Young, Ammi Burnham

Golf Course Architects
Jones, Robert Trent, Sr. *Suppl. 2*
Macdonald, Charles Blair
Travis, Walter John

Landscape Architects
Church, Thomas Dolliver
Downing, Andrew Jackson
Eckbo, Garrett *Suppl. 2*
Eliot, Charles
Farrand, Beatrix Cadwalader Jones
Griffin, Walter Burley
Hubbard, Henry Vincent
Jensen, Jens

King, Mrs. Francis
Nolen, John
Olmsted, Frederick Law
Olmsted, Frederick Law, Jr.
Platt, Charles Adams
Ramée, Joseph
Shipman, Ellen Biddle
Shurcliff, Arthur Asahel
Simonds, Ossian Cole
Taylor, Albert Davis
Vaux, Calvert
Waugh, Frank Albert
Weidenmann, Jacob

Marine Architects
Bushnell, David
Eckford, Henry
Ericsson, John
Herreshoff, L. Francis *Suppl. 2*
Herreshoff, Nathanael Greene
Holland, John Philip
Isherwood, Benjamin Franklin
Lake, Simon
Shreve, Henry Miller
Stevens, Robert Livingston
Taylor, David Watson
Webb, William Henry
Westervelt, Jacob Aaron

Art
Art Connoisseurs
Berenson, Bernard
Greene, Belle da Costa
Laffan, William Mackay
Okakura Kakuzo *Suppl. 1*

Artist's Models
d'Harnoncourt, René
Nesbit, Evelyn Florence
Spreckels, Alma

Cartoonists / Comic Strip Creators
Addams, Charles Samuel
Arno, Peter
Baker, George
Breger, Dave *Suppl. 2*
Briggs, Clare A.
Browne, Carl
Browne, Dik
Buell, Marjorie Henderson *Suppl. 2*
Bushmiller, Ernie
Caniff, Milton Arthur Paul

Art *(cont.)*
Capp, Al
Clay, Edward Williams
Cole, Jack *Suppl. 2*
Cranch, Christopher
  Pearse
Crane, Royston
  Campbell
Darling, Jay Norwood
Doolittle, Amos
Dorgan, Tad
Dumm, Edwina *Suppl. 2*
Dunn, Alan
Feininger, Lyonel
  Charles Adrian
Fisher, Ham
Foster, Hal
Fox, Fontaine Talbot, Jr.
Geisel, Theodor Seuss
Gibson, Charles Dana
Godwin, Frank
Goldberg, Rube
Goldwater, John L.
  Suppl. 1
Gorey, Edward *Suppl. 2*
Gottfredson, Floyd
Gould, Chester
Gray, Clarence
Gray, Harold Lincoln
Gropper, William
Gross, Milt
Harman, Fred *Suppl. 2*
Harrington, Oliver W.
  Suppl. 2
Held, John, Jr.
Herblock *Suppl. 2*
Herriman, George
  Joseph
Hirschfeld, Al *Suppl. 2*
Hokinson, Helen
Irvin, Rea
Johnson, Crockett
Kahles, Charles William
  Suppl. 2
Kane, Bob *Suppl. 2*
Kelly, Walt
Kent, Jack
Keppler, Joseph
Ketcham, Hank *Suppl. 2*
Kirby, Jack *Suppl. 2*
Kirby, Rollin
Knerr, Harold Hering
Kurtzman, Harvey
Lasswell, Fred, Jr.
  Suppl. 2
MacNelly, Jeff *Suppl. 1*
Marston, William
  Moulton
Martin, Don *Suppl. 1*
Mauldin, Bill *Suppl. 2*
McCay, Winsor Zenic

McCutcheon, John T.
  Suppl. 2
McManus, George
Minor, Robert
Moore, Donald
  Wynkoop
Mullin, Willard Harlan
Nast, Thomas
Newell, Peter
Opper, Frederick Burr
Outcault, Richard Felton
Raymond, Alex
Ripley, Robert LeRoy
Schulz, Charles M.
  Suppl. 1
Segar, Elzie Crisler
Siegel, Jerry, and Joe
  Shuster *Suppl. 1*
Smith, Al
Smith, Robert Sidney
Soglow, Otto
Steinberg, Saul *Suppl. 1*
Swinnerton, James
  Guilford, Jr.
Thurber, James
Willard, Frank
Williams, Gluyas
Young, Arthur Henry
Young, Chic
Zimmerman, Eugene

*Children's Book Writers /
Illustrators*
Abbott, Jacob
Adams, Harriet
  Stratemeyer
Adams, William Taylor
Alcott, Louisa May
Alger, Horatio, Jr.
Altsheler, Joseph
  Alexander
Andrews, Jane
Arnold, Elliott
Austin, Jane Goodwin
Baum, L. Frank
Baylor, Frances
  Courtenay
Bee, Clair Francis
Bemelmans, Ludwig
Benchley, Nathaniel
  Goddard
Bontemps, Arna
  Wendell
Bouvet, Marie
  Marguerite
Brooks, Noah
Brown, Abbie Farwell
Brown, Margaret Wise
Burgess, Thornton
  Waldo

Burnett, Frances
  Hodgson
Carruth, Hayden
Clarke, Rebecca Sophia
Cox, Palmer
DeJong, David Cornel
Dodge, Mary Elizabeth
  Mapes
Edmonds, Walter D.
  Suppl. 1
Eggleston, George Cary
Ellis, Edward Sylvester
Ets, Marie Hall
Field, Rachel Lyman
Finley, Martha
Fisher, Dorothy F.
  Canfield
Fujikawa, Gyo *Suppl. 1*
Gág, Wanda
Garis, Howard Roger
Geisel, Theodor Seuss
Goodrich, Charles
  Augustus
Goodrich, Samuel
  Griswold
Goulding, Francis
  Robert
Hale, Lucretia Peabody
Hale, Susan
Harris, Joel Chandler
Henderson, Alice Corbin
Herrick, Sophia
  McIlvaine Bledsoe
Irwin, Inez Leonore
  Haynes Gillmore
James, Will Roderick
Jamison, Cecilia Viets
Janvier, Margaret
  Thomson
Johnson, Crockett
Johnson, Osa
Johnston, Annie Fellows
  Suppl. 1
Judson, Emily Chubbuck
Kelland, Clarence
  Budington
Kelly, Myra
Kent, Jack
Krapp, George Philip
Lathbury, Mary
  Artemisia
Leaf, Munro
McGinley, Phyllis
McIntosh, Maria Jane
Miller, Olive Beaupré
Montgomery, Elizabeth
  Rider
Moore, Clara Sophia
  Jessup Bloomfield
Nash, Ogden
Newcomb, Harvey

O'Hara, Mary
Orton, Helen Fuller
Parish, Peggy
Parrish, Anne
Parrish, Maxfield
Patten, Gilbert
Perkins, Lucy Fitch
Porter, Eleanor
  Hodgman
Prentiss, Elizabeth
  Payson
Pyle, Howard
Rey, H. A.
Richards, Laura
  Elizabeth Howe
Sargent, Epes
Sawyer, Ruth
Scarry, Richard
  McClure
Scudder, Horace Elisha
Selden, George
Stratemeyer, Edward
Tunis, John R.
Very, Lydia Louisa Ann
Wells, Carolyn
White, E. B.
White, Eliza Orne
Wibberley, Leonard
Widdemer, Margaret
Wilder, Laura Ingalls
Woolsey, Sarah Chauncy

Folk Artists
Bad Heart Bull, Amos
  Suppl. 2
Chambers, Thomas
Chandler, Winthrop
Cohoon, Hannah
  Harrison
Hampton, James
Hicks, Edward
Hunter, Clementine
Pinney, Eunice Griswold
Rodia, Simon

Illustrators
Abbey, Edwin Austin
Anderson, Alexander
Ashley, Clifford Warren
Barber, John Warner
Barnes, Djuna
Billings, Charles
  Howland Hammatt
Blashfield, Edwin
  Howland
Blum, Robert Frederick
Blumenschein, Ernest L.
Bodmer, Karl
Borthwick, John David
Bridges, Fidelia
Burgess, Gelett

Art *(cont.)*

Cary, William de la
  Montagne
Chambers, Robert
  William
Chapman, John Gadsby
Chappel, Alonzo
Christy, Howard
  Chandler
Clay, Edward Williams
Cox, Kenyon
Darley, Felix Octavius
  Carr
Day, Clarence Shepard,
  Jr.
Douglas, Aaron
Dove, Arthur Garfield
Dunn, Harvey Thomas
Flagg, James
  Montgomery
Foote, Mary Anna
  Hallock
Frost, Arthur Burdett
Gibson, Charles Dana
Gifford, Robert Swain
Glackens, William
Godwin, Frank
Gray, Clarence
Greatorex, Eleanor
  Elizabeth
Grosz, George
Guérin, Jules Vallée
Gutmann, Bernhard
Hambidge, Jay
Hassam, Childe
Held, John, Jr.
Herford, Oliver
Irvin, Rea
James, Will Roderick
Kappel, Philip
Kent, Rockwell
Kirby, Rollin
La Farge, John Frederick
  Lewis Joseph
Lathbury, Mary
  Artemisia
Lawson, Alexander
Leigh, William Robinson
Le Moyne de Morgues,
  Jacques
Leslie, Frank
Leyendecker, J. C.
Linton, William James
Longacre, James Barton
Lossing, Benson John
Marsh, Reginald
Matteson, Tompkins
  Harrison
Moran, Thomas
Newell, Peter

Nugent, Richard Bruce
  Suppl. 2
O'Neill, Rose Cecil
Parrish, Maxfield
Penfield, Edward
Pennell, Joseph
Proskouriakoff, Tatiana
  Suppl. 2
Pyle, Howard
Reason, Patrick Henry
Reiss, Winold Fritz
Remington, Frederic
Rockwell, Norman
Ruzicka, Rudolph
Sartain, John
Shinn, Everett
Smillie, James
Smith, Francis
  Hopkinson
Strother, David Hunter
Tanner, Benjamin
Taylor, William Ladd
Urban, Joseph
Vargas, Alberto
Warhol, Andy
Waud, Alfred R.
  Suppl. 2
Wyeth, N. C.
  (1882–1945)

Painters

Abbey, Edwin Austin
Albers, Josef
Albright, Ivan
Alexander, Francis
Alexander, John White
Allston, Washington
Ames, Blanche Ames
Ames, Ezra
Anshutz, Thomas
  Pollock
Appleton, Thomas Gold
Aragón, José Rafael
Ashley, Clifford Warren
Audubon, John James
Avery, Milton Clark
Badger, Joseph
Banvard, John
Barney, Alice Pike
Basquiat, Jean-Michel
  Suppl. 1
Bayer, Herbert
Baziotes, William
Beard, James Henry
Bearden, Romare
Beaux, Cecilia
Beckwith, James Carroll
Bellows, George Wesley
Benbridge, Henry
Bennett, Gwendolyn
Benson, Eugene

Benson, Frank Weston
Benton, Thomas Hart
  (1889–1975)
Biddle, George
Bierstadt, Albert
Bingham, George Caleb
Birch, Thomas
Birch, William Russell
Bishop, Isabel
Blackburn, Joseph
Blakelock, Ralph Albert
Blashfield, Edwin
  Howland
Bluemner, Oscar Julius
Blum, Robert Frederick
Blume, Peter
Blumenschein, Ernest L.
Bodmer, Karl
Bolotowsky, Ilya
Borthwick, John David
Bradford, William
  (1823–1892)
Bridges, Fidelia
Bridgman, Frederick
  Arthur
Brooks, James
Brown, John George
Brown, Mather
Brumidi, Constantino
Brush, George de Forest
Bunker, Dennis Miller
Burbank, Elbridge Ayer
Burchfield, Charles
  Ephraim
Cadmus, Paul *Suppl. 2*
Caesar, Doris
Carles, Arthur B.
Cary, William de la
  Montagne
Cassatt, Mary
Catlin, George
Chalfant, Jefferson
  David
Chaplin, Ralph Hosea
Chapman, Conrad Wise
Chapman, John Gadsby
Chappel, Alonzo
Chase, William Merritt
Christy, Howard
  Chandler
Church, Frederic Edwin
Clark, Alvan
Clements, Gabrielle
  DeVaux
Cole, Thomas
Colman, Samuel
Copley, John Singleton
Cox, Allyn
Cox, Kenyon
Crawford, Ralston
Cropsey, Jasper Francis

Cummings, E. E.
Curry, John Steuart
Davies, Arthur Bowen
Davis, Stuart
DeCamp, Joseph
  Rodefer
de Kooning, Elaine
de Kooning, Willem
  Suppl. 1
Demuth, Charles Henry
  Buckius
Dewing, Maria Richards
  Oakey
Dewing, Thomas
  Wilmer
Dickinson, Anson
Dickinson, William
  Preston
Diebenkorn, Richard
Diller, Burgoyne
Dodge, John Wood
Doughty, Thomas
Douglas, Aaron
Dove, Arthur Garfield
Dreier, Katherine Sophie
Drexel, Francis Martin
Du Simitière, Pierre
  Eugène
Dummer, Jeremiah
  (1645–1718)
Duncanson, Robert S.
Dunlap, William
Dunn, Harvey Thomas
Durand, Asher Brown
Durand, John
Durrie, George Henry
Duveneck, Frank
Eakins, Thomas
  Cowperthwait
Earl, James
Earl, Ralph
Eaton, Wyatt
Edmonds, Francis
  William
Eichholtz, Jacob
Eilshemius, Louis
  Michel
Elliott, Charles Loring
Emmons, Chansonetta
  Stanley
Enneking, John Joseph
Enters, Angna
Ernst, Jimmy
Ernst, Max
Evergood, Philip
Feininger, Lyonel
  Charles Adrian
Feke, Robert
Ferris, Jean Leon
  Gerome
Field, Erastus Salisbury

Art *(cont.)*
Fisher, Alvan
Fitzgerald, Zelda
Flagg, James
  Montgomery
Fournier, Alexis Jean
Fraser, Charles
Frost, Arthur Burdett
Fuertes, Louis Agassiz
Fuller, George
Fulton, Robert
Gallatin, Albert Eugene
Getchell, Edith Loring
  Peirce
Gibran, Kahlil
Gifford, Robert Swain
Gifford, Sanford
  Robinson
Gilder, Helena de Kay
Glackens, William
Goodridge, Sarah
Gorky, Arshile
Gottlieb, Adolph
Greatorex, Eleanor
  Elizabeth
Greatorex, Eliza Pratt
Gropper, William
Grosz, George
Guérin, Jules Vallée
Guston, Philip
Gutmann, Bernhard
Gwathmey, Robert
  Suppl. 2
Haberle, John
Hale, Ellen Day
Hale, Lilian Clarke
  Westcott
Hale, Philip Leslie
Hale, Susan
Hanley, Sarah Eileen
Harding, Chester
Haring, Keith Allen
Harman, Fred *Suppl. 2*
Harnett, William
  Michael
Harrison, Alexander
Hartley, Marsden
Hassam, Childe
Hawthorne, Charles
  Webster
Hawthorne, Sophia
  Peabody
Healy, George Peter
  Alexander
Henri, Robert
Hentz, Nicholas
  Marcellus
Herring, James
Hesse, Eva
Hesselius, Gustavus
Hesselius, John

Hill, John Henry
Hofmann, Hans
Homer, Winslow
Hopkinson, Charles
  Sydney
Hopper, Edward
Hovenden, Thomas
Howells, Elinor Mead
Hunt, William Morris
Huntington, Daniel
Ingham, Charles
  Cromwell
Inman, Henry
Inness, George
Jackson, William Henry
Jamison, Cecilia Viets
Jarvis, John Wesley
Jennys, Richard, and
  William Jennys
Jewett, William
Johnson, David
Johnson, Eastman
Johnson, Joshua
Johnston, Henrietta de
  Beaulieu Dering
Johnston, Thomas
Jones, Hugh Bolton
Jonson, Raymond
Jouett, Matthew Harris
Kensett, John Frederick
Kent, Rockwell
King, Charles Bird
Kline, Franz
Knight, Daniel Ridgway
Koehler, Robert
Krasner, Lee
Krimmel, John Lewis
Kuhn, Walt
La Farge, John Frederick
  Lewis Joseph
Laning, Edward
Lathrop, Francis
  Augustus
Lawrence, Jacob *Suppl. 2*
Lazzell, Blanche
Le Clear, Thomas
Le Moyne de Morgues,
  Jacques
Leigh, William Robinson
Lesley Bush-Brown,
  Margaret White
Leslie, Charles Robert
Leutze, Emanuel
  Gottlieb
Liberman, Alexander
  Suppl. 2
Lichtenstein, Roy
  Suppl. 1
Lindner, Richard
Linton, William James
Louis, Morris

Low, Will Hickok
Loy, Mina
Luce, Molly
Luks, George Benjamin
MacCameron, Robert
  Lee
MacMonnies, Frederick
  William
Malbone, Edward
  Greene
Man Ray
Marin, John
Marsh, Reginald
Martin, Homer Dodge
Matteson, Tompkins
  Harrison
Maurer, Alfred Henry
McEntee, Jervis
Meière, Marie Hildreth
  Suppl. 2
Melchers, Gari
Merritt, Anna Massey
  Lea
Metcalf, Willard Leroy
Mifflin, Lloyd
Mignot, Louis Rémy
Miller, Alfred Jacob
Miller, Charles Henry
Miller, Kenneth Hayes
Millet, Francis Davis
Mitchell, Joan
Moholy-Nagy, László
Mondrian, Piet *Suppl. 1*
Moore, Charles Herbert
Moran, Edward
Moran, Mary Nimmo
Moran, Thomas
Morse, Samuel Finley
  Breese
Moses, Grandma
Mosler, Henry
Mostel, Zero
Motherwell, Robert
Mount, William Sidney
Murphy, Gerald Cleary
Neagle, John
Neal, David Dalhoff
Neel, Alice Hartley
Newman, Barnett
Newman, Henry
  Roderick
O'Donovan, William
  Rudolf
O'Keeffe, Georgia
Otis, Bass
Pach, Walter
Page, William
Parrish, Maxfield
Payne, Edgar Alwin, and
  Elsie Palmer Payne
Peale, Anna Claypoole

Peale, Charles Willson
Peale, James
Peale, Raphaelle
Peale, Rembrandt
Peale, Sarah Miriam
Pearson, Marguerite
  Stuber
Pelham, Peter
Pereira, Irene Rice
Peterson, Jane
Peto, John Frederick
Pine, Robert Edge
Pinney, Eunice Griswold
Pippin, Horace
Platt, Charles Adams
Pollock, Jackson
Porter, Fairfield
Porter, James Amos
Pratt, Matthew
Prendergast, Maurice
  Brazil
Quidor, John
Ramage, John
Rand, Ellen Emmet
Ranney, William
Read, Thomas
  Buchanan
Rebay, Hilla
Reid, Robert Lewis
Reinhardt, Ad
Reiss, Winold Fritz
Remington, Frederic
Richards, William Trost
Rideout, Alice Louise
Rimmer, William
Robinson, Theodore
Roerich, Nicholas
  Suppl. 2
Rossiter, Thomas
  Pritchard
Rothermel, Peter
  Frederick
Rothko, Mark
Russell, Charles Marion
Ryder, Albert Pinkham
Ryder, Chauncey Foster
Saint-Mémin, Charles
  Balthazar Julien Févret
  de
Sample, Paul Starrett
Sargent, Henry
Sargent, John Singer
Sartain, Emily
Savage, Edward
Schussele, Christian
Shahn, Ben
Sharples, James
Sheeler, Charles
Shinn, Everett
Shoumatoff, Elizabeth

Art *(cont.)*
Simmons, Edward
  Emerson
Sloan, John
Smibert, John
Smillie, George Henry
Smillie, James David
Smith, Francis
  Hopkinson
Smithson, Robert Irving
Sobel, Janet
Soyer, Raphael
Spencer, Lilly Martin
Spencer, Niles
Stamos, Theodoros
  Suppl. 2
Stanley, John Mix
Stella, Joseph
Stettheimer, Florine
Stevens, Will Henry
Still, Clyfford
Stillman, William James
Stuart, Gilbert
Sully, Thomas
  (1783–1872)
Swinnerton, James
  Guilford, Jr.
Tack, Augustus Vincent
Tanner, Henry Ossawa
Tarbell, Edmund
  Charles
Taylor, William Ladd
Tchelitchew, Pavel
Thayer, Abbott
  Handerson
Theus, Jeremiah
Thompson, Cephas
  Giovanni
Tobey, Mark George
Tomlin, Bradley Walker
Trott, Benjamin
Troye, Edward
Trumbull, John
  (1756–1843)
Twachtman, John Henry
Tworkov, Jack
Vanderlyn, John
Vargas, Alberto
Vedder, Elihu
Vinton, Frederic Porter
Vonnoh, Robert William
Waldo, Samuel Lovett
Warhol, Andy
Way, Mary *Suppl. 2*
Weber, Max
Weir, John Ferguson
Weir, Julian Alden
Weir, Robert Walter
West, Benjamin
  (1738–1820)
West, William Edward

Whistler, James McNeill
White, John
Whitman, Sarah de St.
  Prix Wyman
Whittredge,
  Worthington
Wiles, Irving Ramsey
Williams, William
  (1727–1791)
Wilson, Ellen Axson
Wimar, Carl Ferdinand
Wood, Grant
Wores, Theodore
Wright, Joseph
Wyant, Alexander
  Helwig
Wyeth, N. C.
  (1882–1945)
Wylie, Robert
Young, Mahonri
  Mackintosh

Photographers
Abbott, Berenice
Adams, Ansel
Adams, Marian Hooper
Arbus, Diane
Bachrach, Louis Fabian
Bourke-White, Margaret
Boyd, Louise Arner
Brady, Mathew B.
Callahan, Harry *Suppl. 1*
Capa, Robert
Coolidge, Dane
Crawford, Ralston
Cunningham, Imogen
Curtis, Edward Sheriff
Day, F. Holland
Draper, John William
Edgerton, Harold
  Eugene
Eisenstaedt, Alfred
Emmons, Chansonetta
  Stanley
Evans, Walker
Feininger, Andreas
  Suppl. 1
Fellig, Arthur
Gardiner, Leon
Genthe, Arnold
Gilpin, Laura
Harrison, Gabriel
Hine, Lewis Wickes
Horst, Horst P. *Suppl. 1*
Jackson, William Henry
Johnston, Frances
  Benjamin *Suppl. 1*
Käsebier, Gertrude
  Stanton
Kertész, André
Lange, Dorothea

Le Clercq, Tanaquil
  Suppl. 2
Lee, Russell Werner
Leyda, Jay
Lion, Jules
Lynes, George Platt
Man Ray
Mapplethorpe, Robert
Moholy-Nagy, László
Morgan, Barbara
  Suppl. 1
Morris, Wright *Suppl. 1*
Muybridge, Eadweard
Nutting, Wallace
Orkin, Ruth
O'Sullivan, Timothy H.
Plumbe, John
Porter, Eliot
Riis, Jacob August
Sachse, Julius Friedrich
Shahn, Ben
Sheeler, Charles
Steichen, Edward
Stieglitz, Alfred
Stoddard, Seneca Ray
  Suppl. 2
Strand, Paul
Struss, Karl Fischer
Ulmann, Doris *Suppl. 1*
Van Der Zee, James
  Augustus
Van Vechten, Carl
Washington, Augustus
  Suppl. 2
Weston, Brett
Weston, Edward
  (1886–1958)
White, Minor
Winogrand, Garry
Wolcott, Marion Post

Printmakers
Anderson, Alexander
Arms, John Taylor
Barrymore, Lionel
Bellows, George Wesley
Biddle, George
Birch, William Russell
Bodmer, Karl
Cassatt, Mary
Chapman, John Gadsby
Clements, Gabrielle
  DeVaux
Corita
Doolittle, Amos
Doughty, Thomas
Durand, Asher Brown
Edwin, David
Gág, Wanda
Getchell, Edith Loring
  Peirce

Gifford, Robert Swain
Greatorex, Eliza Pratt
Gropper, William
Hale, Ellen Day
Hall, Frederick Garrison
Hassam, Childe
Hill, John
Hill, John Henry
Hurd, Nathaniel
Kappel, Philip
Kent, Rockwell
Lawson, Alexander
Lazzell, Blanche
Lesley Bush-Brown,
  Margaret White
Lion, Jules
Longacre, James Barton
Marin, John
Marsh, Reginald
Merritt, Anna Massey
  Lea
Moran, Mary Nimmo
Moran, Thomas
Otis, Bass
Pach, Walter
Pelham, Peter
Pennell, Joseph
Potter, Louis McClellan
Reason, Patrick Henry
Roth, Ernest David
Ruzicka, Rudolph
Ryder, Chauncey Foster
Saint-Mémin, Charles
  Balthazar Julien Févret
  de
Sartain, Emily
Sartain, John
Savage, Edward
Shahn, Ben
Sloan, John
Smillie, James
Smillie, James David
Soyer, Raphael
Tanner, Benjamin
Weir, Julian Alden

Scientific Illustrators
Abbot, John
Ames, Blanche Ames
Audubon, John James
Bartram, William
Beard, James Carter
Brödel, Paul Heinrich
  Max
Comstock, Anna
  Botsford
Fuertes, Louis Agassiz
Furbish, Kate
Holmes, William Henry
  Suppl. 1

Art *(cont.)*
Lesueur, Charles
  Alexandre
Peale, Titian Ramsay
Peterson, Roger Tory
  Suppl. 1
Seton, Ernest Thompson
Sinclair, Isabella
  McHutcheson

Sculptors
Adams, Herbert Samuel
Aitken, Robert Ingersoll
Andrei, Giovanni
Archipenko, Alexander
  Porfirevich
Augur, Hezekiah
Bailly, Joseph Alexis
Ball, Thomas
Barnard, George Grey
Barthé, Richmond
Bartlett, Paul Wayland
Bertoia, Harry
Bissell, George Edwin
Bitter, Karl Theodore
  Francis
Borglum, Gutzon
Borglum, Solon
  Hannibal
Boyle, John J.
Brackett, Edward
  Augustus
Brenner, Victor David
Brooks, Richard Edwin
Browere, John Henri
  Isaac
Brown, Henry Kirke
Bush-Brown, Henry
  Kirke
Caesar, Doris
Calder, A. Stirling
Calder, Alexander
Calder, Alexander Milne
Clevenger, Shobal Vail
Cornell, Joseph *Suppl. 1*
Crawford, Thomas
Cresson, Margaret
  French
Dallin, Cyrus Edwin
Davidson, Jo
de Creeft, José
Dehner, Dorothy
De Lue, Donald
  Harcourt
de Rivera, José
Donoghue, John Talbott
Eberle, Abastenia St.
  Leger
Elwell, Frank Edwin
Epstein, Jacob
Ezekiel, Moses Jacob

Flannagan, John Bernard
Fraser, James Earle
Fraser, Laura Gardin
Frazee, John
French, Daniel Chester
Friedlander, Leo William
Frishmuth, Harriet
  Whitney
Fry, Sherry Edmundson
Gabo, Naum
Galt, Alexander
Goldberg, Rube
Grafly, Charles
Greenough, Horatio
Greenough, Richard
  Saltonstall
Gregory, John
Hart, Joel Tanner
Hesse, Eva
Hoffman, Malvina
Hosmer, Harriet
  Goodhue
Hoxie, Vinnie Ream
Hughes, Robert Ball
Huntington, Anna
  Vaughn Hyatt
Ives, Chauncey Bradley
Jennewein, C. Paul
Johnson, Sargent Claude
Judd, Donald *Suppl. 1*
Kemeys, Edward
Kienholz, Edward
  Suppl. 1
Kingsley, Norman
  William
Lachaise, Gaston
Langston, John Mercer
Launitz, Robert
  Eberhardt Schmidt von
  der
Laurent, Robert
Lawrie, Lee Oscar
Lewis, Edmonia
Liberman, Alexander
  Suppl. 2
Lipchitz, Jacques
MacMonnies, Frederick
  William
Manship, Paul Howard
Martiny, Philip
McCartan, Edward
  Francis
Mead, Larkin Goldsmith
Meštrović, Ivan
Mills, Clark
Milmore, Martin
Mozier, Joseph
Myers, Ethel
Nadelman, Elie
Nakian, Reuben
Nevelson, Louise

Newman, Barnett
Niehaus, Charles Henry
Noguchi, Isamu
O'Donovan, William
  Rudolf
Palmer, Erastus Dow
Partridge, William
  Ordway
Persico, Luigi
Potter, Edward Clark
Potter, Louis McClellan
Powers, Hiram
Proctor, Alexander
  Phimister
Prophet, Elizabeth
Read, Thomas
  Buchanan
Remington, Frederic
Rideout, Alice Louise
Rimmer, William
Roberts, Howard
Robus, Hugo
Rogers, John
  (1829–1904)
Rogers, Randolph
Roszak, Theodore
Rumsey, Charles Cary
Rush, William
Saint-Gaudens,
  Augustus
Savage, Augusta
Scudder, Janet
Segal, George *Suppl. 2*
Shrady, Henry Merwin
Shreve, Richmond
  Harold
Simmons, Franklin
Smith, David
Smith, Tony
Smithson, Robert Irving
Stankiewicz, Richard
  Peter
Stone, Horatio
Story, William Wetmore
Taft, Lorado
Thompson, Launt
Valentine, Edward
  Virginius
Volk, Leonard Wells
Vonnoh, Bessie
  Onahotema Potter
Ward, John Quincy
  Adams
Warneke, Heinz
Warner, Olin Levi
Weinman, Adolph
  Alexander
Whitney, Anne
Whitney, Gertrude
  Vanderbilt
Willard, Solomon

Wright, Alice Morgan
Wright, Joseph
Yandell, Enid
Young, Mahonri
  Mackintosh
Zorach, William

**BUSINESS AND
INDUSTRY**

Agriculture
Agriculturists
Armsby, Henry Prentiss
Babcock, Stephen
  Moulton
Bennett, John Cook
Bidwell, John
Bordley, John Beale
Brewer, William Henry
Bromfield, Louis
Buel, Jesse
Callaway, Cason Jewell
Calvert, Charles
  Benedict
Carver, George
  Washington
Chamberlain, William
  Isaac
Cobb, Cully Alton
Colman, Norman Jay
Dabney, Charles William
Davenport, Eugene
Dickson, David
Dymond, John
Emerson, Gouverneur
Fitch, Asa
Furnas, Robert
  Wilkinson
Gale, Benjamin
Garnett, James Mercer
Garst, Roswell
Gaylord, Willis
Hoffmann, Francis
  Arnold
Jenkins, Edward Hopkins
Johnson, Samuel William
Jones, Donald Forsha
Kinloch, Cleland
Knapp, Seaman Asahel
Kolb, Reuben Francis
Ladd, Carl Edwin
Ladd, Edwin Fremont
Ladejinsky, Wolf Isaac
Logan, George
London, Jack
Lowden, Frank Orren
Mangelsdorf, Paul
  Christoph
Mapes, Charles Victor
Mapes, James Jay
McBryde, John McLaren

Agriculture *(cont.)*
Miles, Manly
Norton, John Pitkin
Patrick, Marsena
  Rudolph
Peters, Richard
  (1810–1889)
Piper, Charles
  Vancouver
Powell, G. Harold
Pugh, Evan
Robinson, Solon
Rodale, J. I.
Rosen, Joseph A.
Ruffin, Edmund
Scovell, Melville Amasa
Stakman, Elvin Charles
Stockbridge, Horace
  Edward
Stockbridge, Levi
  Suppl. 2
Strong, Harriet Williams
  Russell
Taylor, John
  (1753–1824)
Thomas, John Jacobs
Tilton, James
Vanderbilt, George
  Washington *Suppl. 1*
Wallace, Henry Agard
Ward, Joshua John
Waring, George Edwin,
  Jr.

Apiarists
Langstroth, Lorenzo
  Lorraine *Suppl. 1*
Palmer, Daniel David

Cattle Raisers / Traders
Allerton, Samuel Waters
Bush, George
  Washington
Harris, William
  Alexander
Lasater, Edward
  Cunningham
Littlefield, George
  Washington
Mackenzie, Murdo
McCoy, Joseph Geiting
McNeill, John Hanson
Morris, Nelson
Renick, Felix

Cowboys
Cortez Lira, Gregorio
Dart, Isom
Doolin, William
Glass, Charlie
James, Will Roderick

Love, Nat
Mix, Tom
Nigger Add
Rogers, Will
Russell, Charles Marion
Siringo, Charles Angelo

*Farmer Organization
Leaders*
Barrett, Charles Simon
Carr, Elias
Garey, Thomas Andrew
Goss, Albert Simon
Gresham, Newt
Kelley, Oliver Hudson
Lemke, William
  Frederick
Mayo, Mary Anne
  Bryant
O'Neal, Edward Asbury,
  III
Peek, George Nelson
Polk, Leonidas
  LaFayette
Reno, Milo
Townley, Arthur Charles
Ware, Harold

Farmers
Aiken, George David
Alden, John
Banneker, Benjamin
Bush, George
  Washington
Carpenter, Cyrus Clay
Clay, Laura
Colden, Cadwallader, II
Cooper, Joseph
  Alexander
Corey, Giles
Deitz, John F.
Delafield, John
  (1786–1853)
Dickson, David
Dummer, William
Favill, Henry Baird
Featherstonhaugh,
  George William
Glidden, Joseph Farwell
Heard, Dwight Bancroft
Heaton, Hannah Cook
Hilgard, Theodor
  Erasmus
Lewis, John Francis
Lloyd, Edward
López, José Dolores
MacDonald, Betty
Mayo, Mary Anne
  Bryant
Murie, James Rolfe
Newton, Isaac

Other Day, John
Perry, Edward
Robinson, Rowland
  Evans
Rodale, J. I.
Sanford, Henry Shelton
Strawbridge, Robert
Wallace, Henry Cantwell
Ward, Samuel
  (1725–1776)
Weare, Nathaniel
Whitehill, Robert
Whittemore, Samuel
Wilbarger, John Wesley
Wolfskill, William
Wood, Carolena
Wood, James
Yount, George
  Concepción

Foresters
Allen, Edward Tyson
Baker, Hugh Potter
Fernow, Bernhard
  Eduard
Hough, Franklin
  Benjamin
Michaux, François-
  André
Pinchot, Gifford

Horticulturists
Bailey, Liberty Hyde
Blackstone, William
Burbank, Luther
Callaway, Cason Jewell
Crockett, James
  Underwood *Suppl. 1*
Downing, Andrew
  Jackson
du Pont, Henry Francis
Fairchild, David
  Grandison
Garey, Thomas Andrew
Hansen, Niels Ebbesen
Logan, Martha Daniell
Longworth, Nicholas
  (1782–1863)
Marshall, Humphry
McFarland, J. Horace
Prince, William
Pursh, Frederick
Waugh, Frank Albert

*Plantation Managers /
Overseers*
King, Roswell

Plantation Owners
Adams, James Hopkins
Aiken, William

Allston, Robert Francis
  Withers
Alston, Joseph
Alston, William
Barbour, James
Bouligny, Dominique
Bowie, Robert
Breckinridge, John
  (1760–1806)
Bryan, Hugh
Byrd, William
  (1652–1704)
Byrd, William
  (1674–1744)
Cabell, William
Carr, Elias
Carroll, Daniel
Carroll of Carrollton,
  Charles
Carter, Robert
  (1663–1732)
Couper, James Hamilton
Dunbar, William
Durnford, Andrew
Dymond, John
Elliott, Stephen
Elliott, William
Ellison, William
Fendall, Josias
Fitzhugh, William
Forstall, Edmond Jean
Gibbons, Thomas
Goldsborough, Robert
Habersham, James
Hampton, Wade
  (1754?–1835)
Harrison, Benjamin
  (1726?–1791)
Heyward, Nathaniel
Izard, Ralph
Jenifer, Daniel of St.
  Thomas
Jones, Allen
Kinloch, Cleland
Lamar, John Basil
Laurens, Henry
LeFlore, Greenwood
Lewis, William Berkeley
Lynch, Charles
Manigault, Gabriel
  (1704–1781)
Manigault, Peter
Marigny, Bernard
Mason, George
Mason, John Young
McIntosh, Lachlan
McMinn, Joseph
Mercer, John Francis
Middleton, Arthur
Middleton, Henry

Agriculture *(cont.)*
(1717–1784)
Middleton, Henry
(1770–1846)
Montgomery, Isaiah
Thornton
Morgan, Sir Henry
Moultrie, John, Jr.
Nelson, Thomas
Nelson, William
(1711–1772)
Page, John
Page, Mann
Parke, Daniel
Percy, William
Alexander
Pickens, Andrew
Pillow, Gideon Johnson
Pinckney, Charles
Cotesworth
Pinckney, Elizabeth
Lucas
Plater, George
Pollock, Oliver
Porter, Alexander
Randolph, Peyton
Ravenel, Henry William
Rayner, Kenneth
Redwood, Abraham
Robinson, John
Rolfe, John
Rost-Denis, Pierre
Adolphe
Ruffin, Thomas
Shelby, Joseph Orville
Smith, Ashbel
Tilghman, Matthew
Tyler, Julia Gardiner
Vann, Joseph
Walker, Thomas
Ward, Joshua John
Washington, George
Berry
Wharton, William Harris
Williams, David
Rogerson
Winchester, James
Yeardley, Sir George

Ranchers
Burt, Struthers
Cassidy, Butch
Chisum, John Simpson
Cortina, Juan
Nepomuceno
Goodnight, Charles
Greene, William Cornell
Ivins, Anthony
Woodward
Jones, Buffalo
King, Richard

Lasater, Edward
Cunningham
Littlefield, George
Washington
Marsh, John
McCrea, Joel
Parker, John Palmer
Ross, C. Ben
Stearns, Abel
Vallejo, Mariano
Guadalupe
Warner, Jonathan
Trumbull
Wolfskill, William

Seedsmen
Burpee, David
Chapman, John
Vick, James

Soil Scientists
Bennett, Hugh
Hammond
Hilgard, Eugene
Woldemar
Kelley, Walter Pearson
Lowdermilk, Walter
Clay *Suppl. 1*
Marbut, Curtis Fletcher

Winegrowers / Vintners
de Latour, Georges
Suppl. 2
Gallo, Julio
Haraszthy de Mokcsa,
Agoston
Mondavi, Rosa Grassi
Petri, Angelo
Petri, Louis
Sbarboro, Andrea

**Clothing, Fashion, and
Textiles**
Clothing Industry Leaders
Blake, Lyman Reed
Carnegie, Hattie
Douglas, William Lewis
Halston
Jarman, W. Maxey
Johnson, George Francis
Kellogg, Charles Edwin
Suppl. 2
King, Stanley
Luchese, Thomas
McKay, Gordon
Nash, Arthur
Sachse, Julius Friedrich
Strauss, Levi

Cosmetics Industry Leaders
Arden, Elizabeth

Ayer, Harriet Hubbard
Cochran, Jacqueline
Factor, Max
Gillette, King Camp
Malone, Annie Turnbo
Nestle, Charles
Niebaum, Gustave
Ferdinand *Suppl. 2*
Noda, Alice Sae
Teshima
Revson, Charles Haskell
Rubinstein, Helena
Van Slyke, Helen Lenore
Vogt
Walker, Madame C. J.

Cotton Brokers / Merchants
Clayton, William
Lockhart
Cullen, Hugh Roy
Maybank, Burnet Rhett
Nolte, Vincent Otto
Thompson, Jeremiah

Modeling Agency Executives
Conover, Harry Sayles
Powers, John Robert

Seamstresses
Keckley, Elizabeth
Hobbs
Parks, Lillian Rogers
Suppl. 1
Ross, Betsy

Textile Industry Leaders
Allen, Philip
Allen, Zachariah
Atkinson, Edward
Bachelder, John
Boit, Elizabeth Eaton
Brown, Lydia
Brown, Moses
Brown, Obadiah
Callaway, Fuller Earle
Cannon, James William
Coleman, Warren Clay
Cone, Moses Herman
Coolidge, Thomas
Jefferson
Crompton, George
Fox, Gustavus Vasa
Goldfine, Bernard
Grover, La Fayette
Hazard, Thomas
Robinson
Howland, William
Dillwyn
Jackson, Patrick Tracy
King, Roswell
Lawrence, Abbott

Love, James Spencer
Lowell, Francis Cabot
Lowell, John
(1799–1836)
Marshall, Benjamin
Maybank, Burnet Rhett
Moody, Paul
Slater, John Fox
Slater, Samuel
Taylor, Myron Charles
Williams, David
Rogerson
Wood, William Madison

Wool Industry Leaders
Grundy, Joseph Ridgway

Communication
Computer Industry Leaders
Cray, Seymour *Suppl. 1*
Packard, David *Suppl. 1*
Wang, An
Watson, Arthur
Kittridge
Watson, Thomas John,
Jr.

*News Agency Owners /
Managers*
Barnett, Claude Albert
Cooper, Kent
Haessler, Carl
Koenigsberg, Moses
Smith, William Henry
(1833–1896)
Stone, Melville Elijah

Telegraph Industry Leaders
Cornell, Alonzo Barton
Eckert, Thomas
Thompson
Edison, Thomas Alva
Fessenden, Reginald
Aubrey
Field, Cyrus West
Green, Norvin
Kendall, Amos
Morse, Samuel Finley
Breese
Orton, William
Sarnoff, David
Sibley, Hiram
Stager, Anson
Wade, Jeptha Homer

Telephone Industry Leaders
Barnard, Chester Irving
Behn, Sosthenes
Bell, Alexander Graham
Blake, Francis
deButts, John Dulany

Communication *(cont.)*
Edison, Thomas Alva
Gifford, Walter Sherman
Hubbard, Gardiner
Greene
McGowan, William
Vail, Theodore Newton
Watson, Thomas
Augustus

Construction
*Building Materials Industry
Leaders*
Avery, Sewell Lee
Coxey, Jacob Sechler
Crown, Henry
Kelly, John Brendan, Jr.
MacNider, Hanford
Meyer, Henry
Coddington
Pope, Generoso
Stearns, George Luther

Carpenters
Ariss, John
Hoadley, David
Jones, Noble
Luther, Seth
Meachum, John Berry

*Construction Industry
Leaders*
Ainslie, Hew
Bogardus, James
Brundage, Avery
Cook, Abner Hugh
Fox, Harry
Greene, Francis Vinton
Kelly, John Brendan
Levitt, Abraham
Levitt, William Jaird
Morrison, Harry
Winford
O'Sullivan, James
Edward
Starrett, Paul
Starrett, William Aiken
Stubbs, Walter Roscoe
Wolfson, Erwin Service

Copper Industry Leaders
Hussey, Curtis Grubb

Lumber Industry Leaders
Alger, Russell Alexander
Fordney, Joseph Warren
Long, George S.
Sage, Henry Williams
Sawyer, Philetus
Washburn, William
Drew

Weyerhaeuser, Frederick
Weyerhaeuser, Frederick
Edward
Weyerhaeuser, Phil

**Entertainment and
Recreation**
*Amusement Park Owners /
Managers*
Disney, Walt
Schenck, Joseph M.
Schenck, Nicholas
Michael
Thompson, Frederic
Tilyou, George
Cornelius

Brothelkeepers
Adler, Polly
Everleigh, Ada, and
Minna Everleigh
Stanford, Sally

Casino Owners / Managers
Crosby, James Morris
Dalitz, Morris B. "Moe"
Suppl. 2
Harrah, William Fisk
Lansky, Meyer

Circus Owners / Managers
Bailey, James Anthony
Barnum, P. T.
Beatty, Clyde Raymond
Forepaugh, Adam
North, John Ringling
Rice, Dan
Ringling, Charles

*Game and Toy
Manufacturers*
Bradley, Milton
Cowen, Joshua Lionel
Duncan, Donald
Franklin
Gilbert, A. C. *Suppl. 2*
Hassenfeld, Merrill
Thomas *Suppl. 2*
Marx, Louis, Sr.
Parker, George S.
Suppl. 1
Ryan, Jack

*Greeting Card
Manufacturers*
Burrell, Berkeley
Graham
Hall, J. C.

Hotel Owners / Managers
Ames, Nathaniel
(1708–1764)
Astor, John Jacob, IV
Crosby, James Morris
Downing, George
Thomas
Fraunces, Samuel
Greenway, Isabella
Grim, David
Grossinger, Jennie
Harvey, Fred
Hilton, Conrad
Marriott, John Willard
Plant, Henry Bradley
Schine, G. David
Suppl. 1
Statler, Ellsworth Milton
Wormley, James

Impresarios
Armitage, Merle
Charlot, André
Conried, Heinrich
Hurok, Sol
Pastor, Tony
Redpath, James
Rose, Billy
Thurber, Jeannette
Meyers
Wikoff, Henry

Motion Picture Distributors
Levine, Joseph Edward
Mayer, Arthur Loeb

*Motion Picture Studio
Executives*
Balaban, Barney
Cohn, Harry
Cohn, Jack
Dietz, Howard
Fleischer, Max, and
Dave Fleischer
Fox, William
Giannini, Attilio Henry
Goldwyn, Samuel
Kalmus, Herbert
Thomas
Laemmle, Carl
Lasky, Jesse Louis
Loew, Marcus
Lyon, Ben
Mayer, Arthur Loeb
Mayer, Louis Burt
Pickford, Mary
Schary, Dore
Schenck, Joseph M.
Schenck, Nicholas
Michael

Skouras, Spyros
Panagiotes
Steel, Dawn *Suppl. 1*
Stein, Jules Caesar
Tartikoff, Brandon
Suppl. 1
Thalberg, Irving G.
Warner, Albert
Warner, Harry Morris
Warner, Jack Leonard
Yates, Herbert John
Zanuck, Darryl F.
Zukor, Adolph

Music Promoters
Abbey, Henry Eugene
Abbott, Emma
Armitage, Merle
Bauer, Marion Eugenie
Bradford, Perry
Childers, Lulu Vere
Condon, Eddie
Damrosch, Leopold
Dorsey, Thomas
Andrew
Engel, Carl
Farwell, Arthur
Feather, Leonard
Flagg, Josiah
Fowler, Wally
Goldkette, Jean *Suppl. 2*
Graham, Bill *Suppl. 1*
Grau, Maurice
Grossman, Albert
Bernard
Hammerstein, Oscar
Hay, George Dewey
Herrmann, Eduard Emil
Howe, Mary
Johnson, Hall
Kellogg, Clara Louise
Lunsford, Bascom
Lamar
Marek, George Richard
Maretzek, Max
Mezzrow, Mezz
Mills, Irving
Nabokov, Nicolas
Nassi, Thomas
Parker, Tom *Suppl. 1*
Petrides, Frédérique
Rice, Helen
Stamps, V. O., and
Frank Henry Stamps
Stark, John, and Eleanor
Stark
Stein, Jules Caesar
Strakosch, Maurice, and
Max Strakosch
Thurber, Jeannette
Meyers

Entertainment and Recreation *(cont.)*
Webb, Thomas Smith
Wiggs, Johnny
Wilburn, Virgil Doyle

Nightclub Owners / Operators
Billingsley, Sherman
Bricktop
Condon, Eddie
Downey, Morton
Durante, Jimmy
Guinan, Texas
Lewis, Ted
Rose, Billy
Rosenbloom, Maxie
Rubell, Steve *Suppl. 1*
Ventura, Charlie

Radio / Television Industry Leaders
Ball, Lucille
Cowles, Gardner, Jr.
Disney, Walt
Goldenson, Leonard H. *Suppl. 2*
Gray, James Harrison
Harbord, James Guthrie
Kent, Atwater
Levy, David *Suppl. 2*
Macy, John Williams, Jr.
McLendon, Gordon Barton
Newhouse, Samuel Irving
Paley, William S.
Sarnoff, David
Scripps, William Edmund
Tartikoff, Brandon *Suppl. 1*
White, Paul Welrose
Wood, Robert D.
Young, Owen D.

Recording Industry Leaders
Asch, Moses
Berliner, Emile
Blesh, Rudi
Drake, Pete
Edison, Thomas Alva
Feather, Leonard
Goldmark, Peter Carl
Hammond, John Henry, Jr.
Johnson, Eldridge Reeves
Kapp, Jack
Marek, George Richard
Pace, Harry Herbert

Peer, Ralph Sylvester
Robey, Don D.
Satherley, Uncle Art
Walker, Frank Buckley
Williams, Clarence

Resort Owners
Wrigley, William, Jr. *Suppl. 1*

Sporting Goods Industry Leaders
Bauer, Eddie
Bean, L. L.
Reach, Alfred James
Spalding, Albert Goodwill
Wright, George

Sports Organization Executives
Barrow, Edward Grant
Bell, Bert
Bell, Matty
Briggs, Walter Owen
Brown, Paul E.
Brundage, Avery
Burke, Michael
Busch, August Anheuser, Jr.
Camp, Walter Chauncey
Carr, Joseph F.
Chandler, Albert Benjamin
Collins, Eddie
Comiskey, Charles Albert
Connor, Roger
Conzelman, James Gleason
Cronin, Joe
Diddle, Edgar Allen, Sr.
Douglas, Robert L.
Ebbets, Charles Hercules
Eckert, William Dole
Evans, Billy
Finley, Charles O. *Suppl. 1*
Foster, Rube
Frick, Ford Christopher
Giamatti, Bart
Giles, Warren Crandall
Gottlieb, Eddie
Greenberg, Hank
Greenlee, William Augustus
Griffith, Calvin *Suppl. 1*
Griffith, Clark Calvin
Gulick, Luther Halsey (1865–1918)
Halas, George Stanley

Hanlon, Ned
Harridge, William
Haughton, Percy Duncan
Hess, Leon *Suppl. 1*
Hofheinz, Roy Mark
Hulbert, William Ambrose
Hulman, Tony
Irish, Ned
Johnson, Ban
Kiphuth, Robert John Herman
Kroc, Ray
Landis, Kenesaw Mountain
Liston, Emil Sycamore
Mack, Connie
MacPhail, Larry
Mara, Timothy James
Marshall, George Preston
Mathewson, Christy
Muldoon, William
Munn, Biggie
Murchison, Clint, Jr.
Navin, Frank
O'Brien, John Joseph
O'Malley, Walter Francis
Posey, Cum
Reach, Alfred James
Rickey, Branch
Rooney, Art
Rozelle, Pete *Suppl. 2*
Ruppert, Jacob
Shaw, Wilbur
Shibe, Benjamin Franklin
Short, Robert Earl
Spalding, Albert Goodwill
St. John, Lynn Wilbur
Stoneham, Horace Charles
Taylor, C. I.
Tower, Oswald
Tunnell, Emlen
Veeck, Bill
Von der Ahe, Christian Frederick Wilhelm
Wade, William Wallace
Ward, Holcombe
Weiss, George Martin
Wilke, Lou
Wrenn, Robert Duffield
Wrigley, Philip Knight
Wrigley, William, Jr. *Suppl. 1*
Yawkey, Tom
Young, Buddy

Sports Promoters
Brady, William Aloysius
Brown, Walter A.
Carbo, Frankie
Carr, Joseph F.
Fox, Richard Kyle
Gottlieb, Eddie
Hitchcock, Thomas, Jr.
Hoff, Max
Holder, Charles Frederick
Irish, Ned
Jacobs, Mike
Kearns, Jack
Lebow, Fred
Pyle, Charles C.
Rickard, Tex
Saperstein, Abe
Sears, Eleonora Randolph
Sullivan, James Edward
Veeck, Bill
Ward, Archibald Burdette
Wightman, Hazel Hotchkiss
Wright, George
Yost, Fielding Harris

Tent Show Owners
Sadler, Harley

Theater Owners / Managers
Aarons, Alfred E.
Abbey, Henry Eugene
Albee, E. F.
Aldrich, Richard (1902–1986)
Ames, Winthrop
Aronson, Rudolph
Baker, Benjamin Archibald
Barrett, George Horton
Barrett, Lawrence
Barry, Thomas
Beck, Martin
Bingham, Amelia
Blake, William Rufus
Bonstelle, Jessie
Booth, Edwin Thomas
Boucicault, Dion
Brown, Gilmor
Brown, William Alexander
Burton, William Evans
Byron, Oliver Doud
Celeste, Mme.
Charlot, André
Christy, Edwin Pearce
Coburn, Charles Douville

Entertainment and Recreation (cont.)
Comstock, F. Ray
Conway, Sarah Crocker
Cooper, Thomas Abthorpe
Daly, Augustin
Darling, Edward V.
Davenport, Benjamin Butler
De Bar, Benedict
Douglass, David
Drake, Frances Ann Denny
Drake, Samuel
Drew, Louisa Lane
Durang, John
Elliott, Maxine
Ford, John Thomson
Frohman, Daniel
Griffith, Robert E.
Hackett, James Keteltas
Hamblin, Thomas Sowerby
Haverly, Jack H.
Hayman, Al
Henderson, David
Henry, John (1746–1794)
Hodgkinson, John
Jacobs, Bernard *Suppl. 2*
Jones, Margo
Keene, Laura
Keith, B. F.
Langner, Lawrence
Lewisohn, Irene
Lortel, Lucille *Suppl. 1*
Ludlow, Noah Miller
Mayer, Arthur Loeb
McCullough, John
Merry, Anne Brunton
Miller, Henry (1859–1926)
Mitchell, William (1798–1856)
Niblo, William
Owens, John Edmond
Palmer, Albert Marshman
Powell, Snelling
Price, Stephen
Proctor, Frederick Francis
Rankin, McKee
Reinagle, Alexander
Rothafel, Roxy
Seymour, William
Shubert, Lee
Simpson, Edmund Shaw
Skinner, Otis
Smith, Solomon Franklin

Smith, William Henry (1806–1872)
Wallack, James William (1795?–1864)
Wallack, Lester
Wemyss, Francis Courtney
Wood, Mrs. John
Wood, William Burke

Theatrical Agents
Aronson, Rudolph
Bennett, Isadora
Brown, Thomas Allston
Darling, Edward V.
Erlanger, Abraham Lincoln
Fiske, Harrison Grey
Hayward, Leland
Janney, Russell Dixon
Kauser, Alice
Klaw, Marc Alonzo
Maney, Richard
Marbury, Elisabeth
Redpath, James
Stein, Jules Caesar
Wikoff, Henry

Finance, Management, Insurance, and Real Estate
Accountants
Andersen, Arthur Edward
Lasser, Jacob Kay
Lybrand, William Mitchell

Advertising Industry Leaders
Ayer, Francis Wayland
Barton, Bruce Fairchild
Bates, Theodore Lewis
Benton, William
Bernbach, William
Bowles, Chester Bliss
Burnett, Leo
Calkins, Earnest Elmo
Collier, Barron Gift
Dietz, Howard
Edge, Walter Evans
Lamb, Theodore Lafayette
Lasker, Albert Davis
Levy, David *Suppl. 2*
Ogilvy, David *Suppl. 1*
Resor, Helen Lansdowne *Suppl. 2*
Resor, Stanley Burnet
Roosevelt, Elliott
Rubicam, Raymond

Thompson, J. Walter
Watson, John Broadus
Young, John Orr

Bankers / Financial Industry Leaders
Adams, Edward Dean
Aldrich, Winthrop
Babson, Roger Ward
Bacon, Robert
Baker, George Fisher
Banks, Charles
Barron, Clarence Walker
Bates, Joshua
Biddle, Nicholas (1786–1844)
Binga, Jesse
Bishop, Charles Reed
Black, Eugene Robert
Bloomingdale, Alfred Schiffer
Brown, Alexander
Browne, William Washington
Bush, Prescott Sheldon
Butterfield, Daniel
Carroll of Carrollton, Charles
Cartwright, Alexander Joy, Jr.
Clark, Georgia Neese *Suppl. 1*
Coffin, Charles Fisher
Colton, George Radcliffe
Cooke, Jay
Corbett, Henry Winslow
Corcoran, William Wilson
Creighton, Edward
Dale, Chester
Davison, George Willets
Davison, Henry Pomeroy
Dawes, Charles Gates
Delafield, John (1748–1824)
Dillon, Clarence
Dodge, Joseph Morrell
Drexel, Anthony Joseph
Drexel, Francis Martin
Dumaine, Frederic Christopher
Dun, Robert Graham
du Pont, Francis Irénée
Eccles, Marriner Stoddard
Edmonds, Francis William
Eells, Dan Parmelee
Emery, Henry Crosby
Few, William

Fish, Stuyvesant
Flint, Charles Ranlett
Forbes, William Cameron
Forstall, Edmond Jean
Funston, George Keith
Gage, Lyman Judson
Gaston, A. G. *Suppl. 1*
Giannini, Amadeo Peter
Giannini, Attilio Henry
Girard, Stephen
Green, Hetty
Hammond, Bray
Harding, William Proctor Gould
Hascall, Milo Smith
Hauge, Gabriel Sylfest
Heard, Dwight Bancroft
Hepburn, Alonzo Barton
Herrick, Myron Timothy
Hertz, John Daniel
Hoffmann, Francis Arnold
Hutton, E. F.
Jones, Jesse Holman
Kahn, Otto Herman
Kelly, Eugene
Knox, John Jay
Ladd, William Sargent
Lamar, Gazaway Bugg
Lamont, Thomas William
Lanier, James Franklin Doughty
Lawson, Thomas William
Lehman, Arthur
Lehman, Herbert Henry
Lehman, Robert
Littlefield, George Washington
Lowden, Frank Orren
Lowell, Ralph
Ludlow, Daniel
Marcus, Bernard Kent
McCloy, John Jay, Jr.
McCulloch, Hugh
McDougall, Alexander
McFadden, Louis Thomas
Merriam, William Rush
Merrill, Charles Edward
Meyer, André Benoit Mathieu
Meyer, Eugene Isaac
Mills, Darius Ogden
Mitchell, John, Jr.
Morgan, John Pierpont
Morgan, John Pierpont, Jr.

Finance, Management, Insurance, and Real Estate *(cont.)*
Morrill, Edmund Needham
Morrow, Dwight Whitney
Paul, Josephine Bay
Peabody, George
Peabody, George Foster
Perkins, George Walbridge
Perry, Heman Edward
Pettiford, William Reuben
Phelan, James Duval
Phillips, Frank
Phillips, John
Powers, Daniel William
Price, Hiram
Riggs, George Washington
Riis, Mary Phillips
Rukeyser, Merryle Stanley
Sbarboro, Andrea
Scammon, Jonathan Young
Schiff, Jacob Henry
Seligman, Jesse
Seligman, Joseph
Seney, George Ingraham
Sewall, Arthur
Smith, Samuel Harrison
Snyder, John Wesley
Spaulding, Elbridge Gerry
Sproul, Allan
Stedman, Edmund Clarence
Stillman, James
Stotesbury, Edward Townsend
Stout, Gardner Dominick
Straight, Willard Dickerman
Streeter, Edward
Strong, Benjamin
Swanwick, John
Taylor, Myron Charles
Thatcher, Mahlon Daniel
Vanderlip, Frank Arthur
Walker, Maggie L. *Suppl. 2*
Ward, Thomas Wren
Ware, Nathaniel A.
Westcott, Edward Noyes
White, Harry Dexter
Wiggin, Albert Henry

Wiggins, A. L. M.
Williams, Samuel May
Willing, Thomas
Wingfield, George
Woodring, Harry Hines
Woods, George David
Wright, Richard Robert, Sr.
Yeatman, James Erwin
Yeatman, Thomas

Business Consultants
Andersen, Arthur Edward
Gantt, Henry Laurence
Gates, Frederick Taylor
Nielsen, A. C.
Rosenberg, Anna Marie Lederer
Vestey, Evelyn *Suppl. 1*

Business Machine Industry Leaders
Burroughs, William Seward
Carlson, Chester Floyd
Dick, A. B. *Suppl. 2*
Hollerith, Herman
Patterson, John Henry
Remington, Philo
Sholes, Christopher Latham
Underwood, John Thomas *Suppl. 1*
Watson, Thomas John

Capitalists / Financiers
Abbott, Horace
Adams, Charles Francis (1866–1954)
Adams, Edward Dean
Addicks, John Edward O'Sullivan
Allerton, Samuel Waters
Ames, Oakes (1804–1873)
Ames, Oliver (1831–1895)
Astor, John Jacob
Astor, John Jacob, III
Astor, William Waldorf
Austell, Alfred
Bache, Jules Semon
Baruch, Bernard Mannes
Belmont, August
Belmont, August, II
Bingham, William
Bluhdorn, Charles G.
Brice, Calvin Stewart
Brown, Alexander

Brown, William (1784–1864), George Brown, John A. Brown, and James Brown
Butterfield, John
Cheves, Langdon
Chisholm, Hugh Joseph
Chisolm, Alexander Robert
Chouteau, Pierre, Jr.
Colgate, James Boorman
Collier, Barron Gift
Colt, Samuel Pomeroy
Cooke, Jay
Coolidge, Thomas Jefferson
Cope, Caleb Frederick
Corbett, Henry Winslow
Corbin, Austin
Cord, Errett Lobban
Cornell, Ezra
Davis, Arthur Vining
DePauw, Washington Charles
Dillon, Sidney
Drew, Daniel
Dunwoody, William Hood
du Pont, Alfred Irénée
Durant, William Crapo
Eaton, Cyrus Stephen
English, James Edward
Evans, John
Fair, James Graham
Field, Cyrus West
Field, Marshall, III
Forbes, John Murray
Garrett, Robert
Glidden, Joseph Farwell
Gould, George Jay
Gould, Jay
Grace, William Russell
Green, Hetty
Green, John Cleve
Greene, Catharine Littlefield
Haggin, James Ben Ali
Hambleton, Thomas Edward
Hanna, Marcus Alonzo
Hatch, Alfrederick Smith
Hirshhorn, Joseph H.
Ho, Chinn
Hopkins, Johns
Hopper, Edna Wallace
Hunt, John Wesley
Huntington, Collis Potter
Inman, John Hamilton
Insull, Samuel
James, Daniel Willis

Keep, Henry
Kennedy, John Stewart
Kennedy, Joseph Patrick
Keys, Clement Melville
Lamont, Daniel Scott
Lamont, Thomas William
Larkin, Thomas Oliver
Leary, John
Lewis, Reginald Francis
Liggett, Louis Kroh
Lord, Eleazar
Mackay, John W. *Suppl. 1*
Mellon, Andrew William
Mellon, Thomas
Moffat, David Halliday
Morgan, Junius Spencer, Sr.
Morris, Robert (1735–1806)
Murchison, Clint, Jr.
Newberry, Truman Handy
Newman, Isidore
Nicholson, John
Odlum, Floyd Bostwick
Payne, Oliver Hazard
Phelan, James
Pittock, Henry Lewis
Pratt, Enoch
Prince, Frederick Henry
Pritzker, Abram Nicholas
Raskob, John Jakob
Ream, Norman Bruce
Roberts, Ellis Henry
Rockefeller, William
Rogers, Henry Huttleston
Rosenwald, Julius
Ryan, Thomas Fortune
Sage, Russell
Salomon, Haym
Seligman, Isaac Newton
Severance, Louis Henry
Simon, Norton Winfred
Smith, Francis Marion
Smith, George
Smith, Stephen
Spreckels, Claus
Stotesbury, Edward Townsend
Stranahan, James Samuel Thomas
Strauss, Lewis Lichtenstein
Sturgis, William
Thatcher, Mahlon Daniel

Finance, Management, Insurance, and Real Estate *(cont.)*
Thompson, William Boyce
Tower, Charlemagne
Trenholm, George Alfred
Vanderbilt, Cornelius
Vanderbilt, William Kissam
Vanderlip, Frank Arthur
Villard, Henry
Wade, Jeptha Homer
Wallace, Hugh Campbell
Warburg, Felix
Warburg, James Paul
Warfield, Solomon Davies
Weightman, William
Weyerhaeuser, Frederick
Whitney, Harry Payne
Whitney, John Hay
Widener, Peter Arrell Brown
Wright, Charles Barstow
Yerkes, Charles Tyson
Young, Robert Ralph

Computer Industry Leaders
Cray, Seymour *Suppl. 1*
Packard, David *Suppl. 1*
Wang, An
Watson, Arthur Kittridge
Watson, Thomas John, Jr.

Entrepreneurs
Allen, Ira
Ames, Nathan Peabody
Annenberg, Moses Louis
Averell, William Woods
Avery, R. Stanton *Suppl. 2*
Ayer, James Cook
Baldwin, John
Barnes, Albert Coombs
Barnett, Claude Albert
Barnum, P. T.
Bedaux, Charles Eugene
Bedinger, George Michael
Benner, Philip
Bennett, John Cook
Birdseye, Clarence
Blackton, James Stuart
Blackwell, Henry Browne
Blodget, Samuel, Jr.

Bloomingdale, Alfred Schiffer
Blow, Henry Taylor
Bluhdorn, Charles G.
Bowen, Thomas Meade
Brady, Mathew B.
Brown, Joseph Emerson
Burden, Henry
Calvert, George
Carse, Matilda Bradley
Chouteau, René Auguste
Church, Robert Reed
Cohen, Walter L.
Coker, James Lide
Collier, Barron Gift
Cone, Moses Herman
Connor, Patrick Edward
Cooper, Kent
Cooper, William
Cornell, Ezra
Couch, Harvey Crowley
Craigie, Andrew
Crosby, James Morris
Crown, Henry
Cuffe, Paul
Daché, Lilly
Dana, William Buck
Davenport, George
DeBaptiste, George
Dorsey, Stephen Wallace
Drake, Samuel
Dreyfus, Camille Edouard
Duncan, Donald Franklin
Durang, John
Eads, James Buchanan
Edison, Thomas Alva
Everleigh, Ada, and Minna Everleigh
Farquhar, Percival
Flora, William
Forbes, Malcolm Stevenson
Ford, Barney Launcelot
Fuller, Alfred Carl
Fulton, Robert
Gates, John Warne
Genovese, Vito
Getty, J. Paul
Gibbs, Mifflin Wistar
Godfroy, Francis
Goldfine, Bernard
Goldkette, Jean *Suppl. 2*
Grace, Charles Emmanuel
Graupner, Gottlieb
Gridley, Richard
Gwin, William McKendree
Hale, James Webster

Hammer, Armand
Henson, Jim
Herndon, Alonzo Franklin
Hertz, John Daniel
Hill, Nathaniel Peter
Hilton, Edward
Hopper, Edna Wallace
Houston, Henry Howard
Insull, Samuel
Johnson, James
Johnson, William (1809–1851)
Kane, Thomas Leiper
Keith, Minor Cooper
Kennedy, Joseph Patrick
Kiralfy, Imre, and Bolossy Kiralfy
Klaw, Marc Alonzo
Knight, Sarah Kemble
Koenigsberg, Moses
Lamar, Gazaway Bugg
Lear, William Powell
Leidesdorff, William Alexander
Liggett, Louis Kroh
Loudon, Samuel
Lyon, Matthew
Marriott, John Willard
Marshall, Andrew Cox
Meachum, John Berry
Merrick, John
Mills, Darius Ogden
Mills, Irving
Moody, Harriet Converse
Munsey, Frank Andrew
Nail, John E.
Napier, James Carroll
Nelson, John
Nichols, William Henry
Nicholson, John
Noyce, Robert Norton
Ogden, Aaron
O'Kelly, Berry
Oliver, Henry William
Osborn, Chase Salmon
Pace, Harry Herbert
Palmer, Albert Marshman
Parker, John P.
Parks, Henry Green, Jr.
Pendleton, Edmund Monroe
Perry, Heman Edward
Phelan, James
Pinchback, P. B. S.
Pleasant, Mary Ellen
Pope, Albert Augustus
Post, Charles William

Pritzker, Abram Nicholas
Putnam, Gideon
Pynchon, John
Reeside, James
Rice, Isaac Leopold
Richardson, Sid Williams
Rothafel, Roxy
Rothstein, Arnold
Sarpy, Peter A.
Sartain, John
Saunders, Clarence
Savage, Edward
Savage, Henry Wilson
Scherman, Harry
Schultz, Dutch
Schuster, Max Lincoln
Smith, Francis Marion
Smith, Peter (1768–1837)
Smith, Venture
Sperry, Elmer Ambrose
Spotswood, Alexander
Sprague, Frank Julian
Sprunt, James
Stearns, Abel
Still, William
Stockton, Robert Field
Stratemeyer, Edward
Tabor, Horace Austin Warner
Tandy, Charles David
Tarascon, Louis Anastase
Thompson, J. Walter
Thompson, Lydia
Thompson, William Boyce
Torrence, Joseph Thatcher
Touro, Judah
Vann, Joseph
Vassall, John
Walker, David (1796?–1830)
Walker, John Brisben
Walton, Samuel Moore
Wang, An
Ward, Henry Augustus
Washburn, Frank Sherman
Watson, Thomas Augustus
Wheelwright, William
Whipper, William
White, Eartha Mary Magdalene
White, Maunsel
Wilburn, Virgil Doyle
Worthington, Thomas

Finance, Management, Insurance, and Real Estate (*cont.*)
Yerkes, Charles Tyson

Financial Managers
Abernethy, George
Ivins, Anthony Woodward
Woolley, Edwin Dilworth

Franchise Industry Leaders
Carvel, Thomas Andreas
Johnson, Howard Dearing
Kroc, Ray
Sanders, Harland David

Insurance Industry Leaders
Batterson, James Goodwin
Bulkeley, Morgan Gardner
Bush, John Edward
Cohen, Walter L.
Delafield, John (1748–1824)
Douglas, Lewis William
Dryden, John Fairfield
Fackler, David Parks
Finley, Charles O. *Suppl. 1*
Gaston, A. G. *Suppl. 1*
Hegeman, John Rogers
Herndon, Alonzo Franklin
Hyde, Henry Baldwin
Kemper, James Scott
Kingsley, Darwin Pearl
Lawson, James
MacArthur, John D.
McCall, John Augustine
McClintock, Emory
McCurdy, Richard Aldrich
Merrick, John
Oliphant, Elmer Quillen
Pace, Harry Herbert
Perkins, George Walbridge
Perry, Heman Edward
Phelps, Guy Rowland
Seward, George Frederick
Upchurch, John Jordan
Wright, Elizur

Land Agents
Troup, Robert

Land Promoters
Alsop, George
Coram, Thomas
Cushman, Robert
Cutler, Manasseh
Filson, John
Greenleaf, Moses
Hammond, John
Imlay, Gilbert
Kelley, Hall Jackson
Peerson, Cleng
Singleton, Benjamin
Smith, John (1580–1631)
Walker, George
White, Andrew
White, Elijah

Real Estate Business Leaders
Astor, John Jacob, IV
Billingsley, Sherman
Binga, Jesse
Binney, Amos
Church, Robert Reed, Jr.
Cooper, William
Corbin, Austin
De Witt, Simeon
Dillingham, Benjamin Franklin
Disston, Hamilton
Ford, Barney Launcelot
Garrard, Kenner
Haggin, James Ben Ali
Hascall, Milo Smith
Hastings, Serranus Clinton
Ho, Chinn
Houston, Henry Howard
Huntington, Henry Edwards
Kenedy, Patrick John
Lafon, Thomy
Lasater, Edward Cunningham
Levitt, William Jaird
McKinlay, Whitefield
Morgenthau, Henry
Nail, John E.
Newberry, Walter Loomis
Otis, Harrison Gray (1765–1848)
Palmer, Potter
Payton, Philip A., Jr.
Putnam, Gideon
Rouse, James *Suppl. 1*
Ruggles, Samuel Bulkley
Savage, Henry Wilson
Starrett, William Aiken

Sutro, Adolph Heinrich Joseph
Torrence, Joseph Thatcher
Van Sweringen, Oris Paxton, and Mantis James Van Sweringen
Wadsworth, James (1768–1844)
Woodward, George
Zeckendorf, William

Speculators
Bowie, Jim
Cazenove, Théophile
Craigie, Andrew
Croghan, George (?–1782)
Davenport, George
Donelson, John
Duer, William
Fisk, James
Fitch, James
Garey, Thomas Andrew
Gilpin, William
Greene, William Cornell
Hagar, Jonathan
Harvey, Coin
Henderson, Richard
Hunter, David
Imlay, Gilbert
Johnson, Sir William
Low, Nicholas
Maverick, Samuel Augustus
Nicholson, John
O'Fallon, James
Patton, James
Preston, William
Smith, Gerrit
Smith, Peter (1768–1837)
Symmes, John Cleves
Waldo, Samuel
Walker, Thomas
Wentworth, Paul

Talent Scouts
Grimes, Burleigh Arland
Lazar, Swifty
Waterfield, Bob

Food and Beverage
Bakers
Clark, Catherine Taft
Ludwig, Christoph
Rudkin, Margaret Fogarty

Bar Owners / Saloonkeepers
Livingstone, Belle

Turpin, Tom

Brewers
Brand, Virgil Michael
Busch, Adolphus
Busch, August Anheuser, Jr.
Coors, Adolph *Suppl. 2*
Ruppert, Jacob
Vassar, Matthew

Chefs
Chen, Joyce
Diat, Louis Felix
Scotto, Charles

Chewing Gum Industry Leaders
Adams, Thomas, Jr.
Harney, William Selby
Wrigley, Philip Knight
Wrigley, William, Jr. *Suppl. 1*

Confectioners
Carvel, Thomas Andreas
Gunther, Charles Frederick *Suppl. 2*
Hershey, Milton Snavely
Hinkle, Samuel Forry
Welch, Robert

Distillers
Daniel, Jack *Suppl. 1*
Fleischmann, Charles Louis
Hammer, Armand
Harnett, Cornelius, Jr.
Lopez, Aaron
Manigault, Gabriel (1704–1781)
O'Hara, James
Thomson, Charles
Whalen, Grover Michael Aloysius Augustine

Fast-Food Business Leaders
Ingram, Edgar Waldo
Kroc, Ray
Sanders, Harland David

Flour Milling Industry Leaders
Bell, James Ford
Bell, James Stroud
Dunwoody, William Hood
Pillsbury, Charles Alfred
Pillsbury, John Sargent
Washburn, Cadwallader Colden

Food and Beverage
(cont.)
Washburn, William
Drew

Food Business Leaders
Bell, James Ford
Birdseye, Clarence
Borden, Gail
Bunker, Ellsworth
Chester, Colby Mitchell,
Jr.
Clark, Catherine Taft
Crowell, Henry Parsons
Danforth, William
Henry
Dole, James Drummond
Dorrance, John
Thompson
Fleischmann, Charles
Louis
Gerber, Daniel Frank
Heinz, Henry John
Heinz, Henry John, II
Hershey, Milton Snavely
Hines, Duncan
Horlick, William
Alexander
Hormel, George Albert
Hutton, E. F.
Kellogg, John Harvey
Kellogg, W. K.
Knox, Rose Markward
Kraft, James Lewis
Lasater, Edward
Cunningham
Perry, Stuart
Pillsbury, Charles Alfred
Post, Charles William
Post, Marjorie
Merriweather
Redenbacher, Orville
Suppl. 2
Rossi, Anthony Talamo
Rudkin, Margaret
Fogarty
Sanford, Henry Shelton
Stuart, Elbridge Amos
Vestey, Evelyn *Suppl. 1*

Grain Dealers
Bacon, Edward Payson
Barnes, Julius Howland
Butler, Hugh Alfred

Grocery Store Owners
Goldman, Sylvan
Nathan
Hartford, George
Huntington, and John
Augustine Hartford

Hartford, George
Ludlum
Kroger, Bernard Henry
Mugar, Stephen Pabken
Saunders, Clarence
Spreckels, Claus

Meatpackers
Allerton, Samuel Waters
Armour, Philip Danforth
Cudahy, Edward
Aloysius, Jr.
Cudahy, Michael
Hammond, George
Henry
Hormel, George Albert
Hormel, Jay Catherwood
Hubbard, Gurdon
Saltonstall
Hussey, Curtis Grubb
Mayer, Oscar Gottfried
Morris, Nelson
Parks, Henry Green, Jr.
Swift, Gustavus Franklin

Restaurateurs
Chen, Joyce
Delmonico, Lorenzo
Downing, George
Thomas
Harvey, Fred
Johnson, Howard
Dearing
Moody, Harriet
Converse
Niblo, William
Shor, Toots
Stanford, Sally

Soft Drink Industry Leaders
Candler, Asa Griggs
Goizueta, Roberto
Suppl. 1
Hires, Charles Elmer

*Sugar Refining Industry
Leaders*
Bunker, Ellsworth
Havemeyer, Henry
Osborne *Suppl. 1*
Kenner, Duncan Farrar
Suppl. 1
Spreckels, Claus
Tulane, Paul *Suppl. 1*

Wine Merchants
Cozzens, Frederick
Swartwout
Gualdo, John
Vaughan, John

**Household Goods and
Appliances**
*Air Conditioning Industry
Leaders*
Carrier, Willis Haviland
Crosthwait, David
Nelson, Jr.

Cabinetmakers
Buckland, William
Goddard, John
Gostelowe, Jonathan
Herter, Gustave, and
Christian Herter
Hitchcock, Lambert
Lannuier, Charles-
Honoré
Marcotte, Léon
Alexandre
Phyfe, Duncan
Quervelle, Anthony
Savery, William
Seymour, John
Seymour, Thomas
Stickley, Gustav
Townsend, John

Ceramists / Potters
Grueby, William Henry
Martinez, Maria
Montoya *Suppl. 2*
Nampeyo
Ohr, George E.
Overbeck, Margaret,
Hannah Borger
Overbeck, Elizabeth
Grey Overbeck, and
Mary Frances
Overbeck
Wood, Beatrice *Suppl. 1*

*Cleaning Aids
Manufacturers*
Colgate, William
Fels, Joseph
Fels, Samuel Simeon
Fuller, Alfred Carl
Procter, William Cooper

*Furniture Designers /
Manufacturers*
Bertoia, Harry
Eames, Charles
(1907–1978)
Hunzinger, George
Jakob
Jelliff, John
Lloyd, Marshall Burns
Stickley, Gustav
Sypher, Obadiah Lum

*Housewares / Household
Appliance Manufacturers*
Crowell, Henry Parsons
Fuller, Alfred Carl
Hoover, Herbert William
Maytag, Frederick Louis
Popeil, Samuel J.
Tupper, Earl Silas
Wampler, Cloud

*Sewing Machine
Manufacturers*
Bachelder, John
Howe, Elias
Singer, Isaac Merritt

Labor
Factory Workers
Bagley, Sarah George
Robinson, Harriet Jane
Hanson

Labor Organizers / Leaders
Anderson, Mary
(1872–1964)
Arthur, Peter M.
Bagley, Sarah George
Bambace, Angela
Barker, Mary Cornelia
Barnum, Gertrude
Barry, Leonora
Beck, Dave
Belanger, Mark *Suppl. 2*
Bellanca, August
Bellanca, Dorothy Jacobs
Berry, George Leonard
Beyer, Clara Mortenson
Biemiller, Andrew John
Bloor, Ella Reeve
Borchardt, Selma
Munter
Boyle, Michael J.
Boyle, William Anthony
Bridges, Harry Renton
Brooks, John Graham
Brophy, John
Browne, Carl
Budenz, Louis
Cameron, Andrew Carr
Carr, Charlotte Elizabeth
Chávez, César Estrada
Chaplin, Ralph Hosea
Christman, Elisabeth
Cohn, Fannia
Coit, Eleanor Gwinnell
Coles, Edward
Collins, Jennie
Conboy, Sara Agnes
McLaughlin
Coxey, Jacob Sechler

Labor *(cont.)*
Crosswaith, Frank
    Rudolph
Curran, Joseph Edwin
Davis, Richard L.
Debs, Eugene Victor
de Graffenried, Mary
    Clare
Dietz, Peter Ernest
Dodd, Bella Visono
Dreier, Mary Elisabeth
Drury, Victor S.
Dubinsky, David
Dudley, Helena Stuart
Duncan, James
Dunn, Robert Williams
Ettor, Joseph James
Evans, George Henry
Fechner, Robert *Suppl. 2*
Fitzpatrick, John
Fitzsimmons, Frank
    Suppl. 2
Fletcher, Benjamin
    Harrison
Flynn, Elizabeth Gurley
Ford, James William
Frey, John Philip
Furuseth, Andrew
Galarza, Ernesto
Germer, Adolph
Giovannitti, Arturo
    Massimo
Gompers, Samuel
Green, William
Gresham, Newt
Grigsby, Snow Flake
Haessler, Carl
Haley, Margaret Angela
Hamid, Sufi Abdul
Harrison, Hubert Henry
Hayes, Max Sebastian
Haywood, Allan Shaw
Haywood, William
    Dudley
Heighton, William
Henry, Alice
Hill, Joe
Hillman, Bessie
    Abramowitz
Hillman, Sidney
Hoffa, Jimmy
Howard, Charles Perry
Hutcheson, William Levi
Hutchins, Grace
Iglesias, Santiago
Jackson, Gardner
Johnston, William Hugh
Jones, Mother
Kallet, Arthur
Kearney, Denis
Kelley, Florence

Kirkland, Lane *Suppl. 1*
Lang, Lucy Fox Robins
Larkin, James
Lens, Sidney
Lewis, Augusta
Lewis, John L.
Litchman, Charles
    Henry
London, Meyer
Lovestone, Jay
Low, Seth
Lundeberg, Harry
Luther, Seth
Lynch, James Mathew
Malkiel, Theresa Serber
Marot, Helen
Mason, Lucy Randolph
Maurer, James Hudson
McDonald, David John
McDowell, Mary Eliza
McGuire, Peter J.
McNeill, George Edwin
Meany, George
Miller, Frieda Segelke
Mitchell, Harry Leland
Mitchell, John
    (1870–1919)
Mooney, Thomas Joseph
Moore, Ely
Moreno, Luisa
Mosessohn, David
    Nehemiah
Murray, Philip
Muste, Abraham
    Johannes
Myers, Isaac
Nestor, Agnes
Newman, Pauline
Norwood, Rose
    Finkelstein
O'Reilly, Leonora
O'Sullivan, Mary
    Kenney
Parker, Julia O'Connor
Parsons, Albert Richard
Parsons, Lucy Eldine
Payne, Virginia
Perkins, Frances
Pesotta, Rose
Petrillo, James Caesar
Phillips, Lena Madesin
Phillips, Wendell
Potofsky, Jacob Samuel
Powderly, Terence
    Vincent
Powell, William Peter
Presser, William
Quill, Mike
Randolph, Asa Philip
Reuther, Walter Philip
Robins, Margaret Dreier

Rodgers, Elizabeth Flynn
Schlesinger, Benjamin
Schneiderman, Rose
Shanker, Albert *Suppl. 1*
Siney, John
Sorge, Friedrich Adolph
Stelzle, Charles
Stephens, Uriah Smith
Stevens, Alzina Ann
    Parsons
Steward, Ira
Swartz, Maud O'Farrell
Swinton, John
Sylvis, William H.
Thomas, Roland Jay
Tobin, Daniel Joseph
Townsend, Willard
    Saxby, Jr.
Tresca, Carlo
Trevellick, Richard F.
Tveitmoe, Olaf Anders
Valesh, Eva McDonald
Vorse, Mary Heaton
Walling, William English
Weitling, Wilhelm
    Christian
Wertheimer, Barbara
    Mayer
Whitney, Alexander Fell
Wilson, William
    Bauchop
Woll, Matthew
Yorke, Peter Christopher
Young, Ruth
Young, William Field
Younger, Maud

Labor Relations Experts
Comey, Dennis J.
    Suppl. 1

Miners
Brophy, John
Burnham, Frederick
    Russell
Davis, Richard L.
Dubuque, Julien
Henry, Andrew
Jones, George Wallace
Siney, John
Tabor, Horace Austin
    Warner

Slaves
Abraham
Albert, Octavia Victoria
    Rogers
Allen, Richard
Ball, Charles
Bayne, Thomas
Bibb, Henry Walton

Billy
Bradley, Aaron Alpeora
Brooks, Walter
    Henderson
Brown, John
    (1810?–1876)
Brown, William Wells
Bruce, Blanche Kelso
Bryan, Andrew
Burns, Anthony
Bush, John Edward
Cary, Lott
Cesar
Clarke, Lewis G.
Coleman, Warren Clay
Cook, George William
Cook, John Francis
Coppin, Fanny Jackson
Councill, William
    Hooper
Craft, Ellen
Craft, William
Cromwell, John Wesley
Dorman, Isaiah
Dorsette, Cornelius
    Nathaniel
Douglas, H. Ford
Douglass, Frederick
Durham, James
Eagleson, William Lewis
Early, Jordan Winston
Ellison, William
Esteban
Ferguson, Katy
Ford, Barney Launcelot
Fortune, Amos
Freeman, Elizabeth
Fuller, Thomas
Gabriel
Garnet, Henry Highland
George, David
Grimké, Archibald
    Henry
Hammon, Jupiter
Haralson, Jeremiah
Hayden, Lewis
Healy, Eliza
Healy, James Augustine
Healy, Patrick Francis
Hemings, Sally
Henson, Josiah
Herndon, Alonzo
    Franklin
Holsey, Lucius Henry
Horton, George Moses
Hyman, John Adams
Jacobs, Harriet
Jasper, John
Jefferson, Isaac
Jeremiah, Thomas
Johnson, Edward Austin

Labor *(cont.)*
Johnson, Joshua
Johnson, William
  (1809–1851)
Keckley, Elizabeth
  Hobbs
Lafayette, James
Laney, Lucy Craft
Lee, Archy
Lee, Samuel J.
Liele, George
Long, Jefferson Franklin
Love, Nat
Lynch, John Roy
Marshall, Andrew Cox
Martin, John Sella
Meachum, John Berry
Merrick, John
Mitchell, John, Jr.
Montgomery, Benjamin
  Thornton
Montgomery, Isaiah
  Thornton
Napier, James Carroll
Northup, Solomon
O'Kelly, Berry
Parker, John P.
Pennington, James
  William Charles
Perry, Rufus Lewis
Plummer, Henry Vinton
Riley, James
Rudd, Daniel
Russell, James Solomon
Scott, Dred
Simmons, William James
Singleton, Benjamin
Smalls, Robert
Smith, James McCune
Smith, Venture
Spencer, Peter
Stockton, Betsey
Tarrant, Caesar
Terry, Lucy
Thompson, Joseph
  Pascal
Tindley, Charles Albert
Truth, Sojourner
Tubman, Harriet
Turner, Benjamin
  Sterling
Turner, Jack
Turner, James Milton
Turner, Nat
Varick, James
Vesey, Denmark
Walls, Josiah Thomas
Washington, Booker T.
Wells-Barnett, Ida Bell
Wheatley, Phillis
Whipple, Prince

Whittaker, Johnson
  Chesnut

**Manufacturing and
Mining**
Aluminum Industry Leaders
Clapp, George Hubbard
Davis, Arthur Vining
Hall, Charles Martin
Hunt, Alfred Ephraim

Barbed Wire Manufacturers
Gates, John Warne
Glidden, Joseph Farwell
Haish, Jacob

Blacksmiths
Davenport, Thomas
Deere, John
Jefferson, Isaac
Yellin, Samuel

Chemical Industry Leaders
Barber, Ohio Columbus
Bell, William Brown
Cabot, Godfrey Lowell
du Pont, Henry Belin
Grasselli, Caesar
  Augustin
Hill, Henry Aaron
Hooker, Elon
  Huntington
Mallinckrodt, Edward
Mallinckrodt, Edward,
  Jr.
McKnight, William
  Lester
Morehead, John Motley
Pfister, Alfred
Plunkett, Roy Joseph
Warren, Cyrus Moors
Washburn, Frank
  Sherman
Weightman, William

Clockmakers
Bond, William Cranch
Thomas, Seth

Computer Industry Leaders
Cray, Seymour *Suppl. 1*
Packard, David *Suppl. 1*
Wang, An
Watson, Arthur
  Kittridge
Watson, Thomas John,
  Jr.

Coopers
Henkel, Paul
Meachum, John Berry

Cork Industry Leaders
Prentis, Henning Webb,
  Jr.

Electronics Industry Leaders
Schmitt, Arthur J.
  Suppl. 2
Tandy, Charles David

Explosives Manufacturers
Bidermann, Jacques
  Antoine
du Pont, Eleuthère
  Irénée
du Pont, Henry
Mowbray, George
  Mordey

Firearms Manufacturers
Blake, Eli Whitney
Colt, Samuel
Garand, John C.
Gatling, Richard Jordan
Lewis, Isaac Newton
Maxim, Hiram Percy
Maxim, Sir Hiram
Remington, Philo
Spencer, Christopher
  Miner
Whitney, Eli
Williams, Carbine
Winchester, Oliver
  Fisher

Glass Industry Leaders
Bakewell, Benjamin
Ball, Frank Clayton
Ball, George Alexander
Carder, Frederick
Craig, Isaac
Houghton, Alanson
  Bigelow
Houghton, Amory
Houghton, Arthur
  Amory, Jr.
Libbey, Edward
  Drummond
Mason, John Landis
  Suppl. 2
O'Hara, James
Owens, Michael Joseph
Stiegel, Henry William
Wistar, Caspar
  (1696–1752)

Gunsmiths
Browning, John M.
  Suppl. 2
Pomeroy, Seth

Hatters
Daché, Lilly
Stetson, John Batterson
Swan, Timothy

*Hemp / Cordage Industry
Leaders*
Fitler, Edwin Henry
Hunt, John Wesley

Industrialists
Acheson, Edward
  Goodrich
Anderson, Joseph Reid
Austin, Moses
Barnes, Julius Howland
Bausch, Edward
Bell, William Brown
Bendix, Vincent Hugo
Brown, Francis
  Donaldson
Buchtel, John Richards
Bueche, Arthur Maynard
Cabot, Godfrey Lowell
Callaway, Cason Jewell
Camden, Johnson
  Newlon
Canaday, Ward
  Murphey
Carnegie, Andrew
Colt, Samuel
Colt, Samuel Pomeroy
Colyar, Arthur St. Clair
Comer, Braxton Bragg
Cooper, Peter
Corey, William Ellis
Couch, Harvey Crowley
Crane, Richard Teller
Crane, Winthrop
  Murray
Crawford, George
  Gordon *Suppl. 1*
Crawford, George
  Washington
Davis, Arthur Vining
Davis, Henry Gassaway
DeBardeleben, Henry
  Fairchild
Dow, Herbert Henry
Duke, Benjamin Newton
Duke, James Buchanan
Duke, Washington
Dumaine, Frederic
  Christopher
du Pont, Alfred Irénée
du Pont, Eleuthère
  Irénée
du Pont, Henry
du Pont, Irénée
du Pont, Lammot
du Pont, Pierre Samuel

Manufacturing and Mining (cont.)
du Pont, T. Coleman
Durant, William Crapo
Eaton, Cyrus Stephen
Elkins, Stephen Benton
Falk, Maurice
Flanders, Ralph Edward
Folger, Henry Clay
Frick, Henry Clay
Gary, Elbert Henry
Girdler, Tom Mercer
Grace, Eugene Gifford
Green, Benjamin Edwards
Guggenheim, Daniel
Guggenheim, Solomon Robert
Hall, Charles Martin
Hanger, James Edward Suppl. 2
Hasenclever, Peter
Heinz, Henry John
Higgins, Andrew Jackson
Hillman, Thomas Tennessee
Hoover, Herbert William
Johnson, Philip Gustav
Jones, Benjamin Franklin
Juilliard, Augustus D.
Kaiser, Henry John
Kohler, Walter Jodok
Letchworth, William Pryor
Mather, Samuel (1851–1931)
Mather, Samuel Livingston
McKay, Gordon
Miller, Lewis Suppl. 2
Mott, Charles Stewart
Murchison, Clinton Williams
Newberry, Truman Handy
Olds, Irving Sands
Pew, John Howard
Pratt, Daniel (1799–1873)
Pratt, George Dupont
Pullman, George Mortimer
Reynolds, Richard Samuel, Sr.
Rice, Edwin Wilbur, Jr.
Rockefeller, John D.
Rockefeller, William
Romney, George
Scripps, William Edmund
Seiberling, Franklin Augustus

Sloan, Alfred Pritchard, Jr.
Stettinius, Edward Reilly
Straus, Roger Williams
Symington, Stuart
Takamine, Jokichi
Talbott, Harold Elstner
Thomson, Elihu
Tompkins, Daniel Augustus
Vanderbilt, William Henry
Vauclain, Samuel Matthews
Washburn, Cadwallader Colden
Weeks, Sinclair
Weston, Edward (1850–1936)
Wharton, Joseph
Widdicomb, John
Wilson, Charles Edward
Wilson, Joseph Chamberlain
Woodruff, George Waldo

Iron and Steel Industry Leaders
Abbott, Horace
Alger, Cyrus
Anderson, Joseph Reid
Benner, Philip
Blough, Roger Miles
Bly, Nellie
Burden, Henry
Carnegie, Andrew
Carroll of Carrollton, Charles
Chisholm, Henry
Cooper, Edward
Corey, William Ellis
Corning, Erastus
Dickerson, Mahlon
Embree, Elihu
Fairless, Benjamin Franklin
Farrell, James Augustine
Frick, Henry Clay
Gary, Elbert Henry
Gates, John Warne
Gayley, James
Girdler, Tom Mercer
Grace, Eugene Gifford
Graff, Everett Dwight
Graham, Joseph
Hasenclever, Peter
Hewitt, Abram Stevens
Hill, William
James, Daniel Willis
Jenks, Joseph

Jones, Benjamin Franklin
Kelly, William
Lukens, Rebecca Webb Pennock
McArthur, John
Mesta, Perle
Metcalf, William
Moxham, Arthur James
Olds, Irving Sands
Oliver, Henry William
Oliver, Peter
Park, James, Jr.
Randall, Clarence Belden
Reese, Abram
Schwab, Charles Michael
Scranton, George Whitfield
Spotswood, Alexander
Stettinius, Edward Reilly, Jr.
Stiegel, Henry William
Taylor, Myron Charles
Torrence, Joseph Thatcher
Verity, George Matthew
Weir, Ernest Tener
Wilkeson, Samuel
Woodin, William Hartman
Yeatman, Thomas

Machinery Manufacturers
Allis, Edward Phelps
Baldwin, Matthias W.
Bettendorf, William Peter
Blake, Eli Whitney
Brown, Alexander Ephraim
Carrier, Willis Haviland
Case, Jerome Increase
Chalmers, William James
Clark, Edward
Corliss, George Henry
Deere, John
Deering, William
Draper, William Franklin
Ellison, William
Esterly, George
Evinrude, Ole
Haish, Jacob
Hartness, James
Hoe, Richard March
Hoe, Robert
Hughes, Howard Robard, Sr.
Hurley, Edward Nash
Jacuzzi, Aldo Joseph
Jacuzzi, Candido

Jacuzzi, Rachele
Lanston, Tolbert
Leffel, James
Marsh, Charles Wesley
Mason, William (1808–1883)
McCormick, Cyrus Hall
McCormick, Cyrus Hall, Jr.
McCormick, Leander James
McCormick, Nettie Fowler
Merrick, Samuel Vaughan
Otis, Charles Rollin
Otis, Elisha Graves
Parker, John P.
Peek, George Nelson
Pratt, Francis Ashbury
Ramage, Adam
Singer, Isaac Merritt
Spencer, Christopher Miner
Tilghman, Benjamin Chew
Worthington, Henry Rossiter

Medical Equipment Manufacturers
Hanger, James Edward Suppl. 2

Mining Industry Leaders
Agassiz, Alexander
Austin, Moses
Bankhead, John Hollis (1872–1946)
Bowen, Thomas Meade
Buell, Don Carlos
Cist, Jacob
Clark, William Andrews
Daly, Marcus
Greene, William Cornell
Guggenheim, Simon
Haggin, James Ben Ali
Hearst, George
Hill, Nathaniel Peter
Mackay, John W. Suppl. 1
Mather, Samuel (1851–1931)
Mills, Darius Ogden
Mondell, Frank Wheeler
Oliver, Henry William
Smith, Francis Marion
Thompson, Robert Means
Thompson, William Boyce
Tod, David
Wingfield, George

Manufacturing and Mining *(cont.)*
Musical Instrument Makers
Babcock, Alpheus
Chickering, Jonas
Gemunder Family
Johnston, Thomas
Steinway, Christian
  Friedrich Theodore
Steinway, Henry
  Engelhard
Steinway, William

Ordnance Manufacturers
Alger, Cyrus
Ames, Nathan Peabody
Anderson, Joseph Reid
Bomford, George
Dahlgren, John
  Adolphus Bernard
Davison, Gregory
  Caldwell
Ford, Hannibal Choate
Miller, George
  Augustus, Jr.
Parrott, Robert Parker
Rains, Gabriel James
Rains, George
  Washington
Taylor, George *Suppl. 1*
Wisner, Henry

Paper Industry Leaders
Chisholm, Hugh Joseph
Crocker, Alvah
Dennison, Henry Sturgis
McCabe, Thomas
  Bayard
Rittenhouse, William
West, George

Pencil Industry Leaders
Faber, John Eberhard
  Suppl. 1

Petroleum Industry Leaders
Archbold, John Dustin
Bard, Thomas Robert
Benedum, Michael L.
  Suppl. 1
Camden, Johnson
  Newlon
Cullen, Hugh Roy
Cullinan, Joseph Stephen
Doheny, Edward
  Laurence
Farish, William Stamps
Flagler, Henry Morrison
Gallagher, Ralph W.
Getty, J. Paul
Gilcrease, Thomas

Guffey, Joseph F.
Hess, Leon *Suppl. 1*
Hoover, Herbert Clark,
  Jr.
Hunt, H. L.
Jones, Samuel Milton
Kerr, Robert Samuel
Lockhart, Charles
Marland, Ernest
  Whitworth
Mellon, William Larimer
Murchison, Clinton
  Williams
O'Brien, John Joseph
Pew, John Howard
Phillips, Frank
Pratt, Charles
Richardson, Sid
  Williams
Rockefeller, John D.
Rogers, Henry
  Huttleston
Roosevelt, Archibald
  Bulloch
Sadler, Harley
Sinclair, Harry Ford
Sterling, Ross Shaw
Teagle, Walter Clark
Wright, Eliphalet Nott

*Pharmaceutical Industry
Leaders*
Barnes, Albert Coombs
Childs, Richard Spencer
Kiss, Max
Lilly, Eli *Suppl. 1*
Lilly, Josiah Kirby
Lloyd, John Uri
Merck, George Wilhelm
Squibb, Edward
  Robinson

*Photographic Industry
Leaders*
Bachrach, Louis Fabian
Eastman, George
Edison, Thomas Alva
Ives, Frederic Eugene
Land, Edwin Herbert

Plastics Industry Leaders
Baekeland, Leo Hendrik
Davis, Francis Breese, Jr.
Dreyfus, Camille
  Edouard
du Pont, Henry Belin
du Pont, Lammot
Ellis, Carleton
Hyatt, John Wesley
Tupper, Earl Silas

Wyeth, N. C.
  (1911–1990)

Prospectors
Fair, James Graham
Marshall, James Wilson
Scott, Walter Edward

Rubber Industry Leaders
Candee, Leverett
Colt, Samuel Pomeroy
Davis, Francis Breese, Jr.
Dodge, Theodore
  Ayrault
Firestone, Harvey
  Samuel
Flint, Charles Ranlett
Goodrich, Benjamin
  Franklin
Goodyear, Charles
Kimball, Dan Able
Litchfield, Paul Weeks
Seiberling, Franklin
  Augustus

Sailmakers
Forten, James

Salt Industry Leaders
O'Hara, James
Richmond, Dean

*Scientific Instrument
Makers*
Anderson, John August
Bayard, James Ashton
Brashear, John Alfred
Clark, Alvan
Clark, Alvan Graham
Hamlin, William
Ritchey, George Willis
Rittenhouse, David
Ross, Frank Elmore
Swasey, Ambrose
Tagliabue, Giuseppe

Silversmiths
Atsidi, Sani
Dummer, Jeremiah
  (1645–1718)
Fitch, John
Hull, John
Hurd, Jacob
Hurd, Nathaniel
Kirk, Samuel Child
Le Roux, Bartholomew
Moore, Edward
  Chandler
Myers, Myer
Revere, Paul
Richardson, Joseph

Stone, Arthur John
Syng, Philip, Jr.
Welles, Clara

*Smelting / Refining Industry
Leaders*
Hussey, Curtis Grubb
Straus, Roger Williams

Tilemakers
Mercer, Henry
  Chapman

Tobacco Industry Leaders
Ginter, Lewis
Hill, George Washington
Reynolds, Richard
  Joshua, Sr.
Reynolds, William Neal

Tool Manufacturers
Ames, Oakes
  (1804–1873)
Ames, Oliver
  (1807–1877)
Deere, John
Disston, Henry
Gleason, Kate
Pratt, Francis Ashbury
Towne, Henry Robinson

Watchmakers
Bulova, Arde
Crosby, Sylvester Sage

Weavers
Bresci, Gaetano
Keyser, Louisa *Suppl. 2*

Woodcarvers
López, José Dolores
Skillin, John, and
  Simeon Skillin, Jr.

Public Utilities
Electricity Industry Leaders
Brush, Charles Francis
Coffin, Charles Albert
Couch, Harvey Crowley
Edison, Thomas Alva
Eickemeyer, Rudolf
Hewitt, Peter Cooper
Rankine, William Birch
Reed, Philip Dunham
Stager, Anson
Swope, Gerard
Tesla, Nikola
Thomson, Elihu
Warren, Henry Ellis
Westinghouse, George

Public Utilities (cont.)
Weston, Edward
(1850–1936)

Gas Industry Leaders
Addicks, John Edward
O'Sullivan

Public Utilities Executives
Copley, Ira Clifton
Cortelyou, George Bruce
Couch, Harvey Crowley
Dawes, Rufus Cutler
Insull, Samuel
O'Sullivan, James
Edward
Sloan, Matthew Scott
Sporn, Philip
Willkie, Wendell Lewis

**Retail / Wholesale
Goods and Services**
Animal Trainers
Adams, Grizzly
Beatty, Clyde Raymond
Rarey, John Solomon

Antique Dealers
Sack, Israel
Sypher, Obadiah Lum

Art Dealers
Avery, Samuel Putnam
Castelli, Leo *Suppl. 1*
Daniel, Charles
Halpert, Edith Gregor
Janis, Sidney
Macbeth, William
Paff, Michael
Sullivan, Mary Quinn

Boardinghouse Operators
Mondavi, Rosa Grassi

Booksellers
Bancroft, Hubert Howe
Beach, Sylvia
Woodbridge
Deinard, Ephraim
Dobson, Thomas
Drake, Samuel Gardner
Dunton, John
Gaine, Hugh
Hall, Samuel
(1740–1807)
Mein, John
Michaux, Lewis H.
Nicholson, Timothy
Rich, Obadiah
Rosenbach, Abraham
Simon Wolf

Sabin, Joseph
Theobald, Paul
Timothy, Elizabeth
Weems, Mason Locke

Department Store Owners
Altman, Benjamin
Avery, Sewell Lee
Bamberger, Louis
Bonwit, Paul J. *Suppl. 1*
Farkas, Alexander S.
Suppl. 2
Filene, Edward Albert
Gimbel, Bernard
Feustman
Hoving, Walter
Hudson, J. L. *Suppl. 1*
Kaufmann, Edgar Jonas,
Sr.
Kirstein, Louis Edward
Lubin, David
Macy, R. H. *Suppl. 1*
May, Morton Jay
Nelson, Donald Marr
Shedd, John Graves
Straus, Isidor
Straus, Jesse Isidor
Wanamaker, John
Wanamaker, Rodman
Whalen, Grover Michael
Aloysius Augustine

Dog Breeders
Eustis, Dorothy Harrison
Little, Clarence Cook
Sloane, Isabel Cleves
Dodge

Drugstore Owners
Liggett, Louis Kroh
Walgreen, Charles
Rudolph

*Dry Cleaning Business
Executives*
Burrell, Berkeley
Graham

Fur Traders
Ashley, William Henry
Astor, John Jacob
Bridger, James
Chouteau, Auguste
Pierre
Chouteau, Jean Pierre
Chouteau, René Auguste
Claiborne, William
Davenport, George
Dickson, Robert
Dubuque, Julien
Faribault, Jean Baptiste

Farnham, Russel
Forsyth, Thomas
Gratiot, Charles
Harmon, Daniel
Williams
Henry, Alexander
Henry, Andrew
James, Thomas
Laclède, Pierre
Larpenteur, Charles
Lisa, Manuel
McLoughlin, John
Mitchell, David Dawson
Navarre, Pierre
Niebaum, Gustave
Ferdinand *Suppl. 2*
Ogden, Peter Skene
Pynchon, William
Ross, Alexander
Sarpy, Peter A.
Smith, Jedediah Strong
Smith, Peter
(1768–1837)
Thompson, David
Tonty, Henri de
Vigo, Joseph Maria
Francesco
Walker, Joseph
Rutherford
Williams, William
Sherley
Wolfskill, William
Young, Ewing

Horse Traders
Nolan, Philip

Ice Merchants
Tudor, Frederic

Locksmiths
Day, Stephen
Yale, Linus, Jr.

*Mail-Order Business
Leaders*
Bean, L. L.
Burpee, David
Lubin, David
Sears, Richard Warren
Vick, James
Ward, Aaron
Montgomery
Wells, Samuel Roberts
Wood, Robert Elkington

Merchants
Alexander, Mary Spratt
Provoost
Allen, James
Allerton, Isaac

Alsop, Richard *Suppl. 1*
Alvarez, Manuel
Aspinwall, William
Henry
Bache, Richard
Bache, Theophylact
Banning, Phineas
Suppl. 1
Bates, Joshua
Bayard, John Bubenheim
Bayard, Nicholas
Biddle, Clement
Bingham, William
Bowdoin, James
(1752–1811)
Bowen, Henry Chandler
Brooks, Peter Chardon
Brown, Alexander
Brown, John
(1736–1803)
Brown, Joseph
Brown, Moses
Brown, Nicholas
Brown, Obadiah
Calef, Robert
Carroll, Daniel
Carter, Henry Alpheus
Peirce
Carter, Robert
(1663–1732)
Chouteau, Pierre, Jr.
Claflin, Horace Brigham
Clark, Daniel
(1766–1813)
Clarkson, Matthew
Clymer, George
Coffin, Levi
Coleman, William Tell
Collins, Edward Knight
Colman, John
Cope, Thomas Pym
Crowninshield,
Benjamin Williams
Crowninshield, George,
Jr.
Cruger, Henry, Jr.
Cupples, Samuel
Cushing, John Perkins
Cushing, Thomas
Cutt, John
Cutts, Samuel
Davis, Alice Brown
De Berdt, Dennys
De Peyster, Abraham
de Vries, David
Pietersen
Delafield, John
(1748–1824)
Delafield, John
(1786–1853)
Derby, Elias Hasket

**Retail / Wholesale
Goods and Services**
(cont.)

Derby, Richard
Dexter, Samuel
Dexter, Timothy
Dodge, David Low
  Suppl. 2
Duer, William
Dugdale, Richard Louis
du Sable, Jean Baptiste
  Point
Eaton, Theophilus
Ellery, William
Etting, Solomon *Suppl. 1*
Evans, William
Faneuil, Peter
Farwell, Charles
  Benjamin
Fell, John
Field, Marshall
Findlay, James
Fiske, John (1744–1797)
Fitzsimons, Thomas
Fleete, Henry
Flint, Charles Ranlett
Folsom, Nathaniel
Forbes, John
  (1767?–1823)
Forbes, John Murray
Forstall, Edmond Jean
Gadsden, Christopher
Gaines, George Strother
Galt, John
Garrett, Robert
Gillon, Alexander
Gilman, John Taylor
Girard, Stephen
Glover, John
Goodwin, Ichabod
Gorham, Nathaniel
Gould, Benjamin
  Apthorp (1787–1859)
Gratz, Barnard, and
  Michael Gratz
Gray, William
Green, John Cleve
Green, Joseph
Grim, David
Grinnell, Henry
Gwinnett, Button
Habersham, James
Habersham, Joseph
Hambleton, Thomas
  Edward
Hamilton, Andrew
  (?–1703)
Hamilton, John
Hammett, Samuel
  Adams

Hancock, John
  (1737–1793)
Hancock, Thomas
Hand, Daniel
Hanson, John, Jr.
Hays, Moses Michael
  Suppl. 1
Hazen, Moses
Heathcote, Caleb
Heco, Joseph
Henry, Alexander
Herrman, Augustine
Hiester, Joseph
Higgins, Frank Wayland
Higginson, Nathaniel
Hillegas, Michael
Holker, John
Hooper, Samuel
Hopkins, Johns
Hubbard, Gurdon
  Saltonstall
Hull, John
Hunt, John Wesley
Hunt, Wilson Price
Irving, William
Jackson, Patrick Tracy
James, Thomas
Jenifer, Daniel of St.
  Thomas
Johnson, Sir William
Jones, George Wallace
Jones, William
  (1760–1831)
Kelly, Eugene
Kilby, Christopher
King, Charles
Kohlberg, Alfred
Laclède, Pierre
Ladd, William Sargent
Langdon, John
Langdon, Woodbury
Larkin, Thomas Oliver
Laurens, Henry
Leacock, John
Leffingwell, Christopher
Leisler, Jacob
Leiter, Levi Zeigler
Lewis, Francis
Livermore, George
Livingston, Peter Van
  Brugh
Livingston, Philip
Livingston, Robert
Lopez, Aaron
Low, Isaac
Low, Nicholas
Ludlow, Daniel
Lunt, Orrington
MacVeagh, Franklin
Malcom, Daniel

Manigault, Gabriel
  (1704–1781)
Marshall, Benjamin
Masters, Sybilla
Matlack, Timothy
Maule, Thomas
Mayhew, Thomas
Mazzei, Philip
McHenry, James
  (1753–1816)
Meade, George
Menard, Pierre
Merry, William
  Lawrence
Mifflin, Thomas
Montgomery, Benjamin
  Thornton
Morgan, Edwin Denison
Morrill, Justin Smith
Morris, Robert
  (1735–1806)
Morrison, William
Moses, Isaac *Suppl. 2*
Mott, James
Murray, John
  (1737–1808)
Murray, Robert
Nelson, Thomas
Nelson, William
  (1711–1772)
Nolte, Vincent Otto
Norris, Isaac
  (1671–1735)
Norris, Isaac
  (1701–1766)
Norton, Joshua Abraham
  Suppl. 2
Oliver, Andrew
  (1706–1774)
Oliver, Peter
Opdyke, George
Orr, Alexander Ector
Osborn, William Henry
Osgood, Samuel
Outerbridge, Eugenius
  Harvey
Palmer, Potter
Panton, William
Parris, Samuel
Partridge, Richard
Peabody, George
Pemberton, Israel
Penhallow, Samuel
Penington, Edward
Penney, J. C.
Pepperrell, Sir William
Perkins, Thomas
  Handasyd
Pettit, Charles
Phelan, James
Philipse, Adolph

Philipse, Frederick
Philipse, Margaret
  Hardenbrook
Phillips, John
Phillips, Jonas *Suppl. 1*
Pintard, Lewis
Pollock, Oliver
Randall, Robert Richard
Rawle, Francis
Read, Daniel
Redwood, Abraham
Reed, Luman
Rice, Abraham Joseph
Rice, William Marsh
Richardson, Thomas
Roberdeau, Daniel
Roberts, William Randall
Rowe, John
Saffin, John
Sage, Henry Williams
Schuyler, Peter
Seligman, Joseph
Sewall, Samuel
Shaw, Henry
Shaw, Nathaniel, Jr.
Shelikhov, Grigorii
  Ivanovich
Sherburne, Henry
Sherman, Roger
Shippen, Edward
Smith, John
  (c.1735–1824)
Smith, Melancton
  (1744–1798)
Stearns, Abel
Steendam, Jacob
Steenwyck, Cornelis
  Jacobsz
Steere, Richard
Stewart, Alexander
  Turney
Stewart, Anthony
Storer, Arthur
Sturgis, William
Swanwick, John
Telfair, Edward
Thatcher, Mahlon
  Daniel
Thompson, Jeremiah
Tome, Jacob
Tracy, Nathaniel
Trumbull, Jonathan
Van Cortlandt,
  Stephanus
van Cortlant, Oloff
  Stevensz
Van Dam, Rip
Van Rensselaer, Jeremias
Vaughan, George
Vespucci, Amerigo

Retail / Wholesale Goods and Services
(cont.)
Vigo, Joseph Maria Francesco
Vizcaíno, Sebastián
Wadsworth, Peleg
Walderne, Richard
Waldron, Richard, Jr.
Wanton, John
Wanton, Joseph
Wanton, William
Ward, Samuel (1725–1776)
Watson, Elkanah
Welsh, John
Wentworth, Mark Hunking
Wharton, Richard
Wharton, Robert
Wharton, Thomas, Jr.
Whipple, William
White, Henry (1732–1786)
Williams, Jonathan
Willing, Thomas
Wistar, Caspar (1696–1752)
Woolley, Edwin Dilworth
Wooster, David
Wyeth, Nathaniel Jarvis
Yeatman, Thomas

Patent Medicine Makers
Ayer, James Cook
Brandreth, Benjamin Cesar
Hartman, Samuel Brubaker
Koch, William Frederick
Perkins, Elisha
Pinkham, Lydia Estes

Press-Clipping Service Owners
Romeike, Henry

Public Relations Business Leaders
Bernays, Doris Elsa Fleischman
Bernays, Edward
Fleischman, Doris E.
Harlow, Bryce
Hill, John Wiley
Husted, Marjorie Child
Lee, Ivy Ledbetter
Swope, Herbert Bayard
Young, John Orr

Scribes
Downer, Silas

Shoemakers
Bean, L. L.
Blake, Lyman Reed
Capezio, Salvatore *Suppl. 2*
Douglas, William Lewis
Evans, Henry
Heighton, William
Mackintosh, Ebenezer

Stenographers
Barrows, Isabel

Taxidermists
Akeley, Carl Ethan

Traders with Indians / Pioneers
Adair, James
Ashley, William Henry
Bent, Charles
Bent, William
Bridger, James
Carson, Kit
Chisholm, Jesse
Chouteau, Auguste Pierre
Claiborne, William
Faribault, Jean Baptiste
Gaines, George Strother
Gratiot, Charles
Harris, John
Hubbell, John Lorenzo
James, Thomas
Lorimier, Louis
McGillivray, Lachlan
McLoughlin, John
Menard, Pierre
Oldham, John
Rice, Henry Mower
Schuyler, Peter
Viele, Aernout Cornelissen
Wolfskill, William

Trappers
Ashley, William Henry
Baker, James
Bent, Charles
Bridger, James
Carson, Kit
Colter, John
Fink, Mike
Glass, Hugh
LaRamee, Jacques
Leonard, Zenas
Pattie, James Ohio

Williams, William Sherley
Wolfskill, William
Young, Ewing
Yount, George Concepción

Undertakers
Gaston, A. G. *Suppl. 1*
Johnson, Andrew N.

Variety Store Owners
Grant, W. T.
Kresge, Sebastian Spering
Kress, Samuel Henry
McCrory, John Graham *Suppl. 2*
Woolworth, Frank Winfield

Whaling Industry Leaders
Rodman, Samuel
Rotch, Joseph
Rotch, William
Rotch, William, Jr.
Russell, Joseph

Transportation
Aerospace Industry Leaders
Allen, William McPherson
Bell, Lawrence Dale
Bellanca, Giuseppe Mario
Berlin, Donovan Reese
Boeing, William Edward
Breech, Ernest Robert
Burnelli, Vincent Justus
Butler, Charles Wilfred
Chamberlin, Clarence Duncan
Crown, Henry
Curtiss, Glenn Hammond
de Seversky, Alexander Procofieff
Douglas, Donald Wills
Egtvedt, Claire
Ehricke, Krafft Arnold
Grumman, Leroy Randle
Hughes, Howard
Hunsaker, Jerome Clarke
Hurley, Roy T.
Ide, John Jay
Johnson, Philip Gustav
Kellett, W. Wallace
Keys, Clement Melville
Kimball, Dan Able
Lear, William Powell

Ley, Willy
Link, Edwin Albert, Jr.
Lockheed, Allan Haines
Martin, Glenn Luther
McDonnell, James Smith, Jr.
Northrop, John Knudsen
Piper, William Thomas
Raymond, Arthur E. *Suppl. 1*
Schroeder, Rudolph William
Vought, Chance
Wright, Theodore Paul

Airline Industry Leaders
Braniff, Thomas Elmer
Chennault, Claire Lee
Coffin, Howard Earle
Damon, Ralph Shepard
Doole, George Arntzen
Frye, William John
Gorrell, Edgar Staley
Henderson, Paul
Hunter, Croil
Patterson, William Allan
Prescott, Robert William
Raymond, Arthur E. *Suppl. 1*
Rickenbacker, Edward Vernon
Six, Robert Forman
Smith, Cyrus Rowlett
Trippe, Juan Terry
Woolman, Collett Everman

Automobile Industry Leaders
Bennett, Harry Herbert
Breech, Ernest Robert
Briggs, Walter Owen
Briscoe, Benjamin
Buick, David Dunbar
Champion, Albert
Chapin, Roy Dikeman
Chrysler, Walter Percy
Cole, Edward Nicholas
Cord, Errett Lobban
Couzens, James
Curtice, Harlow Herbert
Dodge, John Francis, and Horace Elgin Dodge
Donner, Frederic Garrett
Duryea, Charles Edgar
Duryea, Frank
Earl, Harley Jefferson

Transportation *(cont.)*
Fisher, Frederic John,
Charles Thomas
Fisher, William
Andrew Fisher,
Lawrence P. Fisher,
Edward Francis Fisher,
and Alfred Joseph
Fisher
Ford, Edsel Bryant
Ford, Henry
Ford, Henry, II
Frazer, Joseph
Washington
Fuller, Alvan Tufts
Gehringer, Charlie
Haynes, Elwood
Hertz, John Daniel
Hoffman, Paul Gray
Keller, Kaufman Thuma
Knudsen, William
Signius
Leland, Henry Martyn
Macauley, James Alvan
Mason, George Walter
Nash, Charles W.
Olds, Ransom Eli
Packard, James Ward
Pope, Albert Augustus
Roosevelt, Franklin
Delano, Jr.
Sorensen, Charles
Stanley, Francis Edgar,
and Freelan Oscar
Stanley
Stearns, Frank Ballou
Stettinius, Edward
Reilly, Jr.
Studebaker, John Mohler
Stutz, Harry Clayton
Tucker, Preston Thomas
Vance, Harold Sines
Wills, Childe Harold
Willys, John North
Wilson, Charles Erwin
Winton, Alexander

Bicycle Makers
Duryea, Charles Edgar

Canal Builders / Promoters
Fulton, Robert
Lacock, Abner
Watson, Elkanah
Worthington, Thomas

*Car Rental Company
Owners*
Hertz, John Daniel
Jacobs, Walter L.

Elevated Railway Operators
Gilbert, Rufus Henry
Yerkes, Charles Tyson

*Horse-Drawn Vehicle
Manufacturers*
Studebaker, Clement
Studebaker, John Mohler

Keelboatmen
Fink, Mike

Railroad Industry Leaders
Adams, Charles Francis
(1835–1915)
Aldrich, Nelson
Wilmarth
Alexander, Edward
Porter
Ames, Oliver
(1807–1877)
Andrews, Alexander
Boyd
Atterbury, William
Wallace
Austell, Alfred
Baer, George Frederick
Baldwin, William Henry,
Jr.
Ball, George Alexander
Barnes, James
Billings, Frederick
Boteler, Alexander
Robinson
Boyle, Jeremiah Tilford
Brady, Diamond Jim
Suppl. 1
Brice, Calvin Stewart
Brown, William Carlos
Budd, Ralph
Bullock, Rufus Brown
Burnside, Ambrose
Everett
Bush, Benjamin Franklin
Cass, George
Washington
Cassatt, Alexander
Johnston
Clement, Martin
Withington
Corbin, Austin
Corning, Erastus
Crocker, Alvah
Crocker, Charles
Depew, Chauncey
Mitchell
Dillingham, Benjamin
Franklin
Dillon, Sidney
Drake, Francis Marion
Durant, Thomas Clark

Dwight, William
Evans, George
Fink, Albert
Fish, Stuyvesant
Flagler, Henry Morrison
Forbes, John Murray
Gadsden, James
Garrett, John Work
Gowen, Franklin
Benjamin
Green, John Cleve
Guthrie, James
Hall, Thomas Seavey
Harriman, Edward
Henry
Harriman, W. Averell
Haupt, Herman
Hayne, Robert Young
Hill, James Jerome
Hopkins, Mark *Suppl. 2*
Huntington, Collis
Potter
Huntington, Henry
Edwards
Ingalls, Melville Ezra
Jewett, Hugh Judge
Johnston, John Taylor
Johnston, Wayne
Andrew
Joy, James Frederick
Judah, Theodore
Dehone
Keep, Henry
Kelley, Alfred
Kennedy, John Stewart
Kneass, Strickland
Litchfield, Electus
Backus
Logan, Thomas
Muldrup
Lord, Eleazar
Loree, Leonor Fresnel
Lowry, Thomas
Mahone, William
Mason, William
(1808–1883)
McAdoo, William Gibbs
McCallum, Daniel Craig
McKennan, Thomas
McKean Thompson
McLane, Louis
Merrick, Samuel
Vaughan
Mills, Darius Ogden
Moffat, David Halliday
O'Brien, John Joseph
Osborn, William Henry
Packer, Asa
Palmer, William Jackson
Perkins, Charles Elliott
Perlman, Alfred E.

Plant, Henry Bradley
Plumbe, John
Porter, Horace
Rea, Samuel
Richmond, Dean
Ripley, Edward Payson
Ripley, William Zebina
Roberts, George Brooke
Rogers, Henry
Huttleston
Rollins, Edward Henry
Saunders, Stuart
Thomas
Sayre, Robert Heysham
Seney, George Ingraham
Sewall, Arthur
Sloan, Matthew Scott
Sloan, Samuel
Smith, Alfred Holland
Smith, Francis Marion
Smith, John Walter
Spencer, Samuel
Sproule, William
Stanford, Leland
Stevens, Edwin
Augustus
Stickney, Alpheus Beede
Stilwell, Arthur Edward
Strong, William Barstow
Swann, Thomas
Thaw, William
Thomson, J. Edgar
Tod, David
Van Sweringen, Oris
Paxton, and Mantis
James Van Sweringen
Van Winkle, Peter
Godwin
Vanderbilt, Cornelius
Vanderbilt, Cornelius, II
Suppl. 1
Vanderbilt, William
Henry
Vanderbilt, William
Kissam
Villard, Henry
Westinghouse, George
Willard, Daniel
Wright, Charles Barstow
Young, Robert Ralph
Yulee, David Levy

Rubber Industry Leaders
Candee, Leverett
Colt, Samuel Pomeroy
Davis, Francis Breese, Jr.
Dodge, Theodore
Ayrault
Firestone, Harvey
Samuel
Flint, Charles Ranlett

Transportation (cont.)
Goodrich, Benjamin
  Franklin
Goodyear, Charles
Kimball, Dan Able
Litchfield, Paul Weeks
Seiberling, Franklin
  Augustus

Sailors
Attucks, Crispus
Ball, Charles
Barney, Joshua
Equiano, Olaudah
Miller, Dorie
Patten, Mary Ann
  Brown
Pinkney, Edward Coote
Ranger, Joseph
West, Joseph
Young, John
  (1744–1835)

Ship Captains
Álvarez de Pineda,
  Alonso
Barry, John
Boyle, Thomas
Coggeshall, George
Creesy, Josiah Perkins
Decatur, Stephen
  (1752–1808)
Delano, Amasa
Derby, Richard
Gosnold, Bartholomew
Hill, Richard
Low, Charles Porter
Malcom, Daniel
Merry, William
  Lawrence
Morrell, Benjamin
Newport, Christopher
Olmsted, Gideon
Pérez, Juan
Peirce, William
Pound, Thomas
Ribault, Jean
Riley, James
Rogers, Moses
Ropes, Joseph
Teach, Edward
Tucker, Samuel
Tyng, Edward
Waterman, Robert
  Henry
Wooster, Charles
  Whiting

Shipbuilders
Burns, Otway, Jr.
Claghorn, George

Cramp, William
Eckford, Henry
Gibbs, William Francis
Hall, Samuel
  (1800–1870)
Hichborn, Philip
Higgins, Andrew Jackson
Hunley, Horace L.
  Suppl. 2
McKay, Donald
Meserve, Nathaniel
Russell, Joseph
Sewall, Arthur
Slocum, Joshua
Webb, William Henry
Westervelt, Jacob Aaron

Shipping Industry Leaders
Barlow, Joel
Barnes, Julius Howland
Butterfield, John
Casey, James E.
Cheney, Benjamin Pierce
Collins, Edward Knight
Fargo, William George
Grady, Henry Francis
Hale, James Webster
Harriman, W. Averell
Holladay, Ben
Keith, Minor Cooper
King, William
Lamar, Gazaway Bugg
Low, Frederick
  Ferdinand
March, William
Marshall, Benjamin
Merry, William
  Lawrence
Moran, Eugene Francis
Myers, Isaac
Otero, Miguel Antonio
Paul, Josephine Bay
Plant, Henry Bradley
Powell, James Robert
Reeside, James
Roosevelt, Kermit
  (1889–1943)
Short, Robert Earl
Thaw, William
Thompson, Jeremiah
Ward, James Edward
White, Maunsel
Wilkeson, Samuel

*Stagecoach Company
Owners*
Cheney, Benjamin Pierce
Holladay, Ben
Reeside, James

Steamboat Captains / Pilots
Bixby, Horace Ezra
Grimes, Absalom
  Carlisle
Rogers, Moses
Sellers, Isaiah
Shreve, Henry Miller
Twain, Mark
Vanderbilt, Cornelius

*Steamboat Owners /
Operators*
Fitch, John
Fulton, Robert
Gibbons, Thomas
King, Richard
Lamar, Gazaway Bugg
Longstreet, William
Ogden, Aaron
Roosevelt, Nicholas J.
Stevens, John
Thaw, William
Vanderbilt, Cornelius
Yeatman, Thomas

Streetcar Company Owners
Calhoun, Patrick
Holladay, Ben
Johnson, Tom Loftin
Lowry, Thomas
Yerkes, Charles Tyson

Taxicab Company Owners
Hertz, John Daniel
Scull, Robert Cooper

Tramway Company Owners
Heineman, Daniel
  Webster

EDUCATION

Acting Teachers
Adler, Stella
Boleslavsky, Richard
  Valentinovich
Eytinge, Rose
Morgan, Anna
Strasberg, Lee

Art Teachers
Albers, Josef
Anshutz, Thomas
  Pollock
Bennett, Gwendolyn
Carles, Arthur B.
Chase, William Merritt
de Creeft, José
Douglas, Aaron
Eakins, Thomas
  Cowperthwait

Gutmann, Bernhard
Hale, Philip Leslie
Henri, Robert
Hofmann, Hans
Hoyte, Lenon *Suppl. 2*
Luks, George Benjamin
Marsh, Reginald
Miller, Kenneth Hayes
Moholy-Nagy, László
Pitman, Benn
Pyle, Howard
Rimmer, William
Saint-Gaudens,
  Augustus
Stevens, Will Henry
Sullivan, Mary Quinn
Tarbell, Edmund
  Charles
Weir, John Ferguson
Weir, Julian Alden
Weir, Robert Walter
Young, Mahonri
  Mackintosh

*Arts Organization
Administrators*
Batchelder, Alice
  Coleman
Becker, Marion
  Rombauer
Cornish, Nellie
  Centennial
Diller, Burgoyne
Europe, James Reese
Flanagan, Hallie Mae
  Ferguson
Hanks, Nancy
Johnston, Ella Bond
Jones, Margo
Koehler, Robert
Leatherman, LeRoy
Neuendorff, Adolph
  Heinrich Anton
  Magnus
Papp, Joseph
Rush, William
Sartain, Emily
Shelly, Mary Josephine
Spofford, Grace Harriet
Thompson, Helen Lena
  Mulford
Zimbalist, Mary Louise
  Curtis Bok

Dance Teachers
Albertieri, Luigi
Alexander, Dorothy
Balanchine, George
Bales, William
Beatty, Talley
Belcher, Ernest

Bolm, Adolph
Bonfanti, Maria
Camryn, Walter
Cansino, Angel
Celli, Vincenzo
Chalif, Louis Harvey
Christensen, Harold
Colby, Gertrude Kline
Craske, Margaret
Danielian, Leon *Suppl. 2*
Dollar, William
Duncan, Irma
Duport, Pierre Landrin
Englund, Richard
Fort, Syvilla
Gollner, Nana
Gould, Norma
Graham, Martha
Griffiths, John
Herman, Mary Ann
  Suppl. 2
Herman, Michael
  Suppl. 2
H'Doubler, Margaret
  Newell
Hill, Martha *Suppl. 2*
Holm, Hanya
Horst, Louis
Horton, Lester
Hovey, Henrietta
Ito, Michio
La Meri
Le Clercq, Tanaquil
  Suppl. 2
Loring, Eugene
Luahine, Iolani
Mansfield, Portia
Maracci, Carmelita
McRae, Edna
Moore, Charles *Suppl. 2*
Moore, Lillian
Murray, Arthur
Nijinska, Bronislava
Piro, Frank
Schollar, Ludmilla
Shook, Karel
Smith, George
  Washington
St. Denis, Ruth
Stebbins, Genevieve
Stone, Bentley
Trisler, Joyce
Van Tuyl, Marian
Wayburn, Ned
Weidman, Charles
  Edward, Jr.
Wells, Mary Ann
Williams, E. Virginia

Early Childhood Educators
Andrews, Jane

Arbuthnot, May Hill
Blaker, Eliza Ann
  Cooper
Bradley, Milton
Bryan, Anna E.
Cooke, Flora Juliette
Cooper, Sarah Brown
  Ingersoll
Dobbs, Ella Victoria
Fisher, Dorothy F.
  Canfield
Fuller, Sarah
Garrett, Mary Smith
Harrison, Elizabeth
Hill, Patty Smith
Huntington, Emily
Lax, Anneli *Suppl. 2*
Locke, Bessie
Marwedel, Emma
  Jacobina Christiana
Mitchell, Lucy Sprague
Moten, Lucy Ellen
Neef, Francis Joseph
  Nicholas
Putnam, Alice Harvey
  Whiting
Schurz, Margarethe
  Meyer
Sharp, Zerna Addas
Ueland, Clara Hampson
Wheelock, Lucy
White, Edna Noble

*Educational Institution
Officials*
Abbott, Jacob
Adams, John
  (1772–1863)
Adams, Numa
  Pompilius Garfield
Adams, William
Adler, Cyrus
Agassiz, Elizabeth Cabot
  Cary
Alden, Joseph
Alden, Timothy
Alderman, Edwin
  Anderson
Alison, Francis
Allen, William Henry
  (1808–1882)
Allyn, Robert
Ames, James Barr
Anderson, David
  Lawrence
Anderson, Martin
  Brewer
Anderson, Matthew
Andrews, Elisha
  Benjamin
Andrews, Lorin

Angell, James Rowland
Armstrong, Samuel
  Chapman
Atherton, George
  Washington
Aydelotte, Frank
Ayres, Leonard Porter
Baker, Daniel
Baker, Hugh Potter
Baker, James Hutchins
Ballou, Hosea, 2d
Barnard, Frederick
  Augustus Porter
Barnwell, Robert
  Woodward
Barr, Stringfellow
Barrett, Janie Porter
Barrows, John Henry
Bartlett, Samuel Colcord
Bascom, Henry
  Bidleman
Bascom, John
Battle, Kemp Plummer
Baugher, Henry Lewis
Beadle, George Wells
Beardshear, William
  Miller
Beman, Nathan Sidney
  Smith
Bennett, Henry Garland
Benton, Thomas Hart,
  Jr.
Benton, William
Berry, Edward Wilber
Bestor, Arthur Eugene
Birge, Edward Asahel
Blair, James
Blanchard, Jonathan
Blanding, Sarah Gibson
Blaustein, David
Bliss, Daniel
Bliss, Tasker Howard
Blunt, Katharine
Bogardus, Emory
  Stephen
Bogle, Sarah Comly
  Norris
Bolles, Frank
Bond, Horace Mann
Bowman, Isaiah
Bradley, Amy Morris
Branch, Mary Elizabeth
Branner, John Casper
Brewster, Kingman, Jr.
Briggs, LeBaron Russell
Brigham, Mary Ann
Brodbeck, May
Brown, Charlotte
  Eugenia Hawkins
Brown, Elmer Ellsworth

Brownell, Thomas
  Church
Brush, George Jarvis
Bryan, John Stewart
Bryan, William Lowe
Buchanan, Scott Milross
Buck, Paul Herman
Bulkley, John Williams
Burdick, Usher Lloyd
Burgess, John William
Burr, Aaron
  (1716–1757)
Burroughs, Nannie
  Helen
Burton, Marion LeRoy
Butler, Nicholas Murray
Butterfield, Kenyon
  Leech
Calkins, Norman Allison
Camm, John
Campbell, Prince Lucien
Campbell, William
  Henry
Capen, Samuel Paul
Capps, Edward
Cardozo, Francis Louis
Carmichael, Oliver
  Cromwell
Carrick, Samuel Czar
Caswell, Alexis
Caswell, Hollis Leland
Cattell, William Cassady
Cavanaugh, John Joseph
Chandler, Julian Alvin
  Carroll
Chauncy, Charles
  (1592–1672)
Church, Alonzo
  (1793–1862)
Clapp, Margaret
  Antoinette
Clark, Charles Edward
Clark, Mark Wayne
Clement, Rufus Early
Cleveland, Emeline
  Horton
Clewell, John Henry
Cohn, Fannia
Coit, Henry Augustus
Cole, Charles Woolsey
Comstock, Ada Louise
Conant, James Bryant
Cook, John Francis, Jr.
Cook, John Williston
Cook, Vivian E. J.
Cooper, Myles
Cope, Arthur Clay
Coppin, Fanny Jackson
Corby, William
Cotter, Joseph Seamon,
  Sr.

Councill, William
  Hooper
Cox, Samuel Hanson
Crary, Isaac Edwin
Craven, Braxton
Cronkhite, Bernice
  Brown
Cuthbert, Marion Vera
Cutler, Timothy
Dabney, Charles William
Dagg, John Leadley
Danforth, Thomas
Day, Jeremiah
De Koven, James
DeGarmo, Charles
Dennett, Tyler Wilbur
de Schweinitz, Edmund
  Alexander
Deutsch, Gotthard
Dickey, Sarah Ann
Dodds, Harold Willis
Douglass, Mabel Smith
Dow, Blanche Hinman
Duer, William Alexander
Dunster, Henry
Dwight, Sereno Edwards
Dwight, Timothy
Earle, Ralph
Eaton, Nathaniel
Edwards, Jonathan, Jr.
Eisenhower, Milton
  Stover
Eliot, Charles William
Eliot, William Greenleaf,
  Jr.
Elvehjem, Conrad
  Arnold
Ende, Amalie von
Ewell, Benjamin
  Stoddert
Fairchild, George
  Thompson
Fairchild, James Harris
Farrand, Livingston
Faruqi, Isma'il Raji al-
Faunce, William Herbert
  Perry
Felton, Cornelius
  Conway
Ferguson, John Calvin
Few, Ignatius Alphonso
Field, Jessie
Fine, Benjamin
Finley, Samuel
Finney, Charles
  Grandison
Fisk, Wilbur
Ford, Guy Stanton
Foster, William
  Hendrick
Fox, Dixon Ryan

Fred, Edwin Broun
Fromkin, Victoria A.
  Suppl. 1
Fulton, Robert Burwell
Gale, George
  Washington
Gasson, Thomas
  Ignatius
Gates, Caleb Frank
Giamatti, Bart
Gibbs, Jonathan C.
Gilbert, Helen Homans
Gildersleeve, Virginia
  Crocheron
Gill, Laura Drake
Gilman, Daniel Coit
Glueck, Nelson
Goodnow, Frank
  Johnson
Gould, Laurence
  McKinley
Gove, Aaron Estellus
Graham, Frank Porter
Grant, Zilpah Polly
Greene, Jerome Davis
Gregg, John Andrew
Griswold, Alfred
  Whitney
Gross, Paul Magnus
Gulliver, Julia Henrietta
Hadley, Arthur Twining
Hall, Charles Cuthbert
Hardenbergh, Jacob
  Rutsen
Harnwell, Gaylord
  Probasco
Harper, William Rainey
Harris, John Howard
Hart, James D.
Haygood, Atticus
  Greene
Hazard, Caroline
Healy, Patrick Francis
Hentz, Nicholas
  Marcellus
Hibben, John Grier
Hill, Daniel Harvey
Hill, David Jayne
Hill, Thomas
Hitchcock, Roswell
  Dwight
Hoar, Leonard
Holland, Annie Welthy
  Daughtry
Holley, Horace
Holt, Hamilton Bowen
Hopkins, Isaac Stiles
Hopkins, Mark
Horrocks, James
Houghton, Henry
  Spencer

Houston, David Franklin
Howard, Oliver Otis
Humphrey, Heman
Hunt, Henry Alexander,
  Jr.
Hunter, Thomas
Hutchins, Robert
  Maynard
Hyde, William DeWitt
Irwin, Agnes
Jacobson, John Christian
James, Edmund Janes
Jardine, William Marion
Jarrell, Helen Ira
Jay, Allen
Jessup, Walter Albert
Jewett, Milo Parker
Johnson, Mordecai
  Wyatt
Johnson, Samuel
Johnston, William
  Preston
Jordan, David Starr
Judson, Harry Pratt
Junkin, George
Kelly, Robert Lincoln
Kephart, Ezekiel Boring
Keppel, Francis C.
Kildahl, John Nathan
King, Charles
King, Stanley
Kirkland, James
  Hampton
Knapp, Seaman Asahel
Kroeger, Alice Bertha
Landis, James McCauley
Langdon, Samuel
Lange, Alexis Frederick
Leggett, Mortimer
  Dormer
Leverett, John
  (1662–1724)
Lewis, Samuel B.
Lindsley, Philip
Little, Charles Joseph
Little, Clarence Cook
Lloyd, Alfred Henry
Longstreet, Augustus
  Baldwin
Low, Seth
Lowell, A. Lawrence
Lyon, Mary
MacAlister, James
MacCracken, Henry
  Noble
Maddison, Isabel
Madison, James
  (1749–1812)
Magill, Edward Hicks
Magnes, Judah Leon

Magoun, George
  Frederic
Main, John Hanson
  Thomas
Maltby, Margaret Eliza
Mannes, Clara
  Damrosch
Manning, James
Marshall, Louis
  (1773–1866)
Maxcy, Jonathan
Maxwell, William Henry
Mays, Benjamin Elijah
McBride, Katharine
  Elizabeth
McCormick, Samuel
  Black
McCrady, Edward
McKeen, Joseph
McNair, Lesley James
Mead, Elizabeth Storrs
  Billings
Meiklejohn, Alexander
Mennin, Peter
Meyer, Annie Nathan
Middleton, William
  Shainline
Milledoler, Philip
Miller, Thomas Ezekiel
Mills, Susan Lincoln
  Tolman
Minor, Benjamin Blake
Moore, Zephaniah Swift
Morais, Sabato
Morgan, Agnes Fay
Morgan, Arthur Ernest
Morgan, Mary Kimball
Morrison, Nathan
  Jackson
Morton, Henry
Muhlenberg, Frederick
  Augustus
Murray, David
Neilson, William Allan
Nichols, Ernest Fox
Nott, Eliphalet
Oakes, Urian
Olin, Stephen
Otey, James Hervey
Oxnam, Garfield
  Bromley
Painter, Theophilus
  Shickel
Palmer, Alice Elvira
  Freeman
Parker, Francis Wayland
Parrish, Celestia
  Susannah
Parrish, Edward
Payne, Daniel Alexander

Peabody, Endicott *Suppl. 1*
Pease, Arthur Stanley
Pegram, George Braxton
Peirce, James Mills
Pendleton, Ellen Fitz
Phelps, Almira Hart Lincoln
Pierce, Sarah
Pillsbury, John Sargent
Porter, John Addison
Porter, Noah
Potter, Eliphalet Nott
Preston, William Campbell
Pritchett, Henry Smith
Pugh, Evan
Pusey, Nathan *Suppl. 2*
Quincy, Josiah (1772–1864)
Raymond, John Howard
Revels, Hiram Rhoades
Rhees, Rush
Ricketts, Palmer Chamberlaine
Rivera, Tomás
Rogers, John Almanza Rowley
Rosenberry, Lois Carter Kimball Mathews
Ruderman, Yaakov Yitzchak
Russell, Harry Luman
Russell, James Earl
Russell, James Solomon
Ryland, Robert
Sabin, Ellen Clara
Sanchez, George Isidore
Sanders, Daniel Clarke
Sanford, Edmund Clark
Sanford, Terry *Suppl. 1*
Schiff, Leonard Isaac
Schuman, William Howard
Scott, Emmett Jay
Seelye, Julius Hawley
Seldes, Gilbert Vivian
Seymour, Charles
Sharp, Zerna Addas
Sharpless, Isaac
Simmons, William James
Smith, Courtney C. *Suppl. 2*
Smith, Samuel Stanhope
Spencer, Matthew Lyle
Sproul, Robert Gordon
Stebbins, Horatio
Stiles, Ezra
Straus, Roger Williams
Sturtevant, Julian Monson

Summerall, Charles Pelot
Swain, David Lowry
Swain, Joseph
Talbot, Israel Tisdale
Talbot, Marion
Tappan, Henry Philip
Thacher, Thomas Anthony
Thurston, Matilda Smyrell Calder
Thwing, Charles Franklin
Tichenor, Isaac Taylor
Trueblood, Benjamin Franklin *Suppl. 2*
Tucker, William Jewett
Tugwell, Rexford Guy
Van Amringe, John Howard
Van Hise, Charles Richard
Vashon, George Boyer
Waddel, John Newton
Waddel, Moses
Walker, James
Warren, William Fairfield
Washburn, George
Wayland, Francis
Wearn, Joseph T.
Weed, Ella
Wesley, Charles Harris
Wheelock, John
White, Andrew Dickson
Whitehead, John Boswell
Whitsitt, William Heth
Wiesner, Jerome Bert
Wilbur, Earl Morse
Wilbur, Ray Lyman
Willard, Emma Hart
Willard, Joseph
Willey, Samuel Hopkins
Williams, Jonathan
Williams, Nathaniel
Wirt, William Albert
Witherspoon, John
Woolsey, Theodore Dwight
Wriston, Henry Merritt
Wylie, Andrew
Zollars, Ely Vaughn
Zook, George Frederick

Educators
Abbot, Gorham Dummer
Abbott, Edith
Adams, Herbert Baxter
Ain, Gregory *Suppl. 1*

Akeley, Mary Leonore Jobe
Albee, Ernest
Alberty, Harold Bernard
Alexander, Joseph Addison
Allen, Alexander Viets Griswold
Allen, William G.
Allen, William Henry (1808–1882)
Allen, Young John William
Allinson, Anne Crosby Emery
Alston, Melvin Ovenus
Amberg, George
American, Sadie
Ames, Van Meter
Andrews, Eliza Frances
Andrews, George Leonard
Andrews, Lorrin
Andrus, Ethel Percy
Angela, Mother
Angell, James Burrill
Anneke, Mathilde Franziska Giesler
Armour, Richard Willard
Arnett, Benjamin William
Arvin, Newton
Atkins, Mary
Atwater, Lyman Hotchkiss
Atwater, Wilbur Olin
Ayres, Clarence Edwin
Backus, Truman Jay
Bacon, Alice Mabel
Bacon, Benjamin Wisner
Bacon, Leonard
Bagley, William Chandler
Bailey, Ebenezer
Baker, Carlos Heard
Baker, George Pierce
Baker, Osmon Cleander
Baltzell, E. Digby *Suppl. 1*
Bancroft, Cecil Franklin Patch
Bapst, John
Barber, Francis
Barbour, Clarence Augustus
Bard, Samuel
Bardin, Shlomo
Barker, Mary Cornelia
Barnard, Henry
Barnes, Albert Coombs

Barnes, Mary Downing Sheldon
Baron, Salo Wittmayer
Barr, Amelia Edith Huddleston
Barr, Stringfellow
Barton, George Aaron
Bates, Ernest Sutherland *Suppl. 1*
Bates, Katharine Lee
Battle, Kemp Plummer
Bauer, Catherine Krouse
Baugher, Henry Lewis
Beach, Harlan Page
Beach, Joseph Warren
Beckwith, Martha Warren
Beecher, Catharine Esther
Bell, Alexander Graham
Bellamy, Elizabeth Whitfield Croom
Bellini, Carlo
Benezet, Anthony
Bennett, John Cook
Benson, Oscar Herman
Berkson, Isaac Baer
Bettelheim, Bruno
Bickmore, Albert Smith
Bingham, Caleb
Bingham, Sybil Moseley
Bishop, Morris Gilbert
Bishop, Robert Hamilton
Bissell, Richard Mervin, Jr.
Bixler, Julius Seelye
Blackwell, Randolph Talmadge
Blake, Harrison Gray Otis
Blaker, Eliza Ann Cooper
Blanshard, Brand
Blau, Joseph Leon
Bledsoe, Albert Taylor
Blegen, Carl William
Bleyer, Willard Grosvenor
Bloch, Ernest
Blumer, Herbert George
Blunt, Katharine
Bobbitt, Franklin
Bode, Boyd Henry
Bond, Horace Mann
Bonner, Marita Odette
Bonney, Mary Lucinda
Borchardt, Selma Munter
Boswell, John Eastburn
Botta, Anne Charlotte

Bouchet, Edward Alexander

Bouvet, Marie Marguerite

Bowden, John

Bowen, Norman Levi

Bowne, Borden Parker

Boyesen, Hjalmar Hjorth

Boyle, Kay

Brackett, Anna Callender

Bradley, Amy Morris

Bradley, Charles Henry

Brameld, Theodore Burghard Hurt

Brawley, Benjamin Griffith

Breaux, Joseph Arsenne

Breckinridge, Robert Jefferson

Brickman, William Wolfgang

Briggs, LeBaron Russell

Brinton, Howard Haines, and Anna Shipley Cox Brinton

Brinton, Clarence Crane

Broadus, John Albert

Brodbeck, May

Brodie, Fawn McKay

Brooks, Cleanth

Brown, Charles Reynolds

Brown, Elmer Ellsworth

Brown, Emma V.

Brown, Hallie Quinn

Brown, Josephine Chapin

Brown, Samuel Robbins

Brown, Sterling Allen

Brown, Willa *Suppl. 2*

Brucker, Herbert

Buck, Carl Darling

Bulkley, John Williams

Bundy, Elroy Lorraine

Burnham, William Henry

Burns, James Aloysius

Burr, George Lincoln

Butler, James

Butler, Lee Pierce

Butler, Nicholas Murray

Byerly, William Elwood

Cabrini, Frances Xavier

Caldwell, David

Calkins, Norman Allison

Camm, John

Campbell, James Edwin

Campbell, Joseph

Campbell, Lucie E.

Canby, Henry Seidel

Candler, Warren Akin

Cardozo, Michael H. *Suppl. 2*

Carnell, Edward John

Carpenter, Rhys

Carroll, Mother Austin

Carter, Jesse Benedict

Cary, Mary Ann Camberton Shadd

Caswell, Hollis Leland

Chávez, Carlos

Chadwick, George Whitefield

Chamberlain, Joshua Lawrence

Charters, W. W.

Chase, Mary Ellen

Chavis, John

Church, Alonzo (1793–1862)

Clapp, Elsie Ripley

Clark, Peter Humphries

Clark, Septima Poinsette

Clark, Walter Van Tilburg

Clark, William Bullock

Clebsch, William Anthony

Clifford, James Lowry

Cloud, Henry Roe

Cobb, Cully Alton

Cobb, Lyman

Coerne, Louis Adolphe

Coffin, Robert Peter Tristram

Coffman, Lotus Delta

Cohen, Morris Raphael

Coit, Eleanor Gwinnell

Coker, Daniel

Colby, Gertrude Kline

Colton, Elizabeth Avery

Comey, Dennis J. *Suppl. 1*

Commager, Henry Steele *Suppl. 1*

Comstock, Anna Botsford

Conkling, Grace Walcott Hazard

Converse, Frederick Shepherd

Cook, George William

Cook, John Williston

Cook, Vivian E. J.

Cooper, Anna Julia Haywood

Cooper, Jacob

Cooper, Sarah Brown Ingersoll

Cooper, William John

Copeland, Charles Townsend

Cornish, Nellie Centennial

Corson, Juliet

Coulter, Ellis Merton

Covello, Leonard

Cowles, Betsey Mix

Craft, Ellen

Crandall, Prudence

Crane, Thomas Frederick

Craven, Wesley F.

Creighton, James Edwin

Cremin, Lawrence Arthur

Cret, Paul Philippe

Crocker, Lucretia

Cross, Arthur Lyon

Crozet, Claudius

Cubberley, Ellwood Patterson

Curme, George Oliver

Curry, Daniel

Cuthbert, Marion Vera

Da Ponte, Lorenzo

Davidson, Donald Grady

Davidson, James Wood

Davies, Samuel

Davis, Jerome Dean

Davis, Paulina Kellogg Wright

Davis, Raymond Cazallis

Davis, Richard Beale

Dawson, William

Day, Caroline Stewart Bond

Day, Jeremiah

Day, William Howard

Dean, Vera Micheles

de Cleyre, Voltairine

DeGarmo, Charles

Delany, Annie Elizabeth "Bessie", and Sarah Louise "Sadie" Delany *Suppl. 1*

de Lima, Agnes Abinun

Dempster, John

de Schweinitz, Karl

Dett, R. Nathaniel

Deutsch, Gotthard

Dew, Thomas Roderick

Dewey, Alice Chipman

Dewey, John

Dewing, Arthur Stone

Dexter, Franklin Bowditch

De Zavala, Adina Emily

Diaz, Abby Morton

Dickinson, John Woodbridge

Dickson, Samuel Henry

Dillard, James Hardy

Diller, Angela

Doak, Samuel

Dobie, James Frank

Dodds, Harold Willis

Donovan, James Britt

Dorsey, Susan Almira Miller

Douglas, Paul Howard

Douglass, Sarah Mapps

Dow, Blanche Hinman

Doyle, Sarah Elizabeth

DuBose, William Porcher

DuBourg, Louis William Valentine

Dubbs, Joseph Henry

Dubois, John

Ducasse, Curt John

Duffy, Francis Patrick

Dykes, Eva Beatrice

Eaton, Walter Prichard

Eckstein, Otto

Edman, Irwin

Eliot, Charles William

Eliot, Samuel

Elliott, Aaron Marshall

Elliott, Harriet Wiseman

Elliott, John Lovejoy

Emerson, George Barrell

Emerson, Joseph

Emerson, Mary Moody

Emerton, Ephraim

Fainsod, Merle

Fairchild, George Thompson

Fairchild, James Harris

Fall, Bernard B.

Farmer, James *Suppl. 1*

Fauset, Jessie Redmon

Fay, Sidney Bradshaw

Feibleman, James Kern

Fenner, Erasmus Darwin

Ferguson, Katy

Fieser, Louis Frederick

Fillmore, John Comfort

Fincke, William M. *Suppl. 2*

Finley, John Huston

Firth, Roderick

Fischer, Irwin

Fish, Carl Russell

Fisher, Ada Lois Sipuel

Fiske, Fidelia

Fite, Warner

Fithian, Philip Vickers

Flanagan, Hallie Mae Ferguson

Flexner, Helen Thomas

Flexner, Jennie Maas

Flynt, Henry

Foerster, Norman
Folwell, William Watts
Foster, Frank Hugh
Foster, George Burman
Foster, William Trufant
Fowle, William Bentley
Francis, Convers
Frazier, Maude
Frelinghuysen, Theodore
Freund, Ernst
Friedlaender, Israel
Fry, Joshua
Fry, Varian *Suppl. 2*
Fuller, Thomas Oscar
Fulton, Robert Burwell
Galbreath, Charles
  Burleigh
Gardner, John
Garfield, Harry
  Augustus
Garman, Charles
  Edward
Garnet, Sarah Smith
  Tompkins
Garreau, Armand
Gassner, John Waldhorn
Gatzke, Hans Wilhelm
Gauss, Christian
  Frederick
Gerhart, Emanuel Vogel
Gerould, Katharine
  Fullerton
Gill, Mother Irene
Gillett, Emma Millinda
Gilman, Arthur
Ginsberg, Allen *Suppl. 1*
Goldman, Eric
Goldsmith, Grace
  Arabell
Good, James Isaac
Goodnow, Frank
  Johnson
Goodrich, Carter
Goodrich, Chauncey
  Allen
Goodspeed, Thomas
  Wakefield
Goodwin, William
  Watson
Gordin, Jacob
Gordon, Caroline
  Ferguson
Gordy, John Pancoast
Gottheil, Richard James
  Horatio
Goucher, John Franklin
Gould, James
Gouldner, Alvin Ward
Grattan, Clinton Hartley
Gratz, Rebecca
Gray, William Scott, Jr.

Green, Beriah
Green, Edith
Greene, George
  Washington
Greener, Richard
  Theodore
Greenlaw, Edwin
  Almiron
Gregory, John
Grew, Theophilus
Grimké, Angelina Weld
Grimké, Charlotte
  Forten
Grimké, Sarah Moore
Griswold, Alfred
  Whitney
Gropius, Walter
Gros, John Daniel
Gruenberg, Sidonie
  Matsner
Guérin, Anne-Thérèse
Guilday, Peter Keenan
Gunsaulus, Frank
  Wakeley
Guyot, Arnold Henry
H'Doubler, Margaret
  Newell
Hadas, Moses
Haddock, Charles
  Brickett
Hadley, Herbert Spencer
Haid, Leo Michael
Halsted, George Bruce
Hamilton, Clayton
Hamilton, Earl Jefferson
Hamilton, Edith
Hamlin, Alfred Dwight
  Foster
Hamlin, Talbot Faulkner
Hanby, Benjamin Russel
Hanus, Paul Henry
Haring, Clarence Henry
Harpur, Robert
Harris, Abram Lincoln,
  Jr.
Harris, John Howard
Harris, Samuel
Harris, Seymour Edwin
Harris, William Torrey
Hart, James Morgan
Hart, Joseph Kinmont
Hartshorne, Henry
Haskins, Charles Homer
Hatathli, Ned
Hayden, Mother Bridget
Hayden, Robert Earl
Hays, Paul Raymond
Heald, Henry Townley
Hedge, Frederic Henry
Hedge, Levi
Heiss, Michael

Henry, Caleb Sprague
Herrick, Robert Welch
Hewett, Edgar Lee
Hibben, John Grier
Higman, Howard
  Suppl. 1
Hinton, Carmelita Chase
Hocking, William Ernest
Hodges, George
Hoffman, Frederick John
Holley, Sallie
Hoover, Calvin Bryce
Hope, Lugenia D. Burns
Hovey, Henrietta
Howard, Ada Lydia
Howard, Timothy
  Edward
Howe, George
  (1802–1883)
Howison, George
  Holmes
Howland, Emily
Hubbell, Jay Broadus
Huberman, Leo
Huebner, Solomon
  Stephen
Hughan, Jessie Wallace
Hume, Samuel James
Hundley, Mary Gibson
  Brewer
Hung, William
Hunt, Carleton
Hunton, Addie D.
  Waites
Hutchins, Harry Burns
Hutchins, Margaret
Iddings, Joseph Paxson
Inglis, Alexander James
Irwin, Agnes
Irwin, Elisabeth
  Antoinette
Irwin, Robert Benjamin
Jacobson, John Christian
James, Thomas C.
Jameson, John Franklin
Jarrell, Helen Ira
Jarrett, Mary Cromwell
Jessup, Walter Albert
Jewett, Milo Parker
Johnson, Allan Chester
Johnson, Alvin Saunders
Johnson, Bushrod Rust
Johnson, Charles
  Spurgeon
Johnson, Edward Austin
Johnson, Joseph French
Johnson, Richard W.
Johnston, Ella Bond
Johnston, Richard
  Malcolm
Jones, Charles Colcock

Jones, Howard Mumford
Jordan, Barbara *Suppl. 1*
Jordan, Mary Augusta
Judson, Harry Pratt
Kagen, Sergius
Kallen, Horace Meyer
Kefauver, Grayson
  Neikirk
Keller, Fred S. *Suppl. 2*
Kelly, Myra
Keppel, Frederick Paul
Kessen, William *Suppl. 1*
Kilpatrick, William
  Heard
King, Henry Churchill
Kinnersley, Ebenezer
Kirchwey, George
  Washington
Kirkland, James
  Hampton
Kittredge, George
  Lyman
Knopf, Adolph
Koch, Adrienne
Koch, Frederick Henry
Koch, Vivienne
Kohut, Rebekah
  Bettelheim
Kraemer, Henry
Krause, Herbert Arthur
Krauth, Charles Philip
Krauth, Charles
  Porterfield
Krech, David
Kremers, Edward
Kuykendall, Ralph
  Simpson
Ladd, Catherine Stratton
Lane, James Henry
  (1833–1907)
Laney, Lucy Craft
Lange, Mary Elizabeth
Langer, William
  Leonard
Langston, Charles Henry
Langworthy, Edward
Lanman, Charles
  Rockwell
Lanusse, Armand
Larrazolo, Octaviano
  Ambrosio
Lax, Anneli *Suppl. 2*
Lazerowitz, Morris
Le Sueur, Marian
Lee, George Washington
  Custis
Lee, James Melvin
Lee, Porter Raymond
Lee, Stephen Dill
Lee, Ulysses Grant
Leipziger, Henry Marcus

Leith, Charles Kenneth
Leonard, Robert Josselyn
Leonard, Sterling
  Andrus
Lerner, Max
Levenson, Sam
Lieber, Francis
Lilienthal, Max
Lincoln, Mary Johnson
  Bailey
Lindeman, Eduard
  Christian
Lingelbach, Anna Lane
Lloyd, Alice Spencer
  Geddes
Lloyd-Jones, Eleanor,
  and Jane Lloyd-Jones
Lockwood, Belva Ann
  Bennett McNall
Logan, Rayford
  Whittingham
Longfellow, Henry
  Wadsworth
Lord, Asa Dearborn
Lovell, John
Lovett, Robert Morss
Lowell, Robert Traill
  Spence
Lusk, Georgia Lee Witt
MacAlister, James
MacCracken, Henry
  Mitchell
MacCracken, Henry
  Noble
Macgowan, Kenneth
Machen, J. Gresham
Mackay, John Alexander
Maclean, Norman
MacLeish, Martha
  Hillard
Maier, Walter Arthur
Maisch, John Michael
Malone, John Walter
Maltby, Margaret Eliza
Malter, Henry
Mandelbaum, Maurice
  H.
Manly, John Matthews
Mannes, David
Mansfield, Portia
Marcuse, Herbert
Marden, Charles Carroll
Marsh, James
Martin, Everett Dean
Martin, William
  Alexander Parsons
Mason, Lowell
Mathews, Shailer
Mathews, W. S. B.
Matthews, Brander
Matthiessen, F. O.

Mattingly, Garrett
Maxwell, William Henry
Mayes, Edward
Mayo, George Elton
Mazzuchelli, Samuel
  Charles
McAndrew, William
McClellan, George
  Brinton
McClintock, John
McCorkle, Samuel
  Eusebius
McCosh, James
McDowell, John
McGroarty, Sister Julia
McGuffey, William
  Holmes
McIver, Charles Duncan
McNicholas, John
  Timothy
McQuaid, Bernard John
Mead, Elizabeth Storrs
  Billings
Meigs, Josiah
Mercer, Margaret
Messer, Asa
Messersmith, George
  Strausser
Meyer, Lucy Jane Rider
Middleton, William
  Shainline
Miles, Josephine Suppl. 1
Miller, Dickinson
  Sergeant
Miller, Emily Clark
  Huntington
Miller, Kelly
Miller, Lewis Suppl. 2
Miller, Samuel
Millett, Fred Benjamin
Mills, Elijah Hunt
Mills, Susan Lincoln
  Tolman
Miner, Sarah Luella
Mitchell, Lucy Sprague
Mitchell, Maria
Mizener, Arthur Moore
Moley, Raymond
Monis, Judah
Monroe, Paul
Monroe, Will Seymour
Montague, William
  Pepperell
Moody, William Vaughn
Moore, Charles Herbert
Moore, Harry Tyson
Morison, Samuel Eliot
Moron, Alonzo
  Graseano Suppl. 2
Morris, Edward Dafydd
Morrison, Henry Clinton

Morton, Charles
Mott, Frank Luther
Murdock, George Peter
Murie, James Rolfe
Muzzey, David Saville
Nash, Philleo
Niebuhr, H. Richard
Norris, Mary Harriott
Northen, William
  Jonathan
Norton, Alice Peloubet
Notestein, Wallace
Nutting, Mary Adelaide
Nyswander, Dorothy B.
  Suppl. 1
O'Conor, John F. X.
  Suppl. 2
Odell, George C. D.
O'Hara, Edwin Vincent
Olsson, Olof
Ordronaux, John
Orr, Gustavus John
Orton, George
  Washington
Osborn, Sarah Haggar
  Wheaten
Packard, Silas Sadler
Packard, Sophia Betsey
Paine, John Knowles
Palmer, Alice Elvira
  Freeman
Palmer, George Herbert
Parker, Horatio William
Parker, Willard
Parkhurst, Helen
Parks, Oliver Lafayette
Parloa, Maria
Parrish, Celestia
  Susannah
Parrish, Edward
Partridge, Alden
Patri, Angelo
Pattee, Fred Lewis
Payne, William Morton
Peabody, Andrew
  Preston
Peabody, Elizabeth
  Palmer
Peabody, Francis
  Greenwood
Pearson, Eliphalet
Peck, John Mason
Peirce, Cyrus
Peirce, James Mills
Peixotto, Jessica Blanche
Perkins, Dexter Suppl. 1
Perry, Ralph Barton
Peter, Laurence Johnston
Pettingill, Olin Sewall, Jr.
  Suppl. 2
Pettit, Katherine Rhoda

Phelps, Austin
Phelps, William Franklin
Phelps, William Lyon
Plato, Ann Suppl. 2
Plummer, Mary Wright
Pollyblank, Ellen
  Albertina
Pommerel, Celestine
Pormort, Philemon
Porter, Andrew
Porter, Eliza Emily
  Chappell
Porter, Noah
Porter, Sarah
Pottle, Frederick Albert
Presser, Theodore
Price, William
  Thompson
Priestley, Joseph
Procter, William, Jr.
Pugh, Sarah
Purnell, William Henry
Putnam, Caroline F.
Rölvaag, Ole Edvart
Rafferty, Max
Rand, Edward Kennard
Randall, John Herman,
  Jr.
Randolph, Sarah
  Nicholas
Rauch, Frederick
  Augustus
Rautenstrauch, Walter
Ray, Charles Bennett
Ray, Gordon Norton
Raymond, George
  Lansing
Rayner, John Baptis
Reason, Charles Lewis
Redding, J. Saunders
Reed, Henry Hope
Reid, Ira De Augustine
Reilly, Marion
Reinsch, Paul Samuel
Reischauer, Edwin
  Oldfather
Reynolds, Bertha Capen
Rice, John Andrew
Richard, Gabriel
Richards, I. A.
Richardson, Anna
  Euretta
Richter, Curt Paul
Ricord, Frederick
  William
Riley, Isaac Woodbridge
Ripley, Sarah Alden
  Bradford
Roback, A. A.
Robb, Isabel Hampton
Roberts, Lydia Jane

Robie, Thomas
Robinson, Edgar
  Munson
Robinson, James Harvey
Rogers, Elizabeth Ann
Root, Azariah Smith
Rorer, Sarah Tyson
Rosen, George
Rossiter, Clinton
  Lawrence, III
Rowson, Susanna
  Haswell
Royce, Sarah Eleanor
  Bayliss
Rugg, Harold Ordway
Rutherford, Mildred
  Lewis
Rutledge, Archibald
Sabin, Ellen Clara
Sachs, Julius
Sachs, Paul Joseph
Sage, Margaret Olivia
  Slocum
Sampter, Jessie Ethel
Sanford, Maria Louise
Sargent, Irene Jesse
Sartain, Emily
Scammell, Alexander
Schneider, Herbert
  Wallace
Schofield, Martha
Schorer, Mark
Schuschnigg, Kurt Alois
  Josef Johann von
Scopes, John Thomas
Scudder, Vida Dutton
Seeger, Charles
Seligman, Edwin Robert
  Anderson
Sellars, Roy Wood
Sewall, May Eliza
  Wright
Seward, Theodore
  Frelinghuysen
Shanker, Albert *Suppl. 1*
Shannon, Fred Albert
Sharp, Katharine
  Lucinda
Shepard, Odell
Shera, Jesse Hauk
Sherman, Stuart Pratt
Sherwood, Thomas
  Kilgore
Short, Charles
Shuster, George
  Nauman
Sigel, Franz
Sill, Edward Rowland
Skinner, Clarence
  Russell
Sledd, Andrew

Slowe, Lucy Diggs
Smart, James Henry
Smith, Charles Alphonso
Smith, Courtney C.
  Suppl. 2
Smith, David Eugene
Smith, Francis Henney
Smith, Hilda Jane
  Worthington
Smith, Judson
Smith, Lucy Harth
Smith, William
  (1727–1803)
Smith, William Waugh
Snow, Wilbert
Soldan, Frank Louis
Spalding, Henry
  Stanislaus *Suppl. 2*
Spalding, Lyman
Spencer, Anna Garlin
Spencer, Anne
Spencer, Platt Rogers
Spofford, Grace Harriet
Stanley, Albert Augustus
Stanley, Sara G.
Stearns, Marshall
  Winslow
Stegner, Wallace Earle
Sterling, John Whalen
Stevens, William Oliver
Steward, Theophilus
  Gould
Stewart, Alexander Peter
Stewart, George Rippey
Stewart, Maria W.
Stockbridge, Levi
  Suppl. 2
Stockton, Betsey
Stoddard, Charles
  Warren
Stokes, Anson Phelps
Stone, Barton Warren
Stouppe, Pierre *Suppl. 2*
Stowe, Calvin Ellis
Straight, Dorothy Payne
  Whitney
Strang, Ruth May
Strauss, Leo
Strunk, William, Jr.
  Suppl. 1
Sutton, William Seneca
Suzzallo, Henry
Swett, John
Sydnor, Charles Sackett
Syrkin, Marie
Taft, Jessie
Taylor, Alrutheus
  Ambush
Taylor, Fred Manville
Taylor, Nathaniel
  William

Taylor, Peter Hillsman
Tenney, Charles Daniel
Terman, Frederick
  Emmons
Terrell, Mary Eliza
  Church
Thach, Charles Coleman
Thacher, Thomas
  Anthony
Thayer, Amos Madden
Thayer, Sylvanus
Thilly, Frank
Thomas, Dorothy
  Swaine
Thomas, M. Carey
Thompson, Hugh Smith
Thompson, Randall
Thornwell, James Henley
Ticknor, George
Titchener, Edward
  Bradford
Tolson, Melvin
  Beaunorus
Tompson, Benjamin
Torrey, Charles Cutler
Tourjée, Eben
Towle, Charlotte Helen
Towne, Laura Matilda
Trapp, Maria von
Treadwell, Daniel
Trent, William Peterfield
Tucker, William Jewett
Turner, James Milton
Tutwiler, Julia Strudwick
Tuve, Rosemond
Tyler, William Seymour
Upham, Thomas
  Cogswell
Van Amringe, John
  Howard
Van de Velde, James
  Oliver
Van Doren, Carl
Van Doren, Mark
Varela y Morales, Felix
  Francisco
Vashon, George Boyer
Vasiliev, Alexander
  Alexandrovich
Vincent, George Edgar
Vincent, John Heyl
Wade, John Donald
Wait, Samuel
Walker, Amasa
Walker, Francis Amasa
Walker, Maggie L.
  Suppl. 2
Walsh, Edmund
  Aloysius
Ward, John William
Ware, Henry

Warren, Caroline
  Matilda
Warren, Robert Penn
Washington, Booker T.
Washington, Margaret
  Murray *Suppl. 2*
Watson, Goodwin
  Barbour
Weaver, Robert C.
  Suppl. 2
Webb, Frank J. *Suppl. 2*
Webster, John White
Weed, Ella
Welch, Adonijah Strong
Weld, Theodore Dwight
Wertenbaker, Thomas
  Jefferson
Wertheimer, Barbara
  Mayer
Wesley, Charles Harris
Wheeler, Benjamin Ide
White, Emerson
  Elbridge
White, Frances Emily
White, Helen Constance
White, Helen Magill
White, Minor
Whittaker, Johnson
  Chesnut
Wiener, Leo
Wiggin, Kate Douglas
Wildavsky, Aaron
  Bernard
Willard, Frances
  Elizabeth Caroline
Willard, James Field
Willard, Solomon
Willett, Herbert
  Lockwood
Williams, Lucelia Electa
Willier, Benjamin
  Harrison
Wilson, William Lyne
Wimsatt, W. K.
Winslow, Ola Elizabeth
Wirth, Louis
Wolbach, S. Burt
Wolfson, Theresa
Wood, George Bacon
Wood, Mary Elizabeth
Woodberry, George
  Edward
Woodbridge, Frederick
  James Eugene
Woodbridge, William
  Channing
Woodbury, Isaac Baker
Woods, Robert Archey
Woolley, Mary Emma
Woolman, Mary
  Raphael Schenck

Woolsey, Abby Howland
Wright, Richard Robert, Sr.
Wright, Sela Goodrich
Wright, Sophie Bell
Wright, Theodore Paul
Yates, Josephine A.
Yellow Robe, Rosebud *Suppl. 2*
Young, Allyn Abbott
Young, Ella Flagg
Yung Wing
Zachos, John Celivergos
Zirbes, Laura
Zuber, Paul Burgess

Lecturers

Adamski, George
Avery, Martha Gallison Moore
Bacon, Alice Mabel
Bangs, John Kendrick
Banning, Margaret Culkin
Beard, Frank
Bell, James Madison
Bibb, Henry Walton
Blashfield, Edwin Howland
Brown, Hallie Quinn
Brown, John (1810?–1876)
Brown, John Mason, Jr.
Brown, William Wells
Burleigh, Charles Calistus
Burnett, Alfred
Chew, Ng Poon
Clarke, Lewis G.
Coffin, Charles Carleton
Conwell, Russell Herman
Cook, Joseph
Cooke, George Willis
Copway, George
Couzins, Phoebe Wilson
Craft, William
de Cleyre, Voltairine
Devine, Edward Thomas
Dickinson, Anna Elizabeth
Dods, John Bovee
Emerson, Ralph Waldo
Ende, Amalie von
Fields, James Thomas *Suppl. 2*
Fine, Benjamin
Fiske, John (1842–1901)
Fuller, R. Buckminster
Gage, Frances Dana Barker

Gestefeld, Ursula Newell
Goldsmith, Joel Sol
Gougar, Helen Mar Jackson
James, Henry (1811–1882)
Johnson, Osa
Jones, Jane Elizabeth
Keller, Helen
King, Thomas Starr
Kinnersley, Ebenezer
Lowell, Amy
Mitchel, Ormsby Macknight
Morris, Robert (1818–1888)
Newman, Angelia French
Newton, Joseph Fort
Pollock, Channing
Pratt, Daniel (1809–1887)
Rohde, Ruth Bryan Owen
Rukeyser, Merryle Stanley
Salter, William Mackintire
Sampson, Deborah
Sanford, Maria Louise
Sawyer, Ruth
Seton, Ernest Thompson
Sheed, Francis Joseph
Smith, Elizabeth Oakes
Spencer, Archibald
Stearns, Lutie Eugenia
Stefansson, Vilhjalmur
Stone, Horatio
Thompson, Clara Ann
Thompson, Oscar
Thompson, Priscilla Jane
Twain, Mark
Waisbrooker, Lois
Warner, Charles Dudley
Wattles, John Otis
Watts, Alan Wilson
Whipple, Edwin Percy
Williams, Fannie Barrier

Legal Scholars

Ames, James Barr
Angell, Joseph Kinnicutt
Armstrong, Barbara Nachtrieb
Baldwin, Simeon Eben
Battle, William Horn
Beale, Joseph Henry
Bickel, Alexander Mordecai
Bigelow, Harry Augustus

Bigelow, Melvin Madison
Bishop, Joel Prentiss
Borchard, Edwin Montefiore
Bouvier, John
Cahn, Edmond Nathaniel
Cary, William Lucius
Chafee, Zechariah, Jr.
Chamberlain, Joseph Perkins
Clark, Charles Edward
Cobb, Andrew Jackson
Cook, Walter Wheeler
Corwin, Edward Samuel
Crosskey, William Winslow
Dane, Nathan
Daniel, John Warwick
Dickinson, Edwin De Witt
Dickinson, John
Du Ponceau, Pierre Étienne
Dwight, Theodore William
Fairman, Charles
Farrar, Timothy
Frank, Jerome New
Freund, Ernst
Gilmer, Francis Walker
Glueck, Sheldon
Goodhart, Arthur Lehman
Goodnow, Frank Johnson
Goodrich, Elizur (1761–1849)
Gray, John Chipman
Green, Leon
Greenleaf, Simon
Gregory, Charles Noble
Gridley, Jeremiah
Guthrie, William Dameron
Hastie, William Henry
Hilliard, Francis
Hoffman, David
Hohfeld, Wesley Newcomb
Holcombe, James Philemon
Holmes, Oliver Wendell (1841–1935)
Houston, Charles Hamilton
Hudson, Manley Ottmer
Jessup, Philip C.
Keener, William Albert

Langdell, Christopher Columbus
Legaré, Hugh Swinton
Livermore, Samuel (1786–1833)
Llewellyn, Karl Nickerson
Magruder, Calvert
McClain, Emlin
Medina, Harold Raymond
Mentschikoff, Soia
Minor, Raleigh Colston
Morawetz, Victor
Morgenthau, Hans Joachim
Nicolls, Matthias
Oliphant, Herman
Owens, Elisabeth *Suppl. 1*
Parker, Joel (1795–1875)
Parsons, Theophilus (1797–1882)
Paschal, George Washington
Patton, John Mercer
Pfeffer, Leo
Pomeroy, John Norton
Pound, Roscoe
Powell, Thomas Reed
Prosser, William Lloyd
Ransom, Leon Andrew
Redfield, Amasa Angell
Redfield, Isaac Fletcher
Reeve, Tapping
Robinson, Conway
Rodell, Fred
Sayles, John
Schaefer, Walter V.
Schiller, A. Arthur
Sedgwick, Theodore (1811–1859)
Sharp, Malcolm Pitman
Sharswood, George
Stockton, Charles Herbert
Story, Joseph
Taylor, Hannis
Taylor, Telford *Suppl. 1*
Thayer, James Bradley
Tiedeman, Christopher Gustavus
Tucker, Beverley
Tucker, Henry St. George (1780–1848)
Tucker, John Randolph (1823–1897)
Von Moschzisker, Robert
Walker, Timothy (1802–1856)

Ward, Nathaniel
Wheaton, Henry
Wigmore, John Henry
Wright, Austin Tappan
Zeisel, Hans

Medical Educators
Agnew, D. Hayes
Andrews, Ludie
Antony, Milton
Arnstein, Margaret
Augusta, Alexander
  Thomas
Bass, Mary Elizabeth
Beck, Claude Schaeffer
Beck, John Brodhead
Beck, Theodric Romeyn
Bender, Lauretta
Berry, George Packer
Bigelow, Henry Jacob
Blackwell, Elizabeth
Blackwell, Emily
Bodley, Rachel Littler
Bryant, Joseph Decatur
Cabell, James Lawrence
Cabot, Hugh
Caldwell, Charles
Chaillé, Stanford
  Emerson
Chapman, Nathaniel
Cleveland, Emeline
  Horton
Cooke, John Esten
  (1783–1853)
Cope, Oliver
Coxe, John Redman
Crandall, Ella Phillips
Curtis, John Green
Cutler, Elliott Carr
DaCosta, John Chalmers
Dalton, John Call, Jr.
Dana, Israel Thorndike
Davidge, John Beale
Davis, Frances Elliott
Davis, Nathan Smith
Dexter, Aaron
Dock, George
Drake, Daniel
Drew, Charles Richard
Dudley, Benjamin
  Winslow
Dunglison, Robley
Dunham, Carroll
Eberle, John
Edsall, David Linn
Eliot, Martha May
Ellis, Calvin
Fenger, Christian
Flint, Austin
  (1812–1886)
Folin, Otto

Gaillard, Edwin Samuel
Gallup, Joseph Adams
Geddings, Eli
Gerster, Arpad Geyza
  Charles
Gies, William John
Goodrich, Annie
  Warburton
Gorham, John
Gregory, Samuel
Gridley, Selah
Gross, Samuel David
Harrington, Thomas
  Francis
Harrison, John Pollard
Harrison, Tinsley
  Randolph
Hawthorne, Edward
  William
Holmes, Bayard Taylor
Holmes, Oliver Wendell
  (1809–1894)
Holt, Luther Emmett
Hooker, Worthington
Horner, William
  Edmonds
Howe, Percy Rogers
Howland, John
Hubbard, George
  Whipple
Jackson, James
  (1777–1867)
Jackson, Samuel
Jacobi, Abraham
Jacobi, Mary Corinna
  Putnam
Janeway, Edward
  Gamaliel
Jermain, Louis Francis
Joslin, Elliott Proctor
Keeler, Clyde Edgar
Keep, Nathan Cooley
Kelly, Aloysius Oliver
  Joseph
Kempster, Walter
Kent, James Tyler
Kenworthy, Marion
  Edwena
Koplik, Henry
Lahey, Frank Howard
Larsell, Olof
Locke, John
Long, Perrin Hamilton
Lyman, Charles Parker
Macfarlane, Catharine
MacNider, William De
  Berniere
Magoun, Horace
  Winchell
Manning, Isaac Hall
March, Alden

Marshall, Clara
McCaw, James Brown
McDowell, Joseph Nash
McLean, Franklin
  Chambers
McQuillen, John Hugh
Means, James Howard
Meigs, Charles Delucena
Mendenhall, Dorothy
  Reed
Merrick, Myra King
Miller, Edward
Mitchell, Thomas Duché
Moore, Carl Vernon
Mosher, Clelia Duel
Mosher, Eliza Maria
Mott, Valentine
Moultrie, James, Jr.
Moursund, Walter
  Henrik
Mussey, Reuben
  Dimond
Ochsner, Alton
Osler, Sir William
Paine, Martyn
Palmer, Alonzo
  Benjamin
Palmer, Walter Walker
Pancoast, Henry
  Khunrath
Parrish, Joseph
  (1779–1840)
Pearce, Richard Mills, Jr.
Pearson, Leonard
Physick, Philip Syng
Pope, Charles Alexander
Potter, Nathaniel
Preston, Ann
Purvis, Charles Burleigh
Rains, George
  Washington
Roman, Charles Victor
Romayne, Nicholas
Scudder, John Milton
Sedgwick, William
  Thompson
Senn, Nicholas
Shadd, Furman Jeremiah
Shattuck, George
  Cheyne
Shippen, William, Jr.
Short, Charles Wilkins
Sinkler, William H., Jr.
Skene, Alexander
  Johnston Chalmers
Smith, Alban Gilpin
Smith, Harry Pratt
Smith, Nathan
Souchon, Edmond
Steiner, Lewis Henry
Stengel, Alfred

Stillé, Alfred
Strong, Richard Pearson
Thayer, Samuel White,
  Jr.
Thompson, Mary Harris
Warren, Edward
Warren, John
Warren, Stafford Leak
Welch, William Henry
Welsh, Lilian
Wesselhoeft, Conrad
Wheeler, Ruth
Whipple, Allen
  Oldfather
Whipple, George Hoyt
White, Frances Emily
Wilkerson, Vernon
  Alexander
Williams, John Whitridge
Williams, Walter Long
Wistar, Caspar
  (1761–1818)
Wood, Horatio C, Jr.
Wood, William Barry, Jr.
Woodward, Theodore

Music Educators
Bauer, Harold Victor
Bauer, Marion Eugenie
Birge, Edward Bailey
Bonds, Margaret
  Jeannette Allison
Boulanger, Nadia Juliette
Bradbury, William
  Batchelder
Brown, Gertrude Foster
Childers, Lulu Vere
Cowell, Henry *Suppl. 1*
Crawford-Seeger, Ruth
  Porter
Damrosch, Frank Heino
Diller, Angela
Dresel, Otto
Farwell, Arthur
Fay, Amy Muller
Flagg, Josiah
Foster, Sidney
Galamian, Ivan
Godowsky, Leopold
Goldmark, Rubin
Graupner, Gottlieb
Greenfield, Elizabeth
  Taylor *Suppl. 2*
Harris, Johana
Herman, Mary Ann
  Suppl. 2
Herman, Michael
  Suppl. 2
Hewitt, Sophia Henriette
Hommann, Charles
Hughes, Revella Eudosia

Johns, Clayton
Kelley, Edgar Stillman
Klauser, Julius
Kroeger, Ernest Richard
Lewis, John *Suppl. 2*
Mannes, Clara
  Damrosch
Mannes, Leopold
  Damrosch
Mason, Daniel Gregory
Mason, Lowell
Mathews, W. S. B.
Matthews, Artie
Mehegan, John Francis
Moore, Douglas
Moore, Undine
Nabokov, Nicolas
Nassi, Thomas
Oldberg, Arne
Parker, J. C. D.
Parsons, Albert Ross
Persichetti, Vincent
  Ludwig
Root, Frederick
  Woodman
Root, George Frederick
Samaroff, Olga
Schillinger, Joseph
Schnabel, Artur
Schreiber, Frederick
  Charles
Schuman, William
  Howard
Selby, William
Sessions, Roger
  Huntington
Sherwood, William Hall
Sowerby, Leo *Suppl. 2*
Stewart, Slam
Surette, Thomas
  Whitney
Tourjée, Eben
Tristano, Lennie
Tuckey, William
Ussachevsky, Vladimir
Webb, George James
Whiting, George
  Elbridge
Yon, Pietro Alessandro
Ziehn, Bernhard

Orators
Ames, Fisher
Cockran, William
  Bourke
Curtis, George William
Darrow, Clarence
Depew, Chauncey
  Mitchell
Dickinson, Anna
  Elizabeth

Diggs, Annie LePorte
Everett, Edward
Gough, John
  Bartholomew
Grady, Henry Woodfin
Henry, Patrick
Hiawatha
Ingersoll, Robert Green
Jasper, John
Lease, Mary Elizabeth
  Clyens
Maffitt, John Newland
  (1794–1850)
Mazakutemani, Paul
Niebuhr, Reinhold
O'Hare, Kate Richards
Ostenaco
Phillips, Wendell
Randolph, John
  (1773–1833)
Remond, Charles Lenox
Simmons, Roscoe
  Conkling Murray
Simpson, Matthew
Smith, Gerald Lyman
  Kenneth
Taylor, Edward
  Thompson
Teedyuskung
Watson, Thomas
  Edward
Willett, Herbert
  Lockwood

Penmanship Experts
Spencer, Platt Rogers

Physical Culturists
Atlas, Charles
Fixx, James Fuller
Hovey, Henrietta
Macfadden, Bernarr
Muldoon, William
Sandow, Eugen
Stebbins, Genevieve

*Physical Education
Teachers / Leaders*
Ainsworth, Dorothy
  Sears
Baer, Clara Gregory
Berenson, Senda
Blaikie, William
Gulick, Luther Halsey
  (1865–1918)
Kiphuth, Robert John
  Herman
Lee, Mabel *Suppl. 1*
Lewis, Dioclesian
Perrin, Ethel
Ruble, Olan G.

Sargent, Dudley Allen
Walsh, David Henry
Wightman, Hazel
  Hotchkiss

Reading Teachers
Gray, William Scott, Jr.
McGuffey, William
  Holmes
Sharp, Zerna Addas

Religious Educators
Adams, William
Adger, John Bailey
Barber, Virgil Horace
Beard, Richard
Beecher, Edward
Bennett, Belle Harris
Bennett, John Coleman
Boisen, Anton
  Theophilus
Bowen, John Wesley
  Edward
Boyce, James Petigru
Brattle, William
Brawley, Edward
  McKnight
Brown, William Adams
Case, Adelaide Teague
Caulkins, Frances
  Manwaring
Coe, George Albert
Coffin, Henry Sloane
Cook, John Francis
Curtis, Olin Alfred
Dabney, Robert Lewis
Erdman, Charles
  Rosenbury
Fahs, Sophia Lyon
Fenn, William Wallace
Fritschel, Conrad
  Sigmund
Fritschel, Gottfried
  Leonhard Wilhelm
Furman, Richard
Garry, Spokan
Giles, Chauncey
  Commodore
Girardeau, John
  Lafayette
Going, Jonathan
Green, Ashbel
Guiles, Austin Philip
Hare, George Emlen
Hasselquist, Tuve
  Nilsson
Hazelius, Ernest Lewis
Heschel, Abraham
  Joshua
Hiltner, Seward
Hirschensohn, Chaim

Hodge, Charles
Hoge, Moses
Johnson, Paul Emanuel
Jung, Leo
Kaplan, Mordecai
  Menahem
Keith, Reuel
Kidder, Daniel Parish
Knudson, Albert
  Cornelius
Larsen, Peter Laurentius
Livingston, John Henry
Maas, Anthony John
Mayo, Amory Dwight
McCord, James Iley
McGarvey, John William
Miller, Lewis *Suppl. 2*
Mills, Samuel John
Montgomery, Helen
  Barrett
Moore, George Foot
Mullins, Edgar Young
Murray, John Courtney
Nevin, John Williamson
Norton, Andrews
Noyes, George Rapall
Pendleton, James
  Madison
Pieper, Franz August
  Otto
Pond, Enoch
Porter, H. Boone
  Suppl. 2
Rall, Harris Franklin
Raymond, Miner
Reichel, Charles
  Gotthold
Reichel, William
  Cornelius
Reu, Johann Michael
Revel, Bernard
Rice, John Holt
Riddle, Matthew Brown
Riley, William Bell
Russell, Elbert
Scarborough, Lee
  Rutland
Schechter, Solomon
Schenck, Ferdinand
  Schureman
Schmucker, Samuel
  Simon
Sewell, Frank
Shahan, Thomas Joseph
Shedd, William
  Greenough Thayer
Shields, Thomas Edward
Sihler, Wilhelm
Sill, Anna Peck
Sittler, Joseph Andrew,
  Jr.

Smith, Gerald Birney
Smith, Henry Boynton
Sorin, Edward Frederick
Sperry, Willard Learoyd
Staughton, William
Stearns, Oliver
Stone, John Timothy
Strong, Augustus
  Hopkins
Stuart, Moses
Suzuki, D. T. *Suppl. 1*
Sverdrup, Georg
Taylor, Graham
Tennent, William
Terry, Milton Spenser
Tillett, Wilbur Fisk
Tyler, Bennet
Verhaegen, Peter Joseph
Ward, Harry Frederick
Ware, Henry, Jr.
Warfield, Benjamin
  Breckinridge
Wells, Seth Youngs
Wentz, Abdel Ross
Wheelock, Eleazar
Whitsitt, William Heth
Wise, Carroll Alonzo
Witmer, Safara Austin
Wolff, Sister Madeleva
Wood, Thomas Bond
Woods, Leonard
Wright, George Ernest
Zahm, John Augustine

Science Educators
Abell, George Ogden
Adams, Charles Baker
Adams, Comfort Avery
Angell, James Rowland
Anslow, Gladys Amelia
Bache, Alexander Dallas
Bailar, John Christian, Jr.
Bailey, Jacob Whitman
Barbour, George Brown
Bascom, Florence
Bates, Marston
Beach, Frank Ambrose,
  Jr.
Berry, Edward Wilber
Bode, Hendrik Wade
Bouchet, Edward
  Alexander
Brown, Harrison Scott
Buchanan, Herbert Earle
Cain, Stanley Adair
Caldwell, Joseph
Caldwell, Otis William
Campbell, Angus
Carver, George
  Washington
Caswell, Alexis

Chamberlin, Rollin
  Thomas
Chase, Pliny Earle
Chauvenet, William
Clapp, Cornelia Maria
Cleaveland, Parker
Cook, George Hammell
Cooley, Mortimer Elwyn
Cooper, Thomas
Cope, Arthur Clay
Courant, Richard
Crafts, James Mason
Dabney, Charles William
Dana, James Dwight
Davenport, Eugene
Dewey, Chester
Dodge, Bernard Ogilvie
Doremus, Robert Ogden
Draper, John William
Eisenhart, Luther Pfahler
Espy, James Pollard
Farlow, William Gilson
Fowler, Joseph Smith
Frazer, John Fries
Fred, Edwin Broun
Giauque, William
  Francis
Goodale, George
  Lincoln
Gould, Laurence
  McKinley
Greenwood, Isaac
Griffis, William Elliot
Griscom, John
Guilford, Joy Paul
Hall, Granville Stanley
Hamilton, William John,
  Jr.
Harrar, Jacob George
Hildebrand, Joel Henry
Hogness, Thorfin
  Rusten
Houston, Edwin James
Jones, Harry Clary
Jones, Lynds
Judd, Charles Hubbard
Kingsbury, Albert
Ladd, Carl Edwin
Latimer, Wendell
  Mitchell
Law, James
LeConte, John
LeConte, Joseph
Leopold, A. Starker
Leuschner, Armin Otto
Libby, Willard Frank
Loomis, Elias
MacNeven, William
  James
McBryde, John McLaren

McKinney, Roscoe
  Lewis
McMahon, Thomas A.
  Suppl. 2
Merritt, Ernest George
Miles, Manly
Morton, Henry
Murray, David
Nef, John Ulric
Norsworthy, Naomi
Noyes, W. Albert, Jr.
Orton, James
Painter, Theophilus
  Shickel
Parr, Samuel Wilson
Patterson, Robert
Pendleton, Edmund
  Monroe
Peter, Robert
Phelps, Almira Hart
  Lincoln
Pierce, Joseph Alphonso
Pimentel, George Claude
Porter, John Addison
Prager, William
Raper, John Robert
Remsen, Ira
Renwick, James
Richards, Joseph William
Robinson, Edward
  Stevens
Rogers, Robert Empie
Rogers, William Barton
Rose, Mary Davies
  Swartz
Runkle, John Daniel
Rush, Benjamin
Ryan, Harris Joseph
Salisbury, Rollin D.
Sauveur, Albert
Scott, Charlotte Angas
Shaler, Nathaniel
  Southgate
Shepard, Charles
  Upham
Shoup, Francis Asbury
Silliman, Benjamin
Smith, Edgar Fahs
Smith, Edmund Kirby
Smith, Gilbert Morgan
Soderberg, C. Richard
Sperti, George Speri
Stakman, Elvin Charles
St. John, Charles
  Edward
Story, William Edward
Stringham, Irving
Talbot, Arthur Newell
Tarr, Ralph Stockman
Teuber, Hans-Lukas
Thurston, Robert Henry

Timoshenko, Stephen
  Prokofievitch
Turner, Charles Henry
Turner, Thomas Wyatt
Watt, George Willard
Westergaard, Harald
  Malcolm
White, Henry Clay
Whitmore, Frank
  Clifford
Woodward, Robert
  Burns
Zacharias, Jerrold
  Reinach

*Scientific Organization
Administrators*
Adams, Roger
Aitken, Robert Grant
Bache, Alexander Dallas
Bailey, Pearce
Baird, Spencer Fullerton
Barnard, Frederick
  Augustus Porter
Bauer, Louis Agricola
Berelson, Bernard
Bolton, Elmer Keiser
Bowen, Ira Sprague
Buckley, Oliver
  Ellsworth
Bush, Vannevar
Carmichael, Leonard
Carty, John Joseph
Clark, William Bullock
Compton, Karl Taylor
Coolidge, William David
Davenport, Charles
  Benedict
Dryden, Hugh Latimer
Ewing, Maurice
Fisk, James Brown
Fleming, John Adam
Franz, Shepherd Ivory
Goodpasture, Ernest
  William
Haworth, Leland John
Hayes, Charles Willard
Henry, Joseph
Hill, Henry Aaron
Horsfall, Frank Lappin,
  Jr.
Houghton, Henry
  Spencer
Houston, William
  Vermillion
Ipatieff, Vladimir
  Nikolaevich
Jewett, Frank Baldwin
Kellogg, Vernon Lyman
Kelly, Mervin Joseph
Kinzel, Augustus Braun

Lewis, George William
Little, Clarence Cook
Mees, Charles Edward
   Kenneth
Merriam, Clinton Hart
Merriam, John Campbell
Moore, Joseph Haines
Oppenheimer, J. Robert
Osborn, Henry Fairfield
Pickering, Edward
   Charles
Ridenour, Louis Nicot,
   Jr.
Ritter, William Emerson
Rivers, Thomas Milton
Robbins, William Jacob
Sargent, Charles
   Sprague
Spitzer, Lyman, Jr.
   Suppl. 2
Stratton, Samuel Wesley
Thomas, Lewis
Tishler, Max
Waterman, Alan Tower
Whitney, Willis Rodney
Wright, William
   Hammond
Young, Stanley Paul

Singing Teachers
Billings, William
Childers, Lulu Vere
Damrosch, Frank Heino
DeGaetani, Jan
Duncan, Todd *Suppl. 1*
Flagg, Josiah
Holyoke, Samuel Adams
Kieffer, Aldine Silliman
Mason, Lowell
Root, George Frederick
Walker, Edyth

Special Educators
Anagnos, Michael
Barnard, Frederick
   Augustus Porter
Bonner, Marita Odette
Bridgman, Laura Dewey
Churchman, William
   Henry
Crosby, Fanny
Fuller, Sarah
Gallaudet, Edward
   Miner
Gallaudet, Thomas
Gallaudet, Thomas
   Hopkins
Garrett, Mary Smith
Howe, Samuel Gridley
Macy, Anne Sullivan
Nitchie, Edward Bartlett

Peet, Harvey Prindle
Rogers, Harriet Burbank
Russ, John Dennison
Seguin, Edouard O.
Wait, William Bell

Speech Teachers
Brown, Hallie Quinn
Carnegie, Dale
Morgan, Anna

EXPLORATION,
PIONEERING, AND
NATIVE PEOPLES

Adventurers
Boyd, John Parker
Browne, John Ross
Carmichael, William
Cooper, Merian
   Coldwell
de Vries, David
   Pietersen
Halliburton, Richard
Harlan, Josiah
Hayes, Bully
Henry, John
   (1776?–1820?)
Johnson, Osa
Judson, Edward Zane
   Carroll
O'Fallon, James
Panton, William
Ruxton, George
   Augustus Frederick
Salm-Salm, Agnes
   Elisabeth Winona
   Leclercq Joy
Thomas, Lowell
Ward, Samuel
   (1814–1884)
Webber, Charles Wilkins
Wellman, Walter
Wilkinson, James

*American Indian Cultural
Intermediaries*
Adair, James
Bent, George
Brant, Molly
Chisholm, Jesse
Chouteau, Auguste
   Pierre
Cuming, Sir Alexander
Dickson, Robert
Dorion, Marie
Dorman, Isaiah
Dorris, Michael *Suppl. 2*
Eastman, Charles
   Alexander
Fleete, Henry

Folger, Peter
Hiacoomes
Ishi
Lame Deer, John Fire
   Suppl. 2
Logan, James
   (c.1725–1780)
McNickle, D'Arcy
Mouet de Langlade,
   Charles-Michel
Musgrove, Mary
Pocahontas
Sacagawea
Tisquantum
Viele, Aernout
   Cornelissen
Warren, William
   Whipple
Winnemucca, Sarah

American Indian Leaders
Abraham
American Horse
Ann
Arapoosh
Atsidi, Sani
Attakullakulla
Ayres, Jacob
Barboncito *Suppl. 2*
Big Warrior
Black Hawk
Black Hoof
Black Kettle (?–c.1698)
Black Kettle
   (1807?–1868)
Blackfish
Blue Jacket
Bowlegs
Brant, Joseph
Brims
Buckongahelas
Buffalo
Canonchet
Canonicus
Captain Jack
Charlot
Cheeseekau
Cloud, Henry Roe
Coacoochee
Cochise
Colbert, Levi
Colbert, William
Cornplanter
Cornstalk
Crazy Horse
Davis, Alice Brown
Dodge, Henry Chee
Doublehead
Dragging Canoe
Dunquat
Egushawa

Folsom, David
Frechette, James George
Gall
Garacontié, Daniel
Garry, Spokan
George, Samuel
Geronimo
Godfroy, Francis
Grass, John
Gray Lock
Guyasuta
Hagler
Harjo, Chitto
Hatathli, Ned
Hiawatha
Hole-in-the-Day
Hollow Horn Bear
Horse, John *Suppl. 2*
Inkpaduta
Jones, Sam (?–1867)
Joseph
Juh
Kamiakin
Kekewepelethy
Keokuk
La Flesche
LeFlore, Greenwood
Leschi
Little Crow
Little Turtle
Little Wolf
Logan, James
   (1776?–1812)
Lone Wolf *Suppl. 2*
Looking Glass
Lookout, Fred
Mangas Coloradas
Manuelito
Massasoit
Matchekewis
Mathews, John Joseph
Mazakutemani, Paul
McGillivray, Alexander
McIntosh, William
McQueen, Peter
Menewa
Miantonomo
Morgan, Jacob Casimera
Mortar
Moses
Mountain Chief
Mourning Dove
Mushalatubbe
Nampeyo
Nimham, Daniel
Oconostota
Old Briton
Ollokot
Opechancanough
Opothle Yoholo
Orontony, Nicholas

Osceola
Oshkosh
Ostenaco
Other Day, John
Ouray
Parker, Quanah
Pawhuska
Petalesharo
Peters
Philip
Pipe
Pitchlynn, Peter Perkins
Plenty Coups
Pokagon, Simon
Pontiac
Popé
Porter, Pleasant
Powhatan
Pushmataha
Quinney, John Waun-
Nau-Con
Red Cloud
Red Jacket
Red Shoes
Richardville, Jean
Baptiste
Rickard, Clinton
Ridge, John
Ridge, Major
Roman Nose
Ross, John
Roundhead
Saint-Castin, Baron de
Sassacus
Satanta *Suppl. 2*
Sayenqueraghta
Scarouady
Seattle
Set-angya
Shabeni
Shickellamy
Shingas
Sitting Bull
Skenandoa
Snake
Sohappy, David *Suppl. 2*
Spotted Tail
Standing Bear, Luther
Tamaqua
Tammany
Tanacharison
Tarhe
Tecumseh
Teedyuskung
Tendoy
Tenskwatawa
Thomas, William
Holland
Tomochichi
Tsali
Tustenuggee

Two Moon
Uncas
Vann, Joseph
Victorio
Wakara
Wapahasha I
Wapahasha II
Wapahasha III
Ward, Nancy
Washakie
Watie, Stand
Watts, John
Weatherford, William
White Eyes
Young Man Afraid of
His Horse

*American Indian Religious
Leaders*
Black Elk
Deganawidah
Francis, Josiah
Handsome Lake
Kenekuk
Kicking Bear
Main Poc
Neolin
Porcupine
Red Wing
Short Bull
Smohalla
Tavibo
Tenskwatawa
Wilson
Wodziwob

*Captives of American
Indians*
Duston, Hannah
Jemison, Mary
Kelly, Fanny Wiggins
Parker, Cynthia Ann
Rowlandson, Mary
White
Slocum, Frances
Wakefield, Sarah F.
Brown
Williams, John
(1664–1729)

Captivity Narrativists
Jemison, Mary
Kelly, Fanny Wiggins
Rowlandson, Mary
White
Wakefield, Sarah F.
Brown
Williams, John

(1664–1729)
Conquistadors
de Soto, Hernando
Menéndez de Avilés,
Pedro
Narváez, Pánfilo de
Explorers
Akeley, Mary Leonore
Jobe
Alarcón, Hernando de
Álvarez de Pineda,
Alonso
Ambler, James Markham
Marshall
Andrews, Roy Chapman
Anza, Juan Bautista de
Argall, Sir Samuel
Baldwin, Evelyn Briggs
Beltrami, Giacomo
Constantino
Bering, Vitus Jonassen
Bingham, Hiram
(1875–1956)
Block, Adriaen *Suppl. 1*
Bonneville, Benjamin
Louis Eulalie de
Boyd, Louise Arner
Brewer, William Henry
Bridger, James
Bridgman, Herbert
Lawrence
Brierton, John
Burden, William
Douglas
Burnham, Frederick
Russell
Byrd, Richard Evelyn
Cabot, John
Cabot, Sebastian
Carver, Jonathan
Céloron de Blainville,
Pierre Joseph
Champlain, Samuel de
Chouteau, René Auguste
Clark, William
Colter, John
Columbus, Christopher
Cook, Frederick Albert
Coronado, Francisco
Vázquez de
Danenhower, John
Wilson
De Long, George
Washington
Denys de la Ronde,
Louis
de Soto, Hernando
Donelson, John
Drake, Sir Francis
Du Chaillu, Paul Belloni
Dunbar, William

du Sable, Jean Baptiste
Point
Eklund, Carl Robert
Ellis, Henry
Ellsworth, Lincoln
Escalante, Silvestre Vélez
de
Esteban
Fabry De La Bruyère,
André
Farabee, William Curtis
Forbes, Alexander
Frémont, John Charles
Freeman, Thomas
Garcés, Francisco
Tomás Hermenegildo
Gass, Patrick
Gist, Christopher
Gorges, Ferdinando
Gosnold, Bartholomew
Gould, Laurence
McKinley
Greely, Adolphus
Washington
Hall, Charles Francis
Heilprin, Angelo
Hennepin, Louis
Henry, Andrew
Henson, Matthew
Alexander
Hill, Robert Thomas
Hilton, William
Hudson, Henry
Hunt, Wilson Price
Huntington, Ellsworth
Ives, Joseph Christmas
Kane, Elisha Kent
Keating, William
Hypolitus
Kennicott, Robert
Kern, Edward Meyer,
Richard Hovendon
Kern, and Benjamin
Jordan Kern
Kino, Eusebio Francisco
Lander, Frederick West
La Salle, René-Robert
Cavalier de
La Vérendrye, Pierre
Gaultier de
Ledyard, John
Leif Eriksson
Le Moyne, Jean-Baptiste
Le Moyne, Pierre
Lewis, Meriwether
Long, Stephen Harriman
Lummis, Charles
Fletcher
Luna y Arellano, Tristan
de
Mackay, James

Marquette, Jacques
Martínez, Esteban José
Moore, James
  (c.1650–1706)
Morrell, Benjamin
Mullan, John
Nairne, Thomas
Narváez, Pánfilo de
Neighbors, Robert
  Simpson
Nicollet, Joseph Nicolas
Niza, Marcos de
Núñez Cabeza de Vaca,
  Alvar
Ogden, Peter Skene
Ordway, John
Orton, James
Page, Thomas Jefferson
Peary, Josephine
  Diebitsch
Peary, Robert Edwin
Pérez, Juan
Pike, Zebulon
  Montgomery
Ponce de León, Juan
Porter, Russell Williams
Powell, John Wesley
Pryor, Nathaniel Hale
Pumpelly, Raphael
Reynolds, Jeremiah N.
Ribault, Jean
Ronne, Finn
Roosevelt, Kermit
  (1889–1943)
Ross, Alexander
Saint-Denis, Louis
  Juchereau de
Say, Thomas
Schwatka, Frederick
Seton, Grace Gallatin
  Thompson
Siple, Paul Allman
Smith, Jedediah Strong
Stanley, Henry Morton
Stansbury, Howard
Stefansson, Vilhjalmur
Stevenson, Matilda Coxe
  Evans
Strain, Isaac G.
Thompson, David
Thompson, Edward
  Herbert
Tonty, Henri de
Vancouver, George
Verrazzano, Giovanni da
Vespucci, Amerigo
Vial, Pierre
Vizcaíno, Sebastián
Walker, Joseph
  Rutherford
Walsh, Henry Collins

Wilkes, Charles
Wood, Abraham
Wyeth, Nathaniel Jarvis

Frontiersmen / Pioneers
Adams, Grizzly
Allen, Ethan
Allen, Ira
Applegate, Jesse
Austin, Stephen Fuller
Baker, James
Barnwell, John
Bent, Charles
Bent, George
Bent, William
Benton, Thomas Hart,
  Jr. (1816–1879)
Bidwell, John
Birkbeck, Morris
Boggs, Lilburn W.
Boone, Daniel
Bowie, Jim
Bozeman, John M.
Brannan, Samuel
Breen, Patrick
Burleson, Edward
Bush, George
  Washington
Butterfield, John
Calamity Jane
Campbell, Arthur
Carson, Kit
Chapman, John
Clark, George Rogers
Clay, Green
Clayton, William
Cleveland, Benjamin
Cody, William Frederick
Cresap, Michael
Crockett, Davy
Dale, Samuel
Donner Party *Suppl. 1*
Dorman, Isaiah
Duniway, Abigail Jane
  Scott
Dupratz, Antoine Simon
  Le Page
Fay, Jonas
Flower, George
Flower, Richard
Freeman, Frederick
  Kemper
Girty, Simon
Glass, Hugh
Gratiot, Charles
Haraszthy de Mokcsa,
  Agoston
Harrod, James
Hunt, John Wesley
Jeffords, Thomas
  Jonathan

Johnson, John *Suppl. 1*
Jones, Buffalo
Kenton, Simon
Kinzie, Juliette Augusta
  Magill
Lee, Jason
Leidesdorff, William
  Alexander
Lincecum, Gideon
Mathews, George
Maverick, Mary
Maxwell, William
  (1766?–1809)
Meeker, Ezra
California Joe
Newell, Robert
Oñate, Juan de
Patterson, Robert
  Suppl. 2
Patton, James
Peerson, Cleng
Pleasant, Mary Ellen
Poston, Charles Debrille
Preston, William
Putnam, Rufus
Robertson, James
  (1742–1814)
Robinson, Solon
Royce, Sarah Eleanor
  Bayliss
Shelby, Evan
Smith, Jedediah Strong
Spalding, Eliza Hart
Stevens, John Harrington
Stuart, Granville
Sutter, John August
Thornton, Jessy Quinn
Tilghman, William
  Matthew
Walker, Timothy
  (1705–1782)
Washington, George
  (1817–1905)
White, James
Wilbarger, John Wesley
Winchester, James
Wolfskill, William
Wright, Susanna
Zane, Ebenezer
Ziegler, David

Guides / Scouts
Bailey, Ann Hennis
  Trotter
Baker, James
Bridger, James
Burnham, Frederick
  Russell
California Joe
Carson, Kit
Cody, William Frederick

Crawford, John Wallace
Fink, Mike
Grouard, Frank
Hardin, John
Horn, Tom
Navarre, Pierre
Reynolds, Charles
  Alexander
Stilwell, Simpson Everett
Walker, Joseph
  Rutherford
Williams, William
  Sherley

Hawaiian Leaders
Bishop, Bernice Pauahi
Bishop, Charles Reed
Cooper, Henry Ernest
Dole, Sanford Ballard
Emma
Ii, John Papa
Judd, Albert Francis
Judd, Gerrit Parmele
Kaahumanu
Kalakaua, David Laamea
Kamehameha I
Kamehameha II
Kamehameha III
Kamehameha IV
Kamehameha V
Kawananakoa, Abigail
  Wahiikaahuula
  Campbell
Kuhio
Liliuokalani
Luahine, Iolani
Malo, Davida
Pukui, Mary Abigail
  Kawena Wiggin

Indian Agents
Carson, Kit
Chouteau, Jean Pierre
Clark, William
Cocke, William
Croghan, George
  (?–1782)
Davenport, George
Forsyth, Thomas
Gist, Christopher
Hawkins, Benjamin
Jeffords, Thomas
  Jonathan
Johnson, Guy
Lorimier, Louis
McGillycuddy, Valentine
  Trant O'Connell
McKee, John
Mccoy, Isaac
Meigs, Return Jonathan

(1740–1823)
Mitchell, David Brydie
Mitchell, David Dawson
Mouet de Langlade,
  Charles-Michel
Neighbors, Robert
  Simpson
O'Fallon, Benjamin
Schoolcraft, Henry Rowe
Sibley, John
Thompson, Wiley
Tipton, John
White, Elijah
Woodward, Henry

Navigators
Block, Adriaen *Suppl. 1*
Cabot, John
Hudson, Henry
Patten, Mary Ann
  Brown
Slocum, Joshua

Traders with Indians /
Pioneers
Adair, James
Ashley, William Henry
Bent, Charles
Bent, William
Bridger, James
Carson, Kit
Chisholm, Jesse
Chouteau, Auguste
  Pierre
Claiborne, William
Faribault, Jean Baptiste
Gaines, George Strother
Gratiot, Charles
Harris, John
Hubbell, John Lorenzo
James, Thomas
Lorimier, Louis
McGillivray, Lachlan
McLoughlin, John
Menard, Pierre
Oldham, John
Rice, Henry Mower
Schuyler, Peter
Viele, Aernout
  Cornelissen
Wolfskill, William

GOVERNMENT AND
POLITICS

Colonial Government
and Revolutionary
Politics
British Legislators
Coote, Richard
Cruger, Henry, Jr.
Lyttelton, William Henry

Pownall, Thomas

Colonial Agents
Ashmun, Jehudi
Barnwell, John
Bollan, William
Clarke, John
Cooke, Elisha
De Berdt, Dennys
Dummer, Jeremiah
  (1681–1739)
Knox, William
Mazzei, Philip
Partridge, Richard
Weld, Thomas

Colonial Founders /
Officials
Argall, Sir Samuel
Ayllón, Lucas Vázquez
  de
Barradall, Edward
Blathwayt, William
Bridger, Jonathan
Byrd, William
  (1652–1704)
Calvert, Cecilius
Carter, Robert
  (1663–1732)
Carteret, Philip
Cary, Thomas
Clarke, George
Colden, Cadwallader
Conant, Roger
Coxe, Daniel
Cutt, John
Dale, Sir Thomas
de Croix, Teodoro
De Peyster, Abraham
Dinwiddie, Robert
D'Oyley, Edward
Dulany, Daniel
Dummer, William
Eddis, William
Fairfax, Thomas
Fanning, Edmund
Fauquier, Francis
Fenwick, George
Folger, Peter
Gálvez, Bernardo de
Gookin, Daniel
Habersham, James
Heathcote, Caleb
Higginson, Nathaniel
Home, Archibald
Hooker, Thomas
Hudde, Andries
Hull, John
Hutchinson, Thomas
Ingersoll, Jared
Jamison, David

Johnson, Sir William
Jones, Noble
Kennedy, Archibald
Knox, William
Krol, Bastiaen Janszen
Kuskov, Ivan
  Aleksandrovich
Leeds, John
Logan, James
  (1674–1751)
Ludlow, George Duncan
Ludlow, Roger
Ludwell, Philip
Lyman, Phineas
Menéndez de Avilés,
  Pedro
Mézières, Athanaze de
Minuit, Peter
Monckton, Robert
Morgan, Sir Henry
Neve, Felipe de
Nicholas, Robert Carter
Nicolls, Matthias
Norwood, Henry
Oglethorpe, James
  Edward
Oñate, Juan de
Page, Mann
Penn, William
Peters, Richard
  (1704?–1776)
Pierson, Abraham
Povey, Thomas
Randolph, Edward
Randolph, John
  (1727–1784)
Rezanov, Nikolai
  Petrovich
Richardson, Ebenezer
Richardson, Thomas
Robinson, John
Rockingham, Lord
Saint-Denis, Louis
  Juchereau de
Saltonstall, Richard
Sandys, George
Shippen, Edward
Shippen, Edward, IV
Smith, Samuel
  (1720–1776)
Sothel, Seth
Standish, Myles
Steenwyck, Cornelis
  Jacobsz
Stoughton, William
Strachey, William
Stuyvesant, Peter
Temple, John
Valverde Cosío, Antonio
  de

Van Cortlandt,
  Stephanus
van Cortlant, Oloff
  Stevensz
van Curler, Arent
Van der Donck, Adriaen
  Suppl. 1
Van Ilpendam, Jan
  Jansen
van Rensselaer, Kiliaen
Vassall, John
Vaughan, George
Villasur, Pedro de
Weare, Meshech
Wharton, Thomas, Jr.
Williams, Roger
  (1603?–1683)
Wingfield, Edward
  Maria
Wormeley, Ralph
Wraxall, Peter
Youngs, John

Colonial Governors General
Andros, Sir Edmund
Buade, Louis de
Codrington,
  Christopher, Jr.
Gayoso de Lemos,
  Manuel
Smith, James Francis
Vaudreuil, Pierre de
  Rigaud de

Colonial Governors /
Proprietors
Andros, Sir Edmund
Anza, Juan Bautista de
Archdale, John
Basse, Jeremiah
Belcher, Jonathan
Bellingham, Richard
Berkeley, William
Bernard, Sir Francis
Bradford, William
  (1590–1657)
Bradstreet, Simon
Bull, William
Bull, William, II
Burnet, William
  (1688–1729)
Burrington, George
Calvert, Cecilius
Calvert, Charles
  (1637–1715)
Calvert, Charles
  (1699–1751)
Calvert, Frederick
Calvert, George
Calvert, Leonard

**Colonial Government
and Revolutionary
Politics** *(cont.)*
  Campbell, William
    (1730?–1778)
  Carver, John
  Clinton, George
    (1686–1761)
  Coddington, William
  Coote, Richard
  Copley, Lionel
  Cornbury, Viscount
  Coronado, Francisco
    Vázquez de
  Cosby, William
  Cranston, Samuel
  Culpeper, John
  Culpeper, Thomas
  De La Warr, Baron
  Dobbs, Arthur
  Dongan, Thomas
  Dudley, Joseph
  Dudley, Thomas
  Eaton, Theophilus
  Eden, Charles
  Ellis, Henry
  Endecott, John
  Fendall, Josias
  Fitch, Thomas
  Franklin, William
  Gálvez, Bernardo de
  Gage, Thomas
  Gates, Sir Thomas
  Gayoso de Lemos,
    Manuel
  Glen, James
  Gooch, Sir William
  Gorges, Robert, William
    Gorges, and Thomas
    Gorges
  Habersham, James
  Hamilton, Andrew
    (?–1703)
  Harford, Henry
  Harris, William
  Harrison, Benjamin
    (1726?–1791)
  Haynes, John
  Hopkins, Edward
  Howard, Francis
  Hunter, Robert
    (1666–1734)
  Hyde, Edward
  Johnson, Nathaniel
  Johnson, Robert
    (1676?–1735)
  Johnston, Gabriel
  Johnstone, George
  Keith, William
  Kieft, Willem

  Lamothe Cadillac,
    Antoine Laumet de
  Lane, Sir Ralph
  Le Moyne, Jean-Baptiste
  Le Moyne, Pierre
  Leete, William
  Leisler, Jacob
  Leverett, John
    (1616–1679)
  Lovelace, Francis
  Ludwell, Philip
  Lyttelton, William Henry
  Markham, William
  Martin, Josiah
  Mayhew, Thomas
  Mayhew, Thomas, Jr.
  Menéndez de Avilés,
    Pedro
  Minuit, Peter
  Miró, Esteban Rodríguez
  Moore, Sir Henry
  Moore, James
    (c.1650–1706)
  Morris, Lewis
    (1671–1746)
  Murray, John (1730/
    2–1809)
  Nicholson, Francis
  Nicolls, Richard
  Ogle, Samuel
  Parke, Daniel
  Peñalosa, Diego Dionisio
    de
  Percy, George
  Phips, Sir William
  Pitkin, William
  Pott, John
  Pownall, Thomas
  Printz, Johan Bjornsson
  Reynolds, John
    (1713?–1788)
  Rising, Johan Classon
  Robertson, James
    (1717–1788)
  Robinson, Beverly
  Russwurm, John Brown
  Salcedo, Manuel María
    de
  Saltonstall, Gurdon
  Sharpe, Horatio
  Shirley, William
  Shute, Samuel
  Smith, John
    (1580–1631)
  Sothel, Seth
  Spotswood, Alexander
  Stephens, William
  Stone, William
  Trumbull, Jonathan
  Tryon, William
  Ulloa, Antonio de

  Vane, Sir Henry
  Van Twiller, Wouter
  Vargas, Diego de
  Vaudreuil, Pierre de
    Rigaud de
  Vaughan, George
  Vetch, Samuel
  Wanton, William
  Ward, Samuel
    (1725–1776)
  Warren, Sir Peter
  Wentworth, Benning
  Wentworth, John
    (1672–1730)
  Wentworth, John
    (1737–1820)
  West, Joseph
  White, John
  Winslow, Josiah
  Winthrop, John
    (1588–1649)
  Winthrop, John
    (1638–1707)
  Winthrop, John, Jr.
  Wolcott, Roger
  Wright, James
  Wyatt, Sir Francis
  Yale, Elihu
  Yeamans, Sir John
  Yeardley, Sir George
  Zéspedes y Velasco,
    Vicente Manuel de

Colonial Militiamen
  Barnwell, John
  Clay, Green
  McMinn, Joseph
  Meserve, Nathaniel
  Moore, James, Jr.
  Pepperrell, Sir William
  Standish, Myles
  Underhill, John
  Waldo, Samuel
  Williams, Israel
  Winslow, John
  Winslow, Josiah
  Winthrop, John
    (1638–1707)

Colonists
  Alden, John
  Alden, Priscilla Mullins
  Allerton, Isaac
  Austin, Stephen Fuller
  Ballou, Adin
  Baranov, Aleksandr
    Andreevich
  Blackstone, William
  Boehler, Peter
  Brent, Margaret
  Bronck, Jonas *Suppl. 1*

  Bull, Ole
  Champlain, Samuel de
  Coode, John
  Dare, Virginia
  de Vries, David
    Pietersen
  Duston, Hannah
  Endecott, John
  Falckner, Daniel
  Fenwick, John
  Gardiner, Sir
    Christopher
  Gardiner, Lion
  Gardner, Horod Long
    Hicks
  George, David
  Gorton, Samuel
  Graffenried, Christoph,
    Baron von
  Harriman, Job
  Hathorne, William
  Hughes, Pryce
  Hutchinson, Anne
  Lumbrozo, Jacob
  Luna y Arellano, Tristan
    de
  Lyman, Phineas
  Maverick, Samuel
  Moody, Lady Deborah
  Morton, Thomas
  Rich, Charles Coulson
  Robertson, Sterling
    Clack
  Rosen, Joseph A.
  Roye, Edward James
  Scholte, H. P.
  Shelikhov, Grigorii
    Ivanovich
  Van Raalte, Albertus
    Christiaan
  Willard, Simon
  Williams, Samuel May
  Winslow, Edward
  Young, Brigham

Landowners / Patroons
  Beekman, Henry
  Brent, Margaret
  Hazen, Moses
  Heathcote, Caleb
  Livingston, Robert
  Livingston, Robert
    Robert
  Pell, Thomas
  Penn, William
  Philipse, Frederick
  Van Cortlandt, Pierre
  Van Rensselaer, Jeremias
  van Rensselaer, Kiliaen
  Van Rensselaer, Maria
    Van Cortlandt

Colonial Government and Revolutionary Politics *(cont.)*
Van Rensselaer, Nicholas
Van Rensselaer, Stephen

Loyalists (American Revolution)
Allen, Levi
Auchmuty, Robert, Jr.
Auchmuty, Samuel
Bailey, Jacob
Barclay, Thomas
Bates, Walter
Brant, Joseph
Brant, Molly
Brown, Thomas
Browne, William
Butler, Walter
Coffin, Sir Isaac
Coffin, John
Colden, Cadwallader, II
Cooper, Myles
De Lancey, James (1747–1804)
De Lancey, Oliver
Draper, Richard
Dunbar, Moses
Fanning, David
Fanning, Edmund
Franklin, William
Galloway, Joseph
Gardiner, Silvester
Girty, Simon
Hamilton, John
Howard, Martin
Howetson, James
Hutchinson, Thomas
Inglis, Charles
Johnson, John (1741–1830)
Leonard, Daniel
Loring, Joshua (1716–1781)
Loring, Joshua (1744–1789)
Low, Isaac
Ludlow, Gabriel George
Ludlow, George Duncan
Mein, John
Morris, Roger
Odell, Jonathan
Randolph, John (1727–1784)
Richardson, Ebenezer
Robertson, James (1747–1816)
Robinson, Beverly
Ruggles, Timothy
Sewall, Jonathan

Skene, Philip
Trowbridge, Edmund
Wentworth, John (1737–1820)
White, Henry (1732–1786)
Wormeley, Ralph
Worthington, John
Wragg, William
Zubly, John Joachim

Patriots (American Revolution)
Alexander, Abraham
Attucks, Crispus
Bache, Sarah Franklin
Cabell, William
Clarke, Parker
Corbin, Margaret Cochran
Crane, John
Dana, Richard
Dawes, William
Derby, Elias Hasket
Downer, Silas
Faulkner, Thomas
Flora, William
Hale, Nathan
Hall, Prince
Hart, Nancy
Haynes, Lemuel
Howley, Richard
Hull, Agrippa
Izard, Ralph
Lafayette, James
Langdon, Samuel
Leacock, John
Lewis, Andrew
Marshall, Christopher
Moses, Isaac *Suppl. 2*
Nicholas, Robert Carter
Page, John
Paine, Thomas
Pettit, Charles
Pitcher, Molly
Pollock, Oliver
Quincy, Josiah (1744–1775)
Ranger, Joseph
Salomon, Haym
Sampson, Deborah
Sisson, Jack
Tarrant, Caesar
Thompson, Ebenezer
Warren, Joseph
Weare, Meshech
Whipple, Prince
Yates, Abraham, Jr.

Revolutionary Leaders (American Revolution)
Allen, Ethan
Archer, John
Arnold, Jonathan
Ashe, John
Bedford, Gunning (1742–1797)
Bedford, Gunning, Jr. (1747–1812)
Benson, Egbert
Blair, John, Jr.
Bland, Theodorick
Broom, Jacob
Brownson, Nathan
Bulloch, Archibald
Burnet, William (1730–1791)
Butler, Pierce (1866–1939)
Carroll, Charles
Carter, Landon
Cutts, Samuel
Dana, Francis
Dayton, Jonathan
Deane, Silas
Dickinson, John (1732–1808)
Drayton, William Henry
Duer, William
Dyer, Eliphalet
Few, William
Findley, William
Gadsden, Christopher
Gibbons, William (1750?–1800)
Gorham, Nathaniel
Graham, Joseph
Habersham, Joseph
Hanson, John, Jr.
Harnett, Cornelius, Jr.
Henry, Patrick
Hillegas, Michael
Hobart, John Sloss
Holten, Samuel
Houston, William Churchill
Houstoun, John
Jenifer, Daniel of St. Thomas
Johnson, Thomas
Johnson, William Samuel
Jones, Allen
Jones, Noble Wimberly
Jones, Willie
Langworthy, Edward
Laurens, Henry
Livingston, Robert Robert
Livingston, William
Low, Isaac

Lowell, John (1743–1802)
Madison, James (1751–1836)
Martin, Luther
Mason, George
Mathews, John
Matlack, Timothy
McClurg, James
McDougall, Alexander
Mercer, John Francis
Mifflin, Thomas
Morris, Gouverneur
Nelson, Thomas
Osgood, Samuel
Paterson, William
Pendleton, Edmund
Person, Thomas
Pinckney, Charles
Pinckney, Charles Cotesworth
Plater, George
Ramsay, David
Randolph, Peyton
Reed, Joseph
Revere, Paul
Root, Jesse
Schuyler, Philip John
Scott, John Morin
Sears, Isaac
Smilie, John
Smith, Meriwether
Telfair, Edward
Ten Broeck, Abraham
Thompson, Samuel
Thomson, Charles
Tilghman, Matthew
Wadsworth, James (1730–1817)
Ward, Artemas
Warren, James
Wentworth, John (1719–1781)
Willing, Thomas
Yates, Robert

Signers of the Declaration of Independence
Adams, John (1735–1826)
Adams, Samuel
Bartlett, Josiah
Braxton, Carter
Carroll of Carrollton, Charles
Chase, Samuel
Clark, Abraham
Clymer, George
Ellery, William
Floyd, William

Colonial Government and Revolutionary Politics *(cont.)*
Franklin, Benjamin (1706–1790)
Gerry, Elbridge
Gwinnett, Button
Hall, Lyman
Hancock, John (1737–1793)
Harrison, Benjamin (1726?–1791)
Hart, John
Hewes, Joseph
Heyward, Thomas
Hooper, William
Hopkins, Stephen
Hopkinson, Francis
Huntington, Samuel
Jefferson, Thomas
Lee, Francis Lightfoot
Lee, Richard Henry
Lewis, Francis
Livingston, Philip
McKean, Thomas
Morris, Lewis (1726–1798)
Morris, Robert (1735–1806)
Morton, John
Nelson, Thomas
Paca, William
Paine, Robert Treat
Penn, John
Read, George
Rodney, Caesar
Ross, George
Rush, Benjamin
Rutledge, Edward
Sherman, Roger
Smith, James (1719–1806) *Suppl. 1*
Stockton, Richard
Stone, Thomas *Suppl. 1*
Taylor, George *Suppl. 1*
Thornton, Matthew
Walton, George
Whipple, William
Williams, William (1731–1811)
Wilson, James (1742–1798)
Witherspoon, John
Wolcott, Oliver (1726–1797)
Wythe, George

Government (Federal)
Attorneys General (Federal)
Akerman, Amos Tappan
Bates, Edward

Biddle, Francis Beverley
Black, Jeremiah Sullivan
Brewster, Benjamin Harris
Butler, Benjamin Franklin (1795–1858)
Clark, Tom Campbell
Crittenden, John Jordan
Cummings, Homer Stillé
Daugherty, Harry Micajah
Garland, Augustus Hill
Gregory, Thomas Watt
Griggs, John William
Harmon, Judson
Hoar, Ebenezer Rockwood
Johnson, Reverdy
Kennedy, Robert Francis
Kleindienst, Richard G. *Suppl. 1*
Knox, Philander Chase
Lee, Charles (1758–1815)
Legaré, Hugh Swinton
McGranery, James Patrick
McGrath, J. Howard
McReynolds, James Clark
Miller, William Henry Harrison
Mitchell, John Newton
Moody, William Henry
Olney, Richard
Palmer, A. Mitchell
Pierrepont, Edwards
Randolph, Edmund
Richardson, Elliot *Suppl. 1*
Rodney, Caesar Augustus
Rogers, William Pierce *Suppl. 2*
Speed, James
Stanbery, Henry
Stanton, Edwin McMasters
Taft, Alphonso
Taney, Roger Brooke
Wickersham, George Woodward
Willebrandt, Mabel Walker
Williams, George Henry
Wirt, William

Civil Servants
Bulfinch, Charles
Clague, Ewan
Greenhow, Robert

McCarthy, Charles
O'Connor, William Douglas
Thornton, William
Tolley, Howard Ross

Commissioners of Agriculture
Newton, Isaac

Commissioners of Education
Cooper, William John
Keppel, Francis C.

Commissioners / Superintendents of Indian Affairs
Brown, Thomas
Butler, Richard
Dickson, Robert
McKenney, Thomas Loraine
Mitchell, David Dawson
Palmer, Joel
Parker, Ely Samuel
Rice, Henry Mower
Stokes, Montfort
Stuart, John
Wraxall, Peter

Congressional Officers / Staff
Beckley, John James
Miller, Fishbait
Schine, G. David *Suppl. 1*

Diplomats
Adams, Charles
Adams, Charles Francis (1807–1886)
Adams, John (1735–1826)
Adee, Alvey Augustus
Allen, Elisha Hunt
Allen, George Venable
Allison, John Moore
Alvarez, Manuel
Anderson, Larz
Anderson, Richard Clough, Jr.
Andrews, Israel DeWolf
Angell, James Burrill
Armour, Norman
Austin, Warren Robinson
Bacon, Robert
Baker, Jehu
Bancroft, George
Barclay, Thomas
Barlow, Joel

Barnard, Daniel Dewey
Barrett, John
Barringer, Daniel Moreau
Bayard, Richard Henry
Bayard, Thomas Francis
Biddle, Anthony Joseph Drexel, Jr.
Bidlack, Benjamin Alden *Suppl. 1*
Bigelow, John
Bingham, Robert Worth
Bliss, Tasker Howard
Blount, James Henderson
Blue Jacket
Bohlen, Charles Eustis
Boker, George Henry
Borland, Solon
Bowdoin, James (1752–1811)
Bowers, Claude Gernade
Bowles, Chester Bliss
Bragg, Edward Stuyvesant
Breckinridge, Clifton Rodes
Brewster, Kingman, Jr.
Briggs, Ellis Ormsbee
Bristol, Mark Lambert
Broadhead, James Overton
Brodhead, John Romeyn
Brown, Ethan Allen
Brown, James
Bruce, David Kirkpatrick Este
Bullitt, William Christian
Bunche, Ralph Johnson
Bunker, Ellsworth
Burlingame, Anson
Cabot, John Moors
Caffery, Jefferson
Cameron, Simon
Campbell, Lewis Davis
Carmichael, William
Carter, Henry Alpheus Peirce
Carter, William Beverly, Jr.
Castle, William Richards, Jr.
Child, Richard Washburn
Choate, Joseph Hodges
Chouteau, Auguste Pierre
Clapp, Margaret Antoinette
Clark, Daniel (1766–1813)

Government (Federal)
(cont.)

Clark, Joshua Reuben, Jr.
Clay, Cassius Marcellus
Clayton, Powell
Clubb, Oliver Edmund
Coggeshall, William
 Turner
Conger, Edwin Hurd
Coolidge, Thomas
 Jefferson
Cooper, John Sherman
Crosby, John Schuyler
Crowder, Enoch Herbert
Curtin, Andrew Gregg
Daggett, Rollin Mallory
Dallas, George Mifflin
Dana, Francis
Daniel, John Moncure
Daniels, Josephus
Davezac, Auguste
 Genevieve Valentin
Davies, Joseph Edward
Davis, Bancroft
Dayton, William Lewis
Dean, Arthur Hobson
Deane, Silas
Deganawidah
Denby, Charles
Denby, Charles, II
Dennis, Lawrence
Dodge, Augustus Caesar
Donelson, Andrew
 Jackson
Draper, William
 Franklin
Dunquat
Durham, John Stephens
Eames, Charles
 (1812–1867)
Eaton, John Henry
Eaton, William
Egan, Maurice Francis
Egan, Patrick
Ellis, Powhatan
Eustis, George, Jr.
Eustis, James Biddle
Eustis, William
Everett, Alexander Hill
Fairchild, Lucius
Fay, Theodore Sedgwick
Featherstonhaugh,
 George William
Ferguson, Homer
Fletcher, Henry Prather
Foote, Lucius Harwood
Forbes, William
 Cameron
Forsyth, John
Forward, Walter
Foster, John Watson

Gallatin, Albert
Gauss, Clarence Edward
Genet, Edmond Charles
George, Samuel
Gerard, James Watson
Gibson, Hugh Simons
Goldberg, Arthur Joseph
Gore, Christopher
Grady, Henry Francis
Graham, John
Greathouse, Clarence
 Ridgley
Green, Benjamin
 Edwards
Greene, Roger Sherman
Greener, Richard
 Theodore
Gregg, David
 McMurtrie
Grew, Joseph Clark
Grimké, Archibald
 Henry
Griscom, Lloyd
 Carpenter
Guyasuta
Halderman, John Adams
Hale, John Parker
Hamilton, John
Hamilton, Maxwell
 McGaughey
Harriman, Daisy
Harriman, Pamela
 Suppl. 1
Harris, Patricia Roberts
Harvey, George Brinton
 McClellan
Hay, John Milton
Henderson, Loy Wesley
Herrick, Myron Timothy
Herrman, Augustine
Hill, David Jayne
Hilliard, Henry
 Washington
Hise, Elijah
Hitt, Robert Roberts
Holcomb, Thomas
Holcombe, Chester
Holker, John
Hollow Horn Bear
Hoover, Herbert Clark,
 Jr.
Houghton, Alanson
 Bigelow
Hughes, Christopher, Jr.
Humphreys, David
Hunt, William Henry
 (1823–1884)
Hunt, William Henry
 (1869–1951)
Hurley, Patrick Jay
Jarves, James Jackson

Jay, John
Jessup, Philip C.
Joy, Charles Turner
Judd, Norman Buel
Kasson, John Adam
Kavanagh, Edward
Keating, Kenneth
 Barnard
Kemper, James Scott
Kilpatrick, Hugh Judson
King, Rufus
 (1755–1827)
King, Rufus (1814–
 1876)
King, Thomas Butler
Koerner, Gustave
 Philipp
Lane, Arthur Bliss
Langston, John Mercer
Larkin, Thomas Oliver
Laurens, John
Lawrence, Abbott
Lear, Tobias
Lee, Arthur
Lee, William
Leidesdorff, William
 Alexander
Lincoln, Robert Todd
Lind, John
Lodge, Henry Cabot
 (1902–1985)
Long, Breckinridge
Loomis, Francis Butler
Low, Frederick
 Ferdinand
Lowell, James Russell
MacVeagh, Isaac Wayne
MacVeagh, Lincoln
Maney, George Earl
Mann, Ambrose Dudley
Marsh, George Perkins
Mason, James Murray
Mason, John Young
Matthews, Harrison
 Freeman
McCloy, John Jay, Jr.
McCoy, Frank Ross
McLane, Louis
McLane, Robert
 Milligan
McNutt, Paul Vories
Merry, William
 Lawrence
Messersmith, George
 Strausser
Mesta, Perle
Meyer, George von
 Lengerke
Middleton, Henry
 (1770–1846)
Moore, Thomas Patrick

Moran, Benjamin
Morehead, John Motley
Morgenthau, Henry
Morris, Edward Joy
Morris, Gouverneur
Morrow, Dwight
 Whitney
Morse, Freeman Harlow
Motley, John Lothrop
Murphy, Robert Daniel
Murray, William Vans
Nelson, Hugh
Nelson, Thomas Henry
Nicholson, Meredith
Osborn, Thomas
 Andrew
Osten Sacken, Carl
 Robert Romanovich
 von der
Osterhaus, Peter Joseph
Pacheco, Romualdo
Page, Walter Hines
Parker, Peter
 (1804–1888)
Partridge, James
 Rudolph
Patterson, Richard
 Cunningham, Jr.
Peixotto, Benjamin
 Franklin
Pendleton, George Hunt
Pendleton, John Strother
Peurifoy, John Emil
Phelps, William Walter
Phillips, William
Piatt, John James
Pierrepont, Edwards
Pinkney, William
Pitchlynn, Peter Perkins
Poinsett, Joel Roberts
Porter, Horace
Price, Byron
Pruyn, Robert Hewson
Ransom, Matt Whitaker
Reid, Whitelaw
Reinsch, Paul Samuel
Reischauer, Edwin
 Oldfather
Rich, Obadiah
Rives, William Cabell
Robins, Raymond
Robinson, Christopher
Rockhill, William
 Woodville
Rodney, Caesar
 Augustus
Rohde, Ruth Bryan
 Owen
Roosevelt, Eleanor
Root, Joseph Pomeroy
Rush, Richard

Government (Federal)
(cont.)

Russell, Jonathan
Sanford, Henry Shelton
Saunders, Romulus
  Mitchell
Sayenqueraghta
Schenck, Robert
  Cumming
Schurman, Jacob Gould
Schuyler, Eugene
Scott, Hugh Lenox
Sergeant, John
  (1779–1852)
Seward, Frederick
  William
Seward, George
  Frederick
Shaw, Samuel
Short, William
Shufeldt, Robert Wilson
Sickles, Daniel Edgar
Slidell, John
Smith, Walter Bedell
Smith, William
  Loughton
Snake
Soulé, Pierre
Stahel, Julius
Standley, William
  Harrison
Steinhardt, Laurence
  Adolph
Stettinius, Edward
  Reilly, Jr.
Stevens, John Leavitt
Stevenson, Adlai Ewing,
  II
Stevenson, Andrew
Stillman, William James
Straight, Willard
  Dickerman
Straus, Jesse Isidor
Straus, Oscar Solomon
Taft, Alphonso
Taylor, Hannis
Taylor, Myron Charles
Temple, John
Tenney, Charles Daniel
Terrell, Edwin Holland
Thayer, Alexander
  Wheelock
Thayer, Charles Wheeler
Thompson, Llewellyn
  Edward
Thompson, Thomas
  Larkin
Thompson, Waddy
Torbert, Alfred Thomas
  Archimedes

Tousard, Anne-Louis
  Suppl. 2
Tower, Charlemagne
Trist, Nicholas Philip
Turner, James Milton
Vaillant, George Clapp
Van Braam Houckgeest,
  Andreas Everardus
van Curler, Arent
van Dyke, Henry
Vaughan, Benjamin
Vincent, John Carter
Wadsworth, James
  Jeremiah
Wallace, Hugh Campbell
Waller, John Louis
Walton, Lester A.
  Suppl. 2
Warden, David Bailie
Washburne, Elihu
  Benjamin
Watson, Arthur
  Kittridge
Welles, Sumner
Welsh, John
Wharton, Clifton
  Reginald
Wheaton, Henry
White, Andrew Dickson
White, Henry
  (1850–1927)
Whitlock, Brand
Williams, Edward
  Thomas
Williams, G. Mennen
Williams, James
Willis, Albert Shelby
Willis, Frances Elizabeth
Wilson, Henry Lane
Wilson, Hugh Robert
Winant, John Gilbert
Winslow, Edward
Woodford, Stewart
  Lyndon
Wright, Joseph Albert
Young, Owen D.
Young, Pierce Manning
  Butler
Yung Wing

Federal Government
Officials
Abbott, Grace
Albright, Horace
  Marden
Alexander, Will Winton
Altmeyer, Arthur Joseph
Anderson, Joseph Inslee
Anderson, Mary
  (1872–1964)
Anslinger, Harry Jacob

Arnold, Thurman
Austin, Jonathan Loring
Ballantine, Arthur
  Atwood
Barnes, Julius Howland
Bennett, Henry Garland
Bennett, James Van
  Benschoten
Beyer, Clara Mortenson
Bissell, Richard Mervin,
  Jr.
Bradley, Abraham, Jr.
Brown, Walter Folger
Bullard, Arthur
Bundy, Harvey Hollister
Burgess, George Kimball
Burns, Arthur Frank
Cahill, Holger
Caldwell, Captain Billy
Calhoun, John
Caminetti, Anthony
Campbell, Walter
  Gilbert
Cary, William Lucius
Casey, William Joseph
Clinch, Charles Powell
Corcoran, Thomas
  Gardiner
Cotton, Joseph Potter
Crèvecoeur, J. Hector St.
  John de
Creel, George Edward
Daniels, Jonathan
Dean, Gordon Evans
Dennett, Tyler Wilbur
Dickinson, John
  (1894–1952)
Dodge, Joseph Morrell
Donovan, William
  Joseph
Douglas, Lewis William
Douglas, William O.
Dryden, Hugh Latimer
Du Bois, William Ewing
Eastman, Joseph Bartlett
Eccles, Marriner
  Stoddard
Edwards, Corwin D.
Eisenhower, Milton
  Stover
Elliott, Harriet Wiseman
Engen, Donald
  Davenport *Suppl. 2*
Esch, John Jacob
Ewbank, Thomas
Ewing, Oscar Ross
Fechner, Robert *Suppl. 2*
Flagg, Edmund
Flint, Weston
Fly, James Lawrence
Ford, Guy Stanton

Fox, Gustavus Vasa
Frank, Jerome New
Gabrielson, Ira Noel
Gallagher, William Davis
Gardener, Helen
  Hamilton
Goldenweiser, Emanuel
  Alexander
Goodrich, Carter
Grant, Frederick Dent
Haas, Francis Joseph
Hanks, Nancy
Harding, William
  Proctor Gould
Harriman, W. Averell
Haworth, Leland John
Henderson, Leon
Hennock, Frieda Barkin
Henshaw, Henry
  Wetherbee
Hershey, Lewis Blaine
Hoey, Jane Margueretta
Hoffman, Paul Gray
Hopkins, Harry Lloyd
Howard, Oliver Otis
Hunt, Henry Alexander,
  Jr.
Hurley, Edward Nash
Jackson, Hartley Harrad
  Thompson
Johnson, Hugh Samuel
Jones, Jesse Holman
Judd, Gerrit Parmele
Kennedy, Joseph Patrick
Keyserling, Leon
King, Clarence Rivers
Kirlin, Florence
  Katharine
Knox, John Jay
Landis, James McCauley
Lane, Franklin Knight
Lawrence, David Leo
Lewis, George William
Lilienthal, David Eli
Lubin, Isador
MacDonald, Thomas
  Harris
Macy, John Williams, Jr.
Malone, Dudley Field
Maverick, Maury
McCabe, Thomas
  Bayard
McCone, John A.
McDill, James Wilson
Mead, Elwood
Mendenhall, Walter
  Curran
Merriam, Clinton Hart
Merriam, William Rush
Meyer, Eugene Isaac
Miller, James

Government (Federal)
(cont.)
Moore, John Bassett
Morgan, Arthur Ernest
Moron, Alonzo
  Graseano *Suppl. 2*
Morrison, William Ralls
Murray, Thomas
  Edward
Myer, Albert James
Myer, Dillon Seymour
Nash, Philleo
Nelson, Donald Marr
Nelson, Edward William
Niles, David K.
Ohly, John Hallowell
Olds, Leland
Oliphant, Herman
Page, Charles Grafton
Page, Logan Waller
Patterson, Hannah Jane
Paulding, James Kirke
Peek, George Nelson
Pilling, James
  Constantine
Pope, Nathaniel
Post, Louis Freeland
Price, Byron
Prouty, Charles Azro
Raum, Green Berry
Rhees, William Jones
Rice, Stuart Arthur
Richberg, Donald
  Randall
Roberts, Frank H. H., Jr.
Roche, Josephine
  Aspinwall
Rosenberg, Anna Marie
  Lederer
Rowan, Carl T. *Suppl. 2*
Seaborg, Glenn T.
  Suppl. 1
Shaw, Nathaniel, Jr.
Smith, George Otis
Smith, Harold Dewey
Smith, Hilda Jane
  Worthington
Smith, Walter Bedell
Snowden, James Ross
Snyder, John Wesley
Sparks, William Andrew
  Jackson
Stettinius, Edward Reilly
Stewart, Alexander Peter
Strauss, Lewis
  Lichtenstein
Strong, Benjamin
Stryker, Roy Emerson
Switzer, Mary Elizabeth
Talbott, Harold Elstner
Tiffin, Edward

Truman, Benjamin
  Cummings
Tugwell, Rexford Guy
Vance, Harold Sines
Wadsworth, James
  Jeremiah
Walcott, Charles
  Doolittle
Walker, Frank
  Comerford
Warburg, James Paul
Ware, Nathaniel A.
Webb, James Edwin
Wheeler, John Hill
White, Harry Dexter
Wickard, Claude
  Raymond
Wiggins, A. L. M.
Williams, John Foster
Wilson, Charles Edward
Winston, Ellen Black
Woodward, Ellen
  Sullivan
Wrather, William Embry
Wright, Theodore Paul
Yeamans, Sir John
Yellowley, Edward
  Clements

First Ladies of the United States
Adams, Abigail
Adams, Louisa
  Catherine Johnson
Cleveland, Frances
  Folsom
Coolidge, Grace Anna
  Goodhue
Eisenhower, Mamie
  Doud
Fillmore, Abigail Powers
  Suppl. 2
Garfield, Lucretia
  Rudolph
Grant, Julia Dent
Harding, Florence Mabel
  Kling DeWolfe
Harrison, Anna *Suppl. 2*
Harrison, Caroline
  Lavinia Scott
Hayes, Lucy Ware
  Webb
Hoover, Lou Henry
Jackson, Rachel
  Donelson Robards
Johnson, Eliza McCardle
Johnston, Harriet Lane
Lincoln, Mary Todd
Madison, Dolley
McKinley, Ida Saxton

Monroe, Elizabeth
  Kortright
Nixon, Pat
Onassis, Jacqueline
  Kennedy
Pierce, Jane Means
  Appleton
Polk, Sarah Childress
  Suppl. 1
Randolph, Martha
  Jefferson
Roosevelt, Edith Kermit
  Carow
Roosevelt, Eleanor
Taft, Helen Herron
Taylor, Margaret
  Suppl. 1
Truman, Bess
Tyler, Julia Gardiner
Tyler, Letitia Christian
  Suppl. 2
Washington, Martha
  Dandridge Custis
Wilson, Edith Bolling
  Galt
Wilson, Ellen Axson

Foreign Advisers
Bundy, William *Suppl. 1*
Ferguson, John Calvin
Willoughby, Westel
  Woodbury
Young, John
  (1744–1835)

National Park Officials
Langford, Nathaniel Pitt
Mather, Stephen Tyng

Postal Officials
Davis, William
  Augustine
Goddard, Mary
  Katherine
Holbrook, James
Kasson, John Adam
Vail, Theodore Newton

Postmasters General
Barry, William Taylor
Blair, Montgomery
Burleson, Albert Sidney
Campbell, James
Cortelyou, George Bruce
Creswell, John Angel
  James
Dickinson, Donald
  McDonald
Farley, James Aloysius
Gresham, Walter
  Quintin

Habersham, Joseph
Hitchcock, Frank Harris
Holt, Joseph
Howe, Timothy Otis
Jewell, Marshall
Kendall, Amos
Key, David McKendree
Maynard, Horace
Meigs, Return Jonathan,
  Jr.
New, Harry Stewart
Randall, Alexander
  Williams
Reagan, John Henninger
Vilas, William Freeman
Walker, Frank
  Comerford
Wickliffe, Charles
  Anderson

Presidential Advisers
Aldrich, Winthrop
Bennett, John Charles
Blair, Francis Preston
Bloomingdale, Alfred
  Schiffer
Bundy, McGeorge
  Suppl. 1
Corcoran, Thomas
  Gardiner
Cutler, Robert
Dean, Arthur Hobson
Donelson, Andrew
  Jackson
Flynn, Edward Joseph
Gilpatric, Roswell L.
  Suppl. 1
Goldman, Eric
Graham, John
Haldeman, H. R.
Harlow, Bryce
Hauge, Gabriel Sylfest
Heller, Walter Wolfgang
Hopkins, Harry Lloyd
House, Edward Mandell
Howe, Louis McHenry
Hughes, Emmet John
Kistiakowsky, George
  Bogdan
Kleindienst, Richard G.
  Suppl. 1
Lauritsen, Charles
  Christian
Loomis, Francis Butler
Moley, Raymond
Okun, Arthur Melvin
Rosenman, Samuel
  Irving
Rublee, George
Stein, Herbert *Suppl. 1*

Government (Federal)
(cont.)
Taylor, Maxwell
Davenport
Walker, Frank
Comerford
Wallace, Hugh Campbell
Warburg, James Paul
Wiesner, Jerome Bert
Young, Owen D.

Presidential Press Secretaries
Cortelyou, George Bruce
Early, Stephen Tyree
Hagerty, James
Campbell
Reedy, George E.
Suppl. 1
Ross, Charles Griffith
Short, Joseph Hudson,
Jr.

Secret Service Agents
Baker, La Fayette Curry

Secretaries of Agriculture
Anderson, Clinton
Presba
Benson, Ezra Taft
Brannan, Charles F.
Suppl. 2
Colman, Norman Jay
Houston, David Franklin
Jardine, William Marion
Morton, Julius Sterling
Rusk, Jeremiah McClain
Wallace, Henry Agard
Wallace, Henry Cantwell
Wickard, Claude
Raymond
Wilson, James
(1836–1920)

Secretaries of Commerce
Brown, Ron *Suppl. 1*
Chapin, Roy Dikeman
Jones, Jesse Holman
Morton, Rogers C. B.
Richardson, Elliot
Suppl. 1
Roper, Daniel Calhoun
Weeks, Sinclair

*Secretaries of Commerce
and Labor*
Cortelyou, George Bruce
Straus, Oscar Solomon

Secretaries of Defense
Forrestal, James Vincent
Johnson, Louis Arthur

Lovett, Robert
Abercrombie
Wilson, Charles Erwin

*Secretaries of Health and
Human Services*
Harris, Patricia Roberts

*Secretaries of Health,
Education, and Welfare*
Cohen, Wilbur Joseph
Hobby, Oveta Culp
Suppl. 1

*Secretaries of Housing and
Urban Development*
Harris, Patricia Roberts
Weaver, Robert C.
Suppl. 2

Secretaries of Labor
Perkins, Frances
Tobin, Maurice Joseph
Wilson, William
Bauchop

Secretaries of State
Acheson, Dean
Gooderham
Adams, John Quincy
(1767–1848)
Bacon, Robert
Bayard, Thomas Francis
Black, Jeremiah Sullivan
Blaine, James Gillespie
Bryan, William Jennings
Buchanan, James
Byrnes, James Francis
Calhoun, John C.
Cass, Lewis
Clay, Henry
Clayton, John Middleton
Colby, Bainbridge
Day, William Rufus
Dulles, John Foster
Evarts, William Maxwell
Everett, Edward
Fish, Hamilton
(1808–1893)
Forsyth, John
Foster, John Watson
Frelinghuysen, Frederick
Theodore
Gresham, Walter
Quintin
Hay, John Milton
Herter, Christian
Archibald (1895–1966)
Hughes, Charles Evans
Hull, Cordell
Jefferson, Thomas

Kellogg, Frank Billings
Knox, Philander Chase
Lansing, Robert
Livingston, Edward
Marcy, William Learned
Marshall, George
Catlett, Jr.
Marshall, John
McLane, Louis
Monroe, James
Muskie, Edmund S.
Suppl. 1
Olney, Richard
Pickering, Timothy
Randolph, Edmund
Rogers, William Pierce
Suppl. 2
Root, Elihu
Rusk, Dean
Seward, William Henry
Sherman, John
Smith, Robert
(1757–1842)
Stettinius, Edward
Reilly, Jr.
Stimson, Henry Lewis
Upshur, Abel Parker
Van Buren, Martin
Washburne, Elihu
Benjamin
Webster, Daniel

Secretaries of the Air Force
Finletter, Thomas
Knight

Secretaries of the Army
Brucker, Wilber Marion

Secretaries of the Interior
Ballinger, Richard
Achilles
Chapman, Oscar
Littleton
Delano, Columbus
Fall, Albert Bacon
Fisher, Walter Lowrie
Garfield, James Rudolph
Harlan, James
(1820–1899)
Hitchcock, Ethan Allen
(1835–1909)
Ickes, Harold LeClair
Lamar, Lucius Quintus
Cincinnatus
Lane, Franklin Knight
McClelland, Robert
Morton, Rogers C. B.
Noble, John Willock
Schurz, Carl
Smith, Caleb Blood

Stuart, Alexander Hugh
Holmes
Thompson, Jacob
Usher, John Palmer
Suppl. 1
Vilas, William Freeman
West, Roy Owen
Wilbur, Ray Lyman
Work, Hubert

Secretaries of the Navy
Adams, Charles Francis
(1866–1954)
Branch, John, Jr.
Chafee, John H. *Suppl. 2*
Chandler, William Eaton
Connally, John Bowden,
Jr.
Daniels, Josephus
Denby, Edwin
Dickerson, Mahlon
Forrestal, James Vincent
Graham, William
Alexander
Herbert, Hilary Abner
Hunt, William Henry
(1823–1884)
Jones, William
(1760–1831)
Kimball, Dan Able
Knox, Frank
Long, John Davis
Matthews, Francis
Patrick
Meyer, George von
Lengerke
Moody, William Henry
Smith, Robert
(1757–1842)
Stoddert, Benjamin
Thompson, Smith
Toucey, Isaac
Tracy, Benjamin
Franklin
Upshur, Abel Parker
Welles, Gideon
Whitney, William
Collins

Secretaries of the Treasury
Carlisle, John Griffin
Connally, John Bowden,
Jr.
Cortelyou, George Bruce
Crawford, William
Harris
Fessenden, William Pitt
Folger, Charles James
Forward, Walter
Gage, Lyman Judson
Gallatin, Albert

Government (Federal)
(cont.)
Gresham, Walter
  Quintin
Guthrie, James
Hamilton, Alexander
  (1757?–1804)
Houston, David Franklin
Humphrey, George
  Magoffin
MacVeagh, Franklin
Manning, Daniel
McAdoo, William Gibbs
McCulloch, Hugh
Mills, Ogden Livingston
Morgenthau, Henry, Jr.
Morrill, Lot Myrick
Sherman, John
Snyder, John Wesley
Spencer, John Canfield
Walker, Robert John
Windom, William
Wolcott, Oliver
  Woodin, William
  Hartman

Secretaries of War
Alger, Russell Alexander
Baker, Newton Diehl
Belknap, William Worth
Cameron, Simon
Crawford, William
  Harris
Davis, Dwight Filley
Dern, George Henry
Endicott, William
  Crowninshield
Floyd, John Buchanan
Garrison, Lindley Miller
Holt, Joseph
Hurley, Patrick Jay
Knox, Henry
Lamont, Daniel Scott
Lincoln, Robert Todd
Marcy, William Learned
Patterson, Robert Porter
Porter, Peter Buell
Proctor, Redfield
Rawlins, John Aaron
Root, Elihu
Royall, Kenneth
  Claiborne
Spencer, John Canfield
Stanton, Edwin
  McMasters
Stimson, Henry Lewis
Weeks, John Wingate
Woodring, Harry Hines

Solicitors General
Beck, James
  Montgomery
Bowers, Lloyd Wheaton
Fahy, Charles
Perlman, Philip
  Benjamin
Rankin, J. Lee *Suppl. 1*

*Speakers of the U.S. House
of Representatives*
Albert, Carl *Suppl. 2*
Bankhead, William
  Brockman
Banks, Nathaniel
  Prentiss
Barbour, Philip
  Pendleton
Bell, John
Blaine, James Gillespie
Boyd, Linn
Byrns, Joseph
  Wellington
Cannon, Joseph Gurney
Carlisle, John Griffin
Cheves, Langdon
Clark, Champ
Clay, Henry
Cobb, Howell
Colfax, Schuyler
Crisp, Charles Frederick
Davis, John Wesley
Dayton, Jonathan
Garner, John Nance
Gillett, Frederick
  Huntington
Grow, Galusha Aaron
Henderson, David
  Bremner
Hunter, Robert M. T.
  Suppl. 2
Jones, John Winston
  Suppl. 2
Keifer, Joseph Warren
Kerr, Michael *Suppl. 2*
Longworth, Nicholas
  (1869–1931)
Macon, Nathaniel
Martin, Joseph William,
  Jr.
McCormack, John
  William
Muhlenberg, Frederick
  Augustus Conrad
O'Neill, Thomas Philip
  "Tip"
Orr, James Lawrence
Pennington, William
Polk, James Knox
Pomeroy, Theodore
  Medad *Suppl. 2*

Rainey, Henry Thomas
Randall, Samuel Jackson
Rayburn, Sam
Reed, Thomas Brackett
Sedgwick, Theodore
  (1746–1813)
Stevenson, Andrew
Taylor, John W. *Suppl. 2*
Trumbull, Jonathan, Jr.
Varnum, Joseph Bradley
Winthrop, Robert
  Charles

State Department Officials
Brunauer, Esther
Bundy, Harvey Hollister
Cardozo, Michael H.
  Suppl. 2
Carr, Wilbur John
Grew, Joseph Clark
Hiss, Alger *Suppl. 1*
Hornbeck, Stanley Kuhl
Lovett, Robert
  Abercrombie
Miller, David Hunter
Peurifoy, John Emil
Shipley, Ruth Bielaski
Watson, Barbara Mae

Territorial Delegates
Clark, Daniel
  (1766–1813)
Kuhio
Poindexter, George
Pope, Nathaniel
Poydras, Julien
Rice, Henry Mower
Sibley, Henry Hastings

*Treasurers of the United
States*
Clark, Georgia Neese
  Suppl. 1
Hillegas, Michael
Meredith, Samuel
Priest, Ivy Maude Baker
Spinner, Francis Elias

U.S. Presidents
Adams, John
  (1735–1826)
Adams, John Quincy
  (1767–1848)
Arthur, Chester Alan
Buchanan, James
Cleveland, Grover
Coolidge, Calvin
Eisenhower, Dwight
  David
Fillmore, Millard
Garfield, James Abram

Grant, Ulysses S.
Harding, Warren
  Gamaliel
Harrison, Benjamin
  (1833–1901)
Harrison, William Henry
Hayes, Rutherford
  Birchard
Hoover, Herbert Clark
Jackson, Andrew
Jefferson, Thomas
Johnson, Andrew
Johnson, Lyndon Baines
Kennedy, John
  Fitzgerald
Lincoln, Abraham
Madison, James
  (1751–1836)
McKinley, William
Monroe, James
Nixon, Richard Milhous
Pierce, Franklin
Polk, James Knox
Reagan, Ronald Wilson
  Suppl. 2
Roosevelt, Franklin
  Delano
Roosevelt, Theodore
Taft, William Howard
Taylor, Zachary
Truman, Harry S.
Tyler, John
Van Buren, Martin
Washington, George
  (1732–1799)
Wilson, Woodrow

U.S. Representatives
Abzug, Bella *Suppl. 1*
Adams, Henry Cullen
Adams, John Quincy
  (1767–1848)
Aiken, D. Wyatt
Aiken, William
Aldrich, Nelson
  Wilmarth
Alexander, De Alva
  Stanwood
Allen, Elisha Hunt
Allen, William
  (1803–1879)
Ames, Fisher
Ames, Oakes
  (1804–1873)
Anderson, Richard
  Clough, Jr.
Arends, Leslie Cornelius
Arnold, Isaac Newton
Ashbrook, John Milan
Ashe, Thomas Samuel
Ashley, James Mitchell

Government (Federal)
(cont.)
Ashmun, George
Atherton, Charles
  Gordon
Babcock, Joseph Weeks
Bailey, Joseph Weldon
Baker, Jehu
Banks, Nathaniel
  Prentiss
Barbour, Philip
  Pendleton
Barden, Graham Arthur
Barksdale, Ethelbert
Barksdale, William
Barnard, Daniel Dewey
Barnwell, Robert
  Woodward
Barrett, Frank Aloysius
Barringer, Daniel
  Moreau
Bartholdt, Richard
Bartley, Mordecai
Barton, Bruce Fairchild
Bayly, Thomas Henry
Beatty, John
Beck, James
  Montgomery
Bedinger, George
  Michael
Bender, George
  Harrison
Benton, Thomas Hart
  (1782–1858)
Berger, Victor Louis
Bidlack, Benjamin Alden
  Suppl. 1
Bissell, William Henry
Blair, Austin
Blair, Henry William
Bland, Richard Parks
Blount, James
  Henderson
Blow, Henry Taylor
Bolton, Frances Payne
Bonham, Milledge Luke
Bono, Sonny *Suppl. 1*
Bosone, Reva Beck
Boteler, Alexander
  Robinson
Bourne, Benjamin
Boutwell, George Sewall
Boyd, Linn
Boyle, John
Bradbury, Theophilus
Bragg, Edward
  Stuyvesant
Brentano, Lorenz
Briggs, George Nixon
Broadhead, James
  Overton

Brooks, Preston Smith
Brown, Albert Gallatin
Brown, Clarence J.
Brown, George E., Jr.
  Suppl. 2
Brown, John
  (1736–1803)
Brown, John
  (1757–1837)
Burdick, Usher Lloyd
Burke, Aedanus
Burke, James Anthony
Burleson, Albert Sidney
Burlingame, Anson
Burrows, Julius Caesar
Burton, Hutchins
  Gordon
Burton, Phillip
Burton, Theodore Elijah
Butler, William
Butterworth, Benjamin
Cabell, Samuel Jordan
Calhoun, William
  Barron
Cambreleng, Churchill
  Caldom
Caminetti, Anthony
Campbell, James
  Hepburn
Campbell, John Wilson
Campbell, Lewis Davis
Campbell, William
  Bowen
Cannon, Clarence
  Andrew
Cannon, Newton
Carlile, John Snyder
Carlisle, John Griffin
Case, Francis Higbee
Chalmers, James Ronald
Chambers, John
Chandler, John
Cheatham, Henry
  Plummer
Cheves, Langdon
Clay, Matthew
Clayton, Henry De
  Lamar
Clopton, John
Cockran, William
  Bourke
Colfax, Schuyler
Conger, Edwin Hurd
Connally, Thomas Terry
Cook, Philip
Copley, Ira Clifton
Covode, John
Cox, Samuel Sullivan
Crary, Isaac Edwin
Creighton, William

Crittenden, Thomas
  Theodore
Crocker, Alvah
Crockett, Davy
Cross, Edward
Culberson, David
  Browning
Curtis, Charles
Daggett, Rollin Mallory
Dalzell, John
Dana, Samuel
  Whittelsey
Davis, Garret
Davis, Henry Winter
Davis, John Wesley
Dawes, Henry Laurens
Dawson, William Crosby
Dawson, William Levi
Dayton, Jonathan
De Priest, Oscar Stanton
Delano, Columbus
Denby, Edwin
Desha, Joseph
Dickerson, Philemon
Dies, Martin
Dingley, Nelson, Jr.
Dixon, James
Doddridge, Philip
Doughton, Robert Lee
Draper, William
  Franklin
Drayton, William
  (1776–1846)
Dunlap, Robert
  Pinckney
DuVal, William Pope
Duvall, Gabriel *Suppl. 1*
Dworshak, Henry
  Clarence
Edgerton, Sidney
Elliott, Carl A. *Suppl. 1*
Elliott, Robert Brown
Engle, Clair William
  Walter
English, William Hayden
Eppes, John Wayles
Esch, John Jacob
Ewing, Thomas, Jr.
Farrington, Joseph Rider
Fenwick, Millicent
  Suppl. 2
Findlay, James
Findley, William
Fish, Hamilton
  (1888–1991)
Fitzsimons, Thomas
Flower, Roswell
  Pettibone
Flowers, Walter Winkler,
  Jr.
Floyd, William

Foot, Samuel Augustus
Foot, Solomon
Fordney, Joseph Warren
Forward, Walter
Frye, William Pierce
Fuller, Alvan Tufts
Garnett, James Mercer
Gartrell, Lucius Jeremiah
Gayle, John
Gibson, Randall Lee
Giddings, Joshua Reed
Giles, William Branch
Gilman, Nicholas
Gilmer, John Adams
González, Henry B.
  Suppl. 2
Goodenow, John Milton
Goodrich, Chauncey
  (1759–1815)
Goodwin, John Noble
Gore, Albert, Sr.
Grasso, Ella Tambussi
Green, Edith
Greenup, Christopher
Greenway, Isabella
Gregg, Andrew
Grosvenor, Charles
  Henry
Hale, Robert Safford
Halleck, Charles A.
Hamer, Thomas Lyon
Hamilton, James, Jr.
Hamilton, William
  Thomas
Hammond, Jabez Delano
Hampton, Wade
  (1754?–1835)
Hancock, John
  (1824–1893)
Hannegan, Edward Allen
Hanson, Alexander
  Contee (1786–1819)
Haralson, Jeremiah
Hardin, Benjamin, Jr.
Harlan, James
  (1800–1863)
Harper, Robert Goodloe
Harris, William
  Alexander
Harrison, Pat
Hartley, Fred Allan, Jr.
Hastings, William Wirt
Hatch, William Henry
Hayden, Carl Trumbull
Hébert, Felix Edward
Heflin, James Thomas
Hemphill, Joseph
Hendricks, William
Hepburn, William Peters
Herbert, Hilary Abner
Hewitt, Abram Stevens

Government (Federal)
(cont.)
Hill, Joshua
Hill, Lister
Hilliard, Henry
  Washington
Hindman, Thomas
  Carmichael
Hitt, Robert Roberts
Hoar, George Frisbie
Hobson, Richmond
  Pearson
Hoffman, Clare Eugene
Holman, William Steele
Holmes, John
Hooper, Samuel
Hopkinson, Joseph
Houghton, Alanson
  Bigelow
Howard, Benjamin
  Chew
Howard, Jacob Merritt
Hruska, Roman *Suppl. 1*
Huck, Winnifred
  Sprague Mason
Hull, Cordell
Hunt, Carleton
Hunt, Washington
Hunter, Robert M. T.
  Suppl. 2
Hunton, Eppa
Hyman, John Adams
Ingersoll, Charles Jared
Irvine, William
Jackson, James
  (1757–1806)
Jackson, John George
Jenckes, Thomas Allen
Jenkins, Albert Gallatin
Johnson, Albert
Johnson, Richard
  Mentor
Johnson, Robert Ward
Johnston, Josiah
  Stoddard
Jones, John Winston
  Suppl. 2
Jordan, Barbara *Suppl. 1*
Kahn, Florence Prag
Kahn, Julius
Kasson, John Adam
Keating, Kenneth
  Barnard
Keifer, Joseph Warren
Keitt, Laurence
  Massillon
Kelley, William Darrah
Kerr, Michael *Suppl. 2*
Kershaw, Joseph Brevard
Key, Philip Barton
King, Preston

King, Thomas Butler
Kitchin, Claude
Kitchin, William Walton
Knott, James Proctor
Lacey, John Fletcher
Lacock, Abner
La Follette, Robert
  Marion
La Guardia, Fiorello
  Henry
Lamar, Lucius Quintus
  Cincinnatus
Lane, Henry Smith
Langley, Katherine
  Gudger
Lanham, Fritz
Laurance, John
Lawrence, William
  (1819–1899)
Leavitt, Humphrey
  Howe
Lee, Richard Bland
Lee, William Henry
  Fitzhugh
Lemke, William
  Frederick
Lenroot, Irvine Luther
Letcher, John
Letcher, Robert Perkins
Lever, Asbury Francis
Lewis, Dixon Hall
Ligon, Thomas Watkins
Lind, John
Lindbergh, Charles
  August
Lindsay, John Vliet
  Suppl. 2
Long, John Davis
Lovejoy, Owen
Lowenstein, Allard
  Kenneth
Lucas, Robert
Ludlow, Louis Leon
  Suppl. 2
Lundeen, Ernest
Lusk, Georgia Lee Witt
Lynch, John Roy
Lyon, Matthew
Maclay, Samuel
Maclay, William Brown
Mahon, George Herman
Mallary, Rollin Carolas
Mangum, Willie Person
Mankin, Helen Douglas
Mann, James Robert
Marcantonio, Vito
  Anthony
Mason, James Murray
Matsunaga, Spark
  Masayuki

Maxwell, Augustus
  Emmet
May, Andrew Jackson
Maynard, Horace
McArthur, Duncan
McCall, Samuel Walker
McClurg, Joseph
  Washington
McComas, Louis Emory
McCormick, Ruth
  Hanna
McDonald, Lawrence
  Patton
McDuffie, George
McFadden, Louis
  Thomas
McGranery, James
  Patrick
McKee, John
McKennan, Thomas
  McKean Thompson
McLane, Robert
  Milligan
McLemore, Jeff
McPherson, Edward
Mercer, Charles Fenton
Metcalfe, Ralph Harold
Metcalfe, Thomas
Miles, William Porcher
Miller, Stephen Decatur
Miller, William Edward
Mills, Ogden Livingston
Mills, Roger Quarles
Mills, Wilbur Daigh
Mitchell, Arthur Wergs
Mitchell, George
  Edward
Mondell, Frank Wheeler
Money, Hernando de
  Soto
Monroney, Mike
Moody, William Henry
Moore, Andrew
Moore, Ely
Moore, Gabriel
Moore, Thomas Patrick
Morrill, Edmund
  Needham
Morrill, Justin Smith
Morris, Edward Joy
Morrison, William Ralls
Morrissey, John
Morrow, Jeremiah
Morse, Freeman Harlow
Morton, Marcus
Morton, Thruston
  Ballard
Muhlenberg, Henry
  Augustus Philip
Mundt, Karl Earl
Murdock, Victor

Murphy, Henry Cruse
Murray, William Vans
Nash, Charles Edmund
Nelson, Hugh
Nelson, Knute
Newell, William
  Augustus
Newlands, Francis
  Griffith
Nisbet, Eugenius
  Aristides
Norris, George William
Norton, Elijah Hise
Norton, Mary Teresa
  Hopkins
Nott, Abraham
O'Day, Caroline Love
  Goodwin
Orth, Godlove Stein
Owen, Robert Dale
Pacheco, Romualdo
Palmer, A. Mitchell
Paterson, John
Patman, Wright
Payne, Sereno Elisha
Pendleton, George Hunt
Pendleton, John Strother
Pennington, William
Pepper, Claude Denson
Perkins, Carl Dewey
Peters, John Andrew
Phelps, William Walter
Pickering, Timothy
Pleasants, James
Pool, Joe Richard
Porter, Peter Buell
Porter, Stephen Geyer
Potter, Robert
Powell, Adam Clayton,
  Jr.
Preston, William Ballard
Price, Hiram
Prouty, Winston Lewis
Pujo, Arsene Paulin
Quincy, Josiah
  (1772–1864)
Randolph, Jennings
  Suppl. 1
Randolph, John
  (1773–1833)
Randolph, Thomas
  Mann
Rankin, Jeannette
  Pickering
Rankin, John Elliott
Ransdell, Joseph Eugene
Rapier, James Thomas
Reagan, John Henninger
Rhea, John
Ribicoff, Abraham
  Suppl. 1

Government (Federal)
(cont.)

Richardson, James
  Daniel
Rivers, Mendel
Roberts, Ellis Henry
Robertson, Alice Mary
Robinson, George
  Dexter
Robinson, Joseph Taylor
Rogers, Edith Nourse
Rohde, Ruth Bryan
  Owen
Rollins, Edward Henry
Rollins, James Sidney
Rosecrans, William
  Starke
Rousseau, Lovell
  Harrison
Rusk, Jeremiah McClain
Sabath, Adolph Joachim
Saunders, Romulus
  Mitchell
Sawyer, Lemuel, Jr.
Saylor, John Phillips
  Suppl. 2
Schenck, Robert
  Cumming
Seddon, James
  Alexander
Seelye, Julius Hawley
Sergeant, John
  (1779–1852)
Sevier, John
Shellabarger, Samuel
  (1817–1896)
Shepard, William
Sheppard, Morris
Sherman, James S.
  Suppl. 1
Simms, William Elliott
Simpson, Jerry
Slemp, Campbell
  Bascom
Smalls, Robert
Smilie, John
Smith, Caleb Blood
Smith, Howard Worth
Smith, Israel
Smith, Jeremiah
Smith, Margaret Chase
Smith, Meriwether
Smith, Oliver Hampton
Smith, Samuel
  (1752–1839)
Smith, Truman
Smith, William
  Loughton
Smith, William Stephens
Smyth, Alexander
Snell, Bertrand Hollis

Sparkman, John Jackson
Sparks, William Andrew
  Jackson
Spaulding, Elbridge
  Gerry
Speer, Emory
Spence, Brent
Spinner, Francis Elias
Spinola, Francis Barretto
Springer, William
  McKendree
Stanly, Edward
Steed, Thomas Jefferson
Stevens, Thaddeus
Stewart, Bennett McVey
Stewart, John George
St. George, Katharine
  Delano Price Collier
Stone, David
Stone, William Joel
Story, Joseph
Stuart, John Todd
Sullivan, George
Sullivan, Leonor Alice
  Kretzer
Sumter, Thomas
Swanwick, John
Swift, Zephaniah
Taber, John
Tallmadge, Benjamin
Tallmadge, James
Tawney, James Albertus
Taylor, Alfred Alexander
Taylor, John W. *Suppl. 2*
Teague, Olin Earl
Thayer, Eli
Thomas, David
Thomas, Elmer
Thomas, J. Parnell
Thompson, Jacob
Thompson, Thomas
  Larkin
Thompson, Waddy
Thompson, Wiley
Tinkham, George
  Holden
Towne, Charles Arnette
Troup, George Michael
Trumbull, Jonathan, Jr.
Tsongas, Paul Efthemios
  Suppl. 2
Tucker, Henry St.
  George (1780–1848)
Tucker, John Randolph
  (1823–1897)
Turner, Benjamin
  Sterling
Udall, Morris K.
  Suppl. 1
Underwood, Oscar
  Wilder

Vallandigham, Clement
  Laird
Van Rensselaer,
  Solomon
Van Rensselaer, Stephen
Vance, Zebulon Baird
Verplanck, Gulian
  Crommelin
Vinson, Carl
Vinton, Samuel Finley
Volstead, Andrew John
Voorhees, Daniel Wolsey
Voorhis, Horace
  Jeremiah
Wadsworth, Jeremiah
Wallace, David
Walls, Josiah Thomas
Washburn, Israel, Jr.
Washburn, William
  Drew
Washburne, Elihu
  Benjamin
Washington, Harold
Watson, James Eli
Weaver, James Baird
Weeks, John Wingate
Welch, John
Wentworth, John
  (1815–1888)
West, George
White, Albert Smith
White, Edward Douglass
  (1795–1847)
White, George Henry
Whitehill, Robert
Whitman, Ezekiel
Wickliffe, Charles
  Anderson
Williams, John Bell
Williams, John Sharp
Willis, Albert Shelby
Wilmot, David
Wilson, James Falconer
Wilson, William
  Bauchop
Windom, William
Winn, Richard
Winthrop, Robert
  Charles
Wise, Henry Alexander
Wolf, George
Wood, Fernando
Wood, John Stephens
Wright, Hendrick
  Bradley
Wright, Joseph Albert
Wright, Robert
Yancey, William
  Lowndes
Young, Pierce Manning
  Butler

Zablocki, Clement John

U.S. Senators
Abbott, Joseph Carter
Aiken, George David
Alcorn, James Lusk
Aldrich, Nelson
  Wilmarth
Allen, Philip
Allen, William
  (1803–1879)
Allen, William Vincent
Allison, William Boyd
Ames, Adelbert
Anderson, Clinton
  Presba
Anderson, Joseph Inslee
Anthony, Henry Bowen
Ashurst, Henry Fountain
Atchison, David Rice
Atherton, Charles
  Gordon
Austin, Warren
  Robinson
Badger, George Edmund
Bailey, Joseph Weldon
Bailey, Josiah William
Baldwin, Roger Sherman
Bankhead, John Hollis
  (1872–1946)
Barnwell, Robert
  Woodward
Barrett, Frank Aloysius
Bate, William Brimage
Bayard, James Asheton
Bayard, Richard Henry
Bayard, Thomas Francis
Bell, Samuel
Bender, George
  Harrison
Benjamin, Judah Philip
Benton, Thomas Hart
  (1782–1858)
Beveridge, Albert
  Jeremiah
Bibb, William Wyatt
Bible, Alan Harvey
Bigler, William
Bilbo, Theodore
  Gilmore
Bingham, Hiram
Black, Hugo Lafayette
Blaine, John James
Blair, Henry William
Blease, Coleman
  Livingston
Blount, William
Bogy, Lewis Vital
Borah, William Edgar
Borland, Solon
Bouligny, Dominique

Government (Federal)
(cont.)
Bourne, Jonathan, Jr.
Bowen, Thomas Meade
Bradley, Stephen Row
Bragg, Thomas
Branch, John, Jr.
Brice, Calvin Stewart
Bricker, John William
Bridges, Styles
Bright, Jesse David
Bristow, Joseph Little
Broderick, David
  Colbert
Brookhart, Smith
  Wildman
Brown, Benjamin Gratz
Brown, Ethan Allen
Brown, James
Brown, John
  (1757–1837)
Brown, Joseph Emerson
Bruce, Blanche Kelso
Bruce, William Cabell
Buckalew, Charles Rollin
Buckingham, William
  Alfred
Bulkeley, Morgan
  Gardner
Burnet, Jacob
Burr, Aaron
  (1756–1836)
Burrows, Julius Caesar
Burton, Theodore Elijah
Bush, Prescott Sheldon
Butler, Andrew Pickens
Butler, Hugh Alfred
Butler, Marion
Butler, Matthew
  Calbraith
Butler, Pierce
  (1744–1822)
Byrd, Harry Flood
Byrnes, James Francis
Caffery, Donelson
Calhoun, John C.
Camden, Johnson
  Newlon
Cameron, Don
Cameron, Simon
Capehart, Homer Earl
Capper, Arthur
Caraway, Hattie Ophelia
  Wyatt
Carey, Joseph Maull
Carlile, John Snyder
Carlisle, John Griffin
Carlson, Frank
Carpenter, Matthew
  Hale
Carter, Thomas Henry

Case, Clifford Philip
Catron, Thomas Benton
Chafee, John H. *Suppl. 2*
Chandler, Albert
  Benjamin
Chandler, John
Chandler, Zachariah
Chavez, Dennis
Chesnut, James, Jr.
Chiles, Lawton *Suppl. 2*
Chipman, Nathaniel
Christiancy, Isaac
  Peckham
Church, Frank
Clark, Bennett Champ
Clark, Daniel
  (1809–1891)
Clark, William Andrews
Clarke, James Paul
Clay, Clement Claiborne
Clay, Clement Comer
Clayton, John Middleton
Clayton, Powell
Cocke, William
Cockrell, Francis Marion
Coke, Richard
Connally, Thomas Terry
Cooper, John Sherman
Copeland, Royal Samuel
Costigan, Edward
  Prentiss
Couzens, James
Coverdell, Paul *Suppl. 2*
Cowan, Edgar A.
Crane, Winthrop
  Murray
Crawford, William
  Harris
Crittenden, John Jordan
Culberson, Charles Allen
Cummins, Albert Baird
Curtis, Carl T. *Suppl. 1*
Curtis, Charles
Cutting, Bronson
  Murray
Dallas, George Mifflin
Dana, Samuel
  Whittelsey
Daniel, John Warwick
Davis, Garret
Davis, Henry Gassaway
Davis, Jeff
Davis, Jefferson
Dawes, Henry Laurens
Dawson, William Crosby
Deneen, Charles Samuel
Depew, Chauncey
  Mitchell
Dirksen, Everett
  McKinley
Dodd, Thomas Joseph

Dodge, Henry
Dolliver, Jonathan
  Prentiss
Dolph, Joseph Norton
Doolittle, James Rood
Dorsey, Stephen Wallace
Douglas, Paul Howard
Douglas, Stephen
  Arnold
Downey, Sheridan
Drake, Charles Daniel
Duff, James Henderson
du Pont, Henry
  Algernon
du Pont, T. Coleman
Dworshak, Henry
  Clarence
Eastland, James Oliver
Edmunds, George
  Franklin
Edwards, Ninian
Ellis, Powhatan
Engle, Clair William
  Walter
Eppes, John Wayles
Ervin, Sam J., Jr.
Fair, James Graham
Fairfield, John
Fenton, Reuben Eaton
Ferguson, Homer
Fessenden, William Pitt
Fitzpatrick, Benjamin
Flanders, Ralph Edward
Foot, Samuel Augustus
Foot, Solomon
Foote, Henry Stuart
Foraker, Joseph Benson
Fowler, Joseph Smith
Frazier, Lynn Joseph
Frelinghuysen, Frederick
  Theodore
Frye, William Pierce
Fulbright, J. William
Gallinger, Jacob Harold
Garland, Augustus Hill
Gear, John Henry
George, James Zachariah
George, Walter *Suppl. 2*
Geyer, Henry Sheffie
Gibson, Randall Lee
Giles, William Branch
Gilman, Nicholas
Glass, Carter
Goldthwaite, George
Goldwater, Barry
  Suppl. 1
Goodrich, Chauncey
  (1759–1815)
Gore, Albert, Sr.
  Suppl. 1
Gore, Thomas Pryor

Gorman, Arthur Pue
Graham, Frank Porter
Graham, William
  Alexander
Green, Theodore
  Francis
Gregg, Andrew
Gruening, Ernest Henry
Grundy, Joseph Ridgway
Guffey, Joseph F.
Guthrie, James
Hale, Eugene
Hale, John Parker
Hamilton, William
  Thomas
Hamlin, Hannibal
Hammond, James Henry
Hampton, Wade
  (1818–1902)
Hanna, Marcus Alonzo
Hannegan, Edward Allen
Hanson, Alexander
  Contee (1786–1819)
Hardin, Martin D.
Harlan, James
  (1820–1899)
Harper, Robert Goodloe
Harper, William
Harris, Isham Green
Harris, William
  Alexander
Harrison, Pat
Hatch, Carl Atwood
Hawkins, Benjamin
Hayden, Carl Trumbull
Hayne, Robert Young
Hearst, George
Heflin, James Thomas
Hemphill, John
Henderson, James
  Pinckney
Henderson, John Brooks
Hendricks, William
Hickenlooper, Bourke B.
Hicks, Thomas Holliday
Hill, Benjamin Harvey
Hill, Joshua
Hill, Lister
Hill, Nathaniel Peter
Hoar, George Frisbie
Holmes, John
Houston, George Smith
Houston, Sam
Howard, Jacob Merritt
Howard, John Eager
Howe, Timothy Otis
Hruska, Roman *Suppl. 1*
Humphrey, Hubert
  Horatio
Hunt, Lester Callaway

Government (Federal)
(cont.)

Hunter, Robert M. T.
  Suppl. 2
Hunton, Eppa
Ingalls, John James
Ives, Irving McNeil
Izard, Ralph
Jackson, Henry Martin
Jackson, James
  (1757–1806)
James, Ollie Murray
Jarvis, Thomas Jordan
Javits, Jacob Koppel
Johnson, Herschel
  Vespasian
Johnson, Hiram Warren
Johnson, Lyndon Baines
Johnson, Reverdy
Johnston, Josiah
  Stoddard
Johnston, Samuel
Jones, John Percival
Jones, Wesley Livsey
Keating, Kenneth
  Barnard
Kefauver, Estes
Kellogg, William Pitt
Kennedy, Robert Francis
Kenyon, William Squire
King, Rufus
  (1755–1827)
King, William Rufus
  Devane
Knowland, William Fife
Knox, Philander Chase
Lacock, Abner
Ladd, Edwin Fremont
La Follette, Robert
  Marion
La Follette, Robert
  Marion, Jr.
Lamar, Lucius Quintus
  Cincinnatus
Lane, Henry Smith
Lane, James Henry
  (1814–1866)
Langer, William
Larrazolo, Octaviano
  Ambrosio
Laurance, John
Lee, Richard Henry
Lenroot, Irvine Luther
Lewis, Dixon Hall
Linn, Lewis Fields
Livermore, Samuel
  (1732–1803)
Lodge, Henry Cabot
  (1850–1924)
Lodge, Henry Cabot

(1902–1985)
Logan, John Alexander
Long, Huey Pierce
Lucas, Scott Wike
Lundeen, Ernest
Maclay, Samuel
Magnuson, Warren
  Grant
Mahone, William
Mallory, Stephen Russell
Manderson, Charles
  Frederick
Mangum, Willie Person
Marshall, Humphrey
Mason, James Murray
Mason, Jeremiah
Matsunaga, Spark
  Masayuki
McAdoo, William Gibbs
McCarran, Patrick
  Anthony
McCarthy, Joseph
McClellan, John Little
McComas, Louis Emory
McCormick, Medill
McDill, James Wilson
McDuffie, George
McEnery, Samuel
  Douglas
McFarland, Ernest
  William
McGrath, J. Howard
McKinley, John
McLaurin, Anselm
  Joseph
McMahon, Brien
McMillan, James
McNary, Charles Linza
Meigs, Return Jonathan,
  Jr.
Merrimon, Augustus
  Summerfield
Metcalfe, Thomas
Miller, Stephen Decatur
Millikin, Eugene Donald
Mills, Roger Quarles
Minton, Sherman
Mitchell, John Hipple
Money, Hernando de
  Soto
Monroney, Mike
Montoya, Joseph Manuel
Moore, Andrew
Moore, Gabriel
Morgan, John Tyler
Morrill, Lot Myrick
Morris, Thomas
Morrow, Dwight
  Whitney
Morrow, Jeremiah
Morse, Wayne Lyman
Morton, Oliver Perry

Morton, Thruston
  Ballard
Mundt, Karl Earl
Murray, James Edward
Muskie, Edmund S.
  Suppl. 1
Nelson, Knute
Neuberger, Richard
  Lewis
New, Harry Stewart
Newberry, Truman
  Handy
Newlands, Francis
  Griffith
Noble, James
Norbeck, Peter
Norris, George William
North, William
Nye, Gerald Prentice
Nye, James Warren
O'Daniel, W. Lee
O'Mahoney, Joseph
  Christopher
Overman, Lee Slater
Palmer, John McAuley
  (1817–1900)
Palmer, William Adams
Pearce, James Alfred
Peffer, William Alfred
Pendleton, George Hunt
Penrose, Boies
Pepper, Claude Denson
Pepper, George
  Wharton
Pettigrew, Richard
  Franklin
Pickens, Israel
Pickering, Timothy
Pittman, Key
Platt, Orville Hitchcock
Pleasants, James
Plumb, Preston B.
Plumer, William
Poindexter, George
Poindexter, Miles
Pomerene, Atlee
Pomeroy, Samuel Clarke
Pool, John
Porter, Alexander
Preston, William
  Campbell
Proctor, Redfield
Prouty, Winston Lewis
Pugh, George Ellis
Randolph, Jennings
  Suppl. 1
Randolph, John
  (1773–1833)
Ransdell, Joseph Eugene
Ransom, Matt Whitaker
Reagan, John Henninger

Reed, David Aiken
Reed, James Alexander
Reid, David Settle
Revels, Hiram Rhoades
Reynolds, Robert Rice
Ribicoff, Abraham
  Suppl. 1
Rice, Henry Mower
Robinson, Joseph Taylor
Rollins, Edward Henry
Root, Elihu
Ross, Edmund Gibson
Ross, James
Rowan, John
Russell, Richard
  Brevard, Jr.
Saltonstall, Leverett
Sanford, Terry *Suppl. 1*
Saulsbury, Eli
Saulsbury, Willard
Sawyer, Philetus
Schoeppel, Andrew
  Frank
Schurz, Carl
Scott, Kerr
Seward, William Henry
Sheppard, Morris
Sherman, John
Shoup, George Laird
Slidell, John
Smith, Ellison DuRant
Smith, Israel
Smith, John
  (c.1735–1824)
Smith, Margaret Chase
Smith, Oliver Hampton
Smith, Samuel
  (1752–1839)
Smith, William
  (1762–1840)
Smoot, Reed Owen
Soulé, Pierre
Sparkman, John Jackson
Spencer, George Eliphaz
Spooner, John Coit
Stanford, Leland
Stennis, John Cornelius
Stevenson, Adlai Ewing
Stevenson, John White
Stewart, William Morris
Stockton, John Potter
Stokes, Montfort
Stone, William Joel
Sumter, Thomas
Sutherland, George
Symington, Stuart
Taft, Robert Alphonso
Tappan, Benjamin
Taylor, Glen Hearst
Taylor, Robert Love
Thayer, John Milton

Government (Federal)
(cont.)
Thomas, Elmer
Thurman, Allen
  Granberry
Tichenor, Isaac
Tiffin, Edward
Tillman, Benjamin Ryan
Tipton, John
Toombs, Robert
  Augustus
Toucey, Isaac
Tower, John G. *Suppl. 2*
Troup, George Michael
Trumbull, Jonathan, Jr.
Trumbull, Lyman
Tsongas, Paul Efthemios
  Suppl. 2
Tydings, Millard Evelyn
Underwood, Oscar
  Wilder
Vance, Zebulon Baird
Vandenberg, Arthur H.
Van Dyke, Nicholas
  (1769–1826)
Van Winkle, Peter
  Godwin
Vest, George Graham
Vilas, William Freeman
Voorhees, Daniel Wolsey
Wade, Benjamin
  Franklin
Wadsworth, James
  Wolcott, Jr.
Wagner, Robert F.
Walker, Robert John
Walsh, David Ignatius
Walsh, Thomas James
Walthall, Edward Cary
Watkins, Arthur Vivian
Watson, James Eli
Weeks, John Wingate
Weller, John Brown
Wheeler, Burton Kendall
Wherry, Kenneth Spicer
Whitcomb, James
White, Albert Smith
White, Edward Douglass
  (1845–1921)
White, Hugh Lawson
White, Stephen Mallory
Wigfall, Louis Trezevant
Wiley, Alexander
Willey, Waitman
  Thomas
Williams, George Henry
Williams, John
  (1778–1837)
Williams, John Sharp
Wilson, Henry
Wilson, James Falconer

Windom, William
Winthrop, Robert
  Charles
Worthington, Thomas
Wright, Robert
Wright, Silas
Yates, Richard
Young, Milton Rueben
Yulee, David Levy

U.S. Supreme Court Chief Justices
Burger, Warren Earl
Chase, Salmon Portland
Ellsworth, Oliver
Fuller, Melville Weston
Hughes, Charles Evans
Jay, John
Marshall, John
Rutledge, John
Stone, Harlan Fiske
Taft, William Howard
Taney, Roger Brooke
Vinson, Fred
Waite, Morrison Remick
Warren, Earl
White, Edward Douglass
  (1845–1921)

U.S. Supreme Court Justices
Baldwin, Henry
Barbour, Philip
  Pendleton
Black, Hugo Lafayette
Blackmun, Harry A.
  Suppl. 1
Blair, John, Jr.
Blatchford, Samuel
Bradley, Joseph P.
Brandeis, Louis Dembitz
Brennan, William J., Jr.
  Suppl. 1
Brewer, David Josiah
Brown, Henry Billings
Burton, Harold Hitz
Butler, Pierce
  (1866–1939)
Byrnes, James Francis
Campbell, John
  Archibald
Cardozo, Benjamin
  Nathan
Catron, John
Chase, Samuel
Clark, Tom Campbell
Clarke, John Hessin
Clifford, Nathan
Cobb, Howell
Curtis, Benjamin
  Robbins

Cushing, William
Daniel, Peter Vivian
Davis, David
Day, William Rufus
Douglas, William O.
Duvall, Gabriel *Suppl. 1*
Field, Stephen Johnson
Fortas, Abe
Frankfurter, Felix
Goldberg, Arthur Joseph
Gray, Horace
Grier, Robert Cooper
Harlan, John Marshall
  (1833–1911)
Harlan, John Marshall
  (1899–1971)
Holmes, Oliver Wendell
  (1841–1935)
Hughes, Charles Evans
Hunt, Ward
Iredell, James
Jackson, Howell
  Edmunds
Jackson, Robert
  Houghwout
Johnson, Thomas
Johnson, William
  (1771–1834)
Lamar, Joseph Rucker
Lamar, Lucius Quintus
  Cincinnatus
Livingston, Brockholst
Lurton, Horace Harmon
Marshall, Thurgood
Matthews, Stanley
McKenna, Joseph
McKinley, John
McLean, John
McReynolds, James
  Clark
Miller, Samuel Freeman
Minton, Sherman
Moody, William Henry
Moore, Alfred *Suppl. 2*
Murphy, Frank
Nelson, Samuel
Paterson, William
Peckham, Rufus
  Wheeler
Pitney, Mahlon
Powell, Lewis F., Jr.
  Suppl. 1
Reed, Stanley Forman
Roberts, Owen Josephus
Rutledge, John
Rutledge, Wiley Blount,
  Jr.
Sanford, Edward Terry
Shiras, George
Stewart, Potter
Stone, Harlan Fiske

Story, Joseph
Strong, William
Sutherland, George
Swayne, Noah Haynes
Thompson, Smith
Todd, Thomas
Trimble, Robert
Van Devanter, Willis
Washington, Bushrod
Wayne, James Moore
White, Edward Douglass
  (1845–1921)
Whittaker, Charles E.
  Suppl. 1
Wilson, James
  (1742–1798)
Woodbury, Levi
Woods, William
  Burnham

U.S. Vice Presidents
Adams, John
  (1735–1826)
Agnew, Spiro T.
  Suppl. 1
Arthur, Chester Alan
Barkley, Alben William
Breckinridge, John
  Cabell
Burr, Aaron
  (1756–1836)
Calhoun, John C.
Clinton, George
  (1739–1812)
Colfax, Schuyler
Coolidge, Calvin
Curtis, Charles
Dallas, George Mifflin
Dawes, Charles Gates
Fairbanks, Charles
  Warren
Fillmore, Millard
Garner, John Nance
Gerry, Elbridge
Hamlin, Hannibal
Hendricks, Thomas
  Andrews
Hobart, Garret Augustus
Humphrey, Hubert
  Horatio
Jefferson, Thomas
Johnson, Andrew
Johnson, Lyndon Baines
Johnson, Richard
  Mentor
King, William Rufus
  Devane
Marshall, Thomas Riley
Morton, Levi Parsons
Nixon, Richard Milhous

Government (Federal)
(cont.)
Rockefeller, Nelson
  Aldrich
Roosevelt, Theodore
Sherman, James S.
  Suppl. 1
Stevenson, Adlai Ewing
Tompkins, Daniel D.
Truman, Harry S.
Tyler, John
Van Buren, Martin
Wallace, Henry Agard
Wheeler, William Almon
Wilson, Henry

White House Staff
Babcock, Orville Elias
Ehrlichman, John D.
  Suppl. 1
Keckley, Elizabeth
  Hobbs
Lincoln, Evelyn *Suppl. 1*
Nicolay, John George
Parks, Lillian Rogers
  Suppl. 1
Shaw, William Smith
Slemp, Campbell
  Bascom
Tully, Grace George
Vaughan, Harry
  Hawkins

Government (Non-Federal)
Attorneys General (State)
Atherton, Joshua
Innes, James
Martin, Luther
Paine, Robert Treat
Stockton, John Potter
Tucker, John Randolph
  (1823–1897)
Warren, Earl
Wilentz, David
  Theodore

County Officials
Jones, John (1816–1879)
Pelham, Benjamin B.

Mayors
Alioto, Joseph L.
  Suppl. 1
Baker, Newton Diehl
Behrman, Martin
Cermak, Anton Joseph
Clinton, De Witt
Conrad, Robert Taylor
Couzens, James
Cruger, Henry, Jr.

Curley, James Michael
Curtis, Edwin Upton
Daley, Richard Joseph
DiSalle, Michael Vincent
Dow, Neal
Dunne, Edward
  Fitzsimmons
Fagan, Mark Matthew
Fargo, William George
Fitzgerald, John Francis
Gaston, William
Gaynor, William Jay
Grace, William Russell
Hague, Frank
Hall, Abraham Oakey
Hamtramck, John
  Francis
Hardin, William
  Jefferson
Harrison, Carter Henry
Harrison, Carter Henry,
  Jr.
Havemeyer, William
  Frederick
Hewitt, Abram Stevens
Hoan, Daniel Webster
Hoffman, John
  Thompson
Jones, Samuel Milton
Kelly, Edward Joseph
Ladd, William Sargent
La Guardia, Fiorello
  Henry
Landes, Bertha Ethel
  Knight
Lindsay, John Vliet
  Suppl. 2
Low, Seth
Matthews, Nathan, Jr.
McClellan, George
  Brinton
Mitchel, John Purroy
Moore, Alfred *Suppl. 2*
Moscone, George
  Richard
O'Dwyer, William
Pingree, Hazen S.
Quincy, Josiah
  (1772–1864)
Quincy, Josiah
  (1859–1919)
Radcliff, Jacob
Rizzo, Frank Lazzaro
Rolph, James, Jr.
Seidel, George Lukas
  Emil
Skaggs, William H.
  Suppl. 1
Stanford, Sally
Stokes, Carl *Suppl. 1*

Strong, William
  Lafayette
Swann, Thomas
Thompson, William
  Hale
Wagner, Robert F.
Walker, James J.
Washington, Harold
Wentworth, John
  (1815–1888)
Wharton, Robert
Wherry, Kenneth Spicer
Whitlock, Brand
Willett, Marinus
Wood, Fernando
Yorty, Sam *Suppl. 1*
Young, Coleman
  Suppl. 1

Military Governors
Cortina, Juan
  Nepomuceno
Mason, Richard Barnes
Riley, Bennet
Stanly, Edward
Washington, John
  Macrae
Wood, Leonard

Municipal Government Officials
Byrnes, Thomas F.
Connor, Bull
Croker, Richard
Davies, Henry Eugene,
  Jr.
Denton, Daniel
Jackson, Robert R.
McArthur, John
Milk, Harvey
Moses, Robert
Pelham, Benjamin B.
Whalen, Grover Michael
  Aloysius Augustine

Resident Commissioners
Iglesias, Santiago
Muñoz Rivera, Luis

State Government Officials
Adams, Henry Cullen
Anderson, Charles
  William
Austin, Jonathan Loring
Cardozo, Francis Louis
Cheatham, Henry
  Plummer
Daniel, Peter Vivian
Eastman, Joseph Bartlett
Forbes, Stephen Alfred
Gibson, Mary Simons

Gilman, John Taylor
Gregg, David
  McMurtrie
Harpur, Robert
Kennedy, John
  Alexander
Parsons, Lewis Eliphalet
Pettit, Charles
Talmadge, Eugene
Thomas, David
Weinfeld, Edward

State Governors
Adair, John
Adams, James Hopkins
Adams, Samuel
Adams, Sherman
  Llewelyn
Agnew, Spiro T.
  Suppl. 1
Aiken, William
Alcorn, James Lusk
Alger, Russell Alexander
Allen, Henry Justin
Allen, Henry Watkins
Allen, Philip
Allen, William
  (1803–1879)
Allston, Robert Francis
  Withers
Alston, Joseph
Altgeld, John Peter
Ames, Adelbert
Ames, Oliver
  (1831–1895)
Andrew, John Albion
Anthony, Henry Bowen
Armijo, Manuel
Ashe, Samuel
Aycock, Charles
  Brantley
Baldwin, Roger Sherman
Baldwin, Simeon Eben
Banks, Nathaniel
  Prentiss
Barnett, Ross Robert
Barrett, Frank Aloysius
Bartlett, Josiah
Bartley, Mordecai
Bass, Robert Perkins
Bassett, Richard
Bate, William Brimage
Baxter, Elisha
Bedford, Gunning
  (1742–1797)
Bell, Samuel
Bibb, William Wyatt
Bigler, John
Bigler, William
Bilbo, Theodore
Gilmore

Government (Non-Federal) *(cont.)*
Bingham, Hiram
Bissell, William Henry
Black, Frank Swett
Blackburn, Luke Pryor
Blaine, John James
Blair, Austin
Blasdel, Henry Goode *Suppl. 2*
Blease, Coleman Livingston
Bloomfield, Joseph
Blount, Willie
Boggs, Lilburn W.
Boies, Horace
Bond, Shadrach
Bonham, Milledge Luke
Boreman, Arthur Ingram
Bouck, William C.
Boutwell, George Sewall
Bowdoin, James (1726–1790)
Bowie, Robert
Bowles, Chester Bliss
Bradford, Augustus Williamson
Bragg, Thomas
Bramlette, Thomas Elliott
Branch, John, Jr.
Brandon, Gerard Chittocque
Bricker, John William
Bridges, Styles
Briggs, Ansel *Suppl. 2*
Briggs, George Nixon
Brooks, John
Brough, John
Broward, Napoleon Bonaparte
Brown, Aaron Venable
Brown, Albert Gallatin
Brown, Benjamin Gratz
Brown, Ethan Allen
Brown, John Calvin
Brown, John Young
Brown, Joseph Emerson
Brownlow, William Gannaway
Brownson, Nathan
Brucker, Wilber Marion
Bryan, Charles Wayland
Buckingham, William Alfred
Buckner, Simon Bolivar
Bulkeley, Morgan Gardner
Bullock, Rufus Brown
Burke, Thomas (c. 1747–1783)

Burnett, Peter Hardeman *Suppl. 2*
Burnside, Ambrose Everett
Burton, Hutchins Gordon
Butler, Benjamin Franklin (1818–1893)
Butler, David *Suppl. 2*
Butler, Pierce Mason
Byrd, Harry Flood
Cabell, William H.
Campbell, William Bowen
Candler, Allen Daniel
Cannon, Newton
Capper, Arthur
Carey, Joseph Maull
Carlson, Frank
Carnahan, Melvin Eugene *Suppl. 2*
Carney, Thomas
Carondelet, Baron de
Carpenter, Cyrus Clay
Carr, Elias
Carroll, William
Casey, Robert *Suppl. 2*
Caswell, Richard
Chafee, John H. *Suppl. 2*
Chamberlain, Daniel Henry
Chamberlain, George Earle
Chamberlain, Joshua Lawrence
Chandler, Albert Benjamin
Chapman, Reuben
Chase, Salmon Portland
Chittenden, Martin
Chittenden, Thomas
Churchill, Thomas James
Claiborne, William Charles Coles
Clark, Charles
Clark, John
Clark, Myron Holley
Clarke, James Paul
Clay, Clement Comer
Clayton, Powell
Clement, Frank Goad
Cleveland, Grover
Clinton, De Witt
Clinton, George (1739–1812)
Cobb, Howell
Coke, Richard
Coles, Edward
Collier, Henry Watkins
Colquitt, Alfred Holt

Comer, Braxton Bragg
Connally, John Bowden, Jr.
Coolidge, Calvin
Cornell, Alonzo Barton
Corwin, Thomas
Cox, Jacob Dolson
Cox, James Middleton
Crane, Winthrop Murray
Crawford, Samuel Johnson
Crittenden, John Jordan
Crittenden, Thomas Theodore
Cross, Wilbur Lucius
Culberson, Charles Allen
Cullom, Shelby Moore
Cummins, Albert Baird
Curley, James Michael
Curtin, Andrew Gregg
Davie, William Richardson
Davis, Edmund Jackson
Davis, Jeff
Davis, John
Deneen, Charles Samuel
Dennison, William
Derbigny, Pierre Auguste Charles Bourguignon
Desha, Joseph
Dewey, Thomas Edmund
Dickerson, Mahlon
Dickerson, Philemon
Dingley, Nelson, Jr.
DiSalle, Michael Vincent
Dix, John Adams
Dixon, Joseph Moore
Douglas, William Lewis
Drake, Francis Marion
Drayton, John
Dudley, Edward Bishop
Duff, James Henderson
Duncan, Joseph
Dunlap, Robert Pinckney
Dunne, Edward Fitzsimmons
Edge, Walter Evans
Edwards, Ninian
Egan, William Allen
Elbert, Samuel
Ely, Joseph Buell
English, James Edward
Eustis, William
Everett, Edward
Fairbanks, Erastus
Fairchild, Lucius
Fairfield, John

Faubus, Orval
Fenner, Arthur, Jr.
Fenton, Reuben Eaton
Ferguson, James Edward
Ferguson, Miriam Amanda
Fish, Hamilton (1808–1893)
Fishback, William Meade
Fitzpatrick, Benjamin
Flanagin, Harris
Flower, Roswell Pettibone
Floyd, John Buchanan
Folsom, James E.
Foot, Samuel Augustus
Foote, Henry Stuart
Foraker, Joseph Benson
Ford, Thomas
Forsyth, John
Foster, Charles
Frazier, Lynn Joseph
Fuller, Alvan Tufts
Furnas, Robert Wilkinson
Gamble, Hamilton Rowan
Garland, Augustus Hill
Garrard, James
Gaston, William
Gayle, John
Gear, John Henry
Geary, John White
Gerry, Elbridge
Gilman, John Taylor
Gist, William Henry
Goebel, William
Goodwin, Ichabod
Gordon, John Brown
Gore, Christopher
Graham, William Alexander
Grant, James Benton
Grasso, Ella Tambussi
Green, Theodore Francis
Greenhalge, Frederic Thomas
Greenup, Christopher
Griggs, John William
Grimes, James Wilson
Griswold, Matthew
Griswold, Roger
Grover, La Fayette
Hébert, Paul Octave
Hadley, Herbert Spencer
Hagood, Johnson
Hahn, Michael Decker
Haight, Henry Huntley
Hall, Lyman

Government (Non-Federal) *(cont.)*

Hamilton, Andrew
  Jackson
Hamilton, James, Jr.
Hamilton, Paul
Hamilton, William
  Thomas
Hamlin, Hannibal
Hammond, James Henry
Hampton, Wade
  (1818–1902)
Hancock, John
  (1737–1793)
Hardin, Charles Henry
Harmon, Judson
Harriman, W. Averell
Harris, Isham Green
Hartness, James
Hartranft, John
  Frederick
Haskell, Charles
  Nathaniel *Suppl. 2*
Hawley, James Henry
Hawley, Joseph
Hayes, Rutherford
  Birchard
Hayne, Robert Young
Helm, John Larue
Henderson, James
  Pinckney
Hendricks, Thomas
  Andrews
Hendricks, William
Herrick, Myron Timothy
Herter, Christian
  Archibald (1895–1966)
Hickenlooper, Bourke B.
Hicks, Thomas Holliday
Hiester, Joseph
Higgins, Frank Wayland
Hill, David Bennett
Hill, Isaac
Hoadly, George
Hobby, William Pettus
Hoey, Clyde Roark
Hoffman, John
  Thompson
Hogg, James Stephen
Holden, William Woods
Holland, Spessard
  Lindsey
Holmes, David
Houston, George Smith
Houston, Sam
Houstoun, John
Howard, John Eager
Howell, Richard
Howley, Richard
Hughes, Charles Evans

Humphreys, Benjamin
  Grubb
Hunt, George Wylie
  Paul
Hunt, Lester Callaway
Hunt, Washington
Huntington, Samuel
Jackson, Claiborne Fox
Jackson, James
  (1757–1806)
Jarvis, Thomas Jordan
Jay, John
Jenkins, Charles Jones
Jennings, Jonathan
Jewell, Marshall
Johnson, Andrew
Johnson, Herschel
  Vespasian
Johnson, Hiram Warren
Johnson, John Albert
Johnson, Thomas
Johnston, Olin DeWitt
  Talmadge
Johnston, Samuel
Jones, Thomas Goode
  Suppl. 1
Kavanagh, Edward
Kellogg, William Pitt
Kemper, James Lawson
Kent, Edward
Kent, Joseph
Kerner, Otto
Kerr, Robert Samuel
King, William
  Washington
Kirkwood, Samuel
  Jordan
Kitchin, William Walton
Knight, Goodwin Jess
Knott, James Proctor
La Follette, Philip Fox
La Follette, Robert
  Marion
Landon, Alfred
  Mossman
Lane, Henry Smith
Langdon, John
Langer, William
Larrabee, William
Larrazolo, Octaviano
  Ambrosio
Lawrence, David Leo
Lehman, Herbert Henry
Letcher, John
Letcher, Robert Perkins
Lewelling, Lorenzo Dow
Lewis, David Peter
Lewis, Morgan
Ligon, Thomas Watkins
Lincoln, Enoch
Lincoln, Levi

  (1749–1820)
Lincoln, Levi
  (1782–1868)
Lind, John
Livingston, William
Lloyd, Edward
Long, Earl Kemp
Long, Huey Pierce
Long, John Davis
Low, Frederick
  Ferdinand
Lowden, Frank Orren
Lowry, Robert
Lubbock, Francis
  Richard
Lucas, Robert
Lumpkin, Wilson
Magoffin, Beriah
Marcy, William Learned
Marland, Ernest
  Whitworth
Marshall, Thomas Riley
Martin, Alexander
Martin, John Alexander
Marvin, William
Mason, Stevens
  Thomson
Mathews, George
Mathews, John
Maybank, Burnet Rhett
McArthur, Duncan
McCall, Samuel Walker
McClellan, George B.
McClelland, Robert
McClurg, Joseph
  Washington
McDonald, William C.
  Suppl. 2
McDuffie, George
McEnery, Samuel
  Douglas
McFarland, Ernest
  William
McGrath, J. Howard
McKean, Thomas
McKeldin, Theodore
  Roosevelt
McKinley, William
McKinly, John
McLane, Robert
  Milligan
McLaurin, Anselm
  Joseph
McMinn, Joseph
McNutt, Paul Vories
McRae, John Jones
Meigs, Return Jonathan,
  Jr.
Mellette, Arthur Calvin
  Suppl. 2
Mercer, John Francis
Merriam, William Rush

Metcalfe, Thomas
Middleton, Henry
  (1770–1846)
Mifflin, Thomas
Milledge, John
Miller, John
Miller, Nathan Lewis
Miller, Stephen Decatur
Milton, John
Mitchell, David Brydie
Moore, Gabriel
Moore, Thomas Overton
Morgan, Edwin Denison
Morrill, Edmund
  Needham
Morrill, Lot Myrick
Morrow, Jeremiah
Morton, Levi Parsons
Morton, Marcus
Morton, Oliver Perry
Moses, Franklin J., Jr.
Moultrie, William
Murphy, Frank
Murphy, Isaac
  (1799–1882)
Murrah, Pendleton
Murray, William Henry
  David
Muskie, Edmund S.
  Suppl. 1
Nash, Abner
Nelson, Knute
Newell, William
  Augustus
Nicholas, Wilson Cary
Nicholls, Francis
  Redding Tillou
Norbeck, Peter
Northen, William
  Jonathan
Oates, William Calvin
O'Daniel, W. Lee
Ogden, Aaron
Oglesby, Richard James
Olson, Floyd
  Bjornstjerne
Orr, James Lawrence
Osborn, Chase Salmon
Osborn, Thomas
  Andrew
Paca, William
Pacheco, Romualdo
Page, John
Palmer, John McAuley
  (1817–1900)
Palmer, William Adams
Parker, Joel (1816–1888)
Parris, Albion Keith
Parsons, Lewis Eliphalet
Paterson, William
Pease, Elisha Marshall

Government (Non-Federal) *(cont.)*
Peay, Austin Leavell
Pennington, William
Pennoyer, Sylvester
Perry, Benjamin Franklin
Perry, Edward
  Aylesworth
Petersen, Hjalmar
Pettus, John Jones
Phelps, John Smith
Pickens, Francis
  Wilkinson
Pickens, Israel
Pierce, Benjamin
Pierpont, Francis
  Harrison
Pillsbury, John Sargent
Pinchback, P. B. S.
Pinchot, Gifford
Pinckney, Charles
Pinckney, Thomas
Pingree, Hazen S.
Plater, George
Pleasants, James
Plumer, William
Poindexter, George
Polk, James Knox
Price, Sterling
Proctor, Redfield
Quitman, John Anthony
Randall, Alexander
  Williams
Randolph, Edmund
Randolph, Thomas
  Mann
Reagan, Ronald Wilson
  Suppl. 2
Rector, Henry Massey
Reid, David Settle
Reynolds, John
  (1788–1865)
Ribicoff, Abraham
  Suppl. 1
Ritchie, Albert Cabell
Roane, Archibald
Roberts, Oran Milo
Robertson, Thomas
  Bolling
Robinson, Charles
Robinson, George
  Dexter
Robinson, Joseph Taylor
Rockefeller, Nelson
  Aldrich
Rolph, James, Jr.
Romney, George
Roosevelt, Franklin
  Delano
Roosevelt, Theodore
Ross, C. Ben

Ross, Nellie Tayloe
Routt, John Long
  Suppl. 2
Ruger, Thomas Howard
Rusk, Jeremiah McClain
Russell, Richard
  Brevard, Jr.
Russell, William Eustis
Rutledge, Edward
Rutledge, John
Saltonstall, Leverett
Sanford, Terry *Suppl. 1*
Scales, Alfred Moore
Schoeppel, Andrew
  Frank
Scott, Charles
Scott, Kerr
Scott, Robert Kingston
Sevier, John
Seward, William Henry
Seymour, Horatio
Shafroth, John Franklin
Shannon, Wilson
Sharkey, William Lewis
Shelby, Isaac
Shoup, George Laird
Sibley, Henry Hastings
Smallwood, William
Smith, Alfred E.
Smith, Hoke
Smith, Israel
Smith, Jeremiah
Smith, John Cotton
Smith, William
  (1797–1887)
Snow, Wilbert
Snyder, Simon
Southard, Samuel Lewis
Stanford, Leland
Stephens, Alexander
  Hamilton
Sterling, Ross Shaw
Stevenson, Adlai Ewing,
  II
Stevenson, John White
St. John, John Pierce
Stokes, Montfort
Stone, David
Stone, John Marshall
Stone, William Joel
Stoneman, George
Strong, Caleb
Stubbs, Walter Roscoe
Sullivan, James
Sullivan, John
Swain, David Lowry
Swann, Thomas
Talmadge, Eugene
Taylor, Alfred Alexander
Taylor, Robert Love
Telfair, Edward

Thayer, John Milton
Thomas, Philip Francis
Thompson, Hugh Smith
Tichenor, Isaac
Tiffin, Edward
Tilden, Samuel Jones
Tillman, Benjamin Ryan
Tobin, Maurice Joseph
Tod, David
Tompkins, Daniel D.
Toole, Joseph Kemp
Toucey, Isaac
Treutlen, John Adam
  Suppl. 2
Troup, George Michael
Trumbull, Jonathan
Trumbull, Jonathan, Jr.
Van Buren, Martin
Vance, Zebulon Baird
Van Dyke, Nicholas
  (1738–1789)
Van Rensselaer, Stephen
Vardaman, James
  Kimble
Villeré, Jacques Philippe
Vroom, Peter Dumont,
  Jr.
Walker, Gilbert Carlton
Wallace, David
Wallace, George
  Suppl. 1
Wallace, Lurleen Burns
Waller, Thomas
  MacDonald
Walsh, David Ignatius
Walton, George
Wanton, John
Wanton, Joseph
Warmoth, Henry Clay
Warren, Earl
Washburn, Israel, Jr.
Watts, Thomas Hill
Weare, Meshech
Weller, John Brown
Wells, James Madison
Whitcomb, James
White, Edward Douglass
  (1795–1847)
Whiteaker, John *Suppl. 2*
Whitman, Charles
  Seymour
Wickliffe, Charles
  Anderson
Williams, David
  Rogerson
Williams, G. Mennen
Williams, John Bell
Williamson, Isaac
  Halsted
Willson, Augustus
  Everett

Wilson, Woodrow
Wiltz, Louis Alfred
Winant, John Gilbert
Winston, John Anthony
Wise, Henry Alexander
Wolcott, Oliver
  (1726–1797)
Wolcott, Oliver
  (1760–1833)
Wolf, George
Woodbridge, William
Woodbury, Levi
Woodring, Harry Hines
Worth, Jonathan
Worthington, Thomas
Wright, Fielding Lewis
Wright, Joseph Albert
Wright, Robert
Wright, Silas
Yates, Joseph C.
Yates, Richard
Yell, Archibald
Young, John
  (1802–1852)
Youngdahl, Luther
  Wallace

State Legislators
Adair, John
Alston, William
Arnett, Benjamin
  William
Baldwin, John Brown
Barnum, P. T.
Bedinger, George
  Michael
Bingham, George Caleb
Buckalew, Charles Rollin
Burnet, Jacob
Burns, Otway, Jr.
Calhoun, William
  Barron
Caminetti, Anthony
Connor, Henry Groves
Crary, Isaac Edwin
Crockett, Davy
Cruger, Henry, Jr.
Daugherty, Harry
  Micajah
Davis, John Wesley
Day, Albert
Duer, William Alexander
Fauset, Crystal Bird
Few, William
Fournet, John Baptiste
Frazier, Maude
Fuller, Thomas Oscar
Gary, Martin
  Witherspoon
Gilmer, John Adams
Grasso, Ella Tambussi

Government (Non-Federal) *(cont.)*

Haddock, Charles Brickett
Hamlin, Albert Comstock
Hammond, Jabez Delano
Hardin, Benjamin, Jr.
Hooper, Samuel
Hopkins, Samuel (1753–1819)
Howard, Timothy Edward
Hyman, John Adams
Ickes, Anna Wilmarth Thompson
Irvine, James
Jackson, Robert R.
Johnson, Edward Austin
Johnston, Peter
Kearney, Belle
Kelley, Alfred
Kempfer, Hannah Johnson
Kershaw, Joseph Brevard
King, Preston
Lacock, Abner
Laughlin, Gail
Lee, Henry (1787–1837)
Lee, Samuel J.
LeFlore, Greenwood
Maclay, William Brown
Mankin, Helen Douglas
Maxwell, William (1766?–1809)
McLemore, Jeff
Mills, Ogden Livingston
Mitchell, George Edward
Morris, Edward Joy
Moses, Franklin J., Jr.
Musmanno, Michael Angelo
Neuberger, Richard Lewis
O'Neall, John Belton
O'Sullivan, John Louis
Penrose, Boies
Raines, John
Randolph, Benjamin Franklin
Robinson, Joseph Taylor
Root, Erastus
Rosewater, Edward
Russell, Benjamin
Sadler, Harley
Sedgwick, Theodore (1746–1813)
Smith, Meriwether
Somerville, Nellie Nugent

Spencer, Ambrose
Spencer, John Canfield
Steiner, Lewis Henry
Stevens, Thaddeus
Stokes, Carl *Suppl. 1*
Taney, Roger Brooke
Thomas, David
Tucker, Henry St. George (1780–1848)
Turner, Josiah, Jr.
Upshur, Abel Parker
Van Ness, William W.
Van Vechten, Abraham
Van Winkle, Peter Godwin
Wadsworth, James Jeremiah
Walker, Leroy Pope
Ward, Joshua John
Warren, William Whipple
Washington, Harold
Williams, George Washington
Woods, William Burnham

Territorial Delegates

Clark, Daniel (1766–1813)
Kuhio
Poindexter, George
Pope, Nathaniel
Poydras, Julien
Rice, Henry Mower
Sibley, Henry Hastings

Territorial Governors

Abernethy, George
Blount, William
Branch, John, Jr.
Call, Richard Keith
Campbell, John Allen
Chambers, John
Claiborne, William Charles Coles
Clark, William
Colton, George Radcliffe
Connelly, Henry
Crosby, John Schuyler
Cumming, Alfred
Denver, James William
Dodge, Henry
Dole, Sanford Ballard
DuVal, William Pope
Eaton, John Henry
Edgerton, Sidney
Edwards, Ninian
Geary, John White
Goodwin, John Noble
Howard, Benjamin

Hull, William
Izard, George
Jackson, Andrew
Lucas, Robert
Magoon, Charles Edward
McCook, Edward Moody
Medary, Samuel
Miller, James
Muñoz Marín, Luis
Nye, James Warren
Piñero, Jesús Toribio
Reeder, Andrew Horatio
Sargent, Winthrop
St. Clair, Arthur
Walker, Robert John
Winship, Blanton
Young, Brigham

Government of the Confederacy

Confederate Agents

Hotze, Henry
Huse, Caleb
Peyton, John Lewis
Sanders, George Nicholas
Thompson, Jacob

Confederate Legislators / Government Officials

Ashe, Thomas Samuel
Baldwin, John Brown
Barksdale, Ethelbert
Barnwell, Robert Woodward
Benjamin, Judah Philip
Brown, Albert Gallatin
Campbell, Josiah Adams Patterson
Clay, Clement Claiborne
Cobb, Thomas Reade Rootes
Davis, George
Gartrell, Lucius Jeremiah
Gholson, Thomas Saunders
Gilmer, John Adams
Graham, William Alexander
Hill, Benjamin Harvey
Holcombe, James Philemon
Hunter, Robert M. T. *Suppl. 2*
Johnson, Herschel Vespasian
Johnson, Robert Ward
Kenner, Duncan Farrar *Suppl. 1*

Mallory, Stephen Russell
Maxwell, Augustus Emmet
McRae, John Jones
Memminger, Christopher Gustavus
Miles, William Porcher
Oldham, Williamson Simpson
Orr, James Lawrence
Orr, Jehu Amaziah
Pettus, John Jones
Preston, William Ballard
Randolph, George Wythe
Reagan, John Henninger
Seddon, James Alexander
Slidell, John
Staples, Waller Redd
Toombs, Robert Augustus
Trenholm, George Alfred
Vest, George Graham
Walker, Leroy Pope
Watson, John William Clark
Watts, Thomas Hill
Wigfall, Louis Trezevant
Yancey, William Lowndes

First Lady of the Confederacy

Davis, Varina Howell

President of the Confederacy

Davis, Jefferson

Vice President of the Confederacy

Stephens, Alexander Hamilton

Politics

Abolitionists

Allen, William G.
Alvord, John Watson
Andrew, John Albion
Bailey, Gamaliel
Ballou, Adin
Barbadoes, James G.
Bell, James Madison
Bell, Philip Alexander
Beman, Amos Gerry
Benezet, Anthony
Bibb, Henry Walton
Bird, Francis William
Birney, James Gillespie
Bloss, William Clough

Politics (cont.)
Bourne, George
Bowditch, Henry
  Ingersoll
Brooke, Abraham
Brown, John (1800–
  1859)
Brown, William Wells
Burleigh, Charles
  Calistus
Burleigh, William Henry
Burris, Samuel D.
  Suppl. 2
Campbell, Tunis Gulic
Chace, Elizabeth Buffum
Chapman, Maria
  Weston
Chase, Salmon Portland
Cheever, George Barrell
Child, David Lee
Child, Lydia Maria
  Francis
Clarke, Lewis G.
Clay, Cassius Marcellus
Coffin, Levi
Coles, Edward
Collins, John Anderson
Colman, Lucy Newhall
Copeland, John
  Anthony, Jr.
Cowles, Betsey Mix
Craft, Ellen
Craft, William
Crandall, Prudence
Crummell, Alexander
Dargan, Edmund S.
Davis, Paulina Kellogg
  Wright
DeBaptiste, George
Douglas, H. Ford
Douglass, Frederick
Douglass, Sarah Mapps
Downing, George
  Thomas
Earle, Thomas
Embree, Elihu
Equiano, Olaudah
Everett, Robert
Fairbanks, Erastus
Fee, John Gregg
Ford, Barney Launcelot
Foster, Abby Kelley
Foster, Stephen
  Symonds
Gage, Frances Dana
  Barker
Garnet, Henry Highland
Garrett, Thomas
Garrison, William Lloyd
Gatch, Philip
Gay, Sydney Howard

Gibbons, Abigail
  Hopper
Gibbs, Mifflin Wistar
Giddings, Joshua Reed
Goodell, William
  (1792–1878)
Green, Beriah
Grew, Mary
Griffing, Josephine
  Sophia White
Grimké, Angelina Emily
Grimké, Sarah Moore
Grinnell, Josiah Bushnell
Hale, Edward Everett
Hall, Prince
Hamilton, Thomas
Haven, Gilbert
Haviland, Laura Smith
Hayden, Lewis
Helper, Hinton Rowan
Hildreth, Richard
  Suppl. 2
Holley, Myron
Holley, Sallie
Hopkins, Samuel
  (1721–1803)
Hopper, Isaac Tatem
Jackson, James Caleb
Jenkins, David
Jewett, John Punchard
Johnson, Oliver
Jones, Jane Elizabeth
Julian, George
  Washington
Langston, Charles Henry
Lay, Benjamin
Leavitt, Joshua
Lee, Luther
Little, Sophia Louisa
  Robbins
Loguen, Jermain Wesley
Lovejoy, Elijah Parish
Lovejoy, Owen
Lundy, Benjamin
M'Clintock, Mary Ann
  Wilson, and Thomas
  M'Clintock
Malvin, John
Martin, John Sella
Martineau, Harriet
May, Samuel Joseph
McKim, James Miller
Meigs, Return Jonathan
  (1801–1891)
Mercer, Margaret
Mott, James
Mott, Lucretia Coffin
Murray, Orson S.
Nell, William Cooper
Page, Ann Randolph
  Meade

Parker, John P.
Pennington, James
  William Charles
Phillips, Wendell
Post, Amy Kirby
Potter, Ray
Powell, William Peter
Pugh, Sarah
Purvis, Robert
Putnam, Caroline F.
Realf, Richard
Reason, Patrick Henry
Remond, Charles Lenox
Remond, Sarah Parker
Ruggles, David
Scott, Orange
Smith, Gerrit
Smith, James McCune
Smith, Joshua Bowen
Stearns, George Luther
Steward, Austin
Stewart, Alvan
Still, William
Stone, Lucy
Stuart, Charles
Sumner, Charles
Sunderland, La Roy
Swisshelm, Jane Grey
  Cannon
Tappan, Arthur, and
  Lewis Tappan
Torrey, Charles Turner
Truth, Sojourner
Tubman, Harriet
Van Zandt, John
Walker, David (1796?–
  1830)
Ward, Samuel Ringgold
Washington, Augustus
  Suppl. 2
Whitfield, James Monroe
Whittier, John Greenleaf
Williams, Peter, Jr.
Woolman, John
Wright, Elizur
Wright, Henry Clarke
Wright, Theodore
  Sedgwick

Anticommunists
Budenz, Louis
Chambers, Whittaker
Cohn, Roy
Cvetic, Matthew C.
Fischer, Ruth
Kohlberg, Alfred
Schine, G. David
  Suppl. 1
Welch, Robert

Parker, John P.
Antisuffragists
Conway, Katherine
  Eleanor
Dahlgren, Sarah
  Madeleine Vinton
Dodge, Josephine
  Marshall Jewell
Meyer, Annie Nathan
Parker, Jane Marsh
Putnam, Elizabeth
  Lowell
Wells, Kate Boott
  Gannett

Black Nationalists
Blyden, Edward Wilmot
Crummell, Alexander
Cuffe, Paul
Delany, Martin
  Robinson
Garvey, Amy Euphemia
  Jacques
Garvey, Marcus
Logan, Rayford
  Whittingham
Michaux, Lewis H.
Singleton, Benjamin
Whitfield, James Monroe

Civil Rights Activists
Abernathy, Ralph David
Adams, John Quincy
  (1848–1922)
Albert, Octavia Victoria
  Rogers
Albrier, Frances Mary
Alexander, Will Winton
Alston, Melvin Ovenus
Ames, Jessie Daniel
Andrew, John Albion
Apess, William
Baker, Ella Josephine
Baker, Josephine
Barber, Jesse Max
Bass, Charlotta Spears
Bayne, Thomas
Bethune, Mary Jane
  McLeod
Bird, Francis William
Blackwell, Randolph
  Talmadge
Boudinot, Elias
  Cornelius
Bowles, Eva Del Vakia
Braden, Carl James
Bright Eyes
Bruce, John Edward
Bunche, Ralph Johnson
Burnham, Louis Everett
  Suppl. 2

Politics (cont.)
Carmichael, Stokely
  Suppl. 1
Cass, Melnea Agnes
  Jones
Church, Robert Reed, Jr.
Clark, Peter Humphries
Clark, Septima Poinsette
Cleaver, Eldridge
  Suppl. 1
Cohen, Felix Solomon
Collier, John
Comstock, Elizabeth
  Leslie Rous Wright
Converse, Harriet
  Maxwell
Cook, George William
Cook, Vivian E. J.
Cooper, Anna Julia
  Haywood
Dancy, John Campbell,
  Jr.
De Baptiste, Richard
Deming, Barbara
Dillard, James Hardy
Douglass, Frederick
Downing, George
  Thomas
Drake, St. Clair, Jr.
Du Bois, W. E. B.
Durham, John Stephens
Durr, Virginia Foster
  Suppl. 1
Eastman, Charles
  Alexander
Evers, Medgar
Farmer, James *Suppl. 1*
Fauset, Crystal Bird
Fisher, Ada Lois Sipuel
Ford, Barney Launcelot
Fortune, Timothy
  Thomas
Green, Ely
Griffing, Josephine
  Sophia White
Grigsby, Snow Flake
Grimké, Archibald
  Henry
Grimké, Francis James
Groppi, James Edward
Hamer, Fannie Lou
  Townsend
Harrison, Hubert Henry
Hastie, William Henry
Higginbotham, A. Leon,
  Jr. *Suppl. 2*
Hill, Charles Andrew
Holland, Annie Welthy
  Daughtry
Hope, Lugenia D. Burns

Houston, Charles
  Hamilton
Howe, Mark De Wolfe
Hundley, Mary Gibson
  Brewer
Hunter, Jane Edna
  Harris
Hunton, George
  Kenneth
Jackson, Helen Hunt
Jackson, Luther Porter
Jackson, Robert R.
Jemison, Alice Mae Lee
Johns, Vernon Napoleon
Johnson, James Weldon
Jones, Claudia *Suppl. 2*
Jones, John (1816–1879)
Kellogg, Laura Minnie
  Cornelius
King, Carol Weiss
King, Martin Luther
King, Martin Luther, Jr.
LaFarge, John
La Farge, Oliver Hazard
  Perry
Lamb, Theodore
  Lafayette
Lampkin, Daisy
  Elizabeth Adams
Langston, John Mercer
Lanusse, Armand
Lattimore, John Aaron
  Cicero
Logan, Rayford
  Whittingham
Loving, Richard Perry
Lowenstein, Allard
  Kenneth
Majors, Monroe Alpheus
Malcolm X
Malvin, John
Manning, Joseph
  Columbus
Marshall, Thurgood
Mays, Benjamin Elijah
McClendon, James Julius
McGhee, Frederick
  Lamar
McKissick, Floyd Bixler
Miller, Kelly
Mitchell, Clarence
  Maurice, Jr.
Montezuma, Carlos
Moore, Audley "Queen
  Mother" *Suppl. 2*
Moore, Harry Tyson
Morgan, Clement
  Garnett
Morris, Robert
  (1823–1882)
Murray, Pauli

Nixon, Edgar Daniel
Otero, Miguel Antonio
Ovington, Mary White
Patterson, Louise
  Suppl. 2
Peck, James *Suppl. 2*
Pettiford, William
  Reuben
Phillips, Channing E.
Pleasant, Mary Ellen
Pledger, William
  Anderson
Quinton, Amelia Stone
Randolph, Asa Philip
Randolph, Benjamin
  Franklin
Ransom, Leon Andrew
Ransom, Reverdy
  Cassius
Reason, Charles Lewis
Remond, Charles Lenox
Rickard, Clinton
Robeson, Paul
Robinson, Ruby Doris
  Smith
Rosenberg, Anna Marie
  Lederer
Rustin, Bayard
Sanchez, George Isidore
Simmons, William James
Smith, Lucy Harth
Sparer, Edward V.
Spingarn, Arthur Barnett
Spottswood, Stephen
  Gill
Stanley, Sara G.
Stewart, Maria W.
Terrell, Mary Eliza
  Church
Tilly, Dorothy Eugenia
  Rogers
Tobias, Channing
  Heggie
Tourgée, Albion
  Winegar
Trotter, William Monroe
Tucker, Samuel Wilbert
Tureaud, Alexander
  Pierre
Turner, James Milton
Turner, Thomas Wyatt
Walden, Austin Thomas
Walker, Maggie L.
  Suppl. 2
Walling, William English
Walton, Lester A.
  Suppl. 2
Waring, J. Waties
Washington, Booker T.
Washington, Margaret
  Murray *Suppl. 2*

Wells-Barnett, Ida Bell
Whipple, Henry
  Benjamin
White, Walter Francis
Wilkins, Roy
Williams, Aubrey Willis
Willkie, Wendell Lewis
Wilson, J. Finley
Winnemucca, Sarah
Wright, Louis Tompkins
Wright, Muriel Hazel
Young, Whitney Moore,
  Jr.
Zuber, Paul Burgess

Communists
Bentley, Elizabeth Terrill
Browder, Earl Russell
Childs, Morris *Suppl. 2*
Davis, Benjamin
  Jefferson (1903–1964)
Dennis, Eugene
Eisler, Gerhart
Fischer, Ruth
Ford, James William
Foster, William Z.
Gitlow, Benjamin
Gold, Michael
Hall, Gus *Suppl. 1*
Larkin, James
Massing, Hede Tune
Minor, Robert
Patterson, William L.
Perry, Pettis
Stokes, Rose Pastor
Thompson, Robert
  George
Ware, Harold
Winston, Henry

Environmentalists
Adams, Ansel
Brower, David *Suppl. 2*
Denver, John *Suppl. 1*
Douglas, Marjory
  Stoneman *Suppl. 1*
Douglas, William O.
Emerson, George Barrell
Fuller, R. Buckminster
Marsh, George Perkins
Marshall, Robert
Owings, Nathaniel
  Alexander
Udall, Morris K.
  Suppl. 1

Fenians
O'Mahony, John
Roberts, William Randall

Politics *(cont.)*
Lobbyists
Biemiller, Andrew John
Carroll, Anna Ella
Detzer, Dorothy
Dodd, Bella Visono
Galt, John
Greene, Roger Sherman
Grundy, Joseph Ridgway
Mitchell, Clarence
    Maurice, Jr.
Roosevelt, Kermit
    Suppl. 1
Swank, James Moore
Ward, Samuel
    (1814–1884)
Wilson, E. Raymond

Nationalists
Ahn, Chang-ho
Burgos, Julia de
Kosciuszko, Tadeusz
    Andrzej Bonawentura
MacNeven, William
    James
Meagher, Thomas
    Francis
Mitchel, John
Muñoz Marín, Luis
Muñoz Rivera, Luis
Zhitlowsky, Hayim

Nazi Leaders
Rockwell, George
    Lincoln

Political Consultants
Atwater, Lee *Suppl. 1*
Baroody, William Joseph
Brown, Ron *Suppl. 1*
Bryan, Charles Wayland
Chotiner, Murray
Finletter, Thomas
    Knight
Hanna, Marcus Alonzo
Holborn, Hajo Ludwig
    Rudolph
Nutter, Gilbert Warren
O'Brien, Lawrence
    Francis, Jr.
Proskauer, Joseph Meyer
Smith, William Henry
    (1833–1896)

Political Figures
Adams, Charles Francis
    (1807–1886)
Adams, Sherman
    Llewelyn
Addicks, John Edward
    O'Sullivan

Alexander, James
Allen, Henry Justin
Allen, Ira
Allen, James
Allston, Robert Francis
    Withers
Alston, Joseph
Andrews, Israel DeWolf
Armstrong, John
    (1717–1795)
Armstrong, John, Jr.
    (1758–1843)
Ashe, John Baptista
Ashley, William Henry
Aspinwall, William
    (1605–?)
Atwater, Caleb
Axtell, Samuel Beach
Bache, Richard
Bacon, John
Baker, Edward
    Dickinson
Baldwin, Abraham
Ball, George
Bankhead, John Hollis
    (1842–1920)
Barbour, James
Bard, Thomas Robert
Barnard, Kate
Barry, William Taylor
Bartlett, Ichabod
Bartlett, Joseph
Baruch, Bernard Mannes
Bates, Edward
Battle, Cullen Andrews
Bayard, James Ashton
Bayard, John Bubenheim
Bayne, Thomas
Beekman, Henry
Bell, John
Belmont, August
Belmont, Perry
Benton, Thomas Hart,
    Jr.
Benton, William
Berle, Adolf Augustus
Berrien, John
    Macpherson
Bibb, George Mortimer
Bidwell, John
Biffle, Leslie L.
Bingham, John Armor
Bingham, William
Bishop, Abraham
Black, Frank Swett
Blackburn, Joseph Clay
    Stiles
Blair, Emily Newell
Blair, Francis Preston, Jr.
Bland, Richard

Blatchford, Richard
    Milford
Bloodworth, Timothy
Bloomfield, Joseph
Blunt, James Gillpatrick
Bocock, Thomas S.
Bolling, Robert
Bonaparte, Charles
    Joseph
Boudinot, Elias (1740–
    1821)
Bowdoin, James
    (1726–1790)
Bowie, Robert
Bowles, Chester Bliss
Bradley, Aaron Alpeora
Bradley, William Czar
Bradstreet, Simon
Brandegee, Frank
    Bosworth
Brawley, William Hiram
Brayton, Charles Ray
Breckinridge, Clifton
    Rodes
Breckinridge, James
Breckinridge, John
    (1760–1806)
Breckinridge, W. C. P.
Breese, Sidney
Brinkerhoff, Jacob
Bristow, Benjamin Helm
Brokmeyer, Henry
    Conrad
Brooke, Henry
Brooks, Erastus
Brown, Aaron Venable
Brown, Walter Folger
Brownell, Herbert, Jr.
    Suppl. 1
Browning, Orville
    Hickman
Bruce, Blanche Kelso
Bryan, George
Bryan, Hugh
Bryant, John Emory
Bryce, James
Bullitt, Alexander Scott
Bundesen, Herman Niels
Burke, Thomas (c.
    1747–1783)
Burleson, Edward
Burnet, David
    Gouverneur
Burns, John Anthony
Bush, John Edward
Butler, Nicholas Murray
Byrnes, John William
Cain, Richard Harvey
Calhoun, John
Calvert, Charles
    Benedict

Cameron, Don
Campbell, Arthur
Campbell, George
    Washington
Campbell, Tunis Gulic
Candler, Allen Daniel
Carpenter, Cyrus Clay
Castiglioni, Luigi
Catron, Thomas Benton
Celler, Emanuel
Chamberlain, George
    Earle
Chamberlain, Joshua
    Lawrence
Champion, Henry
Chandler, William Eaton
Chapman, Oscar
    Littleton
Chapman, Reuben
Chase, Salmon Portland
Chateaubriand,
    François-René de
Chipman, Nathaniel
Choate, Rufus
Churchill, Thomas
    James
Churchill, Winston
Cilley, Joseph
Clagett, Wyseman
Claiborne, William
Clark, Peter Humphries
Clark, William Thomas
Clay, Cassius Marcellus
Clay, Henry
Clayton, Augustin Smith
Clayton, William
    Lockhart
Clemens, Jeremiah
Clement, Frank Goad
Clingman, Thomas
    Lanier
Cobb, Howell
Cohen, Walter L.
Colden, Cadwallader
    David
Colquitt, Alfred Holt
Colt, LeBaron Bradford
Colyar, Arthur St. Clair
Conkling, Roscoe
Connor, Patrick Edward
Cook, John Francis, Jr.
Cooke, Elisha
Cooke, Elisha, Jr.
Cooper, Edward
Cooper, Henry Ernest
Cooper, William
Corbett, Henry Winslow
Corse, John Murray
Corsi, Edward
Corwin, Thomas
Cox, George Barnesdale

Politics *(cont.)*

Cox, Jacob Dolson
Cox, James Middleton
Cox, William Ruffin
Coxey, Jacob Sechler
Crater, Joseph Force
  Suppl. 1
Creighton, William
Crowninshield,
  Benjamin Williams
Crump, Edward Hull
Cullom, Shelby Moore
Curry, Jabez Lamar
  Monroe
Cushing, Caleb
Cushing, Thomas
Dabney, Wendell
  Phillips
Dallas, Alexander James
Dane, Nathan
Dargan, Edmund S.
Davezac, Auguste
  Genevieve Valentin
Davie, William
  Richardson
Davis, Benjamin
  Jefferson (1870–1945)
Davis, Edmund Jackson
Davis, John
Dawson, John
Dayton, William Lewis
Dearborn, Henry
De Lancey, James
  (1703–1760)
De Lancey, Oliver
DeLarge, Robert Carlos
Devens, Charles, Jr.
Dewson, Molly
Dexter, Samuel
Dick, Robert Paine
Dickerson, Mahlon
Dickinson, Daniel
  Stevens
Dickinson, John
  (1732–1808)
Dingley, Nelson, Jr.
Dix, John Adams
Dixon, Joseph Moore
Dodge, Augustus Caesar
Donelson, Andrew
  Jackson
Donnelly, Ignatius
  Loyola
Duane, James
Duane, William
  (1760–1835)
Dubuclet, Antoine
Dudley, Paul
Dulany, Daniel
Dulany, Daniel, Jr.
Dummer, William

Dunn, Oscar James
Durant, Thomas
  Jefferson
Dymond, John
Eaton, John Henry
Eaton, Peggy
Edwards, Pierpont
Eisler, Gerhart
Elkins, Stephen Benton
Elliot, James
Elliott, Robert Brown
Elmer, Jonathan
English, James Edward
English, Thomas Dunn
Eustis, George, Jr.
Eustis, James Biddle
Eustis, William
Evans, George
Evans, John
Evarts, William Maxwell
Everett, Edward
Ewing, James
  (1736–1806)
Farwell, Charles
  Benjamin
Fayssoux, Peter
Fell, John
Fishback, William
  Meade
Flagg, Azariah Cutting
Floyd, John
Flynn, Edward Joseph
Folsom, Nathaniel
Forsyth, John
Foster, Charles
Franklin, Deborah Read
Frelinghuysen, Theodore
Gadsden, James
Gaines, Matthew
Galloway, Joseph
Garnett, Muscoe Russell
  Hunter
Gaston, William Joseph
Gayarré, Charles Étienne
  Arthur
Gerard, James Watson
Gibbs, Jonathan C.
Gibbs, Mifflin Wistar
Gillett, Frederick
  Huntington
Gillon, Alexander
Gilmer, Thomas Walker
Gilmore, James Roberts
Goldsborough, Robert
Goodloe, William
  Cassius
Goodrich, Elizur
  (1761–1849)
Gordon, John Brown
Gore, Christopher
Graham, James

Granger, Francis
Granger, Gideon
Gray, William
Graydon, Alexander
Grayson, William
Grayson, William John
Greeley, Horace
Green, Duff
Green, James Stephens
Green, John Patterson
Greenhalge, Frederic
  Thomas
Gregg, Maxcy
Grimes, James Wilson
Grinnell, Josiah Bushnell
Griswold, Roger
Grow, Galusha Aaron
Grundy, Felix
Gunther, Charles
  Frederick *Suppl. 2*
Gwin, William
  McKendree
Hadley, Herbert Spencer
Hagar, Jonathan
Hagood, Johnson
Halderman, John Adams
Hale, Robert
Hall, Abraham Oakey
Hamilton, Alexander
  (1757?–1804)
Hamilton, Andrew
  (c.1676–1741)
Hamilton, Andrew
  Jackson
Hamilton, Paul
Hannegan, Robert
  Emmet
Hardin, John J.
Hardin, William
  Jefferson
Harrison, Benjamin
  (1726?–1791)
Harrison, Francis Burton
Harrison, Mary Scott
  Lord Dimmick
Hartranft, John
  Frederick
Hatfield, Henry Drury
Hathorne, William
Haugen, Gilbert Nelson
Hawley, Joseph
Hawley, Joseph Roswell
Hayakawa, S. I.
Haynes, Elizabeth Ross
Hays, Lawrence Brooks
Hays, Will H.
Heath, James Ewell
Henderson, Richard
Heyward, Nathaniel
Hiester, Joseph
Higgins, Frank Wayland

Hill, David Bennett
Hill, Isaac
Hill, Richard
Hill, William
Hillard, George Stillman
Hillhouse, James
Hitchcock, Frank Harris
Hitchcock, Gilbert
  Monell
Hoey, Clyde Roark
Hoffman, Ogden
Hoffmann, Francis
  Arnold
Holden, William Woods
Holland, Spessard
  Lindsey
Holt, Rush Dew
Horsmanden, Daniel
Houston, Sam
Howell, Clark
Howell, Evan Park
Huntington, Jabez
Hurlbut, Stephen
  Augustus
Hyer, Tom
Iredell, James
Irving, William
Jackson, William
Jefferson, Martha Wayles
  Skelton
Jeffries, Edward John, Jr.
Jennings, Jonathan
Jewett, Hugh Judge
Johnson, Andrew N.
Johnson, Cave
Johnson, James
Johnson, Robert Ward
Johnston, Olin DeWitt
  Talmadge
Jones, George Wallace
Jones, Thomas Goode
  Suppl. 1
Judah, Samuel
Judd, Norman Buel
Kavanagh, Edward
Kawananakoa, Abigail
  Wahiikaahuula
  Campbell
Kearsley, John
Kelly, John
Kennedy, John
  Pendleton
Kent, Edward
Kent, Joseph
Kerr, Robert Samuel
Kilgore, Harley Martin
Kinloch, Cleland
Kinsey, John
Kitchin, William Hodge
Koerner, Gustave
  Philipp

Politics *(cont.)*
Kohler, Walter Jodok
L'Hommedieu, Ezra
Labouisse, Henry
 Richardson
Lafayette, Marquis de
Lamar, Mirabeau
 Buonaparte
Lane, Joseph
Langdon, John
Langston, John Mercer
Lansing, John
Law, Richard
Lawrence, David Leo
Leary, John
Lee, William Little
Lehman, Herbert Henry
Leib, Michael
Leigh, Benjamin
 Watkins
Lewis, John Francis
Lewis, Morgan
Lewis, William Berkeley
Lewis, William Henry
Lincoln, Levi
 (1749–1820)
Lincoln, Levi
 (1782–1868)
Livingston, Edward
Livingston, Peter Van
 Brugh
Livingston, Robert
Livingston, Robert R.
Lloyd, David
Lloyd, Edward
Lloyd, Thomas
Logan, Benjamin
Logan, George
Logan, James
 (1674–1751)
Lomasney, Martin
 Michael
Long, Jefferson Franklin
Loucks, Henry Langford
Lovell, James
Lovestone, Jay
Low, Frederick
 Ferdinand
Lowndes, Rawlins
Lowndes, William Jones
Luce, Clare Boothe
Ludlow, Gabriel George
Lumpkin, Wilson
Lynch, James
Lynch, Thomas
Maclay, William
Macon, Nathaniel
Maguire, Patrick
Manigault, Peter
Manning, Joseph
 Columbus

Marigny, Bernard
Marland, Ernest
 Whitworth
Marsh, George Perkins
Marshall, George
 Catlett, Jr.
Marshall, Thomas
 Alexander
Martin, Alexander
Martin, John Bartlow
 Suppl. 2
Masaryk, Charlotte
 Garrigue
Mason, George
Mason, John Young
Mathews, John
Maverick, Maury
Maverick, Samuel
 Augustus
Maybank, Burnet Rhett
McAfee, Robert
 Breckinridge
McClelland, Robert
McClernand, John
 Alexander
McClure, Alexander
 Kelly
McClure, George
McKeldin, Theodore
 Roosevelt
McLane, Allen
McLane, Louis
McNutt, Paul Vories
Medary, Samuel
Mellon, Andrew William
Menard, Pierre
Middleton, Arthur
Middleton, Henry
 (1717–1784)
Middleton, Henry
 (1770–1846)
Miller, Thomas Ezekiel
Mills, Elijah Hunt
Mitchell, Martha
Mitchell, Robert
 Byington
Mitchill, Samuel Latham
Moïse, Edward Warren
Moore, Frederick
 Randolph
Moore, William
More, Nicholas
Morehead, James Turner
Morgan, Edwin Denison
Morril, David Lawrence
Morrill, Justin Smith
Morris, Robert Hunter
Morton, Rogers C. B.
Moultrie, John, Jr.
Muhlenberg, Frederick
 Augustus Conrad

Muhlenberg, John Peter
 Gabriel
Mullen, Arthur Francis
Munford, William
Murphy, Charles Francis
Murphy, Frank
Murphy, George
Murphy, Isaac
 (1799–1882)
Murray, William Henry
 David
Nairne, Thomas
Napier, James Carroll
Nash, Philleo
Nelson, William
 (1711–1772)
Nicholas, Wilson Cary
Niles, Nathaniel
Noah, Mordecai Manuel
Norris, Isaac
 (1671–1735)
Norris, Isaac
 (1701–1766)
Northen, William
 Jonathan
Oates, William Calvin
O'Brian, John Lord
O'Conor, Charles
O'Donnell, Kenneth P.
O'Dwyer, Paul *Suppl. 2*
Ogden, Aaron
O'Hara, James Edward
Oliver, Andrew
 (1706–1774)
O'Neill, Thomas Philip
 "Tip"
Opdyke, George
Osborn, Thomas
 Andrew
Otero, Miguel Antonio
Otero-Warren, Nina
Otis, Harrison Gray
 (1765–1848)
Otis, James
Owen, Chandler
Palfrey, John Gorham
Parker, Isaac Charles
Partridge, James
 Rudolph
Paterson, William
Patton, John Mercer
Pease, Elisha Marshall
Peck, George Wilbur
Pendergast, Thomas
 Joseph
Penhallow, Samuel
Perez, Leander Henry
Perkins, George
 Walbridge
Perkins, Thomas
 Handasyd

Petigru, James Louis
Phelan, James Duval
Phelps, John Smith
Philipse, Adolph
Phillips, Samuel, Jr.
Pierce, William Leigh
Pinchback, P. B. S.
Pinckney, Charles
Pinckney, Thomas
Pinkney, William
Pitkin, Timothy
Platt, Jonas
Pledger, William
 Anderson
Poinsett, Joel Roberts
Poland, Luke Potter
Pomeroy, Theodore
 Medad *Suppl. 2*
Porter, Benjamin Faneuil
Pory, John
Posey, Thomas
Potter, Robert
Poydras, Julien
Prat, Benjamin
Price, Sterling
Pruyn, Robert Hewson
Purnell, William Henry
Pusey, Caleb
Pynchon, John
Quay, Matthew Stanley
Quezon, Manuel Luis
Quick, Herbert
Quitman, John Anthony
Rainey, Joseph Hayne
Randall, Henry Stephens
Randolph, Sir John
Ranney, Rufus Percival
Ransier, Alonzo Jacob
Raymond, Henry Jarvis
Rayner, John Baptis
Rayner, Kenneth
Reid, Whitelaw
Rhett, Robert Barnwell
Richmond, Dean
Ricord, Frederick
 William
Ripley, Eleazar
 Wheelock
Rives, William Cabell
Roberts, William Randall
Robinson, John
Robinson, Moses
Rodney, Caesar
Romney, George
Roosevelt, Alice
 Hathaway Lee
Roosevelt, Elliott
Roosevelt, Franklin
 Delano, Jr.
Roosevelt, Theodore, Jr.
Root, Joseph Pomeroy

Politics *(cont.)*
Ross, C. Ben
Ross, Edmund Gibson
Rowe, John
Rowley, Thomas
Roye, Edward James
Ruby, George T.
Ruef, Abraham
Rush, Richard
Russell, Chambers
Russell, Jonathan
Russell, Richard
  Brevard, Jr.
Rutherford, Griffith
Rutledge, John
Schuschnigg, Kurt Alois
  Josef Johann von
Schwellenbach, Lewis
  Baxter
Scott, Hugh Doggett, Jr.
Seguín, Juan
  Nepomuceno
Settle, Thomas, Jr.
Sevier, Ambrose
  Hundley
Shafroth, John Franklin
Shannon, Wilson
Sharkey, William Lewis
Sherburne, Henry
Sherwood, Isaac Ruth
Sherwood, Lorenzo
Shields, James
Shippen, Edward
Shouse, Jouett
Sickles, Daniel Edgar
Sigel, Franz
Simmons, Furnifold
  McLendel
Skaggs, William H.
  Suppl. 1
Smallwood, William
Smith, Alfred E.
Smith, Ashbel
Smith, Charles Emory
Smith, Charles Perrin
Smith, Daniel
Smith, Harry Clay
Smith, Hoke
Smith, Melancton
  (1744–1798)
Smith, Richard
Snow, Wilbert
Southard, Samuel Lewis
Southwick, Solomon
Spinola, Francis Barretto
Steedman, James Blair
Stephens, Linton
Stevens, Isaac Ingalls
Stimson, Henry Lewis
Stoughton, William
Strong, Caleb

Stuart, Alexander Hugh
  Holmes
Sullivan, James
Sullivan, John
Sullivan, Timothy
  Daniel
Sumner, Charles
Swanson, Claude
  Augustus
Sweeny, Peter Barr
Symmes, John Cleves
Taliaferro, William
  Booth
Tazewell, Littleton
  Waller
Teller, Henry Moore
Thomas, Philip Francis
Thompson, Richard
  Wigginton
Thurston, Lorrin
  Andrews
Tilton, James
Tocqueville, Alexis de
Toulmin, Harry
Tracy, Uriah
Tumulty, Joseph Patrick
Tweed, William Magear
Twitchell, Marshall
  Harvey
Tyler, Ralph Waldo
Upham, Charles
  Wentworth
Vallejo, Mariano
  Guadalupe
Van Buren, Hannah
  Hoes
Van Buren, John
Van Cortlandt, Philip
Van Cortlandt, Pierre
Van Dam, Rip
van der Kemp, Francis
  Adrian
Van Dyke, Nicholas
  (1738–1789)
Van Ness, William Peter
Van Rensselaer,
  Solomon
Van Wyck, Charles
  Henry
Vardaman, James
  Kimble
Varick, Richard
Varnum, Joseph Bradley
Vaughan, Benjamin
Vroom, Peter Dumont,
  Jr.
Waddell, Alfred Moore
Wadsworth, James
  Samuel
Wadsworth, Peleg
Walderne, Richard

Waldron, Richard, III
Waldron, Richard, Jr.
Waller, John Louis
Washburn, Cadwallader
  Colden
Watson, Thomas
  Edward
Watterson, Henry
Weare, Nathaniel
Webb, James Watson
Webster, Daniel
Weed, Thurlow
Wentworth, Mark
  Hunking
Wilkins, William
Williams, David
  Rogerson
Williams, Israel
Williamson, Hugh
Willkie, Wendell Lewis
Wilson, William Lyne
Wise, John Sergeant
Wisner, Henry
Wolcott, Erastus
Woodbridge, William
Woodbury, Levi
Wormeley, Ralph
Worthington, John
Worthington, Thomas
Wright, Jonathan Jasper
Yates, Joseph C.
Young, John
  (1802–1852)
Zavala, Lorenzo de
Zollicoffer, Felix Kirk
Zubly, John Joachim

Powerbrokers
Cohn, Roy
Moses, Robert

Presidential Candidates
Bryan, William Jennings
Cass, Lewis
Crawford, William
  Harris
Davis, John William
Debs, Eugene Victor
Dewey, Thomas
  Edmund
Douglas, Stephen
  Arnold
Frémont, John Charles
Goldwater, Barry
  Suppl. 1
Hancock, Winfield Scott
Kennedy, Robert Francis
La Follette, Robert
  Marion
Landon, Alfred
  Mossman

Lemke, William
  Frederick
McClellan, George B.
Seymour, Horatio
Smith, Alfred E.
Stevenson, Adlai Ewing,
  II
Tilden, Samuel Jones
Udall, Morris K.
  Suppl. 1
Wallace, George
  Suppl. 1
Weaver, James Baird
White, Hugh Lawson
Wirt, William
Woodhull, Victoria
  Claflin

Socialists
Ameringer, Oscar
Berger, Victor Louis
Browne, Carl
Calverton, Victor
  Francis
Carey, James Francis
  Suppl. 2
De Leon, Daniel
Dietzgen, Peter Joseph
Ghent, William James
Gronlund, Laurence
Haessler, Carl
Harriman, Job
Harrington, Michael
Harrison, Hubert Henry
Hillquit, Morris
Hoan, Daniel Webster
Howland, Marie
Hughan, Jessie Wallace
London, Meyer
Maurer, James Hudson
McGrady, Thomas
O'Hare, Kate Richards
Scott, Leroy Martin
Seidel, George Lukas
  Emil
Simons, Algie Martin
Spargo, John
Stokes, Rose Pastor
Stolberg, Benjamin
Thomas, Norman
  Mattoon
Wayland, Julius
  Augustus
Willich, August

Suffragists
Anneke, Mathilde
  Franziska Giesler
Anthony, Susan B.
Avery, Rachel G. Foster

Politics *(cont.)*
Bailey, Hannah Clark
  Johnston
Barron, Jennie Loitman
Belmont, Alva Erskine
  Smith Vanderbilt
Bittenbender, Ada
  Matilda Cole
Blankenburg, Lucretia
  Longshore
Blatch, Harriot Stanton
Boissevain, Inez
  Milholland
Bowen, Louise deKoven
Breckinridge, Madeline
  McDowell
Brown, Gertrude Foster
Brown, Olympia
Catt, Carrie Chapman
Chase, Agnes
Clay-Clopton, Virginia
  Tunstall
Collins, Jennie
Couzins, Phoebe Wilson
Cunningham, Minnie
  Fisher
Decker, Sarah Sophia
  Chase Platt
Dock, Lavinia Lloyd
Dreier, Mary Elisabeth
Duniway, Abigail Jane
  Scott
Ferrin, Mary Upton
Field, Sara Bard
Foltz, Clara Shortridge
Friganza, Trixie
Gage, Matilda Joslyn
Garnet, Sarah Smith
  Tompkins
Gordon, Jean Margaret
Gordon, Kate M.
Gordon, Laura de Force
Gougar, Helen Mar
  Jackson
Grossman, Mary Belle
Harper, Ida Husted
Haskell, Ella Louise
  Knowles
Havemeyer, Louisine
  Waldron
Hay, Mary Garrett
Hazard, Rebecca Ann
  Naylor
Hooker, Isabella Beecher
Howe, Julia Ward
Howland, Emily
Hull, Hannah Hallowell
  Clothier
Ingham, Mary Hall
Jacobs, Pattie Ruffner
Johnston, Mary

Kearney, Belle
Kilgore, Carrie Sylvester
  Burnham
Livermore, Mary
Malkiel, Theresa Serber
Martin, Anne Henrietta
May, Abigail Williams
May, Samuel Joseph
McCormick, Ruth
  Hanna
Mead, Lucia True Ames
Minor, Virginia Louise
Morris, Esther Hobart
Nathan, Maud
Otero-Warren, Nina
Park, Maud Wood
Patterson, Hannah Jane
Pollitzer, Anita Lily
Ricker, Marilla Marks
  Young
Robins, Elizabeth
Robinson, Harriet Jane
  Hanson
Rutherford, Mildred
  Lewis
Seton, Grace Gallatin
  Thompson
Sewall, May Eliza
  Wright
Shaw, Anna Howard
Shaw, Mary
Sherwin, Belle
Shuler, Nettie Rogers
Smith, Julia Evelina, and
  Abby Hadassah Smith
Somerville, Nellie
  Nugent
Stanton, Elizabeth Cady
Stevens, Doris Caroline
Turner, Eliza L. Sproat
Ueland, Clara Hampson
Upton, Harriet Taylor
Valentine, Lila
  Hardaway Meade
Villard, Fanny Garrison
Waite, Catharine Van
  Valkenburg
Wells, Emmeline B.
Welsh, Lilian
Wright, Alice Morgan

Vice Presidential Candidates
Bryan, Charles Wayland
English, William Hayden
Johnson, Herschel
  Vespasian
Miller, William Edward
Muskie, Edmund S.
  Suppl. 1
Thurman, Allen
  Granberry

Wright, Fielding Lewis

Zionists
Blackstone, William E.
Flexner, Bernard
Gottheil, Richard James
  Horatio
Greenberg, Hayim
Lewisohn, Ludwig
Lowenthal, Marvin
  Marx
Mack, Julian William
Magnes, Judah Leon
Mendes, Henry Pereira
Rosenblatt, Bernard
  Abraham
Sampter, Jessie Ethel
Silver, Abba Hillel
Sonneschein, Rosa
Syrkin, Marie
Szold, Henrietta
Weisgal, Meyer Wolfe
Wise, Stephen Samuel

HEALTH AND MEDICINE

Abortionists
Lohman, Ann Trow

Allergists
Schick, Béla

Anesthesiologists
Apgar, Virginia
Long, Crawford
  Williamson

Artificial Heart Recipients
Schroeder, William J.

Cardiologists
Herrick, James Bryan
Hirschfelder, Arthur
  Douglas

Chiropractors
Palmer, Bartlett Joshua
Palmer, Daniel David

Dance Therapists
Boas, Franziska Marie
Chace, Marian
Schoop, Trudi *Suppl. 2*

Dentists
Barber, Jesse Max
Bayne, Thomas

Delany, Annie Elizabeth
  "Bessie". *See* Delany,
  Annie Elizabeth
  "Bessie", and Sarah
  Louise "Sadie" Delany
  Suppl. 1
Evans, Thomas
  Wiltberger
Flagg, Josiah Foster
Freeman, Robert Tanner
Garretson, James
  Edmund
Greenwood, John
Harris, Chapin Aaron
Howe, Percy Rogers
Keep, Nathan Cooley
Kingsley, Norman
  William
McQuillen, John Hugh
Miller, Willoughby
  Dayton
Morton, William
  Thomas Green
Parmly, Eleazar
Taylor, Lucy Beaman
  Hobbs
Wells, Horace

Dermatologists
Duhring, Louis
  Adolphus
Hyde, James Nevins
Klein, Edmund *Suppl. 2*
Morrow, Prince Albert
Pusey, William Allen
Schamberg, Jay Frank
White, James Clarke

Eclectic Physicians
Beach, Wooster
Foote, Edward Bliss
King, John
Newton, Robert Safford
Scudder, John Milton

Gastroenterologists
Ingelfinger, Franz Joseph
Jordan, Sara Claudia
  Murray

Gynecologists
Byford, William Heath
Chadwick, James Read
Dickinson, Robert Latou
Emmet, Thomas Addis
  (1828–1919)
Hurd-Mead, Kate
  Campbell
Hurdon, Elizabeth
Kelly, Howard Atwood
Levine, Lena

Martin, Franklin Henry
Meigs, Charles Delucena
Morris, John McLean
Parvin, Theophilus
Putnam, Helen Cordelia
Sims, J. Marion
Skene, Alexander
  Johnston Chalmers
Storer, Horatio
  Robinson
Taussig, Frederick
  Joseph
Van De Warker, Edward
  Ely

Homeopathic Physicians
Dunham, Carroll
Gram, Hans Burch
Guernsey, Egbert
Hale, Edwin Moses
Hempel, Charles Julius
Hering, Constantine
Kent, James Tyler
Leach, Robert Boyd
Merrick, Myra King
Talbot, Israel Tisdale
Wesselhoeft, Conrad

Hydropathists
Austin, Harriet N.
Baruch, Simon
Kellogg, John Harvey
Nichols, Mary Gove
Nichols, Thomas Low
Trall, Russell Thacher

Hypnotherapists
Erickson, Milton Hyland

Midwives
Ballard, Martha Moore
Van Blarcom, Carolyn
  Conant

Music Therapists
Nordoff, Paul

Naturopaths
Thomson, Samuel

Neonatologists
Dunham, Ethel Collins

Neurologists
Bailey, Pearce
Cobb, Stanley
Dana, Charles Loomis
Denny-Brown, Derek
  Ernest
Dercum, Francis Xavier
Geschwind, Norman

Goldstein, Kurt
Hammond, William
  Alexander
Jelliffe, Smith Ely
Myerson, Abraham
Putnam, James Jackson
Ranson, Stephen Walter
Sachs, Bernard
Seguin, Edward
  Constant
Spitzka, Edward Charles
Tilney, Frederick
Timme, Walter

Neurosurgeons
Cushing, Harvey
  Williams
Dandy, Walter Edward
Elsberg, Charles Albert
Frazier, Charles
  Harrison
Penfield, Wilder Graves

Nurses
Andrews, Ludie
Anthony, Sister
Arnstein, Margaret
Bacon, Georgeanna
  Muirson Woolsey
Beard, Mary
Bickerdyke, Mary Ann
  Ball
Blanchfield, Florence
  Aby
Bradley, Amy Morris
Bragg, Janet *Suppl. 2*
Buckel, C. Annette
Davis, Frances Elliott
Delano, Jane Arminda
Dock, Lavinia Lloyd
Fitzgerald, Alice
Franklin, Martha
  Minerva
Freeman, Elizabeth
Gardner, Mary Sewall
Goodrich, Annie
  Warburton
Haupt, Alma Cecilia
Hawes, Harriet Ann
  Boyd
Henderson, Virginia
  Suppl. 1
Hopkins, Juliet Ann
  Opie
Jean, Sally Lucas
Kenny, Elizabeth
Law, Sallie Chapman
  Gordon
Nutting, Mary Adelaide
Osborne, Estelle Massey
  Riddle

Palmer, Sophia French
Parsons, Emily Elizabeth
Pinn, Petra Fitzalieu
Richards, Linda
Robb, Isabel Hampton
Safford, Mary Jane
Stimson, Julia Catherine
Thompson, John D.
  Suppl. 2
Thoms, Adah Belle
  Samuels
Tompkins, Sally Louisa
Van Blarcom, Carolyn
  Conant
Wald, Lillian D.
Woolsey, Jane Stuart

Nutritionists
Atwater, Wilbur Olin
Blunt, Katharine
Corson, Juliet
Davis, Adelle
Goldsmith, Grace
  Arabell
Hart, Edwin Bret
Hauser, Gayelord
Morgan, Agnes Fay
Pritikin, Nathan
Roberts, Lydia Jane
Rorer, Sarah Tyson
Rose, Mary Davies
  Swartz
Rose, William Cumming
Sherman, Henry Clapp
Wheeler, Ruth
Williams, Robert
  Ramapatnam

Obstetricians
Atkinson, William Biddle
DeLee, Joseph Bolivar
Dewees, William Potts
Guttmacher, Alan
Hodge, Hugh Lenox
Lambright, Middleton
  Huger
Leverton, Ruth M.
  Suppl. 2
Meigs, Charles Delucena
Parvin, Theophilus
Price, Joseph

Oncologists
Chinn, May Edward
del Regato, Juan A.
  Suppl. 1
Lampe, Isadore
Papanicolaou, George
  Nicholas
Soiland, Albert
Sugiura, Kanematsu

Ophthalmologists
Agnew, Cornelius Rea
Barrows, Isabel
Chisolm, Julian John
de Schweinitz, George
  Edmund
Gradle, Henry
Hays, Isaac
Hepburn, James Curtis
Knapp, Hermann Jakob
Stein, Jules Caesar
Williams, Henry Willard

Orthopedic Surgeons
Bradford, Edward
  Hickling
Holmes, Hamilton
  Suppl. 2
Judson, Adoniram
  Brown
Orr, H. Winnett
Sayre, Lewis Albert
Steindler, Arthur
Whitman, Royal

Osteopaths
Sheppard, Sam *Suppl. 1*
Still, Andrew Taylor

Otolaryngologists
Barnes, William Harry
Burnett, Charles Henry
Elsberg, Louis
Green, Horace
Jarvis, William Chapman
Shambaugh, George E.,
  Jr. *Suppl. 1*
Solis-Cohen, Jacob da
  Silva

Parapsychologists
Hyslop, James Hervey
Rhine, J. B.

Pathologists
Andersen, Dorothy
  Hansine
Biggs, Hermann Michael
Cone, Claribel
Cone, Etta
Councilman, William
  Thomas
Delafield, Francis
De Witt, Lydia Maria
Ewing, James
  (1866–1943)
Fenger, Christian
Flexner, Simon
Frantz, Virginia
  Kneeland
Fuller, Solomon Carter

Gardner, Leroy Upson
Gerhard, William Wood
Goldblatt, Harry
Hertzler, Arthur
    Emanuel
Hinton, William
    Augustus
Hurdon, Elizabeth
Kinyoun, Joseph James
Landsteiner, Karl
Larson, Leonard
    Winfield
L'Esperance, Elise
    Strang
Longcope, Warfield
    Theobald
MacCallum, William
    George
Mallory, Frank Burr
Martland, Harrison
    Stanford
Meyer, Karl Friedrich
Minot, George Richards
Murphy, James
    Bumgardner
Opie, Eugene Lindsay
Pearce, Richard Mills, Jr.
Prudden, Theophil
    Mitchell
Rich, Arnold Rice
Ricketts, Howard Taylor
Shope, Richard Edwin
Smith, Harry Pratt
Smith, Margaret Gladys
Smith, Theobald
Warren, Shields
Wells, Harry Gideon
Whipple, George Hoyt
Wolbach, S. Burt
Wollstein, Martha

Pediatricians
Abt, Isaac Arthur
Alexander, Hattie
    Elizabeth
Andersen, Dorothy
    Hansine
Apgar, Virginia
Coit, Henry Leber
Diamond, Louis K.
    Suppl. 2
Eliot, Martha May
Gesell, Arnold Lucius
Hess, Alfred Fabian
Holt, Luther Emmett
Howland, John
Jackson, Edith Banfield
Jacobi, Abraham
Kenyon, Josephine
    Hemenway
Koplik, Henry

Sachs, Bernard
Schick, Béla
Schloss, Oscar
    Menderson
Smith, Job Lewis
Spock, Benjamin
    Suppl. 1
Stokes, Joseph, Jr.
Trask, James Dowling
Van Ingen, Philip

Pharmacists
Browne, Benjamin
    Frederick
Craigie, Andrew
Durand, Élie Magloire
Hurty, John Newell
Kiss, Max
Maisch, John Michael
Marshall, Christopher
Parrish, Edward
Procter, William, Jr.
Rice, Charles
Walgreen, Charles
    Rudolph

Phrenologists
Buchanan, Joseph Rodes
Caldwell, Charles
Fowler, Lorenzo Niles
Fowler, Orson Squire
Sizer, Nelson
Wells, Samuel Roberts

Physicians
Abrams, Albert
Adams, Numa
    Pompilius Garfield
Adler, Alfred
Allen, Nathan
Allison, Richard
Alvarez, Walter Clement
Ames, Nathaniel
    (1708–1764)
Ames, Nathaniel
    (1741–1842)
Antony, Milton
Appleton, Moses
Archer, John
Arnold, Richard Dennis
Aspinwall, William
    (1743–1823)
Atlee, John Light
Atlee, Washington
    Lemuel
Aub, Joseph Charles
Augusta, Alexander
    Thomas
Bache, Franklin
Bagley, Sarah George
Baker, Sara Josephine

Baldwin, William
Bancroft, Edward
Bard, John
Bard, Samuel
Barker, Benjamin
    Fordyce
Barker, Jeremiah
Barnes, William Harry
Barringer, Emily
    Dunning
Barrus, Clara
Bartholow, Roberts
Bartlett, Elisha
Bartlett, Josiah
Barton, Benjamin Smith
Baruch, Simon
Bass, Mary Elizabeth
Bate, Humphrey
Bayley, Richard
Bayne-Jones, Stanhope
Beard, George Miller
Beatty, John
Beaumont, William
Beck, John Brodhead
Beck, Theodric Romeyn
Benjamin, Harry
Bennet, Sanford
    Fillmore
Bennett, Alice
Bennett, John Cook
Berson, Solomon Aaron
Bigelow, Jacob
Biggs, Hermann Michael
Billings, John Shaw
Blackburn, Luke Pryor
Blackwell, Elizabeth
Blackwell, Emily
Blunt, James Gillpatrick
Bond, Thomas
Boswell, Henry
Bousfield, Midian
    Othello
Bowditch, Henry
    Ingersoll
Boylston, Zabdiel
Brackett, Joshua
Branche, George
    Clayton
Brandreth, Benjamin
Brigham, Amariah
Brooke, Abraham
Brown, Charlotte
    Amanda Blake
Brown, Lawrason
Brown, Samuel
Brown, William
    (1748–1792)
Brownson, Nathan
Bruce, Archibald
Buchanan, Joseph Rodes
Buckel, C. Annette

Bulkeley, Gershom
Bundesen, Herman Niels
Burnet, William
    (1730–1791)
Burnett, Waldo Irving
Cabell, James Lawrence
Cadwalader, Thomas
Caldwell, Charles
Caldwell, David
Carlson, Henry Clifford
Carroll, James
Carson, Joseph
Cartwright, Samuel
    Adolphus
Caverly, Charles
    Solomon
Cecil, Russell LaFayette
Cesar
Chaillé, Stanford
    Emerson
Chapin, Henry Dwight
Chapman, Nathaniel
Child, Robert
Chinn, May Edward
Christian, Henry Asbury
Church, Benjamin
    (1734–1778?)
Clapp, Asahel
Clarke, Edward
    Hammond
Cleaves, Margaret
    Abigail
Clendening, Logan
Cochran, Jerome
Cochran, John
Coffin, Nathaniel, Jr.
Cohn, Alfred Einstein
Colden, Cadwallader
Cole, Richard Beverly
Cole, Rufus
Cooke, Elisha, Jr.
Cooke, John Esten
    (1783–1853)
Cooper, James Graham
Copeland, Royal Samuel
Cotzias, George C.
Cournand, André
    Frédéric
Coxe, John Redman
Craik, James
Crawford, John
Crumbine, Samuel Jay
Crumpler, Rebecca
    Davis Lee
Curtis, Austin Maurice
Cutler, Hannah Tracy
Cutter, Ammi Ruhamah
Dale, Thomas
    (1700–1750)
Dameshek, William
Dana, Israel Thorndike

Dandy, Walter Edward
Daniel, Annie Sturges
Darlington, William
Davis, Charles Henry
Stanley
Davis, Edwin Hamilton
Davis, John Wesley
Davis, Nathan Smith
Degrasse, John Van
Surly
Delafield, Edward
Delafield, Francis
Denison, Charles
Dennis, Frederic
Shepard
Dexter, Aaron
Dibble, Eugene Heriot,
Jr.
Dick, Elisha Cullen
Dick, George Frederick
Dick, Gladys Suppl. 1
Dickson, Samuel Henry
Dimock, Susan
Dochez, Alphonse
Raymond
Dock, George
Dods, John Bovee
Donaldson, Mary
Elizabeth
Donnell, Clyde Henry
Dooley, Thomas
Anthony, III
Dorsette, Cornelius
Nathaniel
Douglass, William
Drake, Daniel
Draper, George
DuBois, Eugene Floyd
Dunlap, Livingston
Durham, James
Durnford, Andrew
Eberle, John
Edsall, David Linn
Eliot, Jared
Elmer, Jonathan
Emerson, Gouverneur
Emmons, Ebenezer
Engelmann, George
Ernst, Harold Clarence
Evans, John
Evans, Matilda Arabella
Ewell, James
Faget, Jean Charles
Favill, Henry Baird
Fayssoux, Peter
Ferebee, Dorothy
Boulding
Ferguson, Richard
Babbington
Finlay, Carlos Juan
Fishberg, Maurice

Fisher, Rudolph
Fitz, Reginald Heber
Flick, Lawrence Francis
Flint, Austin
(1812–1886)
Floyd, John
Forbes, Alexander
Forsythe, Albert Edward
Suppl. 2
Forwood, William Henry
Francis, Thomas, Jr.
Frost, Wade Hampton
Gale, Benjamin
Gallup, Joseph Adams
Galt, John Minson, II
Galt, William Craig
Gamble, James Lawder
Gantt, Love Rosa
Hirschmann
Garden, Alexander
(1730–1791)
Gardiner, Silvester
Garvin, Charles Herbert
Geddings, Eli
Gerhard, William Wood
Giannini, Attilio Henry
Gibbes, Robert Wilson
Gibbons, William
(1781–1845)
Girard, Charles Frédéric
Gleason, Rachel Brooks
Goddard, Paul Beck
Goforth, William
Goodale, George
Lincoln
Goodpasture, Ernest
William
Gorham, John
Gorrie, John
Gould, Augustus
Addison
Gray, John Purdue
Green, Asa
Greene, Cordelia Agnes
Gridley, Selah
Griscom, John Hoskins
Guiteras, Juan
Gulick, Luther Halsey
(1828–1891)
Gunn, John C.
Guthrie, Samuel
Hamilton, Alexander
(1712–1756)
Hamilton, Alice
Hand, Edward
Handerson, Henry
Ebenezer
Harlan, Richard
Harrington, Thomas
Francis
Harris, Seale

Harrison, John Pollard
Harrison, Tinsley
Randolph
Hartman, Samuel
Brubaker
Hartshorne, Henry
Hatfield, Henry Drury
Hawthorne, Edward
William
Heiser, Victor George
Hektoen, Ludvig
Hench, Philip Showalter
Hepburn, James Curtis
Herter, Christian
Archibald (1865–1910)
Hertzler, Arthur
Emanuel
Hildreth, Samuel
Prescott
Hinson, Eugene
Theodore
Hirsch, James Gerald
Hoff, John Van
Rensselaer
Holbrook, John Edwards
Holmes, Bayard Taylor
Holmes, Oliver Wendell
(1809–1894)
Holten, Samuel
Holyoke, Edward
Augustus
Hooker, Worthington
Hopkins, Lemuel
Horn, George Henry
Horner, William
Edmonds
Hosack, David
Houghton, Douglass
Hubbard, George
Whipple
Hunt, Ezra Mundy
Hunt, Harriot Kezia
Hunter, William
Huntington, George
Hutchinson, James
Hutchinson, Woods
Jackson, Hall
Jackson, James
(1777–1867)
Jackson, James Caleb
Jackson, James, Jr.
Jackson, Samuel
Jacobi, Abraham
Jacobi, Mary Corinna
Putnam
James, Edwin
James, Thomas C.
Janeway, Edward
Gamaliel
Jarvis, DeForest Clinton
Jeffries, John

Jenison, Nancy Blanche
Jermain, Louis Francis
Johnson, Halle Tanner
Dillon
Johnson, Peter August
Jones, Calvin
Jones, John (1729–1791)
Jones, Joseph
Jones, Mary Amanda
Dixon
Jones, Noble
Joslin, Elliott Proctor
Judd, Gerrit Parmele
Kane, Elisha Kent
Kean, Jefferson
Randolph
Kearsley, John
Keeley, Leslie Enraught
Kelly, Aloysius Oliver
Joseph
Kempster, Walter
Kent, Joseph
Kern, Benjamin Jordan
Killpatrick, James
King, Albert Freeman
Africanus Suppl. 2
Kirtland, Jared Potter
Knowles, John Hilton
Knowlton, Charles
Koch, William Frederick
La Roche, René
Lattimore, John Aaron
Cicero
Lazear, Jesse William
Lee, Charles Alfred
Leib, Michael
Leonard, Charles Lester
Lewis, Henry Clay
Libman, Emanuel
Lining, John
Long, Crawford
Williamson
Lovejoy, Esther Pohl
Lozier, Clemence Sophia
Lumbrozo, Jacob
Lyon, Irving Whitall
Macfarlane, Catharine
Maclean, John
MacNeven, William
James
Mahler, Margaret S.
Major, Ralph Hermon
Majors, Monroe Alpheus
Mallory, Frank Burr
Mann, Frank Charles
Mann, James
Manning, Isaac Hall
Marcy, Henry Orlando
Marsh, John
Marshall, Clara

Marshall, Louis
(1773–1866)
Mayo, Sara
Mayo, William James,
and Charles Horace
Mayo
Mayo, William Starbuck
Mayo, William Worrell
Mazzei, Philip
McCaw, Walter Drew
McClendon, James Julius
McClennan, Alonzo
Clifton
McClurg, James
McCormack, Arthur
Thomas
McCormack, Joseph
Nathaniel
McCrae, Thomas
McCready, Benjamin
William
McDowell, Ephraim
McGee, Anita Newcomb
McGillycuddy, Valentine
Trant O'Connell
McHenry, James
(1753–1816)
McKinly, John
McLean, Franklin
Chambers
McLean, Mary Hancock
Means, James Howard
Mease, James
Meltzer, Samuel James
Mendenhall, Dorothy
Reed
Menninger, Charles
Frederick
Mercier, Alfred
Mergler, Marie Josepha
Metcalfe, Samuel Lytler
Mettauer, John Peter
Middleton, Peter
Middleton, William
Shainline
Miles, Manly
Miller, Charles Henry
Miller, Edward
Minoka-Hill, Lillie Rosa
Minot, George Richards
Mitchell, John
(1690?–1768)
Mitchell, John Kearsley
Mitchell, S. Weir
Mitchell, Thomas Duché
Mitchill, Samuel Latham
Montezuma, Carlos
Moore, Aaron McDuffie
Moore, Joseph Earle
Morgan, John
Morril, David Lawrence

Morris, Caspar
Morrow, Thomas
Vaughn
Morton, Samuel George
Mosher, Clelia Duel
Mosher, Eliza Maria
Mossell, Nathan Francis
Moten, Pierce Sherman
Moultrie, James, Jr.
Moursund, Walter
Henrik
Munson, Aeneas
Murphy, William Parry
Suppl. 2
Murray, Peter Marshall
Neal, Josephine Bicknell
Newell, William
Augustus
Nixon, Pat Ireland
North, Elisha
Nott, Josiah Clark
O'Fallon, James
Ordronaux, John
Osler, Sir William
Otto, Bodo
Otto, John Conrad
Owens-Adair, Bethenia
Angelina
Packard, Francis
Randolph
Paine, Martyn
Palmer, Alonzo
Benjamin
Palmer, Walter Walker
Park, William Hallock
Parker, Peter
(1804–1888)
Parker, Willard
Parrish, Joseph
(1779–1840)
Parrish, Joseph
(1818–1891)
Parsons, Mary Almera
Parsons, Usher
Peck, David Jones
Pell, Thomas
Pendleton, Edmund
Monroe
Pepper, Oliver Hazard
Perry
Pepper, William
Pepper, William, Jr.
Perkins, Elisha
Perrine, Henry
Phelps, Guy Rowland
Physick, Philip Syng
Picotte, Susan La
Flesche
Pitcher, Zina
Plummer, Henry Stanley

Poindexter, Hildrus
Augustus
Pomeroy, John
Porcher, Francis Peyre
Pott, John
Potter, Ellen Culver
Prescott, Oliver
Prescott, Samuel
Preston, Ann
Prevost, François Marie
Prime, Benjamin Youngs
Purvis, Charles Burleigh
Quintard, Charles Todd
Ramsay, Alexander
Randolph, Jacob
Randolph, Paschal
Beverly
Ravenel, Edmund
Redman, John
Redmond, Sidney Dillon
Reed, Walter
Remond, Sarah Parker
Rice, Joseph Mayer
Richards, Dickinson
Woodruff
Richards, Paul Snelgrove
Richmond, John
Lambert
Ridgely, Frederick
Ripley, Martha George
Robbins, Jane Elizabeth
Robertson, Oswald
Hope
Robie, Thomas
Rock, John Charles
Rockwell, Alphonso
David
Roman, Charles Victor
Romayne, Nicholas
Root, Joseph Pomeroy
Roudanez, Louis Charles
Rush, Benjamin
Rush, James
Russ, John Dennison
Sabin, Albert Bruce
Sabin, Florence Rena
Safford, Mary Jane
Salk, Jonas Edward
Sappington, John
Sargent, Dudley Allen
Saugrain De Vigni,
Antoine François
Savage, Thomas
Staughton
Say, Benjamin
Scheele, Leonard A.
Schloss, Oscar
Menderson
Scudder, Ida Sophia
Scudder, John
Seagrave, Gordon Stifler

Seaman, Valentine
Seguin, Edouard O.
Sellaro, Vincenzo
Sewall, Henry
Sewall, Lucy Ellen
Shadd, Furman Jeremiah
Shakespeare, Edward
Oram
Shattuck, George
Cheyne
Shaw, John (1778–1809)
Shecut, John Linnaeus
Edward Whitridge
Sheldon, William
Herbert
Sherwood, Mary
Shippen, William, Jr.
Short, Charles Wilkins
Sibley, John
Sidis, Boris
Simmons, George Henry
Smith, Ashbel
Smith, Elihu Hubbard
Smith, Fred M.
Smith, James
(1771–1841)
Smith, James McCune
Smith, John Lawrence
Smith, Nathan
Smith, Peter
(1753–1815)
Smith, Relliford Stillmon
Snow, Edwin Miller
Solis-Cohen, Jacob da
Silva
Solis-Cohen, Solomon
Soper, Fred Lowe
South, Lillian Herreld
Spalding, Lyman
Squibb, Edward
Robinson
Stein, Jules Caesar
Stengel, Alfred
Sternberg, George Miller
Steward, Susan Maria
Smith McKinney
Still, Andrew Taylor
Stillé, Alfred
Stone, Abraham, and
Hannah Mayer Stone
Storer, David
Humphreys
Sutton, William Loftus
Swain, Clara A.
Tailfer, Patrick
Tarnower, Herman
Taussig, Helen Brooke
Tennent, John
Terry, Charles Edward
Testut, Charles
Thacher, Thomas

Thayer, Samuel White, Jr.
Thayer, William Sydney
Thomas, Lewis
Thompson, Ebenezer
Thompson, Joseph Pascal
Thornton, Matthew
Ticknor, Francis Orray
Tildon, Toussaint Tourgee
Tilton, James
Todd, Eli
Townsend, Francis Everett
Trudeau, Edward Livingston
Tufts, Cotton
Tully, William
Tunnicliff, Ruth May
Twitchell, Amos
Tyson, James
Underwood, Felix Joel
Underwood, Lillias Stirling Horton
Van Beuren, Johannes
Van Dyck, Cornelius Van Alen
Walcott, Henry Pickering
Warren, John Collins (1842–1927)
Warren, Joseph
Waterhouse, Benjamin
Wearn, Joseph T.
Weiss, Soma
Welsh, Lilian
White, James Platt
White, Paul Dudley
Whitman, Marcus
Wilkerson, Vernon Alexander
Williams, Francis Henry
Williams, Joseph Leroy
Williams, Nathaniel
Williams, Stephen West
Williams, William Carlos
Williamson, Hugh
Wilson, Frank Norman
Winthrop, John, Jr.
Wislizenus, Frederick Adolphus
Wistar, Caspar (1761–1818)
Wood, George Bacon
Wood, Horatio C, Jr.
Wood, William Barry, Jr.
Woodhull, Alfred Alexander
Woodward, Henry

Woodward, Joseph Janvier
Woodward, Theodore
Woodworth, John Maynard
Work, Hubert
Wright, Eliphalet Nott
Wright, Joseph Jefferson Burr
Yandell, Lunsford Pitts, Sr.
Yarros, Rachelle
Young, John Richardson
Zakrzewska, Marie Elizabeth

Psychiatrists
Babcock, James Woods
Bell, Luther V.
Bender, Lauretta
Berne, Eric *Suppl. 2*
Blumer, George Alder
Brill, Abraham Arden
Bryce, Peter
Bucke, Richard Maurice
Burrow, Trigant
Campbell, Charles Macfie
Cobb, Stanley
Cotton, Henry Andrews
Deutsch, Helene Rosenbach
Dunbar, Helen Flanders
Earle, Pliny
Erickson, Milton Hyland
Felix, Robert Hanna
Flint, Austin (1836–1915)
Fromm-Reichmann, Frieda
Fuller, Solomon Carter
Goldstein, Kurt
Gray, John Purdue
Greenacre, Phyllis
Healy, William
Hilgard, Josephine Rohrs
Hurd, Henry Mills
Jarvis, Edward
Jones, William Palmer
Kardiner, Abram
Kenworthy, Marion Edwena
Kirkbride, Thomas Story
Levine, Lena
Menninger, Karl Augustus
Menninger, William Claire
Meyer, Adolf
Moore, Merrill
Myerson, Abraham

Nichols, Charles Henry
Nyswander, Marie
Oberndorf, Clarence Paul
Ray, Isaac
Rohé, George Henry
Sackler, Arthur Mitchell
Sakel, Manfred Joshua
Salmon, Thomas William
Sidis, Boris
Southard, Elmer Ernest
Spitzka, Edward Charles
Sullivan, Harry Stack
Thompson, Clara *Suppl. 1*
Tildon, Toussaint Tourgee
White, William Alanson
Williams, Frankwood E. *Suppl. 1*
Woodward, Samuel Bayard

Psychoanalysts
Alexander, Franz Gabriel
Bibring, Grete Lehner
Brill, A. A.
Brunswick, Ruth Jane Mack
Burrow, Trigant
Coriat, Isador Henry
Deutsch, Helene Rosenbach
Dunbar, Helen Flanders
Eissler, K. R. *Suppl. 1*
Erikson, Erik
Fenichel, Otto
Fromm, Erich Pinchas
Fromm-Reichmann, Frieda
Greenacre, Phyllis
Hinkle, Beatrice Moses
Horney, Karen Theodora Clementina Danielsen
Jackson, Edith Banfield
Jelliffe, Smith Ely
Kardiner, Abram
Kohut, Heinz
Mahler, Margaret S.
May, Rollo
Oberndorf, Clarence Paul
Rado, Sandor
Rank, Otto
Reich, Wilhelm
Reik, Theodor
Sachs, Hanns

Williams, Frankwood E. *Suppl. 1*

Psychobiologists
Gantt, W. Horsley
Nissen, Henry Wieghorst
Richter, Curt Paul

Psychologists
Adler, Alfred
Ainsworth, Mary *Suppl. 1*
Allport, Floyd Henry
Allport, Gordon Willard
Angell, James Rowland
Baldwin, James Mark
Beach, Frank Ambrose, Jr.
Bettelheim, Bruno
Bingham, Walter Van Dyke
Boring, Edwin Garrigues
Brigham, Carl Campbell
Bronner, Augusta Fox
Brown, Junius Flagg
Brown, Warner
Bryan, William Lowe
Bühler, Charlotte
Bühler, Karl
Burnham, William Henry
Burrow, Trigant
Calkins, Mary Whiton
Campbell, Angus
Cantril, Hadley
Carmichael, Leonard
Cattell, James McKeen
Coe, George Albert
Curti, Margaret Wooster
Dallenbach, Karl M.
Dearborn, Walter Fenno
Dodge, Raymond
Dollard, John
Downey, June Etta
Dunlap, Knight
Erikson, Erik
Faris, Ellsworth
Festinger, Leon
Franz, Shepherd Ivory
Frenkel-Brunswik, Else
Fromm, Erich Pinchas
Gesell, Arnold Lucius
Gibson, James Jerome
Gilbreth, Lillian Evelyn Moller
Goddard, Henry Herbert
Goodenough, Florence Laura
Guiles, Austin Philip
Guilford, Joy Paul

Guthrie, Edwin Ray
Haggerty, Melvin
  Everett
Hall, Calvin Springer
Hall, Granville Stanley
Harlow, Harry Frederick
Hartmann, George
  Wilfred
Hathaway, Starke
  Rosecrans
Healy, William
Hebb, Donald Olding
Heidbreder, Edna
  Frances
Heider, Fritz
Hilgard, Josephine Rohrs
Hollingworth, Harry
  Levi
Hollingworth, Leta Anna
  Stetter
Holt, Edwin Bissell
Hovland, Carl Iver
Hull, Clark Leonard
Hunter, Walter Samuel
Hyslop, James Hervey
Ichheiser, Gustav
Irwin, Elisabeth
  Antoinette
James, William
Jastrow, Joseph
Johnson, Paul Emanuel
Johnson, Wendell
  Andrew Leroy
Jones, Mary Elizabeth
  Cover
Judd, Charles Hubbard
Kantor, Jacob Robert
Katona, George
Keller, Fred S. *Suppl. 2*
Kelley, Truman Lee
Kessen, William *Suppl. 1*
Klineberg, Otto
Koffka, Kurt
Köhler, Wolfgang
Krech, David
Ladd, George Trumbull
Ladd-Franklin, Christine
Lashley, Karl Spencer
Lazarsfeld, Paul Felix
Leary, Timothy *Suppl. 1*
Lewin, Kurt
Likert, Rensis
Link, Henry Charles
Marston, William
  Moulton
Martin, Everett Dean
Martin, Lillien Jane
Maslow, Abraham
  Harold
McDougall, William

McFarland, Ross
  Armstrong
McGraw, Myrtle Byram
McNemar, Quinn
Meyer, Max Friedrich
Milgram, Stanley
Mowrer, Orval Hobart
Münsterberg, Hugo
Murphy, Gardner
Murray, Henry
  Alexander, Jr.
Newcomb, Theodore
  Mead
Norsworthy, Naomi
Otis, Arthur Sinton
Pace, Edward Aloysius
Pillsbury, Walter Bowers
Prince, Morton Henry
Rand, Marie Gertrude
Rank, Otto
Rapaport, David
Roback, A. A.
Robinson, Edward
  Stevens
Rogers, Carl Ransom
Rokeach, Milton
Sanford, Edmund Clark
Scott, Colin Alexander
Scott, Walter Dill
Scripture, Edward
  Wheeler
Sears, Robert
  Richardson
Seashore, Carl Emil
Shakow, David
Sheldon, William
  Herbert
Sherif, Muzafer
Shinn, Milicent
  Washburn
Sidis, Boris
Skinner, B. F.
Smith, Theodate Louise
Spence, Kenneth
  Wartinbee
Starbuck, Edwin Diller
Stevens, Stanley Smith
Stoddard, George
  Dinsmore
Strong, Charles
  Augustus
Sumner, Francis Cecil
Terman, Lewis Madison
Teuber, Hans-Lukas
Thorndike, Edward Lee
Thurstone, Louis Leon
Titchener, Edward
  Bradford
Tolman, Edward Chace
Warren, Howard Crosby

Washburn, Margaret
  Floy
Watson, Goodwin
  Barbour
Watson, John Broadus
Wechsler, David
Weiss, Albert Paul
Wells, Frederic Lyman
Werner, Heinz
Wertheimer, Max
Whipple, Guy Montrose
Wissler, Clark
Witmer, Lightner
Wolfe, Harry Kirke
Woodworth, Robert
  Sessions
Woolley, Helen Bradford
  Thompson
Yerkes, Robert Mearns

Public Health Officials
Abbott, Samuel Warren
Arnstein, Margaret
Baker, Sara Josephine
Beard, Mary
Bennett, Alice
Biggs, Hermann Michael
Boswell, Henry
Bradley, Charles Henry
Brigham, Amariah
Bryce, Peter
Calderone, Mary S.
  Suppl. 1
Caverly, Charles
  Solomon
Chapin, Charles Value
Cochran, John
Crandall, Ella Phillips
Crothers, Thomas
  Davison
Day, Albert
Dyer, Rolla Eugene
Earle, Pliny
Felix, Robert Hanna
Fitzgerald, Alice
Frost, Wade Hampton
Galt, John Minson, II
Gardner, Mary Sewall
Garrison, Charles Willis
Goldwater, Sigismund
  Schulz
Gray, John Purdue
Guiteras, Juan
Gunn, Selskar Michael
Heiser, Victor George
Hopkins, Juliet Ann
  Opie
Horsfall, Frank Lappin,
  Jr.
Hunt, Ezra Mundy
Hurd, Henry Mills

Kellogg, John Harvey
Knowles, John Hilton
Kolb, Lawrence
Lovejoy, Esther Pohl
Lumsden, Leslie Leon
Mahoney, John Friend
Manning, Isaac Hall
McCaw, James Brown
McCormack, Arthur
  Thomas
McCormack, Joseph
  Nathaniel
Mossell, Nathan Francis
Nichols, Charles Henry
Nyswander, Dorothy B.
  Suppl. 1
Pember, Phoebe Yates
  Levy
Pinn, Petra Fitzalieu
Poindexter, Hildrus
  Augustus
Potter, Ellen Culver
Rauch, John Henry
Rosenau, Milton Joseph
Sawyer, Wilbur
  Augustus
Snow, Edwin Miller
Snow, William Freeman
Soper, Fred Lowe
Stiles, Charles Wardell
Switzer, Mary Elizabeth
Terry, Charles Edward
Thompson, Mary Harris
Todd, Eli
Underwood, Felix Joel
Walcott, Henry
  Pickering
White, William Alanson
Williams, Daniel Hale
Winston, Ellen Black
Woodward, Samuel
  Bayard
Woodworth, John
  Maynard
Wright, Louis Tompkins

Radiologists
Caldwell, Eugene Wilson
Failla, Gioacchino
Kaplan, Henry Seymour
Lampe, Isadore
Lawrence, John Hundale
Pancoast, Henry
  Khunrath
Strax, Philip *Suppl. 2*
Warren, Stafford Leak

Siamese Twins
Chang and Eng

Speech Therapists
Johnson, Wendell
  Andrew Leroy
Scripture, Edward
  Wheeler

Surgeons
Abbott, Anderson Ruffin
Agnew, D. Hayes
Ainsworth, Fred Crayton
Ambler, James Markham
  Marshall
Atlee, John Light
Atlee, Washington
  Lemuel
Bassett, John Young
Battey, Robert
Bayley, Richard
Beck, Claude Schaeffer
Benites, José María
Bevan, Arthur Dean
Bigelow, Henry Jacob
Blalock, Alfred
Bond, Thomas
Boylston, Zabdiel
Brinton, John Hill
Brophy, Truman
  William
Bryant, Joseph Decatur
Buck, Gurdon
Cabot, Hugh
Carnochan, John Murray
Chisolm, Julian John
Chovet, Abraham
Churchill, Edward Delos
Clarke, Parker
Cleveland, Emeline
  Horton
Coley, William Bradley
Cooper, Elias Samuel
Cope, Oliver
Craik, James
Crile, George
  Washington
Crosby, Dixi
Curtis, Austin Maurice
Curtis, John Green
Cutler, Elliott Carr
DaCosta, John Chalmers
Dailey, Ulysses Grant
Davidge, John Beale
Deaver, John Blair
Dennis, Frederic
  Shepard
Dimock, Susan
Dragstedt, Lester
  Reynold
Drew, Charles Richard
Dudley, Benjamin
  Winslow

Emmet, Thomas Addis
  (1828–1919)
Fenger, Christian
Ferguson, Richard
  Babbington
Finney, John Miller
  Turpin
Fowler, George Ryerson
Frantz, Virginia
  Kneeland
Garretson, James
  Edmund
Gerster, Arpad Geyza
  Charles
Gibbon, John Heysham,
  Jr.
Gibson, William
Gihon, Albert Leary
Gilbert, Rufus Henry
Gross, Samuel David
Halsted, William Stewart
Harkins, Henry N.
Hays, Isaac
Hertzler, Arthur
  Emanuel
Huggins, Charles
  Brenton *Suppl. 2*
Hullihen, Simon P.
Hume, David Milford
Hunter, William
Hutchinson, James
Jameson, Horatio Gates
Jeffries, John
Jones, John (1729–1791)
Jones, Mary Amanda
  Dixon
Kazanjian, Varaztad
Keen, William Williams
Kellogg, John Harvey
Kelly, Howard Atwood
Kilty, William
Kingsley, Norman
  William
Ladd, William Edwards
Lahey, Frank Howard
Lloyd, James, II
Long, Crawford
  Williamson
Lovelace, William
  Randolph, II
Lydston, G. Frank
Mann, James
March, Alden
Marchbanks, Vance
  Hunter, Jr.
Martin, Franklin Henry
Mason, James Tate
Matas, Rudolph
Mathews, Joseph
  McDowell

Matson, Ralph Charles,
  and Ray William
  Matson
Mayo, William James,
  and Charles Horace
  Mayo
Mayo, William Worrell
McClellan, George
McDowell, Ephraim
McGuire, Hunter
  Holmes
Mearns, Edgar
  Alexander
Mergler, Marie Josepha
Mott, Valentine
Mumford, James
  Gregory
Murphy, John Benjamin
Mussey, Reuben
  Dimond
Ochsner, Alton
Otis, George Alexander
Otto, Bodo
Pancoast, Joseph
Park, Roswell
Parsons, Usher
Pattison, Granville Sharp
Prevost, François Marie
Price, Joseph
Randolph, Jacob
Ridgely, Frederick
Saugrain De Vigni,
  Antoine François
Seaman, Valentine
Senn, Nicholas
Sinkler, William H., Jr.
Smith, Alban Gilpin
Smith, Nathan
Smith, Stephen
Souchon, Edmond
Stitt, Edward Rhodes
Thompson, Mary Harris
Thorek, Max
Twitchell, Amos
Van Hoosen, Bertha
Warbasse, James Peter
Warren, Edward
Warren, John
Warren, John Collins
  (1778–1856)
Warren, John Collins
  (1842–1927)
Whipple, Allen
  Oldfather
Williams, Daniel Hale
Woodward, Theodore
Wright, Louis Tompkins
Yandell, David Wendel
Young, Hugh Hampton

Surgeons General
Barnes, Joseph K.
Benites, José María
Gorgas, William
  Crawford
Hamilton, John Brown
Lawson, Thomas
Lovell, Joseph
Parran, Thomas
Scheele, Leonard A.
Smith, Ashbel

Syphilologists
Hinton, William
  Augustus
Morrow, Prince Albert
Pusey, William Allen

Teratologists
Apgar, Virginia

Transsexuals
Jorgensen, Christine

Urologists
Flocks, Rubin Hyman
Lydston, G. Frank
Young, Hugh Hampton

Veterinarians
Kelser, Raymond
  Alexander
Law, James
Lyman, Charles Parker
Pearson, Leonard
Salmon, Daniel Elmer
Williams, Walter Long

Veterinary Pathologists
Moore, Veranus Alva

HUMANITIES AND SOCIAL SCIENCES

Criticism
Architectural Critics
Eidlitz, Leopold
Fowler, Orson Squire
Gilman, Arthur Delavan
Hamlin, Alfred Dwight
  Foster
Magonigle, Harold Van
  Buren
Mumford, Lewis
Sturgis, Russell
Van Brunt, Henry

Art Critics
Benson, Eugene
Caffin, Charles Henry
Chávez, Carlos

Criticism *(cont.)*
Coates, Robert Myron
Cook, Clarence
Cortissoz, Royal
Cox, Kenyon
de Kooning, Elaine
Gallatin, Albert Eugene
Greenberg, Clement
Hambidge, Jay
Hartmann, Sadakichi
Heap, Jane
McBride, Henry
Miller, Charles Henry
Pach, Walter
Partridge, William
 Ordway
Pepper, Stephen C.
Perkins, Charles
 Callahan
Phillips, Duncan
 Suppl. 2
Porter, Fairfield
Porter, James Amos
Rosenberg, Harold
Ross, Denman Waldo
Saarinen, Aline
 Bernstein
Sargent, Irene Jesse
Shinn, Earl
Smithson, Robert Irving
Van Dyke, John Charles
Van Rensselaer, Mariana
 Griswold
Wright, Willard
 Huntington

Dance Critics
Amberg, George
Denby, Edwin Orr
Horst, Louis
Martin, John Joseph
Terry, Walter

Film Critics
Agee, James Rufus
Amberg, George
Crowther, Bosley
Macdonald, Dwight
Sherwood, Robert
 Emmet

Literary Critics
Aiken, Conrad
Arvin, Newton
Babbitt, Irving
Bacon, Leonard
Baker, Carlos Heard
Bate, Walter Jackson
 Suppl. 1
Beach, Joseph Warren
Blackmur, R. P.

Bodenheim, Maxwell
Bogan, Louise
Bourne, Randolph
 Silliman
Boyd, Ernest Augustus
Braithwaite, William
 Stanley Beaumont
Brooks, Cleanth
Brooks, Van Wyck
Brownell, William Crary
Burke, Kenneth
Chamberlain, John
 Suppl. 2
Clifford, James Lowry
Cournos, John
Cowley, Malcolm
Cuppy, William Jacob
Dabney, Richard
Dahlberg, Edward
Dell, Floyd James
de Man, Paul *Suppl. 2*
Dennie, Joseph
Dupee, F. W.
Eckman, Frederick
 Suppl. 1
Eliot, T. S.
Ellmann, Richard David
Fadiman, Clifton
 Suppl. 1
Foerster, Norman
Freeman, Joseph
Fuller, Hoyt William
Geismar, Maxwell David
Gilder, Jeannette
 Leonard
Goodman, Paul
Greenslet, Ferris
Gregory, Horace Victor
Harby, Isaac
Harris, Corra
Hayne, Paul Hamilton
Hicks, Granville
Highet, Gilbert
Hillyer, Robert Silliman
Hoffman, Frederick John
Hofstadter, Richard
Howe, Irving
Howells, William Dean
Hyman, Stanley Edgar
Jacobs, Joseph
James, Henry
 (1843–1916)
Jarrell, Randall
Kazin, Alfred *Suppl. 1*
Kirkus, Virginia
Koch, Vivienne
Krutch, Joseph Wood
Lewisohn, Ludwig
Lloyd, Margaret *Suppl. 2*
Locke, Alain Leroy
Loveman, Amy

Lowell, Amy
Matthiessen, F. O.
McCarthy, Mary
McHenry, James
 (1785–1845)
Mencken, H. L.
Millett, Fred Benjamin
Moore, Marianne
Morley, Christopher
 Darlington
Newman, Frances
Noguchi, Yone
Otis, Brooks
Parker, H. T. *Suppl. 2*
Payne, William Morton
Poe, Edgar Allan
Pound, Ezra
Rahv, Philip
Ransom, John Crowe
Redding, J. Saunders
Richards, I. A.
Ripley, George
Rittenhouse, Jessie Belle
Schorer, Mark
Schwartz, Delmore
Scott, Evelyn
Scudder, Horace Elisha
Sherman, Stuart Pratt
Smith, Henry Nash
Spingarn, Joel Elias
Stedman, Edmund
 Clarence
Stoddard, Richard
 Henry
Taggard, Genevieve
Tate, Allen
Thompson, Maurice
Trent, William Peterfield
Trilling, Diana *Suppl. 1*
Trilling, Lionel
Trowbridge, John
 Townsend
Tuve, Rosemond
Van Doren, Carl
Van Doren, Mark
Warren, Austin
Warren, Robert Penn
Whipple, Edwin Percy
Wilson, Edmund
Winters, Yvor
Yourcenar, Marguerite
Zukofsky, Louis

Music Critics
Aldrich, Richard
 (1863–1937)
Apthorp, William Foster
Chávez, Carlos
Chotzinoff, Samuel
Downes, Olin
Dwight, John Sullivan

Feather, Leonard
Finck, Henry Theophilus
Flanagan, William
Fry, William Henry
Gilman, Lawrence
Gleason, Ralph Joseph
Haggin, B. H.
Hammond, John Henry,
 Jr.
Huneker, James Gibbons
Krehbiel, Henry Edward
Mason, Daniel Gregory
Parker, H. T. *Suppl. 2*
Peck, George
 Washington
Peyton, Dave
Rosenfeld, Paul Leopold
Spaeth, Sigmund
Taylor, Deems
Thompson, Oscar
Thomson, Virgil
Van Vechten, Carl

Television Critics
Amory, Cleveland
 Suppl. 1
Gould, Jack

Theater Critics
Atkinson, Brooks
Benchley, Robert
Brackett, Charles
 William
Brown, John Mason, Jr.
Clurman, Harold Edgar
Dale, Alan
Denby, Edwin Orr
Dithmar, Edward
 Augustus
Eaton, Walter Prichard
Freedley, George
Gassner, John Waldhorn
Gibbs, Wolcott
 (1902–1958)
Gilder, Rosamond
Hamilton, Clayton
Hammond, Percy
 Hunter
Hapgood, Norman
Isaacs, Edith Juliet Rich
Kerr, Walter *Suppl. 2*
Kronenberger, Louis
Krutch, Joseph Wood
Leslie, Amy
Macgowan, Kenneth
Mantle, Burns
Matthews, Brander
McCarthy, Mary
Nathan, George Jean
Parker, H. T. *Suppl. 2*

Criticism *(cont.)*
Price, William
    Thompson
Seldes, Gilbert Vivian
Simonson, Lee
Stevens, Ashton
Walton, Lester A.
    Suppl. 2
Winter, William
Woollcott, Alexander
    Humphreys
Young, Stark

**History and Related
Scholarship**
Archaeologists
Abbott, Charles Conrad
Albright, William
    Foxwell
Bandelier, Adolph
    Francis Alphonse
Barton, George Aaron
Bieber, Margarete
Blegen, Carl William
Bowditch, Charles
    Pickering
Carpenter, Rhys
Cotter, John L. *Suppl. 2*
Davis, Edwin Hamilton
Emory, Kenneth Pike
Frothingham, Arthur
    Lincoln
Giddings, James Louis
Glueck, Nelson
Goell, Theresa
    Bathsheba
Goodman, Joseph
    Thompson
Gordon, George Byron
Hawes, Harriet Ann
    Boyd
Heizer, Robert Fleming
Jones, Charles Colcock,
    Jr.
Kelsey, Francis Willey
Kidder, Alfred Vincent
Mercer, Henry
    Chapman
Morley, Sylvanus
    Griswold
Morris, Earl Halstead
Nelson, Nels Christian
Nuttall, Zelia Maria
    Magdalena
Peet, Stephen Denison
Proskouriakoff, Tatiana
    Suppl. 2
Prudden, Theophil
    Mitchell
Richter, Gisela Marie
    Augusta

Roberts, Frank H. H., Jr.
Squier, Ephraim George
Stephens, John Lloyd
    Suppl. 2
Tarbell, Frank Bigelow
Thompson, Edward
    Herbert
Vaillant, George Clapp
Winchell, Newton
    Horace
Wright, George Ernest

Architectural Historians
Brown, Glenn
Frothingham, Arthur
    Lincoln
Hamlin, Alfred Dwight
    Foster
Hitchcock, Henry-
    Russell
Kimball, Fiske
Kocher, A. Lawrence
Moore, Charles Herbert
Tallmadge, Thomas
    Eddy
Tuthill, Louisa Caroline
    Huggins
Warren, Herbert
    Langford

Art Historians
Barr, Alfred Hamilton,
    Jr.
Baur, John I. H.
Belknap, Waldron
    Phoenix
Berenson, Bernard
Bieber, Margarete
Breeskin, Adelyn Dohme
Coomaraswamy, Ananda
    Kentish
Ferguson, John Calvin
Friedlaender, Walter
    Ferdinand
Frothingham, Arthur
    Lincoln
Gardner, Helen
Goodrich, Lloyd
Janson, Horst Woldemar
Jarves, James Jackson
Mather, Frank Jewett, Jr.
Meiss, Millard
Miner, Dorothy Eugenia
Montgomery, Charles
    Franklin
Norton, Charles Eliot
Okakura Kakuzo
    Suppl. 1
Oliver, Andrew
    (1906–1981)
Pach, Walter

Panofsky, Erwin
Park, Lawrence *Suppl. 2*
Porter, James Amos
Richter, Gisela Marie
    Augusta
Schapiro, Meyer
    Suppl. 1
Wittkower, Rudolf

Buddhist Studies Scholars
Suzuki, D. T. *Suppl. 1*

Church Historians
Bacon, Leonard Woolsey
Bainton, Roland Herbert
Beaver, Robert Pierce
Clebsch, William
    Anthony
Corwin, Edward Tanjore
de Schweinitz, Edmund
    Alexander
Dorchester, Daniel
Dubbs, Joseph Henry
Emerton, Ephraim
Engelhardt, Zephyrin
Fisher, George Park
Gavin, Frank Stanton
    Burns
Guilday, Peter Keenan
Hitchcock, Roswell
    Dwight
Jackson, Samuel
    Macauley
Jacobs, Henry Eyster
Jones, Rufus Matthew
Little, Charles Joseph
McAvoy, Thomas
    Timothy
Morini, Austin M.
Pauck, Wilhelm
Perry, William Stevens
Reichel, William
    Cornelius
Reu, Johann Michael
Schaff, Philip
Shahan, Thomas Joseph
Shea, John Dawson
    Gilmary
Smith, Joseph Fielding
    (1876–1972)
Tappert, Theodore
    Gerhardt
Thompson, Ernest Trice
Tigert, John James, III
Walker, Williston
Walls, William Jacob
Whitsitt, William Heth
Wilbur, Earl Morse

Comparatists
Lord, Albert Bates
    Suppl. 1

Dance Historians
Holt, Claire
Kirstein, Lincoln
    Suppl. 1
La Meri
Luahine, Iolani
Moore, Lillian
Primus, Pearl
Selden, Elizabeth S.

*Documentary / Historical
Editors*
Blake, Harrison Gray
    Otis
Boyd, Julian Parks
Emerson, Edward Waldo
Fitzpatrick, John
    Clement
Ford, Paul Leicester
Ford, Worthington
    Chauncey
Hazard, Samuel
Kellogg, Louise Phelps
Knight, Lucian Lamar
Sparks, Jared
Thwaites, Reuben Gold

East Asian Studies Scholars
Fenollosa, Ernest
    Francisco
Holt, Claire
Jones, George Heber
Lattimore, Owen
McCawley, James D.
    Suppl. 1
Morse, Edward Sylvester
Reischauer, Edwin
    Oldfather
Rockhill, William
    Woodville
Wright, Mary Clabaugh

Ethnomusicologists
Cowell, Henry *Suppl. 1*
Curtis, Natalie
Densmore, Frances
    Theresa
Fillmore, John Comfort
Garrison, Lucy McKim
Lomax, John Avery

Film Historians
Kracauer, Siegfried
Mayer, Arthur Loeb

History and Related Scholarship *(cont.)*

Historians

Abel-Henderson, Annie Heloise
Acrelius, Israel
Adams, Charles Francis (1835–1915)
Adams, George Burton
Adams, Herbert Baxter
Alexander, De Alva Stanwood
Alexander, William DeWitt
Alvord, Clarence Walworth
Andrews, Charles McLean
Angle, Paul McClelland
Arnold, Richard Dennis
Atherton, Gertrude Franklin
Bailey, Thomas Andrew
Bancroft, Frederic A.
Bancroft, George
Bancroft, Hubert Howe
Bandelier, Adolph Francis Alphonse
Banvard, Joseph
Bartlett, John Russell
Baxter, James Phinney, III
Beard, Charles Austin
Beard, Mary Ritter
Beer, George Louis
Beer, Thomas
Belknap, Jeremy
Bemis, Samuel Flagg
Bettmann, Otto *Suppl. 1*
Beveridge, Albert Jeremiah
Bickerman, Elias Joseph
Billington, Ray Allen
Binns, Archie
Bolton, Herbert Eugene
Boswell, John Eastburn
Botsford, George Willis
Bowers, Claude Gernade
Boyd, Julian Parks
Bradford, John
Breasted, James Henry
Brickman, William Wolfgang
Brierton, John
Brinton, Clarence Crane
Brodhead, John Romeyn
Brooks, Van Wyck
Brown, Charles Brockden
Brown, Letitia Christine Woods

Bruce, John Edward
Bruce, Philip Alexander
Bruce, William Cabell
Bryce, James
Buck, Paul Herman
Buckmaster, Henrietta
Burdick, Usher Lloyd
Burgess, John William
Burk, John Daly
Burr, George Lincoln
Byrd, William (1674–1744)
Cabell, Nathaniel Francis
Callender, Guy Stevens
Callender, John
Campbell, Walter Stanley
Cantwell, Robert Emmett
Carmer, Carl Lamson
Castañeda, Carlos Eduardo
Catton, Bruce
Caulkins, Frances Manwaring
Chandler, Julian Alvin Carroll
Channing, Edward
Charlevoix, Pierre-François-Xavier de
Cheyney, Edward Potts
Chittenden, Hiram Martin
Collins, James Daniel
Coman, Katharine
Commager, Henry Steele *Suppl. 1*
Coolidge, Archibald Cary
Coues, Elliott
Coulter, Ellis Merton
Craven, Wesley F.
Crawford, F. Marion
Cromwell, John Wesley
Cross, Arthur Lyon
Cubberley, Ellwood Patterson
Cunliffe, Marcus *Suppl. 1*
Curti, Merle *Suppl. 1*
Dabney, Virginius
Davis, Samuel Post
Davis, William Stearns
Deane, Charles
DeBenedetti, Charles Louis *Suppl. 2*
Dennett, Tyler Wilbur
Dennis, Alfred Lewis Pinneo

Dexter, Franklin Bowditch
Dexter, Henry Martyn
Dodge, Theodore Ayrault
Douglass, William
Drake, Benjamin
Drake, Francis Samuel
Drake, Samuel Gardner
Drinker, Sophie Lewis Hutchinson
Dunning, William Archibald
Dupratz, Antoine Simon Le Page
Durant, Will, and Ariel Durant
Earle, Alice Morse
Eggleston, Edward
Eliot, Samuel
Ellet, Elizabeth F.
Ellis, George Edward
English, William Hayden
Fairbank, John King
Fall, Bernard B.
Farrand, Max
Fay, Sidney Bradshaw
Feis, Herbert
Ferguson, William Scott
Filson, John
Finley, Moses
Fish, Carl Russell
Fisher, Sydney George
Fiske, John (1842–1901)
Fitch, Asa
Fleming, Walter Lynwood
Flick, Lawrence Francis
Folwell, William Watts
Forbes, Esther
Ford, Guy Stanton
Ford, Thomas
Fortier, Alcée
Frank, Tenney
Freeman, Douglas Southall
Frei, Hans Wilhelm
Frost, Holloway Halstead
Galbreath, Charles Burleigh
Garden, Alexander (1757–1829)
Gardiner, Leon
Gatzke, Hans Wilhelm
Gayarré, Charles Étienne Arthur
Gibbes, Robert Wilson
Gibbs, George (1815–1873)
Gilbert, Felix

Golder, Frank Alfred
Goldman, Eric
Gordy, John Pancoast
Green, Constance McLaughlin
Greenhow, Robert
Griffis, William Elliot
Grigsby, Hugh Blair
Griswold, Alfred Whitney
Hammond, Bray
Hammond, Jabez Delano
Hansberry, William Leo
Hansen, Marcus Lee
Haring, Clarence Henry
Hart, Albert Bushnell
Hartz, Louis *Suppl. 2*
Haskins, Charles Homer
Haynes, Williams
Haywood, John
Hewat, Alexander
Hildreth, Richard *Suppl. 2*
Hildreth, Samuel Prescott
Holborn, Hajo Ludwig Rudolph
Homans, George Caspar
Horgan, Paul *Suppl. 2*
Howard, George Elliott
Hung, William
Hurd-Mead, Kate Campbell
Hutchinson, Thomas
Ii, John Papa
Jackson, Luther Porter
James, Janet Wilson
James, Marquis
Jameson, John Franklin
Johnson, Allen
Johnson, Edward (1599–1672)
Johnston, Henry Phelps
Jones, John William
Josephson, Matthew
Judd, Laura Fish
Keeler, Clyde Edgar
Kelley, Robert Lloyd
Kellogg, Louise Phelps
Key, V. O.
Kinzie, Juliette Augusta Magill
Knight, Lucian Lamar
Knight, M. M.
Knox, Dudley Wright
Koch, Adrienne
Kohler, Max James
Kramer, Samuel Noah
Kuykendall, Ralph Simpson

History and Related Scholarship *(cont.)*

Lamb, Martha Joanna R. N.
Langer, William Leonard
Larned, Josephus Nelson
Larsen, Jakob Aall Ottesen
Latimer, Elizabeth Wormeley
Latourette, Kenneth Scott
Leech, Margaret Kernochan
Leland, Waldo Gifford
Libby, Orin Grant
Lingelbach, Anna Lane
Lodge, Henry Cabot (1850–1924)
Logan, Rayford Whittingham
Lossing, Benson John
Lowenthal, Marvin Marx
Lynch, John Roy
Lyon, Irving Whitall
Mahan, Alfred Thayer
Malin, James Claude
Malo, Davida
Malone, Dumas
Marshall, Humphrey
Marshall, S. L. A.
Marx, Alexander
Mattingly, Garrett
McAfee, Robert Breckinridge
McElroy, John (1846–1929)
McLaughlin, Andrew Cunningham
Meritt, Benjamin Dean
Middleton, Drew
Miller, David Hunter
Miller, Perry
Moore, Charles
Moorland, Jesse Edward
Morgan, Dale Lowell
Morison, Samuel Eliot
Morris, Richard Brandon
Motley, John Lothrop
Mott, Frank Luther
Murphy, Henry Cruse
Muzzey, David Saville
Myers, Gustavus
Neilson, Nellie
Nell, William Cooper
Nelson, Benjamin
Nevins, Allan
Notestein, Wallace

Nuttall, Zelia Maria Magdalena
Ogg, Frederic Austin
Olmstead, Albert Ten Eyck
Ostroff, Eugene *Suppl. 2*
Owsley, Frank Lawrence
Padover, Saul K.
Parkman, Francis
Parrington, V. L.
Penhallow, Samuel
Perkins, Dexter *Suppl. 1*
Perlman, Selig
Phillips, Ulrich Bonnell
Pierce, Bessie Louise *Suppl. 1*
Pollard, Edward Alfred
Prescott, William Hickling
Prince, Thomas
Ramsay, David
Randall, James Garfield
Randall, John Herman, Jr.
Randolph, Sarah Nicholas
Read, Conyers
Redding, J. Saunders
Rhodes, James Ford
Richardson, James Daniel
Robertson, William
Robinson, Conway
Rollins, Philip Ashton
Ross, Alexander
Rossiter, Clinton Lawrence, III
Rostovtzeff, Michael
Ryan, Cornelius
Saarinen, Aline Bernstein
Sachse, Julius Friedrich
Salisbury, Harrison Evans
Salvemini, Gaetano *Suppl. 2*
Sandoz, Mari
Saposs, David J. *Suppl. 2*
Schlesinger, Arthur Meier, Sr.
Schomburg, Arthur Alfonso
Schuyler, Robert Livingston
Seymour, Charles
Shannon, Fred Albert
Shirer, William Lawrence
Sibley, John Langdon
Simkins, Francis Butler

Skinner, Constance Lindsay
Smith, Henry Nash
Smith, John (1580–1631)
Smith, Samuel (1720–1776)
Sparks, Jared
Stokes, Anson Phelps
Stokes, Isaac Newton Phelps
Stone, William Leete
Strachey, William
Sydnor, Charles Sackett
Tansill, Charles Callan
Tarbell, Ida M.
Taylor, Alrutheus Ambush
Taylor, Lily Ross
Taylor, Telford *Suppl. 1*
Teggart, Frederick John
Thompson, Zadock
Thwaites, Reuben Gold
Trent, William Peterfield
Trumbull, Benjamin
Tuchman, Barbara Wertheim
Turner, Frederick Jackson
Upham, Charles Wentworth
van Heijenoort, Jean
van Loon, Hendrik Willem
Vasiliev, Alexander Alexandrovich
Warden, David Bailie
Ware, Caroline Farrar
Warren, Mercy Otis
Warren, William Whipple
Webb, Walter Prescott
Weeks, Stephen Beauregard
Welles, Charles Bradford
Welles, Sumner
Wertenbaker, Thomas Jefferson
Wesley, Charles Harris
Westermann, William Linn
Wharton, Anne Hollingsworth
White, Leonard Dupee
White, Solomon
White, Theodore H.
Whitehill, Walter Muir, Jr.
Whitmore, William Henry
Wiley, Bell Irvin

Willard, Emma Hart
Willard, James Field
Williams, George Washington
Williams, Mary Wilhelmine
Williams, T. Harry
Williams, William Appleman
Winsor, Justin *Suppl. 1*
Winthrop, John (1588–1649)
Wolfson, Harry Austryn
Woodson, Carter Godwin
Wright, Mary Clabaugh
Wright, Muriel Hazel
Wroth, Lawrence Counselman

Historians of Science
Barker, Jeremiah
Bass, Mary Elizabeth
Bolton, Henry Carrington
Bronowski, Jacob
Cajori, Florian
Coolidge, Julian Lowell
Corner, George Washington
Cushing, Harvey Williams
Deutsch, Albert
Draper, John William
Edelstein, Ludwig
Edwards, Everett Eugene
Ewbank, Thomas
Flick, Lawrence Francis
Fulton, John Farquhar
Garrison, Fielding Hudson
Goode, George Brown
Handerson, Henry Ebenezer
Kessen, William *Suppl. 1*
Kuhn, Thomas S. *Suppl. 1*
Long, Esmond
Major, Ralph Hermon
Miller, William Snow
Nixon, Pat Ireland
Osler, Sir William
Packard, Francis Randolph
Rosen, George
Sarton, George Alfred Léon
Shryock, Richard Harrison
Sigerist, Henry Ernest
Smith, David Eugene

History and Related Scholarship *(cont.)*
Stone, Witmer
Thorndike, Lynn
White, George Willard
Wilder, Raymond Louis
Williams, Stephen West
Wilson, Charles Erwin

History of Religions Scholars
Adams, Hannah
Eliade, Mircea
Evans-Wentz, Walter Yeeling
Moore, George Foot
Nock, Arthur Darby
Smith, Henry Preserved
Wach, Joachim
Warren, William Fairfield

Hymnologists
Beissel, Johann Conrad
Bennet, Sanford Fillmore
Bradbury, William Batchelder
Brown, Phoebe Hinsdale
Campbell, Lucie E.
Clayton, William
Crosby, Fanny
Fletcher, Bridget Richardson
Hatfield, Edwin Francis
Mason, Lowell
Oatman, Johnson, Jr.
Sears, Edmund Hamilton
Swan, Timothy
Thompson, Will Lamartine
Woodbury, Isaac Baker

Legal Historians
Bigelow, Melvin Madison
Curtis, George Ticknor
Howe, Mark De Wolfe
Warren, Charles

Legal Scholars
Ames, James Barr
Angell, Joseph Kinnicutt
Armstrong, Barbara Nachtrieb
Baldwin, Simeon Eben
Battle, William Horn
Beale, Joseph Henry
Bickel, Alexander Mordecai

Bigelow, Harry Augustus
Bigelow, Melvin Madison
Bishop, Joel Prentiss
Borchard, Edwin Montefiore
Bouvier, John
Cahn, Edmond Nathaniel
Cary, William Lucius
Chafee, Zechariah, Jr.
Chamberlain, Joseph Perkins
Clark, Charles Edward
Cobb, Andrew Jackson
Cook, Walter Wheeler
Corwin, Edward Samuel
Crosskey, William Winslow
Dane, Nathan
Daniel, John Warwick
Dickinson, Edwin De Witt
Dickinson, John (1894–1952)
Du Ponceau, Pierre Étienne
Dwight, Theodore William
Fairman, Charles
Farrar, Timothy
Frank, Jerome New
Freund, Ernst
Gilmer, Francis Walker
Glueck, Sheldon
Goodhart, Arthur Lehman
Goodnow, Frank Johnson
Goodrich, Elizur (1761–1849)
Gray, John Chipman
Green, Leon
Greenleaf, Simon
Gregory, Charles Noble
Gridley, Jeremiah
Guthrie, William Dameron
Hastie, William Henry
Hilliard, Francis
Hoffman, David
Hohfeld, Wesley Newcomb
Holcombe, James Philemon
Holmes, Oliver Wendell (1841–1935)
Houston, Charles Hamilton
Hudson, Manley Ottmer
Jessup, Philip C.

Keener, William Albert
Langdell, Christopher Columbus
Legaré, Hugh Swinton
Livermore, Samuel (1786–1833)
Llewellyn, Karl Nickerson
Magruder, Calvert
McClain, Emlin
Medina, Harold Raymond
Mentschikoff, Soia
Minor, Raleigh Colston
Morawetz, Victor
Morgenthau, Hans Joachim
Nicolls, Matthias
Oliphant, Herman
Owens, Elisabeth *Suppl. 1*
Parker, Joel (1795–1875)
Parsons, Theophilus (1797–1822)
Paschal, George Washington
Patton, John Mercer
Pfeffer, Leo
Pomeroy, John Norton
Pound, Roscoe
Powell, Thomas Reed
Prosser, William Lloyd
Ransom, Leon Andrew
Redfield, Amasa Angell
Redfield, Isaac Fletcher
Reeve, Tapping
Robinson, Conway
Rodell, Fred
Sayles, John
Schaefer, Walter V.
Schiller, A. Arthur
Sedgwick, Theodore (1811–1859)
Sharp, Malcolm Pitman
Sharswood, George
Stockton, Charles Herbert
Story, Joseph
Taylor, Hannis
Taylor, Telford *Suppl. 1*
Thayer, James Bradley
Tiedeman, Christopher Gustavus
Tucker, Beverley
Tucker, Henry St. George (1780–1848)
Tucker, John Randolph (1823–1897)
Von Moschzisker, Robert

Walker, Timothy (1802–1856)
Ward, Nathaniel
Wheaton, Henry
Wigmore, John Henry
Wright, Austin Tappan
Zeisel, Hans

Literary Scholars
Bowers, Fredson *Suppl. 1*
Boyesen, Hjalmar Hjorth
Brooks, Cleanth
Canby, Henry Seidel
Child, Francis James
Cross, Wilbur Lucius
De Leon, Thomas Cooper
de Man, Paul *Suppl. 2*
Dupee, F. W.
Dykes, Eva Beatrice
Edel, Leon *Suppl. 1*
Folger, Emily Jordan
Follett, Wilson *Suppl. 1*
Furness, Horace Howard
Giamatti, Bart
Greenlaw, Edwin Almiron
Guiney, Louise Imogen
Hart, James D.
Hubbell, Jay Broadus
Isham, Ralph Heyward
Jakobson, Roman Osipovich
Lord, Albert Bates *Suppl. 1*
Lounsbury, Thomas Raynesford
Lowell, James Russell
Lowes, John Livingston
Matthiessen, F. O.
Miller, Perry
Norton, Charles Eliot
Parry, Milman
Pattee, Fred Lewis
Pottle, Frederick Albert
Preston, Harriet Waters
Reed, Henry Hope
Sanborn, Franklin Benjamin
Smith, Charles Alphonso
Smith, Logan Pearsall
Ticknor, George
Trilling, Lionel
Warren, Austin
Wellek, René
Wilde, Richard Henry
Wimsatt, W. K.
Wolfson, Harry Austryn
Woodberry, George Edward

History and Related Scholarship *(cont.)*

Music Historians
Allen, Walter Carl
Feather, Leonard
Fillmore, John Comfort
Krehbiel, Henry Edward
Moore, John Weeks
Pratt, Waldo Selden
Stearns, Marshall Winslow
Thompson, Oscar

Music Theorists
Cowell, Henry *Suppl. 1*
Klauser, Julius
Schillinger, Joseph
Schoenberg, Arnold
Seeger, Charles
Ziehn, Bernhard

Musicologists
Crawford-Seeger, Ruth Porter
Gilman, Lawrence
Kirkpatrick, Ralph Leonard
Pratt, Waldo Selden
Seeger, Charles
Slonimsky, Nicolas

Mythologists
Bulfinch, Thomas
Campbell, Joseph

Natural Historians
Dall, William Healey
Dixon, Roland Burrage
Lapham, Increase Allen
Shepard, Charles Upham

Orientalists
Davis, Charles Henry Stanley
Salisbury, Edward Elbridge

Religious Studies Scholars
Adams, Hannah
Ahlstrom, Sydney Eckman
Alexander, Joseph Addison
Andrews, Edward Deming
Baron, Salo Wittmayer
Barton, George Aaron
Burrows, Millar
Cadbury, Henry Joel
Carus, Paul

Clebsch, William Anthony
Cohon, Samuel Solomon
Deutsch, Gotthard
Evans-Wentz, Walter Yeeling
Faruqi, Isma'il Raji al-
Feinstein, Moses
Fenn, William Wallace
Freehof, Solomon Bennett
Gavin, Frank Stanton Burns
Ginzberg, Louis
Glatzer, Nahum Norbert
Goddard, Dwight
Grayzel, Solomon
Harper, William Rainey
Haupt, Paul
Heschel, Abraham Joshua
Jacobs, Joseph
Kadushin, Max
Kaplan, Mordecai Menahem
Kent, Charles Foster
Knox, John
Kohut, Alexander
Kotler, Aaron
Leeser, Isaac
Lieberman, Saul
Lyman, Mary Redington Ely
Malter, Henry
Margolis, Max Leopold
Moore, George Foot
Morgan, Abel
Mudge, James
Norton, Andrews
Noyes, George Rapall
Perrin, Norman
Rahman, Fazlur
Rawidowicz, Simon
Riddle, Matthew Brown
Robinson, Edward
Salisbury, Edward Elbridge
Schaff, Philip
Schechter, Solomon
Smith, Henry Preserved
Stowe, Calvin Ellis
Stuart, Moses
Suzuki, D. T. *Suppl. 1*
Terry, Milton Spenser
Torrey, Charles Cutler
Watts, Alan Wilson
Wright, George Ernest
Zeitlin, Solomon
Zwemer, Samuel Marinus

Social Historians / Commentators
Adamic, Louis
Adams, Brooks
Adams, Henry
Adams, James Truslow
Allen, Frederick Lewis
Amory, Cleveland *Suppl. 1*
Asbury, Herbert
Austin, Mary Hunter
Barnes, Harry Elmer
Becker, Carl Lotus
Bontemps, Arna Wendell
Buley, Roscoe Carlyle
Bunche, Ralph Johnson
Calkins, Clinch
Calvert, George Henry
Cram, Ralph Adams
DeVoto, Bernard Augustine
Du Bois, W. E. B.
Eastman, Max
Ford, Henry Jones
Fox, Dixon Ryan
Frank, Waldo David
Galarza, Ernesto
Goodman, Paul
Gunther, John
Hayes, Carlton J. H.
Helper, Hinton Rowan
Herberg, Will
Hofstadter, Richard
Holbrook, Stewart Hall
Howe, Irving
Lasch, Christopher
Lerner, Max
Lindeman, Eduard Christian
Mayo, Katherine
Mencken, H. L.
Mitford, Jessica *Suppl. 1*
Moore, Clement Clarke
Morton, Thomas
Mumford, Lewis
Murat, Achille
Niebuhr, Reinhold
Norton, Charles Eliot
Packard, Vance *Suppl. 1*
Paul, Elliot
Potter, David Morris
Robinson, James Harvey
Rourke, Constance Mayfield
Seldes, Gilbert Vivian
Shotwell, James Thomson
Skaggs, William H. *Suppl. 1*
Smith, Lillian Eugenia

Tocqueville, Alexis de
Trilling, Diana *Suppl. 1*
Turnbull, Robert James
Veblen, Thorstein Bunde
Villard, Oswald Garrison
Wright, Frances

Theater Historians
Barrett, Lawrence
Brown, Thomas Allston
Freedley, George
Hornblow, Arthur, Sr.
Mantle, Burns
Matthews, Brander
Odell, George C. D.

Theologians
Alexander, Archibald
Allen, Alexander Viets Griswold
Ames, Edward Scribner
Anderson, Rufus
Bacon, Benjamin Wisner
Ballou, Hosea
Bellamy, Joseph
Bennett, John Coleman
Berkhof, Louis
Bomberger, John Henry Augustus
Bouquillon, Thomas Joseph
Bowen, John Wesley Edward
Bowne, Borden Parker
Boyce, James Petigru
Breckinridge, Robert Jefferson
Briggs, Charles Augustus
Brown, William Adams
Buckham, John Wright
Bushnell, Horace
Carnell, Edward John
Clarke, William Newton
Cohon, Samuel Solomon
Corcoran, James Andrew
Curtis, Olin Alfred
Dearing, John Lincoln
DuBose, William Porcher
Dwight, Timothy
Emmons, Nathanael
Erdman, William Jacob
Felsenthal, Bernhard
Fenton, Joseph Clifford
Foster, Frank Hugh
Foster, George Burman
Frei, Hans Wilhelm
Fritschel, Conrad Sigmund

History and Related Scholarship *(cont.)*
Fritschel, Gottfried Leonhard Wilhelm
Fuller, Richard
Gavin, Frank Stanton Burns
Geffen, Tobias
Gerhart, Emanuel Vogel
Gmeiner, John
Gordon, George Angier
Gorton, Samuel
Harkness, Georgia Elma
Harris, Samuel
Heschel, Abraham Joshua
Hodge, Archibald Alexander
Hodge, Charles
Hoge, Moses
Hopkins, Samuel (1721–1803)
Horton, Walter Marshall
Hove, Elling
Jacobs, Henry Eyster
Keith, George
Keith, Reuel
King, Henry Churchill
Knox, John
Knudson, Albert Cornelius
Krauth, Charles Porterfield
Ladd, George Trumbull
Lewis, Edwin
Lord, Eleazar
Lyman, Eugene William
Machen, J. Gresham
Macintosh, Douglas Clyde
Mathews, Shailer
Miley, John
Mitchell, Hinckley Gilbert Thomas
Mullins, Edgar Young
Murray, John Courtney
Neumark, David
Nevin, John Williamson
Niebuhr, H. Richard
Niebuhr, Reinhold
Niles, Nathaniel
Norton, Andrews
Noyes, George Rapall
Parham, Charles Fox
Park, Edwards Amasa
Pauck, Wilhelm
Peck, Thomas Ephraim
Pieper, Franz August Otto
Pond, Enoch
Priestley, Joseph

Rall, Harris Franklin
Ralston, Thomas Neely
Ramsey, Paul
Raymond, Miner
Ryan, John Augustine
Schaff, Philip
Schmidt, Friedrich August
Schmucker, Samuel Simon
Shedd, William Greenough Thayer
Sihler, Wilhelm
Sittler, Joseph Andrew, Jr.
Smith, Gerald Birney
Smith, Henry Boynton
Stearns, Lewis French
Stoddard, Solomon
Stone, Barton Warren
Stringfellow, Frank William
Strong, Augustus Hopkins
Summers, Thomas Osmond
Sverdrup, Georg
Talmage, James Edward
Taylor, Nathaniel William
Tillett, Wilbur Fisk
Tillich, Paul
Tucker, William Jewett
Walker, James Barr
Ware, William
Warfield, Benjamin Breckinridge
Warren, William Fairfield
Weigel, Gustave
Wells, Seth Youngs
Whedon, Daniel Denison
Wieman, Henry Nelson
Willard, Samuel
Williams, Daniel Day
Wright, George Ernest
Wright, George Frederick
Wright, John Joseph
Zinzendorf, Nikolaus Ludwig von

Linguistics and Philology
Assyriologists
Barton, George Aaron
Clay, Albert Tobias
Gelb, Ignace Jay
Goetze, Albrecht
Haupt, Paul

Hilprecht, Herman Vollrath

Classicists
Anthon, Charles
Bonner, Campbell
Bonner, Robert Johnson
Bundy, Elroy Lorraine
Calhoun, George Miller
Capps, Edward
Carter, Jesse Benedict
Cherniss, Harold Fredrik
Edelstein, Ludwig
Felton, Cornelius Conway
Fränkel, Hermann Ferdinand
Friedländer, Paul
Gildersleeve, Basil Lanneau
Goodwin, William Watson
Hadas, Moses
Hahn, E. Adelaide *Suppl. 1*
Hamilton, Edith
Highet, Gilbert
Jaeger, Werner Wilhelm
Johnson, Allan Chester
Kelsey, Francis Willey
Lattimore, Richmond Alexander
Lewis, Charlton Thomas
Linforth, Ivan Mortimer
Loeb, James
Macurdy, Grace Harriet
Meritt, Benjamin Dean
Morgan, Morris Hicky
Nock, Arthur Darby
Oldfather, William Abbott
Parry, Milman
Pease, Arthur Stanley
Peck, Harry Thurston
Perry, Ben Edwin
Platner, Samuel Ball
Rand, Edward Kennard
Shorey, Paul
Short, Charles
Smith, Kirby Flower
Smyth, Herbert Weir
Sophocles, Evangelinus Apostolides
Tarbell, Frank Bigelow
Turyn, Alexander
Wheeler, Arthur Leslie
White, John Williams

Cryptanalysts
Friedman, William Frederic, and Elizabeth Smith Friedman

Egyptologists
Breasted, James Henry
Reisner, George Andrew

Epigraphists
Gordon, Arthur Ernest
Morley, Sylvanus Griswold

Grammarians
Follett, Wilson *Suppl. 1*
Murray, Lindley
Strunk, William, Jr. *Suppl. 1*

Hebraists
Monis, Judah

Interpreters
Dorion, Marie
Fleete, Henry
Gallaudet, Thomas
Girty, Simon
Heco, Joseph
Viele, Aernout Cornelissen
Williams, William Sherley

Language Theorists
Bühler, Karl
Hayakawa, S. I.

Lexicographers
Allibone, Samuel Austin
Bartlett, John
Elwyn, Alfred Langdon
Funk, Isaac Kauffman
Goodrich, Chauncey Allen
Hepburn, James Curtis
Moore, Clement Clarke
Ord, George
Robinson, Edward
Rosten, Leo *Suppl. 1*
Vizetelly, Frank Horace
Von Zedtwitz, Waldemar Konrad Anton Wilhelm Ferdinand
Webster, Noah
Wheeler, William Adolphus
Whitney, William Dwight
Worcester, Joseph Emerson

Linguists
Alexander, Joseph Addison

Linguistics and Philology *(cont.)*
Andrews, Lorrin
Avery, John
Bloch, Bernard *Suppl. 2*
Bloomfield, Leonard
Bolling, George Melville
Brickman, William
  Wolfgang
Buck, Carl Darling
Crane, Thomas
  Frederick
Davis, Charles Henry
  Stanley
Deloria, Ella Cara
Fortier, Alcée
Fromkin, Victoria A.
  Suppl. 1
Gatschet, Albert Samuel
Goddard, Pliny Earle
Goodell, William
  (1792–1867)
Hahn, E. Adelaide
  Suppl. 1
Harrington, John
  Peabody
Harriot, Thomas
Hewitt, John Napoleon
  Brinton
Hockett, Charles F.
  Suppl. 2
Jakobson, Roman
  Osipovich
Kellogg, Samuel Henry
Krapp, George Philip
Leonard, Sterling
  Andrus
Lin Yutang
Lounsbury, Thomas
  Raynesford
Marsh, George Perkins
McCawley, James D.
  Suppl. 1
Monis, Judah
Morris, Alice Vanderbilt
  Suppl. 1
Neumark, David
Pareja, Francisco
Pei, Mario Andrew
Percival, James Gates
Pike, Kenneth Lee
  Suppl. 2
Rice, Charles
Riggs, Stephen Return
Roback, A. A.
Sapir, Edward
Sequoyah
Sturtevant, Edgar H.
  Suppl. 2
Townsend, William
  Cameron

Van Name, Addison
Viele, Aernout
  Cornelissen
Whitney, William
  Dwight
Whorf, Benjamin Lee

Papyrologists
Welles, Charles Bradford
Westermann, William
  Linn

Philologists
Adler, George J.
Bloomfield, Maurice
Bolling, George Melville
Child, Francis James
Davis, Charles Henry
  Stanley
Du Ponceau, Pierre
  Étienne
Frank, Tenney
Friedlaender, Israel
Gibbs, Josiah Willard
  (1790–1861)
Hahn, E. Adelaide
  Suppl. 1
Haldeman, Samuel
  Stehman
Krapp, George Philip
Leonard, William Ellery
Manly, John Matthews
Marden, Charles Carroll
Morini, Austin M.
Otis, Brooks
Robinson, Edward
Scott, John Adams
Seymour, Thomas Day
Smith, Logan Pearsall
Solmsen, Friedrich
  Heinrich Rudolph
Turner, William
  Wadden
Whitney, William
  Dwight
Wiener, Leo

Phoneticists
Scripture, Edward
  Wheeler

Phonographers
Pitman, Benn

Sanskritists
Salisbury, Edward
  Elbridge

Semitists
Adler, Cyrus
Friedlaender, Israel

Jastrow, Morris
Montgomery, James
  Alan
Salisbury, Edward
  Elbridge
Torrey, Charles Cutler
Weiss-Rosmarin, Trude
Welles, Charles Bradford
Willett, Herbert
  Lockwood

Slavists
Lord, Albert Bates
  Suppl. 1

Sumerologists
Kramer, Samuel Noah

Translators
Auslander, Joseph
Blackburn, Paul
Boardman, Sarah Hall
Booth, Mary Louise
Campanius, Johan
Ciardi, John
Dabney, Richard
Deutsch, Babette
Du Ponceau, Pierre
  Étienne
Dwight, Theodore
  (1796–1866)
Ferguson, Elizabeth
  Graeme
Fitts, Dudley
George, Grace
Hart, James Morgan
Hearn, Lafcadio
Humphries, Rolfe
Jolas, Maria
Latimer, Elizabeth
  Wormeley
Lattimore, Richmond
  Alexander
Le Gallienne, Eva
Lewisohn, Ludwig
Leyda, Jay
Lowe-Porter, H. T.
Montour, Madame
Moore, Marianne
Morgan, Abel
Morris, Edward Joy
Parsons, Thomas
  William
Payne, William Morton
Phillips, Henry, Jr.
Pike, Albert
Pool, David De Sola
Porter, Charlotte
  Endymion
Preston, Harriet Waters
Rexroth, Kenneth

Rockhill, William
  Woodville
Sandys, George
Schereschewsky, Samuel
  Isaac Joseph
Smith, Julia Evelina, and
  Abby Hadassah Smith
Swenson, David
  Ferdinand
Taylor, Bayard
Townsend, William
  Cameron
Untermeyer, Jean Starr
van der Kemp, Francis
  Adrian
Van Dyck, Cornelius
  Van Alen
Wiener, Leo
Willcox, Louise Collier
Wormeley, Katharine
  Prescott

Philosophy
Ethicists
Ramsey, Paul

Logicians
Gödel, Kurt Friedrich
Ladd-Franklin, Christine
Tarski, Alfred
van Heijenoort, Jean
Whitehead, Alfred North

Philosophers
Abbot, Francis
  Ellingwood
Adorno, Theodor
Albee, Ernest
Andrews, Stephen Pearl
Arendt, Hannah
Ascoli, Max
Baldwin, James Mark
Bentley, Arthur Fisher
Bergmann, Gustav
Berkeley, George
Berkson, Isaac Baer
Bertocci, Peter Anthony
Bjerregaard, Carl Henrik
  Andreas
Black, Max
Blanshard, Brand
Blau, Joseph Leon
Bloom, Allan
Bode, Boyd Henry
Bowen, Francis
Brameld, Theodore
  Burghard Hurt
Bridgman, Percy
  Williams
Brightman, Edgar
  Sheffield

Philosophy *(cont.)*
Brodbeck, May
Brokmeyer, Henry
 Conrad
Bronowski, Jacob
Brownson, Orestes
 Augustus
Bryan, William Lowe
Buchanan, Scott Milross
Cage, John
Cahn, Edmond
 Nathaniel
Calkins, Mary Whiton
Carnap, Rudolf
Carus, Paul
Church, Alonzo
 (1903–1995)
Cohen, Morris Raphael
Coomaraswamy, Ananda
 Kentish
Creighton, James Edwin
Croly, David Goodman
Croly, Herbert David
Davidson, Thomas
de Laguna, Grace Mead
de Laguna, Theodore de
 Leo
Dewey, John
Dietrich, John Hassler
Dietzgen, Peter Joseph
Ducasse, Curt John
Edman, Irwin
Edwards, Jonathan
Eiseley, Loren Corey
Emerson, Ralph Waldo
Farber, Marvin
Feibleman, James Kern
Feigl, Herbert
Feyerabend, Paul K.
 Suppl. 1
Firth, Roderick
Fite, Warner
Frank, Philipp G.
Frankel, Charles
Frankena, William
Fromm, Erich Pinchas
Gestefeld, Ursula Newell
Gordy, John Pancoast
Greenwood, Isaac
Gros, John Daniel
Gulliver, Julia Henrietta
Guthrie, Joseph Hunter
Harris, William Torrey
Hartshorne, Charles
 Suppl. 2
Hibben, John Grier
Hickok, Laurens Perseus
Hildreth, Richard
 Suppl. 2
Hocking, William Ernest
Hoffer, Eric

Holt, Edwin Bissell
Hook, Sidney
Hopkins, Mark
Howison, George
 Holmes
Hutner, Isaac
James, Henry
 (1811–1882)
James, William
Jefferson, Thomas
Johnson, Samuel
Jones, Rufus Matthew
Kallen, Horace Meyer
Kaufmann, Walter
 Arnold
Knight, Frank Hyneman
Kristeller, Paul Oskar
 Suppl. 1
Kuhn, Thomas S.
 Suppl. 1
Ladd, George Trumbull
Langer, Susanne K.
Lazerowitz, Morris
Lewis, Clarence Irving
Lin Yutang
Lloyd, Alfred Henry
Locke, Alain Leroy
Lovejoy, Arthur O.
Lyman, Eugene William
Lynd, Helen Merrell
Malcolm, Norman
 Adrian
Mandelbaum, Maurice
 H.
Marcuse, Herbert
Marsh, James
Martin, Everett Dean
McCosh, James
Mead, George Herbert
Miller, David Louis
Miller, Dickinson
 Sergeant
Montague, William
 Pepperell
Moore, Addison
 Webster
More, Paul Elmer
Morris, George Sylvester
Nagel, Ernest
Newbold, William
 Romaine
Pace, Edward Aloysius
Palmer, George Herbert
Parry, William Tuthill
Peirce, Charles Sanders
Pepper, Stephen C.
Perry, Ralph Barton
Pitkin, Walter Boughton
 Suppl. 2
Porter, Noah
Pratt, James Bissett

Priber, Christian
 Gottlieb
Quine, W. V. *Suppl. 2*
Rader, Melvin
Rand, Ayn
Randall, John Herman,
 Jr.
Randolph, Paschal
 Beverly
Rauch, Frederick
 Augustus
Rawidowicz, Simon
Raymond, George
 Lansing
Reichenbach, Hans
Riley, Isaac Woodbridge
Ritter, William Emerson
Royce, Josiah
Santayana, George
Schneider, Herbert
 Wallace
Schurman, Jacob Gould
Schutz, Alfred
Sellars, Roy Wood
Sellars, Wilfrid Stalker
Stallo, Johann Bernhard
Strauss, Leo
Strong, Charles
 Augustus
Swenson, David
 Ferdinand
Tappan, Henry Philip
Taylor, Fred Manville
Thilly, Frank
Tillich, Paul
Toomer, Jean
Tufts, James Hayden
Varela y Morales, Felix
 Francisco
von Mises, Ludwig
 Suppl. 2
Walker, James
Watts, Alan Wilson
Wayland, Francis
Wertheimer, Max
Whitehead, Alfred North
Wieman, Henry Nelson
Williams, Donald Cary
Woodbridge, Frederick
 James Eugene
Wright, Chauncey
Zhitlowsky, Hayim

Transcendentalists
Alcott, A. Bronson
Cheney, Ednah Dow
 Littlehale
Cranch, Christopher
 Pearse
Emerson, Ralph Waldo
Fuller, Margaret

Hedge, Frederic Henry
Ripley, George
Ripley, Sarah Alden
 Bradford
Ripley, Sophia Willard
 Dana
Thoreau, Henry David
Very, Jones

Social Sciences
Anthropologists
Angel, John Lawrence
Ardrey, Robert
Bartlett, John Russell
Bascom, William Russel
Bateson, Gregory
Benedict, Ruth Fulton
Boas, Franz
Castaneda, Carlos
 Suppl. 1
Chamberlain, Alexander
 Francis
Cobb, William
 Montague
Coon, Carleton Stevens
Cushing, Frank
 Hamilton
Day, Caroline Stewart
 Bond
Dixon, Roland Burrage
Dorsey, George Amos
Dozier, Edward Pasqual
Drake, St. Clair, Jr.
Eiseley, Loren Corey
Emory, Kenneth Pike
Fairbanks, Charles
 Herron
Farabee, William Curtis
Fewkes, Jesse Walter
Fishberg, Maurice
Fletcher, Alice
 Cunningham
Goldenweiser, Alexander
 Alexandrovich
Hallowell, A. Irving
Heizer, Robert Fleming
Herskovits, Melville Jean
Hewett, Edgar Lee
Hockett, Charles F.
 Suppl. 2
Hodge, Frederick Webb
Holmes, William Henry
 Suppl. 1
Hooton, Earnest Albert
Hrdlička, Aleš
Hurston, Zora Neale
Kluckhohn, Clyde Kay
 Maben
Kroeber, Alfred Louis
La Farge, Oliver Hazard
 Perry

Social Sciences *(cont.)*
La Flesche, Francis
Lewis, Oscar
Linton, Ralph
Lowie, Robert Harry
Malinowski, Bronislaw
  Kasper
McGee, William John
McNickle, D'Arcy
Mead, Margaret
Montagu, Ashley
  Suppl. 1
Mooney, James
Morgan, Lewis Henry
Morton, Samuel George
Murdock, George Peter
Parsons, Elsie Clews
Powdermaker, Hortense
Powell, John Wesley
Primus, Pearl
Putnam, Frederic Ward
Radin, Paul
Redfield, Robert
Reichard, Gladys
  Amanda
Roberts, Jack
Sapir, Edward
Sheldon, William
  Herbert
Spier, Leslie
Steward, Julian Haynes
Swanton, John Reed
Todd, Thomas Wingate
Turner, Victor Witter
Verrill, Alpheus Hyatt
Warner, W. Lloyd
Weltfish, Gene
White, Leslie Alvin
Wissler, Clark
Wolf, Eric R. *Suppl. 2*
Wyman, Jeffries

Child Development Experts
Arbuthnot, May Hill
Gruenberg, Sidonie
  Matsner

Criminologists
Bronner, Augusta Fox
Kirchwey, George
  Washington
Smith, Bruce

Demographers
Hagood, Margaret Loyd
  Jarman
Lotka, Alfred James
Spengler, Joseph John
Taeuber, Irene Barnes

Economists
Alexander, Sadie Tanner
  Mossell
Anderson, Benjamin
  McAlester
Ayres, Clarence Edwin
Ayres, Leonard Porter
Bissell, Richard Mervin,
  Jr.
Black, John Donald
Blodget, Samuel, Jr.
Bourneuf, Alice
  Elizabeth
Brown, Harry Gunnison
Burns, Arthur Frank
Callender, Guy Stevens
Campbell, Persia
  Crawford
Cardozo, Jacob Newton
Carey, Henry Charles
Carey, Mathew
Chase, Stuart
Clague, Ewan
Clark, John Bates
Clark, John Maurice
Commons, John Rogers
Coxe, Tench
Currie, Lauchlin
  Suppl. 2
Davenport, Herbert
  Joseph
Dew, Thomas Roderick
Dewing, Arthur Stone
Douglas, Paul Howard
Eckstein, Otto
Edwards, Corwin D.
Ely, Richard Theodore
Emery, Henry Crosby
Feis, Herbert
Fetter, Frank Albert
Fisher, Irving
Foster, William Trufant
George, Henry
Goldenweiser, Emanuel
  Alexander
Grady, Henry Francis
Hadley, Arthur Twining
Hamilton, Earl Jefferson
Hansen, Alvin Harvey
Harris, Abram Lincoln,
  Jr.
Harris, Seymour Edwin
Hauge, Gabriel Sylfest
Haynes, Williams
Heller, Walter Wolfgang
Henderson, Leon
Hollander, Jacob Harry
Hoover, Calvin Bryce
Hotelling, Harold
James, Edmund Janes
Jenks, Jeremiah Whipple

Johnson, Alvin Saunders
Katona, George
Keyserling, Leon
Knight, Frank Hyneman
Knight, M. M.
Koopmans, Tjalling
  Charles
Kuznets, Simon Smith
Ladejinsky, Wolf Isaac
Lerner, Abba
Lewis, W. Arthur
Loucks, Henry Langford
Lubin, Isador
Machlup, Fritz
Means, Gardiner Coit
Mitchell, Wesley Clair
Morgenstern, Oskar
Myrdal, Gunnar Karl
Nearing, Scott
Newcomb, Simon
Nutter, Gilbert Warren
Okun, Arthur Melvin
Rawle, Francis
Ripley, William Zebina
Rogers, James Harvey
Ruggles, Samuel Bulkley
Ruml, Beardsley
Saposs, David J. *Suppl. 2*
Schultz, Henry
Schultz, Theodore W.
  Suppl. 1
Schumpeter, Joseph
  Alois Julius
Seligman, Edwin Robert
  Anderson
Simons, Henry Calvert
Slichter, Sumner Huber
Spengler, Joseph John
Stein, Herbert *Suppl. 1*
Stigler, George J.
Sumner, Helen
Sumner, William
  Graham
Taussig, Frank William
Taylor, Fred Manville
Taylor, Paul Schuster
  Suppl. 2
Tolley, Howard Ross
Tucker, George
Veblen, Thorstein
  Bunde
Vickrey, William S.
  Suppl. 1
Viner, Jacob
von Mises, Ludwig
  Suppl. 2
von Neumann, John
  Louis
Walker, Amasa
Walker, Francis Amasa
Warne, Colston Estey

Weaver, Robert C.
  Suppl. 2
Wells, David Ames
Weyl, Walter Edward
White, Harry Dexter
Wolfson, Theresa
Wolman, Leo
Young, Allyn Abbott

Epidemiologists
Carter, Henry Rose
Chapin, Charles Value
Francis, Thomas, Jr.
Frost, Wade Hampton
Langmuir, Alexander
  Duncan
Lining, John
Lumsden, Leslie Leon
Paul, John Rodman
Potter, Nathaniel
Rosenau, Milton Joseph
South, Lillian Herreld

Ethnographers
Beckwith, Martha
  Warren
Gibbs, George
  (1815–1873)
Grinnell, George Bird
Murie, James Rolfe
Radin, Paul

Ethnologists
Bandelier, Adolph
  Francis Alphonse
Brinton, Daniel Garrison
Deloria, Ella Cara
Dorsey, James Owen
Goddard, Pliny Earle
Hale, Horatio Emmons
Harrington, John
  Peabody
Henshaw, Henry
  Wetherbee
Hewitt, John Napoleon
  Brinton
Hough, Walter
Jones, William
  (1871–1909)
Mallery, Garrick
Mason, Otis Tufton
Nott, Josiah Clark
Pilling, James
  Constantine
Roberts, Jack
Schoolcraft, Henry Rowe
Speck, Frank
  Gouldsmith
Stevenson, James
Stevenson, Matilda Coxe
  Evans

Social Sciences *(cont.)*
Voth, Henry Richert

Ethnomusicologists
Cowell, Henry *Suppl. 1*
Curtis, Natalie
Densmore, Frances
  Theresa
Fillmore, John Comfort
Garrison, Lucy McKim
Lomax, John Avery

Folklorists
Bascom, William Russel
Beckwith, Martha
  Warren
Dobie, James Frank
Eastman, Mary
  Henderson
Faulkner, William John
Jacobs, Joseph
Jaramillo, Cleofas
  Martínez
Jones, James Athearn
La Farge, Oliver Hazard
  Perry
Lord, Albert Bates
  Suppl. 1
Pound, Louise
Randolph, Vance
Scarborough, Dorothy

Home Economists
Atwater, Helen Woodard
Campbell, Helen Stuart
Leverton, Ruth M.
  Suppl. 2
Morgan, Agnes Fay
Norton, Alice Peloubet
Paredes, Américo
  Suppl. 2
Parloa, Maria
Richards, Ellen Henrietta
  Swallow
Richardson, Anna
  Euretta
Roberts, Lydia Jane
Talbot, Marion
Terhune, Mary Virginia
  Hawes
Van Rensselaer, Martha
White, Edna Noble
Woolman, Mary
  Raphael Schenck

Industrial Relations Experts
Bass, Robert Perkins
Kellor, Frances Alice
Slichter, Sumner Huber
Williams, John Elias

Learning Theorists
Tolman, Edward Chace

Market Researchers
Nielsen, A. C.
Roper, Elmo

*Organization and
Management Theorists*
Alford, Leon Pratt
Barnard, Chester Irving
Bedaux, Charles Eugene
Cooke, Morris Llewellyn
Follett, Mary Parker
Gantt, Henry Laurence
Gilbreth, Frank
Kimball, George Elbert
Likert, Rensis
Peter, Laurence Johnston
Taylor, Frederick
  Winslow
Towne, Henry Robinson
van Kleeck, Mary
Whyte, William H.
  Suppl. 1

Parliamentarians
Cannon, Clarence
  Andrew
Robert, Henry Martyn

Policy Analysts
Baroody, William Joseph
Kahn, Herman
Okun, Arthur Melvin

Political Scientists
Adorno, Theodor
Beard, Charles Austin
Bentley, Arthur Fisher
Boudin, Louis Boudinoff
Breckinridge,
  Sophonisba Preston
Brunauer, Esther
Burgess, John William
Dunning, William
  Archibald
Fainsod, Merle
Follett, Mary Parker
Freund, Ernst
Gilpin, William
Hartz, Louis *Suppl. 2*
Kendall, Willmoore
Key, V. O.
Lasswell, Harold Dwight
Lieber, Francis
Mason, Alpheus
  Thomas
Merriam, Charles E.
Moley, Raymond

Neumann, Franz
  Leopold
Ogg, Frederic Austin
Pool, Ithiel de Sola
Simons, Algie Martin
Smith, James Allen
Sorge, Friedrich Adolph
Taylor, John
  (1753–1824)
Walsh, Edmund
  Aloysius
White, Leonard Dupee
Wildavsky, Aaron
  Bernard
Willoughby, Westel
  Woodbury

Pollsters
Campbell, Angus
Cantril, Hadley
Gallup, George Horace
Roper, Elmo

Sex Researchers
Benjamin, Harry
Davis, Katharine
  Bement
Dickinson, Robert Latou
Kinsey, Alfred Charles

*Sexual and Marital
Counselors*
Benjamin, Harry
Stone, Abraham, and
  Hannah Mayer Stone

Sociologists
Balch, Emily Greene
Baltzell, E. Digby
  Suppl. 1
Barnes, Harry Elmer
Becker, Howard Paul
Bentley, Arthur Fisher
Bernard, Luther Lee
Blumer, Herbert George
Bogardus, Emory
  Stephen
Brooks, John Graham
Burgess, Ernest Watson
Butterfield, Kenyon
  Leech
Cayton, Horace Roscoe
Chapin, Francis Stuart
Coleman, James S.
  Suppl. 1
Cooley, Charles Horton
Cummings, Edward
Davis, Katharine
  Bement
Dollard, John
Douglass, Harlan Paul

Du Bois, W. E. B.
Ellwood, Charles Abram
Faris, Ellsworth
Frazier, E. Franklin
Giddings, Franklin
  Henry
Goffman, Erving
  Manual
Gouldner, Alvin Ward
Hagood, Margaret Loyd
  Jarman
Hayes, Edward Cary
Haynes, George
  Edmund
Henderson, Charles
  Richmond
Higman, Howard
  Suppl. 1
Homans, George Caspar
Howard, George Elliott
Johnson, Charles
  Spurgeon
Kerby, William Joseph
Kracauer, Siegfried
Lazarsfeld, Paul Felix
Lee, Rose Hum
Lumpkin, Katharine Du
  Pre
Lynd, Helen Merrell
Lynd, Robert Staughton
MacIver, Robert
  Morrison
Mills, C. Wright
Ming, John Joseph
Nelson, Benjamin
Odum, Howard
  Washington
Ogburn, William
  Fielding
Park, Robert Ezra
Parsons, Elsie Clews
Parsons, Talcott
Reid, Ira De Augustine
Rice, Stuart Arthur
Roberts, Peter *Suppl. 1*
Ross, Edward Alsworth
Sanderson, Ezra Dwight
Schutz, Alfred
Small, Albion Woodbury
Sorokin, Pitirim
  Aleksandrovich
Steiner, Edward Alfred
Stouffer, Samuel
  Andrew
Sumner, William
  Graham
Sutherland, Edwin
  Hardin
Taft, Jessie
Taylor, Carl Cleveland

Social Sciences *(cont.)*
Thomas, Dorothy
  Swaine
Thomas, William Isaac
Thrasher, Frederic
  Milton
Vance, Rupert B.
van Kleeck, Mary
Ward, Lester Frank
Wirth, Louis
Woods, Robert Archey
Work, Monroe Nathan
Young, Donald Ramsey
Znaniecki, Florian

Statisticians
Ayres, Leonard Porter
Babson, Roger Ward
Bryant, Louise Frances
  Stevens
Chandler, Seth Carlo, Jr.
Cochran, William
  Gemmell
Cox, Gertrude Mary
Dorchester, Daniel
Elliott, Ezekiel Brown
Emerson, Gouverneur
Hoffman, Frederick
  Ludwig
Hotelling, Harold
Hourwich, Isaac
  Aaronovich
Jacoby, Oswald
Jarvis, Edward
Koopmans, Tjalling
  Charles
Lotka, Alfred James
Neyman, Jerzy
Olds, Leland
Pearl, Raymond
Rice, Stuart Arthur
Shattuck, Lemuel
Sutton, William Loftus
Swank, James Moore
Sydenstricker, Edgar
Walker, Francis Amasa
Wilks, Samuel Stanley
Zeisel, Hans

**LAW AND
CRIMINOLOGY**
—————
**Crime and Law
Enforcement**
Alleged Assassins
Oswald, Lee Harvey

Alleged Murderers
Borden, Lizzie Andrew
Sacco, Nicola, and
  Bartolomeo Vanzetti

Sheppard, Sam *Suppl. 1*

Assassination Conspirators
Mudd, Samuel
  Alexander *Suppl. 1*
Surratt, Mary

Assassins
Booth, John Wilkes
Czolgosz, Leon F.
Guiteau, Charles Julius
Horn, Tom
Ray, James Earl *Suppl. 2*
Ruby, Jack L.

Bootleggers
Capone, Al
Gordon, Waxey
Guzik, Jack
Hoff, Max
Lansky, Meyer

Detectives
Burns, William John
Horn, Tom
Hume, James B.
Means, Gaston Bullock
Pinkerton, Allan
Ruditsky, Barney
Siringo, Charles Angelo

Forgers
Beer, Thomas
Eaton, Amos
Edwards, Monroe
Griswold, Rufus Wilmot
Mickley, Joseph Jacob

Gangsters
Adonis, Joe
Capone, Al
Carbo, Frankie
Cohen, Mickey
Colombo, Joseph
  Anthony, Sr.
Costello, Frank
Gambino, Carlo
Genovese, Vito
Giancana, Sam
Guzik, Jack
Kelly, Machine Gun
Lansky, Meyer
Luchese, Thomas
Luciano, Lucky
Mackintosh, Ebenezer
Madden, Owen Victor
Profaci, Joseph
Schultz, Dutch
Siegel, Bugsy
Valachi, Joseph

Informants
Bentley, Elizabeth Terrill
Cvetic, Matthew C.
Massing, Hede Tune
Richardson, Ebenezer
Valachi, Joseph

Kidnappers
Chessman, Caryl
  Whittier
Hauptmann, Bruno
  Richard

Law Enforcers
Byrnes, Thomas F.
Curtis, Edwin Upton
Earp, Wyatt
Garrett, Pat
Glassford, Pelham Davis
Hays, Jacob
Hickok, Wild Bill
Hoover, J. Edgar
Hume, James B.
Jones, John B.
Kennedy, John
  Alexander
Masterson, Bat
Ness, Eliot *Suppl. 1*
O'Neill, Buckey
Plummer, Henry
Rizzo, Frank Lazzaro
Ruditsky, Barney
Tilghman, William
  Matthew
Tolson, Clyde Anderson

Murder Victims
Adamson, Joy
Blitzstein, Marc
Bodenheim, Maxwell
Canby, Edward Richard
  Sprigg
Cermak, Anton Joseph
Colvocoresses, George
  Musalas
Cornstalk
Crane, Bob
Crazy Horse
Doublehead
Europe, James Reese
Evers, Medgar
Falkner, William Clark
Faruqi, Isma'il Raji al-
Fisk, James
Fossey, Dian
Frank, Leo Max
Frankel, Charles
Friedlaender, Israel
Garfield, James Abram
Garrett, Pat
Giancana, Sam

Goebel, William
Hardin, John
Harrison, Carter Henry
Hickok, Wild Bill
Hindman, Thomas
  Carmichael
Hole-in-the-Day
Jansson, Eric
Jefferson, Eddie
Johnson, William
  (1809–1851)
Jones, Thomas ap
  Catesby
Jones, William
  (1871–1909)
Kennedy, John
  Fitzgerald
Kennedy, Robert Francis
King, Martin Luther, Jr.
La Salle, René-Robert
  Cavalier de
Lennon, John
Lincoln, Abraham
Logan, James
  (c.1725–1780)
Long, Huey Pierce
Lovejoy, Elijah Parish
Malcolm X
Marsh, John
McIntosh, William
McKinley, William
Milk, Harvey
California Joe
Moore, Harry Tyson
Moscone, George
  Richard
Newton, Huey P.
Oldham, John
Opechancanough
Oswald, Lee Harvey
Plummer, Henry
Polk, George
Pratt, Parley Parker
Randolph, Benjamin
  Franklin
Red Shoes
Rice, William Marsh
Ridge, John
Rockwell, George
  Lincoln
Schultz, Dutch
Scott, William
  Alexander, II
Seghers, Charles Jean
Siegel, Bugsy
Smith, Joseph
  (1805–1844)
Spotted Tail
Tarnower, Herman
Till, Emmett Louis
Tresca, Carlo

**Crime and Law
Enforcement** (cont.)
Turner, Jack
Villa, Pancho
van Heijenoort, Jean
White, Stanford

Murderers
Bundy, Ted
Floyd, Charles Arthur
Gein, Edward
Hardin, John Wesley
Hauptmann, Bruno
  Richard
Leopold, Nathan
  Freudenthal, Jr., and
  Richard Albert Loeb
Thaw, Harry Kendall
Webster, John White

Outlaws
Billy the Kid
Black Bart
Barrow, Clyde, and
  Bonnie Parker
Cassidy, Butch
Dalton, Bob
Deitz, John F.
Dillinger, John
Doolin, William
Earp, Wyatt
Floyd, Charles Arthur
Holliday, Doc
James, Jesse
Mason, Samuel
Murieta, Joaquín
Renfroe, Stephen S.
Slade, Joseph Alfred
Starr, Belle
Starr, Henry George
Sutton, Willie
Vásquez, Tiburcio
Younger, Cole

Perjurers
Hiss, Alger *Suppl. 1*

Pirates
Halsey, John
Ingle, Richard
Kidd, William
Laffite, Jean
Mason, Samuel
Morgan, Sir Henry
Pound, Thomas
Scott, John
Teach, Edward
You, Dominique

Regicides
Bresci, Gaetano

Dixwell, John
Whalley, Edward

Smugglers
Rowe, John

Swindlers
Edwards, Monroe
Means, Gaston Bullock
Musica, Philip Mariano
  Fausto

Thieves
Dart, Isom
Murrell, John Andrews
Railroad Bill
Wyman, Seth

Vigilantes
Coleman, William Tell
Langford, Nathaniel Pitt
Lynch, Charles

Legal Practice
Attorneys General (Federal)
Akerman, Amos Tappan
Bates, Edward
Biddle, Francis Beverley
Black, Jeremiah Sullivan
Brewster, Benjamin
  Harris
Butler, Benjamin
  Franklin (1795–1858)
Clark, Tom Campbell
Crittenden, John Jordan
Cummings, Homer Stillé
Daugherty, Harry
  Micajah
Garland, Augustus Hill
Gregory, Thomas Watt
Griggs, John William
Harmon, Judson
Hoar, Ebenezer
  Rockwood
Johnson, Reverdy
Kennedy, Robert Francis
Kleindienst, Richard G.
  Suppl. 1
Knox, Philander Chase
Lee, Charles
  (1758–1815)
Legaré, Hugh Swinton
McGranery, James
  Patrick
McGrath, J. Howard
McReynolds, James
  Clark
Miller, William Henry
  Harrison
Mitchell, John Newton
Moody, William Henry

Olney, Richard
Palmer, A. Mitchell
Pierrepont, Edwards
Randolph, Edmund
Richardson, Elliot
  Suppl. 1
Rodney, Caesar
  Augustus
Rogers, William Pierce
  Suppl. 2
Speed, James
Stanbery, Henry
Stanton, Edwin
  McMasters
Taft, Alphonso
Taney, Roger Brooke
Wickersham, George
  Woodward
Willebrandt, Mabel
  Walker
Williams, George Henry
Wirt, William

Attorneys General (State)
Atherton, Joshua
Innes, James
Martin, Luther
Paine, Robert Treat
Stockton, John Potter
Tucker, John Randolph
  (1823–1897)
Warren, Earl
Wilentz, David
  Theodore

Court Clerks
Brown, John
  (1750–1810)

Court Reporters
Deming, Philander

Judge Advocates
Crowder, Enoch Herbert
Tudor, William

Jurists / Judges
Adams, Annette Abbott
Alden, John
Allen, Florence
  Ellinwood
Allen, Macon Bolling
Allen, William
  (1704–1780)
Alpern, Anne X.
Amidon, Charles
  Fremont
Anderson, Joseph Inslee
Appleton, John
Arrington, Alfred W.
Ashe, Samuel

Ashe, Thomas Samuel
Atkinson, Theodore
Auchmuty, Robert
  (1687–1750)
Axtell, Samuel Beach
Ayllón, Lucas Vázquez
  de
Baker, Harvey
  Humphrey
Baldwin, Simeon
Baldwin, Simeon Eben
Barron, Jennie Loitman
Barry, William Taylor
Bartelme, Mary
  Margaret
Battle, William Horn
Beatty, William Henry
Bedford, Gunning, Jr.
Benning, Henry Lewis
Benson, Egbert
Bibb, George Mortimer
Biddle, Francis Beverley
Bird, Rose *Suppl. 1*
Bleckley, Logan Edwin
Boldt, George Hugo
Bond, Hugh Lennox
Bosone, Reva Beck
Bourne, Benjamin
Boyle, John
Brackenridge, Hugh
  Henry
Bradbury, Theophilus
Bradley, Stephen Row
Brawley, William Hiram
Brearly, David
Breaux, Joseph Arsenne
Breese, Sidney
Brinkerhoff, Jacob
Browne, William
Bryan, George
Buchanan, John
Buchanan, John
  Alexander
Buck, Carrick Hume
Bullock, Georgia
  Philipps
Burke, Aedanus
Burnet, Jacob
Burnet, William
  (1730–1791)
Butler, Andrew Pickens
Cabell, William H.
Cady, Daniel
Caldwell, Henry Clay
Campbell, James
Campbell, John Wilson
Campbell, Josiah Adams
  Patterson
Carr, Dabney
Casey, Joseph
Chew, Benjamin

Legal Practice (cont.)
Chipman, Nathaniel
Christiancy, Isaac
    Peckham
Clagett, Wyseman
Clark, Bennett Champ
Clark, Charles Edward
Clark, Daniel
    (1809–1891)
Clark, Walter McKenzie
Clayton, Henry De
    Lamar
Cline, Genevieve Rose
Cobb, Andrew Jackson
Collens, Thomas
    Wharton
Collier, Henry Watkins
Connor, Henry Groves
Cooley, Thomas
    McIntyre
Cowen, Esek
Cranch, William
Crater, Joseph Force
    Suppl. 1
Cross, Edward
Dale, Thomas
    (1700–1750)
Daly, Charles Patrick
Dana, Francis
Danforth, Thomas
Dargan, Edmund S.
Davis, Bancroft
De Lancey, James
    (1703–1760)
Deady, Matthew Paul
Dembitz, Nanette
Derbigny, Pierre
    Auguste Charles
    Bourguignon
Devens, Charles, Jr.
Dick, Robert Paine
Dickerson, Philemon
Dill, James Brooks
Dixon, Luther Swift
Doe, Charles Cogswell
Doster, Frank
Drake, Charles Daniel
Drayton, William
    (1732–1790)
Duane, James
Dudley, Paul
Duer, John
Duer, William Alexander
Dyer, Eliphalet
Elliott, Carl A. *Suppl. 1*
Ellis, Powhatan
Elmer, Jonathan
Endicott, William
    Crowninshield
Ewing, Charles
Farrar, Timothy

Fenner, Charles Erasmus
Ferguson, Homer
Fitch, James
Folger, Charles James
Force, Manning
    Ferguson
Fournet, John Baptiste
Frank, Jerome New
Friendly, Henry Jacob
Gamble, Hamilton
    Rowan
Gaston, William Joseph
Gayle, John
Gaynor, William Jay
Geddes, James
George, Walter *Suppl. 2*
Gesell, Gerhard Ansel
Gholson, Samuel
    Jameson
Gholson, Thomas
    Saunders
Gholson, William Yates
Gibson, John Bannister
Gibson, Phil Sheridan
Goldthwaite, George
Goodenow, John Milton
Gookin, Daniel
Gould, James
Grant, Claudius
    Buchanan
Grant, Robert
Gray, Horace
Gresham, Walter
    Quintin
Griffin, Cyrus
Griswold, Matthew
Groesbeck, William
    Slocum
Grossman, Mary Belle
Hale, Robert Safford
Hamtramck, John
    Francis
Hand, Augustus Noble
Hand, Learned
Handy, Alexander
    Hamilton
Hanson, Alexander
    Contee (1749–1806)
Harper, William
Harron, Marion Janet
Hastie, William Henry
Hastings, Serranus
    Clinton
Haynsworth, Clement
    Furman, Jr.
Hays, Paul Raymond
Hemphill, John
Hemphill, Joseph
Henderson, Leonard
Henderson, Richard

Higginbotham, A. Leon,
    Jr. *Suppl. 2*
Hilgard, Theodor
    Erasmus
Hilton, Edward
Hoar, Ebenezer
    Rockwood
Hobart, John Sloss
Holman, Jesse Lynch
Holt, Joseph
Hopkinson, Francis
Hopkinson, Joseph
Horsmanden, Daniel
Hosmer, Hezekiah Lord
Howard, Martin
Howard, Timothy
    Edward
Howe, John Homer
Howe, William Wirt
Hudson, Manley Ottmer
Hughes, Robert William
Hunt, William Henry
    (1823–1884)
Hutcheson, Charles
    Sterling
Ii, John Papa
Jackson, John George
Jenkins, Charles Jones
Jessup, Philip C.
Johnson, Frank, Jr.
    Suppl. 1
Johnston, Josiah
    Stoddard
Johnston, Peter
Jones, Thomas
Jones, Thomas Goode
    Suppl. 1
Judd, Albert Francis
Kane, John Kintzing
Kaufman, Joseph
    William
Keating, Kenneth
    Barnard
Kent, Edward
Kent, James
Kenyon, Dorothy
Kenyon, William Squire
Kerner, Otto
Key, David McKendree
Kilty, William
Kirkpatrick, Andrew
Landis, Kenesaw
    Mountain
Langdon, Woodbury
Lansing, John
Laurance, John
Law, Richard
Leavitt, Humphrey
    Howe
Lee, William Little
Lehman, Irving

Leonard, Daniel
Lewis, Rhoda Valentine
Lindsey, Ben B.
Livermore, Samuel
    (1732–1803)
Lloyd, David
Lockwood, Lorna
    Elizabeth
Logan, Stephen Trigg
Lowell, John
    (1743–1802)
Ludlow, George Duncan
Ludlow, Roger
Lumpkin, Joseph Henry
Lynde, Benjamin
Mack, Julian William
Magruder, Calvert
Malone, Walter
Marshall, Thomas
    Alexander
Martin, François-Xavier
Marvin, William
Mason, Charles
Mason, John
Matthews, Burnita
    Shelton
Maxwell, Augustus
    Emmet
McClain, Emlin
McComas, Louis Emory
McFarland, Ernest
    William
McGranery, James
    Patrick
McKean, Thomas
McKinstry, Elisha
    Williams
Medina, Harold
    Raymond
Mellen, Prentiss
Mellon, Thomas
Merrick, Edwin Thomas
Merrimon, Augustus
    Summerfield
Miller, Nathan Lewis
Mills, Benjamin
Mitchell, Stephen Mix
Mitchell, William
    (1801–1886)
Moore, Alfred *Suppl. 2*
Moore, John Bassett
Moore, Maurice
Moore, William
More, Nicholas
Morris, Lewis
    (1671–1746)
Morris, Richard
Morris, Robert Hunter
Morton, Marcus
Musmanno, Michael
    Angelo

Legal Practice *(cont.)*
Nelson, Hugh
Nicholls, Francis
  Redding Tillou
Nicolls, Matthias
Nisbet, Eugenius
  Aristides
Nixon, John Thompson
Norton, Elijah Hise
Nott, Abraham
O'Brien, Morgan Joseph
Okey, John Waterman
Oliver, Andrew
  (1731–1799)
Oliver, Peter
O'Neall, John Belton
Orr, Jehu Amaziah
Overton, John
Parke, Benjamin
Parker, Isaac
Parker, Isaac Charles
Parker, Joel (1795–1875)
Parker, John Johnston
Parsons, Theophilus
  (1750–1813)
Patterson, Robert Porter
Pecora, Ferdinand
Pendleton, Edmund
Peters, John Andrew
Philips, John Finis
Phillips, John
Pickering, John
Platt, Jonas
Poland, Luke Potter
Pope, Nathaniel
Proskauer, Joseph Meyer
Pryor, Roger Atkinson
Putnam, William
  LeBaron
Pynchon, William
Radcliff, Jacob
Raney, George Pettus
Ranney, Rufus Percival
Redfield, Isaac Fletcher
Reeve, Tapping
Rives, Richard Taylor
Roane, Spencer
Roberts, Oran Milo
Robinson, Moses
Root, Jesse
Rosellini, Hugh J.
Rosenman, Samuel
  Irving
Ross, Erskine Mayo
Rost-Denis, Pierre
  Adolphe
Ruffin, George Lewis
Ruffin, Thomas
Rugg, Arthur Prentice
Ruggles, Timothy
Russell, Chambers

Ryan, Edward George
Saffin, John
Saltonstall, Richard
Sampson, Edith
  Spurlock
Saypol, Irving
Schaefer, Walter V.
Scott, James Brown
  Suppl. 2
Sebastian, Benjamin
Sedgwick, Theodore
  (1746–1813)
Settle, Thomas, Jr.
Sewall, David
Sewall, Samuel
Sewall, Stephen
Sharkey, William Lewis
Sharswood, George
Shaw, Lemuel
Sherwood, Thomas
  Adiel
Shippen, Edward
Shippen, Edward, IV
Shiras, Oliver Perry
Sirica, John Joseph
Slater, Duke
Smith, James Francis
Smith, Jeremiah
Smith, William
  (1697–1769)
Sobeloff, Simon E.
Speer, Emory
Spencer, Ambrose
Springer, William
  McKendree
Stallo, Johann Bernhard
Staples, Waller Redd
Stone, David
Stone, George
  Washington
Stone, Wilbur Fisk
Stuart, Archibald
Swan, Joseph Rockwell
Swift, Zephaniah
Symmes, John Cleves
Taft, Alphonso
Tappan, Benjamin
Taylor, Creed
Taylor, John Louis
Terry, David Smith
Thayer, Amos Madden
Thornton, Jessy Quinn
Tichenor, Isaac
Toulmin, Harry
Tourgée, Albion
  Winegar
Tracy, Benjamin
  Franklin
Traynor, Roger John
Trott, Nicholas
Trowbridge, Edmund

Trumbull, John
  (1750–1831)
Trumbull, Lyman
Tucker, Henry St.
  George (1780–1848)
Tucker, St. George
Tuttle, Elbert P.
Tyler, Royall
Underhill, John
Underwood, John
  Curtiss
Upshur, Abel Parker
Vanderbilt, Arthur T.
Van Ness, William Peter
Van Ness, William W.
Varnum, James Mitchell
Von Moschzisker,
  Robert
Waddy, Joseph C.
Walden, Austin Thomas
Walker, David
  (1806–1879)
Walker, Robert Franklin
Walworth, Reuben Hyde
Ward, Nathaniel
Waring, J. Waties
Watkins, George
  Claiborne
Weare, Meshech
Weinfeld, Edward
Welch, John
Wentworth, John
  (1719–1781)
Wheeler, Royall Tyler
White, Albert Smith
Whitman, Ezekiel
Williamson, Isaac
  Halsted
Wisdom, John Minor
  Suppl. 1
Wolcott, Erastus
Woods, William Allen
Woodward, Augustus
  Brevoort
Wright, J. Skelly
Wright, Jonathan Jasper
Wythe, George
Wyzanski, Charles
  Edward, Jr.
Yates, Joseph C.
Yates, Robert
Yerger, William
Youngdahl, Luther
  Wallace
Zane, Charles Shuster

Justices of the Peace
Dana, Richard
Morris, Esther Hobart

Law Reporters
Cohen, Felix Solomon
Cranch, William
Dane, Nathan
Field, David Dudley, Jr.
Halleck, Henry Wager
Hening, William Waller
Howard, Benjamin
  Chew
Iredell, James
Johnson, William
  (1769–1848)
Kirby, Ephraim
Leigh, Benjamin
  Watkins
Maxwell, William
  (1766?–1809)
McClain, Emlin
Meigs, Return Jonathan
  (1801–1891)
Munford, William
Redfield, Amasa Angell
Root, Jesse
Stockton, Charles
  Herbert
Swift, Zephaniah
Taylor, John Louis
Toulmin, Harry
Wheaton, Henry

Lawyers
Acheson, Dean
  Gooderham
Adams, Annette Abbott
Aldrich, Winthrop
Alexander, Sadie Tanner
  Mossell
Alioto, Joseph L.
  Suppl. 1
Allen, Macon Bolling
Alpern, Anne X.
Appleton, John
Arnold, Thurman
Arvey, Jacob Meyer
Atchison, David Rice
Auchmuty, Robert
  (1687–1750)
Auchmuty, Robert, Jr.
  (1725–1788)
Austin, William
Axtell, Samuel Beach
Aycock, Charles
  Brantley
Baer, George Frederick
Baker, Newton Diehl
Baldwin, Joseph Glover
Baldwin, Roger Sherman
Baldwin, Simeon
Ball, George
Ballantine, Arthur
  Atwood

Legal Practice (cont.)

Ballinger, Richard Achilles

Bankhead, John Hollis (1872–1946)

Bankhead, William Brockman

Barlow, Francis Channing

Barnard, Daniel Dewey

Barron, Jennie Loitman

Bartelme, Mary Margaret

Bartlett, Ichabod

Bartlett, Joseph

Bassett, Edward Murray

Bassett, Richard

Baxter, Elisha

Bayard, James Asheton

Bayard, James Ashton

Bayard, Richard Henry

Beatty, William Henry

Beck, James Montgomery

Bell, Samuel

Benjamin, Judah Philip

Benjamin, Robert Charles O'Hara

Berle, Adolf Augustus

Berrien, John Macpherson

Bettman, Alfred

Biddle, Francis Beverley

Bidlack, Benjamin Alden Suppl. 1

Bigelow, Harry Augustus

Billings, Frederick

Bingham, John Armor

Bingham, Robert Worth

Binney, Horace

Birney, James Gillespie

Birney, William

Bittenbender, Ada Matilda Cole

Black, Frank Swett

Black, Jeremiah Sullivan

Blackford, Charles Minor

Blackmun, Harry A. Suppl. 1

Blackwell, Randolph Talmadge

Blair, Montgomery

Blatchford, Richard Milford

Blennerhassett, Harman

Bloomfield, Joseph

Blount, James Henderson

Blount, Willie

Bocock, Thomas S.

Bogy, Lewis Vital

Boissevain, Inez Milholland

Bollan, William

Bonaparte, Charles Joseph

Bond, Hugh Lennox

Bordley, John Beale

Boreman, Arthur Ingram

Boudin, Leonard B.

Boudin, Louis Boudinoff

Boudinot, Elias Cornelius

Bowers, Lloyd Wheaton

Bradbury, Theophilus

Bradley, William Czar

Bradwell, James Bolesworth

Brandegee, Frank Bosworth

Brandeis, Louis Dembitz

Brannan, Charles F. Suppl. 2

Breckinridge, James

Breckinridge, John (1760–1806)

Briggs, George Nixon

Bristow, Benjamin Helm

Brown, John (1757–1837)

Brown, Walter Folger

Browning, Orville Hickman

Bryan, William Jennings

Buchanan, John Alexander

Buck, Carrick Hume

Buckner, Emory Roy

Bulloch, Archibald

Bundy, Harvey Hollister

Burke, Thomas (1849–1925)

Burlingham, Charles Culp

Burnet, William (1688–1729)

Butler, Pierce (1866–1939)

Butler, William Allen Suppl. 2

Butterworth, Benjamin

Buzhardt, Joseph Fred

Cady, Daniel

Cahn, Edmond Nathaniel

Calhoun, Patrick

Calhoun, William Barron

Campbell, George Washington

Cane, Melville Henry

Cardozo, Benjamin Nathan

Cardozo, Michael H. Suppl. 2

Carlile, John Snyder

Carpenter, Matthew Hale

Carter, Eunice Hunton

Carter, James Coolidge

Cary, Mary Ann Camberton Shadd

Casey, Joseph

Casey, Robert Suppl. 2

Casey, William Joseph

Catron, John

Celler, Emanuel

Chamberlain, George Earle

Chambers, George

Chandler, William Eaton

Chapman, Reuben

Chester, Colby Mitchell, Jr.

Chester, Thomas Morris

Cheves, Langdon

Chew, Benjamin

Choate, Joseph Hodges

Choate, Rufus

Chotiner, Murray

Christiancy, Isaac Peckham

Clagett, Wyseman

Clark, Charles Edward

Clark, Edward

Clark, Grenville

Clayton, Augustin Smith

Cobb, Howell

Cobb, Thomas Reade Rootes

Cohen, Benjamin Victor

Cohen, Felix Solomon

Cohn, Roy

Colby, Bainbridge

Colden, Cadwallader David

Colt, LeBaron Bradford

Conboy, Martin

Cook, Ebenezer

Cooper, Henry Ernest

Cooper, John Sherman

Cooper, Thomas

Costigan, Edward Prentiss

Cotton, Joseph Potter

Coudert, Frederic René

Coudert, Frederic René, II

Coulter, Ernest Kent

Couzins, Phoebe Wilson

Crafts, William

Crater, Joseph Force Suppl. 1

Cravath, Paul Drennan

Creswell, John Angel James

Crittenden, Thomas Leonidas

Cromwell, John Wesley

Cromwell, William Nelson

Crosby, Ernest Howard

Crosskey, William Winslow

Culberson, Charles Allen

Culberson, David Browning

Cummings, Homer Stillé

Curtin, Andrew Gregg

Curtis, Carl T. Suppl. 1

Curtis, George Ticknor

Cushing, Caleb

Dallas, Alexander James

Dalzell, John

Dana, Richard

Dana, Richard Henry, Jr.

Dana, Samuel Whittelsey

Dane, Nathan

Daniel, Peter Vivian

Dargan, Edmund S.

Darrow, Clarence

Daveiss, Joseph Hamilton

Davies, Joseph Edward

Davis, George

Davis, John

Davis, John William

Davison, George Willets

Dean, Arthur Hobson

Dean, Gordon Evans

Dembitz, Lewis Naphtali

Dembitz, Nanette

Denby, Charles

Deneen, Charles Samuel

Denver, James William

DeSilver, Albert

Dickinson, Donald McDonald

Dill, James Brooks

Dillon, John Forrest

DiSalle, Michael Vincent

Dodd, Bella Visono

Doddridge, Philip

Doniphan, Alexander William

Donnelly, Charles Francis

Donovan, James Britt

Donovan, William Joseph

Downer, Silas

Legal Practice (*cont.*)
Doyle, John Thomas
Drake, Benjamin
Drayton, William
  (1776–1846)
Duer, John
Duke, Basil Wilson
Dulany, Daniel
Dulany, Daniel, Jr.
Dulles, John Foster
Du Ponceau, Pierre
  Étienne
Durant, Henry Fowle
Durant, Thomas
  Jefferson
Durham, John Stephens
Durr, Clifford Judkins
Eames, Charles
  (1812–1867)
Earle, Thomas
Early, Jubal Anderson
Eastman, Crystal
Edmunds, George
  Franklin
Edwards, Pierpont
Eisenhower, Edgar
  Newton
Elliott, Walter Hackett
  Robert
Ely, Joseph Buell
Emmet, Thomas Addis
  (1764–1827)
Ernst, Morris Leopold
Eustis, James Biddle
Evans, George
Evarts, William Maxwell
Ewing, Charles
Ewing, Oscar Ross
Ewing, Thomas, Jr.
Fahy, Charles
Fairfield, John
Farnham, Thomas
  Jefferson
Farrar, Timothy
Fessenden, Thomas
  Green
Few, William
Ficke, Arthur Davison
Field, David Dudley, Jr.
Findlay, James
Finletter, Thomas
  Knight
Fish, Hamilton
  (1808–1893)
Fisher, Ada Lois Sipuel
Fisher, Sydney George
Fitch, Thomas
Fitzhugh, George
Fitzhugh, William
Flexner, Bernard
Flint, Weston

Flowers, Walter Winkler,
  Jr.
Fly, James Lawrence
Foltz, Clara Shortridge
Foot, Solomon
Foote, Lucius Harwood
Fortas, Abe
Foster, Judith Ellen
  Horton Avery
Fowler, Joseph Smith
Fraenkel, Osmond
  Kessler
Frelinghuysen, Theodore
Froelich, William
Gaither, Horace Rowan,
  Jr.
Gardiner, John
Gardiner, Robert
  Hallowell, III
Gardner, Erle Stanley
Garfield, Harry
  Augustus
Garfield, James Rudolph
Garnett, Muscoe Russell
  Hunter
Garrison, Lindley Miller
Garvan, Francis Patrick
Gary, Elbert Henry
Gary, Martin
  Witherspoon
Gaston, William
George, James Zachariah
Geyer, Henry Sheffie
Gibbons, Thomas
Gibbons, William
  (1750?–1800)
Gillett, Emma Millinda
Gilmer, Francis Walker
Gilpatric, Roswell L.
  Suppl. 1
Glover, Samuel Taylor
Goldberg, Arthur Joseph
Goldsborough, Robert
Goodhart, Arthur
  Lehman
Goodloe, William
  Cassius
Goodrich, Chauncey
  (1759–1815)
Goodrich, Elizur
  (1761–1849)
Goodwin, John Noble
Gordon, Laura de Force
Gore, Albert, Sr.
  Suppl. 1
Gore, Christopher
Gould, James
Gould, Milton S.
  Suppl. 1
Gowen, Franklin
  Benjamin

Graham, James
Granger, Gideon
Grant, Claudius
  Buchanan
Grant, Madison
Grayson, William
Greathouse, Clarence
  Ridgley
Green, Benjamin
  Edwards
Green, John Patterson
Green, William Thomas
Greener, Richard
  Theodore
Greenhalge, Frederic
  Thomas
Gregg, John
Gregory, Charles Noble
Gridley, Jeremiah
Griffin, Cyrus
Grimké, Archibald
  Henry
Griscom, Lloyd
  Carpenter
Griswold, Roger
Grossman, Mary Belle
Grover, La Fayette
Grundy, Felix
Guthrie, William
  Dameron
Hadley, Herbert Spencer
Haight, Henry Huntley
Hale, Robert
Hale, Robert Safford
Hall, John Elihu
Hamer, Thomas Lyon
Hamilton, Andrew
  (c.1676–1741)
Hammond, John
Hand, Augustus Noble
Hanson, Alexander
  Contee (1749–1806)
Hanson, Alexander
  Contee (1786–1819)
Hardin, Benjamin, Jr.
Hardin, Martin D.
Harlan, James
  (1800–1863)
Harlan, John Marshall
  (1899–1971)
Harley, Herbert Lincoln
Harris, Paul Percy
Harvey, Coin
Haskell, Ella Louise
  Knowles
Hastie, William Henry
Hawley, James Henry
Hay, George
Haynsworth, Clement
  Furman, Jr.
Hays, Arthur Garfield

Hays, Will H.
Haywood, John
Hemphill, Joseph
Hening, William Waller
Hennock, Frieda Barkin
Henry, Patrick
Herndon, William Henry
Herrman, Augustine
Hickenlooper, Bourke B.
Higgins, George V.
  Suppl. 2
Hill, David Bennett
Hill, Joshua
Hillard, George Stillman
Hillhouse, James
Hilliard, Francis
Hillquit, Morris
Hines, Walker Downer
Hise, Elijah
Hitchcock, Gilbert
  Monell
Hoadly, George
Hoffman, David
Hoffman, Ogden
Hogan, Frank Smithwick
Hogan, William
Holland, Spessard
  Lindsey
Holman, Jesse Lynch
Holmes, John
Hooper, Johnson Jones
Hornblower, William
  Butler
Hourwich, Isaac
  Aaronovich
Houston, Charles
  Hamilton
Houstoun, John
Howe, Frederic Clemson
Howley, Richard
Hruska, Roman *Suppl. 1*
Hunt, Carleton
Hunton, George
  Kenneth
Hurley, Patrick Jay
Hutchins, Harry Burns
Imboden, John Daniel
Ingalls, John James
Ingersoll, Charles Jared
Ingersoll, Jared
Ingersoll, Robert Green
Innes, James
Ivins, William Mills
Jackson, Robert
  Houghwout
Jamison, David
Jaworski, Leon
Jenckes, Thomas Allen
Jewett, Hugh Judge
Johnson, Edward Austin
Johnson, Louis Arthur

Legal Practice *(cont.)*
Johnson, Reverdy
Johnson, William Samuel
Jones, Charles Colcock, Jr.
Jones, Hamilton C.
Jones, Samuel
Jones, Scipio Africanus
Jones, Thomas
Jones, Thomas Goode *Suppl. 1*
Jones, Walter
Jordan, Barbara *Suppl. 1*
Joy, James Frederick
Judah, Samuel
Judd, Albert Francis
Kane, Thomas Leiper
Kaufman, Joseph William
Keating, William Hypolitus
Kellogg, Frank Billings
Kent, Benjamin
Kent, Edward
Kenyon, Dorothy
Kepley, Ada Harriet Miser
Kershaw, Joseph Brevard
Key, Francis Scott
Key, Philip Barton
Kilgore, Carrie Sylvester Burnham
Kilgore, Harley Martin
King, Carol Weiss
Kinsey, John
Kirchwey, George Washington
Kirkland, Joseph
Kirkpatrick, Andrew
Kitchin, William Hodge
Koerner, Gustave Philipp
Kohler, Max James
Kunstler, William Moses
Lacey, John Fletcher
La Follette, Philip Fox
Lamb, Theodore Lafayette
Lamon, Ward Hill
Langston, John Mercer
Lanham, Fritz
Lanier, James Franklin Doughty
Lansing, Robert
Larrazolo, Octaviano Ambrosio
Latrobe, John Hazlehurst Boneval
Laughlin, Gail
Lechford, Thomas

Lee, Charles (1758–1815)
Lee, Samuel J.
Lehman, Irving
Leigh, Benjamin Watkins
Leonard, Daniel
Levitt, Abraham
Lewis, Alfred Henry
Lewis, Charlton Thomas
Lewis, Reginald Francis
Lewis, Rhoda Valentine
Lewis, William Henry
L'Hommedieu, Ezra
Lilienthal, David Eli
Lincoln, Enoch
Lincoln, Levi (1782–1868)
Lindbergh, Charles August
Littell, William
Livermore, Samuel (1786–1833)
Livingston, Edward
Livingston, Robert Robert
Lloyd, Thomas
Lockwood, Belva Ann Bennett McNall
Logan, Stephen Trigg
London, Meyer
Long, Breckinridge
Lowenstein, Allard Kenneth
Lowry, Robert
Lucas, Scott Wike
Lunt, George
Lynch, John Roy
Mack, Julian William
MacVeagh, Isaac Wayne
Magoon, Charles Edward
Mahon, George Herman
Mallary, Rollin Carolas
Malone, Dudley Field
Manderson, Charles Frederick
Maney, George Earl
Mankin, Helen Douglas
Mansfield, Arabella
Margold, Nathan Ross
Marshall, Louis (1856–1929)
Marshall, Thomas Alexander
Marshall, Thurgood
Mason, Charles
Mason, Jeremiah
Mason, John Young
Mason, Stevens Thomson

Masters, Edgar Lee
Mayes, Edward
McCall, Samuel Walker
McCloy, John Jay, Jr.
McCook, Edward Moody
McCulloch, Catharine Gouger Waugh
McDowell, John
McGhee, Frederick Lamar
McGrady, Thomas
McKennan, Thomas McKean Thompson
McKinstry, Elisha Williams
McKissick, Floyd Bixler
McWilliams, Carey
Meagher, Thomas Francis
Medina, Harold Raymond
Meek, Alexander Beaufort
Meigs, Return Jonathan (1801–1891)
Mentschikoff, Soia
Mercer, John
Merrick, Edwin Thomas
Miller, David Hunter
Miller, Nathan Lewis
Milligan, Lambdin P.
Mills, Benjamin
Mills, Elijah Hunt
Mills, Ogden Livingston
Milroy, Robert Huston
Minor, Benjamin Blake
Mitchell, John Hipple
Mitchell, John Newton
Mitchell, Stephen Mix
Mitchell, William (1801–1886)
Mondell, Frank Wheeler
Monsky, Henry
Montoya, Joseph Manuel
Moore, John Bassett
Morawetz, Victor
Morehead, James Turner
Morgan, Clement Garnett
Morgenthau, Henry
Morris, Richard
Morris, Robert (1823–1882)
Morton, Ferdinand Quintin
Mullan, John
Mullen, Arthur Francis
Murphy, Henry Cruse
Murphy, Isaac
Murray, James Edward

Murray, Joseph
Murray, Pauli
Mussey, Ellen Spencer
Napier, James Carroll
Nelson, Thomas Henry
Neumann, Franz Leopold
Newsome, Joseph Thomas
Nicholas, George
O'Brian, John Lord
O'Brien, Morgan Joseph
O'Conor, Charles
O'Dwyer, Paul *Suppl. 2*
O'Hara, James Edward
Ohly, John Hallowell
Okey, John Waterman
Olds, Irving Sands
Oliver, Andrew (1906–1981)
Olney, Richard
Ordronaux, John
Osborn, Thomas Andrew
O'Sullivan, John Louis
Otis, Elwell Stephen
Otis, Harrison Gray (1765–1848)
Overman, Lee Slater
Overton, John
Paca, William
Paine, Robert Treat
Paine, Robert Treat, Jr.
Palmer, William Adams
Parker, Isaac Charles
Parker, John Cortlandt
Parker, John Johnston
Parris, Albion Keith
Parsons, Theophilus (1750–1813)
Parsons, Theophilus (1797–1882)
Patman, Wright
Patterson, Thomas McDonald
Patterson, William L.
Patton, John Mercer
Peabody, Oliver William Bourn
Pendleton, Edmund
Pepper, George Wharton
Perez, Leander Henry
Perlman, Philip Benjamin
Peters, John Andrew
Petigru, James Louis
Pettus, John Jones
Pfeffer, Leo
Phillips, Lena Madesin
Pickering, John

Legal Practice (cont.)

Pierce, Edward Lillie
Pierpont, Francis Harrison
Pike, Albert
Pillow, Gideon Johnson
Pinchot, Amos Richards Eno
Pinckney, Charles Cotesworth
Pinkney, William
Pitkin, Timothy
Pitkin, William
Plumb, Preston B.
Poe, L. Marian
Poindexter, Miles
Pollak, Walter Heilprin
Pomeroy, John Norton
Porter, Benjamin Faneuil
Potter, Robert Brown
Pound, Roscoe
Powell, Lewis F., Jr. *Suppl. 1*
Prat, Benjamin
Pressman, Lee
Priber, Christian Gottlieb
Prichard, Edward Fretwell, Jr.
Prouty, Charles Azro
Pruyn, John Van Schaick Lansing
Pugh, George Ellis
Pujo, Arsene Paulin
Putnam, William LeBaron
Quick, Herbert
Quincy, Josiah (1744–1775)
Quincy, Samuel
Quinn, John
Raines, John
Randolph, Sir John
Rankin, J. Lee *Suppl. 1*
Rankine, William Birch
Ranney, Rufus Percival
Ransom, Leon Andrew
Rawalt, Marguerite
Ray, Charlotte E.
Rector, Henry Massey
Redfield, Amasa Angell
Redfield, Isaac Fletcher
Redmond, Sidney Dillon
Reed, David Aiken
Reed, Henry Hope
Reed, James Alexander
Reed, Joseph
Reed, Thomas Brackett
Reeder, Andrew Horatio
Requier, Augustus Julian
Reynolds, Robert Rice

Rice, Isaac Leopold
Richberg, Donald Randall
Ricker, Marilla Marks Young
Roane, Archibald
Robinson, Christopher
Robinson, Conway
Robinson, George Dexter
Robinson, Lelia Josephine
Roe, Gilbert Ernstein
Rogge, O. John
Root, Erastus
Rorer, David
Ross, George
Ross, James
Royall, Kenneth Claiborne
Rublee, George
Ruffin, George Lewis
Rugg, Arthur Prentice
Ruggles, Samuel Bulkley
Ruggles, Timothy
Russell, William Eustis
Rutherford, Joseph Franklin
Rutledge, John
Sampson, Edith Spurlock
Sampson, William
Sapiro, Aaron *Suppl. 2*
Saunders, Stuart Thomas
Sayles, John
Saypol, Irving
Scammon, Jonathan Young
Schaefer, Walter V.
Schroeder, Theodore
Schwellenbach, Lewis Baxter
Scott, John Morin
Sedgwick, Theodore (1811–1859)
Selden, George Baldwin
Sergeant, John (1779–1852)
Sevier, Ambrose Hundley
Sewall, David
Sewall, Jonathan
Shafroth, John Franklin
Shannon, Wilson
Sharp, Malcolm Pitman
Sharswood, George
Shaw, William Smith
Shea, William *Suppl. 1*
Shellabarger, Samuel

(1817–1896)
Sheppard, Morris
Sherwood, Lorenzo
Sherwood, Thomas Adiel
Simmons, Furnifold McLendel
Simms, William Elliott
Slattery, John Richard
Slocum, Henry Warner
Smith, Caleb Blood
Smith, Melancton (1744–1798)
Smith, Oliver Hampton
Smith, Richard
Smith, Richard Penn
Smith, Truman
Smith, William (1697–1769)
Smyth, Alexander
Soulé, Pierre
Southard, Samuel Lewis
Sparer, Edward V.
Spencer, John Canfield
Speranza, Gino Carlo
Spingarn, Arthur Barnett
Springer, William McKendree
Stanbery, Henry
Steinhardt, Laurence Adolph
Stephens, Linton
Sterne, Simon
Stewart, Alvan
Stewart, William Morris
Stickney, Alpheus Beede
Stockton, John Potter
Stockton, Richard
Stringfellow, Frank William
Strong, Caleb
Strong, George Templeton
Stuart, Archibald
Stuart, John Todd
Sullivan, George
Sullivan, James
Swan, Joseph Rockwell
Taber, John
Taft, Charles Phelps
Taliaferro, William Booth
Tallmadge, James
Taney, Roger Brooke
Taylor, Creed
Taylor, Hannis
Taylor, Telford *Suppl. 1*
Tazewell, Littleton Waller
Teller, Henry Moore
Terrell, Edwin Holland
Thomas, Elmer

Thomas, Philip Francis
Thompson, Richard Wigginton
Thompson, Robert Means
Thurston, Lorrin Andrews
Tod, David
Todd, Marion Marsh
Toucey, Isaac
Towne, Charles Arnette
Tracy, Uriah
Train, Arthur
Troup, Robert
Tucker, Samuel Wilbert
Tudor, William
Tumulty, Joseph Patrick
Tureaud, Alexander Pierre
Underwood, Oscar Wilder
Untermyer, Samuel
Usher, John Palmer *Suppl. 1*
Vallandigham, Clement Laird
Van Buren, John
Vanderbilt, Arthur T.
Van der Donck, Adriaen *Suppl. 1*
Van Dyke, Nicholas (1738–1789)
Van Dyke, Nicholas (1769–1826)
Van Schaack, Peter
Van Vechten, Abraham
Van Winkle, Peter Godwin
Van Wyck, Charles Henry
Varnum, James Mitchell
Vinton, Samuel Finley
Vroom, Peter Dumont, Jr.
Waddell, Alfred Moore
Waddy, Joseph C.
Waite, Catharine Van Valkenburg
Walden, Austin Thomas
Waldron, Richard, III
Walker, Frank Comerford
Walker, Gilbert Carlton
Walker, Robert Franklin
Walker, Timothy (1802–1856)
Wallis, Severn Teackle
Walsh, Frank P.
Walsh, Thomas James
Walton, George
Ward, Hortense Sparks

Legal Practice *(cont.)*
Warren, Charles
Watkins, George
  Claiborne
Watson, John William
  Clark
Webb, James Edwin
Webster, Daniel
Welch, Joseph Nye
Wertman, Sarah Killgore
West, James Edward
Wharton, William Harris
Wheeler, Burton Kendall
Wheeler, Everett
  Pepperrell
White, George Henry
White, Stephen Mallory
Whitney, William
  Collins
Wickersham, George
  Woodward
Willebrandt, Mabel
  Walker
Willey, Waitman
  Thomas
Williams, Edward
  Bennett
Williams, John
  (1778–1837)
Williamson, Isaac
  Halsted
Willis, Albert Shelby
Willkie, Wendell Lewis
Wilson, James
  (1742–1798)
Winder, William Henry
Wise, John Sergeant
Wolf, Simon
Wood, Frederick Hill
Wood, L. Hollingsworth
Woodbridge, William
Woodford, Stewart
  Lyndon
Woods, William Allen
Worthington, John
Wragg, William
Wyzanski, Charles
  Edward, Jr.
Yamaoka, George
Yell, Archibald
Yerger, William
Young, Owen D.
Zane, Charles Shuster
Zuber, Paul Burgess

Litigants
Alston, Melvin Ovenus
Crandall, Prudence
Fisher, Ada Lois Sipuel
Freeman, Elizabeth
Gaines, Myra Clark

Gibbons, Thomas
Gideon, Clarence Earl
Loving, Richard Perry
Maffitt, John Newland
  (1794–1850)
Milligan, Lambdin P.
Minor, Virginia Louise
Ogden, Aaron
Ozawa, Takao
Penn, Hannah Callowhill
Plessy, Homer Adolph
Quinlan, Karen Ann
Scopes, John Thomas
Scott, Dred
Truth, Sojourner
Zenger, John Peter

Patent Experts
Carlson, Chester Floyd
Ewbank, Thomas
Jones, Thomas P.
Langner, Lawrence
Leggett, Mortimer
  Dormer
Renwick, Edward Sabine
Selden, George Baldwin

Public Prosecutors
Cohn, Roy
Dewey, Thomas
  Edmund
Garrison, Jim
Jaworski, Leon
Rogge, O. John
Wilentz, David
  Theodore

Solicitors General
Beck, James
  Montgomery
Bowers, Lloyd Wheaton
Fahy, Charles
Perlman, Philip
  Benjamin
Rankin, J. Lee *Suppl. 1*

U.S. Supreme Court Chief Justices
Burger, Warren Earl
Chase, Salmon Portland
Ellsworth, Oliver
Fuller, Melville Weston
Hughes, Charles Evans
Jay, John
Marshall, John
Rutledge, John
Stone, Harlan Fiske
Taft, William Howard
Taney, Roger Brooke
Vinson, Fred
Waite, Morrison Remick

Warren, Earl
White, Edward Douglass
  (1845–1921)

U.S. Supreme Court Justices
Baldwin, Henry
Barbour, Philip
  Pendleton
Black, Hugo Lafayette
Blackmun, Harry A.
  Suppl. 1
Blair, John, Jr.
Blatchford, Samuel
Bradley, Joseph P.
Brandeis, Louis Dembitz
Brennan, William J., Jr.
  Suppl. 1
Brewer, David Josiah
Brown, Henry Billings
Burton, Harold Hitz
Butler, Pierce
  (1866–1939)
Byrnes, James Francis
Campbell, John
  Archibald
Cardozo, Benjamin
  Nathan
Catron, John
Chase, Samuel
Clark, Tom Campbell
Clarke, John Hessin
Clifford, Nathan
Cobb, Howell
Curtis, Benjamin
  Robbins
Cushing, William
Daniel, Peter Vivian
Davis, David
Day, William Rufus
Douglas, William O.
Duvall, Gabriel *Suppl. 1*
Field, Stephen Johnson
Fortas, Abe
Frankfurter, Felix
Goldberg, Arthur Joseph
Gray, Horace
Grier, Robert Cooper
Harlan, John Marshall
  (1833–1911)
Harlan, John Marshall
  (1899–1971)
Holmes, Oliver Wendell
  (1841–1935)
Hughes, Charles Evans
Hunt, Ward
Iredell, James
Jackson, Howell
  Edmunds
Jackson, Robert
  Houghwout

Johnson, Thomas
Johnson, William
  (1771–1834)
Lamar, Joseph Rucker
Lamar, Lucius Quintus
  Cincinnatus
Livingston, Brockholst
Lurton, Horace Harmon
Marshall, Thurgood
Matthews, Stanley
McKenna, Joseph
McKinley, John
McLean, John
McReynolds, James
  Clark
Miller, Samuel Freeman
Minton, Sherman
Moody, William Henry
Moore, Alfred *Suppl. 2*
Murphy, Frank
Nelson, Samuel
Paterson, William
Peckham, Rufus
  Wheeler
Pitney, Mahlon
Powell, Lewis F., Jr.
  Suppl. 1
Reed, Stanley Forman
Roberts, Owen Josephus
Rutledge, John
Rutledge, Wiley Blount,
  Jr.
Sanford, Edward Terry
Shiras, George
Stewart, Potter
Stone, Harlan Fiske
Story, Joseph
Strong, William
Sutherland, George
Swayne, Noah Haynes
Thompson, Smith
Todd, Thomas
Trimble, Robert
Van Devanter, Willis
Washington, Bushrod
Wayne, James Moore
White, Edward Douglass
  (1845–1921)
Whittaker, Charles E.
  Suppl. 1
Wilson, James
  (1742–1798)
Woodbury, Levi
Woods, William
  Burnham

MILITARY AND INTELLIGENCE OPERATIONS

American Revolution
Revolutionary Army Officers
Alexander, William

American Revolution
(cont.)
Allan, John
Angell, Israel
Armstrong, John
 (1717–1795)
Arnold, Benedict
Ashe, John
Ashe, John Baptista
Barber, Francis
Barton, William
Beatty, John
Benner, Philip
Biddle, Clement
Bland, Theodorick
Bloomfield, Joseph
Brearly, David
Brodhead, Daniel
Brooks, John
Brown, John
 (1744–1780)
Buford, Abraham
 (1749–1833)
Burr, Aaron
 (1756–1836)
Butler, Richard
Butler, William
Cabell, Samuel Jordan
Cadwalader, John
Cadwalader, Lambert
Campbell, Arthur
Campbell, William
 (1745–1781)
Caswell, Richard
Champion, Henry
Cilley, Joseph
Claghorn, George
Clark, George Rogers
Clarke, Elijah
Clarkson, Matthew
Cleveland, Benjamin
Clinton, George
 (1739–1812)
Clinton, James
Conway, Thomas
Craig, Isaac
Craik, James
Crane, John
Crawford, William
Davidson, William Lee
 Suppl. 1
Davie, William
 Richardson
Dayton, Jonathan
Dearborn, Henry
Dickinson, Philemon
Eddy, Jonathan
Elbert, Samuel
Ewing, James
 (1736–1806)
Febiger, Christian

Fish, Nicholas
Flagg, Josiah
Forman, David
Franks, David Salisbury
 Suppl. 2
Gansevoort, Peter
 Suppl. 1
Garden, Alexander
 (1757–1829)
Gates, Horatio
Glover, John
Graham, Joseph
Grayson, William
Greene, Nathanael
Hamilton, Alexander
 (1757?–1804)
Hampton, Wade
 (1754?–1835)
Hand, Edward
Hardin, John
Hazen, Moses
Heath, William
Herkimer, Nicholas
Hogun, James
Hopkins, Samuel
 (1753–1819)
Houstoun, John
Howard, John Eager
Howell, Richard
Hull, William
Huntington, Jabez
Huntington, Jedediah
Innes, James
Irvine, James
Irvine, William
Jackson, William
Johnston, Peter
Kalb, Johann
Knox, Henry
Kosciuszko, Tadeusz
 Andrzej Bonawentura
Lafayette, Marquis de
Lamb, John
Laurens, John
Lee, Charles
 (1731–1782)
Lee, Henry (1756–1818)
Lewis, Andrew
Lewis, Morgan
Lincoln, Benjamin
Livingston, James
Logan, Benjamin
Lovell, Solomon
Lyon, Matthew
Machin, Thomas
Marion, Francis
Martin, Alexander
Mathews, George
Maxwell, William
 (1733–1796) *Suppl. 1*
McDonald, Donald

McIntosh, Lachlan
McLane, Allen
Meigs, Return Jonathan
 (1740–1823)
Mifflin, Thomas
Montgomery, Richard
Moore, Alfred *Suppl. 2*
Moore, James
 (1737–1777)
Morgan, Daniel
Moultrie, William
Muhlenberg, John Peter
 Gabriel
North, William
Ogden, Aaron
O'Hara, James
Parke, John
Paterson, John
Pickens, Andrew
Pickering, Timothy
Pierce, William Leigh
Pinckney, Thomas
Polk, Thomas
Polk, William
Pomeroy, Seth
Porter, Andrew
Posey, Thomas
Prescott, Oliver
Prescott, William
Pulaski, Casimir
Putnam, Israel
Putnam, Rufus
Reed, Joseph
Roberdeau, Daniel
Rutherford, Griffith
Sargent, Winthrop
Scammell, Alexander
Schuyler, Philip John
Scott, Charles
Sevier, John
Shaw, Samuel
Shays, Daniel
Shelby, Evan
Shelby, Isaac
Shepard, William
Silliman, Gold Selleck
Smallwood, William
Smith, Daniel
Smith, Samuel
 (1752–1839)
Smith, William Stephens
Spencer, Joseph
Stark, John (1728–1822)
St. Clair, Arthur
Stephen, Adam
Steuben, Friedrich
 Wilhelm von
Sullivan, John
Sumner, Jethro
Sumter, Thomas
Ten Broeck, Abraham

Thomas, David
Thompson, Samuel
Tilghman, Tench
Tousard, Anne-Louis
 Suppl. 2
Trumbull, Joseph
Van Cortlandt, Philip
Van Schaick, Goose
Varick, Richard
Varnum, James Mitchell
Varnum, Joseph Bradley
Wadsworth, James
 (1730–1817)
Wadsworth, Jeremiah
Wadsworth, Peleg
Ward, Artemas
Warner, Seth
Washington, George
 (1732–1799)
Wayne, Anthony
Weedon, George
Wilkinson, James
Willett, Marinus
Williams, Otho Holland
Williamson, Andrew
Winchester, James
Winn, Richard
Woodford, William
Woodhull, Nathaniel
Wooster, David
Ziegler, David

Revolutionary Naval
Officers
 Barney, Joshua
 Barry, John
 Biddle, Nicholas
 (1750–1778)
 Conyngham, Gustavus
 Fiske, John (1744–1797)
 Hopkins, Esek
 Jones, John Paul
 Little, George
 Manley, John
 McNeill, Hector
 Murray, Alexander
 Nicholson, James
 O'Brien, Jeremiah
 Saltonstall, Dudley
 Talbot, Silas
 Tucker, Samuel
 Waters, Daniel
 Whipple, Abraham
 Wickes, Lambert

Civil War
Confederate Army Officers
 Alexander, Edward
 Porter
 Allen, Henry Watkins

Civil War *(cont.)*

Anderson, George Thomas "Tige"
Anderson, Joseph Reid
Anderson, Patton
Anderson, Richard Heron
Archer, James Jay
Armistead, Lewis Addison
Ashby, Turner
Barksdale, William
Barringer, Rufus
Bate, William Brimage
Battle, Cullen Andrews
Beauregard, Pierre Gustave Toutant
Belo, Alfred Horatio
Benning, Henry Lewis
Bonham, Milledge Luke
Bragg, Braxton
Breckinridge, John Cabell
Buckner, Simon Bolivar
Buford, Abraham (1820–1884)
Butler, Matthew Calbraith
Cabell, William Lewis
Capers, Ellison
Chalmers, James Ronald
Cheatham, Benjamin Franklin
Chisolm, Alexander Robert
Churchill, Thomas James
Clark, Charles
Cleburne, Patrick Ronayne
Cobb, Thomas Reade Rootes
Cockrell, Francis Marion
Colquitt, Alfred Holt
Cook, Philip
Cooper, Samuel (1798–1876)
Cox, William Ruffin
Crittenden, George Bibb
Daniel, John Warwick
Duke, Basil Wilson
Early, Jubal Anderson
Elzey, Arnold
Evans, Nathan George
Ewell, Richard Stoddert
Fenner, Charles Erasmus
Floyd, John Buchanan
Forrest, Nathan Bedford
Fry, Birkett Davenport
Garnett, Robert Selden
Gartrell, Lucius Jeremiah

Gary, Martin Witherspoon
Gholson, Samuel Jameson
Gordon, John Brown
Gorgas, Josiah
Govan, Daniel Chevilette
Gregg, John
Gregg, Maxcy
Hagood, Johnson
Hampton, Wade (1818–1902)
Hardee, William Joseph
Hébert, Paul Octave
Herbert, Hilary Abner
Heth, Henry
Hill, A. P.
Hill, Daniel Harvey
Hindman, Thomas Carmichael
Hoke, Robert Frederick
Holmes, Theophilus Hunter
Hood, John Bell
Howell, Evan Park
Humphreys, Benjamin Grubb
Hunton, Eppa
Huse, Caleb
Imboden, John Daniel
Ives, Joseph Christmas
Jackson, Thomas Jonathan
Jackson, William Hicks
Jenkins, Albert Gallatin
Jenkins, Micah
Johnson, Bushrod Rust
Johnson, Edward (1816–1873)
Johnston, Albert Sidney
Johnston, Joseph Eggleston
Johnston, William Preston
Keitt, Laurence Massillon
Kemper, James Lawson
Kershaw, Joseph Brevard
Lane, James Henry (1833–1907)
Lee, Fitzhugh
Lee, George Washington Custis
Lee, Robert E.
Lee, Stephen Dill
Lee, William Henry Fitzhugh
Logan, Thomas Muldrup
Longstreet, James

Loring, William Wing
Lovell, Mansfield
Magruder, John Bankhead
Mahone, William
Maney, George Earl
Manigault, Arthur Middleton
Maury, Dabney Herndon
McCausland, John
McCulloch, Ben
McLaws, Lafayette
McNeill, John Hanson
Moïse, Edward Warren
Morgan, John Hunt
Mosby, John Singleton
Myers, Abraham Charles
Northrop, Lucius Bellinger
Oates, William Calvin
Pelham, John
Pemberton, John Clifford
Pender, William Dorsey
Perry, Edward Aylesworth
Pettigrew, James Johnston
Pickett, George Edward
Pike, Albert
Pillow, Gideon Johnson
Polk, Leonidas
Price, Sterling
Pryor, Roger Atkinson
Rains, Gabriel James
Rains, George Washington
Ramseur, Stephen Dodson
Ransom, Matt Whitaker
Rodes, Robert Emmett
Rosser, Thomas Lafayette
Scales, Alfred Moore
Shelby, Joseph Orville
Shoup, Francis Asbury
Sibley, Henry Hopkins
Smith, Edmund Kirby
Smith, Gustavus Woodson
Smith, William (1797–1887)
Stevenson, Carter Littlepage
Stewart, Alexander Peter
St. John, Isaac Munroe
Stone, John Marshall
Stuart, J. E. B.
Taliaferro, William Booth

Taylor, Richard
Thomas, William Holland
Toombs, Robert Augustus
Trimble, Isaac Ridgeway
Twiggs, David Emanuel
Van Dorn, Earl
Venable, Charles Scott
Walker, William Henry Talbot
Walthall, Edward Cary
Watie, Stand
Wheeler, Joseph
Wilcox, Cadmus Marcellus
Winder, John Henry
Wirz, Henry
Wise, Henry Alexander
Young, Pierce Manning Butler

Confederate Naval Officers

Brooke, John Mercer
Bulloch, James *Suppl. 2*
Buchanan, Franklin
Jones, Catesby ap Roger
Kell, John McIntosh
Maffitt, John Newland (1819–1886)
Maury, Matthew Fontaine
Page, Thomas Jefferson
Parker, William Harwar
Semmes, Raphael
Tattnall, Josiah
Tucker, John Randolph (1812–1883)
Waddell, James Iredell
Wilkinson, John
Wood, John Taylor

Union Army Officers

Abbot, Henry Larcom
Adams, Charles
Ames, Adelbert
Anderson, Robert
Andrews, George Leonard
Asboth, Alexander Sandor
Augur, Christopher Colon
Averell, William Woods
Ayres, Romeyn Beck
Babcock, Orville Elias
Badeau, Adam
Bailey, Joseph
Baird, Absalom
Baker, Edward Dickinson

Civil War *(cont.)*

Banks, Nathaniel
Prentiss
Barlow, Francis
Channing
Barnard, John Gross
Barnes, James
Barnes, Joseph K.
Barnitz, Albert Trorillo
Siders
Barry, William Farquhar
Bendire, Charles Emil
Billings, John Shaw
Birney, David Bell
Birney, William
Blair, Francis Preston, Jr.
Blunt, James Gillpatrick
Bonneville, Benjamin
Louis Eulalie de
Boyle, Jeremiah Tilford
Bragg, Edward
Stuyvesant
Brannan, John Milton
Brayton, Charles Ray
Brisbin, James Sanks
Brooks, William Thomas
Harbaugh
Buell, Don Carlos
Buford, John
Burnside, Ambrose
Everett
Butler, Benjamin
Franklin (1818–1893)
Butterfield, Daniel
Canby, Edward Richard
Sprigg
Carney, William Harvey
Carr, Eugene Asa
Carrington, Henry
Beebee
Carroll, Samuel Sprigg
Carter, Samuel
Powhatan
Casey, Silas
Chaffee, Adna Romanza
Chamberlain, Joshua
Lawrence
Clark, William Thomas
Connor, Patrick Edward
Cooke, Philip St. George
Cooper, Joseph
Alexander
Corse, John Murray
Couch, Darius Nash
Cox, Jacob Dolson
Crawford, Samuel
Johnson
Crittenden, Thomas
Leonidas
Crook, George
Crosby, John Schuyler

Cullum, George
Washington
Curtis, Samuel Ryan
Custer, George
Armstrong
Davies, Henry Eugene,
Jr.
Davis, Jefferson
Columbus
Delafield, Richard
Denver, James William
Devens, Charles, Jr.
Devin, Thomas Casimir
Dix, John Adams
Dodge, Grenville Mellen
Dodge, Theodore
Ayrault
Doubleday, Abner
Douglas, H. Ford
Drake, Francis Marion
du Pont, Henry
Algernon
Dwight, William
Emory, William Hemsley
Ewing, Hugh Boyle
Ewing, Thomas, Jr.
Fairchild, Lucius
Farnsworth, Elon John
Force, Manning
Ferguson
Forwood, William Henry
Foster, John Gray
Foster, Robert Sanford
Franklin, William Buel
French, William Henry
Fry, James Barnet
Garrard, Kenner
Geary, John White
Getty, George
Washington
Gibbon, John
Gillem, Alvan Cullem
Gillmore, Quincy Adams
Granger, Gordon
Grant, Ulysses S.
Greely, Adolphus
Washington
Greene, George Sears
Gregg, David
McMurtrie
Grierson, Benjamin
Henry
Griffin, Charles
Grover, Cuvier
Halderman, John Adams
Halleck, Henry Wager
Halpine, Charles
Graham
Hamlin, Charles
Hancock, Winfield Scott
Hardie, James Allen

Hartranft, John
Frederick
Hascall, Milo Smith
Haskell, Franklin Aretas
Hatch, Edward
Hawley, Joseph Roswell
Hays, Alexander
Hazen, William Babcock
Hecker, Friedrich Karl
Franz
Heintzelman, Samuel
Peter
Henry, Guy Vernon
Herron, Francis Jay
Higginson, Thomas
Wentworth
Hitchcock, Ethan Allen
(1798–1870)
Hooker, Joseph
Howard, Oliver Otis
Howe, John Homer
Humphreys, Andrew
Atkinson
Hunt, Henry Jackson
Hunter, David
Hurlbut, Stephen
Augustus
Johnson, Richard W.
Kane, Thomas Leiper
Kautz, August Valentine
Kearny, Philip
Keifer, Joseph Warren
Keyes, Erasmus Darwin
Kilpatrick, Hugh Judson
Kimball, Nathan
King, Rufus
(1814–1876)
Leggett, Mortimer
Dormer
Logan, John Alexander
MacArthur, Arthur
Mackenzie, Ranald
Slidell
Mallery, Garrick
Mansfield, Joseph King
Fenno
Martin, John Alexander
McArthur, John
McClellan, George B.
McClernand, John
Alexander
McCook, Alexander
McDowell
McCook, Edward
Moody
McDowell, Irvin
McIntosh, John Baillie
McPherson, James B.
Meade, George Gordon
Meagher, Thomas
Francis

Meigs, Montgomery
Cunningham
Merriam, Henry Clay
Miles, Nelson Appleton
Milroy, Robert Huston
Mitchell, Robert
Byington
Mott, Gershom
Mower, Joseph Anthony
Myer, Albert James
Nelson, William
(1824–1862)
Newton, John
Oglesby, Richard James
Ord, Edward Otho
Cresap
Osterhaus, Peter Joseph
Otis, Elwell Stephen
Otis, George Alexander
Parke, John Grubb
Parrott, Robert Parker
Patrick, Marsena
Rudolph
Pleasonton, Alfred
Pope, John
Porter, Fitz John
Porter, Horace
Post, George Browne
Potter, Robert Brown
Ransom, Thomas
Edward Greenfield
Raum, Green Berry
Rawlins, John Aaron
Reno, Jesse Lee
Reynolds, John Fulton
Reynolds, Joseph Jones
Ricketts, James
Brewerton
Ripley, James Wolfe
Roberts, Benjamin Stone
Robinson, John
Cleveland
Rosecrans, William
Starke
Rousseau, Lovell
Harrison
Ruger, Thomas Howard
Russell, David Allen
Schofield, John
McAllister
Schurz, Carl
Scott, Robert Kingston
Scott, Winfield
Sedgwick, John
Seymour, Truman
Shafter, William Rufus
Shaw, Robert Gould
Sheridan, Philip Henry
Sherman, William
Tecumseh
Sherwood, Isaac Ruth

Civil War *(cont.)*
Shields, James
Sibley, Henry Hastings
Sickles, Daniel Edgar
Sigel, Franz
Slocum, Henry Warner
Smith, Andrew Jackson
Smith, Charles Ferguson
Smith, Giles Alexander
Smith, Morgan Lewis
Smith, William Farrar
Stahel, Julius
Stanley, David Sloane
Steedman, James Blair
Steele, Frederick
Stevens, Isaac Ingalls
Stone, Charles Pomeroy
Stone, Roy
Stoneman, George
Sturgis, Samuel Davis
Sumner, Edwin Vose
Sykes, George
Terry, Alfred Howe
Thomas, George Henry
Thomas, Lorenzo
Tilghman, Benjamin
   Chew
Torbert, Alfred Thomas
   Archimedes
Totten, Joseph Gilbert
Trobriand, Régis Dénis
   de
Turner, John Wesley
Twitchell, Marshall
   Harvey
Upton, Emory
Van Wyck, Charles
   Henry
Wadsworth, James
   Samuel
Wallace, Lew
Warren, Gouverneur
   Kemble
Weaver, James Baird
Webster, Joseph Dana
Weitzel, Godfrey
Wheaton, Frank
Willcox, Orlando Bolivar
Williams, Alpheus
   Starkey
Willich, August
Wilson, James Harrison
Wood, Thomas John
Woodhull, Alfred
   Alexander
Woods, Charles Robert
Wool, John Ellis
Wright, Horatio
   Gouverneur
Wright, Joseph Jefferson
   Burr

Young, Samuel Baldwin
   Marks

Union Naval Officers
Alden, James
Ammen, Daniel
Bailey, Theodorus
Bridge, Horatio
Brownell, Henry Howard
Collins, Napoleon
Colvocoresses, George
   Musalas
Craven, Thomas Tingey
Craven, Tunis Augustus
   MacDonough
Cushing, William Barker
Dahlgren, John
   Adolphus Bernard
Davis, Charles Henry
Dewey, George
Drayton, Percival
Du Pont, Samuel
   Francis
Erben, Henry
Evans, Robley
   Dunglison
Farragut, David
   Glasgow
Foote, Andrew Hull
Fox, Gustavus Vasa
Gihon, Albert Leary
Goldsborough, Louis
   Malesherbes
Greene, Samuel Dana
Gridley, Charles Vernon
Howell, John Adams
Jeffers, William
   Nicholson
Jenkins, Thornton
   Alexander
Jouett, James Edward
Kempff, Louis
Lee, Samuel Phillips
Loring, Charles Harding
Luce, Stephen Bleeker
Mahan, Alfred Thayer
McNair, Frederick
   Vallette
Meade, Richard
   Worsam, III
Mullany, James Robert
   Madison
Nicholson, James
   William Augustus
Palmer, James Shedden
Parker, Foxhall
   Alexander, Jr.
Parrott, Enoch
   Greenleafe
Pattison, Thomas
Paulding, Hiram

Porter, David Dixon
Preble, George Henry
Radford, William
Ramsay, Francis
   Munroe
Remey, George Collier
Ringgold, Cadwalader
Rodgers, George
   Washington
   (1822–1863)
Rodgers, John
   (1812–1882)
Rowan, Stephen Clegg
Sampson, William
   Thomas
Sands, Benjamin
   Franklin
Schley, Winfield Scott
Selfridge, Thomas
   Oliver, Jr.
Shufeldt, Robert Wilson
Sicard, Montgomery
Sigsbee, Charles Dwight
Smith, Joseph
   (1790–1877)
Smith, Melancton
   (1810–1893)
Stringham, Silas Horton
Thatcher, Henry Knox
Wainwright, Richard
   (1817–1862)
Walke, Henry
Wilkes, Charles
Winslow, John Ancrum
Wise, Henry Augustus
Worden, John Lorimer

Intelligence
Alleged Traitors
Bayard, Nicholas
   Billy
Hiss, Alger *Suppl. 1*

Informants
Bentley, Elizabeth Terrill
Cvetic, Matthew C.
Massing, Hede Tune
Richardson, Ebenezer
Valachi, Joseph

*Intelligence Operatives /
Officials*
Angleton, James Jesus
Birch, John *Suppl. 1*
Colby, William E.
   Suppl. 1
Dulles, Allen Welsh
Gottlieb, Sidney *Suppl. 2*
Hillenkoetter, Roscoe
   Henry
Lansdale, Edward Geary

Roosevelt, Kermit
   (1916–2000) *Suppl. 1*
Wisner, Frank Gardiner

Spies
André, John
Bancroft, Edward
Bentley, Elizabeth Terrill
Boyd, Belle
Browne, John Ross
Burke, Michael
Childs, Morris *Suppl. 2*
Denys de la Ronde,
   Louis
Digges, Thomas
   Attwood
Fuchs, Klaus Emil Julius
Greenhow, Rose O'Neal
Hale, Nathan
Lafayette, James
Massing, Hede Tune
Means, Gaston Bullock
Moody, James
Powers, Francis Gary
Rosenberg, Ethel, and
   Julius Rosenberg
Tallmadge, Benjamin
Van Lew, Elizabeth L.
Velazquez, Loreta Janeta
Wentworth, Paul

Traitors
Arnold, Benedict
Bedaux, Charles Eugene
Church, Benjamin
   (1734–1778?)
Dunbar, Moses
Gillars, Mildred
   Elizabeth

**Military (General U.S.
and Foreign)**
Blockade Runners
Grimes, Absalom
   Carlisle
Hambleton, Thomas
   Edward
Wilkinson, John

*British Army / Navy
Officers*
Abercromby, James
Amherst, Jeffery
André, John
Bouquet, Henry
Braddock, Edward
Bradstreet, John
Burgoyne, John
Butler, Walter
Coffin, Sir Isaac
Coffin, John

Military (General U.S. and Foreign) *(cont.)*
Cornwallis, Charles
Cunningham, William
Fletcher, Benjamin
Forbes, John
(1707–1759)
Gage, Thomas
Hall, Basil
Howe, George Augustus
Howe, William
Hunter, Robert
(1666–1734)
Johnstone, George
Loring, Joshua
(1716–1781)
Loudoun, Earl of
Monckton, Robert
Morris, Roger
Nicholson, Francis
Parker, Peter
(1721–1811)
Pitcairn, John
Robertson, James
(1717–1788)
Ruxton, George
Augustus Frederick
Sharpe, Horatio
Shute, Samuel
Skene, Philip
Tryon, William
Vancouver, George
Warren, Sir Peter
Webb, Daniel
Webb, Thomas

Colonial Militiamen
Barnwell, John
Clay, Green
McMinn, Joseph
Meserve, Nathaniel
Moore, James, Jr.
Pepperrell, Sir William
Standish, Myles
Underhill, John
Waldo, Samuel
Williams, Israel
Winslow, John
Winslow, Josiah
Winthrop, John
(1638–1707)

Congressional Medal of Honor Recipients
Ames, Adelbert
Bell, James Franklin
Butler, Smedley
Darlington
Carney, William Harvey
Cohan, George M.
Doolittle, James Harold

du Pont, Henry
Algernon
Edison, Thomas Alva
Fletcher, Frank Jack
Funston, Frederick
Furness, Frank
Herron, Francis Jay
Hobson, Richmond
Pearson
Lindbergh, Charles
Augustus
MacArthur, Arthur
MacArthur, Douglas
Merriam, Henry Clay
Meyer, Henry
Coddington
Mitchell, William
Lendrum
Moffett, William Adger
Murphy, Audie
Quay, Matthew Stanley
Rickenbacker, Edward
Vernon
Roosevelt, Theodore, Jr.
Shafter, William Rufus
Shoup, David Monroe
Sickles, Daniel Edgar
Stahel, Julius
Tracy, Benjamin
Franklin
Wainwright, Jonathan
Mayhew, IV
Wood, Leonard
York, Alvin Cullum

Filibusters
Bradburn, Juan Davis
Henningsen, Charles
Frederick
Humbert, Jean Joseph
Amable
Ingraham, Prentiss
Long, James
Nolan, Philip
Walker, William

French Army / Navy Officers
Buade, Louis de
D'abbadie, Bernard-
Anselme
Denys de la Ronde,
Louis
Estaing, Comte d'
Fabry De La Bruyère,
André
Grasse, Comte de
Humbert, Jean Joseph
Amable
Lafayette, Marquis de

La Vérendrye, Pierre
Gaultier de
Le Moyne, Jean-Baptiste
Le Moyne, Pierre
Mézières, Athanaze de
Mouet de Langlade,
Charles-Michel
Noailles, Louis Marie
Rochambeau, Comte de
Saint-Ange de Bellerive,
Louis Groston de
Saint-Castin, Baron de

Guerrillas
Fagen, David
Quantrill, William Clarke
Rogers, Robert
Sisson, Jack

Guides / Scouts
Bailey, Ann Hennis
Trotter
Baker, James
Bridger, James
Burnham, Frederick
Russell
California Joe
Carson, Kit
Cody, William Frederick
Crawford, John Wallace
Fink, Mike
Grouard, Frank
Hardin, John
Horn, Tom
Navarre, Pierre
Reynolds, Charles
Alexander
Stilwell, Simpson Everett
Walker, Joseph
Rutherford
Williams, William
Sherley

Inspectors General
Croghan, George
(1791–1849)
Steuben, Friedrich
Wilhelm von

Judge Advocates
Crowder, Enoch Herbert
Tudor, William

Mercenaries
Bouquet, Henry
Boyd, John Parker
Harlan, Josiah
Henningsen, Charles
Frederick
Ingraham, Prentiss
Kalb, Johann

Loring, William Wing
Ward, Frederick
Townsend

Military Chaplains
Colton, Walter
Duffy, Francis Patrick
Eastman, William Reed
Fithian, Philip Vickers
McCabe, Charles
Cardwell
Plummer, Henry Vinton
Trumbull, Henry Clay

Military Deserters
Fagen, David

Military Engineers
Abbot, Henry Larcom
Abert, John James
Babcock, Orville Elias
Bailey, Joseph
Barnard, John Gross
Bernard, Simon
Casey, Thomas Lincoln
Chittenden, Hiram
Martin
Comstock, Cyrus Ballou
Cone, Hutchinson
Ingham
De Brahm, William
Gerard
Derby, George Horatio
Ericsson, John
Foster, John Gray
Franklin, William Buel
Gaillard, David Du Bose
Gardiner, Lion
Gillmore, Quincy Adams
Goethals, George
Washington
Graham, James Duncan
Gridley, Richard
Groves, Leslie Richard,
Jr.
Gunnison, John Williams
Haupt, Herman
Humphreys, Andrew
Atkinson
Isherwood, Benjamin
Franklin
Ives, Joseph Christmas
Jadwin, Edgar
Lander, Frederick West
Lay, John Louis
L'Enfant, Pierre Charles
Long, Stephen Harriman
Loring, Charles Harding
Machin, Thomas
Mackellar, Patrick
Mahan, Dennis Hart

Military (General U.S. and Foreign) *(cont.)*
Mangin, Joseph François
McPherson, James B.
Meade, George Gordon
Meigs, Montgomery Cunningham
Melville, George Wallace
Milligan, Robert Wiley
Montrésor, James Gabriel
Montrésor, John
Mullan, John
Newton, John
Pick, Lewis Andrew
Rains, George Washington
Roberdeau, Isaac
Robert, Henry Martyn
Shreve, Henry Miller
Sibert, William Luther
Swift, Joseph Gardner
Swift, William Henry
Taylor, Harry
Totten, Joseph Gilbert
Tousard, Anne-Louis *Suppl. 2*
Turnbull, William
Warren, Gouverneur Kemble
Webster, Joseph Dana
Weitzel, Godfrey
Wheeler, George Montague
Wright, Horatio Gouverneur

Military Governors
Cortina, Juan Nepomuceno
Mason, Richard Barnes
Riley, Bennet
Stanly, Edward
Washington, John Macrae
Wood, Leonard

Privateers
Boyle, Thomas
Burns, Otway, Jr.
Decatur, Stephen (1752–1808)
Green, Nathan
Halsey, John
Hunley, Horace L. *Suppl. 2*
Manley, John
McNeill, Daniel
Newport, Christopher
Olmsted, Gideon
Ropes, Joseph

Tracy, Nathaniel
Truxtun, Thomas
Waters, Daniel
Whipple, Abraham
Williams, John Foster
Wooster, Charles Whiting

Soldiers
Bent, George
Berkeley, William
Bowie, Jim
Bradburn, Juan Davis
Brown, Thomas
Church, Benjamin (1639–1718)
Cresap, Michael
Dale, Sir Thomas
Edmonds, Sara Emma Evelyn
Hanger, James Edward *Suppl. 2*
Hayes, Ira
Hull, Agrippa
Lovewell, John
Mason, John
Moore, James (c.1650–1706)
Murphy, Audie
Norwood, Henry
Oglethorpe, James Edward
Ordway, John
Putnam, Rufus
Reynolds, Charles Alexander
Robertson, James (1742–1814)
Seeger, Alan
Tennery, Thomas D.
Travis, William Barret
Vallejo, Mariano Guadalupe
Velazquez, Loreta Janeta
Willard, Simon
Williams, George Washington
York, Alvin Cullum
You, Dominique

Spanish Army / Navy Officers
Anza, Juan Bautista de
Bouligny, Dominique
Gayoso de Lemos, Manuel
Martínez, Esteban José
Miró, Esteban Rodríguez
Núñez Cabeza de Vaca, Alvar
Neve, Felipe de

O'Reilly, Alejandro
Ulloa, Antonio de
Vigo, Joseph Maria Francesco
Zéspedes y Velasco, Vicente Manuel de

War Heroes
Allen, William Henry (1784–1813)
Bailey, Ann Hennis Trotter
Carney, William Harvey
Corbin, Margaret Cochran
Ellsworth, Elmer Ephraim
Flora, William
Hale, Nathan
Hart, Nancy
Jones, John Paul
Kelly, Colin Purdie
Lafayette, James
Logan, James (1776?–1812)
Miller, Dorie
Murphy, Audie
Pitcher, Molly
Ross, Betsy
Sampson, Deborah
Shelby, Isaac
Sisson, Jack
Tarrant, Caesar
Taylor, Zachary
Thompson, Robert George
York, Alvin Cullum
Zane, Betty

U.S. Military Services
Air Force Chiefs of Staff
Brown, George Scratchley
Spaatz, Carl Andrew
Twining, Nathan Farragut

Air Force Officers
Boyd, John R. *Suppl. 1*
Clay, Lucius DuBignon, Jr.
Doolittle, James Harold
Eaker, Ira Clarence
Eckert, William Dole
James, Daniel, Jr.
Lansdale, Edward Geary
LeMay, Curtis Emerson
Marchbanks, Vance Hunter, Jr.
Norstad, Lauris

Stratemeyer, George Edward

Army Air Corps / Army Air Forces Officers
Arnold, Henry Harley
Eatherly, Claude Robert
Ferebee, Thomas *Suppl. 1*
Kelly, Colin Purdie
Kenney, George Churchill
Kurtz, Frank *Suppl. 2*
Tinker, Clarence Leonard
Vandenberg, Hoyt Sanford

Army Air Service Officers
Lufbery, Gervais Raoul Victor
Rickenbacker, Edward Vernon
Twining, Nathan Farragut

Army Chiefs of Staff
Craig, Malin
Hines, John Leonard
Johnson, Harold Keith
McNair, Lesley James
Ridgway, Matthew Bunker
Summerall, Charles Pelot
Wheeler, Earle Gilmore

Army Officers (1784–1860)
Adair, John
Ainsworth, Fred Crayton
Armistead, George
Armstrong, John (1717–1795)
Armstrong, John (1755–1816)
Armstrong, John, Jr. (1758–1843)
Beauregard, Pierre Gustave Toutant
Bedinger, George Michael
Benner, Philip
Bissell, Daniel
Bloomfield, Joseph
Bomford, George
Bonneville, Benjamin Louis Eulalie de
Boyd, John Parker
Brown, Jacob Jennings
Campbell, Arthur
Carroll, William

U.S. Military Services
(cont.)
Carson, Kit
Chandler, John
Childs, Thomas
Claghorn, George
Cocke, William
Connor, Patrick Edward
Cooke, Philip St. George
Cooper, Samuel
(1798–1876)
Craik, James
Crawford, William
Crittenden, Thomas
Leonidas
Croghan, George
(1791–1849)
Crook, George
Dearborn, Henry
Dodge, Henry
Doniphan, Alexander
William
Eaton, William
Elliot, James
Emory, William Hemsley
Fannin, James Walker
Fanning, Alexander
Campbell Wilder
Folsom, Nathaniel
Gadsden, James
Gaines, Edmund
Pendleton
Gass, Patrick
Gilpin, William
Graham, James Duncan
Gridley, Richard
Hamtramck, John
Francis
Hardin, John J.
Hardin, Martin D.
Harmar, Josiah
Harney, William Selby
Harrod, James
Hitchcock, Ethan Allen
(1798–1870)
Hopkins, Samuel
(1753–1819)
Howard, Benjamin
Howard, Oliver Otis
Ives, Joseph Christmas
Izard, George
Jackson, Andrew
Jesup, Thomas Sidney
Johnson, James
Johnston, Albert Sidney
Jones, Calvin
Kearny, Philip
Kearny, Stephen Watts
King, William
Lane, Joseph
Lane, Sir Ralph

Leavenworth, Henry
Lee, Robert E.
Lewis, Andrew
Lewis, Meriwether
Logan, Benjamin
Long, Stephen Harriman
Lyon, Nathaniel
Macomb, Alexander
Mansfield, Joseph King
Fenno
Mason, Richard Barnes
McClure, George
Meigs, Montgomery
Cunningham
Miller, James
Miller, John
Mitchell, George
Edward
Mordecai, Alfred
Mullan, John
Parke, Benjamin
Partridge, Alden
Pike, Zebulon
Montgomery
Pillow, Gideon Johnson
Pomeroy, Seth
Porter, Peter Buell
Pryor, Nathaniel Hale
Quitman, John Anthony
Reid, Mayne
Reynolds, Joseph Jones
Riley, Bennet
Ripley, Eleazar
Wheelock
Sargent, Winthrop
Scott, Winfield
Seguín, Juan
Nepomuceno
Shelby, Evan
Smith, Charles Ferguson
Smith, Francis Henney
Smith, James
(1737–1814)
Smith, Persifor Frazer
Smith, Samuel
(1752–1839)
Smith, Thomas Adams
Smyth, Alexander
Stansbury, Howard
Stevens, Isaac Ingalls
Sumner, Edwin Vose
Swift, Joseph Gardner
Swift, William Henry
Taylor, Zachary
Thayer, Sylvanus
Thomas, David
Thompson, Wiley
Turnbull, William
Twiggs, David Emanuel
Van Dorn, Earl

Van Rensselaer,
Solomon
Waddell, Hugh
Washington, John
Macrae
Wayne, Anthony
Wilkinson, James
Williams, Ephraim
Williams, John
(1778–1837)
Winder, William Henry
Worth, William Jenkins
Wright, Joseph Jefferson
Burr

Army Officers (1866–1995)
Abrams, Creighton
Williams, Jr.
Adams, Charles
Allen, Henry Tureman
Almond, Edward
Mallory
Andrews, Frank Maxwell
Atkinson, Henry
Bacon, Robert
Barnitz, Albert Trorillo
Siders
Beightler, Robert S.
Suppl. 1
Bell, James Franklin
Bendire, Charles Emil
Bennett, John Charles
Billings, John Shaw
Blanchfield, Florence
Aby
Bliss, Tasker Howard
Brereton, Lewis Hyde
Buckner, Simon Bolivar,
Jr.
Bullard, Robert Lee
Carlson, Evans Fordyce
Carr, Eugene Asa
Chaffee, Adna Romanza
Chaffee, Adna Romanza,
Jr.
Chennault, Claire Lee
Clark, Mark Wayne
Clay, Lucius DuBignon
Collins, James Lawton
Collins, Joseph Lawton
Crozier, William
Custer, George
Armstrong
Davis, Benjamin Oliver,
Sr.
Devers, Jacob Loucks
Dickman, Joseph
Theodore
Dix, John Adams
Donovan, William
Joseph

Dutton, Clarence
Edward
Eichelberger, Robert
Lawrence
Eisenhower, Dwight
David
Ely, Hanson Edward
Flipper, Henry Ossian
Forwood, William Henry
Foulois, Benjamin
Delahauf
Funston, Frederick
Gaillard, David Du Bose
Gavin, James Maurice
Glassford, Pelham Davis
Goethals, George
Washington
Grant, Frederick Dent
Graves, William Sidney
Greely, Adolphus
Washington
Greene, Francis Vinton
Grierson, Benjamin
Henry
Groves, Leslie Richard,
Jr.
Gruenther, Alfred
Maximilian
Haan, William George
Harbord, James Guthrie
Hazen, William Babcock
Heintzelman, Stuart
Hershey, Lewis Blaine
Hodge, John Reed
Hodges, Courtney Hicks
Hoff, John Van
Rensselaer
Hunter, Frank
O'Driscoll
Irwin, George Le Roy
Jadwin, Edgar
Johnson, Hugh Samuel
Kautz, August Valentine
Kean, Jefferson
Randolph
Kilmer, Joyce
Krueger, Walter
Kuhn, Joseph Ernst
Lear, Ben
Lee, Ulysses Grant
Lee, William Carey
Lemnitzer, Lyman Louis
Lewis, Isaac Newton
Liggett, Hunter
MacArthur, Arthur
MacArthur, Douglas
MacNider, Hanford
March, Peyton Conway
Marshall, George
Catlett, Jr.
Marshall, S. L. A.

U.S. Military Services
(cont.)
McAlexander, Ulysses
  Grant
McAuliffe, Anthony
  Clement
McCaw, Walter Drew
McClure, Robert Alexis
McCoy, Frank Ross
Mearns, Edgar
  Alexander
Menoher, Charles
  Thomas
Merrill, Frank Dow
Merritt, Wesley
Miles, Nelson Appleton
Mitchell, William
  Lendrum
O'Daniel, Iron Mike
O'Neill, Buckey
Otis, George Alexander
Palmer, John McAuley
  (1870–1955)
Patch, Alexander
  McCarrell, Jr.
Patton, George Smith
Pershing, John Joseph
Pick, Lewis Andrew
Reed, Walter
Ridgway, Matthew
  Bunker
Roosevelt, Archibald
  Bulloch
Roosevelt, Theodore, Jr.
Roosma, John Seiba
Schwatka, Frederick
Scott, Hugh Lenox
Shafter, William Rufus
Sheridan, Philip Henry
Sherman, William
  Tecumseh
Short, Walter Campbell
Simpson, William Hood
Smith, Walter Bedell
Snelling, Josiah
Somervell, Brehon Burke
Squier, George Owen
Stilwell, Joseph Warren
Sutherland, Richard
  Kerens
Taylor, Harry
Taylor, Maxwell
  Davenport
Tipton, John
Trobriand, Régis Dénis
  de
Upton, Emory
Wainwright, Jonathan
  Mayhew, IV
Walker, Walton Harris
Weed, Ethel Berenice

Whitney, Courtney
Winship, Blanton
Wood, Leonard
Wood, Robert Elkington
Woodhull, Alfred
  Alexander
Woodward, Joseph
  Janvier
Young, Charles
Young, Samuel Baldwin
  Marks

Army Signal Corps Aviators
Andrews, Frank Maxwell
Arnold, Henry Harley
Foulois, Benjamin
  Delahauf
Gorrell, Edgar Staley
Kenney, George
  Churchill
Schroeder, Rudolph
  William

Chiefs of Naval Operations
Boorda, Jeremy Michael
  Suppl. 2
Burke, Arleigh *Suppl. 2*
Coontz, Robert Edward
Denfield, Louis Emil
  Suppl. 2
Eberle, Edward Walter
Pratt, William Veazie
Sherman, Forrest
  Percival
Standley, William
  Harrison
Stark, Harold Raynsford

Coast Guard Officers
Waesche, Russell
  Randolph

*Joint Chiefs of Staff
Chairmen*
Bradley, Omar Nelson
Brown, George
  Scratchley
Radford, Arthur William
Twining, Nathan
  Farragut
Wheeler, Earle Gilmore

Marine Corps Aviators
Boyington, Gregory
Cunningham, Alfred
  Austell

*Marine Corps
Commandants*
Burrows, William Ward
Heywood, Charles

Vandegrift, Alexander
  Archer

Marine Corps Officers
Butler, Smedley
  Darlington
Carlson, Evans Fordyce
Cunningham, Alfred
  Austell
Geiger, Roy Stanley
Henderson, Archibald
Holcomb, Thomas
Lee, William Andrew
  Suppl. 2
Lejeune, John Archer
McCutcheon, Keith Barr
Megee, Vernon Edgar
Neville, Wendell
  Cushing
Puller, Lewis Burwell
Puller, Lewis Burwell, Jr.
  Suppl. 2
Shoup, David Monroe
Smith, Holland
  McTyeire
Turner, Thomas
  Caldwell
Walt, Lewis William

Naval Aviators
Bennett, Floyd
Brown, Jesse Leroy
Byrd, Richard Evelyn
Rodgers, John
  (1881–1926)
Rosendahl, Charles
  Emery
Towers, John Henry

*Naval Officers (1784–
1860)*
Alden, James
Allen, William Henry
  (1784–1813)
Bainbridge, William
Barron, James
Biddle, James
Blakeley, Johnston
Bridge, Horatio
Buchanan, Franklin
Burrows, William W.
Carter, Samuel
  Powhatan
Champlin, Stephen
Chauncey, Isaac
Collins, Napoleon
Colvocoresses, George
  Musalas
Conner, David
Crane, William
  Montgomery

Craven, Tunis Augustus
  MacDonough
Dale, Richard
Davis, Charles Henry
Decatur, Stephen
  (1752–1808)
Decatur, Stephen
  (1779–1820)
De Kay, George Colman
Downes, John
Drayton, Percival
Du Pont, Samuel
  Francis
Elliott, Jesse Duncan
Erben, Henry
Farragut, David
  Glasgow
Foote, Andrew Hull
Gihon, Albert Leary
Henley, Robert
Howell, John Adams
Hull, Isaac
Jeffers, William
  Nicholson
Jewett, David
Jones, Jacob
Jones, Thomas ap
  Catesby
Jouett, James Edward
Kearny, Lawrence
Lawrence, James
Lee, Samuel Phillips
Levy, Uriah Phillips
Little, George
Luce, Stephen Bleeker
Macdonough, Thomas
Mackenzie, Alexander
  Slidell
Maffitt, John Newland
  (1819–1886)
McArthur, William Pope
McNair, Frederick
  Vallette
McNeill, Daniel
Mervine, William
Moore, Edwin Ward
Morris, Charles
Mullany, James Robert
  Madison
Murray, Alexander
Nelson, William
  (1824–1862)
Nicholson, James
  William Augustus
Nicholson, Samuel
Page, Thomas Jefferson
Patterson, Daniel Todd
Pattison, Thomas
Paulding, Hiram
Perry, Matthew
  Calbraith

U.S. Military Services
(cont.)
Perry, Oliver Hazard
Porter, David
Preble, Edward
Ramsay, Francis
  Munroe
Reid, Samuel Chester
Ridgely, Charles
  Goodwin
Ringgold, Cadwalader
Rodgers, George
  Washington
  (1787–1832)
Rodgers, John
  (1773–1838)
Rodgers, John
  (1812–1882)
Sands, Benjamin
  Franklin
Shaw, John (1773–1823)
Shubrick, John Templer
Shubrick, William
  Branford
Shufeldt, Robert Wilson
Sloat, John Drake
Smith, Joseph
  (1790–1877)
Somers, Richard
Sterett, Andrew
Stevens, Thomas
  Holdup
Stewart, Charles
Stockton, Robert Field
Strain, Isaac G.
Stringham, Silas Horton
Talbot, Silas
Tarbell, Joseph
Thatcher, Henry Knox
Tingey, Thomas
Truxtun, Thomas
Turner, Daniel
Voorhees, Philip
  Falkerson
Waddell, James Iredell
Ward, James Harmon
Warrington, Lewis
Wedemeyer, Albert C.
  Suppl. 2
Wilkes, Charles
Wilkinson, John
Woolsey, Melancthon
  Taylor

Naval Officers (1866–1995)
Andrews, Philip
Benson, William
  Shepherd
Bloch, Claude Charles

Boorda, Jeremy Michael
  Suppl. 2
Bristol, Mark Lambert
Burke, Arleigh *Suppl. 2*
Caperton, William Banks
Chadwick, French Ensor
Cone, Hutchinson
  Ingham
Danenhower, John
  Wilson
Davis, Charles Henry, II
Davison, Gregory
  Caldwell
De Long, George
  Washington
Denfield, Louis Emil
  Suppl. 2
Dewey, George
Doyle, James Henry
Earle, Ralph
Engen, Donald
  Davenport *Suppl. 2*
Evans, Robley
  Dunglison
Fiske, Bradley Allen
Fletcher, Frank Friday
Fletcher, Frank Jack
Frost, Holloway
  Halstead
Furer, Julius Augustus
Gallery, Daniel Vincent
Gleaves, Albert
Gridley, Charles Vernon
Halsey, William
  Frederick, Jr.
Hancock, Joy Bright
Hichborn, Philip
Hobson, Richmond
  Pearson
Hopper, Grace Brewster
  Murray
Ingersoll, Royal Eason
Ingersoll, Royal Rodney
Ingram, Jonas Howard
Jewell, Theodore
  Frelinghuysen
Jones, Hilary Pollard
Joy, Charles Turner
Kempff, Louis
Kimball, William Wirt
Kimmel, Husband
  Edward
King, Ernest Joseph
Kinkaid, Thomas Cassin
Kirk, Alan Goodrich
Knight, Austin Melvin
Knox, Dudley Wright
Lamberton, Benjamin
  Peffer
Laning, Harris
Leahy, William Daniel

Lee, Willis Augustus, Jr.
Mahan, Alfred Thayer
Mayo, Henry Thomas
McCain, John Sidney
  Suppl. 2
McCalla, Bowman
  Hendry
Meade, Richard
  Worsam, III
Melville, George Wallace
Milligan, Robert Wiley
Mitscher, Marc Andrew
Moffett, William Adger
Niblack, Albert Parker
Nimitz, Chester William
Parsons, Edwin Charles
Pillsbury, John Elliott
Pringle, Joel Roberts
  Poinsett
Radford, Arthur William
Reeves, Joseph Mason
Remey, George Collier
Rickover, Hyman
  George
Rodgers, John
  (1881–1926)
Rodman, Hugh
Ronne, Finn
Sampson, William
  Thomas
Schley, Winfield Scott
Selfridge, Thomas
  Oliver, Jr.
Sherman, Frederick Carl
Sicard, Montgomery
Sigsbee, Charles Dwight
Sims, William Sowden
Sperry, Charles Stillman
Spruance, Raymond
  Ames
Stitt, Edward Rhodes
Stockton, Charles
  Herbert
Taussig, Joseph Knefler
Taylor, David Watson
Taylor, Henry Clay
Towers, John Henry
Turner, Richmond Kelly
Wainwright, Richard
  (1849–1926)
Zacharias, Ellis Mark
Zumwalt, Elmo Russell,
  Jr. *Suppl. 2*

Women's Airforce Service Pilots
Cochran, Jacqueline

Women's Army Corps Officers
Hobby, Oveta Culp
  Suppl. 1

MISCELLANEOUS OCCUPATIONS AND REALMS OF RENOWN

Confidantes
Keckley, Elizabeth
  Hobbs
Randolph, Martha
  Jefferson
Summersby, Kay

"Daughter of the Confederacy"
Davis, Varina Anne
  Jefferson

Duelists
Allen, Henry Watkins
Arnold, Benedict
Austin, William
Barron, James
Bennett, James Gordon,
  Jr.
Benton, Thomas Hart
  (1782–1858)
Broderick, David
  Colbert
Brooks, Preston Smith
Brown, Benjamin Gratz
Burk, John Daly
Burr, Aaron
  (1756–1836)
Cadwalader, John
Campbell, George
  Washington
Carey, Mathew
Carroll, William
Claiborne, William
  Charles Coles
Clark, Daniel
  (1766–1813)
Clark, John
Clay, Cassius Marcellus
Clay, Henry
Clingman, Thomas
  Lanier
Conway, Thomas
Crawford, William
  Harris
Daniel, Peter Vivian
Davis, Jefferson
Decatur, Stephen
  (1779–1820)
Denver, James William
Dudley, Benjamin
  Winslow
Flagg, Edmund
Foote, Henry Stuart
Garreau, Armand
Gates, Horatio
Gibbons, Thomas

Gist, William Henry
Goodman, Joseph
  Thompson
Gwinnett, Button
Hamilton, Alexander
  (1757?–1804)
Hamilton, James, Jr.
Hemphill, John
Hope, James Barron
Hughes, Robert William
Jackson, Andrew
Jackson, James
  (1757–1806)
Jackson, John George
Johnston, Albert Sidney
Laurens, Henry
Laurens, John
Lee, Charles
Lee, Samuel Phillips
Leggett, William
Levy, Uriah Phillips
Livingston, Brockholst
Marigny, Bernard
Marshall, Humphrey
Maverick, Samuel
  Augustus
McDuffie, George
McIntosh, Lachlan
Mitchell, David Brydie
Moore, Gabriel
Morgan, John Hunt
Nolte, Vincent Otto
Otero, Miguel Antonio
Pattison, Granville Sharp
Perry, Benjamin Franklin
Perry, Oliver Hazard
Pierce, Benjamin
Pike, Albert
Placide, Alexandre
Pleasants, John
  Hampden
Porter, Andrew
Porter, Peter Buell
Potter, Robert
Pryor, Roger Atkinson
Rowan, John
Slidell, John
Smyth, Alexander
Soulé, Pierre
Stanly, Edward
Tattnall, Josiah
Temple, John
Terry, David Smith
Van Rensselaer,
  Solomon
Waddell, James Iredell
Walker, William
Webb, James Watson
Wigfall, Louis Trezevant
Wilkinson, James
Wise, Henry Alexander

Wise, John Sergeant
Yancey, William
  Lowndes

Eccentrics
Andrews, Stephen Pearl
Barnett, Jackson *Suppl. 2*
Brooke, Abraham
Calamity Jane
Fort, Charles Hoy
Grace, Charles
  Emmanuel
Green, Hetty
Jumel, Eliza Bowen
Norton, Joshua Abraham
  Suppl. 2
Pratt, Daniel
  (1809–1887)
Scott, Walter Edward
Williams, Eleazar

Eponyms
Birch, John *Suppl. 1*

Family Members
Carter, Maybelle
Eisenhower, Edgar
  Newton
Falkner, William Clark
Fitzgerald, John Francis
Hathorne, William
Irving, Peter
Kennedy, John F., Jr.
  Suppl. 1
Kennedy, Kathleen
  Agnes
Kennedy, Rose
  Fitzgerald
Mecom, Jane Franklin

Feudists
Hatfield, William
  Anderson

Folk Heroes
Billy the Kid
Boone, Daniel
Calamity Jane
Carson, Kit
Chapman, John
Cody, William Frederick
Cortez Lira, Gregorio
Crockett, Davy
Fink, Mike
Jones, Casey *Suppl. 2*
McCrea, Jane
Murieta, Joaquín
Pitcher, Molly
Railroad Bill
Whittemore, Samuel

Gamblers
Earp, Wyatt
Hickok, Wild Bill
Minnesota Fats
Morrissey, John
Rothstein, Arnold
Snyder, Jimmy "the
  Greek" *Suppl. 1*

Holocaust Survivors
Bettelheim, Bruno
Friedländer, Paul
Kadar, Jan

Legendary Figures
Brady, Diamond Jim
  Suppl. 1
Brown, Margaret Tobin
  Suppl. 1
Burroughs, Stephen
  Suppl. 2

Lighthouse Keepers
Lewis, Ida

Nobel Prize Winners
Addams, Jane
Alvarez, Luis Walter
Anderson, Carl David
Anfinsen, Christian B.
  Suppl. 2
Balch, Emily Greene
Bardeen, John
Beadle, George Wells
Békésy, Georg von
Bloch, Felix
Bloch, Konrad E.
  Suppl. 2
Brattain, Walter H.
  Suppl. 1
Bridgman, Percy
  Williams
Brodsky, Joseph *Suppl. 1*
Buck, Pearl S.
Bunche, Ralph Johnson
Butler, Nicholas Murray
Calvin, Melvin *Suppl. 1*
Carrel, Alexis
Chandrasekhar,
  Subrahmanyan
Claude, Albert
Compton, Arthur Holly
Cori, Carl Ferdinand,
  and Gerty Theresa
  Radnitz Cori
Cournand, André
  Frédéric
Dam, Carl Peter Henrik
Davisson, Clinton Joseph
Dawes, Charles Gates

Debye, Peter Joseph
  William
Delbrück, Max
Doisy, Edward Adelbert
du Vigneaud, Vincent
Einstein, Albert
Elion, Gertrude *Suppl. 1*
Eliot, T. S.
Enders, John Franklin
Erlanger, Joseph
Faulkner, William
Fermi, Enrico
Feynman, Richard
  Phillips
Flory, Paul John
Fowler, William Alfred
Franck, James
Gasser, Herbert Spencer
Giauque, William
  Francis
Hartline, Haldan Keffer
Hemingway, Ernest
Hench, Philip Showalter
Hess, Victor Franz
Hitchings, George H.
  Suppl. 2
Hofstadter, Robert
Huggins, Charles
  Brenton *Suppl. 2*
Hull, Cordell
Kellogg, Frank Billings
Kendall, Edward Calvin
King, Martin Luther, Jr.
Koopmans, Tjalling
  Charles
Kusch, Polykarp
Kuznets, Simon Smith
Landsteiner, Karl
Langmuir, Irving
Lawrence, Ernest
  Orlando
Lewis, Sinclair
Lewis, W. Arthur
Libby, Willard Frank
Lipmann, Fritz Albert
Loewi, Otto
Luria, Salvador Edward
Mann, Thomas
Marshall, George
  Catlett, Jr.
Mayer, Maria Gertrude
  Goeppert
McClintock, Barbara
McMillan, Edwin
  Mattison
Meyerhof, Otto Fritz
Michelson, Albert
  Abraham
Millikan, Robert
  Andrews
Minot, George Richards

Moore, Stanford
Morgan, Thomas Hunt
Mott, John R.
Muller, Hermann Joseph
Mulliken, Robert
 Sanderson
Murphy, William Parry
 Suppl. 2
Myrdal, Gunnar Karl
Nathans, Daniel *Suppl. 2*
Northrop, John Howard
Ochoa, Severo *Suppl. 2*
O'Neill, Eugene
Onsager, Lars
Pauling, Linus Carl
Pedersen, Charles John
Purcell, Edward M.
 Suppl. 2
Rabi, I. I.
Rainwater, James
Richards, Dickinson
 Woodruff
Richards, Theodore
 William
Rodbell, Martin *Suppl. 2*
Roosevelt, Theodore
Root, Elihu
Rous, Francis Peyton
Schultz, Theodore W.
 Suppl. 1
Schwinger, Julian
 Seymour
Seaborg, Glenn T.
 Suppl. 1
Segrè, Emilio Gino
Shockley, William
 Bradford
Singer, Isaac Bashevis
Stanley, Wendell
 Meredith
Stein, William Howard
Steinbeck, John
Stern, Otto
Stigler, George J.
Sumner, James
 Batcheller
Sutherland, Earl W.
Szent-Györgyi, Albert
Tatum, Edward Lawrie
Theiler, Max
Urey, Harold Clayton
Van Vleck, John
 Hasbrouck
Vickrey, William S.
 Suppl. 1
Waksman, Selman
 Abraham
Whipple, George Hoyt
Wigner, Eugene Paul
Wilson, Woodrow

Woodward, Robert
 Burns

Press Agents
de Lima, Agnes Abinun
Hannagan, Stephen
 Jerome
Malkiel, Theresa Serber
Michelson, Charles
Redpath, James
Revell, Nellie McAleney
Scott, Emmett Jay
Tully, Jim
Ward, Herbert
 Dickinson

Psychics
Cayce, Edgar
Dixon, Jeane *Suppl. 1*
Green, Ely
Urrea, Teresa

Salon Hostesses
Adams, Marian Hooper
Barney, Natalie Clifford
Botta, Anne Charlotte
Fields, Annie Adams
Le Vert, Octavia Celeste
 Walton
Stein, Gertrude
Stettheimer, Florine

Slave Traders
Edwards, Monroe
Hayes, Bully

Socialites
Astor, Caroline
Berkeley, Lady Frances
Bingham, Anne Willing
Blair, Eliza Violet Gist
Bonaparte, Elizabeth
 Patterson
Brown-Potter, Cora
 Urquhart
Burr, Theodosia
Caldwell, Mary
 Gwendolin Byrd
Clay-Clopton, Virginia
 Tunstall
Douglas, Adèle Cutts
Duke, Doris
Eaton, Peggy
Fish, Marian Graves
 Anthon
Fitzgerald, Zelda
Frankland, Lady Agnes
 Surriage
Frazier, Brenda Diana
 Duff
Hone, Philip

Hutton, Barbara
 Woolworth
Kennedy, John F., Jr.
 Suppl. 1
Longworth, Alice Lee
 Roosevelt
Manville, Tommy
Maxwell, Elsa
McCormick, Edith
 Rockefeller
Mesta, Perle
Palmer, Bertha Honoré
Pickens, Lucy Petway
 Holcombe
Post, Marjorie
 Merriweather
Schuyler, Catherine Van
 Rensselaer
Schuyler, Margarita
Sherwood, Mary
 Elizabeth Wilson
Simpson, Wallis
 Warfield
Smith, Margaret Bayard
Sprague, Kate Chase
Stockton, Annis
 Boudinot
Thaw, Harry Kendall
Vanderbilt, Gloria
 Morgan

Travelers
Karzhavin, Fedor
 Vasil'evich
Keyes, Frances
 Parkinson
Pratt, Daniel
 (1809–1887)
Scidmore, Eliza
 Ruhamah
Vincent, Frank
Waln, Robert, Jr.
White, Stewart Edward

Witchcraft Hysteria Victims
Corey, Martha
Hibbins, Ann
Nurse, Rebecca

PERFORMING ARTS

Dance
*Choreographers / Dance
Directors*
Ailey, Alvin
Albertieri, Luigi
Allan, Maud
Astaire, Fred
Balanchine, George
Beatty, Talley
Belcher, Ernest

Bennett, Michael
Berkeley, Busby
Blunden, Jeraldyne
 Suppl. 2
Bolm, Adolph
Borde, Percival
Bradley, Buddy
Camryn, Walter
Champion, Gower
Christensen, Lew
Cole, Jack
Costa, David
Dafora, Asadata
Danielian, Leon *Suppl. 2*
de Mille, Agnes
Dollar, William
Douvillier, Suzanne
Dunn, Robert Ellis
 Suppl. 2
Durang, John
Field, Ron
Fokine, Michel
Fort, Syvilla
Fosse, Bob
Fuller, Loie
Gennaro, Peter *Suppl. 2*
Goh, Choo San *Suppl. 2*
Gould, Norma
Graham, Martha
Griffiths, John
Haney, Carol
Hawkins, Erick
Holm, Hanya
Horton, Lester
Humphrey, Doris
Ito, Michio
Kinch, Myra
Koner, Pauline *Suppl. 2*
Lee, Sammy
Lichine, David
Limón, José
Littlefield, Catherine
Loring, Eugene
Mansfield, Portia
Massine, Léonide
Mitchell, Julian
Moore, Charles *Suppl. 2*
Nikolais, Alwin
Page, Ruth
Pan, Hermes
Placide, Alexandre
Primus, Pearl
Rasch, Albertina
Robbins, Jerome
 Suppl. 1
Shapero, Lillian
Shawn, Ted
Smith, George
 Washington
St. Denis, Ruth
Stone, Bentley

Dance *(cont.)*
Trisler, Joyce
Tudor, Antony
Waring, James
Wayburn, Ned
Weidman, Charles
  Edward, Jr.
Winfield, Hemsley
Youskevitch, Igor
  Suppl. 2
Zane, Arnie

Dance Company Directors
Alexander, Dorothy
Balanchine, George
Beatty, Talley
Berk, Fred
Bolm, Adolph
Chase, Lucia
Christensen, Lew
de Mille, Agnes
Englund, Richard
Fuller, Loie
Galli, Rosina
Graham, Martha
Hawkins, Erick
Horton, Lester
Joffrey, Robert
Kirstein, Lincoln
  Suppl. 1
Limón, José
Littlefield, Catherine
Mansfield, Portia
Nikolais, Alwin
Page, Ruth
Rasch, Albertina
Shawn, Ted
Shook, Karel
Skibine, George
Trisler, Joyce
Waring, James
Williams, E. Virginia
Winfield, Hemsley
Zane, Arnie

Dance Therapists
Boas, Franziska Marie
Chace, Marian
Schoop, Trudi *Suppl. 2*

Dancers
Ailey, Alvin
Albertieri, Luigi
Alexander, Dorothy
Allan, Maud
Astaire, Adele
Astaire, Fred
Baby Laurence
Baker, Josephine
Bales, William
Bates, Peg Leg *Suppl. 2*

Beatty, Talley
Berk, Fred
Berry, Ananias "Nyas"
  Suppl. 2
Berry, James *Suppl. 2*
Berry, Warren *Suppl. 2*
Blunden, Jeraldyne
  Suppl. 2
Bolger, Ray
Bolm, Adolph
Bonfanti, Maria
Borde, Percival
Bradley, Buddy
Brooks, Louise
Bruhn, Erik
Bubbles, John
Cagney, James
Camryn, Walter
Cansino, Angel
Castle, Irene, and
  Vernon Castle
Celeste, Mme.
Celli, Vincenzo
Chalif, Louis Harvey
Champion, Gower
Chase, Lucia
Christensen, Harold
Christensen, Lew
Cole, Jack
Coles, Honi
Costa, David
Craske, Margaret
Crawford, Joan
Dafora, Asadata
Danielian, Leon *Suppl. 2*
Danilova, Alexandra
  Suppl. 1
Davis, Sammy, Jr.
de Mille, Agnes
Dickson, Dorothy
  Suppl. 1
Dollar, William
Dolly Sisters
Douvillier, Suzanne
Draper, Paul *Suppl. 1*
Duncan, Irma
Duncan, Isadora
Duncan, Maria-Theresa
Durang, John
Eglevsky, André
Fernandez, Royes
Fokine, Michel
Fort, Syvilla
Fosse, Bob
Foy, Eddie
Foy, Eddie, Jr.
Fuller, Loie
Galli, Rosina
Gennaro, Peter *Suppl. 2*
Goh, Choo San *Suppl. 2*
Gollner, Nana

Gould, Norma
Grable, Betty
Graham, Martha
Gray, Gilda
Green, Chuck *Suppl. 2*
Groody, Louise
Haley, Jack
Haney, Carol
Harney, William Selby
Hart, Tony
Hawkins, Erick
Hayworth, Rita
Hill, Martha *Suppl. 2*
Hoctor, Harriet
Humphrey, Doris
Ito, Michio
James, Leon, and Albert
  Minns
Jefferson, Eddie
Kaye, Nora
Keeler, Ruby
Kelly, Gene *Suppl. 1*
Kinch, Myra
Kiralfy, Imre, and
  Bolossy Kiralfy
Koner, Pauline *Suppl. 2*
Kosloff, Theodore
Kriza, John
Laing, Hugh
Lake, Margaret Maiki
  Souza Aiu *Suppl. 2*
La Meri
Lane, William Henry
Le Clercq, Tanaquil
  Suppl. 2
Lee, Mary Ann
Lewis, Ted
Lichine, David
Limón, José
Littlefield, Dorothie
Loring, Eugene
Luahine, Iolani
Magallanes, Nicholas
Mansfield, Portia
Maracci, Carmelita
Massine, Léonide
Maywood, Augusta
McCracken, Joan
Miller, Marilyn
Mills, Florence
Miranda, Carmen
Montez, Lola
Moore, Lillian
Morlacchi, Giuseppina
Murphy, George
Murray, Arthur
Murray, Mae
Nelson, Gene *Suppl. 2*
Nissen, Greta
Nugent, Pete
Page, Ruth

Pan, Hermes
Placide, Alexandre
Powell, Eleanor
Ragini Devi
Rand, Sally
Rasch, Albertina
Rector, Eddie
Reed, Janet *Suppl. 2*
Ritchard, Cyril
Robbins, Jerome
  Suppl. 1
Robinson, Bill
Rogers, Ginger
Rooney, Pat
Schollar, Ludmilla
Selden, Elizabeth S.
Shapero, Lillian
Shawn, Ted
Smith, George
  Washington
St. Denis, Ruth
Stone, Bentley
Stratton, Eugene
Tamiris, Helen
Trisler, Joyce
Tucker, Snake Hips
Tudor, Antony
Turnbull, Julia
Vera-Ellen
Verdon, Gwen *Suppl. 1*
Waring, James
Webb, Clifton
Weidman, Charles
  Edward, Jr.
White, George
Whitman, Alice
Williams, Bert, and
  George Walker
Winfield, Hemsley
Youskevitch, Igor
  Suppl. 2
Zane, Arnie

Film
Cinematographers
Bitzer, Billy
Howe, James Wong
Kalmus, Herbert
  Thomas, and Natalie
  Mabelle Dunfee
  Kalmus
Mohr, Hal
Struss, Karl Fischer

Costume Designers
Alexander, John White
Aronson, Boris
Bernstein, Aline Frankau
Head, Edith
Nikolais, Alwin
Orry-Kelly

Film *(cont.)*
Sharaff, Irene

Documentary Filmmakers
Capra, Frank
Chapin, Harry Forster
de Rochemont, Louis
Ditmars, Raymond Lee
Flaherty, Robert Joseph
Ford, John
Hays, Lee Elhardt
Johnson, Osa
Kees, Weldon
Larsen, Roy Edward
Lorentz, Pare
Maysles, David Carl
Mead, Margaret
Van Dyke, Willard

Film Animators
Avery, Tex
Clampett, Bob *Suppl. 2*
Disney, Walt
Fleischer, Max, and
    Dave Fleischer
Freleng, Friz
Hanna, William *Suppl. 2*
Harman, Hugh N.
    Suppl. 2
Hubley, John
Ising, Rudolf C. *Suppl. 2*
Iwerks, Ub *Suppl. 1*
McCay, Winsor Zenic
Natwick, Grim
Pal, George

Motion Picture Censors
Breen, Joseph Ignatius
Hays, Will H.

Motion Picture Editors
Milestone, Lewis

Motion Picture Producers /
Directors
Aldrich, Robert Burgess
Arzner, Dorothy
Avery, Tex
Blackton, James Stuart
Boleslavsky, Richard
    Valentinovich
Borzage, Frank
Boyd, William
Brackett, Charles
    William
Brenon, Herbert
Brisson, Frederick
Browning, Tod
Capra, Frank
Cassavetes, John
Chaplin, Charlie

Coe, Fred Hayden
Cooper, Merian
    Coldwell
Cromwell, John
Cukor, George
Curtiz, Michael
De Mille, Cecil B.
Deren, Maya
de Rochemont, Louis
DeSylva, B. G.
Disney, Walt
Dmytryk, Edward
    Suppl. 2
Dwan, Allan
Eames, Charles
    (1907–1978)
Eames, Ray
Edison, Thomas Alva
Flaherty, Robert Joseph
Ford, Hugh
Ford, John
Foreman, Carl
Fox, William
Foy, Bryan
Frankovich, Mike
    Suppl. 1
Freed, Arthur
Freleng, Friz
Gershenson, Joseph
Goetz, William *Suppl. 1*
Griffith, D. W.
Hanna, William *Suppl. 2*
Harman, Hugh N.
    Suppl. 2
Hart, William Surrey
Hathaway, Henry
Hawks, Howard
Hitchcock, Alfred
Houseman, John
Hubley, John
Hughes, Howard
Huston, John
Ince, Thomas Harper
Ising, Rudolf C. *Suppl. 2*
Johnson, Osa
Kadar, Jan
Kanin, Garson *Suppl. 1*
Keaton, Buster
King, Henry
    (1886–1982)
Kramer, Stanley *Suppl. 2*
Kubrick, Stanley
    Suppl. 1
Lang, Fritz
Lasky, Jesse Louis
LeRoy, Mervyn
Leisen, Mitchell
Levine, Joseph Edward
Leyda, Jay
Lorentz, Pare
Losey, Joseph

Lubitsch, Ernst
Lupino, Ida
Macgowan, Kenneth
Mamoulian, Rouben
Mankiewicz, Joseph Leo
Mayer, Louis Burt
Maysles, David Carl
McCarey, Leo *Suppl. 1*
Micheaux, Oscar
Milestone, Lewis
Minnelli, Vincente
Muse, Clarence E.
Orkin, Ruth
Pakula, Alan J. *Suppl. 2*
Pal, George
Peckinpah, Sam
Porter, Edwin Stanton
Preminger, Otto
Ray, Nicholas
Reis, Irving
Renoir, Jean
Ritt, Martin
Roach, Hal
Robson, Mark
Rossen, Robert
Schary, Dore
Schine, G. David
    Suppl. 1
Schlesinger, Leon
    Suppl. 2
Schwartz, Arthur
Seaton, George
Selig, William Nicholas
Selznick, David O.
Sennett, Mack
Spiegel, Sam
Sternberg, Josef von
Stevens, George
Sturges, Preston
Todd, Michael
Trotti, Lamar
Turner, Florence
Van Dyke, Willard
Veiller, Bayard
Vidor, King
von Stroheim, Erich
Waller, Frederic
Wallis, Hal B.
Walsh, Raoul
Wanger, Walter
Warhol, Andy
Warner, Jack Leonard
Welles, Orson
Wellman, William
    Augustus
Wyler, William
Zanuck, Darryl F.
Zinnemann, Fred
    Suppl. 1
Zukor, Adolph

Screenwriters
Agee, James Rufus
Akins, Zoë
Arnold, Elliott
Balderston, John Lloyd
Beach, Rex
Bessie, Alvah
Bolton, Guy Reginald
Burnett, W. R.
Caspary, Vera
Cassavetes, John
Chayefsky, Paddy
Clavell, James
Cohen, Octavus Roy
Cohn, Alfred A.
Connell, Richard
Connelly, Marc
Crouse, Russel
    McKinley
de Mille, William
    Churchill
Dix, Beulah Marie
Ephron, Phoebe, and
    Henry Ephron
Epstein, Philip G.
Fante, John Thomas
Foreman, Carl
Frings, Ketti
Furthman, Jules G.
Gleason, James
Hawks, Howard
Haycox, Ernest *Suppl. 1*
Hecht, Ben
Herbert, F. Hugh
Howard, Sidney Coe
Hughes, Rupert
Huston, John
Jarrico, Paul *Suppl. 1*
Johnson, Nunnally
Kalmar, Bert
Kanin, Garson *Suppl. 1*
Kober, Arthur
Lardner, Ring, Jr.
    Suppl. 2
Lawson, John Howard
Loos, Anita
MacArthur, Charles
    Gordon
Maltz, Albert
Mankiewicz, Herman
    Jacob
Mankiewicz, Joseph Leo
March, Joseph Moncure
Marion, Frances
McCoy, Horace Stanley
Milestone, Lewis
Muse, Clarence E.
Nichols, Dudley
Osborn, Paul
Parker, Dorothy
Raphaelson, Samson

Film *(cont.)*
Riskin, Robert
Rossen, Robert
Ryskind, Morrie
Sackler, Howard Oliver
Salt, Waldo
Schary, Dore
Seaton, George
Shaw, Irwin
Sherwood, Robert
  Emmet
Sklar, George
Slesinger, Tess
Smith, Thorne
Steinbeck, John
Stewart, Donald Ogden
St. Johns, Adela Rogers
Sturges, Preston
Tarloff, Frank *Suppl. 2*
Taylor, Charles Alonzo
Thurman, Wallace
Totheroh, Dan
Trotti, Lamar
Trumbo, Dalton
West, Jessamyn
Wexley, John
Wheeler, Hugh
  Callingham

Special Effects Experts
O'Brien, Willis Harold
Pal, George

Stage / Screen Actors
Abbott, Bud, and Lou
  Costello
Adams, Edwin
Adams, Maude
Adler, Jacob Pavlovich
Adler, Luther
Adler, Sara
Adler, Stella
Aiken, George L.
Albertson, Jack
Alda, Robert
Aldrich, Louis
Aldridge, Ira Frederick
Allan, Maud
Allen, Gracie
Allen, Viola
Ameche, Don
Anders, Glenn
Anderson, Broncho Billy
Anderson, Eddie
  "Rochester"
Anderson, Mary
  (1859–1940)
Anglin, Margaret
Arbuckle, Roscoe
  "Fatty" *Suppl. 1*
Arden, Eve

Arlen, Richard
Arliss, George
Arnaz, Desi
Arthur, Jean *Suppl. 1*
Arthur, Julia
Astaire, Fred
Astor, Mary
Atwill, Lionel
Autry, Gene *Suppl. 1*
Ayres, Lew *Suppl. 1*
Backus, Charles
Backus, Jim
Bacon, Frank
Bailey, Pearl
Bainter, Fay
Ball, Lucille
Bangs, Frank C.
Bankhead, Tallulah
Bara, Theda
Barnabee, Henry Clay
Barnes, Binnie *Suppl. 1*
Barnes, Charlotte Mary
  Sanford
Barrett, George Horton
Barrett, Lawrence
Barry, Thomas
Barrymore, Ethel
Barrymore, Georgie
  Drew
Barrymore, John
Barrymore, Lionel
Barrymore, Maurice
Barton, James Edward
Bateman, Kate Josephine
Bates, Blanche
Baxter, Anne
Beavers, Louise
Beery, Wallace
Bellamy, Ralph *Suppl. 1*
Belushi, John
Ben-Ami, Jacob
Benchley, Robert
Bennett, Constance
Bennett, Richard
Bennett, Wilda
Berg, Gertrude
Bergman, Ingrid
Bernard, John
Bernardi, Herschel
Bingham, Amelia
Blackmer, Sidney
Blake, William Rufus
Blanc, Mel
Blinn, Holbrook
Blondell, Joan
Blore, Eric *Suppl. 1*
Bogart, Humphrey
Boleslavsky, Richard
  Valentinovich
Bolger, Ray
Bond, Ward

Bonstelle, Jessie
Boone, Richard
Booth, Edwin Thomas
Booth, John Wilkes
Booth, Junius Brutus
Booth, Marian Agnes
Booth, Shirley
Bordoni, Irene
Boucicault, Dion
Bow, Clara
Bowers, Elizabeth
  Crocker
Bowman, Lee
Boyd, William
Boyer, Charles
Brady, Alice
Breese, Edmund
Brennan, Walter Andrew
Broderick, Helen
Brooke, J. Clifford
Brooks, Louise
Brougham, John
Brown, Gilmor
Brown, Joe E.
Brown, Johnny Mack
Brown-Potter, Cora
  Urquhart
Browne, Maurice
Bryant, Dan
Brynner, Yul
Burgess, Neil
Burke, Billie *Suppl. 2*
Burnett, Alfred
Burns, David
Burns, George *Suppl. 1*
Burr, Raymond
Burton, Richard *Suppl. 2*
Burton, William Evans
Bushman, Francis X.
Butterworth, Charles
Byron, Arthur
Byron, Oliver Doud
Cagney, James
Cahill, Marie
Calhern, Louis
Cambridge, Godfrey
Campbell, Mrs. Patrick
Cantor, Eddie
Carroll, Leo G.
Carter, Caroline Louise
  Dudley
Cassavetes, John
Catlett, Walter L.
Chaney, Lon
Chaney, Lon, Jr.
Chanfrau, Frank
Chanfrau, Henrietta
  Baker
Chaplin, Charlie
Chapman, Caroline
Chase, Ilka

Childress, Alvin
Claire, Ina
Clark, Bobby
Clark, Marguerite
Clarke, Corson Walton
Claxton, Kate
Clift, Montgomery
Clifton, Josephine
Cobb, Lee J.
Coburn, Charles
  Douville
Cody, William Frederick
Coghlan, Rose
Cohan, George M.
Colbert, Claudette
  Suppl. 1
Cole, Bob
Collinge, Patricia
Colman, Ronald
Columbo, Russ
Comingore, Dorothy
Compson, Betty
Conklin, Chester
Conried, Heinrich
Conway, Sarah Crocker
Coogan, Jackie
Cooke, George Frederick
Cooper, Gary
Cooper, Thomas
  Abthorpe
Cornell, Katharine
Cotten, Joseph
Cottrelly, Mathilde
Couldock, Charles
  Walter
Courtenay, William
Coward, Noël
Cowl, Jane
Coyne, Joseph *Suppl. 1*
Crabbe, Buster
Crabtree, Lotta
Crane, Bob
Crane, William Henry
Craven, Frank
Crawford, Broderick
Crawford, Joan
Crews, Laura Hope
Cromwell, John
Crosby, Bing
Crosman, Henrietta
  Foster
Cummings, Bob
Cushman, Charlotte
  Saunders
Dangerfield, Rodney
Daly, Arnold
Dandridge, Dorothy
Daniels, Bebe
Da Silva, Howard
Davenport, Benjamin
  Butler

Film *(cont.)*

Davenport, Edward
  Loomis
Davenport, Fanny Lily
  Gypsy
Davidge, William Pleater
Davies, Marion
Davis, Bette
Davis, Sammy, Jr.
Day, Edith
Dean, James
Dean, Julia (1830–1868)
Dean, Julia
  (1878?–1952)
De Angelis, Thomas
  Jefferson
De Bar, Benedict
Deeter, Jasper
del Río, Dolores *Suppl. 2*
Denham, Reginald
Derwent, Clarence
Desmond, Johnny
Devine, Andy
de Wolfe, Elsie
Dickson, Dorothy
  Suppl. 1
Dietrich, Marlene
Digges, Dudley
Ditrichstein, Leo
Dolly Sisters
Donnelly, Dorothy
  Agnes
Doro, Marie
Douglas, Helen Gahagan
Douglas, Melvyn
Douglass, David
Dowling, Eddie
Drake, Frances Ann
  Denny
Drake, Samuel
Dresser, Louise Kerlin
Dressler, Marie
Drew, John (1827–1862)
Drew, John (1853–1927)
Drew, Louisa Lane
Duff, John R.
Duff, Mary Ann Dyke
Dumont, Margaret
Duncan, Augustin
Dunne, Irene
Duse, Eleonora
Eagels, Jeanne
Eddinger, Wallace
Eddy, Nelson
Elliott, Maxine
Elliston, Grace
Eltinge, Julian
Emmet, J. K.
Errol, Leon
Eytinge, Rose
Fairbanks, Douglas

Fairbanks, Douglas, Jr.
  Suppl. 1
Farnum, Dustin Lancy
Farnum, William
Faversham, William
  Alfred
Fawcett, George
Faye, Alice *Suppl. 1*
Ferguson, Elsie
Ferguson, William Jason
Ferrer, José
Fetchit, Stepin
Field, Joseph M.
Field, Kate
Fields, W. C.
Finch, Peter
Fiske, Minnie Maddern
Flynn, Errol
Fonda, Henry
Foran, Dick
Ford, Paul
Forrest, Edwin
Fox, Della May
Fox, George Washington
  Lafayette
Foy, Bryan
Foy, Eddie, Jr.
Franklin, Irene
Friganza, Trixie
Gable, Clark
Gannon, Mary
Garbo, Greta
Gardner, Ava
Garfield, John
Garland, Judy
Garson, Greer *Suppl. 1*
Gaynor, Janet
Geer, Will
Genn, Leo
George, Gladys
George, Grace
Gersten, Berta
Gibson, Hoot
Gilbert, Anne Hartley
Gilbert, John *Suppl. 2*
Gilbert, John Gibbs
Gilbert, Mercedes
Gillette, William Hooker
Gilpin, Charles Sidney
Girardot, Étienne
Gish, Dorothy
Gish, Lillian
Gleason, Jackie
Gleason, James
Goodwin, Nathaniel C.,
  Jr.
Goodwin, Ruby Berkley
Gordon, Ruth
Gordone, Charles
  Suppl. 2
Grable, Betty

Grahame, Gloria
Grant, Cary
Greenstreet, Sidney
Greenwood, Charlotte
  Suppl. 1
Griffith, Corinne
Guinan, Texas
Hackett, James Henry
Hackett, James Keteltas
Hall, Adelaide
Hall, Juanita
Hall, Pauline
Hallam, Lewis, and Mrs.
  Lewis Hallam Douglass
Halliday, John
Hamblin, Thomas
  Sowerby
Hamilton, Margaret
Hampden, Walter
Hards, Ira
Harlow, Jean
Harrigan, Ned
Harrison, Gabriel
Harrison, Richard Berry
Hart, Tony
Hart, William Surrey
Hayden, Sterling
Hayes, Gabby
Hayes, Helen
Hayward, Susan
Hayworth, Rita
Heggie, O. P.
Held, Anna
Henie, Sonja
Henry, John
  (1746–1794)
Hepburn, Audrey
Hepburn, Katharine
Herne, Chrystal
  Katharine
Herne, James A.
Heron, Matilda Agnes
Hewlett, James S.
Hill, George Handel
Hilliard, Robert
Hitchcock, Raymond
Hodge, William Thomas
Hodgkinson, John
Holden, William
Holland, George
Holliday, Judy
Holloway, Stanley
Holman, Libby
Homolka, Oscar
Hood, Darla Jean
Hopper, DeWolf
Hopper, Edna Wallace
Hopper, Hedda
Horton, Edward Everett
  Suppl. 1
Houseman, John

Howard, Leslie
Hudson, Rock
Hull, Henry
Hull, Josephine
Hunter, Glenn
Huntington, Catharine
  Sargent
Huston, Walter
Illington, Margaret
Irwin, May
Ives, Burl
Jaffe, Sam
James, Louis
Janauschek, Fanny
Jefferson, Joseph, I
Jefferson, Joseph, III
Jessel, George
Jolson, Al
Jory, Victor
Julia, Raul *Suppl. 2*
Kalich, Bertha
Kaminska, Ida
Karloff, Boris
Kaye, Danny
Keaton, Buster
Keeler, Ruby
Keenan, Frank
Keene, Laura
Keene, Thomas Wallace
Kelcey, Herbert
Kellerman, Annette
Kelly, Gene *Suppl. 1*
Kelly, Grace
Kelly, Patsy
Kelly, Walter C.
Kemble, Fanny
Kennedy, Charles Rann
Kennedy, John Arthur
Kessler, David
Kiley, Richard *Suppl. 2*
Kovacs, Ernie
Lackaye, Wilton
Ladd, Alan
La Follette, Fola
Lahr, Bert
Lake, Veronica
Lamarr, Hedy *Suppl. 1*
Lamour, Dorothy
  Suppl. 1
Lancaster, Burt
Lanchester, Elsa
Lander, Jean Davenport
Landon, Michael
Langdon, Harry
  Philmore
Lanza, Mario
Laughton, Charles
Laurel, Stan, and Oliver
  Hardy
Lawford, Peter
Lawrence, Florence

Film *(cont.)*

Lawrence, Gertrude
  Suppl. 1
Lee, Bruce
Lee, Canada
Le Gallienne, Eva
Leigh, Vivien
Lemmon, Jack *Suppl. 2*
Lenya, Lotte
Leslie, Amy
Levant, Oscar
Levene, Sam
Lewis, James
Lillie, Beatrice *Suppl. 1*
Lindsay, Howard
Lloyd, Harold
Loftus, Cissie
Logan, C. A.
Logan, Joshua
Logan, Olive
Lombard, Carole
Long, Sylvester Clark
Loos, Anita
Lord, Pauline
Lorre, Peter
Loy, Myrna
Lubitsch, Ernst
Ludlam, Charles
Ludlow, Noah Miller
Lugosi, Bela
Luke, Keye
Lund, Art
Lunt, Alfred, and Lynn
  Fontanne
Lupino, Ida
Lynde, Paul
Lyon, Ben
MacDonald, Jeanette
MacKaye, Steele
MacMurray, Fred
MacRae, Gordon
Maeder, Clara Fisher
Mann, Erika Julia
  Hedwig
Mann, Louis
Manners, John Hartley
Mansfield, Jayne
Mansfield, Richard
Mantell, Robert Bruce
Marble, Danforth
March, Fredric
Marley, John
Marlowe, Julia
Marsh, Mae
Marshall, E. G. *Suppl. 2*
Martin, Dean *Suppl. 2*
Martin, Mary
Marvin, Lee
Marx Brothers
Mason, James
Massey, Raymond

Matthau, Walter
  Suppl. 2
Mature, Victor *Suppl. 1*
Mayo, Frank
Mayo, Margaret
McAvoy, May
McClendon, Rose
McCrea, Joel
McCullough, John
McDaniel, Hattie
McDowall, Roddy
  Suppl. 1
McElheney, Jane
McFarland, George
McQueen, Steve
Meadows, Audrey
  Suppl. 1
Melmoth, Charlotte
Menjou, Adolphe
Menken, Adah Isaacs
Meredith, Burgess
  Suppl. 1
Merkel, Una
Merman, Ethel
Merry, Anne Brunton
Milland, Ray
Miller, Henry
  (1859–1926)
Miller, Marilyn
Mills, Florence
Miranda, Carmen
Mitchell, Maggie
Mitchell, Thomas
Mitchell, William
  (1798–1856)
Mitchum, Robert
  Suppl. 1
Mix, Tom
Modjeska, Helena
Monroe, Marilyn
Montague, Henry James
Montez, Lola
Montgomery, Elizabeth
  Suppl. 1
Montgomery, Robert
Moore, Clayton *Suppl. 2*
Moore, Grace
Moore, Victor Frederick
Moorehead, Agnes
Morris, Clara
Morris, Elizabeth
Mostel, Zero
Mowatt, Anna Cora
Muni, Paul
Murdoch, James Edward
Murphy, Audie
Murphy, George
Murray, Mae
Muse, Clarence E.
Nazimova, Alla
Negri, Pola

Nelson, Ozzie, and
  Harriet Nelson
Nelson, Rick
Newley, Anthony
  Suppl. 1
Nissen, Greta
Niven, David
Nolan, Lloyd Benedict
Normand, Mabel
Nugent, Elliott
Oberon, Merle
O'Brien, Edmond
O'Brien, Pat
O'Connor, Carroll
  Suppl. 2
Oland, Warner *Suppl. 1*
Olcott, Chauncey
O'Neill, James
Owens, John Edmond
Page, Geraldine
Payne, John Howard
Payne, Virginia
Perkins, Anthony
Perry, Antoinette
Pickens, Slim
Pickford, Mary
Pidgeon, Walter
Placide, Henry
Powell, Dick
Powell, Eleanor
Powell, Snelling
Powell, William
Power, Tyrone
  (1869–1931)
Power, Tyrone
  (1914–1958)
Preston, Robert
Price, Vincent
Prinze, Freddie
Questel, Mae *Suppl. 2*
Radner, Gilda *Suppl. 1*
Raft, George
Rains, Claude
Rankin, McKee
Rathbone, Basil
Ray, Aldo *Suppl. 1*
Raye, Martha *Suppl. 1*
Raymond, John T.
Rehan, Ada
Reignolds, Catherine
  Mary
Remick, Lee
Rice, Thomas
  Dartmouth
Ritter, Tex
Ritz Brothers
Robeson, Paul
Robins, Elizabeth
Robinson, Edward G.
Robson, Stuart
Rogers, Ginger

Rogers, Roy *Suppl. 1*
Rogers, Will
Romero, Cesar *Suppl. 2*
Rose, George
Russell, Annie
Russell, Lillian
Russell, Rosalind
Russell, Sol Smith
Ryan, Robert
Sanders, George
Sands, Diana
Schwartz, Maurice
Scott, George C.
  Suppl. 1
Scott, Randolph
Sellers, Peter
Seymour, William
Shaw, Mary
Shean, Al
Shearer, Norma
Sidney, Sylvia *Suppl. 1*
Sills, Milton
Silverheels, Jay
Simpson, Edmund Shaw
Sinatra, Frank *Suppl. 1*
Skelton, Red *Suppl. 1*
Skinner, Cornelia Otis
Skinner, Otis
Smith, C. Aubrey
Smith, Mamie
Smith, Solomon Franklin
Smith, William Henry
  (1806–1872)
Sothern, Edward Askew
Sothern, Edward Hugh
Standing Bear, Luther
Stanwyck, Barbara
Stevens, Emily
Stewart, James *Suppl. 1*
Stoddart, James Henry
Stone, Fred *Suppl. 1*
Stone, John Augustus
Strasberg, Susan
  Suppl. 2
Sullavan, Margaret
  Suppl. 1
Swanson, Gloria
Sweet, Blanche
Tandy, Jessica
Taylor, Laurette
Taylor, Robert
Templeton, Fay
Thomas, Danny
Thomas, William, Jr.
Thompson, Denman
Three Stooges
Toler, Sidney *Suppl. 1*
Tracy, Spencer
Treacher, Arthur
Tucker, Lorenzo
Tucker, Sophie

Film *(cont.)*
Turnbull, Julia
Turner, Florence
Turner, Lana
Turpin, Ben *Suppl. 2*
Valentino, Rudolph
Vallee, Rudy
Vance, Vivian
Vandenhoff, George
Velez, Lupe *Suppl. 1*
Vera-Ellen
Verdon, Gwen *Suppl. 1*
Vincent, Mary Ann
von Stroheim, Erich
Wakely, Jimmy
Wallack, James William
　(1795?–1864)
Wallack, James William
　(1818–1873)
Wallack, Lester
Waller, Emma
Walsh, Blanche
Walsh, Raoul
Walthall, Henry Brazeale
Ward, Geneviève
Warde, Frederick
　Barkham
Warfield, David
Waters, Ethel
Wayne, John
Webb, Clifton
Webb, Jack
Webster, Margaret
Weissmuller, Johnny
Welles, Orson
Wemyss, Francis
　Courtney
West, Mae
Western, Lucille
Westley, Helen
Whiffen, Blanche Galton
White, George
White, Pearl
Wilson, Flip *Suppl. 1*
Wilson, Francis
Windsor, Marie *Suppl. 2*
Winfield, Hemsley
Wolheim, Louis Robert
Wong, Anna May
Wood, Mrs. John
Wood, Natalie
Wood, William Burke
Woolley, Monty
Wynn, Ed
Young, Loretta *Suppl. 2*
Young, Robert *Suppl. 1*
Yurka, Blanche

Music
COMPOSING AND
CONDUCTING
Bandleaders
　Arnaz, Desi

Barnet, Charlie
Basie, Count
Bate, Humphrey
Blakey, Art
Bolden, Buddy
Bradshaw, Tiny
Brown, Les *Suppl. 2*
Brown, Milton
Butterfield, Paul
Calloway, Cab
Cappa, Carlo Alberto
Celestin, Papa
Clarke, Kenny
Cooley, Spade
Crosby, Bob
Cugat, Xavier
Dameron, Tadd
Davis, Miles
Dickerson, Carroll
Donahue, Sam
Dorsey, Jimmy, and
　Tommy Dorsey
Eckstine, Billy
Ellington, Duke
Erwin, Pee Wee
Europe, James Reese
Evans, Gil
Fox, Roy *Suppl. 2*
Garcia, Jerry
Getz, Stan
Gillespie, Dizzy
Gilmore, Patrick
　Sarsfield
Goldkette, Jean *Suppl. 2*
Goldman, Edwin Franko
Goldman, Richard
　Franko *Suppl. 2*
Goodman, Benny
Grafulla, Claudio S.
Gray, Glen
Grimes, Tiny
Guaraldi, Vince
Hackett, Bobby
Haley, Bill
Hawkins, Erskine
　Suppl. 2
Henderson, Fletcher
Henderson, Horace W.
Herman, Woody
Hines, Earl "Fatha"
Hite, Les
Hopkins, Claude
Hughes, Revella Eudosia
Hutton, Ina Ray
Ives, George
James, Harry
Johnson, Francis
　Suppl. 2
Jones, Spike
Jones, Thad
Kaye, Sammy

Kenton, Stan
Kirby, John
Kirk, Andy
Krupa, Gene
Kyser, Kay
Laine, Papa Jack
Lawson, Yank
Lee, Canada
Lee, George E.
Leonard, Harlan
　Quentin
Lewis, Mel
Lewis, Ted
Lombardo, Guy
Lopez, Vincent
Lunceford, Jimmie
Machito
Marable, Fate
Miller, Glenn
Millinder, Lucky
Monroe, Charlie
Monroe, Vaughn Wilton
Montgomery, Little
　Brother
Montgomery, Wes
Morgan, Sam
Moten, Bennie
Murphy, Turk
Napoleon, Phil
Nelson, Ozzie, and
　Harriet Nelson
Noble, Ray *Suppl. 1*
Oliver, King
Ory, Kid
Page, Walter
Parsons, Gram
Perez Prado, Damaso
Peyton, Dave
Piron, Armand John
Pollack, Ben
Poole, Charlie
Prima, Louis
Pryor, Arthur Willard
Puente, Tito *Suppl. 2*
Raeburn, Boyd
Reeves, David Wallis
Rogers, Shorty
Russell, Luis Carl
Scala, Francis
Sissle, Noble
Sousa, John Philip
Spanier, Muggsy
Spivak, Charlie
Stewart, Slam
Sun Ra
Tanner, Gid
Teagarden, Jack
Thornhill, Claude
Trent, Alphonso
Vallee, Rudy
Ventura, Charlie

Vincent, Gene
Waring, Fred
Watters, Lu
Webb, Chick
Weems, Ted
Welk, Lawrence
Whiteman, Paul
Wiggs, Johnny
Wills, Bob
Wooding, Sam

Choral Directors
　Childers, Lulu Vere
　Gilchrist, William
　　Wallace
　Hughes, Revella Eudosia
　Ives, George
　Johnson, Hall
　Lang, Benjamin Johnson
　Luboff, Norman
　Ritter, Frédéric Louis
　Schreiber, Frederick
　　Charles
　Tuckey, William
　Waring, Fred

Composers / Arrangers
　Acuff, Roy
　Adorno, Theodor
　Alexander, Jeff
　Anderson, Leroy
　Antheil, George
　Aronson, Rudolph
　Austin, Lovie
　Ayler, Albert
　Bacon, Ernst
　Bacon, Thomas
　Baermann, Carl
　Barber, Samuel
　Barrymore, Lionel
　Bartók, Béla
　Basie, Count
　Bauer, Marion Eugenie
　Beach, Amy
　Beck, Johann Heinrich
　Bennett, Robert Russell
　Bergmann, Carl
　Bernstein, Leonard
　Best, Denzil
　Billings, William
　Blake, Eubie
　Bledsoe, Jules
　Blind Tom
　Bliss, Philip Paul
　Blitzstein, Marc
　Bloch, Ernest
　Bonds, Margaret
　　Jeannette Allison
　Boulanger, Nadia Juliette
　Bowles, Paul *Suppl. 1*

Music: *Composing and Conducting (cont.)*

Bradbury, William Batchelder
Bristow, George Frederick
Buck, Dudley
Buckner, Milt
Bull, Ole
Cadman, Charles Wakefield
Cage, John
Carpenter, John Alden
Carr, Benjamin
Caryll, Ivan
Chávez, Carlos
Chadwick, George Whitefield
Churchill, Frank Edwin
Clayton, Buck
Cobb, George Linus
Coerne, Louis Adolphe
Cohn, Al
Coltrane, John
Confrey, Zez
Converse, Frederick Shepherd
Cook, Will Marion
Copland, Aaron
Cowell, Henry *Suppl. 1*
Crawford-Seeger, Ruth Porter
Dailey, Albert Preston
Dameron, Tadd
Damrosch, Walter Johannes
Daniels, Mabel Wheeler
De Koven, Reginald
DeRose, Peter *Suppl. 2*
Dett, R. Nathaniel
Dohnányi, Ernst von *Suppl. 2*
Doráti, Antal
Dragon, Carmen Martin
Dresel, Otto
Dreyfus, Max
Druckman, Jacob *Suppl. 2*
Duke, John Woods
Duke, Vernon
Duport, Pierre Landrin
Durham, Eddie
Dvořák, Antonín
Eddy, Hiram Clarence
Ellington, Duke
Ellis, Don
Engel, Carl
Engel, Lehman
Erwin, Pee Wee
Europe, James Reese
Evans, Gil

Fahey, John *Suppl. 2*
Farwell, Arthur
Feldman, Morton *Suppl. 1*
Fischer, Irwin
Fisher, Fred
Fisher, William Arms
Foote, Arthur William
Freeman, Harry Lawrence
Friedhofer, Hugo Wilhelm
Friml, Rudolf
Frizzell, Lefty
Fry, William Henry
Gaillard, Slim
Garner, Erroll
Gershwin, George
Gifford, Gene
Gilbert, Henry Franklin Belknap
Gilchrist, William Wallace
Gillespie, Dizzy
Godowsky, Leopold
Goldman, Edwin Franko
Goldman, Richard Franko *Suppl. 2*
Goldmark, Rubin
Gottschalk, Louis Moreau
Gould, Morton *Suppl. 1*
Grafulla, Claudio S.
Grainger, Percy Aldridge
Griffes, Charles Tomlinson
Grofé, Ferde
Gruenberg, Louis
Gryce, Gigi
Gualdo, John
Guaraldi, Vince
Guthrie, Jack
Hadley, Henry Kimball
Hanson, Howard Harold
Harline, Leigh
Harris, Bill *Suppl. 2*
Harris, Johana
Harris, Little Benny
Harris, Roy
Hayden, Scott
Heinrich, Anthony Philip
Henderson, Horace W.
Herbert, Victor
Herrmann, Bernard
Herrmann, Eduard Emil
Hewitt, James
Hindemith, Paul *Suppl. 1*
Hirsch, Louis A.
Hockett, Charles F. *Suppl. 2*

Hodges, Edward
Holyoke, Samuel Adams
Hommann, Charles
Hope, Elmo
Hopekirk, Helen
Hopkinson, Francis
Horst, Louis
Hoschna, Karl L.
Hovhaness, Alan *Suppl. 2*
Howe, Mary
Humiston, William Henry
Hupfeld, Charles Frederick
Ives, Charles
Janssen, Werner Alexander
Jenkins, Edmund Thornton
Jenkins, Gordon
Johns, Clayton
Johnson, Budd
Johnson, Francis *Suppl. 2*
Johnson, Hall
Johnson, J. J. *Suppl. 1*
Johnson, James P.
Jones, Thad
Joplin, Scott
Kaiser, Alois
Kaper, Bronislaw
Kay, Hershy
Kelley, Edgar Stillman
Kenton, Stan
Kern, Jerome
Kieffer, Aldine Silliman
Kincaid, Bradley
Korngold, Erich Wolfgang
Kreisler, Fritz
Krenek, Ernst *Suppl. 2*
Kroeger, Ernest Richard
Kubik, Gail Thompson
Lamb, Joseph Francis
Lambert, Dave
Lane, Burton *Suppl. 1*
Lang, Margaret Ruthven
Lange, Arthur William
Larson, Jonathan *Suppl. 1*
Lead Belly
Leginska, Ethel
Lennon, John
Levant, Oscar
Lewis, John *Suppl. 2*
Loeffler, Charles Martin
Loesser, Frank
Loewe, Frederick
Louvin, Ira
Luboff, Norman

Luening, Otto *Suppl. 1*
MacDowell, Edward
Mahler, Gustav *Suppl. 1*
Mana-Zucca
Mancini, Henry
Mannes, Leopold Damrosch
Mantovani
Maretzek, Max
Marshall, Arthur
Martin, Roberta
Mason, Daniel Gregory
Mason, William (1829–1908)
Matthews, Artie
Mayfield, Curtis *Suppl. 2*
McGhee, Howard B.
McMichen, Clayton
Mennin, Peter
Mercer, Johnny
Miley, Bubber
Millinder, Lucky
Mingus, Charles
Mitropoulos, Dimitri
Mobley, Hank
Monk, Thelonious
Moore, Douglas
Moore, Mary Carr
Moore, Undine
Morgan, Lee
Morrison, Jim
Morton, Jelly Roll
Moten, Bennie
Mulligan, Gerry *Suppl. 1*
Nabokov, Nicolas
Neuendorff, Adolph Heinrich Anton Magnus
Nevin, Ethelbert Woodbridge
Newman, Alfred
Nichols, Herbie
Nikolais, Alwin
Niles, John Jacob
Noble, Ray *Suppl. 1*
Nordoff, Paul
Nyiregyházi, Ervin
O'Hara, Mary
Oldberg, Arne
Oliver, Sy
Ory, Kid
Paine, John Knowles
Parker, Charlie
Parker, Horatio William
Parker, J. C. D.
Parsons, Albert Ross
Partch, Harry
Pastorius, Jaco
Perez Prado, Damaso
Perry, Julia

Music: *Composing and Conducting (cont.)*
Persichetti, Vincent Ludwig
Peter, John Frederick
Pettiford, Oscar
Piatigorsky, Gregor
Piron, Armand John
Piston, Walter
Porter, Cole
Price, Florence B.
Pryor, Arthur Willard
Pullen, Don
Rachmaninoff, Sergei
Rapee, Erno
Read, Daniel
Redman, Don
Reeves, David Wallis
Reiff, Anthony, Jr.
Reinagle, Alexander
Revel, Harry
Riddle, Nelson
Riegger, Wallingford
Ritter, Frédéric Louis
Robinson, Earl Hawley
Robinson, J. Russel
Rodgers, Richard
Rogers, Clara Kathleen
Rogers, Shorty
Romberg, Sigmund
Rome, Harold
Ronell, Ann *Suppl. 1*
Root, George Frederick
Rosenblatt, Josef
Rózsa, Miklós *Suppl. 1*
Ruggles, Carl
Rushing, Jimmy
Russell, Luis Carl
Russell, Pee Wee
Rutherford, Leonard C.
Sauter, Eddie
Schelling, Ernest Henry
Schillinger, Joseph
Schnabel, Artur
Schoebel, Elmer
Schoenberg, Arnold
Schreiber, Frederick Charles
Schuman, William Howard
Scott, James
Selby, William
Sessions, Roger Huntington
Shavers, Charlie
Shaw, Arnold
Shields, Larry
Slonimsky, Nicolas
Smith, Fiddlin' Arthur
Smith, Julia
Smith, Paul Joseph

Sobolewski, Edward
Sousa, John Philip
Sowerby, Leo *Suppl. 2*
Stanley, Albert Augustus
Steiner, Max R.
Stevens, Leith
Still, William Grant
Stoessel, Albert Frederic
Stothart, Herbert Pope
Stravinsky, Igor
Strayhorn, Billy
Suesse, Dana *Suppl. 1*
Sun Ra
Swan, Timothy
Swift, Kay *Suppl. 1*
Szell, George
Taylor, Deems
Taylor, Rayner
Thayer, Eugene
Thompson, Randall
Thompson, Will Lamartine
Thomson, Virgil
Thornhill, Claude
Timmons, Bobby
Tiomkin, Dimitri
Tobani, Theodore Moses
Travis, Merle
Tuckey, William
Turpin, Tom
Ussachevsky, Vladimir
Varèse, Edgard
Vincent, Gene
Wakely, Jimmy
Walter, Bruno
Warren, Elinor Remick
Warren, Harry
Warren, Richard Henry
Warren, Samuel Prowse
Watters, Lu
Waxman, Franz
Webb, George James
Weill, Kurt
Weston, Paul *Suppl. 1*
White, Clarence Cameron
Whiting, George Elbridge
Wilder, Alec
Williams, Mary Lou
Willson, Meredith
Winding, Kai
Woodbury, Isaac Baker
Yon, Pietro Alessandro
Young, Victor
Zappa, Frank
Zeuner, Charles

Librettists
Atteridge, Harold Richard
Blossom, Henry Martyn, Jr.
Bolton, Guy Reginald
Caldwell, Anne
Cohan, George M.
Cook, Will Marion
Da Ponte, Lorenzo
Donnelly, Dorothy Agnes
Grey, Clifford *Suppl. 1*
Hammerstein, Oscar, II
Harburg, E. Y.
Hobart, George V.
Klein, Charles
Krenek, Ernst *Suppl. 2*
Larson, Jonathan *Suppl. 1*
Lerner, Alan Jay
Ryskind, Morrie
Stein, Gertrude

Lyricists
Adamson, Harold Campbell
Atteridge, Harold Richard
Blossom, Henry Martyn, Jr.
Caesar, Irving *Suppl. 1*
Caldwell, Anne
Chapin, Harry Forster
DeSylva, B. G.
Dietz, Howard
Donaldson, Walter
Dubin, Al
Fields, Dorothy
Fisher, Fred
Freed, Arthur
Gilbert, Ray
Grey, Clifford *Suppl. 1*
Hammerstein, Oscar, II
Harburg, E. Y.
Hart, Lorenz
Jefferson, Eddie
Kahn, Gus
Kalmar, Bert
Larson, Jonathan *Suppl. 1*
Lerner, Alan Jay
Loesser, Frank
Logan, Joshua
Mercer, Johnny
Parish, Mitchell *Suppl. 1*
Payne, John Howard
Porter, Cole
Razaf, Andy
Rowe, James
Swift, Kay *Suppl. 1*

Willson, Meredith
Wodehouse, P. G.
Young, Rida Johnson

Opera Company Managers
Abbott, Emma
Barnabee, Henry Clay
Bing, Rudolf *Suppl. 1*
Gallo, Fortune
Gatti-Casazza, Giulio
Grau, Maurice
Greenwall, Henry
Hammerstein, Oscar
Johnson, Edward (1878–1959)
Kellogg, Clara Louise
Maretzek, Max
Neuendorff, Adolph Heinrich Anton Magnus
Savage, Henry Wilson
Seguin, Anne
Seguin, Arthur
Strakosch, Maurice, and Max Strakosch

Orchestral Conductors
Alexander, Jeff
Barrère, Georges
Beck, Johann Heinrich
Bergmann, Carl
Bernstein, Leonard
Braham, David
Brico, Antonia
Casals, Pablo
Chávez, Carlos
Damrosch, Leopold
Damrosch, Walter Johannes
Dixon, Dean
Dohnányi, Ernst von *Suppl. 2*
Doráti, Antal
Dragon, Carmen Martin
Engel, Lehman
Englander, Ludwig
Europe, James Reese
Fiedler, Arthur
Fischer, Irwin
Freeman, Harry Lawrence
Gabrilowitsch, Ossip
Gericke, Wilhelm
Gershenson, Joseph
Gilchrist, William Wallace
Gould, Morton *Suppl. 1*
Green, Johnny
Hadley, Henry Kimball
Herbert, Victor
Herrmann, Bernard

Music: *Composing and Conducting (cont.)*

Hewitt, James
Hill, Ureli Corelli
Humiston, William Henry
Hupfeld, Charles Frederick
Iturbi, José
Janssen, Werner Alexander
Jenkins, Edmund Thornton
Jenkins, Gordon
Klemperer, Otto
Kostelanetz, André
Koussevitzky, Serge
Leginska, Ethel
Leinsdorf, Erich
Mahler, Gustav *Suppl. 1*
Mancini, Henry
Mannes, David
Mantovani
Maretzek, Max
Menuhin, Yehudi *Suppl. 2*
Mitropoulos, Dimitri
Monteux, Pierre Benjamin
Munch, Charles
Neuendorff, Adolph Heinrich Anton Magnus
Newman, Alfred
Ormandy, Eugene *Suppl. 2*
Parker, Horatio William
Perry, Julia
Petrides, Frédérique
Pryor, Arthur Willard
Rachmaninoff, Sergei
Rapee, Erno
Reiff, Anthony, Jr.
Reiner, Fritz
Rodzinski, Artur
Schelling, Ernest Henry
Schippers, Thomas
Schneider, Alexander
Seidl, Anton
Shaw, Robert *Suppl. 1*
Simmons, Calvin Eugene
Slonimsky, Nicolas
Sobolewski, Edward
Solti, Georg *Suppl. 2*
Stanley, Albert Augustus
Steinberg, William
Steiner, Max R.
Stevens, Leith
Stock, Frederick August
Stoessel, Albert Frederic

Stokowski, Leopold Anthony
Szell, George
Thomas, Theodore
Timm, Henry Christian
Toscanini, Arturo
Varèse, Edgard
Wallenstein, Alfred
Walter, Bruno
Weston, Paul *Suppl. 1*
Willson, Meredith
Young, Victor
Zach, Max

Songwriters

Ace, Johnny
Ager, Milton
Allen, Steve *Suppl. 2*
Arlen, Harold
Armstrong, Harry
Armstrong, Lil
Ball, Ernest R.
Berlin, Irving
Bland, James Allen
Bond, Carrie Jacobs
Bond, Johnny
Bradford, Perry
Braham, David
Brown, Lew
Brown, Nacio Herb
Bryant, Boudleaux
Burleigh, Henry Thacker
Caesar, Irving *Suppl. 1*
Campbell, Lucie E.
Carlisle, Cliff
Carlisle, Una Mae
Carmichael, Hoagy
Carroll, Earl
Carter, A.P., and Sara Carter
Chapin, Harry Forster
Churchill, Frank Edwin
Cohan, George M.
Cole, Bob
Cooke, Sam
Coots, J. Fred
Coward, Noël
Crawford-Seeger, Ruth Porter
Croce, Jim
Crudup, Arthur
Darin, Bobby
Delmore Brothers
Denver, John *Suppl. 1*
Dixon, Dorsey Murdock
Dixon, Howard Briten
Donaldson, Walter
Dorsey, Thomas Andrew
Downey, Morton
Dresser, Paul

Dreyfus, Max
Duke, John Woods
Duke, Vernon
Emmet, J. K.
Emmett, Daniel Decatur
Englander, Ludwig
Estes, Sleepy John
Fain, Sammy
Feather, Leonard
Fisher, William Arms
Flanagan, William
Flatt, Lester
Fogerty, Tom
Foote, Arthur William
Foster, Stephen
Fowler, Wally
Fuller, Jesse
Gaye, Marvin
Gershwin, Ira
Gilbert, Ray
Golden, John
Green, Johnny
Guthrie, Woody
Hall, Wendall *Suppl. 1*
Hanby, Benjamin Russel
Handy, W. C.
Harline, Leigh
Harris, Charles Kassell
Hays, Lee Elhardt
Hays, Will S.
Helms, Bobby *Suppl. 1*
Henderson, Ray
Hendrix, Jimi
Hill, Joe
Hoffman, Al *Suppl. 1*
Holly, Buddy
Howard, Joe
Jenkins, Andrew
Johnson, James P.
Johnson, Robert (1911–1938)
Kagen, Sergius
Kern, Jerome
Key, Francis Scott
Kummer, Clare Rodman Beecher
Lenoir, J. B.
Lipscomb, Mance
Maxwell, Elsa
McDowell, Mississippi Fred
Mercer, Johnny
Miller, Roger
Morgan, George Thomas
Newley, Anthony *Suppl. 1*
Niles, John Jacob
Nyro, Laura *Suppl. 1*
Ochs, Phil
Olcott, Chauncey

Orbison, Roy
Pastor, Tony
Perkins, Carl *Suppl. 1*
Porter, Cole
Ray, Johnnie
Redding, Otis
Robison, Carson Jay
Romberg, Sigmund
Ronell, Ann *Suppl. 1*
Root, George Frederick
Rose, Billy
Rose, Fred
Sankey, Ira David
Schwartz, Arthur
Shannon, Del
Shaw, Oliver
Shindler, Mary Dana
Sigman, Carl *Suppl. 1*
Sissle, Noble
Smith, Chris
Smith, Samuel Francis
Sosenko, Anna *Suppl. 1*
Speaks, Oley
Spivey, Queen Victoria
Stamps, V. O., and Frank Henry Stamps
Styne, Jule
Suesse, Dana *Suppl. 1*
Swift, Kay *Suppl. 1*
Thompson, Will Lamartine
Tormé, Mel *Suppl. 1*
Tubb, Ernest
Van Heusen, Jimmy
Vaughan, James David
Von Tilzer, Harry, and Albert Von Tilzer
Walker, James J.
Waller, Fats
Warren, Harry
White, Anna
Whiting, Richard *Suppl. 1*
Whitley, Keith
Wilder, Alec
Williams, Hank
Work, Henry Clay
Wynette, Tammy *Suppl. 1*
Youmans, Vincent
Zunser, Eliakum

INSTRUMENTAL PERFORMANCE
Accordionists
Abshire, Nathan

Banjoists
Akeman, Stringbean
Ashley, Thomas Clarence

Music: *Instrumental Performance (cont.)*
Boggs, Dock
Bumgarner, Samantha
Cockerham, Fred
Cousin Emmy
Ford, Whitey
Holcomb, Roscoe
Jarrell, Tommy
Johnson, Bill
Kazee, Buell
Macon, Uncle Dave
Poole, Charlie
Reno, Don
Snowden, Elmer

Bassists
Blanton, Jimmy
Braud, Wellman
Callahan, Walter
Chambers, Paul
Foster, Pops
Hall, Al
Holley, Major Quincy, Jr.
Johnson, Bill
Jones, Sam (1924–1981)
Kirby, John
Kirk, Andy
Koussevitzky, Serge
LaFaro, Scott
Lindsay, John
Mingus, Charles
Page, Walter
Pastorius, Jaco
Pettiford, Oscar
Stewart, Slam
Ware, Wilbur

Buglers
Johnson, Francis *Suppl. 2*

Calliope Players
Marable, Fate

Cellists
Bergmann, Carl
Casals, Pablo
Piatigorsky, Gregor
Rose, Leonard
Wallenstein, Alfred

Clarinetists
Andrews, LaVerne
Andrews, Maxene
Bailey, Buster
Baquet, Achille
Baquet, George
Bechet, Sidney
Bigard, Barney

Burbank, Albert
Caceres, Ernie
Dodds, Johnny
Dorsey, Jimmy. *See Dorsey, Jimmy, and Tommy Dorsey*
Fazola, Irving
Goodman, Benny
Hall, Edmond Blainey
Herman, Woody
Jenkins, Edmund Thornton
Lewis, George
Lewis, Ted
Mezzrow, Mezz
Nicholas, Albert
Noone, Jimmie
Parenti, Tony
Picou, Alphonse Floristan
Procope, Russell
Robinson, Prince
Scott, Cecil
Sedric, Gene
Shields, Larry
Simeon, Omer Victor
Teschemacher, Frank *Suppl. 2*
Tio, Lorenzo, Jr.

Comb Players
McKenzie, Red

Cornetists
Armstrong, Louis
Beiderbecke, Bix
Bolden, Buddy
Celestin, Papa
Davison, Wild Bill
Hackett, Bobby
Jones, Thad
Keppard, Freddie
LaRocca, Nick
Mares, Paul Joseph
McPartland, Jimmy
Mitchell, George
Morgan, Sam
Nichols, Red
Oliver, King
Perez, Manuel
Smith, Joe
Spanier, Muggsy
Stewart, Rex
Wiggs, Johnny

Fiddlers
Carson, John
Choates, Harry
Cockerham, Fred
Cooley, Spade
Cooper, Stoney

Jarrell, Tommy
McMichen, Clayton
Robertson, Eck
Rutherford, Leonard C.
Smith, Fiddlin' Arthur
Tanner, Gid
Wills, Bob

Flugelhorn Players
Jones, Thad
Rogers, Shorty
Sullivan, Maxine

Flutists
Barrère, Georges
Farrell, Joe
Gryce, Gigi
Lanier, Sidney
Willson, Meredith

Guitarists
Ashby, Irving C.
Bond, Johnny
Broonzy, Big Bill
Callahan, Walter
Carlisle, Cliff
Carter, Maybelle
Christian, Charlie
Copas, Cowboy
Davis, Gary D.
Delmore Brothers
Drake, Pete
Fahey, John *Suppl. 2*
Fuller, Blind Boy
Garcia, Jerry
Green, Grant
Grimes, Tiny
Harris, Bill *Suppl. 2*
Holly, Buddy
Hooker, Earl
Hopkins, Lightnin'
House, Son
Hurt, Mississippi John
Hutchinson, Frank
Hutto, J. B.
James, Elmore
Jefferson, Blind Lemon
Johnson, Lonnie
Johnson, Robert (1911–1938)
Lucas, Nick *Suppl. 1*
Magic Sam
Maphis, Joe
McAuliffe, Leon
McDowell, Mississippi Fred
McGee, Sam
McTell, Blind Willie
Memphis Minnie
Monroe, Charlie
Montgomery, Wes

Nighthawk, Robert
Osborne, Mary
Patton, Charlie
Puckett, Riley
Robison, Carson Jay
Snow, Hank *Suppl. 2*
Snowden, Elmer
Stanley, Roba
Tampa Red
Taylor, Eddie
Taylor, Hound Dog
Tharpe, Sister Rosetta
Travis, Merle
Vaughan, Stevie Ray
Walker, T-Bone
Waters, Muddy
White, Clarence J.
White, Josh
Whitley, Keith
Williams, Hank

Harmonica Players
Bailey, DeFord
Bate, Humphrey
Butterfield, Paul
Horton, Walter
Jacobs, Little Walter
Terry, Sonny
Wells, Junior *Suppl. 2*
Williamson, Sonny Boy (1914–1948)

Harpsichordists
Kirkpatrick, Ralph Leonard
Landowska, Wanda

Horn Players
Timm, Henry Christian
Watkins, Julius

Keyboard Players
Sun Ra

Oboists
Graupner, Gottlieb
Hoschna, Karl L.

Organists
Biggs, E. Power
Buck, Dudley
Buckner, Milt
Carr, Benjamin
Eddy, Hiram Clarence
Fox, Virgil Keel
Hewitt, Sophia Henriette
Hodges, Edward
Hughes, Revella Eudosia
Humiston, William Henry
Kroeger, Ernest Richard

Music: *Instrumental Performance (cont.)*

Lang, Benjamin Johnson
Paine, John Knowles
Parker, J. C. D.
Pratt, Waldo Selden
Price, Florence B.
Schreiber, Frederick Charles
Selby, William
Sowerby, Leo *Suppl. 2*
Taylor, Rayner
Thayer, Eugene
Warren, Richard Henry
Warren, Samuel Prowse
Whiting, George Elbridge
Yon, Pietro Alessandro
Zeuner, Charles

Percussionists

Barbarin, Paul
Best, Denzil
Blakey, Art
Boas, Franziska Marie
Bradshaw, Tiny
Catlett, Big Sid
Clarke, Kenny
Cole, Cozy
Dodds, Baby
Green, George Hamilton
Greer, Sonny
Heard, J. C.
Jones, Jo
Jones, Philly Joe
Krupa, Gene
Lewis, Mel
Machito
Manne, Shelly
Morehouse, Chauncey
Pollack, Ben
Pozo, Chano
Puente, Tito *Suppl. 2*
Rich, Buddy
Richmond, Dannie
Singleton, Zutty
Tjader, Cal
Tough, Dave
Waits, Freddie
Walcott, Collin
Webb, Chick
Wettling, George Godfrey
Wilson, Dennis Carl
Wilson, Shadow
Woodyard, Sam

Pianists

Albany, Joe
Ammons, Albert C.
Armstrong, Harry

Armstrong, Lil
Bachauer, Gina
Bacon, Ernst
Baermann, Carl
Ball, Ernest R.
Bartók, Béla
Basie, Count
Batchelder, Alice Coleman
Bauer, Harold Victor
Beach, Amy
Blake, Eubie
Blind Tom
Bonds, Margaret Jeannette Allison
Brown, Gertrude Foster
Brown, Roy James
Buckner, Milt
Carlisle, Una Mae
Carreño, Teresa
Charles, Ray
Chotzinoff, Samuel
Clark, Frederic Horace, and Anna Steiniger
Clark, Sonny
Cole, Nat King
Confrey, Zez
Cornish, Nellie Centennial
Cowell, Henry *Suppl. 1*
Dailey, Albert Preston
Davis, Blind John
Diller, Angela
Dohnányi, Ernst von *Suppl. 2*
Dresel, Otto
Duke, John Woods
Ellington, Duke
Evans, Bill
Fay, Amy Muller
Foster, Sidney
Friml, Rudolf
Gabrilowitsch, Ossip
Garland, Red
Garner, Erroll
Gershwin, George
Godowsky, Leopold
Goldkette, Jean *Suppl. 2*
Gottschalk, Louis Moreau
Grainger, Percy Aldridge
Grofé, Ferde
Guaraldi, Vince
Guarnieri, Johnny
Haig, Al
Harney, Benjamin Robertson
Harris, Johana
Henderson, Fletcher
Henderson, Horace W.
Henderson, Ray

Hewitt, Sophia Henriette
Hines, Earl "Fatha"
Hodes, Art
Hofmann, Josef Casimir
Hope, Elmo
Hopekirk, Helen
Hopkins, Claude
Horowitz, Vladimir
Howe, Mary
Hughes, Revella Eudosia
Huneker, James Gibbons
Hungerford, Bruce *Suppl. 1*
Iturbi, José
Johns, Clayton
Johnson, James P.
Johnson, Pete
Kagen, Sergius
Kapell, William *Suppl. 2*
Katchen, Julius
Kelly, Wynton
Kersey, Kenny
Kraus, Lili
Kroeger, Ernest Richard
Lang, Benjamin Johnson
Lee, Julia
Leginska, Ethel
Leinsdorf, Erich
Levant, Oscar
Lewis, John *Suppl. 2*
Lewis, Meade Lux
Liberace
Lopez, Vincent
Mana-Zucca
Mannes, Clara Damrosch
Mannes, Leopold Damrosch
Marable, Fate
Marshall, Arthur
Martin, Roberta
Mason, William (1829–1908)
Mehegan, John Francis
Memphis Slim
Mitropoulos, Dimitri
Monk, Thelonious
Montgomery, Little Brother
Morton, Jelly Roll
Mullican, Moon
Nevin, Ethelbert Woodbridge
Newborn, Phineas, Jr.
Nyiregyházi, Ervin
Oldberg, Arne
Perez Prado, Damaso
Powell, Bud
Price, Florence B.
Professor Longhair
Pullen, Don

Rachmaninoff, Sergei
Rapee, Erno
Ray, Johnnie
Reinagle, Alexander
Rivé-King, Julie
Roberts, Luckey
Robinson, J. Russel
Rose, Fred
Rubinstein, Arthur
Russell, Luis Carl
Samaroff, Olga
Schelling, Ernest Henry
Schnabel, Artur
Schoebel, Elmer
Scott, Hazel Dorothy
Scott, James
Serkin, Rudolf
Sherwood, William Hall
Smith, Julia
Smith, Pine Top
Smith, Willie "the Lion"
Stacy, Jess Alexandria
Strayhorn, Billy
Sykes, Roosevelt
Tatum, Art
Templeton, Alec
Thornhill, Claude
Timm, Henry Christian
Timmons, Bobby
Trent, Alphonso
Tristano, Lennie
Turpin, Tom
Ussachevsky, Vladimir
Waller, Fats
Walter, Bruno
Warren, Elinor Remick
Wellstood, Dick
Weston, Paul *Suppl. 1*
Williams, Mary Lou
Wilson, Teddy
Wooding, Sam
Zeuner, Charles

Saxophonists

Adams, Pepper
Adderley, Cannonball
Ammons, Gene
Andrews, LaVerne
Andrews, Maxene
Ayler, Albert
Bailey, Buster
Bechet, Sidney
Berry, Chu
Bostic, Earl
Byas, Don
Caceres, Ernie
Carney, Harry Howell
Chaloff, Serge
Cohn, Al
Coltrane, John
Criss, Sonny

Music: *Instrumental Performance (cont.)*
Curtis, King
Davis, Eddie "Lockjaw"
Desmond, Paul *Suppl. 1*
Donahue, Sam
Dorsey, Jimmy. *See* Dorsey, Jimmy, and Tommy Dorsey
Ervin, Booker Telleferro, Jr.
Farrell, Joe
Forrest, Jimmy
Freeman, Bud
Getz, Stan
Gonsalves, Paul
Gordon, Dexter Keith
Gray, Glen
Gray, Wardell
Gryce, Gigi
Hardwick, Toby
Hawkins, Coleman
Henderson, Joe *Suppl. 2*
Henry, Ernie *Suppl. 2*
Herman, Woody
Hite, Les
Hodges, Johnny
Johnson, Budd
Jordan, Louis
Leonard, Harlan Quentin
Lyons, Jimmy
Marsala, Joe
Marsh, Warne Marion
Mezzrow, Mezz
Mobley, Hank
Mulligan, Gerry *Suppl. 1*
Musso, Vido William
Nicholas, Albert
Parenti, Tony
Parker, Charlie
Paul, Emmanuel
Pepper, Art
Procope, Russell
Quebec, Ike Abrams
Quinichette, Paul
Raeburn, Boyd
Redman, Don
Robinson, Prince
Rollini, Adrian
Rouse, Charlie
Scott, Cecil
Sedric, Gene
Sims, Zoot
Snowden, Elmer
Stitt, Sonny
Teschemacher, Frank *Suppl. 2*
Trumbauer, Frankie
Turrentine, Stanley William *Suppl. 2*

Ventura, Charlie
Vick, Harold
Washington, Grover, Jr. *Suppl. 2*
Webster, Ben
Young, Lester

Sitar Players
Walcott, Collin

Trombonists
Archey, Jimmy
Bernhardt, Clyde Edric Barron
Brown, Lawrence
Cappa, Carlo Alberto
De Paris, Wilbur
Dickenson, Vic
Dorsey, Tommy. *See* Dorsey, Jimmy, and Tommy Dorsey
Dutrey, Honore
Harris, Bill *Suppl. 2*
Higginbotham, J. C.
Johnson, J. J. *Suppl. 1*
Jones, Thad
Lindsay, John
Miller, Glenn
Mole, Miff
Morton, Benny
Murphy, Turk
Nanton, Joe "Tricky Sam"
Ory, Kid
Pryor, Arthur Willard
Robinson, Jim
Rosolino, Frank
Smith, Jabbo
Sullivan, Maxine
Teagarden, Jack
Weems, Ted
Wells, Dicky
Winding, Kai
Young, Trummy

Trumpeters
Allen, Henry "Red"
Anderson, Cat
Armstrong, Louis
Austin, Johnny
Baker, Chet
Berigan, Bunny
Bonano, Sharkey
Brown, Clifford
Butterfield, Billy
Carey, Mutt
Celestin, Papa
Clayton, Buck
Coleman, Bill
Davis, Miles
De Paris, Sidney

Dorham, Kenny
Edison, Harry "Sweets" *Suppl. 2*
Eldridge, Roy *Suppl. 1*
Elman, Ziggy
Gillespie, Dizzy
Hackett, Bobby
Hawkins, Erskine *Suppl. 2*
James, Harry
Johnson, Bunk
LaRocca, Nick
Lawson, Yank
Mares, Paul Joseph
McGhee, Howard B.
Méndez, Rafael
Miley, Bubber
Mitchell, George
Morgan, Lee
Nance, Ray Willis
Napoleon, Phil
Navarro, Fats
Newton, Frankie
Oliver, Sy
Page, Hot Lips
Pierce, Billie
Pierce, De De
Prima, Louis
Rodney, Red
Rogers, Shorty
Sauter, Eddie
Shavers, Charlie
Shaw, Woody
Smith, Jabbo
Smith, Joe
Spivak, Charlie
Thomas, Joe
Valentine, Kid Thomas
Watters, Lu
Whetsol, Arthur Parker
Williams, Cootie

Vibraharpists
Jackson, Milt *Suppl. 2*
Norvo, Red *Suppl. 1*

Violinists
Beck, Johann Heinrich
Braham, David
Bristow, George Frederick
Brown, Eddy *Suppl. 2*
Bull, Ole
Dickerson, Carroll
Elman, Mischa
Gilbert, Henry Franklin Belknap
Heifetz, Jascha
Herrmann, Eduard Emil
Hill, Ureli Corelli
Hommann, Charles

Hupfeld, Charles Frederick
Johnson, Francis *Suppl. 2*
Kreisler, Fritz
Lang, Margaret Ruthven
Loeffler, Charles Martin
Mannes, David
Menuhin, Yehudi *Suppl. 2*
Milstein, Nathan
Mironovich
Musin, Ovide
Nance, Ray Willis
Petrides, Frédérique
Piron, Armand John
Powell, Maud
Rice, Helen
Schneider, Alexander
Smith, Stuff
Sobolewski, Edward
Spalding, Albert *Suppl. 2*
Stoessel, Albert Frederic
Urso, Camilla
Venuti, Joe
Weems, Ted
White, Clarence Cameron
Zimbalist, Efrem

Violists
Primrose, William
Zach, Max

TYPES OF MUSIC AND SINGING
Blues Musicians / Singers
Allman, Duane
Bradshaw, Tiny
Broonzy, Big Bill
Brown, Roy James
Carter, Bo
Cox, Ida
Crudup, Arthur
Davis, Gary D.
Dorsey, Thomas Andrew
Estes, Sleepy John
Fuller, Blind Boy
Handy, W. C.
Hegamin, Lucille
Hill, Chippie
Hopkins, Lightnin'
Horton, Walter
Howlin' Wolf
Humes, Helen
Hunter, Alberta
Hutto, J. B.
Jacobs, Little Walter
James, Elmore
James, Skip

Music: *Types of Music and Singing (cont.)*
Jefferson, Blind Lemon
Johnson, Lonnie
Johnson, Tommy
Lenoir, J. B.
Lewis, Furry
Lightnin' Slim
Lipscomb, Mance
Martin, Sara
McDowell, Mississippi Fred
McGhee, Brownie *Suppl. 2*
Memphis Minnie
Memphis Slim
Miles, Lizzie
Montgomery, Little Brother
Patton, Charlie
Professor Longhair
Rainey, Ma
Reed, Jimmy
Rushing, Jimmy
Smith, Bessie
Smith, Clara
Smith, Mamie
Smith, Trixie
Spann, Otis
Spivey, Queen Victoria
Tampa Red
Taylor, Eddie
Taylor, Hound Dog
Terry, Sonny
Thornton, Willie Mae
Turner, Big Joe
Wallace, Sippie
Washington, Dinah
Waters, Ethel
Waters, Muddy
Wells, Junior *Suppl. 2*
White, Bukka
White, Josh
Williams, Big Joe
Williams, Clarence
Williams, Joe *Suppl. 2*
Williamson, Sonny Boy (1899?–1965)
Williamson, Sonny Boy (1914–1948)
Wilson, Edith Goodall
Witherspoon, Jimmy *Suppl. 2*
Yancey, Mama

Cantors
Kaiser, Alois
Rosenblatt, Josef
Seixas, Gershom Mendes

Chanters
Luahine, Iolani

Concert Singers
Anderson, Marian
Bledsoe, Jules
Burleigh, Henry Thacker
DeGaetani, Jan
Eddy, Nelson
Grierson, Francis
Hayes, Roland
Hewlett, James S.
Hughes, Revella Eudosia
MacDonald, Jeanette
Robeson, Paul
Swarthout, Gladys
Thomas, John Charles

Country Musicians / Singers
Abshire, Nathan
Acuff, Roy
Akeman, Stringbean
Anglin, Jack
Autry, Gene *Suppl. 1*
Bailey, DeFord
Bate, Humphrey
Bond, Johnny
Brown, Milton
Bryant, Boudleaux
Callahan, Walter
Canova, Judy
Carlisle, Cliff
Carson, John
Carter, Maybelle
Carter, A.P., and Sara Carter
Choates, Harry
Cline, Patsy
Cooper, Stoney
Copas, Cowboy
Cousin Emmy
Dalhart, Vernon
Delmore Brothers
Dexter, Al
Dixon Brothers
Drake, Pete
Duncan, Tommy
Flatt, Lester
Foley, Red
Ford, Tennessee Ernie
Ford, Whitey
Frizzell, Lefty
Greenfield, Elizabeth Taylor *Suppl. 2*
Guthrie, Jack
Hawkins, Hawkshaw
Horton, Johnny
Hutchinson, Frank
Jarrell, Tommy
Kincaid, Bradley
Louvin, Ira

Luman, Bob
Macon, Uncle Dave
Maddox, Rose *Suppl. 1*
Mainer, J. E.
Maphis, Joe
McGee, Sam
McMichen, Clayton
Miller, Roger
Monroe, Bill *Suppl. 1*
Monroe, Charlie
Morgan, George Thomas
Mullican, Moon
Nelson, Rick
O'Day, Molly
Parsons, Gram
Pearl, Minnie *Suppl. 1*
Poole, Charlie
Puckett, Riley
Reeves, Jim
Reno, Don
Ritter, Tex
Robbins, Marty
Robison, Carson Jay
Rodgers, Jimmie
Rogers, Roy *Suppl. 1*
Rose, Fred
Rutherford, Leonard C.
Smith, Fiddlin' Arthur
Snow, Hank *Suppl. 2*
Sovine, Red
Stanley, Carter
Stanley, Roba
Stoneman, Ernest V.
Tanner, Gid
Texas Ruby
Travis, Merle
Tubb, Ernest
Wakely, Jimmy
White, Clarence J.
Whitley, Keith
Wilburn, Virgil Doyle
Williams, Hank
Williams, Tex
Wynette, Tammy *Suppl. 1*

Folk Musicians / Singers
Ashley, Thomas Clarence
Boggs, Dock
Bumgarner, Samantha
Carson, John
Cockerham, Fred
Cotten, Elizabeth
Guthrie, Woody
Hays, Lee Elhardt
Holcomb, Roscoe
Ives, Burl
Jenkins, Andrew
Kazee, Buell

Lead Belly
Ledford, Lily May
Lipscomb, Mance
Lunsford, Bascom Lamar
Niles, John Jacob
Ochs, Phil
Riddle, Almeda
Sandburg, Carl
White, Josh
Wilson, John (1800–1849)

Gospel Musicians / Singers
Bliss, Philip Paul
Burleigh, Henry Thacker
Campbell, Lucie E.
Carter, Dad
Cooke, Sam
Davis, Gary D.
Dorsey, Thomas Andrew
Fowler, Wally
Jackson, Mahalia
Jenkins, Andrew
Johnson, Blind Willie
Martin, Roberta
Oatman, Johnson, Jr.
Rodeheaver, Homer Alvin
Rowe, James
Sankey, Ira David
Stamps, V. O., and Frank Henry Stamps
Tharpe, Sister Rosetta
Vaughan, James David
Wilson, Orlandus *Suppl. 1*

Jazz Musicians
Adams, Pepper
Adderley, Cannonball
Albany, Joe
Allen, Henry "Red"
Ammons, Albert C.
Ammons, Gene
Anderson, Cat
Andrews, LaVerne
Andrews, Maxene
Archey, Jimmy
Armstrong, Lil
Armstrong, Louis
Ashby, Irving C.
Austin, Johnny
Austin, Lovie
Ayler, Albert
Bailey, Buster
Baker, Chet
Baquet, Achille
Barbarin, Paul
Basie, Count

Music: *Types of Music and Singing (cont.)*

Bechet, Sidney
Beiderbecke, Bix
Berigan, Bunny
Bernhardt, Clyde Edric Barron
Berry, Chu
Best, Denzil
Bigard, Barney
Blakey, Art
Blanton, Jimmy
Bolden, Buddy
Bonano, Sharkey
Bostic, Earl
Bradshaw, Tiny
Braud, Wellman
Broonzy, Big Bill
Brown, Clifford
Brown, Lawrence
Brown, Les *Suppl. 2*
Brown, Roy James
Buckner, Milt
Burbank, Albert
Butterfield, Billy
Butterfield, Paul
Byas, Don
Caceres, Ernie
Calloway, Cab
Carey, Mutt
Carlisle, Una Mae
Carmichael, Hoagy
Carney, Harry Howell
Catlett, Big Sid
Celestin, Papa
Chaloff, Serge
Chambers, Paul
Cheatham, Doc *Suppl. 1*
Cherry, Don *Suppl. 2*
Christian, Charlie
Clark, Sonny
Clarke, Kenny
Clayton, Buck
Cohn, Al
Cole, Cozy
Coleman, Bill
Coltrane, John
Condon, Eddie
Criss, Sonny
Crosby, Bob
Curtis, King
Dailey, Albert Preston
Dameron, Tadd
Davis, Blind John
Davis, Eddie "Lockjaw"
Davis, Miles
Davison, Wild Bill
De Paris, Sidney
De Paris, Wilbur
Desmond, Paul *Suppl. 1*
Dickenson, Vic

Dickerson, Carroll
Dodds, Baby
Dodds, Johnny
Dolphy, Eric
Donahue, Sam
Dorham, Kenny
Dorsey, Jimmy, and Tommy Dorsey
Durham, Eddie
Dutrey, Honore
Eckstine, Billy
Edison, Harry "Sweets" *Suppl. 2*
Eldridge, Roy *Suppl. 1*
Ellington, Duke
Ellis, Don
Elman, Ziggy
Ervin, Booker Telleferro, Jr.
Erwin, Pee Wee
Evans, Bill
Evans, Gil
Farrell, Joe
Fazola, Irving
Forrest, Jimmy
Foster, Pops
Freeman, Bud
Fuller, Blind Boy
Gaillard, Slim
Garland, Red
Garner, Erroll
Getz, Stan
Gifford, Gene
Gillespie, Dizzy
Gonsalves, Paul
Goodman, Benny
Gordon, Dexter Keith
Gray, Glen
Gray, Wardell
Green, Grant
Greer, Sonny
Grimes, Tiny
Gryce, Gigi
Guaraldi, Vince
Guarnieri, Johnny
Hackett, Bobby
Haig, Al
Hall, Al
Hall, Edmond Blainey
Hampton, Lionel *Suppl. 2*
Hardwick, Toby
Harris, Little Benny
Hawkins, Coleman
Hawkins, Erskine *Suppl. 2*
Heard, J. C.
Henderson, Fletcher
Henderson, Horace W.
Henderson, Joe *Suppl. 2*
Henry, Ernie *Suppl. 2*

Herman, Woody
Higgins, Billy *Suppl. 2*
Higginbotham, J. C.
Hines, Earl "Fatha"
Hite, Les
Hodes, Art
Hodges, Johnny
Holley, Major Quincy, Jr.
Hooker, Earl
Hope, Elmo
Hopkins, Claude
Hopkins, Lightnin'
Horton, Walter
House, Son
Hughes, Revella Eudosia
Hurt, Mississippi John
Hutto, J. B.
Hutton, Ina Ray
Jackson, Milt *Suppl. 2*
Jacobs, Little Walter
James, Elmore
James, Harry
Jefferson, Blind Lemon
Jefferson, Eddie
Johnson, Bill
Johnson, Budd
Johnson, Bunk
Johnson, J. J. *Suppl. 1*
Johnson, James P.
Johnson, Lonnie
Johnson, Pete
Johnson, Robert (1911–1938)
Jones, Jo
Jones, Philly Joe
Jones, Sam (1924–1981)
Jones, Thad
Jordan, Louis
Kelly, Wynton
Kenton, Stan
Keppard, Freddie
Kersey, Kenny
Kirby, John
Kirk, Andy
Kirk, Rahsaan Roland
Krupa, Gene
LaFaro, Scott
Laine, Papa Jack
Lambert, Dave
LaRocca, Nick
Lawson, Yank
Lee, George E.
Lee, Julia
Leonard, Harlan Quentin
Lewis, George
Lewis, John *Suppl. 2*
Lewis, Meade Lux
Lewis, Mel
Lewis, Ted

Lindsay, John
Lopez, Vincent
Lunceford, Jimmie
Lyons, Jimmy
Machito
Magic Sam
Manne, Shelly
Marable, Fate
Mares, Paul Joseph
Marsala, Joe
Marsh, Warne Marion
McDowell, Mississippi Fred
McGhee, Howard B.
McPartland, Jimmy
McTell, Blind Willie
Mehegan, John Francis
Memphis Minnie
Memphis Slim
Mezzrow, Mezz
Miley, Bubber
Millinder, Lucky
Mingus, Charles
Mitchell, Blue
Mitchell, George
Mobley, Hank
Mole, Miff
Monk, Thelonious
Montgomery, Little Brother
Montgomery, Wes
Morehouse, Chauncey
Morgan, Lee
Morgan, Sam
Morton, Benny
Morton, Jelly Roll
Moten, Bennie
Mulligan, Gerry *Suppl. 1*
Murphy, Turk
Musso, Vido William
Nance, Ray Willis
Nanton, Joe "Tricky Sam"
Napoleon, Phil
Navarro, Fats
Newborn, Phineas, Jr.
Newton, Frankie
Nicholas, Albert
Nichols, Herbie
Nichols, Red
Nighthawk, Robert
Noone, Jimmie
Norvo, Red *Suppl. 1*
Oliver, King
Oliver, Sy
Ory, Kid
Osborne, Mary
Page, Hot Lips
Page, Walter
Parenti, Tony
Parker, Charlie

Music: *Types of Music and Singing (cont.)*

Pastorius, Jaco
Patton, Charlie
Paul, Emmanuel
Pepper, Art
Perez, Manuel
Pettiford, Oscar
Peyton, Dave
Picou, Alphonse Floristan
Pierce, Billie
Pierce, De De
Piron, Armand John
Pollack, Ben
Powell, Bud
Pozo, Chano
Prima, Louis
Procope, Russell
Professor Longhair
Pullen, Don
Quebec, Ike Abrams
Quinichette, Paul
Raeburn, Boyd
Redman, Don
Rich, Buddy
Richmond, Dannie
Roberts, Luckey
Robinson, J. Russel
Robinson, Jim
Robinson, Prince
Rodney, Red
Rogers, Shorty
Rollini, Adrian
Rosolino, Frank
Rouse, Charlie
Russell, Luis Carl
Sauter, Eddie
Schoebel, Elmer
Scott, Cecil
Scott, Hazel Dorothy
Sedric, Gene
Shavers, Charlie
Shaw, Woody
Shields, Larry
Simeon, Omer Victor
Sims, Zoot
Singleton, Zutty
Smith, Jabbo
Smith, Joe
Smith, Pine Top
Smith, Stuff
Smith, Willie "the Lion"
Snowden, Elmer
Spanier, Muggsy
Spivak, Charlie
Stacy, Jess Alexandria
Stewart, Rex
Stewart, Slam
Stitt, Sonny
Sullivan, Maxine

Sun Ra
Sykes, Roosevelt
Tampa Red
Tatum, Art
Taylor, Eddie
Taylor, Hound Dog
Teagarden, Jack
Terry, Sonny
Teschemacher, Frank *Suppl. 2*
Thomas, Joe
Thornhill, Claude
Timmons, Bobby
Tio, Lorenzo, Jr.
Tjader, Cal
Tough, Dave
Trent, Alphonso
Tristano, Lennie
Trumbauer, Frankie
Turrentine, Stanley William *Suppl. 2*
Valentine, Kid Thomas
Vaughan, Stevie Ray
Ventura, Charlie
Venuti, Joe
Vick, Harold
Waits, Freddie
Walcott, Collin
Walker, T-Bone
Waller, Fats
Ware, Wilbur
Washington, Grover, Jr. *Suppl. 2*
Waters, Muddy
Watkins, Julius
Watters, Lu
Webb, Chick
Webster, Ben
Wells, Dicky
Wellstood, Dick
Wettling, George Godfrey
Whetsol, Arthur Parker
White, Josh
Whiteman, Paul
Wiggs, Johnny
Williams, Clarence
Williams, Cootie
Williams, Mary Lou
Williams, Tony *Suppl. 2*
Williamson, Sonny Boy (1914–1948)
Wilson, Shadow
Wilson, Teddy
Winding, Kai
Wooding, Sam
Woodyard, Sam
Young, Lester
Young, Trummy

Jazz Singers
Anderson, Ivie
Armstrong, Lil
Armstrong, Louis
Bailey, Mildred
Baker, Chet
Bernhardt, Clyde Edric Barron
Boswell, Connee
Bradshaw, Tiny
Burbank, Albert
Calloway, Cab
Carlisle, Una Mae
Carmichael, Hoagy
Carter, Betty *Suppl. 1*
Christy, June
Crosby, Bob
Eckstine, Billy
Fitzgerald, Ella *Suppl. 1*
Gonzales, Babs
Hall, Adelaide
Holiday, Billie
Humes, Helen
Lambert, Dave
Lee, George E.
Machito
McDaniel, Hattie
McKenzie, Red
McRae, Carmen
Page, Hot Lips
Prima, Louis
Rainey, Ma
Scott, Hazel Dorothy
Smith, Stuff
Sullivan, Maxine
Vaughan, Sarah
Waller, Fats

Opera Singers
Abbott, Emma
Anderson, Marian
Baccaloni, Salvatore
Barnabee, Henry Clay
Bishop, Anna Rivière
Bispham, David Scull
Bledsoe, Jules
Braslau, Sophie
Brignoli, Pasquilino
Callas, Maria
Caruso, Enrico
Cary, Annie Louise
De Angelis, Thomas Jefferson
De Cisneros, Eleanora
Duncan, Todd *Suppl. 1*
Eddy, Nelson
Farrar, Geraldine
Fox, Della May
Galli-Curci, Amelita
Garden, Mary
Garrison, Mabel

Gluck, Alma
Homer, Louise
Hopper, DeWolf
Jeritza, Maria
Johnson, Edward (1878–1959)
Kellogg, Clara Louise
Kipnis, Alexander
Lanza, Mario
Lawrence, Marjorie
Lehmann, Lotte
Lewis, Mary
London, George
MacDonald, Jeanette
Mason, Edith
Melchior, Lauritz Lebrecht Hommel
Moore, Grace
Nordica, Lillian
Patti, Adelina
Peerce, Jan
Pinza, Ezio
Pons, Lily
Ponselle, Rosa
Raskin, Judith
Rethberg, Elisabeth
Rogers, Clara Kathleen
Sayão, Bidú *Suppl. 1*
Schumann-Heink, Ernestine
Seguin, Anne
Seguin, Arthur
Shirreff, Jane
Steber, Eleanor
Swarthout, Gladys
Talley, Marion
Tetrazzini, Luisa
Thomas, John Charles
Tibbett, Lawrence
Traubel, Helen Francesca
Treigle, Norman *Suppl. 1*
Troyanos, Tatiana *Suppl. 1*
Tucker, Richard
Van Zandt, Marie
Walker, Edyth
Ward, Geneviève
Warren, Leonard
Whiffen, Blanche Galton
Wilson, John (1800–1849)

Popular Singers
Andrews Sisters
Armstrong, Louis
Bailey, Pearl
Baker, Belle
Baker, Josephine
Bayes, Nora

Music: *Types of Music and Singing (cont.)*
Bledsoe, Jules
Bono, Sonny *Suppl. 1*
Bordoni, Irene
Brice, Fanny
Broderick, Helen
Calloway, Cab
Cantor, Eddie
Carpenter, Karen
Chapin, Harry Forster
Cline, Maggie
Cohan, George M.
Cole, Nat King
Columbo, Russ
Como, Perry *Suppl. 2*
Cooke, Sam
Croce, Jim
Crosby, Bing
Crosby, Bob
Crumit, Frank *Suppl. 2*
Daniels, Bebe
Darin, Bobby
Davis, Sammy, Jr.
De Angelis, Thomas
  Jefferson
Denver, John *Suppl. 1*
Desmond, Johnny
Dietrich, Marlene
Downey, Morton
Dragonette, Jessica
Elliot, Cass
Etting, Ruth
Faye, Alice *Suppl. 1*
Fields, Benny
Foran, Dick
Friganza, Trixie
Froman, Jane *Suppl. 2*
Garland, Judy
Groody, Louise
Haley, Jack
Hall, Pauline
Hall, Wendall *Suppl. 1*
Held, Anna
Helms, Bobby *Suppl. 1*
Holman, Libby
Howard, Joe
Hughes, Revella Eudosia
Hutchinson, Abigail
  Jemima *Suppl. 2*
Hutchinson, Adoniram
  Judson Joseph *Suppl. 2*
Hutchinson, Asa
  Burnham *Suppl. 2*
Hutchinson, Jesse, Jr.
  Suppl. 2
Hutchinson, John
  Wallace *Suppl. 2*
Jessel, George
Jolson, Al
Jones, Sissieretta *Suppl. 2*

Kaye, Danny
Lenya, Lotte
Lewis, Ted
Liberace
Lillie, Beatrice *Suppl. 1*
Lucas, Nick *Suppl. 1*
Lund, Art
MacRae, Gordon
Machito
Mana-Zucca
Martin, Dean *Suppl. 2*
McCormack, John
McRae, Carmen
Mercer, Johnny
Mercer, Mabel
Merman, Ethel
Miller, Roger
Mills, Florence
Mills, Irving
Mills, Harry, and
  Herbert Mills
Miranda, Carmen
Monroe, Marilyn
Monroe, Vaughn Wilton
Newley, Anthony
  Suppl. 1
Nyro, Laura *Suppl. 1*
Olcott, Chauncey
Pastor, Tony
Ray, Johnnie
Robbins, Marty
Rooney, Pat
Russell, Lillian
Shore, Dinah
Sinatra, Frank *Suppl. 1*
Smith, Kate
Speaks, Margaret
Stratton, Eugene
Tanguay, Eva
Taylor, Eva
Tormé, Mel *Suppl. 1*
Trapp, Maria von
Tucker, Sophie
Vallee, Rudy
Waller, Fats
Webb, Clifton
Williams, Bert, and
  George Walker
Williams, Joe *Suppl. 2*
Wilson, Edith Goodall

Ragtime Musicians
Blake, Eubie
Cobb, George Linus
Confrey, Zez
Harney, Benjamin
  Robertson
Hayden, Scott
Joplin, Scott
Lamb, Joseph Francis
Marshall, Arthur

Matthews, Artie
Roberts, Luckey
Robinson, J. Russel
Scott, James
Turpin, Tom
Wayburn, Ned

Reggae Musicians
Marley, Bob

*Rhythm and Blues
Musicians / Singers*
Ace, Johnny
Bostic, Earl
Forrest, Jimmy
Gaye, Marvin
Grimes, Tiny
Humes, Helen
Johnson, Lonnie
Jordan, Louis
Redding, Otis
Washington, Dinah
Wilson, Jackie

Rock Musicians / Singers
Allman, Duane
Burnette, Dorsey
Chapin, Harry Forster
Elliot, Cass
Fogerty, Tom
Garcia, Jerry
Haley, Bill
Hendrix, Jimi
Holly, Buddy
Joplin, Janis
Lennon, John
Luman, Bob
Mayfield, Curtis *Suppl. 2*
Morrison, Jim
Nelson, Rick
Orbison, Roy
Parsons, Gram
Perkins, Carl *Suppl. 1*
Presley, Elvis
Shannon, Del
Texas Ruby
Valens, Ritchie *Suppl. 2*
Vincent, Gene
Wilson, Dennis Carl
Zappa, Frank

Soul Musicians / Singers
Charles, Ray
Gaye, Marvin
Vick, Harold
Waits, Freddie
Wilson, Jackie

Western Swing Musicians
Cooley, Spade
McAuliffe, Leon

Wills, Bob

Radio and Television
Disc Jockeys
Freed, Alan
Hay, George Dewey
Whiteman, Paul

Radio / Television Engineers
Alexanderson, Ernst
  Fredrik Werner
Armstrong, Edwin
  Howard
Berkner, Lloyd Viel
de Forest, Lee
Farnsworth, Philo
  Taylor
Fessenden, Reginald
  Aubrey
Goldmark, Peter Carl
Hogan, John Vincent
  Lawless
Kompfner, Rudolf
Storm, Hans Otto
Zworykin, Vladimir
  Kosma

*Radio / Television
Personalities*
Abbott, Bud, and Lou
  Costello
Ace, Goodman
Ace, Jane
Acuff, Roy
Adams, Franklin P.
Allen, Fred
Allen, Gracie
Ameche, Don
Anderson, Eddie
  "Rochester"
Arden, Eve
Arnaz, Desi
Backus, Jim
Ball, Lucille
Bankhead, Tallulah
Belushi, John
Benny, Jack
Berg, Gertrude
Bergen, Edgar
Bono, Sonny *Suppl. 1*
Boone, Richard
Bowes, Major
Brice, Fanny
Burr, Raymond
Canova, Judy
Cantor, Eddie
Cerf, Bennett Alfred
Cole, Nat King
Como, Perry *Suppl. 2*
Conover, Willis Clark,
  Jr. *Suppl. 2*

Radio and Television
(cont.)
Crane, Bob
Crockett, James
  Underwood *Suppl. 1*
Crosby, Bing
Crosby, Bob
Cross, Milton
Crumit, Frank *Suppl. 2*
Daniels, Bebe
Demarest, William Carl
DeRose, Peter *Suppl. 2*
Dragonette, Jessica
Durante, Jimmy
Eddy, Nelson
Fadiman, Clifton
  Suppl. 1
Faye, Alice *Suppl. 1*
Fields, W. C.
Foley, Red
Ford, Paul
Ford, Tennessee Ernie
Foxx, Redd
Garrett, Leroy
Garroway, Dave
Gillars, Mildred
  Elizabeth
Gleason, Jackie
Godfrey, Arthur
Gosden, Freeman
  Suppl. 1
Goulding, Ray
Hall, Wendall *Suppl. 1*
Hopper, Hedda
Jaffe, Sam
Jolson, Al
Jordan, Jim, and Marian
  Jordan
Kaye, Danny
Kieran, John Francis
Kilgallen, Dorothy
Kovacs, Ernie
Kyser, Kay
Landon, Michael
Lemmon, Jack *Suppl. 2*
Levenson, Sam
Lewis, Shari *Suppl. 1*
Liberace
Livingstone, Mary
Lynde, Paul
Lyon, Ben
McBride, Mary
  Margaret
McNeill, Don *Suppl. 1*
Meadows, Audrey
  Suppl. 1
Monroe, Vaughn Wilton
Montgomery, Elizabeth
  Suppl. 1
Nelson, Ozzie, and
  Harriet Nelson

Nelson, Rick
Oboler, Arch
O'Daniel, W. Lee
Parsons, Louella
  Oettinger
Perkins, Marlin
Popeil, Samuel J.
Prinze, Freddie
Radner, Gilda *Suppl. 1*
Ritter, Tex
Rogers, Will
Rothafel, Roxy
Rowan, Dan
Sagan, Carl *Suppl. 1*
Serling, Rod
Shepherd, Jean *Suppl. 1*
Shore, Dinah
Silvers, Phil
Smith, Kate
Sullivan, Ed
Susskind, David
Swayze, John Cameron
  Suppl. 1
Thomas, Danny
Thomas, Lowell
Tubb, Ernest
Vallee, Rudy
Vance, Vivian
Webb, Clifton
Webb, Jack
Welk, Lawrence
Winchell, Walter
Wolfman Jack
Woollcott, Alexander
  Humphreys
Wynn, Ed

*Radio / Television
Producers / Directors*
Arnaz, Desi
Berg, Gertrude
Bowes, Major
Brown, Eddy *Suppl. 2*
Coe, Fred Hayden
Cowan, Louis George
Funt, Allen *Suppl. 1*
Hammond, John Henry,
  Jr.
Levinson, Richard
  Leighton
Levy, David *Suppl. 2*
Liebman, Max
Mack, Nila *Suppl. 1*
Miner, Worthington
Montgomery, Robert
Nelson, Ozzie, and
  Harriet Nelson
Reis, Irving
Roddenberry, Gene
  Suppl. 1

Schaefer, George Louis
  Suppl. 2
Seldes, Gilbert Vivian
Serling, Rod
Spivak, Lawrence
Susskind, David
Thomas, Danny
Todman, William Selden
Waller, Judith Cary
Webb, Jack

Radio / Television Writers
Backus, Jim
Berg, Gertrude
Carrington, Elaine
  Sterne
Chayefsky, Paddy
Levinson, Richard
  Leighton
Levy, David *Suppl. 2*
Moore, Donald
  Wynkoop
Oboler, Arch
Phillips, Irna
Serling, Rod
Teichmann, Howard
  Miles
Todman, William Selden

Religious Broadcasters
Alamo, Susan
Ayer, William Ward
Barnhouse, Donald Grey
Brown, R. R.
Coughlin, Charles
  Edward
Fosdick, Harry Emerson
Fuller, Charles Edward
Jones, Clarence Wesley
Maier, Walter Arthur
Michaux, Lightfoot
  Solomon
Poling, Daniel Alfred
Rader, Paul
Russell, Clayton
Sheen, Fulton John

**Theater and Live
Entertainment**
Acrobats
Placide, Alexandre
Stratton, Eugene

Burlesque Performers
Cantor, Eddie
Clark, Bobby
Cline, Maggie
Fields, Lewis Maurice
Lee, Gypsy Rose
Thompson, Lydia
Weber, Joseph Morris

Circus Performers
Beatty, Clyde Raymond
Clark, Bobby
Kelly, Emmett
Leitzel, Lillian
Pastor, Tony
Rice, Dan
Rogers, Will
Tripp, Charles B.
  Suppl. 2
Wallenda, Helen
  Suppl. 1
Zacchini, Hugo

Clowns
Clark, Bobby
Hart, Tony
Kelly, Emmett
Patkin, Max *Suppl. 1*
Rice, Dan

Comedians
Abbott, Bud, and Lou
  Costello
Akeman, Stringbean
Allen, Fred
Allen, Gracie
Allen, Steve *Suppl. 2*
Arbuckle, Roscoe
  "Fatty" *Suppl. 1*
Backus, Jim
Bayes, Nora
Belushi, John
Benny, Jack
Bolger, Ray
Brice, Fanny
Brown, Joe E.
Bruce, Lenny
Burns, George *Suppl. 1*
Cambridge, Godfrey
Clark, Bobby
Cousin Emmy
Dangerfield, Rodney
Dooley, Ray
Durante, Jimmy
Errol, Leon
Fay, Frank
Fields, W. C.
Ford, Whitey
Foxx, Redd
Foy, Eddie
Gallagher, Edward
  Francis
Gleason, Jackie
Goodwin, Nathaniel C.,
  Jr.
Goulding, Ray
Haley, Jack
Hewlett, James S.
Holtz, Lou
Howard, Willie

Theater and Live Entertainment (cont.)
Irwin, May
Jessel, George
Kaye, Danny
Kelly, Walter C.
Kovacs, Ernie
Lahr, Bert
Langdon, Harry Philmore
Laurel, Stan, and Oliver Hardy
Levenson, Sam
Lillie, Beatrice *Suppl. 1*
Lloyd, Harold
Lynde, Paul
Mabley, Moms
Marx Brothers
Normand, Mabel
Olsen, Ole, and Chic Johnson
Pearl, Minnie *Suppl. 1*
Picon, Molly
Prinze, Freddie
Radner, Gilda *Suppl. 1*
Raye, Martha *Suppl. 1*
Raymond, John T.
Ritchard, Cyril
Ritz Brothers
Rowan, Dan
Sellers, Peter
Shean, Al
Silvers, Phil
Skelton, Red *Suppl. 1*
Smith, Stuff
Templeton, Fay
Three Stooges
Wilson, Flip *Suppl. 1*
Wynn, Ed
Youngman, Henny *Suppl. 1*

Costume Designers
Alexander, John White
Aronson, Boris
Bernstein, Aline Frankau
Head, Edith
Nikolais, Alwin
Orry-Kelly
Sharaff, Irene

Cowboys
Cortez Lira, Gregorio
Dart, Isom
Doolin, William
Glass, Charlie
James, Will Roderick
Love, Nat
Mix, Tom
Nigger Add
Rogers, Will

Russell, Charles Marion
Siringo, Charles Angelo

Daredevils
Houdini, Harry
Patch, Samuel
Zacchini, Hugo

Impersonators
Dooley, Ray
Eltinge, Julian
Hart, Tony
Janis, Elsie
Loftus, Cissie

Magicians
Blackstone, Harry
Blackstone, Harry, Jr. *Suppl. 1*
Davenport, Ira Erastus, and William Henry Harrison Davenport
Goldin, Horace
Houdini, Harry
Kellar, Harry
Thurston, Howard

Midgets
Tom Thumb

Mimes
Enters, Angna
Fox, George Washington Lafayette
Jackson, Joe
Schoop, Trudi *Suppl. 2*

Minstrel Show Performers
Backus, Charles
Bland, James Allen
Bryant, Dan
Christy, Edwin Pearce
Christy, George N. Harrington
Dixon, George Washington
Dockstader, Lew
Emmett, Daniel Decatur
Hart, Tony
Haverly, Jack H.
Stratton, Eugene

Monologuists
Draper, Ruth
Howe, Helen
Webb, Mary *Suppl. 2*

Orators
Ames, Fisher
Cockran, William Bourke

Curtis, George William
Darrow, Clarence
Depew, Chauncey Mitchell
Dickinson, Anna Elizabeth
Diggs, Annie LePorte
Everett, Edward
Gough, John Bartholomew
Grady, Henry Woodfin
Henry, Patrick
Hiawatha
Ingersoll, Robert Green
Jasper, John
Lease, Mary Elizabeth Clyens
Maffitt, John Newland (1794–1850)
Mazakutemani, Paul
Niebuhr, Reinhold
O'Hare, Kate Richards
Ostenaco
Phillips, Wendell
Randolph, John (1773–1833)
Remond, Charles Lenox
Simmons, Roscoe Conkling Murray
Simpson, Matthew
Smith, Gerald Lyman Kenneth
Taylor, Edward Thompson
Teedyuskung
Watson, Thomas Edward
Willett, Herbert Lockwood

Puppeteers
Baird, Bil *Suppl. 1*
Henson, Jim
Lewis, Shari *Suppl. 1*
Tillstrom, Burr

Rodeo Performers
Pickens, Slim
Pickett, Bill

Sharpshooters
Oakley, Annie

Siamese Twins
Chang and Eng

Stage / Screen Actors
Abbott, Bud, and Lou Costello
Adams, Edwin
Adams, Maude

Adler, Jacob Pavlovich
Adler, Luther
Adler, Sara
Adler, Stella
Aiken, George L.
Albertson, Jack
Alda, Robert
Aldrich, Louis
Aldridge, Ira Frederick
Allan, Maud
Allen, Gracie
Allen, Viola
Ameche, Don
Anders, Glenn
Anderson, Broncho Billy
Anderson, Eddie "Rochester"
Anderson, Mary (1859–1940)
Anglin, Margaret
Arbuckle, Roscoe "Fatty" *Suppl. 1*
Arden, Eve
Arlen, Richard
Arliss, George
Arnaz, Desi
Arthur, Jean *Suppl. 1*
Arthur, Julia
Astaire, Fred
Astor, Mary
Atwill, Lionel
Autry, Gene *Suppl. 1*
Ayres, Lew *Suppl. 1*
Backus, Charles
Backus, Jim
Bacon, Frank
Bailey, Pearl
Bainter, Fay
Ball, Lucille
Bangs, Frank C.
Bankhead, Tallulah
Bara, Theda
Barnabee, Henry Clay
Barnes, Binnie *Suppl. 1*
Barnes, Charlotte Mary Sanford
Barrett, George Horton
Barrett, Lawrence
Barry, Thomas
Barrymore, Ethel
Barrymore, Georgie Drew
Barrymore, John
Barrymore, Lionel
Barrymore, Maurice
Barton, James Edward
Bateman, Kate Josephine
Bates, Blanche
Baxter, Anne
Beavers, Louise
Beery, Wallace

**Theater and Live
Entertainment** *(cont.)*
Bellamy, Ralph *Suppl. 1*
Belushi, John
Ben-Ami, Jacob
Benchley, Robert
Bennett, Constance
Bennett, Richard
Bennett, Wilda
Berg, Gertrude
Bergman, Ingrid
Bernard, John
Bernardi, Herschel
Bingham, Amelia
Blackmer, Sidney
Blake, William Rufus
Blanc, Mel
Blinn, Holbrook
Blondell, Joan
Blore, Eric *Suppl. 1*
Bogart, Humphrey
Boleslavsky, Richard
  Valentinovich
Bolger, Ray
Bond, Ward
Bonstelle, Jessie
Boone, Richard
Booth, Edwin Thomas
Booth, John Wilkes
Booth, Junius Brutus
Booth, Marian Agnes
Booth, Shirley
Bordoni, Irene
Boucicault, Dion
Bow, Clara
Bowers, Elizabeth
  Crocker
Bowman, Lee
Boyd, William
Boyer, Charles
Brady, Alice
Breese, Edmund
Brennan, Walter Andrew
Broderick, Helen
Brooke, J. Clifford
Brooks, Louise
Brougham, John
Brown, Gilmor
Brown, Joe E.
Brown, Johnny Mack
Brown-Potter, Cora
  Urquhart
Browne, Maurice
Bryant, Dan
Brynner, Yul
Burgess, Neil
Burke, Billie *Suppl. 2*
Burnett, Alfred
Burns, David
Burns, George *Suppl. 1*
Burr, Raymond

Burton, Richard *Suppl. 2*
Burton, William Evans
Bushman, Francis X.
Butterworth, Charles
Byron, Arthur
Byron, Oliver Doud
Cagney, James
Cahill, Marie
Calhern, Louis
Cambridge, Godfrey
Campbell, Mrs. Patrick
Cantor, Eddie
Carroll, Leo G.
Carter, Caroline Louise
  Dudley
Cassavetes, John
Catlett, Walter L.
Chaney, Lon
Chaney, Lon, Jr.
Chanfrau, Frank
Chanfrau, Henrietta
  Baker
Chaplin, Charlie
Chapman, Caroline
Chase, Ilka
Childress, Alvin
Claire, Ina
Clark, Bobby
Clark, Marguerite
Clarke, Corson Walton
Claxton, Kate
Clift, Montgomery
Clifton, Josephine
Cobb, Lee J.
Coburn, Charles
  Douville
Cody, William Frederick
Coghlan, Rose
Cohan, George M.
Colbert, Claudette
  Suppl. 1
Cole, Bob
Collinge, Patricia
Colman, Ronald
Columbo, Russ
Comingore, Dorothy
Compson, Betty
Conklin, Chester
Conried, Heinrich
Conway, Sarah Crocker
Coogan, Jackie
Cooke, George Frederick
Cooper, Gary
Cooper, Thomas
  Abthorpe
Cornell, Katharine
Cotten, Joseph
Cottrelly, Mathilde
Couldock, Charles
  Walter
Courtenay, William

Coward, Noël
Cowl, Jane
Coyne, Joseph *Suppl. 1*
Crabbe, Buster
Crabtree, Lotta
Crane, Bob
Crane, William Henry
Craven, Frank
Crawford, Broderick
Crawford, Joan
Crews, Laura Hope
Cromwell, John
Crosby, Bing
Crosman, Henrietta
  Foster
Cummings, Bob
Cushman, Charlotte
  Saunders
Daly, Arnold
Dandridge, Dorothy
Dangerfield, Rodney
Daniels, Bebe
Da Silva, Howard
Davenport, Benjamin
  Butler
Davenport, Edward
  Loomis
Davenport, Fanny Lily
  Gypsy
Davidge, William Pleater
Davies, Marion
Davis, Bette
Davis, Sammy, Jr.
Day, Edith
Dean, James
Dean, Julia (1830–1868)
Dean, Julia
  (1878?–1952)
De Angelis, Thomas
  Jefferson
De Bar, Benedict
Deeter, Jasper
del Río, Dolores *Suppl. 2*
Denham, Reginald
Derwent, Clarence
Desmond, Johnny
Devine, Andy
de Wolfe, Elsie
Dickson, Dorothy
  Suppl. 1
Dietrich, Marlene
Digges, Dudley
Ditrichstein, Leo
Dolly Sisters
Donnelly, Dorothy
  Agnes
Doro, Marie
Douglas, Helen Gahagan
Douglas, Melvyn
Douglass, David
Dowling, Eddie

Drake, Frances Ann
  Denny
Drake, Samuel
Dresser, Louise Kerlin
Dressler, Marie
Drew, John (1827–1862)
Drew, John (1853–1927)
Drew, Louisa Lane
Duff, John R.
Duff, Mary Ann Dyke
Dumont, Margaret
Duncan, Augustin
Dunne, Irene
Duse, Eleonora
Eagels, Jeanne
Eddinger, Wallace
Eddy, Nelson
Elliott, Maxine
Elliston, Grace
Eltinge, Julian
Emmet, J. K.
Errol, Leon
Eytinge, Rose
Fairbanks, Douglas
Fairbanks, Douglas, Jr.
  Suppl. 1
Farnum, Dustin Lancy
Farnum, William
Faversham, William
  Alfred
Fawcett, George
Faye, Alice *Suppl. 1*
Ferguson, Elsie
Ferguson, William Jason
Ferrer, José
Fetchit, Stepin
Field, Joseph M.
Field, Kate
Fields, W. C.
Finch, Peter
Fiske, Minnie Maddern
Flynn, Errol
Fonda, Henry
Foran, Dick
Ford, Paul
Forrest, Edwin
Fox, Della May
Fox, George Washington
  Lafayette
Foy, Bryan
Foy, Eddie, Jr.
Franklin, Irene
Friganza, Trixie
Gable, Clark
Gannon, Mary
Garbo, Greta
Gardner, Ava
Garfield, John
Garland, Judy
Garson, Greer *Suppl. 1*
Gaynor, Janet

Theater and Live Entertainment (*cont.*)

Geer, Will
Genn, Leo
George, Gladys
George, Grace
Gersten, Berta
Gibson, Hoot
Gilbert, Anne Hartley
Gilbert, John *Suppl. 2*
Gilbert, John Gibbs
Gilbert, Mercedes
Gillette, William Hooker
Gilpin, Charles Sidney
Girardot, Étienne
Gish, Dorothy
Gish, Lillian
Gleason, Jackie
Gleason, James
Goodwin, Nathaniel C., Jr.
Goodwin, Ruby Berkley
Gordon, Ruth
Gordone, Charles *Suppl. 2*
Grable, Betty
Grahame, Gloria
Grant, Cary
Greenstreet, Sidney
Greenwood, Charlotte *Suppl. 1*
Griffith, Corinne
Guinan, Texas
Hackett, James Henry
Hackett, James Keteltas
Hall, Adelaide
Hall, Juanita
Hall, Pauline
Hallam, Lewis, and Mrs. Lewis Hallam Douglass
Halliday, John
Hamblin, Thomas Sowerby
Hamilton, Margaret
Hampden, Walter
Hards, Ira
Harlow, Jean
Harrigan, Ned
Harrison, Gabriel
Harrison, Richard Berry
Hart, Tony
Hart, William Surrey
Hayden, Sterling
Hayes, Gabby
Hayes, Helen
Hayward, Susan
Hayworth, Rita
Heggie, O. P.
Held, Anna
Henie, Sonja

Henry, John (1746–1794)
Hepburn, Audrey
Hepburn, Katharine
Herne, Chrystal Katharine
Herne, James A.
Heron, Matilda Agnes
Hewlett, James S.
Hill, George Handel
Hilliard, Robert
Hitchcock, Raymond
Hodge, William Thomas
Hodgkinson, John
Holden, William
Holland, George
Holliday, Judy
Holloway, Stanley
Holman, Libby
Homolka, Oscar
Hood, Darla Jean
Hopper, DeWolf
Hopper, Edna Wallace
Hopper, Hedda
Horton, Edward Everett *Suppl. 1*
Houseman, John
Howard, Leslie
Hudson, Rock
Hull, Henry
Hull, Josephine
Hunter, Glenn
Huntington, Catharine Sargent
Huston, Walter
Illington, Margaret
Irwin, May
Ives, Burl
Jaffe, Sam
James, Louis
Janauschek, Fanny
Jefferson, Joseph, I
Jefferson, Joseph, III
Jessel, George
Jolson, Al
Jory, Victor
Julia, Raul *Suppl. 2*
Kalich, Bertha
Kaminska, Ida
Karloff, Boris
Kaye, Danny
Keaton, Buster
Keeler, Ruby
Keenan, Frank
Keene, Laura
Keene, Thomas Wallace
Kelcey, Herbert
Kellerman, Annette
Kelly, Gene *Suppl. 1*
Kelly, Grace
Kelly, Patsy

Kelly, Walter C.
Kemble, Fanny
Kennedy, Charles Rann
Kennedy, John Arthur
Kessler, David
Kiley, Richard *Suppl. 2*
Kovacs, Ernie
Lackaye, Wilton
Ladd, Alan
La Follette, Fola
Lahr, Bert
Lake, Veronica
Lamarr, Hedy *Suppl. 1*
Lamour, Dorothy *Suppl. 1*
Lancaster, Burt
Lanchester, Elsa
Lander, Jean Davenport
Landon, Michael
Langdon, Harry Philmore
Lanza, Mario
Laughton, Charles
Laurel, Stan, and Oliver Hardy
Lawford, Peter
Lawrence, Florence
Lawrence, Gertrude *Suppl. 1*
Lee, Bruce
Lee, Canada
Le Gallienne, Eva
Leigh, Vivien
Lemmon, Jack *Suppl. 2*
Lenya, Lotte
Leslie, Amy
Levant, Oscar
Levene, Sam
Lewis, James
Lillie, Beatrice *Suppl. 1*
Lindsay, Howard
Lloyd, Harold
Loftus, Cissie
Logan, C. A.
Logan, Joshua
Logan, Olive
Lombard, Carole
Long, Sylvester Clark
Loos, Anita
Lord, Pauline
Lorre, Peter
Loy, Myrna
Lubitsch, Ernst
Ludlam, Charles
Ludlow, Noah Miller
Lugosi, Bela
Luke, Keye
Lund, Art
Lunt, Alfred, and Lynn Fontanne
Lupino, Ida

Lynde, Paul
Lyon, Ben
MacDonald, Jeanette
MacKaye, Steele
MacMurray, Fred
MacRae, Gordon
Maeder, Clara Fisher
Mann, Erika Julia Hedwig
Mann, Louis
Manners, John Hartley
Mansfield, Jayne
Mansfield, Richard
Mantell, Robert Bruce
Marble, Danforth
March, Fredric
Marley, John
Marlowe, Julia
Marsh, Mae
Marshall, E. G. *Suppl. 2*
Martin, Dean *Suppl. 2*
Martin, Mary
Marvin, Lee
Marx Brothers
Mason, James
Massey, Raymond
Matthau, Walter *Suppl. 2*
Mature, Victor *Suppl. 1*
Mayo, Frank
Mayo, Margaret
McAvoy, May
McClendon, Rose
McCrea, Joel
McCullough, John
McDaniel, Hattie
McDowall, Roddy *Suppl. 1*
McElheney, Jane
McFarland, George
McQueen, Steve
Meadows, Audrey *Suppl. 1*
Melmoth, Charlotte
Menjou, Adolphe
Menken, Adah Isaacs
Meredith, Burgess *Suppl. 1*
Merkel, Una
Merman, Ethel
Merry, Anne Brunton
Milland, Ray
Miller, Henry (1859–1926)
Miller, Marilyn
Mills, Florence
Miranda, Carmen
Mitchell, Maggie
Mitchell, Thomas
Mitchell, William (1798–1856)

Theater and Live Entertainment *(cont.)*

Mitchum, Robert *Suppl. 1*
Mix, Tom
Modjeska, Helena
Monroe, Marilyn
Montague, Henry James
Montez, Lola
Montgomery, Elizabeth *Suppl. 1*
Montgomery, Robert
Moore, Clayton *Suppl. 2*
Moore, Grace
Moore, Victor Frederick
Moorehead, Agnes
Morris, Clara
Morris, Elizabeth
Mostel, Zero
Mowatt, Anna Cora
Muni, Paul
Murdoch, James Edward
Murphy, Audie
Murphy, George
Murray, Mae
Muse, Clarence E.
Nazimova, Alla
Negri, Pola
Nelson, Ozzie, and Harriet Nelson
Nelson, Rick
Newley, Anthony *Suppl. 1*
Nissen, Greta
Niven, David
Nolan, Lloyd Benedict
Normand, Mabel
Nugent, Elliott
Oberon, Merle
O'Brien, Edmond
O'Brien, Pat
O'Connor, Carroll *Suppl. 2*
Oland, Warner *Suppl. 1*
Olcott, Chauncey
O'Neill, James
Owens, John Edmond
Page, Geraldine
Payne, John Howard
Payne, Virginia
Perkins, Anthony
Perry, Antoinette
Pickens, Slim
Pickford, Mary
Pidgeon, Walter
Placide, Henry
Powell, Dick
Powell, Eleanor
Powell, Snelling
Powell, William

Power, Tyrone (1869–1931)
Power, Tyrone (1914–1958)
Preston, Robert
Price, Vincent
Prinze, Freddie
Questel, Mae *Suppl. 2*
Radner, Gilda *Suppl. 1*
Raft, George
Rains, Claude
Rankin, McKee
Rathbone, Basil
Ray, Aldo *Suppl. 1*
Raye, Martha *Suppl. 1*
Raymond, John T.
Rehan, Ada
Reignolds, Catherine Mary
Remick, Lee
Rice, Thomas Dartmouth
Ritter, Tex
Ritz Brothers
Robeson, Paul
Robins, Elizabeth
Robinson, Edward G.
Robson, Stuart
Rogers, Ginger
Rogers, Roy *Suppl. 1*
Rogers, Will
Romero, Cesar *Suppl. 2*
Rose, George
Russell, Annie
Russell, Lillian
Russell, Rosalind
Russell, Sol Smith
Ryan, Robert
Sanders, George
Sands, Diana
Schwartz, Maurice
Scott, George C. *Suppl. 1*
Scott, Randolph
Sellers, Peter
Seymour, William
Shaw, Mary
Shean, Al
Shearer, Norma
Sidney, Sylvia *Suppl. 1*
Sills, Milton
Silverheels, Jay
Simpson, Edmund Shaw
Sinatra, Frank *Suppl. 1*
Skelton, Red *Suppl. 1*
Skinner, Cornelia Otis
Skinner, Otis
Smith, C. Aubrey
Smith, Mamie
Smith, Solomon Franklin

Smith, William Henry (1806–1872)
Sothern, Edward Askew
Sothern, Edward Hugh
Standing Bear, Luther
Stanwyck, Barbara
Stevens, Emily
Stewart, James *Suppl. 1*
Stoddart, James Henry
Stone, Fred *Suppl. 1*
Stone, John Augustus
Strasberg, Susan *Suppl. 2*
Sullavan, Margaret *Suppl. 1*
Swanson, Gloria
Sweet, Blanche
Tandy, Jessica
Taylor, Laurette
Taylor, Robert
Templeton, Fay
Thomas, Danny
Thomas, William, Jr.
Thompson, Denman
Three Stooges
Toler, Sidney *Suppl. 1*
Tracy, Spencer
Treacher, Arthur
Tucker, Lorenzo
Tucker, Sophie
Turnbull, Julia
Turner, Florence
Turner, Lana
Turpin, Ben *Suppl. 2*
Valentino, Rudolph
Vallee, Rudy
Vance, Vivian
Vandenhoff, George
Velez, Lupe *Suppl. 1*
Vera-Ellen
Verdon, Gwen *Suppl. 1*
Vincent, Mary Ann
von Stroheim, Erich
Wakely, Jimmy
Wallack, James William (1795?–1864)
Wallack, James William (1818–1873)
Wallack, Lester
Waller, Emma
Walsh, Blanche
Walsh, Raoul
Walthall, Henry Brazeale
Ward, Geneviève
Warde, Frederick Barkham
Warfield, David
Waters, Ethel
Wayne, John
Webb, Clifton
Webb, Jack

Webster, Margaret
Weissmuller, Johnny
Welles, Orson
Wemyss, Francis Courtney
West, Mae
Western, Lucille
Westley, Helen
Whiffen, Blanche Galton
White, George
White, Pearl
Wilson, Flip *Suppl. 1*
Wilson, Francis
Windsor, Marie *Suppl. 2*
Winfield, Hemsley
Wolheim, Louis Robert
Wong, Anna May
Wood, Mrs. John
Wood, Natalie
Wood, William Burke
Woolley, Monty
Wynn, Ed
Young, Loretta *Suppl. 2*
Young, Robert *Suppl. 1*
Yurka, Blanche

Theatrical Designers
Alexander, John White
Aronson, Boris
Ayers, Lemuel Delos
Beck, Julian
Bernstein, Aline Frankau
Geddes, Norman Bel
Hoyt, Henry E.
Hume, Samuel James
Johnson, Albert Richard
Jones, Robert Edmond
Jonson, Raymond
Mielziner, Jo
Nikolais, Alwin
Sharpe, Robert Redington
Simonson, Lee
Tchelitchew, Pavel
Urban, Joseph

Theatrical Producers / Directors
Aarons, Alexander A.
Aarons, Alfred E.
Abbott, George
Aldrich, Louis
Aldrich, Richard (1902–1986)
Ames, Winthrop
Ayers, Lemuel Delos
Belasco, David
Bennett, Michael
Blackmer, Sidney
Bloomgarden, Kermit

Theater and Live Entertainment *(cont.)*
Boleslavsky, Richard Valentinovich
Bonstelle, Jessie
Brady, William Aloysius
Brecht, Bertolt
Brisson, Frederick
Broadhurst, George Howells
Brooke, J. Clifford
Brown, Gilmor
Browne, Maurice
Burnside, R. H.
Caesar, Irving *Suppl. 1*
Campbell, Bartley, Jr.
Carroll, Earl
Charlot, André
Claxton, Kate
Clurman, Harold Edgar
Coburn, Charles Douville
Cody, William Frederick
Coe, Fred Hayden
Cohan, George M.
Cole, Bob
Cole, Jack
Comstock, F. Ray
Conried, Heinrich
Cook, George Cram
Cornell, Katharine
Cowl, Jane
Crabtree, Lotta
Crawford, Cheryl
Cromwell, John
Crothers, Rachel
Da Silva, Howard
Deeter, Jasper
de Liagre, Alfred
Denham, Reginald
DeSylva, B. G.
Digges, Dudley
Dillingham, Charles Bancroft
Dowling, Eddie
Duncan, Augustin
Dunning, Philip Hart
Erlanger, Abraham Lincoln
Ferrer, José
Fields, Lewis Maurice
Fiske, Harrison Grey
Fiske, Minnie Maddern
Flanagan, Hallie Mae Ferguson
Ford, Hugh
Forrest, Sam
Franken, Rose Dorothy
Freedley, Vinton
Frohman, Charles
Frohman, Daniel

Gaige, Crosby
Geddes, Norman Bel
George, Grace
Golden, John
Gordon, Max
Gordone, Charles *Suppl. 2*
Griffith, Robert E.
Hammerstein, Arthur
Hammerstein, Oscar, II
Hards, Ira
Harris, Jed
Harris, Sam Henry
Hart, Moss
Hayward, Leland
Helburn, Theresa
Henderson, David
Hill, Abram
Hirschbein, Peretz
Hopkins, Arthur Melancthon
Houseman, John
Hoyt, Charles Hale
Huffman, J. C.
Hull, Josephine
Hume, Samuel James
Huntington, Catharine Sargent
Janney, Russell Dixon
Jessel, George
Jones, Margo
Jones, Robert Edmond
Kaminska, Ida
Kaufman, George S.
Kennedy, Charles Rann
Kiralfy, Imre, and Bolossy Kiralfy
Klaw, Marc Alonzo
Lee, Canada
Le Gallienne, Eva
Leslie, Lew
Lewisohn, Irene
Leyendecker, J. C.
Liebman, Max
Lindsay, Howard
Logan, Joshua
Lombardo, Guy
Losey, Joseph
Ludlam, Charles
Lunt, Alfred, and Lynn Fontanne
Macgowan, Kenneth
MacKaye, Hazel
MacKaye, Steele
Mamoulian, Rouben
Marbury, Elisabeth
McClintic, Guthrie
Meredith, Burgess *Suppl. 1*
Merrick, David *Suppl. 1*
Miller, Gilbert Heron

Miller, Henry (1859–1926)
Miner, Worthington
Minnelli, Vincente
Moeller, Philip
Montgomery, Robert
Muse, Clarence E.
Nesbitt, Robert *Suppl. 2*
Nichols, Anne
North, John Ringling
Nugent, Elliott
Papp, Joseph
Pemberton, Brock
Perry, Antoinette
Quintero, José *Suppl. 1*
Ritchard, Cyril
Rose, Billy
Sackler, Howard Oliver
Schwartz, Maurice
Seymour, William
Short, Hassard
Shubert, Lee
Shumlin, Herman
Smith, Winchell
Sosenko, Anna *Suppl. 1*
Todd, Michael
Tyler, George Crouse
Vance, Nina Eloise Whittington
Wallack, Lester
Walton, Lester A. *Suppl. 2*
Wanger, Walter
Ward, Theodore James
Wayburn, Ned
Weber, Joseph Morris
Webster, Margaret
Weisgal, Meyer Wolfe
Welles, Orson
White, George
Woolley, Monty
Ziegfeld, Florenz

Toastmasters
Jessel, George

Vaudeville Performers
Armstrong, Harry
Barton, James Edward
Beck, Martin
Bricktop
Bubbles, John
Cantor, Eddie
Clark, Bobby
Cline, Maggie
Cohan, George M.
Coles, Honi
Davis, Sammy, Jr.
Dockstader, Lew
Dolly Sisters
Duncan, Rosetta

Eltinge, Julian
Errol, Leon
Fay, Frank
Fields, Benny
Fields, Lewis Maurice
Fields, W. C.
Ford, Whitey
Franklin, Irene
Gray, Gilda
Guinan, Texas
Hall, Adelaide
Hart, Tony
Hill, Chippie
Holtz, Lou
Houdini, Harry
Howard, Willie
Janis, Elsie
Jessel, George
Jolson, Al
Kalmar, Bert
Kellerman, Annette
Langdon, Harry Philmore
Lee, Gypsy Rose
Lewis, Ted
Loftus, Cissie
Martin, Sara
Mills, Florence
Rainey, Ma
Rooney, Pat
Russell, Lillian
Smith, Chris
Smith, Clara
Smith, Mamie
Smith, Trixie
Tanguay, Eva
Taylor, Eva
Templeton, Fay
Tucker, Sophie
Walker, Edyth
Weber, Joseph Morris
Whitman, Alice
Williams, Bert, and George Walker

Ventriloquists
Bergen, Edgar
Burnett, Alfred

RELIGION AND SPIRITUALITY

Denominations
Adventist Leaders
Miller, William
Smith, Uriah
Ward, Henry Dana
White, Ellen Gould Harmon

Denominations *(cont.)*

African Methodist Episcopal Bishops
Allen, Richard
Arnett, Benjamin William
Brown, John Mifflin
Brown, Morris
Coker, Daniel
Gregg, John Andrew
Payne, Daniel Alexander
Ransom, Reverdy Cassius
Tanner, Benjamin Tucker
Turner, Henry McNeal

African Methodist Episcopal Clergy
Brown, Morris
Cain, Richard Harvey
Corrothers, James David
Early, Jordan Winston
Evans, Henry
Jackson, Rebecca Cox
Revels, Hiram Rhoades
Smith, Stephen
Steward, Theophilus Gould
Thomas, William Hannibal

African Methodist Episcopal Lay Leaders
Coppin, Fanny Jackson

African Methodist Episcopal Zion Bishops
Loguen, Jermain Wesley
Spottswood, Stephen Gill
Thompson, Joseph Pascal
Varick, James
Walls, William Jacob
Walters, Alexander

African Orthodox Bishops
McGuire, George Alexander

Anglican Activists
Heathcote, Caleb

Anglican Bishops
Inglis, Charles

Anglican Clergy
Bacon, Thomas
Bailey, Jacob
Banister, John

Blackstone, William
Boucher, Jonathan
Bowden, John
Bray, Thomas
Camm, John
Checkley, John
Coke, Thomas
Cooper, Myles
Eaton, Nathaniel
Evans, Evan
Evans, Nathaniel
Honyman, James
Inglis, Charles
Jarratt, Devereux
Johnson, Samuel
Le Jau, Francis
MacSparran, James
Odell, Jonathan
Ogilvie, John
Peters, Richard (1704?–1776)
Peters, Samuel Andrew
Smith, William (1727–1803)
Spencer, Archibald
Sterling, James
Stouppe, Pierre *Suppl. 2*
Zouberbuhler, Bartholomew

Baptist Clergy
Abernathy, Ralph David
Andrews, Elisha Benjamin
Ayer, William Ward
Backus, Isaac
Banvard, Joseph
Barbour, Clarence Augustus
Boardman, George Dana
Boyd, Richard Henry
Brawley, Edward McKnight
Broaddus, Andrew
Broadus, John Albert
Brooks, Walter Henderson
Bryan, Andrew
Burns, Anthony
Buttrick, Wallace
Callender, John
Cary, Lott
Clarke, John
Clarke, William Newton
Conwell, Russell Herman
Corrothers, James David
Dagg, John Leadley
Dahlberg, Edwin Theodore
Davis, Gary D.

Dixon, Amzi Clarence
Eddy, Daniel Clarke
Faunce, William Herbert Perry
Fosdick, Harry Emerson
Fuller, Richard
Fuller, Thomas Oscar
Furman, Richard
Gano, John
Garrard, James
Gates, Frederick Taylor
Going, Jonathan
Goodspeed, Thomas Wakefield
Griggs, Sutton E.
Hart, Oliver
Henderson, Charles Richmond
Hill, Charles Andrew
Holcombe, Henry
Holman, Jesse Lynch
Howell, Robert Boyte Crawford
Jasper, John
Jewett, Milo Parker
Johns, Vernon Napoleon
Johnson, Mordecai Wyatt
Jones, John William
King, Martin Luther
King, Martin Luther, Jr.
Lawrence, Joshua *Suppl. 2*
Leland, John
Liele, George
Macintosh, Douglas Clyde
Manly, Basil, Jr.
Manning, James
Marshall, Andrew Cox
Marshall, Daniel
Martin, John Sella
Maxcy, Jonathan
Mccoy, Isaac
Meachum, John Berry
Mercer, Jesse
Morgan, Abel
Moulton, Ebenezer
Moxom, Philip Stafford
Murray, Orson S.
Myles, John
Newton, Joseph Fort
Paul, Thomas
Peck, John Mason
Pendleton, James Madison
Perry, Rufus Lewis
Pettiford, William Reuben
Plummer, Henry Vinton
Potter, Ray

Powell, Adam Clayton
Powell, Adam Clayton, Jr.
Randall, Benjamin
Rauschenbusch, Walter
Rhees, Rush
Rigdon, Sidney
Riley, William Bell
Ross, Martin
Ryland, Robert
Simmons, William James
Smith, Hezekiah
Smith, John (c.1735–1824)
Smith, Peter (1753–1815)
Smith, Samuel Francis
Staughton, William
Stearns, Shubal
Stillman, Samuel
Taliaferro, Hardin Edwards
Tichenor, Isaac Taylor
Tupper, Henry Allen
Wait, Samuel
Walker, Jeremiah
Washington, George Berry
Williams, George Washington
Winchester, Elhanan
Yeaman, William Pope

Baptist Lay Leaders
Coleman, Alice Blanchard Merriam
De Baptiste, Richard
George, David
MacLeish, Martha Hillard
Miller, William
Montgomery, Helen Barrett
Peabody, Lucy Whitehead McGill Waterbury
Rice, Luther
Ross, Martin
Yeaman, William Pope

Christian Connection Leaders
Jones, Abner
Smith, Elias

Christian Science Leaders
Eddy, Mary Baker
Morgan, Mary Kimball
Stetson, Augusta Emma Simmons

Denominations *(cont.)*
Colored Methodist Episcopal
Church Bishops
Holsey, Lucius Henry

Congregational Clergy
Abbott, Lyman
Adams, John
  (1705–1740)
Alden, Timothy
Alvord, John Watson
Atwater, Lyman
  Hotchkiss
Austin, David
Bacon, Leonard, Sr.
Bacon, Leonard Woolsey
Baldwin, John Denison
Barnard, John
Bartlett, Samuel Colcord
Barton, James Levi
Beecher, Edward
Beecher, Henry Ward
Beecher, Lyman
Belknap, Jeremy
Bellamy, Joseph
Beman, Amos Gerry
Blackwell, Antoinette
  Louisa Brown
Bradford, Amory Howe
Bradford, Ebenezer
Brattle, William
Bristol, Sherlock *Suppl. 1*
Brown, Charles Oliver
  Suppl. 1
Brown, Charles
  Reynolds
Bulkeley, Gershom
Burton, Asa
Bushnell, Horace
Byles, Mather
Cardozo, Francis Louis
Chauncy, Charles
  (1705–1787)
Cheever, George Barrell
Clark, Francis E.
Colman, Benjamin
Cook, Russell Salmon
Cooper, Samuel
  (1725–1783)
Croswell, Andrew
Cutler, Manasseh
Davenport, John
Davis, Jerome Dean
Deane, Samuel
DeBerry, William
  Nelson
Dewey, Chester
Douglass, Harlan Paul
Dow, Daniel
Dwight, Louis
Dwight, Sereno Edwards

Dwight, William
  Theodore
Eastman, Annis
Eastman, William Reed
Edwards, Bela Bates
Edwards, Jonathan
Edwards, Jonathan, Jr.
Eliot, Jared
Emerson, Joseph
Emmons, Nathanael
Everett, Robert
Faulkner, William John
Flint, Timothy
Foxcroft, Thomas
Gay, Ebenezer
Gladden, Washington
Goodrich, Charles
  Augustus
Goodrich, Chauncey
  Allen
Goodrich, Elizur
  (1734–1797)
Gordon, George Angier
Green, Beriah
Griffis, William Elliot
Grinnell, Josiah Bushnell
Gunsaulus, Frank
  Wakeley
Haynes, Lemuel
Hemmenway, Moses
Hillis, Newell Dwight
Horton, Douglas
Hume, Robert Allen
Humphrey, Heman
Hyde, William DeWitt
Kirk, Edward Norris
Langdon, Samuel
Lovejoy, Owen
Lyman, Mary Redington
  Ely
Magoun, George
  Frederic
Mather, Samuel
  (1706–1785)
Mayhew, Jonathan
McCulloch, Oscar
  Carleton
McKeen, Joseph
Moore, Zephaniah Swift
Morril, David Lawrence
Morse, Jedidiah
Moxom, Philip Stafford
Munger, Theodore
  Thornton
Nettleton, Asahel
Newcomb, Harvey
Ockenga, Harold John
Peet, Stephen Denison
Peloubet, Francis
  Nathan

Pennington, James
  William Charles
Phelps, Austin
Phillips, Channing E.
Pond, Enoch
Porter, Noah
Prince, Thomas
Proctor, Henry Hugh
Reed, Myron Winslow
Rogers, Daniel
Rogers, John Almanza
  Rowley
Saltonstall, Gurdon
Sanders, Daniel Clarke
Scofield, Cyrus Ingerson
Seccomb, John
Seccombe, Joseph
Sheldon, Charles
  Monroe
Smyth, Newman
Sperry, Willard Learoyd
Sprague, William Buell
Steiner, Edward Alfred
Stiles, Ezra
Stoddard, Solomon
Strong, Josiah
Sturtevant, Julian
  Monson
Taylor, Graham
Tennent, William, III
Thacher, Peter
Thacher, Thomas
Torrey, Reuben Archer
Tracy, Joseph Carter
Trumbull, Benjamin
Tufts, John
Tyler, Bennet
Walker, Timothy
  (1705–1782)
Ware, Henry
Washburn, George
Wheelock, Eleazar
Willard, Joseph
Williams, John
  (1664–1729)
Wise, John (1652–1725)
Woods, Leonard
Worcester, Noah
Wright, Henry Clarke

Disciples of Christ Clergy
Campbell, Alexander
Franklin, Benjamin
  (1812–1878)
McGarvey, John William
McLean, Archibald
Scott, Walter
Smith, Gerald Lyman
  Kenneth
Wharton, Greene
  Lawrence

Willett, Herbert
  Lockwood
Zollars, Ely Vaughn

Dutch Reformed Clergy
Berg, Joseph Frederic
Bertholf, Guiliam
Bogardus, Everardus
Corwin, Edward Tanjore
Freeman, Bernardus
Frelinghuysen,
  Theodorus Jacobus
Griffis, William Elliot
Hardenbergh, Jacob
  Rutsen
Krol, Bastiaen Janszen
Livingston, John Henry
Megapolensis, Johannes
Michaelius, Jonas
Milledoler, Philip
Seelye, Julius Hawley
Selijns, Henricus
Talmage, Thomas De
  Witt
Van Raalte, Albertus
  Christiaan
Van Rensselaer,
  Nicholas
Verbryck, Samuel

Episcopalian Bishops
Brent, Charles Henry
Brooks, Phillips
Brownell, Thomas
  Church
Chase, Philander
Cheney, Charles Edward
Clark, Thomas March
Cobbs, Nicholas
  Hamner
Coxe, Arthur Cleveland
Cummins, George
  David
Doane, George
  Washington
Doane, William Croswell
Gailor, Thomas Frank
Grafton, Charles
  Chapman
Greer, David Hummel
Griswold, Alexander
  Viets
Hale, Charles Reuben
Hare, William Hobart
Hobart, John Henry
Holly, James Theodore
Hopkins, John Henry
Huntington, Frederic
  Dan
Ives, Levi Silliman
Kemper, Jackson

Denominations *(cont.)*
Kip, William Ingraham
Lawrence, William
  (1850–1941)
Madison, James
  (1749–1812)
Manning, William
  Thomas
McIlvaine, Charles Pettit
McVickar, William
  Neilson
Meade, William
Moore, Richard
  Channing
Nash, Norman Burdett
Onderdonk, Benjamin
  Tredwell
Onderdonk, Henry
  Ustick
Otey, James Hervey
Perry, William Stevens
Polk, Leonidas
Potter, Henry Codman
Provoost, Samuel
Quintard, Charles Todd
Ravenscroft, John Stark
Rowe, Peter Trimble
Satterlee, Henry Yates
Schereschewsky, Samuel
  Isaac Joseph
Seabury, Samuel (1729–
  1796)
Slattery, Charles Lewis
Smith, Robert
  (1732–1801)
Spalding, Franklin
  Spencer
Talbot, Ethelbert
Tuttle, Daniel Sylvester
Wainwright, Jonathan
  Mayhew
Whipple, Henry
  Benjamin
White, William
Williams, Channing
  Moore
Williams, Charles David
Wilmer, Richard Hooker

Episcopalian Clergy
Allen, Alexander Viets
  Griswold
Auchmuty, Samuel
Blake, John Lauris
Bliss, William Dwight
  Porter
Brady, Cyrus Townsend
Bragg, George Freeman,
  Jr.
Breck, James Lloyd
Brooks, Phillips

Capers, Ellison
Cheney, Charles Edward
Coit, Henry Augustus
Colton, Calvin
Crapsey, Algernon
  Sidney
Crummell, Alexander
Curtis, Moses Ashley
Cutler, Timothy
De Koven, James
Dix, Morgan
Ewer, Ferdinand
  Cartwright
Ferris, Theodore Parker
Gallaudet, Thomas
Gavin, Frank Stanton
  Burns
Grant, Percy Stickney
Hare, George Emlen
Henry, Caleb Sprague
Hodges, George
Houghton, George
  Hendric
Huntington, William
  Reed
Ingraham, Joseph Holt
Jarratt, Devereux
Jones, Absalom
Jones, Edward
Langdon, William
  Chauncy
Lowell, Robert Traill
  Spence
McVickar, William
  Neilson
Miles, James Warley
Montgomery, James
  Alan
Moore, James
  (1764–1814)
Muhlenberg, William
  Augustus
Murphy, Edgar Gardner
Murray, Pauli
Newton, Joseph Fort
Newton, Richard Heber
Newton, William
  Wilberforce
Ogden, John Cosens
Ogden, Uzal
Potter, Eliphalet Nott
Rainsford, William
  Stephen
Russell, James Solomon
Savage, Thomas
  Staughton
Scarlett, William
Seabury, Samuel
  (1801–1872)
Sherrill, Henry Knox
Shoup, Francis Asbury

Smith, William
  (1754–1821)
Stokes, Anson Phelps
Stuck, Hudson
Tucker, Henry St.
  George (1874–1959)
Tyng, Stephen
  Higginson
Vesey, William
Ward, Henry Dana
Weems, Mason Locke
Williams, Charles David
Williams, Peter, Jr.
Wilmer, William Holland
Worcester, Elwood
Wylie, Andrew

Episcopalian Lay Leaders
Ayres, Anne
Emery, Julia Chester
Gardiner, Robert
  Hallowell, III
Page, Ann Randolph
  Meade
Wedel, Cynthia Clark

Evangelical Clergy
Albright, Jacob
Esher, John Jacob
Seybert, John

*Evangelical and Reformed
Clergy*
Beaver, Robert Pierce

Free Methodist Clergy
Hogue, Wilson Thomas
Roberts, Benjamin Titus

French Reformed Clergy
Rou, Louis *Suppl. 2*

German Reformed Clergy
Berg, Joseph Frederic
Boehm, John Philip
Bomberger, John Henry
  Augustus
Dubbs, Joseph Henry
Goetschius, John Henry
Good, James Isaac
Gros, John Daniel
Harbaugh, Henry
Otterbein, Philip William
Schlatter, Michael

Greek Orthodox Clergy
Callimachos, Panos
  Demetrios

Islamic Leaders
Ali, Noble Drew

Fard, Wallace
Hamid, Sufi Abdul
Malcolm X
Muhammad, Elijah

Jehovah's Witnesses Leaders
Knorr, Nathan Homer
Russell, Charles Taze
Rutherford, Joseph
  Franklin

Jewish Clergy
Adler, Morris
Bernstein, Philip Sidney
Blaustein, David
Carlebach, Shlomo
  Suppl. 2
Cohon, Samuel Solomon
Eckman, Julius
Einhorn, David
Eisendrath, Maurice
  Nathan
Feinstein, Moses
Felsenthal, Bernhard
Freehof, Solomon
  Bennett
Geffen, Tobias
Goldman, Solomon
Goldstein, Herbert S.
Goldstein, Israel
Gottheil, Gustav
Grayzel, Solomon
Gutheim, James Koppel
Heller, Maximilian
Hirsch, Emil Gustave
Hirschensohn, Chaim
Hutner, Isaac
Isaacs, Samuel Myer
Jastrow, Marcus
  Mordecai
Joseph, Jacob
Jung, Leo
Kaplan, Mordecai
  Menahem
Kohler, Kaufmann
Kohut, Alexander
Lazaron, Morris Samuel
Levinthal, Israel Herbert
Liebman, Joshua Loth
Lilienthal, Max
Magnes, Judah Leon
Magnin, Edgar Fogel
Mendes, Henry Pereira
Morais, Sabato
Neumark, David
Philipson, David
Poznanski, Gustavus
Raphall, Morris Jacob
Rice, Abraham Joseph
Ruderman, Yaakov
  Yitzchak

Denominations *(cont.)*

Silver, Abba Hillel
Steinberg, Milton
Szold, Benjamin
Voorsanger, Jacob
Wise, Isaac Mayer
Wise, Stephen Samuel

Jewish Lay Leaders
Adler, Cyrus
Antin, Mary
Bardin, Shlomo
Bernstein, Philip Sidney
Deinard, Ephraim
Dembitz, Lewis Naphtali
Einstein, Hannah
Bachman
Etting, Solomon *Suppl. 1*
Fishberg, Maurice
Ford, Arnold Josiah
Frank, Ray
Goldstein, Israel
Gordin, Jacob
Gratz, Barnard, and
Michael Gratz
Gratz, Rebecca
Harby, Isaac
Hays, Moses Michael
Suppl. 1
Kohler, Max James
Leeser, Isaac
Leipziger, Henry Marcus
Lichtenstein, Tehilla
Rachael
Magnin, Edgar Fogel
Marshall, Louis
(1856–1929)
Masliansky, Zvi Hirsch
Monsky, Henry
Mosessohn, David
Nehemiah
Nathan, Maud
Noah, Mordecai Manuel
Peixotto, Benjamin
Franklin
Phillips, Jonas *Suppl. 1*
Pool, David De Sola
Proskauer, Joseph Meyer
Revel, Bernard
Rosen, Joseph A.
Rubinow, Isaac Max
Schechter, Mathilde
Roth
Schneersohn, Joseph
Isaac
Schneerson, Menachem
Mendel
Seixas, Gershom
Mendes
Solis-Cohen, Solomon
Wolf, Simon

Zhitlowsky, Hayim

Lutheran Clergy
Acrelius, Israel
Bachman, John
Berkenmeyer, Wilhelm
Christoph
Boltzius, Johann Martin
Dahl, Theodor
Halvorson
Dietrichson, Johannes
Wilhelm Christian
Douglas, Lloyd Cassel
Eielsen, Elling
Empie, Paul Chauncey
Esbjörn, Lars Paul
Falckner, Daniel
Falckner, Justus
Fritschel, Conrad
Sigmund
Fritschel, Gottfried
Leonhard Wilhelm
Fry, Franklin Clark
Grabau, Johannes
Andreas August
Graebner, Theodore
Conrad
Hartwick, John
Christopher
Hasselquist, Tuve
Nilsson
Hazelius, Ernest Lewis
Helmuth, Henry
Henkel, David
Henkel, Paul
Hove, Elling
Kildahl, John Nathan
Kocherthal, Josua von
Krauth, Charles Philip
Kunze, John Christopher
Kurtz, Benjamin
Larsen, Peter Laurentius
Lund-Quist, Carl Elof
Morris, John Gottlieb
Muhlenberg, Henry
Muhlenberg, Henry
Augustus Philip
Muhlenberg, Henry
Melchior
Nikander, Juho Kustaa
Nolde, Otto Frederick
Norelius, Eric
Olsson, Olof
Passavant, William
Alfred
Pieper, Franz August
Otto
Schiotz, Fredrik Axel
Schmidt, Friedrich
August

Schmucker, Beale
Melanchthon
Seiss, Joseph Augustus
Sihler, Wilhelm
Swensson, Carl Aaron
Swensson, Jonas
Walther, Carl Ferdinand
Wilhelm
Wentz, Abdel Ross

Lutheran Lay Leaders
Empie, Paul Chauncey
Fry, Franklin Clark
Grabau, Johannes
Andreas August
Hasselquist, Tuve
Nilsson
Loy, Matthias
Muhlenberg, Frederick
Augustus
Reu, Johann Michael
Schiotz, Fredrik Axel
Swensson, Jonas
Wyneken, Friedrich
Conrad Dietrich

Mennonite Bishops
Boehm, Martin
Rittenhouse, William

Methodist Episcopal Bishops
Andrew, James Osgood
Asbury, Francis
Baker, Osmon Cleander
Bashford, James
Whitford
Coke, Thomas
Emory, John
Fisher, Frederick Bohn
Fisk, Wilbur
Fowler, Charles Henry
Hamilton, John William
Hamline, Leonidas Lent
Harris, Merriman
Colbert
Hartzell, Joseph Crane
Haven, Gilbert
Hedding, Elijah
McCabe, Charles
Cardwell
McConnell, Francis John
McKendree, William
McTyeire, Holland
Nimmons
Merrill, Stephen Mason
Oxnam, Garfield
Bromley
Pierce, George Foster
Roberts, Robert
Richford
Simpson, Matthew

Taylor, William
Thoburn, James Mills
Vincent, John Heyl
Waugh, Beverly
Whatcoat, Richard

*Methodist Episcopal
Church, South, Bishops*
Bascom, Henry
Bidleman
Cannon, James, Jr.
Capers, William
Hendrix, Eugene Russell
Paine, Robert
Soule, Joshua
Tigert, John James, III

*Methodist Episcopal
Church, South, Clergy*
Browder, George
Richard
Brownlow, William
Gannaway
Candler, Warren Akin
Haygood, Atticus
Greene
Hopkins, Isaac Stiles
Jones, Samuel Porter
Lane, John
McAnally, David Rice
McFerrin, John Berry
Ralston, Thomas Neely
Rivers, Richard
Henderson
Sledd, Andrew
Tillett, Wilbur Fisk
Winans, William

Methodist Episcopal Clergy
Bowne, Borden Parker
Bresee, Phineas Franklin
Buckley, James Monroe
Cadman, S. Parkes
Cartwright, Peter
Cooper, Ezekiel
Curry, Daniel
Curtis, Olin Alfred
Dorchester, Daniel
Durbin, John Price
Elliott, Charles
Finley, James Bradley
Garrettson, Freeborn
Haskins, Thomas
Henson, Josiah
Inskip, John Swanel
Johnson, Paul Emanuel
Jones, Eli Stanley
Kidder, Daniel Parish
Kynett, Alpha Jefferson
Lee, Jesse
Lee, Luther

Denominations *(cont.)*
Little, Charles Joseph
Lynch, James
Maffitt, John Newland
   (1794–1850)
McClintock, John
Miley, John
Mudge, James
Nast, William
North, Frank Mason
O'Kelly, James
Olin, Stephen
Peck, George
Ray, Charles Bennett
Raymond, Miner
Scott, Orange
Sloan, Harold Paul
Stevens, Abel
Sunderland, La Roy
Taylor, Edward
   Thompson
Terry, Milton Spenser
Tindley, Charles Albert
Tittle, Ernest Fremont
Van Cott, Maggie
   Newton
Way, Amanda
   Whedon, Daniel
   Denison

*Methodist Episcopal Lay
Leaders*
Bennett, Belle Harris
Dickins, John
Jacoby, Ludwig
   Sigismund
Meyer, Lucy Jane Rider
Newman, Angelia
   French
Robinson, Jane Marie
   Bancroft
Willing, Jennie Fowler

*Methodist Pioneers / Lay
Leaders*
Albright, Jacob
Bangs, Nathan
Embury, Philip
Gatch, Philip
Heck, Barbara
Strawbridge, Robert
Watters, William
Webb, Thomas
Williams, Robert

Methodist Protestant Clergy
Apess, William
McCaine, Alexander
Shaw, Anna Howard
Shinn, Asa
Snethen, Nicholas

Moravian Bishops
Boehler, Peter
Boehm, Martin
de Schweinitz, Edmund
   Alexander
Jacobson, John Christian
Kephart, Ezekiel Boring
Reichel, Charles
   Gotthold
Spangenberg, Augustus
   Gottlieb

Moravian Clergy
Beardshear, William
   Miller
Clewell, John Henry
Grube, Bernhard Adam
Newcomer, Christian
Peter, John Frederick
Reichel, William
   Cornelius
Schweinitz, Lewis David
   von
Zeisberger, David

Moravian Lay Leaders
Watteville, Henrietta
   Benigna von
Zinzendorf, Nikolaus
   Ludwig von

Mormon Leaders
Bennett, John Cook
Benson, Ezra Taft
Clark, Joshua Reuben, Jr.
Cowdery, Oliver
Goldsmith, Joel Sol
Grant, Heber Jeddy
Ivins, Anthony
   Woodward
Kane, Thomas Leiper
Kimball, Heber Chase
Kimball, Spencer
   Woolley
Lee, John Doyle
McKay, David Oman
Pratt, Orson
Pratt, Parley Parker
Rich, Charles Coulson
Rigdon, Sidney
Roberts, Brigham Henry
Smith, George Albert
Smith, Joseph, III
Smith, Joseph
   (1805–1844)
Smith, Joseph Fielding
   (1838–1918)
Smith, Joseph Fielding
   (1876–1972)
Smoot, Reed Owen
Snow, Eliza Roxcy

Snow, Lorenzo
Strang, James Jesse
Taylor, John
   (1808–1887)
Wells, Emmeline B.
Whitmer, David
Woodruff, Wilford
Woolley, Edwin
   Dilworth
Young, Brigham

*Polish National Catholic
Bishops*
Hodur, Francis

Presbyterian Clergy
Adams, William
Alexander, Archibald
Alison, Francis
Anderson, Matthew
Armstrong, George Dod
Bacon, John
Baird, Charles
   Washington
Baker, Daniel
Balch, Hezekiah
Barnes, Albert
Barnhouse, Donald Grey
Barrows, John Henry
Beard, Richard
Beecher, Lyman
Beman, Nathan Sidney
   Smith
Biederwolf, William
   Edward
Bishop, Robert Hamilton
Blackburn, Gideon
Blake, Eugene Carson
Boisen, Anton
   Theophilus
Bonnell, John Sutherland
Bourne, George
Breckinridge, John
   (1797–1841)
Briggs, Charles Augustus
Brookes, James H.
Burr, Aaron
   (1716–1757)
Caldwell, David
Campbell, William
   Henry
Carrick, Samuel Czar
Cattell, William Cassady
Cavert, Samuel McCrea
Chafer, Lewis Sperry
Chavis, John
Chew, Ng Poon
Coffin, Henry Sloane
Colton, Calvin
Cook, John Francis
Cornish, Samuel Eli

Corrothers, James David
Cox, Samuel Hanson
Cuyler, Theodore
   Ledyard
Dabney, Robert Lewis
Davenport, James
Davies, Samuel
Dickinson, Jonathan
Doak, Samuel
Donnell, Robert
Duffield, George
Erdman, Charles
   Rosenbury
Erdman, William Jacob
Ewing, Finis
Fee, John Gregg
Finley, Robert
Finley, Samuel
Gale, George
   Washington
Garnet, Henry Highland
Gibbs, Jonathan C.
Girardeau, John
   Lafayette
Goulding, Francis
   Robert
Green, Ashbel
Grimké, Francis James
Hall, Charles Cuthbert
Hatfield, Edwin Francis
Hewat, Alexander
Hillis, Newell Dwight
Hiltner, Seward
Hoge, Moses
Hoge, Moses Drury
Howe, George
   (1802–1883)
Jessup, Henry Harris
Jones, Charles Colcock
Junkin, George
Kellogg, Samuel Henry
Kent, Aratus
Kirk, Edward Norris
Knox, Samuel
Linn, John Blair
Lovejoy, Elijah Parish
Macartney, Clarence
   Edward Noble
MacCracken, Henry
   Mitchell
Makemie, Francis
Matthews, Mark Allison
McBride, F. Scott
McCord, James Iley
McCorkle, Samuel
   Eusebius
McCormick, Samuel
   Black
McGready, James
Miller, Samuel
Morris, Edward Dafydd

Denominations *(cont.)*
Morrison, William
  McCutchan
Palmer, Benjamin
  Morgan
Parker, Joel (1799–1873)
Parker, Thomas
Parkhurst, Charles
  Henry
Pattillo, Henry
Peck, Thomas Ephraim
Pierson, Arthur Tappan
Plumer, William Swan
Prime, Samuel Irenaeus
Rice, David
Rice, John Holt
Roberts, William Henry
Robinson, Stuart
Roe, Edward Payson
Rogers, John Almanza
  Rowley
Ruffner, William Henry
Smith, Benjamin Mosby
Smith, Samuel Stanhope
Smyth, Thomas
Spencer, Ichabod Smith
Sprague, William Buell
Spring, Gardiner
Stelzle, Charles
Stone, John Timothy
Swing, David
Talmage, Thomas De
  Witt
Tennent, Gilbert
Tennent, William
Thompson, Ernest Trice
Thornwell, James Henley
van Dyke, Henry
Waddel, John Newton
Waddel, Moses
Wallace, Henry
Willey, Samuel Hopkins
Wilson, Joshua Lacy
Wines, Frederick
  Howard
Witherspoon, John
Woodrow, James
Wright, Theodore
  Sedgwick
Wylie, Andrew
Yandell, Lunsford Pitts,
  Sr.
Zubly, John Joachim

Presbyterian Lay Leaders
Adger, John Bailey
Bennett, M. Katharine
  Jones
Speer, Robert Elliott

Puritan Clergy
Bulkeley, Peter
Chauncy, Charles
  (1592–1672)
Cotton, John
Eliot, John
Harvard, John
Hiacoomes
Higginson, Francis
Higginson, John
Hoar, Leonard
Hooker, Thomas
Hubbard, William
Lothropp, John
Mather, Cotton
Mather, Increase
Mather, Richard
Mitchell, Jonathan
Morton, Charles
Norris, Edward
Norton, John
Oakes, Urian
Parris, Samuel
Peter, Hugh
Shepard, Thomas
Stone, Samuel
Taylor, Edward
Weld, Thomas
Wigglesworth, Edward
Wigglesworth, Michael
Willard, Samuel
Williams, Roger
  (1603?–1683)
Wilson, John
  (c.1591–1667)

Puritans
Brainerd, David
Brewster, William
  (1567–1644)
Davenport, John
Edwards, Sarah Pierpont
Leverett, John
  (1616–1679)
Vane, Sir Henry

Quaker Clergy
Ashbridge, Elizabeth
Bean, Joel
Bowers, Bathsheba
Coffin, Charles Fisher
Comstock, Elizabeth
  Leslie Rous Wright
Fisher, Mary
Gurney, Eliza Paul
  Kirkbride
Hicks, Elias
Hoag, Joseph
Hume, Sophia
  Wigington
Jay, Allen

Jones, Rebecca
Jones, Sybil
Malone, John Walter
Pemberton, John
Russell, Elbert
Sands, David
Starbuck, Mary Coffyn
Updegraff, David
  Brainerd
Way, Amanda
Wilbur, John

Quakers
Barnard, Hannah Jenkins
Bates, Elisha
Brinton, Howard Haines,
  and Anna Shipley Cox
  Brinton
Brown, Moses
Brown, Obadiah
Dyer, Mary
Eddy, Thomas
Evans, Jonathan
Evans, William
Ferris, Benjamin
Gibbons, William
  (1781–1845)
Hopper, Isaac Tatem
Jansen, Reinier
Keith, George
Kinsey, John
Lay, Benjamin
Lloyd, David
Maule, Thomas
M'Clintock, Mary Ann
  Wilson, and Thomas
  M'Clintock
Murray, John
  (1737–1808)
Murray, Lindley
Murray, Robert
Nicholson, Timothy
Norris, Isaac
  (1671–1735)
Norris, Isaac
  (1701–1766)
Pemberton, Israel
Penington, Edward
Penn, William
Perry, Edward
Pickett, Clarence Evan
Pusey, Caleb
Rodman, Samuel
Rotch, William
Rotch, William, Jr.
Shippen, Edward
Wister, Sarah
Wood, James
Wood, L. Hollingsworth
Woolman, John

*Reformed Church in
America Clergy*
Peale, Norman Vincent
Schenck, Ferdinand
Schureman

Roman Catholic Bishops
Alemany, Joseph Sadoc
Alter, Karl J.
Baraga, Frederic
Bayley, James Roosevelt
Blanchet, Francis
  Norbert
Bruté De Rémur, Simon
  William Gabriel
Byrne, Andrew
Carroll, John
Chapelle, Placide-Louis
Cheverus, John Louis
  Anne Magdalen
  Lefebvre de
Cody, John Patrick
Conwell, Henry
Cooke, Terence
Corrigan, Michael
  Augustine
Cretin, Joseph
Curley, Michael Joseph
Currier, Charles Warren
Cushing, Richard James
David, John Baptist
  Mary
Dearden, John F.
Dougherty, Dennis
  Joseph
Dubois, John
DuBourg, Louis William
  Valentine
Dwenger, Joseph
Eccleston, Samuel
Elder, William Henry
England, John
Feehan, Patrick
  Augustine
Fenwick, Benedict
  Joseph
Fenwick, Edward
  Dominic
Fitzgerald, Edward
Fitzpatrick, John Bernard
Flaget, Benedict Joseph
García Diego y Moreno,
  Francisco
Gibbons, James
Glennon, John Joseph
Haas, Francis Joseph
Haid, Leo Michael
Hallinan, Paul John
Hanna, Edward Joseph
Healy, James Augustine
Heiss, Michael

Denominations *(cont.)*
Hennessy, John
Henni, John Martin
Hughes, John Joseph
Hurley, Joseph Patrick
Ireland, John
Janssens, Francis
Katzer, Frederick Xavier
Keane, James John
Keane, John Joseph
Kenrick, Peter Richard
Krol, John *Suppl. 1*
Lamy, John Baptist
Lefevere, Peter Paul
Loras, John Mathias
 Peter
Lynch, Patrick Neison
Maes, Camillus Paul
Maréchal, Ambrose
McCloskey, John
McCloskey, William
 George
McNicholas, John
 Timothy
McQuaid, Bernard John
Messmer, Sebastian
 Gebhard
Miles, Richard Pius
Mitty, John Joseph
Moeller, Henry
Moore, John
Mundelein, George
 William
Neale, Leonard
Neumann, John
 Nepomucene
Noll, John Francis
O'Connell, Denis
O'Connell, William
 Henry
O'Connor, Michael J.
Odin, Jean-Marie
O'Gorman, Thomas
O'Hara, Edwin Vincent
Purcell, John Baptist
Quarter, William James
Quigley, James Edward
Ready, Michael Joseph
Rese, Frederic
Riordan, Patrick William
Rosati, Joseph
Rummel, Joseph Francis
Schrembs, Joseph
Seghers, Charles Jean
Sheen, Fulton John
Shehan, Lawrence
 Joseph
Spalding, John Lancaster
Spalding, Martin John
Turner, William

Verot, Jean Pierre
 Augustin Marcellin
Walsh, Thomas Joseph
Wigger, Winand Michael
Williams, John Joseph
Wood, James Frederick

Roman Catholic Cardinals
Bernardin, Joseph
 Suppl. 1
Cody, John Patrick
Glennon, John Joseph
Hayes, Patrick Joseph
Krol, John *Suppl. 1*
McCloskey, John
McIntyre, James Francis
Meyer, Albert Gregory
Ritter, Joseph Elmer
Shehan, Lawrence
 Joseph
Spellman, Francis Joseph
Stritch, Samuel
 Alphonsus
Wright, John Joseph

Roman Catholic Clergy
Antoine, Père
Bójnowski, Lucyan
Barber, Virgil Horace
Barzynski, Vincent
Behrens, Henry
Bishop, W. Howard
Bouquillon, Thomas
 Joseph
Cavanaugh, John Joseph
Charlevoix, Pierre-
 François-Xavier de
Comey, Dennis J.
 Suppl. 1
Corby, William
Corcoran, James Andrew
Coughlin, Charles
 Edward
Damien, Father
Davis, Thurston Noble
Dietz, Peter Ernest
Dorsey, John Henry
Doyle, Alexander Patrick
Drumgoole, John
 Christopher
Duffy, Francis Patrick
Elliott, Walter Hackett
 Robert
Feeney, Leonard
 Edward
Fenton, Joseph Clifford
Finn, Francis James
Flanagan, Edward
 Joseph
Gasson, Thomas
 Ignatius

Gmeiner, John
Graessl, Dominic
 Laurence
Greaton, Joseph
Groppi, James Edward
Guthrie, Joseph Hunter
Healy, Patrick Francis
Hecker, Isaac Thomas
Hellriegel, Martin
 Balthasar
Helmpraecht, Joseph
Hessoun, Joseph
Hewit, Augustine
 Francis
Hillenbrand, Reynold
 Henry
Hogan, William
Hudson, Daniel Eldred
Judge, Thomas
 Augustine
Keller, James G.
Kenrick, Francis Patrick
Kerby, William Joseph
LaFarge, John
Lambing, Andrew
 Arnold
Ligutti, Luigi
Maas, Anthony John
Macelwane, James
 Bernard
Machebeuf, Joseph
 Projectus
Malone, Sylvester
Markoe, William
 Morgan
McAvoy, Thomas
 Timothy
McElroy, John
 (1782–1877)
McGivney, Michael J.
McGlynn, Edward
McGrady, Thomas
Ming, John Joseph
Moosmüller, Oswald
 William
Morini, Austin M.
Nerinckx, Charles
O'Conor, John F. X.
 Suppl. 2
Pace, Edward Aloysius
Preston, Thomas Scott
Price, Thomas Frederick
Roseliep, Raymond
Rouquette, Adrien
 Emmanuel
Ryan, Abram Joseph
Ryan, John Augustine
Shahan, Thomas Joseph
Sheil, Bernard James
Shields, Thomas Edward
Slattery, John Richard

Sorin, Edward Frederick
Spalding, Henry
 Stanislaus *Suppl. 2*
Sullivan, William
 Laurence
Tabb, John Banister
Talbot, Francis Xavier
Tolton, Augustus
Van de Velde, James
 Oliver
Varela y Morales, Felix
 Francisco
Verhaegen, Peter Joseph
Walsh, Edmund
 Aloysius
Walsh, James Anthony
Walworth, Clarence
 Augustus
Weigel, Gustave
Williams, John Joseph
Wimmer, Boniface
Yorke, Peter Christopher
Zahm, John Augustine

*Roman Catholic Lay
Leaders*
Avery, Martha Gallison
 Moore
Behrens, Henry
Brownson, Orestes
 Augustus
Burke, John Joseph
Callahan, Patrick Henry
Conboy, Martin
Crowley, Patrick Francis
Day, Dorothy
Doherty, Catherine de
 Hueck
Dougherty, Dennis
 Joseph
Kenedy, Patrick John
Meade, George
Mulry, Thomas Maurice
Preston, Thomas Scott
Rudd, Daniel
Shea, John Dawson
 Gilmary
Shuster, George
 Nauman
Ward, Maisie

*Romanian Orthodox
Bishops*
Trifa, Valerian Dionisie

Russian Orthodox Clergy
Netsvetov, Jacob
Veniaminov, Ivan

Shakers
Allen, Catherine

Denominations *(cont.)*
Avery, Giles Bushnell
Barker, Ruth Mildred
Bishop, Rufus
Cohoon, Hannah
  Harrison
Darrow, David
Evans, Frederick William
Green, Calvin
Jackson, Rebecca Cox
Johnson, Theodore
  Elliott
King, Emma Belle
Lee, Ann
Lindsay, Bertha
Mace, Aurelia
McNemar, Richard
Taylor, Leila Sarah
Wells, Seth Youngs
White, Anna
Whittaker, James
Wright, Lucy

Southern Baptist Clergy
Graves, James Robinson
Hatcher, William
  Eldridge
Jeter, Jeremiah Bell
Norris, J. Frank
Scarborough, Lee
  Rutland
Willingham, Robert
  Josiah

*Southern Baptist Lay
Leaders*
Hays, Lawrence Brooks
Willingham, Robert
  Josiah

Swedenborgian Clergy
Barrett, Benjamin Fiske
Giles, Chauncey
  Commodore
Sewell, Frank

Swedenborgian Lay Leaders
Duché, Jacob
Reed, Sampson

Unitarian Clergy
Abbot, Francis
  Ellingwood
Alger, William
  Rounseville
Bancroft, Aaron
Barrows, Samuel June
Bellows, Henry Whitney
Bentley, William
Blackwell, Antoinette
  Louisa Brown

Blake, James Vila
Buckminster, Joseph
  Stevens
Channing, William
  Ellery
Channing, William
  Henry
Clarke, James Freeman
Collier, Price
Conway, Moncure
  Daniel
Cooke, George Willis
Cummings, Edward
Dall, Charles Henry
  Appleton
Davies, A. Powell
Dewey, Orville
Dietrich, John Hassler
Eliot, Frederick May
Eliot, Samuel Atkins
Eliot, Thomas Lamb
Eliot, William Greenleaf,
  Jr.
Ellis, George Edward
Emerson, William
Fenn, William Wallace
Francis, Convers
Freeman, James
Fritchman, Stephen Hole
Frothingham, Nathaniel
  Langdon
Frothingham, Octavius
  Brooks
Furness, William Henry
Gannett, Ezra Stiles
Gilman, Samuel Foster
Hale, Edward Everett
Harris, Thaddeus Mason
Hedge, Frederic Henry
Higginson, Thomas
  Wentworth
Hill, Thomas
Holley, Horace
Holmes, John Haynes
Jones, Jenkin Lloyd
Judd, Sylvester
Lathrop, John Howland
Longfellow, Samuel
MacCauley, Clay
May, Samuel Joseph
Mayo, Amory Dwight
Palfrey, John Gorham
Parker, Theodore
Peabody, Andrew
  Preston
Peabody, Francis
  Greenwood
Peabody, Oliver William
  Bourn
Potter, Charles Francis
Potter, William James

Reese, Curtis Williford
Ripley, Ezra
Savage, Minot Judson
Sears, Edmund
  Hamilton
Simmons, Henry Martyn
Simons, Minot
Sparks, Jared
Stearns, Oliver
Stebbins, Horatio
Sullivan, William
  Laurence
Sunderland, Jabez
  Thomas
Toulmin, Harry
Tuckerman, Joseph
Upham, Charles
  Wentworth
Vogt, Von Ogden
Ware, Henry, Jr.
Ware, William
Wendte, Charles William
West, Samuel
Wheelwright, John
Woolley, Celia Parker

Unitarian Lay Leaders
Jones, Susan Charlotte
  Barber

*Unitarian Universalist
Clergy*
Greeley, Dana McLean

Universalist Clergy
Ballou, Adin
Ballou, Hosea
Ballou, Hosea, 2d
Brown, Olympia
King, Thomas Starr
Kneeland, Abner
Miner, Alonzo Ames
Murray, John
  (1741–1815)
Newton, Joseph Fort
Skinner, Clarence
  Russell
Soule, Caroline Augusta
  White

Universalist Lay Leaders
Winchester, Elhanan

Wesleyan Methodist Clergy
Lee, Luther

**Spiritual Communities
and Movements**
Alleged Heretics
Bowne, Borden Parker

Crapsey, Algernon
  Sidney
Hutchinson, Anne

*American Indian Religious
Leaders*
Black Elk
Deganawidah
Francis, Josiah
Handsome Lake
Kenekuk
Kicking Bear
Main Poc
Neolin
Porcupine
Red Wing
Short Bull
Smohalla
Tavibo
Tenskwatawa
Wilson
Wodziwob

Antinomian Leaders
Hutchinson, Anne

Buddhist Leaders
Olcott, Henry Steel
Trungpa, Chögyam

Christian Converts
Marrant, John
Occom, Samson
Opukahaia
Other Day, John
Tekakwitha, Kateri

*Christian Fellowship
Members*
Seiberling, Henrietta
  Buckler

Cult Leaders
Divine, Father
Jones, Jim
Koresh, David
Laveau, Marie *Suppl. 1*

Ethical Culture Leaders
Adler, Felix
Coit, Stanton
Elliott, John Lovejoy
Spencer, Anna Garlin

Evangelists
Alline, Henry
Biederwolf, William
  Edward
Bliss, Philip Paul
Brown, R. R.
Bryan, Hugh

**Spiritual Communities
and Movements** *(cont.)*
Chapman, John Wilbur
Croswell, Andrew
Davenport, James
Dixon, Amzi Clarence
Dow, Lorenzo
Eddy, George Sherwood
Finney, Charles
  Grandison
Gillis, James Martin
Goldstein, David
Grace, Charles
  Emmanuel
Haviland, Laura Smith
Henkel, Paul
Inskip, John Swanel
Ironside, Henry Allan
Jones, Abner
Jones, Bob
Jones, Samuel Porter
Kirk, Edward Norris
Lee, Jarena
Livermore, Harriet
Maffitt, John Newland
  (1794–1850)
Matthews, Mark Allison
McIlvaine, Charles Pettit
McNemar, Richard
McPherson, Aimee
  Semple
Miller, George
Mills, Benjamin Fay
Moody, Dwight Lyman
Nast, William
Nettleton, Asahel
Norris, J. Frank
Ockenga, Harold John
Osborn, Sarah Haggar
  Wheaten
Palmer, Phoebe Worrall
Palmer, Sarah Worrall
  Lankford
Parham, Charles Fox
Rader, Paul
Riley, William Bell
Rimmer, Harry
Rodeheaver, Homer
  Alvin
Sankey, Ira David
Scofield, Cyrus Ingerson
Scott, Walter
Smith, Amanda Berry
Smith, Fred Burton
Smith, Hannah Whitall
Stearns, Shubal
Stone, Barton Warren
Sunday, Billy
Taylor, William
Torrey, Reuben Archer

Van Cott, Maggie
  Newton
Webb, Thomas
White, Alma Bridwell
Whitefield, George
Willing, Jennie Fowler
Woodworth-Etter, Maria
  Beulah

Freethinkers
Colman, Lucy Newhall
Kneeland, Abner
Potter, William James
Rose, Ernestine

Gurus
Bhaktivedanta, A. C. P.
Krishnamurti, Jiddu
Prabhavananda
Rajneesh, Bhagwan
Yogananda,
  Paramahansa

Humanists
Hunt, Harriot Kezia
Jaeger, Werner Wilhelm
Loeb, James
MacIver, Robert
  Morrison
Potter, Charles Francis
Rabinowitch, Eugene
Reese, Curtis Williford

Inspirationist Leaders
Heinemann, Barbara
Metz, Christian

Military Chaplains
Colton, Walter
Duffy, Francis Patrick
Eastman, William Reed
Fithian, Philip Vickers
McCabe, Charles
  Cardwell
Plummer, Henry Vinton
Trumbull, Henry Clay

Millennialists
Husband, Herman

Missionaries
Abeel, David
Adger, John Bailey
Allen, Young John
  William
Altham, John
Anderson, David
  Lawrence
Anderson, Rufus
Andrews, Lorrin
Asbury, Francis

Ashmun, Jehudi
Badin, Stephen
  Theodore
Bailey, Jacob
Baird, Robert
Bapst, John
Barton, James Levi
Bashford, James
  Whitford
Beach, Harlan Page
Becker, Abraham Jacob
  Suppl. 2
Becker, Magdalena
  Hergert *Suppl. 2*
Benavides, Alonso de
Biard, Pierre
Bingham, Hiram (1789–
  1869)
Bingham, Sybil Moseley
Blackburn, Gideon
Blanchet, Francis
  Norbert
Bliss, Daniel
Boardman, Sarah Hall
Brainerd, David
Brainerd, John
Bray, Thomas
Breck, James Lloyd
Bressani, Francesco
  Giuseppe
Bridgman, Elijah
  Coleman
Bridgman, Eliza Jane
  Gillette
Brown, Lydia
Brown, Samuel Robbins
Cabrini, Frances Xavier
Cameron, Donaldina
  Mackenzie
Capers, William
Cary, Lott
Cataldo, Joseph Maria
Copley, Thomas
Crawford, Isabel
  Suppl. 1
Dall, Charles Henry
  Appleton
Davis, Jerome Dean
Dearing, John Lincoln
Dempster, John
De Smet, Pierre-Jean
Dooley, Thomas
  Anthony, III
Dorsey, James Owen
Duchesne, Rose
  Philippine
Eliot, John
Elliott, Walter Hackett
  Robert
Engelhardt, Zephyrin

Escalante, Silvestre Vélez
  de
Evans, Nathaniel
Fisher, Frederick Bohn
Fisher, Mary
Fiske, Fidelia
Fitton, James
Flint, Timothy
Frame, Alice Seymour
  Browne
Gallitzin, Demetrius
  Augustine
Garcés, Francisco
  Tomás Hermenegildo
Gates, Caleb Frank
Gilman, Frank Patrick
Goodell, William
  (1792–1867)
Goodrich, Chauncey
  (1836–1925)
Gordon, Andrew
Graessl, Dominic
  Laurence
Greaton, Joseph
Grube, Bernhard Adam
Gulick, John Thomas
Gulick, Luther Halsey
  (1828–1891)
Gulick, Sidney Lewis
Harris, Merriman
  Colbert
Hawley, Gideon
Hayden, Mother Bridget
Haygood, Laura Askew
Henni, John Martin
Hepburn, James Curtis
Hidalgo, Francisco
Holcombe, Chester
Holly, James Theodore
Homes, Henry Augustus
Hume, Robert Allen
Ingalls, Marilla Baker
Jackson, Sheldon
Jacoby, Ludwig
  Sigismund
Jessup, Henry Harris
Jogues, Isaac
Johnson, Samuel
Jones, Charles Colcock
Jones, Edward
Jones, Eli Stanley
Jones, George Heber
Judd, Gerrit Parmele
Judd, Laura Fish
Judson, Adoniram
Judson, Ann Hasseltine
Judson, Emily Chubbuck
Kellogg, Samuel Henry
Kidder, Daniel Parish
Kino, Eusebio Francisco
Kirkland, Samuel

Spiritual Communities and Movements (cont.)

Lamy, John Baptist
Leavitt, Mary Greenleaf Clement
Lee, Jason
Lefevere, Peter Paul
Leiper, Henry Smith *Suppl. 1*
Liele, George
Lowry, Edith Elizabeth
MacCauley, Clay
Mackay, John Alexander
Mackenzie, Jean Kenyon
MacSparran, James
Marquette, Jacques
Martin, William Alexander Parsons
Marty, Martin
Mateer, Calvin Wilson
Mayhew, Experience
Mayhew, Thomas, Jr.
Mazzuchelli, Samuel Charles
McBeth, Susan Law
McLean, Mary Hancock
McNemar, Richard
Mccoy, Isaac
Menetrey, Joseph
Miner, Sarah Luella
Moninger, Mary Margaret
Moon, Lottie
Morrison, William McCutchan
Mudge, James
Nerinckx, Charles
Netsvetov, Jacob
Nevius, John Livingstone
Newell, Harriet Atwood
Niza, Marcos de
Odin, Jean-Marie
Ogilvie, John
Packard, Sophia Betsey
Pareja, Francisco
Parker, Peter (1804–1888)
Peabody, Lucy Whitehead McGill Waterbury
Peck, John Mason
Pierson, Abraham
Pierson, Arthur Tappan
Pierz, Francis Xavier
Pond, Samuel William
Porter, Eliza Emily Chappell
Price, Thomas Frederick
Ravalli, Antonio
Rese, Frederic
Rice, Luther

Richard, Gabriel
Riggs, Stephen Return
Rogers, Elymas Payson
Rogers, John Almanza Rowley
Savage, Thomas Staughton
Scudder, Ida Sophia
Scudder, John
Seagrave, Gordon Stifler
Seghers, Charles Jean
Sergeant, John (1710–1749)
Serra, Junipero
Smith, Amanda Berry
Smith, Arthur Henderson
Smith, Hezekiah
Smith, Judson
Spalding, Eliza Hart
Stouppe, Pierre *Suppl. 2*
Swain, Clara A.
Talcott, Eliza
Taylor, John (1752–1835)
Taylor, William
Tenney, Charles Daniel
Thoburn, James Mills
Thurston, Lucy Goodale
Thurston, Matilda Smyrell Calder
Turner, Fennell Parrish
Underwood, Lillias Stirling Horton
Van Dyck, Cornelius Van Alen
Vautrin, Minnie
Veniaminov, Ivan
Verbeck, Guido Herman Fridolin
Voth, Henry Richert
Washburn, George
Wharton, Greene Lawrence
White, Andrew
White, Elijah
Whitman, Marcus
Whitman, Narcissa Prentiss
Wilder, Robert Parmalee
Williams, Edward Thomas
Williams, Eleazar
Wilson, John Leighton
Wood, Thomas Bond
Wright, Sela Goodrich
Wyneken, Friedrich Conrad Dietrich
Young, Hall
Zeisberger, David

Zinzendorf, Nikolaus Ludwig von
Zwemer, Samuel Marinus

Monks
Huntington, James Otis Sargent
Marty, Martin
Merton, Thomas
Michel, Virgil
Moosmüller, Oswald William
Wimmer, Boniface

Mystics
Deganawidah
Grierson, Francis
Heard, Gerald
Kelpius, Johannes
Urrea, Teresa

Nuns
Angela, Mother
Anthony, Sister
Ayres, Anne
Butler, Mother Marie Joseph
Cannon, Harriett Starr
Clarke, Mary Frances
Connelly, Cornelia
Drexel, Katharine
Duchesne, Rose Philippine
Gill, Mother Irene
Guérin, Anne-Thérèse
Hardey, Mary Aloysia
Hayden, Mother Bridget
Healy, Eliza
Lange, Mary Elizabeth
Lathrop, Rose Hawthorne
Matthews, Ann Teresa
McGroarty, Sister Julia
Pollyblank, Ellen Albertina
Pommerel, Celestine
Powers, Jessica
Rogers, Elizabeth Ann
Warde, Mary Frances

Occultists
Adamski, George
Ballard, Edna Anne Wheeler, and Guy Warren Ballard
Blavatsky, Helena Petrovna
Randolph, Paschal Beverly

Pentecostals
Alamo, Susan
Bell, Eudorus Neander
du Plessis, David Johannes
Seymour, William Joseph
Woodworth-Etter, Maria Beulah

Religious Broadcasters
Alamo, Susan
Ayer, William Ward
Barnhouse, Donald Grey
Brown, R. R.
Coughlin, Charles Edward
Fosdick, Harry Emerson
Fuller, Charles Edward
Jones, Clarence Wesley
Maier, Walter Arthur
Michaux, Lightfoot Solomon
Poling, Daniel Alfred
Rader, Paul
Russell, Clayton
Sheen, Fulton John

Religious Martyrs
Dyer, Mary
Garcés, Francisco Tomás Hermenegildo
Jogues, Isaac

Saints
Netsvetov, Jacob
Neumann, John Nepomucene
Seton, Elizabeth Ann Bayley
Veniaminov, Ivan

Sectarian Leaders
Ballard, Edna Anne Wheeler, and Guy Warren Ballard
Bimeler, Joseph Michael
Brooks, Nona Lovell
Campbell, Thomas
Dowie, John Alexander
Fillmore, Charles Sherlock
Fillmore, Myrtle
Grace, Charles Emmanuel
Harris, Thomas Lake
Holmes, Ernest Shurtleff
Hopkins, Emma Curtis
Hubbard, L. Ron
Jansson, Eric

Spiritual Communities and Movements *(cont.)*
Matthew, Wentworth Arthur
Osgood, Jacob
Randall, Benjamin
Rogers, John (1648–1721)
Sandeman, Robert
Scholte, H. P.
Simpson, Albert Benjamin
Spencer, Peter
White, Alma Bridwell
Winebrenner, John

Separatist Leaders
Bimeler, Joseph Michael

Spiritual Healers
Anderson, Garland
Cayce, Edgar
Evans, Warren Felt
Quimby, Phineas Parkhurst
Urrea, Teresa

Spiritualists
Atkinson, William Walker
Britten, Emma Hardinge
Colby, Luther
Davenport, Ira Erastus, and William Henry Harrison Davenport
Davis, Andrew Jackson
Davis, Mary Fenn Robinson
Dods, John Bovee
Fox, Catherine, Margaret Fox, and Ann Leah Fox
Goldsmith, Joel Sol
Green, Frances Harriet Whipple
Jones, Amanda Theodosia
Richmond, Cora L. V. Scott Hatch Daniels Tappan
Shindler, Mary Dana
Sprague, Achsa W.
Sunderland, La Roy
Whitman, Sarah Helen
Williams, John Shoebridge

Theologians
Alexander, Archibald
Allen, Alexander Viets Griswold

Ames, Edward Scribner
Anderson, Rufus
Bacon, Benjamin Wisner
Ballou, Hosea
Bellamy, Joseph
Bennett, John Coleman
Berkhof, Louis
Bomberger, John Henry Augustus
Bouquillon, Thomas Joseph
Bowen, John Wesley Edward
Bowne, Borden Parker
Boyce, James Petigru
Breckinridge, Robert Jefferson
Briggs, Charles Augustus
Brown, William Adams
Buckham, John Wright
Bushnell, Horace
Carnell, Edward John
Clarke, William Newton
Cohon, Samuel Solomon
Corcoran, James Andrew
Curtis, Olin Alfred
Dearing, John Lincoln
DuBose, William Porcher
Dwight, Timothy
Emmons, Nathanael
Erdman, William Jacob
Felsenthal, Bernhard
Fenton, Joseph Clifford
Foster, Frank Hugh
Foster, George Burman
Frei, Hans Wilhelm
Fritschel, Conrad Sigmund
Fritschel, Gottfried Leonhard Wilhelm
Fuller, Richard
Gavin, Frank Stanton Burns
Geffen, Tobias
Gerhart, Emanuel Vogel
Gmeiner, John
Gordon, George Angier
Gorton, Samuel
Harkness, Georgia Elma
Harris, Samuel
Heschel, Abraham Joshua
Hodge, Archibald Alexander
Hodge, Charles
Hoge, Moses
Hopkins, Samuel (1721–1803)
Horton, Walter Marshall
Hove, Elling

Jacobs, Henry Eyster
Keith, George
Keith, Reuel
King, Henry Churchill
Knox, John
Knudson, Albert Cornelius
Krauth, Charles Porterfield
Ladd, George Trumbull
Lewis, Edwin
Lord, Eleazar
Lyman, Eugene William
Machen, J. Gresham
Macintosh, Douglas Clyde
Mathews, Shailer
Miley, John
Mitchell, Hinckley Gilbert Thomas
Mullins, Edgar Young
Murray, John Courtney
Neumark, David
Nevin, John Williamson
Niebuhr, H. Richard
Niebuhr, Reinhold
Niles, Nathaniel
Norton, Andrews
Noyes, George Rapall
Parham, Charles Fox
Park, Edwards Amasa
Pauck, Wilhelm
Peck, Thomas Ephraim
Pieper, Franz August Otto
Pond, Enoch
Priestley, Joseph
Rall, Harris Franklin
Ralston, Thomas Neely
Ramsey, Paul
Raymond, Miner
Ryan, John Augustine
Schaff, Philip
Schmidt, Friedrich August
Schmucker, Samuel Simon
Shedd, William Greenough Thayer
Sihler, Wilhelm
Sittler, Joseph Andrew, Jr.
Smith, Gerald Birney
Smith, Henry Boynton
Stearns, Lewis French
Stoddard, Solomon
Stone, Barton Warren
Stringfellow, Frank William
Strong, Augustus Hopkins

Summers, Thomas Osmond
Sverdrup, Georg
Talmage, James Edward
Taylor, Nathaniel William
Tillett, Wilbur Fisk
Tillich, Paul
Tucker, William Jewett
Walker, James Barr
Ware, William
Warfield, Benjamin Breckinridge
Warren, William Fairfield
Weigel, Gustave
Wells, Seth Youngs
Whedon, Daniel Denison
Wieman, Henry Nelson
Willard, Samuel
Williams, Daniel Day
Wright, George Ernest
Wright, George Frederick
Wright, John Joseph
Zinzendorf, Nikolaus Ludwig von

Theosophists
Bailey, Alice Anne La Trobe-Bateman
Blavatsky, Helena Petrovna
Judge, William Quan
Krishnamurti, Jiddu
Olcott, Henry Steel
Tingley, Katherine Augusta Westcott

Witchcraft Hysteria Victims
Corey, Martha
Hibbins, Ann
Nurse, Rebecca

Zionists
Blackstone, William E.
Flexner, Bernard
Gottheil, Richard James Horatio
Greenberg, Hayim
Lewisohn, Ludwig
Lowenthal, Marvin Marx
Mack, Julian William
Magnes, Judah Leon
Mendes, Henry Pereira
Rosenblatt, Bernard Abraham
Sampter, Jessie Ethel
Silver, Abba Hillel

Spiritual Communities and Movements *(cont.)*
Sonneschein, Rosa
Syrkin, Marie
Szold, Henrietta
Weisgal, Meyer Wolfe
Wise, Stephen Samuel

SCIENCE AND TECHNOLOGY

Earth Sciences
Cartographers
Bradley, Abraham, Jr.
Darton, Nelson Horatio
De Brahm, William Gerard
De Witt, Simeon
Emory, William Hemsley
Evans, Lewis
Greenleaf, Moses
Harriot, Thomas
Herrman, Augustine
Hutchins, Thomas
Keith, Arthur
Kern, Edward Meyer, Richard Hovendon Kern, and Benjamin Jordan Kern
Kino, Eusebio Francisco
Le Moyne de Morgues, Jacques
Lesley, J. Peter
Romans, Bernard
Snyder, John P. *Suppl. 2*
Tanner, Henry Schenck
Thompson, David
Wood, John

Gemologists
Kunz, George Frederick

Geochemists
Brown, Harrison Scott
Hillebrand, William Francis

Geodesists
Bowie, William
Chandler, Seth Carlo, Jr.
Davidson, George
Hassler, Ferdinand Rudolph
Hayford, John Fillmore
Hilgard, Julius Erasmus

Geographers
Adams, Cyrus Cornelius
Atwood, Wallace Walter
Baker, Oliver Edwin
Bowman, Isaiah

Brown, Ralph Hall
Daly, Charles Patrick
Davis, William Morris
Gannett, Henry
Guyot, Arnold Henry
Hakluyt, Richard
Huntington, Ellsworth
Jefferson, Mark Sylvester William
Morse, Jedidiah
Robinson, Edward
Sauer, Carl Ortwin
Semple, Ellen Churchill
Shaler, Nathaniel Southgate
Tanner, Henry Schenck
Wheeler, George Montague

Geologists
Agassiz, Louis
Ashburner, Charles Albert
Barbour, George Brown
Barrell, Joseph
Bascom, Florence
Becker, George Ferdinand
Blackwelder, Eliot
Boll, Jacob
Bowman, Isaiah
Boyé, Martin Hans
Bradley, Wilmot Hyde *Suppl. 2*
Branner, John Casper
Brooks, Alfred Hulse
Brush, George Jarvis
Bryan, Kirk
Buddington, Arthur Francis
Chamberlin, Rollin Thomas
Chamberlin, Thomas Chrowder
Clapp, Asahel
Clapp, Charles Horace
Clark, William Bullock
Cook, George Hammell
Crosby, William Otis
Cross, Charles Whitman
Daly, Reginald Aldworth
Dana, James Dwight
Darton, Nelson Horatio
Davis, William Morris
Day, David Talbot
Dunbar, Carl Owen
Dutton, Clarence Edward
Eaton, Amos
Emmons, Ebenezer

Emmons, Samuel Franklin
Evans, Lewis
Featherstonhaugh, George William
Fenneman, Nevin Melancthon
Gardner, Julia Anna
Gibbs, George (1815–1873)
Gilbert, Grove Karl
Gilluly, James
Gould, Laurence McKinley
Grabau, Amadeus William
Hague, Arnold
Hall, James (1811–1898)
Hayden, Ferdinand Vandeveer
Hayes, Charles Willard
Hedberg, Hollis Dow
Heezen, Bruce
Heilprin, Angelo
Hess, Harry Hammond
Hilgard, Eugene Woldemar
Hill, Robert Thomas
Hitchcock, Charles Henry
Hitchcock, Edward
Hobbs, William Herbert
Holmes, William Henry *Suppl. 1*
Houghton, Douglass
Hunt, Thomas Sterry
Irving, John Duer
Jackson, Charles Thomas
Jaggar, Thomas Augustus, Jr.
Keith, Arthur
Kennedy, Kathleen Agnes
Keyes, Charles Rollin
King, Clarence Rivers
Knopf, Adolph
Knopf, Eleanora Frances Bliss
Larsen, Esper Signius, Jr.
Lawson, Andrew Cowper
LeConte, Joseph
Leith, Charles Kenneth
Lesley, J. Peter
Lindgren, Waldemar
Lowdermilk, Walter Clay *Suppl. 1*
Mackin, J. Hoover
Maclure, William

Marbut, Curtis Fletcher
Mather, William Williams
McGee, William John
McKelvey, Vincent E. *Suppl. 1*
Meinzer, Oscar Edward
Menard, Henry William
Mendenhall, Walter Curran
Merrill, George Perkins
Mitchell, Elisha
Moore, Raymond Cecil
Newberry, John Strong
Nolan, Thomas B. *Suppl. 1*
Orton, Edward Francis Baxter
Owen, David Dale
Pecora, William Thomas
Percival, James Gates
Pirsson, Louis Valentine
Powell, John Wesley
Price, George McCready
Pumpelly, Raphael
Ransome, Frederick Leslie
Riddell, John Leonard
Rogers, Henry Darwin
Rogers, William Barton
Rubey, William Walden
Ruffner, William Henry
Russell, Israel Cook
Safford, James Merrill
Salisbury, Rollin D.
Shaler, Nathaniel Southgate
Shoemaker, Gene *Suppl. 1*
Smith, George Otis
Smithson, James *Suppl. 2*
Spurr, Josiah Edward
Stevenson, Matilda Coxe Evans
Swallow, George Clinton
Talmage, James Edward
Tarr, Ralph Stockman
Taylor, Frank Bursley
Taylor, Richard Cowling
Troost, Gerard
Ulrich, Edward Oscar
Van Hise, Charles Richard
Vanuxem, Lardner
Vaughan, Thomas Wayland
Veatch, Arthur Clifford
Walcott, Charles Doolittle
Wanless, Harold Rollin

Earth Sciences *(cont.)*
Ward, Lester Frank
White, Charles Abiathar
White, David
White, George Willard
White, Israel Charles
Whitney, Josiah Dwight
Willis, Bailey
Winchell, Horace
  Vaughn
Winchell, Newton
  Horace
Woodworth, Jay Backus
Worthen, Amos Henry
Wright, George
  Frederick

Geomorphologists
Atwood, Wallace Walter
Johnson, Douglas Wilson

Geophysicists
Bauer, Louis Agricola
Benioff, Victor Hugo
Byerly, Perry
Chapman, Sydney
Day, Arthur Louis
Ewing, Maurice
Ferrel, William
Fleming, John Adam
Forbush, Scott Ellsworth
Griggs, David Tressel
Hubbert, M. King
Macelwane, James
  Bernard
Reid, Harry Fielding
Schott, Charles Anthony
Vestine, Ernest Harry
Woodward, Robert
  Simpson

Hydrographers
Davis, Arthur Powell
Davis, Charles Henry
McArthur, William Pope
Newell, Frederick
  Haynes

Hydrologists
Darton, Nelson Horatio

Limnologists
Birge, Edward Asahel
Juday, Chancey

Meteorologists
Abbe, Cleveland
Bjerknes, Jacob Aall
  Bonnevie
Charney, Jule Gregory
Coffin, James Henry

Davis, William Morris
Espy, James Pollard
Gregg, Willis Ray
Harrington, Mark
  Walrod
Hess, Seymour Lester
Loomis, Elias
Marvin, Charles
  Frederick
McAdie, Alexander
  George
Myer, Albert James
Reichelderfer, Francis
  Wilton
Rossby, Carl-Gustaf
  Arvid
Siple, Paul Allman

Mineralogists
Bruce, Archibald
Cleaveland, Parker
Genth, Frederick
  Augustus
Gibbs, George
  (1776–1833)
Grim, Ralph Early
Keating, William
  Hypolitus
Mitchell, Elisha
Saugrain De Vigni,
  Antoine François
Seybert, Henry
Shepard, Charles
  Upham
Silliman, Benjamin
Smith, John Lawrence
Smithson, James
  Suppl. 2

Oceanographers
Agassiz, Alexander
Beebe, William
Bigelow, Henry Bryant
Eckart, Carl Henry
Heezen, Bruce
Hess, Harry Hammond
Iselin, Columbus
  O'Donnell, II
Maury, Matthew
  Fontaine
Pillsbury, John Elliott
Revelle, Roger Randall
  Dougan
Rossby, Carl-Gustaf
  Arvid
Sverdrup, Harald Ulrik
Thompson, Thomas
  Gordon

Paleontologists
Clarke, John Mason

Cope, Edward Drinker
Cushman, Joseph
  Augustine
Dall, William Healey
Dunbar, Carl Owen
Gabb, William More
Grabau, Amadeus
  William
Granger, Walter
Gregory, William King
Hall, James (1811–1898)
Harlan, Richard
Holland, William Jacob
Hyatt, Alpheus
Leidy, Joseph
Marsh, Othniel Charles
Mather, Kirtley Fletcher
Matthew, William Diller
Meek, Fielding Bradford
Merriam, John Campbell
Newberry, John Strong
Osborn, Henry Fairfield
Patten, William
Patterson, Bryan
Romer, Alfred Sherwood
Schuchert, Charles
Scott, William Berryman
Sepkoski, J. John, Jr.
  Suppl. 1
Simpson, George
  Gaylord
Vaughan, Thomas
  Wayland
Wachsmuth, Charles
Walcott, Charles
  Doolittle
Wetmore, Alexander
White, Charles Abiathar
Whitfield, Robert Parr
Wieland, George Reber
Williston, Samuel
  Wendell

Petroleum Geologists
Bell, Alfred H. *Suppl. 2*
DeGolyer, Everette Lee
Pratt, Wallace E.
  Suppl. 1
Wrather, William Embry

Petrologists
Bowen, Norman Levi
Iddings, Joseph Paxson
Washington, Henry
  Stephens

Seismologists
Benioff, Victor Hugo
Byerly, Perry
Gutenberg, Beno
Richter, Charles Francis

Winthrop, John
  (1714–1779)

Soil Scientists
Bennett, Hugh
  Hammond
Hilgard, Eugene
  Woldemar
Kelley, Walter Pearson
Lowdermilk, Walter
  Clay *Suppl. 1*
Marbut, Curtis Fletcher

Volcanologists
Jaggar, Thomas
  Augustus, Jr.

Life Sciences
Anatomists
Brödel, Paul Heinrich
  Max
Chovet, Abraham
Cobb, William
  Montague
Corner, George
  Washington
Danforth, Charles
  Haskell
Detwiler, Samuel
  Randall
Goddard, Paul Beck
Godman, John Davidson
Harlan, Richard
Jameson, Horatio Gates
Kellogg, Charles Edwin
  Suppl. 2
Leidy, Joseph
Lewis, Warren Harmon
Mall, Franklin Paine
McClellan, George
McDowell, Joseph Nash
McKinney, Roscoe
  Lewis
Miller, William Snow
Pancoast, Joseph
Papanicolaou, George
  Nicholas
Pattison, Granville Sharp
Ramsay, Alexander
Ranson, Stephen Walter
Smith, Alban Gilpin
Souchon, Edmond
Spitzka, Edward
  Anthony
Stockard, Charles
  Rupert
Todd, Thomas Wingate
Wyman, Jeffries

Bacteriologists
Avery, Oswald Theodore

Life Sciences *(cont.)*
Bayne-Jones, Stanhope
Biggs, Hermann Michael
Carroll, James
de Kruif, Paul Henry
Dick, George Frederick
Dick, Gladys *Suppl. 1*
Dochez, Alphonse
  Raymond
Ernst, Harold Clarence
Flexner, Simon
Fred, Edwin Broun
Gay, Frederick Parker
Gradle, Henry
Jordan, Edwin Oakes
Kelser, Raymond
  Alexander
Lancefield, Rebecca
  Craighill
Moore, Veranus Alva
Mueller, John Howard
Noguchi, Hideyo
Park, William Hallock
Pearson, Leonard
Perkins, Roger Griswold
Prescott, Samuel Cate
Prudden, Theophil
  Mitchell
Ravenel, Mazÿck
  Porcher
Reed, Walter
Russell, Harry Luman
Shakespeare, Edward
  Oram
South, Lillian Herreld
Sternberg, George Miller
Tunnicliff, Ruth May
Vaughan, Victor
  Clarence
Werkman, Chester
  Hamlin
Williams, Anna Wessels
Zinsser, Hans

Biochemists
Anfinsen, Christian B.
  Suppl. 2
Benedict, Stanley
  Rossiter
Bergmann, Max
Bloch, Konrad E.
  Suppl. 2
Brown, Rachel Fuller
Cannan, Robert Keith
Chittenden, Russell
  Henry
Clarke, Hans Thacher
Cohn, Edwin Joseph
Cori, Carl Ferdinand,
  and Gerty Theresa
  Radnitz Cori

Dakin, Henry Drysdale
Dam, Carl Peter Henrik
Dayhoff, Margaret
  Oakley
Doisy, Edward Adelbert
du Vigneaud, Vincent
Elion, Gertrude *Suppl. 1*
Elvehjem, Conrad
  Arnold
Folin, Otto
Funk, Casimir
Gortner, Ross Aiken
Gottlieb, Sidney *Suppl. 2*
Haagen-Smit, Arie Jan
Hart, Edwin Bret
Hastings, Albert Baird
Haurowitz, Felix
  Michael
Heidelberger, Charles
Henderson, Lawrence
  Joseph
Herter, Christian
  Archibald (1865–1910)
Kendall, Edward Calvin
King, Charles Glen
Koch, Fred Conrad
Kunitz, Moses
Levene, Phoebus Aaron
  Theodor
Lewis, Howard Bishop
Link, Karl Paul Gerhardt
Lipmann, Fritz Albert
Longsworth, Lewis
  Gibson
Lusk, Graham
McCollum, Elmer
  Verner
Meyerhof, Otto Fritz
Mirsky, Alfred Ezra
Moore, Stanford
Murray, Henry
  Alexander, Jr.
Nachmansohn, David
Northrop, John Howard
Ochoa, Severo *Suppl. 2*
Osborne, Thomas Burr
Pauling, Linus Carl
Roberts, Richard Brooke
Rose, William Cumming
Schoenheimer, Rudolph
Stein, William Howard
Sumner, James
  Batcheller
Sutherland, Earl W.
Szent-Györgyi, Albert
Van Slyke, Donald
  Dexter
Vaughan, Victor
  Clarence
Wilkerson, Vernon
  Alexander

Wrinch, Dorothy Maud

Biologists
Allee, Warder Clyde
Bartelmez, George
  William
Binney, Amos
Blinks, Lawrence Rogers
Briggs, Robert William
Castle, William Ernest
Clapp, Cornelia Maria
Cockerell, Theodore
  Dru Alison
Conklin, Edwin Grant
Cope, Edward Drinker
Crozier, William John
Demerec, Milislav
Dobzhansky,
  Theodosius
Eklund, Carl Robert
Evermann, Barton
  Warren
Gabrielson, Ira Noel
Grinnell, Joseph
Harrison, Ross Granville
Harvey, Ethel Nicholson
  Browne
Jennings, Herbert
  Spencer
Keeler, Clyde Edgar
Keeton, William Tinsley
Kellogg, Vernon Lyman
Leopold, A. Starker
Loeb, Jacques
McClung, Clarence
  Erwin
McCrady, Edward
McMahon, Thomas A.
  Suppl. 2
McMurrich, James
  Playfair
Miles, Manly
Miller, Alden Holmes
Minot, Charles Sedgwick
Morgan, Thomas Hunt
Morris, John McLean
Morse, Edward Sylvester
Pearl, Raymond
Robertson, Oswald
  Hope
Rodbell, Martin *Suppl. 2*
Sedgwick, William
  Thompson
Stockard, Charles
  Rupert
Szilard, Leo
Thomas, Lewis
Turner, Charles Henry
Wald, George *Suppl. 1*
Weiss, Paul Alfred

Wilson, Henry Van
  Peters
Winslow, Charles-
  Edward Amory
Young, Stanley Paul

Biometricians
Harris, James Arthur

Biophysicists
Bronk, Detlev Wulf
Cole, Kenneth Stewart
Hartline, Haldan Keffer
Hecht, Selig

Botanists
Allen, Charles Elmer
Ames, Oakes
  (1874–1950)
Anderson, Edgar
Arthur, Joseph Charles
Atkinson, George
  Francis
Bailey, Irving Widmer
Bailey, Liberty Hyde
Baldwin, William
Barton, Benjamin Smith
Bartram, John
Beal, William James
Bessey, Charles Edwin
Bigelow, Jacob
Blakeslee, Albert Francis
Blinks, Lawrence Rogers
Bodley, Rachel Littler
Brandegee, Mary
  Katharine Layne
  Curran
Brandegee, Townshend
  Stith
Bridges, Robert
Britton, Elizabeth
  Gertrude Knight
Britton, Nathaniel Lord
Cain, Stanley Adair
Caldwell, Otis William
Campbell, Douglas
  Houghton
Carson, Joseph
Catesby, Mark
Chamberlain, Charles
  Joseph
Chapman, Alvan
  Wentworth
Chase, Agnes
Clapp, Asahel
Clausen, Jens Christen
Clayton, John
Clements, Frederic
  Edward
Colden, Jane
Coulter, John Merle

Life Sciences *(cont.)*
Cowles, Henry Chandler
Curtis, Moses Ashley
Cutler, Manasseh
Darlington, William
Douglas, David
Durand, Élie Magloire
Eastwood, Alice
Eaton, Amos
Eaton, Daniel Cady
Elliott, Stephen
Emerson, Robert
Engelmann, George
Fairchild, David
    Grandison
Farlow, William Gilson
Ferguson, Margaret Clay
Fernald, Merritt Lyndon
Furbish, Kate
Goodale, George
    Lincoln
Gray, Asa
Greene, Edward Lee
Harris, James Arthur
Harshberger, John
    William
Hosack, David
James, Edwin
James, Thomas Potts
Jepson, Willis Linn
Kalm, Peter
Kellogg, Albert
Mangelsdorf, Paul
    Christoph
Marshall, Humphry
Meeuse, Bastiaan Jacob
    Dirk *Suppl. 2*
Merrill, Elmer Drew
Michaux, André
Muhlenberg, Henry
Neal, Marie Catherine
Nieuwland, Julius Arthur
Pease, Arthur Stanley
Perrine, Henry
Piper, Charles
    Vancouver
Porcher, Francis Peyre
Pursh, Frederick
Raper, John Robert
Ravenel, Henry William
Riddell, John Leonard
Robbins, William Jacob
Rose, Joseph Nelson
Sargent, Charles
    Sprague
Sax, Karl
Schweinitz, Lewis David
    von
Sears, Paul Bigelow
Setchell, William Albert
Shattuck, Lydia White

Shecut, John Linnaeus
    Edward Whitridge
Short, Charles Wilkins
Shull, George Harrison
Sinnott, Edmund Ware
Smith, Gilbert Morgan
Stebbins, G. Ledyard
    Suppl. 1
Sullivant, William
    Starling
Thurber, George
Torrey, John
Trelease, William
Tuckerman, Edward
Walter, Thomas
Watson, Sereno
Webber, Herbert John

Conchologists
Anthony, John Gould
Gould, Augustus
    Addison
Stearns, Robert Edwards
    Carter
Tryon, George
    Washington, Jr.

Cytologists
Claude, Albert
Friend, Charlotte
Mirsky, Alfred Ezra
Stevens, Nettie Maria
Wilson, Edmund
    Beecher

Dendrochronologists
Douglass, Andrew
    Ellicott

Ecologists
Abbey, Edward
Allee, Warder Clyde
Cain, Stanley Adair
Carson, Rachel Louise
Clausen, Jens Christen
Clements, Frederic
    Edward
Cowles, Henry Chandler
Forbes, Stephen Alfred
MacArthur, Robert
    Helmer
Morgan, Ann Haven
Sears, Paul Bigelow
Shelford, Victor Ernest
Vogt, William
Whittaker, Robert
    Harding

Embryologists
Lewis, Warren Harmon
Lillie, Frank Rattray

Mall, Franklin Paine
Nicholas, John Spangler
Streeter, George Linius
Twitty, Victor Chandler
Weiss, Paul Alfred
Willier, Benjamin
    Harrison
Wilson, Edmund
    Beecher

Endocrinologists
Albright, Fuller
Allen, Edgar
Astwood, Edwin Bennett
Benjamin, Harry
Corner, George
    Washington
Evans, Herbert McLean
Hoskins, Roy Graham
Long, Cyril Norman
    Hugh
Moore, Carl Richard
Papanicolaou, George
    Nicholas
Pincus, Gregory
    Goodwin
Russell, Jane Anne
Timme, Walter

Entomologists
Cockerell, Theodore
    Dru Alison
Comstock, John Henry
Dyar, Harrison Gray, Jr.
Edwards, William Henry
Fitch, Asa
Forbes, Stephen Alfred
Glover, Townend
Hagen, Hermann August
Harris, Thaddeus
    William
Hentz, Nicholas
    Marcellus
Horn, George Henry
Howard, Leland Ossian
Kinsey, Alfred Charles
LeConte, John Lawrence
Lutz, Frank Eugene
Morris, John Gottlieb
Osten Sacken, Carl
    Robert Romanovich
    von der
Peck, William Dandridge
Riley, Charles Valentine
Sanderson, Ezra Dwight
Scudder, Samuel
    Hubbard
Smith, John Bernhard
Taylor, Charlotte
    Scarbrough
Uhler, Philip Reese

Walsh, Benjamin Dann
Wheeler, William
    Morton
Williams, Joseph Leroy
Williston, Samuel
    Wendell

Evolutionists
Fiske, John (1842–1901)
Scopes, John Thomas
Stebbins, G. Ledyard
    Suppl. 1

Geneticists
Babcock, Ernest Brown
Beadle, George Wells
Bridges, Calvin
    Blackman
Clausen, Jens Christen
Clausen, Roy Elwood
Davenport, Charles
    Benedict
East, Edward Murray
Goldschmidt, Richard
    Benedict
Lerner, I. Michael
Little, Clarence Cook
Luria, Salvador Edward
Lush, Jay Laurence
Mangelsdorf, Paul
    Christoph
McClintock, Barbara
Muller, Hermann Joseph
Sax, Karl
Schultz, Jack
Shull, George Harrison
Stadler, Lewis John
Stebbins, G. Ledyard
    Suppl. 1
Stern, Curt
Sturtevant, Alfred Henry
Tatum, Edward Lawrie
Wilson, Edmund
    Beecher
Wright, Sewall

Gerontologists
MacNider, William De
    Berniere

Hematologists
Dameshek, William
Moore, Carl Vernon

Herpetologists
Ditmars, Raymond Lee
Schmidt, Karl Patterson
Stejneger, Leonhard
    Hess

Life Sciences (*cont.*)

Immunologists
Berry, George Packer
Friend, Charlotte
Hirsch, James Gerald
Landsteiner, Karl
Sabin, Albert Bruce
Samter, Max *Suppl. 1*

Insect Pathologists
Steinhaus, Edward
Arthur

Malacologists
Dall, William Healey

Mammalogists
Allen, Glover Morrill
Anthony, Harold Elmer
Hamilton, William John,
Jr.
Jackson, Hartley Harrad
Thompson
Mearns, Edgar
Alexander
Miller, Gerrit Smith, Jr.
Tate, George Henry
Hamilton
Young, Stanley Paul

Marine Biologists
Agassiz, Alexander
Bigelow, Henry Bryant
Eigenmann, Carl H.
Eigenmann, Rosa Smith
Fewkes, Jesse Walter
Hubbs, Carl Leavitt
Hyatt, Alpheus
Mayor, Alfred
Goldsborough
Stimpson, William

Medical Scientists
Alvarez, Walter Clement
Aub, Joseph Charles
Beecher, Henry Knowles
Bender, Lauretta
Berson, Solomon Aaron
Carrel, Alexis
Cohn, Alfred Einstein
Cournand, André
Frédéric
Crile, George
Washington
Draper, George
Drew, Charles Richard
Dyer, Rolla Eugene
Gamble, James Lawder
Goldberger, Joseph
Goldblatt, Harry

Goodpasture, Ernest
William
Hektoen, Ludvig
Hess, Alfred Fabian
Holmes, Bayard Taylor
Howe, Percy Rogers
Ivy, Andrew Conway
Janeway, Charles
Alderson
Kolb, Lawrence
Leake, James Payton
Libman, Emanuel
Long, Esmond
Long, Perrin Hamilton
Lovelace, William
Randolph, II
Macklin, Madge
Thurlow
MacLeod, Colin Munro
Mahoney, John Friend
McDermott, Walsh
McLean, Franklin
Chambers
Metcalfe, Samuel Lytler
Michaelis, Leonor
Miller, Willoughby
Dayton
Moore, Joseph Earle
Morris, John McLean
Mosher, Clelia Duel
Richards, Dickinson
Woodruff
Rous, Francis Peyton
Sabin, Florence Rena
Sawyer, Wilbur
Augustus
Smith, Fred M.
Strong, Richard Pearson
Trask, James Dowling
Waterhouse, Benjamin
Welch, William Henry
Whipple, George Hoyt
Wilson, Frank Norman
Wood, William Barry, Jr.

Microbiologists
Alexander, Hattie
Elizabeth
Burkholder, Paul Rufus
Dubos, René Jules
Evans, Alice Catherine
Koplik, Henry
Novy, Frederick George
Poindexter, Hildrus
Augustus
Smith, Theobald
Waksman, Selman
Abraham

Molecular Biologists
Dayhoff, Margaret
Oakley
Delbrück, Max

Morphologists
Spitzka, Edward
Anthony

Mycologists
Dodge, Bernard Ogilvie
Thaxter, Roland

Naturalists
Abbot, John
Abbott, Charles Conrad
Adams, Charles Baker
Akeley, Carl Ethan
Audubon, John James
Bachman, John
Bailey, Jacob Whitman
Banister, John
Barbour, Thomas
Bartram, William
Bates, Marston
Beard, James Carter
Beebe, William
Bendire, Charles Emil
Boll, Jacob
Brugger, Kenneth C.
Suppl. 2
Burden, William
Douglas
Burroughs, John
Castiglioni, Luigi
Catesby, Mark
Cist, Jacob
Colden, Cadwallader
Coolidge, Dane
Cooper, James Graham
Coues, Elliott
Craighead, Frank
Cooper, Jr. *Suppl. 2*
Dewey, Chester
Drake, Daniel
Elliot, Daniel Giraud
Flagg, Wilson
Fossey, Dian
Fuertes, Louis Agassiz
Gabb, William More
Garden, Alexander
(1730–1791)
Gibbons, Euell
Theophilus
Godman, John Davidson
Grant, Madison
Green, Seth *Suppl. 2*
Gulick, John Thomas
Haldeman, Samuel
Stehman

Hamilton, William John,
Jr.
Harlow, Richard
Cresson
Hayden, Ferdinand
Vandeveer
Hildreth, Samuel
Prescott
Holbrook, John Edwards
Holder, Charles
Frederick
Hornaday, William
Temple
Horsfield, Thomas
Hubbs, Carl Leavitt
Jordan, David Starr
Josselyn, John
Kennicott, Robert
Kieran, John Francis
Kirtland, Jared Potter
Krause, Herbert Arthur
Lea, Isaac
Lesueur, Charles
Alexandre
Lincecum, Gideon
Lucas, Frederic
Augustus
Maxwell, Martha Ann
Dartt
McCook, Henry
Christopher
Meeuse, Bastiaan Jacob
Dirk *Suppl. 2*
Miller, Harriet Mann
Mitchell, John
(1690?–1768)
Moyer, Andrew Jackson
Suppl. 2
Muir, John
Nelson, Edward William
Nuttall, Thomas
Ord, George
Orton, James
Osborn, Fairfield
Peale, Titian Ramsay
Peattie, Donald Culross
Suppl. 1
Pickering, Charles
Pourtalès, Louis
François de
Putnam, Frederic Ward
Rafinesque, Constantine
Samuel
Ravenel, Edmund
Ritter, William Emerson
Romans, Bernard
Saugrain De Vigni,
Antoine François
Say, Thomas
Seton, Ernest Thompson
Stevenson, James

Life Sciences *(cont.)*
Stone, Witmer
Storer, David
  Humphreys
Stout, Gardner
  Dominick
Tate, George Henry
  Hamilton
Teale, Edwin Way
Thayer, Abbott
  Handerson
Thompson, Zadock
Thoreau, Henry David
Tryon, George
  Washington, Jr.
Wailes, Benjamin
  Leonard Covington
Ward, Henry Augustus
Williams, Stephen West
Wright, Mabel Osgood
Wyman, Jeffries
Xántus, John

Neuroanatomists
Crosby, Elizabeth
  Caroline

Neurobiologists
Donaldson, Henry
  Herbert

Neuroendocrinologists
Scharrer, Beta *Suppl. 2*

Neuroscientists
Cotzias, George C.
Geschwind, Norman
Herrick, Clarence
  Luther, and Charles
  Judson Herrick
Larsell, Olof
Magoun, Horace
  Winchell
O'Leary, James Lee

Ornithologists
Allen, Arthur Augustus
Allen, Glover Morrill
Bailey, Florence Augusta
  Merriam
Bonaparte, Charles
  Lucien Jules Laurent
Brewer, Thomas Mayo
Brewster, William
  (1851–1919)
Cassin, John
Catesby, Mark
Chapin, James Paul
Chapman, Frank
  Michler
Cory, Charles Barney

Eklund, Carl Robert
Forbush, Edward Howe
Friedmann, Herbert
Griscom, Ludlow
Henshaw, Henry
  Wetherbee
Jones, Lynds
Lawrence, George
  Newbold
Mearns, Edgar
  Alexander
Murphy, Robert
  Cushman
Nice, Margaret Morse
Oberholser, Harry
  Church
Pearson, Thomas
  Gilbert
Peterson, Roger Tory
  Suppl. 1
Pettingill, Olin Sewall, Jr.
  Suppl. 2
Richmond, Charles
  Wallace
Ridgway, Robert
Stejneger, Leonhard
  Hess
Todd, Walter Edmond
  Clyde
Townsend, John Kirk
Vogt, William
Wetmore, Alexander
Wilson, Alexander

Paleobotanists
Berry, Edward Wilber
Lesquereux, Leo
White, David
Wieland, George Reber

Paleoecologists
Edinger, Tilly
Gardner, Julia Anna

Parasitologists
Ward, Henry Baldwin

Pharmacognosists
Kraemer, Henry
Maisch, John Michael
Rusby, Henry Hurd

Pharmacologists
Abel, John Jacob
Auer, John
Brodie, Bernard Beryl
Graham, Helen Tredway
Hatcher, Robert
  Anthony
Hirschfelder, Arthur
  Douglas

Hunt, Reid
King, John
Krayer, Otto Hermann
Loewi, Otto
MacNider, William De
  Berniere
Marshall, Eli Kennerly,
  Jr.
Richards, Alfred Newton
Sutherland, Earl W.
Weiss, Soma

Physiologists
Allen, Edgar
Astwood, Edwin Bennett
Auer, John
Bard, Philip
Bazett, Henry Cuthbert
Beaumont, William
Békésy, Georg von
Benedict, Francis Gano
Best, Charles Herbert
Bishop, George Holman
Bowditch, Henry
  Pickering
Cannon, Walter
  Bradford
Carlson, Anton Julius
Curtis, John Green
Dalton, John Call, Jr.
Dragstedt, Lester
  Reynold
Drinker, Cecil Kent
DuBois, Eugene Floyd
Dunglison, Robley
Erlanger, Joseph
Evans, Herbert McLean
Fenn, Wallace Osgood
Flint, Austin
  (1836–1915)
Forbes, Alexander
Fulton, John Farquhar
Gasser, Herbert Spencer
Harvey, Edmund
  Newton
Hawthorne, Edward
  William
Hecht, Selig
Henderson, Lawrence
  Joseph
Henderson, Yandell
Hooker, Donald Russell
Hoskins, Roy Graham
Howell, William Henry
Hyde, Ida Henrietta
Knowles, John Hilton
Lewis, Warren Harmon
Lusk, Graham
Mann, Frank Charles
Marshall, Eli Kennerly,

  Jr.
Martin, Henry Newell
Meek, Walter Joseph
Meltzer, Samuel James
O'Leary, James Lee
Osterhout, Winthrop
  John Vanleuven
Penfield, Wilder Graves
Porter, William
  Townsend
Robbins, William Jacob
Scholander, Per Fredrik
  Thorkelsson
Sewall, Henry
Smith, Homer William
Visscher, Maurice Bolks
Wiggers, Carl John

Plant Collectors
Bartram, John
Bartram, William
Douglas, David
Fairchild, David
  Grandison
Fraser, John
Hansen, Niels Ebbesen
Mexia, Ynes Enriquetta
  Julietta
Michaux, François-
  André
Rusby, Henry Hurd
Wright, Charles

Plant Geneticists
Blakeslee, Albert Francis
Emerson, Rollins Adams
Wortman, Sterling, Jr.

Plant Pathologists
Arthur, Joseph Charles
Burrill, Thomas
  Jonathan
Dodge, Bernard Ogilvie
Duggar, Benjamin
  Minge
Galloway, Beverly
  Thomas
Harrar, Jacob George
Jones, Lewis Ralph
Kunkel, Louis Otto
Smith, Erwin Frink

Plant Physiologists
Crocker, William
Goddard, David
  Rockwell
Hoagland, Dennis
  Robert

Psychobiologists
Gantt, W. Horsley

Life Sciences *(cont.)*
Nissen, Henry
    Wieghorst
Richter, Curt Paul

Toxicologists
MacNider, William De
    Berniere

Virologists
Enders, John Franklin
Francis, Thomas, Jr.
Horsfall, Frank Lappin,
    Jr.
Paul, John Rodman
Rivers, Thomas Milton
Sabin, Albert Bruce
Salk, Jonas Edward
Shope, Richard Edwin
Stanley, Wendell
    Meredith
Theiler, Max

Zoologists
Agassiz, Louis
Allen, Joel Asaph
Andrews, Roy Chapman
Baird, Spencer Fullerton
Brooks, William Keith
Burnett, Waldo Irving
Calkins, Gary Nathan
Child, Charles Manning
Clapp, Cornelia Maria
Clark, Henry James
Dana, James Dwight
Darlington, Philip
    Jackson, Jr.
Dean, Bashford
De Kay, James Ellsworth
Fernald, Charles Henry
Fossey, Dian
Gardner, Julia Anna
Gill, Theodore Nicholas
Girard, Charles Frédéric
Goode, George Brown
Hall, Eugene Raymond
Harlow, Harry Frederick
Holland, William Jacob
Hyman, Libbie Henrietta
Just, Ernest Everett
Kellogg, Remington
Kofoid, Charles Atwood
Koopman, Karl *Suppl. 1*
Lillie, Frank Rattray
Lyman, Theodore
    (1833–1897)
Merriam, Clinton Hart
Montgomery, Thomas
    Harrison, Jr.
Morgan, Ann Haven
Nathans, Daniel *Suppl. 2*

Packard, Alpheus
    Spring, Jr.
Painter, Theophilus
    Shickel
Parker, George Howard
Patten, William
Rathbun, Mary Jane
Riddle, Oscar
Sonneborn, Tracy
    Morton
Stiles, Charles Wardell
Sumner, Francis Bertody
True, Frederick William
Twitty, Victor Chandler
Verrill, Addison Emery
Ward, Henry Baldwin
Whitman, Charles Otis

Mathematical Sciences
Computer Scientists
Aiken, Howard
    Hathaway
Atanasoff, John Vincent
    Suppl. 2
Hamming, Richard
    Wesley *Suppl. 2*
Hopper, Grace Brewster
    Murray
Kemeny, John George
Mauchly, John William

Mathematicians
Adrain, Robert
Albert, Abraham Adrian
Alexander, James
    Waddell
Artin, Emil
Bartlett, William Holms
    Chambers
Bateman, Harry
Bell, Eric Temple
Bergmann, Gustav
Bing, R. H.
Birkhoff, George David
Blichfeldt, Hans Frederik
Bliss, Gilbert Ames
Bôcher, Maxime
Bochner, Salomon
Bolza, Oskar
Bowditch, Nathaniel
Brauer, Richard
    Dagobert
Bronowski, Jacob
Brown, Ernest William
Buchanan, Herbert Earle
Byerly, William Elwood
Calderón, Alberto P.
    Suppl. 2
Caldwell, Joseph
Chapman, Sydney
Chauvenet, William

Church, Alonzo
    (1903–1995)
Coble, Arthur Byron
Coffin, James Henry
Cole, Frank Nelson
Coolidge, Julian Lowell
Courant, Richard
Cox, Elbert Frank
Craig, Thomas
De Forest, Erastus
    Lyman
Dickson, Leonard
    Eugene
Eisenhart, Luther Pfahler
Ellicott, Andrew
Evans, Griffith Conrad
Feller, William
Fine, Henry Burchard
Forbush, Scott Ellsworth
Fuller, Thomas
Geiringer, Hilda
Gibbs, Josiah Willard
    (1839–1903)
Godfrey, Thomas
    (1704–1749)
Greenwood, Isaac
Grew, Theophilus
Halsted, George Bruce
Hamming, Richard
    Wesley *Suppl. 2*
Harish-Chandra
Hassler, Ferdinand
    Rudolph
Hill, George William
Hille, Einar
Hoffmann, Banesh
Huntington, Edward
    Vermilye
Jackson, Dunham
Johnson, William
    Woolsey
Kac, Mark
Kasner, Edward
Kellogg, Oliver Dimon
Kemeny, John George
Koopmans, Tjalling
    Charles
Lane, Jonathan Homer
Lax, Anneli *Suppl. 2*
Leeds, John
Lefschetz, Solomon
Lewy, Hans
Maddison, Isabel
Martin, Artemas
Maschke, Heinrich
Mason, Max
McClintock, Emory
McShane, Edward James
Miller, George Abram
Minto, Walter
Montroll, Elliott Waters

Moore, Clarence Lemuel
    Elisha
Moore, Eliakim Hastings
Moore, Robert Lee
Morley, Frank
Morse, Marston
Moulton, Forest Ray
Murnaghan, Francis
    Dominic
Neugebauer, Otto
    Eduard
Newton, Hubert Anson
Nicollet, Joseph Nicolas
Osgood, William Fogg
Patterson, Robert
Peirce, Benjamin
Peirce, Benjamin
    Osgood, II
Peirce, James Mills
Pierce, Joseph Alphonso
Pólya, George
Prager, William
Rademacher, Hans
Ritt, Joseph Fels
Rittenhouse, David
Robertson, Howard
    Percy
Robie, Thomas
Robinson, Julia
Runkle, John Daniel
Safford, Truman Henry
Scott, Charlotte Angas
Steenrod, Norman Earl
Stone, Marshall Harvey
Story, William Edward
Stringham, Irving
Strong, Theodore
Sylvester, James Joseph
Tamarkin, Jacob David
Taussky-Todd, Olga
Thaxton, Hubert Mack
Thomas, Tracy Yerkes
Ulam, Stanislaw Marcin
Van Vleck, Edward Burr
Veblen, Oswald
Venable, Charles Scott
von Mises, Richard
    Marten Edler
von Neumann, John
    Louis
Walsh, Joseph Leonard
Weaver, Warren
Weil, André *Suppl. 1*
West, Benjamin
    (1730–1813)
Weyl, Hermann
Wheeler, Anna Johnson
    Pell
White, Henry Seely
Whitehead, Alfred North
Whitney, Hassler

Mathematical Sciences
(cont.)
Whyburn, Gordon
  Thomas
Wiener, Norbert
Wilczynski, Ernest Julius
Wilder, Raymond Louis
Wilson, Edwin Bidwell
Wright, Chauncey
Wright, Sewall
Wrinch, Dorothy Maud
Zariski, Oscar

Statisticians
Ayres, Leonard Porter
Babson, Roger Ward
Bryant, Louise Frances
  Stevens
Chandler, Seth Carlo, Jr.
Cochran, William
  Gemmell
Cox, Gertrude Mary
Dorchester, Daniel
Elliott, Ezekiel Brown
Emerson, Gouverneur
Hoffman, Frederick
  Ludwig
Hotelling, Harold
Hourwich, Isaac
  Aaronovich
Jacoby, Oswald
Jarvis, Edward
Koopmans, Tjalling
  Charles
Lotka, Alfred James
Neyman, Jerzy
Olds, Leland
Pearl, Raymond
Rice, Stuart Arthur
Shattuck, Lemuel
Sutton, William Loftus
Swank, James Moore
Sydenstricker, Edgar
Walker, Francis Amasa
Wilks, Samuel Stanley
Zeisel, Hans

Physical Sciences
Astronomers
Abbe, Cleveland
Abbot, Charles Greeley
Abell, George Ogden
Adams, Walter Sydney
Aitken, Robert Grant
Alexander, Stephen
Baade, Walter
Bailey, Solon Irving
Banneker, Benjamin
Barnard, Edward
  Emerson

Bartlett, William Holms
  Chambers
Blake, Francis
Bok, Bart Jan
Bond, George Phillips
Bond, William Cranch
Boss, Lewis
Bowditch, Nathaniel
Brattle, Thomas
Bressani, Francesco
  Giuseppe
Brouwer, Dirk
Brown, Ernest William
Brown, Joseph
Buchanan, Herbert Earle
Burnham, Sherburne
  Wesley
Caldwell, Joseph
Campbell, William
  Wallace
Cannon, Annie Jump
Chandler, Seth Carlo, Jr.
Coffin, John Huntington
  Crane
Comstock, George Cary
Curtis, Heber Doust
Davidson, George
Dixon, Jeremiah *Suppl. 2*
Douglass, Andrew
  Ellicott
Draper, Henry
Ellicott, Andrew
Fleming, Williamina
  Paton Stevens
Frost, Edwin Brant
Gilliss, James Melville
Godfrey, Thomas
  (1704–1749)
Goldberg, Leo
Gould, Benjamin
  Apthorp (1824–1896)
Hall, Asaph
Harkness, William
Harrington, Mark
  Walrod
Harriot, Thomas
Herget, Paul
Hill, George William
Hill, Thomas
Holden, Edward
  Singleton
Hough, George
  Washington
Hubble, Edwin Powell
Hussey, William Joseph
Hynek, J. Allen
Keeler, James Edward
Kirkwood, Daniel
Kuiper, Gerard Peter
Leavitt, Henrietta Swan
Leuschner, Armin Otto

Loomis, Elias
Lord, Henry Curwen
Lowell, Percival
Mason, Charles *Suppl. 2*
Maury, Antonia Caetana
  De Paiva Pereira
Mitchel, Ormsby
  Macknight
Mitchell, Maria
Mitchell, Samuel Alfred
Moore, Joseph Haines
Morgan, William Wilson
  Suppl. 1
Moulton, Forest Ray
Newcomb, Simon
Newton, Hubert Anson
Nicholson, Seth Barnes
Nicollet, Joseph Nicolas
Olmsted, Denison
Parkhurst, John Adelbert
Peirce, Benjamin
Perrine, Charles Dillon
Peters, Christian
  Heinrich Friedrich
Pickering, Edward
  Charles
Porter, Jermain
  Gildersleeve
Porter, Russell Williams
Rittenhouse, David
Rogers, William
  Augustus
Ross, Frank Elmore
Russell, Henry Norris
Safford, Truman Henry
Schilt, Jan
Schlesinger, Frank
Seares, Frederick Hanley
Shane, Charles Donald
Shapley, Harlow
Shoemaker, Gene
  Suppl. 1
Slipher, Vesto Melvin
Stebbins, Joel
St. John, Charles
  Edward
Stone, Ormand
Storer, Arthur
Strömgren, Bengt
  Suppl. 1
Struve, Otto
Swift, Lewis
Tombaugh, Clyde
  Suppl. 1
Twining, Alexander
  Catlin
Walker, Sears Cook
Watson, James Craig
West, Benjamin
  (1730–1813)
Whiting, Sarah Frances

Whitney, Mary Watson
Winlock, Joseph
Winthrop, John
  (1714–1779)
Wright, William
  Hammond
Young, Charles
  Augustus

Astrophysicists
Babcock, Harold Delos
Bowen, Ira Sprague
Chandrasekhar,
  Subrahmanyan
Goldberg, Leo
Hale, George Ellery
Joy, Alfred Harrison
Langley, Samuel
  Pierpont
Menzel, Donald Howard
Merrill, Paul Willard
Payne-Gaposchkin,
  Cecilia
Rutherfurd, Lewis
  Morris
Spitzer, Lyman, Jr.
  Suppl. 2
Zwicky, Fritz

Biochemists
Benedict, Stanley
  Rossiter
Bergmann, Max
Brown, Rachel Fuller
Cannan, Robert Keith
Chittenden, Russell
  Henry
Clarke, Hans Thacher
Cohn, Edwin Joseph
Cori, Carl Ferdinand,
  and Gerty Theresa
  Radnitz Cori
Dakin, Henry Drysdale
Dam, Carl Peter Henrik
Dayhoff, Margaret
  Oakley
Doisy, Edward Adelbert
du Vigneaud, Vincent
Elion, Gertrude *Suppl. 1*
Elvehjem, Conrad
  Arnold
Folin, Otto
Funk, Casimir
Gortner, Ross Aiken
Haagen-Smit, Arie Jan
Hart, Edwin Bret
Hastings, Albert Baird
Haurowitz, Felix
  Michael
Heidelberger, Charles

Physical Sciences *(cont.)*
Henderson, Lawrence
Joseph
Herter, Christian
Archibald (1865–1910)
Kendall, Edward Calvin
King, Charles Glen
Koch, Fred Conrad
Kunitz, Moses
Levene, Phoebus Aaron
Theodor
Lewis, Howard Bishop
Link, Karl Paul Gerhardt
Lipmann, Fritz Albert
Longsworth, Lewis
Gibson
Lusk, Graham
McCollum, Elmer
Verner
Meyerhof, Otto Fritz
Mirsky, Alfred Ezra
Moore, Stanford
Murray, Henry
Alexander, Jr.
Nachmansohn, David
Northrop, John Howard
Ochoa, Severo *Suppl. 2*
Osborne, Thomas Burr
Pauling, Linus Carl
Roberts, Richard Brooke
Rose, William Cumming
Schoenheimer, Rudolph
Stein, William Howard
Sumner, James
Batcheller
Sutherland, Earl W.
Szent-Györgyi, Albert
Van Slyke, Donald
Dexter
Vaughan, Victor
Clarence
Wilkerson, Vernon
Alexander
Wrinch, Dorothy Maud

Biophysicists
Bronk, Detlev Wulf
Cole, Kenneth Stewart
Hartline, Haldan Keffer
Hecht, Selig

Chemists
Adams, Roger
Adkins, Homer Burton
Alvarez, Francisco
Sanchez
Austen, Peter Townsend
Babcock, James Francis
Babcock, Stephen
Moulton
Bache, Franklin

Bachmann, Werner
Emmanuel
Badger, Richard
McLean
Baekeland, Leo Hendrik
Bailar, John Christian, Jr.
Bancroft, Edward
Bancroft, Wilder Dwight
Benedict, Francis Gano
Blodgett, Katharine Burr
Bodley, Rachel Littler
Bolton, Elmer Keiser
Bolton, Henry
Carrington
Boltwood, Bertram
Borden
Booth, James Curtis
Boyé, Martin Hans
Bridges, Robert
Brode, Wallace Reed
Bueche, Arthur Maynard
Calvin, Melvin *Suppl. 1*
Carothers, Wallace
Hume
Carr, Emma Perry
Chandler, Charles
Frederick
Clark, William Mansfield
Clarke, Frank
Wigglesworth
Conant, James Bryant
Cooke, Josiah Parsons,
Jr.
Cooper, Thomas
Cope, Arthur Clay
Coryell, Charles DuBois
Cottrell, Frederick
Gardner
Crafts, James Mason
Cram, Donald J.
Suppl. 2
Curme, George Oliver,
Jr.
Dana, Samuel Luther
Daniels, Farrington
Day, David Talbot
Debye, Peter Joseph
William
Doremus, Robert Ogden
Dow, Herbert Henry
Dreyfus, Camille
Edouard
Duncan, Robert
Kennedy
du Pont, Francis Irénée
Ellis, Carleton
Eyring, Henry
Fieser, Louis Frederick
Flory, Paul John
Frasch, Herman
Frazer, John Fries

Genth, Frederick
Augustus
Giauque, William
Francis
Gibbs, Josiah Willard
(1839–1903)
Gibbs, Wolcott
(1822–1908)
Gies, William John
Gilchrist, Raleigh
Goessmann, Charles
Anthony
Gomberg, Moses
Griscom, John
Gross, Paul Magnus
Guthrie, Samuel
Hare, Robert
Harkins, William Draper
Harteck, Paul
Hayes, Augustus Allen
Heath, Fred Harvey
Hendricks, Sterling
Brown
Herty, Charles Holmes
Hildebrand, Joel Henry
Hill, Henry Aaron
Hill, Mary Elliott
Hirschfelder, Joseph
Oakland
Hitchings, George H.
Suppl. 2
Hogness, Thorfin
Rusten
Hooker, Samuel Cox
Horsford, Eben Norton
Howe, James Lewis
Hudson, Claude Silbert
Hunt, Thomas Sterry
Ipatieff, Vladimir
Nikolaevich
Jackson, Charles Loring
Jackson, Charles
Thomas
Johnson, Treat Baldwin
Jones, Harry Clary
Julian, Percy Lavon
Kharasch, Morris Selig
Kimball, George Elbert
Kirkwood, John Gamble
Kistiakowsky, George
Bogdan
Kohler, Elmer Peter
Kraus, Charles August
Lamb, Arthur Becket
LaMer, Victor Kuhn
Langmuir, Irving
Latimer, Wendell
Mitchell
Lea, Mathew Carey
Levene, Phoebus Aaron
Theodor

Lewis, Gilbert Newton
Libby, Willard Frank
Loeb, Morris
Longsworth, Lewis
Gibson
Lucas, Howard Johnson
Maclean, John
Mallet, John William
Mallinckrodt, Edward,
Jr.
Mapes, James Jay
Marvel, Carl Shipp
McElvain, Samuel
Marion
Mees, Charles Edward
Kenneth
Mendel, Lafayette
Benedict
Michael, Arthur
Midgley, Thomas, Jr.
Moore, Richard Bishop
Morehead, John Motley
Morley, Edward
Williams
Mowbray, George
Mordey
Mulliken, Robert
Sanderson
Munroe, Charles
Edward
Nef, John Ulric
Nichols, William Henry
Niemann, Carl George
Nieuwland, Julius Arthur
Noyes, Arthur Amos
Noyes, W. Albert, Jr.
Noyes, William Albert
Olsen, Fred
Onsager, Lars
Osborne, Thomas Burr
Ostromislensky, Iwan
Iwanowitch
Parr, Samuel Wilson
Pauling, Linus Carl
Peckham, Stephen
Farnum
Pedersen, Charles John
Pennington, Mary Engle
Peter, Robert
Piccard, Jean Félix
Pimentel, George Claude
Plunkett, Roy Joseph
Porter, John Addison
Power, Frederick
Belding
Priestley, Joseph
Rabinowitch, Eugene
Reese, Charles Lee
Remsen, Ira
Rice, Oscar Knefler

Physical Sciences *(cont.)*
Richards, Ellen Henrietta
  Swallow
Richards, Theodore
  William
Riegel, Byron
Rillieux, Norbert
  Suppl. 1
Rogers, Robert Empie
Sanger, Charles Robert
Scatchard, George
Schlesinger, Hermann
  Irving
Seaborg, Glenn T.
  Suppl. 1
Shepard, Charles
  Upham
Sheppard, Samuel
  Edward
Sherman, Henry Clapp
Silliman, Benjamin
Silliman, Benjamin, Jr.
Slosson, Edwin Emery
Smith, Edgar Fahs
Smith, John Lawrence
Smithson, James
  Suppl. 2
Sparks, William Joseph
Squibb, Edward
  Robinson
Stieglitz, Julius
Stine, Charles Milton
  Atland
Takamine, Jokichi
Taylor, William
  Chittenden
Thompson, Thomas
  Gordon
Thurber, George
Tilghman, Richard
  Albert
Tishler, Max
Tolman, Richard Chace
Troost, Gerard
Urey, Harold Clayton
Venable, Francis Preston
Warren, Cyrus Moors
Washburn, Edward
  Wight
Washington, Henry
  Stephens
Watt, George Willard
Weightman, William
Wetherill, Charles Mayer
White, Henry Clay
Whitmore, Frank
  Clifford
Whitney, Willis Rodney
Wiley, Harvey
  Washington

Williams, Robert
  Ramapatnam
Williams, Roger
  (1890–1978)
Woodhouse, James
Woodward, Robert
  Burns
Wurtz, Henry
Yost, Don Merlin Lee
Young, William Gould

Crystallographers
Corey, Robert Brainard

Geophysicists
Bauer, Louis Agricola
Benioff, Victor Hugo
Byerly, Perry
Chapman, Sydney
Day, Arthur Louis
Ewing, Maurice
Ferrel, William
Fleming, John Adam
Forbush, Scott Ellsworth
Griggs, David Tressel
Hubbert, M. King
Macelwane, James
  Bernard
Reid, Harry Fielding
Schott, Charles Anthony
Vestine, Ernest Harry
Woodward, Robert
  Simpson

Physical Scientists / Natural Philosophers
Bowdoin, James
  (1726–1790)
Chase, Pliny Earle
Franklin, Benjamin
  (1706–1790)
Goddard, Paul Beck
LeConte, John
Mannes, Leopold
  Damrosch
Mitchill, Samuel Latham
Oliver, Andrew
  (1731–1799)
Williams, Jonathan

Physicists
Allison, Samuel King
Alvarez, Luis Walter
Anderson, Carl David
Anderson, Herbert
  Lawrence
Anderson, John August
Anslow, Gladys Amelia
Arnold, Harold DeForest
Babcock, Harold Delos
Bardeen, John

Barus, Carl
Beams, Jesse Wakefield
Birge, Raymond Thayer
Bloch, Felix
Bonner, Tom Wilkerson
Brace, DeWitt Bristol
Brattain, Walter H.
  Suppl. 1
Breit, Gregory
Bridgman, Percy
  Williams
Briggs, Lyman James
Brode, Robert Bigham
Brode, Wallace Reed
Bumstead, Henry
  Andrews
Burgess, George Kimball
Chase, Pliny Earle
Coblentz, William
  Weber
Compton, Arthur Holly
Compton, Karl Taylor
Condon, Edward Uhler
Coolidge, Albert
  Sprague
Coolidge, William David
Cowan, Clyde Lorrain,
  Jr.
Crew, Henry
Darrow, Karl Kelchner
Davis, Bergen
Davisson, Clinton Joseph
Debye, Peter Joseph
  William
Delbrück, Max
Dempster, Arthur Jeffrey
Dennison, David
  Mathias
Dryden, Hugh Latimer
Duane, William
  (1872–1935)
DuMond, Jesse William
  Monroe
Eckart, Carl Henry
Einstein, Albert
Epstein, Paul Sophus
Failla, Gioacchino
Fermi, Enrico
Feynman, Richard
  Phillips
Fisk, James Brown
Foote, Paul Darwin
Fowler, William Alfred
Franck, James
Frank, Philipp G.
Fuchs, Klaus Emil Julius
Gale, Henry Gordon
Gamow, George
Goddard, Robert
  Hutchings
Goudsmit, Samuel

Graves, Alvin Cushman
Gunn, Ross
Hansen, William
  Webster
Harkins, William Draper
Harnwell, Gaylord
  Probasco
Haworth, Leland John
Henry, Joseph
Herzfeld, Karl Ferdinand
Hess, Victor Franz
Hirschfelder, Joseph
  Oakland
Hofstadter, Robert
Houston, William
  Vermillion
Hull, Albert Wallace
Imes, Elmer Samuel
Ives, Herbert Eugene
Kalmus, Herbert
  Thomas
Kemble, Edwin
  Crawford
Kompfner, Rudolf
Kusch, Polykarp
Lane, Jonathan Homer
Laporte, Otto
Lauritsen, Charles
  Christian
Lauritsen, Thomas
Lawrence, Ernest
  Orlando
Lilienfeld, Julius Edgar
  Suppl. 2
Livingston, Milton
  Stanley
Loomis, Francis Wheeler
Luckiesh, Matthew
Lyman, Theodore
  (1874–1954)
Maltby, Margaret Eliza
Marshak, Robert Eugene
Mauchly, John William
Mayer, Alfred Marshall
Mayer, Maria Gertrude
  Goeppert
McMillan, Edwin
  Mattison
Meggers, William
  Frederick
Mendenhall, Charles
  Elwood
Mendenhall, Thomas
  Corwin
Merritt, Ernest George
Michelson, Albert
  Abraham
Miller, Dayton Clarence
Millikan, Robert
  Andrews
Morse, Philip McCord

Physical Sciences *(cont.)*
Mulliken, Robert
  Sanderson
Nichols, Edward
  Leamington
Nichols, Ernest Fox
Nordberg, William
Noyce, Robert Norton
Onsager, Lars
Oppenheimer, Frank
  Friedman
Oppenheimer, J. Robert
Page, Leigh
Pegram, George Braxton
Pfund, August Herman
Pierce, George
  Washington
Pupin, Michael Idvorsky
Purcell, Edward M.
  Suppl. 2
Quimby, Edith Hinkley
Rabi, I. I.
Rainwater, James
Richtmyer, Floyd Karker
Ridenour, Louis Nicot,
  Jr.
Roberts, Richard Brooke
Rogers, William
  Augustus
Rood, Ogden Nicholas
Rosa, Edward Bennett
Rowland, Henry
  Augustus
Sabine, Wallace Clement
  Ware
Schiff, Leonard Isaac
Schwinger, Julian
  Seymour
Segrè, Emilio Gino
Shockley, William
  Bradford
Slater, John Clarke
Smyth, Henry Dewolf
Stern, Otto
Stratton, Samuel Wesley
Street, J. C.
Szilard, Leo
Tate, John Torrence
Thaxton, Hubert Mack
Thompson, Benjamin
Tolman, Richard Chace
Trowbridge, Augustus
Trowbridge, John
Tuve, Merle Antony
Uhlenbeck, George
  Eugene
Van Vleck, John
  Hasbrouck
von Neumann, John
  Louis
Waterman, Alan Tower

Webster, Arthur Gordon
Webster, David Locke
Whiting, Sarah Frances
Wigner, Eugene Paul
Williams, John Harry
Wolff, Irving
Wood, Robert Williams
Wright, Arthur Williams
Zacharias, Jerrold
  Reinach

Phytochemists
Kremers, Edward

Planetary Scientists
Urey, Harold Clayton
Vestine, Ernest Harry

Space Scientists
Sagan, Carl *Suppl. 1*
Zwicky, Fritz

Spectroscopists
Anslow, Gladys Amelia
Badger, Richard
  McLean

**Technological and
Applied Sciences**
AGRICULTURE
Agriculturists
Armsby, Henry Prentiss
Babcock, Stephen
  Moulton
Bennett, John Cook
Bidwell, John
Bordley, John Beale
Brewer, William Henry
Bromfield, Louis
Buel, Jesse
Callaway, Cason Jewell
Calvert, Charles
  Benedict
Carver, George
  Washington
Chamberlain, William
  Isaac
Cobb, Cully Alton
Colman, Norman Jay
Dabney, Charles William
Davenport, Eugene
Dickson, David
Dymond, John
Emerson, Gouverneur
Fitch, Asa
Furnas, Robert
  Wilkinson
Gale, Benjamin
Garnett, James Mercer
Garst, Roswell
Gaylord, Willis

Hoffmann, Francis
  Arnold
Jenkins, Edward Hopkins
Johnson, Samuel William
Jones, Donald Forsha
Kinloch, Cleland
Knapp, Seaman Asahel
Kolb, Reuben Francis
Ladd, Carl Edwin
Ladd, Edwin Fremont
Ladejinsky, Wolf Isaac
Logan, George
London, Jack
Lowden, Frank Orren
Mangelsdorf, Paul
  Christoph
Mapes, Charles Victor
Mapes, James Jay
McBryde, John McLaren
Miles, Manly
Norton, John Pitkin
Patrick, Marsena
  Rudolph
Peters, Richard
  (1810–1889)
Piper, Charles
  Vancouver
Powell, G. Harold
Pugh, Evan
Robinson, Solon
Rodale, J. I.
Rosen, Joseph A.
Ruffin, Edmund
Scovell, Melville Amasa
Stakman, Elvin Charles
Stockbridge, Horace
  Edward
Stockbridge, Levi
  Suppl. 2
Strong, Harriet Williams
  Russell
Taylor, John
  (1753–1824)
Thomas, John Jacobs
Tilton, James
Vanderbilt, George
  Washington *Suppl. 1*
Wallace, Henry Agard
Ward, Joshua John
Waring, George Edwin,
  Jr.

Apiarists
Langstroth, Lorenzo
  Lorraine *Suppl. 1*
Palmer, Daniel David

Cattle Raisers / Traders
Allerton, Samuel Waters
Bush, George
  Washington

Harris, William
  Alexander
Lasater, Edward
  Cunningham
Littlefield, George
  Washington
Mackenzie, Murdo
McCoy, Joseph Geiting
McNeill, John Hanson
Morris, Nelson
Renick, Felix

Cowboys
Cortez Lira, Gregorio
Dart, Isom
Doolin, William
Glass, Charlie
James, Will Roderick
Love, Nat
Mix, Tom
Nigger Add
Rogers, Will
Russell, Charles Marion
Siringo, Charles Angelo

*Farmer Organization
Leaders*
Barrett, Charles Simon
Carr, Elias
Garey, Thomas Andrew
Goss, Albert Simon
Gresham, Newt
Kelley, Oliver Hudson
Lemke, William
  Frederick
Mayo, Mary Anne
  Bryant
O'Neal, Edward Asbury,
  III
Peek, George Nelson
Polk, Leonidas
  LaFayette
Reno, Milo
Townley, Arthur Charles
Ware, Harold

Farmers
Aiken, George David
Alden, John
Banneker, Benjamin
Bush, George
  Washington
Carpenter, Cyrus Clay
Clay, Laura
Colden, Cadwallader, II
Cooper, Joseph
  Alexander
Corey, Giles
Deitz, John F.
Delafield, John
  (1786–1853)

Technological and Applied Sciences:

Agriculture (cont.)
Dickson, David
Dummer, William
Favill, Henry Baird
Featherstonhaugh, George William
Glidden, Joseph Farwell
Heard, Dwight Bancroft
Heaton, Hannah Cook
Hilgard, Theodor Erasmus
Lewis, John Francis
Lloyd, Edward
López, José Dolores
MacDonald, Betty
Mayo, Mary Anne Bryant
Murie, James Rolfe
Newton, Isaac
Other Day, John
Perry, Edward
Robinson, Rowland Evans
Rodale, J. I.
Sanford, Henry Shelton
Strawbridge, Robert
Wallace, Henry Cantwell
Ward, Samuel (1725–1776)
Weare, Nathaniel
Whitehill, Robert
Whittemore, Samuel
Wilbarger, John Wesley
Wolfskill, William
Wood, Carolena
Wood, James
Yount, George Concepción

Foresters
Allen, Edward Tyson
Baker, Hugh Potter
Fernow, Bernhard Eduard
Hough, Franklin Benjamin
Michaux, François-André
Pinchot, Gifford

Horticulturists
Bailey, Liberty Hyde
Blackstone, William
Burbank, Luther
Callaway, Cason Jewell
Crockett, James Underwood *Suppl. 1*
Downing, Andrew Jackson

du Pont, Henry Francis
Fairchild, David Grandison
Garey, Thomas Andrew
Hansen, Niels Ebbesen
Logan, Martha Daniell
Longworth, Nicholas (1782–1863)
Marshall, Humphry
McFarland, J. Horace
Prince, William
Pursh, Frederick
Waugh, Frank Albert

Plantation Managers / Overseers
King, Roswell

Plantation Owners
Adams, James Hopkins
Aiken, William
Allston, Robert Francis Withers
Alston, Joseph
Alston, William
Barbour, James
Bouligny, Dominique
Bowie, Robert
Breckinridge, John (1760–1806)
Bryan, Hugh
Byrd, William (1652–1704)
Byrd, William (1674–1744)
Cabell, William
Carr, Elias
Carroll, Daniel
Carroll of Carrollton, Charles
Carter, Robert (1663–1732)
Couper, James Hamilton
Dunbar, William
Durnford, Andrew
Dymond, John
Elliott, Stephen
Elliott, William
Ellison, William
Fendall, Josias
Fitzhugh, William
Forstall, Edmond Jean
Gibbons, Thomas
Goldsborough, Robert
Habersham, James
Hampton, Wade (1754?–1835)
Harrison, Benjamin (1726?–1791)
Heyward, Nathaniel
Izard, Ralph

Jenifer, Daniel of St. Thomas
Jones, Allen
Kinloch, Cleland
Lamar, John Basil
Laurens, Henry
LeFlore, Greenwood
Lewis, William Berkeley
Lynch, Charles
Manigault, Gabriel (1704–1781)
Manigault, Peter
Marigny, Bernard
Mason, George
Mason, John Young
McIntosh, Lachlan
McMinn, Joseph
Mercer, John Francis
Middleton, Arthur
Middleton, Henry (1717–1784)
Middleton, Henry (1770–1846)
Montgomery, Isaiah Thornton
Morgan, Sir Henry
Moultrie, John, Jr.
Nelson, Thomas
Nelson, William (1711–1772)
Page, John
Page, Mann
Parke, Daniel
Percy, William Alexander
Pickens, Andrew
Pillow, Gideon Johnson
Pinckney, Charles Cotesworth
Pinckney, Elizabeth Lucas
Plater, George
Pollock, Oliver
Porter, Alexander
Randolph, Peyton
Ravenel, Henry William
Rayner, Kenneth
Redwood, Abraham
Robinson, John
Rolfe, John
Rost-Denis, Pierre Adolphe
Ruffin, Thomas
Shelby, Joseph Orville
Smith, Ashbel
Tilghman, Matthew
Tyler, Julia Gardiner
Vann, Joseph
Walker, Thomas
Ward, Joshua John

Washington, George Berry
Wharton, William Harris
Williams, David Rogerson
Winchester, James
Yeardley, Sir George

Ranchers
Burt, Struthers
Cassidy, Butch
Chisum, John Simpson
Cortina, Juan Nepomuceno
Goodnight, Charles
Greene, William Cornell
Ivins, Anthony Woodward
Jones, Buffalo
King, Richard
Lasater, Edward Cunningham
Littlefield, George Washington
Marsh, John
McCrea, Joel
Parker, John Palmer
Ross, C. Ben
Stearns, Abel
Vallejo, Mariano Guadalupe
Warner, Jonathan Trumbull
Wolfskill, William

Seedsmen
Burpee, David
Chapman, John
Vick, James

Soil Scientists
Bennett, Hugh Hammond
Hilgard, Eugene Woldemar
Kelley, Walter Pearson
Kellogg, Charles Edwin *Suppl. 2*
Lowdermilk, Walter Clay *Suppl. 1*
Marbut, Curtis Fletcher

Winegrowers / Vintners
de Latour, Georges *Suppl. 2*
Gallo, Julio
Haraszthy de Mokcsa, Agoston
Mondavi, Rosa Grassi
Petri, Angelo, and Louis Petri

Technological and Applied Sciences:
Agriculture (cont.)
Sbarboro, Andrea

AVIATION
Astronauts
Challenger Shuttle Crew
Conrad, Pete *Suppl. 1*
Lawrence, Robert
Henry, Jr. *Suppl. 2*
Project Apollo Crew
Shepard, Alan *Suppl. 1*
Slayton, Deke *Suppl. 2*

Aviators
Acosta, Bertram
Blanchard
Barnes, Pancho
Boyd, John R. *Suppl. 1*
Bragg, Janet *Suppl. 2*
Brown, Willa *Suppl. 2*
Bullard, Eugène Jacques
Suppl. 2
Cochran, Jacqueline
Coleman, Bessie
Corrigan, Douglas
"Wrong Way" *Suppl. 1*
Curtiss, Glenn
Hammond
Doolittle, James Harold
Earhart, Amelia Mary
Forsythe, Albert Edward
Suppl. 2
Herring, Augustus M.
Hughes, Howard
Julian, Hubert F.
Suppl. 2
Lawrence, Robert
Henry, Jr. *Suppl. 2*
Lindbergh, Anne
Morrow *Suppl. 2*
Lindbergh, Charles
Augustus
Nichols, Ruth Rowland
Niebaum, Gustave
Ferdinand *Suppl. 2*
Omlie, Phoebe Jane
Fairgrave
Pangborn, Clyde
Edward
Parsons, Edwin Charles
Post, Wiley
Powers, Francis Gary
Quimby, Harriet N.
Suppl. 2
Robinson, John C.
Rosendahl, Charles
Emery
Stinson, Katherine

Wright, Wilbur, and
Orville Wright

Balloonists
Jeffries, John
King, Samuel Archer
La Mountain, John
Piccard, Jean Félix
Wise, John (1808–1879)

Test Pilots
Acosta, Bertram
Blanchard
Allen, Edmund Turney
Engen, Donald
Davenport *Suppl. 2*

COMPUTER SCIENCE
Computer Industry Leaders
Cray, Seymour *Suppl. 1*
Packard, David *Suppl. 1*
Wang, An
Watson, Arthur
Kittridge
Watson, Thomas John,
Jr.

Computer Scientists
Aiken, Howard
Hathaway
Atanasoff, John Vincent
Suppl. 2
Hamming, Richard
Wesley *Suppl. 2*
Hopper, Grace Brewster
Murray
Kemeny, John George
Mauchly, John William

ENGINEERING
Acoustical Engineers
Asch, Moses
Olson, Harry Ferdinand

Aerospace Engineers
Berlin, Donovan Reese
Busemann, Adolf
Colley, Russell *Suppl. 2*
de Seversky, Alexander
Procofieff
Douglas, Donald Wills
Draper, Charles Stark
du Pont, Henry Belin
Durand, William
Frederick
Egtvedt, Claire
Ehricke, Krafft Arnold
Flügge-Lotz, Irmgard
Herring, Augustus M.
Hunsaker, Jerome Clarke
Kármán, Theodore von

Lawrance, Charles
Lanier
Lockheed, Allan Haines
Lockheed, Malcolm
Loening, Grover
Cleveland
Malina, Frank Joseph
McDonnell, James
Smith, Jr.
Millikan, Clark
Blanchard
Piccard, Jean Félix
Sikorsky, Igor Ivanovich
von Braun, Wernher
Magnus Maxmillian
Warner, Edward Pearson
Wells, Edward Curtis

Automotive Engineers
Chevrolet, Louis
Coffin, Howard Earle
Kettering, Charles
Franklin
Lockheed, Malcolm
Milton, Tommy

Chemical Engineers
Frary, Francis Cowles
Frasch, Herman
Houdry, Eugene Jules
Lewis, Warren Kendall
Little, Arthur Dehon
Sherwood, Thomas
Kilgore
Teeple, John Edgar

Civil Engineers
Alexander, Archie
Alphonso
Allen, Horatio
Ammann, Othmar
Hermann
Andrews, George
Leonard
Baldwin, Loammi
Baldwin, Loammi, Jr.
Bates, Onward
Burr, William Hubert
Cass, George
Washington
Chanute, Octave
Cone, Russell Glenn
Cooper, Hugh Lincoln
Crowe, Francis
Trenholm
Curtis, Samuel Ryan
Davies, John Vipond
Davis, Arthur Powell
Dodge, Grenville Mellen
Eads, James Buchanan
Eastman, William Reed

Eddy, Harrison Prescott
Ellet, Charles, Jr.
Ferris, George
Washington Gale, Jr.
Suppl. 2
Fink, Albert
Francis, James Bicheno
Freeman, John Ripley
Freeman, Thomas
Fuller, George Warren
Fulton, Robert
Geddes, James
Goethals, George
Washington
Goldmark, Henry
Greene, George Sears
Harrington, John Lyle
Haupt, Herman
Henny, David Christian
Hexamer, Charles John
Hill, Louis Clarence
Hovey, Otis Ellis
Jervis, John Bloomfield
Judah, Theodore
Dehone
Kirkwood, James Pugh
Kneass, Strickland
Latrobe, Benjamin
Henry (1764–1820)
Latrobe, Benjamin
Henry (1806–1878)
Lindenthal, Gustav
Lovell, Mansfield
MacDonald, Thomas
Harris
McCallum, Daniel Craig
Mead, Elwood
Mills, Robert
Modjeski, Ralph
Moisseiff, Leon
Solomon
Moran, Daniel Edward
Morison, George
Shattuck
Mulholland, William
Mullan, John
Newell, Frederick
Haynes
O'Shaughnessy, Michael
Maurice
Othmer, Donald F.
Suppl. 2
Page, Logan Waller
Peters, Richard
(1810–1889)
Purcell, Charles H.
Suppl. 1
Purdy, Corydon Tyler
Rea, Samuel
Roberdeau, Isaac
Roberts, George Brooke

Technological and Applied Sciences:
Engineering (cont.)
Roebling, John Augustus
Roebling, Washington Augustus
Rogers, Fairman
Savage, John Lucian
Sayre, Robert Heysham
Smillie, Ralph
Snow, Jessie Baker
Steinman, David Barnard
Stevens, John Frank
St. John, Isaac Munroe
Stone, Charles Pomeroy
Stone, Roy
Storrow, Charles Storer
Strauss, Joseph Baermann
Strickland, William
Strobel, Charles Louis
Stuart, Francis Lee
Swift, William Henry
Talbot, Arthur Newell
Thomson, J. Edgar
Twining, Alexander Catlin
Waddell, John Alexander Low
Waring, George Edwin, Jr.
Washburn, Frank Sherman
Wegmann, Edward
Westergaard, Harald Malcolm
Weymouth, Frank Elwin
Whipple, Squire
White, Canvass
Williams, John Shoebridge
Wisely, William Homer
Wolman, Abel
Worthington, Henry Rossiter
Wright, Benjamin

Communications Engineers
Bode, Hendrik Wade
Buckley, Oliver Ellsworth
Colpitts, Edwin Henry
Gherardi, Bancroft
Jewett, Frank Baldwin
Stone, John Stone

Construction Engineers
Alexander, Archie Alphonso
Starrett, William Aiken

Consulting Engineers
Adams, Comfort Avery
Eddy, Harrison Prescott
Hunt, Robert Woolston
Steinman, David Barnard
Stuart, Francis Lee
Teeple, John Edgar
Warner, Edward Pearson

Electrical Engineers
Adams, Comfort Avery
Alexanderson, Ernst Fredrik Werner
Armstrong, Edwin Howard
Berkner, Lloyd Viel
Bush, Vannevar
Carty, John Joseph
Clarke, Edith
Cray, Seymour Suppl. 1
Daft, Leo
Dunn, Gano Sillick
Edgerton, Harold Eugene
Emmet, William Le Roy
Engstrom, Elmer William
Friis, Harald Trap
Hammer, William Joseph
Heineman, Daniel Webster
Hewitt, Peter Cooper
Houston, Edwin James
Jansky, Karl Guthe
Latimer, Lewis Howard
Lear, William Powell
Lieb, John William
Luckiesh, Matthew
Rice, Edwin Wilbur, Jr.
Ryan, Harris Joseph
Ryan, Walter D'Arcy
Sperry, Elmer Ambrose
Sperti, George Speri
Sporn, Philip
Squier, George Owen
Steinmetz, Charles Proteus
Stone, Charles Augustus, and Edwin Sibley Webster
Terman, Frederick Emmons
Weston, Edward (1850–1936)
Whitehead, John Boswell
Wiesner, Jerome Bert

Industrial Engineers
Boyden, Uriah Atherton

Consulting Engineers (cont.)
Brugger, Kenneth C. Suppl. 2
Gorrell, Edgar Staley
Gunn, James Newton
Kimball, Dexter Simpson
Rautenstrauch, Walter
Taylor, Frederick Winslow
Torrence, Joseph Thatcher

Mechanical Engineers
Carrier, Willis Haviland
Cooke, Morris Llewellyn
Cooley, Mortimer Elwyn
Crosthwait, David Nelson, Jr.
Emmet, William Le Roy
Fritz, John
Gibbs, George (1861–1940)
Halsey, Frederick Arthur
Hewitt, Peter Cooper
Hodgkinson, Francis
Kimball, Dexter Simpson
Kingsbury, Albert
Lieb, John William
Main, Charles Thomas
McMahon, Thomas A. Suppl. 2
Nordberg, Bruno Victor
Norden, Carl Lukas
Norton, Charles Hotchkiss
Prager, William
Smith, Francis Hopkinson
Soderberg, C. Richard
Swasey, Ambrose
Thurston, Robert Henry

Military Engineers
Abbot, Henry Larcom
Abert, John James
Babcock, Orville Elias
Bailey, Joseph
Barnard, John Gross
Bernard, Simon
Casey, Thomas Lincoln
Chittenden, Hiram Martin
Comstock, Cyrus Ballou
Cone, Hutchinson Ingham
De Brahm, William Gerard
Derby, George Horatio
Ericsson, John
Foster, John Gray

Military Engineers (cont.)
Franklin, William Buel
Gaillard, David Du Bose
Gardiner, Lion
Gillmore, Quincy Adams
Goethals, George Washington
Graham, James Duncan
Gridley, Richard
Groves, Leslie Richard, Jr.
Gunnison, John Williams
Haupt, Herman
Humphreys, Andrew Atkinson
Isherwood, Benjamin Franklin
Ives, Joseph Christmas
Jadwin, Edgar
Lander, Frederick West
Lay, John Louis
L'Enfant, Pierre Charles
Long, Stephen Harriman
Loring, Charles Harding
Machin, Thomas
Mackellar, Patrick
Mahan, Dennis Hart
Mangin, Joseph François
McPherson, James B.
Meade, George Gordon
Meigs, Montgomery Cunningham
Melville, George Wallace
Milligan, Robert Wiley
Montrésor, James Gabriel
Montrésor, John
Mullan, John
Newton, John
Pick, Lewis Andrew
Rains, George Washington
Roberdeau, Isaac
Robert, Henry Martyn
Shreve, Henry Miller
Sibert, William Luther
Swift, Joseph Gardner
Swift, William Henry
Taylor, Harry
Totten, Joseph Gilbert
Tousard, Anne-Louis Suppl. 2
Turnbull, William
Warren, Gouverneur Kemble
Webster, Joseph Dana
Weitzel, Godfrey
Wheeler, George Montague
Wright, Horatio Gouverneur

Technological and Applied Sciences:
Engineering (cont.)
Mining Engineers
Ashburner, Charles Albert
Brunton, David William
Church, John Adams
Emmons, Samuel Franklin
Flipper, Henry Ossian
Gayley, James
Hammond, John Hays
Hoover, Herbert Clark
Kelly, Mervin Joseph
Keyes, Charles Rollin
Sutro, Adolph Heinrich Joseph

Nuclear Engineers
Rickover, Hyman George

Radio / Television Engineers
Alexanderson, Ernst Fredrik Werner
Armstrong, Edwin Howard
Berkner, Lloyd Viel
de Forest, Lee
Farnsworth, Philo Taylor
Fessenden, Reginald Aubrey
Goldmark, Peter Carl
Hogan, John Vincent Lawless
Kompfner, Rudolf
Storm, Hans Otto
Zworykin, Vladimir Kosma

Steam Propulsion Engineers
Fitch, John
Fulton, Robert
Herreshoff, Nathanael Greene
Isherwood, Benjamin Franklin
Loring, Charles Harding
Roosevelt, Nicholas J.
Stevens, John

Structural Engineers
Khan, Fazlur Rahman
Pond, Irving Kane
Purdy, Corydon Tyler
Timoshenko, Stephen Prokofievitch

GENERAL
Ballisticians
Kent, Robert Harrington

Inventors
Acheson, Edward Goodrich
Adler, Charles, Jr.
Akeley, Carl Ethan
Alger, Cyrus
Allen, Zachariah
Alvarez, Luis Walter
Ammen, Daniel
Appleby, John Francis
Armstrong, Edwin Howard
Atanasoff, John Vincent *Suppl. 2*
Avery, R. Stanton *Suppl. 2*
Bachelder, John
Baekeland, Leo Hendrik
Bausch, Edward
Beach, Alfred Ely
Beach, Moses Yale
Bell, Alexander Graham
Bendix, Vincent Hugo
Berliner, Emile
Bettendorf, William Peter
Birdseye, Clarence
Blake, Eli Whitney
Blake, Francis
Blake, Lyman Reed
Blanchard, Thomas
Blodgett, Katharine Burr
Bogardus, James
Borden, Gail
Brooke, John Mercer
Brown, Alexander Ephraim
Browning, John M. *Suppl. 2*
Brush, Charles Francis
Buick, David Dunbar
Burden, Henry
Burroughs, William Seward
Burt, William Austin
Bushnell, David
Carlson, Chester Floyd
Carrier, Willis Haviland
Champion, Albert
Cist, Jacob
Clark, Frederic Horace, and Anna Steiniger
Colley, Russell *Suppl. 2*
Colt, Samuel
Coolidge, William David
Cooper, Peter
Corliss, George Henry

Cottrell, Frederick Gardner
Cowen, Joshua Lionel
Crompton, George
Curtiss, Glenn Hammond
Davenport, Thomas
Davison, Gregory Caldwell
de Forest, Lee
Doremus, Robert Ogden
Dorrance, John Thompson
Draper, William Franklin
Drew, Richard Gurley
du Pont, Francis Irénée
Duryea, Charles Edgar
Duryea, Frank
Eastman, George
Eddison, William Barton
Edgerton, Harold Eugene
Edison, Thomas Alva
Eickemeyer, Rudolf
Ellis, Carleton
Ericsson, John
Esterly, George
Evans, Oliver
Ewbank, Thomas
Farmer, Moses Gerrish
Farnsworth, Philo Taylor
Ferris, George Washington Gale, Jr. *Suppl. 2*
Fessenden, Reginald Aubrey
Fessenden, Thomas Green
Fiske, Bradley Allen
Fitch, John
Fleischmann, Charles Louis
Ford, Hannibal Choate
Frasch, Herman
Fuller, R. Buckminster
Fulton, Robert
Furer, Julius Augustus
Garand, John C.
Gatling, Richard Jordan
Gayley, James
Gernsback, Hugo
Gillette, King Camp
Glidden, Joseph Farwell
Godfrey, Thomas (1704–1749)
Goldman, Sylvan Nathan
Goldmark, Peter Carl
Goodyear, Charles

Gorrie, John
Grainger, Percy Aldridge
Gray, Elisha
Gregg, John Robert
Haish, Jacob
Hall, Charles Martin
Hall, Thomas Seavey
Hammerstein, Oscar
Hanger, James Edward *Suppl. 2*
Hartness, James
Haupt, Herman
Haynes, Elwood
Herreshoff, James Brown
Hewitt, Peter Cooper
Hodgkinson, Francis
Hoe, Richard March
Holland, John Philip
Hollerith, Herman
Houdry, Eugene Jules
House, Royal Earl
Howe, Elias
Howey, Walter Crawford
Hughes, Howard Robard, Sr.
Hunt, Alfred Ephraim
Hyatt, John Wesley
Ives, Frederic Eugene
Ives, Herbert Eugene
Jacuzzi, Candido
Jacuzzi, Rachele
Jenks, Joseph
Johnson, Eldridge Reeves
Jones, Amanda Theodosia
Kalmus, Herbert Thomas
Kelly, William
Kent, Atwater
Kettering, Charles Franklin
Kingsbury, Albert
Knight, Margaret E.
Kraft, James Lewis
Kruesi, John
Lake, Simon
Lamarr, Hedy *Suppl. 1*
Land, Edwin Herbert
Langmuir, Irving
Langstroth, Lorenzo Lorraine *Suppl. 1*
Lanston, Tolbert
Latimer, Lewis Howard
Lay, John Louis
Leffel, James
Lewis, Isaac Newton
Lilienfeld, Julius Edgar *Suppl. 2*
Link, Edwin Albert, Jr.

Technological and Applied Sciences:
General (cont.)
Lloyd, Marshall Burns
Locke, John
Lockheed, Malcolm
Longstreet, William
Marsh, Charles Wesley
Mason, John Landis
  Suppl. 2
Mason, William
  (1808–1883)
Masters, Sybilla
Matzeliger, Jan Earnst
Mauchly, John William
Maxim, Hiram Percy
McCormick, Cyrus Hall
McCoy, Elijah
McKay, Gordon
McTammany, John
Mergenthaler, Ottmar
Morgan, Garrett A.
  Suppl. 1
Morse, Samuel Finley
  Breese
Murray, Thomas
  Edward
Muybridge, Eadweard
Nestle, Charles
Niles, Nathaniel
Nordberg, Bruno Victor
Norton, Charles
  Hotchkiss
Otis, Charles Rollin
Otis, Elisha Graves
Owens, Michael Joseph
Page, Charles Grafton
Parker, John P.
Parrott, Robert Parker
Perry, Stuart
Pierce, George
  Washington
Plunkett, Roy Joseph
Popeil, Samuel J.
Porter, Edwin Stanton
Pratt, Francis Ashbury
Pritikin, Nathan
Pupin, Michael Idvorsky
Rains, Gabriel James
Rains, George
  Washington
Reese, Abram
Renwick, Edward Sabine
Richter, Charles Francis
Rillieux, Norbert
  Suppl. 1
Rogers, John Raphael
Roosevelt, Nicholas J.
Rumsey, James
Rust, John Daniel
Ryan, Jack

Schmitt, Arthur J.
  Suppl. 2
Sholes, Christopher
  Latham
Sickels, Frederick
  Ellsworth
Simjian, Luther *Suppl. 2*
Singer, Isaac Merritt
Sparks, William Joseph
Spencer, Christopher
  Miner
Sperry, Elmer Ambrose
Sperti, George Speri
Sprague, Frank Julian
Stanley, Francis Edgar,
  and Freelan Oscar
  Stanley
Stevens, John
Stevens, Robert
  Livingston
Stone, John Stone
Strauss, Joseph
  Baermann
Strong, Harriet Williams
  Russell
Swasey, Ambrose
Tagliabue, Giuseppe
Tesla, Nikola
Thomson, Elihu
Thorp, John
Tilghman, Benjamin
  Chew
Tilyou, George
  Cornelius
Treadwell, Daniel
Tupper, Earl Silas
Twining, Alexander
  Catlin
Tytus, John Butler, Jr.
Waller, Frederic
Wang, An
Warren, Henry Ellis
Watson, Thomas
  Augustus
Westinghouse, George
Weston, Edward
  (1850–1936)
Whitney, Eli
Willard, Solomon
Williams, Carbine
Wright, Wilbur, and
  Orville Wright
Wyeth, N. C.
  (1911–1990)
Yale, Linus, Jr.
Zworykin, Vladimir
  Kosma

Machinists
Kruesi, John
Thorp, John

Mechanics
Chevrolet, Louis
Moody, Paul

Metallurgists
Becket, Frederick Mark
Campbell, William
  (1876–1936)
Grant, James Benton
Haynes, Elwood
Holley, Alexander
  Lyman
Howe, Henry Marion
Hunt, Alfred Ephraim
Hunt, Robert Woolston
Jeffries, Zay
Kinzel, Augustus Braun
Landis, Walter Savage
Merica, Paul Dyer
Richards, Joseph William
Sauveur, Albert
Wills, Childe Harold

Microscopists
Clark, Henry James
Leidy, Joseph
Riddell, John Leonard
Woodward, Joseph
  Janvier

Millwrights
Lucas, Jonathan

Scientific Instrument Makers
Anderson, John August
Bayard, James Ashton
Brashear, John Alfred
Clark, Alvan
Clark, Alvan Graham
Hamlin, William
Ritchey, George Willis
Rittenhouse, David
Ross, Frank Elmore
Swasey, Ambrose
Tagliabue, Giuseppe

Surveyors
Armstrong, John
  (1717–1795)
Borden, Gail
Bradley, William Czar
Burt, William Austin
Clark, Abraham
Cluskey, Charles Blaney
Davidson, George
De Brahm, William
  Gerard
De Witt, Simeon
Dixon, Jeremiah *Suppl. 2*
Ellicott, Andrew

Emory, William Hemsley
Ferris, Benjamin
Filson, John
Freeman, Thomas
Fry, Joshua
Geddes, James
Gist, Christopher
Hutchins, Thomas
Lawson, John
Leeds, John
Mackay, James
Maclay, Samuel
Maclay, William
Mason, Charles *Suppl. 2*
Mccoy, Isaac
Scammell, Alexander
Smith, Daniel
Taylor, Richard Cowling
Wright, Benjamin

Telegraphers
Creighton, Edward
Eckert, Thomas
  Thompson
Edison, Thomas Alva
Morse, Samuel Finley
  Breese
Sarnoff, David
Stager, Anson
Storm, Hans Otto
Watson, Thomas
  Augustus

SOCIETY AND SOCIAL CHANGE

Civics and Philanthropy
City and Regional Planners
Adams, Thomas
Bassett, Edward Murray
Bauer, Catherine Krouse
Bennett, Edward Herbert
Burnham, Daniel
  Hudson
Coit, Elisabeth
Dealey, George
  Bannerman
Gruen, Victor David
Hubbard, Henry Vincent
Moore, Charles
Moses, Robert
Nolen, John
Olmsted, Frederick Law,
  Jr.
Owings, Nathaniel
  Alexander
Perkins, Dwight Heald
Pratt, Daniel
  (1799–1873)
Putnam, Gideon

Civics and Philanthropy
(cont.)
Smith, Chloethiel
  Woodard
Stein, Clarence Samuel
Wright, Henry

City and Town Founders /
Benefactors
Boott, Kirk
Coddington, William
Estaugh, Elizabeth
  Haddon
Graffenried, Christoph,
  Baron von
Hagar, Jonathan
Harris, John
Heathcote, Caleb
King, Roswell
Lamothe Cadillac,
  Antoine Laumet de
Lane, John
Lorimier, Louis
Menéndez de Avilés,
  Pedro
Montgomery, Isaiah
  Thornton
Pastorius, Francis Daniel
Pierson, Abraham
Powell, James Robert
Pynchon, William
Scholte, H. P.
Stevens, John Harrington
Stilwell, Arthur Edward
Williams, Samuel May

Civic Leaders
Adams, Charles Francis
  (1835–1915)
Albrier, Frances Mary
Alexander, Abraham
Benson, Oscar Herman
Broom, Jacob
Bulova, Arde
Burke, Thomas
  (1849–1925)
Burlingham, Charles
  Culp
Burrell, Berkeley
  Graham
Butler, Selena Sloan
Candler, Asa Griggs
Cass, Melnea Agnes
  Jones
Childs, Richard Spencer
Cooper, Peter
Coppin, Fanny Jackson
Cotter, Joseph Seamon,
  Sr.
Craig, Isaac
Dawes, Rufus Cutler

Decker, Sarah Sophia
  Chase Platt
Desmond, Humphrey
  Joseph
Dunlap, Livingston
Favill, Henry Baird
Fenner, Charles Erasmus
Fisher, Walter Lowrie
Follett, Mary Parker
Gaston, A. G. *Suppl. 1*
Gilbert, Helen Homans
Gordon, Kate M.
Greenway, Isabella
Griffith, Goldsborough
  Sappington
Hallowell, Anna
Hare, Thomas Truxtun
Haynes, Elizabeth Ross
Hinkle, Samuel Forry
Hirsch, Emil Gustave
Hogg, Ima
Hope, Lugenia D. Burns
Hubbard, Gardiner
  Greene
Jennings, May Elizabeth
  Mann
Kaufmann, Edgar Jonas,
  Sr.
Kimball, Heber Chase
Kirstein, Louis Edward
Kittredge, Mabel Hyde
Leffingwell, Christopher
Lingelbach, Anna Lane
Lowell, Ralph
Malone, Sylvester
McClennan, Alonzo
  Clifton
McFarland, J. Horace
Montgomery, Helen
  Barrett
Morris, John Gottlieb
Outerbridge, Eugenius
  Harvey
Palmer, Bertha Honoré
Parks, Henry Green, Jr.
Paul, Thomas
Scammon, Jonathan
  Young
Seligman, Isaac Newton
Seligman, Joseph
Sherwin, Belle
Stranahan, James Samuel
  Thomas
Strong, Harriet Williams
  Russell
Ueland, Clara Hampson
Vladeck, Baruch
  Charney
Walls, William Jacob
Ware, Caroline Farrar
Welsh, John

White, Eartha Mary
  Magdalene
Wilkeson, Samuel
Wilson, J. Finley

Clubwomen
Blankenburg, Lucretia
  Longshore
Bowles, Eva Del Vakia
Brown, Charlotte
  Emerson
Clarke, Grace Giddings
  Julian
Cotten, Sallie Swepson
  Sims Southall
Croly, Jane Cunningham
Decker, Sarah Sophia
  Chase Platt
Diaz, Abby Morton
Doyle, Sarah Elizabeth
Fay, Amy Muller
Gaines, Irene McCoy
Henrotin, Ellen Martin
Laws, Annie
Lawson, Roberta
  Campbell
Moore, Eva Perry
Pennybacker, Anna
  McLaughlin
  Hardwicke
Ruffin, Josephine St.
  Pierre
Severance, Caroline
  Maria Seymour
Sherman, Mary Belle
  King
Shuler, Nettie Rogers
Slowe, Lucy Diggs
Smith, Lucy Harth
Terrell, Mary Eliza
  Church
Turner, Eliza L. Sproat
Walworth, Ellen Hardin
Welsh, Lilian
Williams, Elizabeth
  Sprague
Williams, Fannie Barrier
Winter, Alice Vivian
  Ames
Yates, Josephine A.

Foundation Officials
Barnard, Chester Irving
Buttrick, Wallace
Colcord, Joanna Carver
Gaither, Horace Rowan,
  Jr.
Harrar, Jacob George
Hiss, Alger *Suppl. 1*
Hutchins, Robert
  Maynard

Jessup, Walter Albert
Keppel, Frederick Paul
Knowles, John Hilton
Pritchett, Henry Smith
Ray, Gordon Norton
Trowbridge, Augustus
Weaver, Warren
Woodward, Robert
  Simpson
Young, Donald Ramsey

Freemasons
Bennett, John Cook
Etting, Solomon *Suppl. 1*
Hall, Prince
Hays, Moses Michael
  Suppl. 1
Morris, Robert
  (1818–1888)
Pike, Albert
Reason, Patrick Henry
Webb, Thomas Smith

Institutional Founders /
Benefactors
Baldwin, Abraham
Baldwin, John
Berry, Martha
  McChesney
Blair, James
Bliss, Daniel
Bliss, Lillie P.
Bolton, Frances Payne
Bradley, Amy Morris
Bradley, Lydia Moss
Burr, Aaron
  (1716–1757)
Burroughs, Nannie
  Helen
Butler, Mother Marie
  Joseph
Cataldo, Joseph Maria
Chafer, Lewis Sperry
Cornell, Ezra
Corson, Juliet
Crandall, Prudence
Damrosch, Frank Heino
Davidge, John Beale
Dickey, Sarah Ann
Dobbs, Ella Victoria
Drumgoole, John
  Christopher
Durant, Henry Fowle
Evans, William Thomas
Farmer, Fannie Merritt
Fee, John Gregg
Ferguson, Katy
Fitton, James
Flanagan, Edward
  Joseph
Folger, Emily Jordan

Civics and Philanthropy
(cont.)
Freer, Charles Lang
Fuld, Caroline
  Bamberger Frank
Gallatin, Albert Eugene
Gardner, Isabella
  Stewart
Graham, Isabella
Gregory, Samuel
Guggenheim, Solomon
  Robert
Harvard, John
Huntington, Henry
  Edwards
Jolas, Maria
Jones, Bob
Kander, Lizzie Black
Kent, Aratus
Lange, Mary Elizabeth
L'Esperance, Elise
  Strang
Livermore, George
Lyon, Mary
Mannes, David
Mayo, William James,
  and Charles Horace
  Mayo
McGroarty, Sister Julia
Menninger, Charles
  Frederick
Merrick, Samuel
  Vaughan
Minor, Benjamin Blake
Morais, Sabato
Morrison, Nathan
  Jackson
Mossell, Nathan Francis
Newcomb, Josephine
  Suppl. 1
Palmer, Lizzie Pitts
  Merrill
Parkhurst, Helen
Parks, Oliver Lafayette
Passavant, William
  Alfred
Peabody, Endicott
  Suppl. 1
Peale, Charles Willson
Phillips, John
Phillips, Samuel, Jr.
Pierce, Sarah
Porter, Sarah
Rice, John Holt
Rice, William Marsh
Rogers, John Almanza
  Rowley
Sage, Henry Williams
Schofield, Martha
Scudder, Ida Sophia
Seelye, Laurenus Clark

Seymour, Mary Foot
Sill, Anna Peck
Smith, Sophia
Spreckels, Alma
Starr, Ellen Gates
Surette, Thomas
  Whitney
Thurston, Matilda
  Smyrell Calder
Tompkins, Sally Louisa
Tulane, Paul *Suppl. 1*
Van Rensselaer, Stephen
Vassar, Matthew
Vincent, George Edgar
Warren, Herbert
  Langford
Watteville, Henrietta
  Benigna von
Webb, Electra
  Havemeyer
Wheelock, Lucy
Whitney, Gertrude
  Vanderbilt
Wilbur, Earl Morse
Willard, Emma Hart
Willey, Samuel Hopkins
Williams, Walter
Yale, Elihu
Zimbalist, Mary Louise
  Curtis Bok

Organization Founders /
Officials
Abbott, Grace
Adler, Cyrus
Ainsworth, Dorothy
  Sears
Ames, Fanny Baker
Andrus, Ethel Percy
Baker, Ella Josephine
Bangs, Nathan
Barnard, John Gross
Barrett, Janie Porter
Barton, James Levi
Bauer, Harold Victor
Beebe, William
Bell, Luther V.
Bennett, Belle Harris
Benson, Oscar Herman
Bethune, Joanna
  Graham
Bethune, Mary Jane
  McLeod
Billikopf, Jacob
Blackwell, Randolph
  Talmadge
Boardman, Mabel Thorp
Booth, Maud Elizabeth
  Charlesworth
  Ballington

Booth-Tucker, Emma
  Moss
Bowles, Eva Del Vakia
Breen, Joseph Ignatius
Brown, Josephine
  Chapin
Browne, William
  Washington
Buchman, Frank Nathan
  Daniel
Burrell, Berkeley
  Graham
Capen, Samuel Paul
Caswell, Alexis
Clark, Francis E.
Cook, George Cram
Cratty, Mabel
Cunningham, Ann
  Pamela
Cuthbert, Marion Vera
Dahl, Theodor
  Halvorson
Dancy, John Campbell,
  Jr.
Darling, Flora Adams
Darrow, Karl Kelchner
Davison, Henry
  Pomeroy
Dearden, John F.
Dederich, Charles
  Suppl. 2
Delano, Jane Arminda
Dodge, Grace Hoadley
Dunn, Robert Williams
Dwight, James
Eichelberger, Clark Mell
Eliot, Samuel Atkins
Emery, Julia Chester
Empie, Paul Chauncey
Eustis, Dorothy Harrison
Evans, Luther Harris
Farmer, James *Suppl. 1*
Field, Jessie
Ford, Guy Stanton
Franklin, Martha
  Minerva
Gilder, Rosamond
Going, Jonathan
Gompers, Samuel
Gottheil, Richard James
  Horatio
Greene, Roger Sherman
Gulick, Luther Halsey
  (1828–1891)
Harley, Herbert Lincoln
Harris, Paul Percy
Harrison, Hubert Henry
Hartzell, Joseph Crane
Hatfield, Edwin Francis
Hayes, Edward Cary
Heald, Henry Townley

Heide, Wilma Scott
Hoffman, Paul Gray
Hoover, Lou Henry
Hunton, Addie D.
  Waites
Irwin, Robert Benjamin
Jacobs, Frances Wisebart
Jacobson, John Christian
Joffrey, Robert
Johnson, Rachel Harris
Johnston, Eric Allen
Kallet, Arthur
Keating, William
  Hypolitus
Kefauver, Grayson
  Neikirk
Kelley, Oliver Hudson
Kelly, Robert Lincoln
Knorr, Nathan Homer
Kynett, Alpha Jefferson
Locke, Bessie
Low, Juliette
Lowell, Josephine Shaw
Lowry, Edith Elizabeth
Lund-Quist, Carl Elof
MacDowell, Marian
  Griswold Nevins
Maltby, Margaret Eliza
Martin, Franklin Henry
McBurney, Robert Ross
McDowell, Mary Eliza
McGee, Anita Newcomb
McGivney, Michael J.
McKim, James Miller
McLean, Archibald
Mills, Samuel John
Milner, Lucille
  Bernheimer
Montgomery, Helen
  Barrett
Moore, Charles
Moorland, Jesse Edward
Morris, Alice Vanderbilt
  Suppl. 1
Mott, John R.
Mulry, Thomas Maurice
Murray, William
  Davidson
Nolde, Otto Frederick
Norelius, Eric
Olmsted, Frederick Law,
  Jr.
O'Neal, Edward Asbury,
  III
Osborne, Estelle Massey
  Riddle
Ovington, Mary White
Park, Maud Wood
Parrish, Celestia
  Susannah
Patterson, Robert

Civics and Philanthropy
(cont.)
Peabody, Lucy
Whitehead McGill
Waterbury
Perkins, Charles
Callahan
Perkins, Frances
Phillips, Lena Madesin
Pickett, Clarence Evan
Reason, Patrick Henry
Riley, Alice C. D.
Roberts, William Henry
Robinson, Edgar
Munson
Rosenberg, Anna Marie
Lederer
Rubinow, Isaac Max
Russell, Charles Edward
Russell, Charles Taze
Sayre, John Nevin
Schechter, Mathilde
Roth
Schneider, Herbert
Wallace
Schuyler, Louisa Lee
Scotto, Charles
Sellaro, Vincenzo
Sewall, May Eliza
Wright
Shelly, Mary Josephine
Simmons, George Henry
Simmons, William
Joseph
Simms, Florence
Slowe, Lucy Diggs
Smith, Fred Burton
Smith, Judson
Sommers, Tish
Speer, Robert Elliott
Spottswood, Stephen
Gill
Swift, Linton Bishop
Szold, Henrietta
Tappan, Arthur, and
Lewis Tappan
Taylor, Graham
Terrell, Mary Eliza
Church
Townley, Arthur Charles
Tracy, Joseph Carter
Turner, Fennell Parrish
Upchurch, John Jordan
Verhaegen, Peter Joseph
Walsh, James Anthony
Walworth, Ellen Hardin
Wedel, Cynthia Clark
Weisgal, Meyer Wolfe
Welch, Robert
Wilkins, Roy

Wilson, Bill, and Bob
Smith *Suppl. 1*
Wilson, J. Finley
Wisely, William Homer
Woodsmall, Ruth
Frances
Worcester, Noah

Patrons of Science
Brown, George E., Jr.
Suppl. 2
Gibbs, George
(1776–1833)
Smithson, James
Suppl. 2
Tappan, Benjamin

Patrons of the Arts
Barney, Alice Pike
Bliss, Lillie P.
Chrysler, Walter Percy,
Jr.
Clarke, Thomas
Benedict
Dreier, Katherine Sophie
Force, Juliana Rieser
Gallatin, Albert Eugene
Gardner, Isabella
Stewart
Gilder, Helena de Kay
Guggenheim, Peggy
Harkness, Rebekah West
Havemeyer, Henry
Osborne *Suppl. 1*
Havemeyer, Louisine
Waldron
Herring, James
Johnston, John Taylor
Juilliard, Augustus D.
Kahn, Otto Herman
Kaufmann, Edgar Jonas,
Sr.
Koenigswarter,
Pannonica de
Lewisohn, Irene
Luhan, Mabel Dodge
Mason, Charlotte Louise
McCormick, Edith
Rockefeller
Mellon, Paul *Suppl. 1*
Menil, Dominique de
Suppl. 1
Miller, Charles Henry
Moody, Harriet
Converse
Murphy, Gerald Cleary
Perry, Antoinette
Post, Marjorie
Merriweather
Quinn, John
Reed, Luman

Rockefeller, Abby
Aldrich
Rose, Billy
Sackler, Arthur Mitchell
Saltus, J. Sanford
Sargent, Henry
Scull, Robert Cooper
Spreckels, Alma
Thurber, Jeannette
Meyers
Wallace, Lila Bell
Acheson
Warburg, Edward
Suppl. 1
Whitney, Gertrude
Vanderbilt
Zimbalist, Mary Louise
Curtis Bok

Philanthropists
Altman, Benjamin
Anderson, Larz
Archbold, John Dustin
Arnold, Richard Dennis
Astor, John Jacob, III
Astor, William Waldorf
Babson, Roger Ward
Bacon, Georgeanna
Muirson Woolsey
Bailey, Hannah Clark
Johnston
Baldwin, John
Baldwin, William Henry,
Jr.
Ball, Frank Clayton
Bamberger, Louis
Bancroft, Frederic A.
Barnett, Jackson *Suppl. 2*
Barton, Clara
Bennett, M. Katharine
Jones
Bishop, Bernice Pauahi
Bishop, Charles Reed
Blaine, Anita
McCormick
Bliss, Cornelius Newton
Bok, Edward William
Boudinot, Elias (1740–
1821)
Bowditch, Charles
Pickering
Bowen, Louise deKoven
Brace, Charles Loring
(1826–1890)
Brace, Charles Loring
(1855–1938)
Brookings, Robert
Somers
Brown, John Carter
Brown, Margaret Tobin
Suppl. 1

Brown, Moses
Bruce, Catherine Wolfe
Buchtel, John Richards
Bundy, McGeorge
Suppl. 1
Busch, August
Anheuser, Jr.
Cabot, Godfrey Lowell
Caldwell, Mary
Gwendolin Byrd
Callaway, Cason Jewell
Carnegie, Andrew
Carnegie, Louise
Whitfield
Case, Leonard
Chalmers, William James
Childs, George William
Codrington,
Christopher, Jr.
Coffin, Charles Fisher
Coker, James Lide
Cole, Anna Virginia
Russell
Colgate, James Boorman
Colgate, William
Coolidge, Elizabeth
Sprague
Cooper, Edward
Cooper, Peter
Cope, Caleb Frederick
Cope, Thomas Pym
Copley, Ira Clifton
Coram, Thomas
Corcoran, William
Wilson
Creighton, Edward
Crown, Henry
Cullen, Hugh Roy
Cupples, Samuel
Davis, Arthur Vining
Delano, Jane Arminda
DePauw, Washington
Charles
Dodge, Grace Hoadley
Douglass, William
Draper, Mary Anna
Palmer
Drexel, Anthony Joseph
Drexel, Katharine
Driscoll, Clara
Duke, Benjamin Newton
Duke, Doris
Duke, Washington
Dummer, Ethel Sturges
Eastman, George
Elwyn, Alfred Langdon
Emma
Eno, William Phelps
Eustis, Dorothy Harrison
Falk, Maurice
Faneuil, Peter

Civics and Philanthropy
(cont.)

Fels, Samuel Simeon
Field, Marshall, III
Filene, Edward Albert
Folger, Henry Clay
Fowle, Elida Barker
  Rumsey
Frick, Henry Clay
Fuld, Caroline
  Bamberger Frank
Garrett, Mary Elizabeth
Gerard, James Watson
Ginter, Lewis
Girard, Stephen
Goldman, Sylvan
  Nathan
Goucher, John Franklin
Graff, Everett Dwight
Graham, Augustus
Graham, Isabella
Green, John Cleve
Griffith, Goldsborough
  Sappington
Grinnell, Henry
Griscom, John
Grossinger, Jennie
Guggenheim, Daniel
Guggenheim, Harry
  Frank
Guggenheim, Simon
Gurley, Ralph Randolph
Hammer, Armand
Hand, Daniel
Harkness, Anna M.
  Richardson
Harkness, Edward
  Stephen
Harkness, Mary Emma
  Stillman
Harkness, Rebekah West
Harriman, Mary
  Williamson Averell
Hastings, Serranus
  Clinton
Hearst, Phoebe Elizabeth
  Apperson
Hecht, George Joseph
Heinz, Henry John, II
Hemenway, Mary
Hepburn, Alonzo Barton
Herron, Carrie Rand
Hershey, Milton Snavely
Hogg, Ima
Hoover, Herbert Clark
Howland, Emily
Huntington, Anna
  Vaughn Hyatt
Jackson, Samuel
  Macauley
James, Daniel Willis

Jarman, W. Maxey
Jeanes, Anna Thomas
Jenkins, Helen Hartley
Johnson, George Francis
Kane, Thomas Leiper
Karolik, Maxim
Kearsley, John
Kellogg, W. K.
Kelly, Eugene
Kennedy, John Stewart
Kennedy, Rose
  Fitzgerald
Kettering, Charles
  Franklin
Ladd, Kate Macy
Lafon, Thomy
Lawrence, Abbott
Letchworth, William
  Pryor
Levy, Uriah Phillips
Lewisohn, Irene
Littlefield, George
  Washington
Loeb, James
Loeb, Morris
Longworth, Nicholas
  (1782–1863)
Lowell, John
  (1799–1836)
Ludwig, Christoph
Lunt, Orrington
MacArthur, John D.
MacDowell, Marian
  Griswold Nevins
Mallinckrodt, Edward
Malone, Annie Turnbo
Markey, Lucille Parker
  Wright
Mather, Samuel
  (1851–1931)
May, Abigail Williams
McCormick, Edith
  Rockefeller
McCormick, Katharine
  Dexter
McCormick, Nettie
  Fowler
Mellon, Paul *Suppl. 1*
Morehead, John Motley
Morgan, Anne Tracy
Mott, Charles Stewart
Mugar, Stephen Pabken
Newberry, Walter
  Loomis
Newcomb, Josephine
  Suppl. 1
Newman, Isidore
Oglethorpe, James
  Edward
Osborn, William Henry

Ottendorfer, Anna Behr
  Uhl
Packard, David *Suppl. 1*
Palmer, Lizzie Pitts
  Merrill
Parrish, Joseph
  (1818–1891)
Paul, Josephine Bay
Payne, Oliver Hazard
Peabody, George
Peabody, George Foster
Pemberton, Israel
Perkins, Charles
  Callahan
Perkins, Thomas
  Handasyd
Pew, John Howard
Post, Marjorie
  Merriweather
Poydras, Julien
Pratt, Charles
Pratt, Enoch
Pritzker, Abram
  Nicholas
Procter, William Cooper
Randall, Robert Richard
Reynolds, Richard
  Joshua, Sr.
Reynolds, William Neal
Rindge, Frederick
  Hastings
Rockefeller, Abby
  Aldrich
Rockefeller, John D.
Rockefeller, John D., Jr.
Rockefeller, John D., III
Rollins, Philip Ashton
Rose, Billy
Rosenwald, Julius
Rosenwald, Lessing
  Julius
Rutgers, Henry *Suppl. 1*
Sackler, Arthur Mitchell
Sage, Margaret Olivia
  Slocum
Sanders, Harland David
Schiff, Jacob Henry
Schmitt, Arthur J.
  Suppl. 2
Schuyler, Louisa Lee
Scripps, Ellen Browning
Seligman, Jesse
Severance, Louis Henry
Sewall, Samuel
Seybert, Henry
Shaw, Henry
Sigourney, Lydia
Slater, John Fox
Sloan, Alfred Pritchard,
  Jr.
Speyer, Ellin Prince

Springer, Reuben
  Runyan
Sprunt, James
Stanford, Jane Eliza
Stern, Edith Rosenwald
Stetson, John Batterson
Stewart, Alexander
  Turney
Stokes, Olivia Egleston
  Phelps, and Caroline
  Phelps Stokes
Straight, Dorothy Payne
  Whitney
Straus, Gladys Eleanor
  Guggenheim
Talbot, Emily Fairbanks
Thaw, William
Thomas, Danny
Thompson, Elizabeth
  Rowell
Tome, Jacob
Touro, Judah
Toussaint, Pierre
  Suppl. 2
Trask, Kate Nichols
Tulane, Paul *Suppl. 1*
Vanderbilt, Cornelius, II
Vanderbilt, George
  Washington *Suppl. 1*
Vaughan, John
Vaux, Roberts
Wadsworth, James
  (1768–1844)
Wallace, DeWitt
Wallace, Lila Bell
  Acheson
Warburg, Edward
  Suppl. 1
Warburg, Felix
Ward, Lydia Arms
  Avery Coonley
White, Alfred Tredway
Whitney, Helen Hay
Whitney, John Hay
Widener, George
  Dunton, Jr.
Widener, Peter Arrell
  Brown
Wittenmyer, Annie
  Turner
Wittpenn, Caroline
  Bayard Stevens
Wolfe, Catharine
  Lorillard
Woodruff, George
  Waldo
Woolsey, Jane Stuart
Yawkey, Tom
Yeatman, James Erwin
Zimbalist, Mary Louise
  Curtis Bok

Political Activism and Reform Movements

AIDS Activists
Shilts, Randy Martin

Abolitionists
Allen, William G.
Alvord, John Watson
Andrew, John Albion
Bailey, Gamaliel
Ballou, Adin
Barbadoes, James G.
Bell, James Madison
Bell, Philip Alexander
Beman, Amos Gerry
Benezet, Anthony
Bibb, Henry Walton
Bird, Francis William
Birney, James Gillespie
Bloss, William Clough
Bourne, George
Bowditch, Henry
  Ingersoll
Brooke, Abraham
Brown, John
  (1800–1859)
Brown, William Wells
Burleigh, Charles
  Calistus
Burleigh, William Henry
Burris, Samuel D.
  Suppl. 2
Campbell, Tunis Gulic
Chace, Elizabeth Buffum
Chapman, Maria
  Weston
Chase, Salmon Portland
Cheever, George Barrell
Child, David Lee
Child, Lydia Maria
  Francis
Clarke, Lewis G.
Clay, Cassius Marcellus
Coffin, Levi
Coles, Edward
Collins, John Anderson
Colman, Lucy Newhall
Copeland, John
  Anthony, Jr.
Cowles, Betsey Mix
Craft, Ellen
Craft, William
Crandall, Prudence
Crummell, Alexander
Dargan, Edmund S.
Davis, Paulina Kellogg
  Wright
DeBaptiste, George
Douglas, H. Ford
Douglass, Frederick
Douglass, Sarah Mapps

Downing, George
  Thomas
Earle, Thomas
Embree, Elihu
Equiano, Olaudah
Everett, Robert
Fairbanks, Erastus
Fee, John Gregg
Ford, Barney Launcelot
Foster, Abby Kelley
Foster, Stephen
  Symonds
Gage, Frances Dana
  Barker
Garnet, Henry Highland
Garrett, Thomas
Garrison, William Lloyd
Gatch, Philip
Gay, Sydney Howard
Gibbons, Abigail
  Hopper
Gibbs, Mifflin Wistar
Giddings, Joshua Reed
Goodell, William (1792–
  1878)
Green, Beriah
Grew, Mary
Griffing, Josephine
  Sophia White
Grimké, Angelina Emily
Grimké, Sarah Moore
Grinnell, Josiah Bushnell
Hale, Edward Everett
Hall, Prince
Hamilton, Thomas
Haven, Gilbert
Haviland, Laura Smith
Hayden, Lewis
Helper, Hinton Rowan
Hildreth, Richard
  Suppl. 2
Holley, Myron
Holley, Sallie
Hopkins, Samuel (1721–
  1803)
Hopper, Isaac Tatem
Jackson, James Caleb
Jenkins, David
Jewett, John Punchard
Johnson, Oliver
Jones, Jane Elizabeth
Julian, George
  Washington
Langston, Charles Henry
Lay, Benjamin
Leavitt, Joshua
Lee, Luther
Little, Sophia Louisa
  Robbins
Loguen, Jermain Wesley
Lovejoy, Elijah Parish

Lovejoy, Owen
Lundy, Benjamin
Malvin, John
Martin, John Sella
Martineau, Harriet
May, Samuel Joseph
McKim, James Miller
M'Clintock, Mary Ann
  Wilson, and Thomas
  M'Clintock
Meigs, Return Jonathan
  (1801–1891)
Mercer, Margaret
Mott, James
Mott, Lucretia Coffin
Murray, Orson S.
Nell, William Cooper
Page, Ann Randolph
  Meade
Parker, John P.
Pennington, James
  William Charles
Phillips, Wendell
Post, Amy Kirby
Potter, Ray
Powell, William Peter
Pugh, Sarah
Purvis, Robert
Putnam, Caroline F.
Realf, Richard
Reason, Patrick Henry
Remond, Charles Lenox
Remond, Sarah Parker
Ruggles, David
Scott, Orange
Smith, Gerrit
Smith, James McCune
Smith, Joshua Bowen
Stearns, George Luther
Steward, Austin
Stewart, Alvan
Still, William
Stone, Lucy
Stuart, Charles
Sumner, Charles
Sunderland, La Roy
Swisshelm, Jane Grey
  Cannon
Tappan, Arthur, and
  Lewis Tappan
Torrey, Charles Turner
Truth, Sojourner
Tubman, Harriet
Van Zandt, John
Walker, David
  (1796?–1830)
Ward, Samuel Ringgold
Washington, Augustus
  Suppl. 2
Whitfield, James Monroe
Whittier, John Greenleaf

Williams, Peter, Jr.
Woolman, John
Wright, Elizur
Wright, Henry Clarke
Wright, Theodore
  Sedgwick

Agricultural Reformers
Aiken, D. Wyatt
Dickson, David
Hatch, William Henry
Murray, William Henry
  David

*Alleged Slave Revolt
Leaders*
Cinqué *Suppl. 2*
Jeremiah, Thomas

Alleged Traitors
Bayard, Nicholas
Billy
Hiss, Alger *Suppl. 1*

Anarchists
Berkman, Alexander
Bresci, Gaetano
Ciancabilla, Giuseppe
de Cleyre, Voltairine
Galleani, Luigi
Goldman, Emma
Most, Johann Joseph
Parsons, Albert Richard
Sacco, Nicola, and
  Bartolomeo Vanzetti

Animal Welfare Activists
Amory, Cleveland
  Suppl. 1
Bergh, Henry
Spira, Henry *Suppl. 1*

*Antiabortion Rights
Activists*
Storer, Horatio
  Robinson

Anticommunists
Budenz, Louis
Chambers, Whittaker
Cohn, Roy
Cvetic, Matthew C.
Fischer, Ruth
Kohlberg, Alfred
Schine, G. David
  Suppl. 1
Welch, Robert

*Antimasonic Movement
Leaders*
Morgan, William

Political Activism and Reform Movements
(cont.)

Antinuclear Activists
Rabinowitch, Eugene
Sagan, Carl *Suppl. 1*

Antisuffragists
Conway, Katherine Eleanor
Dahlgren, Sarah Madeleine Vinton
Dodge, Josephine Marshall Jewell
Meyer, Annie Nathan
Parker, Jane Marsh
Putnam, Elizabeth Lowell
Wells, Kate Boott Gannett

Birth Control Advocates
Calderone, Mary S. *Suppl. 1*
Campbell, Loraine Leeson
Cannon, Cornelia James
Dennett, Mary Coffin Ware
Foote, Edward Bliss
Guttmacher, Alan
Levine, Lena
McKinnon, Edna Bertha Rankin
Morris, John McLean
Rock, John Charles
Sanger, Margaret
Stone, Abraham, and Hannah Mayer Stone
Yarros, Rachelle

Black Nationalists
Blyden, Edward Wilmot
Crummell, Alexander
Cuffe, Paul
Delany, Martin Robinson
Garvey, Amy Euphemia Jacques
Garvey, Marcus
Logan, Rayford Whittingham
Michaux, Lewis H.
Singleton, Benjamin
Whitfield, James Monroe

Civil Liberties Activists
Baldwin, Roger Nash
Bonnin, Gertrude Simmons
Chafee, Zechariah, Jr.

Chapman, Maria Weston
Coolidge, Albert Sprague
DeSilver, Albert
Flynn, Elizabeth Gurley
Foltz, Clara Shortridge
Hays, Arthur Garfield
McWilliams, Carey
Meiklejohn, Alexander
Milligan, Lambdin P.
Milner, Lucille Bernheimer
Moore, Audley "Queen Mother" *Suppl. 2*
Ozawa, Takao
Porter, Benjamin Faneuil
Roe, Gilbert Ernstein
Rogge, O. John
Savio, Mario *Suppl. 1*
Schroeder, Theodore
Scopes, John Thomas

Civil Rights Activists
Abernathy, Ralph David
Adams, John Quincy (1848–1922)
Albert, Octavia Victoria Rogers
Albrier, Frances Mary
Alexander, Will Winton
Alston, Melvin Ovenus
Ames, Jessie Daniel
Andrew, John Albion
Apess, William
Baker, Ella Josephine
Baker, Josephine
Barber, Jesse Max
Bass, Charlotta Spears
Bayne, Thomas
Bethune, Mary Jane McLeod
Bird, Francis William
Blackwell, Randolph Talmadge
Boudinot, Elias Cornelius
Bowles, Eva Del Vakia
Braden, Carl James
Bright Eyes
Bruce, John Edward
Bunche, Ralph Johnson
Carmichael, Stokely *Suppl. 1*
Cass, Melnea Agnes Jones
Church, Robert Reed, Jr.
Clark, Peter Humphries
Clark, Septima Poinsette
Cleaver, Eldridge

Suppl. 1
Cohen, Felix Solomon
Collier, John
Comstock, Elizabeth Leslie Rous Wright
Converse, Harriet Maxwell
Cook, George William
Cook, Vivian E. J.
Cooper, Anna Julia Haywood
Dancy, John Campbell, Jr.
De Baptiste, Richard
Deming, Barbara
Dillard, James Hardy
Douglass, Frederick
Downing, George Thomas
Drake, St. Clair, Jr.
Du Bois, W. E. B.
Durham, John Stephens
Durr, Virginia Foster *Suppl. 1*
Eastman, Charles Alexander
Evers, Medgar
Farmer, James *Suppl. 1*
Fauset, Crystal Bird
Fisher, Ada Lois Sipuel
Ford, Barney Launcelot
Fortune, Timothy Thomas
Green, Ely
Griffing, Josephine Sophia White
Grigsby, Snow Flake
Grimké, Archibald Henry
Grimké, Francis James
Groppi, James Edward
Hamer, Fannie Lou Townsend
Harrison, Hubert Henry
Hastie, William Henry
Higginbotham, A. Leon, Jr. *Suppl. 2*
Hill, Charles Andrew
Holland, Annie Welthy Daughtry
Hope, Lugenia D. Burns
Houston, Charles Hamilton
Howe, Mark De Wolfe
Hundley, Mary Gibson Brewer
Hunter, Jane Edna Harris
Hunton, George Kenneth
Jackson, Helen Hunt
Jackson, Luther Porter

Jackson, Robert R.
Jemison, Alice Mae Lee
Johns, Vernon Napoleon
Johnson, James Weldon
Jones, John (1816–1879)
Kellogg, Laura Minnie Cornelius
King, Carol Weiss
King, Martin Luther
King, Martin Luther, Jr.
LaFarge, John
La Farge, Oliver Hazard Perry
Lamb, Theodore Lafayette
Lampkin, Daisy Elizabeth Adams
Langston, John Mercer
Lanusse, Armand
Lattimore, John Aaron Cicero
Logan, Rayford Whittingham
Loving, Richard Perry
Lowenstein, Allard Kenneth
Majors, Monroe Alpheus
Malcolm X
Malvin, John
Manning, Joseph Columbus
Marshall, Thurgood
Mays, Benjamin Elijah
McClendon, James Julius
McGhee, Frederick Lamar
McKissick, Floyd Bixler
Miller, Kelly
Mitchell, Clarence Maurice, Jr.
Montezuma, Carlos
Moore, Harry Tyson
Morgan, Clement Garnett
Morris, Robert (1823–1882)
Murray, Pauli
Nixon, Edgar Daniel
Otero, Miguel Antonio
Ovington, Mary White
Patterson, Louise *Suppl. 2*
Pettiford, William Reuben
Phillips, Channing E.
Pleasant, Mary Ellen
Pledger, William Anderson
Quinton, Amelia Stone
Randolph, Asa Philip

Political Activism and Reform Movements
(cont.)
Randolph, Benjamin Franklin
Ransom, Leon Andrew
Ransom, Reverdy Cassius
Reason, Charles Lewis
Remond, Charles Lenox
Rickard, Clinton
Robeson, Paul
Robinson, Ruby Doris Smith
Rosenberg, Anna Marie Lederer
Rustin, Bayard
Sanchez, George Isidore
Simmons, William James
Smith, Lucy Harth
Sparer, Edward V.
Spingarn, Arthur Barnett
Spottswood, Stephen Gill
Stanley, Sara G.
Stewart, Maria W.
Terrell, Mary Eliza Church
Tilly, Dorothy Eugenia Rogers
Tobias, Channing Heggie
Tourgée, Albion Winegar
Trotter, William Monroe
Tucker, Samuel Wilbert
Tureaud, Alexander Pierre
Turner, James Milton
Turner, Thomas Wyatt
Walden, Austin Thomas
Walker, Maggie L. *Suppl. 2*
Walling, William English
Walton, Lester A. *Suppl. 2*
Waring, J. Waties
Washington, Booker T.
Washington, Margaret Murray *Suppl. 2*
Wells-Barnett, Ida Bell
Whipple, Henry Benjamin
White, Walter Francis
Wilkins, Roy
Williams, Aubrey Willis
Willkie, Wendell Lewis
Wilson, J. Finley
Winnemucca, Sarah
Wright, Louis Tompkins
Wright, Muriel Hazel

Young, Whitney Moore, Jr.
Zuber, Paul Burgess

Civil Service Reformers
Bonaparte, Charles Joseph
Wheeler, Everett Pepperrell

Communists
Bentley, Elizabeth Terrill
Browder, Earl Russell
Childs, Morris *Suppl. 2*
Davis, Benjamin Jefferson (1903–1964)
Dennis, Eugene
Eisler, Gerhart
Fischer, Ruth
Ford, James William
Foster, William Z.
Gitlow, Benjamin
Gold, Michael
Hall, Gus *Suppl. 1*
Larkin, James
Massing, Hede Tune
Minor, Robert
Patterson, William L.
Perry, Pettis
Stokes, Rose Pastor
Thompson, Robert George
Ware, Harold
Winston, Henry

Conscientious Objectors
Firth, Roderick

Conservationists
Adamson, Joy
Albright, Horace Marden
Allen, Edward Tyson
Baker, John Hopkinson
Bass, Robert Perkins
Becker, Marion Rombauer
Bennett, Hugh Hammond
Darling, Jay Norwood
Forbush, Edward Howe
Gabrielson, Ira Noel
Grinnell, George Bird
Hornaday, William Temple
Johnson, Osa
Jones, Buffalo
Leopold, A. Starker
Leopold, Aldo
Lowdermilk, Walter Clay *Suppl. 1*

McCrackin, Josephine
McFarland, J. Horace
Muir, John
Newell, Frederick Haynes
Olmsted, Frederick Law, Jr.
Olson, Sigurd Ferdinand
Osborn, Fairfield
Osborn, Henry Fairfield
Pearson, Thomas Gilbert
Pinchot, Gifford
Pratt, George Dupont
Saylor, John Phillips *Suppl. 2*
Sears, Paul Bigelow
Sherman, Mary Belle King
Shields, George Oliver
Stoddard, Seneca Ray *Suppl. 2*
Van Hise, Charles Richard
Wright, Mabel Osgood
Zahniser, Howard Clinton

Consumer Rights Advocates
Campbell, Persia Crawford
Kallet, Arthur
Kelley, Florence
Lakey, Alice
Rumsey, Mary Harriman
Ware, Caroline Farrar
Warne, Colston Estey

Dress Reformers
Austin, Harriet N.
Bloomer, Amelia Jenks
Hasbrouck, Lydia Sayer

Ecologists
Abbey, Edward
Allee, Warder Clyde
Cain, Stanley Adair
Carson, Rachel Louise
Clausen, Jens Christen
Clements, Frederic Edward
Cowles, Henry Chandler
Forbes, Stephen Alfred
MacArthur, Robert Helmer
Morgan, Ann Haven
Sears, Paul Bigelow
Shelford, Victor Ernest
Vogt, William
Whittaker, Robert Harding

Economic Reformers
Baird, Henry Carey
Fels, Joseph
Harvey, Coin
Macune, Charles William
Warbasse, James Peter

Educational Reform Advocates
Alberty, Harold Bernard
Alcott, A. Bronson
Alderman, Edwin Anderson
Andrews, Fannie Fern Phillips
Antony, Milton
Bardin, Shlomo
Barnard, Henry
Barnes, Mary Downing Sheldon
Berkson, Isaac Baer
Bestor, Arthur Eugene
Bevan, Arthur Dean
Blow, Susan Elizabeth
Brameld, Theodore Burghard Hurt
Bulkley, John Williams
Byford, William Heath
Carter, James Gordon
Clapp, Elsie Ripley
Cobb, Lyman
Cotten, Sallie Swepson Sims Southall
Cubberley, Ellwood Patterson
Curry, Jabez Lamar Monroe
Dennett, Mary Coffin Ware
Dewey, Melvil
Dobbs, Ella Victoria
du Pont, Pierre Samuel
Eaton, Amos
Fahs, Sophia Lyon
Fee, John Gregg
Flesch, Rudolf Franz
Flexner, Abraham
Fuller, Sarah
Garnett, James Mercer
Gill, Laura Drake
Gilman, Daniel Coit
Gould, Benjamin Apthorp (1787–1859)
Greene, Roger Sherman
Gulick, Luther Halsey (1865–1918)
Hallowell, Anna
Hazard, Thomas Robinson

**Political Activism and
Reform Movements**
(cont.)
Hunt, Mary Hannah
  Hanchett
Hunter, Thomas
Huntington, Emily
Inglis, Alexander James
Keppel, Francis C.
Kingsley, Clarence
  Darwin
Knox, Samuel
Kraus-Boelté, Maria
Laws, Annie
Lewis, Samuel B.
Lord, Asa Dearborn
Maclure, William
Magoun, George
  Frederic
Malkiel, Theresa Serber
Mann, Horace
Marwedel, Emma
  Jacobina Christiana
McAndrew, William
Mitchell, Lucy Sprague
Packard, Frederick
  Adolphus
Parker, Francis Wayland
Parkhurst, Helen
Partridge, Alden
Patri, Angelo
Peet, Harvey Prindle
Perkins, Charles
  Callahan
Prichard, Edward
  Fretwell, Jr.
Pugh, Evan
Putnam, Alice Harvey
  Whiting
Raymond, John Howard
Reilly, Marion
Rice, Joseph Mayer
Richman, Julia B.
Rogers, Harriet Burbank
Ruffner, William Henry
Sachs, Julius
Schurz, Margarethe
  Meyer
Scott, Colin Alexander
Sheldon, Edward Austin
Smart, James Henry
Smith, Benjamin Mosby
Snedden, David Samuel
Spencer, Cornelia
  Phillips
Stone, Lucinda Hinsdale
Stowe, Calvin Ellis
Taba, Hilda
Talbot, Emily Fairbanks
Thayer, Eli
Tutwiler, Julia Strudwick

Valentine, Lila
  Hardaway Meade
Vaux, Roberts
Wadsworth, James
  (1768–1844)
Welch, William Henry
White, Edna Noble
Wiley, Calvin Henderson
Woodward, Calvin
  Milton
Woolman, Mary
  Raphael Schenck
Zachos, John Celivergos

Environmentalists
Adams, Ansel
Brower, David *Suppl. 2*
Denver, John *Suppl. 1*
Douglas, Marjory
  Stoneman *Suppl. 1*
Douglas, William O.
Emerson, George Barrell
Fuller, R. Buckminster
Marsh, George Perkins
Marshall, Robert
Owings, Nathaniel
  Alexander
Udall, Morris K.
  Suppl. 1

Eugenicists
Davenport, Charles
  Benedict
Laughlin, Harry
  Hamilton

Evolutionists
Fiske, John (1842–1901)
Scopes, John Thomas
Stebbins, G. Ledyard
  Suppl. 1

Fenians
O'Mahony, John
Roberts, William Randall

Futurologists
Kahn, Herman

Gay Rights Activists
Milk, Harvey
Shilts, Randy Martin

Historic Preservationists
Appleton, William
  Sumner
De Zavala, Adina Emily
du Pont, Henry Francis
Gill, Brendan *Suppl. 2*
Meem, John Gaw

Onassis, Jacqueline
  Kennedy

Human Rights Activists
Cooper, Anna Julia
  Haywood
Green, Paul
Proskauer, Joseph Meyer
Weltfish, Gene

Humanitarians
Blackwell, Alice Stone
Buck, Pearl S.
Chapman, Oscar
  Littleton
Hale, Clara McBride
Keller, Helen
Labouisse, Henry
  Richardson
Mayo, Sara
Nicholson, Timothy
Peter, Sarah
  Worthington King
Salm-Salm, Agnes
  Elisabeth Winona
  Leclercq Joy
Smith, Emma Hale
Stowe, Harriet Beecher
Tutwiler, Julia Strudwick
Wright, Sophie Bell

*Immigration Reform
Advocates*
Abbott, Grace
Bremer, Edith Terry
Kellor, Frances Alice
Kohler, Max James
Roberts, Peter *Suppl. 1*
Speranza, Gino Carlo
Stoddard, Theodore
  Lothrop

Insurgents
Bacon, Nathaniel
Clarke, Parker
Coode, John
Culpeper, John
Ely, Samuel Cullick
Faulkner, Thomas
Fries, John
Girty, Simon
Ingle, Richard
Shays, Daniel
Whipple, Prince
Youngs, John

Internationalists
Brown, Harrison Scott
Holt, Hamilton Bowen
Shotwell, James
  Thomson

Wambaugh, Sarah

Ku Klux Klan Leaders
Forrest, Nathan Bedford
Gholson, Samuel
  Jameson
Gordon, John Brown
Simmons, William
  Joseph

Labor Organizers / Leaders
Anderson, Mary
  (1872–1964)
Arthur, Peter M.
Bagley, Sarah George
Bambace, Angela
Barker, Mary Cornelia
Barnum, Gertrude
Barry, Leonora
Beck, Dave
Belanger, Mark *Suppl. 2*
Bellanca, August
Bellanca, Dorothy Jacobs
Berry, George Leonard
Beyer, Clara Mortenson
Biemiller, Andrew John
Bloor, Ella Reeve
Borchardt, Selma
  Munter
Boyle, Michael J.
Boyle, William Anthony
Bridges, Harry Renton
Brooks, John Graham
Brophy, John
Browne, Carl
Budenz, Louis
Cameron, Andrew Carr
Carr, Charlotte Elizabeth
Chávez, César Estrada
Chaplin, Ralph Hosea
Christman, Elisabeth
Cohn, Fannia
Coit, Eleanor Gwinnell
Coles, Edward
Collins, Jennie
Conboy, Sara Agnes
  McLaughlin
Coxey, Jacob Sechler
Crosswaith, Frank
  Rudolph
Curran, Joseph Edwin
Davis, Richard L.
Debs, Eugene Victor
de Graffenried, Mary
  Clare
Dietz, Peter Ernest
Dodd, Bella Visono
Dreier, Mary Elisabeth
Drury, Victor S.
Dubinsky, David
Dudley, Helena Stuart

Political Activism and Reform Movements
(cont.)
Duncan, James
Dunn, Robert Williams
Ettor, Joseph James
Evans, George Henry
Fechner, Robert *Suppl. 2*
Fitzpatrick, John
Fitzsimmons, Frank *Suppl. 2*
Fletcher, Benjamin Harrison
Flynn, Elizabeth Gurley
Ford, James William
Frey, John Philip
Furuseth, Andrew
Galarza, Ernesto
Germer, Adolph
Giovannitti, Arturo Massimo
Gompers, Samuel
Green, William
Gresham, Newt
Grigsby, Snow Flake
Haessler, Carl
Haley, Margaret Angela
Hamid, Sufi Abdul
Harrison, Hubert Henry
Hayes, Max Sebastian
Haywood, Allan Shaw
Haywood, William Dudley
Heighton, William
Henry, Alice
Hill, Joe
Hillman, Bessie Abramowitz
Hillman, Sidney
Hoffa, Jimmy
Howard, Charles Perry
Hutcheson, William Levi
Hutchins, Grace
Iglesias, Santiago
Jackson, Gardner
Johnston, William Hugh
Jones, Mother
Kallet, Arthur
Kearney, Denis
Kelley, Florence
Kirkland, Lane *Suppl. 1*
Lang, Lucy Fox Robins
Larkin, James
Lens, Sidney
Lewis, Augusta
Lewis, John L.
Litchman, Charles Henry
London, Meyer
Lovestone, Jay
Low, Seth

Lundeberg, Harry
Luther, Seth
Lynch, James Mathew
Malkiel, Theresa Serber
Marot, Helen
Mason, Lucy Randolph
Maurer, James Hudson
McDonald, David John
McDowell, Mary Eliza
McGuire, Peter J.
McNeill, George Edwin
Meany, George
Miller, Frieda Segelke
Mitchell, Harry Leland
Mitchell, John (1870–1919)
Mooney, Thomas Joseph
Moore, Ely
Moreno, Luisa
Mosessohn, David Nehemiah
Murray, Philip
Muste, Abraham Johannes
Myers, Isaac
Nestor, Agnes
Newman, Pauline
Norwood, Rose Finkelstein
O'Reilly, Leonora
O'Sullivan, Mary Kenney
Parker, Julia O'Connor
Parsons, Albert Richard
Parsons, Lucy Eldine
Payne, Virginia
Perkins, Frances
Pesotta, Rose
Petrillo, James Caesar
Phillips, Lena Madesin
Phillips, Wendell
Potofsky, Jacob Samuel
Powderly, Terence Vincent
Powell, William Peter
Presser, William
Quill, Mike
Randolph, Asa Philip
Reuther, Walter Philip
Robins, Margaret Dreier
Rodgers, Elizabeth Flynn
Schlesinger, Benjamin
Schneiderman, Rose
Shanker, Albert *Suppl. 1*
Siney, John
Sorge, Friedrich Adolph
Stelzle, Charles
Stephens, Uriah Smith
Stevens, Alzina Ann Parsons
Steward, Ira

Swartz, Maud O'Farrell
Swinton, John
Sylvis, William H.
Thomas, Roland Jay
Tobin, Daniel Joseph
Townsend, Willard Saxby, Jr.
Tresca, Carlo
Trevellick, Richard F.
Tveitmoe, Olaf Anders
Valesh, Eva McDonald
Vorse, Mary Heaton
Walling, William English
Weitling, Wilhelm Christian
Wertheimer, Barbara Mayer
Whitney, Alexander Fell
Wilson, William Bauchop
Woll, Matthew
Yorke, Peter Christopher
Young, Ruth
Young, William Field
Younger, Maud

Land Reformers
Evans, George Henry
Macune, Charles William

Nationalists
Ahn, Chang-ho
Burgos, Julia de
Kosciuszko, Tadeusz Andrzej Bonawentura
MacNeven, William James
Meagher, Thomas Francis
Mitchel, John
Muñoz Marín, Luis
Muñoz Rivera, Luis
Zhitlowsky, Hayim

Nazi Leaders
Rockwell, George Lincoln

Pacifists
Andrews, Fannie Fern Phillips
Ballou, Adin
Brooke, Abraham
Burritt, Elihu
Cadbury, Henry Joel
Deming, Barbara
Dennett, Mary Coffin Ware
Detzer, Dorothy
Dudley, Helena Stuart

Fincke, William M. *Suppl. 2*
Hartmann, George Wilfred
Holmes, John Haynes
Hughan, Jessie Wallace
Mead, Lucia True Ames
Murray, Orson S.
Muste, Abraham Johannes
Sayre, John Nevin
Schwimmer, Rosika
Smith, Fred Burton
Villard, Fanny Garrison
Villard, Oswald Garrison
Worcester, Noah
Wright, Henry Clarke

Peace Activists
Addams, Jane
Bailey, Hannah Clark Johnston
Balch, Emily Greene
Bartholdt, Richard
Bok, Edward William
Bunche, Ralph Johnson
Catt, Carrie Chapman
Clark, Grenville
Cousins, Norman
Dahlberg, Edwin Theodore
DeBenedetti, Charles Louis *Suppl. 2*
Dodge, David Low *Suppl. 2*
Eichelberger, Clark Mell
Fulbright, J. William
Ginn, Edwin
Ginsberg, Allen *Suppl. 1*
Hooper, Jessie Annette Jack
Hull, Hannah Hallowell Clothier
Ladd, William
Lathrop, John Howland
Love, Alfred Henry
Rankin, Jeannette Pickering
Roerich, Nicholas *Suppl. 2*
Trueblood, Benjamin Franklin *Suppl. 2*
Wilson, E. Raymond
Wood, Carolena
Woolley, Mary Emma

Political Activists
Adams, John Quincy (1848–1922)
Alexander, Will Winton
Allen, Levi

Political Activism and Reform Movements
(cont.)
Ames, Fisher
Ames, Nathaniel
(1741–1842)
Anderson, Charles
William
Arenas, Reinaldo
Arvey, Jacob Meyer
Ashe, Arthur
Austin, Benjamin
Bailey, Gamaliel
Barbadoes, James G.
Barker, James William
Bates, Barnabas
Bellanca, August
Berger, Victor Louis
Bird, Francis William
Boyle, Kay
Bradwell, Myra Colby
Bruce, William Cabell
Burr, Theodosia
Cass, Lewis
Childs, Richard Spencer
Church, Robert Reed, Jr.
Coe, George Albert
Colón, Jesús *Suppl. 2*
Connor, Bull
Coolidge, Albert
Sprague
Coughlin, Charles
Edward
Croker, Richard
Cummings, Homer Stillé
Cunningham, Minnie
Fisher
Dargan, Edmund S.
Dean, Vera Micheles
Dembitz, Lewis Naphtali
Dorr, Thomas Wilson
Douglas, Helen Gahagan
Drury, Victor S.
Du Bois, W. E. B.
Dunbar-Nelson, Alice
Dunn, Robert Williams
Eagleson, William Lewis
Eddy, George Sherwood
Edge, Walter Evans
Edwards, India
Egan, Patrick
Elliott, Harriet Wiseman
Farley, James Aloysius
Faulk, John Henry
Fletcher, Henry Prather
Foster, Judith Ellen
Horton Avery
Gardiner, John
Garfield, Harry
Augustus

Gildersleeve, Virginia
Crocheron
Graham, Shirley *Suppl. 1*
Gray, James Harrison
Gwathmey, Robert
Suppl. 2
Hapgood, Norman
Harper, Frances Ellen
Watkins
Harriman, Daisy
Harriman, Pamela
Suppl. 1
Hays, Lee Elhardt
Haywood, William
Dudley
Hecker, Friedrich Karl
Franz
Hexamer, Charles John
Hines, James J.
Hoffman, Abbie
Howe, Louis McHenry
Hunt, H. L.
Husband, Herman
Ivins, William Mills
Jackson, Gardner
Julian, George
Washington
Kahn, Albert Eugene
Kenyon, Dorothy
Kirby, Ephraim
Kolb, Reuben Francis
Kunstler, William Moses
La Follette, Belle Case
Lash, Joseph P.
Le Sueur, Marian
Lorimer, William
Lovett, Robert Morss
Lowenstein, Allard
Kenneth
Loy, Myrna
Lubin, David
Luscomb, Florence
Hope
MacVeagh, Isaac Wayne
Marcantonio, Vito
Anthony
Marcuse, Herbert
Margold, Nathan Ross
Marley, Bob
Mather, Kirtley Fletcher
Matthews, Joseph Brown
McCormick, Ruth
Hanna
Miller, Emma Guffey
Mitchel, John Purroy
Morgan, Jacob Casimera
Morton, Ferdinand
Quintin
Morton, Julius Sterling
Moulton, Ebenezer
Newton, Huey P.

Niles, David K.
Ogden, John Cosens
Outlaw, Wyatt *Suppl. 2*
Overton, John
Patterson, Louise
Suppl. 2
Pauling, Linus Carl
Penrose, Boies
Pinchot, Amos Richards
Eno
Pinchot, Cornelia Bryce
Platt, Thomas Collier
Pleasants, John
Hampden
Pope, Generoso
Prichard, Edward
Fretwell, Jr.
Priest, Ivy Maude Baker
Putnam, Elizabeth
Lowell
Ramírez, Sara Estela
Raynal, Guillaume-
Thomas-François
Redmond, Sidney Dillon
Reed, Philip Dunham
Ritchie, Thomas
Roberts, Oran Milo
Robins, Raymond
Rockwell, George
Lincoln
Roosevelt, Eleanor
Roudanez, Louis Charles
Rubin, Jerry
Ruffin, Edmund
Russell, Clayton
Rustin, Bayard
Sabin, Pauline Morton
Salvemini, Gaetano
Suppl. 2
Short, Robert Earl
Simmons, Roscoe
Conkling Murray
Sinclair, Upton
Smith, Gerald Lyman
Kenneth
Sterne, Simon
Taylor, Richard
Todd, Marion Marsh
Turner, Jack
Tyler, Robert
Upton, Harriet Taylor
U'Ren, William Simon
Viereck, George
Sylvester
Wallis, Severn Teackle
Weeks, Sinclair
Welch, Robert
West, Roy Owen
Wharton, William Harris
Whitney, Charlotte Anita

Wickersham, George
Woodward
Woodward, George
Wright, Eliphalet Nott
Wright, Hendrick
Bradley
Wright, Theodore
Sedgwick
Yancey, William
Lowndes

Remonstrants
Child, Robert

Revolutionaries
Brentano, Lorenz
Cortina, Juan
Nepomuceno
Digges, Thomas
Attwood
Fannin, James Walker
Fay, Jonas
Garza, Catarino Erasmo
Hecker, Friedrich Karl
Franz
Lea, Homer
Popé
Ramírez, Sara Estela
Rapp, Wilhelm
Reed, John
Sanders, George
Nicholas
van Heijenoort, Jean
Villa, Pancho

Slave Revolt Leaders
Cinqué *Suppl. 2*
Gabriel
Turner, Nat
Vesey, Denmark

Social Reformers
Abbott, Edith
Abbott, Grace
Addams, Jane
Adler, Felix
Alcott, A. Bronson
Alinsky, Saul David
Allen, Nathan
Altgeld, John Peter
American, Sadie
Ames, Fanny Baker
Anderson, Matthew
Andrews, John Bertram
Andrews, Stephen Pearl
Anthony, Susan B.
Atkinson, Edward
Bacon, Leonard, Sr.
Bagley, Sarah George
Baker, Harvey
Humphrey

**Political Activism and
Reform Movements**
(cont.)

Baldwin, Roger Nash
Barnard, Kate
Barnum, Gertrude
Barrett, Janie Porter
Barrows, Isabel
Barrows, Samuel June
Bates, Barnabas
Beecher, Catharine
Esther
Beecher, Henry Ward
Belmont, Alva Erskine
Smith Vanderbilt
Benezet, Anthony
Bethune, Joanna
Graham
Bethune, Mary Jane
McLeod
Birney, Alice Josephine
McLellan
Blackwell, Antoinette
Louisa Brown
Blackwell, Henry
Browne
Blanchard, Jonathan
Bliss, William Dwight
Porter
Bloss, William Clough
Bonney, Mary Lucinda
Booth, Maud Elizabeth
Charlesworth
Ballington
Booth-Tucker, Emma
Moss
Bowen, Louise deKoven
Bowker, R. R.
Brace, Charles Loring
(1826–1890)
Brace, Charles Loring
(1855–1938)
Bradford, Cornelia
Foster
Branch, Anna
Hempstead
Breckinridge, Madeline
McDowell
Breckinridge,
Sophonisba Preston
Brisbane, Albert
Brooks, John Graham
Brown, Margaret Tobin
Suppl. 1
Burleigh, Charles
Calistus
Burlingham, Charles
Culp
Burritt, Elihu
Butler, Elizabeth
Beardsley

Butler, Selena Sloan
Cameron, Donaldina
Mackenzie
Carse, Matilda Bradley
Chávez, César Estrada
Chace, Elizabeth Buffum
Chandler, Lucinda
Channing, William
Henry
Chapin, Henry Dwight
Chapin, Sarah Flournoy
Moore
Cheney, Ednah Dow
Littlehale
Coit, Stanton
Colcord, Joanna Carver
Collier, John
Collins, John Anderson
Coman, Katharine
Comstock, Anthony
Cone, Moses Herman
Conway, Moncure
Daniel
Coulter, Ernest Kent
Cratty, Mabel
Crosby, Ernest Howard
Dargan, Edmund S.
Davis, Frances Elliott
Day, Dorothy
Dennison, Henry Sturgis
de Schweinitz, Karl
Dewson, Molly
Diaz, Abby Morton
Dix, Dorothea Lynde
Dock, Lavinia Lloyd
Dodge, Grace Hoadley
Dodge, Josephine
Marshall Jewell
Doherty, Catherine de
Hueck
Donaldson, Mary
Elizabeth
Dorr, Thomas Wilson
Doster, Frank
Drumgoole, John
Christopher
Dudley, Helena Stuart
Dugdale, Richard Louis
Dummer, Ethel Sturges
Dwight, Louis
Dwight, Theodore
(1796–1866)
Easley, Ralph
Montgomery
Eastman, Crystal
Eastman, Elaine Goodale
Eddy, Thomas
Edson, Katherine Philips
Einstein, Hannah
Bachman

Eliot, Charlotte Champe
Stearns
Elliott, John Lovejoy
Epstein, Abraham
Evans, Elizabeth
Glendower
Evans, Frederick William
Ferebee, Dorothy
Boulding
Field, Sara Bard
Fields, Annie Adams
Filene, Edward Albert
Finley, Robert
Flanagan, Edward
Joseph
Flexner, Bernard
Flower, Benjamin
Orange
Flower, Lucy Louisa
Coues
Folks, Homer
Forten, James
Foster, Stephen
Symonds
Fourier, Charles
Fritchman, Stephen Hole
Fuller, Minnie Ursula
Oliver Scott
Rutherford
Gardiner, Robert
Hallowell, III
Garrett, Mary Smith
George, Henry
Gibson, Mary Simons
Gillette, King Camp
Glenn, John Mark
Goldmark, Josephine
Clara
Gordon, Jean Margaret
Graham, Isabella
Gratz, Rebecca
Green, Frances Harriet
Whipple
Hale, Clara McBride
Hale, Edward Everett
Harman, Moses
Hazard, Thomas
Robinson
Heide, Wilma Scott
Henrotin, Ellen Martin
Herron, Carrie Rand
Herron, George Davis
Heywood, Angela
Fiducia Tilton
Heywood, Ezra Hervey
Higginson, Thomas
Wentworth
Hillenbrand, Reynold
Henry
Hine, Lewis Wickes
Holly, James Theodore

Holmes, John Haynes
Howe, Frederic Clemson
Howe, Samuel Gridley
Howland, William
Dillwyn
Hunter, Robert
(1874–1942)
Hunton, Addie D.
Waites
Hutchins, Grace
Hutchinson, Abigail
Jemima *Suppl. 2*
Hutchinson, Adoniram
Judson Joseph *Suppl. 2*
Hutchinson, Asa
Burnham *Suppl. 2*
Hutchinson, Jesse, Jr.
Suppl. 2
Hutchinson, John
Wallace *Suppl. 2*
Iams, Lucy Dorsey
Ickes, Anna Wilmarth
Thompson
Ingham, Mary Hall
Jacobs, Harriet
Jacobs, Pattie Ruffner
Jennings, May Elizabeth
Mann
Johnson, George Francis
Johnson, Tom Loftin
Jones, Samuel Milton
Kander, Lizzie Black
Kaufmann, Peter
Kehew, Mary Morton
Kimball
Kelley, Florence
Kellogg, Paul
Underwood
Kelpius, Johannes
Kepley, Ada Harriet
Miser
Kerby, William Joseph
Kohut, Rebekah
Bettelheim
Kuhn, Maggie *Suppl. 1*
Lathrop, Julia Clifford
Lee, Elizabeth Blair
Ligutti, Luigi
Lindsey, Ben B.
Lippard, George
Livermore, Mary
Lloyd, Henry Demarest
Lockwood, Belva Ann
Bennett McNall
Loeb, Sophie Irene
Simon
Lovejoy, Owen Reed
Lowell, Josephine Shaw
Lozier, Clemence Sophia
Lumpkin, Joseph Henry

Political Activism and Reform Movements

(cont.)

Lumpkin, Katharine Du Pre
Lundberg, Emma Octavia
Luscomb, Florence Hope
Mann, Horace
Marshall, Robert
Martin, George Madden *Suppl. 1*
Marvin, Cornelia
Mason, Lucy Randolph
Matthews, Mark Allison
Maurin, Peter Aristide
May, Abigail Williams
May, Samuel Joseph
McCarthy, Charles
McCormick, Katharine Dexter
McCulloch, Catharine Gouger Waugh
McCulloch, Oscar Carleton
McDowell, Mary Eliza
McGlynn, Edward
McKelway, Alexander Jeffrey
Mead, George Herbert
Mercer, Charles Fenton
Morrow, Prince Albert
Moskowitz, Belle Lindner Israels
Murphy, Edgar Gardner
Nathan, Maud
Nearing, Scott
Newman, Angelia French
Oberholtzer, Sara Louisa Vickers
O'Connor, Jessie Lloyd
Older, Fremont
Owen, Robert Dale
Owens-Adair, Bethenia Angelina
Oxnam, Garfield Bromley
Parker, Theodore
Parkhurst, Charles Henry
Pinchot, Cornelia Bryce
Potter, Ellen Culver
Pratt, Anna Beach
Pratt, Daniel (1799–1873)
Rainsford, William Stephen
Rauschenbusch, Walter
Reed, Myron Winslow

Ridge, Lola
Riis, Jacob August
Riis, Mary Phillips
Ripley, George
Robbins, Jane Elizabeth
Robins, Margaret Dreier
Robins, Raymond
Rodgers, Elizabeth Flynn
Roosevelt, Eleanor
Rubinow, Isaac Max
Rukeyser, Muriel
Rummel, Joseph Francis
Rumsey, Mary Harriman
Rush, Benjamin
Russ, John Dennison
Ryan, John Augustine
Salmon, Thomas William
Sampson, William
Sanborn, Franklin Benjamin
Saunders, Prince
Savio, Mario *Suppl. 1*
Scott, Leroy Martin
Scudder, Vida Dutton
Sheldon, Charles Monroe
Simms, Florence
Sinclair, Upton
Skaggs, William H. *Suppl. 1*
Solomon, Hannah Greenebaum
Spencer, Anna Garlin
Spingarn, Joel Elias
Sprague, Achsa W.
Starr, Ellen Gates
Stern, Edith Rosenwald
Stevens, Alzina Ann Parsons
Strong, Josiah
Stuck, Hudson
Sunderland, Jabez Thomas
Swift, Linton Bishop
Swope, Gerard
Taylor, Graham
Terrell, Mary Eliza Church
Thomas, Norman Mattoon
Thompson, Benjamin
Townsend, Francis Everett
Turner, Henry McNeal
Van Vorst, Marie Louise
Van Waters, Miriam
Verity, George Matthew
Villard, Fanny Garrison
Wald, Lillian D.
Walters, Alexander

Ward, Harry Frederick
Ward, Henry Dana
Ward, Maisie
Weld, Theodore Dwight
Wells, Marguerite
Whipper, William
White, Eartha Mary Magdalene
Winston, Ellen Black
Wise, Stephen Samuel
Wood, L. Hollingsworth
Wood, Thomas Bond
Woods, Robert Archey
Wright, Theodore Sedgwick
Young, Ann Eliza

Socialists

Ameringer, Oscar
Berger, Victor Louis
Browne, Carl
Calverton, Victor Francis
Carey, James Francis *Suppl. 2*
De Leon, Daniel
Dietzgen, Peter Joseph
Ghent, William James
Gronlund, Laurence
Haessler, Carl
Harriman, Job
Harrington, Michael
Harrison, Hubert Henry
Hillquit, Morris
Hoan, Daniel Webster
Howland, Marie
Hughan, Jessie Wallace
London, Meyer
Maurer, James Hudson
McGrady, Thomas
O'Hare, Kate Richards
Scott, Leroy Martin
Seidel, George Lukas Emil
Simons, Algie Martin
Spargo, John
Stokes, Rose Pastor
Stolberg, Benjamin
Thomas, Norman Mattoon
Wayland, Julius Augustus
Willich, August

Suffragists

Anneke, Mathilde Franziska Giesler
Anthony, Susan B.
Avery, Rachel G. Foster
Bailey, Hannah Clark Johnston

Barron, Jennie Loitman
Belmont, Alva Erskine Smith Vanderbilt
Bittenbender, Ada Matilda Cole
Blankenburg, Lucretia Longshore
Blatch, Harriot Stanton
Boissevain, Inez Milholland
Bowen, Louise deKoven
Breckinridge, Madeline McDowell
Brown, Gertrude Foster
Brown, Olympia
Catt, Carrie Chapman
Chase, Agnes
Clay-Clopton, Virginia Tunstall
Collins, Jennie
Couzins, Phoebe Wilson
Cunningham, Minnie Fisher
Decker, Sarah Sophia Chase Platt
Dock, Lavinia Lloyd
Dreier, Mary Elisabeth
Duniway, Abigail Jane Scott
Ferrin, Mary Upton
Field, Sara Bard
Foltz, Clara Shortridge
Friganza, Trixie
Gage, Matilda Joslyn
Garnet, Sarah Smith Tompkins
Gordon, Jean Margaret
Gordon, Kate M.
Gordon, Laura de Force
Gougar, Helen Mar Jackson
Grossman, Mary Belle
Harper, Ida Husted
Haskell, Ella Louise Knowles
Havemeyer, Louisine Waldron
Hay, Mary Garrett
Hazard, Rebecca Ann Naylor
Hooker, Isabella Beecher
Howe, Julia Ward
Howland, Emily
Hull, Hannah Hallowell Clothier
Ingham, Mary Hall
Jacobs, Pattie Ruffner
Johnston, Mary
Kearney, Belle
Kilgore, Carrie Sylvester Burnham

**Political Activism and
Reform Movements**
(cont.)
Livermore, Mary
Malkiel, Theresa Serber
Martin, Anne Henrietta
May, Abigail Williams
May, Samuel Joseph
McCormick, Ruth
  Hanna
Mead, Lucia True Ames
Minor, Virginia Louise
Morris, Esther Hobart
Nathan, Maud
Otero-Warren, Nina
Park, Maud Wood
Patterson, Hannah Jane
Pollitzer, Anita Lily
Ricker, Marilla Marks
  Young
Robins, Elizabeth
Robinson, Harriet Jane
  Hanson
Rutherford, Mildred
  Lewis
Seton, Grace Gallatin
  Thompson
Sewall, May Eliza
  Wright
Shaw, Anna Howard
Shaw, Mary
Sherwin, Belle
Shuler, Nettie Rogers
Smith, Julia Evelina, and
  Abby Hadassah Smith
Somerville, Nellie
  Nugent
Stanton, Elizabeth Cady
Stevens, Doris Caroline
Turner, Eliza L. Sproat
Ueland, Clara Hampson
Upton, Harriet Taylor
Valentine, Lila
  Hardaway Meade
Villard, Fanny Garrison
Waite, Catharine Van
  Valkenburg
Wells, Emmeline B.
Welsh, Lilian
Wright, Alice Morgan

*Temperance Movement
Leaders*
Arthur, Timothy Shay
Bloomer, Amelia Jenks
Bolton, Sarah Knowles
Boole, Ella Alexander
Brooks, Walter
  Henderson
Burger, Nelle Gilham
  Lemon

Cannon, James, Jr.
Carse, Matilda Bradley
Chapin, Sarah Flournoy
  Moore
Cheever, George Barrell
Cherrington, Ernest
  Hurst
Comstock, Elizabeth
  Leslie Rous Wright
Crothers, Thomas
  Davison
Day, Albert
Delavan, Edward
  Cornelius
Dow, Neal
Everett, Robert
Fairbanks, Erastus
Forsyth, Jessie
Foster, Judith Ellen
  Horton Avery
Funk, Isaac Kauffman
Gage, Frances Dana
  Barker
Goodell, William
  (1792–1878)
Gordon, Anna Adams
Gougar, Helen Mar
  Jackson
Gough, John
  Bartholomew
Hay, Mary Garrett
Hickman, John James
Hunt, Mary Hannah
  Hanchett
Kearney, Belle
Langston, Charles Henry
Leavitt, Mary Greenleaf
  Clement
Lewis, Dioclesian
Little, Sophia Louisa
  Robbins
Lumpkin, Joseph Henry
McBride, F. Scott
Merwin, James Burtis
Miller, Emily Clark
  Huntington
Nation, Carry
Quinton, Amelia Stone
St. John, John Pierce
Stoddard, Cora Frances
Thompson, Eliza Jane
  Trimble
Way, Amanda
Wheeler, Wayne Bidwell
Willard, Frances
  Elizabeth Caroline
Willing, Jennie Fowler
Wittenmyer, Annie
  Turner
Woolley, John Granville

Yellowley, Edward
  Clements

*Traffic Regulation
Reformers*
Eno, William Phelps

Traitors
Arnold, Benedict
Bedaux, Charles Eugene
Church, Benjamin
  (1734–1788?)
Dunbar, Moses
Gillars, Mildred
  Elizabeth

Ufologists
Adamski, George
Hynek, J. Allen

*Utopian Community
Leaders*
Ballou, Adin
Beissel, Johann Conrad
Brisbane, Albert
Brooke, Abraham
Collins, John Anderson
Flower, Richard
Harriman, Job
Harris, Thomas Lake
Ireland, Shadrach
Jansson, Eric
Moody, Lady Deborah
Noyes, John Humphrey
Owen, Robert Dale
Rapp, George
Ripley, George
Ripley, Sophia Willard
  Dana
Rose, Ernestine
Tingley, Katherine
  Augusta Westcott
Wattles, John Otis
Wilkinson, Jemima
Wright, Frances

White Supremacists
Kitchin, William Hodge
Stoddard, Theodore
  Lothrop

Women's Rights Advocates
Abbot, Gorham
  Dummer
Abzug, Bella *Suppl. 1*
Ames, Blanche Ames
Ames, Fanny Baker
Anthony, Katharine
  Susan
Anthony, Susan B.
Austin, Harriet N.

Banning, Margaret
  Culkin
Barney, Nora Stanton
  Blatch
Bascom, Florence
Bernays, Doris Elsa
  Fleischman
Bethune, Mary Jane
  McLeod
Blackwell, Alice Stone
Blackwell, Elizabeth
Blair, Emily Newell
Blake, Lillie Devereux
Bloomer, Amelia Jenks
Bloor, Ella Reeve
Boissevain, Inez
  Milholland
Bradwell, Myra Colby
Carse, Matilda Bradley
Chandler, Lucinda
Claflin, Tennessee
  Celeste
Clarke, Grace Giddings
  Julian
Clay, Laura
Colby, Clara Dorothy
  Bewick
Colman, Lucy Newhall
Coppin, Fanny Jackson
Cotten, Sallie Swepson
  Sims Southall
Cowles, Betsey Mix
Crocker, Hannah
  Mather
Cutler, Hannah Tracy
Dall, Caroline Wells
  Healey
Davis, Mary Fenn
  Robinson
Davis, Paulina Kellogg
  Wright
Dewey, Alice Chipman
Dorr, Rheta Childe
Doyle, Sarah Elizabeth
Drinker, Sophie Lewis
  Hutchinson
Edson, Katherine Philips
Edwards, India
Elliott, Sarah Barnwell
Farnham, Eliza Wood
  Burhans
Felton, Rebecca Latimer
Ferrin, Mary Upton
Foster, Abby Kelley
Fuller, Margaret
Gage, Frances Dana
  Barker
Gardener, Helen
  Hamilton
Gilman, Charlotte
  Perkins

**Political Activism and
Reform Movements**
(cont.)
Goldman, Emma
Grew, Mary
Griffing, Josephine
   Sophia White
Grimké, Angelina Emily
Grimké, Sarah Moore
Heide, Wilma Scott
Hepburn, Katharine
   Martha Houghton
Heywood, Angela
   Fiducia Tilton
Hinkle, Beatrice Moses
Hollingworth, Leta Anna
   Stetter
Hooker, Isabella Beecher
Howland, Marie
Hunt, Harriot Kezia
Hunter, Jane Edna
   Harris
Hutchinson, Anne
Irwin, Inez Leonore
   Haynes Gillmore
Jones, Jane Elizabeth
La Follette, Fola
La Follette, Suzanne
Lampkin, Daisy
   Elizabeth Adams
Landes, Bertha Ethel
   Knight
Laughlin, Gail
Lee, Muna
Lockwood, Belva Ann
   Bennett McNall
Lorde, Audre *Suppl. 2*
Lozier, Clemence Sophia
MacKaye, Hazel
Martin, Anne Henrietta
Matthews, Burnita
   Shelton
M'Clintock, Mary Ann
   Wilson, and Thomas
   M'Clintock
Mesta, Perle
Miller, Elizabeth Smith
Miller, Emma Guffey
Miller, Frieda Segelke
Mott, James
Mott, Lucretia Coffin
Mussey, Ellen Spencer
Neal, John
Nichols, Mary Gove
O'Reilly, Leonora
Owens-Adair, Bethenia
   Angelina
Patterson, Louise
   Suppl. 2
Paul, Alice

Peter, Sarah
   Worthington King
Phillips, Lena Madesin
Phillips, Wendell
Pinchot, Cornelia Bryce
Pollitzer, Anita Lily
Post, Amy Kirby
Rawalt, Marguerite
Reilly, Marion
Remond, Sarah Parker
Ripley, Martha George
Ripley, Sophia Willard
   Dana
Rose, Ernestine
Rosenberg, Anna Marie
   Lederer
Schwimmer, Rosika
Seymour, Mary Foot
Sommers, Tish
Soss, Wilma Porter
Spencer, Anna Garlin
Stevens, Doris Caroline
Stewart, Maria W.
Stone, Lucinda Hinsdale
Stone, Lucy
Swisshelm, Jane Grey
   Cannon
Thomas, M. Carey
Truth, Sojourner
Vorse, Mary Heaton
Waisbrooker, Lois
Ward, Hortense Sparks
Way, Amanda
Weed, Ethel Berenice
Wells, Emmeline B.
Wells, Helena
Willard, Emma Hart
Willard, Frances
   Elizabeth Caroline
Willing, Jennie Fowler
Woodhull, Victoria
   Claflin
Woodsmall, Ruth
   Frances
Woolley, Mary Emma
Wright, Martha Coffin
   Pelham
Younger, Maud
Zakrzewska, Marie
   Elizabeth

Zionists
Blackstone, William E.
Flexner, Bernard
Gottheil, Richard James
   Horatio
Greenberg, Hayim
Lewisohn, Ludwig
Lowenthal, Marvin
   Marx
Mack, Julian William

Magnes, Judah Leon
Mendes, Henry Pereira
Rosenblatt, Bernard
   Abraham
Sampter, Jessie Ethel
Silver, Abba Hillel
Sonneschein, Rosa
Syrkin, Marie
Szold, Henrietta
Weisgal, Meyer Wolfe
Wise, Stephen Samuel

Social Welfare
Charity Workers
Bethune, Joanna
   Graham
Chapin, Harry Forster
Hamilton, Elizabeth
   Schuyler
Hepburn, Audrey
Jacobs, Frances Wisebart
Jessel, George
Kaye, Danny

*Health and Safety
Reformers*
Allen, Nathan
Austin, Harriet N.
Baker, Henry Brooks
Beers, Clifford
   Whittingham
Biggs, Hermann Michael
Billings, John Shaw
Bissell, Emily Perkins
Blackwell, Elizabeth
Bowditch, Henry
   Ingersoll
Breckinridge, Mary
Buckel, C. Annette
Bundesen, Herman Niels
Cabot, Hugh
Coit, Henry Leber
Corson, Juliet
Cramp, Arthur Joseph
Crumbine, Samuel Jay
Daniel, Annie Sturges
Dederich, Charles
   Suppl. 2
Drinker, Cecil Kent
Eliot, Martha May
Farrand, Livingston
Fixx, James Fuller
Fletcher, Horace Page
Flick, Lawrence Francis
Folks, Homer
Gleason, Rachel Brooks
Gradle, Henry
Graham, Sylvester
Greene, Cordelia Agnes
Hamilton, Alice

Harrington, Thomas
   Francis
Haupt, Alma Cecilia
Hoffman, Frederick
   Ludwig
Hutchinson, Woods
Jean, Sally Lucas
Kellogg, John Harvey
Kenny, Elizabeth
Kenyon, Josephine
   Hemenway
Koplik, Henry
Lakey, Alice
Law, James
McCann, Alfred
   Watterson
McClennan, Alonzo
   Clifton
McDermott, Walsh
Mendenhall, Dorothy
   Reed
Merrick, Myra King
Meyer, Henry
   Coddington
Nichols, Thomas Low
Ochsner, Alton
Packard, Elizabeth
   Parsons Ware
Parrish, Joseph
   (1818–1891)
Pennington, Mary Engle
Perkins, Roger Griswold
Poindexter, Hildrus
   Augustus
Putnam, Elizabeth
   Lowell
Putnam, Helen Cordelia
Rauch, John Henry
Ravenel, Mazÿck
   Porcher
Ray, Isaac
Richards, Dickinson
   Woodruff
Richards, Linda
Richards, Paul Snelgrove
Rodale, J. I.
Rorer, Sarah Tyson
Rosen, George
Salmon, Thomas
   William
Seaman, Valentine
Shakespeare, Edward
   Oram
Shattuck, Lemuel
Smith, James
   (1771–1841)
Soper, Fred Lowe
Souchon, Edmond
Squibb, Edward
   Robinson
Sutton, William Loftus

Social Welfare (cont.)
Switzer, Mary Elizabeth
Sydenstricker, Edgar
Todd, Eli
Trall, Russell Thacher
Trudeau, Edward
  Livingston
Valentine, Lila
  Hardaway Meade
Welsh, Lilian
Wiley, Harvey
  Washington
Wilson, Bill, and Bob
  Smith *Suppl. 1*
Winslow, Charles-
  Edward Amory
Wolman, Abel
Wood, Edith Elmer
Yarros, Rachelle

Housing Reformers
Bauer, Catherine Krouse
Dinwiddie, Emily
  Wayland
Flagg, Ernest
Levitt, Abraham
Stokes, Isaac Newton
  Phelps
Veiller, Lawrence
  Turnure
White, Alfred Tredway
Wood, Edith Elmer

Penologists
Bennett, James Van
  Benschoten
Brockway, Zebulon Reed
Van Waters, Miriam
Vaux, Roberts

Prison Officials
Duffy, Clinton T.
Harris, Mary Belle
McClaughry, Robert
  Wilson

Prison Reformers
Booth, Maud Elizabeth
  Charlesworth
  Ballington
Comstock, Elizabeth
  Leslie Rous Wright
Davis, Katharine
  Bement
Farnham, Eliza Wood
  Burhans
Gibbons, Abigail
  Hopper
Griffith, Goldsborough
  Sappington

Hodder, Jessie
  Donaldson
Hopper, Isaac Tatem
Little, Sophia Louisa
  Robbins
McClaughry, Robert
  Wilson
Nicholson, Timothy
Peter, Sarah
  Worthington King
Round, William M. F.
Tutwiler, Julia Strudwick
Wines, Frederick
  Howard
Wittpenn, Caroline
  Bayard Stevens

Public Health Officials
Abbott, Samuel Warren
Arnstein, Margaret
Baker, Sara Josephine
Beard, Mary
Bennett, Alice
Biggs, Hermann Michael
Boswell, Henry
Bradley, Charles Henry
Brigham, Amariah
Bryce, Peter
Calderone, Mary S.
  Suppl. 1
Caverly, Charles
  Solomon
Chapin, Charles Value
Cochran, John
Crandall, Ella Phillips
Crothers, Thomas
  Davison
Day, Albert
Dyer, Rolla Eugene
Earle, Pliny
Felix, Robert Hanna
Fitzgerald, Alice
Frost, Wade Hampton
Galt, John Minson, II
Gardner, Mary Sewall
Garrison, Charles Willis
Goldwater, Sigismund
  Schulz
Gray, John Purdue
Guiteras, Juan
Gunn, Selskar Michael
Heiser, Victor George
Hopkins, Juliet Ann
  Opie
Horsfall, Frank Lappin,
  Jr.
Hunt, Ezra Mundy
Hurd, Henry Mills
Kellogg, John Harvey
Knowles, John Hilton
Kolb, Lawrence

Lovejoy, Esther Pohl
Lumsden, Leslie Leon
Mahoney, John Friend
Manning, Isaac Hall
McCaw, James Brown
McCormack, Arthur
  Thomas
McCormack, Joseph
  Nathaniel
Mossell, Nathan Francis
Nichols, Charles Henry
Nyswander, Dorothy B.
  Suppl. 1
Pember, Phoebe Yates
  Levy
Pinn, Petra Fitzalieu
Poindexter, Hildrus
  Augustus
Potter, Ellen Culver
Rauch, John Henry
Rosenau, Milton Joseph
Sawyer, Wilbur
  Augustus
Snow, Edwin Miller
Snow, William Freeman
Soper, Fred Lowe
Stiles, Charles Wardell
Switzer, Mary Elizabeth
Terry, Charles Edward
Thompson, Mary Harris
Todd, Eli
Underwood, Felix Joel
Walcott, Henry
  Pickering
White, William Alanson
Williams, Daniel Hale
Winston, Ellen Black
Woodward, Samuel
  Bayard
Woodworth, John
  Maynard
Wright, Louis Tompkins

Relief Workers
Billikopf, Jacob
Empie, Paul Chauncey
Hoge, Jane Currie
  Blaikie
Porter, Eliza Emily
  Chappell
Reed, Esther De Berdt
Wood, Carolena
Wormeley, Katharine
  Prescott

Sanitarians
Agnew, Cornelius Rea
Bard, John
Baruch, Simon
Cabell, James Lawrence
Carter, Henry Rose

Chaillé, Stanford
  Emerson
Cochran, Jerome
Gorgas, William
  Crawford
Griscom, John Hoskins
Hunt, Ezra Mundy
Hurty, John Newell
Jones, Joseph
Livermore, Mary
Pearson, Leonard
Smith, Stephen

Social Reformers
Abbott, Edith
Abbott, Grace
Addams, Jane
Adler, Felix
Alcott, A. Bronson
Alinsky, Saul David
Allen, Nathan
Altgeld, John Peter
American, Sadie
Ames, Fanny Baker
Anderson, Matthew
Andrews, John Bertram
Andrews, Stephen Pearl
Anthony, Susan B.
Atkinson, Edward
Bacon, Leonard, Sr.
Bagley, Sarah George
Baker, Harvey
  Humphrey
Baldwin, Roger Nash
Barnard, Kate
Barnum, Gertrude
Barrett, Janie Porter
Barrows, Isabel
Barrows, Samuel June
Bates, Barnabas
Beecher, Catharine
  Esther
Beecher, Henry Ward
Belmont, Alva Erskine
  Smith Vanderbilt
Benezet, Anthony
Bethune, Joanna
  Graham
Bethune, Mary Jane
  McLeod
Birney, Alice Josephine
  McLellan
Blackwell, Antoinette
  Louisa Brown
Blackwell, Henry
  Browne
Blanchard, Jonathan
Bliss, William Dwight
  Porter
Bloss, William Clough
Bonney, Mary Lucinda

Social Welfare *(cont.)*

Booth, Maud Elizabeth Charlesworth Ballington
Booth-Tucker, Emma Moss
Bowen, Louise deKoven
Bowker, R. R.
Brace, Charles Loring (1826–1890)
Brace, Charles Loring (1855–1938)
Bradford, Cornelia Foster
Branch, Anna Hempstead
Breckinridge, Madeline McDowell
Breckinridge, Sophonisba Preston
Brisbane, Albert
Brooks, John Graham
Brown, Margaret Tobin *Suppl. 1*
Burleigh, Charles Calistus
Burlingham, Charles Culp
Burritt, Elihu
Butler, Elizabeth Beardsley
Butler, Selena Sloan
Cameron, Donaldina Mackenzie
Carse, Matilda Bradley
Chávez, César Estrada
Chace, Elizabeth Buffum
Chandler, Lucinda
Channing, William Henry
Chapin, Henry Dwight
Chapin, Sarah Flournoy Moore
Cheney, Ednah Dow Littlehale
Coit, Stanton
Colcord, Joanna Carver
Collier, John
Collins, John Anderson
Coman, Katharine
Comstock, Anthony
Cone, Moses Herman
Conway, Moncure Daniel
Coulter, Ernest Kent
Cratty, Mabel
Crosby, Ernest Howard
Dargan, Edmund S.
Davis, Frances Elliott
Day, Dorothy
Dennison, Henry Sturgis

de Schweinitz, Karl
Dewson, Molly
Diaz, Abby Morton
Dix, Dorothea Lynde
Dock, Lavinia Lloyd
Dodge, Grace Hoadley
Dodge, Josephine Marshall Jewell
Doherty, Catherine de Hueck
Donaldson, Mary Elizabeth
Dorr, Thomas Wilson
Doster, Frank
Drumgoole, John Christopher
Dudley, Helena Stuart
Dugdale, Richard Louis
Dummer, Ethel Sturges
Dwight, Louis
Dwight, Theodore (1796–1866)
Easley, Ralph Montgomery
Eastman, Crystal
Eastman, Elaine Goodale
Eddy, Thomas
Edson, Katherine Philips
Einstein, Hannah Bachman
Eliot, Charlotte Champe Stearns
Elliott, John Lovejoy
Epstein, Abraham
Evans, Elizabeth Glendower
Evans, Frederick William
Ferebee, Dorothy Boulding
Field, Sara Bard
Fields, Annie Adams
Filene, Edward Albert
Finley, Robert
Flanagan, Edward Joseph
Flexner, Bernard
Flower, Benjamin Orange
Flower, Lucy Louisa Coues
Folks, Homer
Forten, James
Foster, Stephen Symonds
Fourier, Charles
Fritchman, Stephen Hole
Fuller, Minnie Ursula Oliver Scott Rutherford
Gardiner, Robert Hallowell, III

Garrett, Mary Smith
George, Henry
Gibson, Mary Simons
Gillette, King Camp
Glenn, John Mark
Goldmark, Josephine Clara
Gordon, Jean Margaret
Graham, Isabella
Gratz, Rebecca
Green, Frances Harriet Whipple
Hale, Clara McBride
Hale, Edward Everett
Harman, Moses
Hazard, Thomas Robinson
Heide, Wilma Scott
Henrotin, Ellen Martin
Herron, Carrie Rand
Herron, George Davis
Heywood, Angela Fiducia Tilton
Heywood, Ezra Hervey
Higginson, Thomas Wentworth
Hillenbrand, Reynold Henry
Hine, Lewis Wickes
Holly, James Theodore
Holmes, John Haynes
Howe, Frederic Clemson
Howe, Samuel Gridley
Howland, William Dillwyn
Hunter, Robert (1874–1942)
Hunton, Addie D. Waites
Hutchins, Grace
Hutchinson, Abigail Jemima *Suppl. 2*
Hutchinson, Adoniram Judson Joseph *Suppl. 2*
Hutchinson, Asa Burnham *Suppl. 2*
Hutchinson, Jesse, Jr. *Suppl. 2*
Hutchinson, John Wallace *Suppl. 2*
Iams, Lucy Dorsey
Ickes, Anna Wilmarth Thompson
Ingham, Mary Hall
Jacobs, Harriet
Jacobs, Pattie Ruffner
Jennings, May Elizabeth Mann
Johnson, George Francis
Johnson, Tom Loftin
Jones, Samuel Milton

Kander, Lizzie Black
Kaufmann, Peter
Kehew, Mary Morton Kimball
Kelley, Florence
Kellogg, Paul Underwood
Kelpius, Johannes
Kepley, Ada Harriet Miser
Kerby, William Joseph
Kohut, Rebekah Bettelheim
Kuhn, Maggie *Suppl. 1*
Lathrop, Julia Clifford
Lee, Elizabeth Blair
Ligutti, Luigi
Lindsey, Ben B.
Lippard, George
Livermore, Mary
Lloyd, Henry Demarest
Lockwood, Belva Ann Bennett McNall
Loeb, Sophie Irene Simon
Lovejoy, Owen Reed
Lowell, Josephine Shaw
Lozier, Clemence Sophia
Lumpkin, Joseph Henry
Lumpkin, Katharine Du Pre
Lundberg, Emma Octavia
Luscomb, Florence Hope
Mann, Horace
Marshall, Robert
Martin, George Madden *Suppl. 1*
Marvin, Cornelia
Mason, Lucy Randolph
Matthews, Mark Allison
Maurin, Peter Aristide
May, Abigail Williams
May, Samuel Joseph
McCarthy, Charles
McCormick, Katharine Dexter
McCulloch, Catharine Gouger Waugh
McCulloch, Oscar Carleton
McDowell, Mary Eliza
McGlynn, Edward
McKelway, Alexander Jeffrey
Mead, George Herbert
Mercer, Charles Fenton
Morrow, Prince Albert
Moskowitz, Belle Lindner Israels

Social Welfare *(cont.)*
Murphy, Edgar Gardner
Nathan, Maud
Nearing, Scott
Newman, Angelia
French
Oberholtzer, Sara Louisa
Vickers
O'Connor, Jessie Lloyd
Older, Fremont
Owen, Robert Dale
Owens-Adair, Bethenia
Angelina
Oxnam, Garfield
Bromley
Parker, Theodore
Parkhurst, Charles
Henry
Pinchot, Cornelia Bryce
Potter, Ellen Culver
Pratt, Anna Beach
Pratt, Daniel
(1799–1873)
Rainsford, William
Stephen
Rauschenbusch, Walter
Reed, Myron Winslow
Ridge, Lola
Riis, Jacob August
Riis, Mary Phillips
Ripley, George
Robbins, Jane Elizabeth
Robins, Margaret Dreier
Robins, Raymond
Rodgers, Elizabeth Flynn
Roosevelt, Eleanor
Rubinow, Isaac Max
Rukeyser, Muriel
Rummel, Joseph Francis
Rumsey, Mary Harriman
Rush, Benjamin
Russ, John Dennison
Ryan, John Augustine
Salmon, Thomas
William
Sampson, William
Sanborn, Franklin
Benjamin
Saunders, Prince
Savio, Mario *Suppl. 1*
Scott, Leroy Martin
Scudder, Vida Dutton
Sheldon, Charles
Monroe
Simms, Florence
Sinclair, Upton
Skaggs, William H.
Suppl. 1
Solomon, Hannah
Greenebaum
Spencer, Anna Garlin

Spingarn, Joel Elias
Sprague, Achsa W.
Starr, Ellen Gates
Stern, Edith Rosenwald
Stevens, Alzina Ann
Parsons
Strong, Josiah
Stuck, Hudson
Sunderland, Jabez
Thomas
Swift, Linton Bishop
Swope, Gerard
Taylor, Graham
Terrell, Mary Eliza
Church
Thomas, Norman
Mattoon
Thompson, Benjamin
Townsend, Francis
Everett
Turner, Henry McNeal
Van Vorst, Marie Louise
Van Waters, Miriam
Verity, George Matthew
Villard, Fanny Garrison
Wald, Lillian D.
Walters, Alexander
Ward, Harry Frederick
Ward, Henry Dana
Ward, Maisie
Weld, Theodore Dwight
Wells, Marguerite
Whipper, William
White, Eartha Mary
Magdalene
Winston, Ellen Black
Wise, Stephen Samuel
Wood, L. Hollingsworth
Wood, Thomas Bond
Woods, Robert Archey
Wright, Theodore
Sedgwick
Young, Ann Eliza

Social Workers
Abbott, Edith
Adie, David Craig
Bayer, Adèle Parmentier
Billikopf, Jacob
Bissell, Emily Perkins
Blaustein, David
Bremer, Edith Terry
Brown, Josephine
Chapin
Cannon, Ida Maud
Carr, Charlotte Elizabeth
Coyle, Grace Longwell
Davis, Katharine
Bement
DeBerry, William
Nelson

de Schweinitz, Karl
Devine, Edward Thomas
Dinwiddie, Emily
Wayland
Falconer, Martha Platt
Ferguson, Katy
Gaines, Irene McCoy
Glenn, Mary Willcox
Brown
Haynes, Elizabeth Ross
Haynes, George
Edmund
Hoey, Jane Margueretta
Hoge, Jane Currie
Blaikie
Hunter, Robert
(1874–1942)
Jarrett, Mary Cromwell
Johnson, Alexander
Kittredge, Mabel Hyde
Lee, Porter Raymond
Levin, Louis Hiram
Lothrop, Alice Higgins
Lovejoy, Owen Reed
McMain, Eleanor Laura
Milner, Lucille
Bernheimer
Pettit, Katherine Rhoda
Pratt, Anna Beach
Reynolds, Bertha Capen
Roche, Josephine
Aspinwall
Smith, Zilpha Drew
Stern, Elizabeth
Gertrude
Taft, Jessie
Towle, Charlotte Helen
West, James Edward
Whitney, Charlotte Anita
Williams, Aubrey Willis
Williams, Elizabeth
Sprague
Wittpenn, Caroline
Bayard Stevens
Woerishoffer, Emma
Carola
Woolsey, Abby Howland
Young, Whitney Moore,

SPORTS AND GAMES

Athletic Coaches /
Managers
Allen, George Herbert
Allen, Phog
Alston, Walter Emmons
Anson, Cap
Bancroft, David James
Bee, Clair Francis
Bell, Matty

Bender, Chief
Bierman, Bernard
William
Blaik, Red
Blood, Ernest Artel
Bowerman, Bill *Suppl. 2*
Brady, William Aloysius
Bresnahan, Roger Philip
Brown, Paul E.
Brown, Walter A.
Bryant, Bear
Camp, Walter Chauncey
Carlson, Henry Clifford
Case, Everett Norris
Chamberlin, Guy
Chance, Frank Leroy
Charleston, Oscar
McKinley
Christiansen, Jack
Clarke, Fred Clifford
Cobb, Ty
Cochrane, Mickey
Collins, Eddie
Combs, Earle Bryan
Connor, Roger
Conzelman, James
Gleason
Crisler, Fritz
Cromwell, Dean Bartlett
Cronin, Joe
Dahlen, Bill
D'Amato, Cus
Daugherty, Hugh Duffy
Davis, George Stacey
Dean, Dizzy
Dehnert, Dutch
De Moss, Elwood
Diddle, Edgar Allen, Sr.
Dobie, Gilmour
Dodd, Bobby
Driscoll, Paddy
Durocher, Leo
Edmundson, Hec
Ewbank, Weeb *Suppl. 2*
Ewing, Buck
Fitzsimmons, Frederick
Landis
Flanagan, John J.
Friedman, Benny
Frisch, Frank Francis
Goslin, Goose
Gottlieb, Eddie
Grange, Red
Griffith, Clark Calvin
Grimes, Burleigh Arland
Grimm, Charlie
Halas, George Stanley
Hamilton, Billy
Hanlon, Ned
Harlow, Richard
Cresson

Harris, Bucky
Harvey, Beatrix
  Loughran
Haughton, Percy
  Duncan
Hayes, Woody
Hayward, William Louis
Healey, Edward Francis,
  Jr.
Hein, Mel
Heisman, John William
Herman, Billy
Hickey, Edgar Sylvester
Hodges, Gil
Hoff, Max
Hooper, Harry
  Bartholomew
Huggins, Miller James
Jennings, Hugh Ambrose
Johnson, Bob
Johnson, Judy
Johnson, Robert Lee
Johnson, Walter
Kearns, Jack
Kelley, Joseph James
Kiphuth, Robert John
  Herman
Lajoie, Napoleon
Lambeau, Curly
Landry, Tom *Suppl. 1*
Lapchick, Joe
Leahy, Frank
Lemon, Bob *Suppl. 1*
Lindstrom, Freddy
Litwack, Harry *Suppl. 2*
Lloyd, John Henry
Lombardi, Vince
Mack, Connie
Mackey, Biz
Martin, Billy
Mathews, Eddie *Suppl. 1*
Mathewson, Christy
McCarthy, Joe
McCormick, Jim
McCracken, Emmett
  Branch
McCracken, Jack
McDermott, Robert
McGraw, John
McGugin, Daniel Earle
McKechnie, Bill
McMillin, Bo
McNally, Johnny Blood
Meanwell, Walter
  Earnest
Millner, Wayne Vernal
Munn, Biggie
Murphy, Michael
  Charles
Murtaugh, Danny

Neale, Alfred Earle
Nevers, Ernie
Neyland, Robert Reese,
  Jr.
Oosterbaan, Bennie
Orton, George
  Washington
Ott, Mel
Owen, Maribel Yerxa
  Vinson
Owen, Stephen Joseph
Peck, Robert Durham
Pilkington, James
Pollard, Fritz
Reese, Pee Wee *Suppl. 1*
Rigney, Bill *Suppl. 1*
Rockne, Knute
Rogan, Bullet
Ruble, Olan G.
Rupp, Adolph Frederick
Sachs, Leonard David
Schabinger, Arthur
  August
Schulz, Adolph George
Selee, Frank Gibson
Shaughnessy, Clark
  Daniel
Shelton, Ev
Sheppard, Melvin
  Winfield
Shevlin, Thomas
  Leonard
Sisler, George Harold
Speaker, Tris
Stagg, Amos Alonzo
Stanky, Eddie *Suppl. 1*
Stengel, Casey
St. John, Lynn Wilbur
Stydahar, Joseph Lee
Sutherland, Jock
Suttles, George "Mule"
Taylor, C. I.
Tebbetts, Birdie *Suppl. 1*
Terry, Bill
Tower, Oswald
Trafton, George
Tunnell, Emlen
Van Brocklin, Norm
Wade, William Wallace
Wagner, Honus
Walsh, David Henry
Warner, Pop
Waterfield, Bob
Wefers, Bernard J.
White, Solomon
Yost, Fielding Harris
Zuppke, Robert Carl

Baseball Players
Alexander, Grover
  Cleveland

Anson, Cap
Ashburn, Richie *Suppl. 1*
Averill, Earl
Baker, Home Run
Bancroft, David James
Beckley, Jake
Belanger, Mark *Suppl. 2*
Bell, Cool Papa
Bender, Chief
Boudreau, Lou *Suppl. 2*
Bresnahan, Roger Philip
Brouthers, Dan
Brown, Mordecai Peter
  Centennial
Browning, Pete
Burkett, Jesse Cail
Campanella, Roy
Carey, Max George
Caruthers, Robert Lee
Chance, Frank Leroy
Charleston, Oscar
  McKinley
Chase, Hal
Chesbro, Jack
Cicotte, Eddie
Clarke, Fred Clifford
Clarkson, John Gibson
Clemente, Roberto
Cobb, Ty
Cochrane, Mickey
Collins, Eddie
Collins, Jimmy
Combs, Earle Bryan
Comiskey, Charles
  Albert
Conlan, Jocko
Connor, Roger
Coveleski, Stanley
  Anthony
Crawford, Sam
Cronin, Joe
Cuyler, Kiki
Dahlen, Bill
Dandridge, Ray
Davis, George Stacey
Day, Leon
De Moss, Elwood
Dean, Dizzy
Delahanty, Edward
  James *Suppl. 1*
Dickey, Bill
Dihigo, Martin
DiMaggio, Joe
Driscoll, Paddy
Drysdale, Don *Suppl. 1*
Durocher, Leo
Evers, Johnny *Suppl. 1*
Ewing, Buck
Faber, Red
Fitzsimmons, Frederick
  Landis

Flick, Elmer Harrison
Flood, Curt *Suppl. 1*
Foster, Rube
Foster, William
  Hendrick
Fowler, Bud
Foxx, Jimmie
Frisch, Frank Francis
Galvin, James Francis
Gehrig, Lou
Gehringer, Charlie
Gibson, Josh
Gomez, Lefty
Goslin, Goose
Grant, Ulysses Frank
Greenberg, Hank
Griffith, Clark Calvin
Grimes, Burleigh Arland
Grimm, Charlie
Grove, Lefty
Guyon, Joseph
  Napoleon
Hamilton, Billy
Hanlon, Ned
Harris, Bucky
Harris, E. Victor
Hartnett, Gabby
Heilmann, Harry Edwin
Herman, Billy
Hill, Pete
Hodges, Gil
Hooper, Harry
  Bartholomew
Hornsby, Rogers
Howard, Elston
Hubbell, Carl
Huggins, Miller James
Hunter, Jim "Catfish"
  Suppl. 1
Jackson, Shoeless Joe
Jennings, Hugh Ambrose
Johnson, Judy
Johnson, Robert Lee
Johnson, Walter
Joss, Addie
Keefe, Timothy John
Keeler, Wee Willie
Kelley, Joseph James
Kelly, Michael Joseph
Klein, Chuck
Lajoie, Napoleon
Lazzeri, Tony
Lemon, Bob *Suppl. 1*
Leonard, Buck *Suppl. 1*
Lindstrom, Freddy
Lloyd, John Henry
Lombardi, Ernesto
  Natali
Lyons, Ted
Mack, Connie
Mackey, Biz

Magee, Sherry
Mantle, Mickey
Manush, Heinie
Maris, Roger Eugene
Martin, Billy
Mathews, Eddie *Suppl. 1*
Mathewson, Christy
Mays, Carl William
McCarthy, Joe
McCormick, Jim
McGinnity, Joe
McGraw, John
McKechnie, Bill
Medwick, Joe
Mendez, José
Meusel, Bob
Mullane, Anthony John
Munson, Thurman Lee
Murtaugh, Danny
Neale, Alfred Earle
Newhouser, Hal *Suppl. 1*
Nichols, Kid
Ott, Mel
Paige, Satchel
Patkin, Max *Suppl. 1*
Pennock, Herb
Plank, Eddie
Poles, Spottswood
Quisenberry, Dan
  Suppl. 2
Reach, Alfred James
Redding, Dick
Reese, Pee Wee *Suppl. 1*
Reulbach, Edward
  Marvin
Rice, Sam
Rigney, Bill *Suppl. 1*
Robinson, Jackie
Rogan, Bullet
Roush, Edd J.
Ruffing, Red
Rusie, Amos Wilson
Ruth, Babe
Sewell, Joe
Simmons, Al
Sisler, George Harold
Smith, Hilton
Sockalexis, Louis M.
  Suppl. 1
Spalding, Albert
  Goodwill
Speaker, Tris
Stanky, Eddie *Suppl. 1*
Stargell, Willie *Suppl. 1*
Stearnes, Turkey
Stengel, Casey
Stovey, Harry Duffield
Sunday, Billy
Suttles, George "Mule"
Taylor, C. I.
Tebbetts, Birdie *Suppl. 1*

Terry, Bill
Thompson, Samuel
  Luther
Tinker, Joe *Suppl. 1*
Torriente, Cristobal
Traynor, Pie
Vance, Dazzy
Vander Meer, Johnny
  Suppl. 1
Vaughan, Arky
Waddell, Rube
Wagner, Honus
Walker, Harry *Suppl. 1*
Walker, Moses
  Fleetwood
Wallace, Bobby
Walsh, Edward
  Augustine
Waner, Paul Glee
Ward, John Montgomery
Welch, Mickey
Wheat, Zack
White, Solomon
Williams, Joe
Willis, Victor Gazaway
Wilson, Hack
Wood, Smoky Joe
Wright, George
Wynn, Early *Suppl. 1*
Young, Cy
Youngs, Ross *Suppl. 2*

Basketball Players
Chamberlain, Wilt
  Suppl. 1
Cooper, Tarzan
Dehnert, Dutch
Douglas, Robert L.
Fulks, Joseph
Johnston, Neil
Lapchick, Joe
Maravich, Pete
McCracken, Emmett
  Branch
McCracken, Jack
McDermott, Robert
Roosma, John Seiba
Tatum, Goose

Billiards Champions
Hoppe, Willie
Mosconi, Willie

Bobsledders
Eagan, Eddie
Grey, Clifford *Suppl. 1*

Bowlers
McCutcheon, Floretta
  Doty

Varipapa, Andrew

Boxers
Armstrong, Henry
Attell, Abe
Baer, Max *Suppl. 1*
Braddock, Jim *Suppl. 1*
Britton, Jack
Canzoneri, Tony
Carnera, Primo *Suppl. 2*
Charles, Ezzard
Choynski, Joseph
  Bartlett
Conn, Billy *Suppl. 1*
Corbett, James John
Coulon, Johnny
Dempsey, Jack
Dempsey, Nonpareil
  Jack
Dixon, George
Dundee, Johnny
Eagan, Eddie
Fitzsimmons, Robert
Flowers, Tiger
Gans, Joe
Graziano, Rocky
Greb, Harry
Heenan, John Carmel
Herman, Pete
Hyer, Tom
Jackson, Peter
Jeffries, James Jackson
Johnson, Jack
Ketchel, Stanley
Kilbane, Johnny
Langford, Samuel
Lee, Canada
Leonard, Benny
Lewis, John Henry
Liston, Sonny
Loughran, Tommy
  Suppl. 1
Louis, Joe
Mandell, Sammy
Marciano, Rocky
McCoy, Kid *Suppl. 1*
McGovern, Terry
Miller, Freddie
Molyneaux, Tom
Moore, Archie *Suppl. 1*
Morrissey, John
Nelson, Battling *Suppl. 1*
Ortiz, Manuel
Robinson, Sugar Ray
Rosenbloom, Maxie
Ross, Barney
Ryan, Tommy
Sharkey, Jack *Suppl. 1*
Stribling, Young
  Suppl. 1
Sullivan, John L.

Tunney, Gene
Villa, Pancho *Suppl. 2*
Walcott, Jersey Joe
Walcott, Joe
Walker, Mickey
Willard, Jess *Suppl. 1*
Wills, Harry
Yarosz, Teddy *Suppl. 2*
Zale, Tony *Suppl. 1*

Bridge Champions
Crawford, John
  Randolph
Culbertson, Ely
Jacoby, Oswald
Von Zedtwitz,
  Waldemar Konrad
  Anton Wilhelm
  Ferdinand

Chess Champions
Marshall, Frank James
Morphy, Paul Charles
Pillsbury, Harry Nelson
Reshevsky, Samuel
  Herman
Steinitz, William

Cyclists
Kramer, Frank Louis
Taylor, Major

Figure Skaters
Blanchard, Theresa
  Weld
Haines, Jackson *Suppl. 1*
Harvey, Beatrix
  Loughran
Henie, Sonja
Owen, Maribel Yerxa
  Vinson

Football Players
Bell, Matty
Brown, Johnny Mack
Chamberlin, Guy
Christiansen, Jack
Clark, Dutch
Conzelman, James
  Gleason
Coy, Ted
Davis, Ernie
Dobie, Gilmour
Driscoll, Paddy
Eckersall, Walter Herbert
Ford, Len
Four Horsemen of Notre
  Dame
Friedman, Benny
Gelbert, Charles Saladin,
  Jr.

George, Bill
Gipp, George
Grange, Red
Guyon, Joseph
  Napoleon
Halas, George Stanley
Harmon, Tom
Healey, Edward Francis,
  Jr.
Heffelfinger, Pudge
Hein, Mel
Herber, Arnold
Heston, William Martin
Hinkey, Frank Augustus
Hogan, Jim
Hubbard, Cal
Kinnick, Nile Clarke, Jr.
Lambeau, Curly
Landry, Tom *Suppl. 1*
Layne, Bobby
Leemans, Tuffy
Lipscomb, Big Daddy
Luckman, Sid *Suppl. 1*
McDonald, Henry
McGugin, Daniel Earle
McMillin, Bo
McNally, Johnny Blood
Millner, Wayne Vernal
Nagurski, Bronko
Neale, Alfred Earle
Nevers, Ernie
Nitschke, Ray *Suppl. 1*
O'Brien, Davey
Oliphant, Elmer Quillen
Owen, Stephen Joseph
Payton, Walter *Suppl. 1*
Peck, Robert Durham
Pollard, Fritz
Rockne, Knute
Schulz, Adolph George
Slater, Duke
Strong, Ken
Stydahar, Joseph Lee
Sutherland, Jock
Thorpe, Jim
Trafton, George
Tunnell, Emlen
Van Brocklin, Norm
Wade, William Wallace
Walker, Doak *Suppl. 1*
Washington, Kenneth
  Stanley
Waterfield, Bob
Young, Buddy

Golf Teachers
Penick, Harvey Morrison

Golfers
Anderson, Willie
Armour, Tommy

Barnes, James Martin
Browne, Mary Kendall
Collett, Glenna
Demaret, Jimmy
Didrikson, Babe
Diegel, Leo H.
Evans, Chick
Ghezzi, Vic
Guldahl, Ralph
Hagen, Walter Charles
Harrison, Dutch
Hogan, Ben *Suppl. 1*
Hoyt, Beatrix
Jones, Bobby
Macdonald, Charles
  Blair
Mangrum, Lloyd
  Eugene
McDermott, John J., Jr.
Ouimet, Francis Desales
Penick, Harvey Morrison
Sarazen, Gene *Suppl. 2*
Shute, Denny
Smith, Alexander
Smith, Macdonald
Travers, Jerome
  Dunstan
Travis, Walter John

Harness Racers
Haughton, Billy
White, Benjamin
  Franklin
Woodruff, Hiram
  Washington

Ice Hockey Players
Baker, Hobey
Goheen, Francis Xavier

Jockeys
Arcaro, Eddie *Suppl. 1*
Murphy, Isaac
  (1861–1896)
Sande, Earle
Simms, Willie
Sloan, Tod

Long-Distance Walkers
O'Leary, Daniel
Weston, Edward Payson

Mountaineers
Workman, Fanny
  Bullock

Olympic Medalists
Blanchard, Theresa
  Weld
Crabbe, Buster
Cunningham, Glenn V.

Daniels, Charles
  Meldrum
DeMar, Clarence
  Harrison
Didrikson, Babe
Eagan, Eddie
Ewry, Ray
Flanagan, John J.
Grey, Clifford *Suppl. 1*
Gutterson, Albert
  Lovejoy
Hahn, Archie
Hardin, Slats
Hare, Thomas Truxtun
Harvey, Beatrix
  Loughran
Hayes, Johnny
Henie, Sonja
Hubbard, William
  DeHart
Jaffee, Irving W.
Johnson, Cornelius
  Cooper
Kahanamoku, Duke
  Paoa
Kealoha, Warren Daniels
Kelly, John Brendan
Kelly, John Brendan, Jr.
Kraenzlein, Alvin
  Christian
Lee, Willis Augustus, Jr.
Madison, Helene Emma
McDonald, Babe
McGrath, Matthew J.
Metcalfe, Ralph Harold
Morris, Glenn Edward
Norelius, Martha
Orton, George
  Washington
Osborn, Harold Marion
Owens, Jesse
Paddock, Charles
  William
Rawls, Katherine Louise
Richards, Vincent
Rose, Ralph Waldo
Rudolph, Wilma
Scholz, Jackson Volney
Sheppard, Melvin
  Winfield
Sheridan, Martin Joseph
Taylor, Frederick
  Morgan
Thorpe, Jim
Tolan, Thomas Edward
Weissmuller, Johnny
Wightman, Hazel
  Hotchkiss
Williams, Dick
Wright, Beals Coleman

Polo Players
Rumsey, Charles Cary

Race Car Drivers
Bettenhausen, Tony
Chevrolet, Louis
De Palma, Ralph
De Paolo, Peter
Milton, Tommy
Oldfield, Barney
Shaw, Wilbur

*Racehorse Breeders /
Trainers*
Belmont, August
Belmont, August, II
Belmont, Perry
Bonner, Robert
Buford, Abraham
Duryea, Harmanus
  Barkulo
Fitzsimmons, Sunny Jim
Haggin, James Ben Ali
Haughton, Billy
Jackson, William Hicks
Jacobs, Hirsch
Kenner, Duncan Farrar
  Suppl. 1
Madden, John Edward
Markey, Lucille Parker
  Wright
Simms, Willie
Sloane, Isabel Cleves
  Dodge
Ten Broeck, Richard
White, Benjamin
  Franklin
Whitney, Harry Payne
Whitney, Helen Hay
Whitney, John Hay
Widener, George
  Dunton, Jr.

Rodeo Performers
Pickens, Slim
Pickett, Bill

Rowers
Kelly, John Brendan
Kelly, John Brendan, Jr.
Pilkington, James

Speed Skaters
Jaffee, Irving W.

Sports Inventors
Cartwright, Alexander
  Joy, Jr.
Doubleday, Abner
Naismith, James

Sports Officials
Ashford, Emmett
Littleton
Conlan, Jocko
Connolly, Thomas
Henry, Sr.
Eckersall, Walter Herbert
Evans, Billy
Hubbard, Cal
Klem, Bill
Liston, Emil Sycamore
Magee, Sherry
Walsh, David Henry

*Sports Organization
Executives*
Barrow, Edward Grant
Bell, Bert
Bell, Matty
Briggs, Walter Owen
Brown, Paul E.
Brundage, Avery
Burke, Michael
Busch, August
Anheuser, Jr.
Camp, Walter Chauncey
Carr, Joseph F.
Chandler, Albert
Benjamin
Collins, Eddie
Comiskey, Charles
Albert
Connor, Roger
Conzelman, James
Gleason
Cronin, Joe
Curtis, William
Buckingham *Suppl. 2*
Diddle, Edgar Allen, Sr.
Douglas, Robert L.
Ebbets, Charles Hercules
Eckert, William Dole
Evans, Billy
Finley, Charles O.
Suppl. 1
Foster, Rube
Frick, Ford Christopher
Giamatti, Bart
Giles, Warren Crandall
Gottlieb, Eddie
Greenberg, Hank
Greenlee, William
Augustus
Griffith, Calvin *Suppl. 1*
Griffith, Clark Calvin
Gulick, Luther Halsey
(1865–1918)
Halas, George Stanley
Hanlon, Ned
Harridge, William

Haughton, Percy
Duncan
Hess, Leon *Suppl. 1*
Hofheinz, Roy Mark
Hulbert, William
Ambrose
Hulman, Tony
Irish, Ned
Johnson, Ban
Kiphuth, Robert John
Herman
Kroc, Ray
Landis, Kenesaw
Mountain
Liston, Emil Sycamore
Mack, Connie
MacPhail, Larry
Mara, Timothy James
Marshall, George
Preston
Mathewson, Christy
Muldoon, William
Munn, Biggie
Murchison, Clint, Jr.
Navin, Frank
O'Brien, John Joseph
O'Malley, Walter
Francis
Posey, Cum
Reach, Alfred James
Rickey, Branch
Rooney, Art
Rozelle, Pete *Suppl. 2*
Ruppert, Jacob
Shaw, Wilbur
Shibe, Benjamin
Franklin
Short, Robert Earl
Spalding, Albert
Goodwill
St. John, Lynn Wilbur
Stoneham, Horace
Charles
Taylor, C. I.
Tower, Oswald
Tunnell, Emlen
Veeck, Bill
Von der Ahe, Christian
Frederick Wilhelm
Wade, William Wallace
Ward, Holcombe
Weiss, George Martin
Wilke, Lou
Wrenn, Robert Duffield
Wrigley, Philip Knight
Wrigley, William, Jr.
Suppl. 1
Yawkey, Tom
Young, Buddy

Surfers
Freeth, George Douglas
Kahanamoku, Duke
Paoa

Swimmers / Divers
Crabbe, Buster
Daniels, Charles
Meldrum
Kahanamoku, Duke
Paoa
Kealoha, Warren Daniels
Kellerman, Annette
Kurtz, Frank *Suppl. 2*
Madison, Helene Emma
Norelius, Martha
Rawls, Katherine Louise
Weissmuller, Johnny

Tennis Players
Ashe, Arthur
Atkinson, Juliette Paxton
Browne, Mary Kendall
Budge, Don *Suppl. 2*
Bundy, May Godfray
Sutton
Campbell, Oliver Samuel
Connolly, Maureen
Catherine
Davis, Dwight Filley
Dwight, James
Gonzalez, Pancho
Jacobs, Helen Hull
Suppl. 1
Johnston, William M.
Larned, William
Augustus
Mallory, Molla Bjurstedt
McLoughlin, Maurice
Evans
Moody, Helen Wills
Suppl. 1
Paret, Jahail Parmly
Richards, Vincent
Riggs, Bobby *Suppl. 2*
Sears, Dick
Sears, Eleonora
Randolph
Talbert, Billy *Suppl. 2*
Tilden, Bill
Ward, Holcombe
Whitman, Malcolm
Douglass
Wightman, Hazel
Hotchkiss
Williams, Dick
Wrenn, Robert Duffield
Wright, Beals Coleman

Track and Field Athletes
Bennett, Lewis

Brundage, Avery
Cunningham, Glenn V.
Curtis, William
Buckingham *Suppl. 2*
DeMar, Clarence
Harrison
Didrikson, Babe
Drew, Howard Porter
Ewry, Ray
Flanagan, John J.
Griffith-Joyner, Florence
Suppl. 1
Gutterson, Albert
Lovejoy
Hahn, Archie
Hardin, Slats
Hayes, Johnny
Hayward, William Louis
Hubbard, William
DeHart
Johnson, Cornelius
Cooper
Kraenzlein, Alvin
Christian
McDonald, Babe
McGrath, Matthew J.
Metcalfe, Ralph Harold
Morris, Glenn Edward
Myers, Lon
Orton, George
Washington
Osborn, Harold Marion
Owens, Jesse
Paddock, Charles
William
Prefontaine, Steve
Rose, Ralph Waldo
Rudolph, Wilma
Scholz, Jackson Volney
Sheppard, Melvin
Winfield
Sheridan, Martin Joseph
Stannard, Henry
Taber, Norman *Suppl. 1*
Taylor, Frederick
Morgan
Thorpe, Jim
Tolan, Thomas Edward
Walsh, Stella
Wefers, Bernard J.

Wrestlers
Gotch, Frank Alvin
Lewis, Strangler
Lipscomb, Big Daddy
Muldoon, William
Wagner, Gorgeous
George *Suppl. 2*

Yachtsmen
Crowninshield, George,
Jr.
Duryea, Harmanus
Barkulo
Stevens, John Cox
Vanderbilt, William
Kissam

WRITING AND PUBLISHING

Editing and Publishing
Anthologists
Alger, William
Rounseville
Asimov, Isaac
Auslander, Joseph
Bontemps, Arna
Wendell
Braithwaite, William
Stanley Beaumont
Brownson, Henry
Francis
Burnett, Whit
Child, Francis James
Clarke, Mary Bayard
Devereux
Coggeshall, William
Turner
Conroy, Jack
Dannay, Frederic
Dunbar-Nelson, Alice
Fadiman, Clifton
Suppl. 1
Foley, Martha
Gassner, John Waldhorn
Griswold, Rufus Wilmot
Hakluyt, Richard
Hall, James (1793–1868)
Hart, James D.
Henderson, Alice Corbin
Kennedy, William
Sloane
Kronenberger, Louis
Lawson, James
Moore, Milcah Martha
O'Brien, Edward Joseph
Harrington
Sargent, Epes
Smith, Elihu Hubbard
Stoddard, Richard
Henry
Teasdale, Sara
Tenney, Tabitha Gilman
Untermeyer, Louis
Zevin, Israel Joseph

Bible Editors
Scofield, Cyrus Ingerson

Book Designers
Armitage, Merle
Conkwright, P. J.
Suppl. 2
Rogers, Bruce
Updike, Daniel Berkeley
Whitman, Sarah de St.
Prix Wyman

Book Editors / Publishers
Abrams, Harry Nathan
Adams, Harriet
Stratemeyer
Aitken, Robert
Alden, Henry Mills
Allen, Paul
Appleton, Daniel
Appleton, William
Henry
Barrett, Benjamin Fiske
Bartlett, John
Beach, Sylvia
Woodbridge
Beadle, Erastus Flavel
Benét, William Rose
Boni, Albert
Bostwick, Arthur Elmore
Bowker, R. R.
Brett, George Platt
Brett, George Platt, Jr.
Brower, David *Suppl. 2*
Bryant, Louise Frances
Stevens
Canfield, Cass
Carey, Henry Charles
Carey, Mathew
Carter, Robert
(1819–1879)
Cerf, Bennett Alfred
Clampitt, Amy Kathleen
Collier, Peter Fenelon
Cooper, Ezekiel
Cooper, Susan Augusta
Fenimore
Covici, Pascal Avram
Cowley, Malcolm
Crain, Gustavus
Dedman, Jr.
Day, F. Holland
de Graff, Robert F.
Derleth, August William
Deutsch, Babette
Dobson, Thomas
Dodd, Frank Howard
Donahoe, Patrick
Doran, George Henry
Doubleday, Frank
Nelson
Doubleday, Nelson
Duyckinck, Evert
Augustus

Duyckinck, George
Long
Evans, Donald
Farrar, John Chipman
Fields, James Thomas
Suppl. 2
Fischer, John
Fodor, Eugene
Folsom, Charles
Ford, Guy Stanton
Funk, Wilfred John
Ginn, Edwin
Godwin, Parke
Green, Bartholomew
Greenslet, Ferris
Haldeman-Julius,
Emanuel
Hall, Samuel
(1740–1807)
Harcourt, Alfred
Harper, Fletcher
Harper, James
Hawthorne, Julian
Hays, Isaac
Henry, Caleb Sprague
Herr, Daniel
Hines, Duncan
Holt, Henry
Houghton, Henry Oscar
Howe, Mark Antony
DeWolfe
Hubbard, Elbert Green
Huberman, Leo
Huebsch, B. W.
Humphreys, James
Jewett, John Punchard
Johnson, Allen
Jovanovich, William
Suppl. 2
Kahn, Albert Eugene
Kaufmann, Peter
Kenedy, Patrick John
Kirkus, Virginia
Klopfer, Donald Simon
Knopf, Alfred A.
Knopf, Blanche Wolf
Lathrop, George Parsons
Laughlin, James *Suppl. 1*
Lea, Isaac
Leventhal, Albert Rice
Lippincott, Joshua
Ballinger
Liveright, Horace
Brisbane
Lothrop, Daniel
Lynes, George Platt
Marquis, Albert Nelson
Massee, May
McAlmon, Robert
Menzies
McGraw, James Herbert

Merriam, Charles
Miller, Olive Beaupré
Moore, Milcah Martha
Morgan, Dale Lowell
Norton, William Warder
Onassis, Jacqueline
Kennedy
Peabody, Oliver William
Bourn
Peck, Harry Thurston
Peloubet, Francis
Nathan
Perkins, Maxwell E.
Porter, Charlotte
Endymion
Putnam, George Haven
Putnam, George Palmer
Redfield, Justus Starr
Revell, Fleming Hewitt,
Jr.
Rinehart, Stanley
Marshall, Jr.
Rudge, William Edwin
Sawyer, Caroline M.
Scherman, Harry
Schuster, Max Lincoln
Scribner, Arthur Hawley
Scribner, Charles
(1821–1871)
Scribner, Charles
(1854–1930)
Scribner, Charles
(1890–1952)
Scribner, Charles, Jr.
Scudder, Horace Elisha
Sheed, Francis Joseph
Simon, Richard Leo
Singer, Isidore
Smith, Lloyd Pearsall
Sparks, Jared
Stoddard, Richard
Henry
Stratemeyer, Edward
Theobald, Paul
Thomas, Robert Bailey
Thomes, William Henry
Thwaites, Reuben Gold
Ticknor, William Davis
Van Nostrand, David
Victor, Orville James
Vizetelly, Frank Horace
Waldman, Milton
Wallace, DeWitt
Ward, Maisie
Warner, Charles Dudley
Webb, Charles Henry
Weeks, Edward
Augustus
Wells, Samuel Roberts
Wheelock, John Hall
Whipple, Guy Montrose

Editing and Publishing
(cont.)
Wilson, Halsey William
Wood, Horatio C, Jr.

Bookbinders
Fortune, Amos

Crossword Puzzle Editors
Farrar, Margaret
Petherbridge

*Documentary / Historical
Editors*
Blake, Harrison Gray
Otis
Boyd, Julian Parks
Emerson, Edward Waldo
Fitzpatrick, John
Clement
Ford, Paul Leicester
Ford, Worthington
Chauncey
Hazard, Samuel
Kellogg, Louise Phelps
Knight, Lucian Lamar
Sparks, Jared
Thwaites, Reuben Gold

Engravers
Ames, Ezra
Johnston, Thomas

Fashion Magazine Editors
Blackwell, Betsy Talbot
Chase, Edna Woolman
Long, Lois
Sheppard, Eugenia
Vreeland, Diana Dalziel

Literary Agents
Hayward, Leland
Norris, Charles Gilman
Smith

Literary Executors
Barrus, Clara
Paine, Albert Bigelow

*Magazine and Journal
Editors / Publishers*
Abbott, Lyman
Adams, Cyrus Cornelius
Adams, William Taylor
Ahern, Mary Eileen
Aiken, D. Wyatt
Aitken, Robert
Alden, Henry Mills
Aldrich, Thomas Bailey
Allen, Frederick Lewis
Allen, Paul

Anderson, Margaret
Angoff, Charles
Armstrong, Hamilton
Fish
Arthur, Timothy Shay
Ascoli, Max
Auslander, Joseph
Ballou, Maturin Murray
Bangs, John Kendrick
Barber, Jesse Max
Barnard, Henry
Barrett, Benjamin Fiske
Baum, L. Frank
Beach, Alfred Ely
Benét, William Rose
Benjamin, Park
Bennett, Gwendolyn
Blackwell, Betsy Talbot
Bliven, Bruce
Bloomer, Amelia Jenks
Bok, Edward William
Booth, Mary Louise
Bostwick, Arthur Elmore
Bowker, R. R.
Bradford, Andrew
Bradwell, James
Bolesworth
Brann, William Cowper
Brickman, William
Wolfgang
Brown, Charles
Brockden
Brownson, Henry
Francis
Brownson, Orestes
Augustus
Bruce, Archibald
Buckingham, Joseph
Tinker
Bunner, Henry Cuyler
Burgess, Gelett
Burnett, Whit
Burnham, James
Burton, William Evans
Calverton, Victor
Francis
Canby, Henry Seidel
Carpenter, Stephen
Cullen
Carus, Paul
Cattell, James McKeen
Catton, Bruce
Chamberlin, Rollin
Thomas
Chambers, Whittaker
Chase, Edna Woolman
Clark, Emily Tapscott
Clark, Lewis Gaylord
Clarke, Mary Bayard
Devereux
Cobb, Cully Alton

Collier, Peter Fenelon
Como, William Michael
Conroy, Jack
Cousins, Norman
Cowles, Gardner, Jr.
Cowley, Malcolm
Crain, Gustavus
Dedman, Jr.
Croly, Herbert David
Crothers, Thomas
Davison
Crowninshield, Frank
Curry, Daniel
Curtis, Cyrus H. K.
Curtis, George William
Dannay, Frederic
Davis, Thurston Noble
De Bow, James
Dunwoody Brownson
Demorest, Ellen Curtis
Dennie, Joseph
Dexter, Henry Martyn
Didier, Eugene Lemoine
Dodge, Mary Elizabeth
Mapes
Donahoe, Patrick
Donovan, Hedley
Williams
Dow, George Francis
Duffy, Francis Patrick
Durant, Thomas
Jefferson
Duyckinck, Evert
Augustus
Dymond, John
Eastman, Max
Eckman, Frederick
Suppl. 1
Edwards, Bela Bates
Eliot, T. S.
Engel, Carl
Everett, Robert
Fairfield, Sumner
Lincoln
Fauset, Jessie Redmon
Fenner, Erasmus Darwin
Fischer, John
Fishbein, Morris
Fixx, James Fuller
Fleischer, Nat
Flower, Benjamin
Orange
Foley, Martha
Forbes, Malcolm
Stevenson
Ford, Paul Leicester
Franklin, Benjamin
(1812–1878)
Freeman, Joseph
French, Lucy Virginia
Smith

Fry, Varian *Suppl. 2*
Fuller, Hoyt William
Fuller, Margaret
Funk, Isaac Kauffman
Funk, Wilfred John
Gaillard, Edwin Samuel
Gaines, William M.
Suppl. 2
Garreau, Armand
Gernsback, Hugo
Gibbs, Wolcott
(1902–1958)
Gilder, Jeannette
Leonard
Gilder, Richard Watson
Gildersleeve, Basil
Lanneau
Gillis, James Martin
Gilman, Caroline
Howard
Gingrich, Arnold
Gleason, Ralph Joseph
Godey, Louis Antoine
Godkin, Edwin
Lawrence
Godwin, Parke
Gold, Michael
Goldwater, John L.
Suppl. 1
Gould, George Milbry
Graebner, Theodore
Conrad
Green, Abel
Griswold, Rufus Wilmot
Grosvenor, Gilbert
Hovey
Hackett, Francis
Hadden, Briton
Hale, Sarah Josepha
Buell
Hall, James (1793–1868)
Hall, John Elihu
Halsey, Frederick Arthur
Hamilton, Earl Jefferson
Hamilton, Thomas
Hapgood, Norman
Harbaugh, Henry
Harland, Henry
Harman, Moses
Harper, Fletcher
Harris, Frank
Harris, Seale
Hart, Joseph Kinmont
Harvey, George Brinton
McClellan
Hasbrouck, Lydia Sayer
Haven, Emily Bradley
Neal
Haynes, Williams
Heap, Jane
Heard, Dwight Bancroft

Editing and Publishing
(cont.)

Hearst, William Randolph, Jr.
Hecht, George Joseph
Henry, Caleb Sprague
Herr, Daniel
Herrick, Clarence Luther, and Charles Judson Herrick
Herrick, Sophia McIlvaine Bledsoe
Hibbs, Ben
Hill, Daniel Harvey
Hoffman, Charles Fenno
Holbrook, James
Holt, Hamilton Bowen
Hopkins, Pauline Elizabeth
Hornblow, Arthur, Sr.
Horst, Louis
Howard, Blanche Willis
Howkins, Elizabeth Penrose
Hubbard, Elbert Green
Huberman, Leo
Hudson, Daniel Eldred
Ingelfinger, Franz Joseph
Isaacs, Edith Juliet Rich
Jameson, John Franklin
Jelliffe, Smith Ely
Jolas, Maria
Jones, Thomas P.
Jordan, Elizabeth Garver
Jordan, John Woolf
Josephson, Matthew
Kellogg, Paul Underwood
Kelly, Aloysius Oliver Joseph
Kendall, Willmoore
Kennedy, John F., Jr. *Suppl. 1*
Kerr, Sophie
Keyes, Charles Rollin
Keyes, Frances Parkinson
Kirkland, Caroline Matilda
Kocher, A. Lawrence
Kreymborg, Alfred Francis
La Follette, Belle Case
La Follette, Suzanne
Lamb, Arthur Becket
Lamb, Martha Joanna R. N.
Lane, Gertrude Battles
Larcom, Lucy
Larsen, Roy Edward
Lawrence, David

Leland, Charles Godfrey
Liberman, Alexander *Suppl. 2*
Liebowitz, Jack S. *Suppl. 2*
Lincoln, Joseph Crosby
Linen, James Alexander, III
Littledale, Clara Savage
Longfellow, William Pitt Preble
Lord, Asa Dearborn
Lorimer, George Horace
Lothrop, Daniel
Loveman, Amy
Lovett, Robert Morss
Loy, Matthias
Luce, Henry Robinson
Lummis, Charles Fletcher
Mabie, Hamilton Wright
Macdonald, Dwight
Macfadden, Bernarr
MacVeagh, Lincoln
Mapes, James Jay
Martin, Franklin Henry
Mathews, Cornelius
Mathews, Joseph McDowell
Matthews, Thomas Stanley
Mayes, Herbert R.
McAlmon, Robert Menzies
McAndrew, William
McClure, Samuel Sidney
McGraw, James Herbert
McQuillen, John Hugh
McWilliams, Carey
Mencken, H. L.
Meredith, Edna C. Elliott
Meyer, Henry Coddington
Miller, Bertha Everett Mahony
Minor, Benjamin Blake
Monroe, Harriet
Moore, Donald Wynkoop
Moore, Frederick Randolph
Morley, Christopher Darlington
Morris, Willie *Suppl. 1*
Mosessohn, David Nehemiah
Moss, Howard
Munsey, Frank Andrew
Munson, Gorham Bert
Myrick, Herbert

Nast, Condé
Nathan, George Jean
Niles, Hezekiah
Noll, John Francis
Norelius, Eric
Oppenheim, James
Osgood, Frances Sargent Locke
O'Sullivan, John Louis
Packard, Frederick Adolphus
Paul, Elliot
Peabody, Oliver William Bourn
Peck, George Washington
Peck, Harry Thurston
Perkins, Frederic Beecher
Perry, Rufus Lewis
Poe, Edgar Allan
Poling, Daniel Alfred
Porter, Charlotte Endymion
Putnam, George Palmer
Rahv, Philip
Redfield, Justus Starr
Rice, Charles
Rice, Charles Allen Thorndike
Rice, Joseph Mayer
Rodale, J. I.
Root, Frederick Woodman
Ross, Harold
Ruffin, Josephine St. Pierre
Sargent, Epes
Sayre, John Nevin
Scribner, Charles (1821–1871)
Scudder, Horace Elisha
Sedgwick, Ellery
Seldes, Gilbert Vivian
Seymour, Mary Foot
Shaw, Albert
Shawn, William
Shields, George Oliver
Shinn, Milicent Washburn
Shull, George Harrison
Simmons, George Henry
Simons, Algie Martin
Skinner, John Stuart
Smart, David Archibald
Smith, Elias
Smith, Lloyd Pearsall
Smith, Samuel Francis
Sonneck, Oscar George Theodore
Sonneschein, Rosa

Sparks, Jared
Spivak, Lawrence
Stallings, Laurence Tucker
Stevens, Abel
Stickley, Gustav
Stieglitz, Alfred
Stoddard, Cora Frances
Straight, Dorothy Payne Whitney
Summers, Thomas Osmond
Thompson, Era Bell
Thompson, John Reuben
Thurman, Wallace
Ticknor, William Davis
Tietjens, Eunice
Tigert, John James, III
Tompkins, Juliet Wilbor
Travis, Walter John
Trowbridge, John Townsend
Turner, George Kibbe
Valesh, Eva McDonald
Van Nostrand, David
Varela y Morales, Felix Francisco
Vick, James
Vinal, Harold
Waite, Catharine Van Valkenburg
Walker, John Brisben
Wallace, DeWitt
Wallace, Lila Bell Acheson
Warren, Edward
Webb, Charles Henry
Weeks, Edward Augustus
Weiss-Rosmarin, Trude
Whipple, Guy Montrose
Whitaker, Daniel Kimball
White, Katharine Sergeant
White, Thomas Willis
Whittelsey, Abigail Goodrich
Whyte, William H. *Suppl. 1*
Williams, John Shoebridge
Williams, Michael
Willis, Nathaniel Parker
Wright, Willard Huntington
Wurtz, Henry
Youmans, Edward Livingston
Youmans, William Jay

Editing and Publishing
(cont.)
Ziff, William Bernard

Music Editors / Publishers
Berlin, Irving
Bond, Carrie Jacobs
Bradbury, William
  Batchelder
Bradford, Perry
Carr, Benjamin
Ditson, Oliver
Donaldson, Walter
Drake, Pete
Dreyfus, Max
Engel, Carl
Fisher, William Arms
Flagg, Josiah
Garrison, Lucy McKim
Graupner, Gottlieb
Harris, Charles Kassell
Hewitt, James
Holyoke, Samuel Adams
Kieffer, Aldine Silliman
Mills, Irving
Pace, Harry Herbert
Peer, Ralph Sylvester
Presser, Theodore
Read, Daniel
Rodeheaver, Homer
  Alvin
Root, Frederick
  Woodman
Rose, Fred
Schirmer, Gustav
Schmidt, Arthur Paul
Shaw, Arnold
Stark, John, and Eleanor
  Stark
Surette, Thomas
  Whitney
Thompson, Will
  Lamartine
Tufts, John
Vaughan, James David
Von Tilzer, Harry, and
  Albert Von Tilzer
Williams, Clarence

*News Agency Owners /
Managers*
Barnett, Claude Albert
Cooper, Kent
Haessler, Carl
Koenigsberg, Moses
Smith, William Henry
  (1833–1896)
Stone, Melville Elijah

*Newspaper Editors /
Publishers*
Abbott, Joseph Carter
Abbott, Robert
  Sengstacke
Abell, Arunah
  Sheperdson
Adams, John Quincy
  (1848–1922)
Allen, Elizabeth Akers
Allen, Henry Justin
Ameringer, Oscar
Anneke, Mathilde
  Franziska Giesler
Annenberg, Moses Louis
Anthony, Henry Bowen
Bache, Benjamin
  Franklin
Bacheller, Irving
Bailey, Francis
Bailey, Gamaliel
Baldwin, John Denison
Ballou, Maturin Murray
Barksdale, Ethelbert
Barron, Clarence Walker
Barrows, Samuel June
Bartholdt, Richard
Bass, Charlotta Spears
Bates, Elisha
Beach, Moses Yale
Beebe, Lucius Morris
Bell, Philip Alexander
Belo, Alfred Horatio
Benét, William Rose
Benjamin, Robert
  Charles O'Hara
Bennett, James Gordon
  (1795–1872)
Bennett, James Gordon,
  Jr. (1841–1918)
Bernstein, Theodore
  Menline
Bibb, Henry Walton
Bingham, Barry
Bingham, Robert Worth
Binns, John
Blackwell, Henry
  Browne
Blair, Francis Preston
Bonfils, Frederick
  Gilmer and Harry
  Heye Tammen
Bonner, Robert
Borland, Solon
Boudinot, Elias (1804?–
  1839)
Bovard, Oliver Kirby
Bowen, Henry Chandler
Bowles, Samuel

(1797–1851)
Bowles, Samuel
  (1826–1878)
Bradford, Andrew
Bradford, John
Bradwell, Myra Colby
Brawley, Edward
  McKnight
Breckinridge, Desha
Breckinridge, John
  (1797–1841)
Brentano, Lorenz
Bridgman, Herbert
  Lawrence
Brisbane, Arthur
Bristow, Joseph Little
Brooks, Noah
Brown, Clarence J.
Brownlow, William
  Gannaway
Brucker, Herbert
Bryan, John Stewart
Bryant, John Emory
Bryant, William Cullen
Buckingham, Joseph
  Tinker
Burk, John Daly
Bush, John Edward
Cahan, Abraham
Callender, James
  Thomson
Callimachos, Panos
  Demetrios
Cameron, Andrew Carr
Campbell, John
Campbell, John *Suppl. 2*
Canham, Erwin Dain
Cantwell, Mary *Suppl. 1*
Capers, William
Carter, Amon G.
Carter, John
Carter, Robert
  (1819–1879)
Carter, William Beverly,
  Jr.
Carter, William
  Hodding, II
Cary, Mary Ann
  Camberton Shadd
Case, Francis Higbee
Catledge, Turner
Chamberlain, William
  Isaac
Chaplin, Ralph Hosea
Chase, William Calvin
Childs, George William
Clarke, Joseph Ignatius
  Constantine
Cobb, Frank
Cockerill, John Albert
Coggeshall, William
  Turner

Colby, Clara Dorothy
  Bewick
Colby, Luther
Collins, Isaac
Colton, Walter
Conway, Katherine
  Eleanor
Copley, Ira Clifton
Cornish, Samuel Eli
Cowles, Gardner
Cowles, Gardner, Jr.
Cox, James Middleton
Croly, David Goodman
Curtis, Cyrus H. K.
Dabney, Virginius
Dabney, Wendell
  Phillips
Dana, Charles Anderson
Dana, William Buck
Daniel, John Moncure
Daniels, Jonathan
Daniels, Josephus
Davis, Benjamin
  Jefferson (1870–1945)
Davis, Samuel Post
Davis, Watson
Day, Dorothy
Day, William Howard
Dealey, George
  Bannerman
Desmond, Humphrey
  Joseph
De Young, Michel
  Henry, Jr.
Dixon, George
  Washington
Donahoe, Patrick
Douglass, Frederick
Draper, John
Draper, Margaret Green
Draper, Richard
Drummond, Roscoe
Duane, Margaret
  Hartman Markoe
  Bache
Duane, William
  (1760–1835)
Dunlap, John
Dwight, Theodore
  (1764–1846)
Eagleson, William Lewis
Eckman, Julius
Evans, George Henry
Farrington, Joseph Rider
Faubus, Orval
Fenno, John
Field, Kate
Field, Marshall, III
Fine, Benjamin
Fiske, Harrison Grey
Flagg, Azariah Cutting

Editing and Publishing

(cont.)

Fleet, Thomas
Ford, Daniel Sharp
Forney, John Wien
Fortune, Timothy
  Thomas
Fowle, Daniel
Fox, Richard Kyle
Franklin, Ann Smith
Franklin, James
Freeman, Douglas
  Southall
Freeman, Frederick
  Kemper
Funk, Isaac Kauffman
Gaine, Hugh
Gales, Joseph
Gallagher, William Davis
Gannett, Frank Ernest
Garreau, Armand
Garrison, William Lloyd
Garza, Catarino Erasmo
Gauvreau, Emile Henry
Gay, Sydney Howard
Gill, John
Glass, Carter
Glenn, William Wilkins
Goddard, Mary
  Katherine
Goddard, Morrill
Goddard, Sarah Updike
Goddard, William
Godkin, Edwin
  Lawrence
Godwin, Parke
Gonzales, Ambrose
  Elliott
Gonzales, Narciso Gener
Goodell, William
  (1792–1878)
Goodman, Joseph
  Thompson
Goodwin, Charles
  Carroll
Gordon, Laura de Force
Graebner, Theodore
  Conrad
Graham, Katharine
  Meyer *Suppl. 2*
Graham, Philip Leslie
Graves, James Robinson
Gray, James Harrison
Greeley, Horace
Green, Anne Catharine
Green, Bartholomew
Green, Duff
Green, Jonas
Greenfield, Meg *Suppl. 1*
Greenleaf, Thomas
Gresham, Newt

Griscom, Lloyd
  Carpenter
Guggenheim, Harry
  Frank
Hackett, Francis
Hale, David
Halstead, Murat
Hanson, Alexander
  Contee (1786–1819)
Harris, Benjamin
Harrison, Hubert Henry
Harvey, George Brinton
  McClellan
Hatcher, William
  Eldridge
Haven, Gilbert
Hawley, Joseph Roswell
Hayes, Max Sebastian
Hays, Will S.
Hearst, William
  Randolph
Hearst, William
  Randolph, Jr.
Heco, Joseph
Henni, John Martin
Hill, Daniel Harvey
Hill, Isaac
Hitchcock, Gilbert
  Monell
Ho, Chinn
Hobby, Oveta Culp
  Suppl. 1
Hobby, William Pettus
Holbrook, James
Holden, William Woods
Holland, Edwin Clifford
Holland, Josiah Gilbert
  Suppl. 1
Holt, John
Hotze, Henry
Hough, Henry Beetle
Howard, Roy Wilson
Howe, Edgar Watson
Howell, Clark
Howell, Evan Park
Howey, Walter
  Crawford
Howkins, Elizabeth
  Penrose
Hudson, Frederic
Hughes, Robert William
Humphreys, James
Isaacs, Samuel Myer
Jenkins, David
Jeter, Jeremiah Bell
Johnson, Albert
Johnson, Andrew N.
Johnson, Gerald W.
  Suppl. 2
Johnson, John Albert
Jones, George

Jones, Hamilton C.
Jones, John Beauchamp
Kaufmann, Peter
Kendall, Amos
Kendall, George Wilkins
King, Charles
King, Henry
  (1842–1915)
King, Rufus
  (1814–1876)
Kirchwey, Freda
Kneeland, Samuel
Knight, John Shively
Knowland, William Fife
Knox, Frank
Kurtz, Benjamin
Laffan, William Mackay
Lawrence, David
Lawson, James
Lawson, Victor Fremont
Leavitt, Joshua
Leland, Charles Godfrey
Leslie, Frank
Leslie, Miriam Florence
  Follin
Litchman, Charles
  Henry
Locke, David Ross
Loeb, William, III
Lovejoy, Elijah Parish
Lundy, Benjamin
Lynch, James
Marble, Manton Malone
Markel, Lester
Martin, John Alexander
Maxwell, William
  (1766?–1809)
Maynard, Robert Clyve
McAnally, David Rice
McCarroll, Marion
  Clyde
McClatchy, Charles
  Kenny
McClure, Alexander
  Kelly
McCormick, Medill
McCormick, Robert
  Rutherford
McElroy, John
  (1846–1929)
McFerrin, John Berry
McGill, Ralph
McKelway, Alexander
  Jeffrey
McLean, William
  Lippard
McLemore, Jeff
McMaster, James
  Alphonsus
Medary, Samuel
Medill, Joseph

Mein, John
Mencken, H. L.
Meredith, Edna C.
  Elliott
Merz, Charles
Meyer, Eugene Isaac
Miller, Henry
  (1702–1782)
Mitchell, Edward Page
Mitchell, John, Jr.
Moore, Frederick
  Randolph
Moore, John Weeks
Mosessohn, David
  Nehemiah
Muñoz Rivera, Luis
Munsey, Frank Andrew
Murdock, Victor
Murphy, John Henry,
  Sr.
Murray, Orson S.
Nast, William
Nelson, William Rockhill
Newcomb, Harvey
Newhouse, Samuel
  Irving
Newsome, Joseph
  Thomas
Nicholson, Eliza Jane
  Poitevent Holbrook
Nicolay, John George
Noyes, Crosby Stuart
Oakes, George
  Washington Ochs
Ochs, Adolph Simon
Older, Fremont
O'Neill, Buckey
O'Reilly, John Boyle
Osborn, Chase Salmon
O'Sullivan, John Louis
Oswald, Eleazer
Otis, Harrison Gray
  (1837–1917)
Ottendorfer, Anna Behr
  Uhl
Ottendorfer, Oswald
Parker, James
Patterson, Alicia
Patterson, Cissy
Patterson, Joseph Medill
Patterson, Thomas
  McDonald
Peck, George Wilbur
Pelham, Benjamin B.
Pendleton, James
  Madison
Perry, Benjamin Franklin
Petersen, Hjalmar
Pinchback, P. B. S.
Pittock, Henry Lewis

Editing and Publishing
(cont.)
Pleasants, John
  Hampden
Pledger, William
  Anderson
Polk, Leonidas
  LaFayette
Pope, Generoso
Porter, William Trotter
Post, Louis Freeland
Potter, Ray
Poynter, Nelson
Price, Thomas Frederick
Pulitzer, Joseph
Pulitzer, Joseph, Jr.
Pulitzer, Ralph
Pulliam, Eugene Collins
Rapp, Wilhelm
Raymond, Henry Jarvis
Regan, John
Reid, Helen
Reid, Ogden Mills
Reid, Whitelaw
Rind, Clementina
Ritchie, Thomas
Rives, John Cook
Rivington, James
Roberts, Ellis Henry
Robertson, James
  (1747–1816)
Rosewater, Edward
Ross, Charles Griffith
Ross, Edmund Gibson
Roudanez, Louis Charles
Rudd, Daniel
Russell, Benjamin
Russell, Charles Edward
Russwurm, John Brown
Schiff, Dorothy
Scott, James Wilmot
Scott, William
  Alexander, II
Screws, William Wallace
Scripps, E. W.
Scripps, Ellen Browning
Scripps, James Edmund
Scripps, Robert Paine
Scripps, William
  Edmund
Scull, John
Seabury, Samuel
  (1801–1872)
Seaton, William Winston
Sengstacke, John H. H.
  Suppl. 2
Seward, Theodore
  Frelinghuysen
Sherwood, Isaac Ruth
Sholes, Christopher
  Latham

Sloan, Harold Paul
Smith, Charles Emory
Smith, Charles Perrin
Smith, Harry Clay
Smith, Samuel Harrison
Smith, Seba
Smith, Uriah
Solis-Cohen, Solomon
Southwick, Solomon
Spink, J. G. Taylor
Stevens, Abel
Stockbridge, Horace
  Edward
Stone, I. F.
Stone, Melville Elijah
Stone, William Leete
Storey, Wilbur Fiske
Sullivan, James Edward
Sulzberger, Arthur Hays
Swank, James Moore
Swinton, John
Swisshelm, Jane Grey
  Cannon
Swope, Herbert Bayard
Talbot, Francis Xavier
Taylor, Charles Henry
Testut, Charles
Thomas, Isaiah
Thompson, John
  Reuben
Tilton, Theodore
Timothy, Ann
Timothy, Elizabeth
Towne, Benjamin
Tracy, Joseph Carter
Tresca, Carlo
Trotter, William Monroe
Trumbull, Henry Clay
Turner, Josiah, Jr.
Tveitmœ, Olaf Anders
Van Anda, Carr Vattel
Van Doren, Irita
  Suppl. 1
Villard, Henry
Villard, Oswald Garrison
Waisbrooker, Lois
Walker, Stanley
Walker, William Otis
Wallace, Henry Cantwell
Walter, Cornelia Wells
Ward, Samuel Ringgold
Ware, William
Warman, Cy
Warner, Charles Dudley
Watterson, Henry
Wayland, Julius
  Augustus
Webb, Charles Henry
Webb, James Watson
Wechsler, James A.
Weed, Thurlow

Wells-Barnett, Ida Bell
Wentworth, John
  (1815–1888)
White, Horace
White, William Allen
Whiteley, L. A.
Williams, John
  (1761–1818)
Winchevsky, Morris
Yorke, Peter Christopher
Young, Plummer
  Bernard
Zenger, John Peter

Printers
Aitken, Robert
Bailey, Francis
Bailey, Lydia R.
Bradford, Andrew
Bradford, John
Bradford, William
  (1663–1752)
Bradford, William
  (1722–1791)
Carter, John
Cassin, John
Collins, Isaac
Currier, Nathaniel
Dawkins, Henry
Day, Stephen
Dobson, Thomas
Donahoe, Patrick
Doolittle, Amos
Draper, John
Draper, Margaret Green
Draper, Richard
Duane, Margaret
  Hartman Markoe
  Bache
Dunlap, John
Edes, Benjamin
Fleet, Thomas
Foster, John
Fowle, Daniel
Franklin, Ann Smith
Franklin, James
Gaine, Hugh
Gales, Joseph
Gill, John
Goddard, Mary
  Katherine
Goddard, Sarah Updike
Goddard, William
Goudy, Frederic William
Green, Anne Catharine
Green, Bartholomew
Green, Jonas
Green, Samuel
Greenleaf, Thomas
Hall, Samuel
  (1740–1807)

Hamlin, William
Hoen, August
Holt, John
Houghton, Henry Oscar
Hugo, E. Harold
Humphreys, James
Hunter, Dard
Ives, James Merritt
Jansen, Reinier
Johnson, Marmaduke
Johnston, Thomas
Keimer, Samuel
Kneeland, Samuel
Loudon, Samuel
Maxwell, William
  (1766?–1809)
McFarland, J. Horace
Mecom, Benjamin
Mein, John
Miller, Henry
  (1702–1782)
Munsell, Joel
Nash, John Henry
Nicholson, Timothy
Nuthead, William
Parker, James
Parks, William
Prang, Louis
Revere, Paul
Rind, Clementina
Rives, John Cook
Rivington, James
Robertson, James
  (1747–1816)
Rudge, William Edwin
Russell, Benjamin
Seaton, William Winston
Sholes, Christopher
  Latham
Sower, Christopher, II
Stevens, Alzina Ann
  Parsons
Tanner, Benjamin
Thomas, Isaiah
Timothy, Ann
Timothy, Elizabeth
Timothy, Lewis
Towne, Benjamin
Updike, Daniel Berkeley
White, Thomas Willis
Zenger, John Peter

Typographers
Goudy, Frederic William
Nash, John Henry
Ruzicka, Rudolph

**Literature and
Journalism**
Almanac Makers
Ames, Nathaniel
  (1708–1764)

Literature and Journalism (*cont.*)
Ames, Nathaniel
(1741–1842)
Collins, Isaac
Foster, John
Franklin, Ann Smith
Franklin, Benjamin
(1706–1790)
Gaine, Hugh
West, Benjamin
(1730–1813)

Autobiographers / Memoirists
Adler, Polly
Alexander, Edward Porter
Allen, Steve *Suppl. 2*
Anderson, Margaret
Antin, Mary
Ashbridge, Elizabeth
Ashe, Arthur
Barr, Amelia Edith Huddleston
Blackford, Charles Minor
Bowers, Bathsheba
Browne, Benjamin Frederick
Burroughs, Stephen *Suppl. 2*
Cantwell, Mary *Suppl. 1*
Chessman, Caryl Whittier
Childs, George William
Church, Benjamin
(1639–1718)
Coggeshall, George
Cohen, Rose Gollup
Conway, Moncure Daniel
Cowley, Malcolm
Crapsey, Algernon Sidney
DeJong, David Cornel
Delany, Annie Elizabeth "Bessie," and Sarah Louise "Sadie" Delany *Suppl. 1*
Dorris, Michael *Suppl. 2*
Dyer, Mary Marshall *Suppl. 2*
Eiseley, Loren Corey
Equiano, Olaudah
Farrar, Elizabeth Ware Rotch
Faulk, John Henry
Finley, James Bradley
Fisher, M. F. K.
Frémont, Jessie Benton

Garcia, Céline Léonie Frémaux
Garland, Hamlin
Gilbreth, Frank B., Jr. *Suppl. 2*
Gill, Brendan *Suppl. 2*
Goodwin, Ruby Berkley
Graham, Sheilah
Graydon, Alexander
Grayson, William John
Gunther, John
Harris, Frank
Harrison, Constance Cary
Heller, Joseph *Suppl. 1*
Holbrook, James
Huncke, Herbert *Suppl. 2*
Hunter, Jane Edna Harris
Isherwood, Christopher
Johnson, Osa
Kazin, Alfred *Suppl. 1*
Keckley, Elizabeth Hobbs
Keller, Helen
Kirkland, Caroline Matilda
Lame Deer, John Fire *Suppl. 2*
Larpenteur, Charles
Lee, Gypsy Rose
Lee, Jarena
Leonard, Zenas
Lincoln, Evelyn *Suppl. 1*
Lindbergh, Anne Morrow *Suppl. 2*
Love, Nat
Luhan, Mabel Dodge
Lumpkin, Katharine Du Pre
Mann, Klaus Heinrich Thomas
Matthews, Thomas Stanley
McAlmon, Robert Menzies
McElroy, John
(1846–1929)
Merton, Thomas
Morris, Willie *Suppl. 1*
Morris, Wright *Suppl. 1*
Murray, Pauli
Ness, Eliot *Suppl. 1*
Nock, Albert Jay
Otero-Warren, Nina
Parks, Lillian Rogers *Suppl. 1*
Pember, Phoebe Yates Levy

Percy, William Alexander
Pringle, Elizabeth Waties Allston
Pryor, Sara Agnes Rice
Puller, Lewis Burwell, Jr. *Suppl. 2*
Riley, James
Robinson, Harriet Jane Hanson
Roerich, Nicholas *Suppl. 2*
Royce, Sarah Eleanor Bayliss
Santayana, George
Seagrave, Gordon Stifler
Simon, Kate
Siringo, Charles Angelo
Smith, James
(1737–1814)
Stein, Gertrude
Thompson, Era Bell
Trapp, Maria von
Trobriand, Régis Dénis de
Vining, Elizabeth Gray *Suppl. 2*
Wallace, Lew
West, Jessamyn
White, William Allen
Wilson, James Harrison
Wodehouse, P. G.
Wolcott, Roger
Wright, Richard
Wyman, Seth

Biographers
Albert, Octavia Victoria Rogers
Aldrich, Richard
(1902–1986)
Alger, William Rounseville
Allen, Hervey
Anthony, Katharine Susan
Arnold, Isaac Newton
Ashe, Arthur
Atherton, Gertrude Franklin
Atkinson, William Biddle
Badeau, Adam
Bainton, Roland Herbert
Baker, Carlos Heard
Baker, Ray Stannard
Baldwin, Joseph Glover
Barrus, Clara
Bate, Walter Jackson *Suppl. 1*
Beer, Thomas

Benchley, Nathaniel Goddard
Bigelow, John
Bishop, James Alonzo
Bolton, Sarah Knowles
Bowen, Catherine Drinker
Bradford, Gamaliel
Bridge, Horatio
Brodie, Fawn McKay
Brown, William Wells
Buck, Pearl S.
Bucke, Richard Maurice
Calvert, George Henry
Campbell, Walter Stanley
Canfield, Cass
Cantwell, Robert Emmett
Chotzinoff, Samuel
Clifford, James Lowry
Considine, Bob
Cullum, George Washington
Custer, Elizabeth Clift Bacon
Darlington, William
De Casseres, Benjamin
de Kruif, Paul Henry
De Leon, Thomas Cooper
Dexter, Franklin Bowditch
Dibble, Roy Floyd
Didier, Eugene Lemoine
Dorsey, Sarah Anne Ellis
Drake, Francis Samuel
Dubos, René Jules
Duyckinck, Evert Augustus
Duyckinck, George Long
Edel, Leon *Suppl. 1*
Elder, Susan Blanchard
Ellmann, Richard David
Emerson, Edward Waldo
English, William Hayden
Fields, Annie Adams
Filson, John
Flint, Timothy
Garvey, Amy Euphemia Jacques
Godwin, Parke
Graham, Shirley *Suppl. 1*
Greenacre, Phyllis
Greenslet, Ferris
Gunther, John
Hagedorn, Hermann Ludwig Gebhard
Haley, Alex

Literature and
Journalism (cont.)
Hatcher, William
  Eldridge
Hendrick, Burton Jesse
Herbst, Josephine Frey
Herndon, William Henry
Howe, Mark Antony
  DeWolfe
Irving, Washington
James, Marquis
Josephson, Matthew
Kelly, Howard Atwood
Kennedy, William
  Sloane
King, Grace Elizabeth
Knapp, Samuel Lorenzo
Kronenberger, Louis
Lash, Joseph P.
Lathrop, George Parsons
Lee, Henry (1787–1837)
Linderman, Frank Bird
Mackenzie, Alexander
  Slidell
Malone, Dumas
Marek, George Richard
Marshall, Catherine
Mason, Alpheus
  Thomas
Miller, Merle
Mizener, Arthur Moore
Mumford, Lewis
Nicolay, John George
Ord, George
Ostenso, Martha
Paine, Albert Bigelow
Parton, James
Pierce, Edward Lillie
Pottle, Frederick Albert
Pringle, Henry Fowles
Randall, James Garfield
Randolph, Sarah
  Nicholas
Ravenel, Harriott Horry
  Rutledge
Richards, Laura
  Elizabeth Howe
Rives, William Cabell
Ross, Ishbel
Ruzicka, Rudolph
Schorer, Mark
Seager, Allan
Sellers, Charles Coleman
  Suppl. 2
Shellabarger, Samuel
  (1888–1954)
Shilts, Randy Martin
Sibley, John Langdon
Skinner, Cornelia Otis
Smith, Chard Powers
Sprague, William Buell

Stegner, Wallace Earle
Stein, Gertrude
Stone, Irving
Taggard, Genevieve
Tate, Allen
Teichmann, Howard
  Miles
Thayer, Alexander
  Wheelock
Van Doren, Carl
Wade, John Donald
Waldman, Milton
Ward, Maisie
Warner, Charles Dudley
Weems, Mason Locke
Williams, Catharine
  Read Arnold
Williams, T. Harry
Winslow, Ola Elizabeth
Wolfe, Linnie Marsh
Wormeley, Katharine
  Prescott

Broadcast Journalists
Agronsky, Martin
  Suppl. 2
Allen, Mel *Suppl. 1*
Barber, Red
Beatty, Bessie
Blesh, Rudi
Caray, Harry *Suppl. 1*
Carter, Boake *Suppl. 1*
Chancellor, John
  Suppl. 1
Clapper, Raymond
  Lewis
Collingwood, Charles
  Cummings
Cosell, Howard
Craig, Elisabeth May
  Adams
Cross, Milton
Davis, Elmer
Dean, Dizzy
Dickerson, Nancy
  Suppl. 1
Eisler, Gerhart
Eliot, George Fielding
Frederick, Pauline
  Annabel
Frick, Ford Christopher
Friendly, Fred W.
Garroway, Dave
Gibbons, Floyd
Grange, Red
Hale, Arthur William
Hard, William
Harmon, Tom
Heatter, Gabriel
Heilmann, Harry Edwin

Howe, Quincy
  Huntington
Huntley, Chet
Husing, Ted
Kaltenborn, H. V.
Kuralt, Charles *Suppl. 1*
Lewis, Fulton, Jr.
Lindstrom, Freddy
McBride, Mary
  Margaret
McCann, Alfred
  Watterson
McGee, Frank
McLendon, Gordon
  Barton
McNamee, Graham
Murrow, Edward R.
Polk, George
Reasoner, Harry
Reynolds, Frank
Rice, Grantland
Robinson, Max
  Cleveland
Rowan, Carl T. *Suppl. 2*
Samuel, Maurice
Savitch, Jessica
Schoenbrun, David
  Franz
Seldes, Gilbert Vivian
Sevareid, Eric
Shirer, William
  Lawrence
Snyder, Jimmy "the
  Greek" *Suppl. 1*
Stern, William
Susskind, David
Swayze, John Cameron
  Suppl. 1
Thomas, Lowell
Thompson, Dorothy
  Celine
Trout, Robert *Suppl. 2*
van Loon, Hendrik
  Willem
Winchell, Walter

Captivity Narrativists
Jemison, Mary
Kelly, Fanny Wiggins
Rowlandson, Mary
  White
Wakefield, Sarah F.
  Brown
Williams, John
  (1664–1729)

Cartoonists / Comic Strip
Creators
Addams, Charles Samuel
Arno, Peter
Baker, George

Breger, Dave *Suppl. 2*
Briggs, Clare A.
Browne, Carl
Browne, Dik
Buell, Marjorie
  Henderson *Suppl. 2*
Bushmiller, Ernie
Caniff, Milton Arthur
  Paul
Capp, Al
Clay, Edward Williams
Cranch, Christopher
  Pearse
Crane, Royston
  Campbell
Darling, Jay Norwood
Doolittle, Amos
Dorgan, Tad
Dumm, Edwina *Suppl. 2*
Dunn, Alan
Feininger, Lyonel
  Charles Adrian
Fisher, Ham
Foster, Hal
Fox, Fontaine Talbot, Jr.
Geisel, Theodor Seuss
Gibson, Charles Dana
Godwin, Frank
Goldberg, Rube
Goldwater, John L.
  Suppl. 1
Gorey, Edward *Suppl. 2*
Gottfredson, Floyd
Gould, Chester
Gray, Clarence
Gray, Harold Lincoln
Gropper, William
Gross, Milt
Harman, Fred *Suppl. 2*
Harrington, Oliver W.
  Suppl. 2
Held, John, Jr.
Herblock *Suppl. 2*
Herriman, George
  Joseph
Hokinson, Helen
Irvin, Rea
Johnson, Crockett
Kahles, Charles William
  Suppl. 2
Kane, Bob *Suppl. 2*
Kelly, Walt
Kent, Jack
Keppler, Joseph
Ketcham, Hank *Suppl. 2*
Kirby, Jack *Suppl. 2*
Kirby, Rollin
Knerr, Harold Hering
Kurtzman, Harvey
Lasswell, Fred, Jr.
  Suppl. 2

Literature and Journalism *(cont.)*

MacNelly, Jeff *Suppl. 1*
Marston, William Moulton
Martin, Don *Suppl. 1*
McCay, Winsor Zenic
McCutcheon, John T. *Suppl. 2*
McManus, George
Minor, Robert
Moore, Donald Wynkoop
Mullin, Willard Harlan
Nast, Thomas
Newell, Peter
Opper, Frederick Burr
Outcault, Richard Felton
Raymond, Alex
Ripley, Robert LeRoy
Schulz, Charles M. *Suppl. 1*
Segar, Elzie Crisler
Siegel, Jerry, and Joe Shuster *Suppl. 1*
Smith, Al
Smith, Robert Sidney
Soglow, Otto
Steinberg, Saul *Suppl. 1*
Swinnerton, James Guilford, Jr.
Thurber, James
Willard, Frank
Williams, Gluyas
Young, Arthur Henry
Young, Chic
Zimmerman, Eugene

Children's Book Writers / Illustrators

Abbott, Jacob
Adams, Harriet Stratemeyer
Adams, William Taylor
Alcott, Louisa May
Alger, Horatio, Jr.
Altsheler, Joseph Alexander
Andrews, Jane
Arnold, Elliott
Austin, Jane Goodwin
Baum, L. Frank
Baylor, Frances Courtenay
Bee, Clair Francis
Bemelmans, Ludwig
Benchley, Nathaniel Goddard
Bontemps, Arna Wendell

Bouvet, Marie Marguerite
Brooks, Noah
Brown, Abbie Farwell
Brown, Margaret Wise
Burgess, Thornton Waldo
Burnett, Frances Hodgson
Carruth, Hayden
Clarke, Rebecca Sophia
Cox, Palmer
DeJong, David Cornel
Dodge, Mary Elizabeth Mapes
Edmonds, Walter D. *Suppl. 1*
Eggleston, George Cary
Ellis, Edward Sylvester
Ets, Marie Hall
Field, Rachel Lyman
Finley, Martha
Fisher, Dorothy F. Canfield
Fujikawa, Gyo *Suppl. 1*
Gág, Wanda
Garis, Howard Roger
Geisel, Theodor Seuss
Goodrich, Charles Augustus
Goodrich, Samuel Griswold
Goulding, Francis Robert
Hale, Lucretia Peabody
Hale, Susan
Harris, Joel Chandler
Henderson, Alice Corbin
Herrick, Sophia McIlvaine Bledsoe
Irwin, Inez Leonore Haynes Gillmore
James, Will Roderick
Jamison, Cecilia Viets
Janvier, Margaret Thomson
Johnson, Crockett
Johnson, Osa
Johnston, Annie Fellows *Suppl. 1*
Judson, Emily Chubbuck
Kelland, Clarence Budington
Kelly, Myra
Kent, Jack
Krapp, George Philip
Lathbury, Mary Artemisia
Leaf, Munro
McGinley, Phyllis
McIntosh, Maria Jane

Miller, Olive Beaupré
Montgomery, Elizabeth Rider
Moore, Clara Sophia Jessup Bloomfield
Nash, Ogden
Newcomb, Harvey
O'Hara, Mary
Orton, Helen Fuller
Parish, Peggy
Parrish, Anne
Parrish, Maxfield
Patten, Gilbert
Perkins, Lucy Fitch
Porter, Eleanor Hodgman
Prentiss, Elizabeth Payson
Pyle, Howard
Rey, H. A.
Richards, Laura Elizabeth Howe
Sargent, Epes
Sawyer, Ruth
Scarry, Richard McClure
Scudder, Horace Elisha
Selden, George
Stratemeyer, Edward
Tunis, John R.
Very, Lydia Louisa Ann
Wells, Carolyn
White, E. B.
White, Eliza Orne
Wibberley, Leonard
Widdemer, Margaret
Wilder, Laura Ingalls
Woolsey, Sarah Chauncy

Cookbook / Food Writers

Beard, James Andrews
Becker, Marion Rombauer
Chen, Joyce
Claiborne, Craig *Suppl. 2*
Corson, Juliet
Farmer, Fannie Merritt
Fisher, M. F. K.
Gaige, Crosby
Gibbons, Euell Theophilus
Herrick, Christine Terhune
Hines, Duncan
Jaramillo, Cleofas Martínez
Kander, Lizzie Black
Leslie, Eliza
Lincoln, Mary Johnson Bailey

Parloa, Maria
Randolph, Mary
Rombauer, Irma
Root, Waverley
Rorer, Sarah Tyson
Terhune, Mary Virginia Hawes
Toklas, Alice B.
Vanderbilt, Amy

Diarists

Andrews, Eliza Frances
Ballard, Martha Moore
Bentley, William
Breen, Patrick
Bridge, Horatio
Browder, George Richard
Burr, Esther Edwards
Carter, Landon
Chesnut, Mary Boykin Miller
Delano, Amasa
Doten, Alfred
Drinker, Elizabeth
Ellis, Edward Robb *Suppl. 1*
Emerson, Mary Moody
Ferguson, Elizabeth Graeme
Fields, Annie Adams
Green, Ely
Grimké, Charlotte Forten
Harmon, Daniel Williams
Heaton, Hannah Cook
Hone, Philip
James, Alice
Johnson, William (1809–1851)
Jones, John Beauchamp
Knight, Sarah Kemble
Langford, Nathaniel Pitt
Larpenteur, Charles
Maclay, William
Manly, William Lewis
Marshall, Christopher
Mencken, H. L.
Merton, Thomas
Miller, David Hunter
Moran, Benjamin
Newcomb, Charles King
Nin, Anaïs
Ramsay, Martha Laurens
Robinson, Harriet Jane Hanson
Sewall, Samuel
Smith, Elihu Hubbard
Smith, Richard

**Literature and
Journalism** *(cont.)*
Strong, George
  Templeton
Thoreau, Henry David
Welles, Gideon
Wister, Sarah

Dramatists
Aiken, George L.
Akins, Zoë
Anderson, Garland
Anderson, Maxwell
Ardrey, Robert
Armstrong, Paul
Asch, Sholem
Bacon, Frank
Baker, Benjamin
  Archibald
Balderston, John Lloyd
Barnes, Charlotte Mary
  Sanford
Barnes, Djuna
Barry, Philip
Barrymore, Maurice
Baum, L. Frank
Behrman, S. N.
Belasco, David
Bernard, John
Biggers, Earl Derr
Bird, Robert
  Montgomery
Blossom, Henry Martyn,
  Jr.
Boker, George Henry
Bolton, Guy Reginald
Bonner, Marita Odette
Boucicault, Dion
Bowles, Jane
Brecht, Bertolt
Broadhurst, George
  Howells
Brougham, John
Brown, Alice
Brown, William
  Alexander
Brown, William Hill
Burgoyne, John
Burk, John Daly
Burnett, Frances
  Hodgson
Burnside, R. H.
Burrows, Abe *Suppl. 1*
Bush-Banks, Olivia
  Ward
Bynner, Witter
Caldwell, Anne
Campbell, Bartley, Jr.
Cannon, Charles James
Carleton, Henry Guy
Caspary, Vera

Chase, Mary Coyle
Chayefsky, Paddy
Clarke, Joseph Ignatius
  Constantine
Cohan, George M.
Cohen, Octavus Roy
Collens, Thomas
  Wharton
Connelly, Marc
Conrad, Robert Taylor
Cook, George Cram
Coward, Noël
Cowl, Jane
Craven, Frank
Crawford, John Wallace
Crothers, Rachel
Crouse, Russel
  McKinley
Cullen, Countée
Custis, George
  Washington Parke
Daggett, Rollin Mallory
Daly, Augustin
Da Silva, Howard
Davenport, Benjamin
  Butler
Davis, Owen Gould
Dazey, Charles T.
de Mille, Henry
  Churchill
de Mille, William
  Churchill
Denham, Reginald
Ditrichstein, Leo
Dix, Beulah Marie
Donnelly, Dorothy
  Agnes
Dunlap, William
Dunning, Philip Hart
Ephron, Phoebe, and
  Henry Ephron
Ferber, Edna
Feuchtwanger, Lion
Field, Joseph M.
Fields, Joseph Albert
Fiske, Minnie Maddern
Fitch, Clyde
Flavin, Martin Archer
Flexner, Anne Crawford
  Suppl. 1
Ford, Harriet French
Franken, Rose Dorothy
Frings, Ketti
Gale, Zona
Gayler, Charles
Gillette, William Hooker
Glaspell, Susan Keating
Godfrey, Thomas
  (1736–1763)
Golden, John

Goodman, Kenneth
  Sawyer
Gordin, Jacob
Gordon, Ruth
Gordone, Charles
  Suppl. 2
Graham, Shirley *Suppl. 1*
Green, Paul
Hansberry, Lorraine
  Vivian
Harrigan, Ned
Hart, Moss
Hatton, Fanny Cottinet
  Locke
Hawkes, John *Suppl. 1*
Hecht, Ben
Heggen, Thomas
Helburn, Theresa
Heller, Joseph *Suppl. 1*
Hellman, Lillian
Herbert, F. Hugh
Herne, James A.
Heyward, DuBose
Hill, Abram
Hirschbein, Peretz
Hobart, George V.
Hodge, William Thomas
Hopwood, Avery
Hornblow, Arthur, Sr.
Howard, Bronson
  Crocker
Howard, Sidney Coe
Hoyt, Charles Hale
Hughes, Hatcher
Hull, Henry
Inge, William
Isherwood, Christopher
Jessop, George H.
Johnson, Georgia
  Douglas
Kanin, Garson *Suppl. 1*
Kaufman, George S.
Keene, Laura
Kelly, George Edward
Kennedy, Charles Rann
Klein, Charles
Kober, Arthur
Kummer, Clare Rodman
  Beecher
Langner, Lawrence
Lawson, James
Lawson, John Howard
Leonard, William Ellery
Lerner, Alan Jay
Lewis, Estelle Anna
  Blanche Robinson
Lindsay, Howard
Logan, C. A.
Logan, Joshua
Long, John Luther
Luce, Clare Boothe

Ludlam, Charles
MacArthur, Charles
  Gordon
MacKaye, Hazel
MacKaye, Percy
MacKaye, Steele
MacLeish, Archibald
Mann, Klaus Heinrich
  Thomas
Mann, Louis
Manners, John Hartley
Markoe, Peter
Marqués, René
Mathews, Cornelius
Mayo, Frank
Mayo, Margaret
McCord, Louisa
  Susannah Cheves
McCullers, Carson
Megrue, Roi Cooper
Miller, Alice Duer
Mitchell, Langdon
  Elwyn
Mitchell, Thomas
Moeller, Philip
Moody, William Vaughn
Morton, Martha
Munford, Robert, III
Muse, Clarence E.
Nash, N. Richard
  Suppl. 2
Nichols, Anne
Noah, Mordecai Manuel
Nugent, Elliott
Odets, Clifford
O'Neill, Eugene
Osborn, Paul
Payne, John Howard
Peabody, Josephine
  Preston
Perelman, S. J.
Piñero, Miguel *Suppl. 2*
Pollock, Channing
Porter, Charlotte
  Endymion
Potter, Paul Meredith
Powell, Dawn *Suppl. 1*
Raphaelson, Samson
Rice, Elmer
Riggs, Lynn *Suppl. 2*
Riley, Alice C. D.
Rinehart, Mary Roberts
Rives, Amélie
Robinson, Harriet Jane
  Hanson
Sackler, Howard Oliver
Saroyan, William
Sawyer, Lemuel, Jr.
Séjour, Victor
Sexton, Anne Gray
  Harvey

Literature and Journalism (*cont.*)

Shaw, Irwin
Sheldon, Edward Brewster
Sherwood, Robert Emmet
Skinner, Cornelia Otis
Sklar, George
Smith, Betty
Smith, Elihu Hubbard
Smith, Richard Penn
Smith, William Henry (1806–1872)
Smith, Winchell
Spewack, Samuel, and Bella Spewack
Stallings, Laurence Tucker
Stone, John Augustus
Strong, Austin
Sturges, Preston
Tarkington, Booth
Taylor, Charles Alonzo
Teichmann, Howard Miles
Thompson, Denman
Thompson, Eloise Alberta Veronica
Thurman, Wallace
Totheroh, Dan
Treadwell, Sophie Anita
Tyler, Royall
Van Druten, John
Veiller, Bayard
Wallack, Lester
Walter, Eugene
Ward, Theodore James
Wexley, John
Wheeler, Hugh Callingham
Wilder, Thornton
Williams, Jesse Lynch
Williams, Tennessee
Wilson, Harry Leon
Woodworth, Samuel
Young, Rida Johnson
Young, Stark

Essayists

Abbey, Edward
Ames, Fisher
Andrews, Eliza Frances
Applegate, Jesse
Appleton, Thomas Gold
Bacon, Leonard Woolsey
Baldwin, James
Behrman, S. N.
Benson, Eugene
Bissell, Emily Perkins
Blake, Mary Elizabeth

Bonner, Marita Odette
Bonner, Sherwood
Brodsky, Joseph *Suppl. 1*
Brown, Sterling Allen
Brown, William Hill
Carruth, Hayden
Chandler, Elizabeth Margaret
Chapman, John Jay
Crafts, William
Dana, Richard Henry
Davidson, Donald Grady
De Casseres, Benjamin
Dennie, Joseph
Dodge, Mary Abigail
Elliott, George Paul
Ellison, Ralph Waldo
Emerson, Ralph Waldo
Fullerton, William Morton *Suppl. 2*
Gerould, Katharine Fullerton
Gilbert, Henry Franklin Belknap
Giles, William Branch
Goldman, Richard Franko *Suppl. 2*
Grimké, Charlotte Forten
Hall, Sarah Ewing
Hanson, Alexander Contee (1749–1806)
Hartley, Marsden
Hayne, Paul Hamilton
Herrick, Robert Welch
Hodes, Art
Hoffer, Eric
Hopkinson, Francis
Huneker, James Gibbons
Huxley, Aldous
Jovanovich, William *Suppl. 2*
Lazarus, Emma
Le Gallienne, Richard
Lindbergh, Anne Morrow *Suppl. 2*
Livingston, William
Lorde, Audre *Suppl. 2*
Lowell, James Russell
Marqués, René
Martin, Anne Henrietta
McGinley, Phyllis
Mencken, H. L.
Merton, Thomas
Miller, Kelly
More, Paul Elmer
Morley, Christopher Darlington
Morris, Willie *Suppl. 1*

Murray, Judith Sargent Stevens
Nye, Bill
O'Conor, John F. X. *Suppl. 2*
Olson, Charles John
Piatt, John James
Plato, Ann *Suppl. 2*
Repplier, Agnes
Richter, Conrad Michael
Robinson, Rowland Evans
Rosenfeld, Paul Leopold
Royce, Josiah
Russell, Charles Marion
Saltus, Edgar Evertson
Smith, Elizabeth Oakes
Smith, Lillian Eugenia
Smith, Logan Pearsall
Smith, William Loughton
Spofford, Harriet Elizabeth Prescott
Stuart, Jesse Hilton
Terhune, Albert Payson
Thaxter, Celia *Suppl. 1*
Thoreau, Henry David
Thornton, William
Tolson, Melvin Beaunorus
Townsend, Mary Ashley
Turnbull, Robert James
Tyler, Royall
Warner, Charles Dudley
West, Anthony
Whitaker, Daniel Kimball
White, E. B.
Whiting, Lilian

Etiquette Writers

Moore, Clara Sophia Jessup Bloomfield
Post, Emily
Tuthill, Louisa Caroline Huggins
Vanderbilt, Amy

Fiction Writers

Aarons, Edward Sidney
Abbey, Edward
Adams, Alice *Suppl. 2*
Adams, Andy
Adams, Henry
Adams, Samuel Hopkins
Agee, James Rufus
Aiken, Conrad
Alcott, Louisa May
Aldrich, Bess Streeter
Aldrich, Thomas Bailey
Alger, Horatio, Jr.

Algren, Nelson
Allen, Henry Wilson, Jr.
Allen, Hervey
Allen, James Lane
Ames, Mary Clemmer
Anderson, Sherwood
Andrews, Eliza Frances
Andrews, Mary Raymond Shipman
Andrews, V. C.
Angoff, Charles
Appel, Benjamin
Ardrey, Robert
Arenas, Reinaldo
Arlen, Michael
Arnold, Elliott
Arnow, Harriette Simpson
Arthur, Timothy Shay
Asch, Nathan
Asch, Sholem
Asimov, Isaac
Atherton, Gertrude Franklin
Austin, Jane Goodwin
Bacheller, Irving
Bailey, Temple
Baker, Dorothy Dodds
Baldwin, Faith
Baldwin, James
Baldwin, Joseph Glover
Ballou, Maturin Murray
Banning, Margaret Culkin
Barnes, Djuna
Barr, Amelia Edith Huddleston
Barthelme, Donald
Basso, Hamilton
Baum, Vicki
Baylor, Frances Courtenay
Beach, Rex
Beers, Ethel Lynn
Bellamy, Edward
Bellamy, Elizabeth Whitfield Croom
Benét, Stephen Vincent
Benchley, Nathaniel Goddard
Bernstein, Aline Frankau
Bernstein, Herman
Bessie, Alvah
Bianco, Margery Winifred Williams
Bierce, Ambrose Gwinnett
Biggers, Earl Derr
Binns, Archie
Bird, Robert Montgomery

**Literature and
Journalism** *(cont.)*
Bishop, John Peale
Bissell, Emily Perkins
Blake, Lillie Devereux
Bleecker, Ann Eliza
Bodenheim, Maxwell
Bolton, Guy Reginald
Bonner, Marita Odette
Bonner, Sherwood
Bonnin, Gertrude
  Simmons
Bontemps, Arna
  Wendell
Bowen, Catherine
  Drinker
Bowles, Jane
Bowles, Paul *Suppl. 1*
Boyd, James
Boyesen, Hjalmar Hjorth
Boyle, Kay
Brackenridge, Hugh
  Henry
Brackett, Charles
  William
Bradford, Ebenezer
Bradford, Roark
  Whitney Wickliffe
Brady, Cyrus Townsend
Brautigan, Richard
Bremer, Fredrika
Brewster, Anne
  Hampton
Bromfield, Louis
Brooks, Gwendolyn
  Suppl. 2
Brown, Alice
Brown, Charles
  Brockden
Brown, William Hill
Brown, William Wells
Buck, Pearl S.
Buckmaster, Henrietta
Bukowski, Charles
Bunner, Henry Cuyler
Burke, Kenneth
Burnett, Frances
  Hodgson
Burnett, W. R.
Burnett, Whit
Burnham, Clara Louise
  Root
Burns, John Horne
Burroughs, Edgar Rice
Burroughs, William S.
  Suppl. 1
Burt, Struthers
Bush-Banks, Olivia
  Ward
Cabell, James Branch

Cable, George
  Washington
Cahan, Abraham
Cahill, Holger
Cain, James M.
Caldwell, Erskine
Caldwell, Taylor
Calkins, Clinch
Calvert, George Henry
Campbell, Walter
  Stanley
Cannon, Charles James
Cannon, Cornelia James
Cantwell, Robert
  Emmett
Capote, Truman
Carr, John Dickson
Carrington, Elaine
  Sterne
Caruthers, William
  Alexander
Carver, Raymond
Cary, Alice
Caspary, Vera
Cather, Willa
Catherwood, Mary
  Hartwell
Chambers, Robert
  William
Chandler, Raymond
  Thornton
Chase, Ilka
Chase, Mary Ellen
Chateaubriand,
  François-René de
Cheever, John
Chesebrough, Caroline
Chesnutt, Charles
  Waddell
Chester, George
  Randolph
Childs, Marquis *Suppl. 2*
Chopin, Kate O'Flaherty
Churchill, Winston
Chute, Beatrice Joy
Clark, Walter Van
  Tilburg
Clavell, James
Clemens, Jeremiah
Coates, Robert Myron
Cobb, Irvin Shrewsbury
Cobb, Sylvanus, Jr.
Coffin, Charles Carleton
Cohen, Octavus Roy
Collens, Thomas
  Wharton
Collinge, Patricia
Comfort, Will Levington
Condon, Richard
  Suppl. 1
Connell, Richard

Conroy, Jack
Cook, George Cram
Cooke, John Esten
  (1830–1886)
Cooke, Philip Pendleton
Cooke, Rose Terry
Coolidge, Dane
Cooper, James Fenimore
Corle, Edwin
Corrington, John
  William
Costain, Thomas
  Bertram
Cozzens, Frederick
  Swartwout
Cozzens, James Gould
Crane, Anne Moncure
Crane, Stephen
Crawford, F. Marion
Cummins, Maria
  Susanna
Curtis, George William
Curwood, James Oliver
Cutler, Lizzie Petit
Daggett, Rollin Mallory
Dahlberg, Edward
Dana, Richard Henry, Jr.
Dannay, Frederic
Dargan, Olive Tilford
Davis, Clyde Brion
Davis, Harold Lenoir
Davis, Mary Evelyn
  Moore
Davis, Rebecca Blaine
  Harding
Davis, Richard Harding
Davis, Samuel Post
Davis, William Stearns
de Camp, L. Sprague
  Suppl. 1
De Forest, John William
DeJong, David Cornel
Deland, Margaret
De Leon, Thomas
  Cooper
Dell, Floyd James
Deming, Philander
Denison, Mary Andrews
Derleth, August William
Dickey, James *Suppl. 2*
Digges, Thomas
  Attwood
Donn-Byrne, Brian
  Oswald Patrick
Dorr, Julia Caroline
  Ripley
Dorris, Michael *Suppl. 2*
Dorsey, Anna Hanson
  McKenney
Dorsey, Sarah Anne Ellis
Dos Passos, John

Douglas, Lloyd Cassel
Dreiser, Theodore
Dromgoole, Will Allen
Duganne, Augustine
  Joseph Hickey
Dunbar, Paul Laurence
Dupuy, Eliza Ann
Eastman, Mary
  Henderson
Eaton, Edith Maude
Eberhart, Mignon G.
  Suppl. 1
Edmonds, Walter D.
  Suppl. 1
Edwards, Harry Stillwell
Edwards, Leo *Suppl. 2*
Eggleston, Edward
Eggleston, George Cary
Elder, Susan Blanchard
Eliade, Mircea
Ellin, Stanley Bernard
Elliott, George Paul
Elliott, Sarah Barnwell
Ellison, Ralph Waldo
Exley, Frederick *Suppl. 2*
Fante, John Thomas
Farrell, James T.
Faulkner, William
Fauset, Jessie Redmon
Faust, Frederick Schiller
Fay, Theodore Sedgwick
Fearing, Kenneth
  Flexner
Ferber, Edna
Fern, Fanny
Feuchtwanger, Lion
Finley, Martha
Finn, Francis James
Fisher, Dorothy F.
  Canfield
Fisher, Rudolph
Fisher, Vardis Alvero
Fitzgerald, F. Scott
Flagg, Edmund
Flavin, Martin Archer
Fletcher, Inglis
Foley, Martha
Foote, Mary Anna
  Hallock
Forbes, Esther
Ford, Paul Leicester
Forester, C. S.
Foster, Hannah Webster
Fox, John, Jr.
Frank, Waldo David
Franken, Rose Dorothy
Frederic, Harold
Freeman, Cynthia
Freeman, Mary Eleanor
  Wilkins
French, Alice

Literature and Journalism *(cont.)*

French, Lucy Virginia Smith
Fuller, Henry Blake
Gaddis, William *Suppl. 1*
Gale, Zona
Gallico, Paul William
Galt, John
Gardner, Erle Stanley
Garland, Hamlin
Gerould, Katharine Fullerton
Gerson, Noel Bertram
Gibbs, Arthur Hamilton
Gill, Brendan *Suppl. 2*
Gilman, Caroline Howard
Gilman, Charlotte Perkins
Glasgow, Ellen
Glaspell, Susan Keating
Gold, Michael
Gonzales, Ambrose Elliott
Gordon, Caroline Ferguson
Gorey, Edward *Suppl. 2*
Grant, Robert
Green, Anna Katharine
Green, Asa
Greene, Sarah Pratt McLean
Grey, Zane
Grierson, Francis
Griffin, John Howard
Griggs, Sutton E.
Guthrie, A. B., Jr.
Haldeman-Julius, Emanuel
Hale, Edward Everett
Hale, Nancy
Haley, Alex
Hall, James (1793–1868)
Hamilton, Alexander (1712–1756)
Hammett, Dashiell
Hammett, Samuel Adams
Harben, William Nathaniel
Harland, Henry
Harper, Frances Ellen Watkins
Harris, Corra
Harris, Frank
Harris, Miriam Coles
Harrison, Constance Cary
Harrison, Henry Sydnor
Harte, Bret

Hatton, Ann Julia Kemble
Hawkes, John *Suppl. 1*
Hawthorne, Julian
Hawthorne, Nathaniel
Haycox, Ernest *Suppl. 1*
Hayes, Alfred
Heard, Gerald
Heath, James Ewell
Hecht, Ben
Heggen, Thomas
Heinlein, Robert Anson
Heller, Joseph *Suppl. 1*
Hemingway, Ernest
Hentz, Caroline Lee Whiting
Herbert, F. Hugh
Herbert, Frank
Herbst, Josephine Frey
Hergesheimer, Joseph
Herrick, Robert Welch
Hersey, John Richard
Heyward, DuBose
Higgins, George V. *Suppl. 2*
Highsmith, Patricia *Suppl. 2*
Hill, Grace Livingston
Hillyer, Robert Silliman
Himes, Chester Bomar
Hobart, Alice Tisdale
Hobson, Laura Keane Zametkin
Hoffman, Charles Fenno
Holland, Josiah Gilbert *Suppl. 1*
Holley, Marietta
Holmes, Mary Jane Hawes
Hopkins, Pauline Elizabeth
Horgan, Paul *Suppl. 2*
Hornblow, Arthur, Sr.
Hosmer, Hezekiah Lord
Hough, Emerson
Howard, Blanche Willis
Howard, Robert E. *Suppl. 1*
Howe, Edgar Watson
Howe, Helen
Howells, William Dean
Hoyer, Linda Grace
Hughes, Rupert
Huie, William Bradford
Hurst, Fannie
Hurston, Zora Neale
Huxley, Aldous
Ingraham, Joseph Holt
Ingraham, Prentiss
Irving, Washington

Irwin, Inez Leonore Haynes Gillmore
Isherwood, Christopher
Jackson, Helen Hunt
Jackson, Shirley
James, Henry (1843–1916)
Jamison, Cecilia Viets
Janney, Russell Dixon
Jessop, George H.
Jewett, Sarah Orne
Johnson, James Weldon
Johnson, Owen McMahon
Johnston, Mary
Johnston, Richard Malcolm
Jones, James
Jones, James Athearn
Jones, John Beauchamp
Jordan, Elizabeth Garver
Judd, Sylvester
Judson, Edward Zane Carroll
Judson, Emily Chubbuck
Kantor, MacKinlay
Kelland, Clarence Budington
Kelley, Edith Summers
Kelly, Florence Finch
Kemp, Harry Hibbard
Kennedy, John Pendleton
Kerouac, Jack
Kerr, Sophie
Kesey, Ken *Suppl. 2*
Keyes, Frances Parkinson
Killens, John Oliver
King, Edward Smith
King, Grace Elizabeth
King, Susan Petigru
Kinzie, Juliette Augusta Magill
Kirkland, Joseph
Knowles, John *Suppl. 2*
Kober, Arthur
Kosinski, Jerzy Nikodem
Krause, Herbert Arthur
Kronenberger, Louis
Kyne, Peter Bernard
La Farge, Oliver Hazard Perry
Lamb, Martha Joanna R. N.
L'Amour, Louis Dearborn
Lanusse, Armand
Larsen, Nella
Lathrop, Rose Hawthorne

Latimer, Elizabeth Wormeley
Latimer, Margery Bodine
Leech, Margaret Kernochan
Le Gallienne, Richard
Lennox, Charlotte Ramsay
Lewis, Alfred Henry
Lewis, Janet *Suppl. 1*
Lewis, Sinclair
Lewisohn, Ludwig
Libbey, Laura Jean
Lin Yutang
Lincoln, Joseph Crosby
Lincoln, Victoria Endicott
Lippard, George
Little, Sophia Louisa Robbins
Lockridge, Richard
Lockridge, Ross Franklin, Jr.
London, Jack
Long, John Luther
Loos, Anita
Lovecraft, H. P.
Lumpkin, Grace
Lumpkin, Katharine Du Pre
Lunt, George
MacDonald, John D.
Macdonald, Ross
MacInnes, Helen
Maclean, Norman
Magruder, Julia
Major, Charles
Malamud, Bernard
Maltz, Albert
Mann, Klaus Heinrich Thomas
Mann, Thomas
March, William
Marqués, René
Marquand, J. P.
Marquis, Don
Marshall, Catherine
Martin, George Madden *Suppl. 1*
Martineau, Harriet
Mason, F. Van Wyck
Mathews, Cornelius
Mayo, William Starbuck
McAlmon, Robert Menzies
McCarthy, Mary
McCoy, Horace Stanley
McCrackin, Josephine
McCullers, Carson

Literature and Journalism *(cont.)*

McCutcheon, George Barr
McElroy, John (1846–1929)
McHenry, James (1785–1845)
McIntosh, Maria Jane
McKay, Claude
McKenney, Ruth
McMahon, Thomas A. *Suppl. 2*
Melville, Herman
Mercier, Alfred
Metalious, Grace
Micheaux, Oscar
Michener, James *Suppl. 1*
Miller, Alice Duer
Miller, Henry (1891–1980)
Miller, Joaquin
Miller, Merle
Mitchell, Edward Page
Mitchell, Margaret
Mitchell, S. Weir
Moore, Clara Sophia Jessup Bloomfield
Moore, John Trotwood
Morley, Christopher Darlington
Morris, Wright *Suppl. 1*
Morrow, Honoré Willsie
Motley, Willard Francis
Mourning Dove
Mulford, Clarence Edward
Munsey, Frank Andrew
Murfree, Mary Noailles
Nabokov, Vladimir
Nash, N. Richard *Suppl. 2*
Nathan, Robert
Neal, John
Nemerov, Howard
Newman, Frances
Nicholson, Meredith
Nin, Anaïs
Niven, David
Nordhoff, Charles Bernard, and James Norman Hall *Suppl. 1*
Norris, Charles Gilman Smith
Norris, Frank
Norris, Kathleen Thompson
Norris, Mary Harriott
Nugent, Richard Bruce *Suppl. 2*

O'Connor, Edwin Greene
O'Connor, Flannery
O'Connor, William Douglas
O'Hara, John Henry
O'Neill, Rose Cecil
Oppenheim, James
O'Reilly, John Boyle
Ostenso, Martha
Page, Thomas Nelson
Pancake, Breece Dexter
Parker, Dorothy
Parrish, Anne
Patchen, Kenneth
Patten, Gilbert
Paul, Elliot
Pennell, Joseph Stanley
Percy, Walker
Perelman, S. J.
Peterkin, Julia Mood
Phelps, Elizabeth Stuart
Phelps, Elizabeth Wooster Stuart
Phillips, David Graham
Pike, Mary Hayden Green
Plath, Sylvia
Poe, Edgar Allan
Pool, Maria Louise
Poole, Ernest
Porter, Eleanor Hodgman
Porter, Katherine Anne
Porter, William Sydney
Post, Melville Davisson
Powell, Dawn *Suppl. 1*
Powers, J. F. *Suppl. 2*
Prentiss, Elizabeth Payson
Prouty, Olive Higgins
Putnam, Nina Wilcox
Puzo, Mario *Suppl. 1*
Rölvaag, Ole Edvart
Rand, Ayn
Raphaelson, Samson
Rawlings, Marjorie Kinnan
Read, Opie Percival
Reece, Byron Herbert
Reed, Myrtle
Reid, Mayne
Renoir, Jean
Rhodes, Eugene Manlove
Rice, Alice Caldwell Hegan
Richter, Conrad Michael
Ridge, John Rollin
Rinehart, Mary Roberts
Rivera, Tomás

Rives, Amélie
Rives, Hallie Erminie
Robbins, Harold *Suppl. 1*
Roberts, Elizabeth Madox
Roberts, Kenneth
Robins, Elizabeth
Robinson, Rowland Evans
Roe, Edward Payson
Roosevelt, Elliott
Rosenfeld, Paul Leopold
Rosten, Leo *Suppl. 1*
Roth, Henry
Rowson, Susanna Haswell
Runyon, Damon
Russell, Charles Marion
Ruxton, George Augustus Frederick
Saltus, Edgar Evertson
Sandoz, Mari
Santayana, George
Saroyan, William
Sarton, May
Scarborough, Dorothy
Schorer, Mark
Scott, Evelyn
Scott, Leroy Martin
Seager, Allan
Sealsfield, Charles
Seawell, Molly Elliot
Sedgwick, Anne Douglas
Sedgwick, Catharine Maria
Seifert, Elizabeth
Seton, Anya
Shaw, Irwin
Shecut, John Linnaeus Edward Whitridge
Sheean, Vincent *Suppl. 1*
Shellabarger, Samuel (1888–1954)
Sheppard, Eugenia
Short, Luke
Simak, Clifford D. *Suppl. 2*
Simms, William Gilmore
Sinclair, Upton
Singer, Isaac Bashevis
Singer, Israel Joshua
Skinner, Constance Lindsay
Sklar, George
Slesinger, Tess
Smith, Betty
Smith, Chard Powers
Smith, Elizabeth Oakes
Smith, Francis Hopkinson

Smith, Lillian Eugenia
Smith, Margaret Bayard
Smith, Thorne
Snelling, William Joseph
Southworth, Emma Dorothy Eliza Nevitte
Spalding, Henry Stanislaus *Suppl. 2*
Spofford, Harriet Elizabeth Prescott
Stafford, Jean
Stallings, Laurence Tucker
Steele, Wilbur Daniel
Stegner, Wallace Earle
Stein, Gertrude
Steinbeck, John
Stephens, Ann Sophia Winterbotham
Stevenson, Robert Louis
Stewart, Donald Ogden
Stockton, Frank Richard
Stoddard, Elizabeth Drew Barstow
Stone, Irving
Storm, Hans Otto
Stout, Rex
Stowe, Harriet Beecher
Stratton-Porter, Gene
Stribling, T. S.
Strother, David Hunter
Stuart, Jesse Hilton
Stuart, Ruth McEnery
Sturgeon, Theodore
Suckow, Ruth
Susann, Jacqueline
Swados, Harvey
Tarkington, Booth
Taylor, Bayard
Taylor, Peter Hillsman
Taylor, Phoebe Atwood
Tenney, Tabitha Gilman
Terhune, Albert Payson
Terhune, Mary Virginia Hawes
Testut, Charles
Thayer, Tiffany
Thomes, William Henry
Thompson, Eloise Alberta Veronica
Thompson, Jim *Suppl. 2*
Thompson, Maurice
Thompson, William Tappan
Throop, George Higby
Thurman, Wallace
Tiernan, Frances Christine Fisher
Tiernan, Mary Spear Nicholas
Tobenkin, Elias

**Literature and
Journalism** *(cont.)*
Tompkins, Juliet Wilbor
Toole, John Kennedy
Toomer, Jean
Tourgée, Albion
  Winegar
Train, Arthur
Trollope, Frances
Trowbridge, John
  Townsend
Trumbo, Dalton
Tully, Jim
Turner, George Kibbe
Twain, Mark
Tyler, Royall
Van Doren, Dorothy
  Suppl. 1
Van Slyke, Helen Lenore
  Vogt
Van Vechten, Carl
van Vogt, A. E. *Suppl. 1*
Verrill, Alpheus Hyatt
Very, Lydia Louisa Ann
Walker, Margaret
  Suppl. 1
Wallace, Irving
Wallace, Lew
Walworth, Jeannette
  Ritchie Hadermann
Ward, Herbert
  Dickinson
Ware, William
Warfield, Catherine Ann
  Ware
Warman, Cy
Warner, Charles Dudley
Warner, Susan Bogert
Warren, Robert Penn
Webb, Frank J. *Suppl. 2*
Webber, Charles Wilkins
Webster, Jean
Wells, Carolyn
Wells, Helena
Welty, Eudora *Suppl. 2*
Wertenbaker, Charles
  Christian
Wescott, Glenway
West, Anthony
West, Jessamyn
West, Nathanael
Weston, Christine
Wexley, John
Wharton, Edith
Wheeler, Hugh
  Callingham
White, Eliza Orne
White, Helen Constance
White, Stewart Edward
White, William Allen
Whitlock, Brand

Wibberley, Leonard
Widdemer, Margaret
Wiggin, Kate Douglas
Wilbarger, John Wesley
Wilder, Thornton
Williams, Ben Ames
Williams, Catharine
  Read Arnold
Williams, Jesse Lynch
Williams, Tennessee
Williams, William
  (1727–1791)
Williams, William Carlos
Willis, Nathaniel Parker
Wilson, Augusta Jane
  Evans
Wilson, Edmund
Wilson, Harriet E.
Wilson, Harry Leon
Winthrop, Theodore
Wister, Owen
Wodehouse, P. G.
Wolf, Emma
Wolfe, Thomas
Wood, Sally Sayward
  Barrell Keating
Woodrow, Nancy Mann
  Waddel
Woods, Katharine
  Pearson
Woolley, Celia Parker
Woolrich, Cornell
Woolson, Constance
  Fenimore
Wright, Austin Tappan
Wright, Harold Bell
Wright, Richard
Wright, Willard
  Huntington
Wylie, Elinor
Wylie, Philip Gordon
Yerby, Frank *Suppl. 1*
Yezierska, Anzia
Yourcenar, Marguerite
Zevin, Israel Joseph
Zugsmith, Leane

Humorists
Adams, Franklin P.
Ade, George
Ameringer, Oscar
Armour, Richard Willard
Bagby, George William
Baldwin, Joseph Glover
Bangs, John Kendrick
Bemelmans, Ludwig
Benchley, Robert
Billings, Josh
Bombeck, Erma *Suppl. 1*
Browne, Charles Farrar
Burgess, Gelett

Carruth, Hayden
Cerf, Bennett Alfred
Clark, Charles Heber
Cobb, Irvin Shrewsbury
Cozzens, Frederick
  Swartwout
Cuppy, William Jacob
Daly, Thomas Augustine
Day, Clarence Shepard,
  Jr.
Delano, Alonzo
De Quille, Dan
Derby, George Horatio
Faulk, John Henry
Field, Joseph M.
Frost, Arthur Burdett
Green, Asa
Hale, Lucretia Peabody
Hammett, Samuel
  Adams
Harris, George
  Washington
Harris, Joel Chandler
Herford, Oliver
Hooper, Johnson Jones
Jones, Hamilton C.
Lamar, John Basil
Landon, Melville De
  Lancey
Lardner, Ring
Leland, Charles Godfrey
Levenson, Sam
Lewis, Charles Bertrand
Lewis, Henry Clay
Locke, David Ross
Longstreet, Augustus
  Baldwin
Loomis, Charles Battell
Lukens, Henry Clay
MacDonald, Betty
Marquis, Don
Mason, Walt
McKenney, Ruth
Nash, Ogden
Newell, Robert Henry
  Suppl. 2
Nye, Bill
Parker, Dorothy
Peck, George Wilbur
Putnam, Nina Wilcox
Read, Opie Percival
Rogers, Will
Shepherd, Jean *Suppl. 1*
Smith, Charles Henry
Smith, H. Allen
Smith, Seba
Smith, Thorne
Streeter, Edward
Sullivan, Frank
Taliaferro, Hardin
  Edwards

Taylor, Bert Leston
Thompson, William
  Tappan
Thomson, Mortimer
  Neal
Thurber, James
Townsend, Mary Ashley
Twain, Mark
Warner, Anne
  Richmond
Wells, Carolyn
Westcott, Edward Noyes
Whitcher, Frances
  Miriam Berry
White, E. B.
Zevin, Israel Joseph

Letter Writers
Adams, Abigail
Agee, James Rufus
Bowne, Eliza Southgate
Bruns, Henriette
Clappe, Louise Amelia
  Knapp Smith
Emerson, Mary Moody
Ferguson, Elizabeth
  Graeme
Fields, Annie Adams
Hayne, Paul Hamilton
Lee, Elizabeth Blair
O'Hanlon, Virginia
Ripley, Sarah Alden
  Bradford
Smith, Margaret Bayard
Trumbull, Maria
Wheatley, Phillis
Winthrop, Margaret
Wright, Susanna

Literary Inspirations
Alden, Priscilla Mullins
Alger, William
  Rounseville
Barney, Natalie Clifford
Bishop, John Peale
Calamity Jane
Cassady, Neal
Cody, William Frederick
Falkner, William Clark
Frietschie, Barbara
  Hauer
Gardiner, Sir
  Christopher
Gein, Edward
Glass, Hugh
Henson, Josiah
Hiawatha
Loeb, Jacques
Mallon, Mary
Mesta, Perle
Murphy, Gerald Cleary

Literature and Journalism *(cont.)*
Oberon, Merle
Revere, Paul
Rezanov, Nikolai Petrovich
Rogers, Robert
Story, William Wetmore
Taylor, Edward Thompson
Toklas, Alice B.
Uncas

Medical Writers
Alvarez, Walter Clement
Bache, Franklin
Barrus, Clara
Buchanan, Joseph Rodes
Coxe, John Redman
Dunglison, Robley
Eberle, John
Gould, George Milbry
Harris, Seale
Holmes, Oliver Wendell (1809–1894)
Horner, William Edmonds
Hutchinson, Woods
Hyde, James Nevins
Jacobi, Mary Corinna Putnam
Kelly, Aloysius Oliver Joseph
Lee, Charles Alfred
Lloyd, John Uri
Mumford, James Gregory
Palmer, Alonzo Benjamin
Smith, Elihu Hubbard
Smith, Homer William
Stitt, Edward Rhodes
Terry, Charles Edward
Thorek, Max
Wood, George Bacon
Youmans, William Jay

Nature Writers
Burroughs, John
Carson, Rachel Louise
Cooper, Susan Augusta Fenimore
Crockett, James Underwood *Suppl. 1*
Ditmars, Raymond Lee
Doubleday, Neltje de Graff
Eifert, Virginia S.
Eiseley, Loren Corey
Elliott, William
Herbert, Henry William

Holder, Charles Frederick
Krutch, Joseph Wood
Leopold, Aldo
Miller, Harriet Mann
Mills, Enos Abijah
Muir, John
Olson, Sigurd Ferdinand
Ord, George
Peattie, Donald Culross *Suppl. 1*
Seton, Ernest Thompson
Stratton-Porter, Gene
Teale, Edwin Way
Thomas, Lewis
Van Dyke, John Charles
Webber, Charles Wilkins
Wright, Mabel Osgood

Pamphleteers
Bishop, Abraham
Bollan, William
Callender, James Thomson
Carroll, Anna Ella
Carter, Landon
Dickinson, John (1732–1808)
Flower, Richard
Hay, George
Ingersoll, Charles Jared
Kennedy, Archibald
Knox, William
Lee, Arthur
Paine, Thomas
Pratt, Orson
Stewart, Maria W.
Van Ness, William Peter
Walker, David (1796?–1830)
Ward, Nathaniel
Zubly, John Joachim

Photojournalists
Bourke-White, Margaret
Chapelle, Dickey
Eisenstaedt, Alfred
Hare, James Henry
Rothstein, Arthur
Stryker, Roy Emerson

Poets
Adams, Charles Follen
Adams, John (1705–1740)
Aiken, Conrad
Ainslie, Hew
Aldrich, Thomas Bailey
Allen, Elizabeth Akers
Allen, Hervey
Allen, Paul

Alsop, Richard *Suppl. 1*
Appleton, Thomas Gold
Arensberg, Walter Conrad
Arrington, Alfred W.
Auden, W. H.
Auslander, Joseph
Bacon, Leonard
Banvard, John
Barlow, Joel
Barnitz, Albert Trorillo Siders
Barr, Amelia Edith Huddleston
Bates, Katharine Lee
Beach, Joseph Warren
Beers, Ethel Lynn
Bell, James Madison
Benét, Stephen Vincent
Benét, William Rose
Benjamin, Park
Bennet, Sanford Fillmore
Bennett, Gwendolyn
Berryman, John
Billings, William
Bishop, Elizabeth
Bishop, John Peale
Bissell, Emily Perkins
Blackburn, Paul
Blake, Mary Elizabeth
Bleecker, Ann Eliza
Bloede, Gertrude
Bodenheim, Maxwell
Bogan, Louise
Bolling, Robert
Bontemps, Arna Wendell
Boyd, James
Bradstreet, Anne
Braithwaite, William Stanley Beaumont
Branch, Anna Hempstead
Bremer, Fredrika
Brodsky, Joseph *Suppl. 1*
Brooke, Henry
Brooks, Gwendolyn *Suppl. 2*
Brooks, Maria Gowen
Brooks, Walter Henderson
Brown, Sterling Allen
Brown, William Hill
Brownell, Henry Howard
Bryant, William Cullen
Bukowski, Charles
Burgos, Julia de
Burt, Struthers
Bush-Banks, Olivia Ward

Butler, William Allen *Suppl. 2*
Byles, Mather
Bynner, Witter
Calkins, Clinch
Calvert, George Henry
Campbell, James Edwin
Cane, Melville Henry
Cannon, Charles James
Carman, Bliss
Carmer, Carl Lamson
Carver, Raymond
Cary, Phoebe
Caulkins, Frances Manwaring
Cawein, Madison Julius
Chandler, Elizabeth Margaret
Channing, William Ellery, II
Chapman, John Jay
Chivers, Thomas Holley
Church, Benjamin (1734–1778?)
Ciardi, John
Clampitt, Amy Kathleen
Clarke, Joseph Ignatius Constantine
Clarke, Mary Bayard Devereux
Clarke, McDonald
Cliffton, William
Coffin, Robert Peter Tristram
Conkling, Grace Walcott Hazard
Cook, Ebenezer
Cooke, Philip Pendleton
Coolbrith, Ina
Corrington, John William
Corrothers, James David
Corso, Gregory *Suppl. 2*
Cotter, Joseph Seamon, Sr.
Crafts, William
Cranch, Christopher Pearse
Crane, Hart
Crane, Stephen
Crapsey, Adelaide
Cromwell, Gladys
Crosby, Fanny
Cullen, Countée
Cummings, E. E.
Dabney, Richard
Daggett, Rollin Mallory
Dale, Thomas (1700–1750)
Daly, Thomas Augustine
Dana, Richard Henry

Literature and
Journalism *(cont.)*
Da Ponte, Lorenzo
Dargan, Olive Tilford
Davidson, Donald
  Grady
Davidson, Lucretia
  Maria, and Margaret
  Miller Davidson
Davies, Samuel
Davis, Harold Lenoir
Dawson, William
De Casseres, Benjamin
Denby, Edwin Orr
Deutsch, Babette
Dickey, James *Suppl. 2*
Dickinson, Emily
Dinsmoor, Robert
Doolittle, Hilda
Dorr, Julia Caroline
  Ripley
Drake, Joseph Rodman
Duganne, Augustine
  Joseph Hickey
Dunbar, Paul Laurence
Dunbar-Nelson, Alice
Duncan, Robert Edward
Dwight, Theodore
  (1764–1846)
Eckman, Frederick
  Suppl. 1
Edwards, Harry Stillwell
Eliot, Charlotte Champe
  Stearns
Eliot, T. S.
Ellet, Elizabeth F.
Elwyn, Alfred Langdon
Evans, Donald
Evans, Nathaniel
Fairfield, Sumner
  Lincoln
Fauset, Jessie Redmon
Fearing, Kenneth
  Flexner
Fenollosa, Ernest
  Francisco
Ficke, Arthur Davison
Field, Eugene
Field, Sara Bard
Fields, James Thomas
  Suppl. 2
Fitts, Dudley
Flagg, Edmund
Fletcher, Bridget
  Richardson
Fletcher, John Gould
Foss, Sam Walter
Freneau, Philip Morin
Frost, Robert
Gallagher, William Davis
Garrigue, Jean

Gay, E. Jane
Gibran, Kahlil
Gilder, Richard Watson
Ginsberg, Allen *Suppl. 1*
Giovannitti, Arturo
  Massimo
Godfrey, Thomas
  (1736–1763)
Goodwin, Ruby Berkley
Gould, Hannah Flagg
Grant, Percy Stickney
Grayson, William John
Green, Joseph
Gregory, Horace Victor
Griffitts, Hannah
Grimké, Angelina Weld
Grosz, George
Guest, Edgar Albert
Guiney, Louise Imogen
Hagedorn, Hermann
  Ludwig Gebhard
Halleck, Fitz-Greene
Hammon, Jupiter
Harper, Frances Ellen
  Watkins
Harris, Thomas Lake
Hartley, Marsden
Hatton, Ann Julia
  Kemble
Hayden, Robert Earl
Hayes, Alfred
Hayne, Paul Hamilton
Hays, Will S.
Henderson, Alice Corbin
Herford, Oliver
Heyward, DuBose
Hillyer, Robert Silliman
Hoffman, Charles Fenno
Holmes, Oliver Wendell
  (1809–1894)
Homans, George Caspar
Home, Archibald
Hooper, Ellen Sturgis
Hope, James Barron
Hopkins, Lemuel
Hopkinson, Francis
Horton, George Moses
Hosmer, William Howe
  Cuyler
Hovey, Richard
Howe, Julia Ward
Hubner, Charles William
Hughes, Langston
Hugo, Richard
Humphreys, David
Humphries, Rolfe
Imber, Naphtali Herz
Janvier, Margaret
  Thomson
Jarrell, Randall
Jeffers, Robinson

Johnson, Georgia
  Douglas
Johnson, James Weldon
Jones, Amanda
  Theodosia
Jones, James Athearn
Kaufman, Bob
Kees, Weldon
Keimer, Samuel
Kemp, Harry Hibbard
Kennedy, William
  Sloane
Kerouac, Jack
Killpatrick, James
Kilmer, Joyce
Knight, Etheridge
Krause, Herbert Arthur
Kreymborg, Alfred
  Francis
Lanier, Sidney
Lanusse, Armand
Lathrop, George Parsons
Lathrop, Rose
  Hawthorne
Latil, Alexandre
Lattimore, Richmond
  Alexander
Laughlin, James *Suppl. 1*
Lawson, James
Lazarus, Emma
Lee, Muna
Le Gallienne, Richard
Leland, Charles Godfrey
Leonard, William Ellery
Levertov, Denise
  Suppl. 1
Lewis, Estelle Anna
  Blanche Robinson
Lewis, Janet *Suppl. 1*
Lewis, Richard
Lincoln, Joseph Crosby
Lindsay, Vachel
Linn, John Blair
Linton, William James
Lockridge, Ross
  Franklin, Jr.
Lodge, George Cabot
Longfellow, Henry
  Wadsworth
Lorde, Audre *Suppl. 2*
Lowell, Amy
Lowell, James Russell
Lowell, Maria White
Lowell, Robert
Lowell, Robert Traill
  Spence
Loy, Mina
MacKaye, Percy
MacLeish, Archibald
Malone, Walter
March, Joseph Moncure

Markham, Edwin
Markoe, Peter
Marqués, René
Marquis, Don
Mason, Walt
Masters, Edgar Lee
Mathews, Cornelius
Mayo, Sarah Carter
  Edgarton
McCord, Louisa
  Susannah Cheves
McGinley, Phyllis
McHenry, James
  (1785–1845)
McKay, Claude
McKinley, Carlyle
Melville, Herman
Mercier, Alfred
Merrill, James *Suppl. 1*
Merton, Thomas
Mifflin, Lloyd
Miles, Josephine *Suppl. 1*
Millay, Edna St. Vincent
Miller, Alice Duer
Miller, Joaquin
Moïse, Penina
Monroe, Harriet
Moody, William Vaughn
Moore, Clement Clarke
Moore, Julia A.
Moore, Marianne
Moore, Merrill
Morley, Christopher
  Darlington
Morris, George Pope
Morris, Robert
  (1818–1888)
Morton, Sarah
  Wentworth Apthorp
Moss, Howard
Moulton, Louise
  Chandler
Munford, William
Muñoz Rivera, Luis
Nash, Ogden
Neihardt, John
  Gneisenau
Nemerov, Howard
Nicholson, Eliza Jane
  Poitevent Holbrook
Nies, Konrad
Noguchi, Yone
O'Brien, Edward Joseph
  Harrington
O'Connor, William
  Douglas
Odell, Jonathan
O'Hara, Frank
Olson, Charles John
O'Neill, Rose Cecil
Oppen, George August

Literature and Journalism *(cont.)*
Oppenheim, James
O'Reilly, John Boyle
Osgood, Frances Sargent Locke
Ostenso, Martha
Otis, Eliza Ann
Pain, Philip
Paine, Robert Treat, Jr.
Parke, John
Parker, Dorothy
Parsons, Thomas William
Patchen, Kenneth
Peabody, Josephine Preston
Percival, James Gates
Percy, William Alexander
Piatt, John James
Piatt, Sarah Morgan Bryan
Piñero, Miguel *Suppl. 2*
Pinkney, Edward Coote
Plath, Sylvia
Plummer, Mary Wright
Poe, Edgar Allan
Pound, Ezra
Powers, Jessica
Preston, Margaret Junkin
Prime, Benjamin Youngs
Ramírez, Sara Estela
Ransom, John Crowe
Read, Thomas Buchanan
Realf, Richard
Reece, Byron Herbert
Reed, Myrtle
Requier, Augustus Julian
Rexroth, Kenneth
Reznikoff, Charles
Richards, I. A.
Ridge, John Rollin
Ridge, Lola
Riley, James Whitcomb
Rittenhouse, Jessie Belle
Rivera, Tomás
Roberts, Elizabeth Madox
Robinson, Edwin Arlington
Roethke, Theodore
Rogers, Elymas Payson
Rose, Aquila
Roseliep, Raymond
Rosenberg, Harold
Rosenfeld, Morris
Rouquette, Adrien Emmanuel

Rouquette, François Dominique
Rowley, Thomas
Rukeyser, Muriel
Russell, Irwin
Ryan, Abram Joseph
Sampter, Jessie Ethel
Sandburg, Carl
Sandys, George
Santayana, George
Sargent, Epes
Sarton, May
Sawyer, Caroline M.
Schwartz, Delmore
Scott, Evelyn
Searing, Laura Catherine Redden
Seeger, Alan
Sexton, Anne Gray Harvey
Shapiro, Karl *Suppl. 1*
Shaw, John (1778–1809)
Sigourney, Lydia
Sill, Edward Rowland
Skinner, Constance Lindsay
Smith, Chard Powers
Smith, Elihu Hubbard
Smith, Samuel Francis
Snow, Eliza Roxcy
Snow, Wilbert
Spencer, Anne
Speyer, Leonora von Stosch
Spofford, Harriet Elizabeth Prescott
Stanton, Frank Lebby
Starbuck, George *Suppl. 1*
Stedman, Edmund Clarence
Steendam, Jacob
Steere, Richard
Sterling, George
Sterling, James
Stevens, Wallace
Stickney, Trumbull
Stockton, Annis Boudinot
Stoddard, Richard Henry
Stuart, Jesse Hilton
Stuckey, Elma
Tabb, John Banister
Taggard, Genevieve
Tappan, Caroline Sturgis
Tate, Allen
Taylor, Bayard
Taylor, Edward
Taylor, Leila Sarah

Teasdale, Sara
Terry, Lucy
Testut, Charles
Thaxter, Celia *Suppl. 1*
Thierry, Camille
Thompson, Clara Ann
Thompson, Eloise Alberta Veronica
Thompson, John Reuben
Thompson, Priscilla Jane
Ticknor, Francis Orray
Timrod, Henry
Tolson, Melvin Beaunorus
Tompson, Benjamin
Toomer, Jean
Townsend, Mary Ashley
Trumbull, John (1750–1831)
Tucker, St. George
Tuckerman, Frederick Goddard
Turell, Jane Colman
Turner, Eliza L. Sproat
Untermeyer, Jean Starr
Untermeyer, Louis
Van Doren, Mark
van Dyke, Henry
Very, Jones
Very, Lydia Louisa Ann
Viereck, George Sylvester
Villagrá, Gaspar Pérez de
Vinal, Harold
Walker, Margaret *Suppl. 1*
Ward, James Warner
Ward, Lydia Arms Avery Coonley
Warfield, Catherine Ann Ware
Warman, Cy
Warren, Mercy Otis
Warren, Robert Penn
Welby, Amelia Ball Coppuck
Wheatley, Phillis
Wheelock, John Hall
White, E. B.
Whitfield, James Monroe
Whiting, Lilian
Whitman, Sarah Helen
Whitman, Walt
Whitney, Anne
Whittier, John Greenleaf
Widdemer, Margaret
Wigglesworth, Edward
Wigglesworth, Michael
Wilcox, Ella Wheeler

Wilde, Richard Henry
Williams, John (1761–1818)
Williams, Tennessee
Williams, William Carlos
Willis, Nathaniel Parker
Wilson, Edmund
Winchevsky, Morris
Winters, Yvor
Wister, Sarah
Wolcott, Roger
Wolff, Sister Madeleva
Woodberry, George Edward
Woodworth, Samuel
Wright, James Arlington
Wright, Susanna
Wylie, Elinor
Yehoash
Zaturenska, Marya Alexandrovna
Zukofsky, Louis
Zunser, Eliakum

Poets Laureate of the United States
Nemerov, Howard
Warren, Robert Penn

Print Journalists
Abell, Arunah Sheperdson
Adams, Franklin P.
Adams, Samuel Hopkins
Agee, James Rufus
Allen, Young John William
Alsop, Joseph
Alsop, Stewart
Alvarez, Walter Clement
Ames, Mary Clemmer
Anderson, Paul Y.
Antheil, George
Asbury, Herbert
Ayer, Harriet Hubbard
Bagby, George William
Baker, Ray Stannard
Balderston, John Lloyd
Barnes, Djuna
Barrett, John
Beatty, Bessie
Beebe, Lucius Morris
Belden, Jack
Bennett, Gwendolyn
Bent, Silas
Bentley, William
Berger, Meyer
Bernstein, Herman
Bierce, Ambrose Gwinnett
Bigart, Homer

Literature and
Journalism *(cont.)*
Birney, William
Bishop, James Alonzo
Black, Winifred Sweet
Blake, Lillie Devereux
Bleyer, Willard
  Grosvenor
Bliven, Bruce
Bly, Nellie
Bourne, Randolph
  Silliman
Bowers, Claude Gernade
Boyle, Hal
Braden, Carl James
Bradford, Roark
  Whitney Wickliffe
Brann, William Cowper
Brewer, Thomas Mayo
Brewster, Anne
  Hampton
Briggs, Emily Pomona
  Edson
Brisbane, Arthur
Bromfield, Louis
Brooks, Erastus
Brooks, Noah
Brough, John
Broun, Heywood
Browne, Carl
Bruce, John Edward
Brucker, Herbert
Bryant, Louise
Buckley, James Monroe
Bugbee, Emma
Bullard, Arthur
Burnett, Alfred
Cable, George
  Washington
Caen, Herb *Suppl. 1*
Cain, James M.
Calhoun, William
  Barron
Cardozo, Jacob Newton
Carpenter, Frank George
Carr, Joseph F.
Carter, Boake *Suppl. 1*
Cash, W. J.
Cayton, Horace Roscoe
Cazneau, Jane Maria
  Eliza McManus
  Storms
Chadwick, Henry
Chamberlain, John
  Suppl. 2
Chapelle, Dickey
Chester, Thomas Morris
Childs, Marquis *Suppl. 2*
Ciancabilla, Giuseppe
Claiborne, Craig

Suppl. 2
Clapper, Raymond
  Lewis
Clark, Charles Heber
Cobb, Irvin Shrewsbury
Coffin, Charles Carleton
Cogley, John
Collens, Thomas
  Wharton
Colman, Norman Jay
Colón, Jesús *Suppl. 2*
Comfort, Will Levington
Connelly, Marc
Considine, Bob
Cooper, Kent
Corrothers, James David
Coxe, Tench
Coy, Ted
Craig, Elisabeth May
  Adams
Creel, George Edward
Creelman, James
Croly, Jane Cunningham
Crouse, Russel
  McKinley
Curtis, Charlotte Murray
Dabney, Wendell
  Phillips
Daggett, Rollin Mallory
Daley, Arthur John
Daly, Thomas Augustine
Daniel, Clifton *Suppl. 2*
Daniel, Daniel
Daniels, Jonathan
Danzig, Allison
Davidson, James Wood
Davis, Clyde Brion
Davis, Elmer
Davis, Rebecca Blaine
  Harding
Davis, Richard Harding
Davis, Samuel Post
De Casseres, Benjamin
de Fontaine, Felix
  Gregory
De Leon, Daniel
de Lima, Agnes Abinun
De Quille, Dan
Deutsch, Albert
DeVoto, Bernard
  Augustine
Diggs, Annie LePorte
Dithmar, Edward
  Augustus
Dix, Dorothy
Dodge, Mary Abigail
Dorr, Rheta Childe
Dos Passos, John
Doten, Alfred
Douglas, Marjory
  Stoneman *Suppl. 1*
Draper, Dorothy

Dromgoole, Will Allen
Drummond, Roscoe
Duffus, Robert Luther
Dunbar-Nelson, Alice
Dunne, Finley Peter
Durham, John Stephens
Eckersall, Walter Herbert
Eggleston, George Cary
Eifert, Virginia S.
Eisler, Gerhart
Eliot, George Fielding
Ende, Amalie von
Enright, James Edward
Evans, Donald
Ewer, Ferdinand
  Cartwright
Fall, Bernard B.
Fern, Fanny
Field, Eugene
Field, Kate
Fine, Benjamin
Finley, John Huston
Fischer, Louis
Flanagan, William
Flanner, Janet
Fleeson, Doris
Fleischer, Nat
Ford, Henry Jones
Frank, Ray
Frederic, Harold
Frick, Ford Christopher
Fry, Varian *Suppl. 2*
Fry, William Henry
Fullerton, William
  Morton *Suppl. 2*
Furman, Bess
Gales, Joseph
Gallico, Paul William
Garvey, Amy Euphemia
  Jacques
Gauvreau, Emile Henry
Gerson, Noel Bertram
Gibbons, Floyd
Gilbreth, Frank B., Jr.
  Suppl. 2
Giovannitti, Arturo
  Massimo
Gobright, Lawrence
  Augustus
Godkin, Edwin
  Lawrence
Godwin, Parke
Golden, Harry
Gonzales, Narciso Gener
Gould, Jack
Grady, Henry Woodfin
Graham, Sheilah
Greeley-Smith, Nixola
Green, Abel
Greenfield, Meg *Suppl. 1*
Griffin, John Howard

Gruening, Ernest Henry
Grund, Francis Joseph
Guest, Edgar Albert
Gunther, John
Guthrie, A. B., Jr.
Hébert, Felix Edward
Haessler, Carl
Hale, Edward Everett
Hall, Abraham Oakey
Hall, Grover Cleveland
Halpine, Charles
  Graham
Halstead, Murat
Hamilton, Thomas
Hapgood, Hutchins
Hard, William
Harman, Moses
Harper, Ida Husted
Harris, Benjamin
Harris, Joel Chandler
Harrison, Henry Sydnor
Harriss, Robert Preston
Hawthorne, Julian
Hayes, Alfred
Hearn, Lafcadio
Hearst, William
  Randolph, Jr.
Hemingway, Ernest
Henderson, David
Hendrick, Burton Jesse
Herbst, Josephine Frey
Hibben, Paxton Pattison
Hickok, Lorena Alice
Higgins, Marguerite
Hildreth, Richard
  Suppl. 2
Hitt, Robert Roberts
Holbrook, Stewart Hall
Holt, Claire
Holt, Rush Dew
Hopper, Hedda
Howe, Edgar Watson
Howe, Quincy
  Huntington
Hoyt, Charles Hale
Huck, Winnifred
  Sprague Mason
Hughes, Emmet John
Huie, William Bradford
Hutton, E. F.
Ingalls, John James
Irish, Ned
Irwin, William Henry
Jackson, Gardner
Jarves, James Jackson
Jemison, Alice Mae Lee
Johnson, Alvin Saunders
Johnson, Ban
Johnson, Oliver
Jordan, Elizabeth Garver

Literature and Journalism *(cont.)*

Kelland, Clarence Budington
Kelly, Florence Finch
Kempton, Murray *Suppl. 1*
Kendall, George Wilkins
Kennan, George
Kieran, John Francis
Kilgallen, Dorothy
King, Edward Smith
Kirchwey, Freda
Kober, Arthur
Kraft, Joseph
LaFarge, John
La Follette, Suzanne
Lanigan, George Thomas
Lardner, Ring
Lash, Joseph P.
Lattimore, Owen
Lawrence, David
Lee, James Melvin
Leggett, William
Lerner, Max
Lernoux, Penny
Levin, Louis Hiram
Lewis, Alfred Henry
Lewis, Augusta
Ley, Willy
Lieb, Frederick George
Liebling, A. J.
Lippincott, Sara Jane Clarke
Lippmann, Walter
Lisagor, Peter Irvin
Lloyd, Henry Demarest
Loeb, Sophie Irene Simon
London, Jack
Long, Lois
Loomis, Francis Butler
Lubell, Samuel
Ludlow, Louis Leon *Suppl. 2*
Lukens, Henry Clay
MacArthur, Charles Gordon
MacGahan, Januarius Aloysius
Mackenzie, Robert Shelton
Manning, Marie
Marcosson, Isaac Frederick
Marquis, Don
Marshall, S. L. A.
Martin, John Bartlow *Suppl. 2*
Martineau, Harriet

Mason, Walt
Masterson, Bat
Matthews, Herbert Lionel
Maxwell, Elsa
Maynard, Robert Clyve
Mayo, Katherine
McBride, Henry
McCann, Alfred Watterson
McCarroll, Marion Clyde
McClain, Leanita
McClellan, George Brinton
McCord, Louisa Susannah Cheves
McCormick, Anne Elizabeth O'Hare
McCrackin, Josephine
McIntyre, O. O.
McKay, Claude
McKinley, Carlyle
Mencken, H. L.
Michelson, Charles
Middleton, Drew
Millet, Francis Davis
Mitchel, John
Moore, John Trotwood
Morford, Henry
Morris, George Pope
Mowrer, Edgar Ansel, and Paul Scott Mowrer
Murdock, Victor
Nettleton, Alvred Bayard
Neuberger, Richard Lewis
Nevins, Allan
Niles, Hezekiah
Nye, Bill
O'Connor, Jessie Lloyd
O'Hare, Kate Richards
Olds, Leland
Osbon, B. S.
Otis, Eliza Ann
Ottley, Roi
Owen, Chandler
Paret, Jahail Parmly
Parker, Jane Marsh
Parsons, Louella Oettinger
Patterson, Ada *Suppl. 1*
Pearson, Drew
Pegler, Westbrook
Perlman, Philip Benjamin
Phillips, David Graham
Pike, James Shepherd
Pitkin, Walter Boughton *Suppl. 2*
Plumb, Preston B.

Polk, George
Pollard, Edward Alfred
Pollock, Channing
Poole, Ernest
Poore, Benjamin Perley
Porter, Sylvia
Povich, Shirley *Suppl. 1*
Prentice, George Dennison
Price, Byron
Pringle, Henry Fowles
Pryor, Roger Atkinson
Pyle, Ernie
Quimby, Harriet N. *Suppl. 2*
Ramírez, Sara Estela
Randall, James Ryder
Rawlings, Marjorie Kinnan
Ray, Charles Bennett
Raynal, Guillaume-Thomas-François
Redpath, James
Reed, John
Reed, Myrtle
Reed, Sampson
Reston, James *Suppl. 1*
Revell, Nellie McAleney
Reynolds, Quentin *Suppl. 2*
Rice, Charles Allen Thorndike
Rice, Grantland
Ridge, John Rollin
Riis, Jacob August
Rinehart, Mary Roberts
Ripley, Robert LeRoy
Roberts, Kenneth
Robinson, Solon
Rodell, Fred
Rogers, Will
Root, Waverley
Ross, Charles Griffith
Ross, Ishbel
Round, William M. F.
Rovere, Richard Halworth
Rowan, Carl T. *Suppl. 2*
Royall, Anne Newport
Royko, Mike *Suppl. 1*
Ruby, George T.
Ruggles, David
Rukeyser, Merryle Stanley
Runyon, Damon
Russell, Charles Edward
Ryan, Cornelius
Salazar, Ruben
Salisbury, Harrison Evans
Sandburg, Carl

Schiff, Dorothy
Scholte, H. P.
Schultz, Sigrid Lillian
Schuyler, George Samuel
Scott, Leroy Martin
Scovel, Sylvester Henry
Scripps, Ellen Browning
Seabury, Samuel (1801–1872)
Searing, Laura Catherine Redden
Seldes, Gilbert Vivian
Sevareid, Eric
Seward, Frederick William
Sheean, Vincent *Suppl. 1*
Sheppard, Eugenia
Shilts, Randy Martin
Shirer, William Lawrence
Short, Joseph Hudson, Jr.
Simmons, Roscoe Conkling Murray
Slosson, Edwin Emery
Smedley, Agnes
Smith, H. Allen
Smith, Jack *Suppl. 1*
Smith, Red
Smith, William Henry (1833–1896)
Snelling, William Joseph
Snow, Edgar Parks
Snyder, Jimmy "the Greek" *Suppl. 1*
Spencer, Matthew Lyle
Spewack, Samuel, and Bella Spewack
Squier, Ephraim George
Stahel, Julius
Stanley, Henry Morton
Stanton, Elizabeth Cady
Stanton, Frank Lebby
Steffens, Lincoln
Stevens, Alzina Ann Parsons
Stevens, John Leavitt
Stillman, William James
St. Johns, Adela Rogers
Stoddard, Elizabeth Drew Barstow
Stolberg, Benjamin
Stone, I. F.
Strong, Anna Louise
Strout, Richard L.
Strunsky, Simeon
Sullivan, Ed
Sullivan, Frank
Sullivan, Mark
Swados, Harvey

Literature and Journalism *(cont.)*

Swope, Herbert Bayard
Tarbell, Ida M.
Taylor, Bert Leston
Taylor, Charles Henry
Thompson, Dorothy Celine
Thomson, Mortimer Neal
Tobenkin, Elias
Treadwell, Sophie Anita
Truman, Benjamin Cummings
Turner, George Kibbe
Tyler, Ralph Waldo
Valesh, Eva McDonald
Vandenberg, Arthur H.
Vanderbilt, Amy
Villard, Oswald Garrison
Vladeck, Baruch Charney
Vorse, Mary Heaton
Wallace, Henry
Walling, William English
Walsh, Henry Collins
Walton, Lester A. *Suppl. 2*
Ward, Archibald Burdette
Watterston, George
Webb, Charles Henry
Wechsler, James A.
Weisgal, Meyer Wolfe
Welles, Gideon
Wellman, Walter
Wertenbaker, Charles Christian
White, Frances Emily
White, Theodore H.
White, William Allen
White, William Lindsay
Whiteley, L. A.
Whiting, Lilian
Whitman, Alden
Whittier, John Greenleaf
Willard, Josiah Flint
Williams, James
Williams, Michael
Williams, Walter
Wilson, Edmund
Wilson, J. Finley
Winchell, Walter
Woodworth, Samuel
Zevin, Israel Joseph
Zollicoffer, Felix Kirk

Radio / Television Writers
Backus, Jim
Berg, Gertrude

Carrington, Elaine Sterne
Chayefsky, Paddy
Levinson, Richard Leighton
Moore, Donald Wynkoop
Oboler, Arch
Phillips, Irna
Serling, Rod
Tarloff, Frank *Suppl. 2*
Teichmann, Howard Miles
Todman, William Selden

Science Writers
Andrews, Eliza Frances
Anthony, Harold Elmer
Asimov, Isaac
Bartram, William
Bates, Marston
Carson, Rachel Louise
Darlington, William
Davis, Watson
Douglas, Marjory Stoneman *Suppl. 1*
Dubos, René Jules
Eiseley, Loren Corey
Fowler, Orson Squire
Gamow, George
Hall, Basil
Herrick, Sophia McIlvaine Bledsoe
Laurence, William Leonard
Lee, Charles Alfred
Ley, Willy
Lloyd, John Uri
Lowell, Percival
Neal, Marie Catherine
Randall, Henry Stephens
Sagan, Carl *Suppl. 1*
Sinclair, Isabella McHutcheson
Sullivant, William Starling
Tarr, Ralph Stockman
Thomas, Lewis
Tuckerman, Edward
Youmans, Edward Livingston

Screenwriters
Agee, James Rufus
Akins, Zoë
Arnold, Elliott
Balderston, John Lloyd
Beach, Rex
Bessie, Alvah
Bolton, Guy Reginald
Burnett, W. R.

Caspary, Vera
Cassavetes, John
Chayefsky, Paddy
Clavell, James
Cohen, Octavus Roy
Cohn, Alfred A.
Connell, Richard
Connelly, Marc
Crouse, Russel McKinley
de Mille, William Churchill
Dix, Beulah Marie
Ephron, Phoebe, and Henry Ephron
Epstein, Philip G.
Fante, John Thomas
Foreman, Carl
Frings, Ketti
Furthman, Jules G.
Gleason, James
Hawks, Howard
Haycox, Ernest *Suppl. 1*
Hecht, Ben
Herbert, F. Hugh
Howard, Sidney Coe
Hughes, Rupert
Huston, John
Jarrico, Paul *Suppl. 1*
Johnson, Nunnally
Kalmar, Bert
Kanin, Garson *Suppl. 1*
Kober, Arthur
Lardner, Ring, Jr. *Suppl. 2*
Lawson, John Howard
Loos, Anita
MacArthur, Charles Gordon
Maltz, Albert
Mankiewicz, Herman Jacob
Mankiewicz, Joseph Leo
March, Joseph Moncure
Marion, Frances
McCoy, Horace Stanley
Milestone, Lewis
Muse, Clarence E.
Nichols, Dudley
Osborn, Paul
Parker, Dorothy
Raphaelson, Samson
Riskin, Robert
Rossen, Robert
Ryskind, Morrie
Sackler, Howard Oliver
Salt, Waldo
Schary, Dore
Seaton, George
Shaw, Irwin

Sherwood, Robert Emmet
Sklar, George
Slesinger, Tess
Smith, Thorne
Steinbeck, John
Stewart, Donald Ogden
St. Johns, Adela Rogers
Sturges, Preston
Tarloff, Frank *Suppl. 2*
Taylor, Charles Alonzo
Thurman, Wallace
Totheroh, Dan
Trotti, Lamar
Trumbo, Dalton
West, Jessamyn
Wexley, John
Wheeler, Hugh Callingham

Slave Narrative Authors
Ball, Charles
Bibb, Henry Walton
Brown, John (1810?–1876)
Clarke, Lewis G.
Jacobs, Harriet
Northup, Solomon
Smith, Venture

Speechwriters
Hughes, Emmet John
Martin, John Bartlow *Suppl. 2*

Sportswriters
Carr, Joseph F.
Chadwick, Henry
Coy, Ted
Daley, Arthur John
Daniel, Daniel
Eckersall, Walter Herbert
Enright, James Edward
Fleischer, Nat
Frick, Ford Christopher
Gallico, Paul William
Johnson, Ban
Kieran, John Francis
Lardner, Ring
Lieb, Frederick George
Masterson, Bat
Povich, Shirley *Suppl. 1*
Rice, Grantland
Smith, Red
Tunis, John R.
Ward, Archibald Burdette

Tract Writers
Blackstone, William E.
Monk, Maria

**Literature and
Journalism** *(cont.)*
Travel Writers
  Birkbeck, Morris
  Blake, Mary Elizabeth
  Bremer, Fredrika
  Browne, John Ross
  Carpenter, Frank George
  Castiglioni, Luigi
  Coggeshall, George
  Collier, Price
  Colton, Walter
  Crèvecoeur, J. Hector St.
    John de
  Delano, Amasa
  Dorr, Julia Caroline
    Ripley
  Dos Passos, John
  Du Chaillu, Paul Belloni

  Farnham, Thomas
    Jefferson
  Fielding, Temple
    Hornaday
  Fodor, Eugene
  Hale, Susan
  Hall, Basil
  Halliburton, Richard
  Harriot, Thomas
  Hines, Duncan
  Hoffman, Charles Fenno
  Irving, Washington
  Josselyn, John
  Le Vert, Octavia Celeste
    Walton
  Mackenzie, Alexander
    Slidell
  Manly, William Lewis
  Martineau, Harriet

  Morford, Henry
  Morris, Edward Joy
  Olmsted, Frederick Law
  Regan, John
  Reynolds, Jeremiah N.
  Royall, Anne Newport
  Ruxton, George
    Augustus Frederick
  Sandys, George
  Scidmore, Eliza
    Ruhamah
  Senn, Nicholas
  Sheean, Vincent *Suppl. 1*
  Simon, Kate
  Smith, Francis
    Hopkinson
  Stefansson, Vilhjalmur
  Stephens, John Lloyd
    Suppl. 2

  Stoddard, Charles
    Warren
  Stuck, Hudson
  Taylor, Bayard
  Thompson, Era Bell
  Trollope, Frances
  Tuckerman, Henry
    Theodore
  Van Braam Houckgeest,
    Andreas Everardus
  Vincent, Frank
  Waln, Robert, Jr.
  Warner, Charles Dudley
  Wislizenus, Frederick
    Adolphus
  Woolson, Constance
    Fenimore
  Workman, Fanny
    Bullock